THE COMMON LAW LIBRARY

LIBEL AND SLANDER

THE COMMON LAW LIBRARY

GATLEY

ON

LIBEL AND SLANDER

TWELFTH EDITION

By

JOINT EDITORS

Professor Alastair Mullis
LLB (Lond), LLM (Cantab)
Head of the School of Law,
University of Leeds

Richard Parkes Q.C., M.A. (Cantab)
A bencher of Gray's Inn,
a circuit judge and a
deputy High Court judge

SENIOR CONTRIBUTING EDITOR
Godwin Busuttil, M.A., M.Phil. (Cantab), of Lincoln's Inn, Barrister

CONTRIBUTING EDITORS
Andrew Scott, LLB MPhil (Belfast) PhD (Wales)
Associate Professor of Law, London School of Economics
Adam Speker, B.A., of Middle Temple, Barrister

PRECEDENTS AND DAMAGES AWARDS
Chloe Strong, LLB (LSE), of the Middle Temple, Barrister

SWEET & MAXWELL   THOMSON REUTERS

Published in 2013 by Sweet & Maxwell, 100 Avenue Road, London NW3 3PF
part of Thomson Reuters (Professional) UK Limited
(Registered in England & Wales, Company No 1679046.
Registered Office and address for service:
Aldgate House, 33 Aldgate High Street, London EC3N 1DL)

Typeset by Interactive Sciences Ltd, Gloucester
Printed and bound by CPI Group (UK) Ltd, Croydon, CR0 4YY

For further information on our products and services, visit
www.sweetandmaxwell.co.uk

ISBN 978-0-41402-843-2

No natural forests were destroyed to make this product; only farmed
timber was used and re-planted

A CIP catalogue record for this book is available from the British Library

PREFACE

The five years since the publication of the 11th edition have seen two parallel, in some senses conflicting, developments in the law of defamation. In the courts, there has been a subtle yet firm drawing back from the prioritising of the right to freedom of speech seen in the late 1990s and early 2000s. The law of defamation prior to that was undoubtedly weighted towards the protection of reputation but in those two decades significant revisions were made to law and practice with the express intention of according greater weight to expression interests. The most obvious development was the emergence of a public interest privilege in *Reynolds v Times Newspapers* but there were other significant developments that went some way towards re-balancing the law.[1] This is not to say that the courts ignored reputation (we should not forget Lord Nicholls' insistence in *Reynolds* that it is not in the public interest for the reputation of public figures to be falsely debased), but rather that freedom of expression was regarded as the 'starting point', as Lord Nicholls himself put it. Reputation interests were considered primarily as a possible limitation on the right to freedom of expression where this could be demonstrated to be necessary in a democratic society.

The years since 2008 have seen the Strasbourg and domestic courts become progressively more pronounced in their recognition that reputation falls to be protected under the art.8 right to respect for private life (see e.g. *Karako v Hungary*, *Axel Springer AG v Germany* and *Re Guardian News and Media Ltd*). If it was thought that freedom of expression would always be the more important right, this is no longer the case. The effect of this shift is potentially very profound, although the full ramifications have yet to become clear. Where the only right engaged is the claimant's art.8 right and the defendant is a public authority, it has been said that the existence of an established duty and interest—the common law requirement for qualified privilege (see ch.14)—is not enough to establish the defence. Instead, the defendant will only be able to rely on qualified privilege if it can show that it has acted compatibly with the art.8 rights of those to whom the information relates, and it can satisfy a proportionality test (see *Clift v Slough Borough Council*). The effect in cases where both arts.8 and 10 are engaged is less clear. While the

---

[1] 'The Swing of the Pendulum: Reputation, Expression and the Recentering of English Libel Law' (2012), Mullis and Scott *Northern Ireland Legal Quarterly*, 63(1), 27–58.

presumptive prioritising of art.10 is no longer acceptable, the courts have yet to take the step of applying the 'ultimate balancing' approach, originally articulated in the privacy context, in every defamation case. Yet, as was perceptively observed by Eady J., that great common law judge whose decency and humanity deserve to be more widely acknowledged, "what seems to be emerging clearly is that the 'new methodology' sanctioned by the House of Lords in 2004, both in *Campbell v MGN* and in *Re S (A Child)*, originally in the context of privacy... is now finding its way inexorably into the application of our well known principles of defamation". The implications of this are potentially profound. Decisions in individual cases may become ever more fact dependent as courts seek to balance the arts.8 and 10 rights on the particular facts of the case. More generally, established principles of defamation may be challenged on the basis that they fail properly to balance the engaged rights. For example, for how much longer can the rule in *Bonnard v Perryman*, unalloyed by art.8 considerations, continue to dictate the outcome of applications for interim injunctions? Or will absolute privilege continue to apply to complaints to police (*Westcott v Westcott*) without reference to the art.8 interests of the person who is the subject of the complaint?

If the last five years have seen the courts developing a more nuanced approach to defamation, involving a careful consideration of the weights of the respective rights, the same cannot be said of the process that has led to the enactment of the Defamation Act 2013. The Act, which is not at the time of writing in force, is the culmination of several years of campaigning for wide-ranging and radical reform that if accepted would have made English law more tolerant of defamatory speech than the United States. The 2013 Act does not deliver everything that the campaigners wanted but it undoubtedly effects a shift of the law in favour of freedom of speech, albeit one that may prove to be no more than slight. Thus, a higher threshold is now set before a defamatory imputation becomes actionable (s.2), honest comment and public interest are liberalised (ss.3 and 4) and some statutory 'report' privileges widened (s.7), a single publication rule is introduced (s.8), and new defences are made available to operators of websites (s.5) and the publishers of peer-reviewed statements in academic journals (s.6). Additionally, the presumption in favour of jury trial is abolished (s.11), new rules are established in relation to jurisdiction (s.9) and new remedial powers are granted to the court (ss.12 and 13).

Precisely how these two developments—the progressive recognition by the courts of the importance of reputation as a protected right and the greater weight accorded to expression rights in some provisions of the Act—will play out is difficult to predict. Inevitably, the short term consequence will be a high volume of litigation as the true effect of the new Act, which in several areas expressly abolishes the common law, is explored through the courts. However, the new Act will have to be interpreted against the background of the rights context underpinned by the European Convention on Human Rights and the Human Rights Act 1998 and consequently, while some movement in favour of expression rights seems probable, any changes are unlikely to prove as significant as the promoters of statutory reform may expect.

The enactment of the Defamation Act 2013 presented us with several difficulties. The fact that the Act is not yet in force, and when in force will only apply with prospective effect, led us to the conclusion that we needed to state the law as it currently is and then separately to consider what the Act says and how it may change the existing law. This approach has been adopted throughout the book. Secondly, we faced the inevitable difficulty that arises with any new piece of legislation, of trying to predict how it will be interpreted. Many of the views expressed in the text are consequently tentative and may subsequently be proved to have been mistaken.

The structure of this edition remains broadly similar to that of the 11th. However, though this edition is not significantly shorter than its predecessor, two chapters have been removed. Though criminal libel remains on the statute books of some Commonwealth jurisdictions, its abolition in England, Wales and Northern Ireland by s.73 of the Coroners and Justice Act 2009 led us to take the decision to remove the chapter on this area of law. We also took the decision to excise the chapter on the European Convention on Human Rights. The general issues covered in the previous edition are dealt with in much greater detail in specialised works on the subject and we felt that the discrete overview offered in that one chapter was less useful than a discussion of specific issues raised by Convention jurisprudence in the chapters to which they are relevant.

As before, we have tried to draw widely on the case law of other common law jurisdictions. Inevitably in a work that focuses on the English law of defamation, the coverage is partial and care must be taken when comparing the approaches taken and results reached by foreign courts. Nevertheless valuable insights can be gained from the decisions of our fellow common law jurisdictions and we have therefore sought to include some of the more significant decisions reached by courts in Australia, Canada, New Zealand, Hong Kong, the USA and other jurisdictions.

The general editors have read the whole text in draft, assisted by Godwin Busuttil, whose generous preparedness to read large tracts of material on request and offer a third view was of huge assistance. Subject to this, the initial responsibility for writing was as follows: Godwin Busuttil, Chapters 25 and 29–31, and updating of the statutes in Appendix 2; Alastair Mullis, Chapters 2–10, 13 & 14, 16–21 and 23; Richard Parkes, Chapters 24 and 32–35; Andrew Scott, Chapters 1, 11 & 12, 15 and 22; Adam Speker, Chapters 26–28 and 36. The precedents and the damages awards were prepared by Chloe Strong, who rejuvenates 5RB's long association with *Gatley*.

Alastair Mullis would like to thank the following for various enlightening discussions and insights they have shared with him over the years: Dr Andrew Scott, Professors Gavin Phillipson and Eric Barendt, and Benjamin Pell. He would also like to thank his family for their patience throughout the writing process. Without their support and forbearance, he would still be writing. Richard Parkes echoes that gratitude for family patience. Long hours of vacation work on past editions of *Gatley* scarred the young lives of his neglected older boys, and his youngest endured its demands this summer, both in Italy and in Winchester, with characteristically good-natured tolerance. We are both grateful to Gregory Smith of Sweet and Maxwell for his admirable patience and stoicism as his deadlines were repeatedly and shamelessly breached.

We have endeavoured to state the law on the basis of the material available to us at the end of July 2013.

Alastair Mullis   **Richard Parkes**
Leeds   Winchester

CONTENTS

PART ONE
THE DEFAMATORY STATEMENT

PART TWO
DEFENCES

PART THREE
OTHER CAUSES OF ACTION AND RELATED MATTERS

CONTENTS

PART FOUR
THE ACTION

CONTENTS

CONTENTS

TABLE OF CASES

TABLE OF CASES

TABLE OF CASES

TABLE OF STATUTES

*[References in **bold** indicate where legislation is reproduced in full]*

TABLE OF STATUTORY INSTRUMENTS

*[References in **bold** indicate where legislation is reproduced in full]*

TABLE OF CIVIL PROCEDURE RULES

TABLE OF PRACTICE DIRECTIONS

TABLE OF PRACTICE DIRECTIONS

TABLE OF NATIONAL (NON UK) LEGISLATION

TABLE OF EUROPEAN AND INTERNATIONAL CONVENTIONS AND TREATIES

TABLE OF EUROPEAN DIRECTIVES

TABLE OF EUROPEAN REGULATIONS

Part One

THE DEFAMATORY STATEMENT

INTRODUCTION

Section 1. Introduction

Reputation and defamation. Whether reflected in Shakespearian lit- **1.1**
erature or modern discussions of internet communications and brand development, the enormous personal and economic value of reputation is universally
appreciated.[1] The laws of libel and slander provide the primary legal means
for defending reputation, and responding to unwarranted and damaging allegations. Such laws possess a long history in English common law,[2] and their
interplay with other torts is complex.[3] They now sit in the rights context
underpinned by the intrinsic values of the common law, the European Convention on Human Rights, and the Human Rights Act 1998.[4] In recent times, a
sustained political campaign has argued that the law places inappropriate and
harmful constraints on the freedom of scientists, academics, and 'normal'
people commenting in online forums to participate in discussions of profound
public importance. Media organisations have been willing participants in this

---

[1] Among other of his plays, reputation and its value provides a key theme in Shakespeare's
Othello. See, for instance, Iago's soliloquy:
"Good name in man and woman, dear my lord, Is the immediate jewel of their souls;
Who steals my purse steals trash; 'tis something, nothing;
'Twas mine, 'tis his, and has been slave to thousands;
But he that filches from me my good name
Robs me of that which not enriches him
And makes me poor indeed."
   Othello, Act 3, Scene 3.
In Act 2, Scene 3, of course, in reply to Cassio's lament that having lost his reputation he has "lost
the immortal part of [himself] and what remains is bestial", Iago says that reputation "is an idle
and most false imposition; oft got without merit and lost without deserving". See also, *Richard
II*, Act 1 Scene 1. In the second respects, see e.g. Solove, *The Future of Reputation: Gossip,
Rumor, and Privacy on the Internet* (Cambridge MA: Yale University Press, 2008); Newmark,
Masum and Tovey, *The Reputation Society: How Online Opinions Are Reshaping the Offline
World* (Boston: MIT Press, 2012).
[2] Mitchell, *The Making of the Modern Law of Defamation* (London: Hart Publishing, 2005).
[3] See paras 1.16–1.21, below.
[4] See paras 1.11–1.15, below.

critique. Whatever the legitimacy of such criticism, this campaign culminated in the Defamation Act 2013.[5] Defamation law has rarely possessed such standing in the public consciousness. That this has been the case is evidence of its importance to the freedom of public sphere deliberation, and ultimately to democratic culture.

1.2 Subject-matter. This book is primarily concerned with the English law of libel and slander (defamation), the torts which protect a person's reputation. For convenience, it also deals with the closely related tort of malicious falsehood,[6] and with the complaints procedures alternative to a civil action which are open to a defamed person.[7] There are also outline accounts of other areas which sometimes overlap with defamation or which may be associated with it: the claim for misuse of private information,[8] contravention of the data protection legislation,[9] harassment,[10] certain wrongs based on copyright,[11] passing off,[12] and negligent misstatement.[13] As well as the substantive law of libel, slander and malicious falsehood, the book also describes the procedural and evidential aspects of these torts.[14] There are a number of special features of procedure and evidence in this area and they have a major effect upon the substantive law. The law of libel and slander is based upon the common law but there have been a number of major statutory modifications.[15] On the coming into force of the Defamation Act 2013, there will be further significant changes to a number of areas of the substantive law. These changes are discussed as appropriate in the text.

1.3 Foreign and international law. Although concerned primarily with English law, this book draws widely on other common law jurisdictions without there being any pretence to offer a comprehensive account of those laws. There is, of course, less uniformity in the rules of defamation within the common law world than there was 100 years ago. This is due mainly to the effect of legislation, but is also attributable to fashioning by courts of local rules to meet different exigencies even as they remain within the same broad

---

[5] Other notable contributions in this process included Culture, Media and Sport Committee [2009–10] *Second Report: Press Standards, Privacy and Libel.* HC 362-I; Second Reading debate on Lord Lester's Defamation Bill—720 HLDeb col 432 et seq, July 9, 2010; Ministry of Justice, *Draft Defamation Bill: Consultation Paper CP3/11* (Cm 8020, Norwich: TSO); Joint Committee on Defamation [2010–12] *Draft Defamation Bill.* HL Paper 203, HC 930-I.

[6] Ch.21, below.
[7] Ch.26, below.
[8] Ch.22, below.
[9] Ibid.
[10] Ch.23, below.
[11] Ch.23, below.
[12] Ibid.
[13] Ibid.
[14] See Pt IV, below.
[15] Principally, the Defamation Acts of 1952 and 1996. These are set out, with other relevant legislation, in Appendix 2.

conceptual structure. The differences first became and remain marked in the case of the United States,[16] where the modern interpretation of the First Amendment to the Constitution radically transformed (indeed in some situations obliterated) the common law relating to privilege, honest comment, and the burden of proof on the issue of falsity.[17] Other areas of US law have been subject to less change, however, and American cases may still usefully be cited. Indeed, at the higher levels, the US First Amendment cases may be called in aid in an attempt to persuade the court to change the direction of English law.[18] Generally speaking, the laws of Australia,[19] Canada,[20] New Zealand,[21] Ireland,[22] Hong Kong,[23] Malaysia, Singapore,[24] and the West Indian jurisdictions remain closer to the English model, although in most

---

[16] See generally, Sack, *Sack on Defamation: Libel, Slander, and Related Problems*, 4th edn (New York: Practising Law Institute, 2013). Subject to constitutional requirements, defamation law is a matter for individual states rather than federal law.

[17] The relevant part of the First Amendment reads: "Congress shall make no law . . . abridging freedom of speech or of the press". The process of the 'constitutionalisation' of US defamation law began with *New York Times v Sullivan*, 376 U.S. 254 (1964). As defamation law is closely linked with social conditions, as long ago as 1908, Lord Macnaghten warned against the dangers of uncritical use of American decisions: *Macintosh v Dun* [1908] A.C. 390 at 401. See also, the majority of the Supreme Court of Victoria in *Hercules v Phease* [1994] 2 V.R. 411 App Div.

[18] Thus *New York Times v Sullivan* is cited in support of the decision of the House of Lords in *Derbyshire CC v Times Newspapers* [1993] A.C. 534, denying a cause of action to a governmental body, while in *British Chiropractic Association v Singh* [2010] EWCA Civ 350; [2011] 1 W.L.R. 133 at [34], the Court of Appeal cited aspects of the judgment of Judge Easterbrook in *Underwager v Salter* 22 Fed. 3d 730 (1994) in an honest comment judgment deriving from science journalism.

[19] For many years, Australian law presented a very diverse picture due to the existence of diverse state legislation. In 2005 and 2006, however, the states each passed uniform legislation to harmonise the respective laws: Defamation Acts 2005 of New South Wales, Queensland, South Australia, Tasmania, Victoria and Western Australia; Defamation Act 2006 of the Northern Territory; and Division 9 of the Civil Law (Wrongs) Act 2002 of the Australian Capital Territory, as inserted by the Civil Law (Wrongs) Amendment Act 2006. All Acts are available at *http://www.austlii.edu.au*.

[20] Except Quebec, which is a Civil Law jurisdiction. For Canadian Law, see Brown, *The Law of Defamation in Canada*, 2nd edn (Toronto: Carswell, 1994) and Brown, *Defamation Law: A Primer* (Toronto: Thomson Canada Ltd, 2003). The guarantee of freedom of speech in the Canadian Charter of Rights has had only a rather limited impact on the law of defamation, but the law must be in line with Charter values: *Grant v Torstar Corp, Toronto Star Newspapers Ltd* [2009] S.C.C. 61; *WIC Radio Ltd v Simpson* [2008] S.C.C. 40; *Hill v Church of Scientology of Toronto* [1995] 2 S.C.R. 1130. There is no completely uniform defamation legislation in Canada but many provinces have Acts based on the work of the Canadian Uniform Law Commissioners. The provincial Acts are: Alberta Defamation Act 2000, British Columbia Defamation Act 1996, Manitoba Defamation Act, C.C.S.M. c. D20, New Brunswick Defamation Act 1973, Newfoundland and Labrador Defamation Act 1990, Northwest Territories Defamation Act 1988, Nova Scotia Defamation Act 1989, Ontario Libel and Slander Act 1990, Prince Edward Island Defamation Act 1988, Saskatchewan Libel and Slander Act 1978, and Yukon Territories Defamation Act 2002. Much of this legislation is available at *http://www.canlii.org/*.

[21] The Defamation Act 1992 (N.Z.) made important changes, but the law retains the essential common law conceptual structure.

[22] See generally, Maher, *The Law of Defamation* (Dublin: Round Hall, 2011). The Irish Defamation Act 2009 came into force on January 1, 2010.

[23] The Defamation Ordinance is substantially based on the Defamation Act 1952.

[24] Evans, *Law of Defamation in Singapore and Malaysia*, 3rd edn (2008). The Defamation Act 1965 is substantially based on the Defamation Act 1952.

cases with a heavy overlay of statute which in some cases comes close to codification.[25] While for the past two decades and more, English libel law has seen reforms oriented towards ensuring greater coherence with the needs of freedom of expression, the European Convention on Human Rights, as interpreted by the European Court of Human Rights and applied by domestic courts, has become more directly influential since the coming into force of the Human Rights Act 1998. Initially, this involved a further impetus in the direction of actualising the requirements of art.10. More recently, there has been a growing recognition of the need for a conscious balancing between free speech and the right to reputation, the latter having been recognised as falling within the ambit of the art.8 right to respect for private life. In this sense, the 'constitutionalisation' of English defamation law proceeds at pace.[26]

SECTION 2. OVERVIEW OF DEFAMATION LAW

1.4 Reputation. The core concern at the heart of defamation law is the deterring and remedying of unwarranted harm to reputation. Yet, the core interest at stake is not precisely understood. Without a satisfactory understanding, there is a risk that elements of the law designed to defend the interest or interests may in time prove misdirected. Disparate explanations of the importance of reputation have been proffered by scholars and others, resting on such values as honour, dignity and property.[27] The matter has resurfaced in a new guise in recent times, as attempts have been made to explain the coverage of reputation—a quintessentially public thing—by the art.8 right to respect for privacy.[28]

1.5 Libel and slander. The term 'defamation' is used as a collective term for the torts of libel and slander. It is committed when a person publishes words

---

[25] The Roman-Dutch systems of South Africa and Sri Lanka have been heavily influenced by English law (see Burchell, *Law of Defamation in South Africa* (1985) and Amerasinghe, *Defamation in the Law of South Africa and Ceylon* (1969)). However, while cases from these jurisdictions are helpful on whether words are defamatory and on aspects of privilege it should be noted that with regard to the state of mind of the defendant these systems are based on different principles from the common law. The underlying principle is that there must be an *animus iniurandi*. That can be presumed from the publication of defamatory words and can be rebutted, e.g. by showing that the defendant had a good reason to speak. South African cases sometimes speak in terms of qualified privilege and malice in the English sense (see para.17.2, below) but the underlying idea of fault is wider.

[26] See para.1.11, below.

[27] A classical investigation is Post, "The Social Foundations of Defamation Law: Reputation and the Constitution" (1986) *California Law Review* 691. See also, Craik, *Reputation: A Network Interpretation* (Oxford: Oxford University Press, 2009); Barendt, "What is the Point of Libel Law" (1999) *Current Legal Problems*, 52, 110.

[28] See, e.g. Mullis and Scott, "The Swing of the Pendulum: Reputation, Expression and the Recentering of English Libel Law" (2012) NILQ, 63(1), 27–58; Howarth, "Libel: its purpose and reform" (2011) *Modern Law Review*, 74(6), 845–877.

or matter[29] to a third party that contain an untrue imputation that harms the reputation of the claimant. Broadly speaking, if the publication is made in a permanent form or is broadcast or is part of a theatrical performance, it is libel.[30] If the publication assumes some transient form, it is slander.[31] The most important distinction between the two is that libel is actionable per se: the law presumes that some damage will flow from it.[32] In contrast, and insofar as it falls outside certain specified categories, the publication of a slander provides a remedy only when some special damage can be proven to flow from it.[33]

Publication. In English law, there is no actionable tort unless the words are   **1.6** "published" to at least one person other than the person defamed: the wrong is injury to reputation, not insult.[34] Publication to one person only will do. Strictly speaking, it is not necessary that the matter should have been "published" in a book, newspaper or broadcast.[35]

The meaning of defamatory. In layman's terms, words are defamatory   **1.7** when they cause harm to reputation.[36] However, there is no wholly satisfactory legal definition of the term.[37] Three formulae have been particularly influential: (1) would the imputation tend to "lower the plaintiff in the estimation of right-thinking members of society generally"?[38] (2) would the

---

[29] Strictly speaking, "matter" is the more accurate term as it encompasses every medium whereby defamatory thought and ideas can be expressed—see Bower, *Actionable Defamation*, 2nd edn (London: Butterworths, 1923), at 226. The great majority of defamation cases, of course, involve imputations expressed in words, whether written, spoken or transmitted. Hence, this book generally uses 'words'. The Defamation Act 1952, s.16(1) defines words as including "pictures, visual images, gestures and other methods of signifying meaning". The Defamation Act 1996 uses "statement", but defines that in the same way: s.17(1).

[30] Broadcasts and theatrical performances are deemed libel by statute—see paras 3.10–3.11, below.

[31] See paras 3.6–3.9, below.

[32] This does not preclude the striking out of a claim where the harm is minimal on the ground of abuse of process—see para.6.2, below.

[33] See para.3.6, below.

[34] See para.6.1, below.

[35] In some cases of limited publication, however, the court may strike out an action as an abuse of process—see para.6.2, below.

[36] Hence, true words can be defamatory although not unlawful—e.g. *Pyke v Hibernian Bank* [1950] I.R. 195 at 203; *Elliott v Freisen* (1982) 136 D.L.R. (3d) 281, where it is noted that non-legal usage may incorrectly incorporate the notion of falsity as part of the issue whether the statement is defamatory.

[37] In *Sim v Stretch* (1936) 52 T.L.R. 669 HL at 671, Lord Atkin said that "judges and textbook writers alike have found difficulty in defining with precision the word 'defamatory' ". Though the test stated in that case has been very influential, Lord Atkin himself declined to lay down any formal definition. It is probable that not all cases are reconcilable with a single principle. This difficulty no doubt relates back to the lack of clarity on the underpinning nature of reputation. See also, Milo, *Defamation and Freedom of Speech* (2008) at 42: "it is probably too optimistic to expect reputation to be fully explained by only one justification. It is better that the influences of property, and dignity, and to a lesser extent, honour, are acknowledged".

[38] *Sim v Stretch* (1936) 52 T.L.R. 669 HL at 671 per Lord Atkin.

imputation tend to cause others to shun or avoid the claimant?[39] and (3) would the words tend to expose the claimant to "hatred, contempt or ridicule"?[40] True words can be defamatory, although not unlawful. Conversely, the mere fact that words are untrue does not make them defamatory as they may not affect the claimant's reputation:

> "The objective truth or falsity of the matter complained of is irrelevant to its defamatory nature. To say of a solicitor that he is dishonest is injurious to his reputation (and thus defamatory of him), and it does not become less injurious because the statement is true. To say of a member of the Bar (irony aside) that he is universally regarded as the best advocate in Sydney is not injurious to his reputation, and does not become injurious because the statement is false."[41]

Non-defamatory untrue words may be actionable as malicious falsehood,[42] or as negligence.[43] However, the scope of damages is more limited in those torts. Libel and some forms of slander are actionable per se because injury to reputation is presumed from the publication, whereas a negligence claimant must always establish the material loss (for example, loss of employment) that the general law regards as "damage".[44] In malicious falsehood, the claimant must either prove 'special damage' (i.e. some pecuniary loss) or bring the case within s.3 of the Defamation Act 1952 (which covers cases where the words are "calculated" to cause such damage).[45] The publication of true words can be actionable if they comprise private information. The law on damages for misuse of private information is not yet very highly developed; court awards have been relatively low when compared with those awarded for defamation.[46]

1.8 Malice, motive, intention and mistake. Fundamentally, and despite many qualifications, defamation is a tort of strict liability.[47] The law looks at the tendency and consequences of the publication rather than the motive or intention of the publisher. In the basic case, it is not relevant to liability that defamatory words were published in error or that the defamation was unintended. The defendant may have published the words in jest,[48] or he may have been actuated by the best of motives in publishing the words.[49] At common

---

[39] *Youssoupoff v Metro-Goldwyn-Mayer* (1934) 50 T.L.R. 581 CA at 587.
[40] *Parmiter v Coupland* (1840) 6 M.&W. 105 at 108, per Parke B.
[41] *Ainsworth v Burden* [2005] NSWCA 174 at [88] per Hunt A.J.A. See also, *John Fairfax Publications Pty Ltd v Gacic* [2007] HCA 28; 235 A.L.R. 402 at [13]; *Adams v Guardian Newspapers Ltd* [2003] ScotCS 131 at [5].
[42] See Ch.21, below.
[43] See Ch.23, below.
[44] See para.23.11, below.
[45] See para.21.13, below.
[46] Ch.9, below.
[47] Malicious falsehood is an entirely different matter: there, as the name implies, malice is a necessary part of the claimant's case.
[48] See para.3.36, below.
[49] *Cook v Ward* (1830) 6 Bing. 409; *R. v Hicklin* (1868) L.R. 3 Q.B. 360; *Bowen v Hall* (1881) 6 Q.B.D. 333 at 343, per Lord Coleridge C.J.

law, the defendant is liable even though he did not intend to refer to the claimant,[50] or to any living person,[51] or had no reason to know that the words were defamatory of the claimant.[52] It is irrelevant (except on an occasion of privilege) that he believed, or even reasonably believed, that the statement was true:

> "A man in good faith may publish a libel believing it to be true, and it may be found by the jury that he acted in good faith, believing it to be true, and reasonably believing it to be true, but that in fact the statement was false. Under those circumstances he has no defence to the action, however excellent his intention."[53]

That said, the 'offer of amends' procedure introduced under the Defamation Act 1996—while not a defence to liability—provides a potential shortcut to a resolution. If the defendant makes an offer of amends that is refused, he has a defence to the action unless it is shown that he had reason to believe that the words referred to the claimant and were false and defamatory of him.[54]

The common law does recognise that it would be unjust to impose strict liability on every person who has communicated the words complained of. In some relatively blameless situations, a person will only be held to have published the words at all if he has been negligent.[55] Under the Defamation Act 2013, it will become impossible to bring an action in defamation against any person other than the author, editor or publisher of the statement complained of unless the court is satisfied that it is not reasonably practicable for an action to be brought against one of those primarily responsible persons.[56]

The publisher's motive is not relevant, and—outside of occasions of privilege—malice will not transform an otherwise legitimate publication into something actionable. Malice in its popular sense signifies spite or ill-will. In the law of defamation, it is often rather broader. A person may act maliciously, for example, if he publishes a statement for an improper purpose rather than

---

[50] *Hulton v Jones* [1909] 2 K.B. 444; [1910] A.C. 20 HL. See para.7.5, below.

[51] E.g. ibid.; *Corrigan v Bobbs-Merrill*, 228 N.Y. 58 (1920).

[52] See para.3.15, below.

[53] *Campbell v Spottiswoode* (1863) 3 B. & S. 769 at 781 per Blackburn J. In *Hodgkinson v Economic Mutual Insurance Co.* (2003) 68 O.R. (3d) 587, the question of intention was considered in the context of an exclusion for any "intentional ... act" in a liability insurance policy. See also *Blanchard v Halifax Insurance Co.* (1996) 184 N.B.R. (2d) 271; *Wilkinson v Security National Insurance Co.* (1999), 81 Alta. L.R. (3d) 149.

[54] See paras 19.1 and 29.39, below. The offer of amends must include an offer to pay compensation to be assessed by a judge.

[55] For instance, where a person has taken only a subordinate part in disseminating a libel as a mere distributor, or has addressed defamatory matter to the person defamed which has come to the notice of a third party, or has in some other way unintentionally published the words, e.g. by dropping a letter in the street—see Ch.6, below. Under the Defamation Act 1996, it is a defence for a person who is not the author, editor or publisher (in the commercial sense) to show that he has taken all reasonable care. There is also a common law defence for the innocent disseminator, albeit that this is somewhat narrower in range.

[56] S.10. See para.6.45, below.

that for which the law permits publication.[57] Malice does become relevant to liability if the defendant contends that the words were published on an occasion of qualified privilege. Then it is incumbent upon the claimant to prove malice (sometimes known as "express malice") in order to rebut the defence. Malice was submerged, if not rendered obsolete, in the development of the *Reynolds* privilege, but it may now emerge as a factor relevant to the new statutory defence of publication on a matter of public interest.[58] Of course, the presence or absence of malice may have a great effect upon the quantum of damages even where it is irrelevant on liability. 'Malice' is also relevant to the defence of honest comment, but in that context the word has a different sense, for it is only established by showing that the opinion expressed was not genuinely held by the defendant.[59]

1.9 Defences. A range of defences is available to defamation defendants. These include justification (truth), honest comment (honest opinion), absolute privilege, qualified privilege, and others. With one exception relating to spent criminal convictions,[60] truth is a complete defence to an action for defamation in English law, even if the publication is made with a malicious desire to injure the claimant.[61] The starting point of the law is that the words complained of are presumed to be false, and it is up to the defendant to rebut that by proving the truth of the defamation[62] or by establishing, in mitigation of damages, that the claimant has a general bad reputation.[63]

The defence of honest comment (or honest opinion as it will be renamed under the Defamation Act 2013) allows a person who comments on a matter of public interest to escape liability for defamatory words, however forceful, unless the claimant can show that those words do not represent his opinion. The defence can extend to inferences of fact from other facts, but it does not extend to "pure" statements of fact which must be justified or protected by privilege.

---

[57] The allegation of malice in the statement of case, though once conventional pleading (and was still so described in *Buchanan v Jennings* [2002] 3 N.Z.L.R. 145 NZCA at [128]), is now surplusage. Old dicta to the effect that malice "is the gist of an action for defamation" no longer represent the law. Nor is it very helpful to say that the law presumes malice from the making of a defamatory statement (see Lord Finlay L.C. in *Adam v Ward* [1917] A.C. 309 at 318; *Shaw v Morgan* (1888) 15 R. 865 at 870), or to speak of "malice in law" which is conclusively established by inference of law from the defamatory character of the publication (*Harris v Arnott (No.2)* (1890) 26 L.R. Ir. 55 at 75).

[58] See para.15.21, below.

[59] Hence the proposition that defamation fundamentally involves strict liability is probably more true in juristic theory than in practice, given the scope of these defences.

[60] See Ch.18, below.

[61] See Ch.11, below.

[62] See para.11.4, below.

[63] See para.27.29, below. The basic rule is that evidence of specific acts, falling short of proving substantial truth of the charge made, is not admissible in mitigation. However, nowadays this is very substantially qualified by the admission of facts going to directly relevant background context: paras 11.21 and 33.43, below.

There are occasions of absolute privilege where the public interest in free speech is such that persons must have the right to speak free from any risk of an action against them for what they say, regardless of the injury to the reputation of others.[64] In order to ensure this freedom, the defence applies even to vindictive statements made with full knowledge of their falsity. Examples of matters covered by absolute privilege are statements made in parliamentary or judicial proceedings.

Much more extensive is the defence of qualified privilege. If a defamatory statement is made on an occasion of qualified privilege, the defendant is protected unless the claimant is able to show that he was actuated by malice (that is to say, that the defendant has abused the occasion).[65] The categories of qualified privilege at common law are not closed, but they can be broadly grouped under the following heads: (a) cases where the statement is made in performance of a duty (which need not be a legally enforceable duty), and (b) cases where the defendant has an interest in the matter which is the subject of the communication. In both cases, the recipient of the communication must have a corresponding interest or duty in receiving it. The requirement of a corresponding interest meant that publications in the mass media were for a long time generally thought to lie outside the scope of qualified privilege at common law. In addition, a wide range of reports of specific matters which are of legitimate public concern have long been given the protection of qualified privilege by statute.[66] In some cases, the privilege is granted "subject to explanation or contradiction" such that the defence is available only if the subject of the statement has been given, upon request, the opportunity to publish a reasonable statement in response. In *Reynolds v Times Newspapers Ltd*, the House of Lords considerably extended qualified privilege for publications on matters of public interest.[67] Malice in the traditional sense is not relevant in these cases. Rather, the primary question is whether the defendant has complied with the standards of "responsible journalism".

Certain other defences of general application in tort (such as consent and limitation) are applicable to defamation. There is also a more or less obsolete defence of apology under the Libel Act 1843.[68]

Trial and remedies. Defamation actions are one of the few categories of   **1.10** civil claim that are still tried with a jury.[69] The starting point is that each side has a right to trial by jury, unless the trial would require prolonged examination of documents or accounts which cannot conveniently be made with a jury.

---

[64] See Ch.13, below.
[65] See Ch.17, below.
[66] See Ch.16, below.
[67] See para.15.2, below. The defence is prospectively abolished and replaced by a defence of publication on a matter of public interest: Defamation Act 2013, s.4. See Ch.15, below.
[68] See paras 19.7–19.9, below.
[69] But not for much longer: the presumption in favour of jury trial (s.69(1), Senior Courts Act 1981) is prospectively repealed by Defamation Act 2013, s.11.

In fact, few cases are now tried in this way. In particular, *Reynolds* privilege cases have proven difficult to manage in jury trials.[70] Where there is a trial by jury, the issues of the meaning of the words, whether they were defamatory, whether they were true and whether, if the defences of qualified privilege or honest comment are raised, the defendant was actuated by malice are for the jury.[71] It is for the judge to rule, first, whether the words are capable of bearing the meanings contended for and of being defamatory, and whether the occasion or matter were such as to be capable of attracting privilege or honest comment.[72]

Under the Defamation Act 1996, moreover, the court may dispose of a claim summarily in the defendant's favour if it has no realistic prospect of success; or in the claimant's favour if there is no defence which has a realistic prospect of success.[73] Damages under the summary procedure are not to exceed £10,000, but the court may in addition make a declaration of falsity, an order that the defendant publish a suitable correction and apology, and an order restraining future publication.

As in the case of other torts, the primary remedy for defamation is an action for damages.[74] In the case of libel or of slander actionable per se, damages are "at large"; the jury is entitled to award substantial damages for injury to reputation even though the claimant is unable to prove any financial loss or even distress. Damages act as a vindication, rather than merely as compensation in the ordinary sense.[75] They also serve as a "necessary and effective deterrent".[76] In addition to such general damages, exemplary damages may be awarded where the defendant has committed the wrong intentionally or recklessly and has calculated that the profit from the publication may exceed the compensatory damages payable to the claimant. Damages must not be awarded at a level which goes beyond what is necessary for the legitimate

---

[70] See *Jameel v Wall Street Journal Europe SPRL (No.3)* [2005] EWCA Civ 74; [2005] Q.B. 904 at [70] (on appeal [2006] UKHL 44; [2007] 1 A.C. 359); *Prince Radu of Hohenzollern v Houston* [2007] EWHC 2328 (QB). Sometimes a trial by judge alone takes place in stages: see, e.g. *Charman v Orion Publishing Group Ltd* [2005] EWHC 2187 (QB) and [2006] EWHC 1756 (QB); [2007] 1 All E.R. 622 (on appeal [2007] EWCA Civ 972; [2008] 1 All E.R. 750).

[71] But in the case of the special category of privilege created by *Reynolds v Times Newspapers Ltd* it is for the judge to rule whether the defendant complied with the "standards of responsible journalism" and the role of the jury will be confined to determining any disputed issues of primary fact.

[72] Between 1995 and 2005 the law of New South Wales was a curious hybrid under which the meaning of words and their defamatory character were for the jury but all other issues of fact and law were for the judge (see *Tucker v Echo Publications Pty Ltd* [2003] N.S.W.S.C. 554). But s.22 of the Defamation Act 2005 (NSW) restored the ultimate decision on defences to the jury. Other state legislation is now in the same terms but there is no jury in South Australia, the Northern Territory or the ACT.

[73] Ss.8–10. See Ch.30, below. The latter power may be exercised without the consent of the claimant if summary relief will adequately compensate him.

[74] *John v MGN Ltd* [1997] Q.B. 586 CA.

[75] *Gleaner Co. Ltd v Abrahams* [2003] UKPC 55; [2004] 1 A.C. 628 at [55]. Hence where a declaration of falsity is made under the summary procedure above, the damages may be lower than they would be if awarded by a jury on the same facts.

[76] Ibid. at [53].

protection of reputation and which might stifle the free expression of opinion. In this regard, the level of damages for personal injuries is a relevant factor and, while it is not possible to equiparate injury to the body and injury to reputation, an award which is manifestly excessive (or, in the case of exemplary damages, an award which goes beyond what is necessary to teach the defendant that tort does not pay) will be set aside by the Court of Appeal, which has power to fix damages itself.[77] Even with these restrictions, damages seem to be substantially higher than in European countries,[78] to some extent perhaps because of the larger role of the criminal law elsewhere and the view that by its nature a court-ordered retraction provides a remedy.[79]

While an interim injunction may be granted in respect of defamation, the practice differs from that applicable to most other torts. Not only must there be strong prima facie evidence that the statement is defamatory and untrue, but it will be refused if the defendant proposes to plead justification or privilege or honest comment.[80] In the nature of things, the law is more liberal in granting an interim injunction where the action is one for misuse of private information, for while a substantial award of damages may act as a vindication in respect of untrue statements, it cannot restore secrecy to what has been made public.[81]

SECTION 3. DEFAMATION AND THE RIGHTS CONTEXT

Introduction: the rights context. The task facing legislators and judges   **1.11**
in the design and implementation of defamation law involves reaching an appropriate accommodation between individual rights and social interests in both freedom of expression and reputation.[82] Under s.3(1) of the Human Rights Act 1998, so far as it is possible to do so, legislation must be read and given effect in a way which is compatible with the Convention rights. As public authorities, the courts must themselves not "act in a way which is incompatible with a Convention right".[83] The result is that defamation law, whether based on statute or the common law, must be understood in a rights-compliant manner. Clearly, this involves assigning a value to art.10 and the

---

[77] See para.9.9, below.

[78] Thus a Dutch court in 1993 awarded about EUR 55,000 against a media organ (on facts which would probably have led to exemplary damages here) for a story that a city councillor had taken bribes; and in 1990 an award of about EUR 22,000 was made to a film director who was accused in a newspaper of having robbed and killed a Jewish refugee in the Second World War: Wissink and Van Boom in Rogers (ed.) *Damages for Non-Pecuniary Loss in a Comparative Perspective* (New York: Springer, 2001), at 170.

[79] See, e.g. with reference to German law, Magnus and Fedtke, ibid. at 125.

[80] See para.25.2, below.

[81] See para.25.33, below.

[82] *Panday v Gordon* [2005] UKPC 36; [2006] 1 A.C. 427 at [12]–[14]. Access to justice is also key, both for defendants and claimants. Indeed, it may be in this respect that the English libel regime can be considered to have been—and to remain—most inadequate.

[83] S.6(1). Courts and tribunals are public authorities by virtue of s.6(3).

importance of free expression in the development and interpretation of the law.[84] It also involves acknowledging the right to reputation that is protected by art.8. In many ways, the move to a rights-based jurisprudence merely emulates values that were already present in the common law. At the very least, however, defamation law is now to be understood and applied through a new lens.

1.12 Emphasis on freedom of expression. English libel law has long been criticised for a perceived failure properly to reflect the importance of freedom of expression.[85] Significant revisions have been made to law and practice in

---

[84] Article 10(1) of the European Convention on Human Rights guarantees the right to freedom of expression, which includes "freedom to hold opinions and to receive and impart information and ideas without interference by public authority". Under art.10(2), however, the exercise of these freedoms "may be subject to such formalities, conditions, restrictions or penalties as are prescribed by law and are necessary in a democratic society, in the interests of", inter alia, "the protection of the reputation or rights of others" or "for preventing the disclosure of information received in confidence".

It has been said that:

"freedom of expression is, of course, intrinsically important: it is valued for its own sake. But it is well recognised that it is also instrumentally important. It serves a number of broad objectives. First, it promotes the self-fulfilment of individuals in society. Secondly, in the famous words of Holmes J. (echoing John Stuart Mill), 'the best test of truth is the power of the thought to get itself accepted in the competition of the market': *Abrams v United States* (1919) 250 U.S., 616, 630, per Holmes J. (dissenting). Thirdly, freedom of speech is the lifeblood of democracy. The free flow of information and ideas informs political debate. It is a safety valve: people are more ready to accept decisions that go against them if they can in principle seek to influence them. It acts as a brake on the abuse of power by public officials. It facilitates the exposure of errors in the governance and administration of justice of the country."

—see *R. v Secretary of State for the Home Department Ex p Simms* [2000] 2 A.C. 115 HL at 126 per Lord Steyn.

In *Reynolds v Times Newspapers Ltd* [2001] 1 A.C. 127 at 200, Lord Nicholls commented that

"at a pragmatic level, freedom to disseminate and receive information on political matters is essential to the proper functioning of the system of parliamentary democracy cherished in this country. This freedom enables those who elect representatives to Parliament to make an informed choice, regarding individuals as well as policies, and those elected to make informed decisions . . . To be justified, any curtailment of freedom of expression must be convincingly established by a compelling countervailing consideration, and the means employed must be proportionate to the end sought to be achieved".

This value extends to the importance of a free press, which has been recognised often in the jurisprudence of the domestic (e.g. *Reynolds v Times Newspapers Ltd* [2001] 2 A.C. 127 HL at 200 per Lord Nicholls) and the Strasbourg court (e.g. *Castells v Spain* (1992) 14 EHRR 445 at [43]).

[85] By the late 1980s, damages awards had become exorbitant (e.g. *Lord Aldington v Count Tolstoy* (1989) *Guardian*, December 1 (£1.5m awarded in respect of an allegation that the claimant was a war criminal); *Stark v Mirror Group Newspapers* (1988) *Times*, November 4 (£300,000 awarded to an actress for an imputation that she retained a 'lingering love' for her former boyfriend and had secret meetings with him after marrying someone else); *Archer v Express Newspapers* (1987) *The Times*, July 25 (£500,000 for an allegation that the claimant had paid a prostitute for sex and subsequently lied about it)), no 'public interest defence' existed, and strict liability was the invariable rule.

the area over the past two decades in the hope of addressing this concern.[86] In recent times, political campaigning has been dedicated towards asserting that problems persist still.[87] Given the egregious restriction that it once imposed on freedom of speech, it is perhaps unsurprising that so much modern thinking and action regarding libel law has emphasised the need to accord a higher value to expression interests. The 'constitutionalisation' of libel law has been viewed largely through the prism of art.10 ECHR alone.

Relative neglect of reputation. One consequence of this orientation has been that the need also to defend reputation has been subordinated in political debate, and—albeit to a lesser extent—in judicial decision-making. In the period before, and for some years after, the passing of the Human Rights Act 1998, the approach of courts to the need to balance expression and reputation interests also focused in large measure on the question of whether existing rules of law were compliant with art.10.[88] The importance of reputation was not ignored,[89] but freedom of expression was regarded as the 'starting point'.   **1.13**

---

[86] The rebalancing of the law by reference to art.10 began well before the passage of the 1998 Act: e.g. *Derbyshire CC v Times Newspapers* [1993] A.C. 534 at 551 per Lord Keith; *Goldsmith v Bhoyrul* [1998] Q.B. 459 at 462 per Buckley J.; *Rantzen v Mirror Group Newspapers* [1994] Q.B. 670 at 691. The judgment most closely associated with the 'constitutionalisation' of libel law is that of the House of Lords in *Reynolds v Times Newspapers Ltd* [2001] 2 A.C. 127 at 200 per Lord Nicholls, at 207–208 per Lord Steyn, and at 223 per Lord Cooke. Lord Steyn stated at 208:

"the starting point is now the right of freedom of expression, a right based on a constitutional or higher legal order foundation. Exceptions to freedom of expression must be justified as being necessary in a democracy. In other words, freedom of expression is the rule and regulation of speech is the exception requiring justification. The existence and width of any exception can only be justified if it is underpinned by a pressing social need. These are fundamental principles governing the balance to be struck between freedom of expression and defamation".

[87] A foundational document in the campaign for libel reform was Index on Censorship / English PEN, *Free Speech is Not For Sale* (2009).

[88] Important shifts in the law reflecting the dominant influence of art.10 included the development of the abuse of process jurisdiction (*Jameel v Dow Jones & Co. Ltd* [2005] EWCA Civ 75; [2005] Q.B. 946 in which the Court of Appeal indicated that it was appropriate to have regard to art.10 in deciding whether a claim should be allowed to proceed, and that such consideration could not be left to be addressed only at the stage when a defendant was serving a defence), the emergence of the defence of reportage (*Al Fagih v HH Saudi Research and Marketing (UK) Ltd* [2001] EWCA Civ 1634; [2002] E.M.L.R. 13 at [26]; see paras 15.15–15.18, below), the abandonment of the strict liability principle in so-called 'look-alike' cases (*O'Shea v MGN Ltd* [2001] E.M.L.R. 40 at [47], and the broadening of the honest comment defence (see Ch.12, below). Moreover, in cases where the courts have held that the existing law was Convention compliant, the special importance of freedom of expression has been specifically recognised: e.g. *Jameel v Wall Street Journal Europe Sprl* [2006] UKHL 44, [2007] 1 A.C. 359 (on right of companies to sue without pleading special damages); *Berezovsky v Forbes (No.2)* [2001] EWCA Civ 1251; [2001] E.M.L.R. 45 at [12] (proof of substantial truth; see Ch.11, below); *Loutchansky v Times Newspapers Ltd and Others (Nos 2–5)* [2001] EWCA Civ 1805; [2002] Q.B. 783 (multiple publication rule).

[89] E.g. in *Reynolds v Times Newspapers Ltd* [2001] 1 A.C. 127 at 201, Lord Nicholls commented that:

"once besmirched by an unfounded allegation in a national newspaper, a reputation can be damaged for ever, especially if there is no opportunity to vindicate one's reputation. When this happens, society as well as the individual is the loser. For it should not be supposed that protection of reputation is a matter of importance only to the affected individual and his family.

Reputation interests were considered only as a possible limitation on the right to freedom of expression where this could be demonstrated to be necessary in a democratic society.[90]

1.14 Recognition of the rights-value of reputation. In the light of more recent developments in European and English jurisprudence, this approach is no longer tenable. The Strasbourg and domestic courts have, since 2004, become progressively more pronounced in recognising that reputation falls to be protected under the art.8 right to respect for private life. They have recognised a Convention right to the protection of reputation.[91] Hence, to the extent that it was thought that freedom of expression would always be the more important right, this is no longer the case. Yet, while this jurisprudential innovation is now embedded at both the European and domestic levels, it is not clear that a coherent intellectual underpinning has been articulated by the courts. Notwithstanding the increasingly consistent message deriving from the case law on the coverage of reputation by art.8, a fundamental question is obviously begged. Reputation, by dint of being determined by aggregating the appraisals made of an individual by other people, is quintessentially public in nature. Different views have been expressed as to why protection is afforded reputation under art.8, relying variously on the public–private divide, the concept of human dignity, the contribution of reputation to psychological integrity, and the impact of libel on personal relationships. A second level question is whether art.8 is invoked by every instance of harm to reputation.[92] Interestingly, when delivering the unanimous decision of the Supreme Court in *Guardian News and Media Ltd*, Lord Rodger suggested that the protection of reputation still falls within Article 8 even where the libel in question is

---

Protection of reputation is conducive to the public good. It is in the public interest that the reputation of public figures should not be debased falsely. In the political field, in order to make an informed choice, the electorate needs to be able to identify the good as well as the bad. Consistently with these considerations, human rights conventions recognise that freedom of expression is not an absolute right. Its exercise may be subject to such restrictions as are prescribed by law and are necessary in a democratic society for the protection of the reputations of others".

[90] Article 10(2) ECHR provides for the subjection of the art.10(1) right to such formalities, conditions, restrictions or penalties as are prescribed by law and are necessary in a democratic society, *inter alia*, for the protection of the reputation or the rights of others.

[91] See, for example, the following Strasbourg decisions: *Chauvy v France* (2005) 40 EHRR 610, at [70]; *Radio France v France* (2005) 40 EHRR 29, at [31]; *Cumpănă and Mazăre v Romania* (2005) 41 EHRR 200, at [91]; *White v Sweden* (2008) 46 EHRR 3; *Lindon, Otchakovsky-Laurens and July v France* (2008) EHRR 35. For English cases, see: *Re Guardian News and Media Ltd* [2010] UKSC 1; [2010] 2 A.C. 697; *Re Attorney-General's Reference No.3 of 1999* [2009] UKHL 34; [2010] 1 A.C. 145; *Clift v Slough Borough Council* [2009] EWHC 1550 (QB); [2009] 4 All E.R. 756; *Flood v Times Newspapers* [2009] EWHC 2375; [2010] E.M.L.R. 8; *Brady v Norman* [2010] EWHC 1215; *Ronaldo v Telegraph Media Group Ltd* [2010] EWHC 2710.

[92] For a discussion of these themes, see Mullis and Scott, "The Swing of the Pendulum: Reputation, Expression and the Recentering of English Libel Law" (2012) NILQ 63(1), 27–58.

deemed insufficiently serious to bear on the claimant's psychological integrity.[93] This would suggest that art.8 will be relevant in almost every case, and may extend the coverage of art.8 too far.[94]

Ramifications: a new methodology. The recognition of the art.8 dimension to reputation is potentially of real significance. Once Article 8 protection for reputation is allowed, the traditional approach to the assessment of an alleged breach of art.10—the presumed priority of freedom of expression over the enunciated social interests, intervention in the pursuit of which must be clearly demonstrated to be necessary by the state authorities—must transmute into a balancing exercise between competing Convention rights. At the level of international law, State parties will henceforth be able to offer rights-based counterpoint where applicants challenged restrictions imposed by libel law on freedom of speech. In addition, because art.8 imposes positive obligations on State parties to secure the substance of the right to its citizens, disgruntled libel claimants will be able to apply to the Strasbourg court to contest the perceived failure of domestic laws to ensure respect for the right to reputation.

    At the domestic level, the fact that the state is under a positive obligation to protect both freedom of expression and reputation requires courts to weigh the competing interests of the claimants under art.8 and the defendants under art.10. They must engage in a careful balancing of the two rights with neither having a presumptive precedence over the other. The days when art.10 could

1.15

---

[93] [2010] UKSC 1; [2010] 2 A.C. 697 at [37]–[42].

[94] It is open to question whether this explanation as to why Article 8 should extend to cover reputation is sustainable or appropriate. Most importantly, it is based upon a misreading of precedent. Despite Lord Rodger's view to the contrary, the reading of *Karako v Hungary* (2011) 52 EHRR 36 presented in *Guardian News and Media Ltd*, ibid., is plainly at odds with the European judgment. His Lordship suggested that *Karako* involved a factual circumstance in which the case for applying Article 8 based on psychological integrity had not been made out. Yet, he considered that the Strasbourg Court had proceeded to balance Articles 8 and 10, on the assumption that Article 8 was engaged on the other basis that he proposed involving the estimation of the claimant in the minds of others. He suggested that a number of paragraphs of the Strasbourg judgment would otherwise not make sense. The problem with this analysis is twofold. First, it appears to run contrary to the clear dicta of the Court to the effect that Article 8 is not concerned with the external evaluation of the subject of a defamatory statement. Secondly, had the Court in fact proceeded on the basis that some Article 8 right had been restricted by the publication then as Lord Rodger noted it would have been in the territory of balancing the Article 8 and 10 rights. Notably, the Court is traditionally cautious in this scenario, tending in all but the most unusual of circumstances to respect assessments made by the domestic court in recognition of the 'margin of appreciation'. Lord Rodger appears to have been untroubled by the absence of any reference to this doctrine in the key paragraphs (cf. the extensive reference to the doctrine in *Petrenco v Moldova* [2011] E.M.L.R. 5 at [54]–[56]). Had the Strasbourg Court in fact been undertaking the balancing exercise that Lord Rodger suggested, it would have been highly irregular for there to have been no such mention. In the paragraphs highlighted by Lord Rodger, the Strasbourg Court in fact undertook only a fleeting analysis under Article 10(2); it did not offer any balancing of Articles 8 and 10. See further, Mullis and Scott, "The Swing of the Pendulum: Reputation, Expression and the Recentering of English Libel Law" (2012) NILQ, 63(1), 27–58.

be considered a trump card are over.[95] The new requirement has begun to have an effect both on the way in which English judges approach their task in defamation cases and in the shape of the substantive law. This will almost certainly not lead to any resiling from the decisions reached in the 1990s and early 2000s, but it does entail that libel laws cannot be designed nor implemented in a manner that privileges freedom of speech over other important interests. While Lord Nicholls spoke in *Reynolds* of the appropriate starting point being freedom of expression and the need for the common law to be developed and applied in a manner consistent with art.10,[96] courts now articulate the need to find a balance between privacy and expression rights. In all cases, societal interests in the protection of individuals' reputations will also be in play. This has prompted one experienced judge to comment that "what seems to be emerging clearly is that the 'new methodology' sanctioned by the House of Lords in 2004, both in *Campbell v MGN Ltd* and in *Re S (A Child)*, originally in the context of privacy ... is now finding its way inexorably into the application of our well known principles of defamation".[97] The same sense that the correct approach is the application of the 'ultimate balancing test' stated in *Re S (a child)* has been articulated in decisions of the High Court,[98] the Court of Appeal,[99] and the Supreme Court.[100] There is a real likelihood that the coming years will see significant questions asked of disparate aspects of the law of defamation as the implications of the new approach are worked through.[101]

SECTION 4. DEFAMATION AND THE LAW OF TORTS

1.16 Principle and precedent in defamation. Nothing so clearly illustrates the proposition that the common law of torts is a collection of torts deeply rooted in their historical origins than the law of defamation. The common law

---

[95] Often, the dictum of Lord Justice Hoffmann in *R. v Central Independent Television Plc* [1994] Fam 192 at 203 is cited in reflecting this erstwhile position. In fairness, however, the full dictum should be offered:
"it cannot be too strongly emphasised that outside the established exceptions [in Article 10(2)], or any new ones which Parliament may enact in accordance with its obligations under the Convention, there is no question of balancing freedom of speech against other interests. It is a trump card which always wins".
[96] *Reynolds v Times Newspapers* [2001] 2 A.C. 127, at 200.
[97] *Hunt v Times Newspapers Ltd* [2012] EWHC 1220 (QB) at [13]. See also, *Flood v Times Newspapers Ltd* [2009] EWHC 2375; [2010] E.M.L.R. 8 at [149] per Tugendhat J.
[98] *Flood v Times Newspapers* [2009] EWHC 2375; [2010] E.M.L.R. 8 at [141]–[142], and *Thornton v Telegraph Media Group* [2010] EWHC 1414; [2011] 1 W.L.R. 1985 at [25] per Tugendhat J.; *Brady v Norman* [2010] EWHC 1215 at [1] per Eady J.; *Ronaldo v Telegraph Media Group Ltd* [2010] EWHC 2710 at [31] per Sharp J.
[99] *Flood v Times Newspapers* [2010] EWCA Civ 804; [2011] 1 W.L.R. 153 at [21].
[100] *Re Guardian News and Media Ltd* [2010] UKSC 1; [2010] 2 A.C. 697.
[101] For some possible outcomes in this respect, see Mullis and Scott, "The Swing of the Pendulum: Reputation, Expression and the Recentering of English Libel Law" (2012) NILQ 63(1), 27–58.

of torts has no "general clause" of liability, though in the last 50 years the tort of negligence has become something which at least reflects that role. Negligence and defamation are, however, poles apart, even if there are factual situations where they overlap. So, there is no general requirement of fault (negligence or otherwise) in defamation.[102] The picture is far more complicated: in some aspects the liability is strict, in other aspects the position is the opposite, so that intention or malice is required, and 'negligence' in the sense of failure to behave like a reasonable person is comparatively rarely in issue. There is no element of 'duty' (save at the unhelpfully general level that you have a duty not to defame others without just cause or excuse). Perhaps most important is the fact that the compensable damage which is at the heart of defamation, injury to reputation, is not even recognised as damage in the tort of negligence.

One may contrast French law. Although there are special provisions for defamation in the law of July 29, 1881, these are primarily criminal and give rise to civil liability only secondarily. What we would call defamation falls in principle, however, like any other sort of damage, within the scope of art.1382 of the *Code civil*, the general liability for damage caused by fault.[103] Indeed,

---

[102] See Mitchell, *The Making of the Modern Law of Defamation* (London: Hart Publishing, 2005) who argues that this state of affairs is really a mid-19th century development and that before that the "malice" which was presumed (or implied) from using defamatory words represented a general requirement of fault which the defendant could rebut by showing that he was not guilty of it. In the modern law, on the other hand, malice only plays a practical role in the specific defences of qualified privilege and honest comment and the burden of proof has been turned on its head so that malice must be established by the claimant in order to defeat the defence which would otherwise arise because the words were spoken on a privileged occasion or were comment on a matter of public interest. Indeed, we now think of the implied malice arising from the publication as a mere obsolete pleader's artifice.

[103] However, this has been thrown into doubt by Cass. 1st Civ., September 27, 2005, D2006, note Hassler. The *Code civil* of Québec is in similar terms to that of France and there is no special provision for defamation, liability resting on the general article (1457) of the Code concerning injury to others by wrongful act. It has been said that it:

"can be seen from the leading cases how often the Quebec courts have, when dealing with defamation and verbal abuse, borrowed from common law concepts (good faith and justification, qualified privilege), from decisions of English or Canadian courts or from common law commentators, such as Odgers. Borrowing from the common law in this manner is totally unnecessary and unwarranted . . . and it has the effect of greatly complicating a subject that, when examined in light of the Civil Code and the general principles of civil law, has the merit of being relatively straightforward"

(Baudouin and Deslauriers, *La responsabilité civile*, 6th edn (2003), p.193). This sentiment was accepted by Le Bel J. in *Gilles E. Nérron Communication Marketing Inc. v Chambre des notaires du Québec* 2004 S.C.C. 53; 241 D.L.R. (4th) 577 at [56]. At [61]–[62] he said:

"In sum, the existence of a fault is the general and fundamental requirement in the law of defamation and fault is measured against professional journalistic standards. A journalist is not held to a standard of absolute perfection; he or she has an obligation [to behave reasonably]. On the one hand, if a journalist disseminates erroneous information, this will not be determinative of fault. On the other hand, a journalist will not necessarily be exonerated simply because the information he or she disseminated is true and in the public interest. If, for other reasons, the journalist has fallen below the standard of the reasonable journalist, it is still open to the courts to find fault. Viewed this way, civil liability for defamation continues to fit nicely within the general framework of art. 1457 C.C.Q. As such, the conduct of the reasonable journalist becomes the all-important guidepost. It is the tool which allows us to assess what

that has even been applied to invasion of privacy, though since 1979 that right has been more specifically recognised by art.9 of the *Code*. German law takes a similarly general approach. The basic, general tort provision of the *Bürger-liches Gezetsbuch* is art.823(1), under which compensation is due from a person who "intentionally or negligently injures life, body, health, freedom, ownership or any other right of another in a manner contrary to law". Since 1954, influenced by the guarantees of human dignity and the right to develop-ment of one's personality in the Constitution, a general "personality right" falls within the scope of "any other right" under art.823(1). Hence, instances of what we would classify as defamation,[104] or breach of confidence,[105] or privacy,[106] or (if we had such a concept) placing someone in a false light,[107] or passing off,[108] all potentially fall within the scope of this right, but so do things which we would be unlikely to think of as connected with the person-ality of the claimant, as where the right was relied on in connection with a hospital's negligent destruction of sperm samples taken from the claimant prior to surgery.[109]

In contrast, the common law has sharply distinguished between defamation and such other heads of liability.[110] Defamation is concerned with statements which are defamatory and untrue, and the core damage compensable is that to reputation (though this includes injury to feelings and consequential loss of a financial nature).[111] Malicious falsehood and negligence are concerned with statements that are untrue and damaging (but not necessarily defamatory), and made with the relevant degree of fault. Here though, it is financial loss rather than reputation which is mainly in issue on damages (though damages for injury to feelings can be awarded).[112] The law of misuse of private informa-tion has grown out of the older equitable wrong of breach of confidence. That was certainly concerned with the revelation of *true* facts (typically trade

---

conduct is reasonable within the context of art. 1457 C.C.Q. It is the ultimate standard against which fault is determined, and the framework through which other important considerations such as truth, falsity and the public interest are filtered."

[104] See, e.g. BGH, October 12, 1993, NJW 1994, 124 (depiction of company's policy as "swindle by misdescription"). Note, however, that under art.824 of the BGB more specific protection is given against false factual statements which endanger the credit or earning capacity of another, provided that the defendant knew or ought to have known that the statement was untrue. In the common law many statements affecting either interest may be defamatory; otherwise it will be a case of malicious falsehood or (subject to the question of duty of care) of negligence.

[105] See, e.g. BGH, April 2, 1957, BGHZ 24, 72 (disclosure of medical records; claim failed because of legitimate interest in detection of fraud).

[106] See, e.g. BGH, December 19, 1995, NJW 1996, 1128.

[107] See, e.g. BGH, May 25, 1954, NJW 1954, 1404.

[108] BGH, March 18, 1959, BGHZ 30, 7.

[109] BGH, November 9, 1993, NJW 1994, 127 (though the reasoning is also based on bodily integrity).

[110] Defamation has been described by Ipp J. in Australia as the "Galapagos Islands Division" of tort law: "Themes in the Law of Torts" (2007) 81 A.L.J. 609 at 615.

[111] Putting aside the quasi-exception of slander not actionable per se.

[112] See para.23.11, below.

secrets) impressed with a duty of confidence. In the nature of things, the law of misuse of private information may trump one fundamental principle of the law of defamation, namely that truth is an absolute defence[113] but it can hardly be the law that by the simple device of framing the claim on the basis of misuse of private information the claimant can sidestep this to the extent of recovering the same damages as in a defamation action. The firm stance of the law of defamation is that, even though in the ordinary use of language one's reputation (what others think of one) may be damaged just as much by the publication of truth as falsehood, one's protected reputation is not the one which one has but the one which one is entitled to. Hence, truth is a defence. It is so far unclear how far an action for misuse of private information lies where the matter published is untrue. If, for example, the claim is for an interim injunction, there would be a conflict with the established principle that one will not be awarded in a defamation case where the defendant proposes to put forward a serious plea of justification. The various statutory wrongs littered about this area (contravention of the data protection legislation, harassment and certain wrongs connected with copyright[114]) have no very clear unifying theme as to what it is they are seeking to protect, though in certain circumstances they all allow damages for "distress". Which is the better approach, a broad theme of protection of personality or a collection of ad hoc torts, is a matter of debate. It may be argued that the common law is more predictable (though this is somewhat weakened by the inevitable uncertainties thrown up by the current developing state of the law on the Human Rights Act 1998 and on misuse of private information),[115] but on the other hand that may produce a undue element of rigidity.

Whatever the truth, the differences between the two approaches are intimately bound up with history and general legal culture, including the tendency in one system to elevate theory and in the other to eschew it. What is undeniable, even by the standards of the common law, is that defamation is conceptually complex, with a multitude of "categories". The law of negligence, by contrast, has comparatively few concepts, even if some of them are notoriously difficult to apply, or even lacking in clear contours. The courts approach possible cases of defamation by asking whether there was publication, was it libel or slander, and if the latter did it fall within the various closed categories of exception to the need for special damage, was there a defamatory imputation, was it justified, did it attract privilege, whether absolute or qualified, common law or statutory, was it honest comment, or published innocently, and was a defence of honest comment or qualified privilege defeated by malice? The courts will also ask whether the defendant authorised

---

[113] Subject to the Rehabilitation of Offenders Act 1974: see Ch.18, below. Some Australian jurisdictions once added a further public interest requirement to the defence of truth but this has now gone.

[114] See Ch.23, below.

[115] The German Supreme Court admitted the ill-defined nature of the general personality right in BGH, April 2, 1957, BGHZ 24, 72. See Ch.22, below.

an actionable publication or was vicariously liable for it. Each publication will be examined along these lines, and there is limited room for approaches from general principle based on policy grounds not embodied in existing categories. Legislative intervention has made matters more, not less, complex: for example, some situations are governed by parallel heads of qualified privilege under the Defamation Act 1996 and the common law,[116] and the question whether the defendant can be ordered to publish a correction and apology is determined by whether an initial decision is taken to deal with the case under the summary procedure rather than by trial by jury.

Even if defamation is regarded as a rather self-contained tort,[117] rather than a coherent structure covering the whole ground of protection of reputation in the broad sense, the courts have sometimes shown themselves willing to allow restrictive rules of defamation to be outflanked by reference to other, overlapping heads of liability.[118] The point that the developing law of misuse of private information goes some way to negate the fundamental principle that truth is a defence to defamation has been made above. However, there are earlier examples. Thus, defamation was always excluded from the provision of legal aid, but where a plaintiff brought an action against a newspaper which had accused her of dishonesty she was allowed to proceed with an action based upon malicious falsehood,[119] which did then fall within the legal aid provisions.[120] Similarly, where a plaintiff claimed that he had lost employment

---

[116] It has been held in Australia that the various defences available to a defamation action under the common law are to be seen as a collection of matters which may be inconsistent one with another. Thus at common law there is a qualified privilege for a fair and accurate report of court proceedings; but a report which is not accurate might in certain circumstances shelter under the general qualified privilege based on duty and interest:

"The appellant's submissions appear to be founded on an assumption that the law of defamation has evolved through reference to a coherent legal policy which implicitly rejects the availability of two or more defences of privilege to a single defamatory imputation. Such an assumption in turn requires acceptance of the proposition that the plurality of common law defences of privilege available in respect of a defamatory imputation exist within a framework which requires each defence to be developed with constant reference to each other defence. Neither that somewhat paradoxical proposition, nor the assumption upon which it is founded, should be accepted":

Bashford v Information Australia (Newsletters) Pty Ltd [2004] HCA 5; 204 A.L.R. 193 at [124], per Gummow J.

[117] See Lord Wilberforce in *Cassell & Co. Ltd v Broome* [1972] A.C. 1027 HL at 1114, 1119, emphasising the distinctiveness of the tort.

[118] Compare the dissenting speech of Lord Keith in *Spring v Guardian Assurance Plc* [1995] 2 A.C. 296. In Australia there was some overlap between defamation and the statutory wrong under s.52 of the Trade Practices Act 1974 (C'th) of engaging in "conduct that is misleading or deceptive or . . . likely to mislead or deceive." However, by s.65A (inserted by the Statute Law (Miscellaneous Provisions) Act (No.2) 1984 (C'th)), s.52 does not apply to a publication by a person who carries on the business of providing information, other than the publication of matter in connection with the supply of goods or services or the publication of an advertisement. See *Australian Ocean Line Pty Ltd v West Australia Newspapers Ltd* (1985) 58 A.L.R. 549; *Switzerland Australia Health Fund Pty Ltd v Shaw* (1988) 81 A.L.R. 111, Fed Ct of Australia; *Bond v Barry* [2007] FCA 1484.

[119] *Joyce v Sengupta* [1993] 1 W.L.R. 337 CA. See para.21.3, below.

[120] Public funding is now also excluded for malicious falsehood claims.

as a result of an inaccurate reference in which he had been accused of dishonesty, the majority of the House of Lords held that notwithstanding that for the purposes of defamation a reference is protected by qualified privilege unless the giver can be shown to have been actuated by *malice*, the plaintiff was owed a duty of *care* in the preparation of the reference for the purposes of the law of negligence.[121] In both these cases the ultimate issue was the same as it would have been for the purposes of the law of libel, that is to say whether the allegation was true. The elements of the torts relied on, however, were different from defamation. For the purposes of libel, the plaintiff could succeed simply by showing that the statements were of a defamatory nature, and he was not required to prove any malice or negligence as part of his initial case,[122] nor to show that it was untrue, nor to show that he had suffered any quantifiable material damage. In contrast, in malicious falsehood the plaintiff would have to show that the statement was made with malice, that it was untrue, and—depending on the nature of the statement[123]—that it had caused material loss. In negligence, the claimant would in every case have to show that there was a duty of care, negligence amounting to a breach of that duty, and material loss.

It would be wrong, however, to conclude that the distinctiveness of defamation means that it travels entirely in a carriage of its own. It is part of the law of torts and therefore many general principles, particularly those of an "ancillary" nature, apply to it. Thus the treatment of consent is similar to that in the rest of the law,[124] as is that of contribution among tortfeasors,[125] release,[126] and res judicata.[127] Defamation cases are governed by no peculiar rule with regard to causation and remoteness of damage,[128] even if the terminology used in some of the cases might give the contrary impression. Furthermore, while some features of defamation law may not be found across the whole field of torts, they are not unique to defamation. Thus, libel is actionable per se and damages are "at large" so that substantial (but not extravagant) sums may be awarded by way of vindication of the claimant's good name and assuagement of his injured feelings, but the same (or very similar) principles apply also to torts based on trespass to the person. There may also be in this group of torts a common 'delictual' element, whereby even if the law is not imposing exemplary damages as such,[129] it is in effect imposing a penalty upon the

---

[121] *Spring v Guardian Assurance Plc* [1995] 2 A.C. 296. See para.23.1, below.
[122] Though once the defendant established an occasion of qualified privilege (as it could easily do in *Spring's* case) the plaintiff would have to show malice.
[123] Defamation Act 1952, s.3(1)—see para.21.13, below.
[124] See para.19.10, below.
[125] See paras 19.28 and 27.44, below.
[126] See para.19.27, below.
[127] See para.19.22, below.
[128] See para.6.36, below.
[129] As to exemplary damages, see para.9.25, below.

defendant as well as "compensating" the claimant.[130] This tends to be obscured (or alternatively regarded as anomalous) by an ahistorical tendency to see tort law as exclusively concerned with physical injury to persons or property in accidents with a limited sub-category of liability for "economic loss".

1.17 Motive and the law of defamation. The motive with which the defendant acts plays a more prominent role in defamation than in most other areas of the law of tort. It is true that even here we follow the general rule that malice or ill-will cannot *of itself* make conduct unlawful,[131] for there must in any case be the publication of an untrue statement tending to injure the claimant's reputation. There is a very large number of occasions, however, on which it is considered to be for the general welfare that people should say what they believe, whether as to matters of fact or as to opinion. In these cases, the protection granted to the defendant (the defences of qualified privilege and honest comment) is lost if it can be shown that he was actuated by "malice". Here again, however, there are some analogies to be found with other torts. Thus, an improper motive may cause an otherwise permissible act to be a nuisance,[132] and may make a combination into an actionable conspiracy even if there is no independently unlawful conduct.[133] Though the burden of proof is different, malicious prosecution has some similarity to the plea of qualified privilege: just as a person incurs liability, even though he publishes on a privileged occasion, if he is actuated by malice, so also a person who lays a criminal charge against another will be liable for malicious prosecution if he is aware that the charge is unfounded even though it might appear to be very well founded to an objective observer.[134] Though the terminology is wholly incompatible with defamation, there is also an analogy to privilege in the defence of 'justification' in the tort of inducing breach of contract,[135] albeit that it is not an exact one as the defence is narrower.[136]

1.18 Verbal torts and falsity. Though this is certainly not a recognised legal category, it may be helpful, in placing defamation in the structure of the law,

---

[130] See Lord Wilberforce in *Cassell & Co. Ltd v Broome* [1972] A.C. 1027 HL at 1114. It has been said that defamation is an assault on reputation analogous to a physical assault on the person: *Att-Gen v Newspaper Publishing* [1988] Ch. 333 CA at 371.

[131] *Bradford Corporation v Pickles* [1895] A.C. 587 HL; *Allen v Flood* [1898] A.C. 1 HL; *Clerk & Lindsell on Torts*, 19th edn (London: Sweet & Maxwell, 2006), para.1–50.

[132] *Christie v Davey* [1893] 1 Ch. 316.

[133] *Crofter Hand Woven Harris Tweed v Veitch* [1942] A.C. 435 HL.

[134] *Clerk and Lindsell on Torts*, 19th edn (London: Sweet & Maxwell, 2006), para.16–33.

[135] *Brimelow v Casson* [1924] 1 Ch. 302; *Clerk and Lindsell on Torts*, above, para.25–63.

[136] Thus there would be a sufficient community of interest between a trade union official and the members to support the defence of qualified privilege in respect of statements made about a wage claim; but (putting aside the protection granted by the trade disputes legislation) there is no justification for inducing breaches of contract in pursuit of the claim: *South Wales Miners Federation v Glamorgan Coal Co.* [1905] A.C. 239 HL. See also the possibility of "justification" in the public interest for misuse of private information: see para.22.15, below.

to compare it with other wrongs in which the agency of harm to the claimant is the defendant's use of words. In the "economic torts" (the various forms of interference with contract, intimidation, conspiracy and unlawful interference with trade or business), the central feature is an inducement or threat or some unlawful action directed at the victim (e.g. intimidation by D of X so as to cause harm to C). The statutory wrong of harassment is rather similar, though there is no requirement of a "threat" or independently unlawful conduct. In misuse of private information cases, there is a—generally true—statement about the claimant, such that what the claimant complains of is the unauthorised revelation of the information in question. In another group of torts (of which defamation is one), the central feature is a *false* statement, but in some of them there is no necessity that the statement should be about the claimant. So, if D induces C to buy shares by falsely representing the company's financial health there may be liability in deceit or for negligent[137] misstatement[138] if the requisite mental element can be established. But there are three torts which have as a common feature that the statement[139] must,[140] directly or indirectly, refer to the claimant, his business or the goods or services in which he deals: they are malicious falsehood, defamation and passing off. In passing off, however, the statement is also about the business, goods or services of the representor, and it has to be false in the connection it alleges with the business, goods or services of the claimant. In addition, the connection has to be such as to take advantage of the reputation attaching to the claimant's business, goods or services, and to suggest that the representor is entitled to that reputation.[141]

---

[137] Where the shares are bought by C from D it is more likely that the statutory liability under s.2(1) of the Misrepresentation Act 1967 will be relied on. But though sui generis and statutory, that liability is fundamentally tortious in nature.

[138] By this terminology it is not meant to suggest that "negligent misstatement" is a tort in its own right. It is, of course, an aspect of the tort of negligence and both statement cases and those where there has been failure to fulfil an undertaking relied on by the claimant have been described as falling under the broad "*Hedley Byrne* principle": see Lord Goff in *Henderson v Merrett Syndicates Ltd* [1995] 2 A.C. 145 at 180, and *Spring v Guardian Assurance Plc* [1995] 2 A.C. 296 at 318.

[139] For a case in which there was no statement about the plaintiff but the damage caused was to the plaintiff's reputation, see *Morrison v NBC*, 227 N.E.2d. 572 (1967) (defendants induced the innocent plaintiff to participate in a rigged television quiz show; the court, which thought there was deceit but the damage was not actionable under that tort, found for the plaintiff under a theory of "prima facie tort").

[140] The other torts *may*, of course, involve a reference to the claimant. So, there may be liability for negligence where D makes an untrue statement about C to X and this causes loss to C (*Spring v Guardian Assurance Plc* [1995] 2 A.C. 296); and a libel or malicious falsehood might be unlawful means for the purposes of the economic torts (*Gulf Oil (GB) Ltd v Page* [1987] Ch. 327 CA).

[141] This may also give rise to fine differences: thus, to suggest that the defendant's goods are the same as the claimant's goods is passing off, since it treats the claimant's reputation as attaching to the defendant's goods; to say that the defendant's goods are as good as or better than the claimant's goods is actionable only, if at all, as malicious falsehood since it does not seek to appropriate, but only to make use of, the claimant's reputation.

1.19 Verbal torts and parties. Deceit and most cases of negligent misstatement involve a "two party" situation: D makes a false statement to C, causing C to act to his loss in reliance on it. Defamation, however, belongs to that class of torts in which the defendant incurs liability by reason of a "transaction" with a third party. It is the publication of the false statement by D to X which causes the harm to C (though this harm is usually presumed and does not need to be proved). So also, in the case of malicious falsehood and passing off, it is the action taken (or likely to be taken[142]) by X in response to the false statement to him which is the source of the injury to C. The same is generally true of the economic torts,[143] as where D intimidates X into taking action detrimental to C or induces X to break his contract with C, and of misuse of private information.

1.20 The mental element in verbal torts. The economic torts all require some form of intention to harm the claimant, though this may vary, according to the context, between a predominant purpose to injure ("disinterested malice"),[144] and the infliction of that harm as a means to a self-interested end.[145] Malicious falsehood of course requires "malice". Typically, this will be found where the defendant is aware of the falsity of the statement, but it seems it may also exist where—although he believes what he says to be true—the defendant's object is to injure the claimant (as opposed, say, to promoting his own business).[146] In passing off and defamation, on the other hand, an intention to injure or deceive is not relevant to liability.[147] Though subject to numerous qualifications at common law and by statute, the fundamental principle in defamation is that a defendant incurs liability even though he reasonably believes in the truth of the statement. In misuse of private information cases, the fundamental duty is to respect the claimant's reasonable expectation of privacy over the information (unless there is some lawful reason for making it public), and there is no need for any further intention to injure the claimant. In practice, the

---

[142] It is necessary to make this qualification in the context of passing off in particular, as the normal claim is for an injunction based upon the risk of confusion among buyers rather than for damages in respect of past loss.

[143] But not always. In some cases there can be liability for "two party" intimidation where D threatens C: *Godwin v Uzoigwe* [1993] Fam. Law 65 CA. Some cases under the Protection from Harassment Act 1997 might be intimidation of this sort.

[144] As in the case of conspiracy to injure: *Crofter Hand Woven Harris Tweed v Veitch* [1942] A.C. 435.

[145] *OBG Ltd v Allan* [2007] UKHL 21; [2008] 1 A.C. 1.

[146] See para.21.8, below.

[147] It now seems, after earlier doubts, that even in the case of innocent passing off there can be an award of substantial damages, though the same does not necessarily apply to an account of profits: *Gillette UK Ltd v Edenwest Ltd* [1994] R.P.C. 297. J.D. Heydon, *Economic Torts*, 2nd edn (London: Sweet & Maxwell, 1978), p.85, suggests that the distinction between malicious falsehood and passing off in this respect is strange, since one is the destruction of business reputation, the other its theft. However, the availability of an action in passing off is subject to substantial limitations in respect of the proof of a relevant reputation and the type of misrepresentation. Nearly all cases of passing off are brought against competitors, but in fact the defendant in an action of malicious falsehood will also often be a competitor.

issue is likely to be the court's assessment of whether the information is such as to attract a reasonable expectation of privacy, rather than the mental element in the defendant.

Verbal torts and interests. The torts of deceit and negligent misstatement **1.21** and the economic torts primarily protect the interest of the claimant in the security of his contractual relationships with others. They are concerned with what is called, in the terminology of negligence law, "economic loss", though there may be rare cases in which damages are recovered under some of these heads for damage to property,[148] or personal injury,[149] or even matters like inconvenience and distress.[150] There is also some authority for an innominate tort, derived from the action on the case, involving liability for the wilful infliction of physical harm, which may be committed by making false statements,[151] though its present status is doubtful.[152] These torts are not focused on injury to reputation, and damages for such injury are not recoverable under them as such.[153] Nor does it assist to frame the claim as one for loss of "business reputation".[154] We must be clear, however, what injury to reputation means in this context. If there is provable and quantifiable injury to a business leading to loss of trade as a consequence of one of the above torts, such loss is recoverable.[155] It is, after all, recoverable for breach of contract in such cases. There are no damages in contract for loss of reputation "at large" as there are in libel cases, but if injury to reputation leads to loss of business that is a different matter. For example, if a supplier of component parts to a motor manufacturer delivers a consignment with a latent defect so that a large number of the manufacturer's cars break down, the manufacturer's "reputation" with motorists may be damaged and it may lose sales. In principle, that loss is recoverable subject to the rules of remoteness and mitigation, even though the case is utterly remote from one of defamation as the supplier has not "said" anything at all about the manufacturer. The distinction between this type of case and a claim for defamation is well put in *Foaminol Laboratories Ltd v British Artid Plastics Ltd*:

> "A claim for mere loss of reputation is the proper subject of an action for defamation, and cannot ordinarily be sustained by means of any other form of action ... However ... if any pecuniary loss is established, the mere fact that the pecuniary loss is brought about by the loss of reputation caused by a breach of contract is not

---

[148] E.g. *Burrows v Rhodes* [1899] 1 Q.B. 816 (deceit).
[149] Ibid.; *Clayton v Woodman & Sons* [1962] 1 Q.B. 537 (negligence).
[150] E.g. *Shelley v Paddock* [1980] Q.B. 348 CA (deceit).
[151] *Wilkinson v Downton* [1897] 2 Q.B. 57.
[152] See *Wainwright v Home Office* [2003] UKHL 53; [2004] A.C. 406, in particular the speech of Lord Hoffmann. Cf. *Austen v University of Wolverhampton* [2005] EWHC 1635 (QB).
[153] *Spring v Guardian Assurance Plc* [1995] 2 A.C. 296 HL (negligence); *Lonrho Plc v Fayed (No.5)* [1993] 1 W.L.R. 1489 CA (conspiracy).
[154] *Lonrho Plc v Fayed (No.5)*, ibid.
[155] See the different formulations in *Lonrho Plc v Fayed (No.5)*, ibid.

sufficient to preclude the plaintiffs from recovering in respect of that pecuniary loss".[156]

Such losses might, of course, be recoverable as special damage where there was an action for libel,[157] but:

"there can be no justification for artificially excising from the damages recoverable for breach of contract that part of the financial loss which might or might not be the subject of a successful claim for defamation ... Furthermore, the fact that the breach of contract injures the plaintiff's reputation in circumstances where no claim for defamation would lie is not, by itself, a reason for excluding from the damages recoverable for breach of contract compensation for financial loss which on ordinary principles would be recoverable."[158]

Loss of business goodwill is the prime concern of the torts of malicious falsehood and passing off, though in the case of malicious falsehood there has to be proof of special damage other than in cases falling within s.3 of the Defamation Act 1952.[159] Defamation, on the other hand, is primarily concerned with reputation and, while actual pecuniary damage which is not too remote is undoubtedly recoverable (and in the case of many slanders is a condition of a claim), in an action for defamation evidence of such loss is in fact rarely given. It is now held that an employer owes an implied duty not to act in a manner destructive of the relationship of trust and confidence between himself and his employees, so that it is a breach of the contract of employment to operate a dishonest and corrupt business. In principle, the employee may recover damages for his handicap in the labour market caused by the "stigma" of being associated with the business.[160] The claimant in such a case, however, may well face formidable difficulties in proving causation of loss,[161] whereas if the defendant had used words to the effect that the claimant was involved in running a dishonest business a jury might well award thousands of pounds damages without any proof of difficulty in the employment market. There

---

[156] [1941] 2 All E.R. 393 at 399, per Hallett J., cited by Lord Nicholls in *Mahmud v Bank of Credit and Commerce International SA* [1998] A.C. 20 HL at 40. See also *Spring v Guardian Assurance* [1995] 2 A.C. 296 at 334; *PT Royal Bali Leisure v Hutchinson & Co. Trust Co. Ltd* [2004] EWHC 1014 (Ch).

[157] The CA in *Wheeler v Somerfield* [1966] 2 Q.B. 94 said that while they would not rule out the recovery of damages for injury to health no such claim had theretofore succeeded. The question of recoverability of damages for psychiatric illness caused by defamation was left open in *Brown v Cole* [1999] 7 W.W.R. 703 BCCA. However, they would have been awarded in *Marsden v Amalgamated Television Services Pty Ltd* [2001] N.S.W.S.C. 510 had such loss been proved (on appeal [2002] N.S.W.S.C. 419). See also *Lloyds Bank v Rogers, The Times*, March 24, 1997 CA; *Sattin v Nationwide News* [1996] 2 V.R. 32 at 45; *Chu Siu Kuk Yuen, Jessie v Apple Daily Ltd* [2002] 1 H.K.L.R.D. 1.

[158] *Mahmud v Bank of Credit and Commerce International SA* [1998] A.C. 20 HL at 40. The same is true of an action for the tort of negligence: *Spring v Guardian Assurance Plc* [1995] 2 A.C. 296 HL. See para.23.3, below.

[159] See para.21.13, below.

[160] *Mahmud v Bank of Credit and Commerce International SA* [1998] A.C. 20 HL.

[161] *Bank of Credit and Commerce International SA v Ali (No.3)* [2002] EWCA Civ 82; [2002] I.C.R. 1258.

could be no better illustration of the nature of defamation damages, as opposed to those which depend upon proof of financial loss.

The line between "pure" loss of reputation damages and damages for loss arising from injury to the claimant's reputation in this sense may, however, sometimes be hard to draw. Indeed, the word "reputation" is sometimes used in a rather broad sense which does not accord exactly with that in defamation. Thus, it is well established that where someone engages an actor for a series of performances he owes him a duty not only to pay his fees, but also to give him the opportunity to appear before the public and for loss of that opportunity of "so enhancing or maintaining his reputation, he is . . . entitled to recover damages".[162] Such loss has been alternatively (and perhaps preferably) referred to as "loss of publicity".[163] Where a bank dishonours a customer's cheque substantial general damages for loss of reputation in the sense of financial standing may be recovered and this is no longer confined to traders.[164] Such a case may be extremely difficult to distinguish from general damages for libel: one reason why damages in defamation are at large is the fact that although some financial loss is a not unlikely consequence it will generally be quite impossible to assess it and the position may be similar in the case of the dishonoured cheque.

---

[162] *Withers v General Theatre Corp* [1933] 2 K.B. 536 CA at 554, per Greer L.J. Although this case decided that there was no liability for *damage* to an *existing* reputation, as opposed to loss of the opportunity to enhance reputation, the distinction is insupportable: *Mahmud v Bank of Credit and Commerce International SA*, above, at 41, 51.

[163] *Clayton v Oliver* [1930] A.C. 209 HL at 220, per Lord Buckmaster.

[164] *Kpohraror v Woolwich Building Society* [1996] 4 All E.R. 119 CA. The claimant was, however, in trade. The general damages were £5,500, even though the error was corrected quickly (the cheque was for £4,500) and the claim for special damages failed.

CHAPTER 2

DEFAMATORY IMPUTATIONS

SECTION 1. WHAT IS DEFAMATORY

The defamatory imputation. The gist of the torts of libel and slander is **2.1** the publication of matter (usually words) conveying a defamatory imputation. In determining whether words are defamatory there are two stages, first to decide what they mean, and then to decide whether that meaning is defamatory. Where there is trial by jury[1] these stages are in practice dealt with separately for the purposes of the judge's decision whether the case should be left to the jury, but at the end of the day they are compressed into a single question for the jury, whether the words are defamatory of the claimant. From a technical point of view "imputation" is to be preferred to "meaning" since extrinsic facts, whether or not they are generally known, may give rise to implications which go beyond the "meaning" of the words in their ordinary sense.[2]

---

[1] For the summary procedure without a jury, see Ch.30, below. S.11 of the Defamation Act 2013, which is not yet in force, abolishes the presumption in favour of trial by jury. Once it is in force, there will be no inhibition on judges determining whether the words complained of are defamatory of the claimant at an early stage in the proceedings. As such, the question of whether words are or are not capable of bearing a defamatory meaning is liable to become an academic one.

[2] See, e.g. the Rehabilitation of Offenders Act 1974, s.8(1). Between 1974 and 2005 in New South Wales "imputation" was more than a preferable variant of "meaning" because the plaintiff had a separate cause of action in respect of each imputation in a publication. However, under s.8 of the Defamation Act 2005 (NSW) a "person has a single cause of action for defamation in relation to the publication of defamatory matter about the person even if more than one defamatory imputation about the person is carried by the matter". Nevertheless, multiple, specific imputations still seem to characterise pleading: see, e.g. *Dobson v MacQuarie Radio Network Ltd* [2007] N.S.W.S.C. 718. The Uniform Civil Procedure Rules still require the plaintiff to specify each imputation upon which he places reliance: *Holmes v Fraser* [2008] N.S.W.S.C. 570 at [58]. For criticism of the former NSW system see Kirby J. in *John Fairfax Pty Ltd v Rivkin* [2003] HCA 50; 201 A.L.R. 77 at [83].

It is not every untrue statement about another person that gives rise to a claim. An untrue imputation is only actionable in English law if it is defamatory. At common law, an imputation will be treated as defamatory if:

(1) the words complained of fall within one, or more, of the several tests that have, at various times, been offered by the courts.[3] That is to say the imputation must be to the claimant's discredit[4]; or tend to lower him in the estimation of others[5]; or cause him to be shunned or avoided[6]; or expose him to hatred, contempt or ridicule.[7]

(2) Whatever definition of defamatory is adopted, "it must include a qualification or threshold of seriousness so as to exclude trivial claims".[8]

When the Defamation Act 2013 comes into force, the law of England and Wales will require the claimant to show that publication of the defamatory statement "has caused or is likely to cause serious harm to the reputation of the claimant".[9] Where the claimant is a "body that trades for profit", harm is not "serious harm" unless "it has caused or is likely to cause the body serious financial loss".[10] Whether the requirement to prove that publication has

---

[3] The difficulty of producing a comprehensive definition has often been remarked. Lord Atkin said in *Sim v Stretch* (1936) 52 T.L.R. 669 HL that "Judges and textbook writers alike have found difficulty in defining with precision the word 'defamatory'". See also Neill L.J. in *Berkoff v Burchill* [1996] 4 All E.R. 1008 CA at 1011. In the Report of the Select Committee of the House of Lords appointed in 1843 to consider the Law of Defamation and Libel Lord Lyndhurst L.C. said (p.11) that he "had never yet seen or been able himself to hit upon anything like a definition of libel which possessed the requisites of a logical definition," and Lord Campbell said (pp.4, 5) that he did not think that there could be any definition of a private libel more specific than "a writing tending to injure and degrade the character of the person who is the object of it". No definition of "what is defamatory" is provided in the current Australian uniform legislation but the Irish Defamation Act 2009 defines a defamatory statement in s.2 as "a statement that tends to injure a person's reputation in the eyes of reasonable members of society . . . ". See also McNamara, *Reputation and Defamation* (Oxford: Oxford University Press, 2007) at 1.

[4] This definition of a defamatory statement, "a false statement about a man to his discredit", was preferred by Scrutton L.J. in *Youssoupoff v Metro-Goldwyn-Mayer* (1934) 50 T.L.R. 581 at 584. For its origin see Cave J. in *Scott v Sampson* (1882) 8 Q.B.D. 491 at 503.

[5] See para.2.16, below.

[6] See paras 2.14–2.15, below.

[7] See paras 2.10–2.13, below.

[8] *Thornton v Telegraph Media Group Ltd* [2010] EWHC 1414 (QB); [2011] 1 W.L.R. 1985; [2010] E.M.L.R. 25 per Tugendhat J. at [89]. The Court of Appeal has not had to consider directly whether words are only defamatory at common law if they satisfy a test of seriousness. But in *Cammish v Hughes* [2012] EWCA Civ 1655 CA; [2013] E.M.L.R. 13 at [38], that court proceeded on the assumption that the claimant's complaint must surmount a threshold of seriousness. See also, *Cook v Telegraph Media Group* [2011] EWHC 1134 (QB) at [3]; *Daniels v British Broadcasting Corporation* [2010] EWHC 3057 (QB) per Sharp J. at [50]; *Dell'Olio v Associated Newspapers Ltd* [2011] EWHC 3472 (QB) per Tugendhat J. at [27]; *Church v MGN Ltd* [2012] EWHC 693 (QB); [2013] 1 W.L.R. 284 per Tugendhat J. at [12]; *McGrath v Dawkins* [2012] EWHC B3 (QB) per H.H.J. Moloney QC, at [520]; *Hamaizia v The Comr of Police for the Metropolis* [2013] EWHC 848 (QB) per Tugendhat J. at [13].

[9] Defamation Act 2013, s.1(1).

[10] Defamation Act 2013, s.1(2).

caused serious harm is in addition to, or substitution for, the requirement that
a qualification of seriousness be met is not entirely clear. The Explanatory
Notes to the Act state that s.1 is intended to build on the consideration given
by the courts in *Thornton v Telegraph Media Group*[11] and the *Jameel*[12] abuse
case law to the question of what is sufficient to establish that a statement is
defamatory. As s.1 and the existing case law are directed to the same question,
the better reading of the provision is that the current seriousness threshold is
replaced by a requirement for the claimant to prove that the harm caused to his
reputation was serious.[13]

   All the definitions offered by the courts present certain difficulties, which
are considered below, and in one respect or another they are each perhaps too
narrow to act as an exclusive test. For example, allegations that the claimant
has been raped, or has an infectious disease or is insane or insolvent have all
been held to be capable of being defamatory, but none of these would expose
the claimant to hatred, contempt or ridicule, nor can they all be discreditable
nor tend to lower him in people's estimation.[14] Possibly the closest to a
comprehensive definition is that adopted by the American Law Institute in the
Second Restatement of Torts[15]: "A statement is defamatory if it tends to harm
the reputation of another so as to lower him or her in the estimation of the
community or to deter third parties from associating or dealing with him or
her".[16] Although this has never been adopted by an English court, and one
must bear in mind that in many respects there are major differences between
American and English defamation law, nevertheless it would seem to provide
a workable test consistent with the case law. In any event, the definitions
which have been stated in the English cases should probably be regarded as

---

[11] [2010] EWHC 1414 (QB).

[12] *Jameel (Yousef) v Dow Jones & Co. Inc.* [2005] EWCA Civ 75; [2005] Q.B. 946 CA.

[13] This appears to have been the view of Tugendhat J. in *Euromoney Institutional Investor Plc v Aviation News Ltd* [2013] EWHC 1505 (QB) at [19].

[14] In the rape case, *Youssoupoff v Metro-Goldwyn-Mayer* (1934) 50 T.L.R. 581, Slesser L.J. thought it was to "shut one's eyes to realities" to hold that a woman's standing in society would not be harmed by an allegation that she had been raped. No doubt that is true, but the difficulty is that this is supposed to be based not on how real people behave but upon the notional views of the "right thinking member of society". It has been suggested that juries "are willing to accept this artificiality (which is insulting to them), no doubt because they see it as doing justice on the facts of the case" and that such cases would be better dealt with as a form of "false light" invasion of privacy: Richard Parkes QC, in Tugendhat and Christie, *The Law of Privacy and the Media* (Oxford: Oxford University Press, 2011), para.7.23. Since the modern law of "misuse of private information" does not appear to be confined to the publication of *true* facts that might be applicable to such a case. The difficulty is that it renders the untruth of the allegation irrelevant and while the claimant might legitimately object to the revelation that she *had* been raped, she might feel a good deal worse about a statement which was untrue.

[15] Para.559.

[16] For a collection of other American formulae, see 50 Am.Jur.2d, *Libel and Slander*, para.118. In the light of *Thornton v Telegraph Media Group Ltd* [2010] EWHC 1414 (QB); [2011] 1 W.L.R. 1985; [2010] E.M.L.R. 25 this definition would also have to be qualified by the addition of the word "seriously": "A statement is defamatory if it tends to harm [seriously] the reputation of another so as to lower him or her in the estimation of the community or to deter third parties from associating or dealing with him or her".

cumulative, so that words which fall within any of them are actionable.[17] They all have the common feature that they look to the likely effect of the words upon the view taken of the claimant by others. For this purpose some standard of opinion has to be set and it is that of "right-thinking persons generally". Words are not defamatory merely because their publication has a damaging effect on the claimant's reputation; there has to be a statement of fact or expression of opinion or imputation conveyed by them which will have this effect.[18] A true imputation may still be defamatory, although its truth may be a defence to an action brought on it[19]; conversely, untruth alone does not render an imputation defamatory even though it may cause damage to the claimant, as where a statement was made that a stud farm had closed because of a virus.[20]

2.2 The impact of the Human Rights Act 1998. As with other aspects of the claim for libel, the courts must view the question whether an imputation is defamatory in light of the rights under art.8 and art.10 of the ECHR. Several consequences flow from this. First, the need to avoid normal social banter, discourtesy or statements of trivial content and import ending up in litigation with the consequential risk of interference to the right to freedom of expression has led the courts to require that a threshold qualification of seriousness be met before words will be treated as defamatory.[21] Secondly, the court must decide on the facts of the case whether art.8 is engaged. Not every case where a person makes an untrue and reputation damaging statement about another person will engage art.8.[22] Thus, it is clear that for art.8 to be engaged the statement must be more than trivial and it should significantly impact a person's psychological integrity[23] or their relationship with others.[24] Where art.8 is not engaged, a court may still find a statement defamatory, as the protection of reputation is a ground for restricting the right to freedom of

---

[17] See, e.g. *Russell v Pressdram*, *The Times*, February 4, 1966, in which Havers J. referred to the first two.

[18] See para.2.18, below.

[19] See Ch.11. *National Roads and Motorists' Association Ltd v Snodgrass* [2002] N.S.W.S.C. 811, where the point was significant because of legislation exempting a company from circulating members' statements which were defamatory.

[20] *Dawson Bloodstock Agency v Mirror Newspapers* [1979] I N.S.W.L.R. 16; *George's Tavern Ltd v Fundy Broadcasting Co.* (1975) 10 N.B.R. (2d) 592. However, such a statement might be actionable as malicious falsehood. See Ch.21.

[21] *Thornton v Telegraph Media Group Ltd* [2010] EWHC 1414 (QB); [2011] 1 W.L.R. 1985; [2010] E.M.L.R. 25 at [89].

[22] See, e.g., *R. (Gillan) v Comr of Police for the Metropolis* [2006] UKHL 12 HL; [2006] 2 A.C. 307 at [28]; *Wood v Comr of Police for the Metropolis* [2009] EWCA Civ 414 CA; [2010] 1 W.L.R. 123 at [22]–[23]; *M v Secretary of State for Work and Pensions* [2006] UKHL 11, [2006] 2 A.C. 91 HL at [93]; *Crow v Johnson* [2012] EWHC 1982 (QB) at [16]; *Raab v Associated Newspapers Ltd* [2011] EWHC 3375 (QB) at [56].

[23] *Karako v Hungary* (2011) 52 EHRR 36.

[24] *In re Guardian News and Media Ltd* [2010] UKSC 1 SC; [2010] 2 A.C. 697; [2010] 2 W.L.R. 325 per Lord Rodger, at [42].

expression under art.10(2), but the absence of any art.8 right will inevitably weigh against such a decision.[25]

Thirdly, in any case where both art.8 and art.10 are engaged, the question whether an imputation is defamatory must be viewed in light of the rights under art.8 and art.10.[26] In this regard, the question whether the threshold of seriousness has been met requires the court to consider the respective interests and rights of the parties so that the threshold may be met more easily in cases where the imputation touches on a person's private or personal life than it may in regard to imputations that touch solely on a person's business or public life. Thus where, for instance, the imputation involves criticism of a politician in his public role, the importance attached by the courts to the value of political debate is likely to weigh heavily in determining whether the statement complained of is defamatory.[27] By way of contrast, the more personal or private the matter complained of, the more likely it will be that the threshold of seriousness will be met.

Business and personal defamation. The various "definitions" of what is defamatory were reviewed by Tugendhat J. in *Thornton v Telegraph Media Group Ltd.*[28] He suggested as a possible ordering of defamation cases the following: **2.3**

> "i) There are two main varieties of each of the torts of libel and slander: (A) personal defamation, where there are imputations as to the character or attributes of an individual and (B) business or professional defamation, where the imputation is as to an attribute of an individual, a corporation, a trade union, a charity, or similar body, and that imputation is as to the way the profession or business is conducted. These varieties are not mutually exclusive: the same words may carry both varieties of imputation. By contrast, if the imputation is as to the product of the business or profession, then it will be the tort of malicious falsehood, not defamation, to which the claimant must look for any remedy.
>
> ii) Personal defamation comes in a number of sub-varieties including: a) Imputations as to what is 'illegal, mischievous, or sinful' in Pollock CB's phrase . . . This would perhaps now be expressed as what is illegal, or unethical or immoral, or socially harmful, but will now cover imputations which are less serious than that . . . ; b) Imputations as to something which is not voluntary, or the result of the claimant's conscious act or choice, but rather a misfortune for which no direct moral responsibility can be placed upon the claimant (such as disease . . .); c) Imputations which ridicule the claimant . . .
>
> iii) Business or professional defamation also comes in a number of sub-varieties . . . : a) Imputations upon a person, firm or other body who provides goods or services that the goods or services are below a required standard in some respect which is likely to cause adverse consequences to the customer, patient or client. In these cases there may be only a limited role for the opinion or attitude of right-

---

[25] *Dell'Olio v Associated Newspapers Ltd* [2011] EWHC 3472 (QB) per Tugendhat J. at [16].

[26] *Dell'Olio v Associated Newspapers Ltd* [2011] EWHC 3472 (QB) per Tugendhat J. at [13].

[27] See, e.g. *Crow v Johnston* [2012] EWHC 1982 (QB).

[28] [2010] EWHC 1414 (QB); [2011] 1 W.L.R. 1985; [2010] E.M.L.R. 25 at [27]–[35].

thinking members of society, because the required standard will usually be one that is set by the professional body or a regulatory authority; b) Imputations upon a person, firm or body which may deter other people from providing any financial support that may be needed, or from accepting employment, or otherwise dealing with them. In these cases there may be more of a role for the opinion or attitude of right-thinking members of society.

[34] In addition to these varieties, there is a distinction between sub-varieties of business defamation in which: (a) The action is brought by an individual, where damage may include injury to feelings, and (b) The action is brought by a corporation, where damage cannot include injury to feelings."[29]

Tugendhat J. explained why a distinction should be drawn between business and personal defamation.[30] First, unlike the case of personal defamation, a claim for business defamation may succeed notwithstanding that the imputation complained of may not involve any adverse reflection upon the personal qualities of a claimant.[31] Where the words denigrate the claimant's business or professional capacity they may be defamatory even though they in no way reflect on the *character* of the claimant. It may be that those "community standards" of "right-thinking people" of which the jury is the ultimate guardian have less of a role in these cases and it has been suggested that the correct approach is to ask whether the tendency of the words is to convey to the reader that the claimant's fitness or competence falls short of what are generally necessary for the business or profession.[32] The second reason given

---

[29] Ibid. at [27]–[35].

[30] Ibid. at [33].

[31] *Drummond-Jackson v British Medical Association* [1970] 1 W.L.R. 688 CA at 698–9; *Derbyshire County Council v Times Newspapers Ltd* [1993] A.C. 534 HL per Lord Keith at 547.

[32] *Radio 2UE Sydney Pty Ltd v Chesterton* [2008] NSWCA 66 at [19]. It should be noted however that the High Court of Australia took a different view on this question in *Radio 2UE Sydney Pty Ltd v Chesterton* [2009] HCA 16. The joint judgment of French C.J. and Gummow, Kiefel and Bell JJ. is based upon the following propositions.

(1) The test for defamation in Australia is whether the words are likely to lead an ordinary reasonable person to think the less of the plaintiff; this is essentially the test stated by Lord Atkin in *Sim v Stretch*.

(2) This test does not necessarily imply the application of any judgment of a moral or ethical nature.

(3) "The concept of 'reputation' in the law of defamation comprehends all aspects of a person's standing in the community . . . In principle therefore the general test for defamation should apply to an imputation concerning any aspect of a person's reputation. A conclusion as to whether injury to reputation has occurred is the answer to the question posed by the general test, whether it be stated as whether a person's standing in the community, or the estimation in which people hold that person, has been lowered or simply whether the imputation is likely to cause people to think the less of a plaintiff. An imputation which defames a person in their professional or business reputation does not have a different effect. It will cause people to think the less of that person in that aspect of their reputation. For any imputation to be actionable, whether it reflects upon a person's character or their business or professional reputation, the test must be satisfied" (at [36]).

(4) It is not therefore correct to say that general community standards are irrelevant to imputations about a person's conduct in a business as opposed to imputations about "character". Moral or ethical standards about honesty or fidelity may of course be relevant to certain imputations about business conduct but this:

by the judge as to why business defamation cases require separate treatment is that in such cases the art.8 right to reputation is less likely to be engaged than in cases involving personal defamation:

> "There is a further reason why cases of business defamation require separate consideration, whether or not there is a separate tort of 'business defamation'. What is at stake in a defamation reflecting on a person's character is now likely to be recognised as engaging that person's rights under Art 8. On the other hand, if an alleged defamation engages only a person's professional attributes, then what is at stake is less likely to engage their rights under Art 8, but may engage only their commercial or property rights (which are Convention rights, if at all, under Art 1 of the First Protocol). See *Pfeifer v Austria* (2009) 48 EHRR 8 para 35 and *Karako v Hungary* 28 April 2009 No 39311/05, para 22–23."[33]

There is much in what the learned judge said in *Thornton*. Although neither party in the case advanced submissions on the issue, most cases of business defamation are unlikely to engage art.8. It has been accepted that corporations do not possess art.8 rights of this type[34] and consequently in domestic proceedings, such claimants are able to rely on art.10(2) arguments only. Moreover, they would be unable to challenge the features of a domestic libel

---

"does not suggest a true dichotomy as between imputations of that kind and those as to character, with different standards applying to each. Rather it confirms as practicable the general test as applying in all cases involving all aspects of reputation. In such cases the ordinary reasonable person may be expected to draw upon such community standards as may be relevant, in order to answer the question whether there has been injury to that reputation. In keeping with that test it may be said such standards are those by which a person's standing in the community, the esteem in which others hold them, is lowered. The focus upon moral or ethical standards, in discussions about standards of the community, no doubt reflects the fact that they are the standards most often identified as relevant in actions for defamation. There are obviously other standards, for example as to the behaviour expected of persons within the community, which may not involve a sense of wrongdoing. In some cases injury to reputation may appear so obvious that a standard, which may unconsciously be applied, is not identified. And in some cases such a conclusion may be possible without the need to identify a standard. It may be obvious that people will be thought the less of simply because of what is said about them. The imputations in *Gacic v John Fairfax* [[2006] NSWCA 175; (2006) 66 N.S.W.L.R. 675] were considered to fall within this latter category. Another example may be the attribution of authorship of a work of very inferior quality, which may be taken to affect an established author's high reputation, without more. Whether a social standard applies to an imputation of a person's lack of competence to carry out a profession or business may not be so clear, particularly where it is also conveyed that the person held themselves out as competent and for reward. It is not necessary to determine such questions; in each case the plaintiff will have been defamed because he or she has suffered a loss of reputation. The applicability of the general test towards that conclusion cannot be denied because a general community standard does not apply in a particular case. The test does not depend for its exercise upon the existence of standards." (at [46]–[48]).

[33] [2010] EWHC 1414 (QB); [2011] 1 W.L.R. 1985; [2010] E.M.L.R. 25 at [38].

[34] See, for example, Tugendhat J. in *Hays v Hartley* [2010] EWHC 1068 (QB): "Companies enjoy certain rights under art.8, and in some cases damage to reputation can be an interference with a person's rights under art.8. But that is not this case. It follows that the only Convention right engaged in these proceedings (which involved a claim brought by a corporate entity) is the right of the Defendant to freedom of expression under art.10." See also, Tugendhat J. in *Thornton v Telegraph Group* [2010] EWHC 1414 (QB); [2011] 1 W.L.R. 1985; [2010] E.M.L.R. 25 at [38].

regime before the Strasbourg court. Whether, however, it is possible to go further and suggest that cases of business defamation will never engage art.8 must be more doubtful. It is sometimes suggested that, like companies, any individual engaged in and criticised in respect of business, professional or public functions should be unable to claim any protection under art.8. To the extent that individuals can be conceived as merely economic actors such that reputational harm will be akin to property loss only, this is sensible. The "psychological integrity" explanation for drawing such reputational concerns within the rights umbrella, however, militates against any generic limitation of the scope of protection. To the extent that a person builds their sense of self-worth in part on an appreciation of their competence, success or importance in an employment, professional or business context, the perception that one has lost the esteem of others in that context can be devastating.[35] The existing jurisprudence on art.8 has adopted a similar line, indicating that harm to economic or professional reputations may indeed fall within the ambit of the Convention right. In *Niemietz v Germany*,[36] for example, the Strasbourg Court asserted that:

> "there appears . . . to be no reason of principle why [the] understanding of the notion of 'private life' should be taken to exclude activities of a professional or business nature since it is, after all, in the course of their working lives that the majority of people have a significant, if not the greatest, opportunity of developing relationships with the outside world . . . it is not always possible to distinguish clearly which of an individual's activities form part of his professional or business life and which do not."[37]

2.4 Threshold of seriousness. In addition to the requirement that the imputation conveyed must have an effect identified in one of definitions discussed above, the imputation must meet the necessary level of seriousness. As Tugendhat J. explained in *Thornton v Telegraph Media Group*[38]: "Whatever definition of 'defamatory' is adopted, it must include a qualification or threshold of seriousness, so as to exclude trivial claims." Such threshold was required for two reasons. First, it is in accordance with the true interpretation of Lord Atkin's speech in *Sim v Stretch*[39] in which his lordship made clear that exhibitions of bad manners or discourtesy were not to be placed on the same level as attacks on character. Secondly, such a threshold is required by the development of the law recognised in *Jameel (Youssef) v Dow Jones & Co.*

---

[35] A parallel can be drawn with the alienation and depression suffered by some individuals who experience unexpected and/or prolonged disengagement from the workplace, for example, on account of redundancy or unexpected incapacity.

[36] (1993) 16 EHRR 97.

[37] Ibid. at [29]. The court proceeded to suggest, questionably, that this was particularly true of a person engaged in a liberal profession for whom "work . . . may form part and parcel of his life to such a degree that it becomes impossible to know in what capacity he is acting at a given moment of time".

[38] [2010] EWHC 1414 (QB); [2011] 1 W.L.R. 1985; [2010] E.M.L.R. 25 at [89].

[39] [1936] 2 All E.R. 1237.

Inc[40] as arising from the passing of the Human Rights Act 1998: "regard for Art 10 and the principle of proportionality both require it".[41]

Whether the threshold of seriousness has been met is a multi-factorial question,[42] that must be viewed in light of the rights in art.8 and art.10,[43] and that will require the court to consider matters such as the nature and inherent gravity of the allegation, whether the publication was oral or written, the status and number of publishees and whether the allegations were believed, the status of the publisher[44] and whether this makes it more likely that the allegation will be believed, and the transience of the publication. The result in each case will depend on the particular facts but some guidance as to how it is likely to be treated can be gleaned from several recent cases. In *Thornton v Telegraph Media Group*,[45] Tugendhat J. concluded that an imputation that the claimant author had engaged in copy approval, that is to say giving interviewees the right to read what the author has said about them and to change it, fell below the threshold required and was not therefore defamatory of the claimant. In *Ecclestone v Telegraph Media Group*,[46] Sharp J. held that an allegation that the claimant was dismissive of the views of several well-known vegetarians was not capable of being defamatory. Such an imputation was at worst a breach of conventional etiquette but did not reach the level of seriousness required to be actionable.[47] Similarly in *Daniels v BBC*[48] Sharp J. again concluded that minor criticisms of the claimant's performance

---

[40] [2005] EWCA Civ 75; [2005] Q.B. 946 CA.

[41] Ibid. While such an explanation is tenable, an alternative way of explaining the decision would have been to say that art.8 is not engaged where the nature of any attack on the claimant's reputation is not sufficiently serious to affect his psychological integrity. Such an approach would have been consistent with other comments that his lordship made in the case in relation to business defamation and also with the privacy jurisprudence. Thus, in *R. (Wood) v Comr of Police of the Metropolis* [2009] EWCA Civ 414 CA; [2010] 1 W.L.R. 123 at [22]–[23] it was said that a requirement that the attack must achieve a certain level of seriousness was necessary to ensure that the core right protected by art.8, "however protean", should not be "read so widely that its claims become unreal and unreasonable". So too in *R. (Gillan) v Comr of Police of the Metropolis* [2006] UKHL 12 HL; [2006] 2 A.C. 307 at [28], Lord Bingham stated "It is true that 'private life' has been generously construed to embrace wide rights to personal autonomy. But it is clear Convention jurisprudence that intrusions must reach a certain level of seriousness to engage the operation of the Convention."

[42] *Cammish v Hughes* [2012] EWCA Civ 1655 CA; [2013] E.M.L.R. 13 at [40]. See also, per Sharp J. in *Haji Ioannu v Mark Dixon, Regus Group Plc* [2009] EWHC 178 (QB) at [30].

[43] *Dell'Olio v Associated Newspapers Ltd* [2011] EWHC 3472 (QB) per Tugendhat J. at [13].

[44] See, e.g., *Haji Ioannu v Mark Dixon, Regus Group Plc* [2009] EWHC 178 (QB) in which Sharp J. refused to strike out a claim as an abuse of process notwithstanding that the publication was made to one person only. The allegation in the case was a particularly serious one (dishonesty) and the publication was made by a respected businessman to a *Financial Times* journalist in the knowledge that it was likely to be believed and republished in the newspaper.

[45] [2010] EWHC 1414; [2011] 1 W.L.R. 1985; [2010] E.M.L.R. 25.

[46] [2009] EWHC 2779 (QB).

[47] See also *Dell'Olio v Associated Newspapers* [2011] EWHC 3472 (QB): imputation that the claimant was a serial "gold-digger" who cynically sought out relationships with older men because they were millionaires and not for any genuine reason held not to reach level of seriousness required for publication to be capable of being defamatory (at [32]).

[48] [2010] EWHC 3057 (QB).

at work would not be defamatory because the necessary threshold of serious-ness was not met.[49]

By way of contrast, in *Church v MGN Ltd*[50] the necessary threshold of seriousness was held to have been met in respect of an imputation that the claimant had made an embarrassingly drunken spectacle of herself as she proposed to her boyfriend while singing karaoke in a pub in the early hours of the morning. So too, in *Cammish v Hughes*[51] the Court of Appeal con-cluded that a charge of serious incompetence against a businessman was sufficient to meet the necessary threshold. Such an imputation "was capable of affecting his livelihood. Reputation is important to a businessperson as he needs to persuade others to trust that he will competently perform commit-ments entered into in the course of business."[52]

2.5 Defamation Act 2013, s.1: introduction. At common law, an imputation need have no actual effect on a person's reputation; the law looks only at its tendency, so there is a cause of action even if the words were not believed by the audience.[53] The position might have been different, however, where the nature of the charge was such that no reasonable person would believe it, e.g. a charge of witchcraft in an advanced society.[54] While this remains the position at common law, s.1(1) of the Defamation Act 2013, when it comes into force, will provide that "A statement is not defamatory unless its publica-tion has caused or is likely to cause serious harm to the reputation of the claimant." Where the claimant is a "body that trades for profit", harm to reputation is not, by virtue of s.1(2), "serious harm" unless it "has caused or is likely to cause serious financial harm."[55] Although the provision appears, in terms, only to deal with the question whether a statement is defamatory, and to require serious harm to be shown in addition to proof that the words complained of lowered the claimant's reputation, the intention of the drafters seems to be to extend the requirement of serious harm to other considerations such as the question of publication and reference to the claimant. In other words, s.1(1) should be read as meaning that a statement is not *actionable*

---

[49] Ibid. at [20].
[50] [2012] EWHC 693 (QB); [2012] E.M.L.R. 28 (QB).
[51] [2012] EWCA Civ 1655 CA; [2013] E.M.L.R. 13.
[52] Ibid, at [41].
[53] In *Hough v London Express* [1940] 2 K.B. 507 CA at 515, Goddard L.J. said:
"If words are used which impute discreditable conduct to my friend, he has been defamed to me, although I do not believe the imputation and may even know it is untrue."
These words were approved by Lord Morris in *Morgan v Odhams Press Ltd* [1971] 1 W.L.R. 1239 HL at 1253. See also per Lord Reid at 1246. *Pratten v Labour Daily* [1926] V.L.R. 115 at 122. See also *Knight v Gibbs* (1834) 1 A. & E. 43. The fact that the claimant's reputation has been tarnished by other publications does not prevent the one in respect of which he complains being actionable: *Mthembi-Mahanyele v Mail & Guardian Ltd* [2004] ZASCA 67; 2004 (11) B.C.L.R. 1182 Sup. Ct of Appeal of South Africa.
[54] *Loukas v Young* [1968] 3 N.S.W.R. 549 (allegation of witchcraft).
[55] Defamation Act 2013, s.1(2).

unless its publication has caused, or is likely to cause, serious harm to the reputation of the claimant.

Defamation Act 2013, s.1: Proof of harm or likely harm to reputa- **2.6**
tion. Under s.1 of the 2013 Act, the claimant must prove that the publication has caused, or is likely to cause, serious harm to his reputation. Proof that serious harm to reputation has *actually* occurred will obviously suffice but the claimant need only prove that such harm was *likely*. The harm need not manifest itself in financial terms, though it may do so: serious harm for the purposes of this provision may also be established by proof that the effect of the libel was to cause others to shun the claimant or that the claimant was caused serious injury to feelings, distress, hurt and/or humiliation.

Section 1(1) will have the effect of putting the burden on the claimant to prove that the defamatory imputation has caused, or is likely to cause, him serious harm. At present, the claimant need only establish that the words complained of have the *tendency* adversely to affect his reputation.[56] The question whether a publication has the tendency adversely to affect a person's reputation can of course be determined by examining the statement on its own: whether a publication has caused, or is likely to cause, serious harm is likely to require a careful investigation of facts of the particular case and in particular the inherent gravity of the allegation, the nature and status of the publisher and publishee, the claimant's current reputation and financial posi- tion, and whether similar allegations have been published before. The claim- ant should therefore include details in his particulars of claim of the harm caused, or likely to be caused, to him by the publication complained of.

Defamation Act 2013, s.1: A "raised" threshold? Beyond requiring   **2.7**
greater particularity by the claimant in his pleadings with regard to the harm suffered, the question arises whether s.1(1) will make it more difficult for claimants to succeed. As stated earlier in the chapter, the law already requires that an imputation meet the necessary threshold of seriousness, and there is also currently the potential for trivial cases to be struck out under the *Jameel*[57] abuse jurisdiction on the basis that they are an abuse of process because so little is at stake.[58] It is true that currently the law only looks to the tendency of the words, but s.1 only requires that harm is likely and it is difficult to think of cases where an imputation has the tendency to adversely affect a person's reputation to a substantial degree that are not also likely to cause serious harm to reputation. It may be that cases that fall within the second and third category of personal defamations identified by Tugendhat J. in *Thornton v*

---

[56] Albeit that in every case the claimant must also establish that the threshold of seriousness has been met: para.2.4, above.
[57] *Jameel (Yousef) v Dow Jones & Co. Inc.* [2005] EWCA Civ 75; [2005] Q.B. 946 CA.
[58] See further, para.30.48, below.

Telegraph Media Group Ltd[59]—that is to say imputations as to something which is not voluntary, but rather a misfortune for which no direct moral responsibility can be placed upon the claimant and imputations which ridicule the claimant—will be less likely to succeed than currently.[60] So far as claims involving misfortunes that cause others to shun and avoid the claimant, as Tugendhat J. explained in *Terry (previously "LNS") v Persons Unknown*,[61] such statements were defamatory when no other cause of action existed. It was consequently understandable that in 1934 the court would find a remedy in libel for Princess Youssoupoff to complain about an allegation that she had been raped.[62] Whether a court today would consider such imputations were likely to cause serious harm must be doubtful especially given that an individual in the position of the Princess would have a statutory right to anonymity and claims for misuse of private information under the Data Protection Act 1998. As for the third category—imputations that are said to ridicule a claimant—few cases are likely to cross the necessary threshold.

2.8 Defamation Act 2013, s.1: Bodies that trade for profit. So far as concerns claims brought by a "body that trades for profit", harm to reputation will not, by virtue of s.1(2) of the Act, be "serious harm" unless it has caused or is likely to cause serious financial harm. S.1(2) will require that a body that trades for profit sets out in its particulars of claim how the imputation has caused or is likely to cause it serious financial harm. Whether this will in fact lead to more cases failing or being struck out is a difficult question. Under the existing law, the necessary threshold of seriousness must be met and the *Jameel*[63] abuse jurisdiction is available where little is at stake.[64] Moreover, a corporate claimant must show that the imputation has the tendency to cause it damage in its own trading reputation. Although a body that trades for profit will have to spell out in more detail than currently what financial harm has been caused or is likely to be caused, there is not a great distance between that and what it currently has to show.

While a trading corporation is clearly a "body that trades for profit", the Act is not limited to such entities: any non-natural person that trades for profit whether that is their only or merely a minor part of their purpose, will be covered. Thus, charities may fall within the provision, in so far as they are involved in trade for profit,[65] as may non-governmental organisations, trade

---

[59] [2010] EWHC 1414 (QB); [2011] 1 W.L.R. 1985; [2010] E.M.L.R. 25.

[60] See, e.g., *Dell'Olio v Associated Newspapers Ltd* [2011] EWHC 3472 (QB) per Tugendhat J. at [27]; *Ecclestone v Telegraph Media Group* [2009] EWHC 2779 (QB); *John v Guardian News and Media Group* [2008] EWHC 3066 (QB).

[61] [2010] EWHC 119 (QB) [2010] E.M.L.R. 16.

[62] *Youssoupoff v Metro-Goldwyn-Mayer Pictures Ltd* (1934) 50 T.L.R. 581.

[63] *Jameel (Yousef) v Dow Jones & Co. Inc.* [2005] EWCA Civ 75 CA; [2005] Q.B. 946.

[64] See further, para.30.48, below.

[65] Non-natural persons such as corporations have different segments of their reputation that may be susceptible to being defamed. A charity that may engage in trade for the purposes of fundraising, may have a reputation, for example, for unbiased reporting on human rights in the developing world. An allegation that it has been biased or prejudiced in its reporting of a

unions[66] and employers' associations, and public bodies. Governmental and some other bodies performing public functions are prevented completely from suing for defamation[67] and s.1(2) does not change the law in this respect.

SECTION 2. CATEGORIES OF DEFAMATORY IMPUTATION

Introduction. In the following section consideration is given to the several   **2.9** categories of defamatory imputation. In considering these categories and their application in particular cases a number of matters should be borne in mind. First, many of these cases were decided before the Human Rights Act 1998 and in particular before the articulation of the requirement that a "threshold of seriousness" must be met[68] for an imputation to be defamatory. This recognition of a "threshold of seriousness" has had the effect of raising the bar in respect of the question "what is defamatory" such that imputations once held to have been defamatory may no longer be treated as such. Secondly, it is important to bear in mind that the judge decides whether the words are *capable* of being defamatory[69] and, on the basis that they are so capable, the jury decides whether they are in fact defamatory. Verdicts of juries do not create binding precedents and even on the issue which is for the judge there is a certain margin within which there may be legitimate disagreement. It is not surprising, therefore, that not all the cases are readily reconcilable and that judges in the same case may differ.[70] If the judge rules that the words are capable of being defamatory it cannot be the law that the jury is therefore compelled to find that they are, for that would be to take away one of the jury's principal functions, which is to apply general community standards. However, there are situations in which a finding for the defendant on this issue would be perverse.[71] It is also important to note that even for the judge the

---

particular matter would undermine its credibility seriously as a reliable source of information but might not cause it serious financial harm. Yet it would appear that s.1(2) would apply as much to such an allegation as it would to an allegation that it had used unethical techniques in fundraising (an allegation that would be much more likely to cause serious financial harm).

[66] A question exists whether a trade union may maintain a claim in defamation. See further para.8.24, below.

[67] *Derbyshire CC v Times Newspapers* [1993] A.C. 534 HL at 551. See further para.8.20, below.

[68] See para.2.4, above.

[69] Under PD 53 an application to determine this question may be made at any time after service of particulars of claim.

[70] See, e.g. *Berkoff v Burchill* [1996] 4 All E.R. 1008 CA.

[71] The matter is fully considered by the High Court of Australia in *John Fairfax Pty Ltd v Rivkin* [2003] HCA 50; 201 A.L.R. 77. In *Saffron v John Fairfax Pty Ltd* [2004] NSWCA 254 the plaintiff, an applicant for a liquor licence, was described as having an unsavoury reputation. The court seems to have been of the view that, standing alone, that would almost inevitably be defamatory but refused to interfere with the verdict that in the context of the publication it was not. The jury might have regarded the imputation as meaning that the plaintiff had once had an unsavoury reputation but no longer had such a reputation. Furthermore, to the allegation of bad reputation were appended the words "all of it undeserved and completely the fault of the media". Many might have regarded that as a sarcastic comment on the argument of the plaintiff's counsel in the liquor licensing proceedings but presumably it was not possible to discount the fact that the

issue is whether the words are capable, *in their particular context*, of being defamatory of *this* claimant so that, e.g. while an accusation of lying is no doubt generally capable of being defamatory, it would not be actionable to say that a parent had told his child that there was a Father Christmas[72] and a statement that a person is ugly may be defamatory of a person to whose occupation appearance is relevant while it may not be of another.[73] The cases in the following sections can therefore be no more than a starting point. They certainly should not be regarded as indicating that particular words are necessarily defamatory or not defamatory as the case may be.

2.10 Hatred, contempt or ridicule. Any imputation that exposes a person to "hatred, contempt, or ridicule" has been said to be defamatory of him.[74] Such statement must however now be qualified by the requirement that the imputation meet the necessary "threshold of seriousness".[75] While this may not be particularly difficult to establish with regard to statements that expose a person to hatred or contempt, more difficulty is likely to arise and indeed has in the past arisen in respect of statements exposing a person to ridicule.[76] In a number of cases, statements exposing a person to ridicule have been treated as defamatory though whether, in the post Human Rights Act world they would today reach the necessary threshold of seriousness must be open to question. Thus in an American case an action lay where an advertising photograph, coupled with the legend, "Get a Lift with a Camel," gave the impression that the plaintiff was exposing himself, even though it was almost instantly

---

jury might have taken it literally. See also *Pavy v John Fairfax Publications Pty Ltd* [2004] NSWCA 177 (verdict that plaintiff "had broken six ribs of his baby son, by doing a similar sort of act to shaking him" not defamatory was not perverse; but pleader had omitted original imputation that plaintiff "had directed physical violence towards his infant son thereby breaking six of his ribs"); *Bennette v Cohen* [2005] NSWCA 341; 64 N.S.W.L.R. 81; and *John Fairfax Publications Pty Ltd v Gacic* [2007] HCA 28; 235 A.L.R. 402. In *Cairns v John Fairfax & Sons Ltd* [1983] 2 N.S.W.L.R. 708 NSWCA a finding that an accusation of adultery was not defamatory was not perverse ("the reputations of Antony and Cleopatra have not been lowered in the eyes of the public by their romance and in other days the title of the King's Mistress was one of honour"). Of course the issue may not arise if the jury are simply invited to give a general verdict and other matters are in contention.

[72] *Greek Herald Pty Limited v Nikolopoulos* [2002] NSWCA 41; 54 N.S.W.L.R. 165, per Mason P.

[73] *Berkoff v Burchill*, above.

[74] This is part of the classic definition of Parke B. in *Parmiter v Coupland* (1840) 6 M. & W. 105 at 108; *Wilson v Reed* (1860) 2 F & F 149; per Lord Blackburn in *Capital and Counties Bank v Henty* (1882) 7 A.C. 741 at 771. For its inadequacy as a complete definition, see para.2.1, above, though there is no doubt that any imputation falling within it would be defamatory.

[75] See para.2.4, above.

[76] The Supreme Court of South Australia in *Brander v Ryan and Messenger Press Pty Ltd* [2000] SASC 446, 78 S.A.S.R. 234 accepted that to expose a person to ridicule could be defamatory but pointed out that the matter had never been tested in the High Court. It is not permissible to add the imputation that the statement makes the claimant appear ridiculous as a rhetorical makeweight unsupported by the pleaded facts: *O'Hara v Channel 7 Sydney Pty Ltd* [2007] NSWDC 181.

apparent that the effect was an optical illusion[77]; in another a newspaper story said that the plaintiff had been served with civil process while in her bath tub[78]; and in *Dunlop Rubber Co. Ltd v Dunlop* it was regarded as clear that the representation of the plaintiff in an advertisement as an absurdly foppish old man was defamatory.[79] In *Berkoff v Burchill*[80] a majority of the Court of Appeal upheld a decision to leave to the jury an imputation that the plaintiff was hideously ugly in a review by the defendant of the film "Frankenstein" in which she had said that "The Creature" was marginally better-looking than the plaintiff. Reputation, for this purpose:

> "is to be interpreted in a broad sense as comprehending all aspects of a person's standing in the community. A man who is held up as a figure of fun may be defeated in his claim for damages by, for example, a plea of fair comment, or, if he succeeds on liability, the compensation which he receives from a jury may be very small. But nevertheless, the publication of which he complains may be defamatory of him because it affects in an adverse manner the attitude of other people towards him."[81]

However, in the view of one member of the majority the case did not rest merely upon the expression of the opinion that the plaintiff was ugly but on the fact that the words were plainly intended to hold the plaintiff up to ridicule.[82] The context in which the statement is made is therefore vital.[83] Furthermore, it is conceivable that a sustained campaign of public abuse might amount to the statutory tort of harassment.[84]

While it remains the case that a statement that causes a person to be exposed to ridicule may be treated as defamatory, it is very likely that many cases involving ridicule will not be of sufficient seriousness to engage art.8 and will fail to meet the necessary threshold of seriousness.[85] Moreover, when s.1 of the Defamation 2013 comes into force, the claimant will have to prove

---

[77] *Burton v Crowell Publishing Co*, 82 F.2d 154 (2 Cir. 1936). Among many other American cases on ridicule see *Zbyszko v NY American*, 228 N.Y. App. Div 277 (1930) (plaintiff like gorilla; see the uncomplimentary remarks on this case by Millett L.J. dissenting in *Berkoff v Burchill* [1996] 4 All E.R. 1008 CA at 1019); *Cherry v Des Moines Leader*, 86 N.W. 323 (Iowa 1901) (review of the Dancing Cherry Sisters); *Triggs v Sun Printing and Publishing Ass'n*, 71 N.E. 739 (N.Y. 1904) (Shakespeare rewritten in mockery of professor's style). See also *Ettinghausen v Australian Consolidated Press Ltd* (1991) 23 N.S.W.L.R. 443.

[78] *Snyder v New York Press Co*, 121 N.Y.S. 944 (1910).

[79] [1920] 1 I.R. 280 at 291; [1921] 1 A.C. 367. See also the old cases of *Cropp v Tilney* (1693) 3 Salk. 225 and *Villers v Monsley* (1769) 2 Wils. 403, recounted by Neill L.J. in *Berkoff v Burchill* [1996] 4 All E.R. 1008 at 1014.

[80] [1996] 4 All E.R. 1008 CA.

[81] [1996] 4 All E.R. 1008 CA at 1018, per Neill L.J.

[82] Phillips L.J. at 1021.

[83] See *Norman v Future Publishing Ltd* [1999] E.M.L.R. 325 CA (see para.3.30, below), where the issue was the meaning of the words.

[84] See para.23.12 below. Note, however, *Trimingham v Associated Newspapers* [2012] EWHC 1296 (QB) in which a series of newspaper articles making fun of and insulting the claimant were held not to give rise to a claim for harassment.

[85] See, e.g. *John v Guardian News and Media Group* [2008] EWHC 3066 (QB). Note however *Dee v Telegraph Media Group* [2010] EWHC 924 (QB).

that the defamatory imputation has caused, or is likely to cause him, serious harm and this may not be easy where the statement complained of has caused him to be subject to ridicule.

2.11 Words must cause ridicule. A difficult line has to be drawn here for two reasons: first, some degree of humour at the expense of others is generally regarded as part of normal life[86]; secondly, insults which do not diminish a person's standing with others do not found an action for defamation.[87] Words which tend to subject the claimant to chaff or banter or "ribbing" but which fall short of tending to make him look ridiculous are not defamatory even if fair comment does not come into play.[88] For example, it was held not defamatory to publish an account of a man's wedding on the day before it happened, even though it was alleged that on the following morning, before the ceremony, he was unable to do his work because of the reaction of his colleagues to the story.[89] It was, however, held to be capable of being defamatory to impute of the claimant that she had made an embarrassingly drunken spectacle of herself as she proposed to her boyfriend whilst singing karaoke in the Robin Hood pub in Cardiff in the early hours of the morning.[90]

2.12 Position of the claimant and circumstances of the publication. Although caricatures and cartoons frequently portray politicians and other public figures in such a way as to make them appear absurd, these publications have figured infrequently in defamation cases. No doubt this is explained by a number of factors which go beyond the narrow question of

---

[86] It is particularly important here to be sensitive to changing public perceptions of what is acceptable. For example, Lord Blanesburgh's description of the advertisement in *Tolley v JS Fry & Sons Ltd* [1931] A.C. 333 HL at 346, as a "piece of offensive vulgarity" seems rather strong to modern eyes. It is hard to imagine his Lordship's reaction to the publication in *Obermann v ACP Publishing Pty Ltd* [2001] N.S.W.S.C. 1022.

[87] *Berkoff v Burchill*, above at 1013.

[88] See *MacLeod v Newsquest (Sunday Herald) Ltd* [2007] Rep. L.R. 5 "In my view it would have been clear to the ordinary reasonable reader that the pursuer, like the other three journalists mentioned, was being chaffed or teased by the diarist in a good-humoured or bantering manner for having written a story which could be described as a 'gaffe'." See also, *John v Guardian News & Media Ltd* [2008] EWHC 3066 (QB) where the issue was the meaning of the words.

[89] *Emerson v Grimsby Times* (1926) 42 T.L.R. 238 CA. Cf. the debated decision in *Blennerhassett v Novelty Sales* (1933) 175 L.T.I. 393, where an advertisement in the terms "Beware of Yo-Yo . . . Take warning by Mr. Blennerhassett. as worthy a citizen as ever ate lobster at Pimms, or holed a putt at Walton Heath . . . Sound Man, Blennerhassett, . . . placed in a quiet place in the country and under sympathetic surveillance . . . after yielding to the fascination" of defendants' toy was held to be incapable of a defamatory meaning. See also *Frank v NBC*, 506 N.Y.S.2d 869 (1986).

[90] *Church v MGN Ltd* [2012] EWHC 693 (QB); [2013] 1 W.L.R. 284. In *Dee v Telegraph Media Group* [2010] EWHC 924 (QB) at [59], Sharp J. accepted that a statement that the claimant, a professional tennis player, was the worst tennis player in the world may be capable of being defamatory in that the claimant was ridiculed by the suggestion that he was absurdly bad at tennis.

whether the publication is defamatory: in many cases even the fiercest criticism falls within the defence of fair comment[91] and the reader may anyway be unlikely to take a cartoon as literally depicting actual events.[92] However, the law of defamation is clearly applicable in principle to publications of this type[93] and it is thought that what will be permissible in respect of a politician or entertainer may not be so if applied to a person in private life.[94] If a person is a public character whose public life or great position is calculated to excite interest, there will be circumstances in which it would be unreasonable to suppose that his portrayal in exaggerated form would tend to injure his reputation in the sense of making him an object of ridicule. For example, an actor could not reasonably object that in an advertisement by way of a poster of a theatrical performance in which he takes a part he is depicted in the garb proper to the part which he plays,[95] whereas an ordinary citizen might legitimately object to notoriety of such a kind, even though he were made to represent a personage of fame and distinction in history, as it would make him merely ridiculous.[96] In such a case a representation of him in a form or appearance entirely different from his real form and appearance or in an absurd costume or attitude might well tend to make him an object of ridicule in the eyes of his friends, and so be defamatory of him.[97]

The issue may also be affected by the nature and scope of the publication. Where a newspaper reported in its columns an after-dinner speech containing

---

[91] *Vander Zalm v Times Publishers* (1980) 109 D.L.R. (3d) 531 BCCA. The limits of permissible criticism in public life are wide: see *Massey v New Zealand Times* (1911) 30 N.Z.L.R. 929; *Chemodurov v Russia* App. no.72683/01; [2007] ECHR 684 and para.12.27, below.

[92] On both issues, see *Ross v New Brunswick Teachers' Association* (2001) 201 D.L.R. (4th) 75. It has been said that cartoons are ordinarily understood by reasonable readers to be rhetorical, exaggerated means of expressing opinions: *Vander Zalm v Times Publishers* (1980) 109 D.L.R. (3d) 531, per Aikin J.A.; *King v Globe Newspaper*, 512 N.E.2d 241 (Mass 1987); *DRT Construction Co. v Lenkei*, 576 N.Y.S.2d 724 (1991). It has been held that to show the claimant in the pillory is capable of being defamatory (see para.3.4, below). But it is submitted that to show in this position a politician who was at the centre of public controversy is not now so capable. From about 1750 to 1830 political caricature in England was generally at a level of ferocity which has not been matched since. For an introduction to this, see J. Wardroper, *Kings, Lords and Wicked Libellers* (1973). For the related question of whether statements made in jest are actionable, see para.3.36, below.

[93] See also *Church v MGN Ltd* (above) in which Tugendhat J. held that "The [drunken] behaviour described might not be defamatory if attributed to some other people, but to attribute such drunken behaviour to a star such as the Claimant is in my judgment clearly capable of defaming her." (at [16]). This is so even in the USA, where freedom of speech on "political" matters is less confined by defamation law: *Dworkin v Hustler Magazine Inc.*, 668 F.Supp. 1408 (C.D. Cal 1987), affirmed. 867 F.2d 867 (CA 9 1989).

[94] *Dell'Olio v Associated Newspapers Ltd* [2011] EWHC 3472 (QB) per Tugendhat J. at [28]: "The public position or character of a claimant is relevant to whether words complained of bear a defamatory meaning." But cf. *Church v MGN Ltd* (above) at [16].

[95] But cf. *Louka v Park Entertainments* 1 N.E.2d (Mass 1936) (actress who played in Greek tragedies portrayed outside burlesque theatre).

[96] *Mazatti v Acme Products* [1930] 4 D.L.R. 601, approving a passage in a previous edition to the same effect (action for libel in respect of a testimonial falsely purporting to have been given by the claimant recommending a patent medicine sold by the defendants); cf. *Tolley v Fry* [1930] 1 K.B. 467 CA at 477, per Greer L.J.

[97] *Dunlop v Dunlop Co* [1920] 1 I.R. 280 at 291; [1921] 1 A.C. 367.

humorous but disparaging remarks about the plaintiff, it was held that an action lay, even though those present might not have understood the speech to have had a defamatory meaning.[98]

> "When anything of that kind is published in a newspaper a man has a right to say: 'I do not care what Mr. A or Mr. B said after dinner. I do not choose to be made an object of ridicule, be it, good-natured or otherwise, merely to amuse a number of people who know nothing of me.'"[99]

In one case it was held libellous to publish a story in which the plaintiff was made to look ridiculous, although the plaintiff had told the story of himself in the first instance.[100]

> "There is a wide distinction between someone's telling a ludicrous story of himself, in the private circle of his friends and acquaintances, and the publication of it to the world at large, through the medium of a newspaper."[101]

2.13 Ridicule and truth. A person may be exposed to ridicule by the revelation of true facts about him, as for example where the defendant publishes an unclothed picture of him. This has been held to be defamatory in two Australian jurisdictions[102] where a requirement of public benefit was then added to that of truth in the defence of justification. At common law, however, the defendant would have no difficulty in making out the defence of justification,[103] unless the publication was capable of further meanings, for example that the claimant had consented to appear in this way.[104] In any event, however, such a case might now lead to liability for misuse of private information.[105]

2.14 Words causing others to shun or avoid one. An imputation may be defamatory even though it does not tend to make others think worse of the person to whom it refers, nor expose him to ridicule. Provided that the necessary "threshold of seriousness" is met,[106] a statement may be defamatory if it would tend to cause others to shun or avoid him,[107] or to exclude him

---

[98] *Dolby v Newnes* (1887) 3 T.L.R. 393.

[99] Per Stephen J. ibid. at 394.

[100] *Cook v Ward* (1830) 4 Moo. & P. 99.

[101] Per Tindall C.J., ibid. at 111.

[102] *Ettingshausen v Australian Consolidated Press Ltd* (1991) 23 N.S.W.L.R. 443; *McDonald v North Queensland Newspaper Co. Ltd* [1997] 1 Qd R. 62 Qd CA; *Obermann v ACP Publishing Pty Ltd* [2001] N.S.W.S.C. 1022.

[103] *Hollinsworth v BCTV* [1999] 6 W.W.R. 54 BCCA (release of film on plaintiff's operation for baldness not actionable as defamation; "the film was true").

[104] See *Obermann v ACP Publishing Pty Ltd.* In *Charleston v News Group Newspapers Ltd* [1995] 2 A.C. 65 HL, a faked photograph pictured the plaintiffs in an obscene position. The only imputations pleaded were that the reader would conclude that the plaintiffs had willingly participated in the production of the photographs.

[105] See Ch.22, below.

[106] See para.2.4, above.

[107] *Youssoupoff v Metro-Goldwyn-Mayer* (1934) 50 T.L.R. 581 CA at 587; *Watkin v Hall* (1868) L.R.3 Q.B. 396 at 399; (semble) *Plumb v Jeyes*, *The Times*, April 15, 1937 (offensive feet). Cf. 3 Black. Comm. 123–124.

from the society of others.[108] It has, for instance, been held to be defamatory to say of someone that he is insane,[109] or is "not quite responsible for what he does".[110] It is true that insanity is a misfortune and not a fault, and that a person suffering therefrom is an object of pity or sympathy rather than of hatred, ridicule or contempt. But it is no less true that the tendency of such an imputation may be to diminish people's confidence in the claimant and even cause them not to associate with him.[111] However, while not denying that an imputation of mental disorder was capable of being defamatory the New South Wales Court of Appeal held in *Mallik v McGeown*[112] that it was open to the jury to conclude that contemporary community attitudes in twenty-first century Australia were such that ordinary reasonable readers would not think less of a person for being described as demented. So too, in *Ibrahim v University of Swansea*[113] Eady J. accepted the submission of the defendant that no reasonable person would nowadays think any the worse of someone who had suffered from either "mental health difficulties" or from "chronic fatigue syndrome and anxiety". Moreover, there can be no doubt, that words like "crazy" or "lunatic" do not necessarily, when taken in context, impute mental disorder.[114]

Similar considerations apply to statements imputing disease.[115] There will be some cases (e.g. where there is an allegation of venereal disease) where the statement is capable of imputing discreditable conduct to the claimant. But it has been held to be defamatory to say that someone has leprosy[116] and it may possibly be defamatory to say that a person was HIV positive even though the statement made it plain that the condition had been acquired innocently, for

---

[108] *Villiers v Monsley* (1769) 2 Wilson 403 at 404.

[109] *Youssoupoff v Metro-Goldwyn-Mayer* (1934) 50 T.L.R. 581 CA at 587; *R. v Harvey* (1823) 2 B. & C. 257 at 258, per Abbott C.J.; *Morgan v Lingen* (1863) 8 L.T. 800; *Totten v Sun Printing*, 109 F. 289 (1901). It is not apparent what it was about the context which led to the opposite conclusion in *Campbell v Preston*, unreported, November 15, 1996, CA.

[110] *Pearce v Symes* (1909) 28 N.Z.L.R. 562; cf. *Bower v Sunday Pictorial, The Times*, July 7, 1962; *Brauer v Globe Newspaper Co*, 217 N.E.2d 736 (Mass. 1966) (mental retardation). For American law see 23 A.L.R. 3d 652. *Justin v Associated Newspapers* (1966) 86 W.N. (Pt.1) (N.S.W.) 17.

[111] In *John v MGN Ltd* [1997] Q.B. 586 CA, a statement that the plaintiff, who had earlier conquered various forms of addiction, followed a bizarre diet which was a form of bulimia was left to the jury and found by them to be defamatory. See also *Berkoff v Burchill* [1996] 4 All E.R. 1008 CA.

[112] [2008] NSWCA 230.

[113] [2012] EWHC 290 (QB).

[114] Cf. *Boaks v South London Press, The Times*, October 27, 1967 ("nutty" found not defamatory by jury); *McGowen v Prentice*, 431 So.2d 55 (55) (students described as "nuts"); *Pretorius v Masilela* [1994] (3) S.A. 167 TPD ("you've gone off your head" not implying mental illness in context of *iniuria*); cf. *Capps v Watts*, 246 S.E.2d 606 (S.C. 1978) ("paranoid son of a bitch" cast doubt on mental competence).

[115] Most of the case law on disease concerns the different issue of whether oral statements are actionable as slander per se: see para.4.13, below.

[116] *Simpson v Press Publishing* 67 N.Y.S. 461 (1900). Certainly it is now quite widely known that leprosy presents very little danger of contagion, but ordinary people must be taken as they are, not as medical experts.

example by a blood transfusion.[117] It can hardly be defamatory of a person to say that he has a bad bout of influenza or heart trouble[118] (except in a context in which that imputes unfitness in his calling) so the line has to be drawn somewhere and it is submitted that (always putting aside the case where the statement carries the imputation of discreditable conduct[119]) a statement relating to a person's physical health should be defamatory wherever ordinary people would, rightly or wrongly, regard it as hazardous to associate with him. Some 70 years ago it was thought to be defamatory to say of a woman that she has been raped,[120] although it involves no moral turpitude on her part.[121] It seems highly unlikely that such a conclusion would be reached today. Sexual behaviour[122] is an area in which there have been enormous changes in public attitudes and the question of what is defamatory must be answered in accordance with current social opinions,[123] but the same opinion about the allegation of rape was expressed in Australia in 1986.[124] An imputation of illegitimacy has been held to be defamatory in quite modern times,[125] but it is doubtful if this is now so.[126]

---

[117] Held arguable in *Serdar v Metroland Printing Publishing and Distributing Ltd* [2001] O.T.C. 318 Ont Sup CJ (story that police officer bitten by HIV-positive suspect). A person who was thought to be HIV positive might suffer adverse discrimination in employment, insurance, etc. However, a person who was said to have a weak heart might suffer disadvantage in insurance and it is thought that this would be actionable, if at all, only as malicious falsehood or negligence. Possibly there is a distinction in the fact that being HIV positive is so closely associated in the public mind with promiscuity and drug-taking that the innocent explanation has little impact, but a better distinction lies in the fact that HIV is perceived as dangerous to others. In *Peters-Brown v Regina District Health Board* [1996] 1 W.W.R. 337, it was held defamatory to put plaintiff on a list of persons with infectious blood conditions.

[118] *Grappelli v Derek Block Holdings* [1981] 1 W.L.R. 822 (not defamatory to say that musician is seriously ill).

[119] Including cases where it is implied that the claimant is malingering.

[120] *Youssoupoff v Metro-Goldwyn-Mayer* (1934) 50 T.L.R. 581 CA at 584, 586, 587 (suffered in social reputation and in opportunities of receiving respectful consideration from the world); *Lewis v Daily Telegraph* [1964] A.C. 234 at 285: *Quigley v Creation Ltd* [1971] I. R. 272; *Lau v Life Publisher Bhd* [2004] 7 M.L.J. 7. For acid comment see the Faulks Committee, Cmnd.5909 (1975) App. V, though it is not clear whether they are saying that the law was wrongly stated in *Youssoupoff*, or that it should be changed. See also para.2.15, below.

[121] To say the contrary was said to be "to shut one's eyes to realities": *Youssoupoff*, above, per Slesser L.J.

[122] See further on this para.2.29, below.

[123] Ibid.

[124] *Krahe v TCN Channel Nine* (1986) 4 N.S.W.L.R. 536 at 546.

[125] *Solomon v Simmons*, *The Times*, April 10, 1954; 3 Black.Comm. 124. *Huth v Huth* [1915] 3 K.B. 32 at 47 seems to turn on reference.

[126] Held not to be defamatory in *Robson v News Group Newspaper Ltd* (unreported, 95/SC/0876, October 9, 1995) Judge Previté QC. The proportion of births outside marriage rose from about 5 per cent in 1960 to about 44 per cent in 2006: see Social Trends (1996 and 2008 edns). Any legal disabilities attaching to the status were removed by the Family Law Reform Act 1987. In those rare cases where legitimate status is relevant (succession to titles of honour) quaere whether a false statement imputing illegitimacy could be defamatory or actionable only as malicious falsehood. In Scotland the status has been formally abolished: Family Law (Scotland) Act 2006 (asp) s.21.

Defamation Act s. 1(1) and the "shun and avoid" test. The "shun   2.15
and avoid" test is the most troublesome of the definitions of "what is
defamatory" in that it appears to permit a claim notwithstanding that the
words complained of have neither caused harm to reputation nor do they have
any tendency so to do. It is true that such a position has some support in a
limited number of older cases[127] but, even at the time *Youssoupoff v Metro-
Goldwyn-Mayer Pictures Ltd*[128] was decided, the leading textbook writers
were divided as to whether such a view was consistent with general principles
of defamation.[129] As Tugendhat J. noted in *Terry (formerly LNS) v Persons
Unknown*,[130] "there was always a difficulty in fitting such cases into defamation, but it was done because of the absence of any alternative cause of
action"—the implication being that such cases should now be "located" in
misuse of private information. In the light of the requirement in s.1(1) of the
Act that the claimant show that the statement has caused serious harm to the
reputation of the claimant, it is submitted that cases where the claimant can
show *only* that he has been shunned or avoided as a consequence of the
publication may in the future fail.

Words lowering a person in the estimation of others. An imputation   2.16
may be defamatory without falling within any of the specific heads so far set
out. Any imputation is defamatory if it would tend to lower the claimant in the
estimation of right-thinking members of society generally or would be likely
to affect a person adversely in the estimation of reasonable people[131]
generally[132]   provided   that   it   meets   the   necessary   "threshold   of

---

[127] See, e.g., *Villers v Monsley* (1769) 2 Wils. 403 (imputation that a person had the "itch");
Morgan v Lingen (1863) 8 L.T. 800 at 801. At the time of *Youssoupoff v Metro-Goldwyn-Mayer
Pictures Ltd* (above), it would certainly have lowered a woman's reputation to have alleged of her
that she had been raped (see Treiger-Bar-Am, "Defamation Law in a Changing Society: The case
of *Youssoupoff v Metro-Goldwyn-Mayer*" (2001) 21 *Legal Studies* 291). The problem with the
decision is that (as McNamara, *Reputation and Defamation* (Oxford: Oxford University Press,
2007) at 144–150 points out) the judges accepted that the fact that the plaintiff would have been
shunned or avoided would be enough.
[128] (1934) 50 T.L.R. 581 CA.
[129] For further details, see McNamara, at 155–158.
[130] [2010] EWHC 119 (QB); [2010] E.M.L.R. 16 at [96].
[131] "In practice, the tribunal of fact, judge or jury, will ask itself about its own response to the
matter complained of. To a very large extent that response will be impressionistic, subjective and
individual to the decision-maker. The point of the invocation of the hypothetical reasonable
person is to remind decision-makers that they may, or may not, reflect the response of the average
recipient of the communication and should make allowance for that possibility": *Chakravarti v
Advertiser Newspapers Ltd* [1998] H.C.A. 37; 93 C.L.R. 519 at [134], per Kirby J.
[132] *Skuse v Granada Television* [1996] E.M.L.R. 278 CA; *Gillick v BBC* [1996] E.M.L.R. 267
CA. The origin of at least part of this is Lord Atkin in *Sim v Stretch* (1936) 52 T.L.R. 669 HL,
who, "after collating the opinions of many authorities", without inviting their Lordships to lay
down a formal definition, proposed as a test in that case: "Would the words tend to lower the
plaintiff in the estimation of right-thinking members of society generally?" (though it has been
pointed out that Lord Atkin may have been concerned simply with the point that on the facts of
the case—a telegram—the jury should not be given the "impression that a standard particular to
the sole recipient of the telegram could have been appropriate": *Radio 2UE Pty Ltd v Chesterton*
[2008] NSWCA 66 at [7]). "That which may tend to lower the plaintiff in the estimation of others

seriousness".[133] For instance, to say of someone that he is ungrateful would scarcely expose him to hatred, ridicule or contempt, or cause him to be avoided, yet it has been held defamatory.[134] Whether it would be today, however, is seriously questionable. To say of a person carrying on any trade or profession, or holding any office, that he is incompetent at it, may not lower him in the estimation of others in the sense that they will think less of his general character, but the words will be defamatory because of the injury to his reputation in his trade, profession or office and that is enough.[135] The same will be true of an imputation on his credit worthiness, even though from some points of view poverty is a virtue.[136]

In *Ecclestone v Telegraph Media Group Ltd*[137] the defendants published a story that the claimant, a fashion designer, had said "I am not a veggie and I don't have much time for people like the McCartneys and Annie Lennox [well-known promoters of vegetarianism]". Sharp J. struck out the claim as being incapable of bearing any defamatory meaning. It was impossible to say that the public generally would think less of the claimant because of the view she was said to have expressed on vegetarianism or because it might be regarded as dismissive or disrespectful of the persons referred to. It was not a case where the view expressed would generally have been regarded as outrageous, nor was there any implication of hypocrisy or of the opinion being expressed in an abusive fashion.

2.17 Relative reputation, comparisons. In the great majority of cases statements such as "A is better at . . . than B" will be so obviously expressions of opinion within the scope of fair comment that no action will be brought. But the question arises whether such statements are capable of being defamatory in the first place. It has been held that it is not defamatory to say that one journalist is less talented than another,[138] or that a lawyer is only of average ability.[139] So too in *Dee v Telegraph Media Group*[140] Sharp J. commented that it was difficult to characterise an imputation of a relative lack of sporting skill

---

we cannot withhold from a jury": *Fray v Fray* (1864) 17 C.B.(N.S.) 603 at 605. "Whatever tends to lower a man in the estimation of the world amounts to a libel, if written": *Archbishop of Tuam v Robeson* (1828) 2 Moo. & P. 32 at 39. See also *O'Brien v Clement* (1846) 15 M. & W. 435 ("Everything which reflects on the character of another"); *Helsham v Blackwood* (1851) 11 C.B. 111 at 130 ("everyone would have thought the worse of him for it"); *Boyd v Mirror Newspapers* [1980] 2 N.S.W.L.R. 449 ("likely to cause ordinary folk in the community to think less of him").

[133] See para.2.4, above.
[134] See para.2.28, below.
[135] See para.2.1, above and paras 2.35–2.49, below. Cf. however *Daniels v BBC* [2010] EWHC 3057 (QB) in which the judge held that minor criticisms of a person's competence at work were not capable of being defamatory (at [49]–[50]).
[136] See para.2.30–2.34, below.
[137] [2009] EWHC 2779 (QB).
[138] *Dowling v Time Inc.*, The Times, April 10, 1954.
[139] *Thompson v Matthiasen*, 135 N.Y. Supp. 796 (1912).
[140] [2010] EWHC 924, at [49] (QB).

as defamatory. That to print a story of inferior quality under the name of a well-known author[141] or to place the name or trademark of a well-known manufacturer on inferior goods not of his manufacture[142] may be defamatory of the person whose name is so used is understandable since the conduct might lead people to think that the author was a hack or that the manufacturer was guilty of exploitation or sharp practice. In any event, the conduct carries an obvious risk of injury to the claimants' business reputations.[143] Similarly, it was no doubt correct to hold that it was defamatory where the defendants sponsored an inferior but recognisable imitation of the voice of the plaintiff, an actor, suggesting that his abilities had deteriorated and that he was reduced to making anonymous television commercials.[144] An action lay where the defendant, who had engaged the plaintiff, a well-known vocalist, to sing at a concert, published a programme in which her name appeared in a position which on the evidence indicated that her reputation was less than that of other artistes.[145]

Statements denigrating the claimant's abilities will almost always be made in the context of some reference, express or implied, to facts about his performance, thus attracting fair comment. In *Dee v Telegraph Media Group Ltd*,[146] however, the assertion that the claimant was the world's "worst tennis player" was regarded as inseparable from and "parasitic" upon his match record. No sensible reader could really think that "the suggestion that the claimant was 'the world's worst . . . professional' was a free standing and objectively verifiable allegation independent of his record of losses in the 54 matches played all around the world".[147] Hence there was a defence of justification and it was unnecessary to consider fair comment.

Words injuring feelings or trade. Words or matter which merely injure   **2.18**
the feelings or cause annoyance but which in no way reflect on character or reputation or tend to cause one to be shunned or avoided or expose one to ridicule are not actionable as defamation.[148] It is quite proper, where words are

---

[141] *Ridge v English Illustrated* (1913) 29 T.L.R. 592. See also para.23.18, below.

[142] *Manton v Bales* (1845) I C.B. 444; *Wilson v Smith* (1902) 2 N.S.W.S.R. 174. See also para.23.11, below.

[143] Similarly where dubious advertisements are published in such a way as to suggest that they are authorised by a reputable trader: *Mount Cook Group Ltd v Johnstone Motors Ltd* [1990] 2 N.Z.L.R. 488.

[144] *Lahr v Adell Chemical*, 300 F.2d 256 (1962). See also, *Beckinsale v Express Newspapers Ltd*, unreported, July 9, 2009 where the defendants agreed to pay damages in settlement where their story gave the impression that an actress's career was in decline.

[145] *Russell v Notcutt* (1896) 12 T.L.R. 195 CA: see para.2.44, below.

[146] [2010] EWHC 924 (QB); [2010] E.M.L.R. 20.

[147] Ibid. at [38]. See further, para.2.35, below.

[148] "That juries should be free to award damages for injuries to reputation is one of the safeguards of liberty. But the protection is undermined when exhibitions of bad manners or discourtesy are placed on the same level as attacks on character and are treated as actionable wrongs": per Lord Atkin in *Sim v Stretch* (1937) 52 T.L.R. 669 at 672; "To cast a slight upon a person is not the same as libelling him", per O'Brien C.J. in *O'Hea v Guardians of Cork Union* (1892) 32 L.R.Ir. at 629; *O'Malley v O'Callaghan* (1992) 89 D.L.R. (4th) 577.

in themselves defamatory, for the jury to take into consideration as a specific element of damages the injury to the claimant's feelings[149]; but one cannot submit such injury as a basis for recovery independent of loss of reputation[150] or some other tort in which such damages may be available.[151] Hence it is not defamatory without more to publish a false report of a person's death or an obituary,[152] or to overstate a person's age,[153] or to use the claimant's family grave as the setting for a scene in a "comedy horror" film.[154] Similarly, it is not defamatory without more to use a person's name without his authority,[155] or to publish his photograph or likeness without his consent,[156] however much annoyance these acts may cause to his personal feelings. Similarly, words which tend to interfere with a person's business are not as such defamatory, unless they tend to injure his reputation (though he may for this purpose have a business reputation which is distinct from his "general character").[157] Of course, in any of the above cases, the words will be defamatory if the context or circumstances of the publication may cause it to convey a defamatory imputation. Thus a false news story about the plaintiff's death was defamatory

---

[149] See para.9.4, below.

[150] Per curiam in *Samuels v Evening Mail* (1875) 6 Hun. (N.Y.) R. 5 at 11, and see the report of the Porter Committee: Cmd.7536 (1949), paras 24–26.

[151] E.g. assault or false imprisonment. The law in the United States recognises a liability for infliction of mental distress by outrageous conduct: see the Restatement 2d, *Torts*, para.46 and Mullany and Handford, *Tort Liability for Psychiatric Damage* (1993), pp.297 et seq. A comparable English principle of *Wilkinson v Downton* [1897] 2 Q.B. 57 has not advanced so far, since there must be some physical or psychiatric injury to amount to damage, not mere distress: *Wainwright v Home Office* [2003] UKHL 53; [2004] 2 A.C. 406. However, see the statutory tort of harassment: para.23.12, below.

[152] *Cohen v New York Times*, 153 N.Y. App. Div. 242 (1912) (even though such a statement might annoy or irk the subject thereof or subject him to chaff or banter even to the extent of affecting his feelings); *Rubinstein v New York Post Corp*, 488 N.Y.S.2d (1985) 331 (death is an honourable estate); for a full discussion see *Decker v Princeton Packet Inc.*, 561 A.2d 1122 (N.J. 1989) and 85 A.L.R. 4th 813.

[153] *Van Baggen v Nichol* (1963) 38 D.L.R. (2d) 654. Cf. a questionable decision concerning an actress at para.2.44, below.

[154] *Bradley v Wingnut Films Ltd* [1993] 1 N.Z.L.R. 415.

[155] *Tolley v Fry* [1930] I K.B. 467 CA at 478.

[156] *Dockrell v Dougan* (1899) 80 L.T. 556; *Corelli v Wall* (1906) 22 T.L.R. 532; *Palmer v NSC* (1906) MacG. Copyright Cas. 15; *Wood v Sandow, The Times*, June 30, 1914: *Sports v Our Dogs* [1916] 2 K.B. 880; [1917] 2 K.B. 125 CA; *Tolley v Fry* [1930] 1 K.B. 467 CA (advertisement showing caricature of the plaintiff, an amateur golfer, with a packet of defendants' chocolate protruding from his pocket and listening to a caddie's doggerel in praise of it), per Greer L.J. at 478:

> "I have no hesitation in saying that in my judgment the defendants in publishing the advertisement in question, without first obtaining Mr. Tolley's consent acted in a manner inconsistent with the decencies of life, and in doing so they were guilty of an act for which there ought to be a legal remedy. But unless a man's photograph, caricature, or name be published in such a context that the publication can be said to be defamatory within the law of libel, it cannot be made the subject-matter of complaint by action at law."

As to the possibility now of misuse of private information or passing off see Ch.22 and para.23.16, below.

[157] *Ratcliffe v Evans* [1892] 2 Q.B. 524 at 529; *Dawson Bloodstock Agency v Mirror Newspapers* [1979] I N.S.W.L.R. 16; *Daniels v BBC* [2010] EWHC 3057. See para.2.36, below.

where it stated that he had committed suicide[158]; to overstate a person's age might suggest that he was guilty of deception; and the use of his likeness might, in the context, expose him to ridicule or convey the imputation that he had consented to its use in circumstances which would be discreditable to him.[159] Furthermore, non-defamatory but damaging statements may be actionable as malicious falsehood[160] or negligence.[161] It is not in itself defamatory to reveal matters about the claimant which he would prefer to be kept secret or private because truth is a defence and in English law there is no independent tort of intrusion into privacy.[162] However, such conduct may be actionable under some other head, such as misuse of private information[163] (which has expanded very significantly in recent times) or the Data Protection Act 1998.[164] Furthermore, where the defendant is a public body, conduct which is intrusively offensive may lead to liability under the Human Rights Act 1998, giving effect to the guarantee in art.8 of the European Convention on Human Rights of private and family life, home and correspondence.

SECTION 3. STANDARD OF OPINION

The community as a whole. Though the issue may need to be further **2.19** considered by the courts,[165] the present position is that to be defamatory in

---

[158] *Dall v Time Inc.*, 300 N.Y.S. 680 (1937); affirmed 16 N.E.2d 297. However, see *Todd v Swan Television and Radio Broadcasting Pty Ltd* [2001] WASC 324; 25 W.A.R. 382 at [74] (imputation of suicide attempt probably no longer defamatory).

[159] In *Tolley v Fry* in the House of Lords ([1931] A.C. 333) the plaintiff succeeded on the basis that the publication compromised his status as an amateur golfer. See also *Ridge v English Illustrated* (1913) 29 T.L.R. 231 (false attribution of inferior work); *Pryce v Pioneer Press* (1925) 42 T.L.R. 29 (imputation of disloyalty to customers). For other quaint or entertaining examples alleging ridicule or imputations of discreditable behaviour see *Griffiths v Bondor, The Times*, December 11, 1935 (advertisement headed Leg Appeal showing plaintiff's head and shoulders and (below) the naked limbs of another female); *Plumb v Jeyes, The Times*, April 15, 1937 (photograph of the plaintiff, a one-time policeman, used as an advertisement of the value of Jeyes Fluid for the feet); *Funston v Pearson, The Times*, March 12, 1915 (actress without teeth as advertisement for dentist); *Debenham v Ancorn, The Times*, March 5, 1921 (photo of unmarried woman "with her little daughter Peggy"); *Dunlop v Dunlop* [1921] 1 A.C. 367; *Honeysett v News Chronicle, The Times*, May 14, 1935 (photograph of married woman in cycling costume, with man not her husband, under title "Unchaperoned Holidays"); *Kirk v Reed* [1968] N.Z.L.R. 801 (picture captioned "reveller with his Christmas beer"; plaintiff not told that picture for publication). See also, *Ettinghausen v Australian Consolidated Press Ltd* (1991) 23 N.S.W.L.R. 443.

[160] See Ch.21, below.

[161] See para.23.1, below.

[162] See para.22.1, below.

[163] See para.22.2, below.

[164] See para.22.19, below.

[165] In *Arab News Network v Jihad Al Khazen* [2001] EWCA Civ 118, Keene L.J. said at [30] that because it had been held that the words were incapable of bearing any of the pleaded meanings it was

"unnecessary to deal with the other issue raised on this appeal, namely whether any of the pleaded meanings would be capable of being held to be defamatory and whether that is to be judged by the reaction of ordinary reasonable people in our society as a whole or by that of such people within a particular community within that society. We were addressed at some length on this issue but for my part I would only add that I can see considerable difficulties in this court departing from the former of those two approaches, endorsed as it has been in a long series of

English law an imputation must tend to lower the claimant in the estimation of right-thinking members of society *generally.*

> "Words are not defamatory, however much they may damage a man in the eyes of a section of the community, unless they also amount to disparagement of his reputation in the eyes of right-thinking men generally. To write or say of a man something that will disparage him in the eyes of a particular section of the community but will not affect his reputation in the eyes of the average right-thinking man is not actionable within the law of defamation."[166]
>
> "It is not enough to prove that the words rendered the plaintiff obnoxious to a limited class: it should be proved that the words are such as would produce a bad impression on the minds of average reasonable men."[167]

A fortiori the words are not defamatory if the standard of opinion of the particular section of the community is one which the courts cannot recognise or approve.[168] The criterion has been said to be "the arbitrium boni: the view which would be taken by the ordinary good and worthy subject of the King",[169] or ordinary reasonable people in our society as a whole,[170] or by "right-thinking people generally"[171] or by "ordinary folk in the community".[172]

2.20 Imputation of disloyalty or hypocrisy. In *Myroft v Sleight*[173] the plaintiff was a trawler skipper and a member of a fisherman's trade union. He voted in favour of a strike at a union meeting but the defendant then told certain union members that the plaintiff had visited one of the owners and asked for

---

powerful authorities. The familiar words of Greer L.J. in *Tolley v Fry . . .* were not an isolated instance but formed part of a lengthy line of authority and dicta to the same effect. This is not to ignore the fact that we are today a much more diverse society than in the past and that the reputation of a person within his own racial or religious community may be damaged by a statement which would not be regarded as damaging by society at large. This is an issue which may need to be addressed at some stage in the future. I merely note the substantial difficulties, at least in this court, in determining it in the way contended for by the claimants."

[166] Per Greer L.J. in *Tolley v Fry* [1930] 1 K.B. 467 CA at 479.

[167] Per Farwell L.J. in *Leetham v Rank* (1912) 57 S.J. 111 CA at 112. Thus whatever may be the differences among Christians it cannot be defamatory to describe adherents of a church as "evangelical": it is the duty of all Christians to spread the gospel: *Campbell v Toronto Star* (1990) 73 D.L.R. (4th) 190.

[168] See para.2.23, below. This may include certain mere prejudice which is in fact widely held. Thus in *Robson v News Group Newspapers* (unreported, 95/SC/0876, October 9, 1995), Judge Previté QC, it was held not to be capable of being defamatory to say that the plaintiff's father was a criminal and a fugitive from justice.

[169] Per Slesser L.J. in *Byrne v Deane* [1937] 1 K.B. 818 CA at 833; cf. *Conroy v Nicol*, 1951 (1) S.A. 653 AD.

[170] *Arab News Network v Jihad Al Khazen* [2001] EWCA Civ 118 per Keene L.J. at [30].

[171] For "right-thinking" see *Sim v Stretch* (1936) 52 T.L.R. 669 HL at 671, per Lord Atkin; *Tolley v Fry* [1930] 1 K.B. 467 CA at 479, per Greer L.J.; *Mawe v Pigott* (1869) I.R. 4 C.L. at 62. In *Slatyer v Daily Telegraph* (1908) 6 C.L.R. 1 disapproval was expressed of the use of "right thinking" except in the sense of a citizen "of fair average intelligence".

[172] *Consolidated Trust v Browne* (1948) 49 S.R.(N.S.W.) 86 at 89; *Gorton v ABC* (1973) 22 F.L.R. 181 at 186–187.

[173] (1921) 90 L.J.K.B. 883. Cf. *McMullan v Mulhall* [1929] I.R. 470; *Murphy v Plasterers Society* [1949] S.A.S.R. 98.

a ship to take to sea. It was contended that no action lay, as the words only conveyed a defamatory imputation to a limited class of persons, namely the members of the trade union. In a considered judgment, McCardie J. said that the cases:

"seem to show that the words complained of must be such as would injure the plaintiff's reputation in the minds of ordinary, just and reasonable citizens"

and, applying that test, he concluded that:

"it would not be defamatory merely to say of an ordinary trade unionist that he had left his union,[174] or that he had openly continued at work in spite of the orders of his union."

On the facts of the case, however, he was able to conclude that the words amounted to a charge of disloyalty or hypocrisy, which was defamatory.[175] It was also held in the 1860s that an allegation that a physician had met homeopaths in consultation (conduct which according to the declaration was considered by medical opinion of the time to be improper or disgraceful) was not actionable.[176] In the course of argument Pollock C.B. said:

"Is it defamation? . . . There is a distinction between imputing what is merely a breach of conventional etiquette, and what is illegal, mischievous or sinful-between, in fact, matters of taste and matters of crime."[177]

No doubt Pollock C.B.'s view that it would not be defamatory of a lady of fashion to state that she had travelled on a bus[178] was correct even in 1863, but there is a considerable gulf between this and allegations of breach of professional etiquette. At any rate, it seems clear that one can draw a distinction between mere breaches of etiquette on the one hand and breaches of professional ethics or codes of conduct on the other: the latter are actionable even if the former are not.[179] Thus, despite some old authority to the contrary,[180] it is submitted that today an allegation that a professional person advertises would be defamatory if that were contrary to the rules of the profession.[181]

---

[174] *McMullan v Mulhall* [1929] I.R. 470 (held by one judge that it would not be defamatory of a printer to say he was not a union member).

[175] An imputation of hypocrisy is still likely to be treated as defamatory: *Cook v Telegraph* [2011] EWHC 1134 (QB) whether it means dishonest pretence or not living up to stated principles though an imputation of hypocrisy will frequently be treated as a statement of opinion.

[176] *Clay v Roberts* (1863) 8 L.T. 397.

[177] These words of Pollock C.B. were quoted with apparent approval by Lord Atkin in *Sim v Stretch* (1936) 52 T.L.R. 669 HL at 672 but the passage was cited by him only "because of its reference to social conditions" in the 1860s. Contrast *Southee v Denny* (1847) 1 Exch. 196 at 203 ("no medical man would meet him professionally"; slander actionable per se). Cf. *Snow v Etty* (1887) 22 L.J.Newspaper 292.

[178] *Clay v Roberts*, above, at 398.

[179] *Angell v Bushell* [1968] 1 Q.B. 813 at 825. Cf. *O'Neill v Christiano* (1961) 31 D.L.R. (2d) 195 ("unethical conduct" not defamatory).

[180] *Beaney v Fitzgerald* (1863) 2 W. & W. (Vict.) 184.

[181] See *Grubb v Bristol United Press* [1963] 1 Q.B. 309 at 337; *Lewis v Daily Telegraph* [1964] A.C. 234 at 271. On the relation between professional codes and the opinions of society, see *Hughes v Architects Registration Council* [1957] 2 Q.B. 550.

2.21 The American approach. It is easy to think of cases in which, if the law looks only to the reaction of persons generally, statements very damaging to reputation would go without legal redress. For example, a statement attributing heretical views to a member of a religious group might excite odium within that group even though it might be a matter of indifference to people in general. It is suggested below that in the majority of cases the problem may be circumvented by pleading that the statement contains further imputations, but should the matter ever come before the Supreme Court it will be necessary to consider whether there may be advantages in the test used in the United States. In a leading case the plaintiff's picture was used in a whiskey advertisement along with a purported testimonial from her about the "great, invigorating, life-giving and curative properties" of the whiskey.[182] The plaintiff was in fact a teetotaller. In holding that the case should have been left to the jury, Holmes J. pointed out that there was clearly no general consensus of opinion that to drink whiskey was wrong but that:

> "if the advertisement obviously would hurt the plaintiff in the estimation of an important and respectable part of the community, liability is not a question of a majority vote . . . No falsehood is thought about or even known by all the world. No conduct is hated by all. That it will be known by a large number and will lead an appreciable fraction of that number to regard the plaintiff with contempt is enough to do her practical harm . . . It seems to be impossible to say that the obvious tendency of what is imputed to the plaintiff by this advertisement is not seriously to hurt her standing with a considerable[183] and respectable class in her community."

This approach may be supported on two grounds: first, what the law is primarily concerned with is to exclude from the law of defamation those cases where the reaction to the statement may be described as anti-social or eccentric[184]; secondly, the English test is arguably based upon the assumption of a consensus of moral opinion in society which, if it ever existed, has now passed away. On the other hand, the American test is not without difficulty[185]: how large is the class of persons to be before it is regarded as "considerable" or "important"? By this test Muslims would presumably qualify as a sufficiently large group in England and presumably so would Jews, though they are less numerous. There are, however, only a very small number of Jains in the

---

[182] *Peck v Tribune Co*, 214 U.S. 185 (1909). See 50 Am.Jur.2d, *Libel and Slander*, para.128.

[183] Cf. *Burrascano v Levi* 452 F.Supp. 452 (1978), affirmed 612 F.2d 1306 (CA5 1979) (minimal element of community).

[184] See para.2.23, below.

[185] Though the point was not in issue, the English test is stated by the High Court of Australia in *Reader's Digest Services Pty Ltd v Lamb* (1982) 150 C.L.R. 500 at 505. In *Hepburn v TCN Channel Nine Pty Ltd* [1983] 2 N.S.W.L.R. 682 NSWCA, Glass J.A. favoured the American test: *Quigley v Creation Ltd* [1971] I.R. 269 at 272 appears to regard the two approaches as the same.

country and it would seem odd if a statement that C, a Jain, had broken a fundamental tenet of that faith were not actionable whereas a similar statement about a Muslim were. Furthermore, would it be enough that the statement reflected upon the claimant only in the eyes of social acquaintances or fellow workers?[186]

Meaning and imputations in these cases. Two factors tend to the result   **2.22**
that there is less difference in practice between these two approaches than might at first appear. First, it is plain that to say that the statement must lower the claimant in the estimation of right-thinking persons generally does not mean that the statement must be readily comprehensible to people in general: a defamatory statement may be made in a foreign language or in a highly technical scientific journal which would be incomprehensible to the great mass of people.[187] Both the "right-thinking person" and the "ordinary reader" are abstractions, things which exist only as an idea, they are not identifiable persons with a standard quantity of knowledge.[188] In such cases there must be a publication to persons (for example, an expert group) who would be capable of understanding the statement in the sense of which the claimant complains. That has led courts in some cases to speak in terms of the likely reaction of the target audience of the publication rather than persons generally.[189] However, that is not difficult to reconcile with the standard approach, for one can pose the question as "if this were explained to the ordinary citizen would it

---

[186] Cf. *Myroft v Sleight*: para.2.20, above.

[187] *Drummond-Jackson v BMA* [1970 1 W.L.R. 698. See also *Ben-Oliel v Press Publishing Co*, 167 N.E. 432 (N.Y. 1929) (false attribution of article, errors in which made plaintiff appear an ignoramus to fellow-experts).

[188] In *Sim v Stretch* no evidence was of course put before the House of Lords to show the effect of the allegation (of borrowing money from a servant) on right thinking people (and the judges below and the jury thought it was defamatory). The "right thinking person", like the "reasonable man", serves as a metaphor for what is in fact the judge's view of what is capable of being recognised as acceptable public opinion. Perhaps the American approach makes this issue more open to argument.

[189] *Drummond-Jackson v BMA* [1970] 1 W.L.R. 698 at 1009, 1106; *Cornelius v De Taranto*, June 30, 2000, (QB); *Gillick v Brook Advisory Centres* [2002] EWHC 829 (QB) at [13]; *Bowker v RSPB* [2011] EWHC 737 (QB) at [39]; *Switzerland Australia Health Fund Pty Ltd v Shaw* (1988) 81 A.L.R. 111 at 119, Fed Ct. of Australia; *FAI General Insurance Co. Ltd v RAIA Insurance Brokers Ltd* (1992) 108 A.L.R. 479 at 496, Fed Ct. of Australia; *Morgan v Mallard* (1997) 68 S.A.S.R. 184 at 193–194. *Al-Fagih v HH Saudi Research & Marketing (UK) Ltd*, July 28, 2000, (QB) is perhaps different. This concerned an alleged libel in an Arabic newspaper circulating among Saudi Arabians in London. Smith J. seems to have accepted the argument of counsel that: "the test to be applied is what the words would mean to the hypothetical ordinary reasonable reader of the newspaper. That would be an Arab speaking reader, living or staying in the UK, probably in London. This would be a reader who understood and shared the values of Islamic culture who put a higher value on the honour of women than we do in this country". The latter part of the formulation strays from "What did the words convey?" to "What would be the effect of these words upon the claimant's reputation?" and the target audience is clearly assumed to have "non-standard" views on this. The case on appeal turned only on the issue of qualified privilege: [2001] EWCA Civ 1634 CA; [2002] E.M.L.R. 13.

reflect on the plaintiff's reputation[190] in his eyes?"[191] Secondly, in many cases it may be possible to show that a charge of conduct which in itself is obnoxious only to a limited group is defamatory because the statement carries the additional imputation that the claimant is thereby guilty of conduct, such as disloyalty or hypocrisy, which is regarded as discreditable by reasonable people generally even though they may be indifferent to the tenets of the group which is directly offended. Hence in *Myroft v Sleight*[192] the statement was defamatory on this basis, as it was in *Shah v Akram*,[193] where the plaintiff was alleged to have insulted Islam.

2.23 Anti-social views. Whether one takes the community as a whole or a substantial group as the point of reference, all are agreed that it is necessary to reject claims which are based upon the claimant's reputation being harmed among persons whose views are wrong-headed and anti-social.

"The fact that the plaintiff is lowered in the eyes of all the members of the Beneficial Burglars' Society by a statement that his reports have greatly reduced the number of professional burglars in active practice, is not defamatory of the plaintiff."[194]

In *Mawe v Pigott*,[195] an Irish priest sued for words charging him with being an informer against a certain class of Irish criminals. He argued that, amongst certain classes who were either themselves criminals or who sympathised with crime, it would expose a person to great odium to represent him as an

---

[190] Hence it may not be very important that, as McColl J.A. says in *Radio 2UE Sydney Pty Ltd v Chesterton* [2008] NSWCA 66 at [128] "none of these cases consider how the tribunal of fact would determine the standards of the discrete target". It can be assumed in the absence of evidence to the contrary that the standards of a professional body will be acceptable to right-thinking persons.

[191] Whether that requires an innuendo in the technical sense is discussed at para.3.27, below. In *Drummond-Jackson v BMA*, above, no innuendo was thought necessary even though the article was "barely intelligible to the ordinary layman". In *Krahe v TCN Channel Nine Pty Ltd* (1986) 4 N.S.W.L.R. 536 at 544, Hunt J. held that:

"where a plaintiff relies upon the existence of a particular attitude towards certain behaviour which is held by one group within the community which is not an attitude held by the general community . . . it is necessary for the plaintiff to plead that sectional attitude as an extrinsic fact or circumstance, and his case will then (within certain limits not here relevant) proceed upon the basis that publication in a defamatory sense is alleged only in relation to members of the particular group."

Quaere whether this takes the "American view" as its starting point, since it does not seem to be concerned only with the meaning of the statement.

[192] (1921) 90 L.J.K.B. 883. See para.2.20, above. *Murphy v Plasterers Society* [1949] S.A.S.R. 98, also seems to proceed on this basis, despite the reference to trade unionists being a large part of the population. *Prinsloo v SA Associated Newspapers*, 1959 (2) S.A. 693 (student alleged to be spy for police; not defamatory) seems to take a narrow view on this approach.

[193] (1981) 79 L.S. Gaz. 814 CA. However, it must be said that to explain some of the cases in this way seems artificial.

[194] Eldredge, *Law of Defamation* (1978), para.7.

[195] (1869) I.R. 4 C.L. 54; *Saunders v WHY-TV*, 382 A.2d 257 (Del 1978) (allegation that prisoner an FBI informant).

informer, or otherwise acting in the detection of crime. "That," said the court, "is quite true, but we cannot be called upon to adopt that standard. The very circumstances which will make a person be regarded with disfavour by the criminal classes will raise his character in the estimation of right-thinking men. We can only regard the estimation in which a man is held by society generally."[196] Again, in *Byrne v Deane*[197] it was held not defamatory to allege that the plaintiff, a member of a club, gave information to the police about illegal gaming machines in the club.[198] It is, however, necessary to pay careful attention to the imputations conveyed by the statement. Thus if in *Byrne v Deane* the statement had been that the plaintiff had (1) informed the police and (2) had thereby behaved in a disgraceful manner, it is difficult to see how the additional comment could have been regarded as other than defamatory.[199] What the majority of the court in that case were not prepared to do was to regard the statement as carrying that additional imputation by implication.[200] There are Scots cases to the effect that calling someone an informer is defamatory because the allegation carries the imputation of base motives.[201] However in the more recent English case of *Williams v MGN Ltd*[202] Eady J. held on the facts that the allegation of being a "grass" was to be regarded, as a matter of public policy, as being incapable of bearing a defamatory meaning.

Illegal activity. The law does not protect a reputation in any illegal calling or activity, no matter how highly certain people think of the claimant for his   **2.24**

---

[196] (1869) I.R. 4 C.L. 54 at 62.

[197] [1937] 1 K.B. 818 CA.

[198] "To say of a man that he has put in motion the proper machinery for suppressing crime is a thing which cannot on the face of it be defamatory": ibid. at 840, per Greene L.J. See also *Blair v Mirror Newspapers* [1970] 2 N.S.W.R. 604. Similarly it is not prima facie defamatory to say that the claimant proposes to enforce a judgment he has obtained: *Trkulja v Ethnic Broadcasting Station of Victoria Ltd* [2000] VSC 219 at [18], Hedigan J.

[199] A point made by Greer L.J. in his dissent. Even where the alleged act of the claimant was reporting an offence which all reasonable people would say should be reported, an additional allegation that the claimant had behaved improperly in doing so would be actionable, e.g. if D said that C had reported suspicions of child abuse to the police without making proper inquiries.

[200] Greer L.J., dissenting, thought this could be read into the statement (a doggerel rhyme). *Berry v Irish Times* [1973] I.R. 368 is a borderline case in which the Irish Supreme Court was divided over whether "20th century felon setter" was capable of being defamatory. The majority took the view that the statement merely imputed participation in securing the conviction of Irish nationals by English courts and was not defamatory.

[201] *Kennedy v Allan* (1848) 10 D. 1293; *Graham v Roy* (1851) 13 D. 634; *Winn v Quillan* (1899) 2 F. 322. In *Graham* there was in fact an express allegation that the plaintiff was motivated by a desire to get a share in the statutory penalties. The view of Greer L.J. in *Byrne v Deane* seems more in accord with the views of real people, but as the majority point out, to accept it would involve drawing distinctions between different types of criminal conduct. Cf. *Hepburn v TCN Channel Nine Pty Ltd* [1983] 2 N.S.W.L.R. 682 NSWCA ("abortionist" defamatory even though abortions capable of being performed lawfully).

[202] [2009] EWHC 3150 (QB).

experience or proficiency in it.[203] In *Wilkinson v Sporting Life*[204] Evatt J. formulated the following principles: (1) If the source of the injured reputation is illegality, the law will not protect it at all, even from injury resulting from imputations travelling far beyond the mere charge of illegality. The law does not regard a reputation illegally attained as proper to be protected however it may be infringed upon and whatever be the precise terms of the libel. (2) A claimant is entitled to recover in respect of imputations injurious to his reputation so far as it is not founded upon or attained by unlawful conduct on his part. (3) Neither general nor special damages can be awarded in respect of an injury to a claimant's business reputation or his business so far as such reputation or business is founded upon or attained by illegality. Hence at a time when it was unlawful for a person to practise medicine without certain legal qualifications, it was held not actionable to say of an unqualified medical practitioner that he was a quack and an impostor.[205] However, a person retains his right to sue for defamatory statements that impugn his personal or his professional reputation *ultra* the illegal calling or activity.[206] Thus, where a libel imputed to the plaintiff an intention to cheat the public in the course of a betting business which was illegal, he was entitled to recover damages in respect of the charge of dishonesty.[207]

"The rule makes it impossible for the party defamed to recover when the defamatory character of the publication consists only in reflections upon his skill, fitness or competence in a business or vocation which he carries on unlawfully . . . In such a case he must set up his illegality in order to complete his cause of action; or stated in another, or perhaps better, way the only reputation which he seeks to protect from disparagement is dependent upon or arises from the illegal course of conduct . . . But when a libel contains reflections upon the private character of the plaintiff calculated to injure his reputation as a man, he has in respect of those implications a complete cause of action and . . . that cause of action is not defeated by the circumstance that they relate to his conduct in the course of an unlawful pursuit or transaction."[208]

2.25 State of public opinion. It is a truism that the state of public opinion at the time and place of publication must be considered in determining whether a

---

[203] *Morris v Langdale* (1800) 2 Bos. & P. 284; *Hunt v Bell* (1822) 1 Bing. 1; *Collins v Carnegie* (1833) 1 Ad. & E. 697 at 705; *Foulger v Newcomb* (1867) L.R. 2 Ex. 327 at 330; *Mackintosh v Truth (NZ) Ltd* [1962] N.Z.L.R. 137; *Woodger v Federal Capital Press of Australia Pty Ltd* (1992) 106 F.L.R. 183 ACTSC.

[204] (1933) 49 C.L.R. 365 at 379.

[205] *Collins v Carnegie* (1833) 1 A. & E. 697, and see *Skirving v Ross* (1880) 31 Up.Can.C.P. 423; *Lathrop v Sundberg*; 104 P. 574 (Wash 1911), held that an osteopath could not recover damages for defamation of him as a quack and charlatan as he was practising osteopathy in violation of the laws of the state. For allegation of quackery, see para.2.43, below.

[206] *Yrisarri v Clement* (1826) 3 Bing. 432; *Smith's Newspapers v Becker* (1932) 47 C.L.R. 279 (unregistered medical practitioner held entitled to sue for libel in respect of qualifications genuinely held by him, and in respect of allegations defamatory of him as a man, apart from as a doctor); *Church of New Faith v Bower* (1977) 18 S.A.S.R. 554 at 562.

[207] *Wilkinson v Sporting Life* (1933) 49 C.L.R. 365.

[208] Ibid. at 376, per Dixon J. See also *Greville v Chapman* (1844) 5 Q.B. 731.

statement is capable of being defamatory.[209] An imputation may make people think worse of the claimant at one time and not at another.[210] For instance, in the time of Charles II it was actionable to call a person a Papist and to say that he went to Mass,[211] but obviously in the existing state of opinion in England no action would lie for such a statement.[212] Again, the place where the words were published may be an important factor in determining whether they are defamatory or not,[213] so that two legally similar systems may come to opposing results at the same time. In Quebec in the late 19th century it was held actionable to publish of a candidate for public office that he was a freemason.[214] In South Africa,[215] and in some of the southern states of America,[216] it was held actionable in the last century to state that a white person was black. Those decisions are now historical curiosities even in those countries and probably never represented the law in England.[217] This process of change is an ongoing[218] and perhaps an accelerating one[219]: e.g. there have

---

[209] If it is so *capable*, the role of the jury in determining whether by current standards it *is* defamatory must be respected: *Cairns v John Fairfax & Sons Ltd* [1983] 2 N.S.W.L.R. 708 NSWCA (extra-marital relationship); *Beran v John Fairfax Publications Pty Ltd* [2004] NSWCA 107 (charge of "profiteering").

[210] *Holdsworth v Associated Newspapers* (1937) 53 T.L.R. 1029 CA at 1033. Contrast this para. with para.3.28, below on the changing sense of words.
"Sometimes words appear to have changed their meanings, when the real change is in the popular estimate of the value of the ideas they stand for. There is no hint in the O.E.D. definitions that appeasement can be anything but praiseworthy":
Gowers, *The Complete Plain Words*, (Pelican edn, 1962), p.59. For a passage in which the two points are considered together see *Row v Clargis* (1683) Raym. 482: "and times alter the law when the sense of words alters; for though formerly [Papist] was not actionable, yet now 'tis grown to be a word of more reproach". The other examples are of the changing use of words. For the effect of fluctuating views of Communism, see para.2.28. See also *Vander Zalm v Times Publishers* (1980) 109 D.L.R. (3d) 531 at 540.

[211] *Row v Clargis* (1683) Raym. 482; cf. *Walden v Mitchell* (1692) 2 Vent. 265 (time when accusation would have exposed man to the rabble). Cf. *Ireland v Smith* (1610) 2 Brownl. 166.

[212] Cf. *Loukas v Young* [1968] 3 N.S.W.R. 549; allegation of witchcraft not defamatory as ordinary man does not now believe in it. But cf. Pennsylvania in 1896: *Oles v Pittsburg Times*, 2 Pa. Super 130.

[213] In *Chen Cheng v Central Christian Church* [1999] 1 Sing. L.R. 94 Sing CA, it was held that calling a church a "cult" was defamatory because in Singapore the word was a pejorative one, meaning a religious group with teachings and practices that are abhorrent and harmful to society. Quaere whether the result would be the same in England.

[214] *Lareau v La Minerve* (1883) 27 Lower Canada Jurist 337.

[215] *Pitout v Rosenstein* (1930) O.P.D. 112 at 117: "There is an impairment of reputation when an imputation is made of poverty, leprosy, bastardy, or anything else which according to the standard prevailing in the country is calculated to bring a person into contempt even though it may not reflect on his moral character. It is, therefore, defamatory to assert that a white man is a Hottentot."

[216] *Natchez Times v Dunigan*, 72 So.2d 681 (Miss 1954).

[217] See *Hoare v Silverlock* (1848) 12 Q.B. 630 at 632. The decision in *Camrose v Action Press*, *The Times*, October 14, 15, 16, 1937 (actionable to call plaintiff "international Jew financier") seems to turn on an imputation of disloyalty.

[218] "A belief which represented unquestioned orthodoxy in Year X may have become questionable by Year Y, and unsustainable by Year Z": *R. v Ministry of Defence Ex p. Smith* [1996] 1 All E.R. 257 at 263, per Sir Thomas Bingham M.R.

[219] To take the situation which is the reverse of that where a person of race A is said to belong to race B, it is now capable of being defamatory to say of a person that he holds "racist" or "anti-

been radical changes in public attitudes towards sexual behaviour in the last 40 years[220] and there is a greater public concern with environmental issues, which is likely to be significant for imputations concerning trade or business.[221]

2.26 State of the law. The state of the law may also determine whether an imputation is defamatory. It will usually be defamatory to impute the commission of a criminal offence, and a change in the law may therefore make words actionable which once were not so.[222] However conduct may still be disapproved of even when legalised.[223]

SECTION 4. INSTANCES OF DEFAMATORY IMPUTATIONS

(a) *General*

2.27 A question of fact. Since the issue whether a particular imputation is defamatory will vary with time, place and the state of public opinion, it is not possible to say that such and such is defamatory and such and such is not. In any case, whether or not any imputation is defamatory is not a matter of law, but a matter of fact for the jury, and no other jury will be bound to reach the same decision. It is similarly a matter of fact whether any words convey the defamatory imputation alleged, and this may depend to a great extent on the circumstances and context of a particular publication.[224] But provided these points are borne in mind, previous decisions are of some value in determining whether particular words are capable of conveying a defamatory imputation.[225] What must be borne in mind however in reading this section, is that

---

Semitic" views ("Jew-hater" was held defamatory in *De Stempel v Dunkels* [1938] 1 All E.R. 238 CA, affirmed (1939) 55 T.L.R. 655). See also *Boyle v Mirror Group Newspapers Ltd http://informm.wordpress.com/2012/10/22/news-frankie-boyle-wins-54650-in-mirror-libel-action/* in which Frankie Boyle won £50,400 in a jury trial for an allegation that he was a "racist comedian". Nowadays opprobrium would attach to a person who called black people "niggers" but this was not necessarily so even in the 1960s: raised in argument in *Mitchell v Book Sales, Independent,* March 25, 1994.

[220] See para.2.29, below.
[221] There have also been changes in attitude towards advertising practices: *Mount Cook Group Ltd v Johnstone Motors Ltd* [1990] 2 N.Z.L.R. 488. In *Robertson v John Fairfax Publications Pty Ltd* [2003] N.S.W.S.C. 473 it does not seem to have been disputed that an imputation of outdated attitudes on sex discrimination to those engaged in trade union activities was defamatory.
[222] See para.2.28, below.
[223] *R. v Bishop* [1975] Q.B. 274 CA at 281. As to homosexuality, see para.2.29, below. In South Africa the "right thinking" person is to be treated as subscribing to the norms and values of the Constitution, which may have implications for cases of this type: *Sokhulu v New African Publications Ltd*, 2001 (4) S.A. 1357 (W).
[224] See para.3.30, below.
[225] This is also the view of Burchell, *Law of Defamation in South Africa* (1985), p.83. Contrast *Mateus v Short* (1919) 40 N.L.R. 193 at 194.

many of these cases were decided before the Human Rights Act 1998 became law and before the requirement that the imputation meet the necessary "threshold of seriousness"[226] was articulated. Consequently, there are many imputations which though once considered defamatory may no longer be treated as such. Defamation is often couched in slang[227] and consideration will have to be given to whether the words are sufficiently clear in their ordinary meaning to be pleaded with no elaboration, or whether it is desirable or even necessary[228] to explain them. Again, considerations of time and place have to be taken into account. For example, the public today is likely to be a good deal less familiar with Biblical allusions than in the past.

Instances of defamatory words. It has been held defamatory to publish   **2.28**
of a person that he is a rogue and a rascal,[229] a swindler or a sharper,[230] a greedy sinecurist,[231] a crook,[232] a shyster,[233] dishonest,[234] a coward,[235] a liar,[236] someone who "rats" on promises,[237] a paedophile,[238] a hypocrite,[239] a

---

[226] See para.2.4, above.

[227] See *Winyard v Tatler Publishing Co, Independent*, August 16, 1991 ("boot" capable of meaning ugly old harridan or promiscuous slut).

[228] For the "true" and "false" innuendo, see para.3.20, below.

[229] *Villers v Monsley* (1769) 2 Wilson 403 at 404; *Massee v Williams* (1913) 207 F. 222. Whether today, without more, such imputations would be treated as defamatory must be doubtful.

[230] *I'Anson v Stuart* (1787) I T.R. 748; *Goldstein v Foss* (1827) 6 B. & C. 1 54, and see *Brown v Beatty* (1862) 12 Up.Can.C.P. 107. Cf. *Shendish Manor Ltd v Coleman* [2001] EWCA Civ 913 ("out to make a fast buck" not reasonably capable of imputing criminality).

[231] *Mitchell v Nanaimo District Teachers' Association* (1994) 94 B.C.L.R. (2d) 81

[232] *Pandolfo v Bank of Benson* 273 F. 48 (1921); *Wells v Puddister* [2007] NLCA 25; [2007] 265 Nfld. & P.E.I.R. 174.

[233] *Wells v Puddister*, above. *Levi v Bates* [2009] EWHC 1495 (QB).

[234] *Austin v Culpepper* (1684) 2 Show. 313; *Mularczyk v John Fairfax Publications Pty Ltd* [2001] NSWCA 467; *Raliphaswa v Mugivhi* [2008] ZASCA 17. Cf. *Macrae v Sutherland* (1889) 16 R. 476 (unpopularity not actionable, but dishonesty is).

[235] *Russel v Sheriffs* (1837) 15 S. 881 (Ct of Sess); *Edmondson v Amery, The Times*, January 28, 1911; *Churchill v Nabarro, The Times*, October 29, 1960; *Baker v Odhams Press, The Times*, March 15, 1966 ("quitter", "funkhole").

[236] *MacLaren v Robertson* (1859) 21 D. 183; *Neill v Henderson* (1901) 3 F. 387; *Drummond v Kwaku* [2000] 1 H.K.L.R.D. 604; cf. *Welgemoed v Cohen* [1937] T.P.D. 134: a statement that P. made "a false representation on the faith of which money had been paid" held not defamatory; *Yates v McRae* [1929] T.P.D. 480; *Whitlock v Smith* [1943] C.P.D. 321; *Daniels v Jackson, The Times*, October 10, 1956 ("Complete misstatement of fact"; not defamatory in circumstances); *Vaughan v Palmer, The Times*, October 26, 1963 (posing as an official); *Carroll v BBC*, 1997 S.L.T. (Sh. Ct.) 23 ("stranger to the truth"—meaning "liar"—merely abusive and not defamatory in Scots law).

[237] *Clark v Express Newspapers* [2004] EWHC 481 (QB).

[238] See, e.g., *Lord McAlpine of West Green v Bercow* [2013] EWHC 1342 (QB): imputation that the claimant was a paedophile who was guilty of sexually abusing boys living in care.

[239] *Thorley v Lord Kerry* (1812) 4 Taunt. 355; *Newby v Times-Mirror Co*, 160 P. 233 (1916); *Griffin v Divers*, 1922 S.C. 605; *McGuiness v J T Publishing Australia Pty Ltd* [1999] N.S.W.S.C. 471; *Mawdsley v Guardian Newspapers Ltd* [2002] EWHC 1780 QB; *Cook v Telegraph* [2011] EWHC 1134 (QB).

fanatic,[240] a villain,[241] a racist,[242] a blackguard,[243] a libeller,[244] a slanderer and a scandalmonger,[245] or an habitual drunkard[246] or a drug addict[247] (and a fortiori a drug dealer)[248]; or indiscreet,[249] or arrogant,[250] or wanting in gratitude,[251] or mistreats his children.[252] It has been held defamatory to write of someone that he has been guilty of oppressive,[253] intolerant,[254] insulting,[255] reprehensible,[256] threatening[257] or unbrotherly conduct,[258] or of a breach of

---

[240] *O'Malley v Callaghan* (1992) 89 D.L.R. (4th) 577.

[241] *Bell v Stone* (1798) 1 Bos. & P. 331.

[242] See e.g., *Boyle v MGN Ltd http://inforrm.wordpress.com/2012/10/22/news-frankie-boyle-wins-54650-in-mirror-libel-action/*. See also *Hays Plc v Hartley* [2010] EWHC 1068, per Tugendhat J., at [9].]

[243] *Brownlie v Thomson* (1859) 21 M. 480.

[244] *Colby v Reynolds* (1834) 6 Vermont R. 489; *Brookes v Tichborne* (1850) 5 Exch. 929; *Wakley v Healey* (1894) 7 C.B. 59, 606.

[245] *Parton v Cruce* (1904) 105 Amer.St. R. 46; *Paterson v Welch* (1893) 20 R. 744 at 746.

[246] *Alexander v Jenkins* [1892] 1 Q.B. 797 at 804; *Ritchie v Sexton* (1891) 64 L.T. 610; or sells moonshine whisky; *Mychajluk v Kolisnyk* [1923] 4 D.L.R. 724; or of a schoolmaster that he is well known for giving riotous parties; *Golding v Torch Printing*, 1949 (4) S.A. 150. Cf. *Kirk v Reed* [1968] N.Z.L.R. 801.

[247] *Miles v McGrath*, 4 F.Supp. 603 (1933).

[248] *Platt v Time International* (1964) 44 D.L.R. (2d) 17; *Entienne v Festival City Broadcasters* [2001] SASC 60; 79 S.A.S.R. 19.

[249] Per Gaselee J. in *Archbishop of Tuam v Robeson* (1828) 5 Bing. 17 at 24.

[250] *Cruise v Express Newspapers Plc* [1999] Q.B. 931 CA; *Brown v Marron* [2001] WASC 100.

[251] *Cox v Lee* (1869) L.R. 4 Ex. 284. "Want of gratitude is a serious imputation": per Lord Denman C.J. in *Hoare v Silverlock* (1848) 12 Q.B. 624 at 630; cf. *Robbins v Western Newspapers* (Bristol Assizes), *The Times*, December 9, 12, 1930 (want of filial devotion); *Greef v Raubenheimer*, 1976 (3) S.A. 37 AD: disloyalty. The transcript of *O'Hara v Channel 7 Pty Ltd* [2007] NSWDC 181 does not reveal the final fate of the pleaded imputation that the plaintiff was "one of Australia's greatest whingers". But see *Ecclestone v Telegraph Media Group Ltd* [2009] EWHC 2779 (QB): imputation that the claimant was dismissive of, or showed a lack of respect to, others, however well-respected they may be, was not capable of being defamatory (at [20]). In the light of *Ecclestone*, the cases suggesting that "want of gratitude" may be defamatory must surely be treated with some care.

[252] *Atkinson v CBC* (1981) 49 N.S.R. (2d) 381.

[253] *Woodard v Dowsing* (1828) 2 Man. & Ry.74. Cf. *Arthur v Clitherow*, *The Times*, June 29, 1963 (cruelty to a horse); cf. *Vander Zalm v Times Publishers* (1980) 109 D.L.R. (3d) 531.

[254] *Teacy v M'Kenna* (1869) I.R. 4 C.L. 374; *Mitchell v Faber & Faber* [1998] E.M.L.R. 807; *Sweeney v Schenectady Union Co*, 112 F. 288 (1941): false allegation that P. had opposed an appointment to the Bench on the ground that the appointee was a Jew and one not born in the United States; *De Stempel v Dunkels* (1938) 54 T.L.R. 289; *Bor-Komorowski v Manchester Guardian*, *The Times*, March 26, 1959; *Caul v Beaverbrook Newspapers*, *The Times*, January 28, 1960, CA; *Templeton v Jones* [1984] 1 N.Z.L.R. 448 NZCA. In Canada, see *Dennison v Sanderson* [1946] 4 D.L.R. 314; *Cherneskey v Armadale Publishers* [1979] 1 S.C.R. 1067; *Christie v Geiger* (1984) 35 Alta. L.R. (2d) 316; affirmed [1987] 1 W.W.R. 357; *Wagner v Lim* (1994) 22 Alta. L.R. (3d) 169 (racist attitudes). Accusations of racial bias in the administration of justice have been held defamatory in modern South African cases (*SA Associated Newspapers v Estate Pelser*, 1975 (4) S.A. 797 AD; *Argus Printing & Publishing Co. Ltd v Esselen's Estate*, 1994 (2) S.A. 1 AD) and it has been held defamatory of a black man to say that he abused a white man by calling him "white trash": *Sindani v Van der Merwe*, 2002 (2) S.A. 38 SCA.

[255] *Clement v Chivis* (1829) 9 B. & C. 172.

[256] *Fox v Boulter* [2012] EWHC 3183 (QB).

[257] *Carter v Gair* (1999) 170 D.L.R. (4th) 204.

[258] *Campbell v Payton* (1898) 17 N.Z.L.R. 91.

duty,[259] or that his actions are motivated by revenge when he asserts other motives,[260] or that he is a "heartless, rude bastard"[261]; or to impute "any dishonourable conduct to another though not involving a breach of positive law"[262] or to impute that a person is motivated by vanity or self-delusion.[263] It is defamatory to suggest that a person's conduct has brought about an undesirable social development, provided that what is imputed to him is culpable.[264] It has been held defamatory to publish of a person that he has falsely accused another of some criminal offence,[265] or that he has cheated at horse-racing[266] or at cards,[267] or that he has been blackballed on seeking admission to a club,[268] or that he has entertained with a view to winning money from his guests by gaming,[269] or that he is not a proper person to be received in society.[270] The imputation of a criminal offence[271] or conviction,

---

[259] *Foulger v Newcomb* (1867) L.R. 2 Ex. 327; *Moffat v London Express*, 1950 S.L.T. (Notes) 46 (disloyalty); *Mohamed Hussain v Chew How Yang Eddie* [1995] 3 S.L.R. 177 ("sell-out" by union).

[260] *Branson v Bower* [2001] E.M.L.R. 32 CA.

[261] *Nail v News Group Newspapers Ltd* [2004] EWCA Civ 1708; [2005] E.M.L.R. 12 at [21] (though the point was not in issue since there had been an unqualified offer of amends). More particular allegations were of indiscriminate sexual encounters, attempting to seduce the fiancée of a friend, eating canned dog meat when pressed for cash, being arrogant to colleagues, being mean, shunning his sick father, exploiting the death of a colleague for financial advantage and illegally financing a property development business.

[262] Per Jervis C.J. in *Helsham v Blackwood* (1851) 11 C.B. 111 at 125 (practising before a duel!); *Holdsworth v Associated Newspapers* (1937) 53 T.L.R. 1029 CA, where a statement that the plaintiffs had refused to accept the interim award of the Joint Conciliation Board for the Road Transport Industry was held to be capable of a defamatory meaning, for it suggested they had gone back on an agreement to accept such awards; *Armstrong v Times Newspapers* [2006] EWHC 1614 (QB) (professional cyclist taking performance-enhancing drugs); *Jones v Skelton* [1963] I W.L.R. 1362 PC (councillor accepting preferential treatment), and contrast *Demmers v Wyllie*, 1978 (4) S.A. 619 (where the plaintiff was a businessman); on appeal 1980 (1) SA 835 AD, possibly differing on this point; *Kennel Union of SA v Park* 1981 (1) S.A. 714 (misconduct at dog show); *Lloyd v Hickley*, 1967 S.L.T. 225 ("unsporting"). Quaere, whether imputation of snobbery would be defamatory: *Gotla v Odhams Press, The Times*, March 21, 1963.

[263] *Branson v Bower* [2002] Q.B. 737.

[264] *Gillick v Brook Advisory Centres* [2002] EWHC 829 QB. Cf. *Gillick v BBC* [1996] E.M.L.R. 267 CA. See also *Field v Local Sunday Newspapers (North) Ltd* [2002] EWHC 336 (QB) at [51]: not defamatory to state that claimant was vicariously responsible for the wrongdoing of others but not personally to blame.

[265] *Pearce v Symes* (1909) 28 N.Z.L.R. 562; cf. *Smith v Levitt*, F.2d 855 (1955) (character assassination).

[266] *Greville v Chapman* (1844) 5 Q.B. 731; *Wilkinson v Sporting Life* (1933) 49 C.L.R. 365.

[267] *Paterson v Shaw* (1830) 8 S. 573.

[268] *O'Brien v Clement* (1846) 16 M. & W. 159. Sed quaere today.

[269] *Digby v Thompson* (1833) 4 B. & Ald. 821.

[270] *Gregory v The Queen* (1845) 15 Q.B. 957; or that he is a queer combination of squalor and dignity: *Schoeman v Potter*, 1949 (2) S.A.L.R. 573. Cf. *Robinson v Jermyn* (1814) 1 Price 11; *Murphy v La Marsh* [1971] 2 W.W.R. 196.

[271] See, e.g., *Bento v Chief Constable of Bedfordshire Police* [2012] EWHC 1525 (QB): imputation that claimant was probably guilty of murder clearly defamatory. See also, *Lord McAlpine of West Green v Bercow* [2013] EWHC 1342 (QB): imputation that the claimant was a paedophile who was guilty of sexually abusing boys living in care. Several cases have been brought in recent years involving allegations of involvement with or funding of terrorism. Unsurprisingly, such imputations have been held to be capable of being defamatory. See, e.g., *Jameel v Wall Street Journal Europe Ltd* [2006] UKHL 44 HL; [2007] 1 A.C. 359; *Al Rajhi*

or attempt to commit such an offence,[272] would usually[273] be defamatory,[274] but not, it is thought in very minor cases: for example, it would not be defamatory to say of someone that he had committed a parking offence or a minor offence of speeding.[275] But the issue cannot turn solely on the penalty[276]: e.g. to say that someone had wilfully failed to obtain a television licence would reflect on his honesty and might be defamatory when an accusation of a traffic offence carrying a similar penalty would not be.[277] It may be defamatory to say that someone is suspected of an offence even where that does not imply guilt[278]; or that he has been charged with an offence.[279] It has been held defamatory to publish of a person that he is an alien enemy.[280] The statement that a person is a "Communist" has resulted in varying conclusions and it presents a good example of the importance of considering time and place in deciding whether words are defamatory.[281] Probably the majority of cases[282] have held it to be so, but Devlin L.J. said in 1960 that he

---

Banking & Investment Corpn v Wall Street Journal Europe [2003] EWHC 1358 (QB). See also *Berezovsky v Russian Television and Radio Broadcasting Co* [2010] EWHC 476 (QB): the claimant was alleged to have been a party to the murder of another.

[272] *Hussein v Hamilton Franks and Co. Ltd* [2013] EWHC 462 (QB).

[273] In *Vroman v Vancouver Daily* [1942] 2 D.L.R. 456, it was held that a reasonable man would not be likely to understand in a defamatory sense a newspaper headline: Husband jailed on wife's plea. Sed quaere, for the husband must have been in breach of some legal duty. See also *Thakers v Chipunguhelo* [1965] E.A. 82 (breach of prison regulations). The imputation of a criminal offence to a young child might be taken as an assertion that the act fell within the technical description of the offence without reference to mens rea or, even if guilt were imputed, a reasonable person might feel no more than pity for the child: *Saunders v Nationwide News Pty Ltd* [2005] NSWCA 404.

[274] In *Berry v BTC* [1961] 1 Q.B. 146 at 164, Diplock J. stated that in an action for malicious prosecution the test of whether a charge affected the fair fame of the plaintiff was: Was the charge one which necessarily and naturally is defamatory of the plaintiff? There was no dissent from this in the CA: [1962] 1 Q.B. 306 at 318, 333. Clearly, then, not all charges of a criminal offence are necessarily defamatory, and in that case Diplock J. held that a charge of pulling a communication cord without reasonable and sufficient cause was capable of a non-defamatory meaning.

[275] *Groom v Crocker* [1937] 3 All E.R. 844 at 848: false imputation that the plaintiff had negligently caused a personal injury accident was defamatory.

[276] Distinguish the question of whether an oral accusation of crime is a slander actionable per se, where the matter turns on whether the offence is punishable by imprisonment: see para.4.3, below.

[277] Cf. *Alexander v NE Ry* (1865) 6 B. & S. 340.

[278] See para.3.28, below.

[279] *Hassen v Post*, 1965 (3) S.A. 562 (W.), and cf. *Cadam v Beaverbrook Newspapers* [1959] 1 Q.B. 413 CA; *Monson v Tussauds* [1894] 1 Q.B. 671 at 686, per Lord Halsbury; *SA Associated Newspapers v Schoeman* (1962) 2 S.A. 613 AD at 617; *Modern Newspapers v Bill* (1978) 4 S.A. 149. In *Lewis v Daily Telegraph* [1964] A.C. 234 at 285, Lord Devlin said that it might be defamatory to say that someone had been acquitted of an offence, which would seem inevitably to follow.

[280] *Hambourg v London Mail, The Times*, October 29, 1914; *Brunner v Palmer, The Times*, December 9, 1914; *Slazengers Ltd v Gibbs* (1916) 33 T.L.R. 35. See also *Fichardt v Friend* [1916] A.D. 1; *Richler v Mack* [1917] A.D. 201; *Van der Merwe v Stalbert* [1921] A.D. 88. The English cases may reflect the strong anti-German feelings in the First World War.

[281] Quaere whether allegation, without more, of membership of British National Party or English Defence League would today be treated as being defamatory.

[282] See *Burns v Associated Newspapers* (1926) 42 T.L.R. 37; cf. *Braddock v Bevins* [1948]1 K.B. 580 CA; *Linklater v Daily Telegraph* (1964) 108 S.J. 992 (saying of man with English name

wished to be guarded against saying that in all circumstances it was defamatory of a man to say that he was a Communist[283] and today it seems
improbable that such an imputation would be treated as defamatory. To call an
aspirant for political honour a Socialist when, in fact, he does not belong to the
Socialist party is no more defamatory than to describe a Free Trader as a
Protectionist or a Protectionist as a Free Trader,[284] for a statement is not
defamatory simply because it is untrue. However, such a charge might support
an imputation of hypocrisy or disloyalty.[285] At the time of apartheid it was
held in the United States that it was defamatory of a corporation to state that
it had dealings with the government of South Africa because of the antipathy
this would cause among many Americans.[286]

Where the claimant has been accused of some discreditable conduct, it is no
answer to say "the article cannot be defamatory because it is made clear that
the law was on the claimant's side".[287] Nevertheless, the legal recognition of
beliefs or of an institution is of some relevance in determining whether an
imputation is capable of being defamatory even if there are widespread hostile
views on the matter.[288]

Sexual conduct. Any imputation of conduct considered by right-thinking   **2.29**
persons to be immoral, provided the necessary "threshold of seriousness"[289]
is met, is necessarily defamatory. In this regard, it has been held defamatory
to publish words to the effect that the plaintiff was a homosexual,[290] a

---

that he was Czech might imply that he was a Communist and disloyal); *Brannigan v Seafarers
International Union* (1963) 42 D.L.R. (2d) 249; *Delaney v News Media Ownership* [1976] 1
N.Z.L.R. 322. Cf. *Morin v Ryan* [1957] Q.B. 296, Quebec (different kinds of communism in
different places). Views in the USA have fluctuated but by 1984 the position was that the
accusation was well-nigh universally held defamatory: Prosser and Keeton, *Torts*, 5th edn, p.778.
See also cases cited in para.50, fn.12 of the 6th edition of this book and 62 A.L.R. (4th) 314. See
Botha v Marais 1974 (1) S.A. 44, AD (not all Communist methods and techniques are reprehensible); *Buthelezi v Poorter* 1975 (4) S.A. 608 (advocacy of violent change); *Marais v Richard*,
1979 (1) S.A. 83; on appeal 1981 (1) S.A. 1157.

   [283] *Kantorowicz v Cookridge*, *The Times*, October 18, 1960, CA.
   [284] *Slatyer v Daily Telegraph* (1907) 7 N.S.W.S.R. 488 at 498, per Street J.
   [285] See para.2.20, above. For allegations against politicians, see para.2.42, below.
   [286] *Southern Air Transport Inc. v American Broadcasting Co*, 877 F.2d 1010 (US App DC,
1989); and see *Partington v Bugliosi*, 825 F. Supp. 906 (DC Hawaii, 1993).
   [287] Per Singleton L.J. in *Clarke v Associated Newspapers*, *The Times*, May 7, 1955, CA;
Roberts v Patillo (1855) 2 N.S.R. 367; *Seested v Post Printing* (1931) 31 S.W.2d 1045. But some
US cases take a contrary line: *Bennett v Williamson* (1850) 4 Sandford (N.Y.) R. 60; *Homer v
Engelhardt* (1875) 117 Mass.R. 539. See Prosser and Keeton, *Torts*, 5th edn, p.774.
   [288] See Brooke L.J.'s view on whether it is defamatory to say someone is a Scientologist in
Cruise v Express Newspapers Plc [1999] Q.B. 931 CA.
   [289] See para.2.4, above.
   [290] *Liberace v Daily Mirror Newspapers Ltd*, *The Times*, June 18, 1959; or, semble, a "pansy":
Thaarup v Hulton Press (1943) 169 L.T. 309. Whatever applies to homosexuality presumably
applies to bisexuality.

lesbian,[291] or a pimp,[292] or has sold pornographic pictures.[293] It has also been held defamatory to publish of an unmarried woman that she has a child,[294] or to record the birth of a child to a woman one month after the date of her marriage,[295] for an imputation of extra-marital intercourse is in either case necessarily conveyed.[296] For the same reason it has been held defamatory of a woman who is known among her acquaintances as the wife of A and who cohabits with him to publish in a newspaper that A is engaged to be married to a different woman.[297] However in this field more than any other standards have changed,[298] and a jury must consider the case on its view of the standards of today.[299] Unmarried cohabitation[300] is now so widespread that it is not looked on as discreditable[301] in large sections (perhaps the greater part) of

---

[291] *Kerr v Kennedy* [1942] 1 K.B. 409. *Weatherhead v Armitage* (1690) 2 Lev 233 (not actionable to call a woman a "hermaphrodite") is unlikely to have much force as a precedent today. See further para.3.29, below.

[292] *Todosichuk v MacLenahan* [1946] 1. D.L.R. 557.

[293] *Garbett v Hazell, Watson and Viney* [1943] 2 All E.R. 359 CA.

[294] *Chattell v Daily Mail* (1901) 18 T.L.R. 165; *Debenham v Ancorn, The Times*, March 5, 1921; *Anderson v Stewart* (1851) 8 Up.Can. Q.B. 243; cf. *Bordeleau v Bonnyville Nouvelle Ltd* (1992) 97 D.L.R. (4th) 764.

[295] *Morrison v Ritchie* (1902) 4 F. 645.

[296] It has been held that an imputation of indelicacy of a gross kind against a Scotswoman "plainly amounts to an actionable wrong": *Cuthbert v Linklater*, 1935 S.L.T. 94 at 98. In *Bingle v EMAP Australia Pty Ltd* [2006] FCA 1704 Edmonds J. held that the imputation that the plaintiff had agreed to pose topless in a "lad's magazine" was capable of being defamatory.

[297] *Cassidy v Daily Mirror* [1929] 2 K.B. 331 CA; *Hough v London Express* [1940] 2 K.B. 507 CA.

[298] For the many (and conflicting) US cases in this area, see 57 A.L.R. (4th) 402. In *CC v AB* [2006] EWHC 3083; [2007] E.M.L.R. 11 at [25] Eady J. said in the context of breach of confidence or misuse of private information: "At one time, when there was, or was perceived to be, a commonly accepted standard in such matters as sexual morality, it may have been acceptable for the courts to give effect to that standard in exercising discretion or in interpreting legal rights and obligations. Now, however, there is a strong argument for not holding forth about adultery, or attaching greater inherent worth to a relationship which has been formalised by marriage than to any other relationship."

[299] Thus cases suggesting that it was defamatory to say of one spouse that the other had brought divorce proceedings, even in a "no-fault" jurisdiction, cited in previous editions of this book as illustrations of the principle in para.2.6, above, would not now be followed.

[300] Though attitudes to adultery have also changed markedly in the last 50 years, the fate of the numerous politicians who lost office in the periodic fits of concern about family values in the 1980s and 1990s shows that an accusation of adultery could be extremely damaging to a public figure. It should be noted however that in *Bowman v MGN Ltd* [2010] EWHC 895 (QB) Eady J. regarded an allegation that an actor, who had been in a serious relationship for 20 years, was "stepping out" with another woman as little more than celebrity gossip and at the less serious end of the scale (an offer of amends had been made so no question arose whether the words were in fact defamatory).

[301] But it is still capable of being defamatory of a man to say that he consorts with a known prostitute: *Dwek v Macmillan Publishers Ltd* [2000] E.M.L.R. 284 CA. In South Africa it has been held that it is not now capable of being defamatory to say of a woman that she has borne a child out of wedlock and has cohabited with the father for two years. The Constitution forbids discrimination on the grounds of birth or marital status and the "right thinking" person is to be treated as subscribing to the norms and values of the Constitution: *Sokhulu v New African Publications Ltd*, 2001 (4) S.A. 1357 (W).

society[302] and attitudes towards homosexuality have also changed markedly.[303] It seems highly unlikely that a judge would find that imputations, without more, that a woman was cohabiting outside marriage[304] or that a man was a practising homosexual,[305] were capable of being defamatory and it would now be proper for a judge to withdraw such allegations from a jury. In

---

[302] In 2011, 29 per cent of non-married women aged between 16 and 59 were cohabiting and of all women aged beteen 14 and 49, 18 per cent were cohabiting (compared to 3 per cent in 1979): 2011 General Lifestyle Survey, Office of National Statistics.

[303] See *R. v Ministry of Defence Ex p. Smith* [1996] 1 All E.R. 257 at 261–262, 270, since when the process has probably accelerated.

[304] While societal views on the propriety of cohabitation outside marriage have changed significantly over the last 30 years, in some sectors of society such a statement could be seriously damaging: see the report in *Independent*, May 3, 1990, of a substantial verdict in favour of a Muslim girl. See also *Lambe v Walsh* (1986) 61 Nfld. & P.E.I.R. 193 (plaintiff 14 years old). In *Khalil v Barakat* [2013] EWHC 85 (QB) Eady J. stated that

> "In our society today an allegation of unchastity would not be taken by most readers to reflect in itself adversely upon a claimant's reputation (by contrast, for example, with the social mores at the time of the Slander of Women Act 1891)."

(at [8]) However, he went to explain that there would in some cases be room for an innuendo meaning to be pleaded:

> "Nevertheless, I can see that there may well be room for an innuendo, if the relevant facts were known to the publishee(s), on the basis that Ms Khalil had given an assurance (e.g. to Dr Barakat and his family) prior to marriage that she was in fact a virgin and/or that it was generally regarded as wrong for a woman purporting to be a practising Muslim to lose her virginity prior to marriage."

(at [8]) For an indication of what sort of allegations about the sexual behaviour of a male actor might now be over the defamation threshold, see *Nail v News Group Newspapers Ltd* [2004] EWCA Civ 1708; [2005] E.M.L.R. 12 at [18] (though the point was not in issue since there had been an unqualified offer of amends). Cf. *King Zwelithini v Mervis*, 1978 (2) S.A. 521 ("ladies' man" not defamatory even of a King).

[305] In *Quilty v Windsor*, 1999 S.L.T. 346, Lord Kingarth said that he was "inclined to agree with counsel for the first defender that merely to refer to a person as being homosexual would not now generally at least be regarded—if it ever was—as defamatory *per se*"; and in *Rivkin v Amalgamated Television Services Pty Ltd* [2001] N.S.W.S.C. 432, Bell J. accepted a submission that:

> "it is no longer open to contend that the shared social and moral standards with which the ordinary reasonable member of the community is imbued include that of holding homosexual men (or men who engage in homosexual sex) in lesser regard on account of that fact alone."

However, Levine J., in *Kelly v John Fairfax Publications Pty Ltd* [2003] N.S.W.S.C. 586, declined to follow this. And in *John Fairfax Publications Pty Ltd v Rivkin* [2003] HCA 50; 201 A.L.R. 77 at [140] Kirby J. said,

> "In most circumstances, it ought not to be the case in Australia that to publish a statement that one adult was involved in consenting, private homosexual activity with another adult involves a defamatory imputation. But whether it does or does not harm a person's reputation to publish such an imputation is related to time, personality and circumstance . . . The day may come when, to accuse an adult of consenting homosexual activity is likewise generally a matter of indifference. However, it would ignore the reality of contemporary Australian society to say that that day has arrived for all purposes and all people. At least for people who treat their sexuality as private or secret, or people who have presented themselves as having a different sexual orientation, such an imputation could, depending on the circumstances, still sometimes be defamatory."

In this context one can hardly ignore the fact that (a) certain forms of discrimination in employment on the ground of sexual orientation are unlawful by regulations made under the Equality Act 2006 and (b) by the Civil Partnership Act 2004 Parliament extended most of the legal incidents of marriage to registered same sex partnerships. By the end of 2006 more than 16,000 such partnerships had been formed, sixty per cent of them male: *Social Trends* (2008 edn).

any event a jury might now be invited with some prospect of success to decide that these allegations were not in fact defamatory.[306] In practice, however, these cases are usually presented as involving some further imputation such as hypocrisy or exploitation.[307] Defamatory imputations about a person's marital or domestic affairs may of course not directly involve sexual conduct. Thus it has been held defamatory to say that a person has married for money,[308] or is willing to betray domestic confidences,[309] or neglects his spouse.[310] It is a grave defamation of a doctor to say that he engages in sexual harassment[311] and it is submitted that such a charge is now defamatory of any person, whether employer or employee.

(b) *Credit*

2.30 **Insolvency and credit.** While it is not defamatory, without more, to say that someone owes money, for that "is to say what is true of every householder . . . on most days of the month"[312] it is defamatory to say that any

---

For a sustained, and it is argued successful, critique of the proposition that it is defamatory to impute homosexuality to another, see McNamara, *Reputation and Defamation* (2007), at 197–218.

[306] In *Cairns v John Fairfax & Sons Ltd* [1983] 2 N.S.W.L.R. 708 NSWCA the article described X as the male plaintiff's "girlfriend". The jury was asked whether (a) there was an imputation of a sexual association and (b) whether it was defamatory. They answered (a) "Yes" (b) "No". The majority of the court held that the verdict, though surprising, was not perverse. Mahoney J.A. said at 721 that:

"at one time a sexual relationship between unmarried persons was, I think, necessarily seen as discreditable. At the present time, at least a substantial part of the community would not see it as discreditable. And, more important for present purposes, the general community view would, in my opinion, be that whether such a relationship should be seen as discreditable will depend upon the case and the circumstances of it."

[307] As in *Random House Australia Pty Ltd v Abbott* [1999] FCA 1538; 167 A.L.R. 224 (granting sexual favours for manipulative purposes). See also, *Khalil v Barakat*, above. Without such further imputation the law is in the difficulty that it can only grant a remedy where the allegation is both hurtful and almost certainly damaging in some quarters by attributing to right thinking people what is now perceived as improper prejudice: see para.2.1, above.

[308] *Polovtsoff v Illustrated Newspapers*, *The Times*, October 25, 1953, and February 26, 1954, CA (plaintiff said to have "landed a rich wife . . . preferring the fleshpots"). It has also been said to be capable of being defamatory to impute that his marriage is "one of convenience only": *Cruise v Express Newspapers plc* [1999] Q.B. 931. Cf. *Dell' Olio v Associated Newspapers* 2011] EWHC 3472 (QB) (The claimant complained of words which she said meant that she was a "serial gold-digger who cynically seeks out relationships with men nor for genuine emotional reasons but because they are millionaires and therefore capable of funding her conspicuously lavish and ostentatious lifestyle". Tugendhat J. held that the words were not capable of substantially affecting (or tending to affect) in an adverse manner the attitude of other people towards this claimant).

[309] *Karjavainean v MacFadden Inc.*, 26 N.E.2d 538 (Mass., 1940).

[310] *Brown v Du Frey*, 134 N.E.2d 469 (1951). On accepted standards of family life, see also *Saleh v Odhams Press*, *The Times*, June 27, 1963; *Moore v News of the World* [1972] 1 Q.B. 441.

[311] *Smith v Houston*, unreported, CA, December 16, 1993 (LEXIS) (appeal on issue of damages only).

[312] Per Begbie C.J. in *Wolfenden v Giles* (1892) 2 Br.Col.R. at 284; *R. v Coghlan* (1865) 4 F. & F. 316; *Sim v Stretch* (1936) 52 T.L.R. 669 HL; *Winstanley v Bampton* [1943] K.B.319; cf.

person (whether or not he is a trader or in business[313] and including a corporation[314]) is insolvent,[315] or cannot[316] or will not pay his debts, or has delayed paying his debts.[317] No element of misconduct is required; even if delay in paying or inability to pay a debt is the result of misfortune, to impute such delay or inability to someone would tend to injure his credit in a financial sense, which the law protects as part of his reputation.[318] A statement may be defamatory without imputing actual insolvency.[319] It is defamatory to suggest that the claimant is given to refusing or delaying to pay his debts in the ordinary and proper course,[320] and it was therefore held that it might be defamatory of a person to say that he had relied on the Statute of Frauds[321] or the Statute of Limitations[322] in order to avoid paying a just debt. An allegation

---

Storey v Challands (1837) 8 C. & P. 234; *McCann v Edinburgh Roperie* (1889) 24 L.R.Ir. 24; *Coomer v Moorosi* [1936] E.D.L. 233.

[313] Cf. the position where the issue is whether a slander is actionable per se: para.4.17, below.

[314] As to whether imputation of insolvency to a corporation is defamatory of directors or officers, see para.7.13, below.

[315] *Aspro Travel Ltd v Owners Abroad Group Plc* [1996] 1 W.L.R. 132 CA; *Kiam v Neil (No.2)* [1996] E.M.L.R. 493 CA; *Eaton v Johns* (1842) 1 Dowl. (N.S.) 602; *Kritzinger v Perskorporasie van Suid-Afrika*, 1981 (2) S.A. 373; cf. *Shepheard v Whitaker* (1875) L.R. 10 C.P. 502; *Boaks v Associated Newspapers, The Times*, June 14, 1967 ("living on national assistance"); *Katapodis v Brooklyn Spectator*, 38 N.E.2d 112 (N.Y. 1941) (plaintiffs' child gone to "pauper's grave"); and contrast *Dennis v Southam* (1954) 12 W.W.R. 379 (appeal allowed on obscure grounds 13 W.W.R. 494).

[316] *Stubbs v Russell* [1913] A.C. 386 HL at 392; *R. v Coghlan* (1865) 4 F. & F. 316; *Brown v Smith* (1853) 22 L.J.C.P. 151.

[317] "A mere statement that the plaintiff was indebted to the defendant could not be held to be defamatory, apart from some special circumstances, but the words which I have quoted seem to me to impute to the plaintiff a deliberate intention to avoid payment of his rent as long as possible, and to suggest that he is not likely to pay unless he was compelled by legal proceedings. Not to pay punctually is a very different thing from refusing to pay at all or only under compulsion"; per Viscount Caldecote C.J. in *Winstanley v Bampton* [1943] K.B. 319 at 321; *Stubbs v Russell* [1913] A.C. 386 at 397–398; *Stubbs v Mazure* [1920] A.C. 66. For payment under compulsion, see also para.2.33, above.

[318] *Borella v Penfolds Wines Pty Ltd* (1992) 7 W.A.R. 492; *Aspro Travel Ltd v Owners Abroad Group Plc* [1996] 1 W.L.R. 132 CA; *AB v CD* (1905) 7 F. 22 at 25.

[319] *Stubbs v Mazure* [1920] A.C. 66 HL per Lord Finlay, at 72; *Lloyd's Ships Holdings Pty Ltd v Davros Pty Ltd* (1987) 72 A.L.R. 643.

[320] *Stubbs v Russell* [1913] A.C. 386 per Lord Shaw at 397–398; *Stubbs v Mazure* [1920] A.C. 66.

[321] Pleading the Statute of Frauds is one of the things a man might not like his neighbours to hear he had done: *Clarke v Associated Newspapers, The Times*, May 7, 1955, CA. There is, of course, nothing left of the Statute of Frauds in England apart from s.4 relating to guarantees. It should not be defamatory to say that a person has relied on s.2 of the Law of Property (Miscellaneous Provisions) Act 1989 (land sales, requirement of written contract) without some superadded imputation of impropriety.

[322] "It is said that it cannot be actionable to say of another that he has availed himself of the Statute of Limitations to refuse payment of a promissory note, for it is merely to assert that he has done just what the law authorised him to do. But that, I apprehend, cannot be a true criterion of what is libellous or not; it may be perfectly lawful for a man to do many things, the imputation of which would subject him to contempt, ridicule or disgrace, and which it would be, therefore, libellous to publish of him. There may be a strictly legal right, the resort to which in some cases would be morally wrong. The Statute of Limitations, though

of refusing to admit liability would not itself be defamatory but in the context it might carry the meaning of wrongful refusal.[323] It is certainly defamatory to say of a person that he has taken any deliberate action to avoid paying his debts.[324] It is defamatory to impute future insolvency to the claimant[325] and may be so to state that he was once in pecuniary difficulties.[326]

2.31 Imputations as to credit. Imputations as to credit, like any others, may arise from the ordinary meaning of words, as their plain meaning or by implication, or from the proof of extrinsic facts.[327] Thus, apart from directly saying that the claimant is a bankrupt or insolvent, or unable to pay his just debts,[328] it would be actionable to say that he has bolted without paying his debts,[329] or that he left a certain place "with his creditors in the lurch"[330] or to warn people not to deal with him in a way which cast doubt upon his credit.[331] It has also been held to be defamatory to say of another that he has a "delinquent or "unauthorised" overdraft, especially if the overdraft is significantly in excess of the limit. In such a case the defamatory meaning would be to the effect that the claimant had shown serious irresponsibility in financial matters by overdrawing money from his bank in grave excess of the limits it had allowed.[332]

2.32 Banks and financial institutions. It would be defamatory to publish of a bank that it has "stopped payment",[333] or is "in liquidation".[334]

---

it offers a legal, and often a most just defence, is capable like every other good of being abused and perverted for an improper end. And there may be occasions in which no one can well make use of it without necessarily having his reputation injured thereby":
per Bliss J. in *Roberts v Patillo* (1855) 2 N.S.R. at 370; *Clarke v Associated Newspapers*, above.

[323] *Kaplan v Go Daddy Inc.* [2006] N.S.W.S.C. 250. See also *Concord Trust v Law Debenture Trust Corp Plc* [2004] EWCA Civ 1001; [2004] All E.R. (Comm) 737 at [83].

[324] See cases cited in para.2.31, below.

[325] See *Whittington v Gladwin* (1825) 5 B. & C. 180; *Brown v Smith* (1853) 13 C.B. 596.

[326] Per Kelly C.B. in *Cox v Lee* (1869) L.R. 4 Ex. 284 at 288, even if it is stated that these difficulties have been overcome: "Anything like inability in respect of pecuniary resources would injure his position in the world". But unless there is a connotation of present or future embarrassment the case may only reflect Victorian social attitudes. Cf. also *Leycroft v Dunker* (1633) Cro Car 317; *Stanton v Smith* (1727) 2 Stra. 762.

[327] See Ch.3, s.3, below.

[328] But where insurance was not required by law, a statement that a company was uninsured was not of itself capable of being defamatory, for it did not impute that it was unable to meet its obligations: *Lions Gate Marketing Co. v Used Car Dealers Assn of Ontario* [2005] BCCA 274; 41 B.C.L.R. (4th) 243.

[329] *O'Brien v Bryant* (1846) 16 M. & W. 168; *Seaborn v Wilson* (1881) 1 N.Z.L.R. 74.

[330] *Brown v Beatty* (1862) 12 Up.Can.C.P. 107 at 113.

[331] *Orpwood v Barkes* (1827) 4 Bing. 261 (though the case turns on a technical point).

[332] *Gatt v Barclays Bank plc* [2013] EWHC 2 (QB) at [37].

[333] *Forster v Lawson* (1826) 3 Bing. 451 at 456, per Best C.J.; and see *Bromage v Prosser* (1825) 4 B. & C. 247.

[334] *London & Northern Bank v George Newnes* (1900) 16 T.L.R. 76.

"A bank, sustained by public confidence,[335] has no better heritage than credit and character; and a false accusation affecting its credit and character, and injuring it by creating distrust and alarm, is surely a wrong of a slanderous description, for which reparation may be sought."[336]

However, in *Capital and Counties Bank v Henty*[337] it was held that a circular published by the defendants that they would not receive in payment cheques drawn on the plaintiff bank was not reasonably capable of supporting the inference that the bank was insolvent.

Decrees and judgments. Whether it is capable of being defamatory to **2.33** state simply that a judgment or writ of execution has been obtained against the plaintiff admits of no simple answer and illustrates how the question "what is defamatory?" is intimately bound up with the question "what does the statement mean?" A person might suffer a judgment for a variety of causes that are perfectly consistent with solvency and honest intention on his part,[338] e.g. that he had forgotten to pay or was absent and knew nothing about the summons, or that having certain opinions as to the injustice of the claim or the full amount of it he was determined not to pay except under compulsion of law.[339] However, it is doubtful if these would be the inferences that would be drawn by most recipients of the information. Two decisions of the House of Lords concerning a "black list" show how close the issue may be. In *Stubbs v Russell*[340] the pursuer's name appeared in error in the defendants' journal in the weekly list of persons against whom decrees in absence had been obtained in the small debt courts. A note explained that in no case did inclusion imply inability to pay. It was held that the entry, read in conjunction with the note, was inacapable of bearing the defamatory meaning the pursuer ascribed to it, namely that he was insolvent.[341] In *Stubbs v Mazure*[342] the facts were similar, but the entry was held capable of bearing the meaning which was this time contended for, namely that the pursuer was given to or had begun to refuse or delay to make payment of his debts, and that he was not a person to whom credit should be given.[343]

---

[335] Obviously, the same principle applies to other financial institutions in which people deposit or invest funds. As to privilege in connection with complaints or reports to regulatory authorities, see Ch.14, below.

[336] Per Lord Ardmillan in *North and Scotland Banking v Duncan* (1857) 19 D. 881 at 885; also *South Hetton v N.E. News* [1894] 1 Q.B. 133 at 141; *Capital and Counties Bank v Henty* (1882) 7 A.C. 741 HL. It might be defamatory of a bank to say, in a time of panic, that X has withdrawn his account from it: ibid. at 786, per Lord Blackburn.

[337] (1882) 7 A.C. 741. See further para.3.24, below.

[338] Per Lord Kinnear in *Stubbs v Russell* [1913] A.C. 386 at 392.

[339] Per Lord Shaw in *Stubbs v Russell* at 397, applied in *Payn v Bowles* (1933) N.P.D. 501.

[340] [1913] A.C. 386.

[341] Had the plaintiff not relied on insolvency as the meaning, Lord Shaw at 398 thought a less serious defamatory meaning was reasonably possible.

[342] [1920] A.C. 66.

[343] In this case Viscount Cave L.C. said that the note could not be relied on because it was so contradictory to the nature of the publication, the purpose of which was for traders to draw inferences about credit.

The manner in which the existence of a debt or judgment is made known may imply that it is impossible to recover the debt in the ordinary course, as for instance where the existence of a debt is shown on a placard,[344] or a letter asking for assistance in its recovery is written to a superior or employer.[345]

2.34 **Cheques and bills.** The wrongful dishonour of a cheque amounts to breach of contract by the bank against its customer and since it will naturally affect the drawer's credit, general damages for loss of reputation relating to creditworthiness may be recovered.[346] However, such dishonour is not, apparently, of itself defamatory,[347] and actions for libel are only brought on the paying bank's answer on or attached to the cheque or on a report of dishonour.[348] The essential questions will be what imputation is conveyed by the answer and whether that is defamatory. Thus "Refer to drawer, incorrectly completed" would clearly not convey any defamatory imputation. It has been held that the words "Reason assigned—not stated" written by collecting bankers on a slip attached to a cheque returned to the payee cannot amount to a libel in the absence of proof of facts and circumstances leading to the reasonable belief that the cheque had been dishonoured through want of funds.[349] In *Flach v L. & S.W. Bank*[350] Scrutton L.J. was of the opinion that the words "refer to drawer"[351] written on a cheque returned to the payee were not defamatory

---

[344] *Wolfenden v Giles* (1892) 2 B.C.L.R. 284 at 290.

[345] *Winstanley v Bampton* [1943] K.B. 319.

[346] *Kpohraror v Woolwich Building Society* [1996] 4 All E.R. 119 CA. Formerly this was only applicable to "traders" but social conditions have changed and a good credit rating is now important to ordinary people: ibid. at 124.

[347] In no English case has importance been attached to the fact of dishonour, although in *Svendsen v State Bank* (1896) 58 Am.St.Rep. 522 (a case which confuses contract and tort) it was said to import "insolvency, dishonesty or bad faith in the drawer of the cheque". Is the refusal by an EFTPOS terminal to accept a transaction on the basis of a debit card a "statement"? Even if it is, it is submitted that it is distinguishable from a notation on a cheque and is not capable of being defamatory. Given the possibility of technical failure it would be wholly unreasonable to treat it as a statement that the customer has no funds to pay.

[348] *M'Nickle v Bank of New South Wales* (1881) 2 N.S.W.L.R. 7; *Hall v Bank of New South Wales* (1889) 10 N.S.W.L.R. 292; *Ballin v Bank of Australasia* (1895) 16 N.S.W.L.R. 15; *Levy v Union Bank* (1896) 21 V.L.R. 738; *Cowan v Bank of Adelaide* [1942] S.A.S.R. 99.

[349] *Frost v London J.S. Bank* (1906) 22 T.L.R. 760 CA. While there was evidence that business men would understand the absence of any explanation as indicating want of funds, *Frost's* case applies the strict interpretation of *Capital and Counties Bank v Henty* (1882) 7 A.C. 741: see para.3.24, below.

[350] (1915) 31 T.L.R. 334. See also *Plunkett v Barclays Bank* [1936] 2 K.B. 107 at 120.

[351] Similar expressions which mean the same thing are "R/D", "Present again", or, in the case of a bill, "R/A", "Refer to acceptor". In *Millward v Lloyd's Bank*, unreported, M. No.86, Wright J. expressed the opinion (obiter) that it was defamatory of a merchant to return a bill drawn by him to the payee marked "R/A" observing that the statements in the House of Lords in the case of *Barber v Deutsche Bank London Agency* [1919] A.C. 304, especially the language of Lord Finlay at 309, justified this view. The words, however, which Sankey J. (after verdict for the plaintiff) and the Court of Appeal held to be defamatory in the *Barber* case were not the words "Refer to acceptor" written on the bill, but the words contained in the cablegram and telegram sent by the defendants to the Banco Aleman Transatlantico: see 1918 House of Lords Printed Cases, p.7. But "R/A" should be on a similar footing to "R/D".

because they were simply a statement by the bank, "We are not paying. Go back to the drawer and ask him why".[352] It is true that such an expression does not *necessarily* imply anything defamatory of the drawer, but this is too severe a test and the weight of the case law indicates that it is capable of being defamatory.[353] The imputation which may reasonably be conveyed would usually be insolvency or want of funds[354] but not normally dishonesty.[355] It can scarcely be defamatory to say that someone has an overdraft[356] and dishonour may occur because of breach or misunderstanding by the claimant of such an arrangement. If a defendant bank was contractually justified in dishonouring a cheque in such circumstances, it is submitted that it could justify an allegation of libel in its answer on the cheque by proving that fact without proving insolvency.[357] Rather more obviously defamatory responses

---

[352] However, judgment was entered for the defendants on another ground.

[353] These words were left to the jury in *Szek v Lloyds Bank*, *The Times*, January 15, 1908. The jury awarded the plaintiff £50 on the claim for breach of contract but gave no damages for libel. In *Jayson v Midland Bank* [1967] 2 Lloyd's Rep. 563, on a submission that the words "Refer to drawer" (no innuendo being pleaded) were incapable of being defamatory, the judge said that he would rule on this submission, if necessary, after the verdict of the jury. In the event the jury found that the words were defamatory, but since they also found justification, no ruling was given. The point did not arise on the appeal: [1968] 1 Lloyd's Rep. 409. The clearest case is *Hill v National Bank of New Zealand* [1985] 1 N.Z.L.R. 736, where the judge, sitting without a jury, found that the words were defamatory in fact since:
"the majority of reasonable people would think that in all probability the bank had [dishonoured] on good grounds founded on some circumstance discreditable to the drawer."
This was so even though the number of cheques now processed may have increased the likelihood of innocent error. In *Pyke v Hibernian Bank* [1950] 1 I.R. 195 the same words were held by the trial judge and two out of four judges in the Supreme Court to be reasonably capable of a defamatory meaning; and in *Baker v Australia and N.Z. Bank* [1958] 1 N.Z.L.R. 907 "refer to acceptor" was held capable of a defamatory meaning. The point was not decided in *Allen v L.C. & W. Bank* (1915) 84 L.J.K.B. 1286, or in *Sterling v Barclays Bank*, *The Times*, July 18, 1930. See also, *Atkas v Westpac Banking Corpn* [2010] HCA 25 where a jury found that "refer to drawer" on cheques was defamatory of the claimant. The High Court of Australia noted that it was the reason given by Westpac for the notice of dishonour, not the mere fact of dishonour or the fate of the cheques in some general sense, which founded the action (at [5]).

[354] In *Hill v National Bank of New Zealand* [1985] 1 N.Z.L.R. 736 the imputations which were conceded to arise from "R/D" were (1) being without funds or failing to make adequate arrangements to cover the cheque (2) being negligent in preparing the cheque to a sufficient degree to lead the bank to refuse to meet it (3) being indifferent in preparing the mandate as to whether it would be honoured. The second cannot have been intended to relate merely to negligence in writing the cheque—it would be surprising if it were defamatory to say someone had forgotten to sign a cheque or inserted the wrong year. A fourth conceded meaning was based on *Baker v Australia and N.Z. Bank* [1958] 1 N.Z.L.R. 907, but the judge found the thrust of it "not easy to follow".

[355] Rejected as a possible meaning in *Hill v National Bank of New Zealand* [1985] 1 N.Z.L.R. 736. See also *Cox v Cox & Co*, *The Times*, March 18, 1921 and *Smith v Cox & Co*, *The Times*, March 9, 1923.

[356] It has however been held to be defamatory to say of another that they have an unauthorised overdraft: *Gatt v Barclays Bank plc* [2013] EWHC 2 at [37] (QB).

[357] Such a justification in fact succeeded in *Jayson v Midland Bank* [1968] I Lloyd's Rep. 409 CA. In *Hill v National Bank of New Zealand* [1985] 1 N.Z.L.R. 736 justification succeeded in respect of one of the accounts but in respect of the other the bank had not given adequate notice of the reduction of the overdraft limit.

on dishonour of a cheque are "No account",[358] "Account closed",[359] "Not sufficient",[360] or "Drawer's estate sequestrated".[361] It should, however, be noted that a mistaken defamatory notation on a cheque may be protected by the defence of qualified privilege.[362]

(c) *Reputation in Business, Trade or Profession*

2.35 Reputation in business, trade or profession. Any imputation which may tend to injure a person's reputation in a business, employment, trade, profession, calling or office carried on or held by him is defamatory[363] provided that such imputation meets the necessary threshold of seriousness.[364] To be actionable, words must impute to the claimant some quality which would be detrimental, or the absence of some quality which is essential, to the successful carrying on of his office, profession or trade. The mere fact that words tend to injure the claimant in the way of his office, profession or trade is insufficient. If they do not involve any reflection upon the personal character, *or* the official, professional or trading reputation of the claimant, they are not defamatory.[365]

Two English cases have given detailed consideration of this area. In *Dee v Telegraph Media Group Ltd*[366] the defendants gave the claimant's match record and on that basis described him as the "world's worst tennis pro". While Sharp J. had no doubt that, in some cases, an imputation of lack of professional skill could be defamatory, she had reservations about translating that proposition to the world of sport. In the case of professional people like architects or solicitors want of competence had clear potential consequences for people who took advantage of their services but that could hardly be said of a professional tennis player: "Losing in sport is . . . an occupational hazard. Shaky hands for a surgeon, or endangering the lives of your dental patients through an unproven anaesthetic cannot be so characterised."[367]

---

[358] Which might suggest that the claimant had committed criminal deception.

[359] These words were held to be defamatory in *Russell v Bank of America*, *The Times*, October 21, 1978.

[360] *Davidson v Barclays Bank* [1940] 1 All E.R. 316.

[361] *Miles v Commercial Banking* (1904) 1 C.L.R. 470.

[362] The defence was rejected in *Davidson v Barclays Bank*, above, but that case was doubted in *Pyke v Hibernian Bank Ltd* [1950] I.R. 195 and is directly rejected in *Aktas v Westpac Banking Corp Ltd* [2007] N.S.W.S.C. 1261. See para.14.43, below.

[363] Such an imputation, if spoken, may be actionable per se: see para.4.15, below. See *Henderson v Thompson* [1934] N.Z.L.R. 444; *A v Ipec Australia* [1973] V.R. 39 for calling no longer exercised.

[364] See para.2.4, above.

[365] One suspects that a statement that a hotel had unwittingly been providing facilities to a terrorist organisation would not help its public relations, but it is not thereby defamatory: *Al Rajhi Banking and Investment Corp v Wall Street Journal Europe SPRL* [2003] EWHC 1358 (QB), per Eady J., at [25].

[366] [2010] EWHC 924 (QB); [2010] E.M.L.R. 20.

[367] Ibid., at [49].

In *Thornton v Telegraph Media Group Ltd*[368] the defendants' review of the claimant's book accused her of the practice of "copy approval" in interviews, something of which journalists disapproved. Tugendhat J. held that this could not be a "personal" libel because there was no plea that it suggested anything like hypocrisy and it imputed nothing disreputable by the standards of ordinary people, whatever journalists might think. Nor could it be a business or professional libel. The position of a writer was comparable to that of a sportsman: writers are free to write to different standards for different readerships and it could not be defamatory of the claimant to say that she did not apply the standards accepted by journalists: "There is no consequence for prospective readers of Dr Thornton's Book which corresponds to the consequences that may be suffered by a patient from the shaky hand or unproven anaesthetic technique of a dental surgeon."[369]

Of course the "effect upon others" point cannot be the end of the argument in all cases. To say of an historian (or, indeed, a journalist) that he is slipshod in checking his sources is plainly defamatory but that is because it imputes that he ignores the standards of his particular branch of the "writing" profession.

Insufficient that words damage claimant in business, etc. To be   **2.36**
defamatory the statement complained of must be reasonably capable[370] of conveying "a personal imputation upon them, either upon their character, or upon the mode in which their business is carried on".[371] If the statement does not satisfy these requirements it may be actionable as a malicious falsehood[372] or as negligence[373] but not as defamation.[374] It is not defamatory to publish that a trader has ceased to carry on his business or that the business has been, or is about to be, acquired or absorbed by another firm, for such statement, though likely to injure the trader in his business by diverting custom, does not

---

[368] [2010] EWHC 1414 (QB); [2011] 1 W.L.R. 1985; [2010] E.M.L.R. 25.

[369] Ibid. at [103].

[370] *Short v Kirkpatrick* [1982] 2 N.Z.L.R. 358 (notice pinned to door of business premises that landlord had terminated lease did not entitle the reader to conclude that this was attributable to anything discreditable on plaintiffs' part).

[371] Per Cozens-Hardy M.R., in *Griffiths v Benn* (1911) 27 T.L.R. 346 CA at 350.
"A malicious falsehood not defamatory but causing damage may in some circumstances be foundation for an action on the case for damages, but unless the untruth is calculated to injure the reputation and character of the person of whom it is written, it cannot give rise to an action for defamation": *Slatyer v Daily Telegraph Co* (1907) 7 N.S.W.S.R. 488 at 498; *Carelse v Van de Schyff* [1928] C.P.D. at 94; *Dawson Bloodstock Agency v Mirror Newspapers* [1979] 1 N.S.W.L.R. 16.

[372] See Ch.21, below.

[373] See Ch.23, below.

[374] Some Australian states formerly had statutory provisions making defamatory "any imputation ... by which [a person] is likely to be injured in his profession or trade": see, e.g. Queensland Defamation Act 1889, s.4(1). This was generally thought to be broader than the common law test: *Sungravure v Middle East Airlines* (1975) 134 C.L.R. 1; *Dawson Bloodstock Agency v Mirror Newspapers* [1979] 1 N.S.W.L.R. 16. The current uniform legislation contains no definition of what is defamatory, which therefore depends on the common law.

reflect on him in his conduct of it.[375] Nor was it in itself defamatory for an association of manufacturers to place on a "stop list" the name of a retailer for selling proprietary articles of their members at prices different from those contained in the "protected price list" published by the association.[376] It is not without more defamatory of a bank to say that accounts it manages have been used without its knowledge to fund terrorism.[377] To state that a trader's goods lack desirable qualities may be very damaging but it is only defamatory if it imputes some deficiency in the way that the business is run.[378] It is not, however, necessary that there should be an imputation of conduct which is morally wrong: an imputation of incompetence will do,[379] for:

" . . . words may be defamatory of a trader or a business man or professional man, though they do not impute any known fault or defect of personal character. They can be defamatory of him if they impute lack of qualifications, knowledge, skill, capability,[380] judgment or efficiency in the conduct of his trade or business or professional activity."[381]

It is defamatory of a surgeon to say that although he is of excellent character he is "past it" and his hands shake[382] and to say of a musical act that its members might not honour their commitments[383]: but it is not defamatory of

---

[375] Per curiam in *Ratcliffe v Evans* [1892] 2 Q.B. 524 CA at 529. See also *Concaris v Duncan* [1909] W.N. 51; *Shapiro v La Morta* (1923) 40 T.L.R. 201 CA; *General Accident Co. v Miller* (1902) 9 S.L.T. 510; *Irish Toys v Irish Times* [1937] I.R. 298; *Grobbelaar v Du Toit* [1917] T.P.D. 433; *Henderson v Thompson* [1934] N.Z.L.R. 444.

[376] *Ware and De Freville v Motor Trade Assn* [1921] 3 K.B. 40 CA; *Auto-Man v Chilton* (1927) 43 T.L.R. 463; *Thorne v Motor Trade Assn* [1937] A.C. 797. Such practices will now generally offend against the Competition Act 1998 or the EC Treaty and price fixing agreements are generally invalid.

[377] *Al Rajhi Banking and Investment Corp v Wall Street Journal Europe SPRL* [2003] EWHC 1358 (QB) at [19].

[378] See para.2.46, below. In *Hackenschmidt v Odhams Press, The Times*, October 23, 24, 1950, Pritchard J. ruled that to say of a one-time champion wrestler that he had been defeated in a particular contest which had in fact resulted in a draw, was capable of a defamatory meaning.
Whether *Hackenschmidt* is consistent with *Dee v Telegraph Media Group Ltd* [2010] EWHC 924 (QB); [2010] E.M.L.R. 20 must be open to doubt.

[379] *Cinevest Ltd v Yirandi Productions Ltd* [2001] NSWCA 68; *Stalyce Holdings (Aust) Pty Ltd v Cetec Pty Ltd* [2002] FCA 278.

[380] *Ravnikar v Bogojavlensky* 782 N.E.2d 508 (Mass. 2003) is a difficult case, because there seems to have been no allegation of present incompetence.

[381] *Drummond-Jackson v BMA* [1970] 1 W.L.R. 688 CA at 698–699, per Lord Pearson; *Hope Technical Developments v BBC*, March 31, 1995, CA. Some American cases take the line that it is not defamatory to accuse another of a single mistake even if negligent, because that does not necessarily imply unfitness (though it may do so). See 50 Am.Jur.2d, *Libel and Slander*, para.213 and 51 A.L.R.3d 1300.

[382] *John Fairfax Publications Pty Ltd v Gacic* [2007] HCA 28; 235 A.L.R. 402 at [2]. See also *Edsall v Russell* 134 E.R. 446; (1842) 4 Man. & G. 1090 (imputation that claimant apothecary had killed a child by improperly and with gross ignorance administering an injection held defamatory); *Botterill v Whitehead* (1879) 41 L.T.N.S. 588 (imputation that architect employed in restoration of an ancient church had no experience in work for which employed held libellous as touching on his professional competence).

[383] *Joseph v Spiller* [2009] EWHC 1152 (QB).

a musician to say that he is at present too ill to fulfil his engagements.[384] The distinction lies, it is suggested, in the fact that in the first two cases the imputations are on the claimant's professional reputation[385] but it would be difficult to say that the other case fell into that category, even though on the particular facts it might cause damage by depriving him of an engagement.[386] The line may, of course, be hard to draw.[387] Though most of the cases concern individuals, the same principles govern trading corporations: if there is an imputation of misconduct or incompetence in the operation of a company's business that would be a libel on the company.[388]

Imputation of unfitness in office. It is defamatory to impute to a person   **2.37** in any office[389] any corrupt,[390] dishonest or fraudulent conduct or other misconduct[391] or inefficiency in it,[392] or any unfitness or want of ability to discharge its duties,[393] and this is so whether the office be public or private, or whether it be one of profit, honour or trust. Thus, it has been held defamatory to charge a senior civil servant with losing a large amount of public money,[394] or a judge with racial bias,[395] or a police officer with being

---

[384] *Grappelli v Derek Block (Holdings)* [1981] 1 W.L.R. 822 CA at 824.

[385] I write of Judge A that he nods off on the bench because he lunches too well. I write that Judge B does the same thing because he is a martyr to narcolepsy. The statement about Judge B may be less harmful to his personal reputation, but not to his reputation as a judge. Of course in this case it might be possible to plead an innuendo of improper behaviour in remaining in office. But that could hardly apply to, say, a statement that an actor forgets his lines.

[386] On this basis it is difficult to agree with the suggestion of Lord Slynn in *Spring v Guardian Assurance Plc* [1995] 2 A.C. 296 HL at 334, that it is not defamatory to say that a labourer is a lame or a secretary arthritic (assuming those matters to seriously affect their permanent capacity for work).

[387] In *Boyd v Mirror Newspapers* [1980] 2 N.S.W.L.R. 449 it was held that it was not defamatory of a footballer to say he was too fat to play except in so far as it was capable of bearing the imputations that the plaintiff was ridiculous or that his condition was his fault; doubted in *Bell v Kingsbay Pty Ltd* [2001] VSC 498 in so far as the case was rejected without these elements. Cf. *Fullam v Associated Newspapers* [1955–1956] Ir.Jr.Rep. 45 (allegation that footballer could not kick with one leg defamatory). See also *Williams v Associated Newspapers, The Times,* November 24, 1937 (umpire's errors of judgment); *Henderson v Thompson* [1934] N.Z.L.R. 444 (jockey's injuries).

[388] See para.8.16, below. For an example, see *Ming Kee Manufactory v Man Shing Electrical Manufactory* [1992] 1 H.K.C. 442.

[389] See also para.4.15, below.

[390] *Broadcasting Corp of New Zealand v Crush* [1988] 2 N.Z.L.R. 234; *Neapetung v Whitehead* [1994] 1 W.W.R. 206; cf. *Evans v John Fairfax & Sons Ltd* (1993) 112 F.L.R. 74 ACTSC (career aided by "patronage of senior politicians" did not impute active and improper seeking of favours by plaintiff).

[391] *Sachs v Werkerspers Bpk*, 1952 (2) S.A. 261 (dictator in office).

[392] *Potts v Moran* (1976) 16 S.A.S.R. 302. But an imputation of an error of judgment may not be defamatory: *Wallachs v Marsh* [1928] T.P.D. 531.

[393] *Random House Australia Pty Ltd v Abbott* [1999] FCA 1538; 167 A.L.R. 224 at [22]. It would be defamatory of a senior civil servant to say that the Minister lacked confidence in his competence, but not to say that he and the Minister "do not get on" because that does not impute incompetence: *Evans v John Fairfax & Sons Ltd* (1993) 112 F.L.R. 74 ACTSC.

[394] *Blackshaw v Lord* [1984] Q.B. 1 CA.

[395] *Argus Printing & Publishing Co. Ltd v Esselen's Estate*, 1994 (2) S.A. 1 AD. See also *Hlophe v Constitutional Court of South Africa* [2009] ZASCA 36 (allegation of improper interference with proceedings).

cruel, rude and threatening,[396] or a parish overseer with oppressive conduct towards the poor of the parish,[397] or a municipal officer with treating workers like dogs,[398] or a vestry clerk with having misappropriated or misapplied the parish moneys,[399] or a mayor of a borough, though retired from office, with ignorance of his duties, partiality and corruption.[400]

2.38 Imputation of unfitness for profession or calling. It is defamatory to impute that a person is unfit for his profession or calling owing to want of ability,[401] mental stability,[402] learning or some other necessary qualification,[403] or that he has been guilty of any dishonest or disreputable[404] conduct or any other misconduct[405] or inefficiency[406] therein. This applies to any profession or calling, however humble,[407] so long as it is not illegal.[408] But to say that a person lacks a qualification which he might usefully have is not defamatory for that does not impute incompetence.[409]

2.39 Dismissals. A person wrongfully dismissed cannot rely on the dismissal itself as conveying a defamatory imputation,[410] nor is it in itself defamatory for a person to publish of one who has ceased to be employed by him that he

---

[396] *Posadas v City of Reno*, 851 P.2d 438 (Nev., 1993). For other American cases, see 50 Am.Jur.2d, *Libel and Slander*, para.232. *Drost v Sunday Herald* (1976) 11 Nfld. & P.E.I.R. 342; *AUPE v Edmonton Sun* (1986) 49 Alta. R. (2d) 141 (prison guards).

[397] *Woodard v Dowsing* (1828) 2 M. & Ry. 74.

[398] *Halluk v Brown* (1982) 41 A.R. 350 Alta. QB.

[399] *May v Brown* (1824) 3 B. & C. 113.

[400] *Parmiter v Coupland* (1840) 6 M. & W. 105. See also *Field v Local Sunday Newspapers (North) Ltd* [2002] EWHC 336 (QB) (local government officer; political bias, on appeal on other grounds sub nom. *Gough v Local Sunday Newspapers (North) Ltd* [2003] EWCA Civ 297; [2003] 1 W.L.R. 1836).

[401] Cf. *May v Greater Kansas City Dental Society*, 863 S.W.2d 941 (Mo., 1993) (to call plaintiff a "yo-yo" did not impute professional incapacity).

[402] *Capps v Watts*, 246 S.E.2d 606 (S.C. 1978); *Rand v Miller* 408 S.E.2d 655 (W Va 1991); *Moores v Salton* (1982) 37 Nfld. & P.E.I.R. 128 (violent displays of temper).

[403] *Botterill v Whitehead* (1879) 41 L.T.N.S. 588.

[404] E.g. to say of a trade unionist that he is a "stooge" and "willing tool of the boss": *Herbert v Jackson* [1950] 2 D.L.R. 538; *O'Neal v Pulp, Paper and Woodworkers of Canada* [1975] 4 W.W.R. 92. See also para.2.20, above.

[405] *Skuse v Granada Television* [1996] E.M.L.R. 278 CA (want of skill, knowledge, care and thoroughness to be expected of forensic scientist).

[406] An imputation of inefficiency or incompetence in a person's profession or calling is usually defamatory of him, though it may not even lower him in the estimation of others: *Pratten v Labour Daily* [1926] V.L.R. 115. For other cases in which it has been so held, see *Edsall v Russell* (1842) 4 Man. & G. 1090; *Lawrence v Hall* (1928) 72 S.J. 87; *Harker v Prewitt* [1937] G.L.R. 663; *Chenning v SA Financial Gazette*, 1966 (3) S.A. 475; *Allsopp v Incorporated Newsagencies* (1975) 26 F.L.R. 238; *Blackshaw v Lord* [1984] Q.B. 1 CA.

[407] See para.4.18, below (whether slander actionable per se).

[408] See para.2.24, above.

[409] *Turner v Metro-Goldwyn-Mayer* [1950] 1 All E.R. 449 HL at 453.

[410] *Cowles v Prudential Assurance* [1957] N.Z.L.R.124, applying *Addis v Gramophone Co* [1909] A.C. 488 HL; *Greyridge Investments v TC Welding & Automotive* (1994) 129 N.S.R (2d) 33. Cf. *Riddick v Thames Board Mills* [1977] Q.B. 881 CA. Of course to publish a defamatory reason for a dismissal is actionable. Some American cases have reasoned that where an employer dismisses a worker for a reason which, if published, is defamatory there is a publication by the employer when the worker is required to reveal the reason in applying for work: *Lewis v*

is no longer so employed and is no longer authorised to do business or to receive moneys on behalf of the person lately employing him. The context however, or extrinsic circumstances may cause the words to be understood in a defamatory sense by those to whom they were addressed, and in that case they are actionable.[411]

> "If special facts were proved to have been known to the persons to whom the words were published which would lead a reasonable person knowing those facts to conclude that the words impliedly stated that the plaintiff had been discharged for misconduct, an action for libel would lie."[412]

The clergy.[413] It has been held defamatory to state of an archbishop of the   **2.40**
Church of Ireland that he has attempted to convert a Catholic priest to Protestantism by an offer of £1,000 in cash and a living of £800 a year,[414] or to state of a clergyman that he is guilty of immorality or drunkenness,[415] or that he preaches sedition,[416] lies,[417] or that he knows less about his religion

---

Equitable Life Assurance Society 389 N.W.2d 876 (Minn. 1986); *contra, Wieder v Chemical Bank,* 608 N.Y.2d 195 (1994). See 50 Am.Jur.2d, *Libel and Slander,* para.242.

[411] *Mulligan v Cole* (1875) L.R. 10 Q.B. 549; *Grundy v Geyer* (1887) 21 S.A.L.R. 3; *Nevill v Fine Arts* [1897] A.C. 68; *Beswick v Smith* (1907) 24 T.L.R. 169; *Russell v Gruar* (1913) 33 N.Z.L.R. 237; *Fowler v Nankin* (1909) 11 W.L.R. 586. Cf. *Gallagher v Murton* (1888) 4 T.L.R. 304, and *Burke v Ellison, The Times,* January 27, 1910, where the words were: "We regret to inform you that we have been obliged to make a change in our representative, and that we have no longer the services of Mr. Burke". Alverstone C.J. allowed the case to go to the jury. It is submitted that such a notice is defamatory if it is prefixed by the word "Caution": see also para.3.29. See also *Morris v Sanders Universal Products* [1954] 1 W.L.R. 67 CA ("dismissed" capable of defamatory meaning); *Birne v NSL, The Times,* April 12, 1957 ("expelled"); *Stewart v Daily Telegraph, The Times,* July 30, 1958; *Munro v Coyne* [1990] W.A.R. 333 (newspaper notice that plaintiff not agent of defendant and had never been authorised to incur liability on behalf of defendant properly left to jury); cf. *D. Miles Griffiths v Woodruff* (1953) 162 E.G. 35; *Nichols v Item Publishers* (1956) 309 N.Y. 596 ("former pastor" not defamatory); *Conrad v Behnsen* 1960 (4) S.A. 760; *Coulson v Rappon Vitgewers* 1979 (3) S.A. 286 AD: "summarily dismissed" not defamatory in context. See also *Monk v Cann Hall Primary School* [2013] EWCA Civ 826; [2013] I.R.L.R. 732 (a claim for negligence). A claim for defamation arising out of the manner of the claimant's dismissal—she was forced to clear her desk and hand over her keys, before being publicly escorted from the premises by a governor of the school—was compromised but there seems little doubt that a dismissal in such circumstances would be capable of being defamatory.

[412] Per Greer L.J. in *Tolley v Fry* [1930] 1 K.B. 467 CA at 480. Cf. *Lones v British Oak* (1931) E.D.L. (S. Africa) 258; *Roberge v Tribune Publishers* (1977) 20 N.B.R.2d 381.

[413] See also para.4.17, below.

[414] *Archbishop of Tuam v Robeson* (1828) 5 Bing. 17.

[415] *Payne v Beaumorris* (1661) 1 Lev. 248; *Evans v Gwyn* (1844) 5 Q.B. 844; *Gallwey v Marshall* (1853) 9 Exch. 294; *Stow v Gardner* (1843) 6 Up.Can.Q.B. (O.S.) 512; *Steltzer v Domm* [1932] 2 W.W.R. 139. Words which, if directed against another would not be defamatory may be so if directed against a clergyman, because of the nature of the calling: *Murphy v Harty,* 393 P.2d 206 (Or 1964).

[416] *Cranden v Walden* (1693) 3 Lev. 17.

[417] *Phillips v Badley* (1582) cited 4 Co. Rep. at 19a; *Drake v Drake* (1652) Style 363. In *Dod v Robinson* (1648) Aleyn 63, it was held that it was defamatory to say that a clergyman preached false doctrine. No doubt this would still be defamatory if, in the circumstances, it imputed hypocrisy. But it cannot be defamatory as such for A, who belongs to one church, to say that B, a minister of another church, preaches false doctrine if the churches are in disagreement about the doctrine.

than an adolescent,[418] or that he has used his pulpit to throw out personal invectives against a member of the congregation,[419] or that he has juggled with the collections,[420] or that he has desecrated a part of his church by turning it into a cooking department.[421] However, the court will not determine doctrinal disputes or the customs and procedures of a religious community, so that, for example, where the alleged libel involved an assertion that the claimant was not a validly consecrated bishop the action was stayed.[422]

2.41   The law.[423]   It is defamatory to publish of a barrister that he knows no law,[424] or that he gives bad advice[425] or ought to be disbarred[426] but not that he is not particularly prominent, or to refer to him as one of average ability.[427] It is defamatory to publish of a solicitor that he has been guilty of "sharp practice" in his profession,[428] or a breach of professional confidence,[429] or other disreputable, dishonest, or incompetent conduct,[430] or that she is "downright crooked",[431] or that he has given his client's case away,[432] or that he has no regard to the interests of his clients,[433] or that he knows no law,[434] but not

---

[418] *Maidman v Jewish Publications* 54 Cal.2d 643 (1960).

[419] *Edwards v Bell* (1824) 1 Bing. 403.

[420] *Curtis v Argus*, 155 N.Y. S. 813 (1915); *Dr Sibthorp's Case* (1628) W. Jones 366.

[421] *Kelly v Sherlock* (1866) L.R. 1 Q.B. 686.

[422] *Blake v Associated Newspapers Ltd* [2003] EWHC 1960 (QB). See also *Baba Jeet Singh Ji Maharaj v Eastern Media Group* [2010] EWHC 1294 (QB) (claim involved reliance on meanings including the concept of an imposter in a religious group and thus the determination of the central issue necessitated the determination of doctrinal issues and was outwith the court's jurisdiction); *Shergill v Purewal* [2010] EWHC 3610 (QB) (libel proceedings stayed as court would otherwise inevitably be bound to abstain from determining doctrinal questions which lay at the heart of the case).

[423] See also para.4.17. And for many more ancient and entertaining examples, see *The Digest*, Vol.32(1), paras 2051–2093.

[424] *Palmer v Boyer* (1594) Cro.Eliz. 342; *Bankes v Allen* (1616) 1 Roll.Abr. 54.; *Peard v Jones* (1634) Cro. Ca. 382 ("he is a dunce and will get little by the law").

[425] *King v Lake* (1672) 2 Vent. 28.

[426] *Gallwey v Marshall* (1853) 9 Exch. 294 at 310.

[427] *Thompson v Matthiasen* 135 N.Y.S. 796 (1912).

[428] *Boydell v Jones* (1838) 4 M. & W. 446; or has been party to "cooking up" evidence: *Drapeau v Langley* [1960] Revue Legale 209. Cf. *De Flamingh v Pakendorf* (1979) 3 S.A. 676. But to describe a lawyer as "sharp" would normally be a compliment.

[429] *Moore v Terrell* (1833) 4 B. & Ad. 870; *Martyn v Burlings* (1597) Cro.Eliz. 589.

[430] *Bishop v Latimer* (1861) 4 L.T.(N.S.) 775; *Woodgate v Ridout* (1865) 4 F. & F. 202; *Lawrence v Hag* (1928) 72 S.J. 87; *Husbands v Advocate* (1968) 12 W.l.R. 454; (1970) 15 W.l.R. at 181–182; *Wiley v Toronto Star* (1985) 51 D.L.R. (4th) 439; *Joceline Tan Poh Choo v Muthusamy* [2003] 4 M.L.J. 494 Mal CA.
    See also, *Bailey, Douglas and Bressington v Kordowski* [2011] EWHC 785 (QB) (serious professional misconduct, dishonesty and incompetence).

[431] *Farrall v Kordowski* [2010] EWHC 2436 (QB).

[432] *Kelly v O'Bierne* (1909) 127 L.T.J. 214.

[433] *MacRostie v Ironside* (1849) 12 D. 74; *Andrews v Wilson* (1845) 3 Kerr N.B.R. 86; *Gluckman v Holford* [1940] T.P.D. 336 ("What I hear about him (a solicitor) is enough for me"); *Cobbett-Tribe v Zambia Publishing* (1973) Z.R. 19 ("money-grabbing desire to benefit themselves"). Alternatively it may be defamatory to state that he will act improperly in pursuit of clients' interests: *Hopwood v Muirson* [1945] K.B. 313 CA: para.4.17, below.

[434] *Baker v Morfue* (1668) Sid. 327.

merely to misstate the date on which he was admitted a solicitor.[435] It is defamatory to say that a solicitor has been struck off the roll,[436] or suspended from practice,[437] or that these things ought to happen to him[438]; but not that he has provided services to a notorious client associated with terrorism.[439]

Politics. There are considerable variations in the law of defamation as it 2.42 applies to political or other "public" figures. However, even those jurisdictions which give greater protection to "political speech" than does English law[440] do not deny that the law of defamation is applicable to statements[441] about politicians.[442] The same is true of the jurisprudence of the European Convention on Human Rights.[443] The European Court of Human Rights has frequently emphasised that the protection of reputations in the political arena has to be weighed against the interests of open discussion of political issues and that politicians must display a greater degree of tolerance of criticism of their conduct than is required of private persons.[444] However, the context of these statements has been accusations which in the common law would fall potentially within the scope of the defence of honest comment (which does not require that the criticism be fair in any objective sense). At common law it may not be easy to distinguish, in discussions of political affairs, between words which are not, in that context, to be taken in a defamatory sense and words which are honest comment[445]; but either way there is:

> "the utmost freedom in the discussion of the conduct and motives of those who take part in its public business, whether in the higher plain of statesmanship or in the

---

[435] *Raven v Stevens* (1886) 3 T.L.R. 67.

[436] Per Cockburn C.J. in *Blake v Stevens* (1865) 11 L.T. 543 at 544.

[437] *Clarkson v Lawson* (1829) 3 Moo. & P. 605; (1830) 4 Moo. & P. 356. See also *D. Miles Griffiths v Woodruff* (1953) 162 E.G. 35, where it was held that the words "We do not care to take instructions from the solicitors concerned" were not capable of a defamatory meaning in their context.

[438] *Phillips v Jansen* (1798) 2 Esp. 623. For striking off for matters unconnected with practice, see para.4.17, below.

[439] *Madden v Sunday Newspapers* [2006] NIQB 18 (aliter perhaps if he is said to have "boasted" of it).

[440] See paras 15.25 et seq., below.

[441] But it is uncertain how far the law in the United States applies to statements of opinion: see para.12.1, below.

[442] In England (and presumably Scotland) the law of defamation is not applicable to statements about governmental bodies as opposed to individuals: see para.8.20, below.

[443] *Lingens v Austria* (1986) 8 EHRR 407; *Oberschlick v Austria* (1995) 19 EHRR 389; *Oberschlick v Austria (No.2)* (1998) 25 EHRR 357.

[444] See, e.g. *Lingens* at [42], *Oberschlick* at [59].

[445] See, for example, *Waterson v Lloyd*, one of several claims that arose out of the MPs' expenses scandal. At first instance (*Waterson v Lloyd* [2011] EWHC 3197 (QB)), Tugendhat J. held that the words complained of meant that the claimant's conduct in making expenses claims had given rise to legitimate outrage, and that the cause was his grave abuse for his own financial advantage of the Parliamentary rules governing such claims. This, he concluded, was a defamatory allegation of fact, not comment. On appeal, the Court of Appeal (*Waterson v Lloyd* [2013] EWCA Civ 136, [2013] E.M.L.R. 17) held, by a majority, that the words complained of meant only that the claimant had claimed nearly £70,000 from the taxpayer in respect of a family home that was 60 miles from Eastbourne, and that this was a scandal. There was no statement to the effect that the claimant had broken the law or the Parliamentary rules governing expenses, or that

conduct of local affairs. In such criticism, ridicule is just as legitimate as any other rhetorical artifice. If . . . this should take the form of rough language and unmannerly jests, the person aggrieved must put up with it."[446]

An accusation of corruption or "hypocrisy",[447] whether or not that imputes dishonesty, against a politician is, however, as much defamatory as the same accusation against a civil servant[448] though it was said not to be defamatory in *Lait v Evening Standard*[449] to suggest that an MP had "milked" the expenses system. In Singapore it has been held defamatory to impute that an advocate who is holder of high public office has lent his name and image to advertising a restaurant.[450] It has been held defamatory to impute lack of commitment[451] or political irresponsibility or involvement with a hostile regime[452] or disloyalty to a politician.[453] In theory one might say that it was

---

he had been required to repay sums previously claimed. On this basis, the claimant's conduct, and the comment made upon it, were clearly identified. In the circumstances, the words complained of were comment, not allegations of fact.

[446] *McLaughlan v Orr Pollock & Co* (1894) 22 R. 38 at 42, per Lord McLaren; *Brooks v Lind*, February 28, 1997, OH ("sheer lunacy" and "gross maladministration" not defamatory in attack on councillor). See also, *Waterson v Lloyd* (above), where Laws L.J. made a similar point (at [66]–[67]): "While of course . . . politicians are entitled to be protected by the law of defamation, 'the limits of acceptable criticism are wider in relation to politicians acting in their public capacity than in relation to private individuals'—*Jerusalem v Austria* (2003) 37 EHRR 25 , para 38" . . . (the Lord Justice referred to *Joseph v Spiller* [2010] UKSC 53; [2011] 1 A.C. 852 per Lord Phillips of Worth Matravers at [78], to Lord Phillips' reference to the Strasbourg court's observation in *Hrico v Slovakia* (2005) 41 EHRR 18 at [40g] that "there was little scope under article 10(2) of the Convention for restrictions on political speech or on debate on questions of public interest", and to his view that: "These expressions of principle are in general consonant with the English law of defamation") The Lord Justice concluded at [67]: "They exemplify, it seems to me, the common law's increasing focus in this area on the balance to be struck between public interest and individual right: between free speech and private claims, rather than on reputation as akin to a right of property . . . A political context—and especially at election time—surely informs this balance."

[447] *Cook v Telegraph Media Group Ltd* [2011] EWHC 1134 (QB).

[448] In *Field v Local Sunday Newspapers (North) Ltd* [2002] EWHC 336 (QB), an accusation of political bias against a local government officer was held defamatory (on appeal on other grounds sub nom. *Gough v Local Sunday Newspapers (North) Ltd* [2003] EWCA Civ 297; [2003] 1 W.L.R. 1836).

[449] [2010] EWHC 642 (QB) at [8] (An imputation that the claimant had been "forced" to pay back sums of money paid out as expenses was however held to be capable of being defamatory because such an allegation introduced connotations of concealment and being underhand (at [9])). Cf. *Miller v Associated Newspapers* [2010] EWHC 700 (QB) at [18] and *Fierravanti-Wells v Nationwide News Pty Ltd* [2010] N.S.W.S.C. 648 (allegation that plaintiff "rorted" her study tour abroad held capable of being defamatory). In *Cook v Telegraph Media Group* [2011] EWHC 1134 (QB) Tugendhat J. held that it was defamatory to suggest that at the time the claimant MP made an expenses claim he did not believe he could justify it but that it was a comment.

[450] *Chiam See Tong v Xin Zhang Jiang Restaurant* [1995] 3 S.L.R. 196.

[451] *Random House Australia Pty Ltd v Abbott* [1999] FCA 1538; 167 A.L.R. 224 (claimant alleged to be so shallow that he would change his allegiance for sexual favours); *Clark v Express Newspapers* [2004] EWHC 481 (QB) ("ratting" on promises). It was said to be defamatory, but also a comment, in *Cook v Telegraph Media Group Ltd* [2011] EWHC 1134 (QB) to impute of a politician that he represented "low value for money" (at [12]–[13]).

[452] *Galloway v Telegraph Group Ltd* [2006] EWCA Civ 17; [2006] E.M.L.R. 11 (see para. 15.13, below).

[453] *Blackburn v London Express, The Times*, January 14, 1953; *Pottle v Evening Telegram* (1954) 34 M.P.R. 101; *Fairbairn v Scottish National Party*, 1980 S.L.T. 149; *Parry v Express*

defamatory to impute incompetence to a Minister in his capacity as such[454] but nowadays such a claim would be likely to be doomed from the start because it would be unlikely to meet the necessary "threshold of seriousness"[455] and in view of the defence of fair comment, bearing in mind (a) that the comment need not be objectively fair and (b) that the motive of damaging your opponent is not "malice" for the purposes of this defence.[456] In any event, it has been suggested that criticism of public figures has less impact than that made of others.[457] Hence while it may be defamatory of a civil servant to say that he has lost the confidence of the Minister[458] it is surely not defamatory of a Minister to say that he has lost the confidence of his party.[459]

Doctors and other medical people. It is defamatory to impute to any   **2.43** doctor[460] want of proper qualification for his profession.[461] It is defamatory to publish of a doctor that he has caused the death or illness of a patient by reckless or careless treatment,[462] or that he has displayed gross ignorance in

---

Newspapers (unreported, March 10, 1995), CA (charge that Labour M.P. supported "Militant" policies). But see *Murphy v Australian Consolidated* [1968] 3 N.S.W.R. 200 (article containing no allegation of disloyalty to party); *Barrow v Target* (1970) 15 W.I.R. at 250; *Minister of Justice v SA Associated Newspapers*, 1979 (3) S.A. 466 (not defamatory to allege involvement with scandal only in political sense). See also *Lawson v Burns* (1975) 56 D.L.R. (3d) 240; *Renouf v Federal Capital Press* (1977) 17 A.C.T.R. 35 at 42; *Fairbairn v John Fairfax* (1977) 21 A.C.T.R. 1; *Baxter v CBC* (1979) 28 N.B.R.(2d) 114.

[454] *Pratten v Labour Daily* [1926] V.L.R. 115; or racial bias: *SA Associated Newspapers v Estate Pelser*, 1975 (4) S.A. 797 AD.

[455] See para.2.4, above.

[456] See paras 12.23 and 12.25, below.

[457] *Gorton v ABC* (1973) 22 F.L.R. 181 at 189; *Bacon v Hansch* [2001] TASSC 42 (union elections). See also *Mutch v Robertson*, 1981 S.L.T. 217.

[458] *Evans v John Fairfax* (1993) 112 F.L.R. 74 ACTSC.

[459] See, *Curran v Scottish Daily Record and Sunday Mail Ltd* [2011] CSIH 86; 2012 S.L.T. 359 (imputation that claimants had failed to give political support and loyalty to S held not capable of being defamatory). But cf. *John Fairfax v Punch* (1980) 31 A.L.R. 624 Fed Ct of Australia.

[460] Want of care or skill charged against a midwife was held actionable at an early date: Flowers' Case (1631) Cro.Car. 211; *Whitehead v Foulkes* (1676) Freem. K.B. 277.

[461] *Southee v Denny* (1847) I Exch. 196.

[462] *Southee v Denny* (1847) I Exch. 196 at 203; *Stevens v Kitchener* (1887) 4 T.L.R. 159; *Sumner v Utley* (1828) 7 Conn. R. 257; *Rogers v Nationwide News Pty Ltd* [2003] HCA 52; or, that he recommends a course of action which could cause harm to part of the public: *Bonham v Pure Water Association* (1970) 74 W.W.R. 617. Cf. *Edsall v Russell* (1842) 4 Man. & G. 1090. It is clearly not defamatory as such of a professional person to state that he took a wrong decision.

"For example, judgments of court are being criticized all the time, particularly by academics, and nobody has even suggested that it is defamatory to say that a judge has gone completely wrong or has failed to take into account this factor or that factor. How could it be defamatory to merely say that a person has erred or made a mistake?":
per Chao Hick Tin J. in *Oversea Chinese Banking Corp v Wright Norman* [1994] 3 S.L.R. 760 at 781. See also the submissions of the defendants in *Skuse v Granada Television* [1996] E.M.L.R. 278 CA. But there must be some risk, particularly in modern conditions and in the case of the medical profession, that an allegation of error made without explanation or qualification could be widely treated as imputing negligence. Whether the court would accept that remains to be seen.

the treatment of a patient,[463] or that he has forged a medical report,[464] or that his treatments are useless and dangerous,[465] or that he is a quack[466] or "not fit to treat a dog"[467] or to use his name without his consent in the advertisement of a medicine or treatment in such a way as to induce the persons to whom it is published to doubt his good faith or competence.[468] In Australia it has been held capable of being defamatory to call a doctor "an abortionist" because even though abortions may be performed lawfully the word has a pejorative sting.[469] It is defamatory to state of a doctor that he has been guilty of unprofessional conduct in the treatment of a case,[470] or of any unethical conduct,[471] but not to impute a mere breach of professional etiquette, unless the act imputed would tend to lower him in the estimation of the general public.[472] An attack on the special technique of a dentist has been held arguably capable of bearing a defamatory meaning.[473]

2.44 Entertainment. It is defamatory to say that a racing man has been "warned off,"[474] or to state that a top level sports player had refused to play in a world championship match,[475] or that a high ranking sports official was involved in a plan to destroy the sport's structure,[476] or to accuse a sportsman of taking

---

[463] *Rodgers v Kilne* (1879) 31 Am.Rep. 389; *Secor v Harris* (1854) 18 Barb. (N.Y.) 425.

[464] *Khalil v Barakat* [2013] EWHC 85 (QB) (claim struck out as an abuse of process on other grounds).

[465] *Gorman v Barber* [2004] NSWCA 402.

[466] *Allen v Eaton* (1630) 1 Roll.Abr. 54; *White v Carrol* (1870) 42 N.Y.R. 161 at 164; *Hunter v Sharpe* (1866) 4 F. & F. 983; *Dakhyl v Labouchere* [1908] 2 K.B. 325n.; *Grant v Chisholm*, 1914 S.C. 239; *Crofton v Lawson, The Times*, May 7, 1953 ("the language of the quack remedy advertisement"); *Arnott v Saskatchewan College* (1953) 9 W.W.R. at 128; *Warren v Green* (1958) 25 W.W.R. 563; and see *Blumberg v Shendan, The Times*, February 14, 1967. There are other meanings of the word "quack" than one who pretends to medical skill he does not have, such as "a person who, however skilled, lends himself to a medical imposture" (per Lord Loreburn L.C. in *Dakhyl v Labouchere* [1908] 2 K.B. at 326n.); or "exploits the timid and the credulous for his own advantage" per Lord Alverstone C.J. in *Bell v Bashford, The Times*, June 15, 1912). See also *Chisholm v Grant* 1914 S.C. 239. See also para.2.20, above.

[467] *Cruickshank v Gordon*, 118 N.Y. 179 (1890).

[468] *Dockrell v Dougall* (1899) 80 L.T. 558; *Noah v Shuba* [1991] F.S.R. 14.

[469] *Hepburn v TCN Channel Nine Pty Ltd* [1983] 2 N.S.W.L.R. 682 NSWCA, per Hutley J.A.; cf. Glass J.A., who adopted the test of defamation set out in para.2.12, above.

[470] *Marion v Courier Publishing* (1906) 125 Ill.App.R. 349.

[471] *Van Pelt v Carter, The Times*, November 21, 1957; *Ross v Bricker* 770 F.Supp. 1038 (1991) (poaching patients); *Smith v Houston*, CA, December 16, 1993 (LEXIS) (sexual harassment, appeal on issue of damages only).

[472] See para.2.16, above.

[473] *Drummond-Jackson v BMA* [1970] 1 W.L.R. 668 CA, per Lord Pearson and Willmer L.J. at 698, 699, 701, 702, Lord Denning M.R. dissenting) where it was doubted whether an analogy sought to be drawn between a trader's goods (see para.2.39, below) and a professional man's technique was sound; per Lord Pearson at 698.

[474] *Cookson v Harewood* [1932] 2 K.B. 478n.; *Demerara Turf Club v Phang* [1961] 3 W.I.R. 454.

[475] *Munro v Brown* [2011] CSOH 117, (2011) SLT 947 (CSOH).

[476] *Modi v Clarke* [2011] EWCA 937 CA. In reaching its decision, the Court of Appeal noted that it was not, without more, defamatory to say of a person that he wished to destroy the structure of a sport. However, where, as was the case here, the claimant was a high ranking official within the sport whom readers would know had agreed to be bound by the rules and practices of those

performance-enhancing drugs,[477] or of cheating or corrupt practices,[478] or a jockey of riding horses unfairly and dishonestly,[479] or favouritism to a referee.[480] However, it is not defamatory, without more, to impute incompetence to a sportsperson.[481] As Sharp J. explained in *Dee v Telegraph Media Group Ltd*: "Losing in sport is . . . an occupational hazard. Shaky hands for a surgeon, or endangering the lives of your dental patients through an unproven anaesthetic cannot be so characterised".[482] It has also been held to be defamatory to write of an actor that he cannot act,[483] of an actress that her performance is vulgar,[484] of a television commentator that he is the only one in town enrolled on a remedial speaking course[485] and of an entertainer that he has a bizarre diet involving chewing food and then spitting it out,[486] though whether the last of these would be held defamatory today must be open to doubt.[487] A statement that an actor is "hideously ugly" has been held to be capable of being defamatory because it may lower him in the estimation of the public and make him the object of ridicule (though this was by a majority and decided before the Human Rights Act 1998 became law),[488] but it must be questionable whether it was right to hold it defamatory to state (without more) that an actress was 10 years older than her actual age.[489] Where the defendant, who had engaged a well-known vocalist to sing at a concert, published a programme in which her name appeared in an inferior position to that of other artistes of lesser reputation, it was held that an action of libel lay.[490] But it is

---

organisations that governed the sport, the words were capable of bearing the defamatory meaning that the claimant had acted dishonourably and disloyally.

[477] *Armstrong v Times Newspapers Ltd* [2006] EWHC 1614 (QB).

[478] *Grobelaar v News Group Newspapers Ltd* [2002] 1 W.L.R. 3024. See also *Cairns v Modi* [2012] EWHC 756 (involvement in match-fixing).

[479] *Wood v Earl of Durham* (1888) 21 Q.B.D. 501, not affected on this point by *Plato Films v Speidel* [1961] A.C. 1090; cf. *Breasley v Odhams Press, The Times,* November 15, 1963.

[480] *Harrigan v Jones* [2001] N.S.W.S.C. 623.

[481] *Dee v Telegraph Media Group Ltd* [2010] EWHC 924 (QB); [2010] E.M.L.R. 20. Note however that in *Hoeppner v Dunkirk Printing*, 227 N.Y.A.D. 130 (1929) a New York court held that it was defamatory to impute incompetence to a football coach.

[482] *Dee v Telegraph Media Group Ltd*, (above) at [49].

[483] *Duplany v Davis* (1886) 3 T.L.R. 184. A libel which attacks an artist's integrity or professional reputation is likely to merit a higher award of damages than one which does not: *John v MGN Ltd* [1997] Q.B. 586 CA. In *Sarma v Federal Capital Press of Australia Pty Ltd* [2002] NSWCA 93 a review stated that the claimant was incompetent as a dancer. There was no evidence that she was a professional dancer and the court declined to interfere with a verdict that the statement was not defamatory, though the implication is that the result would have been different if she had been a professional.

[484] *Cooney v Edeveain* (1897) 14 T.L.R. 34.

[485] *Myers v Boston Magazine Co. Inc.*, 403 N.E.2d (Mass. 1980).

[486] *John v MGN Ltd* [1997] Q.B. 586 CA.

[487] See para.2.14, above.

[488] *Berkoff v Burchill* [1996] 4 All E.R. 1008; [1997] E.M.L.R. 139, CA. It seems that the position might have been different in this case if the statement were that the plaintiff was physically unattractive rather than actually repulsive.

[489] *Chattell v Daily Mail* (1901) 18 T.L.R. 165 CA; cf. para.2.18, above.

[490] *Russell v Notcutt* (1896) 12 T.L.R. 195. See also *Elen v London Music Hall, The Times,* June 1, 1906; *Smith v Elmore* [1938] T.P.D. 18; *Lohr v Adell Chemical*, 300 F.2d 256 (1962). See also para.2.8, above.

not defamatory without more[491] to bill an artist's name for a performance at which he is in fact not appearing.[492]

2.45 **Other professions and callings.** It is defamatory to publish of an editor that he is a libellous[493] or incompetent[494] journalist, or of an architect of a public building that his appointment can be regarded in no other light than a public calamity,[495] or, when employed to restore an ancient building, that he is incompetent or has not the experience to do so.[496] An engineer[497] was defamed by a broadcast which imputed he was unfit for his office and that he had wrongfully caused a worker's death.[498] It has been held to be defamatory to accuse an author of plagiarism,[499] or of being a "paid hack",[500] or to publish falsely in the name of a well-known author any literary work[501] which would tend to injure him in the world of letters,[502] or falsely to attribute to him an obscene or profane article[503] or one which expresses sentiments abhorrent to right-thinking people.[504] It is defamatory falsely to attribute to a well-known teacher and lecturer an article which puts into his mouth or attributes to his pen statements that reveal entire ignorance of the subject on which he professes to teach or lecture,[505] or to state that a teacher unjustifiably struck a

---

[491] *Louka v Park Entertainments*, 1 N.E.2d (Mass.1936) (actress who played in Greek tragedies portrayed outside burlesque theatre); cf. *Grappelli v Derek Block (Holdings)* [1981] 1 W.L.R. 872 CA.

[492] *Renard v Carl Rosa, The Times*, February 15, 1906. If the statement is made maliciously an action on the case may lie: see Ch.21, below.

[493] *Wakley v Cooke* (1849) 4 Exch. 511. An apology by a newspaper may be in terms which imputes incompetence to the journalist: *Tracy v Kemsley Newspapers, The Times*, April 9, 1954. Compare *Oversea Chinese Banking Corp v Wright Norman* [1994] 3 S.L.R. 760, where the words merely meant that the original statement was incorrect.

[494] *Dowling v Time Inc, The Times*, April 10, 1954 and June 25, 1954, CA (editorship brought paper to brink of ruin); *Allsopp v Incorporated Newspapers* (1975) 26 F.L.R. 238.

[495] *Clifford v Cochrane* (1880) 10 Ill.App.R. 570.

[496] *Botterill v Whitehead* (1879) 41 L.T. 588.

[497] See also *A-S v Statewide Roads Ltd* [2007] N.S.W.S.C. 1472.

[498] *Thomas v CBC* [1981] 4 W.W.R. 289.

[499] *McLellan v Dutton, The Times*, May 23, 1906. See also *Reichardt v Allport* (1892) 9 T.L.R. 604 at 605; per Vaughan Williams L.J. in *Joynt v Cycle Trade* [1904] 2 K.B. 292 at 297; *Watts v Times Newspapers Ltd* [1997] Q.B. 650 CA.

[500] *Churchill v Ainsworth, The Times*, October 10, 1956.

[501] In principle, the same must apply to a film or musical work. False attribution may also be actionable as passing off (para.23.14) and there is a statutory right, independent of defamation, not to have a work falsely attributed to one as author or director: Copyright, Designs and Patents Act 1988, s.84. See para.23.18, below.

[502] *Lee v Gibbins* (1892) 67 L.T. 263; *Ridge v English Illustrated* (1913) 29 T.L.R. 592. See also *Archbold v Sweet* (1832) 1 Mood. & R. 162; *Humphries v Thompson, The Times*, May 1, 1908; *Locke v Benton*, 2 N.Y.S.2d 150 (1937); *Karjavainean v MacFadden Inc.*, 26 N.E.2d 538 (Mass, 1940); *Moore v News of the World* [1972] 1 Q.B. 441 at 449.

[503] Per Scott J. in *D'Altomonte v N.Y. Herald* 139 N.Y.S. (1913) 200 at 204; *Gershwin v Ethical* (1937) 1 N.Y.S.2d 904.

[504] *Waugh v Ayrshire Post* (1893) 21 R. 326; *Carter v Gair* (1999) 170 D.L.R. (4th) 204.

[505] *Ben Oliel v Press Publishing*, 167 N.E. 432 (N.Y. 1929). See also para.2.17, above. In *Alexander v Macdonald* (1826) 4 Murr. 94, it was held defamatory of a professor to say that he was unfit for his duties, neglected them and that his class was in a state of insubordination. There

pupil.[506] But it is not defamatory to say that other professional people are better than the claimant or that he lacks a qualification which would be useful.[507]

Defamation in relation to trade. Many imputations defamatory of a   **2.46**
merchant or trader[508] would be equally so of a non-trader. Among these are imputations of fraud and dishonesty[509]; it is defamatory to publish of a trader that he uses false weights,[510] or sells[511] unwholesome[512] or adulterated,[513] or dangerous goods,[514] or worthless or unworkable wares,[515] or fakes,[516] or delivers goods inferior to those contracted for,[517] or infringes hygiene regulations, or has issued a circular giving a false reason for raising his prices.[518] Similarly, to publish of a trader that he employs sweated labour is "calculated to bring him and his business into hatred and contempt, and to deter respectable persons from dealing with him."[519] A trader cannot adopt the position of

---

were perhaps times in the universities in the 1960s when the last imputation alone would not have been defamatory.

[506] *Zelik v Daily News Publishing Co*, 431 A.2d 1046 (Pa., 1981); and see *Kohuch v Wilson* (1988) 71 Sask. R. 33.

[507] See paras 2.17 and 2.36, above.

[508] Generally words which are defamatory of a sole trader will be defamatory of a trading company: see para.8.18, below.

[509] See *Angel v Bushell & Co* [1968] I Q.B. 813 at 825–826 ("not conversant with normal business ethics").

[510] *Prior v Wilson* (1856) I C.B. (N.S.) 95; *Henderson v Marsden* (1863) 22 Up.Can.Q.B. 585.

[511] For the relevance of the trader's knowledge of their character, see para.2.48, below.

[512] *Burnett v Wells* (1700) 12 Mod. 241.

[513] *Solomon v Lawson* (1846) 8 Q.B. 823; *Evans v Harlow* (1844) 5 Q.B. 624 at 635; *Broomfield v Greig* (1868) 6 M. 563; *Kennedy v Press Publishing* (1886) 41 Hun. (N.Y.) R. at 423.

[514] *Camporese v Parton* (1983) 150 D.L.R. (3d) 208; *Ming Kee Manufactory v Man Shing Electrical Manufactory* [1992] 1 H.K.C. 442.

[515] *Empire Typesetting Machine Co. v Linotype Co* (1898) 79 L.T. 8 at 9.

[516] *McManus v Beckham* [2002] 1 W.L.R. 2982 CA.

[517] *Pack's Case* (1616) Roll. Abr. 62; *Thomas v Jackson* (1825) 3 Bing. 104. See also *Robinson v Coulter*, 215 Mass. 566 (1913) (builder alleged to use sub-specification materials). For imputations defamatory of innkeepers and hoteliers see *Plunkett v Gilmore* (1724) 8 Mod. 215; *Riding v Smith* (1876) 1 Ex. D. 91 at 94; *Trimmer v Hiscock* (1882) Hun. (N.Y.) R. 364.

[518] *Initial Services v Putterill* [1968] 1 Q.B. 396 at 407.

[519] *Collard v Marshall* [1892] 1 Ch. 571 at 577. And see *James Gilbert v MGN Ltd* [2000] E.M.L.R. 680 (QB). It was said in *Robinson v Adams* (1924) 56 O.L.R. 227 to be not defamatory to publish of a business man that he will not employ trade union labour. Unless some imputation of hypocrisy can be found in the context (as to which, see para.2.22) it is thought that this represents current English law. First, it is probably necessary that the charge should lower the claimant in the estimation of persons generally (see para.2.19, above). Secondly, ss.144–145 and 186–187 of the Trade Union and Labour Relations (Consolidation) Act 1992 contain statutory wrongs of refusing to deal with a person on the basis of his attitude to union recognition. Though not directly relevant to defamation, it is thought that these provisions demonstrate a legislative intent which is relevant to what is considered "proper" behaviour. Nor is it defamatory to suggest of a businessman or a company that it has used financial muscle to gain an advantage in business circumstances where there is no suggestion of dishonesty, unlawfulness, wrongdoing or lack of ethics, because that would not lower the perpetrator in the eyes of right thinking people generally: *Bell v Kingsbay Pty Ltd* [2001] VSC 498.

"the public be damned" and it is therefore defamatory to impute to him conduct which is unacceptable to public opinion.[520] Imputations on a trader's credit are as defamatory as they are in relation to another person, and may cause more damage.[521] This is illustrated by the special treatment given at common law to oral statements disparaging commercial credit. Slander is not actionable without proof of actual damage, subject to certain exceptions, of which one is a defamatory statement calculated to disparage a person in his trade, profession or calling. The general rule for these cases was[522] that such a slander was only actionable per se if the words were spoken "in the way of" (i.e. with reference to) a profession or calling but there was no such requirement in relation to a trader's credit. Thus it was held actionable per se to impute to a trader that he was bankrupt[523] or not able to pay his debts[524] or that he had compounded with his creditors[525] or to say that he had been bankrupt or insolvent in the past,[526] even though he was carrying on business in a different place in a different trade.[527] It was also actionable per se to impute future insolvency to a trader.[528] The abolition of the "in the way of" requirement of course now means that no special rule is necessary for traders, but all the above examples remain valid.[529] It may be defamatory to suggest of a trader that he does not keep his contracts.[530] However it has been held that a statement by a competitor that the claimant is "not highly regarded in the trade" was not capable of being defamatory.[531]

2.47 Incompetence and want of judgment. It is not enough that words in fact damage a trader in his business,[532] but just as imputations on the competence of a professional person may be injurious to his reputation as such without reflecting on his character,[533] an imputation of incompetence or want of

---

[520] *United States Tobacco Inc. v BBC* [1998] E.M.L.R. 816; *Brown & Williamson Tobacco Corp v Jacobson*, 713 F.2d 262 (CA7 1983) (aiming tobacco advertising at children); *Mayes v Hub Publications Ltd* [1993] N.W.T.R. 174; *Provincial Partitions Inc. v Ashlar Implant Structures Ltd*, (1993) 50 C.P.R. (3d) 497; *Chapman v Allan* (1999) 74 S.A.S.R. 274, Full Court. For the problem that there may be divisions of opinion on an issue, see para.2.12, above.

[521] See para.2.30, above.

[522] No longer: see para.4.15, below.

[523] *Read v Hudson* (1700) 1 Ld. Raym. 610.

[524] *Cook v Tucker* (1695) Carthew 330.

[525] *Stanton v Smith* (1727) 2 Ld. Raym. 1480.

[526] Ibid.

[527] *Hall v Smith* (1813) 1 M. & S. 287.

[528] *Whittington v Gladwin* (1826) 5 B. & C. 180; *Brown v Smith* (1853) 596.

[529] Thus it is defamatory to impute future insolvency to a trading company: *Aspro Travel v Owners Abroad Group* [1996] 1 W.L.R. 132 CA. See also *Kiam v Neill* [1996] E.M.L.R. 493 CA.

[530] See *Holdsworth v Associated Newspapers* (1937) 53 T.L.R. 1029; *Morris v Langdale* (1800) 2 Bos. & P. 284. It may be defamatory to say that although the plaintiff pays his debts he does not do so promptly.

[531] *Schindler Lifts v Debelak* (1989) 89 A.L.R. 275 Fed. Ct. of Australia (negative equivalent of defendant puffing his own wares).

[532] See para.2.18, above.

[533] See para.2.36, above.

judgment in his trade may be defamatory of a trader without reflecting on his character. Such might be an imputation that he had been careless or incompetent[534] in the manufacture of goods or the provision of services,[535] or incompetent in the way in which he ran his business,[536] inefficient in the choice of goods to stock,[537] or that he carelessly ran an unsafe business[538] or that he did not have the proper credentials to engage in the trade.[539] Words which merely disparage a person's goods or property, but in no way reflect on his personal or trading character, are not defamatory.[540] "To disparage a trader's goods," said Cozens-Hardy M.R. in *Griffiths v Benn*[541]:

"which is often (though inaccurately) spoken of as a trade libel, does not give ground for an action of libel, although, if special damage is proved, the plaintiff may recover in an action on the case.[542] On the other hand, the words used, though directly disparaging goods, may also impute such carelessness, misconduct, or want of skill in the conduct of his business by the trader as to justify an action of libel."

It is thus clear that language in disparagement of goods or their quality is defamatory where it reflects on the owner or manufacturer of the goods in his character as a person or as a trader. An excellent illustration is given by Lord Esher M.R.[543]:

"Suppose the plaintiff was a merchant who dealt in wine and it was stated that wine which he had for sale of a particular vintage was not good wine; that might be so stated as only to import that the wine of the particular year was not good in whosesoever hands it was, but not to imply any reflection on his conduct of his

---

[534] *Hope Technical Developments v BBC*, unreported, March 31, 1995, CA.

[535] *John Fairfax Publications Pty Ltd v Gacic* [2007] HCA 28; 235 A.L.R. 402.

[536] In *Cammish v Hughes* [2012] EWCA Civ 1655; [2013] E.M.L.R. 13 CA the Court of Appeal upheld Tugendhat J.'s decision that the words complained of bore the defamatory meaning that the claimant had had to dissolve 15 companies because he was unable to run them and that this showed that he was a seriously incompetent businessman. However, in light of the finding by the court that the words complained of were comment and not allegations of fact and that it was unreasonable to infer from the fact that he had had to dissolve even 15 companies that the claimant was unfit to run them, the court concluded that no better vindication could be obtained by going to trial. Accordingly, they dismissed the proceedings as an abuse of process.

[537] See para.2.48, below.

[538] *Marley's Transport Pty Ltd v West Australian Newspapers Ltd* [2001] WASC 31.

[539] It is defamatory to say of a Kosher butcher that he is not licensed by the Beth Din Court: *Saunderson v Jewish Chronicle, The Times*, April 24, 1953.

[540] *Evans v Harlow* (1844) 5 Q.B. 624; *Linotype Co. Ltd v British Empire Typesetting Machine Co. Ltd* (1899) 81 L.T. 331 HL; *Griffiths v Benn* (1911) 27 T.L.R. 346; *Hein v Canadian Fairbanks* [1938] 4 D.L.R. 63; *John Hall & Co. v Bowden* [1953] C.P.L. 273; *Charterhouse etc. Ltd v Richmond Pharmacology* [2003] EWHC 1099 (QB).

[541] (1911) 27 T.L.R. 346 CA.

[542] I.e. that variety of malicious falsehood known, equally inaccurately, as slander of goods: see Ch.21, below.

[543] *South Hetton Coal v N.-E. News Ass* [1894] 1 Q.B. 133 CA at 139. This statement of the law was expressly approved by Smith L.J. in *Empire Typesetting Machine Co. of New York v Linotype Co. Ltd* (1898) 79 L.T. 8 CA at 9 and by Lord Pearson in *Drummond-Jackson v BMA* [1970] 1 W.L.R. 688 CA at 698.

business. In that case the statement would be with regard to his goods only, and there would be no libel, although such a statement, if it were false and made maliciously, with intention to injure him, and it did injure him, might be made the subject of an action on the case. On the other hand, if the statement were so made as to import that his judgment in the selection of wine was bad, it might import a reflection on his conduct in his business and show that he was an inefficient man of business. If so, it would be a libel. In such a case a jury would have to say which sense the libel really bore; if they thought it related to the goods only, they ought to find that it was not a libel; but, if they thought that it related to the man's conduct of business, they ought to find that it was a libel." [544]

"The question is whether . . . there is an imputation on the maker and not the product." [545]

Care should however be taken not to read too much into Lord Esher's words. Lord Esher spoke of the criticism of the wine as imputing that the merchant's judgment was bad. But, as Tugendhat J. pointed out in *Thornton v Telegraph Media Group Ltd* [546]:

"Merchants may choose to deal in . . . different products directed to different markets. Not all shoppers want vintage wine. Some merchants may choose to sell poorer quality wine, or no wine at all, because if they did not, many of their customers would buy less wine, or no wine at all. Even a wine lover may be happy to drink vintage champagne on one day, and some other sparkling wine (at a fraction of the price) on another. The same supermarket may be proud to sell wines of both types, displaying them within arm's length of each other on the same stacks."

2.48 Examples: disparagement of goods. [547] A statement that the meat sold by a butcher is diseased, rotten, or tubercular, [548] or that the house erected by a builder is jerry-built, [549] is defamatory of them. It is a reflection on a shipowner in the way of his business to state that a ship which he owns and has advertised for a voyage is unseaworthy and likely to go to the bottom. [550]

---

[544] See also *Kennedy v Press Publishing* (1886) 41 Hun.(N.Y.) R. 423, per Cullen J.:
"A libel on a thing may constitute a libel on a person. Thus, to say of a brewer that his beer is adulterated would be a libel upon him in his trade, not because of the allegation that the beer was bad, but because the language would import deceit and malpractice on the part of the brewer."
[545] *Hope Technical Developments Ltd v BBC*, March 31, 1995, CA, per Morritt L.J.
[546] [2010] EWHC 1414 (QB); [2011] 1 W.L.R. 1985; [2010] E.M.L.R. 25 at [42].
[547] In *Tabart v Tipper* (1808) 1 Camp. 353 it was held that it was defamatory to say of a bookseller that he sold immoral books. While this can hardly now be taken *au pied de la lettre*, it is no doubt defamatory to say that a booksellers' trade consists wholly or mainly of pornography.
[548] *Panster v Wasserman*, 190 N.Y. App. Div. 822 (1920).
[549] *Erasmus v Scott* [1933] Natal P.D.271 at 283; or a fire-trap: *Morgenstern v Oakville Record Star* (1962) 33 D.L.R. (2d) 354; but not perhaps that he was late in completing it: *Grande v Chace*, 333 Mass.166 (1955). Cf. para.2.46, above.
[550] *Ingram v Lawson* (1840) 6 Bing. N.C. 212. See, however, *City-County Helicopters v United Telecasters* [1979] A.C.L.D. 581 (three of plaintiffs' helicopters said to have crashed in a month; not defamatory); *Sungravure v Middle East Airlines* (1975) 134 C.L.R. 1 (allegation that travellers by plaintiffs' airline faced a serious risk of hijacking not defamatory at common law).

In *Hatchard v Mege*,[551] a statement that a certain wine sold by the plaintiff "cannot be the wine it is represented to be" was held to be capable of being interpreted as a charge of personal dishonesty on the part of the vendor, though it was also an attack on the plaintiff's trade mark. Moreover, where the defendants stated that a wine which the plaintiff made and advertised as "really genuine nutritive meat wine" contained such a ridiculously small quantity of beef extract that it could not really be strengthening and that the claim for its use on this ground was positively absurd, it was held that such statement imputed either dishonesty or fraudulent incapacity in the conduct of the plaintiff's business, and was therefore defamatory.[552] On the other hand, an advertisement cautioning the public that the plaintiff's "self-acting tallow syphons and lubricators wasted the tallow", was held not to be a libel on the plaintiff either generally or in the way of his trade, but only a reflection on the goods sold by him which was not actionable without proof of (malice and of) special damage.[553] It is not necessary that there should be an express allegation of incompetence or wrongdoing against the claimant but whether such an imputation is implied in statements about his goods or services will depend on the context.[554] It may be easier to draw an inference of fault where the statement is made about the manufacturer of the product rather than a distributor.[555]

It is necessary to treat with caution dicta in some older cases which suggest that there is no defamation unless the claimant *knew* of the bad quality of what he sold[556]: it is clear that an imputation of incompetence in business may be actionable, not merely one of dishonesty.[557]

> "For material to be defamatory of a company there must . . . be some inference of culpable responsibility on the part of the company, whether it be, in ascending order of seriousness, inefficiency, negligence, recklessness, deliberate malpractice of some kind, or plain fraud and dishonesty which is so serious that it is likely to affect the company adversely in the true estimation of reasonable people generally."[558]

Examples: disparagement of newspapers. In modern conditions a **2.49** newspaper will almost always trade as a company and, since a trading company has a reputation for the purposes of defamation, it may bring an action.[559] However, in the past the question has arisen (and may still arise)

---

[551] (1887) 18 Q.B.D. 771.

[552] *Bendle v United Kingdom Alliance* (1915) 31 T.L.R. 403 CA.

[553] *Evans v Harlow* (1844) 5 Q.B. 624; *Charterhouse Clinical Research Unit Ltd v Richmond Pharmacology Ltd* [2003] EWHC 1099 (QB); *Dorset Flint & Stone Blocks Ltd v Moir* [2004] EWHC 2173 (QB).

[554] *John Fairfax Publications Pty Ltd v ACP Publishing Pty Ltd* [2005] ACTCA 12.

[555] *Morford v Rigby*, February 17, 1998, CA.

[556] See, e.g. *Evans v Harlow*, above; *Broomfield v Greig* (1868) 6 M. 563.

[557] See paras 2.36 and 2.47, above.

[558] *Griffiths v Benn* (1911) 27 T.L.R. 346 CA at 350.

[559] For the position of trading companies, see para.8.16, below. In *Chinese Herald Ltd v New Times Media Ltd* [2004] 2 N.Z.L.R. 749 the following meanings were found and were held to be defamatory: that the claimant newspaper.

"behaved in an underhand and devious manner, adopted a biased practice to reporting, was

whether a statement disparaging a newspaper may involve an imputation upon the personal character of those who own or conduct and manage the newspaper.[560] Thus, to write and publish of a newspaper that it is the Daily "Ananias",[561] or that there are inserted in its pages columns of advertisements which were not ordered, but merely copied from other papers,[562] or that it has a column for the advertisements of quack doctors and usurers,[563] or that "it is alleged to have been started for the purposes of plunder",[564] or that "it reports favourably or adversely at ten cents a line", or that it is ignorant, prejudiced or corrupt,[565] may be defamatory of the proprietors of the paper. "To write of a newspaper that its action is a disgrace to journalism, that it has wantonly published a scandalous effusion, that its action is cowardly and despicable, and that it has not the least sense of decency, is undoubtedly tantamount to an attack on those who are responsible for the conduct of the paper."[566] It is defamatory of the proprietors to charge a newspaper with selling its influence to any political party or group and thereby binding itself to deceive the public and its readers by publishing what may be contrary to the honest opinions and convictions of its management,[567] or to allege that the newspaper's policy in advocating some public measure (e.g. prohibition) is mere hypocrisy or pretence[568] or that it is a mere tool of the proprietor's interests and cannot act in a fair and balanced way.[569] It is defamatory of the editor of a newspaper to allege that the paper is manipulated by outside influences,[570] or that in pursuance of a policy of vilification it has deliberately falsified a report of a speech which was correctly taken down by its reporter.[571] But a statement that a newspaper has been purchased by, and will in future be controlled by, some

---

malicious and absurd in its reporting, was a sycophant and acted in an obscene manner, was evil and acted dishonourably, and was a less than upright newspaper".
The statement that it opposed democracy was in the circumstances defamatory but if it had stood on its own without the other comments, it would not have led to more than nominal damages.

[560] For the general question of whether a libel on a company reflects on its officers, see para.7.13, below.

[561] *Bennett v Australian Newspaper* (1891) 12 N.S.W.L.R. 141; [1894] A.C. 284. That is to say, "The Daily Liar": *Acts*, 5:2. But the jury were entitled to find that in the context the imputation did not reflect on the plaintiff proprietor.

[562] *Latimer v Western Morning News* (1871) 25 L.T. 44.

[563] *Russell v Webster* (1874) 23 W.R. 59 at 60. Cf. *Ackrill v RTSA*, *The Times*, February 2, 1965 (allegation of irresponsibility in accepting advertisements); *Rhodesian Printing v Howman*, 1967 (4) S.A. 1 ("fairly high degree of irresponsibility").

[564] *Hart v Townsend* (1884) 67 How Practice (N.Y.) R. 88.

[565] *Journal Printing v Maclean* (1894) 25 O.R. 509; affirmed (1896) 23 O.A.R. 324.

[566] *Kingswell v Robinson* [1913] W.L.D. 129 at 142.

[567] *Albertan Publishing Co. v Munns* (1918) 13 A.R. 533.

[568] *Sentinel Review v Robinson* (1927) 61 O.L.R. 62; cf. *News Media v Finlay* [1971] N.Z.L.R. 1089 at 1095, 1103.

[569] *Oriental Daily Publisher v Ming Pao Holdings Ltd* [1999] 4 H.K.C. 354. But it cannot be the law that it is defamatory of the proprietor to say that he influences its editorial policy: frequently that is why powerful people acquire newspapers.

[570] *Gwynne v Stopes*, *The Times*, January 26, May 3, 4, 1928.

[571] *Nasionale Pers Bpkt v Long* [1930] A.D. 87. It is the editor who guides and controls the policy of a paper, and a statement that the paper deliberately falsified a report correctly taken by its reporter is libellous of the editor though his name is not mentioned.

person other than its present proprietor,[572] or that its circulation is 5,000 when it is in fact much larger, is not defamatory of the proprietors.[573]

Burden of proof. In such cases the onus lies on the claimant to prove that   **2.50** the words are defamatory of him in his personal or business or trading character and not merely a disparagement of his goods.[574] If the words are reasonably capable of either meaning it is a question for the jury which meaning the words really bore.[575] If the jury think that the words reflect on the claimant in his personal or business or trading character, they ought to find for the claimant. If they think that the words disparage only his goods the words are not defamatory.[576]

---

[572] *Wallach's Printing Co. v Noordelike Drukpers* [1921] T. P. D. 441.

[573] *Publishers of The Observer v Advertisers' Protection Society, The Times*, February 3, 4, 1910. Cf. para.2.17, above. In *Heriot v Stuart* (1796) 1 Esp. 437, Erskine (for the plaintiff) admitted that it was not actionable for one newspaper to describe another as "the most vulgar, ignorant and scurrilous journal ever published in Great Britain", but contended that it was actionable to state: "It is the lowest now in circulation, and we submit the fact to the consideration of advertisers", to which, the report says, Lord Kenyon C.J. assented. But in the modern law the first statement would seem prima facie defamatory (though likely to attract a defence of fair comment) and the second would seem to be actionable only as malicious falsehood.

[574] *Griffiths v Benn* (1911) 27 T.L.R. 346 at 350; *South Hetton Coal Co. v N.-E. News* [1894] 1 Q.B. 133 CA at 139.

[575] See the following cases, where, the words being capable of either meaning, the case was properly left, or proper to leave, to the jury: *Salmon v Isaac* (1869) 20 L.T. 885; *Jenner v A'Beckett* (1871) L.R. 7 Q.B. 11; *Société des Asphaltes v Farrell* (1885) Cab. & Ell. 563; *Australian Newspaper Co. v Bennett* [1894] A.C. 284; *Linotype v British Empire Typesetting Machine Co. Ltd* (1899) 81 L.T. 331 HL.

[576] Per Lord Esher M.R. in *South Hetton Coal Co. v N. E. News Ass* [1894] 1 Q.B. 133 CA at 139; *Linotype Co. Ltd v British Empire Typesetting Machine Co. Ltd* (1899) 81 L.T. 331 HL.

CHAPTER 3

THE FORM AND MEANING OF THE DEFAMATORY STATEMENT

SECTION 1. FORM

Defamatory matter. Defamatory imputations are usually conveyed in **3.1** words, written[1] or spoken.[2] But there are many other activities and objects[3] which may convey an imputation defamatory of some person, either of themselves or in their context. Statues, waxworks, pictures, photographs (particularly in collocation with words[4]), cartoons,[5] cinema or television pictures,[6] marks on a pavement,[7] burning a person in effigy, hanging a sign outside his house or hissing him,[8] signs and gestures[9] have all been considered capable of conveying a defamatory imputation. More difficulty is caused by the necessity to classify defamatory matter[10] as libel or as slander, since they

---

[1] See para.3.2, below.

[2] See para.3.3, below.

[3] "Law Update" in the "Press Gazette" of December 15, 2000, reports a case in which Eady J. directed the jury that a series of numbers sent by a building society's computer to a credit reference agency signifying that the claimant had missed payments on his mortgage were capable of being defamatory. However, the jury found for the defendants.

[4] See, e.g. *Burnett v CBC (No.1)* (1981) 48 N.S.R. 2d 1.

[5] For physical representations, see para.3.4, below.

[6] *Youssoupoff v Metro-Goldwyn-Mayer* (1934) 50 T.L.R. 581 at 587; *Merle v Sociological Film Corporation*, 166 N.Y.App.Div. 376 (1915), where the plaintiff successfully brought an action against a film-producing company who had photographed his business premises in a film dealing with the white slave traffic; *Brown v Paramount Corporation*, 240 N.Y.App.Div. 520 (1934).

[7] See para.3.2, fn.13, below.

[8] See para.3.5, below.

[9] See para.3.3, below.

[10] "Matter" is the general expression used in the Australian uniform legislation. It includes (a) an article, report, advertisement or other thing communicated by means of a newspaper, magazine or other periodical, (b) a program, report, advertisement or other thing communicated by means of television, radio, the Internet or any other form of electronic communication, (c) a letter, note or other writing, (d) a picture, gesture or oral utterance, and (e) any other thing by means of which something may be communicated to a person: Defamation Act 2005 (NSW) s.4.

The Irish Defamation Act 2009, s.6 abolishes the distinction between libel and slander and provides that the two separate torts shall, instead, be collectively described, and are referred to in the Act, as the "tort of defamation." The tort of defamation is actionable without proof of damage (s.6(5)) and "consists of the publication, by any means, of a defamatory statement concerning a person to one or more than one person (other than the first-mentioned person) . . . " (s.6(3)). S.2

have different legal consequences.[11]

3.2 Written words. Words, whether printed in a book or newspaper, or written by hand in a letter[12] or on a wall,[13] or inscribed on a tombstone,[14] or conveyed by electronic means to a computer screen[15] or other electronic device, may convey a defamatory imputation, either of themselves in their natural and ordinary meaning,[16] or by reason of their collocation with some other matter (e.g. a photograph),[17] the circumstances of their publication,[18] or some other extrinsic facts known to the persons to whom the words are published.[19]

3.3 Spoken words and gestures. The same applies to spoken[20] words. But their meaning may also be affected by the tone of voice in which they are spoken or by accompanying expressions or gestures.[21] Signs or gestures may themselves also convey a defamatory imputation, either because they express words (e.g. sign language),[22] or because they have a conventional defamatory meaning known to those who see them, or indicate to the ordinary observer that the claimant has done some discreditable act.[23]

3.4 Physical representations. Statues,[24] pictures[25] and other physical repre-

---

defines "Statement" to include "(a) a statement made orally or in writing, (b) visual images, sounds, gestures and any other method of signifying meaning, (c) a statement—(i) broadcast on the radio or television, or (ii) published on the internet, and (d) an electronic communication."

[11] See para.3.6 et seq., below.

[12] 3 Black.Comm. 125 ("printed or written libels").

[13] *Monson v Tussauds* [1894] 1 Q.B. 671 at 692, per Lopes L.J. (chalk marks); *Hellar v Bianco* (1952) 244 P.2d 757; or on a gate: see *Tarpley v Blabey* (1833) 2 Bing. N.C. 437; or on a pavement: see *Haylock v Sparke* (1853) 1 E. & B. 471.

[14] *Ralston v Ralston* [1930] 2 K.B. 238; *Solomon v Simmons, The Times,* April 10, 1954.

[15] *Godfrey v Demon Internet Ltd* [2001] Q.B. 201.

[16] See para.3.17, below.

[17] *Garbett v Hazell, Watson and Viney* [1943] 2 All E.R. 359 CA; *Cassidy v Daily Mirror* [1928] 2 K.B. 331 CA. and see fn.25, below.

[18] See para.3.30, below.

[19] See paras 3.20 et seq., below.

[20] Or, no doubt, sung. See *Smith v Chrysalis Records Ltd,* (QB), February 1, 2008, Claim no.HQ06X02905 (settlement).

[21] See para.3.36, below.

[22] *Gutsole v Mathers* (1836) 1 M. & W. 495 at 501.

[23] "An act of gesticulation, such as holding up an empty purse or the like": *Cook v Cox* (1814) 3 M. & S. 110 at 114. See also *Innes v Visser* [1936] W.L.D. 44, where the declaration alleged:

"On the 8th April,1935, while the plaintiff was seated on a bench in a public place, to wit, in the corridor outside the Council Chamber of the Town Hall, Krugersdorp, the defendant, in the presence of three other persons . . . lifted up his right leg in the direction of and in the immediate vicinity of the plaintiff as if he were a dog urinating upon the claimant."

Piasta v Stewart (1986) 48 Sask. R. 56.

[24] *Monson v Tussauds* [1894] I Q.B. 671 CA; *Corelli v Wall* (1906) 22 T.L.R. 532.

[25] Pictures: 5 Co. Rep. 125; 2 Hawk.P.C., c.73, s.2; *Cropp v Tilney* (1707) 11 Mod. 99. *Du Bost v Beresford* (1810) 2 Camp. 511; *Monson v Tussauds* [1894] 1 Q.B. 671 CA at 678. Photographs: *Dwek v Macmillan Publishers Ltd* [2000] E.M.L.R. 284 CA; *Monkton v Ralph Dunn, The Times,* January 20, 1907; *De Frece v News of the World, The Times,* February 5, 1919; *Beattie v Sphere and Tatler, The Times,* April 12, 1924; *Peck v Tribune,* 214 U.S.185 (1909); *Burton v Crowell*

sentations of a person[26] may convey an imputation defamatory of him, either by their content,[27] as where a person was shown in a pillory[28] or in the company of a prostitute,[29] or by their context (a waxwork near the Chamber of Horrors in Madame Tussauds),[30] or by the circumstances in which they were published[31] and the same applies to a representation of the claimant's product where disparagement of that reflects upon his character.[32] Likewise a representation of a person in a cartoon[33] or caricature[34] in a form or appearance entirely different from his real form and appearance or in an absurd costume or attitude may well tend to expose him to ridicule, and so be defamatory.[35] On the other hand, words which are associated with a picture may take away the defamatory sting which would arise from the publication of the photograph alone.[36]

Other acts. Sometimes a mere act may convey a defamatory imputation, if it would be so understood by reason of a conventional meaning, e.g. hissing at a theatre,[37] or by reason of the inferences to be drawn from it, whether by ordinary people, or by some person with special knowledge to whom it was published.[38] Thus, it has been held defamatory to place a lamp in front of a **3.5**

Publishing Co 82 F.2d 154 (2 Cir. 1936); *Mama Group Ltd v Sinclair* [2013] EWHC 2374 (QB).

[26] Or his business: *Marley's Transport v West Australian Newspapers Ltd* [2001] WASC 31.

[27] In *Ettinghausen v Australian Consolidated Press Ltd* (1991) 23 N.S.W.L.R. 443, a photograph of the claimant, an international rugby league player, in the shower showed "a shape between [his] legs which (despite the defendant's submissions to the contrary) is certainly capable of being interpreted as a penis". This was held to be capable of bearing the defamatory meaning that the plaintiff deliberately permitted a photograph to be taken of him with his genitals exposed for the purposes of publication to a widespread audience. See also *Shepherd v Walsh* [2001] QSC 358; *Obermann v ACP Publishing Pty Ltd* [2001] N.S.W.S.C. 1022.

[28] *Austin v Culpepper* (1684) 2 Show. 313.

[29] *Dwek v Macmillan Publishers Ltd* [2000] E.M.L.R. 284 CA.

[30] *Monson v Tussauds* [1894] 1 Q.B. 671 CA; *Greenwood v D'Arc, The Times,* March 8, 1922; *Marley's Transport v West Australian Newspapers Ltd* [2001] WASC 31 (use of photographs of claimants' trucks in article about drug abuse by truckers); *Nixon v Slater & Gordon* [2000] FCA 531 (photograph of surgeons on cover of booklet about medical malpractice).

[31] See para.3.30, below.

[32] *Modern Products Inc. v Schwarz,* 734 F. Supp. 362 (1990) (photographic association with junk food).

[33] *Datuk Syed Kechik bin Syed Mohamed v Datuk Yeh Pao Tzu* [1977] 1 M.L.J. 56. Cf. *Pitman v Jersey Evening Post* [2012] JRC 92.

[34] *Austin v Culpepper* (1684) 2 Show. 313; *Smith v Wood* (1813) 3 Camp. 323; *Monson v Tussauds* [1894] 1 Q.B. 671 at 692; *Whitehead v Yorkshire Newspaper, The Times,* November 24, 1909; *Dunlop v Dunlop Co* [1920] 11. R. 280; [1921] 1 A.C. 367; *Tolley v Fry* [1931] A.C. 333; *Spider's Web v Pearson, The Times,* April 18, 1953. "A man may be as grossly libelled, as effectively exposed to hatred, contempt and ridicule, by a caricature as by written language": per Shaw C.J. in *Ellis v Kimball* (1834) 33 Mass. R. at 134. See also, *Jarratt v John Fairfax Publications Pty Ltd* [2001] N.S.W.S.C. 739. But for qualifications, see para.2.12, above.

[35] See para.2.10ff, above.

[36] *Charleston v News Group Newspapers Ltd* [1995] 2 A.C. 65 HL.

[37] *Gregory v Duke of Brunswick* (1843) 6 M. & Gr. 953.

[38] *Mason v Jennings* (1680) Raym. 401 (riding Skimmington implying that plaintiff's wife beat him); *Drysdale v Earl of Rosebery,* 1909 S.C. 1121; *Brewer v Dew* (1843) 11 M. & W. 625 (seizure of goods on an unfounded claim for debt).

person's house, to signify that it was a brothel,[39] or to burn him in effigy,[40] or to arrange a charivari which implied marital unfaithfulness.[41] Setting surveillance on a person in a conspicuous manner has been held capable of being defamatory.[42]

SECTION 2. THE DISTINCTION BETWEEN LIBEL AND SLANDER

3.6 The consequences of the distinction. Libel is committed when defamatory matter is published in a "permanent" form or in a form which is deemed to be permanent. Defamation published by spoken word or in some other transitory form is slander. In English law libel is always actionable per se,[43] that is to say the claimant is not required to show any actual damage, and substantial rather than merely nominal damages may be awarded even in the absence of such proof,[44] whereas in slander, with four exceptions, the cause of

---

[39] *Jeffries v Duncombe* (1809) 2 Camp. 3, where damages were recovered against the defendant for suspending in front of the claimant's house a lamp burning during the daytime, "thereby intending to mark out the dwelling-house of the claimant as a bawdy-house". The action was on the case for nuisance, but, as Grose J. said, "it might be considered an action for libelling the claimant". Cf. *Spall v Massey* (1819) 2 Stark. 559.

[40] *Eyre v Garlick* (1878) 42 J.P. 68.

[41] *Varner v Morton* (1919) 53 N.S.R. 180.

[42] *Schultz v Frankfort, Marine etc Insurance Co* 139 N.W. 386 (Wis., 1913); *Molt v Public Indemnity Co*, 161 A. 346 (N.J. 1940); *Miles v Stewarts Supermarkets* (1987) B.N.I.L. 111 (search); *Bennett v Norban* 151 A.2d 576 (Pa., 1959) (search). In *Robertson v Keith*, 1936 S.C. 29 (which was tried by a court of seven judges), the pursuer sued for damages for (inter alia) defamation caused by the wrongful and illegal action of the defendant, a chief constable, in posting a watch of constables outside her premises for a period of five days. The defendant succeeded on a plea that he was privileged in what he did and that he acted without malice and with reasonable and probable cause. On the issue of defamation see per Lord Moncrieff at 32–33, 36; Lord President Normand at 41, 44; Lord Hunter at 50, 54; Lord Murray at 59–60.

[43] In the United States the picture is complicated by a factor unique to that country, the distinction between "libel *per se*" and "libel *per quod*". Some states follow the English rule that libel is actionable per se (subject to the constitutional point in the next note) but the majority hold that libel is only actionable per se if it is defamatory on its face, whereas if the defamatory meaning can be discovered only by those who know extrinsic facts (known as libel *per quod*) it is subject to the same rule as slander. Hence it is libellous per se to write that P is a drunkard but only libellous *per quod* to write that P (whom the reader knows to be a campaigner for total abstention) likes the occasional whisky. This approach (fiercely criticised in Eldredge, *Law of Defamation*, Chs 5 and 6) appears to be a curious offshoot of the quite different English rule of pleading, whereby if the words are not defamatory in their ordinary meaning but only by virtue of extrinsic facts known to the reader (as in the second example given above) an innuendo is required: see para.3.20, below.

[44] This remains generally true in other jurisdictions but in the United States the Supreme Court in *Gertz v Robert Welch Inc.*, 418 US 323 (1974) declared that there could be no recovery of "presumed damages" unless the defendant acted with knowledge that the charges were untrue or with reckless disregard of whether they were true or false. However, there are a number of reasons why this does not necessarily entirely abolish defamation which is actionable per se. First, it seems that it is open to states to allow recovery of presumed damages where the defamatory statement is not about a public figure or a matter of public concern: *Dun & Bradstreet v Greenmoss Builders*, 472 U.S. 749 (1985); *Snead v Redland Aggregates*, 998 F.2d 1325 (CA 5 1993). Secondly, the "actual damage" required under *Gertz* is a good deal wider than the narrow concept of "special damage" in slander: e.g. it covers humiliation and distress (*Time Inc. v Firestone*, 424 U.S. 448 (1976)) and proven harm to reputation or standing. The Irish Defamation Act 2009 provides in s.6 that the torts of libel and slander shall cease to be so described and shall

action is not complete unless there is "special" damage, i.e. some actual, temporal loss.[45] The four exceptional cases are:

(1) Where the words impute a crime for which the claimant can be made to suffer physically by way of punishment.[46]
(2) Where the words are calculated to disparage the claimant in any office, profession, calling, trade or business held or carried on by him at the time of publication.[47]
(3) Where the words impute to the claimant a contagious or infectious disease.[48]
(4) By the Slander of Women Act 1891,[49] where the words impute adultery or unchastity to a woman or girl.

(Note that the Defamation Act 2013, when it comes into force, repeals, by virtue of s.14, the Slander of Women Act 1891 and the common law exception for contagious or infectious diseases abolished.)

Damage is presumed where a libel is established:

"Every libel is of itself a wrong in regard to which the law implies general damage ... Akin to actions of libel are those actions which are brought for oral slander, where such slander consists of words actionable in themselves, and the mere use of which constitutes the infringement of the claimant's right. The very speaking of such words, apart from all damage, constitutes a wrong and gives rise to a cause of action. The law in such a case presumes, and in theory allows proof of, general damage."[50]

However, the fact that damage is presumed does not mean that a substantial award of damages is to be made where on the evidence it is shown that the claimant has suffered limited damage, or no damage at all, as a result of the publication: liability may be for no more than one penny or some other token sum,[51] perhaps with consequences for costs.[52] The rule that proof of damage is unnecessary to found the claim makes pragmatic sense in avoiding having

---

instead be collectively described as the "tort of defamation". The tort of defamation is, by s.6(5), actionable without proof of special damage.

[45] See Ch.5, below.
[46] See para.4.3, below.
[47] See para.4.15, below.
[48] See para.4.13, below.
[49] See para.4.20, below.
[50] Per Bowen L.J. in *Ratcliffe v Evans* [1892] 2 Q.B. 524 at 529–530; *Halls v Mitchell* (1927) 59 O.L.R. 590. Theoretically, one might draw a distinction between a case where the tort was actionable per se and one where damage was presumed, but it would make no difference in practice for the purposes of establishing a cause of action since the presumption is irrebuttable: *Jameel (Yousef) v Dow Jones & Co. Inc.* [2005] EWCA Civ 75; [2005] Q.B. 946.
[51] *Jameel (Yousef) v Dow Jones & Co. Inc.* [2005] EWCA Civ 75; [2005] Q.B. 946 at [36]. In *Reynolds v Times Newspapers Ltd* [1998] 3 W.L.R. 862 the trial judge declined to accept a verdict for the plaintiff with no damages and substituted one penny (on appeal on other issues, [2001] 2 A.C. 127).
[52] See para.35.19, below.

to call witnesses to testify what meaning they put upon the words and how the words affected the claimant's standing in their eyes and it has been said that "English law has been well served by a principle under which liability turns on the objective question of whether the publication is one which tends to injure the claimant's reputation".[53] In *Jameel v Wall Street Journal Europe SPRL*,[54] where the issue was whether the same rule applied to a trading corporation, Lord Hoffmann, who (contrary to the majority) would have applied a different rule to that case, said that in "the case of an individual, his reputation is a part of his personality, the 'immortal part' of himself and it is right that he should be entitled to vindicate his reputation and receive compensation for a slur upon it without proof of financial loss". The present law does not offend art.10 of the European Convention on Human Rights because it does not mean that juries may award damages on a scale incommensurate with any damage likely in fact to have been suffered. Furthermore, where the claimant brings proceedings in circumstances where it is apparent that there has been no, or minimal, actual damage, it is open to the court to dismiss the action as an abuse of process or, where the defendant is based abroad and there has been minimal publication here, to refuse leave to serve process out of the jurisdiction on the ground that England is not an appropriate forum. An application to dismiss on the ground of an abuse of process is now readily entertained in a libel action.[55] Although therefore there is not in England an exact equivalent of the defence of triviality which exists under the unified law of libel and slander in the Australian states,[56] there is considerable similarity in the practical result.[57]

3.7 Defamation Act 2013, s.1 and presumed damage. While s.1 of the Defamation Act 2013, when it comes into force, will require that the claimant must show that the statement has caused, or is likely to cause, serious harm to reputation, it will not get rid of the common law presumed damages rule. The effect of that rule is that where injury to reputation has been shown, or where the words have the tendency to cause such injury, by the publication of a defamatory statement, the law presumes that this has a deleterious financial effect: there is no need for the claimant to go further and establish that the defamatory statement has caused him to suffer actual financial loss. The effect of s.1 is to impose an obligation on the claimant to establish, in order for the words complained of to be defamatory, that they caused serious harm to his

---

[53] *Jameel (Yousef) v Dow Jones & Co. Inc.*, above at [37].

[54] [2006] UKHL 44; [2007] 1 A.C. 359 at [91].

[55] *Jameel (Yousef) v Dow Jones & Co. Inc.* [2005] EWCA Civ 75; [2005] Q.B. 946 at [55]. See also paras 6.2, 8.16, 30.1 et seq., below.

[56] See, e.g. s.33 of the Defamation Act 2005 (NSW). The meaning of a previous version of this is examined in *Jones v Sutton* [2004] NSWCA 439. Furthermore, there is a requirement that damages should bear an "appropriate and rational" relationship with the harm suffered: s.34 of the NSW Act.

[57] See, e.g. *Smith v ADVFN Plc* [2008] EWHC 1797 (QB) para.3.37, below (vulgar abuse on internet bulletin board).

reputation. Absent proof that serious harm to reputation has been caused or is likely to be caused, the statement is not actionable. However, once serious harm to reputation is shown as having been caused, or as being likely to be caused, damages are still presumed though, as under the common law, their extent remains to be assessed. So far as a "body that trades for profit" is concerned, harm to the reputation of such a body is not serious harm unless it has caused, or is likely to cause, the body serious financial loss. This requirement recognises that such bodies can only, unlike human beings, be injured in their pocket and consequently an injury must sound in money. What the provision does not do however is require that a body that trades for profit *must* prove that the statement complained of has caused it actual financial loss. Certainly proof that actual financial loss has been caused will satisfy the provision, but a body that trades for profit need only show that some serious financial loss, whether that be loss of customers, contracts or even a decline in the share price,[58] is *likely*. Once such harm is shown to have been caused or as likely to be caused, by the statement complained of, a body that trades for profit can recover damages even in the absence of any proof that it suffered actual financial loss.

Reason for distinction between libel and slander. The historical pro-   **3.8**
cess whereby the law made this distinction between the written and the spoken word is in some respects obscure[59] but it was certainly well established by the eighteenth century.[60] It was subject to criticism as early as 1812[61] and has

---

[58] At the Committee stage in the House of Commons, Jonathan Djanogly, the Parliamentary Under-Secretary of State for Justice, said the following in response to a proposed amendment to the Bill that would, inter alia, have provided that a "fall in the share price" is not to be treated as such harm:

"Corporations are already unable to claim for certain types of harm, such as injury to feelings. In order to satisfy the serious harm test, a corporation would in practice be likely to have to demonstrate actual or likely financial loss in any event. Given the potential effects on shareholders and management, we see no reason why there should be no redress for a defamatory action that has caused a fall in share price": PBC (Bill 005) 2012–2013, col 206.

It is of course the case that a company cannot recover for a decline in its share price (*Collins Stewart Ltd v Financial Times Ltd* [2004] EWHC 2337 (QB); [2005] E.M.L.R. 64). What Mr Djanogly presumably meant was that a decline in share price could be evidence that "serious financial loss" was likely to occur (or to have occurred), in the sense that the decline in the share price would reflect underlying problems in the business, say loss of customers or contracts. Consequently, a decline in share price can be evidence of serious financial loss.

[59] See, inter alia, Holdsworth, *History of English Law*, Vol.5, pp.205–212 and Vol.8, pp.333–378; Kaye, "Libel and Slander-Two Torts or One?" (1975) 91 L.Q.R. 524; Mitchell, *The Making of the Modern Law of Defamation* (Oxford: Hart Publishing, 2005), Ch.1; Restatement 1st, *Torts*, para.568, comment b.

[60] *Thorley v Lord Kerry* (1812) 4 Taunt. 355 at 364; per Best C.J. in *Archbishop of Tuam v Robeson* (1828) 5 Bing. 17 at 21 ("established too firmly to be shaken").

[61] *Thorley v Lord Kerry* (1812) 4 Taunt. 355 at 364, per Sir James Mansfield C.J.: "I cannot, upon principle, make any difference between words written and words spoken, as to the right which arises on them of bringing an action."

been so regularly since.[62] The law has been modified in a number of other common law jurisdictions.[63]

The distinction did not exist in Roman law,[64] nor is it to be found in Scots law[65] or in the civil law systems. Reasons commonly given for the distinction (and for the greater severity of libel in most cases) are that a libel written and published shows more deliberate malignity than a mere oral slander[66]; and that a greater degree of mischief is probable in the case of a libel, owing to its more durable character, and the fact that it can be more easily disseminated.[67] These arguments are not wholly without merit in so far as they reflect the fact that libels would in general, at that time, have been more widely circulated and more likely to injure than would slanders, but the advent of new technologies made it impossible to maintain the distinction in its original form.[68] In any event, even in the nineteenth century the distinction could operate in an arbitrary manner, as Sir James Mansfield C.J. recognised:

> "it has been argued that writing shows more deliberate malignity; but the action is not maintainable upon the ground of the malignity, but for the damage sustained. So it is argued that written scandal is more generally diffused than words spoken, and is therefore actionable; but an assertion made in a public place, as upon the Royal Exchange, concerning a merchant in London, may be much more extensively diffused than a few printed papers dispersed or a private letter: it is true that a

---

[62] The Select Committee of the House of Lords, appointed in 1843 to consider the Law of Defamation and Libel, before which such eminent judges as Lords Brougham, Denman, Lynd-hurst, Campbell and Abinger gave evidence, advocated the abolition of the distinction, which in their opinion, "rested on no solid foundation", and reported that "whenever an injury is done to character by defamation (of whatever kind) there ought to be redress by action". See also Holdsworth, *History of English Law*, Vol.8, p.378. A majority of the members of the Porter Committee did not favour the assimilation of the law of slander to law of libel (Cmd.7536, para.40), but the Report of the Faulks Committee recommended the abolition of the distinction: Cmnd.5909 (1975), paras 75–91.

[63] The distinction has been abolished (or abolished in practical effect if not in name by providing that slander is actionable per se in all cases) in New Zealand and in the Uniform legislation now prevailing in Australia. In Canada, the majority of provinces have adopted the provision of the Canadian Uniform Defamation Act, which provides that slander is actionable per se, and only British Columbia, Ontario and Nova Scotia maintain the common law distinction. The Irish Defamation Act, s.6, creates a single tort of defamation, actionable per se. Even jurisdictions which have maintained the distinction have, like England, substantially modified its practical effect by providing that broadcasting is libel.

[64] By the Law of the Twelve Tables public affronts and accusations, oral or written, were punishable with death. Defamation as defined by Justinian (*Digest*, xivii 10, *De Injuriis et Famosis Libellis*, s.5) was simply a variety of *injuria*, and might be *re, litteris, verbis*. See Florian, *Injiuria e Difamazione* (1939 edn) 153; Ranchod, *Foundations of the South African Law of Defamation*, pp.21–23.

[65] See *Mackay v M'Cankie* (1883) 10 R. 537. However, the words "libel" and "slander" are often used as synonyms for defamation.

[66] *Clement v Chivis* (1829) 9 B. & C. 172 at 174.

[67] *Ratcliffe v Evans* [1892] 2 Q.B. 524 CA at 530; *De Crespigny v Wellesley* (1829) 5 Bing. 392 at 402. See also *Archbishop of Tuam v Robeson* (1828) 2 Moo. & P. 32 at 39, and per Farwell L.J. in *Hulton v Jones* [1909] 2 K.B. 444 CA at 483.

[68] See para.3.10, below.

newspaper may be very generally read, but that is all casual. These are the arguments which prevail in my mind to repudiate the distinction between written and spoken scandal."[69]

The distinction at common law. Not only does the distinction between   **3.9**
libel and slander rest on unsatisfactory grounds, but how the distinction should be drawn is rather unclear at a number of points,[70] even leaving aside modern technology. There is no doubt that to publish written or printed words by showing them to another is to commit libel. Similarly it is libel to issue or display a defamatory picture or effigy.[71] Equally to speak defamatory words to another is slander.[72] This might suggest that libel is that which appeals to the eye and slander that which appeals to the ear, but this cannot be so because it has never been doubted that gestures are slander.[73] Further, the current English view is that to read out a defamatory letter or script to an audience is libel, and this is so regardless of whether the audience realises that the defamatory matter is being read,[74] though in Australia it was said that the perception of the audience is decisive.[75] Either view might perhaps be justified on the basis that

---

[69] *Thorley v Lord Kerry* (1812) 4 Taunt. 355 at 364. The Restatement, 2d, *Torts*, para.568, provides that libel includes "any other form of communication which has the potentially harmful qualities characteristic of written or printed words" and that "the area of the dissemination, the deliberate and premeditated character of its publication, and the persistence of the defamation are factors to be considered in deciding whether a publication is a libel rather than a slander." Under this formulation a defamatory address to the crowd in a football stadium might be libel, whereas in England it could only be slander.

[70] Some of which were discussed by Sir Alan Herbert in cases collected in *Uncommon Law* and *Codd's Last Case*: *Chicken v Ham* (gramophone record); *Silvertop v Stepney Guardians* (parrot); *Temper v Hume* (flags at sea).

[71] *Monson v Tussauds Ltd* [1894] 1 Q.B. 671 CA (though the issue in the case was whether an interlocutory injunction should be granted and the imputation of the effigy was a charge which would have been actionable per se even if it had been slander); *Du Bost v Bereford* (1810) 2 Camp. 511; *Austin v Culpeper* (1684) 2 Show. 313. According to the Restatement, 2d, *Torts*, para.568, comment d, a picture, etc., is libel because the publication is embodied in physical form. See below.

[72] The defendant may speak the words to X, knowing or intending that X will publish them in written form. If X does so, that does not mean that the initial publication to X was libel, but the defendant may be liable for the further publication of a libel by X: see para.6.41, below.

[73] E.g. sign language, see *Gutsole v Mathers* (1836) 1 M. & W. 495 at 501. "An act of gesticulation, such as holding up an empty purse or the like": *Cook v Cox* (1814) 3 M. & S. 110 at 114. It seems from the brief report of *Miles v Stewarts Supermarkets* (1987) B.N.I.L. 111 that the court regarded a search of the claimant as slander. Accord, *Bennett v Norban*, 151 A.2d 476 (Pa., 1959).

[74] *Forrester v Tyrrell* (1893) 9 T.L.R. 257 CA; *Robinson v Chambers (No.2)* [1946] N.I. 148. See also *Land v Delta Airlines*, 250 S.E.2d 188 (Ga., 1978). In *Longdon-Griffiths v Smith* [1951] 1 K.B. 295 a claim in libel was brought in respect of the reading out of a report by one of the report's authors. It does not appear to have occurred to anyone to argue that this was a slander.

[75] *Meldrum v ABC* [1932] V.L.R. 425 at 429, 434; *Mitchell v ABC* (1958) 60 W.A.L.R. 382. The Faulks Committee, Cmnd.5909 (1975), para.436, considered that no prosecution for criminal libel could be brought in respect of a broadcast unless some listeners realised that words were being read from a script or that the broadcast was recorded. The statutory provisions making broadcasting libel (see para.3.10) were not then applicable to criminal libel. Both *Forrester v Tyrrell* and *Meldrum v ABC* present serious practical problems. Consider, e.g. a lecturer who during one discourse reads directly from his notes, uses his notes as an *aide memoire* and extemporises.

the document was a potential libel and any method of disseminating it should carry the same liability, but this seems inconsistent with the fact that the gist of defamation is publication. It can hardly be the law that if one learns a defamatory message by heart from a document and repeats it, one commits libel.[76]

Where the defendant dictates a defamatory statement to another, who takes it down, the defendant publishes a slander to that other[77]: although a writing then comes into existence, it was not a writing when it was published.[78] So too, it has been held that the recording of defamatory words on a voicemail is plainly a libel.[79] It cannot, however, be wholly true to say that a libel must exist before it is published[80] (though this will commonly be the case) for it must be libel to chalk defamatory matter on a blackboard or send it as an SMS or text message. Where dictated words are read back in the presence of a third party[81] by the person who took them down then, in view of the position where a letter is read to an audience, that should logically be the publication of a libel[82] but there are dicta that it is slander.[83] Of course where the dictated material has been transcribed and sent out there will be a publication of a libel to the recipient by the originator of the material, provided that is intended or authorised by him.[84]

There can be little doubt that in the present law publication of the defamatory matter in a "permanent" form is libel, if only because that was the view of Parliament when it provided that broadcast defamation was to constitute libel[85] and, while that may not be decisive as to the common law,[86] the courts are not likely to treat the legislation as ineffective in that context[87] and are

---

[76] But words spoken in a play are libel by statute: para.3.11, below.

[77] *Angelini v Antico* (1912) 31 N.Z.L.R. 841; *Osborn v Boulter* [1930] 2 K.B. 226, per Scrutton and Slesser L.JJ., *contra* Greer L.J.; *Lawrence v Finch* (1930) 66 O.L.R. 415. However, the Restatement, 2d, *Torts*, para.577, comment h, regards it as libel "even though the notes are never transcribed nor read by the stenographer or any other person"; *Ostrowe v Lee*, 175 N.E. 505 (N.Y., 1931).

[78] Similarly, it has been held slander where a message was dictated to a telegraph company: *Williamson v Freer* (1874) L.R. 9 C.P.

[79] *Cooper v Turrell* [2011] EWHC 3269 (QB) at [78].

[80] As the court said in *Angelini v Antico* (1912) 31 N.Z.L.R. 841.

[81] Where no third party is present it seems that there is no publication at all: see para.6.1, below.

[82] See fn.77, above.

[83] Dicta of Scrutton and Slesser L.JJ. in *Osborn v Boulter* [1930] 2 K.B. 226 (*contra*, Greer L.J.). *Forrester v Tyrrell* (1893) 9 T.L.R. 257 CA was not cited. In *Pullman v Hill* [1891] 2 Q.B. 524 CA, it was held that if a person dictates defamatory matter to a clerk and then asks him to type it out and the clerk then does so, there is publication of a libel. Sed quaere. If, however, the typed material is handed back to the clerk after revision, that ought to be publication of a libel: see Lawton L.J. in *Bryanston Finance v De Vries* [1975] Q.B. 703 CA at 736, though nothing turned on the point and it was not argued. See Mitchell, *The Making of the Modern Law of Defamation* (Oxford: Hart Publishing, 2005), at 25–26.

[84] See para.6.12, below.

[85] Defamation Act 1952, s.1 (see para.3.10, below).

[86] *Mollwo March v Court of Wards* (1869) L.R. 4 P.C. 419 at 437.

[87] *Wainer v Rippon* (1980) 124 A.L.R. 643.

likely to pay deference to the view of Parliament in others. "Permanent" here does not necessarily signify long-lasting: it is defamatory to chalk a defamatory message on a wall[88] and the nature of the tort cannot depend on whether it remains there for weeks or is washed away by the rain a few minutes later. Possibly the residual test of the Restatement is better: is the matter embodied in a physical form?[89] It does not, however, follow that there may not be additional tests of libel at common law, for example the transient publication of matter which is embodied in a permanent form,[90] so that it might be libel to play a record or audio-tape[91] or to call up on screen words or images from a computer memory.[92] The showing of a defamatory cinema film is libel at common law[93] and this cannot turn on the fact that the images are permanently visible on the film, so the same should apply to the showing of a DVD. Hence it is thought that the showing of a film or DVD on television would (even apart from statute) be libel at common law[94] and perhaps the same is true of a recorded radio broadcast.[95]

Broadcasting: statute. In 1948 the Porter Committee commented that "a   **3.10** defamatory statement transmitted over the radio in a broadcast, reaching as it may an audience of many millions, is calculated to cause as much, if not more, damage than a written report in a newspaper, however large its circulation."[96] Since then broadcasting in the form of television has become for many people one of the most important sources of news and entertainment. Clearly the

---

[88] *Monson v Tussauds Ltd* [1894] 1 Q.B. 671 CA.

[89] Restatement, 2d, *Torts*, para.568. This would cover *Eyre v Garlick* (1878) 42 J.P. 68 (libel to burn the claimant in effigy) or *Jeffries v Duncombe* (1809) 2 Camp. 2 (fixing object outside claimant's house which conveyed defamatory imputation) but not mere gestures.

[90] *Forrester v Tyrrell* (1893) 9 T.L.R. 257 CA.

[91] Where the defendant supplies the tape containing the defamatory message so that the publishee may play it repeatedly, it is hard to see how this differs from the sale of a book.

[92] In *Derby & Co. Ltd v Weldon (No.9)* [1991] 1 W.L.R. 652, it was held that a computer database is a "document" for the purposes of R.S.C. Ord. 24. Since it would clearly be libel to print the contents of the screen on paper and show it to another, it is submitted that the same must be so if the other's attention is drawn to the screen.

[93] *Youssoupoff v Metro-Goldwyn-Mayer* (1934) 50 T.L.R. 581 per Slesser L.J. at 587. At least if the defamatory imputation is conveyed in visual form and the words are ancillary.

[94] Cf. *Youssoupoff v Metro-Goldwyn-Mayer.*

[95] *Olowo v Att-Gen* [1972] E.A. 311. Or perhaps one where a script is read: *Meldrum v ABC* [1932] V.L.R. 425. This was the view of the Porter Committee: Cmd.7536, para.42 (1948). It is difficult to see how an unrecorded, unscripted radio broadcast could be libel at common law: neither the publication nor the material is in any way permanent and the matter is addressed entirely to the ear. To hold this to be libel would require a radical change in approach such as that of the Restatement 2d (fn.67, above). Some American courts have gone down this road: see 50 Am.Jur.2d, *Libel and Slander*, para.12. In *Mickelberg v 6 PR Southern Cross Radio Pty Ltd* [2002] WASCA 270 the Full Court considered the position of a live radio transmission via the internet. The local legislation made radio broadcasting libel. At that stage of the proceedings it could not be determined whether the transmission was "broadcasting" but if it was not Ipp J. (agreeing with the judge below) inclined to the view that at common law it would be slander.

[96] Cmd.7536, para.42. Some internet services may fall within s.166 of the Broadcasting Act 1990: para.3.12, below.

broadcast media are closely analogous to those using print[97] and it was necessary to act to cure the uncertainties over the common law position. Parliament first intervened in s.1 of the Defamation Act 1952,[98] which has been replaced by s.166 of the Broadcasting Act 1990. This provides that "for the purposes of the law of libel and slander (including the law of criminal libel so far as it relates to the publication of defamatory matter) the publication of words[99] in the course of any programme included in a programme service shall be treated as publication in a permanent form." Though a more direct method of saying so might have been chosen, there is no doubt that the effect of this is to make such broadcasts libel rather than slander.[100] The principal differences from the Act of 1952 are as follows:

The Act of 1952 applied to broadcasts for general reception by means of wireless telegraphy.[101] The present test is whether the material was published in a programme included in a "programme service". A programme service is defined[102] in s.201(1) of the 1990 Act, as amended, as any of the following services (whether or not it is, or it requires to be, licensed under the Act), namely:

(a) any service which is a programme service within the meaning of the Communications Act 2003, s.145(1);

(b) any other service which consists in the sending, by means of an electronic communications network (within the meaning of the Communications Act 2003) of sounds or visual images or both either (i) for reception at two or more places in the United Kingdom (whether they are so sent for simultaneous reception or at different times in response to requests made by different users of the service) or (ii) for reception

---

[97] But for a recent example of a distinction being drawn between them in favour of the broadcast media, see s.1(3)(d) of the Defamation Act 1996: para.6.34, below.

[98] See also the Nova Scotia Defamation Act 1989, the Ontario Libel and Slander Act 1990 and the British Columbia Libel and Slander Act 1996. The scope of the Ontario legislation was raised but not decided upon in *Bahlieda v Santa* (2003) 68 O.R. (3d) 115 Ont. CA and *Romano v D'Onofrio* (2005) 262 D.L.R. (4th) 181 Ont. CA. There are numerous different common law and statutory provisions in the US: see 50 Am.Jur.2d, *Libel and Slander*, para.10 and 50 A.L.R.3d 1311.

[99] Under the Defamation Act 1952, s.16(1) any reference to words "shall be construed as including a reference to pictures, visual images, gestures and other methods of signifying meaning." Since s.166 of the 1990 Act does not operate by way of textual amendment of s.1 and there is no comparable provision in the 1990 Act it is arguable that in the case of television visual images the 1990 Act throws us back on the common law." This would be curious.

[100] *Wainer v Rippon* (1980) 124 A.L.R. 643, dealing with similar words in the Broadcasting and Television Act 1942–63 (Cwth.); *Anderson v Church of Scientology* [1980] W.A.R. 71 at 76–77. Cf. *Burns v Collins* [1968] V.R. 667, where it was held that it was arguable that the Australian legislation was ineffective since the criterion of libel was not publication in permanent form.

[101] The definition of wireless telegraphy had to be sought in s.19(1) of the Wireless Telegraphy Act 1949. However, simultaneous transmission by wire amounted to broadcasting: s.16(4) of the 1952 Act. There were provisions for cable services in the Cable and Broadcasting Act 1984.

[102] The statutory provisions are extremely complex because they are designed for the regulation of broadcasting and the defamation provision is merely a minor sideshow.

at a place in the United Kingdom for the purpose of being presented there to members of the public or to any group of persons.[103]

A programme service within the meaning of the Communications Act 2003, s.145(1) means

    (a) a television programme[104] service;
    (b) the public teletext service;
    (c) an additional television service;
    (d) a digital additional television service;
    (e) a radio programme service; or
    (f) a sound service provided by the BBC.[105]

Although the "general reception" requirement no longer applies, much the same function is fulfilled as far as category (a) under s.201(1) is concerned by the requirement that the transmission be in a programme service, though category (b) is wider. Hence a radio message sent from an aircraft or a ship or a police car would still be governed by the rule (whatever that may be) of the common law.[106] The effect of the legislation would appear not to be confined to the broadcasting station or programme maker so that a contributor to a programme is liable for libel rather than slander,[107] but the former are not necessarily liable at all in respect of a contribution to an unrecorded programme.[108]

Plays and ballets. By the Theatres Act 1968, the publication of words[109] in **3.11** the course of a performance of a play is treated as publication in permanent form, that is to say, as libel.[110] A play is defined as "any dramatic piece, whether involving improvisation or not, which is given wholly or in part by one or more persons actually present and performing, and in which the whole or a major proportion of what is done by the person or persons performing, whether by way of speech, singing, or acting, involves the playing of a role," and also includes "any ballet given wholly or in part by one or more persons

---

    [103] As substituted by the Communications Act 2003, s.360(1)(a). Category (b) does not apply to certain two-way sound services: s.201(2A), (2B) as substituted for the original subs.(2) by the Communications Act 2003, s.360(2). A podcast presumably falls under (b).
    [104] Any programme (with or without sounds) which (a) is produced wholly or partly to be seen on television and (b) consists of moving or still images or of legible text or of a combination of those things: Communications Act 2005, s.405.
    [105] Communications Act 2003, s.405.
    [106] See para.3.9, above.
    [107] *Wainer v Rippon* (1980) 124 A.L.R. 643.
    [108] See para.6.24, below.
    [109] "words" is defined in s.4(3) to include pictures, visual images, gestures and other methods of signifying meaning. Cf. fn.99, above.
    [110] Theatres Act 1968, s.4(1). See previous note. The provisions, like those for broadcasting, seem to apply to all the performers, and the modifications contained in s.18(2) seem not relevant.

actually present and performing".[111] This provision does not apply to a performance of a play given on a domestic occasion in a private dwelling[112]; nor to a performance given solely or primarily for rehearsal, or to enable a record[113] or cinematograph film[114] to be made from or by means of the performance, or the performance to be broadcast, or included in a programme service.[115]

3.12 The internet. Perhaps surprisingly, the question whether internet communications amount to libel or slander[116] appears to have attracted comparatively little attention in the case law.[117] Communications from an internet site (such as a web page) would seem to come within s.201(1)(b) of the Broadcasting Act 1990[118] (because they are sent by a telecommunications system for reception at two or more places[119]) and are therefore libel by statute. However, email messages (and certain other forms of communication such as relay "chat") are not within the definition and depend upon the common law. It seems likely that an email is a libel at common law since it is very like a paper letter—it is stored on the recipient's machine[120] unless he deletes it and may be read by him any number of times.[121] If an email is a libel then so too are SMSs and text messages. "Tweets" appear to have been assumed to be libel though the issue does not appear to have been the subject of argument.[122] Bulletin board postings, instant messages and contributions to Internet Relay Chat, are no doubt technically libel but in nature are rather like contributions to casual conversation and consequently are more susceptible of being equated with slander for the purposes of abuse of process or the "defence" of vulgar abuse.[123] On the other hand, telephonic communication via the internet (unless perhaps in the form of a "conference call" involving more than two

---

[111] Ibid. s.18(1). Such a ballet counts as a play, regardless of the extent to which the playing of a role is involved, but apart from rather far-fetched examples, it would seem that the playing of a role would be necessary if a defamatory imputation were to be conveyed in the course of a performance.

[112] Ibid. s.7(1).

[113] "Record" means a record or similar contrivance for reproducing sound, including the sound track of a cinematograph film; ibid. s.7(3).

[114] This means any print, negative, tape, or other article on which a performance of a play or any part of such a performance is recorded for the purposes of visual reproduction; ibid., s.7(3) (the film itself is a libel: see fn.92, above).

[115] S.7(2)(b) as amended by the Broadcasting Act 1990, s.203(1), Sch.20.

[116] As to the liability of internet service providers, see para.6.25ff, below.

[117] A usenet (bulletin board) posting was regarded as libel in *Godfrey v Demon Internet Ltd* [2001] Q.B. 201, but the point does not appear to have been contested.

[118] See para.3.10, above.

[119] See further M. Collins, *The Law of Defamation and the Internet*, 2nd edn (USA: Oxford University Press, 2005), para.4.06 et seq.

[120] Or, in the case of web-based email, on a remote server.

[121] Perhaps an email sent to multiple addresses falls within the 1990 Act.

[122] See, e.g., *Lord McAlpine of West Green v Bercow* [2013] EWHC 1342 (QB); *Cairns v Modi* [2012] EWCA Civ 1382 CA; [2013] 1 W.L.R. 1015; *Mama Group Ltd v Sinclair* [2013] EWHC 2374 (QB).

[123] *Smith v ADVFN Plc* [2008] EWHC 1797 (QB), paras 3.3–6.37, below.

persons) would seem to be indistinguishable from a landline or cell phone call and hence would be slander, notwithstanding the theoretical possibility that a record of the communication might be recovered.[124]

Section 3. Interpretation

The meaning of words. Although it has been said that the "question as to the meaning that the words convey to the ordinary person should be a simple and straightforward one, as befits a law that governs the everyday life and actions of all levels of persons in the community"[125] yet, only in a very simple case are words or matter capable of conveying a single, clear, indisputable imputation.[126] To say of a doctor that a patient died while in his care despite the use of all care and skill and the best techniques is clearly not defamatory. To say that a doctor's neglect caused the death of a patient equally clearly is defamatory. But what of a statement that a doctor took a wrong decision and a patient died as a result? To be wrong is not necessarily to be in breach of duty but some people will read into the statement the imputation that there was negligence and the question will be whether it is *reasonably capable* of conveying that imputation.[127] Logically anterior, therefore, to the question of whether the words are capable of being defamatory in law[128] is the question of what meaning or meanings the words are reasonably capable of bearing.[129] Where an action for defamation goes to full trial it may be before a jury[130] and the jury is then the arbiter, subject to the limited powers of the Court of Appeal,[131] of what the words do convey and whether they are defamatory. In this sense, therefore, the meaning of words is a question of fact.[132] But it is for the judge to rule whether the words are capable of bearing the meanings contended for[133] and, if so, whether any of those meanings is capable in law

3.13

---

[124] Collins, *The Law of Defamation and the Internet*, above at para.4.36.

[125] *Gacic v John Fairfax Publications Pty Ltd* [2006] NSWCA 175; 66 N.S.W.L.R. 675 at [113] per Ipp J.A. (on appeal [2007] HCA 28; 235 A.L.R. 402). The information explosion does not help. In *King v Lewis* [2004] EWCA Civ 1329; [2005] E.M.L.R. 4 at [36] it is said that there had been a web search of 900 dictionaries for the meaning of "shyster".

[126] Though even in a very simple case the context in which the statement is made may show that words like "thief" or "killer" are not defamatory: see para.3.31, below. For a fantastic example, see Eldredge, *Law of Defamation* (1978), p.42.

[127] See *Dobson v MacQuarie Radio Network Ltd* [2007] N.S.W.S.C. 718 (sex scandal at police academy; whether report carried imputation that principal bore responsibility).

[128] See Ch.2, above.

[129] Of course it is not necessarily the case that both issues are in dispute and if they are they may be run together, but they are analytically different: *Arab News Network v Jihad al Khazen* [2001] EWCA Civ 118 at [11].

[130] See Ch.31, s.5, below.

[131] See Ch.36, below.

[132] *Lewis v Daily Telegraph* [1964] A.C. 234 at 271, per Lord Hodson.

[133] But even here the issue is not one of construction but of what the words would convey to the ordinary reader: *Grubb v Bristol United Press* [1963] 1 Q.B. 309 CA; *Lewis v Daily Telegraph* [1964] A.C. 234

of being defamatory.[134] The judge's function in this regard is "no more and no less than to pre-empt perversity".[135] If, on the other hand, the court is required, as it has increasingly been required to do, to determine the actual meaning as a preliminary issue,[136] or the case is disposed of under the summary procedure under s.8 of the Defamation Act 1996[137] or otherwise tried without a jury,[138] the questions of whether the words are capable of being defamatory and whether they are in fact so will be run together as the judge will decide both issues.[139]

Issues of meaning are not confined to the simple question of whether the claimant has a triable case.[140] For example, the seriousness of the imputation conveyed will plainly be relevant on damages or for the purpose of evaluating a defence of qualified privilege, particularly where the defendant relies on the principle of *Reynolds v Times Newspapers*.[141] Furthermore, the defendant may be able to justify—i.e. prove the truth of—the words on one possible interpretation but not on another[142]: it may therefore be a question whether the

---

[134] The relationship between the roles of judge and jury on this and other matters is fully considered in Ch.36. As to whether the function of the judge in deciding whether words are capable of bearing a meaning is properly described as one of determining a question of law, see para.36.3. An application to determine whether the statement complained of is capable of having any meaning attributed to it in a statement of case or whether it is capable of bearing any other meaning defamatory of the claimant may be made at any time after service of particulars of claim: PD53 (replacing RSC Ord. 82, r.3A). See paras 32.2 and 36.9, below. By s.7 of the Defamation Act 1996 a court is not to be asked to rule on whether words are *arguably* capable of bearing a particular meaning.

[135] *Jameel v Wall Street Journal Europe SPRL* [2003] EWCA Civ 1694; [2004] E.M.L.R. 6 at [14].

[136] See by way of recent examples, *Lord McAlpine of West Green v Bercow* [2013] EWHC 1342 (QB); *Cruddas v Calvert* [2013] EWHC 1427 (QB) (appeal allowed on "single meaning" for purposes of law of defamation: [2013] EWCA Civ 748 CA); *Fox v Boulter* [2013] EWHC 1435 (QB); *Auladin v Shaikh* [2013] EWHC 157; *Cammish v Hughes* [2012] EWCA Civ 1655; [2013] E.M.L.R. 13. Preliminary hearings to determine the *actual* meaning of words have become much more common in the last couple of years. When the abolition of the presumption in favour of jury trial is effected by the coming into force of s.11 Defamation Act 2013, judges will almost invariably have to consider the actual meaning of the words. See generally Ch.30, below.

[137] See Ch.30, below.

[138] See by way of recent examples, *Thompson v James* [2013] EWHC 515 (QB); *Joseph v Spiller* [2012] EWHC 2958 (QB); *El Naschie v Macmillan Publishers Ltd (t/a Nature Publishing Group)* [2012] EWHC 1809 (QB).

[139] In *Cruddas v Calvert* [2013] EWCA Civ 748 CA, the Court of Appeal said, in a case where the question of actual meaning was decided by the judge on a trial of a preliminary issue, that the meaning of words was not a binary question or a question of being right or wrong but a nuanced question which should be left to the judge (at [18]). It acknowledged that the Court of Appeal should be slow to differ from any conclusion on this issue reached by the judge but "if [the appeal court] is satisfied that the judge's finding is wrong, it is [the court's] duty to reverse him" (at [21]). See also per Sir Thomas Bingham M.R. in *Skuse v Granada Television Ltd* [1996] E.M.L.R. 278 at 286 CA; *Slim v Daily Telegraph* [1968] 2 Q.B. 157 per Salmon L.J. at 186–187 CA; *Waterson v Lloyd* [2013] EWCA Civ 136; [2013] E.M.L.R. 17, at [36], [52]; *Cammish v Hughes* [2012] EWCA Civ 1655 CA; [2013] E.M.L.R. 13 at [31].

[140] *Jameel v Wall Street Journal Europe SPRL* [2003] EWCA Civ 1694; [2004] E.M.L.R. 6 at [13].

[141] See Ch.15, below, and in particular *Flood v Times Newspapers Ltd* [2012] UKSC 11; [2012] A.C. 273 at [48]–[52].

[142] See paras 11.5 et seq., below.

words are reasonably capable of bearing a meaning for which the defendant contends in a plea of justification[143] a matter which may be raised by the claimant.[144]

The general approach. Unless required to determine the actual meaning **3.14** of the words, in ruling on meaning, the court is simply delimiting the outside boundaries of the possible range of meanings and setting the "ground rules" for the trial.[145] Thus in *Shah v Standard Chartered Bank*[146] the allegations were capable of bearing the meaning that the plaintiffs were guilty of money laundering; but the use of miscellaneous qualifying words such as "alleged" or "apparently" meant that in the alternative they were capable of imputing no more than reasonable suspicion.[147] In *McJannett v Armstrong*[148] the words "renegade unionist" when applied to the plaintiff were held to be capable of bearing the meaning that he had deserted the union cause but not that he had engaged in illegal activity. The nature of the exercise has been summarised as follows (citations omitted):

> "(1) The governing principle is reasonableness. (2) The hypothetical reasonable reader is not naive but he is not unduly suspicious. He can read between the lines. He can read in an implication more readily than a lawyer and may indulge in a certain amount of loose thinking but he must be treated as being a man who is not avid for scandal and someone who does not, and should not, select one bad meaning where other non-defamatory meanings are available. (3) Over-elaborate analysis is

---

[143] The traditional rule was that evidence of specific acts of misconduct which were not charged in the libel could not be given in mitigation of damages: *Scott v Sampson* (1882) 8 Q.B.D. 491 CA. It would be improper to plead justification merely in order to get in otherwise inadmissible evidence for the purpose of mitigation; but if the defendant takes the view that the words will bear a meaning to which the evidence of misconduct would be relevant and is allowed to plead that meaning he is likely to get the benefit, on damages, of that evidence having been before the jury even if the plea of justification fails. However, the rule has now been substantially modified. See paras 11.21 and 33.43 et seq., below.

[144] Under PD 53. A "statement of case" under PD 53, para.4.1(1) includes a defence.

[145] *Mapp v News Group Newspapers Ltd* [1998] Q.B. 520 CA.
"The proper role for the judge when adjudicating a question of this kind is to evaluate the words complained of and to delimit the range of meanings of which the words are reasonably capable, exercising his or her own judgment in the light of the principles laid down in the authorities and without any of the former Order 18 Rule 19 overtones. If the judge decides that any pleaded meaning falls outside the permissible range, then it will be his duty to rule accordingly. In deciding whether words are capable of conveying a defamatory meaning, the court should reject those meanings which can only emerge as the produce of some strained or forced or utterly unreasonable interpretation. The purpose of the new rule is to enable the court to fix in advance the ground rules and permissible meanings, which are of cardinal importance in defamation actions, not only for the purpose of assessing the degree of injury to the claimant's reputation but also for the purpose of evaluating any defences raised, in particular, justification and fair comment."
Eady J. at first instance in *Gillick v Brook Advisory Centres* (quoted in judgment of Court of Appeal [2001] EWCA Civ 1263 CA at [7] and said to be an "impeccable synthesis of the authorities in the area").

[146] [1999] Q.B. 240 CA. See also *Hinduja v Asia TV* [1998] E.M.L.R. 517 CA.

[147] Cf. *Berezovsky v Forbes Inc.* [2001] EWCA Civ 1251; [2001] E.M.L.R. 45, where the article could only impute murder, fraud and intimidation, not mere suspicion of them.

[148] [2009] WASC 3.

best avoided. (4) The intention of the publisher is irrelevant. (5) The article must be read as a whole, and any 'bane and antidote' taken together. (6) The hypothetical reader is taken to be representative of those who would read the publication in question. (7) In delimiting the range of permissible defamatory meanings, the court should rule out any meaning which, 'can only emerge as the produce of some strained, or forced, or utterly unreasonable interpretation . . . ' (8) It follows that it is not enough to say that by some person or another the words *might* be understood in a defamatory sense."[149]

The exercise is one of impression,

"provided that the impression is not of what the words mean but of what a jury could sensibly think they meant. Such an exercise is an exercise in generosity, not in parsimony. It is why, once fairly performed, it will not be second-guessed on appeal by [the Court of Appeal]: the longstop is the jury".[150]

Where a judge has to determine meaning it has been said that the correct approach is to ask himself what overall impression the material made on him and then to check that against the detailed textual arguments put forward by the parties. Hence in *Armstrong v Times Newspapers*[151] Gray J. "deliberately read the article complained of before reading the parties' respective statements of case or the rival skeleton arguments".

---

[149] *Jeynes v News Magazines Ltd* [2008] EWCA Civ 130 at [14] per Sir Anthony Clarke M.R. To similar effect and very frequently cited is *Skuse v Granada Television Ltd* [1996] E.M.L.R. 278 at 285–287. But when

"an article is opaquely written, . . . allowance has to be made for this; defences may be advanced on the basis of any meaning which the words are reasonably capable of bearing. Although it may seem unattractive, it follows that an author or his publishers may sometimes take advantage of the lack of clarity in his writing to prolong and complicate the issues . . . ":

Lowe v Associated Newspapers Ltd [2006] EWHC 320 (QB); [2007] Q.B. 580 at [3]. See also *Johnson v MGN Ltd* [2009] EWHC 1481 (QB), though this time the opacity worked in favour of the claimant.

[150] *Berezovsky v Forbes Inc.* at [16]. However,

"if on an application for permission to appeal it appears that the judge has erred on the side of unnecessary restriction of meaning, this court—though it will always be mindful of what Brooke L.J. said in *Cruise v Express Newspapers* [1999] Q.B. 931 about self-denial in libel cases—may be readier to take another look. In those cases where it does so, its decision is akin to (and strictly speaking probably is) a holding of law. It will have careful regard to the judge's view, but the view it comes to on the legitimate ambit of meaning will be its own." (ibid.).

[151] [2006] EWHC 1614 (QB) at [31]. See also the same judge in *Charman v Orion Publishing Group Ltd* [2005] EWHC 2187 (QB) at [11]:

"It appears to me to be particularly important where, as here, a judge is providing written reasons for his conclusion as to the meaning to be attributed to the words sued on, that he should not fall into the trap of conducting an over-elaborate analysis of the various passages relied on by the respective protagonists. The parties are entitled to a reasoned judgment but that does not mean that the court should overlook the fact that it is ultimately a question of the meaning which would be put on the words of the book by the ordinary reasonable reader. Such a hypothetical reader is assumed not to be a lawyer. He or she is very unlikely to read the whole book in a single sitting or to compare one passage with another or to focus on particular phrases. The exercise is essentially one of ascertaining the broad impression made on the hypothetical reader by the book taken as a whole."

On appeal on other issues, [2007] EWCA Civ 972; [2008] 1 All E.R. 750.

Despite the recognition given by the European Convention on Human Rights to the importance of the press in a free society, this has not altered the court's approach to the question of meaning where the defendant puts forward a lesser or different meaning by way of justification from that contended for by the claimant, for "there is no defensible way in which the courts can adjust the meaning of meaning so as to include things which no sensible reading of the words could embrace".[152]

Intention and knowledge of the publisher. It is clearly established at   **3.15**
common law that in determining the meaning of words the intention and knowledge of the publisher are immaterial.[153] To this there was a limited exception in cases where the defendant merely distributed the work of others.[154] This common law exception was supplemented with considerable alterations by s.1 of the Defamation Act 1996.[155] Furthermore, the general rule does not apply where the defendant speaks on a privileged occasion and the issue is whether he was actuated by malice.

> "Meaning is an objective test, entirely independent of the defendant's state of mind or intention. Malice is a subjective test, entirely dependent on the defendant's state of mind and intention. Thus, in a case where words are ultimately held objectively to bear meaning A, if the defendant subjectively intended not meaning A but meaning B, and honestly believed meaning B to be true, then the plaintiff's case on malice would be likely to fail".[156]

The general rule must also be qualified where an innocent defendant makes an offer of amends under the Defamation Act 1996, since if the offer is rejected the defendant has a defence if the claimant cannot prove that the defendant knew or had reason to believe that the words were false and defamatory of the claimant.[157]

Subject to these matters, however, what imputation is conveyed by any particular words is to be determined on an objective test, that is, by the meaning in which the ordinary reasonable person would understand them, and is not to be determined by what the defendant intended to convey. "Liability for libel does not depend on the intention of the defamer, but on the fact of defamation",[158] and the rule is the same for slander.[159] Even where the

---

[152] *Berezovsky v Forbes Inc.* [2001] EWCA Civ 1211; [2001] E.M.L.R. 45 at [14].

[153] Distinguish the issue of whether the defendant intended to publish at all. There liability is governed by a negligence standard: see para.6.9. But it seems that if the defendant intended to publish but published the wrong material in error (e.g. as a result of a typographical mistake) he is liable: *Shepheard v Whitaker* (1875) L.R. 10 C.P. 502; *Upton v Times-Democrat*, 28 So. 970 (La., 1900).

[154] See para.6.30, below.

[155] See para.6.31, below.

[156] *Loveless v Earl* [1999] E.M.L.R. 530 CA at 538–539, per Hirst L.J.

[157] Para.19.6, below.

[158] *Cassidy v Daily Mirror* [1929] 2 K.B. 331 at 354, per Russell L.J; *Jeynes v News Magazines Ltd* [2008] EWCA Civ 130 CA at [14].

[159] *Marks v Samuel* [1904] 2 K.B. 287 at 290.

defendant makes a charge against the claimant and adds that he does not consider the alleged behaviour improper he may be liable: what counts is what the defendant has said the claimant has done and the jury may legitimately disagree with the defendant as to the quality of the act charged.[160] A fortiori therefore he is liable if he makes a defamatory charge but has a secret intention not to defame. "Libel . . . consists in using language which others knowing the circumstances would reasonably think to be defamatory of the person complaining of and injured by it. A person charged with libel cannot defend himself by showing that he intended in his breast not to defame."[161] There are many other judicial statements to similar effect.[162] Hence if the defendant uses words by way of a joke and they are taken seriously by reasonable readers he is liable.[163] Though the intention of the defendant is irrelevant in determining meaning, it has been said that "the perceived intention of the publisher may well colour the meaning" of the words.[164] It

---

[160] *Botham v Khan, The Times*, July 15, 1996, CA ("ball tampering" in cricket, alleged to be widespread).

[161] *Hulton v Jones* [1910] A.C. 20 at 23, per Lord Loreburn L.C. See *Klason v Australian Capital Territory* [2003] ACTSC 104; 177 F.L.R. 216 (statement that allegations of child abuse had been "substantiated"; irrelevant that some child care practitioners might treat the expression as meaning only that there was a risk of abuse).

[162] "It is not the defendant's intention, or the meaning in his own mind, that makes the sense of a libel": *Bolton v O'Brien* (1885) 16 L.R. Ir. 97 at 118, per O'Brien J. The test is "what was the meaning and inference that would naturally be drawn by reasonable and intelligent persons reading it": ibid. at 108, per May C.J.; *Capital and Counties Bank v Henty* (1882) 7 A.C. 741 at 745, per Lord Selborne L.C. See also, *Rothschild v Associated Newspapers Ltd* [2012] EWHC 177 (QB) at [23]; *Haire v Wilson* (1829) 9 B. & C. 643; *Fisher v Clement* (1830) 10 B. & C. 472; *Read v Ambridge* (1834) 6 C. & P. 308; *Hankinson v Bilby* (1847) 16 M. & W. 442; *Atkinson v Newton* (1854) 3 W.R. 14; *Slim v Daily Telegraph* [1968] 2 Q.B. 157 at 172, per Diplock L.J.; *Johnston v Ewart* (1893) 24 O.R. 116; *Stopforth v Goyer* (1978) 87 D.L.R. (3d) 373 at 385; *McCrea v Canada Newspapers Ltd* (1993) 109 D.L.R. (4th) 396 NSCA; *Planned Parenthood Newfoundland/Labrador v Fedorik* (1982) 135 D.L.R. (3d) 714. *Rofe v Smith's Newspapers* (1924) 25 N.S.W.S.R. 423; *Hepburn v TCN Channel Nine Pty Ltd* [1983] 2 N.S.W.L.R. 664; *Baltinos v Foreign Language Publications Pty Ltd* (1986) 6 N.S.W.L.R. 85; *Mouti-Haitsma Enterprises Pty Ltd v Lord* (1988) Aust. Torts R. para.80–200; *Morgan v John Fairfax & Sons Ltd (No.2)* (1991) 23 N.S.W.L.R. 374. The 1996 Constitution of South Africa incorporates an entrenched right of freedom of speech and expression (which includes the freedom of the press). Such right may only be limited so far as reasonable and justifiable in a democratic society and, in the case of speech relating to political activity, so far as is *necessary*. The South African common law has a requirement of *animus injuriandi* for defamation (though this may be presumed from the publication of defamatory words) but media defendants need to show that their publication was reasonable (a test which bears some resemblance to the English law of qualified privilege for media publications (see para.15.30, below)): *National Media Ltd v Bogoshi*, 1998 (4) S.A. 1196 SCASA (replacing a former strict liability under *De Flaminghe v Pakendorf* 1982 (3) S.A. 146). See also *Khumalo v Holomisa* [2002] ZASC 12; 2002 (5) SA 401.

[163] See para.3.36, below.

[164] *Berkoff v Burchill* [1996] 4 All ER 1008 per Neill L.J. at 1018; *Bowker (t/a Lagopus Services) v The Royal Society for the Protection of Birds* [2011] EWHC 737 (QB) at [39]–[40]. In *Bowker* Sharp J. held that because what was said was part of a measured analysis of issues in a scientific context, the *perceived* intention of the publisher that it should be so, may well colour the meaning attributed to the words by an ordinary reasonable reader: "the scientific method itself requires scrutiny and criticism for the advancement of knowledge and as the relevant hypothetical reader might well understand, even the most eminent scientist may be wrong without being incompetent" (at [40]).

may be that what is being said here is no more than that the court must consider the context in determining meaning. If so, that is not contentious.[165] If, however, what is being suggested is that the relevant question for the determination of meaning is not "what imputation would the words convey to the reasonable reader?" but "what would the reasonable reader infer that the defendant intended?" then it is not in line with the approach that has generally been taken by the English courts.[166]

Not only is it irrelevant to the liability of the publisher that he did not intend that his words should convey any defamatory imputation, but if they only convey such an imputation by reason of extrinsic facts known to those to whom the words are published, it will be irrelevant that the publisher did not himself know those facts.[167] So where a newspaper published an announcement of X's engagement without knowing that X was a married man, it was held that reasonable men knowing that fact might conclude that the article conveyed an imputation defamatory of X's wife.[168] In *Baturina v Times Newspapers*[169] the defendant sought to re-open the issue whether a defendant can be liable in defamation where the claim is based on an innuendo which he did not and could not reasonably have been expected to appreciate at the time he made the statement. While counsel accepted that there was authority inconsistent with his argument, he advanced two reasons why the court should not follow them. First, the authorities (*Hulton v Jones*,[170] *Cassidy v Daily Mirror Newspapers Ltd*,[171] *Hough v London Express Newspaper Ltd*,[172] and *Fullam v Newcastle Chronicle*[173]) are in the main *reference* and not *meaning* innuendo cases. Secondly, following the coming into force of the Human Rights Act 1998, these decisions are no longer good law. The Court of Appeal rejected the arguments. While it was true that all but the last case involved reference innuendos, the reasoning adopted in those cases applied equally to

---

[165] See para.3.30, below.

[166] See *Cassidy v Daily Mirror* [1940] 2 K.B. 507 CA. In *Nationwide News Pty Ltd v Heggie* [2001] NSWCA 257, Hodgson J.A. thought that to invite a jury to embark on such an inquiry would be highly confusing.

[167] For such extrinsic facts, see para.3.19, below. There are dicta to the effect that the publisher will not be liable unless he knew the extrinsic facts: *Capital and Counties Bank v Henty* (1880) 5 C.P.D. 514 at 539, per Brett L.J.; *Jones v Hulton* [1909] 2 K.B. 444 at 466, per Fletcher Moulton L.J. These must be taken to have been overruled by the decisions of the Court of Appeal in *Cassidy v Daily Mirror* [1929] 2 K.B. 331; *Newstead v London Express* [1940] 1 K.B. 377, and *Hough v London Express* [1940] 2 K.B. 507. See also *Grubb v Bristol United Press* [1963] 1 Q.B. 309 CA at 338; *Morrison v Ritchie* (1902) 4 F. 645, where it was unsuccessfully contended that the defenders could not be held liable, as the fact that the pursuer had only been married two months was "outwith their knowledge".

[168] *Cassidy v Daily Mirror* [1940] 2 K.B. 507 CA; *Morrison v Ritchie* (1902) 4 F. 645. See also *Ralston v Ralston* [1930] 2 K.B. 238.

[169] [2011] EWCA Civ 308 CA; [2011] E.M.L.R. 19.

[170] [1910] A.C. 20 HL.

[171] [1929] 2 K.B. 331.

[172] [1940] 2 K.B. 507.

[173] [1977] 1 W.L.R. 651.

both forms.[174] So far as the Human Rights Act argument was concerned, the court held that art.10 did not compel or justify changing the law. The development of the law of defamation in *Reynolds v Times Newspapers Ltd*,[175] recognising that there was a defence of "responsible journalism", appeared (except perhaps in exceptional circumstances) to be sufficient acknowledgment by the court of the need for the protection of the press over and above the defence of fair (now honest) comment.[176]

In the closely related situation where the defendant uses words which are defamatory on their face but does not intend to refer to the claimant, the common law rule was similar: what counted was whether a reasonable person could understand the words as referring to the claimant. However, this strict liability is now in some doubt because of art.10 of the European Convention on Human Rights.[177] On that basis, it must be said that it is difficult to distinguish this from the situation where the words are defamatory only by reason of extrinsic facts known to the reader but not to the defendant.

3.16 Reasonable understanding. If words conveyed a defamatory imputation to those to whom they were published, but would not have done so to the hypothetical reasonable person in that position, they are not defamatory.[178] "The essence of libel is the publication of written words to a person or persons by whom they would be reasonably understood to be defamatory of the claimant"[179] so that the "mere fact that the hearers understood the language in a defamatory sense does not make it defamatory unless they were reasonably justified in so understanding it".[180] In the case of words defamatory in their ordinary sense, it is unnecessary to prove that anyone did understand the words in a defamatory sense, as long as it is proved that reasonable people would have so understood them.[181] It is true that the claimant may, by

---

[174] [2011] EWCA Civ 308 CA; [2011] E.M.L.R. 19 at [24]–[25].

[175] [2001] 2 A.C. 127 HL; [2000] E.M.L.R. 1.

[176] [2011] EWCA Civ 308 CA; [2011] E.M.L.R. 19 at [27]–[28].

[177] See para.7.8, below.

[178] For the temperament of the reasonable person see para.3.25, below.

[179] *Fullam v Newcastle Chronicle* [1977] 1 W.L.R. 651 CA at 654, per Lord Denning M.R. "In considering questions of this kind we have to ascertain not exactly the sense in which the words were understood by the hearers, but in what sense they would be reasonably understood": *Barnett v Allen* (1858) 3 H. & N. 376 at 380, per Bramwell B.; *Johnson v Rand Daily Mail* [1928] A.D. 1920. In *Rothschild v Associated Newspapers Ltd* [2012] EWHC 177 (QB) at [23] Tugendhat J. stated:

"the court is not concerned with what the writer or publisher intended, nor with what any actual reader may have understood, still less with what the claimant understood. The meaning (or each of the meanings where there are multiple allegations) must be a single meaning, that is a meaning which the court finds would be understood by the hypothetical reasonable reader."

(An appeal from the judgment was dismissed: [2013] EWCA Civ 197; [2013] E.M.L.R. 18). There are dicta in some older cases inconsistent with this approach: *Hankinson v Bilby* (1847) 16 M. & W. 442 at 443; *Capital and Counties Bank v Henty* (1882) 7 A.C. 741 at 777.

[180] *Rudd v De Vos* [1892] 2 C.T.R. 384, per de Villiers C.J.

[181] Thus where words are published in a newspaper or in a broadcast it is unnecessary for the claimant to show that anyone actually read or heard them: see para.7.3, below. Nevertheless, the standard form of pleading is that the words "in their natural and ordinary meaning meant and

pleading an innuendo, show that the words are defamatory by reason of some special fact outside the statement itself and known to those to whom it was published, and that evidence is admissible as to the sense in which they understood it,[182] but even here the question is the sense which a reasonable person with that knowledge would have given to the words. "It is not proof of a special fact ... merely to call a number of people to say that they understood the words in a defamatory sense; they would have to prove some fact known to them which would be sufficient to entitle any reasonable man with such knowledge to interpret the words in a defamatory sense."[183]

For the purposes of the law of defamation the words have only a single, "right" meaning.[184] This does not mean that more than one meaning cannot

---

were understood to mean ... ". If I make a defamatory statement about X in plain English to an audience of five-year-olds who have no idea what I am talking about it is submitted that I have not committed an actionable defamation. In the case of the newspaper story it is reasonable to assume that someone will have understood the words in the defamatory sense.

X has a neighbour dispute with C. X seeks the assistance of D, the landlord of X and C. After taking some steps D writes to X and the letter contains the words "let me know if [C] is abusive etc.". This comes to C's attention. The Court of Appeal held that on any view this could not be read as an assertion that C was, or was likely to be, abusive but Sedley L.J. referred to the air of unreality in judging the statement by the standards of the hypothetical reasonable reader when X was the only recipient: *Freeguard v Martlet Homes Ltd* [2008] EWCA Civ 1577 CA at [6]. It seems likely that an alternative approach leading to the same result might have been to strike out on the basis that the claim was not worth the candle, para.6.2, below.

[182] *Charleston v News Group Newspapers Ltd* [1995] 2 A.C. 65 HL at 72. Where the claimant relies on an innuendo meaning, he should plead the facts and matters on which he relies in support of such sense (see para.26.23) and should, in general, identify the person or persons to whom the words were published and who are alleged to have had knowledge of the special meaning or the extrinsic facts (see, e.g. *Baturina v Times Newspapers Ltd* [2011] EWCA Civ 308; [2011] E.M.L.R. 19 at [44]ff; *Fullam v Newcastle Chronicle* [1977] 1 W.L.R. 651; *Grappelli v Block* [1981] 1 W.L.R. 822). However, it is not an invariable rule and there may be cases—for example, of publication in a national newspaper—where it is reasonable for a court to draw an inference that some readers of that national newspaper must have the particular knowledge (see, e.g. *Wright v Caan* [2011] EWHC 1978 (QB) at [26]; *Lord McAlpine of West Green v Bercow* [2013] EWHC 1342 (QB) at [54]).

[183] Per Greer L.J. in *Tolley v Fry* [1930] 1 K.B. 467 at 480, approved by Slesser L.J. in *Hough v London Express* [1940] 2 K.B. 507 at 514. See also *Frost v London J.S. Bank* (1906) 22 T.L.R. 760 CA; *Beswick v Smith* (1907) 24 T.L.R. 169 CA; *Major v McCregor* (1903) 6 O.L.R. 528.

[184] *Slim v Daily Telegraph Ltd* [1968] 2 Q.B. 157 CA at 171–172, approved by Lord Bridge in *Charleston v News Group Newspapers Ltd* [1995] 2 A.C. 65 at 71. Determination of the single meaning is important for the assessment of damages but does not preclude consideration of other matters, in particular the credibility of the accuser: *Oriental Daily Publisher Ltd v Ming Pao Holdings Ltd* [2012] HKCFA 59; [2013] E.M.L.R. 7. In the *Oriental Daily Publisher* case the allegations, though serious, had been made by a person who had been convicted of very serious criminal offences and who described himself as the "Hong Kong Bin Laden". The Hong Kong Court of Final Appeal held that the single meaning determined by the court was relevant to the eventual award of damages in that it established the nature and seriousness of the libel but there was no justification for treating that meaning as the sole basis for assessing damages:

"There is a self-evident difference between ascertaining what the ordinary, reasonable, fair-minded reader would understand the defamatory words to mean and considering how far such a reader might be expected to believe or be sceptical about the words so understood. If and in so far as the accuser's low credibility may be capable of reducing the injurious impact of the defamatory words, consideration of such impact is not excluded by the single meaning rule." (at [56]).

See also *Barrick Gold Corp. v Lopehandia* (2004), 71 O.R. (3d) 416 at [49].

be left to the jury; but it does mean that the jury or other fact-finder[185] must ignore the undoubted fact that in many cases it is likely (or even obvious[186]) that different readers will have understood the publication in different ways, some defamatory, others not.[187]

---

[185] *Next Magazine Publishing Ltd v Oriental Daily Publisher Ltd* [2000] 2 H.K.L.R.D. 333 HKCFA (judge sitting alone).

[186] In *Jameel v Wall Street Journal Europe SPRL (No.3)* [2004] EWHC 37 (QB); [2004] E.M.L.R. 11 at [6] Eady J. said that he had

"never known a case in which a jury was asked to set out its definitive meaning or meanings. There may be examples where this has occurred, but it does seem to me that there are potentially serious problems about any such exercise. It is difficult to see how it would be possible to avoid asking the jurors to draft in committee, since they cannot generally be given a finite number of multiple option questions. They are not … bound by either side's contentions on meaning. It is open for them to come up with their own particular meaning or meanings. Also, where there is room for differences between ordinary readers as to the interpretation of a newspaper article, there is no reason to suppose that all 12 jurors are necessarily going to fit into one straitjacket. Any differences between them, which are likely to be relatively minor and limited to matters of shading or emphasis, would not normally have to be revealed. If they are asked to produce a carefully drafted set of meanings, however, which remove any ambiguity which has been left in the article ex hypothesi by the professional journalist or editor, there is much more scope for stalemate."

See also *Joseph v Spiller* [2012] EWHC 2598 (QB) at [12] (judge alone).

[187] *Charleston v News Group Newspapers Ltd* [1995] 2 A.C. 65; *Curistan v Times Newspapers Ltd* [2008] EWCA Civ 432; [2009] Q.B. 231. However the "single meaning" rule does not apply in an unqualified way where the issue is qualified privilege: *Bonnick v Morris* [2002] UKPC 31; [2003] 1 A.C. 300. See para.15.23, below. Nor does the rule mean that where an article reports what X has said and adds D's comments, which are not in the same terms, to that, there must be a single meaning to the whole publication: *Curistan*, above. For the operation of the single meaning rule in the context of chatroom or forum publications see *McGrath v Dawkins* [2012] EWHC B3 at [53] (QB) where H.H.J. Moloney QC considered how the "single meaning" rule operated in the context of chatroom or forum publications:

"a. While the website operator is prima facie liable for all the contents of the thread, individual contributors are of course liable only for their own words.

b. Those individual contributions must be read in the context of the earlier contributions, which may affect the meaning of the latest one.

c. As later contributors add further comments, the context of the thread as a whole will change. This will affect the meaning of the whole thread, for which the operator is liable; but an individual contributor cannot be held liable for a change in the meaning of his contribution, brought about by the later contributions of third parties which alter its context.

d. Strictly speaking, whenever a new contribution was added, the thread would become a new publication with a different meaning. In the case of a thread with more than a few entries, it would rapidly become impracticable for a judge, let alone a jury, to ascribe a separate defamatory meaning at each point, and then apply it to such meaning-dependent issues as justification.

e. The only practicable course here is to adopt the general approach of treating the final thread as a single publication for context and meaning purposes (albeit with several authors of distinct parts), while carefully avoiding the injustice of holding an individual contributor liable for any material changes in the meaning of his contribution brought about by later contributions from others." (at [53]).

As to honest comment see para.12.8, below. Of course, as juries do not reveal their reasoning it may well be that some of them in fact find for the claimant on the basis that some people might rationally have understood the words in defamatory sense A while others might have rationally interpreted it in sense B. Where, as is now more common, the question of the actual meaning is determined by judge alone it is still presumed that there is a "single meaning" and, since judges have to give reasons for their conclusions, that single meaning has to be articulated: *Cruddas v Calvert* [2013] EWCA Civ 748 CA at [14]. See also, Jacob J. in *Vodafone Group v Orange*

For the moment, the single meaning rule remains well established in defamation and indeed it was decided by the Court of Appeal in 2011 that it also applied to the assessment of meaning for the purposes of the honest comment defence.[188] However, its existence owes much to accidents of history and practical concerns[189] rather than legal principle or policy and whenever the rule is examined few can be found to defend it.[190] It was justified in *Ajinomoto Sweeteners Europe SAS v Asda Stores Ltd*[191] by Tugendhat J. as follows:

> "The reason for the rule in defamation is to protect freedom of expression on the one hand, and the right to reputation on the other hand, striking a balance between the two. The rule is a control mechanism . . . An alternative to the single meaning rule would be . . . that the statement was false to a substantial number of people. That test would not, of course, apply when the statement was made only to one, or a few people, as is sometimes the case. In such a case the alternative to the single meaning

---

Personal Communications [1997] F.S.R. 34 (a malicious falsehood case) and *Entienne v Festival City Broadcasters* [2001] SASC 60; 79 S.A.S.R. 19.

[188] *Lait v Evening Standard Ltd* [2011] EWCA Civ 859; [2011] 1 W.L.R. 2973. Lord Neuberger M.R. explained the position as follows:
"The first question is whether the single meaning rule, as explained by Diplock L.J. in *Slim v Daily Telegraph Ltd* [1968] 2 QB 157, 171–174, and as discussed more recently by Sedley L.J. in *Ajinomoto Sweeteners Europe SAS v Asda Stores Ltd* [2011] QB 497, applies where the defence is one of honest comment. In my view, it does. First, given the rationale for the rule in the field of defamation (which has been affirmed in *Charleston v News Group Newspapers Ltd* [1995] 2 A.C. 65, 71–72), it is a little hard to see why, as a matter of principle, it should not apply when the court is assessing a defence of honest comment. Secondly, it appears to me that it would be inconvenient, particularly if the case was being tried by a jury, if the single meaning rule applied in a defamation trial for some purposes, but not for others. Thirdly, a number of authorities support this conclusion: see *Merivale v Carson* 20 QBD 275, 279, 281 and 282, and *Burstein v Associated Newspapers Ltd* [2007] 4 All ER 319, paras 7–8. I also agree with Laws L.J. that the approval in the *Charleston* case [1995] 2 A.C. 65 of Diplock L.J.'s judgment in the Slim case appears to support this conclusion" (at [52]).
See also, Laws L.J. at [31]–[35].
[189] See Mitchell, *The Making of the Modern Law of Defamation* (Oxford: Hart Publishing, 2005), ch.2, and the judgment of Diplock L.J. in *Slim v Daily Telegraph* [1968] 2 Q.B. 157 CA at 171–174.
[190] See, e.g, Diplock L.J. in *Slim v Daily Telegraph* [1968] 2 Q.B. 157 at 171–174; Lord Nicholls in *Charleston v News Group Newspapers* [1995] 2 A.C. 65 at 73–74 HL. However, Lord Neuberger N.P.J. offered a robust defence of the rule in *Oriental Daily Publisher Ltd v Ming Pao Holdings Ltd* [2012] HKCFA 59; [2013] E.M.L.R. 7:
"Although things may be very different in the world of linguistic philosophy, the single meaning rule makes obvious good sense in the world of legal interpretation; indeed it is essential. While the consequences of applying the rule may sometimes seem a little harsh, if a court could hold that a provision in a statute, a contract or a notice could, as a matter of law, have more than one meaning, it would self-evidently lead to chaos and uncertainty in many cases, both in outcome and in procedure . . . If the single meaning rule did not apply in defamation, it would similarly lead to greater uncertainty in outcome and increased legal expenses. Instead of a statement with two possible meanings giving rise to a problem requiring a binary resolution, it would give rise to a problem which had a multiplicity of potential answers, along what might be seen as a continuous spectrum. Abolition of the single meaning rule would also lead to the dispiriting, expensive, and time-consuming prospect of many witnesses being called by each party, to explain how they understood the statement in question." (at [141]–[142]).
[191] [2009] EWHC 1717 (QB); [2009] Q.B. 204.

rule might in effect have to be whatever meaning happens to be attributed to the statement by the person to whom it is made. Either of these alternatives would strike a balance more favourable to protection of reputation, and less to freedom of expression, than the existing rule. They would allow more successful claims in defamation."[192]

Yet it surely fails consistently to strike this balance. By insisting on a single meaning when it is clear that the words may carry more than one meaning, the court will either fail to provide redress for injury that has unquestionably been suffered[193] or overcompensate the claimant by awarding him damages for a meaning that some readers may have found the words to bear whereas others, wholly reasonably, understood the words in a non-defamatory or less-defamatory sense.[194]

The single meaning rule has been held not to apply to malicious falsehood by the Court of Appeal in *Ajinomoto*,[195] which reversed Tugendhat J.'s decision in that respect. Sedley L.J. said that in the libel context what was

> "a pragmatic practice became elevated into a rule of law and has remained in place without any enduring rationale. It is frequently otiose, as counsel's own experience testifies, because in the great majority of defamation cases the choice between libel and no libel, by the time the case goes to a verdict, is an either-or choice."[196]

Referring to Tugendhat J.'s views below, Rimer L.J. said:

> "If the single meaning rule does achieve a fair balance in defamation law between the parties' competing interests, that would appear to be the result of luck rather than judgment; and how the measure of such claimed fairness might be assessed may anyway be questionable. The application of the rule can also be said to carry with it the potential for swinging the balance unfairly against one party of the other, resulting in no compensation in cases when fairness might suggest that some should be due, or in over-compensation in others."[197]

The abolition of the presumption in favour of jury trial that will be effected by s.11 of the Defamation Act 2013 removes the pragmatic reason for retaining the rule and in view of the fact that a multiple meaning rule would strike a better balance between competing rights, the continued existence of the rule seems ripe for challenge.

3.17 Natural and ordinary meaning. At one time words were construed *mitiori sensu*, that is to say the mildest meaning would be attributed to them even if that involved a forced and artificial construction. This was described

---

[192] Ibid. at [29], [31].

[193] In *Entienne P/L v Festival City Broadcasters* [2001] SASC 60, the Supreme Court of South Australia declined to apply the single meaning rule on the ground that, "to insist upon an innocent interpretation where any reasonable person could, and many reasonable people would, understand a sinister meaning is to refuse reparation for a wrong that has in fact been committed."

[194] See, Lord Nicholls in *Charleston v News Group Newspapers* [1995] 2 A.C. 65, at 73–74.

[195] [2010] EWCA Civ 609 CA; [2011] Q.B. 497. See para.21.5, below.

[196] Ibid. at [32].

[197] Ibid. at [43].

as "long since superseded" in 1807.[198] Words are normally construed in their natural and ordinary meaning, i.e. in the meaning in which reasonable people of ordinary intelligence, with the ordinary person's general knowledge and experience of worldly affairs, would be likely to understand them.[199] The question is what would the words convey to the mind of the ordinary, reasonable,[200] fair-minded reader?[201] The natural and ordinary meaning may also include implications or inferences.[202] Where a party contends that the words should not be construed in their natural and ordinary meaning (as where the claimant pleads an innuendo based on an extrinsic fact which makes apparently innocent words defamatory or the defendant claims that the circumstances in which the words were used prevented them being understood in a defamatory sense) the burden of proof lies on him.[203]

Ordinary meaning and implications.   **3.18**

"What the ordinary man would infer without special knowledge has generally been called the natural and ordinary meaning of words. But that expression is rather misleading in that it conceals the fact that there are two elements in it. Sometimes it is not necessary to go beyond the words themselves, as where the claimant has been called a thief and a murderer. But more often the sting is not so much in the words themselves as in what the ordinary man will infer from them,[204] and that is also regarded as part of their natural and ordinary meaning".[205]

---

[198] *Roberts v Cowden* (1807) 9 East 93 at 96; *Pelton v Ward* 3 Cai. R. (N.Y. 1805); *Galloway v Telegraph Group Ltd* [2004] EWHC 2786 (QB); [2005] E.M.L.R. 7 (appeal dismissed [2006] EWCA Civ 17; [2006] E.M.L.R. 11); *Ajinomoto Sweeteners Europe SAS v Asda Stores Ltd* [2010] EWCA Civ 609 CA; [2011] Q.B. 497 at [1]. See also, per Tugendhat J. in *Lord McAlpine of West Green v Bercow* [2013] EWHC 1342 (QB) at [64].

[199] Per Lord Mansfield C.J. in *R. v Horne* (1777) 2 Cowp. 680; per curiam in *Harrison v Thornborough* (1714) 10 Mod. 196; *Hankinson v Bilby* (1847) 16 M. & W. 442 at 445; *Capital and Counties Bank v Henty* (1882) 7 A.C. 741 at 745, 772, 788; *Holdsworth v Associated Press* (1937) 53 T.L.R. 1029 CA; *Cray v Jones* [1939] 1 All E.R. 798; *Liberace v Daily Mirror Newspapers, The Times*, June 17, 18, 1959; *Jones v Skelton* [1963] 1 W.L.R. 1362 PC; *Lewis v Daily Telegraph* [1964] A.C. 234 HL; *Slim v Daily Telegraph* [1968] 1 Q.B. 157 CA at 172–175, per Diplock L.J.; *Corton v ABC* (1973) 22 F.L.R. at 187 (applying this sentence). See also *Demmers v Wylie*, 1980 (1) S.A. 835 AD. For the ordinary person's knowledge and temperament, see paras 3.25 and 3.26, below.

[200] For practical purposes there is no difference between "reasonable" and "ordinary"; contrast *Mollo v BBC, Guardian*, February 2, 1963 ("reasonable men with ordinary intelligence"), with *Russell v Pressdram, The Times*, February 4, 1966 ("ordinary man with reasonable intelligence").

[201] *Charleston v News Group Newspapers Ltd* [1995] 2 A.C. 65 HL at 71, per Lord Bridge.

[202] *Jones v Skelton* [1963] 1 W.L.R. 1362 PC at 1371; see further para.3.18, below.

[203] See paras 3.21–3.22, below.

[204] So if there is a statement that a particular wing of a prison is occupied by child molesters, sexual offenders or those incarcerated there for their own protection and a further statement that the claimant is in that wing it seems that the reader will inevitably infer that he falls into one of those categories: *Hill v Cork Examiner Publications Ltd* [2001] IESC 95; [2001] 4 I.R. 219.

[205] Per Lord Reid in *Lewis v Daily Telegraph* [1964] A.C. 234 at 258; see also ibid., per Lord Devlin at 280. "There must be added to the implications which a court is prepared to make as a matter of construction all such insinuations and innuendoes as could reasonably be read into them by the ordinary man." "One must consider not what the words are, but what conclusion could reasonably be drawn from it, as a man who issues such a document is answerable not only for the terms of it but also for the conclusion and meaning which persons will reasonably draw from and

"The ordinary and natural meaning of words may be either the literal meaning[206] or it may be implied or inferred[207] or an indirect meaning; any meaning that does not require the support of extrinsic facts passing beyond general knowledge but is a meaning which is capable of being detected in the language used can be part of the ordinary and natural meaning. The ordinary and natural meaning may therefore include any implication or inference which a reasonable reader guided not by any special but only by general knowledge, and not fettered by any strict legal rules of construction[208] would draw from the words."[209]

It is immaterial whether the defamatory imputation is conveyed by words of direct assertion or by suggestion, for insinuation[210] may be as defamatory as an explicit statement[211] and even more mischievous.[212] Similarly words may

---

put upon the document": per Cotton L.J. in *Capital and Counties Bank v Henty* (1880) 5 C.P.D. 514 at 536, approved in *Cassidy v Daily Mirror* [1929] 2 K.B. 331 CA and *Grubb v Bristol United Press* [1963] 1 Q.B. 309 CA; *Gillick v BBC* [1996] E.M.L.R. 267 CA (principle applied to television broadcast); *Mirror Newspapers v World Hosts* (1979) 53 A.L.R. 243 HCA at 246 (natural and ordinary meaning includes inferences and conclusions which the ordinary man draws); see also *Slim v Daily Telegraph* [1968] 2 Q.B.157 CA at 172–175, per Diplock L.J. Such a conclusion might be, for instance, that a man who had entered a brothel had done so for an immoral purpose: *Lewis v Daily Telegraph*, above, at 278 (though cf. *Hannah v Scottish Daily Record*, 2000 S.L.T. 673 OH). Cf. *Angel v Bushell* [1968] 1 Q.B. 813 at 825–826: "'Not conversant with normal business ethics' connotes at a minimum dishonourable behaviour". For the pleading in such cases, see para.26.23, below.

[206] However sometimes it is not the literal meaning but a colloquial meaning: *Ayub bin Saud v TS Sambanthamurthi* [1989] 1 M.L.J. 315 ("daylight robbery" means exorbitant pricing).

[207] For the distinction between an implication (what the speaker is understood as intending to convey) and an inference (what the hearer concludes from what the speaker says), see *Amalgamated Television Services Pty Ltd v Marsden* (1998) 43 N.S.W.L.R. 158 NSWCA and *Nationwide News Pty Ltd v Warton* [2002] NSWCA 377.

[208] So, in *Memphis Publishing Co. v Nichols* 569 S.W.2d 412 (Ten. 1978) a newspaper statement that P had been shot by X's wife when the wife found them together at P's house was capable of imputing adultery to P.

[209] *Jones v Skelton* [1963] 1 W.L.R. 1362 PC at 1370–1371, per Lord Morris. "The ordinary and natural meaning or inferred or indirect meaning—any meaning which does not require the support of extrinsic facts passing beyond general knowledge but is a meaning which is capable of being detected in the language used can be part of the ordinary meaning of words": Hirst L.J. in *Mitchell v Faber & Faber Ltd* [1998] E.M.L.R. 807 CA.

In *Fox v Boulter* [2013] EWHC 1435 (QB) there was disagreement as to what is comprised under the heading of "general knowledge". Bean J. held that "general knowledge" means:

"'matters of universal notoriety'—that is to say, matters which any intelligent viewer or reader may be expected to know. Anything which requires assiduous reading and a good memory so as to recall the facts of a story dating back several weeks or months cannot fall within that definition. To give the term 'general knowledge' such a wide interpretation would erode the distinction between ordinary and natural meaning on the one hand and innuendo meaning on the other, and would breach the well established rule that evidence is inadmissible on the issue of the natural and ordinary meaning of the words complained of" (at [16]).

[210] In *Cook v Telegraph Media Group Ltd* [2011] EWHC 1134 (QB) Tugendhat J. held that a statement that an MP's claim for expenses in respect of the cost of a poppy "was particularly embarrassing because he is an official supporter of the campaign to commemorate [a senior officer who commanded Fighter Command at the Battle of Britain]", could only be read as imputing a weakness of character or judgment and not that his support for the campaign was a pretence (at [20]).

[211] The law is the same under the Civil Code of Quebec: *Dimanche-Matin v Fabien* (1983) 20 C.C.L.T. 283 CA (Que).

[212] The use of "emoticons" in text, email or internet communications may affect the meaning that a reasonable reader would attach to the statement complained of. A smiling face—:-)—may

be defamatory even though they are used in an interrogative form,[213] and in principle the same should apply if they are used in a hypothetical way, so long as in the context in which they are used they may reasonably be interpreted to convey the truth.[214] The tendency and effect of the language, not its form, is the criterion and a defendant cannot defame and escape the consequences by dexterity of style.[215] "The results of a calumnious falsehood arise from the impression which it—all of it, including reservations, cautions, and all the rest—makes upon the minds of the readers, an impression which may be quite apart from any artificial restriction which the author of the falsehood sought to impose."[216] Where the defendant invites the reader to adopt a suspicious approach, then it is reasonable to conclude that the words entitle the reader to indulge in some degree of conjecture or guesswork which would not otherwise be permitted.[217]

It has been said that:

"the publisher is not held responsible . . . for an inference which the ordinary reasonable reader, listener or viewer draws from an inference already drawn from the matter complained of, because it is unreasonable for the publisher to be held so responsible . . . An inference is drawn from an inference when . . . the viewer

---

be used to convey the meaning that the statement is not to be read seriously. Whereas a grim face—:-l—might be read as signifying that the statement is to be taken seriously and a winking face— ;-) —as signifying that mischief is intended.

[213] In *Lord McAlpine of West Green v Bercow* [2013] EWHC 1342 (QB) a post on Twitter asked, "Why is Lord McAlpine trending? *Innocent face*". Tugendhat J. held that the reasonable reader would understand the writer's addition of the words "innocent face" after asking the question as insincere and ironical: "The law is clear that words may be defamatory in whatever form they are used. A question, or a rhetorical question, or any other form of words may, in principle, be understood to convey a defamatory meaning" (at [62]). See also, *Jackson v Adams* (1835) 2 Bing. N.C. 408; *Collins v Cooper* (1902) 19 T.L.R. 118 CA; *Jones v Skelton* [1963] 1 W.L.R. 1362 PC ("It is beyond understanding. Or is it?"); *Fox v Goodfellow* (1926) N.Z.L.R. 58, where the words "Have you ever heard that Fox was reported twice as a spy?" were held to be defamatory because "there was implied in the statement that he had committed an offence"; *Collins v Cooper* (1902) 19 T.L.R. 118 CA (is this the woman who . . . ?). See also *Evans v Johns* (1962) 4 W.I.R. 502 (metaphors and rhetorical questions).

[214] It has been said that a statement "If Mr Justice X took a bribe he is not fit to hold office" is not on its face defamatory of Mr Justice X, but would be so if the words gave the impression that he had done so: *Galloway v Telegraph Group* [2004] EWHC 2786 (QB); [2005] E.M.L.R. 7 at [178].

[215] *State v Norton*, 36 A. 290 at 294 (Mne., 1896); *Yarwood v Mirror Newspapers* [1968] 1 N.S.W.R. 720 (ironical publication not to be analysed according to the literal meaning).

[216] *Stubbs v Mazure* [1920] A.C. 66 HL at 80.

[217] *Amalgamated Television Services Pty Ltd v Marsden* (1998) 43 N.S.W.L.R. 158 NSWCA, explaining *Jones v Skelton* [1963] 1 W.L.R. 1362 PC. However, in *Tesla Motors Ltd v BBC* [2013] EWCA Civ 152 CA the Court of Appeal held that no reasonable person could draw the inference from the following statement made on the "Top Gear" programme—"Tesla say it will do 200 miles, we worked out that on our track it would run out after just 55 miles"—that the car's range under normal driving conditions was only 55 miles or that in claiming it had a range of 200 miles Tesla had set out dishonestly to mislead the public. See also *John v Times Newspapers Ltd* [2012] EWHC 2751 (QB) (the defendant had published various articles about tax avoidance, named the founders of the film finance tax avoidance scheme and described one of them as Elton John's former accountant. Tugendhat J. held that the defendant's hypothetical readers would not infer from the articles that Elton John was implicated in immoral tax avoidance measures).

draws an inference which is available in the matter complained of then uses that inference as a basis (at least in part) from which a further inference is drawn".[218]

On the other hand, the view has been taken that there is no special rule about an inference from an inference and that the question is simply one of what the words can reasonably convey; so it would be unreasonable to infer guilt from an inference of suspicion,[219] but that while there

"may be many circumstances ... in which a primary inference could fairly be drawn from the published material but a secondary inference said to arise from the first could not be regarded as an imputation reasonably drawn from that material. At the other extreme, there may be circumstances in which the second inference would be regarded an almost inevitable corollary of the first. In the latter event, there would be no rational reason to act upon some perceived truism that a reasonable reader would lack the intellectual acuity to draw it."[220]

3.19 Defamatory comparisons. An obvious example of defamation by implication arises when the claimant is compared with an animal perceived to be treacherous or disgusting[221] or with odious or disreputable persons, or with people perceived to be incompetent,[222] whether they be historical[223] or fictional.[224] "Nothing is easier than to bring persons into contempt by allusion to

---

[218] *Amalgamated Television Services Pty Ltd v Marsden* (1998) 43 N.S.W.L.R. 158 NSWCA at 167, per Hunt C.J. at C.L.

[219] See *Lewis v Daily Telegraph* [1964] A.C. 234 HL at 247. Indeed, it would be unreasonable to infer guilt from a direct statement of suspicion. See also sub-para.(5) of the proposed amendments in *Bennett v News Group Newspapers Ltd* [2002] E.M.L.R. 39 CA.

[220] *John Fairfax Publications Pty Ltd v ACP Publishing Pty Ltd* [2005] ACTCA 12 at [13]. See also the similar view expressed by Ipp J.A. in *Gacic v John Fairfax Publications Pty Ltd* [2006] NSWCA 175; 66 N.S.W.L.R. 675 at [113] (omitted from the N.S.W.L.R. report) and approved by Callinan and Heydon JJ. on appeal, [2007] HCA 28; 235 A.L.R. 402 at [174]; and *Kelson v David Syme & Co. Ltd* [1998] SCACT 60 at [17], per Crispin J.

[221] *Hoare v Silverlock* (1848) 12 Q.B. 624; *Zbyszko v N. Y. American*, 228 N.Y. App. Div. 277 (1930).

[222] "Perhaps Dee has earned the right to be bracketed with such global sporting icons as ski-jumping's Eddie the Eagle or swimming's Eric the Eel": *Dee v Telegraph Media Group Ltd* [2010] EWHC 924 (QB) [2010] E.M.L.R. 20. While Sharp J. acknowledged that words imputing want of skill or incompetence to a professional person were capable of being defamatory, it was not easy to translate those principles into the sporting arena so that an imputation of relative lack of skill did not necessarily impute incompetence. The judge was however prepared to accept that it was arguable that the words in the present case were defamatory on the grounds that they were capable of suggesting "want of skill", incompetence and/or on the ground that the claimant had been ridiculed by the suggestion that he was absurdly bad at tennis. Summary judgment was however granted to the defendant on the basis that the defence of justification must succeed.

[223] *Ashby v Billingsly* (1671) Carter 231 ("Jezebel"); *Curtis v Massey*, 72 Mass. R. 251 (1856) (Judas); *Bennett v Australian Newspaper* (1891) 12 N.S.W.L.R. 141 (Ananias). The Privy Council set aside the rule absolute for a new trial, on the ground that it was for the jury to determine whether the words complained of did in fact convey an imputation of deliberate falsehood [1894] A.C. 284. The words might have been understood to have been used extravagantly: ibid. at 287; *Gwynne v Wairarapa Times-Age* [1972] N.Z.L.R. 586. As to changes in the public perception of nationalities and races, see para.2.25, above.

[224] *Buckstaff v Viall*, 84 Wisconsin R. 129 (1893) (Pecksniff); *Woodgate v Ridout* (1865) 4 F. & F. 202 (comparison with the firm of Quirk, Gammon & Snap in *Ten Thousand a Year*). "Shylock" is probably defamatory as implying that the claimant is heartless or mean, even though that is a superficial reading of *The Merchant of Venice*. Neither "Ananias" nor "Pecksniff" is likely to mean much to a modern audience.

names well known in history, or by mention of animals to which certain ideas are attached", and the court "will take judicial notice that such words as 'Judas' have an application very generally known indeed, which application is likely to bring into contempt a person against whom it is directed".[225]

Innuendoes, "true" and "false". Hitherto we have been concerned with   **3.20** the ordinary meaning of words, though including within that cases where a defamatory imputation is conveyed by implication.[226] Where, however, the defamatory meaning only arises because of extrinsic facts which are known to the recipients there is said to be an "innuendo".[227] This has two principal consequences. First, the claimant must not only identify in his particulars of claim the defamatory meaning which he contends the words convey (for he must now do that in all cases) but also identify the relevant extrinsic facts[228] and prove that those facts were known to at least one of the persons to whom the words were published.[229] Secondly, the meaning resulting from those facts gives rise to a cause of action separate from that (if any) arising from the words in their ordinary and natural meaning because it is an extended meaning not present in the words themselves.[230] Where the claimant relies on such a meaning:

> "there is one cause of action for the libel itself, based on whatever imputations or implications can reasonably be derived from the words themselves, and there is another different cause of action, namely, the innuendo, based not merely on the libel itself, but on an extended meaning created by a conjunction of the words with something outside them. The latter cause of action cannot come into existence unless there is some extrinsic fact to create the extended meaning."[231]

---

[225] *Hoare v Silverlock* (1848) 12 Q.B. 624 at 633–634. See also *Bennett v Australian Newspaper* (1891) 12 N.S.W.L.R. at 146; *Lawson v Thompson* (1969) 5 D.L.R. (3d) 550; *Husnul bin Abdul Hadi v Bulat bin Mohamed* [1978] 1 M.L.J. 70.

[226] See para.3.18, above. "An innuendo is the technical term for a meaning that would only be understood by a reader who knows facts not stated in the words complained of . . . and the reader interprets the words in the light of those facts": *Waterson v Lloyd* [2013] EWHC 2201 (QB) at [9].

[227] Now defined in PD 53, para.2.3(1)(b) as "a meaning alleged to be conveyed to some person by reason of knowing facts extrinsic to the words complained of". The sense of the word is "nodding": *Smythe v Mackinnon* (1894) 24 R. 1086 at 1093 (from the Latin "*innuere*" nod towards and hence, figuratively, to intimate).

[228] PD 53, para.2.3(2).

[229] See *Grubb v Bristol United Press* [1963] 1 Q.B. 309 CA; *Lewis v Daily Telegraph* [1964] A.C. 234; *Federal Capital Press of Australia Pty Ltd v Edwards* (1992) 108 F.L.R. 118; and para.3.20, below.

[230] *Watkin v Hall* (1868) L.R. 3 Q.B. 396 at 402; *Sim v Stretch* (1936) 52 T.L.R. 669 at 671; *Grubb v Bristol United Press* [1963] 1 Q.B. 309 CA at 327; *Lewis v Daily Telegraph* [1964] A.C. 234 at 277–280, where Lord Devlin reviews the development of the law. This was the effect of the Common Law Procedure Act 1852, s.61, as to which see the 8th edition of this book, para.95, fn.76.

[231] Per Pearce L.J. in *Grubb v Bristol United Press* [1963] 1 Q.B. 309 at 327.
"When read in conjunction with extrinsic facts words may in the law of defamation have some special or secondary meaning additional to or different from, their natural and ordinary meaning. This special or secondary meaning is not one which the words viewed in isolation are capable of sustaining. It is one which a reader acquainted with the extrinsic facts will understand the words in the light of those facts":

A "true"[232] or "legal" innuendo[233] in this sense only exists where the extended meaning arises from facts passing beyond general knowledge.[234] If the defamatory meaning arises indirectly by inference or implication from the words published without the aid of any extrinsic facts there is said to be a "false" or "popular" innuendo[235] and this does not give rise to a separate cause of action.[236]

3.21 True innuendo: extrinsic facts. Such facts[237] have also been referred to as "added",[238] "extraneous"[239] or "special"[240] facts, or "something outside the words".[241] They may, for instance, be the circumstances of publication,[242] any accompanying gestures or expression or tone of voice,[243] a slang or technical meaning or the meaning of a foreign language,[244] or some additional fact which would allow those who knew it to read a defamatory meaning into the words published,[245] as for example where the claimant had told people

---

per Mason and Jacobs JJ. in *Mirror Newspapers v World Hosts* (1979) 53 A.L.J.R. 243 HCA at 246.

[232] *Grubb v Bristol United Press* [1963] 1 Q.B. 309 CA at 333: see also ibid. at 328 ("genuine innuendo"); *Lewis v Daily Telegraph* [1964] A.C. 234 at 258, 263, 264, 271.

[233] *Lewis v Daily Telegraph*, above, at 280–282, per Lord Devlin; see fn.208, above.

[234] See *Byrne v Radio Telefis Eireann* [2006] IEHC 71. For the curious perversion of this in some American jurisdictions into an entirely different rule concerned with damage rather than pleading, see para.3.6, above.

[235] *Grubb v Bristol United Press* [1963] 1 Q.B. 309 CA at 328, 333; *Lewis v Daily Telegraph* [1964] A.C. 234 at 271. Lord Devlin did not care for "false" as a description of what he called the "popular" innuendo (see at 280); "it is the law and not popular usage which gives a false and restricted meaning to the word". He pointed out (at 278) that De Grey C.J., in *R. v Horne* (1777) 2 Cowp. at 684, had used the word for the implication to be derived from the words without extrinsic aid; for such use see also *English and Scottish Co-operative Society v Odhams Press* [1940] 1 K.B. 440 CA at 450, per Slesser L.J.; *Ryan v Ross* (1916) 22 C.L.R. 1 at 11, per Griffith C.J.; *Langlands v John Leng*, 1916 S.C. (H.L.) 102 at 105, per Lord Haldane.

[236] Even before the present rules, the distinction was blurred from a pleading point of view by the practice of requiring the claimant to give particulars of meaning whenever there could be any doubt as to the meaning of the words. This is now required in all cases.

[237] However, the New South Wales CA has said that literally to require "facts" is to misunderstand the nature of an innuendo; the "facts" may exist only as a belief in the minds of the audience, induced for example by what the defendant has previously said: *John Fairfax Publications v Rivkin* [1999] NSWCA 164. It would certainly be curious to require the claimant to prove the truth of the assertions by the defendant on which the claimant founds the innuendo.

[238] *Grubb v Bristol United Press* [1963] 1 Q.B. 309 CA at 327.

[239] *Lewis v Daily Telegraph* [1964] A.C. 234 at 271.

[240] *Tolley v Fry* [1930] 1 K.B. 467 CA at 480.

[241] *Grubb v Bristol United Press* [1963] 1 Q.B. 309 CA at 327.

[242] See para.3.30, below.

[243] See para.3.36, below.

[244] It is not certain that these cases involve an innuendo in the technical sense: see para.3.26, below.

[245] See, e.g. *Baturina v Times Newspapers Ltd* [2011] EWCA Civ 308 CA; [2011] 1 W.L.R. 1526 (knowledge of decree promulgated by the President of the Russian Federation that all officials, civil servants and their families were required to post on official websites certain information about their assets and income). See also *Ronaldo v Telegraph Media Group Ltd* [2010] EWHC 2710 (QB); *Flood v Times Newspapers Ltd* [2013] EWHC 2182 (QB). In *Khalil v Barakat* [2013] EWHC 85 (QB) Eady J. stated that while an imputation that a woman was not a virgin when she married was probably not defamatory in today's society it might be so on the basis of an innuendo if the relevant facts known to the publishees included that the woman had

some matter.[246] The key point is that the matter is not merely one of general knowledge.[247] "Thus, to say of a man that he was seen to enter a named house would contain a derogatory implication for anyone who knew that that house was a brothel but not for anyone who did not."[248] Similarly to say of A that he is engaged to B may in certain circumstances convey to those who know that C has lived with A as his wife an implication that C has done so without being married to him.[249] Facts in the publication containing the words sued on are not extrinsic facts in this sense; they are merely part of the context.[250]

Extrinsic facts may cause words to convey a less rather than a more serious imputation than their ordinary meaning, so the defendant may also wish to rely on such a meaning where the words are in their natural and ordinary meaning defamatory. For instance, they may make it clear, in a case of slanderous words in their natural and ordinary meaning charging a crime, that no such charge was being made. "If at the time the words were uttered there are circumstances (known to the hearers) which clearly show that the words

---

given an assurance (e.g. to her husband and his family) prior to marriage that she was in fact a virgin and/or that it was generally regarded as wrong for a woman purporting to be a practising Muslim to lose her virginity prior to marriage (at [8]).

[246] *Auladin v Shaikh* [2013] EWHC 157 (QB) at [17].

[247] Whether the circumstances of a publication amount to extrinsic facts, which have to be proved as such to support an innuendo, or whether they are general knowledge, which can be relied on in support of its natural and ordinary meaning is not infrequently an issue between the parties. For the meaning of "general knowledge", see *Fox v Boulter* [2013] EWHC 1435 (QB) at [16]. In *Lord McAlpine of West Green v Bercow* [2013] EWHC 1342 (QB) there was disagreement as to whether any followers of Ms Bercow would have remembered the claimant as a leading Conservative Party politician so that it would have been necessary to plead and prove that the tweet was read by one of more persons who remembered Lord McAlpine. Tugendhat J. however held that it was not necessary for readers of the tweet to have had any prior knowledge of the claimant as a leading politician of the Thatcher years in order for them reasonably to have linked the tweet naming him with what he had found they knew about the allegations in the "Newsnight" report.

There could hardly be a better illustration of how the most apparently innocuous statement may become arguably defamatory to persons who know further facts than *Wray v University of the West Indies* [2007] UKPC 14. During a period when the defendant employed the plaintiff as a professor he was described in an official publication of the defendant's as a senior lecturer. With some reluctance (the dispute being primarily contractual) the Privy Council was unable to say that this could not possibly be defamatory (because others might think he was calling himself a professor when he was not entitled to do so) and remitted the issue to the Jamaican court. One could conceive circumstances in which a statement that C is a professor when he is in fact a senior lecturer might also support an imputation of false claims on his part.

[248] Per Lord Devlin in *Lewis v Daily Telegraph* [1964] A.C. 234 at 278.

[249] *Cassidy v Daily Mirror* [1929] 2 K.B. 331 CA. A fortiori, a statement about a woman may be defamatory if it suggests an association with a man and she is known to be married to another: *Honeysett v News Chronicle, The Times*, May 14, 1935; *Sydney v McFadden Newspaper*, 242 N.Y. 208 (1926) (statement that claimant "is Fatty Arbuckle's latest lady love" becomes defamatory on proof that claimant is a married woman); or it suggests that she has a child when she is in fact unmarried or was unmarried when it was conceived: *Debenham v Ancorn, The Times*, March 5, 1921; *Morrison v Ritchie* (1902) 4 F. 645 See also *Fullam v Newcastle Chronicle* [1977] 1 W.L.R. 651 CA. Cf. *Crafter v Webster* (1980) 23 S.A.S.R.

[250] *Grubb v Bristol United Press* [1963] 1 Q.B. 309 CA; and see *Burrows v Knighley* (1987) 10 N.S.W.L.R. 651.

were not used in the sense of imputing a felony, then the charge falls to the ground, and no action will lie."[251]

The claimant cannot rely on facts occurring or becoming known after publication to support a legal innuendo, for the cause of action, if any, is complete upon publication. In *Grappelli v Derek Block (Holdings) Ltd*[252] the defendants, managers of the plaintiff, a musician, booked an appearance for him on December 4, without authority and had to cancel it. They issued a false statement, without his knowledge, to the effect that he was ill. The claimant then played another engagement on the same date. The claimant claimed damages on the basis that the statement was to be understood, by way of innuendo, as meaning that he had knowingly given a false reason for cancelling the engagement. It was held that the initially non-defamatory statement[253] could not be converted into a defamatory one by reason of facts later coming into existence.[254]

It need not be shown that any person knowing the extrinsic facts actually understood the words in a defamatory sense.[255]

3.22 Knowledge of extrinsic facts: (1) relied on by claimant. Where extrinsic facts or circumstances are relied on as showing that the words would not be understood in their primary meaning, such facts and circumstances must have been within the knowledge of the persons to whom the words were published, for they could not have been influenced in their understanding by facts or circumstances of which they were unaware.[256]

> "So far as concerns knowledge on the part of the persons to whom the words complained of are published, no difficulty presents itself. If the defamatory meaning only arises from a knowledge of outside facts, and the persons to whom the words

---

[251] Per Parke B. in *Heming v Power* (1842) 10 M. & W. 564 at 569, cited *Gray v Jones* (1939) 55 T.L.R. 436 at 439. See further para.3.23, below.

[252] [1981] 1 W.L.R. 822 CA; *Baltinos v Foreign Language Publications Ltd* (1986) 6 N.S.W.L.R. 85. For difficulties in the case of "serial" publication, see paras 3.33–4. But if D gives X a note defamatory of C in a language X does not understand and X immediately goes home and deciphers it with the aid of a dictionary, there is surely an actionable publication to X? Perhaps D may be taken to have intended and brought about a republication. In *Vermaalk v Van der Merwe*, 1981 (3) S.A. 78 D, in a telephone conversation with X, called P a lesbian. Moments later X asked her husband what this meant and he told her. D was held to have defamed P.

[253] See para.2.36, above.

[254] If the claimant had been able to identify anyone to whom the false statement was published who then knew that at the time there was another engagement on December 4, the case would have been different.

[255] *Hough v London Express* [1940] 2 K.B. 507 CA; *Mark v Deutsch* (1973) 39 D.L.R. (3d) 568. As to whether it is necessary that the defendant knew the extrinsic facts, see para.3.15, above.

[256] *Read v Ambridge* (1834) 6 C. & P. 308; *Hankinson v Bilby* (1847) 16 M. & W. 442; *Martin v Loei* (1861) 2 F. & F. 654; *Capital and Counties Bank v Henty* (1880) 5 C.P.D. 514 at 539–542, per Brett L.J.; *Tolley v Fry* [1930] 1 K.B. 467 at 480 ("some fact known to them"); *Fullam v Newcastle Chronicle* [1977] 1 W.L.R. 651 CA at 655–658; *Lord McAlpine of West Green v Bercow* [2013] EWHC 1342 at [50] (QB); *Baturina v Times Newspapers Ltd* [2011] EWCA Civ 308 CA; [2011] 1 W.L.R. 1526 at [46]–[47]. But cf. the view of Dunn L.J. in *Grappelli v Derek Block (Holdings) Ltd* [1981] 1 W.L.R. 822 at 830.

are published are ignorant of those facts, those persons could not reasonably attach a defamatory meaning to the words."[257]

"If matter which on the face of it is capable of being regarded as defaming a particular person, who is mentioned by name, is proved to have been published to any one whomsoever the tort of libel is committed; but if the matter on the face of it is not capable of being regarded as defamatory or, if defamatory, as defaming a particular person, it cannot be regarded as having been published unless it is proved to have been published to someone possessing knowledge which would suffice to enable him to realise that the matter was defamatory or defamatory of the plaintiff as the case may be."[258]

The claimant who relies on such extrinsic facts need not show that all of the persons to whom the words were published knew the facts, since he will have been defamed to those who do.[259]

(2) Relied on by defendant. Where it is the defendant who relies on extrinsic facts to show that words defamatory in their natural and ordinary meaning did not convey to those to whom they were published a defamatory meaning, he must show that all the persons to whom the words were published knew the facts, since otherwise the claimant will have been defamed to those persons who did not know the facts.[260] And moreover where the defendant, who had imputed theft and robbery to the claimant, urged that he only intended to express exasperation as to the result of a previous dispute, and not to impute a crime, it was held that it was for the defendant to show that the special circumstances were within the knowledge of the persons to whom the words were published, and as there was no proof that all such persons knew the circumstances, the defendant failed.[261]   **3.23**

More than one meaning possible. Putting aside those cases where words innocent on their face have a defamatory meaning when coupled with facts within the knowledge of the persons to whom they are addressed   **3.24**

---

[257] Per Russell L.J. in *Cassidy v Daily Mirror* [1929] 2 K.B. 331 CA at 353. For an example of a case where the pleader was impaled on a logical dilemma, see *Trkulja v Google Inc. Llc* [2010] VSC 226 at [8].

[258] Per Jordan C.J. in *Consolidated Trust v Browne* (1948) 49 S.R. (N.S.W.) 86 at 90–91, collating the authorities. See also *Simons Proprietary v Riddell* [1941] N.Z.L.R. at 925, per Myers C.J.

[259] See *Cassidy v Daily Mirror* [1929] 2 K.B. 331 CA; *Hough v London Express* [1940] 2 K.B. 507 CA; *Cross v Denley* (1952) 52 S.R. (N.S.W.) 112; *Morgan v Odhams Press Ltd* [1971] 1 W.L.R. 1239 HL. In construing the words complained of the court may take into account the likelihood that those who know the extrinsic facts relied on may also know other facts causing them to put an innocent construction on the words: *Solomon v Simmons*, *The Times*, April 10, 1954.

[260] *Chiam See Tong v Xin Zhang Jiang Restaurant* [1995] 3 S.L.R. 196, seems to be an example of this. A photograph of a holder of a high public office in an advertisement might have been taken as indicating that he was "endorsing" the restaurant. The Chinese text made it clear that this was not so. The advertisement was defamatory because non-Chinese speakers would not know this.

[261] *Hankinson v Bilby* (1847) 16 M. & W. 422. And see *Donoghue v Hayes* (1831) Hayes (Ir. Exch) 265 ("every bystander"); *Maybee v Fisk* (1864) 42 Barb. (N.Y.) R. 326.

("innuendo"), language is such an imprecise tool that many statements may carry a range of reasonable meanings.[262] Where the words complained of are ambiguous, that is, reasonably capable of either an innocent or a defamatory meaning, it is a question of fact for the jury to determine in which of the two meanings they are to be understood[263] and the case should not be withdrawn from them, despite occasional statements proposing a more stringent test.[264] Different (but still reasonable) people may understand words in different ways: the issue is whether any of those people could have understood the words in the sense pleaded.[265] Indeed, the contrary view seems to be inconsistent with the generally accepted view of the respective roles of judge and jury.

3.25 Mere conjectures or strained meanings. Although the judge does not have to be satisfied that the defamatory meaning contended for by the claimant is more probable than an alternative, innocent meaning, yet he should "reject those meanings which can only emerge as the product of some

---

[262] See, e.g. para.3.28, below.

[263] For the proposition that as far as the jury is concerned there is a single, "right" meaning, see para.3.15, above. In *Lord McAlpine of West Green v Bercow* [2013] EWHC 1342 (QB) Tugendhat J. stated that:

"If there are two possible meanings, one less derogatory than the other, whether it is the more or the less derogatory meaning that the court should adopt is to be determined by reference to what the hypothetical reasonable reader would understand in all the circumstances. It would be unreasonable for a reader to be avid for scandal, and always to adopt a bad meaning where a non-defamatory meaning was available. But always to adopt the less derogatory meaning would also be unreasonable: it would be naïve" (at [66]).

See also *Horlick v Associated Newspapers Ltd* [2010] EWHC 1544 (QB) in which Eady J. said at [9]:

"It is sometimes said that the reasonable reader does not, and should not, select one bad meaning where other non-defamatory meanings are available. That is not to be confused, on the other hand, with the untenable proposition that the reasonable reader should be taken as always selecting the least defamatory of the available meanings. It is a question of how the particular article, put in its context, strikes the reader. If he or she thinks that the message conveyed by the article is defamatory, and towards the more serious end of the scale, there would be no reason to opt for an alternative possible meaning just because it is less serious."

[264] See para.34.7, below. Surprising to English eyes is the decision of the majority in *Knievel v ESPN* 393 F.3d 1068 (CA9, 2005) that the caption to a photograph of a stunt celebrity, his wife and an unnamed woman, "[Plaintiff] proves that you're never too old to be a pimp" was incapable of being defamatory because "pimp" is in some circles used as meaning "cool" or "sharp dresser". But First Amendment attitudes may stray over into "common law" issues.

[265] *Aspro Travel Ltd v Owners Abroad Group* [1996] 1 W.L.R. 132 CA at 137, per Schiemann L.J., citing *Mitchell v Faber & Faber Ltd* (1994) [1998] E.M.L.R. 807 CA. The fact that A is said to have conferred on B a benefit which was (or is reasonably to be suspected of being) contrary to some rules governing A's behaviour, does not necessarily impute impropriety (or reasonable suspicion of it) to B: *Miller v Associated Newspapers Ltd* [2010] EWHC 700 (QB). It is necessary to focus on the facts of the case.

"Whether a particular article imputes anything to the discredit of a person who receives favours will inevitably depend, not only on the wording of the article in question, but also upon the status of the protagonists relative to one another and the nature of the relationship between them" (at [11]).

strained or forced or utterly unreasonable interpretation"[266] and "it is not enough to say that by some person or another the words *might* be understood in a defamatory sense."[267] Mere conjectures which some person might possibly, though unreasonably, form are not enough to leave the case to the jury.[268] The line between mere conjecture and reasonable inference is not easily drawn[269] and it is not surprising that opinions may differ on particular cases. In *Capital and Counties Bank v Henty*[270] the defendants, a firm of brewers, having had a squabble with the manager of a branch of the plaintiff's bank, sent to the tenants of their public houses (who knew nothing of the squabble) a printed circular containing the following words: "Messrs. Henty & Sons hereby give notice that they will not receive in payment cheques drawn on any of the branches of the Capital and Counties Bank." The circular became known to other persons and there was a run on the bank causing it loss. The bank brought an action for libel, alleging in their innuendo that the circular

---

[266] *Jones v Skelton* [1963] 1 W.L.R. 1362 PC at 1370; *Keays v Rubython* (1996) unreported, CA April 1; *Gillick v Brook Advisory Centres* [2001] EWCA Civ 1263 at [7]; *ICN Photonics Ltd v Patterson* [2003] EWCA Civ 343; *Fox v Boulter* [2013] EWHC 1435 at [14] (QB). "Fanciful, absurd or factitious": *Jeynes v News Magazines Ltd* [2008] EWCA Civ 130 at [20]. "Dressed up" to look worse than it was: *Dorset Flint & Stone Blocks Ltd v Moir* [2004] EWHC 2173 (QB).

[267] *Nevill v Fine Arts Co* [1897] A.C. 68 at 73, per Lord Halsbury. In *Bennison v Hulton, The Times*, April 13, 1926, Scrutton L.J. said that "suspicious people might get a defamatory meaning out of 'chop and tomato sauce'".

[268] See *Capital and Counties Bank v Henty* (1882) 7 A.C. 741 at 744, per Lord Selborne. *Jeynes v News Magazines Ltd*, above. However, if the defendant invites the reader to adopt a suspicious approach, it is reasonable to conclude that the words entitle the reader to indulge in some degree of conjecture or guesswork which would not otherwise be permitted: *Amalgamated Television Services Pty Ltd v Marsden* [1998] 43 N.S.W.L.R. 158 NSWCA.

In *John v Times Newspapers* [2012] EWHC 2751 *The Times* published several articles about tax avoidance in particular in the context of film tax avoidance schemes. The articles named several accountants as being responsible for such schemes including one who was wrongly described as Sir Elton John's former accountant. Sir Elton sued claiming that a reasonable reader might infer from the articles that he was implicated in immoral tax avoidance. *The Times'* application to have the claim struck out succeeded. Any suggestion that the articles could be read as inferring that the claimant was guilty of, or that there were reasonable grounds to suspect him of engaging in, immoral tax avoidance (Chase levels 1 and 2) was far-fetched and lacking in any possible basis (at [30]). As to the argument that the articles were capable of meaning that there were reasonable grounds to investigate whether he had engaged in immoral tax avoidance schemes or was doing so (Chase level 3), the judge accepted that some readers might infer something to the discredit of the claimant to be investigated by reason of his alleged association with the accountant. But he held that "a hypothetical reader of *The Times* who inferred that would be outside any definition of the reasonable reader which a jury could apply without perversity. There is simply nothing to support the inference other than the alleged association" (at [31]).

[269] It is not to be drawn mathematically, i.e. on the basis that the alleged defamatory meaning is outnumbered by possible non-defamatory or less defamatory meanings. Lord Shaw in *Stubbs v Russell* [1913] A.C. 386 did not accept that the statement could be read as imputing insolvency (which was what the pursuer claimed) but would have been prepared to accept that it could carry the lesser, though still damaging, meaning that he was a person given to failing to pay his debts on time and would have let that go to the jury although there were three other possible non-defamatory meanings. However, in *Mapp v News Group Newspapers* [1998] Q.B. 520 CA, Hirst L.J. referred with approval to Lord Blackburn's statement in *Henty*'s case at 786 that if there were a number of possible meanings it was not reasonable to pick only on the one most defamatory of the plaintiff.

[270] (1882) 7 A.C. 741 HL.

imputed insolvency to them. It was held by the House of Lords (Lord Penzance dissenting) that in their natural meaning the words were not libellous, that the inference suggested by the innuendo was not the inference which reasonable persons would draw, and that as the evidence failed to show that the circular had a libellous tendency there was no case to go to the jury, and that the defendants were entitled to judgment. Passages in the speeches can be read as requiring that the defamatory inference must be a "natural and necessary" one or more likely than innocent meanings[271] but that would be inconsistent with many other statements.[272] Indeed it would be inconsistent with the fundamental rule that the issue for the judge is whether the words are *capable* of a defamatory meaning.[273]

Commenting on this case, Salmon L.J. in *Slim v Daily Telegraph*[274] said that on the question of what words are capable of meaning to the ordinary layman,

"the principles were never better formulated than they were in *Capital and Counties Bank v Henty* nor perhaps ever worse applied. It was there held that the words complained of were incapable of meaning to ordinary men that the bank was in financial difficulties, yet they caused a run on the bank, whose customers, presumably, were ordinary men."[275]

A somewhat more liberal interpretation has in some cases been put on the return of cheques marked "R/D".[276]

The issue of course depends on the words and the context in each case but three further cases illustrate the difficulty of drawing the line. In *Clarke (t/a Elumina Iberica UK) v Bain*[277] it was held that an allegation of breach of a commercial contract could not, without more, impute dishonesty.

"Breaches of a distribution agreement and non-payment of goods sold and delivered can in principle be accompanied by dishonesty, but that is neither necessary nor common. Other explanations are much more likely. Only a person who was unduly suspicious and determined to select a bad meaning where a lesser meaning was available could understand that an allegation of dishonesty was being made."[278]

In *Nevill v Fine Art Insurance Co.*[279] the defendants sent out a circular saying that the agency of the plaintiff "had been closed by the Directors" when in

---

[271] See, e.g. Lord Watson at 788 and Lord Bramwell at 792. For a similarly strict approach, see *McCann v Shell Oil*, 551 A.2d 696 (R.I., 1988) (words "pre-cancellation notice" on outside of envelope identifying P as credit card holder not capable of imputing default or insolvency).

[272] E.g. Scrutton L.J. in *Cassidy v Daily Mirror* [1929] K.B. 331 at 339; Lord Porter in *Turner v MGM Pictures* [1950] 1 All E.R. 449 at 454.

[273] Although not precisely the same point, it is not uncommon for juries to be left the question whether words admittedly defamatory impute guilt or suspicion of guilt: para.3.27, below.

[274] [1968] 2 Q.B. 157 at 187.

[275] Certainly the pleaded meaning in *Henty* comes nowhere near the level of artificiality of that in, for example, *Jeynes v News Magazines Ltd* [2008] EWCA Civ 130.

[276] See para.2.25, above. See also para.2.24, above.

[277] [2008] EWHC 2636 (QB).

[278] Ibid. at [12].

[279] [1897] A.C. 68.

fact the plaintiff had resigned. It was held that the circular was incapable of having any defamatory meaning. But in *Morris v Sanders Universal Products*[280] the defendants in very similar circumstances issued a circular to the effect that the plaintiff, a representative, had been "dismissed" and this was held capable of the defamatory meaning that the plaintiff had been guilty of misconduct, even though literally it was compatible with dismissal on notice without cause.[281]

The ordinary person: temperament. The "ordinary reader" or "ordi-   **3.26**
nary viewer" or "ordinary listener" against whom the court[282] is to judge

---

[280] [1954] 1 W.L.R. 67 CA (not followed on another point in *Keays v Murdoch Magazines* [1991] 1 W.L.R. 1184 CA).

[281] Quaere whether the existence of unfair dismissal protection legislation strengthens the inference of misconduct which would arise from such a statement. The nature of the job may be relevant. To say that a football manager had been sacked might impute no more than lack of success; but to say that a schoolteacher had been sacked might more easily be taken to impute incompetence or misconduct.

[282] In deciding what impression the material complained of would have been likely to have on the hypothetical reasonable viewer the court are entitled (if not bound) to have regard to the impression it made on them: *Gillick v BBC* [1996] E.M.L.R. 267 CA at 273. And see para.3.14, above. The invocation of the ordinary reader has been criticised. See the remarks of Kirby J. in *Favell v Queensland Newspapers Pty Ltd* [2005] HCA 52; 221 A.L.R. 186 at [23]–[24]:

> "In the conventional way, their Honours have invoked the fiction of the 'ordinary reasonable reader' to reinforce the conclusion which they have reached. The resort to this fiction has led appellate courts to define, and refine, the 'ordinary reader' whom the judges have in mind. This has led, in turn, to almost ludicrous elaborations concerned with where the notional 'reasonable, ordinary reader' lives (it is not in an ivory tower) and how he (only recently has a female reader been postulated) will approach the hypothetical task. Older formulae have it that the reader is 'the ordinary good and worthy subject of the King'. Others, more recent, emphasise the ordinariness of the reader or a capacity for what is called 'right-thinking' (whatever that may be). The reader (or listener or viewer) is a person of fair, average intelligence, who is neither perverse, nor morbid or suspicious of mind. However, the 'ordinary reasonable reader' is a layman, not a lawyer, with a capacity for implication that is much greater than that of a lawyer. United States authority conceives of the reader as a disembodied member of the 'respectable' community generally, as distinct from a member of any sub-group. The list is nearly endless.
>
> [24] It would be preferable to drop this fiction altogether. Judges should not hide behind their pretended reliance on the fictitious reasonable recipient of the alleged defamatory material, attributing to such a person the outcome that the judges actually determine for themselves. Appellate judges and judges in the practice list working under their supervision, should acknowledge candidly the reserve function that judges perform in our legal system in rejecting pleaded imputations that are not reasonably arguable by reference to the matter complained of. If the third party fiction were dropped, it is likely that a new formulation would emerge to explain more precisely and accurately the considerations according to which one imputation is accepted and goes to the tribunal of fact for its decision, and why another is not, so that that tribunal is spared the necessity of considering it. Or why one imputation is held defamatory and another is not."

However, while one understands the irritation that can be produced by the various forms of elaboration of the characteristics of the hypothetical reader (cf. Sir Alan Herbert on the reasonable man of negligence law in *Fardell v Potts* (*Uncommon Law*)) it is not apparent what, given the potentially infinite variety of words sued upon, the replacement formulation might be or how the considerations would emerge more clearly. Certainly the judge is exercising a "reserve function" in excluding unacceptably wide meanings; equally certainly he has to proceed largely on the basis of his own experience and intuition on what the audience will read into the words and what, in view of the need for freedom of communication, it may *legitimately* read into them. It may even

whether the words have the meaning contended for is something of an abstraction,[283] for among the actual audience of a defamatory publication there will plainly be a very great variation in the way the words are understood, but there is only one standard recognised by the law.[284] It therefore follows that in the case of a publication in the mass media the claimant may fail even though there is no doubt that as a matter of fact some of the audience (perhaps even a considerable proportion of the audience) will have understood the publication in a defamatory sense.[285] Nevertheless the "ordinary reader" is perhaps a little closer to reality than the "reasonable man"[286] of the law of negligence, for the courts are ready to recognise his weaknesses up to a point.[287] He is a sort of half-way house between the unusually suspicious and the unusually naive.[288] He is essentially fair-minded and reasonable[289] but he may be guilty of a certain amount of loose thinking[290] and does not read a sensational article with cautious and critical care.[291] The court must be alive to the broad impression created by the publication,[292] rather than indulge in

---

be that in the typical case no real reasons could be expressed for what is simply a conclusion, "It does not seem reasonable to me to understand the words in this way". But while it may be the tradition of the Cour de cassation to pronounce so baldly, it is not ours.

[283] The implication in *Jeynes v News Magazines Ltd* [2008] EWCA Civ 130 at [20] seems to be that the court should not adjust its criteria according to the nature of the material and the likely audience ("matters of demotic literature and popular culture" not especially a jury issue). Some differences may however exist between the ordinary "viewer" and the ordinary "reader". The former, "even when watching Sky News, which tends to repeat its news items in the course of a day" will only see the material once. While an ordinary reasonable reader is highly unlikely to read the material more than once, or stop and consider the meaning of particular phrases or passages, or compare different passages, he may nevertheless "flick back" through the article in the course of reading it: *Fox v Boulter* [2013] EWHC 1435 (QB) at [15].

[284] See *Charleston v News Group Newspapers Ltd* [1995] 2 A.C. 65 at 73, per Lord Nicholls. See para.3.16, above.

[285] *Charleston v News Group Newspapers Ltd* [1995] 2 A.C. 65.

[286] But "reasonable man" is sometimes used to describe the "ordinary reader": *Duncan v Associated Scottish Newspapers*, 1929 S.C. 14 at 20. Other expressions are persons "of common and reasonable understanding" (Pollock C.B. in *Hankinson v Bilby* (1847) 16 M. & W. 442 at 445); the "average reader" (Lord Morris in *Morgan v Odhams Press Ltd* [1971] 1 W.L.R. 1239 HL at 1254).

[287] *Independent Newspapers Holdings Ltd v Suliman* [2004] ZASCA 57 at [19]–[20] per Marais J.A. He is of course a device to control liability and strike a balance between free speech and reputation: *Oduro v Time-Life Entertainment Group Ltd* [2003] EWHC 1787 (QB) at [10]. The former *mitiori sensu* rule (see para.3.16, above) arose from a desire to restrict liability for defamation.

[288] See *Lewis v Daily Telegraph* [1964] A.C. 234 at 259, 286, per Lord Reid and Lord Devlin; *Skuse v Granada Television Ltd* [1996] E.M.L.R. 278 CA; *Gillick v BBC* [1996] E.M.L.R. 267 CA.

[289] *Charleston v News Group Newspapers Ltd* [1995] 2 A.C. 65 at 71. Not a person of "morbid or suspicious mind": *Byrnes v John Fairfax Publications Pty Ltd* [2004] N.S.W.S.C. 635 at [11], citing Lord O'Brien C.J. in *Keogh v The Incorporated Dental Hospital of Ireland* [1910] 2 I.R. 577 at 586.

[290] *Morgan v Odhams Press Ltd* [1971] 1 W.L.R. 1239 HL at 1245, per Lord Reid. For an expectation of greater care by those to whom matter is published, see *Coulson v Rapport Uitgewers* 1979 (3) S.A. 286 AD.

[291] *Morgan v Odhams Press Ltd*, at 1254, per Lord Morris.

[292] *Hayward v Thompson* [1982] Q.B. 47 CA; *Gorton v ABC* (1973) 22 F.L.R. 181 (impression of TV broadcast); *Hewitt v WA Newspapers* (1976) 27 F.L.R. 231; *Morosi v Mirror Newspapers*

meticulous analysis of what will have been read quite quickly by the public[293] and a first impression may be lasting.[294] That the material being read is archive material does not mean that the reasonable reader will just treat it as historical and relating only to the original time of publication. Depending on the nature of the archive, the reasonable reader may treat it as speaking as at the date on which it is being read.[295] Moreover the characteristics of the publication itself need to be borne in mind, since the hypothetical reasonable reader is taken to be representative of those who read that publication.[296] The ordinary reader does not construe words as would a lawyer,[297] for he is not inhibited by the rules of construction[298] or of evidence[299] and his capacity for implication or drawing inferences is greater than the lawyer's.[300] "The law-yer's rule is that the implication must be necessary as well as reasonable. The layman reads in an implication much more freely, and unfortunately, as the law of defamation has to take into account, is especially prone to do so when it is derogatory."[301] One should not attribute to him charitable

---

[1977] 2 N.S.W.L.R. 749 at 770; *Mirror Newspapers v World Hosts* (1979) 53 A.L.J.R. 243 HCA at 246, 248; *Parker v John Fairfax* [1980] A.C.L.D. 558 NSWCA (broad effect of television broadcast).

[293] *Slim v Daily Telegraph Ltd* [1968] 2 Q.B. 157 CA at 171; *Keays v Rubython*, April 1, 1996, CA; *Gillick v BBC* [1996] E.M.L.R. 267 CA at 273. But the defendant is entitled to have the article read as a whole, whatever some readers may do: see para.3.31, below.

[294] *Suid-Afrikaanse Uitsaaikorporasie v O'Malley* 1977 (3) S.A. 394 AD at 408; *Hayward v Thompson* [1982] Q.B. 47 CA; *England v CBC* [1979] 3 W.W.R. 193.

[295] *Flood v Times Newspapers* [2013] EWHC 2182 (QB) at [19]. It follows from the passage in the main text that what is read may not bear the same meaning to a reasonable reader who reads it at the original date of publication as it does to the reasonable reader who only reads it for the first time at a later date: "But it must be read on both dates as saying something about the position current as at the date of reading" (at [19]).

[296] *McGrath v Dawkins* [2012] EWHC B3 (QB) at [51]. Readers of *The Times* newspaper were assumed to be amongst the more highly educated and better informed members of the public in *John v Times Newspapers* [2012] EWHC 2751 (QB) at [19]. It has also been suggested that ordinary citizens are now perceived by the courts, both domestic and international, as having more discriminating judgment than was traditionally recognised: *John* at [19]; *Lukowiak v Unidad Editorial SA (No.1)* [2001] E.M.L.R. 46 (QB) at [47]; *Lennon v Scottish Daily Record & Sunday Mail Ltd* [2004] E.M.L.R. 18 (QB) at [18].

[297] In *Waterson v Lloyd* [2013] EWCA Civ 136; [2013] E.M.L.R. 17, McCombe L.J. allowed an appeal against a decision of Tugendhat J. on meaning on the basis that the analysis that the judge had adopted was over-elaborate and utilised "the technique of the lawyer, rather than that of the layman" (at [53]).

[298] *Lewis v Daily Telegraph* [1964] A.C. 234 at 258. See *Winyard v Tatler Publishing Co. Ltd*, *Independent*, August 16, 1991, CA ("personal massage services" connoted sexual services —claim of male claimant).

[299] *Bargold v Mirror Newspapers* [1981] 1 N.S.W.L.R. 9. Hence he may infer from statements that the claimant has misbehaved on previous occasions that he has also done so on the occasion to which the defendant refers.

[300] *Gillick v BBC* [1996] E.M.L.R. 267 CA at 273; *John Fairfax Publications Pty Ltd v Rivkin* [2003] HCA 50; 201 A.L.R. 77 at [23]–[26]; *Somosi v John Fairfax Publications Pty Ltd* [2004] NSWCA 176.

[301] *Lewis v Daily Telegraph* [1964] A.C. 234 at 277, per Lord Devlin; *Hartt v Newspaper Publishing*, *Independent*, October 27, 1989, CA; *Gillick v BBC* [1996] E.M.L.R. 267 CA; *John Fairfax v Hook* (1983) 72 F.L.R. 190 Fed Ct of Australia. However, in *Armstrong v Times Newspapers Ltd* [2005] EWHC 2816 (QB) (where the issue was whether there should be a jury) at [31] Eady J. commented as follows on the words of Lord Devlin quoted above:

decency[302] but neither is he avid for scandal.[303]

3.27 **The ordinary person: knowledge.** Where the words are not defamatory in their natural and ordinary meaning but depend for a defamatory sense upon knowledge of extrinsic facts[304] the claimant must rely on an innuendo and show that the words were published to persons who had such knowledge.[305] But the ordinary person does not live in an ivory tower[306] and will be assumed

---

"Nevertheless, it is necessary to read these words, 40 years on, with some careful reservation. They might, nowadays, be thought to be somewhat patronising to the hypothetical juror—in a way that is rather contrary to the modern approach. Secondly, even if his Lordship's observations are still valid, I can hardly think that it would be to the Defendants' advantage in this case to have a tribunal of fact which was especially susceptible to 'reading in an implication'. A readiness to take 'a nudge and a wink' would surely work to their disadvantage."

[302] *Newstead v London Express* [1940] 1 K.B. 377 CA at 390, per Mackinnon L.J.

[303] *Hartt v Newspaper Publishing, Independent*, October 27, 1989, CA; *Gillick v BBC* [1996] E.M.L.R. 267 CA. That some people will always be willing to take humorous or satirical material seriously is shown by the real life examples in *New Times Inc. v Isaacks* 146 S.W.3d 144 (Tex. 2004) at 158, fn.7 (cert. den. June 6, 2005).

[304] It is sometimes said that an innuendo is required where the words are in a foreign language but it is submitted that this is an over-simplification. Such cases are certainly akin to cases calling for an innuendo in that there is only an actionable publication to persons who understand the language. Furthermore, the meaning which the words would bear in ordinary English may have to be established by testimony (for an ancient example see *Anon.* (1616) Hob. 126, where the Exchequer "took information by Welshmen"). However, once the "standard" meaning has been established it is submitted that (in contrast with the situation where extrinsic facts are relied on) evidence is not admissible of what meanings were in fact conveyed by the words: see para.32.25, below. Thus if a newspaper were published in England in the Serbo-Croat language and contained an article accusing C of fraud, it is submitted that the position is as follows. (1) The requirement that the words should have been published to someone understanding the language is satisfied by proof that copies of the newspaper were sold since it can be inferred that it was bought by Serbo-Croat speakers. (2) The ordinary meaning of the words complained of will have to be established by agreement or by testimony. (3) Once that is done, no further evidence is admissible as to the meaning of the words or the sense in which they were understood, just as such evidence would not be admissible if the words had been published in English: see para.34.25, below. (4) The claimant may, of course, plead an innuendo if he complains of a defamatory meaning in the foreign language which depends upon extrinsic facts known to the readers. In principle, it is difficult to see why words in a local dialect, slang which has not passed into common currency, or words of a scientific or technical nature should be treated differently, since each is in effect a "language" which is not known to the ordinary reader. Even in the case of scientific or technical language it may be easy to infer that they were published to persons who understood them, as where they are published in a professional journal. Where the publication is to a limited class of specialists then, even though the case may not call for an innuendo, the test would seem to be what the words would convey to a reasonable member of that class: *Switzerland Australia Health Fund v Shaw* (1988) 81 A.L.R. 111 Fed Ct of Australia at 119; *FAI General Insurance v RAIA Insurance Brokers* (1992) 108 A.L.R. 479 Fed Ct of Australia. For multi-lingual societies, see *Lok Kwai-Fu v Chan* [1978] Hong Kong L.R. 225; *Chiam See Tong v Xian Zhang Jiang Restaurant* [1995] 3 S.L.R. 196.

[305] See para.3.20, above.

[306] *Lewis v Daily Telegraph* [1964] A.C. 234 at 258, per Lord Reid; *Farquhar v Bottom* [1980] 2 N.S.W.L.R. 380 at 385–386; *Bargold v Mirror Newspapers* [1981] 1 N.S.W.L.R. 9. In *Oriental Daily Publisher Ltd v Ming Pao Holdings Ltd* [2012] HKCFA 59; [2013] E.M.L.R. 7 the Hong Kong Court of Final Appeal held that the reasonable reader recognises on the basis of their general knowledge that some speakers are more credible than others.

to be possessed of general[307] knowledge[308] (which may of course vary from one jurisdiction to another[309]) and ordinary knowledge and experience of worldly affairs.[310] He will also be taken to know the meaning of slang expressions,[311] of allusive terms,[312] and, no doubt of catchphrases and adver-

---

[307] Although the ordinary person is aware of the presumption of innocence (see para.3.28, below) he does not have a "working knowledge of the criminal law": *Channel 7 Sydney Pty Ltd v Parras* [2002] NSWCA 202. The ordinary reader of a specialist political blog is a person with some interest and knowledge of public affairs but is not a lawyer: *Thompson v James* [2013] EWHC 515 at [291] (QB). In *Lord McAlpine of West Green v Bercow* [2013] EWHC 1342 (QB) at [81] Tugendhat J. held that the reasonable reader of Ms Bercow's tweets was someone who shared her interest in politics and current affairs (and who therefore probably knew of certain elements in the "Newsnight" story, in particular that M had been abused at a children's home in Wales by a man he identified as a leading Conservative politician and that the BBC's decision not to name him was the subject of controversy). Occasionally courts recognise that it might be difficult to place themselves in the shoes of a reasonable reader—"reasonable reader who is a member of the Palmer's Green Mosque": *Auladin v Shaikh* [2013] EWHC 157 (QB). Perhaps somewhat surprisingly, knowledge of Baader Meinhof's involvement in political extremism was said to be part of the general knowledge of reasonable readers in *Kaschke v Gray* [2010] EWHC 1907 (QB) at [51].

[308] *Jones v Skelton* [1963] 1 W.L.R. 1362 PC at 1371. Sometimes this is put in terms of the knowledge which the *jury* may apply in determining the meaning of the words but this is only another way of stating the sense which the ordinary reader might give to them.

[309] *Hasnul bin Abdul Hadi v Bulat bin Mohamed* [1978] 1 M.L.J. at 76 (ordinary man's general knowledge of the Islamic religion and experience of worldly affairs). In *National Glass Auto Supplies (Australia) Pty Ltd v Nielsen and Moller Autoglass (NSW) Pty Ltd* [2006] FCA 1386, a claim in Australia arising from publication of an email in China, it is said at [26] that "the hypothetical ordinary reasonable reader, who must be assumed to be without any special knowledge, is also taken to be a person in no particular geographical location for the purpose of deciding whether the [matter] was capable of giving rise to defamatory imputations." Sed quaere, this seems to be taking the abstraction very far. However, nowadays what might be technical publications are liable to run foul of the principle of abuse of process.

[310] *Lewis v Daily Telegraph* [1964] A.C. 234 at 258. Thus the ordinary reader will be aware that reputable advertisers do not use the name or likeness of well-known people without their consent and may therefore conclude from their use that the consent has been given: *Tolley v Fry* [1931] A.C. 333; *Dockrell v Dougall* (1899) 80 L.T. 558; see also *Bowles v Truth (NZ) Ltd* [1965] N.Z.L.R. 768 at 772–773 (knowledge that counsel do not ask questions without foundation). It has been suggested that the ordinary reader must now be credited with having achieved a level of education which was not widely accessible to earlier generations: *Lennon v Scottish Daily Record and Sunday Mail Ltd* [2004] EWHC 359 (QB); [2004] E.M.L.R. 18. See further para.30.5, below. It seems that in Canada in 2006 the ordinary reader is to be taken to have some acquaintance with the Harry Potter books; *Lysko v Braley* (2006) 79 O.R. (3d) 721 at [109] (Ont. CA).

[311] In *Winyard v Tatler Publishing Co. Ltd, Independent*, August 16, 1991, CA, the expression "boot" was regarded as meaning "ugly old harridan" in its ordinary meaning, but a further sense of "promiscuous person" (given only in a specialist dictionary of slang) was pleaded as an innuendo. See also *Haarup v Hulton Press Ltd* (1943) 169 L.T. 309 CA ("pansy"); *Fields v Davis, The Times*, April 18, 1953 ("tramp"); *Boaks v South London Press, The Times*, October 27, 1967 ("nutty"); *Currie v Stairs* (1885) 25 N.B.R. 4; *Major v McGregor* (1903) 6 O.L.R. 528; *French v Smith* [1923] 3 D.L.R. 902; *Doyle v IAM Local 1681* (1991) 110 A.R. 222 ("scab").

[312] "We ought to attribute to the jury and court a knowledge of such terms, whether they be allegorical, historical, or fabulous. If such terms, whether historical, fabulous, or allegorical, have passed so much into common use as to have obtained a fixed meaning to persons of ordinary knowledge, then we should take notice that such is their meaning": per Coleridge J. in *Hoare v Silverlock* (1848) 17 L.J.Q.B. 306 at 309. The phraseology is antique but the proposition remains valid.

tising slogans in common, current[313] use.

3.28 "Levels" of defamatory meanings. A defamatory statement may impute discreditable behaviour to the claimant, for example involvement in crime, but it may be a matter of dispute what level of involvement the statement imputes. The issue is obviously relevant on damages, for "a man's reputation can suffer if it can truly be said of him that although innocent he behaved in a suspicious way; but it will suffer much more if it is said that he is not innocent"[314] but it most often arises at an interlocutory stage in relation to a defendant's plea of justification. If the statement means that the claimant is guilty of a crime that can only be justified by proving that he is[315] (even if the defendant is merely repeating what someone else has said[316]) and the defendant cannot adduce evidence tending merely to show that he was suspected of crime. But if the words are reasonably capable of bearing the meaning that the claimant is under suspicion, the defendant can justify that meaning because he is not confined to justifying the meaning the claimant has pleaded.[317] A statement that the claimant is under suspicion or investigation cannot reasonably be understood as stating that he is guilty,[318] for if the ordinary sensible person was "capable of thinking that wherever there was a police inquiry there was guilt, it would be almost impossible to give accurate information about

---

[313] See para.3.29, below.

[314] *Lewis v Daily Telegraph* [1964] A.C. 234 at 284.

[315] A statement which directly says that the claimant has committed a crime must be justified in that sense even if it is accompanied by a statement that inquiries into the case are in progress: *Ford v John Fairfax & Sons Ltd*, February 27, 1997, N.S.W.S.C.; *Singleton v Hudson* [1998] W.A.R. 191; *Shave v Western Australian Newspapers* [2000] WASC 172.

[316] See para.11.13, below. Perhaps this is a case where we have to depart from the proposition that words are to be interpreted according to their ordinary meaning. To a layman the statement by D "A says C killed B" is exactly that but in law, for reasons of policy, it has equivalent effect to a statement by D that "C killed B": *Hamilton v Clifford* [2004] EWHC 1542 (QB) at [33].

[317] See para.27.8, below. The
"rationale for introducing the graduated levels of meaning . . . is that precision is required of a defendant as to the level at which he is pitching his plea of justification. One reason for this is that the level of meaning sought to be justified will determine the nature of the evidence which is admissible in support of the plea of justification pursuant to the so-called 'conduct' and 'repetition' rules. . . . [T]his reasoning does not apply to the pleading by the Claimant of the defamatory meaning which he contends the words complained of bear. The degree of precision will no doubt depend on the circumstances of the case. It is not necessary in any case to tie a claimant to one or other of the three levels of defamatory meaning":
Jameel v Times Newspapers Ltd [2004] EWCA Civ 983; [2004] E.M.L.R. 31 at [17] per Sedley L.J.

[318] However, in every case the statement has to be examined in its context, which may lead to the conclusion that guilt is implied from a statement of suspicion: "Loose talk about suspicions can very easily convey the impression that it is a suspicion that is well-founded": Lord Devlin in *Lewis v Daily Telegraph* [1964] A.C. 234 at 285. "Likewise, repetitive and loose talk about 'questions' can convey the impression that there are reasonable grounds to suspect": Eady J. in *Armstrong v Times Newspapers* [2004] EWHC 2928 (QB) at [22]. See also the analysis by Glass J.A. in *Sargi v Australian Broadcasting Commission* [1983] 2 N.S.W.L.R. 669 NSWCA; and see *Kelson v David Syme & Co. Ltd* [1998] SCACT 60 (sudden retirement during investigation). See also *Marke v Ewart* [2009] VSC 544 (publication went further than simply reporting that plaintiff under investigation).

anything".[319] In *Lewis v Daily Telegraph* the defendants had each published statements to the effect that the City of London Fraud Squad were inquiring[320] into the affairs of the R Co, and that L was the chairman of the company. L and R Co brought actions alleging that the statements meant and were understood to mean that L and the company were guilty of, or were suspected by the police to be guilty of, fraud. They did not rely on any extrinsic facts passing beyond general knowledge. It was held by the House of Lords (Lord Morris dissenting) that the words complained of were not capable of meaning that the plaintiffs were guilty of fraud, for a person would not, unless he were unduly suspicious or unfair in his approach, draw that conclusion.[321] In *Flood v Times Newspapers Ltd*[322] the defendant published, in 2006, an article in their newspaper and subsequently on their website entitled "Detective accused of Taking Bribes from Russian Exiles". Proceedings were issued and the defendant pleaded justification and *Reynolds* privilege. In 2007, the Metropolitan Police concluded an investigation into the claimant finding no evidence that he was guilty of the conduct alleged by the article. The defendant was notified of this in September 2007. A "qualification" was added to the website that stated, "this article is subject to legal complaint". *Reynolds* privilege was tried as a preliminary issue and after appeals to the Court of Appeal and Supreme Court, it was held that publication up to September 2007 was privileged. The claimant's claim was therefore confined to publications between September 2007 and 2009 when the article was taken down. The claimant argued that the article meant that there were at the date of publication, and remained, strong

---

[319] *Lewis v Daily Telegraph* [1964] A.C. 234 at 286, per Lord Devlin. In *Peregrine Investment Holdings Ltd v The Associated Press* [1997] H.K.L.R.D. 1073, a press release alleging that a securities business had become the repository of illicit funds was held not capable of carrying the imputation that the business knew or had reason to know of their source.

[320] "There would be nothing libellous in saying that an inquiry into [the company's] affairs was proceeding: the inquiry might be by a statistician or other expert. The sting is in inferences drawn from the fact that it is the fraud squad which is making the inquiry": per Lord Reid, ibid. at 258.

[321] [1964] A.C. 234.
   "It may be defamatory to say that someone is suspected of an offence, but it does not carry with it that that person has committed the offence, for this must surely offend against the ideas of justice which reasonable persons are supposed to entertain. If one repeats a rumour one adds one's own authority to it and implies that it is well founded, that is to say that it is true. It is otherwise when one says or implies that a person is under suspicion of guilt. That does not imply that he is in fact guilty, but only that there are reasonable grounds for suspicion, which is a different matter":
at 274–275, per Lord Hodson. See also In *Mirror Newspapers Ltd v Harrison* (1982) 42 A.L.R. 487 HCA; *Ainsworth Nominees v Hanrahan* [1982] 2 N.S.W.L.R. 823; *Sargi v Australian Broadcasting Commission* [1983] 2 N.S.W.L.R. 669 NSWCA; *Whelan v John Fairfax & Sons Ltd* (1988) 12 N.S.W.L.R. 148; *Gummina v Williams (No.2)* (1990) 3 W.A.R. 35. The ordinary person should have in mind the presumption of innocence in criminal proceedings: see *Lewis* at 274–275 and *Lang v Australian Consolidated Press Ltd* [1970] 2 N.S.W.L.R. 408 at 416. But the law is the same in respect of an allegation made, but not yet determined, in civil proceedings: *Ross McConnel Kitchen & Co. Pty Ltd v John Fairfax & Sons Ltd* [1980] 2 N.S.W.L.R. 845. It has been said that "guilt by association" is part of the ordinary reader's perception of things: *Baffsky v John Fairfax & Sons Ltd* (1991) 106 F.L.R. 21 at 32.

[322] [2013] EWHC 2182 (QB).

grounds to believe, or alternatively reasonable grounds to suspect, that the claimant had abused his position as a police officer by corruptly accepting bribes from Russian criminals in return for information and he had thereby committed a very serious criminal offence. The allegation of commission of a serious criminal offence was an innuendo meaning and the claimant pleaded in support of it that where a person who is employed to perform a public duty takes a bribe he is guilty of a criminal offence under the common law. The defendant sought to justify a meaning that the claimant was the subject of an internal investigation and there were grounds that objectively justified such an investigation.

Tugendhat J. held that the actual meaning was the more serious one. Anyone reading the archive would have known that where a person employed to perform a public duty takes a bribe to act corruptly that he commits a criminal offence. Though the article may be read as alleging actual guilt, read as a whole it was clear that it was about an investigation and not just about the making of allegations. As was said in *Lewis*, a statement that a claimant is under investigation cannot reasonably be understood as stating that he is guilty because if that were so it would be almost impossible to get accurate information about anything.[323] Further, because readers of an archive do not just regard it as an historical document, but as also speaking at the date on which it is being read, the addition of the warning in this case did not improve things from the claimant's point of view as it did not indicate where the complaint came from or what it was about and it led to the inference that any more recent information would have been added to the article.

It is usually said that there are two levels of imputation below that of guilt ("Level 1") which are possible in such a situation,[324] both of which are defamatory,[325] though in different degrees: that there are reasonable grounds to suspect that the claimant is involved ("Level 2") or that there are grounds to investigate what the claimant has done ("Level 3").[326] In *Lewis* it was admitted that the words were defamatory in the last sense (or something like

---

[323] Ibid. at [23].

[324] *Chase v News Group Newspapers Ltd* [2002] EWCA Civ 1772; [2003] E.M.L.R. 11; *Musa King v Telegraph Group Ltd* [2004] EWCA Civ 613; [2004] E.M.L.R. 23.

[325] But in the case of slander there must be an imputation of the commission of a crime to render the slander actionable per se and an imputation of suspicion will not do: see para.4.9, below.

[326] The
"harsh reality of the situation is that even mere suspicion, to put it at its lowest, raises doubts in the mind of those to whom it is communicated as to whether the hitherto unsullied reputation which the person enjoyed continues to be deserved or whether it should now be regarded as undeserved. To say that which imperils the continued existence of a person's good reputation and causes people generally to doubt the integrity of that person even though they may not be certain the doubt is justified, is to adversely affect to at least some degree his or her reputation. That the doubt may be temporary and ultimately transient because of the subsequently established innocence of the person concerned cannot cure the loss of esteem which that person endures pending the establishment of his or her innocence":
Independent Newspapers Holdings Ltd v Suliman [2004] ZASCA 57 at [24] and [32], per Marais J.A.

it)[327] but the defendants could justify that by showing that the investigation was taking place.[328]

The line between Level 2 and Level 3 meanings can be somewhat blurred[329] and the judge is not required to place the imputation exactly in one of the three "pigeon holes"[330] but it is nevertheless a useful practical classification.[331] Nor is it necessary to say that the imputation must be placed at *only* one level, for the question is not what the words mean but what they are capable of meaning, so that, for example, the jury may be left with Level 2 or Level 3 as alternative meanings.[332] However, the greater does not include the lesser for this purpose and a defendant will not be allowed to advance a case of justification on the basis of a meaning less serious than the words can legitimately bear. Where the defendant has made a direct charge of wrongdoing he must justify that and the court will not allow him to put forward the meaning that there are reasonable grounds for suspicion.[333] Suspicion of guilt is not a separate or distinct charge when guilt has been directly imputed. Such

---

[327] It is arguable that there is a fourth level, viz. the mere statement that the claimant *is* being investigated. This may have been the view of Lord Devlin in *Lewis* at 285–286, who considered that in principle it was defamatory to state that a person had been charged with a crime and acquitted of it. In practice a statement that C is under investigation will almost always justify the inference that the police have some basis for suspicion, though there are some situations where an investigation might be automatic (e.g. where a person is killed by police firearms). In any event, Lord Devlin was "focusing on the particular facts of the case before him—where it so happened that an inquiry had been under way at the time of publication": *Armstrong v Times Newspapers Ltd* [2004] EWHC 2928 (QB) at [9]. See also *Sargi v Australian Broadcasting Commission* [1983] 2 N.S.W.L.R. 669 NSWCA. See *Cadam v Beaverbrook Newspapers* [1959] 1 Q.B. 413 CA (report of issue of writ for conspiracy to defraud; plea by way of justification that such a writ had been issued not struck out): see para.11.13, below.

[328] See also, *Desmond v Foreman* [2012] EWHC 1900 (QB) (words not capable of meaning that claimant was guilty of assault or attempted rape but were capable of bearing level 2 and 3 meanings); *Horlick v Associated Newspapers* [2010] EWHC 1544 (QB) (article raising, inter alia, questions about claimant's due diligence before investing in Madoff Ponzi scheme. Eady J. held allegations were at level 3 and not, as claimant had argued, level 1).

[329] *Jameel v Wall Street Journal Europe SPRL* [2003] EWCA Civ 1694; [2004] E.M.L.R. 6 at [19]. In *Charman v Orion Publishing Group Ltd* [2005] EWHC 2187 (QB) (on appeal on other issues, [2007] EWCA Civ 972; [2008] 1 All E.R. 750) Gray J. was of the view that on close analysis there may be more than three levels of meaning in such cases: the material, although not imputing guilt, showed "cogent" rather than merely reasonable grounds for suspicion. And he thought that the

"ordinary reasonable reader would not use legalistic concepts such as the existence of 'reasonable grounds for suspicion' when articulating his or her impression of the meaning conveyed by the words complained of. There is in my opinion much to be said for the use of vernacular expressions such as 'probably guilty' or 'a bit suspicious' to indicate the shade of meaning to be contended for at trial."

[330] *Curistan v Times Newspapers Ltd* [2007] EWHC 926 (QB) at [10] (reversed on the facts, [2008] EWCA Civ 432; [2009] Q.B. 231); *Fallon v MGN Ltd* [2006] EWHC 783 (QB); [2006] E.M.L.R. 19 at [1].

[331] *Fallon v MGN Ltd* [2006] EWHC 783 (QB); [2006] E.M.L.R. 19 at [1].

[332] *Jameel v Times Newspapers Ltd* [2004] EWCA Civ 983; [2004] E.M.L.R. 31; *Jameel v Wall Street Journal Europe SPRL*, above, where the CA took the view that it might well be that the jury would find that the level 2 meaning was the natural and therefore the "right" one to place upon the words, but the lesser meaning was not strained or forced or utterly unreasonable.

[333] *Berezovsky v Forbes Inc.* [2001] EWCA Civ 1251; [2001] E.M.L.R. 45; *Windsor v Boycott*, May 9, 2001, QB; *Rakhimov v Jennings*, June 8, 2001, QB.

formulations are regularly prayed in aid by media defendants who recognise difficulty in proving what they have actually published[334] and it is therefore "desirable as a matter of public policy to avoid a situation where journalists, unable to plead justification at the highest level, approach the defence as though it will suffice simply to throw mud at the Claimant in the hope that some of it will stick."[335] The question of the type of evidence the defendant may adduce in order to prove grounds for suspicion or investigation is considered below.[336]

Similar considerations apply to statements that the claimant has been arrested for or charged with an offence: such statements are likely to be defamatory in themselves but will not normally bear the imputation of guilt.[337]

3.29 Meaning to be determined according to time and place. In *Harrison v Thornborough*[338] it was said that "precedents in actions for words are not of equal authority as in other actions, because *norma loquendi* is the rule for the interpretation of words, and this rule is different in one age from what it is in another. The words which 100 years ago did not import a slanderous sense may now; and vice versa." "It is use which makes words have force,"[339] it is current, general usage which should be looked to in determining meaning and the jury should take into account the current general usage of the words. This is particularly important in relation to slang or colloquial language or vulgarisms. Thus the primary popular meaning of "gay" is probably now homosexual,[340] not bright and cheerful, but this would not have been so 50 years ago.[341] "Blackleg" now means a strike-breaker but in 1858 it apparently

---

[334] *Lukowiak v Unidad Editorial SA* [2001] E.M.L.R. 46 at [26], per Eady J.

[335] (1) *Fallon v MGN Ltd,* above at [17]; *Armstrong v Times Newspapers Ltd* [2004] EWHC 2928 (QB) (by subsequent order ([2005] EWHC 2816 (QB) the question of meaning was assigned for determination by judge alone and Gray J. held that the words imputed guilt: *Armstrong v Times Newspapers* [2006] EWHC 1614 (QB))); *Lowe v Associated Newspapers Ltd* [2006] EWHC 320 (QB); [2007] Q.B. 580 at [146]. On damages in "suspicion" cases see *Greig v WIN Television NSW Pty Ltd* [2009] N.S.W.S.C. 632.

[336] See para.11.13, below. A defendant who has to justify an allegation of reasonable grounds to suspect has a lower burden than showing reasonable grounds to *believe*, for facts which can reasonably ground a suspicion may be quite insufficient reasonably to ground a belief: *Sands v Channel Seven Adelaide Pty Ltd* [2009] SASC 215 at [140]. The appeal was dismissed, [2010] SASC 202 but at [120] it is said that the categorisation into three levels "even if rigidly applied in the United Kingdom, has not been so embraced by the Australian courts". See also *West Australian Newspapers Ltd v Elliott,* above at [70].

[337] *Mirror Newspapers Ltd v Harrison* (1982) 42 A.L.R. 487 HCA; *Webbie v Nationwide News* (1968) 12 F.L.R. 271.

[338] 88 E.R. 691; (1713) 10 Mod. 196 at 197.

[339] Per Bridgman C.J. in *Falkner v Cooper* 124 E.R. 821; (1666) Carter at 55. Cf. "Words are the tokens current and accepted for conceits as moneys are for values" quoted by Pearce L.J. in *Lewis v Daily Telegraph* [1963] 1 Q.B. 340 at 374 from Bacon, *The Advancement of Learning.*

[340] Though this may be changing again. In colloquial speech "gay" is often used pejoratively to mean "useless" or "feeble".

[341] Homosexuality is the first meaning given in *The Collins English Dictionary,* 2nd edn (1986). The headline in *Luna v Seattle Times,* 59 P.2d 753 (Wa., 1936) "Consul's Gay Party

meant a gambler.[342] "Truckmaster" was regarded in 1860 as capable of being defamatory in its ordinary sense[343] but it would probably not convey anything at all to most readers today. Similarly, the law has to take into account that English words have different meanings in different places, though nowadays the "internationalisation" of television, films and advertising has probably given the ordinary person a fairly wide knowledge of, say, American and Australian colloquial English. The question of whether a slang expression has become part of ordinary usage is a matter of degree.[344] If the expression has not become part of ordinary usage it may still be defamatory because the meaning was known to those to whom the words were addressed, but in this case it will be an innuendo and the claimant will have to prove publication to persons who had knowledge of the meaning of the expression so that they could have understood it in the defamatory sense.[345]

Context and circumstances of publication. "It is necessary to take into   **3.30** consideration, not only the actual words used, but the context of the words."[346] "Words in themselves apparently innocent may be shown to have a defamatory meaning when they are read with reference to the circumstances in which they were uttered or written, and with reference to the context in which they appear."[347] However, the context in which the words appear may

---

Winds Up as Girls Steal Clothes, Cash" would probably convey a rather more complex message to a reader today. In *Blackman v Bryant* (1872) 27 L.T. 491, it was held that an innuendo was required as to the meaning of "welsher" but this would not, it is thought, be so today.

[342] *Barnett v Allen* (1858) 3 H. & N. 376. "Body snatcher" would probably not now convey the activity of grave robbing to ordinary people but it is still defamatory as dealing with a body without legal justification: *Awa v Independent News Auckland* [1995] 3 N.Z.L.R. 701 (held fair comment on appeal: [1997] 3 N.Z.L.R. 590).

[343] *Homer v Taunton* (1860) 5 H. & N. 661. But the ordinary meaning did not then carry the further connotation of "cheat".

[344] See the differences in the knowledge of "pansy" in the Court of Appeal in *Thaarup v Hulton Press* (1943) 169 L.T. 309. In any event a slang expression may have more than one defamatory meaning. "Bent" connotes sexual deviance or dishonesty: see *Allsop v Church of England Newspaper* [1972] 2 Q.B. 161 CA.

[345] See para.3.21, above.

[346] Per Lord Halsbury L.C. In *Nevill v Fine Arts Co* [1897] 1 A.C. 68 at 72, 78; *English and Scottish Co-op Ltd v Odhams Press Ltd* [1940] 1 K.B. 440 CA at 452; and see *Flanagan v Walton* (1934) E.D.L. 138; *Stewart Printing Co. v Conroy* [1948] 2 S.A.L.R. 707; *Greek Herald v Nikolopoulos* [2002] NSWCA 41; 54 N.S.W.L.R. 165. *English and Scottish Co-op* is a borderline case. The plaintiffs had made a profit return which included the proceeds of sale of a ground rent, an item with which the auditor disagreed. They were charged with wrongfully making a return of profits which was false. The defendants' report of the affair bore the headline in heavy italic type "False Profit Return Charge Against Society". The CA held that the word "false" was ambiguous as capable of meaning either fraudulent (the plaintiffs' sense) or incorrect (the defendants' sense) and that the judge had rightly left the matter to the jury. In *Hamaizia v The Comr of Police for the Metropolis* [2013] EWHC 848 (QB) it was said that, "In ordinary language the words 'their involvement in the lead up to the murder' and 'involved in Marvin Henry's murder' were, in that context, not capable of being understood to mean that either of the Claimants was himself guilty of murder" (at [52]).

[347] Per Lord Kinnear in *Smith v Walker*, 1912 S.C. 224 at 228.
"The manner of publication, and the things relative to which the words were published and which [the person knew or ought to have known] would influence those to whom it was

also have the effect of negativing any defamatory meaning.[348] Words which are not in themselves defamatory may, from the whole context in which they are published,[349] convey a defamatory imputation.[350] So, the statement that C left in a hurry on its face imputes nothing bad to C but wears a different air when the context shows that what he left was his employment and there were disciplinary proceedings pending.[351] Again, where a number of persons are engaged in an activity and they are listed there may normally be no significance in the order in which they are listed, but in *Russell v Notcutt*,[352] where the name of the plaintiff, a well-known singer, appeared in the middle

---

published in putting a meaning on the words, are all material in determining whether the writing is calculated to convey a libellous imputation":
per Lord Blackburn in *Capital and Counties Bank v Henty* (1882) 7 A.C. 741 at 771; see also at 744, per Lord Selborne L.C. Notice also that in *Lewis v Daily Telegraph* [1963] Q.B. 340 at 353, Davies L.J. *arguendo* referred to the "tone" and "heading" of an article as intrinsic facts. See also *Aaron v Cheong Yip Sung* [1996] 1 S.L.R. 623 Sing. CA (juxtaposition of material); *Nationwide News Pty Ltd v Murphy* [1999] NSWCA 118 (statement in a gossip column that the claimant was "a 'celebrity' lawyer better known for getting drug dealers . . . off criminal charges" held capable of bearing the meaning that he had behaved improperly).

[348] By way of example, that the words were spoken in the context of a discussion or disagreement about scientific or academic issues is highly relevant in determining meaning: a critique of a scientist's work will not readily be interpreted as imputing incompetence. See, e.g. *Bowker (t/a Lagopus Services) v The Royal Society for the Protection of Birds* [2011] EWHC 737 (QB).

[349] So a headline may be defamatory when the rest of the publication cannot be attacked: *Crowne v Warden* (1968) 112 S.J. 824 CA; *Leon v Edinburgh Evening News*, 1909 S.C.1014; *Grand Theatre (Glasgow) v Outram* (1908) ibid. at 1018n.; *Bowers v Hutchinson* (1865) 5 N.S.R. 679 ("Lamentable").

[350] *Roberts v Patillo* (1855) 2 N.S.R. 367 (account of claimant's lawful conduct prefaced by "caution"). In *Stubbs Ltd v Mazure* [1920] A.C. 66, it was incorrectly stated in the defendants' publication that a decree had been obtained against the pursuer in his absence. It was the object of the publication that its readers might draw inferences as to the credit of the traders named in it; the section in which the pursuer's name appeared was called the "Black List", and the credit of persons whose names appeared in it was viewed with suspicion. It was held in the House of Lords that these facts could support an innuendo that the pursuer was given to or had begun to refuse to make payment of his debts, and that he was not a person to whom credit should be given. This was so even though such a publication may not impute insolvency (see para.2.33, above) and on the facts certainly did not because it was preceded by a note to the effect that the list did not imply inability to pay.
In *Lord McAlpine v Bercow* [2013] EWHC 1342 (QB) "*innocent face*" was held in context to be insincere and ironical. As counsel for the claimant put it, "People sometimes ask a question to which they already know the answer. They may do that as an indirect way of bringing out into the open something they already know, or believe to be, a fact. They sometimes seek to conceal what they are up to (or pretend to conceal what they are up to) by putting on an expression which suggests that they do not already know the answer to the question" (at [55]).

[351] *W v JH* [2008] EWHC 399 (QB) (where the point is made that context may present more difficulty in a case of slander). In *Auladin v Shaikh* [2013] EWHC 157 (QB) it was held that the words "backed out" when read in the context of a statement that all trustees of a charity had served with "sincerity, integrity and with no personal benefit", could not be understood to be signifying a rejection of the democratic process or an allegation that the claimant failed, in some way, to comply with a pre-existing obligation. It was instead consistent with the interpretation that the claimant chose to resign because he did not approve of the majority decision. "'Backing out' can cover a dignified withdrawal and does not, in my view, in the present context, impute a rejection of the democratic process as such" (at [14]).

[352] (1896) 12 T.L.R. 195 CA. See also *Elen v London Music Hall*, *The Times*, June 1, 1906.

of the programme, the plaintiff proved that in the musical world the order in which the names appeared conveyed a particular meaning, the best singer being usually placed first or last, and the Court of Appeal held that there was evidence upon which the jury could rightly find that the publication of the programme amounted to a libel on the plaintiff in the way of her profession.[353]

To display an effigy or picture of the claimant which did not expose the claimant to ridicule[354] would not normally be actionable as defamation but it would be so if it was displayed in circumstances which impliedly associated the claimant with misconduct, as where an effigy was displayed near the Chamber of Horrors in Tussauds after the plaintiff had obtained a verdict of "not proven" at his trial for murder in Scotland.[355] So also it would plainly be defamatory to say of a local politician that he was associated with the Mafia; but where a newspaper stated that a Scots councillor was part of the "Monklands Mafia" that did not convey at all the same message and was not defamatory.[356] Conversely, the ordinary meaning of "X kills babies" is plainly defamatory as charging a criminal offence, but this imputation was held not to be open when the words were on a placard carried by protesters outside an abortion clinic.[357] Similarly the cumulative effect of a number of individually true statements may be to create a defamatory imputation which is not true. So to say that manufacturers A and B were phasing out the use of a dangerous chemical might imply that manufacturer C was not doing that.[358] It may in some cases be permissible to travel outside the bounds of the particular publication complained of to establish the context. If, for example, a weekly publication is so made up that a particular part of it becomes associated with the exposure of wrongdoing, that may make defamatory the inclusion in that part of material which would not otherwise be so.[359]

In considering the context of a television or radio broadcast it is necessary to bear in the mind the "one-off" nature of the viewer's exposure to a

---

[353] For comparative assessments as capable of being defamatory, see para.2.17, above.

[354] As to which, see para.2.11, above.

[355] *Monson v Tussauds* [1894] 1 Q.B. 671.

[356] *Brooks v Lind, The Times*, March 26, 1997. See also *Crow v Johnson* [2012] EWHC 1982 (QB) for the importance of the context (in this case a "hotly contested election") in determining meaning.

[357] *Att-Gen for Ontario v Dicleman* (1994) 117 D.L.R. (4th) 449. Cf. *Daishowa Inc. v Friends of the Lubicon* (1998) 158 D.L.R. (4th) 699. To call a logging programme "genocide" of local native people without any qualification such as "cultural" was defamatory. However, the plaintiffs sought and received only $1.

[358] *Color Your World Corp v CBC* (1994) 17 O.R. (3d) 308. The decision was reversed on appeal ((1998) 156 D.L.R. (4th) 27 Ont. CA) on the basis that to the reasonably well-informed viewer the footage of mercury-related disasters simply identified the sources of knowledge of the risks of mercury and that it would be obvious to such a viewer that the risks posed by mercury in paint were likely to be of a different order, but without, it is thought, denying the proposition in the text.

[359] *Wheeler v Somerfield* [1966] 2 Q.B. 94 CA (argument failed on facts). See para.3.32, below.

broadcast[360] and the messages that may be conveyed by intercutting aural and visual material.[361] The common legislative provision that broadcasting is deemed to be publication in a permanent form is directed to making it libel rather than slander and should not influence the court's approach to determining the meaning of words in their context.[362] The principles applicable in such cases are the same as those applicable to newspapers or books but in practice the nature of broadcasting may mean that a court is more ready to leave an issue to the jury than if the same words appeared in print.[363]

Where the statement complained of has been made in the context of an ongoing debate, whether in the real or virtual world, the whole of the debate and the context and circumstances in which the debate took place are relevant in determining the meaning of the words complained of. Thus, where the context is a hotly contested election, this has been held to be relevant to the question of the meaning of the words published.[364] So too, Eady J. clearly regarded the more casual, speech-like, characteristics of bulletin board exchanges as relevant to the determination of meaning in *Smith v ADVFN Plc*.[365] In *Baglow v Smith*[366] robust views were expressed in the context of an online debate conducted through the medium of blogs and attached comments. At first instance, Annis J. granted summary judgment to the defendant on the basis that an apparently defamatory statement made in a debate on a blog or internet forum may not be found to be defamatory if the plaintiff previously engaged in the debate but did not respond to the statement despite having the opportunity to do so:

---

[360] *Skuse v Granada Television* [1996] E.M.L.R. 278 CA; *Hinduja v Asia TV Ltd* [1998] E.M.L.R. 516 CA. In *Bond v BBC* [2009] EWHC 539 (QB) at [9] Eady J. said:
"It is important to acknowledge that assessing the meaning(s) of an hour long television programme is to a large extent a matter of impression. Yet it is also necessary to remember that the test is objective, so that one must always have in mind how the reasonable viewer would interpret it. Nonetheless, it is recognised in the authorities that the judge can take into account his or her own subjective reaction as part of the process. Beyond that, one must not be over-analytical, in the sense of subjecting the text to a leisurely or legalistic breakdown: ordinary viewers will not have had that opportunity. The overall flavour of a programme may contribute to an interpretation which would not necessarily be found when subjecting the text to piecemeal analysis. There is a risk that such an exercise will focus on the trees and miss the wood."
See also *Fox v Boulter* [2013] EWHC 1435 (QB) at [15].
[361] See *Channel Seven Sydney Pty Ltd v Parras* [2002] NSWCA 202.
[362] *Amalgamated Television Services Pty Ltd v Marsden* (1998) 43 N.S.W.L.R. 158 NSWCA. On television and radio broadcasts see also *Australian Broadcasting Corp v Reading* [2004] NSWCA 411; *Australian Broadcasting Corp v Obeid* [2006] NSWCA 231.
[363] Ibid. In *Color your World Corp v Canadian Broadcasting Corp* (1998) 156 D.L.R. (4th) 27 Ont. CA, it is said that in the case of an audio-visual presentation the words should be regarded as the primary conveyor of meaning unless they were distorted by the visual aspect. American courts have emphasised that the approach to the interpretation of written words cannot be woodenly applied to television for the script may give a wholly different impression from the programme. See *Southern Air Transport Inc. v American Broadcasting*, 877 F.2d. 1010 (App DC 1989) and 50 Am.Jur.2d., *Libel and Slander*, para.132. See also para.3.31, below.
[364] *Crow v Johnson* [2012] EWHC 1982 (QB); *Baglow v Smith* 2012 ONCA 407.
[365] [2008] EWHC 1797 (QB) at [17].
[366] 2011 ONSC 5131.

"I am not suggesting that defamation can never occur in a live debate. I do say, however, that the live debate forum should be considered as a contextual factor to determine whether the statement is defamatory in so far as whether it is complete ... in essence I am suggesting that the court, in construing allegedly defamatory words in an ongoing debate, should determine whether the context of the comment from the perspective of the reasonable reader or listener is one that anticipates a rejoinder which would eliminate the possible consequences of a statement lowering the reputation of the plaintiff in their eyes. To some extent the court is attempting to decide whether the debate should have gone forward, such that walking off the blogging stage, so to speak, is a form of 'gotcha' contrary to the rules governing the debate. I realize that this sounds like a form of defence of mitigation of a defamatory comment. I see it more as an uncompleted comment, something akin to the plaintiff arguing that he has been defamed by a question, when the response is what the audience was expecting."[367]

The Ontario Court of Appeal subsequently overturned Annis J.'s decision[368] on the basis that this issue was not suitable for determination by summary judgment but should instead be resolved after a trial perhaps with expert evidence. The cautious approach of the Court of Appeal to the important question of whether different rules apply to the determination of meaning in internet debates was understandable and it seems unlikely that an English court would accede to an argument that different rules should apply to the determination of meaning simply because the debate is conducted on the internet. That said, the usual terms of such debates is clearly part of the context that a court should consider in determining meaning.

Publication must be taken as a whole. It follows from the fact that the   **3.31** context and circumstances of the publication must be taken into account, that the claimant cannot pick and choose parts of the publication which, standing alone, would be defamatory.[369] This or that sentence may be considered defamatory, but there may be other passages which take away their sting.[370] In this regard, the reasonable reader is assumed to have read the whole article complained of.[371] If "in one part of the publication something disreputable to the plaintiff is stated, but that is removed[372] by the conclusion, the bane and

---

[367] Ibid. at [61], [65]–[67].

[368] 2012 ONCA 407.

[369] See *Monks v Warwick DC* [2009] EWHC 959 (QB).

[370] Or, of course, the reverse. In *Nationwide News Pty Ltd v Warton* [2002] NSWCA 337 a headline "Bout a Sucker Punch" in an article about boxing might simply have suggested a surprise blow, but the article taken as a whole imputed dishonesty in the promotion of the fight.

[371] In *Cruddas v Calvert* [2013] EWHC 1427 (QB), Tugendhat J. noted (at [93]) that the assumption that the reasonable reader has read the article as a whole is: "as unrealistic an assumption as any that is required to be made, whether in defamation or in malicious falsehood (applying a multiple meaning rule), albeit that that assumption is necessary to do justice to a defendant."

[372] That is necessary: see para.3.32(2), below.

the antidote must be taken together".[373] If that were not so it would be impossible to refute charges made against another person, since the refutation must, in practice, refer to the charges.[374] Thus in the case of a newspaper article the defendant is entitled to have considered as part of the claimant's case the whole of the piece from which the alleged libel is extracted.[375] In *Charleston v News Group Newspapers Ltd*[376] the defendants published in their newspaper a photograph in which the heads of the plaintiffs, actors in a well-known soap opera, had been superimposed on the bodies of two persons engaged in sexual intercourse and which was accompanied by large headlines referring to the series in which they played and the characters portrayed by them. The article as a whole made it plain that the plaintiffs were in fact the victims of persons in Australia who had marketed a pornographic computer game from which the photograph had been taken. It was held that the article as a whole was incapable of conveying to the hypothetical reasonable reader[377] the meaning that the plaintiffs had engaged in the conduct portrayed or had co-operated in the creation of the photograph, despite the fact that many readers of a tabloid newspaper might have drawn such a conclusion by failing to read the article as a whole and that the House of Lords expressed sympathy with the plaintiffs' position.[378]

---

[373] Per Alderson B. in *Chalmers v Payne* (1835) 2 Cr. M. & R. 156 at 159; *Sykes v Southam* [1991] 3 W.W.R. 27. See also para.3.31 and *Golding v Torch Printing*, 1949 (4) S.A.L.R. 150 ("quisling" interpreted in context in a non-defamatory sense). Bane and antidote has become "almost conventional jargon among libel lawyers": *Charleston v News Group Newspapers Ltd* [1995] 2 A.C. 65 at 70, per Lord Bridge. Where the issue is whether the antidote in the article extinguishes the bane it will be rare that there is no issue for the jury: *Cruise v Express Newspapers Plc* [1999] Q.B. 931 CA; *Mark v Associated Newspapers Ltd* [2002] EWCA Civ 772, [2002] E.M.L.R. 839; *Al Fayed v Telegraph Group Ltd* [2002] EWHC 1631 (QB).

[374] See also para.6.51, below. Note, however, that in *Lewis v Daily Telegraph* [1964] A.C. 234, at 285 Lord Devlin considered it defamatory to say that someone had been acquitted of an offence when he had never in fact been charged.

[375] *Polly Peck Plc v Trelford* [1986] Q.B. 1000 at 1032; *Carlton Communications Plc v News Group Newspapers Ltd* [2001] EWCA Civ 1644; [2002] E.M.L.R. 16. In *McGrath v Independent Print Ltd* [2013] EWHC 2202 (QB) Nicola Davies J. noted that if the case had been based solely on the headline there would have been force in the claimant's argument that the article had alleged that he had sued over a book review. However, when the whole of the article was read, it was clear that the subject matter of the earlier libel proceedings was not the review:

"The meaning claimed for by the claimant is not only too narrow an interpretation of this article, it is inaccurate. I find that upon reading the article as a whole, it is clear that it was not the original review which was the subject matter of the libel proceedings but the unpleasant online conversation between the claimant, in one or more guises, and Mr Vaughan Jones" (at [41]).

[376] [1995] 2 A.C. 65 HL. Cf. *Byrd v Hustler Magazine Inc.*, 433 So.2d 593 (Fla., 1983).

[377] See para.3.26, above.

[378] Lord Bridge at [1995] 2 A.C. 69 referred to the fact that the article was couched in self-righteous terms which were at odds with the appeal of the photograph and the style of the headlines and Lord Nicholls, at 73, said that to anyone unversed in defamation the contrary conclusion on meaning "would appear to be the common sense of the matter". The approach in *Charleston* is strongly criticised by Kirby J. in *Chakravarti v Advertiser Newspaper* [1998] HCA 37; 193 C.L.R. 519 at [134].

In *Norman v Future Publishing Ltd*[379] the attribution to a famous black opera singer of the remark, "Honey, I ain't got no sideways" was held incapable of bearing the meanings that she was vulgar and undignified, conformed to a racist stereotype or was a hypocrite who mocked modes of speech stereotypically attributed to a particular racial group. The general tone of the article portrayed her as a person of high standing and impeccable dignity and in the context the attributed remark merely poked gentle fun at her size.[380] Where the alleged defamation takes place in a broadcast no doubt the rule is the same where the antidote is closely placed in time to the bane but it is easy to imagine cases where the "relevant publication" might only be a distinguishable segment of the broadcast. Thus in *Australian Broadcasting Corp v Obeid*[381] the defendants at 9.05am at the commencement of an ongoing news programme broadcast allegations of corruption against the claimant and between 10.05 and 11.50 broadcast various denials by him. The claim pleaded the first broadcast and the New South Wales Court of Appeal held that the defendants were not entitled to "strike in"[382] the later parts of the programme. It was unlikely that many people had listened to the whole programme, there were no indications in the initial part of the broadcast that this was "breaking news" upon which listeners might reasonably be expected to reserve judgment until the end of the programme, there were intervals between the statements about the plaintiff taken up with other matters and it was a case where "some reasonably minded listeners could regard the matter complained of as a separate, self-contained broadcast containing the whole context of what the [plaintiff] was complaining about."[383]

Qualifications. Although the publication must be taken as a whole, the following qualifications must be made: **3.32**

(1) The standard is still that of the ordinary reader, and he may not notice curative words tucked away in the publication or in another publication to which he is referred.[384] "Whether the text of a newspaper article

---

[379] [1999] E.M.L.R. 325 CA.

[380] "There are cases . . . in which the refutation is of such a nature that, taken as a whole, the matter complained of is incapable of conveying the imputation refuted, for example, where the imputation arises by way of inference only and the matter complained of itself contains an express disclaimer of any intention to convey such an imputation: *Stubbs v Russell* [1913] A.C. 386 [as to which see para.2.33, above]; or where the refutation consists of a statement of fact destructive of the entire basis upon which the imputation relies: *Bik v Mirror Newspapers* [1979] 2 N.S.W.L.R. 679." *Bass v McDonald (No.6)* [2001] N.S.W.S.C. 988. See also *Auladin v Shaikh* [2013] EWHC 157 (QB).

[381] [2006] NSWCA 231.

[382] I.e. requiring the plaintiff to plead additional parts of the material complained of.

[383] [2006] NSWCA 231 at [70] per Tobias J.A.

[384] *Charleston v News Group Newspapers Ltd* [1995] 2 A.C. 65 at 74, per Lord Nicholls. "Those who print defamatory headlines are playing with fire": ibid. See *Crowne v Warden & Co. Ltd* (1968) 112 S.J. 824 CA (headlines giving impression that claimant, a witness, was on trial for fraud, impression corrected later in text, claim allowed to proceed).

will, in any particular case, be sufficient to neutralise the defamatory implication of a prominent headline will sometimes be a nicely balanced question for the jury to decide and will depend not only on the nature of the libel which the headline conveys and the language of the text which is relied on to neutralise it but also on the manner in which the whole of the relevant material is set out and presented."[385]

(2) It will be a question in each case whether the antidote is sufficient to offset the bane; the mere presence of a denial of a defamatory charge does not necessarily prevent the article being defamatory, for the reader may be left in the position of having to choose between inconsistent assertions.[386]

3.33 Meaning collected from other parts of same publication or from other publications. Where a newspaper article refers to another report in the same issue either party is entitled to have that read as part of the context in which the meaning of the words complained of is to be determined,[387]

---

[385] [1995] 2 A.C. at 72, per Lord Bridge; *Jameel v Times Newspapers Ltd* [2004] EWCA Civ 983; [2004] E.M.L.R. 31; *Kelson v David Syme & Co. Ltd* [1998] SCACT 60; *John Fairfax Publications Pty Ltd v Rivkin* [2003] HCA 50; 201 A.L.R. 77 at [187–188]; *Stanton v Metro Corp* 438 F.3d 119 (CA 1, 2006) (modestly sized "disclaimer"). However in *Jameel* at [16] Sedley L.J. detected a certain tension in the case law
"between the principle that the feasible range of meanings is to be derived from the article as a whole, read through the eyes of a sensible person, and the principle that if the article contains a defamatory statement or imputation, that will define its meaning unless it is very plainly negatived in the same article."
In *Robertson v Newsquest (Sunday Herald) Ltd* [2006] CSOH 97; 2006 SCLR 792 Lord Reed held that the approach of taking the publication as a whole was the fundamental principle of Scots law. Referring to the view of Sedley L.J. in *Jameel* that "a publication which advances and then purports to dispel a defamatory allegation can be acquitted of any possible defamatory meaning only in the very clearest of cases", he said that
"I accept that the court may sometimes find it difficult to conclude, as a matter of law, that the article as a whole is nevertheless incapable of conveying a defamatory imputation, but I would not myself be inclined, so far as Scots law is concerned, to elevate that practical difficulty into a legal principle of interpretation."
(at [22]).
[386] See, e.g. *Klason v Australian Capital Territory* [2003] ACTSC 104; 177 F.L.R. 216 (document referring without further explanation to inconsistent conclusions in child protection investigation and later court proceedings left reader with impression that there were conflicting views). It is not enough that the defendant publishes the claimant's denial and leaves it to the audience to make up their own minds: *Mark v Associated Newspapers Ltd* [2002] EWCA Civ 772; [2002] E.M.L.R. 839, pointing out that the other approach would be inconsistent with *Reynolds v Times Newspapers Ltd* [2001] 2 A.C. 127 (see para.15.2, below) making publication of the claimant's side of the story a requirement of reliance on qualified privilege in some cases; *Farquhar v Bottom* [1980] 2 N.S.W.L.R. 380.
[387] *Thornton v Stephen* (1837) 2 Mood. & R. 45. See also *Bolton v O'Brien* [1885] 16 L.R. Ir. 97, affirmed ibid. at 483; *Cooke v Hughes* (1824) Ry. & M. 112; *Hedley v Barlow* (1865) 4 F. & F. 224. If a publication contains two distinct and severable charges without a common sting and the claimant chooses to rely only on one of them, the other becomes irrelevant (see para.11.4, below) but that does not mean that the claimant can alter the sense of what the defendant has said.

provided that the various items being considered were sufficiently closely connected as to be regarded as a single publication.[388] Thus, where an article begins on one page of a newspaper and it is made clear that the article continues on a separate page or in a different part of the newspaper, that will usually be enough to establish that the items were sufficiently connected to be regarded as a single publication. In *Dee v Telegraph Media Group Ltd Ltd*[389] Sharp J. said that the same test should be applied regardless of whether the items are "separate" items or one is a continuation page from the other. Ordinarily it is not controversial that two items in the same newspaper or magazine that relate to the same subject matter are to be read together for the purposes of determining meaning. But if the matter is controversial, there is no reason why such a question should not be determined, in an appropriate case, on a CPR Pt 24 application.[390] It may, however, be necessary to go outside the particular vehicle in which the words complained of are contained. For example, in the case of an alleged libel contained in a letter, the whole of the correspondence provides the context,[391] for one may assume that the other party to the correspondence is aware of its contents. Some difficulty arises, however, where the defendant publishes what is in fact one piece but does so as a number of items over a period of time[392] (for example, the serialisation of a book in a newspaper or a series of television programmes[393] on a controversial issue). It is clear that in such a case the publisher invites the public to read or view all of the material and, bearing in mind that in the case of a book published as (and treated by the law as) one unit the information in it can only in fact come to the attention of the reader over a period of hours, days or weeks as he reads it, common sense would indicate that the series should be treated as one unit for the purposes of determining the meaning of

---

[388] *Charleston v News Group Newspapers Ltd* [1995] 2 A.C. 65 per Lord Bridge at 70–71; *Dee v Telegraph Media Group Ltd* [2010] EWHC 924 (QB); [2010] E.M.L.R. 20 per Sharp J. at [29].

[389] [2010] EWHC 924 (QB); [2010] E.M.L.R. 20. In *Dee* itself, the front page article drew attention to the "full story" on the back page of the sports section of the newspaper and it was not arguable that they could be separated for the purposes of determining meaning (at [32]).

[390] Ibid. at [31].

[391] See *Smythe v Mackinnon* (1897) 24 R. 1086.

[392] In *McCann v Scottish Media Newspapers Ltd*, 2000 S.L.T. 256, Lord MacFadyen held that where three articles appeared in one edition of a newspaper and the first ended with a reference to the second and the second with a reference to the third, they should all be read as one; *Beran v John Fairfax Publications Pty Ltd* [2004] NSWCA 107 (two pieces in same issue so interlinked that the ordinary reader would have read them as one publication); *Li v The Herald and Weekly Times Pty Ltd* [2007] VSC 109. In *Galloway v Telegraph Group Ltd* [2004] EWHC 2786 (QB); [2005] E.M.L.R. 7 (on appeal on other issues, [2006] EWCA Civ 17; [2006] E.M.L.R. 11) the claimant sued in respect of a number of articles extending over two days' issues of a newspaper. Eady J. was of the view that the context included reproductions of documents upon which the articles were founded but in respect of which no complaint was made and that in determining the meaning of the material published on the second day one had to bear in mind the impression likely to be left by the first day's coverage.

[393] For a single, extended broadcast see para.3.31, above.

a particular part. If, for example, a book were to say on page 100 that the claimant entered a particular house and on page 110 were to reveal that that house was a brothel, the second statement would make the apparently innocuous first statement defamatory.[394] It would be strange if the position were different if there were a gap of a week between the publication of the two pages in serial form. The difficulty arises from the fact that it is said that the meaning of words must be determined at the time of the publication, when the cause of action is complete.[395] It is submitted that the situation of the series of work,[396] all published by the same person is distinguishable,[397] and there is no good reason for applying this rule to it.[398]

---

[394] See *Lewis v Daily Telegraph* [1964] A.C. 234 at 278; and *Burrows v Knightley* (1987) 10 N.S.W.L.R. 651 containing a full review of this problem in the context of pleading. But there is some danger of over-elaboration in attributing the meaning to be derived by the reasonable reader to passages many pages apart in a book: *Oduro v Time-Life Entertainment Group Ltd* [2003] EWHC 1787 (QB) at [18].

[395] See *Grappelli v Derek Block (Holdings) Ltd* [1981] 1 W.L.R. 822 CA, para.3.21, above. It is possible to conceive of somewhat far-fetched examples where this would obviously give rise to difficulty even in case of publication of a single unit. D publishes a book in 2000 stating falsely that C has done "X" which at that time is not capable of being defamatory. By 2005 "X" has acquired a common slang meaning which is defamatory. It is hard to believe that a sale of the book in 2008 would constitute a defamatory publication. Perhaps this would be a case in which the "ordinary reader" would be deemed to have a somewhat artificially inflated knowledge of etymological development. In *Brown v Marron* [2001] WASC 100, Owen J. accepted that oral material accompanying written words is equally part of the context. On the question of reconciling this with the rule that the cause of action is complete upon publication of the defamatory words (so that a retraction even an hour or so later does not destroy the claim) he said (at [56]):

> "There must be an intimate connection between the primary source of the alleged defamation and the other material which is said to form part of the context. The primary and secondary sources must be so closely connected, interwoven or enmeshed that it is necessary to take them effectively as one transaction in order to arrive at the true import and meaning of what was written and said. The requisite degree of intimacy will usually (although not always, for example in the serialisation situation) demand contemporaneity. It will be necessary to consider all of the surrounding circumstances to decide whether the secondary materials are so intimately connected with the primary sources that they are to be taken to be a part of the context which might affect the way in which the ordinary reasonable reader would understand the words complained of."

[396] For a discussion of the problems of context presented by linked internet pages, see *Buddhist Society of Western Australia Inc. v Bristile Ltd* [2000] WASCA 210.

[397] Sir Stanley Rees in *Hayward v Thompson* [1982] Q.B. 47 CA at 72, described *Grappelli* as involving the principle that: "a writer of innocent matter cannot *by reason of facts which came into existence subsequent to the original innocent publication* become liable in damages for libel because the subsequent material attributes a defamatory meaning to the innocent publication."

[398] See *Burrows v Knightley* (1987) 10 N.S.W.L.R. 651; *Bureya Pty Ltd v McKay Printing* [2003] QCA 284. But the contrary view is expressed in *Galloway v Telegraph Group Ltd* [2004] EWHC 2786 (QB); [2005] E.M.L.R. 7 at [50] (on appeal on other issues, [2006] EWCA Civ 17; [2006] E.M.L.R. 11). In any event the *Grappelli* rule does not apply to separate publications by the same defendant in which material in a later publication is used to identify the victim of an *ex facie* defamatory statement in an earlier one: *Hayward v Thompson* [1982] Q.B. 47 CA; *Misir v Toronto Star Newspapers Ltd* (1997) 105 O.A.C. 270 Ont. CA; *Butler v Southam Inc.*, September 7, 2001, NSCA; cf. *Ballantyne v Television New Zealand* [1992] 3 N.Z.L.R. 455. Hence if one varies the example in the text so that page 100 describes a person entering a brothel and page 110 identifies him, that falls within this principle.

However, there must be a statement *by the defendant* which expressly or impliedly defames the claimant. In *Astaire v Campling*[399] the defendants' article stated that the plaintiff was known as "Mr. X" in the world of boxing, and other publications had contained disparaging references to "Mr. X". The plaintiff was not entitled to rely on those publications in support of an allegation that the defendants' article disparaged him.[400] It would be otherwise in a case in which the defendant's statement expressly or by implication approved, adopted or repeated statements by other persons.[401]

Internet publications. There is no reason to think that when approaching   **3.34** internet publications, the test identified above—whether the various items being considered were sufficiently closely connected as to be regarded as a single publication—should not be applied. Thus where it is clear that an article on one page is continued on another, a court should have no difficulty in concluding that the items were sufficiently closely connected to be regarded as a single publication. Even if the decision of the Canadian Supreme Court in *Crookes v Newton*[402] was to be applied by the English courts it is suggested that the position should be no different. *Crookes*[403] decided that a "hyperlink" by itself does not constitute publication of the content to which it refers. It does not however affect the question whether the person who published the material linked to is liable for it, nor does it affect the question whether in determining the meaning of an item on one webpage it is appropriate to take into account material on another webpage. That question can only be answered by asking whether the two pages are sufficiently closely connected to be regarded as a single publication. The fact that there is a link from one to the other is relevant but not determinative.[404]

Where the hyperlink is to a webpage published by a different author the position is more difficult. If *Crookes* does represent English law, then it would appear that the author of one page (the "linking page") who links to another page (the "page linked to") is not to be treated as the publisher of the content on the page linked to and presumably therefore the content on the page linked to should not be taken into account in determining the meaning of the linking page. Unless by linking to another page, a person is treated as having adopted,

---

[399] [1966] 1 W.L.R. 34 CA; *Ramaiah Naragatha Vally v Singapore Press Holdings* [1966] 2 S.L.R. 497.

[400] Defamatory statements published by other persons were held not to be "facts" within RSC Ord.82, r.3(1) on which the plaintiff might rely to give the defendant's words a meaning other than their natural and ordinary meaning: *Astaire v Campling* [1966] 1 W.L.R. 34 at 39–40; *Hyams v Peterson* [1991] 3 N.Z.L.R. 648 NZCA. However, Sellers L.J. in *Astaire v Campling*, at 39, thought that such other publications were relevant in support of an allegation that defamatory statements referred to the claimant. So held in *Onama v Uganda Argus* [1969] E.A. 92 and *Hyams v Peterson*, above, even though the other publications were privileged.

[401] *Astaire v Campling* [1966] 1 W.L.R. 34 CA at 40–41. See para.6.39, below.

[402] 2011 SCC 47, [2011] 3 S.C.R. 269.

[403] See further, para.6.13, below.

[404] See *Budu v BBC* [2010] EWHC 616 (QB).

approved or repeated statements made on the page linked to, there can be no question that the content on the page linked to is relevant in determining the meaning of the page that contains the hyperlink. *Crookes* however decides that merely linking to another page does not constitute adoption, repetition or approval and consequently there can be no question of the linked to page being relevant to the meaning of the content on the linking page. Whether *Crookes* represents English law remains to be seen. Such English cases as have addressed the question are inconclusive but suggest that it may not. Thus in *Islam Expo Ltd v The Spectator (1828) Ltd*[405] Tugendhat J. was prepared, "without intending to imply any ruling, one way or the other",[406] to approach the case on the basis that text on web pages, to which a reader of the words complained of will be directed if the reader clicks on the hyperlink, is to be treated as parts of the words complained of for the purposes of determining what the words mean. So too, in *McGrath v Dawkins*,[407] H.H.J. Moloney QC stated that even "if the general English rule were to be as recently held in Canada", the decision may well be a fact-sensitive one, especially when, as in *McGrath*, "the two websites [were] very closely associated, the link [was] hidden, and the point of contact [was] the 'Home' button".[408] Certainly the position most consistent with authority would be to ask whether by linking to another page of which he was not the publisher, the publisher of the page that contained the link has adopted, repeated or approved the content on the page linked to.[409] If the answer to any of those questions is yes, then it suggested that the content of the page linked to should be taken into account in determining the meaning of content on the linking page.

3.35 Parts of publication privileged. The defendant publishes material in respect of which his publication is protected by privilege (for example, because it is a fair and accurate report of what was said in Parliament). To that he adds related material of his own. The correct approach to determining the meaning of the non-privileged part is to separate it from the privileged part and interpret it in its own terms. Although the defendant has repeated the defamatory words of another and under the repetition rule the repeater is generally liable for further dissemination, that rule does not apply to privileged statements.[410] Hence the privileged material might make a direct, unequivocal "Level 1"[411] accusation of criminality but the reasonable meaning of the additional material might simply be that this was one factor that

---

[405] [2010] EWHC 2011 (QB).

[406] At [15].

[407] [2012] EWHC B3 (QB).

[408] Ibid. at [26]. See to similar effect, *Ali v Associated Newspapers Limited* [2010] EWHC 100 (QB) at [28].

[409] *Astaire v Campling* [1966] 1 W.L.R. 34 CA.

[410] *Curistan v Times Newspapers Ltd* [2008] EWCA Civ 432; [2009] Q.B. 231. See further para.30.8, below.

[411] On "levels" see para.3.28, above.

gave rise to a "Level 2" reasonable suspicion. However, the privileged material forms part of the context in which the non-privileged material is to be interpreted. So if the article having reported the direct allegation, were to continue, "That is exactly what The Trumpet has believed for years and furthermore we think the following material is worthy of investigation by the police ... " the privileged material would show what allegation the newspaper was "adopting"[412] as its own statement.

Context and circumstances: spoken words and words published in jest. Although the above principles apply to any publication, there are elements of greater subtlety in the case of spoken words because intonation and the expressions or gestures accompanying words may give them a meaning[413] which is not their natural and ordinary meaning.[414] Accompanying gestures may in the words of Dean Swift "convey a libel in a frown, and wink a reputation down".[415] Likewise, even words of praise are actionable on proof that they were published ironically,[416] and words spoken in the form of a question may, by the way in which they were spoken, convey a defamatory imputation.[417] The fact that words are intended by way of jest does not of itself prevent them being actionable for it is not the intention of the publisher that matters but the interpretation that would be put upon the words by the reasonable listener (and the same clearly applies to written words and other forms of publication such as cartoons[418]). If he would understand them as made in jest they are not actionable,[419] but "if a man in jest conveys a serious

3.36

---

[412] There is some disagreement in Curistan between Laws L.J. and the other members of the court as to whether this is truly regarded as a case of "adoption".

[413] For this reason it may be more difficult to attack a jury verdict in respect of spoken than of written words.

[414] Sankey L.J. in *Broome v Agar* (1928) 138 L.T. 698 at 702 said that in slander: "gesture, tone of voice, expression of countenance, all of which are absent in libel, may materially affect the meaning of the spoken words." In principle exactly the same must be true of films, television and to a lesser extent radio (as to which see para.3.30, above) even though they are libel. See also on intonation, gesture, etc. *Penfold v Westcote* (1806) 2 Bos. & P.N.R. 335 ("the manner in which the words were pronounced"); *Halls v Mitchell* (1926) 59 O.L.R. 590 at 603.

[415] Quoted by Pearce L.J. in *Grubb v Bristol United Press* [1963] 1 Q.B. 309 at 328.

[416] "Brutus is an honourable man": Milmo QC *arguendo* in *Lewis v Daily Telegraph* [1964] A.C. 234 at 250. See *Hick's Case* (1619) Hobart 215; *R. v Browne* (1707) Holt 425; *Boydell v Jones* (1838) 4 M. & W. 466; *Daines v Hartley* (1848) 3 Exch. at 206; *Pienaar v Pretoria Works* (1906) Transvaal L.R. 805 at 814; *Lord McAlpine of West Green v Bercow* [2013] EWHC 1342 (QB).

[417] See para.3.18, above.

[418] "Many a true word is spoken in jest; many a false one, too": per Millett L.J. in *Berkoff v Burchill* [1996] 4 All E.R. 1008 CA at 1018. Although this is a dissenting judgment it does not seem that the majority of the court disagreed with the proposition that written words which are clearly not meant to be taken seriously are not defamatory, but merely with the application of that to the facts.

[419] "Even the words 'X is a thief' may have been spoken in play or other circumstances showing that they could not be taken by reasonable persons as imputing an accusation of theft": per Lord Hodson in *Lewis v Daily Telegraph* [1964] A.C. 234 HL at 271. To this there is one qualification and perhaps one exception. The qualification is that in some cases (see, e.g. *Hulton v Jones* [1910] A.C. 20) the courts have not shown much inclination to accept material as humorous. Nowadays, however, juries and (in the light of art.10 of the European Convention on

imputation, he jests at his peril".[420] So where the defendant said, as a joke, that the plaintiff had been detected taking dead bodies out of a churchyard and fined, and the judge directed the jury that if they believed the words to have been spoken jocularly they should find for the defendant, a verdict for the defendant was set aside, for there was no evidence that the persons who heard the words understood them in a jocular sense,[421] and the jury might have inferred from the judge's direction that they had to decide the meaning in which the defendant intended the words to be understood, and not the meaning in which the words would in fact be understood by those who heard them.[422]

> "The principle is clear, that a person shall not be allowed to murder another's reputation in jest. But if words be so spoken that it is obvious to every bystander that only a jest is meant, no injury is done, and consequently no action would lie."[423]

The same applies to written words which the reasonable reader would regard as nothing more than an absurd joke. So, in a modern Australian case a story about a football coach's lack of success being attributable to his lack of "adequate communication and intimacy skills" arising from a deprived childhood was dismissed as, taken as whole, no sensible person would have taken it seriously.[424] So too, in *John v Guardian News and Media Ltd*[425] the words were not reasonably capable of the defamatory meanings complained of because it was obvious to the reasonable reader that they were an attempt at humour by "putting words in the claimant's mouth". The defendants were a

---

Human Rights) perhaps judges are likely to take a more robust attitude to humorous and satirical radio and television broadcasting. The possible exception is that it is by no means clear that the defendant can escape liability in this way if the effect of the publication is to expose the claimant to widespread ridicule.

[420] Per Smith B. in *Donoghue v Hayes* (1831) Hayes (Ir. Ex.) R. 265 at 266; *Beloff v Pressdram* [1973] 1 All E.R. 241 (defence failed). If he has published "what [he knew, or ought to have known] was calculated to injure the claimant, he must (at least civilly) be responsible for the consequences, though his object might have been to injure another person than the claimant, or though he may have written in levity only": per Lord Blackburn in *Capital and Counties Bank v Henty* (1882) 7 A.C. 741 at 772. See also *Hatch v Potter* (1845) 7 Ill. R. 725.

[421] "The whole question is, whether the jocularity was in the mind of the defendant alone, or was shared by the bystanders": per Foster B. in *Donoghue v Hayes* (1831) Haynes (Ir. Ex.) 265 at 267. A good example is *McKethan v Texas Farm Bureau*, 996 F.2d 734 (CA 5 1993).

[422] *Donoghue v Hayes* (1831) Hayes (Ir. Ex.) R. 265; cf. *Masch v Leask* [1916] T.P.D. 114.

[423] Per Joy C.B. in *Donoghue v Hayes*, above, at 266. "Every bystander" should not be taken literally, the audience might contain a humourless, literal-minded person. Jokes cannot be judged by the standards of Malvolio. And see per Solomon J. in *Glass v Perl* [1928] T.P.D. 264. "Jest is not justification unless it is manifest from the language employed that it could in no respect be regarded as an attack upon the reputation of the person to whom it related": per Martin J. in *Triggs v Sun Printing Assn.* (1904) 179 N.Y. 144 at 155. For a review of the U.S. cases, see 57 A.L.R. 4th 520.

[424] *Coleman v John Fairfax Publications Pty Ltd* [2003] N.S.W.S.C. 564. See also *Macleod v Newsquest (Sunday Herald) Ltd* [2007] CSOH 4; *New Times Inc. v Isaacks* 146 S.W.3d 144 at 161 (Tex. 2004), (cert. den. June 6, 2005); *Nikowitz v Austria*, App. no.5266/03 [2007] E.M.L.R. 8.

[425] [2008] EWHC 3066 (QB). See also *Macleod v Newsquest (Sunday Herald) Ltd* [2007] CSOH 4.

serious newspaper and would not be taken to be making serious accusations of misconduct in this way. Even an obvious attempt at humour may, however, be actionable if it rests upon a clear factual assumption of the truth of a defamatory imputation.[426]

Vulgar abuse. Similar principles would apply to vulgar abuse, the question being whether the circumstances in which the words were used would convey a defamatory imputation to those who heard them. Insults or abuse which convey no defamatory imputation are not actionable as defamation[427] though they may be subject to some criminal sanction as tending to a breach of the peace or public order. Even if the words, taken literally and out of context, might be defamatory, the circumstances in which they are uttered may make it plain to the hearers that they cannot regard it as reflecting on the claimant's character so as to affect his reputation because they are spoken in the "heat of passion, or accompanied by a number of non-actionable, but scurrilous epithets, e.g. a blackguard, rascal, scoundrel, villain, etc."[428] for the "manner in which the words were pronounced may explain the meaning of the words."[429]

3.37

---

[426] *Entienne v Festival City Broadcasters* [2001] SASC 60; 79 S.A.S.R. 19 (obvious comic skit nevertheless conveyed the message that claimant was involved in drug dealing).

[427] See, e.g. *Rambo v Cohen*, 587 N.E.2d 147 (Ind. 1992) ("horse's butt"); *Marruchi v Harris* [1943] O.P.D. 15 ("maccaroni bastard"); *Wood v Branson* [1952] 3 S.A. 369 ("cow", "bitch"); *McGuire v Jankiewicz* 290 N.E.2d 675 (Ill. 1972) ("asshole" not defamatory of attorney). For an entertaining disquisition on the various nuances of "son of a bitch" (which alone is mere abuse) when accompanied by qualifying adjectives, see *Ralston v Fomich* [1994] 2 W.W.R. 284. In *Noorani v Calver* [2009] EWHC 561 (QB) Coulson J. rejected the defendant's argument that words alleged to have been spoken in a private conversation (which suggested the publishee was married to an Islamic terrorist) were mere vulgar abuse. Though the context in which the words were allegedly spoken (a shopping street in the middle of the day) provided some support for the suggestion that they were not to be taken seriously, "the alleged description of the claimant as an Islamic terrorist was so serious a matter that I could not conclude that the words were not capable of being defamatory" (at [14]). However, the claim was struck out as an abuse of process.

See also *Clynes v O'Connor* [2011] EWHC 1201 (QB) (abusive words directed by one neighbour to another in front of a small group of bystanders not treated as mere vulgar abuse though the fact that there had been an "admission" by the defendant was clearly relevant to that decision).

[428] *Christie v Robertson* (1899) 1 F. 1155 at 1157. In Scotland, words spoken in *rixa* are not actionable: see *M'Neill v Forbes* (1883) 10 R. 867; *Watson v Duncan* (1890) 17 R. 404; *Christie v Robertson* (1899) 1 F. 1155. To succeed in such a defence, it must be shown (1) that the words were spoken as pointless vituperation or abuse in the heat of an altercation; (2) that the words were not intended to convey the defamatory meaning; and (3) that the words were not understood to convey the defamatory meaning. Proof of (1) alone is not sufficient. "If", said Lord M'Laren in *Christie*, above, at 1157, "a party, under whatever amount of provocation, makes a definite charge of crime or dishonest conduct against another, giving such point in regard to time and circumstances as to lead those who were present to believe that the charge was seriously made, it is not a defence that the words were spoken in heat". *Rixa* in South African law is a somewhat fluid concept but seems best translated as provocation. See Burchell, *Law of Defamation in South Africa* (1985), Ch.20.

[429] *Penfold v Westcote* (1806) 2 Bos. & P.N.R. 335 at 336.

"'Mere vulgar abuse' is not a good or clear vehicle for the expression of the element in the interpretation of the words used that brings about the result that they were not likely to affect reputation. This topic has become associated with the expression 'mere vulgar abuse' in a way which I cannot dispel, but I regard this as unfortunate because the matter under consideration is not whether the publication constitutes mere vulgar abuse, but whether the imputation which

It is generally said that written words[430] cannot be treated as vulgar abuse[431] but while this would commonly be so in practice because they are much more likely to be taken seriously, it is difficult to see why it should be so as a matter of principle. Indeed, it has been held that bulletin board exchanges on the internet (which are almost certainly technically libel) are more susceptible of being equated for this purpose with slander because "it is often obvious to casual observers that people are just saying the first thing that comes into their heads and reacting in the heat of the moment".[432]

---

it conveys has a defamatory meaning: it may not have a defamatory meaning because the terms or the manner in which it is spoken show that it is not likely to injure reputation":
Bennette v Cohen [2005] NSWCA 341; 64 N.S.W.L.R. 81 at [51] per Bryson J.A. At the end of the day it may be just a question of how the claim is disposed of, since in England there must be a high chance of dismissal for abuse of process and under the current Australian legislation of the application of the defence of "triviality".

[430] The distinction cannot turn solely on whether the case is one of slander rather than libel for unscripted broadcast words are libel: see para.3.1, above.

[431] "For mere general abuse *spoken*, no action lies": *Thorley v Lord Kerry* (1812) 4 Taunt. 355 at 365. *Plummer v Charman (No.2)*, *The Times*, October 25, 1962; *Uren v Australian Consolidated* [1969] N.S.W.R. 745 at 752.

[432] *Smith v ADVFN Plc* [2008] EWHC 1797 (QB). *Burns v Pollock* [2001] BCSC 986, may be another example (exchange of emails indicated state of mind of sender but would not have made reasonable people think less of subjects). See also *McGrath v Dawkins* [2012] EWHC B3 (QB); *Tamiz v Google Inc.* [2012] EWHC 449 (QB); [2012] E.M.L.R. 24.

Chapter 4

SLANDERS ACTIONABLE PER SE

Section 1. General

Libel and slander. The distinction between libel and slander has already **4.1** been considered.[1] At common law libel is always actionable per se.[2] Generally speaking, slander is not so actionable[3] and a person defamed can only succeed on proof of "special damage" arising as the direct and natural and reasonable result of the publication of the words.[4] This is so no matter how malicious the publication, how disgraceful the imputation and however likely it is to cause damage to the claimant.[5]

However, in four classes of case slander is actionable per se and the claimant's cause of action is complete upon proof of publication of the defamatory words.

The four categories of slander actionable per se.   4.2

(1) Where the words impute a crime for which the claimant can be made to suffer physically by way of punishment.[6]

(2) Where the words impute to the claimant a contagious or infectious disease.[7]

---

[1] See Ch.3, s.2, above.

[2] See para.3.6, above.

[3] This has been modified in many jurisdictions: see para.3.8, above.

[4] See para.5.1, below.

[5] A defamatory letter read by one person is actionable per se. A slander published to a packed football stadium requires special damage.

[6] See para.4.3, below.

[7] See para.4.13, below. When it comes into force, s.14(2) of the Defamation Act 2013 will abolish, so far as the law of England and Wales is concerned, the common law rule which provides an exemption from the requirement for special damage where the imputation conveyed by the statement complained of is that the claimant has a contagious or infectious disease.

(3) Where the words are calculated to disparage the claimant in any office, profession, calling, trade or business held or carried on by him at the time of publication.[8]

(4) By the Slander of Women Act 1891,[9] where the words impute adultery or unchastity to a woman or girl.[10]

In all the above cases the words are actionable per se: the claimant need not prove that he has suffered any resulting damage, in the sense of actual financial damage,[11] for such damage is presumed.[12]

> "Every libel is of itself a wrong in regard to which the law implies general damage ... Akin to actions of libel are those actions which are brought for oral slander, where such slander consists of words actionable in themselves, and the mere use of which constitutes the infringement of the plaintiff's right. The very speaking of such words, apart from all damage, constitutes a wrong and gives rise to a cause of action. The law in such a case presumes, and in theory allows proof of, general damage."[13]

The first three of these exceptional cases depend upon the common law, but in the case of the third (probably the most important in practice) there has been a substantial statutory modification.

Section 2. Criminal Offences

4.3 Words imputing a criminal offence. Words which impute to the claimant the commission of a crime for which a person may be made to suffer "corporally"—i.e. physically—"by way of punishment"[14] are actionable without proof of special damage.[15] Because a corporation cannot be made to

---

[8] See para.4.15, below.

[9] See para.4.20, below.

[10] The Slander of Women Act 1891 will be repealed by s.14(1) of the Defamation Act 2013 when it comes into force. See below at para.4.22.

[11] Under s.1 of the Defamation Act 2013, the claimant will have to show, if the statement is to be actionable, that the statement complained of caused serious harm to his reputation: para.2.5. This does not affect the common law presumption of damage: para.3.7.

[12] See *M'Pherson v Daniels* (1829) 10 B. & C. 263; *Jones v Jones* [1916] 2 A.C. 481 HL at 500. But where no damage is likely to be suffered the claim is just as susceptible to striking out as an abuse of process as one for libel: see para.3.6, above.

[13] Per Bowen L.J. in *Ratcliffe v Evans* [1892] 2 Q.B. 524 CA at 529, 530; *Halls v Mitchell* (1927) 59 O.L.R. 590.

[14] Cf. the Restatement 2d, *Torts*, para.571—punishable with imprisonment *or* regarded by public opinion as involving moral turpitude. There are varying formulations in the US case law, but none extends to all crimes: 50 Am.Jur.2d, *Libel and Slander*, para.167.

[15] Comyn Dig., *Action on the Case for Defamation*, D. 5, 9; *Webb v Beavan* (1883) 11 Q.B.D. 609 at 610; *Michael v Spiers and Pond* (1909) 101 L.T. 352; *Hellwig v Mitchell* [1910] 1 K.B. 609 at 614; *Ormiston v G.W. Ry* [1917] 1 K.B. 598; *Heimann v Meissner* [1936] N.Z.L.R. Supp. 56. See also *Brady v Norman* [2010] EWHC 1215 (QB) per Eady J. at [11] (allegation of forgery would constitute slander actionable per se, since by reason of s.6(2) of the Forgery and Counterfeiting Act 1981 the offence carries a maximum penalty of ten years' imprisonment).

suffer in this way there is some doubt whether it is actionable per se to impute to a corporation a crime for which an individual could be imprisoned. In *D & L Caterers v D'Ajou*[16] Stable J. decided that it was but the Court of Appeal expressly reserved the point.

The reason why such slander is actionable per se. Although one **4.4** might support the rule that an accusation of crime is actionable per se on the ground that it exposes the claimant to the jeopardy of a prosecution[17] and that would explain why it is not actionable per se to charge criminal intent or proclivity[18] or to charge what, on the proper interpretation of the words, is not capable of being a crime even though the speaker and all the listeners believe it is,[19] it is now settled that the true reason is the obloquy and ostracism to which the charge exposes the claimant. Atkinson J. so held in *Gray v Jones*[20] after a review of the authorities and at an early stage it was held actionable without proof of special damage to impute to the claimant a crime for which he had already been convicted and punished,[21] or to impute to the claimant a crime for which prosecution is barred, either by a Statute of Limitations,[22] or because the statute creating the crime has been repealed.[23] So, in *Fowler v Dowdney*,[24] the plaintiff sued the defendant for calling him "a returned convict". It was contended for the defendant that the words were not actionable without proof of special damage as they imputed no present liability, but rather that the plaintiff had already suffered punishment, but Lord Denman C.J. ruled that the words were actionable as imputing some offence for which the plaintiff was liable to be transported, adding "they import, to be sure, that the punishment has been suffered, but still the obloquy remains".[25]

Crime need not be indictable. The crime imputed need not be indictable; **4.5** it is sufficient if it be triable summarily. However it must be an offence for

---

[16] [1945] K.B. 210.

[17] This was the reason given by Parke B. in *Heming v Power* (1842) 10 M. & W. 564 at 569. See also *Carslake v Mapledoram* (1788) 2 Term Rep. 473 at 475 per Ashurst J. It should be noted, however, that in some of the early cases the basis of the decision appears not to have been the danger of loss of liberty but instead the scandal to which the allegation exposed the victim. See, by way of example, *Boston v Tatam* (1621) Cro Jac 622 (the words spoken were that the plaintiff was a thief who had stolen the defendant's gold. The court overruled the defendant's objection that the theft might have been committed "in former times" since when the plaintiff might have been pardoned. The court stated that, "It was a great slander to be once a thief, for although a pardon may discharge him of the punishment, yet the scandal of the offence remains.").

[18] See para.4.8, below.

[19] See para.4.6, below.

[20] (1939) 55 T.L.R. 437.

[21] *Gainford v Tuke* (1620) Cro.Jac. 536; *Boston v Tatam* (1622) Cro.Jac. 623; *Carpenter v Tarrant* (1736) Cases in K.B. *temp.* Hardwicke 339; *Beavor v Hides* (1766) 2 Wilson 300; *Fowler v Dowdney* (1838) 2 Mood. & R. 119; *Krebs v Oliver* (1858) 78 Mass. R. 239.

[22] *Webb v Fitch* (1793) 1 Root (Conn.) R. 544.

[23] *French v Creath* (1820) 1 Ill. R. 31 at 69.

[24] (1838) 2 Mood. & R. 119.

[25] For numerous examples of accusations held actionable per se, see the 8th edition of this book at para.150. Most of them remain valid today but what counts is the present state of the criminal law and whether the crime in question is punishable with imprisonment.

which a person may be made to suffer physically by way of punishment.[26] It makes no difference that the court may inflict a fine in addition, or in the alternative.[27] But if the offence imputed be punishable by fine only, the words are not actionable per se,[28] even though there is power to commit to prison in default of payment of such fine.[29] It is not enough that the crime, though not punishable by imprisonment, renders the claimant liable to summary arrest and detention.[30]

4.6 Words must impute a criminal offence. To be actionable per se the words must impute a criminal offence. Other conduct, such as a trespass,[31] a breach of contract,[32] or a non-criminal breach of trust[33] will not do, even though the defendant intends to impute a criminal offence and the hearers understand it in this way[34] and even though the obloquy to which the claimant is exposed is just as great as if the conduct charged were criminal. Examples are provided by two old cases, though they would now be decided differently because of changes in the law of theft. Where defendant charged the plaintiff, a churchwarden, with stealing the parish bell-ropes, it was held that inasmuch as a churchwarden had possession of the bell-ropes he could not be guilty of stealing them, and therefore no action would lie.[35] Moreover where the defendant said that the plaintiff had "broken open a box belonging to his (plaintiff's) wife, in her room, and had robbed her of about £75", it was held that the words were not actionable, for they did not impute an offence.[36]

A more modern illustration, which remains valid, is a case where the defendant accused the plaintiff of "stealing" information from a file so as to solicit the defendant's customers.[37] For the same reasons, while it is actionable without proof of special damage to accuse someone of perjury,[38] it is not

---

[26] *Ogden v Turner* (1705) 6 Mod. 104; *Webb v Beavan* (1883) 11 Q.B.D. 609 at 610; *Michael v Spiers and Pond Ltd* (1909) 101 L.T. 352 at 353; *Hellwig v Mitchell* [1910] 1 K.B. 609; *D & L Caterers Ltd and Jackson v D'Ajou* [1945] K.B. 210 CA; *Routley v Hams* (1889) 18 O.R. 405; *McDonald v Mulqueen* (1922) 53 O.L.R. 191.

[27] *McDonald v Mulqueen* (1922) 53 O.L.R. 191.

[28] *Sanders v Percy* [2009] EWHC 1870 (QB) (imputation of driving without a tax disc, punishable only by fine, struck out as disclosing no cause of action); *Gray v Jones* (1939) 55 T.L.R. 437; [1939] 1 All E.R. 798 at 440; *Michael v Spiers and Pond Ltd* (1909) 101 L.T. 352 at 353; *Ogden v Turner* (1705) 6 Mod. 104; *M'Cabe v Foot* (1866) 15 L.T. 115; *Hellwig v Mitchell* [1910] 1 K.B. 609, followed *Heimann v Meissner* [1936] N.Z.L.R.Supp. 56.

[29] *Michael v Spiers and Pond* (1909) 101 L.T.352; *Ormiston v G.W. Ry* [1917] 1 K.B. 598; *Robertson v Robertson* (1921) 67 D.L.R. 496.

[30] *Hellwig v Mitchell* [1910] 1 K.B. 609.

[31] *Herrington v McBay* (1889) 29 N.B.R. 670.

[32] *Christie v Cowell* (1790) Peake 4; *Gray v Chilman (No.2)* [1935] S.A.S.R. 359 (special constable not indictable for general inattention to duty).

[33] *Thompson v Bernard* (1807) 1 Camp. 47.

[34] *Jackson v Adams* (1835) 2 Bing. N.C. 402; *Williams v Stott* (1833) 1 Cr. & M. 675; *Young v Sloan* (1852) 2 Up.Can.C.P. 284; *Lemon v Simmons* (1888) 57 L.J.Q.B. 260.

[35] *Jackson v Adams* (1835) 2 Bing. N.C. 402; *Ferris v Irwin* (1860) 10 Up.Can.L.R. 116.

[36] *Lemon v Simmons* (1888) 57 L.1.Q.B. 260.

[37] *Lawrence v Finch* [1931] 1 D.L.R. 689 Ont. CA. But in modern conditions such a person might commit an offence under s.1 of the Computer Misuse Act 1990.

[38] *Ceely v Hoskins* (1638) Cro.Car. 509; *Roberts v Camden* (1807) 9 East 93.

merely to say that he is "forsworn"[39] or has "taken a false oath",[40] because, though the taking of a false oath may be disgraceful, it is not a criminal offence unless taken under such circumstances as would make it perjury.

It has been held in Canada that words which impute that the plaintiff has committed a criminal offence in a foreign country are actionable without proof of special damage, whether the offence was one for which the plaintiff could be extradited or not, but there is no English decision on the point.[41]

Charge need not be specific. The exact offence need not be specified; **4.7** words involving a general charge of criminality will suffice, provided they impute some offence for which the claimant can be made to suffer corporally by way of punishment.[42] Thus it would be actionable to say of a person in the presence of others "You have committed an act for which I can have you put in prison",[43] or "for which you ought to be put in prison",[44] or "I know enough to put you in prison".[45] Words which impute a crime are actionable though they describe it in popular or even slang terms.[46] "The meaning of the words is to be gathered from the vulgar import, and not from any technical legal sense."[47]

Imputation of intention or proclivity to commit crime. Words which **4.8** merely impute an intention or inclination to commit a crime are not actionable without proof of special damage, for a criminal intention does not amount to

---

[39] *Guerdon v Winterstud* (1593) Cro.Eliz. 308; *Harris v Dixon* (1608) Cro.Jac. 158.

[40] *Holt v Scholefield* (1796) 6 T.R. 691; *Hall v Weedon* (1826) 8 Dowl. & Ry. 140.

[41] *Smith v Collins* (1846) 3 Up.Can.Q.B. 1, and see *Malloch v Graham* (1832) 2 Up.Can. Q.B.(O.S.) 375; *Porter v McMahon* (1885) 25 N.B.R. 211; *Fox v Goodfellow* [1926] N.Z.L.R. 58 at 62; *Furlong v German-American Press Assn*, 189 S.W. 385 (1916).

[42] Com.Dig. *Action on the Case for Defamation*, D. 4; *Donne's Case* (1587) Cro.Eliz. 62; *Webb v Beavan* (1883) 11 Q.B.D. 609; *Munafo v Helfand* (1956) 140 F.Supp. 234; *Odongkara v Astles* [1970] E.A. 374. See also *Noorani v Calver* [2009] EWHC 561 (QB): imputation that the claimant was an "Islamic terrorist" held actionable per se. Being a terrorist is a criminal offence as defined by numerous recent statutes. The fact that the allegation was not to the effect that the claimant was a bomber or an assassin did not prevent them from relating to the commission of serious and specific criminal offences (at [16]); *Sanders v Percy* [2009] EWHC 1870 (QB) ("benefit fraudster"). For the interpretation of ambiguous words, see para.3.24, above.

[43] *Curtis v Curtis* (1834) 10 Bing. 477.

[44] *Francis v Roose* (1838) 3 M. & W. 191.

[45] *Webb v Beavan* (1883) 11 Q.B.D. 609; and see *Johnson v Shields* (1855) 25 N.J. 116 ("I know enough to send him to a penitentiary"). In *Cockburn v Reakie* (1890) 17 R. 568 such an imputation could not be inferred in the context.

[46] *Colman v Godwin* (1782) 3 Doug.K.B. 90; *Bureau v Campbell* [1928] 2 W.W.R. 535; *Merkoff v Pawluk* [1931] 1 W.W.R. 669; *Noorani v Calver* [2009] EWHC 561 (QB) ("Islamic terrorist"). In *Clynes v O'Connor* [2011] EWHC 1201 (QB) defendant in a dispute with her neighbour called him a "wife beater", a "drug dealer" and either (depending on which version is preferred) a "paedophile" or a "perv". The defendant admitted liability and the issue was simply therefore one of damages but Eady J. stated (at [9])) that it would not be right to treat such specific allegations as "mere vulgar abuse."

[47] Per Buller J. in *Colman v Godwin* (1783) 3 Doug.K.B. 90 at 91.

a crime.[48] But to impute an attempt to commit an indictable crime is actionable without proof of special damage, for an attempt to commit an indictable crime is an offence punishable corporally.[49] Thus where the words were "She would have cut her husband's throat and did attempt to do it", it was held that no action lay for the words "She would have cut her husband's throat", but that an action was maintainable for the remaining words which charged an attempt.[50] A fortiori therefore it is not actionable to state an opinion that the claimant will commit a crime in the future[51] or that he would commit a crime if the opportunity presented itself.[52]

4.9 Suspicion and opinion. Words which do not definitely charge a crime, but impute a mere suspicion that the claimant has committed a crime, or has been charged with a crime[53] are not actionable without proof of special damage.[54] But words which are expressive of the belief that the claimant has committed a crime, e.g. "It is my opinion that the claimant is a thief", are equivalent to an allegation that the claimant is a thief, and are actionable per se.[55]

> "Were an objection to be sustained to an action for slanderous words in such a case because of the use of the words 'in my opinion,' it would be easy for one who designed to injure the character of another to effect his malicious purpose without incurring any responsibility. By circulating the slander, clothed in expression of opinion or belief, he might destroy the fairest reputation with impunity. But the law will not permit an injury done to character by such an artifice to be without remedy. Whatever may be the mode of expression used, if an assertion of guilt is implied the words will be actionable."[56]

---

[48] *Dr Poe's Case*, cited 2 Bulstrode at 206; *Stoner v Audley* (1590) Cro.Eliz. 250; *Mayne v Digle* (1762) Freeman K.B. 45; *Harrison v Stratton* (1802) 4 Esp. 217 at 219, per Lord Ellenborough C.J.; *Stone v World Newspaper* (1918) 44 O.L.R. 33; *Conyd v Brekelmans* [1971] 3 W.W.R. 107.

[49] *R. v Roderick* (1837) 7 C. & P. 795; *R. v Butler* (1834) 6 C. & P. 368. An attempt to commit a summary offence is not an offence, in the absence of express statutory provision: Criminal Attempts Act 1981.

[50] *Scot v Hilliar* (1611) Lane 98.

[51] *Annison v Blofield* (1682) Carter 215; *Simon v Shearson Lehman Bros*, 895 F.2d 1304 (CA 11, 1990). But the nature of treason means that it may be committed with little more than intention: see *Odongkara v Astles* [1970] E.A. 374.

[52] *Dubord v Lambert* [1928] 3 D.L.R. 538 ("you can go home now . . . there are no pigs to steal here" incapable of imputing that P *had* stolen pigs even if D had that in mind); *Kaye v Prisma Corp*, 568 N.Y.S. 2d 103 (1991) (statement by D that he wished to watch P pack her belongings to make sure she did not steal company property).

[53] *Le Blanc v l'Imprimerie* [1955] 5 D.L.R. 91 (under New Brunswick statute making libel subject to the rules of slander in the case of certain newspaper publications); *Tucker v Douglas* [1950] 2 D.L.R. 827 Sask. CA, affirmed [1952] 1 D.L.R. 657.

[54] *Frank v Alsop* (1608) Cro.Jac 215; *Tozer v Mashford* (1851) 6 Exch. 539; *Simmons v Mitchell* (1880) 6 A.C. 156; *Gorst v Barr* (1887) 13 O.R. 644 at 651; *Persen v Rainbow* [1922] 1 W.W.R. 592. Cf. the position in libel: see para.3.28, above. Where the words admit fairly of two meanings, the one being an imputation of suspicion only, the other of guilt, the matter should be left to the jury: *Simmons v Mitchell*, above, at 162 and para.3.23, above.

[55] *Stich v Wisedom* (1594) Cro.Eliz. 348; *Peake v Oldham* (1775) 2 Wm. Black 961; *Lowe v Brown* 235 P. 235 (Or., 1925); *Rocca v Manhire* (1992) 57 S.A.S.R. 224.

[56] Per curiam in *Logan v Steele* (1809) 2 K.R. 93 at 95. Although there are constitutional restrictions of somewhat uncertain extent on liability for defamatory "opinion" in the US (see

Context to be considered. As in all cases of defamation, words which are   **4.10**
said to constitute accusations of crime must be considered in the context in
which they are used.[57] Words which prima facie impute a crime are not
actionable without proof of special damage if it is clear from their context, or
from facts stated by the speaker or known to the hearers, that they were in fact
neither used nor understood to convey a criminal imputation.[58] For example,
words may be used figuratively: to charge the plaintiff with highway robbery
is clearly actionable per se but where the plaintiff was said to have "held the
town up" over the price of land needed for a development, this merely
imputed hard bargaining.[59] Similarly such words might be spoken by way of
vulgar abuse.[60] The burden of proving these facts and their effect lies on the
defendant.[61]

Examples. Thus where the words complained of were: "Thompson is a   **4.11**
damned thief, and so was his father before him, and I can prove it", but these
words followed: "Thompson received the earnings of the ship, and ought to
pay the wages", Lord Ellenborough C.J. directed a non-suit on the ground that
it was clear from the whole conversation that the words did not impute a
felony, but only a mere breach of trust.[62] It has been held that it is not
actionable per se to impute to a person a crime which the audience know he
cannot have committed,[63] e.g. to charge A with killing B when, to the
audience's knowledge, B is alive, for, it is said, they could not then have
understood the words to impute murder.[64] If this is the law it is not clear how
it is to be reconciled with the common law principle that a statement may be
actionable even if published only to persons who do not believe it to be true

---

para.12.1, below) they would seem not to be applicable to this sort of opinion, which implies
underlying facts.

[57] For context generally, see para.3.30, above.

[58] *Brittridge's Case* (1602) 4 Co.Rep. 19b; *Christie v Cowell* (1790) Peake 4; *Robin v
Hildredon* (1606) Cro.Jac. 65; *Thompson v Bernard* (1807) 1 Camp. 47; *Day v Robinson* (1834)
1 A. & E. 556; *Beardsley v Dibblee* (1841) 3 Kerr N.B.R. 246; *Herrington v McBay* (1889) 29
N.B.R. 670; cf. *Cockburn v Reekie* (1890) 17 R. 568.

[59] *Holland v Hall* [1912] 3 D.L.R. 722 Ont. CA; *Narvey v Green* [1941] 3 D.L.R. 759; cf. *Taylor
v Carr* (1847) 3 U.C.Q.B. 306 ("public robber" connoted fraud).

[60] See, e.g. *Todosichuk v MacLenahan* [1946] 1 D.L.R. 557 ("pimp"); *Brockley v Maxwell*
[1949] 2 D.L.R. 784 ("bastard, liar and cheat"); *Lever v George* [1950] 2 D.L.R. 85 ("cheap
bastard . . . has a mysterious fire"); *Waymire v de Haven* 858 S.W.2d 69 (Ark. 1993) ("crook");
Williams v Rutherford Freight Lines Inc., 179 S.E.2d 319 (N.C., 1971). Cf. *Clynes v O'Connor*
[2011] EWHC 1201 (QB). See para.3.37, above.

[61] *Stoner v Audley* (1580) Cro.Eliz. 250; *Tomlinson v Brittlebank* (1833) 4 B. & Ad. 630. For
the burden of proof, see also para.3.36, above.

[62] *Thompson v Bernard* (1807) 1 Camp. 47.

[63] Cf. *Clynes v O'Connor* [2011] EWHC 1201 (QB) in which it was said that none of the
people standing nearby "appears to have believed what she said or taken it seriously" (at [3]).
However, liability was not in issue.

[64] *Tenney v Clement* (1838) 10 N.H. 52 at 58. Similarly, it has been said not to be actionable
to charge a tenant in common of a chattel with theft of it where the audience were aware of the
tenancy in common and such a crime was not known to the law: *Carter v Anderson* (1834) 33
Mass. R. 1; *Williams v Miner* (1847) 18 Conn. R. 464. See also *Heming v Power* (1842) 10 M.
& W. 564 at 570.

or who know it to be untrue.[65] It seems artificial to say that in such a case the audience cannot understand the words to impute crime, especially bearing in mind that the defendant might appear to the audience not to know the facts inconsistent with the charge.

4.12 Judge and jury. It is a question of law for the judge whether the acts and conduct imputed to the claimant amount to a crime punishable with imprisonment. If the words are not reasonably capable of being understood as imputing a crime, the judge should withdraw the case from the jury.[66]

SECTION 3. WORDS IMPUTING A CONTAGIOUS DISEASE[67]

4.13 Scope of this category. It is not easy to state a test to determine when an imputation of illness is defamatory[68] and the scope of the category of slanderous imputations of disease which are actionable per se is still more obscure. However three things can be said with some confidence:

(1) the English cases in which the issue has been litigated are all old and date from an era when it would be unsafe to assume that the distinction between libel and slander was as clear as it now is[69];

(2) it is clear that the illness must be contagious or infectious—an imputation of mental illness is not within the category,[70] although such an imputation may be defamatory[71];

---

[65] See para.2.1, above. Defamation Act 2013, s.1 requires a claimant to prove that he has suffered or is likely to suffer serious harm to his reputation. It must therefore be doubtful whether, so far as the law of England and Wales is concerned, a statement published only to people who do not believe it will be actionable.

[66] See paras 34.3, 34.12, below. As to the situation where both a defamatory and an innocent meaning are possible see paras 3.23, above and 34.7, below. Once Defamation Act 2013, s.11 is brought into effect, the presumption in favour of jury trial will be abolished and trial by jury will become vanishingly rare: see para.4.1, above.

[67] S.14(2) of the Defamation Act 2013 will abolish, so far as the law of England and Wales is concerned, the common law rule which provides an exemption from the requirement for special damage to words imputing a contagious disease.

[68] See paras 2.6. and 2.14, above.

[69] See para.3.8, above.

[70] *Countess of Shrewsbury's Case* (1625) Bendloe 155, *Bootham v Smith* (1911) 19 O.W.R. 147: and see per Martin B. in *Morgan v Lingen* (1863) 8 L.T. 800 at 801. But such an imputation might be actionable per se under the next section. See, e.g. *Miles v Record Publishing Co*, 133 S.E. 99 (S.C., 1926) (dairyman stated to be a typhoid carrier). Rather curiously smallpox was excluded in *James v Rutlech* (1599) 4 Co. Rep. 17a.

[71] Imputations of some other non-contagious diseases (e.g. cancer or heart disease) would not generally be defamatory at all: see para.2.6, above. Cf. *Chuy v Philadelphia Eagles*, 595 F.2d (CA 3 1979) (red blood cell condition).

(3) it is only in the case of venereal disease[72] and, perhaps, leprosy[73] that there is clear authority for inclusion.[74]

There are, however, various dicta which go further.[75] Nor is it clear what is the basis of the category. If it were confined to venereal disease it might be explained on the basis of moral censure,[76] but the cases justify the category by reference to the effect of the imputation being to exclude the claimant from society as a person with whom it is unsafe to associate.[77] "It makes no difference whether the disease be owing to the visitation of God, to accident, or to the indiscretion of the party therewith afflicted; for, in every one of the cases, the being avoided, from whence the damage arises, is the consequence."[78] On this basis the category should be extended to cover any serious communicable disease[79] or dropped altogether.[80]

Whatever the scope of this category of slander actionable per se it is not essential that the imputation should be conveyed in direct or technical medical terms; it is sufficient if it is conveyed by a description of its symptoms, or its effects on the sufferer,[81] or by any other words which would lead reasonable persons to understand that a relevant disease is imputed.[82]

---

[72] *Milner v Reeves* (1617) 1 Roll.Abr. 43 (pox); *Bloodworth v Gray* (1844) 7 M. & Gr. 334 (pox); *Houseman v Coulson* [1948] 2 D.L.R. ("VD"); *Derig v Zawadaski* [1943] Que.S.C. 150. See also *Taylor v Perkins* (1607) Cro.Jac. 144. The cases seem to be concerned with syphilis and gonorrhea and there are many less serious sexually communicable diseases. It would, however, be extraordinary if an imputation of being HIV positive were not actionable per se.

[73] *Taylor v Perkins* (1607) Cro.Jac. 144. *Simpson v Press Publishing*, 67 N.Y.S. (1900) and *Lewis v Hayes*, 132 P. 1022 (Cal., 1913) are cases of libel, though the issue is confused by the American doctrine of libel per se and *per quod*: see para.3.6, above.

[74] In *Villers v Monsley* (1769) 2 Wils. 403 Wilmot L.C.J. equates leprosy, the plague and the itch. But the point in that case was whether it was libellous to assert that the plaintiff had the itch and Gould J. and (with some hesitation) Bathurst J. thought that it would not be actionable without more to say that the plaintiff had the itch; see 91 L.Q.R. at 537–538 for a discussion of the context.

[75] In *Watkins v Hall* (1868) L.R. 3 Q.B. 396 at 399, Blackburn J. referred to "infectious disease" without limitation; thus also 3 Black.Comm. 123. See also *Jones v Jones* [1916] 2 A.C. 481 at 490, 500, 507. The reference to scarlet fever in *Riding v Smith* (1876) I Ex.D. at 94 seems not to be relevant.

[76] But not necessarily: a person may contract venereal disease without immoral behaviour.

[77] "The reason why the making of such a charge is actionable is because the having a contagious disorder renders the person an improper member of society": per Buller J. in *Carslake v Mapledoram* (1788) 2 T.R. 473 at 475; *Jones v Jones* [1916] 2 A.C. 481 at 507, per lord Wrenbury ("tending to exclude the plaintiff from society"). See also para.4.14 (words not actionable per se if statement relates to past).

[78] 7 Bac.Abr. tit. *Slander* 266.

[79] Thus it is hard to understand why smallpox may be excluded, as appears from the obscure case of *James v Rutlech* (1599) 4 Co.Rep. 17a. The Restatement 2d., *Torts*, para.527 makes actionable per se imputations of venereal disease or other loathsome and communicable disease.

[80] It will be abolished for England and Wales by Defamation Act 2013, s.14(2). For a full discussion of the problem, see Eldredge, *Law of Defamation* (1978), para.20.

[81] See *Miller's Case* (1618) Cro.Jac. 430.

[82] *French v Smith* [1922] 3 D.L.R. 902; *C v D* [1925] 1 D.L.R. 734; *Monks v Monks*, 20 N.E. 744 (Ind., 1889) ("plaintiff has a loathsome disease and he caught it while in the army").

4.14 Imputation must relate to time when words spoken. To be actionable without proof of special damage the words must impute that the claimant is suffering from the disease at the time when the words were spoken. Words which impute that the claimant has suffered from a contagious disease in the past (unless they import that he is still suffering from the disease)[83] are not actionable without proof of special damage, for they do not show that he is at present unfit for society, and therefore the substance of the action is wanting.[84] "It is the avoiding him for fear of contagion and refusing to keep him company that is the legal notion of damage, and when he is cured those inconveniences will not attend him."[85]

SECTION 4. WORDS CALCULATED TO DISPARAGE IN ANY OFFICE, PROFESSION, CALLING, TRADE OR BUSINESS

4.15 Development of the law: the Defamation Act 1952. At common law slander was actionable per se if it was calculated to disparage the reputation of the plaintiff in any office held by him, or in any lawful[86] profession, calling, trade or business carried on by him. However, the rule generally only applied[87] if the words were spoken "in the way of" the office, etc.[88] Thus in *Jones v Jones*[89] the defendant stated that the plaintiff, a schoolmaster, had committed adultery with the caretaker's wife and a verdict for the plaintiff was set aside because the words were spoken without reference to his profession.[90]

---

[83] *Irons v Field* (1869) 9 Rhode Island R. 216.

[84] *Smith's Case* (1669) Noy 151; *Taylor v Hall* (1743) 2 Strange 1189; *Carslake v Mapledoram* (1788) 2 T.R. 473 at 475; *Halls v Mitchell* [1927] 1 D.L.R 163 Ont. CA (an imputation that the effects of the disease exist is not equivalent to an imputation that the disease remains); *Sungravure v Middle East Airlines* (1974) 134 C.L.R. 1 at 23–24. Since the Slander of Women Act 1891, an imputation that a woman has suffered from a venereal disease in time past is actionable per se if unchastity is imputed thereby; see para.4.20, below.

[85] Per curiam in *Taylor v Hall* (1743) 2 Strange 1189.

[86] Statements disparaging the claimant in an unlawful calling, etc. are not actionable: see para.2.24, above.

[87] There were two exceptions. Words disparaging the credit of a tradesman were actionable without any reference to his business: *Stanton v Smith* (1727) 2 Ld. Raym. 1480; *Jones v Littler* (1841) 7 M. & W. 423; *Jones v Jones* [1916] 2 A.C. 481 at 498, 507. Whether this was a true exception is doubtful because, as Lord Wrenbury pointed out in *Jones v Jones* [1916] 2 A.C. 481 at 507, "solvency is so essential a factor in the existence of a trader that to speak of him as insolvent will necessarily 'touch him in his trade' ". Similarly, it was actionable per se to impute to a clergyman of the Church of England holding a benefice or some other office of temporal profit conduct which, if true, would be a cause of deprivation or degradation from orders, even if there were no reference to the office. See the 8th edition of this book, para.176.

[88] The common law continues to apply in Trinidad and Tobago: *Panday v Gordon* [2005] UKPC 36; [2006] 1 A.C. 427.

[89] [1916] 2 A.C. 481 Lord Sumner pointed out at 495 that the standard form of pleading was that the words were spoken "of and concerning the plaintiff in his profession or calling of . . . ". See also *Weidberg v La Guardia*, 10 N.Y.S.2d 445 (1939) (mayor referred to attorney in political meeting as a "bum [found] in a gin mill").

[90] It was accepted that the words were likely to endanger him in his employment (though they had not in fact harmed him in it) and it is suggested in the case that at that time most employers would have dismissed for such immoral conduct. It seems unlikely now that adultery between

This rule was abolished by s.2 of the Defamation Act 1952, which provides that in "an action for slander in respect of words, calculated to disparage the plaintiff in any office, profession, calling, trade or business carried on by him at the time of the publication it shall not be necessary to allege or prove special damage, whether or not the words are spoken of the plaintiff in the way of his office, profession, calling, trade or business."[91]

Calculated to disparage. There appears to be no direct authority on the **4.16** meaning of "calculated",[92] though there is some on the similar phrase "calculated to cause pecuniary damage" in s.3 of the 1952 Act (which deals with malicious falsehood). Though "calculated to" may have the subjective sense of "intended to bring about a certain result" it is often used in the law in the broader, objective sense of "likely to produce a result"[93] and it has been interpreted in this way in cases under s.3[94] and this seems the most likely sense under s.2.[95] "Disparage" has been said to be synonymous with "discredit".[96] In *Andre v Price*[97] Tugendhat J. noted that there can be degrees both of "likelihood" and "disparagement". However s.2 had to be interpreted in a way that required more than a minimal meaning to be attributed to each of the words to reflect the importance of art.10 rights: "It would be inconsistent with

---

members of staff of a school would endanger their employment unless in some way it brought the school into disrepute (e.g. a religious school).

[91] Presumably in such cases the claimant can recover damages for annoyance and distress, whether or not financial loss is shown. See also para.21.13, below. For the position in the case of slanders not actionable per se, see para.5.10, below.

[92] "Disparage" is synonymous with "discredit": *Maccaba v Lichtenstein* [2004] EWHC 1580 (QB).

[93] See, e.g. *McDowell v Standard Oil* [1927] A.C. 632 (trade mark legislation); *Craften v Webster (No.2)* (1980) 23 S.A.S.R. 321 (electoral legislation). In *Maccaba v Lichtenstein* [2004] EWHC 1580 (QB) it was common ground that the test whether words are likely to disparage the plaintiff is an objective one upon which no evidence is admissible. The facts of *Wilkinson v Downton* [1897] 2 Q.B. 57 suggest that Wright J. intended the latter sense.

[94] *Customglass Boats v Salthouse Boats* [1976] R.P.C. 589 at 602 (interpreting s.5(1) of the New Zealand Defamation Act 1954, which was the equivalent of s.3(1) of the English Act); *Allason v Campbell*, unreported, June 30, 1993 (Morland J.), reversed without deciding this point, February 9, 1995, CA.

[95] This meaning was common ground in *Maccaba v Lichtenstein* [2004] EWHC 1580 (QB) and *Andre v Price* [2010] EWHC 2572 (QB). If the words are not likely to produce the result it seems that the claimant should not be able to rely in the alternative upon an intention to produce the result. Though the statute offers no guidance on the point, it is submitted that the relative roles of judge and jury should be similar to those where the issue is whether the words are capable of bearing a defamatory meaning, that is to say that it should be for the judge to rule whether the words are capable of disparaging the claimant in his calling, etc. in the eyes of the reasonable hearer and, if they are, for the jury to decide whether they in fact do so: see para.34.12, below. Under the old law it was a question of fact for the jury whether the words were spoken of the plaintiff in relation to his office, profession or trade, provided there was any evidence that they were so spoken which was for the judge to determine: *Doyley v Roberts* (1837) 3 Bing. N.C. 835; *Jones v Littler* (1841) 7 M. & W. 423; *Lott v Drury* (1882) 1 O.R. 577; *Ronald v Harper* (1910) 11 C.L.R. 63 at 73; *Dauncey v Holloway* [1901] 2 K.B. 441; *West v Wormell*, *The Times*, November 4, 1926; cf. *Hopwood v Muirson* [1945] K.B. 313 CA.

[96] *Maccaba v Lichtenstein* [2004] EWHC 1580 (QB) per Gray J. at [2].

[97] [2010] EWHC 2572 (QB).

Article 10 to impose liability for slander when the effect upon a Claimant's reputation was below a certain threshold." Having said that, his lordship agreed with counsel that in this context "calculated" must mean something less than "more likely than not".[98] Whether s.2 is satisfied must be considered not only in the light of the words complained of but also the context in which they are spoken.[99]

4.17 Examples. (1) Words will be actionable per se where they are defamatory of the claimant only because of his calling—they then necessarily disparage him in it by imputing unfitness. It is not defamatory to say of the claimant that he knows no law or no surgery or no religion, but it is defamatory to say such things of a lawyer[100] or of a surgeon[101] or of a clergyman.[102] (2) But even if the words do not relate to qualifications peculiar to the claimant's calling and would be defamatory if published of others, they are actionable per se if they would be likely adversely to affect his professional reputation (and not merely his private character) in the eyes of reasonable people.[103] Thus it would be actionable per se under this head to say of a judge that he was inattentive and unable to keep awake on the bench but not, it is submitted, in England in 2013 to say that he had committed adultery.[104] In *Hopwood v Muirson*[105] the defendant depreciated a character reference written by the plaintiff by saying it had been obtained "from that pimp Hopwood ... His very calling as a solicitor makes him write whatever suits his client best. Damn it, he would sue his grandmother for 7s. 6d." The action failed because in writing the reference the plaintiff was not acting in a professional capacity but as a friend and the words were therefore not spoken of him "in the way of" his profession or did not "touch" his professional reputation, even though they mentioned his

---

[98] Ibid. at [97].

[99] *Maccaba v Lichtenstein* [2004] EWHC 1580 (QB) per Gray J. at [9]; *Andre v Price* [2010] EWHC 2572 (QB) per Tugendhat J. at [99].

[100] See para.2.41, above.

[101] See para.2.43, above.

[102] See para.2.40, above.

[103] See also Restatement, 2d, *Torts*, para.573, comment c. Disparagement of a general character, equally discreditable to all persons, is not enough, unless the particular quality disparaged is peculiarly valuable in the plaintiff's business: *Clemente v Espinosa*, 749 F.Supp. 672 (1990).

[104] Note however that in *Maccaba v Lichtenstein* [2004] EWHC 1580 (QB) Gray J. was prepared to accept that imputations of adultery with young Jewish married women against an orthodox Jewish businessman who was chief executive officer and acting chairman of an information technology company should be left to the jury as they were capable of having been likely to disparage the claimant in his business. While his lordship acknowledged that many businessmen would be wholly unaffected, in relation to their business, by an accusation of adultery, the position may be different if, for example, the bookseller specialised in the sale of religious books. In such cases, the particular claimant, the nature of his business, the activities in which he engages in connection with his business and the kind of people with whom he regularly does business had to be taken into account (at [9]). Cf. *Andre v Price* [2010] EWHC 2572 (QB) in which Tugendhat J. held that an imputation made by the claimant's estranged wife, a model and TV personality, that the claimant, a pop singer and TV celebrity, had had an affair with his manager did not meet the necessary level of seriousness to fall within s.2.

[105] [1945] K.B. 313 CA.

profession.[106] The words would have been defamatory of any person because they imputed disregard of the moral, social and even legal duty of candour which attaches to the writing of references but the slander was "on the solicitor as a man, not on the man as a solicitor",[107] the reference to his profession being merely the reason why he acted as alleged. Even at that time it must have been arguable that the words were actionable per se if they had contained an imputation that the plaintiff so acted on behalf of his clients and even without this imputation they might now be actionable per se under the statutory test. A solicitor may be subject to professional discipline in respect of conduct unbecoming a solicitor even though the conduct takes place in circumstances wholly unconnected with practice.[108] In another case[109] the defendant said that the plaintiff, a dissenting minister, had cheated his brother-in-law of £2,000 and the words were again held not actionable per se because they were not spoken with reference to his ministry.[110] Such words would be defamatory of any person but not actionable per se (unless they imputed a crime punishable by imprisonment)[111] but spoken of a clergyman they would impute a characteristic wholly incompatible with his calling. In the case of traders it remains the law that imputations on his credit will be actionable per se even if they relate to his private financial affairs for the words: "must necessarily affect him in his trade ... for if a tradesman be incapable of paying all his debts, whether in or out of trade, his credit as a tradesman, which depends on his general solvency, must be injured."[112] In a modern case the conclusion that "to allege that the plaintiff used ('misused') racism to maintain a monopolistic advantage over competitors in the media business is to convey an imputation of misconduct and impropriety on the plaintiff in his calling in the media business" was described as unanswerable.[113]

Callings. Section 2 of the Defamation Act applies to words calculated to **4.18** disparage the claimant in *any* profession, calling, trade or business carried on

---

[106] The first and last parts of the statement seem to have been treated as mere abuse.

[107] Ibid. at 323.

[108] See *Re Weare* [1983] 2 Q.B. 439; *Re A Solicitor* [1912] 1 K.B. 302; Halsbury's *Laws of England, Solicitors*, para.435.

[109] *Hopwood v Thorne* (1849) C.B. 293.

[110] The position would have been different if he had been a clergyman of the established church: see para.4.15, above.

[111] See para.4.3, above.

[112] Per Parke B. in *Jones v Littler* (1841) 7 M. & W. 423 at 428; *Kiam v Neill* [1996] E.M.L.R. 493. Most substantial traders now trade as corporations. It is thought that a slander on the credit of the controlling director of a "one man company", even in his private capacity, might still be defamatory of the company but not necessarily in other cases. A slander on the credit of a trading company is clearly actionable per se (*D & L Caterers v D' Ajou* [1945] K.B. 210 CA at 364) but such a slander may also defame the directors in respect of the management of the company (see para.7.13) and that, too, would be actionable per se. Nor is the capacity of a company to sue for slander actionable per se confined to cases where its credit is impugned: it is actionable per se to say of a company that it is being run illegally or corruptly: *D & L Caterers v D' Ajou*, above; *Feo v Pioneer Concrete (Vic) Pty Ltd* [1999] VSCA 180.

[113] *Panday v Gordon* [2005] UKPC 36; [2006] 1 A.C. 427 (decided under the common law but that makes no difference).

by him and, as under the old law, it does not matter how modest it is. So, in *Foulger v Newcomb*[114] words imputing breach of duty by a gamekeeper in killing foxes were held actionable per se.[115] In Canada it has been held that being (lawfully) a professional gambler is a legitimate line of work for this purpose.[116] It has been said that the occupation must be, at least in broad terms, a commercial one for which payment can be earned. Thus, in the United States it has been held that parenting as such is not a trade or profession[117] and, in England, an allegation of misconduct in attendance of fire-watching duties has been held not to be actionable per se.[118]

4.19 **Offices of profit and of honour.** With regard to words spoken of a person in the way of his office the old law[119] drew a distinction between (1) offices of profit, i.e. offices which carry with them a salary or some other emolument, the loss of which would necessarily entail pecuniary damage,[120] and (2) offices of honour or credit, i.e. offices to which no salary or emolument is attached and the loss, therefore, of which would not necessarily involve any pecuniary damage, e.g. the office of sheriff, justice of the peace, alderman, or (at that time) town councillor. An action of slander lay without proof of special damage for words imputing general unfitness for an office of profit, e.g. incompetence or want of integrity.[121] In the case of an office of trust, credit or honour[122] an action for slander without proof of special damage generally lay only for words imputing want of integrity or corruption or other

---

[114] (1867) L.R. 2 Ex. 327.

[115] For various other trades and callings, see *Seaman v Bigg* (1638) Cro.Car. 480 (bailiff); *Terry v Hooper* (1663) 1 Lev.115 (lime burner); *Botterill v Whytehead* (1879) 41 L.T. 582 (architect); *Slack v Barr* (1918) 8 J.P. 91 (engineer); *Hirst v Goodwin* (1862) 3 F. & F. 257 (veterinary surgeon); *Blunden v Eustace* (1619) Cro.Jac. 504 (surveyor); *Irwin v Brandwood* (1864) 2 H. & C. 960 (master mariner); *Jones v Jones* [1916] 2 A.C. 481 (schoolmaster); *Ross v Lamport* [1956] S.C.R. 366 (taxi-cab driver and owner); *Johnson v Jolliffe* (1981) 26 B.C.L.R. 176 (ski coach).

[116] *Caldwell v McBride* (1988) 45 C.C.L.T. 150.

[117] *Kennedy v Children's Service Society of Wisconsin* (1994) 17 F.3d 980.

[118] *Cleghorn v Sadler* [1945] K.B. 325, [1945] 1 All E.R. 544 (QB). In *Simba Tola v London Borough of Lewisham*, unreported, November 11, 1993, CA, Otton J., at first instance, appears to have rejected the plaintiff's contention that her being a carer for her disabled sister amounted to a "calling" for the purposes of s.2. See also *Romano v D'Onofrio* [2004] O.J. no.4989 Ont. Sup. Ct and on appeal (2005) 262 D.L.R. (4th) 181 (being law student and "folklore group representative" of folk dancing club).

[119] For many other cases on this somewhat arcane issue see the 10th edition of this book.

[120] "An office of profit does not, as I understand, mean an office that is actually and necessarily profitable, but an office in which, in respect of the work the person does in that office, he receives payment": per Bankes L.J. in *Thomas v Moore* [1918] 1 K.B. 555 at 571, where the CA (Pickford L.J. dissenting) held that a member of the executive committee of a trade union who receives certain payments when engaged on the union's business occupies an office of profit.

[121] The probability of pecuniary loss to the plaintiff ensuing from such an imputation obviated the necessity of proving special damage: per curiam in *How v Prinn* (1702) 2 Salk. 694 at 695; *Alexander v Jenkins* [1892] 1 Q.B. 797 at 800, 801.

[122] It was sometimes said that this was confined to "public offices" but in *Maccaba v Lichtenstein* [2004] EWHC 1580 (QB) (which rejected altogether the distinction between offices of profit and of honour) Gray J. greatly doubted whether this was so.

misconduct in the discharge of the office; but an action also lay without proof of special damage for words imputing incompetence or moral misbehaviour without misconduct in the office where it would be a ground for removal from office.[123] In 1958 it was held that the distinction between offices of profit and of honour had survived s.2 of the Defamation Act 1952[124] but the point does not appear to have been fully argued and in *Maccaba v Lichtenstein*[125] Gray J. held the contrary: despite the possible justification for the distinction in that the holder of an office of profit would be likely to suffer financial loss and the fact that s.2 may have been primarily motivated by the injustice produced by the quite different requirement that the words should have been spoken "in the way of" the office, the words of the statute are too clear to admit any other view.

SECTION 5. WORDS IMPUTING UNCHASTITY TO FEMALE[126]

Slander of Women Act 1891. At common law words which imputed   **4.20**
unchastity to a woman or girl were not actionable "unless they were spoken of her in the way of her calling, or were followed by provable damage".[127] The Slander of Women Act 1891[128] enacted that: "words[129] spoken and published ... which impute unchastity[130] or adultery to any woman or girl,

---

[123] So in *Alexander v Jenkins* [1892] 1 Q.B. 797 CA a statement that a councillor drank so much that he had to be carried home was not actionable per se since such behaviour was no ground for dismissal; but in *Booth v Arnold* [1895] 1 Q.B. 571 CA an allegation that an alderman "put money into his own pocket" was.

[124] *Robinson v Ward, The Times*, June 16, 1958; 108 L.J. 491. See also *Jeyaretnam v Goh*, Sing. CA, (1984).

[125] [2004] EWHC 1580 QBD. The same view seems to have been taken under the Malaysian Defamation Act 1957 in *Dato' Seri Tiong King Sing v Datuk Justine Jinggut* [2003] 6 M.L.J. 433, though the point does not really seem to have been in issue.

[126] Defamation Act 2013, s.14(1), when it comes into force, will repeal the Slander of Women Act 1891.

[127] *Jones v Jones* [1916] 2 A.C. 481 at 495, and see *Wilby v Elston* (1849) 18 L.J.C.P. 320. This was regarded as a defect in the law: see *Jones v Herne* (1759) 2 Wilson 87; Lord Campbell C.J. and Lord Brougham in *Lynch v Knight* (1861) 9 H.L.C. 577 at 593, 594; and Cockburn C.J. in *Roberts v Roberts* (1864) 5 B. & S. 389.

[128] Some common law jurisdictions extended such a provision to the sexual behaviour of men but the point has now almost disappeared because of the general tendency to merge slander with libel, in effect if not in name. In the United States the position is, as always, varied. The Restatement, 2d, *Torts*, para.574 makes actionable per se slander imputing "serious sexual misconduct" to another without distinction of sex. Some states make imputations of unchastity to a female actionable per se; others do not unless the conduct amounts to a criminal offence. It may be that constitutional requirements prohibit any distinction between the sexes: Restatement, 2d, *Torts*, para.574, comment c. Article 14 of the European Convention on Human Rights forbids interference with the rights and freedoms guaranteed by the Convention on the ground of sex.

[129] It would seem difficult to extend this to gestures or transient visual signs: cf. para.3.3, above.

[130] ... Is an allegation of rape equivalent to an imputation of unchastity? Cf. *Youssoupoff v Metro-Goldwyn-Mayer* (1934) 50 T.L.R. 581 at 584, but see at 586, 587 (was it seduction?); and para.2.20. An imputation of lesbianism is an imputation of unchastity within the meaning of the statute; *Kerr v Kennedy* [1942] 1 K.B. 409; followed in *Fotu v Loketi* [2003] TOSC 26, the Tongan legislation being in the same terms. As to the possibility that "unchastity" may have to be interpreted by the standards of the 21st century, not the 1890s, see para.2.29, above.

shall not require special damage to render them actionable." There is a proviso that: "the plaintiff shall not recover more costs than damages, unless the judge shall certify that there was reasonable ground for bringing the action."[131]

4.21 Direct terms unnecessary to constitute slander. It is not essential that the imputation should be made in direct or positive terms[132]; it is sufficient if the expressions used would be understood by persons of ordinary intelligence to convey a specific imputation of unchastity,[133] e.g. "kept woman," "loose woman" or "loose character".[134] The fact that the charge is expressed in slang or in terms too obscene to be found in a dictionary will not prevent its being actionable per se, if the words are understood to convey a specific charge of unchastity.[135] But if the expressions used were understood only as mere vulgar abuse of the claimant, no action will lie.[136]

4.22 Defamation Act 2013. When it comes into force, s.14(1) of the Defamation Act 2013 will repeal for England and Wales the Slander of Women Act 1891.[137] (The 1891 Act originally applied to Ireland but was replaced by the Irish Defamation Act 1961, s.16. That Act was repealed by the Defamation Act 2009 which abolished the distinction between libel and slander (s.6).) Section 14(2) of the Defamation Act 2013 abolishes, again only so far as the law of England and Wales is concerned, the common law rule which provides an exemption from the requirement for special damage where the imputation conveyed by the statement complained of is that the claimant has a contagious or infectious disease.

---

[131] For the application of this proviso, see para.35.37, below.

[132] See para.3.18, above.

[133] Cf. *Saunders v Randolph Hotel* [1945] 4 D.L.R. 420 Ont. CA (refusal of accommodation in hotel in presence of witnesses; jury's verdict in favour of defendants upheld).

[134] See *Woolnoth v Meadows* (1804) 5 East 463; *Howard v Nuttall* [1906] E.D.C. 285; *Mitchell v Clement* [1919] 1 W.W.R. 183 Alta., CA. If the words would in common usage be susceptible of two meanings, one being want of chastity, it is for the jury to say in which sense they were understood by those who heard them: *Moore v Levy*, 191 N.Y.S. 165 (1922); *Rovira v Boget*, 240 N.Y. 314 (1925) ("cocotte"); *contra, Williams v Brown* [1927] 3 W.W.R. 305, and see para.3.23, above.

[135] *French v Smith* (1922) 53 O.L.R. 31; *Houseman v Coulson* [1948] 2 D.L.R. 62; *Salanski v Melville* [1951] 1 D.L.R. 239: "Trying to be in the bush with me—me, another woman's husband"; *Luick v Kelly* (1865) 25 Ind. 278; cf. *Fields v Davis, The Times*, May 25, 1955.

[136] *Fields v Davis*, above ("tramp"); cf. *Winyard v Tatler Publishing Co. Ltd, Independent*, August 16, 1991, C.A; and see para.3.37, above.

[137] The Act remains in force in Northern Ireland but has never applied to Scotland (Slander of Women Act 1891, s.2).

CHAPTER 5

SLANDER ACTIONABLE ONLY ON PROOF OF SPECIAL DAMAGE

Special damage necessary to maintain action. Where spoken words or **5.1** other matter amounting to slander do not fall under one of the four heads set out in the preceding chapter, the claimant can only maintain an action if he has suffered "special damage" which is the natural and probable result of the publication. This is so however disgraceful the imputation may be, however certain it is that it will injure the reputation of the claimant and however malicious be the motive of the defendant.[1]

What constitutes special damage. Special damage for this purpose[2] is **5.2** some "actual temporal loss"[3]—the loss of some "material" or "temporal advantage"[4] which is "pecuniary" or "capable of being estimated in money".[5] Or, to put it another way, in cases of slander not actionable per se, the law does not presume that damage will be suffered from the publication and the distress felt by the claimant at the injury to his reputation is not sufficient to found his cause of action. So, e.g. the requirement of special damage is satisfied where there is the loss or refusal of an office or employment,[6] or the dismissal from a situation,[7] or the loss of a client,[8] or of

---

[1] See *Jones v Jones* [1916] 2 A.C. 481 (though the facts of that case would now be affected by s.2 of the Defamation Act 1952: see para.4.15). For examples, see *Edmunds v Jenkins*, *The Times*, June 23, 1920 (hypocrite); *Black v Hunt* (1878) L.R.Ir. 10 (swindler); *Storey v Challands* (1837) 8 C. & P. 234 (failure to pay debts); *Gibson v McDougall* (1919) O.W.N. 157 (fathering illegitimate child); *Cobb v Tinsley*, 243 S.W. 1009 (Ky., 1922) (bed-wetter). For a number of other old examples see the 8th edition of this work, para.202.

[2] The phrase is used in a number of different senses in different contexts: see Jolowicz, "The Changing Use of 'Special Damage' and its Effect on the Law" [1960] C.L.J. 214; McGregor, *Damages* (17th edn). In the context of slander the Restatement, 2d, *Torts*, uses "special harm": para.575. In at least some cases libel is no longer actionable in the United States without proof of "actual harm" but this is wider than special damage: see para.3.6, above. See also the rule of libel *per quod*, which prevails in some states: ibid.

[3] Per curiam in *Ratcliffe v Evans* [1892] 2 Q.B. 524 CA at 532.

[4] Per Bowen L.J. in *Chamberlain v Boyd* (1883) 11 Q.B.D. 407 CA at 415.

[5] Per Cockburn C.J. in *Roberts v Roberts* (1864) 5 B. & S. 389; per Coleridge C.J. in *Chamberlain v Boyd* (1883) 11 Q.B.D. 407 CA; *Chakravarti v Advertiser Newspapers Ltd* [1998] HCA 37; (1998) 93 C.L.R. 519 at [98].

[6] *Sterry v Foreman* (1827) 2 C. & P. 592; *Ecklin v Little* (1890) 6 T.L.R. 366.

[7] *Coward v Wellington* (1836) 7 C. & P. 531; *Martin v Strong* (1836) 5 A. & E, 535; *Kendillon v Maltby* (1842) 1 Cr. & M. 402; *Rumsey v Webb* (1842) Car. & M. 104; *Longdon-Griffiths v Smith* [1950] 1 K.B. 295. But not where the dismissal is colourable only, e.g. in order that the claimant may be able to show special damage, the employer intending to take him back as soon as the action is over; *Coward v Wellington*, above.

[8] *King v Watts* (1838) 8 C. & P. 614.

[179]

commercial dealing.[9] The loss or postponement of marriage has been held to be special damage.[10] The loss by a husband of the consortium or conjugal society of his wife, as the result of the words complained of, is special damage.[11] If so, it is thought that despite doubts expressed in earlier times so also now is the loss by a wife of the consortium or conjugal society of her husband.[12] If a person is prevented by slanderous words from receiving some gift or income which he would otherwise have received, there is special damage sufficient to support the action.[13] The loss of gratuitous entertainment or the hospitality of friends is special damage,[14] but the mere loss of their "society" or social ostracism or disgrace is not enough even though its effect on the claimant may be very painful.[15] In *Roberts v Roberts* the plaintiff's declaration alleging that she had been turned out of her religious congregation and had been unable to join another one was held bad.[16]

5.3 Accrual of special damage. The special damage must have accrued before the action was brought. Not only is a mere apprehension of temporal loss insufficient,[17] so also is the possibility, or even *likelihood*, of temporal

---

[9] *Brown v Smith* 138 E.R. 1333; (1853) 13 C.B. 596; even though it might have turned out unprofitably: *Storey v Challands* 173 E.R. 475, (1837) 8 C. & P. 234; *Coroneo v Kurri Kurri* (1934) 51 C.L.R. 328.

[10] *Davis v Gardiner* (1593) 4 Co.Rep. 16; *Holwood v Hopkins* (1600) Cro.Eliz. 787; *Mathew v Crass* (1614) Cro.Jac. 323; *Speight v Gosnay* (1891) 60 L.J.Q.B. 231 at 232; *Bordeaux v Jobs* (1913) 6 Alberta R. 440. Marriage is now less of a "commercial" matter but it is thought that this still the law.

[11] Per Lords Campbell and Cranworth in *Lynch v Knight* (1861) 9 H.L.C. 577 at 589, 595; and see also per Crompton J. in *Roberts v Roberts* (1864) 5 B. & S. 384 at 388.

[12] Lord Campbell L.C. thought so in *Lynch v Knight* (1861) 9 H.L.C. 577 at 589 and Lord Cranworth at 595 was "strongly inclined" to agree with him. *Contra*, Lord Wensleydale at 599, with whom Lord Brougham was inclined to agree (at 593). The opinion of Lords Campbell and Cranworth was followed by Darling J. in *Gray v Gee* (1923) 39 T.L.R. 429; and by the Supreme Court of N.S. Wales in *Johnson v The Commonwealth* (1927) N.S.W.S.R. 133; cf. *Newton v Hardy* (1933) 149 L.T.R. 165. The opinion of Lord Wensleydale was preferred by the Full Court in *Wright v Cedzich* [1929] V.L.R. 117; affirmed (1930) 43 C.L.R. 493. That a woman had no action for the loss of her husband's consortium by injury or enticement of him whereas a man did in the reverse situation (*Best v Samuel Fox Ltd* [1952] A.C. 716, the husband's action has now been abolished) hardly seems to be determinative of this issue.

[13] *Hartley v Herring* (1799) 8 T.R. 130; *Corcoran v Corcoran* (1857) 7 Ir.C.L.R. 272 (withdrawal of a promise of financial assistance).

[14] *Moore v Meagher* (1807) 1 Taunt. 39; *Davies v Solomon* (1871) L.R. 7 Q.B. 112; *Campbell v Campbell* (1875) 25 Up.Can.C.P. 368; *Clarke v Morgan* (1877) 38 L.T. 354; *Mitchell v Clement* [1919] 1 W.W.R. 183. But it may be difficult to determine whether the cause is in fact the friends' refusal or the claimant's diffidence: *Stewart v Sterling* (1918) 42 O.L.R. 479; see also *Olmsted v Miller* (1828) 1 Wend.(N.Y.) R. 506 (refusal of "civil treatment" at inn); *Romano v D'Onofrio* [2004] O.J. No.4989 Ont. Sup. Ct.

[15] *Barnes v Bruddell* (1669) 1 Lev. 261; *Weldon v De Bathe* (1884) 54 L.J.Q.B. 113; *Argent v Donigan* (1892) 8 T.L.R. 432; *Palmer v Solmes* (1880) 30 Up.Can.C.P. 481; *Ball v Donnelly* [1918] 3 W.W.R. 55.

[16] (1864) 5 B. & S. 384 (the imputation in the case would, however, now be actionable per se under the Slander of Women Act 1891); *Dwyer v Meehan* (1886) 18 L.R. Ir. 138.

[17] *Corcoran v Corcoran* (1857) 7 Ir.C.L.R. 272 at 275.

loss accruing in the future.[18] "I know," said De Grey C.J. in *Onslow v Horne*[19]: "of no case where ever an action for words was grounded upon eventual damages which may possibly happen to a man in the future."[20] In *Michael v Spiers and Pond*[21] the plaintiff was ejected from the defendants' licensed premises by their servant, who said that he was drunk. The plaintiff told his father, who threatened to remove him from the directorate of a company of which he (the father) had the control, unless he could clear his character. The plaintiff brought an action of slander against the defendants, alleging the threat of removal as special damage. The court ordered such allegation to be struck out of the statement of claim on the ground that a threat of temporal damage in the future did not constitute sufficient special damage to sustain the action. In *Chamberlain v Boyd*[22] the plaintiff alleged that, after his failure to be elected as a member of the Reform Club, the defendant, at a meeting called to consider alteration of the rules, slandered him about his conduct at a club in Melbourne, which induced the members to retain the existing rules and "thereby prevented the plaintiff from again seeking to be elected". On the assumption that failing to gain entry to a club might be special damage[23] the action failed because it was not alleged that the defendant's words prevented the election of the plaintiff, merely that the plaintiff was prevented from again seeking to be elected: "that is, that the determination of the club to retain the regulations under which the plaintiff [had] been rejected, made him think it not worth his while to stand again for election."[24] The plaintiff's case amounted to saying that the refusal to alter the regulations kept him in a position in which a further election might or might not have resulted in his being elected. However, such a case must, it is submitted, be a matter of fact and degree: if (1) the failure in the first election were on some technical ground of qualification and the claimant can show that but for the slander (2) the rule would have been changed and (3) that his election would then have been highly likely, then he ought to succeed.[25]

A person who has been defamed may incur expenditure to counteract the damage to his reputation, e.g. by issuing notices and advertisements. Such expenditure would seem to be a proper head of damages where the defamation

---

[18] *Barmund's Case* (1619) Cro.Jac. 473; *Barnes v Bruddell* (1669) 1 Lev. 261; *Onslow v Horne* (1771) 3 Wils. 177; *Chamberlain v Boyd* (1883) 11 Q.B.D. 407 at 415; *Michael v Spiers and Pond* (1909) 101 L.T. 352; *West v West* (1911) 27 T.L.R. 476 at 478.

[19] (1771) 3 Wils. 177 at 188.

[20] To allow a claim in such a case would be to say that the words were actionable if they were *calculated* to cause pecuniary loss. Cf. para.4.15, above.

[21] (1909) 101 L.T. 352. See also *Barnes v Bruddell* (1669) 1 Lev. 261.

[22] (1883) 11 Q.B.D. 407 CA.

[23] Which Bowen L.J. at 415 was prepared to assume might be the case.

[24] Ibid. at 416.

[25] According to general principles, where a claimant has suffered the loss of the chance of gaining some benefit the granting of which was dependent on the decision of a third party, he may recover damages for the loss of the chance, provided it was not merely speculative: *Chaplin v Hicks* [1911] 2 K.B. 786 CA; *Allied Maples v Simmons & Simmons* [1995] 1 W.L.R. 1602 CA. *Chamberlain v Boyd* suggests that the law on special damage is narrower.

is actionable per se[26] but cannot, it is submitted, constitute special damage in order to make a slander actionable. If that were so, then the restrictive approach to damages in slander cases would be easily subverted.[27]

5.4 Loss of custom. Since the enactment of s.2 of the Defamation Act 1952 it is more likely that words tending to cause loss of custom will be actionable per se.[28] However, where it is necessary to prove special damage the following principles apply[29] and the cases will in any event remain relevant where, although special damage is not necessary, the claimant seeks to prove the damage he has actually suffered.[30] Loss of particular customers constitutes special damage.[31] If the claimant intends to rely on such a loss, he must specially plead it, and give particulars of the names of the customers who have ceased to deal with him.[32] But where, from the nature of the case, it is impracticable for the claimant to give their names, or unreasonable to require him to do so, e.g. his customers are persons who deal with him over the counter, or consist of a "floating or transitory class" such as theatrical audiences or the customers of an inn, he can allege and prove a general loss of custom as special damage.[33]

---

[26] See, e.g. *Australian Broadcasting Corp v Comalco Ltd* (1986) 68 A.L.R. 259 Fed Ct.

[27] In *Lonrho Plc v Fayed (No.5)* [1993] 1 W.L.R. 1489, a case of conspiracy, the CA declined to strike out a claim for staff time spent in investigating and mitigating the effects of the conspiracy, but reference was made to the problem posed by claimants in such cases relying on their own acts to make the defendant's conduct actionable.

[28] See para.4.15, above.

[29] As the test under that statute is whether the words are calculated (i.e. likely) to disparage the claimant in his trade and as at common law it is necessary to show that the special damage was the natural and probable result of the slander (see para.5.6, below) it is not easy to conceive of cases which would satisfy one test but not the other.

[30] As in *McManus v Beckham* [2002] EWCA Civ 939; [2002] 1 W.L.R. 2982, where the loss of custom particulars are described as particulars of special damage (at [4]).

[31] *Bateman v Lyall* (1860) 7 C.B.(N.S.) 638; *Shore v Britski (No.2)* [1942] 2 W.W.R. 343.

[32] *Barnes v Bruddell* (1669) 1 Lev. 261; *Hopwood v Thorn* (1849) 8 C.B. 293; *Bluck v Lovering* (1885) 1 T.L.R. 497. The claim for special damages failed in *Hussein v Farooq* [2008] EWHC 2487 (QB) on the basis that it lacked sufficient particularity:

"[The claim] seems to be based on the propositions that one or more of the persons present when the words were allegedly spoken would have done business with the Claimant and, had it not been for the damaging impact of the slander, that he would have earned commissions on the transaction(s) in question. It is, yet again, for the Claimant to prove that there would have been such transactions and to establish a causal link to the loss claimed."

(per Eady J. at [12]) A claim for special damages failed in *Joseph v Spiller* [2012] EWHC 2958 (QB) because it was based on fabricated documents. See further para.26.30, below.

[33] *Hargrave v Le Breton* (1769) 4 Burr. 2423 at 2424; *Hartley v Herring* (1799) 8 T.R. 130; *Bradley v Youlden* (1867) 4 W.W. & A'B. (Victoria) 205 at 207; *Ratcliffe v Evans* [1882] 2 Q.B. 524 CA at 530; *George v Blow* (1899) 20 N.S.W.L.R. 400; *Worsley v Cooper* [1939] 1 All E.R. 290. In *Tesla Motors Inc. v British Broadcasting Corporation* [2011] EWHC 2760 (QB) Tugendhat J. stated that where the claimant alleges loss, or delay, of sales as a consequence of the alleged falsehood such loss must be proved with sufficient particularity. The claimant's appeal was dismissed ([2013] EWCA Civ 152), Moore-Bick L.J. emphasising the importance of causation, i.e. proving that actual loss was caused by an actionable statement.

"How is a public-house keeper, whose only customers are persons passing by, to show a damage resulting from the slander unless he is allowed to give general evidence of a loss of custom?"[34]

"Suppose a biscuit baker in Regent Street is slandered by a man saying his biscuits are poisoned, and in consequence no one enters his shop. He cannot complain of the loss of particular customers, for he does not know them; and how hard and unjust it would be if he could not prove the fact of the loss under a general allegation of loss of custom."[35]

Illness. Social ostracism does not constitute special damage,[36] nor does the   **5.5** injury to the claimant's feelings or annoyance which flows from it.[37] Furthermore, even physical illness consequent upon the slander is too remote to support an action.[38] "Bodily illness is not the natural or the ordinary consequence of the speaking of slanderous words."[39] "In all the innumerable actions for slander there are no precedents for alleging illness to be sufficient special damage ... it would be of evil consequence to treat it as sufficient, because such a rule might lead to an infinity of trumpery or groundless actions."[40] This is clearly a special rule of causation applicable to this type of slander[41] since injury to health may in principle be compensable in actions for libel and for slander actionable per se.[42] Furthermore, it is not wholly clear what is the position where the defendant is aware that illness is a likely consequence. Where D makes to C a false statement about a third party with whom C has a close relationship (e.g. that the third party has been injured[43] or is wanted for spying[44]) which he knows may cause illness, then C has a cause of action, though not for defamation.[45] It is difficult to see why the same principle should not apply where D makes a false statement about C, directly to C and, if so, why this should not apply to statements to third parties about C, whether in C's presence or not.[46]

Causation. As in the case of all other torts, the special damage must have   **5.6** been caused *in fact* by the defendant's wrong, in the sense that but for the

---

[34] Per Martin B. in *Evans v Harries* (1856) 1 H. & N. 251 at 254.

[35] Per Martin B. in *Evans v Harries* (1856) 26 L.J.Ex. 31 at 32.

[36] See para.5.2, above.

[37] *Weldon v De Bathe* (1884) 54 L.J.Q.B. 113 at 116.

[38] *Allsop v Allsop* (1860) 5 H. & N. 534, approved in *Lynch v Knight* (1861) 9 H.L.C. 577 at 592; *Terwilliger v Wands*, 17 N.Y. 54 (1858).

[39] Per Bramwell B. in *Allsop v Allsop* (1860) 5 H. & N. 534 at 539.

[40] Per Wright J. in *Wilkinson v Downton* [1897] 2 Q.B. 57 at 60.

[41] So held in *Chu Siu Kuk Yuen, Jessie v Apple Daily Ltd* [2002] H.K.L.R.D. 1 HKCFI.

[42] See paras 1.21, above and 34.54, below.

[43] *Wilkinson v Downton* [1897] 2 Q.B. 57 (though on the facts it is most unlikely that the defendant realised illness would ensue and nowadays the case would be one of negligence: see Lord Hoffmann in *Wainwright v Home Office* [2003] UKHL 53; [2004] 2 A.C. 406).

[44] *Janvier v Sweeney* [1919] 2 K.B. 316 CA.

[45] Historically the claim would be classified as an action on the case, though for obvious reasons it is difficult to classify it as "negligence" in the modern law.

[46] See, e.g. *Johnson v Sampson*, 208 N.W. 814 (Minn., 1926) (accusation made to a schoolgirl with threats of sending her to a reformatory, causing nervous shock and impairment of health). However, there is no doubt that the law in the US on liability for "extreme outrage" has developed much further than in England: see Dobbs, *Law of Torts* (2000), Ch.20.

defendant's act the damage would not have occurred.[47] In *Barrett v Associated Newspapers*[48] (a case of malicious falsehood, but the same principles apply) the defendant published a report that the plaintiff's house was haunted. It was proved that the house had diminished in value owing to its having the reputation of being haunted, but that it had acquired such a reputation long before the publication by the defendant, and it was held that the damage was not the result of the defendant's words. However it is not enough that the damage is so caused: it must also be the *natural and probable* result of the defendant's words.

5.7 Response of third party to slander. At one time it was held that where the damage was immediately caused by the illegal or wrongful act of a third party in response to the slander, it was too remote to amount to special damage. In *Vicars v Wilcocks*[49] it was held that where the plaintiff's employer was induced by the slander to dismiss the plaintiff before the end of his contract, that was not the legal consequence of the slander but a mere wrongful act of the employer for which the defendant was not responsible. This case does not represent the modern law.[50] The true test is that to "make the words actionable by reason of special damage the consequence must be such as, taking human nature as it is, with its infirmities, and having regard to the relationship of the parties concerned, might fairly and reasonably have been anticipated and feared would follow from the speaking of the words, not what would reasonably follow, or we might think ought to follow."[51] Not much more can be done than to give examples, bearing in mind that what may seem "natural and probable" in one generation may not seem so in another and vice versa.

5.8 Examples. A father, as a consequence of defamatory words spoken of his daughter, which he entirely disbelieved, refused to furnish her with articles of

---

[47] In *Tesla Motors Inc. v British Broadcasting Corpn* [2013] EWCA Civ 152 CA the Court of Appeal affirmed the decision of Tugendhat J. ([2011] EWHC 310 (QB)) refusing the claimants permission to amend their statement of claim so as to reinstate proceedings for libel and malicious falsehood. The need to distinguish the effect of actionable falsehoods from other unfavourable but true statements raised an acute causation problem that was not properly addressed in the proposed amendments. In particular, the amendment failed to show how the failure to sell 200 additional cars resulted entirely from the statements complained of rather than by one or more statements that was not actionable.

[48] (1907) 23 T.L.R. 666.

[49] (1806) 8 East 1.

[50] See Lord Campbell L.C. and Lord Wensleydale in *Lynch v Knight* (1861) 9 H.L.C. 590 at 600–601; Brett L.J. in *Bowen v Hall* (1881) 6 Q.B.D. 333 at 339. Though no doubt the court's illustration in *Vicars v Wilcocks* remains correct, namely that a slanderer would not be responsible for the decision of hearers to put the plaintiff in the horse pond.

[51] Per Lord Wensleydale in *Lynch v Knight* (1861) 9 H.L.C. 590 at 600, cited as the governing rule by Brett L.J. in *Chamberlain v Boyd* (1883) 11 Q.B.D. 407 CA. The formulation of Lord Campbell at 592 may be more severe: "The act constituting the special damage must be such as might be expected from a reasonable man who believed the truth of the words according to the intention of the slanderer."

clothing or means of education. This was not such special damage as would sustain the action, as such treatment by a parent of his child is not the natural, but highly unnatural, result of a falsehood reported of her.[52]

D falsely told P's father that P had had a child by her master. The father went to the master, repeated the charge, and asked if it were true. The master replied that it was entirely untrue, but dismissed P from her situation as governess to his children on the ground that it might be injurious to her character and unpleasant to them both if she continued in her situation. It was held that it was reasonable that the master should act as he did after such a statement had been made, although he knew it to be untrue, and that the special damage was the natural consequence of D's slander.[53]

D falsely told A that A's wife "was all but seduced by Dr. C before her marriage", whereupon A turned her out of his house and refused to live with her any longer. It was held that A's conduct was not the natural or reasonable consequence of the defendant's slander, as the words did not impute actual criminality before marriage, nor did they contain any imputation which, if true, would induce any reasonable man to turn his wife out of doors.[54]

D falsely told P's employers that P had removed from a house, of which he was tenant, leaving rent due to his landlord, whereupon P's employers dismissed him from their employment. It was held that their conduct was not the natural or reasonable consequence of the speaking of the words.[55] D "might reasonably be supposed to have contemplated, when he spoke the words, that P's employers would remonstrate with him on the subject, but not that they would dismiss him from their employment."[56]

Repetition of the words. The special damage may arise from the repeti- **5.9**
tion of the defamatory words to someone other than the original hearer. The question is whether the defendant knew or should have appreciated that there was a significant risk of repetition and a consequent increase in the damage.[57] This is particularly relevant where the claimant seeks to prove a general loss of custom for such loss would never be recoverable if repetition always broke

---

[52] *Anon* (1875) N.Y. 262. See also, *Chamberlain v Boyd* (1883) 11 Q.B.D. 407 CA in which the Court of Appeal held, as a further reason for giving judgment for the defendant, that the claimed loss was not the natural and probable consequence of the slander:
"In the present case the refusal to alter the rules was not the natural and probable result of the words complained of. It is almost absurd to suppose that because the members of a club in London believed the plaintiff to have misconducted himself at Melbourne, they refused to alter their rules as to the mode of election. Such a result would be absurd and fantastic." (per Brett L.J. at 414).
[53] *Gillet v Bullivant* (1846) 7 L.T. (O.S.) 490; *Knight v Gibbs* (1834) 1 A. & E. 43.
[54] *Lynch v Knight* (1861) 9 H.L.C. 577.
[55] *Speake v Hughes* [1904] 1 K.B. 138 CA.
[56] Per Mathew L.J., ibid. at 141.
[57] *McManus v Beckham* [2002] EWCA Civ 939; [2002] 1 W.L.R. 2982. In *Ratcliffe v Evans* [1892] 2 Q.B. 524 at 530, Bowen L.J. said that there would be liability where the words are: "uttered in such circumstances that their repetition follows in the ordinary course of things from their original utterance."

the chain of causation.[58] In *Speight v Gosnay*[59] the damage was regarded as having been caused by the voluntary act of the plaintiff herself where D made a false imputation on P in the presence of P's mother, and the mother repeated it to P, who repeated it to her fiancée and he thereupon broke off the engagement. This is considered further in connection with the general issue of the responsibility of a defamer for repetition by others.[60]

5.10   Scope of damages for slanders not actionable per se. Where the claimant proves such special damage as to be the foundation of an action for slander, there is some uncertainty as to whether he may then recover further general damages or whether he is confined to the proved special damage.[61] In other words, is the special damage merely a requirement of the claim, which is thereafter like a claim for libel, or is it the sum of the claimant's claim? There is some authority both ways but the matter has never perhaps been fully considered.[62]

---

[58] In fact since the enactment of s.3 of the Defamation Act 1952 the wrong will be likely to be actionable per se and the issue of repetition will arise because the claimant is seeking to prove his actual loss. But the principle is the same.

[59] (1891) 60 L.J.Q.B. 231. See also *Parkins v Scott* (1862) 1 H. & C. 153. Compare *Bordeaux v Jobs* (1913) 14 D.L.R. 451 (repetition by addressee to his daughter, who was engaged to P, slander actionable) and *Merkoff v Pawluk* [1931] 1 W.W.R. 669 (repetition not authorised, not actionable).

[60] See para.6.52, below.

[61] As to the position where a slander is actionable per se by virtue of s.2 of the Defamation Act 1952 or in cases of malicious falsehood where s.3 of the Act applies, see paras 4.15, above and 21.11, below.

[62] The view that the claimant is confined to the proved special damage accords with a number of textbooks. Clerk & Lindsell, *Torts*, 20th edn (2010), para.23–65; Odgers, *Libel and Slander*, 6th edn, pp.315–316; Fraser, *Libel and Slander*, 7th edn, p.185; Spencer Bower, *Actionable Defamation*, 2nd edn, p.1523. For dicta supporting it, see *Jones v Jones* [1916] 2 A.C. 481 at 490 ("ascertainment of actual damage suffered and to a remedy limited to such damage"); per Lord North C.J. in *Townsend v Hughes* (1676) 2 Mod. 150 at 151; per Williams J. in *Brown v Smith* (1853) 13 C.B. at 600; per Martin B. (*arguendo*) in *Dixon v Smith* (1860) 5 H. & N. at 452 (though the *result* of the case may support the other view). The Faulks Committee appears to have thought the law to be otherwise (Cmnd.5909 (1975), para.86) and see Fleming, *Law of Torts*, 9th edn, p.608; Addison, *Law of Torts*, 8th edn, p.503; Salmond & Heuston, *Torts*, 21st edn, p.189. In *Lynch v Knight* (1861) 9 H.L.C. 577 at 598, Lord Wensleydale said that: "mental pain or anxiety the law cannot value, and does not pretend to redress, when the unlawful act complained of causes that alone; though where a material damage occurs, and is connected with it, it is impossible a jury, in estimating it, should altogether overlook the feelings of the party interested." Furthermore, if there is such a rule it seems sometimes to be ignored in practice: *Knott v Jeffrey, The Times*, June 2, 1883 (£400 damages, special damage loss of a dinner). The weight of the American case law is in accord with the view that damages are not confined to the special damage: Prosser and Keeton, *Torts*, 5th edn, p.794. This is also the position under the Restatement 2d, para.622, comment b. McGregor, *Damages* (17th edn), para.39–02, regards the matter as undecided. The issue is also bound up with the question of whether successive actions may be brought if there are different items of special damage: see para.19.25, below.

CHAPTER 6

PUBLICATION

SECTION 1. GENERAL PRINCIPLES

General principles: publication. No civil action can be maintained for **6.1**
libel or slander unless the words complained of have been published.[1] "The
material part of the cause of action in libel is not the writing, but the
publication of the libel."[2] In order to constitute publication, the matter must
be published by the defendant[3] to (communicated to) a third party,[4] that is to

---

[1] "The law of defamation has loaded the word 'publish' with a gloss which would seem bizarre
to all but the cognoscenti": *Tom & Bill Waterhouse Pty Ltd v Racing New South Wales* [2008]
N.S.W.S.C. 1013 at [26] (there is an entertaining gloss on this at [25]; the case concerned an
offence of publishing a race field under the Racing Administration Act 1998 (NSW).

[2] Per Lord Esher M.R. in *Hebditch v Macllwaine* [1894] 2 Q.B. 54 CA at 58, 61, per Davey
L.J. at 64; *Bata v Bata* [1948] W.N. 366 CA; *Thomson v Lambert* [1938] 2 D.L.R. 545 SCC. "The
act of publishing the libellous matter constitutes the cause of action": *O'Keefe v Walsh* [1903] 2
I.R. 706. "It is the publication not the composition of the libel which is the actionable wrong":
Dixon J. in *Lee v Wilson* (1934) 51 C.L.R. 276 at 287. *Lee v Wilson* (1934) 51 C.L.R. 276 at 287.
"The tort of defamation, at least as understood in Australia, focuses upon publications causing
damage to reputation": *Dow Jones & Co. Inc. v Gutnick* [2002] HCA 56; 210 C.L.R. 575 at
[25].

[3] In *Lysko v Braley* (2006) 79 O.R. (3d) 721 Ont. CA it was held that publication must be by
an identified defendant.
  "Proving that one or more of a group of four people, not alleged to be acting in concert and
  not alleged to otherwise be responsible for each other's actions, defamed the plaintiff, does not
  make out a case against any of them. Absent proof of vicarious liability or actions in concert,
  we do not make individuals liable for the anonymous acts of others": at [94].

[4] Is communication to a *human being* necessary in defamation? In certain circumstances there
may be communication between automated systems which leads to consequences adverse to the
claimant, e.g. where a credit application is rejected by the provider's computer because of default
information sent by the system of a credit information provider. In *Dale v Veda Advantage
Information Services and Solutions Ltd* [2009] FCA 305 it was conceded by the claimants that the
report must be read by a human being. However, it has been held that there may be liability for
fraud where false information is given to a machine which processes information so as to grant
or deny a benefit: *Renault UK Ltd v Fleetpro Technical Services* [2007] EWHC 2541 (QB).

say, at least one person other than the claimant.[5] "A cannot sue B for defaming him to A himself, or to B himself; that is to say where B reads to himself his libel on A and then locks it away. A must prove that B defamed him to C."[6] Defamation protects a person's reputation and his reputation is not the good opinion he has of himself but the estimation in which others hold him.[7] A defamatory statement about the claimant communicated to the claimant alone may injure his self-esteem but it cannot injure his reputation.[8] The requirement that there be a publication to a third party is also a requirement of malicious falsehood.[9] It is not sufficient that the matter has been merely communicated to the third party: it is also necessary that it be communicated in such a manner that it may convey the defamatory meaning[10] and that persons acquainted with the claimant could[11] understand it to refer to him. If, therefore, a defamatory letter was handed to a person who could not read or who could not read the language in which it was written, there would be no publication[12] nor would there be where words were spoken in a foreign language not understood by those who heard them[13]; and where a defendant sent to a third person on a privileged occasion a postcard defamatory of the plaintiff, though his name was not mentioned, and no stranger unacquainted with the circumstances would have identified him as the person referred to, it was held that there was no publication to the postman or other persons through whose hands the postcard passed.[14]

---

[5] A shows a letter defaming X to B, C and D. B, C and D then sign the letter and it is shown to E. A is liable for the publication to B, C and D and all four of them are liable for the republication to E: *Trantum v McDowell* [2007] NSWCA 138. Contrast the situation where A, B, C and D jointly compose a letter defamatory of X and send it to X. Held no publication in *Davis v Resources for Human Development Inc.* 770 A.2d 353 (Penn. 2001). But communication to the defendant's wife may not be a publication: see para.6.7, below. As to publication within an organisation see para.6.16, below.

[6] *Riddick v Thames Board Mills* [1977] Q.B. 881 CA at 898, per Stephenson L.J.

[7] "It is damage done to character in the opinion of other men, and not in a party's self-estimation, which constitutes the material element in an action for libel or slander": per Bigelow J. in *Sheffil v Van Deusen* (1859) 79 Mass. R. 304 at 305. But in Scots law publication to the pursuer alone will suffice.

[8] D speaks words defamatory of C1 and C2 in the presence of both of them but of no one else. Has there been a publication to C2 of the slander on C1 and vice versa? There is some American authority that there has not (*Harbison v Chicago, etc. Ry*, 37 S.W.2d 609 (Mo., 1931) and see 92 A.L.R.2d 219, para.9); but the contrary view, taken in *Marble v Chapin* (1882) 132 Mass. 225, seems more in accord with principle. See also *Trantum v McDowell* [2007] NSWCA 138 at [49]. Note that it is irrelevant that the person to whom the publication is made does not believe the charge: see para.2.1, above.

[9] See para.21.6, below.

[10] "To publish a libel is to convey by some means to the mind of another the defamatory sense embodied in the vehicle": *Webb v Bloch* (1928) 41 C.L.R. 331 at 363, per Isaacs J. "Harm to reputation is done when a defamatory publication is comprehended by the reader, the listener or the observer. Until then, no harm is done by it": *Dow Jones & Co. Inc. v Gutnick* [2002] HCA 56; 210 C.L.R. 575 at [26].

[11] "Could", not necessarily "did": para.7.3, below.

[12] *Gambrill v Schooley* (1901) 93 Maryland R. 48 at 60.

[13] *Jones v Davers* (1597) Cro.Eliz. 496; *Price v Jenkings* (1601) Cro.Eliz. 865.

[14] *Sadgrove v Hole* [1901] 2 K.B. 1 CA.

Since publication to one person will suffice[15] it is clearly not necessary that there should be a "publication" in the commercial sense, though the scale of the publication will of course affect the damages.[16] The writer of a defamatory letter is therefore a "publisher" of it and a person who whispers a slander in the ear of an acquaintance also publishes. However, where the publication is to a small number of people any claim risks being struck out as an abuse of process.[17] Further, once the Defamation Act 2013, s.1, comes into effect in England and Wales, a claimant will have to establish that the statement complained of has caused, or is likely to cause, serious harm to his reputation which may be difficult where the publication is limited.[18] Somewhat confusingly, the word "publisher" is now also used in its commercial sense for the purpose of the defence in s.1 of the Defamation Act 1996,[19] but that does not alter its fundamental meaning at common law.

For limitation purposes it is necessary to know *when* a tort is committed[20]; for the purposes of jurisdiction and applicable law it is necessary to know *where* it is committed.[21] Publication being the gist of libel and slander actionable per se[22] the cause of action for those torts arises immediately the publication has taken place; but this is not so in the case of other slanders because the cause of action is not complete until special damage has been suffered.[23] Similarly, the tort is committed in the place where the publication is received by the hearer, reader or viewer,[24] so that, e.g. where internet material is uploaded to a server by the originator in New York and accessed by a person in England, the tort is committed in England.[25] Whatever difficulties this may cause for the defendant,[26] it is a corollary of the proposition that defamation is concerned with reputation, that is to say what others think about the claimant.

General principles: limited publication. Although publication to one **6.2** person will suffice,[27] the scale of the publication will of course affect the damages.[28] However, the proposition that a limited publication is actionable

---

[15] "A libel does not require publication to more than one person": per Lord Penzance in *Capital and Counties Bank v Henty* (1882) 7 A.C. 741 at 765.

[16] *John v Mirror Group Newspapers* [1997] Q.B. 586 CA.

[17] See para.6.2, above.

[18] See para.6.3, above.

[19] See para.6.33, below.

[20] Ch.19, s.4, below.

[21] Ch.26, s.3, below.

[22] As to which see Ch.4, above.

[23] See para.5.1, above.

[24] *Bata v Bata* [1948] W.N. 366 CA; *Longworth v Hope* (1865) 3 MacPh. (Ct. of Sess.) 1049.

[25] *Dow Jones & Co. Inc. v Gutnick* [2002] HCA 56; 210 C.L.R. 575.

[26] He may be exposed to suits in a number of jurisdictions; and in the example, the case would be actionable in English law even if there was no liability under the law of New York.

[27] See para.6.1, above.

[28] *John v Mirror Group Newspapers* [1997] Q.B. 586 CA.

must now be qualified by the principle of abuse of process. In *Jameel (Yousef) v Dow Jones & Co. Inc*[29] there was a worldwide publication but the material had only been published to five subscribers in England and, though there had not been any trial on the facts, it was contended that three of the subscribers were associates of the claimant and therefore "in his camp" and two had never heard of the claimant. The Court of Appeal said that if it had been faced with an application to refuse service outside the jurisdiction it would have done so.[30] Furthermore, any trial was likely to focus on qualified privilege rather than justification and if the claimant succeeded the only vindication he could be said to have obtained was for the very small injury to his reputation in this country and even that would be on the basis only of the presumption of falsity which the law attached to defamatory words, since the truth of the allegation would not have been explored at the trial. The Court also said that *Duke of Brunswick v Harmer*[31] (where the claimant sent his agent to obtain a copy of a newspaper containing a libel long after the initial publication) would not now survive an application to dismiss on the ground of abuse of process for if "his agent read the article he is unlikely to have thought the Duke much, if any, the worse for it and, to the extent that he did, the Duke brought this on his own head".[32]

Abuse of process has been called in aid in several cases since *Jameel (Yousef) v Dow Jones & Co. Inc*[33] and has been applied in some cases involving a purely English publication.[34] Reliance on it has become quite frequent and in *Thornton v Telegraph Media Group Ltd*[35] Tugendhat J. said that "each of the three judges who are currently hearing most of the defamation cases are applying the principle of *Jameel v Dow Jones* with some frequency, and in a number of different, but related, contexts in defamation actions" and in several cases the courts have struck out claims where publication was to a limited number of publishees only. Thus, in *Noorani v Calver*[36] the contention that *Jameel* should be applied was said to be unanswerable where the defendant was said to have stated orally to the claimant's wife and daughter that the claimant was an Islamic terrorist.[37] So too the claim was struck out in *Wallis v Meredith*,[38] another case involving publication to only

---

[29] [2005] EWCA Civ 75; [2005] Q.B. 946. See also *Bezant v Rausing* [2007] EWHC 1118 (QB) and *McBride v Body Shop International Plc* [2007] EWHC 1658 (QB).

[30] Such a decision was made in respect of a minimal publication in England as long ago as 1937: *Kroch v Rossell* [1937] 1 All E.R. 725.

[31] (1849) 14 Q.B. 185.

[32] [2005] EWCA Civ 75; [2005] Q.B. 946 at [56].

[33] [2005] EWCA Civ 75; [2005] Q.B. 946. See also *Bezant v Rausing* [2007] EWHC 1118 (QB) and *McBride v Body Shop International Plc* [2007] EWHC 1658 (QB).

[34] See also paras 2.4, above, 9.2, 30.48, below.

[35] [2010] EWHC 1414 (QB); [2010] E.M.L.R. 25 at [62].

[36] [2009] EWHC 561 (QB).

[37] See also, *Khader v Aziz* [2010] EWCA Civ 716; [2010] 1 W.L.R. 2673; [2011] E.M.L.R. 2 (proved publication to one person only).

[38] [2011] EWHC 75 (QB). Cf. *Sanders v Percy* [2009] EWHC 1870 (QB), a slander case, in which the claim was struck out in so far as it concerned publication to the claimant's solicitor of

one person. Though the allegation was a relatively serious one, the publishee was the claimant's solicitor who was unlikely to have thought the worse of his client on account of it, particularly in the light of his client's denials. Claims have also been struck out where the publication was to a larger, though still limited, number of people. Thus, in *Lonzim Plc v Sprague*[39] a claim for a slander was brought resulting from a publication to about half a dozen people at a company meeting. If the words were defamatory at all they were at the "trivial or innocuous end" of defamatory meaning and it was held that the claim should be struck out as the costs of proceedings would be wholly disproportionate to any damages awarded.[40] So too in *Khalil v Barakat*[41] the claim was struck in a case where the publication was "numerically limited".

However, the question whether there has been a real and substantial tort cannot "depend upon a numbers game, with the court fixing an arbitrary minimum according to the facts of the case"[42] and the *Jameel* jurisdiction should not be pushed too far. It does not mean that any sort of mass publication is always necessary for a successful suit, otherwise claims for slander (which sometimes lead to substantial awards of general damages) would largely disappear. It is not difficult to conceive of claims for slanders or libels with limited circulation which would cause the claimant great embarrassment or distress or which might blight his financial prospects. Thus in *Crossland v Wilkinson Hardware Stores Ltd*[43] (where the context was CPR Pt 24 rather than abuse of process) Tugendhat J. said that:

> "The fact that a libel or slander has been communicated only to very few publishees within an organisation does not of itself give any indication of what is at stake. For example, if one employee makes an allegation of dishonesty or sexual harassment at work against a claimant, then the claimant may have very much at stake in bringing a libel action. Without vindication, that single accusation may seriously impair or destroy his or her prospects of obtaining employment in the future."[44]

---

statements concerning the claimant's resemblance (or lack of it) to Ali G; but not in so far as it concerned benefit fraud. The fact that the accusation was serious and "crucially" that the defendant was a court officer pointed towards allowing the claim to proceed. There was some analogy with the alternative ground under CPR r.24.2 for allowing an action to proceed even if it has no real prospect of success: that there is nevertheless a "compelling reason why the case should be disposed of at a trial".

[39] [2009] EWHC 2838 (QB).

[40] There was also a claim for libel in the online edition of a South African publication, the *Financial Mail*. Whether this had been read by anyone within the jurisdiction was speculative but at best the publication here was minimal and again the claim was an abuse of process.

[41] [2013] EWHC 85 (QB).

[42] *Mardas v New York Times Co* [2008] EWHC 3135 (QB); [2009] E.M.L.R. 8 at [15]. See also, *Cairns v Modi* [2010] EWHC 2859 (QB) at [42]: "There is more to abuse of process than the number of publishees."

[43] [2005] EWHC 481 (QB) at [57].

[44] An early decision on the modern approach to this aspect of abuse of process is *Schellenberg v BBC* [2000] E.M.L.R. 296, where Eady J. had spoken of the game not being worth the candle. However, the same judge in *Howe & Co. v Burden* [2004] EWHC 196 (QB) (a slander case) said.

"It will be remembered that [in *Schellenberg*] there had been a lengthy trial which the claimant

So too, in *Underhill v Corser*[45] which involved a charge of dishonesty made in the editorial of a steam train preservation society magazine, the court refused to strike out the claim in respect of 13 non-privileged publications. Though the number of publishees was relatively small, the charge was a serious one and the aim of the proceedings was vindication[46]: the "fact that a claimant may not be able to pay the costs of a case if he loses is not of itself a reason why he should be denied access to justice".[47] Further, where there is limited publication it may be necessary to consider the defendant's response. If D accuses C of being a charlatan and puts in a defence of justification it may be justifiable to allow the claimant to meet that.[48]

6.3 Publication and Defamation Act 2013, s.1.[49] Section 1 of the Defamation Act 2013, which is not yet in force, provides that "A statement is not defamatory unless its publication has caused or is likely to cause serious harm to the reputation of the claimant." Although the provision appears to deal only with the question whether a statement is defamatory, the intention of the drafters seems to have been to extend the requirement of serious harm to other considerations including publication.[50] If that is right, for a claim to be actionable the claimant will have to prove that the extent of publication was sufficient to cause serious harm to him. Where he cannot prove that the claim will fail. The provision may make a difference in a marginal case where the claim is only just currently sufficiently widely published to overcome a *Jameel* abuse application. It is, however, not likely to make a great deal of difference in the way a case is pleaded. Though a claimant is currently not required to plead or prove publication to particular persons where the material

---

had abandoned without a definitive result having been achieved. The essential point was that he had the opportunity in those proceedings of having a determination on the merits of substantively the same issues as those in the later action which came before me. That was the context of the remarks. It would not be right to elevate that phrase into a general principle of some kind to be applied in other libel actions.

It is important to note [in this case] that the allegations complained of in the recorded telephone conversations . . . are very serious. It was said of the Claimant firm . . . that acts or omissions had regularly taken place with regard to public funding which were not only professionally improper but also tantamount to criminal offences. By contrast with the *Schellenberg* case, the Claimants have not yet had any opportunity of having those matters determined on the merits. It is to be noted that there is no plea of justification and, accordingly, any outcome would be predicated upon the presumption that these serious allegations are false. Mr. Price's submissions, if successful on any of the grounds put forward, would have the consequence that the Claimants would be prevented from achieving vindication in respect of those allegations through the court process" (at [5]–[6]).

[45] [2010] EWHC 1195 (QB).

[46] See also, *Hughes v Alan Dick & Co. Ltd* [2008] EWHC 2695 (QB) (serious slander with limited publication); *Haji-Ioannou v Dixon* [2009] EWHC 178 (QB) (only limited publication complained of but charge against prominent businessman capable of being read as one of dishonesty).

[47] [2010] EWHC 1195 at [143] (QB).

[48] *Mardas v New York Times Co* [2008] EWHC 3135 (QB); [2009] E.M.L.R. 8 at [18].

[49] See further, para.2.5, above.

[50] Ibid.

complained of has been issued within the jurisdiction in the form of a book or newspaper, the same is not true of publications on a website. In the latter situation, there is no presumption of substantial publication within the jurisdiction[51] and the claimant must prove that it has been read.

General principles: multiple publication. At common law, each communication of the material is a separate publication and gives rise to a separate cause of action.[52] So where a newspaper was published 17 years before the action was brought but the defendant supplied a copy to a person within the limitation period (then six years) it was held that an action lay.[53] Technically, in the case of an edition of a newspaper or a broadcast programme or similar widespread dissemination[54] on a single occasion there are separate publications to each person to whom the matter is communicated, but it would be an abuse of process to bring multiple actions in such a case in respect of a publication within the jurisdiction and damages would represent compensation for all loss suffered thereby.[55] A further cause of action arises, however, if the matter is repeated[56] or if the original edition is further distributed on what may fairly be regarded as a separate occasion.[57] So there are separate

6.4

---

[51] *Al Amoudi v Brisard* [2006] EWHC 1062 (QB); [2007] 1 W.L.R. 113. See also, *Nationwide News Pty Ltd v University of Newlands* [2005] NZCA 317 and *Crookes v Yahoo* [2008] BCCA 165.

[52] *Duke of Brunswick v Harmer* (1849) 14 Q.B. 185; *Berezovsky v Michaels* [2000] 1 W.L.R. 1004 HL at 1012: *McLean v David Syme & Co. Ltd* (1970) 92 W.N. (N.S.W.) 611 NSWCA at 616, 625; *Toomey v Mirror Newspapers Ltd* (1985) 1 N.S.W.L.R. 173 at 178. However, Hunt J. in the last case said that where a speech is delivered to an audience there is only one publication. The Irish Defamation Bill, cl.10, provides that a publication to two or more persons, whether contemporaneously or not, gives rise to one cause of action unless the interests of justice lead the court to grant leave to bring more than one action.

[53] *Duke of Brunswick v Harmer*, above. But on the facts, because the publication was procured by the plaintiff to his agent, the claim would now be an abuse of process: see para.6.2, above.

[54] *Godfrey v Demon Internet Ltd* [2001] Q.B. 201 at 208 (internet newsgroup).

[55] "The effect of the rule has been mitigated, if not ignored, to avoid inconvenient results": *Harris v 718932 Pty Ltd (formerly Globe Press Pty Ltd)* [2003] NSWCA 38; 56 N.S.W.L.R. 276 at [20], where it is suggested that the same would apply: "where publication occurs over an extended period, as with books, unless time becomes critical because of a defence under the Limitation Act, or for some other reason." However, the court applied the basic principle so as to allow further action in respect of reprints of a book.

"The substance of the matter is that each print gave rise to separate causes of action or groups of causes of action. They arose at different times, against different defendants, and caused different damage. There is no discernible reason why a judgment in respect of the first print should bar proceedings in respect of the reprints, and as already mentioned any other rule would allow defamatory material to be republished after judgment with impunity" (at [29]). Cf. *Firth v State* 775 N.E.2d 463 (NY 2002) where it was held for the purposes of the New York single publication rule (see below) that the addition of unrelated material to a website after the initial publication of the defamatory matter could not be equated with, say, the publication of a new edition of a book.

[56] Repetition to the same person must in principle create a new cause of action but it can hardly be the law that if A buys a defamatory book or video there is a new publication to him every time he reads or views it. Of course there would be no damage after the first reading.

[57] Some jurisdictions have developed forms of a "single publication" rule. This has two purposes. First, it starts the limitation period running from the time when the material is put into general circulation and, once the period has expired, prevents an action being brought upon an

claims in respect of the paper edition of a newspaper and its publication from an internet archive of the newspaper,[58] or the first and subsequent editions of a book.[59]

6.5 Multiple publication and the European Convention on Human Rights. The application of the multiple publication rule to internet archives was the subject of a challenge before the European Court of Human Rights in *Times Newspapers (nos 1 and 2) v UK*.[60] The case concerned two articles originally published by the applicant and retained by it in its internet archives. When the articles were originally published, the claimant, Mr Loutchansky, had brought libel claims against the applicant in respect of the hard copy publication. Subsequently he brought a second claim in respect of the internet publications. The applicant then added a notice to both articles warning that they were subject to High Court litigation and they should not be reproduced or relied on without reference to the applicant's legal department. The defendant sought to persuade the English courts that the internet claim was time barred on the basis that English law recognised a "single-publication" rule and the claim had been commenced more than one year after that publication.

---

individual sale at a later date. However, it is not easy to determine what amounts to a single publication. The Restatement, 2d, *Torts*, para.577(A)(3) excludes "separate aggregate publications" such as the continual showing of a cinema film as well as more obvious cases like a paperback edition of a book. Secondly, in a federal state with widespread dissemination of news and comment it prevents the defendant being harassed by multiple actions in different jurisdictions. Some states have adopted a Uniform Single Publications Act. See generally 50 Am.Jur.2d, *Libel and Slander*, para.264. A single publication rule has been rejected in Australia (*Dow Jones & Co. Inc. v Gutnick* [2002] HCA 56; 210 C.L.R. 575) and, until the Defamation Act 2013, had also been rejected in England (*Loutchansky v Times Newspapers Ltd (Nos 2–5)* [2001] EWCA Civ 1805; [2002] Q.B. 783, where an argument based on art.10 of the European Convention on Human Rights was rejected). For details of the single publication rule that will become part of English law when the 2013 Act enters into force, see para.6.6, below. However, in Australia a plaintiff will be compelled to bring a claim in respect of a nationwide publication in one jurisdiction and the Jurisdiction of Courts (Cross-Vesting) Act 1987 (C'th) allows transfer of proceedings in the interests of justice. See also the discussion in the (English) Law Commission Scoping Study No.2, *Defamation and the Internet, A Preliminary Investigation* (2002), Pt III. The clear tendency of the Canadian authorities is in favour of the English and Australian position and not in favour of the American single publication rule: *Carter v BC Federation of Foster Parents Association* [2005] BCCA 398 at [18].

[58] *Loutchansky v Times Newspapers Ltd (Nos 2–5)* [2001] EWCA Civ 1805; [2002] Q.B. 783. In *Green v Times Newspapers Ltd*, January 17, 2001, (QB), Gray J. declined to strike out as an abuse of process an action in respect of a publication on a newspaper web site where an offer of amends had been accepted in respect of the publication of the same matter in the paper edition, but had been rejected in respect of the web site publication.

"The action is properly constituted; it is in respect of (at any rate notionally) a separate cause, or separate causes, of action; and, most importantly, I do not think it would be right for me to make an order which would have the effect of compelling the claimant to accept an offer of amends when they have, and have exercised, a statutory right to reject that offer."

However, an order for summary disposal was made in view of the fact that the offer of amends had been accepted in respect of the paper publication (which was regarded as the more serious), thereby allowing damages for both publications to be assessed by the same tribunal.

[59] *Harris v 718932 Pty Ltd (formerly Globe Press Pty Ltd)* [2003] NSWCA 38; 56 N.S.W.L.R. 276.

[60] (2009), App. nos 3002/03 and 23676/03; [2009] E.M.L.R. 14.

This argument was rejected by both High Court and Court of Appeal and judgment was entered for Mr Loutchansky.[61] The applicant newspaper applied to the European Court of Human Rights for a ruling that the domestic courts' refusal to apply a single publication rule to internet publications was an unjustifiable and disproportionate restriction of its art.10 rights. It argued that the internet publication rule restricted its ability to maintain an archive and exposed it to ceaseless liability, and there should not be any obligation to publish qualifications until litigation had been resolved.

The European Court of Human Rights held that the rule that a separate internet publication gave rise to a new cause of action did not infringe art.10 of the Convention. The court agreed that newspaper internet archives made a substantial contribution:

> "to preserving and making available news and information. Such archives constitute an important source for education and historical research, particularly as they are readily accessible to the public and are generally free. The Court therefore considers that, while the primary function of the press in a democracy is to act as a 'public watchdog', it has a valuable secondary role in maintaining and making available to the public archives containing news which has previously been reported. However, the margin of appreciation afforded to States in striking the balance between the competing rights is likely to be greater where news archives of past events, rather than news reporting of current affairs, are concerned. In particular, the duty of the press to act in accordance with the principles of responsible journalism by ensuring the accuracy of historical, rather than perishable, information published is likely to be more stringent in the absence of any urgency in publishing the material."[62]

However, the right to freedom of expression was not absolute and it had to be balanced against the right of individuals to protect their reputations and where necessary have access to the courts to do so. In this case the domestic court had not ordered that the articles be removed altogether, and the obligation to attach a notice to archive material where the newspaper was on notice that a libel action had been initiated in respect of that same article was not a disproportionate interference with art.10.[63] Moreover, on the facts of the case no injustice had been done to the applicant as the claim had been brought in respect of the internet publication within 15 months of the hard copy claim

---

[61] *Loutchansky v Times Newspapers Ltd (Nos 2–5)* [2001] EWCA Civ 1805, [2002] Q.B. 783 CA.

[62] (2009), App. nos 3002/03 and 23676/03; [2009] E.M.L.R. 14, at [45].

[63] In *Loutchansky v Times Newspapers Ltd (Nos 2–5)* [2001] EWCA Civ 1805, [2002] Q.B. 783 CA, the Court of Appeal stated (at [74]) that: "Where it is known that archive material is or may be defamatory, the attachment of an appropriate notice warning against treating it as the truth will normally remove any sting from the material." See also *Budu v BBC* [2010] EWHC 616 (QB) in which "*Loutchansky* notices" had been attached. Cf. *Flood v Times Newspapers* [2013] EWHC 2182 (QB) where Tugendhat J. held that the attachment of the notice did not remove the sting: because readers of an archive do not just regard it as an historical document, but as also speaking at the date on which it is being read, the addition of the warning did not improve things from the claimant's point of view as it did not indicate where the complaint came from or what it was about and it led to the inference that any more recent information would have been added to the article.

and it was not therefore a case in which delay had affected the defendants' ability to defend the claim. However, the court emphasised that:

> " . . . while an aggrieved applicant must be afforded a real opportunity to vindicate his right to reputation, libel proceedings brought against a newspaper after a significant lapse of time may well, in the absence of exceptional circumstances, give rise to a disproportionate interference with press freedom under art.10."[64]

6.6 Defamation Act, s.8—single publication rule. Section 8, when it comes into force, will replace the existing multiple publication rule under which every new publication of a defamatory statement gives rise to a separate claim with a single publication rule. The rule, which will apply to a republication of the same material by the same publisher, prevents any claim being brought in respect of the subsequent publication more than one year from the date of the first publication (subs.(4)). The section provides as follows:

> **"8. Single publication rule**
> (1) This section applies if a person—
>   (a) publishes a statement to the public ('the first publication'), and
>   (b) subsequently publishes (whether or not to the public) that statement or a statement which is substantially the same.
> (2) In subsection (1) 'publication to the public' includes publication to a section of the public.
> (3) For the purposes of section 4A of the Limitation Act 1980 (time limit for actions for defamation etc) any cause of action against the person for defamation in respect of the subsequent publication is to be treated as having accrued on the date of the first publication.
> (4) This section does not apply in relation to the subsequent publication if the manner of that publication is materially different from the manner of the first publication.
> (5) In determining whether the manner of a subsequent publication is materially different from the manner of the first publication, the matters to which the court may have regard include (amongst other matters)—
>   (a) the level of prominence that a statement is given;
>   (b) the extent of the subsequent publication.
> (6) Where this section applies—
>   (a) it does not affect the court's discretion under section 32A of the Limitation Act 1980 (discretionary exclusion of time limit for actions for defamation etc), and
>   (b) the reference in subsection (1)(a) of that section to the operation of section 4A of that Act is a reference to the operation of section 4A together with this section."

6.7 Defamation Act, s.8—conditions for application of single meaning rule. The new rule applies where a person publishes a statement to the public *and* subsequently publishes (whether or not to the public) that statement or a statement that is substantially the same. Only the person who published the

---

[64] (2009), App. nos 3002/03 and 23676/03; [2009] E.M.L.R. 14 at [48].

"first publication" is covered by the provision. Thus, where the original publication is republished by a third party, this will be treated as a new publication and time, for limitation purposes, will only begin to run against him from the date of his publication and not the first publication.

For the provision to apply, there must have been a first publication to the public and then a subsequent publication by the same person of the "statement or a statement that is substantially the same". The purpose of the provision is said in the *Explanatory Notes* to be: "to ensure that the provisions catch publications which have the same content or content which has changed very little so that the essence of the defamatory statement is not substantially different from that contained in the earlier publication".[65] Clearly within the provision would be a standalone republication, whether orally or in writing, of the statement complained of or one that makes substantially the same allegation. Where the statement is contained in a longer work, however, the position may be more difficult. Presumably, it would cover a paperback edition of a book previously published in hardback and a DVD of a cinema released film or rebroadcast of a television programme. In such cases any changes from the original are likely to be minimal. More difficult may be the case where a new edition of a book is published which contains significant changes but the statement complained of remains the same. Subs.(1) focuses attention on the statement itself, not any work in which the statement has appeared. Unless therefore a new edition is treated as a publication in a materially different form (see subss.(4), (5)), which is thereby excluded from the protection of the provision, it is the fact that the *statement complained* of has not changed that it is the relevant issue and not the changes to other material in respect of which no complaint is made.

Defamation Act, s.8—"materially different". Subs.(4) excludes from　**6.8** the provision cases where the manner of the subsequent publication is "materially different" from that of the first publication. In determining whether the manner is "materially different" the matters to which the courts may have regard (subs.(5)) include, but are not limited to, (a) the level of prominence that a statement is given and (b) the extent of the subsequent publication. The *Explanatory Notes* give as an example of a "materially different" publication: "where a story has first appeared relatively obscurely in a section of a website where several clicks need to be gone through to access it, but has subsequently been promoted to a position where it can be directly accessed from the home page of the site, thereby increasing considerably the number of hits it receives."[66] A second example might be the publication on an open access basis of an academic article previously only available by subscription. In such a case not only is the readership likely to increase with the new publication but it may also change. More difficult might be the publication of a paperback

---

[65] Explanatory Notes, Defamation Act 2013, at para.61.
[66] Ibid. at para.63.

edition of a hardback book that has sold only a very small number of copies. If sales of the paperback were many times those of the hardback, would this make the paperback publication materially different? On one view the case is indistinguishable from the website example. Yet not to apply the new rule to such a situation would significantly undermine its utility and it is hard to see, if the need for a single publication rule is accepted, why it should not apply to such an example. Whether the status of the publisher may be relevant is a difficult question. If, for example, a person publishes a defamatory tweet and subsequently becomes embroiled in some public controversy or otherwise becomes well known and as a result acquires thousands more followers, would a republication after this be treated as being in a "materially different" form? "Form" seems to refer to the manner of publication but clearly the extent of any publication is likely to be much greater and therefore it is suggested that the status of the publisher may in suitable cases be a relevant matter. Where however minor modifications are made to a website or new material is added which is unconnected to the libel, or changes are made to the manner in which the site is accessed, these are unlikely to be treated as material differences.

6.9 Defamation Act, s.8—limitation. Where the provision applies, subs.(4) provides that for the purposes of limitation, any cause of action in respect of the subsequent publication is to be treated as having accrued from the date of the first publication. However, subs.(6) specifically provides that where the new rule applies it does not affect the court's discretion under s.32A of the Limitation Act 1980 to disapply the primary one-year limitation period that applies to libel and slander claims. Under Limitation Act 1980, s.32A, the court may disapply the primary limitation period where it appears to the court that it would be equitable to allow an action to proceed notwithstanding that the primary limitation period has expired.[67] In exercising its discretion, the court is required to have regard to the relative prejudice that would be caused to claimant or defendant depending on whether the limitation period was disapplied or not. The court is also required "to have regard to all the circumstances of the case" and in particular to the length of, and the reasons for, the delay on the part of the claimant, and, where the reason for the delay was ignorance of relevant facts, the date on which the facts did become known to him and the extent to which he acted promptly and reasonably once he knew whether or not the facts might be capable of giving rise to a claim.[68]

The courts have thus far regarded disapplication as an exceptional step and there are few examples where s.32A has been successfully relied on.[69] It may be however that the position will change once s.8 becomes law. Reputational harm is not caused by the act of publication, but rather when the reading

---

[67] See further, paras 19.20, 19.21, below.
[68] Limitation Act 1980, s.32A(2).
[69] See further, para.19.21, below.

occurs. Irrespective of when first publication occurs, each reading has the potential to harm the reputation of the person defamed. The problems caused by the perpetual availability of damaging publications online are an increasingly pressing concern.[70] Faced with a claimant who argues credibly that a reading of a defamatory online publication that took place yesterday, and which might be emulated tomorrow, has had adverse consequences for his art.8 right to reputation, it may be difficult for a judge to refuse to disapply the limitation period (at least for the years after first publication when no especial practical difficulty would be caused to the defendant). Moreover, as courts have stated repeatedly, the freedom of expression interest in ongoing publication is comparatively weak.[71] Arguably, the judge will find himself in this position on every occasion that the harm to reputation might be described as 'serious' and this may mean that the supposed safe harbour will prove illusory.

General principles: responsibility for publication. The person who   **6.10** first spoke or composed the defamatory matter (the originator) is of course liable, provided he intended to publish it or failed to take reasonable care to prevent its publication.[72] However, at common law liability extends to any person who participated in, secured[73] or authorised the publication[74] (even the printer of a defamatory work) though this was qualified by special rules for mere distributors, who could escape liability by showing lack of knowledge of the defamatory nature of the publication and the exercise of reasonable care.[75] Under s.1 of the Defamation Act 1996 the defence was recast and somewhat extended so that some persons who at common law would have been primary publishers may now claim the benefit of the defence. Persons other than the "author", "editor" and "publisher" (used here in the commercial sense) may show that they took reasonable care in relation to the publication of the statement and did not know and had no reason to believe that what they did caused or contributed to the publication of a defamatory statement. Additionally, by s.10 of the Defamation Act 2013, a court will not have jurisdiction to

---

[70] Solove, *The Future of Reputation: Gossip, Rumor and Privacy on the Internet* (Yale University Press, 2007).

[71] *Loutchansky v Times Newspapers Ltd (Nos 2–5)* [2001] EWCA Civ 1805 CA; [2002] Q.B. 783 at [74].

[72] See para.6.17, below. For liability of the originator for repetition by others, see para.6.53, below.

[73] "There are various acts that can give rise to legal responsibility, for example, encouraging the primary author, supplying him with information intending or knowing that it will be republished, or, if one is in a position to do so, instructing or authorising him to publish it": *Bataille v Newland* [2002] EWHC 1692 (QB) at 8. Thus a person who demands an apology from a newspaper and dictates its terms is a publisher: *Watts v Times Newspapers* [1997] Q.B. 650 CA (apology defamatory of third party).

[74] This was accepted as an accurate statement of the law in, for example, *Watts v Times Newspapers Ltd (Schilling & Lom (a firm), third party)* [1997] Q.B. 650 (QB) at 670 and *Mahfouz v Brisard* [2005] EWHC 2304 (QB) at [11].

[75] See para.6.18, below.

hear an action for defamation brought against a person who was not the "author", "editor" or "publisher" of the statement complained of unless the court is satisfied that it is not reasonably practicable for an action to be brought against the author, editor or publisher.[76] The common law defence available to distributors is not, in terms, abolished,[77] but in view of the statutory defence it seems unlikely that hereafter it will be relied on. However, it is for the claimant to show that the defendant is guilty of some act or omission which under the common law amounts to a publication—only if that is established does the defence come into play.

The provisions of the 1996 Act apply to internet service providers[78] but since August 2002 these publishers gain additional protection from the Electronic Commerce (E.C. Directive) Regulations 2002, implementing an EU Directive.[79] Though the Defamation Act 1996, s.1 and the Electronic Commerce (E.C. Directive) Regulations 2002 may also apply to an "operator of a website", the Defamation Act 2013, s.5 provides an additional defence where the operator can show that it was not the operator who posted the statement on the website.[80]

6.11   **Joint and several liability.** In accordance with general principle, all persons who procure or[81] participate[82] in the publication of a libel, and who

---

[76] Defamation Act 2013, s.10(1). By subs.(2) "author", "editor" or "publisher" have the same meaning as in s.1 of the Defamation Act 1996. See further para.6.45, below.

[77] This was accepted by Eady J. (at [70]) in *Metropolitan International Schools Ltd v Designtechnica Corp* [2009] EWHC 1765 (QB); [2009] E.M.L.R. 27.

[78] See para.6.34, below.

[79] See para.6.41, below.

[80] See para.6.41, below.

[81] If A procures B (e.g. a television station) to publish defamatory matter about the claimant and the claimant sues in respect of the publication by B, for which A is liable, the claimant is not required to plead the words in which A conveyed the information to B: *De Jong v State of Victoria* [2006] VSC 274.

[82] There is no tort liability for "knowing assistance" (*Credit Lyonnais v ECGD* [1998] 1 Lloyd's Rep. 19 CA; *Douglas v Hello! Ltd* [2002] EWHC 2560 Ch). Statements in the defamation cases about liability for "participation" were:

"directing attention to identifiable defamatory statements, to the publication of which in the completed form the defendant in question was held to have given his authority or approval or to the final form of which he had contributed": *Purcell v Cruising Yacht Club of Australia Ltd* [2001] N.S.W.S.C. 927.

A person who provides material for or even participates in a television programme is not necessarily a co-publisher with the television company of the whole programme: *Thiess v TCN Channel Nine Pty* [1994] 1 Qd. R. 156 Full Court. Whether he bears responsibility for republication of what he conveys to the company (as to which, see para.6.52, below) raises different issues. See also, *Berezovsky v The Russian Television and Radio Broadcasting Co.* [2010] EWHC 476 (QB) in which Eady J. held that the defendants, a state-owned Russian television company and T, were joint tortfeasors in respect of statements expressly made by T about the claimant on a programme made and published by the company. However, on the facts, he held that the claimant, who had the burden of proof on this issue, had not proved that T was also responsible for the overall message conveyed by the programme or other defamatory statements not directly derived from his words.

In *Fish & Fish Ltd v Sea Shepherd UK* [2013] EWCA Civ 544 CA, (not a libel case but applied in *Dar Al Arkan Real Estate Development Co. v Al Refai* [2013] EWHC 1630 (Comm)) Beatson L.J. indicated that there were two requirements that must be met for one person (a participator)

are liable therefor,[83] are jointly and severally liable for the whole damage suffered by the claimant.[84] Thus in the case of the publication of a newspaper the journalist, editor[85] and publisher are all joint tortfeasors.

> "If one repeat, and another write a libel, and a third approve what is wrote they are all makers of it; for all persons who concur, and show their assent or approbation to do an unlawful act, are guilty."[86]

Similarly, the signatories of a petition, praying for the removal from office of a public official, were jointly and severally liable with the person who drafted the petition for any defamatory statements contained therein.[87] However, it has been held that although a wholesale agency and retail vendor may be liable[88] they are not joint tortfeasors with the publishers of the newspaper.[89] It is not consistent with the principles governing joint liability:

> "to contend that a person suffers actionable damage on account of the conduct of one of the joint tortfeasors who participated in the publication, and separate actionable damage in respect of the participation by another joint tortfeasor. Once liability as a joint tortfeasor is established, each of the joint tortfeasors is liable for the whole damage."[90]

---

to be liable for a tort directly committed by another (a perpetrator) because he was a party to a common design with the perpetrator (or concerted action with him). First, there must be a common design that at least one of the putative joint tortfeasors should do the act(s) said to be tortious to which the "actual perpetrator or perpetrators" was or were a party, and, second, the participator must do an act or acts in furtherance of the common design which was or were more than de minimis and did not merely facilitate the tort without it being necessary that the participator did something "essential" or of "real significance to the commission of the tort [at 45ff]. In the *Dar Al Arkan* case, Andrew Smith J. held that it was not appropriate to grant summary judgment in favour of one defendant in defamation and malicious falsehood proceedings in circumstances where there was a sufficient argument that the company was a joint tortfeasor (by virtue of their alleged participation in the creation and publication of a website and an email that libelled the claimants) and there was insufficient evidence to enable the court to determine the responsibility summarily.

[83] For the effect of the Defamation Act 1996, see para.6.31ff, below. Co-publishers are not "infected" by the malice of others where there is a plea of qualified privilege or fair comment: see Ch.17, s.3 and para.12.37, below.

[84] See generally Clerk & Lindsell, *Torts*, 20th edn (2010), Ch.4.

[85] However, in *Allason v Campbell, The Times*, May 8, 1996 (a case of malicious falsehood) Sir Maurice Drake held that a newspaper political editor had not published a piece written by a subordinate. Cf. *Balakrishnan v Nirumalan K Pillay* [1999] 3 S.L.R. 22 Sing. CA (general editor liable at common law for material written by a section editor, whether he had read it or not). See also, *Berezovsky v The Russian Television and Radio Broadcasting Co.* [2010] EWHC 476 (QB).

[86] Per curiam in *R. v Paine* (1696) 5 Mod. 163 at 167.

[87] *Willcocks v Howell* (1885) 8 O.R. 576. Persons who second or vote in favour of a resolution proposed at a meeting are jointly and severally liable with the proposer of the resolution for any defamation contained therein: *Meurant v Raubenheimer* (1882) 1 Buchanan (C. of G. Hope) R. 87, considered in *African Realty v Robinson* [1939] T.P.D. 155 (re-publication by reference).

[88] See para.6.23, below.

[89] *Lambert v Roberts* [1933] 2 W.W.R. 508. See also *Thomson v Lambert* [1938] S.C.R. 253 at 267.

[90] *Bracks v Smyth-Kirk* [2008] N.S.W.S.C. 930 at [52]. On appeal, [2009] NSWCA 401.

SECTION 2. PUBLICATION

6.12 **Acts amounting to publication.** The question is whether the defendant has communicated the defamatory matter to others and this may be done in a variety of ways.[91] Thus, words contained in a letter or email sent to a third person would be published when read and a film or television broadcast would be published when seen. As a general rule, silence is not libel[92] so that a failure to object to a defamatory communication made by another will not, without more, be actionable.[93] However, liability may arise where the defendant deliberately draws the attention of others to an existing libel[94] or even leaves it in a place where they are likely to see it,[95] provided someone does so.[96] It has been held that where defamatory matter is placed in a visible manner on the defendant's property by some third party for whom he is not responsible, he may be treated as publishing the matter if he elects to leave it there.[97] Where, however, the removal of the defamatory matter would involve

---

[91] See Restatement, 2d, *Torts*, para.577, comment a. (precise mode immaterial). "There are no limitations on the manner in which defamatory matter may be published. Any act which has the effect of transferring the defamatory information to a third person constitutes a publication": *Stanley v Shaw*, 2006 BCCA 467, 231 B.C.A.C. 186 at [5]. In *Holding v Howlett* [2003] EWHC 286 QB, the mode of publication was by aerial banners towed by aircraft.

[92] *Stanley v Shaw*, 2006 BCCA 467, 231 B.C.A.C. 186; *Pond v General Electric Co.*, 256 F.2d 824 (9th Cir. 1958) at 827.

[93] Liability may, for example, be imposed where one party is vicariously liable for the acts of the publisher or where, notwithstanding that he does not say anything, he is found to have participated in, adopted or approved the publication. See, for example, *Frawley v State of New South Wales*, [2007] N.S.W.S.C. 1379. Cf. *Underhill v Corser* [2010] EWHC 1195 (QB) in which Tugendhat J. held that although the defendant, who was treasurer and board member of a charity, was aware of the editorial and could have taken steps to stop its publication, he was nevertheless not liable for its publication.

[94] *Hird v Wood* (1894) 38 S.J. 234 CA. In *Smith v Wood* (1813) 3 Camp. 323, it was held not to be a publication to show a libellous caricature to another on request. In *Wolfson v Syracuse Newspapers*, 4 N.Y.S.2d 640 (1938) permission by the original publisher to read a bound volume of a newspaper was held "too passive" to amount to a publication. However, the first case seems difficult to square with principle and the second may be explained by a desire not to subvert the "single publication" rule (see para.6.3, above): see the dissent in the appeal 279 N.Y. 716 (1939). As to internet links see para.6.42, below.

[95] As by leaving a copy on file: *Edgeworth v New York Central* [1936] 2 D.L.R. 577; *Peck v R.* [1964] Ex.C.R. 966.

[96] *Pinkney v District of Columbia*, 439 F.Supp. 519 (DC, 1977): mere filing on record not publication.

[97] *Byrne v Deane* [1937] 1 K.B. 818 CA; *Hellar v Bianco*, 244 P.2d 757 (Cal 1952) (telephone number and "Ask for Isabelle" on wall of men's lavatory); *Tacket v General Motors*, 836 F.2d 1042 (CA 7 1987). Cf. *Sedleigh-Denfield v O'Callaghan* [1940] A.C. 880 (nuisance caused by third party). Section 1 of the Defamation Act 1996 is of no assistance because the defendant is aware of the defamation. However, it has to be said that the section seems to be drafted on the assumption that there can only be publication by positive act. *Urbanchich v Drummoyne Municipal Council* (1991) Australian Torts Reports 81–127 interprets *Byrne v Deane* as requiring that the defendant should have in some way ratified or promoted the libel, though this could be inferred from merely allowing it to remain there. But suppose A paints a defamatory message on D's wall and this can be removed at modest expense. Can D escape liability by adding a line, "I certainly do not agree with this"?

great trouble and expense the occupier will not be liable, for one cannot then draw the inference that he is voluntarily allowing it to remain.[98]

While these principles are well established in relation to traditional forms of communication, their application to online communication is in the process of development. Modern methods of communication, in particular the internet, pose questions of how far those who are not originators of defamatory material should be regarded as having published it when the services they provide have facilitated the distribution of the material. Although, for example, it is clear that the person who is the author of a blog, website or tweet is liable for its publication, what of the situation where a non-defamatory statement is published via the internet, whether on a website, bulletin board or email, that contains a hyperlink that if clicked on takes the reader to a webpage that contains defamatory material? Clearly the author of the page linked to is liable for his original publication, but the question whether the linking author is liable is considered below. An internet service provider upon whose site defamatory material is placed by another may incur liability for failure to remove it, as may the provider of a platform that allows people to communicate online[99] though neither situation is without difficulties. Claims have also been brought against internet search engines which "link" searchers via hyperlinks to websites. While the presence of common law and statutory defences for distributors mitigates the consequences of giving a broad meaning to what amounts to "publication", it is sometimes difficult to draw the line between cases where these defences apply and those where there is no liability for the more fundamental reason that the defendant has not published at all.[100] These issues are considered later in the chapter.

Acts amounting to publication—"hyperlinking". The question whether the publisher of an internet communication—whether that be an email, webpage or bulletin board posting—which contains a link[101] to defamatory content on another webpage should be treated as having published that   6.13

---

[98] *Byrne v Deane* [1937] 1 K.B. at 837 (giving the example of a defamatory imputation carved into stonework). Trustees of a cemetery are not obliged to remove a tombstone: *Solomon v Simmons, The Times*, April 10, 1954. Removing spray painted graffiti may be very expensive but the court in *Scott v Hull*, 259 N.E.2d 160 (Oh, 1970) simply rejected liability for nonfeasance.

[99] See para.6.26, below.

[100] See para.6.28–29, below.

[101] A link (or hyperlink) is a part of a webpage that connects to another webpage or another portion of the same webpage. By clicking on the link, the reader is taken to the second webpage. Links are either "shallow", which take the reader to a webpage where articles are posted, or "deep", which take the reader directly to an article. Both shallow and deep hyperlinks require the reader to click on the link in order to be taken to the content. Almost every webpage contains hyperlinks so that content is endlessly connected to other content. A search engine generates lists of hyperlinks to webpages on related topics around the web. A second form of linking is "framing". This involves the inclusion of a hyperlink on a webpage which, when followed, causes another party's web content to appear within a frame on the original webpage. Unlike ordinary linking, the internet user does not leave the original website when they follow the hyperlink: Collins, *The Law of Defamation and the Internet*, 3rd edn (Oxford: OUP, 2010), at para.2.43.

content has not been directly considered by an English court[102] but was the subject of a decision by the Canadian Supreme Court in *Crookes v Newton*.[103] The defendant in *Crookes* owned and operated a website containing commentary about various issues, including free speech and the internet. One of the articles he posted included shallow and deep hyperlinks to other websites which contained defamatory material about the plaintiff. At first instance,[104] the trial court found there had been no publication and the claimant's appeal was dismissed by both the Court of Appeal[105] and the Supreme Court. Abella J.,[106] who delivered the leading judgment, was definitive in her rejection of liability for hyperlinking: "I would conclude that a hyperlink, by itself, should never be seen as 'publication' of the content to which it refers."[107] Abella J. stated that a hyperlink was, in essence, simply a reference[108]:

---

[102] In *McGrath v Dawkins* [2012] EWHC B3 (QB), one of the defendants contended that it was not responsible for the publication of the forum on which the material was published which was part of a similar but distinct US website, operated by a different entity. H.H.J. Moloney QC refused to grant summary judgment because there was a hyperlink from the UK to the US site. The judge held that:

"The law on liability for hyperlinks is in a state of some uncertainty at present. Even if the general English rule were to be as recently held in Canada, that a mere hyperlink does not render the operator of the linking website liable for the content of the linked site, the decision may well be a fact-sensitive one, especially when, as here, the two websites are very closely associated, the link is hidden, and the point of contact is the 'Home' button which is normally regarded as taking you to the central hub of the same website you are already on. I therefore conclude that I am not satisfied at this stage that the 2nd Defendant was not answerable for the .net forum at the material time, and that it is a question fit for trial" (at [26]).

In *Ali v Associated Newspapers Limited* [2010] EWHC 100 (QB), a summary judgment and strike-out application made on the basis that it would be perverse for a jury to conclude that even in the broad meaning contended for by the claimant the words were not substantially true, Eady J. stated, at [28]:

"It was said that it is so far undecided in the authorities whether, as a matter of generality, any material to which attention is drawn in a blog by this means should be taken to be incorporated as part of the blog itself. I suspect that a general rule of thumb is unlikely to be adopted. Much will depend on the circumstances of the particular case."

See also, *Islam Expo Ltd v Spectator (1828) Ltd* [2010] EWHC 2011 (QB): the allegedly defamatory information in that case was an online text containing four hyperlinks. The court concluded that the words complained of were capable of referring to the claimant and regarded the hyperlinked information as if it was incorporated into the message containing the hyperlinks; *Budu v BBC* [2010] EWHC 616 (QB), which raised issues of meaning in which the judge assumed, without deciding, that pages linked to were part of the context for the purposes of determining meaning.

[103] 2011 SCC 47; [2011] 3 S.C.R. 269. In *International Telephone Link Pty Ltd v IDG Communications Ltd* HC Auckland CP 344/97, February 20, 1998, a reference to a URL in a print media article was held to be sufficient communication of the contents of the website to constitute publication.

[104] (2008) BCSC 1424, 88 B.C.L.R (4th) 395.

[105] 2009 BCCA 392, 96 B.C.L.R. (4th) 315. The Court of Appeal held, by a majority (Prose J.A. dissenting), that hyperlinking to another webpage was analogous to a footnote or card index in a library and should not be found to constitute republication of the defamation.

[106] Binnie, LeBel, Charron, Rothstein and Cromwell JJ. agreed. A concurring judgment was given by McLachlin C.J., with which Fish J. agreed. Deschamps J. dissented.

[107] 2011 SCC 47; [2011] 3 S.C.R. 269 at [14].

[108] Ibid. at [27].

"Both communicate that something exists, but do not, by themselves, communicate its content. And they both require some act on the part of a third party before he or she gains access to the content. The fact that access to that content is far easier with hyperlinks than with footnotes does not change the reality that a hyperlink, by itself, is content-neutral—it expresses no opinion, nor does it have any control over, the content to which it refers."[109]

While the learned Justice noted that the internet had a terrible power to ruin reputations, that a person is entitled to vigorous protection from defamatory content, and that the right to free expression did not confer a licence to ruin another's reputation,[110] she concluded that imposing liability for linking would not ultimately protect reputations[111] and would seriously chill freedom of expression:

"The Internet cannot, in short, provide access to information without hyperlinks. Limiting their usefulness by subjecting them to the traditional publication rule would have the effect of seriously restricting the flow of information and, as a result, freedom of expression. The potential "chill" in how the Internet functions could be devastating, since primary article authors would unlikely want to risk liability for linking to another article over whose changeable content they have no control. Given the core significance of the role of hyperlinking to the Internet, we risk impairing its whole functioning. Strict application of the publication rule in these circumstances would be like trying to fit a square archaic peg into the hexagonal hole of modernity."[112]

Abella J. accepted that individuals may attract liability for hyperlinking if the manner in which they have referred to content conveys defamatory meaning; not because they have created a reference, but because, understood in context, they have actually *expressed* something defamatory.[113] Beyond that, however, hyperlinking could not amount to publication.

In their concurring judgment, McLachlin C.J. and Fish J. proposed a slightly different approach to the question of when combined text and hyper-link may amount to publication, suggesting that publication should be found if the text "indicates *adoption or endorsement of the content of the hyper-linked text*".[114] A mere reference without any adoption or endorsement remains that—a content-neutral reference. Adoption or endorsement of the content accessible by a link in the text:

"can be understood to actually incorporate the defamatory content into the text. Thus, the content of the text comes to include the defamatory content accessed via hyperlink. The hyperlink, combined with the surrounding words and context, ceases

---

109 Ibid. at [30].
110 Ibid. at [37]–[38].
111 Ibid. at [39]–[42].
112 Ibid. at [36].
113 Ibid. at [40].
114 Ibid. at [48].

to be a mere reference and the content to which it refers becomes part of the published text itself."[115]

Deschamps J. dissented and proposed what she regarded as a more nuanced approach to revising the publication rule. In her view, the blanket exclusion of hyperlinks exaggerated the difference between references and other acts of publication and in treating all references alike disregarded the fact that references vary greatly in how they make defamatory information available to third parties and, consequently, the harm they can cause to people's reputations. Canadian law should therefore hold that a reference to defamatory content could satisfy the requirements of publication if "it makes the defamatory information *readily available* to a third party in a comprehensible form."[116] Such an approach was, according to the Justice, more consistent with developing jurisprudence that only deliberate acts can meet the first component of publication.[117]

Abella J. was undoubtedly correct to emphasise the importance of hyperlinking and similar processes to the working of the internet, and the risks that may attach if liability is imposed too readily. Whether an English court would reach the same conclusion must however be questioned. First, even if an English court was not to conclude that this was a new publication by analogy to the cases on publication by reference,[118] it is not entirely clear why the person who creates the hyperlink should not at least be liable as a subordinate publisher.[119] Such a person intentionally participates in the dissemination of the material complained of and, in the absence of proof that he did not know and had no reason to know that the page linked to contained defamatory material, should be liable for its further dissemination.[120] Secondly, such a blanket exclusion of liability may well be held not to give sufficient weight to the art.8 right to reputation.[121] There is of course a strong general freedom of expression interest in protecting the flow of information via the internet, but it is not difficult to think of examples where the harm to a person's reputation is so serious and the malignity of the linker so obvious that a court may conclude that liability should be imposed.[122] Thirdly, it is arguable that English courts would not be prepared to accept Abella J.'s premise that a link is content-neutral that does not in itself communicate its content. While this

---

[115] Ibid. at [51].

[116] Ibid. at [59].

[117] The second being that the statement complained of must have been read or viewed by a third party.

[118] See para.6.50, below.

[119] See further, paras 6.30 and 6.31, below.

[120] If he can prove that he did not know and had no reason to know that the page linked to contained defamatory material he would at least be able to rely on the common law defence of innocent dissemination.

[121] It should be noted that Abella J. did refer to the importance of reputation in her judgment but ultimately concluded that the critical role played by hyperlinking in the facilitation of information transfer justified a blanket exclusion rule (at [33]–[39]).

[122] 2011 SCC 47; [2011] 3 S.C.R. 269, at [36].

may be true in some cases, it is not invariably so. Much will surely depend upon the context in which it appears. Finally, even if a court were to accept that *Crookes v Newton* represents English law, determining its ambit is not without difficulty. Does, for example, the blanket exclusion rule apply where the link is in a tweet, email or bulletin board posting? What about the situation where the hyperlink is hidden and/or automatic and a click on the home page takes the user to another site without any indication that one is changing websites?[123] Abella J. noted that these questions had not been argued in the courts below and therefore did not need to be addressed by the Supreme Court but they nevertheless remain real issues.

Husband and wife. Although it is clear that communication of the defama- **6.14**
tory matter to the spouse of the person defamed is sufficient publication,[124] it was held in *Wennhak v Morgan*[125] that there was no publication where the communication was to the spouse of the *defendant*.[126] One reason for that decision, that husband and wife were one person in law, can no longer stand, but nonetheless there is something dubious in the idea that a person could be sued for defamation in respect of communications to his spouse. The case also turned upon "policy"[127] and it is thought that on the basis of the need to preserve privacy and confidentiality within the family it is still valid.[128] In effect, therefore, such statements would be protected by a form of absolute privilege.[129] In modern conditions the immunity should not be confined to lawfully married spouses, whatever difficulties of definition that might create.

Communication to claimant's agent. There is a publication where the **6.15**
defamatory matter is communicated to the claimant's agent. The best known case, where the plaintiff procured publication of a newspaper to his agent

---

[123] See *McGrath v Dawkins* [2012] EWHC B3 (QB) and fn.102, above.

[124] *Wenman v Ash* (1853) 13 C.B. 536; *Jones v Williams* (1885) 1 T.L.R. 572; *Theaker v Richardson* [1962] 1 W.L.R. 151 CA. But cf. *Wallis v Valentine* [2002] EWCA Civ 103; [2003] E.M.L.R. 8 where, on the facts, a case based only on publication to the claimant's domestic partner was an abuse of process. In *Noorani v Calver* [2009] EWHC 561 (QB), the slander was to the claimant's wife and daughter. While it was accepted that there was a technical publication, the claim was struck out as an abuse of process.

[125] (1880) 20 Q.B.D. 637; *Markisic v Middletons Lawyers* [2005] N.S.W.S.C. 258.

[126] See also *Springer v Swift*, 239 N.W. 171 (1931).

[127] See (1880) 20 Q.B.D. at 639; *Cattanach v Melchior* [2003] HCA 38; 215 C.L.R. 1 at [63].

[128] It is true that there may be a tortious conspiracy between husband and wife (*Midland Bank Trust Co. v Green (No.3)* [1982] Ch. 529 CA) but a civil conspiracy requires some overt act causing damage. The rule of non-liability is maintained in the law of criminal conspiracy (s.2(2) of the Criminal Law Act 1977) and it is thought that this is a better guide as to the rule which should be applied in defamation. However, even if publication only to the defendant's wife were actionable there must be a high chance of a claim being dismissed on the basis of abuse of process: para.6.2, above.

[129] Privilege rather than non publication is the approach of the Restatement 2d, *Torts*, para.592.

many years after its initial publication[130] would nowadays be dismissed as an abuse of process,[131] but there could be publications to an agent, unprovoked by the claimant-principal, which could be damaging.[132] A distinction must be drawn in this context between communications to the agent of a natural person and certain communications to the agent of a company. When, e.g. a communication defamatory of a company is sent to the company secretary as a communication to the company it has not been published to the secretary in his personal capacity: the only publication is to the company, which can only act through human agents.[133] There is some Canadian authority extending the scope of non-publication further than to the situation of the agent of a company. Thus, in *Monument Mining Ltd v Balendran Chong & Bodi*[134] the British Columbia Supreme Court held that an unsolicited communication about the plaintiff to his lawyer was not published.[135] On the other hand, there may be a publication to an employee who is not acting in a representative capacity for the company.[136]

6.16 Communication within organisation. It is clearly established in England that there is a publication when A, an employee of a company, communicates defamatory material to a fellow employee, even if there is no further publication outside the company and even if the matter relates only to the

---

[130] *Duke of Brunswick v Harmer* (1849) 14 Q.B. 185 at 188, 189; and see *Ward v Smith* (1830) 6 Bing. 749 at 752; *Pullman v Hill* [1891] 1 Q.B. 524 at 528, 529.

[131] See para.6.2, above.

[132] See, for example, *Wallis v Meredith* [2011] EWHC 75 (QB) (publication to claimant's solicitor only). Cf. *Sanders v Percy* [2009] EWHC 1870 (QB) and see further para.6.2, above.

[133] *State Bank of New South Wales Ltd v Currabubula Holdings Pty Ltd* [2001] NSWCA 47; (2001) 51 N.S.W.L.R. 399. The point did not arise in *Pullman v Walter Hill & Co. Ltd*, above. See also, *Ontario Ltd v Canadian Uniform Ltd* (1997), 35 O.T.C. 177: Lally J. held that a letter defamatory of a company sent to the sales manager and president of that company was not published. But cf. *Traztand Pty Ltd v Government Insurance Office of New South Wales*, [1984] 2 N.S.W.L.R. 598, 56 A.L.R. 188 in which the court held that a company remains an entity distinct from its members and the fact that the recipient of the defamatory communication was a servant or agent of the plaintiff did not mean there had not been publication in law. In *Currabubula*:

> "the letter was not addressed to the plaintiffs, and the plaintiffs were not a company which could only act through natural persons. In essence, a letter defamatory of A was sent to B in circumstances in which it might be opened by C. Questions of steps to prevent communication to C arose. They cannot arise, however, if, A being a company, the correct view is that a letter defamatory of A is sent to A and is opened by A acting by C" (at [136]).

Plainly it would be absurd to hold that there was a publication about the company when it was a "one man" company effectively controlled by the recipient of the statement. But that was not the case in *Currabubula*. If, as that case holds, a statement to the "authorised officer" of an ordinary company is a statement to the company and only to the company it is perhaps curious that the position seems to be automatically different where the statement is to a person occupying a similar position (e.g. as general manager) in the employment of a sole trader.

[134] 2012 BCSC 1769.

[135] See also, *Grimmer v Carleton Road Industries Assn*, 2009 NSSC 169; 2009 NSSC 169, 282 N.S.R. (2d) 159.

[136] Which may, on the basis of *Currabubula*, be the correct explanation of *Traztand Pty v Government Insurance Office* [1984] 2 N.S.W.L.R. 598. The most likely way in which a company would suffer damage by communication of defamatory statements about it to employees would be where they lost confidence in the company as a result. Where the communication was to a

company's affairs.[137] Similarly, there is a publication where one partner conveys information to another. However, it has been argued that in such cases there is no publication where one servant of a company produces a report which is not read by anyone outside the company, for the acts of the servant making the report and the servant reading it are acts of the company and there is no liability for publication to oneself.[138] This is the view taken in some, but not all, American jurisdictions[139] and the underlying rationale is (as in the previous paragraph) the fact that the company can only operate through its employees.[140] However, it is arguable that there is adequate protection in the fact that if the communication is made in good faith and concerns the company's affairs it will attract qualified privilege.[141]

There is no publication where a printer or clerk merely hands back the document he was instructed to prepare to the person who gave the instructions.[142]

Publication at common law: intention and foresight. As a general **6.17** rule, when a letter is addressed to a particular person, the writer is not responsible except for a publication to that person.[143] However, if in the circumstances of the case the writer knows that the letter will be opened and

---

significant number of employees it is unlikely that they would receive it in their capacity as employees in the sense considered here.

[137] See *Riddick v Thames Board Mills* [1977] Q.B. 893 CA, where the cases are reviewed. *Pullman v Hill* [1891] 1 Q.B. 524; *Bloxsius v Goblet Freres* [1894] 1 Q.B. 842; *Edmondson v Birch* [1907] 1 K.B. 37 CA; *Osborn v Thomas Boulter* [1930] 2 K.B. 226 CA; *Bryanston Finance v De Vries* [1975] Q.B. 703 CA; *Puterbaugh v Gold Medal Co* (1903) 5 O.L.R. 680; *Greenman v Minneapolis Threshing Machine Co* [1929] 4 D.L.R. 501. *Morgan v Wallis* (1917) 33 T.L.R. 495 is out of line with the weight of authority.

[138] By Lord Denning M.R., dissenting, in *Riddick v Thames Board Mills* [1977] Q.B. 893. Alternatively, his Lordship would have revived the doctrine of common employment to prevent the company being vicariously liable for defamation of one servant by another in an internal report. In New South Wales, Hunt J. in *Jones v Amalgamated Television Services* (1991) 23 N.S.W.L.R. 364 left it open whether a company is vicariously liable where the fellow servant to whom the matter is conveyed is acting as agent of the company to receive the information.

[139] See 50 Am.Jur.2d, *Libel and Slander*, para.2.47. The rule is known as that of "intracorporate immunity". The Restatement, 2d, *Torts*, para.577 does not recognise the rule.

[140] *Lovelace v Long John Silver's Inc.*, 841 S.W.2d 682 (Mo., 1992). Hence it must be doubtful if one can in the same breath accept the current English rule about intra-company communications and that about communications by an outsider to an authorised officer about the company: cf. *State Bank of New South Wales Ltd v Currabubula Holdings Pty Ltd* [2001] NSWCA 47; (2001) 51 N.S.W.L.R. 399 at [129]. See also, *Tom & Bill Waterhouse Pty Ltd v Racing New South Wales* [2008] N.S.W.S.C. 1013 at [55].

[141] See para.14.46, below.

[142] *Eglantine Inn v Smith* [1948] N.I. 29.

[143] The Irish Defamation Act 2009 provides in s.6 that:

"(4) There shall be no publication for the purposes of the tort of defamation if the defamatory statement concerned is published to the person to whom it relates and to a person other than the person to whom it relates in circumstances where—
  (a) it was not intended that the statement would be published to the second-mentioned person, and
  (b) it was not reasonably foreseeable that publication of the statement to the first-mentioned person would result in its being published to the second-mentioned person."

Presumably it is not intended that there should be publication where there is no intention to

read by some person other than the person to whom he addresses it, he will be liable for the publication to that person. As it was put by Swinfen Eady L.J. in *Huth v Huth*, if:

> "a person sends a letter to, say, a merchant at his office, knowing that the merchant has a staff of clerks who in the ordinary course of business open all letters sent to the merchant's office, that would clearly be a publication[144] if the letter were opened and perused by a clerk in that way, even although that letter were most carefully sealed."[145]

By analogy with the cases in the next paragraph it is submitted that the true rule is that the defendant will be liable if he has reason to know that the letter may be opened in the ordinary course of business by someone other than the addressee and, probably in modern business conditions, such knowledge will generally[146] be imputed to him, unless the letter carries some clear indication[147] (e.g. by being marked "personal" or "private and confidential") to show that this should not take place.[148] There may also be cases in which the defendant has reason to know that a letter sent to a private address may be opened by someone other than the addressee, though in practice this may be less likely than in the case of a letter sent to a business address. Such a case might arise, e.g. if the writer knew that the addressee was illiterate[149] or blind.[150]

---

publish to anyone at all, as where the defendant believes that he is alone and is talking to himself.

[144] For cases in which publication to an employee of a company may only constitute publication to the company, see para.6.15, above.

[145] [1915] 3 K.B. 32 CA at 43. See also *Delacroix v Thevenot* (1817) 2 Stark. 63, in which case it was proved not only that the clerk was in the habit of opening letters directed to his master which were not marked "Private", but that the defendant was aware of the nature of the clerk's employment. In *Hall v Zeitsman* (1899) 16 C.G.Hope R. 213, the requisite knowledge was not proved.

[146] But no mechanical rule can be laid down. Compare the differing results in the similar cases of *Gomersall v Davies* (1898) 14 T.L.R. 430 CA and *Sharpe v Skues* (1909) 25 T.L.R. 336 CA.

[147] Email messages to business addresses are commonly opened by secretaries and presumably the same principles apply: see Collins, *The Law of Defamation and the Internet*, 3rd edn (Oxford: OUP, 2010), para.5.08. Would some indication such as "private" in the header be the equivalent of a sealed envelope marked in the same way?

[148] In *Pullman v Hill* [1891] 1 Q.B. 524, a letter was addressed to the plaintiff's firm. It was opened by a clerk and there was held to be a publication, but the court suggested that if it had been marked "private" the result would have been different. In *Paul v Holt* (1935) 69 Ir.L.T.Rep. 157, a defamatory letter was addressed equivocally to "Mr. Paul". The Court of Appeal of Northern Ireland held that:

> "it lay with the respondent (defendant) to prove that he had no knowledge of the existence of anyone to whom the address of the letter might equally apply".

[149] In *Jackson v Staley* (1885) 9 O.R. 334, there was no evidence that the defendant knew that the plaintiff was illiterate and there was therefore held to have been no publication by the defendant when the letter was read to the plaintiff by his wife.

[150] *Lane v Schilling*, 279 P. 267 (Or., 1929); or immature: *Davis v Askin's Retail Stores*, 191 S.E. 33 (N.C., 1937).

In *Theaker v Richardson*[151] where the defendant put a letter intended for the plaintiff into an envelope similar to one which would contain an election address and delivered it by hand and the plaintiff's husband picked it up and opened it, there was evidence on which the jury could find, as they did, that the defendant anticipated that someone other than the plaintiff might open and read the letter, and that it was a natural and probable consequence of the defendant's act that the plaintiff's husband would open and read it. There was accordingly held to have been publication.[152] The appearance of the communication is significant in this case: it should certainly not be taken as supporting the view that one must assume that spouses open each other's letters. On the other hand in *Huth v Huth*[153] where the defendant sent through the post in an unclosed[154] envelope a written communication defamatory of the plaintiff which was taken out and read by the plaintiff's butler out of curiosity, the Court of Appeal held that there was no evidence of publication, for there was no evidence that, to the defendant's knowledge, the letter would in the ordinary course be likely to be opened by the butler, or by any other person at the plaintiff's house, before it was delivered to her.

Loss of defamatory document and mistake at common law. The 6.18 defendant is liable for unintentional publication of defamatory matter to a third person unless he can show that it was not due to any want of care on his part. Thus if A drops in the public street a defamatory document, and B picks it up and reads it, A will be liable for the publication to B, for such publication was due to his want of care in the custody of the document.[155] Similarly, A will be liable if he utters defamatory words in so loud a voice that B overhears what he says, whether he knows that B is within hearing or not, unless he can show that he did not know and had no reason to suppose that anyone was within hearing.[156] Again, if A hands to B a letter defamatory of C in mistake

---

[151] [1962] 1 W.L.R. 151 CA. Cf. *Powell v Gelston* [1916] 2 K.B. 615 (letter opened by father of addressee; no publication); *Bezant v Rausing* [2007] EWHC 1118 (QB) (letter opened by daughter of claimant; no publication).

[152] *Bezant v Rausing* [2007] EWHC 1118 (QB) at [73] could be read as denying that there is a publication when the writer knows of a practice of members of a family opening each other's mail; but the explanation probably is that in face of a denial by the author and the absence of a witness statement by the person alleged to have opened the letter there was no prospect of success even for striking out purposes. Furthermore, in many such cases the likely damage will be minimal, attracting the principle of abuse of process: para.6.2, above.

[153] [1915] 3 K.B. 32 CA.

[154] See also *Jackson v Staley* (1885) 9 O.R. 334 where, although the letter was unclosed, there was no evidence of publication to the messenger who carried it to the plaintiff's house.

[155] See *Weld-Blundell v Stephens* [1920] A.C. 956. The duty of taking special care in the custody of a defamatory document is emphasised by Viscount Finlay L.C. at 971–972.

[156] See *McNichol v Grandy* [1932] 1 D.L.R. 225, where (the defendant "being angry raised his voice at a time and place wherein he might be overheard" by unsuspected hearers) the Supreme Court of Canada held that there was evidence of publication proper for submission to a jury. As to the burden of proof in such cases, see per Duff J. (obiter) at 231:

"Publication takes place where the defamatory matter is brought by the defendant or his agent to the knowledge and understanding of some person other than the plaintiff; but when the communication is intended only for one person, and in fact the defamatory matter is, without

for another letter he will be civilly liable, for the publication was by his carelessness.[157] So A will be liable if, intending to send to B a letter in which he has defamed B, he sends it by mistake to C,[158] or if, intending to send to B a letter in which he has defamed C, he sends it in mistake to D,[159] even though in the latter case the letter would have been published on a privileged occasion had it been received and read by B.[160]

However where the publication was neither intentional nor due to any want of care on the defendant's part, he will not be liable for it. Thus a person who reads aloud in the presence of another a letter, not knowing beforehand that it contains a libel, is not liable for such publication[161] nor is there a publication to a person who, unknown to the defendant, hears a telephone conversation.[162] A fortiori, the defendant will not be liable where the defamatory matter is made known by the unanticipated and voluntary act of an independent third person. Thus if A writes a letter defamatory of B, fastens it in an envelope, and sends it to B, and B's servant wrongfully opens the letter and reads it to C, A will not be liable.[163]

> "It would be impossible successfully to contend . . . that if a person, in breach of his duty, were to open a letter, and there was no reason to expect that he would commit that breach of duty, the fact that he had opened it and read it would amount to publication by the person who sent it."[164]

So if the writer of a defamatory letter were to lock it up in his desk, and a thief were to break open the desk, take away the letter, and make its contents

---

any intention on the part of the defendant, communicated to another, the responsibility must, generally speaking, depend upon the answer to the question whether communication to the last-mentioned person or to somebody in a similar situation ought to have been anticipated. Where the communication is the direct result of the defendant's act, it seems reasonable as well as in consonance with the general principles of liability that the burden should be upon the defendant to show that the communication which is the subject of complaint was not the result of his negligence; and that, I think, is the rule."
See also *Paul v Holt* (1935) 69 Ir.L.T.R. 157, and the observations of Hosking J. in *Hill v Balkind* [1918] N.Z.L.R. 740.

[157] In *R. v Paine* (1696) 5 Mod.163, it was held that the "delivering a libel by mistake is no publication", but that was a criminal case. In a footnote to *Mayne v Fletcher* (1829) 4 Man. & Ry. 311 at 312, it is stated that the defendant "would probably be held to be liable civilly in such a case". See also *Fox v Broderick* and *Tompson v Dashwood*, below.

[158] *Fox v Broderick* (1864) 14 Ir.C.L.R. 453; cf. *Paul v Holt* (1935) Ir.L.T.R. 157. So in Scotland (where publication to the pursuer alone is sufficient to sustain an action) the defendant will be liable for a defamatory statement made in a letter sent to the pursuer by inadvertence: *Gordon v Stubbs Ltd* (1895) 3 S.L.T. 10, following *Outram v Reid* (1852) 14 D. 577.

[159] *Tompson v Dashwood* (1883) 11 Q.B.D. 43.

[160] *Hebditch v MacIlwaine* [1894] 2 Q.B. 54 CA, overruling *Tompson v Dashwood*, above, on this point only.

[161] *John Lamb's Case* (1610) 9 Co Rep. at 60.

[162] *Harbridge v Greyhound Lines Inc.*, 294 F.Supp. 1059 (1969).

[163] *Huth v Huth* [1915] 3 K.B. 32 CA; cf. *Weld-Blundell v Stephens* [1920] A.C. 956.

[164] Per Lord Reading C.J. in *Huth v Huth*, ibid. at 38.

known, that would not be a publication for which the writer would be liable.[165]

Unintentional publication and the Defamation Act 1996. Section 1   **6.19**
of this Act (which is dealt with below[166]) is primarily concerned with providing a defence to persons (such as newsvendors or live broadcasters) who do intend to publish the material in respect of which they are sued but who cannot reasonably be held responsible for its *content*. They have a defence if they can show that they did not know and, having taken all reasonable care, had no reason to believe that their acts involved or contributed to the publication of a statement defamatory of the claimant. The author of defamatory material cannot generally rely on this defence but he can do so if he did not intend that his statement be published.[167] Hence if A writes for his own records a document defamatory of B and locks it away and it is then stolen by a thief, the Act would seem to create a further defence for A, though it probably adds nothing to the position at common law.[168]

Publication by claimant. As a general rule if A writes a letter to B   **6.20**
defaming B (which is no publication) and B shows this to C there is no publication for which A is responsible, for the publication is B's own act.[169] However, the position is different where B is under a duty to pass on the charge against him[170] or, probably, where special circumstances, such as the immaturity of the recipient, make a publication by him likely.[171] However, it may be that the responsibility of the defendant does not stretch so far as it does when there has been an initial publication to a third party and that party repeats it to others.[172]

---

[165] Per Lord Esher M.R. in *Pullman v Hill* [1891] 1 Q.B. 524 at 527; *Olson v Molland*, 232 N.W. 625 (Minn., 1930). Or if a computer hacker were to break into the defendant's computer system: Collins, *The Law of Defamation and the Internet*, 2nd edn (2005), para.5.09.

[166] paras 6.31–6.39, below.

[167] S.1(2).

[168] In fact it is, if read literally, rather narrower. If A writes a letter to C defamatory of B and it is stolen by X before it is sent to C and published to Y, then on the principles stated in para.6.18 A would have a defence in respect of the publication to Y. But since he intended his statement to be published (albeit to C, not Y) he cannot rely upon the statutory defence.

[169] *Wilcox v Moon*, 24 A. 244 (Vt., 1892); *Shepard v Lamphier*, 146 N.Y. Supp. 745 (1914).

[170] *Collerton v MacLean* [1962] N.Z.L.R. 1045. Possibly this should extend to a case where in practice the claimant is compelled to repeat the charge in protection of his own interests. Cf. *Chasewood Construction Co. v Rico*, 696 S.W.2d 439 (Tx., 1985) (contractor charged with theft and told to leave site immediately; contractor needed to give explanation to his men). Some courts in the United States hold that there is an actionable publication when a dismissed employee relates the reason for dismissal to a prospective new employer: see 62 A.L.R. 4th 616. If the employee has "at least a moral obligation" to make such disclosure and the dismissing employer must reasonably have anticipated that, such a cause of action has been said to be arguable in New South Wales: *Jones v Amalgamated Television Services* (1991) 23 N.S.W.L.R. 364 at 368–369. But see *Gooley v Westpac Banking Corp* (1995) 129 A.L.R. 628 Ind Ct of Australia (dismissal occasion of qualified privilege).

[171] *Davis v Askin's Retail Stores* 191 S.E. 33 (N.C., 1937). And see *Wen Yue He v Chinese Newspapers Pty Ltd* [2005] N.S.W.S.C. 253.

[172] See para.6.52, below.

6.21 Proof of publication. The fundamental principle is that the matter must be communicated to a third party in such a manner as to be capable of conveying the defamatory imputation about the claimant.[173] Where a publication is innocent on its face but extrinsic facts exist that make the publication defamatory, the claimant must plead and prove that the publication was read by persons who had knowledge of the facts from which the defamatory meaning could be drawn.[174] However, it is not necessary in every case for the claimant to prove directly that the words complained of were brought to the actual attention of some third person in this sense. If he proves facts from which it can be inferred that the words were brought to the attention of some third person, he will establish a prima facie case.[175] This is particularly obviously so where the matter is contained in a book or distributed in the news media[176] where in practice it would seem impossible to rebut the inference[177] and in such a case it would seem that the presumption of publication would be impossible to displace. However, it has been held that in the case of material placed on the internet there is no basis for a presumption of law that there has been a publication to a substantial number of persons[178] within the jurisdiction, though evidence of the number of times the site was accessed may justify the trier of fact in drawing the inference that a substantial number of persons did read the material complained of.[179]

6.22 Telegrams and postal communications: proof of publication. Similarly, there may be reasonable inference of publication in the case of communications which are not distributed to the world at large. In the past telegrams were necessarily communicated to the agents of the telegraph company which transmitted them, though whether that was libel or slander depended on the

---

[173] See para.6.1, above.

[174] See *Baturina v Times Newspapers* [2011] EWCA Civ 308; [2011] 1 W.L.R. 1526, applying *Grappelli v Derek Block (Holdings) Ltd* [1981] 1 W.L.R. 822. In *Baturina*, the defendant published an article alleging that the claimant, a successful Russian businesswoman and wife of former Mayor of Moscow, had purchased, through an offshore company, a house in London for £50m and that she was planning to spend an additional £50m renovating it. The claimant denied having purchased the property and alleged that the article defamed her in the eyes of readers who were aware that a declaration of assets she had made in accordance with Russian anti-corruption law did not include the property. The Court of Appeal held, inter alia, that to succeed the claimant would have to identify, by witness evidence, readers who on reading the article inferred the innuendo meaning that the claimant alleged the words had.

[175] See further paras 32.8–32.9, below.

[176] Communication to others on an internet newsgroup does not seem to have been contested in *Godfrey v Demon Internet Ltd* [2001] Q.B. 201. See also *Bristile v Buddhist Society of Western Australia Inc.* [1999] WASC 259 (on appeal on other points [2000] WASCA 210).

[177] It is assumed that a reference to the claimant is apparent on the ordinary meaning of the words.

[178] This is relevant because of the risk of striking out for abuse of process if the publication is minimal: para.6.2, above.

[179] *Al Amoudi v Brizard* [2006] EWHC 1062 (QB); [2007] 1 W.L.R. 113; *Trumm v Norman* [2008] EWHC 116 (QB).

form of communication[180]; proof that a letter was posted is sufficient prima facie evidence of publication to the person to whom it was addressed; and the sending of a postcard to the claimant is evidence of publication to those through whose hands it passes.[181]

SECTION 3. PARTICULAR PUBLISHERS AND DISTRIBUTORS

Responsibility for publication in newspapers: common law. Lia-   **6.23**
bility arises from participation in[182] the publication of defamatory matter, though even at common law there are special rules for those who act as mere distributors for they can escape liability by showing absence of fault.[183] Thus, where a libel is published in a newspaper everyone who has taken part[184] in publishing it, or in procuring its publication, or has submitted the material complained of published in it, is prima facie liable: the journalist,[185] editor,[186] publisher,[187] printer,[188] or vendor[189] of a newspaper is prima facie liable for any libel which appears in its columns. In an old case a printer's servant "whose business was only to clap down the press" was held liable, though no circumstances were offered of his knowledge of the import of the paper.[190]

---

[180] Telegrams are no longer provided by the postal service in the United Kingdom. However, there are providers of online services which will deliver a paper telegram. Presumably the whole process up to the sealing of the envelope will be automatic and there will be no communication with any human being.

[181] See generally for these and other cases (e.g. faxes, emails and letters in unsealed envelopes), para.32.8, below.

[182] Authorisation may amount to participation but mere facilitation does not: the supplier of newsprint to a newspaper is not liable for a libel contained in it. Cf. *Lobay v Workers and Farmers Pub Co* [1939] 2 D.L.R. 272 (officers of defendant company aware that offending article was being printed on defendants' presses by defendants' employees, and made no effort to prevent it).

[183] See para.6.30, below.

[184] For vicarious liability in this context, see para.8.30ff, below.

[185] But a journalist will not always be responsible for headlines, photographs and captions so it should not be assumed that his liability is on all fours with that of the editor or proprietor: see Hunt J. "Defamation-Pre-Trial Practice", p.14 in *Aspects of Defamation Law in New South Wales* (1990).

[186] *R. v Dover* (1663) 8 How.St.Tr. 547; *Watts v Fraser* (1835) 7 C. & P. 369; *Balakrishnan v Nirumalan K. Pillay* [1999] 3 S.L.R. 22 Sing. CA; see also *Keyzor v Newcomb* (1859) 1 F. & F. 559 at 562.

[187] *Morrison v Ritchie* (1902) 4 F. 645; *Blake v Stevens* (1864) 11 L.T. 543.

[188] *Baldwin v Elphinstone* (1775) Sir W. Black. 1037; *Johnson v Hudson* (1836) 7 A. & E. 233n.; cf. *Marchant v Ford* [1936] 2 All E.R. 1510: an allegation that D "assisted to publish" a libel is equivalent to an allegation that he published it; *Youmans v Smith*, 153 N.Y. 214 at 219 (1897).

[189] Per Lord Esher M.R. in *Emmens v Pottle* (1886) 16 Q.B.D. 354 at 356; per Romer L.J. in *Vizetelly v Mudie's Library* [1900] 2 Q.B. 170 at 179. But for the special position of distributors, see para.6.19, below. In *Day v Bream* (1837) 2 Mood. & R. 54, the porter who picked up parcels of papers from the London coach was held to have published but he escaped upon showing that he was ignorant of the contents.

[190] *R. v Clerk* (1728) 1 Barn. 304.

"Where defamatory matter is contained in a book, periodical or newspaper, there are normally a series of publications each of which constitutes a separate tort. First, there is a publication by the author to the publisher for which the author is solely liable. Secondly, there is the publication by the author and publisher jointly to the printer, for which the author and publisher are jointly liable. Thirdly, there is the publication of the printed work to the trade and the public, for which the author, printer and publisher are jointly liable. It is normally in respect of this last publication that proceedings for libel are brought, although it is open to a plaintiff to sue in respect of the separate publication set out above."[191]

The proprietor of a newspaper is also civilly liable even though the libel may have been published without his knowledge or in his absence,[192] for the editor is his servant and it is within the scope of his employment to send to the printers whatever matter he thinks ought to be published.

6.24 Responsibility for publication in broadcasts and plays: common law. The common law position of broadcasters was stated by the Faulks Committee[193] as follows:

"A broadcasting company is liable for all material broadcast or televised on its network, whether scripted or live, whether it is a studio or an outside broadcast. Consequently they may incur liability for completely unexpected and unforeseeable defamatory statements such as, for example, a derogatory remark made by a contributor to a live studio discussion, or a banner or leaflet thrust before a television camera in a live transmission of a political meeting or demonstration."

It is not to the point that the broadcasting company does not itself make or adopt the defamatory statements because by its broadcast it has published them[194] and this is so even if the company simply simultaneously relays a programme produced by another station.[195] By analogy with the press, liability would also be incurred by those contributing to the broadcast (whether natural persons such as journalists, presenters and interviewees[196] or companies providing programmes under contract) and those assisting in its transmission. The author, director and actors, as well perhaps as the managers of

---

[191] Report of the Committee on the Law of Defamation, Cmd.7536 (1948), p.29, para.116.

[192] *R. v Walter* (1799) 3 Esp. 21; *R. v Gutch* (1829) Moo. & Mal. 433 at 437; *Shepheard v Whitaker* (1875) L.R. 10 C.P. 502; *Levien v Fox* (1890) 11 N.S.W.L.R. 414; *Morrison v Ritchie* (1902) 4 F. 645 (Ct of Sess). Of course in modern conditions the proprietor in law will nearly always be a corporation but the same principle applies. But a director of the publishing company (who may in ordinary speech be referred to as the "proprietor") is not liable unless he has been actively involved: *PGL Research v Ardon International* [1993] F.S.R. 197; *ACP Publishing Pty Ltd v John Fairfax Publications Pty Ltd* [2001] ACTSC 83.

[193] Cmnd.5909 (1975), para.298.

[194] *Australian Broadcasting Corp v Comalco Ltd* (1986) 68 A.L.R. 259 Fed. Ct of Australia; *Nationwide News Pty Ltd v Heggie* [2001] NSWCA 257; *Buck v Jones* [2002] NSWCA 8 (though the last two cases emphasise that the ultimate question is what imputation is conveyed by the matter published by a defendant, so that, e.g. the overall message conveyed by the broadcast might not be the same as that conveyed by an individual contributor).

[195] *Thompson v Australian Capital Television Pty Ltd* (1996) 186 C.L.R. 574. The decision is criticised by Collins, *The Law of Defamation and the Internet*, 3rd edn (2010), paras 18.09 et seq. on the basis that it is difficult to distinguish such defendants from distributors of print media.

[196] *Berezovsky v Russian Television and Radio Broadcasting Co.* [2010] EWHC 476 (QB).

the theatre, would also be joint publishers in the case of a live performance of a play, though it is thought that only the actor would be liable for an unauthorised ad-lib remark,[197] unless perhaps there is an opportunity for the director to intervene.[198]

Internet service providers and other carriers: common law. The   6.25
author (that is to say, originator) of material on the internet clearly publishes it on general principles. So a person who creates a website, publishes a tweet or comments online publishes the information on it when it is accessed by a human being. However, the author (even if he can be traced) may not be worth suing and the question arises of how far the internet service provider the services of which are used to disseminate the material incurs liability. Several cases have considered the issue in different contexts.

Liability of those who host or who provide a platform to allow   6.26
third parties to publish material. It has been held in England that an internet service provider is a publisher of material which it "hosts" where it is aware that the material is defamatory[199] and the judge was of the opinion that the same was true even if there was no such knowledge.[200] In *Godfrey v Demon Internet*[201] the defendant hosted on its news server a particular Usenet newsgroup, storing postings for about a fortnight. A user would request a particular posting from the news server and a copy of the posting would be transmitted (presumably automatically) from the server to the user's computer. The judge held that the defendant was a publisher at common law, because it was not merely the owner of an electronic system through which postings were transmitted, but chose to receive and store the newsgroup containing the offending postings on its computers, and to transmit them in response to requests. In other words, it was not simply a conduit, but it hosted and transmitted the offending material, which it could delete if it chose. When a defamatory posting was transmitted from the defendant's news server to a subscriber, it published the posting. Morland J. decided that liability at common law was strict: there could still be publication even if the publisher was unaware of the defamatory material within a document. The publisher

---

[197] It is submitted that the case of a play cannot be equated with that of a broadcast. In the latter case it can fairly be said that the broadcasting company "publishes" everything which passes through its system. In the case of the play, the director and theatre managers would do no more than provide the setting for the independent act of the actor. The provisions of the Theatres Act 1968, s.18(2) as to who shall be taken to have directed or presented the performance of a play seem not to be relevant to this point.

[198] *Bishop v State of New South Wales* [2000] NSWC 1042 (headmaster of a school where a play was performed which had no published text and involved dumbshow).

[199] This proposition was accepted as correct by the High Court of New Zealand in *Sadiq v Baycorp (NZ) Ltd* [2008] NZHC 403.

[200] *Godfrey v Demon Internet Ltd* [2001] Q.B. 201 (QB) in particular at 212. See also *Silberberg v Builders Collective of Australia Inc.* [2007] FCA 1512 (wrong under race relations legislation).

[201] [2001] Q.B. 201 (QB).

would be liable unless he could establish (the onus was on him) that he was an innocent disseminator.

A rather different conclusion on the question of the liability of those that host material, and one which casts doubt on the correctness of Morland J.'s decision, at least with respect to pre-notification publication, was reached by the Court of Appeal in *Tamiz v Google Inc.*[202] The claimant brought a claim against Google Inc. as operator of the service Blogger.com, in relation to comments that appeared anonymously on the "London Muslim" blog which Google Inc. failed to remove promptly after the claimant notified it of the comments and their defamatory nature. The claimant was initially granted permission to serve the claim form on the defendant in California but on the defendant's application Eady J. held[203] that the court should decline jurisdiction and the order for service out of the jurisdiction was set aside. The claimant appealed. On the issue of publication,[204] the Court of Appeal held, albeit obiter, that so far as the period prior to notification of the defamatory statements was concerned, Google Inc. was not a primary publisher and only doubtfully a secondary or subordinate publisher.[205] The Court of Appeal found that the Blogger service plainly facilitated publication of the blog and its comments. However, Google's involvement was not enough to make it a primary publisher as it was not in a position comparable to an author, an editor or the corporate proprietor of a newspaper in which a defamatory article is published. The court was also doubtful whether Google was a "secondary" publisher facilitating publication in a manner analogous to a distributor. They noted that there was a long established line of authority that a person involved only in dissemination was not to be treated as a publisher unless he knew or ought by the exercise of reasonable care to have known that the publication

---

[202] [2013] EWCA Civ 68 CA; [2013] 1 W.L.R. 2151.

[203] [2012] EWHC 449 (QB).

[204] The appeal was dismissed on the grounds that the defendant would have an unassailable defence under Defamation Act 1996, s.1 and *Jameel* abuse.

[205] In *Davison v Habeeb* [2011] EWHC 3031 (QB) a claim was brought against Google Inc., inter alia, in respect of a publication on its "Blogspot" blog. Google Inc. provided the blog platform (through its website *www.blogger.com*) and hosted the blog on its servers. H.H.J. Parkes QC held that it was at least arguable that Google was liable for publication of the articles at common law, even without notification, on the basis that it had not merely acted as a passive conduit like an ISP but could be seen as a publisher hosting material on its servers and responding to requests for downloads like the defendant in *Godfrey v Demon Internet* [2001] Q.B. 201 (QB); or at least as providing an almost infinitely huge electronic notice board which was within its control, so that it became liable once it refused to take them down. Moreover, it appeared to assume a degree of responsibility for what was published, given its ability to remove offending matter in accordance with its own "contents policy" (see at [38]–[41]). The judge did however note that

"I accept that it is unrealistic to suppose that, absent notification, Blogger.com adopts as its own any of the content which it facilitates. But this is a summary application. In my view it must be at least arguable that the fifth defendant should properly be seen as a publisher responding to requests for downloads like Demon Internet, rather than a mere facilitator, playing a passive instrumental role" (at [41]).

was likely to be defamatory.[206] Since it could not be said that Google Inc. either knew or ought reasonably to have known of the defamatory comments prior to notification of the appellant's complaint, that line of authority told against viewing Google Inc. as a secondary publisher prior to such notification. So far as the position after notification was concerned, the Court of Appeal held that Google Inc was a publisher at least after the moment when it had had a reasonable time in which to act to remove the defamatory comments. The court held that the provision of a platform for the blogs was equivalent to the provision of a notice board; one for which, moreover, Google Inc. provided tools to help a blogger design the layout of his part of the notice board and also enabled a blogger to display advertisements alongside the notices on his part of the notice board. Most importantly, it made the notice board available to bloggers on terms of its own choice and it could readily remove or block access to any notice that did not comply with those terms. Those features brought the case within the authority of *Byrne v Deane*[207] and accordingly by leaving the defamatory material on a Blogger blog after it had been notified of its presence, Google Inc. might be inferred to have associated itself with, or made itself responsible for, the continued presence of the material on the blog and thereby to have become a publisher. While there was clearly a difference in scale between the Blogger set-up and the small club-room in *Byrne v Deane* that was not a matter that was appropriately considered at that stage of the proceedings and therefore the claim would not be struck out on that basis.

In *Oriental Press Group Ltd v Fevaworks Solutions Ltd*[208] the Hong Kong Final Court of Appeal considered whether an internet forum provider was liable for defamatory statements posted by third parties. The Court reviewed case law from other jurisdictions and provided, it is suggested, a statement of the law with regard to internet publications that is consistent with the well-accepted principles of publication. Mr Justice Ribeiro P.J. who delivered the leading judgment held first that the defendants could not be treated as the main or primary publishers. To be treated as the main or primary publisher it has to be established that a person: (1) knows or can easily acquire knowledge of the content of the article being published (although not necessarily of its defamatory nature as a matter of law); and (2) has a realistic ability to control publication of such content, in other words, editorial control involving the ability and opportunity to prevent publication of such content.[209] In the instant case, there could be more than 5,000 postings each hour. The defendants did not know, and nor could he realistically be expected to have known, of the content of each particular discussion thread or group of such threads.[210] Mr

---

[206] [2013] EWCA Civ 68 CA; [2013] 1 W.L.R. 215 at [26]. For a criticism of the Court of Appeal on this issue, see below.
[207] [1937] 1 K.B. 818 CA.
[208] [2013] HKFCA 47.
[209] Ibid. at [76].
[210] Ibid. at [84].

Justice Ribeiro P.J. also concluded that in this "many-to-many" context, the defendants did not have the ability or opportunity to prevent their dissemination.[211]

The learned Justice also concluded that this case did not fall within the *Byrne v Deane*[212] line of authority. In his view, *Byrne v Deane* was authority for the following propositions:

"(1) Where a third person writes or affixes a statement defamatory of the plaintiff on the occupier's property without the occupier's knowledge, the occupier is not treated as a publisher of that statement prior to his becoming aware of it. (2) Once the occupier discovers its existence, he may be treated as a publisher but only if, having the power to do so, he does not remove or obliterate the offending statement in circumstances which justify inferring as a matter of fact that by his inaction he has consented to or ratified its continued publication. (3) Where the occupier becomes aware of the libel but the circumstances show that removal or obliteration is very difficult or very expensive, the fact that the defamatory statement is not expunged may well not justify the inference that it remains in place with his approval."[213]

Contrary to the position taken by the Court of Appeal in *Tamiz v Google Inc*,[214] the Justice concluded that the case could not be applied to internet platform providers like the defendants in that case (and Google Inc. in *Tamiz*). The provider of a discussion forum was in a wholly different position from that of the occupier of premises who was not in the business of publishing or facilitating publication at all, but who had imposed on him the defamatory act of a trespasser. The *Byrne v Deane* line of cases addressed the conditions which must be satisfied before an occupier could be regarded as turning himself into a publisher. This occurred only when he became aware of the libellous statement and did nothing about it in circumstances in which it would not be difficult for him to do so. In this case the defendants actively encouraged and facilitated the postings, as Google Inc. had done in the *Tamiz* case. They were therefore plainly participants in the publication of the postings from the beginning and in that sense the only question was whether they were main or subordinate publishers.

Finally, Mr Justice Ribeiro P.J. concluded, again contrary to the decision of the Court of Appeal in *Tamiz*, that the defendants were to be treated as subordinate publishers. A subordinate publisher is someone who has intentionally participated in the dissemination of the work but who either does not know or could not with reasonable care have known of its content. As providers of the discussion forum, the defendants neither knew, nor could they with the exercise of reasonable care have known, of the content of each and every thread. They were however publishers of the postings since they provided a platform for their dissemination. As subordinate publishers, the defendants could rely on the common law defence of innocent dissemination

---

[211] Ibid. at [89].
[212] [1937] 1 KB 818.
[213] *Oriental Press Group v Fevaworks Solutions Ltd* (above) at [44].
[214] [2013] EWCA Civ 68 CA.

provided that they showed that they did not know and could not with reasonable care have known that the posting contained the libel complained of. On the facts, the court concluded that, until the moment they were notified of the libellous statements, they neither knew nor was it reasonable to expect them to know of them. Once they were notified, a subordinate publisher was afforded the continued protection of the defence if he proved that he took all reasonable steps to remove the offending publication from circulation as soon as reasonably practicable.[215] This the defendants had done, and therefore they could rely on the defence.

Liability of "mere facilitators". In *Bunt v Tilley*[216] three internet service   **6.27** providers were sued for allowing access to the internet to others who, using the service provided, posted defamatory messages on websites hosted by third parties. Eady J. held, on a strike-out application, that an internet service provider which "performs no more than a passive role in facilitating postings on the Internet" and which does not host the defamatory material on its server is not a publisher at common law[217] and the judge took the same view of the position of a telephone company.[218] Although it was by no means always necessary for the defendant to be aware of the defamatory content of the material, "for a person to be held responsible [as a publisher] there must be knowing involvement in the process of the publication of the relevant words. It is not enough that a person plays a passive instrumental role in the process."[219]

There was clearly no question in *Bunt v Tilley* that the defendants could have been treated as main publishers as they had no knowledge of the publications complained of and no realistic ability to exercise effective control over the publications. However it is certainly arguable that, like others innocently involved in the transmission of a defamatory publication, they should have been treated as subordinate publishers. It has been said to be the law that the mere transmission by an intermediary is a publication.[220] If this is correct then not only should the internet service providers in *Bunt v Tilley* have been treated as having published the defamatory statements but it would seem to follow that the Post Office "publishes" a defamatory letter which it

---

[215] [2013] HKFCA 47, at [97].

[216] [2006] EWHC 407 (QB); [2007] 1 W.L.R. 1243.

[217] Ibid. at [37]. As to the hosting issue, there is no suggestion that *Godfrey v Demon Internet Ltd*, above, was wrongly decided. The facts of *Bunt* are not wholly clear. The claimant conducted his own case and it was not pleaded that any of the three ISP defendants had hosted material (at [5]). However, it appears to have been conceded that BT had hosted newsgroups complained of (at [68]) though it escaped liability under reg.19 of the Electronic Commerce Regulations and under s.1 of the Defamation Act 1996 (see paras 6.41 and 6.31, below).

[218] *Bunt v Tilley* at [37].

[219] *Bunt v Tilley* at [23]. On this basis *Day v Bream*, above, seems no longer to be law. Presumably a bookseller or library is to be regarded as intending to publish the material it sells or lends, *whatever its content may be*.

[220] Arguably supported by *Day v Bream* (1837) 2 Mood. & R. 54, para.6.23, above.

delivers[221] and a telephone company publishes a slander when it relays a defamatory telephone call.[222] Of course, in the overwhelming majority of cases internet service providers, the Post Office and telephone companies do not know, nor is it reasonable to expect them to know, of the contents of the publications and therefore they will be able to rely on either the common law defence of innocent dissemination or one of the statutory defences.

6.28 Liability of internet search engine operators. The liability of the operator of an automated internet search engine was considered in *Metropolitan International Schools Ltd v Designtechnica Corp.*[223] Following the line he had taken in *Bunt v Tilley*,[224] Eady J. held that the operator did not at common law publish words in the "snippets" generated by the search engine.

> "It is fundamentally important to have in mind that the [operator] has no role to play in formulating the search terms. Accordingly, it could not prevent the snippet appearing in response to the user's request unless it has taken some positive step in advance. There being no input from the [operator], therefore, on the scenario I have so far posited, it cannot be characterised as a publisher at common law. It has not authorised or caused the snippet to appear on the user's screen in any meaningful sense. It has merely, by the provision of its search service, played the role of a facilitator."[225]

It might be that the compiler of a complex manual library catalogue who included snippets from the books in the catalogue "published" that material but in that case he would at least have taken a conscious decision to include

---

[221] It is perhaps not surprising that the issue of the Post Office's liability as publisher has not arisen as the immunity which it formerly had as an emanation of the Crown is preserved by s.90 of the Postal Services Act 2000, which provides that no action in tort lies against the Post Office (or its servants or agents) in respect of loss or damage suffered by any person by reason of anything done or omitted to be done in relation to anything in the post. The Postal Services Act 2000 replaced s.29 of the Post Office Act 1969. The equivalent provision in s.9 of the Crown Proceedings Act 1947 was applied in *Boakes v Post Office, The Times*, October 27, 1962, CA, even though the allegedly defamatory matter was a postmark applied by the Post Office itself. The liability of a telegraph company has been quite frequently litigated in the United States: it seems to be accepted that the company publishes the matter contained in the telegram but there is support for the view that there is a form of privilege which protects it, even if the message was defamatory on its face, unless it is aware that the sender is acting in bad faith (See *O'Brien v Western Union*, 113 F.2d 539 (CA 1 1940) and Eldredge, *Law of Defamation*, p.440). Telegram services are no longer offered by general postal operators but in some countries (including the United Kingdom) hand-delivered telegrams may still be initiated online. There seems much to be said for treating the operators of such services in the same way as telephone companies.

[222] A telephone company has no statutory immunity equivalent to that of the Post Office for mail. It has been held in the United States that a telephone company was not a publisher even where the defamation was contained in a recorded service provided by a subscriber: *Anderson v New York Telephone Co*, 361 N.Y.S.2d 913 (1974) NYCA. However, the telephone company pleaded that it had no right to terminate the subscriber's facilities.

[223] [2009] EWHC 1765 (QB); [2009] E.M.L.R. 27.

[224] [2006] EWHC 407 (QB); [2007] 1 W.L.R. 1243.

[225] *Metropolitan International Schools Ltd v Designtechnica Corp.* [2009] EWHC 1765 (QB); [2009] E.M.L.R. 27 at [51].

the material. That left open the situation after the operator had been informed that its engine was throwing up the offending material. Here

"It is not possible to draw a complete analogy with a website host. One cannot merely press a button to ensure that the offending words will never reappear on a Google search snippet: there is no control over the search terms typed in by future users. If the words are thrown up in response to a future search, it would by no means follow that the [operator] has authorised or acquiesced in that process."[226]

It was possible for an operator to block particular URLs notified to it and on the facts some steps of this sort had been taken; but the evidence showed that that this would have a limited effect and was easily evaded by the originator of the material moving it. If the operator was required to attempt to block particular words or phrases that would be easily evaded by changes in terminology and would have the effect of depriving the user of access to large numbers of innocent sites. As counsel for the operator put it, "it is practically impossible, and certainly disproportionate, to expect the [operator] to embark on a wild goose chase in order to determine where the words complained of, or some of them, might from time to time 'pop up' on the Web".[227] Eady J. accepted that there might be "room for debate as to what further blocking steps it would be open for [the defendants] to take, or how effective they might be",[228] but that did not alter his conclusion that there was no common law publication on the facts.[229]

A different conclusion on this issue was however reached by an Australian court in *Trkulja v Google Inc.*[230] In that case, the plaintiff sought damages in respect of material described by counsel as the "images matter" and the "web matter" which were generated by Google Inc.'s search engine.[231] The jury

---

[226] Ibid. at [55].

[227] Ibid. at [62].

[228] Ibid. at [64].

[229] The reverse situation was one of the issues in *Budu v BBC* [2010] EWHC 616 (QB) which involved an attempt to make the originator of material liable for the publication of a search engine snippet. The material in the defendant's web archive, taken as a whole, could bear no worse a meaning than that there were questions about the claimant's immigration status, but the Google snippet, which had simply automatically extracted a few words from one of the pieces in the archive, might give the impression that the claimant was a security risk. Sharp J. held that the defendants could not be liable for the snippet. They could not be liable under ordinary principles for republication since the snippet did not "republish" the archive material, it gave a distorted view of it.

[230] [2012] VSC 533. See also, *A v Google New Zealand Ltd* [2012] NZHC 2352 in which Associate Judge Abbott refused to strike out a claim against Google New Zealand in respect of publication of search engine results (snippets) which contained material that allegedly defamed the plaintiff. The liability of search engines as "publishers" was a novel issue and its resolution required determination of complex issues of law in a proper factual context. In particular, it might need to be considered whether there was a "stamp of human intervention" in the way in which search engine programmes were written and to address the public policy issues raised in *Crookes v Newton*. Consequently this was an inappropriate case for summary judgment.

[231] At least one of the photographs was a page not published by any person other than Google Inc. It was a page put together as a result of the Google Inc. search engine working as it was intended to work by those who wrote the relevant computer programs. It was in that sense a cut and paste creation (at [20]).

entered a verdict for the claimant. Subsequently Google Inc. made an application for judgment notwithstanding the jury verdict against it. In rejecting the application, the judge held that it had been open to the jury to find that Google Inc. was a publisher:

> "The question of whether or not Google Inc was a publisher is a matter of mixed fact and law. In my view, it was open to the jury to find the facts in this proceeding in such a way as to entitle the jury to conclude that Google Inc was a publisher even before it had any notice from anybody acting on behalf of the plaintiff. The jury were entitled to conclude that Google Inc intended to publish the material that its automated systems produced, because that was what they were designed to do upon a search request being typed into one of Google Inc's search products. In that sense, Google Inc is like the newsagent that sells a newspaper containing a defamatory article. While there might be no specific intention to publish defamatory material, there is a relevant intention by the newsagent to publish the newspaper for the purposes of the law of defamation."[232]

The judge in *Trkulja* referred to the English cases above and in particular the *Metropolitan Schools* case.[233] In holding that he would not follow that decision, he noted that Eady J. did not appear to have given any consideration to the fact that internet search engines, while operating in an automated fashion from the moment a request is typed into them, operate precisely as intended by those who own them and who provide their services. Moreover, it was not possible to say as a general principle that if an entity's role is a passive one then it cannot be a publisher because that would cut across principles which have formed the basis for liability in the newsagent/library type cases and also in those cases where someone with power to remove a defamatory publication chooses not to do so in circumstances where an inference of consent can be drawn.

6.29 **Applicable principles for internet publications.** It is not easy to reconcile the cases that have been discussed either with each other or with the orthodox common law principles of publication. While the decision of the Hong Kong Court of Final Appeal in *Oriental Press Group Ltd v Fevaworks Solutions Ltd*[234] offers, it is suggested, a model analysis of how well-accepted principles of the common law of publication should apply to internet publications, the decision of the English courts are not so easily reconciled. The following represents an attempt to state those principles:

(1) Where an internet intermediary knows or ought reasonably to be aware of the content of the article complained of, though not necessarily of its defamatory nature as a matter of law, and has a realistic ability to control publication of such content, the intermediary is the main or primary publisher of such content.[235]

---

[232] [2012] VSC 533 at [18].
[233] Ibid. at [27].
[234] [2013] HKFCA 47.
[235] *Tamiz v Google Inc.* [2013] EWCA Civ 68 CA; [2013] 1 W.L.R. 2151 at [25]. It should be noted that the Court of Appeal is not entirely clear in its judgment on the question whether

(2) Where an internet intermediary merely "facilitates" access to websites provided by others by, for example, providing the computer systems through which communications happen to pass on their route from one computer to another, there is, following *Bunt v Tilley*,[236] no publication. Although this proposition has been accepted in several English cases, the better view may be that they should be treated as subordinate publishers in that they intentionally participate in the dissemination of the material complained of.[237] Of course, in most cases the intermediary will be able to rely on the innocent dissemination defence as it will neither know, nor have any reason to know, of the content of the publication. It will also have little difficulty in availing itself of the statutory defence under s.1 of the Defamation Act 1996[238] and still less in relying on the Electronic Commerce Regulations 2002.[239]

(3) Where an internet intermediary hosts a website and has not received notification of the defamatory material then, according to the Court of Appeal in *Tamiz v Google Inc.*,[240] it is neither the primary nor secondary publisher of the material complained of.[241] If this is correct, then it would seem to follow that the common law rule that liability for publication is strict[242] may have been swept away in this jurisdiction certainly so far as concerns internet publications.[243] It should be noted, however, that this view was rejected by the

---

knowledge of the defamatory nature of the statement is required. While Richards L.J. infers (at [25]) that it is effective control (rather than knowledge) that is important, in the paragraphs that follow, he appears to suggest that knowledge of the defamatory nature of the content is a prerequisite for publication (at [27]–[36]). It is possible that the two statements can be reconciled on the basis that (at [25]) he was discussing the pre-requisites for primary, ab initio, publication, while (at [27]–[36]) he was discussing the circumstances in which a person who was not originally liable as publisher might later become so. Even if this is so, it is not obvious why the position should be different between the two, and the better view, and the one consistent with orthodox common law, is that expressed at [25] and also by the Hong Kong Final Court of Appeal in *Oriental Press Group Ltd v Fevaworks Solutions Ltd* [2013] HKFCA 47.

[236] [2006] EWHC 407 (QB).

[237] *Oriental Press Group Ltd v Fevaworks Solutions Ltd* [2013] HKFCA 47. It was however said by the Court of Appeal in *Tamiz v Google Inc.* that it was doubtful that Google Inc. as host was a subordinate or secondary publisher (at [26]). If the proposition is doubtful in relation to hosts, then a fortiori, it is doubtful in relation to mere conduits.

[238] See para.6.31, below.

[239] See para.6.41, below.

[240] [2013] EWCA Civ 68; [2013] 1 W.L.R. 2151.

[241] Ibid. at [25], [26] CA. The conclusion that it was not a secondary publisher was more tentatively expressed (at [26]). The decisions of Morland J. in *Godfrey v Demon Internet Ltd* [2001] Q.B. 201 (QB) and H.H.J. Parkes in *Davison v Habeeb* [2011] EWHC 3031 (QB), to the extent that are inconsistent with this dicta, must now be doubted.

[242] *Day v Bream* (1837) 2 Mood. & R. 54; *Pullman v Hill & Co* [1891] 1 Q.B. 524; *Emmens v Pottle* (1885) 16 Q.B.D. 354.

[243] Richards L.J.'s interpretation (at [27]) of *Emmens v Pottle* (1885) 16 Q.B.D. 354, 357–358; *Vizetelly v Mudie's Select Library Ltd* [1900] 2 Q.B. 170, 177–180; *Bottomley v FW Woolworth and Co. Ltd* (1932) 48 T.L.R. 521 as being authority for the proposition that a person involved only in dissemination is not to be treated as a publisher unless he knew or ought by the exercise of reasonable care to have known that the publication was likely to be defamatory raises the question whether the strict liability rule has also been swept away for offline publications. All three cases involved offline publications, and if his lordship was correct in his interpretation there is no reason to think his decision is not of wider import.

Hong Kong Final Court of Appeal in the *Oriental Press Group Ltd v Feva-works Solutions Ltd* case which treated the website host as a secondary publisher. The court in that case correctly, it is suggested, concluded that a website operator that made facilities available for others to post to, intentionally participated in the dissemination of the defamatory material. It was, therefore, liable as a secondary publisher unless it could bring itself within the innocent dissemination defence which required it to show that it neither knew, nor ought to have been aware of the content of the material. The Court of Appeal in *Tamiz*, appears, however, to have regarded knowledge or imputed knowledge as an essential element of the definition of secondary publisher. The view more consistent with authority is that of the Hong Kong (5) Final Court of Appeal.[244]

(4) When an internet intermediary that hosts a website is notified of the defamatory postings, it is to be treated as a publisher if it fails to disable access to, or take down, the material once it has had reasonable time to do so.[245] Such a conclusion follows from an application of the *Byrne v Deane* line of authority to internet publications. While the conclusion that those who host are not liable in the absence of knowledge of the material is correct, it is more questionable that this is explained by application of *Byrne v Deane*. As the Hong Kong Final Court of Appeal explained in *Oriental Press Group Ltd v Fevaworks Solutions Ltd*,[246] *Byrne v Deane* applies where the occupier of premises has defamatory material forced on him: it does not apply where the defendant actively encourages third parties to post material on the website that it provides. The better view may therefore be that hosts are secondary publishers who will, in the absence of knowledge or imputed knowledge, be able to rely on the innocent dissemination defence.

Though there is Commonwealth authority that reaches a different conclusion,[247] under English law the operator of an automated internet search engine is not, following *Metropolitan International Schools Ltd v Designtechnica Corp.*,[248] liable for publication of the search results as it never has any control over the result of a search and lacks any knowing involvement in publication.

Given the existence of the common law defence of innocent dissemination[249] and the statutory defences under the Defamation Act 1996, the Electronic Commerce Regulations 2002 and, when it comes into force, the Defamation Act 2013, it may be thought that these issues are rather academic and that none of these defendants has anything to fear from being considered

---

[244] See further, para.6.21, above.

[245] *Tamiz v Google Inc.* [2013] EWCA Civ 68 CA; [2013] 1 W.L.R. 2151; *Davison v Habeeb* [2011] EWHC 3031 (QB); *Wishart v Murray* [2013] NZHC 540.

[246] [2013] HKFCA 47.

[247] *Trkulja v Google Inc.* [2012] VSC 533; *A v Google New Zealand Ltd* [2012] NZHC 2352.

[248] [2009] EWHC 1765; [2009] E.M.L.R. 27.

[249] See para.6.30, above.

technically a publisher. However, there is a great deal to be said, absent strong countervailing policy arguments, for bringing internet publications within orthodox common law principles of publication.[250] If Parliament wishes to provide defences for internet intermediaries it should do so, and indeed it has. The importance of promoting certainty in the law should mean, however, that the courts should not create new principles where the old ones are still perfectly serviceable.

Distributors: special defence at common law. As has been said above,   **6.30**
the common law[251] gives some degree of protection to the person who publishes but who is not the author, printer, or the "first or main publisher of a work which contains a libel", but has only taken "a subordinate part in disseminating it", e.g. by selling, distributing or handing to another a copy of the newspaper or book in which it appears.[252] Such a person has a defence[253] if he succeeds in showing:

(1) that he did not know that the book or paper contained the libel complained of; and

(2) that he did not know that the book or paper was of a character likely to contain a libel; and

(3) that such want of knowledge was not due to any negligence on his part.[254]

---

[250] There is much sense, in this regard, in what Sir James Munby P. said in *Re J (a child)* [2013] EWHC 2694 (albeit not in a libel context):
"The law must develop and adapt, as it always has done down the years in response to other revolutionary technologies. We must not simply throw up our hands in despair and moan that the internet is uncontrollable. Nor can we simply abandon basic legal principles" (at [43]).

[251] As to the relationship between the common law defence and s.1 of the Defamation Act 1996, and in particular whether the Act has "abolished" or "superseded" the common law defence, see para.6.38, below.

[252] For the liability of the originator where he knows or has reason to believe that the material will be republished to others (e.g. where a statement is made to the media) see para.6.52, below.

[253] Cf. the judgment of Richards L.J. in *Tamiz v Google Inc.* [2013] EWCA Civ 68 CA; [2013] 1 W.L.R. 2151 where his lordship appears to suggest that a person is not a publisher unless he knew or ought reasonably to have known that the publication was likely to be defamatory. *Tamiz* of course involved an internet publication and it may be that its effect is limited to such publications. However there is little indication (at [27]) that his lordship thought his comments were so limited.

[254] This is a summary of the judgment of Romer L.J. in *Vizetelly v Mudie's Library* [1900] 2 Q.B. 170 CA. In *Sun Life Assurance v WH Smith* (1934) 150 L.T. 211 at 212, Scrutton L.J. said that it might be better if the jury were asked, instead of the second and third questions, only one, whether the defendants were negligent in carrying on their business. Similarly, Bridge L.J. stated the defence as follows:
" . . . it is for him to show that he did not in fact know that the publication contained defamatory matter and that he had no reason to believe that it was likely to contain defamatory matter":
Goldsmith v Sperrings [1977] I W.L.R. 478 at 505. Cf. Denning L.J. (dissenting on this point):
"Common sense and fairness require that no subordinate distributor . . . should be held liable for a libel contained in it unless he knew or ought to have known that newspaper or periodical contained a libel . . . a subordinate distributor has never been held liable to a plaintiff except

On this basis news vendors[255] and proprietors of libraries[256] have escaped liability.

The onus of proving such facts lies on the defendant[257] and the question of liability is one for the jury.[258] In the case of a newspaper, this question depends to a great extent on the character and reputation of the paper.[259] The jury may rightly infer negligence from the fact that the defendant sold or distributed the newspaper after being warned of libellous matter in a former issue.[260] In the case of a book the jury may rightly infer negligence from the title or general nature of the book itself, or from the recognised propensity of the author or publishers to publish libellous matter. The mere fact that the defendant did not have the book read through before he offered it for sale or otherwise distributed it is not in itself evidence of such negligence.[261]

6.31 **The Defamation Act 1996.** By s.1 of this Act[262] it is a defence in proceedings for defamation[263] for the defendant to show that (1) he was not the author, editor or publisher[264] of the statement complained of, (2) he took

---

when prior knowledge of the libel has been brought home to him" (at 487). But the liability of the distributors in this case was conceded and the point was not argued.
[255] *Emmens v Pottle* (1885) 16 Q.B.D. 354 CA.
[256] *Vizetelly v Mudie's Library* [1900] 2 Q.B. 170 CA. The Legal Deposit Libraries Act 2003 added another layer to the story as from February 1, 2004. Under s.10(2) of the Act, a legal deposit library is not liable in damages for defamation in relation to activities related to deposited material unless it knows, or knows of facts or circumstances from which it ought to know, that the material contains a defamatory statement and it has had a reasonable opportunity since obtaining that knowledge to prevent its use. Nor, under s.10(3), is the publisher (i.e. in the commercial sense) liable in damages for defamation in respect of the use of the material unless it has similar knowledge or means of knowledge that the material contains a defamatory statement and has had a reasonable opportunity to inform the library and has not done so. The Act empowers the Secretary of State to make regulations (none have been traced) governing the direct "harvesting" of publications from the internet by the libraries. Where works are copied in this way no person other than the library can be liable in damages for defamation in relation to activities related to copied material and the library is liable on the same basis as for deposited material (s.10(6)). S.10 also contains provisions restricting criminal liability.
[257] However, the *plea* in *Emmens v Pottle* (1885) 16 Q.B.D. 354 was that the defendant did not publish the libel. See the comments of Scrutton L.J. in *Bottomley v Woolworth* (1932) 48 T.L.R. 521.
[258] *Vizetelly v Mudie's Library* [1900] 2 Q.B. 170 CA; *Morrison v Ritchie* (1902) 4 F. 651.
[259] Per Holmes L.J. in *Ross v Winning Post* (1911) 45 Ir.L.T. 89 at 93.
[260] Per Lord Hewart C.J. in *Batten v Pall Mall Deposit, The Times*, June 24, 1927. Cf. *Trimble v Central News* [1934] A.D. 43, where it was held to be from a business point of view impossible to go through certain periodicals in order to make certain there was no libellous matter in them. The periodical in question was stated by the court to be:
"a periodical whose contents are merely of ephemeral interest and which is generally sold 'hot from the press' and one can readily see that the defendants could not possibly exercise any effective supervision over the contents."
[261] Per Cozens-Hardy M.R. in *Weldon v Times Book Co* (1911) 28 T.L.R. 143 at 144; *Bottomley v Woolworth* (1932) 48 T.L.R. 521 CA; *Hood v WH Smith, The Times*, November 4 and 5, 1937.
[262] Which applies to causes of action arising after September 3, 1996: s.19(2). The section applies to Scotland (s.18(2)) and Northern Ireland (s.18(3)).
[263] In practice it seems unlikely that the section will have much application to slander.
[264] Which is used in a narrower sense than its normal defamation meaning: see para.6.1, above.

reasonable care in relation to its publication and (3) he did not know, and had no reason to believe, that what he did caused or contributed to the publication of a defamatory statement.[265] It seems clear that the circumstances must be such that what the defendant has done must be at least capable of amounting to a publication at common law[266] and that the burden of showing this rests upon the claimant. For example, the claimant cannot, without showing that the defendant had anything to do with the publication, cast upon the defendant the burden of establishing the statutory defence. Similarly, if D uses a word processor manufactured and sold by X to create a defamatory document about C, X is not liable quite apart from the statute and even if he had notice before the sale that D was a notorious defamer. He has simply not published the libel.

Author and editor. Author is defined simply as the "originator" of the statement complained of, with the qualification that it does not include a person who did not intend that his statement be published at all.[267] If the author alone were denied the protection of s.1 it might give rise to the same difficulties as occur in applying the similar concept[268] as it is used in the context of copyright.[269] However, these seem likely to be largely avoided by the fact that the protection of s.1 is also denied to the editor, that is to say any person having editorial or equivalent responsibility for the content of the statement or the decision to publish it.[270] Hence whether the "editors" of this book are authors or editors for the purposes of the statute[271] matters

6.32

---

[265] S.1(1). "Statement" means "words, pictures, visual images, gestures or any other method of signifying meaning": s.17(1). This is the same as the definition of "words" in s.16(1) of the Defamation Act 1952.

[266] See para.6.17, above.

[267] S.1(2). As to the person who does not intend that his statement be published, see para.6.18, above.

[268] But copyright is concerned with the author of the *work*. S.1 is concerned with the author of the *statement*. Hence if X recounts his reminiscences to a "ghost-writer" (as opposed to dictating them to an amanuensis) the latter is the author for copyright purposes, even if he sometimes uses X's words verbatim. But if the ghost writer recounts the substance of a defamatory story told by X, then it is submitted that X is author for the purposes of s.1.

[269] Under the Copyright, Designs and Patents Act 1988, s.9(1) the author of a literary, dramatic or musical work is defined as the person who created it. Prior to that the expression was generally not defined in the legislation. The question whether the defendant was the author of words was relevant to the former defence in cases of unintentional defamation under s.4 of the Defamation Act 1952 (see para.19.1, below) because the defence was only available to a person who was not the author if he proved that the words "were written by the author without malice". The only authority appears to be *Solomon v Simmons, The Times*, April 7–10, 1954, a case of a libel on a tombstone, where, not surprisingly, it was held that the trustees of the cemetery were not the author of the inscription but the person who composed it was.

[270] S.1(2). Hence a journalist who inserts a press agency report without attribution may not be the author but he has editorial responsibility.

[271] In the context of copyright it may be difficult to determine who are authors in the case of a compilation such as an encyclopaedia. Under s.1 the contributors of individual entries are authors and the compiler is editor of the whole.

little[272]—they are clearly one or the other.[273] Similarly, where X writes a letter to a newspaper and it is published therein, X is liable as author and the editor of the newspaper as editor, even though X's statement is repeated verbatim.[274]

Although "editor" standing alone might perhaps connote persons engaged in the production of books or newspapers or broadcasts, the inclusion of persons having equivalent responsibility casts the net more widely.[275] However, it is clear from the structure of the section that a person who has a degree of responsibility which is not equivalent to editorial responsibility may take advantage of the defence.[276] The editor of a newspaper obviously may not read every word published in each edition but it is submitted that he has the requisite responsibility for the entire issue. Similarly, it is submitted, the editor of a part of the paper (e.g. the sports or entertainments section) has responsibility for that part but not for others.[277] So also, in the electronic media, a person assigned the task of vetting material for publication would be an editor for this purpose. Whether simply by adopting a policy of limited pre-publication control a person becomes an "editor" is a difficult question. Much, it is suggested, is likely to depend upon the extent of control that person purports to take and the mechanisms used to exercise that control. The creator of a link from one webpage to another is unlikely to be treated as the "author" of the linked statement.[278] However, the creation of a hyperlink will usually be a deliberate act that makes the creator's role more than a passive one. Consequently, the creator will generally satisfy the definition of an "editor".[279] There may, however, be persons who are described as "editors" in the trade but who may be within the scope of the s.1 defence—e.g. if their function is merely to proof read or otherwise check text for purely technical purposes.

---

[272] Except for pleading purposes because it may be necessary to plead in the alternative in case of doubt.

[273] Previous editors clearly cannot be liable for any defamatory statements originating in this edition but the present editors would be liable in respect of the decision to retain any defamatory passages from previous editions.

[274] The newspaper itself is also liable as "publisher".

[275] However, some slight doubt is cast upon this broad approach by s.1(4): see para.6.35, below.

[276] See, e.g. s.1(5)(a) which directs the court, in determining whether the defendant has exercised reasonable care for the purposes of s.1 to have regard to the extent of his responsibility.

[277] Except in so far as he may have participated on a particular occasion in a decision to publish.

[278] This of course assumes that such a person will be treated as having published at all in such a case. Cf. *Crookes v Newton* 2011 SCC 47; [2011] 3 S.C.R. 269 and see further para.6.13, above.

[279] See further, Collins, *The Law of Defamation and the Internet*, 3rd edn (2010), para.16.20. Cf. Law Commission, *Defamation and the Internet, A Preliminary Investigation* (2002), para.2.24, which considers he might be able to take advantage of the s.1 defence. Collins at para.16.21 considers that even if a person who created a link were not an editor he might be under a duty to monitor the linked page for changes.

Publisher. A publisher for this purpose has a narrower meaning than that   **6.33**
normally used in defamation[280]: it means a commercial[281] publisher, that is,
person whose business is issuing material to the public, or a section of the
public, and who issues material containing the statement in the course of that
business.[282] This will obviously cover those who publish newspapers, magazines, books and broadcasts[283] and, it is submitted, those who publish in the
course of business in the electronic media,[284] even though it may be necessary
for recipients to possess special equipment or subscribe to a service: these are
no more than the equivalent of the price paid for a newspaper. It has been
held[285] that book retailers are not publishers within s.1 even if, like Amazon
and other online retailers, they may publish information on their own behalf
online. Internet intermediaries that host or cache material will usually not be
considered publishers within Defamation Act 1996, s.1. They do not themselves issue[286] material to the public and in particular will not usually have
issued the material containing the statement complained of.[287] More difficult
is the position of those that provide platforms that enable others to set up their
own blogs or websites, or websites that allow others to post comments. While
they may not be in the business of issuing material to the public, they may
nevertheless have "control" over the persons whose material is issued either
via their computer system or via their standard terms of business. However, in
Tamiz v Google[288] the Court of Appeal held that in providing the Blogger
service, Google was not a publisher for the purposes of Defamation Act 1996,
s.1. It did not itself issue material to the public or a section of the public.[289]
Moreover, its position in providing the service was treated as of a kind
analogous to, if not identical to, that described in subs.(3)(e) and the existence
of a contractual term about the content of the blog was not capable of giving

---

[280] But "publication" and "publish" in the Act have the meaning they have in defamation
generally: s.17(1).

[281] In *Tamiz v Google Inc.* [2012] EWHC 449 (QB) at first instance, counsel for Google Inc.
had suggested that it was implicit in the statutory notion of "issuing material to the public" in the
course of a business that there was a direct relationship, of a commercial or contractual nature,
between the relevant "publisher" and its readers. Eady J. did not think that was necessarily
correct but did not finally determine the question.

[282] sS.1(2).

[283] But see s.1(3)(d).

[284] But see s.1(3)(c) and (e).

[285] *McGrath v Dawkins* [2012] EWHC B3 at [40] (QB).

[286] In *McGrath v Dawkins* [2012] EWHC B3 (QB), H.H.J. Moloney QC stated at [40]: "So far
as the concept of 'issuing' is concerned, there is no doubt that the 1996 Act was intended to
preserve the established distinction between publishers who originate books and other publications, and distributors and sellers who pass on to the public the books originating from the
publishers . . . 'Issuing' refers to the former process, not the latter one."

[287] See, for example *Godfrey v Demon Internet* [1999] EWHC 244 (QB); [2001] Q.B. 201 at
[19].

[288] [2013] EWCA Civ 68 CA.

[289] Ibid. at [39]–[40]. Twitter and Facebook would presumably also not be treated as publishers
on the same basis.

Google "effective control" over the person who posted the defamatory comments.

The applicability of s.1 of the 1996 Act to an internet search engine was considered in *Metropolitan International Schools Ltd v Designtechnica Corp.*[290] It was not suggested that the operator of the search engine was liable for the material on the sites to which the engine directed users, for the claim was brought only in respect of the "snippets" generated (sometimes with an automatic editing process) from the material through which the engine searched. Eady J. thought that it would be difficult to say that the operator was not a "publisher" in the sense of s.1 but decided in light of his conclusion that Google was not a common law publisher for these purposes that it was unnecessary to decide the question.

The producer of a film for general release is a publisher for the purposes of s.1. In the context of the race relations legislation "section of the public" has been held to exclude members of a private club,[291] so a person who issues material for such persons may not be a publisher (quite apart from the question of whether he is carrying on a business) though the possibility of his being author or editor of the statement must be borne in mind. What amounts to a business is something which depends very much on the context in which the word is used, but in the absence of an extended definition[292] it must be doubtful whether it extends to, e.g. the activities of government organisations in issuing statements.[293]

6.34 Persons not considered as authors, editors or publishers. A number of persons who would or might fall outside the distributor's defence at common law are not to be considered as authors, editors or publishers for the purposes of the s.1 defence and hence may take advantage of it. The categories enumerated in the statute are not exhaustive, for the court is in any other case directed to them by way of analogy in deciding whether a person is considered to be the author, editor or publisher of a statement.[294]

> (1) A person involved only[295] in printing, producing, distributing or selling printed material containing the statement.[296] There is some overlap here with the common law defence but the printer is given protection for the first time. "Producing" has, it is thought, the meaning of being

---

[290] [2009] EWHC 1765 (QB); [2009] E.M.L.R. 27.

[291] *Charter v Race Relations Board* [1973] A.C. 868; *Dockers' Labour Club and Institute v Race Relations Board* [1976] A.C. 285.

[292] Such as that in s.14 of the Unfair Contract Terms Act 1977.

[293] But it is submitted that HMSO is a publisher for the purpose of s.1. One reason for taking a broad approach is that the legal status of government organs may be affected by matters such as privatisation.

[294] S.1(3).

[295] The same person may of course be the publisher and the printer, producer, distributor or seller.

[296] S.1(3)(a).

concerned with the physical production of printed material, as where A binds material published by B. The reference to printed material seems to be for the purpose of distinguishing this category from, e.g. film or electronic media, which are dealt with separately. There is no definition of "printed" but in its ordinary meaning it probably covers any process of reproduction on paper or a similar medium (including photocopying) other than handwriting. Though the provision appears to be directed at giving protection to persons involved in the chain of commercial publication, the literal meaning of the words, coupled with the direction to the courts to apply the particular provisions by analogy, would seem to indicate that a clerk or secretary instructed to copy and circulate a memorandum within a company is covered by the s.1 defence.

(2) A person involved only in processing, making copies of, distributing, exhibiting[297] or selling a film or sound recording (as defined in Pt I of the Copyright, Designs and Patents Act 1988)[298] containing the statement.[299]

(3) A person involved only in processing, making copies of, distributing or selling any electronic medium in or on which the statement is recorded, or in operating any equipment by means of which the statement is retrieved, copied or distributed. This will cover video recordings, CD-ROMs, DVDs and computer software. There is a certain degree of overlap with the previous category (e.g. a video recording of a cinema film would fall under both heads)[300] and they both extend to activities which are analogous to those protected in relation to printed material. The latter part of the definition (relating to retrieval) also means that an internet service provider may fall under this paragraph as well as under para.(e).[301]

(4) A person involved only as the broadcaster of a live programme containing the statement in circumstances in which he has no effective control over the maker of the statement.[302] This involves a complete departure

---

[297] This would allow a cinema to claim the protection of s.1.

[298] By ss.5A and 5B of the 1988 Act (substituted from January 1, 1996 for s.5 by SI 1995/3297, reg.9(1), "film" means a recording on any medium from which a moving image may by any means be produced and the sound track accompanying a film is to be treated as part of the film; "sound recording" means (a) a recording of sounds, from which the sounds may be reproduced, or (b) a recording of the whole or any part of a literary, dramatic or musical work, from which sounds reproducing the work or part may be produced, in either case regardless of the medium on which the recording is made or the method by which the sounds are reproduced or produced.

[299] S.1(3)(b).

[300] A videotape or CD-ROM containing still images would be within (3) but a series of images on film which could not produce a moving image (e.g. a collection of slides) would not be within (2), though no doubt the court would come to a similar conclusion by analogy. Pictures in a book are printed material and so, presumably, are any photographic prints.

[301] See *Godfrey v Demon Internet Ltd* [2001] Q.B. 201 at 206.

[302] S.1(3)(d).

from the common law,[303] though its significance is somewhat reduced by the fact that a very large proportion of broadcast material is pre-recorded.[304] The requirement that the broadcaster has no effective control over the maker of the statement should probably be read as relating to the contractual relationship between them rather than the ability to prevent the making of the statement in question: it is no more possible to prevent an ad-lib defamatory remark in a live broadcast by an employed journalist than by an outside contributor[305] but it would be surprising if the broadcaster were relieved of liability for the former as well as the latter. An obvious case where the broadcaster would be protected would be where a defamatory placard was shown in the case of an outside broadcast,[306] but the same would seem to apply to a contribution to a phone-in programme[307] or to the remarks of a politician during an interview.

(5) A person involved only as the operator or provider of access to a communications system by means of which the statement is transmitted, or made available, by a person over whom he has no effective control. A telephone service[308] would seem to be the simplest example of such a communications system, though it seems that the telephone company may not publish at common law and hence does not need the protection of the provision.[309] More complication arises in the case of networks of computers, particularly the internet. What has been said in the previous section about effective control and employees applies here, too: if a systems operator late one night floods the internet system with defamatory messages his employers should not be able to take advantage of the s.1 defence. Greater difficulty arises, however, over the activities of outsiders. The internet is an international network

---

[303] See para.6.24, above.

[304] There would, e.g. still be liability on the facts of *Australian Broadcasting Commission v Comalco* (1986) 68 A.L.R. 259. If station A produces a live programme and this is relayed by station B, the latter would be a "broadcaster" protected by s.1(3)(d). But if the programme is recorded the protection would be lost by both, even though B was unaware of its nature. Compare *Thompson v Australian Capital Television Pty Ltd* (1996) 186 C.L.R. 574.

[305] It is possible in all cases slightly to delay the transmission of a programme. There may be circumstances surrounding a broadcast which would make this relevant to the exercise of reasonable care, but such steps are only likely to detect the most obvious libels. For a settled case in which this issue arose see Collins, *Law of Defamation and the Internet*, 3rd edn (2010), para.16.14.

[306] Cf. the facts of *Gulf Oil (G.B.) Ltd v Page* [1987] Ch. 327 CA, where the defendants planned to use a plane to tow a defamatory streamer over the Cheltenham Gold Cup meeting. See also, *Oriental Daily Publishers v Ming Pao* [2012] HKCFA 59 (photograph published in a newspaper of a defamatory placard—had the publication been by way of broadcast in the UK, s.1(3)(e) would apply).

[307] As in *Syms v Warren* (1976) 71 D.L.R. (3d) 558, where there was liability at common law.

[308] Whether by wire, cable or radio.

[309] See para.6.27, above.

linking together a very large number of computers which act as "hosts" to the information contained on the network. A large part of the publicly available information on the internet is generated by persons who subscribe to the facilities of "service providers" and is entered on the system (in the form of "newsgroup messages," "home pages" or "www sites"[310]) without any intervention or participation by the providers or hosts,[311] and this category is clearly intended to provide some protection for them.[312] Electronic mail (email) is also carried by the system, though this is not publicly available, even if it may be accessible by those carrying the messages.[313] If material is examined before being made publicly available it is difficult to see how the person who does that is other than an editor for the purposes of the Act, so that the protection of s.1 is lost.[314] In practice, however, material is likely to be reviewed not in advance of publication but afterwards. In *Godfrey v Demon Internet Ltd*[315] it was held that s.1 applied where an internet service provider carried a usenet "news group"[316] which could be accessed by its users. The position is not so clear in the case of a service provider who hosts a subscriber's web page because it is likely that the contract between it and the subscriber will contain conditions about the content of the page, including restrictions on defamatory matter. However, if this were to be held to amount to "effective control" over the originator of the material that would seriously reduce the protection afforded by s.1[317] and, in *Tamiz v Google Inc.*,[318] which was concerned with the question whether in providing the Blogger service, Google was a publisher for the purposes of Defamation Act 1996, s.1, the Court of Appeal stated that the existence of a contractual term about the content of the blog was not capable of giving Google "effective control" over a person who posted the defamatory comments. Where, however, the service provider commissions an independent contractor to make available information via the service provider's site, it is

---

[310] World wide web.

[311] The volume of data is so great that it would be impossible to treat it like a conventional publication.

[312] The host clearly publishes in the common law sense; those playing a more passive role may not do so. See paras 3.26–29, above.

[313] Unauthorised interception may be an offence under the Regulation of Investigatory Powers Act 2000.

[314] cf. *Stratton Oakmont Inc. v Prodigy Services*, 23 Media L. Rep. 1794 (NY., 1995).

[315] [2001] Q.B. 201. See also the position of BT in *Bunt v Tilley* [2006] EWHC 407 (QB); [2007] 1 W.L.R. 1243.

[316] Postings on usenet groups will originate on the server of the originator's internet service provider but all service providers will carry the majority of groups on their servers, usually for a limited time.

[317] Cf. Collins, *The Law of Defamation and the Internet*, 3rd edn (2010), para.16.08.

[318] [2013] EWCA Civ 68 CA.

thought that the service provider should be regarded as a publisher and outside the protection of s.1.[319]

6.35 Employees and agents. Employees or agents of an author, editor or publisher are in the same position as their employer or principal to the extent that they are responsible for the content of the statement or the decision to publish it.[320] This is a curious provision. In practice authors will necessarily be natural persons. This will also be commonly so for editors, though one can conceive of cases in which a corporation (acting via natural persons) could be said to have "editorial responsibility" for a statement. Since a publisher is only such under s.1 if it is a commercial publisher that will mean that in practice it will be a corporation which will act through natural persons. However, since the test used by this provision to equate employees with their employers is the same as that used to determine whether a person has editorial or equivalent responsibility,[321] it is hard to see why it is necessary: if a servant or agent of the author, editor or publisher does have responsibility for the content of the statement or the decision to publish it, that means he has editorial or equivalent responsibility.

6.36 Nature of liability of persons other than author, editor or publisher. A person who is qualified to take advantage of the s.1 defence must show that he did not know, and had no reason to believe, that what he did caused or contributed to the publication of a defamatory statement.[322] This requirement would be satisfied *either* by proof that he had no reason to believe[323] that the statement was defamatory *or* by proof that, although he was aware that the statement was defamatory, he had no reason to believe that his actions caused or contributed to its publication.[324] The defence is not, however, made out if the defendant has reason to believe that the statement is defamatory but has no reason to believe it to be defamatory of the *claimant*,[325]

---

[319] Cf. *Cubby v CompuServe Inc.*, 776 F.Supp. 135 (1991) and *Blumenthal v Drudge*, 992 F.Supp. 44 (1998). A newspaper issues an "insert supplement" on Ruritania, which is prepared by the Government of Ruritania. It would be surprising if the newspaper were treated as a mere distributor of this. However (a) there is no mention of effective control in that part of s.1 dealing with the print media and (b) the possibility of examining material before publication is much greater.

[320] S.1(4).

[321] Under s.1(2).

[322] S.1(1)(c).

[323] To save repetition, this expression will be used to cover the statutory formula, in which absence of knowledge is of course an additional requirement. The protection of s.1 is lost if the defendant knew he was publishing a defamatory statement even if a reasonable person would not have come to that conclusion.

[324] E.g. A shows B a document defamatory of C. Later, A asks B to deliver a letter to X and, unknown to B, this is the defamatory document.

[325] Hence the defence would not apply to a statement like that in *Newstead v London Express* [1940] 1 K.B. 377 CA (true statement that HN had been convicted of bigamy; statement untrue about another HN). However, it would apply to a case like *Cassidy v Daily Mirror* [1929] 2 K.B. 331 CA (statement innocent on its face about C's engagement defamatory of C's wife, of whom

nor by showing that he had reason to believe that the statement was true or protected by privilege or some other defence.[326]

Under s.4 of the Act (the offer of amends procedure) it has been held that a person does not "have reason to believe" something merely because he is negligent in not knowing it: the formula requires that he must at least have chosen to ignore or shut his mind to information in his possession which would have led a reasonable person to the conclusion that the statement was defamatory.[327] However, s.1 incorporates the further requirement that the defendant establish that he took reasonable care in relation to the publication of the statement[328] and these are cumulative requirements which must be established by the defendant. A person may (if he is believed) be unconscious of the defamatory nature of the material but very careless indeed, in which case s.1 does not provide him with a defence. In determining "reason to believe" or reasonable care the court is directed to have regard to a common list of factors, namely:

(1) the extent of the defendant's responsibility for the content of the statement or the decision to publish it;
(2) the nature or circumstances of the publication; and
(3) the previous conduct or character of the author, editor or publisher.[329]

Subject to the point that (1) has to be included because the s.1 defence is open to certain persons who have participated in the creation, as opposed to the mere distribution of the defamatory statement, this does not seem, as far as reasonable care is concerned, very different from the common law test for distributors[330] and in view of (2) confers only limited protection on distributors of controversial publications.[331] For example, the information about the publication in his possession may give him no reason to believe that the statement is defamatory but the circumstances may be such as to put him on further inquiry. On the other hand it would seem impractical to expect an

---

defendants were unaware). The offer of amends "defence" under s.2 is open in both cases but is less favourable to the defendant than the s.1 defence.

[326] The question whether a statement is *defamatory* is not the same as whether it is *actionable*: see para.1.8, above.

[327] *Milne v Express Newspapers Ltd* [2004] EWCA Civ 664; [2005] 1 W.L.R. 772. See para.19.6, below. See also *Bunt v Tilley* [2006] EWHC 407 (QB); [2007] 1 W.L.R. 1243 at [61].

[328] S.1(1)(b).

[329] S.1(5).

[330] See para.6.30, above.

[331] Collins, *The Law of Defamation and the Internet*, 2nd edn (2005), para.16.16 points out that there is a tension between the reasonable care requirement and the very nature of s.1, for if the defendant takes active steps to monitor for defamatory content he risks being held to be an "editor" and outside the scope of s.1 altogether. Nor is it easy to give a clear content to what might be "reasonable care" by an internet service provider. In practice the protection granted by the Electronic Commerce Regulations 2003 will be wider: see para.6.41, below.

internet service provider to institute checks for defamatory material passing through its system,[332] or even hosted on its system, so that in practice there will be no requirement of "proactive inquiry".

6.37 Conduct of distributor after notice. In many cases the question of the defendant's knowledge and care has to be judged once only, at the point of distribution by him, because the defamatory material either has no further existence (e.g. a live radio broadcast) or is then beyond his control (e.g. an issue of a newspaper sold by him). However, in other cases the defendant may be engaged in a number of ongoing, separate publications by further sales or exhibitions of the work (a bookseller, library or cinema) or by maintaining it on a publicly accessible service provided by him (an internet host or teletext service provider) and in such cases the protection of s.1 is lost in respect of publications subsequent to his receiving notice of the defamatory character of the statement.[333] It is thought that the concept of reasonable care should allow him the opportunity to make reasonable inquiries after notice,[334] but in practice it may be expected that defendants, particularly in the electronic media, will err on the side of caution and remove material if there is the slightest risk that it may be defamatory.

6.38 Relationship of the Defamation Act 1996 and the common law. There is no express provision in the 1996 Act to abolish the common law defence for distributors, though it is arguable that it does so by implication.[335] The point is not without significance because, while the Act is plainly wider than the common law in a number of respects (e.g. in relation to printers and live broadcasters) it is possible that the mental element which allows advantage to be taken of the statutory defence is narrower than that under the common law. The defendant loses the protection of the statutory defence if he has reason to believe that he is contributing to the publication of a defamatory statement and it is irrelevant that he has reason to believe that the statement

---

[332] Even assuming it was lawful for it to do so: see the Regulation of Investigatory Powers Act 2000.

[333] *Godfrey v Demon Internet Ltd* [2001] Q.B. 201.

[334] In *Godfrey*, above, liability arose from the day on which the plaintiff notified the defendant of the presence of the posting, but the implication at 205 seems to be that if they had acted promptly to remove it they would not have incurred liability.

[335] Compare s.15(4)(b) (privilege), which provides that nothing in s.15 is to limit or abridge any privilege subsisting apart from the section. The Lord Chancellor, when introducing the Bill, stated that it would "supersede" the common law defence: *Hansard*, HL, col.577 (March 8, 1996). See also para.2.6 of the Consultation on the draft Bill (May 5, 1995): "replace and modernise innocent dissemination". In *Metropolitan International Schools Ltd v Designtechnica Corp* [2009] EWHC 1765 (QB), Eady J. held (at [70]) that the defence was not abolished in 1996 (albeit that it had effectively been superseded) because the statute did not do so expressly and it was a fundamental principle of statutory construction that Parliament should not be taken as effecting a fundamental alteration in the general law unless it made this expressly clear in the statutory wording: see e.g. Bennion on *Statutory Interpretation*, 4th edn (LexisNexis), pp.693–694 and *National Assistance Board v Wilkinson* [1952] 2 QB 648 per Devlin J. at 661.

is true or is protected by privilege.[336] By contrast the judicial formulations of
the common law defence commonly speak in terms of the defendant having
reason to believe that what he is distributing contains a *libel*,[337] so that the
defence might be open to a person who would qualify as a mere distributor at
common law and who believed he had satisfactory evidence that the defamatory matter was not actionable because of some defence available to the
originator.[338] This issue was fully considered in *Metropolitan International
Schools Ltd v Designtechnica Corp.*[339] Having referred to the difficulties
presented by the views of Lord Denning M.R. in *Goldsmith v Sperrings*,[340]
Eady J. said that:

> "[The common law defence] would almost certainly not be available to a defendant
> who has had it drawn to his attention that the words are defamatory or, at least,
> arguably so. To that extent, the common law defence is much more closely in line
> with the statutory defence introduced in s.1 of the 1996 Act."[341]

Defamation Act 2013, s.5. Section 5 of the Defamation Act 2013 will,   **6.39**
when it comes into force, provide a new defence for website operators in
respect of defamatory statements posted on their sites by third parties. Where
the statement complained of is made by an identifiable author, the defence will
be unconditional unless the operator has acted with malice. In respect of
unidentified authors, the defence will be available unless the claimant shows

---

[336] See para.6.36, above.
[337] See *Emmens v Pottle* (1885) 16 Q.B.D. 354 CA at 357, 358; *Ridgway v Smith* (1890) 6
T.L.R. 275 at 276; *Mallon v WH Smith* (1893) 9 T.L.R. 621 at 622; *Vizetelly v Mudie's Select
Library* [1900] 2 Q.B. 170 CA at 176, 180.
[338] This seems to have been the view of Lord Denning M.R., dissenting, in *Goldsmith v
Sperrings* [1977] 1 W.L.R. 478 at 487:
> "Common sense and fairness require that no subordinate distributor . . . should be held liable
> for a libel contained in it unless he knew or ought to have known that newspaper or periodical
> contained a libel on the plaintiff himself; *that is to say, that it contained a libel which could not
> be justified or excused*".
However, there must be some doubt about his Lordship's assertion that para.581 of the Restate-
ment, 2d, *Torts*, supports this view. In the same case, however, Bridge L.J. at 505, formulated the
common law in a manner compatible with the 1996 Act:
> " . . . it is for [the defendant] to show that he did not in fact know that the publication contained
> defamatory matter and that he had no reason to believe that it was likely to contain defamatory
> matter".
But the liability of the distributors in this case was conceded and the point was not argued.
Though the older cases are briefly reported it seems likely that in fact they involved situations
where the defendants were simply unaware of the contents of what they were selling, in which
event perhaps too much weight should not be placed upon the precise words used by the judges,
who did not, after all, say "*actionable* libel".
The Lord Chancellor, responding to an amendment put forward by Lord Lester of Herne Hill,
was of the view that what is now s.1 accorded with the common law in this respect and that to
allow the defendant to rely on his reasonable belief that there would be some defence to an action
in respect of words which he realised were defamatory would be to introduce "an entirely new
defence": *Hansard*, HL, col.214 (April 2, 1996).
[339] [2009] EWHC 1765 (QB).
[340] [1977] 1 W.L.R. 478 at 487 (see fn 338)
[341] [2009] EWHC 1765 (QB) at [70].

that he gave the operator a notice of complaint in relation to the statement, and the operator failed to respond to the notice of complaint in accordance with any provision contained in regulations. The defence will not affect pre-existing statutory and common law defences for website operators which already provide them significant protection.

Section 5 creates a defence where an action for defamation is brought against "an operator of a website" in respect of a statement posted on the website. Where the defendant can show that it was not the operator who posted the statement it has a defence.[342] No definitions are offered for the key terms in the section and it will therefore be for the courts to interpret them. In technical terms, "websites" consist of one or more webpages served from a single web domain that is accessible through a uniform resource locator (URL) via a network such as the internet. Section 5 will presumably therefore apply to retail websites, review and discussion forums and social media networks such as Twitter, Facebook and Blogger so far as they are accessible through a URL. As an "application" or "App" for smartphones and similar devices is simply computer software the defence will not be applicable to the manufacturer of the "App" but it will presumably apply to a site from which such an application can be purchased. Whether an "operator" is the person who has effective control of the site itself or simply the content is not entirely clear though as the provision is concerned with removing content the latter interpretation seems more likely. For many sites, there is likely to be more than one person entitled to rely on the "operator" defence. Thus, not only is the 'owner' of a social networking page an operator for the purposes of s.5 but so would be the entity that owns the website hosting the pages. This would also be the case with most blog platforms. Section 5(12) provides that the fact the operator "moderates" statements posted in the site does not of itself defeat the defence. The intention here is presumably to make clear that merely because an operator has the power, either technically or by the terms of a contract, to remove or delete parts of a post, that it does not thereby lose the defence. That a website automatically removes or blocks certain swearwords or spam would also not defeat the defence. Where the moderation does involve editing or even deletion of part of the post, however, knowledge may stray into participation, and the website operator may become liable as a primary publisher. The consequence may be that websites will choose not to monitor at all. "Post" presumably does not mean "publish" in the legal sense but refers instead to "publish" in its everyday sense, that is to say the process whereby a statement is made available to potential readers in some medium, in this case on a website.

6.40 Defamation Act 2013, s.5—when the defence is defeated. By s.5(3) of the Act, the defence is defeated if: (a) it was not possible for the claimant

---

to identify the person who posted the statement; (b) the claimant gave the operator a notice of complaint in relation to the statement; and (c) the operator failed to respond to the notice of complaint in accordance with any provision contained in regulations. Where the claimant can identify the person who posted the statement without the help of the operator, the operator will have a defence unless the claimant can prove malice.[343] Thus, in cases involving identifiable authors, there is no requirement on a defendant who wishes to rely on the defence to respond to a notice of complaint. Such immunity only exists, however, where the "claimant has sufficient information to bring proceedings against the person".[344] This will generally require an address in order for the claim to be served.[345] Quite how much research a claimant will be required to undertake before he can establish that it was not possible to identify the poster is not clear. Presumably, the fact that there was no physical or other address on the site will not necessarily be enough where other information existed that would have enabled the claimant to find the poster reasonably easily. The time at which the knowledge of the claimant will be tested is the time at which notice of complaint was sent to the website operator.[346]

Where it is not possible for the claimant to identify the person who posted the statement, the defence will be defeated if the claimant can prove that he gave a notice of complaint in relation to the statement[347] and the operator failed to respond to the notice in accordance with any provision contained in the regulations.[348] By s.5(6),[349] the notice of complaint given by the claimant should (a) include the complainant's name; (b) set out the statement concerned explaining why it is defamatory of the complainant; (c) specify where on the website the statement was posted, and (d) such other information as

---

[343] S.5(11).

[344] S.5(4).

[345] CPR r.6.6 (2).

[346] Lord Ahmed, *HL Hansard* January 15, 2013, col. GC193.

[347] S.5(3)(b).

[348] S.5(3)(c).

[349] S.5(7) provides that "Regulations may make provision about the circumstances in which a notice which is not a notice of complaint is to be treated as a notice of complaint for the purposes of this section or any provision made under it." Draft Regulations only had been published at the time of writing (the Defamation (Operators of Websites) Regulations 2013). These provide in reg.2 that a notice of complaint must, in addition to the matters referred to in s.5(6)(a) to (c) of the Act:

    (a) specify the email address at which the complainant can be contacted;

    (b) set out the meaning which the complainant attributes to the statement referred to in the notice;

    (c) set out the aspects of the statement which the complainant believes are factually inaccurate or opinions not supported by facts;

    (d) confirm that the complainant does not have sufficient information about the poster to bring proceedings against that person; and

    (e) confirm whether the complainant consents to the operator providing the poster with the complainant's name and the complainant's email address.

A notice that does not comply with these requirements may be rejected by the website operator provided that it does so within 48 hours of receipt and sets out in its response the requirements of a valid notice. It need not explain why the notice received is deficient (reg.4).

may be specified in regulations. Critically, the notice need not engage substantively with the question whether the statement is in fact unlawful: the only requirement is that the claimant set out why the statement is *defamatory*. This requirement mirrors the practical effect of the defence under s.1 of the Defamation Act 1996 but is a lower legal threshold than is required to defeat the hosting defence provided to internet hosts by reg.19 of the E-Commerce Regulations 2000, which requires a claimant to demonstrate why the information complained of is "unlawful".[350] This approach can be criticised on the basis that a website operator should not be required to reveal identity details or take down the statement complained of on the basis of "half the story". Nevertheless, it has the merit of placing the responsibility on the website operator to investigate if it wishes to leave the statement up. Knowledge should import some responsibility; it is not unreasonable to require a website operator to take steps to ascertain the truth of an allegation that it is knowingly publishing. Somewhat surprisingly, the Act is silent as to the action required of a website operator in response to a notice of complaint. Section 5(5) provides only that regulations may specify the action required; this may include, in particular, "action relating to the identity or contact details of the person who posted the statement and action relating to its removal" and "time limits for the taking of any such action, including a discretion for a court to treat action taken after the expiry of a time limit as having been taken before the expiry".[351]

The defence will be defeated, even in respect of an identifiable author, if the claimant shows that the operator of the website has acted with malice in relation to the posting of the statement.[352] Malice should have the same meaning as it does at common law[353] so that a website operator will be liable if he knew the statement was false or was reckless as to whether it was true

---

[350] See further, para.6.35, above.

[351] The draft Defamation (Operators of Websites) Regulations 2013 provide in reg.3 and the Schedule for the steps which a website operator must take on receiving a valid notice of complaint in order to be able to benefit from the defence in s.5. On receiving the notice, the website operator must within 48 hours send the poster:
    (a) the notice of complaint;
    (b) notification in writing that the statement complained of may be removed unless the operator receives a response from the poster in writing within five days. That response must state whether the poster wishes the statement to be removed and if he does not want it removed he must provide his full name, his postal address and whether he consents to those details being provided to the complainant;
    (c) notification that any information received from the poster will not be released to the complainant unless he consents or the website operator is ordered by a court to release the information.
Where the operator has no means of contacting the poster, or the poster fails to respond within five days, the operator must remove the statement complained of within 48 hours and send notice of this to the complainant. If the poster responds consenting to the removal of the statement, this must be done within 48 hours. If the poster does not consent to the removal, the operator must notify the complainant of this refusal within 48 hours of receiving the response.

[352] S.5(11).

[353] See ch.17, below.

or false. Whether failing to remove a defamatory statement after the website operator becomes aware of its falsity will amount to malice is not clear. The wording of the provision refers to malice with regard to "the posting of the statement" and it is a difficult question whether this refers to the act of posting for the first time or whether "posting" continues while the statement remains on the site. It is suggested that the second meaning is the better one.

The Electronic Commerce (E.C. Directive) Regulations 2002. Dir-   **6.41**
ective 2000/31 deals with many aspects of electronic commerce but arts 12 to 15 restrict the liability of an internet service provider (known as an "information society service provider"). In the words of Recital 42 of the Directive:

> "The exemptions from liability established in this Directive cover only cases where the activity of the information society service provider is limited to the technical process of operating and giving access to a communication network over which information made available by third parties is transmitted or temporarily stored, for the sole purpose of making the transmission more efficient; this activity is of a mere technical, automatic and passive nature, which implies that the information society service provider has neither knowledge of nor control over the information which is transmitted or stored."

The Directive is transposed into English law by the Electronic Commerce (E.C. Directive) Regulations 2002,[354] which closely follow the wording of the Directive.[355] An information society service is defined by reference to art.1(2) of Directive 98/34, as amended by Directive 98/48 and means any service normally provided for remuneration, at a distance, by means of electronic equipment for the processing (including digital compression) and storage of data, and at the individual request of a recipient of a service.[356] Many internet service providers charge no fee to users and derive their revenue from advertising or commission on telephone charges but the remuneration presumably does not have to be provided by the user so the vast majority will be covered, though a business organisation operating an internal network would not.[357]

---

[354] SI 2002/2013. The relevant provisions came into force on August 21, 2002.

[355] However, the Regulations do not transpose art.15 of the Directive, which forbids the imposition of a general duty to monitor information which the service provider transmits or a general duty actively to seek facts or circumstances indicating illegal activity. Presumably the absence of any such duty is considered implicit in the transposed provisions of arts 12, 13 and 14 (see below).

[356] SI 2002/2013, reg.2(1).

[357] Eady J. in *Metropolitan International Schools Ltd v Designtechnica Corp.* [2009] EWHC 1765; [2009] E.M.L.R. 27 (QB) at [81]–[84] stated that if the phrase "for remuneration" stood alone, it would imply that the recipient was directly paying for it, but that, given the context, "on balance" Recital 18 of the Directive indicated that services financed by advertising were covered. It followed, notwithstanding that it did not charge the user directly for its services but instead derived its revenue from advertising, that an internet search engine was an internet society service for the purposes of the Regulations. A number of European countries have enacted legislation specifically protecting the operators of search engines and some of these were reviewed by Eady J. at [97]–[111]. There are some difficulties in classifying such an operator for the purposes of the three categories in the Regulations but Eady J. did not consider it necessary to decide the issue since he had held that the defendants were not publishers at common law. See also, per H.H.J.

The Regulations do not repeal s.1 of the Defamation Act 1996, though they generally confer more protection on service providers than that section does; nor do they abolish the common law defence for distributors (if that still exists). The 1996 Act and the Regulations do not necessarily produce consistent results,[358] so that a defendant may have a defence under the Regulations but not under the Act (or even vice versa). It is for the defendant to prove that he falls within the restrictions of liability provided by the Regulations.[359] The Regulations provide protection against liability for "damages or for any other pecuniary remedy or for any criminal sanction"[360] and do not therefore prevent the issue of an injunction but this does not give the claimant any special right to an injunction. For example, in *Bunt v Tilley*[361] an injunction against an internet service provider to "prevent" defamatory postings by its client was refused because it would be impossible for it to comply short of terminating its service to him and an order to do that would be pointless because it would be easy to obtain equivalent services elsewhere.

6.42 Mere conduits. Where an information society service is provided which consists of the transmission in a communication network of information provided by a recipient of the service or the provision of access to a communication network, the service provider (if he otherwise would) is not liable for damages or for any other pecuniary remedy or for any criminal sanction as a result of that transmission where the service provider (1) did not initiate the transmission; (2) did not select the receiver of the transmission; and (3) did not select or modify the information contained in the transmission.[362] These acts of transmission and of provision of access include the automatic, intermediate and transient storage of the information transmitted where (a) this takes place for the sole purpose of carrying out the transmission in the communication network, and (b) the information is not stored for any period longer than is reasonably necessary for the transmission.[363] The protection is

---

Parkes QC in *Davison v Habeeb* [2011] EWHC 3031 (QB) where the judge held that the provider of the Blogger service was an internet society service notwithstanding that it did not charge directly for its services but derived its revenue from advertisements. That the user may not have had any advertisements on his page was not held to be determinative (at [54]–[56]). In *McGrath v Dawkins* [2012] EWHC B3 (QB), H.H.J. Moloney QC held that Amazon was an internet society service (at [38]) for the purposes of the Regulations. It would seem to follow that any institution that charges fees for services that include the access to a computer network would be treated as an internet society service notwithstanding that no separately identifiable charge is made for the service. Whether the service is provided "at a distance" will vary from case to case, depending on whether there is a facility for external access.

[358] *Bunt v Tilley* [2006] EWHC 407 (QB); [2007] 1 W.L.R. 1243 at [58].

[359] That is to say, they are defences. However, this arises by way of inference from reg.21 (criminal proceedings) rather than any express provision.

[360] Regs 17, 18 and 19. Reg.20 provides that nothing in regs 17 to 19 affects the rights of any party to apply to a court for relief to prevent or stop infringement of any rights.

[361] [2006] EWHC 407 (QB); [2007] 1 W.L.R. 1243.

[362] SI 2002/2013, reg.17(1). Art.12 of the Directive.

[363] Ibid. reg.17(2). The linguistic construction of reg.17 is not easy. Suppose X sends, via gatley.com, an Email defamatory of C to Y at odgers.com. Reg.17 plainly protects gatley.com as transmitter. There can be no reason why odgers.com should be in a different position when it

therefore aimed at transient messages, such as email,[364] or at more permanent material which simply passes through the defendant's system for purposes of access but not at material which is stored by the defendant for significant periods. The knowledge of the defendant is irrelevant, so he is not liable (in contrast to what might be the case under s.1 of the Defamation Act 1996) for failing to take steps to prevent access to another site which he is aware carries defamatory material.

Caching. Caching is a sort of half-way house between mere transmission   **6.43**
and "hosting". It is the storage of information primarily stored on another computer to make retrieval of a web page more efficient.[365] Where a service is provided which consists of the transmission in a communication network of information provided by a recipient of the service, the service provider (if he otherwise would) is not liable for damages or for any other pecuniary remedy or for any criminal sanction as a result of that transmission where:

"(a) the information is the subject of automatic, intermediate and temporary storage where that storage is for the sole purpose of making more efficient onward transmission of the information to other recipients of the service upon their request, and
(b) the service provider—
    (i) does not modify the information;
    (ii) complies with conditions on access to the information;
    (iii) complies with any rules regarding the updating of the information, specified in a manner widely recognised and used by industry;
    (iv) does not interfere with the lawful use of technology, widely recognised and used by industry, to obtain data on the use of the information; and
    (v) acts expeditiously to remove or to disable access to the information he has stored upon obtaining actual knowledge of the fact that the information at the initial source of the transmission has been removed from the network, or access to it has been disabled, or that a court or an administrative authority has ordered such removal or disablement."[366]

As in the case of the service provider acting as no more than a conduit, the caching service provider does not (in contrast with the position under s.1 of the Defamation Act 1996) incur liability in damages merely because he has

---

"shows" the message to Y but that conclusion is not obvious on the wording. Although the "service" referred to in the Regulation may be either (a) the transmission of information provided by the recipient of the service (which covers the act of gatley.com) or (v) the provision of access to a communication network (odgers.com) the immunity is conferred on "that transmission", which, linguistically, can refer only to (a) and even though odgers.com is transmitting X's information, X is not a recipient of odgers.com's service. Nor are the actual (slightly different) terms of the Directive much clearer.

[364] But perhaps not web-based email, which is normally stored on the provider's server until deleted by the customer: Collins, *The Law of Defamation and the Internet*, 3rd edn (OUP, 2010), para.17.08. Some automatic or temporary storage is permitted where that is necessary solely for the purpose of transmitting the transaction (reg.17(2)(a) (see *Bunt v Tilley* (above) at [50]).
[365] Explained in *Bunt v Tilley* (above) at [52].
[366] SI 2002/2013, reg.18. Art.13 of the Directive.

knowledge of the defamatory content of the information: he only does so if he continues to cache the information after he becomes aware that it has been removed or access disabled or that a court has ordered either of those things.

6.44 Hosting. Hosting takes place where an internet service provider stores on its server information (e.g. web pages) supplied by others. Where a service is provided which consists of the storage of information provided by a recipient of the service,[367] the service provider (if he otherwise would) is not, under reg.19, liable for damages or for any other pecuniary remedy or for any criminal sanction as a result of that storage where:

"(a) the service provider—
(i) does not have actual knowledge[368] of unlawful activity or information and, where a claim for damages is made, is not aware of facts or circumstances from which it would have been apparent to the service provider that the activity or information was unlawful; or
(ii) upon obtaining such knowledge or awareness, acts expeditiously to remove or to disable access to the information, and
(b) the recipient of the service was not acting under the authority or the control of the service provider."[369]

---

[367] (1) Sources of information may be combined, as where a newspaper website contains an article and a "Have your say about this" section directed at readers. In *Kaschke v Gray* [2010] EWHC 690 (QB) it was held that:

"When considering in a particular case whether a defendant is entitled to the immunity conferred by Regulation 19 (subject to satisfying the extra conditions) the question to be asked is whether the information society service provided by the defendant in respect of the information containing the defamatory words which would otherwise give rise to liability consists only of and is limited to storage of that information. If the answer to that question is that it does consist only of storage of the information, Regulation 19 immunity is potentially available even if it would not be available in respect of other information also stored by the defendant in respect of which the service provided by the defendant goes beyond mere storage." (at [75]).

See also *Karim v Newsquest Media Group Ltd* [2009] EWHC 3205 (QB) and *Mulvaney v Sporting Exchange Ltd (t/a Betfair)* [2009] IEHC 33. The focus of the reg.19 immunity is upon the particular hosted information of which complaint is made so that if with regard to that the defendant exercises an editorial function the immunity may be lost. In *Kaschke* the Master had found against the defendant on his Pt 24 application based on s.1 of the Defamation Act 1996 and there was no appeal against that.

[368] By reg.22, in determining whether a service provider has actual knowledge for this purpose (or for the purposes of reg.18(b)(v)),

"a court shall take into account all matters which appear to it in the particular circumstances to be relevant and, among other things, shall have regard to—
(a) whether a service provider has received a notice through a means of contact made available in accordance with regulation 6(1)(c) [which requires a service provider to provide information enabling a user to contact it], and
(b) the extent to which any notice includes—
(i) the full name and address of the sender of the notice;
(ii) details of the location of the information in question; and
(iii) details of the unlawful nature of the activity or information in question."

[369] SI 2002/2013, reg.19. Art.14 of the Directive. No doubt para.(b) would cover the case where the service provider commissioned a third party to provide some regular service accessible from its site.

Since defamation cases will generally involve claims for damages, the service provider may be liable even if he does not have actual knowledge of the unlawful nature of the material, provided he is aware of facts or circumstances from which its unlawful nature would have been apparent to him.[370] It is clear that he must have actual knowledge (and not merely constructive knowledge) of the facts and circumstances, but it is less clear what is the meaning of "apparent". Arguably something would be "apparent" to the defendant when he has reason to be aware of it; but it may involve a lower standard, something akin to obviousness.[371] A possibly very significant difference between s.1 of the Defamation Act 1996 and reg.19 is that while the former refers to the defendant's means of knowledge that he is contributing to the publication of a defamatory statement, the latter refers to his means of knowledge that the statement[372] is "unlawful". A statement is defamatory even though there is a perfectly viable defence to a libel action but where there was a defence it would be difficult to say that it was "unlawful" (for example, much of the law of privilege is based upon a *duty* to publish a defamatory statement),[373] which would make the reg.19 defence much wider. At a minimum, it seems that before one can say that it would be apparent to a defendant that a statement is unlawful he would need to know something of the strength or weakness of available defences.[374]

---

[370] Reg.19 (in its original form as art.14 of the Directive) was considered by the European Court of Justice in *Google France SARL v Louis Vuitton Malletier SA* (C 236/08). The context was a reference from the French courts in a trademark infringement dispute. The court said that:

"Article 14 of Directive . . . must be interpreted as meaning that the rule laid down therein applies to an internet referencing service provider in the case where that service provider has not played an active role of such a kind as to give it knowledge of, or control over, the data stored. If it has not played such a role, that service provider cannot be held liable for the data which it has stored at the request of an advertiser, unless, having obtained knowledge of the unlawful nature of those data or of that advertiser's activities, it failed to act expeditiously to remove or to disable access to the data concerned" (at [114]).

The case involved not "natural" searches determined by Google algorithms but a service called Adwords, under which "Google processes the data entered by advertisers and the resulting display of the ads is made under conditions which Google controls. Thus, Google determines the order of display according to, inter alia, the remuneration paid by the advertisers" (at [115]). It would be for the national court to determine whether the terms of Google's arrangements with advertisers prevented the situation falling within the scope of the test stated (at [114]).

[371] Collins, *The Law of Defamation and the Internet*, 3rd edn (Publisher, 2010), para.17.24 points out that the wording of the Directive is "*is* apparent".

[372] Strictly, "activity or information".

[373] cf. the position under the common law innocent dissemination defence: para.6.30, above.

[374] *Bunt v Tilley* [2006] EWHC 407 (QB); [2007] 1 W.L.R. 1243 at [72]. Eady J.'s view was endorsed by Stadlen J. in *Kaschke v Gray* [2010] EWHC 690 (QB); [2011] 1 W.L.R. 452. In *L'Oréal SA and others v eBay International AG* case C-324/09 the Grand Chamber of the European Court of Justice stated (at [120]) that it was sufficient, in order for the provider of an information society service to be denied entitlement to the exemption from liability provided for in art.14 of Directive 2000/31, for it to "have been aware of facts or circumstances on the basis of which a diligent economic operator should have identified the illegality in question". If the rules in art.14(1)(a) of the Directive were not be rendered redundant:

"they must be interpreted as covering every situation in which the provider concerned becomes aware, in one way or another, of such facts or circumstances . . . The situations thus covered

6.45 Defamation Act 2013, s.10—claim against secondary publisher. Under the common law, a secondary publisher could be the subject of a defamation claim, subject to having a defence at common law of innocent dissemination or under s.1 of the Defamation Act 1996 or the Electronic Commerce (E.C. Directive) Regulations 2002. When s.10(1) comes into force it will provide that a court does not have jurisdiction to hear and determine an action for defamation "brought against a person who was not the author, editor or publisher of the statement complained of unless the court is satisfied that it is not reasonably practicable for an action to be brought against the author, editor or publisher".[375] By s.5(2), "author", "editor" and "publisher" will have the same meaning as in s.1 of the Defamation Act 2013.[376]

Questions will inevitably arise as to when it will be "not reasonably practicable" to bring an action for defamation. Would, for example, the fact that the primary author and publisher were in the United States so that any judgment obtained against them in this jurisdiction would, as a consequence of the Securing the Protection of our Enduring and Established Heritage (SPEECH) Act, be unenforceable in the United States, mean that it was not reasonably practicable to bring a claim against them? It cannot surely be required of a claimant that he pursue a claim that even if successful would be of no practical value to him, and consequently it is arguable that a court should have jurisdiction to hear a claim against the secondary publisher in such a case. A similar argument can be made if the primary publisher is insolvent. In both cases, it does not seem just to allow a secondary publisher to continue to distribute a book simply because the claimant has no effective claim against

---

include, in particular, that in which the operator of an online marketplace uncovers, as the result of an investigation undertaken on its own initiative, an illegal activity or illegal information, as well as a situation in which the operator is notified of the existence of such an activity or such information. In the second case, although such a notification admittedly cannot automatically preclude the exemption from liability provided for in Article 14 of Directive 2000/31, given that notifications of allegedly illegal activities or information may turn out to be insufficiently precise or inadequately substantiated, the fact remains that such notification represents, as a general rule, a factor of which the national court must take account when determining, in the light of the information so transmitted to the operator, whether the latter was actually aware of facts or circumstances on the basis of which a diligent economic operator should have identified the illegality." (at [121]–[122]).

In *Davison v Habeeb* [2011] EWHC 3031 (QB) H.H.J. Parkes QC noted that the alternative view (that "unlawful" in reg.19 means "prima facie" unlawful or defamatory) was inconsistent with both *Kaschke* and the *L'Oreal* decision and also gave little weight to the art.10 implications (at [64]). On the facts of *Davison*, the judge held that the claimant had no realistic prospect of establishing that the notification of her complaint fixed the Google Inc., as the provider of the Blogger service, with actual knowledge of unlawful activity or information as Google and was faced with conflicting claims from the claimant and the second defendant between which it was in no position to adjudicate (at [68]).

[375] S.10 was added in light of concerns expressed to the Joint Committee on the Draft Defamation Bill by the Booksellers Association to the effect that s.1 of the Defamation Act 1996 had reduced the protection for secondary publishers (who are not covered by the Electronic Commerce (E.C. Directive) Regulations 2002). Whether or not this was in fact the case, s.10 was introduced to allay their concerns.

[376] See paras 6.32, 6.33, above.

the primary publisher. A second set of concerns might arise in the case where the primary publisher has published under a cloak of anonymity. In such a case, a claimant may only be able to obtain sufficient information to commence a claim by using the *Norwich Pharmacal* jurisdiction. Could it be argued that if the claimant fails to utilise the *Norwich Pharmacal* jurisdiction, then s.10 would prevent a claim being brought against any secondary publisher? Where the secondary publisher is a website operator, the effect of acceding to such an argument would be to render the s.5 notice procedures redundant and that is presumably not what was intended by Parliament. In respect of other secondary publishers, it may however be perfectly reasonable to require the claimant to make a *Norwich Pharmacal* application. This of course entails a difference in treatment for online and offline publications but that is simply a consequence of the language of the relevant provisions.

Defamation Act 2013, s.13—order to remove.[377] A consequence to **6.46** which the enactment of s.10 of the Defamation Act 2013 would have given rise is that even if the claimant successfully sued the primary publisher, he would still be unable to prevent the continued dissemination of the libel by a secondary publisher who might, for example, refuse to remove the libel from a website under his control or continue to distribute the libel in printed form. In order to remedy this potential problem s.13 was introduced. When it comes into force, it will provide that where a successful claim for defamation is made by the claimant and judgment given for him, the court may order (a) the operator of a website on which the defamatory statement is posted to remove the statement, or (b) any person who was not the author, editor or publisher of the statement to stop distributing, selling or exhibiting material containing the statement.[378]

SECTION 4. REPUBLICATION AND REPETITION

(a) *Liability of republisher*

General principles. At common law every republication of a libel is a new **6.47** libel and, if committed by different persons, each one is liable as if the defamatory statement had originated with him.[379] Thus, where A wrote a libellous letter to D, and D republished extracts in a pamphlet, it was held that the fact that the letter was written by A, and that D honestly believed the

---

[377] See further, para.9.47, below.
[378] S.13(1). S.13(2) provides that "author", "editor" and "publisher" have the same meaning as in s.1 of the Defamation Act 1996. See paras 6.23, 6.24, above.
[379] See *Morse v Times-Republican Co* (1904) 124 Iowa R. 700 at 717, quoted with apparent approval in *Truth (NZ) Ltd v Holloway* [1960] 1 W.L.R. 997 PC at 1002–1003; *Chinese Cultural Centre of Vancouver v Holt* (1978) 87 D.L.R. (3d) 744; *Thomas v CBC* [1981] 4 W.W.R. 289.

statements in it to be true, was no defence to an action for such republication.[380] So the mere fact that a libellous article in a newspaper had previously
been published in another paper is no defence to an action against the
proprietor who has republished the article.[381] The same applies even if it is
clear that the defendant is purporting to report what someone else has said: if
the defendant states that someone else has said that the claimant has committed a crime, the defendant's statement is treated as if the defendant himself
had made that charge and to escape liability he must (unless it was a privileged
occasion) show that the claimant did commit the crime, not merely that the
other person said he did.[382] So where the defendant newspaper printed an
article purporting to report a conversation in which J. said that the plaintiff
was prepared to act dishonourably, a direction that the jury could treat the case
as if the defendant had said this was approved.[383] Although J. might have
slandered the plaintiff "if the words had not been repeated by the newspaper,
the damage done by J. would be as nothing compared to the damage done by
this newspaper when it repeated it. It broadcast the statement to the people at
large".[384] This is the "repetition rule", which:

> "reflects a fundamental canon of legal policy in the law of defamation, dating back
> nearly 170 years, that words must be interpreted, and the implications they contain
> justified, by reference to the underlying allegations of fact and not merely by
> reliance upon some second-hand report or assertion of them".[385]

The rule applies even if the defendant believes the statement to be true[386] and
even if he names his source.[387] "For the purposes of the law of libel a hearsay
statement is the same as a direct statement, and that is all there is to it".[388]
These principles apply to the media as much as to private defendants[389] and
have been held to be consistent with art.10 of the European Convention on

---

[380] *Tidman v Ainslie* (1854) 10 Exch. 63. See also *Macdonald v Martin*, 1935 S.C. 621;
Robshaw v Smith (1878) 38 L.T. 423 (passing on anonymous letters).
[381] *Lewis v Walter* (1821) 4 B. & Ald. 605.
[382] See para.11.18, below.
[383] *Truth (NZ) Ltd v Holloway* [1960] 1 W.L.R. 997 PC.
[384] Ibid. at 1003.
[385] *Shah v Standard Chartered Bank* [1999] Q.B. 241 CA at 263; *Curistan v Times Newspapers
Ltd* [2008] EWCA Civ 432 at [80]; [2008] 3 All E.R. 923. The rule is further considered in the
context of justification, para.11.18ff, below.
[386] But such belief may protect him if his publication was on an occasion of qualified privilege:
see Ch.16, below.
[387] "X said that P . . . ". *Lewis v Walter* (1821) 4 B. & Ald. 605; *M'pherson v Daniels* (1829)
10 B. & C. 263; *Bennett v Bennett* (1834) 6 C. & P. 588; *Collis v Bate* (1846) 10 Jur. 647;
Macdonald v Mail Printing Co (1900) 32 O.R. 163, reversed on other grounds (1901) 2 O.L.R.
278; *Trafton v Deschene* (1917) 44 N.B.R. 552 NBCA; *Patterson v Edmonton Bulletin Co* (1908)
1 Alta. L.R. 477.
[388] Per Lord Devlin in *Lewis v Daily Telegraph* [1964] A.C. 234 HL at 284. Cf. Pincus J. in
Australian Broadcasting Corp v Comalco (1986) 68 A.L.R. 259 Fed Ct of Australia at 336.
[389] However, it has to be said that every day newspapers contain stories which would appear
to fall foul of this rule. No doubt many of them are true; in many others the risks of litigation are
a deterrent to action.

Human Rights.[390] In a large number of situations reports of matters of public concern are given the protection of qualified privilege by common law[391] or statute.[392] In many cases this defence can only be defeated by proof of malice so that it is irrelevant that the defendant has not taken care to verify the truth of what has been said. However, in one type of case taking steps to verify may be part of the requirements of what is known as "responsible publication."[393]

The same applies to a repetition of a slander originally uttered by another.[394] As great or greater an injury may accrue from the wrongful repetition as from the first publication of a slander; the first utterer may have been a person of bad character, or insane, or in a state of intoxication when he uttered it. Slander uttered by such a person would not receive much attention, but a person of good character and sound mind who repeats the slander adds weight and credit to it.[395] A party is not the less entitled to recover damages for injurious matter published concerning him, because another person previously published it. That shows merely that the claimant has been wronged by another person as well as the defendant, and may consequently have an action for damages against that person also.

To say that a person who repeats a defamatory allegation originated by another is liable is not to say that the nature and extent of his liability is necessarily the same as that of the originator.

"[T]he nature and quality of the defamatory publication may vary, dependent upon whether it is a report of what another has said and whether it is adopted, repudiated or discounted. The purpose of the republication will also have a significant bearing ... When a defamatory publication purports to repeat or report the defamatory statement of another it is an essentially different libel from one where the same imputation is conveyed directly. It may require to be charged or defended differently".[396]

It may also be relevant on damages.

Effect of Defamation Act 1996. This Act does not affect the principle   **6.48** that a person who repeats a defamatory statement first published by another also publishes it. However the question arises whether the liability of the

---

[390] *Chase v News Group Newspapers Ltd* [2002] EWCA Civ 1772; [2003] E.M.L.R. 11.
[391] See Chs 14 and 15, below.
[392] See Ch.16, below.
[393] See para.15.11, below.
[394] *M'Pherson v Daniels* (1829) 10 B. & C. 263; *De Crespigney v Wellesley* (1829) 5 Bing. 392; *Watkin v Hall* (1868) L.R. 3 Q.B. 396; *Douglas v Tucker* [1952] 1 S.C.R. 275; *McCauley v John Fairfax* (1933) 34 N.S.W.S.R. 339. For a strong statement of this rule, see *Duke of Windsor v Heinemann, The Times*, November 23, 1937.
[395] *M'Pherson v Daniels* (1829) 10 B. & C. 263 at 273, 276. See also *Truth (NZ) Ltd v Holloway* [1960] 1 W.L.R. 997 PC, where the newspaper lent credence to a report by basing a call for a public inquiry on it.
[396] *Wake v John Fairfax* [1973] 1 N.S.W.L.R. 43 at 49–50; *Nationwide News Pty Ltd v Heggie* [2001] NSWCA 257; *Buck v Jones* [2002] NSWCA 8.

republisher is ameliorated by the Act. Persons other than the author, editor or publisher of a statement may rely on the defence under s.1 if they show that they took reasonable care in relation to the publication and did not know and had no reason to believe that what they did caused or contributed to the publication of a defamatory statement.[397] So, if X slanders C to D and D repeats that slander to Y, D is not the author of the statement because only the originator is the author[398]; and he is not a publisher because in this context that means a commercial publisher.[399] However, he is very arguably a person who has editorial or equivalent responsibility for the publication. The concept of editorial responsibility is not confined to journalism, rather it seems to mean a person who takes a decision to publish the material instead of merely obeying the instructions of someone else to do so. In any event, the protection of s.1 is only available where the statement is not defamatory on its face.[400] In practice most cases will be actions for libel against the media and the republisher will be either an editor or (commercial) publisher and hence unprotected by s.1. This is assumed in what follows.

6.49 Effect of Defamation Act 2013, s.8.[401] Section 8 of the Defamation Act 2013 will replace the existing multiple publication rule under which every new publication of a defamatory statement gives rise to a separate claim with a single publication rule. The rule which applies to a republication of the same material by the publisher will prevent any claim being brought in respect of the subsequent publication more than one year from the date of the first publication (subs.(4)). The rule, however, will only apply where the *original publisher* republishes the statement complained of in substantially the same form: it will not apply where a third party repeats or republishes the original statement. Section 8 will not therefore change the common law where the republication is by a third party. Nor will there be any change to the common law where the republication by the original publisher is in a form different from the original publication. Where the republication is by the original publisher, the effect of s.8 will only be to prevent a claim being brought in respect of a subsequent publication (the republication) more than one year after the date of the first publication. It will not otherwise prevent the claimant from bringing an action in respect of the republication. Nor, where the claimant sues in relation to the first publication only, will it prevent the claimant seeking to recover, as a consequence of that original publication, the damage which he has suffered by reason of its repetition.[402]

---

[397] See para.6.36, above.
[398] S.1(2).
[399] See para.6.33, above.
[400] See para.6.36, above.
[401] See para.6.6ff, above.
[402] See para.6.52, above.

Publication by reference. It is clear that a defendant may be liable for   **6.50**
publication by referring to a statement originally published on another occasion by himself or another: e.g. if A writes a defamatory publication of C and
D then writes, "A description of C may be found in A's work".[403] Whether
a defendant is liable on this basis will be a matter of fact and degree.[404] In such
cases it may be that the correct analysis is not so much that D *republishes* what
A has written but that he procures a publication of it by leading readers to it,
for what they see is the original work of A,[405] though that makes no difference
to D's liability. An obvious modern instance would be where the defendant
incorporates on a website a link to another site containing material defamatory
of the claimant.[406]

Expressions of doubt. The fact that the defendant expressed a doubt or   **6.51**
disbelief as to the truth of defamatory assertions which he repeats may not
relieve him of liability.[407]

> "No character or reputation would be safe, if a mere statement of a person's
> disbelief of a rumour which the speaker was engaged in circulating could be made
> to defeat the right of recovery for the slander."[408]

It is not therefore necessary that the defendant should have adopted the
statement,[409] though that is very relevant where the occasion of publication
was privileged. Where the defendant publishes an article defamatory of the

---

[403] *Buchanan v Jennings* [2004] UKPC 36; [2005] 1 A.C. 115 at [12] PC; *Makudi v Baron
Triesman of Tottenham in the Borough of Haringey* [2013] EWHC 142 (QB) at [71] (statements
made in Parliament and referred to before an FA inquiry); *Lawrence v Newberry* (1891) 64 L.T.
797 (where the reference to the plaintiff was more indirect but still sufficient). See also *Peters v
TV New Zealand*, December 20, 2007 CIV 2004–404–003311, applying *Buchanan v Jennings*;
Spike v Golding (1895) 27 N.S.R. 370 NSCA; *African Life v Robinson* [1938] N.P.D. 277; *African
Realty v Robinson* [1939] T.P.D. 155; cf. *Astaire v Campling* [1966] 1 W.L.R. 34 CA, para.3.32,
above.

[404] *Makudi v Baron Triesman of Tottenham in the Borough of Haringey* [2013] EWHC (QB) at
[71].

[405] See Collins, *Law of Defamation and the Internet*, 2nd edn (2005), para.5.27.

[406] The linker would probably be an "editor" and therefore have no protection under the
Defamation Act 1996, s.1: Collins, *Law of Defamation and the Internet*, para.16.20. However, in
Crookes v Newton 2011 SCC 47; [2011] 3 S.C.R. 269 the Supreme Court of Canada held that
hyperlinking did not amount to publication (see further para.6.13, above).

[407] *Bransetter v Borrough* (1882) 81 Indiana R. 527; *Morse v Times-Republican Co* (1904) 124
Iowa R. 701; cf. *Duke of Windsor v Heinemann*, *The Times*, November 23, 1937; *Parker v John
Fairfax* [1980] A.C.L.D. 558 NSWCA.

[408] *Nicholson v Merritt* (1909) 109 Kentucky R. 369 at 371; *Syms v Warren* (1975) 71 D.L.R.
(3d) 588 at 563.

[409] *Stern v Piper* [1997] Q.B. 123 CA; *Curistan v Times Newspapers Ltd* [2008] EWCA Civ
432 at [2]; [2008] 3 All E.R. 923; *Wake v John Fairfax* [1973] 1 N.S.W.L.R. 43; *Nationwide News
Pty Ltd v Heggie* [2001] NSWCA 257; *Buck v Jones* [2002] NSWCA 8; *John Fairfax Publications Pty Ltd v Obeid* [2005] NSWCA 60; 64 N.S.W.L.R. 485 and *Yoon Shin Lee v Bob Chae-
Sang Cha* [2005] NSWCA 279.

claimant, even a contrary statement in the article will not necessarily prevent a claim for defamation.[410] The question is whether, taken as a whole, the article conveys a defamatory imputation, whether the antidote takes away the bane, and this is for the jury,[411] although there will be some cases where it is clear that it could not convey such an imputation to a reasonable person and the issue will be withdrawn from them. So, in *Bik v Mirror Newspapers*[412] a report of a statement by a Minister[413] completely exonerating the plaintiff from the charges of wrongdoing which had been made against him was held incapable of a defamatory meaning, even though it necessarily referred to the charges. If the law were otherwise it would be most unwise, except in so far as the reports were privileged, to report an acquittal without being in a position to prove that the acquittal was wrong.

(b) *Liability of the original publisher*

6.52 General principle. Where a defendant's defamatory statement is voluntarily republished by the person to whom he published it or by some other person, the question arises whether the defendant is liable for the damage caused by that further publication. In such a case the claimant may have a choice: he may (1) sue the defendant both for the original publication and for the republication as two separate causes of action, or (2) sue the defendant in respect of the original publication only, but seek to recover as a consequence of that original publication the damage which he has suffered by reason of its repetition, so long as such damage is not too remote.[414]

The cases do not always distinguish clearly between the two situations and in many cases it will make no practical difference whether the defendant's liability is based upon one rather than the other. However, it has been said that the second principle is wider than the first. Thus, in *Slipper v BBC*,[415] the defendant showed a television film defamatory of the plaintiff and the plaintiff was allowed to rely on the effect of newspaper reviews of the film as damage

---

[410] *Savige v News* [1932] S.A.S.R. 240 (refutation by third party); *Hopman v Mirror Newspapers* [1961] S.R. (N.S.W.) 632; *Gotla v Odhams Press, The Times*, March 21, 1963 (plaintiff's denial of charge printed, followed by "be that as it may"); *Australian Broadcasting Corp v Comalco* (1986) 68 A.L.R. 259 (progamme containing refutation by plaintiffs); *Keramianakis v Regional Publishers Pty Ltd* [2007] NSWCA 375 at [43].

[411] Para.3.30, above. *Montereale v Longmans Green, The Times*, February 23, 1965; *Bowles v Truth (NZ) Ltd* [1965] N.Z.L.R. 768 (denials of damaging questions), approved [1966] N.Z.L.R. 303 NZCA.

[412] (1971) [1979] 2 N.S.W.L.R. 679n., NSWCA.

[413] In the legislature, reports of which will normally be privileged: para.16.9, below.

[414] *Toomey v Mirror Newspapers* (1985) 1 N.S.W.L.R. 173 at 182–183; *Sims v Wran* [1984] 1 N.S.W.L.R. 317.

[415] [1991] 1 Q.B. 283 CA.

flowing from the broadcast of the film,[416] but the differences between the film and the reviews were such that he could not have relied on the reviews as amounting to a republication of the film.[417] Read at its widest,[418] this might seem to suggest that damages can be recovered for the republication regardless of whether the later publication would be actionable by the claimant. Thus, even if the publisher of the later publication would have had a defence, or had been released as a joint tortfeasor,[419] in respect of that publication, damages may still be recovered by the claimant for the republication. As Eady J. pointed out in *Baturina v Times Newspapers*,[420] the juridical basis of the proposition that a claimant can recover damages flowing from a publication in respect of which he could not establish primary liability on the part of the defendant is difficult to ascertain. It is submitted therefore that the correct view is that where no claim would lie against the defendant in respect of the later publication, the claimant should not as a matter of principle be allowed to recover damages in respect of that publication.[421] If the later publication is not actionable then, even if it was caused by the original publication, it would be unjust to make the defendant liable for any harm caused by that publication. If that is right, then regardless of whether a claimant relies on a republication as a cause of action or in aggravation of damages, a defendant would be entitled to meet the claim in respect of that publication with any relevant defence. That is not to say however that the original statement must be repeated word for word in the republication. Provided a media report of the initial publication conveys the sting of the original, in whole or in part, it may be relied on to increase the damages flowing from the initial publication even

---

[416] *Slipper v BBC* [1991] 1 Q.B. 283 CA.

[417] Ibid. at 296, per Bingham L.J. However, in *Kirby-Harris v Baxter* [1995] E.M.L.R. 516 CA, the plaintiff's claim was based on both (1) and (2).

[418] In both *Baturina v Times Newspapers* [2010] EWHC 696 (QB) at [53] and *Budu v BBC* [2010] EWHC 616 (QB) at [65] the judges suggested that the Court of Appeal in *Slipper v BBC* recognised implicitly that it would have been open to the claimant to sue in respect of the reviews in so far as they simply republished the words of the libel itself.

[419] But see *Cutler v McPhail* [1962] 2 Q.B. 292 CA (publication by D to editor of association journal and republication in journal; release of the claim against the journal released D as joint tortfeasor in respect of that publication; but a claim still lay in respect of the publication to editor and D was liable for the damage flowing from the republication). Criticised in *Timms v Clift* [1998] 2 Qd. R. 100 Qd CA at 108:

> "if, as was held, the plaintiff had no right to recover in respect of the cause of action for the second publication, that in the magazine, it is difficult to understand why the cause of action in respect of the first publication should have included a right to damages in respect of the second publication."

[420] [2010] EWHC 696 (QB) at [60] (rev'sd in part, *Baturina v Times Newspapers* [2011] EWCA Civ 308; [2011] 1 W.L.R. 1526. The Court of Appeal did not address this issue which was not the subject of the appeal).

[421] *Baturina v Times Newspapers* [2010] EWHC 696 (QB). This issue was raised in *Hays v Hartley* [2010] EWHC 1068 (QB) where it was argued by counsel that it was contrary to art.10 for the publisher of the original publication to be liable in damages for later publications where the re-publisher might have had a defence to any claim. Tugendhat J. noted that it was a "difficult issue" and that since he did not have to address it, it was better that he did not do so (at [67]).

if it cannot be said to "repeat" what was then said.[422] Moreover, there may be differences between the two for limitation purposes.[423]

It is clear that if the republication was by a person for whom the defendant is vicariously liable under the principles of master and servant or agency then the defendant is liable for that. Beyond this it may be that the original publisher should only be liable *as a publisher* of the republished statement where he authorised or intended it, but some of the cases speak in broader terms and assume that the same principles relating to the responsibility of the defendant apply to both situations.[424] In any event,

> "the law would part company with the realities of life if it held that the damage caused by publication of a libel began and ended with publication to the original publishee. Defamatory statements are objectionable not least because of their pro- pensity to percolate through underground channels and contaminate hidden springs."[425]

The question is essentially the same as that in any other tort case where it is sought to make the defendant liable for harm which is directly attributable to the voluntary act of a third person. That is a question of causation but it is not a pure question of fact, nor is the inquiry a value-free one: the "reality is that the court has to decide whether, on the facts before it, it is *just* to hold [the defendant] responsible for the loss in question."[426] No doubt it is still true that the starting point is that the defendant is prima facie not liable for the further damage,[427] because it is incumbent on the claimant to show that there is an adequate causative link between the tort and the damage, but subject to that, the defendant will be liable if he is actually aware that what he says or does is likely to be reported or if a reasonable person in his position should have appreciated that there was a significant risk that what he said would be repeated in whole or in part and that that would increase the damage caused by what he said.[428] For reasons of clarity it is better not to direct the jury in

---

[422] *McManus v Beckham* [2002] EWCA Civ 939; [2002] 1 W.L.R. 2982.

[423] So if the limitation period in respect of the original publication had expired that would bar a claim under that in respect of damage arising from the republication; but the limitation period might still be running in respect of the cause of action arising from the republication. See *Weaver v Beneficial Finance Co*, 98 S.E.2d 687 (Va., 1957); *Wiggins v Creary* 475 So.2d 780 (La., 1985). But see Defamation Act 2013, s.8.

[424] See, e.g. *Broxton v McClelland* [1995] E.M.L.R. 485 CA, where the claim was plainly based on the defendants' liability as publishers in respect of the republication by the intermediary. See also *Basse v Toronto Star Newspapers* (1983) 4 D.L.R. (4th) 381.

[425] Per Bingham L.J. in *Slipper v BBC* [1991] 1 Q.B. 283 CA at 300. See also, *Cairns v Modi* [2012] EWCA Civ 1382; [2013] 1 W.L.R. 1015 at [26]–[27].

[426] *McManus v Beckham* [2002] EWCA Civ 939; [2002] 1 W.L.R. 2982 at [39], per Laws L.J. (emphasis added). See also Waller L.J. at [34] ("just and reasonable result"). And see, *Budu v BBC* [2010] EWHC 616 at [59]–[80] (QB).

[427] *Ward v Weeks* (1830) 7 Bing 211; *McManus v Beckham* [2002] EWCA Civ 939 CA; [2002] 1 W.L.R. 2982 at [15]–[26].

[428] *McManus v Beckham* [2002] EWCA Civ 939 at [34] CA; [2002] 1 W.L.R. 2982; *Baturina v Times Newspapers* [2010] EWHC 696 (QB) at [55].

terms of reasonable foreseeability,[429] though as a matter of principle that is the underlying concept.[430]

The older cases on this topic tended to speak in terms of "natural and probable consequence".[431] While that formula may not have been intended to convey any different idea, it is open to the objection that it does not necessarily convey that the defendant must be aware of the risk of repetition.[432]

It is unlikely that this matter can be dealt with on an application to strike out: as a question of causation it is one for the jury[433] subject to the usual rule that there must be sufficient evidence for the issue to be left to the jury —though that issue in its turn might require findings of fact from the jury.[434] The Defamation Act 1996 provides a procedure for summary disposal or relief[435] but the court is unlikely to utilise this in favour of either party if there is an arguable issue of responsibility for republication.

Authority to repeat. Although one should now avoid any tendency to state **6.53** the law in rigid categories,[436] it may still be useful to recognise that there are certain situations in which it will very readily be held that the defendant is responsible for the consequences of further publications. In some cases the original publisher authorises or intends the republication. Thus if a person submits material to a newspaper[437] or tells a reporter a story defamatory of the claimant[438] without restriction on its publication,[439] makes statements at a press conference[440] or issues a press release,[441] he will be liable for the

---

[429] Ibid. at [34].

[430] Ibid. at [44]. And see *Slipper v BBC* [1991] 1 Q.B. 283 CA at 310, per Slade L.J. Cf. *Peters-Brown v Regina District Health Board* [1996] 1 W.W.R. 337 at 344.

[431] Or occurring "in the ordinary course of things": *Ratcliffe v Evans* [1892] 2 Q.B. 524 CA at 530.

[432] *McManus v Beckham*, above, at [43].

[433] *Slipper v BBC* [1991] 1 Q.B. 283 CA at 296, 300; *McManus v Beckham*, above, at [30].

[434] *Slipper v BBC*, above, at 296, 300.

[435] See para.30.18, below.

[436] *McManus v Beckham*, above, at [41].

[437] *Slipper v BBC* [1991] 1 Q.B. 283 CA; *Timms v Clift* [1998] 2 Qd. R. 100 Qd. CA; *Cock v Hughes* [2001] WASC 24 (radio interview).

[438] *Adams v Kelly* (1824) Ry. & M. 157; *Parkes v Prescott* (1869) L.R. 4 Ex. 169; *Richards v New South Wales* [2004] VSC 198 at [20]. Similarly a film company which distributes its films authorises their showing: *Kelly v Loew's Inc.*, 76 F.Supp. 473 (1948).

[439] E.g. "off the record": *Thomas v McMullan* [2002] BCSC 22 at [101]. In *Mahfouz v Brisard* [2005] EWHC 2304 (QB) the defendant granted a general licence to LED to publish a book, including in translation. LED then granted publication rights to T, excluding the UK. In an action in respect of copies circulated here, Tugendhat J. held that the restriction in the second agreement was concerned with intellectual property rights and, even though as a practical matter it would be likely to reduce the numbers of persons who read the book in the UK, it did not of itself prevent the defendant being liable for the publication of copies of the book in England. Whether the defendant foresaw or had reason to foresee publication in the libel sense in the UK would be a question of fact.

[440] *Sims v Wran* [1904] 1 N.S.W.L.R. 317; *Dato' Seri Tiong King Sing v Datuk Justine Jinggut* [2003] 6 M.L.J. 433 (political meeting).

[441] *Kirby-Harris v Baxter* [1995] E.M.L.R. 516 CA.

publication in the newspaper.[442] An express authority or request to publish is unnecessary.[443] Similarly, one who writes a libel in one edition of a newspaper knowing that it will be republished in other editions of that paper in other jurisdictions will be liable in respect of those too.[444]

6.54 Alteration of defamatory matter. Where it is alleged that the defendant is liable as a publisher, on the ground that he has authorised another to publish, he is not necessarily protected because the material has been altered. The correct principle is that:

> "where a man makes a request to another to publish defamatory matter, of which, for the purpose, he gives him a statement, whether full or in outline, and the agent publishes that matter, adhering to the sense and substance of it, although the language be to some extent his [the agent's] own, the man making the request is liable to an action as the publisher.[445] If the law were otherwise, it would in many cases throw a shield over those who are the real authors of libels, and who seek to defame others under what would then be the safe shelter of intermediate agents."[446]

The question is whether the defendant authorised the substance and the sting.[447] Hence the defendants were liable when they requested the press to publish an account of a meeting of a board of guardians and a condensed but correct account of the proceedings was published[448]; and the mere fact that the editor of a newspaper has struck out the stronger passages or altered the article in places will not affect the liability of the sender.[449] It would be otherwise if the alterations affected the sense of what the defendant had stated.[450] The mere furnishing by one person of some of the materials used by another in the preparation of a libellous article does not constitute a publication of it by the

---

[442] Clearly the same goes for the broadcast media. See, e.g. *Australian Consolidated Press v Bond* (1984) 56 A.C.T.R. 14; and see *Allan v Bushnell Television Co* [1969] 1 D.L.R. (3d) 534 (liability of feeder news service for broadcast by TV company).

[443] *Bond v Douglas* (1836) 7 C. & P. 626; *Hay v Bingham* (1905) 11 O.L.R. 148 Ont. CA; *Douglas v Tucker* [1952] 1 S.C.R. 275; *St Michael's Extended Care Society v Fort* [1994] 6 W.W.R. 718 and lxxi; *Stoneking v Briggs*, 62 Cal. Rptr. 249 (1967); *Australian Consolidated Press v Bond* (1984) 56 A.C.T.R. 14.

[444] *Whitney v Moignard* (1890) 24 Q.B.D. 630 CA. For repetition in *other* newspapers, see para.6.47, above.

[445] This sentence was cited with approval in *Boston v Bagshaw, The Times*, November 27, 1965 affirmed [1966] 1 W.L.R. 1126 CA.

[446] *Parkes v Prescott* (1869) L.R.4 Ex. 169 at 179, per Montagu Smith J.

[447] *Payton v Daily Sketch, The Times*, May 2, 1967. The same principle applies to broadcasts: *Boston v Bagshaw, The Times*, November 27, 1965; [1966] 1 W.L.R. 1126 CA.

[448] *Parkes v Prescott*, above.

[449] *Adams v Kelly* (1824) Ry. & M. 157; *Tarpley v Blabey* (1836) 2 Bing. N.C. 437; *R. v Cooper* (1846) 8 Q.B. 533; *Pierce v Ellis* (1856) 6 Ir.C.L.R. 55.

[450] *Tarpley v Blabey* (1836) 2 Bing. N.C. 440 at 442, 443; *Douglas v Tucker* [1952] I S.C.R. 275. Cf. *Wilson v Nooman* (1871) 27 Wis.R. 598; (1874) 35 Wis.R. 321 (translation). Indeed, the alteration by A of material which B has furnished so as to put B in a false light may defame him: *Carter v Gair* (1999) 170 D.L.R. (4) 204.

former if, when printed, the article as a whole is something very different from the material so furnished by him.[451]

Republication as a duty. The fact that the recipient of the defendant's   **6.55** initial publication was under a duty to convey the information to others also points towards liability, whether that duty is legal, social or moral. Where the plaintiff was treasurer of a charity and had prepared a list of subscribers and the defendant, whose name was not on the list, told persons that he had given the plaintiff contributions, the defendant was responsible for the publication by them to the president of the charity for it was their duty to pass on the information.[452]

> "Where an actual duty is cast upon the person to whom the slander is uttered to communicate what he has heard to some third person, as when a communication is made to a husband, such as, if true, would render the subject of it unfit to associate with his wife and daughters, the slanderer cannot excuse himself by saying: 'True, I told the husband, but I never intended that he should carry the matter to his wife.' In such a case ... the originator of the slander, and not the hearer of it,[453] is responsible for the consequences."[454]

He must, however, be aware at the time he published the words of the circumstances which give rise to the duty to repeat them.[455]

Examples where there is evidence[456] that republication should   **6.56** **have been within contemplation of defendant.** In *Slipper v BBC*[457] the statement of claim alleged that the defendants gave a private view to members of the press of a film which they broadcast a few days later and that reviews of this film in the press (which were likely to come to the attention of persons who had not seen the broadcast) repeated the sting of defamatory references to the plaintiff in the film. It was held by the Court of Appeal that these allegations provided a basis upon which the jury would be entitled to come to the conclusion that the defendants anticipated that there would be reviews and that they would repeat the sting.[458] The defendants in that case had clearly

---

[451] *Howland v Blake Manufacturing Co* (1892) 156 Mass.R. 543. See also *Klos v Zahorik* (1901) 113 Iowa R. 161.

[452] *Cooper v Warburton* (1931) 44 B.C.R. 328.

[453] I.e. the person who repeats the statement. Of course, the liability of the original publisher does not of itself relieve the republisher.

[454] Per Cockburn C.J. in *Derry v Handley* (1867) 16 L.T. 263 at 264.

[455] See, e.g. *Derry v Handley*, above (D told A that P, who was a dressmaker to A's wife, was a woman of immoral character, and A repeated the words to his wife, who thereupon ceased to employ P; held that D was liable, for he knew at the time he uttered the words that P was dressmaker to A's wife). Cf. *Speight v Gosnay* (1891) 60 L.J.Q.B. 231 CA.

[456] In some cases where the principle that the original publisher may be liable for the effects of a repetition has been accepted, the plaintiff has failed on the facts, e.g. *Lynch v Knight* (1861) 9 H.L.C. 577 and *Speight v Gosnay* (1891) 60 L.J.Q.B. 231 CA.

[457] [1991] 1 Q.B. 283 CA.

[458] If only because it would be impossible to review the film without recounting the basic story. None of the newspapers was sued. On the situation where a book is published in jurisdiction A and copies find their way to jurisdiction B see *Hunter v Gerald Duckworth Ltd* [2000] I.R. 510 and *Mahfouz v Brisard* [2005] EWHC 2304 (QB).

invited others to comment on what they had published[459] but this is not necessary. In *Baturina v Times Newspapers*[460] the claimant, a Russian businesswoman and wife of the former Mayor of Moscow, brought a libel claim against the defendant for their publication of an article which stated that she had purchased a large mansion in Highgate for £50m through an offshore company based in the British Virgin Islands and that she was planning to spend a further £50m renovating and extending the property. The claimant denied purchasing any such property and claimed that the articles defamed her in the eyes of readers who were aware of her declaration of assets made a few months previously in accordance with Russian anti-corruption legislation. Her declaration had not included this property. Unsurprisingly, the story was widely repeated and embellished in the Russian media. So far as the republications in the Russian media were concerned, Eady J. permitted her to sue in respect of republication of the articles by third parties in Russia where they merely repeated the allegations (category 4)[461] but not in respect of any republications to which a direct allegation of illegality had been added on the grounds that such re-publications constituted a *novus actus interveniens* (category 3).[462] In *McManus v Beckham*[463] the particulars of claim alleged that the defendant, the celebrity wife of a star footballer, entered the shop of the claimants, sellers of autographs, and "in a rude, loud and unreasonable way" advised the three customers present that the autograph on a photograph of her husband was a fake. This led to widespread newspaper and internet reporting of the incident, which the claimants complained of as causing them loss of trade as a result of the initial slander. The Court of Appeal reinstated the claimants' particulars alleging that the defendant was a person who courted the media, spoke for the protection of customers generally and knew that it was likely that reports of what she said would spread well beyond the confines of the shop into the media.

The relationship between the various persons involved may be important. Thus, where the defendant told the father of A, who was known to be engaged to marry the plaintiff, that the plaintiff had "a wife in the States", and the father repeated the statement to his daughter, in consequence of which the marriage was postponed until the plaintiff had vindicated his character, it was held that the repetition and the postponement of the marriage were the natural

---

[459] Quaere whether the preliminary press viewing was a necessary part of the plaintiff's case: any broadcast other than a news report would seem to invite review. However, it is thought that it is still the law that where a defamatory story is published in newspaper A the defendant is not without more liable in respect of republication of the story in other newspapers: *Basse v Toronto Star Newspapers* (1983) 4 D.L.R. (4th) 381. As a practical matter, however, it may be difficult to prevent the jury taking account of the general notoriety of a news story rather then simply awarding damages in respect of the publication by the defendant.

[460] [2010] EWHC 696 (QB). That aspect of the judge's order was not appealed to the CA ([2011] EWCA Civ 308, [2011] 1 W.L.R. 1526).

[461] Ibid. at [59] and [61].

[462] Ibid. at [60].

[463] [2002] EWCA Civ 939 CA; [2002] 1 W.L.R. 2982.

and probable consequence of the slander.[464] Again, where the defendant falsely told the plaintiff's father that the plaintiff had had a child by A, and the father repeated the words to A, who dismissed the plaintiff from her situation as governess to his children on the ground that it might be injurious to her character, and would be unpleasant to them both if she remained, it was held that the repetition of the words by the father was the legitimate and natural consequence of the original publication by the defendant.[465] Where a person submits information to a credit reference agency he must be taken to be aware of the likelihood of republication, for that is the function of the agency.[466]

Examples where no sufficient causative link. In *Parkins v Scott*[467] D **6.57** accused the plaintiff, a married woman, of unchastity, and the plaintiff voluntarily repeated the charge made against her to her husband, who refused to cohabit with her in consequence; it was held that such repetition was not the natural or probable consequence of the defendant's original publication. The issue of responsibility for republication arose in an indirect way in *Weld-Blundell v Stephens*.[468] A wrote a letter to his accountant B in which he libelled P1 and P2. B gave the letter to C, a colleague. C left the letter lying around and it was read by X. X communicated the contents to P1 and P2, who successfully sued A in libel. A then sued B in contract, alleging breach of a professional duty of confidence and claiming as damages the sums he had been ordered to pay P1 and P2. The majority of the House of Lords held that it was the independent, voluntary act of X which was the effective cause of the libel actions and A's claim for an indemnity therefore failed.[469] In *Campbell v News Group Newspapers Ltd*[470] the defendants published a defamatory story about the claimant. X, a freelance journalist who had supplied information to the defendants, also fed information to a television company, which ran a

---

[464] *Bordeaux v Jobs* (1913) 6 Alberta R. 400. The manner in which the initial publication takes place may be important. In *Broxton v McClelland* [1995] E.M.L.R. 485 CA, D sent the intermediary, a French speaker resident in a popular English holiday area of Spain and landlord of a bureau de change with which he was in dispute, an English translation of a notice defamatory of the bureau and P.

[465] *Gillett v Bullivant* (1846) 7 L.T. (O.S.) 490. See also *Friend v Civil Aviation Authority* [1998] I.R.L.R. 253 CA (republication of charges in disciplinary proceedings).

[466] *Schneider v United Airlines Inc.*, 256 Cal. Rptr. 71 (1989); cf. *Oberman v Dun & Bradstreet Inc.* 586 F.2d 1173 (CA 7 1978) (confidential information for subscribers only).

[467] (1862) 1 H. & C. 153; *Speight v Gosnay* (1891) 60 L.J.Q.B. 231 CA; *Merkoff v Pawluk* [1931] 1 W.W.R. 669.

[468] [1920] A.C. 956.

[469] Lord Sumner said at [1920] A.C. 986:
"It is quite plain that when [C] dropped the letter and found out his loss, the matter would have ended there but for the idle hands of [X]. He gave the letter a fresh start, and on his original impulse it came to be sued on."
In *Shendish Manor Ltd v Coleman* [2001] EWCA Civ 913, it was not the natural and probable consequence of a statement to one councillor that the statement would be repeated a year later to a business acquaintance of his who was not currently involved in the work of the council; *Cunningham v Essex CC*, June 28, 2000, (QB).

[470] [2002] EWCA Civ 1143; [2002] E.M.L.R. 43.

programme on the allegations. The defendants were not responsible for the damage done by the television programme.

6.58 Privileged occasion. If D, without malice, makes a statement to X on a privileged occasion and X repeats the statement to Y, again on a privileged occasion,[471] D has a defence in respect of both the original publication and the republication. The same is true where X is actuated by malice and therefore loses the protection of the privilege, for it is necessary to consider the state of mind of each defendant separately.[472] If X is unprotected because he repeats the statement on an occasion which is not privileged (e.g. because he republishes it more widely than is permissible) D should still be protected unless he requested the manner or scope of the publication by X.[473] If the statement by D to X was not on a privileged occasion but the republication by X was,[474] D is obviously liable in respect of the publication to X, but what is his position in respect of the republication by X? The difficulty is that if D is to be treated as a publisher on the occasion of the republication there is simply no wrong on that occasion. There is less difficulty where D is actuated by malice because then when X republishes he has the protection of privilege but D does not.

---

[471] As where a complaint is passed up the hierarchy of an organisation.

[472] See para.17.22ff, below.

[473] See *Willman v Dooner*, 770 S.W.2d 275 (Mo., 1988). It is submitted that in this context D should not necessarily lose the protection merely because he foresees that X may publish more widely than the occasion allows (e.g. because X is a notorious gossip): D's privilege will be based upon a duty or interest (see Ch.14, below) and he should not be hampered in discharging or protecting it because of what X may do. X may, e.g. be the only proper person to whom the allegation may be made.

[474] This is most likely to arise under one of the statutory privileges in Sch.1 of the Defamation Act 1996. The matter is discussed, though without a conclusive result, in *Belbin v McLean* [2004] QCA 181, where the claimant was relying on the second publication as increasing the damages in his suit arising from the first (i.e. she took the second course described at para.6.36, above) and where the second publication was protected by absolute privilege. Muir J. expressed the view that as a general rule the original publisher could shelter behind the defence available to the republisher and that he could see no reason why the defence was not capable of operation so as to meet a claim for damages "in respect of a publication" under the statute even if the effect of the defence is only to reduce the quantum of damages. However, *Erglis v Buckley* [2004] QCA 223; [2004] Qd. R. 599 (republication in Parliament) seems to proceed upon a different assumption, though this point was not in issue there and in later proceedings ([2005] QCA 404) it was held that the initial publication was protected by absolute privilege.

CHAPTER 7

IDENTITY OF THE PERSON DEFAMED

|---|---|---|
1. Reference to the claimant		7.1
2. Intention to refer to claimant		7.5
3. Claimant member of a class		7.9

SECTION 1. REFERENCE TO THE CLAIMANT

Words must be published "of the claimant". To succeed in an action **7.1** of defamation the claimant must not only prove that the defendant published the words and that they are defamatory: he must also identify himself as the person defamed. "No writing whatsoever is to be esteemed a libel unless it reflects upon some particular person."[1] "It is an essential element of the cause of action for defamation that the words complained of should be published 'of[2] the plaintiff'."[3] There is no cause of action, for instance, if words are defamatory of the claimant's relatives, unless they reflect on the claimant.[4]

It is usually clear enough that the words are published of the claimant because he is named in the statement and the defendant intends to refer to him, but neither of these elements is necessary.[5] The question in all cases is whether the words might be understood by reasonable people to refer to the claimant, subject to the qualification that where the words are published to persons who have special knowledge the issue will be decided by reference to what reasonable persons possessing that knowledge would understand by them.[6] However, it has been held in England that the defendant is not liable for an unintended reference caused by a photographic likeness.[7]

Although in most cases it is irrelevant, in establishing that the defendant is prima facie liable, that he did not intend to refer to the claimant (and may

---

[1] Hawk. P.C. Bk. 1, c.28, para.6, s.9.
[2] Or "of and concerning".
[3] *Knupffer v London Express* [1944] A.C. 116 HL at 120.
[4] See para.7.13, below.
[5] D publishes material which would be defamatory of C but C cannot be identified from it. C identifies himself as the subject to others. No actionable publication about C: *Scelfo v Rutgers University* 282 A.2d 445 (NJ 1971). Cf. *Craven v Hidding* [2004] TASSC 247 (prior identification).
[6] See para.7.3, below.
[7] See para.7.8, below.

never have heard of the claimant) this is qualified by the fact that in such cases he will have a defence if he makes a statutory offer of amends.[8]

7.2 Claimant need not be referred to by name. The test is whether the claimant may reasonably be understood to be referred to by the words. Thus, e.g. it is sufficient if he is described by a nickname,[9] his initial letters,[10] by photograph, drawing or caricature,[11] his office,[12] or by the first and last letter of his name,[13] or even by asterisks,[14] or blanks,[15] or if he is referred to under the guise of an allegorical, historical, fictitious or fanciful name,[16] or by means of a description of his status,[17] physical peculiarities,[18] or by a recognisable likeness[19] or caricature[20] or his residence,[21] the places which he has visited on his travels,[22] his products[23] or, indeed, if he is not mentioned at all; there need be no "peg or pointer" for his identification in the words complained of themselves.[24] Thus if there is a statement that X is illegitimate that is a

---

[8] First under s.4 of the Defamation Act 1952 and now under s.2 of the Defamation Act 1996: para.19.1, below.

[9] *Every Evening Printing Co. v Buller*, 144 F. 916 (CA 3 1906).

[10] *Roach v Garvan* (1742) 2 Atk. 469; *O'Brien v Clement* (1846) 16 M. & W. 159; *Hellar v Bianco* 244 P.2d 757 (Cal., 1952) (Christian name and telephone number).

[11] *Tolley v J.S. Fry & Sons Ltd* [1931] A.C. 333, 100 L.J.K.B. 328 HL.

[12] Thus, a reference to the President of the United States or the managing director of a named company would usually be sufficient to identify the current holder as the person referred to.

[13] *Hurt's Case* (1714) Selwyn's N.P. (13th edn) 989.

[14] *Bourke v Warren* (1826) 2 C. & P. 307.

[15] *Levi v Milne* (1827) 4 Bing. 195.

[16] *R. v Clerk* (1729) 1 Barn. 304. More difficulty arises where the claimant adopts a pseudonym and his real identity is not known. Thus few readers at the time will have been aware that George Eliot was Mary Ann Evans. It is arguable that in such a situation the claimant has two reputations: one under the publicly recognised pseudonym and another under his true identity as far as concerns people who know of his use of the pseudonym. In *John v MGN* [1997] Q.B. 586 CA, the plaintiff had adopted the name "Elton John" by deed, but even if he had not done so and had continued to use his real name in private life, his reputation as a performer would have existed under the name Elton John, not "Reg Dwight". In *Channel 7 Sydney Pty Ltd v Parras* [2002] NSWCA 202, Mason P., speaking of an entertainer who was known to the public by his stage name, said that if "defamatory matter was published of and concerning the plaintiff by his stage name then he should be able to recover damages without calling witnesses who know his private name". Normally a claimant has to sue in his true name (PD 7A, para.4.1(3)) but the court has power to allow him to sue under an alias where there is good reason (e.g. danger): *McNab v Associated Newspapers*, unreported, CA, May 17, 1996.

[17] *Grant v Cormier-Grant* (2001) 56 O.R. (3d) 215, Ont. CA.

[18] *J'Anson v Stuart* (1787) 1 T.R. 748.

[19] *Dwek v Macmillan Publishers Ltd* [2000] E.M.L.R. 284 CA (book); *Dojas v TCN Channel Nine Pty Ltd* [2001] NSWCA 398 (telecast).

[20] *Louka v Park Entertainments*, 1 N.E.2d (Mass., 1936).

[21] "The man who lives in that house is a paedophile" is actionable by the occupier even if he is a recluse whose name is unknown: *Channel 7 Sydney Pty Ltd v Parras* [2002] NSWCA 202.

[22] *Harrison v Smith* (1869) 20 L.T. 317.

[23] *Orion Pet Products Pty Ltd v Royal Society for the Prevention of Cruelty to Animals (Vic) Inc.* [2002] FCA 860.

[24] *Morgan v Odhams Press Ltd* [1971] 1 W.L.R. 1239 HL; *Sandison v Malayan Times* [1964] M.L.J. 332. See para.7.3, below.

sufficient reference to X's mother[25]; and where statements suggested that a man was married to, or free to, marry Y, C, his real wife, could sue on the basis that the statements cast a slur upon her.[26]

"The test of whether words that do not specifically name the claimant refer to him or not is this: Are they such as reasonably in the circumstances would lead persons acquainted with the claimant to believe that he was the person referred to?[27] That does not assume that those persons who read the words know all the circumstances or all the relevant facts. But although the claimant is not named in words, he may, nevertheless, be described so as to be recognised; and whether that description takes the form of a word-picture of an individual or the form of a reference to a class of persons of which he is or is believed to be a member, or any other form, if in the circumstances the description is such that a person hearing or reading the alleged libel would reasonably believe that the plaintiff was referred to, that is a sufficient reference to him."[28]

Thus a corporation may be defamed and its business damaged even though the persons to whom the words are published have no idea of its formal legal name[29]:

---

[25] *Morgan v Odhams Press Ltd* [1971] 1 W.L.R. at 1243. See also *Cassidy v Daily Mirror* [1929] 2 K.B. 331 at 338–339, per Scrutton L.J; *Hodgkins v Corbet* (1722) 1 Stra. 545: *Anderson v Stewart* (1851) Up.Can.Q.B. 243; *Solomon v Simmons, The Times*, April 10, 1954. See also para.7.13, below.

[26] *Cassidy v Daily Mirror* [1929] 2 K.B. 331 CA; *Hough v London Express* [1940] 2 K.B. 507 CA. See, however, *Solomon v Simmons*, above, where the plaintiff, daughter of the legitimate union, did not seek to argue that the inference was that her parents were not married and she was thus illegitimate, but rather argued (unsuccessfully) that those who knew of the illegitimate union would think that she was the offspring of it.

[27] Hence the fact that a mistake is obvious may prevent the reasonable reader drawing this conclusion: *Landsman v Tonawanda Pub Corp*, 558 N.Y.S.2d. 480 (1992).

[28] Per Isaacs J. in *David Syme v Canavan* (1918) 25 C.L.R. 234 at 238; *Lawrence v Newberry* (1891) 64 L.T. 797; *Shah v United African Press* [1961] E.A. 93; *Raul Amon International Pty Ltd v Telstra Corp Ltd* [1998] 4 V.R. 798 Vict. CA. Cf. the entertaining case of *Clark v Vare* [1930] N.Z.L.R. 430, where a placard with the legend "one Man one Trade one Wife" was held to be defamatory of a next-door trade rival who carried on business under the name "Uno" and lived apart from his wife and had a housekeeper who was living apart from her husband.

[29] *Channel 7 Sydney Pty Ltd v Parras* [2002] NSWCA 202; *Universal Communication Network t/as New Tang Dynasty v Chinese Media Group (Aust) Pty Ltd* [2008] NSWCA 1. In *Euromoney Institutional Investor plc v Aviation News Ltd* [2013] EWHC 1505 (QB) Tugendhat J. accepted that reference could be established even in the absence of knowledge of the corporate claimant's name on the part of the publishee (at [62]). The test to be applied in respect of such unnamed corporations was that set out by the editors of *Duncan & Neill on Defamation*, 3rd edn (London: Butterworths, 2009) at para.10.02:

"Where the publication relates to a business with a complex corporate structure care should be taken to bring the claim in the name of a company which (1) would be identified by reasonable readers as the subject of the allegations and (2) is apt to suffer damage to its own trading reputation as a result of the publication." (at [61]).

For a case where there was sufficient identification by the corporation number even though the name itself was incorrect, see *AIFME '97 Pty Ltd v Norley Pty Ltd* [1999] NSWCA 259. See also, *Islam Expo Ltd v The Spectator (1828) Ltd* [2010] EWHC 2011 (QB) in which Tugendhat J. held that though the words "Islam Expo" were the name both of the claimant corporation and of the events which the claimant corporation organised, a finding that "Islam Expo" referred to the claimant corporation would not be perverse and the words were therefore capable of referring to it.

"(A) person's reputation adheres to more than his, her or its name. It is an attribute of (legal) personality itself. It would be anomalous that, if it were said falsely that a David Jones store was riddled with cockroaches, David Jones Pty Ltd could recover substantial damages in defamation (if it were the owner) but ACN 346 Pty Ltd could not (if it were the owner) absent evidence that a reader knew the obscure name of the corporate owner of the well known business."[30]

However, where the words complained of do not specifically identify the claimant company and that company is one of several in a larger group with similar names, the claim may fail unless a reasonable person could think that the claimant company was sufficiently referred to[31] or that the words sufficiently identified all, or some of, the companies in the group.[32]

It is no bar to a claim that the work purports to be fiction if reasonable people could think the claimant was referred to.[33] No doubt it would be prima facie unreasonable to conclude that a character in fiction represented a real person rather than a type,[34] but everything depends on the facts of the case.[35]

7.3 Statement capable of referring to the claimant. The issue of identification is to be decided on the same principles as those which govern the question of whether the words are capable of a defamatory meaning.[36] Where the claimant is expressly identified by name, it is not necessary to produce evidence that anyone to whom the statement was published did identify the

---

[30] *Channel 7 Sydney Pty Ltd v Parras*, above at [49]; *Universal Communication Network Inc. v Chinese Media Group (Aust) Pty Ltd* [2008] NSWCA 1.

[31] Thus, in *Palace Films Pty Ltd v Fairfax Media Publications Pty Ltd* [2012] N.S.W.S.C. 1136 in which it was held that reference in the statement complained of to "Palace Films" was not enough, without resort to extrinsic facts, to establish sufficient reference to the plaintiff company. As any person with knowledge of the extrinsic facts would also have known that Palace Films Pty Ltd permitted the name "Palace Films" to be used in connection with film distribution to another corporate entity, Palace Enterprises Pty Ltd, which conducted the film distribution business discussed in the matters complained of, the particulars provided were not capable of identifying the plaintiff. See also *Craftsman Homes Australia Pty Ltd v TCN Channel Nine Pty Ltd* [2003] N.S.W.S.C. 124.

[32] See, for example, *Elite Model Management Corpn v British Broadcasting Corpn*, unreported, May 24, 2001 in which Eady J. allowed three companies forming part of the Elite Models Group to proceed to trial as a result of a documentary purporting to show that models under their care were sexually exploited. See further para.8.16, below.

[33] *Hulton v Jones* [1910] A.C. 20; *Bindeim v Mitchell*, 155 Cal. Rptr. 2d. 29 (1979). The usual disclaimer about "no resemblance to persons living or dead" is not conclusive, the issue is whether reasonable people could rationally suspect that the protagonist in the fiction is the claimant: *Geisler v Petrocelli*, 616 F.2d 636 (CA 2 1980).

[34] See *Flanders v Forrester, The Times*, January 31, 1912; *Seymour v Heinemann, The Times*, November 24, 1917; *Buckmaster v Wimperis, The Times*, April 30, 1921; *Montague v Hepworth, The Times*, May 11 and 12, 1921. Cf. *Youssoupoff v Metro-Goldwyn-Mayer* (1934) 50 T.L.R. 581 CA.

[35] See *Ross v Hopkinson, The Times*, October 17, 1956 (points of reference in novel so numerous as to go beyond coincidence).

[36] See paras 3.16, above, 32.18ff, below. This is to be inferred from the speeches in *Morgan v Odhams Press* [1971] 1 W.L.R. 1239 especially at 1243, 1264, 1269–1270. See also, *Islam Expo Ltd v Spectator (1828) Ltd* [2010] EWHC 2011 (QB) per Tugendhat J. at [6]; *Tilbrook v Parr* [2012] EWHC 1946 (QB) per Tugendhat J. at [9].

claimant. The question is not whether anyone *did* identify the claimant but whether persons who were acquainted with the claimant *could* identify him from the words used.[37] Thus if a local newspaper in Cornwall publishes a false story to the effect that "John Smith of 24 Acacia Avenue, Carlisle, has been convicted of fraud" that is actionable by John Smith even though no one who knew him read the story.[38] However, where a common name and no more is included in an article, the name itself will not suffice to identify any individual who bears that name, though the context in which the name appears, coupled with the name may, however, do so.[39]

Where the claimant is referred to in an indirect way or by implication it will be a question of degree how far evidence will be required to connect the libel with him.[40] At one extreme, if there is a libel on "the Prime Minister" that officer does not need to produce witnesses to testify that they know who he is.[41] At the other extreme, the claimant may only be identifiable by reason of extraneous facts which are not generally known, in which case there is no actionable publication unless it is shown that the words were communicated to persons with such knowledge.[42] Even in the latter type of case, however, it is not enough that the recipients of the statement did understand it to refer to the claimant: the issue is whether reasonable people with their knowledge would so understand it.[43]

It is uncertain whether there is any difference of principle between identifying a claimant by using his name and by publishing his photograph[44] without

---

[37] Cf. *Freer v Zeb* [2008] EWHC 212 (QB) at [47] (a case of slander where only the claimant's first name was used and the judge considered that there would be no publication to persons who did not know who was being spoken of; would the position really have been different if his full name had been used? But the greater modern willingness to strike out trivial claims as an abuse of process comes into the picture).

[38] The same is true where the identification is by description: *Grant v Cormier-Grant* (2001) 56 O.R. (3d) 215 Ont. CA ("uncle of X"). In *Multigroup Bulgaria Ltd v Oxford Analytica Ltd* [2001] E.M.L.R. 28, Eady J. said that he did not believe it could be seriously suggested that under English law an individual human being has to surmount a preliminary hurdle in order to bring defamation proceedings by showing an established reputation, i.e. he could sue even if he first came to readers' attention by the publication, provided he was sufficiently identified in it. The question of whether the claimant was lowered in the estimation of persons who knew him may, of course, be very relevant on damages. For pleading publication in the mass media, see para.26.5, below.

[39] *Jameel (Yousef) v Dow Jones & Co. Inc.* [2005] EWCA Civ 75; [2005] Q.B. 946 at [45]. See also *Carter-Clark v Random House Inc.* 793 N.Y.S.2d 394, affirming 768 N.Y.S.2d 290 (librarian in work of fiction purportedly seduced by Presidential candidate; plaintiff employee of library visited by Presidential candidate).

[40] For evidence on the reference issue, see generally paras 32.18–32.24, below.

[41] *Consolidated Trust v Browne* (1948) 49 S.R. (N.S.W.) 86 at 91; *Cross v Denley* (1952) 52 S.R. (N.S.W.) 112 at 116. Cf. *Bonighton v Nationwide News Pty Ltd* [2006] ACTSC 7.

[42] See para.32.19, below. See also para.26.26, below. For an example of such a case where the claim was dismissed as having no reasonable prospect of success, see *Mosley v Focus Magazin Verlag GmbH* [2001] EWCA Civ 1030.

[43] *Morgan v Odhams Press* [1971] 1 W.L.R. 1239. See para.32.19, below.

[44] It has been said that:

"when there is a question of recognition of a plaintiff from a visual image rather than from words, it is not possible adequately to put into words what are the matters known by people

his name.[45] One view is that the latter case involves an innuendo and that the claimant must therefore show that persons who knew him saw the photograph.[46] However, even on that basis, that conclusion may be arrived at by inference, as in the case where the publication is in a national newspaper with a wide circulation.[47]

7.4 Identification from other material. The general rule is that a statement is to be understood in the way in which a reasonable recipient would understand it at the time it is published: subsequent knowledge which makes the recipient look back on it in a different light will not make it defamatory.[48] Exceptionally, however, a subsequent publication may be introduced in evidence to establish identification. Thus, in *Hayward v Thompson*[49] it was held, in a case where the words in the first publication were defamatory on their face and the second publication that identified the plaintiff was published by the defendant, that reference could be made to a second publication in order to establish identification.[50] In *Chase v News Group Newspapers*[51] Eady J. refused to strike out a claim in which the claimant sought to establish identification from subsequent publications by third parties. In so doing, he indicated that it was not possible to lay down a bright line rule as to the circumstances in which the general rule could be departed from.[52] Nor did his lordship think that the only exception to the general rule was where the words were defamatory on their face and the subsequent publication was made by the defendant. Ultimately, whether evidence from subsequent publication should be allowed to establish identification in these cases depends upon a

---

acquainted with the plaintiff that enable them to identify the plaintiff from an image. Furthermore, mere acquaintance with a plaintiff is not really an adequate description of the qualification of the persons who must reasonably be able to identify the plaintiff. There are degrees of acquaintance, and plainly people who know a plaintiff very well indeed may reasonably identify that plaintiff from an image which would be inadequate for such identification by other persons who are merely acquainted with the plaintiff":
Dojas v TCN Channel Nine Pty Ltd [2001] NSWCA 398, per Giles J.A.
[45] Contrast *Marley's Transport Pty Ltd v West Australian Newspapers Ltd* [2001] WASC 31 (montage containing trucks in plaintiff company's livery).
[46] *Dwek v Macmillan Publishers Ltd* [2000] E.M.L.R. 284 CA at 291, per May L.J., approving Hunt J. in *Barbaro v Amalgamated Television Services* [1985] 1 N.S.W.L.R. 30. Contrast Sedley L.J. at 294.
[47] *Dwek v Macmillan Publishers Ltd* at 291, 294, where, however, all claims were allowed to go forward even though one related to publication in a book.
[48] *Grappelli v Derek Block (Holdings) Ltd* [1981] 1 W.L.R. 822 CA. See para.3.21, above.
[49] [1982] 1 Q.B. 47 (QB).
[50] See also, *Misir v Toronto Star Newspapers Ltd* (1997) O.A.C. 105; *Butler v Southam Inc.* [2001] NSCA 121; 197 N.S.R. 2d 97. So also, it seems, previous publications by the defendant or impending publications by another to which the defendant refers: *Baltinos v Foreign Language Publications* (1986) 6 N.S.W.L.R. 85. See further para.32.21, below. Whether *Grapelli* and *Hayward* are truly reconcilable, even though the first is about "meaning" and the second "identification" must be doubtful: see para.32.21, below.
[51] [2002] EWHC 2209 (QB).
[52] See also, *Ballantyne v Television New Zealand Ltd* [1992] 3 N.Z.L.R. 455 per Williamson J. at 462.

careful consideration of the facts of each case. Eady J. gave as examples where it may be possible to lead evidence from subsequent publications to establish reference, cases where it is possible to infer from the subsequent publications that the defendant intended to refer to the claimant and cases where the defendant starts a train of events the foreseeable consequences of which include the identification of the claimant.

SECTION 2. INTENTION TO REFER TO CLAIMANT

The common law rule: intention immaterial. At common law it is   **7.5**
immaterial that the defendant did not intend to refer to the claimant, or did not even know of his existence. The question is: Would the words complained of be understood by reasonable people who knew the claimant to refer to him? If so, they are published of, and concerning, the claimant, no matter what the intention of the defendant may have been.[53] In *Hulton v Jones*[54] the defendants published an article defamatory of a named person believed by the author and the editor to be a fictitious personage with an unusual name. The name was in fact that of the plaintiff, who had at one time been on the staff of the paper and had contributed signed articles to it, and was therefore known to the readers of the paper. Neither the author of the article nor the editor intended to refer to the plaintiff; indeed, they both swore that they did not know of his existence, and this was accepted as true by the plaintiff's counsel. The plaintiff called five witnesses who stated that they had read the article, and thought that it referred to him. Channell J. directed the jury that if they thought that reasonable people reading the article would think it referred only to a fictitious person, it was not actionable at all; but that, if they thought that reasonable persons who knew of the existence of the plaintiff would think that it referred to him, they ought to find for the plaintiff; and that it was immaterial whether the article was intended by the author or editor to refer to the plaintiff or not. The jury found for the plaintiff for £1,750 damages, and judgment was entered for that amount. This judgment was affirmed by the Court of Appeal (Fletcher Moulton L.J. dissenting) and by the House of Lords.

Same rule where statement true of X but false and defamatory of   **7.6**
C. A logical application of the law laid down in *Hulton v Jones* is—as

---

[53] *Hulton v Jones* [1910] A.C. 20; *Cassidy v Daily Mirror* [1929] 2 K.B. 331 CA; *Newstead v London Express* [1940] 1 K.B. 377 CA; *Lee v Wilson* (1934) 51 C.L.R. 276; *Richards v New South Wales* [2004] VSC 198; *Stelzer v Domm* [1932] 2 W.W.R. 139 Sask. CA; *Planned Parenthood Newfoundland v Federik* (1982) 135 D.L.R. (3d) 714. *Corrigan v Bobbs-Merrill Co*, 126 N.E. 260 (N.Y., 1920). However, constitutional developments in the US would seem now to require at least negligence by the defendant as to reference to the plaintiff: *New England Tractor-Trailer v Globe Newspaper*, 480 N.E.2d 1005 (Mass., 1985).
[54] [1910] A.C. 20. Mitchell, *The Making of the Modern Law of Defamation* (2005), Ch.5 attributes the decision to distrust of popular journalism.

Fletcher Moulton L.J. pointed out in the Court of Appeal[55]—to impose liability on a defendant who makes a statement true of A, but which, by an unfortunate coincidence, is equally descriptive of B, of whom it is false and defamatory. Moreover it has been so held in Australia,[56] and in England.[57] "If", said Sir Wilfrid Greene M.R., "there is a risk of coincidence, it ought, I think, in reason to be borne not by the innocent party to whom the words were held to refer but by the party who puts them in circulation."[58] In *Lee v Wilson*[59] there was a public inquiry as to charges of bribery against certain police officials at Melbourne, Victoria, and A gave evidence that "First Constable Lee of the Motor Registration branch" had accepted a bribe. The defendant newspaper reported A as having said that "Detective Lee" had accepted a bribe. There were in the Melbourne police three officers named Lee, one in the Motor Registration branch and two in the Detective branch. Each of the two detectives brought an action of libel against the newspaper and each called evidence of persons who understood the published matter to refer to him. The defendants tendered evidence to show that the words did not in fact refer to either of the plaintiffs but to another member of the police force

---

[55] [1909] 2 K.B. 444 at 471–472. Cf. Pollock, *Torts* (1929 edn), p.259n.:
"It seems to follow that if the same words may reasonably be understood by different persons to apply to A, B and C . . . there is no reason why A, B and C should not all have simultaneous and independent causes of action."
Cf. Holmes J. in *Hanson v Globe*, 159 Mass. 293 at 305 (1893):
"If an article should describe the subject of its statements by two sets of marks, one of which identified one man, and one of which identified another, and a part of the public naturally and reasonably were led by the one set to apply the statements to one plaintiff and another part were led in the same way by the other set to apply them to another, I see no absurdity in allowing two actions to be maintained."
[56] *Lee v Wilson* (1934) 51 C.L.R. 276. See also *Bruton v Estate Agents Licensing Authority* [1996] 2 V.R. 274, where the issue of identification was reserved for trial.
[57] *Newstead v London Express* [1940] 1 K.B. 377 CA, "Harold Newstead, 30-year-old Camberwell man, who was jailed for nine months, liked having two wives at a time". There were two persons named Harold Newstead living at Camberwell, of whom one (who was not the plaintiff) was convicted of bigamy. Held, by the Court of Appeal, that the fact that the words were true of another person did not afford a good defence to an action for defamation. The verdict was for one farthing. In *Murphy v Times Newspapers Ltd* [2000] 1 I.R. 522 the defendants wrote that one "SM" was involved in the IRA. This name was commonly used in the locality of two brothers of the name of M. The defendants were sued by M1 and the jury found that the words were true. They were also sued by M2, his brother and the argument that in view of the finding in the other action the defendants could not seek to show that the words were true was described as:
"wholly unsustainable. If the defendants are in the position that two plaintiffs in successive actions can satisfy the jury that an article, although clearly written about one person was capable of being understood, and was understood, to refer to each of the plaintiffs, the defendant is entitled to rely on whatever defences are open to him at law, including a defence in these proceedings that, although he never intended the words to refer to the plaintiff in these proceedings, they are nonetheless true concerning him, so far as the allegation of being a prominent member of the I.R.A. is concerned. That conclusion flows inevitably from the fact that the intention of the writer is immaterial when one is determining whether the words complained of are not only defamatory but were understood to refer to the particular plaintiff concerned":
Keane J. at 530.
[58] Ibid. at 388.
[59] (1934) 51 C.L.R. 276.

named Lee. The evidence was objected to and was rejected[60]; and judgment was given for each of the plaintiffs. The Full Court of Victoria held that the evidence was wrongly rejected and ordered a new trial. On appeal, it was held by the High Court of Australia that if words capable of referring to more than one person are found to defame each of them, each may recover, although the words may have been intended to refer to quite a different person. In their joint judgment Evatt and McTiernan JJ., assuming that in *Hulton v Jones* the publisher's intent was to refer to no existing person whatever, stated that:

> "the case is *a fortiori* where, as here, there is an admitted attempt to libel one person, but each of several groups of readers reasonably attributes the defamatory imputation to several other persons";

and Dixon J. said:

> "I am altogether unable to believe that the truth and honesty of the statements made about one man can be a criterion of liability to another whose reputation has actually been adversely affected by words capable of referring to him."[61]

Statutory defence. Though by no means solely concerned with the issue of reference to the claimant, it should be noted that a defendant may be able to take advantage of the "offer of amends" procedure under the Defamation Act 1996.[62] Such an offer must be to make and publish a suitable correction and apology and to pay such compensation (if any) as may be agreed or determined. However, a defence of offer of amends is not available where the   **7.7**

---

[60] Such evidence is admissible in mitigation of damages: see para.33.47, below. Cf. *Shaw v London Express* (1925) 41 T.L.R. 475, where in a fantastic claim for libel the trial judge, rightly it is submitted, dismissed the action at the close of the plaintiff's case on the apparent ground that no jury could reasonably find that the libel referred to the plaintiff, cf. a like ruling by Lord Hewart L.C.J. in *Lord v Croydon Advertiser, The Times*, March 2, 1935, and see *Thomson v McNulty*, 71 S.J. 744; *The Times*, July 29, 1927, HL, where the only question was whether the plaintiff in the action was entitled to have an issue approved to be put before the jury. Their Lordships decided on the principle of *Hulton v Jones* that the plaintiff was entitled to an issue. For an explanation of certain obiter dicta of Lord Dunedin in what is manifestly an imperfect report, see *Lee v Wilson*, at 295, 298; *Lambros v BBC, The Times*, June 27–28, 1935. And see 51 L.Q.R. 572–573.

[61] (1934) 51 C.L.R. 276 at 298, referring to Holmes J. in *Peck v Tribune Co*, 214 U.S. 185 (1909) and Lord Mansfield in *R. v Woodfall* (1774) Lofft at 781. D makes a public statement about X which is protected by the qualified privilege established by *Reynolds v Times Newspapers* (see para.15.1, below). By some extraordinary coincidence this can be reasonably understood to refer to C, of whom D was unaware. Does D have a defence against C? It might seem hard if he did not, since he is informing the public of matters in which they have a legitimate interest. The objective single meaning rule does not apply in this context for the purpose of determining whether D has complied with the standards of responsible journalism (see para.15.23, below) and identification is an aspect of meaning. On the other hand D is at liberty to follow what may be a fairly painless escape route against C by making an offer of amends. It was held that privilege would not apply in such a "mistaken identity" situation in *Rogers v Allen* (1989) 154 LSJS 95 (South Australia). In *Peek v Channel Seven Adelaide Pty Ltd* [2003] SASC 346 it was contemplated that the Australian version of the *Reynolds* privilege might nevertheless apply, though on appeal, [2006] SASC 63, it was held that there was no privilege because there was no "government or political matter" involved.

[62] See para.19.1, below.

defendant does not admit that the words complained of referred to the person making the allegation.[63] An offer to publish a suitable correction must refer to the person making the allegation and contain an acceptance that the original statement referred to that person: "A statement cannot be defamatory in the abstract. In my judgment 'a specific defamatory meaning' in s.2(2) must mean a specific meaning defamatory of the person making the allegation."[64] If a duly made offer is rejected it provides a defence to an action unless it is shown that the defendant knew or had reason to believe that the statement referred to was likely to be understood as referring to the claimant and was false and defamatory of him. "Had reason to believe" is not to be equated with "negligence".[65]

7.8 The European Convention on Human Rights. It has been held that the application of the common law rule of strict liability to the publication of a "look-alike" photograph would impose an impossible burden on the media and would infringe the guarantee of freedom of expression in art.10 of the European Convention on Human Rights.[66] The offer of amends procedure under the Defamation Act 1996 was not regarded as providing sufficient protection because it was not a defence in the strict sense. *Hulton v Jones* and *Newstead v London Express* were distinguished in that it was "theoretically" possible to have discovered the existence of the plaintiffs in those cases,[67] but despite the fact that the decision is concerned with photographic resemblance it seems likely that an attempt will be made to extend it to other cases. The view was expressed that the law of malicious falsehood would provide a sufficient protection for reputation in "look alike" cases.[68] However, a claim for malicious falsehood would require proof that the publisher knew that the photograph, although of someone else, would be likely to be taken as that of the claimant. In that event the reference would no longer be unintentional and it is difficult to see why the law of libel should not apply, bearing in mind the difficulties which the law of malicious falsehood might present for the claimant on damages.[69]

---

[63] *Club La Costa (UK) Ltd Plc v Gebhard* [2008] EWHC 2552 (QB).

[64] Ibid. per Tugendhat J. at [23].

[65] See para.19.6, below.

[66] *O'Shea v MGN Ltd* [2001] E.M.L.R. 40 (photograph in advertisement for pornographic internet services). Quaere, however, whether Morland J.'s decision that at common law a reasonable jury could have decided that the photograph was a sufficient reference to the claimant was not unduly generous to her. If the defendant publishes a defamatory article about "John Smith" that does not mean that anyone called John Smith can sue without more material to indicate that he is the person referred to. So also sensible people must be aware that close facial similarities are common.

[67] A better reason for distinguishing *Newstead* is surely that it would have been easy to tie the story to the convicted person by publishing his address.

[68] At [46].

[69] Except in cases falling within s.3 of the Defamation Act 1952 (which, it seems, would have been inapplicable in *O'Shea*) a claim may not be founded upon mere loss of reputation or distress: the claimant must show actual loss of a pecuniary nature (see para.21.13, below). Furthermore, there may be cases in which the defendant is unaware of the resemblance but clearly ought to be

SECTION 3. CLAIMANT MEMBER OF A CLASS

Words referring to a class. The criminal law contains a number of   **7.9**
offences of using threatening, abusive or insulting words or behaviour with
intent to stir up racial or religious hatred or which is likely to have this effect[70]
and this may include words which, if directed against an individual (and
published to a third party) would be civilly actionable. However, the civil law
of defamation does not allow an individual to sue in respect of words directed
only at a group.[71] Where the words complained of reflect on a body or class
of persons generally, such as lawyers, clergymen, publicans, or the like, no
particular member of the body or class can maintain an action.[72] "If", said
Willes J. in *Eastwood v Holmes*,[73] "a man wrote that all lawyers were thieves,
no particular lawyer could sue him unless there was something to point to the
particular individual". As this statement makes plain there is no special rule
about "class libel", it is simply a question of whether a reasonable reader
could conclude that the claimant as an individual was pointed at and the
broader the "class" the less likely this is.[74] The leading case is *Knupffer v
London Express Newspaper*[75] in which a war-time article accused a Russian
émigré group, "Mlado Russ", of being instruments of Hitler. The group
numbered 24 members in England and about 2,000 in the world and the
plaintiff was head of the British branch. Although four of the plaintiff's
witnesses said that their minds went to him when they read the article, the

---

aware of it and even the limited relief from being required to show actual damage provided by
s.3 is inapplicable to a claim for negligence.

[70] See, e.g. Pt III of the Public Order Act 1986, Racial and Religious Hatred Act 2006.

[71] There is an excellent account of the law in this area, with many useful illustrative cases, in
Eldredge, *The Law of Defamation* (1978), para.10.

[72] Cited with approval by Lord Mackey in *Campbell v Wilson* 1934 S.L.T. 249.

[73] (1858) 1 F. & F. 347 at 349. The actual decision concerned the sale of antiquities alleged to
be fakes and Lord Atkin in *Knupffer v London Express Newspaper* [1944] A.C. 116 doubted its
correctness on the "class" point. Similarly, in *Campbell v Ritchie*, 1907 S.C. 1097, Lord Ardwell,
while agreeing with the principle in *Wardlaw v Drysdale* (1898) 25 R. 879 that "intemperate and
foolish language directed against a class will not entitle an individual belonging to that class to
sue for slander in respect of such language", stated that he had "some difficulty in holding that
the words in *Wardlaw's* case did not sufficiently identify individuals so as to take that particular
case out of the category to which the doctrine applies".

[74] In *Orme v Associated Newspapers*, *The Times*, February 4, 1981, Comyn J., referring to the
speeches of Lords Atkin and Porter in *Knupffer v London Express Newspaper* [1944] A.C. 116,
said that "identifiability" would be more satisfactory as a classification or heading than "class
libel"; there would be sub-headings of generalisation, and then down the line, class libel. There
was no particular usage in "class libel" save that wide-ranging generalisations made individual
identification all the harder. S.10 of the Irish Defamation Act 2009 provides that where:
    "a person publishes a defamatory statement concerning a class of persons, a member of that
    class shall have a cause of action ... if—(*a*) by reason of the number of persons who are
    members of that class, or (*b*) by virtue of the circumstances in which the statement is published,
    the statement could reasonably be understood to refer, in particular, to the member con-
    cerned."

[75] [1944] A.C. 116.

House of Lords held that as a matter of law the words were incapable of referring to the plaintiff as an individual.[76] According to Lord Atkin, the:

"reason why a libel published of a large or indeterminate number of persons described by some general name generally fails to be actionable is the difficulty of establishing that the plaintiff was, in fact, included in the defamatory statement, for the habit of making unfounded generalisations is ingrained in ill-educated or vulgar minds, or the words are occasionally intended to be facetious exaggeration."[77]

There may also be a risk that discussion of matters of public concern may be inhibited if the law is too ready to hold that an individual is identified by an attack on a group.[78]

In the Supreme Court of Canada's decision in *Bou Malhab v Diffusion Métromédia CMR Inc.*,[79] Deschamps J. identified seven non-exhaustive factors that may provide guidance in determining whether some or all members of the group have been sufficiently referred to by the impugned statements. (1) *The size of the group.* Deschamps J. noted that the larger the group the less likely reference and/or damage will be established[80] but that the size of the group is not a decisive factor and must be balanced against other factors including the "intensity of suspicion"[81] that the comments could create in the

---

[76] Stable J. sitting without a jury, had awarded the plaintiff £3,500 damages.

[77] Cf. paras 3.36 and 3.37 (jest and vulgar abuse).

[78] In *Butler v Southam Inc.* [2001] NSCA 121; 197 N.S.R. 2d 97, Cromwell J.A. said at [75]:

"The allegations in the articles are concerned with the systemic failings of government. To permit a jury to reach the conclusion that these general statements refer to every one of the hundreds of employees at provincial institutions over 50 years and thus to these plaintiffs would, in my respectful view, pose an unacceptable risk of improperly stifling the sort of hard-hitting critique of government institutions which is at the core of constitutionally protected free speech. This consideration, too, supports the respondents' rather than the appellants' position."

However, certain allegations were held capable of referring to members of a small senior management group. See also *Ryckman v Delavan* 25 Wend. 186, at 1999 (NY, 1840).

[79] 2011 CarswellQue 383; 2011 SCC 9. The case was decided applying the Civil Law of Quebec but extensive reference was made to common law authorities. In considering whether liability could be established for a group libel, three specific rules of Quebec law were relevant. First, the claimant must have suffered personal injury, that is to say injury to reputation that was direct and personal. An objective test of damage to reputation is applied. Secondly, the claimant must prove he has a right to sue and this is possessed only by the "victim" of the interference. Thirdly, the defamation must have affected the claimant personally and not merely the wider group of which he is part.

[80] *Rowan v Cornwall (No.5)* [2002] SASC 160; 82 S.A.S.R. 152 at [480] (on appeal, sub nom, *Cornwall v Rowan* [2004] SASC 384; 90 S.A.S.R. 269). Note, however, that in *Orme v Associated Newspapers*, The Times, February 4, 1981 Comyn J. held that an article about the Moonies was capable of referring to the leader in England of that new minority religion. In that case, the grave charges must have been capable of referring to the plaintiff if only because people might say that he must have known what went on.

[81] Thus, in *Knupffer v London Express Newspapers Ltd* [1944] A.C. 116 Lord Porter said (at 124) that he:

"could imagine it being said that each member of a body, however large, was defamed where the libel consisted in the assertion that no one of the members of a community was elected as a member unless he had committed a murder".

Lord Porter would appear to have had in mind a case in which, because of the specific nature of the charge, it is more likely to be taken seriously than "all lawyers are thieves". Another way of

mind of a sensible person.[82] (2) *The nature of the group*. In general, the more strictly organised and homogenous the group the easier it will be to establish that the injury is personal to each member of the group.[83] Conversely, the imputing of a single characteristic to all members of a group that is highly heterogeneous, has no specific organisation or has flexible, broadly defined admission criteria would make an allegation of personal injury implausible.[84] (3) *The plaintiff's status, duties, responsibilities or activities in the group*. A person who is a well-known member of the group, of high rank within the group,[85] or someone who occupies a leading role[86] is more likely to suffer damage to his reputation as a result of comments made about the group.[87] (4) *The real target of the defamation*. The more general, evasive and vague the allegations, the more difficult it will be to go behind the screen of the group.[88] So too, where allegations apply to only one part of the group, it will be more

---

expressing the issue is to ask what is the intensity of suspicion cast on the individual member: *Butler v Southam Inc.* [2001] NSCA 121; 197 N.S.R. 2d 97 at [59] (this case contains a very full discussion of "group defamation"). In *Sauls v Hendrickse*, 1992 (3) S.A. 912 AD, a statement imputing behaviour to "office bearers" of an organisation was held not to refer to any individual; but the court said the case would have been different if the statement had referred to *all* the office bearers and possibly if it had referred to *the* office bearers. In *Botham v Khan, The Times*, July 15, 1996, CA, the words complained of were: "all the leading bowlers of the last 20 years . . . The biggest names in English cricket . . . I mean as big as you can get." However, the interlocutory appeal was solely on the question of whether the words were capable of being defamatory: para.3.15, above.

[82] 2011 CarswellQue 383; 2011 SCC 9 at [64].

[83] See, for example, *Jackson v TCN Channel 9 Pty Ltd* [2001] NSWCA 108 in which the New South Wales Court of Appeal found that the group's structure was a significant factor:

"While 'all lawyers' are members of the same profession, they are not members of a cohesive and disciplined group with a command structure such as a gang. The statement about 'all lawyers' is an obvious over-generalisation which no reasonable reader or listener would understand applied or was intended to apply literally to every single member of the group . . . On the other hand outlaw bike gangs of the type described in the programme would only attract and retain members who accepted and were willing to conform to the prevailing culture and ethos of the gang. In my judgment the statements made in this programme are akin to statements about organised groups such as the SS, the Klu Klux Klan or the Mafia, rather than statements such as: 'all lawyers are thieves'. It would be well open to a jury to conclude that general statements made about groups such as those applied, and would be understood to apply, to every member of those groups." (at [23]–[24]).

See also, *Butler v Southam Inc.* [2001] NSCA 121; 197 N.S.R. 2d 97 at [62]; *A.U.P.E. v Edmonton Sun* 1986 CarswellAlta 269 at 49.

[84] 2011 CarswellQue 383; 2011 SCC 9 at [66]. See, for example, *Zhang v Chau* 2008 QCC 961.

[85] *Booth v British Columbia Television Broadcasting System Ltd* (1982) 139 D.L.R. (3d) 88 (allegations made about narcotics squad officers "that are high up" had defamed two senior detectives but not nine lower-ranking employees of the narcotics squad.

[86] *Trahan v Imprimerie Gagné Ltée* [1987] R.T.R. 2417 (Que. S.C.).

[87] See, for example, *Fawcett Publications, Inc. v Morris* (1962), 377 P.2d 42 (U.S. Sup. Ct); *Trahan v Imprimerie Gagné Ltée* [1987] R.T.R. 2417 (Que. S.C.).

[88] Thus, in a French decision, the Cour de Cassation held that a document challenging right-wing extremism in general and associating it with criminal purposes was not defamatory because it 'contained no imputation or allegation about a specific natural or legal person.' (Cass. Crim. September 16, 2003, *Bull. Crim., No.161*).

difficult to reflect personally on all members of the group.[89] Where, however, though directed at a group, the words point at a particular individual,[90] reference will be more readily established. For this purpose the knowledge of the recipients of the statement about whom the defendant is aiming at is relevant. In *Le Fanu v Malcolmson* a newspaper article imputed that "in some of the Irish factories" cruelties were practised upon the employees, and the plaintiffs, who were the owners of a factory in Ireland, proved to the satisfaction of the jury that the newspaper was referring especially to their factory, the House of Lords refused to arrest judgment for the plaintiff. In giving judgment Lord Campbell said:

> "Where a class is described it may very well be that the slander refers to a particular individual. That is a matter of which evidence is to be laid before the jury, and the jurors are to determine whether, when a class is referred to, the individual who complains that the slander applied to him is, in point of fact, justified in making such complaint. That is clearly a reasonable principle, because whether a man is called by one name, or whether he is called by another, or whether he is described by a pretended description of a class to which he is known to belong, if those who look on, know well who is aimed at, the very same injury is inflicted, the very same thing is in fact done as would be done if his name and Christian name were ten times repeated."[91]

(5) *The seriousness or extravagance of the allegations.* As a general rule, the more serious or inflammatory the allegation, the more likely it is that reference will be established. However, where the most serious allegations are exaggerated, excessive, generalised or extravagant, that may lead to them being given less credence. Thus, where there is no rational connection between an allegation and the members of a group, the statements made will not be accepted by an ordinary person because, as Lord Atkin explained in *Knupffer*, "the habit of making unfounded generalizations is ingrained in ill-educated or vulgar minds [and] the words are occasionally intended to be a facetious exaggeration".[92] (6) *The plausibility of the comments and tendency to be believed.* "Generally speaking, a plausible or convincing allegation will capture the ordinary person's attention more and thus make it easier for that

---

[89] 2011 CarswellQue 383; 2011 SCC 9 at [72]. Deschamps J. noted however that a claim may still be brought by one, some or all members of the group in such a case, "since what is required is not certainty that the allegation relates to each member, but a suspicion that takes root in the mind of the ordinary person" (at [72]). See also, *Farrington v Leigh*, *The Times*, December 10, 1987.

[90] See the example in Eldredge, fn.71, above, of the person who defames surgeons as a class while glaring at an individual member of that profession. Of course a statement may make an attack on a class and specifically refer to the claimant at the same time: *Sykes v Fraser* (1974) 39 D.L.R. (3d) 321 SCC; *Christchurch Press v McGaveston* [1986] 1 N.Z.L.R. 610 NZCA, but in *Fullerton v Thompson* 143 N.W. 260 (Minn., 1913) the plaintiff recovered in respect of an attack on a board of which he was a member even though the article included a list of members without his name.

[91] (1848) 11 H.L.C. 637 at 668. See also *Marr v Putnam*, 246 P.2d 509 at 519 (Or., 1952); *Taylor v Massey* (1891) 20 O.R. 429 Ont. CA.

[92] [1944] A.C. 116 at 122.

person to connect the allegation with each or some of the group's members personally. Conversely, the ordinary person will quickly brush aside implausible allegations without connecting them with the group's members personally."[93] (7) *Extrinsic factors*. Other factors, related to the maker or target of the comments, the medium used and the general context may be relevant.[94] Thus where there have been previous incidents between the claimant and defendant this may be a highly relevant factor in determining reference.[95] Ultimately, however, the court should not conduct a compartmentalised analysis[96] but should instead ask whether, in light of all the circumstances and taking the specific context in which the statements were made into account a reasonable person would conclude that the claimant was sufficiently referred to.

Examples: sufficient reference. A very early case offers a plain example   **7.10** of a sufficient reference to the claimant. In *Foxcroft v Lacey*[97] a suit was pending against one Foxcroft and 16 other persons and, a discourse being had concerning the suit, Lacey said: "These defendants helped to murder H.F.". It was held that this charge was "sufficient to entitle every one of the defendants to a several action as if they were specially named".[98] Similarly, where the plaintiff was a member of a jury, and the defendant in a newspaper article pronounced the verdict of the jury to be "infamous", and added that "we cannot express the contempt which should be felt for those twelve men who have thus not only offended public opinion, but have done injustice to their oaths", it was held that the plaintiff could maintain an action.[99] Where the defendant, commenting in his newspaper on the proceedings of a presbytery in deposing a minister for intemperance, insinuated that the members of the presbytery were themselves so given to excess that it was unbecoming in them to take the proceedings, it was held that each member of the presbytery was

---

[93] 2011 CarswellQue 383; 2011 SCC 9 at [76].

[94] Ibid. at [78].

[95] *Assoc. des Policiers de Sherbrooke v Delorme* [1997] R.J.Q. 2826 (Que. S.C.).

[96] 2011 CarswellQue 383; 2011 SCC 9 at [79].

[97] (1614) Hobart 89.

[98] In *Riches v News Group Newspapers* [1986] 1 Q.B. 265 CA, a charge against the "Banbury C.I.D." (consisting of 12 officers) was held at the trial to refer to all 10 plaintiffs. This issue was not the subject of appeal. So too, in *Mapp v News Group Newspapers Ltd* [1998] Q.B. 520; [1997] E.M.L.R. 397 there was no dispute that allegations against ex-colleagues of a police sergeant who had killed himself were actionable at the instance of eight officers (at 406). The issue on appeal was meaning. See also *Aiken v Police Review Publishing Co* (unreported, April 12, 1995), CA (27 officers in dog handling squad); *Farrell v Triangle Publications, Inc.* 159 A.2d 734 (U.S. Pa. SC. 1960) (article accused 13 municipal commissioners of criminal behaviour of a scandalous nature).

[99] *Byers v Martin*, 25 Am.Rep. 755 (Colo., 1875). See the similar case of *Le Roux v Cape Times* [1931] C.P.D. 316, distinguished in *Visser v Wallach's Printing Co* [1946] T.P.D. 441; and *McKay v Southam Co. Ltd* [1956] I D.L.R. (2d) 1, where a newspaper columnist, in attacking capital punishment by a figurative arraignment of society for the "murder" of an accused sentenced at a recent trial, referred to the jury "who planned the murder"; this was held not simply an attack on society in general but defamatory of each juror.

entitled to an issue in an action.[100] In an extreme example, decided under the Civil Law of Quebec, but referring to common law cases, the defendant, in a lecture delivered in the City of Quebec, violently assailed and abused the Jewish race, its religious doctrines and social practices, the object being to put the public of Quebec on guard against the Jews of Quebec, who numbered only 75 families in a total population of 80,000 souls. It was held that although not assailed individually, the plaintiff being one of the "restricted collectivity" of the Jews of Quebec was entitled to maintain an action of defamation against the defendant.[101]

7.11 Examples: insufficient reference.[102] Where comments of an alleged defamatory character were made upon an association called the Ancient Order of Hibernians, it was held that an individual member of the order, who was not named, nor in any way referred to, could not maintain an action of libel[103]; and where an article alleged that saleswomen (of whom there were 382) were call girls, claims brought by 30 of them were dismissed.[104] So too, in *Bou*

---

[100] *McPhail v Macleod* (1895) 3 S.L.T. 91. Cf. *Fawcett Publications v Morris* (1962) 377 P.2d 42 (1 out of 60 or 70); *Farrell v Triangle Publications* (1960) 399 Pa.102 (1 out of 13); *Shah v Uganda Argus* [1970] E.A. 362 (1 out of 10); *Dasani v Uganda African Newspapers* [1971] E.A. 450 (1 out of up to 9); *Cobbett-Tribe v Zambia Publishing* (1973) Z.R. 19 (1 out of 7); *AUPE v Edmonton Sun* (1986) 49 Alta. L.R. (2d) 141 (all guards in a prison); cf. *Butler v Southam Inc.* [2001] NSCA 121, 197 N.S.R. (2d) 97; *Trahan v Imprimerie gagné Ltée* (1987) 44 C.C.L.T. 33 SCC (attack on fur traders; plaintiff with semi-monopoly in trade); *Hyams v Peterson* [1991] 3 N.Z.L.R. 648 (member of group of 29 persons known as the "gang of 20"). *Taylor v Network Ten (Perth) Pty Ltd* [1999] WASC 264 (charge against council capable of referring to all members); *Bryant v Nationwide News Pty Ltd* [1999] N.S.W.S.C. 360 (school class of 26); *Bacon v Hansch* [2001] TASSC 42 at [78] (13 members of committee); *DHKW Marketing v Nature's Farm Pte Ltd* [1999] 2 S.L.R. 400 (distributors and sellers of drug); *Balakrishnan v Nirumalan K Pillay* [1999] 3 S.L.R. 22 Sing. CA (10 members of organising committee of Tamil Language week). In *Browne v Thomson*, 1912 S.C. 359, 7 Roman Catholic clergymen defamed as a group were held to be referred to and this was said by Lord Mackay in *Campbell v Wilson*, 1934 S.L.T. 249, to have gone "as far as the law may safely go". Sed quaere, since the issue cannot depend simply on numbers.

[101] *Ortenburg v Plamondon* (1914) 24 Quebec K.B. 69. Taken considerably further under the law of Québec in *Malhab v Metromedia CMR Montreal Inc.* (2003) 226 D.L.R. (4th) 772 Québec CA (class action allowed on behalf of 1,000 Arab and Haitian taxi drivers). See also *Prud'homme v Prud'homme* 2002 SCC 85; [2002] 4 S.C.R. 663 and compare, under the common law, *Kenora (Town) Police Services Board v Savino* (1997) 20 C.P.C. (4th) 13 Ont. CA. Manitoba law makes a collective race libel civilly actionable but only for an injunction: *Courchene v Marlborough Hotel Co* (1972) 22 D.L.R. (3d) 157 Man. CA.

[102] Somewhat optimistic claims which failed are *Elliott v Canadian Broadcasting Corp* (1993) 108 D.L.R. (4th) 385 (one of 25,000 survivors of Bomber Command); *McCann v Ottawa Sun* (1993) 16 O.R. (3d) 672 (mayor of town of 13,500, behaviour of fans at hockey match had been criticised); *Gintert v Howard Publications Inc.*, 565 F.Supp. 829 (1983) (inhabitants allegedly defamed by disparaging comments on environmental conditions in the area); *Mann v Medicine Group Pty* (1992) 38 Fed. Ct. R. 400 (criticism of bulk-billing doctors of whom 18,000); *Yahong Bai v Sing Tao Daily Ltd*, May 20, 2003 Ont. CA (Falun Gong adherents numbering 100m).

[103] *O'Brien v Easson* (1913) 47 Ir. L.T. 266; *Knupffer v London Express* [1944] A.C. 116; *Aiken v Premier of Ontario* (1999) 177 D.L.R. (4th) 489 (advertisements attacking teachers' industrial action); cf. *Lennon v Premier of Ontario* (1999) 45 O.R. (3d) 84 ("union bosses").

[104] *Neiman-Marcus v Lait* (1952) 13 F.R.D. 311 (N.Y.); but the claims of 15 salesmen out of 25 suing on an allegation that "most of them are fairies" was allowed to proceed.

Malhab v Diffusion Métromédia CMR Inc.[105] the Canadian Supreme Court held, Abella J. dissenting, that a class action for libel by Arabic and Creole speaking Montreal taxi drivers in respect of seriously insulting, racist and defamatory statements made about Montreal taxi drivers was not maintainable. The court noted that the relevant group of taxi drivers was about 1,100 strong, the group was heterogeneous, the remarks were subjective in tone and the defendant was a well-known polemicist. Deschamps J. explained the position thus:

> "In light of these factors, ... an ordinary person would have understood the extravagant nature of the comments made. [The defendant's] allegations were undoubtedly serious and infuriating, but an ordinary person would nonetheless have recognized that they were an excessive generalization on the part of the host, based on an unpleasant personal experience. An ordinary person would not have believed the offensive allegations and would not have thought that [the defendant] was vouching for the validity of his racist and contemptuous insults. An ordinary person certainly would not have associated the allegations of ignorance, incompetence, uncleanliness, arrogance and corruption with each taxi driver whose mother tongue is Arabic or Creole personally."[106]

A statement that "office bearers of N.A.A.W.U." were behind unrest in schools was, following *Knupffer's* case, held insufficient to identify the plaintiff officers[107]; a poster attacking the fur trade was held incapable of referring to any member of the trade[108]; and where some hundreds of buildings in a town had been burned, a statement that arson had become common in the town in order to claim insurance money was held incapable of referring to two plaintiffs whose buildings had been burned.[109]

Words incapable of referring to whole group. If a statement would be capable of referring to the members of a group as individuals, what is the position where it is plain that the charge is made against only one, or some, but not all of the group?[110] This could arise in an extreme form if the defendant said, "Either A or B stole my watch". Where a statement indicated that at least two of a team of seven police officers had acted dishonestly it was held arguable, for the purposes of striking out, that each member of the team

7.12

---

[105] 2011 CarswellQue 383; 2011 SCC 9.

[106] Ibid. at [90].

[107] *Sauls v Hendrickse* 1992 (3) S.A. 912 AD; *Aiken v Premier of Ontario* (1999) 177 D.L.R. (4th) 489 (advertisements attacking teachers' industrial action). A police officer had no claim in respect of an allegation that the force was infected with "systemic racism": *Gauthier v Toronto Star Daily Newspapers Ltd* (2004) 245 D.L.R. (4th) 169 Ont. CA. See also *Friends of Falun Gong v Pacific Cultural Enterprise Inc.* 288 F.Supp. 2d 273 (E.D.N.Y. 2003), affirmed 109 Fed. Appdx. 442.

[108] *A. Neumann CC v Beauty Without Cruelty International*, 1986 (4) S.A. 675.

[109] *Grainger v Time Inc.*, 568 P.2d 535 (Mont., 1977).

[110] Graphically illustrated by *Blaser v Krattiger*, 195 P. 359 (Or., 1921). P was sitting with 25 men and D said, "Someone has stolen $1,000 worth of my jewellery from my bedroom, and I know who it is and the son of a bitch sits here in this room". P failed. See also *Arcand v Evening Call*, 567 F.2d 1163 (1977).

had a cause of action[111]; and in South Australia it has been held that a statement referring to one of four commissioners is capable of referring to any of them,[112] but the contrary has been held in New South Wales,[113] as unless the statement refers to *all* of them (which it plainly does not) then in the absence of any identifying evidence,[114] it is incapable of bearing the imputation that any particular *one* of them did the act charged. This is logical, though it means that it may be easy to escape liability by scattering the charge more widely and may make the liability depend on the form of the libel rather than its substance.[115]

It is undoubtedly defamatory[116] to say of a person that he is suspected of wrongdoing[117] (though less so than if he is said to be guilty) and an accusation of wrongdoing against one or some of a small group may be as damaging[118] as a statement that they are all under suspicion, but it is difficult to apply this to our situation because the suspicion about the claimant is not directly stated by the defendant but is an inference stemming entirely from the reader.[119] However there may be situations in which such an accusation is actionable on the separate ground that it imputes to the claimant association with persons guilty of wrongdoing.[120]

---

[111] *Farrington v Leigh, The Times*, December 10, 1987, CA, doubting *Sir John Browne's Case, Jones v Davers* (1597) Cro.Eliz. 496; *James v Rutlech* (1599) 4 Co.Rep. 17; *Falkner v Cooper* (1666) Carter 55; *Harrison v Thornborough* (1714) 10 Mod. 196; and *Chomley v Watson* [1907] V.L.R. 502.

[112] *Pryke v Advertiser Newspapers* (1984) 37 S.A.S.R. 175 Full Court. But the point seems not to have been argued: *Cornwall v Rowan* [2004] SASC 384; 90 S.A.S.R. 269 at [563], where a statement that "some staff" at a shelter had harassed inmates could not be read as referring to all staff. See also *Hardy v Williamson*, 22 S.E. 784 (Ga., 1890); *Sin Cho Chiu Charles v Tin Tin Publication Development Ltd* [2001] 1196 HKCU 1: claimant one of seven members of delegation "most" of whom were "tainted"—capable of referring to claimant.

[113] *McCormick v John Fairfax & Sons* (1989) 16 N.S.W.L.R. 458, not following *Pryke* and distinguishing *Bjelke-Petersen v Warburton* [1987] 2 Qd. R. 465 on the ground that the court was not there concerned with the nature of the slur cast. Distinguished in *Vitale v Bednall* [2000] WASC 207, as a reader could have understood the words to mean that each member of the small group had indulged in the conduct charged. See also *Owens v Clark*, 6 P.2d 755 (Ok., 1932).

[114] Which might take the form of the circumstances in which the words were published.

[115] *Farrell v Triangle Publications Inc.*, 159 A.2d 734 (Pa., 1960). The position would be different if D intended to refer to P and the recipients knew that: see para.7.9, above. Where neither A nor B is specifically indicated, it has been said that either A or B has an action if he can prove that the words were spoken falsely of him and that the other did not commit the offence: see *Harrison v Thornborough* (1714) 10 Mod.196; *Albrecht v Burkholder* (1889) 18 O.R. at 291.

[116] But a slanderous statement of suspicion of crime is not actionable per se: see para.4.9, above.

[117] *Lewis v Daily Telegraph* [1964] A.C. 234 HL. See para.3.28, above.

[118] In *Forbes v Johnson* (1850) Ky. 48 at 50, it was said that an accusation against one of two "is equivalent to the assertion that it is as probable as not that each is guilty".

[119] *McCormick v John Fairfax & Sons* (1989) 16 N.S.W.L.R. 458, disagreeing with Spencer Bower, *Actionable Defamation*, 2nd edn, p.12.

[120] *McCormick v John Fairfax & Sons* (1989) 16 N.S.W.L.R. 458; *Aiken v Police Review Publishing Co* (unreported, April 12, 1995), CA. See also *Cornwall v Rowan* [2004] SASC 384; 90 S.A.S.R. 269.

Reference by association. There are cases in which a statement which is   **7.13**
directly defamatory of A may be regarded as also carrying a defamatory
reference to B because of B's connection with A.[121] So to say that A is a
brothel keeper is also defamatory of A's spouse, who lives on the premises.[122]
Where it is stated that a "family" company is insolvent, this may be capable
of bearing the defamatory imputation that directors of the company have
permitted it to trade[123] in this condition.[124] There are two issues: (1) Does the
statement about the company refer to the directors?[125] (2) Is the statement
defamatory of the directors?[126] As to the first issue, the same does not
necessarily apply to directors, and particularly non-executive directors, of
large companies.[127] In the case of governmental entities the point has gained
importance since it has been held that they do not have standing to sue for
defamation[128] for fear that would inhibit free discussion of political matters.
Too great a readiness to hold that defamatory statements about a council or a
department impliedly defamed its senior officers would risk outflanking this
protection. In a Canadian case it was held that an article accusing the
Canadian and US governments of being accomplices in bringing about a
miscarriage of justice by suppression of evidence, was not capable of a
defamatory reference to counsel acting for the US government because the
ordinary reader would have read the article as an attack on the governments
and the extradition laws and not on counsel (who was not named).[129] However, there will be cases in which the inference will be irresistible that the

---

[121] It will be necessary, except where the matter is notorious, to show that the words were
published to persons who knew of the connection between A and B: *Consolidated Trust Co. v
Brown* (1948) 49 S.R. (N.S.W.) 86 NSWCA and para.7.3, above.

[122] *Huckle v Reynolds* (1859) 7 C.B. (N.S.) 114. The words were said directly of the *wife*, who
in 1859 would have been more subordinated to the husband than now, but now it is thought it
would be equally defamatory of the wife if said directly of the husband. But a husband had no
right of action for words which imputed that his wife was a prostitute: *Finburgh v Moss' Empires*,
1908 S.C. 928; a man's children had no right of action for words which imputed that they had to
be placed in a charitable institution owing to the neglect occasioned by their father's drunken
habits: *Knox v Spencer* (1922) 50 N.B.R. 69; and it was not defamatory to describe the plaintiff
as brother of a communist: *Pogany v Chambers*, 137 N.Y.S.2d 828 (1955); *Livingstone-Thomas
v Associated Newspapers* (1969) 90 W.N.(Pt. I) (N.S.W.) 223.

[123] But it does not impute anything about the directors' personal solvency.

[124] *Aspro Travel Ltd v Owners Abroad Group Plc* [1996] 1 W.L.R. 132 CA.

[125] It was common ground in the *Aspro Travel Ltd* case that it did. See also *Woodger v Federal
Capital Press of Australia* (1992) 106 F.L.R. 183; *Bashford v Information Australia* [2000]
N.S.W.S.C. 665, on appeal on other issues, [2004] HCA 5; 204 A.L.R. 193 (director and company
"one and the same"); *Harding v Essey* [2005] WASCA 30. For the question of whether statements
about directors refer also to the company, see para.8.17, below.

[126] Stuart Smith L.J. was doubtful on this issue since the allegation against the company was
simply that it was insolvent and insolvency of the company because of matters beyond the
directors' control was not a charge that would be defamatory of directors. However, he decided
to allow the action to go forward because of the absence of any exculpatory words in the
statement about the company. In *Kaplan v Go Daddy Group Inc.* [2006] N.S.W.S.C. 250 an
imputation about quality of service given by employees of company was capable of reflecting on
proprietor.

[127] *Aspro Travel Ltd v Owners Abroad Group Plc* [1996] 1 W.L.R. 132 CA at 136.

[128] *Derbyshire CC v Times Newspapers* [1993] A.C. 534: see para.8.20, below.

[129] *Halprin v Sun Publishing Co* [1978] 4 W.W.R. 658.

words refer to an individual employed by the person directly named by the words. For example, to say that "the financial affairs of the University of X have been allowed to fall into chaos" would be defamatory of the finance director and perhaps of the Vice-Chancellor.[130]

---

[130] This example is accepted in *Chee v Minister for Home Affairs* [2005] SGHC 216; [2006] 1 S.L.R. 582 (not a libel case). Note, however, the decision of Eady J. in *Duke v University of Salford* [2013] EWHC 196 (QB) in which he struck out a claim brought by a University because there was no real or substantial tort so far as the university was concerned as the libellous allegations focussed on the conduct of academic staff rather than the university itself.

PARTIES: WHO MAY SUE AND BE SUED

SECTION 1. GENERAL

(a) *Right to sue*

General rule. The general rule is that any natural or juristic person (except **8.1**
a governmental entity) may sue for defamation: particular cases are discussed
in the following sections.

An action for defamation is a purely personal action. The proper person to
sue as claimant is the person defamed, and the proper person to be sued as
defendant is the person who published the defamatory words or caused them
to be published (though this may include a person vicariously liable for
another). A cannot bring an action of libel or slander against B for words
defamatory of C,[1] even though C has purported to assign to him his right of

---

[1] But words directly defamatory of C may also be defamatory by implication of A: see
para.7.13, above.

action; a right of action for damages for libel or slander cannot be assigned.[2] If A suffers damage as a result of a defamatory statement maliciously made about C, who is associated with A's business, A may have an action for malicious falsehood,[3] but that is not the same thing as an action for defamation.

Where several persons are jointly injured by a libel or slander they may all join as co-claimants in an action, but it is not necessary that they should do so; any one of them may sue without joining the others.[4]

(b) *Liability*

8.2 Who may be sued. Any natural or juristic person may be sued for defamation, subject to the qualifications (e.g. as to diplomatic agents or foreign sovereigns) which are general to the law of torts. Since the Crown proceedings Act 1947 there appears to be no obstacle in principle to an action for defamation being brought against the Crown, though none is known to have succeeded.[5]

Where several persons are jointly concerned in the publication of a libel they may all be joined as co-defendants, or any of them may be sued separately.[6] If the claimant elects to sue one of them separately, it is no defence that others are jointly liable with him, nor will such fact mitigate the damages recoverable.[7] Judgment against the one defendant will not bar the claimant from bringing an action or actions against any other person or persons who joined in the publication which produced the damage; but the claimant will not be entitled to the costs of any such subsequent action unless the court is of opinion that there was a reasonable ground for bringing it.[8]

---

[2] *Trendtex Trading v Credit Suisse* [1982] A.C. 679; *May v Lane* (1894) 64 L.J.Q.B. 236 at 238, *Dawson v G.N. Ry* [1904] 1 K.B. 281; *Defries v Milne* [1913] 1 Ch. 98 at 109. It has been held to be arguable in Canada that where there is a libel on a corporation, which can only affect its goodwill, then,

"although the [claim is] . . . nominally personal, because [its] effect is a business effect only, an assignee can have the type of interest in the claim that can be assigned, if it is shown at trial that there is no champertous aspect or effect of the assignment":

PSC Industrial Services Canada Inc. v Ontario (Ministry of the Environment) (2005) 258 D.L.R. (4th) 320. The rule does not prevent an assignment of the damages if and when recovered in such an action, even though the assignment is made before the action has commenced or before judgment has been recovered: *Glegg v Bromley* [1912] 3 K.B. 474.

[3] See *Riding v Smith* (1876) 1 Ex.D. 91: *Knox v Spencer* (1922) 50 N.B.R. 69, and Ch.21, below.

[4] For consolidation of separate actions, see para.33.53ff, below.

[5] But in Canada claims have been brought against the Canadian Broadcasting Corporation as an agent of the Crown: *Lougheed v CBC* (1978) 86 D.L.R. (3d) 229; *United Assn. etc. v CBC* (1979) 97 D.L.R. (3d) 56.

[6] For consolidation see para.33.53ff, below.

[7] See para.33.58, below.

[8] See para.35.60, below.

Section 2. Diplomatic Agents and Foreign Sovereigns

(a) *Right to sue*

Generally. A diplomatic agent (an ambassador or member of the mission) **8.3**
has the same right to sue for defamation as any other person present in
England, but if he does initiate proceedings that precludes him from invoking
his diplomatic immunity[9] in respect of any counterclaim directly connected
with the principal claim.[10] As the Crown cannot sue for defamation in any
circumstances[11] it is arguable that the same rule applies to the government of
a foreign sovereign state.[12] There was no express limitation imposed by the
House of Lords in *Derbyshire CC v Times Newspapers* to UK institutions and
there is much to be said for prohibiting foreign states from suing because of
the desirability of allowing free and uninhibited discussion of their actions and
also because of their ready access to the media to correct any inaccuracies
published about them.

(b) *Liability*

Diplomatic agents. A diplomatic agent, that is the head of a mission or a **8.4**
member of the diplomatic staff who has been accepted or received here,[13] is
immune from civil jurisdiction, except in three cases, none of which is likely
to be relevant to libel and slander.[14] This applies generally to all torts[15] and is
an immunity from suit rather than from liability.[16] It therefore subsists only

---

[9] See para.8.4, below.

[10] Diplomatic Privileges Act 1964, Sch.1, art.32(3); cf. *High Comr for India v Ghosh* [1960]
1 Q.B. 134 CA, where the counterclaim was for an unrelated slander.

[11] *Derbyshire CC v Times Newspapers* [1993] A.C. 534. See para.8.20, below.

[12] But the reasoning in *Derbyshire* rests largely upon the importance of free public criticism of
government. It does not necessarily follow that the same considerations apply to matters in
foreign states.

[13] The immunity from suit also extends to: the family of a diplomatic agent (Diplomatic
Privileges Act 1964 (DPA), Sch.1, art.37(1)); members of the administrative and technical staff
of the mission, together with members of their families (DPA Sch.1, art.37(2)) members of the
service staff of the mission (DPA Sch.1, art.37(3)); and, private servants of members of the
mission (DPA Sch.1, art.37(4)). However, their immunity is more limited than that of a diplomatic
agent in that if any person falling within the latter three categories is a national or permanently
resident in the receiving state no immunity attaches as of right and any immunity is at the
discretion of the receiving state (DPA Sch.1, art.38(2)). Moreover the immunity will only attach
to members of the mission staff where they are acting within the course of their duties.

[14] Diplomatic Privileges Act 1964, s.2(1), Sch.1, art.31(1). The only exception which could
possibly be relevant is that of an action relating to a professional or commercial activity by the
agent outside his official functions. There are a number of other provisions dealing with
diplomatic immunity. See, e.g. the Commonwealth Secretariat Act 1966, the Consular Relations
Act 1968, the Diplomatic and other Privileges Act 1971; and the International Organisations Acts,
1968, 1981 and 2005.

[15] See Clerk and Lindsell, *Torts*, 20th edn (2010), Ch.5, s.4.

[16] As to art.6(1) of the European Convention on Human Rights, see para.8.5, below.

until he leaves the country, or for a reasonable period in which to do so after his functions end, but it continues to have effect even after his duties have ceased "with respect to acts performed by [him] in the exercise of his functions as a member of the mission".[17] The immunity may be waived by the head of the mission or the sending state.[18] Independent of diplomatic immunity is the public policy, arising out of the comity of nations, which will lead an English court to refrain from examining disputes which are properly within the sphere of a foreign state, as for instance an alleged libel in an embassy document.[19] This may be applicable even if the immunity has been waived.

8.5 Foreign states. The liability of foreign states is governed by the State Immunity Act 1978.[20] The immunity of a foreign state is no longer absolute and general as it once was at common law. In particular, it does not apply to any transaction or activity (whether of a commercial, industrial, financial, professional or other similar character) into which a state enters or in which it engages otherwise than in the exercise of sovereign authority.[21] While a government of a state and any department of that government are treated as if they are the state,[22] an entity which is distinct from the executive organs of the government of the state and capable of suing and being sued is immune from the jurisdiction if and only if the proceedings relate to anything done by it in the exercise of sovereign authority and the circumstances are such that a state would have been so immune.[23] The foreign state is entitled to claim immunity

---

[17] Diplomatic Privileges Act 1964, Sch.1, art.39(2).

[18] Ibid. art.32(1) and (2). But where the defendant is head of a mission, a defence formulated on his behalf qua individual litigant is not the correct vehicle for the renunciation of the immunity, which belongs to the foreign sovereign: *Fayed v Al-Tajir* [1988] Q.B. 712 CA. For the effect if the diplomat initiates proceedings, see para.8.3, above.

[19] *Fayed v Al-Tajir* [1988] Q.B. 712 CA. The case also deals with the question of privilege in such cases: see para.13.27, below. *Komarek v Ramco Energy* [2002] EWHC 2501 (QB) (double actionability rule).

[20] See Clerk and Lindsell, *Torts*, 20th edn (2010), Ch.5, s.4. The non-contractual liability of the European Communities under art.215 of the EEC Treaty is a matter for the Court of Justice of the Communities: art.178. In Case C-201/89, *Le Pen v Puhl* (1990), the plaintiff brought an action in a French court in respect of an allegedly defamatory pamphlet distributed in the premises of the European Parliament in France. The ECJ held that the acts of a political group in the Parliament could not be imputed to the Parliament as an institution of the Communities and held that it had no jurisdiction to hear the action simply on the basis that the act complained of took place on Parliament premises.

[21] State Immunity Act 1978 (SIA) s.3(1)(a), (3)(c).

[22] SIA s.14(1)(b) and (c). The head of state and his family and household are equated with the head of a diplomatic mission: s.20.

[23] SIA s.14(2). *Grovit v de Nederlandsche Bank* [2005] EWHC 2944 QB; [2006] 1 Lloyd's Rep. 636 (appeal on another issue, [2007] EWCA Civ 953; [2008] 1 W.L.R. 51) (the Central Bank of the Netherlands, an autonomous administrative authority and part of European system of central banks, and two of its employees were held to be covered by state immunity in respect of an allegedly malicious libel published in the course of the bank's business). An allegation of malice in a libel claim does not prevent the invocation of this immunity: [2005] EWHC 2944 QB; [2006] 1 Lloyd's Rep. 636 at [66].

for its servants or agents and the immunity of the state cannot be circumvented by suing them.[24]

In *Holland v Lampen-Wolfe*[25] the claimant, an American university professor seconded to an American forces base in England to provide a course in international relations for military personnel, sued for libel in a memorandum written by the defendant, a civilian officer of the United States Department of Defense, reporting criticisms of her performance and questioning her competence. The defendant applied to have the proceedings set aside, contending that they impleaded a foreign sovereign state and were covered by state immunity both at common law and under the State Immunity Act 1978. The House of Lords upheld the dismissal of the claim for the following reasons:

(1) The publication of the memorandum was an act done "in relation to" the armed forces of a state under s.16(2) of the 1978 Act, a matter excluded from the operation of Pt I of the Act. Accordingly, the case fell to be dealt with under the common law.

(2) The educational course was provided *jure imperii* (i.e. in the exercise of the state's sovereign authority) since in modern conditions the provision of education for military personnel was a normal part of the maintenance of armed forces, and the immunity at common law therefore applied.

(3) The immunity is part of, and required by, public international law and prevailed over the guarantee of access to the courts under art.6 of the European Convention on Human Rights.

Lord Millett would also have held, had it been necessary to do so, that even if Pt I of the 1978 Act had not been disapplied by s.16(2) there would still have been immunity under the Act. Although the contract between the United States and the plaintiff's employers was of a "commercial" nature, the proceedings did not "relate to" the contract under s.3(1)(a); and if (which he thought unlikely) the production of the memorandum was an "activity" within s.3(3)(c) it was still immune because the act was performed in the exercise of sovereign authority. In *Grovit v de Nederlandsche Bank*[26] immunity was applied to a Central Bank and its employees in respect of statements impugning the trustworthiness of the claimant directors.[27]

---

[24] *Jones v Saudi Arabia* [2006] UKHL 26; [2007] 1 A.C. 270 (not a libel case).

[25] [2000] 1 W.L.R. 1573 HL.

[26] [2005] EWHC 2944 QB; [2006] 1 Lloyd's Rep. 636.

[27] The alternative ground for the decision, that the claim was not a "civil matter" for the purposes of Council Regulation (EC) 44/2001, is the only matter dealt with by the CA, which upheld the decision: [2007] EWCA Civ 953; [2008] 1 W.L.R. 51.

The European Court of Human Rights has subsequently considered sovereign immunity and art.6 of the European Convention on Human Rights and has held that in such cases art.6 is engaged because the immunity creates a "procedural bar"[28] but that since it is based on a generally recognised principle of public international law it cannot be regarded as a disproportionate restriction on the right of access to a court for the purposes of art.6.[29]

Section 3. Foreign Subjects and Companies

8.6 Capacity to sue or liability to be sued. With regard to capacity to sue or liability to be sued, a foreign subject is generally subject to no disability and entitled to no immunity. However, where he is abroad when sued, or where the tort is committed abroad, there are issues of jurisdiction and choice of law which are considered elsewhere.[30] Persons domiciled in states with which this country is at war are "alien enemies" and cannot generally sue here during hostilities.[31] The same principles apply to foreign companies, though there are special provisions as to service.

Section 4. Bankrupts and Insolvent Companies

(a) *Right to sue*

8.7 Generally. Upon bankruptcy the estate of the bankrupt vests in the trustee in bankruptcy. This means the bankrupt's property, which is defined so as to include[32] "things in action".[33] Furthermore, the trustee may claim property acquired by the bankrupt after the commencement of the bankruptcy. The effect of this is that the bankrupt ceases to have an interest in either his assets or his liabilities except in so far as there may be a surplus to be returned to him upon his discharge.[34] However,

> "there are certain causes of action personal to the bankrupt which do not vest in his trustee. These include cases in which 'the damages are to be estimated by immediate

---

[28] Cf. Lord Bingham in *Jones v Saudi Arabia* [2006] UKHL 26; [2007] 1 A.C. 270 at [14].
[29] *Al-Adsani v United Kingdom* App. no.35763/97; ECHR 2001-XI.
[30] See Ch.24, s.3, below.
[31] See the 8th edition of this book, para.927.
[32] With certain exceptions such as books, clothing or items for the bankrupt's personal use.
[33] Insolvency Act 1986, s.436.
[34] *Heath v Tang* [1993] 1 W.L.R. 1421 CA, at 1423 per Hoffmann L.J.

reference to pain felt by the bankrupt in respect of his body, mind, or character, and without immediate reference to his rights of property'".[35]

On this basis it has been held or stated in a number of cases that a bankrupt can sue for defamatory words published before or after his adjudication,[36] and such damages as he may recover will not belong to his trustee.[37] "The trustee can maintain no action for libel, although the injury occasioned thereby to the man's reputation may have been the sole cause of his bankruptcy,"[38] nor can the trustee obtain an order directing that the damages be paid to him, nor prevent the bankrupt, if he has got the damages, from spending them in the maintenance of himself or his family.[39] If, however, the bankrupt has invested the money in the purchase of property, the trustee may be entitled to the property.[40] However, the older cases either do not examine the issue very closely or proceed upon assumptions about the nature of a cause of action which are not consistent with those now prevailing.

Damages for defamation may include both elements for actual and potential pecuniary loss and for "injury to feelings".[41] In *Wilson v United Counties Bank*[42] (an action for injury to credit and reputation arising from failure to supervise the bankrupt's business during his absence on military service) the view was expressed that:

"the negligence of the defendants gave rise to two distinct causes of action, the one consisting of injury to the bankrupt's estate, the other personal and consisting of injury to his character, credit and repute; the first passing to his trustee, the second remaining vested in himself."[43]

However, the modern view is that in such a case there is only one cause of action with different heads of damages. So where the bankrupt brings an action for personal injuries and recovers damages for (1) loss of amenities and

---

[35] Ibid., citing *Beckham v Drake* (1849) 2 II.L.Cas. 579 at 604, per Erle J. and *Wilson v United Counties Bank Ltd* [1920] A.C. 102. In *Vaidya v General Medical Council* [2010] EWHC 984 (QB) Sir Charles Gray accepted that a claim in defamation was a personal one but held that claims in malicious falsehood and negligent misstatement were not and accordingly they passed to the claimant's trustee in bankruptcy (at [54]–[55]).

[36] *Benson v Flower* (1630) W. Jones 215; *Howard v Crowther* (1841) 8 M. & W. 601; *Beckham v Drake* (1849) 2 H.L.C. 579; *Dowling v Browne* (1854) 4 Ir.C.L.R.265; *Rose v Buckett* [1901] 2 K.B. 449 CA; *Wilson v United Counties Bank* [1920] A.C. 102. In *Kordowski v Hudson* [2011] EWHC 2667 (QB) Tugendhat J. acknowledged that a bankrupt had a right to sue in slander but noted that "since bankruptcy may mean that a claimant does not have to decide whether or not the costs of proceedings are proportionate to the reputational issues and financial risks involved, the court is more likely to have to make that decision itself, in the exercise of its case management powers, in accordance with the Overriding Objective (CPR Part 1)" (at [5]). See also the Scottish case of *Ewing v Times Newspapers Ltd* [2008] CSOH 169.

[37] *Ex p. Graham, re Job* (1870) 21 LT. 802; *Ex p. Vine* (1878) 8 Ch. D. 364 CA.

[38] Per Alderson B. in *Howard v Crowther* (1841) 8 M. & W. 601 at 604.

[39] *Ex p. Vine* (1878) 8 Ch D. 364 CA.

[40] Ibid.

[41] See para.9.4, below.

[42] [1920] A.C. 102 HL.

[43] [1920] A.C. 102 HL at 119 and 131, per Viscount Finlay and Lord Atkinson.

pain and suffering and (2) loss of earnings, the cause of action vests in the trustee but he holds the damages under (1) on constructive trust for the bankrupt.[44] However, in such a case the damages under the two heads will be awarded separately,[45] whereas in the typical defamation case, at least if tried by jury, there will probably be one global award of general damages. Indeed, it would be difficult or impossible even for a judge sitting alone to separate out those elements of the general damages which relate to the injury to the claimant's feelings and those which relate to pecuniary harm which has occurred or may occur, because the latter element may be unquantifiable. The better view, therefore, is probably that the trustee has no claim on any part of the damages awardable to a natural person for a libel.

(b) *Liability*

8.8 Generally. Formerly, claims for unliquidated damages for tort were not provable as bankruptcy debts, but this was altered by the Insolvency Act 1986[46] so that there is no remedy against the person or property of the bankrupt.[47] The same is true in the case of insolvent companies.[48] Claims in respect of a defamatory statement published after the commencement of the bankruptcy may be brought against the bankrupt personally, but if proceedings for bankruptcy are pending or an individual has been adjudged bankrupt, the court may stay any action against the property or person as the court thinks fit.[49]

In some cases defendants may carry insurance against liability for defamation. Under the Third Parties (Rights Against Insurers) Act 1930, in the event of the insured becoming bankrupt or being wound up, the rights of the insured against the insurer are transferred to the claimant. The claimant therefore stands in the shoes of the insured and if the insured has been wound up before

---

[44] *Ord v Upton* [2000] Ch. 352 CA.

[45] But see *Re Kavanagh; Ex p. the Bankrupt v Jackson (The Trustee)* [1949] 2 All E.R. 264 CA, a case of a settlement by the bankrupt of her claims for breaches of confidence and contract leading to injury to her reputation and credit and to her business. Jenkins L.J. was of the view at 268 that:

"if there is a sum which is apportionable between the two heads of claim and if there is no evidence to show in what particular shares it should be apportioned, the only possible solution is to make the apportionment equally between the two heads of claim."

[46] Insolvency Act 1986, s.382 and SI 1986/1925, r.12.3(1).

[47] Insolvency Act 1986, s.285(3).

[48] See SI 1986/1925, r.13.12.

[49] Insolvency Act 1986, s.285(1), (2). In practice, there is little point in bringing a claim in defamation against a bankrupt except to prevent repetition of the libel. See, for example, *The Law Society of England and Wales v Kordowski* [2011] EWHC 3185 (QB) in which perpetual injunctions were granted against the publisher of the website "Solicitors from Hell" requiring him to cease its publication and restraining him from transferring it to anyone else or from publishing any similar website.

its liability has been established it will be necessary to seek the restoration of the insured to the register of companies.[50]

Section 5. Minors

Capacity. The capacity of a minor to sue for defamation is governed by the **8.9** ordinary rules of the law of torts. From a procedural point of view a minor must sue by a litigation friend unless the court directs otherwise[51] and damages must be dealt with as the court shall direct.[52] Infancy as such is no defence to defamation any more than to any other tort, though in practice what a very young child says will not reasonably be understood as defamatory and he will lack the requisite mental capacity for malice. A minor will defend an action by a litigation friend.[53]

Section 6. Married Persons

Capacity. The special common law treatment of married women with **8.10** regard to civil actions disappeared in 1935.[54] Now, as a result of the Law Reform (Husband and Wife) Act 1962,[55] marital status has no effect upon capacity to sue or liability to be sued for defamation and a wife may sue her husband for defamation of her (and vice versa). However, a defamatory statement by one spouse to another about a third party does not amount to a publication of the statement,[56] but each can be sued in respect of defamatory matter which he or she has published to a third party, and if the publication is a joint publication, they can be made co-defendants. Although a husband may be liable for the publication of defamatory matter by his wife if, for example he authorised the publication, a husband is not by reason only of the marriage liable for his wife's torts no matter when they were committed.[57] A husband

---

[50] Companies Act 2006, s.1030.

[51] See CPR r.21.2(2).

[52] See CPR r.21.11.

[53] See CPR r.21.2(2).

[54] Law Reform (Married Women and Tortfeasors) Act 1935, s.1.

[55] Which abolished a rule to the effect that spouses could not sue each other in tort during marriage. Until the 1962 Act neither spouse could, even after divorce, sue each other for defamation during marriage: *Phillips v Barnet* (1876) 1 Q.B.D. 436. However, where any action in tort brought by one spouse against the other during the subsistence of the marriage the court may stay the action if it appears that no substantial benefit would accrue to either party from the continuation of the proceedings: s.1(2). The Civil Procedure (Modification of Enactments) Order 1998, SI 1998/2940, para.4 repealed s.1(3), requiring the court to consider a stay at an early stage of the proceedings. However, s.1(2) remained untouched, so the power to order a stay still exists.

[56] See para.6.14, above.

[57] Law Reform (Married Women and Tortfeasors) Act 1935, s.3.

and wife who have been defamed have independent causes of action, and if both have been defamed in the same publication, they may be co-claimants, but neither can sue a third party for defamation of the other.

Section 7. Deceased Persons and Representatives

(a) *Right to sue*

8.11 No defamation of the dead. A defamatory statement about a person who is dead when it is made does not give rise to a civil action for defamation on behalf of his estate,[58] no matter how malicious the statement.[59] Nor is it possible to obtain a declaration to vindicate the deceased's reputation and his relatives have no claim unless the words used reflect on their reputations.[60]

8.12 Defamation of person who subsequently dies. The general rule is that where a deceased person had a cause of action in tort at the date of his death

---

[58] The position is the same in Scotland, even though the law is there different with regard to defamatory words used while the person was alive but in respect of which he has not recovered judgment at the time of his death: see the Faulks Committee, paras 424–426, Cmnd.5909 (1975) and the Damages (Scotland) Act 1976, s.2 (as substituted by the Damages (Scotland) Act 1993). A Consultation Paper (*Death of a Good Name—Defamation and the Deceased: A Consultation Paper*) (*www.scotland.gov.uk/Publications/2011/01/11092246/4*) was issued in 2011 to consider the question whether additional protections could reasonably be developed in order to deter and, where necessary, to provide redress in response to false posthumous allegations. By the Irish Defamation Act 2009, s.39(2), amending s.7 of the Civil Liability Act 1961, a cause of action for defamation vested in a person immediately before his death shall survive for the benefit of his estate but "the damages recoverable for the benefit of the estate of that person shall not include general damages, punitive damages or aggravated damages". The matter of the death of the person about whom the words are published is now specifically dealt with in the uniform Australian legislation. See, e.g. s.10 of the NSW Defamation Act 2005:

"A person (including a personal representative of a deceased person) cannot assert, continue or enforce a cause of action for defamation in relation to: (a) the publication of defamatory matter about a deceased person (whether published before or after his or her death)."

[59] The matter (including the associated issue in the next paragraph) has been considered by committees on several occasions, most recently (and most fully) by the Supreme Court Procedure Committee under Neill L.J. (1991) which recommended no change. Cf. the Faulks Committee, Cmnd.5909 (1975) para.423(b) (action for declaration by relatives within five years of death). An amendment that was moved by Helen Goodman MP during the Committee Stage of the Defamation Act 2013 would have allowed a dead person's spouse or partner, relatives, siblings or children to sue the publisher of a defamatory article up to 12 months after the death but this was rejected. The position is not necessarily the same in a claim framed as breach of confidence/ misuse of private information: *Bluck v Information Comr* EA/2006/0090, September 17, 2007, Information Tribunal (application under Freedom of Information Act 2000).

[60] However, if the statement was (a) known to be false and (b) intended to cause and (c) did cause illness to, say, the deceased's widow, all the elements of the principle of *Wilkinson v Downton* [1897] 2 Q.B. 57 are arguably present. Of course, the burden of proof on all these issues would be on the claimant.

the claim survives for the benefit of his estate.[61] However, this does not apply to claims for defamation,[62] which therefore represent the last relic of the common law rule that *actio personalis moritur cum persona*. The rule does not apply to malicious falsehood,[63] even though since 1952 pecuniary damage is presumed and need not be proved in some cases.[64] If the deceased commenced an action for defamation before death the action abates,[65] even if special damage has accrued to the claimant's estate.[66]

(b) *Liability*

General rule. Here, too, the rule *actio personalis moritur cum persona* is **8.13** followed: no action can be commenced against the estate of a deceased defamer and if the defendant dies before verdict the action abates.[67] Neither rule affects claims against other persons liable for the publication (e.g. the employer of the person who created the libel).[68] It has been held in America that an action will lie against an executor in his representative capacity for damages for a libel contained in the probate of a will, the maxim *actio personalis moritur cum persona* not applying, since the right of action did not exist in the lifetime of the testator.[69] Such a case has never arisen in England.[70]

---

[61] Law Reform (Miscellaneous Provisions) Act 1934, s.1.

[62] Ibid.

[63] *Hatchard v Mêge* (1887) 18 Q.B.D. 771.

[64] See para.21.14, below.

[65] In *Smith v Dha* [2013] EWHC 838 (QB) the claimant died after the defendant's application for a ruling on meaning was heard and written and oral submissions were received by the court but before judgment had been handed down. Nicola Davies J. held that the cause of action abated at the date of the death and CPR r.40.7(1) did not allow judgment to take effect from a day earlier than the day on which it was given.

[66] *Pulling v Great Eastern Railway Co* (1882) 9 Q.B.D. 110; *Hatchard v M'ge* (1887) 18 Q.B.D. 771; *Lendon v London Road* (1884) 4 T.L.R. 448. The dicta in *Twycross v Grant* (1878) 4 C.P.D. 40 must be construed with reference to the cause of action in that case which was in respect of the pecuniary damage done to the testator's estate by reason of the failure to perform certain contracts. In Scotland the representatives of the deceased may carry on an action begun by him and recover as the deceased could have done: *Neilson v Rodger* (1853) 16 D. 325. If he had not sued they may commence an action but only for the pecuniary loss suffered by him: *Smith v Stewart & Co*, 1960 S.C. 329.

[67] The matter of the death of the defamer is now specifically dealt with in the uniform Australian legislation. See, e.g. s.10 of the NSW Defamation Act 2005:
"A person (including a personal representative of a deceased person) cannot assert, continue or enforce a cause of action for defamation in relation to: . . . (b) the publication of defamatory matter by a person who has died since publishing the matter."

[68] Which casts some doubt upon the reason given by the Neill Committee, para.VI. 19 (fn.43) for maintaining the present law, namely, that the "accused" is in no position to defend himself.

[69] See Prosser and Keeton, *Torts*, 5th edn pp.801–802. For a full account, see Eldredge, *Law of Defamation*, para.43. The difficulty about the maxim in relation to events occurring after the death of the "wrongdoer" is not confined to defamation: if a modern-day, non-corporate Stevenson died before Mrs Donoghue drank the ginger beer how could the 1934 Act apply?

[70] The executor could safeguard himself by obtaining an order of the court that the libellous matter be omitted from probate (though this could cause difficulty where the libel was inextrica-

SECTION 8. MENTALLY DISORDERED AND DRUNKEN PERSONS

8.14 Mentally disordered persons. Mental disorder has no effect upon a person's ability to sue for defamation, save that proceedings by (or against) a mentally disordered person are conducted on his behalf by his litigation friend.[71] There appears to be no reported English decision as to whether a mentally disordered person is liable for defamation,[72] but in *Hanbury v Hanbury*[73] Lord Esher M.R. said that:

> " . . . whenever a person did an act which . . . if done by a person with a perfect mind, would make him civilly or criminally responsible to the law, if the disease in the mind of the person doing the act was not so great as to make him unable to understand the nature and quality of the act which he was doing, that was an act for which he would be civilly and criminally responsible."

It is submitted, however, that the fact that the defendant was unaware, because of his state of mind, that what he was uttering was defamatory is not, as such, a defence.[74] In cases, however, where liability depends on the existence of some specific state of mind, e.g. where the words were published on a privileged occasion and proof of actual malice is necessary[75] or where the mental disorder is so notorious or apparent that those who read or heard the words cannot reasonably attach to them any defamatory meaning, the state of mind of the defendant would negative liability. It would also seem that the

---

bly entangled with the dispositive words). However, the grant of probate of a will is the act of the High Court and it is thought it would anyway be protected by absolute privilege.

[71] See CPR r.21.2(1). In principle, a mentally disordered person may be defamed, though the fact of the mental disorder may affect the damages because he may not suffer the same distress as a person of sound mind. However, in relation to statements made in the context of diagnosis and treatment, quite apart from the likely impact of qualified privilege, no action may be brought in respect of an act done in purported discharge of functions under the Mental Health Act 1983 without the leave of the High Court: *Lebrooy v London Borough of Hammersmith and Fulham* [2006] EWHC 1976 (QB) (Mental Health Act 1983, s.139(2)). The test that the court should apply in determining whether to give leave was said to be "whether, on the material immediately available to the court, which, of course, can include material furnished by the proposed defendant, the applicant's complaint appears to be such that it deserves the fuller investigation which will be possible if the intended applicant is allowed to proceed" (at [16], applying the test articulated by Donaldson L.J. in *Winch v Jones* [1986] 1 Q.B. 296 at 305). However, s.139 does not apply to proceedings against the Secretary of State or NHS Trusts: s.139(4).

[72] The observations of Kelly C.B. in *Mordaunt v Mordaunt* (1870) 39 L.J.P. & M. 57 are not *ad rem*, for they had related solely to a case of a person becoming insane after the commission of the wrong, and so being unable properly to instruct his advisers to defend him.

[73] (1892) 8 T.L.R. 559 CA at 560 See also *Emmens v Pottle* (1885) 16 Q.B.D. 354 CA at 356.

[74] This would seem consistent with *Morriss v Marsden* [1952] 1 All E.R. 925 (assault; irrelevant that D did not know that what he was doing was wrong) and see *Hulton v Jones* [1910] A.C. 20.

[75] This is the view of Prosser and Keeton, *Torts*, 5th edn (1984), p.1074, criticising the failure in some American cases to distinguish this from the "malice" implied as a fiction wherever defamatory matter is published: see para.1.8, above.

mentally disordered state of the defendant may be taken into account in mitigation of damages[76] where no actual financial loss is shown.

Drunken persons. There is no English authority on the liability of drunken persons for defamation.[77] Plainly it is no defence that the defendant, under the influence of drink, spoke in a way that he would not have adopted in a sober condition.[78] Otherwise, however, it would seem sensible to adopt the same approach as is suggested above for mentally disordered persons, that is to say, that evidence of drunkenness might negative actual malice, might affect the audience's understanding of the words or might be offered[79] in mitigation of damages.   **8.15**

SECTION 9. CORPORATIONS AND GOVERNMENTAL BODIES

(a) *Right to sue*

Trading corporations. A trading corporation or company "has a trading character, the defamation of which may ruin it".[80]   **8.16**

> "The reputation of a corporate body is capable of being, and will usually be, not simply something in which its directors and shareholders may take pride, but an asset of positive value to it."[81]

---

[76] Ibid. and *Vaughan v Ford* 1953 (4) S.A. 486. There is no English decision.

[77] The issue of drunkenness is obviously more likely to arise in actions for slander and broadcast libel than in others.

[78] Even, it is submitted, if the intoxication was involuntary: cf. *R. v Kingston* [1995] 2 A.C. 355 HL.

[79] Of course the jury might not receive it in the same way in a case of drunkenness.

[80] Per Kay L.J. in *South Hetton Coal Co. v N.-E. News* [1894] 1 Q.B. 133 at 145; *D & L Caterers Ltd v D'Ajou* [1945] K.B. 364 CA. The proposition that such a corporation can maintain an action for defamation was central to the decision in *Derbyshire CC v Times Newspapers* (see para.8.20, below) that a governmental organisation could not. Nor is it open to the CA to:
"invent a category of commercial corporation which, as an exception to a state of the law binding on us, should not be able to maintain an action for libel. Some corporations may be very powerful commercially and in homely terms well able to look after themselves. But we consider that there is no principled basis upon which a line might be drawn between strong corporations and weaker corporations":
McDonald's Corp v Steel, March 31, 1999, CA. Despite some earlier doubts the law is the same in South Africa: *Dhlomo v Natal Newspapers*, 1989 (1) S.A. 945 AD. The Supreme Court of South Africa in *Media 24 Ltd v SA Taxi Securitisation (Pty) Ltd* [2011] ZASCA 117 held by a majority that corporations, both trading and non-trading, had a right to their good name and reputation which included a claim to general damages under the law of defamation. Moreover, such a claim did not constitute an unjustified limitation to the right to freedom of expression.

[81] *Jameel v Wall Street Journal Europe SPRL* [2006] UKHL 44; [2007] 1 A.C. 359 at [120] per Lord Scott.

Accordingly it[82] may maintain an action of libel or slander for any words

[82] A parent company and its subsidiary may each have a distinct reputation and each have a distinct goodwill within a jurisdiction in which only the subsidiary carries on day-to-day business: *McDonald's Corp v Steel*, March 31, 1999, CA. Cf. *Multigroup Bulgaria Ltd v Oxford Analytica Ltd* [2001] E.M.L.R. 28. Where several companies together form a group of companies with very similar names or where there is a holding company and several subsidiaries which share similar names, identifying which company or companies should bring the claim is important because unless the defamatory imputation reflects upon the company which brings the claim no action will lie (see, per Tugendhat J. in *Club La Costa UK Plc v Gebhard* [2008] EWHC 2552 (QB) at [23]–[25]). Companies are individual entities: one company cannot recover losses incurred by another and one libel claimant cannot recover in respect of injuries to another's reputation. For a successful claim, it is not enough that the imputation has a tendency to cause damage to the business of one of the other companies in the group or even to the directors of the company which sues; the imputation must reflect upon the company which brings the claim and have a tendency to damage it in the way of its business. By way of example, in *Elite Model Management Corp v BBC*, unreported, May 24, 2001, claims were commenced by three companies in the Elite Models Management group (one of which was not in existence at the time of publication of the programme complained of) in respect of allegations that they had failed properly to protect young models with whom they worked. Eady J. refused to strike out the claims, holding that it was possible that two of the companies could be treated as "mother agencies" and identified as having failed to protect the models when they were in their jurisdiction. As to the company not in existence at the time of the programme, the imputations could be treated as continuing ones and authority existed that a claim might be brought in respect of a libel that effectively damaged or destroyed a young company's chance of profitable trading. While Eady J. concluded that the companies could continue their claim he did make clear (at [27]) that "the court needs to be alert to the possibility of corporate entities being 'put up' to bring claims for libel in respect of allegations truly reflecting upon individuals". Should this be found to be the case at trial, his lordship indicated that "one sanction that will have to be considered is that of indemnity costs". See also, the judgment of Sedley L.J. in *Jameel v Times Newspapers* [2004] EWCA Civ 983, CA; [2004] E.M.L.R. 31 at [35]. In *Euromoney Institutional Investor plc v Aviation News Ltd* [2013] EWHC 1505 (QB), Tugendhat J. refused to strike out the claim against the holding company because the draft pleading did not state that the claimant was "a mere holding company" and in any event "the issue in relation to claims in libel by corporations that do not trade may be in a state of development" (at [71]). In *Club La Costa UK v Gebhard* [2008] EWHC 2552 (QB) it was held that to comply with the regime in Defamation Act 1996, ss.2–4 an offer to make amends had to be made to the person making the complaint. The offer failed in that case because it had been made in respect of "a company" within the claimant's group of companies, rather than in respect of the claimant itself. See also, *Multigroup Bulgaria Holding AD v Oxford Analytica Ltd* [2001] E.M.L.R. 28 (QB) in which a claim brought by a Bulgarian holding company, which had subsidiaries involved in banking and other financial activities, failed because no properly directed jury could have found that the holding company had been defamed as there was no evidence that it had played any role in the management of the trading companies to which the impugned publications referred. See also, *Atlantis World Group of Companies NV v Gruppo Editoriale L'Espresso SPA* [2008] EWHC 1323 (QB); [2009] E.M.L.R. 15 (claimant company not entitled to damages as it had not started trading at the time of publication and it would not have been understood by any reader that the article complained of referred to it).

Not only has it been made clear that no claim can be brought unless the imputation reflects upon the company that brings the claim, but the courts have also refused to allow a holding company to claim on behalf of subsidiary companies (though cf. *Euromoney Institutional Investor plc v Aviation News Ltd* [2013] EWHC 1505 (QB) above). Thus, in *Adelson v Associated Newspapers* [2007] EWHC 997 (QB); [2008] 1 W.L.R. 585; [2008] E.M.L.R. 324 the claimants' application to amend the corporate claimant's claim to include compensation for injury to its subsidiaries failed because the proposed amendment was inconsistent with established principles of law under which one claimant is not permitted to recover libel damages in respect of injury to other legal entities, whether subsidiaries or otherwise. For the principles to be applied in interpreting the provisions of the CPR in respect of the substitution of parties, see *Adelson v Associated Newspapers Ltd* [2007] EWCA Civ 701 CA; [2008] E.M.L.R. 324.

which have a tendency to damage it in the way of its business[83] and it is not necessary for it to prove special damage.[84] However, by virtue of the Defamation Act 2013, s.1, when it comes into force, a statement will only be defamatory when it refers to a "body that trades for profit" where serious financial harm is caused or likely to be caused by the words complained of.[85] Although a company cannot be injured in its feelings,[86] only in its pocket, and an injury must sound in money, the injury need not be confined to accrued loss of income, for the company's goodwill may be injured.[87] If proof of actual damage were required the causative link between the libel and a downturn in

---

[83] *Derbyshire CC v Times Newspapers Ltd* [1993] A.C. 534 at 547 per Lord Keith. Not, as in the case of a natural person, its "reputation as such": *Heytesbury Holdings Pty Ltd v City of Subiaco* (1998) 19 W.A.R. 440; *Kay v Chesser* [1999] VSCA 83; [1999] 3 V.R. 55; *Feo v Pioneer Concrete (Vic) Pty Ltd* [1999] VSCA 180; [1999] 3 V.R. 417. The Irish Defamation Act 2009 may be wider: a body corporate may sue "whether or not it has incurred or is likely to incur financial loss as a result of the publication of [the] statement" (cl.11). It is not necessary that the corporation should trade within the jurisdiction, but it is:
  "likely in practice that a foreign corporation which trades outside this jurisdiction but does not trade within it will have greater difficulty in establishing that it has a trading reputation within this jurisdiction. If it succeeds, however, the interests of justice require that the same principles of law should apply to its claim for defamation"
(*Jameel v Wall Street Journal Europe SPRL* [2005] EWCA Civ 74; [2005] Q.B. 904 at [117]). And see *McDonald's Corp v Steel*, March 31, 1999, CA; *Multigroup Bulgaria Ltd v Oxford Analytica Ltd* [2001] E.M.L.R. 28; *Atlantis World Group of Companies NV v Gruppo Editoriale L'Espresso SpA* [2008] EWHC 1323 (QB); [2009] E.M.L.R. 15.
  [84] This proposition is reaffirmed by the majority of the HL in *Jameel v Wall Street Journal Europe SPRL* [2006] UKHL 44; [2007] 1 A.C. 359. However, even the judges in the minority would not have gone to the lengths of requiring a company to prove actual special damage resulting from the libel. Thus Baroness Hale (at [157]) seems to have favoured adopting the recommendation of the Faulks Committee that a trading company should be required to show that the words were likely to cause it financial damage. Indeed, there is very little distance between that and the present law, since the company may only recover damages without proof of actual loss if the words have a tendency to damage it in the way of its business: see the *Derbyshire* case, above. *Journal Printing v Maclean* (1896) 23 O.A.R. 324; *Price v Chicutimi Pulp* (1915) 23 D.L.R. 116 SCC; *Mount Cook Group v Johnston Motors* [1990] 2 N.Z.L.R. 488; *BG Rice Marketing v Taylor* (1967) 11 W.I.R. 208. Cf. *Red Man's Syndicate v Associated Newspapers* (1910) 26 T.L.R. 394 (possible inference from verdict that no commercial damage suffered justifying refusal of plaintiff's costs). It is true that some cases of slander are not actionable without proof of special damage (see para.4.1, above). But since words are only actionable at the suit of a trading corporation if they reflect on it in its business capacity, any slander against it which is actionable at all must also in its nature, since the Defamation Act 1952, be actionable per se.
  [85] See further paras 2.5 and 2.8, above.
  [86] *Adelson v Associated Newspapers Ltd* [2007] EWHC 997 (QB); [2008] 1 W.L.R. 585; [2008] E.M.L.R. 324 at [4]. It has been said that an unsuccessful plea of justification against a company could increase the damages payable to it: *Associated Leisure v Associated Newspapers* [1970] 2 Q.B. 450 CA at 455. However, that cannot be on the usual basis that it increases the claimant's feelings of hurt and aggravated damages are not available in favour of a corporation: *Collins Stewart Ltd v Financial Times Ltd* [2005] EWHC 262 (QB); [2006] E.M.L.R. 5; *Midland Metals Overseas Pte Ltd v Christchurch Press Co. Ltd* [2001] NZCA 321; [2002] N.Z.L.R. 289. Cf. *Hiltz and Seamone Co. v Att-Gen (Nova Scotia)* (1999) 172 D.L.R. (4th) 488 NSCA at 530, where a rather broader basis for aggravated damages is contemplated,
  [87] Lord Reid in *Lewis v Daily Telegraph* [1964] A.C. 234 HL at 262. S.6 of the New Zealand Defamation Act 1992 provides that a body corporate must prove pecuniary loss or a likelihood of pecuniary loss but this is regarded as restating the common law: *Midland Metals Overseas Pte Ltd v Christchurch Press Co. Ltd* [2001] NZCA 321; [2002] N.Z.L.R. 289. See *Chinese Herald*

trade might be difficult or impossible to establish.[88] The law is now different under the Uniform Australian legislation and a trading corporation may not sue at all for defamation (even if actual damage can be established) unless it has fewer than 10 employees and is not related to another corporation.[89]

Thus an action will lie for an imputation that a trading company is in an insolvent condition,[90] or that the company or its directorate is composed of alien enemies.[91] So an imputation on the goods sold or manufactured by a trading company may involve a reflection on the company in the way of its business[92]; and if a statement be made as to the mode in which a trading company conducts its business, such as to lead people of ordinary sense to the opinion that it conducts its business in a dishonest, improper or inefficient manner, the law is the same as in the case of an individual, and the company can maintain an action without proof of special damage.[93] Similarly, a false statement about a company's treatment of its workers may hamper its ability to recruit staff,[94] but since a company can only sue for defamation if the words reflect on its trading reputation or in the way of its business, the company must be actually engaged in business[95] or about to commence business[96] when the defamatory words are published.

The European Court of Human Rights does not regard as objectionable the application to companies of this general rule of English libel law that damage is presumed from publication, for:

Ltd v New Times Media Ltd [2004] N.Z.L.R. 749, where there was no evidence of actual loss and an inference of likely loss could not be drawn.

[88] For further difficulties presented by an attempt to assess damage to a company by reference to its market share value see *Collins Stewart Ltd v Financial Times Ltd* [2004] EWHC 2337 (QB); [2005] E.M.L.R. 5.

[89] For the full formula see, e.g. s.9 of the Defamation Act 2005 (NSW). See *Redeemer Baptist School v Glossop* [2006] N.S.W.S.C. 1201. The bar does not apply to a claim by a natural person associated with the corporation: s.9(5). Nor does it prevent a claim for malicious falsehood.

[90] *Metropolitan Saloon v Hawkins* (1859) 4 H. & N. 87; *Aspro Travel Ltd v Owners Abroad Group Plc* [1996] 1 W.L.R. 132 CA, where the action by the corporate plaintiff was settled. See also paras 2.30–2.34, above.

[91] *Lyons v Lipton* (1914) 49 L.J. 542; *Slazengers v Gibbs* (1916) 33 T.L.R. 35.

[92] *British Empire Machine v Linotype* (1898) 79 L.T. 8 CA; (1899) 81 L.T. 331 HL. See also paras 2.37–2.39, above.

[93] See paras 2.46–2.48, above.

[94] *Derbyshire CC v Times Newspapers* [1993] A.C. 534 at 547. In *Elite Model Management Corp v BBC*, unreported, May 24, 2001, (QB), Eady J. refused to strike out a claim against the corporate defendants in respect of an allegation that they had failed to take steps to protect young models entrusted into the care of their senior executives though he noted that the sting alleged was somewhat "artificial" and "tenuous": "It seems curious that these men who are 'principals' should instigate proceedings on the basis that their 'vehicles' are accused of not keeping them in order" (at [21]).

[95] *Dupont Co. v Nashville Banner Co*, 13 F.2d 186 (CA 6 1925).

[96] *Scott v Fourth Estate* [1986] 1 N.Z.L.R. 336. See also *Elite Model Management Corp v BBC*, unreported, May 24, 2001, (QB), where it is accepted in principle at [25] that a libel may effectively damage or destroy a young company's chance of profitable trading. But cf. *Atlantis World Group of Companies NV v Gruppo Editoriale L'Espresso SpA* [2008] EWHC 1323 (QB); [2009] E.M.L.R. 15 (claimant company not entitled to damages as it had not started trading at the time of publication). See also, *Gidney v Anglo-Indian Federation* (1930) I.L.R. (8 Rangoon) 250,

"in addition to the public interest in open debate about business practices, there is a competing interest in protecting the commercial success and viability of companies, for the benefit of shareholders and employees, but also for the wider economic good,"[97]

though on the facts of the case the absence of legal aid rendered the proceedings by the company unfair for the purposes of art.6 of the Convention.

A corporation or company can maintain an action of libel or slander against one of its members.[98]

Defamatory statements against company's officers. It is necessary in all cases that the defamatory words are capable of being understood as referring to the claimant.[99] A company cannot, therefore, maintain an action for defamation in respect of words which reflect solely upon its individual officers or members[100] and not upon the company itself.[101] To take an extreme case, a trading company could clearly have no action in respect of a statement imputing sexual promiscuity to its managing director[102] or alleging that he had murdered his wife.[103] Where the imputation concerns a "business" matter more difficult questions of degree will arise but the extent to which the person directly defamed controls the company and can therefore be regarded as its

8.17

---

in which it was held that an unincorporated body cannot sue even after incorporation for libel published before incorporation.

[97] *Steel and Morris v United Kingdom* (2005) App. no.68416/01; [2005] E.M.L.R. 15 at [94]–[95]. See also, *Kulis v Poland* (2009) App. No.27209/03 at [35]. On the facts (which would plainly have amounted to honest opinion in English law) the imposition of liability on the applicants was disproportionate.

[98] *Metropolitan Saloon v Hawkins* (1859) 4 H. & N. 87.

[99] See generally Ch.7. The reverse case, where it is contended that a statement about a company refers to its officers or members, is discussed at para.7.13, above.

[100] See, for example, *Duke v University of Salford* [2013] EWHC 196 (QB). Nor, of course, can an officer sue in respect of words which reflect solely upon the company.

[101] See *Church of Scientology v Globe and Mail* (1978) 84 D.L.R. (3d) 239 and *Ahmadiyya etc. v Muslim Judicial Council*, 1983 (4) S.A. 855 (both cases of non-trading corporations but the principle is the same). Provided that the words reflect on the company, a campaign of defamation against officers of the company may cause damage to the company as well as to them as individuals: *Barrick Gold Corp v Lopehandia* (2004) 71 O.R. (3d) 416 Ont. CA. Cf. *John Holland Group Pty Ltd v John Fairfax Publications Pty Ltd* [2006] ACTSC 34 (allegations against senior employee who was not controller of company did not defame the company).

[102] Unless perhaps it was alleged that the company was a "front" for sexual services offered by the director. In *Li v The Herald and Weekly Times Pty Ltd* [2007] VSC 109 the basis of the dismissal of the company's claim really seems to have been that it was not sufficiently referred to. Cf. *Elite Model Management Corp v BBC*, May 24, 2001, (QB) (allegations of sexual exploitation by management of model agency); *Neiman-Marcus v Lait*, 107 F.Supp. 96 (1952) (charges of widespread prostitution among employees of store left to jury). In *Beijing Television v Brightec Ltd* [1999] 2 H.K.C. 665 HKCA, it was held to be arguable for the purposes of a striking out application that an article headed "Adulterous Scandal Coming Out of Beijing Television" and dealing with an alleged affair between the station's female "anchor" and a high-ranking official, which was said to have been exposed in dramatic circumstances, might be defamatory of the station in view of the prominence of the anchor's role.

[103] *Todd v Swan Television and Radio Broadcasting Pty Ltd* [2001] WASC 324; 25 W.A.R. 382 (partnership).

alter ego will be a relevant consideration.[104] Thus, in *David Regan & Co. Pty Ltd v West Australian Newspapers Ltd*[105] the publication was alleged to mean that the plaintiff company, an estate agency, had employed an estate agent who was guilty of dishonesty. The Court of Appeal of Western Australia held that this was capable of being defamatory of the company. Pullin J.A. held that it was not decisive that the plaintiff might not be "at fault"—it would plainly have been defamatory to allege that the plaintiff was insolvent; and Buss J.A. said that it was:

> "reasonably arguable that an imputation that a small corporation (such as the first appellant), which carries on the business as a real estate agent in a small country town, employs an agent who has been found guilty of acting dishonestly or deceptively constitutes a reflection upon the business reputation of the corporation".[106]

It has been said that "the court needs to be alert to the possibility of corporate entities being 'put up' to bring claims for libel in respect of allegations truly reflecting upon individuals".[107]

Where it is alleged that a company was incorporated for a fraudulent or improper purpose that will, it is submitted, generally be defamatory of the company but there may be circumstances in which the statement imputes misconduct only to the incorporators.[108]

8.18   Imputations actionable by company. There are obiter dicta from which it might be inferred that a trading corporation or company could not maintain

---

[104] *Bargold v Mirror Newspapers* [1981] 1 N.S.W.L.R. 9; *Hunt Australia Pty Ltd v Davidson's Arnhemland Safaris* (2000) 179 A.L.R. 738 Fed Ct of Australia (allegation that company owned and operated by a liar reflected on company). Cf. *Shendish Manor Ltd v Coleman* [2001] EWCA Civ 913 (T said to be "a crook" and "out to make a fast buck"; T was known to be executive chairman of S. Co. but at least in the absence of evidence that he was known to be the owner of the company the statement could not reasonably be understood as referring to it).

[105] [2007] WASCA 14.

[106] Ibid. at [35].

[107] *Elite Model Management Corp v BBC*, May 24, 2001, (QB) at [27]; *Al Rajhi Banking and Investment Corp v Wall Street Journal Europe SPRL* [2003] EWHC 1358 QB; *Duke v University of Salford* [2013] EWHC 196 (QB) per Eady J. at [8]; *Tiscali UK Ltd v British Telecommunications Plc* [2008] EWHC 2927 (QB) per Eady J. at [16]; *Multigroup Bulgaria Holding AD v Oxford Analytica Ltd* [2001] E.M.L.R. 28 (QB) per Eady J. at [41]. But an imputation may reflect upon the company even if the charge against the individual does not relate to the way he carries out his duties: *Al Rajhi* at [8] (where the issue was the permissible scope of justification). The sentiments in *Elite Model Management* are echoed by Sedley L.J. in *Jameel v Times Newspapers Ltd* [2004] EWCA Civ 983; [2004] E.M.L.R. 31 at [35]. This concerned allegations that funds derived by the natural claimant from the company had found their way into terrorist hands and that implied no wrongdoing by the company. If, however, the allegation were to be that the natural claimant, being the controller of the company, had procured funds to be diverted directly from the company to the terrorists, the conclusion must be that the company, too, is defamed, for the diversion would be the company's act. Indeed, if the company suffered a serious loss of business as a result of the allegations, it is difficult to see how the natural claimant could recover damages for that (as opposed to the injury to his reputation stemming from the procurement) since the loss is the company's and the diminution in the value of the natural claimant's shareholding is merely a reflection of the loss suffered by the company: *Johnson v Gore-Wood* [2002] 2 A.C. 1.

[108] As in *Anderson v Church of Scientology* [1981] W.A.R. 279 Full Court.

an action of libel in respect of an imputation of corruption.[109] It is submitted that these dicta state the law too widely,[110] and that a trading corporation or company can maintain an action in respect of an imputation of corruption, or, indeed, of any other wrongful conduct, provided always (and this will need to be carefully scrutinised)[111] that the words published reflect on the company and not merely upon individual human beings.[112] It has also been said that there are:

> "statements which, with regard to some plaintiffs, would undoubtedly constitute a libel, but which, if published of another kind of plaintiffs, would not have the same effect. For instance, it might be stated of a person that his manners were contrary to all sense of decency or comity, and such that, if the statement were true, they would render him deserving in the minds of persons of ordinary sense of contempt, hatred, or ridicule; but, if the same thing were said with regard to a firm or company, it would be impossible that it should have the same effect, because a firm or company as such cannot have indecent or vulgar manners."[113]

Similarly, it has been said that a corporation or company:

> "could not sue in respect of a charge of murder, or incest, or adultery, because it could not commit those crimes."[114]

As to the first statement it is not a very convincing example. If, for example, it were said that a company dealt with complaints by customers in an insolent and high-handed manner that would be very damaging to its reputation and, it is submitted, actionable even though it might be said to concern the company's "manners". As to the second statement, there is no obvious reason why the questions whether a company could be convicted of a particular crime and whether it is defamatory to charge the crime against a company should in all cases require the same answer[115]; the criminal liability of corporations is now very much wider than it was 100 years ago and it must be remembered that the issue would not be whether the company could physically commit the crime (because on that basis it could never be convicted of any crime) but

---

[109] See per Pollock C.B. in *Metropolitan Saloon v Hawkins* (1859) 4 H. & N. 87 at 90; per Lopes L.J. in *South Hetton Co. v N.-E. News* [1894] 1 Q.B. 133 at 143.

[110] *Multigroup Bulgaria Ltd v Oxford Analytica Ltd* [2001] E.M.L.R. 28. Cf. *D & L Caterers Ltd v D'Ajou* [1945] K.B. 364 CA, where the company was accused of dealing in the "black market".

[111] *Multigroup Bulgaria Ltd v Oxford Analytica Ltd* [2001] E.M.L.R. 28.

[112] See *Derbyshire CC v Times Newspapers* [1993] A.C. 534 at 547. See also *Proprietors of Selby Bridge v Sunday Telegraph*, *The Times*, February 17, 1966 (avarice); *Waverley Housing Management v BBC*, 1993 G.W.D. 17–117; *Journal Printing v Maclean* (1894) 25 O.R. 509; (1896) 23 O.A.R. 324 (corruption in newspaper corporation); *Sentinel v Robinson* (1927) 61 O.L.R. 62; *Barnes v Sharpe* (1910) 11 C.L.R. 462; *News Media v Finlay* [1971] N.Z.L.R. 1089 at 1095, 1102, 1103.

[113] Per Lord Esher M.R. in *South-Hetton Coal Co. v N.-E. News* [1894] 1 Q.B. 133 CA at 139.

[114] Per Lopes L.J. ibid. at 141. Cf. *D & L Caterers v D'Ajou* [1945] K.B. 364 at 366, per Lord Goddard C.J.

[115] See *Barnes v Sharpe* (1910) 11 C.L.R. 462.

whether the acts of the "directing mind" of the company are to be imputed to it.[116] In any event, the interpretation of defamatory words should not be constrained by technical rules of criminal law. Thus, an allegation of racism made against a company in *Hays Plc v Hartley*[117] was said to be seriously defamatory. So too, if after a disaster causing loss of life, a statement were made that a company had "murdered" the victims, the hypothetical reader would no doubt treat that as a charge of gross neglect of duty, for which the company could be criminally liable.[118]

8.19 Non-trading corporations (other than governmental). Where a corporation, though not engaged in business for profit, is authorised to acquire property which may be the source of income or revenue, the transaction of the business incidental thereto creates a reputation similar to that of a corporation engaged in business for profit, and entitles the non-profit corporation to maintain an action for libel in respect of charges which tend injuriously to affect its property or financial position.[119] In the case of a charity, for example, defamatory statements may discourage subscribers or otherwise impair its ability to carry on its charitable objects.[120]

8.20 Governmental bodies. The former view that a local government corporation had a "governing" reputation which was protected by the law of defamation[121] no longer represents English law. In *Derbyshire CC v Times Newspapers*[122] the House of Lords held that at common law, and without

---

[116] Hence a company could be convicted of manslaughter at common law and, from April 6, 2008 of the offence of corporate manslaughter under the Corporate Manslaughter and Corporate Homicide Act 2007. Arguably, were it not for the fact that the crime is punishable only by imprisonment, a company whose board decided to kill the director of a rival would be guilty of murder. See generally Smith and Hogan, *Criminal Law*, 11th edn (2006), p.241 (which contains an example where a company might be guilty of bigamy!).

[117] [2010] EWHC 1068 (QB). The claim was struck out as an abuse of process as the claimant had already received vindication by a public statement republished on the newspaper website to the effect that the allegations were unfounded, there was no realistic prospect of the agent republishing the allegations and the value of the damages made them not worth pursuing.

[118] See *R. v P & O European Ferries Ltd* (1990) 93 Cr. App. R. 72.

[119] *Chinese Empire v Chinese Newspaper* (1907) 13 British Columbia R.141 (non-trading corporation created under the Benevolent Societies Act, R.S.B.C.,1897, c.13): "Benevolent, religious and other like corporations have interests connected with property and its management which should have the same protection in court in case of injury as corporations engaged in business for profit": per curiam at 170–171; applied *Church of Scientology v Globe and Mail* (1978) 84 D.L.R. (3d) 239; *St Michael's Extended Care Society v Frost* [1994] 6 W.W.R. 718 and lxxi. And see *Finnish Temperance v Finnish Socialist*, 130 N.E. 845 (1921); *New York Society v McFadden*, 183 N.E. 284 (1932) (non-trading society supported by voluntary contributions); Restatement, 2d, *Torts*, para.561 (b); *Gorman v Swaggart* 524 So.2d 915 (La., 1988).

[120] *Derbyshire CC v Times Newspapers* [1993] A.C. 534 at 547. Under the uniform Australian legislation a corporation of which the objects "do not include obtaining financial gain for its members or corporators" continues to be able to sue for defamation: see, e.g. s.9 of the Defamation Act 2005 (NSW).

[121] See the 8th edition of this book, para.958, and *Bognor Regis Urban DC v Campion* [1972] Q.B. 169.

[122] [1993] A.C. 534.

reference to the guarantee of freedom of expression in art.10 of the European Convention on Human Rights,[123] an organ of local government may not bring an action for defamation. This rests not upon any absence of likely damage to such a body, for in many cases the considerations which apply to a trading or charitable corporation may also apply to a government body,[124] but upon the likely chilling effect on free speech of granting a right of action. Though the case concerned a local authority the same rule applies to an organ of central government: neither the Crown nor a government department which has corporate status may sue for defamation. It:

> "would be a serious interference with the free expression of opinion hitherto enjoyed . . . if the wealth of the State, derived from the State's subjects, could be used to launch against those subjects actions for defamation because they have, falsely and unfairly it may be, criticised or condemned the management of the country."[125]

However, the mere fact that the body concerned is in receipt of public money and may be a public authority for the purposes of the Human Rights Act 1998 is not enough to mean that it should not be entitled to sue in defamation. Thus, a university has been held to be entitled to maintain an action for libel[126] and it has also been said that a state school has a reputation that it may vindicate by a claim for libel.[127] The question in the *Derbyshire* case was said to be whether the authority was entitled to maintain an action for words which reflected on its "governmental and administrative functions" and its operation of its pension fund, to which the alleged libel related, was clearly thought to fall within that, but it is submitted that the same rule applies even where the activity referred to could properly be described as trading.[128]

It has for long, however, been the case that activities once carried on by central or local governmental bodies have been transferred to statutory corporations[129] and in recent years this process has been taken further by the

---

[123] In contrast, the Court of Appeal had relied on the Convention: [1992] Q.B. 770.

[124] [1993] A.C. at 547; e.g. a false statement about a local authority's treatment of its workers might hamper its ability to recruit staff.

[125] Per Schreiner J.A. in *Die Spoorbond v South African Railways* [1946] A.D. 999 at 1012–1013, cited in *Derbyshire* [1993] A.C. at 549.

[126] *Duke v University of Salford* [2013] EWHC 196 (QB) at [5]: "Of course, it is true that universities receive large sums of public money and that they have to comply with various statutory provisions, but that is not to say that they are to be equated with central or local government" (per Eady J. at [4]); *Hong Kong Polytechnic University v Next Magazine Publishing Ltd* [1997] H.K.L.R.D. 514 HKCA.

[127] *Hill v Governing Body of Great Tey Primary School* [2013] I.C.R. 691 (EAT) at [61], [62] (not a libel case). Tugendhat J. left the issue open in *McLaughlin v London Borough of Lambeth* [2010] EWHC 2726 (QB) [2011] E.M.L.R. 8 at [53].

[128] See *Die Spoorbond v South African Railways* [1946] A.D. 999 at 1013, seemingly approved by Lord Keith [1993] A.C. 550.

[129] Thus the Post Office became a statutory corporation independent of the Crown by the Post Office Act 1969.

transfer of functions to "agencies" and ordinary registered companies,[130] albeit that their functions remain subject to statutory regulation. Such bodies lack the characteristic of being democratically elected, which is regarded as an important factor pointing away from liability in *Derbyshire*, but it is not, it would seem, a necessary feature in all cases.[131] No doubt everything must turn upon a careful examination of the legal nature and functions of the body in question and the fact that it is in form a company limited by shares is not decisive.[132] It remains to be seen whether one can treat the privatised[133] utility suppliers as "organs of government" rather than as ordinary trading companies for the purpose of the *Derbyshire* case.[134] The *Derbyshire* decision was followed in Australia[135] on similar facts, that is to say, in cases involving local government bodies,[136] but under the current uniform legislation lack of capacity to sue has a statutory basis.[137] The *Derbyshire* case makes clear that the decision does not affect the right to sue of an individual member or officer

---

[130] Thus telecommunications were first severed from the Post Office in 1981 and "privatised" by the Telecommunications Act 1984.

[131] "The most important of these features is that it is a governmental body. Further, it is a democratically elected body, the electoral process nowadays being conducted almost exclusively on party political lines. It is of the highest importance that a democratically elected governmental body, or indeed any governmental body, should be open to uninhibited public criticism":

[1993] A.C. 534 at 547. See *British Coal Corp v NUM*, unreported, June 28, 1996 (French J.). The issue was raised but not decided in *Sunderland Housing Co. v Baines* [2006] EWHC 2359 (QB) (see also *Gentoo Group Ltd v Hanratty* [2008] EWHC 627 (QB) at [24]).

[132] Thus the "arrangements" made under the authority of the Student Loans Act 1990 took the form of a company with two shareholders, the Secretary of State for Education and the Secretary of State for Scotland.

[133] In *Posts and Telecommunications Corp v Modus Publications (PNT) Ltd* 1998 (3) S.A. 1114, the Supreme Court of Zimbabwe held that the Posts and Telecommunications Corporation had no capacity to sue for defamation. It was a statutory corporation over which the Minister for Information, Posts and Telecommunications exercised extensive control. Its funds were administered by the state and its pricing policy was subject to the approval of the Minister.

[134] They tend to have (but not necessarily, as in the case of telecommunications) a local monopoly and to be regulated in some aspects of their commercial policy but otherwise resemble ordinary companies. In *British Coal Corp v NUM*, unreported, June 28, 1996, French J. held that British Coal was a governmental body for the purposes of the *Derbyshire* rule. However, that body does not seem to have been truly analogous, in public law terms, to utility suppliers. While it might be arguable that Network Rail was "government" (though its predecessor Railtrack was held not to be so for the purposes of the Human Rights Act 1998 in *Cameron v Network Rail Infrastructure Ltd* [2006] EWHC 1133 (QB); [2007] 1 W.L.R. 163) it would be surprising if that were held of a train operating company.

[135] *Ballina Shire Council v Ringland* (1994) 33 N.S.W.L.R. 680 NSWCA (Mahoney J.A., dissenting, emphasised the lack of factual evidence to support the assumptions on which *Derbyshire* is based); *New South Wales Aboriginal Land Council v Jones* (1998) 43 N.S.W.L.R. 300 NSWCA.

[136] Compare *Robertson v John Fairfax Publications Pty Ltd* [2003] N.S.W.S.C. 473 (trade union).

[137] See, e.g. the Defamation Act 2005 (NSW) s.9. A public body is "a local government body or other governmental or public authority constituted by or under a law of any country". Canadian law precludes a governmental body from suing for defamation: *Halton Hills (Town) v Kerouac* (2006) 270 D.L.R. (4th) 479; *Montague (Township) v Page* (2006) 79 O.R. (3d) 515; *Dixon v Powell River* 2009 CarswellBC 762, 2009BCSC 406. The Irish Defamation Act 2009 appears to have no equivalent of the English law rule that a government body (being a corporation) may not

of a governmental body if the statement about the body is capable of being interpreted as referring to the individual.[138] Indeed, the ability of the individual to sue seems to be regarded as a reason for denying such a right to the body.[139] The governmental body may have power to give an indemnity to an officer in respect of libel proceedings brought by him in respect of statements about the discharge of his duties.[140] To do so is lawful, but if the body's true purpose is to sue for damage to its own reputation, and it gives its officers an indemnity in respect of the costs of defamation in order to circumvent the rule that it has no right to commence such proceedings itself, then it will have acted for an improper purpose and/or taken irrelevant considerations into account and its decision will be liable to be quashed on normal public law principles. The court should be astute to prevent any attempt to circumvent the *Derbyshire* decision.[141] However, while there is no special privilege for

---

sue for defamation in that Defamation Act 2009, s.12 provides that the provisions of the Act apply to a body corporate as they apply to a natural person.

[138] *McLaughlin v London Borough of Lambeth* [2010] EWHC 2726 (QB); [2011] E.M.L.R. 8 per Tugendhat J. at [46]. In *McLaughlin* Tugendhat J. rejected (at [47]–[50]) the submission of counsel for the defendants that the *Derbyshire CC* case prevents a public servant from suing, even if he is referred to and defamed, if the meaning relates in some way to the carrying out of his official functions, rather than to his private life.

Moreover, the fact that the resources of the individual are likely to be less than those of the public body presumably reduces any chilling effect of the right of action. There is no principle in South African law barring a claim by a cabinet minister without proof of malice: *Mthembi-Mahanyele v Mail & Guardian Ltd* [2004] ZASCA 67; 2004 (11) B.C.L.R 1182 Sup. Ct of Appeal of South Africa. The right of action of the individual is clear in Singapore: *Tang Liang Hong v Lee Kuan Yew* [1998] 1 S.L.R. 97; *Lee Hsien Loong v Singapore Democratic Party* [2006] SGHC 220; [2007] 1 S.L.R. 675.

[139] [1993] A.C. 534 at 550. It is said that:
   "(a) publication attacking the activities of the authority will necessarily be an attack on the body of councillors which represents the controlling party, or on the executives who carry on the day-to-day management of its affairs. If the individual reputation of any of these is wrongly impaired by publication any of these can himself bring proceedings for defamation."
It is submitted that the second sentence is important and shows that not every statement about the body will necessarily be taken as capable of referring to an individual: see para.7.13, above.

[140] E.g. under s.111 of the Local Government Act 1972. See also the Local Authorities (Indemnities for Members and Officers) Order 2004, SI 2004/3082, conferring power to grant indemnity in relation to the defence by him of any allegation of defamation made against an officer).

[141] *R. (on the application of Comninos) v Bedford BC* [2003] EWHC 121 Admin. See also, *McLaughlin v London Borough of Lambeth* [2010] EWHC 2726 (QB); [2011] E.M.L.R. 8 at [40]. In *Thompson v James* [2013] EWHC 515 (QB) the Chief Executive of Carmarthenshire County Council brought a libel claim against the defendant who sought, *inter alia*, to have the claim struck out on the basis that it was an abuse of process. In particular, the defendant argued, following the *Derbyshire CC* case, that civil servants acting in their official capacity were required to show a greater degree of tolerance to public scrutiny and that the receipt of an indemnity by the claimant from his County Council employer in respect of his legal costs was a breach of her art.10 right to freedom of expression. Tugendhat J. rejected these arguments, holding that there was nothing in the suggestion that it was contrary to art.10 that a member or officer of a local authority should be able to sue for libel: "On the contrary, there would be a serious gap in the law if members and officers of a local authority (and others who work in or for other public authorities) could not sue for libel (at [405]). So far as the argument based on the indemnity was concerned that was also without foundation. There are procedures by which the

criticism of "politicians"[142] or "public officers"[143] a claim by an officer is now much more likely to be affected by privilege as a result of *Reynolds v Times Newspapers*.[144]

8.21 Malicious falsehood. The Court of Appeal in the *Derbyshire* case[145] observed that a claim for malicious falsehood would still be available and reference was made to this without apparent disapproval by the House of Lords.[146] Such a claim of course presents the claimant with a more serious hurdle than a claim for libel for he has to show that the words were false and that they were published with actual malice.[147] There may also be difficulties for a governmental claimant in showing that it has suffered actual damage or (since it is likely that the words will be in writing or broadcast) that they are "calculated to cause pecuniary damage" to it.[148] "Customers" for many governmental services may not be in a position to withdraw their business and look elsewhere.[149]

(b) *Liability*

8.22 Generally. A corporation or company can be sued for defamatory words published by its servants or agents in the same circumstances as any other principal.[150]

8.23 Defamation Act 2013. Defamation Act 2013, s.1 will provide, when it comes into force, that, in the case of a "body that trades for profit", a

---

grant of an indemnity by a public authority can be challenged and the fact that the claimant had received an indemnity could not make the claim an abuse (at [414]).

[142] But the *Derbyshire* principle was employed so as to deny a claim to a political party in *Goldsmith v Bhoyrul* [1998] Q.B. 459.

[143] Reference was made by the House of Lords in *Derbyshire* to US constitutional law and in particular to *New York Times v Sullivan*, 376 U.S. 254 (1964) under which statements about public figures are actionable only if the plaintiff can prove actual malice (see para.15.31, below). In denying a right to sue *Derbyshire* goes further in respect of governmental bodies, but some American cases adopt a *Derbyshire* approach to governmental bodies. See, e.g. *City of Chicago v Tribune Co*, 307 Ill. 595 (1923).

[144] See para.15.1, below.

[145] [1992] Q.B. 770.

[146] [1993] A.C. 534 at 551. Ralph Gibson and Butler-Sloss L.JJ. also adverted to the possibility of proceedings for criminal libel though this would of course now be precluded so far as England, Wales and Northern Ireland are concerned: Coroners and Justice Act 2009, s.73. This is mentioned by Lord Keith at [1993] A.C. 551 without disapproval, even though one of the decisions relied on by him (*Hector v A-G of Antigua and Barbuda* [1990] 2 A.C. 312) involved the use of a constitutional guarantee of free speech to strike down a law having certain affinities with criminal libel.

[147] See para.21.1, below.

[148] Defamation Act 1952, s.3(1)(a).

[149] See Kirby P. dissenting on this point in *Ballina Shire Council v Ringland* (1994) 33 N.S.W.L.R. 680 NSWCA.

[150] *Whitfield v S.E. Ry* (1858) E.B. & E. 115; *Abrath v N.E. Ry* (1886) 11 A.C. 247 at 253, 254; *Donato v Legion Cabs* (1966) 85 W.N. (Pt.1) (N.S.W.) 242 at 256; see para.8.30, below.

statement is not defamatory unless its publication has caused or is likely to cause the body serious financial harm.[151]

Section 10. Trade Unions

(a) *Right to sue*

Generally. Under s.10 of the Trade Union and Labour Relations (Con- **8.24**
solidation) Act 1992 a trade union[152] is not a body corporate and is not to be
treated as if it were except to the extent authorised by the Act. However, it is
capable of suing in its own name for a tort. Under the legislation governing
trade unions before 1971 it was accepted that although they were not corporations, they could sue for libel[153] but in *EEPTU v Times Newspapers*[154] it was
held that the Act (the Trade Union and Labour Relations Act 1974[155]), on
which s.10 of the 1992 Act is based, precluded such a claim. Whether this
decision represents the law must be regarded as doubtful for a number of
reasons. Prior to 1971[156] there was a tendency to treat unions as "quasi-
corporations" and this was regarded as giving them sufficient legal personality
to sue for defamation. In the *EEPTU* case O'Connor J. held that this approach
was precluded by the provision that the trade union should not be or *be treated
as if it were* a body corporate. Although these words appear in s.10 of the 1992
Act[157] it should be noted that the side note to the section reads "quasi-
corporate status of trade unions". Little weight should probably be placed on
this, particularly in the context of a consolidating Act.

However there are two other matters which may be of greater moment.
First, whatever the meaning of the italicised words they cannot exclude any
incident of status simply because it is one which also attaches to corporations.
For instance, the inference from the fact that a trade union can sue in its own
name in proceedings founded on contract[158] is that contracts can be made in
the name of the union, and this inference cannot be excluded simply because
corporations can also contract in their own name. Similarly, it is submitted
that to hold that a trade union can sue in libel is not to treat it as if it were a
corporation. Secondly, even if one rejects the notion of "quasi-corporate"
personality, it is surely arguable that once the legislature has allowed for the
unincorporated entity to sue in its own name for a tort no separate or quasi-

---

[151] See further paras 2.5 and 2.8, above.
[152] Except a "special register body".
[153] *NUGMW v Gillian* [1946] K.B. 81 CA; *Willis v Brooks* [1947] 1 All E.R. 191.
[154] [1980] Q.B. 585.
[155] S.2(1).
[156] Under the Industrial Relations Act 1971, repealed by the 1974 Act, trade unions had briefly
been corporate bodies.
[157] Albeit that the structure is different from that of the 1974 Act: the reference to "treated"
appears in subs.(2) not in the main words of subs.(1).
[158] S.10(1)(b).

separate personality is necessary: this is, after all, the position in the case of a partnership,[159] where it is well established that the firm may sue for damages for libel likely to injure the firm as a body. Whatever the technical position it should be noted that the denial to the union of the right to sue was described in the *EEPTU* case itself as absurd[160] and the earlier cases are referred to in *Derbyshire CC v Times Newspapers*[161] (where the *EEPTU* case is not referred to[162]) as: "understandable upon the view that the defamatory matter may adversely affect the union's ability to keep its members or attract new ones or to maintain a convincing attitude towards employers".[163]

(b) *Liability*

8.25 Generally. Between 1906 and 1982 trade unions enjoyed total or near total immunity from liability in tort. This was removed by s.15(1) of the Employment Act 1982 so that a trade union (which may be sued in its own name[164]) is now in the same position as any natural or corporate person.[165] The question whether the union is vicariously liable for defamatory words used by an officer or agent is to be determined by common law principles[166] and not by the special code of vicarious liability for the "economic torts" under the Trade Union and Labour Relations (Consolidation) Act 1992.[167] There are, however, restrictions on the union's liability: first, damages may not exceed a maximum sum related to the number of members of the union[168]; secondly, certain

---

[159] See para.8.26, below. It may be argued that this is supported by *Bonsor v Musicians' Union* [1956] A.C. 104 in which the House of Lords held that a member could sue the union in damages for breach of contract. The majority view seems to have been that it was not necessary to ascribe a separate personality to the union to reach this result.

[160] [1980] Q.B. 585 at 601. The law is different in Canada: *Pulp & Paper Workers of Canada v International Brotherhood of Pulp, etc. Workers* (1973) 37 D.L.R. (3d) 687; *Re International Association of Bridge etc. Workers (Local 97) v Campbell* (1997) 152 D.L.R. (4th) 547.

[161] [1993] A.C. 534 at 545. See para.8.20, above.

[162] Furthermore, Lord Hope in *Jameel v Wall Street Journal Europe SPRL* [2006] UKHL 4; [2007] 1 A.C. 359 at [96], [100], [101] seems to assume that a union can sue. See also *Goldsmith v Bhoyrul* [1998] Q.B. 459 per Buckley J. at 462: "It is common ground that a corporation may sue in defamation, albeit with some obvious limitations. It is likewise established that a trade union and a charity may sue."

[163] In New South Wales it was held in *Robertson v John Fairfax Publications Pty Ltd* [2003] N.S.W.S.C. 473; 58 N.S.W.L.R. 246 that a trade union could sue for libel and was not affected by the *Derbyshire* principle. However, it is said that a trade union in NSW is a corporation (at [23]) and now the matter might be affected by the restriction referred to in para.8.16, above.

[164] Trade Union and Labour Relations (Consolidation) Act 1992, s.10(1)(b).

[165] But where certain action is taken in contemplation or furtherance of a trade dispute (as to which see s.219 of the 1992 Act) the union will enjoy the same immunity as its natural servants or agents.

[166] See *Heatons Transport v TGWU* [1973] A.C. 15, a case of industrial action under the repealed Industrial Relations Act 1971.

[167] S.20. But an action for conspiracy to defame would be governed by that code: s.20(1)(b).

[168] Fewer than 5,000 members, £10,000; between 5,000 and 24,999, £50,000; between 25,000 and 99,999, £125,000; 100,000 or more, £250,000: 1992 Act, s.22. The Secretary of State has power to vary these limits. None of the exceptions in s.22(1) is applicable to defamation. It is not clear how these provisions apply to a case of co-claimants.

property of the union is protected against enforcement proceedings under a judgment.[169]

Section 11. Firms

(a) *Right to sue*

Generally. Although in English law a partnership (other than a limited   **8.26** liability partnership) is not a person separate from its members, an action may be brought in the firm's name for damage suffered by the firm.[170] Hence partners can sue jointly for defamatory words calculated to injure the firm as a body,[171] but they cannot in such joint action recover damages for any injury caused by the words to an individual member of the firm.[172] Such partner can, however, join his separate claim for such injury with the joint claim of the firm.[173] If defamatory words are published of one partner, he can maintain an action for libel or slander in respect of such words,[174] but he cannot recover for any special damage resulting to the firm; all the partners should sue jointly for such injury.[175] However words which reflect directly on one partner may equally be defamatory of the firm as a body, quite apart from the question whether the firm has suffered any special damage. An illustration is an imputation of insolvency to an individual partner in a firm. Such an imputation reflects on the credit of the individual partner; it is submitted that it is also calculated to injure the business of the firm of which he is a member,[176] and therefore both he and the firm may properly join in one action their separate claims for damages.

---

[169] S.23.

[170] See CPR PD7A, para.5A.3.

[171] *Coryton v Lithbye* (1670) 2 Wm.Saund., 5th edn, 115; *Cook v Batchellor* (1802) 3 Bos. & P. 150; *Forster v Lawson* (1826) 3 Bing. 452; *Le Fanu v Malcolmson* (1848) 1 H.L.C. 637 at 669, per Lord Campbell; *EEPTU v Times Newspapers* [1980] Q.B. 585 at 595. The Restatement, 2d, *Torts*, para.562 provides that one who publishes defamatory matter concerning a partnership is liable to it as though it were a corporation. Though less direct, our law appears to reach the same result. As to the nature of imputations actionable by a partnership, there seems in general no reason to distinguish it from a company. So if it is defamatory to say of a company that it mistreats its workers, so also should it be of a partnership. Such a statement about a firm of solicitors or accountants could be very damaging.

[172] *Haythorn v Lawson* (1827) 3 C. & P. 196; *Vogel v Bushnell*, 221 S.W. 819 (Mo., 1920); *Maxwell-Smith v Warren* [2007] NSWCA 270 (which would not seem to be affected by the subsequent s.8 of the Defamation Act 2005 (NSW)).

[173] This seems to be the effect of CPR r.19.1 and 7.3, though RSC Ord.15, r.4(1) was more explicit.

[174] *Harrison v Bevington* (1838) 8 C. & P. 708; *Robinson v Marchant* (1845) 7 Q.B. 918; *Bricker v Campbell* (1891) 21 O.R. 204. See also, *Ayan v Islamic Council of Victoria Pty Ltd* [2009] VSC 119.

[175] *Bricker v Campbell*, above, at 211.

[176] Though the contrary seems to have been held in *Davis v Ruff* (1839) 25 S.C.L. 17.

If one partner in a firm publishes words calculated to injure the firm, the other partners can probably maintain an action of libel against him.[177]

As a limited liability partnership is a body corporate with legal personality separate from that of its members,[178] it is to be treated in the same manner as a company for the purposes of the right to sue for defamation.

(b) *Liability*

8.27 Generally. Partners can be sued in the name of the firm.[179] Under s.10 of the Partnership Act 1890 where, by any wrongful act or omission of any partner acting in the ordinary course of business of the firm, or with the authority of his co-partners, loss or injury is caused to any person not being a partner in the firm, the firm is liable[180] therefor to the same extent as the partner so acting or omitting to act. This assimilates the vicarious liability of partners to that of employers for the torts of their servants,[181] which is also relevant here, for the firm is also liable for torts committed by any agent or servant of the firm acting with their authority and consent, or within the scope of his employment.[182] Partners can therefore be sued jointly for any defamatory words published by one of their number with their authority or while acting in the ordinary course of the firm's business. The fact that a partner acts dishonestly or with the intention of causing harm to the claimant or to serve his personal ends does not preclude the act being in the ordinary course of business of the firm.[183] If there is any doubt as to the liability of a firm for a libel published by one partner, or an agent or servant, it is advisable to join a claim against the individual partner, or agent, or servant with the joint claim against the firm.

8.28 Limited liability partnerships. In the case of a limited liability partnership except as far as otherwise provided by the Limited Liability Partnerships Act 2000 or any other enactment (including regulations made under the Act), the law relating to partnerships does not apply.[184] The Act contains no general provision akin to s.10 of the Partnership Act 1890 on the tort liability of a

---

[177] *Metropolitan Saloon v Hawkins* (1859) 4 H. & N. 87 at 92–93 (obiter, Pollock B. dissenting), citing *Longman v Pole* (1828) Moo. & Mal. 223.

[178] Limited Liability Partnerships Act 2000, s.1(2).

[179] CPR PD7, r.5A.3. It is usual to issue the claim against the firm and not against the individual partners, so as to secure a right of execution against the property of the firm. "A writ of execution shall not issue against the partnership property except on a judgment against the firm": Partnership Act 1890, s.23.

[180] The liability of the partners is joint and several: s.12.

[181] *Dubai Aluminium Co. Ltd v Salaam* [2002] UKHL 48; [2003] 2 A.C. 366 at [106].

[182] See para.8.29, below.

[183] *Dubai Aluminium Co. Ltd v Salaam*, above (a case of an equitable wrong of dishonest participation in breach of a fiduciary duty).

[184] S.1(5).

limited partnership. Under s.6 of the 2000 Act: (1) every member of the partnership is the agent of the limited liability partnership, but (2) the partnership is not bound by anything done by a member in dealing with a person if (a) the member in fact has no authority to act for the partnership by doing that thing, and (b) the person knows that he has no authority or does not know or believe him to be a member of the limited liability partnership. The second part of this proposition seems to be aimed at the partnership's liability for misrepresentation and fraud by a member but can hardly apply to a case of defamation. Accordingly, the first proposition alone will be applicable and the question will be whether the agent acted within the scope of his authority, which will have to be determined according to common law principles.

SECTION 12. UNINCORPORATED ASSOCIATIONS

Generally. The special position of trade unions and firms has already been   **8.29**
considered.[185] Where members of an unincorporated group publish a libel each one who authorised or participated in it is personally liable in the normal way. Where the members of such a group are defamed, each has his own action if sufficiently identified by the libel.[186] An action for libel will not lie against an unincorporated association or body of persons in its collective name,[187] for as an entity it can neither publish nor authorise the publication of a libel.[188] Nor can it sue, for it lacks sufficient personality.[189] Thus, in *North London Central Mosque Trust v The Policy Exchange*[190] it was held that the claimant, an unincorporated charitable trust responsible for the management of a mosque, could not sue in its own name nor could trustees sue on its behalf. While Eady J. accepted that a non-corporate charity could "in a loose sense have a good or bad reputation which might encourage or discourage people from giving it money" that is not good enough if it comes to a claim

---

[185] See the two previous sections.

[186] See para.7.9, above. Note also the example given by O'Connor J. in *EEPTU v The Times Newspapers* [1980] Q.B. 585 (QB) at 595.

[187] *London Association v Greenlands* [1916] 2 A.C. 15 at 20, 30, 39; *Bloom v National Federation* (1918) 35 T.L.R. 50 CA.

[188] Per Lord Buckmaster L.C. in *London Association v Greenlands*, above, at 20.

[189] *EEPTU v The Times Newspapers* [1980] Q.B. 585 (but see the criticism of this case in the context of trade unions in para.8.26, above); *Campbell v Toronto Star* (1990) 73 D.L.R. (4th) 190. In Singapore an unincorporated association registered under the Societies Act (Ch.311) has sufficient personality to sue and be sued for defamation: *Chen Cheng v Central Christian Church* [1996] 1 S.L.R. 313 Sing. CA (which considers the English cases on trade unions). Similarly in some states in the US, unincorporated associations have been held to be entitled to sue. See, for example, *Operation Rescue Nat'l v United States* 975 F.2d 612 at 624 (7th Cir., 1965); *Washburn v Wright* 261 Cal. App.2d 789 (1968). Some courts have however indicated that they can only recover for statements that directly attack their finances or business: *Cont'l Nut Co. v Robert L. Berner Co.* 345 F.2d 395 at 397 (7th Cir., 1965).

[190] [2009] EWHC 3311.

for libel.[191] The only way in which an unincorporated association can sue or be sued is under a representative action under CPR, r.19.6(1)[192]:

> "Where more than one person has the same interest in a claim (a) the claim may be begun or (b) the court may order that the claim be continued, by or against any one or more of the persons who have the same interest as representatives of any other persons who have that interest."

Attempts to use this procedure both to allow an unincorporated association to sue and to allow it to be sued have failed under the old rules. In an action of libel brought by the president, treasurer and secretaries of the Salford Civic League of Help "on behalf of themselves and all other members of the said league" against the proprietors and editor of a newspaper, Phillimore J. struck out those parts of the statement of claim which related to "all others, the members of the said league".[193]

---

[191] [2009] EWHC 3311 (QB) at [7].

[192] For a rare, and unsuccessful, attempt to use a representative action in the context of libel, see *The Law Society of England and Wales v Kordowski* [2011] EWHC 3185 (QB). Claims for libel, harassment and under the Data Protection Act 1998 were brought arising out of publications by the defendant on the "Solicitors from Hell" website in a representative capacity by: (1) the Law Society on behalf of all law firms and individuals involved in or connected with the legal profession that are at serious risk of being named on the website; (2) a named law firm on its behalf but also in a representative capacity on behalf of all law firms and organisations presently listed on the Website, and; (3) a named individual solicitor on his own behalf and also on behalf of all solicitors in England and Wales and other individuals involved with or connected to the legal profession that were at serious risk of being named on the website. Tugendhat J. held that the proceedings brought by the second and third claimants for harassment and under the Data Protection Act (DPA) 1998 should be continued as representative actions (at [162]). Consent to be represented was not required. The class was readily identifiable once persons or firms were named on the website and an injunction would be equally beneficial to all. The common interest arose from the fact that the claim was made in respect of a course of conduct which was the same or similar in relation to all the represented parties. The common grievance arose from the facts pleaded regarding the operation of the website. There was at least a threat to cause distress to all represented parties in circumstances where no defence had ever been raised by the defendant, nor could be raised by him. The question whether that course of conduct constituted a breach of the Protection from Harassment Act 1997 (PHA) and the DPA was common to all represented parties because the same course of conduct was used in respect of all of them (at [163]). The position with regard to libel was different. To the extent that they complained of words which referred to all solicitors named in the website (that is both words already published and words which the defendant threatens to publish in the future) there was a common interest. However, whether publication of those words was, or might be, unlawful depended on the conduct of the defendant. It depended upon whether the words were true or false, or whether they could be defended under one of the other established defences in libel. In the circumstances therefore judgment would have to be obtained before it could be said of any person that they would qualify as someone entitled to an injunction against the defendant, or to any remedy other than damages. It followed that in respect of the libel claims, the claimants could not act in a representative capacity (at [166]–[169]).

[193] *Jenkins v John Bull, The Times*, April 20, 1910. In *EEPTU v The Times Newspapers* [1980] Q.B. 585 a representative action was refused because the relief sought is damages, and each member has an individual reputation. See also *Campbell v Toronto Star* (1990) 73 D.L.R. (4th) 190 applying similar reasoning to the equivalent Ontario provision. "To my mind," said Fletcher Moulton L.J. in *Markt v Knight & Co* [1910] 2 K.B. 1021 at 1040:

> "no representative action can lie where the sole relief sought is damages, because they have to be proved separately in the case of each plaintiff, and, therefore, the possibility of representation ceases."

In *Mercantile Marine v Toms*[194] the plaintiff complained of a libel contained in a journal published by an unincorporated association of 15,000 members called "The Imperial Mutual Service Guild", and brought an action against the chairman, vice-chairman and secretary of the Guild, and then applied for an order that the three defendants should be appointed to represent all the other members of the Guild; the Court of Appeal affirmed an order refusing the application. Swinfen Eady L.J. said[195]:

> "I have great difficulty in seeing that in this case there are numerous persons having the same interest in this cause or matter within the meaning of the rule. The action is for libel, and the plaintiffs must prove who published the libel, and prima facie only those who have published it either by themselves or their servants or agents or have authorised its publication are liable. The various members of the association may be in a wholly different position. If the members of the management committee were sued, and if in fact they had authorised the publication of the libel, they could raise such defences as might be open to them . . .   The other members of the association, if sued might say that, however defamatory the words complained of might be, they did not authorise their publication . . . In my opinion, the rule is not intended to apply to such a case."[196]

Section 13. Vicarious Liability

Vicarious liability: its scope. Two principles are as much applicable to **8.30** defamation as to any other tort. First, that where A procures or authorises B to commit a tort, A is liable with B as a joint tortfeasor. Secondly, that where there is a relationship in the nature of employment (formerly referred to as that of "master and servant" and signifying a contract of service) between A and B and "in the course of" that employment, B (the employee) commits a tort, A is vicariously liable for B's act. However, with regard to the second category there has, in the context of defamation, been a tendency to speak in the more general language of principal and agent and this has sometimes been reflected in statute.[197] This causes some difficulty, for while there are undoubtedly examples of vicarious liability in tort for persons who are not employees but who can be described as agents,[198] such a liability is not of universal

---

Though a representative action can be brought in tort for a declaration joined with a personal claim for damages (*Prudential Assurance v Newman Industries* [1981] Ch. 229) it is unlikely that a claim for defamation could be conducted in this way.

[194] [1916] 2 K.B. 243 CA; *Hardie v Chiltern* [1928] 1 K.B. 663 CA; *Ricci v Chow* [1987] 1 W.L.R. 1658 CA.

[195] [1916] 2 K.B. at 246–247.

[196] However, observations here and in *Temperton v Russell* [1893] 1 Q.B. 435 CA at 438, that the procedure can never be applicable to a claim in tort for damages may go too far. See *Prudential Assurance v Newman Industries* [1981] Ch. 229; *EMI Records v Riley* [1981] 1 W.L.R. 923.

[197] See, e.g. s.4(5) of the Defamation Act 1952, repealed by the Defamation Act 1996. The New Zealand Defamation Act 1992, s.20(4) preserves whatever liability exists at common law for the acts of employees or agents but does not state what that is.

[198] E.g. the special liability of the owner of a vehicle (*Morgans v Launchbury* [1973] A.C. 127).

application[199]: an independent contractor may be described as an agent because he is engaged to bring about a result for a principal,[200] but it is fundamental that his "employer" is not liable (with certain exceptions relating to non-delegable duties) for torts committed by the contractor but not authorised by the employer. One view is that agency is primarily a contractual concept which has no general relevance to the law of tort[201]; another is that there is no distinction in principle and the differences in result are explained by the fact that the authority of an agent will commonly be more restricted than that of an employee.[202]

In practice the issue is less important than might appear because of the rule[203] that any person who has authorised[204] or participated in the publication of a libel is treated as publishing the libel and hence is liable in his own right. Thus if B writes a book and A publishes it, A is liable for his own act of publication whether B is his employee or agent or neither.[205] The position is the same where newspaper[206] A publishes an article or letter submitted by B.[207] Where, however, privilege or fair comment is in issue it may not be possible to avoid the issue in this way. Where A publishes material by B on

---

[199] See the criticism by the Faulks Committee, Cmnd.5909 (1975), para.266, fn.162, of the tendency in earlier editions of this book to equate "master and servant" and "principal and agent".

[200] But it was held in *Gros v Cook* (1969) 113 S.J. 408 that a person might be an agent though neither a servant nor an independent contractor; and see *Cornwall v Rowan* [2004] SASC 384; 90 S.A.S.R. 269. Clearly there may be a relationship of agency without a contract of agency. However in *Bishop v State of New South Wales* [2000] N.S.W.S.C. 1042, it was regarded as self-evident that the State was not vicariously liable for the acts of pupils performing a school play, though failure by the headmaster to stop the performance might involve the vicarious liability of the state.

[201] Most forcefully put by Clerk and Lindsell, *Torts*, 20th edn (2010), para.6.75. The undoubted fact that a principal is vicariously liable for the fraud of his agent (although many of the cases in fact involve servants) is explained by the fact that fraud commonly takes place in a contractual context. See also the discussion in *Wong Wai Hing v Hui Wei Lee* [2001] 1 H.K.L.R.D. 736, HKCA.

[202] *Heatons Transport v TGWU* [1973] A.C. 15 at 99–100.

[203] Subject to the restrictions imposed by the Defamation Act 1996: para.6.10, above.

[204] While a client may be liable for authorised communications on his behalf by his solicitor, he is certainly not automatically liable for anything which the solicitor purports to say on his behalf: *Bezant v Rausing* [2007] EWHC 1118 (QB).

[205] "An agreement between A and B for B to speak on A's television programme about a particular topic in whatever terms he chooses could not constitute B as A's agent. It cannot be converted into an authority of itself from A to B to speak for and on behalf of A": *Osmose New Zealand v Wakeling* [2007] 1 N.Z.L.R. 841 at [77]. Where, as in that case, B has sought A's assistance to provide a platform for B's views, the position is, if anything, rather the reverse.

[206] A broadcasting company is also treated as publishing everything transmitted by it, though it may have a defence of innocent dissemination in some cases: para.6.30, above. The position in respect of internet service providers and providers of publication platforms like Blogger and Twitter is more complicated. See further paras 6.25–6.29, above.

[207] Earlier editions of this book quoted the statement in *Crane v Bennett*, 177 N.Y. 106 at 109 (1904) that a proprietor of a newspaper was liable for libels appearing in its columns without his knowledge or consent because his "liability is not upon the ground of his being the publisher, but because he is responsible for the acts of the actual publisher". However, this statement is made in the context of a proprietor who is a natural person. Nowadays the newspaper is likely to be a

an occasion of qualified privilege, if B was actuated by malice and A was unaware of this state of mind, A will have a defence unless the relationship between A and B was such as to make A responsible (i.e. vicariously liable) for B's actions. Plainly A will be responsible where A is a newspaper and B is a journalist employed by it; equally plainly, the publisher of a book is not the agent of the printer to prepare the work to be printed.[208] But is the malice of a (non-employed) contributor of an article[209] to a newspaper or magazine to be attributed to the publisher? Cases on reviewers have suggested that it is,[210] though there is also support for the contrary view.[211]

In the context of misrepresentation it is clearly established that a principal is identified with an agent (not being an employee) acting within the scope of his authority.[212] Where defamation is committed by an agent in the context of negotiating with a third party on behalf of his principal (e.g. an insurance agent canvassing business) it seems that vicarious liability similarly extends beyond employees in the strict sense.[213]

---

corporation and it is submitted that it is simpler and more accurate to say that the *newspaper* publishes the story than that it is vicariously liable for the act of the editor. Of course, what is said in the American case remains perfectly correct as a proposition of vicarious liability. In *Tamiz v Google Inc.* [2013] EWCA Civ 68; [2013] 1 W.L.R. 2151 CA, the Court of Appeal stated (at [25]) that, as the provider of the Blogger service, Google Inc. facilitated the publication of blogs including any comments published on them. However, "there is no relationship of employment or agency between Google Inc. and the bloggers or those posting comments on the blogs: such people are plainly independent of Google Inc and do not act in any sense on its behalf or in its name." There could therefore be no question of Google Inc. being vicariously liable for what the bloggers and/or those who comment had written. Presumably, a similar conclusion would be reached with regard to Twitter and the providers of other platforms on which people may publish.

[208] This is the clear implication of *Egger v Chelmsford* [1965] 1 Q.B. 248 CA in overruling *Smith v Streatfield* [1913] 3 K.B. 764. This is quite independent of the defence accorded to the printer by s.1 of the Defamation Act 1996: para.6.31, above.

[209] Distinguish the case of a "letter to the editor": *Lyon v Daily Telegraph* [1943] K.B. 746 at 752. The controversial decision in *Chernesky v Armadale Publishers* [1979] 1 S.C.R. 1067 did not turn on the newspaper being responsible for the malice of the writer of the letter but upon the defence of fair comment not being available if the originator of the statement was actuated by malice. This is not English law: *Telnikoff v Matusevitch* [1992] 2 A.C. 343, para.12.37, below.

[210] *Gros v Cook* (1969) 113 S.J. 408 (though note that the Faulks Committee (Cmnd.5909, 1975) para.272 expressed some doubt whether the writer was correctly classed as an agent and not an independent contractor); *Falcke v Herald* (1924) V.R. 56 (a good example of the tendency to equiparate servants and agents). In *McLeod v Jones* [1977] 1 N.Z.L.R. 441 it was conceded that the operator of a "talk-back" show for a radio station was an independent contractor and therefore any malice could not be imputed back to the radio station.

[211] *McKenna v MGN Ltd*, July 16, 2007, (QB), HQ04X03315 at [12] (QB) (where the issue was costs). Intuitively, there is much to be said for the view that a newspaper should bear responsibility for the malice of a regular columnist, even if elements of his contract point away from the usual indicia of a contract of service (e.g. because he has freedom to choose what he writes about and is simply contracted to produce a certain number of pieces over a period). Arguably an important factor should be whether material is solicited (which a review or pieces in a regular column will be—it is not known whether the article in *McKenna* was).

[212] Clerk and Lindsell, *Torts*, 20th edn (2010), para.6.75.

[213] See the judgment of Dixon J. in *Colonial Mutual v Producers and Citizens* (1931) 46 C.L.R. 41 at 48–50, in particular at 49:

Generally in this section the terminology of employer and employee is adopted, without meaning to suggest that liability is necessarily limited to that relationship.

8.31 General principles. The principles upon which vicarious liability will arise for the acts of an employee are part of the general law of tort and will not be examined in detail here.[214] The fundamental principle is that the employer is liable[215] where the employee was acting within the scope of his employment and that is as applicable to defamation as to any other tort.[216] In practice because we are concerned with the making of a statement by the employee, and this must almost of necessity be a deliberate act on his part,[217] it may be more natural to speak of the scope of the employee's authority rather than the scope of employment, but that does not involve any difference of principle.[218] Vicarious liability applies to slander as much as to libel,[219] despite some hesitation in the Scots cases[220] on the ground that opening the door to liability for rashly uttered words opens it very wide indeed.[221]

8.32 The scope of employment. Having ascertained what it is that the employee was employed to do,[222] it may be taken that he has authority to do and say anything which may be reasonably necessary for effectively carrying out his duties. Within these limits he will be taken to have a discretion as to the manner in which he will discharge his duties.[223]

"I think that in performing these services for the company, [the agent] does not act independently, but as a representative of the company, which accordingly must be considered as itself conducting the negotiations in person."

[214] See Clerk and Lindsell, *Torts*, 20th edn (2010), Ch.6.

[215] Vicarious liability extends to making an employer liable for words published by one employee to another, and the defence of common employment is not available even where the claimant is another employee: *Riddick v Thames Board Mills* [1977] Q.B. 881 CA, Lord Denning M.R. dissenting on this point; note that the plaintiff was no longer a fellow-servant when the words were published. See also, *Cunningham v Essex County Council*, unreported, June 26, 2000 (QB).

[216] *Citizens' Life Assurance Co. v Brown* [1904] A.C. 423 PC.

[217] There may, however, be cases of accidental actionable publication (see para.6.10, above) to which the ordinary principles of vicarious liability for negligence would apply.

[218] So, the principle stated in *Citizens' Life v Brown* was applied in Scotland in *Ellis v National Free Association* (1905) 7 F. 629, where Lord Dunedin said: "The question is always, Was the servant, in doing what is complained of, acting within the scope of his authority or not?" and the court altered the issue so as to leave it open to either side to prove, either that the writing of the defamatory letter fell within the scope of the secretary's employment, or that it was merely a private letter, and one for which the employers were in no way responsible.

[219] In *Finburgh v Moss' Empires*, 1908 S.C. 928 Lords Stormonth-Darling and Ardwell said that there was no sound reason why the principle should not apply to slander as well as to libel. Cf. *Craig v Inveresk Paper Merchants*, 1970 S.L.T. (Notes) 50. See also *Richards v Australasian Temperance* (1931) N.Z.L.R. 618; *Harrison v Joy Oil* [1938] 4 D.L.R. 360.

[220] Scots law does not require special damage for oral defamation.

[221] See para.8.32, below. Some American jurisdictions restrict liability of the employer for slander to cases where the words are uttered at his direction: 50 Am.Jur.2d, *Libel and Slander*, para.359.

[222] As to which, see *Neville v C & A Modes Ltd*, 1945 S.C. 175.

[223] *NSW County Press v Stewart* (1911) 12 C.L.R. 481 at 500 (a case where the authority of the servant was limited to the obtaining of a copy of an advertisement order).

"A person who puts another in his place to do a class of acts in his absence, necessarily leaves him to determine, according to the circumstances that arise, when an act of that class is to be done, and trusts him for the manner in which it is done; and consequently he is held answerable for the wrong of the person so entrusted either in the manner of doing such an act, or in doing such an act under circumstances in which it ought not to have been done; provided that what was done was done, not from any caprice of the servant, but in the course of the employment."[224]

The employee is not necessarily outside the scope of his employment because he has been expressly forbidden to publish any defamatory matter[225] or because he has been forbidden to publish the material in question.[226] The employee will be deemed to have acted within the scope of his employment when the publication, although itself unauthorised, is so directly incidental to some act which he was authorised to do that it may be said to be a mode, though no doubt an improper mode, of performing such authorised act.[227] This approach of asking whether the act is an improper method of doing what the employee was employed to do has been criticised as artificial where an intentional tort is involved,[228] although it has also been said to be a convenient rule of thumb which provides the answer in very many cases.[229] The ultimate question is whether there is a sufficiently close connection between the employment and the wrongdoing.[230] It is not, however, sufficient that the publication of the libel takes place while the employee is on the employer's premises[231] or making use of information acquired during the employment; it must be possible to say that the employee had express or implied or apparent

---

[224] Per Willes J. in *Bayley v Manchester Ry* (1872) L. R.7 C.P. 415 at 420 (not a case of defamation).

[225] *Colonial Mutual v Producers and Citizens* (1931) 46 C.L.R. 41; cf. *Crescent Sales v British Products* [1936] V.L.R. 336. There is a close analogy with such cases as *Limpus v L.G.O. Co* (1862) 1 H. & C. 526 (prohibition on racing did not prevent employer being liable for accident caused by racing).

[226] Obviously this is so where the disobedience of the order is a mistake. But it is submitted that the employer may be liable even if the disobedience with regard to the particular material is deliberate, so long as publication of material is part of the employee's duty.

[227] Per Stephen J. in *Brown v Citizens Life Assurance Co* (1902) 2 N.S.W.S.R. at 212. "The law upon this subject cannot better be expressed," said Lord Lindley in the Privy Council: sub nom. *Citizens Life Assurance Co. v Brown* [1904] A.C. 423 at 428. Thus it is submitted that the employer is liable for an accusation of theft made by a shop assistant against a customer: *Neville v C & A Modes*, 1945 S.C. 175; *Bonette v Woolworths* (1937) 37 N.S.W.S.R. 142 NSWCA; *Southwest Drugstores Inc. v Garner* 195 So.2d 837 (Miss., 1967). Cf. *Mandelston v North British Ry*, 1917 S.C. 442 HL; *Freer v Zeb* [2008] EWHC 212 (QB).

[228] *Lister v Hesley Hall Ltd* [2001] UKHL 22; [2002] 1 A.C. 215.

[229] Ibid. at [60].

[230] See *Freer v Zeb* [2008] EWHC 212 (QB): words spoken at work by employees were held not to be in the course of employment as they had nothing to do with their employment as, respectively, an order taker for pizzas and a delivery driver, but instead related to their personal lives and in particular "the question of whether they were in a relationship".

[231] *Linebaugh v Sheraton Mich. Corp*, 497 N.W.2d 585 (Mich., 1993) (defamatory cartoon about co-workers).

authority to communicate with others on behalf of the employer[232] and that the publication was within the scope of that authority.[233]

In *Pena v Tameside Hospital NHS Foundation Trust*[234] it was held that the defendant Hospital Trust was not vicariously liable for emails written by a consultant in response to an email sent by the claimant, the chairman of the hospital's staff committee, proposing a vote of no confidence in the Trust's board. While the subject matter of the emails was clearly concerned with the way the hospital was run and the way the claimant was behaving as a representative of the interests of senior clinical staff, that did not mean that the consultant was acting, in any sense, on the Trust's behalf in giving vent to his personal views. The writing of the emails by the consultant could not be said to be in any way part of or incidental to the performance of the clinical function to which his employment related. Nor would it in any way be "just" that the Trust should be held liable for anything said by these doctors by way of participating in the debate.

Some Scots cases on slander take a narrow view of the scope of authority. Thus in *Craig v Inveresk Paper Merchants*[235] statements made by the defendants' sales representatives, while canvassing for orders, to the effect that the pursuer was going out of business were held not to be the responsibility of the employer on the ground that it was not within the authority of sales staff to make statements about competitors. This is not easy to reconcile with the leading Australian case.[236]

8.33 Malice on the part of the employee. It is not enough to take the employee outside the scope of his employment that he is guilty of malice, otherwise there could never be vicarious liability for a statement published by an employee on a privileged occasion, and it is clearly established that there can be. In *Falcke v Herald*[237] the defendants' art critic wrote a malicious article about the plaintiff's work. In holding that the critic's malice in writing

---

[232] In *Brown v Marron* [2001] WASC 100, it was held that a letter written on company notepaper by a director objecting to a golf club membership application could not, on the facts, be understood as written on behalf of the company.

[233] See, e.g. *Leitch v Switchenko*, 426 N.W.2d 804 (Mich., 1988); *Hensley v Armstrong World Industries*, 798 F.Supp. 653 (1992); *Cameron v Young's Express Deliveries*, 1950 S.L.T. (Sh. Ct.) 40.

[234] [2011] EWHC 3027 (QB).

[235] 1970 S.L.T. (Notes) 50. See also *Glasgow Corp v Lorimer* [1911] A.C. 209 (accusation by rate collector of falsifying receipt not within course of employment). In *Cumming v G.N. Ry of Scotland*, 1916 1 S.L.T. 179, the servant had accused the pursuer of travelling twice on the same ticket. Lord Ormidale would have been prepared to hold this within the scope of employment if it had taken place on railway premises rather than at a distance. See also *Eprile v Caledonian Ry* (1898) 6 S.L.T. 65; *Cameron v Yeats* (1899) 1 F. 456 at 463; *Agnew v British Life* (1906) 8 F. 422 at 427; *Aiken v Caledonian Ry* 1913 S.C. 66.

[236] *Colonial Mutual v Producers and Citizens* (1931) 46 C.L.R. 41 (though note that the minority would have followed the more restrictive approach).

[237] (1924) V.R. 56; *Citizens' Life Assurance Co. v Brown* [1904] A.C. 423 PC.

the piece was imputable to the defendants in publishing it, McArthur J. said:

> "Instead of writing the comment himself he employs a servant or agent to write it for him. *Qui facit per alium facit per se.* It seems to me that he must be responsible for both the acts and the state of mind of his servant or agent. It is true that until the words are published, the plaintiff has no cause of action, but once they are published, and once the question arises as to whether or not they are fair comment, the circumstances under which they were written become important, and if it be shown that they were written dishonestly or maliciously by the servant or agent employed by the defendant to write then it seems to me that that dishonesty or malice is imputable to the defendant so as to destroy the fair comment."

In the case of other torts (e.g. assault) the employer may not be vicariously liable for an act which, although within the course of employment from the point of view of objective appearance, is in fact solely an act of personal vengeance[238] and a similar approach has been adopted in a case of slander.[239] On general principles, however, an employee should not be outside the scope of his employment merely because he was not seeking to advance the employer's interests[240] but to advance his own in publishing the libel: an employer may, for example, be liable for fraud by an employee whom he has clothed with authority to deal with customers,[241] or for theft by an employee to whom bailed goods have been entrusted[242] or for sexual assault on a child who has been committed to the employee's care.[243]

It seems, however, that where an employee has "nothing whatever to do with the composition of the libel or the approval of its contents", but "in obedience to the command of his principal merely does the mechanical act of distributing it when handed to him complete", malice on his part is irrelevant, and will not destroy any privilege the employer may have in respect of the publication.[244]

In the contrary case, where the employee innocently publishes defamatory material on a privileged occasion he will escape liability for he is not guilty of malice[245]; but if the employee is guilty of malice the employer will be liable, provided that he authorised or directed the publication. However if he does not so authorise or direct, then he will not, it seems, become liable

---

[238] See *Warren v Henlys Ltd* [1948] 2 All E.R. 935. But see now *Mattis v Pollock* [2003] EWCA Civ 887.

[239] *Aiken v Caledonian Ry*, 1913 S.C. 66 (P dismissed by D's manager for stealing takings, charge motivated by P's rejection of manager's advances. See in particular Lord Salvesen at (77)). See also the dissenting judgment of Evatt J. in *Colonial Mutual v Producers and Citizens* (1931) 46 C.L.R. 41.

[240] Though the leading case of *Citizens' Life Assurance Co. v Brown* [1904] A.C. 423 PC, is a very clear example of the servant seeking to do just this.

[241] *Lloyd v Grace Smith & Co* [1912] A.C. 716 HL.

[242] *Morris v CW Martin & Sons* [1966] 1 Q.B. 716 CA.

[243] *Lister v Hesley Hall Ltd* [2001] UKHL 22; [2002] 1 A.C. 215.

[244] See para.17.23, below.

[245] See para.17.25, below.

merely because he was aware of the facts which showed that the statement was untrue, for it is not possible to add the guilty mind of A to the act of B.[246] Similarly, where one employee publishes the material innocently, the employer is not liable merely because another employee had a malicious mind: "a company's mind is not to be assessed on the totality of knowledge of its servants".[247]

8.34 Ratification of unauthorised act. Though most of the cases are about contracts, the doctrine of ratification applies as much to unauthorised acts which are torts. If the publication of the libel was outside the scope of the employment, ratification by the employer will make him liable for it.

> "That an act done, for another, by a person not assuming to act for himself, but for such other person, though without any precedent authority whatever, becomes the act of the principal, if subsequently ratified by him, is the known and well-established rule of law. In that case the principal is bound by the act, whether it be for his detriment or his advantage, and whether it be founded on a tort or a contract, to the same extent as by, and with all the consequences which follow from, the same act done by his previous authority."[248]

So where a letter was written by a building inspector employed by a council to a building owner containing a defamatory statement about the contractor for the building and at the request of the contractor the letter was considered by the council, who resolved to indorse the action of the inspector in writing and sending the letter, it was held that the resolution of the council amounted to an approval and adoption by it of the action of the inspector and was the same as if the council had expressly authorised the inspector to act as he did.[249] But the employee must in publishing the libel have acted, or assumed to act, on behalf of the principal or employer,[250] and there must be such an unqualified adoption on the part of the principal or employer as to lead to the inference that he intended to take upon himself responsibility for its publication.[251]

---

[246] This is the rule in fraud: *Armstrong v Strain* [1952] 1 K.B. 232 CA.

[247] Per Sellers L.J. in *Broadway Approvals v Odhams Press* [1965] 1 W.L.R. 805 CA at 813; *Webster v British Gas Services Ltd* [2003] EWHC 1188 (QB) at [30]; *Pinniger v John Fairfax* (1979) 26 A.L.R. 55; *Waterhouse v Broadcasting Station 2GB Pty* (1985) 1 N.S.W.L.R. 58 at 72; *Bruton v Estate Agents Licensing Authority* [1996] 2 V.R. 274. Thus, where a non-malicious employee of a company publishes a report on a privileged occasion, the malice of other employees who provided information for the report would not be relevant unless they contemplated or must have contemplated its republication: *Riddick v Thames Board Mills* [1977] Q.B. 881 CA at 900, 908–910. But cf. *Krakowski v Eurolynx Properties* (1995) 183 C.L.R. 563 at 583 (fraud).

[248] *Wilson v Tumman* (1843) 6 M. & Gr. 236 at 242.

[249] *Dawson v County of Bulli* (1927) 27 N.S.W.S.R. 509.

[250] At least this is the case in contract (*Keighley, Maxsted v Durrant* [1901] A.C. 240) where the requirement is obviously connected with privity, but some such requirement is explicit in the general statement in *Wilson v Tumman*.

[251] *Marsh v Joseph* [1897] 1 Ch. 213 CA at 246. Despite a tendency in some of them to use the terminology of ratification, the cases holding that A may be liable for failing to take steps to remove defamatory matter deposited on his premises by B (see para.6.12, above) do not, it is submitted, rest upon this doctrine.

Personal liability. To say that the employer is liable for defamation by the   **8.35**
employee is not to say that the employee is not liable, for:

> "it is a fundamental principle of English law that no tortfeasor can excuse himself
> from the consequences of his acts by setting up that he was acting only as the agent
> of another."[252]

To this, however, three qualifications must be made. First, where an employee, acting on instructions from his employer, publishes a libel on an occasion which is privileged as between the employer and the person to whom the libel is published, such privilege will enure for the benefit of the employee,[253] and even proof that the principal is malicious will not defeat the agent's privilege.[254] Secondly, where the act done by the employee was not manifestly unlawful he may be entitled to an indemnity at common law[255]; and in any case where the employee is liable along with the employer he may seek a contribution or indemnity under the Civil Liability (Contribution) Act 1978.[256] Thirdly, a person who is not the author, editor or commercial publisher of defamatory matter but who has done some subordinate act contributing to publication, who had no reason to know that he was contributing to a defamatory publication and who has taken reasonable care, may have a defence under s.1 of the Defamation Act 1996.[257]

---

[252] Per Lord Moulton in *Vacher v London Society of Compositors* [1913] A.C. 107 at 131. See also *De Crespigny v Wellesley* (1829) 5 Bing. 392 at 405; *Adam v Ward* [1917] A.C. 309 at 341; *Mount Cook Group v Johnstone Motors* [1990] 2 N.Z.L.R. 483. Where liability is for negligence and turns on assumption of responsibility, the fact that a director of a company is actually to carry out the work for the company does not necessarily mean that he incurs personal liability: *Williams v Natural Life Health Foods Ltd* [1998] 1 W.L.R. 830 HL (though cf. *Merrett v Babb* [2001] EWCA Civ 214; [2001] Q.B. 1174 (employee)). But this does not mean that a director, acting fraudulently on behalf of a company, can say, "It was not my fraud but only the company's fraud": *Standard Chartered Bank v Pakistan National Shipping Corp (No.2)* [2002] UKHL 43; [2003] 1 A.C. 959. So also a director or employee who authorises or participates in the publication of a libel incurs personal liability, subject to s.1 of the Defamation Act 1996.

[253] *Baker v Carrick* [1894] 1 Q.B. 838; *Smith v Streatfield* [1913] 3 K.B. 764; *Adam v Ward* [1917] A.C. 309.

[254] *Egger v Chelmsford* [1965] 1 Q.B. 248 CA. See para.17.24, below.

[255] *Adamson v Jarvis* (1827) 4 Bing. 66.

[256] See para.27.44, below. But where the issue is a contribution between the employer and some tortfeasor other than the employee, the employer cannot claim to be judged as innocent of wrongdoing, for he is identified with the employee for whom he is vicariously liable: *Dubai Aluminium Co. Ltd v Salaam* [2002] UKHL 48; [2003] 1 All E.R. 97.

[257] See para.6.31ff, above. But in practice the liability of the employer in cases to which s.1 applies will not be truly vicarious in the sense used in this section.

CHAPTER 9

REMEDIES

SECTION 1. COMPENSATORY (GENERAL) DAMAGES

Damages the primary remedy: vindication and other reme- 9.1
dies. Since defamation is an injury to a person's reputation, it might be
thought that the primary remedy would be an order declaring the calumny
false or requiring the defendant to undo the injury by a corrective publication,
all the more so when proof of loss measurable directly in financial terms is not
required by the law and is anyway rarely obtainable.[1] In fact, however, the

---

[1] English law is, comparatively speaking, unusual in not providing discursive remedies for
defamation. Most European, and many non-European, states have right of reply and correction
provisions that apply in defamation claims. For a survey of international and national discursive
remedies, see Youm, "Rights of Reply and Freedom of the Press: An International and Comparative Perspective" 6 *Geo. Wash. L. Rev.* 1017 (2007–2008). See also, Fleming, "Retraction and
Reply: Alternative Remedies for Defamation" (1978) *University of British Columbia Law Review*
12; Jerome A. Barron, "Access to the Press—A New First Amendment Right" *Harvard Law
Review* (1967) 80, 1641; Dario Milo, *Defamation and Freedom of Speech* (Oxford: OUP, 2008),
ch.VIII.
  While the right to reply and/or require correction is well established in the law of many
jurisdictions, states whose law are based on English law do not usually provide such a right. A
right of reply was rejected as incompatible with the First Amendment by the US Supreme Court
in *Miami Herald Publ'g Co. v Tornillo*, 418 U.S. 241, 259 (1974). For an overview of the media
access and reply rights in US law, see Barron, "Rights of Access and Reply to the Media in the
United States Today" 25 Comm. & L. 1, 2 (2003). The New Zealand Defamation Act 1995 makes
provision for a retraction or reply in s.25 and allows the court to make a recommendation as to
correction and its content (ss.26, 27). In both cases, the remedy must be triggered by an
application by the plaintiff. The South African Law Commission rejected a general right of reply
in 1991 (South African Law Commission Interim Report *Group and Human Rights* (Project 58,
1991). The Irish Defamation Act 2009 does not contain a right of reply provision but does contain
two non-damages restorative remedies. First, by s.28 a person who claims to be the subject of a
defamatory statement may apply to the Circuit Court for a declaratory order that the statement is
false and defamatory. The court is to make an order to that effect if the statement satisfies those
conditions, the respondent has no defence and the respondent has failed to make, at the applicant's
request, an apology, correction or retraction. The applicant is not required to prove that the
statement was false. No damages may be awarded on such an application, nor may the applicant
bring any other proceedings in respect of any cause of action arising out of the statement.

primary remedy of the common law is not correction but damages and there is no general power either to require the defendant to correct or for the court to declare that the claimant was defamed[2] or that the statement was false. The only situation in which there is a power to make a declaration of falsity is under the summary procedure governed by the Defamation Act 1996.[3] Where the court disposes of the claim under the summary procedure it may also order

---

Secondly, by s.30 the court may, on the application of a successful plaintiff in a defamation action, make an order directing the defendant to publish a correction of the statement in such a manner as will ensure (unless the plaintiff otherwise requests) "that it is communicated to all or substantially all of those persons to whom the defamatory statement was published". Such an order may also be made in a Circuit Court application for a declaratory order under s.28. No right of reply or correction is available in Australian law. There is no specific mention in the European Convention on Human Rights of a right of reply but the Court has considered the validity of reply/ rectification provisions in a number of cases. In *Melynychuk v Ukraine* App. Nos 28851/95, 28852/95, January 16, 1998 a newspaper published a highly critical review by P of a book of poetry written by the applicant. The newspaper refused to publish a reply as required by Ukrainian Law and the applicant complained that his art.10 right had been infringed. The court rejected the applicant's complaint as unfounded. The applicant had been offered such an opportunity but his proposed reply contained obscene and abusive remarks about the book reviewer's personality and consequently the newspaper was justified in refusing to publish it. The court did however note that, while newspapers and other privately owned media must be free to exercise editorial discretion in deciding whether to publish articles, comments and letters submitted by private individuals, there may be exceptional circumstances in which a newspaper may legitimately be required to publish, for example, a retraction, an apology or a judgment in a defamation case. Consequently, there will be situations when a positive obligation may arise for the state to ensure an individual's freedom of expression in such media. So too in *Czanics v Hungary* (2009) App. No.12188/06 a remedy to rectify assertions was not disapproved though the remedy was held to be in breach of art.10 because of the disproportionate finding by the court that the applicant had overstepped the bounds of tolerable criticism rather than because of the "relatively mild sanction" (at [46]). Cf. *Karsai v Hungary* (2009), App. no.5380/07, in which it was held that the obligation placed on a historian to publish a rectification breached art.10. The applicant was a university professor of history who published an article critical of a named author. The author brought a civil action, and the Court of Appeal ordered the publication of a rectification. The European Court depicted the debate as of utmost public interest which had a bearing on responses to Hungary's totalitarian era. The author had himself widely published on the subject and so had voluntarily exposed himself to public comment. Thus, harsh criticism was to be permitted between such protagonists. The obligation to publish a rectification was judged to affect unduly the applicant's professional credibility as a historian and was therefore capable of producing an intimidating effect which would dampen public debate to the detriment of art.10.

[2] In *Bracks v Smyth-Kirk* [2009] NSWCA 410 the New South Wales Court of Appeal discussed but left undecided whether a declaration that the claimant has been defamed might be available in Australian law. A declaration is available under the law of New Zealand (Defamation Act 1992, s.24) but Elias J. in *Lange v Atkinson* [1997] 2 NZLR 22 at 48 said that it was quite unclear whether privilege and the like would be defences to applications for a declaration: "If the defendant is protected against liability for damages, a balance in keeping with the pragmatic approach of the common law may be that the defence does not apply to a claim for declaration."

[3] See s.9(1)(a) and Ch.30, below. The summary procedure has its origin in a draft Defamation Bill prepared by Lord Hoffmann. One purpose of the procedure is to assist persons who want a swift vindication of reputation rather than substantial damages. The Neill Committee was against such a procedure: see its report (1991), Ch.XVII. Declarations of falsity have been granted in a number of cases under the summary procedure. See, for example, *Mahfouz v Brisard (No.1)* [2004] EWHC 1735 (QB); *Bin Mahfouz v Ehrenfeld* [2005] EWHC 1156 (QB); *Lloyd v Ratnatunga,* unreported, March 7, 2007 (QB).

that the defendant publish or cause to be published a suitable correction and apology.[4] If the parties cannot agree on the time, manner, form or place of publication the court may direct the defendant to take such reasonable and practicable steps as it considers appropriate. However, if the parties cannot agree on the content, all the court can do is to order the defendant to publish a summary of its judgment.[5] If the defendant wishes to take advantage of the offer of amends procedure under the Act of 1996[6] the offer must include an offer of a suitable correction and apology, but if the parties do not agree on the steps to be taken in fulfilment of this, the defendant may take such steps as he thinks appropriate,[7] the suitability of such steps being a matter which will affect compensation.[8] Nor is there any power to compel the defendant to publish a counter statement or reply by the claimant[9] though a court will be able, under Defamation Act 2013, s.12, (when it comes into force) to order the defendant to publish a summary of the judgment "where the court gives judgment for the claimant in an action for defamation".[10] So too, under s.13 of the 2013 Act, a court that has given judgment for a clamant will be able to order the operator of a website on which a defamatory statement is posted to remove the statement or any person who was not the author, editor or publisher of the defamatory statement to stop distributing, selling or exhibiting material containing the statement.[11] However, in the case of certain reports

---

[4] *Loutchansky v Times Newspapers Ltd (Nos 2–5)* [2002] EWCA Civ 1805; [2002] Q.B. 321 at [98]–[99]. A declaration of falsity and an order for an apology:

"are not available ordinarily, so, in this case, the claimant would not be able to obtain an order for an apology if his claim for damages was not disposed of summarily. This is an anomaly but it is an anomaly which applies to any summary disposal at whatever stage this takes place. The defendant's position however will always be protected by the fact that the judge has a discretion as to whether to make such an order."

[5] Defamation Act 1996, s.9(2). In any case, of course, failure to accept a proper, published apology may amount to failure to mitigate loss. A defendant television company's offer of an interview in which he can defend himself should not be treated like an apology for this purpose. That allows the defendant to maintain his original stance and in effect reverses the burden of proof on falsity: *Television New Zealand Ltd v Ah Koy* [2002] 2 N.Z.L.R. 616, NZCA.

[6] See para.19.1, below.

[7] S.3(4).

[8] S.3(5).

[9] The Faulks Committee rejected the introduction of such a "right of reply": paras 623–624, Cmnd.5909 (1975). Pointing out that damages played a greater role in the common law than in other systems, they continued:

"We do not think a more general right of reply imposed by statute could be introduced into our system of law without creating new criminal offences and punishments, which we do not consider desirable in this field. Furthermore, we find objectionable a principle which entitles a person, who may be without merits, to compel a newspaper to publish a statement extolling his non-existent virtue."

See further fn.1, above.

[10] See para.9.46, below. It is unclear whether that power is intended to be limited to the final judgment in the action, or whether it includes interlocutory judgments. Presumably the intention of the section is to provide the court with a new tool for vindication of the claimant, which might be more effectively provided by (say) summary judgment on justification than by a final judgment which rules on a plea of Reynolds privilege.

[11] See para.9.47, below.

granted qualified privilege by s.15 of the Defamation Act 1996[12] the privilege may only be relied on if the defendant is willing to publish a reasonable statement from the claimant by way of explanation or contradiction.

A shift towards a general practice of declaring falsity, allowing a right of reply, or ordering correction would have a significant effect on the general structure of defamation law and litigation, which has been largely shaped on the assumption that the remedy is an award of damages.[13] At the moment the issue of the truth of the statement may never be in issue at all, the most obvious case being that where the defendant relies solely on absolute privilege: the basic elements of that being established (e.g. that the words were spoken as a witness or complainant in criminal matters or in Parliament) the claim will simply be struck out.[14] Even in the much more common situation where the defence is qualified privilege the truth of the allegation is not the central issue (it could not be, since the whole purpose of the privilege is to protect the defendant even if the allegation is untrue) though it may come in tangentially, as where the defendant claims to have relied on sources for the story and the claimant seeks to adduce evidence that the story is untrue in order to impugn the credibility of the defendant's case on that.[15] Indeed, even where the sole defence is justification, a verdict in the claimant's favour amounts, strictly, not to a finding that the statement was untrue but that the defendant (upon whom the burden of proof lies) has failed to prove that the statement was true, although no doubt the award of substantial damages will be an indication that the jury thought it *was* untrue.[16] Even in the limited

---

[12] See para.16.2, below. This replaced similar provisions in the Defamation Act 1952, which in its turn replaced the Law of Libel Amendment Act 1888.

[13] Other common law jurisdictions now have more extensive powers to declare falsity. The New Zealand Defamation Act 1992 introduced a declaratory remedy with solicitor and own client costs and the Irish Defamation Act, ss.28, 30 enable a court to declare the statement false or make a correction order. However, these are remedies which are only triggered on the application of the plaintiff. In South African law the *amende honorable*, or apology, is an available remedy. In *Mineworkers Investment Co. (Pty) Ltd v Modibane*, 2002 (6) SA 512 (W) the defendant was given the choice between paying 30,000 Rand damages or an apology with costs. See further *Dikoko v Mokhatla* [2006] ZACC 10; 2006 (6) SA 235, where the Constitutional Court was divided on the relative roles of damages and "restorative" remedies. For a full discussion see D. Milo, *Defamation and Freedom of Speech* (Oxford: OUP, 2008), Ch. VIII.

[14] However, it has been suggested that, in so far as art.8 of the European Convention on Human Rights now gives protection to a person's reputation, it might be that the court, in an action against a public authority, could grant a declaration of falsity under s.7 of the Human Rights Act 1998, even if a claim for damages were defeated by absolute or qualified privilege: *W v Westminster City Council* [2004] EWHC 2866 (QB) at [103]. And see the suggestion by Elias J. in *Lange v Atkinson* [1997] 2 N.Z.L.R. 22 at 48 that the declaratory remedy under s.24 of the 1992 Act (fn.9, above) might still be available even though the publication was privileged for the purpose of damages and s.24 involves a declaration of *liability* rather than of *falsity*.

[15] See para.15.11, below. In *Underhill v Corser* [2010] EWHC 1195 (QB) Tugendhat J. noted that where a defendant is able to rely on qualified privilege, the prospect of the claimant achieving any vindication is significantly diminished even if he is wholly innocent (at [90], [141]).

[16] On the burden of proof, see para.11.4, below. Compare the proposal of the N.S.W. Law Reform Commission in Report no.75, *Defamation* (not implemented), to put the burden of proof of falsity on the plaintiff. The Commission thought that vindication should rest on a finding of falsity, not on an inference to be drawn from the award of damages: para.2.8. of the Report.

circumstances in which a declaration of falsity is now available, a court might find difficulty in making a declaration of falsity on the basis of proceedings which have not been primarily directed to the question of whether the allegation is true and that is a good reason for declining to do so. Certainly if damages remained generally available (as they would surely have to, in order to take account of the distress suffered by the claimant and any provable financial loss) a general power to make a declaration on falsity would shift the tactical positions of the parties in very many cases.

> "It is very much on the cards that in every case where a defendant has a viable defence of qualified privilege, the claimant would (if so permitted) add a claim for a declaration of falsity. The newspaper would then find itself on the horns of a dilemma: whether to concede falsity to a perhaps unworthy claimant or whether to spend possibly considerable sums of money resisting the claim for a declaration. As has been remarked, the cost of defending defamation claims can have the effect of blighting the right of the media to freedom of expression."[17]

At the moment therefore the remedy of damages serves the purpose not only of remedying the claimant's distress and loss flowing from the libel, but of "vindicating" his reputation: a substantial award is regarded as sending a message to the world[18] that the imputation was untrue,[19] even if it does so indirectly. There remains, however, the question of the impact of any finding of a declaratory nature, where that is made under the present system, on any award of damages. There is a limit of £10,000 on an award of damages under the summary procedure and summary relief is only available (unless the claimant asks for it) if it would adequately compensate him,[20] but the impact of a declaration of falsity in addition under the procedure must be borne in mind, so that, e.g.:

> "whereas an award of £30,000 damages from a jury, might be inadequate compensation on its own, it does not follow that an award of £10,000 damages, by way of summary relief, coupled with a declaration and an apology... would not be adequate compensation as a whole."[21]

---

[17] *Loutchansky v Times Newspapers Ltd* [2002] E.M.L.R. 44 at [3] per Gray J. This decision has been criticised by Jonathan Coad in an article entitled "The price of truth found to be too high in the new law of libel" but it was not appealed and remains the law (*http://www.swanturton.com/articles/JKCPriceofTruth.aspx*).

[18] "An outward and visible sign": *Cleese v Clark* [2003] EWHC 137 (QB); [2004] E.M.L.R. 3 at [37] per Eady J.

[19] *The Gleaner Co. Ltd v Abrahams* [2003] UKPC 55; [2004] 1 A.C. 628 at [55]; *Broome v Cassell & Co. Ltd* [1972] A.C. 1027 at 1071.

[20] S.8(3). Under s.9(1)(c) of the Defamation Act 1996 the Lord Chancellor has power to vary the figure of £10,000. By s.9(2A) inserted by Pt I of the Schedule to the Constitutional Reform Act 2005, he is required to consult the Lord Chief Justice (or the Lord Chief Justice of Northern Ireland in relation to that jurisdiction) before doing so. For examples of the maximum award on the claimant's request for summary disposal see *Mahfouz v Ehrenfeld* [2005] EWHC 1156 (QB) and *Mahfouz v Brisard* [2006] EWHC 1191 (QB) (allegations of funding terrorism).

[21] *Mawdsley v Guardian Newspapers Ltd* [2002] EWHC 1780 (QB). This would substantially extend the scope of the summary procedure. It has also been suggested that where there is an accepted offer of amends under the Defamation Act 1996, which will involve an apology (see para.19.1, below), injury to feelings rather than injury to reputation will be an especially

9.2 Vindication and reasoned judgment. Outside the context of the summary procedure, the question of how far a prior reasoned judgment in the claimant's favour on the issue of justification may affect damages was considered in *Purnell v Business F1 Magazine Ltd*,[22] where at one stage a defence of justification had been struck out because there was no evidential basis for it and there was no other defence involved. The case then proceeded to trial on damages before a jury, which awarded £75,000. On appeal against that, Laws L.J. said that there:

> "are in theory, no doubt, three possible positions to be considered where damages for defamation have to be assessed in a case where there is also a previous judgment dismissing a justification defence with reasons. First, the earlier judgment should always be taken into account by the tribunal assessing damages as extinguishing the need for any element of vindication to be reflected in the damages. Secondly, the earlier judgment should never be so taken into account. Thirdly, the earlier judgment may be taken into account by the damages tribunal depending on the latter's view of its impact on the vindication issue".[23]

The third is the correct position.

> "The effect of such an earlier judgment no doubt depends on all the circumstances and, generally speaking, the effect in relation to vindication will I think most likely be marginal. Where there has been a fiercely contested trial on the facts, perhaps attended with much publicity, and the defendant's witnesses have been roundly disbelieved and there is a positive and unequivocal finding in the claimant's favour on the merits, those circumstances will be relevant as amounting to some vindication ... But there are also cases where the judgment will provide no or no significant or reckonable vindication. They will perhaps arise where the justification has been struck out for some technical reason in circumstances where, in truth, no consideration whatever has been given to the merits. Those circumstances will have to be regarded. Cases in between may include strike-outs, they may include trials. There will be cases where, for one reason or another, the vindication is real but very faint."[24]

It is not the law that the reasoned judgment in all cases in principle exhausts the need for vindication,[25] nor is there any necessary symmetry between the degree of vindication required and the contents of the reasoned judgment. The award was upheld.[26]

---

prominent element in the assessment of compensation under the Act: *Turner v News Group Newspapers Ltd* [2006] EWCA Civ 540; [2006] 1 W.L.R. 3469 [2006] E.M.L.R. 24.

[22] [2007] EWCA Civ 744; [2008] 1 W.L.R. 1.

[23] At [24], [29].

[24] At [29]–[30].

[25] *Cairns v Modi* [2012] EWCA Civ 1382; [2013] 1 W.L.R. 1015; [2013] E.M.L.R. 8 at [30].

[26] Nowadays it is quite likely that the issue will arise in a case where the judge who gives the reasoned judgment in the claimant's favour also assesses the damages (whether after a full trial or on summary disposal). In *Cairns v Modi* the Court of Appeal rejected (at [30]–[32]) the defendant's argument that the damages awarded should be reduced to take account of the express elements of vindication in Bean J.'s judgment ([2012] EWHC 756 (QB)). There are examples of a judge explicitly making a lower award because his judgment offered vindication. See, *Rackham v Sandy* [2005] EWHC 1354 at [13] (QB); *Coad v Cruze* [2009] EWHC 3782 (QB) at [38] (effect marginal only); *Al Amoudi v Kifle* [2011] EWHC 2037 (QB) at [38] ("fairly marginal factor"). In

Abuse of process and prospect of vindication. Abuse of process has 9.3
been considered above in connection with the questions whether a statement
is defamatory and limited publication.[27] However, it is not possible so to
confine the jurisdiction, since the informing principle is that on the particular
facts of the case there is no "real and substantial tort" or that "the game will
not merely not have been worth the candle, it will not have been worth the
wick"[28] and this may extend beyond those situations. Another factor that has
been said to be relevant to the *Jameel*[29] abuse jurisdiction is the level of
damages recoverable. Where any damages that may be recovered are likely to
be nominal when set against the costs of the proceedings that is a matter that
should be taken into account.[30] It is plainly not the law that there is an abuse
of process simply because the costs involved in establishing a contested claim
will exceed any damages likely to be awarded,[31] otherwise many claims
attracting damages in five or even six figures would constitute an abuse (the
same must apply a fortiori to claims based on misuse of private information,
where damages are generally substantially lower than for libel). Nor is it the
case that, because damages are likely to be low, as a result for example of the
limited extent of publication, the claim will always be struck out.[32]

However, it may be necessary to consider whether the claimant has
achieved his aim in some other way than by pursuing an action for damages.
In *Hays Plc v Hartley*[33] A, B and C, former employees of the claimant, made
serious accusations against it to persons including the defendant; he passed
them on to a journalist and they found their way to the *Sunday Mirror*, which

---

Cruddas v Adams [2013] EWHC 145 (QB), Eady J., after referring to the decision of the Court
of Appeal in *Cairns v Modi* stated (at [43]): "any such observations [relating to the innocence of
the claimant], contained in a judgment of the court, are unlikely to achieve very much in
themselves. What most interested observers will want to know is, quite simply, 'how much did
he get?'"

[27] See paras 2.4, 6.2, above.

[28] *Jameel v Dow Jones & Co. Ltd* [2005] EWCA Civ 75; [2005] Q.B. 946 at [69].

[29] Ibid.

[30] See, for example, *Jameel v Dow Jones & Co. Ltd* (above) at [69]; *Cammish v Hughes* [2012]
EWCA Civ 1655 at [60]; *Khader v Aziz* [2010] EWCA Civ 716 at [32]; *Lonzim Plc & others v
Sprague* [2009] EWHC 2838 (QB) at [31]; *Williams v MGN Ltd* [2009] EWHC 3150 (QB);
Davison v Habeeb [2011] EWHC 3031 (QB) at [26]; *Wallis v Meredith* [2011] EWHC 75
(QB).

[31] *Ronaldo v Telegraph Media Group Ltd* [2010] EWHC 2719 (QB).

[32] See, for example, *Sanders v Percy and the Ministry of Justice* [2009] EWHC 1870 (QB)
(publication to claimant's solicitor only). In *Mardas v New York Times Co.* [2008] EWHC 3135
(QB), Eady J. stated (at [15]): "whether there has been a real and substantial tort within the
jurisdiction (or arguably so) . . . cannot depend upon a numbers game." Cf. *Wallis v Meredith*
[2011] EWHC 75 (QB).

[33] [2010] EWHC 1068 (QB). See also, *Citation Plc v Ellis Whittam Ltd* [2013] EWCA Civ 155
(claim for slander in respect of words allegedly spoken by an employee of the defendant to a
prospective client, who nevertheless went on to enter into a contract with the claimant. It was
accepted by the claimant that it had not, and was unlikely to, suffer any loss from the publication
complained of or any similar publications. The defendant offered undertakings in pre-action
correspondence not to repeat the slander and issued instructions to their sales force along similar
lines. The Court of Appeal upheld Tugendhat J.'s decision to strike out the claim as an abuse of
process. See also, *Wallis v Meredith* [2011] EWHC 75 (QB).

published them. The claimant sued A, B and C but this claim was settled without payment of damages or costs along with employment tribunal proceedings, which A, B and C were pursuing against the claimant. This settlement included a public statement in which it was accepted that there was no basis for the charges against the claimant. The claimant did not sue the *Sunday Mirror* but did sue the defendant, alleging publication to the *Sunday Mirror* and relying on the republication in the newspaper on damages. The claimant had no prospect of recovering its substantial costs against the defendant even if it won, but wished to avoid the likely liability for his costs if it discontinued. Tugendhat J. struck out the claim:

> "In my judgment the significant facts are that the Claimant is a corporation, that the Defendant is a professional intermediary and not the originator of the words complained of, that the action is brought on the publication to a single individual, the Journalist, that the republication gave proper coverage to the Claimant's case (so any damages would be likely to be modest) and that the Claimant has received vindication both from the originators of the words (in the form of the Public Statement) and from MGN (in the form of the republication on their website of the Public Statement). That damages would on any view be modest is accepted . . . In so far as the damages may have value as money they are not worth pursuing. If the Claimant pursued this action to trial and won, there is little prospect that it would be able to enforce any award that it might have. The defendant would be unable to pay any significant part of the damages and costs that might be awarded against him. Damages in defamation actions have an additional value: they are symbolic. They mark the seriousness of the defamation and are a part of the vindication. But in the present case, the sum itself could not be so high as to add any value in terms of vindication to the Public Statement."[34]

9.4 General damages compensatory. The purpose of general damages is to compensate the claimant for the effects of the defamatory statement,[35] but compensation here is a more complex idea than it is in the case of injury to person or property by negligence. General damages serve three functions,[36] albeit that the emphasis placed on each will vary from case to case[37]: to act as a consolation to the claimant for the distress he[38] suffers from the publication of the statement[39]; to repair the harm to his reputation (including, where

---

[34] [2010] EWHC 1068 (QB) at [59].

[35] As to interest, see para.26.39, below.

[36] For the extent to which the principles governing defamation damages can be applied to cases of misuse of private information see Ch.22, below.

[37] *Cairns v Modi* [2012] EWCA Civ 1382, [2013] E.M.L.R. 8 at [22].

[38] It seems that where there is more than one victim of a libel each one may be compensated not only for his own distress but for having to observe the distress of the others, though the court must beware of double counting: *Culla Park Ltd v Richards* [2007] EWHC 1850 (QB) at [26].

[39] See *Kiam v Neil (No.2)* [1996] E.M.L.R. 493 CA (irresponsible attack on businessman's solvency; prolonged and significant effect on him personally). Cf. *Downtex Plc v Flatley* [2004] EWHC 333. Similar libel on a corporation, so that distress was irrelevant. Proper figure would have been not less than £30,000 had the summary procedure cap not applied.

relevant, his business reputation); and as a vindication of his reputation.[40] As Windeyer J. said in a passage approved in the House of Lords[41]:

"It seems to me that, properly speaking, a man defamed does not get compensation *for* his damaged reputation. He gets damages *because* he was injured in his reputation, that is simply because he was publicly defamed. For this reason, compensation by damages operates in two ways—as a vindication of the plaintiff to the public, and as a consolation to him for the wrong done."[42]

"Compensatory damages . . . may include not only actual pecuniary loss and anticipated pecuniary loss or any social disadvantages which result, or may be thought likely to result, from the wrong which has been done. They may also include the natural injury to his feelings—the natural grief and distress which he may have felt at having been spoken of in defamatory terms,[43] and if there has been any kind of high-handed, oppressive, insulting or contumelious behaviour by the defendant which increases the mental pain and suffering caused by the defamation and may constitute injury to the plaintiff's pride and self-confidence, these are proper elements to be taken into account in a case where the damages are at large."[44]

---

[40] *Carson v John Fairfax & Sons Ltd* (1993) 113 A.L.R. 577 HCA at 589; *Cleese v Clark* [2003] EWHC 137 (QB) at [37]; [2004] E.M.L.R. 3. In *Clarke (t/a Elumina Iberica UK) v Bain* [2008] EWHC 2636 (QB) at [55] Tugendhat J. said:
"Defamation actions are not primarily about recovering money damages, but about vindication of a Claimant's reputation. If a successful libel Claimant recovers, say, £30,000, that figure does not represent the measure of his success. In many cases, after paying his irrecoverable costs, he will be out of pocket if he recovers that amount as damages. That does not mean the litigation is not worthwhile. A Claimant wrongly accused of some serious fault, such as malpractice or dishonesty in business, may well suffer very large unquantifiable loss if he does not recover his reputation. The value of the verdict in his favour is expected to consist substantially in the future loss that it is hoped will be avoided by the vindication. Where, as here, the publication complained of is on an internet news service, a verdict in his favour may provide him with a means of persuading the publishers of an archive to edit it."
In the US and to some extent in England, restraints upon the "chilling" effect of libel law on political and public debate have come via the imposition of restrictions on liability: see paras 8.20, above, and 15.1, below. However, in British Columbia an approach has been made via damages. In *Derrickson v Tomat* (1992) 88 D.L.R. (4th) 401 BCC at 411, Wood and Taylor JJ.A. said that general damages for a public official should be limited "to an amount sufficient to bring clearly to public attention the fact that the allegations were unwarranted and that no lawful excuse for them existed". However, the same considerations did not necessarily apply to media defendants.
[41] In *Broome v Cassell & Co. Ltd* [1972] A.C. 1027 at 1071, per Lord Hailsham L.C.
[42] *Uren v John Fairfax & Sons Pty Ltd* (1966) 117 C.L.R. 118 at 150; *Vacik Distributors Pty Ltd v Australian Broadcasting Corp* [2000] NSWC 732 at [100].
[43] "The harm caused to the plaintiff by the publication of the defamation often lies more in his own feelings, what he thinks other people are thinking of him, than in any actual change made manifest in their attitude towards him."
Hence an award "for injured feelings, however innocent the publication by the defendant may have been, forms a large element in the [general compensatory] damages": citing *Cassell & Co. Ltd v Broome* [1972] A.C. 1027 at 1124–25. For this purpose it has been said that the defendant must take the plaintiff as he finds him: *Ali v Nationwide News Pty Ltd* [2008] NSWCA 183 at [77]. See also, *Cleese v Clark* [2003] EWHC 137 (QB) at [40]; *Bowman v MGN Ltd* [2010] EWHC 895 (QB). But this cannot mean that a genuine but exaggerated reaction to a minor libel leads to a large award of damages.
[44] Per Pearson L.J. in *McCarey v Associated Newspapers (No.2)* [1965] 2 Q.B. 86 at 104–105. As this passage makes clear, "aggravated" damages (see s.2 of this Chapter) are compensatory in nature. In *Andrews v Aylott* [2010] EWHC 597 (QB) (not a libel case), Tugendhat J. appears to have accepted (at [38]) the submission that libel damages include compensation to the

Although deterrence may not be a formal *purpose* of general damages for defamation, yet where such damages are substantial (as they are in England) deterrence is an *effect* of them.[45] Indeed, the law goes further and in some cases allows damages which are designed to punish.[46]

While actual financial loss (such as loss of business or employment) which is not too remote is clearly recoverable[47] (and in some cases of slander has to be shown in order to establish a cause of action[48]) it is a comparatively rare case in which evidence of such loss is given,[49] simply because it is not available.[50] It has been said that the most serious defamations are those that touch the "core attributes of the plaintiff's personality",[51] matters such as integrity,[52] honour, courage, loyalty and achievement[53] and in these cases it is most unlikely that he will be able to point to provable items of loss flowing from the words. Even where the libel goes to the claimant's financial credit it may be virtually impossible to prove financial loss but the damage is insidious and merits a substantial award.[54] As has been said in the Supreme Court of Canada:

---

successful claimant for the inconvenience, anxiety and distress of having to resort to and pursue proceedings.

[45] *The Gleaner Co. Ltd v Abrahams* [2003] UKPC 55; [2004] 1 A.C. 628 at [42] PC.

[46] See para.9.25, below.

[47] As is generally the case in tort law, the wrong needs to be *a* cause of the loss but need not be *the* cause: *Selecta Homes and Building Co. Pty Ltd v Advertiser-Weekend Publishing Co Pty Ltd* [2001] SASC 140, 79 S.A.S.R. 451.

[48] See Ch.5, above.

[49] For a case where it was given, involving a company operating in a very limited geographical area see *Culla Park Ltd v Richards* [2007] EWHC 1850 (QB), though even here the figure suggested by the expert evidence and described by the judge as perhaps "near the mark" was discounted by nearly 50 per cent.

[50] "The strict requirements of proving causation are relaxed in return for moderation in the overall figure awarded": *The Gleaner Co. Ltd v Abrahams* [2003] UKPC 55; [2004] 1 A.C. 628 at [56]. See also, *Blakeney-Williams v Cathay Pacific Airways Ltd* [2012] HKFCA 61; [2013] E.M.L.R. 6. Subject to this, "factual causation" of damage is no doubt a necessary part of establishing a claim for substantial damages for libel and that involves a hypothetical question of what would have happened if the defendant had not published the defamatory words, but a claimant is not to be deprived of the substance of his remedy merely because the words might have been published by others or in circumstances in which there would have been a defence to a claim. If a Member of Parliament defames the claimant in an interview, he cannot contend that the damages should be nominal because he might (or even would) have published the words in a speech in the House: *Galloway v Telegraph Group Ltd* [2004] EWHC 2786 (QB); [2005] E.M.L.R. 7 at [216]. Affirmed [2006] EWCA Civ 17; [2006] E.M.L.R. 11.

[51] *John v MGN Ltd* [1997] Q.B. 586 CA at 607.

[52] "In some cases, a person's reputation is, in a relevant sense, his whole life. The reputation of a clerk for financial honesty and of a solicitor for integrity are illustrations of this. The reputation of a doctor is, I think, of this character: at least, it is so where a substantial part of his work is in an area where he acts on reference from or with the recommendation of other doctors":
Crampton v Nugawela (1997) 41 N.S.W.L.R. 176 NSWCA at 193.

[53] *Kiam v Neil (No.2)* [1996] E.M.L.R. 493 CA. See *Campbell-James v Guardian Media Group Plc* [2005] EWHC 893 (QB); [2005] E.M.L.R. 24 at [10].

[54] *Kiam v Neil (No.2)*, above. "Vindication includes the ability at some future date, if the libel resurfaces, to show by reference to a substantial award that it has been decisively rejected by the court" (*Downtex Plc v Flatley* [2004] EWHC 333 at [27], per Tugendhat J.). However, in that

"a defamatory statement can seep into the crevasses of the subconscious and lurk there ever ready to spring forth its cancerous evil. The unfortunate impression left by a libel may last a lifetime.[55] Seldom does the defamed person have the opportunity of replying and correcting the record in a manner that will truly remedy the situation."[56]

In cases of libel and slander actionable per se the law therefore presumes damage arising from the publication and the claimant is entitled to look to an award of damages sufficient to vindicate his reputation according to the seriousness of the defamation, the range of its publication[57] and the extent to which the defendant has persisted with the charge.[58]

Our system does not regard the claimant's reputation as vindicated by a symbolic award of a token or conventional sum of damages and the jury in a serious case is entitled to award a large sum perhaps equalling or exceeding the damages in a case of serious personal injury[59]: While the level of damages should not be so high as unduly to curtail freedom of expression, "the court should be careful not to drive down damages in libel cases to a level which publishers might with equanimity be tempted to risk having to pay".[60] Nevertheless, "the figure of Justice carries a pair of scales, not a cornucopia"[61] and "it serves no public purpose to encourage plaintiffs to regard a successful libel action, risky though the process undoubtedly is, as a road to untaxed riches".[62]

---

case the claimant company had, before the trial, been restructured, changed its name and no longer traded in the same line. It was accepted that this would have been relevant to reduce the damages had the £10,000 cap under the summary procedure not been applicable. On damages and the effect of libel on a company's share price see *Collins Stewart Ltd v Financial Times Ltd* [2004] EWHC 2337 (QB); [2005] E.M.L.R. 5; para.8.16, above.

[55] For a practical example of the insidious effect of a libel in the media on a private citizen, even after a full correction and apology, see *Todd v Swan Television and Radio Broadcasting Pty Ltd* [2001] WASC 324; 25 W.A.R. 382 at [36]–[39].

[56] *Hill v Church of Scientology of Toronto* [1995] 2 S.C.R. 1130. See also Lord Atkin in *Ley v Hamilton* (1935) 153 L.T. 384 at 386:

"It is precisely because the real damage cannot be ascertained and established that the damages are at large. It is impossible to track the scandal, to know what quarters the poison may reach: it is impossible to weigh at all closely the compensation which will recompense a man or a woman for the insult offered or the pain of a false accusation. No doubt in newspaper libels juries take into account the vast circulations which are justly claimed in present times."

[57] See *Kiam v Neil (No.2)* [1996] E.M.L.R. 493 CA.

[58] A prompt apology and offer of amends will commonly mitigate the damages but they do not necessarily prevent a substantial award: *Kiam v Neil (No.2)* [1996] E.M.L.R. 493 CA. (irresponsible attack on plaintiff's solvency to "gild" story; award of £45,000); *Humphries v TWT* (1993) 120 A.L.R. 693 Fed Ct of Australia.

[59] See para.9.9, below.

[60] *Nail v News Group Newspapers Ltd* [2004] EWCA Civ 1708; [2005] E.M.L.R. 12 at [39]. In *Klason v Australian Capital Territory* [2003] ACTSC 104; 177 F.L.R. 216 at [95] Crispin J. remarked of a government department sued for libel that:

"if [it] is prepared to assume that the award of a modest sum justifies an assumption that any criticism of its conduct must have been comparatively trivial, it may be appropriate for judges to ensure that any future awards of damages are so large that even the most defensive executives will be obliged to take them seriously."

[61] Per Greenberg J. in *Innes v Visser* [1936] W.L.D. 44.

[62] *John v MGN Ltd* [1997] Q.B. 586 CA at 611. Libel damages are a good deal lower now than in the early 1990s (see further para 9.5, below). The Porter Committee concluded that when trial by jury was suspended during WWII the level of awards fell substantially: Cmd.7536 (1948)

The jury may, of course, take the view that the libel is not very serious in its nature or effect and award a low or even token sum, but it is contrary to

---

para.157. By today's standards the level of awards in the 1960s was modest (the highest award in 1967–69—£7,000—was by a judge: Faulks Committee, Cmnd.5909 (1975) App.XVII). But there have been very large awards in the past, e.g. the £25,000 in *Youssoupoff v Metro-Goldwyn-Mayer* (1934) 50 T.L.R. 581, perhaps worth £1,000,000 today. In view of the defendants' refusal to withdraw the film because of the potential financial loss (see (1934) 50 T.L.R. 586–587) it is plain that the case would have justified a substantial exemplary award under today's practice but at that time the distinction between compensatory and exemplary damages was not so clear.

According to the Media Law Resource Center's 2012 *Report on Trials and Damages*, the average initial award in the United States (over the 32 years the survey has been in operation) for plaintiffs was $2.86m, thanks to a few very large verdicts. The median was $300,000. However, after post-trial motions and appeals, total damage awards dropped 86.6 per cent from the initial amount awarded at trial. The average damages award at trial was reduced to an average final award of only $674,168 while the median dropped to $100,000. Across the report's 32-year history, the vast majority of initial awards—69.9 per cent—have been under $1m. However, the percentage of awards over $1m has been increasing from decade to decade: it was 22.4 per cent in the 1980s, then 29.5 per cent in the 1990s, and 36.8 per cent in the first decade of the 2000s. During 2010 and 2011, 45.5 per cent (5 of 11 awards) were over $1m.

For damages in Singapore see *Tang Liang Hong v Lee Kuan Yew* [1998] 1 S.L.R. 97 Sing. CA; *Goh v Jeyaretnam* [1998] 3 S.L.R. 337 Sing. CA; *Arul Chandran v Chew Chin Aik Victor JP* [2001] 1 S.L.R. 505 Sing. CA; *Ei-Nets Ltd v Yeo Nai Meng* [2003] SGCA 48; [2004] 1 S.L.R. 153. The Singaporean courts have in general adopted a policy of following established benchmarks though a number of political figures have recovered significant damages awards relating to alleged nepotism and/or corruption in running the country. In Hong Kong in *Chu Siu Kuk Yuen, Jessie v Apple Daily Ltd* [2002] 1 H.K.L.R.D. 1. HK$3 million (about £275,000) plus HK$177,000 medical costs was awarded by a judge for an accusation that a solicitor had been guilty of fraud. However, this contained an element for depression and pre-term delivery caused by the libel. Cf. *Blakeney-Williams v Cathay Pacific Airways Ltd* [2012] HKFCA 61; [2013] E.M.L.R. 6 in which the Hong Kong Final Court of Appeal affirmed the decision of the Court of Appeal to reduce compensatory damages awarded to the claimant airline pilots in respect of allegations that they were "troublemakers upon whom Cathay could not rely" and "bad and disloyal employees" from $3m (approximately £240,000) to $700,000 (c. £60,000). In reaching its decision the Court adopted a similar approach to the "control" of libel awards to that taken by the English courts (see especially at [82]) and see also *Oriental Daily Publisher Ltd v Ming Pao Holding Ltd* [2012] HKCFA 59; [2013] E.M.L.R. 7 at [42]–[46].

The pattern of Malaysian awards in recent years is summarised in *Karpal Singh v DP Vijandran* [2001] 4 M.L.J. 161. A steep upward rise has been checked though large awards to political figures are not uncommon. See also *Chin Choon Chin Tee Fut v Chua Jui Meng* [2005] 3 M.L.J. 494 and *Ummi Hafilda bte Ali v Ketua Setiausaha Parti Islam Se Malaysia* [2006] 4 M.L.J. 761. In 2012, the High Court in Kuala Lumpur entered judgment for a total of MYR500,000 (£101,000) in a defamation claim brought by Mohamad Salim against the well-known journalist, R. Nadeswaran over two postings on Twitter. The Privy Council in *The Gleaner Co. Ltd v Abrahams* [2003] UKPC 55; [2004] 1 A.C. 628 upheld an award equivalent to £533,000, which had been substituted by the Court of Appeal of Jamaica for a jury award of £1.2 million. To some extent this was because of the practice of allowing the local court a wide margin of appreciation (see also *Panday v Gordon* [2005] UKPC 36; [2006] 1 A.C. 427), but there was also a significant, though unquantifiable, financial loss and the defendants had maintained their allegations for years after it became clear they had no evidence to support them. For South Africa see *Mogale v Seima* [2005] ZASCA 101. Australian states now have uniform defamation legislation (see para.1.3). See, e.g. the Defamation Act 2005 (NSW). (1) Damages are awarded by the judge, not the jury, where there is a jury: s.22; (2) the court is to "ensure that there is an appropriate and rational relationship between the harm sustained by the plaintiff and the amount of damages awarded": s.34; (3) damages for non-economic loss are subject, by s.35(1), to an indexed statutory cap which is reviewed annually (A$355,500 in 2013) unless the circumstances of the publication justify aggravated damages: s.35; the court is to:

"disregard the malice or other state of mind of the defendant at the time of the publication of the defamatory matter to which the proceedings relate or at any other time except to the extent

principle for it to find that the claimant has been defamed and to award no damages.[63]

Matters affecting the level of award.[64] Damages are "at large" in the sense that they cannot be assessed by reference to any mechanical, arithmetical or objective formula[65] and they are peculiarly the province of the jury (where there is a trial by that method).[66] The jury (or judge if sitting alone) is

9.5

---

that the malice or other state of mind affects the harm sustained by the plaintiff": s.36; exemplary damages are not available: s.37; and apology, correction, prior suit and recovery of compensation in relation to any other publication of matter having the same meaning or effect are made matters in mitigation of damages: s.38. It has been held in New South Wales that the statutory cap on damages for non-economic loss applies to a proceeding regardless of the number of causes of action that are pleaded or upheld in the proceeding: *David v Nationwide News Pty Ltd* [2008] N.S.W.S.C. 693. And see *Buckley v Herald and Weekly Times Pty Ltd* [2009] VSCA 118 (consolidation).

Damages in European jurisdictions seem much lower than in the Commonwealth: see Rogers (ed.) *Damages for Non-Pecuniary Loss in a Comparative Perspective* (2001), p.280. But the criminal law and power to order a correction play a greater role in some systems.

[63] *Reynolds v Times Newspapers Ltd* [1998] 3 W.L.R. 862 CA (on appeal [2001] 2 A.C. 127). In *Television New Zealand v Keith* [1994] 2 N.Z.L.R. 84 the jury awarded as damages "all legal expenses". This was held (1) to amount to a finding that the plaintiff was entitled to more than nominal damages but (2) to be a usurpation of the judge's function on costs.

[64] The Irish Defamation Act 2009, s.31(4) requires the court in assessing damages to have regard to all the circumstances of the case and the following matters:
   (a) the nature and gravity of any allegation in the defamatory statement concerned,
   (b) the means of publication of the defamatory statement including the enduring nature of those means,
   (c) the extent to which the defamatory statement was circulated,
   (d) the offering or making of any apology, correction or retraction by the defendant to the plaintiff in respect of the defamatory statement,
   (e) the making of any offer to make amends under s.22 by the defendant, whether or not the making of that offer was pleaded as a defence,
   (f) the importance to the plaintiff of his or her reputation in the eyes of particular or all recipients of the defamatory statement,
   (g) the extent (if at all) to which the plaintiff caused or contributed to, or acquiesced in, the publication of the defamatory statement,
   (h) evidence given concerning the reputation of the plaintiff,
   (i) if the defence of truth is pleaded and the defendant proves the truth of part but not the whole of the defamatory statement, the extent to which that defence is successfully pleaded in relation to the statement,
   (j) if the defence of qualified privilege is pleaded, the extent to which the defendant has acceded to the request of the plaintiff to publish a reasonable statement by way of explanation or contradiction, and
   (k) any order made under s.33 (an order prohibiting the publication of a defamatory statement), or any order under that section or correction order that the court proposes to make or, where the action is tried by the High Court sitting with a jury, would propose to make in the event of there being a finding of defamation.

[65] See *Broome v Cassell & Co. Ltd* [1972] A.C. 1027 HL at 1071, per Lord Hailsham L.C.; *Campbell v News Group Newspapers Ltd* [2002] EWCA Civ 1143; [2002] E.M.L.R. 43 at [32]; *Cairns v Modi* [2012] EWCA Civ 1382; [2013] 1 W.L.R. 1015 at [24].

[66] "The rough and ready process by which juries assess damages in a defamation action is not one which appeals to the many sophisticated minds of the spreadsheet generation": McHugh J. in *Carson v John Fairfax* (1993) 113 A.L.R. 577 HCA at 632. On the powers of the CA, see para.9.4, below.

entitled to take into consideration a wide range of matters[67] including the conduct of the claimant,[68] his credibility,[69] his position and standing[70] and the subjective impact that the libel has had on him,[71] the nature of the libel, its

---

[67] In *Jones v Pollard* [1996] EWCA Civ 1186, [1997] E.M.L.R. 233, Hirst L.J. stated that he found the following list of factors suggested by counsel a helpful checklist to be considered when approaching the assessment of damages in defamation cases:

"1. The objective features of the libel itself, such as its gravity, its prominence, the circulation of the medium in which it was published, and any repetition.

2. The subjective effect on the plaintiff's feelings (usually categorised as aggravating features) not only from the publication itself, but also from the defendant's conduct thereafter both up to and including the trial itself.

3. Matters tending to mitigate damages, such as the publication of an apology.

4. Matters tending to reduce damages, e.g. evidence of the plaintiff's bad reputation, or evidence given at the trial which the jury are entitled to take into account in accordance with the decision of this court in *Pamplin v Express Newspapers Ltd* [1988] 1 W.L.R. 116.

5. Special damages.

6. Vindication of the plaintiff's reputation past and future."

This checklist was approved by Buxton L.J. in *Gur v Avrupa Newspaper Ltd* [2008] EWCA Civ 594 at [31]–[35].

[68] E.g. offensive remarks which have provoked the libel: *Burstein v Times Newspapers Ltd* [2001] 1 W.L.R. 579 CA; *Trumm v Norman* [2008] EWHC 116 (QB).

[69] *Morgan v Odhams Press* [1971] 1 W.L.R. 1239 at 1250; *Farmer v Hyde* [1937] 1 Q.B. 728 at 737–738; *Randall v Weich* 1982 Carswell BC 2254 at [23]–[24]. See also, *Oriental Daily Publisher Ltd v Ming Pao Holding Ltd* [2012] HKCFA 59; [2013] E.M.L.R. 7. The defendants published an article reporting on a demonstration by Ma Chiu Sing, a person who had been convicted of serious crimes including making terrorist threats. During the course of Ma's demonstration, he displayed a banner, which the defendants' article pictured so that the words on it were legible. The plaintiffs sued for libel, purely on the words which appeared on the banner, which they contended were repeated by the defendants' publication of the photograph. They claimed the words meant that they had forged evidence in order falsely to incriminate Ma Chiu Sing, entered into a conspiracy with a prosecution witness, bribing him to give false evidence against Ma, and perverted the course of justice, resulting in Ma's imprisonment for criminal intimidation. The plaintiffs succeeded at first instance and were awarded compensatory and aggravated damages which were reduced at first appeal on the basis that very few readers would have believed Ma Chiu Sing's allegations, given his notoriety and criminal record. The five judge court (which included Lord Neuberger of Abbotsbury, sitting as a Non-Permanent Judge of the HKCFA) unanimously dismissed the plaintiffs' appeal. The credence of the allegations, if capable of being established as a fact, was a relevant factor in the assessment of damages and would not be excluded as a matter of law (see at [78]–[84]).

[70] In *Gorman v Mudd*, unreported, October 15, 1992, (QB), the court held that the fact that the publication was made to "prominent, influential and knowledgeable members of the local constituency party" was a matter properly to be taken into account in assessing damages. In *Neeld v Western Broadcasting Co* (1976) 65 D.L.R. (3d) 574 at 576, Bouck J. stated that "The measure of damages must bear some relation to the actual standing and reputation of the plaintiffs in the community prior to the libel. The higher the reputation, the greater the damages."

[71] *Jones v Pollard* [1996] EWCA Civ 1186. See also, *Cruddas v Adams* [2013] EWHC 145 (QB) at [49].

gravity[72] and the mode and extent of its publication,[73] the absence or refusal of any retraction or apology,[74] and the conduct of the defendant from the time when the libel was published down to[75] the verdict. The conduct of the

---

[72] In assessing the damages recoverable for injury to reputation, the most important factor is the gravity of the libel; the "more closely it touches the claimant's personal integrity, professional reputation, honour, courage, loyalty and the core attributes of his personality, the more serious it is likely to be": *John v MGN Ltd* [1997] Q.B. 586 at 607. See also *Lillie & Reed v Newcastle City Council (No.2)* [2002] EWHC 1600 (QB) at [1536]; *Campbell-James v Guardian Media Group plc* [2005] EWHC 893; *Galloway v Telegraph Group Ltd* [2004] EWHC 2786 (QB), [2005] E.M.L.R. 7.

[73] On Internet publication see *Barrick Gold Corp v Lopehandia* (2004) 71 O.R. (3d) 416 Ont. CA at [34]. The majority of the Court observed that the "style" of the internet was not that of a traditional medium of communication and readers of bulletin boards might well take seriously attacks which might appear exaggerated or ludicrous in a newspaper. It should not necessarily be assumed that Emails are equivalent to private letters.

"[T]he present case is concerned with emails which, given their content and ease of communication, may remain in circulation for the indefinite future. It is thus even more important for the plaintiff to be able to point to the sum awarded to 'convince a bystander of the baseness of the charge' in case 'the libel, driven underground, emerges from its lurking place at some future date' (see Hailsham L.C. in *Broome v Cassell*)":

Levine J. in *Markovic v White* [2004] N.S.W.S.C. 37 at [21]. While some tweets and other online publications are ephemeral in nature, their damaging potential has been recognised in a number of cases. In *Cairns v Modi* (above) the Court of Appeal referred with approval (at [26]) to the following statement of Bingham L.J. in *Slipper v BBC* [1991] 1 Q.B. 283 at 300

"the law would part company with the realities of life if it held that the damage caused by publication of a libel began and ended with publication to the original publishee. Defamatory statements are objectionable not least because of their propensity to percolate through underground channels and contaminate hidden springs."

These considerations have been identified in Australian case law, where the convenient expression, "the grapevine effect" has been adopted: see e.g. *Crampton v Nugawela* [1996] N.S.W.S.C. 651. See also *ZAM v CFW* [2013] EWHC 662 (QB): "a website publication will remain accessible in ways that a hard copy publication never did. In some cases (where the fame of a person has increased) it may even be viewed with increasing frequency. So a person's reputation may be 'damaged forever' . . . " (per Tugendhat J. at [61]–[62]). In *Clarke (t/a Elumina Iberica UK) v Bain & Anor* [2008] EWHC 2636 (QB), Tugendhat J. noted that what is found on the internet may "become like a tattoo" (at [55]).

In cases of internet or online publications the courts do not, however, simply presume that because the potential audience is the whole online world the extent of the publication has been significant: see para.6.21, above.

[74] A statement in open court made by another party in respect of the same allegations was said by Eady J. in *Cruddas v Adams* [2013] EWHC 145 (QB) at [41] to go "some way to mitigate the effect of the defamatory imputations against Mr Cruddas, including those made by [the defendant]".

[75] Thus, the fact that the allegations were repeated several times and persisted in up until trial is likely to increase the level of damages. So too, evidence of malice on the part of the defendant (*Farrar v Tribune Publishing Co* 358 P. 2d 792 at 797), the fact that the claimant was subjected to a particularly hostile, lengthy and demanding cross-examination during the trial (*Cairns v Modi* [2012] EWCA Civ 1382; [2013] 1 W.L.R. 1015 at [32]) and the fact that the truth is significantly different from that alleged to be the case by the defendant (*Lillie & Reed v Newcastle City Council (No 2)* [2002] EWHC 1600 (QB) at [1541]) are all factors that have been held to justify an increase in the award. By way of contrast, a failure to accept a reasonable settlement offer (*Garfoot v Walker The Times*, February 8, 2000), a swift offer of (or actual) genuine apology and retraction by the defendant whether or not under the offer of amends procedure (*Nail v News Group Newspapers Ltd* [2004] EWCA Civ 1708; [2005] E.M.L.R. 12 at [41]; *Turner v News Group Newspapers* [2006] EWCA Civ 540; [2006] 1 W.L.R. 3469 at [81]; *Angel v Stainton* [2006] EWHC 637 (QB) at [29]) are all factors that may justify a significant discount. In *Popovic*

claimant[76] is relevant not only in respect of matters which go to "partial justification" of the libel[77] but also to his conduct in the course of the litigation, as where he engages in an elaborate and long-lasting attempt to pervert the course of justice involving making and procuring false testimony and making the most damaging allegations of corruption and lying against innocent third parties.[78]

The European Court of Human Rights has accepted that a jury award for defamation is "prescribed by law" within the meaning of art.10 of the European Convention on Human Rights and that the absence of any overt reasons for such awards is an unavoidable concomitant of the need to allow flexibility to deal with particular cases.[79] However, considerably greater control is now exercised than was formerly the case over immoderate awards by juries, and cases decided before the passing of s.8 of the Courts Act 1990[80] are of limited value in relation to current practice.

9.6 Damages awards and the European Court of Human Rights. The European Court of Human Rights has considered the question of the proportionality of libel awards in several decisions. In *Tolstoy Miloslavsky v United Kingdom*[81] the size of the award (£1.5 m) in favour of Lord Aldington (for the libels accusing him of involvement in war crimes against Cossak and Yugoslav prisoners-of-war and refugees at the end of the Second World War) was held not to be proportionate to the legitimate aim of the protection of a reputation and therefore not necessary in a democratic society. The court was heavily influenced by the fact that it was three times higher than any previous award and that at the time when the award was made the prevailing view was that the Court of Appeal could only interfere if it was irrational, not just because it viewed the award as excessive.[82] However, the court recognised

---

v *Herald and Weekly Times Ltd* [2002] VSC 220, the defendant's conduct between the jury's verdict on the facts and the assessment of damages was taken into account.

[76] Any directly relevant background material that puts the claimant generally in a bad light may be taken into account, though, if a *Burstein v Times Newspapers* [2001] 1 W.L.R. 579 plea is relied upon, any additional hurt caused by factual allegations that cannot ultimately be made out will be reflected in the award of damages (see further paras 33.43–33.46, below). For a somewhat unusual case in which A recovered $85,000 damages against B and B recovered $25,000 against A on a cross-claim in respect of statements arising out of the same controversy, see *Orion Pet Products Pty Ltd v RSPCA (Vic) Inc.* [2002] FCA 860.

[77] See para.11.21, below.

[78] *Campbell v News Group Newspapers Ltd* [2002] EWCA Civ 1143; [2002] E.M.L.R. 43.

[79] *Tolstoy Miloslavsky v UK* (1995) App. no.18139/91; [1996] E.M.L.R. 152. The decision arose from the common law as it was before the changes stemming from the Courts Act 1990 but takes account of that enactment.

[80] See para.9.4, above.

[81] App. no.18139/91, Ser. A, Vol.316, 323 (1995) 20 EHRR 442.

[82] App. no.18139/91, Ser. A, Vol.316, 323, (1995) 20 EHRR 442, *The Times*, July 19, 1995 at [49]–[51], [55]. However, an injunction against repetition of the libel was sufficiently proportionate: [54].

that even before its own decision in *Tolstoy* the Court of Appeal had concluded in *Rantzen v MGN*[83] that the courts should be readier to reduce awards under the Courts and Legal Services Act 1990 because of the requirement of proportionality under art.10. The size of damage awards was also considered in *Independent News & Media and Independent Newspapers Ireland Ltd v Ireland*,[84] when the newspapers published stark allegations of criminal activities and sympathies with violent Communist oppression and anti-Semitism against Proinsias de Rossa, a political leader engaged in negotiations to form a coalition government in 1992. The original jury award of 300,000 Irish pounds was confirmed by the Supreme Court, which was determined to be more respectful of jury discretion than it believed was evident in contemporary English jurisprudence. The European Court took due account of the gravity of the libel, the effect on the libelled person, the extent of the publication and the conduct of the litigation which required the libelled person to endure three long and difficult trials; all in all, this award, "going to the top of the bracket", was within the margin of appreciation.[85]

In *Steel and Morris v United Kingdom*[86] the two applicants defamed a major "fast food" chain in respect of its business methods. Awards of £36,000 and £40,000 were set by the Court of Appeal, which reduced Bell J.'s awards somewhat in view of the applicants' success on some aspects of their appeal. The applicants were unwaged or in low-paid part-time work and so far as is known no part of the damages or the much larger costs had been paid. On an application under the European Convention on Human Rights the primary ground of the applicants' success[87] was that the denial of legal aid to them as defendants constituted a violation of art.6 of the Convention. However, the Court also held that there had been a violation of art.10 by reason of the size of the awards of damages.

> "Under the Convention, an award of damages for defamation must bear a reasonable relationship of proportionality to the injury to reputation suffered . . . The Court notes on the one hand that the sums eventually awarded in the present case . . .

---

[83] [1994] Q.B. 670 CA. See also *Gleaner Co. Ltd v Abrahams* [2003] UKPC 55; [2004] 1 A.C. 628.

[84] App. no.55120/00, June 16, 2005.

[85] Ibid. at [129]. The quantum of damages was also considered in *Armoniene v Lithuania* (2008), App. no.36919/02. The problem was the opposite to that encountered in cases such as *Tolstoy Miloslavsky v UK* (App. no.18139/91, Ser.A, Vol.316, 323 (1995) 20 EHRR 442 in that the libel laws were attacked as unduly restricting damages and so failing to allow the courts to vindicate a person's reputation under art.8. In the case, a leading daily newspaper in a front-page story article alleged that the applicant's husband was HIV-positive and had had a relationship with a woman who had AIDS. The statutory maximum award (which had been granted) was LTL2,896 (approximately £700). Even recognising that heavy sanctions on press transgressions could have a chilling effect, this sum was deemed by the European Court to be insufficient to redress the damage suffered by the applicant and deter the recurrence of such abuses. The court's own award was LTL6,500 (about £1,600) for non-pecuniary damage (the applicant had claimed LTL26,065).

[86] App. no.68416/01; ECHR 2005-II

[87] They received £20,000 and £15,000 for "non-pecuniary damage".

although relatively moderate by contemporary standards in defamation cases in England and Wales, were very substantial when compared to the modest incomes and resources of the two applicants. While accepting, on the other hand, that the statements in the leaflet which were found to be untrue contained serious allegations, the Court observes that not only were the plaintiffs large and powerful corporate entities but that, in accordance with the principles of English law, they were not required to, and did not, establish that they had in fact suffered any financial loss as a result of the publication of the 'several thousand' copies of the leaflets found to have been distributed by the trial judge . . .

"While it is true that no steps have to date been taken to enforce the damages award against either applicant, the fact remains that the substantial sums awarded against them have remained enforceable since the decision of the Court of Appeal. In these circumstances, the Court finds that the award of damages in the present case was disproportionate to the legitimate aim served."[88]

No indication is given of what might have been a suitable figure in the circumstances. Given that it is extraordinarily difficult to prove consequential pecuniary loss in such cases, that there was no question in the original proceedings of exemplary damages and that a corporate claimant cannot suffer worry or distress one could not have stigmatised as perverse a jury which awarded one-tenth of the sums which were in fact awarded. However, the damages were set by the Court of Appeal. The libels were undoubtedly serious and the Court of Appeal's award could not possibly be regarded as extravagant. Furthermore, there is no indication that the Strasbourg court would have objected to the awards if they had been made against, say, a national newspaper. As well as overall quantum, another factor of relevance in the application of proportionality was the relation to the ability of the defendant to pay. Though the sums awarded were modest in objective terms (£36,000 and £40,000), they became disproportionate when compared to the meagre incomes and resources of the two applicants. The case was a very untypical libel action but it seems clear that the Strasbourg Court's reasoning, in so far as it rests on the defendants' means, is entirely inconsistent with English law's approach to general damages. These are compensatory and are based on the claimant's loss (difficult as it may be to assess what that is) and have nothing to do with whether the defendant can afford to pay them.[89] This can only be changed by the House of Lords.[90]

---

[88] At [96]–[97].

[89] See also, *ZAM v CFW* [2013] EWHC 662 (QB) at [72]. Some European legal systems have provisions—apparently very rarely used—allowing a court to reduce tort damages if they would have a disproportionately damaging effect on the defendant (see, e.g. art.6:109 of the Dutch Civil Code).

[90] *Gur v Avrupa Newspaper Ltd* [2008] EWCA Civ 594; [2009] E.M.L.R. 4 at [25]. In *Gentoo Group Ltd v Hanratty* [2008] EWHC 627 at [17] it was said that "it is well settled that the means of a party, as such, are irrelevant both on liability and on quantum of damages." It may readily be accepted that the threat of an award of £10,000 may operate more effectively to "chill" the freedom of expression of a poor person than that of a wealthy person but a general approach of moderating awards of damages in relation to the defendant's means would be very difficult to operate as a general principle and would put the claimant in an awkward position in responding to a Pt 36 offer.

Role of the Court of Appeal. As general damages for defamation are at   **9.7**
large, they are less susceptible of precise calculation than, say, damages for
personal injury[91] or damage to property, and the question of quantum is
therefore dominated by what the Court of Appeal will regard as a justifiable
award. Formerly, that court would only interfere with the award of damages
by a jury in a defamation case if it was extravagant or "divorced from
reality".[92] Now, influenced by its power to substitute a proper award rather
than order a new trial,[93] it has held that the threshold for intervention has come
down: the question now is whether a reasonable jury could have thought the
award necessary to compensate the claimant and re-establish his reputation.[94]
Plainly, therefore, the levels of awards which existed in the 1980s would not
now be tolerated.[95]

The level of damages for non-pecuniary loss in personal injury cases is now
a relevant "comparator" for libel damages[96] and in that area the maximum
award is about £275,000 (adjusted for inflation). That can be awarded for an
outrageously bad case of libel,[97] but it seems safe to assume that, putting aside
exemplary damages and proved financial loss, no higher figure would now be
tolerated[98] and there are few examples since 2000 of that amount being

---

[91] It is true that damages for loss of amenity and pain and suffering are as *arbitrary* in quantum
as general damages for defamation, but it is generally possible to compare like injuries with like
and a judicial "tariff" has developed: see para.9.9, below.

[92] *McCarey v Associated Newspapers (No.2)* [1965] 2 Q.B. 86 CA at 111. See further
para.36.25ff, below. For the position in Hong Kong, which is very similar to that in English law,
see *Blakeney-Williams v Cathay Pacific Airways Ltd* [2012] HKFCA 61; [2013] E.M.L.R. 6 at
[82] and *Oriental Daily Publisher Ltd v Ming Pao Holding Ltd* [2012] HKCFA 59; [2013]
E.M.L.R. 7 at [42]–[46]. On the approach of the New South Wales Court of Appeal, see *Ali v
Nationwide News Pty Ltd* [2008] NSWCA 183.

[93] See para.36.30, below. In *Grobbelaar v News Group Newspapers Ltd* [2002] UKHL 40,
[2002] 1 W.L.R. 3024, the House of Lords held that it also had a power to substitute for a sum
awarded by a jury such sum as appeared to it to be proper instead of ordering a new trial.
Although the power conferred by the Courts and Legal Services Act 1990, s.8(2) is a power
exercisable only by the Court of Appeal, the Supreme Court has, in any case in which it has
jurisdiction to hear an appeal, an inherent power to exercise any power vested in the Court of
Appeal and this, a fortiori, includes the power to substitute an appropriate sum by way of damages
in place of a jury award.

[94] *Rantzen v Mirror Group Newspapers (1986) Ltd* [1994] Q.B. 670 CA at 692; see para.38.26,
below. Most of the controversy in modern times has been in relation to excessive damages. As to
inadequate awards see paras 36.25 and 36.28, below.

[95] However, it should be noted that some of the more notorious examples were not
appealed.

[96] See para.9.9, below.

[97] See para.9.9, below.

[98] In saying this we are speaking of a very bad "one-off" case. It does not follow that the same
considerations apply where the claimant is the target of a sustained campaign by a whole sector
of the press. In *Murat v Associated Newspapers* (Statement in Open Court, July 16, 2008) there
was a settlement very substantially in excess of this figure in favour of the first claimant by four
newspaper groups arising from over 100 articles alleging child abduction and paedophilia. Of
course the possibility of exemplary damages may have entered into the quantum of the settlement.
So too, Lord McAlpine recovered considerably in excess of this sum from media outlets and
private individuals after entirely untrue allegations of paedophilia and child abuse were made
against him.
Modern considerations of the relevance of personal injury damages as providing a ceiling for

exceeded.[99] Subject to this, it is not, however, enough to set aside an award that the sum is more than would have been awarded by the members of the Court of Appeal sitting as a tribunal of fact, for that would be to remove from the jury its function of assessing damages.[100] The test is what the jury could reasonably have thought necessary, not what the court, wholly uninfluenced by the jury's view, thinks appropriate.[101] Nor is a jury award to be overturned merely because it is outside the "bracket" which, under current practice, the trial judge may suggest.[102]

Even if the Court of Appeal is unable to say that the damages awarded are so large or so small as to be outside the powers of the jury, the award may be set aside if the jury has been misdirected[103] on damages by the trial judge or if it is plain that the jury has made a mistake in the calculation of figures or must have taken irrelevant matter into account.[104] In the past comparatively few defamation actions were tried by judge alone, but now jury trials are extremely rare.[105] Since general damages are a matter of impression, the Court of Appeal will not readily interfere with the award of a judge unless there has been some error.[106]

---

libel have been in the context of the defamation of natural persons. In *Collins Stewart Ltd v Financial Times Ltd* [2004] EWHC 2337 (QB); [2005] E.M.L.R. 5 it was conceded that a decline in the share price of a claimant company could be relevant to general damages on the footing that it was evidence of damage to the goodwill of the company but it was contended that the ceiling applicable to claims by natural persons would still apply. No decision was necessary on this point. On the one hand, an element in general damages for a natural person will be injury to feelings and that cannot be relevant to a company; but on the other hand in so far as general damages represent likely but unquantifiable financial loss, the potential loss to a company might be much greater.

[99] There have been three very large jury awards: *Garfoot v Walker, The Times*, February 8, 2000 (false accusation of rape against a doctor—jury award of £400,000); *Campbell v News Group Newspapers* [2002] EWCA Civ 1143, [2002] E.M.L.R. 43 (jury award of £350,000 reduced on appeal to £30,000); *Lowe v Times Newspapers, The Times*, October 27, 2005 (jury award of £250,000; parties settled at £50,000).

[100] "More than I would award" is not necessarily the same as "too much", though it may be if it is a great deal more. No formula is possible. If the CA would have awarded £50,000 an award of £150,000 will plainly be struck down, but it does not follow that the same result will be reached if the respective figures are £1,000 and £3,000. For Scotland see *Baigent v BBC* 2001 S.C. 281.

[101] *Kiam v MGN Ltd* [2002] EWCA Civ 43; [2003] Q.B. 281 at [48].

[102] Ibid. Bracket of £40,000 to £80,000 suggested. Verdict for £105,000 upheld.

[103] Prima facie a misdirection gives rise to a new trial, but if the parties ask the CA to determine a proper sum of damages that may involve the court in interpreting what imputations the jury found and what conclusions they could have come to if properly directed: *Jones v Pollard* [1997] E.M.L.R. 233 CA; *Campbell v News Group Newspapers Ltd* [2002] EWCA Civ 1143; [2002] E.M.L.R. 43.

[104] See para.36.27, below.

[105] See para.34.1, below.

[106] See para.36.32, below. Perhaps in modern practice there is little difference in the principles applicable to appeals on damages from judge or jury. In Scotland the Court of Session in *Baigent v BBC* 2001 SC 281 observed that:

"counsel for the reclaimers accepted that if the awards made in this case had been made by a jury they could not attack them successfully in this court, a concession in our opinion rightly made and not without significance."

Awards are always by judges under the procedure introduced by s.8 of the Defamation Act 1996 (see Ch.30). Since the maximum sum under that procedure is at present only £10,000, awards are

Modern awards made by judges or upheld by the Court of Appeal across a wide range of factual situations are set out in Appendix 3.

Guidance for the jury: general. It has been said that the phenomenon of **9.8** excessive awards:

> "has not been the fault of the juries. Judges, as they were bound to do, confined themselves to broad directions of general principle, coupled with injunctions to the jury to be reasonable. But they gave no guidance on what might be thought to be reasonable or unreasonable, and it is not altogether surprising that juries lacked an instinctive sense of where to pitch their awards. They were in the position of sheep loosed on an unfenced common, with no shepherd."[107]

The current practice is to give more specific guidance in a number of ways, subject to the overriding principle that the award is proportionate to the damage suffered by the claimant.[108]

Relevance of personal injury damages. An important factor in direct- **9.9** ing the jury may be the level of awards in personal injury cases. The assessment of damages for defamation bears some resemblance to the assessment of damages for loss of amenities and pain and suffering in personal injury cases in that in neither case can damages be an exact substitute for the harm suffered. However, in the period since awards in personal injury cases have come to be assessed by judges, there has developed a broad judicial tariff of awards for different types of standard injuries, with a maximum (in

---

perhaps unlikely to attract appeals, still less intervention by the CA. However, "compensation" under the offer of amends procedure (see para.19.5, below) created by the Act is also to be assessed by a judge and "on the same principles as damages in defamation proceedings". That involves taking as starting point the award that would be made after a trial, with a discount for the offer. In *Campbell-James v Guardian Media Group Plc* [2005] EWHC 893 (QB); [2005] E.M.L.R. 24 the starting point was £90,000. See also, *Cairns v Modi* [2012] EWCA Civ 1382, [2013] 1 W.L.R. 1015 in which the Court of Appeal reduced a damages award made under the offer of amends regime.

[107] *John v MGN Ltd* [1997] Q.B. 586 CA at 608. The guidance given in *John v MGN* is equally applicable to a judge assessing contribution under the Civil Liability (Contribution) Act 1978: *Skrine & Co. v Euromoney Publications Plc* [2001] E.M.L.R. 18.

[108] *Rantzen v Mirror Group Newspapers (1986) Ltd* [1994] Q.B. 670 CA at 696. The Irish Supreme Court in *De Rossa v Independent Newspapers* [1999] IESC 63; [1999] 4 I.R. 432 rejected the *John* approach as an undue interference with the sanctity of the jury verdict (where it does interfere, it does not substitute its own figure but orders a retrial). It upheld an award of IR£300,000, which was not the highest award ever made by an Irish libel jury but was three times the amount in any case which had been appealed to and upheld by the Supreme Court. The ECtHR dismissed the defendants' application: *Independent News and Media Plc v Ireland* (2005) App. no.55120/00. The direction to the jury had been marginally more specific than that in *Tolstoy Miloslavsky v UK* (1995) App. no.18139/91; [1996] E.M.L.R. 152 and in the ECtHR's opinion the Irish Supreme Court more clearly enunciated the requirement of proportionality than the English courts did in the past. Meanwhile, the Supreme Court in *O'Brien v Mirror Group Newspapers Ltd* [2001] 1 I.R. 1 had declined to depart from *De Rossa* but on the facts of *O'Brien* set the award aside as too high. See also *Hill v Cork Examiner Ltd* [2001] 4 I.R. 219.

2013[109]) of about £275,000 for the worst injuries such as quadriplegia or severe brain damage. The essential principle underpinning this system is that of comparability: that similar injuries should receive broadly similar awards and that there should be a sensible relationship between the awards for injuries of differing severity.[110]

Until 1996, however, the attitude of the English courts was that such damages were not relevant to assessments in defamation cases and that awards could not be cited to juries even in a general way. It is still the law that it is not possible to equiparate personal injury and defamation damages[111] and this is for a number of reasons. First, one is not comparing like with like. The loss of a leg and the loss of an eye are injuries of the same broad type, but even if one takes the view that it is undesirable that the victim of a libel should receive more in damages than the victim of quadriplegia there is no way in which one can use any particular point on the personal injury tariff as a guide to a correct figure for a particular libel. Secondly, damages for defamation contain an element of vindication which is not directly comparable with personal injury compensation.[112] Thirdly, even leaving aside cases where there is a claim for exemplary damages, damages in defamation cases may be aggravated to take account of the wounding effect of the defendant's behaviour upon the hurt suffered by the claimant,[113] but almost all personal injury cases arise from negligence, where such damages are not possible.[114] Fourthly, damages in personal injury cases are in total very much larger than libel damages and raise issues of what "society can afford".

---

[109] In *Simmons v Castle* [2012] EWCA Civ 1039; [2013] 1 W.L.R. 1239 the Court of Appeal announced that as from April 1, 2013 the proper level of general damages in all civil claims (including defamation and misuse of private information) for (i) pain and suffering, (ii) loss of amenity, (iii) physical inconvenience and discomfort, (iv) social discredit or (v) mental distress would be 10 per cent higher than previously. The increase was made as part of the change in the civil costs regime initiated by Sir Rupert Jackson's reforms (*Final Report on Civil Litigation Costs* (December 2009)) and enacted by the legislature in Legal Aid, Sentencing and Punishment of Offenders Act 2012 (LASPO). The increase was recommended by Sir Rupert as an integral part of his proposed reforms and it was on the basis that the 10 per cent increase would be formally adopted by the judiciary that the 2012 Act was introduced and enacted. See 35.13, below on the delay in bringing into force the relevant sections of LASPO 2012 as far as defamation is concerned.

[110] See Kemp and Kemp, *The Quantum of Damages* and, for convenient ready reference, the Judicial Studies Board's *Guidelines for the Assessment of General Damages in Personal Injury Cases* (11th edn, 2012).

[111] *John v MGN Ltd* [1997] Q.B. 586 CA at 613; *Gur v Avrupa Newspaper Ltd* [2008] EWCA Civ 594; [2009] E.M.L.R. 4 at [18]; *Mosley v News Group Newspapers Ltd* [2008] EWHC 1777 (QB); [2008] E.M.L.R. 20 at [220]. In Scotland the Court of Session observed that:
"we do not find in cases of defamation comparison with awards made in cases of personal injuries particularly helpful or useful. The comparative examples given by senior counsel for the reclaimers are dramatic but also, in our view, unhelpful. Every case of defamation is unique in respect of both the content of the slander and its effect upon the victims and it therefore follows in our view that even comparison with other decided cases in that area is of very limited value": *Baigent v BBC* 2001 SC 281 at [22].

[112] *The Gleaner Co. Ltd v Abrahams* [2003] UKPC 55; [2004] 1 A.C. 628 at [55].

[113] See para.9.18, below.

[114] *Kralj v McGrath* [1986] 1 All E.R. 54.

"General damages in personal injury cases are . . . conventional figures influenced by the overall amount which a society considers it reasonable to pay in compensation to accident victims and fairness between successful tort plaintiffs and other accident victims on state benefits. Defamation awards, on the other hand, are also conventional figures, but influenced (among many other things) by society's views on the need to use private litigation as a means of controlling irresponsible behaviour by the media."[115]

Furthermore, personal injury damages are generally awarded on the basis of negligence or breach of statutory duty and are paid for the most part from the funds of insurers and public bodies on a basis which tends to be comparatively insensitive to the claim record of an individual defendant. Libel damages on the other hand have a significant deterrent effect (even where they are based on a purely compensatory measure) because the damages are likely to be paid from the defendant's own funds or from a policy of insurance which is likely to be sensitive to the incidence of claims.[116] The matter is one on which different opinions may be legitimately held.[117] However, in England in *John v MGN Ltd*,[118] the Court of Appeal held that it was legitimate to draw the attention of the jury to the level of the standard tariff awards in personal injury cases though the importance of this in practice is diminishing as few cases are now heard by juries.[119] Even under the former regime it is possible that jurors' perceptions of personal injury awards may have played a part in driving defamation damages up, for they may have read newspaper reports of multi-million pound payments in serious personal injury cases without realising that

---

[115] *The Gleaner Co. Ltd v Abrahams* [2003] UKPC 55; [2004] 1 A.C. 628 at [62]. The former NSW practice under the Defamation Act 1974, s.46A(2) required the court to take account of the level of personal injury damages (there is now a statutory cap, see para.9.4, above) and in *Rogers v Nationwide News Pty Ltd* [2003] HCA 52; 216 C.L.R. 327 at [191] Heydon J. remarked that statutory restrictions on personal injury damages are:

"not to be explained by reason of a different perception of 'value'. [They are] . . . to be explained as resulting from a perception by the legislature that some classes of compensation have become too substantial and have gone beyond the capacity of those bodies which have to fund them to do so . . . The motivations are financially based, not value based."

See also Hayne J. at [76].

[116] *The Gleaner Co. Ltd v Abrahams* above at [53].

[117] Ibid. at [50].

[118] *John v MGN Ltd* [1997] Q.B. 586.

[119] On the rarity of jury awards, see para.34.1, below. The Hong Kong Final Court of Appeal has also held (see *Blakeney-Williams v Cathay Pacific Airways Ltd* [2012] HKFCA 61; [2013] E.M.L.R. 6 at [100]–[101]) that there is nothing wrong with a court referring to damages for non-pecuniary loss in personal injury claims at least as a sort of cross-check where it has decided to award a large sum. However, Lord Neuberger of Abbotsbury N.P.J. doubted that such a check would be any more than of minimal use:

"While those considerations do not undermine the force of the point made in *John*, I accept that they do emphasise the very limited extent to which the level of personal injury damages can assist a court when it is assessing general damages for defamation. I doubt that personal injury damages would be of any legitimate assistance beyond providing a sort of cross-check in a case where a judge is minded to award a relatively large amount by way of general damages for defamation (and even then I am far from saying that a judge should, as opposed to may, find such an exercise helpful)."

most of these sums represented provable loss of earnings and expenses.[120] The court in *John* said that:

> "it is . . . offensive to public opinion, and rightly so, that a defamation plaintiff should recover damages for injury to reputation greater, perhaps by a significant factor, than if that same plaintiff had been rendered a helpless cripple or an insensate vegetable."[121]

The tenor of the judgment is arguably that the personal injury figures should be brought to the jury's attention by way of guidance[122] for the jury—which is, after all, the law's approximation to public opinion—but not so as to bind the jury.[123] However, in *Jones v Pollard*[124] Hirst L.J. (with whom the other members of the Court of Appeal agreed) said:

> "I cannot accept that the main purpose of *John* was to establish a ceiling, if by that is meant that in the most serious cases awards of general damages at the very top of the JSB range would normally be appropriate. Such cases comprise quadriplegia, very severe brain damage . . . and total blindness and deafness. For my part, save possibly in the most exceptional case, I find it difficult to imagine any defamation action where even the most severe damage to reputation, accompanied by maximum aggravation, would be comparable with such appalling physical injuries. The purpose of the personal injuries comparison sanctioned in *John* is in my judgment to assist juries and the Court of Appeal to maintain a sense of proportion, by drawing a comparison between any prospective award of damages for defamation with the type of personal injury which would lead to a similar award, without of course seeking any precise correlation."

Nevertheless, the maximum figure in personal injury cases has been treated as an effective ceiling[125] and awarded by a judge sitting alone in a case of widely publicised allegations of child abuse, in which he said that the claimants had "earned it several times over because of the scale, gravity and persistence of

---

[120] *Carson v John Fairfax* (1993) 113 A.L.R. 577 at 588.

[121] [1997] Q.B. 586 CA at 614.

[122] The passage is immediately followed by the sentence: "The time has in our view come when judges, and counsel, should be free to draw the attention of juries to these comparisons."

[123] The Court of Appeal in *Rantzen v Mirror Group Newspapers (1986) Ltd* [1994] Q.B. 670, CA in exercising its powers to fix damages on appeal, fixed a sum of £110,000. At the time that was very near the top of the level of awards in personal injury cases. The libel was a very serious one but not the most serious that can be imagined. There is no suggestion of disapproval in *John*.

[124] [1997] E.M.L.R. 233 CA at 257.

[125] *Cairns v Modi* [2012] EWCA Civ 1382: [2013] 1 W.L.R. 1015 at [25]; "It has now become conventional also to recognise in effect a 'ceiling' figure, allowing periodically for inflation, corresponding to the current maximum level of damages for pain and suffering and loss of amenity in personal injury cases": *Campbell-James v Guardian Media Group Plc* [2005] EWHC 893 (QB); [2005] E.M.L.R. 24 at [19]; *Tierney v News Group Newspapers Ltd* [2006] EWHC 3275 (QB); *Cooper v Turrell* [2011] EWHC 3269 (QB) at [93]; *Al Amoudi v Kifle* [2011] EWHC 2037 (QB) at [43].

the allegations and of the aggravating factors".[126] A judge has awarded
£150,000 for newspaper allegations of disloyal dealings with an enemy of this
country and this was upheld on appeal[127] and £180,000 was regarded as a
proper figure for allegations of being involved in terrorist bombings published
in an Albanian language newspaper.[128] The real difficulties probably lie below
that level, and it has been suggested[129] that the sort of libel which may now
attract an award of £50,000 or £100,000 cannot really be compared in gravity
with a personal injury attracting a similar sum.[130] The statutory sum for
damages for bereavement, for example, is only slightly higher (£12,980)[131]
than the sum thought appropriate for the sort of less serious libel suitable for
the summary procedure.[132] Ultimately, it has to be recognised that damage to

---

[126] *Lillie v Newcastle City Council* [2002] EWHC 1600 (QB). In *Campbell v News Group
Newspapers Ltd* [2002] EWCA Civ 1143; [2002] E.M.L.R. 43, another child abuse allegation
case, the jury's award of £350,000 was clearly too high, quite apart from the matters relating to
the claimant's reputation and his conduct of the case which went to reduce the award to £30,000.
In *Kiam v MGN Ltd* [2002] EWCA Civ 43; [2003] Q.B. 281, Simon Brown L.J. at [53] also seems
to be of the view that awards might reach £200,000. In *Hill v Church of Scientology of Toronto*
[1995] 2 S.C.R. 1130, the Supreme Court of Canada declined to impose a cap analogous to that
for non-pecuniary loss in personal injury cases. However, the decision treats such damages as less
relevant than they now are in England.
[127] *Galloway v Telegraph Group Ltd* [2004] EWHC 2786 (QB); [2005] E.M.L.R. 7; [2006]
EWCA Civ 17; [2006] E.M.L.R. 11. There was an element of aggravation in the conduct of the
trial; however, the maximum personal injury figure was a little lower then.
[128] *Veliu v Mazrekaj* [2006] EWHC 1710 (QB); [2007] 1 W.L.R. 495 (the actual award was
£175,000, there being a small discount for a very belated apology). See also *Ghannouchi v Al
Arabiya* [2007] EWHC 2855 (QB) (£165,000 for a libel broadcast to an Arabic-speaking audience
measured in hundreds of thousands, alleging that the claimant was an extremist linked to
Al-Qaeda); *Veliu v Mazrekaj* [2006] EWHC 1710 (QB) (an offer of amends case, the starting
point was fixed at £180,000 for a libel alleging that the claimant was closely involved in the
London bombings in July 2005, published by an Albanian-language newspaper widely read by
the 20,000 strong Albanian community in London); *Berezovsky v Terluk and Russian State
Television* [2010] EWHC 476 (QB) (the claimant was awarded damages of £150,000 for a
television broadcast likely to have been seen by subscribers numbered in the thousands. The
relevant allegation was that he was a knowing party to a criminal conspiracy to avoid his
extradition and to obtain asylum by trying to procure a false confession from the defendant Terluk
by bribery and drugs.)
[129] See, e.g. Sedley L.J. dissenting in *Kiam v MGN Ltd* [2002] EWCA Civ 43; [2003] Q.B. 281.
This was certainly a bad case of:
"a spiteful, insolent and damaging story, based on slapdash research, published without any
justification and without even asking the claimant about it . . . [and which] was repeated more
than once and was defended in one way or another until the end of the trial":
(at [70]). Nevertheless the matter was dealt with within 14 months of publication and the figure
of £105,000 was at the time comparable to the sum for below-knee amputation of both legs. Even
the judge's top of bracket suggestion of £80,000 was comparable to total amputation of one
leg.
[130] Even in *Lillie*, above, is an intensely pressed allegation of child abuse a worse experience
than quadriplegia? It is impossible to say. If we have taken a decision of policy that libel victims
should never get more than quadriplegia victims that still does not make any libel case and any
personal injury case truly comparable.
[131] Damages for Bereavement (Variation of Sum) (England and Wales) Order 2013.
[132] It may of course be objected that the bereavement sum is a classic example of an arbitrary,
conventional figure for a loss which it is impossible to assess, all the more so because the same
figure is awarded whether the survivor is emotionally ruined or rather glad to see the back of the
deceased.

reputation is very different from personal injury and any comparison between the two is of limited utility. Nevertheless, the ceiling figure in personal injury awards does at least provide a useful "reality" check where a court is minded to award a large sum by way of damages.

9.10 Relevance of awards in other defamation cases. Juries should not be told about the awards of other juries in defamation cases as a means of indicating a figure.[133] Past awards would be wholly unreliable because they date from the days when juries received little or no guidance on damages and the Court of Appeal applied only the lightest restraint on excessive awards, and even more recent jury awards would give very little assistance. Cases where the Court of Appeal has approved awards or substituted other sums or where awards have been made by a judge will provide *some* guidance to juries.[134] This corpus of awards is growing, particularly as fewer cases are now heard by juries than was previously the case but even as it develops its value will be limited. This is another respect in which defamation differs from personal injury practice. The non-pecuniary effects of loss of an eye or a leg will be (or at least can sensibly be deemed to be) sufficiently similar from one case to another to allow the award to be contained within a fairly narrow bracket, but the circumstances of defamation cases are almost infinitely various.[135] For example, in *Houston v Smith*[136] the defendant slandered her partner, another medical practitioner, by accusing him of sexual harassment, repeating the charge and, at the trial, persisting in a defence of justification. The Court of Appeal substituted an award of £50,000 for the jury's £150,000, stating that its award was at the top of the range and was based upon the aggravating factors and that if the slander had not been repeated,[137] and the defendant had promptly apologised, the appropriate sum would have been a "very small fraction" of £50,000. Had the defamatory accusation been published as a libel in the media, with similar aggravating factors, the general damages would presumably have been higher.[138] However, there is no reason

---

[133] *Rantzen v Mirror Group Newspapers (1986) Ltd* [1994] Q.B. 670 CA; *John v MGN Ltd* [1997] Q.B. 586 CA. In Canada in *Hill v Church of Scientology of Toronto* [1995] 2 S.C.R. 1130 the jury asked what were the "realistic maximums awarded in recent history" (at 175) and the court, with the agreement of counsel for the defendants, declined to answer.

[134] *John v MGN Ltd* [1997] Q.B. 586 CA at 612. Judicial awards under the summary procedure introduced by s.8 of the Defamation Act 1996 will be of limited relevance since they are made in cases which are often too minor to justify trial by jury. However, cases where a judge has to set compensation in default of agreement between the parties under the offer of amends procedure are not limited to "minor libels". See para.19.5, below.

[135] *Applause Store Productions Ltd v Raphael* [2008] EWHC 1781 (QB) at [77]. In the context of South African law, see *Van der Berg v Coopers & Lybrand Trust (Pty) Ltd* 2001, (2) S.A. 242 SCA.

[136] [1993] CA Transcript 1544.

[137] See also *McCluskie v Summers*, 1988 S.L.T. (Notes) 55 (limited publication a mitigating factor).

[138] For other cases in which the CA has substituted a sum see Appendix 3. In *Khodaparast v Shad* [2000] 1 W.L.R. 618 CA, the court indicated that had the claim been one for libel (it was

why the jury should not be advised of reasoned awards made by first instance judges sitting alone.[139]

Other guidance to jury. Matters such as the seriousness of the libel, the range of publication and the behaviour of the parties are likely to be relevant to the assessment of damages in any case and will no doubt be brought to the attention of the jury. However, in contrast to previous practice[140] it was held in *John v MGN* to be permissible for the judge and counsel for both parties to indicate to the jury the level of award they respectively consider or contend to be appropriate.

9.11

> "The plaintiff will not wish the jury to think that his main object is to make money rather than to clear his name. The defendant will not wish to add insult to injury by underrating the seriousness of the libel. So . . . the figures suggested by responsible counsel are likely to reflect the upper and lower bounds of a realistic bracket."[141]

However, in practice it has been rare for counsel to address the jury in any detail on this and it has been said to be desirable that the only detailed guidance on figures should come from the judge.[142] The jury should be told that they are not bound by any of the suggested figures and that the final word is theirs[143]; and if they award a sum higher than that suggested by the judge then real consideration must be given on any appeal to the possibility that their judgment is to be preferred to that of the judge.[144]

In *Sutcliffe v Pressdram*[145] the Court of Appeal said that to guard against the danger of juries not appreciating the true value of large capital sums they might be asked to consider, once they had a particular sum in mind, what that would mean

> "in terms of weekly, monthly or annual income if the money were invested in a building society deposit account without touching the capital, or, if they have in mind smaller sums, to consider what they could buy with it"[146]

---

for malicious falsehood) £50,000 would not have been excessive (Iranian female represented as advertising telephone sex lines).

[139] *Gur v Avrupa Newspaper Ltd* [2008] EWCA Civ 594; [2009] E.M.L.R. 4 at [28].

[140] For the previous practice and the reasons which were then thought to support it, see the direction of Michael Davies J. in *Sutcliffe v Pressdram*, quoted by Russell L.J. in the CA [1991] 1 Q.B. 153.

[141] [1997] Q.B. 586 at 616.

[142] *Kiam v MGN Ltd* [2002] EWCA Civ 43; [2003] Q.B. 281 at [55]. This is the suggested practice in actions for false arrest and malicious prosecution: *Thompson v MPC* [1998] Q.B. 498.

[143] [1997] Q.B. 586 at 616.

[144] As was the case in *Kiam v MGN Ltd* [2002] EWCA Civ 43; [2003] Q.B. 281. See also *Thornberry v Coleman* [2001] EWCA Civ 1858 (sum well below suggested bracket upheld).

[145] [1991] 1 Q.B. 153 CA.

[146] *Sutcliffe v Pressdram Ltd* [1991] 1 Q.B. 153 CA at 179. In *Rantzen v Mirror Group Newspapers (1986) Ltd* [1994] Q.B. 670 CA, the trial judge's direction was solely in terms of what the award might buy, coupled with the injunction to "be reasonable, keep your feet on the ground". The CA held that the absence of a reference to investment income was not fatal, although the judge "might have gone further" (at 682).

in terms of things like homes, cars and holidays. This practice may now have been superseded,[147] although no doubt judges may still feel it necessary to remind juries in some way of the value of money.

9.12 Jury to deal with damages on the evidence. The jury should not take into account in assessing damages any part of the words complained of in respect of which the defendant has made out a defence,[148] or any damage done to the claimant's reputation or feelings by any defamatory matter or other wrong for which the defendant is not responsible.[149] Where the court has jurisdiction against a foreign publisher it should award damages only for harm suffered within its own jurisdiction.[150] The jury should not consider the question of or the effect of costs, which are entirely a matter for the judge.[151] The judge should direct the jury that costs are not their concern and, if asked questions on the matter, the proper course[152] is to decline to answer. It is for the jury, if they find for the claimant, to say to what extent he has been damaged, irrespective of the effect, if any, which their verdict may have on the action of the judge in dealing with costs.[153]

---

[147] Para.35.3, below. But cf. *The Gleaner Co. Ltd v Abrahams* [2003] UKPC 55 at [45].

[148] But not that the defendant could, by publishing in a different way, have gained the protection of privilege for some of the material: *Galloway v Telegraph Group Ltd* [2004] EWHC 2786 (QB); [2005] E.M.L.R. 7; affirmed [2006] EWCA Civ 17; [2006] E.M.L.R. 11. In *Clift v Slough BC* [2009] EWHC 1550 (QB); [2010] E.M.L.R. 4 where the defendants had run defences of justification and qualified privilege and it had been held that the latter did not apply to all the publications, the jury were required to return a special verdict on justification and malice. They found that the imputations were not justified but that there was no malice, awarding damages for the non-privileged publications. The defendant's appeal against the verdict was dismissed: [2010] EWCA Civ 1484; [2011] 1 W.L.R. 1774.

[149] *Associated Newspapers v Dingle* [1964] A.C. 371 HL; *Harrison v Pierce* (1859) 1 F. & F. 567; *Basse v Toronto Star* (1983) 4 D.L.R. (4th) 381. Note the possibility that the defendant may be responsible for repetition by others: see para.6.52, above. Where there are a number of publications by different persons to similar effect, then even though the defendants are not joint tortfeasors the damage to reputation may nevertheless be indivisible and each will be liable in full, though s.12 of the Defamation Act 1952 goes some way to meet this point (see para.9.14, below).

"If a man reads four newspapers at breakfast and reads substantially the same libel in each, liability does not depend on which paper he opens first. Perhaps one newspaper influences him more than another, but unless he can say he disregarded one altogether, then each is a substantial cause of the damage done to the plaintiff in his eyes":
Dingle v Associated Newspapers Ltd [1961] 2 Q.B. 162 at 189, per Devlin L.J. (and see Lord Denning on appeal [1964] A.C. 371 at 410–411). See also *Television New Zealand Ltd v Ah Koy* [2002] 2 N.Z.L.R. 616 NZCA and *Cornwall v Rowan* [2004] SASC 384; 90 S.A.S.R. 269 at [790] et seq.

[150] *Shevill v Presse Alliance SA* [1995] 2 A.C. 18 ECJ. See also *Hussein v Hamilton Franks & Co. Ltd* [2013] EWHC 462 (QB): damages reduced to take account of fact that this jurisdiction though significant to the Claimants was not the main locus of their reputations or of those with whom they mostly dealt (at [33]).

[151] *Mears v Griffin* (1840) 1 Man. & G. 796; *Poole v Whitcombe* (1862) 12 C.B.N.S. 770; *Kelly v Sherlock* (1866) L.R. 1 Q.B. 686; *Russell v Weniweser* (1868) 16 W.R. 710; *Pamplin v Express Newspapers (No.2)* [1988] 1 W.L.R. 116 CA.

[152] Followed in *Kelly v Sherlock*, above.

[153] Per Bramwell B. in *Kelly v Sherlock* (1866) L.R. 1 Q.B. 691. In *Pamplin v Express Newspapers (No.2)* [1988] 1 W.L.R. 116 CA, the jury, in response to a question, had been told that costs normally follow the event and had awarded one-half penny. The judge, in accordance

Greater sum awarded than claimed.[154] If the claimant has claimed a   **9.13**
specific sum as damages and the jury assess the damages at more than that
sum, the claimant should ask the judge to amend the statement of claim by
altering the sum named to the sum awarded; a judgment for the larger sum
without amendment is irregular.[155] The judge has power to make such amendment, and after amendment to enter judgment for the larger sum,[156] but the
judge will not re-assess damages in relation to material of which evidence
might have been, but was not, given at the trial.[157]

Several libels or slanders alleged. Where two or more libels or slanders   **9.14**
are alleged in separate paragraphs of the statement of claim, it is now a
question for the judge's discretion whether there should be one award of
damages or several awards.[158]

Separate actions for defamation.[159] Section 12 of the Defamation Act   **9.15**
1952 provides that the defendant:

> "may give evidence in mitigation of damages that the plaintiff has recovered
> damages, or has brought actions for damages, . . . in respect of the publication of
> words to the same effect as the words on which the action is founded, or has received
> or agreed to receive compensation in respect of any such publication."[160]

---

with common practice on "contemptuous" damages, ordered the plaintiff to pay the costs of the
action. The Court of Appeal took the view that the jury had concluded that the plaintiff was not
entitled to recover any damages and as the only reason for awarding a half penny must have been
to protect the plaintiff's position on costs, that was an impermissible reason which meant that the
misdirection had caused no miscarriage of justice.

[154] For an example of such a case heard before a judge, see *Hussein v Hamilton Franks & Co.
Ltd* [2013] EWHC 462 (QB) at [33].

[155] *Chattell v Daily Mail* (1901) 18 T.L.R. 165.

[156] *Wyatt v Rosherville* (1885) 2 T.L.R. 282; *The Dictator* [1892] P.D. 64; *Modera v Modera*
(1893) 10 T.L.R. 69. Cf. *Dougherty v Nationwide News* [1971] 1 N.S.W.L.R. 313.

[157] *Stewart v Daily Telegraph, The Times,* August 1, 1958, where an application was made
before judgment was formally drawn up.

[158] See para.35.6, below.

[159] In such a case, the claimant can bring separate claims in respect of each publication though
where this amounts to an abuse the claims may be struck out or stayed (see, e.g., *Smith v ADVFN
Plc* [2010] EWCA Civ 657). Should he succeed in respect of all the allegations he is entitled to
separate damages for each one subject only to the requirement that the judge had directed the jury
(or himself) to take care to avoid double-counting (*Collins-Stewart Ltd v Financial Times Ltd
(No.2)* [2005] EWHC 262 (QB); [2006] E.M.L.R. 100 at [24]). Second, if the claimant chooses
to sue only in respect of the first publication, no damages may be directly awarded for any
defamatory imputations that are not the subject-matter of the claim (*Pearson v Lemaitre* [1845]
5 M. & Gr. 700 at 720; *Collins-Stewart Ltd v Financial Times Ltd (No.2)* [2005] EWHC 262
(QB); [2006] E.M.L.R. 100 at [24]; *Clarke t/a Elumina Iberica UK v Bain & Prolink Holdings
Corp* [2008] EWHC 2636 (QB) at [41]. Thirdly, evidence of subsequent publications may be
admissible in aggravation of damages but the jury should be warned that they should not award
separate damages in respect of the later publications (*Clarke t/a Elumina Iberica UK v Bain &
Prolink Holdings Corp* [2008] EWHC 2636 (QB) at [41]).

[160] Outside s.12 the defendant cannot seek to show that the claimant's reputation has been
damaged by publications by other persons to the same effect: *Associated Newspapers v Dingle*
[1964] A.C. 371 HL, paras 9.12, above and 33.58, below.

Where such evidence is given it is not sufficient to tell each jury to make such allowance as they think fit for the damages the claimant is likely to recover in the other action.

> "They ought to be directed that in considering the evidence submitted to them they should consider how far the damage suffered by the plaintiff can reasonably be attributed solely to the libel with which they are concerned and how far it ought to be regarded as the joint result of the two libels. If they think that some part of the damage is the joint result of the two libels they should bear in mind that the plaintiff ought not to be compensated twice for the same loss. They can only deal with this matter on very broad lines and they must take it that the other jury will be given a similar direction. They must do the best they can to ensure that the sum which they award will fully compensate the plaintiffs for the damage caused by the libel with which they are concerned, but will not take into account that part of the total damage suffered by the plaintiffs which ought to enter into the other jury's assessment."[161]

9.16 Tax and damages. General damages awarded to an individual for defamation are not subject to income tax in the hands of the recipient.[162] However, damages for defamation may represent loss of income, as where such loss is directly proved to have flowed from the wrong or, in the case of a company, because the claimant can only be injured in its pocket,[163] even if that is expressed as injury to goodwill rather than directly as loss of income. In some cases the damages for lost income will not be taxable in the claimant's hands and then, in determining what those damages should be, account must be taken, in computing the loss, of the fact that the claimant would have been subject to tax on the income.[164] In other cases, however, damages awarded to a trader for a libel which has caused loss of business may constitute a trading receipt and be taxable in his hands,[165] in which case the damages should obviously be calculated without any deduction.[166]

---

[161] Per Lord Reid in *Lewis v Daily Telegraph* [1964] A.C. 234 at 261. Cf. also *Uren v John Fairfax* (1966) 117 C.L.R. 118 at 155. For another form of overlap, see *Moore v News of the World* [1972] 1 Q.B. 441 CA; cf. *Longdon-Griffiths v Smith* [1950] 2 All E.R. at 678; *Beloff v Pressdram* [1973] 1 All E.R. 241. In principle a similar direction would be appropriate where damage is caused partly by the publication complained of and partly by the tortious act of another. Libels three months apart can be treated separately: *Kapwepwe v Zambia Publishing* [1978] S.C.Z. No.7.

[162] Whether purely compensatory, aggravated or exemplary. Nor, even if there could be said to be a disposal of a capital asset, are they subject to capital gains tax: Taxation of Chargeable Gains Act 1992, s.51.

[163] Per Lord Reid in *Lewis v Daily Telegraph* [1964] A.C. 234 at 262.

[164] *Lewis v Daily Telegraph* [1964] A.C. 234 at 262, applying *BTC v Gourley* [1956] A.C. 183 HL (damages for personal injury).

[165] See generally *Deeny v Gooda Walker (No.2)* [1996] 1 W.L.R. 426 HL (not a defamation case).

[166] It seems that in *Beta Construction v Channel Four TV* (reported on another point [1990] 1 W.L.R. 1042 CA) Jupp J.'s initial award of £90,000 for libel to the company was recalculated to some £125,000 when the Revenue indicated that it regarded it as carrying a tax liability: Neill L.J. on appeal on another point, unreported, July 31, 1992, CA.

Corporate claimants and damages. While substantial damages may be   **9.17**
awarded to a corporate entity notwithstanding a failure to prove any specific
damage, in practice, in the absence of at least a general loss of business,[167] a
limited company is unlikely to be entitled to a really substantial award of
damages. As was made clear by Lord Reid in *Lewis v Daily Telegraph Ltd*,[168]
"A company cannot be injured in its feelings; it can only be injured in its
pocket. Its reputation can be injured by a libel but that injury must sound in
money." Whilst Lord Reid went on to say, "The injury need not necessarily
be confined to loss of income; its goodwill may be injured", a company which
is unable at trial to point to the slightest hiccup in its trading figures may be
hard pressed to persuade a court that even an unpleasant libel has seriously
injured its reputation. Unlike a personal claimant, it cannot tug the jury's
heart-strings by describing its distress and humiliation on reading the defamatory words. This presents a problem for a limited company which has been
defamed, since it is often difficult to prove that the publication caused either
a specific or a general loss of business. That there is an entitlement to general
damages which are more than nominal damages is certain, but the amount
likely to be awarded to a corporation may be small in commercial terms,
unless the defendant's refusal to retract or apologise makes it possible to argue
that the only way in which the reputation of the company can be vindicated
in the eyes of the world is by way of a really substantial award of damages.[169]

SECTION 2. AGGRAVATED DAMAGES

Aggravated damages. The conduct of the defendant, his conduct of the   **9.18**
case, and his state of mind[170] are all matters which the claimant may rely on
as aggravating the damages in so far as they bear on the injury to him.

> "[I]t is very well established that in cases where the damages are at large the jury
> (or the judge if the award is left to him) can take into account the motives and
> conduct of the defendant where they aggravate the injury done to the plaintiff. There
> may be malevolence or spite or the manner of committing the wrong may be such
> as to injure the plaintiff's proper feelings of dignity and pride.[171] These are matters

---

[167] *Ratcliffe v Evans* [1892] 2 Q.B. 524. This should be expressly pleaded: *Perestrello e
Companhia Ltda v United Paint Co. Ltd* [1969] 1 W.L.R. 570 CA.

[168] [1964] A.C. 234 at 262; [1963] 2 All E.R. 151 at 156 HL.

[169] In *Applause Store Productions v Raphael* [2008] EWHC 1721 H.H.J. Parkes QC made clear
that notwithstanding the lack of evidence of any financial loss, substantial damages may be
justified on the basis of the need to vindicate the claimant's reputation: "A company's good name
is a thing of value, but it can only be hit in its pocket, and there is no evidence here of actual
financial loss. That is not to say that it may not merit vindication."

[170] In Scotland malice in itself is not a ground for increasing the damages: *Stein v Beaverbrook
Newspapers*, 1968 S.C. 272.

[171] Hence aggravated damages are not available to a corporate claimant, which has no feelings
to be hurt: *Collins Stewart Ltd v Financial Times Ltd* [2005] EWHC 262 (QB), [2006] E.M.L.R.
5. Cf. *Hiltz and Seamone Co. v Att-Gen (Nova Scotia)* (1999) 172 D.L.R. (4th) 488 NSCA.

which the jury can take into account in assessing the appropriate compensation."[172]

"The conduct of a defendant which may often be regarded as aggravating the injury to the plaintiff's feelings, so as to support a claim for 'aggravated' damages, includes a failure to make any or any sufficient apology and withdrawal[173]; a repetition of the libel; conduct calculated to deter the claimant from proceeding; persistence, by way of a prolonged or hostile cross-examination of the claimant,[174] or in turgid speeches to the jury,[175] in a plea of justification which is bound to fail[176]; the general conduct either of the preliminaries or of the trial itself in a manner calculated to attract wide publicity; and persecution of the plaintiff by other means."[177]

9.19 Aggravated damages and subsequent publications. The question whether, and if so in what circumstances, a claimant in a libel action is entitled

---

[172] Per Lord Devlin in *Rookes v Barnard* [1964] A.C. 1129 at 1221.
"In awarding 'aggravated damages' the natural indignation of the court at the injury inflicted on the plaintiff is a perfectly legitimate motive in making a generous, rather than a more moderate award to provide an adequate *solatium* . . . that is because the injury to the plaintiff is actually greater, and, as the result of the conduct exciting the indignation, demands a more generous *solatium*":
per Lord Hailsham L.C. in *Broome v Cassell* [1972] A.C. 1027 at 1073.
[173] A majority of the High Court of Australia has said that, while an apology may mitigate damages, the absence of one cannot logically aggravate them, though it may be evidence of the defendant's desire to hurt the plaintiff: *Carson v John Fairfax* (1993) 178 C.L.R. 44. Cf. Lord Guest in *Morgan v Odhams Press Ltd* [1971] 1 W.L.R. 1239 HL at 1262, who did not regard failure to apologise as evidence of malice. In *Rantzen v Mirror Group Newspapers (1986) Ltd* [1994] Q.B. 670 CA at 683, the availability of aggravated damages on the ground of failure to apologise was regarded as firmly settled, even where the defendant believed his statement to be justified. However, it was said that this would not always be so, as where the defendant's defence was that the words were not reasonably capable of being understood as referring to the plaintiff, citing *Morgan v Odhams Press Ltd* [1971] 1 W.L.R. 1239 HL. See also para.34.57, below.
[174] In *Cairns v Modi* [2012] EWHC 756 (QB) Bean J. awarded an extra £20,000 by way of aggravated damages for a "sustained and aggressive assertion of the plea of justification" at the trial (at [137]). The award was upheld on appeal: [2012] EWCA Civ 1382; [2013] 1 W.L.R. 1015.
[175] It may be difficult to distinguish between "improper" pressure and forceful advocacy, but it seems clear that the way counsel conducts a case may be an aggravating factor even though it does not amount to a breach of professional ethics: *Cairns v Modi* (above); *Galloway v Telegraph Group Ltd* [2004] EWHC 2786 (QB); [2005] E.M.L.R. 7; affirmed [2006] EWCA Civ 17; [2006] E.M.L.R. 11. See also *Kiam v MGN Ltd* [2002] EWCA Civ 43; [2003] Q.B. 281; and *Harbour Radio Pty Ltd v Tingle* [2001] NSWCA 194.
[176] See also *Applause Store Productions Ltd v Raphael* (above) (persistence in defence as to responsibility for publication founded on lie). If a defendant has not relied on justification and a claim for aggravated damages is based on the allegation that he callously persisted with the charge in face of the claimant's denial, he cannot meet that by contending that the charge was true; but it is very relevant on the issue of damages for him to show that he believed and had reason to believe the charge to be true: *Warren v Random House Group Ltd* [2008] EWCA Civ 834; [2009] Q.B. 600 at [91].
[177] *Sutcliffe v Pressdram Ltd* [1991] 1 Q.B. 153 CA at 184, per Nourse L.J. In *Rogacki v Belz* (2004) 243 D.L.R. (4th) 585 at [52] the Ontario CA said that it saw
"no difficulty conceptually with the notion that a defendant can act without malice at the time of publication and with malice thereafter. That holds true regardless of the fact that the disparate findings may (and often will) rest upon the same evidence. Illogical though that may seem, it makes sense once it is understood that the focus of the inquiry into malice at the liability stage (the time of publication) is much narrower than the focus of the inquiry at the damages stage (pre-publication to the conclusion of the trial)."

to increase the damages recoverable in respect of the single publication complained of by relying on subsequent publications which are not themselves sued on as separate causes of action[178] has been considered in two important cases: *Collins Stewart Ltd v The Financial Times (No.2)*[179] and *Clarke t/a Elumina Iberica UK v Bain & Prolink Holdings.*[180] The effect of these two decisions is, it is suggested, as follows. First, subject to general case management principles,[181] evidence of subsequent publications in respect of which no claim is brought is admissible in so far as the later publications substantially repeat the same imputation[182] and shed light on the motive or state of mind of the defendant in making the imputation in respect of which the claim is brought. Thus where the subsequent publications help to prove the existence of a malicious motive or establish the existence of malice they may be led in evidence. Second, where the evidence also establishes another cause of action, then the jury must be cautioned against giving damages in respect of that cause of action.[183] Moreover, in such a case the defendant is entitled to plead matters which would afford him a defence to that cause of action, if it had been pleaded as a separate cause of action, including issues of meaning.

Aggravated damages and corporate claimants. There is some uncertainty whether aggravated damages can be recovered by a corporate or other   **9.20**

---

[178] It so clearly established that publications by a defendant subsequent to those which are relied as causes of action can be relied on by the claimant to prove malice, and thus the injury to a claimant's feelings: *Pearson v Lemaitre* [1843] 5 M. & Gr. 700. See also, *ZAM v CFW* [2013] EWHC 662 (QB).

[179] [2005] EWHC 262, [2006] E.M.L.R. 100 (QB). Tugendhat J. did not finally have to decide the question whether subsequent publications not sued on could aggravate damages because he refused the application to amend to plead the later publications in aggravation of damage on case management grounds alone (at [61]). He did however reconsider the issue in *ZAM v CFW* [2013] EWHC 662 (QB) and although noting that the claimant in *Clarke t/a Elumina Iberica UK v Bain & Prolink Holdings Corp* [2008] EWHC 2636 (QB) was a corporate entity which could not, unlike a natural person, recover damages for injury to feelings, nevertheless held that he would follow Gray J.'s decision in *Clarke.*

[180] [2008] EWHC 2636 (QB) was a case where the claimant was a corporation followed the decision (at [66]–[74]).

[181] In *Clarke t/a Elumina Iberica UK v Bain & Prolink Holdings Corp* (above), Tugendhat J. noted, at [41], that even if evidence of subsequent publications is in principle admissible "the court may, in exercise of its case management powers, determine to exclude such evidence".

[182] In *Collins Stewart v Financial Times (No.2)* [2005] EWHC 262 (QB); [2006] E.M.L.R. 100 at [26] (QB) Gray J. made clear that where the subsequent publications did not repeat the imputation then evidence of such imputations could not be led:
"Assume that the defendant publishes three defamatory articles referring to the claimant, articles A, B and C . . . If . . . articles B and C, whilst defamatory of and damaging to the claimant, do not repeat the libel which was contained in article A, it appears to me to be objectionable in principle to allow the claimant to rely on articles B and C in connection with damages recoverable for the publication of article A. Articles B and C would be separate torts giving rise to separate claims for damages."

[183] *Collins Stewart v Financial Times (No.2)* at [27]; *Clarke t/a Elumina Iberica UK v Bain & Prolink Holdings Corp* at [41]. See also, *Pearson v Lemaitre* [1845] 5 M. and Gr. 700 at 720.

inanimate legal entity. In *Collins Stewart Ltd v The Financial Times (No.2)*[184] Gray J. concluded that such damages could not be recovered by a corporate claimant because:

> "the defining characteristic of an award of aggravated damages is that its function is to provide a claimant with compensation ('solatium') for injury to his or her feelings caused by some conduct on the part of the defendant or for which the defendant is responsible. The concept of injury to feelings runs through the cases, whether caused by the high-handed or insulting behaviour of the defendant either before or after publication or by repetition of the libel, or by persistence in a plea of justification or by a failure to apologise. It seems to me that the essence of an award of aggravated damages in libel is not making good damage to the claimant's reputation as such but rather compensating the claimant for the extra injury to his or her feelings."[185]

It followed from this that a corporate claimant, which has no feelings, should not be allowed to recover aggravated damages. A different view was however taken by Caulfield J. *in Messenger Newspapers Ltd v National Graphical Association*[186] who awarded what he characterised as aggravated damages to a corporate claimant. However, the judge made clear that he was eliminating from the award the element of injury to feelings.[187] That fact, together with the tenor of the passage which emphasised the need to punish the defendant for his deliberate wrongdoing, "suggests that the additional damages which the judge awarded to the corporate claimant in that case were in truth what would nowadays be labelled exemplary damages".[188] It is therefore submitted, notwithstanding Caulfield J.'s decision in *Messenger*, that the more convincing view is that a corporate claimant cannot recover aggravated damages in a defamation claim.[189]

9.21 Relationship of aggravated and other damages. There are a number of problems with aggravated damages, though they are more theoretical than practical. First, it is difficult to draw a clear line between them and compensatory general damages, simply because the latter are anyway "at large"[190] and,

---

[184] [2005] EWHC 262, [2006] E.M.L.R. 100 (QB).

[185] Ibid. at [30]. See also *Applause Store Productions v Raphael* [2008] EWHC 1781 (QB) at [76].

[186] [1984] I.R.L.R. 397.

[187] Ibid. at [78].

[188] *Collins Stewart Ltd v The Financial Times (No 2)* (above) at [32].

[189] The Hong Kong Court of Final Appeal in *Oriental Daily Publisher Ltd v Ming Pao Holding Ltd* [2012] HKCFA 59; [2013] E.M.L.R. 7, held that the law as stated by Gray J. in *Collins Stewart Ltd v Financial Times Ltd* represented the law applicable in Hong Kong (at [111]–[125]).

[190] See Lord Diplock in *Broome v Cassell & Co. Ltd* [1972] A.C. 1027 at 1125. Hence in cases of battery the correct course is to bring the element of aggravation for injured feelings into account as part of the general damages awarded "except possibly in a wholly exceptional case": *Richardson v Howie* [2004] EWCA Civ 1127; [2005] P.I.Q.R. Q3. In *Martins v Choudhary* [2007] EWCA Civ 1379, a harassment case, Smith L.J. said at [20]:

> "The judge did not make separate awards for injury to feelings and aggravated damages. No ground of appeal arises from that and I wish to say that I think she was right not to do so. It seems to me that, in the context of a case of this kind (and for that matter in a discrimination

in the case of claimants who are natural persons, contain an inbuilt element for injury to feelings. It may be that, as a general rule outside the area of defamation, something in the nature of malicious or wilful, outrageous conduct on the part of the defendant is required for an award of aggravated damages and they cannot therefore be awarded in a case of negligence, however gross,[191] nor, even where such conduct is present, where the claimant is unaware of the defendant's state of mind,[192] in which case the line would be easy to draw in theory even if it presented evidential difficulties in practice. However, in the context of defamation that would be inconsistent with the fact that in England[193] the failure of the defendant to apologise[194] or his persistence with a plea of justification may aggravate the damages even though he honestly believes that what he said is true.[195] The reason is that:

> "if one looks at the matter not from the point of view of the state of mind of the defendant but for the purpose of assessing the injury to the plaintiff's feelings,[196] it is easy to see that a contest which involves justification or fair comment may increase the injury and add greatly to the anxiety caused by the proceedings which the plaintiff has had to bring to clear his name."[197]

---

case) where damages fall to be awarded for injury to feelings, the quantum of damage should reflect the aggravating features of the Defendant's conduct as they have affected the Claimant. As 'aggravated damages' are supposed to be compensatory, that seems to me to be the most satisfactory way of dealing with them. If a separate award of 'aggravated damages' is made, it looks like a punishment; in other words it looks like exemplary damages. I appreciate that differing views have been expressed on this issue in this court. I have expressed my view and, in the context of this appeal, it is obiter."

[191] *Kralj v McGrath* [1986] 1 All E.R. 54; cf. *Barbara v Home Office* (1984) N.L.J. 888.

[192] *Alexander v Home Office* [1988] 1 W.L.R. 968 CA at 976. For a similar suggestion in the context of defamation, see *Cook v Beaverbrook Newspapers* [1975] B.L.T. 98A CA and *Henry v News Group Newspapers Ltd* [2011] EWHC 1058 (QB) per Eady J. at [7]:

"The purpose of aggravated damages is to compensate the claimant for any salt that the relevant defendant has rubbed in the wound over and above the injury caused by the defamatory publication(s) complained of. It follows that the aggravating conduct must have been known to the claimant. It cannot be relevant to enquire into what was going on behind the scenes ('What the eye does not see . . . ')."

[193] Cf. Toohey J. in *Coyne v Citizen Finance Ltd* (1991) 172 C.L.R. 211 at 237:

"Mere persistence, or even vigorous persistence, in a bona fide defence, in the absence of improper or unjustifiable conduct, cannot be used to aggravate compensatory damages."

[194] See fn.173, above.

[195] *Rantzen v Mirror Group Newspapers (1986) Ltd* [1994] Q.B. 670 CA. It seems to be clearly assumed in *Galloway v Telegraph Group Ltd* [2004] EWHC 2786 (QB); [2005] E.M.L.R. 7 at [203] that pursuit of a bona fide defence of justification may be an aggravating factor (affirmed [2006] EWCA Civ 17; [2006] E.M.L.R. 11). Cf. *Blakeney-Williams v Cathay Pacific Airways Ltd* [2012] HKCFA 61; [2013] E.M.L.R. 6, in which the Hong Kong Court of Final Appeal stated (at [105]) that

"it is wrong in principle to award aggravated damages to a plaintiff in a defamation case, solely because the defendant has decided in good faith to raise a defence of justification, which is then run in a reasonable way. The fact that the defence fails, even in a case where the court regards it as not merely wrong but weak, is not enough, on its own, to bring aggravated damages into play."

[196] But compare s.32 of the Irish Defamation Act 2009, which bases aggravated damages upon the aggravation of the injury to the plaintiff's reputation

[197] *Rantzen*, above at 684.

Though the expression "aggravated damages" is often used, it might be better if instead we simply said that certain features of the case might aggravate the damages. There would then be no difficulty in saying that a vigorously conducted bona fide defence might increase the hurt suffered by the claimant and that a defence conducted in bad faith might increase the hurt still further.[198] In actions against the police for false imprisonment and malicious prosecution separate awards should be made for "basic" and aggravated damages.[199] Even if it is not necessary to make separate awards in a defamation case[200] it has been said to be desirable, if a single award is made, that it should be indicated how that is made up between general and aggravated damages.[201]

Secondly, there is the relationship between aggravated and exemplary damages. Even where aggravated damages are based upon the malice of the defendant they are in principle compensatory[202] because they are concerned

---

[198] This might also explain the apparent distinction between defamation and other torts, for the conduct of the case may be seen as a prolongation of the libel: Law Commission Consultation Paper no.132, *Aggravated, Exemplary and Restitutionary Damages* (1993), para.3.5.

[199] *Thompson v MPC* [1998] Q.B. 498 CA (though cf. *Richardson v Howie* [2004] EWCA Civ 1127; [2005] P.I.Q.R. Q3).

[200] See *Keith-Smith v Williams* [2006] EWHC 860 (QB), where the judge was in doubt on this point.

[201] *Conway v Ratiu* [2005] EWCA Civ 1302 (not reported on this point in [2006] 1 All E.R. 571). Aggravated damages were awarded as a separately identifiable item in *Campbell v Mirror Group Newspapers* [2002] EWHC 499 (QB), a breach of confidence and data protection case (on appeal on other matters [2002] EWCA Civ 1373; [2003] Q.B. 633 and [2004] UKHL 22; [2004] 2 A.C. 457). CPR r.16.4(1)(c), which requires the claimant specifically to plead a claim for aggravated damages and his grounds for claiming them, seems clearly to contemplate that they are a separate category (there was no such requirement under the RSC). However, it must be observed that defamation claims do differ from those at issue in *Thompson v MPC*, above. The nature of the "basic" injury to reputation and the circumstances of aggravation are likely to differ much more from case to case than in false imprisonment and the two elements are likely to be more difficult to disentangle. A judge may well reason

"I would have given the claimant about £X,000 for this in normal circumstances but the way the defendant has behaved means that the claimant has suffered much more so that justifies £X,000 plus 30 per cent",

but quaere whether that should necessitate a separate award. Indeed, to make one might suggest, contrary to the truth, that there was a clear tariff for libel. In *Cairns v Modi* [2012] EWCA Civ 1382; [2013] 1 W.L.R. 1015, the Court of Appeal rejected (at [37]) an argument of counsel that having regard to the need for consistency and proportionality a similarly analytical approach would be appropriate in the context of defamation:

"Because there are the three elements of hurt feelings, injury to reputation and the need for vindication, there would arise almost infinite opportunities to appeal based on criticism of the judge's allocation of particular sums under these respective headings and for arguments that one of them ought to have received more or less monetary recognition relative to the others. It is not unrealistic to put forward three broad bands in the limited context of hurt feelings for discrimination in the workplace. By contrast, the combination of circumstances and the different features which fall for consideration in libel claims vary enormously and do not lend themselves to straightforward categorisation."

As to exemplary damages, see para.9.25, below, but those are not concerned with the impact on the claimant.

[202] In *Clarkson v Gilbert*, unreported, February 26, 2001, (QB) at [27] Eady J. said:

"Aggravated damages in defamation actions are merely an aspect of compensation. It is well established that any conduct by a defendant calculated to add to the hurt to the claimant's

with the way in which the injury to the claimant is increased by the motive or conduct of the defendant[203]: a libel which is maliciously published and persisted in is likely to be more hurtful than one which is published in error and promptly corrected. Hence aggravated damages survive in jurisdictions which have abolished exemplary damages.[204] However, from the point of view of the defendant, it appears that his liability is increased because of his improper conduct[205] and the fact that there is therefore an inbuilt punitive element in aggravated damages means that this has to be taken into account if there is a claim for exemplary damages, which are overtly punitive in their purpose.

Crime and Courts Act 2013. In *The Report of An Inquiry into the*   **9.22**
Culture, Practices and Ethics of the Press[206] Leveson L.J. made a range of recommendations to reform the regulatory framework for the press, creating a new framework for press regulation. The new framework proposed was for a system of voluntary self-regulation, overseen by a recognition body established by Royal Charter and strengthened by a series of incentives for members of the press in the application of costs and exemplary damages, encouraging them to join a recognised regulator. At the time of writing, no agreement had been reached on the final form of the Royal Charter but the Crime and Courts Act 2013 has introduced in ss.34–42 and Sch.15 a new system that covers aggravated and exemplary damages, and costs, as well as defining those who meet the definition of a "relevant publisher" to whom the new system of aggravated and exemplary damages and costs will apply. When the new regulatory scheme is in place it is intended that those who are subject to the regulatory regime will be able to avail themselves of the provisions in the Crime and Courts Act which restrict the circumstances in which aggravated and exemplary damages and costs can be awarded. The Crime and Courts Act 2013 is not yet in force.

"Relevant publisher". The provisions on aggravated and exemplary dam-   **9.23**
ages apply only in respect of claims made against a person who was, at the

---

feelings caused by the publication of the defamatory words can be taken into account by way of aggravation."

Aggravated damages may be awarded in a case of malicious falsehood and may take account of the way the defendant has conducted the case: *Khodaparast v Shad* [2000] 1 W.L.R. 618 CA. Although Stuart-Smith L.J. at 631 distinguished between what he called "compensatory" and "aggravated" damages, it is unlikely that he was implying that aggravated damages were other than compensatory. See Otton L.J. at 632:

"it is important to emphasize that any sum to be awarded is a single sum and any aggravated damages are intended as compensation and not as a form of punishment of the defendant."

[203] Under the uniform Australian legislation the court is to disregard the malice or other state of mind of the defendant except to the extent that the malice or other state of mind affects the harm sustained by the plaintiff. See, e.g. s.36 of the Defamation Act 2005 (NSW).

[204] E.g. Australia.

[205] See Windeyer J. in *Uren v John Fairfax* (1966) 117 C.L.R. 118 at 151–152 and McHugh J. in *Carson v John Fairfax* (1993) 178 C.L.R. 44.

[206] No.0780 2012–13, November 29, 2012.

material time,[207] a "relevant publisher". Thus unless the defendant is a "relevant publisher" as defined in the Act, the common law rules on aggravated and exemplary damages will continue to apply. "Relevant publisher" is defined in s.41 as a person who "in the course of a business (whether or not carried on with a view to profit), publishes[208] news-related material[209]—(a) which is written by different authors, and (b) which is to any extent subject to editorial control".[210] Clearly within this provision would be publishers of newspapers, both national and local, and news magazines. The publishers of blogs and websites which publish news-related material would also potentially fall within the provision. Thus, the websites of national and local newspapers will fall within the provision as they carry news-related material which is written by different authors and subject to editorial control. Small-scale bloggers should not fall within the definition. Certain publishers are excluded from the operation of the provisions by s.41(5) and (6). Under s.41(5) a person is not a relevant publisher if specified by name in Sch.15 of the Act.[211] Section 41(6) also excludes publishers who do not fall within Sch.15 if their publication of news-related material is in a capacity or case of a description specified in Sch.15.

9.24 Aggravated damages and the Crime and Courts Act 2013. Under s.39(1) and (2) of the Act, where a relevant claim[212] is made against a person

---

[207] "Material time" is defined in s.42(6) as "the time of the events giving rise to the claim."

[208] Publication of material includes publication on a website, in hard copy or by other means: s.42(9).

[209] "News-related material" means "(a) news or information about current affairs, (b) opinion about matters relating to the news or current affairs, or (c) gossip about celebrities, other public figures or other persons in the news": s.42(7).

[210] News-related material is, by virtue of s.41(2) of the Act, "subject to editorial control" if there is a person (whether or not the publisher of the material) who has editorial or equivalent responsibility for—(a) the content of the material, (b) how the material is to be presented, and (c) the decision to publish it.

A person who is the operator of a website "is not to be taken as having editorial or equivalent responsibility for the decision to publish any material on the site, or for content of the material, if the person did not post the material on the site": s.41(3).

[211] Sch.15 includes various broadcasters (the BBC, Sianel Pedwar Cymru and the holder of a licence under the Broadcasting Act 1990 or 1996 who publishes news-related material in connection with the broadcasting activities authorised under the licence. Also within Sch.15 are the publishers of certain special interest titles (that is to say titles that relate to particular pastimes, hobbies, trades, business, industries or professions and which only contain news-related material on an incidental basis that is relevant to the title), the publishers of scientific or academic journals, public bodies and charities (which publish news related material in connection with the carrying out of their functions), the publishers of company news publications and "micro-businesses". A "micro-business" is a business with fewer than ten employees with an annual turnover not exceeding £2m. A person who is carrying on a "micro business" publishes news-related material where either (a) the news related material is contained in a multi-author blog or (b) the news-related material is published on an incidental basis that is relevant to the main activities of the business.

[212] A "relevant claim" includes claims for libel and slander but also includes breach of confidence, misuse of private information, malicious falsehood and harassment.

who was at the material time a "relevant publisher", the claim is in respect of news-related material and the defendant is found liable in respect of the claim, aggravated damages[213] may only be awarded against the defendant to compensate for mental distress and not for the purposes of punishment. So far as the law of libel and slander is concerned, s.39 does not appear to effect any change in the common law as aggravated damages can only be awarded to compensate the claimant for "injury to feelings" suffered as a consequence of exceptional conduct by the defendant.[214] So far as a claim for aggravated damages is concerned, it should not therefore matter, once the Act comes into effect, whether the defendant is, or is not, a "relevant publisher". The rules governing recovery of such damages are, so far as libel and slander are concerned, the same.

Section 3. Exemplary Damages

Nature of exemplary damages. Exemplary[215] damages are intended to   **9.25** punish the defendant for the wilful commission of a tort[216] or to teach him that tort does not pay. They are controversial (and not merely in the context of defamation[217]) because on one view they confuse punishment and compensation; but another view is that these two functions are like oil and vinegar,

---

[213] Aggravated damages are defined as damages that were commonly called aggravated before the passing of the Act, which are awarded against a person in respect of the person's motive or exceptional conduct but are not exemplary damages.

[214] See para.9.18, above.

[215] This is now the usual terminology in England, though "punitive" is still widely used elsewhere.

[216] They are not available for breach of contract. Nor are they available, at common law, for misuse of private information, something which to some extent arises from the doubt over whether that wrong can be classified as "tort". Exemplary damages may, after the relevant provisions of the Crime and Courts Act come into effect, be awarded in misuse of private information claims: see paras 9.32–9.33, below.

[217] The evidence received by the Law Commission and published in its report (LC 247, 1997) "Aggravated, Exemplary and Restitutionary Damages", was to the effect that exemplary damages are "seldom sought in libel actions". Three reasons were offered for this:

> "First, it is difficult, in the context of defamation by the press, to prove that a defendant calculated that a particular libel was likely to boost sales of the publication. Secondly, a plaintiff pleading exemplary damages will bear the burden of such proof. This effectively reverses the burden of proof in defamation actions, so that there is a tactical disadvantage in seeking exemplary damages. Thirdly, practitioners may often perceive a punitive element in awards of (supposedly compensatory) 'aggravated damages' by juries in defamation actions; they therefore feel that little is to be gained by claiming exemplary damages in addition" (at para.1.97).

The Law Commission (at para.1.98) noted that it thought claims for exemplary damages might increase as a result of the steps taken in *John v MGN Ltd* [1997] Q.B. 586, [1996] 2 All ER 35 to keep compensatory damages awards to reasonable levels. This does not appear to have happened and indeed the reverse appears to be the case as there does not appear to have been a single example post-2000 in which an award of exemplary damages has been made in a defamation claim.

which may not mix in solution but nevertheless make an acceptable liaison.[218] They are not, even in an attenuated sense, concerned with compensation of the claimant.[219] Until *Rookes v Barnard*[220] they were not clearly differentiated from aggravated damages but that case restricted them to three situations:

(1) Where they are recognised by statute. Whether or not there are any examples of this,[221] none applies to defamation.
(2) Where the wrong involves oppressive, arbitrary or unconstitutional[222] action by servants of the government.[223] In practice the cases have tended to concern matters such as false imprisonment and malicious prosecution. As a matter of principle there seems no reason why this head should not apply to defamation, provided there is some abuse of

---

[218] *Gleaner Co. Ltd v Abrahams* [2003] UKPC 55; [2004] 1 A.C. 628 at [54]. See the contrasting views of Lords Reid and Wilberforce in *Broome v Cassell & Co. Ltd* [1972] A.C. 1027 and Lords Nicholls and Hutton and Lord Scott in *Kuddus v Chief Constable of Leicestershire* [2001] UKHL 29; [2002] 2 A.C. 122. See also the Law Commission's Report on *Aggravated, Exemplary and Restitutionary Damages*, Law Com. no.247 (1997). The Commission (which preferred the adjective "punitive") proposed that such damages should be available in any case of tort wherever the defendant in committing a wrong, or in conduct subsequent to a wrong, deliberately and outrageously disregarded the claimant's rights in such a way as to deserve punishment which could not be imposed by other remedies at the court's disposal (punishment for this purpose to include the deterrence of the defendant and others). However, such damages would never be awarded by a jury. The Government stated that it had deferred a decision on implementing the report: HC Debates, col.502 (November 9, 1999). Exemplary damages are, by statute, not now available for defamation in any Australian state but Mahoney A.C.J. in *Crampton v Nugawela* (1997) 41 N.S.W.L.R. 176 NSWCA, said that "defamation is a tort different in kind from the general run of tortious wrongs. There are aspects of the harm caused by defamation which cannot be effectively dealt with except by punitive damages." Callinan J. in *Gray v Motor Accident Commission* (1998) 158 A.L.R. 455 HCA at 519, said that exemplary damages were "perhaps indispensable" in defamation cases.

[219] "The difference between compensatory and punitive damages is that in assessing the former the jury . . . must consider how much the plaintiff ought to receive, whereas in assessing the latter they must consider how much the defendant ought to pay": *Broome v Cassell* [1972] A.C. 1027 at 1089, per Lord Reid.

[220] [1964] A.C. 1129.

[221] The additional damages under s.97 of the Copyright, Designs and Patents Act 1988 are probably not exemplary. See *Redrow Homes v Betts* [1999] A.C. 197 HL at 209; *Nottinghamshire Healthcare NHS Trust v News Group Newspapers Ltd* [2002] EWHC 409 (Ch) at [51] per Pumfrey J.

[222] These words are to be read disjunctively so that exemplary damages may be awarded, e.g. for acts which are unconstitutional but not oppressive: *Holden v Chief Constable of Lancs* [1987] Q.B. 380 CA. However, this seems inconsistent with the view that the underlying rationale is "outrageousness": *A v Bottrill* [2002] UKPC 44; [2003] 1 A.C. 449.

[223] This expression is wider than servants of the Crown; e.g. it includes the police and local government officers: *Broome v Cassell & Co. Ltd* [1972] A.C. 1027 at 1077–1078, 1088, 1120, 1130, 1134. However to attract this category the defendant must be exercising something in the nature of a governmental function; it is concerned with abuse of power, not with commercial activities carried out by a "public body": *AB v South West Water Services Ltd* [1993] Q.B. 507 CA, overruled on other grounds in *Kuddus v Chief Constable of Leicestershire* [2001] UKHL 29; [2002] 2 A.C. 122. It was said in *Muuse v Secretary of State for the Home Department* [2010] EWCA Civ 453 that the requirement of oppressive, arbitrary or unconstitutional conduct does not need to be qualified by further looking for malice, fraud, insolence, cruelty or similar specific conduct.

official power,[224] as perhaps where a government official libelled a
person through official channels to bring pressure on him in a dispute
with his department.[225]

(3) Where the defendant's tortious act has been done "with guilty knowledge, for the motive that the chances of economic advantage outweigh
the chances of economic, or perhaps physical penalty".[226]

Other common law jurisdictions[227] have tended to reject these restrictions so
exemplary damages tend to be more readily available elsewhere.[228] The
House of Lords[229] and Privy Council[230] have stated that the underlying
rationale of exemplary damages lies in the sense of outrage which a defendant's conduct sometimes evokes, "a sense not always assuaged fully by a
compensatory award of damages, even when the damages are increased to

---

[224] *Shendish Manor Ltd v Coleman* [2001] EWCA Civ 913 at [61] (appeal against decision to
strike out claim for exemplary damages was dismissed); cf. *Riches v News Group Newspapers Ltd*
[1986] Q.B. 256 CA at 269, accepting the narrower formulation in Duncan and Neill, *Defamation*,
2nd edn (1983), para.18.27; *John v MGN Ltd* [1997] Q.B. 587 CA at 616. In *Lillie v Newcastle
CC* [2002] EWHC 1600 (QB), there was no claim for exemplary damages and Eady J. at [328]
said: "I assume that this decision was made because of the difficulty of establishing any financial
or similar motive for publication by these Defendants." There was a claim for exemplary
damages against the Newcastle Chronicle but it withdrew partway through the proceedings on
undisclosed terms.
[225] In *Shendish Manor*, a statement made by a councillor at a planning meeting did not satisfy
the requirements for exemplary damages:
  "What power was being exercised and abused here by the respondent when she allegedly made
  these remarks? I cannot see that she was exercising any power as such. She may have been
  seeking to influence the exercise of power by the council, but that is not the same thing. This
  case is too remote from the type of case which falls within Lord Devlin's first category"
(at [62]). See also *Monks v Warwick DC* [2009] EWHC 959 (QB) and *MOD v Fletcher* [2010]
I.R.L.R. 25 EAT (a discrimination case).
[226] Per Lord Hailsham of Marylebone L.C. in *Broome v Cassell* [1972] A.C. 1027 at 1079,
explaining Lord Devlin's formulation in *Rookes v Barnard* [1964] A.C. 1129 at 1227 ("Where a
defendant with a cynical disregard for a plaintiff's rights has calculated that the money to be made
out of his wrong doing will probably exceed the damages at risk") as being not exhaustive but
merely illustrative of the principle that a wrongdoer should be taught that tort does not pay.
[227] Exemplary damages do not exist in Scots law, but aggravated damages do. Though neither
French nor German law recognise exemplary damages as such, the nature of the conduct of the
defendant may play a large role in the assessment of damages for "intangible" loss: see Law
Commission Consultation Paper no.132, *Aggravated, Exemplary and Restitutionary Damages*
(1993), paras 4.19–4.20.
[228] Canada: *Hill v Church of Scientology of Toronto* [1995] 2 S.C.R. 1130; *Barrick Gold Corp
v Lopehandia* (2004) 71 O.R. (3d) 416 Ont. CA. New Zealand: Defamation Act 1992, s.28, under
which the test is whether the defendant has behaved with "flagrant disregard" of the plaintiff's
rights: *Television New Zealand v Quinn* [1996] 3 N.Z.L.R. 24 NZCA (as to other torts, see *A v
Bottrill* [2002] UKPC 44; [2003] 1 A.C. 449). The Irish Defamation Act 2009, s.30 makes
punitive damages available whenever the defendant: "(a) intended to publish the defamatory
statement concerned to a person other than the plaintiff, (b) knew that the defamatory statement
would be understood by the said person to refer to the plaintiff, and (c) knew that the statement
was untrue or in publishing it was reckless as to whether it was true or untrue".
[229] *Kuddus v Chief Constable of Leicestershire* [2001] UKHL 29; [2002] 2 A.C. 122 (misfeasance in a public office).
[230] *A v Bottrill* [2002] UKPC 44; [2003] 1 A.C. 449.

reflect emotional distress".[231] A majority of the Privy Council has gone so far as to accept that therefore, "considered as a matter of legal principle, the arguments against restricting the jurisdiction to cases of intentional or consciously reckless conduct are to be preferred".[232] However England is in this respect "still toiling in the chains of *Rookes v Barnard*".[233]

For some time the view was taken that at common law not only did the case have to fall within category (2) or (3)[234] above, but that there was a further requirement that the tort must be one for which such damages had been awarded[235] before the decision in *Rookes v Barnard* in 1964, i.e. the "cause of action" test.[236] This view has now been rejected by the House of Lords[237] and, provided the case can be brought into one of the categories, they should be available for malicious falsehood as well as defamation. So far they are not available for misuse of private information.[238] Historically, that is an "equitable wrong" growing from breach of confidence rather than a tort, but it has now been extended to provide de facto protection for privacy in the form of misuse of private information[239] and it is questionable whether remedies should turn on history rather than on the nature of the interest to be protected[240]; on the other hand, the very equitable origin of the liability may make it easier to award an account of the defendant's profits.[241] However, exemplary damages may not be awarded in proceedings under the Human Rights

---

[231] *Kuddus* at [65].

[232] *A v Bottrill*, above, at [40].

[233] Ibid. at [41]. Cf. *Stallwood v Smith*, July 1, 2003, (QB).

[234] It is assumed that category (1) is of no practical importance: see above.

[235] Defamation cases clearly fell within (3), indeed they were the exemplar of it. Do *Kuddus* and *A v Bottrill* mean that there is now a further requirement of outrageousness? That seems to have been the view of Lindsay J. in *Douglas v Hello! Ltd (No.3)* [2003] EWHC 786 Ch D; [2003] 3 All E.R. 996. However, on the other side of the coin, the present state of the authorities does not support the view that the categories are redundant and the only issue is whether there has been outrageous conduct: *Mosley v News Group Newspapers Ltd* [2008] EWHC 1777 (QB) at [180].

[236] *AB v South West Water Services Ltd* [1993] Q.B. 507 CA. A somewhat paradoxical rule in view of the fact that it is a major premise of *Rookes v Barnard* that the distinction between exemplary and aggravated damages had not been clearly made before that case.

[237] *Kuddus*, above.

[238] *Mosley v News Group Newspapers Ltd* [2008] EWHC 1777 (QB); [2008] E.M.L.R. 20. Where a misuse of private information claim is brought against a "relevant publisher" (para.9.23), the Crime and Courts Act 2013 will, when it comes into force, exceptionally permit claims for exemplary damages (see paras 9.32–9.33, below).

[239] See para.22.2, below.

[240] Cf. in another context, Lord Walker in *Watkins v Secretary of State for the Home Department* [2006] UKHL 17; [2006] 2 A.C. 395 at [74]. The Law Commission recommended that exemplary damages should be available for equitable wrongs: Law Com. no.247, *Aggravated, Exemplary and Restitutionary Damages* (1997), para.5.55. They are available in Canada for breach of fiduciary duties (*Norberg v Wynrib* (1992) 92 D.L.R. (4th) 440 SCC) and in New Zealand for breach of confidence (*Aquaculture Corp v NZ Green Mussel Co. Ltd* [1990] 3 N.Z.L.R. 299 NZCA). See the strongly contrary view of the majority of the NSWCA in *Harris v Digital Pulse Pty Ltd* [2003] NSWCA 10; 197 A.L.R. 626.

[241] As to which, see para.9.31, above.

Act 1998.[242] Nor may they be awarded for a tort which is not actionable per se if there is no proof of damage sufficient to support a claim.[243]

The defendant's state of mind in relation to the statement. The   9.26
defendant may of course know that he is committing the tort of defamation but this is not necessary. Recklessness will do[244] and recklessness here has a meaning analogous to that of the mental element of deceit,[245] that is to say, the statement must be made without belief in its truth. "The publisher must have suspected that the words were untrue and have deliberately refrained from taking obvious steps which, if taken, would have turned suspicion into certainty."[246] However mere negligence will not do[247] and therefore the formula that the defendant must have acted "not caring whether the publication be true or false", while technically accurate, should not be used to instruct the jury because there is a risk that they may confuse "not caring" with "carelessness".[248] Conduct which shows a high degree of negligence is, of course, capable of being evidence of recklessness.[249]

At the moment it is established that there is vicarious liability for exemplary damages,[250] though the House of Lords has indicated that the matter needs further consideration[251] and it has been said that "vicarious punishment, via an award of exemplary damages, is contrary to principle and should be rejected".[252] However, since the reach of vicarious *liability* in tort law is much wider than in the criminal law, it may be asked why this should not be carried through into damages. In most libel cases the defendant, or the principal defendant, will be a media corporation but the state of mind of the journalist

---

[242] Human Rights Act 1998, s.9(3). Nor are they awarded by the European Court of Human Rights: Law Com. no.266, *Damages Under the Human Rights Act 1998* (2001).

[243] *Watkins v Secretary of State for the Home Department* [2006] UKHL 17; [2006] 2 A.C. 395.

[244] *Broome v Cassell & Co. Ltd* [1972] A.C. 1027 at 1079, 1094, 1130, 1133.

[245] *Derry v Peek* (1889) 14 A.C. 337 at 374, per Lord Herschell.

[246] *John v MGN Ltd* [1997] Q.B. 586 CA at 618; *Manson v Associated Newspapers* [1965] 1 W.L.R. 1038 at 1041.

[247] A claim for exemplary damages which omits any allegation of intention or recklessness is therefore bad: *Maxwell v Pressdram Ltd* [1987] 1 W.L.R. 298 CA. Cf. *A v Bottrill*, above, a case of personal injury by negligence.

[248] *John v MGN Ltd* [1997] Q.B. 586 CA at 618. Lord Herschell's formula in *Derry v Peek*, "recklessly, careless whether it be true or false", while equally accurate, would appear to be even more risky.

[249] As it was in *John*, above. Under s.10 of the Contempt of Court Act 1981 a court is not to order a person to disclose his sources unless it is established that this is necessary in the interests of justice. For this in the context of the defendant's state of mind on exemplary damages, see *Maxwell v Pressdram Ltd* [1987] 1 W.L.R. 298 CA.

[250] *Thompson v Metropolitan Police Comr* [1998] Q.B. 498 CA. Vicarious liability cannot on the present state of the authorities be confined to Lord Devlin's category of oppressive behaviour by state servants: *Mosley v News Group Newspapers Ltd* [2008] EWHC 1777 (QB); [2008] E.M.L.R. 20 at [201].

[251] *Kuddus v Chief Constable of Leicestershire* [2001] UKHL 29, [2002] 2 A.C. 122.

[252] Ibid. at [137], per Lord Scott.

and a fortiori of any higher officer such as an editor[253] will, of course, be imputed to the corporation[254] and it is irrelevant that the intended gain will come to the corporation rather than to the individual.[255]

9.27 The defendant's purpose. To attract exemplary damages under the third category in *Rookes v Barnard* the publisher must have acted in the hope or expectation of material gain.[256] It is not enough that he is motivated by a desire to injure or ruin the claimant, though that is equally deserving of punishment.[257] The fact that the defendant is engaged in an activity aimed at profit (e.g. publishing a newspaper or a television show) does not of itself justify an award of exemplary damages: there must be something more specific than that; but it is not necessary that there should have been a *detailed* calculation.[258] There must be something in the nature of what is described in one direction approved by the Court of Appeal:

> "Well, it will help the circulation of our newspaper. He may sue, he may not.[259] If he does not so much the better. If he does we will try to settle and get out as quickly

---

[253] In *John v MGN Ltd* [1997] Q.B. 586 CA, the person whose failure to check amounted to recklessness appears to have been a journalist, despite several references to "Mr. Scott and other executives".

[254] A policy of insurance covering *vicarious* liability for exemplary damages is enforceable: *Lancashire CC v Municipal Mutual Insurance Co* [1997] Q.B. 897 CA (a case of police misconduct). It will, of course, be a question of construction whether the policy covers exemplary damages.

[255] In practice it may be that only the corporation is sued. If the journalist or editor is sued, too, can exemplary damages be awarded against him? In *Daley v Ramdath, The Times*, January 21, 1993, CA it was held that in an eviction case exemplary damages could not be awarded against the agent of the landlord since the agent did not stand to profit from the tort. To similar effect is *Sampson v Wilson* [1996] Ch. 39 CA, where it was held that under s.27 of the Housing Act 1988 (damages for eviction to be measured by gain to landlord) while damages based on the statutory measure could be awarded against the landlord in respect of acts committed by the agent, they could not be awarded against the agent personally on the basis that the agent would not receive the gain. As to the means of the individual wrongdoer, see para.9.28, below.

[256] *John v MGN Ltd* [1997] Q.B. 586 CA at 618. This will usually be money but could be other property, e.g. where A libels B to destroy B's chance of bidding for land which A covets, or to obtain possession of land which B holds as tenant of A: compare *AB v South West Water Services Ltd* [1993] Q.B. 507 CA at 526 (example of harassment of tenant). Because New Zealand does not follow *Rookes v Barnard* a purpose to profit is not necessary there: *Television New Zealand v Quinn* [1996] 3 N.Z.L.R. 24 NZCA.

[257] Thus it would seem that exemplary damages could not be awarded on such facts as those of *Hill v Church of Scientology of Toronto* [1995] 2 S.C.R. 1130, where the SCC upheld an exemplary award of $800,000 (in addition to the same amount in general and aggravated damages). The English approach supports the view that a function of exemplary damages is to strip the defendant of the profits of his wrongdoing, but if that is right they only do so in a very rough and ready manner: see para.9.31, below.

[258] The claim for exemplary damages was withdrawn from the jury in *Kiam v MGN Ltd* [2002] EWCA Civ 43; [2003] Q.B. 281 on the basis that there was insufficient evidence of "calculation".

[259] In *Broome v Cassell & Co. Ltd* [1972] A.C. 1027 at 1079, Lord Hailsham L.C. said:
"It is not necessary that the defendant calculates that the plaintiff's damages if he sues to judgment will be smaller than the defendant's profit . . . The defendant may calculate that the plaintiff will not sue at all because he has not the money . . . or because he may be physically or otherwise intimidated."

as we can. If we cannot do that and it goes to court we still think that the total cost to us, adding everything, damages . . . and the legal costs, all the lot, will make it worth the gain for us to publish it. So we will go ahead."[260]

The prominence given to the story containing the libel is a feature which is relevant in determining whether there is evidence of such calculation,[261] as would be advertising of books or "trailers" of broadcasts.

Where the libel is published without the requisite mental element for exemplary damages, they may not be claimed on the basis of the defendant's subsequent conduct of the case (though aggravated damages may be[262]): the essence of this category of exemplary damages is that the tort is committed for the purpose of gaining pecuniary or other advantage, not that the defendant has attempted to cover up the fact that he has committed a tort[263] and the same reasoning would seem to apply to a case where, by the manner of his defence, he attempts to drive the claimant from the field.[264]

Means, etc. of the defendant. The means of the defendant, as in any other   **9.28**
tort case, are irrelevant in the assessment of compensatory damages[265] but they are relevant on exemplary damages. However, the practice is not to give evidence of the state of accounts of a newspaper but merely to put to the jury in a general way its size, circulation and apparent resources.[266] In a case of vicarious liability the relevant means are those of the employer-defendant, not the individual wrongdoer,[267] although the House of Lords has said that this may need to be further considered.[268]

Burden and standard of proof. The claimant bears the burden of proof   **9.29**
of the defendant's state of mind and purpose in publishing the defamatory material. This is on the civil standard of proof, but subject to the qualification

---

[260] The direction in *John v MGN Ltd* [1997] Q.B. 586 CA. See also *Maudling v Stott, The Times*, March 18, 1978.

[261] *John v MGN Ltd*, above; *Riches v News Group Newspapers Ltd* [1986] Q.B. 256 CA. Front page headlines sell newspapers.

[262] See para.9.19, above.

[263] *AB v South West Water Services Ltd* [1993] Q.B. 507 CA at 526 (overruled on other grounds, *Kuddus v Chief Constable of Leicestershire* [2001] UKHL 29; [2002] 2 A.C. 122).

[264] But cf. *Maxwell v Pressdram (No.2), The Times*, November 22, 1986, CA, and *Roberts v Bass* [2002] HCA 57; 212 C.L.R. 1 at [287].

[265] Though cf. the view of the ECtHR, para.9.6, above. Of course in practice, as damages are at large, justifiable within a large bracket and no reasons are given, a jury may well decide to award more against a media defendant than it would against a private individual.

[266] See the direction in *John v MGN Ltd* [1997] Q.B. 586 CA at 625, where it was widely believed that the newspaper may have been in financial difficulties following the death of Robert Maxwell, but there was no evidence of that. Carswell J. in *McCartney v Sunday Newspapers Ltd* [1988] N.I. 565 said that the court would not allow detailed evidence of a newspaper's financial position. Cf. *Singh v London Underground, The Independent*, April 25, 1990.

[267] *Thompson v Metropolitan Police Comr* [1998] Q.B. 498 CA.

[268] *Kuddus v Chief Constable of Leicestershire* [2001] UKHL 29; [2002] 2 A.C. 122.

that as the charge is grave so should the proof be clear,[269] and an inference of such reprehensible conduct should not be lightly drawn.[270]

9.30 Relationship with other damages.

"In a case in which exemplary damages are appropriate, a jury should be directed that if, but only if, the sum which they have in mind to award as compensation (which may, of course, be a sum aggravated by the way in which the defendant has behaved to the plaintiff) is inadequate to punish him for his outrageous conduct, to mark their disapproval of such conduct and to deter him from repeating it, then it can award some larger sum."[271]

There must be no double counting.

"The only practical way to proceed is first to look at the case from the point of view of compensating the plaintiff. He must not only be compensated for proved actual loss but also for any injury to his feelings and for having had to suffer insults, indignities and the like. And where the defendant has behaved outrageously very full compensation may be proper for that. So the tribunal will fix in their minds what sum would be proper as compensatory damages. Then if it has been determined that the case is a proper one for punitive damages the tribunal must turn its attention to the defendant[272] and ask itself whether the sum it has already fixed as compensatory damages is or is not adequate to serve the second purpose of punishment or deterrence. If they think that that sum is adequate for the second purpose as well as the first they must not add anything to it. It is sufficient both as compensatory and punitive damages. But if they think that sum is insufficient as a punishment[273] then they must add to it enough to bring it up to a sum sufficient as punishment. The one thing which they must not do is to fix sums as compensation and as punitive damages and add them together. They must realise that the compensatory damages are always part of the total punishment."[274]

---

[269] *John v MGN Ltd* [1997] Q.B. 586 CA at 619. This is the usual formula stemming from *Hornal v Neuberger Products* [1957] 1 Q.B. 247 CA.

[270] See the seemingly approving reference in *John* to the way in which Widgery J.'s direction in *Manson v Associated Newspapers* [1965] 1 W.L.R. 1038 at 1044 referred to "inescapable" inferences.

[271] Per Lord Devlin in *Rookes v Barnard* [1964] A.C. 1129 at 1228, quoted with approval by Lord Hailsham in *Broome v Cassell* [1972] A.C. 1027 at 1059–1060.

[272] For cases where there is more than one defendant, see para.9.36, below.

[273] As did the CA in *John v MGN Ltd* [1997] Q.B. 586.

[274] Per Lord Reid in *Broome v Cassell* [1972] A.C. 1027 at 1089; *John v MGN Ltd* [1997] Q.B. 586 CA at 619. The suggested guidance to juries in cases of malicious prosecution and false imprisonment in *Thompson v Metropolitan Police Comr* [1998] Q.B. 498 CA, seems very much in line with this. But cf. *Amalgamated Television Services Pty Ltd v Marsden (No.2)* [2003] NSWCA 186 at [18]:
"It can be said with some force that what is compensatory is not punitive, because the defendant is not punished by having to pay compensation properly due to the plaintiff. Put another way, to be punitive damages must be more than compensatory, so that it can be said that exemplary damages are necessarily over and above what has been assessed in compensatory damages. Particularly can that be said in the case of ordinary compensatory damages, and while aggravated compensatory damages have a punitive element that is because the solatium calls for infliction of some punishment on the defendant. Fulfilling the purpose of teaching the defendant that defamation does not pay, and of marking curial disapprobation of the defendant's conduct by punishment, is doing something other than compensate the plaintiff."

Although the incidence of costs upon an unsuccessful defendant may be regarded as having a serious punitive effect[275] this should not be taken into account in assessing exemplary damages.[276]

It has been said that compensatory and exemplary damages should not be awarded as separate sums,[277] but it is hard to see how proper control can be exercised by the Court of Appeal unless the award is itemised into these two categories and it is thought that the jury should always be asked whether they have made an exemplary award and, if so, what the damages would have been without the exemplary element.[278]

The quantum of exemplary damages: miscellaneous. The sum awarded by way of exemplary damages should be the minimum necessary to punish the defendant, to show that tort does not pay and to deter others.[279] While this is straightforward in the case of oppressive behaviour by servants of the state[280] there is a complication in the other category of case because at least an indirect purpose of an exemplary award (and certainly the effect of

9.31

---

[275] *Broome v Cassell* [1972] A.C. 1027 per Lord Wilberforce at 1114.

[276] *John v MGN Ltd* [1997] Q.B. 586 CA at 619.

[277] *Rookes v Barnard* [1964] A.C. 1129 at 1228; *Broome v Cassell* [1972] A.C. 1027 at 1072, 1082, 1094, 1099, 1126. The reason is said to be the risk of double counting.

[278] A course suggested in the case of co-claimants in *Riches v News Group Newspapers Ltd* [1986] Q.B. 256 CA at 268, (see para.9.37, below). In *John v MGN Ltd* [1997] Q.B. 586 CA, the award appears to have been itemised and was treated in the same way by the CA. Compare the remarks of Lord Cooke in *Television New Zealand v Quinn* [1996] 3 N.Z.L.R. 24 NZCA at 36. In *Thompson v Metropolitan Police Comr* [1998] Q.B. 498 CA, it is said that there should be a separate award of exemplary damages in actions for false imprisonment and malicious prosecution. As to aggravated damages in relation to this point, see para.9.21, above.

[279] *Rookes v Barnard* [1964] A.C. 1129 at 1228.
"Principle requires that an award of exemplary damages should never exceed the minimum sum necessary to meet the public purpose underlying such damages, that of punishing the defendant, showing that tort does not pay and deterring others . . . Freedom of speech should not be restricted by awards of exemplary damages save to the extent shown to be strictly necessary for the protection of reputations":
John v MGN Ltd [1997] Q.B. 586 CA at 619. While the NZCA has emphasised the importance of preventing extravagant awards of exemplary damages it has said that in the different conditions of New Zealand there is at present no call for giving more explicit directions: *Television New Zealand v Quinn* [1996] 3 N.Z.L.R. 24 NZCA at 36 (award of $400,000 upheld; award of $1,100,000 struck down).

[280] In actions for false arrest and malicious prosecution against the police the CA has said that £50,000 exemplary damages should be the "absolute maximum": *Thompson v Metropolitan Police Comr* [1998] Q.B. 498 CA. *John* would seem to indicate that libel may justify a higher award since the exemplary sum substituted by the CA was £50,000 and on its facts the case was plainly not at the top end of the scale. Of course in libel cases there is a profit motive and the public purse is not at stake. In *Thompson* it is said that in actions against the police an exemplary award is never likely to be *less* than £5,000. In *Thompson*, Lord Woolf M.R. said (at 517) that it should be explained to the jury that an award of exemplary damages is in effect a windfall for the claimant and that where the damages were payable out of public funds (as by the police), avoidance of providing the claimant a windfall at the public expense provided an even stronger reason for ensuring moderation of awards. That the damages are likely to be paid by insurers should not however be taken into account.

one) may be regarded as stripping the defendant of the gain he has made from his wrongful act.[281] The amount of the profit actually made by the defendant is a relevant consideration[282] but it is not determinative, for an award may be made even when no profit is attributable to the libel provided the defendant acted from mercenary motives. Although it will not necessarily be impossible in a case of libel to show what profit is attributable to the tort, it will in practice be a rare case where this can be done with anything approaching precision[283] and such issues would in any case be very unsuitable for trial by jury.[284]

An award of exemplary damages may properly exceed the award of compensatory damages by a large margin[285] but there should be some proportion between the two.[286] It would seem that just as the Court of Appeal is now more ready to interfere with excessive awards of general damages,[287] so too will it interfere with exemplary awards, though reference to other awards[288] would seem to present even greater difficulties than in the case of general

---

[281] Cf. the Proceeds of Crime Act 2002, under which the proceeds of crime may be confiscated from the defendant; and ss.27 and 28 of the Housing Act 1988, which measure a tenant's damages in case of unlawful eviction by reference not to his loss but to the difference between the value of the premises with and without vacant possession. The House of Lords has also considered the question of disgorgement of wrongfully acquired gains at common law in *Att-Gen v Blake* [2001] 1 A.C. 268. The issue in the case was on damages for breach of contract and it was held, Lord Hobhouse dissenting, that in limited circumstances, where the claimant had a legitimate interest in preventing the defendant profiting from his wrong, an account of profits was available in an action for breach of contract. The tort cases discussed by the court (those where "fair rental" or "wayleave" damages have been awarded or where the claimant has been allowed to waive the tort and sue for money had and received) are based on interference with property rights and have no relevance to defamation. In *Kuddus v Chief Constable of Leicestershire* [2001] UKHL 29; [2002] 2 A.C. 122 at [109], Lord Scott refers to "restitutionary damages" being available in "many" tort actions. However, many of the contract cases are best analysed as being based on damages for loss of the opportunity to bargain and the same is true of the wayleave cases. There is certainly no generally applicable rule in tort cases that the claimant may pursue a remedy based on the defendant's gains: see *Devenish Nutrition Ltd v Sanofi-Aventis SA* [2007] EWHC 2392 Ch; [2008] 2 W.L.R. 637. See now on appeal [2008] EWCA Civ 1086.

[282] *John v MGN Ltd* [1997] Q.B. 586 CA at 619.

[283] However, in *Att-Gen v Guardian Newspapers Ltd (No.2)* [1990] 1 A.C. 109, the HL ordered an account of profits in respect of publication in a newspaper of extracts from a book produced in breach of confidence. Cf. *Att-Gen v Blake* [2001] 1 A.C. 268, where the proceeds of the book itself were in issue.

[284] Cf. *Singh v London Underground, The Independent*, April 25, 1990, where investigation of the defendants' accounts on a claim for exemplary damages seems to have been regarded as militating aginst trial by jury.

[285] In *Broome v Cassell* [1972] A.C. 1027, a verdict for £15,000 general damages and £25,000 exemplary damages was upheld. In *John v MGN Ltd* [1997] Q.B. 586 CA, the jury had awarded £75,000 compensatory damages and £275,000 exemplary damages. The CA substituted £25,000 compensatory damages and £50,000 exemplary damages.

[286] *Riches v News Group Newspapers* [1985] Q.B. 256 CA.

[287] See para.9.4, above. Although the Supreme Court of Canada shows greater deference to the jury on compensatory damages it has said it has greater freedom to intervene on exemplary damages: *Hill v Church of Scientology of Toronto* [1995] 2 S.C.R. 1130.

[288] See para.9.7, above.

damages.[289] If there is to develop here something akin to the "principles of sentencing" in criminal cases it can only be at the most general level.

Exemplary damages and the Crime and Courts Act 2013. By s.34(1) and (2) of the Crime and Courts Act 2013,[290] where a relevant claim is made against a person who was, at the material time a "relevant publisher",[291] the claim is related to the publication of "news-related material"[292] and the defendant is found liable in respect of the claim, exemplary damages may not, subject to certain exceptions, be awarded against a defendant if it was a member of an "approved regulator"[293] at the material time. However, under s.34(3), this exemption from having to pay exemplary damages may be disregarded by a court if: **9.32**

> "(a) the approved regulator imposed a penalty on the defendant in respect of the defendant's conduct or decided not to do so, (b) the court considers, in light of the information available to the approved regulator when imposing the penalty or deciding not to impose one, that the regulator was manifestly irrational in imposing the penalty or deciding not to impose one, and (c) the court is satisfied that, but for subsection (2), it would have made an award of exemplary damages under this section against the defendant."

The bar imposed by s.34(3) for disregarding the exemption in subs.(2) is a high one and presumably requires the claimant to persuade a court that in imposing, or failing to impose, a penalty in respect of the relevant publisher's conduct, the approved regulator acted in a way that no reasonable approved regulator could possibly have acted in either imposing a penalty or not doing so. The court should also be satisfied that, but for the exemption contained in subs.(2) it would have made an award of exemplary damages under the section.

Conditions for the award of exemplary damages. If a court decides that the test in subs.(3) is met and that it should disregard the exemption from having to pay exemplary damages (subs.(2)), or that subs.(2) does not apply because the defendant was not, at the material time, a member of an approved regulator, a court may make an award of exemplary damages if it considers it appropriate to do so in all the circumstances of the case but may only do so   **9.33**

---

[289] If only because the means of the defendant is a relevant consideration on exemplary damages.

[290] See para.9.22, above.

[291] See para.9.22, above.

[292] For the definitions of "relevant claim", "material time", and "news-related material" see para.9.23, above.

[293] "Approved regulator" means a body recognised as a regulator of relevant publishers: s.42(2). By s.42(3) a body is "recognised" as a regulator of relevant publishers if it so recognised by any body established by Royal Charter with the purpose of carrying on activities relating to the recognition of independent regulators of relevant publishers.

under this section.[294] The effect of this is that where a defendant is a "relevant publisher" for the purposes of the Act, any award of exemplary damages must be considered under this Act and not under the common law, regardless of whether the relevant publisher is a member of an approved regulator. For publishers that are not "relevant publishers" the common law relating to exemplary damages will continue to apply.

Exemplary damages can only be awarded[295] under s.34 if they are claimed[296] and, by subs.(6), the court is satisfied that:

"(a) the defendant's conduct has shown a deliberate or reckless disregard of an outrageous nature for the claimant's rights, (b) the conduct is such that the court should punish the defendant for it, and (c) other remedies would not be adequate to punish that conduct."

These are high hurdles that are unlikely to be surmounted save in rare cases. The minimum threshold requires that the defendant's conduct be shown, at least, to have been subjectively reckless. The notion of outrage will inevitably introduce an element of judicial discretion but factors that no doubt will be considered relevant to this question will include whether the wrong was deliberately committed, the extent and type of the harm or potential harm to the claimant and the motive of the defendant.[297] Whether conduct subsequent to the wrong may be taken into account is not entirely clear. If for example the defendant was not aware of the falsity of a publication before publication, but later became so but continued to insist on the truth of what it had published, there seems no reason why, in principle, this might not be treated as a reckless or deliberate disregard of the claimant's art.8 rights. Proving that such disregard was outrageous is unlikely however to be easy.

In deciding whether the circumstances of the case make it an appropriate one in which to award exemplary damages, the court must have regard to the principle that exemplary damages must not usually be awarded if, at any time before the decision comes to be made, the defendant has been convicted of an offence involving the conduct complained of.[298] Further, where the "relevant publisher" was not a member of an approved regulator at the material time the court must, under s.35(3), take account of the reasons why the defendant was not a member and, so far as is relevant in the case of the conduct complained

---

[294] S.34(4) Crime and Courts Act 2013.

[295] The question whether exemplary damages are to be awarded and the amount of any such award is a matter for a judge and must not be left to a jury: s.34(8).

[296] S.34(5) Crime and Courts Act 2013.

[297] This test was that recommended by the Law Commission in its report *Aggravated, Exemplary and Restitutionary Damages* LC247 (1997), at para.5.44. The test of "outrageousness" is drawn from Commonwealth and US case law (see para.9.25, above for the Commonwealth authorities). However, the Law Commission recommended that the test should apply generally and not just to claims against "relevant publishers". A consequence of "singling out" relevant publishers may well be that any award of exemplary damages will be challenged as a violation of art.10.

[298] S.35(2) Crime and Courts Act 2013.

of, whether internal compliance procedures[299] of a satisfactory nature were in place and, if so, the extent to which they were adhered to. The court may, however, have regard to deterring the defendant and others from similar conduct as an object of punishment.[300]

In determining the amount of any exemplary damages to be awarded the court must take account of (a) the nature and extent of any loss or harm caused, or intended to be caused, by the defendant's conduct and (b) the nature and extent of any benefit the defendant derived or intended to derive from such conduct.[301] Any amount awarded must be no more than the minimum needed to punish the defendant for the conduct complained of and the amount awarded must be proportionate to the seriousness of the conduct.[302] The need to deter the defendant and others from similar conduct may however be taken into account in assessing damages.[303]

SECTION 4. MULTIPLE PARTIES

Co-defendants: general. In an action against two or more persons as **9.34** co-defendants in respect of a joint libel there must be one verdict and one judgment against all for the total damages awarded and the jury may not discriminate between them in finding separate damages against the different defendants.[304] Even though the defendants sever their defences, the jury have no power, jurisdiction or authority to apportion the damages, and if they do so, judgment cannot be entered against the several defendants for the amounts so apportioned.[305]

> "The unity of the verdict and of the judgment where the tort is joint is founded on and must stand with the legal theory of the liability of joint tortfeasors. It is the necessary and logical result of the legal principles applicable to this kind of action. What the plaintiff is entitled to receive is a sum representing the damage that he has suffered from a single wrong inflicted by all. The defendant has no right to say that his contribution to the injury was smaller than that of the others. Small though it may

---

[299] The reference to "internal compliance procedures" being in place is a reference to any procedures put in place by the defendant for the purpose of ensuring that—(a) material is not obtained by or on behalf of the defendant in an inappropriate way, and (b) material is not published by the defendant in inappropriate circumstances: s.35(4).

[300] S.35(5) Crime and Courts Act 2013.

[301] S.36(3) Crime and Courts Act 2013.

[302] S.36(2) Crime and Courts Act 2013.

[303] S.36(4) Crime and Courts Act 2013.

[304] *Heydon's Case* (1613) 11 Co.Rep. 56; *Onslow v Orchard* (1721) 1 Strange 422; *Dawson v McClelland* [1899] 2 Ir.R. 486; *O'Keefe v Walsh* [1903] 2 Ir.R. 681 at 684, 726; *Damiens v Modern Society* (1911) 27 T.L.R. 164; *Greenlands v Wilmshurst* [1913] 3 K.B. 507 CA; *Broome v Cassell* [1972] A.C. 1027 at 1089, 1105; *Johnson v Larkin* [1926] 2 Ir.R. 40; *Veliu v Mazrekaj* [2006] EWHC 1710 (QB); [2007] 1 W.L.R. 495.

[305] *Greenlands v Wilmshurst* [1913] 3 K.B. 507 CA. Because of the nature of the liability of joint tortfeasors, where judgment is given against some in default of defence, damages should be assessed at the ultimate trial of the action: *Vasta v Dynwest Pty Ltd* [1988] 1 Qd. R. 79.

have been, the wrong might not have been committed at all if he had not taken part in it."[306]

One tortfeasor may, of course, be able to recover a contribution or indemnity from another[307] but that does not affect the solidary liability of the defendants to the claimant. The position is different where the defendants commit separate libels even though they may be closely related and arise from the same factual background: even if the damage attributable to each libel cannot be separately identified the court must do its best to make a sensible apportionment of the overall damage suffered by the claimant.[308]

9.35 Co-claimants: general. Similarly, in an action brought by two or more persons as co-claimants in respect of a libel in which they are jointly defamed, e.g. as partners, there can be only one verdict and one judgment in their favour. However where two or more persons sue as co-claimants in respect of a libel in which they are separately defamed, "as their damages are several, their damages ought to be severally assessed".[309]

9.36 Co-defendants: exemplary and aggravated damages. An award of exemplary damages where a number of defendants is sued in respect of the same publication should reflect only the lowest figure for which any of them can be held liable.[310]

> "The jury . . . must consider each defendant separately. If any one of the defendants does not deserve punishment or if the compensatory damages are in themselves sufficient punishment for any one of the defendants, then they must not make any addition to the compensatory damages. If each of the defendants deserves more punishment than is involved in payment of the compensatory damages then they must determine which deserves the least punishment and only add to the compensatory damages such additional sum as that defendant ought to pay by way of punishment."[311]

It may therefore be important that the claimant does not cast the net of his claim too widely.[312]

---

[306] Per Hamilton L.J. in *Greenlands v Wilmshurst* at 531, citing Holmes L.J. in *Dawson v McClelland* [1899] 2 Ir.R. at 501.

[307] See para.27.44–45, below.

[308] *Culla Park Ltd v Richards* [2007] EWHC 1850 (QB).

[309] Per Bramwell L.J. in *Booth v Briscoe* (1877) 2 Q.B.D. 496 at 498. If, however, in such a case, the jury return a single verdict for one amount of damages in favour of all the plaintiffs, the Court of Appeal will not disturb their verdict: ibid.

[310] Per Lord Hailsham L.C. in *Broome v Cassell & Co. Ltd* [1972] A.C. 1027 at 1063.

[311] Per Lord Reid in *Broome v Cassell*, above, at 1090. This rule may lead to the result that the profit-stripping function of exemplary damages is wholly frustrated. In Ireland exemplary damages may be awarded against one of concurrent tortfeasors: Civil Liability Act 1961, s.14(4)(5). Likewise, damages may be mitigated in favour of one of them: ibid. s.14(6). The rule has also been rejected by judicial decision in Australia (*XL Petroleum v Caltex Oil* (1985) 57 A.L.R. 639, though exemplary damages are no longer available for libel there) and Canada (*Townsview Properties v Sun Construction and Equipment Co* (1974) 56 D.L.R. (3d) 330).

[312] "Plaintiffs who wish to differentiate between the defendants can do so in various ways, for example by electing to sue the more guilty only, by commencing separate proceedings against each and then consolidating, or in the case of a book or newspaper article, by suing

The position with regard to aggravated damages is not clear.[313] They are compensatory in their nature and look to the injury suffered by the claimant and therefore the "true criterion of damages is the whole injury that the plaintiff has sustained from [the] joint act".[314] On the other hand in the proper sense such damages are based upon the fact that the conduct of the defendants has increased that injury[315] and it has therefore been said that the same rule applies as in the case of exemplary damages.[316]

Co-claimants: exemplary and aggravated damages. Where exem-   **9.37**
plary damages are appropriate, it is clear that a defendant may deserve to be punished more severely for libelling several persons than for libelling one. However, it is wrong to fix a punishment figure and then multiply it for the number of claimants, for that is likely to lead to an excessive award. The proper direction to the jury is that they should proceed in the following steps. First, they should assess the compensatory (including aggravated) damages which each claimant should receive and then aggregate those sums. Secondly, assuming that the case is one suitable for an exemplary award, they should ask themselves whether the aggregate of compensatory damages is sufficient to punish the defendant. Thirdly, if they consider it is not enough, they should ask themselves what is the total sum which the defendant should pay in order

---

separately in the same proceedings for the publication of the manuscript to the publisher by the author. Defendants . . . have their ordinary contractual or statutory remedies for contribution or indemnity . . . But these may be inapplicable to exemplary damages":
per Lord Hailsham L.C. in *Broome v Cassell & Co. Ltd* [1972] A.C. 1027 at 1063–1064. However, it is plain that where an employer is sued as being responsible for the acts of his servant the relevant state of mind is that of the servant and exemplary damages may be awarded even if the employer is entirely innocent of wrongdoing: para.9.17, above. The rule must be the same as far as the employer is concerned where the employer and the servant are both sued.
   [313] *Berezovsky v Russian Television and Radio Broadcasting Co.* [2010] EWHC 476 (QB) at [174].
   [314] *Clarke v Newsam* (1847) 1 Exch. 131 at 140, per Alderson B.
   [315] See para.9.18, above.
   [316] *Broome v Cassell & Co. Ltd* [1972] A.C. 1027 at 1063; *Egger v Chelmsford* [1965] 1 Q.B. 248 CA at 263; *Jensen v Clark* [1982] 2 N.Z.L.R. 268; *Veliu v Mazrekaj* [2006] EWHC 1710 (QB); [2007] 1 W.L.R. 495 at [11] ("the general practice"). The passage in *Hayward v Thompson* [1982] 1 Q.B. 47 CA at 62, seems to take a contrary view, at least for "newspaper" cases. In *Woods v Chalfee* (or *Chaleff*-subsequent proceedings, May 28, 1999), May 14, 1999, the CA declined to strike out particulars of aggravated damages which were not of equal application to all defendants and held that it was arguable that, even in non-newspaper cases (see *Hayward v Thompson*), there was no rule that such damages must be assessed by reference to the conduct of the least blameworthy defendant. While Eady J. noted in *Berezovsky v Russian Television and Radio Broadcasting Co.* [2010] EWHC 476 that the law could not be definitively stated, he expressed (at [175]) the opinion that the lowest common denominator approach was "likely to be preferred by a modern appellate court—not least because it is more compatible with Article 10 of the European Convention on Human Rights. There would seem to be an inhibiting or 'chilling' effect on freedom of expression in so far as the law may render each individual contributor to an investigative story liable for the words or conduct of other people." This appears to be the position in Australia: *Konstantinidis v Foreign Media Pty Ltd* [2004] N.S.W.S.C. 835 (earlier proceedings [2003] N.S.W.S.C. 1135); see also *De Reus v Gray* [2003] VSCA 84; 9 V.R. 432 (not a defamation case). As to the position where one defendant has made an offer of amends see para.20.37, below.

to achieve the objective of punishment. Finally, they should divide among the claimants the difference between that total sum and the aggregate sum of compensatory damages.[317] Where the compensatory damages differ from one claimant to another, a case can be made for dividing the exemplary damages rateably rather than equally, but it has been said that that would unduly complicate the process.[318]

Since aggravated damages in the true sense depend upon the aggravating effect of the defendant's behaviour on the injury suffered by the claimant, it must follow that this element may vary from one co-claimant to another, since some people are more thick-skinned than others. In practice, however, it is likely to be a rare case in which this will be an issue.

9.38 Crime and Courts Act 2013 and multiple claimants. Where a "relevant publisher" is found liable to two or more persons, in deciding whether to award exemplary damages under s.34 or the amount of such damages to award, the court must take into account, if the defendant agrees,[319] any settlement or compromise by any persons of a claim in respect of the conduct complained of.[320] If the court does decide to award damages to two or more persons, the total amount awarded must be such that it does not punish the defendant excessively.

9.39 Crime and Courts Act 2013 and multiple defendants. In any claim brought against two or more defendants that includes exemplary damages, the liability of the defendants for exemplary damages awarded under s.34 of the Act is several only[321] and no contribution in respect of damages may be recovered by any of them under s.1 of the Civil Liability (Contribution) Act 1978.[322]

SECTION 5. INJUNCTIONS

9.40 General. The availability of an interim injunction to restrain the defendant from publication pending the trial of the action is more restricted in defamation than in the case of other torts and is dealt with elsewhere.[323] This section is concerned with final injunctions after trial.

9.41 Libel and slander actionable per se. At the trial of an action for libel, or slander actionable per se, after the jury have found the verdict for the

---

[317] *Riches v News Group Newspapers Ltd* [1986] Q.B. 256 CA at 268. As to "itemisation" see para.9.21, above.
[318] *Riches v News Group Newspapers Ltd*, above at 269, where the compensatory awards were all equal (and very much smaller in total than the exemplary damages).
[319] S.37(3) Crime and Courts Act 2013.
[320] S.37(2) Crime and Courts Act 2013.
[321] S.38(1) Crime and Courts Act 2013.
[322] S.38(3) Crime and Courts Act 2013.
[323] See Ch.25, below.

claimant,[324] or the judge has decided in his favour, the court has jurisdiction to grant an injunction restraining any further or future publication[325] of the words complained of or any similar[326] defamatory matter.[327] The jurisdiction is not confined to cases where the defamatory words affect the trade, business or property of the claimant.[328] The court will grant such an injunction if it is satisfied that the words are injurious to the claimant, and there is reason to apprehend further publication by the defendant[329]; and it may do so even though the claimant has not claimed such relief in his particulars of claim.[330] However, a failure on the part of the defendant to plead a justification does not necessarily amount to an admission that the words are false, so as to entitle the claimant to an injunction merely on the basis that the defendant intends to repeat them.[331]

In principle, the grant of a final injunction is subject to s.12 of the Human Rights Act 1998,[332] since it is relief which "affects the Convention right to freedom of expression". In practice, however, this provision is much more

---

[324] An undertaking to the court given as part of a settlement has the same effect as an injunction.

[325] Where publication has been made on a website and there is a significant risk that the defendant might transfer the website to a third party who operates overseas, an injunction may be granted to prevent such a transfer: *The Law Society of England and Wales v Kordowski* [2011] EWHC 3185 (QB): (the injunction in that case was granted on the basis that transfer would constitute unlawful data processing and harassment).

[326] See *Bentinck v Associated Newspapers Ltd* [1999] E.M.L.R. 556 (undertaking).

[327] Supreme Court Act 1981, s.37(1); *Saxby v Easterbrook* (1878) 3 C.P.D. 339; *Thomas v Williams* (1880) 14 Ch.D. 864; *Thorley's Co. v Massam* (1880) 14 Ch.D. 763; *Kerr v Gandy* (1886) 3 T.L.R. 75; *Hayward v Hayward* (1886) 34 Ch.D. 198; *Bonnard v Perryman* [1891] 2 Ch.D. 269 CA; *Dunlop v Dunlop* [1920] 1 Ir.R. 280. In the case of default judgments, a claimant must make an application for an injunction in accordance with Pt 23 (CPR r.12.4(2)).

[328] "[I]n all cases where the court thinks it just and convenient the remedy exists": per Lord Halsbury L.C. in *Monson v Tussauds* [1894] 1 Q.B. 671 at 690. See also, *The Law Society of England and Wales v Kordowski* [2011] EWHC 3185 (QB) at [138]. "There is no logical distinction between a case affecting trade or property and one affecting character only": *Dunlop v Dunlop* [1920] 1 Ir.R. 280 at 310.

[329] *Procter v Bayley* (1889) 42 Ch.D. 390 CA, "An injunction is granted for prevention, and where there is no ground for apprehending the repetition of a wrongful act there is no ground for an injunction": per Fry L.J. ibid. at 401; and see *Pryce Ltd v Pioneer Press Ltd* (1923) 42 T.L.R. 29, where an injunction was refused on this ground. However, a claim for an injunction is

"standard form in a defamation action; though whether there is any real risk that a defendant will repeat the libel so justifying the grant of an injunction will vary greatly according to the circumstances of the case":

Stuart-Smith L.J. in *Roache v News Group Newspapers Ltd* [1998] E.M.L.R. 161 CA at 173. In *Citation Plc v Ellis Whittam Ltd* [2013] EWCA Civ 155, the Court of Appeal affirmed the decision of the trial judge who had struck out an application for a permanent injunction by a company in relation to an alleged slander made by a competitor company, in the form of comments made by a member of its sales force to a prospective client, as there was no real risk of repetition following an instruction by the competitor to its entire sales force and therefore no utility to the proceedings.

[330] CPR r.16.2(5). Although a libel is a personal matter it has been held in Canada that the Attorney General may obtain an injunction against a libel that is part of a harassing campaign of nuisance: *Att-Gen v Dicleman* (1994) 117 D.L.R. (4th) 449.

[331] *Bryanston Finance v De Vries* [1975] Q.B. 703 CA at 725, 740–741, Lord Diplock dissenting on this point at 735–736.

[332] Except s.12(3).

important in relation to interim injunctions and, at least where the libel is a serious one and the injunction is expressed only in terms necessary to prevent repetition, the grant of one after trial will be legitimate and proportionate.[333]

Despite the absence of a specific power to order a retraction of a defamatory statement[334] it has been held in New Zealand that there is power to grant a mandatory injunction ordering publication of a correction of libellous statements and malicious falsehoods.[335] Defamation Act 2013, s.12, when it comes into force, will give courts power to order publication of a summary of any judgment.[336]

9.42 Slander not actionable per se. In cases of slander actionable only on proof of special damage, the claimant will not in general be entitled to an injunction unless he can prove that he has suffered some resulting special damage. The mere fact that the words are calculated or likely to cause special damage is not enough.[337]

> "To say that an injunction could be granted under circumstances where an action for damages would not lie . . . is a proposition with which I should not agree."[338]
> "The right to an injunction depends upon the legal right to sue, and if there is no legal right to sue there can be no right to an injunction."[339]

---

[333] See, e.g. *McVicar v UK* App. no.46311/99; ECHR 2002-III. In *ZAM v CFW* [2013] EWHC 662 (QB) Tugendhat J., in granting the claimant a final injunction (inter alia), said the following:
" . . . once a final judgment has been entered, whether after a trial, or summarily, a defendant's right to freedom of expression does not preclude the grant of an injunction. On the contrary, a claimant who succeeds in obtaining a final judgment is normally entitled to a permanent injunction to vindicate the right that he has proved that he has . . . Freedom of expression is valued, amongst other reasons, because it tends to lead to discovery of the truth: *R v Secretary of State for the Home Department ex parte Simms* [2000] A.C. 115, 126E-G. So where a defamatory allegation has been proved to be false (as has happened in the present case) there is no public interest in allowing it to be republished, and a strong public interest in preventing the public from being further misinformed. Final or permanent injunctions have been routinely granted after final judgments" (at [22]–[23]).

[334] See para.9.1, above.

[335] *TV 3 Network v Eveready New Zealand* [1993] 3 N.Z.L.R. 435 N.Z.CA. Gault J. referred to *Hermann Loog v Bean* (1884) 26 Ch.D. 306, though it is not clear whether in that case the mandatory injunction was directed at a cause of action in slander or malicious falsehood.

[336] See para.9.46, below.

[337] *White v Mellin* [1895] A.C. 154; *Royal Baking v Wright, Crossley* (1900) 18 R.P.C. 95; *Dunlop Tyre v Maison Talbot* (1904) 20 T.L.R. 579; *Lyne v Nichols* (1906) 23 T.L.R. 86; see also *Cundey v Lerwill* (1908) 99 L.T. at 275. In *Dunlop v Maison Talbot* (1903) 20 T.L.R. 88, an action for slander of title, Walton J. granted an injunction, although no actual damage had been sustained, on the ground that such damage "would be the natural result likely to follow, and so highly probable that it might be properly described as imminent". The decision was reversed by the Court of Appeal (1904) ibid. at 579, on the grounds (1) that there was no evidence of malice and (2) no evidence of actual damage. The cases on slander of title or of goods must now be read subject to the Defamation Act 1952, s.3.

[338] Kay J. in *Burnett v Tak* (1882) 45 L.T. 743 at 745. See also *Garden Cottage Foods v Milk Marketing Board* [1984] A.C. 130.

[339] Chitty J. in *De Francesco v Barnum* (1889) 43 Ch.D. 165 at 172.

In *White v Mellin*,[340] an action for slander of goods, the plaintiff did not prove
that he had suffered any special damage as the result of the words complained
of, but contended that the court should grant an injunction if there was a
reasonable probability of such damage accruing. It was held by the House of
Lords that, even if such probability of damage were proved, the plaintiff
would not be entitled to an injunction. In his judgment Lord Herschell
said[341]:

> "Obviously to call for the exercise of that power [i.e. to grant an injunction] it would
> be necessary to show that there was an actionable wrong well laid, and if the
> statement only showed part of that which was necessary to make up a cause of
> action—that is to say, if special damage was necessary to the maintenance of the
> action, and that special damage was not shown—a tort in the eye of the law would
> not be disclosed, the case would not be within those provisions,[342] and no injunction
> would be granted. I think, therefore, for these reasons that the plaintiff would not be
> entitled to an injunction, any more than he would be entitled to maintain an action
> unless he established all that was necessary to make out that a tort had been
> committed."

However, in cases of slander of title, slander of goods or other malicious
falsehood a claimant will now be entitled to an injunction without proof of
special damage if he can show (1) that the words upon which the action is
founded are calculated to cause him pecuniary damage and were published in
writing or other permanent form, or (2) that the words are calculated to cause
him pecuniary damage in respect of any office, profession, calling, trade or
business held or carried on by him at the time of the publication.[343]

Future damage. The above statements must, however, be read against the **9.43**
background that as a general principle there is an undoubted jurisdiction to
grant an injunction *quia timet* where there is a very high likelihood of damage.
In *White v Mellin* Lord Watson, while agreeing with the order of the court on
the ground that no attempt had been made to prove that the plaintiff had
suffered, or was likely to suffer in the future, any special damage as the result
of the words complained of, expressed the view (obiter) that a plaintiff would
be entitled to an injunction if he could "satisfy the court that damage would
necessarily be occasioned to him in the future".[344] In reference to this dictum
of Lord Watson, McCardie J.[345] made the observation (also obiter) that:

---

[340] [1895] A.C. 154.

[341] Ibid. at 163. See also per Lord Morris at 170: "It would certainly be a strange and novel
chapter in equity if a party could get a perpetual injunction to restrain an act which is not an illegal
act."

[342] I.e. ss.79 and 82 of the Common Law Procedure Act 1854, which conferred on the courts
of common law the power to grant injunctions in all actions of contract and tort.

[343] Defamation Act 1952, s.3; and see para.21.13, below. There must in addition be a real risk
of repetition: *Citation Plc v Ellis Whittam Ltd* [2013] EWCA Civ 155: (application for final
injunction for slander and malicious falsehood refused on the basis that there was not real risk of
repetition).

[344] [1895] A.C. 154 at 167

[345] In *British Railway Traffic v CRC* [1922] 2 K.B. 260 at 272–273.

"Apart from authority, I should have been prepared to hold that by virtue of section 25(8) of the Judicature Act 1873 an injunction might properly be granted in a case of threatened slander of title where damage would either necessarily or probably result. This, I think, is the just and common-sense view of the matter ... It would be strange to hold that no injunction can be granted where the plaintiff proves only that damage will necessarily or probably arise, and yet to grant an injunction where the plaintiff proves a small item of special damage and further claims an injunction to restrain future publications. Surely in such action the only reason for the grant of an injunction can be that damage will necessarily or probably arise from the further publications threatened by the defendant."

9.44 The summary procedure under the Defamation Act 1996. Where the court disposes of the claim in the claimant's favour by the summary procedure under the Defamation Act 1996,[346] it may make an order "restraining the defendant from publishing or further publishing the matter complained of",[347] that is to say, grant an injunction.

9.45 Position of third parties. If an injunction is granted after trial or an order made under the summary procedure restraining the defendant from further publication, it may be that the same defamatory statement is then published, or threatened to be published, by another person. Where A has obtained an injunction against B (whether interim or permanent) to restrain the commission of an unlawful act, then if C does the forbidden act on B's instructions C is in contempt (as is B). C may also be in contempt if, without instructions from B, he does the forbidden act with the purpose of frustrating the order of the court[348] or if the act may interfere with course of justice between A and B.[349] These principles are not easy to apply in the context of defamation.

---

[346] See para.30.20, below.

[347] S.9(1)(d).

[348] *Wellesley v Earl of Mornington* (1848) 11 Beav. 181, explained in *Att-Gen v Times Newspapers* [1992] 1 A.C. 191.

[349] *Att-Gen v News Group Newspapers* [1987] Q.B. 1 CA. Note however that Gray J. concluded (at [23]–[27]) in *Jockey Club v Buffham* [2003] QB 462—a case in which a third party sought an order that it was not bound by the terms of a consent order between the Jockey Club and a former employee restraining the employee from revealing confidential information—that the principle did not apply where a final injunction was granted. The judge held that while interim injunctions did bind third parties (the "Spycatcher principle"), if and when a final injunction was granted in favour of a claimant, any interim injunction was discharged and replaced by the final injunction, and a third party, even one who had notice of the final injunction (as in the instant case), was not at risk of being in contempt of court if he acted inconsistently with the injunction. However doubt was cast on Gray J.'s decision by the Court of Appeal in *Hutcheson v Popdog Ltd* [2011] EWCA Civ 1580; [2012] 1 W.L.R. 782 and in *Ambrosiadou v Coward* [2013] EWHC 58 (QB). Tugendhat J., in granting a final injunction to the claimant restraining her husband from disclosing or publishing certain private information, refused to include a penal notice addressed to third parties warning them that if they knew of and disobeyed the order they may be held in contempt of court. The judge held that there was no evidence of a threat from any third party to publish, nor of a real risk that any third party may publish, the private information. Further, having referred to *Hutcheson v Popdog Ltd*, the judge said: "if any third party might otherwise have been in doubt as to whether they could lawfully publish the information which the Claimant seeks to protect, they will now have to consider the contents of the judgment of the Court of Appeal (in *Hutcheson v Popdog Ltd*), and now of this judgment" (at [29]).

Ambrosiadou was a case where the parties had agreed to submit to a final injunction in settlement of the claim and the Court of Appeal had already determined (*Ambrosiadou v Coward*

Where A has a pending suit for libel against B and C publishes the same libel that may be a contempt by C, whether or not A has obtained an interim

---

[2011] EWCA Civ 409; [2011] E.M.L.R. 21) that the information in issue was private and confidential. Consequently it would have been highly unlikely for a third party to publish the material. What, however, of the situation where there has been no determination of whether the information was private and confidential yet the parties agree to a final injunction preventing future publication by the defendant? If *Jockey Club v Buffham* remains good law, then it would appear that a third party who acquired knowledge of the information and who had notice of the injunction could nevertheless publish it without risk of being in contempt of court. In the absence of a clear decision from the Court of Appeal that *Jockey Club v Buffham* was wrongly decided, a claimant is therefore likely, in such a situation, to want the additional protection of an order binding third parties and this is particularly the case where the private information is newsworthy.

An opportunity to reconsider the *Jockey Club* decision and, if necessary, the principles applicable to the issue of a final injunction binding third parties arose in *Hutcheson v Popdog Ltd* [2011] EWCA Civ 1580; [2012] 1 W.L.R. 782. The claimant had issued proceedings in anonymised form as *WER v REW* against Popdog Ltd seeking to restrain it from publishing or communicating certain information relating to his private life. Sir Charles Gray issued an interim injunction restraining Popdog Ltd from publishing the information ([2009] EWHC 1029 (QB); [2009] E.M.L.R. 17). Subsequently the claimant and Popdog Ltd reached a compromise whereby they agreed that the interim injunction would continue for the foreseeable future, and that Mr Hutcheson's claim against Popdog would not otherwise proceed. NGN then wished to publish the information and applied to the court to set aside the interim injunction. Eady J. held ([2010] EWHC 3156 (QB): the "first" decision) that the proceedings to set aside the injunction represented an "unnecessarily circuitous route" because the interim injunction had in practice ceased to be interim once the claimant and Popdog Ltd made their agreement and it had therefore ceased to bind third parties. The claimant therefore brought fresh proceedings against NGN and other newspapers seeking an order restraining them from publishing the information. This injunction was refused (*KGM v News Group Newspapers Ltd* [2010] EWHC 3145 (QB): The "second" decision) and an appeal dismissed (*Hutcheson v News Group Newspapers Ltd* [2011] EWCA Civ 808; [2012] E.M.L.R. 38). In *Hutcheson v Popdog Ltd* [2011] EWCA Civ 1580; [2012] 1 W.L.R. 782 the claimant sought permission to appeal against the "first" decision. The Court of Appeal refused permission on the ground that the outcome of the appeal was academic between the parties as even if the court were to conclude that Eady J. ought not to have concluded that NGN was free to publish the information, despite the existence of the interim injunction, NGN would still be free to publish information because of the "second" decision (now upheld by this court) that the art.10 (of the Convention for the Protection of Human Rights and Fundamental Freedoms) rights of NGN should prevail over the art.8 rights of the claimant. Consequently, it remains unclear, at least so far as proceedings in breach of confidence or misuse of private information are concerned, whether a person with knowledge of a final injunction preventing publication of information can do so without risk of being in contempt of court.

Even if the Court of Appeal were to conclude that the decision in *Jockey Club v Buffham* was wrong, and that a third party who published private information subject to a final injunction could be in contempt of court, it is suggested that the position with regard to libel should be different. While it is arguable that the publication by C of private information subject to a final injunction obtained in proceedings between A and B would have the effect of frustrating the order of the court the same cannot be said of a libel claim. The purpose of the order in the misuse of private information proceedings was to keep that information private and to protect the claimant's art.8 rights. Publication by whomsoever has the effect of frustrating that purpose and the order of the court. In a libel context republication by a third party of the libel complained of does not frustrate the order of the court or interfere with the course of justice between the claimant and defendant. The purpose of the grant of an injunction against repetition of libel is not to give the claimant a character permanently good against the whole world. The third party may have better evidence of the truth of the allegation than the defendant had and to say that because of the order made against the defendant all persons with knowledge of that order were forbidden to publish the allegation would be a serious restraint upon the freedom of speech.

injunction against B,[350] as tending to interfere with the course of justice between A and B.[351] C may therefore be restrained where such a publication is threatened because the law of contempt overrides the rule against prior restraint in libel proceedings.[352]

It is submitted, however, that the same rule should not apply in the case where C proposes to publish the libel after the termination of proceedings between A and B in which A has obtained a permanent injunction against B.[353] The basic rule, after all, is that an injunction does not bind a person who is not a party[354] and in so far as such a person may be affected by it the juridical basis lies in the law of contempt, the essence of which consists in the interference by the third party with the course of justice in the proceedings in which the order was made.[355] There is no longer any risk of interference with the course of justice between A and B and it must be doubtful if it could be said that C's act would frustrate the court's order: the purpose of the grant of an injunction against repetition of libel is not to give the claimant a character permanently good against the whole world. C may have better evidence of the truth of the allegation than B did (or may simply be more ready to fight) and to say that because of the order made against B all persons with knowledge of that order were forbidden to publish the allegation would be a serious restraint upon the freedom of the press. In such a case it is thought that the publication by C should be treated simply as an independent tort which C may seek to defend.[356] It is true that there is power to grant an injunction which has the effect of binding non-parties,[357] but these are exceptional and it is difficult to conceive how they could have any application to libel, where a further publication after a verdict in the claimant's favour would presumably, in the absence of proof of justification, lead to a large award of damages, including perhaps exemplary damages. Furthermore, it is submitted that the same approach should be taken in a case where an order has been made under the summary procedure, even though the court may also have made a declaration of falsity of the allegation made by B and now repeated by C.[358]

---

[350] Which is perhaps unlikely: para.25.2, below.

[351] *Att-Gen v News Group Newspapers* [1987] Q.B. 1 CA.

[352] Ibid.

[353] It is assumed that C is not acting to assist B to evade the order.

[354] *Att-Gen v Punch* [2001] EWCA Civ 403; [2001] Q.B. 1028 at [86].

[355] *Jockey Club v Buffham* [2002] EWHC 1866; [2003] Q.B. 462, holding that a third party is not bound by a final injunction even in a confidence case.

[356] See *Att-Gen v Newspaper Publishing* [1988] Ch. 333 CA at 371, per Donaldson M.R.

[357] See, e.g. *Venables v News Group Newspapers Ltd* [2001] Fam. 430; *Carr v News Group Newspapers Ltd* [2005] EWHC 971 (QB) (threats to personal safety by revelation of confidential information).

[358] Mainly because there may well have been only a limited investigation of the facts. It would seem odd that an order made in respect of what is, *ex hypothesi*, not a serious libel should have more effect than one made after a full trial of a more serious one. Of course the absence of a full investigation may be a reason for the exercise of caution in making declarations under the summary procedure. See Shillito (1997) 147 N.L.J. 24.

Section 6. Summary of Court's Judgment

Power of court to order a summary of its judgment to be pub-   9.46
lished. Defamation Act 2013, s.12(1) (when it comes into force) will give
the court a general power where judgment has been given for the claimant[359]
to order the defendant to publish a summary of the judgment. The wording of
any summary, and the time, manner, form and place of its publication are to
be for parties to agree (s.12(2)) but if they cannot agree on the wording, the
wording is to be settled by the court (s.12(3)) and if they cannot agree on the
time, manner, form and place of its publication, the court may give such
directions as to those matters as it considers reasonable and practicable in the
circumstances (s.12(4)). At common law, courts had no power to order the
defendant to publish a correction or apology, or to publicise any judgment.
Such a position was no doubt explained by an unwillingness on the part of
courts to tell the press what to publish and also the fact that a jury was not well
suited to give a narrative verdict. However, the power to direct the defendant
to make an order publishing, or causing to be published, a suitable correction
or apology was made available to the courts by the summary disposal provisions of ss.8 and 9 of the Defamation Act 1996. Under these provisions, where
the parties cannot agree on the content of the correction and apology, a court
is empowered to direct the defendant to publish a summary of its judgment,
the contents of which may be agreed by the parties or settled by the court in
accordance with rules of court. Failing agreement on the time, manner, form
or place of publication, the court may direct the defendant to take such
reasonable and practicable steps as the court considers appropriate. Section 12
of the 2013 Act builds on this jurisdiction and gives a court the general power
to grant an order that a summary of its judgment be published. Following the
reversal of the current presumption in favour of jury trials by s.11 of the 2013
Act, judge only trials will become the almost invariable position and consequently orders under s.12 may be expected to become standard where judgment is given in favour of the claimant. Where such relief is granted it will of
course go some way to vindicating the claimant's reputation and this may
have the effect that the vindication element of damages will be reduced,
leaving only damages for injury to reputation and feelings. It should be noted
however that currently the courts have treated the existence of a reasoned
judgment in the claimant's favour as a fairly marginal factor in assessing
damages,[360] and while s.12 offers considerable scope for wide publication of
the essence of the judgment, there is much in what Eady J. said in *Cruddas v*

---

[359] Whether the power is intended to be limited to the final judgment in the action, or whether
it includes interlocutory judgments, is unclear. Presumably the intention of the section is to
provide the court with a new tool for vindication of the claimant, which might be more effectively
provided by (say) summary judgment on justification than by a final judgment which rules on a
plea of Reynolds privilege.

[360] See further, para.9.2, above.

Adams[361]: "Any such observations [relating to the innocence of the claimant], contained in a judgment of the court, are unlikely to achieve very much in themselves. What most interested observers will want to know is, quite simply, 'how much did he get?'"

SECTION 7. ORDER TO REMOVE STATEMENT OR CEASE DISTRIBUTION

9.47 Order to remove statement or cease distribution. When it comes into force, s.13 of the Defamation Act 2013 will provide that where a court has given judgment for the claimant[362] in a defamation action, the court may order—(a) the operator of a website on which the defamatory statement is posted to remove the statement, or (b) any person who was not the author, editor or publisher[363] of the defamatory statement to stop distributing, selling, or exhibiting material containing the statement. The enactment of s.13 is arguably a necessary complement to ss.5 and 10 of the Act. Section 5 of the 2013 Act, when it comes into force, will grant wide immunity from suit to a website operator which publishes a defamatory statement posted by a third party.[364] Section 10[365] will provide that a court does not have jurisdiction to hear and determine an action for defamation "brought against a person who was not the author, editor or publisher of the statement complained of unless the court is satisfied that it is not reasonably practicable for an action to be brought against the author, editor or publisher."[366] A consequence to which both ss.5 and 10 would have given rise, in the absence of the power granted by s.13, is that even if the claimant successfully sued the person who posted the defamatory statement on the website operator's website or in the case of offline publications, the author, editor or publisher of the statement, he might still be unable to get the posting taken down by the website operator or prevent the further dissemination of the libel by a secondary publisher. Section 13 provides a mechanism by which this consequence can be avoided. The

---

[361] [2013] EWHC 145 (QB).

[362] As is the case with s.12 of the Act, it is unclear whether the power is intended to be limited to the final judgment in the action, or whether it includes interlocutory judgments. Might for example summary judgment for claimant on justification justify the court in ordering a secondary publisher to remove the statement even if a *Reynolds* defence remained? Though the issue is not without difficulty, it is suggested that no such order should be made until final judgment has been given. While requiring publication of a summary of an interim judgment on justification (under s.12) may be justified by the need to make clear that the truth of the allegation has not been proved (even if there may have been a public interest in publishing the article complained of), requiring a secondary publisher to remove the statement in the absence of final judgment risks serious interference with that publisher's art.10 rights. On balance therefore s.13 should be interpreted as applying to final judgments only.

[363] "Author", "editor" and "publisher" have the same meaning for the purposes of this provision as they do in Defamation Act 1996, s.1. See further, paras 6.32 and 6.33, above.

[364] See further, para.6.39ff, above.

[365] See further, para.6.45, above.

[366] By s.5(2), "author", "editor" and "publisher" have the same meaning as in s.1 of the Defamation Act 2013. See further, paras 6.32 and 6.33.

court need not of course exercise the power granted by s.13 and presumably will not do so where the non-party indicates that it wishes to raise a defence not raised by the defendant in the action in which the claimant has obtained judgment.

Part Two

DEFENCES

CHAPTER 10

DEFENCES: GENERAL

Defences. This part is concerned with defences in the proper sense, that is **10.1** to say, matters which justify or excuse conduct which is otherwise tortious and in respect of which the onus of pleading and proof lie upon the defendant.[1] It is not, therefore, concerned with matters such as a contention by the defendant that the words were never published[2] or are not capable of a defamatory meaning[3]: although a defendant may have to adduce evidence and argument to rebut a prima facie case on such issues and may therefore be said to have "defended" himself, he has in fact shown that the claimant's prima facie case is unfounded.[4] Nor does it deal with all matters which are defences in the true sense: for reasons of convenience the provisions of the Defamation Act 1996, the Defamation Act 2013 (in so far as it deals with the defences specifically available to subordinate publishers and website operators), and the common law before the Act on "innocent dissemination" have been considered in relation to publication.[5] However, a classification based upon matters which it is for the defendant to plead and prove breaks down because in the case of qualified privilege and fair comment a defendant who shows that his words were published on a privileged occasion or were capable of being comment on a matter of public interest may yet lose the case if the claimant can prove that they were published with "malice": the absence of malice is a condition of the defence but the onus of establishing its presence is upon the claimant.[6]

Defences covered. Subject to the above points, the defences dealt with in **10.2** this Part are:

　1. That the words were true in substance and in fact ("justification").

---

[1] The Irish Defamation Act 2009 comes close to being a code of defamation law. Sections 17 and 18 preserve defences of absolute and qualified privilege which existed before the passing of the Act (though they also contain detailed provisions on those matters). Otherwise, however, and subject to statute or European law, "any defence that, immediately before the commencement of [Part 3 of the Act], could have been pleaded as a defence in an action for libel or slander is abolished": s.15(1).

[2] See para.6.1, above.

[3] See para.3.13, above.

[4] Other matters which may be said to be defences in this loose sense include: that the words did not refer to the claimant (para.7.1, above) and that the words are not actionable without special damage and that has not been established (para.5.1, above).

[5] See paras 6.30–6.46, above.

[6] Contrast the position in US law where "actual malice" is required under the First Amendment to the Constitution in a claim by a public figure: para.15.31, below.

2. That the words were honest comment, without malice towards the claimant, on a matter of public interest.[7]
3. That the publication was absolutely privileged.
4. That the publication was made bona fide and without malice towards the claimant[8] on a privileged occasion.
5. That the publication was of matter which was the subject of legitimate public interest and the defendant complied with the standards of "responsible publication" (so-called *Reynolds* privilege).[9]
6. That the defendant did not know and had no reason to believe that the words referred to the claimant and were false and defamatory of him[10] and he has duly made an offer of amends for the purposes of s.2 of the Defamation Act 1996 which has not been accepted by the claimant.
7. Apology and payment into court under Lord Campbell's Acts 1843 and 1845 (libel in newspaper or periodical publication).

The above defences are unique to defamation proceedings.[11] The following are, or are related to, general tort defences.

(a) That the publication was authorised by the claimant or with his consent.
(b) Release or accord and satisfaction.
(c) Limitation.
(d) Previous action for the same words.

---

[7] The onus is upon the claimant to prove that the defendant was malicious.

[8] In the case of *Reynolds* privilege malice is of no practical significance: para.17.21, below. But malice is for the claimant to prove.

[9] In terms of the development of the law this is an outgrowth of qualified privilege but it differs so much from classical qualified privilege, which is essentially concerned with limited publications, that it requires separate treatment.

[10] It is for the claimant to prove that the defendant did know or have reason to believe the matters stated.

[11] Or virtually so. Words spoken in judicial proceedings or in Parliament would be incapable, because of art.9 of the Bill of Rights, of founding any other verbal tort, such as malicious falsehood. While no one would suggest that it is wholly beyond the powers of the courts to develop new defences to defamation (especially under the influence of art.10 of the European Convention on Human Rights) the defences are looked upon as a *numerus clausus*. In South Africa, by contrast, it has been said that:

"It is hardly necessary to add that the defences available to a defendant in a defamation action do not constitute a *numerus clausus*. In our law the lawfulness of a harmful act or omission is determined by the application of a general criterion of reasonableness based on considerations of fairness, morality, policy and the Court's perception of the legal convictions of the community. In accordance with this criterion . . . it is the task of the Court to determine in each case whether public and legal policy requires the particular publication to be regarded as lawful."

(Hefer J.A. in *National Media Ltd v Bogoshi*, 1998 (4) S.A. 1196 at 1204, approved in *Khumalo v Holomisa*, 2002 (8) B.C.L.R. 771 CC, but with the observation that the court's perception of the legal convictions of the community as a test for determining wrongfulness in delict might well have to be reconsidered in the context of the new constitutional order).

CHAPTER 11

TRUTH (JUSTIFICATION)

SECTION 1. INTRODUCTION

Terminology and policy. It is a defence for a defendant to establish that **11.1** the imputation in respect of which he or she is sued is substantially true. This defence is known as justification, but will be called truth when s.2 of the Defamation Act 2013 enters into force.[1] While its meaning may be clear to lawyers, the name "justification" may convey to lay people the idea that there must be some good reason for the publication, whereas in fact—with the exception of the special rule under the Rehabilitation of Offenders Act 1974—it is not actionable as defamation maliciously to publish the truth. Whether truth should be a defence in all circumstances has long been controversial.[2] Most recently, and speaking extra-judicially, Eady J. asked

---

[1] This change reflects long-standing criticism—e.g. Faulks Committee, Cmnd.5909 (1975), at [129]—and mirrors changes made previously in other jurisdictions: e.g. s.8(1) of the New Zealand Defamation Act 1992; s.16 of the Irish Defamation Act 2009. Compare the position under the claim for misuse of private information—see Ch.22, below. It was foreshadowed in the Defamation Bill introduced to the House of Lords by Lord Lester in 2010. In this text, "justification" will continue to be used to refer to the common law defence and pre-Act jurisprudence, and "truth" to refer to the statutory defence.

[2] The Select Committee of the House of Lords appointed in 1843 to consider the Law of Defamation and Libel expressed their opinion that the law was defective in permitting the truth of the imputation by itself to be an absolute bar to a civil action. They considered that there were many cases in which a wrong might be maliciously done to an individual by making public what might be true, as where the imputation referred to some personal defect or error of conduct long since atoned for and forgotten, and that a remedy should be given for such a wrong. They recommended (p.viii) that the truth of the imputation should not be an absolute defence to an action of libel or slander, unless it was proved that it was for the benefit of the community that the truth should be made known. This recommendation was not adopted, except in so far as criminal proceedings for libel are concerned; see Lord Campbell's Libel Act 1843, s.6. In this way, Sir Valentine Holmes QC said (*Journal of the Institute of Journalists*, November 1949), "an anomaly was perpetuated" for which the Porter Committee Cmd.7536 (1948) paras 74–78, pp.20–21 were unable to propose a remedy. The Faulks Committee also suggested no change on this point: Cmnd.5909 (1975), paras 137 et seq., 428 et seq.

Before the introduction of the uniform legislation, the law in a number of Australian states was that the defence was confined to cases where the publication was "for the public benefit"

whether the absolute nature of the defence could be sustained in light of the new art.8 jurisprudence that draws reputation with the ambit of the Convention right.[3] For the moment, however, the English law of defamation remains committed to the proposition that a claimant is not entitled to recover damages for injury to a reputation which he ought not to possess,[4] and for this purpose the reputation he ought to possess is determined as a matter of objective fact.

11.2 The Defamation Act 2013. S.2(1) of the Defamation Act 2013 provides that "it is a defence to an action for defamation for the defendant to show that the imputation conveyed by the statement complained of is substantially true". This is said in the Explanatory Notes to reflect the "current law as established in the case of *Chase v News Group Newspapers Ltd*,[5] where the Court of Appeal indicated that in order for the defence of justification to be available "the defendant does not have to prove that every word he or she published was true. He or she has to establish the "essential" or "substantial" truth of the sting of the libel".[6] Subss. (2) and (3) provide a new version of the rule applicable where an action for defamation relates to a statement that conveys two or more distinct imputations and the defendant proves the substantial truth of one or more but not all of them.[7] As with s.2(1), these provisions are intended to have the same effect as the existing law—here, that found in s.5 of the 1952 Act—but are expressed in more modern terminology.[8] The common law defence of justification is expressly abolished by s.2(4).

(Queensland, Tasmania and the Australian Capital Territory) or "in the public interest" (New South Wales). The equivalent position has been established in a number of American States. Such statutes may be unconstitutional, even in the case of private plaintiffs, if the matter is of public concern: *Shaari v Harvard Student Agencies*, 691 N.E.2d 925 (Mass., 1998).

[3] Speech delivered at City University, London, March 11, 2010 (*http://www.judiciary.gov.uk/Resources/JCO/Documents/Speeches/eady-j-city-university-10032010.pdf*). The judge suggested that "compared with the distress and embarrassment it would occasion, the prospective exercise of freedom of speech [in publishing some true but seriously embarrassing fact] would not be sufficiently valuable or important. We might find ourselves losing one of our reasonably clear black and white distinctions (that between truth and falsehood)." While it is clearly possible to construct an argument to this effect, and good reasons exist in some circumstances for allowing private and embarrassing information to be "forgotten", truth should remain a complete defence to a defamation claim. Where the matter published is private or personal information, a claim already exists for misuse of private information. Little is to be gained by allowing a claimant also to sue in defamation. The international obligations of the state do not need to be satisfied in every particular in each cause of action, just satisfied somehow. Defamation law need not be considered in isolation. Where information published is true and not private in nature, the public policy interest in always allowing publication is very strong. On reputation as part of the art.8 right, see para.1.14, above.

[4] *McPherson v Daniels* (1829) 10 B & C 263 at 272. *Chase v News Group Newspapers Ltd* [2002] EWCA Civ 1772; [2003] E.M.L.R. 218 at [33].

[5] [2002] EWCA Civ 1772; [2003] E.M.L.R. 218.

[6] Explanatory Notes, at para.14.

[7] The pre-existing rule is stated in s.5 of the Defamation Act 1952. It is repealed by s.2(4) of the Defamation Act 2013.

[8] Explanatory Notes, at para.17.

It appears that the intention of Parliament in s.2 was largely to clarify and "modernise" the existing law rather than effect significant change. Consequently, it seems likely that the new defence of truth will be interpreted largely to conform with existing jurisprudence. There are a number of aspects of the new provision, however, that differ at least in terms of form. This could herald a period of uncertainty in an area of law that has been in large part settled and uncontroversial (if still difficult).[9]

First, while s.2(1) reflects the requirement of substantial truth precisely, in adopting the word "imputation" the provision introduces terminology that English lawyers have not commonly used. The general usage in this context is to refer to the "words or statement complained of", and the term "meaning" is used rather than "imputation". "Imputation" is the terminology in use in Australia. It is arguably more apt than "meaning", as it encompasses not just natural and ordinary meanings but also meanings that can only be conveyed by inference. Extrinsic facts, whether or not they are generally known, may give rise to implications that go beyond the "meaning" of words in their ordinary sense.

Secondly, as stated above, subss.(2) and (3) of s.2 are intended to replace s.5 of the 1952 Act. The new provisions adopt more modern terminology, but are intended to have the same effect as the existing provisions. It should be noted, however, that s.5 of the 1952 Act provides that where an action is brought in respect of words containing two or more distinct charges against the claimant, a defence of justification shall not fail by reason only that the truth of every charge is not proved if the words not proved to be true do not *materially injure* the plaintiff's reputation having regard to the truth of the remaining charge. In contrast, s.2 provides that the defence shall not fail if the words not proved true do not *seriously harm* the defendant's reputation. This change in language was said to be necessary to ensure consistency with the test in s.1 of the Act which provides a higher threshold for liability in defamation.[10] The effect will be to make it easier for a defendant to prove truth in cases where he cannot prove the truth of all the allegations made.

Thirdly, the Explanatory Notes state that s.2(1), by focussing on the imputation conveyed by the statement, incorporates the long-standing common law rule that it is no defence to an action for defamation for the defendant to prove that he was only repeating what someone else had said (known as the "repetition rule").[11] Whether or not that is right, it draws attention to a point which may be important. The "repetition rule", under which a publication which conveys rumour, hearsay or allegation is treated in the same way as a direct allegation, is a rule about the meaning of words—"where it applies, [it] dictates the meaning to be given to the words".[12] It is the common law

---

[9] E.g. 546 HCDeb col 216, June 12, 2012 per David Lammy MP.
[10] Explanatory Notes, at para.17. See para.2.5, above.
[11] Explanatory Notes, at para.15.
[12] *Stern v Piper* [1997] Q.B. 123 at 138.

defence of justification specifically that is abolished by s.2(4), not related aspects of the common law such as those which govern the ascertainment of meaning, about which the Act says nothing explicit.

Fourthly, on a closely related point, given that s.2(4) abolishes the common law defence of justification and repeals s.5 of the 1952 Act, the provision presages a new start for the defence of truth. As the Explanatory Notes state: "This means that where a defendant wishes to rely on the new statutory defence the court would be required to apply the words used in the statute, not the current case law. In cases where uncertainty arises the current case law would constitute a helpful but not binding guide to interpreting how the new statutory defence should be applied".[13] Precisely what the impact of this will be is difficult to predict. It would seem likely that whenever a case involving a "rule" of law relevant to the defence of truth arises, the court will have to consider whether it has survived abolition. A rule will survive either because it was not in fact part of the "common law defence of justification", or because the court determines positively that it should continue to be followed. Some rules are clearly part of the common law of justification: for instance, the rule that the defendant need only prove the main charge or gist of the libel,[14] or the "conduct rule" relevant to *Chase* level 2 pleas of justification.[15] More difficulty may arise, however, with respect to *Chase* levels of meaning,[16] and the repetition rule.[17] Both are of very significant importance to the defence of justification, but each is really a rule about the meaning of words. Yet the Court of Appeal in *Shah v Standard Chartered Bank* described the repetition rule as a "rule of law which governs not only meaning, but also the pleading and proof of a defence of justification".[18] It seems likely that the consequence of abolition of the common law rule will be uncertainty while the courts decide whether a rule is properly classified as part of the common law of justification. If it is so classified, the question inevitably arises how the statute is to be interpreted. It might be expected that counsel will challenge the continuing utility of each rule that is thought disadvantageous to their client in the circumstances of individual cases. This promises a period of ad hoc reappraisal of the detail of the law, one in which conservatism may, but will not necessarily, hold sway. Uncertainty will remain until well-traversed issues are re-litigated.

11.3 Other torts. Defamation overlaps with other heads of tortious liability. A claimant cannot evade the rule that truth is a defence by suing for negligence,[19] and in malicious falsehood the burden of proof of falsity is squarely

---

[13] Explanatory Notes, at para.18.
[14] See para.11.7, below.
[15] See para.11.13, below.
[16] See para.11.13, below.
[17] See paras 11.18–11.19, below.
[18] [1999] Q.B. 241 at 263 CA.
[19] *Lawton v BOC Transhield Ltd* [1987] 2 All E.R. 608. See also, *Spring v Guardian Assurance Plc* [1995] 2 A.C. 296: para.23.3, below.

upon him.[20] Truth is not a defence to a claim for breach of confidence or misuse of private information. The publication of true information may, if it is repeated and so offensive and insulting as to be oppressive, amount to a course of conduct punishable criminally and actionable in private law under the Protection from Harassment Act 1997.[21] Furthermore, conduct by a public authority which infringes the right to respect for a person's private life may be actionable under the Human Rights Act 1998. If two defendants combine to reveal information about the claimant with the sole or predominant purpose of injuring the claimant, then truth as such is not a defence to conspiracy to injure.[22]

The burden of proof. In England and Wales and most other common law   **11.4**
jurisdictions,[23] a defamatory imputation is presumed to be false. Therefore, the burden is on the defendant to show that the imputation is substantially true.[24] It is a common critique of English defamation law that it is inappropriate for the falsity of an impugned statement to be presumed, and for the defendant to be required to justify the statement if he or she is to avoid liability.[25]

---

[20] See para.21.7, below.

[21] E.g. *Trimingham v Associated Newspapers Ltd* [2012] EWHC 1296 (QB) at [70] and [268] (although it was found that there was no harassment on the facts of that case). See para.23.13, below.

[22] *Gulf Oil (GB) Ltd v Page* [1987] Ch. 327 CA. This is offset by the fact that a claim for conspiracy requires proof of actual financial loss and cannot be founded on loss of reputation—see *Lonrho v Fayed (No.5)* [1993] 1 W.L.R. 1489 CA. The same is presumably true of misfeasance in a public office, which was called in aid in *Elliott v Chief Constable of Wiltshire, The Times*, December 5, 1996.

[23] In Canada it has been said that the onus of proof on the issue of falsity under the common law rule does not violate the Canadian Charter of Rights (*Pressler v Lethbridge* (1997) 153 D.L.R. (4th) 537), and is too well established to be changed except by the Supreme Court of Canada (*Bank of British Columbia v Canadian Broadcasting Corp* (1993) 108 D.L.R. (4th) 178). Given the Supreme Court's conservative approach to the Canadian Charter of Rights shown in *Hill v Church of Scientology of Toronto* [1995] 2 S.C.R. 1130, this seems unlikely to happen. The Constitution has not affected the onus on falsity in South Africa: *National Media Ltd v Bogoshi*, 1998 (4) S.A. 1196 Sup Ct App; *Khumalo v Holomisa*, 2002 (8) B.C.L.R. 771 Constitutional Ct. Irish law is the same as English law, and s.16 of the Defamation Act 2009 makes no change. The uniform Australian legislation enshrines the common law concept of justification, and it "should be inferred that the choice was made cognisant of the existence of the presumption [of falsity], and of the law as it had differently developed in non-common law jurisdictions"—*The Age Co. Ltd v Elliott* [2006] VSCA 168; 14 V.R. 375 at [22]. The clearest example of departure from the common law is the US, where a public figure plaintiff or any plaintiff in a case against the media arising from a statement about a matter of public concern must prove that the statement is substantially false: *Philadelphia Newspapers v Hepps*, 475 U.S. 767 (1986).

[24] *Belt v Lawes* (1882) 51 L.J.Q.B. 359 at 361. Where the imputation is one of criminal conduct, if the question whether the claimant did or did not commit a criminal offence is relevant to an issue arising in an action for libel or slander, then proof that at the time when that issue falls to be determined he stands convicted of that offence shall be conclusive evidence that he committed that offence—s.13 of the Civil Evidence Act 1968. A person stands convicted of an offence for this purpose even though there is an appeal pending against conviction: *Sarayiah v Suren* [2004] EWHC 1981 (QB). It seems unlikely, however, that a court would allow the claim to proceed to verdict if an appeal was pending.

[25] E.g. "A wretched law that threatens our free speech", *The Sunday Times*, December 20, 2009. It should be noted, however, that the practical benefit of the presumption of falsity to the

From a theoretical point of view there are arguments both ways.[26] However, the fact is that as a matter of law, the presumption of falsity is firmly entrenched. In *Jameel (Mohammed) v Wall Street Journal Europe SPRL (No.3)*, the Court of Appeal refused permission to argue the point.[27] The court observed that the suggestion to the contrary was a far-reaching submission which would require a major change in the law of defamation.[28] Change to the presumption of falsity was rejected by the Faulks Committee and the Neill Committee, and the Defamation Act 2013 makes no change in this respect. The European Court of Human Rights has also stated that "in principle it is not incompatible with art.10 to place on a respondent in defamation proceedings the onus of proving to a reasonable civil standard of proof (that is, on the balance of probabilities) that the defamatory statements were substantially true".[29]

11.5 Determination of meaning and the defence of truth. The defence of truth is closely associated with the determination of the meaning of publications.[30] Disputes about meaning are common in libel actions, and such disputes regularly play out in the context of attempts to deploy a defence of truth. The claimant will plead one or more meanings. In response, the defendant may suggest that the publication is true in a lesser or different meaning. Ultimately, the court has to decide what the reasonable reader would infer as the "single meaning" that the words complained of bear in their natural and ordinary sense. What that meaning actually is can remain opaque, as where a jury determines meaning the issue is obscured in the fog of jury deliberations with no reasons for the outcome subsequently being given. One potentially profound change that may flow from the Defamation Act 2013, is that judges acting alone will more frequently—perhaps almost invariably—determine the actual meaning at an early stage as a preliminary issue.[31] As this approach

---

claimant is less than might be supposed. As noted by Tugendhat J. in *Rothschild v Associated Newspapers Ltd* [2012] EWHC 177 (QB) at [18],

> "since 2000 the claimant has had to disclose, by a letter written under the Pre-Action Protocol, sufficient explanation to enable the defendant to appreciate why words are inaccurate or unsupportable. And in advance of a trial both parties have to disclose the statements of the witnesses on whose evidence they intend to rely. These reforms thus represent a very significant alteration in the effect of the presumption of falsity. In practice a claimant can rarely, if ever, expect to rely on that presumption to conceal the true position".

[26] For a full review see Milo, *Defamation and Freedom of Speech* (2008), Ch.V, in which reversal of the current rule for statements about public matters is favoured.

[27] [2005] EWCA Civ 74; [2005] Q.B. 904 at [57]. Moreover, it was far too late for the defendant to raise the point. The first instance hearing had been conducted on the premise that the presumption applied. (For the appeal to the HL on other issues, see [2006] UKHL 44; [2007] 1 A.C. 359).

[28] Ibid. at [55].

[29] *EuropaPress Holding DOO v Croatia* (2011) 53 EHRR 27 at [63]. See also *McVicar v UK* (2002) 35 EHRR 22; *Steel and Morris v UK* (2005) 41 EHRR 22 at [93].

[30] See e.g. paras 3.13ff and 3.28, above.

[31] In fact, even before the advent of the 2013 Act meaning has often been determined as a preliminary issue by judges sitting alone—see e.g. para.30.14, below. Further advantages of judge only cases is that they ensure that a reasoned decision on meaning is delivered by the court (e.g.

becomes commonplace it will have significant repercussions for pleading practices. It may see a proportion of cases resolved without further recourse to court. It will also focus attention on the "single meaning" rule and prompt the courts to address the issue of whether it is an appropriate device for the legal determination of public sphere disputes.[32]

At present, what is required of, or open to, a defendant in seeking to establish the truth can be slightly different depending on the type of imputations that a given publication is understood to have. A range of scenarios might arise. In the first, simple, and relatively unusual scenario, a given form of words may be susceptible to only one possible interpretation. A second scenario arises where a single publication includes a number of separate and distinct imputations. In principle, each such imputation is separately actionable.[33] In these first two scenarios, the defence of truth is straightforward in concept: each imputation is either substantially true or not and the dispute will be determined by reference to the evidence that each party adduces.

This seeming simplicity, however, may be complicated in a number of ways:

(1) A defendant may have made some more or less significant error of fact. In such a case, the extent of the error will determine whether the defence will be available. A minor inaccuracy may not preclude the defence.[34]

(2) With regard to an imputation that is general in nature and alleges a pattern of questionable behaviour, a question may arise as to how far proof of only one specific instance of misconduct can be sufficient to justify the more general allegation. This issue may arise because only

---

Rothschild v Associated Newspapers Ltd [2012] EWHC 177 (QB) at [29]–[31]; *Bento v Chief Constable of Bedfordshire* [2012] EWHC 1525 (QB) at [10]; *El Naschie v Macmillan Publishers Ltd (t/a Nature Publishing Group)* [2012] EWHC 1809 (QB) at [20]–[30]; *Mengi v Hermitage* [2012] EWHC 3445 (QB) at [49]–[50]), and provide an opportunity for negotiation between the parties as to the meaning of the imputation on which the case will proceed. In *Rothschild*, since the judge had given a reasoned ruling on meaning, the Court of Appeal was in a position to assess the correctness of the judge's determinations—see [2013] EWCA Civ 197; [2013] E.M.L.R. 18 at [9]–[11].

[32] See para.3.16, above.

[33] Where a number of distinct allegations are made, it is up to the claimant to decide in respect of which he or she will sue—see *Polly Peck (Holdings) Plc v Trelford* [1986] Q.B. 1000 CA at 1020; *Cruise v Express Newspapers Plc* [1999] Q.B. 931 CA at 948; *Carlton Communications Plc v News Group Newspapers Ltd* [2001] EWCA Civ 1644; [2002] E.M.L.R. 16. A claimant accused of being a thief and an adulterer, for instance, can choose to sue on the accusation of adultery only and the defendant cannot then seek to justify the charge of theft. It is no defence to a charge that "You called me A" to say, "Yes, but I also called you B on the same occasion and that was true"—see *Cruise*, at 954; *Warren v Random House Group Ltd* [2008] EWCA Civ 834; [2009] Q.B. 600. For this purpose, the claimant does not "complain" of the charge of theft merely because that charge is set out in his statement of case: severability is a question of substance, not of whether the charges are textually intermingled in the libel—see *United States Tobacco International Inc. v BBC* [1998] E.M.L.R. 816 CA at 825.

[34] See paras 11.8–11.9, below.

a general allegation has been made and the defendant can prove only one instance. It may also arise because a defendant's publication involved a series of separate allegations, but—finding that he or she is able to prove only some of these—the defendant wishes to contend that the apparently separate "stings" in fact comprise aspects of the same general, single imputation.[35]

(3) Conversely, the words complained of may allege an instance of specific misbehaviour, and the defence may seek to rely on general evidence of misconduct in proving the case.[36]

(4) In cases where more than one imputation is levelled, a defendant may be able to prove the truth of one allegation only. In some such cases, it may be possible for the defendant to contend that the provable imputation is relatively so important that the claim of libel lacks real substance.[37] Even if the defendant cannot go this far, it may be permissible for him to seek to justify only part of what he has alleged.[38]

In the remaining scenarios, the same words may be capable of more than one meaning. Where this is the case, the defendant will usually seek to persuade the court to select the least serious of the available meanings as the natural and ordinary meaning of the words that would be inferred by the reasonable reader.

(5) The words complained of may admit of both a literal meaning and an innuendo meaning that can be inferred from the words themselves. This is known as a 'false' innuendo. Whether the words in fact bear the additional meaning is treated as a straightforward question of interpretation.

(6) The same form of words might be understood as being semantically capable of bearing a number of slightly differing interpretations. That is, consideration of the same phrase may elicit a number of "shades of meaning".[39] Here, the defendant may plead and seek to prove a lesser meaning in the hope that the court selects that interpretation of the publication.

---

[35] This is the basis of the *Polly Peck* justification defence in which the defendant contends that supposedly separate imputations are no more than variants on a generalised theme—see paras 11.11–11.12, below.

[36] See para.11.11, below.

[37] This scenario is contemplated in s.2(2)–(3) of the Defamation Act 2013, and in s.5 of the Defamation Act 1952. There is no equivalent in English law to the Australian defence of contextual truth, however, and the statutory defence operates only where multiple imputations are complained of. See paras 11.16–11.17, below.

[38] See para.11.21, below.

[39] E.g. a statement that a man is "helping police with their inquiries into a murder" could be argued to mean that he murdered someone else, that he was complicit in the murder, that he knew about the murder, that the police believe that he might know something about the murder or about its surrounding circumstances, or that he was a forensic psychologist involved in suspect profiling.

(7) In a related scenario, an imputation may be read as importing a number of different strengths of allegation: the *Chase* levels of meaning.[40] These strengths of allegation are (i) that the claimant is guilty of X, (ii) that there are grounds to suspect that the claimant is guilty of X, and (iii) that there are grounds for investigating whether the claimant is guilty of X.

(8) A seemingly anodyne form of words may bear an innuendo meaning for a section of the wider audience whose members possess some special extraneous knowledge that informs only their interpretation of the phrase in question.[41] This is known as "true" or "legal" innuendo. It differs from false innuendo in that it requires the extraneous knowledge: the additional meaning cannot be deciphered from the words alone.

Case management considerations, as well as the substantive law and the meaning of words, are significant in determining what may legitimately be advanced under a defence of truth. Libel actions should not descend into uncontrolled and wide-ranging investigations akin to public inquiries, where that is not necessary to determine the real issues between the parties.[42] Nevertheless, a claimant brings an action to vindicate his reputation, and it is a poor form of vindication if it is only obtained by half muzzling the other side in what it may seek to prove true.[43]

---

[40] *Chase v News Group Newspapers* [2002] EWCA Civ 1722; [2003] E.M.L.R. 218. See further para.11.13, below.

[41] See para.3.21, above and para.11.15, below.

[42] *McPhilemy v Times Newspapers* [1999] 3 All E.R. 775 at 791. Thus had the defendants' proposed case been allowed in *Cruise v Express Newspapers Plc* [1999] Q.B. 931 CA, it would have required a wide-ranging investigation into Scientology, which would have gone far beyond the imputations about their private affairs of which the plaintiffs complained. Similarly, in *McKeith v News Group Newspapers Ltd* [2005] EWHC 1162 (QB); [2005] E.M.L.R. 32 at [21], the action was brought for an imputation that the claimant was a charlatan who had misrepresented her qualifications. In striking out a defendant's pleaded meaning that she made claims about nutrition which were not scientifically based, Eady J. said:

"the claimant is entitled to confine the dispute to whether she has made false claims about her qualifications. That is an important and serious charge. She should not be saddled with having also to enter into an expensive open-ended inquiry about the merits of various nutritional theories. I apprehend that if the defendant's allegations in the newspaper had been addressed solely to those the claimant would not be litigating on the subject. If such an inquiry were permitted, the wealthy defendant with all its resources will be placed in a position of unacceptable tactical and financial advantage over an individual litigant. In any event, these scientific issues may not all be capable of a definitive resolution through the judicial process".

However, there

"is a degree of circularity in looking to the real issue between the parties to determine whether a proposed meaning should be excluded because it is separate and distinct ... the real issue between the parties is whether the words complained of, read in their proper context, are capable of bearing the ... meaning contended for"

—see *Warren v Random House Group Ltd* [2008] EWCA Civ 834; [2009] Q.B. 600 at [112].

[43] *Basham v Gregory*, unreported, February 21, 1996, CA, *Turult v Times Newspapers Ltd*, unreported, December 7, 1999, CA.

Section 2. Basic Requirements of the Defence

11.6 Truth of particular imputation. It is the particular imputation that the words are decided to bear that must be proved substantially true. The defendant will not avoid liability by proving the truth of other facts that might be damaging to the claimant's reputation, but which were not presented or implied in the publication made (or which were not complained of).[44] This is the case even if the other facts relate to the same sector of the claimant's life, and are no less damaging to the claimant's reputation.

A defendant should plead justification only if he or she has reasonable evidence to support the defence or reasonable grounds for supposing that sufficient evidence will be available at trial:

> "If a defendant has no evidence at the time of pleading the defence, and there is no solid basis for assuming that evidence will emerge by way of disclosure of documents or the supply of further information pursuant to a request, the court should be astute to prevent a weak plea going forward and thus wasting everyone's time and money. There must be something going beyond bare Micawberism ... it is not a legitimate tactic to proceed to court on vague allegations of wrongdoing in the hope that cross-examination will elicit some bonus admission".[45]

In pleading the defence, the facts relied upon must be set out clearly and succinctly.[46]

11.7 Substantial truth of particular imputation. For the purposes of justification, only the "substantial" truth of the imputation must be proved.[47] The defendant can rely on the defence of justification if he proves that "the main charge, or gist, of the libel" is true.[48] This is an objective requirement: it is the facts as they were, not the facts as they appeared to be to the defendant or some other observer that must be proved.[49] If the gist of the libel can be proved, then there is no need also to prove peripheral facts that do not add to

---

[44] But as to mitigation of damages, see para.11.21, below.

[45] *Hunt v Times Newspapers Ltd* [2012] EWHC 110 (QB) at [28]–[29] per Eady J. See also, *McDonald's Corp v Steel* [1995] 3 All E.R. 615 at 621. An interesting issue arose in *Raab v Associated Newspapers Ltd* [2011] EWHC 3375 (QB), in which a defendant's access to evidence that might have enabled it to plead justification was precluded by a confidentiality clause in a settlement that the claimant had concluded with a former employee (whom it was alleged the claimant had bullied). It was held that the claimant's refusal to release the former employee from the confidentiality obligation did not prevent the entering of a justification plea nor interfere with the defendant's Convention rights.

[46] *Prince Radu of Hohenzollern v Houston* [2009] EWHC 398; *Ashcroft v Foley* [2012] EWCA Civ 423; [2012] E.M.L.R. 25, particularly at [49]–[59].

[47] This will remain the case under s.2(1) of the Defamation Act 2013.

[48] *Sutherland v Stopes* [1925] A.C. 47 HL. See also, *Chase v News Group Newspapers Ltd* [2002] EWCA Civ 1772; [2003] E.M.L.R. 218 at [34] ("the 'essential' or 'substantial' truth of the sting of the libel").

[49] E.g. *Cambridge v Makin* [2011] EWHC 12 (QB) at [45] (an appeal was dismissed: [2012] EWCA Civ 85; [2012] E.M.L.R. 19). See also, *National Assembly for Wales v Condron* [2006] EWCA Civ 1573 at [50].

the sting of the charge or introduce any matter that is separately actionable: "it is sufficient if the substance of the libellous statement be justified . . . as much must be justified as meets the sting of the charge, and if anything be contained in a charge which does not add to the sting of it, that need not be justified."[50] Hence, when considering substantial truth it is important to "isolate the essential core of the libel and not to be distracted by inaccuracies around the edge—however substantial".[51] In *Clarke v Taylor*, for example, the defendants charged the plaintiff with having been connected with a "grand swindling concern".[52] The whole of the alleged libel related to transactions said to have taken place at Manchester with the exception of the following passage:

> "As we have already stated, Clarke had been at Leeds for one or two days before his arrival in this town, and is supposed to have made considerable purchases there. It is hoped, however, that the detection of his plans in Manchester will be learnt in time to prevent any very serious losses from taking place."

The defendants in their plea justified the whole libel with the exception of this passage. The declaration contained no allegation that the defendants intended to impute to the plaintiff the commission of any fraud at Leeds. A jury having found for the defendants on the part of the libel which was justified the court refused to enter a verdict for the plaintiff on the passage not justified, adding that it was not libellous in itself. According to Vaughan J., the question was:

> "whether the libel is not substantially justified. All that part of it which directly imputes fraud to the plaintiff relates solely to what took place at Manchester, and that is covered by the justification. With respect to Leeds there is no averment or innuendo in the declaration to point the libel . . . I cannot discover in the alleged libel any distinct and clear substantive act of criminality charged, which the defendant's plea does not cover."[53]

Publishers can be permitted a degree of exaggeration even in the context of factual assertions, and—provided the sting of a libel has been established— "it is no part of the court's function to penalise a defendant for sloppy

---

[50] *Edwards v Bell* (1824) 1 Bing. 403 at 409 per Burrough J. See also *Clarke v Taylor* (1836) 3 Scott 95; *Morison v Harmer* (1837) 4 Scott 524; *Walker v Brogden* (1865) 19 C.B.(N.S.) 65 (second plea); *Rofe v Smith's Newspapers Ltd* (1924) 25 N.S.W.S.R. 4 at 23; *Sutherland v Stopes* [1925] A.C. 49; *Hoare v Jessop* [1965] E.A. at 227; *Aaron v Cheong Yip Seng* [1996] 1 S.L.R. 623 Sing. CA. In *Berezovsky v Forbes Inc. (No.2)* [2001] EWCA Civ 1251; [2001] E.M.L.R. 45 at [12], the Court of Appeal affirmed that the requirement to prove the sting of a libel was not a disproportionate restriction of the art.10 right to freedom of expression.

[51] *Turcu v News Group Newspapers Ltd* [2005] EWHC 799 (QB) at [105].

[52] (1836) 3 Scott 95.

[53] Ibid. at 109. See also *Edwards v Bell* (1824) 1 Bing. 403; *Morrison v Harmer* (1837) 3 Bing. N.C. 759. Contrast *O'Brien v Bryant* (1846) 16 M. & W. 168 (charge of bolting from neighbourhood not justified by proof of quitting the neighbourhood since the charge of fraudulent evasion of creditors was not made out); and *Baxter v CBC* (1980) 30 N.B.R. 2d 102 (political contributions not "kickbacks").

journalism, still less for tastelessness of style".[54] A charge of "organizing bands of hecklers to go about wrecking performances of modern, atonal music", however, was not justified by evidence of booing *after* one performance.[55]

The whole context of the imputation complained of is relevant to the determination of meaning and can provide the basis for the defence of truth. The nature of the sting of the libel can be shaped by the context of the publication as a whole. This can be particularly important, for example, should a claimant seek to sue on one allegation only when it might be argued that this comprised only part of a wider imputation. Words cannot be taken out of context. The claimant is not entitled to take a blue pencil to the article so as to change its meaning, and then prevent the defendant from seeking to prove the truth of the words in their unexpurgated form.[56] If the defendant were to write of the claimant, "he is a thief . . . he received fees from his business and failed to pay his workers", the claimant could not, by suing on the first part of the sentence alone, prevent the defendant contending that the words as a whole were true in substance (even though the offence of theft was not made out in the technical sense), and proving true the more general allegation as it was understood in light of the second sentence.[57] In their context, the meaning of the words as a whole is that the claimant behaved discreditably in taking the fees and not paying the workers.[58] It should be noted, however, that the reference to context is about qualifying or explaining the imputation conveyed, not introducing other matters from the same publication.[59]

11.8 Slight inaccuracy. The requirement that the defendant need prove only the substantial truth of what has been published entails that a defence of truth may succeed even though the publication was inaccurate in a number of respects. If the defendant can prove that the main charge or gist of the libel is true, a slight inaccuracy in one or more of its details will not prevent him from succeeding in a defence of truth. In *Alexander v N.E. Railway Co.*, for example, the defendants published a notice at their stations stating that the plaintiff had been convicted of riding in a train with no ticket and sentenced to a fine of £1 with the alternative of three weeks' imprisonment in default of payment. In their plea of justification, the defendants explained that the

---

[54] *Turcu v News Group Newspapers Ltd* [2005] EWHC 799 (QB) at [111].

[55] *Burstein v Times Newspapers Ltd* [2001] 1 W.L.R. 579 CA. In *Heytesbury Holdings Pty Ltd v City of Subiaco* (1998) 19 W.A.R. 440, there was an allegation that the plaintiff company had not paid its debts to the City. In fact it was a subsidiary company which was indebted and the plaintiff company was a guarantor which had not been called upon to pay. The fact that a parent company exercises control over its subsidiary does not of itself justify treating acts of the subsidiary as those of the parent and that precluded the defence of justification.

[56] *Polly Peck (Holdings) Plc v Trelford* [1986] Q.B. 1000 CA.

[57] The example is based on *Thompson v Bernard* (1807) 1 Camp. 48.

[58] *Polly Peck (Holdings) Plc v Trelford* [1986] Q.B. 1000 CA at 1023, per O'Connnor L.J.

[59] *Warren v Random House Group Ltd* [2008] EWCA Civ 834; [2009] Q.B. 600 at [111].

plaintiff had indeed been convicted and fined, but that the alternative was in fact 14 days' imprisonment. It was held that the inaccuracy as to the length of the alternative imprisonment did not necessarily make the notice libellous, and that it was a question for the jury whether the notice was substantially true notwithstanding the inaccuracy.[60]

Material inaccuracy. It follows from the above that, subject to s.5 of the   **11.9**
Defamation Act 1952,[61] any statement which alters the character of the main imputation or adds to its sting must be proved to be true. Otherwise, the defendant will fail in the plea of justification.[62] Thus, where a defendant had charged the plaintiff with various acts of cruelty to a horse, including knocking out its eye, proof that the charge was true in all particulars except that the injury to the eye had not occurred was held to be insufficient.[63] The court observed that:

> "Here, the statement that he knocked out the horse's eye imputed a much greater degree of cruelty than a charge of beating him on other parts of the body. If we were to hold this a sufficient justification, exaggerated accounts of any transaction might always be given with impunity."[64]

Where the sting of the words lies in the inferences which would ordinarily be drawn from them, to succeed in his justification the defendant will have to prove the truth of the facts which would be so inferred, not merely the literal truth of what is expressly stated, as the defamatory imputation extends to reasonable inferences.[65]

---

[60] (1865) 6 B. & S. 340. c.f. *Gwynn v S. E. Rly* (1868) 18 L.T. 738, a case on all fours on the facts, but in which the reference was to an alternative sanction of three-days' imprisonment with hard labour. In that case, the plaintiff recovered £250 damages on the basis—presumably—that the inaccurate words were not only untrue, but must, in the opinion of the jury, have produced a wholly false impression of the gravity of the offence committed. A similar, albeit hypothetical, illustration was given in *Sutherland v Stopes* [1925] A.C. 47 at 79. See also, *Patching v Howarth* [1930] 4 D.L.R. 489; *Modern Newspapers v Bill*, 1978 (4) S.A. 149; *Truth (NZ) Ltd v Avery* [1959] N.Z.L.R. 274 at 288; *Rothschild v Associated Newspapers Ltd* [2012] EWHC 177 (QB) (and on appeal at [2013] EWCA Civ 197; [2013] E.M.L.R. 18).

[61] See para.11.16, below.

[62] *Weaver v Lloyd* (1824) 2 B. & C. 678; *Cooper v Lawson* (1838) 1 A. & E. 746; *Helsham v Blackwood* (1851) 11 C.B. 111; *Walker v Brogden* (1865) 19 C.B.(N.S.) 65 (third plea).

[63] *Weaver v Lloyd* (1824) 2 B. & C. 678.

[64] (1824) 2 B. & C. 678 at 679, distinguishing *Edwards v Bell* (1824) 1 Bing. 403. *Helsham v Blackwood* (1851) 11 C.B. 111, rests upon the same principle though the facts of the case are hardly apt for modern conditions (plaintiff accused of practising all night for a duel): "[I]t certainly would create a very different impression upon the public mind, whether the duel was honestly conducted or not" (Jervis C.J. at 125);
"If the libel had imputed murder simpliciter it would have been enough to show in the plea that the plaintiff had committed murder. But, if the libel goes further, and states something besides which is injurious to the plaintiff's character, it is clear, upon every principle of the law of libel, that that must be justified as well as the rest, or the defence fails. Nobody can doubt that, if the plaintiff had been guilty of the atrocity which the libel imputes to him, every one would have thought the worse of him for it." (Maule J. at 129–130).

[65] *Gorton v ABC* (1973) 22 F.L.R. 181 at 193; *Lang v Australian Consolidated Press* [1970] 2 N.S.W.L.R. 408, especially at 414–415.

11.10 Evidence subsequent to publication. What evidence can be adduced
before the court is dependent on the nature of the imputation that has been
published? Most commonly, perhaps, a general charge against character may
be justified by subsequent events, so that "if a libel accuses a man of being a
'scoundrel', the particulars of justification can include facts which show him
to be a scoundrel, whether they occurred before or after the publication". But
even where the charge is specific, it is submitted that evidence of matters
arising after the date of publication may be admissible to justify it, as for
example evidence of similar facts.[66] In other circumstances, an imputation
may be proved only by reference to the facts as they were at the time when
it was published. Hence, if a *Chase* level 2 imputation was published to the
effect that there were, objectively speaking, reasonable grounds for suspecting
that the claimant performed certain actions, a defendant may not rely on
matters which occurred after the date of publication complained of in order to
support a defence of truth.[67] Conversely, the "viability of [such] a plea of
justification cannot . . . be weakened if subsequent events reveal that it is no
longer reasonable to hold that suspicion".[68]

SECTION 3. PARTICULAR CASES AND THE DEFENCE OF TRUTH

11.11 Specific and general meanings. A charge which upon its proper construction is one of general bad conduct cannot be justified by proof of a single
act or instance.[69] Thus, proof that one person had recovered damages for libel
against a newspaper was no justification of the statement that the proprietor
was a "libellous journalist".[70] As noted by Parke B., "the words 'libellous
journalist' do not mean that the plaintiff has been guilty, upon one occasion

---

[66] *Cohen v Daily Telegraph Ltd* [1968] 1 W.L.R. 916 CA at 919; *Maisel v Financial Times Ltd*
[1915] 3 K.B. 336 (events within a reasonable time after publication); *Bennett v News Group
Newspapers Ltd* [2002] E.M.L.R. 39 CA; *Chase v News Group Newspapers Ltd* [2002] EWCA
Civ 1772; [2003] E.M.L.R. 218; *Raul Amon International Pty Ltd v Telstra Corp Ltd* [1998] 4
V.R. 798 Vict. CA. In *State of New South Wales v Deren* [1999] NSWCA 22, Priestley J.A. in
accepting that the same considerations probably apply whether the facts occur before or after
publication said at [96] that the basis of the "reasonable time" requirement stated in *Maisel* was
that:
> "it is open to a judge to rule that evidence of an act or acts by a plaintiff could not rationally
> enable a conclusion of fact to be drawn and therefore should not as a matter of law be allowed
> to go before a jury considering that issue of fact when the time between the act or acts the
> defendant wished to rely on and the defamation was such that there was no relation between
> that act or acts and the imputation the defendant was seeking to justify."
See also, *Habib v Nationwide News Pty Ltd* [2010] NSWCA 34 at [313]–[335].
[67] *Chase v News Group Newspapers Ltd* [2002] EWCA Civ 1772; [2003] E.M.L.R. 11 at
[52].
[68] Ibid at [55].
[69] *Wakley v Cooke* (1849) 4 Exch. 511; *Bishop v Latimer* (1861) 4 L.T. (N.S.) 775; *Fitch v
Lemmon* (1868) 27 Up.Can.Q.B. 273; *Scott v Cudsell* (1884) 3 N.Z.L.R. 119; *Eastwood v Harper
Collins Publishers Ltd* [2002] NICA 46. See also *Milne v Walker* (1893) 21 R. 155; *Penton v
Calwell* (1945) 70 C.L.R. 219 at 240–241.
[70] *Wakley v Cooke* (1849) 4 Exch. 511.

only, of having merely published a libel, but that he has been guilty of gross misconduct as a journalist, by the habit of libelling others."[71] If a claimant frames his case on the basis of a general charge (for example, of dishonesty), however, "he can hardly be surprised if the defendant seeks to justify by reference to relevant aspects of his conduct irrespective of whether they find mention in the words complained of".[72]

The converse case is that where it is contended that a specific allegation carries a broader imputation of misconduct. In such cases, the general charge may be justified, and the action successfully defended, by reference to other examples of conduct that are shown to be true. These may be facts which are not even asserted in the publication.[73] It may be difficult to determine to what extent a specific charge of wrongdoing is capable of carrying a wider imputation. There was some tendency in older cases to treat defamatory words as if they were an indictment so that pleading and proof had to follow them more or less exactly.[74] Sensibly, this is no longer current practice, but specific allegations do not automatically attract a wider meaning.[75] In *Bookbinder v Tebbit*, the defendant alleged that the plaintiff had spent £50,000 on over-printing local authority stationery with the message "Support Nuclear Free Zones", but an attempt to plead as justification that the plaintiff had squandered public funds in a number of other, unrelated matters was struck out.[76] In contrast, in *Williams v Reason* an allegation that the plaintiff had broken the code of Rugby Union in writing a book for money was held reasonably capable of bearing the wider meaning of a charge of "shamateurism".[77]

---

[71] Ibid. at 516–517.

[72] *Warren v Random House Group Ltd* [2007] EWHC 3062 (QB) at [10] per Eady J.

[73] *Rothschild v Associated Newspapers Ltd* [2013] EWCA Civ 197; [2013] E.M.L.R. 18 at [22] per Laws L.J.

[74] An extreme example is the American case of *Downes v Hawley* (1873) 112 Mass. 237, where, on charging the plaintiff with sodomy with a mare, the defendant was not allowed to prove sexual connection with a cow. Perhaps still more absurd is *Swann v Rary*, 3 Blackf. 298 (Ind., 1833) where, in an action for a charge of "stealing hogs", the court sustained a demurrer to a plea of justification that the plaintiff had stolen one hog. Of course this is not to say that on a specific charge of dishonesty the defendant should be allowed to produce evidence of any dishonest act by the plaintiff at any time. If a libel charges a financier with fraudulently obtaining £1,000,000 the defendant should not be allowed to produce evidence that 20 years before he had falsified a mileage claim. A more difficult case is where the evidence shows that on the occasion in question he did obtain £1,000. Cf. *Plato Films v Speidel* [1961] A.C. 1090 at 1142–1143.

[75] Defendants have been known to contend for a wider (and even more serious) meaning on the basis that this would enable him or her to get in, even if the plea of justification fails, evidence which may go in mitigation of damages, notwithstanding the rule in *Scott v Sampson* (1882) 8 Q.B.D. 491: however, on that rule, see para.11.21, below.

[76] [1989] 1 W.L.R. 640 CA. See also, *Walker v Shehan*, unreported, July 20, 1995, CA (charge of exaggerating quality of yacht not capable of being regarded as general charge of dishonesty so as to allow in evidence of tax affairs in another country); *Eastwood v Harper Collins Publishers*, unreported, March 5, 2002, QB (charges levelled only in context of relationship between claimant and author of publication; accusation of having behaved shabbily on one occasion does not necessarily import a general charge of untrustworthiness).

[77] [1988] 1 W.L.R. 96 CA. See also *Maisel v Financial Times (No.1)* (1915) 84 L.J.K.B. 2145 HL, in which the plaintiff alleged that a charge of fraud meant that he was unfit to be the director of any company; *Loveless v Earl* [1999] E.M.L.R. 530 CA (parts of statement capable of being

Hence, evidence that the plaintiff had taken "boot money" could be adduced by way of justification.[78] Each case depends very much on its own facts,[79] and the question of whether a particular allegation of wrongdoing carries a general charge may depend on the context in which the words are used,[80] and the gravity of the misconduct imputed in the particular charge.[81] In any event, the defendant is entitled to insist that the jury see the whole publication to determine the context.[82] Notably, "if the sting of the example(s) prayed in aid to justify the general accusation is less sharp than that of the unproved specific charge, the justification plea will fail (though the proved examples may have effect to mitigate the damage)"; "the sting of the instance or instances which are proved must in essence be as sharp as the published, unproved libel: so that the claimant has no more reputation to lose by force only of the published, false accusation".[83]

---

read disjunctively). Cf. *Dering v Uris* [1964] 2 Q.B. 669, where the defence argued, apparently successfully, that a charge of operating without anaesthetics could be justified by evidence of operating callously in other respects.

[78] In *Williams v Reason* the statement of claim pleaded the meaning that the plaintiff was guilty of infringing his amateur status. In *Bookbinder v Tebbit* the original statement of claim pleaded a meaning of general wrongdoing but was amended. See also, *Rothschild v Associated Newspapers Ltd* [2012] EWHC 177 (QB)—affirmed on appeal, [2013] EWCA Civ 197; [2013] E.M.L.R. 18.

[79] *Loveless v Earl* [1999] E.M.L.R. 530 CA at 537.

[80] *State of New South Wales v Deren* [1999] NSWCA 22.

[81] "While a person can do a dishonest thing without being thought a dishonest person, some things are so dishonest that one can infer that only a dishonest person would do them. The activities attributed to the plaintiff in the article are so extensive, serious and risky that it is open to ordinary reasonable readers to infer that only a dishonest person would have done them":

Nationwide News Pty Ltd v Warton [2002] NSWCA 377, per Heydon J.A.

[82] *Polly Peck (Holdings) Plc v Trelford* [1986] Q.B. 1000 CA at 1020; *Bookbinder v Tebbit* [1989] 1 W.L.R. 640 CA at 647, per Ralph Gibson L.J. (the case involved words spoken at a political meeting. It was common ground that context was also relevant to spoken words but neither party had relied on context); *United States Tobacco International Inc. v BBC* [1998] E.M.L.R. 816 CA at 825; *Carlton Communications Plc v News Group Newspapers Ltd* [2001] EWCA Civ 1644; [2002] E.M.L.R. 16. However, it seems that the proposition that the jury are to see the whole publication, although described as "unchallenged" in *Polly Peck*, cannot, in view of the court's case management powers to control issues of relevance, any longer be taken literally where there is a large publication like a book: *Warren v Random House Group Ltd* [2008] EWCA Civ 834; [2009] Q.B. 600 at [103].

[83] *Rothschild v Associated Newspapers Ltd* [2013] EWCA Civ 197; [2013] E.M.L.R. 18 at [23]–[24] per Laws L.J. While McCombe L.J. leaned towards agreement with Laws L.J., he concluded that the point did not have to be decided. However, it was doubted by Eady J. In his view, "there could easily be a case . . . in which a defendant sought to prove a general defamatory charge by reference to a particular example of misconduct which . . . [was] notably less serious than the instance originally published". He was concerned that in such a case, the rule stipulated by Laws L.J. "would appear to entail that the defence of justification *in relation to the general charge* should fail for that reason". He considered that this should not necessarily be the case. This view appears to be premised on the notion that the general allegation of which the specific instance was an example and the specific allegation were separate and distinct imputations, such that they might in principle be covered by s.2(3) of the Defamation Act 2013 (at [57]). It is submitted that this is not the case, and that the approach of Laws L.J. is preferable. If the additional particular example(s) on which the defendant relies are not as serious as the false illustration given in the publication, then the separate particular instances should not be treated as

Common sting. A further, closely related scenario is that seen in the *Polly*   **11.12**
Peck variant of the defence in which the defendant contends that apparently
separate allegations in the publication are no more than variants on a generalised theme, and that the generalised allegation can be proved to be substantially true.[84] The seemingly separate allegations are said to possess a
"common sting". The rule is that the defendant is "entitled to justify a
common sting derived from parts of a publication, taken as a whole, of which
the claimant does not complain, in so far as they are relevant to the meaning
of the words complained of and to the sting of the alleged libel".[85] A useful
illustration is that where failure to prove one specific allegation of adultery on
which the claimant sued may be deemed not to defeat a defence of truth if a
number of separate instances of adultery that have been alleged can be proven
and the common sting of the allegations is read as one of adulterous promiscuity.[86] The question of whether the seemingly separate allegations are best
treated as severable and distinct,[87] or as possessing a common sting, is one of
fact and degree.[88] If there is a common sting in the allegations that may
prevent the claimant asserting that they are distinct.[89]

Defence of truth and levels of meaning. An allegation can be published   **11.13**
in such a way that it is made with varying degrees of certainty. This variation

---

being enough to prove a common, general allegation (or a common sting where the allegations
are published together).

[84] *Polly Peck v Trelford* [1986] QB 1000.

[85] *Warren v Random House Ltd* [2008] EWCA Civ 834; [2009] Q.B. 600 at [103] per Sir
Anthony Clarke M.R.

[86] *Khashoggi v IPC Magazines Ltd* [1986] 1 W.L.R. 1412. See also, *Carlton Communications
Plc v News Group Newspapers Ltd* [2001] EWCA Civ 1644; [2002] E.M.L.R.16 (allegations
capable of meaning that defendants had faked a whole series of programmes, not merely the one
in respect of which complaint was made); *Birchwood Homes Ltd v Robertson* [2003] EWHC 293
(QB) (allegations of aggressive methods and sharp practice both aspects of general charge of
"cowboy" methods); *Bennett v BBC* [2003] EWHC 553 (QB) (article a comprehensive critique
of claimant's project).

[87] E.g. *Warren v Random House Ltd* (above).

[88] *Polly Peck (Holdings) Plc v Trelford* [1986] Q.B. 1000 CA at 1032; *S & K Holdings Ltd v
Throgmorton Publications Ltd* [1972] 1 W.L.R. 1036 CA.

[89] In *Mosley v News Group Newspapers Ltd* [2008] EWHC 1777 (QB), the story was (a) that
C played dominant and submissive roles at sado-masochistic parties, and (b) that these had a
"Nazi" flavour. If D could prove (a) but not (b) it would be very difficult to argue that there was
a common sting, although the allegations are undoubtedly factually connected. No doubt most
claimants would blanch at the prospect of suing for libel in respect of (b) for the case could hardly
be run without exposing (a). However, the claimant did sue but for misuse of private information,
not libel. It has been said that it is not necessary for this purpose that the common sting should
involve an allegation of generalised wrongdoing: if the defendant accuses the claimant of three
murders, A, B and C and the claimant sues only in respect of C, the defendant may, on a plea of
justification, offer proof of guilt in cases A and B without showing that the defendant has accused
him of being a serial killer—see *Carlton Communications Plc v News Group Newspapers Ltd*
[2001] EWCA Civ 1644; [2002] E.M.L.R. 16 at [47] per Simon Brown L.J. No doubt that is true
in the sense that there need be no such express accusation, but it is submitted that being a "serial
killer" is a charge that the ordinary reader could find in the express allegation. While the
"common sting" principle is not an issue about the meaning of the words complained of (at [42]),
it does relate to the meaning of the publication as a whole.

was analysed in *Chase v News Group Newspapers*, in which the Court of Appeal offered three distinct levels: (i) that the claimant is guilty of some impugned behaviour; (ii) that there are grounds to suspect that the claimant is guilty of the impugned behaviour; and (iii) that there are grounds for investigating whether the claimant is guilty of the impugned behaviour.[90] The approach to the defence of truth in these respective scenarios is somewhat different. When an allegation is made with the highest degree of certitude, then the imputation of guilt must be defended.[91]

The approach to proof of the defence of truth in *Chase* level 2 "reasonable grounds to suspect" cases was summarised by Eady J. in a passage approved by the Court of Appeal in *Musa King v Telegraph Group Ltd*.[92] In such cases, it is necessary for the defendant to prove the primary facts and matters giving rise to reasonable grounds of suspicion objectively judged. It is impermissible to plead as a primary fact the proposition that some person or persons (e.g. law enforcement authorities) announced, suspected or believed the claimant to be guilty.[93] A defendant may adduce hearsay evidence to establish a primary fact, but this in no way undermines the rule that the statements or beliefs of any individual cannot themselves serve as primary facts.[94] Generally, it is necessary to plead allegations of fact tending to show that it was some conduct on the claimant's part that gave rise to the grounds of suspicion. This is the so-called "conduct rule". This rule is not absolute, however, such that—for example—"strong circumstantial evidence" can contribute to reasonable grounds for suspicion, albeit that such evidence must permit an inference to be

---

[90] [2002] EWCA Civ 1722.

[91] In *Hunt v Times Newspapers Ltd* [2012] EWHC 110 (QB), Eady J. described as "elementary" the proposition that "where a plea of justification asserts that the relevant claimant has committed a criminal offence, or offences, it is necessary to set out the nature of the facts relied upon "with the same precision as an indictment", citing *Hickinbotham v Leach* (1842) 10 M&W 361, 363. This suggestion was criticised by counsel, but the criticism was rejected with a full explanation by the Court of Appeal in *Ashcroft v Foley* [2012] EWCA Civ 423; [2012] E.M.L.R. 25 at [56]–[59]:

"[the phrasing] does no more than require a defendant to comply with the well-established principle that in pleading a defence of justification he must identify the acts which the claimant is said to have committed and which are relied on to justify whichever imputation they are directed to support".

[92] [2003] EWHC 1312 (QB) at [32] (on appeal at [2004] EWCA Civ 613; [2005] 1 W.L.R. 2282). This set of principles has become know as the "*Musa King* principles". Subject to one elaboration the Supreme Court of New Zealand adopted as New Zealand law the principles stated in *Musa King*—see *APN New Zealand Ltd v Simunovich Fisheries Ltd* [2009] NZSC 93; [2010] 1 N.Z.L.R. 315. The elaboration concerns the relevance of circumstantial evidence to the conduct rule (at [35]). The principles were also applied in *Greig v WIN Television NSW Pty Ltd* [2009] N.S.W.S.C. 632. See also, *Shah v Standard Chartered Bank* [1999] Q.B. 240 CA at 263 and *Chase v News Group Newspapers Ltd* [2002] EWCA Civ 1772; [2003] E.M.L.R. 218.

[93] This a fortiori is the case where the libel is a direct "level 1" charge of wrongdoing, and it does not assist to argue that such matters go to the "severity" of the allegation: *Sharma v Singh* [2007] EWHC 2988 (QB).

[94] E.g. *Chase v News Group Newspapers Ltd* [2002] EWCA Civ 1772; [2003] E.M.L.R. 218 at [39] et seq.

drawn regarding the conduct of the plaintiff and will not be sufficient by itself.[95] Importantly, a defendant cannot rely on post-publication events in order to establish the existence of reasonable grounds: the issue has to be judged as at the time of publication.[96] But the defendant may rely upon facts subsisting at the time of publication, even if he or she was unaware of them at that time. A defendant may not confine the issue of reasonable grounds to particular facts of his own choosing, since the issue has to be determined against the overall factual position as it stood at the material time (including any true explanation the claimant may have given for the apparently suspicious circumstances pleaded by the defendant). Finally, a defendant may not plead particulars in such a way as to have the effect of transferring the burden to the claimant of having to disprove them.[97]

The position where the defendant seeks to justify a *Chase* level 3 meaning—the lesser imputation that there are grounds for investigation of the claimant's conduct—is less clear. It would seem, however, that such grounds may exist independently of the conduct of the claimant. Indeed, they may be based on pure hearsay, as in the case of a complaint which a police officer investigates. Certainly, it has been suggested that the proposition that law enforcement authorities announced, suspected or believed the claimant to be

---

[95] In *Miller v Associated Newspapers Ltd* [2012] EWHC 3721 (QB) at [14]–[16], Sharp J. explained that

"it is an essential requisite of a defence of justification to [level 2] charge that it should focus on some conduct on the claimant's part giving rise to reasonable suspicion, albeit it may be necessary in a complicated case to portray some of the background and to set out the material which connects the main facts relied on. But the essential question remains whether the claimant has by his conduct brought suspicion upon himself. I respectfully agree therefore with what was said by the New Zealand Supreme Court in *APN & TVNZ v Simunovich Fisheries Ltd* [2009] NZSC 93 at [34]: "circumstantial evidence cannot contribute to reasonable grounds for suspicion unless it gives rise to an available inference concerning the conduct of the plaintiff. The circumstantial evidence suggestion was first made by Brooke L.J. himself in *Chase* (at [51]) where he said that a defendant could 'rely on strong circumstantial evidence implicating [the plaintiff]' as grounds for reasonable suspicion. The circumstantial evidence could hardly have any value unless it 'implicated' the plaintiff by means of an available inference as to the plaintiff's conduct . . . While strong circumstantial evidence may contribute to the reasonable grounds for suspicion, such evidence is merely an adjunct (rather than an alternative) to the conduct rule. It is also necessary . . . to prove the primary facts which are relied on to support such a defence: it is not sufficient . . . to prove reasonable grounds to suspect the existence of those primary facts".

With regard to the hearsay evidence in that case, Sharp J. also commented that

"selective snippets of hearsay from individuals who have not been called, particularly where it has been 'cherry picked' from material which casts it in a different light, provides an obviously unsatisfactory evidential basis upon which to invite a court to find facts and/or draw adverse inferences whether as to the conduct of those individuals or anyone else. In a sense, it is Hamlet without the Prince" (at [37]).

Much of the evidence related to other persons, such that the case against the claimant seemed "unconvincing and contrived" (at [40]).

[96] Note, however, *Sarayiah v Suren* [2004] EWHC 1981 (QB) at [45] (criminal conviction subsequent to publication; application of the Civil Evidence Act 1968, s.13).

[97] This was one of the general criticisms of the defence pleadings raised by the claimant in *Hunt v Times Newspapers Ltd* [2012] EWHC 110 (QB).

implicated may be enough on which to base a defence of reasonable suspicion.[98] In *Jameel v Times Newspapers Ltd*,[99] Gray J. held that in such a case the plea of justification need not be based upon conduct by the claimant unless the basis asserted for the need for investigation was such conduct.[100] If this is correct, then it would imply that the repetition rule does not apply to *Chase* level 3 imputations. Reflecting on this matter, Sedley L.J. explained:

> "If a level (iii) libel is to have any legal existence distinct from the first two levels, it has to be because it asserts something less than either guilt or conduct founding reasonable suspicion. If so, it ought to be possible in principle to justify it by pleading and proving no more than that a third party has alleged enough to warrant an investigation of the claimant's activities ... the consequences of so holding are disquieting. It means that, so long as a slur on an individual's reputation is cast in level (iii) terms, it can be justified by reliance on the bare fact of assertions made by others, without any need to make them good ... there [is] no prior reason why the repetition rule should apply to this third and novel class of libel ... [and] there [are] defensible theoretical reasons why it should not; but ... there [are] strong practical reasons why it should—among them that disapplying the rule will place a premium upon formulating slurs as level (iii) allegations and defending them unembarrassed by the otherwise general restraint on repeating the allegations of others."[101]

11.14 Defence of truth and shades of meaning. When pleading a defence of truth, the defendant is not obliged to specify what he or she considers the imputations conveyed to mean.[102] Where the defendant asserts that the words

---

[98] *Musa King v Telegraph Group Ltd* [2004] EWCA Civ 613; [2005] 1 W.L.R. 2282 at [22]–[23].

[99] [2003] EWHC 2609 (QB).

[100] The matter was not argued on appeal, where it was held that the words were also capable of meaning that there were reasonable grounds to suspect the claimant's guilt—see, [2004] EWCA Civ 983; [2004] E.M.L.R. 31.

[101] [2004] EWCA Civ 983; [2004] E.M.L.R. 31 at [29]–[30]. This disquiet was shared by Eady J. in *Armstrong v Times Newspapers Ltd* [2004] EWHC 2928 (QB) where the article referred to and summarised a book (written by another journalist on the same newspaper) raising "questions" about whether the claimant, a professional cyclist, had taken performance-enhancing drugs. The judge said (at [28]):

> "The scattering throughout the article of the 'questions' formula suggests that this may have been the very strategy anticipated by Sedley L.J. Be that as it may, whenever a defendant seeks to rely on 'neutral reportage', whether for purposes of setting up a case of *Reynolds* privilege or to justify by reference to a 'level (iii)' libel, it is important to determine whether the public policy considerations which have led to the need for reportage to be protected are truly engaged, or whether it is simply a situation where the journalist is seeking to by-pass the constraints of the repetition rule and the well-established principles in English defamation law relating to the burden of proof. These rules are equally defensible in terms of public policy considerations which should be given their proper weight."

In the event, it was held that, taken as a whole, the minimum the article could convey was the higher, level 2, meaning that there were reasonable grounds to suspect that the claimant had used drugs. The striking out of the plea of *Reynolds* privilege was reversed but not on this basis: [2005] EWCA Civ 1007.

[102] *Viscount de L'Isle v Times Newspapers* [1988] 1 W.L.R. 49 CA at 60, per Mustill L.J.; *Prager v Times Newspapers* [1988] 1 W.L.R. 77 CA at 86 per Purchas L.J and per Nicholls L.J. at 91. Nevertheless, in *Armstrong v Times Newspapers (No 3)* [2006] EWHC 1614 at [15], Gray J. suggested that it would be desirable if defendants did in fact indicate the meaning they contend that the words have in the same way that claimants are required to do.

have a meaning different from that contended for by the claimant, however, he or she must set out in the statement of case the defamatory meaning that is to be proved substantially true.[103] This is generally known as the pleading of *Lucas-Box* meanings.[104] The aim is to allow the claimant (and the court) to know what the defendant is seeking to justify: "It is axiomatic that the function of pleadings is to define the issues between the parties, so that both the plaintiff and the defendant know what is the other side's case and thus everyone, counsel, judge and jury, are able to focus upon the real nature of the dispute. Although to some it may seem a startling observation, we can see no reason why libel litigation should be immune from ordinary pleading rules".[105] If the pleading of a different meaning and the particulars on which it is based are not clear then the situation must be made unequivocal.[106] The defendant must give proper particulars of the facts on which he relies to justify that meaning.[107] This requirement was forcefully demonstrated in *Ashcroft v Foley.*[108]

---

[103] PD 53 para.2.5. See also, *Lucas-Box v News Group Newspapers Ltd* [1986] 1 W.L.R. 147 at 152; *Cruise v Express Newspapers plc* [1999] Q.B. 931; *Polly Peck v Trelford* [1986] Q.B. 1000.

[104] *Lucas-Box v News Group Newspapers Ltd* [1986] 1 W.L.R. 147.

[105] *Lucas-Box v News Group Ltd*, above, at 157 per Ackner L.J.

[106] Ibid., at 153; *Ashcroft v Foley* [2012] EWCA Civ 423; [2012] E.M.L.R. 25 at [49]: "The vice of a vague and general meaning is that it is liable to lead to a loose and ineffective pleading with excessive and irrelevant particulars, a state of affairs which is not permissible and which has been deprecated, particularly in libel actions, for many years".

[107] *McPhilemy v Times Newspapers Ltd* [1999] 3 All E.R. 775 at 788; *Raduv Houston* [2009] EWHC 398 (QB).

[108] [2011] EWHC 292 (QB) (upheld on appeal: [2012] EWCA Civ 423; [2102] E.M.L.R. 25). Having considered the pleaded *Lucas-Box* meanings and supporting particulars offered by the defendants, Eady J. observed that a number of the *Lucas-Box* meanings presented cited purported "associations" between the claimant and other entities, and commented that "the word 'associated' was notoriously vague and was often used in pleas of justification to gloss over exactly what was being said as to the claimant's involvement in disreputable conduct".

"In order to pass muster, a pleaded 'association' in particulars of justification must itself be 'guilty'. To put it another way, any association on the part of a claimant must itself be in some way reprehensible before it can play a legitimate part in a plea of justification . . . where it is intended . . . to allege that some particular association has been instrumental in obtaining or bestowing corrupt benefits, the impropriety should be spelt out" (at [29] and [49]).

He insisted that "facts need to be spelt out with the utmost clarity" (at [39]), and derided one *Lucas-Box* meaning as "as vague a defamatory meaning as one can imagine" (at [37]). Further, he noted that

"the sensitive, and potentially scandalous, nature of [some of] these allegations plainly demands that the claimant is entitled to be told exactly what is alleged against him . . . a case cannot be conducted, whether to be tried by jury or by judge alone, on the basis of 'nods and winks' " (at [52]).

The justification defence was struck out. On an application for reinstatement of the defence of justification with new pleaded meanings, Eady J. considered that one such meaning remained "a fudge" and that the defendants were "trying to make [the pleaded meaning] wide enough to embrace a whole range of possible scenarios but, in their concern to leave nothing out, have presented the claimant and his advisers with a moving and indistinct target"—[2011] EWHC 1710 (QB) at [22] and [38]. The Court of Appeal pronounced itself "surprised at the failure of the defendants to particularise their pleadings sufficiently", and suspected, "in the absence of a different explanation, that there were tactical reasons for keeping it as general as possible"; it chided,

11.15 Defence of truth and true innuendo. A "true" or "legal" innuendo arises where a particular form of words may bear a hidden meaning for a section of the wider audience whose members possess some special extraneous knowledge that informs only their interpretation of the phrase in question.[109] A "true" innuendo gives rise to a separate cause of action. The defendant may contend that there is no such innuendo, or may plead the defence of truth in respect of the natural and ordinary meaning of the words, the innuendo meaning, or both.[110]

11.16 Partial truth: section 5 of the Defamation Act 1952. S.5 of the Defamation Act 1952 applies where a defendant has made a number of separate and distinct imputations, but is unable to prove that all of them are true. It provides that:

> In an action for libel or slander in respect of words containing two or more distinct charges against the plaintiff, a defence of justification shall not fail by reason only that the truth of every charge is not proved if the words not proved to be true do not materially injure the plaintiff's reputation having regard to the truth of the remaining charges.

By way of illustration, if a newspaper article alleges that a person committed murder, committed adultery and on one occasion falsified his expenses, then if only the third imputation remains unproven the defendant will not be precluded by that from establishing a total defence of truth.[111] Should the

---

"repeated satellite litigation on pleadings for tactical reasons is not, in our view, the best use of court resources and we would expect that to be recognised in this as in other areas of the law. There must come a point at which repeated attempts at amendment, necessary because of the defendants' wish to keep the pleading as general as they can, become an abuse of the process of the court"
—see [2012] EWCA Civ 423; [2013] E.M.L.R 25 at [42]–[43]. Ultimately, the defence was able to proceed after further refinement—[2012] EWHC 2214 (QB); [2012] E.M.L.R. 32. See also, *Hunt v Evening Standard Ltd* [2011] EWHC 272 (QB); *Hunt v Times Newspapers Ltd* [2012] EWHC 110 (QB).
[109] True innuendo is to be distinguished from 'popular' or 'false' innuendo which relies upon a 'play on words' such that no knowledge of extrinsic facts is necessary for the reasonable reader to infer the innuendo meaning, and which is no more than the part of the natural and ordinary meaning of the words that can be inferred by the reasonable reader.
[110] See *Watkin v Hall* (1866) L.R. 3 Q.B. 396 at 402; *Maisel v Financial Times* (1915) 31 T.L.R. 192.
[111] In *Jackson v John Fairfax* [1981] 1 N.S.W.L.R. 36, under s.16 of the Defamation Act (N.S.W.) 1974 Hunt J. gave the following examples. If a publication describes the plaintiff (falsely) as having been charged with an offence and (truly) as being guilty of that offence, the truth of the latter imputation would lead to a verdict for the defendant notwithstanding the falsity of the first. However, if the publication describes him (falsely) as a blackmailer and (truly) as a person who has remained in the country on an expired visa, then the trial judge should take the defence away from the jury because there would be no rational basis upon which the jury could find in favour of the defendant. See also, *Cornelius v De Taranto* [2001] E.M.L.R. 12 (untrue allegation of dated criminal behaviour saved by proven imputation of recent deliberate duplicity and mental instability); *Henry v BBC* [2006] EWHC 386 (QB) (falsification of waiting list figures and complicity in waiting list fraud proved; allegation of bullying not proved); *Irving v Penguin Books Ltd*, unreported, April 11, 2000, (QB) (persistent and deliberate misrepresentation and manipulation of historical evidence, unwarrantedly favourable portrayal of Hitler in relation to his attitude towards and responsibility for the treatment of the Jews, active Holocaust denial; anti-

claimant sue only in respect of the third imputation, however, then the section has no application.

Evidently, s.5 postulates that there can be a standard or scale of values by which the relative worth of multiple defamatory charges may be weighed or measured. No guidance is given, however, on how this scale is to be calibrated. If D alleges that C is an adulterer and a thief, and proves only that he is a thief, it is not clear by what reasoned scheme a judge or jury is to determine whether the unproved charge of adultery does or does not materially injure C's reputation. The logic of the provision is that the harm to reputation caused by the allegation(s) found to be true, in respect of which no damages may be recovered, is such as to render any injury to reputation that notionally might have been caused by the unproven allegation nugatory to the point of irrelevance. It may be that s.5 will have greater utility the more that the imputations relate to one specific aspect of the claimant's conduct or character. If, for instance, the publication in question is concerned exclusively with imputations that the claimant has a tendency to commit fraud, alleging some serious but also other minor frauds, then, provided that the more serious allegations can be substantiated, the need to prove the less serious ones is likely to be excused by s.5.[112] In contrast, if the publication embraces one imputation relating to the claimant's marital fidelity and another to his or her business dealings, each imputation is liable to be treated as independently harmful, and s.5 less likely to be of assistance to the defendant.

Defamation Act 2013, section 2(3). S.2(3) of the Defamation Act 2013   **11.17**
provides a new version of this rule.[113] It will replace s.5 of the Defamation Act 1952, which is explicitly repealed by s.2(4) of the 2013 Act. The new rule provides that:

> "If one or more of the imputations is not shown to be substantially true, the defence under this section does not fail if, having regard to the imputations which are shown to be substantially true, the imputations which are not shown to be substantially true do not seriously harm the claimant's reputation".

The text of this provision—read together with s.2(2)—effectively emulates its predecessor except that while s.2(3) of the 2013 Act speaks of the unproven imputations not "seriously harming" the claimant, s.5 of the 1952 Act

---

semitism and racism, and association with right-wing, neo-Nazi extremists proven; scheduling to speak at an anti-Zionist conference which was to be attended by representatives of terrorist organisations, possession and prominent displaying of a self-portrait by Hitler, and guilt of misconduct in relation to the Goebbels diaries not proven but saved by s.5); *Mengi v Hermitage* [2012] EWHC 3445 (QB) (false allegation of lying saved by proof of orchestration of a campaign of vilification and facilitation of a "grab" of a property).

[112] E.g. *Robson v News Group Newspapers* (unreported, 95/SC/0876) October 9, 1995, Judge Previté QC (plainly defamatory of a person to say that he has defrauded the DSS, but in light of s.5 deemed justified when coupled with a true allegation that he had been convicted of a £4 million mortgage fraud).

[113] S.2(2) of the Defamation Act 2013.

employed the terminology of "materially injuring". This would appear to involve a slight lowering of the threshold in terms of the availability of the defence. As such, it is consonant with the requirement in s.1 of the Defamation Act 2013 that a statement be likely to cause serious harm to reputation before an action for defamation can be brought.[114] Under s.5, the distinct imputations should be founded on separate words.[115] It is not clear whether the new version does likewise, or whether it would cover two separate defamatory meanings carried on one hand by the ordinary and natural meaning of words and on the other hand in a true innuendo.[116]

The s.2(3) defence does not go as far as the "contextual truth" defence familiar to Australian jurisdictions. Nor does the Defamation Act 2013 as enacted include the proposal that featured in cl.5(3) of Lord Lester's Defamation Bill whereby a defence similar to that of "contextual truth" would have been extended to situations where a publication contained a single defamatory allegation that might be characterised as possessing several different shades of meaning.

SECTION 4. THE REPETITION RULE

11.18 **The basic rule.** As a general rule, the law does not allow a person to evade liability by attributing a statement to some other person. If D states, "C murdered X", then a defence of truth requires D to show that C did murder X. If, however, D states that "A told me that C murdered X" or that "there is a rumour that C murdered X", D is still required to prove that C did murder X in order to establish the defence. It does not matter that, taken literally, the statement is true in the sense that D can show that he or she was told the information by A or that such a rumour does exist. In short, "If you repeat a rumour you cannot say it is true by proving that the rumour in fact existed; you have to prove that the subject matter of the rumour is true".[117] The

---

[114] See para.3.7, above.

[115] *Polly Peck (Holdings) Plc v Trelford* [1986] Q.B. 1000 CA at 1033, per O'Connor L.J.

[116] For the purposes of the predecessor rule in s.5 of the 1952 Act, should a statement have been capable of bearing the meaning either that the claimant was guilty of an offence or that there were reasonable grounds for suspecting him, those were not treated as distinct charges—see *Armstrong v Times Newspapers Ltd* [2004] EWHC 2928 (QB). This interpretation is likely to persist.

[117] *Cookson v Harewood* [1932] 2 K.B. 478 at 485 per Greer L.J., approved by Lord Devlin in *Lewis v Daily Telegraph* [1964] A.C. 234 at 283–284. In *Aspro Travel v Owners Abroad Group* [1996] 1 W.L.R. 132 CA, it was said that "in the abstract" there can be circumstances in which the statement "there is a rumour . . . " could be justified by proof that the rumour existed. In *Shah v Standard Chartered Bank* [1999] Q.B. 240 CA, Hirst L.J. doubted whether the view expressed in the *Aspro Travel* case was reconcilable with the authorities and said that the case "should be confined to its own facts"(at 263). May L.J. said that *Stern v Piper* [1997] Q.B. 123 CA and *Aspro Travel* did not sit happily together and that he preferred *Stern v Piper* (at 268). He suggested, however, that the repetition of a rumour might in some cases fall under the protection of a recognised privilege, giving the example of a broker telling his client of a market rumour so that the client could decide what action to take.

"repetition rule" "reflects a fundamental canon of legal policy in the law of defamation ... that words must be interpreted, and the implications they contain justified, by reference to the underlying allegations of fact and not merely by reliance upon some second-hand report or assertion of them".[118] This is because "repeating someone else's libellous statement is just as bad as making the statement directly",[119] and therefore "for the purpose of the law of libel a hearsay statement is the same as a direct statement".[120] This would seem to accord with reality, for if:

> "A says to B that C says that D is a scoundrel, B will think just as ill of D as if he had heard the statement directly from C. If, moreover, A is a respectable newspaper, D's position will be worse than if B had merely heard the statement directly from C. It will be worse in part because there will be many more Bs, and in part because responsible newspapers do not generally repeat serious allegations unless they think there is something in them so that the very fact of publication carries a certain weight."[121]

The same approach is taken where D, rather than purporting to report what someone else has said, simply asserts that he believes that C murdered X—no matter how honest that belief and no matter how accurately it states the "fact" of his state of mind, again he must prove that C murdered X.[122] This does not mean that wherever D makes a statement implicating C with wrongdoing it must be proved that C was guilty of the wrongdoing: on its proper interpretation, the statement may convey merely that there are reasonable grounds to suspect C or grounds for investigation of his conduct,[123] and then D succeeds on justification by proving the truth of the words in that level of meaning rather than guilt. It is, therefore, necessary to determine what meaning the words can convey to the reasonable person for it is only such a meaning that the defendant is required to justify.[124] Thus it would seem that

---

[118] *Shah v Standard Chartered Bank* [1999] Q.B. 241 CA at 263; *Curistan v Times Newspapers Ltd* [2008] EWCA Civ 432; [2009] Q.B. 231 at [80]. See also para.27.11, below.

[119] *Lewis v Daily Telegraph* [1964] A.C. 234 at 260 per Lord Reid.

[120] Ibid. at 284 per Lord Devlin.

[121] *Mark v Associated Newspapers Ltd* [2002] EWCA Civ 772; [2002] E.M.L.R. 839 at [29]. Of course, if B thinks that C is a knave or a fool this may not in fact lower B's estimation of D, but it is well established that words are still defamatory even if the recipient is unaffected by them: para.2.1, above.

[122] *Kerr v Force* (1826) 3 Cranch C.C. 8 at 24.

[123] Nowadays it is common to refer to a direct charge as a Level 1 meaning and to the other two as Level 2 and Level 3 meanings respectively—see para.3.28, above. In the latter two cases, the usual question asked is what can the statement be reasonably understood to mean? But where the defendant is repeating a direct charge made by another the policy of the law *dictates* that he is to be treated as making the charge rather than merely repeating it: *Stern v Piper* [1997] Q.B. 123 CA at 136; *Mark v Associated Newspapers Ltd* [2002] EWCA Civ 772; [2002] E.M.L.R. 38 at [29].

[124] In *Hamilton v Clifford* [2004] EWHC 1542 (QB), a statement "all I would say is that when it comes to judging who's telling the truth I totally believe what the young lady told me" was regarded as a clear endorsement or adoption by the defendant of her allegation of criminality against the claimants. Other statements, however, were regarded as potentially capable of meaning only that there were reasonable grounds to suspect the claimants.

a statement that proceedings for conspiracy have been issued against the claimant may be justified by proof that proceedings have been issued, and the defendant is not required to prove that the claimant has committed the wrong alleged in them.[125]

11.19 The repetition rule and privilege. Even if the defendant fails on justification because of the repetition rule does not mean that he may not rely on privilege. The law of privilege (or at least those parts of it concerned with reports of what others have said) presupposes the existence of the repetition rule, because if it did not exist the privilege would be unnecessary.[126] So if D's statement that "A said that C murdered X" was part of a fair and accurate report of judicial proceedings D would be protected by absolute privilege under s.14 of the Defamation Act 1996.[127] It is true that most of the "reporting privileges" are qualified rather than absolute but it is likely to be a rare case, at least in claims against the media, in which the claimant would be in a position to defeat the defence by proof of malice. The repetition rule is concerned with meaning and justification, not with privilege, but particularly important for the practical impact of the rule is the doctrine which is an outgrowth of the "public interest" privilege established by *Reynolds v Times Newspapers*[128] and which is commonly known as "reportage". *Reynolds* privilege generally requires some attempt by the publisher to verify the truth of the allegations published, but this is not true of reportage, where it is only the fact that the allegations have been made which must be verified. The limits

---

[125] *Cadam v Beaverbrook Newspapers* [1959] 1 Q.B. 413 CA (where it was only necessary to establish that the proposition was arguable); *Stern v Piper* [1997] Q.B. 123 CA. The point is important because the absolute (para.13.35, below) or qualified (paras 15.35 and 16.10, below) privilege for reports of court proceedings attaches only to reports of what is done in court, so if justification were not available in this situation it would in practice be impossible to report the issue of proceedings until the trial began: *Stern v Piper* [1997] Q.B. 123 CA at 133, where justification was held not to be available in respect of a report of an affirmation made by a party to other civil proceedings against the plaintiff. More difficulty is caused by reports of judicial statements. In *Waters v Sunday Pictorial Newspapers* [1961] 1 W.L.R. 967, the defendants published, eight years after the event, remarks made by Lord Goddard C.J. during the plaintiff's appeal against conviction. The Court of Appeal refused to strike out a plea of justification. The absolute privilege for reports of judicial proceedings (first under the Law of Libel Amendment Act 1888, now under s.14 of the Defamation Act 1996) was inapplicable because the report was not contemporaneous. The qualified common law privilege (see now Sch.1, para.2 of the Defamation Act 1996) was arguably inapplicable on the ground (also relevant to the absolute privilege) that it was not fair and accurate, since it omitted to state that the plaintiff's appeal had succeeded (albeit on the ground of misdirection). Possibly, there is a special rule which equates reports of public judicial pronouncements with reports of the issue of proceedings, but the decision should not be followed save on similar facts: *Stern v Piper* at 134, 137.

[126] *Stern v Piper* [1997] Q.B. 123 CA at 137; *Wake v John Fairfax & Sons Ltd* [1973] 1 N.S.W.L.R. 43 NSWCA at 50. So in *Coull v Nationwide News Pty Ltd* [2008] NTCA 10, where the reporting privilege failed because the report was not fair and accurate, the fact that a reader might have concluded that all that was being reported was what witnesses said did not affect the fact that the material was defamatory.

[127] See para.13.35, below.

[128] [2001] 2 A.C. 127, para.15.2, below.

of this aspect of *Reynolds* are far from clear[129] but it certainly covers the situation where a newspaper in an even-handed manner reports accusation and counter-accusation in an ongoing dispute between A and B.[130] This resembles what is sometimes known as "neutral reporting". However, there is no *general* doctrine in English law that a report of an accusation made by another is not actionable unless the reporter endorsed or "adopted" the accusation.[131] Although the European Court of Human Rights has said that under art.10 of the Convention a "general requirement for journalists systematically and formally to distance themselves from the content of a quotation that might insult or provoke others or damage their reputation was not reconcilable with the press's role of providing information on current events, opinions and ideas",[132] the Court of Appeal has held that there is no inconsistency between this and the repetition rule, given the current scope of the defence of privilege where the press reports matters of public interest.[133]

It may be that the words published by the defendant consist in part of material protected by privilege and in part of material added by the defendant. In determining the meaning of the non-privileged part it is wrong to take the article as a whole for that might be to bypass the protection conferred on the privileged part: the part protected by privilege forms no more than the context in which the meaning of the non-privileged part must be determined. If the meaning of the non-privileged part is that the defendant asserts that the allegations in the privileged part are true then he is liable for that notwithstanding the protection of the report itself; but it is unnecessary for him to make some ritual incantation to the effect that the truth of the allegations cannot be determined.[134]

---

[129] See para.15.16, below.

[130] For a case where at one stage the argument was advanced that the reporting of accusation and counter-accusation could bear no defamatory meaning at all, see *Milne v Telegraph Group Ltd* [2001] E.M.L.R. 30. Such a case might now simply be run by the defence on the basis of reportage.

[131] Nor in Australia: "for most practical purposes a person who republishes a libel can only escape a finding of publication of the defamatory imputations in it if he has added further material which refutes or undermines those imputations": *Yoon Shin Lee v Bob Chae-Sang Cha* [2005] NSWCA 279 at [6] per Handley J.A. The

"unexplained use of the concept [of adoption] is likely to mislead a jury because, in its ordinary meaning it may be understood as requiring some positive element of acceptance of the allegation as one's own. There are of course obvious differences between affirmatively adopting an allegation, repeating it without comment and repeating it in order to refute it. (These are given by way of example, rather than as covering the field of possibilities.) For the purposes of a defamation action, the critical point is that both the first and second alternatives may convey the imputations, as indeed may the third, although usually it would not":

Keramianakis v Regional Publishers Pty Ltd [2007] NSWCA 375 at [44] per Basten J.A.

[132] *Thoma v Luxembourg* App. no.38432/97; ECHR 2001-III at [64]. See the remarks in *Lukowiak v Unidad Editorial* [2001] E.M.L.R. 46 at [58]–[59].

[133] *Mark v Associated Newspapers Ltd* [2002] EWCA Civ 772; [2002] E.M.L.R. 839 at [29]; *Curistan v Times Newspapers Ltd* [2008] EWCA Civ 432; [2009] Q.B. 231 at [36].

[134] *Curistan v Times Newspapers Ltd*, above.

Section 5. Defence of Truth and the Mixing of Fact and
Opinion

11.20 Fact and opinion. Under the defence of truth, if a publication contains defamatory statements both of fact and of opinion,[135] then the defendant must prove that the statements of fact are true and that the statements of opinion are correct.[136] Hence, if an article in a newspaper is introduced by a defamatory headline in the nature of a comment, evidence that the facts stated in the article were true was not sufficient to support a plea of justification unless the defendant could show that the headline was a true view of the state of affairs disclosed by the facts.[137] It may be, of course, that the comment can be defended as honest opinion: "comment may be defended as honest opinion, or it may be defended as the truth. The fact that words complained of are comment does not preclude their being defended as true".[138]

A defence of truth in respect of an opinion may (in theory, at any rate) succeed where the defence of honest opinion would fail because the defendant was actuated by malice. Contrariwise, a plea of justification may fail in circumstances in which a plea of honest opinion would succeed because the comment, though untrue, was such as an honest person might have made and was made without malice.[139]

Section 6. Defence of Truth and Damages

11.21 Truth and damages. A successful defence of truth provides a complete defence to a claim, but evidence that does not show that the statement is substantially true may nevertheless be damaging to the claimant's character. There has been a substantial change in practice here, though its scope remains somewhat unclear. The original position was that evidence of the claimant's *general* bad reputation was admissible in mitigation of damages,[140] because the   state   of   that   reputation   is   necessarily   an   element   in

---

[135] As to the distinction see para.12.8, below.

[136] *Sutherland v Stopes* [1925] A.C. 47 at 62–63 per Lord Findlay. See also, *Cooper v Lawson* (1838) 8 A. & E. 746; *Howden v Truth and Sportsman* (1937) 58 C.L.R. 416; *Goldsborough v Fairfax* (1934) 34 S.R.(N.S.W.) 524 at 546–547; *Gardiner v Fairfax* (1942) 42 S.R.(N.S.W.) 171 at 179; *Hare and Grolier v Better Business (No.2)* [1947] 1 W.W.R. 25.

[137] See *Lewis v Clement* (1820) 3 B. & Ald. 702, affirmed (1822) 3 Brod. & Bing. 297; *Bishop v Latimer* (1861) 4 L.T. (N.S.) 775; *Pratt v Pioneer Press*, 14 N.W. 62 (Minn., 1882). Similarly the headline could not be protected by the fact that the report of the facts was absolutely privileged.

[138] *Sharma v Singh* [2007] EWHC 2988 (QB) at [24] per Tugendhat J.

[139] The ECtHR has several times emphasised that proving the truth of value judgments is impossible to fulfill and to require the defendant to do so would violate art.10 of the Convention (see, e.g. *Lingens v Austria* (1986) 8 EHRR 407). This may be answered, however, on the basis that English law offers the defence of honest opinion and does not therefore *require* the defendant to prove the truth of an opinion, even though it allows him the opportunity to do so.

[140] But it is extremely rare for such evidence to be called: *Davy v Dilnot* [2006] EWHC 1404 (QB) at [12]. May a defendant say, "Your reputation is so bad that there is nothing left of it worthy to be compensated and the claim should be struck out altogether"? Such an argument failed on the facts in *Magee v MGN Ltd* [2003] IEHC 27. Cf. *Ewing v News International Ltd* [2008]

deciding what damage it has sustained as a result of the libel. However, the defendant was not allowed to put in evidence, by way of mitigation, of specific acts of misconduct tending to show the reputation the claimant deserved (the rule in *Scott v Sampson*).[141] In this sense the defendant was not allowed to plead specific facts in "partial justification" of the meaning advanced by the claimant with the purpose of mitigating damages.[142]

If the libel contained more than one distinct charge, however, the defendant might seek to justify some of the charges in full without justifying all of them.[143] Furthermore, the defendant might be able to advance a different meaning to that contended for by the claimant and justify that.[144] In either event, even if the plea of justification ultimately failed, the relevant evidence would have been before the jury. It is not therefore surprising that defendants might be inclined to take a somewhat optimistic view of the meaning of words in order to extend the plea of justification as widely as possible.[145] In *Burstein v Times Newspapers Ltd*,[146] it was held that *Scott v Sampson* rests at least in

---

EWHC 1390 (QB) at [99]. In *Australian Broadcasting Corp v O'Neill* [2006] HCA 46; 229 A.L.R. 457 one factor playing a role in the majority view that there should be no interlocutory injunction was that the plaintiff's status as a prisoner serving a life sentence for murder might well lead to his recovering only nominal damages even if the allegation in question were untrue. In *Williams v MGN Ltd* [2009] EWHC 3150 (QB), where the allegation was that the claimant was a henchman of a notorious gun criminal the claim was struck out as an abuse of process "because having regard to the Claimant's background and serious criminal convictions ... it would be inappropriate to regard the article ... and its references to him as constituting a 'real and substantial tort' ". For a full discussion of evidence in mitigation of damages see para.35.29 et seq., below.

[141] *Scott v Sampson* (1882) 8 Q.B.D. 491. A clause to reverse this rule was a central feature of the Defamation Bill introduced in 1995, but the clause was lost in the Commons. A clause to the same effect in the Defamation Bill 1952 was lost for lack of time: Report of the Supreme Court Procedure Committee (the Neill Committee) 1991, III. 13. The Faulks Committee made a similar proposal: Cmd.5909 (1975) para.372. Contrast New Zealand law: s.30 of the Defamation Act 1992, discussed in *Television New Zealand Ltd v Ah Koy* [2002] 2 N.Z.L.R. 616.

[142] *Prager v Times Newspapers* [1988] 1 W.L.R. 77 CA at 88–89.

[143] Ibid. It has to be admitted that some judicial statements go further and allow the defendant to plead partial justification of a single, non-severable charge. See, e.g. Lord Denning in *Plato Films Ltd v Speidel* [1961] A.C. 1090 HL at 1141:

"suppose a newspaper said of a man: 'He has been convicted six times for dishonesty', but, on being sued, the newspaper finds that he has in fact only been convicted twice. The newspaper cannot justify, [counsel] said, because it cannot prove the words were true. Nor can it bring forward the two convictions in mitigation of damages because they are specific misconduct. So the plaintiff will get damages on the footing that he has never been convicted at all. If such were the law, I would agree with [counsel] that it would be most unjust and ought to be remedied. But it is not the law. Although the newspaper cannot justify in whole it can justify in part. It can plead that, insofar as the words meant that he had been convicted twice, they were true and thus bring the two convictions before the jury."

It might also attempt to justify a general meaning that the claimant was dishonest.

[144] See para.11.14, above.

[145] *Atkinson v Fitzwalter* [1987] 1 W.L.R. 1201 CA; *Pamplin v Express Newspapers (No.2)* [1988] 1 W.L.R. 116 CA; *Prager v Times Newspapers* [1988] 1 W.L.R. 77 CA. See *Warren v Random House Group Ltd* [2008] EWCA Civ 834; [2009] Q.B. 600 at [110] where the defendants' meaning was described by counsel for the claimant as "artificially cast into a convoluted mouthful to introduce extraneous material in justification with a view to reducing damages."

[146] [2001] 1 W.L.R. 579 CA. See further para.33.43, below.

part upon what today would be called "case management" factors, for example, the undesirability of prolonging proceedings with a multitude of collateral issues.[147] That remains a valid policy but should not be used so as to put the jury in blinkers when assessing damages. Thus the evidence which *Scott v Sampson* excludes is: "particular evidence of general reputation, character or disposition which is not directly connected with the subject matter of the defamatory publication. It does not exclude evidence of directly relevant background context".[148] While it is not permissible to advance an unsustainable defence of justification and thereby, under the guise of particulars of justification, seek to rely on particulars which *Scott v Sampson* would not permit, that: "does not prevent a defendant from frankly accepting that there is no proper plea of justification, but seeking to rely in reduction of damages on particulars which *Scott v Sampson* . . . [does] not exclude".[149]

The *Burstein* principle applies in the context of the offer of amends procedure,[150] as well as on a plea of justification. It was considered by the Court of Appeal in that context in *Turner v News Group Newspapers Ltd*.[151] The argument that the policy of allowing evidence of particular acts of misconduct was based upon the difficulty the jury would have in ignoring evidence which they had heard on an unsuccessful plea of justification or honest comment was rejected, for it:

> "is a fundamental proposition of English law that juries, when directed to ignore evidence which they have heard, will faithfully do so, a proposition which operates as much in the criminal context as it does in the civil, and where any doubts as to its validity would have far-reaching consequences."[152]

It is probably not possible to state any simple "test" for the application of *Burstein* and although the Court of Appeal has subsequently said that the phrase "directly relevant background context" is the best possible encapsulation of the principle within a single phrase,[153] Moses L.J. in *Turner* was unhappy with it, preferring simply to say that:

> "a defendant may seek to reduce damages by adducing evidence which is directly relevant to a claimant's conduct or reputation in the particular sector to which the defamatory material relates."[154]

---

[147] This includes the risk of the claimant being driven from the field by the prospect of increased costs, though Moses L.J. in *Turner v News Group Newspapers Ltd* [2006] EWCA Civ 540; [2006] 1 W.L.R. 3469 at [90] appears to regard the risk of the claimant being "terrorised into submission" as a separate reason. For examples of how an action could potentially be enlarged by collateral issues see *Davy v Dilnot* [2006] EWHC 1404 (QB).

[148] *Burstein v Times Newspapers Ltd* [2001] 1 W.L.R. 579 CA at 598.

[149] Ibid., at 600.

[150] See para.19.5, below. *Abu v MGN Ltd* [2002] EWHC 2345 (QB); [2003] 1 W.L.R. 2201; *Turner v News Group Newspapers Ltd* [2006] EWCA Civ 540; [2006] 1 W.L.R. 3469.

[151] [2006] EWCA Civ 540; [2006] 1 W.L.R. 3469.

[152] Ibid., at [46].

[153] *Warren v Random House Group Ltd* [2008] EWCA Civ 834; [2009] Q.B. 600 at [79].

[154] Ibid., at [89].

It is admitted in *Turner* that it is "inevitable that cases will occur where it is not easy to determine whether the test in *Burstein* is met or not".[155] It is accepted that the new approach should be applied with some caution,[156] but it is not confined to cases where the claimant provoked the libel.[157] Nor is it necessary that the background facts should have had some causal connexion with the publication,[158] nor that the defendant should have had the matters in mind when he published.[159] The case has been relied on to admit evidence in mitigation of a charge of improper sexual advances that the claimant carried on an adulterous affair seven or eight years before.[160] In *Burstein* itself, although the defendant was unable to justify the direct allegation that the claimant had organised the wrecking of performances, evidence was admissible on damages that the claimant was closely associated with a group known as "The Hecklers" because that went directly to the reputation he had courted as a militant opponent of atonal music; but the judge had been correct to exclude evidence of grandiose comparisons he had made of his own music with that of great romantic composers.[161] In *Warren v Random House Group Ltd*,[162] the charge made in the words complained of was that the claimant had "conned" a boxer into accepting a pitifully low purse but the particulars which were properly struck out related to matters occurring subsequent to the contract and relating to the payment of the agreed sum. The evidence might have suggested that the claimant was a hard man but it did nothing at all to show that he was a fraud. Although, therefore, it is clear that the *Burnstein* principle is confined to matters in the same "sector" of the claimant's reputation as that to which the libel refers,[163] that fact alone is not necessarily

---

[155] *Turner v News Group Newspapers Ltd* [2006] EWCA Civ 540; [2006] 1 W.L.R. 3469 at [56] per Keene L.J. See also *Tesco Stores Ltd v Guardian News and Media Ltd* [2009] E.M.L.R. 5.

[156] Ibid, at [56] and [91].

[157] *Turner v News Group Newspapers Ltd* (above), per Keene L.J. at [53]; *Windsor v Boycott*, May 9, 2002, (QB) (leave to appeal [2001] EWCA Civ 1321, action settled July 12, 2002). But failure to complain about a previous publication of the same libel by the defendant is not within *Burstein*: *Rath v Guardian News and Media Ltd* [2008] EWHC 398 (QB).

[158] *Turner v News Group Newspapers Ltd* [2006] EWCA Civ 540; [2006] 1 W.L.R. 3469 at [54].

[159] Ibid.

[160] *Carpenter v Associated Newspapers*, January 16, 2001, (QB).

[161] See *Warren v Random House Group Ltd* (above) at [81].

[162] Ibid.

[163] *Turner v News Group Newspapers Ltd* (above) at [89]. "Private life" would be too broad a category: ibid. at [90]; *Australian Broadcasting Corp v McBride* [2001] NSWCA 322 (reputation was that for care of and compassion for patients; evidence of scientific fraud in drug testing not admissible). Consider facts like those in *Mosley v News Group Newspapers Ltd* [2008] EWHC 1777 (QB); [2008] E.M.L.R. 20 (para.22.12, below). D states that C (a) plays dominant and submissive roles at sado-masochistic parties and (b) these have a "Nazi" flavour. D can prove (a) but not (b) and the statement as a whole may not be substantially true. Is (a) "directly relevant background context" to (b)? On the facts there was no claim for defamation, (a) being demonstrably true and the untruth of (b) went only to defeat D's argument in a claim for misuse of private information that the story was in the public interest.

enough to bring it into play and care must be taken not to stray too far from the charge the defendant has made in the words complained of at the risk of enlarging the damages inquiry with peripheral issues.

CHAPTER 12

HONEST COMMENT

SECTION 1. INTRODUCTION

The basis of the defence. It is a defence to an action of libel or slander that **12.1** the words complained of are honest comment on a matter of public interest.[1] The right to comment honestly on important matters has been considered a "bulwark of free speech"[2]; "one of the fundamental rights of free speech and writing . . . and . . . of vital importance to the rule of law on which we depend for our personal freedom".[3] The defence of honest comment is intended to promote vigorous free speech, so that "a critic need not be mealy-mouthed in denouncing what he disagrees with . . . [but rather is] entitled to dip his pen in gall for the purposes of legitimate criticism".[4] It is one of the principal means by which the common law attempts to comply with the guarantee of freedom of expression found in art.10 of the European Convention on Human

---

[1] The traditional name for the defence—"fair comment"—has been gradually superseded. In *Joseph v Spiller* [2010] UKSC 53; [2011] 1 A.C. 852, the Supreme Court preferred "honest comment" (at [117]). That nomenclature had previously been adopted by Lord Nicholls in *Reynolds v Times Newspapers Ltd* [2001] 2 A.C. 127 HL at 165, and in *Panday v Gordon* [2005] UKPC 36; [2006] 1 A.C. 427. See also *Tse Wai Chun v Cheng* [2000] HKCFA 86; [2001] E.M.L.R 31 at [15]. The defence was termed "honest opinion" by the Court of Appeal in *British Chiropractic Association v Singh* [2010] EWCA Civ 350; [2011] 1 W.L.R. 133 at [36]. The new statutory defence to be introduced by s.3 of the Defamation Act 2013 is also labelled "honest opinion". "Honest opinion" is used in the NZ Defamation Act 1992, in the uniform Australian legislation (see e.g. the Defamation Act 2005 (NSW) s.31) and in s.20 of the Irish Defamation Act 2009. In this text, the term "honest comment" will be used to refer to the common law version of the defence, albeit that "fair comment" will be retained in direct quotation from earlier sources. The term "honest opinion" will be reserved for references to the statutory defence.

[2] Faulks Committee, Cmnd.5909 (1975) at para.151.

[3] *Lyon v Daily Telegraph* [1943] 1 K.B. 746 CA per Scott L.J. at 753. See also, *Slim v Daily Telegraph* [1968] 2 Q.B. 157 CA per Lord Denning M.R. at 170.

[4] *Tse Wai Chun Paul v Albert Cheng* [2000] HKCFA 86; [2001] E.M.L.R 31 per Lord Nicholls at [20].

Rights.[5] There are matters on which the public has a legitimate interest or with which it is legitimately concerned, and on such matters it is desirable that any person should be able to comment freely, and even harshly, so long as he does so honestly and without "malice".[6]

12.2 The elements of the defence. In *Spiller* v *Joseph*, the Supreme Court offered a review of the historical development of the defence of honest comment before restating the five elements that must be proven by a defendant who wishes to rely upon it.[7] Paraphrasing, these five elements are:

(1) the comment must be on a matter of public interest[8];
(2) the comment must be recognisable as comment, as distinct from an imputation of fact[9];
(3) the comment must be based on facts which are true or protected by privilege[10];
(4) the comment must explicitly or implicitly indicate, at least in general terms, the facts on which it is based,[11] and

---

[5] *Lowe v Associated Newspapers Ltd* [2006] EWHC 320 (QB); [2007] Q.B. 580 at [20]. The law is similar in Scotland. So is the law in South Africa (*Marais v Richard*, 1981 (1) S.A. 1157 A.D.), and Canada (*WIC Radio Ltd v Simpson* [2008] SCC 40; [2008] S.C.R. 420 at [28]). The law in the United States is complex, difficult to state, and may vary from one jurisdiction to another. In *Gertz v Robert Welch Inc*, 418 U.S. 323 (1974), there are dicta to the effect that under the First Amendment there is no such thing as a false idea. This has sometimes been interpreted as confining the law of defamation to verifiable imputations of fact. Thus, in *Lifton v Board of Education of the City of Chicago* 416 F.3d 571 (CA7, 2005) saying of a teacher that she was "lazy", "burnt out", "looking for sympathy", "unstable", "resting on her laurels", and that she "doesn't want to work" was held to be unverifiable and non-actionable opinion. In *Milkovich v Lorain Journal*, 497 U.S. 1 (1990), however, the Supreme Court stated that *Gertz* was not intended to create a wholesale exception for opinion. There are at least three scenarios in which an opinion may be actionable: (1) where it implies a provably false fact; (2) where the opinion takes the form of a deduction from facts; (3) where it is based on facts which are provably untrue: *Moldea v New York Times*, 22 F.3d 310 (DC App 1994).

[6] The malice which rebuts the defence does not mean ill-will or spite, but rather lack of belief in the opinion expressed: see para.12.36, below.

[7] [2010] UKSC 53; [2011] 1 A.C. 852. The leading speech was given by Lord Phillips. The five elements had previously been stated by Lord Nicholls in *Tse Wai Chun Paul v Albert Cheng* [2000] HKCFA 86; [2001] E.M.L.R 31 at [16]–[21]. The claimants in the case were a musical act, The Gillettes, and the defendant their former agent. Following a dispute, the defendant published a note on his website purporting to quote from an email from the claimants and suggested that they would not abide by contracts. The original email had stated that the claimants' contract with the defendant did not hold water. On the website, however, the defendant quoted the claimant as having said that "contracts hold no water". The case involved pleas of justification and of fair comment. That relating to fair comment concerned the words "'The Gillettes' c/o Craig Joseph are not professional enough to feature in our portfolio ... it may follow that the artists' obligations for your booking may also not be met. In essence, Craig Joseph who performs with/ arranges bookings for 'The Gillettes' and 'Saturday Night at the Movies' may sign a contract for your booking but will not necessarily adhere to it."

[8] See para.12.32, below.
[9] See para.12.7, below.
[10] See para.12.15, below.
[11] See para.12.24, below.

(5) the comment must be one which could have been made by an honest person, however prejudiced he might be, and however exaggerated or obstinate his views.[12]

Where malice can be established by the claimant this will defeat the defence of honest comment, albeit that the concept of malice is somewhat circumscribed in this context.[13] The defence was said by Lord Phillips in *Spiller* to be consistent with Strasbourg jurisprudence[14] and in *Waterson v Lloyd*, Laws L.J. reflected that these expressions of principle "exemplify . . . the common law's increasing focus in this area on the balance to be struck between public interest and individual right: between free speech and private claims".[15]

Lord Phillips' restatement of the five key elements of the defence involved the revision of the fourth element.[16] This involved the dropping of the rider that "the reader or hearer should be in a position to judge for himself how far the comment was well founded". Instead, Lord Phillips offered a different explanation of why the comment must include some allusion to the underpinning facts, and correspondingly—at a deeper level—emphasised the nature of the rationale that underpins the honest comment defence. Lord Phillips considered that identification of the facts with sufficient particularity was required not in the first instance to enable the reader to judge for himself whether the comment was well founded, but rather to allow the reader to understand what the comment was about.[17]

Honest comment is a defence that is open, in principle, to every defendant. While it has been used constantly by media defendants, the right of comment which the press and broadcasters have is one which they share with every member of the public.[18] That said, the "elevated" position of the media as a

---

[12] See para.12.26, below.

[13] See para.12.36, below. In short, for this purpose, malice means that the defendant was not expressing his genuine opinion.

[14] [2010] UKSC 53; [2011] 1 A.C. 852.

[15] [2013] EWCA Civ 136; [2013] E.M.L.R. 17 at [67].

[16] Lord Nicholls in *Tse Wai Chun Paul v Albert Cheng* [2000] HKCFA 86; [2001] E.M.L.R 31 at [19] had stated, so far as the fourth element was concerned, that "the comment must explicitly or implicitly indicate, at least in general terms, what are the facts on which the comment is being made . . . the reader or hearer should be in a position to judge for himself how far the comment was well founded" (at [19]). The requirement that the facts be sufficiently set out to allow the reader to judge for himself whether the comment was well founded was questioned by Eady J. in *Lowe v Associated Newspapers Ltd* [2006] EWHC 320 (QB); [2007] Q.B. 580 at [21]–[60]. See especially at [57].

[17] [2010] UKSC 53; [2011] 1 A.C. 852 at [104]. A slight awkwardness in the means by which Lord Phillips expressed this idea—he referred to the possibility that the person who had originally made the comment might, if challenged, explain his view further (ibid.)—perhaps masked somewhat the clarity of the restatement of this fourth element of the defence.

[18] *Campbell v Spottiswoode* (1863) 32 L.J.Q.B. 185 at 201; *Kane v Mulvany* (1866) 1.R. 2 C.L. 402; *Anderson v Fairfax* (1883) 4 N.S.W.L.R. 183. There are many dicta to this effect: "Who is entitled to comment? The answer to that is 'everyone'. A newspaper reporter or a newspaper editor has exactly the same rights, neither more or less, than every other citizen" (*Silkin v Beaverbrook Newspapers* [1958] 1 W.L.R. 743 at 746 per Diplock J.); "a newspaper has the right, and no greater or higher right, to make comment upon a public officer or person occupying a public situation than an ordinary citizen would have" (*Langlands v Leng*, 1916 S.C.(H.L.) 102 at

vehicle for the expression of opinions by members of the public is, arguably, given some recognition in the law.[19] However, the advent of social media platforms has opened a new field of public discussion in which the defence might become more important to the average person. Indeed, one explicit motivation that underpinned the court's restatement of the elements of the defence in *Joseph v Spiller* was to allow greater flexibility over how commentators express their views while yet being able to resort to the legal safe harbour. The need to accommodate the advent of social media platforms—and the way in which people relate to one another thereon—in the construction of the defence was explicitly recognised.[20] Fundamentally, people have a right to hold opinions and to express them to others; they have a right to respond to the world as they find it (even if this involves them in reaching wrong conclusions).[21]

12.3 **Reform: common law.** The defence of honest comment has long been considered "one of the most difficult areas of the law of defamation".[22] In *Joseph v Spiller*, the Supreme Court was invited by counsel to consider options for the reform of the defence.[23] These included, the proposals that it should be expanded to permit the defendant to rely on underpinning facts that were not known to him—or even in existence—when the comment was made[24]; that its scope should be widened by removing the requirement that it must be on a matter of public interest[25]; that it should cover inferences of fact

---

110 per Lord Shaw); "to whatever lengths the subject in general may go, so also may the journalist . . . the range of his assertions, his criticisms, or his comments, is as wide as, and no wider than, that of every other subject" (*Arnold v King-Emperor* (1914) 83 L.J.P.C. 299 at 300 per Lord Shaw).

[19] See para.12.37, below.

[20] In *Spiller*, above, Lord Phillips noted that

"today the internet has made it possible for the man in the street to make public comment about others in a manner that did not exist when the principles of the law of fair comment were developed, and millions take advantage of that opportunity. Where the comments that they make are derogatory it will often be impossible for other readers to evaluate them without detailed information about the facts that have given rise to the comments. Frequently these will not be set out" (at [99]).

Lord Walker concurred:

"the creation of a common base of information shared by those who watch television and use the internet has had an effect which can hardly be overstated. Millions now talk, and thousands comment in electronically transmitted words, about recent events of which they have learned from television or the internet. Many of the events and the comments on them are no doubt trivial and ephemeral, but from time to time . . . libel law has to engage with them. The test for identifying the factual basis of honest comment must be flexible enough to allow for this type of case, in which a passing reference to the previous night's celebrity show would be regarded by most of the public, and may sometimes have to be regarded by the law, as a sufficient factual basis" (at [131]).

[21] As Lord Phillips put it in *Joseph v Spiller*, above, at [86], "the right to make honest but derogatory expressions of opinion on such matters was and is an important safeguard for freedom of expression".

[22] *Joseph v Spiller*, above, per Lord Phillips at [1].

[23] Ibid. at [106]–[117].

[24] Ibid. at [108] and [110].

[25] Ibid. at [113].

drawn from underpinning facts,[26] and that it should be possible to rely on *Reynolds* privilege as well as true facts.[27] Lord Phillips concluded, however, that "reforms of this nature would [not] do anything to simplify defamation actions . . . the scope of the defence . . . would be widened, but at the price of continued complexity of process".[28] He also noted that "the proposed reforms go beyond changes that could properly be made by this court in the orderly development of the common law",[29] and suggested that "the whole area merits consideration by the Law Commission . . . or an expert committee".[30]

Reform: section 3 of the Defamation Act 2013. Reform of the honest   **12.4** comment defence has been undertaken by Parliament and a revised defence is contained in s.3 of the Defamation Act 2013. When brought into force, that provision will abolish the common law defence,[31] and replace it with a new statutory defence labelled "honest opinion".

The perception motivating the reform was that honest comment suffers from "complex case law limiting [its] practical value",[32] and this notwithstanding the fact that the Supreme Court had only recently offered its thoroughgoing review of the area.[33] The intention behind the revisions was "to strip out unnecessary technical difficulties and make the renamed defence . . . user-friendly . . . [to] update and simplify . . . clarifying what the defendant must prove . . . and stating the elements of the defence in clear terms".[34] The Explanatory Notes to the Act state that the new defence "broadly reflects the current law while simplifying and clarifying certain elements".[35]

Section 3 provides as follows:

"3 Honest opinion
(1) It is a defence to an action for defamation for the defendant to show that the following conditions are met.
(2) The first condition is that the statement complained of was a statement of opinion.
(3) The second condition is that the statement complained of indicated, whether in general or specific terms, the basis of the opinion.
(4) The third condition is that an honest person could have held the opinion on the basis of—
       (a) any fact which existed at the time the statement complained of was published;

---

[26] Ibid. at [114].
[27] Ibid. at [115].
[28] Ibid. at [111].
[29] Ibid.
[30] Ibid. at [117]. Lord Phillips noted further that the proposals also pushed implicitly at broader questions in the law of defamation, including the sustainability of the repetition rule and of trial by jury (at [115]–[116]).
[31] S.3(8).
[32] Explanatory notes to the Lester Bill, at [62].
[33] *Joseph v Spiller* [2010] UKSC 53; [2011] 1 A.C. 852.
[34] Explanatory notes to the Lester Bill, at [68].
[35] Explanatory notes to the Defamation Act 2013 at [19].

(b) anything asserted to be a fact in a privileged statement published before the statement complained of.

(5) The defence is defeated if the claimant shows that the defendant did not hold the opinion.

(6) Subsection (5) does not apply in a case where the statement complained of was published by the defendant but made by another person ('the author'); and in such a case the defence is defeated if the claimant shows that the defendant knew or ought to have known that the author did not hold the opinion.

(7) For the purposes of subsection (4)(b) a statement is a 'privileged statement' if the person responsible for its publication would have one or more of the following defences if an action for defamation were brought in respect of it—

(a) a defence under section 4 (publication on matter of public interest);

(b) a defence under section 6 (peer-reviewed statement in scientific or academic journal);

(c) a defence under section 14 of the Defamation Act 1996 (reports of court proceedings protected by absolute privilege);

(d) a defence under section 15 of that Act (other reports protected by qualified privilege).

(8) The common law defence of fair comment is abolished and, accordingly, section 6 of the Defamation Act 1952 (fair comment) is repealed."

In summary, the new provision will involve substantive changes to the common law defence. First, it will remove the first of the five requirements for the common law defence: the requirement that the comment be on a matter of public interest. Secondly, it expands the types of privileged statement on which an honest opinion can be based, most notably to permit opinion based on facts that benefit from the new defence under s.4. Thirdly, it will allow the defendant to rely on any fact that existed at the time of publication, whether or not known to the defendant. When the Act is brought into force, the common law defence will be abolished under s.3(8). In general terms, this gives rise to the same general reservation concerning the creation of uncertainty in respect of the operation of the new s.3 defence that was highlighted with regard to the new s.2 defence of truth.[36] In addition, there is real concern that—for a provision that was purportedly introduced to make the defence more simple and user-friendly—s.3 will require significant litigation and judicial interpretation before its contours are fully understood.[37]

---

[36] See para.11.2, above. Here also, a likely consequence of abolition will be that the courts will be asked to decide whether a rule is properly classified as part of the common law of honest comment. Rules will definitely survive the entry into force of the Act only in so far as they are not part of the common law defence. One area in which this question may be of particular moment is in regard to the operation of the single meaning rule in relation to the new defence—see para.12.8, below. The concern regarding uncertainty may be less with regard to s.3 in the sense that relatively more of the common law rule is explicitly reflected in the statutory provision, and there was very much more legislative and pre-legislative discussion on this theme. Conversely, the recasting of this provision involves relatively more by way of reform.

[37] One particular area of concern is the seeming loss of clarity that ensues from the conflation of the third and fifth requirements set out in *Joseph v Spiller* in the third statutory condition stated in s.3(4).

Relationship between honest comment and justification. Justifica-   **12.5**
tion is a defence to any imputation contained in the words complained of,
whether of comment or of fact. To avail himself of that defence, the defendant
must show that his comment is "true". The defendant who pleads honest
comment does not take on this burden: the issue is not whether the jury agrees
with his opinion, but whether it is an opinion which might fairly be held on
the facts referred to.[38] Facts may be proved, but to subject opinion to the same
requirement of proof would be a significant inhibition on free speech.[39]
Honest comment is narrower than justification in that it is not applicable to
pure statements of fact, as opposed to opinions or inferences. In the case of
justification, the state of mind of the defendant at the time when the words
were published is in general immaterial, so the presence of malice is irrelevant
to that defence.[40] In the case of honest comment, however, the defendant's
state of mind can be material. If the defendant does not hold the stated
opinion, then the defence is not available, even if many other people would
hold that opinion. Moreover, he cannot rely on any facts that were not in
existence or of which he was not, at least in a general way, aware when the
comment was made.[41]

Relationship between honest comment and qualified privi-   **12.6**
lege. Although a separate defence of fair comment in relation to criticism of
writings and plays was long recognised, it was not until well on in the
nineteenth century that the defences of fair comment and privilege became
clearly separated in the field of public discussion of public matters.[42] Fair
comment became a defence to comment only (including inferences of fact and
of motive),[43] and was open to all. In contrast, qualified privilege was also a
defence to misstatements of fact, but was confined to those individuals who
stood in such relation to the circumstances as to be entitled to say or write
what would have been libellous or slanderous on the part of anyone else:

---

[38] See *Sutherland v Stopes* [1925] A.C. 47 at 62 per Lord Finlay. See also *Burton v Board* [1929] 1 K.B. 301 CA at 305; *Sharma v Singh* [2007] EWHC 2988 (QB) at [24]; *Rath v Guardian News and Media Ltd* [2008] EWHC 398 (QB) at [48].

[39] *Branson v Bower* [2002] Q.B. 737 at 747; *Lingens v Austria* (1986) 8 EHRR 407 at [46].

[40] The exception is under the Rehabilitation of Offenders Act 1974: see para.18.1, below.

[41] See para.12.29, below.

[42] See Mitchell, *The Making of the Modern Law of Defamation* (2005), Ch. 8. The critical case was *Campbell v Spottiswoode* (1863) 3 B. & S. 769 Ex Ch but it was some time before it was clearly established as a separate defence properly so-called. There are dicta to the effect that, like qualified privilege, honest comment is not defamatory: see *Campbell v Spottiswoode* (1863) 3 B. & S. 769; *Minister of Justice v SA Associated Newspapers*, 1979 (3) S.A. 466 at 475. But the better view is probably that honest comment is defamatory but not actionable: *Pratten v Labour Daily* [1926] V.L.R. 115 at 128; *Augustine Automatic Rotary Engine Co v Saturday Night* (1917) 34 D.L.R. 439 Ont. CA; *Vander Zalm v Times Publishers* [1980] 4 W.W.R. 259 BCCA.

[43] *Augustine Automatic Rotary Engine Co v Saturday Night* (1917) 34 D.L.R. 439 Ont. CA: "fair comment is a weapon which comes into action when justification has failed. Upon the plea of fair comment the substratum must . . . be laid by showing that, notwithstanding that the words are defamatory, yet the facts upon which the comment is based were truly stated, and that the comment was honest and not without foundation".

"For instance, if a master is asked as to the character of a servant, and he says that the servant is a thief, he has a privilege which no one else would have."[44]

"A privileged occasion is one on which the privileged person is entitled to do something which no one who is not within the privilege is entitled to do on that occasion. A person in such a position may say or write about another person things which no other person in the kingdom can be allowed to say or write. But, in the case of a criticism upon [a matter of public interest whether it be the conduct of a public man or] a published work, every person in the kingdom is entitled to do, and is forbidden to do exactly the same things, and therefore the occasion is not privileged."[45]

SECTION 2. RECOGNISABILITY AS COMMENT

12.7 Centrality of recognisability as comment. It is a fundamental rule that the honest comment defence applies to comment and not to imputations of fact. If the imputation is one of fact, the defence must be justification or privilege. Hence, recognisability of a statement as comment is a key determinant of the availability of the defence.[46]

12.8 The distinction between fact and comment. The ultimate determinant of whether the words are comment or fact is how they would strike the ordinary, reasonable reader.[47] That said, the question is in the first instance to be answered by the judge. If satisfied that the words complained of must fall into one or other category, the judge will rule to that effect. If the judge considers that reasonable people could take either view, then the matter must be left to the jury.[48] The matter is not simple.[49] There may be significant

---

[44] *Campbell v Spottiswoode* (1863) 32 L.J.Q.B. 185 at 201 per Blackburn J. See also *Thomas v Bradbury Agnew* [1906] 2 K.B. 627 CA at 640; *Peter Walker v Hodgson* [1909] 1 K.B. 239 CA at 250.

[45] *Merivale v Carson* (1887) 20 Q.B.D. 275 CA at 280 per Lord Esher M.R. (see also at 282–283). This was said by Cartwright J. in *Banks v Globe and Mail* [1961] S.C. R. 474 at 482 to be an accurate statement of the law. All this must now be read, however, in the light of the much extended privilege for media reports: see para.15.2, below.

[46] In *Thornton v Telegraph Media Group Ltd* [2011] EWHC 159 (QB); [2011] E.M.L.R. 25 per Tugendhat J. at [25], the suggestion that the distinction was also relevant in the context of claims for malicious falsehood was said to be "irrelevant and wrong in law".

[47] *Grech v Odhams Press* [1958] 2 Q.B. 275 CA at 313; *London Artists v Littler* [1969] 2 Q.B. 375 CA at 398 (condemning an invitation to bring to the interpretation "a subtlety and perspicacity well beyond that reasonably to be expected of the ordinary reader"); *Smith's Newspapers v Becker* (1932) 47 C.L.R. 279 at 302; *Petritsis v Hellenic Herald* [1978] 2 N.S.W.L.R. 174 at 182; *England v CBC* (1979) 97 D.L.R. (3d) 472; *Harrigan v Jones* [2001] NSWSC 623.

[48] *Telnikoff v Matusevitch* [1992] 2 A.C. 343 at 351; *Branson v Bower* [2001] EWCA Civ 791; [2001] E.M.L.R. 32. Clearly, this will change with the move away from jury trials envisaged under the Defamation Act 2013.

[49] In *Joseph v Spiller* [2010] UKSC 53; [2011] 1 A.C. 852 at [5], Lord Phillips acknowledged that "jurists have had difficulty in defining the difference between a statement of fact and a comment in the context of the defence of fair comment".

practical difficulty in distinguishing comment and fact.[50] The first step is to determine the meaning of what the defendant has said in its context.[51] For this purpose, the law adheres to the normal rule that words are treated as having a single meaning.[52] It is possible to distinguish three general situations:

(1) A statement may be a "pure" statement of evaluative opinion which represents the writer's view on something which cannot be meaningfully verified: for example, "I do not think Jones is attractive".[53]

---

[50] See the differences of judicial opinion in *Crawford v Albu* 1917 A.D. 102, where the words were: "All this strife has been caused by men who are fanatics—no, they are not fanatics—they are criminals in the fullest sense of the word"; the conclusions on the different publications in *Chen Cheng v Central Christian Church* [1999] 1 Sing. L.R. 94 Sing. CA, and the divergence of view between the judge at first instance and the Court of Appeal in *British Chiropractic Association v Singh* [2010] EWCA Civ 350; [2011] 1 W.L.R. 133.

[51] *Burstein v Associated Newspapers Ltd* [2007] EWCA Civ 600; [2007] E.M.L.R. 21; *Lowe v Associated Newspapers Ltd* [2006] EWHC 320 (QB); [2007] Q.B. 580 at [15]. See para.3.13ff, above. By PD 53, para.2.5, when pleading the defence of honest comment, the defendant must, first, set out the defamatory comment contained in the words complained of that he or she intends to defend, and then identify the facts on the basis of which it is asserted that a person could honestly express the relevant comment. The first of these elements is sometimes described as setting out the *Control Risks* meanings (derived from *Control Risks v New English Library* [1990] 1 W.L.R. 183)—e.g. *Ashcroft v Foley* [2011] EWHC 292 (QB) at [60] (upheld on appeal: [2012] EWCA Civ 423; [2012] E.M.L.R. 25); *Schellenberg v BBC* [2000] E.M.L.R. 296 at 304; *Lait v Evening Standard Ltd* [2011] EWCA Civ 859; [2011] 1 W.L.R. 2973 at [14]; *El Naschie v Macmillan Publishers Ltd (t/a Nature Publishing Group)* [2012] EWHC 1809 (QB) at [29]. There is a risk in this usage of conflating the related but distinct tasks of the determination of meaning and the distinguishing of fact from comment. The separateness of these tasks was emphasised in *Buckley v Herald and Weekly Times Pty Ltd* [2008] VSC 459 at [28] per Kaye J.:

"[the] recipient of the publication is not confined to an understanding of the words conveyed in their literal sense; rather . . . the law takes into account that the recipient of the material may indulge in deduction, inference or implication. However, to postulate that an imputation may derive from a publication by a process of implication or inference by the reader or listener of the publication, is not to say that the imputations, thus derived, were understood by the ordinary reasonable reader or listener as the comment or opinion of the publisher. That is, there is an important distinction between inferences or implications by the hypothetical ordinary reasonable reader of the publication complained of, on the one hand, and, on the other hand, an understanding by the ordinary reasonable reader of the publication that imputations, pleaded by a plaintiff, were conveyed to that reader as the opinion or comment of the writer of the articles".

[52] *Lait v Evening Standard Ltd* [2011] EWCA Civ 859; [2011] 1 W.L.R. 2973 at [31]–[35] per Laws L.J. and at [52] per Lord Neuberger M.R.; *Lowe*, above, at [14]; *Simpson v Mair* [2006] BCCA 287; [2006] 10 W.W.R. 460. Lord Cooke had suggested the contrary might be the case in *Next Magazine Publishing Ltd v Ma Ching Fat* [2003] HKCFA 10; [2003] H.K.L.R.D. 751 at [145]. In *Lait*, the Court of Appeal heard an appeal against the granting of summary judgment that had been based on an incontestable defence of honest comment. The court was asked to consider words complained of that might bear any of three different meanings, of which two were particularly at issue in the appeal. Only one of these meanings would be clearly met with an honest comment defence. It was suggested that if the single meaning rule applied, then the judge should have left it to the jury to determine which meaning the words had, and thus whether there was a good defence. The CA found that the single meaning rule did apply, but that where a comment might reasonably be thought to carry a second imputation, not grounded on a sufficient factual basis, the defendant should not normally be held liable for it unless it was maliciously advanced or so grave that the claim should be allowed to go forward. The CA held that the judge had been right to rule that, in light of the ruling on the main meaning, it would be an abuse of process to let the possible additional meaning go forward to trial.

[53] Cf. *Berkoff v Burchill* [1996] 4 All E.R. 1008 CA, para.2.10, above.

(2) A statement which is potentially one of fact or one of evaluative opinion according to the context: for example, "Jones is a disgrace".

(3) A statement which is only capable of being regarded as one of fact and is in no sense one of opinion, but which may be an inference drawn by the writer from other facts: for example, "Jones took a bribe".

Honest comment clearly applies to the first situation.[54] It also obviously applies to the second situation if the statement is best read as an evaluative opinion in the context of the publication as a whole (for example, because the writer has just described some controversial act of Jones).[55]

A statement that may be regarded as an assertion of fact may yet be comment for the purposes of the defence if it comprises an inference from other facts stated or referred to. Though "comment" is often equated with "opinion", this is an over-simplification. Comment is "something which is or can reasonably be inferred to be a deduction, inference, conclusion, criticism, remark, observation, etc.".[56] Hence, the defence can also apply to the third situation above if the statement of fact can be understood as an inference from supporting facts.[57] In this sense, fact and comment are not dichotomous.[58] While it elides any easy distinction between fact and comment, an author can

---

[54] Although it may reasonably be questioned whether such an opinion should ever be actionable at all; whether it differs in any sense from "vulgar abuse". Of course, any publication of the supporting facts on which the evaluative comment is based, if false, may be actionable.

[55] See *Burstein v Associated Newspapers Ltd* [2007] EWCA Civ 600; [2007] E.M.L.R. 21. In *Pervan v North Queensland Newspaper Co Ltd* (1993) 178 C.L.R. 389 HCA, an advertisement published by the defendants read: "Councillors feathering their own nests? Funds being mis-appropriated? This is doing irreparable damage to the image of our shire. It is now more important than ever to attend the ratepayers and residents meeting at the Grand Central Hotel, Tuesday, 12th August at 8pm." This was found to be capable of falling within the defence of honest comment because a legitimate interpretation was that the questions were not merely rhetorical but that the publisher was attempting to raise the accuracy of the charges for public debate.

[56] *Clarke v Norton* [1910] V.L.R. 494 per Cussen J. at 499. Adopted in *Branson v Bower* [2001] EWCA Civ 791; [2001] E.M.L.R. 32; *Skrine v Euromoney Publications Plc* [2001] EWCA Civ 1479; [2002] E.M.L.R. 15 at [26]. *Mitchell v Sprott* [2002] 1 N.Z.L.R. 766 NZCA at [19] ("the defence applies when the words appear to a reasonable reader to be conclusionary"); *Orion Pet Products Pty Ltd v RSPCA (Vic) Inc.* [2002] FCA 860. For a heterodox view that how the words appear to the recipient is to be determined by asking whether the author had authority to make a conclusive decision on the matter of which he speaks see Kirby J. dissenting in *Channel 7 Adelaide Pty Ltd v Manock* [2007] HCA 60; 241 A.L.R. 468.

[57] For instance, in *Branson v Bower* [2001] EWCA Civ 791; [2001] E.M.L.R. 32, a newspaper article was alleged to mean that in making a bid to run the National Lottery the claimant was motivated not by charity but by revenge and financial self-interest. The Court of Appeal held that the judge below was entitled to conclude that this statement was, in its context, one which the jury could only reasonably regard as a comment, because a reader could be in no doubt that the imputation was an inference drawn by the defendant from the facts set out in the article. Yet, the state of a person's mind is unquestionably a fact. Indeed, the criminal courts determine it as a question of fact every day. See also, *Keays v Guardian Newspapers Ltd* [2003] EWHC 1565 (QB); *Nilsen and Johnsen v Norway* (1999) 30 EHRR 878; *Field v Local Sunday Newspapers (North) Ltd* [2002] EWHC 336 (QB) at [82]–[95] (reversed, principally on other grounds, sub nom *Gough v Local Sunday Newspapers (North) Ltd* [2003] EWCA Civ 297; [2003] 1 W.L.R. 1836).

[58] In *British Chiropractic Association v Singh* [2010] EWCA Civ 350; [2011] 1 W.L.R. 133 at [17], one criticism offered by counsel of the decision at first instance was that the judge "treat[ed]

defend as a comment on facts stated or referred to in the publication some
other fact the existence of which he infers or deduces from those facts:

> "Comment may sometimes consist in the statement of a fact, and may be held to be
> comment if the fact so stated appears to be a deduction or conclusion come to by the
> speaker from other facts stated or referred to by him, or in the common knowledge
> of the person speaking and those to whom the words are addressed, and from which
> his conclusion can be reasonably inferred ... If, although stated as a fact, it is
> preceded or accompanied by such other facts, and it can be reasonably based upon
> them, the words may be reasonably regarded as comment, and comment only, and
> if honest and fair, excusable; and whether it is to be regarded as a fact or comment
> is a question for the jury, to be determined by them upon all the circumstances of the
> case."[59]

"Bare comment". On occasion, a statement might be intended as a com-   **12.9**
ment but fails for want of some other element of the defence. For instance, a
publisher might state "on the basis of what I know, Jones is a thief", without
giving any indication of what the underpinning facts are. This situation has
become known as "bare comment".[60] Although it has been recognised that
there are policy reasons either way,[61] such a statement will be treated as a
statement of fact: "a bald comment, made in circumstances where it is not
possible to understand it as an inference ... is likely to be treated as an
assertion of fact which will only be susceptible to a defence of justification or
privilege".[62]

Inferences of verifiable and unverifiable fact. An inference from other   **12.10**
facts may involve an inferred fact that is essentially verifiable or unverifiable.
This has sometimes been treated as the dividing line between statements of
fact and comments, with defendants being required to prove the truth of
inferences of verifiable fact. In *Hamilton v Clifford*, for instance, the defendant—having made statements which were held capable of bearing the meaning that there were reasonable grounds to suspect the claimants of
criminality—sought to rely on a plea of honest comment that presented the

---

'verifiable fact' as antithetical to comment, so that any assertion which ranks as the former cannot
qualify as the latter. This ... is a false dichotomy".

[59] *O'Brien v Salisbury* (1889) 54 J.P. 215 at 216 per Field J. See also, *Channel 7 Adelaide Pty
Ltd v Manock* [2007] HCA 60; 241 A.L.R. 468 at [35].

[60] *Joseph v Spiller* [2010] UKSC 53; [2011] 1 A.C. 852 at [5] and [87]–[89].

[61] In *Joseph v Spiller* ibid. at [88], Lord Phillips commented that
"the damage that such a comment can do is relatively limited. Actions speak louder than words.
Most people judge their fellow men by the way that they behave, not on the basis of general
opinions expressed by others. The common law might have held that bare comments were not
actionable at all. Or it might have held that a defence of fair comment would lie in respect of
a bare comment provided that the defendant could identify the factual basis for his comment
by giving evidence of what it was that he had had in mind. It did not, however, take either
course".

[62] *Lowe v Associated Newspapers Ltd* [2006] EWHC 320 (QB); [2007] Q.B. 580 at [55] per
Eady J.; *Joseph v Spiller* [2010] UKSC 53; [2011] 1 A.C. 852 per Lord Phillips at [5]; "for such
a comment the defence of fair comment does not run".

statement as an inference from the fact of the police investigation into the claimants.[63] Eady J. struck out the defence. In his view, the allegation made by the defendant was verifiable and thus had to be treated as one of fact.[64] He distinguished *Branson v Bower* on the basis that what was in issue in that case had been the nature of the claimant's motive for his actions, something which, although a question of fact, was unverifiable as an objective matter.[65] In *British Chiropractic Association v Singh*, having classified the published remarks as factual assertions rather than the mere expression of opinion, Eady J. stated that "one is not permitted to seek shelter behind a defence of fair comment when the defamatory sting is one of verifiable fact. Here the allegations are plainly verifiable and that is the subject of the defence of justification . . . an issue capable of resolution in the light of the evidence called . . . is a matter of verifiable fact".[66]

In other cases, courts have appeared to be less reluctant to hold that inferences of verifiable fact could be dealt with as comment. In *Jeyaretnam v Goh Chok Tong*, for example, the Privy Council appeared to have no difficulty in holding that a statement that the plaintiff had engineered a supposedly spontaneous exodus of the audience at a meeting was capable of being

---

[63] [2004] EWHC 1542 (QB).

[64] In refusing permission to appeal, Pill L.J. said that it was not arguable that Eady J. had been wrong on this issue: [2004] EWCA Civ 1407 at [22]. This approach would appear to be supported by the formulation in *London Artists v Littler* [1968] 1 W.L.R. 607 at 621: "in comment is included inference, provided it appears that the writer is offering the inference as no more than his personal opinion and not as an assertion of fact from his premises". See also, *Fawcett v John Fairfax Publications Pty Ltd* [2008] NSWSC 139; *Nilsen and Johnsen v Norway* (1999) 30 EHRR 878 at [50]. On the facts of *Hamilton*, it is not difficult to see why a court would wish to be cautious about treating such an inference as comment. If it were comment to say, "the police are taking this charge against C seriously and because in my view the police do not waste their time that probably means that C is guilty", that would make a large inroad into the repetition rule. Far from the defendant having to prove that C was guilty, the claimant would be faced with the burden of showing that the defendant's belief in C's guilt was not his honest opinion. Of course, the whole affair upon which the allegation of suspicion of criminality was based was shown to be a figment of the "victim's" imagination.

[65] This basis for distinguishing *Branson v Bower* was further explained by Eady J. in *Pena v Tameside Hospital NHS Foundation Trust* [2011] EWHC 3027 (QB) at [27]:
"attribution of motive can often, depending on context, be properly classified as comment. It is true, of course, that the state of a man's mind can also, on occasion, be regarded as being as much a fact as the state of his stomach. On the other hand, we can rarely establish definitively what is going on in the mind of another person and are thus dependent on inference. Where it is clear to a listener or reader that someone is drawing an inference as to another person's motivation, it is reasonable to classify whatever he has to say in that context as comment rather than fact".

[66] [2009] EWHC 1101 (QB) at [14]. The words complained of were that:
"the British Chiropractic Association claims that their members can help treat children with colic, sleeping and feeding problems, frequent ear infections, asthma and prolonged crying, even though there is not a jot of evidence. This organization is the respectable face of the chiropractic profession and yet it happily promotes bogus treatments".
The judge read these words as "the plainest allegation of dishonesty." The Court of Appeal overturned Eady J.'s decision that the words complained of were facts: *British Chiropractic Association v Singh* [2010] EWCA Civ 350; [2011] 1 W.L.R. 133. On dishonesty as a provable fact, see also *Harounoff v Baker* [2012] EWHC 1443 (QB) at [37].

comment.[67] While that might be difficult to verify, it is hard to see how it could be regarded as "unverifiable". The issue was referred to explicitly by the Court of Appeal in *British Chiropractic Association v Singh* as counsel presented a direct challenge to the "unwarranted verifiable fact test" that had been deployed at first instance.[68] The court considered that there was "force in [this] critique", but proceeded to determine the appeal on the basis that in the context of publication the words complained of could only be comment.[69] In *Spiller v Joseph*, Lord Phillips was even more circumspect. He noted the divergence of opinion in the jurisprudence before stating that:

> "careful consideration needs to be given to . . . [the] proposition that the defence of fair comment should extend to inferences of fact. Jurisprudence both in this jurisdiction and at Strasbourg . . . has held that allegations of motive, which is inherently incapable of verification, can constitute comment. Some decisions have gone further and treated allegations of verifiable fact as comment . . . it is questionable whether this is satisfactory. Prejudiced commentators can draw honest inferences of fact, such as that a man charged with fraud is guilty of fraud. Should the defence of fair comment apply to such inferences? Allegations of fact can be far more damaging, even if plainly based on inference, than comments on true facts".[70]

This is an issue ripe for judicial determination. Indeed, it is to be regretted that the Court of Appeal in *Singh* did not grasp the nettle and explain whether the divide between verifiable and unverifiable fact is the border between fact and comment; whether inferences of verifiable fact can be the subject matter of a defence of honest comment. The division between verifiable and unverifiable fact is one possible determinant of when the defence of honest comment should cease to be available. There may be policy reasons in favour of such a conclusion, but if so these need to be set out with some clarity. If the ability of an audience to recognise words as comment is key, then it is not obvious why the verifiability or otherwise of the inference should be important. It might be suggested that prejudiced or unwarranted inferences from supporting facts—when recognisable—are generally appreciated as such, with the "fall-out" landing on the speaker rather than his or her subject.

Importance of context. Words must always be read in their context and **12.11** the context of the piece as a whole may point to the conclusion that words which could, taken literally, be a statement of fact, are comment. It has been said that comment is often distinguished by the use of metaphor,[71] but a jury

---

[67] [1989] 1 W.L.R. 1109. It was doubted in *Joseph v Spiller* (above) at [114] whether the Privy Council's preparedness to treat an inference of verifiable fact as comment was satisfactory.

[68] *British Chiropractic Association v Singh* [2010] EWCA Civ 350; [2011] 1 W.L.R. 133 at [8].

[69] Ibid. at [20]–[30].

[70] [2010] UKSC 53; [2011] 1 A.C. 852 at [114].

[71] *Grech v Odhams Press* [1958] 2 Q.B. 275 CA at; *Churchill v Ainsworth, The Times*, October 10, 1956, *Associated Leisure v Associated Newspapers* [1970] 2 Q.B. 450 at 455–456.

is not obliged to treat simile as comment.[72] Matter in editorials or leaders is perhaps more likely to be treated as comment than matter in news stories,[73] and a fortiori in a "Comment" section,[74] though the heading is not of course conclusive.[75] Headlines may clearly be comment[76] but there is no reason for any presumption to that effect.[77] It has been said that a statement cast in the form of a prophecy of future events cannot rank as anything other than comment,[78] but it is possible that such a statement might contain an implied imputation of present defamatory fact.[79] The fact that the words are introduced by expressions such as "in my opinion" may be an indication that they are comment, but is not of itself sufficient to make them so.[80] To say, "in my opinion Jones is a thief" clearly carries the implication that the defendant has some knowledge of wrongdoing upon which that opinion is based.[81] Unless clearly an inference from other facts stated or referred to, this would require justification by proof that Jones *is* a thief.

A particular type of publication that can cause difficulty is the review. Often in such publications, assertions are made that, read literally, appear to state hard facts. It is unlikely, however, that a reader of a restaurant review would regard a statement that a dish was "inedible" as meaning that it was unfit for human consumption rather than being, in the reviewer's opinion, unpalatable.[82] In *Burstein v Associated Newspapers Ltd*, the Court of Appeal granted

---

[72] *Truth (NZ) v Avery* [1959] N.Z.L.R. 274 at 292.

[73] *Marais v Richard*, 1979 (1) S.A. 83 at 89. See also e.g. *Waterson v Lloyd* [2011] EWHC 3197 (QB) at [43], although on appeal Richards L.J. stated that on the facts, that is the wider context of the party political nature of the publications in question, little weight should have been afforded to this issue: [2013] EWCA Civ 136; [2013] E.M.L.R. 17 at [42].

[74] *Keays v Guardian Newspapers Ltd* [2003] EWHC 1565 (QB); *John Fairfax Publications Pty Ltd v O'Shane* [2005] NSWCA 164.

[75] In *British Chiropractic Association v Singh* [2010] EWHC 1101 at [14], Eady J. found there to be statements of fact "despite the fact that the words complained of appear[ed] under a general heading 'comment and debate'", and noted that "it is a question of substance rather than labelling".

[76] *Kemsley v Foot* [1952] A.C. 345.

[77] For the dangers of punchy headlines, the "eye-catching imperative", see *Galloway v Telegraph Group Ltd* [2004] EWHC 2786 (QB); [2005] E.M.L.R. 7 at [181].

[78] *Renouf v Federal Capital Press* (1977) 17 A.C.T.R. 35 at 41.

[79] For instance, if D were to write, "now that C has been appointed treasurer members may expect shortages in the funds" that would seem to be an imputation of dishonesty or incompetence. The subtlety of the distinction between fact and comment in this context is illustrated by *Grant v Torstar Corp, Toronto Star Newspapers Ltd* [2009] SCC 61. One of the imputations was that an application for development approval was a "done deal", the context being that the plaintiff had political influence. The SCC said that it was arguable that this was a comment as "an idiomatic expression of an opinion about the *likelihood* of something, namely government approval, that had not yet come to pass" (at [137]). Alternatively, "it can be taken as an assertion that government approval for the development was actually already sealed, either formally behind closed doors or by tacit understanding" (at [139]). Arguably, this it is not simply a matter of futurity: if read as meaning "his political influence is so great that it is bound to happen", the words would appear to be a statement of present fact.

[80] "Prima facie" may be a weak indicator of comment: *Oversea Chinese Banking Corp v Wright Norman* [1994] 3 S.L.R. 760.

[81] An example given in *Milkovich v Lorain Journal*, 497 U.S. 1 (1990).

[82] *Convery v Irish News* [2008] NICA 14 at [34].

summary judgment to the defendant on the basis that it would be perverse to regard the words—a review of an opera which was held to be "just" capable of meaning that the author admired terrorism—as anything other than comment.

> "Insofar as the final sentence in the review might be said to be capable of being read as a statement of fact, it was patently intended as a summary of and a commentary on the factual description of the opera set out in the preceding part of the review . . . Moreover, the words complained of were contained in a review by a critic, as any reader would appreciate, and which the reader would expect to contain a subjective commentary by the critic."[83]

None of this is to suggest, of course, that a straightforward allegation of fact can never be published in such a context.

Context provided by the particular publication only. The judge or jury is confined to the context of the particular publication in respect of which the action is brought. It is not legitimate to look outside the publication in which the statement complained of is made for "wider" context. In *Telnikoff v Matusevitch*, the plaintiff wrote an article critical of the recruitment policy of the BBC Russian service, and the defendant responded with a letter to the editor of the newspaper accusing him of racism.[84] If the letter alone was looked at, the statement was capable of being read as an assertion of fact,[85] but if looked at along with the article was plainly comment. The majority of the House of Lords held that the question had to be judged solely in the context of the letter.[86] The decision does not mean that the defence of honest comment in such circumstances is confined to those passages which are set out in the criticism,[87] for it is clearly established that the supporting facts may be indicated by reference.[88] What is necessary is that language must be used which conveys to the reader who has not read the article that is the subject of

12.12

---

[83] [2007] EWCA Civ 600; [2007] E.M.L.R. 21 at [22] per Keene L.J. The importance of looking at the words in the context of the whole statement rather than engaging in a linguistic analysis of them in isolation is also emphasised in *Television New Zealand Ltd v Haines* [2006] 2 N.Z.L.R. 433. See also *Mitchell v Sprott* [2002] 1 N.Z.L.R. 766 at 772.

[84] [1992] 2 A.C. 343; *Oversea Chinese Banking Corp v Wright Norman* [1994] 3 S.L.R. 760.

[85] Or so thought Glidewell and Woolf L.JJ. and the majority of the House of Lords. Lloyd L.J. thought the words could only be comment, even if interpreted in the restricted context of the letter: see [1991] 1 Q.B. 102.

[86] Hence, the case should not have been withdrawn from the jury on the ground that the defence of honest comment was bound to succeed as there was no evidence of malice. *Kemsley v Foot* [1952] A.C. 345 was distinguished on the ground that it was never contended in that case that the words were other than comment, the issue being whether there was any reference to facts supporting the comment. However, it is not clear that Lord Porter in *Kemsley v Foot* would have regarded these as two different issues.

[87] So much is conceded in the dissent offered by Lord Ackner, though he suggests that it would be "forensically expedient to set out, *ipsissima verba*, the entire contents" of the article: [1992] 2 A.C. 343 at 361.

[88] See para.12.24, below.

criticism, that the defendant is commenting on what the writer of the article has said, rather than recounting what he has said.[89]

12.13 Comment and fact confused. Occasionally, a publisher will fail to distinguish clearly between the facts on which the intended comment is made, and the comment that is made on those facts. In such circumstances, the audience for the publication might be expected to regard the words either as statements of fact or as seeming to be comment founded upon unrevealed information in the possession of the publisher (bare comment). The publication may then stand in the same position as any ordinary allegation of fact.[90] Where the comment is not clearly identified there is a tendency to hold the entire statement to be one of fact.[91] In *Hunt v Star Newspaper*, Fletcher-Moulton L.J. explained that:

> "In the first place, comment in order to be justifiable as fair comment must appear as comment and must not be so mixed up with the facts that the reader cannot distinguish between what is report and what is comment: see *Andrews v. Chapman* [(1853) 3 C. & K. 286 at 288]. The justice of this rule is obvious. If the facts are stated separately and the comment appears as an inference drawn from those facts, any injustice that it might do will be to some extent negatived by the reader seeing the grounds upon which the unfavourable inference is based. But if fact and comment be intermingled so that it is not reasonably clear what portion purports to be inference, he will naturally suppose that the injurious statements are based on adequate grounds known to the writer, though not necessarily set out by him. In the one case the insufficiency of the facts to support the inference will lead fair-minded men to reject the inference. In the other case it merely points to the existence of extrinsic facts which the writer considers to warrant the language he uses . . . Any matter, therefore, which does not indicate with a reasonable clearness that it purports to be comment, and not statement of fact, cannot be protected by the plea of fair comment."[92]

12.14 Defamation Act 2013: retention of the rule on recognisability. The first condition for the new statutory defence is stated in s.3(2). This provides

---

[89] [1992] 2 A.C. 343 at 356.

[90] For a vigorous pronouncement on journalism which does not separate fact from defamatory expressions of opinion, see *Smith's Newspapers v Becker* (1932) 47 C.L.R. 279 at 303. Cf. *Jones v Bennett* (1967) 59 W.W.R. 449 at 459; [1969] S.C.R. 277; *Telegraph Newspapers v Bedford* (1934) 50 C.L.R. 632 at 653; *Antonovich v WA Newspapers* [1960] W.A.R. 176 at 180; *Ager v Canjex Publishing Ltd* [2005] BCCA 467; 259 D.L.R. (4th) 727.

[91] *Australian Ocean Line v Western Australia Newspapers* (1985) 58 A.L.R. 549 Fed Ct of Australia at 594.

[92] [1908] 2 K.B. 309 CA at 319–320. This dictum was commented on in *Kemsley v Foot* [1952] A.C. at 359–360, and cited with approval in *London Artists v Littler* [1969] 2 Q.B. 375 CA at 395. It should be read in the light of what was said of it in *Kemsley v Foot* [1952] A.C. 345 at 359–360, where they were thought not to controvert the view that the facts on which comment was made could be implied from the terms of the publication if indicated with sufficient clarity. Thus, it is not the case that the publication must contain within itself all the material needed in order for the reader to decide whether the comment was justified. It should be noted, however, that parts of the passage in *Hunt* proceed on a different assumption from that taken in *Lowe v Associated Newspapers Ltd* [2006] EWHC 320 (QB); [2007] Q.B. 580 to the effect that the function of any facts stated in the article is not to enable the reader to make a judgment but to indicate that the words are comment.

that for the defence to be available the defendant must show that "the statement complained of was a statement of opinion". This would appear to retain the existing common law rules. Indeed, that result is presaged in the Explanatory Notes to the Act:

> "condition 1 is intended to reflect the current law and embraces the requirement . . . that the statement must be recognisable as comment as distinct from an imputation of fact. It is implicit in condition 1 that the assessment is on the basis of how the ordinary person would understand it".[93]

The Explanatory Notes also state that "as an inference of fact is a form of opinion, this would be encompassed by the defence".[94] There is no differentiation here between inferences of verifiable and inferences of unverifiable fact.[95] This is suggestive of an inclusive approach, although such a note can hardly be determinative of the question of whether the courts will in future take one view or the other on the question of whether that dichotomy provides the fault line between opinion and fact.

Section 3. Based on True or Privileged Facts

Basic rule: facts must be true. One of the five tests set out in *Joseph v   **12.15** Spiller* is that the facts that are said to underpin a comment must be true or privileged.[96] Examples are legion.[97] The truth of the supporting facts must be

---

[93] Explanatory Notes to the Defamation Act 2013 at [21].
[94] Ibid.
[95] See para.12.10, above.
[96] See para.12.2, above. See also *Hunt v Star Newspaper* [1908] 2 K.B. 309 at 320 per Fletcher Moulton L.J. ("in order to give room for the plea of fair comment the facts must be truly stated. If the facts upon which the comment purports to be made do not exist the foundation of the plea fails"); *Joynt v Cycle Trade Co* [1904] 2 K.B. 292 at 294 per Kennedy J. ("the comment must not misstate facts, because a comment cannot be fair which is built upon facts which are not truly stated"). The latter was quoted with approval by Cozens-Hardy M.R. and Fletcher Moulton L.J. in *Hunt v Star Newspaper* [1908] 2 K.B. 309 CA at 317 and 320, and by Vaughan Williams L.J. in *Peter Walker Ltd v Hodgson* [1909] 1 K.B. 239 CA at 252; *Burton v Board* [1929] 1 K.B. 301 CA; *Kemsley v Foot* [1952] A.C. 345. For a discussion of reliance on privileged facts, see para.12.21, below.
[97] For instance, in *Russell v Pawley* [1987] 3 W.W.R. 442 Man. CA, a minister published a statement criticising the plaintiff civil servant for assisting a political group while on sick leave when in fact he was seriously ill and on unpaid leave. In *Davis v Shepstone* (1886) 11 A.C. 187 PC, the defendants published serious allegations concerning a purported assault perpetrated by the Resident Commissioner of Zululand and allied this reporting with severely critical commentary. In fact, the allegations were absolutely without foundation, and no attempt had been made to support them by evidence. Similarly, if a critic, in reviewing a book or a play, were to misquote from it, or misdescribe its contents, the defence of honest comment would fail—*Tabart v Tipper* (1808) 1 Camp. 350; *Merivale v Carson* (1887) 20 Q.B.D. 275 CA; *Marks v Sunday Times Co* (1915) 15 N.S.W.S.R. 490; *Wilson v Manawatu Daily Times* [1957] N.Z.L.R. 735; *O'Shaughnessy v Mirror Newspapers* (1970) 125 C.L.R. 166; *Thornton v Telegraph Media Group Ltd* [2009] EWHC 2863 (QB); [2012] E.M.L.R. 8.

established by the defendant.[98] Moreover, if these purported facts are themselves defamatory, the defendant may have to plead justification also.[99] A writer may not suggest or invent facts, or treat as true the untrue statements of fact made by others,[100] and then comment on them on the assumption that they are true. If the facts upon which the comment purports to be made do not exist, the defence of fair comment must fail.[101] Comment based on matters of opinion only, which may or may not be true, equally affords no defence.[102] The requirement that a defendant prove the facts that underpin a comment has been held to be not incompatible with art.10.[103]

---

[98] *Branson v Bower* [2002] Q.B. 737 at 748–749 per Eady J. (on appeal [2001] EWCA Civ 791; [2001] E.M.L.R. 32):
"When the . . . question [whether the facts on which the comment is based are true] can be answered will obviously vary from case to case. Sometimes the facts themselves will be uncontroversial and the point at issue is simply whether the opinion could be held or the inference drawn. On other occasions, there may be no doubt that on certain factual assumptions a defamatory opinion could be honestly expressed, but the truth of those assumptions can only be established at trial. In this latter case, there does not seem to be any reason as a matter of logic why the court should not rule that the objective test for a fair comment defence has been satisfied . . . while leaving the jury to decide whether the defendant has proved the facts . . . and, if so, whether he was malicious . . . It may not always be a practical option, on the other hand, for a judge to resolve the objective test where the facts cannot be determined as a black and white issue (for example, whether or not the particular claimant had been guilty of stealing the petty cash)."
[99] *Broadway Approvals v Odhams Press* [1965] 1 W.L.R. 805 CA, approving *Truth (NZ) Ltd v Avery* [1959] N.Z.L.R. 289. See also, *Peter Walker Ltd v Hodgson* [1909] 1 K.B. 239 CA at 256 per Kennedy L.J. ("where the words which are alleged to be defamatory allege, or assume as true, facts concerning the plaintiff which the plaintiff denies, and which either involve a slanderous imputation in themselves, or upon which the comment bases imputations or inferences injurious to the plaintiff, it is settled law that the defence of fair comment fails unless the comment is truthful in regard to its allegation or assumption of such facts"); *R. v Carden* (1879) 5 Q.B.D. 1 at 8 per Cockburn C.J. ("to say that you may first libel a man and then comment upon him is obviously absurd").
[100] *Galloway v Telegraph Group Ltd* [2004] EWHC 2786 (QB); [2005] E.M.L.R. 7 at [45]. See also [2006] EWCA Civ 17; [2006] E.M.L.R. 11 at [88].
[101] *Lefroy v Burnside (No.2)* (1879) 4 L.R.Ir. 556 at 565–566. See also *Davis v Shepstone* (1886) 11 A.C. 187 per curiam PC at 190; *London Artists v Littler* [1969] 2 Q.B. 375 CA; *Stewart v M Kinley* (1885) 9 V.L.R. 802; *Clancy v Roland* [1923] 2 D.L.R. 288 Man CA; *Boys v Star Printing & Publishing* [1927] 3 D.L.R. 847 Ont. CA; *Morgenstern v Oakville Record Star* (1962) 33 D.L.R. (2d) 354; *Lawson v Burns* (1975) 56 D.L.R. (3d) 240; *Holt v Sun Publishing* (1979) 100 D.L.R. (3d) 447 ("definite discrepancy" between facts stated and what happened); *Planned Parenthood Federation v Fedorik* (1982) 135 D.L.R. (3d) 714; *Christie v Geiger* (1984) 35 Alta. L.R. (2d) 316; *Hasnul bin Abdul Hadi v Bulat bin Mohamed* [1978] I M.L.J. 75; *Price Waterhouse Intrust v Wee Choo Keng* [1994] 3 S.L.R. 801 Sing. CA; *Tse Wai Chun v Cheng* [2000] HKCFA 86; [2001] E.M.L.R 31 at [18], per Lord Nicholls; *Versace v Monte* [2002] FCA 190; *Rogacki v Belz* (2004) 243 D.L.R. (4th) 585 Ont. CA. Again, this point is made subject to the right to comment on privileged facts—see para.12.21, below.
[102] *Shenkman v O'Malley*, 157 N.Y.S. (2d) 290 (1956) at 295–296; *Thomas v CBC* [1981] 4 W.W.R. 289; *Australian Ocean Lines v Western Australia Newspapers* (1985) 58 A.L.R. 549 Fed Ct of Australia.
[103] *Alithia Publishing Co Ltd v Cyprus* App. no.17550/03, May 22, 2008 at [69]. The case was based on the law of Cyprus, where the defence of honest comment appears to have been basically the same as English law. The ECtHR said that,
"even where a statement amounts to a value judgment, there must exist a sufficient factual basis to support it, failing which a value judgment may be excessive . . . The Court considers that

Misstatement and omission of facts. The omission of a highly relevant   **12.16**
fact may amount to a misstatement of the supporting facts: "it is not comment ... grossly to misrepresent the conduct of a public man, and then to
hold him up to execration for his alleged wrong-doing".[104] The defence of
honest comment will fail if the defendant omits from the statement of facts on
which the comment purports to be based some important fact that would
falsify or alter the complexion of the facts that are stated. For example, if A
states that B was convicted by a jury of a serious crime and comments
adversely on the fact, but omits to state that the conviction was quashed by the
Court of Appeal, then the defence will not be available.[105] Comment on facts
inaccurately reported cannot be honest comment,[106] as "in those circumstances ... the underlying factual substratum of the comment ... would have
collapsed".[107]

Extent of proof required: common law. At common law it has been   **12.17**
thought necessary for the defendant to prove that all the allegations of fact in
the words complained of are true, and that the comment upon those facts is
bona fide and honest comment on a matter of public interest.[108] Thus, if a
defendant failed to prove the truth of any of the statements of fact, he or she
necessarily failed in his defence.[109] The position was different where the facts
on which the comment was alleged to be based were contained not in the
defamatory words complained of, but instead were merely indicated in the
words and then provided in the particulars of defence in the action. In such a
case:

---

it is not, in principle, incompatible with art.10 to place the onus of proving, to the civil
standard, the truth of the factual basis on which a value judgment was based."

[104] *Christie v Robertson* (1889) 10 N.S.W.L.R. 157 at 163 per Windeyer J.

[105] *Harris v White Ltd* (1926) O.P.D. 104; *Branson v Bower* [2002] Q.B. 737 at [36]–[39]. In
Creative Salmon Co Ltd v Staniford [2009] BCCA 61 at [61] this illustration was said to
exemplify the general principle that:
"the requirement to state the facts truly means in the present context that the commentator may
not omit to state important or material facts that would falsify or alter the complexion of the
facts stated in the commentary. It is not necessary to state all facts of a nature that may
influence the opinion of the person hearing or reading the commentary. In order to defeat the
defence, the omitted facts must be sufficiently fundamental that they undermine the accuracy
of the facts expressed in the commentary to the extent the stated facts cannot be properly
regarded as a true statement of the facts."

[106] *Williams v Spowers* (1882) 8 V.L.R. 85, approved in *Stewart v M'Kinless* (1885) 11 V.L.R.
802 at 806.

[107] *Branson v Bower* [2002] Q.B. 737 at [37]. Failure to mention relevant facts does not go to
the question of whether words may be recognisable as comment, or to the objective test of
capability. However, a deliberate failure to mention known exculpatory facts may evidence malice
(at [38]).

[108] *Sutherland v Stopes* [1925] A.C. 47 at 62–63, 99–100; *Burton v Board* [1929] 1 K.B. 301;
Kemsley v Foot [1952] A.C. 345; *ABC v Comalco* (1986) 68 A.L.R. 259 per Neaves and Smithers
JJ., Fed Ct of Australia.

[109] E.g. *Peter Walker Ltd v Hodgson* [1909] 1 K.B. at 256 CA; *Kemsley v Foot* [1952] A.C. 345
at 357.

"Twenty facts might be given in the particulars and only one justified, yet if that one fact were sufficient to support the comment so as to make it fair, a failure to prove the other nineteen would not of necessity defeat the defendant's plea."[110]

It may be questioned whether so sharp a distinction should be made between cases in which the facts are stated in the publication and those in which extrinsic facts supporting the comment are included in particulars. Arguably, honest comment should accord with the defence of justification where it is enough that the facts stated and sued on are substantially accurate. After all, art.10 allows for some degree of exaggeration and inaccuracy in journalism.[111]

12.18 Extent of proof required: Defamation Act 1952. In s.6 of the Defamation Act 1952, it is provided that:

"In an action for libel or slander in respect of words consisting partly of allegations of fact and partly of expression of opinion, a defence of fair comment shall not fail by reason only that the truth of every allegation of fact is not proved if the expression of opinion is fair comment having regard to such of the facts alleged or referred to in the words complained of as are proved."[112]

This provision did not alter the rule that honest comment is a defence to comment only.[113] The section does not require that all the facts upon which the comment is made are proven substantially true, although that will often be its effect.[114] Rather, the defendant must prove the truth of enough of the supporting facts for the comment to be said to be honest (in the sense of being an opinion that an honest person could hold on those facts). The court is only concerned with the comment in the statement complained of: if that is fair in relation to such of the facts on which it is based as are proved, the defence of honest comment is made out. It is in principle irrelevant whether the facts which are proved true are a substantial part of the facts relied on. Substantial inaccuracies may be evidence of malice, however, and in any event the allegation of a number of facts which cannot be substantiated may make the jury disinclined to believe that the comment was honestly made on the basis of what can be established.

---

[110] *Kemsley v Foot*, ibid. at 358.

[111] *Lowe v Associated Newspapers Ltd* [2006] EWHC 320 (QB); [2007] Q.B. 580 at [35].

[112] See also the same wording in s.8 of the New Zealand Defamation Act 1954, discussed in *Truth (NZ) Ltd v Avery* [1959] N.Z.L.R. 274 and applied *Derrett v Christchurch Press* [1976] N.Z. Recent Law 172 (now replaced by the defence of honest opinion in s.9 of the New Zealand Defamation Act 1992; the equivalent provision is in s.11). See further, *Anders v Gas*, *The Times*, March 1, 1960 per Ashworth J. ("the new section was introduced to protect a defendant whose conduct was fair, who might get a date or place wrong, or misrepresent an incident—nonetheless it would be fair comment if his conduct was fair").

[113] *Broadway Approvals v Odhams Press* [1964] 2 Q.B. 683 (Lawton J.) and [1965] 1 W.L.R. 805 CA at 818 per Sellers L.J. approving *Truth (NZ) Ltd v Avery*, ibid. See also, *London Artists v Littler* [1969] 2 Q.B. 375 CA.

[114] *London Artists v Littler*, ibid. at 391–392 per Lord Denning M.R. (the defendant must "prove the basic facts to be true").

Scope of section 6 and relationship with the common law. The scope   12.19
of s.6 and its relationship with the common law are not wholly clear. The
section applies to "an action . . . in respect of words consisting partly of
allegations of fact and partly of expression of opinion". The case to which it
undoubtedly applies is that where the words complained of contain defamatory allegations of fact and defamatory comment. The charges of fact must be
substantially justified (including, where necessary, by reliance on s.5 of the
Act),[115] and must be shown to be sufficiently true to support the comment
under s.6. It does not, however, appear to apply to a case such as *Kemsley v
Foot*,[116] where the only "fact" stated in the publication was an indication of
the subject-matter of the comment. This does not matter as the common law
allows the defence to succeed on the basis of any proven particulars which are
a sufficient basis for the comment.[117]

Another scenario is possible where this route cannot be taken, and where
the section cannot be applied without some strain. The words published may
contain a number of severable allegations of fact and it is then open to the
claimant to choose those on which he sues. Section 5 of the 1952 Act does not
displace this.[118] The claimant accordingly might sue on only some of the
imputations and on the comment. The allegations of fact omitted by the
claimant may be those which are most directly relevant as a basis for
the comment. If so, s.6 does not literally apply because it only allows the
comment to be judged by "such of the facts alleged or referred to *in the words
complained of* as are proved." One case seems to support this view.[119] In
another, where s.6 was not in issue, however, it was said that s.6 was probably
not so restricted as s.5.[120] The section could even be read as inapplicable
where the supporting facts are fully set out in the publication, and it is only the
comment which is defamatory, for the facts are again not "the words complained of".

It may be that the common law has now advanced far enough to cover this
case, but it seems strange that one should have to revert to this when the
statute was supposed to clarify and reform the law of honest comment. It is
submitted that reliance on the defence should not be restricted by artificialities
of pleading (especially bearing in mind that if the defendant merely "indicates
his subject matter", he has a free run on the introduction of relevant material
by way of particulars).

In this context it may be worth recalling the alternative form of s.6, which
was proposed in 1975.[121] This would have provided that:

---

[115] See para.11.16, above.
[116] [1952] A.C. 345.
[117] See para.12.21, below.
[118] See para.11.16, above.
[119] *United States Tobacco International Inc. v BBC* [1998] E.M.L.R. 816 CA at 825, 830.
[120] *Polly Peck (Holdings) v Trelford* [1986] Q.B. 1000 CA at 1033.
[121] Faulks Committee, Cmnd.5909 (1975), at paras 171–175.

"in an action for defamation in respect of words including or consisting of expression of opinion, a defence of [fair] comment shall not fail by reason only that the defendant has failed to prove the truth of very relevant assertion of fact relied on by him as a foundation for the opinion, provided that such of the said assertions as are proved to be true are relevant and afford a foundation therefor".[122]

Perhaps in view of art.10, the existing provision could be read in this way under s.3 of the Human Rights Act 1998.

12.20 Defamation Act 2013: rationalisation of the truth requirement. The third condition set out in the new statutory defence of honest opinion recasts the requirement that the comment must be based on facts which are true or protected by privilege. Section 3(4) will require the defendant to show that "an honest person could have held the opinion on the basis of (a) any fact which existed at the time the statement complained of was published; (b) anything asserted to be a fact in a privileged statement published before the statement complained of". As with the second statutory condition regarding indication of the basis of the opinion, the Explanatory Notes state that the aim of the legislation is "to simplify the law by providing a clear and straightforward test", while "retain[ing] the broad principles of the current common law defence".[123] The meaning of the provision, and its ramifications for the operation of the honest opinion defence relative to its common law forebear, are relatively difficult to discern. The difficulty arises in large measure from the apparent conflation of the third and fifth requirements set out in *Spiller v Joseph*.[124]

It is clear that the requirement that the supporting facts be true or privileged is retained. Use of the word "fact" without qualification must entail that the facts exist; that is, they must be demonstrated to be true facts. The drafters have sought to require only the minimum factual basis, through use of the phrase "any fact" and the requirement that an honest person would have been able to hold the opinion on the basis of the fact in question.[125] Interpreted in line with the stated intentions of the drafters, this provision may allow the courts to preserve and extend the benefits of s.6 of the 1952 Act, and avoid the limitations of the existing common law.[126] For this to be the result, however, it may be that the phrase "any fact" will have to be interpreted so as to mean "any of the facts on which the claimant has based his or her opinion". It will

---

[122] Though departing from traditional terminology, this seems to be the effect of the Australian uniform legislation. The defence of honest opinion covers an opinion based on "proper material". Proper material includes material which is substantially true and an opinion "does not cease to be based on proper material only because some of the material on which it is based is not proper material if the opinion might reasonably be based on such of the material as is proper material". See, for example, the Defamation Act 2005 (NSW), s.31.

[123] Ibid. at [22].

[124] See para.12.2, above.

[125] Explanatory Notes to the Defamation Act 2013, at [23].

[126] S.6 of the Defamation Act 1952 will be abolished under s.3(8) when the 2013 Act comes into force.

no doubt be argued that there must be some link between the fact expressed to be the basis of the opinion and the fact relied on under s.3(4); otherwise an opinion expressed on facts which were plainly false could be defended by reference to other facts wholly unconnected to the words complained of. However, if the provision is construed literally, then contrary to the stated intention broadly to reflect the common law the new provision could have profound and far-reaching ramifications. It would, for example, enable a defendant who had stated an opinion on the basis of wholly false facts to succeed in his defence if he was able to discover, after the event, some fact of which he previously had no knowledge, and which perhaps related to a wholly different and distant phase of the claimant's life, on which an honest person could have based the comment.

Comment on privileged statement. The foregoing discussion has pro-   **12.21**
ceeded on the premise that the factual basis for comment must be proved true. In fact, privileged statements can also provide the necessary basis at common law. The rule that a defence of honest comment will fail unless the facts commented on are truly stated, does not apply where comment is made on matters stated on a privileged occasion,[127] for example in a parliamentary paper,[128] or report,[129] or judicial proceedings.[130] However, the commentator who seeks to rely upon a privileged statement which he is unable to show to be true must give a fair and accurate account of the occasion on which the statement was made.[131] If the statement has been shown to be untrue, and the commentator is aware of this but uses it as a basis for comment, then the defence might fail on the ground of malice.[132]

---

[127] In *Galloway v Telegraph Group Ltd* [2004] EWHC 2786 (QB); [2005] E.M.L.R. 7, the honest comment defence based on the defendants' own articles fell with the privilege defence.
[128] *Mangena v Wright* [1909] 2 K.B. 958.
[129] *Wason v Walter* (1868) L.R. 4 Q.B. 73.
[130] *Grech v Odhams Press* [1958] 2 Q.B. 275 CA; *Antonovich v WA Newspapers* [1960] W.A.R. 176 at 180; *Petritsis v Hellenic Chronicle* [1978] 2 N.S.W.L.R. 174 (proceedings not referred to, nor did publication purport to comment on them).
[131] *Brent Walker Group Plc v Time Out* [1991] 2 Q.B. 33 CA; *Thompson v Truth and Sportsman (No.4)* (1932) 34 S.R. (N.S.W.) 21 PC. Despite suggestions in *Bailey v Truth and Sportsman* (1938) 60 C.L.R. 700 that only the report as a report might be the subject of comment, it is clear that the rule extends to a fact stated by a witness in a judicial proceeding even though it was hearsay and not within his own knowledge: *Grech v Odhams Press* [1958] 2 Q.B. 275 CA. In *Brent Walker* at 46, Parker L.J. gave the example of two inaccurate reports of judicial proceedings, one with no comment, the other with added comment. To hold that a fair and accurate report was not a necessary part of the defence of honest comment "would mean that . . . the defendant who abstained from damaging comment would be liable whilst the defendant who went further would not". However, even the commentator would be liable in so far as the article contained unprivileged statements of fact.
[132] But only if that means that the opinion was not honestly held. The mere fact that the report was inaccurate would not amount to malice. See, *Brent Walker* (above) at 45, per Bingham L.J.: "It is not hard to imagine circumstances in which a report, although not fair and accurate, would be untainted by any improper motive. The reporter might, for example, have heard and recorded a damaging accusation but left before its convincing refutation". Improper motive is no longer regarded as malice for the purposes of honest comment (see para.12.36, below) but in any event

This principle presents some difficulties in other contexts. First, the requirement that there should be a fair and accurate account of the privileged occasion on which the matter commented on was published is a derogation from the principle applicable where true facts are commented on. Those facts need only be "indicated" in the defendant's words. No doubt it is correct that the defendant should not be allowed to rely on a partial and misleading account of the context in which the original statement was made.[133] Furthermore, a fair and accurate account need not be a verbatim account.

It is unclear whether the requirement of a fair and accurate account would be held to apply in the very different context of public discussion of matters the publication of which was protected on the basis of *Reynolds v Times Newspapers Ltd*.[134] Decided cases have involved facts where the privileged status of the original publication (e.g. evidence given in court) could not be seriously contested. That will not necessarily be so in respect of the broader privilege granted by *Reynolds*. The defendant who seeks to rely on honest comment might find himself in the impossible position of being asked to demonstrate that what was said by another person on another occasion was the fruit of responsible journalism and hence privileged.

12.22 Defamation Act 2013: opinion based on privileged statement. Under s.3(4)(b) of the Defamation Act 2013 it will remain possible for a defendant to base an opinion on anything asserted to be a fact in a privileged statement published before the statement complained of. Indeed, the range of privileged statements that is relevant for this purpose will be expanded. For the purposes of s.3(4)(b), privileged statements are those in respect of which the responsible publisher would have had a defence under:

(1) s.4 of the 2013 Act (publication on matter of public interest);
(2) s.6 of the 2013 Act (peer-reviewed statement in scientific or academic journal);
(3) s.14 of the Defamation Act 1996 (reports of court proceedings protected by absolute privilege), or
(4) s.15 of the 1996 Act (other reports protected by qualified privilege).[135]

12.23 Defamation Act 2013: potential problems with s.3(4)(b). There are two potential problems that may arise for certain defendants who seek to rely on s.3(4)(b). The first issue may arise due to the requirement that any privileged statement upon which a defendant bases an opinion should be

---

the mere fact that the report is inaccurate does not necessarily show that the commentator did not hold the opinion expressed.

[133] In *Brent Walker* ibid. the defendants relied on one sentence in the evidence of a prosecution witness in the claimant's trial for theft.

[134] See ch.15, below.

[135] Defamation Act 2013: s.3(7).

published "before" the statement complained of. The language of s.3(4)(b)—the use of "before"—would appear to preclude the defence of a comment on privileged facts that was published *contemporaneously* with the privileged statement. This might occur, for example, when a press release is issued alongside a larger document, or where a journalist or blogger comments on facts that he or she has published in the same article. These are not infrequent events. As a matter of principle, it is difficult to explain why such opinions should not be protected by the Act. It is not immediately obvious why the law should treat contemporaneous publication of facts mixed with opinion any differently from a press release published one minute after a report, or a comment piece published moments after a news item or investigative findings.[136] Prospectively, the problem may be addressed by a construction of "before" as meaning "not after", that is to say "before, or contemporaneous with".

The second concern with the drafting of s.3(4)(b) concerns the position of the publisher who bases an opinion on facts published by someone else. This is, of course, the common position of the social media commentator. Should those facts subsequently prove to be false, the publisher of the opinion faces potential liability, and will in effect be asked to prove the validity of the privilege (which might entail a s.4 public interest defence) by proxy.[137] This might be a virtually impossible feat.[138] Hence, the utility of the honest opinion defence to social media commentators and others is likely to be significantly less than might have been the case.[139]

---

[136] Two possible explanations as to why s.3(4)(b) was drafted in this manner can be suggested. The first is that it is a quirk of the legislative history of the Act. There was no insistence that the privileged statement be published *before* the statement complained of in the equivalent clause —cl.3(4)(b)—in the Private Member's Bill introduced by Lord Lester. That Bill would have included facts defensible under a public interest defence as a legitimising basis for comment. When the Government published its draft bill, the range of privileged statements that could be relevant for the purposes of the honest comment defence was more limited. Statements privileged under the equivalent of s.4 were not to be included in the s.3 defence, and the draft bill adopted the "before" terminology. This was attributed to a desire not to over-complicate the relationship between the two defences—see Ministry of Justice, *Draft Defamation Bill: Consultation Paper CP3/11* (Cm.8020), at [47]. Other forms of privileged statements are unlikely often to include commentary or critique alongside the privileged content. Hence, the language of the provision merely reflected the then-expected actuality. The Government then resiled from this position, and included facts asserted in statements privileged by s.4. Thus, it seems that the requirement that the privileged statement be published "before" the statement complained of may have been carried through by way of oversight. It should have been excised, however, when it was decided to re-extend the bases on which opinions might be expressed to include statements defensible under s.4. Of course, a second possible explanation is that the authors of the Bill did contemplate this theme, but considered the apparent lacuna unimportant in light of the extension of the s.4 defence to cover opinions.

[137] Depending on how rigorously the new s.4 defence is interpreted, it may also become possible for such an individual to rely instead on that defence.

[138] That such difficulties would be faced was recognised by the Government during the development of the Act—see Ministry of Justice, *Government's Response to the Report of the Joint Committee on the Draft Defamation Bill* (Cm.8295, 2012) at [41].

[139] A preferable option might have been for s.4 to have been reserved for the defence of statements of fact on matters of public interest, for the definition of "privileged statement" in

Section 4. Indication of Facts

12.24 Sufficient reference. A key requirement of the honest comment defence set out in *Joseph v Spiller* was that "the comment must explicitly or implicitly indicate, at least in general terms, the facts on which it is based".[140] The defendant may choose to set out explicitly the details of the matter upon which he comments (as where he says, "the Prime Minister is not fit to hold office because he lied on the *Today* programme yesterday").[141] He may also rely on the defence if his statement imputes unfitness "because of what he said on the *Today* programme yesterday".[142] No reference at all will be necessary if the matter is notorious and the general subject matter is indicated, as where—for example—a person who is widely known to have been convicted of perjury is simply said to be unfit to hold public office.[143] Hence, the common shorthand that the comment must be "on facts truly stated" does not express a requirement that the facts *are* stated but the different proposition that *if* the facts are stated and are not true the defence is unavailable.[144] As Lord Oaksey said in *Kemsley v Foot*: "what is meant in cases in which it has been said that

s.3(7) to have excluded reference to s.4, and for a new s.3(4)(c) to have been introduced to read, "any fact that he or she reasonably believed to be true at the time the statement complained of was published". The defence would then have been available when the factual basis for opinion expressed was either true, privileged, or reasonably believed to be true. This might have had significant ramifications in terms of the operation of the repetition rule. That the introduction of such a defence was an option was recognised by the Government during the development of the Act. Alongside its draft bill, it consulted on the advisability of allowing an honest opinion defence on the basis of an "honest mistake"—see Ministry of Justice, *Draft Defamation Bill: Consultation Paper CP3/11* (Cm 8020) at [46]. In the face of majority support for this development, the Government decided not to proceed. It contended that the offer of amends procedure would normally be available in such circumstances, and that such a provision could complicate the law and undermine the need for a factual basis to the opinion—Ministry of Justice, ibid. at [36]. It is likely, however, that a claimant would still be incentivised to sue by the expectation of compensation under the offer of amends process, whereas a fully effective honest opinion defence might deter the launching of action.

[140] See para.12.2, above.

[141] These examples are based on *Lowe v Associated Newspapers Ltd* [2006] EWHC 320 (QB); [2007] Q.B. 580 at [58]. The first two examples given there might, however, raise issues of Parliamentary privilege.

[142] At least if what is referred to is well-known or easily ascertainable. In *Kemsley v Foot* [1952] A.C. 345 at 356, Lord Porter reserved his position on "how far criticism without facts upon which to base it is subject to the same observation in the case of an obscure publication".

[143] *Lowe v Associated Newspapers Ltd* [2006] EWHC 320 (QB); [2007] Q.B. 580 at [42]. See also, *Lait v Evening Standard Ltd* [2010] EWHC 642 (QB) at [8]; *Waterson v Lloyd* [2013] EWCA Civ 136 (two cases arising out of the Parliamentary expenses scandal); [2013] E.M.L.R. 17 at [43]; *Kemsley v Foot* [1952] A.C. 345 at 357; *Hawke v Tamworth Newspaper* [1983] 1 N.S.W.L.R. 699 at 704 ("contemporary history or general notoriety"); *Bjleke-Petersen v Burns and ABC* [1988] Qd. R. 129. In *Moyle v Mujuru*, 1999 (3) S.A. 39 at 49 the Full Court of the Zimbabwe Supreme Court was of the view that the requirement of reference means "facts expressly stated or referred to in the document or speech, or generally known to the relevant audience". Or there may be a case which straddles the two categories, as where a cartoon depicts a politician in a bad light over some current controversy. Cf. *Vander Zalm v Times Publishers* [1980] 4 W.W.R. 259 BCCA.

[144] *Lowe*, ibid. at [46].

comment to be fair must be on facts truly stated is . . . that the facts so far as they are stated in the libel, must not be untruly stated".[145]

In *Joseph v Spiller*, Lord Phillips explained that:

> "There are a number of reasons why the subject matter of the comment must be identified by the comment, at least in general terms. The underlying justification for the creation of the fair comment exception was the desirability that a person should be entitled to express his view freely about a matter of public interest . . . if the subject matter of the comment is not apparent from the comment this justification for the defence will be lacking. The defamatory comment will be wholly unfocussed . . . More fundamentally . . . it may be thought desirable that the commentator should be required to identify at least the general nature of the facts that have led him to make the criticism. If he states that a barrister is 'a disgrace to his profession' he should make it clear whether this is because he does not deal honestly with the court, or does not read his papers thoroughly, or refuses to accept legally aided work, or is constantly late for court, or wears dirty collars and bands."[146]

The requirement that the publication should at least indicate the facts on which a comment is based is closely related to the requirement that such facts be true. The latter "requirement is better enforced if the comment has to identify, at least in general terms, the matters on which it is based".[147]

What is required of publishers is often influenced by context. For example, a critic can satisfy the requirement that the publication should indicate the underpinning facts by citing the subject of the review. In *Thornton v Telegraph Media Group Ltd*, Gray J. explained that:

> "In appropriate circumstances the publisher of a review of a literary work or dramatic or artistic work will be held to have complied with the requirement that words should indicate, at least in general terms, the factual basis for the comment if the reviewer identifies for the benefit of his or her readers the book or play or film or picture as the case may be . . . In such a case the Defendant reviewer may freely comment on the dramatic quality of the play or film or the literary or artistic merits or demerits of the book or picture . . . The reader of the review can then, if so inclined, buy the book and read it or go to see the play or film or see the picture at an exhibition or gallery. The reader of the review is then in a position to make up his or her own mind whether the comment is a fair one."[148]

Defamation Act 2013: retention of the indication requirement. The   **12.25** new statutory defence of honest opinion sets out as its second condition an obligation on the defendant to show that "the statement complained of indicated, whether in general or specific terms, the basis of the opinion".[149] The Explanatory Notes to the Act indicate that this was intended to "[reflect] the test approved by the Supreme Court in *Joseph v Spiller* that 'the comment

---

[145] [1952] A.C. 345 at 361.
[146] [2010] UKSC 53; [2011] 1 A.C. 852 at [101]–[103].
[147] Ibid. at [102].
[148] [2009] EWHC 2863 (QB) at [44]–[45]. On the facts, however, the defence failed because the review significantly misdescribed what the book had said about the claimant's methods.
[149] S.3(3).

must explicitly or implicitly indicate, at least in general terms, the facts on which it is based'".[150] They also provide, however, that the aim of this condition is "to simplify the law by providing a clear and straightforward test", by "retaining the broad principles of the current common law defence as to the necessary basis for the opinion expressed but avoid the complexities which have arisen in case law".[151] While retention of the test essentially as it has been in the common law will no doubt be helpful, it is not altogether clear what the restatement does that will meet the aspiration to increase clarity set out in the Notes. There are complexities of fact and context that arise with every individual circumstance; these complexities cannot be removed by rhetoric alone.

SECTION 5. OBJECTIVE LIMIT OF DEFENCE

12.26 General. A fourth requirement of the honest comment defence set out by Lord Phillips in *Spiller v Joseph* involves an assessment of whether the comment is one that a "fair" or "honest-minded" person could hold. This has been referred to as the "objective stage", or as the test that sets "the objective limits of the defence".[152] The burden of proof is upon the defendant. This test has been closely associated with the issue of "malice"—sometimes described as the "subjective stage" in the sense that it directs attention to the state of mind of the author of the comment—that would unseat the defence if proven by the claimant.[153] As the nature of honest comment has developed over time, this objective element has become a primary focus for analysis.[154]

12.27 Objective limits of comment. The limits of criticism are exceedingly wide. The question that the jury must answer is this: "[c]ould any [honest] man, however prejudiced he might be, or however exaggerated or obstinate his views, have written this criticism?"[155] A comment may be honest however

---

[150] Explanatory Notes to the Defamation Act 2013 at [22].

[151] Ibid. The Notes add further that "these are areas where the common law has become increasingly complicated and technical, and where case law has sometimes struggled to articulate with clarity how the law should apply in particular circumstances".

[152] *Tse Wai Chun v Cheng* [2000] HKCFA 86; [2001] E.M.L.R 31 at [16] per Lord Nicholls. In *Thornton v Telegraph Media Group Ltd* [2011] EWHC 159 (QB); [2011] E.M.L.R. 25 at [24] the test was labelled the "objective criterion".

[153] See para.12.36, below.

[154] *Joseph v Spiller* [2010] UKSC 53; [2011] 1 A.C. 852 at [107]–[108].

[155] *Merivale v Carson* (1887) 20 Q.B.D. 275 CA at 280–281 per Lord Esher M.R. In *Convery v Irish News Ltd* [2008] NICA 14 at [65], Girvan L.J. pointed out that "could" is preferable to "would", which had been the original usage. Moreover, Lord Esher in fact said "fair", but Lord Porter in *Turner v MGM* [1950] 1 All E.R. 449 at 461 said that in adopting these words he: "would substitute 'honest' for 'fair' lest some suggestion of reasonableness instead of honesty should be read in". Only honesty, and not reasonableness or fair-mindedness, is required (at 462–463). See also, *Tse Wai Chun v Cheng* [2000] HKCFA 86; [2001] E.M.L.R 31 at [24] per Lord Nicholls; *Buffery v Guardian Newspapers Ltd* [2004] EWHC 1514 (QB).

exaggerated or even prejudiced is the language of the criticism.[156] A comment may be honest even if it is irrational, stupid or obstinate,[157] or expressed in pungent and offensive tones.[158] For these reasons, the terminology of "fair" comment was rightly considered "meaningless and misleading".[159]

From the use of such words as "reasonable", "moderate", "temperate", "just", in some of the earlier judgments, it might be inferred that there is a certain measure of violence or perverseness on the part of a critic which will of itself render his criticism unfair and actionable. In so far as mere invective is concerned, this is correct: "criticism cannot be used as a cloak for mere invective".[160] Similarly, a number of older dicta refer to the comment being "warranted" by the facts or as being such as a "fair-minded" person might make. These expressions, however, are potentially misleading. If the statement complained of is recognisable as comment, the lawful limits are wide:

> "[if] the language complained of is such as can be fairly called criticism, the mere circumstance that it is violent, exaggerated, or even in a sense unjust, will not render it unfair. It is at the most evidence that it was not an honest expression of real opinion, but was inspired by malice".[161]

---

[156] In *Eastern Express Publisher Ltd v Mo* [1999] HKCFA 61; [1999] 3 H.K.L.R.D. 530, the Hong Kong Court of Final Appeal upheld the trial judge's finding that matter fell within the scope of fair comment even though she had described it as "cynical and even possibly prejudiced against the plaintiff". See also, *Grundmann v Georgeson* (1996) Aust. Torts Rep. 81–39; *Carleton v ABC* [2002] ACTSC 127.

[157] Nor do these states of mind amount to malice and a clear direction to that effect is required: *Turner v MGM* [1950] 1 All E.R. 449 HL at 463.

[158] *Keays v Guardian Newspapers Ltd* [2003] EWHC 1565 (QB) at [21].

[159] *Reynolds v Times Newspapers Ltd* [2001] 2 A.C. 127 HL per Lord Nicholls at 193. In *WIC Radio Ltd v Simpson* [2008] SCC 40; [2008] S.C.R. 420, the Supreme Court of Canada held that the "objective" element of fair comment was whether an honest person could hold the opinion. Speaking for the court, Binnie J. said at [28]:
> "In my respectful view, the addition of a qualitative standard such as 'fair minded' should be resisted. 'Fair-mindedness' often lies in the eye of the beholder. Political partisans are constantly astonished at the sheer 'unfairness' of criticisms made by their opponents. Trenchant criticism which otherwise meets the 'honest belief' criterion ought not to be actionable because, in the opinion of a court, it crosses some ill-defined line of 'fair-mindedness'. The trier of fact is not required to assess whether the comment is a reasonable and proportional response to the stated or understood facts."

[160] *McQuire v Western Morning News* [1903] 2 K.B. 100 CA at 109 per Collins M.R. See also, *Reynolds v Times Newspapers Ltd* [2001] 2 A.C. 127 HL at 193. In *Baumann v Turner* (1993) 105 D.L.R. (4th) 37 BCCA at 52, Southin J.A. said that:
> "the defence of fair comment provides wide scope for knock down, no holds barred, public debate. It does require . . . that he who relies upon it get his facts straight and state his facts . . . Having done so, he can heap invective, assuming he has some command of the language, upon his opponent".

This is not necessarily inconsistent with what is said in *McQuire*: powerful sarcasm or even ridicule (Southin J.A.'s sense) is one thing, personal abuse (Collins M.R.'s sense) another.

[161] *McQuire v Western Morning News*, ibid. at 110. See also, e.g. *Bergman v Macadam* (1941) 191 L.T.J. 131 (where the comment was judged not unfair: "though couched in the language of exaggerated jocosity which seemed to characterise criticism of boxing contests"); *Gardiner v John Fairfax Ltd* (1942) 42 S.R.N.S.W. 171.

It has been suggested that to pass beyond the bounds of honest comment there must be "something which no honest person could really believe".[162]

Hence, in deciding an issue of honest comment the judge or jury has no right to apply the standard of its own taste and measure the right of the critic accordingly.[163] Such an approach could entail an end of all just and necessary criticism, for there would be a temptation to find a criticism unfair merely because the court did not agree with the views expressed by the critic[164]: "The basis of our public life is that the crank, the enthusiast, may say what he honestly thinks as much as the reasonable man or woman who sits on a jury".[165] The judge or jury is not asked the question "do you agree with what he has said?"[166]

12.28 Requirement of pertinence. Notwithstanding the generosity of the objective limits of honest comment, there is a minimum requirement of relevance to the facts upon which the comment purports to be made.[167] Criticism "must be germane to the subject matter criticised. Dislike of an artist's style would not justify an attack upon his morals or manners."[168] This requirement was described as "pertinence" by Lord Phillips in *Spiller v Joseph.*[169]

12.29 Facts relied on in support of the defence. For the purpose of determining whether the words complained of are capable of being regarded as comment, the defendant is not confined to reliance on facts to which he or she has referred in the publication. Indeed, the publication itself may in some cases contain no "facts" beyond an indication of the matter of public interest in question.

> "Where the facts are set out in the alleged libel, those to whom it is published can read them and may regard them as facts derogatory of the plaintiff, but where, as here, they are contained only in particulars and are not published to the world at large, they are not the subject-matter of the comment, but facts alleged to justify that comment. In the present case, for instance, the substratum of fact on which comment is based is that Lord Kemsley is the active proprietor of and responsible for the

---

[162] *Awa v Independent News Auckland* [1995] 3 N.Z.L.R. 701 at 710.

[163] See *Awa v Independent News Auckland Ltd* [1997] 3 N.Z.L.R. 590 NZCA (comment on practice of racial group not deprived of defence because insensitive). This matter will become an issue for a judge alone under the Defamation Act 2013.

[164] *McQuire v Western Morning News* [1903] 2 K.B. 100 CA at 109.

[165] *Silkin v Beaverbrook Newspapers* [1958] 1 W.L.R. 743 per Diplock L.J. at 747; *Cornwell v Myskow* [1987] 1 W.L.R. 630 CA.

[166] Based upon the summing up of Lord Hewart C.J. in *Stopes v Sutherland*, HL printed Cases, 1924 at 375.

[167] *McQuire v Western Morning News* [1903] 2 K.B. 100 CA at 110: "I think 'fair' embraces the meaning of honesty and also of relevancy. The view expressed must be honest and must be such as can fairly be called criticism". This must be judged as at the time the statement is made, not on the basis of the claimant's reputation later: *Cornwell v Myskow* [1987] 1 W.L.R. 630 CA.

[168] *Tse Wai Chun v Cheng* [2000] HKCFA 86; [2001] E.M.L.R 31 per Lord Nicholls at [20].

[169] [2010] UKSC 53; [2011] 1 A.C. 852 at [6].

Kemsley Press. The criticism is that that Press is a low one. As I hold, any facts sufficient to justify that statement would entitle the defendants to succeed on a plea of honest comment. Twenty facts might be given in the particulars but only one justified, yet if that one fact was sufficient to support the comment so as to make it fair, failure to prove the other nineteen would not of necessity defeat the respondents' plea."[170]

For this purpose, it is sufficient if the defendant knew the existing facts in a general way. He may rely on them even if at the time of publication he had forgotten them, because they may have contributed to his opinion. He may use specific examples of general facts even if he was unaware of those examples at the time.[171] Hence, if the defendant criticises a newspaper as indulging in "low journalism" it is enough that this is an impression he has obtained from specific instances which he has forgotten but which he can find by going through the files.[172]

The defendant may not rely on a fact which came into existence after the time of publication for that would be inconsistent with the idea of comment. One cannot "look into the future and comment on facts which have not yet happened".[173] Nor may a commentator rely on facts of which he or she was unaware at the time of the publication, even if it is clear that they would have reinforced the decision to make the statement.[174] One cannot comment on facts about which one is ignorant.

Imputation of corrupt or dishonourable motives. Historically, the **12.30** courts had tended to deploy a more severe test in the context of comment imputing corrupt or dishonourable motives to the claimant. Some of these went so far as to suggest that the defence was not available unless the view expressed by the defendant was the *correct* one upon the facts.[175] No such rule now persists.[176]

Defamation Act 2013: relaxation of the objective limits. The third **12.31** condition set out in the new statutory defence of honest opinion recasts the

---

[170] *Kemsley v Foot* [1952] A.C. 345 per Lord Porter at 357.
[171] *Lowe v Associated Newspapers Ltd* [2006] EWHC 320 (QB); [2007] Q.B. 580 at [74].
[172] *Kemsley v Foot* [1952] A.C. 345.
[173] *Cohen v Daily Telegraph Ltd* [1968] 1 W.L.R. 916 per Lord Denning M.R. at 918.
[174] *Lowe v Associated Newspapers Ltd* [2006] EWHC 320 (QB); [2007] Q.B. 580.
[175] E.g. *Campbell v Spottiswoode* (1869) 3 B. & S. 769 at 776–777; *Dakhyl v Labouchere* [1908] 2 K.B. 325n HL at 329n; *Hunt v Star Newspaper Ltd* [1908] 2 K.B. 309 CA at 320–321; *Homing Pigeon Co v Racing Pigeon Co* (1915) 29 T.L.R. 389. For a slightly less rigorous version, see e.g. *Wason v Walter* (1868) L.R. 4 Q.B. 73 at 96; *Hunt v Star Newspaper Ltd* [1908] 2 K.B. 309 CA at 317; *Peter Walker v Hodgson* [1909] 1 K.B. 239 CA at 253.
[176] *Branson v Bower* [2002] Q.B. 737 per Eady J. at 746; *Eastern Express Publisher Ltd v Mo* [1999] HKCFA 61; [1999] 3 H.K.L.R.D. 530 at 543 per Sir Anthony Mason. In New Zealand any special rule was ejected by statute: Defamation Act 1992, s.12. There does not appear to be any trace of a special rule in the Australian uniform legislation (see, e.g. Defamation Act 2005 (NSW) s.31) or in the Irish Defamation Act 2009. The position appears to be different, however, in Canada: *Wells v Puddister* [2007] NLCA 25; 265 Nfld & P.E.I.R. 174 at [47]. For further discussion on this theme, see the 11th edition of this work at para.12.24, and the 9th edition at paras 12.24–12.26.

objective criterion in the common law that words complained of are capable of being comment. Section 3(4) states that "an honest person could have held the opinion on the basis of (a) any fact which existed at the time the statement complained of was published; (b) anything asserted to be a fact in a privileged statement published before the statement complained of". The meaning of the provision, and its ramifications for the operation of the honest opinion defence relative to its common law forebear, are relatively difficult to discern. The difficulty arises in large measure from the apparent conflation of the third and fifth requirements set out in *Spiller v Joseph*.[177]

As regards the objective limits of the defence, the provision appears to involve a change from the position in the common law. The reference to "any fact" in this context would appear to entail that the assessment of capability will no longer need to rest only on facts that the defendant knew when publishing the opinion. If so, the test is greatly relaxed. The defendant would still have to have done enough to indicate the factual basis for the opinion (that is, to satisfy the second condition of the statutory defence), but there would no longer be any necessary correlation between the facts that were actually the basis of the comment and the objective test. It is possible, although perhaps less likely, that the phrase "any fact" will be construed to mean "any of the facts on which the claimant has based his or her opinion". If so, then the rule would appear to be coherent with the existing law.

SECTION 6. MATTER OF PUBLIC INTEREST

12.32 General. The first requirement of the defence of honest comment set out in *Joseph v Spiller* is that the comment must be on a matter of public interest.[178] The question as to whether the matter commented on is one of public interest is solely for the judge.[179] That said, often the question of whether the subject matter is a matter of public interest will be uncontested between the parties on the basis that publication at issue obviously satisfies the requirement.[180] Precisely what does and what does not fall within the concept of the public

---

[177] See para.12.2, above.

[178] See para.12.2, above. The Australian defence of honest opinion requires that the opinion relate "to a matter of public interest" (see e.g. the Defamation Act 2005 (NSW) s.31(1)(b)) and under the Irish Defamation Act, s.20(2)(c) the opinion must relate to a matter "of public interest". The New Zealand Defamation Act 1992 makes no mention of a requirement of public interest but, given the form of s.9 ("the defence known before the commencement of this Act as the defence of fair comment shall, after the commencement of this Act, be known as the defence of honest opinion"), it is perhaps arguable that it survives, though the implication in *Awa v Independent News Auckland Ltd* [1997] 3 N.Z.L.R. 590 NZCA at 594 and *Mitchell v Sprott* [2002] 1 N.Z.L.R. 766 NZCA, may be that it does not.

[179] See para.34.17, below; but compare public concern and public benefit under Sch.1 to the Defamation Act 1996: para.34.22, below.

[180] E.g. *El Naschie v Macmillan Publishers Ltd (t/a Nature Publishing Group)* [2012] EWHC 1809 (QB) at [320]; *Ashcroft v Foley* [2011] EWHC 292 (QB) at [55].

interest for these purposes is not entirely clear. It is possible to offer catalogues of decided cases that fall within identifiable categories, but few points of principle can be drawn from them.[181] One general principle is that matters of public interest are very numerous and should not be confined within narrow limits.[182] The types of subject matter that have been treated as involving matters of public interest for the purposes of *Reynolds* privilege may safely be said also to satisfy the public interest requirement for the purposes of the defence of honest comment.[183] The reverse is not, however, necessarily true; the concept of the public interest in the context of the honest comment defence is almost certainly wider than that used in Reynolds privilege or the claim for misuse of private information.

Basis for identifying matters of public interest. The basis on which **12.33** matters are held to be of public interest has not recently been discussed in detail in the English courts, but at least two approaches can be drawn from the

---

[181] Previous editions of this work have catalogued the variegated manifestations of the public interest reflected in decided cases—see the 11th edition of this work, at paras 12.28–12.41. The categories of public interest that have been found in honest comment cases include the conduct of a person who holds or seeks a public office or a position of public trust (e.g. *Parmiter v Coupland* (1840) 6 M. & W. 105 per Parke B. at 108; *Seymour v Butterworth* (1862) 3 F. & F. 372 per Cockburn C.J. at 376–377; *Campbell v Spottiswoode* (1863) 3 B. & S. 769 per Cockburn C.J. at 777–778; *Silkin v Beaverbrook Newspapers Ltd* [1958] W.L.R 743; *Branson v Bower* [2002] Q.B. 735 per Eady J. at 747; *Lait v Evening Standard Ltd* [2011] EWCA Civ 859; [2011] 1 W.L.R. 2973; *Cook v Telegraph Media Group Ltd* [2011] EWHC 763 (QB); *Waterson v Lloyd* [2013] EWCA Civ 136; [2013] E.M.L.R. 17); political and state matters (e.g. *Minister of Justice v SA Associated Newspapers*, 1979 (3) S.A. 466; *Hedley v Barlow* (1865) 4 F. & F. 224; *Dalban v Romania* (2000) 8 B.H.R.C. 91; *Culnane v Morris* [2005] EWHC 2438 (QB); [2006] 1 W.L.R. 2880); the management of institutions and companies (e.g. *Lowe v Associated Newspapers* [2006] EWHC 320 (QB), [2006] 3 All E.R. 357; *Levi v Bates* [2009] EWHC 1495 (QB) per Gray J. at [158]; *Oliver v Chief Constable of Northumbria* [2003] EWHC 2417 (QB), [2004] E.M.L.R. 32; *Nilsen and Johnsen v Norway* (1999) 30 EHRR 878; *Horlick v Associated Newspapers Ltd* [2010] EWHC 1544 (QB) at [25]); the provision and advertisement of goods and services (e.g. *Showerings v Postgate, The Times*, November 4, 1965; *Broadway Approvals v Odhams Press* [1965] 1 W.L.R. 805 CA; *Ratus Mesra S/B v Shaikh Osman Majid* [1999] 3 M.L.J. 529 Malaysia HC; *Joseph v Spiller* [2009] EWCA Civ 1075; [2010] E.M.L.R. 7 at [37]); religious affairs (e.g. *Kelly v Tinling* (1865) L.R. 1 (QB) 699; *Aaron v Cheong Yip Seng* [1996] 1 S.L.R. 623 Sing. CA; *Klos v Zahorik* (1901) 113 Iowa R. 161; *Awa v Independent News Auckland Ltd* [1997] 3 N.Z.L.R. 590 NZCA); public health, science, and education (e.g. *Rath v Guardian News and Media Ltd* [2008] EWHC 398 (QB); *Hertel v Switzerland* (1999) 28 EHRR 534, at [47]; *Selisto v Finland* (2006) 42 EHRR 8 at [63]; *Dunne v Anderson* (1825) 3 Bing. 88; *South Hetton Coal Co Ltd v North-Eastern News Association Ltd* [1894] 1 Q.B. 133; *Reaves v Foster* 200 So 2d 453 (1967); *British Chiropractic Association v Singh* [2010] EWCA Civ 350; [2011] 1 W.L.R. 133); the administration of justice (e.g. *Hibbins v Lee* (1865) 11 L.T. 541 at 542 per Cockburn C.J; *R. v Sullivan* (1868) 11 Cox C.C. 44; *Woodgate v Ridout* (1865) 4 F. & F. 202); literary and artistic criticism (e.g. *Carr v Hood* (1808) 1 Camp 355n; *Merivale v Carson* (1887) 20 Q.B.D. 275; *McQuire v Western Morning News* [1903] 2 K.B. 100 CA; *Vassiliev v Amazon.com Inc.* [2003] EWHC 2302 (QB); *Campbell v Safra* [2006] EWHC 819 (QB); *Thornton v Telegraph Media Group Ltd* [2011] EWHC 159 (QB); [2011] E.M.L.R. 25), and anything which may fairly be said to "invite comment" or "challenge public attention" (e.g. *Campbell v Spottiswoode* (1863) 3 B & S 769 per Blackburn J. at 781; *Keays v Guardian Newspapers Ltd* [2003] EWHC 1565 QB).

[182] *London Artists v Littler* [1969] 2 Q.B. 375 CA per Lord Denning M.R. at 391.

[183] See para.15.6, below. See also the discussion of categories of public interest in the context of the claim for misuse of private information—para.22.16, below.

jurisprudence. The older of these is that matters of public interest are "matters which are expressly or impliedly submitted to public criticism or attention".[184] A second approach has seen courts recognise that the public has a legitimate concern in matters or events which the claimant might even be seeking to keep from the public gaze, or which have taken place in contexts formerly regarded as private. On this view, which has become the more dominant, the basic rule is that:

> "[W]henever a matter is such as to affect people at large, so that they may be legitimately interested in or concerned at what is going on or what may happen to them or to others; then it is a matter of public interest on which everyone is entitled to make fair comment."[185]

The result is that the courts now treat many more matters as being of legitimate public concern or interest than would have been the case in the nineteenth century. In *Joseph v Spiller*, Lord Phillips acknowledged that in this context "the concept of public interest has been greatly widened".[186]

12.34 Reform in the common law. A possible third option can be seen most clearly by inverting the question to ask what types of subject matter should fall outside the domain of the public interest. Here, it might be suggested that comment on information that is private or confidential should not be protected under the defence of honest comment.[187] If the basis of the defence is the promotion of free expression and recognisability as comment its primary mechanism, then it is difficult to see what other categories of information should necessarily fall outside the possibility of protection.[188] That consideration may have led Lord Phillips to suggest in *Joseph v Spiller*—apparently not on the basis of argument—that "there may be a case for widening the scope of the defence of fair comment by removing the requirement that it must be on a matter of public interest".[189]

12.35 Defamation Act 2013: removal of the public interest criterion. Perhaps the most obvious point of difference between the new statutory defence of honest opinion and the common law equivalent is that the new statutory defence makes no reference to the need for the comment to be on a matter of

---

[184] *London Artists v Littler* [1968] 1 W.L.R. 607 at 623 per Cantley J.

[185] *London Artists v Littler* [1969] 2 Q.B. 375 CA per Lord Denning M.R. at 391. Earlier instances of this approach can be seen in *Seymour v Butterworth* (1862) 3 F. & F. 372; *South Hetton Coal Co v North Eastern News* [1894] 1 Q.B. 133 CA.

[186] [2010] UKSC 53; [2011] 1 A.C. 852 at [101].

[187] This is the position currently: e.g. *Andre v Price* [2010] EWHC 2572 (QB) (comment on the claimant's relationship with his step-son not on a matter of public interest).

[188] Even with regard to comment on private or confidential information, it is clear that any such publication must necessarily include the supporting facts, and hence that such instances would be actionable on grounds other than defamation—see ch.22, below. Comment on the private lives of others might not be seemly, but without more that does not mean that it should be unlawful.

[189] [2010] UKSC 53; [2011] 1 A.C. 852 at [113].

public interest. Some commentators have voiced concern regarding this shift.[190] In contrast, the Joint Committee on the Draft Bill considered the public interest dimension "an unnecessary complication".[191] In light of the general movement of the common law defence over time, this change can be seen as merely the end-point of an existing direction of travel. Fundamentally, the basis for excluding liability in respect of opinions is their recognisability as individual viewpoints only. Whether those viewpoints relate to matters of public interest is arguably neither here nor there.

SECTION 7. MALICE

Words not the defendant's opinion. The defence of honest comment is **12.36** defeated by "malice".[192] The burden of proof of malice is upon the claimant.[193] The conception of malice in this context, however, is not the same as that in qualified privilege.[194] The particular conception of malice relevant to the defence of honest comment was explained by Lord Nicholls in *Tse Wai Chun v Cheng*:

"A comment which falls within the objective limits of the defence of fair comment can lose its immunity only by proof that the defendant did not genuinely hold the view he expressed. Honesty of belief is the touchstone. Actuation by spite, animosity, intent to injure, intent to arouse controversy or other motivation, whatever it may

---

[190] E.g. Phillipson, 'The "Global Pariah", the Defamation Bill and the Human Rights Act' (2012) *Northern Ireland Legal Quarterly*, 63(1), 149–186.

[191] Joint Committee on the Defamation Bill [2010–12] *First Report: Draft Defamation Bill* (HL Paper 203/HC930) at [69a].

[192] This has sometimes been referred to as the "subjective" element of the test for honest comment, with the question of whether the words complained of were capable of being comment providing the objective dimension.

[193] *Telnikoff v Matusevitch* [1992] 2 A.C. 343 at 354–355. Cf the position in New Zealand, where under s.10(3) of the NZ Defamation Act 1992 a "defence of honest opinion shall not fail because the defendant was motivated by malice" but it is for the defendant to prove that he held the opinion: s.10(1).

[194] On malice in that context, see Ch.17, below. In *Tse Wai Chun v Cheng* [2000] HKCFA 86; [2001] E.M.L.R 31 at [57], Lord Nicholls explained that:
"The rationale of the defence of qualified privilege is the law's recognition that there are circumstances when there is a need, in the public interest, for a particular recipient to receive frank and uninhibited communication of particular information from a particular source . . . Traditionally, these occasions have been described in terms of persons having a duty to perform or an interest to protect in providing the information. If, adopting the traditional formulation for convenience, a person's dominant motive is not to perform this duty or protect this interest, he is outside the ambit of the defence . . . the rationale of the defence of fair comment is different, and is different in a material respect. It is not based on any notion of performance of a duty or protection of an interest . . . [Its] basis is the high importance of protecting and promoting the freedom of comment by everyone at all times on matters of public interest, irrespective of their particular motives. In the nature of things the instances of misuse of privilege . . . (for example, 'some private advantage unconnected with the duty or interest which constitutes the reason for the privilege') are not necessarily applicable to fair comment."
See also *Joseph v Spiller* [2010] UKSC 53; [2011] 1 A.C. 852 at [68]–[69] (citing the 11th edition of this work); *French v Triple M Melbourne Pty Ltd* [2008] VSC 553.

be, even if it is the dominant or sole motive, does not of itself defeat the defence. However, proof of such motivation may be evidence, sometimes compelling evidence, from which lack of genuine belief in the view expressed may be inferred."[195]

Correspondingly, it has been said that "in practice this issue is seldom likely to be explored" and hence that "the subjective nature of the defence of fair comment has diminished" in light of the difficulty facing the claimant in proving what the defendant thought.[196]

As regards value judgments, this view of malice would require the defendant to show that the claimant did not genuinely hold the opinion. In the context of inferences of fact, it entails that the claimant must prove that the defendant did not honestly believe in the truth of what he or she said.[197] In *Cook v Telegraph Media Group Ltd*, Tugendhat J. equated the standard to "an allegation of dishonesty".[198] As the primary ordinary meaning of malice is probably something in the nature of spite or ill-will, and this will not now defeat a defence of honest comment, it has been suggested that the word should no longer be used, at least in instructions to juries.[199] Removing it from the vocabulary of lawyers as a convenient shorthand may prove more difficult.

In principle, malice may be evidenced in a number of ways. For instance, a publisher's deliberate failure to mention known exculpatory facts may suggest that the defendant did not genuinely hold a stated opinion,[200] as may

---

[195] Ibid. at [79]. In *Joseph v Spiller*, ibid. at [67], this explanation was said to have "broke[n] new ground in holding that malice in the context of fair comment had a different meaning from malice in the context of qualified privilege". Elsewhere, Lord Nicholls himself explained the development on the footing that "freedom of speech does not embrace freedom to make defamatory statements out of personal spite or without having a positive belief in their truth"—see *Reynolds v Times Newspapers Ltd* [2001] 2 A.C. 127 HL at 201. See also, *Sugar v Associated Newspapers*, February 6, 2001, (QB); *Branson v Bower* [2002] Q.B. 737; *Oei v Ban* [2005] SGCA 35; [2005] 3 S.L.R. 608. In the Australian uniform legislation the defence of honest opinion is only defeated if it is proved that the opinion was not honestly held by the defendant: see, e.g. Defamation Act 2005 (NSW), s.31. In *WIC Radio Ltd v Simpson* [2008] SCC 40 at [103], LeBel J. specifically rejected this approach to malice in honest comment. However, (a) he was dissenting (though not as to the result) and (b) the meaning of malice was not a central issue in the case. The matter is not explored by the majority, but the formulations at [1] and at [63] indicated that they regarded "indirect or improper motive" as a form of malice in honest comment. The scenario confronting the court in *WIC Radio Ltd v Simpson* [2008] SCC 40; [2008] S.C.R. 420 was an unusual one in which "the defendant had intended to convey one meaning in his comments but was objectively held to have conveyed a different meaning. He honestly believed the opinion he intended to convey but did not honestly believe the meaning he was taken to have conveyed" (see *Creative Salmon Co Ltd v Staniford* [2009] BCCA 61 at [24]). See also, albeit in the context of qualified privilege, *Loveless v Earl* [1999] E.M.L.R. 530, *Bonnick v Morris* [2002] UKPC 31; [2003] 1 A.C. 300 (*Reynolds* privilege), and paras 17.20 and 15.23, below.
[196] *Joseph v Spiller* [2010] UKSC 53; [2011] 1 A.C. 852 at [108].
[197] *Thornton v Telegraph Media Group Ltd* [2011] EWHC 159 (QB); [2011] E.M.L.R. 25 at [24].
[198] [2011] EWHC 1519 (QB) at [27].
[199] *Tse Wai Chun v Cheng* [2000] HKCFA 86; [2001] E.M.L.R 31 at [80].
[200] *Branson v Bower* [2002] Q.B. 737 at [36]; *Cook v Telegraph Media Group Ltd* [2011] EWHC 763 (QB) at [47]. See also e.g. *Waterson v Lloyd* [2011] EWHC 3197 (QB) at [19].

publication notwithstanding knowledge of compelling evidence contrary to the comment,[201] or the fact that there was no factual basis for the comment. This is not to suggest that such evidence will be easy to come by in many cases.

Comment of another. The honest comment defence is not generally avail-   **12.37**
able if the defendant has simply regurgitated the opinions of others without knowledge of the underlying facts upon which those opinions are based.[202] Hence, the statement that "X has said that C is unfit to hold office and I agree with him for the reasons he has given" is capable of being comment; but "X says that C is unfit to hold office" may not be.

A different scenario arises where A bona fide publishes the comment of B (e.g. a newspaper publishes a letter to the editor). A may rely upon the defence even though he or she does not share the opinion expressed in the comment. Once it is established that the words fall within the objective limits of the defence, then the defence is only defeated if the claimant establishes "malice", and publishing a letter from another with which you do not agree does not amount to that.[203] It does not matter to the liability of A that the originator of the comment, B, was actuated by malice.[204] A may take advantage of the defence of honest comment (unless he is aware of B's malice or is vicariously liable for B). Otherwise, the news media would be placed in an intolerable position in publishing letters and opinions on matters of public concern. The contrary view seems inconsistent with the modern view of honest comment in which the defendant establishes the defence by showing that the words are capable, considered objectively, of being comment and loses its protection only if he is actuated by malice.

Defamation Act 2013: retention of the malice issue. Section 3 of the   **12.38**
Defamation Act 2013 does not restate the malice requirement in terms. It does, however, provide at s.3(5) that "the defence is defeated if the claimant shows that the defendant did not hold the opinion". This amounts to a clear exposition of malice as it applies to the common law defence of honest

---

[201] E.g. *Cook v Telegraph Media Group Ltd* [2011] EWHC 763 (QB) (albeit that the claimant's contention in this respect was not accepted by the court).

[202] *Lowe v Associated Newspapers Ltd* [2006] EWHC 320 (QB); [2007] Q.B. 580 at [74].

[203] *Telnikoff v Matusevitch* [1992] 2 A.C. 343 at 355, disapproving the view of the majority of the Supreme Court of Canada in *Chernesky v Armadale Publishers* (1978) 90 D.L.R. (3d) 321. See also *Pervan v John Fairfax* (1993) 178 C.L.R. 309 HCA. (in context of Queensland Criminal Code). *Telnikoff* was not actually concerned with this situation but the issue arose because the plaintiff argued that it was always incumbent upon the defendant to prove that the comment represented his own honest opinion.

[204] *Egger v Chelmsford* [1965] 1 Q.B. 248 CA at 265 per Lord Denning M.R. ("If the plaintiff seeks to rely on malice . . . to cause a comment, otherwise fair, to become unfair, then he must prove malice against each person whom he charges with it") See also, *Lyon v Daily Telegraph* [1943] K.B. 746 CA at 752; *Gros v Cook* (1969) 113 S.J. 408; *Mcleod v Jones* [1977] 1 N.Z.L.R. 441. Cf. the view of Davies L.J. (at 269).

comment as set out by Lord Nicholls in *Tse Wai Chun v Cheng*.[205] Moreover, the caveat to the common law rules on malice in respect of publication of the comment of another is retained by s.3(6). This provides that the general rule stated in s.3(5) does not apply in circumstances "where the statement complained of was published by the defendant but made by another person". In that case, the defence is defeated if the claimant shows that the defendant knew or ought to have known that the primary author did not hold the opinion in question.

---

[205] [2000] HKCFA 86; [2001] E.M.L.R 31 at [79]. Manifestly, the shift also accords with the mandate in that decision to drop the usage of the term malice.

CHAPTER 13

ABSOLUTE PRIVILEGE

SECTION 1. INTRODUCTION

General principles. The law recognises that there are certain situations **13.1**
("privileged occasions") in which it is for the public benefit that a person
should be able to speak or write freely and that this should override or qualify
the protection normally given to reputation by the law of defamation. In most
cases the protection of privilege is qualified, i.e. the defence is displaced by
"malice", but there are certain occasions on which public policy and convenience require that a person should be wholly free from even the *risk* of
responsibility for the publication of defamatory words and no action will
therefore lie even though the defendant published the words with full knowledge of their falsity and even with the express intention of injuring the
claimant. A statement of case which alleges publication on any such occasion
of "absolute privilege" will be struck out as disclosing no legally recognisable
claim[1] (or as it would formerly have been said, disclosing no cause of action).[2]
The basis of such privilege has been explained, in the context of judicial
proceedings, in terms which are applicable, mutatis mutandis, to the other
heads of absolute privilege.

---

[1] CPR r.3.4(2)(a), PD 3, para.1.4(3).
[2] See, e.g. *Law v Llewellyn* [1906] 1 K.B. 487; *Burr v Smith* [1909] 2 K.B. 306; *Beresford v White* (1914) 30 T.L.R. 591 CA and para.30.38, below.

"The rule of law exists, not because the conduct of those persons ought not of itself to be actionable, but because, if their conduct was actionable, actions would be brought against judges and witnesses in cases in which they had not spoken with malice, in which they had not spoken with falsehood. It is not a desire to prevent actions from being brought in cases where they ought to be maintained that has led to the adoption of the present rule of law; but it is the fear that if the rule were otherwise, numerous actions would be brought against persons who were merely discharging their duty ... If such actions were allowed, persons performing their duty would be constantly in fear of actions."[3]

Again,

" ... the rule of law is one which involves the balancing of conflicting public policies; one general, that the law should provide a remedy to the citizen whose good name and reputation is traduced by malicious falsehoods uttered by another; the other particular, that witnesses before tribunals recognised by law should ... give their testimony free from any fear of being harassed by an action on an allegation whether *true or false* that they acted from malice."[4]

In the case of privilege in connection with the evidence of witnesses there is the additional reason of a desire to avoid the impeachment of completed proceedings by a subsequent collateral challenge.[5] An absolute privilege attaches to the following statements:

(1) Statements made in or in connection with judicial proceedings.[6]
(2) Statements made in the course of other proceedings having judicial characteristics.[7]
(3) Statements made by one officer of state to another in the course of his official duty.[8]
(4) Statements made in the course of parliamentary proceedings.[9]

---

[3] Per Pigot C.B. in *Kennedy v Hilliard* (1859) 10 Ir. C.L.R. 195 at 209; cited with approval by Farwell L.J. in *Burr v Smith* [1909] 2 K.B. 306 CA at 315–316, and by Sellers L.J. in *Lincoln v Daniels* [1962] 1 Q.B. 237 at 247–248, CA. See also Lord Esher M.R. in *Anderson v Gorrie* [1895] 1 Q.B. 668 at 670; Crompton J. in *Fray v Blackburn* (1863) 3 B. & S. 576 at 578; and Martin B. in *Scott v Stansfield* (1868) L.R. 3 Ex. 220 at 224. See also, *Mann v O'Neill*, [1997] H.C.A. 28, 71 A.L.J.R. 903 at 907; *Amato v Welsh*, 2013 ONCA 258 at [37]. But Cockburn C.J. seems to have had his doubts in *Dawkins v Paulet* (1869) L.R. 5 Q.B. 94 at 110; and cf. South African law in relation to judicial proceedings: para.13.5, below.

[4] *Trapp v Mackie* [1979] 1 W.L.R. 377 HL at 379, per Lord Diplock, referring to *Dawkins v Lord Rokeby* (1875) L.R. 7 H.L. 744 at 753. *Buchanan v Jennings* [2004] UKPC 36; [2005] 1 A.C. 115 at [8]. Cf. the restrictions on the duty of care in negligence, e.g. *Hill v Chief Constable of W. Yorks* [1989] A.C. 53.

[5] *Roy v Prior* [1971] A.C. 470 at 480. Cf. *Hunter v Chief Constable of W. Midlands* [1982] A.C. 529. Outside the area of defamation the immunity given to persons involved in court proceedings rests as much (or perhaps more) on the need for finality as on encouraging persons to speak freely.

[6] See para.13.5, below.
[7] See para.13.17, below.
[8] See para.13.25, below.
[9] See para.13.29, below.

(5) Statements contained in reports published by order of either House of Parliament.[10]

(6) Fair and accurate reports of proceedings publicly heard before a court exercising judicial authority within the United Kingdom and of certain courts and tribunals abroad.[11]

(7) Statements contained in reports of various statutory officers and bodies.[12]

It has been held that absolute privilege attaches to communications between a solicitor and his client, but this is doubtful.[13]

Although it was once said that the courts are unwilling to extend the number of these occasions on which no action will lie,[14] and the test is a strict one, a test of necessity,[15] the categories are not closed,[16] nor are the contents of the categories fixed. For example in *Hasselblad (GB) v Orbinson*[17] an action was brought in respect of a letter forwarded to the Commission of the European Communities during an investigation of allegations of anti-competitive practices. The Court of Appeal held that the procedure used by the Commission was not of a judicial nature and the letter did not therefore attract the established absolute privilege for statements in judicial proceedings. However, the majority of the court went on to hold that the public interest in favour of assisting the Commission to carry out its duties prevented the letter being used as the basis for a libel action.[18] In *S v Newham LBC*[19] the Court of Appeal said that in the absence of previous authority the following factors should be considered in determining whether a communication was protected by absolute privilege:

---

[10] See para.13.34, below.
[11] See para.13.35, below.
[12] See para.13.50, below.
[13] See para.13.51, below.
[14] See Lopes L.J. in *Royal Aquarium v Parkinson* [1892] 1 Q.B 431 CA at 451.
[15] *Taylor v Director of the Serious Fraud Office* [1999] 2 A.C. 177 HL at 214 per Lord Hoffmann; *Mann v O'Neill* [1997] H.C.A. 28, 71 A.L.J.R. 903, at 907 HCA; *Amato v Welsh*, 2013 ONCA 258 at [38]; *Waple v Surrey CC* [1998] 1 W.L.R. 860.
[16] *Merricks v Nott-Bower* [1965] 1 Q.B. 57 CA at 73. Much the same effect is produced as far as a particular group of claimants is concerned by *Derbyshire CC v Times Newspapers* [1993] A.C. 534: para.8.20, above.
[17] [1985] Q.B. 475 CA.
[18] The majority relied on the cases on public interest immunity (see para.13.28, below) dealing with balancing of competing interests, but as Lord Donaldson M.R. admitted those cases were concerned with whether disclosure should be ordered, not with the use which might be made of what was voluntarily disclosed: [1985] Q.B. at 503 (though see *Riddick v Thames Board Mills* [1977] Q.B. 881 CA). Lord Donaldson did not call this a defence of absolute privilege, but May L.J., dissenting, thought that this was what the majority was doing:
"In the end, therefore, I come back to what I think is the only point in this appeal, namely are we prepared to extend the scope of absolute privilege in defamation litigation in this country and hold that it attaches to Mr. Orbinson's letter . . . ":
at 507.
[19] [1998] E.M.L.R. 583 CA.

(a) What is the nature and importance of the interest which the defendant is seeking to protect?

(b) Whether the scale and risk of damage to that interest is sufficiently serious to create a pressing need to protect that interest?

(c) What is the breadth of the immunity which will have to be granted in order to provide protection for that interest?

(d) As a matter of principle would it be appropriate to extend to this situation the immunity from suit which has been applied in other situations?

(e) Is the risk to the public interest which the defendant is seeking to protect so great that it should over-ride the public interest that a person should be entitled to have access to the courts to seek a remedy for a wrong which he alleges he has suffered?

The plaintiff sued for libel in respect of a report made on him by the defendants, his employers, to the Department of Health, which maintained an index designed to enable local authorities to check the suitability of those applying for child-care posts. The court was not convinced that the denial of absolute (as opposed to qualified) privilege would deter persons like the defendants from providing appropriate information; if absolute privilege were to be effective it would be necessary to extend it both to communications received by the defendants which were the source of its reports and to communications by the defendants to persons who made inquiries of it as a result of the inclusion of the plaintiff's name on the Index; and there was a substantial public interest in allowing persons in the plaintiff's position some means of vindicating their reputations. Parliament has provided for absolute privilege in numerous modern enactments[20]; where an activity is carried on under a statutory scheme and Parliament has not made such a provision, that is a reason for caution in extending the common law.

13.2 Privilege and immunity. It has now become common to speak of at least some of the categories of absolute privilege in terms of "immunity" or "immunity from suit",[21] perhaps because (1) the phrase conveys the meaning more clearly than the traditional usage and (2) because the protection of the defendant may go beyond defamation into other areas of tort law.[22] However, in the context of defamation the practical effect of immunity from suit seems the same as that of absolute privilege.[23]

---

[20] See para.13.50, below.

[21] See, e.g. *Taylor v Director of the Serious Fraud Office* [1999] 2 A.C. 177 HL at 207; *Darker v CC West Midlands* [2001] 1 A.C. 435 HL at 444; *Medcalf v Mardell* [2002] UKHL 27; [2003] 1 A.C. 120 at [53]; *Mahon v Rahn (No.2)* [2000] 1 W.L.R. 2150 CA at 2187; *Frankson v Home Office* [2003] EWCA Civ 655 at [51]. Cf. sovereign immunity, which attaches to a person, not a type or occasion of communication: para.8.5, above.

[22] On the latter point, see generally *Darker v CC West Midlands* [2001] 1 A.C. 435.

[23] It is expressly equated with absolute privilege in *S v Newham LBC* [1998] E.M.L.R. 583 CA at 586. It should be noted however that a statement may be protected by absolute privilege but not immune from suit. Thus, an advocate cannot be sued in defamation in respect of what he says

Absolute privilege and the Human Rights Act 1998. While the   13.3
categories of privilege are well established and justifications for their existence well rehearsed, a question exists whether all categories can be supported
as consistent with the Convention. First, Article 6(1) of the Convention
requires that: "in the determination of his civil rights and obligations . . .
everyone is entitled to a fair and public hearing within a reasonable time by
an independent and impartial tribunal established by law." This does not:

> "in itself guarantee any particular content for civil rights and obligations in national
> law . . . [and] it is not enough to bring [it] . . . into play that the non-existence of
> a cause of action under domestic law may be described as having the same effect as
> an immunity, in the sense of not enabling the applicant to sue for a given category
> of harm."[24]

On the other hand:

> "it would not be consistent with the rule of law in a democratic society or with the
> basic principle underlying Article 6(1)—namely that civil claims must be capable of
> being submitted to a judge for adjudication—if, for example, a State could, without
> restraint or control by the Convention enforcement bodies, remove from the jurisdic-
> tion of the courts a whole range of civil claims or confer immunities from civil
> liability on large groups or categories of persons."[25]

If art.6 is engaged, then the restriction on access to the court has to be justified
even though the right which it is sought to enforce is not one which is
protected by the Convention.[26] Even on the basis that art.6 is concerned with
"procedural" rather than "substantive" matters, it is possible that the grant of
privilege to a publication might be regarded in Convention terms as engaging
art.6 and therefore open to examination on the ground of fairness and proportionality.[27] However, in *A v United Kingdom*[28] the majority of the European Court of Human Rights found it unnecessary to decide whether the
absolute privilege for statements in Parliament engaged art.6 in this way since
it was regarded as justifiable for the purposes of the applicant's substantive
claim under art.8 of the Convention.[29]

---

in court but a claim may lie in negligence: *Arthur Hall & Co. v Simons* [2002] 1 A.C. 615 HL;
[2000] 3 W.L.R. 543.
[24] *Z v UK* (2002) 34 EHRR 3, explaining *Osman v UK* (2000) 29 EHRR 245.
[25] *Fayed v UK* (1994) 18 EHRR 393 at [65], repeated in *Fogarty v UK* App. no.37112/97;
ECHR 2001-XI, after *Z v UK*.
[26] There is a certain tension in suggesting that the Convention may cut down the scope of
privilege since the defence is one of the ways of promoting freedom of expression, which the
Convention guarantees.
[27] If so, the same must apply to qualified privilege. However, in *Friend v Civil Aviation
Authority (No.2)*, December 21, 2000, (QB), Sir Oliver Popplewell said at [78]:
"I see no reason to hold that Art.6 has in some way affected the distinction between absolute
and qualified privilege and the category or class of reasons entitled to privilege must be a matter
of domestic law though necessarily involving proportionality."
[28] (2003) 36 EHRR 51.
[29] Respect for private and family life. However, the court observed at para.64:
"that Article 9 of the Bill of Rights is framed not in terms of a substantive defence to civil
claims, but rather in terms of a procedural bar to the determination by a court of any claim
which derives from words spoken in Parliament."

Secondly, it is now recognised that art.8 of the Convention protects a person's reputation.[30] The right to reputation must not only be recognised in principle but should also be enforceable in reality and the contracting state has the responsibility under art.13 to ensure effective remedies are realistically available at a national level. The essential problem in respect of both absolute and qualified privilege is, of course, that they may not allow for any proper balancing exercise between rights. This general need was recognised by Tugendhat J. in *Clift v Slough Borough Council*,[31] a case raising issues of qualified privilege:

> "The historical cases show that the values set down in the Convention in 1950 as rights under Articles 8 (including the right to reputation) and Article 10 (including the right of freedom of expression in the giving of references and warnings) were not invented in 1950. These and some other Convention rights can be traced back, not only to the American Bill of Rights and the French Declaration in the eighteenth century, but also to the very beginnings of English law. So one thing that [the Human Rights Act] has achieved is to provide a means through which the courts can review the relative priority that the common law gave to those rights (which it already recognised), and adjust those priorities to meet contemporary needs."[32]

An area in which the new jurisprudence has already had some effect is that of the use of qualified privilege by public authority defendants. In *Clift v Slough Borough Council*, the fundamental issue was whether the usual principles of qualified privilege should still apply where the defendant is a public authority. If they did, then the public authority need show only that an established relationship requiring the flow of free and frank communications existed between publisher and publishee to satisfy the "duty-interest" test. The alternative view was that as a public authority, the defendant must go further and demonstrate that it has complied with its public law duties under the Human Rights Act 1998 (and, incidentally, the Data Protection Act 1998). Both Tugendhat J. at first instance, and the Court of Appeal[33] held that the latter view was correct. Under s.6(1) of the Human Rights Act 1998, it is unlawful for a public authority to act in a way that is incompatible with a Convention right. It follows that where a public authority publishes information about an individual that interferes with his or her right to reputation under art.8(1), this could only be lawful if justified under art.8(2). The publication must be necessary and proportionate in a democratic society in pursuit of a legitimate aim such as the protection of the rights of others. Given that a

---

For convincing criticism of a procedural/substantive approach, see Lord Millett in *Matthews v Ministry of Defence* [2003] UKHL 4; [2003] 1 A.C. 1163 at [105].

[30] See para.1.14ff, above.

[31] [2009] EWHC 1550 (QB); [2010] E.M.L.R. 4. Tugendhat J.'s decision was affirmed by the Court of Appeal [2010] EWCA Civ 1484 CA. See, paras 14.5–14.6 below.

[32] [2009] EWHC 1550, at [112].

[33] [2010] EWCA Civ 1484.

public authority does not possess human rights,[34] there was no question in that case of balancing countervailing rights in line with the approach set out in *Re S (A child)*.[35]

Hence, the new jurisprudence on the right to reputation has dictated that a different approach must now be taken to the existence of qualified privilege where the defendant is a public authority. There is no reason to think that the position would have been any different had absolute privilege been in question and *Clift* may therefore mark the first in a series of developments in relation to privilege. Importantly, because the Convention imposes a positive obligation on the state to secure art.8 rights to every person, it may be expected that the general development of the law on privilege must in future also be reviewed for coherence with the right to reputation. Each privilege will require assessment to determine whether the policy reflected in its structure is now Convention compliant. An exercise of this type has been undertaken with regard to the absolute privilege granted to MPs in respect of statements made in Parliament, which found that the current rule is consistent with both arts 6 and 8 of the Convention.[36] However, in other respects English law may be unduly indulgent towards publication. By way of example, in *Lindon, Otchakovsky-Laurens and July v France*,[37] the Strasbourg Court upheld a decision of a French Court which had convicted the publication director of the newspaper, *Libération*, because of its report of a petition criticising the conviction of the other applicants and reproducing the passages of the novel that had been found to be defamatory. The French court had condemned the newspaper of acting in bad faith, and the Strasbourg Court concurred with the outcome, suggesting that it was not necessary to reproduce the extracts. Whether the

---

[34] *Parochial Church Council of the Parish of Aston Cantlow and Wilmcote with Billesley Warwickshire v Wallbank* [2003] UKHL 37 at [8] HL [2004] 1 A.C. 546; [2003] 3 W.L.R. 283; *R (Mayor of the City of Westminster) v Mayor of London* [2002] EWHC 2440, at [93]–[6] (QB).

[35] [2004] UKHL 47 HL.

[36] *A v United Kingdom* (2003) 36 EHRR 51. See also *Young v Ireland* and *O'Faolain v Ireland* App. no.25646/94, 29099/95, [1996] E.H.R.L.R. 326. In *Young's* case a member of the Dáil (the Irish Parliament) had raised in a question to the Minister of Health the case of a boy who had died of serious head injuries after admission to hospital because, it was said, of "the failure of staff . . . to operate standard international neurological practices" and "questionable neurological management practices". The applicant had been the sole neurosurgeon on duty at the time and was subsequently exonerated by a coroner's jury of any blame. *O'Faolain's* complaint arose out of a statement by a member of the Dáil in which he accused the former Minister of Education of colluding in irregularities in the running of a vocational education scheme and of a cover-up. In both cases, the Dáil itself had concluded that there was no breach of parliamentary privileges for which it would take disciplinary action. It was clear to both applicants that they could not challenge the Dáil's decisions in court nor could they challenge the offending statements, as they would be protected by absolute privilege. However, the Commission declared inadmissible their complaints under, inter alia, arts 6 and 8 as being manifestly ill-founded. The notion of parliamentary privilege was viewed as the legitimate furtherance of the public interest of facilitating debate and the representation of constituents' interests, while the absolute grant of privilege and the statements made under it (which did not actually name either applicant) were proportionate to those objectives.

[37] App. nos 21279/02 and 36448/02, October 22, 2007.

absolute privilege for reports of judicial proceedings is always consistent with the need to protect art.8 when it is engaged remains to be seen. It is likely therefore that some categories of privilege will be subjected to challenge on the basis that the public policy that originally justified their existence does not apply today or must give way, in a particular case, the claimant's art.8 rights. The availability of privilege in any particular case must become more fact-sensitive, and the courts must find means of weighing the claimant's art.8 rights in the balance.

13.4 Onus of proof. Where a defence of absolute privilege is set up, it is for the defendant to allege and prove all such facts as are necessary to bring the words complained of within the privilege, unless such facts are disclosed in the statement of case, or otherwise admitted before or at the trial of the action.[38] Whether the facts so proved or admitted are or are not such as to render the occasion absolutely privileged is a question of law for the judge.[39]

SECTION 2. STATEMENTS MADE IN OR IN CONNECTION WITH JUDICIAL PROCEEDINGS

13.5 General rule. No action will lie for defamatory statements, whether oral or written, made in the course of judicial proceedings before a court of justice[40] or a tribunal exercising functions equivalent to those of an established court of justice.[41]

---

[38] But the court must act of its own motion if there would be an infringement of Parliamentary privilege.

[39] *Hebditch v MacIlwaine* [1894] 2 Q.B. 54 at 58 (a case of qualified privilege); *Hope v J'Anson* (1901) 18 T.L.R. 201 at 205. See para.34.20, below.

[40] On foreign proceedings, see *Bell Group Ltd v Westpac Banking Corp Ltd* [2004] WASC 162; 208 A.L.R. 491, considering *Anderson v Gorrie* [1895] 1 Q.B. 668.

[41] The law is generally the same in the US (except, seemingly, Louisiana: *Oakes v Alexander*, 135 So.2d 513 (1961); *Freeman v Cooper*, 414 So.2d 355 (1982)); in the common law provinces of Canada; in Australia (see, e.g. Defamation Act 2005 (NSW) s.27(2)(b)) and in New Zealand (Defamation Act 1992, s.14). For Ireland see s.14 of the Irish Defamation Act 2009. The law of Scotland is to the same effect as regards judges (*Haggart's Trustees v Hope* (1821) 2 Shaw App. Cas. 125; *Harvey v Dyce* (1876) 4 R. 265; *Primrose v Waterston* (1902) 4 F. 783) counsel (*Williamson v Umphray* (1890) 17 R. 905; *Rome v Watson* (1898) 25 R. 733; *Hester v McDonald* 1961 S.C. 370) and witnesses (*Mackintosh v Weir* (1875) 2 R. 877; *AB v CD* (1904) 7 F. 72). It differs from the law of England as regards the privilege of parties to a suit. In Scotland parties only enjoy a qualified privilege (*Forteith v Earl of Fife* (1821) 2 Murray 463; *Ewing v Cuden* (1833) 6 W. & S. 566; *Williamson v Umphray* (1890) 17 R. 905; *Neill v Henderson* (1901) 3 F. 387), and may be sued for damages in an action of judicial slander in respect of defamatory statements maliciously made: per Lord Anderson in *Slack v Barr* (1918) 82 J.P. 91 at 92. See further article in [1980] Jur.Rev. 88. In South Africa it has been held that advocates and attorneys enjoy a qualified and not an absolute privilege in drawing pleadings and in conducting cases: *Findlay v Knight* [1935] App.Div. 58; *Pogrund v Yutar* 1967 (2) S.A. 564 AD, where the limits of the privilege are discussed. The same rule has been applied to a magistrate's reasons for judgment: *Udwin v May* 1981 (1) S.A. 1 AD. Witnesses also enjoy a qualified privilege for words spoken in their character as witnesses: *Joubert v Venter*, 1985 (1) S.A. 654; *Van der Berg v Coopers & Lybrand Trust (Pty) Ltd*, 2001 (2) S.A. 242 SCA.

"The authorities establish beyond all question this: that neither party, witness, counsel, jury, nor judge, can be put to answer civilly or criminally[42] for words spoken in office; that no action for libel or slander lies whether against judges, counsel, witnesses, or parties for words spoken in the course of any proceeding before any court recognised by law and this although the words were written or spoken maliciously, without any justification or excuse, and from personal ill will or anger against the party defamed."[43]

The policy justifying this immunity has been said to be to encourage freedom of speech[44] and to prevent a multiplicity of actions against people who are merely discharging their public duty. As Lord President Inglis explained in *Williamson v Umphray and Robertson*[45]:

"It is essential to the ends of justice that persons in such positions should enjoy freedom of speech without fear of consequences, in discharging their public duties in the course of a judicial inquiry. But the motive of the law is not to protect corrupt or malevolent judges, malicious advocates, or malignant and lying witnesses, but to prevent persons acting honestly in discharging a public function from being harassed afterwards by actions imputing to them dishonesty and malice, and seeking to make them liable in damages."

It is immaterial whether such proceedings take place in open court or in private,[46] whether they are of a final or preliminary character,[47] and whether they are ex parte[48] (without notice to other parties) or inter partes[49] (with notice). In *O'Connor v Waldron*[50] Lord Atkin said:

"The law as to judicial privilege has in process of time developed. Originally it was intended for the protection of judges sitting in recognised courts of justice established as such ... The doctrine has been extended to tribunals exercising functions equivalent to those of an established court of justice. In their lordships' opinion ... the privilege applies wherever there is an authorised inquiry which though not

---

[42] The immunity for statements made in Parliament rests on the principle that proceedings in Parliament cannot be called into question elsewhere. It is a broader consequence of this principle that if an outsider defames a member in respect of what the member did in the House, the former may not raise what happened in the house by way of defence (e.g. justification): see para.13.31, below. But there is no such principle in relation to the immunity of those engaged in court proceedings: *Mallick v Mcgeown* [2007] N.S.W.S.C. 1414.

[43] Per Lopes L.J. in *Royal Aquarium v Parkinson* [1892] 1 Q.B. 431 CA at 451. See also Kelly C.B. in *Dawkins v Rokeby* (1873) L.R. 8 Q.B. 255 at 263; Lord Mansfield C.J. in *R. v Skinner* (1772) Lofft 55 at 56; Scrutton L.J. in *More v Weaver* [1928] 2 K.B. 520 CA at 522.

[44] See, e.g., *Taylor v Director of the Serious Fraud Office* [1999] 2 A.C. 177 per Lord Hoffmann HL; [1998] 3 W.L.R. 1040; [1999] E.M.L.R. 1 at 208. See also, *Westcott v Westcott* [2008] EWCA Civ 818; [2009] Q.B. 407, per Ward L.J. at [32].

[45] (1890) 17 R. 905 at 911.

[46] *Taafe v Downes* (1812) 3 Moo.P.C. 37n at 47n. See also per Day J. in *Pedley v Morris* (1891) 61 L.J.Q.B. at 22.

[47] *Bottomley v Brougham* [1908] 1 K.B. 584 at 588.

[48] "A judge in hearing an ex parte application is still acting as a judge and the absolute privilege applies quite as much as when he is hearing a case in which both parties appear": per Channell J. in *Bottomley v Brougham* at 588.

[49] Ibid. As to jurisdiction and excess thereof, see para.13.9, below.

[50] [1935] A.C. 76 PC at 81.

before a court of justice is before a tribunal which has similar attributes ... This doctrine has never been extended further than to courts of justice and tribunals acting in a manner similar to that in which such courts act."[51]

Mere irregularity in proceedings or any incidental document does not remove the privilege.[52]

The absolute privilege for defamation may be compared with other immunities in the administration of justice. For example, no action generally lies against a judge for a wrongful order[53] and no action for negligence lies against a witness of fact in respect of the giving of his evidence, nor is there civil liability even for perjury.[54] The immunity:

> "attaches to anything said or done by anybody in the course of judicial proceedings[55] whatever the nature of the claim made in respect of such behaviour or statement, except for suits for malicious prosecution and prosecution for perjury and proceedings for contempt of court. That is because the rule is there, not to protect the person whose conduct in court might prompt such a claim, but to protect the integrity of the judicial process and hence the public interest. Given that rationale for the rule, there can be no logical basis for differentiating between different types of claim in its application."[56]

The former immunity from claims in negligence of an advocate to his client for the conduct of the case in court has now been removed (at least in respect of the conduct of civil cases),[57] but this has not affected the position as to defamation.[58] The immunity from suit for breach of duty that expert witnesses had enjoyed in relation to their participation in legal proceedings has also been abolished by the Supreme Court,[59] albeit again this has not affected the position with respect to defamation.[60] The scope of "witness immunity" has also been curtailed in other contexts.[61] Whether this greater scepticism about

---

[51] Citing Lord Esher in *Royal Aquarium v Parkinson* [1892] 1 Q.B. 431 CA at 442. For tribunals other than regular courts, see para.13.17, below.

[52] *Addis v Crocker* [1961] 1 Q.B. 11 CA at 27–28; *Scott v Stansfield* (1868) L.R. 3 Ex. 220; *Dawkins v Lord Rokeby* (1875) L.R. 7 H.L. 744; *Munster v Lamb* (1883) 11 Q.B.D. 588 CA. As to jurisdiction, see para.13.9, below.

[53] Though the issue is complicated in the case of inferior courts by the question of jurisdiction and in the case of magistrates is governed by statute: *Re McC* [1985] A.C. 528. However, an award of damages in respect of a judicial act may in certain circumstances be made against the Crown under s.9 of the Human Rights Act 1998.

[54] *Hargreaves v Bretherton* [1959] 1 Q.B. 45 CA.

[55] Cf. *Meadow v General Medical Council* [2006] EWCA Civ 1390; [2007] Q.B. 462 (what is done in court does not preclude professional disciplinary action).

[56] *Heath v Metropolitan Police Comr* [2004] EWCA Civ 943; [2005] I.C.R. 329 at [17] (members of police disciplinary board immune from suit in respect of allegation of sex discrimination in conduct of proceedings).

[57] *Arthur JS Hall & Co. v Simons* [2002] 1 A.C. 615 HL; *Chamberlains v Lai* [2006] NZSC 70. But not in Australia: *D'Orta-Ekenaike v Victoria Legal Aid* (2005) HCA 12; 223 C.L.R. 1.

[58] See para.13.14, below. *Medcalf v Mardell* [2002] UKHL 27; [2003] 1 A.C. 120 at [53].

[59] *Jones v Kaney* [2011] UKSC 13, [2011] 2 A.C. 398 SC.

[60] Ibid. per Lord Phillips at [62]; Lord Collins at [72].

[61] See, e.g. *Darker v CC West Midlands* [2001] 1 A.C. 435 HL; *L v Reading BC* [2000] 1 W.L.R. 1575 CA.

the need for immunity from suit for those involved in judicial proceedings will in due course be carried over into defamation claims remains to be seen. Several of their Lordships in *Arthur JS Hall & Co. v Simons*[62] and *Jones v Kaney*[63] emphasised the importance of ensuring that any exception to the general rule that every wrong should have a remedy had to be justified as being in the public interest. Given that the public policy justifications offered for absolute privilege for statements made in judicial proceedings are to a large extent the same as those formerly said to justify advocate and expert witness immunity, an argument can clearly be made that circumstances have changed such that the public policy arguments that once justified absolute privilege may no longer do so.

Categories of privilege. It has been said that the absolute privilege which covers proceedings in or before a court of justice can be divided into three categories.   **13.6**

> "The first category covers all matters which are done *coram judice*.[64] This extends to everything that is said in the course of proceedings by judges, parties, counsel and witnesses, and includes the contents of documents put in as evidence. The second covers everything that is done from the inception of the proceedings onwards and extends to all pleadings and other documents brought into existence for the purpose of proceedings and starting with the writ or other document which institutes the proceedings. The third category is the most difficult of the three to define. It is based on the authority of *Watson v M'Ewan*[65] in which the House of Lords held that the privilege attaching to evidence which a witness gave *coram judice* attached to the precognition or proof of that evidence taken by a solicitor. It is immaterial whether the proof is or is not taken in the course of proceedings".[66]

The privilege will attach to any matter incidental to the proceedings "practically necessary for the administration of justice". That it is convenient is insufficient.[67] However, with the exception of proofs of evidence of witnesses or inquiries in criminal cases, it is not enough that proceedings are contemplated: they must be actually on foot or the matter in issue must be an act which initiates them. In the case of proceedings of regular courts this is not likely to cause any difficulty since the initiation of the proceedings will

---

[62] [2002] 1 A.C. 615 HL.

[63] [2011] UKSC 13 HL; [2011] 2 A.C. 398 SC.

[64] In the presence of the court.

[65] [1905] A.C. 480.

[66] Per Devlin L.J. in *Lincoln v Daniels* [1962] 1 Q.B. 237 CA at 257–278.

[67] Per Devlin L.J. in *Lincoln v Daniels* [1962] 1 Q.B. 237 CA at 263 explaining the speech of Lord Halsbury in *Watson v McEwan* [1905] A.C. 480; *Mann v Attwood* [1914] 3 K.B. at 287. Devlin L.J. concluded after a careful examination of the authorities:

> "that the privilege that covers proceedings in a court of justice ought not to be extended to matters outside those proceedings except where it is strictly necessary to do so in order to protect those who are to participate in the proceedings from a flank attack."

But "necessary" includes the usual inter partes correspondence and is not confined to documents required by rules of court: *Wong Shui Kee v Chu* [2002] HKEC 1570 HKCA.

involve a well-recognised formal step such as the issue of a claim form,[68] but the matter may be more difficult in the case of other tribunals exercising functions of a judicial nature. In *Lilley v Roney*,[69] a letter of complaint against a solicitor in respect of his professional conduct, with affidavit of alleged charges in conformity with the Solicitors Act 1888, forwarded to the Registrar of the Law Society, was held to be so essentially a step in a judicial proceeding that statements made in such letter or affidavit were absolutely privileged. However a letter containing charges of misconduct against a barrister addressed to the Bar Council did not initiate proceedings, and so was not within the absolute privilege which then attached to the disciplinary proceedings of the Benchers of an Inn,[70] even though in practice the Bar Council received complaints about conduct and acted as a "filter" to pass apparently well-founded ones on to the Inns.[71] For Devlin L.J. the letter to the Bar Council was comparable to a complaint to the police about a crime, which at that time was regarded as the subject of qualified privilege.[72] The Court of Appeal left open whether absolute privilege would have applied to the submission of the complaint to the Inn, but it seems that it probably would have,[73] notwithstanding that it would have lacked the comparative formality of the complaint in *Lilley v Roney*. However, the mere fact that the complaint may not lead to formal proceedings because of the interposition of some preliminary investigation and discretion does not necessarily mean that there is no absolute privilege.[74]

(a) *Privilege of Judges and Jurors*

13.7 Privilege of judges. No action will lie[75] against a judge for defamatory words used by him while acting in his judicial capacity, even though such

---

[68] "On such a point form is of the first importance; it is by form rather than by the substance of the complaint that a writ is to be distinguished from a letter before action":
Lincoln v Daniels [1962] 1 Q.B. 237 CA at 259.

[69] (1892) 61 L.J.Q.B. 727.

[70] *Lincoln v Daniels* [1962] 1 Q.B. 237 CA; *Mann v O'Neill* (1997) C.L.R. 204 HCA (complaint to Attorney-General about magistrate).

[71] In fact the defendant had been advised to complain to the Bar Council. This complaint was clearly the subject of qualified privilege but his conduct was malicious and this defence was not pleaded.

[72] [1962] 1 Q.B. at 262. Such a complaint is now subject to absolute privilege: *Westcott v Westcott* [2008] EWCA Civ 818; [2009] Q.B. 407, para.13.12, below. But there is no suggestion in *Westcott* that *Lincoln v Daniels* would be decided differently.

[73] *Lincoln v Daniels* at 252, 258, 263.

[74] *Hercules v Phease* [1994] 2 V.R. 411. See also *Teletax Consultants v Williams* [1989] 1 N.Z.L.R. 698. The *Hercules* case contains a valuable survey of the area, with the majority (per Ormiston J.) adhering to the traditional view and Marks J. relying on the somewhat broader US approach.

[75] While not connected with defamation and unlikely to give rise to damages in municipal law because of s.9 of the Human Rights Act 1998, judicial statements in criminal proceedings may no longer be without legal consequences: see *Minelli v Switzerland* (1983) 5 EHRR 554 and the remarks of Eady J. in *B v H Bauer Publishing Ltd* [2002] E.M.L.R. 8 at [42].

words were spoken maliciously and without any reasonable or probable cause.[76]

> "A judge is not privileged to be malicious, but he is privileged from inquiry as to whether he is malicious."[77]
>
> "If his judicial duty is transgressed, there is a remedy of a constitutional character through the action of Parliament, but there is no remedy by way of an action at law[78] . . . If the judge were to be exposed to the risk of having his observations made the subject of inquiry by a common jury he would be seriously hampered in the performance of his duty."[79]

The privilege being not for the individual, but for the sake of the public and the advancement of justice, a judge, if impleaded, should rely on his privilege.[80]

The extent of the privilege. The privilege has been held to extend to[81]:   **13.8**

(1) Judges of superior courts of record, e.g. judges of the House of Lords, Judicial Committee of the Privy Council, Court of Appeal, High Court of Justice,[82] High Court of a colony,[83] Court of Session[84] and sheriff's court in Scotland.[85]

(2) Judges of inferior courts of record, e.g. county court judge,[86] recorder[87] or coroner.[88]

---

[76] *Scott v Stansfield* (1868) L.R. 3 Ex. 220; *Anderson v Gorrie* [1895] 1 Q.B. 668; *Sturrock v Greig* (1849) 11 D. 1220; *Tughan v Craig* [1918] 1 Ir.R. 245.

[77] Per Scrutton L.J. in *More v Weaver* [1928] 2 K.B. 520 at 522.

[78] In *Nadeau v Texas Co*, 69 P.2d 586 (Mon., 1937) the court ordered that a "scandalous, scurrilous and defamatory" opinion by one of the judges should be struck from the record and not published.

[79] Per Lord Young in *M'Murchy v Campbell* (1887) 14 R. at 728. Cf. the manner in which judicial remarks quite frequently stir up minor storms in the media. As to the reasons for the present position, see further the cases cited in para.13.1, above. The Faulks Committee was firmly against any change: Cmnd.5909 (1975) para.195.

[80] *Tughan v Craig* [1918] 1 Ir.R. 245.

[81] Judges of the European Court of Justice enjoy immunity from legal proceedings during office and thereafter retain that immunity in respect of acts performed by them in their official capacity, including spoken or written words: EC Treaty, Protocol on the Statute of the Court of Justice, arts 3, 47.

[82] *Fray v Blackburn* (1863) 3 B. & S. 576. Also when sitting in chambers, *Taafe v Downes* (1812) 3 Moo. P.C. 36n, or in bankruptcy, *Dicas v Lord Brougham* (1833) 6 C. & P. 249. Similarly in the past, courts of nisi prius or assize: *Ex p. Fernandez* (1861) 30 L.J.C.P. 321.

[83] *Anderson v Gorrie* [1895] 1 Q.B. 668.

[84] *Haggart's Trustees v Hope* (1824) 2 Shaw A.C. 125.

[85] *Harvey v Dyce* (1876) 4 R. 265.

[86] *Scott v Stansfield* (1868) L.R. 3 Ex. 220; *Houlden v Smith* (1850) 14 Q.B. 841.

[87] *Hamond v Howell* (1689) 2 Mod. 219; *Tughan v Craig* [1918] 1 Ir.R. 245. However, a recorder will now sit in the Crown Court, as to which see *Sirros v Moore* [1975] Q.B. 118 CA.

[88] *Thomas v Churton* (1862) 2 B. & S. 475. As to the Vice-Chancellors of Oxford and Cambridge, see *Kemp v Neville* (1861) 10 C.B.(N.S.) 523.

(3) Judges of inferior courts not of record, e.g. president of a court-martial,[89] stipendiary magistrate (district judge, magistrates' court) or justice of the peace,[90] judge of a consular court having plenary jurisdiction over British subjects.[91]

The same privilege applies to a statement made in performance of his duty by an officer of the court, for:

> "where an officer of any court, in the performance of his official duty, has to draw up a report, he is entitled to the same amount of protection as is extended to a judge who, after a judicial inquiry, performs his duty by fearlessly pronouncing judgment as to matters brought before him, and therefore his report is absolutely privileged."[92]

The delivery by a court of its reasons for judgment is part of the proceedings of the court and does not constitute a "report" of the proceedings to which the judgment relates; court officials who take part in acts necessary for the publication of the judgment are covered by this privilege and not that applicable to reports of court proceedings.[93]

13.9 The scope of the privilege. Even at the highest level the privilege should, it is thought, have some theoretical limits of relevance to the proceedings. This may well be the law in the case of witnesses[94] and the arguments for subjecting the judicial immunity to such a restriction are stronger. If a member of the Supreme Court were to open the hearing of an appeal with defamatory statements about his creditors that should be actionable. In such a case, the Supreme Court Justice would be acting outside his status or character as a judge and his words would no doubt be covered by Lord Coleridge C.J.'s remark that:

---

[89] *Jekyll v Sir John Moore* (1806) 6 Esp 63; *Dawkins v Lord Rokeby* (1873) L.R. 8 Q.B. 255; (1875) L.R. 7 H.L. 744; *Dawkins v Prince Edward of Saxe-Weimar* (1876) 1 Q.B.D. 499; *Hovell v Holland, The Times*, May 6, 1920.

[90] *Law v Llewellyn* (1906) 1 K.B. 487 CA; *Primrose v Waterston* (1902) 4 F. 783. Semble, the decision in *Allardice v Robertson* (1830) 4 W. & S. A.C. 102, that a justice of the peace is not protected against an action for damages for a slander averred to have been uttered maliciously, is no longer law. See also per Connolly J. in *Jellicoe v Haselden* (1902) 22 N.Z.L.R. 343 at 379–380; *Schwartz v Smith* (1964) 45 D.L.R. (2d) 316.

[91] *Haggard v Pelicier Freres* [1892] A.C. 61 PC.

[92] *Burr v Smith* [1909] 2 K.B. 306 CA at 311 (receiver). See also *Bottomley v Brougham* [1908] 1 K.B. 584; *Li v Official Receiver* [1995] 1 H.K.C. 133 HKCA.

[93] *Rogers v Nationwide News Pty Ltd* [2003] HCA 52; 216 C.L.R. 327 at [21]. In *Thomson v Ross* [2000] Scot. CS 202, Lord Eassie held that in Scots law the issuing or publishing of its findings or decision by a judicial tribunal was clearly within the scope of its judicial functions and protected by absolute privilege (on appeal, 2001 S.L.T. 807 on another issue). See also *Garfield v Palmieri*, 297 F.2d 526 (2d Cir., 1962). For the statutory privilege applicable to reports see para.13.35, below.

[94] See para.13.13, below.

"The authority of *Scott v Stansfield*, and of every case, so far as I am aware, to be found in the books, applies only to words spoken by a judge in his judicial capacity, and in the exercise of his functions as judge."[95]

What is perhaps less clear is the relationship between the absolute privilege for defamation purposes and the general judicial immunity from suit in respect of judicial acts.

As a result of the decision of the House of Lords in *Re McC*[96] this may be summarised as follows:

(1) Judges of the Supreme Court (i.e. the High Court and above)[97] are immune from liability for any act of a judicial character even though the act is in excess of or outside their jurisdiction and whether this arises from mistake of fact or of law. However, such a judge would be liable for an act in excess of jurisdiction if done in bad faith, e.g. ordering the imprisonment of an accused after a verdict of not guilty by the jury.[98]

(2) For acts within their jurisdiction judges of inferior courts (other than magistrates) are protected even if actuated by malice; but they have no such protection for acts in excess of their jurisdiction (though not every procedural irregularity will destroy the court's jurisdiction) at least if they have knowledge or means of knowledge of the want of jurisdiction.

(3) Although magistrates were governed by the decision in *Re McC*, now statute provides that no action lies against them for acts within their jurisdiction and they are only liable for acts in excess of their jurisdiction if in bad faith.[99] What will usually be complained of in such cases is lack of power to make a particular order, leading, e.g. to the imprisonment of the claimant or the invasion of his property and there is then an obvious link between the want of jurisdiction and the act complained of. However, in the case of defamation not only would the introduction of these subtleties greatly complicate the position but it is hard to see how the concept of want of jurisdiction could be relevant

---

[95] *Seaman v Nethercliff* (1876) 1 C.P.D. 540 at 544. No privilege would attach to defamatory words spoken by any judge out of office, or when the business of the court is over: *Paris v Levy* (1860) 9 C.B.(N.S.) 342. Cf. *Glick v Hinchcliffe* (1967) 111 S.J. 927 CA, where words spoken at the end of the proceedings by the judge were still part of the proceedings. Cf. the position of witnesses: para.13.13.

[96] [1985] A.C. 528. The case was a claim for false imprisonment in respect of a sentence passed without informing the plaintiff of his right to legal aid.

[97] Under the Constitutional Reform Act 2005 the title of "Supreme Court" was conferred on what used to be the Appellate Committee of the House of Lords, and the Court of Appeal and High Court became known as the "Senior Courts of England and Wales". The Supreme Court Act 1981 was re-named as the Senior Courts Act 1981.

[98] Ibid. at 540, per Lord Bridge.

[99] Courts Act 2003 ss.31, 32.

unless the court had no power to deal with the case at all[100] and in such
a case, at least if this was apparent, the judge would not be acting
judicially.[101] None of the cases discussed in *Re McC* concerned defamation and the tort is not mentioned in the judgments.

13.10 Privilege of jurors. The liability of jurors for defamatory statements made
when acting as such has never been made the subject of judicial decision in
this country, but it is submitted that the principle requisite to secure a free and
independent administration of justice applies to render jurors, no less than
judges, inviolable.[102]

(b) *Privilege of Witnesses*

13.11 Privilege of witnesses. No action will lie against a witness (whether an
expert witness[103] or a witness of fact) for defamatory words used in his
character of witness with reference to the inquiry upon which he is called or
required to give evidence, even though such words were irrelevant and spoken
maliciously and without reasonable or probable cause.[104]

> "If there is anything as to which authority is overwhelming it is that a witness is
> privileged to the extent of what he says in the course of his examination. Neither is

---

[100] But in *MacKenzie v McArthur* [1981] 4 W.W.R. 692, the concept of excess of jurisdiction
was applied in the context of defamation to an inferior (coroner's) court. In *Desmond v Riordan*
[2000] 1 I.R. 505 it was held in Ireland that once a coroner acted beyond the exercise of his
functions, as stated in s.30 of the Coroners Act 1962, he ceased to perform within his jurisdiction
and he no longer enjoyed judicial privilege.

[101] Cf. *Bradley v Fisher*, 80 U.S. 335 (1871) at 351–352:
"A distinction must be here observed between an excess of jurisdiction and the clear absence
of all jurisdiction over the subject-matter. Where there is clearly no jurisdiction over the
subject-matter any authority exercised is a usurped authority, and for the exercise of such
authority, when the want of jurisdiction is known to the judge, no excuse is permissible."

[102] This is the rule of the Restatement, 2d, *Torts*, para.589, providing the matter has some
relation to the proceedings. The same is true in that jurisdiction of pronouncements of a grand
jury, which are perhaps more likely to give rise to the issue: see 48 A.L.R. 2d 716.

[103] *Tufano v Vincenti* [2006] EWHC 1496 (QB). Although this relies on *Meadow v General
Medical Council* [2006] EWHC 146 (Admin); [2006] 1 W.L.R. 1452, which was partially
reversed by [2006] EWCA Civ 1390; [2007] Q.B. 462, that case concerned professional disciplinary proceedings and does not affect the position in civil actions. The immunity from suit for
breach of duty that expert witnesses had enjoyed in relation to their participation in legal
proceedings was abolished by a majority decision of the Supreme Court: *Jones v Kaney* [2011]
UKSC 13 SC; [2011] 2 A.C. 398. However, the immunity of expert witnesses to a defamation
claim is expressly unaffected by the decision: see Lord Phillips at [62], Lord Collins at [72], Lord
Dyson at [125] and Lady Hale at [178].

[104] *Dawkins v Lord Rokeby* (1873) L.R. 8 Q.B. 255; affirmed (1875) L.R. 7 H.L. 744; *Seaman
v Netherclift* (1876) 1 C.P.D. 53; (1876) 2 C.P.D. 53; *Goffin v Donnelly* (1881) 6 Q.B.D. 307;
Watson v McEwan [1905] A.C. 480 HL at 486; *Hargreaves v Bretherton* [1959] 1 Q.B. 45 CA;
Marrinan v Vibart [1963] 1 Q.B. 528 CA; *Rondel v Worsley* [1969] 1 A.C. 191 HL at 268–270;
Taylor v Director of the Serious Fraud Office [1999] 2 A.C. 177 HL; *Darker v CC West Midlands*
[2001] 1 A.C. 435 HL; *Iqbal v Mansoor* [2013] EWCA Civ 149. See also *Cabassi v Vila* (1940)
64 C.L.R. 130 HCA; *Geyer v Merritt* (1980) 26 B.C.L.R. 374 BCCA.

that privilege affected by the relevancy[105] or irrelevancy of what he says; for then he would be obliged to judge of what is relevant or irrelevant, and questions might be, and are, constantly asked which are not strictly relevant to the issue."[106]

Like the judicial immunity the rule is established not for the benefit of malicious witnesses but for the public benefit to prevent honest witnesses being deterred from telling the truth by fear of action.[107] It has also been pointed out that the trial process contains in itself, in the subjection to cross-examination and confrontation with other evidence, some safeguard against careless, malicious or untruthful evidence.[108]

Extent of privilege. The privilege which protects a witness from an action   **13.12**
for defamation in respect of his evidence in a judicial proceeding applies not only to evidence given *viva voce*, but also to statements contained in an affidavit,[109] a witness statement,[110] or in a document handed in by a witness at the close of his examination.[111] However, privilege extends a good way beyond what is said or done in court. It has long been the case that if the person making the statement was called or was proposed to be called as a witness then the protection of absolute privilege would extend to what he said while a proof of his evidence was being taken[112] and the same was so in respect of interviews with the object of possibly calling him at the trial.[113]

However, in the past the position was less clear in respect of statements made during criminal or regulatory investigations. Now there has been a shift towards the promotion of the public interest in being protected against crime and other wrongdoing by extending the scope of this form of privilege to persons involved in such investigations. At one time, unless made the subject of evidence, such statements were unlikely to have seen the light of day, but

---

[105] Relevancy here is being used in the evidential sense: statements unrelated to the proceedings will not be privileged: see para.13.13, below.

[106] Per Cockburn C.J. in *Seaman v Netherclift* (1876) 2 C.P.D. 53 at 56. See also per Pigot C.B. in *Kennedy v Hilliard* (1859) 10 Ir.C.L.R. 195 at 211.

[107] *Seaman v Netherclift* (1876) 2 C.P.D. 53 at 62. See also *Goffin v Donnelly* (1881) 6 Q.B.D. 307 at 308; *Gompas v White* (1890) 6 T.L.R. 20 at 21.

[108] *Roy v Prior* [1971] A.C. 470 HL at 480; *Trapp v Mackie* [1979] 1 W.L.R. 377 HL at 385.

[109] Per Brett M.R. in *Munster v Lamb* (1883) 11 Q.B.D. 588 at 601; *Kennedy v Hilliard* (1859) 10 Ir.C.L.R. 195; *Smeaton v Butcher* [2000] E.M.L.R. 985 CA.

[110] *Darker v CC West Midlands* [2001] 1 A.C. 435 HL at 468.

[111] *Dawkins v Rokeby* (1875) L.R. 7 HL 744.

[112] *Watson v McEwan* [1905] A.C. 480, reversing, on this point only, ibid. sub nom. *AB v CD* (1904) 7 F. 72; *Ronald v Harper* (1913) V.L.R. 311; *Halls v Mitchell* [1928] S.C.R. 125; *Rondel v Worsley* [1969] 1 A.C. 191 at 253. It was held in *Thompson v Turbott* [1962] N.Z.L.R. 298 that the privilege attaching to the giving of a proof by a witness was not lost by the presence of third parties.

[113] *Beresford v White* (1914) 30 T.L.R. 591; *Robinson v Dowling* (1916) O.P.D. 161:
"If a person who is approached by a solicitor collecting evidence is liable to an action for defamation for any statements which he makes and which may turn out to be defamatory, it is clear that no information would be obtained and that the administration of justice would be brought to a standstill":
Web Offset Publications Ltd v Vickery (1999) 43 O.R. (3d) 802 Ont. CA.

the increased burden of disclosure upon the prosecution in a criminal case, extending not merely to material which the prosecution proposes to use but to any material which might be useful to the defence, makes it more likely that they will come to the attention of an accused. A considerable degree of protection is given by the fact that the disclosure of the material to the defence generates an implied undertaking that it will not be used for any purpose other than the conduct of the defence.[114] However, this, coupled with the defamation defence of qualified privilege, is not regarded as a sufficient protection for persons providing information (e.g. the claimant may have discovered what they said in a different way than upon disclosure). Accordingly, the law is that there is immunity from suit in respect of any:

> "statement or conduct [which] is such that it can fairly be said to be part of the process of investigating a crime or a possible crime with a view to a prosecution or a possible prosecution in respect of the matter being investigated".[115]

This protects not only those who provide information but also those who are conducting the investigation. As Lord Hoffmann said in *Taylor v Director of the Serious Fraud Office*[116]:

> "The policy of the immunity is to enable people to speak freely without fear of being sued, successfully or not. If this object is to be achieved, the person in question must know at the time he speaks whether or not the immunity will attach. If it depends upon the contingencies of whether he will be called as a witness, the value of the immunity is destroyed. At the time of the investigation it is often unclear whether any crime has been committed at all. Persons assisting the police with their inquiries may not be able to give any admissible evidence; for example, their information may be hearsay, but none the less valuable for the purposes of the investigation. But the proper administration of justice requires that such people should have the same inducement to speak freely as those whose information subsequently forms the basis of evidence at the trial."
>
> "When one turns to the position of investigators, it seems to me that the same degree of necessity applies. It would be an incoherent rule which gave a potential witness immunity in respect of the statements which he made to an investigator but offered no similar immunity to the investigator if he passed that information to a colleague engaged in the investigation or put it to another potential witness. In my view it is necessary for the administration of justice that investigators should be able to exchange information, theories and hypotheses among themselves and to put

---

[114] *Taylor v Director of the Serious Fraud Office* [1999] 2 A.C. 177 HL. See further para.33.13, below.

[115] Drake J. in *Evans v London Hospital Medical College* [1981] 1 W.L.R. 184 at 192, adopted in *Taylor's* case by Lords Hoffmann, Hope and Hutton. Lord Goff agreed with Lord Hoffmann. Lord Lloyd declined to decide the immunity point. *Evans'* case was a claim for negligence in respect of a post-mortem investigation which led to the claimant's arrest on suspicion of murder.

[116] [1999] 2 A.C. at 214. In *Baxendale-Walker v The Law Society of England and Wales* [2011] EWHC 998 (QB), absolute immunity was held to apply in civil proceedings brought against the Law Society, to protect the statements and conduct of the Law Society defendants in the course of an investigation in anticipation of disciplinary proceedings.

them to other persons assisting in the inquiry without fear of being sued if such statements are disclosed in the course of the proceedings."

Taylor's case arose out of an investigation into a fraud for which D and F were eventually convicted and in which various defamatory statements were made against the claimants, who at that time were suspected to be implicated but against whom no charges were preferred, and the majority of the House of Lords regarded the immunity as applying to the Serious Fraud Office, to its officers and to outsiders who gave them assistance with the investigation. The immunity applies to statements made to the police by a person who makes a complaint[117] and applies to the initial complaint[118] as well as to a witness statement.[119] It was also held by Eady J. in *White v Southampton University Hospitals NHS Trust*[120] to apply to a letter sent by a medical director of the defendant hospital to the GMC's Fitness to Practice Directorate expressing concerns about a doctor's probity. Whether the absolute immunity applies to all complaints made by a person in the course of their employment is an open question, though in *Hughes v Alan Dick & Co. Ltd*[121] Eady J. held that it was arguable, for the purpose of setting aside a default judgment, that absolute privilege would apply.[122]

---

[117] On persons who are mere informants rather than complainants, see para.14.37, below.

[118] *Westcott v Westcott* [2008] EWCA Civ 818; [2009] Q.B, 407; *Alexandrovich v Khan* [2008] EWHC 594 (QB). If a prosecution ensues and the complainant can be shown to be a prosecutor there may be a claim for malicious prosecution (see below). Otherwise, it has been said that the claimant

"has a degree of vindication by virtue of the decision of the CPS that the evidence was insufficient to create a reasonable prospect of his conviction and a man is considered to be innocent unless proved guilty":

Westcott at [46]. This statement might be considered in the light of the travails of the claimants in *Hamilton v Clifford* [2004] EWHC 1542 (QB) where the accuser was a fantasist and received a sentence of three years' imprisonment. She was presumably not worth powder and shot but the claimants had another target.

[119] *Buckley v Dalziel* [2007] EWHC 1025 (QB); *Daniels v Griffiths* [1998] E.M.L.R. 488 CA at 501; *Westcott v Westcott*, above. Under earlier law the complainant had only the protection of qualified privilege: *Shufflebottom v Allday* (1857) 28 L.T.O.S. 292 (though some doubt is expressed about this case in *Westcott*); *Hasselblad (GB) v Orbinson* [1985] Q.B. 475 CA at 503 (instancing a complaint to the Director-General of Fair Trading); *Canada v Lukasik* (1985) 18 D.L.R. (4th) 245.

[120] [2011] EWHC 825 (QB).

[121] [2008] EWHC 2695 (QB).

[122] The statement complained of in *Hughes v Alan Dick & Co. Ltd* was made by a fellow employee of the claimant's to an immigration officer and later conveyed to a police officer. Whether Eady J. would have held it arguable that absolute privilege would apply if the statement had been made solely to the employer is more doubtful. Compare *P and W v Manny* [2010] ACTSC 50. In *Coles Myer Ltd v Webster* [2009] NSWCA 299 the assistant was found to have concocted a story to the police about fraud because she had taken offence at their behaviour. This was held to be malice for the purposes of qualified privilege, which was assumed to be the only defence applicable (there was a concurrent, successful claim for false imprisonment). In *P and W v Manny* it was said that *Taylor v Director of the Serious Fraud Office* and *Westcott v Westcott* involved extensions of absolute privilege in a way rejected by the High Court of Australia in *Mann v O'Neill* (1997) 191 C.L.R. 204 (though on the facts the statement could not fairly be said to be part of the process of investigating crime).

In *Mahon v Rahn (No.2)*[123] the Securities Association was conducting inquiries into a firm of stockbrokers, of which the claimants were officers, with a view to obtaining evidence for its authorisation tribunal and obtained a statement from the defendants, Swiss bankers, which was alleged to be defamatory of the claimants. A criminal prosecution brought against the claimants by the Serious Fraud Office subsequently collapsed and it was in this that the claimants obtained disclosure of the defendants' statement. The Court of Appeal held that the principle of immunity in *Taylor v Director of the Serious Fraud Office* applied not only to a criminal investigation properly so-called but to inquiries made in connection with potential proceedings before any tribunal the proceedings of which are protected by absolute privilege and that the authorisation tribunal was such a body.[124]

The immunity from suit granted in these cases is not confined to an action for libel: it will apply, e.g. to malicious falsehood or conspiracy or misfeasance in a public office,[125] though it does not extend to the fabrication of evidence. So if a police officer knowingly falsely testifies that he found the claimant in possession of a prohibited substance, he may not be sued for libel because his evidence is absolutely privileged; but if he plants the substance in order to give credence to the testimony he proposes to give he is liable for misfeasance in a public office.[126] Nor does immunity apply to a claim for malicious prosecution. The gist of the complaint then is not what was said but the putting of the law in motion for an improper purpose.[127] However, only a "prosecutor" is liable for malicious prosecution. The meaning of this was considered in *Martin v Watson*[128] and it has since been said in *Mahon v Rahn (No.2)*[129] that the starting point should be the following questions: (1) Did the defendant desire and intend that the claimant should be prosecuted? (2) If so, were the facts so peculiarly within the defendant's knowledge that it was virtually impossible for the professional prosecutor to exercise any independent discretion or judgment? (3) Has the defendant procured the institution of

---

[123] [2000] 1 W.L.R. 2150 CA. The issue of the implied undertaking was not raised in this case. *Ayangma v NAV Canada* [2001] PESCAD 1; (2001) 203 D.L.R. (4th) 717 (human rights investigation).

[124] See further para.13.23, below.

[125] *Darker v CC West Midlands* [2001] 1 A.C. 435 HL. The question whether *Arthur JS Hall v Simons*, para.13.14, below, has any effect on the immunity of expert witnesses in respect of *negligence* is considered in *Karling v Purdue* [2004] ScotCS 221; [2005] P.N.L.R. 13 OH (where the point is made that although *Arthur JS Hall* and *Darker* were decided within seven days of each other and there were common elements in the panels, neither case appears to refer to the other). However, if, as is submitted in para.13.14, below *Arthur JS Hall v Simons* does not affect an advocate's liability for defamation, nor should it affect that liability of any sort of witness.

[126] *Darker*, above. Cf. *Commonwealth v Griffiths* [2007] NSWCA 370.

[127] The malicious prosecution claimant has to prove malice and want of reasonable and probable cause. But if the prosecutor is aware that the charge is unfounded, the claim would succeed even if an outside observer might regard it as justified: *Shrosbery v Osmaston* (1877) 37 L.T. 792 at 794.

[128] [1996] A.C. 74 HL.

[129] [2000] 1 W.L.R. 2150 CA.

the proceedings by the professional prosecutor, either by furnishing information which he knew to be false or by withholding information which he knew to be true, or both?[130] However, absolute privilege applies in civil as well as criminal litigation and malicious prosecution does not extend to the institution of civil proceedings in general.[131]

Limits of privilege. No privilege would attach to defamatory words spoken by a witness while waiting to be called into the witness-box, or after he has left it and become divested of his character of witness,[132] unless, in the latter case, he spoke the words for the information of the court, and while still under the sanction of an oath.[133] It is also the case that no privilege will attach to words spoken by a witness that have no kind of reference to the inquiry, but are introduced maliciously for his own purposes.[134]

13.13

> "I am very far from desiring to be considered as laying down as law that what a witness states altogether out of the character and sphere of a witness, or what he may say dehors the matter in hand, is necessarily protected ... What he says before he enters or after he has left the witness-box is not privileged ... Or if a man when in the witness-box were to take advantage of his position to utter something having no reference to the cause or matter of inquiry in order to assail the character of another, as if he were asked: Were you at York on a certain day? and he were to answer: Yes, and A B picked my pocket there; it certainly might well be said in such a case that the statement was altogether dehors the character of witness and not within the privilege."[135]

---

[130] In *Mahon* the Serious Fraud Office acquired a substantial body of evidence independently of the defendants and was exercising its own independent discretion as a skilled organisation set up to investigate cases of fraud; accordingly, the Court of Appeal dismissed the claim under Pt 24 on the ground that the claimants had no reasonable prospect of success.

[131] *Gregory v Portsmouth CC* [2000] 1 A.C. 419 HL at 427. It is actionable maliciously to institute winding-up or bankruptcy proceedings, to procure the issue of a search warrant or warrant for arrest and to set in motion execution against property. There is also a tort of "abuse of process" (*Speed Seal Products Ltd v Paddington* [1985] 1 W.L.R. 1327) but that is not concerned with the issue of unfounded proceedings but with the use of legal process as an instrument of extortion in some collateral matter. Lord Steyn in *Gregory* at 432 thought that:
> "any manifest injustices arising from groundless and damaging civil proceedings are either already adequately protected under other torts or are capable of being addressed by any necessary and desirable extensions of those torts."

It is not clear what the last might be. However, the case concerned local authority disciplinary proceedings, statements in which would only be protected for defamation purposes by qualified privilege: see para.13.24, below.

[132] Per Lord Ellenborough C.J. in *Trotman v Dunn* (1815) 4 Camp. 211; approved by Cockburn C.J. in *Seaman v Netherclift* (1876) 2 C.P.D. 53 at 56. See also *Lynam v Gowring* (1880) 6 L.R. Ir. 259.

[133] *Hope v Leng Ltd* (1907) 23 T.L.R. 243.

[134] "Statements which are wholly extraneous to the investigation—irrelevant and gratuitous libels" are excluded from the immunity: *Taylor v Director of the Serious Fraud Office* [1999] 2 A.C. 177 HL per Lord Hoffmann at 215.

[135] Per Cockburn C.J. in *Seaman v Netherclift* (1876) 2 C.P.D. 53 at 56. See also Clarke J. in *Smeaton v Butcher* [2000] E.M.L.R. 985 CA at [26]. The Court of Appeal in *Iqbal v Mansoor* [2013] EWCA Civ 149; [2013] C.P. Rep. 27 treated Clarke J.'s statement of principle as an accurate statement of the law. It should be noted however that Bramwell L.J. in *Seaman v Netherclift* was more doubtful. Without deciding the issue he said that it
> "might be held that it was better that everything a witness said as a witness should be protected,

But "reference to the proceedings" should be given a generous interpretation lest the underlying purpose of the privilege be destroyed.[136] In *Seaman v Netherclift*[137] the defendant, a handwriting expert, had given evidence in another case against the validity of a will. The will had been held valid and the judge had criticised the defendant's evidence. In a subsequent case counsel had put this to the defendant to attack his credit as a witness and, despite being instructed to say no more by the court, the defendant declared that he still believed the will to be a forgery. In an action for defamation by one of the witnesses of the will it was held that the statement by the defendant was absolutely privileged since it related to his credit as a witness. So too, in *Iqbal v Mansoor*[138] the appellant had been employed as a part-time assistant solicitor by the respondent, before leaving to set up his own practice. Subsequently, the respondent took exception to the appellant representing a former client whom the respondent was suing. This led to the respondent writing several letters, copied to the court, raising issues as to the appellant's professional conduct in acting for the client, which in turn led the appellant to issue harassment proceedings. In the course of costs proceedings relating to the claim brought by the respondent against his former client, witness statements were served on behalf of the respondent which repeated earlier allegations of professional misconduct against the appellant and alleged that he had deliberately held himself out as operating from a wrong address for service. In an action for libel by the appellant, the Court of Appeal upheld the trial judge's decision that absolute privilege applied to the witness statements. The test to be applied was not whether the statements were relevant to the proceedings,

---

than that witnesses should be under the impression that what they said in the witness-box might subject them to an action.":

ibid. at 60. In *M (MJ) v M (DJ)* (2000) 187 D.L.R. (4th) 473, Sask CA, the court declined to strike out a statement of claim in respect of a complaint by D to a provincial law society about C's lawyer, in which D asserted that C had sexually assaulted her son. See also *Duke v Puts* [2004] SKCA 12; [2004] 6 W.W.R. 208; *Rybachuk v Dyrland* [2007] MBQB 305. Of course there are cases in which a statement about a third party is relevant: *Hodson v Pare* [1899] 1 Q.B. 455.

[136] *Smeaton v Butcher* [2000] E.M.L.R. 985 CA. In this case one of the defendants swore an affidavit in connection with a claim against them for unlawful eviction (the Watford proceedings). The claimant in that action then brought proceedings against a Mrs D in connection with another housing dispute (the Brentford proceedings). The defendants in the Watford proceedings made available to Mrs D the affidavit in those proceedings, which alleged that the claimant was operating a "scam" whereby, having failed to comply with the conditions of various tenancy agreements, he then made unwarranted demands for compensation. The claimant sued the defendants for libel in respect of the publication of the affidavit to Mrs D. In upholding the striking out of the libel claim on the ground that it was bound to fail, Clarke L.J. (with whom Latham L.J. agreed) held that on the facts, whether or not the affidavit was "relevant" in the Brentford proceedings, it had reference to them when published to Mrs D because it was intended to be used, and was used in those proceedings in support of an application to strike them out; if Mrs D's solicitors had taken a fresh affidavit (or even a statement) from the defendants that would clearly have been protected by absolute privilege and it could make no difference that the affidavit was already in existence and was simply provided.

[137] (1876) 2 C.P.D. 53.

[138] [2013] EWCA Civ 149, [2013] C.P. Rep. 27 CA. See also, *King v Grundon* [2012] EWHC 2719 (QB).

but whether they could be said to "make no reference at all to the subject matter of the proceedings". Here the respondent's complaint was that the receiving party's solicitor, the appellant, had a conflict of interest that was relevant to the assessment of costs. It was also suggested that a vendetta by the appellant against the respondent, illustrated by his harassment claim which had been struck out but was subject to appeal, was equally relevant to the assessment of costs and its timing.

No privilege attaches to voluntary and officious observations made in court by persons other than those whose duty calls upon them to make them, e.g. strangers and bystanders.[139] Thus, where on the investigation of a charge before the Lord Mayor in his magisterial capacity, an observation was made in open court by his chief clerk reflecting on the character of the accused, it was held that the observation was not privileged; it was not made in the course of any judicial proceeding by anyone whose duty called upon him to make it; it was uttered by a person who, for this purpose, must be considered as an entire stranger; it was the same as if made by any bystander in the court.[140]

(c) Privilege of Lawyers

Privilege of advocates. No action will lie for defamatory words spoken by   **13.14**
an advocate in his professional capacity in the course of an inquiry before a judicial tribunal, even though they were uttered maliciously and not with the object of supporting the case of his client and were entirely irrelevant to the subject-matter of the inquiry.[141] The law is the same whether the defendant be a barrister or a solicitor.[142]

> "With regard to counsel, the questions of malice, bona fides, and relevancy, cannot be raised; the only question is whether what is complained of has been said in the course of the administration of the law."[143]

---

[139] *Lynam v Gowring* (1880) 6 L.R.Ir. 259. See also *Trotman v Dunn* (1815) 4 Camp. 211; *Wilson v Collins* (1932) 5 C. & P. 373; *Cowan v Landell* (1886) 13 O.R. 13.

[140] *Delegal v Highley* (1837) 3 Bing.N.C. 950; cf. *Farmer v Hyde* [1937] 1 K.B. 728 CA (report of interruption).

[141] *Munster v Lamb* (1883) 1 Q.B.D. 588 CA; *Richardson v Harley* (1911) 31 N.Z.L.R. 464. *Munster v Lamb* was cited with approval in *Rondel v Worsley* [1969] 1 A.C. 191 at 229, 252, 266–267, 271. The Faulks Committee, Cmnd.5909 (1975), paras 196–201 rejected suggestions that this immunity should be modified. If a person not involved in the proceedings is aggrieved at statements by counsel (or a witness) he may apply for leave to make a statement in open court. Advocates before the European Court of Justice enjoy immunity in respect of words spoken or written concerning the case of the parties: Rules of Procedure of the Court of Justice 1974, art.32(1).

[142] *Mackay v Ford* (1860) 5 H. & N. 792; *Munster v Lamb* (1883) 1 Q.B.D. 588 CA; *Geyer v Merritt* (1979) 16 B.C.L.R. 27. No action will lie against a solicitor for defamatory statements made by him during proceedings in a taxation of costs by a master: *Weldon v Maples* (1888) 4 T.L.R. 529. Semble, even a stranger, when permitted by a litigant to act on his behalf with the judge's sanction, is protected: *Cowan v Landell* (1886) 13 O.R. 13 at 16.

[143] *Munster v Lamb* (1883) 11 Q.B.D. 588 CA at 605.

It is true that the former immunity from suit for negligence in the conduct of a case before the court or matters intimately connected therewith has now disappeared, at least in civil cases,[144] but it is probably the case that the absolute privilege remains.[145] As in the case of judges and witnesses, the law rests upon the need for free speech in the due administration of justice[146] but it has been said that in the case of the advocate the argument for privilege is even stronger:

"If upon the grounds of public policy and free administration of the law the privilege be extended to judges and witnesses, although they speak maliciously and without reasonable and probable cause, is it not for the benefit of the administration of the law that counsel also should have an entirely free mind? Of the three classes—judge, witness, and counsel—it seems to me that a counsel has a special need to have his mind clear from all anxiety. A counsel's position is one of the utmost difficulty. He is not to speak of that which he knows; he is not called upon to consider whether the facts with which he is dealing are true or false. What he has to do is to argue as best he can, without degrading himself, in order to maintain the proposition which will carry with it either the protection or the remedy which he desires for his client. If amidst the difficulties of his position he were to be called upon during the heat of his argument to consider whether what he says is true or false, whether what he says is relevant or irrelevant, he would have his mind so embarrassed that he could not do the duty which he is called upon to perform. For, more than a judge, infinitely more than a witness, he wants protection on the ground of benefit to the public. The rule of law is that what is said in the course of the administration of the law is privileged; and the reason of that rule covers a counsel even more than a judge or a witness . . . The reason of the rule is, that a counsel who is not malicious and who is acting bona fide, may not be in danger of having actions brought against him. If the rule of law were otherwise, the most innocent of counsel might be unrighteously harassed with suits, and therefore it is better to make the rule of law so large than an innocent counsel shall never be troubled, although by making it so large counsel are included who have been guilty of malice and misconduct."[147]

Nonetheless, although *Munster v Lamb* clearly strengthened the immunity of advocates,[148] there seems no reason why there should not be a minimal requirement that what is said has some reference to the proceedings.[149]

---

[144] *Arthur JS Hall & Co. v Simons* [2002] 1 A.C. 615 HL; *Chamberlains v Lai* [2006] NZSC 70. But not in Australia: *D'Orta-Ekenaike v Victoria Legal Aid* (2005) HCA 12; 223 C.L.R. 1.

[145] This seems to be the view of Lord Hobhouse in *Medcalf v Mardell* [2002] UKHL 27; [2003] 1 A.C. 120 at [53]. Cf. *Clarke v Davey* [2002] EWHC 2342 (QB), though that case concerned communications between lawyer and client out of court, as to which see para.13.51, below.

[146] *Flint v Pike* (1825) 6 Dowl & Ry. K.B. 528 at 532.

[147] Per Brett M.R. in *Munster v Lamb* (1883) 11 Q.B.D. 588 CA at 603–604.

[148] Cf. the earlier cases of *Brook v Montague* (1606) Cro.Jac. 90; *Hodgson v Scarlett* (1818) 1 B. & Ald. 232; *Needham v Dowling* (1845) 15 L.J.C.P. 9; *Higginson v O'Flaherty* (1854) 4 Ir.C.L.R. 125.

[149] This appears to be the view of the Restatement, 2d, *Torts*, para.586: "if [the statement] has some relation to the proceedings." *Demopolis v People's National Bank*, 796 P.2d 426 (Wash., 1990) accusation of perjury during recess not sufficiently pertinent to proceedings simply because plaintiff's credibility in issue). In *Munster v Lamb* the alleged defamatory statements took the form of suggestions that drugs the defendant's client had been charged with administering were kept by the plaintiff at his house for criminal or immoral purposes, which would clearly satisfy this test. It may be objected that there is clearly no such requirement in the case of proceedings in Parliament. But there are several answers to this. First, that rests upon statute rather than the

Extent of privilege. The privilege is not confined to words spoken by an **13.15**
advocate; it extends also to any statements contained in a pleading or other
document incidental to the action[150] settled by a lawyer engaged in litigation,
including inter partes correspondence,[151] even though such statements are
irrelevant for the purposes of the action and introduced unnecessarily and
without any instructions from his client and without any information which
would justify them.[152] But proceedings must be on foot or the statement must
be part of their initiation: no absolute (as opposed to qualified) privilege
attaches to a letter before action or response to an inquiry in a matter from
which litigation may arise.[153]

(d) *Privilege of parties*

Privilege of parties. No action will lie against a party to an action for any **13.16**
defamatory statement made by him in the documents brought into being for
legal proceedings when being used for that purpose,[154] e.g. a pleading,[155]
answer to a request for further information, or affidavit.[156] Of course there is
no privilege (other than that attaching to reports[157]) for the publication of
pleadings to others than the parties and the court[158] and, therefore,

---

common law. Secondly, it is a constitutional matter designed to stop the courts intruding into
Parliament. Thirdly, courts decide defined issues between litigants; Parliament is the "great
inquest" of the nation where anything may be discussed.

[150] *Pedley and May v Morris* (1891) 61 L.J.Q.B. 21 (objection lodged on taxation of costs).

[151] *Wong Shui Kee v Chu* [2002] HKEC 1570 HKCA.

[152] *Rome v Watson* (1898) 25 R. 733. Or a letter properly sent to the court concerning the
litigation: *Richeson v Kessler*, 255 P.2d 707 (Id. 1953). If sending such a letter is irregular and
improper it will not be privileged: *Gould v Hulme* (1829) 3 C. & P. 625; *Thomas v Nield* (1911)
30 N.Z.L.R. 1208.

[153] *Waple v Surrey CC* [1998] 1 W.L.R. 860 CA. It is not thought that this is affected by *Taylor
v Director of the Serious Fraud Office* [1999] 2 A.C. 177 HL, para.13.12, above. *Dashtgard v
Blair* (1990) 4 C.C.L.T. (2d) 284.

[154] *Stern v Piper* [1997] Q.B. 123 CA at 136; *Big Pond Communications 2000 Inc. v Kennedy*
(2004) 236 D.L.R. (4th) 727 (irrelevant pathname at bottom of statement of claim privileged). In
Liboiron v Majola [2007] ABCA 18 (2007); 72 Alta. L.R. (4th) 222 the defendant pleaded guilty
by post to a speeding charge and his letter made defamatory accusations against the relevant
officer. It was held that the letter was not protected by absolute privilege. Although made
contemporaneously with the plea the statement was not "part of the process".

[155] *Lord Beauchamp v Sir R. Croft* (1595) Dyer 285a; *Lann v Third National Bank*, 277 S.W.2d
439 (Tenn., 1955); *Hall v Baxter* (1922) 22 O.W.N. 207; *Razzell v Edmonton Mint* [1981] 4
W.W.R. 5. That pleadings are absolutely privileged and open to abuse was the court's justification
for imposing confidentiality in *Dr A v Mr C* (1994) 113 D.L.R. (4th) 726. There is a tort of abuse
of process but this covers misuse of legal proceedings for some ulterior object and not the
institution of malicious proceedings as such: *Speed Seal Products v Paddington* [1986] 1 All E.R.
91 CA; *Metall und Rohstoff v Donaldson Lufkin & Jenrette Inc.* [1990] 1 Q.B. 391 CA.

[156] *Astley v Young* (1759) 2 Burr. 807; *Henderson v Broomhead* (1859) 28 L.J.Ex. 360; *Kennedy
v Hilliard* (1859) 10 Ir.C.L.R. 195, where Pigot C.B. reviewed the authorities; *Gompas v White*
(1890) 6 T.L.R. 20; *Smeaton v Butcher* [2000] E.M.L.R. 985 CA.

[157] See para.13.35, below.

[158] But cf. *Dingwall v Lax* (1988) 47 D.L.R. (4th) 604 (draft statement of claim sent to lawyers
for third parties).

"though a litigant is privileged in the statements he makes therein, he is not privileged if he sends his pleading to a newspaper for publication. If the pleadings so published are [defamatory], then the paper publishing them[159] and the person sending them for publication are liable in damages"[160]:

nor is there absolute privilege for statements by a litigant to the media about the merits of his case.[161] Similarly, absolute privilege protects anyone conducting his own case in person, either in a civil or criminal court,[162] at least to the extent that statements by an advocate acting on his behalf[163] would be protected. Nor will any action lie for the instructions given by the party for the preparation of a pleading or like document.[164] Again no action will lie in respect of any defamatory statement made by a party applying to a magistrate for a warrant for the apprehension of a person against whom a complaint is made or for the issue of a summons directed to such person requiring him to appear before the magistrate.[165]

SECTION 3. STATEMENTS MADE BEFORE OTHER TRIBUNALS HAVING FUNCTIONS OF A JUDICIAL NATURE

13.17   General. The doctrine that an absolute immunity exists in respect of statements made in the course of proceedings before a court of justice has been held to apply to statements made in the course of any proceedings before a tribunal (which word covers a commission or inquiry) recognised by law which, though not a court in the ordinary sense, exercises judicial functions,

---

[159] For the purposes of the defence of justification the newspaper is likely to run foul of the "repetition rule" (para.11.18): *Stern v Piper* [1997] Q.B. 123 CA.

[160] Per Lord Young in *MacLeod v Ross* (1892) 20 R. at 221; *Richardson v Wilson* (1879) 7 R. 237. See also paras 11.18, above and 13.48, below.

[161] *Kleier Advertising v Premier Pontiac*, 921 F.2d 1036 (CA 10 1990).

[162] *Boulton v Clapham* (1640) Sir W. Jones 431; *Trotman v Dunn* (1815) 4 Camp. 211. See also the judgments of Holroyd J. in *Hodgson v Scarlett* (1818) 1 B. & Ald. at 244; of Pigot C.B. in *Kennedy v Hilliard* (1859) 10 Ir.C.L.R. 195 at 201; and of Lord Coleridge C.J. in *Seaman v Netherclift* (1876) 1 C.P.D. 53 at 54; *Henderson v Scot* (1892) 24 N.S.R. 232. See also *King v Grundon* [2012] EWHC 2719 (QB): though the matter was not the subject of detailed legal argument, Sharp J. "saw nothing" in such argument as she had heard to make her doubt that absolute privilege protects a litigant in person conducting his own case in a civil or criminal court as much as it would extend to an advocate or lawyer instructed on his behalf. To be privileged, the words must be spoken by the party while actually conducting his case. No privilege would attach to any defamatory statement spoken by a party while waiting for his case to come on for hearing, though uttered in the room where the court was sitting: *Trotman v Dunn* (1815) 4 Camp. 211. But words uttered by a party while accusing a judge of corruption in deciding against him have been held not actionable: *Troughton v Mcintosh* (1896) 17 N.S.W.L.R. 334.

[163] See para.13.14, above.

[164] *Lincoln v Daniels* [1962] 1 Q.B. 237 CA at 260, per Devlin L.J., where he distinguishes this category of absolute privilege from the possible category referred to in para.13.51, below.

[165] *Cutler v Dixon* (1585) 4 Co.Rep. 14b; *Ram v Lamley* (1632) Hutt. 113; *Johnson v Evans* (1800) 3 Esp. 32; *Kimber v Press Association* [1893] 1 Q.B. 65 at 69. However, nowadays even a complaint to the police is absolutely privileged: para.13.12, above.

that is to say, acts in a manner similar to that in which a court of justice acts in respect of an inquiry before it.[166]

> "Where a tribunal is a court of justice, *or a body acting in a manner similar to that in which a court of justice acts*, any statement made by a member thereof is absolutely privileged, and no action can be brought thereon"[167]

but the doctrine has never been extended further.[168] The absolute privilege extends also to advocates, litigants, and witnesses, in the same way as in the case of proceedings before courts proper.[169]

The Inquiries Act 2005[170] set up a framework for inquiries set up by Ministers to look into matters of public concern. Although such inquiries are not courts, their findings do not have legal effect, they have no power to determine civil or criminal liability and their proceedings are not necessarily public, s.37(3) of the Act provides that for the purposes of the law of defamation, the same privilege attaches to:

(a) any statement made in or for the purposes of proceedings before the inquiry (including the report and any interim report of the inquiry); and

(b) reports of proceedings before the inquiry as would be the case if those proceedings were proceedings before a court in the relevant part of the United Kingdom.

Immunity from any civil liability is granted to a member of the inquiry panel, assessors, counsel and solicitors to the inquiry and persons engaged to provide assistance to the inquiry in respect of any act done or omissions made during the course of the inquiry in the execution of their duties as such, or any act done or omission made in good faith in the purported execution of their duties as such.[171]

Judicial functions. Though nothing really turns on the point it would seem that foreign courts operating under the civil law system or the European Court   **13.18**

---

[166] *Trapp v Mackie* [1979] 1 W.L.R. 377 HL; *Slack v Barr*, 1918 2 S.L.T. 133; *Keenan v Auckland Harbour Board* [1946] N.Z.L.R. 97; *Stark v Auerbach* [1979] 3 W.W.R. 563.

"In this extension, the common law has done no more than to reflect the reality of the large numbers of quasi-judicial inquiries and tribunals which have been established in all jurisdictions, which inquiries and tribunals have similar needs for the protection of participants to those which first gave rise to absolute immunity for what occurred in courts":
Mann v O'Neill (1997) 191 C.L.R. 204 HCA, per Kirby J.

[167] Per Sankey J. in *Co-partnership Farms v Harvey-Smith* [1918] 2 K.B. 405 at 408.

[168] *Royal Aquarium v Parkinson* [1892] 1 Q.B. 431 CA at 442, per Lord Esher, which is said accurately to state the law on this subject: *O'Connor v Waldron* [1935] A.C. 76 PC at 81; *Trapp v Mackie* [1979] 1 W.L.R. 377 HL at 379, 385–386. See also *Addis v Crocker* [1961] 1 Q.B. 11 CA.

[169] Per Sankey J. in *Co-partnership Farms v Harvey-Smith* [1918] 2 K.B. 405 at 408.

[170] The Act came into force on June 7, 2005: Inquiries Act (Commencement) Order 2005, SI 2005/1432.

[171] S.37(1), (2). As to ad hoc local authority inquiries, see para.16.28, below.

of Justice[172] are to be regarded for this purpose as "courts" within the previous section even though their procedures may be very different from those of the common law systems.[173] Beyond that, the line between those bodies which do and do not exercise judicial functions "is not capable of very precise limitation".[174]

> "[T]o decide whether a tribunal acts in a manner similar to courts of justice and thus is of such a kind as will attract absolute, as distinct from qualified privilege for witnesses when they give testimony before it, one must consider *first* under what authority the tribunal acts, *second* the nature of the question into which it is its duty to inquire; *third* the procedure adopted by it in carrying out the inquiry; and *fourthly* the legal consequences of the conclusion reached by the tribunal as a result of the inquiry."[175]

There is, however, no single element the presence or absence of which will be conclusive as showing whether it has attributes sufficiently similar to those of a court of law to create absolute privilege.[176] Absolute privilege may be available for the proceedings of bodies where a contempt power is not.[177]

13.19 Authority of tribunal. It is a sine qua non of the grant of absolute privilege that the tribunal is one recognised by law[178]: there is no absolute privilege for the proceedings of domestic tribunals established by contract.[179] Commonly the tribunal will be established by statute, but this is not necessary.[180]

---

[172] And, no doubt, the Court of Auditors and the European Court of Human Rights. Reports of proceedings of all these bodies are protected by s.15, Sch.1 to the Defamation Act 1996.

[173] See *Hasselblad (GB) v Orbinson* [1985] Q.B. 475 CA at 497, 507.

[174] Per Lord Diplock in *Trapp v Mackie* [1979] 1 W.L.R. 377 HL at 379, citing Lord Atkin in *O'Connor v Waldron* [1935] A.C. 76 PC at 81.

[175] Per Lord Diplock in *Trapp v Mackie* [1979] 1 W.L.R. 377.

[176] Per Lord Fraser of Tullybelton in *Trapp v Mackie* [1979] 1 W.L.R. at 388; see also per Lord Diplock, ibid. at 383–384 (presence or absence of any relevant characteristic taken in isolation not decisive); *Mahon v Rahn (No.2)* [2000] 1 W.L.R. 2150 CA. Nor should *Trapp v Mackie* be seen as laying down "rules".

[177] *Att-Gen v BBC* [1981] A.C. 303. A statutory definition of "court" which is sometimes found is "any tribunal or body exercising the judicial power of the State": see, e.g. Contempt of Court Act 1981, s.19; Defamation Act 1996, Sch.1, para.19. This is wider than the "popular" sense of the term, e.g. a Mental Health Review Tribunal is a court for the purposes of contempt: *P v Liverpool Daily Post* [1991] 2 A.C. 370 HL. But the Disciplinary Committee of the Law Society would not seem to be a court, though absolute privilege applies to its proceedings.

[178] *Lincoln v Daniels* [1962] 1 Q.B. 237 CA; *Trapp v Mackie* [1979] 1 W.L.R. 377 HL at 394; *Royal Aquarium v Parkinson* [1892] 1 Q.B. 431 CA, at 446–448.

[179] See *Hope v I'Anson* (1901) 18 T.L.R. 201; cf. *Chapman v Ellesmere* [1932] 2 K.B. 431 at 452; *Green v Blake* [1948] Ir.R. 242; *Russell v Norfolk* [1949] 1 All E.R. 109. Under s.29 of the Arbitration Act 1996 an arbitrator is not liable for anything done or omitted in the discharge or purported discharge of his functions as arbitrator unless the act or omission is shown to have been in bad faith. As to the similar immunity of an arbitral institution, see s.74.

[180] *Lincoln v Daniels* [1962] 1 Q.B. 237 CA. Disciplinary and appeal tribunals in both chartered and "new" universities are probably recognised by law for this purpose and in *Foecke v University of Bristol*, unreported, July 30, 1996, CA, Ian Kennedy J. appears to have held at first instance that statements made to such a tribunal were the subject of absolute privilege. However, in the CA the only issue dealt with was the exclusive jurisdiction of the visitor.

Nature of question to be determined. It is relevant that the question to   **13.20**
be decided is in the nature of a *lis inter partes*,[181] raising the kind of issues
which are the daily subject-matter of civil cases in courts of justice.[182] The
fact that its decision affects the status of those who come before it is also of
importance.[183] That the body is exercising a power given for the benefit of the
public has also been said to be relevant[184]:

" . . . in any case of doubt the overriding factor is whether there will emerge from
the proceedings a determination the truth and justice of which is a matter of public
concern, for it is public policy that justifies absolute privilege."[185]

Procedures.   **13.21**

"Courts of law are, for the most part, controlled and presided over by some person
selected as specially qualified for the purpose; and they have generally a fixed and

---

[181] In *Hasan v Comr of Police for the Metropolis* [2006] Po. L.R. 295 EAT, Elias J. held that
a decision by a chief police officer under reg.13 of Police Regulations 2003 to dispense with the
services of a probationer police officer on the grounds that "he is not fitted, physically or
mentally, to perform the duties of his office, or that he is not likely to become an efficient or well
conducted constable" was not to be protected by absolute immunity in part because the question
to be resolved was not sufficiently judicial in nature. As Elias J. explained (at [28]–[29]):
"The Assistant Commissioner is not resolving some dispute between contending parties
according to certain established legal principles. He is exercising a very different and far more
subjective judgment, assessing whether the probationer is sufficiently efficient and well
behaved to remain in the police at all. This requires consideration of a wide range of materials,
much wider than those typically considered in a court of law . . . what we have here is akin to
an employer deciding whether a particular employee (or as in this case, office holder) should
remain in employment. There is no *lis* between the parties in the sense in which that is
traditionally used in the context of legal proceedings. Of course, in a general sense there is a
dispute as to whether the employee has the requisite qualities, character and temperament to
remain in employment. Plainly that involves the exercise of judgment by the officer charged
with the task of making that decision. But it is not in my opinion akin to a judicial judgment;
it is a far cry from the kind of issue which courts and tribunals typically have to determine."
Compare the decision in *Lake v British Transport Police* [2007] EWCA Civ 424; [2007] I.C.R.
1293; [2007] Po. L.R. 40 in which it was held that a police disciplinary board when undertaking
an investigation into a complaint into alleged breaches of the police code of conduct was
exercising a judicial function and its proceedings were protected by absolute immunity (see also
Heath v Comr of Police for the Metropolis [2004] EWCA Civ 943; [2005] I.C.R. 329; [2005]
I.R.L.R. 270).
[182] Per Lord Diplock in *Trapp v Mackie* [1979] 1 W.L.R. 377 HL at 380. In *Collins v Whiteway
Ltd* [1927] 2 K.B. 378, cited without disapproval by Lord Fraser of Tullybelton in *Trapp v Mackie*
at 387, a communication to a body held not to be deciding between parties, was not entitled to
absolute privilege. But there seems no reason to hold that because a body is determining
entitlements as against the state and not another individual, its proceedings do not on that account
attract absolute privilege.
[183] *Co-partnership Farms v Harvey-Smith* [1918] 2 K.B. 405 at 412; *Collins v Whiteway Ltd*
[1927] 2 K.B. 378; *Smith v National Meter Co* [1945] K.B. 543. Cf. *Hodson v Pare* [1899] 1 Q.B.
455.
[184] Per Sellers L.J. in *Lincoln v Daniels* [1962] 1 Q.B. 237 CA at 250.
[185] Per Devlin L.J. ibid. at 255–256.

dignified course of procedure, which tends to minimise the risks that might flow from this absolute immunity."[186]

Thus, it will be relevant to what extent the procedure resembles that of a court of justice trying a contested issue in a civil case,[187] or gives "as fair a trial as would be available in a court of justice".[188] In determining whether the procedure resembles that of a court of justice, due regard must be paid in modern conditions to the fact that the procedure of courts operating under the civil law may differ markedly from that usual under the common law.[189] Furthermore, the fact that the body has an investigatory or inquisitorial function does not mean that it cannot be equated with a court for this purpose.[190] That the body has the power to compel the presence of witnesses is very relevant[191] and whether or not it holds its proceedings in public is a fact "of great importance".[192] But the procedure need not correspond exactly to that of a court of law,[193] and the mere fact that a tribunal cannot compel witnesses[194] to attend and give evidence,[195] or that it has no power to administer an oath,[196] or that it may exclude the parties and the public during the hearing for the purpose of conferring upon any question affecting its decision,[197] or that it has its hearings in private and gives its finding and order publicly,[198] or even that there is no oral hearing at all, the proceedings being

---

[186] Per Fry L.J. in *Royal Aquarium v Parkinson* [1892] 1 Q.B. 431 CA at 447, cited as "illuminating for the present case", by Lord Fraser of Tullybelton in *Trapp v Mackie* [1979] 1 W.L.R. 377 at 387:
"The commissioner was a Queen's Counsel. He was to sit in public. His power to compel witnesses and others to attend (and the provision for privilege and confidentiality) and his power to administer the oath all point to a 'fixed and dignified course of procedure.'" (ibid.).
[187] Cf. *Trapp v Mackie*, above, at 381 (procedure undistinguished from that of court of law).
[188] Per Sellers L.J. in *Lincoln v Daniels* [1964] 1 Q.B. 237 CA at 249. Cf. *Hodson v Pare* [1899] 1 Q.B. 455 at 459.
[189] *Hasselblad (GB) v Orbinson* [1985] Q.B. 475 CA.
[190] *Gray v Avadis* [2003] EWHC 1830 (QB).
[191] *Dawkins v Lord Rokeby* (1873) L.R. 8 Q.B. 255 at 267, cited by Lord Fraser of Tullybelton in *Trapp v Mackie* [1979] 1 W.L.R. 386; *Perry v Hetherington* [1971] 5 W.W.R. 670 at 672. The power to award costs was also held to be relevant in *Trapp v Mackie*.
[192] *Addis v Crocker* [1961] 1 Q.B. 11 CA at 29.
[193] If statutory rules of procedure are not so strict as those of the Supreme Court this does not mean that the procedure is not judicial: *Addis v Crocker* [1961] 1 Q.B. at 23. But that proceedings are conducted with less formality than a court of law, without pleadings or discovery or evidence on oath, are factors to be taken into account: per Devlin L.J. in *Lincoln v Daniels* [1962] 1 Q.B. 237 CA at 255.
[194] As to disclosure of documents see *Mahon v Rahn (No.2)* [2000] 1 W.L.R. 2150 CA, where the power to override the normal rules was regarded as significant.
[195] Per Sellers L.J. ibid. at 250; *Slack v Barr* 1918 1 S.L.T. 133 (statutory arbitration proceedings); per Lord Fraser of Tullybelton in *Trapp v Mackie* [1979] 1 W.L.R. at 386–387.
[196] Per Cozens-Hardy M.R. in *Barratt v Kearns* [1905] 1 K.B. 504 at 511; per Chitty L.J. in *Hodson v Pare* [1899] 1 Q.B. 455 at 459; per Sankey J. in *Co-partnership Farms v Harvey-Smith* [1918] 2 K.B. 405 at 411; *Currie v Chief Constable of Surrey* [1982] 1 W.L.R. 215; *Mahon v Rahn (No.2)* [2000] 1 W.L.R. 2150 CA.
[197] Per Sankey J. in *Co-partnership Farms v Harvey-Smith*, above, at 413.
[198] *Addis v Crocker* [1961] 1 Q.B. 11 CA.

conducted on paper,[199] is not conclusive as showing that its functions are not judicial. If the proceedings are otherwise sufficiently like those of a court, the mere fact that a party whose rights are in question is "not personally before the tribunal will not make any difference to the question of privilege".[200] The fact that the tribunal must have regard to the principles of natural justice in arriving at a decision does not indicate that it is to be regarded as performing a judicial function because many purely administrative decisions attract those principles.[201]

In *Hasselblad (GB) v Orbinson*[202] the Court of Appeal was concerned with an investigation and adjudication by the Commission of the European Communities on a complaint of behaviour infringing arts 85 and 86 of the EC Treaty. Although this might involve a hearing at which the infringer and the complainant had the opportunity to put their cases, the final decision was taken by the members of the Commission, who played no part in that hearing, and after receiving the views of an advisory committee of representatives of Member States. The result was that the Commission was held to be acting in a manner dissimilar to that of a court of justice, whether under the common law or civil law systems,[203] though the claim was dismissed on another basis.[204]

Consequences of decision. Although a court decision usually results in a binding determination,[205] the proceedings of a body may be held to be quasi-judicial, and so to attract absolute privilege, even though their object is to enable another person or body to decide a definite issue which is in dispute, provided that the proceedings are "an essential step towards an effective decision"[206] or the report of the body in question "though not necessarily decisive as a matter of legal theory nevertheless in practice has a major influence upon the final decision that in law is binding and authoritative".[207]   **13.22**

---

[199] *Gray v Avadis* [2003] EWHC 1830 (QB).

[200] Per A.L. Smith L.J. in *Hodson v Pare* [18991 1 Q.B. 455 at 458.

[201] *Hasselblad (GB) v Orbinson* [1985] Q.B. 475 CA at 497; *O'Neill v Mann* (1994) 126 A.L.R. 364 Fed Ct of Australia. s.14(1)(b) of the New Zealand Defamation Act 1992 extends absolute privilege to tribunals which have a duty "to act judicially". This is a narrower concept than a duty to observe the rules of natural justice: *Gray v M* [1998] 2 N.Z.L.R. 161 NZCA.

[202] Ibid.

[203] See also *Tadd v Eastwood* [1985] I.C.R. 132 CA (consensual conciliation proceedings not of a judicial nature); *Hasan v Comr of Police for the Metropolis* [2006] Po. L.R. 295. EAT (decision by chief officer of police under reg.13 of Police Regulations 2003 to dispense with services of probationer police officer not protected by absolute immunity as the taking of such a decision was accompanied by almost none of the procedures that would be expected in judicial proceedings).

[204] See para.13.1, above.

[205] The decision of the Commission in *Hasselblad (GB) v Orbinson*, above, amply satisfied this requirement since it was enforceable here and elsewhere as a Community judgment.

[206] Per Lord Fraser of Tullybelton in *Trapp v Mackie* [1979] 1 W.L.R. 377 HL at 389.

[207] Per Lord Diplock in *Trapp v Mackie* at 383, applying the same cases as Lord Fraser of Tullybelton (see previous note). The two formulations differ, but presumably not in substance, since the other three members of the House of Lords stated their agreement with the reasons in each speech.

So in *Trapp v Mackie*[208] the proceedings in question were an inquiry set up by the Secretary of State under the Education (Scotland) Act 1946, which authorised the Secretary of State to make such inquiry as he saw fit into the reasons for a teacher's dismissal: and if as a result of such inquiry he was of opinion that the dismissal was not reasonably justifiable he was to communicate his opinion to the education authority with certain consequences. It was held by the House of Lords that the proceedings attracted absolute privilege.[209] So too, in *Baxendale-Walker v Middleton*[210] Supperstone J. held that a forensic investigation report and case report on the claimant's law practice that was prepared by the Law Society and an accountancy firm and which led subsequently to an adjudication and appeal and subsequent proceedings against the claimant before the Solicitors Disciplinary Tribunal (SDT) were protected by absolute immunity. Absolute immunity extended not just to things said or done before the adjudication panel and SDT, both of which were tribunals exercising functions equivalent to a court of justice,[211] but also to statements or conduct connected with the preparation of the case to be presented before the adjudication panel and the SDT.[212] Moreover the reports prepared by the Law Society and the accountancy firm[213] were also protected as if they were not that "would be inconsistent with the purpose of the privilege which is to protect the integrity of the judicial process from collateral attacks."[214] On the other hand, where an inquiry, however formally conducted, amounts to no more than a preliminary investigation, its proceedings will not attract absolute privilege.[215]

---

[208] Ibid.

[209] Lord Fraser of Tullybelton said at 388:
"Cases such as *Dawkins v Lord Rokeby* L.R. 7 (H.L.) 744 and *Barratt v Kearns* [1905] 1 K.B. 504 show that absolute privilege may apply if the inquiry is a step leading directly towards determination of an issue by the authority who appointed it. In each case, the object of the tribunal, its constitution and its manner of proceeding must all be considered before the question can be answered."

[210] [2011] EWHC 998 (QB). It should be noted that in *Adams v The Law Society of England and Wales* [2012] EWHC 980 Foskett J. suggested (at [155]), obiter, that *Baxendale-Walker v Middleton* may need to be reconsidered in the light of the decision of the Court of Appeal in *Accident Exchange Ltd v Autofocus Ltd* [2010] EWCA 788, in particular with regard to the issue whether immunity could arise where a preliminary report was prepared with the kind of malevolence necessary to sustain the tort of misfeasance.

[211] Ibid. at [91].

[212] Ibid. at [90].

[213] While Supperstone J. accepted that the accountancy firm's report fell under the category of expert witness report, he nevertheless held that the report was protected by absolute immunity notwithstanding the decision of the Supreme Court in *Jones v Kaney* [2011] UKSC 13. Supperstone J. concluded that *Jones v Kaney* applied only to claims made by clients against their *own* expert in negligence and left unaltered the law applicable to experts sued on similar grounds by the opposing party.

[214] Ibid. at [127].

[215] See *O'Connor v Waldron* [1935] A.C. 76 PC, as explained in *Trapp v Mackie* [1979] 1 W.L.R. 387–388; *Medical Practitioners Board of Victoria v Mann* [2000] VSCA 89; [2000] 1 V.R. 609.

Examples: tribunals of a judicial nature. Most tribunals with which   **13.23**
the central government is concerned (but not Employment Tribunals or the
Immigration and Asylum Tribunal) have been absorbed into a unified tribunal
system under the Tribunals, Courts and Enforcement Act 2007, with a mainly
appellate Upper Tribunal and a First Tier Tribunal sitting in specialised
"chambers". There is no express provision in the Act for defamation but the
Upper Tribunal has the same "powers, rights, privileges and authority" as the
High Court (or the Court of Session in Scotland) in relation to the attendance
and examination of witnesses, the production and inspection of documents
and "all other matters incidental to its functions",[216] which must equate it
with the High Court for the purposes of defamation. The position of the First
Tier Tribunal will no doubt have to be considered in the light of specific
procedural rules,[217] but it may still be helpful to give examples of tribunals the
proceedings of which have been held to attract absolute privilege.

An employment tribunal is exercising a judicial function for this purpose[218]
and the same was held of an Authorisation Tribunal of the Securities Association under the Financial Services Act 1986[219] and of a police disciplinary
tribunal established by Regulations made under the Police Act 1964.[220] It was
held that a military court of inquiry:

> "though not a court of record, nor a court of law, nor coming within the ordinary
> definition of a court of justice, was nevertheless a court duly constituted and
> recognised by the Articles of War and the Mutiny Act",

and that oral or written statements made by a witness summoned before such
court were absolutely privileged.[221] Similarly, a military service tribunal
under the Military Service Acts during the First World War was held to be

---

[216] S.25(1).

[217] The procedural rules for first tier tribunals are available at: *http://www.justice.gov.uk/
tribunals/rules*.

[218] *Wilson v Westney* [2001] EWCA Civ 839 at [11]. Cf. *Tadd v Eastwood* [1985] I.C.R. 132
CA.

[219] *Mahon v Rahn (No.2)* [2000] 1 W.L.R. 2051 CA. See also *Hamouth v Edwards & Angell*
[2005] BCCA 172; 253 D.L.R. (4th) 372 (Securities and Exchange Commission inquiry).

[220] *Heath v Metropolitan Police Comr* [2004] EWCA Civ 943; [2005] I.C.R. 329. *Heath* was
a discrimination case. In *Currie v Chief Constable of Surrey* [1982] 1 W.L.R. 215, where a
subpoena was issued to compel attendance at a hearing under the Police (Discipline) Regulations
1977 under the High Court's power to assist inferior tribunals, McNeill J. was of the opinion that
the witness was probably protected by absolute privilege.

[221] *Dawkins v Lord Rokeby* (1873) L.R. 8 Q.B. 255; affirmed (1875) L.R. 7 H.L. 744. The court
of inquiry in this case by Queen's Regulations was not to be considered as a judicial body, could
not administer an oath, sat in private and could only report to the commander-in-chief. See also
Jekyll v Sir John Moore (1806) 6 Esp. 63. Similarly a commission issued by the bishop of a
diocese under the Pluralities Acts 1838 to 1885 to inquire into the performance by an incumbent
of his ecclesiastical duties was held to be performing a judicial function: *Barratt v Kearns* [1905]
1 K.B. 504 CA. In *Thompson v Turbott* [1962] N.Z.L.R. 298 it was held that the proceedings of
the Public Service Board of Appeal in determining appeals from the rejection of applications for
certain positions attracted an absolute privilege; see also *Fitherbert v Acheson* [1921] N.Z.L.R.
265 (Maori Land Board a court of record by statute).

discharging a judicial function.[222] Proceedings before a justice of the peace under the Lunacy Act 1890 for the reception and detention of an insane person were held to be of a judicial nature.[223] The Disciplinary Committee constituted under the Solicitors Act 1974 is a judicial tribunal within the meaning of the rule,[224] as was the Office for the Supervision of Solicitors,[225] and the Fitness to Practise Panel (formerly the Professional Conduct Committee) of the General Medical Council,[226] and accordingly an absolute privilege attaches to statements made before such bodies when holding an inquiry as to the professional conduct of those over whom they have jurisdiction, and also to statements contained in any petition, information or letter of complaint by which such bodies are set in motion, or in any statutory declaration made in support or in answer.[227] The rule was also applied to an inquiry and decision of the Benchers of an Inn of Court, in the exercise of their disciplinary powers over a member of the Bar (now replaced in this respect by the Council of the Inns of Court), or by the judges on appeal from such a decision, even though their powers were not statutory.[228]

---

[222] *Co-partnership Farms v Harvey-Smith* [1918] 2 K.B. 405.

[223] *Hodson v Pare* [1899] 1 Q.B. 455 CA; and see *Everett v Griffiths* [1920] 3 K.B. 163 at 206; [1921] 1 A.C. 631.

[224] *Addis v Crocker* [1961] 1 Q.B. 11 CA (then Solicitors Act 1959, now Solicitors Act 1974 and SI 1994/228). *Lilley v Roney* (1892) 61 L.J.Q.B. 727; *Voratovic v Law Society of Upper Canada* (1978) 87 D.L.R. (3d) 140; *Hercules v Phease* [1994] 2 V.R. 386. See also, *Baxendale-Walker v Middleton* [2011] EWHC 998 (QB).

[225] *Gray v Avadis* [2003] EWHC 1830 (QB). But see *Murtough v Betham* [2004] N.S.W.S.C. 753 at [23]–[25], where the issue arose in Australian proceedings.

[226] *Ahari v Birmingham Heartlands, etc. NHS Trust* (2008) UKEAT 0355/07/CEA (a discrimination case). The decision in *Ahari* was accepted as correct by Eady J. in *White v Southampton University Hospitals NHS Trust* [2011] EWHC 825 (QB) at [16]. See also, *Vaidya v General Medical Council* [2010] EWHC 984 (QB) per Gray J. at [48] (refusal to strike out defence of absolute privilege in respect of publication by GMC on its website of the decision of a Fitness to Practice Panel) and the observations of Fry, Cotton and Bowen L.JJ. in *Leeson v General Council of Medical Education* (1889) 43 Ch.D. 366, 386, 379 and 383 respectively. See also *Allbutt v General Council of Medical Education* (1889) 23 Q.B.D. 400; *Thompson v NSW Branch of the BMA* [1924] A.C. 764. In *Royal Aquarium v Parkinson* [1892] 1 Q.B. at 447 there is an obiter dictum of Fry L.J. to the contrary. See also Report of the Faulks Committee, Cmnd.5909 (1975), para.202. The Panel is equated with the solicitors' disciplinary body in *Gregory v Portsmouth CC* [2000] 1 A.C. 419 HL. See also *D v Kong* [2003] SGHC 165; [2003] 3 S.L.R. 146 (Complaints and Disciplinary Committees of Singapore Medical Council). In *Hackethal v Weisbein*, 592 P.2d 1175 (Cal. 1979) absolute privilege was held not to apply to a medical peer review proceeding.

[227] *Lilley v Roney* (1892) 61 L.J.Q.B. 727. In *Hung v Gardiner* [2003] BCCA 257; 227 D.L.R. (4th) 282 the BCCA held that letters to the Law Society of British Columbia and the Certified General Accountants Association of British Columbia informing them of disciplinary action against the plaintiff were protected by absolute privilege even though neither body elected to take any further action.

[228] *Lincoln v Daniels* [1962] Q.B. 237 CA, differing from the obiter dictum referred to in fn.201, above. If Davies L.J. suggested otherwise in *Egger v Chelmsford* [1965] 1 Q.B. 248 at 272–273, it is submitted that he did so per incuriam. In *Poland v Maitland* (1994) 27 C.P.C. (3d) 334 the statutory disciplinary procedure for the Royal Canadian Mounted Police was held to be of a judicial nature.

Examples: not judicial functions. In *Gregory v Portsmouth CC*[229] it was   **13.24**
held that a disciplinary committee appointed by a local authority to investigate
the conduct of a councillor was not a judicial body for this purpose and was
therefore covered only by qualified privilege; nor is a communication to the
Parole Board protected as a step in a judicial proceeding.[230] As has already
been pointed out, a domestic forum which derives its authority solely from the
submission or consent of the parties, e.g. the committee of a club called to
inquire into the alleged misconduct of a member, is not a judicial tribunal
within the meaning of the rule, no matter how closely its procedures may be
modelled on those of the courts for it is not "recognized by law".[231] The
following activities of a public nature have been held to be discharging
administrative rather than judicial functions so that the proceedings attracted
only qualified privilege: a social security adjudication,[232] a planning appeal
inquiry,[233] a Royal Commission,[234] an investigation by a commissioner under
monopolies legislation in Canada,[235] a meeting of the old London County
Council for granting music and dancing licences,[236] and a meeting of justices
of the peace for granting or renewing licences for the sale of intoxicating
liquors.[237]

---

[229] [2000] 1 A.C. 419 HL.

[230] *Daniels v Griffiths* [1998] E.M.L.R. 488 CA.

[231] See para.13.19, above. See also *Tertiary Institutes Allied Staff Association v Tahana* [1998] 1 N.Z.L.R. 41 NZCA; *Gray v M* [1998] 2 N.Z.L.R. 161 NZCA.

[232] *Purdew v Serres-Smith, The Times*, September 9, 1992; *Hearts of Oak Ass Co. v Att-Gen* [1932] A.C. 392 at 405 (inquiry by inspector appointed by the Industrial Assurance Commissioner under s.17(1) of the Industrial Assurance Act 1923 held not to be a judicial proceeding so as to confer an absolute privilege); *Smith v National Meter Co* [1945] K.B. 543 (medical referee under Workmen's Compensation Act not performing judicial function). In *Collins v H. Whiteway Ltd* [1927] 2 K.B. 378 it was held that a Court of Referees constituted under s.15 of the Unemployment Insurance Act 1920 for deciding claims made upon the unemployment insurance funds was not exercising judicial functions. Though the nature of the two statutory schemes was very different, the *Purdew* case indicates a continuing unwillingness to regard social security adjudications as "judicial". Cf. *Stark v Auerbach* [1979] 3 W.W.R. 563 (Board of Review under Workmen's Compensation Act performed a function like a court, applying *Perry v Hetherington* [1971] 5 W.W.R. 670—Court of Review (of property assessments) performing judicial function).

[233] *Richards v Cresswell, The Times*, April 24, 1987. In *Atkins v Mays* [1974] 2 N.Z.L.R. 459 the hearing of objection and counter-objection to a town-planning scheme before a town-planning committee attracted absolute privilege; sed quaere, for the tests applied were more appropriate to administrative law. Cf. *Tertiary Institutes Allied Staff Association v Tahana* [1998] 1 N.Z.L.R. 41 NZCA.

[234] *Douglas v Lewis* (1982) 30 S.A.S.R. 50 (but the court referred to statutory provisions in the Commonwealth of Australia and in N.S.W.). Cf. *Bretherton v Kaye* [1971] V.R. 111 (board of inquiry into police malpractice: counsel's opening absolutely privileged).

[235] *O'Connor v Waldron* [1935] A.C. 76 PC. See also *Re Pergamon Press* [1971] Ch. 388 at 400, 404 (witnesses at Department of Trade inquiry not absolutely privileged).

[236] *Royal Aquarium v Parkinson* [1892] 1 Q.B. 431 CA; *R. v LCC, Re Empire Theatre* (1894) 71 L.T. 638; cf. *R. v East Riding QS* [1968] 1 Q.B. 32 CA at 53.

[237] *Mann, Crossman v Binhorn, The Times*, February 1, 1910; *Attwood v Chapman* [1914] 3 K.B. 275. Under the Licensing Act 2003 licensing of the sale of alcoholic liquor is dealt with by the local authority, though there is an appeal to the magistrates' court, and it would be surprising if this were not a "judicial" proceeding for this purpose. Even under the old regime there were decisions that were arguably contrary to the view that the proceedings of licensing justices were

SECTION 4. STATEMENTS MADE BY ONE OFFICER OF STATE TO
ANOTHER IN THE COURSE OF HIS OFFICIAL DUTY

13.25 General. Though the limits of the principle are difficult to define, absolute privilege attaches to certain communications made between officers of state acting in an official capacity. A similar but not identical principle confers absolute privilege upon foreign state documents because the comity of nations renders claims based upon them not justiciable in the English courts. Under a quite different principle, a party may object to the production of documents in his possession on the ground that production would be injurious to the public interest.

13.26 The scope of absolute privilege: municipal officers of state. In *Chatterton v Secretary of State for India*[238] the plaintiff, an army officer, sued for a libel in a communication sent by the Secretary of State for India to the Parliamentary Under-Secretary in order to enable the latter to answer a Parliamentary question. The claim was dismissed on the ground of absolute privilege. The basis of this was stated to be that it:

> "would be injurious to the public interest that such an inquiry should be allowed, because it would tend to take from an officer of state his freedom of action in a matter concerning the public weal. If an officer of state were liable to an action of libel concerning such a communication as this, actual malice could be alleged to rebut a plea of privilege, and it would be necessary that he should be called as a witness to deny that he acted maliciously. That he should be placed in such a position, and that his conduct should be questioned before a jury, would clearly be against the public interest, and prejudicial to the independence necessary for the performance of his functions as an official of the state."[239]

The fact that the report relates to a commercial rather than to a political, diplomatic or military matter does not take the case outside the area of absolute privilege,[240] nor does the fact that the communication is made from the senior to the junior official or vice versa.[241] It will be observed that in *Chatterton's* case the communication was at a very high level. In *Gibbons v*

---

not judicial (see *Jeffrey v Evans* [1964] 1 W.L.R. 505; *R. v East Riding QS* [1968] 1 Q.B. 32 CA and the 10th edition of this book). However, the distinction between the administrative and judicial powers of justices is still drawn in the Defamation Act 1996, Sch.1, para.11(b).

[238] [1895] 2 Q.B. 189 CA.

[239] [1895] 2 Q.B. 189 at 191, per Lord Esher M.R.

[240] *M. Isaacs v Cook* [1925] K.B. 391, where absolute privilege was held to attach to a statement in a report made by the High Commissioner of Australia, in the UK, in his official capacity, to the Prime Minister of Australia, though the report related to a commercial matter, namely, the sale of fruit in the English market. Since this case concerned a communication between officials of a "foreign" state it arguably falls within para.13.27: *Fayed v Al-Tajir* [1988] Q.B. 712 CA at 727, but the point stated here is unaffected.

[241] *Peerless Bakery v Watts* [1955] N.Z.L.R. 339.

Duffell[242] the High Court of Australia declined to apply the same rule to a report made in the course of his duty by an inspector of police to his superior officer which contained defamatory references to a subordinate, Evatt J. remarking that:

> "absolute immunity from the consequences of defamation is so serious a derogation from the citizen's right to the state's protection of his good name that its existence at all can only be conceded in those few cases where overwhelmingly strong reasons of public policy of another kind cut across this elementary right of civic protection, and any extension of the area of immunity must be viewed with the most jealous suspicion and resisted until its necessity is demonstrated."[243]

On somewhat similar facts, arising from a report to the Commissioner of Metropolitan Police, the Court of Appeal declined to strike out the claim for libel.[244] It is not clear how far the absolute privilege extends below ministerial level[245] but it seems plain that there is no blanket immunity for communications between civil servants.[246]

It has also been held that absolute privilege attaches to a communication made by a military or naval officer for any defamatory statement in a report made by him in the course of duty to his superior officer,[247] though here again

---

[242] (1932) 47 C.L.R. 520. See also *Jackson v Magrath* (1947) 75 C.L.R. 293: in report of Taxation Commissioner it was stated there were cases of evasion of tax which, it was considered, were due to unreasonable carelessness in the circumstances. The plaintiff (respondent on appeal) had understated his taxable income by a large amount and an additional tax by way of penalty had been imposed. In an action of libel against the Commissioner, held (by two judges) that the report was absolutely privileged, and (by three judges), on the footing of qualified privilege, that there was no evidence of malice. Latham C.J. (at 307) expressly declined to extend the rule of absolute privilege to the Department of Taxation.

[243] (1932) 47 C.L.R. 520 at 534.

[244] *Merricks v Nott-Bower* [1965] 1 Q.B. 57 (referring to the "very small category" of cases attracting absolute privilege). Canadian law may be more generous to defendants with regard to police reports: *McCarthy v City of Regina* (1921) 60 D.L.R. 205; *Dowson v R.* (1981) 124 D.L.R. (3d) 260, Fed CA.

[245] *Szalatnay-Stacho v Fink* [1946] 1 All E.R. 303 (on appeal [1947] K.B. 1). In *Friend v Civil Aviation Authority (No.2)*, December 21, 2000, (QB), it was held that letters from the Civil Aviation Authority to the Secretary of State in order to allow the latter to respond to a Member of Parliament were absolutely privileged. So were ancillary publications to civil servants in the ordinary course of business.

[246] In *Fayed v Al-Tajir* [1988] Q.B. 712 CA at 732. Mustill L.J. referred to the "high officers of state contemplated by the *Chatterton* line of authority". Compare the law in the US, where the privilege appears to apply to all communications between federal officers: *Barr v Mateo*, 360 U.S. 564 (1959). But state law with regard to state officials is not necessarily so generous: 50 Am. Jur. 2d, *Libel and Slander*, paras 270 et seq. The Restatement, 2d, *Torts*, para.591 extends absolute privilege only to governors and or other superior executive officers of a state.

[247] *Dawkins v Lord Paulet* (1869) L.R. 5 Q.B. 94; *Home v Bentinck* (1806) 2 Brod. & Bing. 130. The report must be an official report. A private letter written by a military or naval officer to his superior officer on military or naval matters would at the most be entitled to a qualified privilege: *Dickson v Earl of Wilton* (1859) 1 F. & F. 419; *Dickson v Combermere* (1863) 3 F. & F. 527; and see *Wright v Cantrell* (1943) 44 S R N S W 45 (statement defamatory of civilian made in course of duty by member of armed force of friendly foreign power, not absolutely privileged).

the scope of the circumstances in which privilege exists is uncertain,[248] and it has been suggested that the leading case may no longer even be good law.[249]

Whether or not the existence of these forms of absolute privilege is determined solely by the status of the persons between whom the communication is made, different principles govern the disclosure of documents where objection is made on the ground of the public interest. This is dealt with below.[250]

13.27 Officials of foreign states. Even though a claim for defamation may be formally subject to the jurisdiction of the English courts, the comity of nations requires that the court should be cautious in meddling in the affairs of a foreign sovereign state. Accordingly, in *Fayed v Al-Tajir*[251] a libel action based upon a memorandum circulated within a foreign embassy was dismissed.[252] While qualified privilege might confer adequate protection upon the defendant, the issue of malice which might be opened up by that defence would require the sort of inquiry into the workings of the foreign embassy that an English court ought to abjure.[253] Nor was it to the point that the immunity from suit might extend more widely than the privilege accorded to English officials discussed above, for the policy considerations were different.[254] On the facts the requirements of comity were given effect to by declaring the document to be the subject of absolute privilege but where the action had not gone to trial that might be done in other ways, e.g. by seeking a stay of the action, by applying to strike it out or by objecting to the admissibility of the document.[255]

This principle goes beyond the immunity granted to diplomatic personnel and to foreign sovereign states.[256] The European Court of Human Rights has

---

[248] See *Richards v Naum* [1967] 1 Q.B. 620 CA (which in fact concerned the armed forces of a friendly foreign power).

[249] *S v Newham LBC* [1998] E.M.L.R. 583 CA at 594, referring to *Dawkins v Lord Paulet* (1869) L.R. 5 Q.B. 94.

[250] See para.13.28, below.

[251] [1988] Q.B. 712 CA.

[252] Diplomatic immunity was waived, though the CA expressed doubts as to the correctness of this on the facts. In *Komarek v Ramco Energy Plc*, unreported, November 21, 2002, Eady J. held (at [25]) that the operation of any such bar against a remedy based on diplomatic considerations, whether of personal immunity or the inviolability of archives, documents or correspondence, was properly to be classified as procedural and not as an absence of right.

[253] Ibid. at 731.

[254] Ibid. at 732.

[255] Ibid. at 735. In *Skrine v Euromoney Publications Plc* [2001] E.M.L.R. 16, Morland J. held, in a contribution claim arising out of litigation in Malaysia, that an English court had to exercise judicial restraint or abstention and not adjudicate upon the acts or transactions of the sovereign, executive or judiciary of a friendly foreign state; but that it would consider and pass judgment upon the laws, court judgments and administration of litigation of a friendly foreign state when not to do so would be manifestly unjust. The CA declined to embark on a full examination of these matters: [2001] EWCA Civ 1479; [2002] E.M.L.R. 15.

[256] para.8.4, above.

held that sovereign immunity creates a "procedural bar" which engages art.6(1) of the European Convention on Human Rights, but as it is based on a generally recognised principle of public international law it cannot be regarded as a disproportionate restriction on the right of access to a court.[257] It remains to be seen whether the same applies to the principle in this paragraph.

Privileged documents and public interest immunity. In some cases a **13.28** party may be able to object to the production of a document or the public interest may require that a document should not be disclosed or that evidence of its contents should not be given ("public interest immunity"). This has nothing to do with the defence of absolute privilege[258] as such[259] and is by no means confined to the law of defamation,[260] but if the claimant is unable to produce evidence of a defamatory communication his action will fail just the same.[261]

If disclosure is ordered, under the common law the party to whom it is disclosed is treated as giving an undertaking[262] that it will be used only for the purpose of the proceedings in which it is disclosed.[263] In *Riddick v Thames Board Mills*[264] the plaintiff was unable to bring an action for defamation on the basis of a memorandum disclosed on discovery in an action by the plaintiff against the defendants for false imprisonment.[265] A similar restriction applies to information disclosed to the defence in a criminal case.[266]

---

[257] *Fogarty v United Kingdom* App. no.37112/97; (2002) 34 EHRR 12. See para.8.5, above.

[258] However, such a right to object to the admission of evidence is commonly called a privilege—e.g. the right to prevent evidence being given of what was said or done in the context of obtaining legal advice is known as "legal professional privilege". What is now called public interest immunity was formerly called "Crown privilege" but the expression ceased to be used after *Rogers v Secretary of State for the Home Department* [1973] A.C. 388.

[259] But in *Hasselblad (GB) v Orbinson* [1985] Q.B. 475 CA reliance was placed upon the cases in this area in support of what was in effect a novel head of absolute privilege: see para.13.1, above.

[260] Hence details should be sought in specialised works such as Matthews and Malek, *Disclosure*.

[261] See *M. Isaacs v Cook* [1925] K.B. 391 at 398–399; *Buttes Gas & Oil Co. v Hammer (Nos 2 & 3)* [1982] A.C. 888 at 930–931; *Gibbons v Duffell* (1932) 47 C.L.R. 520 at 530. But the distinction may be important where a document is disclosed and put in evidence at the trial without objection: *Fayed v Al-Tajir* [1988] Q.B. 712 CA at 726.

[262] In reality it is an obligation imposed by law: *Prudential Assurance Co. Ltd v Fountain Page Ltd* [1991] 1 W.L.R. 756 CA at 764.

[263] See now CPR r.31.22 and para.31.13, below.

[264] [1977] Q.B. 881 CA. Under CPR r.31.22 it is provided that the party to whom disclosure is made may not use the document for other purposes unless it has been read to or by the court or referred to at a public hearing or the court gives permission or the other party consents. However, the court may prohibit the collateral use of a document even if it has been read or referred to in a public hearing, as to which see *McBride v Body Shop International Plc* [2007] EWHC 1658 (QB) at [42].

[265] This principle is not applicable where a document is disclosed voluntarily rather than under compulsion: *Hasselblad (GB) v Orbinson* [1985] Q.B. 475 CA, but the court dismissed the action nevertheless: see para.13.1, above.

[266] *Taylor v Director of the Serious Fraud Office* [1999] 2 A.C. 177 HL.

SECTION 5. PROCEEDINGS IN PARLIAMENT

13.29 The Bill of Rights. Article 9 of the Bill of Rights (1688)[267] provides "That the freedom of speech, and debates or proceedings in Parliament ought not to be impeached or questioned in any court, or place out of Parliament."[268] Accordingly, no action will lie against a member of either House of Parliament for defamatory words, no matter how malicious, spoken in the course of any parliamentary debate or proceeding.

> "It is clear that statements made by members of either House of Parliament in their places in the House, though they might be untrue to their knowledge, could not be made the foundation of civil or criminal proceedings, however injurious they might be to the interest of a third person."[269]

The European Court of Human Rights has left undecided whether the Bill of Rights creates a "procedural immunity" which requires to be justified under art.6(1) of the European Convention on Human Rights, though it observed that[270] the Bill of Rights:

> "is framed not in terms of a substantive defence to civil claims, but rather in terms of a procedural bar to the determination by a court of any claim which derives from words spoken in Parliament".[271]

In any event, the immunity could not be said to exceed the margin of appreciation allowed to states in limiting an individual's right of access to court and the creation of exceptions to the immunity, "the application of which depended upon the individual facts of any particular case, would seriously undermine the legitimate aims pursued".[272]

13.30 Extent of the privilege. What, besides a speech, is a protected "proceeding" is not wholly clear. If the statement is contained in a document tabled in

---

[267] Given the force of law by 1 Will. & Mar. c.2. Although the Bill is a pre-Union measure and the Scots Claim of Right is less specific on freedom of speech, the law is the same on both sides of the border: *Adams v Guardian Newspapers Ltd* [2003] ScotCS 131; 2003 S.L.T. 1058. Members of the European Parliament enjoy the same immunities in their own country as national parliamentarians and elsewhere are immune from legal proceedings.

[268] Art.9 applies in other Commonwealth countries (*Prebble v Television New Zealand* [1995] 1 A.C. 321 PC at 333) but sometimes there is further specific provision (e.g. Defamation Act (NSW) 2005, s.27). Art.I, s.6 of the Constitution of the United States provides that: "for any speech or debate in either House [the Senators and Representatives] shall not be questioned in any other place."

[269] Per Cockburn C.J. in *Ex p. Wason* (1869) L.R. 4 Q.B. 573 at 576; *Dillon v Balfour* (1887) 20 L.R. Ir. 600 (see now for Ireland, Constitution Act 1937, art.15, and Committees of the Houses of the Oireachtas (Privilege and Procedure) Act 1976; see also cl.15(2) of the Irish Defamation Bill); *Gipps v McElhone* (1881) 2 N.S.W.L.R. 18. As in the case of the other absolute privileges, this is granted for the benefit of the public in ensuring freedom of debate in the legislature: per Parsons C.J. commenting on the Bill of Rights in the Massachusetts Constitution of 1780 in *Coffin v Coffin* (1808) 4 Mass. 1 at 27.

[270] *A v UK* App. no.35373/97; (2003) 36 EHRR 51.

[271] At [64].

[272] At [88].

Parliament it is protected and this extends to the publication of it to a typist for preparation in the ordinary course of business.[273] It has been said that the privilege is limited to what is said or done by a member in the exercise of his functions as a member and in the transaction of Parliamentary business,[274] so that it would not cover delivery to members of the House of a letter relating to a private dispute between members[275] or a casual conversation.[276] A letter written by a member to a Minister, criticising the conduct of a statutory board, is probably not a proceeding in Parliament.[277] Under s.13 of the Defamation Act 1996[278] the protection of any enactment or rule of law for words spoken or things done *in the course of*, or *for the purposes of* or *incidental to* proceedings in Parliament[279] extends (without prejudice to the generality of the foregoing) to:

"(a) the giving of evidence before either House or a committee[280];

---

[273] *Holding v Jennings* [1979] V.R. 289.

[274] Per Corbett C.J. in *Poovalingam v Rajbani*, 1992 (1) S.A. 283 at 290, AD. The case turned on ss.2 and 8 of the Union of South Africa Act but (a) this was based on the Bill of Rights and (b) the above statement is made in the context of English law, of which there is a full review. See also Erskine May, *Parliamentary Practice*, 22nd edn, p.95 and De Smith (1958) 21 M.L.R. 465 at 472.

[275] *Poovalingam v Rajbani* 1992 (1) S.A. 283 AD. In *Adams v Guardian Newspapers Ltd* [2003] ScotCS 131; 2003 S.L.T. 1058 an article accused an MP of leaking the confidential suicide note of another MP. The note was not a "proceeding in Parliament" even though it was addressed to some other MPs.

[276] *Coffin v Coffin* (1808) 4 Mass. 1 seems more marginal (defamatory statement by member after closure of debate in response to further information provided in conversation by proposer of resolution; liable).

[277] The Committee of Privileges of the House of Commons considered that it was, the Attorney-General, however, dissenting: see House of Commons Sessions Papers 1956 57, no.305. However, the House resolved not to treat it as such: C.J. (1957–58) 260. See also H.L. 227, 1957–58. In *Re Parliamentary Privilege Act 1770* [1958] A.C. 331 PC, the board expressly declined to answer the question, or the further question whether the mere issue of a writ for libel against the member would be a breach of parliamentary privilege; they held that the House would not be acting contrary to the 1770 Act if they treated the issue of a writ as such a breach. See also Report on Parliamentary Privilege (1967) H.C. 34, para.93. A similar letter was held not privileged in Quebec: *Vezina v Lacroix* (1936) 40 Q.P.R. 1.

[278] Cf. s.16(2) of the Australian Parliamentary Privileges Act 1987 (C'wth):
"all words spoken and acts done in the course of, or for purposes of, or incidental to, the transacting of the business of a House or of a committee";
and the submissions of the Solicitors General in *Dingle v Associated Newspapers* [1960] 2 Q.B. 405 at 411–412 and *Rost v Edwards* [1990] 2 Q.B. 460 at 462–463.

[279] S.13(4). The subsection does not itself create the privilege. The purpose of s.13 as a whole is to allow a member to waive privilege when that would render impracticable the trial of a claim brought by him (see para.13.32, below). This subsection makes it clear that such a waiver does not affect his own immunity from suit (or that of any other member) for words spoken in the House etc. Without prejudice to the generality of subsection (4), subsection (5) provides that the matters listed therein fall within subsection (4). If the matter were *tabula rasa* the expression "incidental to any proceedings in Parliament" would be a very wide one. It might cover, e.g. communications with persons outside Parliament, but it is submitted that the context makes this impossible. Chapter 2 of the Report of the Joint Committee on Parliamentary Privilege (HL Paper 43/HC 214–1, 1998–99) proposed a new statutory definition.

[280] This was protected by privilege before the Act: *Goffin v Donelly* (1881) 6 Q.B.D. 307; more fully reported 50 L.J.Q.B. 303. Under s.13(5) "a committee" means a committee of either House or a joint committee of both Houses.

(b) the presentation or submission of a document to either House[281] or a committee[282];

(c) the preparation of a document for the purposes of or incidental to the transacting of any such[283] business;

(d) the formulation, making or publication of a document, including a report, by or pursuant to an order of either House or a committee[284]; and

(e) any communication with the Parliamentary Commissioner for Standards or any person having functions in connection with the registration of members' interests."[285]

As the section contemplates that the protection of Parliamentary privilege is granted to "a person" who acts for the purposes of or incidentally to the proceedings in Parliament it extends beyond members, to officials of the House and perhaps to certain others.[286]

---

[281] In *Bruton v Estate Agents Licensing Authority* [1996] 2 V.R. 274, without any such definition the submission of a report by a statutory body was not a proceeding "of the Parliament" for the purposes of s.3A of the Wrongs Act 1958 (Vict.).

[282] Petitions to the House or a committee were privileged before the Act: *Lake v King* (1680) 1 Saund. 131; *Kane v Mulvaney* (1866) I.R. 2 C.L. 402. Cf. *Rivlin v Bilainkin* [1953] 1 Q.B. 485 (delivery to member of document unconnected with proceedings of House not privileged). It is not possible for an outsider to manufacture Parliamentary privilege by the artifice of sending the document to an M.P.

"The privilege is not attracted to a document [under section 16(2) of the Australian Act] until at least the Parliamentary member or his agent does some act with respect to it for purposes of transacting business in the House. Junk mail does not, merely by its being delivered, attract privilege of Parliament":

McPherson J.A. in *Rowley v O'Chee* [2000] 1 Qd. R. 207 Qd CA at 221; *Thomson v Broadley* [2000] QSC 100.

[283] The word "business" occurs nowhere else in s.13. It therefore means the matters mentioned in (a) and (b). The Select Committee on the Official Secrets Act thought that a draft of a question sent by a member to a Minister, or to another member with a view to obtaining advice, was privileged: May, *Parliamentary Practice*, 22nd edn, p.95. Under s.16(2) of the Australian Parliamentary Privileges Act 1987 (C'th) it has been held that where a document comes into the possession of a Senator and he elects to keep it with a view to using it for the purpose of a question or debate, his procuring, obtaining or retaining it is an act done "for the purposes of or incidental to the transacting of the business" of the Senate: *Rowley v O'Chee* [2000] 1 Qd. R. 207 Qd CA. But where a document is prepared otherwise than with a view to submission to Parliament, parliamentary privilege does not attach to all copies of the document under the Australian Act merely because a member proposes to table it in Parliament.

"[W]hilst ... a document containing allegedly defamatory statements retained by a Member for a relevant purpose can not be obtained on discovery and used to prove such possession, the Member's possession for that purpose would not give rise to a wholesale application of privilege to other copies. If copies had also been supplied to newspapers for publication, the fact that the Member had decided to keep the copy in his or her possession for a relevant purpose would not prevent the copies supplied to the newspapers from being tendered in defamation proceedings against others":

Szwarcbord v Gallop (2002) 167 F.L.R. 262 at [22].

[284] There is some overlap here with the Parliamentary Papers Act 1840: para.13.34, below.

[285] S.13(5).

[286] E.g. if a member's researcher were to produce a background paper for the member on a matter relating to Parliamentary business and this contained a libel he would be protected. This seems to have been the view of the Joint Committee on Parliamentary Privilege (HL Paper 43/HC 214–1, 1998–99, para.115) provided the material was "directly related to proceedings in Parliament ... such as preparatory material related to a member's participation in debate or in committee". In *Erglis v Buckley* [2005] QCA 404 under the similar but not identical Parliament of Queensland Act 2001 (Qd.), s.9(2) the defendants had, at a Minister's invitation, prepared a

Statements made outside Parliament are not protected by absolute[287] privilege[288] even if they simply repeat what has been said therein.[289]

"The right of members of Parliament to speak their minds in Parliament without any risk of incurring liability as a result is absolute, and must be fully respected. But that right is not infringed if a member, having spoken his mind and in so doing defamed another person, thereafter chooses to repeat his statement outside Parliament."[290]

This is so even if the extra-Parliamentary statement does not literally repeat the words used in Parliament but merely adopts them by reference,[291] for even

---

document which the Minister then, pursuant to an undertaking by her, read out in Parliament and the publication to the Minister was held to be within the protection of the statute. Below ([2005] QSC 25) it was held that the position would have been different had the document been unsolicited (*R. v Grassby* (1991) 55 A. Crim. R. 419 on the NSW legislation) or had the Minister merely undertaken to consider it, but Jerrard J.A. did not think "solicitation" was a necessary element. At an earlier stage of the proceedings (*Erglis v Buckley* [2004] QCA 223; [2004] Qd. R. 599) the issue was whether the plaintiff could rely on the reading of the document in Parliament as a matter affecting damages, though no attempt was made to found a claim on that. The majority of the CA declined to strike out this element of the claim.

[287] However, now that the statutory "reporting privilege" is not confined to newspapers and broadcasts, there may be cases where a member who afterwards circulates a report of his speech to persons outside the House may rely on the qualified privilege granted by Sch.1 to the Defamation Act 1996; but cf. *Rogers v Nationwide News* [2003] HCA 52; 216 C.L.R. 327.

[288] Save in so far as they might fall within s.13(4) (e.g. para.(e)). Cf. in Canada *Re Clark and Att-Gen* (1977) 81 D.L.R. (3d) 33.

[289] *Buchanan v Jennings* [2004] UKPC 36; [2005] 1 A.C. 115; *Duncombe v Daniell* (1838) 2 Jur. 32; *R. v Abingdon* (1794) 1 Esp. 226; *R. v Creevy* (1813) 1 M. & S. 273; *Stopforth v Goyer* (1978) 87 D.L.R. (3d) 373. Hence the frequent challenge to repeat something outside the House. But although in certain cases a person who makes a statement to A will be liable for a further publication by A to B which he knows is a likely consequence (para.6.52) a member is still clearly protected by privilege even though he is aware that what he says will be reported outside the House or even broadcast live. Those who report Parliamentary proceedings are protected by qualified privilege: see paras 15.35 and 16.9, below.

[290] *Buchanan v Jennings*, above at [17]. Although this was an appeal from New Zealand it was accepted that the law was the same as that of England.

[291] *Buchanan v Jennings*, above ("I do not resile from what I said in the House about [the plaintiff]" or words to that effect). See also *Makudi v Baron Triesman of Tottenham in the London Borough of Haringey* [2013] EWHC 142 (QB) ("I have covered it all in the evidence to the select committee and I do invite you to rely on the transcript"); *Beitzel v Crabb* [1992] V.R. 121; *Laurence v Katter* (1996) 141 A.L.R. 447 Qd CA at 490. The Faulks Committee Cmnd.5909 (1975), paras 204–210 were also of that view. It should be noted that the decision in *Buchanan v Jennings* has been the subject of significant adverse comment in New Zealand. Having stated its dissatisfaction with the decision, the Privileges Committee of the House of Representatives noted that:

"[o]ne of the principal aims of Parliament's freedom of speech, acknowledged by the courts as much as by Parliament itself, is to avoid the courts being drawn into examining and making judgments on parliamentary proceedings. There is a longstanding principle of mutual restraint between the courts and the legislature whereby one does not interfere in the work of the other... There is a grave danger of this principle breaking down in a case of 'effective repetition'. In defamation a claimant is alleging that false statements have been published with an intent to defame. Certainly if a member repeats a parliamentary statement outside the House it is no protection against the liability that a finding of defamation is tantamount to a finding that the member on the earlier occasion spoke falsely in the House. That may be an inevitable, though unexpressed, conclusion. But in an 'effective repetition' case the parliamentary statements are being put directly to the court because they are the only or the main evidence of the defamation. In these circumstances the principle of mutual restraint breaks down completely, though in such a case the record of Parliament must be examined to determine what the member said there and is treated as now repeating by implication, that does not amount to "questioning" the proceedings in Parliament. However, if a member made defamatory statements outside the House about an unidentifiable person and then identified him in the House, he would be protected by privilege[292]: until the identification there is no actionable libel and when the identification is made, even though it adopts what was said outside, it is a "proceeding in Parliament".

13.31 Broader scope of Bill of Rights. While the particular historical context of art.9 of the Bill of Rights may have been a desire to ensure that members were not subjected to legal liabilities for their conduct as such,[293] it is clear that there is a broader principle, of which this is but one manifestation, under which the courts and Parliament are both astute to recognise their respective constitutional roles.[294] The law is that proceedings in Parliament are not to be "questioned" elsewhere (that is to say, their propriety may not be called in question in the sense that what was said or done was untrue or misleading or actuated by improper motives[295]) and this has implications for defamation law which go beyond the grant of a simple immunity to members. Thus where a member of the New Zealand House of Representatives brought an action for libel in respect of a television programme which accused him of conspiring with businessmen to sell off state assets at unduly low prices, the Privy Council struck out particulars of justification relating to allegedly misleading statements made in the House[296]; and where a claim was made in respect of defamatory words spoken by a member outside the House of Commons (and hence not within the protection of art.9) it was held that the plaintiff was

---

as the court directly judges the quality of the parliamentary proceedings. This has major implications for the relationship between the legislature and the courts."
(*Questions of Privilege Referred 21 July 1998 Concerning Buchanan v Jennings—Report of Privileges Committee* (May 2005) 5).

[292] *Buchanan v Jennings*, above at [19].

[293] *R. v Murphy* (1986) 5 N.S.W.L.R. 18 at 30. The same approach is taken by Lord Browne-Wilkinson in *Pepper v Hart* [1993] A.C. 593 at 638 (which concerned the admissibility of what was said in Parliament as an aid to the construction of legislation) but compare the same judge in *Prebble v Television New Zealand* [1995] 1 A.C. 321 at 334, in the context of libel.

[294] *Prebble v Television New Zealand* [1995] 1 A.C. 321 PC at 332; *Buchanan v Jennings* [2004] UKPC 36; [2005] 1 A.C. 115 at [18].

[295] *Prebble* at 332. However, in *R. v Secretary of State for the Home Dept Ex p. Brind* [1991] 1 A.C. 696 HL, the validity of reasons given in Parliament was examined in judicial review proceedings. In *Pepper v Hart* [1993] A.C. 593 HL, it was held that a clear ministerial statement in Parliament might be called in aid for the construction of legislation. To put forward a statement in Parliament as evidence of the *truth* of what was said in it would not, literally, be to "question" it, but would be just as unacceptable as calling its truth into question: *Mees v Roads Corp* [2003] FCA 306; *Szuty v Smyth* [2004] ACTSC 77.

[296] *Prebble v Television New Zealand* [1995] 1 A.C. 321 PC, disapproving *News Media Ownership v Finlay* [1970] N.Z.L.R. 1089; *R. v Murphy* (1986) 5 N.S.W.L.R. 18 (the effect of which was reversed by the Parliamentary Privileges Act 1987 (C'wth); and *Wright and Advertiser Newspapers v Lewis* (1990) 53 S.A.S.R. 416.

unable to adduce evidence of what the defendant had said in the House in support of a plea of express malice.[297]

The principle applies even though there is no challenge to the validity of any Parliamentary decision or conclusion and the relief claimed in the action before the court does not conflict with the authority of Parliament:

> "The normal impact of parliamentary privilege is to prevent the court from entertaining any evidence, cross-examination or submissions which challenge the veracity or propriety of anything done in the course of the parliamentary proceedings. Thus, it is not permissible to challenge by cross-examination in a later action the veracity of evidence given to a parliamentary committee."[298]

There is, however, no objection to proof, as a matter of history, of what was said or done in Parliament, provided there is no examination of the propriety of those matters.[299]

---

[297] *Church of Scientology v Johnson-Smith* [1972] 1 Q.B. 522, approved in *Pepper v Hart* [1993] A.C. 593. For the same reasons it is thought the member would at common law be precluded from calling evidence of what was said in the House to rebut a plea of malice. Cf. the position where there is no issue of malice and the claim is in respect of a later republication by reference to what was said in the House: para.13.30, above.

[298] *Hamilton v Al Fayed* [2001] A.C. 395 HL at 407. Section 16(3) of the Australian Parliamentary Privileges Act 1987 (C'th) is more explicit in stating the impact of privilege. It provides that:

> "in proceedings in any court or tribunal, it is not lawful for evidence to be tendered or received, questions asked or statements or submissions or comments made, concerning proceedings in Parliament by way of, or for the purpose of (a) questioning or relying on the truth, motive, intention or good faith of anything forming part of those proceedings in Parliament; (b) otherwise questioning or establishing the credibility, motive, intention or good faith of any person; or (c) drawing, or inviting the drawing of, inferences or conclusions wholly or partly from anything forming part of those proceedings in Parliament."

In *Prebble v Television New Zealand* [1995] 1 A.C. 321 at 333 this is said to represent the true principle under the Bill of Rights. The provision was considered in *Rann v Olsen* [2000] SASC 83; [2000] S.A.S.R. 450, Full Court. The claimant told a Parliamentary committee that the defendant had leaked information to the opposition party, the defendant said this was a lie and the claimant sued him in respect of that. It was held that the defendant was precluded by this from advancing a defence of justification, i.e. showing that the claimant had lied to the committee. However, it was open to him to advance a defence of qualified privilege, either at common law or in the extended *Lange* sense (see para.15.26, below). Far from requiring the defendant to show that the charge he had made against the claimant was true, the defence started from the assumption that that could not be shown and was therefore not concerned with the accuracy or otherwise of what the claimant had said to the committee.

> "Nor, in terms of Article 9 of the Bill of Rights will the Court impeach proceedings in Parliament by making a finding about [the defendant's belief], whatever the finding might imply about [the claimant's] truthfulness. In my opinion a court does not impeach proceedings in Parliament by making a finding on a matter which has been the subject of consideration in Parliament, so long as the finding which it makes does not require it to make a finding about what I might call the Parliamentary treatment of the issue"

(Doyle C.J. at [80]).

[299] *Prebble v Television New Zealand* [1995] 1 A.C. 321 PC at 337. In *Buchanan v Jennings (A-G of New Zealand intervening)* [1995] 1 A.C. 321 the Privy Council allowed reference to be made to what had been said in Parliament where the defendant had affirmed outside Parliament a statement that he had previously made within Parliament. Lord Bingham stated (at [18]):

> "In a case such as the present . . . reference is made to the parliamentary record only to prove the historical fact that certain words were uttered. The claim is founded on the later extra-parliamentary statement. The propriety of the member's behaviour as a parliamentarian will not

13.32 The Defamation Act 1996. Where a Member of Parliament brings proceedings for libel the effect of the above principles may seriously hamper the conduct of the defence. The matter was put by an Australian court[300] in the following way:

> "A Member of parliament could sue for defamation in respect of criticism of his statements or conduct in the Parliament. The defendant would be precluded, however, from alleging and proving that what was said by way of criticism was true.[301] This would amount to a gross distortion of the law of defamation . . . Defamation in law is an *untrue* imputation against the reputation of another . . . If the defendant were precluded from proving the truth of what is alleged, the Member of Parliament would be enabled to recover damages, if no other defence applied, for an imputation which was perfectly true. Moreover the defence of fair comment would often be unavailable . . . because it would not be permissible to prove the factual foundation for the expression of opinion. The defence of qualified privilege might be seriously inhibited because the defendant would be prevented from answering an allegation of express malice by proving facts known to him."

If the exclusion of the privileged material would make the fair determination of the case "quite impossible" the correct course would be to stay the proceedings but this is not a step lightly to be taken.[302]

Now, under s.13[303] of the Defamation Act 1996, where the conduct of a person in or in relation to proceedings in Parliament is in issue in defamation proceedings, he may waive the protection of privilege for the purposes of those proceedings.[304] Hence if a member is accused of accepting money to ask

---

be in issue. Nor will his state of mind, motive or intention when saying what he did in Parliament. The situation is analogous with that where a member repeats outside the House, in extenso, a statement previously made in the House. The claim will be directed solely to the extra-parliamentary re-publication, for which the parliamentary record will supply only the text."
In *Rost v Edwards* [1990] 2 Q.B. 460 the plaintiff M.P. sued for libel on an article imputing improper behaviour for personal gain. He wished to call evidence of (1) the effect of the libel in causing him to be deselected from a standing committee (2) the effect of the libel in causing him not to be chosen as chairman of a select committee (3) a letter from an M.P. complaining about his conduct and (4) the criteria for registration of members' interests. Only (4) was allowed. In *Prebble* at 337 it is said that it is questionable whether this case was rightly decided. Presumably the criticism relates to items (1) to (3) but quaere whether it is well founded. While perhaps not relating to "impropriety", examination as to members' motives would seem to be "questioning" proceedings in Parliament.
[300] Supreme Court of South Australia in *Wright and Advertiser Newspaper v Lewis* (1990) 53 S.A.S.R. 416 at 421–422, per King C.J.
[301] Perhaps not entirely so. If the libel was that the member neglected his duties evidence of, e.g. his attendance record, would presumably be simply a matter of historical fact within para.13.31, above.
[302] It was not taken in *Prebble v Television New Zealand* [1995] 1 A.C. 321 PC, where the impact on the defence was said to be only limited. However, the action in *Hamilton v The Guardian, Financial Times*, July 22, 1995 was stayed.
[303] By far the most controversial provision of the Bill in Parliament. What is now s.13 had formed no part of the strands of law reform which had led up to the Bill but was introduced by Lord Hoffmann. For the background and the various arguments pro and con, see *Hansard*, HL cols 24–29 (May 7, 1996). The section extends to the whole UK (s.18) and came into force on September 4, 1996.
[304] S.13(1).

Parliamentary questions[305] he may waive the privilege of the Bill of Rights and in that event evidence may be given and questions asked about his conduct without infringing the privilege of Parliament. Although Parliamentary privilege exists for the better discharge of the function of Parliament as a whole and belongs to Parliament as a whole,[306] the plain meaning of s.13 is that once a member has waived the protection of privilege, that overrides the privilege of Parliament as a whole.[307] However, the waiver concerns the member alone and does not affect another person who has not waived the protection of privilege.[308] Accordingly, where the member is accused of acting jointly with others it may still be necessary to stay the proceedings because there cannot be a fair trial.[309] A waiver does not affect the non-liability of the

---

[305] The basis of the suit in *Hamilton v The Guardian*, *Financial Times*, July 22, 1995, which lay behind s.13. During the debates on the Bill, Lord Lester of Herne Hill expressed the view that the case could be distinguished from *Prebble* on the basis of *US v Brewster*, 408 U.S. 501 (1972) where it was held that the speech and debate clause of the Constitution did not prevent the prosecution of a senator for accepting bribes related to his official duties.

[306] In *Prebble v Television New Zealand* [1995] 1 A.C. 321 PC, the Privileges Committee of the N.Z. House of Representatives held that it had no power to waive the art.9 privilege. In the debates on the Defamation Bill Lord Simon of Glaisdale was of the opinion that the privilege was that of Parliament and could not be waived by either House: *Hansard*, HL col.32 (May 7, 1996).

[307] *Hamilton v Al Fayed* [2001] A.C. 395 HL. The claimant, a former M.P., sued the defendant in respect of accusations made by him in a television interview that the claimant had accepted money and hospitality in return for asking Parliamentary questions in the defendant's interest. After the interview the Parliamentary Commissioner for Standards reported that these charges were substantially true. The House of Commons Committee on Standards and Privileges, after giving the claimant the opportunity to make oral representations, resolved to approve the report, though it was unable to come to any independent conclusion on the main charge of receiving money. The House of Lords upheld a decision to reject the defendant's application for an order staying the action on the ground that it could not be fairly tried by reason of the exclusion of relevant evidence because of parliamentary privilege. In view of the s.13 waiver by the claimant there was nothing to prevent the defendant from challenging the truth of what had been said by the claimant to the Committee on Standards and Privileges. S.13 was strongly criticised by the Joint Committee on Parliamentary Privilege (HL Paper 43/HC 214-1, 1998–99, Ch.2) on the ground that:

"it undermines the basis of privilege: freedom of speech is the privilege of the House as a whole and not of the individual member in his own right, although an individual member can assert and rely on it"

and in "seeking to remedy a perceived injustice, [it] has created indefensible anomalies of its own which should not be allowed to continue." It should be replaced by a new provision under which either House, on the advice of a committee, would make a general waiver of art.9 in an appropriate case (not necessarily a defamation action). It would not do so if waiver would expose the member or other person concerned to any risk of legal liability.

[308] S.13(3).

[309] A problem also arises if another member is called as a witness (by either side) in proceedings brought by a member. Since the conduct of the witness would not appear to be "in issue" in the proceedings it would seem that the witness would have no power (he certainly could not be compelled) to waive his privilege and the form of s.13(3) would seem to prevent the member called being asked questions about proceedings in Parliament. But even if that is not so, such questions could only be about the conduct of the claimant member: s.13(2). In any event, no member may be compelled to give evidence in court regarding proceedings in the Commons and no official may do so without leave of the House: May, *Parliamentary Practice*, 22nd edn, p.90.

person making it.[310] Accordingly, if a member sues a journalist for libel and waives his privilege there could be no counterclaim for defamatory remarks made by the member in the House.

13.33 **Subordinate legislatures.** Devolution has produced legislatures of varying degrees of competence for Scotland, Wales and Northern Ireland. In each case the legislation provides absolute privilege for the purposes of the law of defamation[311] for statements[312] made in the legislatures.[313]

SECTION 6. REPORTS, ETC. PUBLISHED BY ORDER OF PARLIAMENT

13.34 **The Parliamentary Papers Act.** Under s.1 of the Parliamentary Papers Act 1840,[314] all reports, papers, votes and proceedings published by, or under the authority of, either House of Parliament[315] are absolutely privileged,[316] and the court will stay any proceedings in respect of defamatory statements

---

[310] S.13(4). Hence if a Member were sued for a slander uttered in the chamber and wished to waive his privilege and plead justification he could not do so. The use of the word "protection" in s.13(1) is in fact apt to mislead in view of s.13(4). However, on facts such as those in *Church of Scientology v Johnson-Smith* [1972] 1 Q.B. 522 it would seem that the member could—though it is unlikely he would do so—waive his privilege since the cause of action would not be for "words spoken or things done in the course of, or for the purposes of or incidental to, any proceedings in Parliament."

[311] The fact that they are subordinate legislatures, of course, precludes the "proceedings impeached or questioned" formula of the Bill of Rights. However, the restriction of the immunity to defamation seems curiously limited.

[312] In each case "statement" has the same meaning as in the Defamation Act 1996.

[313] Scotland: Scotland Act 1998, s.41; Wales: Government of Wales Act 2006, s.42; Northern Ireland: Northern Ireland Act 1998, s.50.

[314] This statute was passed in consequence of the decision in *Stockdale v Hansard* (1839) 9 A. & E. 1, an action for a libel contained in the official publication of a report by the inspectors of prisons. Cf. *Harlow v Hansard, Houghton v Plimsoll* (both cited in May's *Parliamentary Practice*, 21st edn, p.88); *Mangena v Edward Lloyd* (1908) 89 L.T. 640; *Mangena v Wright* [1909] 2 K.B. 758.

[315] As to reports of Parliamentary proceedings in the news media, see paras 15.36 and 16.9, below. An absolute privilege attaches to a report ordered to be printed by the Australian Senate or House of Representatives and circulated under the authority of the Australian Parliamentary Papers Act 1908. The same applies under state legislation to documents published by order, or under the authority, of a parliamentary body (see, e.g. Defamation Act (NSW) 2005, s.27. Similarly, documents published by, or under the authority, of the House of Representatives are given absolute privilege in New Zealand by the Defamation Act 1992, s.13 and to any official report or publication of either House of the Parliament of the Republic of Ireland (Constitution Act 1937, arts 15, 12). It also attaches to publications of subcommittees of the United States Senate: *Methodist Federation v Eastland*, 141 F.Supp. 729 (1956); and to material placed on the Congressional Record by a congressman with the consent of Congress: *McGovern v Martz*, 182 F.Supp. 343 (1960). There is an extensive discussion of the English law by Batt J. in *Bruton v Estate Agents Licensing Authority* [1996] 2 V.R. 274, though the law in Victoria on what amounts to authorisation by the legislature is different.

[316] Publication of any statement under the authority of the Scottish Parliament and the Welsh and Northern Irish Assemblies is also subject to absolute privilege under the legislation referred to in para.13.33, above.

contained therein.[317] A defendant who wishes to apply for such a stay must give 24 hours' notice to the claimant, and bring before the court in which the proceedings have been commenced, or before a judge of the High Court, a certificate under the hand of the Lord Chancellor, or of the Lord Keeper of the Great Seal, or of the Speaker or Clerk of the House of Commons, stating that the report, paper, etc. was published by order, or under the authority, of the House of Lords or of the House of Commons.[318] If proceedings have been taken in respect of the publication, not of the original report, paper, etc. but of a copy, no such certificate is necessary; the defendant may obtain a stay on laying before the court the original report or paper, with an affidavit verifying the original and the correctness of the copy.[319] To the publication of any extract from, or abstract of, a parliamentary report, paper, etc. only a qualified privilege attaches under the Act, and the defendant must prove that he published such extract, or abstract, bona fide and without malice.[320]

SECTION 7. REPORTS OF JUDICIAL PROCEEDINGS

Defamation Act 1996.   **13.35**

> "The principle of open justice puts, as has often been said, the judge and all who participate in the trial under intense scrutiny. The glare of contemporaneous publicity ensures that trials are properly conducted."[321]

At common law there is a qualified privilege for fair and accurate reports of judicial proceedings of legitimate public interest.[322] Section 3 of the Law of Libel Amendment Act 1888 conferred a statutory privilege for contemporaneous newspaper reports of judicial proceedings, which was generally thought to be absolute. The Defamation Act 1952 extended this to broadcast reports but the privilege was limited by the statute to reports of proceedings of courts

---

[317] Command papers do not enjoy absolute privilege and the Faulks Committee, Cmnd.5909 (1975), paras 223–225 recommended that this should continue to be the case. See also Leopold, "Recent Use of Unopposed Return Parliamentary Procedure to Ensure Privilege from Defamation" (1993) 56 M.L.R. 690.

[318] S.1. For a form of certificate and order of the court, see *Stockdale v Hansard* (1840) 11 A. & E. 297. The Joint Committee on Parliamentary Privilege (HL Paper 43/HC 214–1, 1998–99, Ch.8) thought that the words of s.1 might be interpreted to cover radio and television broadcasting of debates since these are authorised by the Houses.

[319] S.2.

[320] Ibid. s.3 (as partially repealed by S.L.R. Act 1958). The onus of disproving malice is not usually on the defendant: see para.17.1, below. The provisions of s.3 of the Parliamentary Papers Act 1840 were extended to cover extracts from or abstracts of Parliamentary Papers broadcast by means of wireless telegraphy: see Defamation Act 1952, s.9(1). However, s.3 now appears to be redundant in view of Sch.1, para.7 of the Defamation Act 1996: see para.16.15, below.

[321] *Re S (A Child) (Identification: Restrictions on Publication)* [2004] UKHL 47; [2005] 1 A.C. 593 at [30] per Lord Steyn (not a defamation case and spoken with reference to reports of criminal trials, but clearly of general application).

[322] See para.15.35, below.

exercising judicial authority within the United Kingdom. Now the law is contained in s.14[323] of the Defamation Act 1996.[324] A fair and accurate[325] report[326] of proceedings in public[327] before a court to which s.14 applies is absolutely privileged[328] if published contemporaneously with the proceedings.[329] The relevant courts are (1) any court[330] in the United Kingdom (including any tribunal or body exercising the judicial power of the state[331]); (2) the European Court of Justice or any court attached thereto[332]; (3) the European Court of Human Rights; and (4) any international criminal tribunal established by the Security Council of the United Nations or by an international agreement to which the United Kingdom is a party.[333]

---

[323] The section extends to the whole United Kingdom: s.18.

[324] S.3 of the 1888 Act was repealed by the Defamation Act 1996, Sch.2 and again by the Coroners and Justice Act 2009, Sch.23. The common law qualified privilege would still apply to a case where the proceedings were of a court not mentioned in s.14 or where the report was not contemporaneous. However, since under Sch.1, para.2 of the 1996 Act, qualified privilege is conferred, without explanation or contradiction, on a fair and accurate report (in any form and without any requirement of contemporaneity) of proceedings in public before a court anywhere in the world, the common law privilege seems to be largely redundant. See para.16.10, below.

[325] For this, see para.13.38, below.

[326] It must be recognisable as a report; it is not enough that it repeats accurately what was said in the proceedings but without attribution to them: *Grech v Odhams Press Ltd* [1958] 2 Q.B. 275 at 285; *Rogers v Nationwide News Pty Ltd* [2003] HCA 52; 216 C.L.R. 327 at [18]; *MacQuarie Radio Network Pty Ltd v Dent* [2007] NSWCA 261 at [27].

[327] This reflects the position under the common law qualified privilege for reports. No privilege attaches to a report, however fair and accurate, of judicial proceedings properly held in camera: *Scott v Scott* [1913] A.C. 417 at 452. As to material not read out in court during a public trial see para.13.47, below. Hence also the privilege does not cover a report of the initiation of proceedings (or so it is assumed in *Stern v Piper* [1997] Q.B. 123 CA) and the same is true of the qualified privileges. But see para.13.48, below.

[328] However, in Australia reports of judicial proceedings, whether at home or abroad, are not privileged if the plaintiff proves that they were "not published honestly for the information of the public or the advancement of education". See, e.g. Defamation Act 2005 (NSW) s.29. This is different from the form of words used in s.30 (headed "qualified privilege") which refers to "malice". However, the effect seems to be that the privilege under s.29 is not absolute. It may be recalled that in *Toogood v Spyring* (1834) 1 Cr. M. & R. 181 at 193 Parke B. referred to statements without malice as being "honestly made". So, too, in New Zealand reports are subject only to qualified privilege: Defamation Act 1992, Sch.1, Pt I, para.6. S.17(2)(i) of the Irish Defamation Act 2009 provides for absolute privilege but there is no requirement of contemporaneity. The most frequently encountered Canadian scheme, following the Uniform Defamation Act, gives absolute privilege but requires that the reporter shall not have commented and shall have acceded to a request to publish a statement by way of explanation or contradiction: see, e.g. Ontario, Libel and Slander Act, RSO 1990. However, in British Columbia the privilege is absolute without these requirements.

[329] S.14(1). For a report which was neither fair nor contemporaneous, see *Waters v Sunday Pictorial* [1961] 1 W.L.R. 967 CA.

[330] As in the case of the qualified privilege for reports at common law, the standing of the court is immaterial. "On such a question the dignity of the court cannot be regarded; and we must look only to the nature of the alleged judicial proceeding which is reported": per Lord Campbell C.J. in *Lewis v Levy* (1858) E.B. & E. 537 at 544.

[331] Cf. paras 13.17 et seq., above.

[332] E.g. the Court of First Instance established in 1986.

[333] E.g. the tribunal at The Hague in relation to war crimes in the former Yugoslavia.

The former provision in the Law of Libel Amendment Act 1888 added a proviso that nothing in it should authorise the publication of any blasphemous or indecent matter, but there is nothing to that effect in the 1996 Act. Although there are quite extensive restrictions on reporting of various matters and various types of proceedings,[334] these (including the law of contempt) involve criminal penalties and it must be doubtful[335] that their infringement could restrict or withdraw the protection of absolute privilege in libel proceedings conferred by the unqualified words of s.14.[336]

Unlike the previous legislation, s.14 is not confined to newspaper or broadcast reports but the requirement of contemporaneity in practice restricts it to the news media.[337]

Defamation Act 2013, s.7. Section 7 of the Defamation Act 2013, when   **13.36** it comes into force, will substitute the following for s.14(3) of the 1996 Act:

"This section applies to—
   (a) any court in the United Kingdom;
   (b) any court established under the law of a country or territory outside the United Kingdom;
   (c) any international court or tribunal established by the Security Council of the United Nations or by international agreement;
   and in paragraphs (a) and (b) 'court' includes any tribunal or body exercising the judicial power of the State."

The new provision will extend the ambit of the defence so that it covers proceedings in any court established under the law of a country or state outside the United Kingdom, and any international court or tribunal established by the Security Council of the United Kingdom or by international agreement. The overlap with statutory qualified privilege[338] and the vestigial common law qualified privilege[339] is consequently greater than at present though the absolute privilege continues to have a requirement of contemporaneity as well as fairness and accuracy.

---

[334] Beginning with the Judicial Proceedings (Regulation of Reports) Act 1926.

[335] Unless the meaning of s.14 can be "read down" in the light of art.8 of the European Convention on Human Rights. But see *Nicol v Caledonian Newspapers Ltd*, below.

[336] It would not seem possible to reach this result via the word "fair". The position is different in relation to the qualified privilege under Sch.1 to the Defamation Act 1996 (para.16.10, below) and perhaps common law qualified privilege (para.15.35, below). However, in *Nicol v Caledonian Newspapers Ltd* [2002] ScotCS 106; 2003 S.L.T. 109 contravention of the 1926 Act was held not to affect the qualified privilege under Scots common law, nor was this affected by the Human Rights Act 1998.

[337] Arguably the previous law did not confer absolute privilege on publication by a reporter in delivering his copy to the newspaper (though clearly there would have been qualified privilege), but s.14 would apply to that publication since the report no longer needs to be in a newspaper, etc.

[338] See para.16.10, below.

[339] See para.15.35, below.

13.37 Meaning of "contemporaneously". In order to be privileged under s.14 of the 1996 Act, the report must be published "contemporaneously" with the proceedings. There are only two English decisions[340] on the meaning of the word "contemporaneously" in s.14— there were none under its predecessor s.3 of the Law of Libel Amendment Act 1888—and neither provides a complete definition. It is submitted that at the very least the word means:

> "as nearly at the same time as the proceedings as is reasonably possible, having regard to the opportunities for preparation of the report and the time of going to press or of making the broadcast."

So a report published in the next edition of a daily paper,[341] or in the issues from day to day, if the proceedings were extended, would be "contemporaneous" so, too, perhaps would be a report in the next issue of a weekly paper, even though published six or seven days after proceedings. A report has also been held to have been published contemporaneously when published three days after the proceedings even though that was not the next available issue.[342] However, if a daily paper delayed its report for 10 or 12 days, it would be difficult to say that the report was "published contemporaneously" with the proceedings.[343] Where a report published contemporaneously refers to earlier hearings, it may still amount to a contemporaneous report provided that such reference was necessary to give context to the report of the later proceedings and to enable readers to understand it. Thus, in *Crossley v Newsquest (Midlands South) Ltd*[344] a report of proceedings held on July 20 that was published on July 23 but which referred to earlier hearings held in May and June of the same year, was held to have been published contemporaneously. Eady J. thought that to treat the references to the earlier hearings as not contemporaneous would be unduly technical, especially in a context in which art.10 would be relevant as an aid to interpretation.[345] Nonetheless he recognised that there was no authority on the question and he acknowledged that "it might subsequently be held by an appellate tribunal that a stricter interpretation should be applied; that is to say, that a blue pencil should be applied to remove sentences, or parts of sentences, making reference back to earlier hearings so as to exclude them from absolute protection".[346]

---

[340] See *Crossley v Newsquest (Midlands South) Ltd* [2008] EWHC 3053 (QB) and *Qadir v Associated Newspapers Ltd* [2012] EWHC 2606 (QB); [2013] E.M.L.R. 15.

[341] Report on following day held contemporaneous under the similar Malaysian legislation: *Joceline Tan Poh Choo v Muthusamy* [2003] 4 M.L.J. 494 Mal. CA.

[342] *Crossley v Newsquest (Midlands South) Ltd*, above.

[343] In *Bunker v James* (1980) 24 S.A.S.R., a report several weeks after trial was not "published contemporaneously" under Wrongs Act 1936–1975 (S.A.), s.6 (in terms like the 1888 Act), but with Cox J. holding that the report was contemporaneous.

[344] [2008] EWHC 3053 (QB).

[345] Ibid. at [27].

[346] Ibid. at [28].

Where a report is published in an electronic database or on the internet, it may remain available for access for a considerable period of time. Technically, there would be a fresh publication each time the database or website containing the report was accessed and the question therefore arises whether a report originally published contemporaneously loses its privilege after some (not precisely definable time). In *Qadir v Associated Newspapers*[347] Tugendhat J. was prepared to accept, correctly it is suggested, that online publications which were originally contemporaneous do not cease to be so, for the purposes of this privilege, merely because they remain accessible. However, as the judge decided that the report was not a fair and accurate one the issue cannot be considered to be definitively determined. Where, as is commonly the case with reports of legal proceedings published in newspapers or the law reports proper, the report is not published until several weeks or months after the proceedings, the report is likely to be protected by qualified privilege only but for that purpose a finding of malice would be far-fetched.[348]

Where a report is required to be postponed by an order of the court[349] or as a consequence of any statutory provision,[350] it shall be treated as published contemporaneously if it is published as soon as practicable after publication is permitted.

Fairness and accuracy. Most of the case law on this is concerned either with the common law qualified privilege for reports or with the preceding statutory privilege under the Law of Libel Amendment Act 1888. There is no reason to believe that the authority of these cases on fairness and accuracy is affected in any way by s.14 of the 1996 Act. Indeed, fairness and accuracy are elements in a wide range of qualified reporting privileges under Sch.1 to the 1996 Act, for example in relation to reports of Parliamentary proceedings.[351]   **13.38**

It is not necessary that the report should be verbatim[352]; an abridged or condensed report will be privileged, provided it gives a correct and just

---

[347] [2012] EWHC 2606 (QB); [2013] E.M.L.R. 15.

[348] A report may be "contemporaneous" where it is published in one of the numerous internet services for lawyers. While a newspaper tends to be an ephemeral thing (or at least tended to be so in the days before online editions) and even law reports pass beyond the control of their publishers once they are sold, such an internet service may retain an archive of reports for long periods. According to orthodox theory there is a fresh publication each time the archive is accessed (*Loutchansky v Times Newspapers Ltd (Nos 2–5)* [2001] EWCA Civ 1805; [2002] Q.B. 783, paras 6.4–6.5, above). But it would be odd if a report initially protected under s.14 lost the protection of absolute privilege at some (not precisely definable) time after it was issued. It is submitted that "publication" under s.14 should be read as referring to the initial issue of the material. See also para.16.3, below.

[349] E.g. under s.4 of the Contempt of Court Act 1981.

[350] E.g. the Criminal Justice Act 1967 dealing with restrictions on reporting of committal proceedings.

[351] See Ch.16, below.

[352] Per Lord Campbell C.J. in *Lewis v Levy* (1858) E.B. & E. 537 at 553.

impression of what took place in court.[353] It is sufficient to publish "a fair summarised account".[354]

> "The privilege—a valuable privilege for the public—of publishing reports of proceedings in courts of justice, would be useless if it were necessary to set out every word of the evidence and of the speeches and of what was said by the judge ... that is not necessary; if what is stated is substantially a fair account of what took place, there is an entire immunity for those who publish it."[355]

The report should provide a fair and accurate "presentation of what took place so as to convey to the reader the impression" the proceedings would have made to someone sitting in court[356]: "The theory is that the reporter represents the public—he is their eyes and ears and he has to do his best, using his professional skill, to give them a fair and accurate picture of what he saw and heard."[357]

It is sufficient if the reporter gives the result of the litigation truly and correctly without narrating the steps which led up to the judgment. So where a newspaper reported that the plaintiff had brought an action for slander against B and had failed in the action, it was held that as the report did not purport to be a report of the proceedings in the action, but merely of the result of the action, and the result was accurately stated, the newspaper could not be liable to damages merely because it omitted to state the grounds on which the

---

[353] *Hoare v Silverlock* (1850) 9 C.B. 20; *Andrews v Chapman* (1853) 3 C. & K. 286; *Turner v Sullivan* (1862) 6 L.T.(N.S.) 130; *Jones v John Fairfax & Sons Ltd* (1986) 4 NS.W.L.R. 466 at 471; cf. *Thompson v Truth Ltd* (1934) 34 N.S.W.S.R. 21 PC. In *Cook v Alexander* [1974] Q.B. 279 CA (see para.15.37, below), it was held that a "Parliamentary sketch" giving a fair account of the impression made on hearers can be a fair and accurate report. Nothing in the judgments refers to reports of court proceedings, but at common law there has been thought to be a close analogy between reports of Parliamentary and judicial proceedings: see para.15.33, below. While the law probably protects a report which does not amount to a précis of the court proceedings, it must be fair in relation to the claimant, and the same considerations will not apply where the claimant is a person casually mentioned in the proceedings as where the proceedings are directed towards establishing his guilt or innocence on a serious charge. In *Bunkey v James* [1980] A.L.M.D. 4508 the Wrongs Act 1936–1975 (S.A.) s.6 was held to apply a "sketch" provided that it was not so garbled or short as to be a misrepresentation or give a false and unjust impression, affirmed on appeal [1981] A.C.L.D. 94.

[354] Per Bowen L.J. in *Macdougall v Knight* (1886) 17 Q.B.D. at 642. Does it convey an impression that is substantially different from the impression which would be gained if present in the court when the judgment was given?: *Nationwide News Pty Ltd v Rogers* [2002] NSWCA 171 at [113] (on appeal, [2003] HCA 52; 216 C.L.R. 327); *Curistan v Times Newspapers Ltd* [2008] EWCA Civ 432; [2008] 3 All E.R. 923 at [26] (a case on reports of Parliamentary proceedings).

[355] Per Lord Campbell C.J. in *Andrews v Chapman* (1853) 3 C. & K. 286 at 289.

[356] *Cook v Alexander* [1974] Q.B. 279 CA per Denning M.R. at 288. In *Macdougall v Knight* (1890) 25 Q.B.D. 1 Lord Esher M.R. stated that the basis of the privilege is that "the publication of what took place is merely a means of putting those who were not present in the court in the position of those who were present" (at 9).

[357] *Cook v Alexander* [1974] Q.B. 279 CA per Lord Denning M.R. at 288. Cited with approval by Ward L.J. in *Tsikata v Newspaper Publishing plc* [1997] 1 All E.R. 655 CA; [1997] E.M.L.R. 117 at 670.

plaintiff failed, namely that the occasion on which the slander was uttered was a privileged one.[358] Moreover, the claimant cannot complain if an otherwise accurate report presents a one-sided story because he did not participate in the proceedings.[359]

Whether a report of proceedings is a fair and accurate one must be determined as at the time the proceedings took place.[360] Thus, the fact that events subsequent to the proceedings cast doubt on, or invalidate, the findings of the original proceedings does not make a report that fails to mention the subsequent events unfair or inaccurate.

Slight inaccuracy. If the whole report is a substantially accurate account of what took place, the fact that there are a few slight inaccuracies or omissions[361] is immaterial[362]: "You do not go through a report with a toothcomb and say: "If I can find that little inaccuracy that is the end of the defence." Minor and irrelevant inaccuracies are of no consequence. This principle that you are free to report anything provided it is fair and accurate would not be worth much—human nature being what it is—if, through some slight, inconsequential slip, you were to be deprived of the defence."[363] A report in a daily newspaper is "not to be judged by the same strict standard of accuracy" as a "report coming from the hand of a trained lawyer".[364] "Unless a fair and reasonable latitude is given there would be no safety in reporting the proceedings in courts of justice".[365] "It would be impossible to exercise the privilege of reporting if every trifling slip in a report deprived it of privilege."[366]

13.39

---

[358] *Duncan v Associated Scottish Newspapers Ltd*, 1929 S.C. 14. If a conviction is accurately reported in the terms used by the legislature, it would impose too high a standard on the media to require it to explain that words used by the legislature should not, in a particular case, be given their ordinary meaning: *MD Mineralsearch Inc. v East Kootenay Newspapers Ltd* [2002] BCCA 42; (2002) 209 D.L.R. (4th) 375.

[359] *Karim v Newsquest Media Group Lrd* [2009] EWHC 3205 (QB).

[360] *Tsikata v Newspaper Publishing plc* [1997] 1 All E.R. 655 per Ward L.J. CA at 670. See also per Neill L.J. at 667.

[361] A failure fully to give the claimant's side of the story will not necessarily affect the substantial accuracy of the report: *Karim v Newsquest Media Group Ltd* [2009] EWHC 3205 (QB) per Eady J. at [13].

[362] *Andrews v Chapman*, above; *Kimber v Press Association* [1893] 1 Q.B. 65 at 72; *Thom v Associated Newspapers Ltd* (1964) 64 S.R. (N.S.W.) 376 at 380; *Karim v Newsquest Media Group Ltd* [2009] EWHC 3205 (QB) per Eady J. at [14].

[363] *Burnett & Hallamshire Fuel Ltd v Sheffield Telegraph and Star Ltd* [1960] 1 W.L.R. 502 (QB) per Salmon J. at 505.

[364] Per Collins M.R. in *Hope v Leng Ltd* (1907) 23 T.L.R. 243 CA. And see *Vroman v Vancouver Daily* [1942] 2 D.L.R. 456.

[365] Per Byles J. in *Turner v Sullivan* (1862) 6 L.T.(N.S.) 130 at 131. "It is of public importance that fair and accurate reports should be published and the importance of that overweighed the occasional errors made by reporters": per Scrutton L.J. in *Hales v Times Co. Ltd, The Times*, November 27, 1929; cf. *Farmer v Morning Post* (1936) 80 S.J. 345 CA; *Farmer v Hyde* [1937] 1 K.B. 728 CA.

[366] Per Bramwell L.J. in *M'Wade v Goodlake, The Times*, June 23, 1881.

13.40 Substantial inaccuracy. However where the inaccuracy is of a substantial kind, the report is not privileged[367] although the publisher exercised reasonable care and diligence in endeavouring to ascertain the facts, and though the mistake was an honest mistake.[368] A report of judicial proceedings which states that counsel said things which were not said at all is not a fair and accurate report.[369] In *Geary v Alger*[370] A pleaded guilty to assaulting a police officer in the execution of his duty. In mitigation, counsel sought to excuse A's violence as due to resentment against a person of whom he used very abusive language, but whose name he did not mention. The defendants in their newspaper gave the plaintiff's name as that of the person abused and thus imputed to him the conduct censured by counsel. It was held that the report was not a fair and accurate report. So too, an article that reported comments made by counsel in mitigation for an offender convicted of fraud that the claimant had been "intimately involved in Britain's biggest mortgage fraud" but failed to state that the judge had rebuked counsel, stating that he could not determine the complicity of the claimant, was not a fair and accurate report.[371] Again, a report (based upon assertions in the prosecution's opening) was not fair or accurate which stated that "it appeared from the evidence that the plaintiff had often beaten his wife black and blue, and that witnesses were present to prove it", when there was no evidence given of such facts at the hearing, or they were disproved by the evidence adduced.[372] Moreover,

> "if the evidence of a witness containing matter defamatory to an individual were published, and the cross-examination which showed the witness to be a person unworthy of belief were suppressed, it would obviously be a partial and inaccurate account of what took place."[373]

Although a fair and accurate report of the statement of a witness in the witness box is privileged, even if the statement is afterwards shown to be false, the report is not privileged where the false statement is not attributed to the witness but stated as a fact.[374]

---

[367] *Blake v Stevens* (1864) 11 L.T. 543; *Furniss v Cambridge News Ltd (No.1), The Times,* January 14, 1907; *Mitchell v Hirst Kidd* [1936] 3 All E.R. 872 (charge and conviction of driving motor-car without owner's consent reported as motor-car theft through failure of reporters to note that the charge of theft had been dropped); cf. *Harper v Provincial Newspapers*, 1937 S.L.R. 462 (address on charge sheet not read out in court); *Kavanagh v Argus Printing Co* [1939] W.L.D. 284 (handing annexure to charge sheet to judge for his information, held to be tantamount to reading it in open court); *Anderson v Nationwide News* [1970] 1 N.S.W.R. 317.

[368] *Smith v Scott* (1847) 2 C. & K. 580 at 585; *Sweet v Post Publishing Co*, 102 N.E. 660 (1913). Cf. in a related context *Eyre v N.Z. Press Association* [1968] N.Z.L.R. 736.

[369] *D'Auxy v Star Co*, 64 N.Y.S. 283 (1900).

[370] (1925) 57 O.L.R. 218; affirmed (1925) 58 O.L.R. 39.

[371] *Qadir v Associated Newspapers* [2012] EWHC 2606 (QB); [2013] E.M.L.R. 15.

[372] *Ashmore v Borthwick* (1885) 2 T.L.R. 113, affirmed 209, CA. See also *Young v Toronto Star Newspapers Ltd* (2005) 259 D.L.R. (4th) 127.

[373] Per Lord Halsbury L.C. in *Macdougall v Knight* (1889) 14 A.C. 194 at 200.

[374] *Grech v Odhams Press Ltd* [1958] 2 Q.B. 275 CA, where the evidence on the point was not fairly reported in general.

Abridged reports. An abridged or condensed report of judicial proceed-   **13.41**
ings must be fair, not garbled so as to produce misrepresentation,[375] nor by
suppression of some portion of the evidence giving an entirely false and unjust
impression to the prejudice of one of the parties concerned.[376] A report which
accurately sets out one part of the proceedings and omits another which gives
a different complexion to the whole case will not be privileged.[377] It is not
enough to report part of the proceedings correctly if, by leaving out other
parts, you thereby create a false impression.[378] So, where the defendant, in
publishing a report of proceedings for perjury against the plaintiff, omitted
certain parts of the cross-examination of the Crown witnesses which were
favourable to the plaintiff, it was held that such omission raised a question for
the jury whether the report was partial or inaccurate, Lord Campbell C.J.
observing that "partiality and inaccuracy might be made out by suppression of
true as well as by insertion" of untrue matter.[379]

Reports must be impartial. The report should fairly state the effect of the   **13.42**
evidence, and the statements made on behalf of both parties.[380] A report is not
fair and impartial which gives the statements of counsel on one side, they
being injurious, and not the statements on the other side in denial,[381] or which
sets out an affidavit which played no part in the proceedings[382] or a speech
made by counsel containing observations defamatory of a party, solicitor or
witness without stating any of the evidence given at the trial,[383] or which, after
setting out such speech, asserts that a witness was called who proved all that
counsel had stated.[384] At one time it was said that the evidence ought to be

---

[375] Inaccurate reporting may also render the persons responsible for its publication in a
newspaper liable to proceedings for contempt of court: *R. v Evening Standard Ex p. the Attorney-
General* [1954] 1 Q.B. 578.

[376] *Wright v Outram* (1890) 17 R. 596, where a newspaper, in reporting an examination in
bankruptcy, quoted statements which tended to show that the pursuers were insolvent, but failed
to mention evidence which was produced to refute those charges; *Thompson v Truth Ltd* (1934)
34 N.S.W.S.R. 21, where the Privy Council held that a report which omitted explanations given
by the plaintiff in cross-examination was not fair or accurate. Cf. *Montereale v Longmans Green,
The Times*, February 21 and 23, 1965; *Bowler v Pogonoski* [1967] 1 N.S.W.R. 249.

[377] Per Byles J. in *Turner v Sullivan* (1862) 6 L.T.(N.S.) 130 at 131.

[378] Per Hawke J. in *Farmer v Daily News Ltd, The Times*, May 18, 1935; and see *McGrath v
Wellington Publishing* [1932] G.L.R. 181; *Mitchell v Victoria Daily Times* [1944] 2 D.L.R. 239
(article assumes guilt of accused and omits reference to his denial of charge); *Street v NBC*, 645
F.2d 1227 (C.A. 6 1981).

[379] *Lewis v Levy* (1858) E.B. & E. 537 at 551; cf. *Van Leggelo v Argus Co* (1935) T.P.D.
230.

[380] *Dodson v Owen* (1885) 2 T.L.R. 111; *Ashmore v Borthwick* (1885) 2 T.L.R. 113 at 209;
Grech v Odhams Press [1958] 2 Q.B. 275 CA; *Field v Local Sunday Newspapers (North) Ltd*
[2002] EWHC 336 (QB) (reversed on other grounds, sub nom. *Gough v Local Sunday Newspapers (North) Ltd* [2003] EWCA Civ 297; [2003] 1 W.L.R. 1836).

[381] *M'Wade v Goodlake, The Times*, June 23, 1881.

[382] *Gobbart v WA Newspapers* [1968] W.A.R. 113.

[383] *Flint v Pike* (1825) 4 B. & C. 473; *Saunders v Mills* (1829) 6 Bing. 213; *Kane v Mulvany*
(1866) I.R.2 C.L. 402 at 420. See also per Cockburn C.J. in *Woodgate v Ridout* (1865) 4 F. & F.
202 at 212–215.

[384] *Lewis v Walter* (1821) 4 B. & Ald. 605.

stated in order that those who read the report may be able to form their own judgment as to how far the observations of counsel are well founded,[385] but it is unlikely that literal compliance with this standard could be demanded in modern conditions.

The entire suppression of the evidence of a single witness may render the report unfair.[386] Where a report of a preliminary investigation before a magistrate set out at length the opening speech of counsel for the prosecution, but omitted the examination and cross-examination of the prosecutor, who was the only witness, merely stating that "his testimony supported the statement of his counsel", the jury found that the report was not fair and accurate.[387] The report of statements by an advocate in court, however, does not cease to be privileged by reason only of the statements not having been verified, or by their not being warranted by the facts.[388]

13.43 Reports assuming a verdict not privileged. A report of the proceedings before a magistrate which assumes the truth of the depositions and guilt of the accused, and asserts that "he is likely to meet the legal punishment of his villainy", was not a fair report[389]; nor is a report which insinuates the guilt of a person who has been tried for an offence and acquitted.[390]

13.44 Reports of judgments. A report which contains an untrue statement as to the effect of the judgment in an action is not a fair and accurate report,[391] but a report which accurately sets out the summing-up or the judgment of a judge, without setting out any of the evidence on which the summing-up or judgment is founded, is privileged, even though the summing-up or judgment may contain libellous statements. Thus, where an action by the plaintiff against the defendant had been dismissed with costs, and the defendant published in the form of a pamphlet a verbatim report of the whole judgment, which contained observations reflecting on the plaintiff's character, but omitted all the evidence given at the trial, it was held by the Court of Appeal that the report was privileged.[392]

---

[385] *Lewis v Walter* at 612; *Flint v Pike* (1825) 4 B. & C. 473 at 479. It would be otherwise if the evidence of the witness corresponded closely to the report of the speech.

[386] *Duncan v Thwaites* (1824) 3 B. & C. 556; *Rumney v Walter* (1892) 8 T.L.R. 256.

[387] *Pinero v Goodlake* (1867) 15 L.T. 676.

[388] *Burnett & Hallamshire Fuel Ltd v Sheffield Telegraph Ltd* [1960] 2 All E.R. 157, per Salmon J., disapproving the observations of Bayley J. in *Flint v Pike* (1825) 4 B. & C. 473 at 479–480.

[389] *R. v Fisher* (1811) 2 Camp. 563; cf. *Mitchell v Victoria Daily Times* [1944] 2 D.L.R. 239; *Kelly v Daily Telegraph* (1897) 18 N.S.W.L.R. 358 (account of arrest mentioning evidence and assuming guilt not privileged).

[390] *Risk Allah Bey v Whitehurst* (1868) 18 L.T.(N.S.) 615.

[391] *Hayward v Hayward* (1886) 34 Ch.D.198; cf. *Richards v Sun Newspapers Ltd* [1931] N.Z.L.R. 631, where a newspaper prematurely misstated the result of proceedings taken by the plaintiff for slander.

[392] *Macdougall v Knight* (1886) 17 Q.B.D. 636. Though the decision was affirmed by the House of Lords on other grounds (see (1889) 14 A.C. 194), doubts were expressed by Lord Halsbury L.C. (at 200) and Lord Bramwell (at 203) as to whether the publication of a summing-up or judgment was privileged if unaccompanied by the evidence on which it was founded. These

"The judgment of a judge of the land is in itself an act of such a public and distinct character as to make it to the interest of the commonwealth that they should know it in toto, and provided it is either given verbatim correctly or correctly summarised, it seems to me that the public policy requires that to be the law, and I have no hesitation in saying that I believe that to be the law at the present day. In coming to that conclusion we are arriving at a decision in accordance with the ordinary practice of the public Press, with the usages of society, and with the convenience of Her Majesty's subjects ... It appears to me that it would be to put an undue fetter on the Press to hold that the publication of a judgment is not privileged unless the judgment fairly summarises the evidence ... The judgments of courts must be presumed to be fair, accurate, and adequate, and to make a person who reports such a judgment prove that it is so[393] would be to put on him a burden inconsistent with the interests of the commonwealth."[394]

A report of a judgment is protected by absolute privilege even though it is not read out in open court.[395]

Trials lasting several days. Where a trial lasts more than one day the **13.45**
proceedings of each day may be published separately at the time,[396] unless the court has in the interests of the due administration of justice prohibited any part of the proceedings from being published until the whole trial is concluded, or unless the publication, say, of evidence ruled inadmissible, was likely to prejudice a fair trial.

"The privilege applies to a fair and correct account of proceedings published before the final decision is arrived at, if in the end there must be a final decision. If it were otherwise, the ridiculous result would follow that, where the trial of a case of the greatest public interest lasted fifty days, no report could be published until the case was ended."[397]

However, while disobedience of a court order restricting publication may attract penalties for contempt or other offences it does not seem that this alone can deprive the report of privilege.[398]

---

doubts are referred to in *Macdougall v Knight* (1890) 25 Q.B.D. 1, an action between the same parties for the publication of another part of the same judgment. The Court of Appeal firmly upheld their judgment in the former action, Lopes L.J. observing that:
"there is no decision in the House of Lords which impeaches the law as laid down in the court in the previous action between the present litigants. There are reservations of opinion by two of the learned lords, but such reservations cannot be taken as in any sense decisions."
See also per Lord Esher M.R. at 8; and see *Morriss v Gollancz, The Times*, April 17, 1937.

[393] On the same principle privilege has been held to attach to a fair and accurate report of a judge's charge to a grand jury: *R. v Evening News Ex p. Hobbs* [1925] 2 K.B. 158.

[394] Per Fry L.J. in *Macdougall v Knight* (1890) 25 Q.B.D. at 11. A Court in issuing its reasons for its decision (or a copy thereof) is not "reporting" its judgment. That is part of the judicial process: see para.13.8, above.

[395] This rather obvious proposition (which does not fit very well with the words of the statute) is supported by *Tsikata v Newspaper Publishing* [1997] 1 All E.R. 655 CA.

[396] *Lewis v Levy* (1858) E.B. & E. 537; *Kane v Mulvany* (1866) Ir.R. 2 C.L. 402 at 420; *Kimber v Press Association* [1893] 1 Q.B. 65 CA.

[397] Per Lord Esher M.R. in *Kimber v Press Association* at 71.

[398] See para.13.35, above.

If a trial lasting several days is accurately reported on, say, days one, two and three is a newspaper liable if it omits to report the conclusion of the proceedings (leading to the acquittal of the accused)? Logic might incline one to say yes, but this conclusion puts a potentially serious restraint upon editorial discretion as to what is newsworthy. On the other hand, if after a trial is over the publishers of a newspaper were to pick out and publish an accurate report of one particular portion of the proceedings to the detriment of one of the parties the report would not seem to be fair and accurate.[399]

13.46   **Statements relevant to the case.** The privilege of reporting what takes place in a court of justice extends not only to evidence given on oath, but also, semble, to statements not on oath made in the course of a case and relevant thereto.[400]

> "Suppose a person called as a witness appears in the witness-box, but by oversight has not had the oath administered, and yet gives his testimony, and it is published in a newspaper. Technically and substantially that testimony would not be legal evidence, but can it be said that if a newspaper published it, and it contained matter defamatory of a third person, that person could maintain an action of libel for the publication? It would be throwing an unreasonable burden on the newspapers if they had to inquire whether, or had to be certain that, every proceeding in the ordinary course, or every part of one, in a court of justice was technically correct, and it would probably result in the refusal of newspapers to publish reports of judicial proceedings, and thus lead to a serious injury to the public in not knowing what had taken place in courts of justice."[401]

However, except for a law report, the defendant may not rely on this defence if the report contains a reference to a spent conviction which the court ruled inadmissible in the proceedings reported.[402]

13.47   **Report and comment.** It was once said that for privilege to apply a report

> "must be strictly confined to the actual proceedings in court, and must contain no defamatory observations or comments from any quarter whatever, in addition to what forms strictly and properly the legal proceedings."[403]

This is true if, e.g. the report contains comment inextricably mixed with what happened in court[404] or remarks plainly unconnected with the proceedings,[405]

---

[399] Left open in *Pope v Outram Ltd* 1909 S.C. 230. In *Macdougall v Knight* (1889) 14 A.C. 194 at 207 it was suggested that such behaviour would show malice but (a) the privilege is now absolute (b) the incomplete report may be a result of error. For subsequent republication of contemporaneous privileged reports see para.16.4, below.

[400] *Hutchison v Robinson* (1900) 21 N.S.W.L.R. 130.

[401] Per Cohen J. in *Hutchison v Robinson* at 144; cf. per Simpson J. ibid. at 143.

[402] Rehabilitation of Offenders Act 1974, s.8(3), (6), (7), for which see para.18.14, below. But note that unless the publication was made with malice (ibid. s.8(5)), the defendant would still be able to rely on a justification in relation to a mention of the conviction itself.

[403] *Delegal v Highley* (1837) 3 Bing.N.C. 950 at 960.

[404] As in *Lewis v Levy* (1858) E.B. & E. 537 (report published by defendant).

[405] Which may be an explanation of *Delegal v Highley* (1837) 3 Bing.N.C. 950.

but the proposition needs to be qualified in two ways. First, if an article contains an accurate report[406] and comment which is recognisably distinct from it,[407] the report may be defended as a fair and accurate report and the comment as honest comment[408]; though even where report and comment are distinguishable, it seems that "excessive" comment may deprive the report of its quality of fairness.[409]

Thus, if a reporter wishes to ensure that his report is fair he should avoid inflammatory, offensive or sensationalised language.[410] As Cockburn C.J. told the jury in *Risk Allah Bey v Whitehurst*[411]:

> "As soon as the reporter departs from the usual manner, he is apt to draw on his imagination, to become fantastic; and if he happens to have particular impressions, he is apt to convey those impressions. Therefore, so far as proceedings in the English courts of justice are concerned, I trust we shall adhere to the simple and honest plan that is now in force ... Is this a fair and impartial report of the whole proceedings, or is there in it that sensational and offensive character to which I have referred?"
>
> "Excessive commentary or misleading headlines which amount to commentary

---

[406] A comment cannot be defended if based on an inaccurate report: see para.12.15, above.

[407] E.g. a law textbook or casebook (though that is unlikely to attract s.14—as opposed to the qualified privilege under s.15 or at common law—because of the requirement of contemporaneity). The requirement that purported comment be recognisable as such is part of the general law of honest comment: para.12.7, above.

[408] *Thompson v Truth and Sportsman Ltd* (1934) 34 N.S.W.S.R. 21 PC; *Ager v Canjex Publishing Ltd* [2005] BCCA 467; 259 D.L.R. (4th) 727.

[409] *Curistan v Times Newspapers Ltd* [2008] EWCA Civ 432; [2009] Q.B. 231 at [47]–[51] (a case of a report of Parliamentary proceedings under s.15 of the Defamation Act 1996). It is not entirely clear how this idea is to be applied. In *Curistan* the additional material extended to "most" of 13 paragraphs of an 18 paragraph article ([2007] EWHC 926 (QB); [2008] 1 W.L.R. 126 at [58]) and the report element was still protected. But one can conceive of a case in which, say, a legal commentary on a decision might be many times longer than the included passages from the decision. It might be unlikely that the commentary part would attract the law of defamation, but if the privilege is lost the writer is liable for the defamatory elements in the material reported.

> "[I]f [the publisher] adds its own spice and prints a story to the same effect as the parliamentary paper, and garnishes and embellishes it with circumstantial detail, it goes beyond the privilege and becomes subject to the general law. None of its story on that occasion is privileged. It has 'put the meat on the bones' and must answer for the whole joint":

Lord Denning in *Dingle v Associated Newspapers* [1964] A.C. 371 at 411. In *Curistan* at [51] it is said to be "of some materiality that the additional material was factual, not comment" but again it is not clear why this should be so. No doubt the reporting privilege is primarily aimed at "straight reports" but it is necessary for the protection of other material which merely takes the court proceedings as a launching point and matters like the quantity or nature of the additional material should not be decisive in determining the overall question of whether the court proceedings are fairly reported.

[410] Cockburn C.J. in *Risk Allah Bey v Whitehurst* (1868) 18 L.T. 615 warned the jury that a sensationalised report of judicial proceedings, "akin to those published in 'foreign newspapers'", might not amount to a fair and accurate report. In *Field v Local Sunday Newspapers (North) Ltd* [2002] EWHC 336 (QB), the defence failed at least in part because of the unbalanced nature of the report

[411] (1868) 18 L.T. 615 at 618.

run the risk of depriving the text of the quality of fairness essential to attract the privilege."[412]

Secondly, a more liberal view is now taken of what forms the "legal proceedings" than was once the case. In *Hope v Leng Ltd*[413] W, a witness, shouted out from the well of the court that the evidence given by the plaintiff was "a pack of lies". It was held by the Court of Appeal that a report of the proceedings in which this observation appeared was nevertheless privileged. In the course of a judgment in which Cozens-Hardy and Fletcher Moulton L.JJ. concurred, Collins M.R. said:

> "It was contended that the observation made by Mr. W. was not made by him from the witness-box, and that therefore the report of it did not come within the protection accorded to reports of legal proceedings. I am not prepared to hold that an observation made by a litigant in a case when he was not actually in the witness-box could not be reported without risk of liability on the part of the reporter, if it was in fact made in court in the course of legal proceedings. It may be that a more liberal view of the immunity of reporters is taken now than in former times. The law has accommodated itself to prevailing conditions, and common sense is allowed a larger share in determining the right of parties to litigation of this sort. However that may be, it seems to me to be clear on the uncontroverted facts that the statement made by Mr. W. was made after he had taken the oath, and he thought it might have been elicited by questions directed to him. It was a comment made by him when he was still under the obligation of the oath. It would be too nice to exclude from the privilege accorded to the fair reports a report of an observation made under those circumstances."[414]

13.48 Publication of contents of documents not brought up in open court. Privilege does not attach to a statement that proceedings have been commenced but if that statement is accurate it will be covered by the defence of justification.[415] Privilege will, of course, attach not only to a report of oral evidence but to the publication in the report of a document read out in open court and filed as an exhibit in an action or to a fair and accurate statement of

---

[412] *Chakravarti v Advertiser Newspapers* (1998) 193 C.L.R. 519 at [153] per Kirby J., cited in *Curistan*, above.

[413] (1907) 23 T.L.R. 243 CA. See also *Farmer v Hyde* [1937] 1 K.B. 728, where a report of legal proceedings containing an application made to the judge by a stranger to the action, who had been criticised, in the opening and in the evidence, was held by the CA to be privileged; *Farmer v Morning Post* (1936) 80 S.J. 345; *Leslie v Mirror Newspapers* (1971) 125 C.L.R. 332, where a discussion after judgment was held relevant. The general public interest in what goes on in courts of justice cannot be confined to the regular course of proceedings: the occurrence of irregularities may be of great public concern. Comment on the merits of the case or the conduct of the parties before the conclusion of the case may be, but is not necessarily, contempt of court: *Att-Gen v Hislop* [1991] 1 Q.B. 514 CA.

[414] However, it may be that a report of the remarks of a bystander wholly unconnected with the case would still not be privileged: *Hughes v WA Newspapers* (1940) 43 W.A.L.R. 12 at 13–14.

[415] *Cadam v Beaverbrook Newspapers* [1959] 1 Q.B. 413 CA (where it was only necessary to establish that the proposition was arguable); *Stern v Piper* [1997] Q.B. 123 CA.

the contents of such document,[416] but the general view has been that privilege will not attach to the publication in a newspaper of the contents of pleadings, affidavits, or other papers filed in civil proceedings and not brought up in open court.[417]

> "It would be carrying privilege farther than we feel prepared to carry it, to say that, by the easy means of entitling and filing a statement of claim in a cause, a sufficient foundation may be laid for scattering any libel broadcast with impunity."[418]

The same rule has been regarded as applying to the publication of the contents of documents filed in pending criminal proceedings, and not brought up in open court.[419] The fact that the public is bound to become aware of the contents of the documents at the trial does not justify their prior dissemination on the ground of public interest.[420] The law is the same in Scotland. No privilege attaches to the publication in a newspaper of a summons which has been called in court, but upon which no other step of procedure has followed.[421] If it were otherwise

> "a pursuer who has nothing to lose, and cannot be criminally punished, might by raising a summons (which is a mere *ex parte* writ) and handing it, or causing it to be handed, to the newspapers, ruin irretrievably the character of anyone he chose."[422]

---

[416] *Butler v Saskatoon* [1930] 1 D.L.R. 1009.

[417] This was common ground between counsel in *Stern v Piper* [1997] Q.B. 123 CA, which was fought entirely on justification (see para.11.19, above) but neither Hirst L.J. nor Simon Brown L.J. indicated any doubt on the matter. *R. v Astor* (1913) 30 T.L.R. 10 at 12–13; *Cleary v Leniham* (1874) 8 Ir.L.T. 146; *Lucas & Son v O'Brien* [1978] 2 N.Z.L.R. 289 NZCA; *Gobbart v WA Newspapers* [1968] W.A.R. 113; *Abt v Registrar of Supreme Court* (1889) 9 Cape Times R. 513; *Transvaal Chronicle v Roberts* (1915) T.P.D. 188; *Joceline Tan Poh Choo v Muthusamy* [2003] 4 M.L.J. 494, Mal. CA.

[418] Per Holmes J. in *Cowley v Pulsifer* (1884) 137 Mass.R. 392 at 394, cited by Hirst L.J. in *Stern v Piper*, above. Privilege would attach to a report of a *judgment* which was handed down rather than read out (para.13.44, above). Notwithstanding *Cowley v Pulsifer* many American courts now take the opposite view: see 50 Am.Jur.2d, *Libel and Slander*, para.320. Elder, *The Fair Report Privilege* (1988) para.1.04 regards privilege as the majority view and is critical of *Cowley*. However, the Restatement 2d, *Torts*, para.611 comment e. prefers the old rule.

[419] *Smith v Harris* [1996] 2 V.R. 335; *Furniss v Cambridge News Ltd* (1907) 23 T.L.R. 705, where it was held that no privilege attached to the publication of an abstract from a charge-sheet which was not read in court.

[420] *Kingswell v Robinson* (1913) W.L.D. (S.A.) 129 at 146; distinguished in *Kavanagh v Argus Printing Co* (1939) W.L.D. 284. Cf. *Cowie v Robinson* (1928) 62 O.L.R. 35, where privilege was held to attach to a report of a preliminary inquiry before a magistrate which summarised the facts contained in the information, although the information was not read aloud at the inquiry.

[421] *Richardson v Wilson* (1879) 7 R. 237; *Macleod v Ross* (1892) 20 R. 218; cf. *Harper v Provincial Newspapers*, 1937 S.L.T. 462. But privilege attaches to reports of pleadings which are made the basis of a decision, even though not read out in open court: *Cunningham v The Scotsman*, 1987 S.L.T. 698; and see *Homestead Award Winning Homes Pty Ltd v South Australia* (1997) 72 S.A.S.R. 299 at 307.

[422] Per Lord Deas in *Richardson v Wilson* at 243.

"Though a litigant is privileged in the statements he makes on record, he is not privileged if he sends his pleadings (whether the record is closed or not) to a newspaper for publication. If the pleadings so published are slanderous, then the paper publishing them, and the person sending them for publication, are liable in damages for slander": per Lord Young in *Macleod v Ross* (1892) 20 R. 218 at 221.

It was never the case that a false statement could be made in an affidavit "with impunity" since it was subject to the law of perjury; and in current procedure false statements in witness statements or statements of case are subject to penalties for contempt of court.[423] However, even if the traditional view be accepted in relation to documents which have merely been lodged, what of the case where there has been some sort of public hearing? In *Church of Scientology of Toronto v Hill*[424] the Supreme Court of Canada departed from the previous law under which no (qualified) privilege attached to publication of pleadings or other documents which had not been filed or read out in court.[425] That was under a regime where there was a general public right of access to documents filed in court proceedings unless the court ordered otherwise[426] but the present position in England is that a non-party has access as of right to any statement of case and access to any other filed document with the permission of the court.[427] Nowadays much evidence-in-chief is taken in the form of witness statements rather than being elicited by oral question and answer in court and there appears to be a presumption in favour of granting permission for access to such material. The press and public should not be deprived of access to material which in former times would have been available via a transcript (to which there is an absolute right on payment of the relevant charges) because of changes in court practice and a party opposing disclosure will not succeed with a bald, unparticularised assertion of confidentiality.[428]

---

[423] CPR r.32.14.

[424] [1995] 2 S.C.R. 1130.

[425] However, in *Taylor-Wright v CHBC-TV* [2000] BCCA 629; (2000) 194 D.L.R. (4th) 621, Esson J.A. (with whom Newbury and Saunders JJ.A. agreed), speaking with reference to the law in Canada after *Hill's* case, said at [33] that the evils identified early in the 20th century in denying privilege to reports of documents which have not been subject to a hearing are now more serious.

"The volume of litigation has grown enormously as has the number and proportion of lawyers who show little concern to exercise decent restraint in drafting court documents. The number of litigants in person is much greater. As a result, court registries have in their files an untold and unknowable number of documents containing all sorts of statements potentially damaging to others which have no relevance to anything except the aroused feelings of the litigant, deponent or overly partisan lawyer."

However, the court held that the reporting only of the affidavits of one side without any reference to the detailed denials filed by the other side in the action deprived the report of the necessary quality of being fair as well as accurate. Esson J.A. said at [55] that the weapon put in the hands of the media by *Hill's* case:

"has great capacity for causing harm to innocent people. On the law as it stands, that potential damage can be kept within reasonable limits only by requiring of the media a greater effort to achieve balance than is expected in ordinary reporting of court proceedings where the evidence that is reported on is that which the judge allows to be heard after both parties have had an opportunity, normally through counsel, to raise issues of relevancy."

[426] Ibid. at [153].

[427] CPR r.5.4C.

[428] See *Chan U Seek v Alvis Vehicles* [2004] EWHC 3092 Ch; [2005] 1 W.L.R. 2965. In that case the newspaper was allowed to have copies of pleadings and witness statements even though the judge was satisfied that its purpose was not to prepare a full report of the case but to follow up a newsworthy "spin-off" story from the proceedings. See also *Cleveland Bridge UK Ltd v Multiplex Constructions Ltd* [2005] EWHC 2101 TCC.

Although the Civil Procedure Rules say nothing in this context about privilege, it would seem odd if a newspaper which relied on a witness statement to prepare a report were to be deprived of the protection of privilege.[429]

Burden of proof. The onus of proving that the report is fair and accurate **13.49** lies on the defendant, but it is sufficient if this clearly appears from the claimant's own evidence.[430] If the defendant fails to prove that the report is fair and accurate, the claimant is entitled to succeed, however honestly it may have been published. Whether the report is a fair and accurate report is a question of fact for the jury, provided always there is some evidence of unfairness or inaccuracy to go to the jury. This is a question for the judge to determine, and it is also for the judge to decide whether the matter complained of can fairly be said to be a report of judicial proceedings.[431]

SECTION 8. MISCELLANEOUS STATUTORY HEADS OF ABSOLUTE PRIVILEGE

Various statutory provisions[432] confer absolute privilege upon reports, state- **13.50** ments and determinations of a number of persons and bodies performing investigative or regulatory functions which would not (or might not) be regarded as of a judicial nature. The details and scope of the privilege vary considerably from one case to another but by way of illustration we take the Parliamentary Commissioner Act 1967, s.10 of which confers an absolute privilege on the following:

    (1) the publication of any matter by the Commissioner in making a report to either House of Parliament for the purposes of the Act[433];

    (2) the publication of any matter by a member of the House of Commons in communicating with the Commissioner for those purposes[434] or by

---

[429] Furthermore, as is pointed out in para.16.13, below, a report of the contents of a statement of case would seem to fall under para.5 of Pt I of Sch.1 to the Defamation Act 1996 (qualified privilege) but since access to other documents requires the court's permission, it may be difficult to say that they "are required by law to be open to public inspection". In *Jameel v Times Newspapers Ltd* [2005] EWHC 1219 (QB) it was accepted that the particulars of claim in an American civil action and the "proffer" in a criminal prosecution fell within both para.2 (reports of court proceedings) and para.5 of Sch.1, but not a sealed appendix to the proffer which was not available to the public.

[430] *Kimber v Press Association* [1893] 1 Q.B. 65 at 71.

[431] See para.34.22, below.

[432] These are scattered around the statute book. Compare the way in which such matters are collected together in the Defamation Act 2005 (NSW) Sch.1.

[433] That is, either a special report where injustice has been caused by maladministration and has not been or will not be remedied (s.10(3)), or his annual general report on the performance of his functions under the Act (s.10(4)), or any other report he thinks fit in respect to his functions (ibid.).

[434] This relates primarily to the reference by such a member of a complaint made by a member of the public (s.5(1)(b)): the member cannot be made liable for such a complaint. It would also seem to cover anything said by a member acting as a friend or adviser to a complainant during an investigation: see the Commissioner's 1969 Annual Report, para.17. Notice that the complainant has no absolute privilege.

the Commissioner or his officers in communicating with such a member for those purposes[435];

(3) the publication by a member to the person by whom a complaint was made under the Act of the report or statement[436] sent by the Commissioner to the member in respect of the complaint;

(4) the publication by the Commissioner of a report on a complaint to the principal officer of the department or authority concerned and to any other person alleged in the complaint to have taken or authorised the action complained of.

While no claim is made that the list is comprehensive, the following extant legislation (not necessarily yet in force) conferring absolute privilege on notices, determinations, reports, etc. by regulators, ombudsmen and the like has been found as at June 2013.

Legal Services Act 2007, s.57, 154.

Government of Wales Act 2006, s.42(1).

Courts and Legal Services Act 1990, ss.18A(8), 23(5).

Commissioner for Older People (Wales) Act 2006, s.19.

Scottish Commission for Human Rights Act 2006 (asp), s.17

Public Services Ombudsman (Wales) Act 2005, s.32.

Inquiries Act 2005, s.37.

Higher Education Act 2004, s.17.

Children Act 2004, Sch.1.

Care Standards Act 2000, s.76(7).

Public Finance and Accountability (Scotland) Act 2000, s.23A.[437]

Assembly Members (Independent Financial Review and Standards (Act (Northern Ireland) 2011, s.32.

Welsh Language (Measures) 2011, s.140.

Water Act 2003, s.55.

Housing Act 1996, Sch.2.

Pensions Act 2004,[438] s.216.

Communications Act 2003, Sch.11.

Commissioner for Children and Young People (Scotland) Act 2003 (asp), s.15.

---

[435] That is, either a statement in the course of an investigation when the member is acting as friend or adviser (see previous note), or a report of the result of his investigation or a statement of his reasons for not conducting an investigation (s.10(1)). What, however, would not be privileged would be the publication by the Commissioner of his reports in the press: see Second Report of the Select Committee 1970–71, H.C. 513, p.13, Q.34. Nor, semble, is there an absolute privilege for words published by the Commissioner or his staff in the conduct of the investigation.

[436] That is, the report or statement referred to in the previous note.

[437] As amended by the Public Services Reform (Scotland) Act 2010.

[438] As amended by the Financial Assistance Scheme (Modifications and Miscellaneous Amendments) Regulations 2005, SI 2005/3256.

Water Act 2003, s.55, Sch.4.

Enterprise Act 2002, ss.108, 173, Sch.25.

Scottish Public Services Ombudsman Act 2002 (asp), s.18.

Scottish Parliamentary Standards Commissioner Act 2002 (asp), s.17.

Financial Services and Markets Act 2000, ss.160, 304, Schs 14, 17.

Care Standards Act 2000, s.76.

Local Government Act 2000, s.74, Sch.4.

Transport Act 2000, ss.13, 18.

Postal Services Act 2000,[439] ss.16A, 19A.

Railways Act 1993, ss.14(3), 15C(1), Sch.4A, paras 11(5), 15(1).

Health Act 2009, Sch 5.

Local Government Act 1974, s.32.[440]

Transport Act 2000,[441] ss.13, 18, Sch.10.

Financial Provisions Act (Northern Ireland) 2009, s.1.

Police, Public Order and Criminal Justice (Scotland) Act 2006, s.46A.

Political Parties, Elections and Referendums Act 2000, Sch.2.

Police and Fire Reform (Scotland) Act 2012, s.70.

Ethical Standards in Public Life, etc. (Scotland) Act 2000 (asp), s.27.

Competition Act 1998, ss.16, 57.

Health and Social Care Act 2012, Schs 10, 9(5)

Housing Act 1996, Sch.2.

Consumers, Estate Agents and Redress Act 2007, Sch.6.

Commissioner for Children and Young People (Scotland) Act 2003, s.15.

Health Service Commissioners Act 1993, s.14.

Pension Schemes Act 1993, s.151.

Scotland Act 1998, ss.41, 50.

Northern Ireland Act 1998, s.50.

Railways Act 1993,[442] s.14.

Water Industry Act 1991,[443] ss.15, 16B, 17N, 17Q.

Law Reform (Miscellaneous Provisions) (Scotland) Act 1990, s.40

Electricity Act 1989,[444] ss.13, 14A, 56D.

Airports Act 1986,[445] s.44A(4). See also Airports (Northern Ireland) Order 1994, SI 1994/426) art.36(4).

Gas Act 1986,[446] ss.25, 26A, 41F.

Rehabilitation of Offenders Act 1974, s.8.

Competition Act 1980, s.16(2).

Payment Services Regulations 2009/209, reg.108.

---

[439] As amended by the Enterprise Act 2002, s.278(1), Sch.25.
[440] As amended by the Local Government and Housing Act 1989, Sch.11.
[441] See fn.439, above.
[442] See fn.439, above.
[443] As amended by the Enterprise Act 2002, s.278(1), Sch.25 and the Water Act 2003.
[444] See fn.439, above.
[445] See fn.439, above.
[446] See fn.439, above.

Water and Sewerage Services (Northern Ireland) order 2006/3336, arts 6, 7, 10.

Enterprise Act 2002 (Consequential and Supplemental Provisions) Order 2003/419, art.36.

Energy (Northern Ireland) Order 2003/419, arts 36, 37.

The Solicitors (Scotland) Act 1980, s.64A, inserted by the Law Reform (Miscellaneous Provisions) (Scotland) Act 1990, s.43.

Local Government (Scotland) Act 1973, s.103H, inserted by Ethical Standards in Public Life, etc. (Scotland) Act 2000 (asp) s.33.

Public Services Ombudsman for Wales (Standards Investigations) Order 2006.[447]

Water Services etc. (Scotland) Act 2005 (Consequential Provisions and Modifications) Order 2005.[448]

Transport (Scotland) Act 2001 (Conditions Attached to PSV Operator's Licence and Competition Test for Exercise of Bus Functions) Order 2001.[449]

Visiting Forces and International Headquarters (Application of Law) Order 1999, Sch.7.[450]

Gas (Northern Ireland) Order 1996/275, arts 16, 17A.

Victim and Survivors (Northern Ireland) Order 2006/2953, art.9.

Higher Education Act 2004, s.17.

Parliamentary Commissioner Act 1967, s.10.

SECTION 9. COMMUNICATIONS BETWEEN SOLICITOR AND CLIENT

13.51 **Communications between solicitor and client.** An evidential privilege attaches to communications between solicitor and client for the purposes of actual contemplated litigation ("litigation privilege") or for the purposes of obtaining legal advice, even if no litigation is contemplated, if the purpose of the communication is the obtaining of legal advice[451] by the client ("legal advice privilege"). The first is a product of the adversarial system,[452] the second of the special nature of the relationship of confidence between solicitor and client.[453] In other words, unless the client waives the privilege, the

---

[447] SI 2006/949.

[448] SI 2005/3172.

[449] SI 2001/2748.

[450] SI 1999/1736.

[451] This is not confined to advice about rights and duties *stricto sensu*, but extends to "what should prudently and sensibly be done in the relevant legal context": *Three Rivers DC v Bank of England* [2004] UKHL 48; [2005] 1 A.C. 610.

[452] Cf. *Re L (a Minor)* [1997] A.C. 16.

[453] On the distinction between the two categories see *Three Rivers DC v Bank of England* [2004] UKHL 48; [2005] 1 A.C. 610 at [10]. Other relationships of confidence do not attract this rule, which is based on the special nature of legal advice in a society founded on the rule of law: ibid. at [34], [86].

solicitor cannot give evidence relating to the communication nor are documents relating to it subject to disclosure. The privilege is "absolute", that is to say is not capable of being overridden on any public interest ground.[454] In practice that will protect *the client* against any action for defamation for statements made by him, unless they are provable *aliunde*. However, it has been said that an absolute privilege (in the sense of a defence to a claim for defamation) applies to such communications,[455] the effect of which would be to protect the solicitor in respect of statements made by him, even where the client waived the evidentiary privilege.[456] However, in *Minter v Priest* an opinion was strongly indicated (though it was not necessary to decide the point) that the privilege is qualified, not absolute.[457] An absolute privilege may also attach to defamatory statements in a solicitor's bill of costs, provided they are relevant in the widest sense and are reasonably necessary to enable the client to understand what he is being asked to pay for,[458] but not to wholly unnecessary statements contained therein.[459]

---

[454] *Three Rivers DC*, above at [25].

[455] The evidential privilege may extend to information supplied by a third party to the solicitor and passed on to the client in advice (*Re Sarah C. Getty Trust* [1985] Q.B. 956), but the defamation privilege could not apply to the statement by the third party to the solicitor.

[456] *More v Weaver* [1928] 2 K.B. 520 CA, disapproving *Morgan v Wallis* (1917) 33 T.L.R. 495.

[457] [1930] A.C. 558, per Lord Dunedin at 574, and per Lord Atkin at 586. Although this was an action for defamation, it was the evidential privilege which was in issue. See also *Waple v Surrey CC* [1998] 1 W.L.R. 860 CA. In *Clarke v Davey* [2002] EWHC 2342 (QB), Gray J. refused summary judgment on the grounds that there was a realistic prospect that the claimant would be able to establish at trial that the principle in *More v Weaver* could no longer stand in the light of subsequent authorities. In Scotland only a qualified privilege attaches to instructions given by a client to his solicitor (*Williamson v Umphray* (1890) 17 R. 905); but Lord Shand appears to have doubted whether the privilege was not absolute. The Faulks Committee, Cmnd.5909 (1975), para.243, thought that *More v Weaver* would not be followed in Scotland. *More v Weaver* has statutory force in New Zealand by s.14(2) of the Defamation Act 1992:
"A communication between any person (in this subsection referred to as the client) and a barrister or a solicitor for the purpose of enabling the client to seek or obtain legal advice, and a communication between that solicitor and any barrister for the purpose of enabling legal advice to be provided to the client, are protected by absolute privilege."
In Hong Kong the issue was left open in *Wong Shui Kee v Chu* [2002] HKCA 421.

[458] *More v Weaver* [1928] 2 K.B. 520 CA, overruling on this point *Morgan v Wallis* (1917) 33 T.L.R. 495; but see *Minter v Priest* [1930] A.C. at 574, 586.

[459] *Bruton v Downes* (1859) 1 F. & F. 668.

CHAPTER 14

QUALIFIED PRIVILEGE AT COMMON LAW

SECTION 1. INTRODUCTION

Introduction: the "classical" forms of qualified privilege. There are **14.1** circumstances in which, on grounds of public policy and convenience, less compelling than those which give rise to absolute privilege, a person may yet, without incurring liability for defamation, make statements of fact about another which are defamatory and in fact untrue. These are cases of qualified privilege (or "conditional privilege" as it is sometimes called in the United States[1]). For a very long time these cases primarily concerned communications of a "private" nature, commonly arising out of the necessities of some existing relationship between the maker of the statement and the recipient.

---

[1] Or "qualified protection" in the legislation of some Australian states, though the phrase is no longer used in the uniform defamation legislation. The Irish Defamation Act 2009, s.18(1) provides that:

"it shall be a defence to a defamation action for the defendant to prove that the statement in respect of which the action was brought would, if it had been made immediately before the commencement of this section, have been considered under the law (other than the [Defamation] Act of 1961) in force immediately before such commencement as having been made on an occasion of qualified privilege"

but without prejudice to the generality of that, there is a defence of qualified privilege under s.18(2) if the defendant proves that:

"(a) the statement was published to a person or persons who—

(i) had a duty to receive, or interest in receiving, the information contained in the statement, or

(ii) the defendant believed upon reasonable grounds that the said person or persons had such a duty or interest, and

(b) the defendant had a corresponding duty to communicate, or interest in communicating, the information to such person or persons."

By s.18(7) duty and interest mean a legal, moral or social duty or interest. In other words, there is a statutory restatement of the classical duty/interest model. Compare the similar technique with regard to absolute privilege, para.13.1, above. S.18(3) and (4) make provision for the equivalents

Protection was granted if the statement was "fairly warranted by the occasion" (that is to say, fell within the scope of the purpose for which the law grants the privilege) and so long as it was not shown by the person defamed that the statement was made with malice, i.e. with some indirect or improper motive, which was typically established by proof that the defendant knew the statement to be untrue, or was recklessly indifferent as to its truth. It was customary to classify the cases as turning on either the performance of a duty or the protection of an interest existing between the maker of the statement and the recipient. Because the grounds for protection were regarded as less compelling than in cases where absolute privilege was conferred, it depended generally on the honesty of purpose with which the defamatory statement was made, but it was not defeated by fault in the sense of carelessness in failing to make inquiries or arriving at a conclusion.

There was another category of qualified privilege at common law, of equally respectable antiquity, which covered reports to the public at large of certain matters of legitimate concern to them, for example the proceedings of courts[2] or of Parliament.[3] Such privilege was also defeated by malice but there was an "objective" element in the defence in the requirement that the report should be "fair and accurate".[4] This category still exists, though in practice it has largely been replaced by the absolute privilege for reports of judicial proceedings in s.14 of the Defamation Act 1996[5] and the qualified privilege for many other reports in Sch.1 of the Act.[6] No doubt the theory which underlay these "reporting privileges" was (and is) that the information was already "public" and a newspaper carrying the report was doing no more than bringing it to the attention of its legitimate audience: they offered no protection to material originated by the newspaper or to "investigative journalism". However, until the very end of the twentieth century there was otherwise in England (and, indeed, in the rest of the Commonwealth) a strong reluctance to extend the protection of qualified privilege to publications in the news media. The fundamental principle was that a statement was protected by privilege only if the publication of it was to persons who had a proper interest or duty in the matter with which it was concerned, and the public as a whole was not generally regarded as having a relevant interest or duty. The media defendant (or other defendant who caused his statement to be published in that

---

of the statutory forms of qualified privilege under Sch.1 of the English Defamation Act 1996 (see further para.16.1 (fn.1).

[2] See para.15.35, below.

[3] See para.15.36, below.

[4] If I make an honest statement on a privileged occasion and I get the facts wrong I am protected—that is what the privilege is all about. If I make a report of X's words and this falls under one of the reporting privileges I am protected if X got it wrong, but not if I misreport what X said. See *Bray v Deutsche Bank AG* [2008] EWHC 1263 (QB); [2008] E.M.L.R. 12.

[5] See para.13.35, above.

[6] See Ch.16, below.

way) was in no different position from anyone else[7] and had to show the relevant reciprocity of duty and interest. Such a duty only arose:

> "where it is in the interests of the public that the publication should be made and will not arise simply because the information appears to be of legitimate public interest."[8]

A privilege for publication to the world at large was, in English law, the exception rather than the rule,[9] even if the subject-matter was politics or public affairs. Nor was there any defence of "fair information upon a matter of public interest,"[10] still less of "fair attributed report" of what someone else has stated or of "neutral reportage".

Reynolds v Times Newspapers Ltd. As a result of *Reynolds v Times*   **14.2**
Newspapers Ltd[11] there is now a much more extensive protection for publications to the public at large where the matter is of sufficient public concern.[12] Although this category is classified as one of qualified rather than absolute privilege, it is of rather a different nature[13] from the "classical" privilege founded on a relationship. In very many cases of the latter type the existence of a privileged "occasion" will be well-established by previous case law

---

[7] Report of the Faulks Committee, Cmnd.5909 (1975), para.215. Under the Schedule to the Defamation Act 1952 the statutory protection for reports was confined to newspapers and broadcasters. That restriction has now been removed: para.16.3, below.

[8] Per Cantley J. in *London Artists v Littler* [1968] 1 W.L.R. 607 at 619 (on appeal [1969] 2 Q.B. 375 CA); *Banks v Globe & Mail* [1961] S.C.R. 474 at 484; *Morosi v Mirror Newspapers* [1977] 2 N.S.W.L.R 749 NSWCA (which contains a valuable review of the common law at 772 792).

[9] See *Chapman v Ellesmere* [1932] 2 K.B. 431 CA. There was, of course, no such restriction on fair comment and comment may include inferences of fact.

[10] *Blackshaw v Lord* [1984] Q.B. 1 CA. There had been a suggestion to that effect in *Webb v Times Publishing Co* [1960] 2 Q.B. 535, the decision in which related to a report of foreign judicial proceedings and was hence closely analogous to an existing head of common law qualified privilege.

[11] [2001] 2 A.C. 127 HL, para.15.1, below.

[12] This is essential.
"Many people hold forth about 'the beautiful game' [soccer] from a variety of stand points and with varying degrees of authority and knowledge. When the readership runs into millions, as in the case of this newspaper, there must be some cogent reason of public policy why defamatory remarks need to be accorded a cloak of privilege. If [the writer] wishes to attribute or spread responsibility for the Club's woes, that is his entitlement; but I do not accept that public policy requires that he should be allowed to attack whomsoever he pleases to millions of people under cover of privilege":
Blackwell v News Group Newspapers Ltd [2007] EWHC 3098 (QB) at [10] per Eady J.

[13] A "different jurisprudential creature from the traditional form of privilege from which it sprang": *Loutchansky v Times Newspapers Ltd (Nos 2–5)* [2001] EWCA Civ 1805; [2002] Q.B. 783 at [35]; *Jameel v Wall Street Journal Europe SPRL* [2006] UKHL 44; [2007] 1 A.C. 359 at [146]. In *Flood v Times Newspapers Ltd* [2012] UKSC 11 SC; [2012] 2 A.C. 273; [2012] 2 W.L.R. 760 Lord Phillips stated (at [27]) that the use of the term "privilege" in this context was misleading and it should be more accurately described as a "public interest defence". The other Justices use the terms interchangeably (see e.g. Lord Mance at [122] and Lord Brown at [118]). See further, para.15.2.

dealing with standard situations (e.g. the writing of a reference, the making of a complaint about the provision of services or the transmission of information within a group or organisation which affects the interests of its members) and the protection does not depend upon the extent to which the maker of the statement has made proper investigations: once the occasion is held to be a privileged one, the issue is whether the defendant acted honestly (i.e. without malice) not whether he behaved reasonably or took due care.[14]

The *Reynolds* category is not confined to publication through the "media",[15] though in practice that will be the context of almost all the cases. The very existence of the privilege in this type of case, however, is a matter which involves a closer scrutiny of the facts of the particular case. It involves questions like the extent to which the defendant took steps to verify the information he imparts, the urgency of the matter, the extent of the public's "right to know" about it and whether the defendant has sought any explanation or comment from the person about whom the statement is made. Thus while one can say that the writer of a reference has privilege for any statement which is relevant to the proposed employment, one cannot say, in the abstract, that a newspaper does or does not have privilege at common law for a news story. That question has been described as one of whether the newspaper conformed to the standards of "responsible journalism".[16]

> "The ... duty on the journalist (and equally his editor) ... is to behave as a responsible journalist. He can have no duty to publish unless he is acting responsibly any more than the public has an interest in reading whatever may be published irresponsibly. That is why in this class of case the question whether the publisher has behaved responsibly is necessarily and intimately bound up with the question whether the defence of qualified privilege arises. Unless the publisher is acting responsibly privilege cannot arise. That is not the case with regard to the more conventional situations in which qualified privilege arises.[17] A person giving a reference or reporting a crime[18] need not act responsibly: his communication will be privileged subject only to relevance and malice."[19]

Here it is not so much the "occasion" which is privileged (which has been the

---

[14] The extent to which this proposition needs to be reconsidered in light of the Human Rights Act 1998, especially with respect to cases involving public authority defendants, is considered below.

[15] *Seaga v Harper* [2008] UKPC 9 (speech at meeting).

[16] *Reynolds v Times Newspapers Ltd* [2001] 2 A.C. 202 HL, per Lord Nicholls.

[17] Similarly in Australia the privilege created for media publications about political matters in *Lange v Australian Broadcasting Corp* (1997) 189 C.L.R. 520, and requiring "reasonableness" (see para.15.26, below) does not import this element into cases which can be brought within a traditional category of qualified privilege: *Makeig v Derwent* [2000] NSWCA 136; *Roberts v Bass* [2002] HCA 57; 212 C.L.R. 1.

[18] But the latter case is now regarded as attracting absolute privilege: para.13.12, above.

[19] *Loutchansky v Times Newspapers Ltd (Nos 2–5)* [2001] EWCA Civ 1805; [2002] Q.B. 783 at [36]; *Fox v Wokingham DC* [2003] EWCA Civ 499 at [29].

traditional approach[20]) as the publication.[21] If, on the other hand, the news-paper's case passes the test of responsible journalism that will determine the issue in its favour. Writing a reference is a privileged occasion but the writer may or may not be guilty of malice; but it is hard to see how a person who complied with the standards of responsible journalism could at the same time be malicious.[22]

> "There is no question of the privilege being defeated by proof of malice because the propriety of the conduct of the defendant is built into the conditions under which the material is privileged."[23]

So far as the law of England and Wales is concerned, s.4 of the Defamation Act 2013 abolishes the *Reynolds* common law defence and replaces it with a new public interest defence. However, the new defence was stated in the Explanatory Notes to be based on the existing common law defence estab-lished in *Reynolds* and as intended to reflect the principles established in that case and in subsequent case law. This is considered in detail in Ch.15.

Arrangement of the material. There has been some disagreement as to   **14.3**
whether the *Reynolds* principle rests on the foundation of duty and interest[24] and indeed whether *Reynolds* should properly be described as recognising the existence of a public interest "qualified privilege" or a "public interest defence". However, the "classical" model, *Reynolds* and the traditional reporting privileges, have all been called "qualified privileges"[25] and that

---

[20] See Lord Shaw in *Adam v Ward* [1917] A.C. 309 HL at 348: Privilege "is a term which is applied in two senses. There is a privileged occasion, and there is said to be a privileged communication. The former expression is correct; the latter, strictly viewed, tends to error. What is meant with regard to a privileged communication is that it was protected as being within the scope of the privilege attaching to the occasion. The occasion is privileged, the communication is protected."

[21] *Loutchansky v Times Newspapers Ltd (Nos 2–5)* [2001] EWCA Civ 1805; [2002] Q.B. 783 at [33].

[22] Ibid. See para.17.21, below.

[23] *Jameel v Wall Street Journal Europe SPRL* [2006] UKHL 44; [2007] 1 A.C. 359 per Lord Hoffmann at [46].

[24] Compare on the one hand Lord Bingham and Lord Hope and on the other Lord Hoffmann and Baroness Hale in *Jameel v Wall Street Journal Europe SPRL*, above. For Lord Scott, "I am unable to discern any real differences of principle. If, however, there are any, I want to express my full agreement with the reasons given by my noble and learned friend, Lord Hoffmann": at [144]. In *Flood v Times Newspapers Ltd* [2012] UKSC 11 SC; [2012] 2 A.C. 273; [2012] 2 W.L.R. 760, Lord Phillips (at [38]) stated that he had no doubt that the *Reynolds* public interest defence was "sui generis" and a different "jurisprudential creature" from the traditional form of duty / interest privilege whence it sprang (see also Lord Mance (at [125])).

[25] Perhaps we should have new terminology but there are two objections to "public interest privilege" for the new development: (1) there is a risk of confusion with the principles applicable to non-disclosure of documents (para.13.28, above); (2) even the classical, private communication privilege rests on the "public interest". Confusingly, the only thing in the Australian uniform legislation which is called "qualified privilege" is what is in effect the *Reynolds* principle: see, e.g. Defamation Act 2005 (NSW) s.30. But classical privilege still exists there under the common law: s.24. In the Irish Defamation Act 2009 qualified privilege is defined in s.16 in terms of duty or interest. The *Reynolds* principle (s.26) is called "Fair and reasonable publication on a matter of public interest". Some may object to the rather imprecise expressions "classical" or "tradi-tional" privilege which are frequently used in this text, but the difficulties of terminology may be

presents problems for the arrangement of the material. The course which has
been adopted is as follows: this chapter deals with the situations, predominantly private communications, covered by the classical concept; Ch.15 is
mainly concerned with *Reynolds* and the developments from that case. It is
more difficult to know where to place the common law categories of reporting
privilege. On the one hand, like private communications they are defeated by
malice; on the other hand, the reporter must meet the requirements of fairness
and accuracy, they are almost always invoked by the media and duty and
interest are not in issue in the same way as they are in private communications. On balance it seems better to place them in the next chapter with
Reynolds. In any event they are now of limited practical importance in view
of statutory developments.[26]

The material has been arranged in a way which, it is hoped, may be
convenient in the present state of the law. But it should be noted that the line
between the classical and *Reynolds* privileges cannot be sharply drawn. Thus
it is perfectly possible that a case may fall into the category based on a
relationship even though the audience to which the statement is addressed is
much larger than that for some media publications. In one case, for example,
a privilege existed on the traditional model between the General Council of
the Bar and 10,000 barristers,[27] whereas a newspaper circulating among only
1,500 Saudi nationals in this country had to satisfy the further requirements
under *Reynolds*[28]; and a public body may be under a duty in the traditional
sense to explain to the public its position on a matter which has come into the
public domain.[29] If the requisite duty and interest can be found in a public
communication the defendant is not obliged to satisfy the further *Reynolds*
requirements,[30] though in determining whether qualified privilege applies

---

illustrated by the fact that there are signs we are beginning to speak even of "classic Reynolds
privilege" as opposed to its offshoot of reportage: *Prince Radu of Hohenzollern v Houston* [2007]
EWHC 2735 (QB) at [26] (affirmed [2008] EWCA Civ 921).

[26] See para.14.1, above.

[27] *Kearns v General Council of the Bar* [2003] EWCA Civ 331; [2003] 1 W.L.R. 1357.

[28] *Al-Fagih v HH Saudi Research Marketing (UK) Ltd* [2001] EWCA Civ 1634; [2002]
E.M.L.R. 215.

[29] In *Alexander v Arts Council of Wales* [2001] EWCA Civ 514; [2001] 1 W.L.R. 514, Eady J's
decision on the existence of a privileged occasion was not challenged on appeal. See also *Lillie
v Newcastle CC* [2002] EWHC 1600 (QB) at [1450]–[1451]; *Seray-Wurie v Charity Commission*
[2008] EWHC 870 (QB). However, it should be noted that in *Clift v Slough Borough Council*
[2010] EWCA Civ 1171; [2011] 1 W.L.R. 1774 (see, para.14.5 below), it was held that proof of
an established, existing relationship was not, of itself, sufficient to entitle a public authority
defendant to rely on qualified privilege. As a public authority it was bound to act compatibly with
Convention rights, in particular with its duty not to interfere with the claimant's art.8 rights. Its
public law duties required it to publish information only to the extent necessary for the performance of those duties and in accordance with its obligations under the Human Rights Act 1998.
Consequently, unless any interference could be justified under art.8(2) as necessary and proportionate to a legitimate aim, the public authority could not rely on qualified privilege.

[30] *Kearns v General Council of the Bar* [2003] EWCA Civ 331; [2003] 1 W.L.R. 1357; *Seray-
Wurie v Charity Commission*, above. In *Hewitt v Grunwald* [2004] EWHC 2959 (QB) the
defendants published statements on the internet to the effect that the claimants' organisation was

questions of reasonableness of conduct may be relevant and this may require a court to take account of factors such as whether any steps have been taken to verify the information being communicated.[31] Furthermore, the law does not recognise a simple division between cases where the touchstone is simply honesty of communication and those where a standard of reasonable conduct has to be met. No doubt there are standard categories of privilege[32] where by reason of an established relationship[33] or other circumstances, the necessary conditions may generally be satisfied without further inquiry into the particular circumstances surrounding the publication in question. But of course qualified privilege is not limited to communications made between parties who have a pre-existing relationship, and the ultimate question is whether what was done was warranted (i.e. necessary) by the occasion and all the circumstances surrounding the publication including questions of reasonableness of conduct,[34] and not simply honesty, may enter into this. So, for example, a local authority might be privileged in reporting to the ratepayers the result of an investigation into theft of its property but not privileged in reporting the evidence in its possession before the inquiry had been completed.[35] So too, defamatory statements made by the defendant as part of a campaign to encourage support for a motion of no confidence brought by him against the claimant in her position as a director of the National Register of Public Service Interpreters were protected by qualified privilege only so far as they were made to those interpreters who could vote on the motion of no

---

involved in the support of terrorism. The plea of qualified privilege (which Eady J. declined to strike out) was:

"based upon a more traditional form of common law qualified privilege, uncomplicated by the refinements of their Lordships in [*Reynolds*]. In other words, the case is expressed in terms of a duty, owed to the Jewish community to inform them of developments, and/or upon a common and corresponding interest between the Jewish community and the Defendants in the subject matter of the website postings": at [69].

[31] *Cambridge v Makin* [2012] EWCA Civ 85; [2012] E.M.L.R. 19; *Downtex v Flatley* [2003] EWCA Civ 1282 CA; *Kearns v General Council of the Bar* [2003] EWCA Civ 331; [2003] 1 W.L.R. 1357.

[32] See para.14.12, below.

[33] *Kearns v General Council of the Bar* above at [34], per Simon Brown L.J.

[34] In *Cambridge v Makin* [2012] EWCA Civ 85; [2012] E.M.L.R. 19 the Court of Appeal held in a case where there was not a pre-existing relationship between the maker and recipient of the statement complained of, that in determining whether qualified privilege existed the court should look to all the circumstances of the case and one of the factors which may be relevant is whether steps have been taken to verify the information being communicated. See also *Downtex v Flatley* [2003] EWCA Civ 1282.

[35] *De Buse v McCarthy* [1942] K.B. 156 CA. But see, *Clift v Slough Borough Council* [2010] EWCA Civ 1171; [2011] 1 W.L.R. 1774. At first instance in *Flood v Times Newspapers* [2009] EWHC 2375 (QB); [2010] E.M.L.R. 8, Tugendhat J. pointed out (at [189]), that the freedom of any public authority to disclose information to the public would now fall to be considered, not under the head of Reynolds public interest privilege, but under the Human Rights Act 1998 and art.8 of the Convention or the Data Protection Act 1998. This was approved by the Court of Appeal ([2010] EWCA Civ 804 at [42]; [2011] 1 W.L.R. 153) and the Supreme Court ([2012] UKSC 11 at [59] SC; [2012] 2 A.C. 273).

confidence but not otherwise.[36] In *Guise v Kovelis*[37] the defendant accused the plaintiff in a loud voice in a club of cheating at cards. Clearly persons playing cards at a club have a common interest in the honesty of those who frequent the club and all members of the High Court of Australia seem to have been willing to accept that this community of interest might extend to visitors as well as members. However, the majority held that there was no privilege, as the defendant could have reported the matter to the Committee, which clearly would have been privileged. Latham C.J. said that:

"The basis of the privilege in question is social welfare and I am not prepared to hold that it is conducive to social welfare to lay down a rule that a member of a club who is doubtful of the honesty, or is satisfied of the dishonesty, of another person who is in the club on a particular occasion is privileged in expressing his opinion to members of the club in general. To hold the contrary would amount to granting a wide licence to officious and interfering mischief-makers."[38]

Dixon J. thought otherwise:

"The defendant ... was faced with the embarrassing choice between taxing the plaintiff at once with what he believed he had done and passing it for the time being in silence and subsequently raising the question elsewhere. If he chose the latter, he would or might be met with doubts and denials based on his failure to speak at the time. Why was not his situation a reasonable occasion or exigency fairly warranting an honest challenge of the plaintiff's conduct?"[39]

14.4 No pre-existing relationship. In *Downtex Plc v Flatley*[40] the defendant, who was in dispute with the claimants about the sale of a business, sent letters to suppliers of the claimants casting doubt upon the claimants' solvency and suggesting the calling of a creditors' meeting. The Court of Appeal allowed an appeal against a refusal to strike out a defence of qualified privilege and granted judgment for damages to be assessed. Potter L.J. said[41]:

"Summarising the position, therefore, it does not appear to me that, objectively, any imputation of insolvency or near insolvency could be ... justified from the material which the defendants themselves relied upon as founding the plea of qualified privilege. With respect to the judge, it seems to me that, having rightly identified the necessity for the statement to be 'fairly warranted by the occasion', and having indicated that he understood the strength of the arguments of the claimants to the effect that it was not so warranted, he should have gone further ... it seems to me that the judge should have grasped the nettle and dealt with the question of whether

---

[36] *Cambridge v Makin* [2012] EWCA Civ 85; [2012] E.M.L.R. 19.
[37] (1947) 74 C.L.R. 102 HCA. Compare *Bridgman v Stockdale* [1953] 1 W.L.R. 704 (accusation of cheating in examination).
[38] At 112.
[39] At 124. The defendant may have an undoubted privilege to publish to A but it may be contended that he has exceeded the bounds of the privilege by publishing to B as well: see para.14.69, below.
[40] [2003] EWCA Civ 1282.
[41] At [47].

or not [the defendant's] concerns were objectively justified by the material on which he relied."

The approach in *Downtex*, by introducing as it does an objective element into the defendant's perception of the facts upon which he acts,[42] may mean that the defence is destroyed at the outset before the stage of malice is reached, by the decision that the communication was not fairly warranted by the occasion. This may appear inconsistent with the classical view of qualified privilege that it is only defeated by malice and not lack of reasonable care. Yet it may be explained as recognising a difference between cases where there is an established, pre-existing relationship between maker and recipient and cases where no such relationship exists. With regard to the first of these categories, one does not need to assess the interests of society afresh in each case. The law is relatively well settled on the basis that the balance would fairly be struck if liability in such situations was confined to those cases where the occasion of communication was abused—in the sense that malice could be established. Nothing short of malice will undermine the law's protection. However, in cases where there is no pre-existing relationship, the ultimate question is whether what was done was warranted by the occasion and all the circumstances surrounding the publication, including questions of reasonableness of conduct, the quality of the information and not simply honesty, may enter into this.[43]

The limits of privilege for public authorities. If it was difficult before **14.5** the Human Rights Act 1998 to reduce the law of qualified privilege to a set of simple mechanical rules, that Act has added a further layer of complexity. The classic "off the peg" situation of qualified privilege is the giving of a reference but even here it has been suggested that since reputation as well as freedom of expression is protected by the European Convention on Human Rights the law may have to adapt to ensure a more flexible balancing of these rights even in such a case.[44] More recently, the potential significance of the 1998 Act for qualified privilege has been highlighted by the decision of the Court of Appeal in *Clift v Slough BC*.[45] The claimant in *Clift* witnessed some

---

[42] In this respect the case is distinguishable from *Guise*, where it was the reasonableness of the course of action taken by the defendant which was challenged, not his belief that there were grounds to suspect cheating. See also *Wood v Chief Constable of the West Midlands* [2004] EWCA Civ 1638; [2005] E.M.L.R. 20: para.14.37, below.

[43] See, e.g. *Cambridge v Makin* [2012] EWCA Civ 85 at [52]; [2012] E.M.L.R. 19.

[44] *W v JH* [2008] EWHC 399 (QB) per Tugendhat J. at [48].

[45] [2010] EWCA Civ 1171; [2011] 1 W.L.R. 1774 (on appeal from [2009] EWHC 1550 (QB); [2010] E.M.L.R. 4). See also *Bento v The Chief Constable of Bedfordshire Police* [2012] EWHC 1525 (QB) in which Bean J. held that a chief constable was not able to rely on qualified privilege in a defamation claim. The claim had been brought following a press release stating the view that a CPS decision not to pursue a murder prosecution against the claimant was wrong because he was probably guilty. It was in the public interest for the police to communicate with the public, including through media briefings, during an investigation into a suspicious death, to retain the community's confidence that the case was being taken seriously and to encourage the flow of information that might be of assistance. However, the public interest in maintaining confidence in the criminal justice system would not be served by encouraging the police to issue statements

anti-social behaviour in a park in Slough. Flower-beds were damaged and she was herself threatened when she intervened. On the advice of the police, who had been called to the park, she rang the council's anti-social behaviour co-ordinator, Ms Rachid. The conversation went very badly, words were exchanged and Ms Clift terminated the call. She subsequently wrote a very strongly worded letter of complaint about Ms Rachid's conduct to the council. An investigation was conducted by the council and the complaint was rejected. However, Ms Clift was also informed that her behaviour on the phone and in subsequent letters amounted to violent and threatening behaviour, as a consequence of which a "marker" was to be placed against her name for 18 months and shared with other council departments and government agencies within the borough by email and by placing her name on a register (the potentially violent persons register). Ms Clift's name was duly placed on the register and emails sent to the following:

(1) customer-facing staff (and their managers) in departments where it was possible that they might have to deal with the claimant;
(2) customer-facing staff (and their managers) in other departments where it was unlikely they would have to deal with the claimant;
(3) community wardens, certain trade union officials and various partner organisations that provided services on behalf of the council;
(4) various other publishees including environmental health officers and head of environmental services and policy, head of customer services team, strategic director for social services and an additional number (approximately 150) of publishees who were not identified.

As a consequence of these publications, Ms Clift commenced a claim for libel alleging that they meant that she was a violent person who had engaged in threatening behaviour on a number of occasions. The defendants pleaded, inter alia, qualified privilege. At first instance, Tugendhat J. held that to be able to rely on qualified privilege where the defendant was, as here, a public authority, it must show that it has complied with its public law duties under the Human Rights Act 1998 and, incidentally, the Data Protection Act 1998. Under Human Rights Act, s.6(1) it is unlawful for a public authority to act in a way that is incompatible with a Convention right. It follows that where a public authority publishes information about a person which interferes with her rights under art.8(1) then, unless the publication of such information is in

---

suggesting that a CPS decision not to pursue a prosecution was wrong because the individual concerned was, or probably was, guilty. On the contrary, such statements reduced confidence in the criminal justice system, as well as seriously damaging the right to reputation of the individual. The police could perfectly well have issued a statement which protected their own interests without defaming Mr Bento. The chief constable accepted that it would not have been necessary or proportionate for the purposes of balancing Mr Bento's rights under art.8 with the public's art.10 rights to say that he was guilty of the deceased's murder. The same applied to a statement whose meaning was that he probably killed her (at [95]–[100]). See further para.14.37, below.

accordance with law and is necessary and proportionate in a democratic society for one of the legitimate aims set out in art.8(2) such as protection of the rights of others, such a publication will be unlawful. In short, unless a local authority establishes that it has complied with its public law duties under Human Rights Act 1998, it will not be able to assert the protection of privilege.

Applying that approach to the facts, the judge held that the claimant's art.8 right to reputation was clearly engaged and that no other rights were engaged. While the council had acted with a legitimate aim of protecting the safety of its staff, the circulation of the publications was greater than was necessary to accomplish that objective. Though a reasonable council could have concluded that the claimant's conduct did give rise to a risk to some council employees, the risk was a very limited one and certainly did not exist to those who worked in departments which the claimant was not likely to approach.[46] Beyond that, they certainly owed no duty to the staff of partner organisations from which the claimant might seek services or supplies. There was simply no evidence of risk in such a case. Tugendhat J. was of the view that if the case had not been affected by the Human Rights Act 1998, privilege would have covered publication to all the defendants' staff.

"The ruling I made would have been different if I had followed *Kearns v General Council of the Bar*.[47] So far as publication to fellow Council employees is concerned, there was an existing relationship, and so no occasion to enquire into the circumstances. Publication to all employees of the Council would have been on an occasion of qualified privilege, including to those employees who did not need to know, such as those in the Licensing Department. In the case of publication to partner organisations, or non-employees, these were not with in an existing relationship, and the ruling would have been the same. These were not on an occasion of qualified privilege."[48]

In reaching this conclusion Tugendhat J made a number of additional important comments. First, in determining whether the extent of the publication was necessary and proportionate, the Human Rights Act 1998 requires that an objective test of relevance should be applied: "The effect of my decision has been to 'involve application by the court of an objective test of relevance to every part of the defamatory matter published'."[49]

---

[46] [2009] EWHC 1550 (QB); [2010] E.M.L.R. 4 at [84].
[47] [2003] EWCA Civ 331; [2003] 1 W.L.R. 1357.
[48] [2009] EWHC 1550 (QB); [2010] E.M.L.R. 4 at [99].
[49] Ibid. at [102]. Tugendhat J. indicated that in his view this represented a departure from what Lord Diplock had said in *Horrocks v Lowe* [1975] A.C. 135 HL but that such a departure was justified and required by the Human Rights Act 1998. The Court of Appeal agreed that an objective test of relevance (or as Ward L.J. put of "necessity or reasonableness") should be applied to the question of proportionality but denied that this meant that an examination of proportionality involved any application by the court of an "objective test of relevance to every part of the defamatory matter published":
"The proportionality issue may have involved "an objective test of relevance" (or I would say

It followed that the state of mind of the relevant council officer who had responsibility for employee protection was not relevant either to the question of the existence of the privilege or its extent. Of course, the consequence of testing relevance by reference to an objective standard will often mean, as indeed was the case here, that the defence is destroyed at the outset, before the question of malice has been reached, by the decision that the extent of the communication was wider than was reasonably necessary.

Secondly, as this was a case in which the information disclosed amounted to sensitive personal data under Data Protection Act 1998, s.2, a useful check on the decision as to the existence, and appropriate extent, of any privilege determined to exist could be made by looking at the compliance advice offered by the Information Commissioner. Such advice is not binding in law, but as Tugendhat J. pointed out "it comes from the Information Commissioner, and it is carefully reasoned". Where, as here, both the Human Rights Act 1998 and the Data Protection Act 1998 are relevant, the duties imposed by both pieces of legislation on a public authority with respect to the disclosure of sensitive data should be equivalent.[50]

The defendant's appeal against the decision of Tugendhat J. was dismissed by the Court of Appeal. Ward L.J., who gave a judgment with which Thomas and Richards L.JJ., agreed, noted that traditionally the defence of qualified privilege is rooted in public policy. Its existence depends upon:

> "showing either a duty situation or an interest situation, the former where the maker of the communication was under some legal or social or moral duty to speak out and the recipient had an interest in receiving the information or in the latter case where the maker of the statement was acting in furtherance of some interest or his which the recipient has a reciprocal interest in receiving or was acting under a common interest in the subject matter shared with the recipient."[51]

However, there is additionally the duty of public authorities to act compatibly with individual's convention rights, which include the right to reputation recognised in art.8 jurisprudence. Slough Borough Council is a public authority and here the claimant's art.8 right to reputation was engaged. The council was accordingly bound to respect it unless its interference could be justified under art.8(2). As to the council's argument that this would create immense

---

"necessity or reasonableness") of the publication to various categories of recipients, but that is not questioning the relevance of 'every part of the defamatory matter' itself which is that with which Lord Diplock was dealing. The relevance of the content of the e-mail and the register was not in issue at all. It might have been different if, to use [counsel's] example, the offending communication informed the employees: 'Beware of Ms Clift because she is a violent woman and what is more, she is an habitual drug-taker.' The employees' interest was limited to the risk she posed to them as a violent person; her drug-taking was irrelevant. Here the content of the defamatory statement was not under scrutiny at all: the court's concern was focused on whether the recipients needed to know the information and whether or not it could reasonably be said that they were at risk. For my part I do not see why *Horrocks v Lowe* was relevant at all" (at [44]).
[50] Ibid. at [51].
[51] [2010] EWCA Civ 1171; [2011] 1 W.L.R. 1774 at [25].

practical difficulties for local authority officials required to make an individual assessment of the propriety of each and every proposed publication, Ward L.J. concluded:

> "Ill-considered and indiscriminate disclosure is bound to be disproportionate and no plea of administrative difficulty in verifying the information and limiting publication to those who truly have the need to know or those reasonably thought to be at risk can outweigh the substantial inference with the right to protect reputations. In my judgment the judge's ruling on proportionality is beyond challenge. To publish as widely as the Council did was to breach Ms Clift's Article 8 rights . . . If the Council were in breach of Article 8, it would be unlawful to publish the information. If it was unlawful to publish the information, then the Council's duty was not to publish. If the duty was not to publish, the Council could no longer claim to be under a duty to impart the information to those who did not need to know it. Not being under a duty to publish, the foundation of the claim to qualified privilege falls away."[52]

The question was therefore whether or not the council had a duty to publish the material as widely as it had done. Answering this question required consideration of the proportionality of the council's actions. The Court of Appeal agreed with the judge that the decision to publish the material about the claimant as widely as the council had done was disproportionate and dismissed the appeal.

The Court of Appeal also rejected a number of other arguments put forward by the defendant. First, it held that the judge had not failed to take into account the art.8 rights of the publishees since any risk to them was not significant enough to engage art.8. Secondly, the court held that the claimant's case did not invoke Convention rights to create a new defence. As Ward L.J. explained:

> "In my judgment the fallacy in this argument is that no new defence is being created in this case. The defence is the common law defence of qualified privilege. To support the defence the Defendant must first establish that it is under a duty to communicate the information to those who have a corresponding interest or duty to receive it. The issue is whether or not the Council are under such a duty. Whilst they may, on the one hand, be entitled to say they are under a duty of care to their employees to alert them to risks, they are equally under a duty imposed upon them, it is true, by the Human Rights Act to respect Ms Clift's art 8 right to her reputation and thus under a duty to her not to publish the offending material. The court is equally under a duty to ensure that Convention rights are respected. It follows that the duty to Ms Clift not to publish trumps the duty to the supernumerary employees to distribute the entry on the Violent Persons Register."[53]

Finally, the argument that the claimant should have been confined to bringing a freestanding claim under the Human Rights Act for breach of her Convention rights was also rejected:

---

[52] Ibid. at [35] [36].
[53] Ibid. at [39].

"Damages awarded in defamation claims are bound to exceed damages (if any are awarded at all) for a breach of a party's human rights. Since s 6 of the Human Rights Act requires the court to act compatibly with a Convention right, the court is bound to give effect to art 8 if the point arises as it squarely does in this case. We simply cannot duck it, rule it irrelevant or ignore its implications for qualified privilege, leaving the Claimant with her human rights claim only."

It follows from the decision of the Court of Appeal in *Clift* that where the defendant is a public authority, the Human Rights Act 1998 dictates that a different approach be taken to the existence of qualified privilege. That a relationship exists between the maker of the statement and the publishee under which the maker can be said to have a duty to inform the recipient of some matter and the recipient a corresponding interest to receive that information is not of itself enough.[54] A public authority will only be able to rely on qualified privilege if it can show that it has acted compatibly with the art.8 rights of those to whom the information relates, and must satisfy a proportionality test.[55] In determining this question an objective test of relevance should be applied and, where the matter published is sensitive personal data under Data Protection Act 1998, s.2, a useful check on the decision as to the existence, and appropriate extent, of any privilege determined to exist can be made by looking at the compliance advice offered by the Information Commissioner.

14.6 Impact of *Clift v Slough BC* where defendant not a public authority. What impact *Clift* has beyond cases where the defendant is a public authority is not entirely easy to predict. Of course, strictly speaking it is only public authorities that are under a duty not to act incompatibly with a Convention right. However, it is clear that even in cases where the claim is between private persons the courts cannot ignore the Convention and must seek to ensure that any principle or rule of English law is consistent with it.

---

[54] See also, per H.H.J. Parkes QC in *Morrison v Buckinghamshire County Council* [2011] EWHC 3444 (QB): "In my judgment [*Clift*] . . . shows that it is not enough, even where there would pre-Human Rights Act, have been an established relationship between publisher and publishee, for a defendant public body to rely on that relationship as necessarily establishing qualified privilege." (at [60]).

[55] In *Thompson v James* [2013] EWHC 515 (QB) Tugendhat J. held that a local authority and its chief executive could rely on qualified privilege in respect of a letter sent to councillors and comments on a blog. In the letter and the blog, the chief executive responded to criticisms made of the council and chief executive and accused the claimant of running a campaign of harassment, defamation and intimidation against council staff. Although it was strictly unnecessary to consider the qualified privilege issue as the defence of justification had succeeded, the judge held that the claimant's art.8 right were not engaged as the chief executive had not written about the claimant's private life but had focused on her public behaviour and the claimant had willingly entered the arena of public debate when she published her complaints about the Planning Department and other officers of the council to the public at large, and when she informed the public that she would stand for election. Further, the council and chief executive had a legitimate interest in explaining its actions which had been publicly called into question. What the chief executive had said and done by way of response was no more than was necessary and proportionate. He published his response no more widely than the claimant had herself published her own false version of events and therefore the council and chief executive could rely on qualified privilege.

The state is under a positive obligation to protect both freedom of expression and reputation. This requires the courts to engage in a careful balancing of the two rights with neither having a presumptive precedence over the other. The days when art.10 could be considered a trump card are over. Whether in this new era all the established categories of privilege can survive must be open to question. Generally, in the areas covered by privilege, there will be an expression right countervailing the right to reputation. The essential problem is that the blanket nature of the privileges does not allow for any proper balancing exercise between rights. Yet this general need for privilege to reflect an appropriate balance was recognised by Tugendhat J. in *Clift:*

> "The historical cases show that the values set down in the Convention in 1950 as rights under Articles 8 (including the right to reputation) and Article 10 (including the right of freedom of expression in the giving of references and warnings) were not invented in 1950. These and some other Convention rights can be traced back, not only to the American Bill of Rights and the French Declaration in the eighteenth century, but also to the very beginnings of English law. So one thing that [the Human Rights Act] has achieved is to provide a means through which the courts can review the relative priority that the common law gave to those rights (which it already recognised), and adjust those priorities to meet contemporary needs."[56]

Each privilege will require assessment to determine whether the policy reflected in its structure is now Convention compliant. Precisely how the courts will deal with this remains to be seen, but it is likely that some categories of privilege will be subject to challenge on the basis that the public policy that originally justified their existence does not apply today. Further, in each case, the courts should now consider, even if there is an established relationship between the maker of the statement and its recipient, whether publication pursued a legitimate aim and was proportionate or reasonable. The availability of privilege in any particular case must become more fact-sensitive, and the courts must find means of weighing the claimant's art.8 rights in the balance.

All that said, there are a number of reasons to believe that the practical effect of the Convention may not be particularly significant in cases where the defendant is not a public authority. First, and most importantly, while a public authority does not have any human rights,[57] that is not true of other legal persons. Thus, in cases not involving public authorities any court taking into account the Convention will have to weigh the claimant's art.8 right to reputation, assuming the case is one in which the claimant's art.8 right is engaged, against the rights of the maker of the statement and in particular his art.10 right to freedom of expression. Moreover, art.10(1) not only protects the

---

[56] [2009] EWHC 1550 at [112] (QB); [2010] E.M.L.R. 4.

[57] *Parochial Church Council of the Parish of Aston Cantlow and Wilmcote with Billesley Warwickshire v Wallbank* [2003] UKHL 37 SC; [2004] 1 A.C. 546, at [8]. This principle was given effect to in relation to local authorities in *R (Mayor of the City of Westminster) v Mayor of London* [2002] EWHC 2440 at [93] [96] (QD), *R (Medway Council and others) v Secretary of State for Transport* [2002] EWHC 2516 at [20] (QB).

right to impart information but also the right to receive information. This includes the right of the public (and media on its behalf) to receive information. That the right now appears to be of wider scope than originally thought, in particular where the media are involved and genuine public interest is raised, was acknowledged by the Court of Appeal in *R (Guardian News and Media Ltd) v City of Westminster Magistrates' Court; Guardian News and Media Ltd v Government of the United States of America*[58] and *Independent News and Media Ltd v A.*[59] The wider scope of art.10(1) is plainly of general application where it is the public which has a legitimate interest in receiving the information in question and much of the information in question is already in the public domain. Secondly, there is of course a very well-established jurisprudence on classical qualified privilege and much to be said for certainty. The public policy justifications in favour of granting qualified privilege in certain circumstances have been well rehearsed and several decades of authority are unlikely to be swept away lightly. Thirdly, any movement in favour of restricting the application of qualified privilege would run counter to developments such as *Reynolds v Times Newspapers* which made it substantially easier for a defendant to rely on qualified privilege at least where the matter published is of public interest and made clear that the right to freedom of expression was of very greatest importance. At any rate one can say that the law of qualified privilege deals with so many situations in which a balance has to be struck between the protection of reputation and freedom of speech that it would be idle to hope for it to be reduced to a set of simple, mechanical rules.

SECTION 2. EXISTING RELATIONSHIPS: DUTY AND INTEREST, GENERAL PRINCIPLES

14.7 The reason for the defence. Statements published on an occasion of qualified privilege "are protected for the common convenience and welfare of society".[60]

> "It was in the public interest that the rules of our law relating to privileged occasions and privileged communications were introduced, because it is in the public interest that persons should be allowed to speak freely on occasions when it is their duty to

---

[58] [2011] EWCA Civ 1188; [2011] 1 W.L.R. 3253 at [53].

[59] [2010] EWCA Civ 343; [2010] 1 W.L.R. 2262 at [35]–[38].

[60] Per Parke B. in *Toogood v Spyring* (1834) 1 C.M. & R. 181 at 193. The "first classic exposition": *Watts v Times Newspapers* [1997] Q.B. 650 CA at 659. For the 19th century development from *Toogood v Spyring* see Mitchell, *The Making of the Modern Law of Defamation* (2005), Ch.7, which attributes the origin of the judgment to the 2nd edn of Starkie's *Treatise on the Law of Slander and Libel* (1830).

speak, and to tell all they know or believe, or on occasions when it is necessary to speak in the protection of some (self or) common interest."[61]

"In such cases no matter how harsh, hasty, untrue, or libellous the publication would be but for the circumstances, the law declares it privileged because the amount of public inconvenience from the restriction of freedom of speech or writing would far out-balance that arising from the infliction of a private injury."[62]

"It may be unfortunate that a person against whom a charge that is not true is made should have no redress, but it would be contrary to public policy and the general interest of business and society that persons should be hampered in the discharge of their duty or the exercise of their rights by constant fear of actions for slander."[63]

"It is better for the general good that individuals should occasionally suffer than that freedom of communication between persons in certain relations should be in any way impeded. But the freedom of communication which it is desirous to protect is honest and kindly freedom. It is not expedient that liberty should be made the cloak of maliciousness."[64]

"The principle on which these cases are founded is a universal one, that the public convenience is to be preferred to private interests and that communications which the interests of society require to be unfettered may freely be made by persons acting honestly without actual malice notwithstanding that they involve relevant comments condemnatory of individuals."[65]

If the defendant is malicious, that is, if he uses the occasion for some other purpose than that for which the law gives protection, he will not be able to rely on the privilege.[66] It must, however, be observed that the House of Lords has held that there may be liability for negligence in one of the paradigm situations of qualified privilege and this, to some extent, represents a reversal of the law's policy of encouraging frankness of expression.[67] Moreover, as discussed above, the new balancing methodology required by the Human Rights Act 1998 requires the court in determining whether privilege attaches in any case to give careful consideration to the particular facts, and the courts must find means of weighing the claimant's art.8 rights in the balance.[68]

Position of defendants may have to be considered separately. Al- **14.8** though we commonly speak of a statement being made on a privileged occasion it is important, where there is more than one defendant who contributes to a single publication, to consider the individual position of each. This is so, e.g. where one is guilty of malice and the other one is not,[69] but quite

---

[61] Per Bankes L.J. in *Gerhold v Baker* [1918] W.N. 368 CA at 369.

[62] Per Willes J. in *Huntley v Ward* (1859) 6 C.B.(N.S.) 514 at 517.

[63] Per Lord Sands in *Dunnet v Nelson*, 1926 S.C. at 769; and see *Rogers v Orr*, 1939 S.C. 121.

[64] Per Lord Coleridge C.J. in *Bowen v Hall* (1881) 6 Q.B.D. 333 at 343.

[65] Per Willes J. in *Henwood v Harrison* (1872) L.R. 7 C.P. 606 at 622, approved by Lord Shaw in *Adam v Ward* [1917] A.C. 309 at 349, and cited in *Justin v Associated Newspapers* [1967] 1 N.S.W.R. 61 at 75; *Thompson v Australian Consolidated* [1968] 3 N.S.W.R. 642 at 645.

[66] See Ch.17, below generally.

[67] See para.23.3, below.

[68] See paras 14.5–14.6, above.

[69] See para.17.24, below.

apart from the question of malice it may be that the privilege extends to one defendant but not to another. Where all the defendants share the same circumstances and have the same reason for the publication then their position as to privilege will be the same.

> "However, where there are . . . two parties with very different circumstances and very different origins of their respective publications, it would . . . be impossible to do justice or to meet the general interest of society as a whole, if they were not entitled to separate consideration."[70]

Thus where a newspaper published an apology to A, the terms of which had in effect been dictated by A, and this contained a statement defamatory of B, A was protected by privilege because of the latitude afforded to persons responding to attacks upon them, but the newspaper was not because the statement went beyond what was necessary for it to do by way of apology to A.[71]

14.9 Duty and interest. "The occasions [of qualified] privilege can never be catalogued and rendered exact"[72] but the tendency of the courts has been to

---

[70] *Watts v Times Newspapers* [1996] Q.B. 650 CA at 667 per Hirst L.J.
[71] Ibid. at 668.
[72] Fleming, *Torts*, 9th edn (1998), p.622. In *Bushara v Nobananas Pty Ltd* [2013] N.S.W.S.C. 225 the Supreme Court of New South Wales distilled the classical form of qualified privilege in Australia as follows (at [113]):

"(i) Qualified privilege is based upon public policy, namely, in certain circumstances freedom of communication is a more important aspect of democratic government than an individual's right to protection of his or her reputation: *Cush v Dillon; Boland v Dillon* [2011] HCA 30; (2011) 85 ALJR 865 at [12];

(ii) It is first necessary for a trial judge to determine whether there was a duty of a kind which created the occasion to make the statement to which qualified privilege attaches: *Dillon* at [13];

(iii) The determination of whether the occasion arose to which qualified privilege attaches is determined by consideration of the nature and importance of the matters conveyed, the relationship of the defamatory statement to those matters and the relationship between the maker of the statement and the person to whom the statement is made: *Dillon* at [13];

(iv) The relationship between the maker and receiver of the statement is a requirement of a reciprocity of duty or interest necessary to attract the defence of qualified privilege, meaning, that the maker of the statement has a duty or interest in making it and the receiver of the statement has a duty or interest in receiving it: *Dillon* at [12], [13], [32], [54]; *Bashford v Information Australia (Newsletters) Pty Ltd* [2004] HCA 5; (2004) 218 C.L.R. 366 at [9], [10], [137]; *Aktas v Westpac Banking Corp Limited* [2010] HCA 25; (2010) 241 C.L.R. 79 at [22], [41];

(v) Qualified privilege, if it were to exist, is defeated by an improper motive, otherwise termed 'express malice', being a reason for the making of a statement not referable to the duty or interest pursued: *Dillon* at [14], [29];

(vi) Qualified privilege is also lost for so much of the statement that is not relevant and pertinent to the discharge of the duty or the safeguarding of the interest: *Dillon* at [19];

(vii) While knowledge that a statement is untrue may be evidence of malice, neither lack of belief in the truth of the statement nor objective falsity of the statement is sufficient to destroy qualified privilege: *Dillon* at [28], [29]."
So far as the question whether the necessary duty and interest exist, Ipp J.A. in *Bennette v Cohen* [2009] NSWCA 60 identified the following matters as relevant (at [25]):

"(a) The test for common law qualified privilege is usually expressed at a very high level of generality and abstraction;

(b) In practice, however, the close scrutiny required of all the circumstances of each case

regard most privileged occasions under the common law as very broadly classifiable into two categories: first, where the maker of the statement has a duty (whether legal, social or moral) to make the statement and the recipient has a corresponding interest[73] to receive it; or, secondly, where the maker of the statement is acting in pursuance of an interest of his[74] and the recipient has such a corresponding interest or duty in relation to the statement, or where he is acting in a matter in which he has a common interest with the recipient.[75] "It may be accepted as a well-established rule that some duty or interest must exist in the party to whom the communication is made as well as in the party making it. The duty or interest may be common to both parties, but this is not essential. It is enough if there is a duty or interest on one side, and a duty or interest, or interest or duty (whether common or corresponding or not) on the other."[76]

Two formulations have become almost canonical in this area. First, in *Toogood v Spyring*[77] Parke B. stated the law in the following terms:

"In general, an action lies for the malicious publication of statements which are false in fact, and injurious to the character of another, and the law considers such publication as malicious, unless it is fairly made by a person in the discharge of

---

results in common law qualified privilege having a relatively limited or narrow practical application;

(c) The scrutiny required depends on the facts of each case and there is no closed set of criteria that must be applied or considered, and;

(d) Guidelines have been established that assist in the scrutiny that is required. These include:

(i) As a matter of public policy, it must be in the general interest of the whole community that the type of material in question be published, notwithstanding that it is defamatory of a third party;

(ii) The occasion must not be used for some purpose or motive foreign to the interest that protects the making of the statement. Further, there must be a significant connection between the defamatory material and the privileged occasion;

(iii) The interest that gives rise to qualified privilege must be real and direct;

(iv) Ordinarily, a volunteered statement is privileged only where there is a pressing need to protect the interests of the defendant or a third party, or where the defendant has a duty to make the statement;

(v) If a publication is made to a large audience, a claim of qualified privilege at common law will fail unless the members of the audience all have an interest in knowing the truth, and;

(vi) The interest should not give officious and interfering persons a wide licence to defame."

It should be noted that the High Court of Australia has subsequently held (*Papaconstuntinos v Holmes a Court* [2012] HCA 53) that the defendant need not prove, in addition to the requirement that it has some identified interest to protect, the existence of an "urgency" or "pressing need" which requires publication of the defamatory statements in protection of its interests.

[73] A simple example is the giving of an employment reference where the former employer is regarded as having a duty and the new employer obviously has an interest.

[74] E.g. informing workers of the fact that a fellow-worker was dismissed for misconduct.

[75] E.g. communications between shareholders or employees of a company about a takeover.

[76] Per Murray J. in *Mallan v Bickford* (1915) South Australia L.R. 47 at 84.

[77] 149 E.R. 1044; (1834) 1 C.M. & R. 181 at 193. Some statements are couched only in terms of duty (or interest) because of the facts of the case: *Pullman v Hill* [1891] 1 Q.B. 524 CA at 528.

some public or private duty whether legal or moral, or in the conduct of his own affairs, in matters where his interest is concerned. In such cases the occasion prevents the inference of malice which the law draws from unauthorised communications, and affords a qualified defence depending on the absence of actual malice. If fairly warranted by any reasonable occasion or exigency, and honestly made, such communications are protected for the common convenience and welfare of society."

This passage has been frequently quoted, and always with approval.[78] It:

"not only defines the occasion that protects a communication otherwise actionable, but enunciates the principle on which the protection is founded. The underlying principle is 'the common convenience and welfare of society'—not the convenience of individuals or the convenience of a class, but, to use the words of Erle C.J. in *Whiteley v Adams*,[79] 'the general interest of society'".[80]

Secondly, and more briefly, Lord Atkinson said in *Adam v Ward*[81]:

"A privileged occasion is . . . an occasion where the person who makes a communication has an interest, or a duty, legal, social or moral, to make it to the person to whom it is made, and the person to whom it is so made has a corresponding interest or duty to receive it. This reciprocity is essential."[82]

14.10 Imprecision and overlap of duty and interest. These two categories are imprecise. Certainly there are cases which might be indifferently analysed as involving duty and interest or common interests. Thus in a case where there was held to be privilege for an inspector of social services having passed on to the local authorities information about an irregularity in an adoption

---

[78] Per Lindley L.J. in *Stuart v Bell* [1891] 2 Q.B. 341 CA at 346. See *Loutchansky v Times Newspapers Ltd (Nos 2–5)* [2001] EWCA Civ 1805; [2002] Q.B. 783 at [28]. It should be noted, however, that the "inference of malice" which Parke B. refers to as arising from a defamatory publication is now recognised as mere form. To the modern way of thinking one would say that a defamatory statement is actionable unless there is a privileged occasion. If there is a privileged occasion it is not actionable unless (express) malice is proved. There is, however, no difference of substance.
[79] (1863) 15 C.B. (N.S.) 392 at 418.
[80] Per Lord Macnaghten in *Macintosh v Dun* [1908] A.C. 390 at 399; *Halls v Mitchell* [1928] S.C.R. 125.
[81] [1917] A.C. 309 at 334. See Lord Campbell C.J. in *Harrison v Bush* (1855) E. & B. 344 at 348–349:
   "A communication made bona fide upon any subject-matter in which the party communicating has an interest, or in reference to which he has a duty, is privileged, if made to a person having a corresponding interest or duty, although it contain a criminatory matter, which, without this privilege, would be slanderous and actionable . . . ."
[82] "At common law, a defamatory statement receives qualified protection when it is made in discharge of a duty or the furtherance or protection of an interest of the maker of the statement or some person with whom the publisher has a direct business, professional or social connection, and the recipient of the statement has a corresponding duty to receive or interest in receiving it":
   Bashford v Information Australia (Newsletters) Pty Ltd [2004] HCA 5; 218 C.L.R. 366 at [53] per McHugh J. Compare *Toyne v Everingham* (1993) 117 N.T.R. 1, referring to Dixon J. in *Mowlds v Fergusson* (1940) 64 C.L.R. 206 at 215 and contending that only Lord Atkinson in *Adam v Ward* had emphasised reciprocity.

application, the judge said that the communication was on "a matter of legitimate common and corresponding interest between" the defendant and the addressee, but one might as well say that it was the defendant's duty to pass on the information[83]; and in *Kearns v General Council of the Bar*, where the defendants issued a circular of guidance on the propriety of accepting instructions from the claimants, Simon Brown L.J. said that it mattered:

> "not at all whether the . . . Bar Council are properly to be regarded as owing a duty to the Bar to rule on questions of professional conduct such as arose here, or as sharing with the Bar a common interest in maintaining professional standards."[84]

Duty, interest and relationships. It was said in *Kearns* that attempts to   **14.11**
slot every case into one or the other category can lead to sterile disputes[85] and that the important points are that in these cases some relationship between the maker of the statement and the recipient is normally the foundation of the privilege[86] and the reason for the requirement of reciprocity. Nevertheless, bearing this in mind, the broad classification of duty and interest is adhered to here for several reasons. First, that represents the approach of the vast majority of cases both here and abroad and *Kearns* does not suggest that they have proceeded on some fundamentally wrong principle. Secondly, it provides some sort of structure under which the cases can be organised, for they are more than a random collection of ad hoc judgments that the public good required such and such a communication to be protected by privilege. Thirdly, the theoretical foundation of an "existing relationship" suggested in *Kearns*, while a helpful explanation of many cases, has problems of its own. In the first place, it is rather artificial to say that in some common situations where privilege is well recognised there is any *existing* relationship. The paradigm case of a duty-interest privilege is the giving of an employment reference: one may say that there is a relationship between the provider and the recipient but it is hardly an *existing* one, for the provider may never have heard of the recipient until he receives the request.[87] Furthermore, in some cases it is even more difficult to say that there is such an existing relationship. For example it has never been doubted that a complaint to the police about the commission

---

[83] *Patrick v Secretary of State for Health*, June 19, 2001, QB.

[84] [2003] EWCA Civ 331; [2003] 1 W.L.R. 1357 at [39]. In *Akinleye v E. Sussex Hospitals NHS Trust* [2008] EWHC 68 (QB) X hospital trust dismissed C. X wrote to D hospital trust, a former employer of C, because it was concerned to assess any risk to patient safety arising from C's work. Not surprisingly D's reply was held to be privileged. In the ordinary employment reference case (see para.14.25, below) one normally says that the giver of the reference acts in pursuance of a duty and the one who requests it acts in pursuance of an interest. But on the facts one could equally (or perhaps preferably) say that the one who requested it acted from a duty to the public. The defence was pleaded on the basis that the publication was made "pursuant to a social and moral duty, and/or in the furtherance of a legitimate interest to persons sharing that interest, and/or having a corresponding duty or interest to receive those statements."

[85] At [45], per Keene L.J.

[86] At [30] and [45].

[87] See *W v IH* [2008] EWHC 399 (QD) at [37]. Contrast a case in which the provider of the reference afterwards discovers further facts and communicates those: see para.14.26, below.

of a crime would be protected[88] by qualified privilege[89] but in what real sense is there an existing relationship between the complainant and the police? There is a somewhat shadowy category of privilege at common law between electors for the purpose of communications concerning the suitability of candidates for office. If this is based on a "relationship" that nowadays involves 60,000 or 70,000 people.[90] So also it has long been recognised that if A is attacked in the media by B, A has a qualified privilege to reply in the same manner, but again it is difficult to say, except with great artificiality, that there is any existing relationship between A and the public. What is certain (and this is accepted in *Kearns*) is that it is the volunteered statement between strangers that presents the greatest difficulty for the law of qualified privilege.[91]

14.12 **"Off the peg" categories.** Certain situations attracting qualified privilege occur so frequently that we speak of them as standard categories: for example, the writing of an employment reference, the making of a complaint to the proper authority and so on. These have been called the "off the peg" cases.[92] Very often the establishment of such a situation will establish the privileged occasion without more. However, as has been pointed out above[93] the ultimate question is whether the communication was "fairly warranted by the occasion" and therefore, as a matter of principle, where:

> "the court has to consider whether a particular occasion is privileged, it is necessary to take into account 'every circumstance associated with the origin and publication of the defamatory matter, in order to ascertain whether the necessary conditions are satisfied by which alone protection can be obtained.'"[94]
>
> "The correct approach in determining the issue of qualified privilege is [that] . . . the court must consider all the circumstances and ask whether *this* publisher had a duty to publish or an interest in publishing *this* defamatory communication to *this* recipient. It does not ask whether the communication is for the common convenience and welfare of society. It does not, for example, ask whether it is for the common convenience and welfare of society to report that an employee has a criminal conviction. Instead, it asks whether this publisher had a duty to inform this recipient that the latter's employee had been convicted of a particular offence and whether this recipient had an interest in receiving this information. That will depend

---

[88] Where the complainant is the victim this could be regarded as an example of action taken in protection of an interest. But this is not necessary: a disinterested informant could be regarded as performing a public duty.

[89] However, the current view is that such a case attracts absolute privilege: see para.13.12, above.

[90] Because, as is thought, there is a connection between this and the *Reynolds* privilege, it is considered in Ch.15, below.

[91] [2003] EWCA Civ 331; [2003] 1 W.L.R. 1357 at [30].

[92] *Komarek v Ramco Energy Plc* [2002] EWHC 2501 (QB) at [46]; *Howe v Burden* [2004] EWHC 196 (QB) at [15].

[93] See para.14.3, above.

[94] *Watts v Times Newspapers* [1997] Q.B. 650 CA at 660, per Hirst L.J., quoting Lord Buckmaster L.C. in *London Association v Greenlands* [1916] 2 A.C. 15 at 23.

on all the circumstances of the case. Depending on those circumstances, for example, there may be no corresponding duty and interest where the conviction occurred
many years ago or where it could not possibly affect the employment."[95]

Moreover, even if it is possible to say for "off-the-peg" categories that at a
general level they reflect an appropriate balance between art.8 and art.10,[96] it
has to be recognised that the notion of public interest changes over time. The
courts must therefore in developing the law keep under review the question
whether generally, and on the facts of the particular case, the application of
privilege strikes an appropriate balance between the two rights.[97]

What is a duty. It is plain that a legal duty (in the sense of one backed by   **14.13**
some sanction for its non-performance) is a duty for this purpose. Such a duty
might be one to inform the public as a whole,[98] in which case the traditional
reluctance to extend qualified privilege beyond private communications
would always have been irrelevant. But the expression is not confined to legal

---

[95] *Bashford v Information Australia (Newsletters) Pty Ltd* [2004] HCA 5; 218 C.L.R. 366 at
[63] per McHugh J. (a dissenting judgment but this, it is submitted, does not affect the correctness
of the general thesis). In *Howe & Co v Burden* [2004] EWHC 196 (QB), a case of communication
between co-employees about their employer's conduct, Eady J. held that it was not inevitable that
qualified privilege would apply without investigation of the facts in all "off the peg" categories.

[96] In *Kay v Lambeth BC* [2006] UKHL 10 HL; [2006] 2 A.C. 465 at [54], [55] the House of
Lords said that the courts should in the first instance proceed on the assumption that domestic law
meets the requirement of art.8.

[97] In *Thour v The Royal Free Hampstead NHS Trust* [2012] EWHC 1473 (QB) B, the
claimant's former manager at the Royal Free Hampstead NHS Trust, wrote a reference about the
claimant in response to a request from another hospital trust with whom the claimant was seeking
employment. The reference stated that the claimant had been under investigation following
allegations of aggressive behaviour but "he resigned during the investigation process and
therefore no formal action was taken". The question was raised whether the fact that the
defendant was a public authority would make a material difference to its plea of qualified
privilege. Eady J. held that it did not. On the facts of this case, that the defendant was a public
authority would not make a material difference to its plea of qualified privilege unless, at the least,
the effect of the HRA was that a public authority could not rely on qualified privilege if it had
been negligent. That was not a reference to negligence which constitutes a breach of a common
law duty of care, but of a breach of a public law duty which did not involve the dishonesty which
must be proved to make good the plea of malice that defeats a defence of qualified privilege. As
the claimant could not prove malice or bad faith, then a finding of a breach of a public law duty
could be based only on the statement that the claimant resigned "during the process", being an
innocent mistake. And that erroneous statement had been rectified within a few days, and
immediately upon the claimant asking for it to be rectified:
"As counsel submits, the inaccuracy in the reference (that [the claimant] resigned while under
investigation) is not to the substance and is not material for the purposes of any possible
allegation of a breach of [the claimant's] rights under art.8. There is a strong public interest in
employers such as Barts being able to ask for and receive honest employment references. That
public interest has long been recognised by the common law defence of qualified privilege ...
a public authority is not required in every case to plead and prove that domestic law meets the
requirements of art.8. The courts should in the first instance proceed on the assumption that
domestic law strikes a fair balance and that it is compatible with the requirements of art.8 (see
Kay v Lambeth BC [2006] UKHL 10; [2006] 2 A.C. 465 paras [54] and [55])" (at [27]).
Consequently the defence of qualified privilege was made out.

[98] See, e.g. *Bray v Deutsche Bank AG* [2008] EWHC 1263 (QB); [2008] E.M.L.R. 12.

duties. For example, there is no legal duty to inform a relative about the character of the person he proposes to marry[99] nor is there in general a duty to a prospective employer to provide him with a character reference on someone he proposes to engage,[100] but both are well established occasions of qualified privilege. The duty may be a moral or social[101] one. In *Stuart v Bell*[102] Lindley L.J. said:

> "I take moral duty to mean a duty recognised by English people of ordinary intelligence and moral principle, but at the same time not a duty enforceable by legal proceedings, whether civil or criminal."

In that case the defendant, Mayor of Newcastle, had received information from the Edinburgh police that the plaintiff, valet to H.M. Stanley, the explorer, was suspected of theft at Edinburgh. Stanley had been the defendant's guest at the Mansion House and just before his departure the defendant told him of the suspicion. A few days later Stanley dismissed the plaintiff. In an action for slander the majority of the Court of Appeal held that the occasion was a privileged one and that there was no evidence of malice. Lindley L.J. said that he was satisfied that:

> "all or, at all events, the great mass of right-minded men[103] in the position of the defendant would have considered it their duty, under the circumstances, to inform Stanley of the suspicion which had fallen on the plaintiff. My own opinion is clear and strong that it was his moral or social, although not his legal, duty to do so; in other words, the occasion was privileged, and the judge should have directed the jury to this effect."[104]
>
> "In considering the question whether the occasion was an occasion of privilege, the court will regard the alleged libel and will examine by whom it was published, to whom it was published, when, why, and in what circumstances it was published, and will see whether these things establish a relation between the parties which gives rise to a social or moral right or duty, and the consideration of these things may involve the consideration of questions of public policy."[105]

---

[99] See para.14.41, below.

[100] In *Spring v Guardian Assurance Plc* [1995] 2 A.C. 296, there was a statutory duty to provide the reference. It was common ground between the parties that there was no legally enforceable duty owed to the subject to provide a reference (at 320 and see *Redmond v Kelly* (1894) 28 Ir. L.T. 555). Lord Slynn thought there was "at least a moral" obligation to provide one (at 335) and Lord Woolf thought there was a contractual obligation to do so (at 354).

[101] See Greer L.J. in *Watt v Longsdon* [1930] 1 K.B. 130 CA at 152.

[102] [1891] 2 Q.B. 341 CA at 350, cited and applied in *Watt v Longsdon*, per Scrutton L.J. at 144. Cf. *Howlett v Holding* [2003] EWHC 286 (QB) (accusation of theft communicated to public over five years after the incident on which it was based). See also *Howe v Lees* (1910) 11 C.L.R. 361 at 369; *Guise v Kouvelis* (1947) 74 C.L.R. 102 at 114. In *de Waal v Ziervogel* [1938] A.D. 112, Watermeyer C.J. concluded that the duty of the judge in these cases is to apply the standard of the ordinary reasonable man.

[103] "People of ordinary intelligence and moral principles": *Halls v Mitchell* [1928] S.C.R. 125; *Arnott v College of Physicians and Surgeons (Saskatchewan)* [1954] S.C.R. 538.

[104] The Restatement, 2d, *Torts*, para.595 Comment J. asks whether "the publication to the particular recipient is within current standards of socially desirable or at least permissible conduct".

[105] Per Earl Loreburn in *James v Baird* 1916 S.C.(H.L.) 158 at 163–164, referring to *Macintosh v Dun* [1908] A.C. 390; applied *Mowlds v Fergusson* (1940) 64 C.L.R. 206; *Wells v Wellington* [1952] N.Z.L.R. 312; *Brooks v Muldoon* [1973] N.Z.L.R. 1.

It is for the judge to determine whether an occasion is privileged and therefore to decide whether the defendant was under a duty to make the communication.[106] The judge will have no difficulty in determining whether there was a legal duty to make the communication, but there is no sure and unfailing criterion of what does or does not constitute a moral or social duty; indeed, as was pointed out by Erle C.J. in *Whiteley v Adams*,[107] "Judges . . . have all felt great difficulty in defining what kind of social or moral duty will afford a justification and, ultimately, it must depend on the circumstances of each case, the nature of the information, and the relation of speaker and recipient."[108]

Illustrations. The difficulty which may arise where there is no legally   **14.14**
enforceable duty is illustrated by *Stuart v Bell*, where Lindley and Kay L.JJ. were firmly of the opinion that the occasion was privileged, whereas Lopes L.J. described the defendant's conduct as "officious and uncalled for" and emphasised that he had been told the grounds for suspicion were slender.[109] In *Coxhead v Richards*[110] D received from the mate of a ship a letter containing imputations against P, who was captain of the ship, of constant drunkenness and unfitness for command. After consulting with his friends D forwarded the letter to W, the owner of the ship, who dismissed P. D did not know W, and had no interest in the ship. Tindal C.J. and Erle J. held that the occasion was privileged, Tindal C.J. on the ground that D forwarded the letter to the shipowner in the full belief that the information was true and that he was under a duty:

> "not to keep the knowledge he gained by this letter to himself and thereby make himself responsible, in conscience, if his neglect of the warnings of the letter brought destruction upon the ship or crew",

---

[106] *Toogood v Spyring* (1834) 1 C.M. & R. 181 at 193; *Stuart v Bell* [1891] 2 Q.B. 341 at 350; *Adam v Ward* (1915) 31 T.L.R. at 304; [1917] A.C. 309; *Minter v Priest* [1930] A.C. 558.
"In a secular English court . . . [the question of privilege] is ultimately one of public policy and public interest as identified in the English authorities. The answer to that question may be affected by some other system of law but it cannot and in my view should not be determined by a system of law other than English law":
Gray J. in *Maccaba v Lichtenstein* [2004] EWHC 1577 (QB); [2005] E.M.L.R. 9 at [17] (contended—though not established—that defendant, a Rabbi and an officer of the Beth Din of the Federation of Synagogues, was forbidden by Jewish law to use the words alleged and that therefore he could not be regarded as being under a duty to use them for the purposes of qualified privilege in the law of defamation).
[107] (1863) 15 C.B.(N.S.) 392 at 418; and see *Andrews v Nott-Bower* [1895] 1 Q.B. 888 CA: duty imposed by order of competent court; *Mihaka v Wellington Publishing* [1975] 1 N.Z.L.R. 10 at 19 (duty imposed by contract). It is thought that the mere fact that A is under a contractual obligation to B to make statements about C's affairs does not necessarily give rise to privilege: see *Macintosh v Dun* [1908] A.C. 390 and para.14.31, below. A's contract might be to dig out scandal about C. Many statutes make the communication of particular information an offence, and it is conceived that the law could not recognise a privilege in such cases.
[108] See per Scrutton L.J. in *Watt v Longsdon* [1930] 1 K.B. 130 CA at 149, 150.
[109] [1891] 2 Q.B. at 356.
[110] (1846) 2 C.B. 569.

for the rule of law is not so restricted that a person having information materially affecting the interest of another and honestly communicating it in the full belief, and with reasonable grounds for the belief, that it is true, will not be excused, though he has no personal interest in the subject-matter; and Erle J. on the ground that the information was given for the purpose of preventing considerable damage to the property of the shipowner and saving the lives of his crew, and that in furnishing such information it is not essential that the giver of the information should stand in any relation to the other parties. Coltman and Cresswell JJ., on the other hand, held that the communication was not privileged, Coltman J. on the ground that there was no legal duty to make the communication, and that the moral duty was plainly the other way-the duty of not slandering your neighbour on insufficient grounds is so clear that a violation of that duty ought not to be sanctioned in the case of voluntary communications, except under circumstances of great urgency and gravity which did not (in his opinion) exist in the actual case; and Cresswell J. on the ground that there was no legal duty to make the communication; that as regards moral duty, if the property of the shipowner on the one hand was at stake, the character of the plaintiff was at stake on the other, and the moral duty not to publish defamatory matter which the defendant did not know to be true was quite as strong as the duty to communicate to the shipowner that which he believed to be true.

In *Watt v Longsdon*[111] one B, the foreign manager of a company which carried on business abroad, wrote to D, a director of the company in England, a letter containing gross charges of immorality, drunkenness and dishonesty on the part of P, who was managing director of the company abroad. Without obtaining corroboration and without communicating with P, D, who was a friend of P s wife, showed B' s letter to her. The allegations in the letter were unfounded but D believed them to be true. It was held that the publication of the letter to P's wife was not a privileged occasion; the fact that the person to whom defamatory matter is published has an obvious interest in the matter published being not of itself enough to render the occasion privileged.

The problem in these cases lies in the assessment of the relative claims of moral, social and economic values.[112] In *Coxhead v Richards* the competition was between the safety of the ship and crew, and the good name of the captain; in *Watt v Longsdon* the court had to weigh in the balance the several claims of family unity, of professional reputation, and of economic interest. There is no easy or mechanical way of solving this problem and, as *Stuart v Bell* and *Coxhead v Richards* show, judicial opinions may differ on the same (or at least very similar[113]) facts.

---

[111] [1930] 1 K.B. 130 CA; *Hertlein v Hertlein* (1913) 9 D.L.R. 72.

[112] For the opinion of a leading moralist on the relative values of these things, see, e.g. Aquinas, S.T. 2a, 2ae, Q. 73 A. 3: whether defamation is the greatest wrong a man may do to his neighbour.

[113] A careful reading of the judgments in *Coxhead v Richards* seems to show that Tindal C.J. and Erle J. had prominently before their minds the danger which existed to the *lives* of the crew;

One thing, however, is certain. The question of duty must be determined in the light of the attitudes and opinions of society at the time.[114] By current standards the decision in *Watt v Longsdon* is, it is thought, plainly correct; but issues of safety might now be given a higher priority than at the time of *Coxhead v Richards*.[115]

Protection of interests. In *Hunt v Great Northern Ry*,[116] Lord Esher M.R.   **14.15** said:

> "A privileged occasion arises if the communication is of such a nature that it could be fairly said that those who made it had an interest in making such a communication, and those to whom it was made had a corresponding interest in having it made to them. When those two things co-exist the occasion is a privileged one."

Anyone, said Lord Denman C.J. in *Tuson v Evans*,[117]

> "in the transaction of business with another, has a right to use language *bona fide* which is relevant to that business and which a due regard to his own interest makes necessary, even though it should directly, or by its consequences, be injurious or painful to another; and this is the principle on which privileged communication rests."

The law does not restrict the interests which the defendant may protect by asserting freely what he believes to be true. In the majority of the cases, the interests protected have been business interests; thus, the defendant may write freely to claim money he believes to be due to him,[118] may complain to the employer of a person who has done work for him about the negligence or

---

while Coltman and Creswell JJ., not accepting the existence of the urgency of this danger, were unwilling that the reputation of the plaintiff should be sacrificed to the *property interest* of the shipowner. See the argument of Terence O'Connor K.C. in *Watt v Longsdon* [1930] 1 K.B. 130 at 135–136:

> "Is it for the common convenience and welfare of society that a shipowner should be informed of the conduct of his captain which is endangering the lives of his crew? The law has answered in the case of *Coxhead v Richards* that it was. The question whether it is for the common convenience and welfare of society that a wife should be informed of her husband's misconduct is a very different question ... The answer must depend on the circumstances."

In such a case the law has to weigh and measure the several interests, life, family, reputation, property and the rest, that are involved.

[114] *James Gilbert Ltd v MGN Ltd* [2000] E.M.L.R. 680 at 691.

[115] Compare *Peters-Brown v Regina District Health Board* [1996] 1 W.W.R. 337 (notes of patient's infectious condition) and the majority in *Bashford v Information Australia (Newsletters) Pty Ltd* [2004] HCA 5; 218 C.L.R. 366.

[116] [1891] 2 Q.B. 189 CA at 191.

[117] (1840) 12 A. & E. 733 at 736. See also Lord Young in *Shaw v Morgan* (1888) 15 R. 865 at 870:

> "if the statement is made ... in the reasonable attention to a man's own business and affairs, which gives him legitimate cause to write or speak of his neighbour, the occasion displaces the presumption of malice ... and he is only answerable if malice be shown to have existed in fact."

[118] *Blackham v Pugh* (1846) 15 L.J.C.P. 290.

misconduct of the worker[119] or may inform his employees of his reason for dismissing another employee.[120] But any legitimate interest (that is to say, an interest that is recognised by the law as meriting protection[121]) is protected; thus, in *Laughton v Bishop of Sodor and Man*[122] a bishop was held to have a legitimate interest in publishing to his clergy his answer to an attack made on him by the plaintiff, and a daughter has been held to have a legitimate interest in answering remarks about her deceased father.[123]

14.16 Reciprocity of duty and interest. Where the statement is made in purported discharge of a duty, it is essential that the person receiving it should have a legitimate interest in doing so. A statement as to the character of a former employee will be privileged when made to a prospective employer but not when made to acquaintances of the speaker. There are no rigid, closed categories of interest.[124]

> "The word 'interest' is not used in any technical sense. It is used in the broadest popular sense, as when we say that a man is 'interested' in knowing a fact-not interested in it as a matter of gossip or curiosity,[125] but as a matter of substance apart from its mere quality as news."[126]
> "So long as the interest is of so tangible a nature that for the common convenience and welfare of society it is expedient to protect it, it will come within the rule."[127]

14.17 Reciprocity of interest. Similarly, where the statement is made in protection of an interest, reciprocity of interest[128] or some duty to protect the interest is essential to found the privilege.[129] In *Aspro Travel v Owners Abroad Group*[130] the defendants circulated information to hoteliers to the effect that the plaintiffs were about to go out of business and offering their services instead. The Court of Appeal held that it was arguable that the occasion was privileged in view of the interest of the defendants as members of ABTA in keeping claims on the ABTA compensation fund to a minimum and the

---

[119] *Toogood v Spyring* (1834) 1 C.M. & R. 181.
[120] *Hunt v G.N.Ry* [1891] 2 Q.B. 189 CA.
[121] *Bryanston Finance v De Vries* [1975] Q.B. 703 CA at 726, 728. Cf. *Murphy v Plasterers' Society* [1949] S.A.S.R. 98 (no legitimate interest in pursuing illegal strike).
[122] (1872) L.R. 4 P.C. 495.
[123] *Bowen-Rowlands v Argus Press Ltd, The Times*, February 10 and March 26, 1926.
[124] *Beach v Freeson* [1972] 1 Q.B. 14 at 25.
[125] *Rumsey v Webb* (1842) Carr. & M. 104 at 105; *London Association v Greenlands Ltd* [1916] 2 A.C. 15 HL at 35; *R. v Rule* [1937] 2 K.B. 375.
[126] Per Higgins J. in *Howe v Lees* (1910) 11 C.L.R. 361 at 398.
[127] Per O'Connor J., ibid. at 377.
[128] I.e. legitimate interest not mere interest in gossip: see para.14.16, above.
[129] Per Lord Atkinson in *Adam v Ward* [1917] A.C. 309 HL at 334; *Watt v Longsdon* [1930] 1 K.B. 130 CA at 147, 151, 157; *White v F. Stone* [1939] 2 K.B. 827 CA; *X v Y* [1947] 2 W.W.R. 1011; *Kosovich v Andreyevich* (1947) 73 C.L.R. 665.
[130] [1996] 1 W.L.R. 132 CA. For another aspect of this case, see para.11.18, above. Cf. *Urbanowski v Harkins* [2006] BCSC 1741 (no evidence that trade association publishee had any role in disputes between body shop owners and customers).

possible effects on their own business of the collapse of another operator together with the interest of hoteliers in knowing that another operator would take over in the event of problems.

Reality of duty. Whether there is a duty for this purpose is a question of law and it is not therefore sufficient that the defendant honestly believed it was his duty to speak.   **14.18**

> "The question is, what is the defendant's duty; not what he thinks to be his duty."[131]
>
> "That the defendant acted under a sense of duty, though important on the question of malice, is not, I think, relevant to the question whether the occasion was or was not privileged. That question does not depend on the defendant's belief, but on whether he was right or mistaken in that belief."[132]
>
> "An occasion which in point of fact is not privileged cannot become privileged because the defendant in good faith and on grounds which commended themselves to him, considered it privileged. Good faith, however strong its foundation, cannot convert a non-privileged occasion into a privileged occasion, although it may afford excellent evidence of the absence of malice."[133]

The fact, however, that the defendant is mistaken as to the facts in the statement does not deprive him of his privilege[134]: the very purpose of the defence is to allow the making, in good faith, of untrue statements.[135]

Existence of privileged occasion to be judged at time statement is made. Though most likely to be relevant in cases of media publications, where the apparent reliability or otherwise of the information acted upon by the publisher will almost always be a central issue, it is a general principle that the question of privilege is to be judged by reference to the circumstances known at the time the statement is made and the defendant cannot rely, in order to establish privilege, on information which subsequently comes to his   **14.19**

---

[131] *Whiteley v Adams* (1863) 15 C.B.(N.S.) 392 at 412.

[132] Per Lindley L.J. in *Stuart v Bell* [1891] 2 Q.B. 341 CA at 349 (rejecting *Waller v Loch* (1881) 7 Q.B.D. 615 at 621), quoted with approval by Lord Esher M.R. in *Hebditch v MacIlwaine* [1894] 2 Q.B. 54 CA at 60–61. See also *Stuart v Bell* at 356–357; *Phelps v Kemsley* (1943) 168 L.T. 18 CA at 20–21; *Wade & Wells & Co. v Laing* (1957) 11 D.L.R. (2d) 276 BCCA; *Hare v Better Business Bureau of Vancouver* [1946] 2 W.W.R. 630 (defendant thought he was performing public service; new trial on other grounds [1947] 1 W.W.R. 25). In *Adam v Ward* [1917] A.C. 309 at 334, Lord Atkinson said:

> "While on the question of malice the bona fide belief of the defendant that he was under a moral or social duty to make the communication is relevant and important, the existence, in fact, of this duty or interest, not merely the defendant's belief in its existence, is the thing which is relevant to the question whether the occasion was or was not privileged."

[133] Per Lord Strathclyde in *James v Baird*, 1916 S.C. 510 at 517. See also per Lord Anderson at 531.

[134] Cf. *Aktas v Westpac Banking Corp Ltd* [2010] HCA 25. See, further, para.14.46.

[135] Black J. in *Pyke v Hibernian Bank* [1950] I.R. 195 at 222 rightly points out that the privilege, e.g. attaching to statements seeking redress of a grievance (a case of protection of interest rather than discharge of a duty) would be nugatory if there had in fact to be a grievance. However, cf. para.14.3, above.

attention.[136] A communication which might have been privileged at one time may not be so at the time of publication because of the passage of time, as where the requisite relationship between the parties has ceased before publication[137] or where the defendant delays for a long period before making it.[138] But where privilege subsisted at the time of the original publication it is not lost in respect of later publications which have come about because the communication is available in some widely accessible source such as a website or a library. Despite the general rule that these form separate causes of action,[139] any other approach would make the law unworkable.[140]

14.20 **Reality of interest.** Where the issue is whether the recipient of the statement had a legitimate interest (or some duty to act) in the matter, it is not enough that the defendant believed that to be the case. If, in fact, he had none, there is no privileged occasion.[141] "The defendant cannot create a privilege

---

[136] *GKR Karate (UK) Ltd v Yorkshire Post Newspapers Ltd* [2000] 1 W.L.R. 2571 CA; *Loutchansky v Times Newspapers Ltd (No.1)* [2001] EWCA Civ 536; [2002] Q.B. 321; *Howlett v Holding* [2003] EWHC 286 QB.

[137] *Ley v Hamilton* (1935) 153 L.T. 384 HL. The plaintiff in *Ley v Hamilton* alleged that the defendant had libelled him in connection with a business enterprise, in which the two men were jointly interested, in two letters written on 15 August and 27 August, 1932. The defendant pleaded that the words complained of had been published on a privileged occasion but at a trial before the Lord Chief Justice and a special jury, the Lord Chief Justice ruled that the plaintiff and defendant were not jointly interested in the business on the dates when the letters were published. An award of £5,000 damages was made. The defendant's appeal was dismissed, the House of Lords holding that the ruling of the Lord Chief Justice that the occasions were not privileged was correct and inevitable.

[138] *Howlett v Holding*, above. However,
"the time that has elapsed since events referred to in a defamatory publication does not necessarily take that publication outside the scope of common law qualified privilege . . . . An allegation of sexual abuse by a teacher many years before would not, for that reason alone, be outside the privilege, and the same would apply to allegations of past financial misconduct by a person in a position of trust.":
Goyan v Motyka [2008] NSWCA 28 at [120] per Handley A.J.A.

[139] See para.6.4, above.

[140] *Bray v Deutsche Bank AG* [2008] EWHC 1263 (QB); [2008] E.M.L.R. 12. The material appears to have been on the defendant-originator's website. If at the time of the republication it could be shown that he had discovered it to be untrue that should be malice. On passage of time and privileged reports see para.16.4, below.

[141] *Hebditch v MacIlwaine* [1894] 2 Q.B. 54 CA; *Beach v Freeson* [1972] 1 Q.B. 14; *Halls v Mitchell* [1928] S.C.R. 125. The majority of the Irish Supreme Court followed *Hebditch v MacIlwaine* in *Hynes-Sullivan v O'Driscoll* (1989) 9 I.L.R.M. 349 but Finlay C.J. and Griffin J. were prepared to assume (without deciding) that an honest and reasonable belief might do. Cl.16(2)(a)(ii) of the current Irish Defamation Bill makes reasonable belief a defence.
Harrison v Bush (1858) 5 E. & B. 344 and *Scarll v Dixon* (1864) 4 F. & F. 250 were cited in *Hebditch v MacIlwaine* as authorities for the contention that a person who, in seeking redress, mistakenly applies to the wrong person, is protected if his error was a natural and not unreasonable one. The court did not overrule, but explained both cases, and it is submitted that they only justify the contention of the defendant in *Hebditch v MacIlwaine* if the person to whom the communication is made is an intermediary for communicating with the person whose duty it in fact is to inquire into and redress the grievance complained of. However, though there is no doubt that *Hebditch v MacIlwaine* represents the law, there are judicial statements since which seem to assume the opposite. See, e.g. the dictum of Scrutton L.J. in *Watt v Longsdon* [1930] 1 K.B. at 147 ("which is not . . . an accurate statement of the law" per Geoffrey Lane J. in *Beach v Freeson*, above, at 24); and *Jenoure v Delmege* [1891] A.C. 73, where the trial judge directed the jury that

for himself because of honest belief on his part that the person to whom he made a slanderous communication had an interest or duty in respect of the subject-matter of such statement."[142]

So, in *Hebditch v MacIlwaine*,[143] after the plaintiff had been elected guardian of the poor for a parish, the defendants, ratepayers of the parish who had opposed the election of the plaintiff, signed and sent to the new board of guardians a letter in which they alleged that the plaintiff had been guilty of bribery and other illegal practices and suggested an inquiry. The jury found that the defendants honestly and reasonably believed that the board of guardians were the proper authority to whom to apply. It was held that the letter was not privileged as the board of guardians had in fact no jurisdiction in the matter, and no duty or interest in connection therewith. In his judgment, Lord Esher M.R. said:

> "It was argued that, although the board of guardians had no power or duty or interest in the matter, nevertheless the occasion was privileged, because the defendants honestly and reasonably believed that the board had such a duty or power or interest, and were asking them for redress in the matter, which they believed they could give. Assuming that the defendants had such a belief . . . the argument, in substance, seems to come to this: that the belief of the defendants that the occasion was privileged makes it privileged. I cannot accept the proposition . . . The belief of the defendant might have bearing on the question of malice; . . . but I do not think it has anything to do with the question whether the occasion was privileged."[144]

Qualifications to the rule in Hebditch v MacIlwaine.   14.21

(1) While in no way affecting the principle that the interest of the recipient must be real rather than imagined, cases from the nineteenth century

---

if they thought that the defendant had addressed the letter to the inspector of constabulary by an honest unintentional mistake as to the proper authority to deal with the complaint, then the communication would not be deprived of any privilege to which it would have been entitled had it been addressed to the superintending medical officer. Lord Macnaghten observed that this direction seemed not to be open to any objection, although it appears to be not reconcilable with *Hebditch v MacIlwaine*. Perhaps it is to be explained as being as favourable as possible to the defendant in a defendant's appeal.

[142] Per Lord Hunter in *Cochrane v Young* 1922 S.C. 696 at 703–704. *Harwood v Green* (1827) 3 C. & P. 141; *Blagg v Sturt* (1847) 10 Q.B. 899; *Henderson v Henderson* (1855) 17 D. 348; *Currigan v Ryan* (1867) 15 W.R. 61; *Dickeson v Hilliard* (1874) L.R. 9 Ex. 79; *Harrison v Fraser* (1881) 29 W.R. 652; *Hebditch v MacIlwaine* [1894] 2 Q.B. 54 CA; *James v Baird*, 1916 S.C. 510; *Sevenoaks v Latimer* (1920) 54 Ir.L.T. 11.

[143] [1894] 2 Q.B. 54 CA. Under the Australian uniform legislation there is a defence of "qualified privilege for provision of certain information" (see, e.g. s.30 Defamation Act 2005 (NSW) and "a recipient has an apparent interest in having information on some subject if, and only if, at the time of the publication in question, the defendant believes on reasonable grounds that the recipient has that interest". However, the defence has much more similarity to *Reynolds* privilege and the classical form of privilege is still governed by the common law.

[144] Ibid. at 59. See also per Davey L.J. at 64. Although not binding on the Court of Session the reason was said in *James v Baird*, 1916 S.C. 510 at 517 to be "unassailable". Mitchell, *The Making of the Modern Law of Defamation* (2005), Ch.7 argues that in considering the question of whether a duty must exist in fact the courts failed to get to grips with what, at least at that time, was the underlying question: whether qualified privilege was a special defence to a liability which was fundamentally strict or whether the underlying basis of liability was fault and privilege was merely a way of rebutting the presumption of malice which arose from the publication of

may rely heavily on formal powers of control as the foundation of the necessary interest whereas it is submitted that at the present day courts would pay greater attention to continuing concerns and the legitimacy of interests not accompanied by formal powers. In *Beach v Freeson*[145] the defendant was a Member of Parliament who forwarded to the Law Society and to the Lord Chancellor complaints by a constituent about the plaintiff solicitors. Although the Lord Chancellor had no formal disciplinary powers over solicitors, it was held that in view of his position and his functions in the legal system he was sufficiently interested in their behaviour to make the communication to him privileged. Again in *Mowlds v Ferguson*[146] the defendant, a police officer whose conduct had been criticised, produced a report for his superiors making defamatory allegations against the plaintiff and showed it to a former superior, at that time retired. It was held that this publication was privileged in view of the continuing concern which the retired officer had in matters relating to his own past service. In the light of these cases, *Dickenson v Hilliard*,[147] where it was held that an election agent was not, in the absence of an election petition, sufficiently interested in allegations, after the election, of bribery by a supporter, may not now represent the law.[148]

(2) D receives a request for information about the character of C from X, who purports to be a person considering employing C; or from Y, who purports to be about to advance credit to C. In both cases the inquirer is in fact a person with no such intention but D replies in good faith making statements defamatory of C. It is not the law that the absence of any interest in the inquirer destroys C's privilege, for if that were so it would not be possible to reply to inquiries without undertaking extensive and embarrassing investigations and it would strike at the convenience of society which is at the root of all privilege. The true rule, it is submitted, is that the privilege exists if the defendant bona fide (and perhaps reasonably) believes that the facts are such that on the basis of them the inquirer would have a relevant interest. This is consistent with the formulations of Lord Parker[149] and Lord Atkinson[150] in *London Association v Greenlands*. It has been said that "no

---

defamatory words (rather on the lines of South African law). At any rate we can say that English law, rightly or wrongly, now takes its stance on the first position.

[145] [1972] 1 Q.B. 14.

[146] (1940) 64 C.L.R. 206.

[147] (1874) L.R. 9 Ex. 79.

[148] Though it was followed in *Hasnul bin Abdul Hadi v Bulat bin Mohamed* [1978] 1 M.L.J. at 78.

[149] [1916] 2 A.C. 15 HL at 42 ("bona fide believes that the person making the inquiry has an interest which justifies it").

[150] Ibid. at 35 ("if one person makes an inquiry of another touching the position or character of a third, and the person inquired of makes a reply which he bona fide believes to be true, and

protection can be afforded to a person who wrongly assumes the facts which constitute a privileged occasion."[151] However this refers to a mistake as to the appropriate body to whom a complaint should be made: if a person is mistaken as to certain facts, but complains to the body which would have jurisdiction if the facts were as he supposed, it is submitted that his complaint is privileged.[152]

Representatives. The defence extends also to communications made by or   **14.22** to a representative of the parties directly interested. For instance if A, who has a legitimate interest in making a communication, makes it to B, who is acting as a representative of C, who has a legitimate interest in receiving it, the communication is privileged. Thus where the defendant, who was tenant of a farm, made a complaint to an agent of his landlord as to the conduct of the plaintiff while executing repairs as servant of the landlord, such complaint was privileged.[153] Again, if A, acting as a representative of B, who has a legitimate interest in making the communication, makes it on B's behalf to C, who has a legitimate interest in receiving it, or to D, who is acting as C's representative, the communication will be privileged.[154] Thus, where a solicitor, acting in the ordinary and proper course of his duty to his client,[155] gave a written notice to an auctioneer not to part with the proceeds of the sale of certain goods which the plaintiff had entrusted to him for sale, on the ground that the plaintiff had committed an act of bankruptcy, upon which an order might be made against him, it was held that the notice was privileged.[156] And where A, acting on behalf of B, a member of the plaintiff's congregation, addressed a communication to C, who was acting on behalf of the plaintiff, with reference to the conduct of the plaintiff when in partnership with his

---

also bona fide believes that the inquiry desires the information, not merely to gratify idle curiosity, but for some purpose in which he, the inquirer has a legitimate interest, the occasion upon which the answer is communicated to him is a privileged occasion."). Cf. the dictum of Scrutton L.J. in *Watt v Longsdon* [1930] 1 K.B. at 147, which should apparently be limited to such cases.

[151] Per Lord Buckmaster L.C. in *Baird v Wallace-James* (1916) 85 L.J.P.C. 193; also reported, sub tit. *James v Baird*, 1916 S.C. (H.L.) 158. See also Hilbery J. in *Davidson v Barclays Bank* [1940] 1 All E.R. 316, criticised by Black J. in *Pyke v Hibernian Bank* [1950] I.R. 195 at 222. In *Lloyds Bank v Rogers*, unreported, December 20, 1996, CA, Simon Brown L.J. referred to *Davidson's* case as "doubted but never yet tested".

[152] By parity of reasoning, if D is under a duty to pass on to a disciplinary body complaints about members of a profession or group and a complaint is made about C, who is not a member, D should be protected if he reasonably, though mistakenly, believes that he is.

[153] *Toogood v Spyring* (1834) 1 C.M. & R. 181.

[154] *Blackham v Pugh* (1846) 2 C.B. 611; *Baker v Carrick* [1894] 1 Q.B. 838 CA; *Smith v Streatfield* [1913] 3 K.B. 764; *Wee Richard v Wong Meng Meng* [1995] 3 S.L.R. 68; cf. *Longdon-Griffiths v Smith* [1951] 1 K.B. 295. See also *London Association v Greenlands* [1916] 2 A.C. 15 at 32, 42, 43.

[155] As to the scope of a solicitor's retainer, which may include communications not expressly authorised by the client, see *Regan v Taylor* [2000] E.M.L.R. 549 CA, para.14.57, below.

[156] *Baker v Carrick* [1894] 1 Q.B. 838 CA; *Groom v Crocker* [1939] 1 K.B. 194 CA, *Watts v Times Newspapers* [1997] Q.B. 650 CA.

brother, and with reference to an investigation of the dealings of the plaintiff in such partnership, the occasion was privileged.[157]

SECTION 3. DUTY AND INTEREST: PARTICULAR SITUATIONS

(a) *Communications made in discharge of a duty*

14.23 Introduction. Whether there is a duty to communicate which the law will recognise as creating a privileged occasion depends on all the circumstances and no previous decisions can be conclusive.[158] Nevertheless, some circumstances have regularly been recognised as giving rise to such a duty and are likely to continue to be so.

14.24 Answers to inquiries. Where a person is asked a question about a matter by or on behalf of someone who appears to have a legitimate interest in knowing the answer, the law has recognised that he is under a duty to answer, and that the occasion is privileged; so long as he speaks honestly, he is protected,[159] and the law will not usually inquire into the reasonableness or otherwise of his beliefs.[160] The mere fact that an inquiry is made about the character or position of another does not necessarily render the answer privileged.[161] "It is no part of a man's duty to go into the confessional to every chance person who may choose to ask impertinent questions."[162] But where a person who is asked a question touching the character, financial position, or responsibility of another, bona fide believes[163] that his inquirer is asking the question, not to gratify idle curiosity, but for some other purpose in which he has a legitimate interest of his own, it is not merely his right but his duty to answer, and if he does so in the honest belief that his answer is true and without any malice towards the person whose character or position is the subject-matter of the inquiry, his answer is a privileged communication.[164] "It

---

[157] *Hopwood v Thorn* (1849) 8 C.B. 293. And see *Maccaba v Lichtenstein* [2004] EWHC 1577 (QB); [2005] E.M.L.R. 9 at [25].

[158] See para.14.12, above.

[159] So if A applies to D for a contract to maintain machinery installed by C, D's explanation that he has found defects which lead him to refuse the contract is privileged even though it may reflect on C: *Webster v British Gas Services Ltd* [2003] EWHC 1188 (QB) at [24].

[160] As to malice in defeating qualified privilege see Ch.17. As to circumstances in which a statement may be volunteered, see paras 14.34–14.35, below.

[161] The statement in *Robshaw v Smith* (1878) 38 L.T. 423, that "Everyone owes it as a duty to his fellow men to state what he knows about another person when inquiry is made", must, as was pointed out by Hamilton L.J. in *Greenlands v Wilmshurst* [1913] 3 K.B. 507 at 541 be taken "as limited to the facts of that case. If treated as of universal application it certainly goes beyond any other case and is inconsistent with many. It would be a mere charter for gossip."

[162] Per Erle C.J. in *Force v Warren* (1864) 15 C.B.(N.S.) 806 at 808.

[163] See para.14.21, above.

[164] Per Cresswell J. in *Coxhead v Richards* (1846) 2 C.B. 569 at 606; *Davis v Reeves* (1855) 5 Ir.C.L.R. 79 at 90; *Owens v Roberts* (1856) 6 Ir.C.L.R. 386 at 392: *Robshaw v Smith* (1878) 38 L.T. 423 at 424; *Waller v Loch* (1881) 7 Q.B.D. 615 CA; *Leutner v Merfield, The Times*, May 6. 1880; *Greenlands Ltd v Wilmshurst* [1913] 3 K.B. 507 CA at 546–548; per Lord Atkinson and Lord Parker in *London Association v Greenlands Ltd* [1916] 2 A.C. 15 HL at 35, 42; *Oana v Marwell Construction* (1957) 8 D.L.R. (2d) 377.

is in the general interest of society that correct information should be obtained as to the character of persons in whom others have a legitimate interest,"[165] and that the person who is asked for such information should be able to give it without exposing himself to an action of libel or slander.[166]

The inquiry itself will be privileged if there is a legitimate interest in the person making it, and a moral duty to make answer, or a mutuality of interest.[167]

Employment references. A common illustration of this head of privilege is a reference for a former employee given by a former employer to a possible new employer.[168] The law has held it to be the moral and social duty[169] of the former employer on inquiry being made by an intending employer as to the character, fitness, or capacity of such employee, or as to the cause of his dismissal, to state all that he knows either for or against him, and if he does so honestly and without malice towards him his answer will be privileged.[170]   **14.25**

> "It is so manifestly for the advantage of society that those who are about to employ a servant should be enabled to learn what his previous conduct has been, that it may be well deemed the moral duty of the former employer to answer inquiries to the best of his belief."[171]
> "In the case of master and servant, the convenience of mankind requires that what is said in fair communication between man and man, upon the subject of character, should be privileged, if made *bona fide* and without malice. If, however, the party giving the character knows what he says to be untrue, that may deprive him of the protection which the law throws around such communications."[172]

As honesty is the test, if a reference were to contain a bona fide, but completely erroneous, assertion that the claimant had been convicted of a

---

[165] Per Erle C.J. in *Whiteley v Adams* (1863) 15 C.B. (N.S.) 392 at 148, cited by Lindley L.J. in *Stuart v Bell* [1891] 2 Q.B. 341 CA at 348.

[166] *Robshaw v Smith* (1878) 38 L.T. 423 at 424; per Lord Parker in *London Association v Greenlands Ltd* [1916] 2 A.C. 15 HL at 42.

[167] *Redmond v Kelly* (1894) 28 Ir.L.T. 555.

[168] On a somewhat similar basis, it has been held to be the duty of those having knowledge to communicate it when asked by a person who wishes to know whether an applicant for charitable relief is a deserving object: *Waller v Loch* (1881) 7 Q.B.D. 619 CA.

[169] As to whether there can ever be a legal duty to provide a reference in such a case, see para.14.13, above.

[170] *Edmonson v Stephenson* (1766) Buller's N. P. 8; *Weatherston v Hawkins* (1786) 1 T.R. 110; *Kelly v Partington* (1833) 4 B. & Ad. 700; *Fountain v Boodle* (1842) 3 Q.B. 5; *Waring v M Caldin* (1873) Ir.R. 7 C.L. at 288; *Doane v Grew* 107 N.E. 620 at 621 (Mass., 1915) ("the typical case of a privileged occasion").

[171] Per Cresswell J. in *Coxhead v Richards* (1846) 2 C.B. 569 at 605. Cf. *Holder v C & J Hirst, The Times*, December 20, 1962, CA (reply to Ministry of Labour). See also *Thour v The Royal Free Hampstead NHS Trust* [2012] EWHC 1473 at [27] (QB).

[172] Per Lord Ellenborough C.J. in *Hodgson v Scarlett* (1818) 1 B. & Ald. 232 at 239–240.

criminal offence, the defendant would be protected by this category of privilege even though it is a requirement both at common law and by statute, that "reports" of judicial proceedings should be fair and accurate.[173]

The privilege does not, however, insulate the defendant from liability for the tort of negligence, which is concerned with proven financial loss arising from a misstatement rather than injury to reputation.[174] It has also been said that it is arguable that the simple honesty test no longer applies where the former employer has given an assurance that the information communicated will be removed from the employee's records after a time or its retention infringes the Data Protection Principles or even in any case where the former employer is a public authority and the employee's rights under art.8 of the Human Rights Convention are engaged.[175]

The same principles apply to other persons providing references, e.g. school-teachers or university tutors.

14.26 Subsequent communications. Any communication made subsequently to the inquirer in relation to the same subject-matter will also be protected.[176]

> "Suppose a person goes to inquire the character of a servant, and gets it, and the parties afterwards meet, when the person of whom the inquiry was made says, 'I did not tell you of a particular circumstance to which I ought to call your attention,' surely if made *bona fide* that communication is privileged."[177]

The privilege extends to facts afterwards discovered though at the time of giving the reference they were unknown to the referee. Thus, if A, after giving a former employee a reference discovers that he is dishonest, and that the reference was misleading, it is his duty to communicate his discovery to anyone who has relied on the reference, and such a communication, though apparently volunteered, is privileged.[178] So, in *Gardener v Slade*,[179] P, a domestic servant, was engaged by M on a character given by D. A short time

---

[173] *Bashford v International Australia (Newsletters) Pty Ltd* [2001] NSWCA 470 at [46]. The statutory privilege under the Defamation Act 1996 (para.13.35) is absolute but is unlikely to be relevant, since the report must be contemporaneous. For the common law qualified privilege, see para.15.35, below.

[174] *Spring v Guardian Assurance Plc* [1995] 2 A.C. 296. See paras 23.1–23.8, below.

[175] *W v JH* [2008] EWHC 399 (QB). See also, *Thour v The Royal Free Hampstead NHS Trust* [2012] EWHC 1473 (QB) in which Eady J. stated that the fact that the defendant was a public authority would make a difference to its plea of qualified privilege if it had been negligent in the sense of in breach of a public law duty which did not involve the dishonesty which must be proved to make good a plea of malice.

[176] *Beatson v Skene* (1860) 5 H. & N. 838. See also para.14.36, below. An action in negligence may however exist: *Mckie v Swindon* [2011] EWHC 469 (QB) and see para.23.7, below.

[177] Per Pollock C.B., ibid. at 850.

[178] *Gardener v Slade* (1849) 18 L.J.Q.B. 334; *Adoko v Pal* [2004] EWHC 25 (QB); and see *Child v Affleck* (1829) 9 B. & C. 403. Not to disclose might be actionable at the suit of the new employer: *Brownlie v Campbell* (1880) 5 A.C. 925 HL at 950.

[179] (1849) 18 L.J.Q.B. 334.

afterwards D, having reason to believe that the character was undeserved, wrote to M a letter containing an allusion to P and to having been deceived. M accordingly called on D and made more inquiries, in answer to which D imputed dishonesty to P. It was held that the whole of the communications were privileged. In giving judgment Lord Denman C.J. said:

> "The privilege attaching to answers given to questions of this sort must continue as long as anything remains unknown on the part of the person requiring the knowledge. If a servant gets a good place on a character given by you, but which you afterwards discover to be undeserved, you are bound, in my opinion, to say you have been deceived, in what you previously asserted."[180]

Moreover Coleridge J. said:

> "If I had given a servant a good character, and I afterwards find that I have been deceived, and that the servant is dishonest, I am bound to make the same communication then as I should have made before if the facts had been known to me. If I answer a question asked of me incorrectly, from ignorance, it is my duty as an honest man to set it right directly I have the means of doing so."[181]

Inquiries about crime. Where an inquiry is made of a person with a view   **14.27**
to the detection of a criminal offence,[182] it is his duty in the sense here used[183] to give such information as he may possess, and such information, if given bona fide and without malice, will be privileged.[184] "I cannot doubt", said Parke B. in *Kine v Sewell*[185]:

> "that it is a perfectly privileged communication, if a party who is interested in discovering a wrongdoer, comes and makes inquiries, and a person in answer makes a discovery, or a *bona* fide communication, which he knows, or believes, to be true, although it may possibly affect the character of a third person."

However, answers to inquiries by the police are now protected by absolute privilege even though no proceedings have yet been started.[186]

Inquiries as to credit. It is in the interests of society generally that those   **14.28**
who are proposing to deal with any person or organisation should be able to have such information as they can secure as to the other's character, credit or commercial solvency. Thus, if they make inquiry of another as to the information which that other has about the person with whom they propose to deal, it becomes the duty of that other to give such information as he has. The occasion, therefore, is a privileged one, and no action can be brought on the

---

[180] Ibid. at 336.
[181] Ibid.
[182] As to volunteering information about crime, see para.14.37, below.
[183] Though not, of course, generally in the sense of a legally enforceable duty.
[184] *Kine v Sewell* (1838) 3 M. & W. 297; *Cockayne v Hodgkisson* (1833) 5 C. & P. 542; *Force v Warren* (1864) 15 C.B.(N.S.) 806; *Nelson v Irving* (1897) 24 R. 1054; *Hutchinson v New England Telephone Co.*, 214 N.E.2d 57 (Mass., 1966).
[185] (1838) 3 M. & W. 297 at 302.
[186] See para.13.12, above.

answer provided it is made bona fide and without malice. Thus, where a trader makes inquiries with regard to the character, credit or commercial solvency of any person with whom he proposes to have dealings, the information given in answer to such inquiries will be privileged. "If," said Brett L.J. in *Waller v Loch*[187]:

> "a person who is thinking of dealing with another in any matter of business asks a question about his character from someone who has means of knowledge, it is for the interests of society that the question should be answered, and if answered *bona fide* and without malice, the answer is a privileged communication."
>
> "It is surely as much to the interest of the community that the trader or other person making the inquiry should not be swindled or make a bad debt as it is to the interest of the community that a master should not engage a bad servant . . . I can see no distinction in principle between such a case and the case of the master who is asked for the character of a late servant."[188]

Lord Parker in *London Association v Greenlands Ltd*,[189] defined the conditions under which privilege will attach:

> "In this country occasions must arise in which it is not only legitimate, but necessary, for one trader to inquire into the financial circumstances and credit of another. A person asked for information under such circumstances may be said to be under a social duty to communicate it, and it is in the interests of society generally that he should be able to do so without fear of an action for libel. It is therefore a principle of law that a person asked for information affecting the credit of another is justified in giving it, provided (1) that he bona fide believes in the truth of the information which he gives; (2) that he bona fide believes that the person making the inquiry has an interest which justifies it;[190] and (3), if *Macintosh v Dun*[191] is to be considered good law that he is not actuated by motives of private gain or other motives excluding the possibility of the communication being made under a sense of social duty. Under such circumstances the implication of malice arising out of a false statement to the discredit of another is displaced, and the communication is privileged."

The principles articulated by Lord Parker in *London Association v Greenlands Ltd*[192] were applied by H.H.J. Moloney QC in *Gatt v Barclays Bank.*[193] The defendant, Barclays Bank, gave information to credit reference agencies about

---

[187] (1881) 7 Q.B.D. 619 CA at 622; *Smith v Thomas* (1835) 2 Bing. N.C. 372 at 381; *Storey v Challands* (1837) 8 C & P. 234; *Robshaw v Smith* (1878) 38 L.T. 423.
[188] . . . per Bray J. in *Greenlands v Wilmshurst* [1913] 3 K.B. 507 at 546. See also ibid. at 548. "It is obvious", said Pring J. in *Macintosh v Dun* (1905) 5 N.S.W.S.R. at 717,
> "that it is for the convenience and welfare of a trading community that a merchant should be able to make inquiries with respect to the financial standing and credit of another with whom he is dealing or about to deal. and that the answers to such inquiries, if given honestly and bona fide, should not subject the person giving them to an action for defamation. If the law were otherwise, the position of traders would be intolerable: their business would materially suffer, and the whole community would in its turn feel the effects of the check thus imposed on trade and commerce."
[189] [1916] 2 A.C. 14 HL at 42.
[190] See para.14.21, above.
[191] See para.14.30, below.
[192] [1916] 2 A.C. 14 HL.
[193] [2013] EWHC 2 (QB).

the claimant's husband, stating that an account, which was a joint account held with the claimant, was "delinquent" because the overdraft exceeded the agreed limit. This information was later published to another bank from whom the claimant and her husband were seeking a mortgage. Even if it could be said that the publication referred to and was defamatory of the claimant,[194] the communication was held to have been published on an occasion of privilege. Barclays was a subscriber to a system by which financial institutions shared, through the medium of credit reference agencies, various categories of customer financial performance data. As a subscriber it agreed to share data about its customers with other subscribers. The judge held that it was plainly in the public interest that such authoritative credit information could be obtained and relied on by banks and other financial institutions. This was not a case where the information was provided simply for motives of pecuniary gain and the elements of mutuality, reciprocity, and self-protection emphasised in *London Association v Greenlands Ltd* were clearly present. Moreover, it was inherently likely that the information provided in this well-regulated system was accurate. The judge therefore concluded that the passing of the information by Barclays into the credit reference agency pool, and its onward transmission by the agencies to any other subscribers who may have accessed it for the purpose of deciding whether or not to accept an application from the Gatts for finance, plainly took place on occasions of common-law qualified privilege.

On the analogy of *Spring v Guardian Asurance Plc*,[195] where it was held that a former employer might owe a former employee a duty of care in the preparation of a reference, notwithstanding the existence of qualified privilege for the purposes of defamation, it would seem that a person answering an inquiry as to credit might be liable to the subject of the reference for negligence in respect of his response.

Inquiries made and information obtained through agents. If a **14.29** person may legitimately inquire as to the character or credit of another, it follows that he is justified in making the inquiry through an agent confidentially employed for that purpose. In such a case the agent "is under a legal duty to communicate the result of his inquiries to the person who has employed him to make them, and his duty is the basis of a distinct privilege arising out of the relationship of principal and agent."[196] So, where a member of a trade protection association applied to the secretary for information as to the commercial credit of a trading company with whom he proposed to deal, and the secretary having applied to X for the information and, having received

---

[194] The judge held that the statement did not refer to the claimant (at [49]) and was not defamatory of her (at [50]).

[195] [1995] 2 A.C. 296 HL; para.23.3, below. The liability to the inquirer was of course established in *Hedley, Byrne v Heller* [1964] A.C. 465.

[196] Per Lord Parker in *London Association v Greenlands* [1916] 2 A.C. 15 at 42–43; per Lord Atkinson, ibid. at 36.

"It is beyond doubt that a merchant or trader is entitled to make inquiries with regard to the credit of those with whom he is dealing. He may make those inquiries himself, or he may send

a report, sent a report in substantially the same terms to the member, it was held that the secretary in making the inquiry and report was acting, not as the agent of the association, but as the confidential agent of the particular member, and that the publication was therefore made on a privileged occasion.[197] Similarly, if a person asked for information may himself give it, he may give it through an agent employed for that purpose. In such a case the privilege will normally enure for the benefit of the agent.[198]

14.30 **Credit agencies.** In *Macintosh v Dun*,[199] it was held that where a mercantile agency or trade protection society carries on the business of collecting information as to the credit and financial standing of other persons and supplying such information for reward to any trader who may become a subscriber of the agency or society, the information given to a subscriber, though given bona fide and in answer to a confidential inquiry on his part, is not privileged, for, it was said, it is not in the interests of the community or the welfare of society that:

> "the protection which the law throws around communications made in legitimate self-defence or from a bona fide sense of duty should be extended to communications made from motives of self-interest by persons who trade for profit in the characters of other people."[200]

Macintosh v Dun has been criticised[201] and distinguished,[202] and does not represent the predominant view of the law in the United States,[203] but there does not seem any doubt that it represents English law[204] where credit

---

his clerk or his servant to make them, and, if they are made by his clerk or his servant, it is the duty of the clerk or servant—a legal duty arising out of his employment—to make a communication of everything he knows fairly and honestly, with regard to the credit of the person about whom he is inquiring":
per O'Connor J. in *Dun v Macintosh* (1906) 3 C.L.R. at 1165.

[197] *London Association v Greenlands* [1916] 2 A.C. 15.

[198] See para.14.22, above.

[199] [1908] A.C. 390 PC, reversing the High Court of Australia, and, it is submitted, overruling *Bayne v Stubbs Ltd* (1901) 3 F. 408; *Fitzsimmons v Duncan Ltd* [1908] 2 Ir.R. 483, and *Todd v Dun, Weiman* (1887) 15 O.A.R. 85; *Robinson v Dun* (1897) 24 O.A.R. 287.

[200] [1908] A.C. at 400, per Lord Macnaghten.

[201] Per Scrutton L.J. in *Watt v Longsdon* [1930] 1 K.B. 130 CA at 148.

[202] See, e.g. *Gatt v Barclays Bank* [2013] EWHC 2 (QB) (see further para.14.28, above). In *Dale v Veda Advantage Information Services and Solutions Ltd* [2009] FCA 305 Lindgren J. held that qualified privilege applied to statements made via the defendants' credit database to providers of credit, notwithstanding *Macintosh v Dun*. The defendants had begun as mutual association of credit providers but had become a profit-making company, though the credit providers were still the sole sources of information to the defendants and the sole recipient of information from them. That in itself was sufficient to distinguish the case from *Macintosh*, where the information appears to have been gathered from a range of undisclosed sources. No claim was made for breach of statutory duty under the Privacy Act 1988. See also, *Walker v Veda Advantage Information Services and Solutions Ltd* [2011] QSC 316 (credit reporting agency covered by qualified privilege).

[203] See 15A Am.Jur.2d, *Collections and Credit Agencies*, para.28 and *Re Retailers Commercial Agency Inc.*, 174 N.E.2d 376 (Mass., 1961). However, see the criticism in *Hood v Dun & Bradstreet Inc.*, 486 F.2d 25 (CA5 1973).

[204] It was applied in Canada in *Gillett v Nissen Volkwagen* [1975] 3 W.W.R. 520. See also *Informa Confidential Reports v Abro*, 1975 (2) S.A. 760. Under the Australian uniform legislation

agencies[205] which act for reward give information in the ordinary course of their business.[206] Even if *Macintosh v Dun* were not law, there would be no privilege of this type between a financial journal providing general business information and its subscribers for this would be indistinguishable from a serious newspaper with a financial section. Such an organisation would have to bring itself within the limits of the *Reynolds* variety of privilege.[207]

Mutual protection associations. *Macintosh v Dun*:   **14.31**

> "leaves untouched the wider question as to whether groups of people, however large, may not combine together in order to provide the necessary information for carrying on business."[208]

It is submitted that where a number of traders form themselves into an association for the protection of their mutual trading interests and one of their number makes an inquiry of the association as to the commercial solvency or trustworthiness of a person or firm with whom he is about to deal, the information given in answer is privileged.[209] Similarly, where, for the purpose

---

the defence of qualified privilege "for provision of certain information" is not defeated merely because the information was published for reward (see, e.g. s.30(5) of the Defamation Act 2005 (NSW). However, the relevant defence is aimed primarily at public communications of the *Reynolds* variety and the purpose of the provision is presumably to make it clear that it covers newspapers.

[205] Compare *Bashford v Information Australia (Newsletters) Pty Ltd* [2004] HCA 5; 218 C.L.R. 366, where privilege was found to exist for a subscription newsletter on occupational health and safety.

[206] The Committee on Privacy (Cmnd.5012, para.275) recommended that as a corollary of having to disclose any data they had on a person, they should be given qualified privilege. The Faulks Committee, Cmnd.5909 (1975) agreed that there should be privilege for communications by such an agency (para.237). When the Consumer Credit Act 1974 was originally introduced as a Bill, it gave a privilege to publications both by and to a licensed credit agency, but the Act as finally passed did not contain any such provision. The Consumer Credit Act and the Data Protection Act 1998 impose a duty on a credit reference agency to give a copy of the data they hold on any person to that person on certain conditions. Since this is a legal duty, any publication reasonably incidental to its fulfilment will be privileged, but possible liabilities are mentioned in the Report of the Faulks Committee (p.62, fn.145).

[207] *Gutnick v Dow Jones & Co. Inc. (No.4)* [2004] VSC 138; 9 V.R. 369. The court distinguished *Bashford v Information Australia (Newsletters) Pty Ltd* [2004] HCA 5; 218 C.L.R. 366, where a majority of the HCA found privilege between a health and safety newsletter and its subscribers (but see the strong dissent of McHugh J.). However, the majority in *Bashford* accepted that *Macintosh* does stand for the proposition, as was said in *Howe v Lees* (1910) 11 C.L.R. 361 at 373, that: "an individual, or an association or corporation, that makes a business of collecting information about traders' credit and selling it for reward to other traders has no privilege to communicate defamatory matter in the information": at [17].

[208] Per Lord Buckmaster L.C. in *London Association v Greenlands* [1916] 2 A.C. 15 at 27.

[209] It is true that in *London Association v Greenlands* [1913] 3 K.B. 507 CA, the majority (Vaughan Williams and Hamilton L.JJ.) held that no privilege attached to such a communication. But Bray J. delivered a strong dissenting judgment, in which (at 556) he distinguished *Macintosh v Dun* on the ground that the defendants in that case

> "were not an association of persons who had combined together for their mutual protection, but were a firm carrying on for profit the business of obtaining information with reference to the commercial standing and position of other people . . . . They held themselves out as collectors of information about other people which they were ready for such profit to sell to any customer who asked for it."

In the House of Lords [1916] 2 A.C. 15 the association was struck out of the proceedings, having

of protecting themselves in their business, the members of such an association agree to inform the secretary of the association, and through him the members of the association generally,[210] of any default on the part of a person or firm with whom they have business dealings, such information will be privileged.[211] In *Barr v Musselburgh*,[212] a local association of traders at their own expense and for the protection of their mutual trading interests caused to be circulated among its members a list of the names and addresses of certain persons in the district. The list bore no title and contained no comment on the names included in it, but it was admittedly compiled from "black lists". The pursuer, whose name appeared in the list, brought an action against the association, in which he averred that the list was known in the district as a "black list", and that the insertion of his name in it meant that he was unworthy of credit. The Court of Session held that the publication of the list was privileged, and as facts showing malice had not been averred, the action was dismissed as irrelevant. In his judgment, Lord Dundas distinguished *Macintosh v Dun*, observing that:

> "the information complained of was circulated by the defenders among their own members in legitimate self-defence; they are not persons who trade for profit in the characters of other people."[213]

---

been wrongly sued as if it were an incorporated body. The decision did not proceed on the main question whether a communication made by an association of persons who combine together for their mutual protection is privileged, but only on the point that the secretary acted, not as the agent for the association, but only as the confidential agent for the particular member who made the inquiry. Lord Buckmaster L.C. and Lords Atkinson and Parker, however, distinguished the position from that in *Macintosh v Dun* on the same grounds as Bray J. had done and pointed out that the member making the inquiry was perfectly justified in making it through an agent, and it would appear from their observations at 26, 37 and 42–44, that, had the secretary of the association been proved to have been acting as its agent, they would have held the occasion privileged as between the association and the particular member in view of the fact that the secretary bona fide believed in the accuracy of the information which he conveyed to such member, and that the association was not created or worked from motives of pecuniary gain, but solely for the protection in trade and business of each of its members. In *David Jones v Basma House*, reported only in the *Shoe and Leather Record*, March 8, 1907, cited by Bray J. in his dissenting judgment at 549, 552, the association was identical with that in *London Association v Greenlands*, except in one respect, namely that it was confined to members of the boot and shoe trade. The question of privilege was not argued, but it was clearly in the mind of the Court of Appeal. Cozens-Hardy M.R. said: "It was formally admitted in the court below, and could not be disputed, that the alleged libel in question was published on a privileged occasion."

[210] For the general question of volunteered information, see para.14.34, below. Cases of mutual protection associations fall logically under community of interest rather than discharge of a duty, but it is convenient to deal with them here.

[211] *Keith v Lauder* (1905) 8 F. 356 (Ct of Sess); *Howe v Lees* (1910) 11 C.L.R. 361, overruling in effect *Peatling v Watson* 1 [1909] V.L.R. 198, and distinguishing *Macintosh v Dun*. And see *Bashford v Information Australia (Newsletters) Pty Ltd* [2004] HCA 5; 218 C.L.R. 366.

[212] 1912 S.C. 174. Cf. *Harper v Hamilton* (1901) 32 O.R. 295. Note that though the information was general, the association was local: for cases possibly on the other side of the line, see *Getting v Foss* (1827) 3 C. & P. 160; *Lemay v Chamberlain* (1886) 10 O.R. 638; *Todd v Dunn & Co* (1887) 15 O.A.R. 85.

[213] 1912 S.C. at 180.

The broad distinction between the two kinds of trade protection societies is here very plainly drawn.

Banking references.   **14.32**

"Everyone will admit that in carrying on the business of banking, confidential inquiries are necessary with regard to the character and credit of customers applying for advances of money. In general the answer to such inquiries will be privileged."[214]

Thus, when a bank takes up the non-banking references of a new customer, a person giving information to the bank relevant to the customer's credit will be protected. But as the privilege rests on a duty to answer an inquiry, no privilege attaches to an answer given by a bank to an inquiry as to the financial position or responsibility of a customer where such answer discloses information acquired by the bank from the customer's account, or while the relationship of banker and customer exists and in its character of banker, unless the information is given with the express or implied consent of the customer, e.g. the customer authorises a reference to his bank.[215] Without such consent, an answer is in breach of duty, not in pursuance of one.

Inquiry by the claimant. Where the claimant invites or procures the **14.33** publication of a defamatory statement with a view to making it the foundation of a claim (for example to avoid the effect of the limitation period) that is likely to be an abuse of process.[216] However, if the claimant hears he has been slandered by the defendant and goes to the defendant and, in the presence of others, challenges him with this and the defendant admits that he has[217] and repeats the substance of what he has before said, that is a different case[218] and the publication is not privileged. So, in *Griffiths v Lewis*[219] P asked D if he had

---

[214] Per Lord M'Laren in *Ingram v Russell* (1893) 20 R. 771 at 777.

[215] *Tournier v National Provincial Bank* [1924] 1 K.B. 461 CA.

[216] See para.6.2, above.

[217] This, it seems, is not enough to constitute a cause of action, though it has been said to be evidence of the former slander: *Kine v Sewell* (1838) 3 M. & W. 297; *Griffiths v Lewis* (1845) 14 L.J.Q.B. 196 at 198; *Freeman v Poppe* (1905) 25 N.Z.L.R. 529; *Bade v Bade* (1912) 17 E.D.C. 26. Compare para.6.50, above.

[218] See para.19.12, below. This would not fall within the defence of consent. Consent would not seem to be the basis of an independent head of privilege. It seems best to read the references to the plaintiff's consent in *Chapman v Ellesmere* [1932] 2 K.B. 431 at 450–452 and 467–468 and in *Duke of Norfolk v Russell* [1949] 1 All E.R. 109 at 115, as indicating that the plaintiff could not, after assenting to publication of a decision in the Racing Calendar, be heard to argue that that was not a proper medium through which the Stewards could perform their duty of informing the racing public of their decision. See also per Denning L.J. in *Duke of Norfolk v Russell* above, at 120 ("consent cannot create a privilege where none would otherwise exist"); *Loveday v Sun Newspapers* (1938) 59 C.L.R. 503 at 523 et seq.; *Church of Scientology v Anderson* [1980] W.A.R. at 81 (no privilege where claimant has provoked controversy, but not made attack-reversed on other grounds [1981] W.A.R. 279).

[219] (1845) 14 L.J.Q.D. 197. See also, to similar effect, *Maas v Tweedie* (1906) Transvaal L.R. 897.

accused her of using false weights in her trade and D, in the presence of a third person, replied: "Yes, you have used them for years, and I can prove it". The reply was not privileged. "An attempt by a person who deems himself injured to ascertain truly what slanderous imputations have already been cast upon him can hardly be allowed to justify their renewal."[220] A fortiori, therefore, if the statement is made to a third party who has heard of the accusation from the claimant but who is not the claimant's agent. In *Force v Warren*[221] D, suspecting that P had stolen meat from his shop, accused her of having done so (no one being present at the time). A friend of P, to whom she mentioned the accusation, called at D's shop and asked him if he had accused P of stealing. D replied: "Yes, and I believe it to be true". D's reply was not privileged.

In these cases, far from being a ground for privilege, the repetition has been regarded as an aggravation of the slander.[222] However, this approach, if taken too far, would cause serious problems for legitimate ventilation by the defendant of his grievance and cases like *Griffiths v Lewis* are, it is submitted, ones where the proper interpretation of the situation is that the "request" to the defendant in effect amounts to a challenge to repeat the statement without the protection of privilege. Suppose that C is dismissed by D for theft, wrongly as he alleges, and interests a television or radio station in his complaint. The broadcaster dare not publish C's allegations of wrongful dismissal without making inquiry of D, but if D's answer is not privileged he will not respond. It is submitted that privilege attaches in such a situation.[223] So, in *Taylor v Hawkins,*[224] D, having dismissed P for dishonesty, refused to give him a character, stating to those who asked that he had discharged him for dishonesty, and on P's brother inquiring of D why he had treated P so, and was keeping him out of a situation, replied: "He has robbed me; and I believe for years past"; it was held that D's answer was privileged.[225]

In any event, the position is different where the defendant does not originate the slander but repeats in answer to an inquiry by the claimant what he has been told by another. In *Warr v Jolly*[226] P, a probationary minister at a certain chapel, went with a friend to D to inquire why the congregation had refused to appoint him their permanent minister. D replied that his (the defendant's)

---

[220] Per curiam in *Thorn v Moser* (1845) 1 Denio (N.Y.) R. 488 at 495.

[221] (1864) C.B. (N.S.) 806.

[222] Per Lord Denman C.J. in *Griffiths v Lewis* (1845) 14 L.J.Q.B. 197 at 199.

[223] It did in *Sutherland v British Telecommunications*, 1989 S.L.T. 531. See also *Hanley v Pisces Productions* [1981] 1 W.W.R. 369 (inquiry by P's union; privileged).

[224] (1851) 16 Q.B. 308. It is suggested in *Mims v Metropolitan Life Ins Co*, 200 F.2d (C.A.5 1952) that where the claimant causes a third party to make inquiry on his behalf the statement is to be treated as if it were made to the claimant himself.

[225] This case was distinguished in *Anderson v Ginn (No.2)* [1933] N.Z.L.R. 1073 (D accused P of certain misconduct and refused to listen to any explanation. P subsequently requested his brother to go to D's house and ask him to give P an opportunity of saying what D had refused to hear. Held that D's repetition of the accusation to P's brother was not privileged because D's role was only to arrange a meeting, not hear an explanation).

[226] (1834) 6 C. & P. 495.

wife had been cautioned against him as a man of intemperate habits. This answer was privileged. The distinction is clearly made in *Smith v Matthews*.[227] D originated a false report to the effect that P, a builder, in erecting certain schoolrooms, had used timber inferior to that which the contract required. P demanded an inquiry. The committee of the school instituted one and employed D to survey and report. D reported falsely that inferior timber had been used. Lord Lyndhurst C.B. directed the jury that, if they believed the reports originated with D, and that what he had said produced the inquiry, D's report to the committee was not privileged, but that if they believed that the reports originated themselves elsewhere, and that D, being called on to report, had bona fide made the statement, they should find for D.

Volunteered statements in performance of a duty. It must not be   **14.34** thought that a statement may only be privileged if made in response to an inquiry. Circumstances may exist which make it the moral duty of A to inform B of certain facts derogatory of C, even though B has made no inquiry of A in the matter. Relevant circumstances may be the importance of the interest to be protected,[228] the urgency of the communication,[229] and the nature of the relationship between A and B, especially if it be an existing one of trust and reliance.[230] Thus, it has been held that there may be a duty to furnish information without previous inquiry about the wrongdoing of an employee,[231] in furtherance of justice,[232] to a younger person about the character of an associate,[233] and where there was concern among residents about possible environmental pollution, privilege was accorded not only to the publication of the report of an expert investigation to the public body which commissioned it but also to the publication of the report by the public body to the residents.[234] Where a person engaged in the inspection of an adoption agency discovered irregularities in the documentation concerning an adoption and reported the matter to the local authority whose employee was implicated, the situation was described as being "as clear a case of qualified privilege as

---

[227] (1831) 1 Moo. & Rob. 151.

[228] See para.14.14, above.

[229] Thus, it has been suggested ((1930) 43 Harv. L.Rev.966–967) that if the plaintiff in *Watt v Longsdon* [1930]1 K.B.130 (for which see para.14.14, above) had been about to return to his wife the risk of her contracting venereal disease "would have created an emergency justifying disclosure". Cf. *Simonsen v Sevenson* 177 N.W. 831 (Neb., 1920) (doctor warning hotel owner of venereal disease of plaintiff).

[230] See para.14.42, below.

[231] See para.14.35, below.

[232] See para.14.37, below.

[233] See para.14.41, below.

[234] *Fox v Wokingham DC* [2003] EWCA Civ 499. In *Alexander v Arts Council of Wales* [2001] EWCA Civ 514; [2001] 1 W.L.R. 1840 it was held that the defendant body was under a duty to inform the public of its reasons for declining to make a grant when the issue had been brought into the public domain and this was not challenged on appeal.

one could well imagine".[235] However, in *W v JH*[236] Tugendhat J. declined to grant summary judgment to the defendant in respect of a volunteered statement made by the defendant, a social work practice assessor, who had informed a university that employed the claimant as a practice assessor that the claimant had been due to appear before a disciplinary hearing regarding an allegation of sexual harassment but that he had left in a hurry before the hearing. The judge held that the relationship between the parties was not so clear that no investigation of the circumstances was required in order to determine whether this was an occasion of qualified privilege. Where, as here, the information that was the subject of the communication might engage rights of an individual under art.8, the claimant should be afforded the opportunity to argue that there should be reconsideration of the test by which to answer the question whether the defendant's right to freedom of expression (afforded in such a case by the defence of qualified privilege) prevails over the claimant's rights. Determination of this issue may require a court to adopt the approach set out for resolving such conflicts in *Re S (A Child)*.[237] Although there is "no general rule that statements which would be privileged if made in answer to an inquiry cease to be so when the informant has not waited to be asked"[238] yet ordinarily:

> "the occasion for making a volunteered statement will be privileged only where there is a pressing need to protect the interests of the defendant or a third party or where the defendant has a duty to make the statement to the recipient. The common law has generally perceived no advantage to society in giving qualified privilege to volunteered statements in the absence of a pre-existing reciprocity of interest between the defendant and the recipient."[239]

---

[235] *Patrick v Secretary of State for Health*, June 19, 2001, QB (the claimant did not contest the issue).

[236] [2008] EWHC 399 (QB); [2009] E.M.L.R. 11.

[237] [2004] UKHL 47 at [17] HL; [2005] 1 A.C. 593.

[238] *Greenlands Ltd v Wilmshurst* [1913] 3 K.B. 507 CA at 535–536 per Hamilton L.J.

[239] In *Papaconstuntinos v Holmes a Court* [2012] HCA 53 the High Court of Australia rejected the appellant's submission that the respondent could only make out the defence of qualified privilege if he could show that there had been a "pressing need" for him to make the statements. The requirement of "pressing need" was said to arise from the fact that the respondent's statements were made voluntarily and in the protection of interests that were purely personal. The High Court, by a majority, rejected that contention. The defence of qualified privilege requires the maker of a defamatory statement to demonstrate reciprocity of duty and interest: that the maker had a duty to make, or an interest in making, the statement and that the recipient of the statement had a duty to hear, or an interest in hearing, that statement. There is no superadded requirement of "pressing need" that arises in circumstances where a defamatory statement was made voluntarily and to protect personal interests.

It should be noted that *Papaconstuntinos* was concerned solely with the question whether a "pressing need" was necessary to make out the defence of qualified privilege where the protection of interests was *purely personal*. Where a legitimate personal interest existed then the absence of a pressing need could not disqualify the defendant from being able to rely on the privilege. The court did not, however, cast doubt on the following statement of McHugh J. in *Bashford v Information Australia (Newsletters) Pty Ltd* [2004] HCA 5; 218 C.L.R. 366:

> "Ordinarily the occasion for making a volunteered statement will be privileged only where there is a pressing need to protect the interests of the defendant or a third party or where the defendant has a duty to make the statement to the recipient. The common law has generally

"Thus, the customer of a shopkeeper in answer to a request by a potential customer is entitled to give his or her opinion as to the quality of the shopkeeper's goods, and when he or she does so, the reply will be published on an occasion of qualified privilege. But the case is different where the customer voluntarily defames the character or reputation of the shopkeeper to potential customers."[240]

While one cannot rule out the possibility that a statement volunteered to a stranger about the claimant's credit could be privileged, such a case would, it is thought, be rare.[241]

The real test is whether, having regard to all other circumstances of the particular case, it was the moral or social duty of the defendant to volunteer the communication.

"It may be that the interest of the person receiving the communication is of such a character as by its very nature to create a social duty in another under the circumstances to make the communication that he does in fact make."[242]

What must be emphasised is that it is not enough that the communication was made with the honest purpose of protecting the interests of the recipient: the interest must be such that in the eyes of the law it creates a moral duty in the defendant to protect it. The cause of the privileged occasion is not merely the interest of the recipient; it is that interest *plus* the corresponding moral or social duty which arises in the circumstances of the case by reason of the nature of the interest.[243]

---

perceived no advantage to society in giving qualified privilege to volunteered statements in the absence of a pre-existing reciprocity of interest between the defendant and the recipient. It has taken the view that the reputation of the defamed should be preferred over the freedom to publish volunteered but defamatory statements that may or may not be true."
Indeed the court in *Papaconstuntinos* expressly noted that the case did not involve any question of a duty or interest of the kind dealt with in *Bashford v Information Australia*:
"This case does not raise questions of whether a stranger can come under a duty to speak, so as to protect defamatory statements made in that process, as occurred in *Coxhead v Richards*. This case has been conducted only upon the basis that the respondent's own interests were sufficient to found the privilege." (at [23]).
[240] Ibid. at [77].
[241] In *Storey v Challands* (1837) 8 C. & P. 234 and in *King v Watts* (1838) 8 C. & P. 614, it was held that no privilege attached to such a communication. On the other hand, in *Bennett v Deacon* (1846) 2 C.B. 628, where the same question came before the Common Pleas, the judges were equally divided. In that case the defendant asked X, who was about to sell some timber to the plaintiff, whether he was going to be paid cash for it. On X replying in the negative, the defendant said: "Then you'll lose your timber, for the plaintiff owes me about £25, and I am going to arrest him next week for my debt." Tindal C.J. and Erle J. held that the communication was privileged; Cresswell and Coltman JJ. held that it was not.
[242] *Watt v Longsdon* [1930]1 K.B. 130 CA at 152, per Greer L.J.
[243] In *Whiteley v Adams* (1863) 15 C.B.(N.S.) 392 at 418, Erle C.J. is reported as using language from which it might be inferred that a communication to a person having an interest is sufficient to create a privileged occasion. But if the reports of the case in 33 L.J.C.P. at 94; 9 L.T. at 485; and 12 W.R. at 154 are consulted, it will be seen that the learned judge considered that the existence of a duty or interest, both in the defendant and in the person receiving the communication, was necessary. In any case all earlier cases must be read subject to the categorical statement of Lord Atkinson in *Adam v Ward* [1917] A.C. 309 at 334:
"A privileged occasion is . . . an occasion where the person who makes a communication has an interest or a duty, legal, social or moral, to make it to the person to whom it is made and

14.35 Volunteered communications: employees. Thus the mere fact that a communication as to an employee's character is made voluntarily, and not in answer to any inquiry, will not necessarily render it unprivileged. In an old case it was said:

> "If a servant were strongly suspected of having committed a felony while in his master's service, the master is at liberty to warn others from taking him into their service, for it is the duty of every person to guard the public against admitting such servants into their houses."[244]

Where an employer wrote a first letter without a previous inquiry as to the plaintiff's character, Lord Tenterden C.J. left it to the jury to say whether the communication was made bona fide acting under the belief that he was discharging a duty[245] to the party who was about to take the plaintiff into his service, or whether it was made maliciously, with an intention of doing an injury to the plaintiff.[246] Similarly, notification to an employer that an employee presented a danger to the public (e.g. a worker in catering who was believed to carry typhoid[247]) would be privileged.

14.36 Prior relationships. As previously explained,[248] the existence of some earlier dealing or relationship between the defendant and the person with whom he proposes to communicate is a common, though not exclusive, basis for the existence of this classical form of privilege which depends upon honesty of purpose rather than making adequate inquiry. Thus, if someone takes on an employee on the basis of a reference from A, and then discovers that he is dishonest, he may inform A of the fact, so that he may avoid writing misleading references in the future.[249] Similarly, where an employer, after dismissing a servant whom she had engaged through a registry office, wrote a letter to the registry office in which she stated that the servant was most unsatisfactory and incompetent, it was held that such letter, though volunteered, was privileged.[250] Where an employer discharged one of his domestic

---

the person to whom it is so made has a corresponding interest or duty to receive it. This reciprocity is essential."

[244] *Rogers v Clifton* (1803) 3 Bos. & P. 587 at 592, 595; *Pattison v Jones* (1828) 8 B. & C. 578; and see *Anderson v Smythe* (1935) 50 British Col.R. 113 at 118.

[245] I.e. with the purpose of discharging the duty. If the law does not recognise a duty it is not enough that the defendant believes there is one: para.14.18, above.

[246] *Pattison v Jones* (1828) 8 B. & C. 578. Bayley J. at 584 would go no further than allowing the party making the communication to induce an inquiry.

[247] Assuming that to be defamatory: see Ch.2, above. If not, the only claim would be one for malicious falsehood, where the claimant would have to prove malice anyway. Cf. *W v JH* [2008] EWHC 399 (QB); [2009] E.M.L.R. 11.

[248] See para.14.11, above.

[249] *Dixon v Parsons* (1856) 1 F. & F. 24; *Fryer v Kinnersley* (1863) 15 C.B.(N.S.) 422; cf. *Lawrence v Barker* (1968) 68 D.L.R.(2d) 597; *Angell v Bushell* [1968] 1 Q.B. at 830 (a business introduction). See also para.14.26, above.

[250] *Farquhar v Neish* (1890) 17 R. 716; and see *Hambrosak v Law Society, The Times*, March 1, 1967. But see, *W v JH* [2008] EWHC 399 (QB); [2009] E.M.L.R. 11.

servants and told the others why he has done so, such communication was privileged[251]; and where the defendant, who had dismissed the plaintiff on suspicion of stealing, told two other servants that he had dismissed the plaintiff for robbing him, it was held a privileged communication,[252] for:

> "it was the duty of the defendant, and also his interest, to prevent his servants from associating with a person of such a character as the words imputed to the plaintiff; inasmuch as such association might reasonably be apprehended to be likely to be followed by injurious consequences, both to the servants and to the defendant himself."[253]

The first reason is no doubt rather too paternalistic for the changed relationship of employer and employee, but the reason relating to the protection of the employer's interests no doubt remains valid. Where an employee is subject to a fidelity bond, it is the employer's duty and interest to report a suspected fraud by the employee to the person who has given the bond.[254]

Volunteered statements in aid of justice. Although it is not generally an   **14.37**
offence (or any other wrong) to fail to reveal information[255] about a crime, it is, for the purpose of privilege, the public duty of everyone who knows or believes that a crime has been committed to assist in the discovery of the wrongdoer. "A report, made to the appropriate authorities, that a person has or may have committed a crime attracts qualified privilege"[256] and the mere fact that the defendant volunteered the information will make no difference.[257]

> "When a person has reason to believe that a crime has been committed, it is his duty and his right to inform the police."[258]
> "When it comes to the knowledge of anyone that a crime has been committed, a duty is laid on that person, as a citizen of the country, to state to the authorities what he knows respecting the commission of the crime; and if he states only what he knows and honestly believes, he cannot be subjected to an action of damages merely

---

[251] *Somerville v Hawkins* (1850) 10 C.B. 583. See also *Hunt v G.N. Ry* [1891] 2 Q.B. 189 CA; *Bryant v Edgar*, 1909 S.C. 1080; *AB v XY*, 1907 S.C. 15.
[252] *Somerville v Hawkins* (1850) 10 C.B. 583. Such a case could probably be decided on the basis of common interest: see para.14.48, below.
[253] Per Maule J. at 589. *Fisher v Rankin* [1972] 4 W.W.R. 705.
[254] *Dundas v Livingstone & Co* (1900) 3 F. 37. Cf. *Ginsberg v Union Society* (1902) 63 N.Y.App.Div. 141 (communications by surety company to persons on the faith of whose statements a fidelity bond had been given in respect of an employee now in default).
[255] There may, of course, be particular enforceable duties to reveal information, not necessarily about crime, whether by statute (e.g. in relation to money laundering) or office or contract.
[256] *JD v East Berkshire Community Health NHS Trust* [2005] UKHL 23; [2005] 2 A.C. 373 at [77] per Lord Nicholls.
[257] *Johnson v Evans* (1800) 3 Esp. 32; *Shufflebottom v Allday* (1857) 3 W.R. 315; *Hasselblad (GB) v Orbinson* [1985] Q.B. 475 CA; *Ferguson v Colquhoun* (1862) 24 D. 1428; *Thomson v Adam* (1865) 4 R. 29; *Lightbody v Gordon* (1882) 9 R. 934; *Hassan v Paterson* (1885) 12 R. 1164; *M'Falden v Lynch* (1883) 17 Ir.L.R. 93; *Lupee v Hogan* (1920) 47 N.B.R. 492 NBCA; *Bowles v Armstrong* (1912) 32 N.Z.L.R. 409; *Otten v Schutt*, 113 N.W.2d 152 (Wis., 1962).
[258] *Croucher v Inglis* (1889) 16 R. 774 at 778.

because it turns out that the person as to whom he has given the information is, after all, not guilty of the crime."[259]

Nowadays it has come to be held that where a person complains to the police about a crime against him the privilege is absolute[260] but no case so holding appears to have involved a mere informant who is not involved in the matter,[261] nor a complainant who complains other than to the investigatory authorities, though such persons may still claim qualified privilege. Even when statements by persons who conceived themselves to be the victims of crime were protected only by qualified privilege they were in fact typically not made to fulfil any social or moral obligation but in the interests of the maker,[262] but that did not prevent them being privileged.[263] Privilege on the grounds of the interest of the maker clearly goes far beyond reports of *crime* and it is suggested that the privilege of persons who have no interest, while no doubt narrower, extends to other forms of wrongdoing. For example, if in the course of investigations a newspaper discovers evidence of non-criminal infractions of the rules governing the provision of financial services and it reports it to the relevant regulatory body, that, it is submitted, would be on a privileged occasion, even if the publication of the same information in the newspaper might be required to meet other conditions.[264]

Statements about suspected crimes may, of course, be made by the authorities rather than to them. No doubt there are circumstances in which it is legitimate for the police to disclose pre-conviction information for the purpose of preventing crime[265] but in *Wood v Chief Constable of the West Midlands* H had been arrested in connection with handling stolen vehicles found at his home (though in the event he was not convicted). The police communicated the fact of the arrest to various persons connected with vehicle salvage and added that H had been working for a company known as VSG, of which the claimant was a director. The Court of Appeal rejected an appeal based on the argument that the communications were privileged. The disclosure was in contravention of official guidelines and police regulations and the police:

---

[259] *Lightbody v Gordon* (1882) 9 R. 934 at 937, per Lord President Inglis.
"It is a settled rule or principle of law that where an individual gives information or makes a statement to an officer of the law, whose duty it is to detect and prosecute criminals . . . to the effect that someone has committed a crime, such information or statement has the protection of privilege. This is so in the best interests of society, and the repression of crime could not otherwise be enforced": *Green v Chalmers* (1878) 6 R. 318 at 320.
[260] See para.13.12, above.
[261] However, a person who answers police questions *is* protected by absolute privilege: ibid.
[262] See *Collins v Cooper* [1902] 19 T.L.R. 118 CA.
[263] See para.14.49, below.
[264] See para.15.21, below. Contrast *Adamson v Ede* [2007] N.S.W.S.C. 829 where D sent false information about one party to litigation, C, to the other. Adams J. doubted whether such intervention by a stranger in a civil suit could be an occasion of privilege but in any event found that D was motivated by malice.
[265] See, e.g. *R. v Chief Constable of North Wales Ex p. Thorpe* [1999] Q.B. 396 (not a defamation case).

"had no business, let alone duty, to make statements anticipating that [H] would be convicted . . . Nor did the police have secure information sufficient to justify statements that VSG were complicit with [H's] alleged criminality. Factual statements about [H's] arrest were one thing. But defamatory statements about VSG and, as it turned out, [the claimant] were quite another. These statements were . . . ill-considered and indiscriminate. They did not, as the judge held, sufficiently contribute to the prevention of crime or the protection of victims of crime to sustain a duty of disclosure".[266]

So too, it was held in *Bento v The Chief Constable of Bedfordshire Police*[267] that the defendant could not rely on qualified privilege in respect of statements made in a press statement regarding the CPS's decision not to proceed with a second prosecution of the claimant after the Court of Appeal had quashed the original conviction and ordered a retrial. Bean J. held that the press statement meant: (a) that a jury had already found that the claimant murdered K; (b) that the evidence as it stood in July 2009 showed that he probably killed her, which was sufficient to justify proceeding with a retrial; and (c) that the CPS's decision to offer no evidence was therefore wrong.[268] The defendant based his claim to qualified privilege on two alternative grounds. First, the police had a duty to keep the local public informed about the status of an investigation into a serious crime and the local public had a corresponding right and interest to receive this information. Secondly, that the press release was protected because it was distributed in defence or rebuttal of an anticipated attack in the media about the police's handling of the investigation into K's death. The judge rejected both arguments. In relation to the first of these, Bean J. accepted that there was a high public interest in maintaining confidence in the criminal justice system. However, he did not accept that the public interest was served by encouraging the police to issue statements indicating their opinion that the decision of the CPS not to pursue a prosecution (or, for that matter, the decision of a judge that a defendant has no case to answer) was wrong because the individual concerned was or was probably guilty. On the contrary, such statements reduced confidence in the criminal justice system, as well as seriously damaging the right to reputation of the individual.[269] In addition, the defendant accepted that it would have been a disproportionate interference with the claimant's art.8 rights to say that he was *guilty* of K's murder and the same analysis must apply to a statement that the claimant *probably* killed her.[270]

The judge also rejected the second ground. In *Bhatt v Chelsea and Westminster NHS Trust,*[271] Sir Maurice Drake had accepted that qualified privilege could extend to a statement made in rebuttal of an anticipated attack. Bean J.,

---

[266] [2004] EWCA Civ 1638; [2005] E.M.L.R. 20 at [64].
[267] [2012] EWHC 1525 (QB).
[268] [2012] EWHC 1525 at [10] (QB).
[269] Ibid. at [98].
[270] Ibid. at [100].
[271] Unreported, October 16, 1997.

however, doubted that that decision was correct: "I can see no policy reason to extend qualified privilege to people who believe they are about to be criticised and decide to get their public retaliation in first."[272] However, even if *Bhatt* was correctly decided, the judge held that the principle must be confined to cases where the defamatory statement is both: (i) in reasonable anticipation of an imminent attack on the conduct of the maker of the statement; and (ii) limited to a proportionate rebuttal of that anticipated attack.[273] Here the trigger for the July 2009 press statement was a telephone request from a BBC current affairs programme asking whether the police had a photograph of K. There had been a previous item on the programme about the case in February 2009, at the time of the appeal, which included a strong attack on the evidence of an expert witness, but no express criticism of the police investigation. Moreover, the invariable practice of the BBC before criticising the police was to give them an opportunity to put their side of the story. Consequently, it was not reasonable for the police to have anticipated a public attack on their conduct. Moreover, a proportionate rebuttal of that anticipated attack would have been limited to explaining what the police had done, and would not have extended to saying that the claimant was probably guilty.[274]

As *Bento* makes clear, any statement made by the police, as a public authority, must be consistent with their public law duties and in accordance with their obligations under the Human Rights Act 1998.[275] Thus, if the publication is apt to seriously damage a person's reputation, that person's art.8 right to respect for private life applies and the public authority must not interfere with that right unless the publication can be justified under art.8(2). In order to be justified, the publication must be necessary for a legitimate aim and proportionate to that aim. Ultimately the court must strike a fair balance between the rights of the individual and the interests of the community. While the police do not have any art.10 rights, art.10(1) protects the right of the public (and media on its behalf) to receive information. That the right now appears to be of wider scope than originally thought, in particular where the media are involved and genuine public interest is raised, was acknowledged by the Court of Appeal in *Regina (Guardian News and Media Ltd) v City of Westminster Magistrates' Court; Guardian News and Media Ltd v Government of the United States of America*[276] and *Independent News and Media Ltd v A.*[277] While the facts of those cases were different from *Bento*, the wider scope of art.10(1) is plainly of general application where it is the public which has a legitimate interest in receiving the information in question and much of

---

[272] [2012] EWHC 1525 at [103] (QB).
[273] Ibid. at [104]. See further, para.14.51, below.
[274] Ibid. at [105]–[106].
[275] *Wood v Chief Constable of the West Midlands Police* [2004] EWCA Civ 1638; [2005] E.M.L.R. 20; *Clift v Slough Borough Council* [2010] EWCA Civ 1171; [2011] 1 W.L.R. 1774.
[276] [2011] EWCA Civ 1188; [2011] 1 W.L.R. 3253 at [53].
[277] [2010] EWCA Civ 343; [2010] 1 W.L.R. 2262 at [35]–[38].

the information in question is already in the public domain. In considering whether privilege exists, the court should therefore seek to reach a decision that strikes an appropriate balance between the claimant's art.8 rights and the more general art.10 rights of the public to receive information.

Public representatives. Those who are appointed or elected[278] to serve on   **14.38** a public body have a duty to express themselves freely and to say what they believe to be true at meetings of that body, and thus what they say in pursuance of that duty will be privileged.[279]

> "If in the conduct of public business any member of a public body which is considering and deliberating for the public benefit thinks right in the public interest to make use of expressions which are pertinent to the matter in hand, though they may bear hardly on individuals, that occasion is nevertheless privileged unless malice is proved ... A town council is a typical instance of a public body the members of which enjoy a privilege in the language they use in dealing with the public affairs of the borough."[280]
>
> " ... [W]hat is said by members of a local council at meetings of the council or any of its committees is spoken on a privileged occasion. The reason for the privilege is that those who represent the local government electors should be able to speak freely and frankly, boldly and bluntly,[281] on any matter which they believe affects the interests or welfare of the inhabitants. They may be swayed by strong political prejudice, they may be obstinate and pig-headed, stupid and obtuse; but they were chosen by the electors to speak their minds on matters of local concern and as long as they do so honestly they run no risk of liability for defamation of those who are the subjects of their criticism."[282]

However, while the public have a right under art.10 to receive information from those appointed or elected to serve on a public body, if the public body is sued as vicariously liable for the publications of those appointed or elected to it, then if the publication is apt to damage a person's reputation, his art.8(1) right to respect for private life applies and the public authority must not interfere with that right unless the publication can be justified under art.8(2).

---

[278] As to statements about candidates for public office, see para.15.32, below.

[279] *George v Goddard* (1861) 2 F. & F. 609: *Bennett v Barry* (1863) 8 L.T. 857; *Pittard v Oliver* [1891] 1 Q.B. 474 CA (board of guardians); *Horrocks v Lowe* [1975] A.C. 135 HL; *Shaw v Morgan* (1888) 15 R. 865; *Neilson v Johnston* (1890) 17 R. 442; *Teague v Russell* (1900) 8 S.L.T. 253; *Mapey v Baker* (1909) 73 J.P. 289; *McLean v Murray* (1923) A.D. 406; *Campbell v Weir*, 1924 S.L.T. 14 at 16; *Edwards v Gatman* [1928] 3 D.L.R 187. Cf. *Senior v Medland* (1838) 4 Jur. (N.S.) 1039; *Craig v Jex-Blake* (1871) 9 M. 973, where no privilege attached to the statement as it was irrelevant to the matter under discussion at the meeting. A Premier addressing his political supporters is probably not within this rule: *Jones v Bennett* [1969] S.C.R. 277; but a meeting to discuss planning proposals may attract the privilege: *Robertson v McBride* [1931] 4 D.L.R. 132 SCC.

[280] Per Lord Moncreiff L.J-C. in *Shaw v Morgan* (1885) 15 R. 865 at 869; *Savidant v Day* (1933) 5 M.P.R. 554; *Smith v District of Matsqui* (1986) 4 B.C.L.R. (2d) 342; *McKinnon v Dauphin* [1996] 3 W.W.R. 127.

[281] "[Councillors] have no need to be mealy mouthed and should call a spade a spade": *Ward v McBride* (1911) 24 O.L.R. 555 Ont CA.

[282] Per Lord Diplock in *Horrocks v Lowe* [1975] A.C. 135 at 152. See also *Neilson v Johnson* (1890) 17 R. 442 at 448.

In order to be justified the publication must be necessary for a legitimate aim and proportionate to that aim.[283] Even though such persons may be perfectly well aware that what they say during the deliberations of the public body may be reported in the press, they are not required to meet the additional requirements laid down by *Reynolds v Times Newspapers Ltd*.[284]

14.39 **Participants in proceedings of domestic, etc. tribunals.** Participants in proceedings of a court or of a tribunal recognised by law having the characteristics of a court enjoy absolute privilege.[285] But participants in a wide range of other proceedings (e.g. domestic proceedings established by contract or proceedings established under the authority of statute or by executive action) are recognised as having a duty to say what they know in relation to matters relevant to these proceedings and publications in the course of the proceedings are therefore made on an occasion of qualified privilege.[286]

14.40 **Statements made in discharge of a duty to protect another's interests.** Sometimes a duty to give information may arise not from any public interest but merely from the interests of another, with whom the informant has some close relationship, either a family relationship, or one of trust and reliance, or perhaps one of friendship. If the information is sufficiently important there may be a duty to give information to someone with whom there is no previous relationship of such a kind, or even to a stranger, but in every case it is submitted that the court will weigh the strength of the information which the informant believes himself to have, its relevance to the interests of the person to whom it is to be communicated, the damage which it may do to the reputation of the person to whom it relates and the extent to which the person to whom the information is communicated is likely to rely on the informant for information of this kind.[287]

While no doubt honesty of purpose provides a defence if the occasion is found to be privileged and the defendant is not liable merely because he has not behaved "reasonably", yet the fact that the privilege is not based on clear-cut categories of relationship will call for a close examination of the facts of the particular case, particularly where the art.8 rights of the claimant are

---

[283] See, *Clift v Slough Borough Council* [2010] EWCA Civ 1171; [2011] 1 W.L.R. 1774; *Morrison v Buckinghamshire CC* [2011] EWHC 3444 (QB). See also *Thompson v James* [2013] EWHC 515 (QB) in which it was held that the claimant's art.8 rights were not engaged.

[284] See para.15.1, below. For qualified privilege for those who report local authority meetings, see para.16.19, below.

[285] See paras 13.5–13.24, above.

[286] See *Re Pergamon Press* [1971] Ch. 388 at 400 (Department of Trade inquiries) citing *O'Connor v Waldron* [1935] A.C. 76. There is not much direct authority in relation to domestic proceedings though since the announcement of the decision to those concerned is privileged (see para.14.45, below) and public reports of certain such decisions may also be privileged (see para.16.22, below), it is submitted that it would be wrong in principle if no similar privilege applied to those giving evidence or acting as advocates.

[287] Previous cases should be read with caution since the court must decide whether a duty exists now and not whether it was held to exist previously: see para.14.19, above.

engaged. In *Watt v Longsdon*[288] the court had no doubt that the defendant's passing of the letter alleging misconduct by the plaintiff to the chairman of the board of the company, which employed him, was privileged on account of the employment relationship; but the same was not true in respect of passing the letter to the plaintiff's wife, at any rate in view of the seriousness of the charges, the absence of any corroboration and the failure to confront the plaintiff with the accusations.[289]

Family relationship. The fact that a close family relationship exists   **14.41**
between A and B may make it the especial duty of A to inform B of facts which he knows about C, in order that B's interests may be protected, and any such information, though volunteered, will be privileged, provided it is given bona fide and with the honest purpose of protecting B's interests. Thus, it has been held that a father or near relative may warn a young man as to the character of an associate[290] and that a near relative of a lady may warn her about the character of the man whom she proposes to marry[291]; and it has been said that such communication should be viewed liberally by a jury.[292] So where the defendant, son-in-law of a widow lady to whom the plaintiff was paying his addresses, wrote a letter to the lady charging the plaintiff with various acts of misconduct and desiring a diligent and extensive inquiry into his character, Alderson B. ruled that the letter, though based on erroneous information, was privileged, and directed the jury that:

> "if the defendant has used expressions however harsh, hasty, or untrue, yet *bona fide* and believing them to be true, he was justified in so doing. It is for the good of all that communications of this kind should be viewed liberally by juries, and unless you see clearly that this letter was written with a malicious intention of defaming the plaintiff, your verdict ought to be for the defendant."[293]

Similarly, the defendant may act for the protection of the interest of a member of his family by making statements to another, e.g. to a school.[294] Although there have been dramatic changes in the nature of family relationships since the time these cases were decided, it is submitted that the principle remains

---

[288] [1930] 1 K.B. 130 CA; para.14.14, above. And see the difference of opinion in *Stuart v Bell* [1891] 2 Q.B. 341 CA, para.14.14, above.

[289] "The decision must turn on the circumstances of each case, the judge being much influenced by the consideration that as a general rule it is not desirable for anyone, even a mother in law, to interfere in the affairs of man and wife": Scrutton L.J.

[290] *Moffatt v Coats* (1906) 44 S.L.R. 20.

[291] *Todd v Hawkins* (1837) 8 C. & P. 88; *Adams v Coleridge* (1884) 1 T.L.R. 84; *Nelson v Irving* (1897) 24 R. 1054; *Atkinson v Congreve* (1857) 7 Ir.C.L.R.109; *Fick v Watermeyer* (1874) 4 Buchanan (Cape of G. Hope) R. 86. The same would plainly be true of a warning to a man about his proposed wife.

[292] *Todd v Hawkins* (1837) 8 C. & P. 88 at 92; *Adams v Coleridge* (1884) 1 T.L.R. at 87.

[293] *Todd v Hawkins* (1837) 8 C. & P. 88 at 92.

[294] *Hansen v Hansen*, 148 N.W. 457 (Min., 1914).

valid even if its application may now differ in particular circumstances[295] and it is thought that "family" should be broadly interpreted so as to cover de facto relationships which are equivalent to legal ones.

14.42 **Relationships of trust and reliance.** Where there is a relationship between A and B such that B relies on A for advice and information or otherwise should be able to trust A to act in his best interests, it will be the duty of A to communicate to B information relevant to his interests, and any such communication will be privileged.[296] Thus, a professional adviser has a duty to warn a client of any danger to his interests, even without being consulted,[297] and it has been held (though a good many years ago) that it may be the duty of a clergyman to warn a parishioner as to the character of a person with whom the parishioner's daughter is associating,[298] or of a host to warn a guest of a report that his personal servant may be dishonest.[299]

14.43 **Friendship.** Varying views of the significance of friendship between the maker and recipient of the statement may be found but nowadays[300] the best view is probably that the existence of a close friendship may be taken into account by the court in considering whether A has a duty to communicate to B information relevant to B's interests: friendship is not so important as to excuse any communication, or so irrelevant that communications between friends should stand on the same footing as communications between strangers. In *Watt v Longsdon*[301] the fact that there was a friendship between the

---

[295] Thus in *Watt v Longsdon* [1930] 1 K.B. 130, Scrutton L.J. posed the case of a doctor who attended the claimant and concluded that she had had miscarried a child of whom her absent husband, his brother, could not be the father. He thought that most people would hold that it was the doctor's duty to communicate that fact to the husband. But nowadays it is hard to see how that could be other than a breach of confidence, in which case the communication can hardly be on a privileged occasion.

[296] There is no direct authority for the proposition in these terms, but it seems to underlie the particular cases.

[297] *Davis v Reeves* (1855) 5 Ir.C.L.R. 79; *Baker v Carrick* [1894] 1 Q.B. 838 CA. "It is the duty of a solicitor to do all he can to protect the interests of his client": per Lopes L.J., ibid. at 841.

[298] *Gilbert v Waldy*, The Times, November 19, 1909 (Bristol Assizes). See also *Maccaba v Lichtenstein* [2004] EWHC 1577 (QB); [2005] E.M.L.R. 9. Cf. *Mellor v Parker* (1902) 2 N.S.W.S.R. 156; *M'Carogher v Franks*, The Times, November 25, 1964 (duty of secretary of Old Boys Association to inform senior schoolboys about temperament of dismissed teacher). See also Restatement 2d, *Torts*, para.597, Illustration 2.

[299] *Stuart v Bell* [1891] 2 Q.B. 341 CA at 350, 359–360.

[300] Some early cases expressing strong views in favour of friendship on this issue (e.g. *Herver v Dowson* (1765) Buller's N.P. 7 and *Fairman v Ives* (1822) 5 B. & Ald. 642) are perhaps to be explained as dating from an era when the law was less concerned with "duty and interest" and resting on the view that the issue was whether the presumption of malice from defamatory words had been rebutted. For a narrower view see *Krebs v Oliver* (1858) 78 Mass.R. 239 at 243, holding that friendship, of however long standing, does not, in the absence of pressing emergency,

"impose a duty of communicating charges of a defamatory character concerning a third person, although they may be told to one who has a strong interest in knowing them. The duty of refraining from the utterance of slanderous words, without knowing or ascertaining their truth, far outweighs any claim of mere friendship": per Bigelow J.

[301] [1930] 1 K.B. 130 CA.

defendant and the claimant's wife, she having nursed him during an illness, did not prevent the communication of the unverified charges to her being unprivileged. However, in a modern case where D, an orthodox Jewish religious adviser, had been consulted about unwelcome sexual advances alleged to have been made by C to X and had been told that C was also thought to pose a risk to another woman, Y, D was privileged in raising the matter with Y's father rather than going directly to her in view of the long friendship between him and the father.[302]

Statement made "in confidence" not sufficient for defence. Where **14.44** there is no sufficient relationship between the parties to create a duty to speak, the mere fact that the defendant expressly states that he writes or speaks "in confidence" will not render a communication privileged if there is no moral duty to make the communication.[303]

> "A communication is not privileged merely because it is confidential.[304]
>
> "It is material to distinguish between communications which are privileged in the eye of the law, and may, therefore, be made with impunity unless there be express malice, and communications which are merely confidential. To hold that a communication which the writer may intend to be confidential may, for the reason that it is confidential. be made a vehicle for injuring the reputation of a third person, would be most mischievous. It would afford malicious persons the opportunity of conveying slander to the quarter where it would inflict the greatest injury upon the object of it, and at the same time shut him out from the power of vindicating himself."[305]

(b) *Communications in pursuance of an interest*

Common and reciprocal interests. Where a communication is made by **14.45** someone with an interest in the subject-matter to someone who has a corresponding interest in receiving the communication[306] it is made on a privileged occasion. Such a situation is often referred to as one in which the parties have a common interest. Often their interests will be identical, or arise out of the same set of circumstances, as in the case of communications between employees in a business or shareholders in a company, but a common interest, in this sense, is not an essential ingredient in the defence: the interests of the parties can be quite different in kind, but the occasion may still be privileged.[307] A publication made on a particular occasion may even be privileged notwithstanding that the person was acting solely in pursuit of his own interests

---

[302] *Maccaba v Lichtenstein* [2004] EWHC 1577 (QB); [2005] E.M.L.R. 9.

[303] *Picton v Jackman* (1830) 4 C. & P. 257; *Andrews v Wilson* (1845) 3 Kerr N.B.R. 86; *Carvill v McLeod* (1859) 4 Allen N.B.R. 332; *Curneen v Sweeney* (1969) 103 I.L.T.R. 29.

[304] Per Lord Lyndhurst C.B. in *Brooks v Blanshard* (1833) I Cr. & M. 779 at 783.

[305] Per Chipman C.J. in *Andrews v Wilson* (1845) 5 Kerr N.B.R. 86 at 91.

[306] See *De Buse v McCarthy* [1942] 1 K.B. 156 CA at 164, per Lord Greene M.R. (preferring to speak of common interest in the communication rather than in the subject-matter).

[307] See, e.g. *Aspro Travel v Owners Abroad Group* [1996] 1 W.L.R. 132 CA at 143 (interest of defendants as members of ABTA funding compensation scheme and of hoteliers in knowing that another company will take over responsibilities of an insolvent trader).

provided that the communication is made to someone who has a legitimate interest to receive the communication.[308] In some cases, as where the statement is made to the proper authority by way of grievance, the recipient might be regarded as having a duty rather than (or in addition to) an interest in receiving it but the distinction makes no difference. As in cases where the maker of a statement is acting in performance of a duty it is impossible to draw up a complete catalogue of cases but the following paragraphs deal with situations that have been considered by the courts. We have seen that in cases based on duty the traditional form of common law privilege tends to be confined to limited publications, though where there is a *legal* duty to inform or some pressing emergency it may extend to publication to the public as a whole.[309] In practice communications which can be defended on the basis of community of interest will be similarly confined. Thus in Australia it was held that publication to the Ukrainian community there of information about a person who held a position in one of its representative organisations was "far too wide to satisfy the requirement of reciprocity".[310] That does not of course preclude the application of the *Reynolds* variety of privilege.

14.46 Business and commercial interests. It has often been held that the shareholders of a company have a common interest in the affairs of the company, as do the officers of the company.[311] The Department of Trade and Industry and the Committee of the Stock Exchange (in relation to a quoted company) and other regulatory bodies also have an interest in the company's affairs, although their interest is supervisory, and thus a communication by a shareholder to either body relating to those affairs will prima facie be written on a privileged occasion.[312] A more indirect interest may be sufficient, as where the defendant holds shares in a company which, via a subsidiary, holds shares in the company about whose affairs the statement is made.[313] In *Aspro Travel v Owners Abroad Group*[314] the defendants were alleged to have made

---

[308] *Papaconstuntinos v Holmes a Court* [2012] HCA 53.

[309] See para.14.2, above.

[310] *Goyan v Motyka* [2008] NSWCA 28. But Handley A.J.A. preferred to reserve his opinion on this issue. Cf. *Hyer v Cabbie Pty Ltd* [2007] N.S.W.S.C. 795 (community of interest among cab operators and "cabbie" magazine). The first instance decision was upheld by the NSWCA, sub nom *Lindholdt v Hyer* [2008] NSWCA 264, but only on the basis that there was malice. Only one judge addressed the issue of whether there was a privileged publication. See para.14.70, below.

[311] See *Harris v Thompson* (1853) 13 C.B. 333; *Parsons v Surgey* (1864) 4 F. & F. 247; *Lawless v Anglo-Egyptian Co* (1869) L.R. 4 Q.B. 262: *Quartz Hill Co. v Beal* (1882) 20 Ch.D. 501 CA; *Allan v Clarke, The Times*, January 17, 1912; *McGillivray v Davidson*, 1934 S.L.T. 45; *Horne v Milne* (1881) 7 V.L.R. 296.

[312] *Bryanston Finance v De Vries* [1975] Q.B. 703 CA at 736, per Lawton L.J., the only member of the Court of Appeal actually to decide this point, though he considered that in that case there was no privilege, since the publication was not " fairly warranted". There is in this case perhaps some confusion between the existence of a privileged occasion and malice. See also *Downtex Plc v Flatley* [2003] EWCA Civ 1282, para.14.3, above.

[313] *Price Waterhouse Intrust v Wee Choo Keng* [1994] 3 S.L.R. 801 Sing CA.

[314] [1996] 1 W.L.R. 132 CA.

statements to hoteliers abroad to the effect that the plaintiffs were "going bust" or would be "bankrupt in a few days", these statements being a prelude to offers to take over the plaintiffs' bookings.[315] It was held[316] to be arguable[317] that the publications were privileged on the basis that the hoteliers had an interest in knowing that the bookings would be covered in the event of default and the defendants had an interest in keeping down claims on the ABTA compensation fund and in protecting the reputation of the trade. In *Blackham v Pugh*[318] D sold goods to P on credit and, discovering that the

---

[315] See also *Switzerland Australia Health Fund v Shaw* (1988) 81 A.L.R. 111 Fed Ct of Australia. But compare *Lawrence v Finch* [1931] 1 D.L.R. 689 Ont CA (one estate agent accusing another of stealing business; not privileged):

"If one member of the Law Society . . . were to slander another member . . . by dictating to his stenographer a letter addressed to plaintiff accusing him of practising his profession in a manner which was unethical and improper, he could not in my opinion establish that the occasion was privileged merely because the sender and the receiver of the letter had, or ought to have had, a common interest in the ethics of the legal profession."

[316] The action by the corporate plaintiff was settled and the reported case concerns the action of its directors: see para.7.13, above.

[317] The question of privilege could not be determined until evidence had fleshed out the precise nature of the interests claimed.

[318] (1846) 15 L.J.C.P. 290. *Alexander v Clegg* [2004] NZCA 91; [2004] 3 N.Z.L.R. 586 (common interest of members of distribution network). It has been suggested that there is a duty to draw the attention of possible purchasers to a defect in a title which the defendant asserts: see *Pitt v Donovan* (1813) 1 M. & S. 639 at 648; *Watson v Reynolds* (1826) Moo. 8 Mal. 1; *Steward v Young* (1870) L.R. 5 C.P. 122 at 126. See also *Hamon v Falle* (1879) 4 A.C. 247 (insurers of ship and owner); *Taylor v Despond* (1956) 6 D.L.R. (2d) 161 (finance company and applicant for loan from "crooked dealer"). The position of paying and collecting bankers in communicating the dishonour of a cheque may be seen as based on either a common interest or on a duty, in the case of a paying banker to explain the dishonour, or in the case of a collecting banker, one arising out of the relationship of banker and customer. In *Davidson v Barclays Bank* [1940] 1 All E.R. 316 privilege was rejected for the paying bank because it could not create a privileged occasion by its own mistake. However, that seems inconsistent with principle (see para.14.21, above) and the case has been doubted (*Pyke v Hibernian Bank* [1950] Ir.R. 195). However, the High Court of Australia in *Aktas v Westpac Banking Corp Ltd* [2010] HCA 25 has held, by a majority, that qualified privilege does not apply where a bank wrongly communicates the dishonour of a cheque to a payee. The court stated that there was no public interest protecting the bank's communications to the payees, as payees have no interest in receiving notice of a refusal to pay a cheque where the drawer has sufficient funds to meet the payment:

"The bank has an interest in communicating because it refuses to pay. But the payee has no interest in receiving a communication of refusal to pay a cheque which is regular on its face in a case where the drawer of the cheque has funds sufficient to meet its payment. And where a notice of dishonour is defamatory, the defamation will lie in the assertion either that the cheque is not regular, or that the drawer does not have funds sufficient to meet the payment ordered on the cheque. When a notice of dishonour is defamatory, the communication goes beyond informing the recipient that the bank refuses to pay the cheque; the communication gives the bank's reason for refusal. The defamatory imputation will be found in that reason, not in the bare fact of refusal. That being so, it is wrong to identify some community of interest in the communication actually made as arising out of a need or desire on the part of the bank to say that payment is refused or as founded in some more general notion of the payee needing or wanting to know 'the fate' of the cheque. As explained earlier, the bank acts as it does in what it perceives to be *its* interests. And for the payee of the cheque, there will be no need for any communication from the bank about the fate of the cheque, if it is met on presentation." (at [41])

The decision is based on the view that to "hold banks responsible to their customers not only in contract, but also for damage to reputation, is conducive to maintaining a high degree of accuracy

whole of P's stock in trade had been sold by auction and that P had quitted without leaving his address, told the auctioneer not to pay the proceeds of sale to P because he had committed an act of bankruptcy. P had in fact committed no act of bankruptcy, the goods having been sold on his retiring from business. It was held that the notice was privileged as it was sent in good faith and in the honest protection of D's own interests.

14.47 Interests arising out of employment. Employees in a business, or employer and employee, have common interests in the success of the business,[319] or the way in which it is carried on,[320] and in the terms and conditions of the employment relationship.[321] Thus, the plaintiff in *Hunt v G.N.Ry*[322] was

---

in the decisions that banks must make about paying cheques" (at [42]). No doubt there is something to be said for that from a policy point of view but against the background of the general law of qualified privilege the decision is surprising. To say that "the payee has no interest in receiving a communication of refusal to pay a cheque which is regular on its face in a case where the drawer of the cheque has funds sufficient to meet its payment" is in effect to follow the view of Hilbery J. in *Davidson v Barclays Bank* that the bank could not create a privileged occasion by its own mistake, but as Heydon J. pointed out, dissenting, the occasion:

"commenced when cheques were drawn on the first respondent by the second respondent and continued at least until the time when the first respondent informed payees and collecting banks of its decision not to honour those cheques. The first respondent was not mistaken about those facts. A mistake underlay what it communicated to its customers and the collecting banks. But that mistake was not a mistake about the occasion" (at [62]).

The approach of Hilbery J. in *Davidson* "creates an exception, in the case of banker and customer, to the application of settled principle" (Keifel J., dissenting, at [113]).

[319] See *Bryanston Finance v De Vries* [1975] Q.B. 703 CA. But unless a communication concerns one of these interests, there is no common interest between the person dictating a letter and the secretary taking dictation, so as to give rise to a privilege; the communication is privileged, if at all, only as ancillary to the intended publication outside the business: ibid. at 726, 728, 738; see also per Lord Denning M.R., ibid. at 719, dissenting on this point. See further paras 14.74–14.76, below.

[320] In *Pena v Tameside Hospital NHS Foundation Trust* [2011] EWHC 3027 (QB) the claimant was a surgeon employed by the first defendant who had served for some years as chairman of the Senior Medical Staff Committee (SMSC) at the hospital. The object of the body was to represent the interests of consultants and other senior medical staff. He had for many years expressed concerns about the standard of care at the hospital and in his role of chairman circulated an email to members of the SMSC expressing no confidence in the Board of the Trust, proposing a vote of no confidence in the Trust's board, and asking those who had confidence to email him saying so. An email debate ensued and the second defendant wrote an email suggesting that the vote of confidence was the result of anger that the Trust had stopped an initiative and another suggesting that the claimant had a personal vendetta against the board. The claimant sued. Eady J. held that this was a classic case of traditional qualified privilege: the debate was largely a natural consequence of the claimant's own communication with colleagues who were communicating at his invitation on a subject matter in which they all clearly had a legitimate common and corresponding interest. The defence was reinforced since P himself generated the exchanges and created the occasion for a free and frank exchange of views.

[321] It is submitted that the officials of a trade union, some of whose members are employed in a business, would also have an interest in the last, and probably all, of the matters mentioned in the text. There is sufficient community of interest between a union secretary and members in respect of statements about a strike (*Wells v Wellington etc. Union of Workers* [1952] N.Z.L.R. 312) and between union members in respect of the behaviour of its officers (*Duane v Granrott* [1982] V.R. 767).

[322] [1891] 2 Q.B. 189 CA. See also *Tench v G.W. Ry* (1873) 33 Up.Can.Q.B. 8, where the facts were similar; *Costello v Bremner* (1961) 31 D.L.R. (2d) 537; *Fisher v Rankin* (1972) 27 D.L.R.

a guard in the service of the defendant company. The company dismissed him for alleged gross neglect of duty, and published his name in a printed monthly circular addressed to their servants, stating that he had been dismissed, and the reasons for this dismissal. The decision of Stephen J. that the occasion was privileged and that, for lack of evidence of malice, no action would lie was upheld by the Court of Appeal. Lord Esher M.R. said[323]:

> "Can any one doubt that a railway company, if they are of opinion that some of their servants have been doing things which, if they were done by their other servants, would seriously damage their business, have an interest in stating this to their servants? And how can it be said that the servants to whom that statement is made have no interest in hearing that certain things are being treated by the company as misconduct, and that, if any of them should be guilty of such misconduct, the consequence would be dismissal from the company's service? I cannot imagine a case in which the reciprocal interest could be more clear."

In *Hunt's* case the circumstances were such as to justify publication to all fellow employees, but there may be many other occasions in employment where there may be a privileged publication to a narrower range of persons,[324] e.g. where statements are made in the course of probation or work evaluation[325] or by a supervisor after a reprimand.[326] An employer may also have an interest, if not a duty, in the health and welfare of an employee.[327]

Other common interests. Any other legitimate common interest will also   **14.48**
be protected.[328] Any continuing transaction is likely to give rise to such an

---

(3d) 746; *Neame v Yellow Cabs Ltd* (1930) S.A.S.R. 267; *Phillips v Boyce* (2006) 71 W.I.R. 14 Barbados CA.

[323] [1891] 2 Q.B. at 191; see also per Fry L.J., ibid. at 192.

[324] On the range of publication generally see paras 14.69–14.81, below. An employer may also, of course, be privileged to make statements to his employees about an outsider, as where he warns them of fraud: *Pleau v Simpsons-Sears* (1976) 75 D.L.R. (3d) 747 Ont CA, though there was a question about excessive publication in the case.

[325] *Louisville & Nashville R. v Marshall* 586 S.W.2d 274 (Ky., 1979).

[326] *Moores v Salter* (1982) 37 Nfld. & P.E.I.R. 128. Breach of an internal disciplinary code by the employer does not necessarily remove the protection of qualified privilege: *Halpin v Oxford Brooks University* (unreported, November 30, 1995), CA.

[327] *Phelps v Kemsley* (1942) 168 L.T. 18 CA.

[328] See, e.g. *Wilson v Robinson* (1845) 7 Q.B. 68; *Horne v Milne* (1881) 7 V.L.R. 297; *De Buse v McCarthy* [1942] 1 K.B. 156 CA (common interest of council and ratepayers in decisions, but not preliminary investigations); *Bridgman v Stockdale* [1953] 1 W.L.R. 704 (interest in examination); *Mangat v Sharma* [1968] E.A. 620; *Angell v Bushell* [1968] 1 Q.B. at 830 (common interest in integrity of person introduced); *Peter v Nio* [1980] 1 M.L.J. 226 (insurance company, agents and policy-holders); *Hahn v Katten* 331 N.E.2d 713 (Oh., 1975) (similar); *Bennette v Cohen* [2007] N.S.W.S.C. 739 ("fundraiser" to support environmental activist—the first instance decision was reversed by the NSWCA in *Bennette v Cohen* [2009] NSWCA 60. The purpose of the meeting at which the statement was made was to raise funds for a party to a legal dispute; there was no reciprocal interest in making and receiving statements about the other party and even if there had been what was said was foreign to the occasion); *Vassiliev v Frank Cass & Co. Ltd* [2003] EWHC 1428 (QB) (small group having interest in intelligence matters). See also *Bowker (t/a Lagopus Services) v The Royal Society for the Protection of Birds* [2011] EWHC 737 (QB); *Underhill v Corser* [2010] EWHC 1195 (QB) (publication to members of a charitable train preservation society about the financial affairs of the society was protected by privilege in so far

interest in the parties concerned.[329] Nor does the interest have to be financial. For instance, in *Laughton v Bishop of Sodor and Man*[330] the plaintiff, in a speech against a private bill before the House of Keys, vesting additional ecclesiastical patronage in the bishop, imputed to him improper motives and conduct in the exercise of his church patronage. The bishop in a written charge read to his clergy in convocation, commenting on the plaintiff's speech, made observations defamatory of the plaintiff. It was held that the charge was published on a privileged occasion, for:

> "the bishop had manifestly an interest in explaining and defending his conduct, if indeed it were not strictly his duty to do so, and the clergy were deeply interested in that explanation and defence."

So too, where the Royal Society of Protection of Birds published statements critiquing a peer-reviewed scientific paper written by the claimant about black grouse in an internal email sent to individuals with an interest in black grouse, in a report critiquing the paper and in a letter to the owner of the site that was the subject of the research, it was held that all the publications were written on an occasion of qualified privilege.[331] It was plainly for "the common convenience and welfare of society" that persons within the defendant's organisation should be free to communicate their concerns internally about the merits or otherwise of a study which had been published in a peer-reviewed scientific journal relevant to the work of the organisation itself; and that they should be able to discuss such matters outside their organisation with people who had a legitimate interest in the subject matter of the communication.[332] Similarly, the communication of complaints and adjudications between members of an association and a domestic tribunal within the association have long been held to be privileged[333] though the publication must be to a person who

---

as the publication was made to members of the society but not where it was made to those who had no interest in the society's financial affairs).

[329] *Sadgrove v Hole* [1902] 2 K.B. 1 (building owner and builder); *Hines v Davidson*, 1935 S.C. 30 at 37 (litigants and litigation); *Smythson v Cramp* [1943] 1 All E.R. 326 CA (similar); *John Hall v Bowden* (1953) C.P.L. 273 (architect and builder).

[330] (1872) L.R. 4 P.C. 495 at 504. For other cases on churches and lodges, see *R. v Hart* (1762) 1 W.Black. 386; *Botterill v Whitehead* (1879) 41 L.T. 588 (local clergyman not a parishioner: no duty or interest); *Robinson v Ward, The Times*, June 16,1958; *Saunderson v Jewish Chronicle, The Times*, April 24, 1953 (Beth Din and Jewish community); *Volitsky v Ottawa Vaad* (1926) 31 O.W.N. 189. See also *Barbaud v Hookham* (1804) 5 Esp. 109 (volunteer corps); *Hackett v Tierney* [1952] Ir.R. 185 (president and bursar of college); *Gallant v West* [1955] 4 D.L.R. 209 (military commander).

[331] *Bowker (t/a Lagopus Services) v The Royal Society for the Protection of Birds* [2011] EWHC 737 (QB).

[332] Ibid. at [130].

[333] *Hay v Australian Institute* (1906) 3 C.L.R. 1002; *Thompson v BMA* [1924] A.C. 764 at 782; *Chapman v Ellesmere* [1932] 2 K.B. 431 CA (extending to racing community); *Cookson v Harewood* [1932] 2 K.B. 478 CA; *Pritchard v GRA* (1933) 176 L.T.J. 382 at 395; (1934) 177 L.T.J. 90 CA; *Green v Blake* [1948] Ir. R. 242.

has a legitimate interest in the subject matter of the communication.[334] It is common practice in a recreational club to post the names of applicants for membership. This impliedly invites communications by members on the merits of the application and these are generally protected by qualified privilege.[335]

Where there is a relationship between A and B such that B relies upon A to protect his interests, that may impose a duty upon A to volunteer information to B.[336] It must follow that where such a relationship exists there is also privilege for information imparted by B to A in seeking assistance or advice.[337] Thus there would be privilege between a traveller and a British consul for communications about a lost passport[338]; and it has been held in South Africa that qualified privilege attached to a statement by the defendant to her priest that she believed the plaintiff to have sexually abused her daughter.[339]

---

[334] In *Cambridge v Makin* [2012] EWCA Civ 85; [2012] E.M.L.R. 19 the Court of Appeal affirmed the decision of the first instance judge that a publication by the appellant professional interpreter was protected by qualified privilege in so far as it was published to other professional interpreters able to vote in a no confidence motion brought against the claimant and other members of the leadership of the National Register of Public Service Interpreters Ltd (NRPSI) but not in respect of publication to other professional interpreters not able to vote. The mere fact of shared membership of NRPSI was not sufficient to invoke qualified privilege: "The simple fact that the other recipients happened also to be public service interpreters created no necessity in the public interest that they should be able to receive such a communication provided only that it was not actuated by malice." (at [50])

In *Ryan v Premachandran* [2009] N.S.W.S.C. 1186 privilege was denied for publication of complaints about the competence of a teacher to other parents of children in a class (though on the facts it had not been proved that all publishees were such). Nicholas J. said:

"The recipients were not persons with authority over, or responsible for, the plaintiff's performance as the principal. Thus they were not persons to whom a complaint about her conduct might properly be directed as having the relevant interest in knowing of its existence, or were persons capable of acting so as to further or protect the defendant's interest. In other words, in my opinion, it cannot be said that the defendant was under a social or moral duty to make the publication to the recipients or had an interest to protect in doing so, or that they had a relevant interest in knowing of defamatory statements relating to his personal concerns in support of his call for the plaintiff's resignation . . . Furthermore, in my opinion, the defendant did not show the existence of any occasion or exigency which warranted publication of his grievances against the plaintiff." (at [84]–[85])

[335] *Brown v Marron* [2001] WASC 100.

[336] See para.14.40, above.

[337] The well-established privilege for communications between solicitor and client (which may, however, be absolute: see para.13.51, above) is therefore it is submitted, a special example of a wider principle.

[338] *Komarek v Ramco Energy Plc* [2002] EWHC 2501 (QB) at [46]. The claimants and defendants in this case were in dispute about a commercial venture in the Czech Republic and the action arose from allegations of corruption against the claimants made by the defendants in communications to British Embassy staff in Prague. Eady J. held that it was not possible, for the purposes of an application for summary judgment, to say that the case inevitably fell within the bounds of qualified privilege.

[339] *O v O*, 1995 (4) S.A. 482. Had such a statement been made to the child care authorities or to the police it would plainly have been privileged under paras 14.37, above or 14.49, below. See also *N v S* (1993) 120 N.S.R. (2d) 228 (complaint by child of sexual abuse by father).

14.49 Statements concerning suspected crimes. Though there is no *common interest* involved, the courts have long held that statements are privileged if made bona fide for the purpose of detecting and bringing to punishment a suspected criminal, or of recovering stolen goods.[340] It is now held that a complaint to the police is protected by absolute privilege[341] but no case so far extends that to other statements. A person who suspects another of a particular theft may, with a view to inquiry, tax that individual with the theft, and although the suspicion turns out to be erroneous, the law gives no redress to the party accused.[342] There could of course be no liability unless some third party were present, but the law has been fairly liberal in allowing charges to be made in the presence of others.[343] If the defendant could not lawfully accuse the person suspected, though wrongly, of having committed the theft, it would be quite impossible for a person who is robbed to inquire with any safety after the stolen goods.[344]

A person who suspects another of theft is not only privileged in asking questions of him with a view to finding out whether his suspicions are true, but may also approach any other person who he has reason to believe will be able to help in his inquiry, so long as he acts bona fide. Accordingly, if a victim of theft has suspicions of a particular person and were to ask a third person who was present at the time when the particular article was stolen whether he saw that person steal the article, both the question,[345] and the answer,[346] are privileged. So, in *Collins v Cooper*,[347] the defendant missed from his house certain articles which he suspected to have been stolen by the governess of his children, and sold to the plaintiff, a ladies' wardrobe-dealer. At his invitation the plaintiff called at his house. On the plaintiff denying that she had done so, the defendant said: "Would it surprise you if I could bring five people to say that you had taken the things from here?" The plaintiff said it would surprise her. Four boys and a servant were then sent into the room, and the defendant said to them: "Is this the person who came and took the things away?" The boys replied, "Yes". It was held that all these statements were made on a privileged occasion. Similarly:

---

[340] *McCormack v Olsthoorn* [2004] IEHC 431; [2004] 3 I.R. 632, overruling *Coleman v Keanes Ltd* [1946] Ir. Jur. Rep. 5, which had denied privilege because the statement was made with the desire to recover the property, instead of a desire to bring a thief to justice.

[341] See para.13.12, above.

[342] *Fowler v Homer* (1812) 3 Camp. 294; *Padmore v Lawrence* (1840) 11 A. & E. 380; *Howe v Jones* (1884) 1 T.L.R. 19; (1885) ibid. 461: *Collins v Cooper* (1902) 19 T.L.R. 118 CA; *Bowles v Armstrong* (1912) 32 N.Z.L.R. 409. See also, *LVMH Watch & Jewellery Australia Pty Ltd v Michael Lassanah* [2011] NSWCA 370 (police officers who accused the claimants of intending to steal from a shop were protected by qualified privilege).

[343] See para.14.76, below.

[344] Per Lord Ellenborough C.J. in *Fowler v Homer* (1812) 3 Camp. 294 at 295.

[345] *Force v Warren* (1864) 15 C.B.(N S.) 806; *Collins v Cooper* (1902) 19 T.L.R. 118 CA; *Amann v Damm* (1860) 8 C.B. (N.S.) 597 (approach to suspect's employer).

[346] *Kine v Sewell* (1838) 3 M. & W. 297. See also *Kleinhaus v Usmar* (1929) A.D. 127; *Van Zyle v Erasmus* [1938] E.D.L. 185.

[347] (1902) 19 T.L.R. 118 CA.

"an employer is entitled to make a bona fide investigation of alleged dishonesty or other misconduct among his employees . . . and should not be penalised for communications made to his employees supposed to have knowledge of such matters where they are made in good faith and for the honest purpose of discovering the truth or of protecting the business."[348]

The privilege is not confined to the victim of the crime: it may extend to someone who reasonably becomes involved in the inquiry, e.g. a police officer[349] or the occupier of the premises where the alleged theft takes place. In *Henderson v Patrick Thomson*[350] the pursuer came into the millinery department of the defenders' shop and tried on a hat. When she left, a lady, beside whom she had been standing, alleged that her purse had been stolen. The manager of the department followed the pursuer downstairs, and before she had left the shop informed her of the alleged theft, and told her that she would have to come back and clear herself. The pursuer returned with the manager to the millinery department and was there confronted with the lady and questioned by the manager. In an action for slander it was held that the questions were asked on a privileged occasion, and, as there was no averment of malice, the action must be dismissed.

Reply to demand. Where a person receives a letter making a demand, such   **14.50** as one threatening him with legal proceedings unless he settles an account or apologises for a slander alleged to have been uttered by him, he is entitled to state his reasons for refusing to comply with the demand, and his reply will be privileged provided the statements it contains are made in good faith and are "relevant to the matter in hand".[351]

A strong example is *Stevens v Kitchener*.[352] P, a doctor, had attended D's wife in her confinement. The wife and her sister contracted scarlet fever, as the result of which the wife died. P's solicitor wrote to D for the fees. D wrote in answer to the letter saying that P had no claim "as through his carelessness he caused Mrs. Kitchener's death and also the illness of her sister," and concluded: "I shall never pay him unless the law compels me, and that I do not fancy it can as I could more easily indict Dr. Stevens for manslaughter." It was held that the letter was written on a privileged occasion and was confined to

---

[348] *Montgomery Co. v Watson*, 55 F.2d 184 at 187 (CA 4 1932); *Kroger Grocery v Yount*, 66 F.2d 700 (CA 8 1933).

[349] *LVMH Watch & Jewellery Australia Pty Limited v Michael Lassanah* [2011] NSWCA 370. If the claim was brought in England against the police authority as employer of the police officers, the police authority as a public authority would only be able to rely on qualified privilege if it could show that it had acted compatibly with the art.8 rights of those to whom the information relates, and must satisfy a proportionality test. See further, para.14.5, above.

[350] 1911 1 S.L.T. 284.

[351] *Sayer v Begg* (1864) 15 Ir.C.L. R. 458; *Jacob v Lawrence* (1879) 4 L.R. Ir. 579 at 584; *Hobbs v Bryers* (1878) 2 L.R. Ir. 496 at 499; *Stevens v Kitchener* (1887) 4 T.L.R. 159; *Laidlaw v Gunn* (1890) 17 R. 394; *Sherrif v Denholm* (1898) 15 S.L.T. 234 at 346; *Campbell v Cochrane* (1906) 8 F. 205; *Hanton v Hatje* (1907) 15 S.L.T. 531; *Ward v Mcintyre* (1920) 48 N.B.R. 233; *Hussey v Bank of Australasia* (1889) 15 V.L.R. 9.

[352] (1887) 4 T.L.R. 159.

the matter in hand. Similarly, in *Campbell v Cochrane*,[353] where P had instructed his law agent to claim damages for wrongful dismissal from D, statements by D to the agent that P had been dismissed for theft were privileged.

14.51 Reply to attack. Similar to the principle in the last paragraph is one whereby a person whose character or conduct has been attacked[354] is entitled to answer such attack, and any defamatory statements he may make about the person who attacked him will be privileged, provided they are published bona fide and are fairly relevant to the accusations made.[355] Whether this form of privilege extends to a statement in rebuttal of an anticipated attack is not clear. Sir Maurice Drake held that it did in *Bhatt v Chelsea and Westminster NHS Trust*,[356] but this was doubted by Bean J. in *Bento v The Chief Constable of Bedfordshire Police*[357]: "I can see no policy reason to extend qualified privilege to people who believe they are about to be criticised and decide to get their public retaliation in first."[358] However, even if *Bhatt* was correctly decided, Bean J. held that the principle must be confined to cases where the defamatory statement was both: (1) in reasonable anticipation of an imminent attack on the conduct of the maker of the statement[359]; and (2) limited to a proportionate rebuttal of that anticipated attack.[360]

> "The law justifies a man in repelling a libellous charge by a denial or an explanation. He has a qualified privilege to answer the charge; and if he does so in good faith, and what he publishes is fairly an answer,[361] and is published for the purpose of repelling the charge, and not with malice, it is privileged, though it be false."[362]

---

[353] (1906) 8 F. 205. See also *Meekins v Henson* [1964] 1 Q.B. 472 (reply to accusation of responsibility for delay in settling accounts).

[354] There is no privilege however, where the claimant has merely provoked controversy, without making an attack: *Church of Scientology v Anderson* [1980] W.A.R. at 81 (reversed on other grounds [1981] W.A.R. 279).

[355] See also paras 14.67–14.68, below. A challenge to sue does not exclude a plea of privilege if action is brought: *Penton v Calwell* (1945) 70 C.L.R. 219.

[356] Unreported, October 16, 1997.

[357] [2012] EWHC 1525 (QB). See also, para.14.37, above.

[358] [2012] EWHC 1525 (QB) at [103].

[359] If the defendant is mistaken that he is danger of an imminent attack, it is suggested, by analogy with self-defence in the tort of trespass to the person, that a defendant can only rely on the privilege if his mistake is an honest and reasonable one in all the circumstances: an honest but unreasonable belief is not enough (*Ashley v Chief Constable of Sussex Police* [2008] UKHL 25, [2008] 2 W.L.R. 975 HL).

[360] Ibid. at [104].

[361] D newspaper defames C. C sues D and recovers damages. D then repeats the allegations. D cannot rely on this head of privilege by contending that what it has said is a reply to attacks made on him by C's counsel (under protection of absolute privilege) in the trial: *Baldwin v Rusbridger* [2001] E.M.L.R. 47.

[362] Per curiam in *Brewer v Chase*, 80 N.W. 575 at 577 (Mich., 1899). For the US cases, see *Dickens v International Brotherhood of Teamsters*, 171 F.2d 21 (D.C. App. 1948); *Reynolds v Pegler*, 223 F.2d 429 (C.A.2 1955) and 41 A.L.R. 3d 1083. *Botiuk v Candian Free Press* (1995) 126 D.L.R. (4th) 609, SCC is a Canadian example of excessive response.

"The defendant would be entitled to protect his reputation by a proportionate response which was appropriate both in terms of subject matter and scale of publication. In order for a defendant to avail himself of this form of privilege, the response should not go into irrelevant matters or, in particular, cross over into an attack on the integrity of the claimant if it is not reasonably necessary for defending his own reputation."[363]

"The foundation of the privilege is the necessity of allowing the party attacked free scope to place his case before the body whose judgment the attacking party has sought to affect . . . The purpose is to prevent the charges operating to his prejudice. It may be conceded that to impugn the truth of the charges contained in the attack and even the general veracity of the attacker may be a proper exercise of the privilege, if it be commensurate with the occasion. If that is a question submitted to or an argument used before the body to whom the attacker has appealed and it is done bona fide for the purpose of vindication, the law will not allow the liability of the party attacked to depend on the truth or otherwise of defamatory statements he so makes by way of defence."[364]

Mere retaliation, which cannot be described as an answer or explanation, is not protected,[365] but the defendant is not required to be diffident in protecting himself and is allowed a considerable degree of latitude in this respect[366] and the law does not concern itself with niceties in such matters.[367] Thus in *Mengi v Hermitage*[368] the defendant was held to be able to rely on the privilege notwithstanding that she had "replied" more than once to the attack. Bean J. held that provided the responses were reasonable, proportionate and relevant there is no rule of English law that restricts the defendant to one response.[369] The central difficulty here is to distinguish between mere retaliation and attacking the credibility of your opponent in legitimate self-defence.[370] The longer the time between the attack and the reply, the more likely that the

---

[363] *Hamilton v Clifford* [2004] EWHC 1542 (QB) at [65] per Eady J.

[364] *Penton v Calwell* [1945] HCA 51; (1945) 70 C.L.R. 219 at 242–243. Referred to with approval by the High Court of Australia in *Harbour Radio Pty Ltd v Trad* [2012] HCA 44.

[365] *Brewer v Chase* at 577. See *Whitaker v Huntington* (1980) 15 C.C.L.T. 19; *Bennett v Stupich* (1981) 125 D.L.R. (3d) 743.

[366] *Watts v Times Newspapers* [1997] Q.B. 650 CA. It seems that the same is true for the ECtHR: *Sanocki v Poland*, July 17, 2007, App. no.28949/03 at [65].

"La Cour considère qu'alors que la liberté d'expression d'un journaliste comprend le recours possible à une dose d'exagération, voire même de provocation . . . un homme politique qui répond par la voie de la presse à des critiques émises à son encontre doit pouvoir le faire selon les mêmes principes."

[367] Per Lord Oaksey in *Turner v MGM Pictures* [1950]1 All E.R. 449 at 470–471. See further para.14.68, below.

[368] [2012] EWHC 3445 (QB).

[369] Ibid. at [102]–[103]. Cf. *Heytesbury Holdings Pty Ltd v City of Subiaco and Costa* [1998] WASC 183 (Defendant council under attack from the claimants had responded twice over a three day period in newspaper articles and five days later issued a news release to similar effect. Steytler J. held that the news release was not privileged as it was not issued with the purpose of vindicating their reputation: "[It] was merely a further shot in the battle which shot had been provoked, to some extent at least, by the [first article]. It did not thing new to vindicate the character or action of the [defendants]" (at 83). In *Mengi*, Bean J. held that to the extent Steytler J. intended to lay down a rule of law that the person replying to an attack has only one shot in response to each "salvo" from the attacker, it did not represent English law (at [103]).

[370] See paras 14.67, 14.68, below.

response will be treated as retaliation. Thus in *Henry v BBC*,[371] one of the reasons for rejecting the claim to privilege was that the response was made a year after the attack and in the circumstances this was too long.[372]

For the privilege to apply the defendant must actually be replying to an attack either on himself or his opinions.[373] The attack need not, however, be a direct one: an indirect attack whether by hints, suggestions or implications may also legitimise a response.[374] That a person comments on a matter of public interest in which the defendant has been involved by denying his personal responsibility or defending his own competence in the matter does not necessarily mean that he is attacking the defendant.[375] Nor will the defendant be able to avail himself of the defence where the claimant was merely provoking general controversy or "holding forth" about matters of public interest without targeting the defendant. There must be something in the nature of a charge against, or assault on, the character, integrity, good faith or reputation of the defendant for the defence to apply.[376]

If the defendant is responding to an attack which he knows to be justified he is guilty of malice,[377] though the view has also been expressed that in such a case one might equally well say that there was no privileged occasion.[378]

14.52 Reply to retort. A publishes words which B considers defame him. B publishes a response in self-defence. A then publishes further defamatory material, purportedly by way of rejoinder to B's response. It has been held in Australia that A's second publication is not protected by qualified privilege because (1) it would inhibit B's right of self-defence, since by exercising it he would be laying himself open to further privileged attacks; and (2) assuming the original attack to be unjustified, A would be gaining a benefit from his own wrong.[379]

---

[371] [2005] EWHC 2787 (QB).

[372] Cf. *Mengi v Hermitage* [2012] EWHC 3445 (QB) in which it was held that a delay between the "attack" and the response of over two years did not prevent the defendants from being able to rely on the privilege. On the facts of the case, it was unsurprising that the defendants had not "dared" to respond until they had left Tanzania and were back in the safety of the United Kingdom. The further delay after leaving Tanzania was explained by the breakdown in one of the defendant's health.

[373] *Blackwell v News Group Newspapers Ltd* [2007] EWHC 3098 (QB) per Eady J. at [7]; *Vassiliev v Frank Cass & Co* [2003] EWHC 1428 (QB); [2003] E.M.L.R. 33; *Watts v Times Newspapers* [1997] Q.B. 650 CA.

[374] *Campbell v Safra* [2006] EWHC 819, at [23] (QB).

[375] *Blackwell v News Group Newspapers Ltd* [2007] EWHC 3098 (QB).

[376] Ibid.

[377] *Fraser-Armstrong v Hadow & Nelson* [1995] E.M.L.R. 140 CA per Staughton L.J. at 143; *Oliver v Chief Constable of Northumbria* [2003] EWHC 2417 (QB); [2004] E.M.L.R. 32.

[378] Simon Brown L.J. in *Fraser-Armstrong v Hadow & Nelson*, above at 143.

[379] *Kennett v Farmer* [1988] V.R. 991; *Amalgamated Television Services Pty Ltd v Marsden* [2002] NSWCA 419 (where, however, the defendant was a media "bystander"). *Kennett v Farmer* is considered in *Echo Publications Pty Ltd v Tucker* [2007] NSWCA 73. While Hodgson J.A. accepted that, in at least some cases, a "riposte to a response" would not have the benefit of qualified privilege, the limits of this had not been clearly established, particularly in view of the

Reply to attack in media. While before *Reynolds v Times Newspapers*   **14.53**
Ltd[380] a publication in the mass media would not often be protected by
privilege at common law because the communication would reach a large
number of people with no legally recognised interest in the matter, it has
always been an important qualification to this that a person whose character
or conduct has been attacked in the public press is entitled to have recourse to
the press in his defence and vindication. If, in answering such attack, he makes
relevant[381] defamatory statements about the person who has attacked him,
such statements are prima facie privileged.[382]

Although *Reynolds* made a considerable extension of qualified privilege for
statements published in the media, this category of privilege remains significant because under *Reynolds* the defendant will have to satisfy certain
additional conditions (beyond honesty) before privilege will arise.[383]

By way of an example of a privileged reply to an attack in the press, where
the plaintiff published in a local paper an article charging the defendant, who
was parliamentary candidate for the county of Waterford, with harsh and
tyrannical conduct towards his tenants and particularly towards himself, a
former tenant, and the defendant wrote and published in the same paper, by
way of answer to the article and in vindication of his character, a letter
containing reflections on the character of the plaintiff, such letter, being an
answer to the attack, and relevant thereto, was privileged.[384]

> "Where a party publishes charges affecting the conduct and character of another, the
> public at large have, as against him, such a right of judgment upon those charges as
> render that public interested in anything material to their judgment being just and
> true, and the party aggrieved, having an interest in vindicating his character, has a
> privilege to publish matter of vindication and defence, and all such matter as is
> material to the public forming, such just and true judgment."[385]

The privilege attaches even though the claimant did not write in his own
name.

> "A person libelling another in the public Press cannot by sheltering himself under
> anonymity, or under the name of another, abridge the right of his adversary to defend

---

possible practical difficulties of establishing the actionability of the initial publication. See also,
French v Herald and Weekly Times Pty Ltd [2010] VSC 155.

[380] See para.15.1, below.

[381] As to relevance and how far one may counterattack, see paras 14.67, 14.68, below.

[382] *Hemmings v Gasson* (1858) E.B. & E. 346; *O'Donoghue v Hussey* (1871) Ir. R.5 C.L. 124;
Laughton v Bishop of Sodor and Man (1872) L.R. 4 P.C. 495 at 504; *Dwyer v Esmonde* (1878)
2 L.R.Ir. 243 at 252; *Gray v SPCA* (1890) 17 R. 1185; *Nevin v Roddy* [1935] Ir.R.397 CA; *Wilson
v Deane* (1910) 3 Alberta R. 186; *Mallett v Clarke* (1968) 70 D.L.R. (2d) 67; *Daniel v Mt. Allison
University* (1976) 15 N.B.R. (2d) 373; *Wooding v Little* (1982) 24 C.C.L.T. 37; *Loveday v Sun
Newspapers* (1938) 59 C.L.R. 503; *Penton v Calwell* (1945) 70 C.L.R. 219.

[383] See *Alexander v Arts Council of Wales* [2001] EWCA Civ 514; [2001] 1 W.L.R. 1840,
though Eady J. below preferred to rest the privilege on a duty to explain to the public.

[384] *Dwyer v Esmonde* (1878) 2 L.R.Ir. 243.

[385] *Dwyer v Esmonde* (1877) Ir. R. 11 C.L. 542.

himself. The privilege arises not from the use of the plaintiff's name but from the appeal to the public having been made by him".[386]

In answering an attack made upon his character the defendant should only resort to the press if such attack was made upon him in the press or in public. If it is made in private before two or three persons only, the defendant has no right "to enlarge the constituency" and publish his defence to the general public through the newspapers, and if he does so his answer will not be privileged.[387] It is necessary to show that the defendant responded on an appropriate scale and went no further than was necessary for legitimate defence.[388]

The privilege of a person whose character or conduct has been attacked in the public press to reply to such attacks extends to protect the newspaper which publishes his reply; and in the absence of proved malice neither will be held liable in damages.[389]

> "A privilege would be of no value if the means of exercising it were not also protected. If the party attacked is given a privilege to reply through the public press, the publisher . . . must also enjoy an attendant privilege."[390]

In the older cases the standard pattern was that A published an attack on B in newspaper X and B then responded in kind. However, in *Loveday v Sun Newspapers Ltd*,[391] it was held to make no difference that the newspaper sought B's response first and published it along with A's attack. That situation is now commoner in the broadcast media, where a programme on a controversial issue is likely to be prepared over a period of time; indeed, in such cases the role of the media organ has changed from being a mere conduit for the transmission of the remarks of the two protagonists and it may instigate the confrontation by approaching the person who makes the initial attack.

> "(It) has complete control, not only over the 'playing field', but also over the material included in the programme. The editing can tilt the 'playing field' in favour of one party or the other. The station can select the weakest part of the attack and the strongest part of the reply or vice versa. Its control over the programme enables it to select the party who will be the attacker and the party who will be the target, and bestow qualified privilege on the party of its choice."[392]

---

[386] Per Palles B., ibid. at 550.

[387] *Murphy v Halpin* (1874) Ir.R. 8 C.L. 127, distinguished in *Nevin v Roddy* [1935] Ir.R. 397; *Hopewell v Kennedy* (1904) 9 O.L.R. 43 at 48; *Oei v Ban* [2005] SGCA 35; [2005] 3 S.L.R. 608.

[388] *Campbell v Safra* [2006] EWHC 819 (QB) at [23]. See also *Vassiliev v Frank Cass & Co. Ltd* [2003] EWHC 1428 (QB); [2003] E.M.L.R. 33 and *Fraser-Armstrong v Hadow* [1995] E.M.L.R. 140 (QB).

[389] As to malice in this context, see para.17.22, below.

[390] *Loveday v Sun Newspapers Ltd* (1938) 59 C.L.R. 503 at 519, per Dixon J.

[391] See previous footnote.

[392] *Bass v TCN Channel Nine Pty Ltd* [2003] NSWCA 118, per Handley J.A.

Nevertheless it has been held the media organ retains its derivative privilege in such cases. Inversion of the natural roles of "attacker" and "respondent", or manipulation of the content of the programme so as to produce a one-sided picture are matters which go to malice.[393] Such situations might now fall more easily under the reportage form of privilege stemming from *Reynolds v Times Newspapers*, which requires fair and disinterested reporting.[394]

Responses to attacks on others. The privilege here discussed is not   **14.54**
confined to attacks on the defendant, but extends to action taken by him to defend his family, friends,[395] or even employees.[396] In *Bowen-Rowlands v Argus Press*[397] the defendants, in a newspaper review of a book written by the plaintiff, quoted from the book a story told by the plaintiff about A, a well-known public man then deceased, which story, if not actually defamatory of A, was clearly calculated to injure his daughter's feelings. A's daughter wrote a letter to the defendants in which she said that the story was "pure invention from beginning to end; it is absolutely false both as to matter and manner". The defendants published this letter, without comment, in their newspaper. The plaintiff brought an action for libel alleging that the publication of this letter imputed that he had invented the story and told a deliberate lie, and was a slur upon his character as an author. It was held by the Court of Appeal that the letter, even if defamatory of the plaintiff, was published on a privileged occasion, for A's daughter was entitled to contradict the story, and the defendants were entitled to publish such contradiction in their columns. However, where the plaintiff had been accused of criminal conduct by X under cover of Parliamentary privilege and made a vigorous public denial,

---

[393] *Bass v TCN Channel Nine Pty Ltd*, above. It may be a difficult question where the line is to be drawn between this type of case and one falling under the *Reynolds* privilege (para.15.1, below) where a newspaper or other media organ may be required to publish the response of a person about whom it publishes defamatory material. That response may be an imputation that the newspaper's source has lied: see, e.g. *Milne v Telegraph Group Ltd* [2001] E.M.L.R. 30 (where, however, qualified privilege was waived).

[394] See para.15.18, below.

[395] *Vassiliev v Frank Cass & Co. Ltd* [2003] EWHC 1428 (QB); [2003] E.M.L.R. 33. In *Vassiliev*, the claimant wrote a book in which he alleged that H, who had been accused during his lifetime of being a Soviet spy, was indeed a spy. H had died before the book was published still protesting his innocence. The defendant, a publisher of a specialist academic journal, published a peer-reviewed article by L, a professional historian and long-term friend of H. The article questioned the reliability of the new evidence put forward by some commentators and in particular argued that the Russian documents relied on by the claimant did not support the proposition that H was a spy. On the question of qualified privilege, Eady J. held that the publication was protected as a reply to an attack. The claimant had, in effect, thrown down a gauntlet to H's friends and supporters and in the circumstances it was entirely reasonable for L to respond. See also, *French v Herald and Weekly Times Pty Ltd* [2010] VSC 155 at [62] (though on the facts the statement was a reply to questions rather than a response to an attack).

[396] *Oliver v Chief Constable of Northumbria Police* [2003] EWHC 2417 (QB); [2004] E.M.L.R. 32.

[397] *The Times*, February 10 and March 26, 1926, explained: *Standen v South Essex Recorders* (1934) 50 T.L.R. 365; see also *Wright v Gladstone, The Times*, February 4, 1927. the facts of which are set out in para.17.14, below; *Israel v Portland News*, 53 P.2d 529 (Or., 1936).

calling for X to be dismissed, a television company which broadcast a programme containing similar allegations could not claim privilege on the ground that it was "defending" X, nor upon the basis that it had a "duty" to inform the public so as to enable it to know where the truth lay in relation to the assertions of X and the plaintiff.[398] As to the latter, of course, there might be circumstances in which privilege might be claimed on the alternative basis of *Reynolds v Times Newspapers Ltd*[399] if the requirements of that case could be met.

14.55 Defence of property. The privilege is not confined to statements made in answer to an attack on personal character. A statement made by a person bona fide and without malice in defence of his property against injurious statements concerning it is also privileged.[400]

14.56 Redress of grievances. Where a person believes that he has suffered a grievance at the hands of another, he is entitled to bring his grievance to the notice of the person or body whose power or duty it is to grant redress or to punish or reprimand the offender, or merely to inquire into the subject-matter of the complaint,[401] and any statement so made is privileged, if made in good faith and not for the purpose of defaming the claimant.[402]

> "If, without express malice, I make a defamatory charge, which I bona fide believe to be true, against one whose conduct in the respect defamed has caused me injury, to one whose duty it is . . . to inquire into and redress such injury, the occasion is privileged."[403]

Thus privilege was held to apply to a petition addressed to the Secretary of War by the creditor of an army officer complaining of unjust conduct on the part of the officer, and seeking, through the action of the Secretary, payment of a debt due by him.[404] It is not, however, enough that the defendant believes he is warranted in addressing his complaint to the quarter in which he does so.

---

[398] *Amalgamated Television Services Pty Ltd v Marsden* [2002] NSWCA 419.

[399] See para.15.1, below.

[400] *Norton v Hoare (No.1)* (1913) 17 C.L.R. 310.

[401] See *Adoko v Lewis* [2002] EWHC 848 (QB) (complaint to ISP about website of claimant containing allegations about defendant). As is so often the case with qualified privilege, there is no sharp line between this and the "attack" category.

[402] *R. v Bayley* (1735) 5 Bac.Abr. 199; *R. v Baille* (1778) 21 How. St. Tr. 1; *Fairman v Ives* (1822) 5 B. & Ald. 642; *Woodward v Lander* (1834) 6 C. & P. 548 at 550; *Rogers v Spalding* (1844) 1 Up.Can.Q.B. 258; *Des Barres v Tremaine* (1883) 16 N.S.R. 215. Where the claimant holds public office or has authority over or responsibilities to the public, this head of privilege overlaps with that discussed in para.14.59, below because it is not possible in practice to draw a sharp distinction between those who act out of public spirit or in protection of their own interests.

[403] *Waring v M'Caldin* (1873) Ir.R. 7 C.L. 282 at 288; *Fairman v Ives* (1822) 5 B. & Ald. 642 at 648.

[404] *Fairman v Ives* (1822) 5 B. & Ald. 642; *Winstanley v Bampton* [1943] K.B. 319 (where malice was shown). See also *R. v Baillie* (1778) 21 How.St.Tr.1.

In modern conditions it is submitted that a person is not necessarily entitled to complain to the claimant's employer about a private debt.[405]

Defence of principal's interests. There is a general principle that an   **14.57**
agent acting on behalf of his principal shares any privilege his principal has with regard to the occasion. Similarly, there is an independent privilege for any statement made by an agent bona fide for the protection of the rights or interests,[406] or in defence of the character of his principal.[407] Thus, no action will lie against a solicitor for any relevant defamatory statements contained in a letter written by him in the ordinary course of his duty to his client unless express malice is proved.[408] "If a communication made by a solicitor to a third party is reasonably necessary and usual in the discharge of his duty to his client, the occasion is privileged."[409] So where a solicitor, in vindication of the character of a client and in answer to certain charges of conspiracy preferred against him, wrote and published a letter which contained very defamatory imputations on the prosecutor and among them one of perjury, it was ruled by Cockburn C.J. that:

> "if the jury were of opinion that the defendant wrote and published the letter honestly and for the vindication of his client's character, and in answer to the charges published and mentioned against him, then the occasion was privileged or protected; and if the jury were further of opinion that the terms of the letter were such as under all circumstances might well be deemed warranted then the publication would be protected."[410]

The solicitor is not personally responsible for the truth of statements made to him on the authority of his client[411]; he has a right to advise and act upon such

---

[405] So *Wong Sui Fung v Yip Siu Keung* [2003] HKEC 1711, Ct of First Instance would probably be decided differently here (complaint by neighbour to plaintiff's superior about un-neighbourly behaviour and non-payment of management fees).

[406] *Hargrave v Le Breton* (1769) 4 Burr. 2423; *Steward v Young* (1870) L.R. 5 C.P. 122; *Baker v Carrick* [1894] 1 Q.B. 838; *Hyver Holdings v Schilling & Lom* (1996) (unreported, LTA 95/6425/E, CA).

[407] *R. v Veley* (1867) 4 F. & F. 1117; *Penton v Calwell* (1945) 70 C.L.R. 219 at 242–243. See also *Khader v Aziz* [2010] EWCA Civ 716; [2011] E.M.L.R. 2.

[408] *Wright v Woodgate* (1835) 2 C.M. & R. 573; *Stephens v Lowndes*, *The Times*, April 22, 1886; *Boxsius v Goblet Freres* [1894] 1 Q.B. 842 CA; *Watts v Times Newspapers* [1997] Q.B. 650 CA. See also *Longdon-Griffiths v Smith* [1951] 1 K.B. 295 at 303; *Egger v Chelmsford* [1965] 1 Q.B. 248 at 261. In Scotland, where a solicitor writes a letter on the instructions or on behalf of his client, any pertinent statements which he may bona fide make in his client's interests will be privileged: *Ramsey v Nairne* (1833) 11 Shaw 1033 at 1045; *Crawford v Dunlop* (1900) 2 F. 987.

[409] Per Lopes L.J. in *Boxsius v Goblet Freres* [1894] 1 Q.B. 842 CA at 846; *Baker v Carrick* [1894]1 Q.B. 838 CA.

[410] *R. v Veley* (1867) 4 F. & F. 1117 at 1122.

[411] It has been suggested that there is no privilege if he personally adopts and corroborates the charge his client makes: per Lords Trayner and Moncreiff, in *Crawford v Dunlop* (1900) 2 F. 987 at 997, 998. On this case, see *Regan v Taylor* [2000] E.M.L.R. 549 CA.

information as his client reveals to him[412]; but if he knows that his client's statements are false and that he has no just claim, he will not be protected.[413] A solicitor must not make himself "a conduit pipe for every defamatory allegation of a chagrined or indignant client . . . he is bound to exclude anything defamatory that is not relevant to the occasion".[414]

Although everything depends upon the terms of his retainer, it is likely in modern conditions that where the client is engaged in litigation or under attack a solicitor will be treated as having the authority of the client to make statements to the media in defence of the client's interests which are not explicitly authorised by the client and which contain matter derived from the solicitor's own experience.[415] In *Regan v Taylor*[416] the claimant magazine editor sued in respect of a statement in the press made by the defendant, solicitor for A, A having been accused in the magazine of involvement in sexual abuse and to be subject to prosecution for rape of a minor. The defendant's statement said that A was considering criminal libel proceedings because there was no purpose claiming damages for civil libel against the magazine, which consistently claimed to have no money, and that criminal libel was the only remedy against the organisation, who simply sought publicity for themselves, were not interested in accuracy even less fair reporting and were a disgrace to the profession of journalism. The Court of Appeal, by a majority,[417] upheld Gray J.'s decision to grant summary judgment to the defendant under CPR Pt 24 since the statement was made on a privileged occasion, being a frank answer to a question by the journalist as to why criminal libel proceedings were contemplated and there was no evidence of malice.

14.58 Apology. A defendant who has defamed another may apologise, but it may be that the apology defames someone else.[418] If this is done by means of a statement in open court[419] (which has to be approved by a judge, who may hear third parties[420]) it is protected by absolute privilege. In some other cases

---

[412] A attacks the character of B. B responds by way of defence in a manner which is defamatory of A, but B knows the charge against him is well-founded. B is not protected by privilege because he is malicious: see para.14.51, above. But suppose B's response is delivered via his agent C, who is unaware of the truth. The "correct analysis would almost certainly be" that C would be protected by privilege: *Richardson v Schwarzenegger* [2004] EWHC 2422 (QB) at [14] (the assumption in *Hamilton v Clifford* [2004] EWHC 1542 (QB) at [79] may be to the contrary but *Richardson* is more in accord with general principle about malice).

[413] *Stockley v Hornidge* (1837) 8 C. & P. 11; *McKeogh v O'Brien Moran* [1927] Ir.R. 348.

[414] *McKeogh v O'Brien Moran* [1927] Ir.R. 348 at 359.

[415] *Khader v Aziz* [2010] EWCA Civ 716; [2011] E.M.L.R. 2 at [19].

[416] [2000] E.M.L.R. 549 CA. Contrast *Hamilton v Clifford* [2004] EWHC 1542 (QB) at [79] where the court refused to allow a repetition of the defamatory words of another to be dressed up as an act in protection of the reputation of the other.

[417] Chadwick L.J. dissented because he considered that the decision would expose the client to an unreasonable liability if the solicitor misjudged how far he could go.

[418] See, e.g. *Tracy v Kemsley, The Times*, April 9, 1954.

[419] PD 53 para.6.2. See para.29.10, below (more correctly now "statement in court").

[420] *Watts v Times Newspapers* [1997] Q.B. 650 CA at 669.

there may be a qualified privilege, for example where A publishes material defamatory of B in a newspaper and the newspaper, in apologising to B, makes statements which are critical of A.[421] However, no privilege was established in *Watts v Times Newspapers*.[422] The newspaper published two pieces concerning alleged plagiarism by P in a novel written by him. The second piece was accompanied by a photograph which was in fact of a property developer, X, with the same name. X demanded that an apology be published in the newspaper and this, which was essentially dictated by X, contained a further reference to plagiarism by P. A simple apology which made no further reference to P was, in the view of the Court of Appeal, all that it was necessary for the newspaper to provide in protection of its interests against a potential suit by X. In an action by P against the newspaper on the apology, X's solicitors were joined as third parties and it was held that X's participation in the publication (and therefore that of the solicitors acting on his behalf) was privileged since he was responding to an attack on him by the newspaper and whether the publication was "warranted by the occasion" was to be judged by the liberal standards which are applied to statements made in self-defence.[423] However, it was necessary to consider the position of the newspaper separately and it had no privilege: (1) as the perpetrator of the libel on X, it could not rely on the privilege based on self-defence; (2) the simple, unembellished apology was sufficient; (3) while the newspaper no doubt had a financial interest in the speedy settlement of the dispute with X and the reduction in its risk of exposure to damages, that could not be the basis of a privilege because there was no reciprocity of interest in this respect with the readers, the problem stemmed from the newspaper's own wrong and the interest was, in comparison with the harm to P, modest.[424]

---

[421] *Oversea Chinese Banking Corp v Wright Norman* [1994] 3 S.L.R. 760, where, however, the statement was held not to be defamatory of A.

[422] [1997] Q.B. 650 CA.

[423] See para.14.51, above.

[424] Times Newspapers Ltd (TNL) went to Strasbourg. In *Times Newspapers Ltd v UK* App. No.31811/96; (1997) 23 E.H.R.R. CD200 the European Commission of Human Rights held inadmissible TNL's complaint that the Court of Appeal's refusal to afford a defence of common law qualified privilege for its bona fide apology to the developer was in violation of art.10 of the Convention. Additionally the Commission found that there was no violation of arts 13 and 14 of the Convention when read in conjunction with art.10:

"A newspaper publishing an apology is not in the same position as the plaintiff to defamation proceedings (or his solicitor) who drafts such an apology: whilst the newspaper is under its ordinary duty to check its facts before publishing, the aggrieved plaintiff is, reasonably, entitled to express his opinions in more robust terms, and still to benefit from qualified privilege because it is in the public interest that a person should have a right to reply to rebut an accusation made against him. Moreover, the ultimate decision as to whether to publish the apology rests solely with the newspaper, which may prefer to have the matter settled in court if the demands being made are in its opinion unreasonable having regard to its duties and responsibilities". (at [2])

Further, TNL was not in a "relevantly similar" situation to the plaintiff (and his solicitors), and there was therefore no discrimination within the meaning of Article 14 of the Convention.

(c) *Complaints about public officers, persons in authority or with responsibilities towards the public*

14.59 Complaints and redress. Just as statements made in order to recover stolen property or find a criminal may be seen as made out of duty and in aid of public justice or in furtherance of the interests of the victim,[425] so too complaints about the conduct of those in authority or with responsibilities to the public may be seen as made from a duty to bring the facts to the attention of those who control or are concerned with the conduct in question, or in furtherance of the interests of those affected in securing redress. They are treated here separately only for convenience and the precise basis of duty or interest is immaterial. What is certain is that the law is liberal in protecting such communications, if they are made bona fide, and to a person with a proper interest in the subject-matter.

Thus, it is not only for the victim, in his own interests, but it is the duty of everyone, in the interests of public efficiency and good order, to bring any misconduct or neglect of duty on the part of a public officer or employee, or any public abuse, to the notice of the proper authority for investigation. Any complaint or information as to such misconduct, neglect of duty, or abuse is privileged, provided it is made in good faith to the person or body who has the power or duty to remove, punish or reprimand the offender, or merely to inquire into the subject-matter of the complaint.[426] Any citizen who bona fide believes that wrong has been done has the right and duty to bring the alleged fact before the proper authority for investigation.[427] In doing so he exercises an undoubted privilege which it is not in the public interest to penalise.[428]

14.60 *Harrison v Bush.* In *Harrison v Bush*[429] the defendant, an elector and inhabitant of a borough, bona fide signed (with other persons) and sent to the Home Secretary a memorial complaining of the conduct of the plaintiff, a magistrate for the county in which the borough was situate. The memorial imputed that the plaintiff had made speeches inciting to a breach of the peace, and, after reading the Riot Act, had given orders to a man to strike a person in the streets. It prayed that the Home Secretary would cause an inquiry into the plaintiff's conduct, and recommend the Queen to remove him from the

---

[425] See para.14.37, above.

[426] *Harrison v Bush* (1855) 5 E. & B. 344; *Woodward v Lander* (1834) 6 C. & P. 548; *Rogers v Spalding* (1844) 1 Up.Can.Q.B. 258; *Sutton v Plumridge* (1867) 16 L.T. 741; *Proctor v Webster* (1885) 16 Q.B.D. 112 at 114; *Beach v Freeson* [1972] 1 Q.B. 14.

[427] Per Lord Dundas in *Couper v Lord Balfour*, 1913 S.C. 492 at 501.

[428] Per Lord Salvesen, ibid. at 504; *Mowlds v Fergusson* (1940) 64 C.L.R. 206; *Somerville v Cliff* (1942) 15 L.G.R. 40 (N.S.W.).

[429] (1855) 5 E. & B. 344, followed in *R. v Rule* [1937] 2 K.B. 375. In *Mann v O'Neill* (1997) 191 C.L.R. 204 HCA, it was conceded that letters to the Federal Attorney-General and Minister of Justice complaining that the plaintiff, a special magistrate, was suffering from senile dementia, were the subject of qualified privilege. The defendant unsuccessfully contended that they were the subject of absolute privilege.

commission of the peace, should the allegations in the memorial be substantiated and verified. It was held that the memorial was privileged. "If", said Lord Campbell C.J.:

> "Dr. Harrison had so misconducted himself as a magistrate, he had committed an offence; and it was the *duty* of those who witnessed it to try by all reasonable means in their power that it should be inquired into and punished . . . In this land of law and liberty all who are aggrieved may seek redress, and the alleged misconduct of any who are clothed with public authority may be brought to the notice of those who have the power and the duty to inquire into it and to take steps which may prevent the repetition of it."[430]

Examples.[431] So, a letter written to the Postmaster-General or to the Secretary of the General Post Office complaining of the conduct of a postmaster,[432] or post office employee,[433] or to a Member of Parliament by one of his constituents asking for his assistance in bringing to the notice of the appropriate Minister a complaint of improper conduct in relation to his office of some public official in the constituency,[434] or to the chief constable concerning the conduct of a police officer,[435] or to a bishop as to the conduct of or as   **14.61**

---

[430] (1855) 5 E. & B. 344 at 349.

[431] Although this class of qualified privilege is recognised by the common law in the United States (see, e.g. *Hathaway v Bruggink* 170 N.W. 244 (Wis., 1919) (failure to enforce liquor laws); *Dempsky v Double*, 126 A 2d 915 (Pa., 1956) (corruption in local government); *Swaaley v US*, 376 F.2d (Ct of Claims 1967) (procedures in Navy shipyards); Restatement 2d, *Torts* para.598) the matter is complicated by the First Amendment protection given after *NY Times v Sullivan*, 376 U.S. 254 (1964) (see para.15.31, below) to statements about "public officials" and "public figures". Under this, the plaintiff must prove that the defendant knew the statement was untrue or was (subjectively) reckless as to its truth or falsity. Despite a somewhat confusing tendency (see *Masson v New Yorker Magazine*, 501 U.S. 416 (1991)) to refer to this as "actual malice" it is narrower than common law malice, which may embrace publication for an improper purpose of a statement believed to be true. Furthermore, a publication in the mass media will not necessarily be protected by qualified privilege, whereas the range of publication is irrelevant under *NY Times v Sullivan*. In *Rosenblatt v Baer*, 383 U.S. (1966) the Supreme Court said that the *Sullivan* rule did not necessarily apply to all public employees but would apply where:
> "his position in government has such apparent importance that the public has an independent interest in the qualifications and performance of the person who holds it, beyond the general public interest in the qualifications and performance of all government employees"
(at 85–86). However, this does not mean that the official must hold a high position or be in charge of policy making and it seems that in some areas of public administration (e.g. law enforcement) any officer will be a "public official". See generally, 50 Am.Jur.2d, *Libel and Slander*, para.46 et seq. The result is that this head of common law qualified privilege would seem to be of little practical importance.

[432] *Warren v Falconer* (1771) Morrison 13933; *Woodward v Lander* (1834) 6 C. & P. 548.

[433] *Blake v Pilfold* (1832) 1 Moo. & Rob. 198.

[434] *R. v Rule* [1937] 2 K.B. 375; explained and distinguished, *De Buse v McCarthy* [1942] 1 K.B.156 CA at 170. *Graham v Crozier* (1879) 44 Up.Can.Q.B. 378, in which one's M.P. seems to have been regarded as a last resort, is probably not now good authority; cf. *R. v Rule* [1937] 2 Q.B. 375; *Beach v Freeson* [1972] 1 Q.B. 14.

[435] *Cassidy v Connochie* (1907) 9 F. 1112; *Fraser v Mirza*, 1993 S.C. (H.L.) 27. See also *Anderson v Palombo*, 1986 S.L.T. 46.

to any bad report respecting a clergyman in his diocese,[436] have all been held to have been written on a privileged occasion. On the same principle, privilege has been held to attach to a petition signed by the residents of a school district and addressed to the school board requesting the removal of a school-teacher for immorality or intemperance[437]; to a letter written by a commanding officer of a regiment to his immediate superior as to the conduct of the colonel[438]; or by the president of a charitable association, founded for the benefit of the sick poor of a parish to the chairman of the parish council concerning the failure of the medical officer of the parish to obey directions he had received as to the use of the district nurse in cases in which her services might have been of value[439]; or by a ratepayer to the watch committee of a borough as to the conduct of a police superintendent in the borough.[440]

14.62 Public responsibilities. The principle is not confined to public officers or persons in authority but extends to statements about the conduct of any person who has responsibilities to the public for the way in which he deals with them. For instance, complaints about the conduct of professional men in their calling are on the same footing as those about the conduct of public officials.[441] Thus, an M.P. has been held to have both an interest and a duty to communicate to the appropriate body at the request of a constituent any substantial complaint from him about a professional person at the service of the public.[442] A complaint to the relevant local authority about a breach of statutory obligation by a trader would similarly be protected, and it is suggested that a complaint to a trade association which undertook to mediate on complaints by customers[443] would also be privileged, as it is now clear that the recipient of the complaint need not have power to discipline or grant redress.[444]

---

[436] *James v Boston* (1845) 2 C. & K.4; *Elmke v Grimewald* (1921) E.D.L. 31 Sup Ct of S. Africa. See also *A v B* (1895) 22 R. 984, and *Barclay v Manuel* (1903)10 S.L.T. 450 (parish minister privileged in bringing before his presbytery a charge of misconduct against another minister, which it may be the duty of the presbytery to inquire into, and, if necessary, punish).

[437] *Mcintyre v McBean* (1866) 13 Up.Can.Q.B. 534.

[438] *Dickson v Earl of Wilton* (1859) 1 F. & F. 419.

[439] *Baird v Wallace-James* (1916) 85 L.J.P.C.193.

[440] *Bannister v Kelty* (1895) 59 J.P.793; *Couper v Lord Balfour*, 1913 S.C. 492; *Knight v Hill* (1879) 43 J.P. 176 (clerk of guardians to the board); *Sutton v Plumridge* (1867) 16 L.T. 741 (complaint to relieving officer as to conduct of a medical officer.)

[441] Nor, given the broad nature of the underlying principle of qualified privilege, is it confined to statements arising out of complaints. It is thought that the decision in *Crandall v Atlantic School of Theology* (1993) 120 N.S.R. (2d) 219, that qualified privilege attached to assessments of the progress of a student for a profession is plainly correct. Indeed, it would seem that any assessment of any student or pupil would be privileged on the ground of common interest between the assessor and those to whom he reports. In *Meade v Pugh* [2004] EWHC 408 (QB) at [11], it was said to be clear beyond argument that a report on the progress of a student under training was made on an occasion of qualified privilege.

[442] *Beach v Freeson* [1972] 1 Q.B. 14 (communication by M.P. to Law Society about conduct of constituent's solicitors).

[443] Cf. *Urbanowski v Harkins* [2006] BCSC 1741.

[444] See para.14.21, above.

(d) *Relevance*

Irrelevant statements and privilege: general principle. It has been   **14.63**
said that privilege will not protect matter which cannot be said, broadly
speaking, to be relevant to the occasion. There is, however, some theoretical
difficulty here about the relationship between the occasion and malice. In
Adam v Ward there are statements to the effect that irrelevant matter is simply
outside the privilege. "The fact that an occasion is privileged", said Lord
Loreburn[445]:

> "does not necessarily protect all that is said or written on that occasion. Anything
> that is not relevant and pertinent to the discharge of the duty or exercise of the right
> or the safeguarding of the interest which creates the privilege [or, in the words of
> Lord Atkinson,[446] 'foreign and irrelevant subjects not pertinent to the discharge of
> the duty, or the protection of the interest which forms the basis of the privilege'] will
> not be protected . . . The judge has to consider the nature of the duty or right or
> interest and to rule whether or not the defendant has published something beyond
> what was germane and reasonably appropriate to the occasion . . . A man ought not
> to be protected if he publishes what is in fact untrue of someone else when there is
> no occasion for his doing so."
>
> "If, accordingly, and in so far as the communication deals with matter not in any
> reasonable sense germane to the subject-matter of the occasion, the protection is
> gone: the occasion with its privilege does not reach a communication upon this
> foreign and totally unconnected matter."[447]
>
> "The exercise of privilege on one matter gives no protection to irrelevant libels
> introduced into the same communication."[448]

The *occasion* remains privileged and protection is conferred (in the absence of
malice) upon those portions of the statement which relate to the occasion: it
is only the irrelevant and foreign matter which is not privileged.[449]

However, in *Horrocks v Lowe*,[450] a case on malice and qualified privilege,
Lord Diplock spoke in the following terms of the inclusion of irrelevant
matter in a statement otherwise privileged[451]:

---

[445] [1917] A.C. 309 HL at 320–321. In *Blumenthal v Shore* [1948] 3 S.A.L.R. 671, reference
is made to the "simple objective test of what could fairly be regarded as reasonably necessary . . .
to protect the interest or discharge the duty, which was the foundation of the privilege."

[446] [1917] A.C. 309 at 339–340.

[447] Ibid. at 348, per Lord Shaw; and see *Loutchansky v Times Newspapers Ltd (Nos 2–5)* [2001]
EWCA Civ 1805; [2002] Q.B. 783 at [36]: "[the] communication will be privileged subject only
to relevance and malice".

[448] Ibid. at 318, per Lord Finlay.

[449] Ibid. at 340, per Lord Atkinson; *Dunford Publicity v New Media* [1971] N.Z.L.R. 961; *El
Azzi v Nationwide News Pty Ltd* [2005] N.S.W.S.C. 247; *Goyan v Motyka* [2008] NSWCA 28 at
[94]. Unless one says that "the inclusion of the irrelevant part in the communication affords
evidence of malice and can destroy the privilege attaching to the relevant part": *Bellino v
Australian Broadcasting Corp* (1996) 185 C.L.R. 183 at 228.

[450] [1975] A.C. 135 HL.

[451] Ibid. at 151. Lord Diplock's was the leading speech, with which three other members of the
House of Lords agreed.

"Logically it might be said that matter [which is irrelevant because it is not necessary for the fulfilment of the particular duty or the protection of the particular interest upon which the privilege is founded] falls outside the privilege altogether. But if this were so it would involve the application by the court of an objective test of relevance to every part of the defamatory matter published on the privileged occasion; whereas, as everyone knows, ordinary human beings vary in their ability to distinguish that which is logically relevant from that which is not and few, apart from lawyers, have had any training which qualifies them to do so. So the protection afforded by the privilege would be illusory if it were lost in respect of any defamatory matter which upon logical analysis could be shown to be irrelevant to the fulfilment of the duty or the protection of the right upon which the privilege was founded. As Lord Dunedin pointed out in *Adam v Ward*[452] the proper rule as respects irrelevant defamatory matter incorporated in a statement made on a privileged occasion is to treat it as one of the factors to be taken into consideration in deciding whether, in all the circumstances, an inference that the defendant was actuated by express malice can properly be drawn. As regards irrelevant matter the test is not whether it is logically relevant but whether, in all the circumstances, it can be inferred that the defendant either did not believe it to be true or, though believing it to be true, realised that it had nothing to do with the particular duty or interest on which the privilege was based, but nevertheless seized the opportunity to drag in irrelevant defamatory matter to vent his personal spite, or for some other improper motive."

On the face of it, this amounts to saying that even irrelevant matter does not fall outside the privilege (which would be a question for the judge), but can only be evidence of malice (a question for the jury); or that the test of irrelevance is not "objective" but "subjective", which in practical terms has much the same effect because it would blur the boundaries between irrelevance and malice. This is difficult to reconcile with the clear terms of four of the five judgments in *Adam v Ward*[453] and even Lord Dunedin, upon whom Lord Diplock relies, admitted that:

"if the defamatory statement is quite unconnected with and irrelevant to the main statement which is *ex hypothesi* privileged, then I think it is more accurate to say that the privilege does not extend thereto, than to say, though the result may be the same, that the defamatory statement is evidence of malice."[454]

Moreover, it seems clear,[455] at least with regard to cases where a public authority seeks to rely on privilege, that the Human Rights Act 1998 requires that an objective test of relevance should be applied to the question of

---

[452] [1917] A.C.309 at 326–327.

[453] The distinction between lack of privilege and abuse of privilege is clearly drawn by Earl Loreburn in *Adam v Ward* [1917] A.C. 309 at 321:
"Language has been used in some cases which seems somewhat to confuse the two separate points, namely, whether the defendant has gone beyond the privilege which the occasion creates, and whether the defendant has forfeited the privilege by malice. Excess of privilege in part of a defamatory publication may of course be evidence of malice as to the whole of it, but the two things are different."

[454] Ibid. at 327.

[455] *Clift v Slough BC* [2010] EWCA Civ 1171; [2011] 1 W.L.R. 1774 (on appeal from [2009] EWHC 1550 (QB); [2010] E.M.L.R. 4).

proportionality.[456] Thus, the inclusion of material that failed an objective test of relevance would have the effect of making the publication disproportionate and consequently privilege could not be relied upon.[457]

If the statement is "obviously and wholly extraneous"[458] to the matter in question, it is difficult to see why protection should be granted even if the defendant, from eccentric reasons of his own, believes it is relevant, bearing in mind that even "gross, unreasoning prejudice" does not amount to malice.[459] Thus if D in answer to an inquiry by X as to P's solvency, were not only to say that P was insolvent but were to add, "I suppose you know that P was convicted of indecent assault two years ago" it is submitted that no privilege should attach to the additional information, which is wholly irrelevant to the inquiry.[460] If, on the other hand, D were to exaggerate the facts of C's insolvency—or even perhaps to impute to P improper conduct in the transaction of business—that would be merely evidence of malice to take the case out of the privilege.[461] But the more extreme view would seem to strike at the very purpose for which privilege is granted. It is not the law that a person is protected in making statements about another which he believes to be true but that he is so protected where he is acting in the discharge of a duty or interest which the law considers to outweigh the protection of reputation and it is well established that where that duty or interest does not exist (or there is no reciprocal interest in the person addressed), privilege is not created merely because the defendant believes it to exist.[462] It is difficult to see why this principle should be abandoned merely because the defendant has an interest or duty in respect of some entirely different matter about which, on that occasion, he speaks.

---

[456] See further, para.14.5, above.

[457] In *Clift*, the relevance of the material was not in issue but Ward L.J. indicated (at [44]) that the position might have been different if the offending communication, in addition to warning the Council's employees that the claimant was a violent woman, had stated that she was an habitual drug-taker. Such material would have been objectively irrelevant and the privilege would not have applied at all to them.

[458] *Cunningham v Essex CC*, June 26, 2000 at [73], per Eady J. As was the case in *Warren v Warren* (1834) 1 C.M. & R. 250 and *Huntley v Ward* (1859) 6 C.B.(N.S.) 514.

[459] *Horrocks v Lowe* [1975] A.C. 135 at 153. See para.17.3, below.

[460] *Marks v Construction, Mining etc. Union of Australia (W.A. Branch)* (1995) 14 W.A.R. 360 is perhaps a marginal case in this respect (attack by union on plaintiff's attitude to a development; article made allegations about plaintiff's attitude to asbestos manufacture 30 years before; not privileged).

[461] In *Cush v Dillon; Boland v Dillon* [2011] HCA 30; (2011) 85 ALJR 86 the High Court of Australia considered whether qualified privilege attached to a statement sent to the chairperson of a Catchment Management Authority (CMA), that read: "it is common knowledge among people [on the CMA] that Les and Amanda [the plaintiffs, being Board members of the CMA] are having an affair" [which they were not]. The High Court held that qualified privilege attached. It had been conceded, correctly, that the occasion of the privilege extended to the communication of the existence of the rumour and once that concession was made it could not be suggested that the communication of the fact of an affair was less relevant to the matters discussed than a rumour. The error inherent in the statement does not deny the privilege (at [13]).

[462] See paras 14.17–14.18, above.

14.64 A limited role for relevance. The issue seems to be of limited practical importance, which is perhaps why it has not proved necessary to make it a matter of *decision*, although it is quite frequently the subject of argument.[463] Perhaps the two approaches can be reconciled (though there is some difficulty in accommodating the last sentence of the passage quoted from Lord Diplock above[464]) by saying that what Lord Diplock is concerned with is what is "logically relevant", i.e. that which is relevant when subjected to a close analysis[465] such as would be given to the relevance or admissibility of evidence. This is a valuable caution against too restrictive an approach to the language which may be used on a privileged occasion, which would seriously reduce the protection of qualified privilege, for a

> "person speaking on a privileged occasion should not be regarded as a tightrope walker without a safety net, with the judge waiting underneath with bated breath hoping for a tumble".[466]

It must also be borne in mind that there may be cases in which "the inclusion of the irrelevant part in the communication affords evidence of malice and can destroy the privilege attaching to the relevant part".[467] Although it has been said that:

> "in so far as there may be any inconsistency between Lord Diplock's approach [in *Horrocks v Lowe*] and that of their Lordships in *Adam v Ward*, it would appear to be appropriate to lean towards the later interpretation, which is the more generous in favour of free speech",[468]

yet the weight of the modern case law seems to continue to accept a limited role for relevance in satisfying the conditions of a privileged occasion as opposed to malice and that therefore:

> "there may be circumstances in which it would be possible for the judge to rule, on uncontroversial facts, that the allegations against the claimant were in no sense germane to the subject matter and thus exclude privilege . . . But the irrelevance would need to be plain and obvious".[469]

---

[463] See, e.g. *Alexander v Clegg* [2004] NZCA 91; [2004] 3 N.Z.L.R. 586. It might gain more significance if malice in the form of improper motive were to be restricted: see para.17.4, below.

[464] Indeed, this is hard to reconcile with Lord Dunedin's view in *Adam v Ward*.

[465] A "cool and objective analysis as to logical relevance": *Hamilton v Clifford* [2004] EWHC 1542 (QB) at [75].

[466] *Birchwood Homes Ltd v Robinson* [2003] EWHC (QB) 293 at [27], per Eady J.

[467] *Bellino v Australian Broadcasting Corp* (1996) 185 C.L.R. 183 at 228.

[468] Eady J. in *Hamilton v Clifford* [2004] EWHC 1542 (QB) at [77]. See also *Lillie v Newcastle CC* [2002] EWHC (QB) 1600 at [1089]; *W v Westminster City Council* [2004] EWHC 2866 (QB).

[469] *Hamilton v Clifford* [2004] EWHC 1542 (QB) at [74]; *Maccaba v Lichtenstein* [2004] EWHC 1577 (QB); [2005] E.M.L.R. 9 at [12]; *Akinleye v E Sussex Hospitals NHS Trust* [2008] EWHC 68 (QB) at [18].

This continuing role for relevance also seems to be the position elsewhere.[470]

On any view, the test of relevance is not whether the statement complained of is strictly necessary for or logically relevant to the discharge of the duty or protection of the interest which is the foundation of the privilege. One should not take the approach that the defendant is only protected in doing the "bare minimum" necessary to comply with his duty. Where the statement has any reference to the subject-matter of the privilege, or is in any way pertinent or germane to it, it is material only as evidence of malice to take the case out of the privilege. In *Halford v Chief Constable of Hampshire* the police received an inquiry as to the state of an investigation of a child assault allegation from the claimant's employers (who were also responsible for the welfare of the child). The court rejected the argument that they should simply have replied that the investigation was at an end and that there had been no prosecution. The additional statements that there was a conflict of evidence and that the matter was being treated as "undetected", far from being irrelevant, were well within the scope of the police duty in relation to the occasion of privilege.[471]

"There may be an excess of the privilege in the sense that something has been published which is not within the privileged occasion at all, because it can have no

---

[470] "In my opinion, the correct principle ... is that a matter which is irrelevant to and unconnected with the privileged occasion does not have the protection of privilege at all, and that the inclusion of such matter may also base an inference of malice which will deprive even the relevant part of the communication of the protection of privilege. In so far as the passage from *Horrocks v Lowe* suggests otherwise, in my opinion it is not supported by *Adam v Ward* . , . . However, ... I think the cumulative effect of the passages ... from *Adam v Ward* and *Horrocks v Lowe* do indicate that, unless malice is inferred, material communicated on the privileged occasion will have the protection of the privilege unless it is truly unconnected with the subject matter of the occasion."
Bashford v Information Australia (Newsletters) Pty Ltd [2001] NSWCA 470 at [43], per Hodgson J.A (on appeal [2004] HCA 5; 218 C.L.R. 366, though there is little discussion of this issue); *Goyan v Matykos* [2008] NSWCA 28. See also *Sands v Channel Seven Adelaide Pty Ltd* [2009] SASC 215 at [246] (appeal dismissed [2010] SASC 202); and *Aktas v Westpac Banking Corp Ltd* [2009] NSWCA 9, where McClellan C.J. said at [75]:
  "If a bank returned a cheque to the payee having correctly determined that there were insufficient funds with two endorsements, one being 'Refer to Drawer' and the other, the 'drawer is a thief', the imputations arising from the publication of the first statement, made necessary by the bank's decision to refuse payment, will be an occasion of qualified privilege. The publication of the second will not, there being no interest or duty on the part of the bank to publish that the drawer is a thief, with whatever defamatory imputation may be found to arise from the publication of that statement. An occasion on which matter which gives rise to defamatory imputations is published may not be used for some purpose or motive foreign to the duty or interest that protects the making of the statement."
On appeal the majority of the HCA held that the first statement in the example would not be privileged if the determination had been incorrectly made: para.14.46, above.
[471] [2002] EWCA Civ 102 at [39]. In fact the statements were true but the claimant maintained that they implied guilt. Sedley L.J. remarked that the case was an example of a claimant seeking to inflate "the words complained of into something far beyond their obvious meaning and then saying that the defendant cannot have believed" them to be true (at [64]). Cf. *Bento v The Chief Constable of Bedfordshire Police* [2012] EWHC 1525 (QB). See further para.14.37, above.

reference to it . . . But when there is only an excessive statement having reference to the privileged occasion, and which, therefore, comes within it, then the only way in which the excess is material is as being evidence of malice. In none of the cases on the subject, so far as I know, has it been held that the privilege is taken away when there has been such an excessive statement, unless the jury has found that there was malice."[472]

In *Jacob v Lawrence*[473] a solicitor wrote to D, on behalf of a client P, complaining of a defamation of his client's character, and requesting an apology and retraction, and in the alternative threatening legal proceedings. D wrote in reply refusing to withdraw the charge, and requesting him to inform his client that unless the sum of £6 which he had lent P was paid he would again publicly expose P, concluding as follows: "I should suggest to you the advisability of looking after your costs, as a man guilty of such baseness as he had been to me in repudiating this debt cannot be trusted." It was held, on demurrer, that the occasion was privileged; that the contents of D's letter were sufficiently relevant and pertinent to the occasion to sustain the defence upon demurrer.[474] In *Watts v Times Newspapers*[475] the defendants insisted, on behalf of their client, who had been defamed by a newspaper, in the insertion of an apology which contained defamatory reference to the plaintiff. Although this reference was objectively unnecessary when considered from the point of view of whether the newspaper had made a sufficient apology to the client, yet from the point of view of the client (and hence his representatives) the matter had to be considered as a response to an attack and the words were therefore privileged because they were "not unconnected with the theme" and did not include "entirely irrelevant and extraneous material".[476]

14.65 Defamatory statement affecting third person.

"Where a defendant on an occasion which is privileged as between himself and some other person, makes some defamatory statement affecting a third person which has nothing to do with the privileged occasion, that third person would have a right of action against the defendant, and, as between him and the defendant, there would be no privileged occasion."[477]

---

[472] Per Lord Esher M.R. in *Nevill v Fine Arts Co* [1895] 2 Q.B. 156 CA at 170; approved by Lord Dunedin in *Adam v Ward* [1917] A.C. 309 at 327.

[473] (1879) 4 L.R. Ir. 579.

[474] However, the court's view of the relevant functions of judge and jury would not conform to modern practice.

[475] [1997] Q.B. 650 CA.

[476] Ibid. at 671. However, the newspaper failed on privilege: see para.14.58, above.

[477] Per Lord Esher M.R. in *Nevill v Fine Arts Co* [1895] 2 Q.B. 156 at 170; *Rose v Brennan* [1936] E.D.L. 35 (advantage taken of privileged occasion to attack committee of trade union). Lord Esher's phrasing is somewhat misleading, if it suggests that an occasion has in some sense to be privileged between the claimant and defendant. It is the reciprocal interest and duty of the defendant and the person to whom the defamatory matter is published which creates the privileged occasion, and then the defendant must show that the publication is relevant to the matters which create the privilege.

The question whether a privileged occasion protects a statement involving the character of one who is only indirectly concerned in the charge made depends on its relevancy to the privileged part of the statement and the circumstances in which it was made.[478] Usually, if no attack or demand was made by the claimant and no inquiry was made about him, so much of the statement as concerns him will not be protected. In particular circumstances this may not be true. Thus, if in the reply to an attack it is necessary to bring in the claimant's name in explanation, the publication will certainly remain privileged.[479] Similarly, where there is an imputation against two persons jointly, so that the charge of misconduct against one cannot well be made or rebutted without introducing the name of the other, then, if circumstances exist which make the communication privileged as regards one person, it will be privileged as regards both.[480] In *Alexander v Clegg*, even though the imputations against the viability of the defendant's business had been made by A, the other persons closely associated with A in the competitor enterprise "were within the lawful range of the [defendant's] counterpunch"[481] and it would have been unrealistic not to regard the position of them all as synonymous for the purposes of privilege.

Examples. D discharged his footman and at the same time his cook, and, on   **14.66**
their separately inquiring the reason, told each (in the absence of the other) that his reason was that both of them had been robbing him. Held, the statement was privileged as against both, for what was said to each was part of, and inseparably connected with, the charge against the other.[482]

D mentioned to A, who was rector of her parish, a rumour she had heard impugning his conduct and the conduct of his solicitor, P, in the administration of a certain trust. It was held that privilege extended to the alleged slander of P, since the communication to A could not have been made without introducing P's name.[483] "It was impossible", said Lush J.[484]:

> "to sever the slander affecting A from that affecting P. If the name of P had been maliciously introduced into the conversation, the matter would have assumed a different aspect. But this cannot be suggested; the charge against P was inseparable from that against the clergyman."

---

[478] *Sefton v Baskin* (1918) 37 N.Z.L.R. 157.

[479] "If A accuses B of negligence that caused a building to collapse, and B's [honest] response is that the omissions of C caused the collapse, B can raise the defence against C": *Oei v Ban* [2005] SGCA 35; [2005] 3 S.L.R. 608 at [36].

[480] *Manby v Witt* (1856) 18 C.B. 544; *Davis v Snead* (1870) L.R. 5 Q.B. 608; and see *Findley v Foulds* (1893) 19 V.L.R. 447 at 454, where it was impossible to make the relevant statement without implicating the plaintiff. Cf. *Sefton v Baskin* (1918) 37 N.Z.L.R. 157, where there was no need to bring in the plaintiff's character at all.

[481] [2004] NZCA 91; [2004] 3 N.Z.L.R. 586 at [62].

[482] *Manby v Witt* (1856) 18 C.B. 544.

[483] *Davies v Snead* (1870) L.R.5 Q.B. 608.

[484] In the report in 39 L.J.Q.B. at 202. Cf. *Knapp v McLeod* (1926) 58 O.L.R. 605.

14.67 Answers to attacks. A person responding to an attack upon him must not make countercharges or unnecessary imputations on the private life of the person who has attacked him wholly unconnected with the attack and irrelevant to his vindication.[485] The privilege "extends only so far as to enable him to repel the charges brought against him—not to bring fresh accusations against his adversary."[486]

> "In order for a defendant to avail himself of this form of privilege, the response should not go into irrelevant matters or, in particular, cross over into an attack on the integrity of the claimant if it is not reasonably necessary for defending his own reputation."[487]
>
> "If, for example, A should charge B with theft, a denial by B of the charge would not warrant an action for damages by A however vigorous or gross the language might be in which B's denial was couched. But if B should go on to charge A with theft[488] that would be actionable, and it would not be protected or privileged to any extent on account of A's previous attack."[489]

In *Murphy v Halpin*[490] P, who was a poor law guardian, at a meeting of the board at which the press were present, stated that D, the medical officer to the union, had acted improperly with reference to the seizure of some unsound meat and the prosecution of a person by whom it had been exposed for sale, and that his costs incurred ought not to be paid by the guardians. These statements were afterwards published in a newspaper as part of the proceedings at the board meeting. D, with the view of vindicating himself and showing that credit ought not to be attached to P's statements, wrote to the newspaper a letter in which he imputed to P untruthfulness, inability to discharge his debts, and other discreditable conduct in his office of guardian. It was held that such letter was not privileged.

The question whether a response was sufficiently connected to the initial attack was considered by the High Court of Australia in *Harbour Radio Pty Ltd v Trad*.[491] The plaintiff, Mr Trad, sued in respect of remarks made by a Radio 2GB host after a speech made by him after "race" riots in Cronulla (the "Cronulla Riots"). The speech was delivered at a "peace rally" with around 5,000 people in attendance. In the speech, the plaintiff attributed a proportion of blame to Radio 2GB (Harbour Radio Pty Ltd), claiming the station, was

---

[485] *Senior v Medland* (1858) 4 Jur.(N.S.) 1039; *Murphy v Halpin* (1874) Ir.R. 8 C.L. 127; *O'Brien v Freeman's Journal* (1907) 41 Ir.L.T. 35 CA; *Pearce v Symes* (1909) 28 N.Z.L.R. 562; *News Media v Finlay* [1970] N.Z.L.R. 1089; *Rhodes University College v Field* [1947] 3 S.A.L.R. 437. See also *Huntley v Ward* (1859) 6 C.B.(N.S.) 514; *Simmonds v Dunne* (1871) Ir.R. 5 C.L. 358.

[486] Per May C.J. in *Dwyer v Esmonde* (1878) 2 L.R.Ir. 243 at 254.

[487] *Hamilton v Clifford* [2004] EWHC 1542 (QB) at [66]. See also, *Penton v Calwell* [1945] HCA 51; (1945) 70 C.L.R. 219 at 242–243. Referred to with approval by the High Court of Australia in *Harbour Radio Pty Limited v Trad* [2012] HCA 44.

[488] It appears to be assumed that B is not charging A with the theft with which A charged B.

[489] Per Lord Kincairney in *Milne v Walker* (1898) 21 R. 155 at 157.

[490] (1874) Ir. R. 8 C.L. 127, distinguished in *Nevin v Roddy* (1935) Ir. R. 397 CA.

[491] [2012] HCA 44.

" . . . winning the ratings, it is whipping up fears". As a result, Mr Trad stated that Muslims in Australia were "suffering as a result of the racist actions of predominantly one radio station [2GB]." A jury found that the 2GB broadcast contained the following eight imputations that were defamatory of the plaintiff:

"(a) the plaintiff stirred up hatred against a 2GB reporter which caused him to have concerns about his own personal safety;
    (b) the plaintiff incites people to commit acts of violence;
    (c) the plaintiff incites people to have racist attitudes;
    (d) the plaintiff is a dangerous individual;
    (g) the plaintiff is a disgraceful individual;
    (h) the plaintiff is widely perceived as a pest;
    (j) the plaintiff deliberately gives out misinformation about the Islamic community;
    (k) the plaintiff attacks those people who once gave him a privileged position."[492]

In its defence the defendant radio station sought to rely, inter alia, on the reply to attack privilege. The High Court held that if the privilege was to apply, the response had to be sufficiently connected with the initial attack: to impugn the truth of the charges contained in the attack and even the general veracity of the attacker may be a proper exercise of the privilege, if it be commensurate with the occasion. That the matter complained of is sufficiently connected to the privileged occasion to attract the defence may appear upon any one of several considerations. The matter may be sufficiently connected with the content of the attack, or it may go to the credibility of the attack, or to the credibility of the person making that attack. Questions of degree inevitably will be presented.[493]

The court found that the defence of privilege applied to six of the eight defamatory imputations: (a), (b), (c), (d), (g) and (j).[494] So far as (a), (b) and (c) were concerned, the plaintiff had attacked 2GB by placing at least part of the blame for the riots upon the "tabloid journalism" practised by one particular talk-back radio station, namely 2GB. It was a relevant and reasonable response by 2GB to direct attention to the credibility of the attacker by imputing hypocrisy to Mr Trad as one who himself incited people to commit acts of violence and to have racist attitudes, and as one who at the peace rally had stirred up hatred against a 2GB reporter, causing him concern about his personal safety which revealed the true purpose behind Mr Trad's attack which was to incite racism and violence. As such, 2GB's response was deemed reasonable and relevant. So far as imputations (d), (g) and (j) were concerned, these were linked to the statements that Mr Trad did not represent

---

[492] Ibid. at [9].
[493] Ibid. at [35].
[494] Ibid. at [36]–[38].

the views of the Muslim community and presented misinformation, particularly about issues concerning that community. This, the Court concluded, undermined the credibility of the plaintiff's assertion that the "suffering" of the Islamic community was in part due to 2GB. However, the High Court concluded that imputations (h) and (k) were not sufficiently connected to the attack on 2GB. So far as the charge of being a "pest" (imputation (h)) was concerned, this in no way reflected on Mr Trad's credibility in making the charges against 2GB and no link could therefore be established between this statement and the attacks. Imputation (k) also exceeded the occasion of the privilege as it was not a retort by way of vindication that was fairly warranted by the occasion.

14.68 Counter-attack on credibility. Mere retaliation, which cannot be described as an answer or explanation,[495] is not protected,[496] but the defendant is not required to be diffident in protecting himself.

> "There is an analogy between the criminal law of self-defence and a man's right to defend himself against written or verbal attacks. In both cases he is entitled, if he can, to defend himself effectively, and he only loses the protection of the law if he goes beyond defence and proceeds to offence. That is to say, the circumstances in which he defends himself, either by acts or by words, negative the malice which the law draws from violent acts or defamatory words. If you are attacked with a deadly weapon you can defend yourself with a deadly weapon or with any other weapon which may protect your life. The law does not concern itself with niceties in such matters. If you are attacked by a prize-fighter, you are not bound to adhere to the Queensberry rules in your defence."[497]

Though the authorities are not completely clear, it seems to be a relevant, and indeed, sometimes necessary, means of repelling a charge to state that the person who made it should not be believed. In response to an attack one is given a considerable degree of latitude, and may go on to the offensive so long as one does not include entirely irrelevant and extraneous material.[498] Thus in *O'Donoghue v Hussey*[499] it was held that it was a reasonable mode of defence for a person, whose conduct and character had been assailed in a public newspaper, to state publicly that his assailant was known to be a person in the

---

[495] A "countercharge or diversionary attack wholly unconnected with the original . . . attack": *Regan v Taylor* [2000] E.M.L.R. 549 CA at 574, per Henry L.J.

[496] *Brewer v Chase*, 80 N.W. 575 at 577 (Mich., 1899). See *Whitaker v Huntington* (1980) 15 C.C.L.T. 19; *Bennett v Stupich* (1981) 125 D.L.R. (3d) 743; *Heytesbury Holdings Pty Ltd v City of Subiaco* (1998) 19 W.A.R. 440.

[497] Per Lord Oaksey in *Turner v MGM Pictures* [1950]1 All E.R. 449 HL at 470–471; *Muller v Hatton* (1952) Queensland S.R. 150; *Netupsky v Craig* (1971) 14 D.L.R. (3d) 387 Ont. CA; *Hamilton v Clifford* [2004] EWHC 1542 (QB).

[498] *Watts v Times Newpapers* [1997] Q.B. 650 CA at 671; *Curran v Scottish Daily Record and Sunday Mail Ltd* [2011] CSIH 86; 2012 Rep L.R. 30. The court in *Brewer v Chase*, above, seems to take a narrower view, denying the right to attack the initiator's credibility.

[499] (1871) Ir. R. 5 C.L. 124.

habit of making misstatements.[500] So too, in *Curran v Scottish Daily Record and Sunday Mail Ltd*[501] the Scottish equivalent of the reply to attack privilege —"fair retort"—was successfully relied upon by the defendants. After Mr Sheridan, then the leader of the Scottish Socialist Party, brought a successful action of defamation against the *News of the World*, the pursuer, who was also a member of the Scottish Socialist Party, and two other party members, issued a press statement claiming that Mr Sheridan had committed perjury, that he was no longer wanted by certain parts of the party but that there was no plot against him. The *Daily Record* then published a series of articles said to be based on interviews with Mr Sheridan in which various comments were made about the pursuer and others. The comments accused the pursuer and other fellow members of being "political blackmailers", being "enemies" of the Party and "political scabs". The Extra Division of the Inner House of the Court of Session held that Mr Sheridan had been entitled in law to give a robust response to the serious allegations made against him and it came within the parameters of fair retort.[502] The defenders were therefore entitled to qualified privilege on the occasion that they reported it.

Where a policy-holder in the course of a dispute with an insurance company published a pamphlet accusing the directors of fraud, and the directors published a pamphlet in answer to an intending policy-holder declaring the charges to be false and calumnious and also asserting that, in a suit which he had instituted, the plaintiff had sworn (in support of those charges) in opposition to his own handwriting, Cockburn C.J. ruled that the directors' pamphlet was privileged, and directed the jury that if they were of opinion that it was:

> "published *bona fide* for the purpose of the defence of the company, and in order to prevent these charges from operating to their prejudice, and with a view to vindicate the character of the directors, and not with a view to injure or lower the character of the plaintiff"

they ought to find for the defendants.[503]

(e) *Excessive publication*

Publication to uninterested persons. Publication must be proportionate   **14.69** to the necessity of the occasion. There may be cases of great urgency where, even under the classical form of privilege, publication to the public as

---

[500] Contrast *Milne v Walker* (1893) 21 R. 155, in which a reply accusing the attacker of general mendacity was held to go beyond the bounds of retort. The authority of the latter case is doubtful considering the language used and held to be within the privilege in *Loughton v Bishop of Sodor and Man* (1872) L.R.4 P.C. 495.

[501] [2011] CSIH 86; 2012 Rep. L.R. 30.

[502] Ibid. at [56]–[60].

[503] *Koenig v Ritchie* (1862) 3 F. & F. 413 at 420.

a whole is the only practical method of bringing information to the attention of persons in whose interests the defendant acts.[504] If the defendant is attacked in the public media and responds in the same manner the response is privileged.[505] Otherwise, however, it follows from the fundamental requirement of reciprocity of duty and interest that publication to a person who does not share in this reciprocity is not generally privileged.[506] In determining this question, the Human Rights Act 1998 now requires consideration of the proportionality of the publication. Where the art.8 rights of the claimant are engaged the publication must be no wider than is necessary to ensure that these rights are respected. Thus, in *Clift v Slough BC*[507] while the council had acted with a legitimate aim of protecting the safety of its staff, the circulation of the publications was greater than was necessary to accomplish that objective. Though a reasonable council could have concluded that the claimant's conduct did give rise to a risk to some council employees, the risk was a very limited one and certainly did not exist to those who worked in departments which the claimant was not likely to approach. Beyond that, they certainly owed no duty to the staff of partner organisations from which the claimant might seek services or supplies. There was simply no evidence of risk in such a case.

As a general rule therefore the defendant should be careful to make his communication only to those persons who have a legitimate interest or duty in relation to the subject-matter. The fact that a communication between A and B is privileged does not justify A in making the communication in a manner, or at a time, which would necessarily involve its publication to other persons who have no such interest or duty, and no privilege would prima facie attach[508] to any such publication.[509]

> "A man ought not to be protected if he published what is in fact untrue of someone else when there is no occasion for his doing so, or when there is no occasion for his publishing it to the persons to whom he in fact publishes it."[510]

However, if *strict* reciprocity were essential, society and its business could not be conducted, as others without a direct interest in the communication are regularly employed in helping to make the communication and it would be

---

[504] See, e.g. *Hewitt v Grunwald* [2004] EWHC 2959 (QB), para.14.76, below.
[505] See para.14.53, above.
[506] See para.14.16, above.
[507] [2003] EWCA Civ 331; [2003] 1 W.L.R. 1357.
[508] *Brown v Croome* (1817) 2 Stark. 297; *Duncombe v Daniell* (1838) 2 Jur. 32; *Parsons v Surgey* (1864) 4 F. & F. 247; *Simpson v Downs* (1867) 16 L.T. 391; *Murphy v Halpin* (1874) Ir. R. 8 C.L. 127; *Hopewell v Kennedy* (1904) 9 O.L.R. 43; *Standen v South Essex Recorders* (1934) 50 T L.R. 365; *Guise v Kouvelis* (1947) 74 C.L.R. 102; *Pearce v Hailstone* (1992) 58 S.A.S.R. 240.
[509] But the publication between A and B would still be privileged: *Mutch v Robertson*, 1981 S.L.T. 217. This might be relevant to the question of damages where the publication to uninterested third parties had been very limited.
[510] Per Earl Loreburn in *Adam v Ward* [1917] A.C. 309 at 321.

impossible to communicate if every defamatory communication had to be confined to those with a direct duty or interest in relation to its subject-matter. For these reasons, communications to persons without such an interest or duty are nevertheless privileged if they are published reasonably, in the ordinary course of business, and no more widely than is required for the effective making of the communication, and if they would be privileged but for such incidental publication.[511] Such a privilege has been referred to as an "ancillary" or "incidental" privilege. For this purpose we must of course put aside those cases where a person is responding to a public attack on him, for there he may respond in kind.[512] Furthermore, there is now a wider privilege for statements of certain matters of public concern, which are considered in the next chapter. It should also be noted that some of the older cases in this chapter involved what would be technical publications unlikely to cause any harm and which might nowadays fall foul of the concept of abuse of process.[513] Thus in *Bezant v Rausing*[514] there was a claim for libel in a letter addressed to the claimant and alleged to have been opened by the claimant's daughter. Even if a publication to her had been established it was privileged as having been sent in the ordinary course of business in pursuance of a dispute between the claimant and the defendant; but in any event the minimal nature of the publication and the unlikelihood of damage meant that the claim was an abuse of process.

Unnecessary publication. A simple example of a publication which was   **14.70** unprotected by privilege because of unnecessarily wide dissemination is *Williamson v Freer*,[515] where a communication which would have been privileged if sent in a sealed letter was sent by telegram, so that the libel was unnecessarily published to those through whose hands it passed. "It was", said Brett L.J.[516]:

> "never meant by the legislature that these facilities for postal and telegraphic communication should be used for the purpose of more easily disseminating libels. Where there is such a communication it avoids the privilege, because it is communicated through unprivileged persons."[517]

---

[511] See paras 14.72–14.78, above.
[512] See para.14.53, above.
[513] See para.6.2, above.
[514] [2007] EWHC 1118 (QB).
[515] (1884) L.R. 9 C.P. 393.
[516] Ibid. at 395.
[517] Where transmission by telegram is the necessary or reasonable and usual course to adopt in the circumstances of the case, it will not avoid the privilege: *Edmondson v Birch Ltd* [1907] 1 K.B. 371 at 380–381. In *Hewitt v Grunwald* [2004] EWHC 2959 (QB) at [73] Eady J. referred to the words of Brett L.J. quoted above as sounding "a little quaint in the context of the internet and Article 10 of the European Convention on Human Rights". However, in fairness to Brett L.J. the telegrams in that case contained accusations of theft by the plaintiff from her employer, not the international terrorism involved in *Hewitt*.

Similarly, it has been held that the transmission of an uncovered postcard, containing matter libellous of the addressee, is an actionable publication[518]; and it is no defence that the writer had an interest in making, and the person addressed a corresponding interest in receiving, the communication, or that it was made bona fide and without malice, in the belief that the communication was reasonable. "I decline", said Palles C.B.

> "to be a party to allowing a libeller to extend the sphere of the publication of his libel beyond the necessity or exigency of the case, for the purpose of saving himself a small difference in postage. Postcards were intended to be the vehicle of ordinary communications, not of defamatory matter. I entirely concur in the reasoning in *Williamson v Freer*, and think it as applicable to a postcard as to a post office telegram. Indeed, the case of a postcard is stronger: for I can conceive many cases in which transmission by telegraph would be, not only a reasonable mode, but the only effective mode, of making a communication to the person privileged to receive it. It is difficult to conceive any case in which there can be a necessity to substitute a postcard for a closed letter."[519]

Although there is a possibility that electronic mail may be read by persons operating the various systems through which it will pass, the likelihood of this is remote and, unless the defendant has some reason to suspect interception, it is submitted that this form of communication should be treated like a sealed letter, though the same might not be true if the complaint were of publication to some uninterested person within an organisation to which it was sent.

14.71 *Examples.* Certain members of a town council caused to be published in a local newspaper a letter in which they charged the plaintiffs, contractors for the erection of the borough gaol, with serious omissions and deviations from their contract. It was held that, although such a charge would have been privileged had it been preferred at a meeting of the town council, no privilege attached to its publication in a public newspaper, for the general public, unlike the members of the town council, had no corresponding interests in the matter.[520]

In *Cambridge v Makin*[521] defamatory statements made by the defendant as part of a campaign to encourage support for a motion of no confidence brought by him against the claimant in her position as a director of the National Register of Public Service Interpreters were protected by qualified privilege only so far as they were made to those interpreters who could vote

---

[518] *Robinson v Jones* (1879) 4 L.R.Ir. 391; *Sadgrove v Hole* [1901] 1 2 K.B. 1 CA.
[519] *Robinson v Jones* (1879) 4 L.R.Ir. 391 at 396. A more modern example would be a fax sent to an open business line.
[520] *Simpson v Downs* (1867) 16 L.T. 391; and see *Hopewell v Kennedy* (1904) 9 O.L.R. 43; *Holliday v Ontario Farmers' Co* (1877) 1 O.A.R. 483.
[521] [2012] EWCA Civ 85; [2012] E.M.L.R. 19. See also *Clift v Slough BC* [2003] EWCA Civ 331; [2003] 1 W.L.R. 1357; *Underhill v Corser* [2010] EWHC 1195 (QB) (publication to members of a charitable train society about financial affairs of the society was protected by privilege in so far as the publication was made to members of the society but not where it was made to those who had no interest in the society's financial affairs).

on the motion of no confidence but not otherwise. So too in *Brady v Norman*,[522] a case rather similar to *Trumm v Norman*,[523] it was held that publication in ASLEF's *Loco Journal* to 131 persons (of a total circulation of approximately 18,000) who were not members or ex-members of the union was not privileged.[524] In *Levi v Bates*[525] a publication in football programmes sold to club members was held to be privileged but not in so far as it was included in programmes sold to others (e.g. away supporters). In *Lindholdt v Hyer*[526] the publication was a magazine for cab drivers but was easily accessible to the public, indeed drivers were encouraged to show it to them. At trial the judge had found that there was qualified privilege but that it was defeated by malice. Upholding the latter finding, the majority of the NSWCA declined to deal with the argument in the defendant's Notice of Contention that the finding of privilege was wrong. However, McColl J.A. thought the defendant's argument was correct:

> "Many . . . mono-topic magazines exist. A glance along a newsagent's shelf reveals magazines dedicated to sports, computers etc. Publishers of such magazines do not have a 'community of interest' with their subscribers in the sense required for an occasion of qualified privilege. The interests of society in general do not require that a communication made to any person with an interest in such topics should be protected . . . Once it is concluded that *Cabbie* is published to the general public, then . . . it cannot be said that the interests of society in general required the publication to it of matters concerning the economic welfare of taxi drivers/operators. Such publications were not made for the welfare of society. The fact that some readers may have been interested in the subject matter does not elevate it to that level . . . This was not a case where publication to the public beyond the taxi industry was reasonable, and no wider than was necessary for the effective communication of the imputations."[527]

The defendant town clerk sent out a notice convening a meeting of the defendant borough council to consider inter alia the report of a committee of the council regarding the loss of petrol from one of the council's depots. The notice contained a long agenda and a complete copy of the report of the committee. Copies of the notice were sent to certain public libraries in the borough where they were open to perusal by ratepayers and others. In an action for defamation by persons whose names appeared in the report, it was held by the Court of Appeal that there was no common interest between the council and the ratepayers to have what was only a preliminary stage in an

---

[522] [2008] EWHC 2481 (QB).
[523] *Trumm v Norman* [2008] EWHC 116 (QB). See further, at para.14.76, below.
[524] Note that the defendant accepted that he could, if he wished, communicate with ASLEF members alone (at [15]).
[525] [2009] EWHC 1495 (QB).
[526] [2008] NSWCA 264
[527] Ibid. at [160]–[161].

investigation communicated to the ratepayers in the form in which it was communicated, and the occasion was not privileged.[528]

14.72 Ordinary course of business. Defamatory but privileged words do not lose their privilege by being dictated and transcribed or copied or printed or communicated to the recipient's employees in the reasonable and ordinary course of business.[529]

> "If a business communication is privileged, as being made on a privileged occasion, the privilege covers all the incidents of the transmission and treatment of that communication which are in accordance with the reasonable and usual course of business,"[530]

and it is in accordance with the reasonable and usual course of business to dictate business letters to a typist even though these letters contain statements defamatory of a third person.[531]

> "The fact that, in making the communication on a privileged occasion in the reasonable and usual business manner having regard to the subject-matter of the communication, you bring it before other subordinates, either your own or those of the receiver, does not destroy the privilege."[532]

To hold otherwise would practically destroy the defence of privilege in the case of companies and large mercantile firms, because, as a matter of business, it is impossible that a business document can be written by and pass through the hands of one partner or person only.[533] However, in deciding what is reasonable, the gravity of the charge must be taken into account so that, e.g.

---

[528] *De Buse v McCarthy* [1942] 1 K.B. 156 CA. The publication of such an agenda would now be privileged in certain circumstances under Pt VA of the Local Government Act 1972, as to which see *Lillie v Newcastle CC* [2002] EWHC 1600 (QB). See also *Pulp & Paper Workers of Canada v International Brotherhood of Pulp etc. Workers* (1973) 37 D.L.R. 687 (excessive publication by placards); *Westbank Band of Indians v Tomat* (1989) 50 C.C.L.T. 257 (excessive circulation of petition); *Wagner v Lim* (1994) 22 Alta. L.R. (3d) 169 (excessive publication of complaint).

[529] *Lawless v Anglo-Egyptian Co* (1869) L.R. 4 Q.B. 262; *Boxsius v Goblet Freres* [1894] 1 Q.B. 842 CA; *Harper v Hamilton Retail Association* (1901) 32 O.R. 295; *Edmondson v Birch & Co* [1907] 1 K.B. 371 CA at 380; *Roff v British and French, etc. Co* [1918] 2 K.B. 677 CA; *Osborne v Boulter* [1930] 2 K.B. 226; *Bryanston Finance v De Vries* [1975] Q.B. 703 CA at 727, 736–737; *Greenan v Minneapolis Co* (1929) 4 D.L.R 501 Alta, CA; *Lacarte v Toronto Board of Education* [1959] S.C.R. 465.

[530] Per Fletcher Moulton L.J. in *Edmondson v Birch & Co* [1907] 1 K.B. 371 CA at 382. See also ibid. at 380.

[531] *Osborn v Boulter* [1930] 2 K.B. 226 CA, where *Pullman v Hill* [1891] 1 Q.B. 524 is explained as a mere decision of fact that in 1890 it was not a usual or reasonable thing for a member of a business firm to dictate a letter containing defamatory statements to, and to have it copied by a clerk. *Osborn v Boulter* was treated as settled law in *Bryanston Finance v De Vries* [1975] Q.B. 703 CA. In modern office conditions things like network distribution of files and messages and use of remote printing facilities have probably increased the risk of excessive publication within an organisation as a result of error. But privilege would not be lost if the document were deliberately "leaked" by an employee.

[532] Per Scrutton L.J. in *Roff v British and French, etc. Co* [1918] 2 K.B. 677 at 684.

[533] *Edmondson v Birch* [1907] 1 K.B. 371 at 381–382.

special care should be taken that a document containing a statement imputing criminality only comes to the attention of the recipient and is not exposed to casual examination in the post room.[534]

Examples. The auditors of a company, in making up the year's accounts, **14.73** issued to the shareholders a report containing statements defamatory of the plaintiff, who was manager of the company. The directors presented their report to the shareholders at the annual meeting, and it was resolved that the report should be printed and forwarded to all the shareholders. It was held that the delivery of the report of the printers for the purpose of having it printed was protected by the privilege of the occasion, because the printing of the report was "a necessary and reasonable mode of communicating it to the shareholders" and "the usual course having regard to the exigencies of business and the necessary means of making known that which they thought ought to be made known to the shareholders at large".[535]

A solicitor, acting on behalf of his client, sent to P a letter containing statements defamatory of her. The letter was dictated to a clerk and transcribed by him and signed by the solicitor and then copied by another clerk into the letter-book. Held, that the publications to the clerks were privileged because they were made in the ordinary course of a solicitor's business, and were "reasonably necessary and usual in the discharge of his duty to his client, and in the interests of the client".[536]

P was temporarily engaged by a company in Japan as their mining engineer, the engagement to be continued permanently if their correspondents, a London company, approved. The former company having consulted the latter, the managing director of the latter sent a letter and a cablegram in code containing statements defamatory of P and advising them not to employ him. The letter was dictated by the managing director to a clerk, by whom it was taken down in shorthand, typewritten, and copied into the company's open letter-book. The cablegram was dictated to a clerk, by whom it was typewritten, and, with its translation, copied into the company's cable-book. It was then delivered to the telegraph company's employees, by whom it was transmitted to Japan. It was held that the occasion of the sending of the letter and cablegram being privileged, their incidental publication to the clerks of the London company and of the telegraph company was also privileged, as the course followed in both cases was "the reasonable and usual course to adopt under the circumstances" to give effect to the privilege.[537]

---

[534] *Cunningham v Essex CC*, June 26, 2000, (QB), applying remarks of Scrutton L.J. in *Roff v British and French, etc. Co*, above at 684.

[535] *Lawless v Anglo-Egyptian Co* (1869) L.R.4 Q.B. 262 at 268, 270; followed in *Harper v Hamilton Retail Association* (1900) 32 O.R. 295.

[536] *Boxsius v Goblet Freres* [1894] 1 Q.B. 842. This case expressly rejects a dictum of Kay L.J. in *Pullman v Hill* [1891] 1 Q.B. at 531

[537] *Edmondson v Birch & Co* [1907] 1 K.B. 371 CA; followed in *Osborn v Boulter* [1930] 2 K.B. 226 CA; *Bryanston Finance v De Vries* [1975] Q.B. 703 CA; *Chapman v Barber*, 1989

14.74 Publication to uninterested person: ancillary privilege. While the
policy of the above decisions is obviously correct, the nature of the privilege
presents certain difficulties which were examined by the Court of Appeal in a
case in which a letter was published to employees by being dictated and
copied with a view to sending it to the plaintiff (to whom alone it was in fact
sent), to various City institutions and to the press.[538] It was said that:

> " . . . if under current business practice the reasonable and ordinary way of getting
> [a letter] written is to dictate it to a typist, the publication of its defamatory contents
> to the typist attracts the same privilege as that attaching to its subsequent publication
> to the addressee. This, however, is not an original privilege but one ancillary to, and
> dependent on, the existence of a privilege for the publication of the defamatory
> contents of the letter to its addressee."[539]

As there is at that stage no actual publication of the letter to the addressee, it
"is the use which the author of the defamatory matter intends to make of it at
that time that attracts whatever ancillary privilege there may be".[540] Thus, if
further publication is restrained by injunction, as it was in that case, or the
letter is lost in the post, the defendant may still succeed. Similarly, it does not
matter that there is no communication other than to the person defamed, and
so in law no publication (other than to the typist): nevertheless, qualified
privilege covers "all incidents of the transmission of the letter sent in the
course of a dispute between two parties which were in accordance with the
reasonable and usual course of business".[541]

**14.75 Publication by uninterested person: ancillary and independent
privilege.** Where a publication is made on an occasion which is privileged
by reason of a duty or interest in one of the publishers in making the
communication, any other person whose participation in the publication is
reasonably necessary or in the ordinary course of business is also protected by
the privilege.[542] However, a distinction has been drawn between such ancillary, incidental or derivative privilege and an independent or personal privilege. In some cases, although the communication serves to forward the

---

S.L.T. 830; *Greenan v Minneapolis Co* [1929] 4 D.L.R. 501. See also *Dorn v Peterson*, 512 N.W.
2d 902 (Minn., 1994).

[538] *Bryanston Finance v De Vries* [1975] Q.B. 703, in which the Court of Appeal held that there
was no privilege on the facts of the case, in particular because of the nature of the publication to
the plaintiff, on which the privilege discussed here would have been dependent; it was also
relevant that the letter dictated and copied was intended to be sent to newspapers, which would
not have been a privileged publication.

[539] Per Diplock L.J., ibid. at 727.

[540] Ibid. at 729.

[541] Per Lawton L.J., ibid. at 736. See also *Bezant v Rausing* [2007] EWHC 1118 (QB),
para.14.69, above. Contrast *White v Stone* [1939] 2 K.B. 827 CA, for which see para.14.80,
below.

[542] *Smith v Streatfeild* [1913] 3 K.B. 764, not overruled on this point by *Egger v Chelmsford*
[1965] 1 Q B. 248 CA. See also paras 17.22–17.25, below.

interests of someone other than the person who makes it, the latter is recognised as himself having a duty to make the communication or an interest in making it. Thus, a solicitor or other agent is recognised as having such a duty or interest in relation to the affairs of his client or principal, whereas a printer or typist may not.[543] The distinction is not without significance because while it is plainly established that among joint tortfeasors the malice of one does not infect the others,[544] it might be argued that if the privilege of one defendant was merely ancillary to that of another who was malicious, then it could not survive the loss of the "main" privilege, though this is probably not the law.[545]

Reasonable to take risk of publication to uninterested persons: 14.76
libel. Apart from cases of publication to typists, printers and the like, where the occasion on which a libel is published is otherwise privileged the person exercising the privilege is entitled to take all necessary or reasonable means of so doing and, provided the publication does not go beyond the exigency of the occasion, the mere fact that the defamatory matter is communicated to persons who have no legitimate interest in its subject-matter will not avoid the privilege. So where the general manager of a railway company which had dismissed the plaintiff, a conductor, for alleged dishonesty, directed printed placards describing the offence to be posted up in the company's private offices (in some of which they were seen by strangers), for the information and warning of the company's employees, 2,000 in number, it was held that the evidence showed a reasonable mode of publication having regard to the

---

[543] The distinction was first explicitly drawn by Slade J. in *Longdon-Griffiths v Smith* [1951] 1 K.B. 295 at 303. In his discussion of *Smith v Streatfeild* [1913] 3 K.B. 764, he said that in that case it had been recognised, both in the arguments and in the judgment, that there was a distinction between an independent privilege, such as solicitors enjoy in the protection of their clients' interests (for which, see para.14.22, above), and the derivative privilege of the printers in that case, who had no privilege other than such as they derived from the privilege of Canon Streatfeild. Bankes J. had rejected the argument on behalf of the printers that mere printing and publication in the ordinary course of business was sufficient to constitute an independent privilege, and held that their privilege was defeated by Canon Streatfeild's malice. One anomaly is that the printer's privilege was founded on the decision in *Baker v Carrick* [1894] 1 Q.B. 838 (privilege for a solicitor). Slade J. thus distinguished *Smith v Streatfeild* from the case before him by pointing out that each of the trustees had an independent privilege, so as not to be affected by the malice of another. The distinction drawn by Slade J. was accepted by Winn J. in *Meekins v Henson* [1964] Q.B. at 480, where he held that each partner had a "personal" privilege, and that a non-malicious partner was not affected by the malice of another partner. Comparison should be made with *Bryanston Finance v De Vries* [1975] Q.B. 703 (for which see para.14.74, above) in which the Court of Appeal distinguished between the privilege which would arise between employer and typist if the typist had an interest in the communication being typed, and the privilege which was ancillary to and dependent on the existence of a privileged occasion for the making of the communication to the person for whom it is intended.
[544] *Egger v Chelmsford* [1965] 1 Q.B. 248 CA. See further para.17.24, below.
[545] See para.17.25, below. If instead of malice the claimant were seeking to establish irrelevance of the matter published to the privileged occasion, it does not seem that it would make any difference whether the particular defendant was claiming an independent or a derivative privilege.

circumstances of the case, and that this being so it made no difference that, in imparting the information to persons within the privilege, the libellous matter was also communicated to others not so included.[546] It has been held that, although publication in a newspaper of general circulation might have been excessive, privilege was not lost where the medium used was one circulating among persons with a legitimate interest, even though it might be seen by others.[547] However, whether these cases would be decided in the same way today must be doubtful, particularly if the claimant's art.8 rights are engaged. In principle privilege may extend to publication of a notice in protection of an interest or performance of a duty[548] in an ordinary newspaper or on the internet if that is the only possible and effectual mode of discharging the duty or protecting the interest which gives rise to the privilege.[549] Such a case will, however, be rare.

14.77 Slander: presence of uninterested bystanders not necessarily fatal to defence. In cases of slander, where the defendant spoke the words complained of with honesty of purpose to a person or persons who had some

---

[546] *Tench v G. W. Ry* (1873) 33 Up.Can.Q.B. 8. This decision seems entirely in accord with the principle of the cases in para.14.72, above. However, in the similar case of *Hunt v G.N.Ry.* [1891] 2 Q.B. 189 CA, it is clear from the report on 60 L.J.Q.B.498 that the notice was posted up in rooms occupied by the company's staff, and not in any rooms to which the public had access. In *Neame v Yellow Cabs Ltd* [1930] S.A.S.R. 267, the only evidence of publication to anyone other than the company's staff was to a person who had no business in the part of the company's premises where the notice was posted up, and was a mere trespasser, which publication was held insufficient to found an action. See also *Gallant v West* [1955] 4 D.L.R. 209. The decision in *Pleau v Simpsons-Sears* (1976) 75 D.L.R. (3d) 747 must be close to the borderline since the imputation could have been reduced or eliminated by a change of wording (P's wallet and cards had been stolen; notice on cash register in store, "Wayne Pleau. If any cheque is presented detain person and call security"; the notice was visible to customers).

[547] *Star Gems v Ford* [1980] C.L.Y. 1671 (Russell J; letter in "The Retail Chemist" alleging dubious sales practices by P). There are a number of comparable and more fully reported decisions in other jurisdictions: *Redgate v Roush*, 59 P. 1050 (Kan., 1900) (sectarian paper); *Bereman v Power Publishing Co*, 27 P.2d 749 (Colo., 1933) (union paper); *Sheehan v Tobin*, 93 N.E.2d 524 (Mass., 1950) (similar); *Fisher v Rankin* (1972) 27 D.L.R. (3d) 746 (similar); *Wells v Croskery* [1952] N.Z.L.R. 312 (similar); *Chen Cheng v Central Christian Church* [1999] 1 Sing. L.R. 94 Sing. CA (magazine with a circulation of about 6,000 among the evangelical community):
"Often the only practicable means of communicating defamatory matter involves a probability or even a certainty that it will reach many persons whose knowledge of it is of no value in accomplishing the purpose for which the privilege is given. In this case, the publication is not excessive or an abuse of the privilege, if the importance of the interest involved, the gravity of the harm threatened to it and the inconvenience of any other means of communication make the publication reasonable": Restatement, 2d, *Torts*, para.604, comment b.

[548] This head of privilege should be distinguished from those cases in which it is held that publication in a newspaper is privileged because the newspaper is under a "duty" to communicate the information and the public at large has an "interest" in receiving it: see para.15.2, below.

[549] *Hewitt v Grunwald* [2004] EWHC 2959 (QB). *Chapman v Ellesmere* [1932] 2 K.B. 431 at 456. Cf. *Trumm v Norman* [2008] EWHC 116 (QB) and *Harding v Essey* [2005] WASCA 30 (newsletter addressed to 178 school canteens defamed the plaintiff company; plaintiffs, not knowing to which it had been sent, circulated response to all 1,000 school canteens; plea of qualified privilege based on reply to attack failed: the company should have first sought information from those who issued the newsletter about its distribution).

legitimate interest, or some duty in the matter, the mere fact that one,[550] or even several,[551] (legally) uninterested persons happened to be present and heard what was said will not necessarily prevent the occasion from being a privileged occasion. The business of life could not well be carried on if such restraints were imposed on these communications, and if they were never protected unless the occasion were strictly private.[552] The fact, however, that some other person or persons who had no common interest or duty in the matter were present is a circumstance which may be left to the jury, who are to determine whether the defendant was acting bona fide in speaking the words or was influenced by improper motives.[553]

Examples. P was employed to carry out some repairs at a farm house of which the defendant was tenant. During the progress of the repairs P got drunk, and circumstances induced D to believe that he had broken open the cellar door and obtained access to his cider. Two days afterwards D met P in the presence of X, and charged him with having broken open his cellar door and with having got drunk and spoilt the work. It was held that the mere fact that the charge was made in the presence of X did not destroy the privilege, provided it was made honestly and bona fide, and that it was for the jury to determine from the circumstances, including the style and character of the language used, whether D acted bona fide or was actuated by malice.[554]

14.78

P was about to be sworn in as a paid constable by the justices, when D, a parishioner, objected and made a statement to the justices in the presence of other persons imputing perjury to P. The jury found that D made the statement bona fide believing it to be true. It was held that the fact that other persons

---

[550] *Toogood v Spyring* (1834) 1 C.M. & R. 181; *Padmore v Lawrence* (1840) 11 A. & E. 380; *Howe v Jones* (1885) 1 T.L.R.461 at 462; *M'Falden v Lynch* (1883) 17 Ir.L.T. 93; *Jones v Thomas* (1885) 53 L.T. 678 at 680; *Shaumer v Mayer*, *The Times*, June 20, 1919.

[551] *Kershaw v Bailey* (1848) 1 Exch. 743; *Wallace v Carroll* (1860) 11 Ir.C.L.R. 485; *Hodges v Glass* (1879) O.B. & F. (N.Z. Sup Ct) 66; *Pittard v Oliver* [1891] 1 Q.B. 474 CA; *Gildner v Busse* (1902) 3 O.L.R. 561; *Stewart v Biggs* [1928] N.Z.L.R. 28, reversed by CA at 673; *Kleinhaus v Usmar* (1929) A.D. 121; *Van Zyl v Erasmus* [1938] E.D.L.185. In *Adams v Templeman*, 1913 2 S.L.T. 241, where an employee was stopped by his employer's foreman a few yards from the gates of the employer's premises and accused of theft in the hearing of other employees who were leaving the premises, it was held by Lord Ormidale that the accusation was not privileged. This narrow view of the scope of the privilege is contrary to the English decisions. Cf. *Watson v Burnet* (1862) 24 D. 494.

[552] Per Parke B. in *Toogood v Spyring* (1834) 1 C.M. & R. 181 at 194.

[553] Ibid.; *Richards v Australasian Temperance Co* [1913] N.Z.L.R. 618. See para.34.42, below, on evidence of malice in these situations.

[554] *Toogood v Spyring* (1834) 1 C.M. & R. 181. *McCormack v Olsthoorn* [2004] IEHC 431; [2004] 3 I.R. 632 on rather similar facts. In this aspect *Toogood v Spyring* involves an "ancillary privilege" in the sense described in para.14.74, above. There were three slanders in this case, the first a statement to the plaintiff in the presence of X, the ancillary privilege; the second, a statement to X in P's absence; the third, a statement to B, the plaintiff's superior and agent of D's landlord. The third is an example of the standard privilege situation. The second statement was not privileged, X having nothing to do with the matter. The trial judge having correctly directed that the third publication was privileged and no separate awards having been made between the first and the second slanders, the order was for a new trial.

besides the justices were present did not destroy the privilege.[555] "I think D chose the most proper occasion for making his objection, and that it was his bounden duty to do so. Was he to stand by and see a person elected whom he believed to be perjured, and not take any objection?"[556]

At a meeting of a board of guardians at which reporters were present in accordance with custom, and also persons who were not guardians, the defendant, a member of the board, in a discussion concerning the plaintiff's accounts, made defamatory statements concerning the plaintiff, who had been their clerk. The jury found the statements were made "honestly in the discharge of a public duty, and without malice". It was held that the privilege attaching to such statements was not taken away by the presence of the reporters and the other persons who were not guardians.[557] In his judgment Lord Esher M.R. said:

> "Was the defendant's duty to the guardians and to the ratepayers generally taken away by the presence of these other persons, who were not called in by him[558] and over whose presence he could exercise no control? The question answers itself: the presence of these persons left his duty[559] to discuss the matter untouched, the occasion was privileged for the performance of that duty, and the privilege was not taken away by the presence of such people under such circumstances."[560]

14.79 Unnecessary publication. An example of unnecessary publication in the presence of third parties[561] is *Rankine v Roberts*,[562] where the defendant, a bank agent, charged a customer with forging a signature to a bill and it was held that while he would have been privileged in making the charge to the customer or bank official whom he might have to consult, there could be no privilege if it were made in the public office of the bank in the hearing of the bank clerks and members of the public. However, a number of judicial

---

[555] *Kershaw v Bailey* (1848) 1 Exch.743.

[556] Ibid. at 748. See also *Padmore v Lawrence* (1840) 11 A. & E. 380.

[557] *Pittard v Oliver* [1891] 1 Q.B. 474 CA. See also *Hopewell v Kennedy* (1904) 9 O.L.R. 43; *Restall v Malloch* (1904) 18 E.D.C. 77; *Stewart v Biggs* [1928] N.Z.L.R. 28, reversed by CA, at 673; and see *McIntosh v Scott* [1938] 1 W.W.R. 74; *Broughton v McGrew* (1889) 39 F. 672, where the presence at a shareholders' meeting of the attorneys of the company at the invitation of the directors did not destroy the privilege.

[558] The position where the defendant has himself called in reporters and the public is unclear. In *Parsons v Surgey* (1864) 4 F. & F. 247, as distinguished in *Hodges v Glass* (1879) O.B. & F. 66 N.Z.Sup Ct at 69, it was suggested that this would make the occasion unprivileged.

[559] Compare *Jones v Bennett* [1969] S.C.R. 277, where D was defending himself to supporters rather than discharging a duty and any privilege which existed was lost by knowledge that reporters were present and words would be communicated to general public.

[560] [1891] 1 Q.B. 474 CA at 478; and see per Sir J. Hannen at 480; *Gorst v Barr* (1887) 13 O.L.R. 644. Compare *Parkes v Prescott* (1869) L.R. 4 Ex. 169, where a request was made that the press would take note of what was said and there was evidence of authorisation of a republication. However, in such cases a report of the proceedings would now be privileged: para.16.17, below.

[561] Although it is not clear that all the hearers in *Guise v Kouvelis* (1947) 74 C.L.R. 102 HCA, were "interested" the decision that there was no privilege does not seem to turn on this but on the view that it was unnecessary to make the accusation so publicly.

[562] (1873) 1 R. 230.

statements in these cases of slander treat the unnecessary presence of third parties not as taking the case outside the privilege but as evidence of malice (which will be a question for the jury). So, in *Pittard v Oliver*[563] Lord Esher M.R. said:

> "If a person whose duty it is to make a statement to certain persons calls in other persons to whom he owes no duty to make the statement, in order that those other persons may hear it, I should be inclined to say that it would not become his duty to refrain from making his statement to the proper persons, but that there would be evidence of malice in his making it in the presence of others who might promulgate it."[564]

Plainly there will be cases in which excessive publication takes the case out of the privilege altogether and the defendant's lack of malice is irrelevant. Just as, in a case of libel, D would not be privileged in raising a private dispute with C in the national press, so also he would be unprotected if he used the public address system in Wembley Stadium to air his views. Perhaps it is a question of fact and degree for the judge which approach should be taken and a judge may be more inclined to hold that the case is outside the privilege if the defendant is not acting under a duty but in protection of an interest of his own. Arguably this is not a very satisfactory position for two reasons. Where the publication to uninterested persons is very limited there is a danger that a jury which is told that it *may* regard it as evidence of malice will attach too much importance to it; equally, where the publication to uninterested persons is wide, there is a risk that what ought to be an issue of law will be passed to the jury.[565]

Charges of crime. The question of publication of slanderous words to   **14.80** uninterested third persons has often arisen in relation to charges of crime. The defendant does not lose the protection of privilege if he is unaware that uninterested parties are within earshot. Thus in *Shaumer v Mayer*[566] D sent to P a pearl necklace to be restrung. On the necklace being returned he suspected P of having changed and stolen some of the pearls, so he went to P's office and charged him with the theft. It was held by Lord Reading C.J. that the mere fact that another person was (unknown to the defendant) present in an adjoining room in P's office and happened to overhear the words complained of did not destroy the privilege, the learned judge observing that:

---

[563] [1891] 1 Q.B. 474 CA at 477–478.

[564] See also *Toogood v Spyring* (1834) 1 C.M. & R. 181 at 194; *Jones v Thomas* (1885) 53 L.T. 678 at 679–680. This may be connected with the fact that the original view of qualified privilege looked upon it as rebutting an implied malice which no longer has any significance: see Mitchell, *The Making of the Modern Law of Defamation* (2005).

[565] The point is essentially the same as that which is discussed in para.14.63, above in relation to relevance.

[566] *The Times*, June 20, 1919.

"were it otherwise no one could make a business complaint to anyone without running the serious risk of being subjected to damages, if he were accidentally overheard by a stranger on the premises."[567]

However, the law goes further and protection is not lost even if the defendant is aware that others are present.[568] "The exigencies of a society could never permit such a restriction. If I stop a party suspected may I not say why I do so?"[569] Indeed:

"If money has been suspected to have been stolen in a house from two different persons who live in the same house, and a charge is made against a suspected person of stealing from one of them, it is right and proper that the other should be present when the charge is made. It is not an unreasonable inference that the person who stole from the one stole also from the other. Each has a common interest in discovering the thief."[570]

14.81 Reasonable precaution. Where the defendant, in making a statement on a privileged occasion, as a reasonable precaution and in order to protect his own interests, calls in third persons to hear what he says, the presence of such third persons will not destroy the privilege. Thus where D, who was about to dismiss his servant for dishonesty, called in a friend to hear what passed, the presence of such third party did not avoid the privilege, for it was material to D's interest that a third person should be present who could bear witness to the dissolution of the contract, and so safeguard D against any imputation of having dismissed P for reasons other than those he then assigned.[571]

---

[567] Cf. *McManus v Beckham* [2002] EWCA Civ 939; [2002] 1 W.L.R. 2982.

[568] "If made with honesty of purpose to a party who has any interest in the inquiry (and that has been very liberally construed), the simple fact that there has been some casual bystander cannot alter the nature of the transaction": per Parke B. in *Toogood v Spyring*, above, at 193–194. In *White v Stone* [1939] 2 K.B. 827 CA, the application of the principle in *Toogood's* case was brought into question, and it was held that there could not be any privilege for publication to bystanders unless there was also an independently privileged publication; there was none in that case, it was held, since a communication to the plaintiff himself was not a publication in law. This, however, was also the position in *Toogood v Spyring* itself, and the decision also seems inconsistent with *Bryanston Finance v De Vries* [1975] Q.B. 703, for which see para.14.74, above. It is submitted that *White v Stone* is best explained as a case in which there was no evidence that it was reasonable to make the communication in the presence of bystanders. The decision is also criticised in *Guise v Kouvelis* (1947) 74 C.L.R. at 124.

[569] Per Coleridge J. in *Padmore v Lawrence* (1840) 11 A. & E. 380 at 382. For examples of privileged accusations against shoppers notwithstanding the presence of others, see *McCormack v Olsthoorn* [2004] IEHC 431; [2004] 3 I.R. 632; *Kroger v Yount*, 66 F.2d 700 (C.A. 8 1933); *Ridgeway v Safeway Stores*, 139 F. Supp. 290 (1948).

[570] Per Williams J. in *Bowles v Armstrong* (1912) 22 N.Z.L.R. 409 at 442. So the mere fact that third persons come up of their own accord and listen to what is said when the charge is made is no evidence of abuse of the occasion: *Kleinhaus v Usmar* [1929] A.D. 127. As to the distinction between the presence of third parties taking the case out of the privilege or being evidence of malice, see para.14.79, above.

[571] *Taylor v Hawkins* (1851) 16 Q.B. 308. See also *Somerville v Hawkins* (1851) 10 C.B. 583; *Jones v Thomas* (1885) 53 L.T. 678.

CHAPTER 15

PUBLICATION ON A MATTER OF PUBLIC INTEREST

SECTION 1. INTRODUCTION

Background. Historically, the tendency of the common law was to confine **15.1** qualified privilege to restricted or "private" communications. The according of privilege to communications made to the public generally was, however, very limited[1] and the widespread publication of matters of public interest was not privileged. In *Perera v Peiris*,[2] however, the Privy Council held that publication by a newspaper of an extract from a government report on bribery that accused the plaintiff of lack of candour was privileged because the public interest of Ceylon required that it be widely communicated to the public.[3] Subsequently, in *Blackshaw v Lord*,[4] the Court of Appeal commented, *obiter*, that there might be "extreme cases where the urgency of communicating a warning is so great, or the source of the information so reliable, that publication of suspicion or speculation is justified; for example, where there is danger to the public from a suspected terrorist or the distribution of contaminated

---

[1] There was a comparatively limited, though much extended by statute from the 1880s, category of privileged reports (for example of judicial proceedings or proceedings in Parliament), and a line of cases concerning statements by and about candidates for election. Moreover, in *Allbutt v General Council of Medical Education* (1889) 23 Q.B.D. 400 CA the publication of minutes of council proceedings was afforded privilege.

[2] [1949] A.C. 1 PC. The case concerned the Roman-Dutch law of Ceylon, but this does not seem to have been thought different in this respect from the common law. Compare *Chapman v Ellesmere* [1932] 2 K.B. 431 CA (report of disqualification of trainer published in *Racing Calendar* privileged, not the report in *The Times*. *Allbutt's* case was distinguished because the interest there was regarded as general, rather than sectional. (See now Sch.1, para.14(c), Defamation Act 1996.)

[3] [1949] A.C. 1 at 21. Nowadays in England such a report would, of course, be privileged under Sch.1 to the Defamation Act 1996, either under para.7 or para.9 for reports originating in England. Para.7 would cover the publication of an extract from the Ceylon report in England.

[4] [1984] 1 Q.B. 1 CA. The fact that Parliament had in earlier similar legislation conferred privilege on a wide range of reports was regarded as a reason for being cautious about extending the common law (at 25).

[633]

food or drugs".[5] There was no general privilege for "fair information on a matter of public interest".

This position changed with the decision of the House of Lords in *Reynolds v Times Newspapers Ltd*.[6] In a unanimous decision,[7] their Lordships established a new variant of qualified privilege in which less emphasis was placed on the traditional, reciprocal duty and interest test, and more on the question of whether the publication was on a matter of public interest and whether it was the product of responsible journalism (with the issue of malice being subsumed within this latter element). Thus, qualified privilege extended to cover the situation where a media organisation sought to communicate information regarding matters of public concern to a general audience. It was heralded as a "constitutionalisation" of defamation law.[8] The purpose underpinning the development of the *Reynolds* privilege, in the words of Lord Bingham C.J. in the Court of Appeal, was to recognise that:

> "the common convenience and welfare of a modern plural democracy such as ours are best served by an ample flow of information to the public concerning, and by vigorous public discussion of, matters of public interest to the community. By that we mean matters relating to the public life of the community and those who take part in it, including within the expression 'public life' activities such as the conduct of government and political life, elections . . . and public administration, but we use the expression more widely than that, to embrace matters such as (for instance) the governance of public bodies, institutions and companies which give rise to a public interest in their disclosure, but excluding matters which are personal and private . . . As it is the task of the news media to inform the public and engage in public discussion of matters of public interest, so is that to be recognized as its duty . . . In modern times what we have called the duty test should, in our view, be rather more

---

[5] [1984] 1 Q.B. 1 at 27. On the facts, nothing of that sort was involved and caution was required in approaching a publication "which tries and fails to come within statutory privilege" (at 25). On the point regarding danger from terrorists, cf. *Hewitt v Grunwald* [2004] EWHC 2959 (QB), though the urgency there—whether the claimant charity was a terrorist organisation—was not of the same order as that contemplated by the Court of Appeal.

[6] [2001] 2 A.C. 127 HL. The case had arisen after *The Sunday Times* published an article that chronicled the demise of the coalition government in Ireland in November 1994 (Ruddock and Burns, "Goodbye Gombeen Man", *The Sunday Times*, November 20, 1994). The plaintiff, Albert Reynolds, had been the erstwhile *Taoiseach*. The article alleged that Reynolds had knowingly misled both the *Dáil* and his former coalition partners over the handling of a controversial extradition case by the then Attorney General, whom he wished to appoint as President of the High Court. While the jury agreed that he had been libelled it refused to award any damages. The judge, French J., later altered the award to one pence, and ordered Reynolds to pay the defendants' costs as from the date of payment into court. Reynolds appealed seeking a new trial on the basis that the judge had erred in his summing-up. The defendants cross-appealed, raising questions as to the defence of qualified privilege and costs. There were more or less contemporaneous developments in other parts of the Commonwealth which extended qualified privilege to statements about political matters—see para.15.25, below—and in the United States the law has for many years required "actual malice" for a successful suit in respect of public officials or public figures (see para.15.31, below).

[7] The only point of difference between their Lordships was on a procedural point, that of whether there needed to be a retrial on the facts—see ibid. at 216 per Lord Steyn, and at 237 per Lord Hope.

[8] I. Loveland, "The Constitutionalisation of Political Libels in the English Common Law" [1998] *Public Law* 633.

readily be held to be satisfied . . . We have no doubt that the public also have an interest to receive information on matters of public interest . . . published in a newspaper, so satisfying what we have called the interest test. In modern conditions the interest test should also, in our view, be rather more readily held to be satisfied."[9]

In the House of Lords, Lord Nicholls—giving the leading speech—concurred: "the elasticity of the common law principle enables interference with freedom of speech to be confined to what is necessary in the circumstances of the case. This elasticity enables the court to give appropriate weight, in today's conditions, to the importance of freedom of expression by the media on all matters of public concern".[10]

In the ensuing years, the *Reynolds* privilege was pleaded on a sizeable number of occasions—although rarely successfully—and the issue returned to the highest court twice more: in *Jameel (Mohammed) v Wall Street Journal Europe SPRL*,[11] and in *Flood v Times Newspapers Ltd*.[12] These later decisions were intended to reiterate and explain the development following a period

---

[9] *Reynolds v Times Newspapers Ltd* [1998] 3 W.L.R. 862.

[10] *Reynolds v Times Newspapers Ltd* [2001] 2 A.C. 127 at 204–205.

[11] [2006] UKHL 44; [2007] 1 A.C. 359. In the *Jameel* case, the article that gave rise to the proceedings had been published on 6 February 2002 (it was reproduced in large part in the speech of Lord Hoffmann, at [40]). The gist of it, as presented by Lord Bingham (at [4]), was that at the request of US law enforcement agencies the Saudi Arabian central bank was monitoring accounts associated with some of the country's most prominent businessmen in a bid to prevent them from being used, wittingly or unwittingly, for the funnelling of funds to terrorist organisations. The accounts of the Abdullatif Jamil Group of companies were named as being among this group. The information on which the story was based was attributed to US officials and a number of Saudi contacts.

[12] [2012] UKSC 11; [2012] 2 A.C. 273. The defendants in June 2006 published a story to the effect that there were reasonable grounds to suspect that the claimant, a serving police officer, had corruptly received payments from a security company with Russian clients in return for providing confidential information about the possible extradition of Russians here. The allegations were said to have originated with an insider at the security firm who had passed a dossier to the police anti-corruption squad. The story went on to say that the police were investigating the claimant. The article was also published on the defendants' website. The claimant began proceedings for libel in respect of both publications in May 2007. The police investigation concluded in December 2006 and was unable to find any evidence of wrongdoing on the part of the claimant, though this was not communicated to the parties until September 2007. On an appeal and cross-appeal from Tugendhat J.'s decision on a preliminary issue the higher courts had to consider whether the publications were covered by *Reynolds* privilege, the main publication in June 2006, the website publication on a continuing basis thereafter. There was no doubt that allegations of police corruption were a matter of serious public interest and concern; so was the publication of the fact that there was a police investigation into those allegations, if only because that gave the public confidence that the police would pursue "one of their own" (see [2010] EWCA Civ 804; [2010] E.M.L.R. 26 at [116] per Moses L.J.). Indeed, the reporting of the investigation would have fallen squarely within para.9 of Sch.1 of the Defamation Act 1996 since it was based on a police press statement and, while strictly speaking that would not have covered the identification of the claimant (since that information was not in the press notice), the claimant was prepared to concede that this would have been privileged (a sort of "combination" of *Reynolds* and Sch.1). On that basis, the facts would quite closely resemble those of *Jameel*, where the story (a) identified the claimant and (b) reported the fact of the monitoring of the accounts. However, the story in *Flood* went considerably further than this in including details of the allegations which underlay the investigation.

when judges at first instance were said to have engaged in an over-heavy scrutiny of journalistic practices.[13] They emphasised the flexibility of the new principles, and the scope afforded under them to editorial judgment. In addition, a variant of *Reynolds* privilege developed to cover 'reportage'.[14]

When s.4 of the Defamation Act 2013 comes into force, the *Reynolds* privilege will be revised and recast in statutory form as the defence of "publication on a matter of public interest". Until late in the legislative process, this element of the Bill was essentially unremarkable. It did little more than reiterate *Reynolds* privilege in statutory form.[15] For that reason, it was criticised by campaigners for libel reform who proposed a defence based on a "good faith" or "absence-of-malice" standard equivalent to that familiar in US law. The defence ultimately passed by Parliament, however, is different. It has been altered so that it is now focused on whether, first, the statement complained of was on a matter of public interest, and secondly whether the defendant reasonably believed that publishing was in the public interest.[16] This new form of defence was initially mooted by Lord Lester during the Second Reading debate in the House of Lords.[17] It was subsequently adopted by the Government with necessary amendments introduced at the Committee Stage.

SECTION 2. CONCEPTUAL BASIS

15.2 The conceptual basis of the *Reynolds* privilege. In *Reynolds*, the new law was said to rest on the foundation of duty and interest like the older cases on qualified privilege.[18] Later, Lord Cooke said that it had been less a "breakthrough" than a reminder of the width of the basic common law principles, although it was much more encouraging of their invocation than previous English decisions.[19] Lord Nicholls referred to duty as the "conventional phraseology" for the issue whether the publication was in the public interest,[20] however, and said that the:

> "requirement that both the maker of the statement and the recipient must have an interest or duty draws attention to the need to have regard to the position of both parties when deciding whether an occasion is privileged. But this should not be allowed to obscure the rationale of the underlying public interest on which privilege is founded. The essence of this defence lies in the law's recognition of the need, in

---

[13] *Jameel (Mohammed) v Wall Street Journal Sprl* [2006] UKHL 44; [2007] 1 A.C. 359 at [38] per Lord Hoffmann.

[14] See para.15.15, below.

[15] For a discussion of the defence as it was envisaged in Lord Lester's Defamation Bill, see the First Supplement to the 11th edition of this work, at 84–85 and 91.

[16] S.4(1).

[17] 739 HL Deb 953–954 (October 9, 2012). Its authorship is attributed to Sir Brian Neill.

[18] [2001] 2 A.C. 127 at 224, 229, and 239.

[19] *McCartan Turkington Breen v Times Newspaper Ltd* [2001] 2 A.C. 277 at 301.

[20] [2001] 2 A.C. 127 at 196.

the public interest, for a particular recipient to receive frank and uninhibited communication of particular information from a particular source. That is the end the law is concerned to attain. The protection afforded to the maker of the statement is the means by which the law seeks to achieve that end."[21]

The views expressed by some of their Lordships in the *Jameel* case more strongly emphasised the distinctiveness of the *Reynolds* principle. While for Lord Bingham and Lord Hope the essential basis was still that of duty and interest,[22] for Lord Hoffmann:

"In answering the question of public interest, I do not think it helpful to apply the classic test for the existence of a privileged occasion and ask whether there was a duty to communicate the information and an interest in receiving it. The *Reynolds* defence was developed from the traditional form of privilege by a generalisation that in matters of public interest, there can be said to be a professional duty on the part of journalists to impart the information and an interest in the public in receiving it. The House having made this generalisation, it should in my opinion be regarded as a proposition of law and not decided each time as a question of fact. If the publication is in the public interest, the duty and interest are taken to exist."[23]

For Baroness Hale:

"It should by now be entirely clear that the *Reynolds* defence is a 'different jurisprudential creature' from the law of privilege, although it is a natural development of that law. It springs from the general obligation of the press, media and other publishers to communicate important information upon matters of general public interest and the general right of the public to receive such information. It is not helpful to analyse the particular case in terms of a specific duty and a specific right to know . . . In truth it is a defence of publication in the public interest."[24]

Although Lord Scott would not accept that *Reynolds* "turned its back" on the reciprocal duty and interest test,[25] or that it was "a different jurisprudential creature" from traditional qualified privilege,[26] in other passages he seemed in effect to adhere to Lord Hoffmann's view:

"To insist on a reciprocity of duty and interest between the publisher of a newspaper and the reader of the newspaper, who may be in New York, London, Rome, or anywhere, either makes the requirement of reciprocity meaningless or deprives any

---

[21] Ibid. at 195.

[22] *Jameel (Mohammed) v Wall Street Journal Europe SPRL* [2006] UKHL 44; [2007] 1 A.C. 359 at [30] and [105] respectively. See also *Prince Radu of Hohenzollern v Houston* [2008] EWCA Civ 921; [2009] E.M.L.R. 13 at [2].

[23] *Jameel (Mohammed) v Wall Street Journal Europe SPRL* (above) at [50]. Counsel in *Henry v BBC* [2005] EWHC 2787 (QB) went so far as to describe the duty and interest test in this context as no more than an "archaeological relic", though Gray J. was not inclined to agree: at [83].

[24] *Jameel (Mohammed) v Wall Street Journal Europe SPRL* (above) at [146]. See also, Lord Hoffmann at [46]: "It might more appropriately be called the *Reynolds* public interest defence rather than privilege."

[25] Ibid. at [130].

[26] Ibid. at [135].

defamatory statement in the paper, no matter how important as a matter of public interest the content of the statement may be, of the possibility of the protection of qualified privilege . . . [the] touchstone of a reciprocal interest and duty between the receiver and the giver of the defamatory statement was a judicial construct of the 20th century designed to produce certainty as to the circumstances in which a defamatory statement made by A to B could be accorded the protection of qualified privilege. It is a touchstone that makes little sense in relation to statements, typically those contained in the pages of newspapers, made to the world at large. *Reynolds* was not supplanting the duty/interest touchstone for situations to which that touchstone was intended to apply and could sensibly be applied. It was supplementing that touchstone in order to provide the protection of qualified privilege, where the circumstances warranted that protection, to statements published to the world at large."[27]

Furthermore, he stated that having

"had the advantage of reading the respective opinions of my noble and learned friends on the qualified privilege point I am unable to discern any real differences of principle. If, however, there are any, I want to express my full agreement with the reasons given by my noble and learned friend, Lord Hoffmann".[28]

The traditional form of privilege based on duty often (perhaps more often than not) involves a duty that is not legally enforceable but even in such a case it may be that the maker of the statement would be subject to criticism for not performing it, moral or social as it might be. But in the *Reynolds* context it is wrong to decide the issue of privilege by asking whether the publisher would be open to legitimate criticism for *not* publishing the material.[29]

"If, indeed, the publisher would have been open to legitimate criticism had he not published, his claim to privilege will be indisputable. But the converse is not true. That would be to impose too stringent a test. There will undoubtedly be occasions when one newspaper would decide to publish and quite properly so, yet a second newspaper, no less properly, would delay or abstain from publication."[30]

To equate "a responsible journalist reporting on matters of public interest with an employer who has a moral duty to include in his reference the fact that his former employee was regularly drunk on duty, is quite unrealistic."[31]

15.3 The impact of the European Convention on Human Rights. When *Reynolds* was decided the Human Rights Act 1998 had been passed but was not in force. Nevertheless, art.10 of the Convention played a major formative role in the decisions of both the Court of Appeal and the House of Lords. Both

---

[27] Ibid. at [129] and [137].

[28] Ibid. at [144].

[29] Or even to ask that question as "useful cross-check": ibid. at [57].

[30] *Loutchansky v Times Newspapers Ltd (Nos 2–5)* [2001] EWCA Civ 1805; [2002] Q.B. 783 at [49].

[31] *Jameel (Mohammed) v Wall Street Journal Europe SPRL* [2006] UKHL 44; [2007] 1 A.C. 359 at [57] per Lord Hoffmann.

Lord Nicholls and Lord Steyn referred to the fact that the right of freedom of expression was shortly to be buttressed by the implementation of the Act, and it was common ground that in considering the issues the House should proceed on the basis of the reality that the Act would soon be in force.[32] For Lord Steyn, it was a "new landscape" in which the:

> "starting point is now the right of freedom of expression, a right based on a constitutional or higher legal order foundation. Exceptions to freedom of expression must be justified as being necessary in a democracy. In other words, freedom of expression is the rule and regulation of speech is the exception requiring justification. The existence and width of any exception can only be justified if it is underpinned by a pressing social need. These are fundamental principles governing the balance to be struck between freedom of expression and defamation."[33]

Nevertheless, the protection of reputation was recognised as a major value, for the reputations of politicians no less than of others. Reputation:

> "forms the basis of many decisions in a democratic society which are fundamental to its well-being: whom to employ or work for, whom to promote, whom to do business with or to vote for. Once besmirched by an unfounded allegation in a national newspaper, a reputation can be damaged for ever, especially if there is no opportunity to vindicate one's reputation. When this happens, society as well as the individual is the loser. For it should not be supposed that protection of reputation is a matter of importance only to the affected individual and his family. Protection of reputation is conducive to the public good. It is in the public interest that the reputation of public figures should not be debased falsely. In the political field, in order to make an informed choice, the electorate needs to be able to identify the good as well as the bad."[34]

In *Loutchansky v Times Newspapers Ltd (No.1)*, Brooke L.J. said:

> "To talk of a public right to know, without more, is misleading. The Convention explicitly states that the right to freedom of expression carries with it duties and responsibilities, and its jurisprudence shows how the right to freedom of expression is circumscribed by what is strictly necessary and proportionate in a democratic society for the protection of individuals' reputations. In *Reynolds* Lord Nicholls said . . . that 'reputation is an integral and important part of the individual . . . protection of reputation is conducive to the public good'. If the public 'right to know' was to be adopted, as it has not, as the sole criterion for conferring immunity from liability for damaging and untrue statements, then the courts would be turning their back on their duty to prescribe such restrictions on freedom of expression as are needed in order to achieve that public good."[35]

Indeed, in *Reynolds* the case did, of course, concern a statement about a political matter, but the defendants' contention for a *New York Times v Sullivan* style defence—that a defamatory statement of fact made in the course

---

[32] *Reynolds v Times Newspapers Ltd* [2001] 2 A.C. 127 at 207.
[33] Ibid. at 208.
[34] Ibid. at 201 per Lord Nicholls.
[35] [2001] EWCA Civ 536; [2002] Q.B. 321 at [45].

of political discussion should be free from liability if published in good faith—was specifically rejected for that "would not provide adequate protection for reputation.[36]

It is also the case, now recognised very much more clearly than at the time of *Reynolds*, that reputation is itself a right protected by the Convention in the context of respect for private and family life under art.8.[37] For this reason, in *Hunt v Times Newspapers Ltd*, Eady J. described as "unhelpful" the relabeling of a *Reynolds* argument as a "public interest speech/Article 10 defence".[38] In a later judgment in the same case, he commented further that "what seems to be emerging clearly is that the 'new methodology' sanctioned by the House of Lords in 2004, both in *Campbell v MGN Ltd* and in *Re S (A Child)*, originally in the context of privacy, where we had little established jurisprudence of our own, is now finding its way inexorably into the application of our well known principles of defamation".[39] He added that *"Reynolds* privilege provides fertile ground for this development . . . not least because it was introduced partly to take account of the provisions of the European Convention".[40]

Despite the influence of the Convention on *Reynolds*, the Strasbourg case law does not figure large in the cases interpreting and applying it[41]:

> "The reasoning and guidance given in the appellate courts in England over recent years, including that in *Reynolds* itself, is supposed to be Convention compliant . . . it is not, therefore, for individual judges in any case which comes along to apply and interpret the Convention afresh. If one applies the English law of defamation properly, there should be no reason to think that the principles underlying the Convention are infringed . . . This is more particularly so with the regard to appellate decisions which expressly advert to the Convention and its compatibility with English law".[42]

One frequently finds statements on the theme that "we walk in tune and in step with the Convention and the Strasbourg jurisprudence and no radical

---

[36] [2001] 2 A.C. 127 at 191.
[37] See para.1.14, above.
[38] [2012] EWHC 110 (QB) at [3]–[4].
[39] [2012] EWHC 1220 (QB) at [13]. See also, *Flood v Times Newspapers Ltd* [2009] EWHC 2375; [2010] E.M.L.R. 8 at [149] per Tugendhat J.
[40] Ibid. at [14].
[41] That said, in *Flood v Times Newspapers Ltd* [2010] EWCA Civ 804; [2010] E.M.L.R. 26 the attention of the Court of Appeal was drawn to *A v Norway* (2009) App. No.28070/06, unreported, ECtHR, April 9, 2009. The facts were much more extreme, involving the attribution by the media of serious suspicion of two sex murders to A, who had been convicted of a murder 13 years before and who had served his sentence, although at the time he was still subject to "security measures". A was not named but was identifiable from the material; he had been given the opportunity to declare his innocence on the front page of the newspaper. The ECtHR found that there had been a violation of art.8 and that the Norwegian courts in dismissing (by majority) his claim for defamation had not struck a fair balance between his rights and those of the media under art.10. The reasoning and conclusion are very brief but the case is perhaps a corrective to the not uncommonly held view that under art.8(2) the media are always protected provided they are dealing with matters of public concern and make no egregious errors of fact. Lord Neuberger M.R. said in that while the case might well provide some support for the result in *Flood*, it was unnecessary to say anything more about it (at [85]).
[42] *Galloway v Telegraph Ltd* [2004] EWHC 2786 QBD; [2005] E.M.L.R. 7 at [132].

departure from our approach is necessary".[43] It has been said that "the approach of the European Court is an essentially pragmatic one which focuses on the particular facts of each case",[44] and it is therefore unlikely that one will find in the Strasbourg jurisprudence a "rule" incompatible with *Reynolds* and the subsequent English cases.[45] In any case there is a "margin of appreciation" within which the Strasbourg court leaves it to domestic law to determine how the balance is to be struck between the competing objectives of freedom of expression and protection of reputation.[46]

New statutory basis. The transposition of the *Reynolds* privilege into   **15.4** statutory form in s.4 of the Defamation Act 2013 will see a notable change, at least in form. Section 4 provides:

> "4 Publication on matter of public interest
> (1) It is a defence to an action for defamation for the defendant to show that—
>> (a) the statement complained of was, or formed part of, a statement on a matter of public interest; and
>> (b) the defendant reasonably believed that publishing the statement complained of was in the public interest.
> (2) Subject to subsections (3) and (4), in determining whether the defendant has shown the matters mentioned in subsection (1), the court must have regard to all the circumstances of the case.
> (3) If the statement complained of was, or formed part of, an accurate and impartial account of a dispute to which the claimant was a party, the court must in determining whether it was reasonable for the defendant to believe that publishing the statement was in the public interest disregard any omission of the defendant to take steps to verify the truth of the imputation conveyed by it.
> (4) In determining whether it was reasonable for the defendant to believe that publishing the statement complained of was in the public interest, the court must make such allowance for editorial judgement as it considers appropriate.
> (5) For the avoidance of doubt, the defence under this section may be relied upon irrespective of whether the statement complained of is a statement of fact or a statement of opinion.
> (6) The common law defence known as the Reynolds defence is abolished."

It remains an open question whether the move from the common law privilege to the statutory defence will entail any substantive change. It was intended by

---

[43] *Roberts v Gable* [2007] EWCA Civ 721; [2008] 2 W.L.R. 129 at [52]. See also *Galloway v Telegraph Ltd* [2006] EWCA Civ 17; [2006] E.M.L.R. 11 at [80].

[44] *Galloway v Telegraph Ltd* [2006] EWCA Civ 17; [2006] E.M.L.R. 11 at [78].

[45] If there is a conflict between a binding English precedent and a Strasbourg decision it is the duty of the English court to follow the English precedent: *Kay v Lambeth LBC* [2006] UKHL 10; [2006] 2 A.C. 465.

[46] *Jameel (Mohammed) v Wall Street Journal Europe SPRL* [2006] UKHL 44; [2007] 1 A.C. 359 at [99]. However, in the partial admissibility decision of *Times Newspaper v UK* App. Nos 23676/03 and 3002/03, October 11, 2005 the ECtHR seemingly approved the *Reynolds* regime at a time when it was perhaps being applied more restrictively than now. The Court in *Alithia Publishing Co. Ltd v Cyprus*, App. No.175550/03, May 22, 2008 *http://www.bailii.org/eu/cases/ECHR/2008/420.html* upheld what appears to have been an essentially *Reynolds* approach to qualified privilege for accusations against a Minister.

Parliament that the new defence should build on the *Reynolds* privilege. Speaking for the Government in the Second Reading debate on the Bill in the House of Commons, Jonathan Djanogly explained that the proposed defence "[was] based on existing common law and the defence established in *Reynolds . . .* intended to reflect the principles established in that case and in subsequent case law . . . matches the case law and gives the court appropriate flexibility".[47] Lord McNally confirmed that "my absolute intention is for this part of the legislation to embrace and reflect *Flood*".[48] Similarly, the *Explanatory Notes* to the Act explain that the new defence "is based on . . . and . . . is intended essentially to codify the common law defence".[49] Moreover, they state that "the current case law would constitute a helpful (albeit not binding) guide to interpreting how the new statutory defence should be applied".[50]

The rights context is also likely to be influential in the interpretation of the new defence. It is likely to exert a particular bearing on the crucial s.4(1)(b) question of whether the "the defendant reasonably believed that publishing the statement complained of was in the public interest". There are two tenable interpretations of this provision. On the one hand, it might be said that it requires only a belief that is based on rational grounds. This would entail that the defence would fail only in the unusual circumstance where the belief was proven false, capricious or irrational. Interpreted in this way, the reasonableness standard would differ little from that of good faith or honesty. On the other hand, the test might be thought equivalent to the more onerous responsible publication requirement under *Reynolds* privilege, such that a publisher could not *reasonably* believe that publication was in the public interest unless he had not first done what was necessary and would have been done by a reasonable publisher, to stand up a story.

The second interpretation will almost certainly be that adopted by the courts. Any statutory public interest defence would have to be interpreted by judges in light of the need to balance the Article 8 right to reputation against the Article 10 right to freedom of expression.[51] In such circumstances, as elucidated by Lord Steyn in *Re S*, a court would have to engage in a two-way balancing exercise in light of an intense scrutiny on all the circumstances of the case.[52] Only the second interpretation of "reasonableness" would appear to allow for the balancing exercise to be undertaken. The first interpretation is

---

[47] 546 HC Deb col 260, June 12, 2012.

[48] 743 HL Deb col 198, February 5, 2013. Somehow, ministers at times appeared to think that the new defence could also involve "lifting the bar or moving the goal posts" and that the new proposal was "a genuine attempt to strengthen freedom of speech and should be seen as such"—741 HC Deb GC558, December 19, 2012 per Lord McNally. It may be that such comments can be best understood as playing to the gallery.

[49] Explanatory Note to the Defamation Act 2013, at [29].

[50] Ibid. at [35].

[51] See para.1.15, above. See also, Mullis and Scott, 'The Swing of the Pendulum: Reputation, Expression and the Recentering of English Libel Law' (2012) 63)(1) NILQ 27–58.

[52] *Re S (A Child) (Identification: Restrictions on Publication)* [2004] UKHL 47; [2005] 1 A.C. 593 at [17].

likely to be rejected for the same reasons, strengthened in light of the advent of the art.8 protection for reputation, as those developed by Lord Nicholls in rejecting the argument for a good faith political issue defence contended for by counsel in *Reynolds*.[53]

Ultimately, it appears likely that the new defence can be expressed succinctly in the same words as Lord Brown deployed in *Flood v Times Newspapers Ltd* when depicting the *Reynolds* privilege: "could whoever published the defamation, given whatever they knew (and did not know) and whatever they had done (and had not done) to guard so far as possible against the publication of untrue defamatory material, properly have considered the publication in question to be in the public interest?"[54]

SECTION 3. ELEMENTS OF THE PUBLIC INTEREST DEFENCE

Introduction. The development of the *Reynolds* privilege saw the tradi-   **15.5**
tional duty and interest test come to be reflected in—or supplanted by—three key issues: the issue whether the subject matter of the publication was of sufficient public interest; the question whether it was reasonable to include the particular material complained of, and whether the publisher had met the standards of responsible journalism or publication. With the advent of the new statutory defence, in general terms, the first of these issues remains as s.4(1)(a), while the latter two seem likely to be subsumed in the assessment of whether the publisher had a reasonable belief that publishing the statement complained of was in the public interest under s.4(1)(b). A range of further issues are also worthy of comment, and are addressed below.

Subject matter of public interest. The first component of the *Reynolds*   **15.6**
privilege is the requirement that there must be a real public interest in the matter about which the material is published. An equivalent requirement is included as part of the defence of publication on a matter of public interest, and is set out in s.4(1)(a) of the Defamation Act 2013. Even though the question of public interest is a matter of law for the judge, it would be idle to attempt to state any "test" by which the issue is to be decided. It is not possible exhaustively to delimit in advance the range of subject matters that fall within the amorphous concept of the "public interest". A number of somewhat trite statements are regularly rehearsed, most notable of which is the truism that "what engages the interest of the public may not be material

---

[53] The two interpretations were considered by the Human Rights Joint Committee in its legislative scrutiny of the Defamation Bill: *http://www.publications.parliament.uk/pa/jt201213/jtselect/jtrights/84/8402.htm*, at paras 20–28. It concluded that the second interpretation was the correct one.

[54] *Flood v Times Newspapers* [2012] UKSC 11; [2012] 2 A.C. 273 at [113].

which engages the public interest", or that "the public tends to be interested in many things which are not of the slightest public interest".[55] The courts have offered some general guidance. In its ruling in *Reynolds*, the Court of Appeal explained that by matters of public interest they meant:

> "matters relating to the public life of the community and those who take part in it, including . . . activities such as the conduct of government and political life, elections and public administration . . . [and] more widely . . . the governance of public bodies, institutions and companies which give rise to a public interest in disclosure, but excluding matters which are personal and private, such that there is no public interest in their disclosure."[56]

In the House of Lords, Lord Nicholls' view was that the definition of the public interest proposed by the Court of Appeal "has the merit of elasticity . . . [in that the] principle can be applied appropriately to the particular circumstances of individual cases in their infinite variety".[57] Lord Nicholls also emphasised that "it would be unsound in principle to distinguish political discussion from discussion of other matters of serious public concern".[58] Lord Cooke agreed that the defence could not sensibly be confined to party political discussion. He explained that, "there are other public figures who exercise great practical power over the lives of people or great influence in the formation of public opinion".[59] Furthermore, he noted that "the rights and interests of citizens in democracies are not restricted to the casting of votes . . . matters other than those pertaining to government and politics may be just as important in the community".[60] In one of the first decisions to apply *Reynolds*, privilege was found in respect of a local newspaper article warning the public against the defendants' doorstep selling: the matter did not in any sense concern politics and the defendants could hardly be said to be public figures.[61] In another early case the matter reported was of interest only to the small Saudi community in this country.[62] It seems, therefore, that what is of

---

[55] *Jameel (Mohammed) v Wall Street Journal Europe Sprl* [2006] UKHL 44; [2007] 1 A.C. 359 at [31] per Lord Bingham and at [49] per Lord Hoffmann respectively. Baroness Hale was most imaginative in making this point: "the most vapid tittle-tattle about the activities of footballers' wives and girlfriends interests large sections of the public but no-one could claim any real public interest in our being told all about it" (at [147]).

[56] [2001] 2 A.C. 127 at 176–177 per Lord Bingham.

[57] Ibid. 202.

[58] Ibid. at 204. Lord Nicholls also suggested that this would be in any event at variance with the approach of the European Court of Human Rights which is based on the individual evaluation of each case rather than on categories of speech (at 211; see also at 204, 223).

[59] Ibid. 220.

[60] Ibid.

[61] *GKR Karate Ltd v Yorkshire Post Newspapers Ltd (No.2)* [2000] E.M.L.R. 410. See also *GKR Karate Ltd v Yorkshire Post Newspapers Ltd (No.1)* [2000] 1 W.L.R. 2571 CA and *Lukowiak v Unidad Editorial SA* [2001] E.M.L.R. 46.

[62] *Al-Faghi v HH Saudi Research & Marketing (UK) Ltd* [2001] EWCA Civ 1634; [2002] E.M.L.R. 215.

legitimate public interest is to be gauged by reference to the audience at which the publication is aimed. The international nature of many publications must be borne in mind, however, and it may not be right to have in mind merely the narrow perspective of the public interest in this jurisdiction.[63] In practice, of course, it is stories about political matters which provide the most obvious field for the application of *Reynolds*.

In *Jameel*, their Lordships rejected the suggestion proffered by counsel that the test should be satisfied when material was considered "newsworthy".[64] This was thought too easily met; it was "too subjective a test, based on the target audience, inclinations and interests of the particular publication".[65] Conversely, the idea that material should be privileged only when it was such that the public "needed to know" was rejected as too onerous.[66]

Further insight can be drawn from the wide array of previous decisions regarding the concept of public interest in the areas of copyright, defamation, breach of confidence and misuse of private information. These have included the business of government and political conduct[67]; the promotion of animal welfare[68]; the protection of public health and safety[69]; the dealings of a Member of Parliament with a foreign regime hostile to this country[70]; the fair and proper administration of justice[71]; the conduct of religious groups[72]; discipline in schools[73]; the conduct of the police[74]; cheating, corruption and the pressure on elite athletes from an early age in sport[75]; breach of charitable

---

[63] *Lukowiak v Unidad Editorial SA* [2001] E.M.L.R. at [45]; *Prince Radu of Hohenzollern v Houston* [2007] EWHC 2735 (QB) at [12] (affirmed [2008] EWCA Civ 921).

[64] [2006] UKHL 44; [2007] 1 A.C. 359 at [147].

[65] Ibid.

[66] Ibid.

[67] *Attorney General v Jonathan Cape Ltd* [1976] Q.B. 752; *Reynolds v Times Newspapers Ltd* 2001] 2 A.C. 127 HL ; *London Regional Transport Ltd v Mayor of London* [2001] EWCA Civ 1491; *Al Fagih v HH Saudi Research and Marketing (UK) Ltd* [2001] EWCA Civ 1634; [2002] E.M.L.R. 13; *Roberts v Gable* [2007] EWCA Civ 721; [2008] Q.B. 502; *Galloway v Telegraph Newspapers* [2006] EWCA Civ 17; [2006] E.M.L.R. 11; *Henry v BBC* [2005] EWHC 2787 (QB); *Malik v Newspost* [2007] EWHC 3063 (QB); *Cook v Telegraph Media Group Ltd* [2011] EWHC 763 (QB).

[68] *Imutran Ltd v Uncaged Campaigns Ltd* [2001] 2 All E.R. 385.

[69] *Hubbard v Vosper* [1972] 2 Q.B. 84; *McKeith v News Group Newspapers Ltd* [2005] EWHC 1162 (QB); [2005] E.M.L.R. 32; *W v Egdell* [1990] Ch. 359.

[70] *Galloway v Telegraph Ltd* [2006] EWCA Civ 17; [2006] E.M.L.R. 11.

[71] *Lion Laboratories Ltd v Evans* [1985] Q.B. 526; *Istil Group Inc. v Zahoor* [2003] EWHC 165 (Ch).

[72] *Hubbard v Vosper* [1972] 2 Q.B. 84.

[73] *Leeds City Council v Channel Four Television Corp* [2005] EWHC 3522 (Fam).

[74] *Flood v Times Newspapers* [2012] UKSC 11; [2012] 2 A.C. 273; *Charman v Orion Group Publishing Group Ltd* [2007] EWCA Civ 972; [2008] E.M.L.R. 16; *Miller v Associated Newspapers* [2003] EWHC 2799 (QB); [2004] E.M.L.R. 33; *Hunt v Times Newspapers Ltd* [2013] EWHC 1868 (QB).

[75] *Jockey Club v Buffham* [2002] EWHC 1866 (QB); *Armstrong v Times Newspapers* [2005] EWCA Civ 1007; [2005] E.M.L.R. 33; *Grobbelaar v News Group Newspapers* [2001] EWCA Civ 33; [2001] E.M.L.R. 18; *Spelman v Express Newspapers* [2012] EWHC 355 (QB) at [22].

fiduciary rules[76]; involvement in serious crimes[77]; corporate malpractice[78]; and the correction of prior statements or misrepresentations by others.[79] The public interest is also discussed in a number of "relevant privacy codes", although in substance such listings offer little guidance beyond that available in jurisprudence.

Notably, one piece of guidance offered by the courts has been declared obsolete. In *Reynolds*, Lord Nicholls remarked that "the court should be slow to conclude that a publication was not in the public interest and, therefore, the public had no right to know, especially when the information is in the field of political discussion. Any lingering doubts should be resolved in favour of publication."[80] With the recognition that reputation is an interest protected directly by art.8, there must in any case be a balancing exercise between the protection of that interest and of freedom of expression and Lord Nicholls' statement can no longer stand.[81]

The concept of the public interest is not defined in the Defamation Act. Insofar as it is cited in s.4(1)(a), it might be expected that the concept will operate in essentially the same as that familiar in the common law. Indeed, the Explanatory Notes to the Act provide that "this is a concept which is well-established in the English common law".[82] The Explanatory Notes also state that either the whole or part only of the publication need be on a matter of public interest, such that the specific statement complained of may not itself fall into that category. This reflects the idea that editorial judgment may see some items included for journalistic reasons that it may not be strictly "necessary" for the public to learn.

15.7 Inclusion of the material complained of. Under *Reynolds* privilege, the fact that the general subject matter of the piece is of proper public interest does not necessarily mean that the defence applies to the entire contents. It has been said that in this context there has been a shift of emphasis from the traditional approach of asking whether there was a duty to publish the words complained of, to asking whether—given that the subject matter as a whole is

---

[76] *Seray-Wurie v Charity Commission of England and Wales* [2008] EWHC 870 (QB).

[77] *Hunt v Times Newspapers Ltd* [2013] EWHC 1868 (QB); *Lukowiak v Unidad Editorial SA* [2001] E.M.L.R. 46; *Loutchansky v Times Newspapers Ltd (Nos 2–5)* [2001] EWCA Civ 1805; [2002] Q.B. 783; *Jameel (Mohammed) v Wall Street Journal Europe Sprl* [2006] UKHL 44; [2007] 1 A.C. 359.

[78] *Cream Holdings Ltd v Banerjee* [2004] UKHL 44; [2005] 1 A.C. 253; *GKR Karate (UK) Ltd v Yorkshire Post Newspapers Ltd* [2000] 1 W.L.R. 2571; *Gilbert v Mirror Group Newspapers Ltd* [2000] E.M.L.R. 680; *Loutchansky v Times Newspapers Ltd (Nos 2–5)* [2001] EWCA Civ 1805; [2002] Q.B. 783; *KGM v News Group Newspapers Ltd* [2010] EWHC 3145 (QB) at [39].

[79] *Prince Radu of Hohenzollern v Houston* [2007] EWHC 2328 (QB); *Hyde Park Residence Ltd v Yelland* [1999] E.M.L.R. 654 at 663; *KGM v News Group Newspapers Ltd* [2010] EWHC 3145 (QB) at [39]; *Ferdinand v MGN Ltd* [2011] EWHC 2454 (QB).

[80] [2001] 2 A.C. at 205. In *Prince Radu of Hohenzollern v Houston* above at [15] this is treated as a general presumption in favour of publication, not confined to politics.

[81] *Flood v Times Newspapers Ltd* [2010] EWCA Civ 804; [2011] 1 W.L.R. 153 at [21].

[82] Explanatory Notes to the Defamation Act at [30].

a matter of public interest—it was reasonable to include the material complained of as part of the overall picture.[83]

> "The fact that the material was of public interest does not allow the newspaper to drag in damaging allegations which serve no public purpose. They must be part of the story. And the more serious the allegation, the more important it is that it should make a real contribution to the public interest element in the article."[84]

But it is not necessary to find a separate public interest justification for each item in the story.[85] For this purpose the story must be looked at as a whole in order to determine whether it is published in the public interest, with due allowance for editorial judgement about how it should be presented. Thus in *Jameel* some might have thought that it was enough to refer to "prominent Saudi companies" but it was certainly legitimate for the editor to think that an article which named five groups would be far more effective in showing that the heartland of Saudi business was thought to be involved.[86] This idea of leaving room for editorial discretion was a key feature of their Lordships' speeches in *Flood v Times Newspapers Ltd*.[87] Lord Dyson considered it an "important principle" that:

> "although the question of whether the story as a whole was a matter of public interest must be determined by the court, the question of whether defamatory details should have been included is often a matter of how the story should have been presented. On that issue, allowance should be made for editorial judgment".[88]

A defendant who makes a specific charge, however, will not be allowed to dress up his defence with a plea of *Reynolds* privilege simply because the background to the charge involves a matter of public interest. Otherwise:

> "there is a danger that any plea citing a few generalities about the duty of the media to be a public watchdog will be allowed to pass muster and thus to prolong and complicate unnecessarily a significant number of libel actions in which qualified privilege has no legitimate role to play."[89]

---

[83] *Prince Radu of Hohenzollern v Houston* [2007] EWHC 2735 (QB) [14].

[84] *Jameel (Mohammed) v Wall Street Journal Europe SPRL* [2006] UKHL 44; [2007] 1 A.C. 359 at [51] per Lord Hoffmann.

[85] Ibid. at [48] and [108].

[86] Ibid. at [52] and [148]; *Charman v Orion Publishing Group Ltd* [2007] EWCA Civ 972; [2008] E.M.L.R. 16 at [75]. Cf. *Henry v BBC* [2005] EWHC 2787 (QB). It is of course impossible to be sure how earlier cases would have been decided after *Jameel*, but *Henry* is arguably distinguishable. The named claimant was a hospital administrator in a hospital which was implicated in "fiddling" of waiting list data. One factor in the decision that there was no privilege was that it was not necessary to name her. In *Jameel* the named companies would have been well known to those acquainted with business in Saudi Arabia and there is much therefore to be said for the view that the naming was what really gave the story its impact. In *Henry* on the other hand the core "target" of the story was the hospital and the names of the individuals would have meant nothing to the readership in general.

[87] [2012] UKSC 11; [2012] 2 A.C. 273.

[88] Ibid. at [192].

[89] *Miller v Associated Newspapers Ltd* [2003] EWHC 2799 (QB); [2004] E.M.L.R. 33 at [33]; *McKeith v News Group Newspapers Ltd* [2005] EWHC 1162 (QB); [2005] E.M.L.R. 32 at [55].

In *Baldwin v Rusbridger*,[90] the newspaper had published an article for which the claimant recovered £15,000 libel damages after a trial in which the newspaper pleaded fair comment and justification. The newspaper than published an account of the proceedings in which it quoted its editor to the effect that:

> "We fought this case because we considered it was a responsible and careful piece of journalism on a difficult but important subject. Nothing that happened in court detracted from my faith in the two journalists involved, and it is a sad reflection on the libel laws that they offer so little protection to reporting of such matters which are clearly in the public interest".

After a ruling that this article was capable of meaning that the claimant had in fact done what was alleged in the first article, but that the newspaper had been unable to win the action because the libel laws are unfair and prevent the truth from emerging, the newspaper sought to introduce a qualified privilege argument based on *Reynolds*. Eady J. held that reliance on the *Reynolds* privilege was entirely misplaced. In so far as the article was critical of the present state of libel law the editor was perfectly entitled to express his views, which did not need to be founded on any "duty". His personal opinions on law reform, however, were by the way to the question of whether the newspaper was entitled to repeat the allegations in respect of which the defence of justification had been rejected by the jury in the earlier proceedings. The principles explored in *Reynolds* were "tailored to fit the needs of different customers",[91] and the fact that the Code of the Press Complaints Commission required the newspaper to report a decision adverse to it:

> "could hardly be used . . . as a shelter for undermining that decision itself. A defendant who wishes to repeat a libel must, in general (and subject to issue estoppel), be prepared to defend it afresh and risk a further (no doubt higher) award of damages."[92]

Under s.4 of the Defamation Act 2013, there is no specific mention of this second element of the *Reynolds* privilege. The provision does require that the defendant reasonably believed that publishing the statement complained of was in the public interest,[93] and in determining this matter the court must both have regard to all the circumstances of the case[94] and make such allowance for editorial judgement as it considers appropriate.[95] In that context, it would seem that insofar as the issue remains relevant it has been subsumed within the question that equates to whether the journalism involved met the standards of responsible journalism.

---

[90] [2001] E.M.L.R. 47.
[91] Ibid. at [22].
[92] Ibid. at [36].
[93] S.4(1)(b).
[94] S.4(2).
[95] S.4(4).

Standards of responsible journalism. Once it has been affirmed that the   **15.8**
publication concerned a matter of public interest and the first stage has been
passed, the "inquiry [under *Reynolds* privilege] then shifts to whether the
steps taken to gather and publish the information were responsible and
fair"—whether there has been "responsible journalism".[96] In *Reynolds*, Lord
Nicholls famously set out a non-exhaustive list of circumstances which would
be relevant to the issue of whether the standards of responsible journalism had
been met in a given case.[97] He stated that:

> "the list is not exhaustive. The weight to be given to these and any other relevant
> factors will vary from case to case. Any disputes of primary facts will be a matter
> for the jury, if there is one. The decision on whether, having regard to the admitted
> or proved facts, the publication was subject to qualified privilege is a matter for the
> judge. This is the established practice and seems sound. A balancing operation is
> better carried out by a judge in a reasoned judgment than by a jury. Over time, a
> valuable corpus of case law will be built up."[98]

The ten listed factors were:

"1. The seriousness of the allegation. The more serious the charge, the more the
    public is misinformed and the individual harmed, if the allegation is not
    true.
  2. The nature of the information, and the extent to which the subject-matter is a
    matter of public concern.
  3. The source of the information. Some informants have no direct knowledge of
    the events. Some have their own axes to grind, or are being paid for their
    stories.
  4. The steps taken to verify the information.
  5. The status of the information. The allegation may have already been the subject
    of an investigation which commands respect.
  6. The urgency of the matter. News is often a perishable commodity.
  7. Whether comment was sought from the plaintiff. He may have information
    others do not possess or have not disclosed. An approach to the plaintiff will
    not always be necessary.
  8. Whether the article contained the gist of the plaintiff's side of the story.
  9. The tone of the article. A newspaper can raise queries or call for an investiga-
    tion. It need not adopt allegations as statements of fact.
 10. The circumstances of the publication, including the timing."

A key element in the judgment of the House of Lords in *Jameel* was the
emphasis that the 'Nicholls factors' must be approached in a practical and
flexible manner with due deference to editorial discretion. Certainly, the
factors were not to be seen as a series of hurdles to be negotiated in succession

---

[96] *Jameel (Mohammed) v Wall Street Journal Europe SPRL* [2006] UKHL 44; [2007] 1 A.C.
359 at [53] per Lord Hoffmann.
[97] The phrase, "responsible journalism", was never more than convenient shorthand because
the defence is not confined to the press. The standard is not "high quality journalism": *Jameel v
Wall Street Journal Europe SPRL* [2006] UKHL 44; [2007] 1 A.C. 359 at [109].
[98] [2001] 2 A.C. 127 at 205.

by the defendant with loss of the defence if he cannot pass one of them.[99] As Gray J. had noted previously[100]:

> "If one focuses too closely on those ten matters [set out by Lord Nicholls], there is some danger of missing the wood for the trees: the central underlying question is always whether in the particular circumstances the public interest in freedom of expression should yield to the public interest in an individual being able to vindicate his or her reputation."

15.9 Reasonable belief that publishing is in public interest. The transposition of the *Reynolds* privilege into statutory form in s.4 of the Defamation Act 2013 has seen a notable change, at least in form. Section 4(1)(b) provides that, "it is a defence to an action for defamation for the defendant to show that . . . (b) the defendant reasonably believed that publishing the statement complained of was in the public interest". In determining whether the defendant has shown that he or she held the reasonable belief, "the court must have regard to all the circumstances of the case".[101] Moreover, the "court must make such allowance for editorial judgement as it considers appropriate".[102] Aside from the shift in language from "responsible journalism" to "reasonable belief", the most notable change is that the checklist of factors that reflected the Nicholls factors—and which had been included in the original version of the proposed statutory defence—was excised. Nevertheless, in general terms, it can be expected that this new test will produce very similar analyses to those seen under *Reynolds* privilege.

The need for the provision to be rights compliant is likely to lean in favour of an interpretation of s.4 that emulates *Reynolds* privilege in large measure.[103] Moreover, during the Committee stage debate, Lord McNally affirmed that "in determining whether in all the circumstances the test is met, we would expect the courts to look at many of the same sorts of considerations as they have done before", and that "the courts will need to look at the conduct of the publisher in deciding that question".[104] Presciently, in *Flood v Times Newspapers Ltd*, Lord Mance noted that "it will not be, or is unlikely to be, in the public interest to publish material which has not been the subject of responsible journalistic enquiry and consideration".[105]

Lord McNally also asserted that the reasonable belief test "brings out more clearly the subjective element in the test—what the defendant believed at the time rather than what a judge believes some weeks or months later—while

---

[99] [2006] UKHL 44; [2007] 1 A.C. 359 at [53]. Interestingly, this was also the stated view of the judge at first instance in that case: "[Lord Nicholls' factors should not be approached] artificially as though they occupied separate compartments"—see [2004] EWHC 37 (QB); [2004] E.M.L.R. 11 at [37].

[100] *Henry v BBC* [2005] EWHC 2787 (QB) at [92].

[101] S.4(2).

[102] S.4(4).

[103] See para.15.4, above.

[104] 741 HL Deb GC534, December 19, 2012.

[105] [2012] UKSC 11; [2012] 2 A.C. 273 at [123].

retaining the objective element of whether the belief was a reasonable one for the defendant to hold. The courts will need to look at the conduct of the publisher in deciding that question."[106]

Given that the defendant must show that he reasonably "believed" that publishing was in the public interest, there will be an assessment of the subjective state of mind of the defendant at the time of publishing. In the normal case, this should be relatively straightforward to evidence, but it will have to be demonstrated. In some cases, it may be that the proof of malice "override" that was submerged in the move from the duty and interest test to *Reynolds* privilege will resurface.

Whether these explicit emphases in fact bring anything new to the assessment to be undertaken is doubtful; at the very least, they direct attention towards the fact that the issue is to be considered as at the time when the publishing decision was taken. There are limits to this editorial freedom. As Moses L.J. noted in the Court of Appeal in *Flood v Times Newspapers Ltd*:

> "Of course, the details in the *Times'* article added spice to the story; of course those details might make it more likely that a reader would notice the article. Editors know how to attract the attention and interest of their readers and the courts must defer to their judgement of how best to achieve that result . . . But non sequitur that it can be left to them to judge whether publication of the impugned details is of public interest".[107]

The courts are pushed by s.4(2) and s.4(4) into recognising the scope of the function that should be left to publishers, but ultimately the determinative task is not transferred away from judges.

Application of the responsible journalism test: general. The assess-   **15.10** ment of responsible journalism—or test of reasonable belief that publishing was in the public interest—is an open-textured issue which involves balancing factors which may point in different directions.[108] It is unlikely that the

---

[106] See fn.104, above. It should be noted, however, that in *Hunt v Times Newspapers Ltd* [2012] EWHC 1220 (QB) at [12], Eady J. identified as a key principle of the common law privilege after *Flood* the idea that "verification involves a subjective and an objective element. The journalist must believe in the truth of the defamatory allegation and that must be a reasonable belief to hold." That observation reflected Lord Phillips' words in *Flood* (above) at [79].

[107] [2010] EWCA Civ 804; [2010] E.M.L.R. 26 at [117]–[118].

[108] The recognition that reputation is protected by art.8 (see para.1.14, above) means that particular factors in the responsible journalism or reasonable belief tests will have to be considered from the point of view of both the claimant and the defendant. In *Flood v Times Newspapers Ltd* [2009] EWHC 2375; [2010] E.M.L.R. 8 at [149], for example, Tugendhat J. mooted:

> "So, for example, Lord Nicholls states that 'the more serious the charge, the more the public is misinformed and the individual harmed'. That is focussing on the right to reputation. But as he also said, investigative journalism is part of the vital role of the press. Investigative journalism tends to result in serious allegations. The seriousness of the allegation may also support the journalist's contention that there is a public interest in the making of the allegation. A recent example may be certain allegations that MPs have been claiming as expenses money spent for private purposes."

This point was not mentioned on appeal and nothing was said in the courts above which could be taken as disapproval of it.

decision in one case will provide an automatic template for that in another.[109] The principle is elastic and elasticity means a degree of uncertainty,[110] but "in other professions and callings the law is content with the standard of reasonable care and skill in all the circumstances. The fourth estate should be as capable of operating within general standards".[111] The concept is inherently no more vague and uncertain than the test of reasonable care which is used in other branches of the law, and is made more concrete by (a) the case law, (b) the codes adopted by bodies like the Press Complaints Commission, and (c) the factors set out by Lord Nicholls in *Reynolds* itself.[112] There is no doubt that in English law, after paying due regard to editorial discretion and the need to avoid the advantages of detached hindsight, the court is the final arbiter of what is "responsible journalism". Hence, on the face of it, the view of the European Court of Human Rights in *Selistö v Finland* may seem surprising:

> "The methods of objective and balanced reporting may vary considerably, depending among other things on the medium in question; *it is not for the Court, any more than it is for the national courts, to substitute its own views for those of the press as to what techniques of reporting should be adopted by journalists.*"[113]

This probably simply means, however, that the court should allow a wide margin of professional appreciation to journalists: a sort of journalistic *Bolam* approach.[114] Rather different considerations apply to so-called "reportage" cases, which are dealt with separately below.[115]

15.11 Application of the responsible journalism test: source, status and steps taken to verify. While particular cases do not involve a hurdle race over Lord Nicholls' ten factors, which in any event do not claim to be exhaustive, it may be helpful nevertheless to look at how the case law has

---

[109] In *Flood v Times Newspapers Ltd* [2010] EWCA Civ 804; [2011] 1 W.L.R. 153; [2010] E.M.L.R. 26 at [22], Lord Neuberger M.R. said,
"*Jameel* was fairly heavily referred to in argument before us, as both parties were keen to identify differences or similarities between that case and the instant case. Given that the law relating to *Reynolds* privilege is at a relatively early stage of development, and in the light of Lord Nicholls's reference to 'a valuable corpus of case law [being] built up', this is understandable. However, there is a risk of unnecessarily protracting hearings and losing sight of the wood for the trees if there is too minute a comparison of the various factors in previous decided cases and those in the case at issue. Each case turns on its own facts, and the court has to apply the normal sharp focus on the competing factors, which is required where there are tensions between Convention rights. Too much concentration on the facts of other cases can distract from the exercise."
[110] *Reynolds v Times Newspapers Ltd* [2001] 2 A.C. 127 at 202, 214; *Jameel v Wall Street Journal Europe SPRL* [2006] UKHL 44; [2007] 1 A.C. 359 at [107].
[111] *Reynolds v Times Newspapers Ltd*, above, at 224 per Lord Cooke.
[112] *Jameel v Wall Street Journal Europe SPRL* [2006] UKHL 44; [2007] 1 A.C. 359 at [55]–[56] and [107].
[113] (2004) App. no.56767/00; [2005] E.M.L.R. 8 at [59].
[114] *Bolam v Friern Hospital Management Committee* [1957] 1 W.L.R. 582.
[115] See para.15.16, below.

approached some of the individual factors. In most cases, the reliability of the source from which the published material was obtained as it appeared to the defendant at the time,[116] and the steps that were taken to verify that material, will play a significant role in deciding whether there is privilege. It is established, however, that the court will not generally require a newspaper to reveal the identity of its sources at a preliminary stage, and that s.10 of the Contempt of Court Act 1981 gives protection against disclosure at any stage.[117] The claimant is therefore to a large extent deprived of the opportunity to assess the strength of the defendant's case on this issue.[118] In general, any unwillingness to disclose the identity of sources is not to weigh against the defendant. That is not to say that every claim made by the journalist as to the reliability of his unnamed source is to be taken at face value,[119] and "care should be taken not to give the benefit of the privilege too readily to persons or organizations whose sources of information are themselves protected to an extent which renders the issue of malice inscrutable"[120]:

> "There is always a risk that anonymous sources will acquire, in the eyes of a jury, an aura of saintliness, wisdom, or infallibility when they are not permitted to take on human form, especially having regard to the natural tendency of journalists to buff up the quality of their character or experience—for example, by using the standard description for anonymous sources, which is 'impeccable'. In such circumstances there is room, potentially, for injustice if the claimant is not permitted to introduce evidence capable of casting doubt on the accuracy of the journalist's evidence, or the reliability of his source of information."[121]

---

[116] *GKR Karate (UK) Ltd v Yorkshire Post Newspapers Ltd (No.1)* [2000] 1 W.L.R. 2571 CA at 2578–2579.

[117] See para.31.36, below.

[118] In this respect there is a marked difference between the law in England and Wales and the law in the US, where there is extensive pre-trial discovery of such matters (see *Reynolds v Times Newspapers Ltd* [2001] 2 A.C. 127 at 211, 219).

[119] Ibid. at 205.

[120] Ibid. at 230 per Lord Hope.

[121] *Jameel v Wall Street Journal Europe SPRL* [2003] EWHC 2322 (QB) at [19]. Although the decision was reversed by the HL ([2006] UKHL 44; [2007] 1 A.C. 359) there is no indication that anyone would have quarrelled with this proposition. See also the remarks of Hirst L.J. in *Gaddafi v Telegraph Group Ltd* [2000] E.M.L.R. 431 CA (decided after the decision of the Court of Appeal in *Reynolds* but before that of the House of Lords), where defendants' particulars simply referred to "agents of western governments". In *Hunt v Times Newspapers Ltd* [2012] EWHC 110 (QB) at [31], Eady J. pointed out that
  "of course, it is necessary to take full account of source protection . . . but that does not mean that a claimant is precluded from having the opportunity of making an assessment of the weight to be attributed to the sources in question . . . for example, if a journalist is relying upon a source from the criminal underworld, that may be highly material for the court to take into account in assessing how much reliance can be placed upon it".
In some cases, courts have made it effectively impossible for a claimant to succeed in a disclosure application by accepting assurances given to them by counsel for the defendant that the sources deserve s.10 (of the Contempt of Court Act 1981) protection and refusing to examine the matter further. Thus in *Pell v Express Newspaper* [2003] EWHC 649, at [2] Eady J. refused an application for specific disclosure on the ground that he was satisfied that there were no circumstances which would justify him going behind the assurances given by the defendants through leading counsel and his instructing solicitor. The judge declined to proceed on the basis they had not conscientiously applied the appropriate principles. With all due respect, it is

One must be realistic about what the defendant can do in these cases,[122] however, since a newspaper is not a secret service and if the defendant has pursued what other inquiries are open to him he is not deprived of the protection of privilege because the original source had an obvious axe to grind.[123] Nor is the defendant concerned with proof to a forensic standard that the story is true and he may therefore be protected even if he receives contradictory answers to his inquiries.[124] As Eady J. pointed out in *Hunt v Times Newspapers Ltd*:

> "it may sometimes be legitimate to rely upon the cumulative effect of material to the same or similar effect—even though the quality of the individual sources may not be as high as one would normally expect. 'Responsible journalism' may be judged partly on quality and, perhaps, partly on quantity".[125]

It has been said that "in most cases the *Reynolds* defence will not get off the ground unless the journalist honestly and reasonably believed that the statement was true",[126] though reportage cases are a clear exception to this. In applying this, however, it is important to bear in mind what the words sued on mean (or, in this context, what they were intended to mean): there is a great difference between believing, say, that there are grounds to suspect that a person is involved in funding terrorism or that there are grounds for investigation of the matter and believing that he is so involved.

The status of the information is listed separately from the reliability of its source among Lord Nicholls' factors in *Reynolds*, but the two are obviously closely connected.[127] An "interim progress report" of an internal inquiry was held not to enjoy sufficient status as a source in *Miller v Associated Newspapers Ltd*.[128] In *Henry v BBC* one factor militating against privilege was that,

---

submitted that judicial reliance in an application for disclosure on an assertion by counsel for the defendant that the source deserved protection under s.10 is not acceptable and that such an approach may fail to sufficiently protect the claimant's arts 6 and 8 rights. At the very least, it is suggested that the judge should examine the documents in respect of which disclosure is sought in order to assess for himself whether source protection is deserved.

[122] E.g. *HH Sheikha Mouza Al Misnad v Azzaman Ltd* [2003] EWHC 1783 (QB).

[123] *Charman v Orion Publishing Group Ltd* [2007] EWCA Civ 972; [2008] E.M.L.R. 16.

[124] In *Jameel*, the jury finding was that the defendants had not received confirmation from certain sources. That finding was flawed by the direction they received (see [2005] EWCA Civ 74; [2005] Q.B. 904 at [59] and [2006] UKHL 44; [2007] 1 A.C. 359 at [62]) but in any event they had received confirmation from the US Treasury. The uncontradicted evidence of this was lost sight of the trial, perhaps because of the "coded" form in which it was given.

[125] [2012] EWHC 1220 (QB) at [18].

[126] *Jameel* [2006] UKHL 44; [2007] 1 A.C. 359 at [62] per Lord Hoffmann.

[127] In *Loutchansky v Times Newspapers Ltd (No.4)* [2001] E.M.L.R. 38 at [47], Gray J. thought that as a general rule one media organ was not entitled to treat a story in another as a reliable source.

[128] [2004] EWHC 2799 (QB); [2004] E.M.L.R. 33. Nor was there any urgency about the disclosure. Furthermore, little had been done to verify the information, no attempt had been made to seek comment (even though the claimant would have been barred from responding to an inquiry, the police press office could have been approached) and the tone of the article was sensational. The imputations in the article were subsequently found to be substantially true: *Miller v Associated Newspapers Ltd* [2005] EWHC 557 (QB).

although the employer hospital had been implicated in wrongdoing by an inquiry, no such finding had been made against the named claimant, and the question of disciplinary proceedings against her was still under consideration.[129]

Whether the defendant has behaved responsibly is to be judged by reference to the circumstances known at the time the statement is made by him. The defendant cannot rely, in order to establish privilege, on information which subsequently comes to his attention.[130] The question is whether the defendant has conformed with the standards of responsible journalism, not whether a person who did behave responsibly would have come to the decision to publish.

Application of the responsible journalism test: failure to seek   15.12
claimant's version. This is perhaps the core *Reynolds* factor. Not only does simple fairness require that a person who is going to publish a story without being required to show that it is true should give the subject of the story the opportunity to put his side, but it is often one of the best ways to seek to verify the story: "it should not be taken for granted that a person accused of dishonesty will say 'No comment' or merely give a bare denial."[131] The publisher must allow a reasonable opportunity for the subject of the story to put their side.[132] Where the defendant already has the claimant's version of events, failure to publish that will almost inevitably count against the defendant.[133] In *Reynolds* itself, the plaintiff had given his side in his statement to the *Dáil*, but this was omitted from the article.

---

[129] [2005] EWHC 2787 (QB). As in *Miller*, ibid., after a trial of the justification defence the imputations were found to be substantially true and the claim failed: [2006] EWHC 386 (QB).

[130] *GKR Karate (UK) Ltd v Yorkshire Post Newspapers Ltd* [2000] 1 W.L.R. 2571 CA; *Loutchansky v Times Newspapers Ltd (No.1)* [2001] EWCA Civ 536; [2002] Q.B. 321; *Howlett v Holding* [2003] EWHC 286 (QB). That is one reason why the "sloppy cross-over technique" (*Armstrong v Times Newspapers* [2004] EWHC 2928 (QB) at [94]) of treating particulars in support of a plea of privilege as interchangeable with those in support of justification should be avoided:

"one can often legitimately plead facts subsequent to publication in support of a plea of justification (in particular, to justify a defamatory allegation about general character traits) . . . facts relied upon to support a plea of *Reynolds* privilege need to have been known to the relevant defendant or journalist prior to publication—which is not the case with a plea of justification":

McKeith v News Group Newspapers Ltd [2005] EWHC 1162 (QB); [2005] E.M.L.R. 32 at [53]. In *Henry v BBC* [2005] EWHC 2787 (QB) the trial of the issue of justification was postponed until after that on privilege, which was said to have the advantage of avoiding the risk of account being taken of evidence which, though relevant on justification, was not relevant on the question of privilege.

[131] *Prince Radu of Hohenzollern v Houston* [2007] EWHC 2735 (QB) at [73].

[132] In *Cook v Telegraph Media Group Ltd* [2011] EWHC 763 (QB) at [72], Tugendhat J. refused to give a summary judgment requested on the basis that the claimant had no real prospect of unseating, inter alia, a *Reynolds* privilege argument as the claimant had been given only three hours to comment before publication.

[133] Unless it is unintelligible or obvious nonsense: *Reynolds v Times Newspapers Ltd* [2001] 2 A.C. 127 at 214.

"It goes without saying that a journalist is entitled and bound to reach his own conclusions and to express them honestly and fearlessly. He is entitled to disbelieve and refute explanations given. But this cannot be a good reason for omitting, from a hard-hitting article making serious allegations against a named individual, all mention of that person's own explanation . . . by omitting Mr Reynolds's explanation English readers were left to suppose that, so far, Mr Reynolds had offered no explanation. Further, it is elementary fairness that, in the normal course, a serious charge should be accompanied by the gist of any explanation already given. An article which fails to do so faces an uphill task in claiming privilege if the allegation proves to be false and the unreported explanation proves to be true." [134]

So also where the defendant puts part of the story to the claimant, but not the most damning allegation.[135] It is clear, however, that putting the proposed story to the claimant and seeking his version is not in all cases a requirement of reliance on privilege.[136] Failure to do so (or to make adequate efforts to do so) will generally weigh in the scales against the defendant,[137] but the ultimate issue depends upon the facts of the case. Thus, it is obvious that the defendant is not to be penalised for failing to put the story to the claimant if the latter has "gone to ground" and is inaccessible. It may also be the case that the refusal of the subject to respond at earlier stages may justifiably lead one to conclude that he would not behave any differently now.[138] Similarly, the reverse proposition that putting the case will generally count in the defendant's favour is no doubt true, accepting that one must consider the background and how that is done.[139]

The proposition that this issue depends on all the facts comes out very clearly in *Jameel (Mohammed) v Wall Street Journal Europe SPRL*.[140] The defendants had contacted the personal claimant's organisation the evening before publication but had declined to hold off publication for 24 hours to

---

[134] [2001] 2 A.C. 127 at 206.

[135] *Galloway v Telegraph Group Ltd* [2004] EWHC 2786 (QB); [2005] E.M.L.R. 7 and [2006] EWCA Civ 17; [2006] E.M.L.R. 11 at [75].

[136] *Reynolds v Times Newspapers Ltd* [2001] 2 A.C. 127 at 205; *GKR Karate v Yorkshire Post (No.2)* [2000] E.M.L.R. 410; *Armstrong v Times Newspapers Ltd* [2005] EWCA Civ 1007; [2005] E.M.L.R. 97.

[137] The factor will, of course, commonly be linked with others. In *English v Hastie Publishing Ltd*, January 31, 2002 (QB), the allegation was serious, and the source of the story was anonymous, but the defendant had reason to think it came from a person in dispute with the claimant. It was not put to the claimant and, despite his assertion to the contrary, the defendant had done barely anything else to verify it. See also *Malik v Newspost Ltd* [2007] EWHC 3063 (QB) at [16].

[138] *Charman v Orion Publishing Group Ltd* [2007] EWCA Civ 972; [2008] E.M.L.R. 16 at [83(7)]. But cf. *Galloway v Telegraph Group Ltd* [2006] EWCA Civ 17; [2006] E.M.L.R. 11 at [75].

[139] E.g. *Amalgamated Television Services Pty Ltd v Marsden* [2002] NSWCA 419 (serious allegations of sexual misbehaviour; offer to plaintiff to allow him to see programme without identifying accusers, defendants to retain editorial control of interview with plaintiff; offer unreasonable). In *Brander v Ryan and Messenger Press Pty Ltd* [2000] SASC 446; 78 S.A.S.R. 234 (Full Court) it seems that the reason for not requiring an approach to the plaintiff was that the article held him up to ridicule.

[140] [2006] UKHL 44; [2007] 1 A.C. 359.

enable him to be contacted. The Court of Appeal had regarded this as fatal to the defence but the House of Lords disagreed. Even if the claimant had been able to obtain a denial from the Saudi authorities (which had declined to make any comment to the defendants) that would have meant very little and would not have significantly affected the value of the story since if the monitoring of the accounts was going on the authorities were hardly likely to admit it. Nor could the claimant have had any personal knowledge which could have cast any light on the matter and he could only have said that he knew of no reason why anyone should wish to monitor the accounts.[141] Accordingly, the failure to give a longer opportunity to respond did not invalidate the defence. Indeed, it seems likely that the result would have been the same even if the defendants had made no attempt at all to contact the claimants. It is doubtful if one can now categorically support the proposition from that a "responsible journalist cannot avoid his obligation to contact the person he intends to criticise by saying that he does not suppose that the person . . . would have anything useful to say".[142] To go forward without seeking comment may be a risky course to take and may suggest a certain arrogance, but if that opinion represents a realistic assessment of the situation the defence should be available. Arguably, the same should apply in a case where, although everyone would conclude that the claimant could contribute nothing of value by way of response yet, because of some extraordinary circumstances, he has information which would amount to a refutation of the story.

Application of the responsible journalism test: tone of the article.   **15.13**
The article in *Jameel (Mohammed) v Wall Street Journal Europe SPRL* was a measured and unsensational one, in an unsensational newspaper.[143] In *Grobelaar v News Group Newspapers Ltd*,[144] the claimant was accused by the defendants of having taken bribes to fix football matches. With regard to the *Reynolds* considerations, first the charge was extremely serious—"hugely damaging"[145]—but equally the subject-matter of the charge was a matter of very substantial public concern. It was unreasonable to expect the defendants to confine themselves to making their information available to the appropriate authorities: "the prospect of the . . . 'scoop' . . . [is] part and parcel of the process of investigative journalism."[146] A major basis of the story was the

---

[141] Cf. *Henry v BBC* [2005] EWHC 2787 (QB) where the likely response of a flat denial would at least have come from the claimant's own knowledge.

[142] *Loutchansky v Times Newspapers Ltd (No.6)* [2002] EWHC 2490 (QB) at [50].

[143] [2006] UKHL 44; [2007] 1 A.C. 359.The newspaper "is, as the journalist quoted by [Lord Hoffmann] said, 'gravely serious' (indeed some might find it seriously dull)": at [150] per Baroness Hale.

[144] [2001] EWCA Civ 33; [2001] E.M.L.R. 18.

[145] Ibid. at [33], per Simon Brown L.J.

[146] Ibid. at [201] per Jonathan Parker L.J.

tape recordings secretly made by the source at the instigation of the defendants, in which the claimant made many admissions which coincided with the source's allegations.[147] On the other hand, while the matter was urgent from the point of view of getting a scoop, it was less so from the point of view of the public interest. The defendants had embroidered the story with some features which had not even featured in the source's allegations; there was a massive and relentless campaign of front page abuse and vilification over seven days, just as if "the *Sun* had placed Mr. Grobelaar in the stocks to be publicly mocked, abused and derided for the amusement of the populace"[148]; and the defendants engaged in a simultaneous campaign of harassing intrusion on the claimant's wife and children. The campaign against the claimant "carried the prejudgment of guilt to its uttermost limits"[149] and while such conduct was no longer contempt there was no reason why the law of libel should be adapted along the same lines.

> "If newspapers choose to publish exposés of this character, unambiguously asserting the criminal guilt of those they investigate, they must do so at their own financial risk. Given the obvious commercial benefits attending this style of journalism—the editor here ordered an increase in the Sun's print run in advance of its Grobelaar exclusive—and the substantially reduced level of damages under modern libel law, it seems to me absurd to suggest that the Sun will be discouraged from pursuing its investigatory role unless protected by qualified privilege."[150]

In *Galloway v Telegraph Group Ltd*,[151] the claimant Member of Parliament was accused of being in the pay of a hostile foreign regime. The story was based in part on papers found in Baghdad. No stronger example of a matter of public concern could be found, but the claimant was political anathema to the defendants and they went for him with "relish and fervour" drawing conclusions from the Baghdad documents which they failed to put to him.[152]

This does not mean that only calm and measured pieces can fall within the scope of *Reynolds* privilege: a newspaper is entitled to write hard-hitting pieces about matters of real public concern and to say that it finds the

---

[147] It was not until a later stage that the claimant vouchsafed his story that he had been trying to entrap and expose the source.

[148] *Grobelaar v News Group Newspapers Ltd* [2001] EWCA Civ 33; [2001] E.M.L.R. 18 at [211] per Jonathan Parker L.J.

[149] Ibid. per Simon Brown L.J at [38].

[150] Ibid. per Simon Brown L.J at [40]. There seems to be some disagreement between Simon Brown and Jonathan Parker L.JJ. over the legitimacy of the "ambush" at the airport, which the newspaper contended fulfilled the requirement of allowing the claimant to put his side of the story. Although the court rejected the defence of privilege it went on to hold that on the evidence the jury's finding in favour of the claimant was perverse and quashed the verdict. The HL held ([2002] UKHL 40; [2002] 1 W.L.R. 3024) that this was an error, but that an award of substantial damages was perverse and substituted an award of £1.

[151] [2006] EWCA Civ 17; [2006] E.M.L.R. 11, affirming [2004] EWHC 2786 (QB); [2005] E.M.L.R. 7.

[152] Ibid. at [73] (and see at [77]).

claimant's denials or explanations unconvincing. What it does mean is that the publisher cannot treat matters which would call for investigation as proof of guilt.[153]

Application of the responsible journalism test: post-publication   **15.14**
behaviour. When it was first mooted by Lord Lester, the proposal that became s.4 of the Defamation Act 2013 included an additional element compared with the provision that reached the statute book. This was the requirement that, if a publisher was to avail itself of the defence, it would have to be able to demonstrate that it had not unreasonably refused or applied conditions to the publication of a correction of the statement complained of.[154] That proposal was withdrawn without reference by the Government before the Committee Stage in the House of Lords, and there is no such requirement in the Act.

A similar issue can arise, however, with regard to the availability of previously published material in archives, primarily on the internet but also to some extent in physical form. Where there is litigation it is common to attach a qualification to internet material which may have the effect of removing the sting from the material, but it will not necessarily do so. The issue arose in the *Reynolds* privilege context in *Flood v Times Newspapers Ltd*.[155] Internet publication was continuing at the time of the hearing. It was significant that, although the claimant had been cleared by the police investigation some two to three years earlier, in 2009 the website version still had a note stating only that "this article is subject to legal complaint". Tugendhat J. held that the qualified website article was not protected by privilege from the time of the release of the report of the police investigation.[156] The qualification failed to make clear who had made the complaint, the status of the information relied on in relation to the paper publication had changed for the worse, or that the article could no longer be regarded as a fair representation of the claimant's

---

[153] In *Roberts v Gable* [2007] EWCA Civ 721; [2008] Q.B. 502 at [74], Sedley L.J. was of the view that "tone" went only to the question whether it undermined the claim to be publishing in the public interest.

[154] See 739 HL Deb col 954, October 9, 2012 per Lord Lester. This was the proposal that was then considered by the Joint Committee on Human Rights in its report on the human rights impact of the Defamation Bill.

[155] [2010] EWCA Civ 804; [2011] 1 W.L.R. 153.

[156] [2009] EWHC 2375; [2010] E.M.L.R. 8. The defendants had offered to publish a "news in brief" item referring to the report, but this had been rejected by the claimant on the wording. That fact might be relevant on any eventual award of damages, but it could not support privilege:
"the risk in relation to the *Reynolds* public interest defence lay on [the defendant], and not on the Claimant. It is for a defendant to make good his defence. It may well be good practice to seek to agree a form of follow-up publication in a case such as this. But if there is no agreement, then the publisher must take his own course, and then defend it if he can at trial. He cannot offer the claimant a form of words which the claimant refuses to accept, and then rely on that refusal to relieve him of the obligation of acting responsibly and fairly, at least when the claimant's refusal is reasonable, as it was here" (at [244]).

position. This finding was upheld in large measure by the Court of Appeal.[157]

It is a moot point how this scenario might be affected by the advent of the "single publication rule" for internet (and other) publication in s.8 of the Defamation Act 2013.[158] Should a change in circumstances arise outside of the effective one year limitation period, it must be assumed that no claim would lie and no correction need be made.

15.15 Application of the responsible journalism test: reportage. It is a first principle of the English law of defamation that if D repeats allegations made by X about C, then D cannot defend himself by showing that X made the statement in question. Rather, he must prove that what X said is true, or bring himself within some other defence. This is the repetition rule.[159] To a limited extent, this rule has long been qualified by specific reporting privileges granted by the common law or by statute, for example in relation to fair and accurate reports of court proceedings and of public meetings. The question arises whether the law admits a more general privilege, not tied to pre-defined situations, based on neutral reporting.

It seems that it now does, under the label "reportage".[160] Indeed, reportage has been described as "a special, and relatively rare, form of *Reynolds* privilege".[161] The doctrine first surfaced in *Al-Fagih v HH Saudi Research & Marketing (UK) Ltd.*[162] The majority of the Court of Appeal held that the

---

[157] [2010] EWCA Civ 804; [2011] 1 W.L.R. 153 per Lord Neuberger M.R. at [81]:
"The fact that the claimant's refusal (to agree the defendant's form of words) is unreasonable will, save perhaps in the most unusual circumstances, not be enough to justify the defendant doing nothing if responsible journalism would otherwise require him to retract or modify a website publication if further relevant information comes to light. The essential point is that it is for a defendant to decide on the appropriate course to take. As well as being contrary to principle, it seems to me to be literally adding insult to injury to enable a defendant to require a claimant, after new evidence has come to light, to agree a form of words to amend a publication, which is defamatory of him but against which he cannot protect himself in law, so as to ensure he still cannot protect himself against it in law."
Time did not permit the Supreme Court to hear argument on the defendant's appeal on the issue of whether the website publication continued to be privileged after publication of the report of the police investigation, and the matter was adjourned generally, to be pursued, if appropriate, after judgment had been given on the first limb of the appeal.
[158] See para.6.6, above.
[159] See paras 6.47 and 11.18, above.
[160] A "fancy word": Ward L.J. in *Roberts v Gable* [2007] EWCA Civ 721; [2008] Q.B. 502 at [34]. One which we are presumably supposed to pronounce in a quasi-French manner, but no longer, it seems, to italicise: ibid. at [68].
[161] *Flood v Times Newspapers Ltd* [2012] UKSC 11; [2012] 2 A.C. 273 at [77] per Lord Phillips M.R.
[162] [2001] EWCA Civ 1634; [2002] E.M.L.R. 13. The claimant sued in respect of a report in the defendants' newspaper of defamatory allegations made by X to the effect that the claimant had made imputations of a sexual nature about X's mother. The claimant and X had been members of a group, based in London, that was seeking to bring about change in Saudi Arabia. A feud had developed between them. The newspaper was partly owned by members of the Saudi royal family, and had a London circulation of about 1,500 among members of the Saudi community based there. The claimant conceded that news of a split within the group was of interest to the Saudi community in London. On the facts, it should have been obvious to the newspaper that X

publication was privileged. The defendants had not adopted or endorsed the allegation; the report was of a stage in an ongoing political dispute of legitimate interest to the readership; and the failure of the defendants to take steps to verify the allegation did not in such a case prevent the report from being privileged. The court explained that:

" . . . there will be circumstances where, as here . . . both sides to a political dispute are being fully, fairly and disinterestedly reported in their respective allegations and responses. In this situation . . . the public is entitled to be informed of such a dispute without having to wait for the publisher, following an attempt at verification, to commit himself to one side or the other."[163]

In *Jameel (Mohammed) v Wall Street Journal Europe SPRL*, the defendants relied explicitly on such a doctrine but only at a late stage before the Court of Appeal. The Court was prepared to accept that the ninth of Lord Nicholls' factors in *Reynolds* suggests "the possibility that *Reynolds* privilege may attach to the neutral reporting of allegations made by a third party, notwithstanding that the publisher does not believe that the allegations are true".[164] In the event, however, the Court was of the view that even if the matter had been specifically raised, Eady J. would have rejected it in view of his general conclusions under *Reynolds* that the circumstances were not such as to create a duty to publish. In the House of Lords, the matter was not pursued but the doctrine is referred to as one where "the public interest lies simply in the fact that the statement was made, when it may be clear that the publisher does not subscribe to any belief in its truth".[165] Similarly, in *Galloway v Telegraph Group Ltd* such a doctrine was relied on and acknowledged but rejected on the facts because the defendants had embraced and embellished the allegations.[166]

In *Roberts v Gable*,[167] upholding the decision of Eady J.,[168] the Court of Appeal held that reportage is a form of the *Reynolds* qualified privilege. Hence, it is said not to contradict the repetition rule. The rule is concerned with meaning and justification, whereas privilege as a whole assumes the existence of the rule and is a qualification of it. As Ward L.J. put it:

---

had an axe to grind and could not safely be accepted as a reliable source and the steps that could have been taken to seek verification were not difficult.

[163] Ibid. per Simon Brown L.J. at [52].

[164] [2005] EWCA Civ 74; [2005] Q.B. 904 at [19].

[165] [2006] UKHL 44; [2007] 1 A.C. 359 at [62]. See also, *Flood v Times Newspapers Ltd* (above).

[166] [2006] EWCA Civ 17; [2006] E.M.L.R. 11.

[167] [2007] EWCA Civ 721; [2008] Q.B. 502. The case bears some resemblance to *Al-Fagih* and involved a story in an anti-far-right magazine that one claimant had stolen money collected at a British National Party event, that both claimants had threatened to injure or kill certain other dissident supporters of the party, and that both claimants might be subject to police investigation.

[168] [2006] EWHC 1025 (QB); [2006] E.M.L.R. 23.

"to qualify as reportage the report, judging the thrust of it as a whole, must have the effect of reporting, not the truth of the statements, but the fact that they were made . . . If upon a proper construction of the thrust of the article the defamatory material is attributed to another and is not being put forward as true, then a responsible journalist would not need to take steps to verify its accuracy. He is absolved from that responsibility because he is simply reporting in a neutral fashion the fact that it has been said without adopting the truth".[169]

Section 4(3) of the Defamation Act 2013 sets out a specific version of the reportage test. It provides that:

If the statement complained of was, or formed part of, an accurate and impartial account of a dispute to which the claimant was a party, the court must in determining whether it was reasonable for the defendant to believe that publishing the statement was in the public interest disregard any omission of the defendant to take steps to verify the truth of the imputation conveyed by it.

This test sets out a more or less consonant version of the mainstream of the common law doctrine. It does not leave scope, in itself, for much by way of further development of reportage as a legal concept.

15.16 Reportage: adoption of a position reported. Whether the test for reportage is fulfilled is for the judge to decide. The case law has developed a number of rules regarding availability of the privilege to reportage. The first of these is that the special protection "will be lost if the journalist adopts the report and makes it his own or if he fails to report the story in a fair, disinterested and neutral way".[170] In *Charman v Orion Publishing Ltd*,[171] Ward L.J. offered a graphic differentiation between the book *Bent Coppers* and reporting that might be covered by the reportage doctrine. The two were described as being "miles removed" because the book was:

"a piece of investigative journalism where [the author] was acting as the bloodhound sniffing out bits of the story from here and there, from published material and unpublished material, not as the watchdog barking to wake us up to the story already out there."[172]

Hence, in the English cases the defence of reportage is lost if the defendant has adopted the charges as his own.[173] So long as the reporting is fair and balanced, however, this does not mean that it must be bland. Nor does it require that the defendant should be denied the opportunity of showing pleasure in reporting the matter.[174]

---

[169] [2007] EWCA Civ 721; [2008] Q.B. 502 at [61(3)].
[170] Ibid. at [61(5)].
[171] [2007] EWCA Civ 972; [2008] E.M.L.R. 16.
[172] Ibid. at [49].
[173] *Charman v Orion Publishing Ltd* [2007] EWCA Civ 972; [2008] E.M.L.R. 16 at [48]; *Roberts v Gable* [2007] EWCA Civ 721; [2008] Q.B. 502 at [53] and [61(5)]; *Prince Radu of Hohenzollern v Houston* [2007] EWHC 2735 (QB) at [20] (see, on appeal, [2008] EWCA Civ 921; [2009] E.M.L.R. 13 at [5]).
[174] *Roberts v Gable*, above at [74]. And see at [65]–[66].

Failure to maintain a neutral stance does not necessarily mean that the defendant loses the claim to privilege under *Reynolds* altogether, but he or she is no longer dispensed from the general requirement to try to verify the story and give the subject his or her say. Even where it is a true reportage situation the other factors mentioned in *Reynolds* will continue to apply, where relevant, though they will have to be substantially modified. Although in *Charman* the defendants were able to bring themselves within the general cover of *Reynolds* because, taken as a whole, their conduct amounted to responsible journalism, that may not always be the case. As Sedley L.J. pointed out, it is:

"the very dependence of a reportage defence on the bald retailing of libels which makes it forensically problematical to fall back upon an alternative defence of responsible journalism. Pleaders may need to decide which it is to be".[175]

If the English case law has become clear on this point, the Strasbourg jurisprudence in this general area is somewhat less interpretable. On the basis of the Strasbourg case law there is no requirement that the defendant should formally distance himself from the charges reported,[176] but in *Verlagsgruppe News GMBH v Austria* the court said that:

"It is certainly true that the article at issue [which it described as reportage] reflected a rather critical approach . . . This cannot, however, justify the conclusion that the article identified and adopted the content of the impugned statements of the quoted passage."[177]

The defendants in *Galloway* unsuccessfully relied on the decision of the European Court of Human Rights in *Selistö v Finland*,[178] a "striking decision",[179] in which the majority of the Court held that the criminal conviction of a journalist in respect of stories (which, in the general context of patient safety, imputed by way of example that an unnamed but identifiable surgeon, who had been given no prior opportunity to comment, had been drunk on duty) violated art.10 of the Convention. Perhaps it is best to say overall, as Eady J. did,[180] that the Court was concerned with the particular facts. However, it is also the case that the imputations were based upon a public police investigation document, albeit one which had not led to any proceedings, so the source had some "status" in *Reynolds* terms. Overall, there is probably little to be gained from any close linguistic analysis of the Strasbourg cases, and it is not even clear that in the Strasbourg cases (or, indeed, in the French

---

[175] [2007] EWCA Civ 972; [2008] E.M.L.R. 16 at [91].
[176] *Thoma v Luxembourg* App. No.38432/97; ECHR 2001–III.
[177] App. No.76918/01 at [33].
[178] App. No.56767/00, [2005] E.M.L.R. 8.
[179] *Galloway v Telegraph Group Ltd* [2004] EWHC 2786; [2005] E.M.L.R. 7 per Eady J. at [136].
[180] Ibid. at [148].

language) the word reportage has any of the overtones which it appears to be acquiring in English libel law.[181]

15.17 Reportage: requirement for an ongoing dispute. The second particular test in the area of reportage concerns the issue of whether it is necessary that the material should be a report of a stage in some existing public controversy. Whether this is always a requirement is less clear. There is much to suggest that the existence of an ongoing dispute is a feature of this variant of privilege. In *Roberts*, Ward L.J. offered a narrow line. Thus:

> "the best description of [reportage] which [can be] gleaned from these cases is that it is the neutral reporting without adoption or embellishment or subscribing to any belief in its truth of attributed allegations of both sides of a political and possibly some other kind of dispute".[182]

Although the word "dispute" seems to fit best the case where there is regular reporting of volley and counter-volley, "where the story unfolds day by day as in the *Al Fagih* case",[183] the existence of a dispute generally explains the derogations from the normal *Reynolds* requirements. If A and B are each saying bad things about the other the reporter may not be able realistically to attempt verification without ending up taking sides.

Conversely, there has been some suggestion that the existence of an ongoing dispute need not be a requirement. No such requirement was mentioned in the relevant passages in *Roberts v Gable* which were placed under the heading "The proper approach to the reportage defence". Furthermore, in *Galloway* the court was clearly of the view that the doctrine would have entitled the defendants to publish the documents found in Baghdad without embellishment. There is no doubt that the invasion of Iraq which was the background to that case was *controversial* and so were the opinions and behaviour of the claimant about that and other matters. There was nothing resembling the reporting of the dispute in *Al-Fagih*.[184]

In *Charman v Orion Publishing Ltd*, Ward L.J. repeated his view in *Roberts v Gable* that there was an analogy with the concept of hearsay evidence, that is to say, there was reportage when what was being reported was the mere fact

---

[181] Thus in *Tonsbergs Blad AS v Norway* App. No.510/04 it is used in the translation of the Norwegian court's decision in the sense of "reported matter". Indeed, it is used in the judgment of Arden L.J. in *Curistan v Times Newspapers Ltd* [2008] EWCA Civ 432; [2009] Q.B. 231 to describe material protected by the standard reporting privileges.

[182] [2007] EWCA Civ 721; [2008] Q.B. 502 at [53].

[183] Ibid. at [61(9)]. *Malik v Newspost Ltd* [2007] EWHC 3063 (QB) might have been a case of this type as far as the media defendants were concerned had they reported in a fair and disinterested way: at [15]. So also *Prince Radu of Hohenzollern v Houston* [2007] EWHC 2735 (QB) where the reporting was found to be heavily slanted against the claimant.

[184] In *Mark v Associated Newspapers Ltd* [2002] EWCA Civ 772; [2002] E.M.L.R. 38 at [35] Simon Brown L.J. said: "I am certainly prepared to recognise that the approach adopted in *Al-Fagih* may need to be taken further still—rather than perhaps confined merely to the reporting of statements (attributed and unadopted) by both sides to a political dispute."

that the allegation had been made but not where the report could be said to adopt the allegation.[185] The illustrations he gave of how the line might be drawn are somewhat far removed from the "reporting of a dispute" scenario of *Al-Fagih* and *Roberts*.[186] Sedley L.J. expressed the similar view that "the reportage doctrine . . . cannot logically be confined to the reporting of recip-rocal allegations. A unilateral libel, reported disinterestedly, will be equally protected".[187] In both *Roberts* and *Charman* reportage is linked with the American case of *Edwards v National Audubon Society*,[188] which Sedley L.J. in *Charman* described as a "classic limb of First Amendment jurispru-dence".[189] *Edwards* is certainly a case which gives some support to immunity for the reporting of allegations of legitimate public interest about public figures emanating from "responsible, prominent organizations" regardless of the reporter's belief in the allegations. However, two points must be made about the case. First, as far as the media defendant was concerned it was a "report of a dispute" case. Secondly, it has certainly not gained universal acceptance, some courts considering it inconsistent with the Supreme Court's general approach to defamation of public figures.[190] Furthermore, it is also narrower than the current English doctrine as applied to the reporting of disputes: the sources in *Al-Fagih* and *Roberts* came nowhere near satisfying the "responsible, prominent organization" test. Of course, the basic *New York Times v Sullivan* requirement of "actual malice" towards public figures makes the reportage issue less significant than it is here.[191]

If the requirement of a dispute is excised, reportage has the potential for considerable expansion of a more media-friendly version of *Reynolds*, espe-cially where the newspaper chooses its words carefully and explicitly dis-tances itself from making a judgment. In fact, it becomes rather difficult to

---

[185] [2007] EWCA Civ 972; [2008] E.M.L.R. 16.
[186] Ibid. at [54].
"If J, the journalist, simply reports that S, the source, says that C, the claimant, is corrupt, then the objective meaning of the source allegation and the report is the same, guilt. However, the fact that in so far as J simply repeated the allegation and, to the extent that he did may be said to have adopted it, . . . cannot determine the real question whether he made the allegation his own. If, for example, J adds to his report, 'and I agree', then the meaning remains the same, but adoption is clear from the added words . . . What if J adds to his report, 'X says that C is not guilty, Y says that he does not know and Z says it might be true'? Here the objective meaning of S's statement is at *Chase* level 1 [i.e. an imputation of guilt] but J's report is probably, say, at *Chase* level 2 [i.e. an imputation of reasonable suspicion]. But that difference cannot determine whether J has adopted S's report. As a matter of textual analysis, J was maintaining a position of neutrality and did not adopt S's words as his own. If J reports that S says that C is corrupt and adds, 'so there are reasonable grounds to suspect him' the meanings are different but one can find this time, again as a matter of textual analysis, at least a partial adoption of the allegation."
[187] Ibid. at [91].
[188] 556 F.2d 113 (CA 2 1977).
[189] [2007] EWCA Civ 972; [2008] E.M.L.R. 16 at [91].
[190] See Dobbs, *Torts* (2000), para.415.
[191] See para.15.31, below.

avoid ending up with a general privilege to report "matters of public concern", provided the source of the information comes from outside the newspaper. This would be a very significant step for the law to take, and not one that should be undertaken readily. In *Flood v Times Newspapers Ltd*, while no attempt had been made before the Court of Appeal to rely on the reportage principle,[192] Lord Neuberger M.R. stated that:

> "the fact that an unidentified insider has given specific information which, if true, may incriminate a claimant, will very rarely be justifiable reportage. Of course, it will add something to the substance and newsworthiness of the story that the police are investigating the claimant, but it seems to me that it would be tipping the scales too far in favour of the media to hold that not only the name of the claimant, but the details of the allegations against him, can normally be published as part of a story free of any right in the claimant to sue for defamation just because the general subject matter of the story is in the public interest. The fair balancing of Article 8 and Article 10 would normally require that such allegations should only be freely publishable if to do so is in the public interest and the journalist has taken reasonable steps to check their accuracy. If they are true, a claim for defamation will fail; if they are untrue, but their publication was in the public interest, and a reasonable check was carried out, there is good reason why a claim for defamation should fail, even though it is hard on the claimant; if they are untrue and their publication cannot be said to be in the public interest or no reasonable check was carried out, it seems quite unjust that the claimant should have no remedy in law... [these were] as the journalists must have appreciated, no more than unsubstantiated unchecked accusations, from an unknown source, coupled with speculation".[193]

It is probably fair to say that there is some way to go in setting the proper bounds of reportage. It seems, however, to be accepted on all sides that it would be going too far to give a general, automatic media privilege for repetition of charges originated by others (which would be practically inconsistent with the repetition rule and with the rejection in *Reynolds* of a generic privilege for political reporting). There also seems to be agreement that the defence should be applied "restrictively".[194] The new statutory variant in s.4(3) would appear to set out one version—a relatively strict one—of the range of possibilities. It is not clear how far the more generous thinking of some judges might still be accommodated within the more general reasonable belief test.

15.18 Reportage: the statutory version. The transposition of the *Reynolds* privilege into statutory form in s.4 of the Defamation Act 2013 will see the reiteration of the particular rule on reportage. Section 4(3) provides:

---

[192] [2010] EWCA Civ 804; [2011] 1 W.L.R. 153 at [88].
[193] Ibid. at [63] and [73].
[194] *Charman v Orion Publishing Ltd* [2007] EWCA Civ 972; [2008] E.M.L.R. 16 at [74] per Sedley L.J. (who, it will be recalled, would not confine the defence to the reporting of disputes). At least the matter is now out in the open; in fact there must have been countless thousands of news stories which have infringed the law as until now it has been thought to be, even if they were often covered in the inadequate fig leaf of quotation marks or "it is alleged".

"If the statement complained of was, or formed part of, an accurate and impartial account of a dispute to which the claimant was a party, the court must in determining whether it was reasonable for the defendant to believe that publishing the statement was in the public interest disregard any omission of the defendant to take steps to verify the truth of the imputation conveyed by it".

Application to facts and opinion. One clear difference with the advent   **15.19** of the statutory defence is that it will apply to opinions as well as statements of fact.[195] It will thereby produce some overlap with honest comment (or "honest opinion" as honest comment is to be relabelled under s.3 of the Act). While the Court of Appeal in *British Chiropractic Association v Singh* regarded it as an open question whether *Reynolds* privilege applies also to opinion,[196] both Lord Nicholls and Lord Hobhouse had stated in the seminal case itself that statements of opinion were to be protected, if at all, only by fair comment.[197] As a matter of principle, the position stated in the House of Lords is preferable to that mooted by the Court of Appeal and reflected in the s.4(5) of the Defamation Act 2013, although for some this distinction is no more than a "technicality".[198]

Not solely a news media defence. In the great majority of cases the   **15.20** defendant seeking to rely on the *Reynolds* variety of privilege will be a newspaper or other organ of the news media. Hence, "responsible journalism" is a convenient shorthand description of its requirements. However, *Reynolds* privilege is not confined to the news media.[199] It applies as much to a publication in the form of a book,[200] or a speech at a public meeting.[201] Typically, the defence will be attracted by what is called "investigative journalism" or "reportage", but that is not a necessary element. However, a member of the public who launches serious allegations into the public arena may fall foul of the fact that there may be other effective ways of initially raising the issue, e.g. by informing the proper authority.[202]

Irrelevance of malice. The traditional form of qualified privilege is   **15.21** defeated by proof by the claimant of malice on the part of the defendant. This has become irrelevant in the context of *Reynolds*: the defendant must establish not only that the matter was of sufficient public interest, but that he acted in accordance with the tenets of responsible journalism. There is therefore "no

---

[195] Defamation Act 2013, s.4(5).

[196] [2010] EWCA Civ 350 at [31].

[197] [2001] 2 A.C. 127 at 201 and 193–5 per Lord Nicholls, and 237–238 per Lord Hobhouse. In *Cook v Telegraph Media Group Ltd* [2011] EWHC 763 (QB) at [69], Tugendhat J., referred to the issue as one that is "not yet established" and "left open".

[198] Explanatory notes to the Lester Defamation Bill at [54].

[199] *Jameel v Wall Street Journal Europe Sprl* [2006] UKHL 44; [2007] 1 A.C. 359 at [54].

[200] *Charman v Orion Publishing Group Ltd* [2007] EWCA Civ 972; [2008] E.M.L.R. 16 at [83].

[201] *Seaga v Harper* [2008] UKPC 9; [2009] 1 A.C. 1.

[202] *Malik v Newspost Ltd* [2007] EWHC 3063 (QB) (letter to newspaper).

question of the privilege being defeated by proof of malice because the propriety of the conduct of the defendant is built into the conditions under which the material is privileged."[203] That said, one judge has suggested that malice has survived as a factor capable of defeating the privilege.[204] The irrelevance of malice may be more a matter of practicality than doctrine. In principle, moreover, there seems no reason why there should not be a case which might be approached either from the *Reynolds* angle or from that of traditional privilege,[205] for example in cases where the only practicable way of fulfilling a duty to the public or protecting an interest was to publish generally.[206] In such a case, the defendant should succeed if malice cannot be shown, even though his conduct did not meet the requirements under *Reynolds*. The common law is used to overlapping, alternative defences, nowhere more so than in the context of defamation.[207]

Interestingly, the subjective dimension to the "reasonable belief" element of the defence of publication on a matter of public interest in s.4(1)(b) of the

---

[203] *Jameel (Mohammed) v Wall Street Journal Europe SPRL* [2006] UKHL 44; [2007] 1 A.C. 359 at [46] per Lord Hoffmann. See also, *Loutchansky v Times Newspapers Ltd* (Nos 2–5) [2001] EWCA Civ 1805; [2002] QB 783 at [34] per Lord Phillips M.R.:

"it may be doubted whether in truth there remains room for such a principle in a case of *Reynolds* privilege. Once the publication of a particular article is held to be in the public interest on the basis of the public's right to know, can the privilege really be lost because the journalist (or editor?) had the dominant motive of injuring the claimant rather than fulfilling his journalistic duty? It is a surprising thought".

[204] *Cook v Telegraph Media Group Ltd* [2011] EWHC 763 (QB) at [61], [70] and [121(f)].

[205] See para.14.3, above. One must bear in mind that although usually invoked by the media, *Reynolds* is not a "newspaper defence".

[206] See para.15.1, above. In *Prince Radu of Hohenzollern v Houston* [2007] EWHC 2735 (QB) there was a plea of *Reynolds* privilege and an alternative plea of classical "common interest" privilege. Eady J. said at [9] that if the former failed "it is difficult to see how 'common interest' privilege could survive on its own". A plea based on community of interest between a magazine and its readers would prima facie be a weak one.

[207] In *Henry v BBC* [2007] EWHC 2787 (QB) there were allegations of "fiddling" NHS treatment waiting lists and *Reynolds* was at the heart of the defendant's privilege case, the NHS being so dear to the public heart that its "right to know" could hardly be contested, provided there was "responsible journalism". However, aspects of the claim were also potentially capable of being covered by (a) traditional common law privilege based on reply to attack since the person making the allegations reported by the defendants had been the subject of accusations by her employers and (b) certain statutory "reporting" privileges under Sch.1 to the Defamation Act 1996. Gray J. took the view that: "in the context of the present case, where the action is brought on a media publication, the preferable course seems to me to be to treat the issue of reply to attack as being one of the matters to be taken into account in deciding *Reynolds* privilege rather than as a free-standing ground on which privilege at common law may be established" (at [94]). The claim to statutory reporting privilege failed but it was held that the fact that the broadcast consisted in part at least of a report of the conclusions of an official inquiry and of what was a public meeting for the purposes of the 1996 Act were at least relevant factors in considering the *Reynolds* defence (at [95]). With regard to reply to attack, perhaps little turned on it in this case since the claim to privilege on that ground seems to have been a weak one (see [103]) and the line taken by the judge had the agreement of both counsel, but it would be unfortunate if the view taken were to be regarded as a signal that the media must always rely on *Reynolds* in this type of case. It is well established that if A is attacked in public he may respond in the media if that is a proportionate way to defend himself and he only loses this defence if he can be shown to have common law malice; if the media organ, B, he uses to do so is not treated in the same way he may find it hard to get an outlet.

Defamation Act 2013 may see the re-emergence of proof of malice as a feature of the defence in future come the appropriate case.

Respective roles of jury, judge, and appeal court. Under *Reynolds* **15.22** privilege, the question of whether the publication was protected by privilege (the evaluation of the defendant's conduct against the standard of responsible journalism as well as the issue of public interest) is for the judge. This has not proved easy to operate with trial by jury:

> "the division between the role of the judge and that of the jury when *Reynolds* privilege is in issue is not an easy one; indeed it is open to question whether jury trial is desirable at all in such a case."[208]

In the "classical" common law qualified privilege case, there may be disputed facts going to the existence of the privileged occasion but the jury's role is likely to be mainly concerned with determining the issue of malice. On this they are likely to be required (if they are required to do more than return a general verdict) to simply say "yes" or "no". Under *Reynolds*, however, disputed issues of fact may be at the heart of the very existence of the privilege; questions such as, "What was the nature and background of the source of the story? What did the newspaper do to verify it? What did the newspaper do to enable the claimant to respond?" A possible scenario, therefore, is that at the end of the trial the jury will be presented with a series of questions going first to meaning and reference (if those are in dispute), then to the *Reynolds* factors, and then to damages, the *Reynolds* issue then being reserved for ultimate determination by the judge, who has to evaluate the effect of the jury's answers to determine whether there was the requisite basis for privilege.[209] The matter may be determined as a preliminary issue with a jury determining issues of disputed fact, but there is then a danger that the jury may be mystified by the limited role that they are playing in the proceedings.[210] Hence, in some cases the preliminary issue[211] or even the whole proceedings[212] have been decided by judge alone.

Difficulties surrounding the respective roles of the judge and jury are obviously very substantially reduced in importance in the context of the general move toward trial by judge only in the Defamation Act 2013.

---

[208] *Jameel (Mohammed) v Wall Street Journal Europe SPRL* [2005] EWCA Civ 74; [2005] Q.B. 904 at [70]. See also, *Cook v Telegraph Media Group Ltd* [2011] EWHC 763 (QB) at [68].

[209] See *Jameel (Mohammed) v Wall Street Journal Europe SPRL* [2004] EWHC 37 (QB); [2004] E.M.L.R. 11.

[210] See *Charman v Orion Publishing Group Ltd* [2006] EWHC 1756 (QB); [2007] 1 All E.R. 622 at [4].

[211] *Jameel (Yousef) v Times Newspapers Ltd* [2005] EWHC 1219 (QD).

[212] *Galloway v Telegraph Group Ltd* [2004] EWHC 2786 (QB); [2005] E.M.L.R. 7; *Charman v Orion Publishing Group Ltd* [2006] EWHC 1756 (QB); [2007] 1 All E.R. 622.

A separate issue concerns the role of the appeal court on hearing appeals in *Reynolds* privilege cases. It was said in *Galloway v Telegraph Group Ltd* that:

> "[t]he right to publish must . . . be balanced against the rights of the individual. That balance is a matter for the judge. It is not a matter for an appellate court. This court will not interfere with the judge's conclusion after weighing all the circumstances in the balance unless he has erred in principle or reached a conclusion which is plainly wrong."[213]

This was held by the Court of Appeal in *Flood* to be an incorrect approach. The applicability of *Reynolds* is not a matter of "discretion" but a decision on a matter of law so that in principle there can only be one correct answer, even if one has to recognise that in practice sensible people may come to different conclusions. Lord Neuberger M.R. stated that:

> "a decision in a case such as this does not involve the exercise of a discretion and cannot therefore be approached as the court suggested in *Galloway* . . . Where a first instance court carries out a balancing exercise, the appeal process requires the appellate court to decide whether the judge was right or wrong, but it should bear in mind the advantage that the trial judge had in the ways described [by Lord Bingham] in *Jameel* . . . [at [36]]. Where the determination is a matter of balance and proportionality, it is, generally speaking, difficult for an appellant to establish that the judge has gone wrong."[214]

15.23 Reynolds privilege and meaning. The general rule in defamation law is that words are treated as having a single meaning even though people might in fact read them differently.[215] This rule does not, however, apply where the

---

[213] [2006] EWCA Civ 17; [2006] E.M.L.R. 11 at [68].

[214] [2010] EWCA Civ 804; [2011] 1 W.L.R. 153. at [49]. Moore-Bick L.J. concurred (at [107]):

"there is an intrinsic difference between exercising a discretion and deciding a question of law. In cases where the court is called upon to exercise its discretion views may legitimately differ about the order that should be made. For that reason the judge's decision cannot be overturned otherwise than on well-recognised grounds which, if established, undermine the basis on which the discretion was exercised.

When a question of law is to be decided there is only one correct answer, however difficult it may be to find. Thus, if the true meaning of a document is in issue, the fact that the construction preferred by the judge is plausible does not prevent an appellate court from deciding the matter for itself. Nonetheless, where newspapers and broadcasters are involved striking a balance between freedom of speech and the protection of reputation will often depend to a large extent on an assessment of the behaviour of the journalists involved in the publication. Factors of the kind identified by Lord Nicholls require a careful assessment of the evidence and an appellate court should be cautious before overturning the decision of the judge below, particularly since it has not itself had the advantage of seeing the witnesses."

The apparent view of the CA in *Flood*, namely that the exercise does not involve an exercise of discretion, was confirmed by Lord Phillips in the Supreme Court: [2012] UKSC 11; [2012] 2 A.C. 273 at [104]. But the Supreme Court declined, not having heard argument on the point, to lay down any general principle to the approach to be adopted by appellate courts to the evaluation by the first instance judge of the elements of *Reynolds* privilege: see [106], [182], [203]. Note also *Prince Radu of Hohenzollern v Houston* [2008] EWCA Civ 921; [2009] E.M.L.R. 13 at [20]: "The balance is a matter for the judge. It is not a matter for the appellate court. This Court will not interfere with a judge's conclusion after weighing all the circumstances in the balance unless he has erred in principle or reached a conclusion which is plainly wrong."

[215] See para.3.16, above.

issue is whether the defendant is guilty of malice for the purposes of qualified privilege.[216] In *Bonnick v Morris*,[217] the Privy Council held that a similar rule applied for the purposes of the *Reynolds* privilege under the law of Jamaica so that, if the words used might readily convey different meanings to ordinary reasonable readers, the court could take the meaning reasonably put upon the words by the journalist into account when considering whether the standards of responsible journalism have been met. A similar point has been made in the English High Court:

> "[in] determining whether it was reasonable or responsible not to have made further pre-publication checks, it might well be relevant to consider how the journalist understood the allegations he was making and, if he genuinely thought the words bore no defamatory imputation at all, it would be difficult to criticise him for not addressing such a meaning for the purpose of checks or (say) giving an opportunity to comment upon it."[218]

Bonnick is "more than persuasive" for the purposes of the law of England.[219] However, this:

> "should not be pressed too far. Where questions of defamation may arise ambiguity is best avoided as much as possible. It should not be a screen behind which a journalist is 'willing to wound, and yet afraid to strike'. In the normal course a responsible journalist can be expected to perceive the meaning an ordinary, reasonable reader is likely to give to his article. Moreover, even if the words are highly susceptible of another meaning, a responsible journalist will not disregard a defamatory meaning which is obviously one possible meaning of the article in question. Questions of degree arise here. The more obvious the defamatory meaning, and the more serious the defamation, the less weight will a court attach to other possible meanings when considering the conduct to be expected of a responsible journalist in the circumstances."[220]

Reynolds privilege and justification. As with other, more traditional **15.24** forms of qualified privilege, the ultimate issue is not whether the defamatory

---

[216] See para.17.20, below.

[217] [2002] UKPC 31; [2003] 1 A.C. 300.

[218] *Jameel (Mohammed) v Wall Street Journal Europe SPRL* [2004] EWHC 37 (QB); [2004] E.M.L.R. 11 at [73] per Eady J.

[219] *Charman v Orion Publishing Group Ltd* [2007] EWCA Civ 972; [2008] E.M.L.R. 16 at [55] (where, however, the issue was whether the defendants had adopted the allegation reported). *Bonnick* is clearly assumed to be the law in *Armstrong v Times Newspapers Ltd* [2005] EWCA Civ 1007; [2005] E.M.L.R. 97 at [77] and this also seems to be the view of Lord Scott in *Jameel* [2006] UKHL 44; [2007] 1 A.C. 359 at [136]. The difficulty felt by Eady J. in *Jameel* that *Bonnick* might lead to a court having to hold that there was a duty to publish non-defamatory information would now seem to have disappeared in view of the guidance given by the HL in *Jameel* on the general approach to *Reynolds* privilege.

[220] [2002] UKPC 31; [2003] 1 A.C. 300 at [25]. *Bonnick* was not in fact relevant in *Jameel* because on any view, there was an express statement about the claimant which bore the meaning either that his conduct gave grounds for suspicion or that there were grounds for investigation and whatever the defendants may have intended the statement to mean, no responsible journalist could conceivably disregard the first and more serious meaning, something which was not challenged in the HL. See also, *Flood v Times Newspapers Ltd* [2012] UKSC 11; [2012] 2 A.C. 273 at [51] per Lord Phillips M.R.: "when deciding whether to publish, and when attempting to verify the content of the publication, the responsible journalist should have regard to the full range of meanings that a reasonable reader might attribute to the publication".

imputation is true but whether, upon an objective consideration of the information possessed by the publisher at the time, it is legitimate to publish it even if it may be untrue. The proposition that the truth of the allegation is irrelevant to privilege,[221] however, has to be read subject to the qualification that it may be relevant to an issue of fact necessary to establish a successful *Reynolds* defence. Thus, suppose D publishes a story to the effect that there are grounds for suspicion (or at least investigation) as to C's involvement in criminality. D says that he received this information from X and Y, described as impeccable sources. Although C cannot compel D to reveal who X and Y are, C may seek to introduce evidence from A and B to the effect that X and Y are unlikely to have told D what he claims they told him. In doing so, he is not introducing irrelevant material, nor embarking on a pointless exercise in proving untrue what is already presumed to be untrue. Rather, he is using the evidence of A and B to rebut the evidence of D that what X and Y told him was a basis for legitimate publication: the evidence of A and B may show that D's understanding or recollection of what X and Y told him is incorrect or, possibly, that D's evidence is fabrication.[222] Where, however, the truth of such facts is in issue, the court should not apply the presumption of falsity in regard to the defamatory statement sued on and alleged to have been confirmed which is used for the purposes of the defence of justification and damages: the fact that the truth of the statement has not been proved is a "neutral circumstance".[223]

15.25 The wider context. The law in other common law jurisdictions has been affected by local constitutional guarantees of freedom of speech and of the press and they have tended to follow their own paths.[224] Plainly, cases from

---

[221] *GKR Karate (UK) Ltd v Yorkshire Post Newspapers Ltd* [2001] 1 W.L.R. 2571 CA.

[222] *Jameel v Wall Street Journal Europe SPRL (No.1)* [2003] EWCA Civ 1694; [2004] E.M.L.R. 6.

[223] *Jameel (Mohammed) v Wall Street Journal Europe SPRL* [2006] UKHL 44; [2007] 1 A.C. 359 at [62]. And see [2005] EWCA Civ 74; [2005] Q.B. 904 at [59]–[61]. As is observed in the CA, "it follows that the jury are required to perform some mental gymnastics". There may be a concurrent plea of justification and on that the court may allow justification to be advanced only in respect of one distinct charge on which the claimant has sued. However, where *Reynolds* privilege is pleaded it might not be right to shut out the defendant's belief that the words complained of are true in some wider meaning which the words are reasonably capable of bearing, a factor which might be material to verification (see e.g. per Lord Phillips in *Flood* [2012] UKSC 11; [2012] 2 A.C. 273 at [79]). Such questions as whether there a public interest in publication need to be assessed in the light of the words complained of as a whole, rather than artificially confining the court's attention to one particular meaning, even if there may be difficulties in shutting out evidence on the issue of justification while admitting it for the purpose of establishing one of the *Reynolds* factors: *McKeith v News Group Newspapers Ltd* [2005] EWHC 1162 (QB); [2005] E.M.L.R. 32 at [33]. These problems illustrate the unsuitability of the jury for cases in which *Reynolds* privilege is in issue.

[224] *Reynolds* has been applied in Hong Kong (*Yaqoob v Asia Times Online Ltd* [2008] 3 HKC 589) Malaysia (*Uttley v Wong* [2002] 4 M.L.J. 371), Brunei Darussalam (*Rifli Bin Asli v Ahmed Kawari Isa*, September 10, 2001, HC) and, it seems, in Cyprus (see *Alithia Publishing Co. Ltd v Cyprus* App. No.17550/03, May 22, 2008), but rejected in Singapore: *Lee v Singapore Democratic Party* [2006] SGHC 220; [2007] 1 S.L.R. 675, applying *Jeyaretnam v Lee* [1992] 2 SLR 310 Sing CA. A non-common law system may approach these issues (at least linguistically) in

these countries have no direct application here, particularly now that we have our own "constitutional" basis for freedom of expression in the form of art.10 of the European Convention on Human Rights. Indeed, the Convention is a factor which in its turn restricts the influence of *Reynolds* on those other jurisdictions.[225] However, both the nature of the problems and the structure of the general law are sufficiently similar to make the developments in these countries of continuing interest here.

Australia. There is no explicit guarantee of freedom of speech in the Austra-   **15.26**
lian Constitution, but it is founded upon the idea of representative government and the High Court therefore concluded that freedom of communication on matters of government and politics is an indispensable incident of Australian law. In *Theophanous v Herald & Weekly Times*[226] a majority of the High Court held that where a defamatory publication concerned political matters it was a defence for the defendant to show that he was unaware of the falsity of the statement, that he did not publish recklessly (i.e. not caring whether it was true or false) and that he acted reasonably, either by taking steps to check the accuracy of the matter or by establishing that he had other justification for publishing without taking such steps. The majority also held in the alternative that discussion of political matters was an occasion of privilege at common law, though the relationship between the two defences was not fully pursued. The relationship between defamation and political discussion was subject to further review in *Lange v Australian Broadcasting Corporation*,[227] a unanimous decision of the High Court. The position of Australian law as a result of this case may be summarised as follows.

(1) The guarantee of freedom of political discussion which is implicit in the Constitution means that the common law of defamation and any statutory modifications of it must be compatible with that guarantee.

(2) The correct approach to this is not the recognition of a direct "constitutional defence" but the adaptation of the common law and in particular the concept of qualified privilege.[228]

---

much the same way. Section 6 § 2 lit.2(a) of the Austrian Media Act states that no claim for damages can be made in cases of defamation when a true statement of facts had been published, or (b), *when the statement's publication was of preponderant public interest and the publisher, having complied with the ethics of journalism, had sufficient evidence before him to consider the statement as true.* The Salzburg Oberlandgericht was of the view that this did not allow the raking up of matters relating to the appointment of an archbishop eight years before. However, the majority of the Strasbourg court considered there had been a violation of art.10. *Albert-Engelmann Gmbh v Austria*, App. No.46389/99.

[225] See, e.g. *Roberts v Bass* [2002] HCA 57; 212 C.L.R. 1 at [124]; *Amalgamated Television Services Pty Ltd v Marsden* [2002] NSWCA 419.

[226] (1994) 182 C.L.R. 104; *Stephen v Western Australia Newspapers* (1994) 182 C.L.R. 211.

[227] (1997) 189 C.L.R. 520.

[228] Although the defence of fair comment is not discussed by the High Court, it is clear that it, too, plays a part in ensuring that the common law complies with the minimum constitutional standard.

(3) The traditional approach in most Australian jurisdictions (inherited from England) had been that with certain comparatively rare exceptions the requirements of reciprocal duty and interest had been interpreted so as to limit qualified privilege to comparatively limited publications and to deny it to those in the media. That is now too narrow for the "common convenience and welfare of society" as perceived in modern conditions and in the light of the Constitution.

"In the last decade of the twentieth century, the quality of life and the freedom of the ordinary individual in Australia are highly dependent on the exercise of functions and powers vested in public representatives and officials by a vast legal and bureaucratic apparatus funded by public moneys. How, when, why and where those functions and powers are or are not exercised are matters that are of real and legitimate interest to every member of the community. Information concerning the exercise of those functions and powers is of vital concern to the community. So is the performance of the public representatives and officials who are invested with them. It follows . . . that the general public has a legitimate interest in receiving information concerning matters relevant to the exercise of public functions and powers vested in public representatives and officials."[229]

Consequently, the common law in Australia recognises publication on a "government or political matter" as an occasion of qualified privilege and the necessary reciprocity exists between the media and the public.

(4) Although the Australian Constitution is directly concerned only with federal government, political affairs at federal, state and local level are inextricably intertwined and the qualified privilege will cover all of these. It may also extend further so as to protect, e.g. discussion of matters concerning the United Nations or other countries, even if those discussions cannot realistically be said to illuminate the choice for voters at Australian elections or throw light on the administration of government there.[230]

(5) At common law, the defence of qualified privilege is defeated only if the plaintiff can show that the publication was actuated by malice on the part of the defendant. For the "private" communications to which qualified privilege has traditionally been applied it is legitimate to make

---

[229] McHugh J. in *Stephens v Western Australia Newspapers* (1994) 182 C.L.R. 211 at 264, cited in *Lange*. His Honour instanced:

"the scientist who discovers that lack of government action is threatening the environment, the 'whistle-blower' who observes the bureaucratic or ministerial 'cover-up' and the investigative journalist who finds that grants of public money have been distributed contrary to the public interest."

[230] *Lange* was an action by a New Zealand politician. The pleadings did not disclose a privileged occasion but the High Court said that by reason of:

"matters of geography, history and constitutional and trading arrangements . . . the discussion of matters concerning New Zealand may often affect or throw light on government or political matters in Australia. That being so, it may be that further and better particulars can be provided which bring the publications within the extended defence."

such honesty of purpose the criterion but a more severe standard should be applied to the extended qualified privilege because the damaging potential of media publication is so much greater. Accordingly, the defendant must not only establish that the publication related to a government or political matter but also that he satisfied the requirements of reasonable conduct. This means that as a general rule he must show that he:

"had reasonable grounds for believing that the imputation was true, took proper steps, so far as they were reasonably open, to verify the accuracy of the material and did not believe the imputation to be untrue. Furthermore, the defendant's conduct will not be reasonable[231] unless the defendant has sought a response from the person defamed and published the response made (if any) except in cases where the seeking or publication of a response was not practicable or it was unnecessary to give the plaintiff an opportunity to respond."

(6) If the defendant establishes these elements of the defence, it is still open to the plaintiff to defeat it by showing that the publication was actuated by malice, which in this context is to be understood as "signifying a publication made not for the purpose of communicating government or political information or ideas but for some improper purpose". But "having regard to the subject matter of government and politics, the motive of causing political damage to the plaintiff or his or her party cannot be regarded as improper".[232]

The law stated in *Lange* is clearly an indigenous Australian product and owes little or nothing to US developments.[233] It is clearly a narrower defence than that under *New York Times v Sullivan*[234] because it rests upon a test of reasonable conduct and the burden of proof of the elements of this is upon the defendant. Furthermore, the core determining factor for the application of the privilege is "government and politics" and not "public figure", a category which in the US extends beyond politics. It is also narrower in this respect than the English *Reynolds* privilege, which is attracted not by "political matters" but "matters of public concern".[235]

---

[231] Which is for the defendant to plead and establish.

[232] See also *Roberts v Bass* [2002] HCA 57; 212 C.L.R. 1.

[233] US law is briefly touched on for the purpose of demonstrating the differences in the relationship between the constitutions and the common law in the two countries. The majority in *Theophanous* also disclaimed any intention to "adopt" US law.

[234] See para.15.31, below.

[235] See Kenyon, "*Lange* and *Reynolds* Qualified Privilege: Australian and English Defamation Law and Practice" [2004] *Melbourne University Law Review* 13, which concludes that *Lange* has not had a major effect in improving the position of the media. A comparison with protections in Australian and US constitutional law is made in R. Weaver, A.T. Kenyon, D.F. Partlett, C. Walker, *The Right to Speak Ill* (Durham: Carolina Academic Press, 2005).

There is a substantial body of Australian case law on what constitutes "government and politics" for this purpose,[236] though in 2006 it was said that the:

"meaning of the expression [government or political matter] is imprecise: *APLA Ltd v Legal Services Cmr (NSW)* (2005) 219 ALR 403; [2005] HCA 44 at [27] per Gleeson CJ and Heydon J. That is perhaps the only thing that can be said with any certainty about the expression".[237]

However, the applicable law in *Lange* was that of New South Wales and the statutory qualified privilege in s.22 of the Defamation Act 1974 (NSW) was held to satisfy the constitutional requirements. Under this:

"Where, in respect of matter published to any person: (a) the recipient has an interest or apparent interest in having information on some subject; (b) the matter is published to the recipient in the course of giving to him information on that subject; and (c) the conduct of the publisher in publishing that matter is reasonable in the circumstances there is a defence of qualified privilege."

The equivalent provision in New South Wales is now s.30 of the Defamation Act 2005 (NSW) and each state now has legislation in the same terms. Section 30 provides:

"30 Defence of qualified privilege for provision of certain information
(1) There is a defence of qualified privilege for the publication of defamatory matter to a person (the recipient) if the defendant proves that:
   (a) the recipient has an interest or apparent interest in having information on some subject, and
   (b) the matter is published to the recipient in the course of giving to the recipient information on that subject, and
   (c) the conduct of the defendant in publishing that matter is reasonable in the circumstances.[238]
(2) For the purposes of subsection (1), a recipient has an apparent interest in having information on some subject if, and only if, at the time of the publication in question, the defendant believes on reasonable grounds that the recipient has that interest.

---

[236] See, e.g. *Heytesbury Holdings Pty Ltd v City of Subiaco* (1998) 19 W.A.R. 440; *Harkianakis v Skalkos* [1999] N.S.W.S.C. 505; 47 N.S.W.L.R. 302; *Nationwide News Pty Ltd v International Financing and Investment Pty Ltd* [1999] WASCA 95; *Lam v Nationwide News Pty Ltd* [2000] N.S.W.S.C. 792; *McMullen v TCN Channel Nine Pty Ltd* [2000] N.S.W.S.C. 925; *Cock v Hughes* [2002] WASC 108; *Amalgamated Television Services Pty Ltd v Marsden* [2002] NSWCA 419; *Orion Pet Products Pty Ltd v RSPCA (Vic) Inc.* [2002] FCA 860; *Gutnick v Dow Jones & Co. Inc. (No.2)* [2003] VSC 79; *Herald & Weekly Times v Popovic* [2003] VSCA 161; *Shave v West Australian Newspapers Ltd* [2003] WASC 83; *Conservation Council of SA Inc. v Chapman* [2003] SASC 398; 87 S.A.S.R. 62; *Cornwall v Rowan* [2004] SASC 384; 90 S.A.S.R. 269; *John Fairfax Publications Pty Ltd v O'Shane* [2005] NSWCA 164; *Peek v Channel Seven Adelaide Pty Ltd* [2006] SASC 63 (Full Court).

[237] *Peek v Channel Seven Adelaide Pty Ltd* [2006] SASC 63 (Full Court) at [6].

[238] This is a question for the judge, though the legislation lacks clarity on the point: *Davis v Nationwide News Pty Ltd* [2008] N.S.W.S.C. 699.

(3) In determining for the purposes of subsection (1) whether the conduct of the defendant in publishing matter about a person is reasonable in the circumstances, a court may take into account:
   (a) the extent to which the matter published is of public interest, and
   (b) the extent to which the matter published relates to the performance of the public functions or activities of the person, and
   (c) the seriousness of any defamatory imputation carried by the matter published, and
   (d) the extent to which the matter published distinguishes between suspicions, allegations and proven facts, and
   (e) whether it was in the public interest in the circumstances for the matter published to be published expeditiously, and
   (f) the nature of the business environment in which the defendant operates, and
   (g) the sources of the information in the matter published and the integrity of those sources, and
   (h) whether the matter published contained the substance of the person's side of the story and, if not, whether a reasonable attempt was made by the defendant to obtain and publish a response from the person, and
   (i) any other steps taken to verify the information in the matter published, and
   (j) any other circumstances that the court considers relevant.
(4) For the avoidance of doubt, a defence of qualified privilege under subsection (1) is defeated if the plaintiff proves that the publication of the defamatory matter was actuated by malice.
(5) However, a defence of qualified privilege under subsection (1) is not defeated merely because the defamatory matter was published for reward."

It is too early to say how this will be applied in Australia[239] but it will be observed (a) that it is not confined to matters of government and politics and (b) subsection (3)[240] bears a not inconsiderable resemblance to the *Reynolds* "factors".[241] At the moment the position may be that there are three qualified privilege defences: (1) the classical category at common ("general") law, (2) the extended common law for government and politics under *Lange*, and (3) the less restricted statutory privilege under s.30. Perhaps in the longer term (2)

---

[239] But see, *Belbin v Lower Murray Urban and Rural Water Corp* [2012] VSC 535; *Daily Examiner Pty Ltd v Mundine* [2012] NSWCA 195; *LVMH Watch & Jewellery Australia Pty Ltd v Lassanah* [2011] NSWCA 370.

[240] Most of the subsection was in fact introduced in NSW by the Defamation Amendment Act 2002 (NSW).

[241] In fact the Explanatory Notes to the Bill as introduced state that "these factors largely mirror the factors relevant at general law as stated by the House of Lords in *Reynolds v Times Newspapers Ltd* [2001] 2 A.C. 127." Before the Act in *John Fairfax v Vilo* [2001] NSWCA; 52 N.S.W.L.R. 373 at 380 the NSWCA said:
"Either *Reynolds*' case extended the law beyond the traditional law as modified in *Lange's* case or it did not. If it did not, it is not necessary to consider the detail of the formulation in *Reynolds'* case, because there are many Australian cases . . . stating the received common law principles, and *Lange's* case is a unanimous decision of seven justices stating a modification of them. If, on the other hand, *Reynolds'* case did move English law beyond the traditional law as modified in *Lange's* case, this Court should not adopt the change in preference to the perceived law stated in cases directly binding this Court."

will be absorbed into (3),[242] with *Lange* ensuring that government and political matters remain matters in which the recipient has the necessary interest. However, there would still be a substantial difference between English and Australian law because both under *Lange* and s.30 malice remains a matter which can defeat the defence.

15.27 *Canada.* Canadian courts have traditionally tended to follow the former English approach to qualified privilege and the media.[243] Section 2(b) of the Canadian Charter of Rights and Freedoms states that there is to be freedom of "thought, belief, opinion and expression, including freedom of the press and other media of communication". The Charter is *directly* concerned only with governmental action in so far as it affects citizens and gives rise to no rights between private litigants.[244] However, as a restatement of the fundamental values of the legal system the Charter has a role to play when the court is called upon to develop or reconsider the common law, because the common law should reflect the values of the Charter, so far as it can be made to do so by the incremental powers of change available to the courts.[245] In *Hill v Church of Scientology of Toronto*,[246] the Supreme Court of Canada declined to receive into Canadian common law the approach of *New York Times v Sullivan*[247] in a case where the plaintiff, a lawyer employed by the Crown, was alleged to have breached an order of the court and misled a judge. The view was expressed that the common law of defamation was neither unduly restrictive nor inhibiting of free speech,[248] though the court remarked that issues involving the media and political comment on governmental policies, such as had been in issue in *Theophanous v Herald & Weekly Times*[249] did not call for consideration on the facts.

However, the Court of Appeal of Nova Scotia espoused a more liberal doctrine in *Campbell v Jones,*[250] in allowing privilege for statements made at a press conference by lawyers for school students who had been body

---

[242] Note, however, that the extent to which the matter is of public interest under s.30 goes to reasonableness of conduct rather than being a preliminary question as under *Reynolds*.

[243] See, e.g. *Globe & Mail v Boland* (1960) S.C.R. 203; *Jones v Bennett* [1969] S.C.R. 277. On the law under the Civil Code of Québec, see *Gilles E.Nérron Communication Marketing Inc. v Chambre des notaires du Québec* 2004 SCC 53; 241 D.L.R. (4th) 577, para.1.14, above.

[244] *RWDSU, Local 580 v Dolphin Delivery Ltd* (1986) 33 D.L.R. (4th) 174 SCC; *McKinney v University of Guelph* (1990) 76 D.L.R. (4th) 545 SC; *Hill v Church of Scientology of Toronto* [1995] 2 S.C.R. 1130.

[245] *Hill v Church of Scientology of Toronto* [1995] 2 S.C.R. 1130; *WIC Radio Ltd v Simpson* [2008] SCC 40.

[246] Above. See also *Coates v The Citizen* (1988) 85 N.S.R. (2d) 146; *Bank of British Columbia v Canadian Broadcasting Corp* (1993) 108 D.L.R. (4th) 178.

[247] 376 U.S. 254 (1964): see para.15.31, below.

[248] Per Cory J., La Forest, Gonthier, McLachlin, Iacobucci and Major JJ. concurring. Since L'Heureux-Dubé J. agreed on this point, the court was unanimous. *Goddard v Day* (2000) 194 D.L.R. 559.

[249] Para.15.26, above.

[250] [2002] NSCA 128; 220 D.L.R. (4th) 201. See also *Wells v Puddister* [2007] NLCA 25; 265 Nfld. & P.E.I.R. 174.

searched, even though a formal complaint procedure had been initiated only two days before. While not all public statements made by a lawyer should be privileged merely by invoking the duty to improve the administration of justice, lawyers faced with a patent injustice, such as the violation of their clients' Charter rights by law enforcement officers, had a substantial and compelling duty to ensure such injustice was remedied. The lawyers, in accordance with the principles of their professional ethics, had a duty to speak about the events at the school, the complaints filed against the officer, and the Charter breaches. The members of the public in attendance at the meeting had a reciprocal interest in hearing about the exercise of the authority of the police in a neighbourhood school. In the whole context, including the Charter rights and values implicated, the previous press coverage and the resulting community interest in the matter, and given the position of the lawyers as counsel for the students, the occasion ought to have the protection afforded by the defence of qualified privilege.

The Ontario Court of Appeal in *Cusson v Quan*[251] held that the broad principle of law stated by the House of Lords in *Reynolds* and *Jameel* should be adopted in Ontario:

"in a manner that best reflects Canada's legal values and culture. The defence rests upon the broad principle that where a media defendant can show that it acted in accordance with the standards of responsible journalism in publishing a story that the public was entitled to hear, it has a defence even if it got some of its facts wrong. That standard of responsible journalism is objective and legal, to be determined by the court with reference to the broader public interest. The non-exhaustive list of ten factors from *Reynolds*, applied in the manner directed in *Jameel*, provides a useful guide. The defence is plainly intended to shift the law of defamation away from its rigidly reputation-protection stance to freer and more open discussion on matters of public interest and should be interpreted accordingly."[252]

In 2009, the Supreme Court of Canada restated the law in *Grant v Torstar Corp, Toronto Star Newspapers Ltd* so as to incorporate a new defence, separate from qualified privilege, of "responsible communication on matters of public interest".[253] Speaking for eight members of the court, McLachlin C.J. said that she would

"formulate the test as follows. First, the publication must be on a matter of public interest. Second, the defendant must show that publication was responsible, in that he or she was diligent in trying to verify the allegation(s), having regard to all the relevant circumstances . . . the public interest is not synonymous with what interests the public. The public's appetite for information on a given subject—say, the private lives of well-known people—is not on its own sufficient to render an essentially private matter public for the purposes of defamation law. An individual's reasonable expectation of privacy must be respected in this determination. Conversely, the fact that much of the public would be less than riveted by a given subject matter does not

---

[251] [2007] ONCA 771; 286 D.L.R. (4th) 196. Leave to appeal April 3, 2008.
[252] At [143].
[253] [2009] SCC 61; (2009) 314 D.L.R. (4th).

remove the subject from the public interest. It is enough that some segment of the community would have a genuine interest in receiving information on the subject."[254]

On the other hand, the defence is not confined to government or political matters or the actions of public figures (at [106]) and guidance may be found in the cases on fair comment and on s.2(b) of the Canadian Charter of Rights (which deals with freedom of expression).

> "Public interest may be a function of the prominence of the person referred to in the communication, but mere curiosity or prurient interest is not enough. Some segment of the public must have a genuine stake in knowing about the matter published".[255]

The question of public interest was for the judge: although the focus was on the publication rather than the occasion (as in traditional privilege), the judge had an analogous "gatekeeper" function. But the question of whether the defendant acted responsibly was for the jury and the judge should assess the publication in a broad way and not editorially excise particular passages on the basis that they were not necessary to the communication.

> "Deciding whether the inclusion of the impugned statement was justifiable involves a highly fact-based assessment of the context and details of the publication itself. Whereas a given subject matter either is or is not in law a matter of public interest, the justifiability of including a defamatory statement may admit of many shades of gray. It is intimately bound up in the overall determination of responsibility and should be left to the jury. It is for the jury to consider the need to include particular defamatory statements in determining whether the defendant acted responsibly in publishing what it did".[256]

At the second stage, the jury was to be guided by a list of factors resembling those in *Reynolds*, the issue being whether "the publisher was diligent in trying to verify the allegation", having regard to

"(a) the seriousness of the allegation;
(b) the public importance of the matter;
(c) the urgency of the matter;
(d) the status and reliability of the source;
(e) whether the plaintiff's side of the story was sought and accurately reported;
(f) whether the inclusion of the defamatory statement was justifiable;
(g) whether the defamatory statement's public interest lay in the fact that it was made rather than its truth ('reportage'); and
(h) any other relevant circumstances."[257]

As under *Reynolds*, malice disappears from the picture: a "defendant who has acted with malice in publishing defamatory allegations has by definition not

---

[254] Ibid. at [98] and [102].
[255] Ibid. at [105].
[256] Ibid. at [109].
[257] Ibid. at [126].

acted responsibly".[258] It may be noted that factor (g) is focused, like a number of the English cases cited in the judgment, firmly on the reporting of *disputes*, so there is the same uncertainty as there is in England and Wales on how far reportage can be applied more extensively.[259] Although the application of all these factors would be for the jury, it would remain the case, as in the analogous context of malice and qualified privilege, that the judge could withdraw the defence on the basis that the facts were incapable of supporting it in law.[260] Under the new defence, it is not necessary for the jury to find a single meaning: it is to assess whether responsibility has been shown in the light of the range of meanings the words are reasonably capable of bearing.[261]

Abella J. expressed herself in complete agreement with the Chief Justice's judgment except on the role of the jury. She would have made the whole issue of the applicability of the defence one for the judge alone, leaving to the jury only the determination of disputed matters of fact. Although "the jury's participation in defamation cases is firmly entrenched in the psyche of defamation law",[262]

> "by adopting the responsible communication defence, we are recognizing the sophistication and constitutional complexity of defamation cases involving communications on matters of public interest. What is most important is protecting the integrity of the interests and values at stake in such cases. This defence is a highly complex legal determination with constitutional dimensions. That takes it beyond the jury's jurisdiction and squarely into judicial territory".[263]

The article in *Grant* concerned an application for permission for a golf course development by the plaintiff, a person of political influence, which was being opposed by local residents. On the facts the Canadian Supreme Court seems to have regarded it as more or less self-evident that the material complained of was capable of falling within the new defence. Indeed, there is little reference to the facts beyond the statement that:

> "Overly narrow characterization [of the subject matter] may inappropriately defeat the defence at the outset. For example, characterizing the subject matter in this case simply as 'Peter Grant's business dealings' would obscure the significant public interest engaged by the article and thus restrict the legitimate scope of public interest. Similarly, characterizing the subject matter too broadly as 'Ontario politics' might render the test a mere rubber stamp and bring unworthy material within the protection of the defence."[264]

---

[258] Ibid. at [125].
[259] Ibid. at [120]–[121].
[260] Ibid. at [129].
[261] Ibid. at [124].
[262] Ibid. at [144].
[263] Ibid. at [145]. cf. the view of the majority at [127]–[135].
[264] Ibid. at [107].

On the same day the Supreme Court of Canada decided *Quan v Cusson* and applied the new *Grant* law to that.[265] The allegation was that in the aftermath of "9/11" the plaintiff, an Ontario police officer, had without permission, gone to New York, had purported to assist at "Ground Zero" and had possibly hampered the rescue efforts. The Supreme Court regarded it as plain that the public interest test was met ("the Canadian public has a vital interest in knowing about the professional misdeeds of those who are entrusted by the state with protecting public safety")—and ordered a new trial on the issue of "diligence". The lower appellate court had in fact accepted "*Reynolds* law" into Ontario, but had refused to allow the defendants to rely on it because it had not been raised at trial.

15.28 Ireland. In *Hunter v Gerald Duckworth & Co. Ltd*[266] the plaintiffs were two of the "Birmingham Six", whose convictions in respect of a bombing had been quashed, and who sued in respect of the publication of passages in a book the meaning of which, they alleged, was that they were not entitled to be treated as presumed to be innocent of the crime. On preliminary issues O'Caoimh J. rejected the contention of the second defendant, the author, that the claim should be struck out as an unwarranted interference with his right of freedom of expression under the Irish Constitution but concluded that:

> "the flexible approach represented by the decision of the House of Lords in *Reynolds v Times Newspapers Ltd* is the most appropriate way of approaching the problems in the instant case, in the absence of a clear legislative framework ... The approach adopted by the House of Lords has the merit of enabling the law to be developed on a case by case basis having regard to the requirements of the Constitution and the Convention which may inform the court in its approach to the interpretation of the Constitution."

Later, in *Leech v Independent Newspapers (Ireland) Ltd*,[267] Charleton J. held that the *Reynolds-Jameel* approach was part of Irish law.

With the coming into force of the Defamation Act 2009, there is now a statutory version of the defence in Irish law. Section 26 of the Act provides:

> "26.—(1) It shall be a defence (to be known, and in this section referred to, as the 'defence of fair and reasonable publication') to a defamation action for the defendant to prove that—
>   (*a*) the statement in respect of which the action was brought was published—
>   (i) in good faith, and

---

[265] [2009] SCC 62.

[266] [2003] IEHC 81.

[267] [2007] IEHC 223. The defendants had published a story about an incident in which a live radio caller had made an accusation of impropriety between the plaintiff and a government minister and for which the broadcaster had to apologize. While it might have been just about arguable that the way the broadcaster handled its "call in" programmes was a matter of public concern the defendants had failed to produce any evidence at all that they had taken steps to verify the allegations about the plaintiff and the defence was rejected.

(ii) in the course of, or for the purpose of, the discussion of a subject of public interest, the discussion of which was for the public benefit,

(b) in all of the circumstances of the case, the manner and extent of publication of the statement did not exceed that which was reasonably sufficient, and

(c) in all of the circumstances of the case, it was fair and reasonable to publish the statement.

(2) For the purposes of this section, the court shall, in determining whether it was fair and reasonable to publish the statement concerned, take into account such matters as the court considers relevant including any or all of the following:

(a) the extent to which the statement concerned refers to the performance by the person of his or her public functions;

(b) the seriousness of any allegations made in the statement;

(c) the context and content (including the language used) of the statement;

(d) the extent to which the statement drew a distinction between suspicions, allegations and facts;

(e) the extent to which there were exceptional circumstances that necessitated the publication of the statement on the date of publication;

(f) in the case of a statement published in a periodical by a person who, at the time of publication, was a member of the Press Council, the extent to which the person adhered to the code of standards of the Press Council and abided by determinations of the Press Ombudsman and determinations of the Press Council;

(g) in the case of a statement published in a periodical by a person who, at the time of publication, was not a member of the Press Council, the extent to which the publisher of the periodical adhered to standards equivalent to the standards specified in *paragraph (f)*;

(h) the extent to which the plaintiff's version of events was represented in the publication concerned and given the same or similar prominence as was given to the statement concerned;

(i) if the plaintiff's version of events was not so represented, the extent to which a reasonable attempt was made by the publisher to obtain and publish a response from that person; and

(j) the attempts made, and the means used, by the defendant to verify the assertions and allegations concerning the plaintiff in the statement.

(3) The failure or refusal of a plaintiff to respond to attempts by or on behalf of the defendant, to elicit the plaintiff's version of events, shall not—

(a) constitute or imply consent to the publication of the statement, or

(b) entitle the court to draw any inference therefrom.

(4) In this section—

'court' means, in relation to a defamation action brought in the High Court, the jury, if the High Court is sitting with a jury;

'defamation action' does not include an application for a declaratory order."

Like the Australian provision set out above, this clearly has great similarities with *Reynolds*. It seems unlikely that the addition of "public benefit" to "public interest" will make any difference on the core issue. Like the Australian provision, "malice" was originally retained in the legislative Bill with the burden of showing its absence being placed upon the defendant. This additional provision did not become law, and the malice issue would appear to have been subsumed into the concept of responsible journalism as under *Reynolds* privilege. Similarly, a provision in the Bill to the effect that the defendant would be required to show that he or she believed the publication to be true has been excised, thereby opening the door to the equivalent of the reportage variant of the common law privilege.

15.29 *New Zealand.* The New Zealand Court of Appeal created a New Zealand version of privilege for media publications about persons elected or seeking election to Parliament in *Lange v Atkinson.*[268] The Privy Council[269] set aside the earlier decision in this case[270] so that the New Zealand court could take into account the House of Lords decision in *Reynolds*, but it emphasised that the New Zealand court was not bound to accept either the English or Australian approaches on this matter. However, the New Zealand court declined to modify its previous views because:

> "the *Reynolds* decision appears to alter the structure of the law of qualified privilege in a way which adds to the uncertainty and chilling effect almost inevitably present in this area of law. We are not persuaded that in the New Zealand situation matters such as the steps taken to verify the information, the seeking of comment from the person defamed, and the status or source of the information, should fall within the ambit of the inquiry into whether the occasion is privileged. Traditionally such matters are not of concern to that question in the kind of setting presently under discussion."[271]

The law in New Zealand may now be summarised as follows:

(1) The defence of qualified privilege may be available in respect of a statement which is published generally.

(2) The nature of New Zealand's democracy means that the wider public may have a proper interest in respect of generally-published statements which directly concern the functioning of representative and responsible government, including statements about the performance or possible future performance of specific individuals in elected public office.

(3) In particular, a proper interest does exist in respect of statements made about the actions and qualities of those currently or formerly elected to Parliament and those with immediate aspirations to such office, so far as those actions and qualities directly affect or affected their capacity (including their personal ability and willingness) to meet their public responsibilities.

(4) The determination of the matters which bear on that capacity will depend on a consideration of what is properly a matter of public concern rather than of private concern.

---

[268] [2000] NZCA 95; [2000] 3 N.Z.L.R. 385. See also, for Samoa, *Alesana v Samoa Observer Co. Ltd* [1998] WSSC 1.

[269] [2000] 1 N.Z.L.R. 257.

[270] [1998] 3 N.Z.L.R. 424.

[271] [2000] NZCA 95; [2000] 3 N.Z.L.R. 385 at [38].

(5) The width of the identified public concern justifies the extent of the publication.[272]

(6) To attract privilege the statement must be published on a qualifying occasion.[273]

While this appears closer to a "generic" privilege than that laid down in *Reynolds*, it is not wholly so for two reasons. First, the circumstances and context of the publication are relevant.

"Ordinarily it can be expected that [statements about those elected or seeking election] will warrant protection, but it is still necessary to take into account the circumstances of the publication. Those circumstances will include such matters as the identity of the publisher, the context in which the publication occurs, the likely audience, as well as the actual content of the information. As an example of circumstances where the subject matter may not be determinative, it is questionable whether a one line reference to alleged misconduct of a grave nature on the part of a parliamentary candidate reflecting on his or her suitability, appearing in an article in a motoring magazine about that person's activities in motor sport, should receive protection. By contrast, the inclusion of such material in a lengthy serious article on a coming election may justifiably attract the protection."[274]

Secondly, despite the fact that the case was concerned political discussion, it has been interpreted as having a wider scope. In *Osmose New Zealand v Wakeling*[275] newspaper articles and broadcast programmes were critical of a building authority for approving the claimants' wood preservative product and the claimants considered that this defamed them. It was held that the statement was protected by *Lange* privilege since the problem of rot in timber houses was a matter of great public concern in New Zealand, giving grounds to believe in a systemic failure in the building industry and the publications were a legitimate way of communicating information to the public.

However, unlike the English and Australian positions, there is no requirement of reasonable inquiry or steps in verification or to give the person attacked a chance to put his side. Once the occasion is privilege is established, it is only defeated by the state of mind specified in s.19 of the Defamation Act 1992 (N.Z.), i.e. that the defendant was predominantly motivated by ill will against the plaintiff or otherwise took improper advantage of the publication. Although the court accepted that s.19 was broadly equivalent to malice at common law, it is suggested in *Lange* that in the context of qualified privilege

---

[272] Ibid. at [10].

[273] Ibid. at [41].

[274] [2000] NZCA 95; [2000] 3 N.Z.L.R. 385 at [13].

[275] [2007] 1 N.Z.L.R. 841. The litigation took a curious form, the plaintiffs having sued only the individuals (W and S) who had campaigned on the matter. The individuals then issued third party notices against the media parties, the reported case being a successful application by the media parties to have the third party notices set aside on the ground that, being protected by *Lange* privilege, they would not be liable to make contribution to any damages awarded against the individuals. The tactical difficulties of the latter may be appreciated from the fact that one of their defences was *Lange* privilege.

for statements on political matters it may not have quite the same "pure subjective" meaning as the common law. The Court said[276]:

> "Lord Diplock [in *Horrocks v Lowe*] gave a gave a helpful description of reckless-ness in the present field when he spoke of someone who publishes defamatory material 'without considering or caring' whether it was true or false. Indifference to truth is, of course, not the same thing conceptually as failing to take reasonable care with the truth but in practical terms they tend to shade into each other. It is useful, when considering whether an occasion of qualified privilege has been misused, to ask whether the defendant has exercised the degree of responsibility which the occasion required.
>
> "What constitutes recklessness is something which must take its colour from the nature of the occasion, and the nature of the publication . . . If it is reckless not 'to consider or care' whether a statement be true or false, as Lord Diplock indicated, it must be open to the view that a perfunctory level of consideration (against the substance, gravity and width of the publication) can also be reckless . . . It is within the concept of misusing the occasion to say that the defendant may be regarded as reckless if there has been a failure to give such responsible consideration to the truth or falsity of the statement as the jury considers should have been given in all the circumstances. In essence the privilege may well be lost if the defendant takes what in all the circumstances can fairly be described as a cavalier approach to the truth of the statement.
>
> "No consideration and insufficient consideration are equally capable of leading to an inference of misuse of the occasion. The rationale for loss of the privilege in such circumstances is that the privilege is granted on the basis that it will be responsibly used. There is no public interest in allowing defamatory statements to be made irresponsibly—recklessly—under the banner of freedom of expression. What amounts to a reckless statement must depend significantly on what is said and to whom and by whom. It must be accepted that to require the defendant to give such responsible consideration to the truth or falsity of the publication as is required by the nature of the allegation and the width of the intended dissemination, may in some circumstances come close to a need for the taking of reasonable care. In others a genuine belief in truth after relatively hasty and incomplete consideration may be sufficient to satisfy the dictates of the occasion and to avoid any inference of taking improper advantage of the occasion."

While certain portions of this passage can be read as supporting the uncontroversial proposition that lack of belief in truth may be inferred as a matter of evidence from failure to inquire,[277] taken as a whole it may support the view that at least in some circumstances honesty of belief is not decisive.[278]

---

[276] Ibid. at [46] et seq.

[277] The view of Eady J. in *Lillie v Newcastle CC* [2002] EWHC 1600 (QB) at [1291] et seq.

[278] Which may have been the view of the CA in *Loutchansky v Times Newspapers Ltd (Nos 2–5)* [2001] EWCA Civ 1805; [2002] 2 Q.B. 783 at [25]. In *W v Westminster City Council* [2004] EWHC 2866 (QB); [2005] 1 F.L.R. 816, although of the view that *Horrocks v Lowe* rather than *Lange* provided the basis of malice in English law, Tugendhat J. did refer (at [92]–[93]) to a passage in *Lange* (at [49]) which said that a greater degree of responsibility would be required for a statement to the world than for a statement to a limited group on a "no attribution" basis and, with reference to the facts of the case before him, went on:

"What is included in a Report for a Child Protection Conference is for publication in confidence to a small group of people with specific roles in the life of a child. While the

The New Zealand Court of Appeal declined to extend *Lange* in *Vickery v McLean*.[279] The defendant, a disgruntled ratepayer, advised the news media that he had good reason to contend that three senior servants of a local authority had been guilty of corruption and that he had asked the Serious Fraud Office to investigate. In rejecting the defendant's argument that the publication was privileged, the court said[280]:

"It is of major moment to notice that those who have been defamed are not politicians, whether national or local. They are paid servants of a local body. They may contribute to policy making but they are not the ultimate policy makers. The subject matter of Mr Vickery's publications cannot sensibly be regarded as political discussion, much less political discussion of a kind contemplated by *Lange* ... or any rational extension of that decision. What is more, the subject matter, even if capable of being regarded as political discussion, involves an allegation of serious criminality. The law has been clear for many years that such allegations or complaints, provided they are bona fide, may be made to the appropriate authorities under qualified privilege. But the privilege is lost if the allegations are disseminated beyond those whose proper function it is to investigate and, if appropriate, to act upon them ... Thus, even if this case could be brought within the first five of the six *Lange* criteria, it does not satisfy the sixth, as we will shortly indicate. This is because publications which are disseminated too widely are not made on a qualifying occasion (*Lange* ... at paras [21] and [22])."

"If, as we hold, the present case cannot be brought within any appropriate development of *Lange* ... it is necessary for Mr Vickery to establish his asserted privilege by reference to first principles. He must show that it is in the public interest, (for the common convenience and welfare of society ... that on an occasion such as the present, freedom of expression should prevail over protection of reputation. More specifically he must show that it is in the public interest for people to be able to make allegations of serious criminal offending, albeit in a bona fide way, to or through the news media."

"Even if such allegations were responsibly made, it would be contrary both to settled law and to the public interest to allow such communications to be made under qualified privilege. We do not consider that society has changed in such a way as to justify a departure from previous perceptions of the public interest in this respect. It is, in our view, demonstrably not in the public interest to have criminal allegations, even if bona fide and responsibly made, ventilated through the news media. That could only encourage trial by media and associated developments which would be inimical to criminal justice processes. Society has mechanisms for investigating crime and determining guilt or innocence. It is not in the public interest that these mechanisms be bypassed or subverted. Parliament's view, in the context of Serious Fraud Office matters, and it is a view of which the common law should take notice, can be found in ss.36 to 44 of the Serious Fraud Office Act 1990. These provisions are, broadly speaking, designed to prevent or limit disclosure of matters under investigation by the Office, and specified aspects of such investigations. Parliament has thereby recognised that the very fact that a Serious Fraud Office investigation is

---

publication can still cause grave harm, the extent of that harm can be mitigated by the subsequent actions of the defendants, and by the denials of the Claimant himself. It may not be a context in which the same very high degree of responsibility would be required as in, say, publication to all the world."

[279] [2000] NZCA 338.
[280] At [17] et seq.

taking place can, of itself, cause serious damage to reputations and possible subversion of criminal justice processes. Thus, freedom of expression in this area has been curtailed to reflect Parliament's assessment of how to balance the competing interests."

The Court emphasised that while the background was public concern over the arrangements for water supply, the immediate context was an accusation of corruption against the officials. Although under English law *Reynolds* does not confine privilege to statements about politicians or politics, it is thought that the answer would be the same, bearing in mind in particular that the defendant had put his charges to the Serious Fraud Office.

15.30 *South Africa.* The Supreme Court of Appeal of South Africa (formerly the Appellate Division) in *National Media Ltd v Bogoshi*[281] recast the common law of South Africa in respect of media publications in terms which are rather similar to *Reynolds*:

> "The publication in the press of false defamatory allegations of fact will not be regarded as unlawful if, upon a consideration of all the circumstances of the case, it is found to have been reasonable to publish the particular facts in the particular way and at the particular time.
>
>   "In considering the reasonableness of the publication account must obviously be taken of the nature, extent and tone of the allegations. We know, for example, that greater latitude is normally allowed in respect of political discussion ... What will also figure prominently is the nature of the information on which the allegations were based and the reliability of their source, as well as the steps taken to verify the information. Ultimately there can be no justification for the publication of untruths, and members of the press should not be left with the impression that they have a licence to lower the standards of care which must be observed before defamatory matter is published in a newspaper ... "
>
>   "[Other matters] such as the opportunity given to the person concerned to respond, and the need to publish before establishing the truth in a positive manner, also come to mind. The list is not intended to be exhaustive."[282]

The onus is on the defendant to show that the required standard has been met. If a media defendant is unable to establish that it has measured up to the required standard it cannot in the alternative fall back on the defence of showing that it lacked an *animus injurandi*, though that defence may possibly be open to non-media defendants.

The decision was arrived at without relying on s.15(1) of the then interim Constitution guaranteeing "freedom of speech and expression, which shall include freedom of the press and other media". Section 16 of the present Constitution, guaranteeing freedom of expression, does not specifically refer to reputation as a countervailing consideration, but reputation is an aspect of

---

[281] 1998 (4) S.A. 1196.
[282] 1998 (4) S.A. 1196 at 1212–1213.

human dignity, which is a foundational value.[283] In *Khumalo v Holomisa*[284] the Constitutional Court held that the common law as restated in *Bogoshi* conformed with the Constitution and rejected an argument that it should be part of the plaintiff's case to show that the statement was false.

Subsequently in *Mthembi-Mahanyele v Mail & Guardian Ltd*[285] the Supreme Court of Appeal considered *National Media v Bogoshi* at some length, but was divided in its conclusions. In the majority in favour of the defendants, the thrust of the judgment of Lewis J.A. seems to be towards putting "political" speech in a separate category; whereas the decision of Ponnan A.J.A. turns on the view that in its context the publication could not be given a defamatory meaning. Mthiyane J.A. dissented: political speech was not in a special category, though in practice greater latitude might be allowed to it, and it was important not to downgrade the media's duty to seek comment or corroboration before publishing allegations.

The United States.[286] The First Amendment to the United States Constitu-   **15.31** tion provides that: "Congress shall make no law ... abridging the freedom of speech, or of the press." Though for the better part of two centuries the common law (in a form broadly similar to that prevailing in England) was regarded as compatible with this,[287] in *New York Times v Sullivan*[288] the Supreme Court held that it required a radical change in the law on defamation of public officials.[289] Plaintiffs in this category could not succeed unless they were able to establish by "clear and convincing evidence" that the defendant published the statement with knowledge of its falsity or in reckless disregard of its truth or falsity—the alternative states of mind being described as "actual malice".[290] While this has some affinity with common law malice it is clearly narrower: the constitutional defence can only be defeated by knowledge or recklessness as to falsity and not, as at common law, by proof of an improper purpose in publishing.[291] The same principles apply to claims brought by candidates for public office[292] and by "public figures". The last category is

---

[283] S.1.

[284] [2002] ZACC 12; 2002 (5) S.A. 401.

[285] [2004] ZASCA 67; 2004 (11) B.C.L.R 1182.

[286] See Dobbs, *The Law of Torts* (2000), Ch.28, Topic C, paras 417 et seq.

[287] Indeed, the wording suggests that the framers had in mind legislation.

[288] 376 U.S. 254 (1964). The constitutional guarantees have implications for the recognition and enforcement of English judgments in the US: *Bahchem v India Abroad Publications*, 585 N.Y.S.2d 661 (1989). See also The Securing the Protection of our Enduring and Established Constitutional Heritage Act (SPEECH Act) Public Law 111–223 111th Congress.

[289] Who is a "public official" admits of no simple answer; but the courts have interpreted the phrase widely: see *Rosenblatt v Baer*, 383 U.S. 75 (1966); *Mandel v The Boston Phoenix Inc.* 456 F.3d 198 (CA1, 2006) and 50 Am.Jur.2d, *Libel and Slander*, paras 46 et seq.

[290] 376 U.S. 254 at 280.

[291] *Journal Publishing Co. v McCullough*, 743 So.2d 352 (Miss., 1999); *Rotkiewicz v Sadovsky*, 730 N.E.2d 282 (Mass., 2000). The Supreme Court in *Masson v New Yorker Magazine*, 501 U.S. 416 (1991) recognised that "actual malice" was an unfortunate term and suggested that juries be instructed in terms of knowledge or recklessness.

[292] *Monitor Patriot Co. v Roy*, 401 U.S. 265 (1971).

difficult to define but a distinction has to be drawn between "general purpose" and "limited purpose" public figures. The former are politicians and celebrities who are household names[293]; the latter are persons who voluntarily enter into the forefront only of a particular controversy.[294] With regard to the latter, the scope of the defendant's constitutional protection will be narrower, since it will be confined to matters relevant to the controversy into which the plaintiff has entered. While the defendant cannot, by his own conduct, make the plaintiff a limited purpose public figure,[295] a person may become a public figure by voluntarily engaging in a course of conduct even though he wishes to avoid public attention.[296] Where the plaintiff falls into one of these categories attracting the "actual malice" rule he faces a formidable task in establishing liability.[297]

In the case of persons who are not public figures, the lowest standard which state courts may apply is one of negligence as to falsity,[298] but it seems that where the matter in respect of which the statement is made is not one of public concern, it is open to a state to adopt the common law position, that is to say, strict liability tempered by qualified privilege where applicable.[299] A further significant effect of the First Amendment is that it puts the burden of proof of falsity upon the plaintiff.[300]

Section 4. Candidates for Election

15.32 Candidates for election. *Reynolds* does not create a privilege confined to communications on political or governmental matters, but those matters undoubtedly lie at the heart of it. Long before *Reynolds* there were authorities

---

[293] See *Partington v Bugliosi*, 825 F. Supp. 906 (1993) and 50 Am.Jur.2d, *Libel and Slander*, paras 71 et seq.

[294] One pervasive difficulty is that the First Amendment lays down a minimum standard of constitutional protection for speech below which the states may not go, but there is nothing to prevent the states giving a higher protection to speech than the Constitution requires, e.g. by expanding the concept of public figure. In view of this, it is not surprising that many cases are irreconcilable.

[295] *Hutchinson v Proxmire*, 443 U.S. 111 (1979).

[296] *Marcone v Penthouse*, 754 F.2d 1072 (CA3 1985).

[297] White J., who had participated in *New York Times v Sullivan*, had second thoughts in *Dun & Bradstreet v Greenmoss Builders*, 472 U.S. 749 (1985) describing it at 767 as having "struck an improvident balance . . . between the public's interest in being fully informed about public officials and public affairs and the competing interest of those who have been defamed in vindicating their reputation."

[298] *Gertz v Robert Welch Inc.*, 418 U.S. 323 (1974).

[299] *Dun & Bradstreet v Greenmoss Builders*, 472 U.S. 749 (1985). According to 50 Am.Jur.2d, *Libel and Slander*, para.101, a majority of courts adopt a negligence standard. New York has an intermediate standard of "gross irresponsibility" for matters of public concern: *Chapadeau v Utica Observer-Dispatch*, 341 N.E.2d 569 (1975).

[300] *Philadelphia Newspapers v Hepps*, 475 U.S. 767 (1986).

which supported a privilege for wide-ranging publication of statements concerning the suitability of candidates[301] for election[302] to public office.

> "It is contrary to public policy that electors should not have considerable latitude in discussing the qualifications of those who solicit their suffrages, and so long as they do not speak maliciously they ought to be protected."[303]

The limits of these cases are not clear[304] but at a minimum they supported the view that there was a privilege so long as the defendant and the recipient were both electors in the relevant constituency.[305] Whether and how far they would extend to statements made by or to persons who were not electors or to publications in the media remains rather unclear.[306] In *Braddock v Bevins*[307] the privileged statement was in an election address delivered only to persons on the electoral roll and in Australia there has been held to be privilege for statements in "how to vote" cards distributed near the polling booth.[308] But it is not clear that the same would apply even to a statement at an election meeting.[309] However, it has been held that where an "election special newsletter" was distributed in the area of impending parish council elections the privilege was not lost because it was quite likely to come into the hands of persons not eligible to vote.[310]

Most of the cases now wear the somewhat antique air of a time when politics were conducted on the local hustings and involved an electorate which was more limited than that of today.[311] No doubt it will not be difficult for a

---

[301] Or their supporters: *Braddock v Bevins* [1948] 1 K.B. 580 CA (Mrs Braddock was the only person sufficiently identified but Mr Clitherow was the candidate).

[302] There is less difficulty in the case of an appointment to an office as there may be a communication of relevant facts to those with the power to make the appointment without a public disclosure of the facts. In *M'Kerchar v Cameron* (1892) 19 R 383 privilege was denied for criticism of an established public servant published in a local newspaper.

[303] *Bruce v Leisk* (1892) 19 R. 482 at 485.

[304] The Representation of the People Act 1983, s.106(3), provides a summary remedy in the case of false statements of fact in relation to the personal character or conduct of candidates: see para.27.35, below.

[305] In *Brims v Reid & Sons* (1885) 12 R. 1016, the defendant local newspaper published an anonymous letter attacking a council candidate. In rejecting a plea of privilege Lord President Inglis said at 1020:
"the answer to [the question of privilege] will depend upon who the writer was, and what his connection was with the matters on which he writes. But in the present case we cannot ascertain who the writer was, whether he was a ratepayer in Wick, whether he ever was in Wick in his life, or whether he is even a subject of Her Majesty. In short, we know nothing about him; he is a mere umbra."

[306] *Duncombe v Daniell* (1838) 8 C. & P. 222 suggests a negative answer to the second question, but in *Reynolds v Times Newspapers Ltd* [2001] 2 A.C. 127 at 233 Lord Hope suggests that by the end of the 19th century a Scots court might have taken a different view.

[307] [1948] 1 K.B. 580 CA.

[308] *Roberts v Bass* [2002] HCA 57; 212 C.L.R. 1.

[309] See *Lang v Willis* (1934) 52 C.L.R. 637 HCA.

[310] *Greenaway v Poole* [2003] EWHC 1735, (QB).

[311] In *Anderson v Hunter* (1891) 18 R. 467 the communication was held not privileged, as the defendant was not an elector in the division, though he was an elector in a neighbouring division and a ratepayer in the local authority area to which the pursuer was seeking to be elected. In *Reynolds* at 234 Lord Hope remarks that in modern conditions the emphasis is much more on the

newspaper (or a member of the public) to make out that the fitness of a candidate for public office is a matter of public concern under *Reynolds*, but the price of that will be taking on the other requirements of establishing privilege under that decision, whereas the old cases were to the effect that privilege, if it existed, could be defeated only by malice. It may be that this category of cases has been "absorbed" into *Reynolds*,[312] but that would mean that there was now less protection than formerly for political speech, which would be a surprising result, and in Australia the view that the traditional common law privilege has lapsed after *Lange v Australian Broadcasting Corporation*[313] (which creates an "extended privilege" for generally published statements on government and politics and which bears some resemblance to *Reynolds* in that it imports a requirement of reasonable conduct) has been rejected.[314] Furthermore, the traditional privilege has been held applica-

---

performance of the party than of the individual candidate, increased by the system of "party lists" used in the elections for the European and Scottish Parliament and Welsh Assembly, developments which "show that the case law which confined the privilege to comment on individual candidates at election time and to the electoral process within their own constituencies has become outdated".

[312] That is a reasonable inference from the speech of Lord Hope in *Reynolds*. In *Howlett v Holding* [2003] EWHC 286 (QB); (2003) 147 S.J.L.B. 269, the defendant published (in part by means of streamers towed behind an aircraft!) accusations of theft against the claimant, a councillor. Eady J. struck out the plea of qualified privilege as the facts available to the defendant could at the highest only have supported the view that she had at one time been suspected of theft.

[313] (1997) 189 C.L.R. 520: para.15.22, above

[314] *Roberts v Bass* [2002] HCA 57; 212 C.L.R. 1. That was clearly the view of Gaudron, McHugh, Gummow and Kirby JJ. at [161]. Gleeson C.J. and Hayne J. were uncommitted. The case was fought on the basis that the "pure" common law privilege among electors and candidates survived in parallel with the extended *Lange* privilege, but Gleeson C.J. said:

"There is a substantial difference between them. Why this should be so, as a matter of principle, is difficult to understand. The law of defamation, including the law as to qualified privilege, strikes a balance between competing interests. Those interests include the public interest in freedom of political debate, which is essential to the functioning of representative democracy. Why should the balance that applies when a newspaper with a wide circulation publishes an article about the Prime Minister, or the Leader of the Opposition, differ from the balance that applies when someone distributes throughout an electorate a pamphlet urging electors to vote against the sitting member?" (at [4]).

Hayne J. said:

"[T]here appears much to be said for the view that widespread publication about government or political matters, even if restricted to electors, should not be found to be a publication invoking the pre- *Lange* principles of qualified privilege. The better view may well be that a publication about government and political matters made to a large audience, even if it is drawn only from the body of electors, should fall for consideration on the same basis as publications made to both electors and others. A publication to electors generally, despite what was said in *Braddock* about the common interest which electors have, might be thought not to be an occasion of qualified privilege as those occasions were understood at common law before *Lange*. That would be consistent with what was said in *Lang v Willis* [(1934) 52 C.L.R. 637)] and it would be consistent with the coherent development of the common law after *Lange*. The development of the common law which *Lange* made was scarcely necessary if qualified privilege would be attracted to every case where the communication of political matter was said to have been *aimed* at electors generally or even where the communication was *made* only to those who, together, formed the body of electors. Further, and very importantly, to distinguish between the principles to be applied in cases where a how-to-vote card or other form of

ble in England since *Reynolds*.[315] Notably, in *Shavluk v Green Party of Canada,* an election press release regarding termination of the claimant's party candidacy was held to fall both under qualified privilege and the defence of responsible communication established in *Grant v Torstar*.[316]

It should also be recalled that, while it has nothing to do with privilege, the House of Lords has held that a governmental body has no standing to sue for defamation,[317] no matter what the state of mind of the defendant in publishing the statement complained of. Since the decision rests upon the necessity for free discussion of public affairs, it may appear curious that it explicitly rejects any parallel limitation upon the right of an individual politician or public servant to sue for defamation, though as a practical matter individual claimants are of course more likely to be constrained by the risks of litigation than would be the public body which they serve.

Defamation Act 1952, section 10. This section provides that a defama-   **15.33**
tory statement published by or on behalf of a candidate in any election to a local government authority, to the National Assembly for Wales, to the Scottish Parliament[318] or to Parliament shall not be deemed to be published on a privileged occasion on the ground that it is material to a question in issue in the election, whether or not the person by whom it is published is qualified to vote in the election.[319] In *Plummer v Charman* the effect was said to be that: "if the candidate himself publishes a statement or anyone publishes a statement on his behalf to the electors in support of his candidature, then it is no longer a privileged occasion."[320] However, that view of the law has not been followed. The court in *Plummer v Charman* did not have the benefit of the Parliamentary debates on s.10, which indicate that the section was not intended to deprive a candidate of any protection he had at common law but

---

political advertising is handed to voters as they approach the polling booth, rather than published in the local newspaper or dropped in letterboxes in the electorate, would be to draw a distinction which would be very difficult to justify if it required the application of a different criterion of operation. I am nonetheless precluded by the course that the proceedings have taken from having the benefit of argument on these questions" (at [224]–[225]).
It has been held that this form of privilege in Australia is not confined to a statement by one candidate with respect to another candidate: *Fraser v Holmes* [2009] NSWCA 36 at [30] (statement about union leader opposed to candidate). See also *Megna v Marshall* [2010] N.S.W.S.C. 686.

[315] *Greenaway v Poole* [2003] EWHC 1735 (QB). However, the point was conceded on one aspect of the case and there does not seem to have been full argument on another: at [6] and [8]. See also *Culnane v Morris* [2005] EWHC 2438 (QB); [2006] 1 W.L.R. 2880, below, where the meaning of s.10 of the Defamation Act 1952 was a preliminary issue.

[316] [2010] BCSC 804.

[317] *Derbyshire CC v Times Newspapers* [1993] A.C. 534; para.8.20, above.

[318] The Welsh and Scottish provisions were inserted by the Government of Wales Act 2006, Sch.10, para.5 and the Scotland Act 1998, Sch.8, para.10.

[319] In *Templeton v Jones* [1984] 1 N.Z.L.R. 448 NZCA, although there was no equivalent of s.10 in New Zealand, the court struck out a defence of qualified privilege where the defendant circulated his speech more widely than was necessary to communicate with his electors.

[320] [1962] 1 W.L.R. 1469 CA at 1472. This view seems to have been assumed to be correct by Lord Nicholls in *Reynolds v Times Newspapers Ltd* [2001] 2 A.C. 127 at 197.

simply to ensure that the candidate had no special privilege of his own merely by being a candidate. Furthermore, s.3 of the Human Rights Act 1998 now requires the section to be construed so far as possible to conform with the guarantee of freedom of expression in the European Convention on Human Rights. Eady J. therefore held that he would:

> "construe [s.10] in accordance with what seems to me to be the natural meaning of the words: a candidate cannot claim a special privilege by virtue only of publishing words that are 'material to a question in issue in the election'. On the other hand, a candidate like any other citizen may be able to establish a defence of qualified privilege if the ingredients recognised at common law are present on the facts of the case. The 1952 Act does not specify that a candidate should be confined to the defences of fair comment and justification."[321]

Section 5. Privileged Reports at Common Law

15.34 General. Notwithstanding the general earlier reluctance to accord qualified privilege to material published to the public as a whole, the common law from an early stage granted such protection to fair and accurate reports of judicial proceedings and of proceedings in Parliament and to copies and extracts from public registers. The legitimate public interest in and the educative value of the reports is obvious and, in the case of the reports of court proceedings, the reporting is "simply an enlargement of the audience which hears them in court, but which is limited by the size of the court-room."[322] Since 1888 various statutory provisions have reduced the importance of these common law heads of privilege and the Defamation Act 1996 has taken this further. However, they still exist because that Act does not abolish any common law privilege. Most of the case law on reports of judicial proceedings relates to the question of what is a fair and accurate report and that is considered in the context of the absolute statutory privilege which will, in the case of contemporaneous reports of United Kingdom and certain other proceedings, effectively obliterate the common law privilege.[323]

(a) *Reports of judicial proceedings*

15.35 Reports of judicial proceedings. At common law, qualified privilege attached to publication of a fair and accurate report of judicial proceedings: "The rule of law is that, where there are judicial proceedings before a properly constituted judicial tribunal exercising its jurisdiction in open court,[324] then

---

[321] *Culnane v Morris* [2005] EWHC 2438 (QB); [2006] 1 W.L.R. 2880 at [32].
[322] Lord Young in *Macleod v Justices of Lewis* (1892) R. 218 at 221. Reports of proceedings in Parliament would seem to be a fundamental part of the process of democratic government.
[323] See paras 13.35–13.49, above.
[324] See para.13.47, above.

the publication without malice of a fair and accurate report of what takes place before that tribunal is privileged."[325]

The relevant law is now contained in the Defamation Act 1996, s.14 of which confers absolute privilege on fair and accurate contemporaneous reports of proceedings in public before a court in the United Kingdom or before certain tribunals of an international or supranational character.[326] In these cases, the common law privilege is clearly redundant.

Furthermore, s.15 and Sch.1 to the 1996 Act confer qualified privilege without explanation or contradiction[327] on a fair and accurate report of proceedings in public before a court anywhere in the world,[328] which in practice will be applicable only to cases not falling within s.14. There is no requirement of contemporaneity or of the publisher being a newspaper or broadcaster. In practice this has further diminished the importance of the common law privilege but may not have wholly extinguished it.[329] The statutory qualified privilege does not apply to the publication of matter which is not of public concern and the publication of which is not for the public

---

[325] *Kimber v Press Association* [1893] 1 Q.B. 65 CA at 68.

[326] See para.13.35, above. The report need not be in a newspaper or broadcast. S.7(1) of the Defamation Act 2013 will amend s.14 of the 1996 Act when it comes into force. The effect of s.7(1) will be to widen the categories of the courts, reports of proceedings of which will be protected. See para.16.7, below.

[327] See para.16.6, below.

[328] See para.16.8, below.

[329] It does not formally abolish it: see Defamation Act 1996, s.15(4)(b). There may also be cases in which an account of a court decision may be privileged on some ground other than that it is a report in the ordinary sense. If so, there may be privilege even though the account is neither fair nor accurate.

"For example, if there was an enquiry by a prospective employer, who was considering placing a prospective employee in a position of trust, made of a person with knowledge of that prospective employee, and the person of whom the enquiry was made knew that the prospective employee had been convicted of an offence involving dishonesty, and that person honestly but mistakenly communicated to the prospective employer that the prospective employee had been convicted of obtaining money by false pretences, whereas the conviction was in fact for larceny by a servant, the qualified privilege would not in my opinion be lost because the communication happened to be an inaccurate report of court proceedings":
Hodgson J.A. in *Bashford v Information Australia (Newsletters) Pty Ltd* [2001] NSWCA 470. The decision in *Bashford* was upheld by the High Court of Australia ([2004] HCA 5; 218 C.L.R. 366). The facts are, however, far removed from the illustration by Hodgson J.A., since the publication in question *was* a report of proceedings in the ordinary sense but it was inaccurate because it attributed to the plaintiff a liability which had not in fact been found (he was not even a party to the proceedings). In effect there is an irrebuttable presumption that publication of a fair and accurate report is in the interest of society, whereas the hurdles which have to be surmounted to establish a privileged occasion on the basis of duty and interest impose more severe demands on the publisher. This reasoning is entirely convincing in the context of the situation in Hodgson J.A.'s example of the reference, less so perhaps where, as in *Bashford*, the statement for which privilege is claimed is a volunteered one made to a large number of people as mere "background" to the general matter in which there is a reciprocity of interest. The communication in that case was about the law of copyright in safety data sheets, which was plainly a matter of legitimate interest to persons subscribing to a health and safety newsletter; the inaccurate statement sued on was that the plaintiff had been held liable for misleading or deceptive conduct in proceedings which had involved that copyright issue, whereas in fact he had not even been sued.

benefit.[330] As a matter of substance this may not differ from the position at common law since that was founded upon public policy and benefit and advantage to the community and therefore had such elements "built in".[331] However, the question whether an occasion is privileged at common law is entirely a matter for the judge,[332] whereas under the statutory privilege the questions of public concern and public benefit are for the jury.[333] It is therefore conceivable that a defendant might run the common law defence in parallel with that under the statute in the hope of getting a ruling that the occasion was privileged, so that the defence could only be defeated by proof of malice rather than by the jury's view of public concern and benefit.[334] In *Webb v Times Publishing Co.*[335] the following observations were made on the circumstances in which, at common law, there would be a legitimate public interest in England in foreign court proceedings.

> "Sometimes a report of foreign judicial proceedings will have intensive world-wide importance so that a reasonable man in any civilised country, wishing to be well informed, will be glad to read it, and would think he ought to read it if he has the time available. Sometimes a report of foreign judicial proceedings will not have such intrinsic world-wide importance, but will have special connection with English affairs, so that it will have a legitimate and proper interest for English readers, and the reasonable man in England will wish to read it or hear about it.[336] For instance, a report of foreign proceedings may throw light upon, or be related to or connected with, the administration of justice in England."[337]

(b) *Reports of proceedings in Parliament*

15.36 Reports of parliamentary proceedings.[338] A fair and accurate report[339] in a newspaper or otherwise of any debate or proceeding in either House of

---

[330] Ibid. s.15(4)(a).

[331] Thus the legitimate public interest in foreign proceedings was more limited than in English proceedings: *Webb v Times Publishing Co* [1960] 2 Q.B. 535.

[332] See para.34.18, below.

[333] See para.16.5, below.

[334] Equally, of course, the jury under the 1996 Act might take a more generous view than the common law.

[335] [1960] 2 Q.B. 535, disregarding on this point the previous decisions in *Risk Allah Bey v Whitehurst* (1868) 18 L.T. 615; *Riddell v Clydesdale Horse Society* (1885) 12 R. 976; and *Pope v Outram*, 1909 S.C. 230, in all of which it had been assumed without argument that qualified privilege attached to fair and accurate reports of foreign judicial proceedings in general.

[336] There could be no public interest in England in knowing what two lying witnesses had said of the plaintiff at the trial in Italy: *Montereale v Longmans Green, The Times*, February 23, 1965. On the other hand, a case concerned with the smuggling of heroin into New York with passports obtained in New South Wales on flights starting in N.S.W. was of "real concern" to the people of N.S.W.: *Thompson v Australian Consolidated* [1968] 3 N.S.W.R. 642.

[337] As in *Webb's* case. The case in question, in which the plea of privilege was upheld, related to a British subject prosecuted in a Swiss court, during which he confessed to having committed a murder for which he had been previously acquitted in an English court, and also crimes for which he was wanted by the English police.

[338] For extracts from reports, papers, etc. see paras 13.34, above and 16.13, below.

[339] See para.16.4, below.

Parliament, or in any committee thereof, is privileged at common law.[340] The publication is privileged on the same principle as a fair and accurate report of the proceedings in a court of justice, namely that the advantage of publicity to the community at large outweighs any private injury resulting from the publication.[341] It is not clear whether at common law there is privilege for reports of proceedings of a foreign legislature,[342] but it is submitted that there is, on the lines of that for reports of foreign judicial proceedings.[343] As s.15 and Sch.1, para.1 to the Defamation Act 1996 accord qualified privilege without explanation or contradiction to a fair and accurate report of proceedings in public of a legislature anywhere in the world it may be asked whether the common law privilege (which is not abolished by the Act) retains any importance.[344] The answer, it is submitted, is essentially similar to that given above to the similar question about reports of judicial proceedings.[345] The 1996 Act does not protect the publication of matter which is not of public concern and the publication of which is not for the public benefit and this is a question for the jury[346] whereas, provided the report is fair and accurate, any report of the proceedings of the United Kingdom Parliament is privileged at common law, no matter what the subject-matter of the debate.

Fairness and accuracy. There is a great deal of case law on the meaning   **15.37**
of a fair and accurate report[347] in the context of judicial proceedings[348] but comparatively little on Parliamentary proceedings, but it has been said[349] that:

> "the analogy between the two [types of report] is in every respect complete[350] ...
> all the limitations placed on the one, to prevent injustice to individuals, will
> necessarily attach to the other; a garbled or partial report, or of detached parts of
> proceedings, published with intent to injure individuals will equally be disentitled to
> protection ... whatever would deprive a report of the proceedings in a court of
> justice of immunity, will equally apply to a report of proceedings in Parliament."

---

[340] *Wason v Walter* (1868) L.R.4 Q.B. 73.

[341] See *R v Wright* (1799) 8 T. R. at 298, and *Wason v Walter*, above; *Perera v Peiris* [1949] A.C. 1 PC.

[342] Held not in *Benson v Robinson*, 1967 (1) S.A. 420 AD.

[343] See para.15.31, above.

[344] In *Curistan v Times Newspapers Ltd* [2008] EWCA Civ 432; [2009] Q.B. 231 only the statutory privilege was relied on.

[345] See para.15.31, above.

[346] Ibid.

[347] On reports which contain comment see *Curistan v Times Newspapers Ltd* [2008] EWCA Civ 432; [2009] Q.B. 231 and para.13.46, above. On what is substantial enough to be a "report" see *Nationwide News Pty Ltd v Moodie* [2003] WASCA 273; *Cornwall v Rowan* [2004] SASC 384; 90 S.A.S.R. 269.

[348] See para.13.37, above.

[349] Per Cockburn C.J. in *Wason v Walter* (1868) L.R. 4 Q.B. 73 at 93.

[350] However, it is suggested ibid. that a report would still be privileged even if the House forbade publication or the debate was held in secret, but such restrictions would render unprivileged at common law a report of court proceedings.

Older cases say that no protection is allowed to a report of a single speech out of several delivered in a debate, or in a day's proceedings,[351] but nowadays Parliamentary proceedings are reported much more briefly even in the most serious newspapers and it is submitted that the real question is whether the report is unbalanced or misleading. In *Cook v Alexander* the Court of Appeal held that privilege attached to a "parliamentary sketch".[352] The judgments emphasise that the reporter may present the impression the debate made[353] and select its memorable features.[354] The judgment of Lord Denning M.R. places particular emphasis on the subjective impression of the reporter.[355] The whole court agreed that what was needed was fairness in relation to the impression left by the debate, and that while the defendant could select part of the proceedings as being of particular public interest, he could not fairly omit reference to a rebuttal of charges made against the claimant.

Where Parliamentary proceedings are broadcast or televised the broadcasting company enjoys the same qualified privilege as in the case of a newspaper report.[356]

(c) *Extracts from registers*

15.38 Privilege for fair and accurate copy or extract. The publication of a fair and accurate copy of, or extract from, any register, kept pursuant to statute, and which by law the public are entitled to inspect, is privileged at common law. Thus, a copy of, or extract from, the register of county court judgments,[357] decrees in absence,[358] bills of sale,[359] or a copy of an entry as to the appointment of a receiver of a company contained in the register of joint-stock companies pursuant to the Companies Act 1948[360] have been held to be privileged. It is clear from the decisions that a trade protection society is entitled to publish in its journal, for the information of its subscribers, extracts from the public registers of county court judgments and matters

---

[351] *R. v Abingdon* (1794) 1 Esp. 226; *R. v Creevy* (1813) 1 M. & S. 273; approved in *Davison v Duncan* (1857) 7 E. & B. 229, and in *Wason v Walter* (1868) L.R.4 Q.B. 73 at 95.

[352] [1974] Q.B. 279.

[353] Ibid. at 288–289, 290.

[354] Ibid. at 291.

[355] Ibid. at 288–289.

[356] It would seem to be somewhat academic that the broadcaster could take advantage of s.1 of the Defamation Act 1996: see para.6.23, above. Compare s.13(2) of the Defamation Act 1992 (N.Z.) conferring absolute privilege on live broadcasting. The Faulks Committee recommended absolute privilege for live radio broadcasting and the sound element of live television broadcasting: Cmnd.5909 (1975), para.222. However, it is arguable that sound broadcasts are already absolutely privileged: para.16.7, below. The member whose words are broadcast of course enjoys absolute privilege under the Bill of Rights: para.13.30, above.

[357] *Fleming v Newton* (1848) 1 H.L.C. 363; *Cosgrave v Trade Co* (1874) Ir.R. 8 C.L. 349; *Annaly v Trade Co* (1890) 26 L.R.Ir. 394; *Searles v Scarlet* [1892] 2 Q.B. 56 CA.

[358] *Stubbs v Russell* [1913] A.C. 386 HL.

[359] *Cohen v Merchants' and Traders' Assn* (1900) 21 N.S.W.L.R. 241.

[360] *Jones, John and Sons v Financial Times* (1909) 25 T.L.R. 677.

relating to insolvency, and is not responsible, in the absence of malice, for any error or inaccuracy in the register, or for any defamatory suggestion in the matter so abstracted.[361] The rationale is similar to that underlying privilege for reports of court proceedings, that is to say that the defendant is only reporting what others might find themselves by inspecting the registers. In *Searles v Scarlett*,[362] Lord Esher M.R. said:

> "The law provides that the register shall be a public document which anybody may consult for this purpose. That being so, the publisher of such a list . . . is only doing for the public what they may do for themselves, and is only giving that information to the public and to tradesmen which the legislature has thought it right they should have. Therefore it is said that the publication of such a list is privileged and an action will not lie for it, unless the privilege has been abused . . . as long as the publication is bona fide, and without actual malice, it is privileged."

As in the situations covered by the preceding paragraphs these cases are covered by s.15 and Sch.1 to the Defamation Act 1996, which grant qualified privilege to a copy of or extract from any register or other document required by law to be open to public inspection. For the reasons explained above the common law privilege may continue to have some theoretical significance.

Inaccurate extracts.[363] No privilege attaches to the publication of an   **15.39**
inaccurate extract from a public register,[364] even though such extract was officially supplied and thought by the defendant to be a correct copy.[365]

> "If a person publishes an extract from a public document he is responsible if he has not correctly extracted it, or if it has not been correctly copied. It is no answer that he has been misled by a public official . . . This fact may go to diminish the damages, but it is no answer to an action for defamatory publication."[366]

So a newspaper was entitled to publish a list of bankrupts taken from the *Gazette*, and was immune from action if it printed the list accurately. However if the proprietor of a newspaper varied or abridged the description of a person whose name was gazetted, and that abridgment had the effect of attaching the stigma of bankruptcy to some other person, he would be liable.[367]

---

[361] *Fleming v Newton* (1848) 1 H.L.C. 363; *Annaly v Trade Co* (1890) 26 L.R.Ir. 11 CA at 394: *Searles v Scarlett* [1892] 2 Q.B. 56; *Jones, John and Sons v Financial Times* (1909) 25 T.L.R. 677; *Smith v Dun* (1911) 19 W.W.R. 17. There are dicta that if the defendant knew that the register was incorrect, he would be liable even though he published a correct copy of, or extract from, the register: see per Palles C.B. in *Annaly v Trade Co*, above at 23; per Fitzgibbon L.J., ibid. at 403.

[362] [1892] 2 Q.B. 56 CA at 60.

[363] For fairness and accuracy in the context of statutory qualified privilege, see para.16.4, below.

[364] E.g. the inclusion in a list of "decrees of absence" of a decree which was in fact taken *in foro* (*Crabbe v Stubbs Ltd* (1895) 22 R. 860) or a decree of consent (*Hunter v Stubbs Ltd* (1903) 5 F. 920).

[365] *Reis v Perry* (1895) 64 L.J.Q.B. 566.

[366] Per Day J. at 567.

[367] *Outram v Reid* (1852) 14 D. 577 at 581, followed in *Gordon v Stubbs Ltd* (1895) 3 S.L.T. 10.

CHAPTER 16

QUALIFIED PRIVILEGE: STATUTE

SECTION 1. INTRODUCTION

In general. It will be seen from the previous chapters that while in the pre-   **16.1**
Reynolds era the common law occasions of qualified privilege were primarily
those relating to statements in the performance of a duty or in pursuit of a
common interest or made to secure the redress of grievances, qualified
privilege was not confined to those situations but embraced certain reports of
matters in which the public had a legitimate interest, a category which has
been considerably expanded in modern times. However, the limited scope and
imprecision of the common law led to legislation in Victorian times which
conferred a *statutory* qualified privilege on a wide range of reports. Most such
occasions are now governed by Sch.1 to the Defamation Act 1996.[1] Nothing
in the Act is to abridge any privilege subsisting apart from Sch.1[2] but it
renders some aspects of privilege[3] of little practical importance.[4] The 1996

---

[1] This came into force on April 1, 1999: SI 1999/817. Broadly equivalent provisions are often found in other jurisdictions. See, e.g. Defamation Act 2005 (NSW) s.29 and Sch.3: New Zealand Defamation Act 1992, s.16 and Sch.1. However, in Australia there is no category of statement subject to explanation or contradiction such as is found in the English and New Zealand legislation. The Irish equivalent of Sch.1 is now to be found in the Irish Defamation Act 2009, Sch.1. The structure is similar, i.e. Part 1 cases are privileged without explanation or contradiction; under Part 2 the privilege is lost if the defendant has failed to comply with a request to publish a reasonable statement by way of explanation or contradiction (see s.18(4)). Similarly, the privilege is lost by proof of malice (s.19(1)). There are many differences of detail. Part 1 is considerably longer than the English version, having 19 paragraphs, but five of them relate to the Press Council and the Press Ombudsman (as to which see Sch.2 of the Act). Part 2 is rather shorter than the English version, mainly because all "associations" are put in one category under para.1, rather than being enumerated at length as in para.14 of the English version. Reports of notices issued for the information of the public fall under Pt 1, not Pt 2 as in the English Act.
[2] S.15(4)(b).
[3] E.g. the common law privilege for reports of judicial (para.15.35, above) or Parliamentary proceedings (para.15.36, above).
[4] See para.15.34, above.

Act modified and rationalised similar provisions in the Schedule to the Defamation Act 1952, which in its turn replaced earlier legislation. When it comes into force, the Defamation Act 2013 will update and extend in a number of respects the existing statutory privileges. The Act also creates, by s.6, a new qualified privilege for peer-reviewed statements in scientific or academic journals.[5]

SECTION 2. PRIVILEGE CONFERRED BY SCHEDULE 1 TO THE DEFAMATION ACT 1996

16.2 Background. A common law privilege for the reporting of meetings of public bodies, or of public meetings held to discuss matters of public concern, developed more slowly than the practice of reporting such meetings. After some debate, a statutory privilege was introduced[6]: the Newspaper Libel and Registration Act 1881, s.2, gave a qualified privilege to newspaper reports of public meetings.[7] This section was replaced by the Law of Libel Amendment Act 1888, s.4, which spelled out the protected categories in greater detail.[8] Both these sections required the defendant to publish, if so required, a letter or statement of explanation or contradiction as a condition of the privilege. Section 4 of the 1888 Act was repealed for the purposes of civil proceedings by the Defamation Act 1952, s.18(3) and so far as criminal libel is concerned[9] by the Coroners and Justice Act 2009, s.178 and Sch.23, Pt 2. The 1952 Act substituted a longer list of protected reports, only some of which continued to require the publication of a letter or statement of explanation or contradiction. The updating of the law which had been recommended by two committees[10] was effected by the Defamation Act 1996. However, the updated provisions

---

[5] See para.16.24, below.

[6] The only preceding statutory privilege was that conferred by the Parliamentary Papers Act 1840, s.3, for which, see para.16.27, below.

[7] The Act was based on the report of a Select Committee which sat from 1879 onwards; the Bill was delayed in the Commons, and was finally rushed through the House of Lords at the end of the Session: see 7 B.J.L.S. 31–33. In return for the privilege to report public meetings, and certain relaxations in the criminal law, newspapers accepted a system of registration of proprietors, which is still in force, but does not apply to limited companies, and so is now of little or no importance. S.2 provided a defence for a report in a newspaper of the proceedings of a public meeting lawfully convened for a lawful purpose and open to the public, if the report was fair and accurate and published without malice, and if the publication of the matter complained of was for the public benefit. The defence was not available if the defendant refused to insert in the newspaper a reasonable letter or statement of explanation or contradiction.

[8] It offered a defence to reports of public meetings and of meetings of a wide range of specified bodies except where neither the public nor a newspaper reporter was admitted. It specifically excluded blasphemous and indecent matter and "any matter not of public concern and the publication of which is not for the public benefit". The defence was not to be available:

"if the defendant has been requested to insert in the newspaper in which the report or other publication complained of appeared a reasonable letter or statement by way of contradiction or explanation of such report or other publication and has refused or neglected to insert the same."

[9] The criminal offences of sedition and seditious libel, defamatory libel and obscene libel were abolished for England, Wales and Northern Ireland by Coroners and Justice Act 2009, s.73.

[10] The Faulks Committee, Cmnd.5909 (1975) and the Neill Committee (1991).

were in many respects identical with the old[11] and most of the authorities on the latter remain valid.[12]

Now that a much wider common law qualified privilege on matters of public interest is available (particularly, but by no means exclusively) to media organs[13] there is some potential overlap between the common law and Sch.1.[14] Where a case falls clearly within Pt I of Sch.1 the only possible tactical element for the defendant in relying on the common law rather than the statute would seem to be that the judge will determine the applicability of the common law privilege, whereas in the present state of the law[15] the questions of public concern and public benefit are for the jury. Whether that

---

[11] Perhaps the major change is that the privileges are "internationalised". Under the 1952 Act they tended to be confined to matters occurring in the UK or the Commonwealth. The Defamation Act 2013, s.7 will 'internationalise' the privileges further still.

[12] *Tsikata v Newspaper Publishing* [1997] 1 All E.R. 655 CA, is a particularly important authority, decided under the 1952 Act after the passing of the 1996 Act. The relevant provisions of the 1996 Act apply to the whole of the UK: s.18.

[13] See *Reynolds v Times Newspapers Ltd* [2001] 2 A.C. 127; [1999] 3 W.L.R. 1010 and its progeny. See generally, Ch.15.

[14] There was a partial overlap in *Flood v Times Newspapers Ltd* [2010] EWCA Civ 804; [2010] E.M.L.R. 26 (the Supreme Court [2012] UKSC 11; [2012] 2 A.C. 273 did not consider the overlap issue). In that case the publication of a police notice announcing an investigation would have fallen within para.9 of Pt II (subject to the publication of a statement by way of explanation or contradiction on request) but not the publication of the ex parte allegations which had led to the investigations. The argument that this meant that common law *Reynolds* privilege could not apply because it was inconsistent with s.15 and Sch.1 was rejected. Lord Neuberger M.R. said:

"Subject to complying with section 15(2) and being unmalicious, publication by a defendant of a statement made by the police will be privileged irrespective of whether publication of the statement is in the public interest, and without the defendant being under any duty to check the accuracy of the statement. On the other hand, if it is potentially covered by *Reynolds* privilege, publication of an allegation made to the police will only attract privilege if it is in an article which, taken as a whole, is on a matter of public interest, if its inclusion in the article is justifiable, and if the steps taken to gather and publish the information were responsible and fair.

While these seem to be two conceptually rather different sets of criteria, I accept Mr Price's point that, if one considers the matter more closely, there is, in practice, more overlap between the section 15(1) criteria and the *Reynolds* privilege criteria than may at first appear. Thus, reporting a police statement unmaliciously might well normally be expected to satisfy all the *Reynolds* privilege criteria. However, that rather misses the point; in some cases, absent section 15, it is quite conceivable that the court might take the view that publicising such a statement would not be in the public interest, or even that a competent journalist would have checked the original source of the contents of the statement before publishing it. One can analyse the legislative balancing exercise as involving section 15(2) being a quid pro quo for removing the risk of such a possibility in a case where the publication is of a police statement, and there is nothing inconsistent with that analysis in the notion that *Reynolds* privilege can apply to publication of the information which led to the statement." (at [31]–[32])

"Public interest" must of course here be read in the *Reynolds* sense, though Sch.1 is inapplicable to matter which is not of public concern and the publication of which is not for the public benefit. The meaning of this is not entirely clear (see para.16.5, below) but it is thought that it is inconceivable that publication of a copy of a notice issued by the English police for the information of the public could fall within this restriction. See, also e.g. *Henry v BBC* [2005] EWHC 2787 (QB); and *Charman v Orion Group Publishing Ltd* [2006] EWHC 1756; [2007] 1 All E.R. 622 (QB) (it was not necessary fully to consider statutory privilege on appeal, [2007] EWCA Civ 972; [2008] 1 All E.R. 750).

[15] But see para.16.5, below.

will prove to be an advantage is likely to be unpredictable. However, the Defamation Act 2013, s.11, reverses the existing burden of proof in favour of jury trial and consequently, when the Act comes into force, this question will almost invariably be decided by a judge alone. If the case falls clearly within Pt II of the Schedule and within the common law privilege, the former requires the defendant to publish a statement from the claimant by way of explanation or contradiction and there is no such requirement for the common law privilege. However, in the majority of cases the common law will require the defendant before publication to seek the claimant's side of the story and to give a suitable account of that, so the difference is less great than might at first sight appear.

16.3 Publications protected. Under the previous law the statutory privilege was confined to publication in newspapers[16] or broadcasts.[17] There is no such restriction in the Defamation Act 1996,[18] which applies to any publication, e.g. in a book, in a periodical appearing too infrequently to be a newspaper, in an internet message, a blog post, or even on a placard, and, at least in the case of reports,[19] to an oral statement, for example on radio,[20] or television,[21] or in conversation.[22] It is no part of the definition of a report that it should be self-contained in the sense that it appears in a piece which contains nothing else,[23] nor that it be contemporaneous with the proceedings or events.[24]

Plainly the privilege under the Schedule does not protect the original publication of the matter which is reported (though that may well be protected by some other privilege).[25] Nor, it is submitted, should it protect the originator

---

[16] Defined as "any paper containing public news or observations thereon, or consisting wholly or mainly of advertisements, which is printed for sale and published in the United Kingdom either periodically or in parts or numbers at intervals not exceeding thirty-six days": Defamation Act 1952, s.7(5). Note, however, that there was never any requirement that the report should be contemporaneous with the matter reported. Cf. para.13.37 (reports of judicial proceedings).

[17] Defamation Act 1952, s.9(2).

[18] In *MXB v East Sussex Hospitals NHS Trust* [2012] EWHC 3279 (QB) Tugendhat J. noted at [23] that "The Contempt of Court Act 1981 and the Defamation Act 1996 simply refer to a report. Neither Act limits the reports to which it relates to reports in any specified medium."

[19] The Schedule applies to certain copies and extracts. While an oral statement could hardly be a copy in the ordinary sense of the word there seems to be no reason why it could not be an extract. Thus, if, say, a TV company broadcast a still of a page of a register (see para.5 of Sch.1) that would be privileged as a copy, while the reading of the extract in a radio broadcast would be privileged because it would fall to be treated as an extract. See *Qadir v Associated Newspapers Ltd* [2012] EWHC 2606 at [46]–[50] (QB); [2013] E.M.L.R. 15 .

[20] See previous note.

[21] *McKeown v Attheraces Ltd* [2011] EWHC 179 (QB) (refusal to strike out or dismiss a libel claim brought in respect of a television broadcast that reported that the claimant had been found guilty by a disciplinary panel of the British Horseracing Authority of deliberately failing to ride a horse on its merits).

[22] However, such a "report" might find difficulty in satisfying the requirement of fairness and accuracy.

[23] *Tsikata v Newspaper Publishing* [1997] 1 All E.R. 655 CA; *Curistan v Times Newspapers Ltd* [2008] EWCA Civ 432; [2008] 3 All E.R. 923, para.13.47, above.

[24] *Tsikata v Newspaper Publishing*, above.

[25] *McCartan Turkington Breen v Times Newspapers Ltd* [2001] 2 A.C. 277 HL (NI) at 291, 295. The legislation in question was the Schedule to the Defamation Act (Northern Ireland) 1955, the

of the matter if he is sued in respect of the publication in the report,[26] though the words are literally capable of bearing the contrary interpretation[27]: the policy of the statute would seem to be aimed at protecting the reporter and the originator cannot fairly be said to be "reporting" his own words.[28] However, it is not inconceivable that the originator of the matter might report it for the purposes of the Act. For example, if a Member of Parliament made a speech in the House (protected by absolute privilege) and then circulated an account of it to party members or constituents,[29] that would seem to fall within Pt 1, para.1 of Sch.1.[30] Of course the questions of public interest and public benefit would remain and the privilege would only be qualified, not absolute.

Fairness and accuracy. The reports, copies and extracts[31] referred to in   **16.4** Sch.1 must be "fair and accurate"[32] to gain the protection of privilege.[33]

---

equivalent of the English Act of 1952. However, there is no material difference between the 1952 and 1955 Acts on the one hand and the 1996 Act on the other for the purposes of the issues considered in the appeal.

[26] As to the circumstances in which the originator of a statement may be liable for republication by others, see paras 6.52–6.58, above.

[27] Because the provision says that "the publication" is privileged. In fact the position seems to have been essentially the same under the previous law because the privilege was for publication *in* a newspaper, not *by* a newspaper.

[28] See *Forster v Watson* (1944) 44 S.R. (N.S.W.) 399. But in *Lloyd-Allen v Adams* (unreported, 1977), referred to in the 8th edition of this book at para.667, it was held that the statutory privilege applied to a councillor in respect of a newspaper report of her speech which she had caused or authorised. The point was raised in *Macintyre v Phillips* [2002] EWCA Civ 1087; [2003] E.M.L.R. 9, but the CA upheld the trial judge's refusal to deal with privilege as a preliminary issue.

[29] Which would be outside the scope of the absolute privilege under the Bill of Rights: para.13.31, above.

[30] Para.16.9, below. Cf. *Rogers v Nationwide News* [2003] HCA 52; 216 C.L.R. 327.

[31] In *Qadir v Associated Newspapers Ltd* [2012] EWHC 2606 (QB); [2013] E.M.L.R. 15 Tugendhat J. held that words do not fail to qualify as an "extract" on the ground only that they are not word-for-word citations. An "extract" may mean "excerpt or quotation" but it also has wider meanings of "summary" or "outline": "to interpret an "extract" in the wider sense of "summary" or "outline" distinguishes the word "extract" from the word "copy". That appears likely to reflect the intention of Parliament, whereas "a narrow linguistic approach" would not." (at [48])

Whether in light of the amendments that will be made to s.15 and Sch.1 when the Defamation Act 2013 comes into force, Tugendhat J.'s interpretation of the provision will remain sustainable is open to doubt. In addition to qualified privilege attaching to fair and accurate "copies of or extracts from" various types of publication, subss.(4), (7)(b) and (10) of s.7 of the 2013 Act extends the scope of qualified privilege to cover fair and accurate "summaries" of material. This would seem to suggest that "extract" is intended to have a more limited meaning that "summary" and that it may be restricted to "word for word" citations.

[32] See also paras 13.38, 13.48 and 15.37, above. Though these adjectives are treated as involving separate issues (see, e.g. *Kingshott v Associated Kent Newspapers* [1991] 1 Q.B. 88 CA at 98), they are clearly aspects of the same idea, bearing in mind that "accurate" means "substantially accurate". See *Bruton v Estate Agents Licensing Authority* [1996] 2 V.R. 274 at 309 (omission of full name of subject of inquiry not a fair and accurate report because it led to plaintiff's being confused with the subject).

[33] It has been said that publication of an inaccurate report is not "for the public benefit": *Eyre v N.Z. Press Assn* [1968] N.Z.L.R. 736 at 742. Under the Australian uniform legislation (see, e.g. Defamation Act 2005 (NSW) s.29) a person who republishes material which was contained in an earlier report of a matter of public concern has a defence if at the time he does not have

However, although the report must be fair and accurate, it need not be verbatim; a fair, even if very brief, summary of the proceedings will be privileged[34] and where the report forms part of a publication focusing only on certain aspects of the proceedings reported the reporter is entitled to be selective about what he includes, so long as overall the report is not unfair.[35] In *Qadir v Associated Newspapers Ltd*[36] a claim was brought in respect of two newspaper articles. The first article consisted, for the most part, of an extract from particulars of claim in an action brought against Mr Qadir, though the precise words were not used. The article also contained extraneous information and did not mention the fact that the claimant was disputing the claim. In respect of this article, the defendant sought to rely on, inter alia, s.15 and and Sch.1 para.5 of the Defamation Act 1996.[37] The second article asserted that the claimant had been "intimately involved" in "Britain's biggest mortgage fraud". Those allegations had been made during a sentencing hearing by counsel for an offender convicted of fraud, but the judge had rebuked counsel, stating that he could not determine the complicity of others not before the court. In respect of the second article, the defendant pleaded both absolute privilege for a fair and accurate contemporaneous report of court proceedings and qualified privilege (under Defamation Act 1996, ss.14 and 15 and Sch.1 para.2 respectively). So far as the first article was concerned, Tugendhat J. held that the failure in a report of a statement of claim to state that the claimant was disputing the claim was not unfair and inaccurate.[38] The fairness and accuracy of a report has to be measured by reference to that to which it purports to relate (in this case, the particulars of claim):

"What is fair and accurate is to be judged by comparing the words complained of with the document from which the words complained of are said by the defendant

---

knowledge which should make him aware that the earlier report was unfair. Under English law it would seem that the unfairness or inaccuracy of the original would be fatal to the statutory defence.

[34] In *Tsikata v Newspaper Publishing* [1997] 1 All E.R. 655 CA, two sentences summarising the report of a tribunal of inquiry were held protected under the 1952 equivalent of para.3 of Sch.1. See also *Cook v Alexander* [1974] Q.B. 279 CA, protection for Parliamentary "sketch"; equivalent requirement for common law privilege in relation to report of parliamentary proceedings: para.15.37, above. See the overview of fairness and accuracy by Kirby J. in *Chakravarti v Advertiser Newspapers Ltd* [1998] HCA 37; 93 C.L.R. 519 at [153] (Wrongs Act 1936 (S.A.), which was similar to Sch.1 of the 1996 Act).

[35] *Charman v Orion Group Publishing Ltd* [2006] EWHC 1756; [2007] 1 All E.R. 622. The CA had no quarrel with this view of the law but disagreed with the judge's conclusion that the report fell below this standard: [2007] EWCA Civ 972; [2008] 1 All E.R. 750. On the question of how far editorialising and comment prevents something being a "report" see para.13.47, above.

[36] [2012] EWHC 2606 (QB); [2013] E.M.L.R. 15.

[37] Sch.1 para.5 Defamation Act 1996 provides that "a fair and accurate copy of or extract from any register or other document required by law to be open to public inspection" has qualified privilege without explanation or contradiction. See further para.16.13, below.

[38] Privilege was, however, held not to apply to this article because to publish defamatory allegations made in a claim form or particulars of claim without at the same time stating that the defendant to that claim had denied or was disputing the allegations was not for the public benefit. See para.16.5 fn.67, below.

to be an extract. Where the complaint is of unfairness arising out of the omission to publish information extraneous to that document, such as another document or comments of the complainant, then that issue is to be decided under s.15(3) (public concern and public benefit) or s.15(1) (malice)."[39]

However, the part of the second article which related to the comments made in the sentencing hearing was not a fair and accurate report of those proceedings. The judge had stated very clearly that there was no evidence that the claimant was complicit in the fraud. The omission of the judge's comments seriously unbalanced the report, to the extent that the defendant could not rely upon the privilege, whether absolute or qualified.[40]

"The theory is that the reporter represents the public-he is their eyes and ears and he has to do his best, using his professional skill to give them a fair and accurate picture."[41] However, where the reporter "adopts" the statements in the report as his own, the privilege may be lost.[42] The report need not be accurate in every detail. A bit of "tabloid tweaking" or editorialising will not, unless excessive, make the report unfair and inaccurate.[43] If the report be as a whole a substantially fair and correct account of the proceedings,[44] a few slight inaccuracies, or the addition of a few inaccurate, but non-defamatory statements,[45] will not deprive it of protection,[46] but where the inaccuracies are of a substantial kind, there is no immunity.

The requirement that the reports, copies and extracts referred to in Sch.1 be "fair and accurate" is identical with, and has the same meaning as, the requirement in s.14 of the Act (which protects reports of judicial proceedings with absolute privilege). There is, however, a contemporaneity requirement in s.14 that does not exist in s.15 and the Schedule.[47] It seems that the requirement of fairness and accuracy is to be determined solely by reference to the time at which the matter reported first appeared.[48] It might be argued that if there is a subsequent republication which is misleading in the light of subsequent developments the protection of privilege is lost because such a

---

[39] Ibid. at [68].

[40] The judge also concluded that it was not of "public concern" and "public benefit" to publish allegations made in court against the claimant by defence counsel while omitting to publish the judge's rebuttal. See para.16.5 fn.67, below.

[41] *Tsikata v Newspaper Publishing* [1997] 1 All E.R. 655 CA at 670, per Ward L.J.

[42] *Curistan v Times Newspapers Ltd* [2008] EWCA Civ 432; [2009] Q.B. 231 (a decision on s.14 of the Defamation Act 1996 but accepted as applying to s.15 by Tugendhat J. in *McKeown v Attheraces Limited* [2011] EWHC 179 (QB)).

[43] *Ismail v News Group Newspapers Ltd* [2012] EWHC 3056.

[44] *Andrews v Chapman* (1853) 3 C. &. K. 286 at 289.

[45] *Qadir v Associated Newspapers Ltd* [2012] EWHC 2606 (QB); [2013] E.M.L.R. 15. See further, para.13.47.

[46] See *Kimber v Press Association* [1893] I Q.B. 65 at 72; *de Normanville v Hereford Times Ltd, The Times*, May 20, 1936 (minor amendments by editor); *Nowlan v Moncton Publishing* [1952] 4 D.L.R. 808; *Cavanagh v NT News Services* (1989) 96 F.L.R. 268 NTSC.

[47] See para.16.3, above.

[48] *Tsikata v Newspaper Publishing* [1997] 1 All E.R. 655 CA. See the discussion of a comparable issue in the context of common law privilege in *Bray v Deutsche Bank AG* [2008] EWHC 1263 (QB), para.14.19, above.

"partial" publication may not be for the public benefit[49] or there might be evidence of malice, though care is needed not to impose unreasonable burdens on the holder of widely accessible information.[50]

The onus of proving that the report is fair and accurate lies on the defendant,[51] but it is sufficient if this clearly appears from the claimant's own evidence.[52] If the defendant fails to prove that the report is fair and accurate, the claimant is entitled to succeed, however honestly it may have been published.[53] Whether the report is a fair and accurate report is a question of fact for the jury,[54] provided always there is some evidence of unfairness or inaccuracy to go to the jury. This is a question for the judge to determine.[55]

16.5 Public concern and public benefit. Section 15(3) provides that the protection of the Schedule does not apply to "the publication to the public, or a section of the public, of matter which is not of public concern and the

---

[49] See para.16.5, below. Whether or not the republication is of matter which is of public benefit or concern has to be answered objectively: on the basis of what ought to have been know by a reasonable person at the time of publication, was publication of matter complained of for the public benefit or of public concern: *Qadir v Associated Newspapers Ltd* [2012] EWHC 2606 (QB); [2013] E.M.L.R. 15 at [106]–[108]. Inevitably this creates potential difficulties regarding continuing online publications and, Tugendhat J. made clear, in *Qadir* that nothing he said was in conflict with what the Ward said in *Tsikata v Newspaper Publishing Ltd* [1997] 1 All E.R. 665: "A newspaper may not know what happened subsequently nor may a newspaper be in a position to assess the quality or effect of any denials or refutations" (at 667) and "To require a newspaper to investigate subsequent events and report them in order to place the whole picture before the public in order to exclude damage to individual reputation is to make unacceptable inroads into the press's role as the public watchdog. It transforms investigative journalism from a virtue to a necessity" (at 671). That is not to say however that where there is a continuing publication the publisher will be able to ignore developments in the story. If a reasonable person ought to have known that circumstances have changed from the time of original publication that make clear that what was in the original report was wrong or is contested the report ought to be changed to reflect that or the report risks losing the privilege.

[50] C is convicted of fraud and his trial is widely reported. Six months later his conviction is overturned because he was the victim of perjured evidence. D out of spite then publishes an accurate account of the original trial. That is clearly malice. But it may be unreasonable to expect the holder of widely accessible but out of date information to be in possession of all subsequent relevant information (e.g. where the matter took place abroad) or to expect him to do anything about it.

[51] See para.13.49, above. In *Qadir v Associated Newspapers Ltd* [2012] EWHC 2606 (QB); [2013] E.M.L.R. 15 the judge accepted an argument that because the defendant bears the burden of proving the elements of the defences of statutory qualified privilege there was no basis for submitting that the 1996 Act in this respect failed to strike a fair balance between the art.10 rights of defendants and the art.8 or reputation right of a complainant (at [67]–[68]).

[52] *Kimber v Press Association* [1893] 1 Q.B. 65 at 71.

[53] See *Huntley v Ward* (1859) 6 C.B.(N.S.) 514. Where the report is contained in a TV broadcast, what must be interpreted in determining whether the report is fair and accurate "includes not just the words spoken, but the tone of voice and the body language of the speaker": *McKeown v Attheraces Limited* [2011] EWHC 179 (QB) at [28].

[54] *Kingshott v Associated Kent Newspapers* [1991] 1 Q.B. 880 CA; *Turner v Sullivan* (1862) 6 L.T.(N.S.) 130; *Street v Licensed Victuallers' Society* (1874) 22 W.R. 553.

[55] See para.36.21, below. However, where there is no evidence on which a jury could reasonably find that the report is not fair and accurate, e.g. where it is shown to be a verbatim copy of a shorthand note, or to differ so little that no reasonable jury could say that the difference affected the claimant, the judge should withdraw the question from the jury.

publication of which is not for the public benefit." This is substantially identical with s.7(3) of the Defamation Act 1952 and s.4 of the Law of Libel Amendment Act 1888.[56] What is of public benefit and of concern to the public is to be decided objectively and does not depend upon what the publisher thinks to be the case.[57] Thus where, for example a reasonable person would have been aware of facts contradicting those published in the report or that there was another side of the story, publication of the report without the contradictory facts or the other side of the story is highly unlikely to be for the public benefit.[58]

The question has been raised whether it is sufficient for the defendant to prove either that the subject-matter of the report is of public concern or that its publication is for the public benefit, or whether he must prove both of these facts to satisfy this section of the Act. In *Kelly v O'Malley*[59] Huddleston B. said that: "the publication must be for the public benefit besides being of public interest." It is submitted that this is the correct construction of the statute,[60] although in any event the statutory word is "concern" not "interest".[61] It certainly does not necessarily follow from the fact that the public are interested in the subject-matter of the report that it is for their benefit that such report should be published. In practice it is likely to be a rare case in which the public are concerned with the matter, but the publication will not be for their benefit.[62] So far as reports of court proceedings are concerned, these are absolutely privileged when contemporaneous. Other reports fall within s.15 and Sch.1 and on the face of it there is the further requirement that the publication be of public concern and for the public benefit (s.15(3)). However, in *Crossley v Newsquest (Midlands South) Ltd*[63] Eady J. held that the further requirement did not, at least so far as English proceedings were concerned, have to be established:

> "It may be that the significance of s 15(3) is to be found in the different wording of s 14. Absolute privilege is confined to reports of domestic and European courts. It does not extend to courts elsewhere. The categories covered by s 15, by contrast, are very wide indeed: see the contents of Sch 1 to the 1996 Act. Thus, it may be that the

---

[56] But neither the 1888 nor the 1952 Act contained the words "to the public or a section of the public".

[57] *Qadir v Associated Newspapers Ltd* [2012] EWHC 2606 (QB); [2013] E.M.L.R. 15, at [60].

[58] Ibid. at [100]–[101].

[59] (1889) 6 T.L.R. 62 at 64. In *Sharman v Merritt* (1916) 32 T.L.R. 360, Shearman J. apparently held the same view. In *Crossley v Newsquest (Midlands South) Ltd* [2008] EWHC 3054 (QB), Eady J. seemed to accept that both elements had to be met but noted, in the context of privilege claimed in respect of a non-contemporaneous court report, that such a burden was onerous and that the court's construction of the meaning of the provision would have to be informed by due regard to art.10.

[60] See *Boston v Bagshaw* [1966] 1 W.L.R. 1126 CA.

[61] "That is not your concern" implies something about legitimacy. "You are not interested in that" may be simply an assertion of fact.

[62] Some obvious cases (e.g. the publication of the names of juvenile offenders) will be caught by s.15(4)(a). Nevertheless the two categories are distinct.

[63] [2008] EWHC 3054 (QB).

additional hurdles set up in s 15(3) would have to be overcome in relation to matters taking place elsewhere in the world. For example, the privilege would attach to reports of 'proceedings in public before a court anywhere in the world'. If a British citizen were to be defamed in the course of such proceedings, it may be that the Defendant would have to show 'public concern' and 'public benefit' before being entitled to rely on the statutory privilege . . . That is a possible clue to Parliament's intention in the enactment of s 15(3). Be that as it may, I am quite satisfied that the present Defendant does not require to overcome any additional hurdles in relation to a report of proceedings in the Worcester County Court. Citizens in this jurisdiction are entitled to know what goes on in public hearings before any of Her Majesty's courts."[64]

While it is clear that irrelevant defamatory matter about an individual introduced during a discussion (e.g. at a public meeting) of an issue of public concern is not generally privileged,[65] that is adequately dealt with by the fact that it is the matter published which must be of public concern and for the public benefit.

The questions of public concern and public benefit are for the jury.[66] This means that earlier cases on what might satisfy these tests are of limited value as precedents and the protection of Sch.1 is rather less predictable than it might otherwise be.[67] However, the question of a privileged occasion may be

---

[64] Ibid. at [25]–[26]. Defamation Act 2013, s.7, when it comes into force, will amend s.14 of the 1996 Act and extends its ambit so that it covers contemporaneous reports of proceedings in any court outside the United Kingdom and Europe (see para.13.36, above). Whether, in light of this amendment, the additional hurdles of "public concern" (or public interest, as it will become) and "public benefit" must be met before a defendant can rely on s.15 for non-contemporaneous reports of such courts must be open to doubt. It is at least arguable that by extending the range of courts covered by s.14 Parliament intended to make clear that the public is entitled not only to hear what goes on and how justice is administered in the United Kingdom but also elsewhere in the world.

[65] *Pankhurst v Sowler* (1887) 3 T.L.R.193; per Huddleston B. in *Kelly v O'Malley* (1889) 6 T.L.R. 62 at 64. But in some contexts the fact that irrelevant defamatory statements are made may be of importance for the public to know.

[66] *Qadir v Associated Newspapers Ltd* [2012] EWHC 2606 at [78] (QB); [2013] E.M.L.R. 15 See also, *Kingshott v Associated Kent Newspapers* [1991] 1 Q.B. 880 CA. The court reverted to the view expressed in the early cases dealing with the equivalent provisions under the Newspaper Libel and Registration Act 1881 and the Law of Libel Amendment Act 1888: *Pankhurst v Sowler* (1887) 3 T.L.R. 193; *Kelly v O'Malley* (1889) 6 T.L.R. 62; *Chaloner v Lansdown* (1894) 10 T.L.R. 290; *Rickards v Bartram* (1908) 25 T.L.R. at 183; *M'Inerney v Clareman Printing Co* [1903] 2 Ir.R.347 at 356; see also *Ponsford v Financial Times Ltd* (1900) 16 T.L.R. 248. The assumption in *Boston v WS Bagshaw & Sons* [1966] 1 W.L.R. 1126 and *Hefferman v Regina Daily Star* [1930] 3 W.W.R. 665 that these cases were overruled in *Adam v Ward* [1917] A.C. 309 is incorrect: that case was concerned with a common law head of privilege and the predecessor of Sch.1 never fell to be considered. Presumably there will be some cases in which the judge is justified in directing the jury that they cannot find that the matter is of public concern and for the public benefit.

[67] In *Sharman v Merritt* (1916) 32 T.L.R. 360, the report of the agenda of a borough council meeting which imputed incompetence to an officer was held privileged. In *Ponsford v Financial Times Ltd* (1900) 16 T.L.R. 248 Matthew J. ruled that a report of a company meeting to discuss the need for new capital (see now para.13 of Sch.1 to the 1996 Act) at which fraud had been imputed to the chief cashier was not protected: the "charges against the plaintiff were of grave importance to him and to his accuser, but were no more of public concern than any other defamatory statements which might or might not be true." Today, however, such a report would be covered by para.13 of Sch.1 of the 1996 Act, as amended by s.7(7) of the 2013 Act. At the time

tried as a preliminary issue, in which case the matter will be determined by a judge.[68]

The Defamation Act 2013, s.7(2), when it comes into force, will substitute the phrase "public interest" for "public concern" so that the provision will read: "This section does not apply to the publication to the public, or a section of the public, of matter which is not of public interest and the publication of which is not for the public benefit". This is intended to ensure conformity of terminology within the Act and to prevent any possible confusion arising from the use of two different terms with the same meaning in the Act and in the 1996 Act.[69]

Publication of matter prohibited by law. Section 15(4)(a) of the Defa-   **16.6**
mation Act 1996 provides that the protection of Sch.1 does not extend to the publication of matter the publication of which is prohibited by law.[70] No privilege therefore attaches to a publication in contravention of an order of the court restricting reporting[71] nor, it is submitted, to a publication which amounts to a contempt of court apart from any such order.[72]

---

of *Ponsford* company meetings were not specifically mentioned in the legislation. While it is clearly of "public concern" and "public benefit" for the public to hear about proceedings before English courts (*Crossley v Newsquest (Midlands South) Ltd* [2008] EWHC 3054 (QB)), it will not, as a general rule, be for the public benefit to publish defamatory allegations made in a claim form or particulars of claim without at the same time stating that the defendant to that claim had denied or was disputing the allegations (*Qadir v Associated Newspapers Ltd* [2012] EWHC 2606 (QB); [2013] E.M.L.R. 15 at [100]), nor will it be of "public concern" and "public benefit" to publish allegations made in court against the claimant by defence counsel while omitting to publish the judge's rebuttal (*Qadir* at [174]). Reports of matters occurring abroad may, of course, be of public concern in England: *Tsikata v Newspaper Publishing* [1997] 1 All E.R. 655 CA (human rights and fundamental freedoms in Commonwealth country). The question of whether public concern and public benefit are matters for the judge or the jury is adverted to by Lord Cooke in *Reynolds v Times Newspapers Ltd* [2001] 2 A.C. 127 HL at 225, but only for the purpose of emphasising that the decision in *Kingshott* should not be taken as affecting the allocation of function at common law. *Kingshott* is also referred to by Lord Steyn at 216, but he does not seem to be expressing a view on the point at issue in that case. Lord Cooke returned more directly to the point in *McCartan Turkington Breen v Times Newspapers Ltd* [2001] 2 A.C. 277 HL (NI) at 302, but, while noting the expressed preference of counsel for the defendant newspaper for a return to the pre-*Kingshott* law (because the test should be the same for both common law and statutory privilege), said that the case was not an appropriate one in which to resolve the issue. However, he thought that on the facts a finding that a fair and accurate report would not have been within the statute would have been perverse.

[68] *Tsikata v Newspaper Publishing*, above. In any event, it is now more common for all stages of a case to be handled by judge alone: *Henry v BBC* [2005] EWHC 2787 (QB); *Charman v Orion Group Publishing Ltd* [2006] EWHC 1756; [2007] 1 All E.R. 622 (on appeal [2007] EWCA Civ 972; [2008] 1 All E.R. 750).

[69] See para.51 of the Explanatory Notes to the Act.

[70] The same provision previously appeared in s.7(3) of the Defamation Act 1952.

[71] E.g. under the Contempt of Court Act 1981.

[72] "There will be some cases when the question whether a publication is prohibited by law . . . will be a pure question of law and therefore one for the judge": *Kingshott v Associated Kent Newspapers* [1991] 1 Q.B. 88 CA at 101. Does this mean that there are some cases where it will be for the jury? Cf. the issues of public concern and benefit, below.

16.7 Defamation Act 2013—Amendments to s.15 and Sch.1 of the 1996 Act. When it comes into force, the Defamation Act 2013 will amend in a number of respects s.15 and Sch.1 of the 1996 Act. The main effect of these provisions will be to further "internationalise" the existing provisions extending the protection afforded by qualified privilege to reports of the proceedings of various institutions outside the European Union. This change was originally proposed in Lord Lester's Defamation Bill on the footing that there was no good reason why the statutory privilege should be restricted, as it was, to publications relating to legislatures, governments, courts, public meetings and associations in the European Union. In view of this and in response to concerns expressed by a number of organisations that they were regularly threatened by libel proceedings for quoting or citing public documents published in non-European Union countries, the government decided that it would be in the public interest to extend the scope of Pt II qualified privilege to publications beyond the confines of the United Kingdom and European Union. Section 7 will also internationalise the provision relating to reports of proceedings at company meetings so that it will cover the meetings of companies worldwide. The current restriction to meetings of UK public companies will also be removed and the protection will apply to the meeting of any listed company.[73] In addition to qualified privilege attaching to fair and accurate *copies of or extracts from* various types of publication, subss.(4), (7)(b) and (10) of s.7 of the Act extend the scope of qualified privilege to cover fair and accurate *summaries* of material.[74] In response to concerns raised by the science community, the 2013 Act will also introduce specific protection for reports of proceedings of an academic or scientific conference held anywhere in the world.[75] Additionally a qualified privilege will attach, by virtue of s.6, to peer-reviewed statements in scientific or academic journals.[76] These changes are considered at the appropriate points below.

16.8 Reports subject to explanation or contradiction. In the case of statements falling within Pt I of Sch.1 to the Defamation Act 1996 it is simply a question of whether the "occasion" was privileged within the statute and whether the matter is of public concern and for the public benefit; but s.15(2) of the Act provides that:

> "In defamation proceedings in respect of a report or other statement mentioned in Part II of the Schedule [to this Act], there is no defence [of privilege] if the plaintiff shows that the defendant (a) was requested by him to publish in a suitable manner a reasonable letter or statement by way of explanation or contradiction, and (b) refused or neglected to do so."

---

[73] See para.16.21, below.
[74] If Tugendhat J. was correct in *Qadir v Associated Newspapers Ltd* [2012] EWHC 2606 (QB); [2013] E.M.L.R. 15 (see fn.31, above) the 1996 Act already covers summaries in that his lordship defined "extract" as including "summary".
[75] See para.16.23, below.
[76] See para.16.25, below.

For this purpose "in a suitable manner" means "in the same manner as the publication complained of or in a manner that is adequate and reasonable in the circumstances". Though there is no general *droit de réponse*, this is English law's closest approach to it. The request must set out the terms of the letter or statement to be inserted, and a general demand for a full apology is not sufficient.[77]

Where the libel has appeared in a newspaper it is submitted that the defendant should insert such letter or statement in the same part of the newspaper as that in which the report complained of appeared. In the case of an offending broadcast, a statement by way of explanation or contradiction should prima facie be broadcast from the same station as part of the same programme or service. A letter should not be inserted in a part of the paper not likely to be read by the general public, or in smaller type than the rest of the printed matter, and care should be taken that it contains no reflections on persons who are strangers to the proceedings. Now that the statutory privilege extends more widely than publications in the news media, it may be more difficult in some cases to determine what is a reasonable "venue" for the publication of the statement, for example in the case of a book. Conceivably, e.g. the statement might have to be published in every journal in which the book was reviewed. The letter should be moderate in tone and length. A letter which is unduly long, or likely to expose the newspaper to actions at the suit of other persons, is not a "reasonable letter", and the defendant would be justified in refusing to insert it.[78] It is not unlikely that there will be objections to the letter proffered by the claimant and in that event it is incumbent on the defendant to raise these and endeavour to reach an agreement.[79]

---

[77] *Khan v Ahmed* [1957] 2 Q.B. 149. Nor is a request for a retraction; *Hansen v Nugget Publishers* [1927] 4 D.L.R. 791 at 795. See also *Nowlan v Moncton Publishing* [1952] 4 D.L.R. 808; *Cavanagh v NT News Services* (1989) 96 F.L.R. 768 NTSC.

[78] Speaking of the comparable South Australian statute in *Chakravarti v Advertiser Newspapers Ltd* [1998] HCA 37; 93 C.L.R. 519 at [161], Kirby J. said that "the purpose of the publication envisaged by the proviso is not to afford the complainant, or anyone else, the opportunity to insult the publisher, to extract an apology or to defame others". In *Melynychuk v Ukraine* App. Nos 28851/95, 28852/95, January 16, 1998, a newspaper published a highly critical review by P of a book of poetry written by the applicant. The newspaper refused to publish a reply as required by Ukrainian law and the applicant complained that his art.10 rights had been infringed. The court rejected the applicant's complaint as unfounded. The applicant had been offered such an opportunity but his proposed reply contained obscene and abusive remarks about the book reviewer's personality and consequently the newspaper was justified in refusing to publish it.

[79] *Henry v BBC* [2005] EWHC 2787 (QB) at [91]. The meaning of a "reasonable" response received some consideration, obiter, in the High Court of Australia in *Chakravarti v Advertiser Newspapers Ltd* [1998] HCA 37; 93 C.L.R. 519 in the context of proviso (b) to the former s.7 of the Wrongs Act 1936 (S.A.), which was similar to s.15 and Sch.1 to the 1996 Act. A difficulty arises because, while the fairness and accuracy of the report in question is a pre-condition of the statutory defence, that question may be in dispute at the time when the potential claimant proffers his statement. Gaudron and Gummow JJ. considered that while it would not ordinarily be reasonable to controvert the fairness of a report on a basis which is factually incorrect, yet it did not automatically follow that the measured assertion of a belief which was subsequently shown to be incorrect was unreasonable and, contrariwise, it was conceivable that a letter might be held

(a) *Statements privileged under Schedule 1 without explanation or contradiction*

16.9 Legislative proceedings. A fair and accurate[80] report of proceedings in public of a legislature[81] anywhere in the world.[82] A fair and accurate report of the proceedings of the Westminster legislature is privileged at common law[83] and in this respect Sch.1 would seem virtually[84] to duplicate the common law.[85] A legislature includes a local legislature[86] (e.g. of the states of Australia and the US). It does not seem necessary that the legislature be democractically elected or that its proceedings should allow freedom of debate, speech and voting. However a purely formal body which gives formal approval to the edicts of a dictator may not[87] be a legislature for this purpose.[88]

---

to be unreasonable because of some misstatement of fact, although the letter was thought by all concerned to be accurate at the time it was written: at [85]–[86]. Kirby J. at [161] said:

"Because the publication advances freedom of expression and enhances the public's entitlement to make its own judgments on reputation, courts (and therefore editors) should err on the side of upholding publication of such letters. It can rarely be in the public interest or for the public benefit to deny a person claiming to have been defamed an opportunity to put his or her contradictory or explanatory statement before the same public as has heard the matter complained of. In some circumstances such a denial would evidence an arrogance of power, deprive the publisher of the privilege otherwise applicable and perhaps even illustrate actual malice."

[80] As to fairness and accuracy, see para.16.4, above.
[81] Under para.16(4) the European Parliament is a legislature (also for the purposes of paras 3 and 7). Without this specific provision it might not be such. S.77(4) of the Government of Wales Act 1998 provided that the Welsh Assembly is also a legislature. There appears to be no comparable provision in the Government of Wales Act 2006 but since the Assembly may pass laws (s.93) which, within its legislative competence, may contain any provision which could be made by Act of Parliament (s.94) and it may acquire further law making powers (s.103) the former provision was presumably regarded as unnecessary.
[82] Defamation Act 1996, Sch.1, para.1. The equivalent provision of the Defamation Act 1952 was confined to "the legislature of any part of Her Majesty's dominions outside Great Britain". However, this phrase included for this purpose India and Ireland: Pt III, para.14 of the Schedule to the 1952 Act.
[83] See para.15.36, above. As to fairness and accuracy, see para.15.37, above.
[84] But see paras 15.35 and 15.36, above. On the basis of *Curistan v Times Newspapers Ltd* [2008] EWCA Civ 432; [2008] 3 All E.R. 923 it seems that para.1, rather than the common law, is the primary basis of privilege for reports of English Parliamentary proceedings. In *Curistan* at [24] it is said that para.1 is derived from s.3 of the Parliamentary Papers Act 1840. However, in the view of the Joint Committee on Privilege:

"Newspaper reports are not usually taken from *Hansard*. Accordingly, since they are not taken from a report published by order of the House, they do not fall within the (qualified) protection afforded by section 3 of the 1840 Act": HL Paper 43/HC 214–1, 1998–99, para.356.

[85] It has always been assumed that broadcast reports (whether live or recorded) were covered by the common law privilege and they would clearly also fall within the 1996 Act. The Faulks Committee recommended that the sound element of a live broadcast (but not the pictures) should be protected by absolute privilege: Cmnd.5909 (1975), para.222. However, the Joint Committee on Privilege thought it arguable that broadcast reports were protected by absolute privilege under the Parliamentary Papers Act 1840: see para.13.34, above. The member whose words are reported is, of course, protected by absolute privilege. Live broadcasts are protected by absolute privilege in New Zealand: Defamation Act 1992, s.13(2).
[86] Sch.1, para.16(1).
[87] But see para.16.15, below.
[88] Such a body may well not meet in public.

Judicial proceedings. A fair and accurate report of proceedings in public   **16.10**
before a court anywhere in the world.[89] A court for this purpose includes[90] any
tribunal or body exercising the judicial power of the state.[91] Where the report
of proceedings in public is contemporaneous, absolute privilege applies,[92] so
this provision is of no importance as far as contemporaneous reports are
concerned. There is a common law qualified privilege for reports of proceedings in UK and foreign courts where the matter is of legitimate public interest
here[93] but the statutory provision is certainly no narrower.

When it comes into force, the Defamation Act 2013 will amend the
definition of a "court" so that it will include—"(a) any tribunal or body
established under the law of any country or territory exercising the judicial
power of the State; (b) any international tribunal established by the Security
Council of the United Nations or by an international agreement; (c) any
international tribunal deciding matters in dispute between States."[94]

Public inquiries. A fair and accurate report of proceedings in public[95] of a   **16.11**
person[96] appointed to hold a public[97] inquiry[98] by a government[99] or legislature anywhere in the world.[100] The fact that there are doubts about the
correctness of the conclusions does not remove the privilege.[101] The omission
of countervailing information may be relevant to the question of public
concern and public benefit,[102] but the law should take care not to impose too

---

[89] Sch.1, para.2. The equivalent provision of the Defamation Act 1952 applied only to courts
within Her Majesty's Dominions outside the UK and to courts-martial held outside the UK under
UK military law.

[90] "includes" not "means". For the avoidance of doubt the International Court of Justice and
other judicial or arbitral tribunals deciding matters in dispute between states are included within
the definition of court: para.16(3)(d).

[91] Sch.1, para16(1).

[92] See paras 13.37, 13.38, above.

[93] See para.15.35, above.

[94] Defamation Act 2013, s.7(11).

[95] Which includes the report of the inquiry, even though that may be delivered to a government
officer and released by him: *Tsikata v Newspaper Publishing* [1997] 1 All E.R. 655 CA.
"Common sense informs us that the proceedings of public inquiry begin with the evidence but
end with the findings": per Ward L.J. at 669.

[96] The equivalent provision (para.5) of the 1952 Act referred to "a *body or* person appointed".
It is inconceivable that any change of substance was intended and no doubt a body is merely a
number of persons. Compare the wording of para.11(1)(c), which in this respect is identical to that
of the 1952 Act.

[97] In *Bruton v Estate Agents Licensing Authority* [1996] 2 V.R. 274, it was held that this
expression in s.3A(2A) of the Wrongs Act 1958 (Vict.) meant that the person was obliged to hold
the inquiry in public.

[98] In *Bruton v Estate Agents Licensing Authority*, above, the phrase "public inquiry" in the
Victoria legislation was said to connote an appointment for the specific purpose of holding an
inquiry and not to extend to a body which had investigative functions among others.

[99] Reports of proceedings of an inquiry under the Inquiries Act 2005 are protected by absolute
privilege: para.13.17, above.

[100] Sch.1, para.3. There is an overlap between this para. and para.11(1)(c): see para.16.17,
below.

[101] *Tsikata v Newspaper Publishing* [1997] 1 All E.R. 655 CA.

[102] See para.16.5, above.

high a duty upon the press and to transform "investigative journalism from a virtue to a necessity"[103] and it may be that only an authoritative refutation will defeat the privilege for the report of the original conclusions.[104]

16.12 International organisations or conferences. A fair and accurate report of proceedings in public anywhere in the world of an international organisation or an international conference.[105] An international organisation means an organisation of which two or more governments are members, and includes any committee or other subordinate body of such an organisation; and an international conference means a conference attended by representatives of two or more governments.[106]

16.13 Registers, etc. A fair and accurate[107] copy of or extract[108] from any register or other document required by law[109] to be open to public inspection.[110] This largely duplicates a common law head of qualified privilege.[111]

16.14 Notices and advertisements. A notice or advertisement published by or on the authority of a court, or of a judge or officer of a court, anywhere in the world.[112]

16.15 Government publications. A fair and accurate copy of or extract from[113] matter published by or on the authority of a government or legislature anywhere in the world.[114] In accordance with the general pattern of the 1996

---

[103] *Tsikata v Newspaper Publishing*, above, per Ward L.J. at 671.

[104] See also para.16.4, above.

[105] Sch.1, para.4. The equivalent provision of the 1952 Act was confined to international organisations of which the UK was a member or conferences to which the UK sent a representative.

[106] Sch.1, para.16(1). It is submitted that what is envisaged is a conference the purpose of which is negotiation between governments (e.g. the Hague Conference on Private International Law). The proceedings of an academic or scientific conference will be protected by qualified privilege when s.7(9) of the Defamation Act 2013 (which inserts a new s.14A in the Defamation Act 1996) comes into force, as will be a copy of, extract from or summary of matter published by such a conference (see para.16.22, below).

[107] *Annaly v Trade Auxiliary Co* (1890) 26 L.R. Ir. 394 at 403.

[108] See para.16.3, above.

[109] Under the equivalent provision of the 1952 Act the privilege was only applicable where the right to inspect was conferred by UK law. Note, however, that all the other paragraphs of Pt I of the Schedule (two of which are concerned with copies or extracts) contain the phrase "anywhere in the world".

[110] See *Jameel v Times Newspapers Ltd* [2005] EWHC 1219 (QB). CPR r.5.4(2) gives a right to any person to inspect a claim form but other documents may only be inspected with the permission of the court: see further para.13.48. See also, *Qadir v Associated Newspapers Ltd* [2012] EWHC 2606 (QB); [2013] E.M.L.R. 15; *Ismail v News Group Newspapers Limited* [2012] EWHC 3056 (QB).

[111] See para.15.38, above.

[112] Sch.1, para.6. The 1952 Act confined the protection to notices, etc. of UK courts.

[113] It should be noted, that Sch.1, para.7 is confined to copies or extracts and does not extend to *reports* of material published by foreign governments.

[114] Sch.1, para.7.

Act, this provision internationalised the provision in para.12 of the Schedule to the Defamation Act 1952 (which covered copies, etc. of any notice or other matter issued for the information of the public by a British government department or various other bodies) but went considerably further[115] as para.12 was only a head of privilege subject to explanation or contradiction.

Matter published by international organisations and confer-   **16.16**
ences. A fair and accurate copy of or extract from matter published anywhere in the world by an international organisation or an international conference.[116]

(b) *Statements privileged under Schedule 1 subject to explanation or contradiction*

Notices from governments, etc. A fair and accurate copy of, or extract   **16.17**
from, a notice or other matter issued for the information of the public by or on behalf of (1) a legislature in any member state[117] or the European Parliament[118]; (2) the government of any member state, or any authority performing governmental functions[119] in any member state or part of a member state, or the European Commission; (3) an international organisation or international conference.[120] This follows through the policy of the Act in extending the protection formerly given by the 1952 Act to such matter issued by or on behalf of a government department, officer of state, local authority or chief officer of police.[121]

The privilege covers matter "issued"[122]—i.e. volunteered rather than extracted by questioning[123] but not mere gossip supplied to journalists by the publicity officer of a Ministry for the purpose of keeping the Minister or

---

[115] There is also a substantial overlap between para.7 and para.9 of the 1996 Schedule, which causes problems: see para.16.17, below.

[116] Sch.1, para.8. See para.16.12, above. There was no equivalent provision in the 1952 Act.

[117] I.e. of the European Union.

[118] Cf. para.16.9, above.

[119] This includes police functions: para.9(2). So, e.g. a notice of a reward would be covered: *Boston v WS Bagshaw* [1966] 1 W.L.R. 1126 CA. *Henry v BBC* [2005] EWHC 2787 (QB) (strategic health authority performing governmental functions).

[120] Sch.1, para.9.

[121] Defamation Act 1952, Schedule, para.12.

[122] But not necessarily in writing: *Blackshaw v Lord* [1984] Q.B. 1 CA; *Loveday v Sun Newspapers* (1938) 59 C.L.R. 503. The fact that the matter is supplied in response to a request does not of itself take it outside the section: *Blackshaw v Lord*; *Ferrymead Tavern Ltd v Christchurch Press Ltd* [1999] NZAR 529 NZ High Ct (under provision of NZ Defamation Act 1992). But "information which is put out on the initiative of a government department falls more easily within the paragraph than information pulled out of the mouth of an unwilling officer": *Blackshaw v Lord* at 24.

[123] *Blackshaw v Lord* [1984] Q.B. 1 CA.

department in the public eye.[124] There appears to be a very substantial overlap with para.7, which deals with copies or extracts privileged *without explanation or contradiction*,[125] since where the source of a publication is a government[126] it seems inevitable in the great majority of cases that "a notice or other matter issued for the information of the public by or on behalf of . . . a government of any member State"[127] (para.9) will also be "matter published by or on the authority of a government" (para.7).[128]

Defamation Act 2013, s.7(4) will further "internationalise" s.15 by extending Sch.1 para.9 to include a fair and accurate copy of, extract from or summary[129] of a notice or other matter issued for the information of the public by or on behalf of—(a) a legislature or government anywhere in the world; (b) an authority anywhere in the world performing governmental functions (c) an international organisation or international conference.

16.18 Courts. A fair and accurate copy of or extract from a document made available by a court in any member state or the European Court of Justice (or any court attached to that court[130]), or by a judge or officer of any such court.[131]

Section 7(4) of the Defamation Act 2013, when it comes into force, will extend Sch.1, para.10 to include fair and accurate *summaries* of a document made available by a court *anywhere in the world*, or by a judge or officer of such a court.

16.19 Local authority meetings, inquiries, etc. A fair and accurate report of proceedings at any public meeting or sitting in the United Kingdom (or corresponding proceedings[132] in any of the Channel Islands or the Isle of Man or in another Member State[133]) of (1) a local authority or local authority

---

[124] *Forster v Watson* (1944) 44 S.R. (N.S.W.) 399 at 403.

[125] It seems likely in the case of governments that the Neill Committee wished merely to extend to statements by foreign governments the protection (subject to explanation or contradiction) of para.12 of the 1952 Act: para.XII.8 of its report.

[126] The position would be different in the case of other sources: a local authority or a police force would not be a government for the purposes of para.7.

[127] Which clearly includes the United Kingdom.

[128] It might be argued that "matter" in para.9 is narrower than in para.7 and that under para.7 "matter" might be published by the government in the technical, defamation sense without being for the information of the public. But that would be to ignore the fundamental requirement that to be protected by the Schedule the matter must be of public concern and its publication for the public benefit: s.15(3). In any event, para.9 can hardly be wider than para.7. In *Tsikata v Newspaper Publishing* [1997] 1 All E.R. 655 CA, the parties seem to have agreed that the report of a tribunal of inquiry did not fall within para.12 of the 1952 Act.

[129] See further fn.31.

[130] See para.13.38, above.

[131] Sch.1, para.10. There was no equivalent provision in the 1952 Act. Copies etc. of pleadings obtained with permission under CPR r.5.4C (see para.13.47, above) would be privileged.

[132] The Lord Chancellor and Secretary of State for Scotland are given power to identify these by statutory instrument: para.17.

[133] Sch.1, para.11(3).

committee[134]; (2) a justice or justices of the peace acting otherwise than as a court exercising judicial authority[135]; (3) a commission, tribunal, committee or person appointed for the purpose of any inquiry[136] by any statutory provision, by Her Majesty or by a Minister of the Crown, a member of the Scottish Executive,[137] the Welsh Ministers or the Counsel General to the Welsh Assembly Government[138] or a Northern Ireland Department[139]; (4) a person appointed by a local authority to hold a local inquiry in pursuance of any statutory provision; (5) any other board, committee or body constituted by or under, and exercising functions under, any statutory provision.[140]

Section 7(5) of the Defamation Act 2013, when it comes into force, will insert a new para.11A into Sch.1 of the 1996 Act which has the effect of protecting a fair and accurate report of proceedings at a press conference held anywhere in the world for discussion of a matter of public interest. This amendment was arguably unnecessary as most press conferences would in any event be protected by para.12 of Sch.1. It was nevertheless added for the avoidance of doubt.[141]

In the case of a local authority operating executive arrangements within the meaning of Pt II of the Local Government Act 2000, a fair and accurate record of any decision made by any member of the executive where that record is

---

[134] Both of which are defined in Sch.1, para.2. In the case of a local authority operating executive arrangements within the meaning of Pt II of the Local Government Act 2000, the executive of that authority or a committee of that executive: para.11(1)(aa), inserted in relation to England by the Local Authorities (Executive Arrangements) (Modification of Enactments) (England) Order 2002, SI 2002/1057, arts 2(h), 12(b); a corresponding amendment has been made in relation to Wales by the Local Authorities (Executive Arrangements) (Modification of Enactments and Other Provisions) (Wales) Order 2002, SI 2002/808, arts 2(p), 30(a).

[135] The most obvious example of this at the time of enactment was licensing justices but under the Licensing Act 2003 licensing of sale of alcohol is a matter for the local authority.

[136] See *Bruton v Estate Agents Licensing Authority* [1996] 2 V.R. 274, fn.79, above.

[137] Inserted by the Scotland Act 1998, s.125, Sch.8, para.33(3).

[138] Inserted by the Government of Wales Act 2006, s.160(1), Sch.10, para.40.

[139] There is an overlap here with para.3. Though para.11 does not cover reports of proceedings of foreign inquiries, para.3 plainly covers reports of proceedings of UK inquiries as well as foreign ones. Compare, under the 1952 Act, *Tsikata v Newspaper Publishing* [1997] 1 All E.R. 655 CA. On the basis of *Tsikata*, para.3 covers reports of the sittings *and* the conclusions of the inquiry (see para.16.9); but as a matter of language para.11 appears to cover the sittings but not the conclusions (unless publicly delivered at a sitting). It is curious that (as is the case in relation to paras 7 and 9) the privilege which requires no opportunity of explanation or contradiction appears to cover more ground than the one that does. Note also that para.3 refers only to proceedings by a "person" whereas para.11 refers to a "commission, tribunal, committee or person".

[140] Sch.1, para.11(1). Para.10 of the 1952 Act excluded meetings or sittings admission to which was denied to the press and other members of the public. Now the same result is achieved simply by providing that the meeting or sitting must be public.

[141] An amendment introduced by Robert Flello M.P. in the Committee Debates (*Hansard*, HC col.139 (June 26, 2012)) to make explicit that the privilege would attach to the contents of a press release was withdrawn when the government said it was unnecessary as subs.(5) was intended to reflect the law as it existed, the courts having recognised in *McCartan Turkington Breen v Times Newspapers Ltd* [2001] 2 A.C. 277 HL (NI) that a report based on the material in such a document was a report of the proceedings of the meeting even though the relevant portion had not been read out at the meeting (Jonathon Djanogly M.P., *Hansard*, HC col.141 (June 26, 2012)).

required to be made and available for public inspection by virtue of s.22 of the Local Government Act 2000 or of any provision in regulations made under that section.[142]

16.20 Public meetings in Member States. A fair and accurate report of proceedings at any public meeting held in a Member State. A public meeting means a meeting bona fide and lawfully held for a lawful purpose and for the furtherance or discussion of a matter of public concern, whether admission to the meeting is general or restricted.[143] The statute must be interpreted in a manner which gives effect to the intention of the legislature in the social and other conditions which obtain today. A meeting is public if those who organise it open it to the public or, by issuing a general invitation to the press, manifest an intention or desire that the proceedings of the meeting should be communicated to a wider public. Press representatives may be regarded either as members of the public or as the eyes and ears of the public to whom they report.[144] This reflects the function of the press in a modern democracy to alert and inform the public on matters of public concern.[145]

A public meeting does not require any participation or opportunity for participation by those attending it.[146] No doubt an ordinary lecture at a university is still not a public meeting because there is no intention to invite the public as opposed to registered students, who are invited by virtue of their contractual nexus; but a public lecture, such as an inaugural lecture, would seem now to be potentially within the Act, though in many cases its subject matter would probably not be such as to meet the requirement of "furtherance . . . of a matter of public interest". A meeting held by a student organisation in memory of a famous statesman, not confined to members of the organisation, has been held to be a "public meeting" within the section.[147] A meeting to which the ratepayers of a borough are admitted to consider and discuss a subject of common interest would be the clearest possible example of a "public meeting" within the section. So would a meeting of the electors

---

[142] Sch.1, para.11(1A), inserted in relation to England by SI 2001/2237, arts 1(2), 2(q), 31(b), and in relation to Wales by SI 2002/808, arts 2(p), 30(b).

[143] Sch.1, para.12(2). This is identical in substance with the definition in the 1952 Act.

[144] *McCartan Turkington Breen v Times Newspapers Ltd* [2001] 2 A.C. 277 HL (NI) at 292, per Lord Bingham. The case concerned para.9 of the Schedule to the Defamation Act (Northern Ireland) 1955 but there is no material difference between this and the current English provision.

[145] On the facts the general invitation was issued only to the press, though members of the public attended and were admitted. The policy reasoning indicates, however, that the result would be the same even if only the press were admitted. The difficulty is that if this is so, why is not report of a press *release* automatically privileged as far as the newspaper is concerned even if there is no meeting of any sort?

[146] *McCartan Turkington Breen* [2001] 2 A.C. 292. Cf. *Silva v Toronto Star Newspapers Ltd* (1999) 167 D.L.R. (4th) 554, but there the relevant statute said "furtherance *of* discussion". At an earlier stage in *McCartan Turkington Breen*, Carswell L.J. expressed the view that "or" in the original English legislation may have been an error.

[147] *Khan v Ahmed* [1957] 2 Q.B. 149.

of any constituency to hear an address by their parliamentary representative. A meeting of "passive resisters" in the streets, called for the purpose of protesting against the seizure and sale of their goods for non-payment of rates, is a public meeting.[148]

On the other hand, it has been held that a meeting of a congregation for public worship at a chapel is not a "public meeting", and therefore a report of the sermon preached during the service is not privileged.[149] The meeting of a religious congregation may still not be a public meeting. While it may be true that de facto the assembly is open to anyone who cares to walk in and the incumbent may even hope that people will do that, is it possible to say that the purpose of the exercise is imparting information or views to the public at large? It is submitted that the mere fact that admission to a meeting is restricted to those members of the public who purchase a ticket does not prevent it from being a public meeting within the meaning of the Act, unless perhaps the price of the ticket is so exorbitant as to exclude the general public. However, even though the Act provides that admission may be restricted, if admission to the meeting can only be obtained by virtue of some personal qualification, then (putting aside perhaps the special case of the press conference where admission is restricted to journalists) it is not a "public meeting". Thus a meeting which only those belonging to a certain political party or religious sect can attend would probably not be deemed a "public meeting". A meeting, though in public, held to discuss a business transaction between two private individuals is not a meeting held for the discussion of a matter of public concern.[150] The meeting must have been "bona fide and lawfully held for a lawful purpose". It must be bona fide held; not for the mere purpose of defamation. Again, no privilege will attach to a report of the proceedings at an unlawful meeting, e.g. a meeting held for the purpose of vilifying any person, or discussing any seditious or other unlawful project. A meeting may clearly be unlawful if its holding would contravene the law relating to public order or even, it seems, if it is a breach of some regulation or byelaw,[151] but it is not unlawful merely because it provokes violent opposition which leads to the commission of public order offences by those attending.[152]

The report must be of "proceedings at" the public meeting. Nowadays it is common for persons attending a meeting to be given some form of "handout" relating to the matter under consideration in order to save time and to provide

---

[148] *Spearing v Wandsworth News, The Times*, July 3, 1906.

[149] *Chaloner v Lansdown* (1894) 10 T.L.R. 290. *Contra* the ruling in *Hope v Morris, The Times*, March 14, 1935.

[150] *M'Inerny v Clareman Printing Co* [1903] 2 Ir.R. 347 at 403.

[151] *Bailey v Williamson* (1873) L.R. 8 Q.B. 118 (Hyde Park regulations). But it is hardly good policy that the liability of the press should be affected by some such infringement (possibly in another European Union state) of which it may know nothing.

[152] Cf. *Beatty v Gillbanks* (1882) 9 Q.B.D. 308.

them with a reliable record. In *McCartan Turkington Breen v Times Newspapers Ltd*[153] a report based in part on the material in such a document was held to be a report of the proceedings of the meeting even though the relevant portion had not been read out at the meeting.[154]

The Defamation Act 2013, when it comes into force, will by s.7(6) extend the ambit of the privilege to fair and accurate reports of proceedings at any public meeting held *anywhere in the world*. In subs.(2) public meeting has the same meaning as under the existing provision save that "public interest" is substituted for "public concern".[155]

16.21 Companies. A fair and accurate report of proceedings at a general meeting of a UK public company[156] or a fair and accurate copy of or extract from any document circulated to members of such a company (1) by or with the authority of the board of directors of the company or (2) by the auditors or (3) by any member of the company in pursuance of a right conferred by statutory provisions[157]; or a fair and accurate copy of or extract from any document circulated to members of a United Kingdom public company which relates to the appointment, resignation, retirement or dismissal of directors of the company.[158] The same protection is conferred in relation to corresponding meetings of or documents circulated to members of a public company formed under the law of any of the Channel Islands or the Isle of Man or of another Member State.[159]

Section 7(7) of the Defamation Act 2013 will extend the ambit of the privilege to "listed" companies[160] and will also apply to *summaries* of the protected documents and reports.

16.22 Associations. A fair and accurate report of the findings or decision[161] of any of the following associations formed in the United Kingdom or another member state, or of any committee or governing body of such an association[162]:

(1) an association formed for the purpose of promoting or encouraging the exercise of or interest in any art, science, religion or learning, and empowered by its constitution to exercise control over or adjudicate

---

[153] *McCartan Turkington Breen v Times Newspapers Ltd* [2001] 2 A.C. 277 HL (NI).
[154] See fn.146, above.
[155] See para.16.5, above.
[156] Sch.1, para.13(1).
[157] Sch.1, para.13(2).
[158] Sch.1, para.13(3).
[159] Sch.1, para.13(5). The Lord Chancellor and Secretary of State for Scotland are given power to identify such corresponding matters by statutory instrument: para.17.
[160] "Listed company" is defined as having the same meaning as in Part 12 of the Corporation Tax Act 2009, s.1005" s.7(7)(b)(4).
[161] Not, therefore, the proceedings: compare the New Zealand Defamation Act 1992, Sch.1, Pt 2, para.6.
[162] Sch.1, para.14.

upon matters of interest or concern to the association, or the actions or conduct of any persons subject to such control or adjudication;

(2) an association formed for the purpose of promoting or safeguarding the interests of any trade, business, industry or profession, or of the persons carrying on or engaged in the same, and empowered by its constitution to exercise control over or adjudicate upon matters connected with the trade, business, industry or profession or the actions or conduct of those persons;

(3) an association formed for the purpose of promoting or safeguarding the interests of any game, sport or pastime to the playing or exercise of which members of the public are invited or admitted, and empowered by its constitution to exercise control over or adjudicate upon persons connected with or taking part in the game, sport or pastime;

(4) an association formed for the purpose of promoting charitable objects or other objects beneficial to the community and empowered by its constitution to exercise control over or to adjudicate on matters of interest or concern to the association, or the actions or conduct of any person subject to such control or adjudication.

The broad effect of this provision is to extend the protection of qualified privilege to fair and accurate reports of findings and decisions of tribunals of the kinds of association specified in the Schedule. For example, if the Stewards of the Jockey Club, having made an inquiry into the performance of a horse trained by A for a particular race, announce their decision:

"The Stewards satisfied themselves that a drug had been administered to the horse for the purpose of the race in question. They disqualified the horse for this race and for all future races under their rules, and suspended the licence of A, the trainer,"

a fair and accurate report of this decision will be privileged.[163] It may be, however, that it extends somewhat more widely, to reports on matters of general concern to the association.[164]

The Defamation Act 2013, s.7(8) will, when it comes into force, "internationalise" the privilege, extending its ambit to a report of findings or decisions of associations "anywhere in the world". This will have the effect of bringing a huge range of internationally based organisations and associations within the provision. By way of example, reports of findings or decisions of the International Cricket Council, the governing body of cricket and based in Dubai, will now fall within the provision, as will findings and decisions of the International Chamber of Commerce.[165]

---

[163] Compare the contrary decision of Horridge J. and the Court of Appeal at common law in *Chapman v Ellesmere* [1932] 2 K.B. 431 CA.

[164] It is not necessary that the finding or decision should relate to a person who is a member of the association or subject to its rules: cf. para.8 of the 1952 Act. Quaere, however, whether "finding or decision" implies some sort of adjudication on an issue.

[165] Which describes itself as the World Business Organisation. Its headquarters are located in Paris.

16.23 Proceedings of a scientific or academic conference. Section 7(9) of the Defamation Act 2013, when it comes into force, will insert a new provision into Sch.1 of the 1996 Act which will protect by qualified privilege a fair and accurate report of a scientific or academic conference held anywhere in the world, or a copy of, extract from, or summary of matter published by such a conference.[166] As the *Explanatory Notes*[167] to the Act suggest, Pt II qualified privilege may already apply to academic and scientific conferences (either where they fall within the description of a public meeting in para.12, or where findings or decisions are published by a scientific or academic association: para.14). The amendments made by s.7(9) of the 2013 Act are intended to ensure that there is not a gap in coverage. "Scientific" and "academic" are not defined in the Act but the intention is clearly to spread the net of coverage widely, encompassing not just academic conferences the subject matter of which is pure science, but also conferences in the social sciences, humanities and arts. Whether any quality threshold is implied is more difficult. Would, for example, a conference on a subject that has been conclusively rejected by the mainstream academic community fall within the provision? The view of the Joint Committee on the Draft Defamation Bill was that inclusion of a provision protecting such conferences was welcome "provided the conference is reputable".[168] Though consideration was given to including a peer-review requirement for conferences, no such provision was eventually incorporated and it is therefore difficult to conclude that any quality threshold needs to be met. The provision in s.7(9) is one of two provisions that will be introduced by the Defamation Act 2013 aimed specifically at protecting scientific and academic speech. The second provides qualified privilege to a publication of a statement in a peer-reviewed scientific or academic journal.[169] The reasons for the introduction of these two new privileges and the conditions for the application of the privilege for statements in a peer-reviewed scientific or academic journal are considered below (at para.6.25).

16.24 Designated bodies, etc. The Lord Chancellor and Secretary of State for Scotland have power to designate, by statutory instrument, bodies, officers or persons, fair and accurate reports[170] of whose adjudications, reports, statements or notices will be protected by the Sch.1 privilege.[171] This provision enables the law to be more effectively kept in line with changing circumstances.[172]

---

[166] Para.14A Defamation Act 2013 as inserted by s.7(9) of the Defamation Act 2013.
[167] At para.58.
[168] HL Paper 203, HC 930–I at [48].
[169] S.6 Defamation Act 2013.
[170] Copies or extracts from adjudications, etc. are treated in the same way.
[171] Sch.1, para.15.
[172] Even by 1975 the Faulks Committee found that the Schedule to the 1952 Act had become seriously out of date: Cmnd.5909 (1975).

Para.15 will, when the Defamation Act 2013 comes into force, provide qualified privilege to a fair and accurate report or summary of, copy of or extract from, any adjudication, report, statement or notice issued by a body, officer or other person designated for the purpose of this paragraph by order of the Lord Chancellor.

Section 3: Peer Reviewed Statements in Scientific or Academic Journals

Peer reviewed statements. Calls for greater protection for scientific and **16.25** academic speech are not new and indeed in 1975 the Faulks Committee proposed a new statutory qualified privilege for articles of a technical or scientific nature in technical and scientific journals.[173] In order to prevent journals pretending to be technical or scientific from enjoying this privilege, the Committee further recommended that there should be an appropriate authority charged with the responsibility of approving and registering journals. This proposal was never enacted. Renewed calls for special protection featured prominently in the period leading up to the passing of the Defamation Act 2013. Much play was made of scientific causes célèbres such as *BCA v Singh*,[174] *Bowker v RSPB*,[175] *Rath v Guardian Newspapers*,[176] *El Naschie v MacMillan Publishers Ltd*[177] and *NMT v Wilmshurst*.[178] That these claims all ultimately failed, albeit that some of the scientists faced large bills of unrecoverable costs, and albeit that there is no convincing reason for treating academic and scientific speech any more favourably than other types of public interest speech, did not ultimately prevent Parliament from legislating on the matter.[179] Section 6 of the Defamation Act 2013 Act, which is not yet in force, provides qualified privilege for peer-reviewed statements[180] published in scientific or academic journals (whether published in electronic form or otherwise[181]). Under this provision, a publication will be privileged, unless shown

---

[173] *Report of the Committee on Defamation*, Cmnd.5909, para.232.
[174] [2010] EWCA Civ 350 CA; [2011] 1 W.L.R. 133.
[175] [2011] EWHC 737 (QB).
[176] [2008] EWHC 398 (QB).
[177] [2012] EWHC 1809 (QB).
[178] (*http://www.pressgazette.co.uk/node/47627*).
[179] No such argument is made by the leading theoreticians on academic freedom (see Barendt, *Academic Freedom and the Law, a comparative study* (Oxford: Hart Publishing, 2010), and Finkin and Post, *For the Common Good: Principles of American Academic Freedom* (Yale University Press, 2009).
[180] The protection of the privilege also extends to the publication in the same journal (though not necessarily the same volume or edition) of any assessment of the statement's scientific or academic merit if—(a) the assessment was written by one or more of the persons who carried out the independent review of the statement; and (b) the assessment was written in the course of that review: s.6(4).
[181] Defamation Act 2013, s.6(1).

to have been made with malice,[182] where two conditions are met: first, that the statement relates to "a scientific or academic matter"[183] and, secondly, that before the statement was published in the journal "an independent review of the statement's scientific or academic merit was carried out by—(a) the editor of the journal, and (b) one or more persons with expertise in the scientific or academic matter concerned".[184]

Section 6 will undoubtedly provide greater protection to scientific and academic speech than is currently the case, at least where the form of the speech is the conventional means of academic discourse. However, the scope of the privilege is a relatively narrow one. It would not have assisted any of the defendants in the recent scientific causes célèbres[185] and only applies to peer-reviewed publications that meet the stringent conditions set out in subss.(2) and (3). It is certainly not a general protection for academic speech. Thus, when academics speak in the media or communicate their research through other less formal means than a peer-reviewed journal, they will have to rely on the general defences available.

16.26 **Conditions for application of the privilege.** For the privilege to attach, the statement must have been published in a "scientific *or* academic journal"[186] and it must relate to a "scientific *or* academic matter".[187] Neither "scientific" nor "academic" is defined in the Act but the intention to spread the net widely seems clear. Thus, the Explanatory Notes state that the term "scientific journal" would include "medical and engineering journals"[188] and the use of the word "academic" is sufficiently broad to include journals on subjects in the arts, humanities and social sciences. However, the requirement that the statement relate to a "scientific or academic" matter is unlikely to be treated as encompassing a statement that impugns the bona fides or competence of the claimant.[189]

---

[182] S.6(6).

[183] S.6(2).

[184] S.6(3).

[185] Thus, in *Bowker v RSPB* [2011] EWHC 737 (QB), the defendant was sued in respect of emails critical of a paper written by the claimant. In *BCA v Singh* [2010] EWCA Civ 350 CA; [2011] 1 W.L.R. 133 and *Rath v Guardian Newspapers* [2008] EWHC 398 (QB) the defendants were sued in respect of newspaper articles. In *El Naschie v MacMillan Publishers Ltd* [2012] EWHC 1809 (QB), the statements complained of were published in an academic journal but in the editorial section, and the case turned on the integrity of editorial self-publication and peer review, not a scientific or academic matter. Finally, in *GE v Thomsen* (*http://www.propublica.org/ documents/item/ge-v-thomsen-a-british-libel-case*) the claim was brought in respect of comments made at an academic conference and in *NMT v Wilmshurst* (*http://www.pressgazette.co.uk/node/ 47627*), the defendant was sued, inter alia, in respect of statements he made in a radio programme.

[186] S.6(1).

[187] S.6(2).

[188] Para.44.

[189] In *El Naschie v MacMillan Publishers* [2012] EWHC 1809 (QB), Sharp J. noted (at [10]) that the case concerned the integrity of editorial self-publication and peer review in scientific peer-reviewed journals by reference to the editorial practices of the Claimant. It was not a

The publication must be in a journal (which can be online) but the privilege cannot attach to a statement in a book, even if peer reviewed. Where the publication of the statement or assessment is privileged under the section then, by virtue of s.6(5), "the publication of a fair and accurate copy of, extract from or summary of the statement or assessment is also privileged". A newspaper or other report summarising, or containing an extract from, the statement would consequently be privileged. For the privilege to attach, there will also have to have been an "independent"[190] review of the *statement's* scientific or academic merit carried out before publication by the editor of the journal *and* one or more other persons with expertise in the scientific or academic matter concerned.[191] Presumably this will require proof by the defendant that the *statement* complained of (and not just the article) was the subject of a review by at least two people, one of whom must have been the editor, with the necessary academic expertise. This may not be easy to establish. So far as expertise is concerned, will a person who for example has written on the law of tort but not defamation be possessed of the necessary expertise? In an appropriate case, expert evidence could presumably be led challenging the expertise of the reviewer.

A publication will not be privileged under this section if it is shown to have been made with malice. Lord McNally stated in the House of Lords that "a defendant would forfeit the defence if they could be shown to have acted with ill will or improper motive."[192] In other words, malice here refers to the form established by the common law as defeating qualified privilege.[193]

SECTION 4. MISCELLANEOUS STATUTES CONFERRING QUALIFIED PRIVILEGE

Parliamentary Papers Act 1840. Under s.3 of this Act the publication in   **16.27** print[194] of an extract from, or abstract of,[195] any parliamentary report, paper, vote, or proceedings, published by or under the authority of either House of

---

"scientific matter" that could and should have been capable of being addressed (if not resolved) within the scientific community by ordinary scientific discourse and debate.

[190] What conditions must be satisfied for the review to be independent are not defined. A journal would be well-advised to develop a peer-review policy that articulates the basis on which they conduct reviews and in particular how they avoid potential conflicts of interest.

[191] Defamation Act 2013, s.6(3).

[192] January 15, 2013, GC239.

[193] See Ch.17.

[194] The Defamation Act 1952, s.9(1) extended the protection conferred by s.3 of the Parliamentary Papers Act 1840 to extracts from and abstracts of parliamentary papers broadcast by means of wireless telegraphy. The Act would not apply to publication of extracts, etc. on the internet. However, such publication by HMSO would fall under s.1 of the Act: see para.13.34, above.

[195] The statute does not extend to a defamatory headline: *Mangena v Edward Lloyd* (1908) 98 L.T. 640; (1909) 99 L.T. 824.

Parliament[196] is privileged, provided the defendant prove that he published such extract or abstract bona fide and without malice. The burden of proof on the issue of malice under this is the reverse of that in all other cases of qualified privilege, whether at common law or under statute. However, as, under the Defamation Act 1996 there is qualified privilege for a fair and accurate copy of or extract from matter published by or on the authority of a legislature anywhere in the world,[197] s.3 would seem to be largely obsolete.[198]

16.28 Other statutory provisions. A number of statutory provisions grant qualified privilege to reports, determinations or the issue of material to which the public have a right of access. These include[199]:

Legal Profession and Legal Aid (Scotland) Act 2007 (asp), s.42.
Scottish Commission for Human Rights Act 2007 (asp), s.17.
Scottish Parliamentary Standards Commissioner Act 2002, s.17.
Scottish Parliamentary Commissions and Commissioners etc. Act 2010 asp, 11, s.5.
Education and Inspection Act 2006, s.151.
Education Act 2005, s.29.
Children Act 2004, Sch.1.
Childcare Act 2006, s.50.
Commissioner for Children and Young People (Scotland) Act 2003, s.15.
Protection of Children (Scotland) Act, s.9.
Pensions Act 2004, s.89, 205.
Mental Health (Care and Treatment) (Scotland) Act 2003 (asp), s.20.
Education Act 2002, s.163 as substituted by the Education Act 2005.
Scottish Parliamentary Standards Commissioner Act 2002 (asp), s.17.
Freedom of Information (Scotland) Act 2002 (asp), s.67.
Freedom of Information Act 2000, s.79.
Learning and Skills Act 2000, s.88.
Broadcasting Act 1996, s.121.
School Inspections Act 1996, s.42A as inserted by s.134, School Standards and Framework Act 1998.
Law Reform (Miscellaneous Provisions) (Scotland) Act 1990, s.34A, as inserted by the Scottish Legal Services Ombudsman and Commissioner for Local Administration in Scotland Act 1997.

---

[196] Reports of debates and proceedings are privileged at common law: see para.15.36, above.

[197] See para.16.15, above.

[198] However, an "abstract" is not covered by the 1996 Act. The 1840 Act covers matter emanating from either House. It could be argued that the "legislature" in the 1996 Act covers only matter issued by *both* Houses. Indeed, technically, the legislature comprises the sovereign as well. It is submitted that in this context "legislature" must include "part of a legislature" if only because otherwise privilege for copies of matter emanating from foreign legislatures would turn on whether they were bi-cameral or uni-cameral.

[199] No claim is made that this list is comprehensive.

Legal Profession and Legal Aid (Scotland) Act 2003, s.20.

Northern Ireland Act 2006, Sch.1.

Local Government Act 1972, s.100H, inserted by Local Government (Access to Information) Act 1985.[200]

Public Bodies (Admission to Meetings) Act 1960, s.1.

Local Authorities (Executive Arrangements) (Decisions, Documents and Meetings) (Wales) Regulations 2001.[201]

Local Authorities (Executive Arrangements) (Access to Information) (England) Regulations 2000.[202]

Assembly Members (Independent Financial Review and Standards) Act (Northern Ireland) 2011, s.32.

Pensions Act 2004, ss..89, 205.

Pensions (Northern Ireland) Order 2005, arts 84, 187.

Religious Education (Meetings of Local Conferences and Councils) Regulations 1994.[203]

Although not conferring qualified privilege as such, s.29 of the Arbitration Act 1996 provides that an arbitrator is not liable for anything done or omitted in the discharge or purported discharge of his functions as arbitrator unless the act or omission is shown to have been in bad faith; and s.74 confers a similar immunity on an arbitral institution or person appointing or nominating an arbitrator.

---

[200] For a detailed analysis of this, see *Lillie v Newcastle CC* [2002] EWHC 1600 (QB). The Law Commission examined and reported on the problems arising from ad hoc local authority inquiries in *In the Public Interest: Publication of Local Authority Inquiry Reports*, Law Com. no.289 (2004)). The draft Bill attached to the Law Commission's Report would create a new form of statutory privilege for the publication by the authority of the inquiry report. In summary, the privilege would apply where (a) before publication the authority took all reasonable steps to satisfy themselves that the inquiry was conducted fairly, or (b) even though they did not, the inquiry was conducted fairly (cl.12(1)). An inquiry is not to be treated as conducted fairly unless the person holding it bases his conclusions upon findings of fact, gives every person criticised in the report the opportunity to respond and fairly represents that response in the report (cl.12(4)). There are comparable provisions for publication of part of the report or a summary. Furthermore, a publication is not privileged if proved to be made with malice (cl.12(7)). The Bill would not limit or restrict a privilege which exists apart from it (e.g. at common law-see *Lillie v Newcastle City Council* [2002] EWHC 1600 (QB)) but if the report is published to the public and the conditions in cl.12(1) are not satisfied, the authority would also lose the protection of the statutory qualified privilege under s.100H(5) of the Local Government Act 1972 or regulations made under s.22 of the Local Government Act 2000.

See also Law Commission Consultation Paper No.163, *Publication of Local Authority Reports* (2002).

[201] SI 2001/2290.

[202] SI 2000/3272.

[203] SI 1994/1304.

MALICE AND QUALIFIED PRIVILEGE

SECTION 1. GENERAL

Malice and qualified privilege. This chapter deals with the loss of the **17.1** defence of qualified privilege by reason of the defendant's malice. Honest comment is also defeated by proof of "malice" (if the term should be used at all in that context) but it is now clear that this is narrower than in the context of qualified privilege and it has been dealt with in Ch.12.[1]

"Presumed" and "express" malice. Proof of malice defeats the defence **17.2** of qualified privilege,[2] though the concept has no relevance to the "media"

---

[1] Para.12.36, above.

[2] The common law is losing its unity on this point, at least in relation to terminology. Under the Defamation Act 1992 (N.Z.) common law malice is abolished. In the case of qualified privilege the defence fails if the plaintiff proves that the defendant was predominantly motivated by ill-will towards him or otherwise took improper advantage of the occasion of publication (s.19). In practical terms the latter is much the same as common law malice. In the Australian uniform legislation privilege for publication of public documents and fair reports of proceedings of public concern is defeated only if it is proved that the defamatory matter was not published honestly for the information of the public or the advancement of education: see, e.g. ss.28 and 29 of the Defamation Act 2005 (NSW). The "defence of qualified privilege for provision of certain information" (s.30 of the NSW Act) (which is broadly equivalent to *Reynolds* privilege) requires that the defendant have behaved reasonably but is defeated by proof of malice. There are no provisions in the legislation governing traditional "private communication" privilege but this continues to exist at common law: see ss.6 and 31(5)(b). So far as Ireland is concerned, the defence of qualified privilege fails, by virtue of s.19 of the Defamation Act 2009 Act when the defendant is found to have acted with malice:

"19 (1) In a defamation action, the defence of qualified privilege shall fail if, in relation to the publication of the statement in respect of which the action was brought, the plaintiff proves that the defendant acted with malice.

(2) The defence of qualified privilege shall not fail by reason only of the publication of the statement concerned to a person other than an interested person if it is proved that the statement was published to the person because the publisher mistook him or her for an interested person.

(3) Where a defamation action is brought against more than one defendant, the failure of the defence of qualified privilege in relation to one of the defendants by virtue of the application of *subsection (1)* shall not cause the failure of the defence in relation to another of the defendants unless that other defendant was vicariously liable for such acts or omissions of the first-mentioned defendant as gave rise to the cause of action concerned.

(4) [Repeal of s.11(4) of the Civil Liability Act 1961].

(5) In this section 'interested person' means, in relation to a statement, a person who, under

privilege created by *Reynolds v Times Newspapers Ltd*,[3] where the emphasis is on reasonable or responsible conduct.[4] This section is concerned with the conventional, pre-*Reynolds* categories of qualified privilege. The traditional approach was put very clearly by Bankes J. in *Smith v Streatfeild*.[5]

"The principle upon which the law of qualified privilege rests is this: that where words are published which are both false and defamatory the law presumes malice on the part of the person who publishes them. The publication may, however, take place under circumstances which create a qualified privilege. If so, the presumption of malice is rebutted by the privilege, and . . . the plaintiff has to prove express malice on the part of the person responsible for the publication. The effect of proving express malice is sometimes spoken of as defeating the privilege . . . Although the occasion remains a privileged occasion, the privilege afforded by the occasion ceases to be an effective weapon of defence . . . Qualified privilege is a defence only to the extent that it throws on the plaintiff the burden of proving express malice. Directly the plaintiff succeeds in doing this the defence vanishes, and it becomes immaterial that the publication was on a privileged occasion."[6]

However, the "presumption of malice" is no longer reflected in pleading[7] and it is submitted that we might with advantage now drop the concept of presumed malice arising from a defamatory publication and simply say that the defendant is liable for the publication of defamatory matter without just

---

section 18(2)(a), had a duty or interest in receiving the information contained in the statement."

In the US the "actual malice" required in cases of defamation of public figures is not the same as common law malice (see para.15.27, above). Where common law qualified privilege is in issue the earlier cases used the English terminology. However, since the first Restatement of Torts (1938) the tendency has been instead to speak of the defendant "abusing" the privilege or the occasion, though the core idea of improper purpose appears to be the same: see Eldredge, *Law of Defamation* (1978), para.93. The position in the Roman-Dutch law of South Africa is rather different. The starting point is that the plaintiff must show an *animus injuriandi* which may be presumed from the making of a defamatory statement. The presumption of *animus injuriandi* may be rebutted by a good reason for the making of the statement, what in England would be called qualified privilege. But although modern cases at the highest level continue to speak of "qualified privilege" (indeed to the extent of using the English terminology of duty and interest, e.g. *Naylor v Jansen* [2005] ZASCA 58; *National Education etc. Union v Tsatsi* [2005] ZASCA 125) it is important to remember that the process of rebuttal of the *animus injurandi* is not confined to qualified privilege in the English sense. See *Joubert v Venter*, 1985 (1) S.A. 654 AD.

[3] Para.17.21, above.

[4] Para.15.8, below.

[5] [1913] 3 K.B. 764 at 769–770. The overruling of the case by *Egger v Chelmsford* [1965] 1 Q.B. 248 CA, does not affect this proposition.

[6] See also Parke B. in *Wright v Woodgate* (1835) 2 C.M. & R. 573 at 577:

"The proper meaning of a privileged communication is only this: that the occasion on which the communication was made rebuts the inference [of malice] prima facie arising from a statement prejudicial to the character of the plaintiff, and puts it upon him to prove that there was malice in fact-that the defendant was actuated by motives of personal spite or ill will, independent of the occasion on which the communication was made."

Cited and approved in *Somerville v Hawkins* (1851) 10 C.B. 583; *Laughton v Bishop of Sodor and Man* (1872) L.R. 4 P.C. 495; *Jenoure v Delmege* [1891] A.C. 73; *Adam v Ward* [1917] A.C. 309 HL; *Harris v Arnott (No.2)* (1890) 26 L.R.Ir. at 75.

[7] Para.26.10, below.

cause or excuse.[8] One just cause or excuse is that the words were published on a privileged occasion. This, however, is not an absolute defence and the function of malice is to allow the claimant to defeat it by proving that.

Malice is a question for the jury, if there is one, provided there is evidence of it to be left to them.[9]

The law reviewed in Horrocks v Lowe. The speech of Lord Diplock in   **17.3**
Horrocks v Lowe,[10] with which three other of the Law Lords agreed,[11] restated the law in the context of qualified privilege in what were clearly intended to be authoritative terms. The following is offered as a summary[12]:

(1) Improper motives
   (a) There is some special reason of public policy for giving immunity in all cases of qualified privilege. If the maker of a statement uses the occasion for some other reason he loses the protection of the privilege.[13]
   (b) The defendant is entitled to be protected unless some dominant improper motive on his part is proved.[14]
   (c) (i) The usual motive relied on is that of injuring the claimant, but there may be others.[15]

---

[8] However, Lord Hope holds to more traditional patterns of expression in *Reynolds v Times Newspapers Ltd* [2001] 2 A.C. 127 HL at 229:
   "The foundation of an action of defamation is malice. If words are used which are defamatory and untrue the law implies malice. That presumption is rebutted if the occasion when the words were used is privileged. The privilege destroys the presumption. But it remains open to the claimant to prove that there was malice in fact."
See also *Roberts v Bass* [2002] HCA 57, 212 C.L.R. 1 at [75]; *Cush v Dillon; Boland v Dillon* [2011] HCA 30 at [14]; *Lyons v Chief Constable of Strathclyde Police* [2012] CSOH 46; 2012 Rep. L.R. 108 at [29]. There was, however, a time when the presumption of malice expressed a fundamental requirement of "fault": para.1.8 above.
[9] See para.36.21, below. Allegations of malice "should not be made formulaically by way of bare assertion or used as a tactical weapon to try to bludgeon people into submission or compromise": *Dorset Flint & Stone Blocks Ltd v Moir* [2004] EWHC 2173 (QB) at [49]. The context is honest comment but the proposition must be equally applicable to qualified privilege. Alleging malice is the equivalent of alleging dishonesty: *Bray v Deutsche Bank AG* [2008] EWHC 1263 (QB) at [35]; *Henderson v London Borough of Hackney* [2010] EWHC 1651 (QB) at [35]; *Thompson v James* [2013] EWHC 585 (QB) at [16]; *Ibrahim v Swansea University* [2012] EWHC 290 (QB) at [19].
[10] [1975] A.C. 135 HL.
[11] Lords Wilberforce, Hodson and Kilbrandon, none of whom delivered a separate speech. Viscount Dilhorne was also for dismissing the appeal.
[12] The speech is clearly intended to be so closely connected in its argument that it would be difficult to say of any part of it that it is obiter dictum. The actual ratio decidendi seems to be contained in Lord Diplock's speech at 151 C-D, 152 B-G: where conduct extraneous to the privileged occasion is not relied on, and the only evidence of improper motive is the content of the defamatory matter or the steps taken by the defendant to verify its accuracy, the claimant, in order to succeed, must, with one exception not here relevant, show that the defendant did not honestly believe the truth of what he said or was indifferent to its truth or falsity.
[13] [1975] A.C. 135 HL at 149.
[14] Ibid.
[15] Ibid.

     (ii) Knowledge that a statement will injure the claimant does not destroy the privilege if the defendant was using the occasion for its proper purpose.[16]

(2) Absence of honest belief

   (a) If it can be proved that the defendant did not believe that what he published was true, that is generally conclusive evidence of express malice, "for no sense of duty or desire to protect his own legitimate interests can justify a man in telling deliberate and injurious false-hoods about another".[17] The burden of proof, at least where conduct extraneous to the privileged occasion is not relied on, is not a light one.[18]

   (b) If the defendant publishes untrue matter recklessly, without considering or caring whether it be true or not, he is treated as if he knew it to be false, but carelessness, impulsiveness or irrationality in arriving at a belief is not to be equated with indifference to truth.[19]

   (c) There are exceptional cases where a person may be under a duty to pass on defamatory reports made by another even if he believes them to be untrue: he is not then malicious.[20]

(3) Positive belief

   (a) Positive belief in the truth of what is published will usually protect the defendant unless he can be proved to have misused the occasion. Judges and juries should be slow to draw the inference that he has misused the occasion, and the defendant's desire to use the occasion for its proper purpose must be shown to have played no significant part in his motives if malice is to be found.[21]

   (b) Where the defendant believes in the truth of what he has published and conduct extraneous to the privileged occasion is not relied on, the claimant can only succeed if he shows that the publication contains irrelevant matter, and that it can be inferred that the defendant did not believe it to be true or realised that it was irrelevant, and brought it in for some improper motive. Judges and juries should be slow to draw this inference, too.[22]

17.4 Malice as "improper" or "indirect" motive. Because proof that the defendant knew that what he said was untrue or was indifferent to its truth produces the clearest case of malice,[23] there is a tendency in some modern

---

[16] Ibid. at 149–150.
[17] Ibid.
[18] Ibid. at 151.
[19] [1975] A.C. 135 HL at 150.
[20] Ibid. at 151.
[21] Ibid.
[22] Ibid.
[23] Putting aside those cases where there is a duty to publish an untruth.

cases to say that malice is established *either* by showing knowledge of or recklessness as to falsity *or* the presence of an improper motive,[24] and even to question the continuing validity of "improper motive" malice[25]; but in the High Court of Australia it has been convincingly argued that this is neither historically correct nor consistent with *Horrocks v Lowe*.[26] On this view, malice arises only where the defendant acts from an improper motive: knowledge of or recklessness as to falsity is not a separate head of malice, it is simply a way of establishing that the defendant was acting from an improper motive and relieves the claimant from the burden of showing what that was.[27] The claimant will succeed in proving the existence of express malice if he can show that the defendant was not using the occasion honestly for the purpose for which the law gives protection, but was actuated by some indirect motive not connected with the privilege.[28]

There are certainly many statements supporting this "classical" view.

---

[24] *Loutchansky v Times Newspapers Ltd (Nos 2 5)* [2001] EWCA Civ 1805; [2002] Q.B. 783 at [33]; *Lillie v Newcastle CC* [2002] EWHC 1600 (QB) at [1090]; *Barbaro v Amalgamated Television Services Pty Ltd* (1985) 1 N.S.W.L.R. 30 at 51; *Hanrahan v Ainsworth* (1990) 22 N.S.W.L.R. 73 at 102–103.

[25] "An endangered species": Eady J. in *Lillie v Newcastle CC* at [1093]. This form of malice has disappeared in the context of honest comment: para.12.25, above.

[26] *Roberts v Bass* [2002] HCA 57; 212 C.L.R. 1. *Roberts v Bass* was summarised by the NSWCA in *Gross v Weston* [2007] NSWCA 1 at [52] as follows:

"(1) Except where the defendant was under a legal duty to publish the matter complained of, the defendant's knowledge that it was false is ordinarily conclusive evidence that the publication was actuated by an improper motive.

(2) Recklessness in the publication of the matter complained of does not establish knowledge of its falsity unless it amounts to wilful blindness on the part of the defendant which the law equates with knowledge.

(3) Recklessness—when present with other evidence—may nevertheless be relevant to whether the defendant had an improper motive which actuated the publication.

(4) If a plaintiff's case rises no higher than evidence that the defendant did not have a positive belief in the truth of what he published, there is no evidence that its publication was actuated by an improper motive.

(5) The absence of a positive belief in the truth of what was published may nevertheless be relevant—with other evidence—to whether the defendant's improper motive actuated the publication, but it will not establish that fact by itself.

(6) Where the plaintiff relies on the defendant's knowledge of the falsity of the matter complained of to establish an improper motive, it is unnecessary to identify that improper motive, as there can be no proper motive in those circumstances unless the defendant has a duty to publish the matter complained of."

In the NSWCA's view wilful blindness should be equated with knowledge of falsity for the purposes of proposition (6): at [54]. See also *Conservation Council of South Australia Inc. v Chapman* [2003] SASC 398; 87 S.A.S.R. 62 at [301].

[27] *Roberts v Bass* at [77]–[78], per Gaudron, McHugh and Gummow JJ. See also Gleeson C.J. at [13]:

"It would be inconsistent with the purpose of the privilege to use the occasion, not for the honest expression of views, but for the publication of defamatory matter, knowing it to be false, or not caring whether it was true or false".

Kirby J.'s "reservation" at [185] seems to relate not to this issue but to whether, outside the electoral context, absence of belief in truth might be equated with knowledge of untruth: see at [195].

[28] It is not the existence of ill will, but that the publication complained of was actuated by ill will, that is relevant to express malice: *Mowlds v Fergusson* (1939) 40 S.R. (N.S.W.) 311

"The defendant is only entitled to the protection of the privilege if he uses the occasion in accordance with the purpose for which the occasion arose. He is not entitled to the protection of the privilege if he uses the occasion for some indirect or wrong motive."[29]

" . . . the privilege is not absolute but qualified. It is lost if the occasion which gives rise to it is misused. For in all cases of qualified privilege there is some special reason of public policy why the law accords immunity from suit-the existence of some public or private duty, whether legal or moral, on the part of the maker of the defamatory statement which justifies his communicating it or of some interest of his own which he is entitled to protect by doing so. If he uses the occasion for some other reason he loses the protection of the privilege. So the motive with which the defendant on a privileged occasion made a statement defamatory of the plaintiff becomes crucial."[30]

"It is obviously right that a person should not be allowed to abuse a privileged occasion by making it the opportunity of indulging in some private spite, or for using the occasion for some indirect purpose or under the influence of some indirect motive."[31]

"Malice means making use of the occasion for some indirect purpose."[32]

"If the occasion is privileged it is so for some reason, and the defendant is only entitled to the protection of the privilege if he uses the occasion for that reason. He is not entitled to the protection if he uses the occasion not for the reason which makes the occasion privileged, but for an indirect or wrong motive;"[33]

"an improper motive;"[34]

"some motive other than that which alone would excuse him;"[35]

"some indirect motive not connected with the privilege;"[36]

"some other dominant and improper motive."[37]

"To entitle a person to the protection of qualified privilege, he has to have a positive belief in the truth of what he published. Such a belief is presumed unless the contrary is proved, and so the burden of establishing malice lies on the person who asserts it, in this instance the claimant. What the claimant has to establish is a dominant and improper motive on the part of the defendant comprising a desire to injure the claimant. This dominant motive can only be inferred from what the defendant did or said or knew. If it is proved that he did not believe that what he published was true, that is generally conclusive evidence of express malice."[38]

NSWCA at 327–329; *Roberts v Bass* [2002] HCA 57; 212 C.L.R. 1 at [76]; *Hoare v Jessop* [1965] E.A. 218 at 222.

[29] Per Lopes L.J. in *Royal Aquarium v Parkinson* [1892] 1 Q.B. 431 CA at 454.

[30] Per Lord Diplock in *Horrocks v Lowe* [1975] A.C 135 at 149. See also *Angel v Bushell* [1968] 1 Q.B. 813 at 830–831.

[31] Per Bankes L.J. in *Gerhold v Baker* [1918] W.N. 368 CA at 369.

[32] Per Lord Herschell in *Browne v Dunn* (1893) 6 R. 67 at 72.

[33] Per Brett L.J. in *Clark v Molyneux* (1877) 3 Q.B.D. 237 CA at 246. And see *Groom v Crocker* [1939] 1 K.B. 194 at 206–207, 226.

[34] Per Cotton L.J., *Clark v Molyneux*, above, at 249.

[35] Per Bramwell L.J., ibid. at 245; *Rose v Brewer* (1933) C.P.D. 49 (where the improper motive for a charge of theft was to exert pressure on a third person to replace or pay for an article alleged to have been stolen by the plaintiff).

[36] Per Lopes L.J. in *Nevill v Fine Arts* [1895] 2 Q.B. 156 CA at 171; cf. *Turner v MGM* [1950] 1 All E.R. 449 HL; *Beach v Freeson* [1972] 1 Q.B. 14 at 26.

[37] *Horrocks v Lowe* [1975] A.C. 135 HL at 149.

[38] *Alexander v Arts Council of Wales* [2001] EWCA Civ 514; [2001] 1 W.L.R. 1840 at [34], per May L.J. After the Australian decision in *Roberts v Bass*, Gray J. in *Rackham v Sandy* [2005] EWHC 482 (QB) said:

"[18] . . . [Counsel for the defendants] submits that malice arises if and only if it can be shown

Furthermore, the modern development whereby it has come to be recognised that the defence of honest comment is defeated only by proof that the defendant was not expressing his true opinion, proceeds upon the assumption that malice in the context of qualified privilege is wider and includes a statement made with an improper motive.[39]

Matter believed to be true but purpose to injure. There is no doubt 			**17.5** that Lord Diplock's speech in *Horrocks v Lowe* contemplates that even if the defendant firmly believes his statement to be true[40] he is guilty of malice if his sole or dominant purpose[41] is to harm the claimant.[42]

---

that the defendant was actuated by some improper motive. Knowledge of falsity is not a separate head of malice, still less is recklessness, it is simply a way of establishing an improper motive.

[19] I am of course bound by the decision in *Horrocks v Lowe*. But I respectfully agree with Gleeson CJ [in *Roberts v Bass*] that there is nothing in Lord Diplock's speech in that case which supports treating the defendant's knowledge of falsity or lack of belief in truth as being probative, of itself and without more, of malice. It may be said that the point is of limited practical significance since knowledge of falsity will almost always establish the existence of an improper motive. Nevertheless I accept that the question which I have ultimately to decide in this case is whether or not each of the Defendants was actuated by the improper motive of improperly removing [the claimant] from the Board of WRG or saving his own job with the company or preventing Candover from taking over WRG."

[39] *Tse Wai Chun v Cheng* [2000] HKCFA 86; [2001] E.M.L.R 31, para.12.36, above.

[40] For reckless indifference, see para.17.16, below.

[41] Para.17.5, below. In *Qadir v Associated Newspapers Ltd* [2012] EWHC 2606 (QB); [2013] E.M.L.R. 15I Tugendhat J. stated at [191]:

"[A plea] that [the defendant] has misused the occasion is, so far as it goes, a good plea of malice. It is not necessary to plead in addition that [the defendant] had an improper motive. That is implicit in the plea of misuse of the occasion. But I accept that misuse, or abuse, in this context require proof that the purpose, reason or motive of the defendant must be his dominant one before malice can be proved."

[42] Whether malice can be established by an intention to injure someone other than the claimant is not entirely settled. In *Cruddas v Calvert* [2013] EWHC 1096 (QB) Nicol J. refused to allow a pleaded malice case in libel and malicious falsehood to include an intention to injure a third party, namely the Prime Minister. The judge noted that in several cases the courts had assumed that the intention must be to injure the claimant (see, e.g. *Horrocks v Lowe* [1975] A.C. 135 HL at 149; *Wilts United Dairies v Thomas Robinson Sons and Co. Ltd* [1957] R.P.C. 220 at 234, 237; *Halsey v Brotherhood* (1881) 19 Ch. D. 386 at 388). However, in none of these cases was the issue confronted directly. Nor was there any other authority on the question. The judge was not, however, persuaded by the analogy drawn by counsel to the transferred malice principle in criminal law (that a defendant will be guilty of intentional injury if his intention was to injure X and, inadvertently, he injures Y):

"The purpose of the criminal law is to protect the public interest. In that context it makes obvious sense for the law to be indifferent whether the intention was to injure the actual victim or someone else. The purpose of tort law is different: it is to provide redress to individual claimants for individual wrongs to them. In any case, the limits of the tort of trespass are different to those of malicious falsehood. Malice is an essential ingredient of the latter but not of the former. Furthermore, the other elements of the tort of malicious falsehood must clearly relate to the Claimant. Thus the words published must concern *the Claimant*, or his property or his economic interests and the publication must have caused *him* pecuniary loss (or in circumstances covered by Defamation Act 1952, s.3(1) be calculated to cause *him* pecuniary loss). I consider that it would be anomalous if the third element, malice, could be sufficiently established by an intention to injure, not the Claimant, but some third person. Thus, in my judgment, what the Claimant is here seeking would be a novel extension of the law and that is not a step which I would be justified in taking. I consider also that it would be particularly

"Even a positive belief in the truth of what is published on a privileged occasion
—which is presumed unless the contrary is proved—may not be sufficient to
negative express malice if it can be proved that the defendant misused the occasion
for some purpose other than that for which the privilege is accorded by the law. The
commonest case is where the dominant motive which actuates the defendant is not
a desire to perform the relevant duty or to protect the relevant interest, but to give
vent to his personal spite or ill will towards the person he defames. If this be proved,
then even positive belief in the truth of what is published will not enable the defamer
to avail himself of the protection of the privilege to which he would otherwise have
been entitled."[43]

Another possible case, in his Lordship's view, was where it could be shown
that the defendant's dominant motive may have been to obtain some private
advantage unconnected with the duty or the interest on which the privilege
was based.[44] All this is consistent with the view that the essence of malice *is*
an improper purpose, knowledge of falsity being merely a means of proving
the impropriety.[45] However, in a modern case a judge has said that he has
never heard of a finding of mere "purpose" malice, though it was "there in the
jurisprudence as a possible outcome".[46] An old example is *Stevens v Sampson*,[47] where the solicitor for a party to an action sent a fair and accurate report
of the proceedings to a newspaper with, the jury found, "a certain amount of
malice" against the plaintiff and, the privilege at that time for reports being

---

inappropriate to do so in a context where the third party in question is the Prime Minister. Of
course, he, like anyone else has individual rights which he is entitled to protect, but in the
present case it is the private rights of Mr Cruddas, not Mr Cameron, which are in issue. The
courts should be particularly careful about novel extensions of the law which impinge on areas
of political debate, as *Horrocks v Lowe* itself was at pains to emphasise" (at [18]).
While the judge's observations are directed at malice in the context of malicious falsehood, it is
also the case that the elements of the claim in defamation must clearly be related to the claimant.
There is no reason to think therefore that the position should be any different with respect to
defamation.

[43] [1975] A.C. 135 at 150. See also *Cush v Dillon; Boland v Dillon* [2011] HCA 30:
"[Q]ualified privilege, which attaches to a defamatory statement, can only be destroyed by the
existence of an improper motive that causes the person to make the statement. Thus, lack of
belief in the truth of the statement, or even ill-will felt towards the person defamed, will not be
sufficient. There must be evidence that the making of the statement was actuated by improper
motive. As Cotton L.J. said in *Clark v Molyneux*, the question is 'whether [the defendant] acted
as he did from a desire to discharge his duty' . . . Knowledge on the part of a defendant that a
statement is untrue may be almost conclusive evidence of malice. This is because a person who
knowingly publishes false and defamatory material will usually have an improper motive. A
lack of belief in the statement may stand in a different category. But in neither event is there
warrant for equating knowledge or lack of belief with actual malice" (at [28]–[29]).

[44] Ibid. See, e.g. *Clover Bond Pty Ltd v Carroll* [2004] WASC 216 (defendant's purpose to get
plaintiff's service and maintenance business rather than to protect public, though the court treated
the matter primarily as something outside the scope of the privilege).

[45] Para.17.4, above.

[46] Eady J. in *Branson v Bower* [2002] Q.B. 737 at [8]; and see *Lillie v Newcastle CC* [2002]
EWHC 1600 (QB) at [1091]; *Friend v Civil Aviation Authority* [2005] EWHC 201 (QB) at [237];
and *Meade v Pugh* [2004] EWHC 408 QBD. See also *Hughes v Risbridger* [2010] EWHC 491
at [25] (QB).

[47] See fn.104, below.

qualified,[48] was held unable to rely on the privilege,[49] for "the defendant did not send this report to be published for the benefit of the public in a matter as to which they ought to be informed, but from a desire to injure the plaintiff".[50] However, even at that time Bramwell L.J. was of the view that if the report had been sent by a journalist he should be regarded as performing his duty even if he was motivated by spite against the claimant.[51] In practice, of course, there are likely to be formidable problems of proof in establishing that the improper purpose was dominant where the defendant believed in what he said.

Improper motive. The approach which rests malice upon improper motive **17.6**
perhaps makes it easier to explain why mere absence of positive belief in truth is not malice (there must be knowledge of or reckless indifference as to falsity)[52] and why, although the intention of the defendant is not determinative of the meaning of the words complained of, that intention does govern the question of whether he was malicious.[53] The reason why the significance of improper motive has come to be questioned may be the frequency of litigation against the press. Malice is of no significance in cases about the "media privilege" created by *Reynolds v Times Newspapers Ltd*, where the main issue is reasonable conduct.[54] Where the press relies on "traditional" qualified privilege it is likely to be of the variety (predominantly statutory) which is concerned with reporting official or quasi-official decisions and determinations.[55] There is a basic requirement that the report be fair and accurate[56] but once that is shown it is rather unlikely that a case of malice could be made out anyway. The newspaper is not likely to have reason to believe that what it reports may be untrue,[57] nor to have a purpose of injuring the claimant (as opposed to reporting news). Indeed, even if the newspaper is conducting a "campaign" against the claimant it is thought that the courts should not be overly receptive to argument that it was actuated by an improper motive, since there is a clear Parliamentary intention that it is in the public interest that

---

[48] As to the present law, see para.13.38, above.

[49] (1879) 5 Ex. D. 53 CA.

[50] Ibid. at 56, per Brett L.J. On the similarity (though not exact congruence) of malice in defamation and the absence of the "good faith" which is required where an employee makes a "protected disclosure" under the Employment Rights Act 1996 (as amended) see *Street v Derbyshire Unemployed Workers' Centre* [2004] EWCA Civ 964; [2005] I.C.R. 97.

[51] Ibid. Nowadays that might be regarded as a case of mixed motives.

[52] Para.17.16, below.

[53] *Roberts v Bass* [2002] HCA 57; 212 C.L.R. 1 at [82]. For the proposition as to malice and meaning, see *Loveless v Earl* [1999] E.M.L.R. 530 CA: para.17.20, below.

[54] Para.17.21, below.

[55] See Ch.16, above.

[56] And in some cases a requirement that the subject be offered a "right of reply".

[57] But cf. *Qadir v Associated Newspapers Ltd* [2012] EWHC 2606 (QB); [2013] E.M.L.R. 15, albeit that in *Qadir* the judge found in respect of one of the reports that it was not fair and accurate and the privilege was therefore held not to apply on that basis. See further, para.17.15, below.

material of this type should be made widely known.[58] In other words, in media cases we have (1) a new type of privilege to which malice is irrelevant and (2) a "traditional" privilege which is theoretically qualified but in practice is close to absolute.

17.7 Mixed motives. People commonly act from a mixture of motives and it will be impossible to attribute any precise degree of causative effect to one or another. However, for this purpose the improper purpose must be the dominant motive[59] and it is only where the defendant's desire to comply with the relevant duty or to protect the relevant interest plays no significant part in his motives for publishing what he believes to be true that malice can properly be found.[60]

> "[T]o destroy the privilege the desire to injure must be the dominant motive for the defamatory publication; knowledge that it will have that effect is not enough if the defendant is nevertheless acting in accordance with a sense of duty or in bona fide protection of his own legitimate interests."[61]
>
> "Qualified privilege would be illusory, and the public interest it is meant to serve defeated, if the protection it affords were lost merely because a person, although acting in compliance with a duty or in protection of a legitimate interest, disliked the person whom he defamed or was indignant at what he believed to be that person's conduct and welcomed the opportunity of exposing it."[62]

17.8 Ill will or desire to injure not necessary. Malice does not necessarily mean personal spite or ill will against the claimant, which is malice in the popular sense. "Malice in the actual sense may exist even though there be no spite or desire for vengeance in the ordinary sense."[63] "Any indirect motive other than a sense of duty is what the law calls malice."[64] Since it is the misuse of the occasion which takes away the privilege it is not essential that the defendant should be actuated by malice towards the claimant in the ordinary sense. He might, e.g. be acting solely to further his own interests[65] in a manner not allowed by the privilege and without thought of harm to the

---

[58] In *Qadir v Associated Newspapers Ltd* [2012] EWHC 2606 (QB); [2013] E.M.L.R. 15 malice was proved against the defendant on the grounds, first, that the defendant had, through its journalist, acquired knowledge that a report it had published on its website was not fair and accurate but took no steps to amend the website that contained the report and, secondly, the journalist had deliberately published a report that was unfair to the claimant in failing to include certain exculpatory words of the claimant made by a judge in the hearing reported on. See further, para.17.15, below.

[59] [1975] A.C. 135 at 149.

[60] [1975] A.C. 135 at 151. Compare Callinan J. in *Roberts v Bass* [2002] HCA 57; 212 C.L.R. 1 at [292].

[61] *Horrocks v Lowe* [1975] A.C. 135 at 149, per Lord Diplock. This was applied in *Dobson v Donkin* [1975] B.L.T. 253 CA, where it was held that a finding of malice against a person who passed on information that it was his duty to pass on was not compatible with a finding that he passed it on accurately.

[62] [1975] A.C. 135 at 151. And see *Klason v Australian Capital Territory* [2003] ACTSC 104; 177 F.L.R. 216.

[63] Per McCardie J. in *Pratt v BMA* [1919] 1 K.B. 244 at 275.

[64] Per Lord Campbell C.J. in *Dickson v Wilton* (1859) 1 F. & E. 419 at 427.

[65] E.g. to boost ratings: *Vogel v Canadian Broadcasting Corp* [1982] 3 W.W.R. 97.

claimant.[66] However, the nature and context of the privilege must be taken into account where the defendant is seeking to advance his own interests. At common law communications by a candidate to electors may be privileged.[67] Although the contrary view was once held,[68] it is not the law that the privilege is lost because one candidate makes the statement to draw votes away from the other and to "damage" his reputation before the electorate.[69] The privilege may also apply to communications between electors[70] and in that context it is not malice to "target" a candidate and seek to persuade people not to vote for him because you disagree with his views.[71] If the defendant did not use the occasion for the purpose for which the privilege is granted, but to gratify his animosity against a *third person*, and in so doing libelled the claimant, the defence of privilege will fail.[72]

Malice, duty and interest: general. The following paragraphs give **17.9** examples of the principle that when an occasion is privileged by reason of the duty of the defendant to make a statement, or his interest in making it, the defendant will be held to be malicious if he does not use the occasion to fulfil his duty or serve his interest.

The line between the two questions "Is the occasion privileged?" and "Is there evidence that the defendant was actuated by malice?" is clear in those cases where the scope of the privilege is defined with precision (e.g. certain reports privileged by statute[73]) but in other cases there may be great difficulty in distinguishing between conduct which takes the case outside the privileged occasion and conduct which is evidence upon which a jury may find malice even though the occasion is privileged. For example, material which is irrelevant to the discharge of the duty or protection of the interest, for the sake of which privilege is conferred may in one case be treated as affecting the scope of the privilege and in another as an issue of malice.[74]

---

[66] In *Bray v Deutsche Bank AG* [2009] EWHC 1356 (QB) the form of malice alleged (but not established) was not that the defendant "was aware that he was saying anything false about the Claimant, but . . . that he abused the occasion by saying something which he knew was false in circumstances where (unknown to him) his words referred to, and defamed, [the claimant]".

[67] On the effect of s.10 of the Defamation Act 1952 see para.15.33, above. A candidate has no special privilege qua candidate, but nor is he deprived of one he would otherwise have.

[68] *Pankhurst v Hamilton* (1887) 3 T.L.R. 500.
"The element of malice may be found in the very fact that the person speaking is endeavouring by what he says to draw votes to himself or to the candidate whom he favours":
per Turgeon J.A. in *Bureau v Campbell* (1928) 23 Saskatchewan L.R. 79 at 91, citing *Pankhurst v Hamilton.*

[69] *Braddock v Bevins* [1948] 1 K.B. 580 CA; *Roberts v Bass* [2002] HCA 57; 212 C.L.R. 1.

[70] Para.15.32, above.

[71] *Roberts v Bass*, above. However, it is important to note the electoral context of this proposition: *Amalgamated Television Services Pty Ltd v Marsden* [2002] NSWCA 419.

[72] *Stewart v M'Kinley* (1885) 11 V.L.R. 802. See also *Gwynne v Stopes, The Times*, January 26, May 4, 1928, CA, though in other respects that case may not be reconcilable with *Horrocks v Lowe*: para.17.17, below.

[73] See paras 16.9–16.28, above.

[74] See especially paras 14.63–14.64, above. See also the discussion in *Cush v Dillon; Boland v Dillon* [2011] HCA 30 at [17]–[23].

17.10 Redress of grievance. A complaint made as to the misconduct of a public servant or official is made on an occasion which is privileged on the grounds of the duty of the complainant to draw the attention of the proper authorities to such misconduct, or his interest in securing redress for his grievance.[75] However, the privilege will be destroyed if the complaint was not made from a sense of duty, or with a view to redress, but with the intention of unjustly defaming the plaintiff.[76] In such cases juries have been directed that they should consider whether a letter was written "to slander the plaintiff, or whether it was written honestly, to call attention to a rumour in the parish that was bringing scandal on the church"[77] or whether a memorial "was got up and signed honestly for the purpose which is stated in it, or whether the defendant had any by-motive."[78] That the maker of a complaint would only do so anonymously when he had to continue to work with the person about whom he complained was held not to be evidence of malice in *Nordeen v Hill*.[79]

17.11 Information as to crime. Charges of crime, whether made to the claimant in the presence of other persons, or to the proper authorities,[80] will only be privileged if made with the honest desire of promoting investigation into the alleged crime, or prosecuting the alleged offender, or, it is submitted, recovering property or proper compensation.[81] No privilege will attach where they are proved to have been made with the object of obtaining some improper personal advantage. Thus, where D, having cause for suspicion, went to P's relations and charged him with theft, but it appeared from the evidence that his object was rather to induce P's relations to give him £50 to say no more about the matter than to promote inquiry or enable the relations to redeem P's

---

[75] See para.14.59, above.

[76] *Fairman v Ives* (1822) 5 B. & Ald. 642; *Warman v Hine* (1837) 1 Jur. 820; *Dickson v Earl of Wilton* (1859) 1 F. & F. 419. Summary judgment was granted to the defendant on a plea of malice in *Morrison v Buckinghamshire CC* [2011] EWHC 3444 (QB) on the basis that the claimant, who had been selected to work as a "national challenge adviser" with a view to improving certain schools' performance, had no possible prospect of showing that letters that had been sent to five individuals, including the Director of National Strategies, and which alleged that she had lied in her "pen portrait", were published maliciously (at [97]–[103]).

[77] *James v Boston* (1845) 2 C. & K. 4.

[78] *Harrison v Bush* (1855) 5 E. & B. 344.
"A person is not to be allowed with impunity maliciously to defame another, merely because he does it under the cover of an assumed necessity of preferring a complaint against a public officer or other individual, in order to obtain redress. The motives to such a complaint may be brought in question before a jury":
per Robinson C.J. in *Corbett v Jackson* (1844) 1 Up.Can.Q.B. 128 at 129. "A complaint lodged through mere meddling officiousness cannot be said to be protected by any interest which the law recognises": per Tindall J. in *Holzgen v Woollwright* (1928) T.P.D. at 12. For Scots law, see *Macdonald v Martin*, 1935 S.C. 621 and *Notman v Commercial Bank*, 1938 S.C. 522, denying a requirement of want of probable cause.

[79] [2012] EWHC 2847 (QB).

[80] However, complaints to the police now carry absolute privilege: para.13.12, above.

[81] In *Elms v Crane*, 170 A. 852 (Me., 1919), the protection was lost, as the motive of the defendant was not the public motive of vindicating the law and punishing the criminal, but rather the purely private motive of recovering lost property. This case would probably not be followed in England now; cf. the reasoning in *Abbott v Refuge Assurance* [1962] 1 Q.B. 432, in which it

character, it was held that such communication was altogether unprivileged.[82] In *Lyons v Chief Constable of Strathclyde Police*[83] Strathclyde Police objected to the pursuer's application to Glasgow City Council for a second-hand car dealer's licence by sending a letter to the council which stated that their intelligence showed that he was "involved in serious and organised crime including the trafficking and supply of Class A drugs". Subsequently, Strathclyde police wrote a further and similar letter to the Vehicle and Operator Services Agency suggesting that the pursuer was not a fit and proper person to hold an operator's licence to carry out MOT tests. The Outer House of the Court of Session held that the letters sent by the police were communications sent in the furtherance of their function to enable other bodies to perform their functions and were therefore privileged. Further, the letters sent by the police could not be said to be improper or excessive in nature, and could not themselves be demonstrative of malice, nor could the fact that the pursuer's averments that he had not been charged with any crime give rise to an inference of malice, and the pursuer had not therefore pled a relevant case of actionable defamation.[84]

References. Similarly, the privilege attaching to communications as to an **17.12** employee's character is based on the duty to communicate information to a person whose interest it is to know it.[85] However, that privilege will be lost if, for instance, the defendant's real motive in giving a defamatory answer to an inquiry was spite at the claimant's leaving his employment,[86] or an intention to slander the claimant,[87] and not a desire to give proper information. If the communication was volunteered by the defendant, the jury may be asked "was he a fussy busybody acting 'ultroneously', or a person discharging a genuine moral duty?"[88] Where a jury held that a letter had been written to a woman on the character of her intended husband with some other motive than the desire to prevent the marriage, this was held to be a finding of malice.[89]

Refutation of charges. A person whose character or conduct has been **17.13** attacked may make statements defamatory of his attacker to refute the charges

---

[82] *Hooper v Truscott* (1836) 2 Bing. N.C. 457.
[83] [2012] CSOH 46; 2012 Rep. L.R. 108.
[84] Ibid. at [50]–[55].
[85] See para.14.25, above.
[86] *Jackson v Hopperton* (1864) 16 C.B.(N.S.) 829.
[87] *Hodgson v Scarlett* (1818) 1 B. & Ald. 232 at 240; *Macdonald v M'Coll* (1901) 3 F.1082. A plea of malice failed in *Thour v The Royal Free Hampstead NHS Trust* [2012] EWHC 1473 (QB).
[88] Per Hamilton L.J. in *Greenlands Ltd v Wilmshurst* [1913] 3 K.B. 507 CA at 585–586; *Pattison v Jones* (1828) 8 B. & C. 578
[89] *Coughlan v Jones* (1915) 35 N.Z.L.R. 41. See also *Parks v Canadian Association of Industrial etc. Workers* (1981) 122 D.L.R. (3d) 366 (pique).

made against him and to vindicate his character,[90] but if his motive in making such statements is not refutation or vindication, but a desire to blacken the character of the person who has made the charges, he will be held malicious. So, in *Koenig v Ritchie*[91] a policy-holder, in the course of a dispute with an insurance company, published a pamphlet accusing the directors of fraud, and the directors published a pamphlet in answer declaring the charges to be false and calumnious and also asserting that, in a suit which he had instituted, the plaintiff had sworn (in support of those charges) in opposition to his own handwriting. Cockburn C.J. ruled that the directors' pamphlet was privileged, and directed the jury that if they were of opinion that it was:

> "published *bona fide* for the purpose of the defence of the company, and in order to prevent these charges from operating to their prejudice, and with a view to vindicate the character of the directors, and not with a view to injure or lower the character of the plaintiff"

they ought to find for the defendants. From this direction it is clear that the privilege must be used as a shield of defence, not as a weapon of attack.

Unnecessarily violent language may on occasion be evidence of an improper motive,[92] but where the defendant's character has been publicly attacked by the claimant the tendency of the courts is not to submit the language of the answer to too strict scrutiny and hold every expression which goes beyond what is necessary for self-defence evidence of malice.[93]

> "It is the privilege of every citizen to express his opinion freely in matters which have been brought before the public, and that is specially true where a person is writing to a newspaper to defend himself against charges affecting his own character and conduct. Great latitude must be allowed to a person so put on his defence and endeavouring to meet the case which has been brought against him."[94]
>
> "The language in which a defamatory charge is repudiated is not to be weighed in nice scales."[95]

Allowances should be made for the indignation which the defendant might naturally feel at the attack ever having been made.[96] If the defendant's language, though violent or excessively strong, is, having regard to the nature of the attack made upon him and all the circumstances of the case, such as he

---

[90] See para.14.51, above.

[91] (1862) 3 F. & F. 413.

[92] See para.32.40, below.

[93] Per curiam in *Laughton v Bishop of Sodor and Man* (1872) L.R. 4 P.C. 495 at 508. See also paras 14.51 and 14.67, above.

[94] Per Lord M'Laren in *Gray v SPCA* (1890) 17 R. 1185 at 1200.

[95] *Adam v Ward* [1917] A.C. 309 at 330, 347; *Turner v MGM* [1950] 1 All E.R. 449 HL at 470–471.

[96] *R. v Veley* (1867) 4 F. & F. 1117 at 1122. See also *Hibbs v Wilkinson* (1859) 1 F. & F. 608 at 610.

might have honestly and reasonably believed to be necessary for his vindication, though in fact it was not so,[97] the judge ought, in the absence of any extrinsic evidence of malice, to withdraw the case from the jury and direct a verdict for the defendant.[98]

Example. P wrote and published a book which contained a passage imputing   **17.14**
hypocrisy and gross immorality to Mr Gladstone, the statesman and prime
minister, then deceased. Thereupon D, who was Gladstone's son, with the
view to vindicating his father's name, wrote a letter to the secretary of a club
of which P was a member saying that the plaintiff was a liar, a coward and a
foul fellow. Avory J. ruled that the letter was written on a privileged occasion,
and directed the jury that:

> "they ought not to find D guilty of malice if the words were only such as a man
> moved by righteous indignation might use, or if they were only used in the discharge
> of D's moral duty to vindicate his father's reputation. The mere fact that the
> language was intemperate would not, in the absence of evidence that it was not used
> bona fide, be evidence of malice, if C was actuated by righteous indignation or a
> desire to do his duty he would be protected even if his language was violent or
> excessively strong. They must bear that in mind in deciding whether D was actuated
> by malice, *i.e.* a desire to do something other than that which it was his duty to
> do-namely, refute this calumny and vindicate his father's name."[99]

Reports. The object of the qualified privilege which attaches by common   **17.15**
law and by statute to a fair and accurate report is the information of the
public.[100]

---

[97] In *Harbour Radio Pty Ltd v Trad* [2012] HCA 44, the High Court of Australia upheld the
finding of the trial judge and Court of Appeal that a reply to an attack was not actuated by malice.
A Radio 2GB "host" responded vigorously to an attack by Mr Trad on Radio 2GB referring in
particular to one of his colleagues, G, having been put in fear and having to retreat at a "Peace
Rally" as a consequence of what Mr Trad had said at the rally. This was not true. The High Court
held qualified privilege applied to six of the eight defamatory imputations that the jury had found
the response to bear. However, the majority denied the Mr Trad's application for leave to file a
notice of cross-appeal on the question of malice as there was insufficient prospects of success in
demonstrating error by the Court of Appeal in its conclusions on the question of malice, and no
ground of general importance involved. Heydon J. dissented on this issue. The evidence presented
admitted of only two possibilities both of which were evidence of malice. The first possibility was
that the radio host falsely and knowingly told his audience that his colleague, G, had been put in
fear, and retreated, because the respondent gestured at him. The alternative was that the radio host
truthfully told the audience of G's complaint, while the chief operating officer at 2GB knew that
G had not been put in fear and retreated. Both alternatives fixed Harbour Radio which owned
Radio2GB, with malice and consequently, Heydon J. would have dismissed the appeal, granting
Mr Trad leave to cross-appeal on the issue of malice.
[98] *Spill v Maule* (1869) L.R. 4 Ex. 232 at 235–236; *Laughton v Bishop of Sodor and Man*
(1872) L.R. 4 P.C. 495 at 509–510; *Adam v Ward* [1917] A.C. 309 at 339; *Geere v Gladwin* [1945]
W.L.D. 65; *Lotter v de Villiers* [1946] T.P.D. 569; *Muller v Hatton* [1952] Q.S.R. 150. See also
para.32.40, below.
[99] *Wright v Gladstone, The Times*, February 4, 1927; *Falk v Smith* [1941] 1 D.L.R. 156 Ont
CA.
[100] For contents of registers, see *Annaly v Trade Auxiliary Co* (1890) 26 L.R.Ir. 394 at 403, per
Fitzgibbon L.J.: "the legitimate object of giving information to those to whom he is entitled to
give it." And see the privilege in the Australian uniform legislation governing publication of
public documents and fair reports of proceedings of public concern, which is defeated by proof

"But if you can infer from the circumstances attending the publication that it was really made not with a view to the information of the public, the publisher will be liable in damages to the person whose character he has injured."[101]

"If a newspaper publishes a correct report, but not *bona fide*, for the purpose of injuring a person, and thus with malice, the publisher is liable."[102]

As is explained below, the traditional concept of malice is nowadays of limited significance in media cases.[103] However, where the defendant assumed the character of a reporter, and sent to several local newspapers a report (containing matter defamatory of the plaintiff) of a case in which he had acted as solicitor for the other party, and the jury found that the defendant, in sending the report to the newspapers, was activated by malice towards the plaintiff, it was held by the Court of Appeal (affirming Cockburn C.J.) that the plaintiff was entitled to judgment, although the jury found also that the report "was in substance a fair report".[104] Similarly, the privilege attaching to the publication of a fair and accurate copy of a register open to public inspection[105] will be destroyed on proof that the defendant published the copy or extract:

"from an indirect motive, e.g. for the purpose of extorting money, or if there were any actual malice, e.g. if the publication were to gratify a feeling of revenge . . . but as long as the publication is *bona fide* and without actual malice it is privileged."[106]

In *Qadir v Associated Newspapers Ltd*,[107] Tugendhat J. considered , at a trial to determine preliminary issues, whether malice existed in respect of two articles published by the defendant, and whether absolute and qualified privilege attached. The first article consisted of a report of defamatory allegations

---

that the "matter was not published honestly for the information of the public or the advancement of education": Defamation Act 2005 (NSW) ss.28 and 29.

[101] Per Hannen J. in *Salmon v Isaac* (1869) 20 L.T. 885 at 886. Cf. *Dawson v Dover Chronicle Ltd* (1913) 108 L.T. 481 CA.

[102] *Hutchison v Robinson* (1900) 2 N.S.W.L.R. 130 at 145.

[103] Para.17.21, below.

[104] *Stevens v Sampson* (1879) 5 Ex.D. 53. In *Qadir v Associated Newspapers Ltd* [2012] EWHC 2606 (QB); [2013] E.M.L.R. 15 Tugendhat J. commenting on the previous edition of this book, noted (at [207] that

"The passage in *Gatley* para.17.5 may suggest that [*Stevens v Sampson*] should be decided differently today. In *Stevens* the report is short, and since it was a jury trial, it is not said what facts had been found. The evidence of an improper motive appears to have been no more than the simple fact that the defendant had been solicitor acting for the plaintiff in the proceedings the subject of the report, while the plaintiff in the libel action was the debt collector employed by the other party to that case. But it may be that there was other evidence before the jury."

Cf. *Anderson v Calvert* (1908) 24 T.L.R. 399.

[105] See paras 15.38 and 16.13, above.

[106] Per Lord Esher in *Searles v Scarlett* [1892] 2 Q.B. 56 at 60.

[107] [2012] EWHC 2606 (QB); [2013] E.M.L.R. 15. See further, para.16.4, above.

made in a claim form. The judge held that the defendant could not rely on s.15 and Sch.1, para.5 of the Defamation Act 1996[108] because it was not for the public benefit to publish defamatory allegations made in a claim form or particulars of claim available to the public under CPR r.5.4C without at the same time stating that the defendant to that claim had denied or was disputing the allegations.[109] The second article reported submissions made during a sentencing hearing by counsel for an offender convicted of fraud that the claimant had been "intimately involved" in "Britain's biggest mortgage fraud". However, the article failed to make clear that the judge had replied that there was no evidence of the claimant's complicity. The defendant's plea of qualified (under s.15, Sch.1, para.2 of the Defamation Act 1996) and absolute privilege (under s.14 of the Defamation Act 1996) failed because the report was not a fair and accurate one, nor was publication for the public benefit.[110] Given the court's conclusions on privilege, the question of malice did not strictly arise, but the judge nevertheless went on to consider it in case his conclusions were found to be incorrect. While it may be rare that malice is proved in cases involving the publication of reports, it could nevertheless be established in principle by proof that the defendant knew that what it published was disputed but knowingly published the false statement that it was not disputed, or knew that the form in which it reported an extract or summary of a report was misleading or unfair. Alternatively, though there was no suggestion of this, proof of an ulterior motive such as revenge or extortion or anything of that kind would suffice.[111] On the facts, publication of the first article was malicious once the defendant learned that a defence had been served but took no steps to amend the website that contained the report of the particulars of claim. Failing to notify the website editor of the fact that a defence had been served was reckless and it did not matter what motive the journalist might have had for not informing him.[112] So far as the second article was concerned, malice was established because the journalist deliberately published a report that was unfair to the claimant in failing to include certain exculpatory words of the claimant made by a judge in the hearing reported on.[113]

Untruth, belief and wilful blindness. Where words are published on an **17.16** occasion of qualified privilege the mere proof that they are untrue is not

---

[108] Sch.1 para.5 Defamation Act 1996 provides that "a fair and accurate copy of or extract from any register or other document required by law to be open to public inspection" has qualified privilege without explanation or contradiction. See further para.16.13, above.

[109] See para.16.5, above.

[110] See para.16.4, above.

[111] [2012] EWHC 2606 at [212] (QB).

[112] Ibid. at [230]–[231].

[113] Ibid. at [252].

malice, nor even evidence of malice,[114] but proof that the defendant was aware that what he published was not true is normally conclusive evidence of malice. The burden of proof here is squarely upon the claimant: honesty is presumed and the claimant has the burden of negativing it.[115] A number of statements formulate the issue as being whether the defendant acted "without an honest belief" in the truth of what he published but this, read literally, is a good deal narrower because it would require a positive belief in truth. For example, take a person who has agreed to hand out leaflets in support of a political campaign attacking the record of a candidate.[116] He may have various states of mind about the statements contained in the leaflets: he may have examined them carefully, checked them against the evidence and firmly concluded that they are true; he may have given them a cursory examination, knowing nothing about the evidence supporting them, and concluded that he is not required to make any further inquiry, being content to accept the view of those running the campaign; or he may not have read them at all. Only in the first case could it truly be said that he had an "honest belief" in the truth of the statements, but to deny the protection of privilege in the second case and perhaps even in the third would be a serious restraint upon political campaigning.[117] "Lack of honest belief in the law of qualified privilege does not mean lack of belief; it means a belief that the matter is untrue."[118] In *Horrocks v Lowe*, Lord Diplock spoke of "lack of belief" in the truth of what was published as conclusive evidence of malice but in the same sentence he said that this was because "telling deliberate and injurious falsehoods" could not be within the scope of a duty.[119]

---

[114] *Caulfield v Whitworth* (1868) 18 L.T. (N.S.) 527; *Fountain v Boodle* (1842) 3 Q.B. 5. However, in practice, proof by the claimant that the words are untrue may also suggest that the defendant could not have believed them to be true, which is evidence of malice, as was the case in *Fountain v Boodle*.

[115] See paras 32.33ff, below.

[116] It is assumed that on the facts the elements of qualified privilege are established.

[117] See *Roberts v Bass* [2002] HCA 57, 212 C.L.R. 1. Exactly what the defendant believed is rather unclear; what is certain is that at best he had unthinkingly accepted the statements in the leaflets at face value.

"In a case like the present, persons handing out how-to-vote cards may honestly believe that they are informing the electorate of their candidate's views and may not themselves have thought about whether much or any of the content of the how-to-vote card is true. Such persons will not lose the protection of the occasion because they had no positive belief in the truth of any defamatory matter in the how-to-vote card. It is proper for them to communicate their candidate's views to voters, and they do not lose their protection because, although acting for the purpose of the privileged occasion, they had no positive belief in the truth of the defamatory matter":

at [100].

[118] Ibid. at [96], per Gaudron, McHugh and Gummow JJ. Their Honours suggest that the "absence of belief" formula has come about because (1) honesty is presumed in the defendant's favour and (2) in most cases a person who does not believe that a statement is untrue will know or believe it is untrue.

[119] [1975] A.C. 135 at 149–150.

However, malice may be found even if the defendant does not know the statement is untrue if he is recklessly indifferent whether it is true or false.[120] This is clearly "subjective recklessness"—one cannot be indifferent to a risk of which one is not conscious.[121]

> "[I]f it be proved that out of anger, or for some other wrong motive, the defendant has stated as true that which he does not know to be true, and he has stated it whether it is true or not, recklessly, by reason of his anger or other motive, the jury may infer that he used the occasion, not for the reason which justifies it, but for the gratification of his anger or other indirect motive."[122]

This state of mind has been said to be "wilful blindness".[123]

> "Such cases . . . are likely to be rare. Usually, they will be cases where the defendant had or was given information which gave a reason for supposing that what the defendant intended to publish was false but the defendant nevertheless published the matter without further inquiry or investigation. Failure to inquire is not evidence of recklessness unless the defendant had some indication that what he or she was about to publish might not be true."[124]

Whether there is reckless indifference will also be affected by what the defendant knows of the contents of what he is publishing. If we return to the example of the leaflet distributor it would be difficult to say that he was recklessly indifferent if he failed to make any inquiry about charges in the leaflet that a candidate was incompetent or untrustworthy; it does not follow that the same should be true if the leaflet accused the candidate of serious crime.[125]

---

[120] Ibid. at 150. Cf. *Culnane v Morris* [2005] EWHC 2438 QBD; [2006] 1 W.L.R. 2880 at [28]:
> "if a candidate has on an occasion of prima facie qualified privilege abused his position by saying something which he knows to be false or, *perhaps*, has behaved recklessly, then the defence will not be available"
(emphasis added).
    In *Cambridge v Makin* [2012] EWCA Civ 85; [2012] E.M.L.R. 19 the Court of Appeal upheld the decision of the judge at first instance that the defendant was malicious in that he was wilfully blind to the truth or falsity of the statements he had published. There was ample material on the basis of which it had been open to the judge to conclude that the defendant had simply thrown caution to the wind and crossed the line, as he had realised, from debating policies to making a personal charge. There was no basis upon which the defendant could have believed to be true the allegation that the claimant had abused her position as an office holder by acting on a conflict of interest to her own financial benefit. Indeed he had reached no conclusion that it was true. His conduct could properly be characterised as wilful blindness: he had had in his hands the documents upon which he relied as substantiating his charge and had closed his eyes to that which had been obvious to him two months earlier, namely, that they did no such thing.
[121] Or what is known in the criminal law as "*Cunningham* recklessness" (after *R. v Cunningham* [1957] 2 Q.B. 396). Curiously, Lord Diplock was the principal architect of another form of recklessness used in the criminal law which has an objective element: *R. v Caldwell* [1982] A.C. 341.
[122] *Clarke v Molyneux* (1877) 3 Q.B.D. 237 CA at 247, per Brett L.J.
[123] *Roberts v Bass* [2002] HCA 57, 212 C.L.R. 1 at [84]; *Gross v Weston* [2007] NSWCA 1 at [54]. See also, *Cambridge v Makin* [2012] EWCA Civ 85 at [63]; [2012] E.M.L.R. 19.
[124] *Roberts v Bass* at [109].
[125] Ibid. at [39], per Gleeson C.J.

17.17 Unreasonable belief or carelessness in arriving at belief not malice. In *Horrocks v Lowe* Lord Diplock said that:

> "indifference to the truth of what [the defendant] publishes is not to be equated with carelessness, impulsiveness or irrationality in arriving at a positive belief that it is true. The freedom of speech protected by the law of qualified privilege may be availed of by all sorts and conditions of men. In affording to them immunity from suit if they have acted in good faith in compliance with a legal or moral duty or in protection of a legitimate interest the law must take them as it finds them. In ordinary life it is rare indeed for people to form their beliefs by a process of logical deduction from facts ascertained by a rigorous search for all available evidence and a judicious assessment of its probative value. In greater or in less degree according to their temperaments, their training, their intelligence, they are swayed by prejudice, rely on intuition instead of reasoning, leap to conclusions on inadequate evidence and fail to recognise the cogency of material which might cast doubt on the validity of the conclusions they reach. But despite the imperfection of the mental process by which the belief is arrived at it may still be 'honest,' that is, a positive belief that the conclusions they have reached are true. The law demands no more."[126]

In *Horrocks v Lowe* the defendant made a speech which was defamatory of the plaintiff on a privileged occasion, a meeting of the local borough council. The judge found that while the defendant believed that everything he said was true and justifiable, his state of mind was one of "gross and unreasoning prejudice". The Court of Appeal[127] and the House of Lords held that this did not amount to malice. "[Members of a local council] may be swayed by strong political prejudice, they may be obstinate and pig-headed, stupid and obtuse; but they were chosen by the electors to speak their minds on matters of local concern and so long as they do so honestly they run no risk of liability for defamation."[128] If the defendant honestly believed his statement to be true, he is not to be held malicious merely because such belief was not based on any reasonable grounds[129]; or because he has done insufficient research[130] or was

---

[126] [1975] A.C. at 150. *Davies & Davies Ltd v Kots* [1979] 2 S.C.R. 686 at 697–698; *Camporese v Parton* (1983) 150 D.L.R. (3d) 208 at 226.

[127] See [1972] 1 W.L.R. 135.

[128] [1975] A.C. 135 at 152. Cf. *Cambridge v Makin* [2012] EWCA Civ 85; [2012] E.M.L.R. 19 where the defendant gave evidence that he had carefully satisfied himself that the allegation was true. The Court of Appeal however upheld the judge's finding of malice, noting that "as a highly intelligent man [the defendant] cannot have believed that the documents bore out the charge of abuse of office by the claimant because they do not come within hailing distance of so doing" (at [58]).

[129] *Clark v Molyneux* (1877) 3 Q.B.D. 237 CA, more fully reported 47 L.J.Q.B. 230; *Pitt v Donovan* (1813) 1 M. & S. 639; *Howe v Jones* (1885) 1 T.L.R. 461; *Hesketh v Brindle* (1888) 4 T.L.R. 199; *Collins v Cooper* (1902) 19 T.L.R. 118 CA; *Horrocks v Lowe* [1975] A.C. 135. "An error of judgment has never, so far as I know, been held to be tantamount to malice": Lord Alness in *Hayford v Forrester-Paton*, 1927 S.C. 740 at 756. And see *Korach v Moore* (1991) 76 D.L.R. (4th) 506; *Lawrence v Death* (1908) 28 N.Z.L.R. 620, per Isaacs J. in *Webb v Bloch* (1928) 41 C.L.R. at 369; and see *Wright v McCallum* [1941] 2 D.L.R. 752; *Broom v Stirling* (1952) 4 S.A.L.R. 798 (test is subjective, not objective).

[130] *Camporese v Parton* (1983) 150 D.L.R. (3d) 208.

hasty,[131] credulous,[132] or foolish in jumping to a conclusion,[133] irrational,[134] indiscreet,[135] stupid,[136] pig-headed or obstinate[137] in his belief.

> "The law of qualified privilege requires the defendant to use the occasion honestly in the sense of using it for a proper purpose; but it imposes no requirement that the defendant use the occasion carefully."[138]
>
> "Lack of care for the consequences of exuberant reporting is not malice."[139]
>
> "The only question is whether the defendant did, in fact, believe what he said, and not whether a reasonable man [i.e. a man of rational understanding] would have believed it."[140]
>
> "If gross and unreasoning prejudice causes] the defendant honestly to believe what a more rational or impartial person would reject or doubt he does not thereby lose the protection of the privilege."[141]
>
> "It is clear from the exposition of the law by Lord Diplock in *Horrock v Lowe* that malice is to be carefully distinguished from other states of mind such as carelessness, excessive zeal, pig-headedness, stupidity, or a failure to arrive at rational conclusions. In practice, a claimant has to demonstrate that the words were published without any honest belief in their truth or that the defendant was genuinely indifferent to their truth or falsity."[142]

Despite the argument of simplicity, one may feel some doubt about the wisdom of so liberally protecting assertions of fact[143] which are the product of unreasoning prejudice. In the current state of the law, for example, if a person is anxious for someone not to get a particular job because of his religion or politics, and by dwelling on the subject he comes to believe that that person lacks a qualification for the job, it is not obvious what public

---

[131] Per Willes J., arguendo, in *Amann v Damm* (1860) 8 C.B.(N.S.) 597 at 600: "It matters not how harsh or hasty the defendant may have been [in making the charge] or how untrue the charge, if he bona fide made it." Per Cave J. in *Brown v Hawkes* [1891] 2 Q.B. 718 at 722:
"He may have been hasty both in his conclusion that the plaintiff was guilty and in his proceedings; but hastiness in his conclusion as to the plaintiff's guilt, although it may account for his coming to a wrong conclusion, does not show the presence of any indirect motive."

[132] Per Bramwell L.J. in *Clark v Molyneux* (1877) 3 Q.B.D. 237 CA at 244.

[133] *Krill v Kruger* (1928) E.D.L. 282 at 290.

[134] Per Lord Ellenborough C.J. in *Pitt v Donovan* (1813) 1 M. & S. 639 at 645, 648; per Bayley J., ibid. at 649; *Mumba v Singoyi* [1975] S.C.Z. 79.

[135] *Restall v Mallock* (1904) 18 E.D.C. 77 at 86.

[136] "Mere stupidity is not of itself malice": per Cotton L.J. in *Capital and Counties Bank v Henty* (1880) 5 C.P.D. 514 CA at 538.

[137] Per Brett L.J. in *Clark v Molyneux* (1877) 3 Q.B.D. 237 at 248; *Turner v MGM* [1950] 1 All E.R. 449 HL at 463.

[138] *Roberts v Bass* [2002] HCA 57, 212 C.L.R. 1 at [103]; *Oliver v Chief Constable of Northumbria* [2004] EWHC 790 QBD.

[139] Per Barwick C.J. in *Pinniger v John Fairfax* (1979) 26 A.L.R. 55 HCA; *Barbaro v Amalgamated Television Services* (1985) 1 N.S.W.L.R. 30 (on appeal (1989) 20 N.S.W.L.R. 493).

[140] Per Brett L.J. in *Clark v Molyneux* (1877) 3 Q.B.D. 237 CA at 248.

[141] Per Lord Diplock in *Horrocks v Lowe* [1975] A.C. 135 at 152.

[142] *Hughes v Risbridger* [2010] EWHC 491 (QB) per Eady J. at [24].

[143] The same considerations do not necessarily apply to what is recognisably a statement of opinion: para.12.8, above.

interest is served by protecting[144] the publication of what he has come to believe.[145] However, the fact that the defendant genuinely believes that the claimant is guilty of misconduct does not entitle him to claim the protection of privilege if he knowingly or recklessly makes misstatements of fact to buttress his conclusion.[146]

17.18 Unreasonableness of claimed belief may be evidence of malice. All this is not to say that a defendant who asserts a belief that others find absurd will necessarily succeed in the defence of privilege, for the unreasonableness of the belief may lead the jury to reject his contention that in fact he holds it.[147] Similarly, failure to make available inquiries may be evidence from which it may be inferred that the defendant was consciously indifferent to the truth or falsity of the statement.[148]

17.19 Matter not believed to be true: exceptional cases. While awareness of the falsity or likely falsity of the statement is normally fatal to the defence of privilege it is not so if the defendant is under a duty to pass on the information to a third party. In the course of his summing-up in *Vanbergen v Bosshard*[149] McCardie J. gave as an illustration of such a case an accountant employed to audit the accounts of a company, who:

> "when going through the books ... finds that a cashier in the employ of the company has, to the best of his belief, embezzled £100 of the company's money. The accountant may say, 'I cannot think that young Richardson has really embezzled this £100 ... '. It does not matter what he can think or cannot. If the facts are such

---

[144] Though it has to be said that there may now be liability for negligence in such a case if damage can be proved: para.23.3, below.

[145] In *Gwynne v Stopes*, *The Times*, May 4, 1928, CA, Scrutton L.J. said that there was a state of mind in which a person might have so brooded on a matter and have become so obsessed with the rightness of his case that he was incapable of forming a reasonable judgment. Such a state of mind, if the jury found it to exist, was, he thought, equivalent to malice which destroyed the privilege. If the matter were open, it is thought that there is much to be said for Scrutton L.J.'s view. See also *Royal Aquarium v Parkinson* [1892] 1 Q.B. 431 CA, a honest comment case. *Gwynne v Stopes* is not mentioned in *Horrocks v Lowe* and must be taken to be inconsistent with it, though Legoe J. in *Pearce v Hailstone* (1992) 58 S.A.S.R. 240 thought that *Gwynne v Stopes* still represented the position in Australia.

[146] *Lillie v Newcastle CC* [2002] EWHC 1600 (QB). See also, *Cambridge v Makin* [2012] EWCA Civ 85; [2012] E.M.L.R. 19.

[147] There is of course nothing peculiar to malice or defamation in this proposition: see *Derry v Peek* (1889) 14 A.C. 337 at 376 (fraud). For the same reason the jury in a criminal case may conclude that D foresaw an obvious risk even if he denies that he did.

[148] However, it seems that the courts in New Zealand have abandoned the sharp line between subjective honesty and objective carelessness (from which lack of honesty may be-but need not be-inferred), saying that malice is a flexible concept turning on the risk of injury from the publication: *Lange v Atkinson* [2000] NZCA 95; [2000] 3 N.Z.L.R. 385; *Att Gen v Wright* [2007] NZAR 40. Perhaps there are signs of a wish to move in that direction in *W v JH* [2008] EWHC 399 (QB) at [49].

[149] Unreported, April 4, 1924, from shorthand note.

as to indicate what may be a case of embezzlement, it is clearly his duty to report the matter to the directors of the company." [150]

As Kelly C.B. said in *Botterill v Whitehead* [151]:

"A person may honestly make on a particular occasion a defamatory statement without believing it to be true; because the statement may be of such a character that on that occasion it may be proper to communicate it to a particular person who ought to be informed of it."

In principle this extends to a case where the defendant in performance of a duty passes on a statement *which he knows to be untrue* but he would not be protected if he failed to include contradictory evidence in his possession.

The same principle may be applicable in the case of privileged reports even though the "duty" to convey the information may be the more shadowy one owed by the press to the public. If the claimant is acquitted in a criminal trial in circumstances which show beyond all doubt that he is not guilty, [152] a fair

---

[150] The facts in *Stuart v Bell* [1891] 2 Q.B. 341 CA, illustrate the point. See also the example in *Australian Broadcasting Corp v Comalco* (1986) 68 A.L.R. 259 Fed Ct of Australia at 282. In *W v Westminster City Council* [2004] EWHC 2866 (QB) a claim was brought in respect of statements made by a social worker about the claimant to a child protection conference. In Tugendhat J.'s opinion this was one of the "exceptional cases in which a person may be under a duty to pass on, without endorsing, defamatory reports made by some other person" identified by Lord Diplock in *Horrocks v Lowe*:
"Cases that come before social workers include ones where the adults in the family are at loggerheads. Allegations of sexual abuse, or risk of sexual abuse, can be made by a mother against a father or recent boyfriend who she wishes not to have contact with her child. A social worker might not know whether or not to believe the mother in such a case. In a rare case the social worker might have a very strong belief that the mother is lying. The mother might even have admitted lying. Nevertheless, in all these cases, it might still be the duty of the social worker to raise these matters at a Child Protection Conference, in an appropriate case, and in an appropriate manner. What the mother says on such a topic, even if believed to be false, may have relevance to decisions which are to be made about the child's future. An experienced social worker will know that such allegations made by a mother may be true, even if improbable, and may be withdrawn by her, even if they are true, depending upon what, for the time being, she hopes or fears that she or the child may receive from the man in question" (at [81]).
Tugendhat J. said that the true test in these cases was that posed by Lindley L.J. in *Stuart v Bell* at 351: "What, therefore, has to be ascertained is whether the defendant acted bona fide in the discharge of [the] moral duty which he owed . . . or whether he acted from some other unjustifi-able motive—from some motive other than a sense of duty."
In a subsequent hearing, *W v Westminster City Council (No.2)* [2005] EWHC 102 (QB); [2005] 4 All E.R. 96, the judge held that malice was not made out. He found that the defendants had deliberately published defamatory words as to the truth or falsity of which they had no belief one way or the other. He also found that they were not in fact under a duty to publish the words that they had on the occasion on which way they did (and for that reason the case was not strictly speaking one of Lord Diplock's exceptional cases). What they were doing was acting in good faith and attempting to perform the council's statutory duty (under the Children Act 1989, s.17) to S, by communicating with individuals who had a common and corresponding duty. Their error was in exceeding the limits of what should, in accordance with the guidelines, have been communicated on that occasion. However, there was no motive to injure the claimant, whether dominant or at all and for that reason the allegation of malice failed.
[151] (1879) 41 L.T. 588 at 590. See also *Clark v Molyneux* (1877) 3 Q.B.D. 237 CA at 244.
[152] An acquittal does not necessarily show this, it may simply mean that the prosecution has failed to discharge the onus of proof beyond a reasonable doubt.

and accurate report of the whole trial after the event would still be privileged[153] even if the evidence had contained imputations of guilt and the reporter was aware, in view of the outcome, that these were unfounded. If the law were otherwise the reporter would have to censor his report and risk losing the protection of privilege because it was not fair and accurate.[154] Of course, that case might in the alternative be dealt with on the basis that the publication must be taken as a whole and the antidote outweighs the bane.[155]

Other situations involving the press present more difficulty. As has been explained, if A attacks B in the press, then B has a qualified privilege to respond in kind in his own defence and this also avails the newspaper which publishes B's response.[156] Suppose, however, (unlikely as it may be) that the newspaper knows or believes that what B says about A is not true or knows that B is actuated by malice because he believes it to be untrue. Since awareness of, or even reckless indifference as to, falsity is normally conclusive evidence of malice, general principle would suggest that the newspaper itself is then malicious and it has been so held,[157] the position of the press not being equivalent to that of, e.g. a person under a legal duty to pass on a charge to a superior. Indeed, to hold the contrary would be to say that what is essentially an ancillary or derivative privilege was stronger than an original privilege.[158] On the other hand, it has been said that:

> "the social duty underlying the ancillary privilege is not served if a third party publisher suppresses a reply to an attack because he or she has formed a view about the truth or falsehood of the statements made or the motives of those who made them."[159]

---

[153] Some reports will be the subject of absolute privilege: see para.13.35, above.

[154] See the remarks of Hunt J. in *Waterhouse v Broadcasting Station 2 GB* (1985) 1 N.S.W.L.R. 58, accepting the proposition in the 8th edn, para.786, that such a report was privileged but criticising the reasoning upon which it was then based.

[155] See para.3.31, above.

[156] See para.14.53, above.

[157] *Bass v TCN Channel Nine Pty Ltd* [2003] NSWCA 118; and see *Australian Broadcasting Corp v Comalco* (1986) 68 A.L.R. 259 Fed Ct of Australia.

[158] If the newspaper were the originator of the material and knew it to be untrue that would clearly defeat any of the traditional common law heads of qualified privilege. But as to *Reynolds* privilege, see para.17.21, below.

[159] Spigelman C.J. dissenting in *Bass v TCN Channel Nine Pty Ltd*, above. In *Milne v Telegraph Group Ltd* [2001] E.M.L.R. 30 the defendant published an article about an investigation by the Parliamentary Commissioner for Standards into an allegation by the claimant that V had accepted payments from Z. Although the claimant was not named in the article, the article stated that he was a former senior partner of Z & Co. The article quoted V as denying that he had received any payments. It also quoted Z as denying that he had paid V any money and as saying that the claimant "will make up anything to try and embarrass me because he is vindictive". The defendant in fact waived privilege under the summary procedure but Sit Oliver Popplewell was of the view that there could be a distinction, albeit a thin one, between reporting a bare denial and reporting specific allegations.

Furthermore, the developing idea of privilege for "reportage" may mean that we have to approach such a case from a different angle.[160]

Malice and variant meanings. The fundamental principle is that liability **17.20** is based upon the meaning which the defamatory words will reasonably bear, not upon the meaning intended by the defendant.[161] If D published words on a privileged occasion intending them in defamatory sense A, which he knew to be untrue, malice is established even though on their proper interpretation they carry defamatory sense B, for the privileged occasion has been mis-used.[162] However, where the defendant intended the words in sense A, which he did believe to be true, his privilege is not defeated because they are found to convey defamatory sense B, for "malice is a subjective test, entirely dependent on the defendant's state of mind and intention".[163] Where D publishes a defamatory statement about X on an occasion of qualified privilege and believes that to be true, but the manner of his expression conveys to the reasonable reader that the statement also refers to C, about whom D does not hold that belief, he may not rely on the privilege against C: D's carelessness lies in the expression of what he wishes to convey, not in the formation of a belief.[164]

Section 2. Reynolds Privilege

The House of Lords in *Reynolds v Times Newspapers Ltd*[165] created a form of **17.21** qualified privilege for publications to the general public on matters of public concern. However, while the *Reynolds* defence is still generally described as

---

[160] See para.15.15, above.

[161] See para.3.15, above.

[162] *Fraser v Mirza*, 1993 S.C. (H.L.) 27.

[163] *Loveless v Earl* [1999] E.M.L.R. 530 CA at 538, per Hirst L.J.; *Bray v Deutsche Bank AG* [2008] EWHC 1263 QBD; *Klason v Australian Capital Territory* [2003] ACTSC 104; 177 F.L.R. 216. Hence the claimant should plead that the defendant knew that readers would understand the words in the sense complained of or was indifferent to that risk: *Bray* at [43]. See also para.15.23, above (*Reynolds* privilege).

[164] *Leverman v Campbell Sharp* (1987) 36 D.L.R. (4th) 401 BCCA (bankruptcy notice intended to refer to former partner in firm couched in such a way as to refer to firm). In *Loveless v Earl*, above, at 540, the following passage is quoted from *Leverman*,

"Carelessness in forming an honest belief does not take away the defence of qualified privilege. The honest belief can be formed on the slimmest of evidence. The questions are whether it is honestly held and whether there is a duty to make the statement. But carelessness in the publication of the statement so that it does not express the honest belief, or shows that the honest belief was never formed, takes away the defence of qualified privilege."

Then it is said, "[Counsel] agrees that the word 'carelessness' at the start of the last sentence just quoted must be interpreted as equivalent to recklessness." This is rather difficult to support because the word "carelessness" in the first sentence plainly does not mean recklessness. It is one thing to say that if there is a privilege for what D says about C then D is entitled to be judged by reference to what he meant. It is another thing to apply the same thing where the claimant is X, against whom there is no basis for privilege in the first place.

[165] [2001] 2 A.C. 127: para.15.1, above.

a privilege, its existence requires that the defendant has adhered to the standards of "responsible publication" and this involves matters like the nature of the steps taken to verify the information and whether comment was sought from the claimant. In other words, the mere fact that the defendant honestly believes in the truth of what he says does not of itself provide a basis for the privilege. However, the defendant must show that he complied with the standards of responsible publication, how can there ever be a case where, the defendant having done that, the defence is rebutted by proof of malice?

> "If the judge decides that the occasion was not privileged, the issue of malice does not arise. If the judge decides that the occasion was privileged, he must have decided that, in all the circumstances, at the time of the publication, including the extent of [the defendant's] inquiries, the public was entitled to know the particular information available to [the defendant] without her making further inquiries. It is a little difficult to see how the same inquiries which objectively sustained the occasion as privileged would be capable of contributing to a conclusion that subjectively she was recklessly indifferent to the truth or falsity of her publication."[166]

It is true that, irrespective of honest belief, a desire to injure the claimant is a basis of malice, but:

> "it may be doubted whether in truth there remains room for such a principle in a case of *Reynolds* privilege. Once the publication of a particular article is held to be in the public interest on the basis of the public's right to know, can the privilege really be lost because the journalist (or editor?) had the dominant motive of injuring the claimant rather than fulfilling his journalistic duty? It is a surprising thought."[167]

Of course it may be that the defendant puts forward a convincing prima facie case which the claimant has to meet by showing, e.g. that the defendant shut his eyes to available means of verification, but if the claimant does so he has not, technically, shown malice but shown that the material is not in fact privileged. In short, therefore, "[t]here is no question of the privilege being defeated by proof of malice because the propriety of the conduct of the defendant is built into the conditions under which the material is privileged."[168]

A not dissimilar issue arose under the "extended" qualified privilege created by the High Court of Australia in *Lange v Australian Broadcasting Corporation*.[169] That was confined to discussion of political or governmental matters but had a requirement of "reasonable conduct" by the publisher,

---

[166] *GKR Karate (UK) Ltd v Yorkshire Post Newspapers Ltd* [2000] 1 W.L.R. 2571 CA at 2580.

[167] *Loutchansky v Times Newspapers Ltd (Nos 2–5)* [2001] EWCA Civ 1805; [2002] Q.B. 783 at [34].

[168] *Jameel v Wall Street Journal Europe SPRL* [2006] UKHL 44; [2007] 1 A.C. 359 per Lord Hoffmann at [46]. "If a particular publication passes the privilege test now [i.e. under *Reynolds*], it is very difficult to envisage circumstances where there would be room for it to be overridden by malice": *Miller v Associated Newspapers Ltd* [2004] EWHC 2799 QBD; [2004] E.M.L.R. 33 at [10] per Eady J.

[169] (1997) 189 C.L.R. 520: para.15.26, above.

which is part of the basis of the privilege. Like *Reynolds*, it generally required reasonable steps to verify the information and the opportunity for response by the claimant. However, the High Court clearly considered that malice still had some role to play, so that, e.g. "we see no reason why a publisher who has used the occasion to give vent to its ill will or other improper motive should escape liability for the publication of false and defamatory statements".[170] Perhaps the explanation is that *Lange* was more akin to a "generic" privilege in the sense that it was not necessary to show that the material is of legitimate public interest: that was automatically satisfied if it concerned government or politics. As far as concerned matters like verification and affording a right of response are concerned, however, the position was much as it is in England under *Reynolds*.

> "The protection of [the] . . . reputations [of those defamed by widespread publica-
> tions] will be further enhanced by the requirement that the defence will be defeated
> if the person defamed proves that the publication was actuated by common law
> malice *to the extent that the elements of malice are not covered under the rubric of
> reasonableness*."[171]

The actual decision in *Lange* was that s.22 of the Defamation Act 1974 (NSW), creating a statutory form of qualified privilege for matters of public concern (but not confined to politics) and containing a requirement of reason-ableness as opposed to mere honesty, satisfied the constitutional requirement for protection of political debate.[172] That has now been replaced by s.30 of the Defamation Act 2005 (NSW) which is broadly similar to its predecessor but which is in some ways more closely modelled on *Reynolds*.[173] There is now also an equivalent provision in the legislation of the other states and territo-ries.[174] However, s.30 provides (as does each of its equivalents) that "[f]or the avoidance of doubt, [the] defence . . . is defeated if the plaintiff proves that the publication of the defamatory matter was actuated by malice."

---

[170] But the motive of causing political damage to the plaintiff or his or her party cannot be regarded as improper (see also *Roberts v Bass* [2002] HCA 57; 212 C.L.R. 1).

[171] Emphasis added.

[172] In *Griffith v Australian Broadcasting Corp* [2010] NSWCA 257 the New South Wales Court of Appeal held that the statutory qualified privilege defences created by the 1974 Act (which have now been replaced by the 2005 Uniform legislation albeit that the defence in s.30 of the 2005 Act (NSW) is modelled on s.22 of the 1974 Act) are different from common law qualified privilege. S.22 of the 1974 Act requires that the defendant show that his conduct in publishing the matter is reasonable in the circumstances and as part of establishing reasonableness, the onus is on the defendant to exclude malice. That is an onus to show that his purpose in publishing the matter, in its character of conveying the defamatory imputation, was to give the audience information which the audience had an interest (or apparent interest) in having, and that the defendant did not have any other reason for this publication which was the dominant reason. As Hodgson J.A. notes at [110]: "This view has consequences that are not necessarily favourable to defendants." Whether s.30 will be interpreted in the same way remains to be seen.

[173] See para.15.26, above.

[174] See para.1.3, above.

As we have seen, publication of what the defendant knows or believes to be untrue is normally conclusive evidence of malice.[175] Can it ever be consistent with the tenets of responsible journalism to publish what you know or believe to be untrue? There must be some cases where it is, as for example where a newspaper, as it may be required to do if it is to rely on privilege, publishes a version of events by the claimant which its editor and journalists find unconvincing. Or where it is a case of reportage in which accusations and counter-accusations are being reported. The newspaper's attitude may often be "a plague on both your houses"; but its opinions may favour one side and it should not be at risk of losing protection so long as it reports the matter in a neutral manner.[176]

Section 3. Concurrent Tortfeasors

17.22　Nature of the problem. Words are published by A and B on a privileged occasion.[177] A is actuated by malice and B is not (and B is unaware of A's motives). There are three possible situations. First, A is someone for whom B is vicariously liable. Secondly, A and B each has an independent privilege. Thirdly, A has a privilege based upon duty or interest and B has a merely derivative privilege, as where B types or prints material created by A.

17.23　Vicarious liability. Where an agent or servant,[178] acting within the scope and in the course of his employment,[179] publishes a libel on a privileged occasion, and it is proved that the agent or servant was actuated by malice,[180] the principal or employer is liable.[181] However, where an agent or servant has "nothing whatever to do with the composition of the libel or the approval of

---

[175] See paras 17.16, 17.19, above.

[176] See para.15.15, above.

[177] That is to say, a case falling within s.1 of this Chapter.

[178] For the question of how far this extends to agents who are not servants, see para.8.30, above.

[179] For this in the context of defamation, see para.8.32, above.

[180] Some identifiable person. A company's mind is not to be assessed on the totality of knowledge of its employees: *Broadway Approvals v Odhams Press* [1965] 1 W.L.R. 805 CA at 813; *Webster v British Gas Services* [2003] EWHC 1188 QBD; *Akinleye v East Sussex Hospitals NHS Trust* [2008] EWHC 68 QBD; *Bray v Deutsche Bank AG* [2008] EWHC 1263 QBD.

[181] *Citizens' Life Co. v Brown* [1904] A.C. 423; *Egger v Chelmsford* [1965] 1 Q.B. 248 CA; *Fitzsimmons v Duncan & Co* [1908] 2 Ir.R. 483; *Dawson v The Council of Bulli* (1927) 27 N.S.W.S.R. 509. A, for whom D is vicariously liable, makes a defamatory statement to X about C on a privileged occasion and is not actuated by malice. It is likely that A was misled by some other person unknown, for whom D would also be vicariously liable. In a suit for the publication by A, Crispin J. in *Klason v Australian Capital Territory* [2003] ACTSC 104; 177 F.L.R. 216 at [113] said that he was:

> "unaware of any principle that would enable malice to be imputed to a defendant on the basis that the maker of the relevant statement had been misled by some other person for whose conduct the defendant was also vicariously responsible".

Presumably the position would be different if the evidence showed that the other employee had procured A to make the statement.

its contents," but "in obedience to the command of his principal merely does the mechanical act of distributing it when handed to him complete," malice on his part is (semble) irrelevant, and will not destroy the privilege of his principal or employer.[182] So, a trade union, to which the plaintiff belonged, published to its members, in accordance with its rules, the report and minutes of a conference of an unregistered association, of which the union was the successor. The report contained the terms of a resolution passed at the conference, embodying certain allegations against the plaintiff. The terms of the resolution were accurately stated, but the allegations made against the plaintiff were untrue and defamatory. The occasion was admittedly privileged. It was held that in the absence of evidence of any malicious motive on the part of the union or its governing body, the privilege was not destroyed by the fact that the secretary of the union, whose duty it was to hand the report to the members, was aware that the defamatory statements were untrue, nor by the fact that he himself entertained feelings of personal ill will against the plaintiff.[183]

Independent privilege. It is now firmly established that where words are published by a number of people, each of whom has an independent privilege (e.g. the members of a committee) they are each to be judged individually and the malice of one does not infect the others.[184] In *Egger v Chelmsford*,[185] on the instructions of a subcommittee of the Kennel Club, the assistant secretary wrote a letter which was held to be defamatory of the plaintiff. The letter was written on an occasion of qualified privilege. The jury found that seven out of the 10 members of the committee were malicious, but not the other three, or the assistant secretary, and assessed the damages at £750. Marshall J. gave judgment for £750 against all the members of the committee and the assistant secretary, on the authority of *Smith v Streatfeild*.[186] On an appeal by those defendants who were held not to have been malicious, it was held that they were entitled to rely on the defence of privilege, and *Smith v Streatfeild* was overruled.

17.24

> "It is a mistake to suppose that, on a joint publication, the malice of one defendant infects his co-defendant. Each defendant is answerable severally, as well as jointly, for the joint publication; and each is entitled to his several defence, whether he be sued jointly or separately from the others. If the plaintiff seeks to rely on malice to

---

[182] *Hay v Australasian Institute* (1906) 3 C.L.R. 1002. Per Lord Atkinson in *Adam v Ward* [1917] A.C. 309 at 341; per Lord Dunedin, ibid. at 331, see also *Longdon-Griffiths v Smith* [1951] 1 K.B. 295; *Iwi v Montesole, The Times*, March 14, 1955. See para.8.32, above.

[183] *Hay v Australasian Institute* (1906) 3 C.L.R. 1002.

[184] There is no doctrine of "transferred malice" in the law of defamation: *Egger v Chelmsford* [1965] 1 Q.B. 248 CA; *Curran v Scottish Daily Record and Sunday Mail Ltd* [2012] S.L.T. 359. As the Court of Session Outer House noted in *Curran* there is virtual uniformity across the Commonwealth that there could be no "cross-infection" of malice: at [37].

[185] [1965] 1 Q.B. 248 CA, overruling *Smith v Streatfeild* [1913] 3 K.B. 764 and not following dicta in *Adam v Ward* [1917] A.C. 309 at 320, 331, 340–341.

[186] [1913] 3 K.B. 764.

aggravate the damages, or to rebut a defence of qualified privilege . . . then he must prove malice against each person whom he charges with it. A defendant is only affected by express malice if he himself was actuated by it, or if his servant or agent concerned in the publication was actuated by malice in the course of his employment."[187]

17.25 Derivative privilege. Where a defendant has no personal interest or duty in the matter but merely acts as a mechanical agent for a person with such an interest or duty[188] (as in the case of a printer[189]) it is easy to advance a logical argument that if the principal's privilege is destroyed by malice so must be that of the agent which derives from it. However, in *Egger v Chelmsford*[190] Lord Denning M.R.[191] equated all agents, as, for instance, a solicitor or typist, and both he and Harman L.J. (who did not refer to the original nature of the secretary's privilege) took the view that if he were held liable for the malice of the members of the committee, it would be a case of *respondeat inferior*. This, it is submitted, is plainly the better view.

---

[187] . . . per Lord Denning M.R. in *Egger v Chelmsford* [1965] 1 Q.B. 248 CA at 265; *Pillay v Balakrishnan* [1997] 3 S.L.R. 25 Sing. CA; *Cornwall v Rowan* [2004] SASC 384; 90 S.A.S.R. 269 (Full Ct.); *Roberts v Bass* [2002] HCA 57; 212 C.L.R. 1 at [182], per Kirby J. (Callinan J. at [306], while leaving the point open, seems more inclined to the older view, which was accepted in *Webb v Bloch* (1928) 41 C.L.R. 331 HCA).

[188] See para.14.75, above.

[189] It is true that such agents now have some protection under s.1 of the Defamation Act 1996 (see paras 6.31–6.38, above). However, this is considerably narrower than that provided by a plea of privilege.

[190] [1965] 1 Q.B. 248 CA.

[191] Ibid. at 261; *Richardson v Schwarzenegger* [2004] EWHC 2422 QBD.

CHAPTER 18

REHABILITATION OF OFFENDERS ACT 1974

SECTION 1. INTRODUCTION

The common law. The law of misuse of private information is in a state of **18.1**
development so it is not possible to state categorically that there is no redress
at common law for the revelation of past criminal convictions[1] However, as
far as the law of defamation is concerned it is clear that no such claim lies at
common law, since it gives an absolute defence in respect of the publication
of matter which is true,[2] however much the wrongdoer may have reformed,
and for however long he has led an honest and socially valuable life.[3]

Rehabilitation of Offenders Act 1974. The Rehabilitation of Offenders **18.2**
Act 1974 modified the common law in a number of respects. There are special

---

[1] In *KJO v XIM* [2011] EWHC 1768 (QB) at [16] Eady J. refused to grant summary judgment
in an application brought by a nephew who was attempting to prevent his uncle from informing
potential employers of his spent convention for forgery. It would, he said, require clear authority,
either in Strasbourg or domestic jurisprudence, to justify using the policy behind the Rehabilitation of Offenders Act 1974 to extend the misuse of private information claim to cover the
revelation of past criminal convictions. See para.22.5 fn.43, below.

[2] It was suggested by Lord Shaw of Dunfermline in *Sutherland v Stopes* [1925] A.C. 47 HL at
74, that:

"A statement of fact or of opinion which consists in the raking up of a long-buried past may,
without an explanation (and, in cases which are conceivable even with an explanation), be
libellous or slanderous if written or uttered in such circumstances as to suggest that a taint upon
character and conduct still subsists ... "

The Faulks Committee cited this passage as suggesting that "muck-raking publications may well
be actionable if they imply that a taint on the plaintiffs character still remains" (Cmnd.5909,
para.140); though there is no case in which this has been held, it seems correct in principle, and
would apply to any past wrongdoing, not merely to the subject-matter of a conviction. It has been
held that since a person who had served his term for felony was in the same position as if he had
been given a pardon under the Great Seal, it would be actionable to describe him as a "felon
editor": *Leyman v Latimer* (1878) 3 Ex.D. 15 at 352; even in that case, it seemed to be taken for
granted that the fact of the conviction could be mentioned.

[3] Some of the situations in which people have been adversely affected by knowledge or the
possibility of knowledge of their past conviction are listed in *Living It Down*, Justice (1972).
Cases in which there might have been a defamation action had the law been otherwise are only
some of them. For comment and bibliography on the Rehabilitation of Offenders Act 1974 see 8
Anglo-American L.R. 60.

provisions relating to defamation[4] but they cannot be understood without a knowledge of the scheme of the Act. The Act defines a "spent conviction" as one for which a sentence of no more than 30 months imprisonment was passed on an individual and since which there has elapsed a "rehabilitation period" which varies according to the age of the person concerned, the type of proceeding and the sentence imposed or the order made.[5] Once the rehabilitation period has elapsed the individual is treated for the purposes of the Act as a rehabilitated person in respect of the conviction. The basic scheme of the Act is that once someone has become a rehabilitated person in respect of a conviction[6] he is to be treated for all purposes as a person who has not committed or been charged with or prosecuted for or convicted of or sentenced for the offence or offences which were the subject of that conviction.[7]

The main consequences are two-fold; first, in court proceedings evidence to that effect is not generally admissible, and questions which would elicit spent convictions are not to be admitted, while secondly various rules of law are modified so as to remove obligations to admit the existence of spent convictions in answering questions or to disclose the spent convictions of another, and to make a spent conviction not a proper ground for dismissing a person from an occupation or employment or prejudicing him in any way in any occupation or employment. The Act does not render the spent convictions "confidential".[8]

18.3 Defamation actions and spent convictions. If no special provision had been made for actions for libel and slander, the effect would have been, whether rightly or wrongly, that there would have been no defence of justification available in the case of an allegation of a conviction which was in fact spent, and the defence of privilege would have been affected, in that evidence of such a conviction would not have been admissible if the honesty of the defendant were challenged. The Act thus provides that a defendant may rely on such evidence in support of a defence of justification unless the publication is proved to have been made with malice.[9] Similarly, with certain restrictions, the defendant may also rely on such evidence in support of a plea of absolute or qualified privilege, or of honest comment.

18.4 Reform of the Rehabilitation of Offenders Act. The Act has been criticised for many years on the ground that it does not do enough to rehabilitate offenders. In 2002, the then Labour Government published a

---

[4] See para.18.14, below.
[5] See para.18.7, below.
[6] As to cautions, see para.18.5, below.
[7] See para.18.12, below.
[8] *L v Law Society* [2008] EWCA Civ 811; *KJO v XIM* [2011] EWHC 1768 (QB).
[9] See para.18.16, below.

review of the Act.[10] The review did not make any proposals for alteration in the law on the admissibility or use of convictions in court proceedings nor on defamation and court reporting. The purpose of the review exercise was to increase employment opportunities and it was felt to be inappropriate to seek to further restrict media reporting, where the interest of rehabilitation had to be balanced against freedom of speech.[11] However, no draft bill emerged and in April 2009 it was announced that although the Government remained committed to reform no timescale could be set. In 2010, a further consultation paper, *Breaking the Cycle: Effective Punishment, Rehabilitation and Sentencing of Offenders*,[12] was issued. The Government's response to the consultation[13] did not mention the 1974 Act but amendments were introduced in the House of Lords to what became the Legal Aid, Sentencing and Punishment of Offenders Act 2012. The first key change was to extend the scope of the Act to cover custodial sentences of up to 48 months, and the second was to change the length of some of the rehabilitation periods (in most cases by reducing them). The new clause has now been enacted as s.139 of the 2012 Act. However this provision is not yet in force and the Government informed a rehabilitation charity in February 2013 that it will not commence until November of that year.[14]

SECTION 2. SPENT CONVICTIONS

Conviction needed. The Act at present applies to *convicted* offenders, not,   **18.5** as the title might suggest, to offenders; to be entitled to its protection a person must have been convicted[15] and sentenced and have served or otherwise undergone or complied with his sentence.[16] Thus it has no application where a person is alleged to have committed an offence for which he was not convicted, even if he was charged with the offence, and the prosecution was

---

[10] *Breaking the Circle*, July 2002, Home Office.

[11] Ibid. para.7.12.

[12] Cm 7972, December, 2010.

[13] *Breaking the Cycle: Government Response*, Cm.8070, June 2011.

[14] *http://www.unlock.org.uk/staticpage.aspx?pid=69*.

[15] Hence it does not apply where a person has received a caution: *Lincolnshire CC v R-J* [1998] 1 W.L.R. 1679 (where, however, there is an extended consideration of the Act because it was sought to rely on it by analogy). But see below as to the future effect of the Criminal Justice and Immigration Act 2008.

[16] Rehabilitation of Offenders Act 1974, s.1(2). Non-payment of a fine and breaches of a condition of a recognisance or bond of caution, or of a condition or requirement applicable in relation to a sentence which renders the person to whom it applies liable to be dealt with for the offence for which the sentence was imposed, or liable to be dealt with in respect of a suspended sentence of imprisonment (whether or not in any case, he is in fact so dealt with) or failure to comply with any requirement of a suspended sentence or supervision order, do not prevent a person becoming a rehabilitated person (ibid.). However, the reference to a fine or other sum adjudged to be paid by or imposed on a conviction does not include a reference to an amount payable under a confiscation order made under Pt 2 or 3 of the Proceeds of Crime Act 2002: s.1(2B), inserted by s.456, Sch.11 of the Proceeds of Crime Act 2002.

dropped, or even if he was ultimately acquitted. However, the Act does apply to a conviction by or before a court outside Great Britain,[17] and to any finding (other than a finding linked to a finding of insanity) in criminal proceedings that a person has committed an offence or done the act or made the omission charged.[18] Although convictions followed by a conditional or absolute discharge are deemed not to be convictions for other purposes, they are to be treated as convictions which may become spent for the purposes of the Act.[19] The Act has always applied to certain convictions in service disciplinary proceedings but by the Armed Forces Act 1996 all service convictions were brought within the ambit of the rehabilitation principle so that they became capable of being spent in the same way as civilian convictions.[20] By virtue of amendments made by s.49 of the Criminal Justice and Immigration Act 2008 the Act applies to adult and youth conditional cautions, other cautions (for example, "simple" cautions issued by the police), reprimands and warnings given to children and young people, and cautions given in a jurisdiction outside England and Wales

18.6 Sentences excluded from rehabilitation. Some sentences are excluded from rehabilitation; they are (a) imprisonment for life,[21] (b) imprisonment (or youth custody, detention in a young offender institution or corrective training) for a term exceeding 30 months,[22] and (c) certain equivalent sentences.[23] If such a sentence is imposed in respect of a conviction then the conviction cannot become spent and the individual cannot become a rehabilitated person in respect of that conviction.[24] The same consequences follow if the individual receives a sentence excluded from rehabilitation on a subsequent conviction before the expiry of the rehabilitation period applicable to the first mentioned conviction.[25] Thus, if X was convicted in 1996 and sentenced to two years' imprisonment (for which the rehabilitation period is 10 years)[26] and in 2005 was convicted again and sentenced to three years' imprisonment, he cannot become a rehabilitated person in respect of either conviction. If, on the other

---

[17] S.1(4)(a).

[18] S.1(4)(b).

[19] S.1(4).

[20] Armed Forces Act 1996, s.13, amending the Rehabilitation of Offenders Act 1974. The definition of service disciplinary proceedings is amended from a date to be appointed by the Armed Forces Act 2006, s.378(1), Sch.16, para.64(a).

[21] Rehabilitation of Offenders Act 1974, s.5(1)(a).

[22] S.5(1)(b).

[23] See s.5(1)(b), (c), (d), (da), (e) and (f) as amended or inserted by the Armed Forces Act 1976, the Criminal Justice (Scotland) Act 1980, the Criminal Justice Act 1982, the Powers of Criminal Courts (Sentencing) Act 2000, the Criminal Justice Act 2003, the Armed Forces Act 2006 and the Criminal Justice and Immigration Act 2008.

[24] Rehabilitation of Offenders Act 1974, s.1(1)(a). However, in exceptional cases where there is a risk to the life or health of a convicted person the court may be prepared to protect his identity by injunction even though rehabilitation under the 1974 Act is not possible: para.22.5, below.

[25] Ibid. s.1(1)(b).

[26] See para.18.7, below.

hand, the second conviction is not until 2007, he will have become a rehabilitated person in respect of the first conviction, but cannot become so in respect of the second.

Rehabilitation period: substantial sentences. The rehabilitation period applicable to any conviction is based not on the nature of the offence for which the individual was convicted, but on the nature and length of the sentence imposed. The main periods[27] are found in Table A of s.5(2) of the Act, but all are subject to reduction by half where the sentence was imposed on a person who was under the age of 18 at the date of his conviction.[28] Where the sentence is of imprisonment[29] for a term exceeding six months but not exceeding 30 months, or of cashiering, discharge with ignominy or dismissal with disgrace from Her Majesty's service the period is 10 years from the date of the conviction. Where the sentence is of imprisonment[30] for a term not exceeding six months or of dismissal from Her Majesty's service, the period is seven years. For any sentence of detention in respect of a conviction in service disciplinary proceedings or for a fine the period is five years. There are also periods specified by Table B for certain sentences confined to young offenders. **18.7**

Other sentences. The period applicable to an absolute discharge is six months from the date of the conviction.[31] The period applicable where a person is conditionally discharged, bound over to keep the peace or be of good behaviour is one year from the date of the conviction, or until the order, recognisance or bond ceases or ceased to have effect, whichever is the longer.[32] Similar provisions are applicable to certain orders and requirements relating to children and young persons.[33] Where a probation order or a community service order under s.177 of the Criminal Justice Act 2003 is made **18.8**

---

[27] Consecutive sentences and sentences wholly or partly concurrent are to be treated as a single term: s.5(9)(b). No account is to be taken of a subsequent variation of a suspended term of imprisonment: s.5(9)(c).

[28] S.5(2)(a).

[29] Or of detention in a young offender institution or youth custody or corrective training.

[30] Again including the youth sentences mentioned in the previous note.

[31] Rehabilitation of Offenders Act 1974, s.5(3)(a). The same period applies to the discharge by a children's hearing under the Children (Scotland) Act 1995 of the referral of a child's case: s.5(3)(b). The rehabilitation periods for spent cautions are as follows. In the case of a conditional caution (that is to say, one under the Criminal Justice Act 2003, s.22 or the Crime and Disorder Act 1998, ss.66A and 66ZA) three months from the date of the caution. If the person cautioned is subsequently convicted of the offence in respect of which the conditional caution was given the caution becomes spent at the end of the period for the offence but if the conviction occurs after the end of the initial caution rehabilitation period the caution is not treated as having become spent before the end of the period for the offence: In the case of any other caution it becomes spent when it is given. Rehabilitation of Offenders Act 1974, Sch.2. Para.1, inserted by the Criminal Justice and Immigration Act 2008.

[32] S.5(4).

[33] S.5(4B), (4C) (inserted by the Youth Justice and Criminal Evidence Act 1999 and amended by the Powers of Criminal Courts (Sentencing) Act 2000) and 5(5).

the period of rehabilitation is five years from the date of conviction, except in the case of a person under the age of 18 at the date of his conviction, in which case it is two and one-half years from the date of the conviction or a period beginning with the date of conviction and ending when the order ceases or ceased to have effect, whichever is the longer.[34] In the case of an order for custody in a remand home, an approved school order, an attendance centre order or a secure training order the period is that beginning with the date of conviction and ending one year after the order ceases to have effect.[35] Where a hospital order is made,[36] the period is five years from the date of conviction, or until two years after the hospital order ceases or ceased to have effect, whichever is the longer.[37] Where any disqualification, disability, prohibition or other penalty is imposed the applicable period ends when the penalty imposed ceases or ceased to have effect.[38]

18.9 Period applicable to conviction. The periods mentioned so far are those applicable to particular sentences, and whenever only one sentence is imposed in respect of a conviction, the rehabilitation period applicable to the conviction is that applicable to the sentence.[39] Special provisions are, however, made for the cases in which more than one sentence is imposed in respect of a conviction (whether or not in the same proceedings), either because two sentences are imposed at the same time (e.g. fine and disqualification), or because a person is brought back subsequently to be dealt with on breach, say, of probation. In such cases, the rehabilitation period is the longer or the longest of the periods applicable to each of the sentences.[40]

18.10 Subsequent offences. Where a person during the rehabilitation period is convicted of a further offence (other than one which is to be disregarded for these purposes)[41] and no sentence excluded from rehabilitation is imposed on

---

[34] S.5(4A), added by the Criminal Justice and Public Order Act 1994 and amended by the Criminal Justice Act 2003.

[35] S.5(6). There are further provisions in respect of a detention and training order under s.100 of the Powers of Criminal Courts (Sentencing) Act 2000: s.5(6A), inserted by the Crime and Disorder Act 1998 and amended by the 2000 Act.

[36] Under Pt III of the Mental Health Act 1983 or Pt V of the Mental Health (Scotland) Act 1960.

[37] Rehabilitation of Offenders Act 1974, s.5(7).

[38] S.5(8). If a defendant is given a conditional discharge and disqualified from driving for a longer period, s.5(8) extends the one year period that would otherwise apply: *Re Hamill* [2001] EWHC Admin 762. But an endorsement on a driving licence is not a "disability, prohibition or other penalty" for this purpose: *Power v Provincial Insurance* [1998] R.T.R. 60 CA.

[39] S.6(1).

[40] S.6(2). If a person is dealt with for breach of conditional discharge or a probation order at a time after the rehabilitation period, and is given a sentence for which the applicable period is longer, he is treated as not having become a rehabilitated person in respect of that conviction until the end of that longer period; i.e. he is not temporarily rehabilitated in the time between the end of the original period and the date of the new sentence: ibid. s.6(3).

[41] Under the Act as originally enacted no conviction in service disciplinary proceedings was to be disregarded for these purposes: ibid. s.6(7). However, this was altered by the Armed Forces Act 1996, s.13. See s.6(6)(bb) and Schedule, both inserted by s.13 of the Armed Forces Act 1996. Any conviction in England and Wales of a summary offence or of a scheduled offence (within the

him in respect of the later conviction,[42] whichever of the two applicable rehabilitation periods would have ended earlier is extended to end at the same time as the other.[43] Thus, if a person was convicted and sentenced to two years' imprisonment in 1996 (for which the period is 10 years) and was convicted and fined in 2000 (for which the period is five years), both rehabilitation periods would have ended in 2006. If on the other hand he had been fined on the first occasion and sentenced to two years' imprisonment on the second, both periods would end in 2010. Where, however, the rehabilitation period applicable to one of the convictions is that applicable to an order imposing any disqualification, disability, prohibition or other penalty,[44] the period of the other conviction is to be extended, if at all, only by reference to the longest period applicable to any other sentence imposed along with the penalty.[45] Thus, if the person in the first example above had been disqualified from driving for 10 years on his second conviction as well as being fined, the rehabilitation period for the first conviction would still end in 2006, even though that for the second conviction would continue until 2010.

Convictions outside Great Britain. The Act also applies to convictions   **18.11** by or before a court outside Great Britain,[46] so that a person may become a rehabilitated person in respect of such a conviction, and it may become a spent conviction for the purposes of the Act. The rehabilitation period applicable to such a conviction is determined by reference to the sentence imposed by the court, which is to be treated as a sentence of one of the descriptions mentioned in s.5 of the Act which most nearly corresponds to the sentence imposed.[47]

Section 3. Effects of Rehabilitation

Effects of rehabilitation. While there are special provisions in relation to   **18.12** defamation actions,[48] they act by modifying the general provisions in s.4(1) of

---

meaning of s.22 of the Magistrates' Courts Act 1980 tried summarily in pursuance of subs.(2) of that section (summary trial where value involved is small), or of an offence under s.17 of the Crime (Sentences) Act 1997 (breach of conditions of release supervision order) is to be disregarded, as is any conviction in Scotland of an offence which is not excluded from the jurisdiction of inferior courts of summary jurisdiction by virtue of the Criminal Procedure (Scotland) Act 1975 or any conviction outside Great Britain of an offence in respect of conduct which would not have constituted an offence in Great Britain: Rehabilitation of Offenders Act 1974, s.6(6).

[42] For sentences excluded from rehabilitation. see para.18.6, above. In such a case the person will never become a rehabilitated person in respect of either conviction.

[43] S.6(4).

[44] Under s.5(8).

[45] S.6(5).

[46] S.1(4)(a).

[47] S.5(9)(d). See paras 18.7, 18.8, above.

[48] See para.18.14, below.

the Act on the effects of rehabilitation: these are as follows.[49] A person who has become a rehabilitated person in respect of a conviction shall be treated for all purposes in law as a person who has not committed or been charged with or prosecuted for or convicted of or sentenced for the offence or offences which were the subject of that conviction.[50] Accordingly, notwithstanding the provisions of any other enactment or rule to the contrary,[51] no evidence is admissible in any proceeding before a judicial authority exercising its jurisdiction or functions in Great Britain[52] to prove to the contrary.[53] Nor is a person to be asked and, if asked, he is not to be required to answer, any question relating to his past which cannot be answered without acknowledging or referring to a spent conviction or convictions or any circumstances ancillary thereto.[54] However, nothing in s.4(1) affects the determination of any issue or prevents the admission or requirement of any evidence in any criminal proceedings before a court in Great Britain (including any appeal or reference in a criminal matter) or in the other proceedings specified in the Act.[55] Additionally, if a judicial authority is satisfied that justice cannot be done in a case without admitting or requiring evidence relating to a person's spent convictions or to circumstances ancillary thereto, the authority may admit or

---

[49] Similar provisions apply to cautions: Rehabilitation of Offenders Act 1974, Sch.2 para.3, inserted by the Criminal Justice and Immigration Act 2008.

[50] S.4(1).

[51] This appears to be a reference to such provisions as the Theft Act 1968, s.27(3), or perhaps to the Civil Evidence Act 1968, ss.11–13.

[52] For the purposes of this section, this includes any tribunal, body or person having power (1) by virtue of any enactment, law, custom or practice; (2) under the rule governing any association, institution, profession, occupation or employment; or (3) under any provision of an agreement providing for arbitration with respect to questions arising thereunder, to determine any question affecting the rights, privileges, obligations or liabilities of any person. or to receive evidence affecting the determination of any such question. It thus includes the ordinary domestic tribunal, as well as the kind of inquiry which makes recommendations to someone who can determine the question as in *Trapp v Mackie* [1979] 1 W.L.R. 377 HL. It is not clear that it applies to a tribunal of inquiry, or a body which can exercise only a reporting or critical function.

[53] S.4(1)(a).

[54] S.4(1)(b). "Circumstances ancillary to a conviction" are defined in subs.(5) as any of the following: (a) the offence or offences which were the subject of that conviction; (b) the conduct constituting that offence or those offences; and (c) any process or proceedings preliminary to that conviction, any sentence imposed in respect of that conviction, any proceedings (whether by way of appeal or otherwise) for reviewing that conviction or any such sentence, and anything done in pursuance of or undergone in compliance with any such sentence.

[55] S.7(2)(a). However, under *Practice Direction (criminal: consolidated)* [2002] 1 W.L.R. 2870 it is recommended that both court and advocates should give effect to the general intention of Parliament under the Act by never referring to a spent conviction when such reference can reasonably be avoided and further guidance is given: at [6]. See also *Practice Note* [1975] 2 All E.R. 1072. The other proceedings specified in s.7(2) are service disciplinary proceedings and appeals therefrom, proceedings under Pt 2 of the Sexual Offences Act 2003 and appeals therefrom, certain proceedings related to minors, proceedings under the Children Act 1989, proceedings relating to supervision orders or youth rehabilitation orders and proceedings in which the person is a party or witness and consents: s.7(2)(b)–(f). The Secretary of State may also exclude by order the application of s.4(1) in relation to any proceedings specified in the order to such extent and for such purposes as may be so specified: s.7(4). This power has been exercised in the Rehabilitation of Offenders Act 1974 (Exceptions) Order 1975, SI 1975/1023, para.5, Sch.3, as amended.

require the evidence and determine any issue to which the evidence relates in disregard, so far as necessary, of the provisions of s.4(1).[56]

Extrajudicial consequences. The Act also provides that when a question **18.13** seeking information with respect to a person's previous convictions, offences, conduct or circumstances is put to him or any other person otherwise than in proceedings before a judicial authority,[57] (1) the question shall be treated as not relating to spent convictions or to any circumstances ancillary to spent convictions, and the answer may be framed accordingly; and (2) the person questioned shall not be subjected to any liability or otherwise prejudiced in law by reason of any failure to acknowledge or disclose a spent conviction or any circumstances ancillary to a spent conviction in his answer to the question.[58]

The application of these provisions is by Order excluded[59] in relation to questions asked in order to assess the suitability of a person for admission to a specified profession, for a specified office or employment, to pursue a specified occupation or pursue it subject to a particular condition or restriction, to hold a specified licence, certificate or permit or to hold it subject to a particular condition or restriction. The person questioned must be informed at the time the question is asked that by virtue of the relevant Order spent convictions are to be disclosed. It should also be noted that subject to similar

---

[56] S.7(3). On the question of relevance and the exercise of discretion under s.7(3) see *Thomas v MPC* [1997] Q.B. 813 CA; and on procedure see *Adamson v Waveney DC* [1997] 2 All E.R. 898.

[57] There are similar provisions for cautions: Rehabilitation of Offenders Act 1974, Sch.2 para.3, inserted by the Criminal Justice and Immigration Act 2008.

[58] S.4(2).

[59] By the Rehabilitation of Offenders Act 1974 (Exceptions) Order 1975, SI 1975/1023 para.3, as amended. The Order also excepts certain questions asked for the purpose of safeguarding national security. With regard to Scotland the law is now to be found in the Rehabilitation of Offenders Act 1974 (Exclusions and Exceptions) (Scotland) Order 2003, SSI 2003 no.231. There is a similar power to exclude the comparable provisions in relation to spent cautions: Rehabilitation of Offenders Act 1974, Sch.2 para.4, inserted by the Criminal Justice and Immigration Act 2008. Part V of the Police Act 1997 provides for disclosure to persons entitled to ask exempted questions of convictions recorded in police records (see also the Safeguarding of Vulnerable Groups Act 2006), thereby providing a check on the applicant's answers. In *CC Humberside v Information Comr* [2009] EWCA Civ 1079; [2010] 1 W.L.R. 1136 the court reversed the decisions of the Information Tribunal (*CC Humberside v Information Comr*, EA/2007/0096,98,99,108,127, July 21, 2008—the Information Tribunal had upheld enforcement notices requiring police forces to remove records of old convictions which contravened the Data Protection Principles in the Data Protection Act 1998 in relation to the removal of records of old convictions. The case turned on the interpretation of the Data Protection Act 1998 and this aspect of the case is considered at para.22.21, below. However, the gravamen of the complaints of the data subjects was not simply about the *retention* of the data but the effects of its *disclosure*. In four cases the issue had arisen because the convictions had been disclosed to employers who were exempt under the 1975 Exceptions Order and had been entitled to obtain disclosure. In Hughes L.J.'s concurring judgment, a number of serious concerns were identified about the range of those who have access, directly or indirectly, to the database of conviction information (at [112]–[113]).

exclusions[60] any obligation imposed on any person by any rule of law or by the provisions of an agreement or arrangement to disclose any matters to any other person shall not extend to requiring him to disclose a spent conviction or any circumstances ancillary to a spent conviction,[61] and that a conviction which has become spent or any circumstances ancillary thereto, or any failure to disclose a spent conviction or any such circumstances shall not be a proper ground for dismissing or excluding a person from any office, profession, occupation or employment, or for prejudicing him in any way in any occupation or employment.[62]

SECTION 4. DEFAMATION PROCEEDINGS

18.14 **Defamation proceedings.** Section 8 of the Act contains special provisions, which apply to any action for libel or slander begun after the commencement of the Act by a rehabilitated person and founded upon the publication of any matter imputing that the claimant has committed or been charged with or prosecuted for or convicted of or sentenced for an offence which was the subject of a spent conviction.[63] The general scheme of these provisions is that s.4(1)[64] is not to apply adversely to the defendant in such proceedings, but it is necessary to consider them in detail.[65]

---

[60] SI 1975/1023, para.4, as amended. Spent convictions and offences in respect of which a person has been cautioned are disclosable under the National Care Standards Commission (Registration) Regulations 2001, SI 2001/3969, as amended, and under the Fostering Services Regulations 2002, SI 2002/57.

[61] Rehabilitation of Offenders Act 1974, s.4(3)(a).

[62] Ibid. s.4(3)(b). This has consequences for the rules as to qualified privilege, for which see para.18.20, below. The wording suggests that it may not be an improper ground for prejudicing a person in an office or profession, though why this should be so is unclear. A body which, before the expiry of the rehabilitation period, imposes a disqualification for a period which extends beyond the rehabilitation period does not act in contravention of the Act: *Colgan v The Kennel Club*, October 26, 2001, (QB).

[63] S.8(1). Actions to which s.8 applies are here referred to as "defamation proceedings". Note that s.8 does not apply to proceedings for malicious falsehood or to proceedings in which the conviction of someone other than the claimant is relevant as, for instance, if the claimant were accused of having abetted someone else in the commission of an offence the subject of a conviction in respect of which that other was a rehabilitated person. There was considerable opposition in Parliament to the idea that a successful defamation action might be brought against someone who had told the truth about a spent conviction and the Faulks Committee in an interim report in fact recommended that the Act should not apply to defamation proceedings at all: Cmnd.5571 (1974), para.23.

[64] See para.18.12, above.

[65] In *Silkman v Heard*, February 28, 2001, (QB), Eady J. made the following remarks about the scheme of the 1974 Act:

"[This is] . . . a very unusual case because, although [the Act] has been on the statute book for a quarter of a century, these provisions rarely surface in libel litigation and there is naturally very little authority on their interpretation. There is a potential question as to whether or not this statutory regime, in restricting freedom of communication and in particular inhibiting those who wish to tell the truth, is compatible with Article10 of the European Convention on Human Rights. No doubt one argument would be that, because it is intended to protect those who wish to put a criminal past behind them, it can be justified by reference to a right of privacy in accordance with Article 8. Two factors would tend to undermine such an argument. For one thing, convictions are in the public domain at least until such time as they become spent. For

Publication before conviction becomes spent. Nothing in s.4(1) is to   **18.15**
affect defamation proceedings where the publication complained of took place
before the conviction became spent, and the other provisions of s.8[66] do not
apply in any such case. Thus, in such cases, if the defendant had truly stated
that the claimant had been convicted, and the action was brought after the
conviction became spent the defendant could prove the conviction even if the
publication is proved to have been made with malice.[67]

Justification. In actions to which s.8 of the Act applies, nothing in s.4(1)   **18.16**
shall prevent the defendant from relying on any defence of justification which
is available to him, or to restrict the matters he may establish in support of the
defence,[68] except that a defendant shall not by virtue of this provision be
entitled to rely upon the defence of justification if the publication is proved to
have been made with malice.[69] Where the publication is not proved to have
been made with malice, the ordinary rules as to justification will apply.[70] The
defendant will be able to produce proof of the conviction if the imputation was
that the claimant was convicted of an offence, and that proof will be conclusive evidence of guilt if the allegation was that the claimant was guilty of
the offence for which he was convicted.[71] However, if the publication is

---

another, the very fact that the Rehabilitation of Offenders Act has been relied upon so rarely
in libel actions must at least raise doubts as to whether the concomitant restrictions on freedom
of speech can be described as 'necessary in a democratic society' within the meaning of Article
10.2. This is not, however, the sort of issue that should be determined on a Part 24 application
or, at least, without the benefit of full and considered argument."

[66] See para.18.14, above.

[67] S.8(2).

[68] S.8(3) Though not yet in force, s.16(2) of the Defamation Act 2013 substitutes the words
"under section 2 or 3 of the Defamation Act 2013 which is available to him or any defence [of]"
for "of justification or fair comment". How the provisions inserted by the Criminal Justice and
Immigration Act 2008 that apply to spent cautions will affect defamation is not entirely clear.
Sch.2 para.3(1) replicates s.4(1) of the 1974 Act in providing that a:

"person who is given a caution for an offence shall, from the time the caution is spent, be
treated for all purposes in law as a person who has not committed, been charged with or
prosecuted for, or been given a caution for the offence"

and no evidence to that effect is admissible in any proceedings. However, there is no amendment
of s.8. Since the deemed "conclusive innocence" therefore arises from para.3(1), not from s.4(1)
the literal effect of the language would seem to be that in no circumstances can the defendant raise
any defence in respect of a statement about the spent, cautioned offence. It is difficult to see why
this should be so. The court's power to disregard s.4(1) and admit evidence of a spent conviction
under s.7(3) (see para.18.12, above) does not apply to defamation proceedings because, in view
of s.8, it is unnecessary. However, the wording of para.6 of the Sch.2 appears to have the result
that that power does apply to defamation cases arising from spent convictions. It is not obvious
what is the basis on which such a power would be exercised.

[69] S.8(5). Though not yet in force, s.16(3) of the Defamation Act 2013 substitutes the words "a
defence under section 2 of the Defamation Act 2013" for "the defence of justification". See
para.18.17, below. In *Elliott v Chief Constable of Wiltshire, The Times*, December 5, 1996, there
was an allegation of malice since a claim for misfeasance in a public office was allowed to go
forward but even though some convictions disclosed were false and others were spent, there
appears to have been no claim for libel.

[70] See Ch.11, above.

[71] Civil Evidence Act 1968, s.13. See para.33.17, below.

proved to have been made with malice, the claimant will have to be treated for all purposes as a person who has not committed or been charged with, prosecuted for, convicted of or sentenced for the offence, and no evidence to prove to the contrary will be admissible.[72] Thus, the claimant will be treated to all intents and purposes as an innocent person, and, semble, damages will be assessed accordingly.

18.17 Malice and justification. In no other context in the English law of defamation is it necessary to determine whether a person has been malicious in publishing something which is true. Malice as a common law concept exists in the areas of qualified privilege[73] and (though in a rather different sense) honest comment,[74] but in neither of these cases is the statement true, though where qualified privilege is in issue the defendant may believe what he said to be true. In *Herbage v Pressdram*[75] the Court of Appeal held that malice here meant some irrelevant, spiteful or improper motive, which is essentially the meaning of malice at common law in connection with qualified privilege. In addition, it is submitted that by analogy with malice in the context of qualified privilege, the improper motive must be the dominant reason for the publication.[76] The difficulty is to determine what is an improper motive, since there is no clear "special reason of public policy why the law accords immunity from suit".[77]

---

[72] That the Civil Evidence Act 1968 is inapplicable in this case is shown by s.4(1)(a), which provides that no evidence shall be admissible that a person has been convicted of any offence which was the subject of a spent conviction "notwithstanding the provisions of any other enactment . . . to the contrary".

[73] See para.14.1 and Ch.17, above.

[74] See para.12.36, above. There is also a statutory reference to malice in s.3 of the Parliamentary Papers Act 1840, as there once was in s.4 of the Defamation Act 1952.

[75] [1984] 1 W.L.R. 1160.

[76] See para.17.7, above. Lord Diplock, proposing s.8(5) in the House of Lords (353 HL Deb., 1807 et seq.) referred to disclosures "actuated by spite" or "dragged in gratuitously" and considered "malice" to be "a well-known concept in the law of defamation . . . In a sentence it means taking improper advantage of the occasion of the publication" (col.1812: see also per Viscount Dilhorne at cols 1834–1835). Lord Diplock also referred to the analogy of the statutory privilege for reports and although the comparison is somewhat unsatisfactory (see the next note), this seems to be the closest analogy available. Although the House of Lords in *Horrocks v Lowe* [1975] A.C. 135 laid down strict requirements (for which see para.17.3, above) for the proof of improper motive when a person believed the truth of what he said on a privileged occasion, it was clearly stated that belief in the truth could co-exist with an improper motive: ibid. at 150.

[77] Per Lord Diplock in *Horrocks v Lowe* at 149, in explaining that such a reason exists in all cases of qualified privilege, and if the maker of the defamatory statement uses the occasion for some other reason he loses the protection of the privilege. It is this which makes the qualified privilege for reports an unsatisfactory analogy, since the reason of public policy in such cases is that the public are entitled to such information either because of its intrinsic importance or because the matters reported took place in public. See, for instance, *Webb v The Times* [1960] 2 Q.B. 535 for the various reasons for the privilege in reporting English judicial proceedings. Except in relation to the specified employments (see para.18.13, above) there is no such public policy in the Rehabilitation of Offenders Act 1974: the competing interests are the non-disclosure of spent convictions and an individual interest in being able to tell the truth. Nevertheless, it is submitted, with some hesitation, that the legislature had in mind that there were good and bad

It seems likely that the court will distinguish proper from improper reasons for disclosure.[78] Where a defendant discloses a spent conviction merely in order to damage the claimant or to further some interest of his own, or perhaps where he knows that the information cannot be legally relevant,[79] he should be held to be malicious. Where on the other hand he is seeking to give information which can reasonably be regarded as relevant to the recipient, he should not be held to be malicious.[80] For example, it has been suggested that if the defendant, believing that the claimant was unfit for some office by reason of a spent conviction which he disclosed, he should not necessarily be regarded as malicious.[81]

Honest comment. Similarly nothing in s.4(1) of the Act shall prevent the **18.18** defendant in defamation proceedings from relying on any defence of honest comment which is available to him, or restrict the matters he may establish in support of any such defence.[82] Thus, if the defendant has recalled a past spent conviction of the claimant, and commented on it, the provision seems to enable the defendant to prove the conviction as the facts on which his comment is based. Since the definition of defamation proceedings includes only those brought by the rehabilitated person, it is not by reason of this provision permissible to comment adversely on A on the basis of what was said at the trial which resulted in B's spent conviction. Similarly it is not completely clear that the defendant can rely on the claimant's spent conviction as a matter referred to but not contained in the words complained of.[83]

---

reasons for disclosing spent convictions and that a defendant whose reason was bad might be held to be malicious.

[78] The fact that the court in *Herbage v Pressdram* [1984] 1 W.L.R. 1160 CA, was not prepared to find clear and convincing evidence of malice for the purposes of proceedings for an interlocutory injunction in respect of admittedly spent convictions clearly implies that there may be good reasons for such disclosure. In *KJO v XIM* [2011] EWHC 1768 (QB) Eady J. suggested that it might be possible on the facts of that case to establish malice but determining such an issue was not suitable for summary judgment.

[79] As in the case where a person giving a reference discloses a spent conviction which he knows cannot be of relevance to a potential employer.

[80] In applying this test to newspaper publications it may be of assistance to bear in mind the distinction drawn by Pearson J. in *Webb v The Times*, above, at 569 between "a legitimate and proper interest as contrasted with an interest which is due to idle curiosity or a desire for gossip". Though the context is somewhat different, the distinction seems an appropriate way of drawing a line between proper and gratuitous disclosures.

[81] *Silkman v Heard*, February 28, 2001, (QB). However, Eady J., referring to the difficulty of applying the idea of malice to justification, said: "I find it hard to see where propriety (or impropriety) comes into it in relation to a plea of justification."

[82] S.8(3). Though not yet in force, s.16(2) of the Defamation Act 2013 substitutes the words "under section 2 or 3 of the Defamation Act 2013 which is available to him or any defence [of]" for "of justification or fair comment".

[83] The actions to which s.8 applies are those: "founded upon the publication of any matter imputing that the plaintiff has committed [etc.] an offence which was the subject of a spent conviction." Suppose the defendant refers in general terms to the claimant's "appalling record" as disqualifying him from election to a public office. In ordinary circumstances the defendant may give particulars of the facts referred to which could include a conviction, but if the conviction is spent, the action is not on the face of it founded on the publication of any matter containing the imputation of a spent conviction, since the complaint is of the comment.

Although s.8(4) makes special provision in relation to malice in qualified privilege the wording of s.8(3) seems wide enough to allow a defendant pleading honest comment in defamation proceedings to prove a spent conviction in relation to an issue of malice.[84]

18.19 Absolute privilege. Though there are special provisions as to reports of judicial proceedings[85] nothing in s.4(1) prevents the defendant in defamation proceedings from relying on any defence of absolute or qualified privilege which is available to him, or restrict the matters he may establish in support of such a defence. Thus a claimant who sues in defamation not in relation to the allegation of a spent conviction but on the evidence given by the prosecution witnesses can be met with the defence that the words were published on an occasion of absolute privilege, namely, the proceedings which resulted in the conviction.

18.20 Qualified privilege. Subject to some modification in relation to reports of judicial proceedings[86] nothing in s.4(1) of the Act prevents the defendant in proceedings to which s.8 applies from relying on any defence of qualified privilege available to him, or restricts the matters he may establish in support of such a defence.[87] Thus, where the fact of a spent conviction is relevant either to the existence of a qualified privilege or is communicated on an occasion of qualified privilege, the defendant may prove that fact either as a basis for the privilege on which he relies[88] or as evidence that he communicated matter he believed to be true.[89] For the most part, however, the defendant could equally plead justification in such cases. The subject of qualified privilege and references is further discussed below.[90]

18.21 Reports of judicial proceedings. However, where there have been judicial proceedings in which evidence has been ruled to be inadmissible by virtue of s.4(1), and the claimant proves that the matter published contains a reference to that evidence the defendant will not normally be entitled, by virtue of s.8(3), to rely on any matter or adduce or require any evidence for the purpose of establishing (whether under s.14 of the Defamation Act 1996[91]

---

[84] Malice in the context of honest comment means only lack of belief in the comment, not "improper purpose": para.17.1, above.

[85] See para.18.21, below.

[86] See para.18.21, below.

[87] S.8(3). Without prejudice to the generality of s.8(3) where in an action to which s.8 applies malice is alleged against a defendant who is relying on a defence of qualified privilege, nothing in s.4(1) shall restrict the matters he may establish in rebuttal of the allegation: ibid. s.8(4).

[88] Provided that is, that the action is brought on the imputation of a spent conviction: see para.18.14, above.

[89] Evidence of the spent conviction as evidence of bona fides would be admissible under both s.8(3) and (4).

[90] See para.18.22, below.

[91] I.e. absolute privilege. Previously s.3 of the Law of Libel Amendment Act 1888. See para.13.35, above.

or otherwise[92]) the defence that the matter constituted a fair and accurate report of judicial proceedings.[93] The general effect of this provision is to prevent any mention of evidence of a spent conviction if that evidence has been ruled inadmissible. As this would prevent a law report from reporting the argument and ruling on a point of admissibility of such evidence, the provision does not apply to any report of judicial proceedings contained in any bona fide series of law reports which does not form part of any other publication[94] and consists solely of reports of proceedings in courts of law[95] or to any report or account of judicial proceedings published for bona fide educational, scientific or professional purposes, or given in the course of any lecture, class or discussion given or held for any of these purposes.[96]

References. Whether or not a person who has knowledge of a spent convic-   **18.22** tion should disclose it if asked to give information about the rehabilitated person or can be made liable for disclosing or failing to disclose it are questions only partly to be answered by reference to the provisions relating to defamation actions.[97] The provisions of s.4(2) and (3)[98] should also be borne in mind. From these it is plain that someone who is asked for a reference need not mention spent convictions even if he is specifically asked about them.[99] On the other hand, the provisions do not in themselves prevent disclosure. However, such information will arguably[100] usually be irrelevant since a spent conviction is not, in the absence of special provision, a proper ground for

---

[92] I.e. qualified privilege either under Sch.1 to the Defamation Act 1996 (see para.16.10, above) or at common law (see para.15.35, above).

[93] S.8(6). Although the provision as to inadmissibility of evidence of a spent conviction applies to all proceedings before a judicial authority exercising its jurisdiction or functions in Great Britain (an expression which by reason of s.4(6) is wider than the ordinary courts of law and extends to domestic tribunals: see para.18.12, above) s.8(6) applies only to reports of "judicial proceedings". The reporting privileges under the Defamation Act 1996 apply to reports of proceedings of a "court", which "includes any tribunal or body exercising the judicial power of the state" (plus certain international tribunals.) This would not cover reports of findings of the domestic tribunals of the kinds of association specified in para.14 of Sch.1 to the Defamation Act 1996. Thus, if the findings of such an association included reference to a ruling that evidence of a spent conviction was inadmissible it would apparently be possible for a newspaper to report the finding with the protection of qualified privilege.

[94] The daily law report in *The Times* would not be protected under this head, though it might be under the next.

[95] S.6(8)(a).

[96] S.6(8)(b). This provision protects, for instance, reports in professional journals or in case-books.

[97] I.e. the provisions of s.8. This paragraph does not deal with the various occupations, etc. for which special provision is made by the Rehabilitation of Offenders Act 1974 (Exceptions) Orders (for which see para.18.13, above).

[98] See para.18.13, above.

[99] S.4(2)(a) provides that the question as to previous convictions "shall be treated as not relating to spent convictions", and in the context this includes even specific inquiries. Similarly, no action for misrepresentation or breach of duty could be brought against him (s.4(2)(b), (3)(a)).

[100] The matter is further complicated by some degree of uncertainty as to the test of relevance in the context of qualified privilege: see para.14.63, above.

excluding a person from any office, profession, occupation or employment. This will have consequences in relation to a plea of qualified privilege such as is usually relied on by those who give references. For if he discloses a spent conviction he has done so in answer to a question which is to be treated as not relating to it, and the information itself will not be such that a potential employer can properly act on it. On this basis, it is difficult to see how the information can be relevant to the privilege. Section 8(3)[101] merely provides that "nothing in s.4(1) . . . shall prevent the defendant . . . from relying on any defence of . . . qualified privilege which is available to him or restrict the matters he may establish" in support of such a defence. However, the spent conviction is irrelevant by reason of s.4(2) and (3), not s.4(1), and so, semble, s.8(3) does not allow a defence of qualified privilege. However, the defendant may well be able to rely on a defence of justification,[102] and the point at issue will be whether it is "malice" to disclose irrelevant matter.[103]

---

[101] See para.18.20, above.
[102] See s.8(3) and (5).
[103] See para.18.17, above. It is submitted that it can be, but this will require an examination of the knowledge and motives of the defendant.

CHAPTER 19

OTHER DEFENCES

SECTION 1. THE OFFER OF AMENDS PROCEDURE

Background. Unless the words are spoken on an occasion of qualified **19.1** privilege or are fair comment on a matter of public interest, the fundamental rule of the common law is that the defendant's liability is strict: he is liable even though he did not intend to refer to the claimant and had no reason to know that his words would be so understood[1]; even though he did not know, and had no reason to know, of circumstances by reason of which, the words, innocent on their face, might be understood in a defamatory sense[2]; and a fortiori, in the case of words defamatory on their face, even though he believed-and reasonably believed-them to be true.[3]

The first two principles were modified by s.4 of the Defamation Act 1952. If the defendant published the matter complained of innocently as defined by the section (that is to say that he did not intend to publish the words of and concerning the plaintiff and did not know of circumstances by virtue of which they might be understood to refer to him; or that the words were not defamatory on the face of them, and he did not know of circumstances by virtue of which they might be understood to be defamatory of the plaintiff; and that in either case he had taken all reasonable care) he might make an offer of amends under the section.[4] If the offer was accepted and duly performed, that precluded the bringing of any proceedings for defamation and terminated any that were on foot. If the offer was not accepted, the defendant might defend any action by showing that the offer complied with the terms of the section.

---

[1] See para.7.5, above.
[2] See para.3.15, above.
[3] *Campbell v Spottiswoode* (1861) 3 B. & S. 769 at 781, per Blackburn J.
[4] Involving in any case, an offer to publish or join in the publication of a suitable correction and apology and, where copies had been distributed, to notify holders of those copies that the words were alleged to be defamatory of the person aggrieved.

Section 4 was complex,[5] cumbersome in operation and difficult to comply with[6] and was rarely used.[7]

19.2 The Defamation Act 1996. As from February 28, 2000, s.4 of the Defamation Act 1952 was repealed and replaced by the more extensive provisions of the Defamation Act 1996.[8] These provisions originate in[9] the Report of the Neill Committee, which concluded that it seemed:

> "desirable to have some more streamlined defence [than section 4 of the 1952 Act] available (rather than merely the opportunity of mitigating damages) in circumstances where a defendant has behaved fairly and reasonably after the tort has been committed. Putting it bluntly, there is a need to discourage that small minority of plaintiffs who wish to proceed to trial from purely financial motives, rather than being motivated by a desire for vindication, especially in circumstances where the defendant is conceived to be 'over a barrel'."[10]

The offer of amends procedure is closely connected with other aspects of settlement. Only an outline is given here and it is considered in more detail in Chapter 29. An offer of amends does not provide a "defence" in the simple sense of justification or privilege or consent. There must be an offer by the defendant complying with the statute. If it is accepted that will bar the bringing of proceedings for defamation or terminate any existing suit. If the claimant[11] does not accept it and the defendant relies on the offer, the claimant

---

[5] It is considered in detail in the 8th edition of this book, Ch.18.

[6] The following were particularly problematical: the requirement that the offer had to be made as soon as practicable after the defendant had notice that the words might be defamatory of the plaintiff; the requirement to specify the facts relied on in support of the defence in an affidavit which was definitive in that no other evidence could be relied on; and, where the defendant was not the author of the words, the requirement that he be able to show that the author was not malicious, a task which it might be impossible for a newspaper or a printer to discharge. For criticism, see the Faulks Report, Cmnd.5909 (1975), para.281 and the Neill Report (1991), Ch.7.

[7] The members of the Neill Committee, with a combined experience of over 100 years, could not recall one instance where the defence succeeded, though they received testimony that its existence played some modest part in producing settlements in minor cases: para.VII.1.

[8] Similar provisions exist in the Irish Defamation Act 2009, ss.22–23, though there appears to be a difference in substance from English law in that the defence can be defeated by proof that the defendant knew or ought reasonably to have known at the time of the publication of the statement to which the offer relates that: (a) it referred to the plaintiff or was likely to be understood as referring to the plaintiff, and (b) it was false and defamatory of the plaintiff (s.23(2)). Cf. s.4(2) of the Defamation Act 1996 which uses the phrase "knew or had reason to believe" and see further para.19.6. See also the uniform Australian legislation (e.g. Defamation Act 2005 (NSW), ss.12–19). Under the Australian legislation, if an offer of amends is made but not accepted, the defendant can rely on an offer of amends as a defence if: (a) the publisher made the offer as soon as practicable after becoming aware that the matter is or may be defamatory; and, (b) at any time before the trial the publisher was ready and willing, on acceptance of the offer by the aggrieved person, to carry out the terms of the offer; and, (c) in all the circumstances the offer was reasonable. There is otherwise no provision similar to s.4(2) of the Defamation Act 1996.

[9] However, this part of the Defamation Bill was subject to much detailed amendment.

[10] Para.VII.12.

[11] Defendant and claimant are used here for brevity. Strictly one should speak of "the person who published the allegedly defamatory statement" and "the person aggrieved" because the procedure may be invoked before any action is on foot.

will only win his action if he can show that the defendant did not merely make an innocent mistake.[12] But because it is not a defence of mistake simpliciter it was held that it was an insufficient protection of freedom of expression in one case of "mistaken identity".[13]

Requirements of statutory offer of amends. An offer of amends must **19.3** be in writing and expressed to be made under s.2 of the Act.[14] The offer may be made in relation to the statement generally or it may be a qualified offer, i.e. in relation to a specific defamatory meaning which the defendant accepts that the statement conveys.[15] The offer must state whether[16] it is a qualified offer and, if so, set out the defamatory meaning in relation to which it is made.[17] Hence if an article concerned involvement with crime D might make a qualified offer in respect of the defamatory meaning that C had so conducted himself as to give rise to suspicion, but might refuse to make an offer in respect of C's contention that the words imputed guilt to him.

To comply with the section the offer must be (a) to make a suitable correction and a sufficient apology; (b) to publish the correction and apology in a manner that is reasonable and practicable in the circumstances; and (c) to pay the aggrieved party such compensation (if any) and such costs as may be agreed or determined.[18] The fact that the offer may need to include an offer of compensation (or at least may lead to an award of compensation) is the most obvious difference between this and the former procedure under the Defamation Act 1952. The Neill Committee concluded that it would be:

> "unsatisfactory that defendants should have a defence available, based on their reasonable behaviour after publication, which would leave the plaintiff with no compensation at all, in respect of hurt feelings or injury to reputation, to take account of what was *ex hypothesi* a defamation. Indeed, it could well be a serious defamation, and we see no overriding public interest in depriving plaintiffs of all compensation merely because the defendants have seen the error of their ways."[19]

While the defendant need not spell out the precise terms of any offer he makes, the offer of amends must be made to the person aggrieved, that is say the person making the claim,[20] and the defendant must have understood that

---

[12] See para.19.6, below.

[13] *O'Shea v MGN Ltd* [2001] E.M.L.R. 40: para.7.8, above.

[14] Defamation Act 1996, s.2(3). The procedure applies to the whole of the United Kingdom: s.18.

[15] S.2(2).

[16] Which should be read, in effect, as "if": *SD Marine Ltd v Powell* [2006] EWHC 3095 (QB).

[17] S.2(3)(c).

[18] S.2(4). The fact that the offer is accompanied by an offer to take specific steps does not affect the fact that an offer to make amends under this section is an offer to do all the things specified in (a), (b) and (c): ibid.

[19] Para.VII.17.

[20] *Club La Costa (UK) Plc v Gebhard* [2008] EWHC 2552 (QB).

he was making an offer complying with s.2.[21] An offer may be made after action brought but not after the defendant has served a defence in the action.[22] An offer of amends may be withdrawn before it is accepted[23]; and a renewal of an offer which has been withdrawn is to be treated as a new offer.[24]

19.4 If offer accepted. If the party aggrieved accepts[25] the offer of amends he may not bring or continue defamation proceedings[26] in respect of the publication concerned[27] against the person making the offer[28] but this does not affect his cause of action against any other person in respect of the same publication.[29] Hence if the printer of a book makes an offer of amends[30] and this is accepted, the claimant may still continue his action against the author and commercial publisher. Any compensation paid under the offer is to be treated as paid in bona fide settlement or compromise of the claim[31] so that the offeror may recover contribution from another person liable without regard to whether he (the payer) was in fact liable.[32]

If the parties agree on the steps to be taken in fulfilment of the offer and the offeror fails to comply with them, the aggrieved party may apply to the court for an order requiring the offeror to take the steps agreed.[33] However, it is an important feature of the offer of amends procedure that the parties do *not* need to agree on the content of the offer at all: if the defendant has offered to pay

---

[21] In *S D Marine Ltd v Powell* [2006] EWHC 3095 (QB) Eady J. concluded that there was no offer of amends capable of acceptance because it ought to have been apparent to a reasonable onlooker that the defendant did not understand the structure of the procedure and importantly what he was consenting to in making a purported "offer of amends".

[22] S.2(5).

[23] The Act contains no specific concept of "rejection" of an offer: *Moore v Scottish Daily Record and Sunday Mail Ltd* [2007] CSOH 24; 2007 S.L.T. 217. However, the claimant cannot be allowed to "hold" an offer to see how the trial goes and he must accept or reject the offer within a reasonable time: *Tesco Stores Ltd v Guardian News and Media Ltd*, [2009] E.M.L.R. 5. An "acceptance" which reserves the right to claim special damages when they have been investigated is not an acceptance of the offer within the Act: *Loughton Contracts Plc v Dun & Bradstreet Ltd* [2006] EWHC 1224 (QB).

[24] S.2(6).

[25] It is thought that this occurs when the acceptance is communicated to the offeror.

[26] The claimant will not be allowed to pursue a tactical advantage by concurrent proceedings for malicious falsehood: *Tesco Stores Ltd v Guardian News and Media Ltd*, [2009] E.M.L.R. 5 (QB).

[27] This does not necessarily mean the whole publication. The defendant may select a particular passage and make an offer in respect of that, and the claimant may accept that without foregoing his right of action in respect of other defamatory passages: *Warren v Random House Group Ltd* [2007] EWHC 2856 (QB); [2008] 2 W.L.R .1033 (aff'd on different grounds: [2008] EWCA Civ 834; [2009] Q.B. 600).

[28] S.3(2).

[29] S.3(7).

[30] It is assumed that the printer does not have a complete defence under s.1: para.6.34, above.

[31] Ibid. s.3(8)(a).

[32] Civil Liability (Contribution) Act 1978, s.1(4). For contribution provisions in relation to Scotland see Defamation Act 1996, s.3(9)(b).

[33] Ibid. s.3(3). On procedure see para.29.32, below.

an unspecified sum as compensation the court has power to fix the amount.[34] Additionally it has been held that the court has power under the offer of amends regime to allow the person aggrieved to make a statement in court.[35] As far as the correction and apology is concerned the ball is in the defendant's court and there is no question of either the person aggrieved or the court being able to dictate what the defendant does in these respects,[36] for s.3(4) provides that if the parties do not agree "on the steps to be taken by way of correction, apology and publication, the party who made the offer may take such steps as he thinks appropriate," and may in particular make a statement in court in terms approved by the court or give an undertaking as to the manner of publication. No matter how unsuitable may be the correction, how insufficient the apology and how unsuitable the manner of their publication, these do not invalidate the offer, which is binding once accepted. Rather, the court is to take account of these matters in assessing compensation under the procedure.[37] An accepted offer probably does not amount to a contract in the strict sense since the court will have a continuing role in the dispute, but matters like misrepresentation, which would give rise to a right to resile from a contract, may be a basis on which an accepted offer could be set aside.[38] However, a defendant who has chosen to make an offer on the basis of legal advice and who has chosen not to make further investigations which were open to him will not be allowed to resile.[39]

---

[34] S.3(5).

[35] *Winslet v Associated Newspapers Ltd* [2009] EWHC 2735 (QB); [2010] E.M.L.R. 11; *Broccoli v Associated Newspapers* SIOC/11/0706, June 15, 2011.

[36] A matter which had concerned the media in the consultation on the draft Defamation Bill in 1995: see *Hansard*, HL, cols 20–22 (May 7, 1996).

[37] S.3(5).

[38] *Warren v Random House Group Ltd* [2008] EWCA Civ 834; [2009] Q.B. 600. At first instance ([2007] EWHC 2856 (QB); [2008] 2 W.L.R. 1033), Gray J. had treated the acceptance of an offer of amends as giving rise to a binding and legally enforceable contract. The Court of Appeal, however, disagreed:
  "While the statutory scheme has many of the attributes of a contract, and is certainly consensual, we are inclined to think that it is not a contract in the sense of creating contractual rights and obligations, because it contains express provisions as to what should or should not happen next and the court retains a role." (at [17])
Instead, the court thought that the offer of amends procedure was more akin to circumstances in which a party voluntarily gives an undertaking to the court in the course of litigation. Thus, a court retained a discretion to relieve a party of the consequences of his bargain. This discretion was not, however, the general discretion governing late applications for permission to amend a case after service. It was instead a much more limited discretion which recognised the policy that as a general rule a party should be held to any undertaking he gives voluntarily to the court. The questions to be asked therefore were:
  "the questions posed by Potter L.J. in *Di Placito v Slater*, namely whether it would be just to deprive the [claimant] of the benefit of the bargain made with the [defendant] and whether the circumstances are so different from those contemplated at the time of the agreement that it would be just to allow the [defendant] to resile from the agreement. This involves a consideration of the relevant circumstances, including a consideration of the question whether the circumstances which have subsequently arisen were circumstances which were intended to be covered or ought to have foreseen at the time the agreement was made" (at [42]).

[39] *Warren v Random House Group Ltd* [2008] EWCA Civ 834; [2009] Q.B. 600.

19.5 The amount of compensation. If the amount of the compensation has not been agreed it is determined by the court (which for the purposes of all proceedings under s.3 sits without a jury) "on the same principles as damages in defamation proceedings".[40] The procedure is not to be confused with that for summary disposal under ss.8 to 10 of the Act, which is intended for "minor" libels and where there is a cap of £10,000 on the award. "There should thus be nothing in any senses 'rough and ready' about the assessment of a claimant's reputation under the offer of amends procedure."[41] The usual practice is to make an assessment of what the libel would "deserve" without an offer and then make a discount (which in practice seems to have been between one half and one third[42]) determined in the light of matters like the promptness of the offer and the sincerity and co-operation shown by the defendant.[43]

Hence the court may have to take account of matters which go to the mitigation,[44] aggravation and causation of the loss and there may be cases in which there needs to be pleading or other form of notification of matters to be relied upon (e.g. where reliance is placed upon the claimant's general bad

---

[40] S.3(5).

[41] *Abu v MGN Ltd* [2002] EWHC 2345 (QB); [2003] 1 W.L.R. 2201 at [22]. An award of £120,000 was made in *Veliu v Mazrekaj* [2006] EWHC 1710 (QB); [2007] 1 W.L.R. 495.

[42] Precisely why the discount should be so large has never been made clear in the case law. While an offer of amends swiftly made is no doubt welcome, it is to be doubted whether it really justifies the significant discounts applied. Whether avoiding the tribulations, stresses and risks of a trial justifies a 50 per cent discount is also debatable particularly as that argument cuts both ways: both claimant and defendant benefit from the fact that there is no trial. Is it right to require the claimant to pay for this by a significant discount on his damages? The benefit might be thought to accrue to both parties in having to pay less by way of costs. Nevertheless, the making of a "healthy discount", as Eady J. put it (at [41]) in *Nail v News Group Newspapers Ltd* [2004] EWHC 647 (QB); [2004] E.M.L.R. 20 appears to be a well-established part of the procedure (aff'd [2004] EWCA Civ 1708; [2005] E.M.L.R. 12: in the Court of Appeal, May L.J. said (at [41])"'A healthy discount" may be a more colourful phrase than "substantial mitigation", but they mean the same thing.')

[43] See *Turner v News Group Newspapers Ltd* [2006] EWCA Civ 540; [2006] 1 W.L.R. 3469 at [66]; *Cairns v Modi* [2012] EWCA Civ 1382 CA; [2013] 1 W.L.R. 1015; [2013] E.M.L.R. 8 at [45]; *Campbell-James v Guardian Media Group Plc* [2005] EWHC 893 (QB); [2005] E.M.L.R. 542 ("unaccountable delay" in acknowledging the mistake and dismissive references to qualified privilege and fair comment led to judge discounting by 35 per cent only); *Angel v Stainton* [2006] EWHC 637 (40 per cent discount applied where apology published at last possible moment, references made to possibility of fair comment defence and still unclear the way defendant would present case in court). *Veliu v Mazrekaj*, above deals with the position where there are joint defendants and only one of them makes an offer.

[44] Including evidence of the "directly relevant background context" under *Burstein v Times Newspapers Ltd* [2001] 1 W.L.R. 579 CA: para.11.21, above. In *Abu*, above at [17] and in *Warren v Random House Group Ltd* [2007] EWHC 2860 (QB) the view was taken that the defendant should not, via the *Burstein* principle be allowed to show that the allegation is substantially true, for that would be to allow justification by the back door. However, the CA disagreed.

"The fact that it is no longer open to the defendant to deploy material as part of a substantive defence to liability would seem to us to be no reason to debar it from deploying it in relation to the assessment of compensation if legal principles were otherwise so to permit":
Warren v Random House Group Ltd [2008] EWCA Civ 834 at [85].

reputation or where the circumstances of the incident from which the statement arises reflect badly upon the claimant) or even disclosure.[45]

If offer not accepted. If a duly made offer is not accepted by the party   **19.6**
aggrieved it provides a defence to defamation proceedings by him in respect
of the publication in question against the party making the offer,[46] though if
the latter takes advantage of this[47] it may not be combined with any other
defence.[48] However, by s.4(3) there is:

> "no such defence if the person by whom the offer was made knew or had reason to
> believe that the statement complained of (a) referred to the aggrieved party or was
> likely to be understood as referring to him, and (b) was both false and defamatory
> of that party."[49]

However, it is presumed until the contrary is shown by the claimant that the
defendant did not know and had no reason to believe in these matters.[50] Apart
from the different burden of proof[51] a major change from s.4 of the Defamation Act 1952 is that lack of knowledge or means of knowledge of falsity will
enable the defendant to use this defence even though the words are defamatory on their face and obviously refer to the claimant. It will therefore cover
a much wider range of cases. In this respect the statutory defence is more akin
to privilege.

Under s.4 of the 1952 Act the defendant was required to show that he had
taken all reasonable care in relation to the publication. Quite apart from the
changed burden of proof, the formula in the 1996 Act that the defendant must
have known or had reason to believe that the statement referred to the person
aggrieved and was false and defamatory of him is more favourable to the

---

[45] *Abu* at [21].

[46] S.4(2). A qualified offer is only a defence in respect of the meaning to which the offer
related: ibid.

[47] He is not required to do so: s.4(4). Of course even if he does not do so he may still rely on
the offer in mitigation of damages, as indeed he may do under the general law even if the defence
was not open to him, e.g. because at the time of publication he knew or had reason to believe that
the words were false.

[48] S.4(4). Where the statement was made on an occasion of absolute privilege there would seem
to be no circumstances in which the defendant would ever wish to utilise the procedure. Similarly
if the words were plainly comment or plainly made on a traditional occasion of qualified privilege
the procedure would seem to offer no advantage to the defendant (beyond the prospect of buying
his way out of the proceedings if the offer is accepted) since in order to defeat those defences the
claimant would have to show malice, which he will in effect have to do to defeat the s.4 defence.
However, where the defendant has a potential defence of privilege under *Reynolds v Times
Newspapers Ltd* an offer of amends might be a suitable tactical alternative, since the standard of
"responsible journalism" under that case is plainly higher than the standard under s.4.

[49] An offer of amends which is accepted is plainly effective to terminate existing proceedings
and prevent the commencement of proceedings even though the offeror would fail under s.4(3),
which is directed solely at the situation where the offer is refused.

[50] S.3(3).

[51] Under the 1952 Act it was for the defendant to show that he had published the words
"innocently".

defendant.[52] The expression "had reason to believe" in s.4(3) is equivalent to the recklessness or conscious indifference which amounts to malice for the purposes of qualified privilege.[53] The contrary view would put a defendant who reported a controversy in which there were conflicting assertions at serious risk and would render the defence as ineffective as its predecessor in the 1952 Act.

> "It is quite clear that it was intended that the balance should be significantly shifted in favour of defendants, and journalists in particular, from the position adopted in the 1952 Act . . . . It has to be remembered that, if this defence is relied upon, no other defence may be pleaded . . . . If the jury were persuaded that greater care could or should have been taken, in any given case, then on the claimant's case the defence would fail and the defendant would be left naked on the issue of liability. It would not have been possible to plead, for example, justification or fair comment. In particular, the defendant would have been precluded from pleading justification even on the basis of reasonable grounds to suspect . . . . If claimants were able to challenge a section 4 defence routinely, in the absence of bad faith, the whole offer of amends regime would be rendered ineffective . . . . The main purpose of the statutory regime is to provide an exit route for journalists who have made a mistake and are willing to put their hands up and make amends."[54]

SECTION 2. LORD CAMPBELL'S ACT

19.7 Libel Act 1843, section 2. This provision was obsolete in England even before the introduction of the offer of amends procedure. However, it is still formally part of the law and has some life in other jurisdictions.[55] It is considered in more detail in the ninth edition of this book.

Section 2 of this Act, commonly known as Lord Campbell's Act, provides that:

> "in an action for a libel contained in any public newspaper or other periodical publication, it shall be competent to the defendant to plead that such libel was

---

[52] Occasionally an offer of amends is refused (see, e.g. *Milne v Express Newspapers* [2004] EWCA Civ 664 CA; *John v Associated Newspapers* [2006] EWHC 1740 (QB); *Pell v Express Newspapers* [2003] EWHC 3489 (QB); *Thornton v Telegraph Media Group* [2011] EWHC 1884 (QB); [2012] E.M.L.R. 8 (QB) and the claim brought by Danielle Lloyd against Mirror Group Newspapers, though Lloyd's claim was settled before trial. In *Thornton*, the claimant was able to rely successfully on s.4(3) and in *John*, Eady J. refused an application by the defendant to grant summary judgment under CPR r.24 or strike out the claim on the basis that the claimant had no real prospect of satisfying the s.4(3) test. On the basis of the facts pleaded by the claimant, the judge held that he could not say that a jury would be perverse if its members concluded that the journalist who had written the article was recklessly indifferent to the truth of what he wrote (at [22]).

[53] *Milne v Express Newspapers* [2004] EWCA Civ 664; [2004] E.M.L.R. 24. Cf. s.23(2) of the Irish Defamation Act 2009: "knew or ought reasonably to have known". See, fn.8, above.

[54] *Milne v Express Newspapers* [2002] EWHC 2564 (QB); [2003] 1 W.L.R. 927 at [37]–[41], per Eady J. And see to similar effect the Court of Appeal in *KC v MGN Ltd* [2013] EWCA Civ 3; [2013] 2 Costs L.R. 269 at [13].

[55] Thus it is part of the Hong Kong Defamation Ordinance and was considered in *Chu Siu Kuk Yuen, Jessie v Apple Daily Ltd* [2001] 1375 HKCU 1.

inserted in such newspaper or other periodical publication without actual malice, and without gross negligence, and that before the commencement of the action, or at the earliest opportunity afterwards, he inserted in such newspaper or other periodical publication a full apology for the said libel, or, if the newspaper or periodical publication in which the said libel appeared should be ordinarily published at intervals exceeding one week, had offered to publish the said apology in any newspaper or periodical publication to be selected by the plaintiff in such action; [. . . [56]] and to such plea to such action it shall be competent to the plaintiff to reply generally denying the whole of such plea."[57]

Under s.2 of the Libel Act 1845:

"it shall not be competent to any defendant in such action, whether in England or in Ireland, to file any such plea, without at the same time making a payment of money into court[58] by way of amends [. . . [59]] but every such plea so filed without payment of money into court shall be deemed a nullity and may be treated as such by the plaintiff in the action."

The Act does not apply to slander, but to libel only; and exclusively to such libels as are contained in a "public newspaper" or "periodical publication". The terms are not otherwise defined by statute and it has not been extended to broadcasting.

Requirements of section 2. If there has been the requisite payment into **19.8** court, in order to succeed in a defence under s.2 three things must therefore be proved:

(1) that the libel was inserted in the newspaper "without actual malice".[60]
(2) that the libel was inserted in the newspaper "without gross negligence".[61]

---

[56] The omitted words were repealed by the Civil Procedure Acts Repeal Act 1879, Sch., Pt 11, as to the Supreme Court of Judicature in England, and generally throughout the UK, by the Statute Law Revision Act 1892, s.1.

[57] See *Chadwick v Herapath* (1857) 3 C.B. 885, where it was held that the plaintiff might deny the whole or any part of the plea.

[58] Even if all the requirements are fulfilled, the defendant cannot rely on the provision unless the amount paid in meets the award of damages: *Chu Siu Kuk Yuen, Jessie v Apple Daily Ltd* [2001] 1375 HKCU 1 at [39].

[59] The omitted words were repealed by the Civil Procedure Acts Repeal Act 1879, Sch., Pt 11, as to the Supreme Court of Judicature in England, and generally throughout the UK, by the Statute Law Revision Act 1892, s.1.

[60] In *Allan v Bushnell TV* (1969) 4 D.L.R. (3d) 212, where the defendants pleaded in mitigation of damages, as provided by s.9(2) of the Ontario Libel and Slander Act, that the libel was broadcast without actual malice and without gross negligence, it was held that they were not liable for the malice or negligence of a news agency which was not their agent.

[61] As to which, see *Peters v Edwards* (1887) 3 T.L.R. 423; *Bell v Northern Constitution Ltd* [1943] N.I. 108 (failure of newspaper to inquire into the authenticity of a telephone "birth notice" held gross negligence); *Levien v Fox* (1890) 11 N.S.W.L.R. 414; *Chu Siu Kuk Yuen, Jessie v Apple Daily Ltd* [2001] 1375 HKCU 1 (failure to take steps to verify that the claimant was the solicitor who had absconded with client money held to be gross negligence).

(3) that the defendant inserted a full apology[62] for the libel either before the commencement of the action or at the earliest opportunity afterwards.[63]

The onus of proving a defence under s.2 rests entirely on the defendant.[64] If the defence is not proved, the jury are entitled to take the apology into consideration in mitigation of damages.[65] The absence of actual malice and gross negligence, and the sufficiency of the apology, are distinct and separate issues for the jury to decide.[66]

19.9 Reason the provision is obsolete. It is better for a defendant who has no other defence and who cannot or does not wish to rely on the offer of amends procedure to publish an apology in the newspaper in which the libel appeared, make an offer under CPR Pt 36, and, if this is not accepted, plead the apology in mitigation of damages.[67] For if the defendant fails in a defence under s.2 of the Libel Act, he may have to pay all the costs of the action, even though the jury award the claimant an amount less or no greater than the sum paid in.[68] Whereas if the defendant makes an offer under Pt 36, and the jury award an amount less advantageous than the offer,[69] the defendant will usually receive his costs from the end of the period (not less than 21 days) specified in the offer.[70]

SECTION 3. CONSENT

19.10 Consent. It is a defence to an action for defamation that the claimant consented[71] to the publication of which he now complains by participating in

---

[62] That is, effectually inserted an apology sufficient in its terms in a proper manner as to type and position: *Lafone v Smith* (1858) 28 L.J. Ex. 33.

[63] Regard being had to all the circumstances: see *Ravenhill v Upcott* (1869) 33 J.P. 299; *Cotton v Beatty* (1863) 13 Up.Can.C.P. 243.

[64] *Hope v Brash* [1897] 2 Q.B. 188; *Chu Siu Kuk Yuen, Jessie v Apple Daily Ltd* [2001] 1375 HKCU 1; *Popovich v Lobay* (1937) 2 W.W.R. 64, where the plaintiff was held entitled to discovery on the issues of malice and negligence.

[65] *Limon v Bennett* (1900) 21 N.S.W.L.R. 164.

[66] *Risk Allah Bey v Johnstone* (1868) 18 L.T. 620 at 621.

[67] See para.33.55, below.

[68] *Oxley v Wilkes* [1898] 2 Q.B. 56 CA; *Sley v Tillotson* (1898) 14 T.L.R. 545.

[69] However, in determining this question there is no longer any automatic rule that an award greater in monetary terms than the offer is "more advantageous": *Carver v BAA Plc* [2008] EWCA Civ 412; [2008] 3 All E.R. 911.

[70] See para.29.17, below.

[71] It has been suggested that the expression volenti non fit injuria should be avoided since that is often translated as "assumption of risk". The Irish Defamation Act, s.25 makes the plaintiff's consent to publication a defence.

"The introduction of the word 'risk' into the principle creates an ambiguity which could lead to error if used in that sense with respect to the intentional tort of libel. When a plaintiff consents to being defamed in the way in which it is alleged this plaintiff consented, he consents to the commission of an actual tort, the boundaries of which can be drawn by reference to the terms of his consent. He does not consent to the 'risk' of being libelled. He consents to the libel itself. He may, perhaps, consent to the risk of *injury* as, although injury is presumed to be the

or authorising it.[72] Thus, if the claimant has consented, expressly or impliedly or by conduct, to the publication of the words substantially as they were used,[73] or to the findings of a tribunal in a specified newspaper, whatever the findings might be,[74] there is a good defence to the action; but the proof of consent must be clear and unequivocal.[75] *Carrie v Tolkien*[76] neatly illustrates this defence. The defendant published a potentially defamatory comment on the claimant's blog. The claimant discovered this a maximum of four hours 19 minutes later but allowed it to remain there for 22 months. He had therefore acquiesced in the publication of the libel from the time of discovery and there was no evidence in the short, initial period of any substantial publication to others.

Limits of doctrine. Consent, as in other areas of the law of tort, is a narrow defence.[77] Thus, it has been held not to apply where the publication was not

19.11

---

consequence of the publication of a libel, it is not inevitable that such publication will always lead to actual injury":
Frew v John Fairfax Publications Pty Ltd [2004] VSC 311 at [16]–[17] per Bongiorno J.

[72] The defence is a quite separate defence from privilege, though dicta in *Chapman v Ellesmere* [1932] 2 K.B. 431 CA, may confuse the two defences; *Loveday v Sun Newspapers* (1938) 59 C.L.R. 503 at 523–524. For earlier cases in which consent and privilege (or absence of malice) are not distinguished see *Rogers v Clifton* (1803) 3 Bos. & P. 587; *King v Waring* (1803) 5 Esp. 13 at 15. See more generally *Monson v Tussauds* [1894] 1 Q.B. 671 CA at 691, 697; *Burnett v Greig, The Times*, February 23, 1967; *Abbott v National Coursing* [1941] S.A.S.R. 140; *Cowan v Bank of Adelaide* [1942] S.A.S.R. 140. On principle, consent should not be a defence in a prosecution for criminal libel, though in practice the courts would no doubt lean against a prosecution for a publication to which the claimant had clearly consented. Cf. para.24.6, below.

[73] *Moore v News of the World* [1972] 1 Q.B. 441 at 448; *Friend v Civil Aviation Authority* [1998] I.R.L.R. 253 CA (republication of memoranda in disciplinary proceedings); *Spencer v Sillitoe* [2003] EWHC 1651 (QB); *Crossland v Wilkinson Hardware Stores Ltd* [2005] EWHC 481 (QB) at [70]. Agreement to be referred for examination by a consultant does not, however, amount to consent to publication of the consultant's report: *Cornelius v De Taranto* [2001] EWCA Civ 1511 CA [2001] E.M.L.R. 12.

[74] *Cookson v Harewood* [1932] 2 K.B. 478n CA; *Chapman v Ellesmere* [1932] 2 K.B. 431 CA; *Pritchard v GRA* (1933) 176 L.T.J. 382; (1934) 177 L.T.J. 90 CA. See also *Wilson v Jones* [1979] N.Z. Recent Law 302.

[75] *Mihaka v Wellington Publishing* [1975] 1 N.Z.L.R. 10 at 17; applying *Cook v Ward* (1830) 6 Bing. 409. It is suggested in *Mount Cook Group v Johnstone Motors* [1990] 2 N.Z.L.R. 488 at 499 that there might be defences of estoppel and acquiescence to a claim for damages (independently of the Limitation Act) but it is not clear how far these differ from the defence of consent.

[76] [2009] EWHC 29 (QB); [2009] E.M.L.R. 9. See also, *Flood v Times Newspapers Ltd* [2010] EWCA Civ 804; [2011] 1 W.L.R. 153; [2010] E.M.L.R. 26. Dealing with a situation of non-correction of internet material after a change of circumstances, Lord Neuberger M.R. said at [82]:

"If a claimant says in clear terms that he does not want the publication to be amended or withdrawn, or even that he does not care whether it is amended or withdrawn, then, at least as at present advised, I consider that he could be held to have lost any right to contend that the defendant's failure to amend or withdraw the article was actionable: it could be a simple case of waiver or estoppel, or even, if there was consideration, of contract."

This would seem to be consent under another name.

[77] *Syms v Warren* (1976) 51 D.L.R. (3d) 558 at 563 (awareness that discussion of matter might continue in programme after plaintiff's departure). On the other hand, once consent is established

substantially the same as that to which the claimant consented,[78] nor where the publication was to a wider audience.[79] While republication by the claimant himself would not usually ground an action, it has been held otherwise where the claimant was under a duty to republish the matter of which he complained.[80] The mere submission by the claimant of a matter to public discussion neither authorises a defamatory response, nor even necessarily gives rise to any qualified privilege, unless he has been party to an attack on the defendant which justifies a public reply.[81] A person who authorises publicity for his book does not authorise every statement made in publicising it,[82] and while a person who comes to a "talk-show" to rebut rumours assents to their repetition for that purpose, he does not consent to telephoned repetitions from listeners.[83] Refusal to respond to an accusation is not consent to its repetition.

19.12   **Traps and challenges.** In *Duke of Brunswick v Harmer*[84] the plaintiff succeeded in his claim for publication of a libel to his servant when he procured the latter to obtain a copy of the offending newspaper from the defendant, seventeen years after the initial publication. It is plain that nowadays such a claim would be dismissed as an abuse of process.[85] But it does not follow that a challenge to repeat a defamatory statement before witnesses bars a claim, for that may be the only way the claimant has of putting a stop to defamatory statements about him. Thus while the 2nd Restatement of Torts provides that consent is generally a complete defence,[86] it goes on to say that an:

---

to the publication of a true statement, it is irrelevant that an innuendo meaning is untrue: *Cookson v Harewood*, above, *Chapman v Ellesmere*, above.

[78] *Moore v News of the World* [1972] 1 Q.B. 441. *Frew v John Fairfax Publications Pty Ltd* [2004] VSC 311. See also *Kelly v William Morrow & Co*, 231 Cal.Rptr. 497 (1986).

[79] *Cook v Ward* (1830) 6 Bing. 409.

[80] *Collerton v MacLean* [1962] N.Z.L.R. 1045; *Jones v Amalgamated TV Services* (1991) 23 N.S.W.L.R. 364. Thus a number of cases in the US have held A liable where he wrongfully discharges B for a defamatory reason and knows that B will have to publish that reason to a prospective new employer: see *Lewis v Equitable Life Assurance*, 389 N.W.2d 876 (Minn., 1986) and 50 Am.Jur.2d, Libel and Slander, paras 241 et seq. *Contra, Wieder v Chemical Bank*, 608 N.Y.S.2d 195 (1994).

[81] *Loveday v Sun Newspapers* (1938) 59 C.L.R. 503 at 513–514 applied. *Church of Scientology v Anderson* [1980] W.A.R. at 81, reversed on another point [1981] W.A.R. 279. For qualified privilege in cases where inquiry is made by or on behalf of the claimant, see para.14.33; for replies to an attack, see paras 14.51 and 14.67, above. The European Court of Human Rights has held that the context in which defamatory words are spoken may be relevant in determining their permissibility. Thus, those involved in debate can expect harsher words than others: "a degree of exaggeration should be tolerated in the context of such a heated and continuing public debate of affairs of general concern where on both sides professional reputations are at stake" (*Giniewski v France* App. No.64016/00, January 31, 2006 at [52]. See also *Klein v Slovakia* App. No72208/01, October 31, 2006; *Vilsen and Johnsen v Norway* App. No.23118/93, 1999-VIII).

[82] *Mihaka v Wellington Publishing* [1975] 1 N.Z.L.R. 10.

[83] *Syms v Warren* (1976) 71 D.L.R. (3d) 558.

[84] (1849) 14 Q.B. 185.

[85] See para.6.2, above.

[86] Para.583.

"honest inquiry or investigation by the person defamed to ascertain the existence, source, content or meaning of a defamatory publication is not a defense to an action for its republication by the defamer."[87]

SECTION 4. LIMITATION

Basic principle and history. Like any other cause of action in tort one for **19.13** defamation is barred by the passage of time.[88] Under the Limitation Act 1939, re-enacted by the Limitation Act 1980, the period was the general period in tort, that is to say six years from the date of the accrual of the cause of action.[89] In the case of libel and slander actionable per se that point is the date of publication[90] because that is the first moment at which the claimant can bring proceedings; but in the case of slander actionable only on proof of special damage[91] the cause of action accrues and time begins to run at the time when the damage is sustained, for until then the cause of action is incomplete.[92] In all cases the running of the period might be postponed because the claimant was under a disability[93] or because of concealment by the defendant.[94] By virtue of the Administration of Justice Act 1985 the period for actions for libel or slander was reduced to three years from the accrual of the cause of action,[95] but with power in the court to give leave for the commencement of an action after that time but within one year of the claimant's knowledge of all the facts relevant to the cause of action.[96] In the case of

---

[87] Para.584. Comment (d) says, "The rule stated in this Section has no application when the inquiry is not an honest inquiry or investigation to ascertain the facts, and the republication is invited only for the purpose of decoying the defendant into a lawsuit."

[88] Under the Irish Defamation Act 2009, amending the Statute of Limitations 1957, a defamation action shall be brought within one year of the accrual of the cause of action or such longer period, not exceeding two years, as the court may direct where the interests of justice so require and the prejudice that the plaintiff would suffer if the direction were not given would significantly outweigh the prejudice that the defendant would suffer if the direction were given (see s.38(1)). Furthermore, the date of accrual of the cause of action "shall be the date upon which the defamatory statement is first published and, where the statement is published through the medium of the internet, the date on which it is first capable of being viewed or listened to through that medium".

[89] Limitation Act 1980, s.2.

[90] Under Defamation Act 2013, s.8, which is not yet in force, where a person publishes a statement to the public and subsequently publishes (whether or not to the public) that statement or a statement in substantially the same form, any cause of action in respect of the subsequent publication is treated as having accrued from the first date of publication (s.8(3)).

[91] The same is generally true of actions for malicious falsehood, but not for those in which damage is presumed by virtue of s.3 of the Defamation Act 1952: *Farnham v CEGB* [1976] B.L.T. 104.

[92] *Saunders v Edwards* (1663) 1 Sid. 95; *Littleboy v Wright* (1674) 1 Lev. 69; *Roberts v Read* (1812) 16 East 215.

[93] Limitation Act 1980, s.28.

[94] Limitation Act 1980, s.32(1)(b).

[95] Limitation Act 1980, s.4A, added by the Administration of Justice Act 1985, s.57(2).

[96] Limitation Act 1980, s.32A, added by the Administration of Justice Act 1985, s.57(4). See *C v Mirror Group Newspapers Ltd* [1997] 1 W.L.R. 131 CA.

causes of action arising after September 3, 1996 the period was further reduced by the Defamation Act 1996[97] to one year and this applies also to malicious falsehood. There is power to allow an action to be commenced outside the one-year period, but that is of a different nature from that under the previous law. The cause of action is complete and time begins to run even though the claimant was unaware of the libel or of the identity of the person who published it. In such a case the claimant must rely on the provisions relating to the court's power to disapply the limitation period.[98]

The rationale of these reductions in the basic limitation period is that a person whose reputation has been traduced should pursue legal redress with vigour: "Memories fade. Journalists and their sources scatter and become, not infrequently, untraceable. Notes and other records are retained only for short periods."[99] Where claimants have legitimate reasons for wishing to commence action after a longer period these, it has been argued, can be met by judicial discretion to override the time limit.[100]

> "It is normally anticipated that a victim of defamation will pursue, and will want energetically to pursue, the vindication of his good name. That is why the limitation period in actions for defamation is limited to one year."[101]

The defendant must plead limitation if he intends to rely on it,[102] but if he does so the burden is on the claimant to show that his cause of action arose within the limitation period.[103]

19.14 Subsequent publications. Each and every publication of a libel gives a distinct and separate cause of action, and an action may be brought against the publisher within the limitation period thereafter, although by reason of the lapse of time no action would lie for the original publication.[104]

---

[97] Limitation Act 1980 substituted by s.5 of the Defamation Act 1996, which came into force on September 4, 1996: s.19(2). This has no application to Scotland. S.6 contains equivalent provisions amending the Limitation (Northern Ireland) Order 1989, SI 1989/1339.

[98] *Edwards v Golding* [2007] EWCA Civ 416.

[99] The Neill Report (1991), para.VIII.2.

[100] Ibid. at paras VIII.3 et seq.

[101] *Austin v Newcastle Chronicle and Journal Ltd* [2001] EWCA Civ 834 at [38], per Judge L.J.; *Mullan v Edwards* [2004] NIQB 83. See also the Pre-Action Protocol for Defamation.

[102] PD 16, para.13.1.

[103] *London Congregational Union v Harriss and Harriss* [1988] 1 All E.R. 15 CA (not a defamation case).

[104] This proposition remains true even though the clearest authority for and example of it, *Duke of Brunswick v Harmer* (1849) 14 Q.B. 185, would now be regarded as involving an abuse of process: see para.19.12, above. While for the purpose of assessing damages for a live cause of action (for example where it is alleged that the defendant was actuated by malice) it may be permissible to consider the whole history of matters between the parties, the court should not award damages in respect of the effect of a prior libel or slander which is statute barred (*Murphy v Alexander* (2004) 236 D.L.R. (4th) 302 Ont. CA). For the "single publication" rule in some US jurisdictions, see para.6.4, above. In Australia where a person has brought proceedings for defamation against any person in respect of the publication of any matter, that person shall not bring further proceedings for defamation against the same defendant in respect of the same or any other publication of the same or like matter, except with the leave of the court. See, e.g. Defamation Act 2005 (NSW) s.23.

Defamation Act 2013, s.8—single publication rule and accrual of   **19.15**
cause of action. Under Defamation Act 2013, s.8, which is not yet in force,
where a person publishes a statement to the public and subsequently publishes
(whether or not to the public) that statement or a statement in substantially the
same form, any cause of action in respect of the subsequent publication is, for
the purposes of s.4A of the Limitation Act 1980, treated as having accrued
from the date of the first publication.[105] Thus, where the defendant publishes
a statement about the claimant in a book and, sixth months later, the book is
reprinted and the statement republished, any claim in respect of the subsequent publication is treated as having accrued at the date of first publication.

Cases governed by the law as amended in 1985. Although the basic   **19.16**
limitation period for claims arising before the 1996 Act expired in September
1999 it is still theoretically possible that a claim originating before 1996 might
be brought[106] because, e.g. the claimant was subject to a disability when the
cause of action arose or (perhaps more likely in a defamation case) because he
was unaware of the facts. In either event, the claim is not a matter of judicial
discretion but of entitlement.[107] However, such claims seem highly unlikely
now and the law is fully considered in the ninth edition of this book.

Causes of action arising after September 3, 1996: the one-year   **19.17**
period. Under s.4A of the Limitation Act 1980, as substituted by s.5(2) of
the Defamation Act 1996, a claim for libel or slander or malicious falsehood[108] must be brought within one year[109] from the date on which the cause
of action accrued, that is to say from the date of publication where the words
are actionable per se or from the date when damage is suffered in other
cases.[110]

---

[105] Defamation Act 2013, s.8(3). See para.6.6ff, above.

[106] Indeed, theoretically a claim could arise from publications before 1985, e.g. D libelled C in
1984 at a time when C was insane and C has just recovered his reason. However, such cases are
the fantasy of the examination hall.

[107] Despite the requirement of leave of the High Court in s.32A of the Limitation Act 1980.

[108] The statutory wording is "slander of title, slander of goods or other malicious falsehood".
For an unsuccessful attempt to dress malicious falsehood up as a tort of "interference with rights"
to evade the one-year limit, see *Cornwall Gardens Pte Ltd v RO Garrard & Co. Ltd* [2001]
EWCA Civ 699. Limitation has of course always been a fertile source of "classification"
issues.

[109] Since the period is three years in Scotland, the protection afforded to the national media is
less strong than might at first sight appear.

[110] See para.19.13, above. But a claim for negligent misstatement like that in *Spring v Guardian
Assurance* [1995] 2 A.C. 296 HL (para.23.3, below) which "overlapped" a claim for defamation
would be governed by the six-year basic period of the 1980 Act. S.11 of the Act prescribes a
three-year period for actions for damages for personal injuries, with provision for postponing the
running of time (s.14) and a power to "disapply" the period (s.33). The distress and humiliation
which are commonly said to ensue from defamatory words are not, it is thought, "impairment of
a person's physical or mental condtion" (s.38(1)) for this purpose. But if, in a particular case, a
physical or mental illness were held to be a non-remote consequence of the libel, the three-year
period (and its attended qualifications) only applies to actions arising from "negligence, nuisance

19.18 Claimant under a disability. It is a general principle of the law of limitation that time does not begin to run against a person who is subject to a disability when the wrong against him is committed.[111] Minority (infancy) and unsoundness of mind are the only disabilities recognised by law for this purpose.[112] A person subject to a disability who is defamed may bring an action for libel or slander before the expiration of one year from the date when he ceased to be under a disability.[113] A disability which arises after time has begun to run has no effect,[114] but if a person is a minor when the cause of action accrues and unsoundness of mind supervenes without any interval, then (semble) time does not begin to run until the last disability ceases.[115]

No disability on the part of the defendant prevents the period of limitation from running.[116]

19.19 Concealment. Under s.32(1)(b) of the Limitation Act 1980 where "any fact relevant[117] to the plaintiff's right of action has been deliberately concealed from him by the defendant . . . the period of limitation shall not begin to run until the plaintiff has discovered the . . . concealment . . . or could with reasonable diligence have discovered it." While this will not often in practice apply to a case of defamation, there is no reason in principle why it should not do so,[118] as where the defendant destroys files which are the only physical evidence of a libel. The concealment need not be contemporaneous with the commission of the tort[119]: if, while the claimant is unaware of the existence of his cause of action the defendant conceals it, the normal limitation period

---

or breach of duty". In *A v Hoare* [2008] UKHL 6; [2008] 2 W.L.R. 311 those words were held to include battery. Could they include libel?

[111] See Limitation Act 1980, s.28(1).

[112] Limitation Act 1980, s.38(2).

[113] Ibid. s.28(1) as modified by s.28(4A), which was inserted by the Defamation Act 1996, s.5(3).

[114] Ibid. s.28(1). *Sheldon v RHM Outhwaite (Underwriting Agencies)* [1996] A.C. 102 at 146, per Lord Lloyd. This is a dissenting judgment, but the issue was the meaning of s.32 of the Act. The majority held that under that section concealment by the defendant might interrupt the running of a period which had begun and give the plaintiff a fresh limitation period from the date when he knew or ought to have known of the concealment. But there is no suggestion in the majority that this affects s.28.

[115] The words used in s.28(1) of the Limitation Act 1980 are "after the date when the person ceased to be under *a* disability" which seem to give statutory effect to the decision of *Borrows v Ellison* (1871) L.R.6 Ex. 128.

[116] Since the Limitation Act 1939 the absence of the defendant beyond the seas no longer operates to prevent time from running.

[117] A fact is only "relevant" for this purpose if it is necessary for the claimant to prove it in order to plead a cause of action: *C v Mirror Group Newspapers Ltd* [1997] 1 W.L.R. 131 CA (a case under s.32A as it stood before the Defamation Act 1996). Whether the defendant's concealment of his identity is relevant under this provision is debatable, since knowledge of his identity is not essential to there being a cause of action. But in any event, the provision does not cover a mere anonymous publication: *Edwards v Golding* [2007] EWCA Civ 416.

[118] That it might apply is accepted in *C v Mirror Group Newspapers Ltd* at 139 and it was raised (unsuccessfully on the facts) in *McBride v Bodyshop International Plc* [2007] EWHC 1658 (QB).

[119] Despite the use of the words "shall not begin to run".

commences from the date of his actual or constructive knowledge of it.[120] However, "there is a distinction between not revealing a confidential document (until disclosed under compulsion of law) and deliberately concealing it. It is implicit in the notion of 'deliberate concealment' that a document has been concealed from someone who would otherwise have a right of access to it."[121] No permission is required under s.32(1)(b) and it is as much applicable to malicious falsehood as to defamation.

Discretionary exclusion of time limit. A new s.32A of the Limitation   **19.20**
Act 1980 was substituted by s.5(4) of the Defamation Act 1996[122]:

"(1) If it appears to the court that it would be equitable to allow an action to proceed having regard to the degree to which—
   (a) the operation of section 4A[123] of this Act prejudices the plaintiff or any person whom he represents, and
   (b) any decision of the court under this subsection would prejudice the defendant or any person whom he represents,
the court may direct that that section shall not apply to the action or shall not apply to any specified cause of action to which the action relates.[124]
   (2) In acting under this section the court shall have regard to all the circumstances of the case and in particular to—
   (a) the length of, and the reasons for, the delay on the part of the plaintiff;
   (b) where the reason or one of the reasons for the delay was that all or any of the facts relevant to the cause of action did not become known to the plaintiff until after the end of the period mentioned in section 4A—
      (i) the date on which any such facts did become known to him, and
      (ii) the extent to which he acted promptly and reasonably once he knew whether or not the facts in question might be capable of giving rise to an action; and

---

[120] *Sheldon v RHM Outhwaite (Underwriting Agencies)* [1996] A.C. 102.

[121] *McBride v Bodyshop International Plc*, above at [54]. See also, *Apsion v Butler* [2011] EWHC 844 (QB) at [47]. An allegation of concealment has been said to be of some gravity and it should be properly particularised. Thus, the claimant should: (1) identify the facts alleged to have been concealed; (2) the basis for the allegation of concealment should be explained; and (3) the claimant should identify the dates on which those facts became known to him: *Vaidya v General Medical Council* [2010] EWHC 984 (QB).

[122] Although they are different in many important respects, the basic structure of s.32A is like that of s.33 of the 1980 Act (discretionary exclusion of time limit in personal injury cases).

[123] I.e. the one-year period of limitation. Under s.33 of the Act, dealing with personal injury claims, it was once held that where an action has been started within the limitation period but has then been dismissed (e.g. for want of prosecution) the discretion would not avail the claimant, for the prejudice to him then arose not from the operation of the limitation period but his own dilatoriness: *Walkley v Precision Forgings Ltd* [1979] 1 W.L.R. 606 HL. This was applied to s.32A in *Oldie Publications v Brinn*, February 12, 2001, (QB). However, the HL has subsequently departed from *Walkley*: *Horton v Sadler* [2006] UKHL 27; [2007] 1 A.C. 307.

[124] For addition or substitution of parties after expiry of the limitation period, see *Adelson v Associated Newspapers Ltd* [2007] EWCA Civ 701; [2008] 1 W.L.R. 585 (where s.32A was not relied on) and para.31.62, below. Since s.32A performs a similar function to s.33, the omission of any reference to it in s.35 of the Limitation Act may be an oversight: *Wood v CC West Midlands* [2004] EWCA Civ 1638; [2004] E.M.L.R. 17 at [76] (adding new cause of action).

(c) the extent to which, having regard to the delay, relevant evidence is likely—
    (i) to be unavailable, or
    (ii) to be less cogent than if the action had been brought within the period mentioned in section 4A."

Section 32A of the 1980 Act differs from the former provision introduced by the Administration of Justice Act 1985 in that it is no longer a precondition of allowing the claim to proceed that the failure to comply with the basic limitation period arises from the claimant's ignorance of relevant facts. The ultimate question now is whether it is "equitable" to allow the action to proceed. Given that s.32A gives a quite general discretion[125] it is somewhat strange that subs.(2)(b) refers to the claimant's ignorance of "facts relevant to the cause of action," an expression which in the context of s.32(1)(b) and of the former s.32A has the narrow meaning of facts which the claimant has to plead and prove to establish a prima facie case.[126] If the court is to have regard to all the circumstances of the case and in particular to the effect of delay on the availability and cogency of evidence,[127] it is difficult to see why, e.g. it should have regard to the extent to which the claimant acted promptly on discovering that the defendant had published a prima facie defamatory story about him but should not have regard to the promptness of the claimant's action on discovering evidence that what appeared to be a privileged report was inaccurate or was actuated by malice.

Ignorance of "relevant facts" in relation to s.32(1)(b) is not relevant to the exercise of any discretion and under the former s.32A it was a preliminary test that had to be passed by the claimant before the court could exercise its discretion to allow the action to proceed. In the current s.32A there is no such preliminary issue: ignorance and the action taken by the claimant upon discovery of the facts are merely matters to be considered in the exercise of the discretion.[128] It is, therefore, submitted that "facts relevant to the cause of

---

[125] Lord Mackay L.C. described it as "a completely open discretion to extend the period" and "a very ample judicial discretion": *Hansard*, HL, cols 638–639 (April 16, 1996). "Largely unfettered": *Steedman v BBC* [2001] EWCA Civ 1534; [2002] E.M.L.R. 17 at [17].

[126] *C v Mirror Group Newspapers Ltd* [1997] 1 W.L.R. 131 CA.

[127] S.32A(2)(c). This refers to "relevant evidence" but this, it is submitted, is evidence which will be relevant in the case if it is tried, not merely to evidence of "relevant facts" in the narrow "cause of action" sense.

[128] Indeed, it is difficult to see how the position can rationally be otherwise. Suppose C does not know that D has published. Presumably the court's readiness to allow an action out of time will, putting aside other factors, be closely related to the speed with which the claimant acts when he discovers the truth. Suppose instead that after the expiry of the one-year limitation period P discovers cast-iron evidence that what appeared to be a fair comment was in fact actuated entirely by spite. P then delays for three years before starting proceedings. Is the court to say that it must allow the action to proceed because it cannot take this delay into account? Alternatively, suppose similar facts but with proceedings commenced the day after the discovery. Is the court to say that it must dismiss the action because it can only reward promptness where the matter goes to the "cause of action". Both approaches would seem to be inconsistent with the requirement to have regard to all the circumstances of the case.

action" in s.32A should not be given the narrow meaning which is established in s.32(1)(b).[129]

Exercise of the discretion. The discretion granted by the Act is a wide one[130] and has been said to be "largely unfettered".[131] However, the courts have made clear that its exercise is exceptional.[132] As Eady J. explained in *Adelson v Associated Newspapers*[133]: **19.21**

> "I accept that Parliament . . . decided to put in place a more flexible regime, in the sense that the much reduced period of limitation should be balanced by a broader discretion on the court's part having regard to what is perceived to be 'equitable' in all the circumstances. But genuine libel claims must still be pursued with vigour: that is the most important policy consideration underlying the legislative change."[134]

The essential question in a case when there is an application to disapply the primary limitation period is whether it would be equitable to allow the claim to proceed having regard to the prejudice that would be caused to the claimant on the one hand in not allowing the claim to proceed and, on the other hand, to the prejudice that would be caused to the defendant in allowing the claim to proceed. In answering this question the courts are required to have regard to all the circumstances of the case and in particular to the matters identified in s.32A(2). As with the exercise of any discretion, the precise weight to be given to any particular factor will vary from case to case and particular care therefore needs to be taken in seeking to identify any general principles from the cases. That said, a few general principles emerge.

The effect that the delay has on the defendant's ability to mount a defence is of paramount importance.[135] Where the cogency of the evidence is affected by the delay in commencing proceedings or where evidence or witnesses favourable to the defendant are no longer available this is likely to be treated as highly relevant.[136] However, whilst the effect of the delay on the ability of the defendant to defend an action remains important, it is not decisive (save

---

[129] This despite the fact that s.32A(2)(b)(ii) refers to "facts [which] might be capable of giving rise to an action".

[130] *Edwards v Golding* [2007] EWCA Civ 416 at [23].

[131] *Steedman v BBC* [2001] EWCA Civ 1534; [2002] E.M.L.R. 17 at [15]. See also, per Eady J. in *Adelson v Associated Newspapers* [2007] EWHC 3028 (QB) at [20].

[132] *Steedman v BBC* [2001] EWCA Civ 1534; [2002] E.M.L.R. 17 at [41]; *Hinks v Channel 4 Television Corp*, unreported, March 3, 2000 at 3; *Clarkson v Gilbert*, unreported, February 26, 2001 at [14]; *Maccaba v Lichtenstein* [2003] EWHC 1325 (QB) at [11].

[133] [2007] EWHC 3028 (QB).

[134] Ibid. at [20].

[135] *Steedman v BBC* [2001] EWCA Civ 1534; [2002] E.M.L.R. 17 at [18].

[136] While several judgments refer to the relevance of these factors (see e.g. *Gentoo Group Ltd (formerly known as Sunderland Housing Co. Ltd) v Hanratty* [2008] EWHC 627 (QB) at [32]; *Maccaba v Lichtenstein* [2003] EWHC 1325 (QB)), in no case has it been held that the delay significantly affected the cogency or availability of evidence to the defendant.

perhaps where the defence can be fairly described as a complete windfall).[137] The defendant's ability to defend the claim is a significant factor to be taken into account in assessing the likely prejudice, but it is simply one of several relevant factors and the fact that the defendant's ability to defend the claim is not prejudiced by the delay is certainly not a trump card for the claimant.[138]

The seriousness of the alleged defamation[139] and the extent of publication are relevant factors, as are the length of, and the reasons for, the delay on the part of the claimant. In *Cornwall Gardens PTE Ltd v RO Garrard & Co. Ltd*[140] Lord Phillips M.R. accepted the following statement of H.H.J. Chambers QC at first instance as correct:

" . . . this requirement is no more than confirmatory of the fact that where a party has put itself in a position by its own conduct that it requires a discretion of the court to be allowed to continue in those proceedings it must proffer an explanation to the court as to how the state of affairs has arisen."[141]

So far as the length of the delay is concerned, this is to be considered in relation to the primary limitation period[142] though prior delay is "part of the circumstances of the case".[143] Thus, while a few days or even weeks may in

---

[137] *Steedman v BBC* [2001] EWCA Civ 1534; [2002] E.M.L.R. 17 at [23]. In *Cain v Francis* [2008] EWCA Civ 1451; [2009] Q.B. 754, a personal injury claim, the Court of Appeal stated (at [57]), in respect of the similar provision in s.33 of the 1980 Act, that: "in a case where the defendant has had early notice of the claim the accrual of a limitation defence should be regarded as a windfall and the prospect of its loss, by the exercise of the section 33 discretion, should be regarded as either no prejudice at all or only a slight degree of prejudice." In *Brady v Norman* [2011] EWCA Civ 107; [2011] E.M.L.R. 16 the Court of Appeal treated *Steedman* as binding on it but rejected the argument that *Cain* could not be reconciled with *Steedman*:
"Certainly in a personal injury case where the defendant has had proper opportunity to investigate the facts and has admitted liability, the loss of a fortuitous windfall limitation defence will often, depending on the facts, be regarded as of little or no prejudicial weight and likely to be outweighed by the prejudice of the claimant in accidentally losing his claim. Considerations in defamation claims are likely to be different. The policy behind the much shorter limitation period is clear. The defamatory impact of libel or slander is likely to be transient and Parliament evidently intended that a claimant should assert and pursue his need for vindication speedily" (at [21]).
[138] *Gentoo Group Ltd (formerly known as Sunderland Housing Co. Ltd) v Hanratty* [2008] EWHC 627 (QB) at [12]. Permission to appeal on various points in the *Gentoo* case was refused but the limitation point was not pursued in these proceedings: [2008] EWCA Civ 968.
[139] *Buckley v Dalziel* [2007] EWHC 1025 (QB); [2007] 1 W.L.R. 2933 at [35]. Where damage to reputation is slight or non-existent, the court is also likely to consider the potential impact on the lives of the participants of allowing the claim to continue: *Buckley v Dalziel* at [36]. See also *Khalil v Barakat* [2013] EWHC 85 (QB); *Zinda v Ark Academies (Schools)* [2011] EWHC 3394 (QB) (refusal to exercise discretion as there was limited publication, no further risk of publication and defendant would be put to enormous inconvenience in defending the claim); *Vaidya v GMC* [2010] EWHC 984 (QB).
[140] [2001] EWCA Civ 699; [2002] E.M.L.R. 17 (a malicious falsehood claim).
[141] Ibid. at [56].
[142] *Woodruffe v Fallows* [2007] EWHC 3206 at [31] (QB); *Cornwall Gardens PTE Ltd v RO Garrard & Co. Ltd* [2001] EWCA Civ 69 at [56].
[143] *Thompson v Brown* [1981] 1 W.L.R. 744 HL.

appropriate circumstances be readily overlooked,[144] a delay of several months, when considered in the context of a primary limitation period which is only one year, would be considered a lengthy delay.[145] Where the claimant does not offer a reason for failing to commence the claim within the primary limitation period, this is not necessarily fatal to an application to disapply[146] but any explanation that shows that the claimant was not at fault in failing to commence the claim in time or, better still, that the defendant's behaviour was in fact wholly or partly to blame for the claimant's failure is likely to be accorded considerable weight.[147]

The existence of intervening professional disciplinary or criminal proceedings prompted by the libel (provided at least that a prompt complaint is made)[148] or even, possibly, difficulty in obtaining funding to launch the action were suggested by the Neill Committee as legitimate reasons leading to the exercise of the discretion in the claimant's favour.[149] That the claimant has an alternative claim against the defendant, for, by way of example, negligent misrepresentation or harassment,[150] or against his lawyer for negligently failing to commence the claim within the limitation period,[151] is a matter that

---

[144] In *Maccaba v Lichtenstein* [2003] EWHC 1325 (QB) the period of delay, of just over five weeks, was described as "very short" (at [23]) and the claim was allowed to proceed. However, in *Buckley v Dalziel* [2007] EWHC 1025 (QB); [2007] 1 W.L.R. 2933 the period of delay was approximately six weeks, but the court refused to allow the claim to proceed as other factors meant prejudice to the defendant outweighed that to the claimant.

[145] *Cornwall Gardens PTE Ltd v RO Garrard & Co. Ltd* [2001] EWCA Civ 699 at [56] ("Ten months might, in appropriate circumstances, not seem terribly much in relation to a three-year limitation period, but in relation to a 12-month limitation period it is a lengthy delay"); *Woodruffe v Fallows* [2007] EWHC 3206 (QB) at [31]; *Vaidya v GMC* [2010] EWHC 984 (QB) (delay of nearly a year).

[146] See, e.g. *Maccaba v Lichtenstein* [2003] EWHC 1325 (QB).

[147] That the defendant had published the offending allegation anonymously and great difficulty was experienced identifying the author (See, e.g. *Gentoo Group Ltd (formerly known as Sunderland Housing Co. Ltd) v Hanratty* [2008] EWHC 627 (QB); *Edwards v Golding* [2007] EWCA Civ 416) or that the defendant only escaped being sued within the limitation period by lying, either have been, or would be likely to be, treated as reasons that would go some way to justifying a late commencement of the claim. Even if the reason offered for the delay is a reasonable one, other factors may still mean that the prejudice to the defendant in allowing the claim to proceed outweighs that to the claimant. Where the claimant offers no reason (or an inadequate one) this militates against exercising the discretion (*Vaidya v GMC* [2010] EWHC 984 (QB)). See also *Buckley v Dalziel* [2007] EWHC 1025 (QB); [2007] 1 W.L.R. 2933 (claimant devoting himself to other aspects of the litigation not a good reason); *Woodruffe v Fallows* [2002] EWHC 3206 (claimant seriously concerned about his financial position brought about by alleged defamation not a good reason).

[148] See *Steedman v BBC* [2001] EWCA Civ 1534; [2002] E.M.L.R. 17 at [20] and [44]. In the related area of dismissal for want of prosecution it has been said that it can be a reasonable ground for delaying defamation proceedings to await the outcome of pending criminal or disciplinary proceedings which affected the reputation which the claimant was seeking to protect, though there can be no hard and fast rule about it: *Khalili v Bennett* [2000] E.M.L.R. 996 CA. Cf. *Hinks v Channel 4 Television Corp*, unreported, March 3, 2000, (QB) (a s.32A case: libel proceedings should have been issued and a stay applied for).

[149] See paras VIII.4 et seq., of the Neill Report (1991). However, this is a slippery slope.

[150] *Maccaba v Lichtenstein* [2003] EWHC 1325 (QB); *Iqbal v Mansoor* [2011] EWHC 2261 (QB).

[151] *Steedman v BBC* [2001] EWCA Civ 1534; [2002] E.M.L.R. 17.

should be taken into account in determining whether to allow the claim to proceed. However, the existence of the alternative claim, and the consequent amelioration of the extent of the prejudice suffered by the claimant, must be balanced against the prejudice that might be caused to the claimant in not being able to vindicate his reputation by a defamation claim.[152]

Where several claims are commenced by a claimant against the same defendant of which at least one is commenced outside the primary limitation period, the fact that even if the claim commenced outside the period is dismissed on limitation grounds the others will still proceed is a factor that will significantly reduce any prejudice to the defendant particularly where it can be said that the defamatory imputations are part of a course of conduct.[153] That the claim has appeared "out of the blue" with no, or no significant, complaint having been made until after the primary limitation period has expired or until late in the primary limitation period, has also been held to be a factor that militates against allowing the claim to proceed.[154] Where, however, the claimant notifies the defendant of the likelihood of a claim soon after the publication, this is a matter that can be relied upon in support of an application to disapply the limitation period.[155]

SECTION 5. JUDGMENT RECOVERED AND RES JUDICATA

19.22 The nature of the defences. It is a general principle[156] that a person may only recover damages once in respect of the same cause of action[157]; similarly, where a person's claim has been dismissed by a competent court,[158] he may

---

[152] *Steedman v BBC* [2001] EWCA Civ 1534; [2002] E.M.L.R. 17. This is less true in libel cases than in personal injury cases under s.33 because it does not provide the same vindication as judgment against the defendant; but a long delayed vindication may be a rather watered down thing anyway. Cf. *Adelson v Associated Newspapers Ltd* [2007] EWHC 3028 (QB) at [16] (where the claim sought to be made was for corporate financial loss). So also the fact that the claimant has good claims for libel against others (*Sarayiah v Suren* [2004] EWHC 1981 (QB); *Gentoo Group Ltd v Hanratty* [2008] EWHC 627 (QB)) or against the defendant (*Maccaba v Lichtenstein* [2003] EWHC 1325 (QB)) are factors to be considered but are not decisive.
[153] *Maccaba v Lichtenstein* [2003] EWHC 1325 (QB) at [19].
[154] See, for example, *Steedman v BBC* [2001] EWCA Civ 1534 at [20]; [2002] E.M.L.R. 17, (referring with approval to the following statement in the Supreme Court Procedure Committee's *Report on Practice and Procedure in Defamation* (July 1991), at VIII.5: "We would not expect a plaintiff to receive much sympathy if no relevant complaint had been made within the 12-month period."); *Vaidya v GMC* [2010] EWHC 984 (QB); *Buckley v Dalziel* [2007] EWHC 1025 (QB); [2007] 1 W.L.R. 2933 at [34]; *Woodruffe v Fallows* [2007] EWHC 3206 (QB) at [39]; *Muter v Newcastle Upon Tyne Aero Club Ltd* [2001] EWHC 7 (QB) at [52].
[155] *Maccaba v Lichtenstein* [2003] EWHC 1325 (QB) at [24].
[156] Which has to be qualified in the case of personal injury actions by the system of provisional damages: Clerk & Lindsell, *Torts*, 20th edn (2010), para.29–69.
[157] *Fetter v Beale* (1701) 1 Ld. Raym. 339.
[158] In *McKeown v Attheraces Ltd* [2011] EWHC 179 (QB), an attempt to strike out a libel claim on the basis that it amounted to a re-litigation of findings made by a disciplinary panel of the British Horseracing Authority failed as the matters raised in the libel claim went beyond those dealt with by the panel.

not bring a further claim in respect of the same cause of action for he is estopped *per rem judicatam*; furthermore, even where there are distinct rights and hence distinct causes of action, or even different parties a claim may be dismissed on the ground that it is an abuse of process.[159]

"Abuse of process may arise where there has been no earlier decision capable of amounting to *res judicata* (either or both because the parties[160] or the issues are different) for example, where liability between new parties and/or determination of new issues should have been resolved in the earlier proceedings. It may also arise where there is such an inconsistency between the two that it would be unjust to permit the later one to continue."[161]

So, in *Schellenberg v BBC*[162] abuse of process was a[163] ground for the dismissal of an action for libel arising from a radio programme which had dealt with the claimant's treatment of tenants on the Island of Eigg. Previous actions against two newspapers in respect of statements about the claimant's stewardship of the Island had been settled on terms disadvantageous to the claimant and, while the issues in those actions were not identical to those in the action against the BBC, there was a good deal of overlap between them. The issue of the claimant's treatment of the tenants had been squarely in play

---

[159] In *El Diwany v Ministry of Justice and Police* [2011] EWHC 2077 (QB) claims in libel brought by a solicitor resident in the United Kingdom against a Norwegian police officer living in Norway, her employer and a Norwegian journalist were struck out, inter alia, as an abuse of process. The claimant had wanted to pursue proceedings in this jurisdiction against a Norwegian police officer in respect of words spoken by her to a journalist more than five years ago. The police officer had investigated the claimant over a long period of time in respect of allegations of harassment made by a Norwegian woman who had worked as an au pair in the United Kingdom. The claimant had been convicted by the Norwegian courts of harassing the woman. It was also clear that the claimant had harassed the police officer as well. While the claimant's conviction was not conclusive evidence that he committed the offence, he had had an opportunity to contest the issues and a court in this jurisdiction was entitled to have regard to the fact of the convictions in particular in light of the claimant's admission of guilt. The proceedings were also an attempt to undermine the judgments of the Norwegian courts and demonstrate that they were wrong. They were a further aspect of the claimant's harassment of the police office and were not brought to vindicate his reputation. For these reasons, the claimant's action against the police officer were struck out and consequently those against her employer failed as well, based as they were on their vicarious liability for the police officer's conduct.

[160] See *Aldi Stores Ltd v WSP Group Plc* [2007] EWCA Civ 1260; [2008] P.N.L.R. 14.

[161] *Bradford & Bingley BS v Seddon* [1999] 1 W.L.R. 1482 CA per Auld L.J. at 1490. The distinction between the two was explained by Auld L.J. as follows:

"[Res judicata], in its cause of action estoppel form, is an absolute bar to re-litigation, and in its issue estoppel form save in the 'special cases' or 'special circumstances' ... [Abuse of process] which may arise where there is no cause of action or issue estoppel is not subject to the same test, the task of the court being to draw the balance between the competing claims of one party to put his case before the court and of the other not to be unjustly hounded given the earlier history of the matter."

[162] [2000] E.M.L.R. 296. See also, *Apsion v Dilnot* [2013] EWHC 2428 (QB) in which the court held that the claimant was seeking to re-litigate matters which had already been concluded against him and this amounted to an abuse of process. The allegations made were essentially the same as those already made in previous litigation, and were made on the same factual basis as those previous actions. In so far as the allegations were not res judicata, it would have been unfair to allow the claimant to proceed with them.

[163] The other was that the claim had no reasonable prospect of success.

in those actions and its resolution there would have determined it for the purposes of the claim against the BBC. Although it had not been resolved by verdict, the reality of the situation was that the claimant had abandoned his case on the treatment of tenants when he settled the previous actions. Plainly there is a public interest in having finality to litigation and in encouraging the efficient use of the judicial system, but there can be no hard and fast rules about this. The law was reviewed by the House of Lords in *Johnson v Gore Wood & Co.*, a professional negligence claim. Lord Bingham said[164]:

> "The bringing of a claim or the raising of a defence in later proceedings may, without more, amount to abuse if the court is satisfied (the onus being on the party alleging abuse) that the claim or defence should have been raised in the earlier proceedings if it was to be raised at all. I would not accept that it is necessary, before abuse may be found, to identify any additional element such as a collateral attack on a previous decision or some dishonesty, but where those elements are present the later proceedings will be much more obviously abusive, and there will rarely be a finding of abuse unless the later proceeding involves what the court regards as unjust harassment of a party. It is, however, wrong to hold that because a matter could have been raised in early proceedings it should have been, so as to render the raising of it in later proceedings necessarily abusive. That is to adopt too dogmatic an approach to what should in my opinion be a broad, merits-based judgment which takes account of the public and private interests involved and also takes account of all the facts of the case, focusing attention on the crucial question whether, in all the circumstances, a party is misusing or abusing the process of the court by seeking to raise before it the issue which could have been raised before. As one cannot comprehensively list all possible forms of abuse, so one cannot formulate any hard and fast rule to determine whether, on given facts, abuse is to be found or not. Thus while I would accept that lack of funds would not ordinarily excuse a failure to raise in earlier proceedings an issue which could and should have been raised then, I would not regard it as necessarily irrelevant, particularly if it appears that the lack of funds has been caused by the party against whom it is sought to claim. While the result may often be the same, it is in my view preferable to ask whether in all the circumstances a party's conduct is an abuse than to ask whether the conduct is an abuse and then, if it is, to ask whether the abuse is excused or justified by special circumstances. Properly applied, and whatever the legitimacy of its descent, the rule has in my view a valuable part to play in protecting the interests of justice."

19.23 Libel: actions in respect of one publication. In the case of libel (and of slander actionable per se) it is a good defence that the claimant has already brought and pursued to judgment an action against the defendant for the same words, whether the claimant won or lost that action. "A man slandered or libelled by words actionable in themselves must sue, if at all, for all his damages in one action."[165] A second action cannot in such a case be brought for any damage that may subsequently accrue from the same words.[166] In such cases the jury are entitled and bound to take into their consideration, not only

---

[164] [2002] 2 A.C. 1 at 31; *Stuart v Goldberg* [2008] EWCA Civ 2; [2008] 1 W.L.R. 823.
[165] Per Lord Bramwell in *Darley Main Co. v Mitchell* (1886) 11 A.C. 127 HL at 145.
[166] *Fetter v Beal* (1701) 1 Ld. Raym. 339.

the damage that has accrued, but also such damage as is likely to accrue in the future from the defamatory words.[167]

For this purpose the claimant cannot select passages for the first action and then evade the rule by suing on other passages in the second action.[168] Thus where D published in the form of a pamphlet a verbatim report of a judgment which reflected on P's conduct, and P unsuccessfully brought an action in respect of certain passages in the pamphlet, it was held that he could not maintain a second action in respect of other passages in the same pamphlet which expressed the same charges in another language.[169]

> "The injustice of allowing a litigant to select one portion of a libel as the ground for one action, and another as the ground for a second action, and so on indefinitely, is obvious. The whole publication would be before the jury in each case, and it would be quite impossible for the jury in each case to separate the damages due to the particular part of the libel relied on in that case from the damages arising from other parts of the libel. I think, therefore, that a plea of *res judicata* would succeed, and that we are bound to stay the action. Suppose, however, this to be otherwise, still in such a case, I do not hesitate to say that such successive actions in respect of the same libel would be an abuse of the process of the court, and so, *quacunque via*, the application should succeed and the action be stayed."[170]

This shows a broad and non-technical approach which would, it is submitted, be extended so as to prevent a subsequent suit for defamation even though the first action was in respect of another tort. On this basis, the fact that the claimant has recovered judgment in an action for malicious prosecution would be a defence to a subsequent action of slander for the accusation uttered for the purpose of having the arrest made, and on the occasion when it was made.[171]

Effect of fresh publication. Though the defamatory words may be the same, that is, an allegation of the same defamatory matter, yet a different publication will give another cause of action, for it is a new and distinct   **19.24**

---

[167] Per Lord North C.J. in *Townsend v Hughes* (1676) 2 Mod. 150 at 151; *Ingram v Lawson* (1840) 8 Scott 471 at 477; *Gregory v Williams* (1844) 1 C. & K. 568; *Darley Main Co. v Mitchell* (1886) 11 A.C. 127 HL at 133, 144; *Mallan v Bickford* [1915] South Australia L.R. 47. In so far as Grey C.J. said in *Onslow v Horne* (1771) 3 Wils. at 188 that damages could not be awarded for the possibility of future loss, this would not now be the law.

[168] However, this does not prevent the claimant accepting an offer of amends by the defendant in respect of part of a publication without foregoing his rights in respect of other passages: para.19.4, above.

[169] *Macdougall v Knight* (1890) 25 Q.B.D. 1 CA; *Williams v Hunt* [1905] 1 K.B. 512 at 514; and see *Thomson v Lambert* [1938] 2 D.L.R. 545 SCC.

[170] Per Fry L.J. in *Macdougall v Knight* (1890) 25 Q.B.D. 1 CA at 10; cf. *Montgomery v Russell* (1894) 11 T.L.R. 112; *Greenhalgh v Mallard* [1947] 2 All E.R. 255 CA; *Wright v Bennett (No.2)* [1948] 1 All E.R. 227 CA; *Yat Tung Investment v Dao Heng Bank* [1975] A.C. 581 PC. For an attempt to establish an "issue" estoppel see *Justin v Associated Newspapers* [1967] 1 N.S.W.R. 61 at 74. See also para.30.46, below.

[171] *Sheldon v Carpenter* (1851) 4 N.Y.R. 579; *Rockwell v Brown* (1867) 36 N.Y.R. 207.

injury.[172] If after a recovery and satisfaction for slander or libel the defendant again utters the same slander, or publishes the same libel, there is a new injury and a fresh cause of action.[173] In a New York case, D was the owner of two newspapers, the *Enquirer*, published in the morning, and the *Courier*, published in the afternoon, of each day. On a certain date there was published in the *Courier* an article defamatory of P, and the next day an article the same in substance and effect, though not in identical language, in the *Enquirer*. P brought two actions against D, a separate action for each publication, and recovered judgment in the action based on publication in the *Courier*. It was held that such judgment was not a bar to the action based on publication in the *Enquirer*.[174] Similarly it was held that a news-collecting agency which transmitted to each of the newspapers to which it furnished news a libellous article, which was published in each of such newspapers, incurred two distinct liabilities, first for the transmission of the article to the newspapers, and secondly that of a joint tortfeasor with each newspaper which published the article; and that the recovery and satisfaction of a judgment obtained against the news-collecting agency, in an action based upon the original publication, was not a bar to a subsequent action against the publishers of a particular newspaper for the publication of the article.[175]

This "long established principle of English libel law that each publication is a separate tort"[176] also has the consequences that separate actions may be brought in different jurisdictions where the libel is published[177] and that the second and subsequent publications are governed by new limitation periods.[178]

19.25 Slanders actionable only on proof of special damage. There are dicta to the effect that where special damage is essential to the claimant's cause of action, he can bring a second action for the same words if he can prove that he has suffered fresh special damage since judgment was given in the former action. In *Darley Main Co. v Mitchell*[179] Lord Bramwell said: "For example,

---

[172] Thus, a judgment for libel against a wholesale news agency is no bar to a subsequent action against retail selling agents for subsequent publication of the same defamatory matter: *Lambert v Roberts* (1933) 2 W.W.R. 508 Man. CA; but see *Thomson v Lambert* [1938] 2 D.L.R. 545 SCC. Cf. the judgment of Holmes L.J. in *Ross v Eason* [1911] 2 I.R. 459 CA.

[173] *Brunswick v Pepper* (1848) 3 C. & K. 683; *McElhone v Bennett* (1885) 6 N.S.W.L.R. 262. A fortiori if a different defendant republishes the libel: *Harris v 718932 Pty Ltd (formerly Globe Press Pty Ltd)* [2003] NSWCA 38). For the current Australian position see para.19.14, above.

[174] *Cook v Conners*, 215 N.Y.R. 175 at 179.

[175] *Union Press v Heath*, 49 N.Y. App.Div. 247 (1900).

[176] *Berezovsky v Michaels* [2000] 1 W.L.R. 1004 HL at 1012.

[177] *Berezovsky v Michaels*, above.

[178] *Loutchansky v Times Newspapers Ltd (Nos 2–5)* [2002] EWCA Civ 1805; [2002] Q.B. 783. So far as the England and Wales are concerned, this will be subject to Defamation Act 2013, s.8 when it comes into force: see further, para.6.6.

[179] (1885) 11 A.C. 127 HL at 15. See also Lord O'Brien C.J. in *O'Keefe v Walsh* [1903] 2 I.R. at 700, a case of conspiracy: "Each time damage accrues there is a new cause of action, because damage is the gist of the action."

A says to B that C is a swindler; B refuses to enter into a contract with C; C has a cause of action against A. D, who was present and heard it, also refuses to make such a contract; surely another action would lie. And so one would think if B subsequently refuses another contract." However, *Darley Main* is a case of withdrawal of support, which may fairly be regarded as a continuing wrong. There can be no general rule that a new cause of action arises in the case of a tort not actionable per se whenever further damage is suffered, for if this were so there would have been no need to create a scheme of provisional damages to guard against potential deterioration of the claimant's condition in cases of personal injury.[180] Lord Bramwell's view seems to be based on the proposition that, in an action for slander actionable only on proof of special damage, the claimant is confined to recovery of that special damage.[181] However, there are dicta the other way[182] and it is submitted that Lord Bramwell's view should not be followed.

Concurrent liability. A person who has suffered damage is not now, by   **19.26**
recovering judgment against any persons liable in respect of that damage, barred from bringing or continuing an action against any other person who is jointly liable with him in respect of the same damage.[183] However, if he brings more than one action in respect of the damage he has suffered against persons liable in respect of it (whether jointly or otherwise), the claimant shall not be entitled to costs in any of these actions, other than that in which judgment is first given, unless the court is of opinion that there was reasonable ground for bringing the action.[184]

Section 6. Release, Accord and Satisfaction

Generally. The statutory offer of amends procedure has already been dealt   **19.27**
with.[185] Quite independently of this the parties may of course settle a claim for

---

[180] Clerk & Lindsell, *Torts*, 20th edn (2012), para.32–15 also gives the example of a person who buys a number of parcels of shares as a result of a fraudulent misrepresentation, contending that there is not a separate action for each amount.

[181] See para.5.10, above.

[182] Manisty J. in *Lamb v Walker* (1878) 3 Q.B.D. 389 at 395; *Darley Main Co. v Mitchell* (1885) 11 A.C. 127 at 143, per Lord Blackburn; *Watson v Powles* [1968] 1 Q.B. 596 CA at 603.

[183] Civil Liability (Contribution) Act 1978, s.3, replacing the Law Reform (Married Women and Joint Tortfeasors) Act 1935, s.6(1)(a), which had abrogated the common law rule that judgment (even unsatisfied) against one joint tortfeasor extinguished the cause of action against the others. As to the effect of payment in satisfaction of the judgment, see para.19.28, below.

[184] Civil Liability (Contribution) Act 1978, s.4, replacing Law Reform (Married Women and Joint Tortfeasors) Act 1935, s.6(1)(b), but not re-enacting that part of the earlier section which had provided that the sums recoverable under the judgments given in these actions by way of damages should not in the aggregate exceed the amount of the damages awarded by the judgment first given (which remains the law in N.S.W.: *Harris v 718932 Pty Ltd (formerly Globe Press Pty Ltd)* [2003] NSWCA 38).

[185] See paras 19.1–19.6, above. See also Ch.29, s.4, below.

defamation on such terms as they see fit. If the claimant surrenders his claim by deed this is commonly known as a "release"[186] though there seems no reason why the word should not be used for any binding surrender of a claim. If there is no deed some consideration is necessary and a transaction extinguishing a claim in this way is commonly known as an "accord and satisfaction".[187] So where the claimant has agreed to accept an apology in satisfaction of his claim, and the defendant does publish an apology in accordance with the agreement, this will be a good defence even though the agreement was made after action brought.[188] Satisfaction made by a third party on a defendant's behalf, and accepted by the claimant, may be pleaded in defence to an action.[189] Although at one time it may have been the law that the right of action was not discharged until the promised satisfaction was performed (leaving the promisor of the satisfaction to a claim for damages for breach of the contract if the promisee sought to enforce the claim) the position now is that this is a question of the construction of the agreement.[190]

19.28 Concurrent tortfeasors. Where several persons are jointly liable for the publication of a libel, the basic rule is that a release given to one[191] or an accord and satisfaction made with one[192] is a defence to an action against the others, "the reason being that the cause of action, which is one and indivisible, having been released, all persons otherwise liable thereto are consequently released."[193] The rule does not therefore apply to a case where the defendants are several concurrent tortfeasors liable in respect of the same damage.[194] However, even the basic rule about joint tortfeasors is of limited importance[195] because a claimant can agree to release one or more of several defendants jointly liable for a libel and expressly or by implication reserve his right of action against the others. Such a release will be construed as merely a

---

[186] See *Phillips v Clagett* (1843) 11 M. & W. 84.

[187] See generally Clerk & Lindsell, *Torts*, 20th edn (2010), paras 32–07 et seq.

[188] *Boosey v Wood* (1865) 34 L.J.Ex. 65.

[189] *Jones v Broadhurst* (1850) 9 C.B. 173.

[190] *British Russian Gazette v Associated Newspapers* [1933] 2 K.B. 616 CA.

[191] *Cocke v Jennoe* (1614) Hobart 66; *Howe v Oliver* (1908) 24 T.L.R. 781. Strangely enough, this rule has not been affected by modern English legislation. *Aliter* in Eire: Civil Liability Act 1961, s.17; Tasmania: Tortfeasors and Contributory Negligence Act 1954, s.3(3).

[192] *Thurman v Wild* (1840) 11 A. & E. 453; *Dufresne v Hutchinson* (1810) 3 Taunt. 117; *Re WEA (A Debtor)* [1901] 2 K.B. 642 CA.

[193] Per A. L. Smith L.J. in *Duck v Mayeu* [1892] 2 Q.B. 511 CA at 513; per Stout C.J. in *Kelliher v Bridges* (1911) 31 N.Z.L.R. 203 at 204.

[194] It seems to be commonly assumed that co-participants in the publication of a libel are joint tortfeasors in the technical sense, but in *Gardiner v Moore* [1969] 1 Q.B. 55, Thesiger J. expressed doubt whether, since *Egger v Chelmsford* [1965] 1 Q.B. 248 CA, it is possible to hold that persons are joint tortfeasors: "unless it is proved in a case, where that is necessary to constitute a tort, that all . . . had, at the time of the common act, a common state of mind, such as malice."

[195] Where it does apply it may be important to analyse carefully what exactly are the causes of action available. In *Cutler v McPhail* [1962] 2 Q.B. 292, D had written a letter to a journal and the effect of P's granting a release to the journal in respect of the publication was to release D. But P was allowed to sue for the publication to the editor, including within this claim the damage flowing from the republication. Criticised in *Timms v Clift* [1998] 2 Qd. R. 100 Qd CA.

covenant not to sue the particular defendant or defendants with whom the agreement is made.[196] It has been said that:

" . . . courts nowadays are reluctant to construe an agreement with one tortfeasor as a release rather than a covenant not to sue him, unless it is plain that the agreement was intended by the plaintiff to operate also as a release of the other joint tortfeasors from their liability."[197]

Thus, in *Ansari v Knowles*,[198] which involved claims for libel in respect of serious allegations of professional incompetence against a university lecturer, it was held that a settlement of his claim against one university joint tortfeasor did not dispose of claims against his own employer university or a fellow lecturer. On the issue of release, the judge stated that it was a matter of interpreting the settlement agreement against the particular factual matrix. It was far from clear that the settlement agreement by its terms included the claims against the other parties. Moreover, extensive pleas of justification and malice had been raised by the claimant's employer and fellow lecturer and there was no basis to think that a reasonable bystander, with relevant knowledge, would conclude that these highly contentious issues were included in the settlement without their even being informed. It would be contrary to public policy and the entitlements to freedom of expression and a fair trial in the European Convention on Human Rights to reach such a conclusion.[199]

---

[196] *Duck v Mayeu* [1892] 2 Q.B. 511 CA; *Apley Estates v De Bernales* [1947] Ch. 217. In *Gardiner v Moore* [1969] 1 Q.B. 55, it was held that where claims against some joint tortfeasors were discharged by agreement in circumstances in which it was clear to both parties that the plaintiff's intention was to go on against another joint tortfeasor, there was an implied term reserving the plaintiffs right of action against him which had the same effect as an express term. See also *Watts v Aldington* [1999] L. & T.R. 578 CA (the terms of the release included: "That Lord Aldington undertakes to accept the said sum in full and final settlement of the judgment and orders referred to above and any liability howsoever arising before today's date which could involve any payment by you directly or indirectly to Lord Aldington." The Court of Appeal nevertheless concluded that it was necessary to imply a reservation of Lord Aldington's right to enforce the judgment against Count Tolstoy. Neill L.J. said (at 594) that any other construction would offend against common sense).

[197] Per Lord Diplock in *Bryanston Finance v De Vries* [1975] Q.B. 703 CA at 732. In *Ansari v Knowles* [2012] EWHC 3137 (QB), Eady J. stated (at [30]):
"If it is helpful to speak at all of such a 'rule' as still subsisting, it is nevertheless necessary to recognise that any rigidity it once had has been so eroded by judicial interpretation that it is probably better simply to take into account the policy considerations underlying it (such as the desirability of finality) when construing the individual settlement agreement before the court. It should not be allowed to override what would otherwise be the common sense interpretation of the particular factual matrix. The words of Lord Diplock in *Bryanston Finance*, several decades ago, would appear to support a flexible approach; moreover, that is surely reinforced by the need to pay due regard to the balancing exercise now required when applying Strasbourg jurisprudence."

[198] [2012] EWHC 3137 (QB).

[199] Eady J. also held that the settlement agreement could not be read as having determined the maximum compensation for the cause of action and that it was not an abuse for the claimant to continue the claim as it had the potential to vindicate his reputation in respect of the allegations that were the subject of the justification plea, which itself was a document accessible to the public under the CPR.

Even where the defendants are several, rather than joint, tortfeasors, where money has been paid in satisfaction of a settlement between the claimant and one defendant[200] that must be brought into account so as to diminish the liability of any other defendant subsequently sued, since the claimant cannot recover his loss twice over[201]; and it may be that a settlement with one discharges the other because the settlement must be taken as conclusively determining that the claimant is recovering his full loss and even the rule allowing successive actions against several tortfeasors is subject to the principle that this level of recovery may not be exceeded.[202] However, it has been doubted whether this can be applied to a case where, e.g. a libel is published by A and then republished by B, because the notion of "full satisfaction" cannot necessarily be applied in the same way as in a personal injury or property damage case.[203]

Where there are proceedings against a number of defendants sued as jointly and severally liable the claimant may require the permission of the court to accept a Part 36 offer from one of them without discounting his claim against the others.[204]

---

[200] A defendant who has compromised an action may be able to recover contribution from a joint tortfeasor, even if the latter is no longer liable to the claimant: Civil Liability (Contribution) Act 1978, s.1(3),(4).

[201] *Bryanston Finance v De Vries* [1975] Q.B. 703 CA; *Townsend v Stone Toms & Partners (No.2)* (1984) 27 B.L.R. 26. In *Jameson v CEGB*, 1995 (unreported) Sir Tudor Evans summed up the position as follows:

"the plaintiff with a concurrent claim in tort may, by settlement or by accepting money in Court or by judgment, receive payment from one tortfeasor and still continue against another but that he can never recover more than the full amount of his damages: if he recovers an equal or a lesser amount than he has already received then he loses and pays the costs."

While a settlement sum might commonly be less than the full amount of the claimant's loss, if the causes of action against D1 and D2 are identical then a *judgment* in C's favour will be a conclusive determination of the amount of C's loss and if paid in full will extinguish the action against D2, though without prejudice to D1's right to seek contribution against D2.

[202] *Jameson v CEGB* [2000] 1 A.C. 455 HL (a fatal accident case); *Heaton v Axa Equity and Law Life Assurance Society Plc* [2002] UKHL 15; [2002] A.C. 329 (a contract case).

[203] *Heaton v Axa Equity and Law Life Assurance Society Plc* [2001] Ch. 173 CA at [77], per Robert Walker L.J. (on appeal 2002] UKHL 15; [2002] A.C. 329).

[204] See para.29.20, below.

Part Three

OTHER CAUSES OF ACTION AND RELATED MATTERS

CHAPTER 20

SCOPE OF THIS PART

Introduction. This book is primarily about the protection of reputation via **20.1**
the law of defamation, but the lawyer who is called on to advise or represent
a person who believes his reputation to have been damaged or to be at risk
cannot simply consider libel and slander. Although the historical development
of the law means that there are a number of separate torts rather than one all-
embracing principle of liability for unlawfully inflicted harm,[1] a number of
other heads of liability overlap with defamation law and may offer an avenue
of approach which outflanks a restriction of defamation law. Thus where A
writes to B an employment reference about C, that will be an occasion of
qualified privilege and A will not be liable for a defamatory statement in the
reference unless he is actuated by malice,[2] but if the statement is inaccurate
and was made negligently, B may have a claim for negligence if he has
suffered damage as a result of it. Similarly, a false and malicious statement
which is not defamatory (e.g. that the claimant is ill or has ceased business)
may be actionable as malicious falsehood, even in some cases without proof
of damage.

Malicious falsehood is considered in most detail because it most frequently
overlaps with defamation.[3] In a work of this nature it would be impossible to
give a full account of all the other heads of liability but an outline is given of
them, with particular reference to their relationship with defamation. These
heads of liability are: negligence[4]; passing off[5]; and the statutory wrongs of
derogatory treatment of an author's work and false attribution of work.[6] In
addition, consideration is given to the jurisdiction to grant an injunction or a
declaration against untrue statements which, although not attracting any particular cause of action, are likely to injure the property of, or cause pecuniary
damage to the claimant.[7] Libel as a crime has been abolished by s.73 of the
Coroners and Justice Act 2009 but the criminal law still has a limited role to
play in the protection of reputation through the Protection from Harassment
Act 1997. As well as being a crime, harassment may have civil consequences

---

[1] Indeed, this is also true of civil law systems, though to a much lesser extent than in the case
of the common law.
[2] See para.14.25, above.
[3] See Ch.21, below.
[4] See para.23.1, below.
[5] See para.23.16, below.
[6] See para.23.20, below.
[7] See para.23.15, below.

which overlap with those of defamation.[8] Most importantly, statements about a person which are not defamatory (or which are defamatory but can be proved to be true and hence are not actionable as defamation) may be damaging or wounding because they intrude upon that person's privacy. At present English law still recognises no general tort of invasion of privacy as such but the impact of that proposition is now much curtailed because of direct remedies under the Human Rights Act 1998 and the development out of the law of confidence of liability for misuse of private information. These and related matters concerning the data protection legislation are also considered in this Part.[9]

The potential range of causes of action which may be available may be illustrated by a simple and by no means far-fetched case.[10] C, a television personality, gives an interview without payment to a reporter of a national newspaper and talks about her matrimonial problems. During the course of the interview she gives the reporter some documents by way of background information but says that she does not want them or their contents included. The article which eventually appears is in the first person and hence purports to be written by her. It contains factual inaccuracies (damaging to her reputation) invented by the reporter to make a better story and includes the information she said she wanted withheld, along with further information about her private life which the reporter discovered by investigation. This situation raises at least the possibility that C may have all of the following causes action. (1) Libel in respect of the factual inaccuracies and a possible "false innuendo" that she is willing to wash her dirty linen in public for payment. (2) Breach of confidence and misuse of private information in respect of the material ordered to be withheld and the material discovered. (3) Breach of copyright in respect of the material ordered to be witheld. (4) Malicious falsehood in respect of the factual inaccuracies. (5) A claim for breach of statutory duty under s.84 of the Copyright, Designs and Patents Act 1988 in respect of the way the article purports to have been written by her.

---

[8] See para.23.12, below.
[9] Ch.22, below.
[10] Based on *Moore v News of the World* [1972] 1 Q.B. 441 CA, with some embellishments.

CHAPTER 21

MALICIOUS FALSEHOOD

SECTION 1. INTRODUCTION

Generally. At common law the claimant may maintain an action for mali-   **21.1**
cious falsehood if he can show that: (1) the defendant published to third
parties words which are false; (2) that they refer to the claimant[1] or his
property[2] or his business; (3) that they were published maliciously; and (4)
that special damage has followed as a direct and natural result of their
publication.[3] In *Ratcliffe v Evans*[4] the plaintiff alleged that he and his father
had carried on an engineering business under the name Ratcliffe & Sons, that
the father had died but the plaintiff had continued the business, and that a
newspaper published by the defendant had falsely and maliciously published
a story to the effect that the plaintiff was no longer in business. The jury's
verdict for the plaintiff proceeded on the basis that the story was a "false
statement purposely made about the manufactures of the plaintiff, which was
intended to, and did in fact cause him damage".[5] In upholding this verdict
Bowen L.J. said[6] that:

> "an action will lie for written or oral falsehoods, not actionable *per se* or even
> defamatory, where they are maliciously published, where they are calculated in the
> ordinary course of things to produce, and where they do produce, actual damage.

---

[1] For reference to the claimant, see para.21.4, below.
[2] It is not uncommon to add a claim for malicious falsehood to one for trade mark infringement.
In *British Airways Plc v Ryanair Ltd* [2001] F.S.R. 32, Jacob J. said:
"I suspect the real reason to be this: that victory in a trade mark infringement claim does not
sound so good as victory in a malicious falsehood claim. If the latter can be proved the wronged
trade mark owner can trumpet: judge says my competitor's advertisement was not only false,
it was malicious!"
See also *Cable & Wireless v BT* [1998] F.S.R. 383.
[3] For the equivalent action in Scots law for verbal injury see *Barratt International Resorts Ltd
v Barratt Owners' Group* [2002] ScotCS 318 at [24]–[26]. See also Defamation Act 1952,
s.14.
[4] [1892] 2 Q.B. 524 CA.
[5] Ibid. at 527.
[6] Ibid.

Such an action is not one of libel or slander, but an action on the case for damage wilfully and intentionally done without just occasion or excuse . . . To support it, actual damage must be shown, for it is an action which only lies in respect of such damage as has actually occurred."

Now, however, by statute it is unnecessary to show special damage in certain cases of malicious falsehood where the words are published in writing or other permanent form.[7]

21.2 Slander of goods and slander of title. It is actionable falsely and maliciously to disparage another's goods or another's title to goods. These are not separate torts but particular applications of the generic tort of malicious falsehood.[8] The names are misleading in at least two respects.[9] First, they might be taken as implying that they were confined to oral statements, which is certainly not the case.[10] Secondly, in the case of "slander of goods" the principle is plainly applicable to disparagement of other types of property, e.g. land[11]: it would not be very sensible to say that disparagement of goods was one tort and disparagement of land was another. In this chapter the general principles are discussed under the heading of malicious falsehood but it is convenient to treat separately those matters which are characteristic of claims based on disparagement of title and property.

21.3 Malicious falsehood and other torts. Many cases of malicious false-hood are not cases of defamation.[12] For example, to say that the claimant has retired from business[13] is not capable of being defamatory unless there is some

---

[7] See para.21.14, below.

[8] "This cause of action embraces particular types of malicious falsehood such as slander of title and slander of goods, but it is not confined to those headings": *Joyce v Sengupta* [1993] 1 W.L.R. 337 CA at 341, per Nicholls V.C. This seems to have been the view of the Parliamentary draftsman: s.3 of the Defamation Act 1952 and s.5 of the Defamation Act 1996 (amending the Limitation Act 1980) refer to "an action for slander of goods, slander of title or other malicious falsehood". For the development of the law see Prosser & Keeton, *Torts*, 5th edn (1984), para.128 and 63 Yale L.J. 65 (1953). In the US the expression "injurious falsehood" (coined by Sir John Salmond) is more popular: Prosser & Keeton, above and Restatement 2d, *Torts*, para.623A.

[9] Another, and equally confusing, name for malicious falsehood is "trade libel". Lawyers seem to have a compulsion to attach defamation labels to things which are not defamation. A number of American states have "agricultural disparagement" statutes which permit damages claims based on false statements about food products. They are popularly known as "veggie libel" or "sirloin slander" laws: see Dobbs, *Law of Torts* (2000), para.407.

[10] Indeed, s.3 of the Defamation Act 1952 removes the requirement of special damage where these "torts" are committed in writing.

[11] See *Barrett v Associated Newspapers* (1907) 23 T.L.R. 666 CA, where the plaintiff complained of an article to the effect that his house was haunted, though the claim failed for absence of proof of damage. Such a "haunting" claim succeeded in *Manitoba Free Press v Nagy* (1907) 39 S.C.R. 340. The early cases on slander of title concerned disparagement of the plaintiff's title to land but it is equally applicable to personalty: *Wren v Weild* (1869) L.R. 4 Q.B. 730.

[12] In *Khodaparast v Shad* [2000] 1 W.L.R. 618 CA at 630, Stuart-Smith L.J. said that malicious falsehood is a species of defamation. It is submitted that this should not be taken literally.

[13] See para.21.1, above.

innuendo, for the statement is completely neutral as to the claimant's character.[14] Indeed, it is possible to conceive of cases actionable as malicious falsehood in which the statement would be such as to *improve* the claimant's reputation in the eyes of sensible people.[15]

An action for malicious falsehood will in many cases lie as an alternative to one for defamation. However, it is not very likely that a claimant will embark on the generally more onerous task of establishing a claim for malicious falsehood, though he may occasionally have tactical reasons for doing so. Thus, in *Joyce v Sengupta*[16] the statement that the plaintiff had been dismissed from the service of the Princess Royal for theft of letters was plainly a most serious libel but, on the assumption that the plaintiff was able to prove that the statement was false and was published out of malice (neither of which would of course be necessary in a case of libel) it was also the tort of malicious falsehood. The point was practically significant in *Joyce* because malicious falsehood, unlike defamation, was then not outside the legal aid scheme.[17] *Ajinomoto Sweeteners Europe SAS v Asda Stores Ltd*,[18] which decided that the single meaning rule which applies in defamation is not applicable to malicious falsehood, adds another possible tactical reason.[19] Where the words complained of may be understood by reasonable readers in different ways, some more serious than others, the court in a defamation claim must decide what is the single meaning that the words bear. In a malicious falsehood claim, however, the claimant is entitled to recover in respect of any

---

[14] See also *Kaye v Robertson* [1991] F.S.R. 62 CA (false claim to have interviewed plaintiff depriving him of chance to sell story as "exclusive"). This is perhaps a rather strained application of the law of malicious falsehood, prompted by a desire to deal with an outrageous invasion of privacy. Compare *Bradley v Wingnut Films* [1993] 1 N.Z.L.R. 416. A case of libel was held to be arguable in *Kaye v Robertson* on the analogy of *Tolley v Fry* [1931] A.C. 333 HL, presumably on the basis of the notoriously poor reputation of the newspaper, but was not strong enough to support an interlocutory injunction.

[15] In the course of the argument in *Kelly v Partington (No.2)* (1834) 5 B & Ad. 645, Littledale J. put to Sir John Campbell S.G. the following question:

"Suppose a man had a relation of penurious disposition, and a third person, knowing it would injure him in the opinion of that relation, tells the latter a generous act which the first has done, by which he induces the relation not to leave him money, would that be actionable?"

Sir John Campbell answered: "If the words were spoken falsely, and with intent to injure, they would be actionable." This answer was not controverted by the court.

[16] [1993] 1 W.L.R. 337 CA.

[17] In addition to *Joyce v Sengupta* on this point see *Spring v Guardian Assurance Plc* [1993] 2 All E.R. 273 CA at 286, reversed, but not on the issue of malicious falsehood, [1995] 2 A.C. 296. On April 1, 2000, the legal aid scheme was replaced by the Community Legal Service. Under s.6(6) and Sch.2 of the Access to Justice Act 1999, malicious falsehood joined defamation among the categories of matters which may not be funded as part of the Service. See, however, s.6(8).

[18] [2010] EWCA Civ 609; [2011] Q.B. 497 (reversing Tugendhat J., [2009] EWHC 1717 (QB); [2010] Q.B. 204). See para.21.5, below.

[19] There is the further point that claims for malicious falsehood survive the death of either party: *Hatchard v Mege* (1887) 18 Q.B.D. 771, where there were combined claims for libel and slander of title, the former dying with the plaintiff, the latter surviving him. There is also a "more generous" reference requirement in malicious falsehood than exists in defamation: see para.21.4, below.

meaning or meanings that a substantial number of readers would understand the words to bear. Thus, if, for example, the words can be understood as bearing three meanings—A, B and C—the most serious of which is A and the least, C, then if the court decides that the actual single meaning is C and concludes that it is true no claim will lie in defamation. However, a claim in malicious falsehood may still exist if the claimant can establish that a substantial number of readers would conclude that the words bear either meaning A or B (or both) and that in either or both of those meanings the words are false. The claimant will of course still have to establish the other elements of the claim, which is not easy, but the abolition of the single meaning rule in malicious falsehood does offer claimants the possibility of recovering substantial damages for injury to reputation[20] even where no such claim exists in defamation.

Overlapping causes of action are frequent in English law[21] and there is no requirement that the claimant should pursue the most "appropriate" claim; nor, in domestic law, is any concept that a claim may be barred because it would deprive the defendant of a "legitimate juridical advantage".[22] However, the claimant may not recover general damages for injury to reputation as such[23] in malicious falsehood.[24] In *Khodaparast v Shad*,[25] where on the facts the falsehood was undoubtedly defamatory, though no action for libel was brought, an award of £20,000 was upheld, including an element for injury to the claimant's feelings. Otton L.J. indicated that a sum of £50,000 would have been justified in an action for libel, which is some indication of the value of the "reputation", loss of which is recoverable in defamation but not in malicious falsehood.[26]

There may also be cases in which, although the claimant is unable to pursue a malicious falsehood claim because he is unable to establish malice, yet the defendant owes him a duty of care under the tort of negligence and is in

---

[20] However, see fn.22, below.

[21] See the examples in *Joyce v Sengupta* (above) at 342. Malicious falsehood may also overlap with passing off (as to which see para.23.16, below). In *Bristol Conservatories v Conservatories Custom Build* [1989] R.P.C. 380 CA, the defendants had shown customers photographs of the plaintiff's goods, intending to fill orders with their own. Since the CA found an arguable case of passing off it did not need to consider the plaintiffs' alternative argument on malicious falsehood, which had been rejected at first instance on the ground of (1) absence of a sufficient reference to the plaintiffs and (2) absence of malice.

[22] *Joyce v Sengupta* [1993] 1 W.L.R. 337 CA. As Sedley L.J. observed in *Ajinomoto Sweeteners Europe SAS v Asda Stores Ltd* [2010] EWCA Civ 609 CA; [2011] Q.B. 497 at [28], "A great many fact situations are able to be litigated through more than one cause of action, and the choice of them is as often tactical as jurisprudential."

[23] As opposed to loss of business goodwill with customers which leads or is likely to lead, to loss of trade. As Evans L.J. points out in *Lonrho Plc v Fayed (No.5)* [1993] 1 W.L.R. 1489 CA at 1509, there is some risk of semantic confusion, for this, too, may be described as "loss of reputation".

[24] *Joyce v Sengupta* [1993] 1 W.L.R. 337 CA at 348, per Nicholls V.C.; *Lonrho Plc v Fayed (No.5)* [1993] 1 W.L.R. 1489 CA at 1495, 1504, 1509.

[25] [2000] 1 W.L.R. 618 CA.

[26] Ibid. at 633.

breach of it. However, putting aside the mental element, the reach of negligence is shorter than that of malicious falsehood: e.g. there would not be liability for negligence on facts like those in *Ratcliffe v Evans*.[27]

SECTION 2. MALICIOUS FALSEHOOD

Reference to the claimant. For a claim to exist in malicious falsehood, **21.4** the words complained of must, as in a defamation claim, have been published "about the claimant".[28] However, as H.H.J. Moloney QC made clear in *Marathon Mutual Ltd v Waters*,[29] "reference to the claimant" does not have the same meaning in malicious falsehood as it does in defamation. What is required in malicious falsehood is that there must be "some reference, direct or indirect, in the words complained of to the claimant or to his business, property or other economic interests, though it is not necessary to go further and establish identification of the claimant in the minds of the publishees".[30] The judge in that case rejected a lesser reference requirement suggested by counsel for the claimant that he need only prove that the words were false and malicious of someone or something other than the claimant, his business, his goods or his property, provided that they are also calculated to injure the claimant's economic interests through a direct causal route. To have accepted such an argument would have opened up the risk of a plethora of parasitic

---

[27] See para.23.5, below.

[28] Some older cases do not specifically mention the identification issue though they do emphasise the central importance of the tendency of the words to cause damage. Thus, in *Ratcliffe v Evans* [1892] 2 Q.B. 524 at 527, Bowen L.J. stated it to be established law "that an action will lie for written or oral falsehoods, not actionable per se nor even defamatory, where they are maliciously published, where they are calculated in the ordinary course of things to produce, and where they do produce, actual damage". So too, in *Riding v Smith* (1875–6) L.R. 1 Ex. D. 91 Pollock B. stated (at 95): "where you find that the nature of the words is such that damages would naturally follow from their being uttered, and that damage has arisen, then there is a cause of action" (it should be noted that in the same case, Kelly C.B. did refer (at 93) to the requirement that the words should be about the plaintiff: " . . . if a man states *of another*, who is a trader earning his livelihood by dealing in articles of trade, anything, be it what it may, the natural consequence of uttering which would be to injure the trade and prevent persons from resorting to the place of business, and it so leads to loss of trade, it is actionable" (emphasis added)). In neither case, however, was identification specifically in issue. In some later cases, for example *Kaye v Robertson* [1991] F.S.R. 62 at 67 (accepted as correct in *Tesla Motors Ltd v BBC* [2011] EWHC 2760 (QB) at [5]; *Cruddas v Calvert* [2013] EWHC 2298 (QB) at [191]; *Euromoney Institutional Investor plc v Aviation News Ltd* [2013] EWHC 1505 (QB) at [79]), the courts have said that in malicious falsehood the words must be "about the plaintiff", but again identification was not in issue and what is meant by "about" in this context was not further analysed.

[29] [2009] EWHC 1931 (QB); [2010] E.M.L.R. 3.

[30] Ibid. at [9c]. Where this condition is not satisfied (e.g. where D tells lies to X about himself (D) in order to induce X to deal with him rather than with P) that may be the tort of causing loss by unlawful means or unlawful means for the purposes of other economic torts: *Lonrho Plc v Fayed* [1990] 2 Q.B. 479 CA, and [1992] 1 A.C. 448 HL. From a purely logical point of view, every statement about a trader which amounts to malicious falsehood and causes damage should amount to causing loss by unlawful means, given the requirement of intention in that tort (as to which see *OBG Ltd v Allan* [2007] UKHL 21; [2008] 1 A.C. 1).

claims for secondary economic loss consequent on malicious falsehoods directed at other persons or businesses.[31] On the facts of *Marathon Mutual*, the judge refused to strike out the claim. While the claimant company was nowhere mentioned in the letter or telephone conversation complained of, it was arguable on the pleadings that there was sufficient reference for the purposes of malicious falsehood. The claimant's business was the management of mutual protection funds, in particular Marathon. Those funds could be viewed as "the subject-matter or materials of its business, standing in a position in relation to the claimant closely analogous to the goods of a manufacturer or the properties of a landowner".[32] If so, an attack on them might therefore also be an attack on the claimant's business. It followed that it was a possibility that the words complained of, relating as they did to commercial problems within a fund managed by the claimant as part of its own business, might sufficiently refer to the claimant's own business to bring the claimant within the wide reference limits applicable to malicious falsehood.[33]

21.5 Meaning and malicious falsehood. Prior to the decision of the Court of Appeal in *Ajinomoto Sweeteners Europe SAS v Asda Stores Ltd*[34] the law on the determination of meaning was the same in malicious falsehood as it was, and remains, in defamation,[35] that is to say what was the "single meaning" that the words would have conveyed to the ordinary reader? However, the court in *Ajinomoto* held that the single meaning rule of defamation does not apply to malicious falsehood. Although the rule seemed to have caused little

---

[31] Ibid. at [9b].

[32] Ibid. at [9d].

[33] The question whether the words sufficiently referred to the claimant for the purposes of malicious falsehood was also raised in *Euromoney Institutional Investor plc v Aviation News Ltd* [2013] EWHC 1505 (QB) which involved claims for both libel and malicious falsehood. Tugendhat J. held that sufficient reference existed for the purposes of the law of libel (see para.7.2) and so, a fortiori, sufficient reference existed for malicious falsehood (at [92]). See also Copinger and Skone James, *Copyright*, 13th edn (1991), para.21–50 where reference is made to an unreported (and unidentified) case where a translator obtained damages for malicious falsehood against a publisher when the latter attributed his translation to someone else (malicious falsehood is not dealt with in later editions of the book). In *Tilbrook v Parr* [2012] EWHC 1946 (QB) concurrent claims were brought in libel and malicious falsehood. The judge held that there was insufficient reference for the purposes of defamation and for malicious falsehood "as both depend upon the Claimant establishing that the words complained of are reasonably capable of referring to him" (at [18]). This seems to suggest that Tugendhat J. thought that the test for reference was the same for defamation and malicious falsehood though it is probably the case that even the more attenuated test for reference that H.H.J. Moloney QC articulated in *Marathon Mutual Ltd v Waters* [2009] EWHC 1931 (QB); [2010] E.M.L.R. 3 would not have been satisfied on the facts of *Tilbrook*.

[34] [2010] EWCA Civ 609 CA; [2011] Q.B. 497 (reversing Tugendhat J., [2009] EWHC 1717 (QB); [2010] Q.B. 204). Permission to appeal was granted by the Supreme Court (UKSC 2010/0161) but the parties settled shortly before the hearing.

[35] In *British Sky Broadcasting Group Plc v Microsoft Corp* [2013] EWHC 1826 (Ch) Asplin J. held that that there is in general no single meaning rule in European trade mark law (at [213]).

practical difficulty in defamation,[36] application of the single meaning rule would have the effect, in the context of malicious falsehood, of "denying any remedy to a claimant whose business has been injured in the eyes of some consumers on the illogical ground that it has not been injured in the eyes of others, or alternatively . . . giving such a claimant a clear run to judgment when in the eyes of many customers the words have done it no harm"; whereas "trial of plural meanings permits the damaging effect of the words to be put in perspective and both malice and (if it comes to it) damage to be more realistically gauged".[37]

The claimant in *Ajinomoto* had complained of legends on the defendant's "Good for You" product line that read "No hidden nasties" and "No artificial colours or flavours and no aspartame". The claimant, a major supplier of aspartame, contended that this was capable of meaning at least that there was a risk that aspartame was harmful or unhealthy and the judge had found that a substantial body of consumers would so understand it; but a substantial body would have read it as meaning simply that it was a product for customers

---

[36] [2010] EWCA Civ 609 at [4]; [2011] Q.B. 497 See also, para.3.16, above.

[37] Ibid. at [34]. In *Interflora Inc. v Marks and Spencer Plc* [2013] EWHC 1291 (Ch) Arnold J. held that there was no single meaning rule in European trade mark law. Having concluded that there was no authority that clearly stated that there was, the judge continued:

"given that the single meaning rule which exists in English defamation law is widely regarded as anomalous, that the Court of Appeal forcibly ejected the single meaning rule from the English law of malicious falsehood in *Ajinomoto Sweeteners Europe SAS v Asda Stores Ltd* . . . (thereby bringing that part of English unfair competition law into line with the Court of Justice's jurisprudence in that field) and that there is no such rule in passing off, it would be very surprising if Lewison LJ [in *Interflora Inc. v Marks & Spencer Plc* [2012] EWCA Civ 1501; [2013] F.S.R. 21] had intended to adopt such a rule unless it was clearly required by the case law of the Court of Justice. Thirdly, Lewison LJ expressly accepts that a trade mark is distinctive if a significant proportion of the relevant public identify goods as originating from a particular undertaking because of the mark. Thus he accepts that there is no single meaning rule in the context of validity. As I have said, that is logically inconsistent with a single meaning rule when one comes to infringement. Fourthly, the reason why it is not necessarily sufficient for a finding of infringement that 'some' consumers may be confused is that, as noted above, confusion on the part of the ill-informed or unobservant must be discounted. That is a rule about the standard to be applied, not a rule requiring the determination of a single meaning. If a significant proportion of the relevant class of consumers is confused, then it is likely that confusion extends beyond those who are ill-informed or unobservant. Fifthly, Lewison LJ does not refer to many of the authorities discussed above, no doubt because they were not cited. Nor does he discuss the nature of the test for the assessment of likelihood of confusion laid down by the Court of Justice. The legislative criterion is that 'there exists a likelihood of confusion on the part of the public'. As noted above, the Court of Justice has held that "the risk that the public might believe that the goods or services in question come from the same undertaking or, as the case may be, from economically-linked undertakings, constitutes a likelihood of confusion". This is not a binary question: is the average consumer confused or is the average consumer not confused? Rather, it requires an assessment of whether it is likely that there is, or will be, confusion, applying the standard of perspicacity of the average consumer. It is clear from the case law that this does not mean likely in the sense of more probable than not. Rather, it means sufficiently likely to warrant the court's intervention. The fact that many consumers of whom the average consumer is representative would not be confused does not mean that the question whether there is a likelihood of confusion is to be answered in the negative if a significant number would be confused" (at [224]).

who found aspartame objectionable. Applying the single meaning rule, Tugendhat J. had found that the latter was the meaning to be ascribed.[38] Rimer L.J. said:

> "If the case were allowed to go to trial and the claimant were able to prove that [the former] . . . meaning was false, uttered with malice and calculated to damage it, why should it not be entitled to damages for the injury which the falsehood will have caused it? More importantly—and this is the primary remedy the claimant wants —why, if it can prove its case, should it not be entitled to have the defendant restrained by injunction from doing that which it wants to do, namely (presumably for its own commercial benefit) to continue to publish a falsehood that will continue to damage the claimant in the eyes of a substantial body of consumers? The result, however, of the application by the judge of the single meaning rule is that that body of consumers is removed from the court's radar. The court instead satisfies itself with the fiction, contrary to its own finding, that the entire consuming public will interpret the defendant's packaging as bearing a single innocuous meaning."[39]

In view of the above, and also that the court considered there were no really good practical reasons for continuing to use the single meaning rule,[40] it was held that the rule should no longer be applied in malicious falsehood cases. A court should therefore now identify the reasonably available meanings and decide if a "substantial number"[41] of, or "many", people[42] would reasonably have understood the words complained of in one or more damaging ways. If they would have done, then a viable claim for malicious falsehood exists, and the court should then go on to decide in respect of any meanings which are in fact false and damaging, whether the author was actuated by malice.

---

[38] [2009] EWHC 1717 (QB); [2010] Q.B. 204.

[39] [2010] EWCA Civ 609 at [41]; [2011] Q.B. 497.

[40] The court was not persuaded that getting rid of the rule would make trials of malicious falsehood claims unwieldy or over-complex (at [34]), nor was it persuaded by the "untidiness" in the law that would be created:

> "The common law has . . . never worried about tidiness. It has always been more concerned with meeting the justice of the particular case and developing itself accordingly. If the single meaning rule did not exist, I doubt if any modern court would invent it, either for defamation or any other tort." (at [43]).

[41] In *Cruddas v Calvert* [2013] EWCA Civ 748 the Court of Appeal stated (at [30]) that the duty of a trial judge in a malicious falsehood case is

> "to indicate the reasonably available meanings, decide if a substantial number of persons would reasonably have understood the words to have such a meaning and then decide, in respect of a meaning which is in fact false and damaging, whether the author was actuated by malice."

> "In a case in which the court has found that the statement complained of would be read by many in a damaging sense, the single meaning rule should not be allowed to bar a claim that the defendant has maliciously disparaged the claimant's goods." Per Rimer L.J. at [43].

[42] Where a malicious falsehood claim is brought in respect of comparative advertising the point of reference is the "average consumer": *British Airways Plc v Ryanair Ltd* [2001] F.S.R. 32. So too, where publication was in a specialist magazine serving a specialist group of people, the test should be applied by judging the effect on that audience rather than the general public: *Macmillan Magazines Ltd v RCN Publishing Co. Ltd* [1998] F.S.R. 9. See also *Emaco Ltd & Aktiebolaget Electrolux v Dyson Appliances* [1999] E.T.M.R. 903.

Publication. The falsehood must be communicated to third persons[43] since **21.6**
the tort consists of interference with the claimant's relations with those
persons.[44] Malicious false statements to the claimant causing damage to him
may be actionable as deceit or, where his loss does not arise from action taken
by him in reliance on them, by another variety of action on the case.[45] Though
there may, in the case of defamation, be liability for a publication brought
about by want of due care,[46] it is thought that this should not be the case in
malicious falsehood,[47] but where the defendant has made an initial, deliberate
publication he should be liable for further publications which are the natural
and probable consequence of that.[48]

Falsity. It is essential that the statement should be false and the burden of **21.7**
pleading and proving falsity is on the claimant[49] who must prove that a
statement conveying one or more particular meanings has been published and
that the meaning or meanings complained of were untrue.[50] In a case concerning disparagement of the plaintiff's title Maule J. said:

---

[43] "There does not seem . . . to be any relevant distinction between the concept of publication
for the purpose of defamation and for the purpose of injurious falsehood": *Australand Holdings
Ltd v Transparency and Accountability Council Inc.* [2008] N.S.W.S.C. 669 at [98].

[44] *Horning v Hardy* 373 A.2d 1273 (Md., 1977); *Title Insurance v Howes* 135 N.Y.S. 608
(1912). But these need not be business relations: *Procor v USWA* (1989) 65 D.L.R. (4th) 287
(malicious accusation to customs authorities); *Al Raschid v News Syndicate*, 131 N.E. 713 (N.Y.,
1934) (malicious accusation to immigration authorities).

[45] *Wilkinson v Downton* [1897] 2 Q.B. 57; *Janvier v Sweeney* [1919] 2 K.B. 316 CA (though
see the critical comments in *Wainwright v Home Office* [2003] UKHL 53; [2004] 2 A.C. 406).
Although the statement was initially made to third parties (as in the case of malicious falsehood)
Bielitski v Obadisk [1922] 2 W.W.R. 238 seems to be a case of this type. See also *Austen v
University of Wolverhampton* [2005] EWHC 1635 QBD.

[46] See para.6.18, above.

[47] But compare Restatement 2d, *Torts*, para.630.

[48] *Cellactite and British Uralite v Robertson, The Times*, July 23, 1957, CA. As in the case of
libel, there is a technical distinction between (1) liability for a further publication as a new cause
of action and (2) liability for the damage flowing from the first publication by reason of repetition:
para.6.36, above.

[49] *Pater v Baker* (1847) 3 C.B. 831; *Brook v Rawl* (1849) 4 Exch. 521; *Young v Macrae* (1862)
3 B. & S. 264; *Hatchard v Mege* (1887) 18 Q.B.D 771; *Burnett v Tak* (1892) 45 L.T. 743; *Royal
Baking Powder Co. v Wright, Crossley* (1900) 18 R.P.C. 95; *British Railway Traffic Co. v CRC*
[1922] 2 K.B. 260; *Greers v Pearman* (1922) 39 R.P.C. 410; *Joyce v Sengupta* [1993] 1 W.L.R.
337 CA. In a case in which concurrent claims are brought in defamation and malicious falsehood,
the burden cannot be taken to be discharged merely because the defence of justification to the
defamation claim has been struck out: *Culla Park Ltd v Richards* [2007] EWHC 1687 (QB) at
[13].

[50] In *Cruddas v Calvert* [2013] EWHC 2298 (QB) concurrent claims were brought in libel and
malicious falsehood. The words published were held, in a trial on a preliminary issue, to have
three natural and ordinary meanings (*Cruddas v Calvert* [2013] EWHC 1427 (QB); upheld on this
point by the Court of Appeal in [2013] EWCA Civ 748). At the trial of the claims ([2013] EWHC
2298 (QB)), Tugendhat J. found that that the words were untrue in all three meanings for the
purposes of the claim in libel. Having noted that the burden in malicious falsehood of proving
falsity was on the claimant, so that it would therefore be theoretically possible for the claimant
to fail in his malicious falsehood claim notwithstanding his success in the libel claim, he
continued (at [201]):
"It is the experience of judges in practice that the burden of proof is very rarely decisive of the
outcome of an action. In the present case it is not because of the burden of proof that I have

"It is essential, to give a cause of action, that the statement should be false . . . If the statement is true, if there really be the infirmity in the title that is suggested, no action will lie, however, malicious the defendant's intention might be."[51]

The question of how far statements of opinion will found a claim for this tort has been mainly litigated in the context of disparagement of goods and there it is clear that mere general assertions that the claimant's goods are inferior to those of the defendant will not be enough. However, in such cases there is an obvious policy that the courts should not be made into a tribunal to adjudicate the comparative quality of competing products.[52] In *Euromoney Institutional Investor Plc v Aviation News Ltd*[53] Tugendhat J. accepted that a statement of opinion cannot be complained of as a falsehood for the purposes of a claim in malicious falsehood[54] but whether this rule admits of any exceptions is not clear.[55]

21.8 **Malice.** There is no liability in malicious falsehood for a statement published in good faith.[56] In *Shapiro v La Morta*[57] the defendant's manager, ignorant of the fact that an arrangement under which it was agreed that the plaintiff, a professional pianist, should accompany a singer at the defendant's music hall had fallen through, issued posters and programmes in which the plaintiff's name appeared, and consequently the plaintiff lost an engagement elsewhere. In an action for injurious falsehood to recover damages for loss of this engagement it was held by the Court of Appeal that as the statement causing damage to the plaintiff was published bona fide, the plaintiff could not recover. Mere negligence is not malice (though in certain circumstances it may amount to a separate basis for liability[58]). A statement false in fact and calculated to produce actual damage will therefore not support such an action

---

decided that the defence of truth failed for the purposes of the libel action. I would have reached the same conclusion if the burden of proof had lain on Mr Cruddas. Mr Cruddas has more than satisfied me that the three meanings were all false."

[51] *Pater v Baker* (1847) 3 C.B. 831 at 868.

[52] See para.21.21, below.

[53] [2013] EWHC 1505 (QB).

[54] Prosser & Keeton, *Torts*, 5th edn (1984), para.128 regard the question of whether an opinion can be complained as a malicious falsehood as unsettled, though in the US there are First Amendment problems about holding a statement of opinion actionable.

[55] In the *Euromoney* case Tugendhat J. referred to the last edition of this book (para.21.5) and to the following example which was given as a possible exception to the general principle:
"Suppose for example that an influential theatre critic were to say that the claimant's play was a bad play and not worth seeing and that the claimant was able to show that that was not the critic's opinion at all but the statement was made in pursuit of a vendetta against the claimant, is there any reason why the critic should not be liable?"
Tugendhat J. thought that this was not a true exception: "The statement that a person holds an opinion is for the purposes of the law of misrepresentation and fraud treated as a statement of fact about that person's state of mind" (at [103]).

[56] *Friend v Civil Aviation Authority* [2005] EWHC 201 (QB) at [235]. In *Assured Quality Construction Ltd v Thompson* [2006] EWHC 2440 Ch D the erroneous advice of the defendant's solicitors that he had the beneficial interest which he asserted prevented a finding of malice.

[57] (1923) 40 T.L.R. 201 CA.

[58] See para.23.1, below.

if it was made in the belief, even a careless belief, that it was true.[59] The defendant may have acted stupidly in asserting a right, yet if he bona fide believed such right to exist, no action lies.

> "If what the defendant has written be most untrue, but nevertheless he believed it, if he was acting under the most vicious of judgments, yet if he exercised that judgment *bona fide*, it will be a justification to him in this case. Whether his belief be such as a man of sound sense and knowledge of business would have formed is not the question."[60]
> "The question here is not what judgment a sensible or reasonable man would have formed in this case, but whether the defendant did or did not entertain the opinion he communicated."[61]

Again, "the mere absence of just cause or excuse is not of itself malice. Malice in its proper and accurate sense is a question of motive, intention, or state of mind."[62]

In *Spring v Guardian Assurance Plc*[63] the Court of Appeal held that malice for this purpose was the same as malice where it arises in a claim for defamation in relation to the plea of qualified privilege.[64] In other words, the defendant will be guilty of malice if he is actuated by some improper motive,[65] and knowledge or recklessness as to the falsity of the statement will be virtually conclusive as to malice.[66] Thus in *Joyce v Motor Surveys Ltd*[67]

---

[59] *Balden v Shorter* [1933] 1 Ch. 427; following *Greers v Pearman* (1922) 39 R.P.C. 406; *Langdon's Coach Lines v Toronto Transit Commission* [1956] 1 D.L.R. (2d) 319 (mistake of law); affirmed 5 D.L.R. (2d) 110. See also *Loudon v Ryder (No.2)* [1953] Ch. 423; *Customglass Boats v Salthouse Boats* [1976] R.P.C. 589 at 602 (N.Z.).

[60] Per Lord Ellenborough C.J. in *Pitt v Donovan* (1813) 1 M. & S. 639 at 645. Nor is it a wrongful interference with contract: *Granby Marketing Services v Interlego AG* [1984] R.P.C. 209.

[61] *Pitt v Donovan* (1813) 1 M. & S. 639 at 649.

[62] Per McCardie J. in *British Rail Traffic Co. v CRC* [1922] 2 K.B. 260 at 269.

[63] [1993] 2 All E.R. 273 CA. The decision was reversed on the issue of negligence, but malicious falsehood was not in contention in the HL: [1995] 2 A.C. 296. The fact that the defendant did not seek to contest that if there was malice, the case fell within malicious falsehood ([1993] 2 All E.R. at 286) should not, it is submitted, detract from the authority of the CA's decision on malice.

[64] See Ch.17, above. Accepted as correct by Tugendhat J. in *Cruddas v Calvert* [2013] EWHC 2298 (QB) at [204]. Strictly speaking, the court held that malice was the same as malice "in relation to the torts of libel and slander" (at 288) but since *Spring* it has been held that malice in honest comment cannot be equated with malice in qualified privilege: para.12.36, above.

[65] "Some indirect object": Bankes L.J. in *Greers Ltd v Pearman and Corder Ltd* (1922) 39 R.P.C. 406 at 417; "some indirect or dishonest motive": Scrutton L.J. ibid.

[66] If defendant "knew . . . that [the words] were false or was reckless as to whether they were false or not": Glidewell L.J. in *Kaye v Robertson* [1991] F.S.R. 62 CA at 67.
"A statement made by a man who knows that it is likely to injure and knows that it is false is made maliciously. So also if he knows that it is likely to injure and has no belief whether it is true or false and makes it recklessly, not caring whether it is true or false": Atkin L.J. in *Shapiro v La Morta* (1923) 40 T.L.R. 201 CA at 203. There are exceptional cases in defamation where the defendant is not guilty of malice in publishing a statement he knows or suspects to be untrue because it is his duty to do so: para.17.19, above. In principle the same must be true in malicious falsehood.

[67] [1948] Ch. 252.

liability was found where the defendants, landlords of the plaintiff, in an effort to break his resistance to a notice to quit, returned his mail and published statements to various clients of his to the effect that he had gone away and ceased to trade. So too, in *Cruddas v Calvert*[68] the judge found that the journalists knew and understood the meaning of the words they wrote and knew that they were untrue.[69] In *Wilts United Dairies v Thomas Robinson Sons & Co.*,[70] Stable J. said that:

> "if you publish an injurious falsehood which you know to be false, albeit that your only object is your own advantage and with no intention or desire to injure the person in relation to whose goods the falsehood is published,[71] then provided it is intrinsically injurious—I say 'intrinsically,' meaning not deliberately aimed with intent to injure but as being inherent in the statement itself, the defendant is responsible, the malice consisting in the fact that what he published he knew to be false."

In cases where a defendant did not intend to convey a meaning which the court later found his words to bear, it is the defendant's subjective understanding of the meaning which is relevant to determining whether he knew the words to be false.[72] This may be of some significance where concurrent claims are brought in defamation and malicious falsehood and the court finds that there is more than one reasonable meaning and that some, but not all, of the meanings are false. In such a case, if the words are true in the "single meaning" determined for the purposes of the law of libel, a claim for

---

[68] [2013] EWHC 2298 (QB).

[69] See also *Thornton v Telegraph Media Group Ltd* [2011] EWHC 1884 (QB); [2012] E.M.L.R. 8. The claimant sued in libel and malicious falsehood in respect of a book review which implied that the claimant had falsely and dishonestly stated that she had interviewed the book reviewer for the purposes of the book and that she gave her interviewees "copy approval", a practice disapproved of by other journalists. That a journalist gives her interviewees "copy approval" had been held not to be defamatory in an earlier hearing (*Thornton v Telegraph Media Group Ltd* [2010] EWHC 1414 (QB)) but the defendants accepted that to attribute the practice to a person who was writing for journalism in a serious newspaper, or for academic readers, was damaging and therefore if false and malicious would be actionable in malicious falsehood. The judge held that the allegation that the claimant gave copy approval was false and that the reviewer knew that it was false and therefore that the claim succeeded.

[70] [1957] R.P.C. 220; on appeal, where malicious falsehood was not dealt with [1958] R.P.C. 94.

[71] The defendants had acquired a large quantity of old stock of the plaintiff's condensed milk and presented it to customers as milk of current production.

[72] *Loveless v Earl* [1999] E.M.L.R 530 at 538–541; *Cruddas v Calvert* [2013] EWHC 2298 (QB) at [206]. In *Bonnick v Morris* [2002] UKPC 31 PC; [2003] 1 A.C.300 the Privy Council said (at [25]) this point should not be pressed too far as:
"In the normal course a responsible journalist can be expected to perceive the meaning an ordinary, reasonable reader is likely to give his article. Moreover, even if the words are highly susceptible of another meaning, a responsible journalist will not disregard a defamatory meaning which is obviously one possible meaning of the article in question. Questions of degree arise here. The more obvious the defamatory meaning, and the more serious the defamation, the less weight will a court attach to other possible meanings when considering the conduct to be expected of a responsible journalist in the circumstances."
In *Cruddas*, Tugendhat J. commented that the same applies to "an irresponsible journalist" (at [215]).

malicious falsehood may still succeed if the claimant can prove that the words are false in another meaning that the words are found to bear provided that the meaning is one which the defendant understood the words to bear.[73]

Improper motive as malice is not easy to apply in the context of malicious falsehood.[74] In defamation an occasion is held to be privileged because some particular legal policy requires diminution of the normally high standard of protection afforded to reputation and the privilege covers only statements which are made in furtherance of that legal policy. So if a privilege is accorded to D to make a report to A for the protection of the interests of A or the public, D would lose the protection of the privilege if it could be shown that he made the report, believing in its contents, in order to injure C or to further his (D's) own business interests.[75] In the case of malicious falsehood, as in the case of defamation,[76] an intention to damage another may be malice even if the statement is believed to be true.

> "If you publish a statement which turns out to be false but which you honestly believed to be true, but you publish the statement, not for the purpose of protecting your own interests and achieving some advantage to yourself, but for the purpose of doing harm, and it transpires, contrary to your belief, that the statement that you believed to be true has turned out to be false, notwithstanding the bona fides of your belief because the object you had in mind was to injure him and not to advantage yourself, you would be liable for an injurious falsehood."[77]

The pursuit of self-interest (as opposed to doing harm to another) will not, however, be malice in the context of malicious falsehood where the statement is believed to be true. In *Dunlop v Maison Talbot*[78] Collins M.R. said that:

> "it [is] not malice if the object of the writer was to push his own business. To make the act malicious it must be done with the direct object of injuring that other person's business. Therefore, the mere fact that it would injure that other person's business [is] no evidence of malice."

In *Cruddas v Calvert*[79] it was alleged in newspaper articles written after covertly recorded meetings had been held between journalists and the claimant, then treasurer of the Conservative Party, that the claimant would accept

---

[73] As Tugendhat J. pointed out (at [207]) in *Cruddas v Calvert* [2013] EWHC 2298 (QB) this point might have been significant in that case had he not found that each of the three libel meanings that the Court of Appeal ([2013] EWCA Civ 748) had found the words to bear were false. The judge also found that the journalists did understand the meaning of the words they wrote (at [215]–[218]).

[74] See *Hong Kong Wing On Travel Services Ltd v Hong Thai Citizens Travel Services Ltd* [2001] 420 HKCU 1.

[75] Of course a particular head of privilege may be created to allow the defendant to protect his own interests.

[76] See para.17.5, above.

[77] *Wilts United Dairies v Thomas Robinson Sons & Co* [1957] R.P.C. 220 at 237. Cf. *Australand Holdings Ltd v Transparency and Accountability Council Inc.* [2008] N.S.W.S.C. 669 at [156]–[157].

[78] (1904) 20 T.L.R. 579 CA at 581.

[79] [2013] EWHC 2298 (QB).

cash for access and influence and would be prepared to break electoral law to receive such donations. The judge found the words to be false in the meanings that the words were held to bear[80] and also held that the journalists knew what their words meant and knew they were false. Additionally, the judge held that a dominant intention to injure the claimant was made out. The journalists, for whom the newspaper was vicariously liable, had expressed delight upon learning that they had caused the claimant's resignation and one of the journalist nominated himself for a prize with *Private Eye*, and did so in terms which led the editors of *Private Eye* to report the matter in a manner that caused further damage to Mr Cruddas, saying that he was "even prepared to receive a donation illegally from a Liechtenstein fund". They had done nothing to limit the damage to the claimant's reputation, by giving him a proper opportunity to comment until just before the publication deadline, and what they did tell him about the articles at that time was too vague to enable him to comment effectively; nor did they subsequently make it clear that the corruption meaning was not intended by them to impute criminality, even though it soon became clear that many readers had understood the articles in that way.[81]

And in *White v Mellin*,[82] Lord Herschell L.C., after pointing out that Lopes L.J. (in the court below) had said that "it is actionable to publish maliciously without lawful occasion a false statement disparaging the goods of another person," continued:

> "by that it may be intended to indicate that the object of the publication must be to injure another person, and that the advertisement is not published *bona fide* merely to sell the advertiser's own goods, or at all events, that he published it with the knowledge of its falsity. One or other of these elements, it seems to me, must be intended by the addition of the word 'maliciously'."

21.9 Evidence of malice. The fact that the defendant has no reasonable or probable cause for his claim is evidence from which a judge or jury may infer that he was not acting bona fide.[83] It does not, however, necessarily lead to such an inference.[84] In other words the law here merely follows the normal approach to drawing inferences about a person's knowledge, belief or intention.

---

[80] See, para.21.7 fn.50, above.
[81] [2013] EWHC 2298 at [276]–[278] (QB).
[82] [1895] A.C. 154 at 160.
[83] "Honest belief in an unfounded claim is not malice. But the nature of the unfounded claim may be evidence that there was not an honest belief in it. It may be so unfounded that the particular fact that it is put forward may be evidence that it is not honestly believed": per Scrutton L.J. in *Greers Ltd v Pearman and Corder Ltd* (1922) 39 R.P.C. 406 at 417.
[84] See *Pater v Baker* (1847) 3 C.B. 831 at 868; *C v Mirror Group Newspapers* [1997] 1 W.L.R. 131 CA, a case very near the line on a striking out application. See also, *Kaye v Robertson* [1991] F.S.R. 62 at 67.

"Privilege" and malicious falsehood. Some cases speak in terms of **21.10**
non-malicious statements being privileged. Thus in *Halsey v Brotherhood*[85]
Lord Coleridge C.J. said:

> "if a statement is made in defence of the defendant's own property, although it
> injures and is untrue, it is still what the law calls a privileged statement; it is a
> statement that the defendant has a right to make, unless, besides its untruth and
> besides its injury, express malice is proved, that is to say, want of *bona fides* or the
> presence of *mala fides*."

There is no doubt that such statements are not actionable,[86] but it seems
unhelpful to refer to privilege, which is a device used in the law of defamation
to cast the burden of showing actual malice upon the claimant in a limited
class of cases against a general background of strict liability. In malicious
falsehood the burden of proof of malice is upon the claimant from the outset
in all cases.[87] On the other hand, where a statement is made in circumstances
in which an absolute privilege would attach to the words for the purpose of the
law of defamation (e.g. a statement in Parliament or in judicial proceedings[88])
there is also a complete defence to a claim for malicious falsehood.

Malicious falsehood and honest comment. In *Thornton v Telegraph* **21.11**
Media Group Ltd,[89] Tugendhat J. held that honest comment is not available as
a defence to malicious falsehood. This stage of the *Thornton* litigation
involved an application by the defendant to amend its case[90] and to rely on a
defence akin to honest comment. According to the judge, the question posed
by the proposed amendment was: "is it the law that the words complained of
cannot be regarded as false if they are comment which an honest person could
express on the basis of the contents of the book which are identified?"[91] The
judge noted that in defamation, where honest comment is raised, the defendant

---

[85] (1881) 19 Ch. D. 386 CA at 388–389, referring to *Wren v Weild* (1869) L.R. 4 Q.B. 730.
[86] See para.21.8, above.
[87] In *CHC Software v Hopkins & Wood* [1993] F.S.R. 241, Mummery J. said that:
"the fact that the defence served in this action pleads certain defences, such as qualified
privilege and fair comment, which may constitute defences to a claim for libel, but not to a
claim for malicious falsehood, cannot convert the tort which is pleaded in such a statement of
claim from one of malicious falsehood into one of libel." *Bresden v Johnson* [1945] 1 W.W.R.
273 (complaint to proper officer; no malice).
[88] *Tersigni v Fagan* [1959] O.W.N. 94 Ont. CA. But the malicious procuring of a prosecution
amounts to the tort of malicious prosecution. Malicious commencement of civil proceedings is
probably not a tort in general (*Gregory v Portsmouth CC* [2000] 1 A.C. 419 HL) but to employ
a civil process, not itself unfounded, for an improper collateral purpose may amount to the tort
of abuse of process: *Speed Seal Products v Padington* [1985] 1 W.L.R. 1327 CA.
[89] [2011] EWHC 159 (QB); [2011] E.M.L.R. 25.
[90] The proposed amendment was in the following terms:
"For the avoidance of doubt, the Defendant will allege that the words on which the malicious
falsehood claim is based ("which means that her interviewees have the right to read what she
says about them and alter it. In journalism we call this 'copy approval' and disapprove") were
comment and that an honest person could express comment on the basis of the facts set out
below. Accordingly, the words cannot be regarded to be false" (ibid. at [17]).
[91] Ibid. at [20].

must prove that the words are comment based on correct facts and that the comment is one that an honest person could have made. This latter criterion is an "objective criterion" but the defence can be defeated, even if this criterion is met, by proving malice.[92] The effect of the objective criterion in defamation is that if a defendant draws a false inference of fact, then provided an honest person could have believed that inference to be true, the defendant is not liable, unless the claimant can prove that the defendant did not believe the inference to be true. The effect of introducing the objective test into malicious falsehood would be the opposite: if a defendant draws a false inference of fact, then provided an honest person could have believed that inference to be true, he is not liable, *even if* the claimant could prove that the defendant did not believe the inference to be true. Consequently, the proposed amendment was wrong in law and permission to amend was refused.

21.12 Damage: the common law. Save in cases falling within the provisions of s.3(1) of the Defamation Act 1952,[93] the claimant must allege and prove that he has suffered special damage.[94]

> "The damage is the gist of the action, and therefore . . . it must be especially alleged and proved."[95]
> "The essential ground, the gist, of the action is special damage, done maliciously. Unless the plaintiff has in fact suffered loss, which can be and is specified, he has no cause of action. The fact that the defendant has acted maliciously cannot supply the want of special damage, nor can a superfluity of malice eke out a case wanting in special damage."[96]

21.13 Damage must be pecuniary. Special damage here means the same as in the context of slander not actionable per se[97]: it is pecuniary or capable of being estimated in money[98] rather than being merely (as in the case of defamation) *compensated* by an award of money. Typically (but not necessarily[99]) it is loss of trade,[100] but a case may not be founded on general loss

---

[92] Ibid. at [24].

[93] See para.21.14, below.

[94] See, e.g. *Evans v Harlow* (1844) 5 Q.B. 624, declaration held bad because there was no averment of special damage.

[95] *Royal Baking Powder Co. v Wright, Crossley* (1900) 18 R.P.C. 95 HL at 99; *Lyne v Nichols* (1906) 23 T.L.R. at 88.

[96] Per Lord Robertson in *Royal Baking Powder Co. v Wright, Crossley*, above, at 103; *Joyce v Sengupta* [1993] 1 W.L.R. 337 CA at 347.

[97] See Ch.5, particularly para.5.2, above.

[98] *Chamberlain v Boyd* (1883) 11 Q.B.D. 407.

[99] One of the old cases involved the plaintiff losing her prospective marriage as a result of the defendant representing to her fiancée that she was married: *Sheperd v Wakeman* (1662) 1 Sid. 79.

[100] It is thought that the claimant should be able to recover the cost of steps reasonably taken to investigate and counteract the damaging effects of the falsehood (e.g. the costs of publicity). Such losses were held recoverable in *BMTA v Salvadori* [1949] Ch. 556, a case of unlawful means conspiracy, where, however, there was other damage. A claim for such costs without any other actionable damage was held arguable in *Lonrho v Fayed (No.5)* [1993] 1 W.L.R. 1489 CA, a case of lawful means conspiracy. Tugendhat J. appeared to assume that such losses were recoverable in *Tesla Motors Ltd v BBC* [2011] EWHC 2760 at [66] (QB). Although such damages were

of reputation, nor on mental anxiety and distress.[101] However, once a person can establish a cause of action for malicious falsehood, whether by proof of actual pecuniary damage or by reliance on s.3 of the Defamation Act 1952[102] he may recover aggravated damages for injury to feelings in the same way as he can in an action for defamation and the award may take account of the conduct of the defendant during the litigation, e.g. in trying to blacken the claimant's name.[103] The matter was put in this way by Nicholls V.C. in *Joyce v Sengupta*[104]:

> "Take the example ... of a person who maliciously spreads rumours that his competitor's business has closed down. Or the rumour might be that the business is in financial difficulty and that a receiver will soon be appointed.[105] The owner of the business suffers severe financial loss. Further, because of the effect the rumours are having on his business he is worried beyond measure about his livelihood and his family's future. He suffers anxiety and distress. Can it be right that the law is unable to give him any recompense for this suffering against the person whose malice caused it? Although injury to feelings alone will not found a cause of action in malicious falsehood, ought not the law to take such injury into account when it is connected with financial damage inflicted by the falsehood?"

By virtue of the Crime and Courts Act 2013,[106] the relevant provisions of which are not yet in force, aggravated and exemplary damages may also be available in a harassment claim brought against a "relevant publisher".

At common law the fact that the words are calculated or likely to cause damage (e.g. that some intending purchaser may be deterred from buying the claimant's goods) is not sufficient: actual damage must have accrued whether the claim be for damages or (it seems) an injunction.[107] Where a false and malicious statement is in its very nature intended or reasonably likely to produce, and in the ordinary course of things does produce, a general loss of custom, evidence of such general loss of custom is admissible, and, if uncontradicted, sufficient to support the action.[108] In *Ratcliffe v Evans*, where the

---

described as "self-serving" if the steps are not taken and loss is suffered, the claimant risks being accused of failure to mitigate. The Restatement 2d, *Torts*, para.633 allows recovery of such costs.

[101] *Joyce v Sengupta* [1993] 1 W.L.R. 337 CA at 348; *Fielding v Variety Inc.* [1967] 2 Q.B. 841 CA at 851, 855. D makes a malicious false statement about C. The distress caused by this causes C to be less active in business and the business declines. A claim which seems to have been on this basis was not struck out in *James v Faddoul* [2007] N.S.W.S.C. 821 (see at [17]).

[102] See para.21.14, below.

[103] *Khodaparast v Shad* [2000] 1 W.L.R. 618 CA. The Restatement 2d, *Torts*, para.633, comment j., denies recovery of such damages even where pecuniary loss has been established.

[104] [1993] 1 W.L.R. 337 CA at 347–348. Cf. *Murtough v Betham* [2004] N.S.W.S.C. 753.

[105] This would seem likely to be defamatory: see para.2.30, above.

[106] See paras 9.22–9.24 and 9.32–9.33, above.

[107] *White v Mellin* [1895] A.C. 154 HL; *British Railway Traffic Co. v CRC* [1922] 2 K.B. 260; *Christie, Owen and Davies v Sears, The Times*, November 26, 1952. But as to injunctions, see para.9.30, above.

[108] *Ratcliffe v Evans* [1892] 2 Q.B. 524 CA; *George v Blow* (1899) 20 N.S.W.L.R. 395. Compare *Glo-Klen Distributors v British Columbia Chemicals* (1959) 19 D.L.R. (2d) 635 BCCA (statement not generally distributed; plaintiff should prove loss by testimony).

complaint was of a falsehood appearing in the press, Bowen L.J. said that it had been:

"probably read, and possibly acted on, by persons of whom the plaintiff never heard. To refuse with reference to such a subject-matter to admit such general evidence would be . . . an absolute denial of justice and of redress for the very mischief which was intended to be committed."[109]

21.14 Damage: cases falling within the Defamation Act 1952. Under the provisions of s.3(1) of the Defamation Act 1952,[110] it is not necessary to allege or prove special damage:

"(a) if the words upon which the action is founded are calculated to cause pecuniary damage to the plaintiff[111] and are published in writing or other permanent form; or
(b) if the said words are calculated to cause pecuniary damage to the plaintiff in respect of any office, profession, calling, trade or business held or carried on by him at the time of the publication."[112]

Broadcasting is publication in permanent form,[113] and so is publication of words in the course of a performance of a play.[114] "Calculated to" in this context[115] has been accepted as meaning "more likely than not".[116] The claimant must plead and prove with sufficient particularity that it was more

---

[109] [1892] 2 Q.B. at 533.

[110] As to Scotland, see s.14 of the Act.

[111] In applying s.3 it is necessary to bear in mind the basic principle of company law that a wrong to a company is actionable by the company and not its individual members. So if a malicious falsehood is calculated to cause damage to a company that does not mean it is calculated to cause damage to the directors: *Dorset Flint & Stone Blocks Ltd v Moir* [2004] EWHC 2173 QBD.

[112] In *Joyce v Sengupta* [1993] 1 W.L.R. 337 CA, the plaintiff appears to have relied on para.(a) because she had ceased, and had no intention of resuming, the type of employment to which the statement related.

[113] Broadcasting Act 1990, s.166(2) replacing the Defamation Act 1952, s.3(2).

[114] Theatres Act 1968, s.4(1), (2).

[115] See also para.4.16, above.

[116] *Tesla Motors Ltd v BBC* [2013] EWCA Civ 152 at [27]. See also, *IBM v Web-Sphere Limited* [2004] EWHC 529 (Ch) at [74] (Lewison J). In *Ferguson v Associated Newspapers Ltd*, unreported, December 3, 2001, Gray J. stated:
"In my opinion, the word "calculated", where it appears in the Defamation Act, should be given the meaning of "likely" or "probable" rather than such as might well happen, or something which is a possibility. I say that for the reasons advanced by [counsel]. Namely, firstly that the purpose of s.3(1) Defamation Act is to relieve a claimant of having to shoulder the evidential difficulties of proving actual damage. Secondly, that Article 10 requires that any restriction on freedom of expression must be strictly justified as necessary in a democratic society. And a wider interpretation of "calculated" in s.3(1) would constitute an additional restriction on freedom of expression. Thirdly, that the word "calculated" which one finds in the statute, of itself suggests a higher rather than a lower degree of likelihood."
At first instance in *Tesla Motors Ltd v BBC* [2012] EWHC 310 (QB), Tugendhat J. held that nothing in his decision turned on the issue of the appropriate standard of proof under s.3(1) but that if he had to decide the issue he found the decisions of Gray and Lewison JJ. at the very least persuasive and still good law and the proposition that s.3(1) introduces a lower standard of proof than the normal civil standard was "insupportable".

likely than not that the damage referred to in s.3 was caused by "the words upon which the action is founded". This requires him to give particulars of the nature of the allegedly probable damage and the grounds relied on for saying that it is more likely than not.[117] However, since the claim is one for general damages it is unnecessary for the claimant to identify the amount of pecuniary loss that it is said the falsehoods were calculated to cause. All that is required in order to make the nature of the case clear is identification of the nature of the loss and the mechanism by which it is likely to be sustained.[118]

Where the words fall within the statute the claimant may recover damages representing the loss which he is likely to suffer as the direct and natural consequence[119] of the falsehood. The fact that the claimant cannot adduce evidence of loss which has actually occurred does not mean that he recovers only nominal damages, for that would be to deprive s.3 of all practical effect.[120]

Damage must be natural result. Whether the claim is made for special   **21.15**
damage or under s.3, the damage must be such as directly and naturally (or naturally and probably[121]) results from the words.[122] The defendant will not be liable where the damage is attributable not to his words but to some other unconnected fact or circumstance.[123] In *Palmer Bruyn & Parker Pty Ltd v Parsons*[124] the claimants were acting for M in connection with a planning application. The defendant, who opposed the application, sent to members of

---

[117] *Tesla Motors Ltd v BBC* [2011] EWHC 2760 (QB) at [66].

[118] Ibid. at [37].

[119] *Brady v Express Newspapers, The Times,* December 31, 1994 (possible loss of discretionary weekly allowance to prisoner. Claim struck out because no reasonable prison authority would withdraw the privilege without a proper inquiry); *Sallows v Griffiths* [2001] F.S.R. 15 CA.

[120] *Joyce v Sengupta* [1993] 1 W.L.R. 337 CA. *Fielding v Variety Inc.* [1967] 2 Q.B. 841 CA at 851, 855, is not authority to the contrary: the court simply decided that the falsehood about the plaintiff's show's reception in London was not likely to prejudice its chances in the US. See also *Masood v Zahoor* [2008] EWHC 1034 Ch D.

[121] *Palmer Bruyn & Parker Pty Ltd v Parsons* [2001] HCA 69; 208 C.L.R. 388.

[122] *Kaye v Robertson* [1991] F.S.R. 62 CA at 67; *Sallows v Griffiths* [2001] F.S.R. 15 CA; *Haddan v Lott* (1854) 15 C.B. 411. The Restatement 2d, *Torts,* para.633 requires that the loss be the "direct and immediate" consequence of the falsehood. See Illustration 2:
   "A's business is in a precarious financial position. In order to protect himself from bankruptcy, A offers land to B at $20,000. B is about to accept this offer but is prevented from doing so by C's false statement that A's title to the land is bad. In consequence of A's failure to consummate the sale and receive the agreed price his business goes into bankruptcy. A cannot recover from C the loss that he has sustained by the bankruptcy of the business."
This is broadly in accord with the attitude formerly taken to impecuniosity in *Liesbosch Dredger v Edison SS* [1933] A.C. 449. But it is not clear now that the same rule would be followed here where the defendant was aware of the claimant's financial position.
   It has been said that the fact that a speedy correction and apology was made shortly after the malicious falsehood was published may mean that pecuniary loss is not the natural consequence of the falsehood: *Allason v Campbell, The Times,* May 8, 1996 (based on transcript; new trial ordered, February 26, 1998).

[123] *Barrett v Associated Newspapers* (1907) 23 T.L.R. 666 (house already had reputation as haunted).

[124] [2001] HCA 69; 208 C.L.R. 388.

the council a letter, which was plainly a hoax, purporting to come from the claimants and to offer and make absurd inducements and threats in connection with the application. When a newspaper published an accurate account of this, emphasising that it was a hoax, M terminated the claimants' retainer. The purpose of the hoax letter was to influence council members to reject the application. A majority of the High Court of Australia held that the damage suffered by the claimants was not a natural and probable result of the letter.

In *Tesla Motors Ltd v BBC*[125] the claimant, a manufacturer of electric cars, appealed against a refusal of permission to amend its particulars of claim so as to reinstate a claim for libel and malicious falsehood and add a claim for special damages. The claim arose out of a "Top Gear" programme of the claimant's Roadster car. The programme made a number of favourable comments about the car but also showed the car slowing, stopping and being pushed back to a hangar. This was accompanied by a commentary which stated that the claimant had said the car would do 200 miles but "on our track it would run out after 55 miles and . . . it is not a quick job to charge it up again." The claimant alleged that the mileage statement inferred that the true range was 55 miles not 200 and that the claimant had grossly misled potential customers, intentionally or recklessly, about the range. So far as the malicious falsehood claim was concerned, Tugendhat J. found it was insufficiently particularised and ordered it to be struck out unless the claimant obtained permission to amend its particulars of claim.[126] Permission was subsequently denied[127] and the claimant appealed.

One difficulty faced by the claimant was that, over a period of some 15 months between the first broadcast and the beginning of the one-year limitation period, there had been numerous further broadcasts of the programme, so that there had been very wide publication of unfavourable statements in respect of which a claim could no longer be brought. Added to that was the potential for damage to have been caused by any unfavourable statements about the Roadster that were admitted to be true (for example, the time required to re-charge the batteries and the consequences of overheating). The need to distinguish the effect of false but no longer actionable statements and damaging but true statements from actionable falsehoods raised issues of causation that were acute.[128] However, so far as the proposed amendments were concerned, Tugendhat J.'s concern that they failed to distinguish between damage flowing from actionable falsehoods and damage flowing from unfavourable statements that for one reason or another were not actionable was misplaced. Since the claim was for general damages it was unnecessary for the claimant to identify the amount of pecuniary loss which it is said

---

[125] *Tesla Motors v BBC* [2013] EWCA Civ 152.
[126] *Tesla Motors Ltd v BBC* [2011] EWHC 2760 (QB).
[127] *Tesla Motors Ltd v BBC* [2012] EWHC 310 (QB).
[128] *Tesla Motors v BBC* [2013] EWCA Civ 152 at [36].

the falsehoods were calculated to cause. All that was required in order to make the nature of the case clear was identification of the nature of the loss and the mechanism by which it is likely to be sustained and this the claimant had done.[129] However, even though the claim might have been sufficiently particularised, the allegations identifying pecuniary loss said to have been caused, far from supporting the claimant's case, tended to emphasise that it would be very difficult to persuade the court that the actionable statements, coming so long after the first showing as they did, were calculated to cause any significant loss.[130] Because the claimant had not persuaded the court that the case it sought to make by the proposed amendments had any real prospect of success or, if successful, was likely to yield any benefit to the claimant that would justify the devotion of substantial resources in terms of costs and court time, the judge had been right to refuse permission to amend.[131]

SECTION 3. DISPARAGEMENT OF TITLE

Slander of title. At common law an action for malicious falsehood, commonly known as slander of title[132] lies whenever a person maliciously publishes a false statement in disparagement of another person's title to his property and thereby causes special damage. Where the words are in writing and are calculated to cause pecuniary damage they are actionable by statute without proof of special damage.[133] The court has power to make a declaration of right as to the claimant's title to the property even if the claim itself fails, for example because the defendant honestly believes in the truth of his claim (so there is no malice) and persists in it even though it is false.[134] The disparagement may consist in denying, or casting doubts upon, the existence or the validity of the other person's right, claim, title, or interest to or in property. It may be in writing or by word of mouth. "The fact that the slander of title is written or printed and not oral makes no difference in the ground of action, but goes only to the question of dissemination and consequent damages."[135] It is immaterial what is the nature of the property the title to which is disparaged. It may be real or personal property. It may be property of a

21.16

---

[129] Ibid. at [37].

[130] Ibid. at [47].

[131] Ibid. at [50].

[132] See para.21.2, above.

[133] See para.21.14, above.

[134] See *Loudon v Ryder (No.2)* [1953] Ch. 423, where the defendant continued to maintain his wrongful claim up to the date of the action.

[135] *Malachy v Soper* (1836) 3 Bing.N.C. 386. Per curiam in *Meyrose v Adams* (1882) 12 Missouri App.R. n.332. In *Boulton v Shields* (1846) 3 Up.Can.Q.B. 21 the slander was both written and oral.

tangible or intangible nature, e.g. an option to purchase property,[136] or a right to a patent,[137] copyright,[138] trade mark,[139] or trade name.[140] The interest of the claimant in the property may be either legal or equitable,[141] in possession or reversion.[142]

21.17 Protection of own property. Because the wrong requires malice, no action for slander of title will lie if the defendant published the words in the bona fide, though wrongful, assertion, protection, or defence of his own title or claim to the property, right or interest,[143] or in the assertion, protection or defence of the title or claim of his father, or other near relative to whom he is heir-apparent.[144] Similarly no action will lie where the defendant published the words as an agent,[145] or solicitor,[146] in the bona fide assertion, protection, or defence of the rights of his principal or client. But to assert a title or claim in someone who is a complete stranger is evidence of malice and an action will lie for damage caused by such intrusive and unnecessary interference.[147]

Threats to bring unjustified proceedings for infringement of a patent,[148] registered design,[149] design right,[150] or registered trade mark[151] are actionable by statute independently of malice.

---

[136] *Potosi Zinc Co. v Mahoney*, 135 P. 1078 (Nev., 1913); *Hubbard v Scott* 166 P. 33 (Or., 1917).

[137] *Wren v Weild* (1869) L.R. 4 Q.B. 730; *Cousins v Merrill* (1865) 16 Up.Can.C.P. 114; *Halsey v Brotherhood* (1881) 19 Ch.D. 386; *Andrew v Deshler* (1883) 45 New Jersey L.R. 167.

[138] *Dicks v Brooks* (1880) 15 Ch.D. 22.

[139] *Greers Ltd v Pearman and Corder Ltd* (1922) 39 R.P.C. 406 CA; *McElwee v Blackwell* (1886) 94 N. Carolina R. 261

[140] *Royal Baking Powder Co. v Wright, Crossley* (1900) 18 R.P.C. 95 HL. The claim for a sporting title in *Serville v Constance* [1954] 1 All E. R. 662 at 664, obiter, seems better regarded as an example of the broad, generic malicious falsehood.

[141] *Dunlop Tyre Co. v Maison Talbot* (1903) 20 T.L.R. 88, per Walton J. See also *Lover v Pearce* (1961) 178 E.G. 333.

[142] *Vaughan v Ellis* (1609) Cro.Jac. 213. See also *Baker v Piper* (1886) 2 T.L.R. 733.

[143] *Gerrard v Dickenson* (1589) Cro.Eliz. 196; *Smith v Spooner* (1810) 3 Taunt. 246; *Boulton v Shields* (1847) 3 Up.Can.Q.B. 21; *Carr v Duckett* (1860) 5 H. & N. 785; *Wren v Weild* (1869) L.R. 4 Q.B. 730 (assertion of a right to a patent); *RJ Reuters v Mulhens* [1954] Ch. 50 CA; *Siopiolsz v Taylor* [1944] 2 D.L.R. 92 Ont. CA; *Assured Quality Construction Ltd v Thompson* [2006] EWHC 2440 Ch D.

[144] *Pitt v Donovan* (1813) 1 M. & S. 639; *Gutsole v Mathers* (1836) 1 M. & W. 495.

[145] *Steward v Young* (1870) L.R. 5 C.P. 122; *Baker v Piper* (1886) 2 T.L.R. 733.

[146] *Watson v Reynolds* (1826) 1 Moo. & Mal. 1, where it was held that the attorney of a party claiming title to premises put up for sale was not liable to an action for slander of title if he bona fide, though without authority, made such objections to the vendor's title as the purchaser would have been authorised in making. See also *Hargrave v Le Breton* (1769) 4 Burr. 2422.

[147] *Mildmay's Case* (1582–1584) 1 Co. Rep. 174b, 177b; *Pennyman v Rabanks* (1596) Cro.Eliz. 427; *Northumberland (Earl of) v Byrt* (1606) Cro.Jac. 163; *Rowe v Roach* (1813) 1 M. & S. 304 at 310; cf. *Ontario Loan Co. v Lindsey* (1883) 4 O.R. 473.

[148] Patents Act 1977, s.70.

[149] Registered Designs Act 1949, s.26.

[150] Copyright, Designs and Patents Act 1988, s.253.

[151] Trade Marks Act 1994, s.21.

SECTION 4. DISPARAGEMENT OF GOODS

Slander of goods. An action for that variety of malicious falsehood com-   **21.18**
monly known as slander of goods[152] lies whenever a person maliciously
publishes a false statement in disparagement of another person's goods,[153] and
thereby (save in the cases specified in s.3(1) of the Defamation Act 1952[154])
causes him special damage. Except in so far as concerns s.3(1)(a) of the
Defamation Act 1952, it makes no difference whether the falsehood is oral or
in writing.[155] This type of case is more likely than slander of title to overlap
with defamation since disparagement of the claimant's wares will commonly
also impute some dishonesty or incompetence to the claimant.[156]

Mere puffing not actionable. A trader may always commend his own   **21.19**
goods, and state that they are better than the goods of another trader, and,
provided he does not make any false representation as to the quality or
character of the latter, no action will lie,[157] whatever damage may ensue.[158]

> "If the only false statement complained of is that the defendant's goods are better
> than the plaintiff's, such a statement is not actionable, even if the plaintiff is
> damnified by it."[159]
>   "Moreover, an allegation that the statement was made maliciously is not enough
> to convert what is prima facie a lawful into a prima facie unlawful statement. It is
> not unlawful to say that one's own goods are better than other people's; and *Allen
> v Flood*[160] shows that malice in such a case is immaterial."[161]

To hold such puffing actionable:

---

[152] See para.21.4, above.
[153] Which includes false comparative price advertising: *DSG Retail Ltd v Comet Group Plc*
[2002] F.S.R. 58.
[154] See para.21.14, above.
[155] *Ratcliffe v Evans* [1892] 2 Q.B. 532 CA.
[156] See para.2.48, above.
[157] Such a conclusion was justified in *Vodafone Group Plc v Orange Personal Communications
Services Ltd* [1997] E.M.L.R. 84 (Ch) by Jacob J. as follows:
  "The public are used to the ways of advertisers and expect a certain amount of hyperbole. In
  particular the public are used to advertisers claiming the good points of a product and ignoring
  others, advertisements claiming that you can "save £££££ . . . " are common, carrying with
  them the notion that "savings" are related to amount of spend, and the public are reasonably
  used to comparisons—"knocking copy" as it is called in the advertising world. This is
  important in considering what the ordinary meaning may be. The test is whether a reasonable
  man would take the claim being made as one made seriously . . . the more precise the claim
  the more it is likely to be so taken—the more general or fuzzy the less so." (at 89).
See also *DSG Retail Ltd v Comet Group plc* [2002] EWHC 116 (QB); [2002] F.S.R. 58.
[158] *Harman v Delany* (1731) 2 Str. 898; *Young v Macrae* (1862) 3 B. & S. 264; *White v Mellin*
[1895] A.C. 154 HL; *Hubbuck v Wilkinson* [1899] 1 Q.B. 86 CA; *Alcott v Millar's Karri, etc.*
(1904) 91 L.T. 723 CA.
[159] Per Lindley M.R. in *Hubbuck v Wilkinson* [1899] 1 Q.B. at 93.
[160] [1898] A.C. 1 HL. The reference is to the "chasm" stated in *Allen v Flood* to exist between
lawful and unlawful acts.
[161] Per Lindley M.R. in *Hubbuck v Wilkinson* [1899] 1 Q.B. at 91.

"would open a very wide door to litigation, and might expose every man who said his goods were better than another's to the risk of an action."[162]

"Indeed, the courts of law would be turned into a machinery for advertising rival productions by obtaining a judicial determination which of the two was the better."[163]

A fortiori it is not actionable if the defendant, without any reference at all to the claimant's wares, makes exaggerated claims for his own products.[164]

21.20 *Examples.* The defendant, who sold food manufactured by the plaintiff and known as "Mellin's Food for Infants", affixed to the bottles containing such food a label to the following effect:

"Notice. The public are recommended to try Dr. Vance's Prepared Food for Infants and Invalids [in which the defendant had a proprietary interest], it being far more nutritious and healthful than any other preparation yet offered... Local agent, Timothy White, Portsmouth."

It was held that no action lay, for even if special damage had resulted (which was not proved), such conduct amounted to nothing more than a puffing advertisement of his own goods.[165]

The defendants printed and published a circular containing a report of experiments testing the plaintiff's zinc paint and comparing it with the zinc paint which they manufactured, which report gave particulars of the mode of comparison, and concluded:

---

[162] Per Denman C.J. in *Evans v Harlow* (1844) 5 Q.B. 624 at 631. It would appear from Lord Herschell's judgment in *White v Mellin* [1895] A.C. 154 at 164 that he considered that *Evans v Harlow* was decided not merely on the ground that there was no allegation of special damage, but also on the ground that the words were a mere puffing by the defendant of his own goods, and Lindley M.R. in *Hubbuck v Wilkinson* ([1899] 1 Q.B. 86) expressly states (at 92) that the latter "was the ground of the decision". From a careful examination of the case it seems clear that the ground of the decision was (as is expressed in the headnotes to the case in 5 Q.B. 624 and 8 Jur. 571 and in the judgment in 5 Q.B. at 633) that the words did not amount to a libel on the plaintiff either generally or in the way of his trade, but were only a reflection upon goods sold by him which was not actionable without proof of special damage.

[163] Per Lord Herschell L.C. in *White v Mellin* [1895] A.C. at 165. Note, however, that comparative advertising will almost inevitably involve use of the competitor's trade mark. Such a use is not an infringement unless it is not "in accordance with honest practices in industrial or commercial matters" and "takes unfair advantage of, or is detrimental to the distinctive character or repute of the trade mark": Trade Marks Act 1994, s.10(6). Under the Advertising Standards Authority's Code (which is presumably relevant to "honesty") comparative advertisements that include points of comparison must be capable of substantiation and should not include generalised superiority claims based on selective comparisons.

[164] *Schulke & Mayr UK Ltd v Alkapharm UK Ltd* [1999] F.S.R. 161. In Australia the common law has been virtually extinguished by s.52 of the Trade Practices Act 1974, which makes it a wrong for a corporation in the course of trade to engage in misleading or deceptive conduct. Jacob J. in *Schulke & Mayr UK Ltd* at 164, remarked that "members of the Australian bar have much to say by way of thanks to the short section 52". The Consumer Protection from Unfair Trading Regulations 2008, SI 2008/1277 implementing Directive 2005/29/EC impose criminal sanctions for unfair trading practices.

[165] *White v Mellin* [1895] A.C. 154 HL. See also, *Euromoney Institutional Investor plc v Aviation News Ltd* [2013] EWHC 1505 (QB) at [104]–[105].

"Exactly nine pounds of paint were used in each case, and each coat took the same quantity of paint. Judging from the finished work, it is evident that WH & Co's zinc has a slight advantage over Hubbuck's, but for all practical purposes they can be regarded as being in every respect equal."

It was held that the statement was a mere puff and gave the plaintiffs no cause of action, even if it could be proved that the statement was untrue, was maliciously made, and had caused special damage.[166]

Where puffing is exceeded. However where a trader does not limit   **21.21**
himself to a comparison of his goods with those manufactured by another trader and a mere statement that they are inferior to his own, but makes some untrue statement of fact about his rival's goods, e.g. states that they are rotten or contain deleterious ingredients, or that their prices are always higher,[167] an action for malicious falsehood will lie. Hodson L.J. said that "The general position in law is: Comparison—yes; but Disparagement—no"[168] and in one case Walton J. said that " . . . in order to draw the line, one must apply this test, namely, whether a reasonable man would take the claim being made as being a serious claim."[169]

Examples. The defendants published a detailed analysis of the plaintiffs'   **21.22**
artificial manure and their own, in which it was stated that the plaintiffs' manure "appeared to contain a considerable quantity of coprolites, and was altogether an article of low quality". It was held, on proof of special damage, that an action lay.[170]

The defendants, importers of wood blocks for street paving, wrote to a local authority, who were considering a tender by the plaintiffs for paving a street with American gum blocks, a letter advising them before accepting the tender to go and see certain roads which had been paved with American wood blocks, and which the defendants stated were "in a rotten condition", and would remove from their minds any idea of using such material. It was held

---

[166] *Hubbuck v Wilkinson* [1899] 1 Q.B. 86 CA.
[167] *DSG Retail Ltd v Comet Group plc* [2002] EWHC 116 (QB); [2002] F.S.R. 58.
[168] *Cellactite and British Uralite v Robertson, The Times,* July 23, 1957, CA. See also per Cockburn C.J. in *Young v Macrae* (1862) 32 L.J.Q.B. 6 at 9 ("if the declaration had averred that the defendant had falsely represented that the oil of the plaintiffs had a reddish brown tinge, was much thicker, and that it had a more disagreeable odour an action might have been maintained"); per Lord Shand in *White v Mellin* [1895] A.C. 154 at 171 ("if there had been in this case a statement that Mellin's Food was positively injurious, or that it contained deleterious ingredients, and would be hurtful if it were used, I think there would have been a good ground of action"); per Lindley M.R. in *Hubbuck v Wilkinson* [1899] 1 Q.B. 86 at 94 ("if the defendants had made untrue statements concerning the plaintiffs' goods beyond saying that they were inferior to those of the defendants . . . it would not have been right summarily to strike out the statement of claim as disclosing no cause of action"); *Schindler Lifts v Debelak* (1989) 89 A.L.R. 275 Fed Ct of Australia.
[169] *De Beers v International General Electric* [1975] 1 W.L.R. 972 at 978. See also, *Vodafone Group Plc v Orange Personal Communications Services Ltd* [1997] E.M.L.R. 84 (Ch) at 89.
[170] *Western Counties Manure Co. v Lawes Chemical Manure Co* (1874) L.R. 9 Ex. 218.

by the Court of Appeal that such statement was not a mere puffing by the defendants of their own goods, but amounted to an untrue disparagement of the plaintiff's goods, and that, as special damage had been proved, an action lay.[171]

The defendants, manufacturers of equipment for testing industrial materials, circulated a report that the rival equipment of the plaintiffs had been tested by the US government, had been found to be only 40 per cent as effective as the defendants' products and that the government was withdrawing its custom. Holding for the plaintiff the court, having referred to *White v Mellin*, said that:

> "there is a readily observable difference between saying that one's product is, in general, better than another's . . . and asserting, as here, that such other's is only 40% as effective as one's own. The former, arguably, merely expresses an opinion, the truth or falsity of which is difficult or impossible of ascertainment. The latter, however, is an assertion of fact, not subject to the same frailties of proof, implying that the party making the statement is fortified with the substantive facts necessary to make it."[172]

The defendants circulated a pamphlet purporting to present the results of laboratory studies on the comparative performance of their product and that of the plaintiff and concluding that the plaintiff's was inferior. The defendants sought to strike out the action on the basis that every trader is entitled to claim that his product was superior. It was held that the purported scientific basis of the conclusions could lead a reasonable person to think that the claim was being seriously made.[173]

The claimants and defendants were rival retailers of electrical goods. Posters published by the defendants asserted that their prices were invariably lower than those of the claimants, even taking account of special offers and promotions. This was false to the defendants' knowledge. The claimants established a likelihood that customers would be lured away from their stores by the advertising campaign and an injunction was granted on the basis of malicious falsehood.[174]

---

[171] *Alcott v Millar's Karri, etc.* (1904) 91 L.T. 722 CA.
[172] *Testing Systems Inc. v Magnaflux Corp* 251 F.Supp. 286 (1966).
[173] *De Beers v International General Electric* [1975] 1 W.L.R. 972.
[174] *DSG Retail Ltd v Comet Group Plc* [2002] EWHC 116; [2002] F.S.R. 58.

CHAPTER 22

MISUSE OF PRIVATE INFORMATION

SECTION 1. INTRODUCTION

Scope of this chapter. In many cases, the claim for misuse of private **22.1** information now provides an alternative or complementary cause of action to defamation. While the latter is focused on harm to reputation occasioned by false statements, the former is more concerned with harms caused by the communication of personal information. The overlap is most apparent in those cases that involve the publication of false and defamatory details regarding a claimant's private life. An invasion of privacy may take many forms, such as surveillance or the violation of the privacy of one's home, one's correspondence or one's body. The primary aim of this chapter, however, is to consider the variety that involves the wrongful disclosure of information concerning which an individual has a reasonable expectation of privacy.

While there is no general tort of invasion of privacy in English law,[1] there is now effective protection in law against wrongful publication of private information. Under the influence of the Human Rights Act 1998, judges have developed the equitable claim for breach of confidence better to protect the art.8 Convention right to respect for one's private and family life. The past decade has seen an intense period of development in which the general parameters and many particular details of this protection have been set.[2] The claim for misuse of private information is now generally recognised as providing a distinct cause of action. It comprises a two-stage methodology. First, the court will assess whether the claimant held a "reasonable expectation of privacy" over the information in question. If so, in a second stage the

---

[1] *Wainwright v Home Office* [2003] UKHL 53; [2004] 2 A.C. 406. The European Court of Human Rights found a violation of art.8 of the Convention: *Wainwright v UK* (2007) 44 E.H.R.R. 40.

[2] The fact that the legal principles are now well established is reflected in the fact that the House of Lords refused leave to appeal in four key Court of Appeal decisions—*CTB v News Group Newspapers Ltd* [2011] EWHC 1232 (QB) at [21] per Eady J.

court will consider all relevant factors when undertaking an "ultimate balancing test" to determine whether, in light of an intense scrutiny on the circumstances of the case, a remedy should be allowed. Almost invariably in such cases, the claimant is intent on preventing the publication of the information in question. The result is that most cases are effectively determined at the interim stage, with the preferred remedy being an interim order. While final trials of claims for misuse of private information have occurred, they have been few in number.

In addition, through the Data Protection Act 1998, Parliament has provided legal remedies that, while ostensibly oriented towards addressing other problems, can also serve to ameliorate some publication harms. Claims under the Act are sometimes linked with claims at common law.

22.2 Development of the claim. The equitable claim for breach of confidence rests upon a threefold test. It requires that information that has the "necessary quality of confidence" about it has been "imparted in circumstances importing an obligation of confidence", and that there has been an "unauthorised use" of that information to the detriment of the party who imparted it.[3] In some cases involving the disclosure of private—as opposed to confidential—information, claimants were able to prove these elements of the test without difficulty. In many other cases, however, claimants had difficulty in satisfying the second requirement. Availability of the claim was dependent on whether the private information had been imparted in the course of a pre-existing relationship of confidence. This was considered unsatisfactory by many, and even prior to the advent of the Human Rights Act judges had mooted the possibility of extending the cause of action. In 1990, in a government secrets case, Lord Goff said that it was:

> "well settled that a duty of confidence may arise in equity independently of [information being imparted in confidence] and I have expressed the circumstances in which the duty arises in broad terms, not merely to embrace those cases where a third party receives information from a person who is under a duty of confidence in respect of it, knowing that it has been disclosed by that person to him in breach of his duty of confidence, but also to include certain situations, beloved of law teachers—where an obviously confidential document is wafted by an electric fan out of a window into a crowded street, or where an obviously confidential document, such as a private diary, is dropped in a public place, and is then picked up by a passer-by."[4]

In *Hellewell v Chief Constable of Derbyshire*, Laws J. suggested further that:

---

[3] *Coco v AN Clark (Engineers) Ltd* [1968] F.S.R. 415 per Megarry J.at 419.
[4] *Att-Gen v Guardian Newspapers (No.2)* [1990] 1 A.C. 109 HL at 218.

"if someone with a telephoto lens were to take from a distance and with no authority a picture of another engaged in some private act, his subsequent disclosure of the photograph would, in my judgment, as surely amount to a breach of confidence as if he had found or stolen a letter or diary in which the act was recounted and proceeded to publish it. In such a case, the law would protect what might reasonably be called a right of privacy, although the name accorded to the cause of action would be breach of confidence."[5]

The acceptance that a prior relationship is not a necessary element of a claim has been a major basis of the expansion (or transformation) of the law of confidence to embrace the protection of private information.

An important and necessary step in the development of the claim for misuse of private information was the judicial recognition that Convention rights might influence relationships between not only the individual and the state, but also between private individuals. That is, encouraged by the Strasbourg court's insistence that art.8 entails positive obligations for the state,[6] the English courts recognised that Convention rights should enjoy some measure of "horizontal effect".[7] Much invasion of informational privacy is perpetrated by private individuals, whether on an individual basis, by institutionalised media organisations, or by others who wish subsequently to engage with the media. Without the horizontal effect of Convention rights, the English law would remain largely blind to such wrongs. The result, as Lord Nicholls explained, was that:

"the cause of action has now firmly shaken off the limiting constraint of the need for an initial confidential relationship . . . the law imposes a 'duty of confidence' whenever a person receives information he knows or ought to know is fairly and reasonably to be regarded as confidential . . . the values enshrined in Articles 8 and 10 are now part of the cause of action for breach of confidence . . . and are as much applicable in disputes between individuals or between an individual and a non-governmental body such as a newspaper as they are in disputes between individuals and a public authority."[8]

---

[5] *Hellewell v Chief Constable of Derbyshire* [1995] 1 W.L.R. 804 at 807. For a practical example, see *Donnelly v Amalgamated Television Services Pty Ltd* (1998) 45 N.S.W.L.R. 570.

[6] In *Von Hannover v Germany* (2005) 40 E.H.R.R. 1, for example, the European Court reiterated that

"although the object of Article 8 is essentially that of protecting the individual against arbitrary interference by the public authorities, it does not merely compel the State to abstain from such interference: in addition to this primarily negative undertaking, there may be positive obligations inherent in an effective respect for private or family life. These obligations may involve the adoption of measures designed to secure respect for private life even in the sphere of the relations of individuals between themselves" (at [57]).

See also, *Glaser v United Kingdom* (2001) 33 E.H.R.R. 1 at [63].

[7] *Campbell v Mirror Group Newspaper Ltd* [2004] UKHL 22; [2004] 2 A.C. 457.

[8] Ibid at [14]–[17]. See also, at [50] per Lord Hoffmann; *Mosley v News Group Newspapers Ltd* [2008] EWHC 1777 (QB); [2008] E.M.L.R. 20 at [7] per Eady J., and *McKennitt v Ash* [2006] EWCA Civ 1714 per Buxton L.J. at [11].

Under the new methodology, emphasis is placed, first, on the particular circumstances of the case, and secondly on the proportionality of any restrictions permitted upon the privacy and/or expression rights. The analysis of rights has infused the legal doctrine.

22.3 Other systems of law. In terms of the protection of privacy, there has been a sharp doctrinal contrast between the English common law and the common law in the United States where, in the twentieth century, there developed a general tort of invasion of privacy[9] under the four categories of offensive disclosure of private facts,[10] offensive intrusion into seclusion,[11] placing the plaintiff in a "false light" in the public eye[12] and wrongful appropriation of the plaintiff's name or personality.[13] The reach of the American law of privacy is significantly limited by a number of factors. For example, the plaintiff is unable to claim absolute seclusion or freedom from observation.

> "On the public street, or in any other public place, the plaintiff has no legal right to be let alone . . . Neither is it . . . an invasion to take his photograph in such a place, since this amounts to nothing more than making a record, not differing essentially from a full written description, of a public sight which anyone would be free to see. On the other hand, when the plaintiff is confined to a hospital bed, and when he is merely in the seclusion of his home, the making of a photograph is an invasion of a private right, of which he is entitled to complain."[14]

Furthermore, even before the development of the influence of the First Amendment on defamation law[15] it was plain that prevention of intrusion and disclosure of private facts had to be balanced against the public's legitimate interest in news[16] or in the lives and activities of public figures in so far as they

---

[9] See Dobbs, *Law of Torts* (2000). The origin is the influential article by Warren and Brandeis, "The Right to Privacy" (1890) 4 *Harvard L. Rev* 193. There is no express recognition of a right of privacy in the US Constitution but the Supreme Court has recognised certain specific constitutional guarantees as creating "zones of privacy" which impose limits on governmental power. See, e.g. *Griswold v Connecticut*, 381 U.S. 479 (1965) and *Roe v Wade*, 410 U.S. 113 (1973).

[10] E.g. the revelation that the claimant has a shady past which he has long since lived down: *Melvin v Reid*, 297 P. 91 (Cal. 1931). Cf. the Rehabilitation of Offenders Act 1974, Ch.18, above.

[11] E.g. telephone tapping: *La Crone v Ohio Bell Telephone Co*, 182 N.E.2d 15 (Oh., 1961).

[12] E.g. by falsely presenting the financial position of a family so as to make it an object of pity: *Cantrell v Forest City Publishing Co*, 419 U.S. 245 (1974). There is a considerable overlap here with the law of defamation, but the false light theory does not require the plaintiff to show that people would think less of him, merely that the way he was portrayed would be highly offensive to a reasonable person. Consider, e.g. *Youssoupoff v MGM* (1934) 50 T.L.R. 581 CA para.2.6, above (false imputation that plaintiff had been raped).

[13] E.g. by using the plaintiff's likeness in a non-defamatory way in an advertising campaign: *Flake v Greenboro News Co*, 195 S.E. 55 (N.C. 1938).

[14] Prosser and Keeton, *Torts*, 5th edn (1984), pp.855–856 (citations omitted).

[15] See para.15.31, above.

[16] See, e.g. *Jacova v Southern Radio and Television*, 83 S.2d 34 (Fla., 1955) (P, an innocent customer, caught up in televised gambling raid on cigar store; no cause of action); *Shulman v Group W Products Inc.*, 955 P.2d 469 (Cal., 1998) (videotape of accident). This may extend to the family of a person caught up in newsworthy events. See e.g. *Jenkins v Dell Publishing*, 143 F.Supp. 952; 251 F.2d 447 (CA. 3 1958).

bore on public activity. In the "false light" cases the First Amendment restrictions on defamation liability have been applied by analogy to invasion of privacy, the recklessness or negligence of the defendant having relation not to the falsity of the stated "facts" but to the "light" which they cast on the plaintiff.

For many years New Zealand followed the same line as English law but in *Hosking v Runting*[17] a majority of the New Zealand Court of Appeal held that a tort of invasion of privacy should be recognised as part of the common law of New Zealand.[18] In Australia the High Court in *Australian Broadcasting Corporation v Lenah Game Meats Pty Ltd*[19] held that there was no bar to the development of such a liability but the only superior court decision since then has rejected a tort of invasion of privacy.[20] In South Africa privacy is recognized as falling under the *actio injuriarum* and also receives constitutional protection.[21]

Section 2. Reasonable Expectation of Privacy

Elements of the first stage test. The first step in the analysis of a claim   **22.4** for misuse of private information asks whether the claimant has a "reasonable expectation of privacy" in the information that has been or may be disclosed. This is an objective question. Necessarily, a preliminary task must be to ascertain whether the disclosure comprises information that relates to, or identifies, the particular claimant at all. This issue will normally be straightforward to determine. It may become important, however, in cases where a claimant has not been specifically named but has been identified by reference to a category of persons, or where attempts have been made to obscure the identity of the person to whom personal information relates.[22] Beyond this, a

---

[17] [2004] NZCA 34; [2005] 1 N.Z.L.R. 1.

[18] The New Zealand Bill of Rights Act deliberately omits any guarantee of privacy and the New Zealand Privacy Act 1993 does not create a remedy by civil action.

[19] [2001] HCA 63; 208 C.L.R. 199.

[20] *Giller v Procopets* [2004] VSC 113. *Contra*, two lower court decisions: *Grosse v Purvis* (2003) Aust Torts Reports 81–706 and *Doe v Australian Broadcasting Corp* [2007] VCC 281. On appeal in *Giller v Procopets,* equitable damages for breach of confidence were awarded and it was not thought necessary to consider whether a general tort of invasion of privacy should be recognised: [2008] VSCA 236. See also, *Doe v Yahoo!7 Pty Ltd* [2013] QDC 181 (refusal to strike out claims for breach of confidence and invasion of privacy)

In 2006, a Privacy Bill was introduced into the Irish Seanad but this has not so far been taken further. It would become a tort to violate the privacy to which an individual is reasonably entitled in all the circumstances by subjecting him to surveillance, disclosing information obtained by surveillance, using his name, likeness or voice without consent for advertising or financial gain or disclosing documents about the individual or information obtained therefrom.

[21] See *NM v Smith* [2007] ZACC 6; 2007 (5) SA 250.

[22] See, e.g. *Green Corns Ltd v CLA Verley Group Ltd* [2005] EWHC 958 (QB) at [61].

claimant must show that the information at issue is somehow private in character. As Lord Hope put it in *Campbell v MGN Ltd*, "the question is what a reasonable person of ordinary sensibilities would feel if she was placed in the same position as the claimant".[23] Usually, this involves demonstrating that the information falls into one of a number of categories that are widely acknowledged as comprising private information.[24] The Court of Appeal has said that "in the majority of cases the question of whether there is an interest capable of being the subject of a claim for privacy should not be allowed to be the subject of detailed argument", and that "usually the answer . . . will be obvious".[25] Generalisations are not determinative, however, and the information in question will be considered by the court in its own context.[26] The court will engage in a close assessment of all the circumstances of the case at hand[27]; "there is no bright line which can be drawn between what is private and what is not."[28] In particular, the relevance of a number of "limiting principles" will also be assessed.[29] Potentially relevant matters will include the extent to which the information in question is already in the "public domain", is "trivial or anodyne", or has been published with "consent".

22.5 **What information is private.** Accepting that there are dangers in generalisation, certain situations may be recognised as prima facie involving private information. These include the state of a person's physical or mental

---

[23] [2004] UKHL 22; [2004] 2 A.C. 457 at [99].

[24] Insight can be drawn from a range of sources: first, the growing body of legal precedent to be found in domestic first instance and appeal courts; secondly, the categories of "sensitive personal data" set out in s.2 of the Data Protection Act 1998—see ibid. at [62] per Tugendhat J.; thirdly, useful inferences can be drawn from the Strasbourg jurisprudence under art.8, and finally, given that under s.12(4)(b) of the Human Rights Act 1998 the court is to have particular regard to any "relevant privacy code" where proceedings relate to journalistic, literary or artistic material, the PCC *Editors' Code of Practice* or the *Ofcom Broadcast Code* (although note the comment of Lord Woolf in *A v B plc* [2002] EWCA Civ 337; [2003] Q.B. 195 at [11(xv)]).

[25] *A v B Plc* [2002] EWCA Civ 337; [2003] Q.B. 195 at [11(vii)].

[26] *Lord Browne of Madingley v Associated Newspapers Ltd* [2007] EWHC 202 (QB); [2007] E.M.L.R. 19 per Eady J. at [40]–[42].

[27] *Murray v Big Pictures (UK) Ltd* [2008] EWCA Civ 446 per Sir Anthony Clarke M.R. at [36]. In *A v B* [2005] EWHC 1651 (QB), [2005] E.M.L.R. 36 at [21], Eady J. noted that consideration of the nature of the information alone "would mean that everyone would pass that test automatically and the only scope for differentiation between individual applicants would arise at the stage of assessing proportionality."

[28] *Australian Broadcasting Corp v Lenah Game Meats Pty Ltd* [2001] HCA 63 per Gleeson C.J. at [43], cited with approval in *A v B plc* [2002] EWCA Civ 337; [2003] Q.B. 195 per Lord Woolf M.R. at [11(vii)].

[29] This was the language adopted by Lord Goff in his consideration of the *Spycatcher* breach of confidence case: *Attorney General v Guardian Newspapers Ltd (No 2)* [1990] 1 A.C. 109 at 282. Lord Goff referred to three limiting principles, concerning information that is already in the public domain, trivial or anodyne information, and information that it is in the public interest should be disclosed. Of these, only the first two are relevant to the first stage assessment of a claim for misuse of private information, whereas the third is relevant to the second stage ultimate balancing test.

health or condition,[30] a person's physical characteristics (nudity),[31] a person's racial or ethnic characteristics,[32] a person's emotional state (in particular in the context of distress, injury or bereavement),[33] the generality of personal and family relationships,[34] a person's sexual orienta-

---

[30] Information concerning the state of an individual's health is widely considered to "fall firmly" within the category of private matters *McKennitt v Ash* [2005] EWHC 3003 (QB) per Eady J. at [142], and [2006] EWCA Civ 1714; [2008] Q.B.73 per Buxton L.J at [23]. See also, *X Health Authority v Y* [1988] 2 All ER 648 (doctors' HIV status); *W v Egdell* [1990] Ch. 359 (psychiatric report); *Archer v Williams* [2003] EWHC 1670 (QB) at [34]–[35] (details of cosmetic surgery); *Campbell v MGN Ltd* [2004] UKHL 22; [2004] 2 A.C. 457 (treatment for drug addiction); *Cornelius v De Taranto* [2001] EWCA Civ 1511; [2002] E.M.L.R. 6 (mental health); *British Pregnancy Advisory Service v The Person Using the Alias Pablo Escobar* [2012] EWHC 572 (QB) (advice sought from advisory service). See also *Editions Plon v France* (2006) 42 E.H.R.R. 36 (treatment for cancer); *Z v Finland* (1997) E.H.R.R. 371 (HIV status and other medical information); *PG and JH v United Kingdom* (2008) 46 E.H.R.R. 51 (gender dysphoria). The Information Tribunal has held that an obligation of confidence in respect of medical records may survive the patient's death: *Bluck v Information Comr* (2007) 98 B.M.L.R. 1; [2008] W.T.L.R. 1. The law will sometimes defend privacy interests of this type even when there are relatively strong countervailing public interest considerations in play—see, e.g. *A v B* [2005] EWHC 1651 (QB), [2005] E.M.L.R. 36 at [32].

[31] *Holden v Express Newspapers,* unreported, June 7, 2001 (QB); *AMP v Persons Unknown* [2011] EWHC 3454 (TCC); *Rocknroll v News Group Newspapers Ltd* [2013] EWHC 24 (Ch) at [6]; *ABK v KDT* [2013] EWHC 1192 (QB). See also, *Douglas v Hello! Ltd* [2005] EWCA Civ 595 at [105].

[32] Such information is considered sensitive personal data in s.2 of the Data Protection Act 1998.

[33] In *McKennitt v Ash* [2005] EWHC 3003 (QB) at [80], Eady J. stated that "one's reactions and communications to a friend in the immediate aftermath of personal bereavement are surely a classic example of material in respect of which there would [be] a 'reasonable expectation' that one's privacy would be respected". See also on appeal: [2006] EWCA Civ 1714, [2008] Q.B.73 per Buxton L.J. at [20]; *Campbell v Mirror Group Newspapers Ltd* [2004] UKHL 22; [2004] 2 A.C. 457 per Lord Hoffmann at [75]; *Peck v United Kingdom* (2003) 36 E.H.R.R. 41 at [62]–[63]; *Egeland v Norway* (2010) 50 E.H.R.R. 2.

[34] While the matter of how far the law will protect different variations on the theme of personal relationships as private (heterosexual or homosexual; marital or extra-marital; faithful or adulterous; fleeting or permanent) has been somewhat "turbulent" in jurisprudential terms, the law has now settled on the position that it is not appropriate, aside from instances of manifest criminality (e.g. *BUQ v HRE* [2012] EWHC 774 (QB) at [61]), for the courts to adopt a priori perspectives on the moral appropriateness of disparate forms of human behaviour—see *CC v AB* [2006] EWHC 3083 (QB) per Eady J. at [22]–[28]; *Mosley v News Group Newspapers Ltd* [2008] EWHC 1777 (QB); [2008] E.M.L.R. 20. An individual's "relationship status" is private information—see *Applause Store Productions Ltd v Raphael* [2008] EWHC 1781 (QB) per H.H.J. Parkes QC at [4]; *CC v AB* [2006] EWHC 3083 (QB) at [39]. Of course, in some cases even the privacy associated with intimate personal relationships might be outweighed by some competing public interest or other limiting principle—see *CC v AB* [2006] EWHC 3083 (QB) at [37]; *KGM v News Group Newspapers Ltd* [2010] EWHC 3145 (QB) at [39]. Moreover, an individual's privacy interest in preventing disclosure of the basic facts of his personal life will usually be much less strong than that in the details thereof—e.g. *A v B plc* [2001] 1 W.L.R. 2341 at 2355; *Lord Browne of Madingley v Associated Newspapers Ltd* [2007] EWHC 202 (QB); [2007] E.M.L.R. 19 at [53]; *Terry (originally LNS) v Persons Unknown* [2010] EWHC 119 (QB) at [68]–[69]; [2010] E.M.L.R. 16; *X and Y v Persons Unknown* [2006] EWHC 2783 at [38]; *Trimingham v Associated Newspapers Ltd* [2012] EWHC 1296 (QB) at [285].

While not normally a matter of privacy, the general character of familial relationships may sometimes be sufficiently private as to warrant protection in law—e.g. *T (by her litigation friend the Official Solicitor) v BBC* [2007] EWHC 1683; *Gold v Cox* [2012] EWHC 272 (QB). It may be that matters of parentage may sometimes be similarly private—e.g. *SKA v CRH* [2012] EWHC

tion,[35] the intimate details of personal relationships,[36] information conveyed in the course of personal relationships,[37] a person's political opinions and affiliations,[38] a person's religious commitment,[39] personal financial and tax-related information,[40] personal communications and correspondence,[41] mat-

---

766 (QB); *AAA v Associated Newspapers Ltd* [2012] EWHC 2103 (QB) ; [2013] E.M.L.R. 2. For the future, the impact of the Welfare Reform Act 2009—which would appear to require the name of the father of the child to be included on the public record in form of the child's birth certificate save in very limited circumstances—may have a bearing. This was mentioned in *AAA v Associated Newspapers Ltd* (at [106]) but deemed irrelevant as the Act was not in force at the relevant time.

[35] *Applause Store Productions Ltd v Raphael* [2008] EWHC 1781 (QB) at [4]; *CBL v Persons Unknown* [2011] EWHC 904 (QB); *Laskey, Jaggard and Brown v United Kingdom* (1997) 24 EHRR 39 at [36]; *PG and JH v United Kingdom* (2008) 46 E.H.R.R. 51 at [56].

[36] In *Mosley v News Group Newspapers Ltd* [2008] EWHC 1777 (QB); [2008] E.M.L.R. 20, Eady J. stated that

"one is usually on safe ground in concluding that anyone indulging in sexual activity is entitled to a degree of privacy—especially if it is on private property and between consenting adults (paid or unpaid) . . . people's sex lives are to be regarded as essentially their own business" (at [98]–[100]).

See also, *Applause Store Productions Ltd v Raphael* [2008] EWHC 1781 (QB) at [4]; *Archer v Williams* [2003] EWHC 1670 (QB) at [34]–[35]; *Stephens v Avery* [1988] Ch. 449 at 454; *CC v AB* [2006] EWHC 3083 (QB); *DFT v TFD* [2010] EWHC 2335 (QB); *AMM v HXW* [2010] EWHC 2457 (QB); *Ntuli v Donald* [2010] EWCA Civ 1276; [2011] 1 W.L.R. 294; *MNB v News Group Newspapers Ltd* [2011] EWHC 528 (QB); *NEJ v Wood* [2011] EWHC 1972 (QB); *ETK v News Group Newspapers* [2011] EWCA Civ 439, [2011] 1 W.L.R. 1827; *MJN v News Group Newspapers Ltd* [2011] EWHC 1192 (QB); *Contostavlos v Mendahun* [2012] EWHC 850 (QB). See also, *Dudgeon v United Kingdom* (1981) 4 E.H.R.R. 149; *Laskey, Jaggard and Brown v United Kingdom* (1997) 24 E.H.R.R. 39; *Tammer v Estonia* (2003) 37 E.H.R.R. 43. The case of *Theakston v MGN Ltd* [2002] EWHC 137 (QB), [2002] E.M.L.R.22 can by now be considered to have been wrongly decided on this point, due no doubt to a conception of the cause of action that was over-wedded to the traditional notion of confidentiality.

[37] E.g. *Lord Browne of Madingley v Associated Newspapers Ltd* [2007] EWCA Civ 295; [2008] Q.B. 103 at [34]–[37]; (see also, Eady J. at first instance: [2007] EWHC 202 (QB), [2007] E.M.L.R. 19 at [33]–[42] and [45]–[46]); *WXY v Gewanter* [2012] EWHC 496 (QB) at [78]. In this regard, legal protection may extend even to cover information communicated between close friends or dinner party guests—e.g. *Lord Browne of Madingley v Associated Newspapers Ltd* [2007] EWHC 202 (QB), [2007] E.M.L.R. 19 at [59]; *HRH Prince of Wales v Associated Newspapers Ltd* [2006] EWCA Civ 1776; [2008] Ch. 57; *McKennitt v Ash* [2005] EWHC 3003 (QB) at [17] and [132] (although, with regard to the facts underpinning some elements of the claim in that case, note comments at [147], [149], [152], [154] and [158]).

[38] E.g. *Applause Store Productions Ltd v Raphael* [2008] EWHC 1781 (QB) at [4]. See also, s.2 of the Data Protection Act 1998. Affiliations may include those with political parties, trades unions, charities, campaigning organisations, and so on.

[39] E.g. *Applause Store Productions Ltd v Raphael* [2008] EWHC 1781 (QB) at [4]. See also, s.2 of the Data Protection Act 1998.

[40] E.g. *AB v Barristers Benevolent Association Ltd (Rev 1)* [2011] EWHC 3413 (QB); *Lord Browne of Madingley v Associated Newspapers Ltd* [2007] EWHC 202 (QB), [2007] E.M.L.R. 19 at [61]–[65]; *John Reid Enterprises Ltd v Pell* [1999] E.M.L.R. 675; *McKennitt v Ash* [2005] EWHC 3003 (QB) at [124] and [157]. Whether the judge was correct in the last of these cases to find that such information was private in nature was one basis on which the application for permission to appeal was granted—see *McKennitt v Ash* [2006] EWCA Civ 778 at [7]. The Court of Appeal ultimately affirmed the judge's rulings—see [2006] EWCA Civ 1714 at [74]–[77] and [84].

[41] One's correspondence with others, whether conducted by means of letter, telephone conversation, email, SMS text messaging, or other forms of digital communication, is presumptively private in nature—see e.g. *Maccaba v Lichtenstein (misuse of private information)* [2004] EWHC

ters pertaining to the home,[42] past involvement in criminal behaviour,[43] and involvement in crime as a victim or a witness.[44] Information relating to children may be of such particular sensitivity such that it is generally deemed to be private in character.[45] Conversely, the courts have considered certain types of information not to be private. These categories include corporate

---

1579 (QB) per Gray J. at [4]; *Archer v Williams* [2003] EWHC 1670 (QB) at [34]–[35]; *SKA v CRH* [2012] EWHC 766 (QB); *Abbey v Gilligan* [2012] EWHC 3217 (QB), [2013] E.M.L.R. 12; *Goldsmith v BCD* [2011] EWHC 674 (QB).

[42] E.g. *McKennitt v Ash* [2005] EWHC 3003 at [135]–[138] (expressly confirmed on appeal—see [2006] EWCA Civ 1714 per Buxton L.J. at [22]. See also, *Archer v Williams* [2003] EWHC 1670 (QB) at [34]–[35] (residential security arrangements).

[43] From one perspective, that of "open justice", it is anathema to suggest that the disclosure of prior convictions or alleged criminality should be prevented by law. Conversely, it can be argued that, at least in some circumstances, public policy demands that such information be protected. In *Green Corns Ltd v CLA Verley Group Ltd* [2005] EWHC 958 (QB) at [58] (citing *R v Chief Constable of North Wales Police ex p Thorpe* [1998] 3 W.L.R. 57), Tugendhat J. noted that where a person is a sexual offender, the public policy in restricting disclosure is reflected in Home Office guidance. If the individuals involved are juveniles, then specific protections may be afforded to them. In such cases, the interest that is balanced against freedom of expression is derived less from the concept of privacy per se and more from a deeper concern for the autonomy and vulnerability of the individual concerned—e.g. *Venables v News Group Newspapers Ltd* [2001] Fam. 430.

A similar argument can be built upon the passage of time. Arguably, once a sufficient period of time has passed, the autonomy of the individual and the public interest in their capacity to reintegrate into society might require that details of his or her prior criminal involvement should be considered private, and disclosable only in circumstances where some countervailing public interests requires it—see, e.g. the views expressed by Lords Hope and Neuberger in *R. (on the application of L) (FC) v Comr of Police of the Metropolis* [2009] UKSC 3; [2010] 1 A.C. 410. In *A v B* [2005] EWHC 1651 (QB), [2005] E.M.L.R. 36 at [33], Eady J. allowed that "there might be circumstances in which the court would think it right for spent convictions or past acquittals not to be revealed to the general public". In *Elliott v Chief Constable of Wiltshire, The Times*, December 5, 1996, however, it was held that details of the plaintiff's convictions, having been announced in open court, could not be the subject of confidence. See also, *KJO v XIM* [2011] EWHC 1768 (QB) at [16].

The Rehabilitation of Offenders Act 1974 protects the convicted person from having to answer questions about them, prohibits his being prejudiced by his failure to reveal them and limits the availability of justification in defamation proceedings to cases where the statement about the spent conviction is made without malice—see above Ch.18—but notably it does not provide any general sanction for disclosure of such a conviction and it has been held that it does not make information about them confidential—see *L v Law Society* [2008] EWCA Civ 811.

Information regarding the commission or alleged commission of any offence, information regarding any proceedings in respect of committed or alleged offence, or information regarding the disposal of or the sentence in any proceedings falls within the definition of sensitive personal data in s.2 of the Data Protection Act 1998, e.g. *Chief Constable of Humberside v Information Comr* [2009] EWCA Civ 1079.

[44] E.g. s.1 of the Sexual Offences (Amendment) Act 1992.

[45] In *Murray v Big Pictures (UK) Ltd* [2007] EWHC 1908 (Ch); [2007] E.M.L.R. 22, Patten J. struck out a claim brought on behalf of a child photographed while being pushed in a pram along a street by his parents. The Court of Appeal rejected the view that the law should apply in the same way to children as it does to adults—[2008] EWCA Civ 446; [2009] Ch. 481—and reinstated the claim (which was subsequently settled). As a "relevant privacy code" for the purposes of s.12(4) of the Human Rights Act 1998, it is noteworthy that cl.6 of the PCC Editors' Code provides that the interests of the child should normally be paramount. The interests of the child, however, do not have an automatic precedence over the Convention rights of others. Rather, the court will accord particular weight in the balance to the rights of any children likely to be affected by disclosure—e.g. *K v Newsgroup Newspapers* [2011] EWCA Civ 439; [2011] 1 W.L.R.

information,[46] a person's physical location,[47] involvement in current criminal activity,[48] and the identity of an author.[49]

22.6 Limiting factors: public domain in general. Even if seemingly private in nature, there will usually be no reasonable expectation of privacy in information that is already in the public domain.[50] This principle has carried over to the claim for misuse of private information from that for breach of confidence.[51] The determination as to precisely when information will be deemed already to be in the public domain is more nuanced in this new context however; it is less automatic in the context of privacy than confidentiality of government secrets.[52] The matter will often be a question of degree.[53]

1827 at [19]. The age and relative vulnerability of the child in question will influence the weight of the factor in the analysis—e.g. *Spelman v Express Newspapers* [2012] EWHC 355 (QB) at [55] and [72]; *BUQ v HRE* [2012] EWHC 774 (QB) at [68].

[46] E.g. *Lord Browne of Madingley v Associated Newspapers Ltd* [2007] EWHC 202 (QB); [2007] E.M.L.R. 19 at [43]–[44]. The Court of Appeal appeared more willing to interpret the judge's determinations on this point as involving an outweighing of the interest in confidentiality or privacy by a stronger public interest in disclosure—see [2007] EWCA Civ 295; [2008] Q.B. 103 at [52]–[55]. Individuals may in some cases have a reasonable expectation of privacy in relation to their business affairs. but "companies' rights of confidentiality will usually be governed by the equitable principles of 'old-fashioned' breach of confidence or by specific contractual provisions"—*Ambrosiadou v Coward* [2010] EWHC 1794 (QB), [2010] 2 F.L.R. 1775 at [33].

[47] E.g. *Applause Store Productions Ltd v Raphael* [2008] EWHC 1781 (QB) at [4]. The addition of some further information—for example, that the address that an individual was visiting was that of a brothel or an abortion clinic—would likely be sufficient to see the law treat such information as private in character—e.g. *AM v News Group Newspapers Ltd* [2012] EWHC 308 (QB) (a property let to the family of Abu Qatada).

[48] Two possible means of approaching the question of current alleged criminality exist under the claim for misuse of private information. On one hand, it could be argued that the criminality of impugned behaviour provides a public interest justification for denying a claim. On the other hand, it could be argued that for reasons of public policy criminal behaviour is not to be understood as "private" at the first stage of analysis—for an analysis on these lines, see *A v B* [2005] EWHC 1651 (QB), [2005] E.M.L.R. 36 at [32] per Eady J.

[49] E.g. *The author of a blog v Times Newspapers Ltd* [2009] EWHC 1358 (QB), [2009] E.M.L.R. 22. See also, *Mahmood v Galloway* [2006] EWHC 1286 (QB).

[50] E.g. *McKennitt v Ash* [2006] EWCA Civ 1714, [2006] EWCA Civ 1714 at [53] per Buxton L.J.; *Douglas v Hello! Ltd* [2005] EWCA Civ 595, [2006] Q.B. 125 per Lord Phillips M.R. at [105]; *Green Corns Ltd v CLA Verley Group Ltd* [2005] EWHC 958 (QB) at [78] per Tugendhat J. The rule is reflected in the fact that interim orders restricting publication generally include a "public domain proviso" permitting publishers to reiterate material that is already publicly available—see *A v B* [2005] EWHC 1651 (QB), [2005] E.M.L.R. 36 at [16]; *Kelly v BBC* [2001] Fam. 59 at 91–93; *X and Y v Persons Unknown* [2006] EWHC 2783 (QB) at [62]–[67]; *AMM v HXW* [2010] EWHC 2457 (QB) at [7]; *POI v Lina, The Person Known As* [2011] EWHC 25 (QB) at [3]; *CTB v News Group Newspapers Ltd* [2011] EWHC 1232 (QB) at [27].

[51] *Attorney General v Guardian Newspapers Ltd (No.2)* [1990] 1 A.C. 109 per Lord Goff at 282; *Coco v AN Clark (Engineers) Ltd* [1968] F.S.R. 415 per Megarry J. at 419.

[52] *CTB v News Group Newspapers Ltd* [2011] EWHC 1232 (QB) at [28].

[53] *Attorney General v Guardian Newspapers Ltd (No.2)* [1990] 1 A.C. 109 per Sir John Donaldson M.R. at 177. In *OBG v Allan* [2007] UKHL 21, [2008] 1 A.C. 1 at [122], Lord Hoffmann explained that "once information gets into the public domain . . . there is no point in the law providing protection . . . but . . . whether there is still a point in enforcing the obligation of confidence depends on the facts". See also, *Re X and Y (Children)* [2004] EWHC 762 (Fam) at [66]. Section 12(4) of the Human Rights Act 1998 emphasises this point when requiring courts

There is a qualitative difference, for instance, between appearing physically in a public place with the natural exposure to others present that this brings, and the publication of photographs of the occasion in some mass media platform.[54] Similarly, the fact that information is known to some people does not mean that wider publication would have no significant effect.[55] Another similar factual scenario arises increasingly often in the context of the reproduction in the mainstream media of personal information published on social networking websites.[56]

At some tipping point, however, the general availability of some given information will expunge any reasonable expectation of privacy. For instance, in *Mosley v News Group Newspapers Ltd*—a case in which an online article had already been viewed several hundred thousand times and a video more than 1.5 million times—both items were incontrovertibly in the public domain such that no interim order enjoining further publication was awarded.[57]

A range of additional factors may influence the determination of whether information is sufficiently in the public domain so as to preclude a claim for misuse of private information. These include whether the information has been published in other jurisdictions,[58] the extent to which "jigsaw" revela-

---

to "have particular regard to . . . the extent to which the material has . . . become available to the public" whenever the proceedings relate to journalistic material.

[54] *Campbell v Mirror Group Newspapers Ltd* [2004] UKHL 22; [2004] 2 A.C. 457 at [74]; *Peck v United Kingdom* (2003) 36 E.H.R.R. 41 at [62]. See also, *Blair v Associated Newspapers Ltd*, unreported, March 10, 2000 (QB); *West v BBC*, unreported, June 10, 2002 (QB). Notably, in *B v H Bauer Publishing Ltd* [2002] E.M.L.R. 8 at [25]–[26], Eady J. entertained the possibility that even publication in a national newspaper may sometimes be insufficient to introduce private information into the public domain. Conversely, there is no "general rule . . . that there is always a reasonable expectation of privacy in respect of any personal information merely because it has not been widely published in a newspaper"—*KGM v News Group Newspapers Ltd* [2010] EWHC 3145 (QB) at [22] per Eady J.

[55] E.g. *A v B plc* [2001] 1 W.L.R. 2341 at 2355; *Green Corns Ltd v CLA Verley Group Ltd* [2005] EWHC 958 (QB) at [81]; *HRH the Prince of Wales v Associated Newspapers Ltd* [2006] EWCA Civ 1776; [2008] Ch. 57 at [42]; *Terry (originally LNS) v Persons Unknown* [2010] EWHC 119 (QB); [2010] E.M.L.R. 16 at [130]; *WXY v Gewanter* [2012] EWHC 1601 (QB); *EWQ v GFD* [2012] EWHC 2182 (QB).

[56] E.g. *Rocknroll v News Group Newspapers Ltd* [2013] EWHC 24 (Ch) at [25].

[57] [2008] EWHC 687 (QB). Eady J. noted that
"the Court must always be conscious of the practical realities and limitations as to what can be achieved . . . a point *may* be reached where the information sought to be restricted, by an order of the Court, is so widely and generally accessible 'in the public domain' that such an injunction would make no practical difference . . . the Court should guard against slipping into playing the role of King Canute . . . even though an order may be desirable for the protection of privacy . . . there may come a point where it would simply serve no useful purpose and would merely be characterised, in the traditional terminology, as a *brutum fulmen*. It is inappropriate for the Court to make vain gestures . . . the dam has effectively burst" (at [33]–[35]).

[58] Historically, the view has been that even widespread publication of private information in a foreign jurisdiction may be insufficient to see it enter the public domain for the purposes of English law—e.g. *Attorney General v Guardian Newspapers Ltd (No.2)* [1990] 1 A.C. 109 per Lord Keith at 260; *Venables v News Group Newspapers* [2001] Fam. 430 at 470–471 per Dame Elizabeth Butler-Sloss P, cf. *Long Beach Ltd v Global Witness Ltd* [2007] EWHC 1980 (QB). Clearly, the ready availability of material on the internet may sometimes affect the position.

tion allows the general public access to new information,[59] the conduct of the publisher,[60] the specificity of information already in the public domain,[61] and the passage of time.[62]

A further issue with regard to the public domain concerns whether the test should be that information is actually known by a sufficiently large number of people in the given audience, or whether it is enough that it is merely accessible to them. In *Spycatcher*, Lord Goff suggested a criterion of "general accessibility".[63] Other judges have viewed the matter differently, and concluded that the mere fact that information is accessible somewhere in public records or from some other esoteric source will not be enough to disqualify the information from being private.[64] The same point can be made with regard to unheralded publication on the internet.[65] It is submitted that Lord Goff's concept of "general accessibility" should in this context be understood as meaning 'being known or easily knowable to a substantial number of people'.

---

[59] Courts have increasingly conceded the possibility that the combination of two separate items of information that are themselves both in the public domain can amount to the creation of new information—e.g. *Re X and Y (Children)* [2004] EWHC 762 (Fam) at [66]; *Green Corns Ltd v CLA Verley Group Ltd* [2005] EWHC 958 (QB) at [81]. Courts have regularly acted to avert the risk of jigsaw identification through the publication of the fact that an injunction has been imposed—e.g. *DFT v TFD* [2010] EWHC 2335 (QB); *AMM v HXW* [2010] EWHC 2457 (QB) at [40]–[41]; *JIH v News Group Newspapers Ltd (No.2)* [2010] EWHC 2979 (QB); *MNB v News Group Newspapers Ltd* [2011] EWHC 528 (QB) at [16]. On the specific issue of the granting of anonymity to parties as a means of avoiding jigsaw identification, see *JIH v News Group Newspapers Ltd* [2011] EWCA Civ 42; [2011] 1 W.L.R. 1645 at [21].

[60] For instance, the designation of a story as an "exclusive" might indicate that the publisher considers the information concerned to have been previously unknown to its readership—see *Barrymore v News Group Newspapers Ltd* [1997] F.S.R. 600 at 603; *Attorney General v Parry* [2002] EWHC 3201 (Ch) at [15]; *HRH The Prince of Wales v Associated Newspapers Ltd* [2006] EWCA Civ 1776; [2008] Ch. 57 at [39].

[61] Courts now regularly distinguish between general information that may be in the public domain—perhaps even by the person's own hand—(e.g. one's general ill health) and particular details the privacy of which has been retained (e.g. the fact that one is suffering from cancer), or between different strands of detailed information (e.g. one's suffering from cancer as distinct from one's HIV status)—see *McKennitt v Ash* [2005] EWHC 3003 (QB) at [79]–[80]; *HRH The Prince of Wales v Associated Newspapers Ltd* [2006] EWCA Civ 1776; [2008] Ch. 57 at [39]; *Theakston v Mirror Group Newspapers Ltd* [2002] EWHC 137 (QB), [2002] E.M.L.R.22 at [66]; *X and Y v Persons Unknown* [2006] EWHC 2783 (QB), [2007] E.M.L.R. 10 at [28]. The old "zonal" argument associated with *Woodward v Hutchins* [1977] 1 W.L.R. 760 which suggested that any discussion of an area of one's private life would justify all future discussion in that area, is now obsolete, having been "discredited since at least the decision of the Court of Appeal in *McKennitt*—*KGM v News Group Newspapers Ltd* [2010] EWHC 3145 (QB) at [38] per Eady J.

[62] *A v B* [2005] EWHC 1651 (QB), [2005] E.M.L.R. 36 at [33].

[63] *Attorney General v Guardian Newspapers Ltd (No 2)* [1990] 1 A.C. 109 at 282.

[64] *Stephens v Avery* [1988] Ch 449 at 454; *Green Corns Ltd v CLA Verley Group Ltd* [2005] EWHC 958 (QB) at [78]; *Venables v News Group International (breach of injunction)* [2001] EWHC 530 (QB) at [32]–[33]; *CC v AB* [2006] EWHC 3083 (QB) at [57]; *Venables v News Group Newspapers* [2001] Fam. 430; [2001] 2 W.L.R. 1038 at 470–471.

[65] E.g. *KGM v News Group Newspapers Ltd* [2010] EWHC 3145 (QB) at [30]; *WXY v Gewanter* [2012] EWHC 1601 (QB).

Limiting factors: public domain and photographs. Photographs and   **22.7**
video recordings are special in the manner in which they are able to convey
information. This form of publication of private information can result in the
most poignant invasions of privacy. The proper approach to be taken towards
them in particular cases has, however, been a matter of some disagreement
between judges. One approach sees photographs as just one of a range of
communicative modes that might be used to convey private information. The
publication of a photograph may infringe a reasonable expectation of privacy,
but—in principle—only in the same way as might the publication of a written
narrative, or a voice recording. What is special about visual representations,
then, is *only* their capacity to convey tremendously detailed information
extremely efficiently. As Lord Hoffmann put it in *Campbell*:

> "a photograph is in principle information no different from any other information.
> It may be a more vivid form of information than the written word . . . that has to be
> taken into account in deciding whether its publication infringes the right to privacy
> of personal information. The publication of a photograph cannot necessarily be
> justified by saying that one would be entitled to publish a verbal description of the
> scene . . . but the principles by which one decides whether or not the publication of
> a photograph is an unjustified invasion of the privacy of personal information are in
> my opinion the same as those [for written material]."[66]

From this perspective the oft-cited metaphor of the "picture painting a
thousand words" is an appropriate one: the distinction between the modes of
communication is one of efficiency and degree, not category.[67]

Some judges have discerned a more qualitative difference between photographs and other modes of communication. In *Douglas v Hello! Ltd*, for
example, Lord Phillips M.R. asserted that "[it is not] right to treat a photograph simply as a means of conveying factual information", and that "a
photograph can certainly capture every detail of a momentary event in a way
which words cannot".[68] The Court of Appeal identified four different scenarios involving misuse of private information in the form of audio-visual
content. The first scenario is that where the photograph has not previously
been published or the private information it contains publicly described. Here,
there can obviously be no public domain argument. The second scenario is
where an account of the information depicted in a photograph has been
previously published in written form. In that case, there may still be a
reasonable expectation of privacy in the photograph as it could provide a more

---

[66] *Campbell v Mirror Group Newspapers Ltd* [2004] UKHL 22; [2004] 2 A.C. 457 at [72].
[67] E.g. *Campbell v Mirror Group Newspapers Ltd* [2004] UKHL 22; [2004] 2 A.C. 457 per
Lord Nicholls at [31], per Lord Hoffmann at [72], per Baroness Hale at [155].
[68] [2005] EWCA Civ 595; [2006] Q.B. 125 at [106]. He noted further that
"special considerations attach to photographs in the field of privacy. They are not merely a
method of conveying information that is an alternative to verbal description. They enable the
person viewing the photograph to act as a spectator, in some circumstances voyeur would be
the more appropriate noun, of whatever it is that the photograph depicts" (at [84]).
See also, *D v L* [2003] EWCA Civ 1169 at [23].

full account. Similarly, as the information conveyed in one photograph of a given subject or event will not necessarily be the same as that conveyed in another photograph, the publication of one depiction does not obviate any expectation of privacy attendant over the other.[69] The third scenario arises where republication of a photograph allows someone to see it for the first time; the fourth scenario when republication allows someone who has previously seen the photograph to review it afresh. Lord Phillips M.R. explained that "there will be a fresh intrusion of privacy when each additional viewer sees the photograph and even when one who has seen a previous publication of the photograph . . . is confronted by a fresh publication of it".[70] Hence, there was no public domain argument available. By way of illustration he posited:

> "if a film star were photographed, with the aid of a telephoto lens, lying naked by her private swimming pool, we question whether widespread publication of the photograph by a popular newspaper would provide a defence to a legal challenge to repeated publication on the ground that the information was in the public domain."[71]

These contentions are difficult to credit. The special efficiency of photography and other audio-visual formats in conveying information justifies the especial public domain rule applicable in the second scenario. Those posited by the Court of Appeal with regard to the third and fourth scenarios tend towards the creation of a novel cause of action that would be proprietorial in nature. Such a restriction of the public domain limitation is also unnecessary. Any compensatory award arising from a misuse of private information that was perpetrated under either of the first two of the outlined scenarios above could also include a measure for additional harms caused by foreseeable republication. The significant potency of a publication of this type would also likely see the court award significant damages. The claimant may also have a claim based upon a newsgathering tort, such as trespass or protection from harassment.

22.8　Limiting factors: public domain and harassment. In a series of cases, the courts have deployed a new analysis based on art.8 that may serve to obviate the public domain principle. The basis for this development is that if an interim order has been imposed in a claim for misuse of private information, then to remove it and permit publication would result in harassment and

---

[69] *Douglas v Hello! Ltd* [2005] EWCA Civ 595; [2006] Q.B. 125 at [106]. As Lord Phillips M.R. noted, however, that "to the extent that an individual authorises photographs taken on a private occasion to be made public, the potential for distress at the publication of other, unauthorised, photographs, taken on the same occasion, will be reduced" (at [107]). Hence, the strength of the privacy interest would be weakened in the second stage analysis.

[70] *Douglas v Hello! Ltd*, above, at [105]. This view was cited with approval in the House of Lords (*OBG Ltd v Allan* [2007] UKHL 21, [2008] 1 A.C. 1 at [288] per Lord Walker).

[71] [2005] EWCA Civ 595 at [105].

unjustified intrusion into the lives of the claimant and often his or her family.[72] In *CTB v News Group Newspapers*, Eady J. explained that "it is important always to remember that the modern law of privacy is not concerned solely with information or 'secrets': it is also concerned importantly with intrusion" and that in the instant case removing the non-disclosure order would see the claimants suffer "wall-to-wall excoriation in national newspapers . . . [as they were] engulfed in a cruel and destructive media frenzy".[73] In the same case, Tugendhat J. emphasised that:

> "if the purpose of this injunction were to preserve a secret, it would have failed in its purpose . . . but in so far as its purpose is to prevent intrusion or harassment, it has not failed . . . the claimant and his family need protection from intrusion into their private and family life . . . the order has not protected the claimant and his family from taunting on the internet . . . [but] it is still effective to protect them from taunting and other intrusion and harassment in the print media."[74]

Before adopting this course, the courts have insisted on the provision of evidence of the prospective harm.[75]

The moral sense of these judgments is obvious, but there is undeniably a sense of horses being changed in midstream. Unquestionably, the reading of art.8 that underpins the judgments is correct. It is less clear whether it is possible to deploy an interim remedy granted in a claim for misuse of private information to achieve goals focused on intrusion. On one hand, by removing an order the judge might be said effectively to be facilitating the envisaged breach of the Convention right. This raises concerns with regard to obligations placed on the courts as public authorities under s.6(3) of the Human Rights Act 1998. On the other hand, in the Protection from Harassment Act 1997, Parliament has established the circumstances in which harassment can justify the imposition of an injunction to avoid that type of harm. A recent decision of the High Court indicates that in addition to involving a course of conduct, harassment by publication must satisfy the high hurdle of being "oppressive" before a remedy will be afforded.[76] Moreover, as has been established by the House of Lords, there is no single cause of action that is adequate to cover all aspects of art.8.[77] In the somewhat different circumstances of *AAA v Associated Newspapers Ltd*—a case in which a representative claim was brought

---

[72] *JIH v News Group Newspapers Ltd* [2010] EWHC 2818 (QB); [2011] E.M.L.R. 9 at [59]; *TSE v News Group Newspapers Ltd* [2011] EWHC 1308 (QB) at [29]–[30].

[73] *CTB v News Group Newspapers Ltd* [2011] EWHC 1326 (QB) at [23]–[26]. Other elements in this judgment suggested, however, that the intrusion that the judge had in mind was that caused by "wall-to-wall excoriation in national newspapers" that would see the claimants "engulfed in a cruel and destructive media frenzy", and not specifically physical attention from journalists and photographers.

[74] *CTB v News Group Newspapers Ltd* [2011] EWHC 1334 (QB) at [3].

[75] In *Spelman v Express Newspapers* [2012] EWHC 355 (QB) at [81]–[82], for instance, the judge was unable to make an order as the evidence was insufficiently strong to allow the conclusion that harassment and intrusion would otherwise ensue.

[76] *Trimingham v Associated Newspapers Ltd* [2012] EWHC 1296 (QB), citing *Majrowski v Guy's and St Thomas's NHS Trust* [2006] UKHL 34; [2007] 1 A.C. 224.

[77] *Wainwright v Home Office* [2003] UKHL 53; [2004] 2 A.C. 406.

in order to *obtain* an order—"there is no tort which protects the privacy of individuals in all respects . . . any claim for physical intrusion into a person's life has to be made by reliance on existing and established torts such as harassment, assault, or in exceptional circumstances, intentional infliction of harm."[78] Clearly, any problem of this nature might be avoided if claimants were to base applications upon both the claim for misuse of private information and the 1997 Act. There is no guarantee, however, that factual circumstances would permit the courts always to make orders on both bases.

22.9 Limiting factors: consent. Should a claimant have consented to publication of private information, there will be no reasonable expectation of privacy. In principle, there are no forms of invasion of privacy to which a person may not consent. In some circumstances, however, a valid consent cannot be given by certain vulnerable individuals.[79] To prove consent, a defendant must usually show some positive conduct on the part of the claimant. This must relate to the particular information and form of publication involved. Mere acquiescence is not sufficient, and a court will be slow to infer implicit consent. In practice, therefore, consent is an issue only rarely.[80] It is conceivable that in the age of celebrity-media symbiosis, public figures may on occasion engineer the disclosure of private information in order to enhance their notoriety and income.[81] The consent of the subject of publications is also important in the context of relevant privacy codes.[82]

22.10 Limiting factors: trivial or anodyne information. In general, there will be no reasonable expectation of privacy in trivial or anodyne information. As Eady J. explained in *A v B*, "human rights are concerned with matters of substance . . . to publish that someone in the public eye has a bout of flu or a broken wrist is generally likely to do no harm . . . the potential to cause harm is likely to be 'an important factor' for the court to weigh".[83] This accords with the general understanding that interference with private life must

---

[78] [2012] EWHC 2103 (QB); [2013] E.M.L.R. 2 at [9]–[11].

[79] *T v British Broadcasting Corp* [2007] EWHC 1683 (QB); *E v Channel Four Television Corp* [2005] EWHC 1144 (Fam).

[80] E.g. *A v B and C* (unreported, March 2, 2001), (QB), cited in *Theakston v Mirror Group Newspapers Ltd* [2002] EWHC 137 (QB); [2002] E.M.L.R 22 at [41]. Similar issues have arisen in different legal contexts, e.g. *Moore v News of the World Ltd* [1972] 1 QB 441; *Cook v Ward* 130 ER 1338.

[81] Such an argument was presented, albeit abortively, by the defendant in *Contostavlos v Mendahun* [2012] EWHC 850 (QB).

[82] E.g. Ofcom, *Broadcast Code* (London: Ofcom, 2013), [8.6]–[8.8].

[83] [2005] EWHC 1651 (QB): [2005] E.M.L.R. 36 at [33]. In *McKennitt v Ash* [2005] EWHC 3003 (QB); [2006] E.M.L.R. 10, Eady rejected claims in respect of a large number of such items, for example, details of a shopping trip in Italy for the purchase of furniture and other household items (at [139]). Similarly, see *Lord Browne of Madingley v Associated Newspapers Ltd* [2007] EWHC 202 (QB); [2007] E.M.L.R. 19 at [61] (visit to a friend's flat in Venice). See also, *Attorney General v Guardian Newspapers Ltd (No 2)* [1990] 1 A.C. 109 at 282; *Coco v A N Clark (Engineers) Ltd* [1968] F.S.R. 415 at 421.

be of some seriousness before art.8 is engaged.[84] The minority view in *Campbell v Mirror Group Newspapers Ltd* was that the additional information published beyond the fact that the claimant was a drug addict receiving treatment for her addiction, being "relatively anodyne", was not worthy of the protection of the law.[85]

Nothing can be presumed, however, and in some circumstances even trivial information can warrant a reasonable expectation of privacy.[86] Anodyne information derived from a private venue, from a mobile phone, or from correspondence, for example, may generate a reasonable expectation of privacy. In *McKennitt v Ash*, Eady J. found that "it is intrusive and distressing for [the applicant's] household minutiae to be exposed to curious eyes", and that such information was therefore protectable by a reasonable expectation of privacy.[87] The basis for this expectation is not the subject matter of the information concerned, but rather the circumstances in which the opinions or information are imparted.[88] Should a reasonable expectation of privacy be found on such facts, the issue of triviality would still also speak at the second stage of analysis to the question of whether any remedy would be necessary or proportionate in light of the countervailing arguments.[89]

There has also been particular debate over the question whether the publication of photographs taken in public places containing images that depict scenes that are not private in nature will nevertheless generate a reasonable expectation of privacy. The longstanding position in English law was that there could be no breach of confidence in publishing photographs taken of people in public places. Photographs taken at private events,[90] or for private purposes were protected.[91] This position has changed with the advent of the claim for misuse of private information, so that the actual content of the photograph has become determinative. The essential rule is now that where

---

[84] *M v Secretary of State for Work and Pensions* [2006] 2 A.C. 91 at [83] per Lord Walker.

[85] [2004] UKHL 22; [2004] 2 A.C. 457 at [60] per Lord Hoffmann.

[86] *McKennitt v Ash* [2005] EWHC 3003 (QB); [2008] Q.B. 73, at [58].

[87] [2005] EWHC 3003 (QB); [2006] E.M.L.R. 10 at [135]–[138]. This was confirmed expressly by the Court of Appeal ([2006] EWCA Civ 1714 at [22]). See also, *Lady Archer v Williams* [2003] EWHC 1670 (QB); [2003] E.M.L.R. 38 at [34] and [67]; *Campbell v Mirror Group Newspapers Ltd* [2004] UKHL 22; [2004] 2 A.C. 457 at [75].

[88] *Lord Browne of Madingley v Associated Newspapers Ltd* [2007] EWHC 202 (QB); [2007] E.M.L.R. 19 at [46]; *R v Broadcasting Standards Commission, ex parte BBC* [2001] QB 885 at 900.

[89] *McKennitt v Ash* [2005] EWHC 3003; [2006] E.M.L.R. 10 at [58] and [67]. In *Hutcheson (Formerly Known As "KGM") v News Group Newspapers Ltd* [2011] EWCA Civ 808; [2012] E.M.L.R. 2 at [36]–[38], the Court of Appeal was asked whether art.8 could be engaged on the facts of a case without this then being necessarily followed by a finding that there was a reasonable expectation of privacy. Gross L.J. considered the issue to be little more than an "exercise in semantics": on the facts, the claimant would lose either at the first or second stage of analysis (at [41]).

[90] *Shelley Films Ltd v Rex Features Ltd* [1994] E.M.L.R. 134.

[91] *Pollard v Photographic Co* (1888) 40 Ch. D. 345.

photographs taken of adult people in public places do not convey obviously private information, but rather show the person concerned engaged in mundane or routine behaviours, there will be no reasonable expectation of privacy.[92] This was confirmed by the House of Lords in *Campbell v Mirror Group Newspapers Ltd*: "the famous and even the not so famous who go out in public must accept that they may be photographed without their consent, just as they may be observed by others without their consent".[93] There is no reasonable expectation of privacy in photographs of a person "going about [their] business in a public street" or "pop[ping] out to the shops for a bottle of milk".[94] It may be, however, that in this respect English law remains out of step with the developing jurisprudence under the European Convention of Human Rights.[95] The position is different where the subjects of photographs are children.[96]

---

[92] E.g. *John v Associated Newspapers Ltd* [2006] EWHC 1611 (QB); [2006] E.M.L.R. 27.

[93] [2004] UKHL 22; [2004] 2 A.C. 457 at [73] per Lord Hoffmann.

[94] [2004] UKHL 22; [2004] 2 A.C. 457 at [154] per Baroness Hale. One disagreement between their Lordships on the facts of *Campbell* concerned whether the photographs in question were themselves anodyne or conveyed additional private information. The minority view was that the photographs added nothing of an essentially private nature (per Lord Nicholls at [31], and Lord Hoffmann at [76]. This had also been the view of the Court of Appeal (see [2002] EWCA Civ 1373; [2003] Q.B. 633 at [33]–[34]). Their Lordships in the majority did not speak with one voice on this specific issue (at [121]–[123], [154]–[155], and [170] per Lord Hope, Baroness Hale, and Lord Carswell respectively).

[95] E.g. *von Hannover v Germany* (2005) 40 EHRR 1; *Sciacca v Italy* (2006) 43 EHRR 20, at [28]–[29]. The European Court of Human Rights can be criticised for adopting a rather high-minded view of the proper role of the media in *von Hannover*, tending to view the decisive factor in balancing the protection of private life against freedom of expression as the contribution that the published photos and articles make to a debate of general interest (at [76]–[77]). It insisted upon there being

"a fundamental distinction . . . between reporting facts—even controversial ones—capable of contributing to a debate in a democratic society relating to politicians in the exercise of their functions, for example, and reporting details of the private life of an individual who, moreover, as in this case, does not exercise official functions. While in the former case the press exercises its vital role of 'watchdog' in a democracy by contributing to 'impart[ing] information and ideas on matters of public interest' it does not do so in the latter case" (at [63] et seq)

Compare the German *Bundesversfassungsgericht* in the case:

"Nor can mere entertainment be denied any role in the formation of opinions. That would amount to unilaterally presuming that entertainment merely satisfies a desire for amusement, relaxation, escapism or diversion. Entertainment can also convey images of reality and propose subjects for debate that spark a process of discussion and assimilation relating to philosophies of life, values and behaviour models. In that respect it fulfils important social functions . . . When measured against the aim of protecting press freedom, entertainment in the press is neither negligible nor entirely worthless and therefore falls within the scope of application of fundamental rights . . . the same is true of information about people. Personalization is an important journalistic means of attracting attention. Very often it is this which first arouses interest in a problem and stimulates a desire for factual information. Similarly, interest in a particular event or situation is usually stimulated by personalised accounts."

[96] *AAA v Associated Newspapers Ltd* [2012] EWHC 2103 (QB); [2013] E.M.L.R. 2 at [50]–[61] and [121]–[122], as affirmed by the Court of Appeal ([2013] EWCA Civ 554). See also, *Murray v Big Pictures (UK) Ltd* [2008] EWCA Civ 446; [2009] Ch. 481 (which involved only the reinstatement of a claim previously struck out at first instance, and not its final determination). Contrast *Hosking v Runting* [2004] NZCA 34; [2005] 1 N.Z.L.R. 1.

SECTION 3. ULTIMATE BALANCING TEST

Elements of the second stage exercise. If a claimant has a reasonable **22.11**
expectation of privacy in the information at issue, the second stage in analysing a claim for misuse of private information requires the balancing of all
relevant factors. The court must consider whether it is necessary and proportionate to limit the privacy right in the interests of the expression rights of
others. Simultaneously, it must ask whether the restriction on publication
sought by the claimant is necessary for and proportionate to the protection of
privacy or other rights. Neither right enjoys a presumptive priority over the
other.[97] This requires the "intense focus" on the circumstances of the case to
be further pursued, and the existence, strength and comparative importance of
disparate factors to be determined by the court. In *Mosley v News Group
Newspapers Ltd*, Eady J. stated that:

> "this modern approach . . . is thus obviously incompatible with making broad
> generalisations of the kind to which the media often resorted in the past such as, for
> example, 'public figures must expect to have less privacy' or 'people in positions of
> responsibility must be seen as role models and set us all an example of how to live
> upstanding lives'. Sometimes factors of this kind may have a legitimate role to play
> when the 'ultimate balancing exercise' comes to be carried out, but generalisations
> can never be determinative. In every case 'it all depends' . . . upon what is revealed
> by the intense focus on the individual circumstances."[98]

This exercise will often be complicated by the fact that it must proceed at an
interim stage when the evidence before the court will be unavoidably untested
and hence under-determined.[99]

Relevant factors: strength of the claimant's privacy interest. There **22.12**
is no uniform weighting given to a reasonable expectation of privacy in every
case. The claimant's privacy interest can be more or less strong depending on
variables such as nature of the information itself, the attitude of the claimant,
and the mode of communication envisaged or used. There is, of course, also
a *public* interest in the protection of individual privacy.

Some categories of personal information deserve higher levels of protection
than others; there are "different degrees of privacy".[100] Medical information
and salacious or prurient details of sexual relationships, for example, are

---

[97] *Re S (a child)* [2004] UKHL 47 at [17] per Lord Steyn.

[98] [2008] EWHC 1777 (QB); [2008] E.M.L.R. 20 at [12]. See also, *Douglas v Hello! Ltd* [2001]
QB 967 at 1006 per Sedley L.J.

[99] The artificiality of this task given the untested character of the evidence available has been
noted often, e.g. *CC v AB* [2006] EWHC 3083 (QB), at [34]; *The author of a blog v Times
Newspapers Ltd* [2009] EWHC 1358 (QB); [2009] E.M.L.R. 22 at [12]; *Lord Browne of
Madingley v Associated Newspapers Ltd* [2007] EWHC 202 (QB); [2007] E.M.L.R. 19 at [16];
CDE v MGN Ltd [2010] EWHC 3308 (QB); [2011] 1 F.L.R. 1524 at [2]; *CTB v News Group
Newspapers Ltd* [2011] EWHC 1232 (QB) at [9].

[100] *Campbell v Mirror Group Newspapers Ltd* [2004] UKHL 22; [2004] 2 A.C. 457 at [118] per
Lord Hope; *Douglas v Hello! Ltd* [2001] QB 967 at 1012 per Keene L.J.

generally understood to be relatively very private. The more intimate the aspect of private life concerned, the more weighty must be the justification for their publication.[101]

Other variables can also influence outcomes. For instance, the format of the disclosure—specifically whether it comprises (audio-)visual material—has been considered important. In *Mosley v News Group Newspapers Ltd*, Eady J. explained that while "there may be a good case for revealing the fact of wrongdoing to the general public . . . it will not necessarily follow that photographs of 'every gory detail' also need to be published to achieve the public interest objective . . . [ultimately] it is a question of proportionality".[102] The value accorded to the private interest by the particular claimant can also have a bearing. Those who have taken steps to defend their personal information might expect the courts to be more ready to assist them.[103] In contrast, should a particular claimant be shown to have been relatively unconcerned whether the privacy of information was maintained, then the court may be less willing to provide protection.[104] This factor is likely to be particularly relevant where the claimant has previously engaged with the media, and evidenced a relative lack of sensitivity regarding certain facets of his or her private life.[105]

22.13 Relevant factors: other interests of the claimant. There may be "more at stake" for the claimant than his or her privacy alone. The claimant's right to life or freedom from arbitrary punishment may also be engaged. If relevant, such interests can be especially poignant. They might include the right to life or freedom from serious physical or psychological injury. In *Venables v News Group Newspapers Ltd*, for example, Butler-Sloss P. held

---

[101] *A v B plc* [2002] EWCA Civ 337; [2003] Q.B. 195 at [11(vii)] per Lord Woolf C.J.; *Campbell v Mirror Group Newspapers Ltd* [2004] UKHL 22; [2004] 2 A.C. 457 at [60] per Lord Hoffmann.

[102] [2008] EWHC 1777 (QB); [2008] E.M.L.R. 20 at [16] and [21]. Similarly, an injunction was granted by Ouseley J. in *Theakston v Mirror Group Newspapers Ltd* [2002] EWHC 137 (QB); [2002] E.M.L.R. 22 in respect of photographs taken inside a brothel, even though he considered that it was not appropriate to restrain verbal descriptions of what the claimant did there. See also, *Terry (originally LNS) v Persons Unknown* [2010] EWHC 119 (QB); [2010] E.M.L.R. 16 at [11] and [69].

[103] E.g. *McKennitt v Ash* [2005] EWHC 3003 (QB); [2006] E.M.L.R. 10.

[104] E.g. *Terry (originally LNS) v Persons Unknown* [2010] EWHC 119 (QB); [2010] E.M.L.R. 16 at [127]–[128]; *Hutcheson (Formerly Known As KGM) v News Group Newspapers Ltd* [2011] EWCA Civ 808; [2012] E.M.L.R. 2 at [47]. See also *Douglas v Hello! Ltd* [2005] EWCA Civ 595; [2006] Q.B. 125 at [107] per Lord Phillips M.R.. Interestingly, this approach appears to persist even where it is the interests of a child and the attitude of the parents at issue—compare *Murray v Big Pictures (UK) Ltd* [2007] EWHC 1908 (Ch); [2007] E.M.L.R. 22 and *AAA v Associated Newspapers Ltd* [2012] EWHC 2103 (QB) ; [2013] E.M.L.R. 2 at [101].

[105] Notably, even in cases where a very large volume of personal information has been put into the public domain, courts will not automatically assume that further disclosure of personal information would not be harmful—e.g. *Price v Powel* [2012] EWHC 3527 (QB) at [43]. That case concerned an application for the striking out of a claim as an abuse of process, and the judge was unwilling to obviate the claim without an opportunity for further assessment of the evidence.

that courts are under a positive duty to take steps to protect individuals from the criminal acts of others and consequently granted injunctive relief to the claimants.[106] She considered that there was a real possibility that the claimants would be in danger of not merely harassment or intrusion but revenge attacks if their true identities were disclosed.

Relevant factors: interests of third parties. The privacy or other **22.14** interests of third parties may also be affected by publication such that the court must also take them into account when determining a claim. The courts have increasingly been willing to countenance arguments of this nature on the basis that the Convention rights of all potentially affected persons must be respected. Hence, the rights of spouses and children are regularly factored into the ultimate balancing exercise.[107] If this is to happen, however, the courts have generally required that evidence of expected harm be adduced.[108] Less is required in this respect, more will be presumed, where the affected third party is a child.[109]

One problem with this approach is that often the third party in question will be the primary person from whom the claimant wishes to keep the information concerned. There is a risk that a court may be co-opted by the claimant in the deceit of his or her partner. Recognising this, the courts have required that

---

[106] [2001] Fam. 430 at 461 and 466. The decision was an application of the principle established in *Osman v United Kingdom* (2000) 29 EHRR 245. In *X (a woman formerly known as Mary Bell) and Y v O'Brien* [2003] EWHC 1101 (QB); [2003] E.M.L.R. 37, a similar injunction was awarded notwithstanding the fact that there was no proven threat to the art.2 right to life of either the mother or the daughter to whom it would relate. There was a lengthy history of press intrusion and identity loss. Medical evidence demonstrated that the mother was a vulnerable personality with mental health problems, and that the prospect of identification had caused an adverse effect upon the mother's mental and physical health which could be expected to be further exacerbated in the absence of injunctive relief. Butler-Sloss P. again deemed the case "exceptional".

[107] E.g. *CC v AB* [2006] EWHC 3083 (QB); *KGM v News Group Newspapers Ltd* [2010] EWHC 3145 (QB) at [28]; *CDE v MGN Ltd* [2010] EWHC 3308 (QB); [2011] 1 F.L.R. 1524 at [7]; *Rocknroll v News Group Newspapers Ltd* [2013] EWHC 24 (Ch) at [36]–[37]; *Ambrosiadou v Coward* [2011] EWCA Civ 409; [2011] E.M.L.R. 21; *ETK v News Group Newspapers Ltd* [2011] EWCA Civ 439; [2011] 1 W.L.R. 1827 at [14]–[19]; *CTB v News Group Newspapers Ltd* [2011] EWHC 1232 (QB) at [3]; *SKA v CRH* [2012] EWHC 766 (QB) at [24]. In cases involving children, the age and relative vulnerability of the child in question will influence the weight of the factor in the analysis—e.g. *Spelman v Express Newspapers* [2012] EWHC 355 (QB) at [55] and [72]; *BUQ v HRE* [2012] EWHC 774 (QB) at [68].

[108] In *CC v AB* [2006] EWHC 3083 (QB); [2007] E.M.L.R. 11, for example, the claimant adduced medical evidence of his wife's "stress and anxiety which requires medical attention . . . and which [was] quite likely to be made worse by press exposure", and "non-medical evidence of self-harm and of threats to commit suicide" (at [10]). cf. *A v B plc* [2002] EWCA Civ 337; [2003] Q.B. 195 at [43(v)] per Lord Woolf C.J. ("the judge should not . . . assume that it was in the interests of A's wife to be kept in ignorance of [his] relationships . . . this is an issue on which the court is not in a position to reach a judgment"); *Terry (originally LNS) v Persons Unknown* [2010] EWHC 119 (QB); [2010] E.M.L.R. 16 at [66].

[109] Even in this context, however, the interests of the child do not have an automatic precedence over the Convention rights of others. Rather, the court will accord particular weight in the balance to the rights of any children likely to be affected by disclosure—e.g. *K v Newsgroup Newspapers* [2011] EWCA Civ 439; [2011] 1 W.L.R. 1827 at [19].

normally such third parties should present evidence on their own behalf.[110] They have also sometimes enjoined widespread publication of information without similarly restricting the informing of spouses.[111]

22.15 **Relevant factors: expression rights of the defendant.** As with privacy interests, the expression interests that will be weighed in the balance can be more or less strong. They may comprise the desire of an individual somehow to "tell their own story", or the commercial interest on the part of a media organisation in selling news or entertainment to an audience of consumers. They may instead, or in addition, involve a cumulative interest on the part of the wider public in receiving information on important matters of public concern. Quite which factors are in play in a given case, and how strong the expression interest is, will be determined by reference to the specific facts of the case in hand. There is an intrinsic value in freedom of speech. There is also a general public interest in freedom of expression. It can no longer be contended, however, that such expression rights should "trump" other rights in the legal analysis.[112] In the privacy context, as opposed to that of defamation law, it cannot be said "without qualification, that there is a 'public interest that the truth should out".[113] Free speech is not an absolute good; the importance of speech must be measured against the reasonable expectation of privacy.

Courts have occasionally differentiated between different potential audiences when determining the legitimacy of communication. Thus, speech that is more important to a particular defendant may be permitted, whereas speech that is more general may be enjoined. For instance, the general importance of freedom of expression may justify the drawing of a distinction between personal communications by the defendant or source and mass-mediated transmission of the same information. The former may sometimes remain permissible, whereas the latter would be enjoined. Thus, it may be left permissible for a defendant to discuss a spouse's adultery with a close friend, or with members of the family, or with a family doctor, counsellor or social worker, or with his lawyers, notwithstanding the imposition of a constraint on publishing the impugned information to the world at large through the mass

---

[110] *Terry (originally LNS) v Persons Unknown* (above) at [66]; *Hutcheson (Formerly Known As "KGM") v News Group Newspapers Ltd* [2011] EWCA Civ 808; [2012] E.M.L.R. 2 at [47]; *BUQ v HRE* [2012] EWHC 774 (QB) at [67].

[111] E.g. *SKA v CRH* [2012] EWHC 766 (QB) at [31].

[112] E.g. *Mosley v News Group Newspapers Ltd* [2008] EWHC 1777 (QB); [2008] E.M.L.R. 20 at [10]; *Re S (a child) (identification: restriction on publication)* [2003] EWCA Civ 963; [2004] Fam. 43 at [52] and [2004] UKHL 47; [2005] 1 A.C. 593 at [17]; *Douglas v Hello! Ltd* [2001] Q.B. 967 at 1005. The notion that freedom of expression should operate as a 'trump card which always wins' is often traced—inappropriately—to the judgment of Hoffmann L.J. in *R v Central Television plc* [1994] Fam 192 at 203.

[113] *Mosley v News Group Newspapers Ltd* [2008] EWHC 1777 (QB); [2008] E.M.L.R. 20 at [10] per Eady J., quoting *Fraser v Evans* [1969] 1 QB 349 at 360 per Lord Denning M.R.

media.[114] This point should not, however, be pushed too far. If the balancing exercise leans in favour of publication, the law does not require publishers only to inform other parties who are immediately or directly affected.[115]

In general terms, the basic interest of a media organisation in freedom of expression is little different to that of any other individual. In consequence, and in the absence of any bolstering by reference to some particular public interest aspect to the message communicated, such freedom of expression in the media is likely to outweigh only relatively weak privacy interests. There is, however, a societal interest in the existence and sustainability of a 'free press'; a public interest in media freedom as such. This truism has generate two arguments: first, that the public importance of the continuing viability of commercial media organisations requires a degree of latitude over the invasion of privacy; that without the freedom to convey prurient, invasive stories, the ability also to deliver public interest stories will be undermined.[116] Secondly, that where the generality of particular stories can be justified by reference to the public interest in receiving the information concerned, the courts should leave professional scope for journalists and editors to decide how best they should be narrated. These arguments are related, but distinct. The first contention has been rejected by the courts. The second argument suggests that in order to attract a readership, legitimate stories must themselves be conveyed in the most arresting manner possible. This assertion has been accepted by the courts. Judges have agreed the self-denying ordinance that should not seek to prescribe precisely how information is communicated.[117] This may sometimes mean that peripheral private details may be publishable, even where they are not core to the main thrust of a public interest story but merely somehow enhance its authenticity, credibility or appeal.

Importantly, in undertaking the ultimate balancing exercise the courts have been ready to discount the weight of speech interests if their exercise can be

---

[114] *Attorney General v Guardian Newspapers Ltd (No.2)* [1990] 1 A.C. 109 at 282, citing *Francome v Mirror Group Newspapers Ltd* [1984] 1 W.L.R. 892; *CC v AB* [2006] EWHC 3083 (QB) at [35].

[115] *Theakston v Mirror Group Newspapers Ltd* [2002] EWHC 137 (QB); [2002] E.M.L.R. 22 at [69].

[116] Society of Editors, 'Paul Dacre launches conference with explosive speech', press release, November 9, 2008 (includes full text); *A v B plc* [2002] EWCA Civ 337; [2003] Q.B. 195 at [11(xii)] per Lord Woolf C.J.; *Campbell v Mirror Group Newspapers Ltd* [2004] UKHL 22; [2004] 2 A.C. 457 at [143] per Baroness Hale.

[117] *Campbell v Mirror Group Newspapers Ltd* [2002] EWCA Civ 1373; [2003] Q.B. 633 at [62]–[64] per Lord Phillips M.R., and [2004] UKHL 22; [2004] 2 A.C. 457 at [59] per Lord Hoffmann ("judges are not newspaper editors"), and at [143] per Baroness Hale; *AAA v Associated Newspapers Ltd* [2012] EWHC 2103 (QB); [2013] E.M.L.R. 2 at [102]–[103]; *Terry (originally LNS) v Persons Unknown* [2010] EWHC 119 (QB); [2010] E.M.L.R. 16 at [62]–[64]; *In re BBC* [2009] UKHL 34; [2010] 1 A.C. 145 at [25]–[26] per Lord Hope, and [65]–[66] per Lord Brown; *Re Guardian News & Media Ltd* [2010] UKSC 1; [2010] 2 A.C. 697 at [63]; *Re S (A Child) (Identification: Restriction on Publication)* [2004] UKHL 47; [2005] 1 A.C. 593 at [34]. See also, *Jersild v Denmark* (1995) 19 EHRR 1 at [31]; *News Verlags GmbH & Co. KG v Austria* (2000) 31 EHRR 246 at [39]; *Fressoz and Roire v France* (2001) 31 EHRR 2 at [54].

shown to be motivated by an intention to cause harm. The right is not expunged, but rather accorded less weight in the balancing exercise. This approach reflects the traditional equitable maxim that 'he who comes to equity must come with clean hands'. In *CC v AB*, for example, the court found that the defendant was motivated by a desire for revenge, and was indifferent to the "incidental fallout" on third parties with the result that an order was made enjoining publication.[118] This approach has also been deployed often in the context of attempts by defendants to blackmail claimants using the threat of exposure of private information. In *AMM v HXW*, Tugendhat J. explained that "if a person is making unwarranted demands with threats to publish, that is a factor in deciding whether that person has any Art.10 rights, and, if so, then the weight to be accorded to them in balancing them with the applicant's Art 8 rights".[119] In *DFT v TFD*, Sharp J. warned that "the expression rights of blackmailers are extremely weak (if they are engaged at all)".[120]

22.16 Relevant factors: matters of public interest generally. Aside from the immediate rights of the defendant and others, the interests of the wider public in receiving information on important matters of public concern must also be taken into account. Indeed, the existence of a tenable argument to the effect that information should be published in the public interest has often been decisive in seeing courts refuse a remedy.[121] The availability through the media of the fullest range of information on matters of public concern and controversy is presumed to facilitate the emergence of the informed public opinion on which democratic participation rests. This watchdog function of the media has been recognised often by the courts.[122] As the second stage in the analysis of a purported misuse of private information involves a balancing exercise, however, any reference to the public interest as a 'defence' is

---

[118] [2006] EWHC 3083 (QB); [2007] E.M.L.R. 11.

[119] [2010] EWHC 2457 at [38] (and see generally, [19]–[39]). See also, *KJH v HGF* [2010] EWHC 3064 (QB); *OPQ v BJM* [2011] EWHC 1059 (QB); [2011] E.M.L.R. 23; *CTB v News Group Newspapers Ltd* [2011] EWHC 1232 (QB); *EWQ v GFD* [2012] EWHC 2182 (QB); *SKA v CRH* [2012] EWHC 766 (QB); *NNN v Ryan* [2013] EWHC 637 (QB). Blackmail has also been an important factor in respect of whether notice of an application for an order should be given to the respondents—e.g. *ASG v GSA* [2009] EWCA Civ. 1574 at [3]; *TUV v Persons Unknown* [2010] EWHC 853 (QB); [2010] E.M.L.R. 19 at [23]–[26]; *JIH v News Group Newspapers Ltd* [2010] EWHC 2818 (QB); [2011] E.M.L.R. 9; *POI v Lina, The Person Known As* [2011] EWHC 25 (QB). If publication occurs following the failure of a blackmailing attempt, the attitude of the courts may be affected by the choice of defendant—e.g. *Theakston v Mirror Group Newspapers Ltd* [2002] EWHC 137 (QB); [2002] E.M.L.R. 22 at [70].

[120] [2010] EWHC 2335 (QB) at [23].

[121] The public interest comprised the third of the "limiting principles" on the equitable cause of action for breach of confidence that were set out by Lord Goff in *Attorney General v Guardian Newspapers Ltd (No 2)* [1990] 1 A.C. 109 at 282.

[122] E.g. *Reynolds v Times Newspapers Ltd* [1999] 2 A.C. 127 at 205 per Lord Nicholls, and 214 per Lord Steyn. See also *Sunday Times v United Kingdom* (1979–80) 2 E.H.R.R. 245 at [65]; *Lingens v Austria* (1986) 8 EHRR 407 at [41]–[42]; *Bladet Tromso v Norway* (2000) 29 EHRR 125 at [59]; *Jersild v Denmark* (1995) 19 EHRR 1 at [31]; *Goodwin v United Kingdom* (1996) 22 EHRR 123 at [60]; *Gaweda v Poland* (2004) 39 EHRR 4 at [34].

misleading. The defendant must substantiate the public interest argument in evidence,[123] but even if he or she does so the existence of a public interest argument will not necessarily see the ultimate balancing exercise play out in favour of publication.[124] Not only the existence of a public interest argument that the defendant seeks to invoke, but also its relative strength and the extent of contribution of the impugned information thereto must be assessed by the court. As Lord Phillips explained in *HRH Prince of Wales v Associated Newspapers Ltd*, "the test to be applied . . . is not simply whether the information is a matter of public interest but whether, in all the circumstances, it is in the public interest that the duty of confidence should be breached".[125]

It is not possible exhaustively to delimit the range of scenarios in which a public interest argument might arise: "the circumstances in which the public interest may override [a claim] are probably not capable of precise categorisation or definition".[126] A number of somewhat trite statements are regularly rehearsed, most notable of which is the truism that "what engages the interest of the public may not be material which engages the public interest", or that "the public tends to be interested in many things which are not of the slightest public interest".[127] In *Reynolds v Times Newspapers Ltd* and *Jameel v Wall Street Journal Europe*, the courts offered some further general guidance. In its ruling in *Reynolds*, the Court of Appeal spoke of the need for an ample flow of information to the public concerning, and for vigorous public discussion of, matters of public interest to the community, by which it meant:

> "matters relating to the public life of the community and those who take part in it, including . . . activities such as the conduct of government and political life, elections and public administration . . . [and] more widely . . . the governance of public bodies, institutions and companies which give rise to a public interest in disclosure, but excluding matters which are personal and private, such that there is no public interest in their disclosure."[128]

In *Jameel*, the House of Lords rejected the suggestion that the test was satisfied when material was "newsworthy" as a test too easily met. Conversely, the idea that the category included only material that the public "needed to know" was rejected as too onerous.[129]

---

[123] *Goodwin v News Group Newspapers Ltd* [2011] EWHC 1309 (QB) at [14]–[15].

[124] E.g. *Mosley v News Group Newspapers Ltd* [2008] EWHC 1777 (QB); [2008] E.M.L.R. 20 at [111]; *Rocknroll v News Group Newspapers Ltd* [2013] EWHC 24 (Ch).

[125] [2006] EWCA Civ 1776; [2008] Ch. 57 at [68].

[126] *Hyde Park Residence Ltd v Yelland* [2001] Ch 143 at 172 per Mance L.J.

[127] *Jameel v Wall Street Journal Europe Sprl* [2006] UKHL 44; [2007] 1 A.C. 359 at [31] per Lord Bingham and at [49] per Lord Hoffmann respectively. Baroness Hale was most imaginative in making this point: "the most vapid tittle-tattle about the activities of footballers' wives and girlfriends interests large sections of the public but no-one could claim any real public interest in our being told all about it" (at [147]).

[128] [1998] 3 W.L.R. 862 at 909 per Lord Bingham.

[129] [2006] UKHL 44; [2007] 1 A.C. 359 at [147].

Further insight can be drawn from the wide array of previous decisions regarding the concept in the areas of copyright, defamation, breach of confidence and misuse of private information. These have included the business of government and political conduct[130]; the promotion of animal welfare[131]; the protection of public health and safety[132]; the fair and proper administration of justice[133]; the conduct of religious groups[134]; discipline in schools[135]; the conduct of the police[136]; cheating, corruption and the pressure on elite athletes from an early age in sport[137]; breach of charitable fiduciary rules[138]; involvement in serious crimes[139]; corporate malpractice[140]; and the correction of prior statements or misrepresentations by others.[141] The public interest is also discussed in a number of "relevant privacy codes", although in substance such listings offer little guidance beyond that available in jurisprudence.

22.17 Relevant factors: role models and the public interest. A particularly controversial question has been the position of individuals who might be considered to be "public figures" or "role models". It has sometimes been asserted that the mere fact that a person holds that status should entail that he or she should necessarily expect a lesser degree of legal protection for personal information than might the average person. This would depend on

---

[130] *Attorney General v Jonathan Cape Ltd* [1976] QB 752; *Reynolds v Times Newspapers Ltd* [2001] 2 A.C. 127 ; *London Regional Transport Ltd v Mayor of London* [2001] EWCA Civ 1491; [2003] E.M.L.R. 4; *Al Fagih v HH Saudi Research and Marketing (UK) Ltd* [2001] EWCA Civ 1634; [2002] E.M.L.R. 13; *Roberts v Gable* [2007] EWCA Civ 721; [2008] Q.B. 502; *Galloway v Telegraph Newspapers* [2004] EWHC 2786 (QB); [2005] E.M.L.R. 7; *Henry v BBC* [2005] EWHC 2787; *Malik v Newspost* [2007] EWHC 3063.

[131] *Imutran Ltd v Uncaged Campaigns Ltd* [2001] 2 All E.R. 385.

[132] *Hubbard v Vosper* [1972] 2 Q.B. 84; *McKeith v News Group Newspapers Ltd* [2005] EWHC 1162 (QB); [2005] E.M.L.R. 32; *W v Egdell* [1990] Ch 359.

[133] *Lion Laboratories Ltd v Evans* [1985] Q.B. 526; *Istil Group Inc. v Zahoor* [2003] EWHC 165 (Ch).

[134] *Hubbard v Vosper* [1972] 2 Q.B. 84.

[135] *Leeds City Council v Channel Four Television Corp* [2005] EWHC 3522 (Fam).

[136] *Flood v Times Newspapers* [2012] UKSC 11; [2012] 2 A.C. 273; *Charman v Orion Group Publishing Group Ltd* [2007] EWCA Civ 972; [2008] E.M.L.R. 16; *Miller v Associated Newspapers* [2003] EWHC 2799 (QB); [2004] E.M.L.R. 33; *Hunt v Times Newspapers Ltd* [2013] EWHC 1868 (QB).

[137] *Jockey Club v Buffham* [2002] EWHC 1866 (QB); [2003] Q.B. 462; *Armstrong v Times Newspapers* [2005] EWCA Civ 1007; [2005] E.M.L.R. 33; *Grobbelaar v News Group Newspapers* [2001] EWCA Civ 33; [2001] E.M.L.R. 18; *Spelman v Express Newspapers* [2012] EWHC 355 (QB) at [22].

[138] *Seray-Wurie v Charity Commission of England and Wales* [2008] EWHC 870 (QB).

[139] *Hunt v Times Newspapers Ltd* [2013] EWHC 1868 (QB); *Lukowiak v Unidad Editorial SA* [2001] E.M.L.R. 46; *Loutchansky v Times Newspapers Ltd* [2001] EWCA Civ 1805; [2002] Q.B. 783; *Jameel v Wall Street Journal Europe Sprl* [2006] UKHL 44; [2007] 1 A.C. 359.

[140] *Cream Holdings Ltd v Banerjee* [2004] UKHL 44; [2005] 1 A.C. 253; *GKR Karate (UK) Ltd v Yorkshire Post Newspapers Ltd* [2000] 1 W.L.R. 2571; *Gilbert v Mirror Group Newspapers Ltd* [2000] E.M.L.R. 680; *Loutchansky v Times Newspapers Ltd* [2001] EWCA Civ 1805; [2002] Q.B. 783; *KGM v News Group Newspapers Ltd* [2010] EWHC 3145 (QB) at [39].

[141] *Prince Radu of Hohenzollern v Houston* [2007] EWHC 2328 (QB); *Hyde Park Residence Ltd v Yelland* [1999] E.M.L.R. 654 at 663; *KGM v News Group Newspapers Ltd* [2010] EWHC 3145 (QB) at [39]; *Ferdinand v MGN Ltd* [2011] EWHC 2454 (QB).

whether there could be said to be a public interest in the manner in which such individuals conduct themselves. This contention has enjoyed some measure of judicial support in the past. In *A v B plc*, for instance, Lord Woolf C.J.asserted that:

> "it is not self-evident that how a well-known premiership football player... chooses to spend his time off the football field does not have a modicum of public interest ... footballers are role models for young people and undesirable behaviour on their part can set an unfortunate example ... the fact is that someone holding his position was inevitably a figure in whom a section of the public and the media would be interested."[142]

Such bald contentions now hold less weight; no blanket rule applies.[143]

It is trite to note that any public position or popular fame will necessarily expose an individual's life and conduct to closer scrutiny than would otherwise be the case. It is not clear, however, precisely how it is supposed that the *public interest* might be served by the disclosure of personal information regarding a public figure in the absence of some further, extraneous, validating justification. In *Campbell v Mirror Group Newspapers Ltd*, Lord Phillips M.R. observed that:

> "the fact that an individual has achieved prominence on the public stage does not mean that his private life can be laid bare by the media. We do not see why it should necessarily be in the public interest that an individual who has been adopted as a role model, without seeking this distinction, should be demonstrated to have feet of clay."[144]

Public figures remain entitled to a private life.[145] If an expectation of privacy held by a public figure is to be outweighed, this can be only on account of specific reasons that emerge out of the analysis of the circumstances of the particular case (for instance, because the particular information is already in the public domain, because the general theme has been discussed by the claimant in such a way as to indicate that he or she does not hold such information to be particularly private, or because publication would serve the public interest specifically by exposing some past misrepresentation or by evidencing hypocrisy on the part of the claimant).

---

[142] [2002] EWCA Civ 337; [2003] Q.B. 195 at [43(vi)]. See also, *Theakston v Mirror Group Newspapers Ltd* [2002] EWHC 137 (QB); [2002] E.M.L.R. 22 at [69].

[143] For this reason the analysis conducted in *McClaren v News Group Newspapers Ltd* [2012] EWHC 2466 (QB) at [34] can be criticised as a superficial analysis that appears to abjure the requirement that the court undertake a fact-intensive evaluation.

[144] [2002] EWCA Civ 1373; [2003] Q.B. 633 at [41].

[145] *McKennitt v Ash* [2006] EWCA Civ 1714; [2008] Q.B. 73 at [56] and [62]–[64]; *Mosley v News Group Newspapers Ltd* [2008] EWHC 1777 (QB); [2008] E.M.L.R. 20 at [12]; *A v B plc* [2002] EWCA Civ 337; [2003] Q.B. 195 at [11(xii)] per Lord Woolf C.J.; *Campbell v Frisbee* [2002] EWHC 328 (Ch); [2002] E.M.L.R. 31 at [32] per Lightman J.; *CC v AB* [2006] EWHC 3083 (QB); [2007] E.M.L.R. 11 at [52] per Eady J. See also, *Craxi (No.2) v Italy* (2004) 38 EHRR 995 at [65].

22.18   Relevant factors: hypocrisy, correction and the public interest. A controversial issue has concerned the extent to which a claimant's own previous contributions to the public sphere should influence the ultimate balancing test. Three scenarios can be identified. First, an individual may have made direct public representations in respect of some specific fact or subjective view drawn from his or her private life. The publisher may then wish to "correct" supposed misrepresentations in such statements; to 'put the record straight'. In *Campbell v Mirror Group Newspapers Ltd*, Lord Phillips M.R. appeared to affirm the legitimacy of such publication: "one principle . . . is that, where a public figure chooses to make untrue pronouncements about his or her private life, the press will normally be entitled to put the record straight".[146] If a publisher were always free in law to correct any false impression, however, this would tend towards a form of "justification defence" in the claim for misuse of private information. Yet, if the right to respect for privacy entails anything, it is the freedom to determine for oneself when and to what extent others might learn one's private information. Hence, it should normally be entirely possible to deny the accuracy of some alleged private fact, or to misrepresent one's private details to the extent that one feels appropriate. In normal circumstances, for example, one should be free misleadingly to state one's HIV status or sexual orientation without fear of subsequent correction. For correction to generate a public interest, there must be some additional feature to the original misrepresentation. For instance, the misrepresentation must somehow permit the person concerned to gain some advantage relative to others.

In a second scenario, an individual may have implicitly or explicitly offered normative prescriptions for the manner in which other people should conduct themselves in private life. In a third scenario, a claimant may have directly criticised the conduct of some other person. In the latter two scenarios, the claimant risks charges of hypocrisy if it can be shown that he or she is also guilty of the failings with which others are charged. The scenarios involving correction of previous misrepresentations and/or hypocrisy each potentially generate a public interest in subsequent publication.

The nuance in these points can be seen in a number of decided cases. In *Campbell v Mirror Group Newspapers Ltd*, for example, it was not merely the fact that the claimant had previously denied taking drugs that permitted the defendant to publish the fact of her drug addiction, but also the fact that she had gone out of her way to emphasise that her purported abstinence positively distinguished her from the many fashion models who were less abstemious.[147]

---

[146] [2002] EWCA Civ 1373; [2003] Q.B. 633 at [43]. Similar statements were made in the House of Lords—[2004] UKHL 22; [2004] 2 A.C. 457 at [58] and [129] per Lord Hoffmann and Baroness Hale respectively.

[147] [2004] UKHL 22; [2004] 2 A.C. 457 at [24] and [82] per Lords Nicholls and Hope respectively. Lord Phillips' seemingly more basic point in the Court of Appeal may have amounted to the same idea: consider the inflection that may be given to the word 'pronouncement'.

A similar approach was adopted both at first instance and by the Court of Appeal in *McKennitt v Ash*.[148] In *Ferdinand v MGN Ltd*, the claimant was found to have engaged extensively with the media to create a false image of himself as a reformed character who had forsworn his past ways.[149] In addition, by accepting the England football captaincy when the manager, the FA chief executive, the sports minister and numerous commentators had insisted that the incumbent must maintain high standards both on and off the field, he was making a strong, if implicit, assertion that his private conduct by that time met the prescribed norms. In *KGM v News Group Newspapers Ltd*, the claimant had engaged in a public haranguing match with another person but tried to enjoin publication of what was possibly a central factor in the dispute.[150] When available, the correction of misrepresentation or exposure of hypocrisy argument comprises a public interest rationale for publication. It would not, however, serve as a defence to alleged breach of privacy. It could still be the case that the public interest generated would not be sufficient to outweigh the privacy interests in the balancing exercise.

SECTION 4. DATA PROTECTION

The Data Protection Act 1998.[151] Another strand in the privacy web is   **22.19** the statutory law of data protection.[152] The Data Protection Act 1984 was confined to data processed by automated means but this was replaced by the Data Protection Act 1998, which implemented Directive 95/46 and extends considerably further in that it applies to many non-automated records. The Act gives the data subject certain rights of access to data held concerning him and compensation where he suffers damage because, e.g. it is inaccurate or improperly used. It extends further than the law of defamation in that there is

---

[148] [2005] EWHC 3003 (QB); [2006] E.M.L.R. 10 at [98]–[100]; [2006] EWCA Civ 1714; [2008] Q.B. 73 at [67]–[70]. While the claimant in that case had espoused a series of 'compass points' to govern her personal and professional choices, the courts viewed these as clearly aspirational only: no one else had been in any way strongly urged to abide by them and there was little evidence that she had herself failed to meet them. See also *CC v AB* [2006] EWHC 3083 (QB); [2007] E.M.L.R. 11 at [52].

[149] [2011] EWHC 2454 (QB).

[150] [2010] EWHC 3145 (QB) at [39]. The Court of Appeal noted that "those who choose to conduct their quarrels in such a fashion take the risk that they may not be able to insist thereafter on clear boundary lines between what is public and what is private"—[2011] EWCA Civ 808; [2012] E.M.L.R. 2 at [45].

[151] "A cumbersome and inelegant piece of legislation": *Campbell v MGN Ltd* [2002] EWCA Civ 1373; [2003] Q.B. 633 at [72]. When the subordinate legislation is added, the picture is one of quite amazing complexity. See, with particular reference to the media, Warby, Speker and Hirst, Ch.5 in Tugendhat and Christie (eds), *The Law of Privacy and the Media*, 2nd edn (2011).

[152] The protection of privacy is usually regarded as "central mission" of the Data Protection Act 1998 Act and the underlying Directive: *Johnson v Medical Defence Union* [2007] EWCA Civ 262; [2008] Bus. L.R. 503 at [1], per Buxton L.J.

not necessarily any requirement of falsity; and further than the law of confidence or misuse of private information in that there is no requirement that the information be of a confidential or private nature. It is in fact a more severe constraint upon freedom of expression than either. There are further provisions on the processing of personal data and privacy in the electronic communications sector implementing EC Directive 2002/58.[153] Concurrent claims under the Data Protection Act and under the law of misuse of private information seem to be brought not infrequently.

22.20 Data and systems to which the Act applies. The Act is primarily a regulatory regime, administered by the Information Commissioner[154] and data controllers are, subject to certain exemptions,[155] required to notify him of matters relating to processing of data, which are then recorded in a public register.[156] The Act applies to personal data, that is to say, data relating to an identifiable living individual.[157] The meaning of personal data was considered by the Court of Appeal in *Durant v Financial Services Authority.*[158]

> "Not all information retrieved from a computer search against an individual's name or unique identifier is personal data within the Act. Mere mention of the data subject in a document held by a data controller does not necessarily amount to his personal data. Whether it does so in any particular instance depends on where it falls in a continuum of relevance or proximity to the data subject as distinct, say, from transactions or matters in which he may have been involved to a greater or lesser degree. It seems to me that there are two notions that may be of assistance. The first is whether the information is biographical in a significant sense, that is, going beyond the recording of the putative data subject's involvement in a matter or an event that has no personal connotations, a life event in respect of which his privacy could not be said to be compromised. The second is one of focus. The information should have the putative data subject as its focus rather than some other person with whom he may have been involved or some transaction or event in which he may have figured or have had an interest, for example, as in this case, an investigation into some other person's or body's conduct that he may have instigated. In short, it

---

[153] Privacy and Electronic Communications (EC) Directive Regulations 2003, SI 2003/2426.

[154] The Act refers to the Data Protection Commissioner but the Information Commissioner now oversees both the Data Protection Act 1998 and the Freedom of Information Act 2000. Although the interpretation of the Act lies with the courts, in practice the view of the Commissioner will determine many issues under the Act. Technical documents giving Guidance to the Act are available at *http://www.ico.gov.uk*.

[155] E.g. there is in general no requirement of notification if there is only non-automated processing of data.

[156] In *Murray v Express Newspapers* [2007] EWHC 1908 (Ch); [2007] E.M.L.R. 22 Patten J. considered that failure to register did not give rise to a civil action. The matter was not in issue on appeal: *Murray v Big Pictures (UK) Ltd* [2008] EWCA Civ 446; [2009] Ch. 481; [2008] E.M.L.R. 12 (sub nom *Murray v Express Newspapers Plc*).

[157] See *Common Services Agency v Scottish Information Comr* [2008] UKHL 47; [2008] 1 W.L.R. 1550, which concerned whether anonymisation of data could take them out of the category of "personal".

[158] [2003] EWCA Civ 1746; [2004] F.S.R. 28.

is information that affects his privacy, whether in his personal or family life, business or professional capacity."[159]

The Act applies not only to computerised[160] data but also to certain paper records, namely to data which are recorded as part of a relevant filing system[161] or which forms part of an "accessible record"[162]: s.1(1). A relevant filing system means:

"any set of information relating to individuals to the extent that, although the information is not processed by means of equipment operating automatically, . . . the set is structured either by reference to individuals or by reference to criteria relating to individuals, in such a way that specific information relating to a particular individual is readily accessible."[163]

This was interpreted in *Durant* as being limited to a system:

"1) in which the files forming part of it are structured or referenced in such a way . . . as clearly to indicate at the outset of the search whether specific information capable of amounting to personal data of an individual requesting it under s.7 is held within the system and, if so, in which file or files it is held; and

2) which has, as part of its own structure or referencing mechanism, a sufficiently sophisticated and detailed means of readily indicating whether and where in an individual file or files specific criteria or information about the applicant can be readily located."[164]

"Parliament intended to apply the Act to manual records only if they are of sufficient sophistication to provide the same or similar ready accessibility as a computerised filing system. That requires a filing system so referenced or indexed that it enables the data controller's employee responsible to identify at the outset of his search with reasonable certainty and speed the file or files in which the specific data relating to the person requesting the information is located and to locate the relevant information about him within the file or files, without having to make a manual search of them. To leave it to the searcher to leaf through files, possibly at great length and cost, and fruitlessly, to see whether it or they contain information relating to the person requesting information and whether that information is data within the Act bears . . . no resemblance to a computerised search. It cannot have been intended by Parliament—and a filing system necessitating it cannot be 'a

---

[159] Per Auld L.J at [28]. It is debatable whether the Information Commissioner's Guidance (see above) on "Determining Personal Data" is reconcilable with *Durant*. Thus para.6 states:
"It is important to remember that it is not always necessary to consider 'biographical significance' to determine whether data is personal data. In many cases data may be personal data simply because its content is such that it is 'obviously about' an individual. Alternatively, data may be personal data because it is clearly 'linked to' an individual because it is about his activities and is processed with the purpose of determining or influencing the way in which that person is treated. You need to consider 'biographical significance' only where information is not 'obviously about' an individual or clearly 'linked to' him."
[160] Data processed by means of equipment operating automatically in response to instructions given for that purpose or data recorded with the intention that it should be so processed: s.1(1)(a)–(b).
[161] S.1(1)(c).
[162] S.1(1)(d). i.e. certain health, educational and public records are covered even though they are "unstructured": s.68.
[163] S.1(1).
[164] [2003] EWCA Civ 1746; [2004] F.S.R. 28 per Auld L.J. at [50].

relevant filing system' within the Act. The statutory scheme for the provision of information by a data controller can only operate with proportionality and as a matter of common-sense where those who are required to respond to requests for information have a filing system that enables them to identify in advance of searching individual files whether or not it is 'a relevant filing system' for the purpose"[165]

By s.1(1)(e) (inserted by the Freedom of Information Act 2000, s.68(1), 2(a)) data includes information which is held by a public authority[166] and which does not fall within any of the other provisions of s.1(1). However, such manual data are exempt from the Data Protection Principles except as concerns accuracy and data subject access.[167]

The context of *Durant* is the provisions in s.7 of the Act for access by data subjects.[168]

22.21 The Data Protection Principles. Data controllers (persons who determine the purposes for which and the manner in which personal data are processed[169]) must, subject to the exceptions contained in Pt IV of the Act, comply with the Data Protection Principles,[170] set out in Sch.1, Pt I of the Act.

---

[165] Ibid. at [48].

[166] For which see s.3(1) of the Freedom of Information Act 2000.

[167] S.33A of the 1998 Act, as inserted from January 1, 2005 by s.70(1) of the Freedom of Information Act 2000.

[168] The claimant had lost litigation against a bank and made a complaint to the FSA against the bank. He sought from the FSA records of its investigation of his complaint. The effect of the decision is put as follows:

"Just because the FSA's investigation of the matter emanated from a complaint by [the claimant] does not . . . render information obtained or generated by that investigation, without more, his personal data . . . . In short, Mr Durant does not get to first base in his claim against the FSA because most of the further information he sought, whether in computerised form or in manual files, is not his 'personal data' within the definition in s 1(1). It is information about his complaints and the objects of them, [the bank] and the FSA respectively. His claim is a misguided attempt to use the machinery of the Act as a proxy for third party discovery with a view to litigation or further investigation, an exercise, moreover, seemingly unrestricted by considerations of relevance. It follows that much of [the claimant's] complaint about redaction of other individual's names and details falls away, regardless of the outcome of the correct application of the provisions of s 7(4)–(6) for protection of the confidentiality of other individuals"

(at [30][31]).

The question of the form in which the data is held is to be answered at the time of the request so that data which was once automatically processed but is now held in unstructured manual files is not covered. Nor is such data in manual files within the scope of the Act because it could easily be scanned into automatic equipment: *Smith v Lloyds TSB Bank Plc* [2005] EWHC 246 (Ch).

Under the Freedom of Information Act 2000 a person may request access to personal information about a third party held by a public authority. However, such information is exempt if, inter alia, it is personal data and its disclosure other than under the Freedom of Information Act would contravene any of the Data Protection Principles, or would involve a breach of confidence: ss.40, 41.

[169] S.1(1).

[170] S.4(4).

"*First principle*. Personal data shall be processed fairly and lawfully and, in particular, shall not be processed unless—
(a) at least one of the conditions in Schedule 2 is met, and
(b) in the case of sensitive personal data, at least one of the conditions in Schedule 3 is also met."

Processing is very widely defined. It means:

"obtaining, recording or holding the information or data[171] or carrying out any operation or set of operations on the information or data, including—
(a) organisation, adaptation or alteration of the information or data,
(b) retrieval, consultation or use of the information or data,
(c) disclosure of the information or data by transmission, dissemination or otherwise making available, or
(d) alignment, combination, blocking, erasure or destruction of the information or data".[172]

It has been said that: "in short, 'processing' appears to cover any imaginable treatment of information or data."[173] However, the Court of Appeal held by a majority in *Johnson v Medical Defence Union Ltd*[174] that it did not cover assessing information and deciding whether to forward it as the basis of a decision even though the information was called up from computerised data and the report for forwarding was then converted into computerised form. The consequence of the majority view is that the legislation would be largely inapplicable to control decisions on what should be input into the electronic record.[175] On the other hand, the apparent consequence of the minority view is that if a judge prepares his judgment (something which will be very likely to contain personal data) on his computer, it would be necessary, in order protect him from the First Data Protection Principle, to fall back upon a presumed intention in the Act (and the Directive) that it should be subject to the overriding principle of judicial immunity.

"And that defence would not avail parties who do not benefit from special immunities, unconnected with data protection, provided by domestic law. Thus, employers assess employees for promotion on the basis of their personal qualities, which involves decision-making based on personal data. If that personal data is held on a computer, alternatively once the decision is typed up on a computer, it follows from the [claimant's] argument that the fairness of that decision becomes justiciable not in terms of employment law, but in terms of data protection."[176]

---

[171] For most purposes "information" and "data" are synonymous and it is not clear when, as the definition implies, this is not so.
[172] S.1(1).
[173] Tugendhat and Christie (eds), *The Law of Privacy and the Media*, 2nd edn (2011), para.6.33.
[174] [2007] EWCA Civ 262; [2008] Bus. L.R. 503.
[175] At [86].
[176] At [47].

However, it has been held that if there has been processing of data within the meaning of the Act, then the publication of hard copy forms of that data, e.g. in a newspaper, may be regarded as part of the processing operation.[177]

Further provision as to when data are processed fairly[178] is to be found in Pt II of Sch.1. Thus regard is to be had to the method by which the data are obtained[179] (including whether the person from whom they are obtained is misled as to the purpose of processing)[180] and data are not to be treated as processed fairly unless, so far as practicable,[181] the data subject has been informed of the identity of the data controller and the purpose of processing[182]; but subject to this data is to be treated as obtained fairly if they were obtained from a person who was authorised or required by law to supply them.[183] To satisfy the requirement of fairness one of the conditions in Sch.2 must be met and these are (1) that the data subject has consented to the processing or that the processing is: (2) necessary[184] to perform a contract to which the data subject is a party or for the taking of steps at the request of the data subject with a view to entering into a contract[185]; or (3) necessary to comply with a non-contractual obligation of the data processor; or (4) necessary to protect the vital interests of the data subject[186]; or (5) necessary for various public functions, such as the administration of justice or a governmental function; or (6) necessary for the purposes of legitimate interests pursued by the data controller or by the third party or parties to whom the data are disclosed, except where the processing is unwarranted in any particular case because of prejudice to the rights and freedoms or legitimate interests of the data subject.[187]

---

[177] *Campbell v MGN Ltd* [2002] EWCA Civ 1373; [2003] Q.B. 633. The CA in *Johnson* was divided on the implications of *Campbell* for that case. But see s.32, para.22.25, below.

[178] There is no definition of "lawfully" but if, e.g. the publication of a digital photograph amounted to misuse of private information at common law then it would also be unlawful for the purposes of the Act: *Murray v Big Pictures (UK) Ltd* [2008] EWCA Civ 446; [2008] E.M.L.R. 12 (sub nom *Murray v Express Newspapers Plc*) at [62]. The *Guidance*, fn.258, above, para.3.1.4. suggests that a data controller must comply with all relevant rules of law whether derived from statute or common law, e.g. the law of confidence, the law of ultra vires and the Human Rights Act 1998.

[179] In *Douglas v Hello! Ltd (No.6)* [2003] EWHC 786 Ch D; [2003] E.M.L.R. 31 the underhand way in which the photographs were obtained made the processing unfair.

[180] Para.1(1).

[181] In the context of industrial safety legislation "practicable" has generally been treated as narrower than "reasonably practicable".

[182] Para.2(1),(3). See also the Data Protection (Conditions under para.3 of Pt II of Sch.1) Order 2000, SI 2000/185.

[183] Para.1(2).

[184] Not "convenient".

[185] Clearly there is some overlap here with the "consent" basis.

[186] The Commissioner considers that reliance on this condition may only be claimed where the processing is necessary for matters of life and death.

[187] Legitimate interests includes the business interests of the data controller and his freedom of expression. But if the publication of material produced by the processing amounts to misuse of private information that will mean that the processing is unfair for the purposes of the Act: *Murray v Big Pictures (UK) Ltd* [2008] EWCA Civ 446; [2009] Ch. 481 (sub nom *Murray v Express Newspapers Plc*) at [62]. The *Guidance* para.3.1.1 states:

In *Johnson v Medical Defence Union Ltd*,[188] where the majority held that there was no "processing", the court was unanimous that even if there had been it was not unfair. The case was not the usual "data privacy" claim but in effect an attempt to attack the policy of the defendants on risk assessment in relation to members' insurance cover. In terms of this policy no criticism could be made of the way in which the data had been handled. The fact that the relationship of the parties is contractual:

> "is a relevant factor even if a party's consent to the terms of the contract does not amount to the giving by the data subject of an explicit consent to data processing in accordance with provisions for giving such consent in the directive. This factor is likely to be a critical one where the parties have freely entered into a contract, the data user intended to do no more by way of processing of the information than he was entitled to do with it manually under the terms of the contract and the data subject should reasonably have foreseen that the data user might wish to process the information for this purpose. In this situation, the question of fairness has to be approached on the basis that the parties have made their agreement. If this were not so, the 'privacy' interest protected by the directive would be privileged over the contractual rights of the other contracting party."[189]

"Sensitive personal data" is defined in s.2 to include information on, inter alia, the data subject's racial origin, political opinions, religious beliefs, health, sexual life or criminal record. It is difficult to escape the surprising conclusion that a photograph of a person is sensitive personal data because it more or less inevitably reveals the person's racial origin.[190] The additional conditions applicable to the processing of such data are elaborately defined in Sch.3 and by statutory instrument[191] and cannot be adequately summarised here. While, as under Sch.2, the consent of the data subject is a basis for processing, under Sch.3 it must be his "explicit" consent. The lawyer tends to say that consent may be express or implied and which exactly it is on the facts of a particular case does not matter; but here a line must be drawn between explicit and non-explicit consent and how that is to be done remains to be seen. An alternative condition is that the information contained in the data has

---

"The Commissioner takes a wide view of the legitimate interests condition and recommends that two tests be applied to establish whether this condition may be appropriate in any particular case. The first is the establishment of the legitimacy of the interests pursued by the data controller or the third party to whom the data are to be disclosed and the second is whether the processing is unwarranted in any particular case by reason of prejudice to the rights and freedoms or legitimate interests of the data subject whose interests override those of the data controller. The fact that the processing of the personal data may prejudice a particular data subject does not necessarily render the whole processing operation prejudicial to all the data subjects."

This is likely to be of limited assistance to the data controller, but that is the nature of the Act.

[188] [2007] EWCA Civ 262.

[189] at [143].

[190] *Murray v Express Newspapers Plc* [2007] EWHC 1908 (Ch) [2007] E.M.L.R. 22 (not mentioned on appeal, *Murray v Big Pictures (UK) Ltd* [2008] EWCA Civ 446; [2008] E.M.L.R. 12 (sub nom *Murray v Express Newspapers Plc*).

[191] Data Protection (Processing of Sensitive Personal Data) Order 2000, SI 2000/417.

been made public as a result of steps deliberately taken by the data subject.[192] Among the other alternative conditions[193] are that the processing is necessary for the purposes of obtaining legal advice or that it is necessary for medical purposes and is undertaken by a health professional or person subject to an equivalent obligation of confidentiality. A number of further alternative conditions for processing sensitive personal data are found in the Data Protection (Processing of Sensitive Personal Data) Order 2000,[194] e.g. that the processing is necessary for carrying on an insurance business or the prevention or detection of an unlawful act. Many of these contain the requirement that the processing is "in the substantial public interest".

Second principle. Personal data shall be obtained only for one or more specified and lawful purposes and shall not be further processed in any manner incompatible with that purpose or those purposes.

The purposes are those notified either to the data subject or to the Commissioner and in determining compatibility regard is to be had to the purpose for which they are to be processed by a person to whom they are disclosed.[195]

Third principle. Personal data shall be adequate, relevant and not excessive in relation to the purpose or purposes for which they are processed.[196]

Fourth principle. Personal data shall be accurate and, where necessary,[197] kept up to date.

However, this Principle is not to be taken as being contravened because of any inaccuracy in personal data which accurately record information obtained by the data controller from the data subject or a third party in a case where (a) taking account of the purpose or purposes for which the data were obtained and further processed, the data controller has taken reasonable steps to ensure the accuracy of the data, and (b) if the data subject has notified the data controller of the data subject's view that the data are inaccurate, the data indicate that fact.[198]

---

[192] Para.5. The wording of the Directive (art.8.2(e)) is "data which are manifestly made public by the data subject". On the possible difference, see Tugendhat and Christie (eds), *The Law of Privacy and the Media*, 2nd edn (2011), para.6.49 et seq. In *Murray v Express Newspapers Plc*, above Patten J. held that this condition is satisfied, in the case of a photograph, when a person goes into a public place where it can be taken. On appeal (above) it was held that it was arguable that there was a threatened misuse of private information in publishing the photograph and that meant that processing was necessarily unfair. However, had that not been so, presumably Patten J.'s view remains valid.

[193] Some of which duplicate those in Sch.2, e.g. necessary for the administration of justice.

[194] SI 2000/417.

[195] Sch.1, Pt II, paras 5, 6.

[196] See *Chief Constable of Humberside v Information Comr*, EA/2007/0096,98,99,108,127. July 21, 2008, Information Tribunal ([2009] EWCA Civ 1079; [2010] 1 W.L.R. 1136).

[197] Not for example where the data is simply a historical record of a transaction.

[198] Para.7.

Fifth principle. Personal data processed for any purpose or purposes shall not be kept for longer than is necessary for that purpose or those purposes.[199]

Sixth principle. Personal data shall be processed in accordance with the rights of data subjects under the Act.

Under Sch.1, Pt II, para.8 this Principle is to be regarded as infringed only by contravention of the provisions relating to the subject's right of access to the data,[200] his right to prevent processing likely to cause damage or distress,[201] his right to prevent processing for the purposes of direct marketing[202] or his right in certain cases to require that decisions significantly affecting the data subject are not based solely on processing by automatic means.[203]

Seventh principle. Appropriate technical and organisational measures shall be taken against unauthorised or unlawful processing of personal data and against accidental loss or destruction of, or damage to, personal data.

Guidance on this is given by Pt II of Sch.1, so that, e.g. the magnitude of the likely harm must be balanced against the cost of prevention and effective steps must be taken to ensure the reliability of staff and of any data processor used by the data controller.[204]

Eighth principle. Personal data shall not be transferred to a country or territory outside the European Economic Area unless that country or territory ensures an adequate level of protection for the rights and freedoms of data subjects in relation to the processing of personal data.[205]

Inaccuracy of data. Apart from the compensation right for damage and distress under s.13, the court may, on the application of the data subject, order the rectification, blocking, erasure or destruction of inaccurate personal data[206] and this may extend, where the court considers it reasonably practicable, to informing third parties to whom the data have already been disclosed.[207] If the data are incorrect but accurately record the information given to the data controller, the court may, if the data controller took reasonable   **22.22**

---

[199] See *Chief Constable of Humberside v Information Comr*, above. It may be necessary to keep data long after a relationship has ended, e.g. for reference purposes.

[200] S.7.

[201] S.10.

[202] S.11.

[203] S.12.

[204] Sch.1, Pt II, paras 9–12. For details see *Guidance*, fn.154, above, para.3.7.

[205] Sch.4 of the Act provides for circumstances in which the Eighth Principle does not apply to a transfer. In addition to the general *Guidance*, fn.154, above, the Commissioner has published *The Eighth Data Protection Principle and international data transfers*.

[206] Including other personal data containing an opinion which appears to be based on the inaccurate data.

[207] S.14.

steps to ensure that the data were correct, order that the data be supplemented by a court approved statement of the true facts.[208]

22.23 Compensation. Section 13 provides for compensation as follows:

"(1) An individual who suffers damage by reason of[209] any contravention by a data controller of any of the requirements of this Act is entitled to compensation from the data controller for that damage.

(2) An individual who suffers distress by reason of any contravention by a data controller of any of the requirements of this Act is entitled to compensation from the data controller for that distress if—

(a) the individual also suffers damage by reason of the contravention, or

(b) the contravention relates to the processing of personal data for the special purposes.[210]

(3) In proceedings brought against a person by virtue of this section it is a defence to prove that he had taken such care as in all the circumstances was reasonably required to comply with the requirement concerned."

This is somewhat wider than the equivalent provision under the 1984 Act, as that was confined to damage or distress suffered as a result of inaccuracy, loss, destruction or wrongful disclosure of the data, whereas s.13 applies to any actionable contravention of the Act. Where the information is false, this may provide an alternative to a claim for libel (without any need to show that the matter reflected adversely on the claimant's reputation) or malicious falsehood (without the need to prove malice or falsity)—though in both cases damages are not necessarily the same. Even if the information is not false the Act may provide an alternative to a claim for misuse of private information or breach of confidence[211] (without the necessity to show that the information

---

[208] S.14(2).

[209] Damage and distress must therefore be caused by the contravention of the Act. In *Douglas v Hello! Ltd (No.3)* [2003] EWHC 786 (Ch); [2003] 3 All E.R. 996; [2003] E.M.L.R. 31, the defendants were in breach of the first Principle in publishing unauthorised photographs of the claimants' wedding without their consent. In earlier proceedings (*Douglas v Hello! Ltd* [2001] Q.B. 967) founded on breach of confidence and where the data protection argument was not deployed, the CA had held that damages were an adequate remedy and no injunction should be granted. In the later proceedings Lindsay J. was of the view that even if the data protection argument had been raised the result would still have been the same, the defendants would have published, and on this basis the distress had not been suffered by reason of the contravention of the Act. See also *Ogle v Chief Constable, Thames Valley* [2001] EWCA Civ 598 (a claim under s.22 of the 1984 Act arising out of failure to correct the claimant's record on the Police National Computer, which led to his arrest and detention by another force. The claim failed because of his recovery of damages from the other force). Is it enough that the damage or distress is caused in a "but for" sense by contravention of the Act? Tort law normally requires foreseeability of the event of harm, if not of its quantum, and although the cause of action here is a statutory one, policy would seem to point the same way.

[210] See para.22.23, below.

[211] There were concurrent claims in *Campbell v MGN Ltd* [2002] EWCA Civ 1373; [2003] Q.B. 633; *Douglas v Hello! Ltd (No.3)* [2003] EWHC 786 (Ch); [2003] 3 All E.R. 996; [2003] E.M.L.R. 31; and *Murray v Big Pictures (UK) Ltd* [2008] EWCA Civ 446; [2009] Ch. 481 (sub nom *Murray v Express Newspapers Plc*).

was impressed with a common law obligation of confidence or was private[212]) or, in the case of a public authority, to a claim based on the Human Rights Act 1998 and art.8 of the Convention: although the word "privacy" does not seem to occur in the Data Protection Act, in effect it provides a remedy for infringement of privacy in many cases.[213] It may also avoid the need for artificial extensions of the tort of negligence in cases of failure to handle personal data carefully.[214]

Compensation for non-pecuniary loss. The "special purposes" referred   **22.24** to in s.13 are purposes of journalism and artistic and literary purposes.[215] The structure of the section makes it clear that "distress" is not "damage" because compensation for distress is only recoverable where there is also damage or where the special purposes are involved. Damage in this context, it has been held, means "special or financial damages in contra-distinction to distress in the shape of injury to feelings,"[216] though where the claimant's art.8 rights are affected by the contravention of the Act damages for distress might be recoverable without more.[217] However, it has been said that in other cases, since Community laws differ widely in regard to the concept of "damage" there is no compelling reason why that word should have to go beyond its root meaning of pecuniary loss and extend to distress or injury to reputation.[218] That, of course, resembles the general position in English tort[219] law: apart from statute,[220] distress itself is not damage and damages for distress are only recoverable where the tort is actionable per se and damages are at large (as in the case of libel or those cases of malicious falsehood where damage is presumed) or where there is damage and that is exacerbated by the claimant's

---

[212] Information might be personal data under the Act without being private (e.g. information about a person's racial origins).

[213] *Johnson v Medical Defence c*; at [1].

[214] In *Ogle v Chief Constable, Thames Valley* [2001] EWCA Civ 598, although the claim failed for other reasons, Simon Brown L.J. remarked that in such a situation the law of data protection provided "an altogether better basis" for a claim than the common law of negligence.

[215] S.3.

[216] *Campbell v MGN* [2002] EWHC 499 (QB); [2002] E.M.L.R. 30 at [123].

[217] *Johnson v Medical Defence Union Ltd* [2007] EWCA Civ 262; [2008] Bus. L.R. 503 at [74]. But in no sense was *Johnson* a "privacy" or "reputation" case.

[218] Ibid. This case was applied by Patten J. in *Murray v Express Newspapers Plc* [2007] EWHC 1908 (Ch); [2007] E.M.L.R. 22. On appeal (*Murray v Big Pictures (UK) Ltd* (above) (sub nom *Murray v Express Newspapers Plc*) (para.22.9, above) it is said at [63] that "it seems to us at least arguable that the judge has construed 'damage' too narrowly, having regard to the fact that the purpose of the Act was to enact the provisions of the relevant Directive". Clearly Art. 8 rights were engaged in *Murray*. Patten J. in *Murray* also rejected the view that the principle of account of profits in *Att-Gen v Blake* [2001] 1 A.C. 268 should apply.

[219] Damages in contract for "disappointment" are more restricted still since damages for breach of contract are never at large in the same way. See *Farley v Skinner* [2001] UKHL 49; [2002] 2 A.C. 732.

[220] E.g. the Protection from Harassment Act 1997 (para.23.12, below) and the various statutory discrimination wrongs.

distress.[221] The underlying Directive merely refers to "damage"[222] but it would be hard to say that there was any general European concept of damage which could be called in aid and we should perhaps be cautious about encouraging claims in this area.[223] In the only known case in which substantial[224] compensation has been awarded for distress under s.13[225] (which involved processing for the "special purposes") £2,500 was awarded, plus £1,000 aggravated damages.

On the other hand, distress which amounts to the level of a recognised psychiatric illness is damage in the general sense, albeit damage which presents more problems to the law than physical injury. It is unclear whether such loss is recoverable in an action for libel[226]; if the answer is No, then it would be odd if it were recoverable under the Data Protection Act. However, it may be that the rule in libel simply turns on whether the damage is too remote, in which case it is submitted that it almost always will be and the same should be true under the Act, and that, unless the defendant is aware of some unusual weakness of the data subject, it would not be reasonably foreseeable that such consequences could ensue from contravention of the Act.[227]

22.25 Exemptions. The width of the definitions of data and processing is such that it would be impossible, in the absence of further provision, to deal with almost any automated or structured information about an individual without his consent—the preparation and publication of a newspaper story, for example, will inevitably involve many acts which amount to processing of the data which go into the story; furthermore, there are many situations where it would be unreasonable or even undesirable to have to notify an individual about data

---

[221] E.g. where the claimant's life expectancy is reduced by an accident and this causes him distress. It seems better not to regard ordinary pain and suffering/loss of amenity damages in personal injury cases as awarded for "distress" since they are basically awarded on a tariff basis.

[222] Art.23.

[223] But the European Court of Human Rights awarded damages for non-pecuniary loss for injury to reputation in an art.8 case which involved misuse of data in *Rotaru v Romania* App. no.28341/95; ECHR 2000-V.

[224] Only a nominal award was made in *Douglas v Hello! Ltd (No.6)* [2003] EWHC 786 (Ch); [2003] E.M.L.R. 31.

[225] *Campbell v MGN* [2002] EWHC 499 (QB) [2002] E.M.L.R. 30. Breach of confidence was an alternative basis of liability for the one award. The decision on data protection was reversed on the basis that s.32 of the Act exempted the defendants from liability but nothing was said about damages, save that it would have been open to the judge to award aggravated damages if his finding on liability had been correct: *Campbell v MGN Ltd* [2002] EWCA Civ 1373; [2003] Q.B. 633. The judge's decision on confidence was also reversed by the CA but restored by the HL: *Campbell v MGN Ltd* [2004] UKHL 22; [2004] 2 A.C. 457. The data protection claim was not the subject of argument in the HL.

[226] Para.1.20, above.

[227] For the potential consequences of a liberal approach to this issue see *Tame v New South Wales* [2002] HCA 35; 211 C.L.R. 317 (para.23.5, below). It is submitted that the standard analysis of "primary" and "secondary" victim, which has been developed in the context of accidents, is not helpful in this context. Nor is it necessarily decisive that there is no "sudden shock": *W v Essex CC* [2001] 2 A.C. 592 HL.

held on him or to allow him access. The Act therefore provides a range of exemptions from the obligation to comply with the Data Protection Principles and other provisions of the Act. Thus data are exempt from the Data Protection Principles and the rights of data subjects if the exemption is required for the purpose of safeguarding national security, this being determined by a certificate from a Minister, subject to an appeal to the Information Tribunal[228]; data processed for the prevention of crime, the apprehension of offenders or the assessment or collection of tax are exempt from the first Data Protection Principle (except in so far as it requires compliance with the conditions in Schs 2 and 3) and from the subject right of access to the extent that they would prejudice the crime or taxation purposes, and subject to certain conditions, they are also exempt from the non-disclosure provisions[229]; the Lord Chancellor[230] has power to exempt from or modify the subject information provisions (i.e. information to the data subject about the identity of the data controller and the purpose of processing) and the subject right of access where the data concern the physical or mental health or condition of the subject or educational or social work records and these powers have been exercised[231]; data processed for the purposes of a wide range of regulatory functions are exempt from the subject information provisions where the application of those provisions would be likely to prejudice the proper discharge of those functions[232]; the second and fifth Principles are modified in relation to data processed only for research (which includes history and statistics) purposes, which are exempt from the subject access provisions if they are processed in compliance with the relevant conditions and the results are not made available in a form which identifies data subjects[233]; data which are available to the public by or under any enactment (other than the Freedom of Information Act 2000) are exempt from the subject information provisions, the fourth Data Protection Principle, s.14 and the non-disclosure provisions[234]; data are exempt from the non-disclosure provisions where disclosure is required by law or disclosure is necessary in connection with legal proceedings or the establishment, exercise or defence of legal rights[235]; data processed by an individual only for the purposes of his personal family or household affairs are exempt from the Data Protection Principles and from Pts II and III of the Act[236]; and Sch.7 contains various exemptions in connection with confidential

---

[228] S.28.

[229] S.29.

[230] Substituted for the Secretary of State by SI 2001/3500, art.8, Sch.2, Pt I, para.6.

[231] S.30 and the Data Protection (Subject Access Modification) (Health) Order 2000, SI 2000/413, the Data Protection (Subject Access Modification) (Education) Order 2000, SI 2000/414 and the Data Protection (Subject Access Modification) (Social Work) Order 2000, SI 2000/415).

[232] S.31.

[233] S.33.

[234] S.34.

[235] S.35.

[236] S.36.

references, the armed forces, judicial appointments, Crown employment, management forecasts, corporate finance, negotiations with the data subject, examination marks and scripts, legal professional privilege and self-incrimination. In addition, since the Act was passed, exemptions have been added for certain manual data held by public authorities[237] and any data if the exemption is required for the purpose of avoiding an infringement of the privileges of either House of Parliament[238]; and the Lord Chancellor has power to make further exemptions by order.[239]

22.26 **The special purposes exemption.** Data protection infringements by the media are perhaps most likely to lead to major litigation and the special purposes exemption is therefore of particular importance. The "special purposes" are purposes of journalism and artistic and literary purposes.[240] Under s.32(1):

> "Personal data which are processed only for the special purposes are exempt from any provision to which [subsection (1)] relates if—
> (a) the processing is undertaken with a view to the publication[241] by any person of any journalistic, literary or artistic material,
> (b) the data controller reasonably believes that, having regard in particular to the special importance of the public interest in freedom of expression, publication would be in the public interest, and
> (c) the data controller reasonably believes that, in all the circumstances, compliance with that provision is incompatible with the special purposes."

The exemptions to which this subsection relates are all the Data Protection Principles except the seventh,[242] the rights to subject access,[243] to prevent processing likely to cause damage or distress[244] or automated decision making[245] and to have inaccurate data rectified, blocked, erased or destroyed.[246] Despite the reference to processing "with a view to publication" the exemption covers not only the preliminary processing of information by way of recording and preparation but also the publication of the information in "hard copy" form.[247] The media are therefore protected not only from "prior restraint" by interim injunction against proceeding with the processing of information with a view to publication, but also from claims for compensation

---

[237] S.33A, inserted by the Freedom of Information Act 2000, s.70(1).
[238] S.35A, inserted by the Freedom of Information Act 2000.
[239] S.38, as amended by SI 2001/3500, art.8, Sch.2, Pt I, para.6.
[240] S.3.
[241] Which means to make the material available to the public or any section of the public: s.32(6).
[242] Security of the data.
[243] S.7.
[244] S.10.
[245] S.12.
[246] S.14.
[247] *Campbell v MGN Ltd* [2002] EWCA Civ 1373; [2003] Q.B. 633.

once publication had taken place. The contrary view would lead to an absurdity:

> "Exemption is provided in respect of all steps in the operation of processing up to publication on the ground that publication is reasonably believed to be in the public interest—yet no public interest defence [would, on the contrary view, be] available to a claim for compensation founded on the publication itself. . . . Under section 32(1) it is the *data* which is exempt from the provisions of the Act specified in subsection (2). The Act only applies in relation to data. If, as we have held, the Act applies to publication, as part of the processing operation, it does so because the information published remains 'data', as defined by the Act. Where, by reason of section 32, the data becomes exempt as a result of the reasonable belief of the journalist that the publication *will be* in the public interest, the data remains subject to that exemption thereafter."[248]

In considering for the purposes of subs.(1)(b) whether the belief of a data controller that publication would be in the public interest was or is a reasonable one, regard may be had to his compliance with any designated code of practice which is relevant to the publication in question.[249] In practice the issue of whether the data controller reasonably believed the publication to be in the public interest is likely to be very similar to that of whether it is in the public interest for the purposes of a claim for breach of confidence,[250] even if, in theory at least, the issue in breach of confidence is whether the disclosure *is* in the public interest, rather than whether the defendant reasonably believes it to be so.[251]

---

[248] Ibid. at [128]–[129].

[249] S.32(3). For example the Codes of the Press Complaints Commission or the Broadcasting Standards Council. See the Data Protection (Designated Codes of Practice) (no.2) Order 2000, SI 2000/1864.

[250] See *Campbell v MGN Ltd* [2002] EWCA Civ 1373; [2003] Q.B. 633 at [133].

[251] In *Campbell* the HL allowed the appeal and restored the judgment of Morland J. in the claimant's favour: *Campbell v MGN Ltd* [2004] UKHL 22; [2004] 2 A.C. 457. Data protection was not the subject of argument but at [32] Lord Nicholls said that the parties "were agreed that [the data protection] claim stands or falls with the outcome of the main claim".

CHAPTER 23

OTHER CAUSES OF ACTION ARISING FROM STATEMENTS

SECTION 1. NEGLIGENCE

Introduction. Negligence by word may give rise to liability on the basis **23.1** that the claimant has relied on the defendant's statement to his loss in circumstances where he was owed a duty of care by the defendant and it was reasonable so to rely. This is an aspect of the liability flowing directly from *Hedley, Byrne & Co. v Heller & Partners*[1] and is not the concern of this chapter[2] because in no sense can the statement be said to be about the claimant or his property or his business. What this section is concerned with is those cases where the defendant makes a negligent statement to third parties which affects the claimant's relations with those third parties.[3]

Duty of care: general. In order to establish liability for negligence[4] the **23.2** claimant must show[5] (1) that the defendant owed him a duty of care, (2) that the defendant was in breach of that duty by failing to achieve the standard of

---

[1] [1964] A.C. 465 HL.

[2] Any more than Ch.21 was concerned with deceit.

[3] But both types of case may arise on similar facts. If D writes a careless employment reference on C which leads to C not getting the job, D may be liable to C. But if D's reference carelessly omits matters to C's discredit, X gives C the job and the matters omitted by D subsequently cause loss to X, D may be liable to X for negligence. Lord Goff in *Spring v Guardian Assurance Plc* [1995] 2 A.C. 296 HL at 320, seems concerned to say that this will not necessarily be so rather than to say that it cannot be so. These two categories of case do not exhaust the potential of non-contractual statements for causing harm. Thus D may make a statement to C which injures him by frightening him (*Wilkinson v Downton* [1897] 2 Q.B. 57) or make a statement about C to X which causes C psychiatric injury because C perceives (wrongly) that his reputation will suffer in X's eyes (*Tame v New South Wales* [2002] HCA 35; 211 C.L.R. 317, para.23.5, below). The latter case intersects closely with defamation.

[4] In the sense of a tort. "Professional negligence" is sometimes used in a loose sense to comprehend breach of a contract requiring care and skill. In such a case it is not necessary to establish a duty of care (though the existence of the contract fulfils much the same function) and the content of the defendant's obligation will generally be the same as in negligence. But there may be differences over limitation: see *Henderson v Merrett Syndicates* [1995] 2 A.C. 145.

[5] Only a very abbreviated account of this very large topic is given here. See Clerk and Lindsell, *Torts*, 20th edn (2010), Ch.8.

reasonable care required by law, (3) that as a result he suffered damage which is recognised by the law and is not too remote. Of these elements, by far the most complex is the first. It is necessary in all cases that the claimant should be foreseeably harmfully affected by the act or omission of the defendant which is complained of, but this is not necessarily sufficient to give rise to a duty of care.

There have been many decisions at the highest level on the duty of care issue in recent years and the judicial statements are not perhaps all reconcilable. Three broad approaches have figured in the case law. The first is stated by Lord Bridge in *Caparo Industries v Dickman*[6]:

> "What emerges is that, in addition to the foreseeability of damage, necessary ingredients in any situation giving rise to a duty of care are that there should exist between the party owing the duty and the party to whom it is owed a relationship characterised by the law as one of 'proximity' or 'neighbourhood' and that the situation should be one in which the court considers it fair, just and reasonable that the law should impose a duty of a given scope on the one party for the benefit of the other."

Some judicial statements add a further ground of "policy" but it is not clear that this is in fact any different from the notion of what is fair, just and reasonable. Indeed, some judicial statements run together all considerations under the broad rubric of proximity.[7] *Caparo* was a case of negligent misstatement leading to reliance by the plaintiff receiving the information. In such a situation, however, the courts have sometimes approached the question of duty by asking whether the defendant assumed responsibility to the claimant for what he said (or must be treated in law as having done so).[8] The third approach is the so-called "incremental test", that is to say to ask whether the duty sought to be established can be regarded as sufficiently analogous to existing categories of duty. There is no single touchstone for liability,[9] though there is some support for the view that the incremental approach is really only important as a cross-check on one of the other two approaches[10] and whether it is fair, just and reasonable to impose liability may determine the answer to the question of whether the defendant should be regarded as having assumed responsibility in the legal sense.[11]

It is important to have in mind three points when dealing with cases in this area. First, "proximity" is an elastic or variable concept which varies from

---

[6] [1990] 2 A.C. 605 HL at 617–618.
[7] See, e.g. Lord Goff in *Davis v Radcliffe* [1990] 2 All E.R. 536 PC at 540: proximity is "an expression which refers to such a relation between the parties as renders it just and reasonable that liability in negligence may be imposed on the defendant for loss or damage suffered by the plaintiff by reason of the act or omission of the defendant of which complaint is made."
[8] See in particular *Hedley, Byrne & Co. v Heller & Partners* [1964] A.C. 465 HL; *Henderson v Merrett Syndicates* [1995] 2 A.C. 145 HL at 178.
[9] *Customs and Excise Comrs v Barclays Bank Plc* [2006] UKHL 28 HL; [2007] 1 A.C. 181.
[10] [2006] UKHL 28; [2007] 1 A.C. 181 at [7], [84].
[11] Ibid.

one type of damage to another. A duty of care is readily established on the basis of foreseeability in cases of direct[12] physical injury or damage[13] but in cases of psychiatric injury[14] or pure economic loss, where there is a fear of an excessively wide range of liability, there is a tendency to require a closer relationship between claimant and defendant[15] or to impose other requirements before a duty of care arises.[16] Secondly, the courts must be alert to the general structure of the law: while, e.g. there is no rule barring concurrent claims in contract and in tort,[17] it would be wrong to allow the operation of the law of negligence to subvert the allocation of responsibility made by the parties' contract.[18] The latter point, however, has not been effective to prevent the intrusion of negligence into an area formerly thought to be the exclusive preserve of defamation. Thirdly, the existence of a duty of care is a question of law and it is therefore possible to strike out a claim on the basis that a duty of care cannot exist in cases of this type because it is not fair, just and reasonable for it to do so. After some uncertainty,[19] it is now clear that this does not infringe art.6 of the European Convention on Human Rights,[20] though in many cases the issue is "fact-sensitive" and the courts are now more cautious than before in striking out without hearing evidence.

Spring v Guardian Assurance Plc. In *Spring's* case[21] the plaintiff had **23.3** been employed by Corinium and had been a "company representative" of Guardian, selling Guardian's policies. He was dismissed by Guardian when Guardian took over Corinium. The plaintiff then went into business and sought to gain authority to sell Scottish Amicable policies. In accordance with the rules of the regulatory body under the Financial Services Act 1986, Scottish Amicable sought a reference on the plaintiff and this was very uncomplimentary, asserting inter alia that the plaintiff was "of little or no integrity and could not be regarded as honest".[22] Scottish Amicable thereupon declined to authorise the plaintiff to sell its policies. The trial judge held that while the plaintiff had certainly been guilty of incompetence he had not been dishonest and that the sources in Guardian who had supplied information to

---

[12] Compare *Marc Rich AG v Bishop Rock Marine Co* [1996] A.C. 211 HL.

[13] *Caparo Industries v Dickman* [1990] 2 A.C. 605 at 632, per Lord Oliver.

[14] See *Alcock v Chief Constable of S. Yorks* [1992] 1 A.C. 310 HL; *Frost v Chief Constable of S. Yorks* [1999] 2 A.C. 455 HL.

[15] As in the cases on reliance on statements such as *Hedley, Byrne & Co. v Heller & Partners* [1964] A.C. 465 and *Caparo Industries v Dickman* [1990] 2 A.C. 605.

[16] E.g. C can generally only sue in respect of damage to property if he had ownership or possession at the time the damage was done and it is not enough that he had a contractual right in respect of the property: *Leigh and Sillavan v Aliakmon Shipping Co* [1986] A.C. 786 HL.

[17] *Henderson v Merrett Syndicates* [1995] 2 A.C. 145 HL.

[18] [1955] 2 A.C. 145 HL at 191; and see *Marc Rich AG v Bishop Rock Marine Co* [1996] A.C. 211 (wider contractual framework in which damage arose).

[19] *Osman v UK* 1998-VIII, fasc. 95.

[20] *Z v UK* App. No.29392/95; ECHR 2001-V.

[21] [1995] 2 A.C. 296 HL.

[22] [1995] 2 A.C. 296 at 306.

the compiler of the reference had failed to exercise reasonable care, although they were not malicious.[23] There was some dispute as to whether the plaintiff's status was that of employee or independent contractor, but nothing was thought to turn upon that and for convenience the judgments were largely couched in terms of the former status.[24] The words were plainly defamatory but the provision of a reference at the request of a prospective employer is the classic occasion of qualified privilege[25] and the finding of lack of malice was therefore fatal to the plaintiff's libel claim, as it was to the alternative claim for malicious falsehood. However, a majority of the House of Lords[26] held that if causation could be established[27] the plaintiff had a cause of action in negligence.

23.4 Negligence and defamation. The majority of the House of Lords rejected the contention that defamation and malicious falsehood provided an exclusive legal regime for the resolution of the plaintiff's claim and that the introduction of liability for negligence would improperly subvert the policy of the law in respect of those other torts.[28] The following reasons or justifications for this conclusion may be extracted from the speeches.[29]

(1) Defamation and negligence are different torts with different requirements: negligence requires the claimant to establish a duty of care and to prove a breach of it on a balance of probabilities, whereas in defamation the claimant establishes a case simply by showing that the words were defamatory, it then being for the defendant to prove that they were true or to demonstrate the applicability of qualified privilege or fair comment[30]; defamation protects a person's reputation and in most cases is actionable per se, whereas in negligence the claimant

---

[23] The above is a somewhat simplified account, since the reference was in fact compiled by an employee of GRE, the parent company of Guardian, on the basis of information supplied by other employees of GRE and an employee of Corinium (which was itself two associated companies) but this was treated as the responsibility of Guardian. Lord Goff did not think GRE were under any duty of care to the plaintiff but the other members of the majority treated all four companies as one unit.

[24] See, e.g. at [1995] 2 A.C. 340 and 341.

[25] See para.14.25, above.

[26] Lord Keith dissenting.

[27] For which purpose the case had to be remitted to the Court of Appeal.

[28] This had been the view of the Court of Appeal [1993] I.C.R. 412 and of the New Zealand Court of Appeal in *Bell-Booth Group v A-G* [1989] 3 N.Z.L.R. 148; *Balfour v A-G* [1991] 1 N.Z.L.R. 519; and *South Pacific Manufacturing Co. v New Zealand Security Consultants and Investigations* [1992] 2 N.Z.L.R. 282. See, however, *Midland Metals Overseas Pte Ltd v Christchurch Press Co. Ltd* [2001] NZCA 321; [2002] N.Z.L.R. 289 at [34] on the particular situation in *Spring*.

[29] For clarity only defamation is referred to in the following section. Malicious falsehood presents an even more hostile face to the claimant since the defendant does not even have to show that the words were published on a privileged occasion.

[30] [1995] 2 A.C. 296 at 325, 334, 351. Lord Goff's reasoning is somewhat different from that of his brethren. For him the duty of care arises from an "assumption of responsibility" (see also *Henderson v Merrett Syndicates* [1995] 2 A.C. 145) and therefore "I cannot see that principles of the law of defamation are of any relevance": [1995] 2 A.C. 296 at 324.

must prove some actual loss recognised by law (such as loss of property or employment[31]) and that it was caused by the negligence of the defendant[32]; and there may be cases of damaging statements which cannot be actionable as defamation because they do not reflect upon the claimant's character.[33]

(2) The effect of an incorrect employment reference may be very damaging and in modern conditions it may be impossible to obtain employment without one. There have been very considerable changes in the relationship of employer and employee since the defamation rule was established and it is no longer a fair balance to require the employee to undertake the task (commonly impossible) of proving malice.[34] In effect this largely undermines the reason for granting qualified privilege in this particular situation.

> "There would be no purpose in extending the tort of negligence to protect the subject of an inaccurate reference if he was already adequately protected by the law of defamation. . . . The result of [the requirement of malice in such cases] is that an action for defamation provides a wholly inadequate remedy for an employee who is caused damage by a reference which due to negligence is inaccurate. This is because it places a wholly disproportionate burden on the employee. Malice is extremely difficult to establish. . . . If the law provides a remedy for references which are inaccurate due to carelessness this would be beneficial. It would encourage the adoption of appropriate standards when preparing references."[35]

The contrary argument relies largely upon the proposition that if liability for negligence is imposed that will either lead to refusals to supply references or to references which are not written with candour and honesty but in a bland, defensive way so as to minimise the risk of liability to the subject.[36] Although this is to some extent countered by the fact that a liability for negligence may already exist to the recipient of the reference,[37] the force of the argument is not capable of accurate measurement.[38] All one can say is that the majority of the House of Lords[39] has found the argument unconvincing.[40]

---

[31] Although in a case like *Spring* it may in one sense be said that the claimant suffers loss because his "reputation" is damaged, the damages are not of the same nature as in an action of libel: see para.1.21.

[32] [1995] 2 A.C. 296 at 334, 350.

[33] Ibid. at 334. However, such case may fall within malicious falsehood: para.21.1, above.

[34] Ibid. at 335, 346.

[35] [1995] 2 A.C. 296 at 346, per Lord Woolf.

[36] This was the view of Lord Keith: ibid. at 309.

[37] Ibid. at 352. But compare Lord Goff's caution at 320.

[38] This is true of most "policy" arguments on the duty of care. Compare the warning of Lord Lloyd, dissenting in *Marc Rich AG v Bishop Rock Marine Co* [1996] A.C. 211. Note, however, that Lord Woolf refers at [1995] 2 A.C. 352 to the much greater openness in modern employment relationships and this seems incontrovertible.

[39] Who presumably do not write many references.

[40] For a case which, there being "not a scrap" of evidence of malice, would not have got off the ground pre-*Spring* but which required a substantial trial before the defendant was vindicated, see *Dike v Rickman* [2005] EWHC 3071 (QB).

The Supreme Court of Canada has gone further in applying the law of negligence[41] but the courts in Australia[42] and New Zealand[43] have warned against the dangers of applying negligence where it "intersects" with defamation, though the cases have generally involved relationships more remote than that in *Spring* (for example statements about the plaintiff in police databases) and the New Zealand Court of Appeal has recognized the desirability of

---

[41] See para.23.8, below.

[42] *Sullivan v Moody* [2001] HCA 59; 207 C.L.R. 562; *Tame v New South Wales* [2002] HCA 35; 211 C.L.R. 317; *Mohamed v Victoria* [2007] VSC 538. See also *Gacic v John Fairfax Publications Pty Ltd* [2005] N.S.W.S.C. 1210 (on appeal on other issues [2007] HCA 28; 235 A.L.R. 402). Cf. *Wade v Victoria* [1999] V.R. 121. The High Court of Australia in *Sullivan v Moody* had declined to find a duty of care in relation to the investigation and reporting of suspicions of child abuse against the plaintiff. In *Stewart v Ronalds* [2009] NSWCA 277 the NSWCA similarly declined to find a duty of care in senior counsel retained to investigate allegations against a member of the NSW Parliament. However, at [104] Hodgson J.A. said:

"I do not read [*Sullivan*] as altogether ruling out a duty of care in all cases where the law of defamation might apply. In a footnote to that paragraph, the joint judgment referred, without expressing either approval or disapproval, to *Spring v Guardian Assurance Plc* . . . in which the House of Lords, by a four/one majority, held that an employer giving a reference in respect of a former employee owed that employee a duty to take reasonable care in its preparation. The majority considered that the fact that, in an action for defamation based on an inaccurate reference, the employer would have a defence of qualified privilege, did not bar an action in negligence where no such defence was available. In my opinion, while it is by no means clear that this case would be followed in Australia, it is at least arguable that, because defamation applies irrespective of any particular relationship between a defendant and a plaintiff and irrespective of any particular vulnerability of a plaintiff to injury by defamatory assertions by a defendant, defamation does not necessarily cover the field and exclude a duty of care in cases where there is some particular relationship created by assumption of responsibility by a defendant and where the plaintiff has particular vulnerability to injury from defamatory assertions by the defendant."

See also, *Norris v Gittos* [2011] WASC 295 and in England: *JD v East Berkshire Community Health NHS Trust* [2005] UKHL 23 HL; [2005] 2 A.C. 373; [2005] 2 W.L.R. 993. Cf. *Young v Bella* [2006] SCC 3; [2006] 1 S.C.R. 108.

In *Reeves v New South Wales* [2010] N.S.W.S.C. 611 the plaintiff police officer alleged negligence in failing to give information to protect him from adverse comment in relation to evidence given to a Royal Commission. The defendants' argument that there was no duty of care because the exclusive remedy lay in the law of defamation was rejected. This was not a case, like *Sullivan v Moody,* where there was an "intersection" between defamation and negligence.

"Given the nature of the harm which flowed from the duties Mr Reeves was given; his statutory obligation to pursue them; his resulting vulnerability to allegations of corruption; the adverse attention to which he came before the Royal Commission as the result of the Police Service investigation . . . ; the resulting position into which he was placed at work and before the Police Board from . . . [the] false evidence about this investigation; that Mr Reeves undoubtedly had to rely on the Police Service to provide accurate information about the position into which he had been placed cannot be doubted. He was not in a position where he could protect himself without its support. That a duty of care existed in this situation must be accepted" (at [380]).

See, however, *Dale v Veda Advantage Information Services and Solutions Ltd* [2009] FCA 305, where a duty of care was denied in respect of privileged credit reports (para.14.28, above). See also, *Walker v Veda Advantage Information Services Ltd* [2011] QSC 316, at [18].

[43] *Bell-Booth Group v A-G* [1989] 3 N.Z.L.R. 148; *Balfour v A-G* [1991] 1 N.Z.L.R. 519; and *South Pacific Manufacturing Co. v New Zealand Security Consultants and Investigations* [1992] 2 N.Z.L.R. 282; *Midland Metals Overseas Pte Ltd v Christchurch Press Co. Ltd* [2001] NZCA 321; [2002] 2 N.Z.L.R. 289 at [34] on the particular situation in *Spring*. See also *Mauli v University of the South Pacific* [2007] WSSC 23.

providing a remedy on facts like those in *Spring* and emphasised that the case was based on provable economic loss and not mere injury to reputation.[44]

Limits on liability for negligence. It does not follow from *Spring v*   **23.5**
Guardian Assurance that there will always be liability in negligence where D makes a careless statement to X about C which causes loss to C; nor, to put it another way, is there liability in negligence wherever there would be liability for malicious falsehood if the statement were made with malice. For example, if in *Ratcliffe v Evans*[45] the newspaper had carelessly reported that the plaintiff's firm had gone out of business, it is thought that there would still be no liability. Even in the case where liability arises from reliance by the claimant on false information given by the defendant (the simple *Hedley Byrne* situation) the law requires close proximity between the claimant and the defendant and is reluctant to impose liability (at least for pure economic loss) in respect of generally published information.[46] Certainly the principal fear in those cases, of liability to a large number of unidentified persons is generally absent here,[47] but the imposition of liability would impose a serious burden on the reporting of news.

Media defendants and negligence. In *Spring* one of the judges in the   **23.6**
majority, Lord Goff, based the duty of care on an assumption of responsibility by the employers to the plaintiff[48] but the others relied on more general negligence principles. Nevertheless, there is considerable emphasis upon the close proximity between the plaintiff and the defendant in the case.[49] In *Midland Metals Overseas Pte Ltd v Christchurch Press Co. Ltd*[50] the plaintiffs were a Singaporean company supplying underground cables to X, a subsidiary of the second defendants in New Zealand. Employees of the second defendants made remarks to the press about the poor quality of "Chinese cables" and these were reported by the first defendants and other newspapers. The

---

[44] See *Midland Metals Overseas Pte Ltd v Christchurch Press Co. Ltd,* above at [33]–[35].

[45] [1892] 2 Q.B. 524 CA. See para.21.1, above.

[46] See *Caparo Industries v Dickman* [1990] 2 A.C. 605 HL.

[47] Though it is possible to imagine cases where there might be a very large class of persons. Suppose, e.g. a negligent report that a particular product, sold by thousands of traders, was a danger to health.

[48] This would be so even though the request comes from the prospective new employer, because even then the reference "will (apart from special circumstances) be made with either the express or tacit authority of the employee": [1995] 2 A.C. 296 at 319.

[49] The discussion in the judgments of Lords Lowry, Slynn and Woolf is closely focused on the employment reference situation. See also Lord Lowry at [1995] 2 A.C. 325 (contrasting negligence with defamation) and Lord Woolf at 342 and 344 (referring to the fact that proximity is beyond dispute). Lord Woolf, referring at [1995] 2 A.C. 349 to the N.Z. case of *Bell-Booth Group v A-G* [1989] 3 N.Z.L.R. 148 NZCA, said:
"I can well understand why Sir Robin Cooke P. should have made the comment that he did [concerning the distorting effect of the introduction of negligence liability] about the case which was before him where there was publication on television, but in the case of a reference there is unlikely to be other than limited publication."

[50] [2001] NZCA 321; [2002] 2 N.Z.L.R. 289.

New Zealand Court of Appeal held that the plaintiffs' claim for negligence had been properly struck out. The newspaper story might or might not be sufficient to identify the plaintiffs and if it did it might or might not reflect upon their reputation for the purposes of defamation. The plaintiffs' argument would in effect produce a number of fundamental changes in the balance of the law: it would render the notion of a duty of care based on proximity largely otiose; it would in effect create a liability akin to that for malicious falsehood but based on negligence rather than malice; and it would bypass the law of defamation with its specific defences crafted to produce a balance between freedom of speech and protection of reputation. As far as media defendants were concerned, the court was being asked:

> "to permit [the plaintiffs] to sue the defendants for damage caused by breach of alleged duties of care, namely, in the case of the newspapers, to adequately investigate the subject matter of the publication and to seek comment before publishing.[51] . . . It would appear that these duties would apply in the case of any media defendant. It seems also that any person being interviewed by a journalist in connection with a forthcoming story would be under a duty to refer the journalist to any person potentially affected by it. So, where there was to be a statement about goods in the story, the person being interviewed would be under a duty to refer the journalist to the supplier of the goods. These would be far reaching duties which a newspaper, its reporters and their interviewees would have to fulfil many times every day."[52]

A similar conclusion was reached by the Ontario Court of Appeal in *Shtaif v Toronto Life Publishing Co. Ltd.*[53] The plaintiffs in that case sued the defendants in respect of an internet version of an article originally published in the June 2008 edition of its magazine. The article, "How to Piss Off a Billionaire", was a profile on Canadian businessman Alex Shnaider and part of the article referred to a business dispute between Shnaider and the plaintiffs. The plaintiffs complained about the print version of the article but did not sue over it. However, when they became aware of the internet version of the article in late August 2008, they sued claiming damages both for defamation and negligence. So far as the claim for negligence was concerned, the Ontario Court of Appeal noted that the Supreme Court of Canada had said in *Young v Bella*[54] that a claim for negligence can proceed alongside a defamation claim

---

[51] The judge at this point remarked that "an alleged duty to publish only the truth was not pursued".

[52] Ibid. at [54], per Blanchard J. See also *Fleming v Securities Commission* [1995] 2 N.Z.L.R. 514 NZCA. The combined judgment of Gault, Keith and McGrath JJ. in *Midland Metals* states at [35]:

> "It must be emphasised that in the present case . . . . we are concerned only with claims in negligence for injury to reputation. We are not required to deal with claims in negligence giving rise to economic loss."

However, the plaintiffs had pleaded that they had "suffered serious harm in that orders were cancelled and [their] business in cables has been effectively destroyed" (at [21]).

[53] 2013 ONCA 405.

[54] [2006] SCC 3; [2006] 1 S.C.R. 108. See, para.23.8 below.

provided that the necessary elements of a cause of action in negligence have been established. On the facts, however, a sufficiently close relationship of proximity was not made out. There were only two telephone interviews between the plaintiffs and the defendants, and no other pre-existing relationship between the parties. While in a general sense the media has, or should have, an obligation to adequately investigate a story to ensure the accuracy of the facts about any person referred to in the story, and to obtain that person's side of the story, to say that these contacts by themselves gave rise to a duty of care would mean that in virtually every case a plaintiff could proceed with a negligence claim as well as a defamation claim. The principle in *Young v Bella* does not go that far.[55]

Duties in reference-like situations. The question therefore is how far   **23.7**
Spring is to be extended beyond the narrow situation of a reference by a former employer to another potential employer.[56] For example, because a former employer will generally be under a duty of care in the preparation of a reference it does not follow that the same is true of a social acquaintance.[57] It has been held that an employer does not owe a duty of care to a former employee, who had been dismissed, to ensure that future possible employers were aware of the actual reasons for the dismissal.[58] Duties of care have, however, been held to exist in English law beyond the straightforward situation of a requested employment reference. Thus, in *Gatt v Barclays Bank*[59] it was held that a duty of care was owed by a bank to the wife of the person about whom a credit reference was given. While the court thought that ordinarily this would not be so, where to the bank's knowledge the wife was a joint holder of the same account and a co-director of the family business which largely depended on her husband's credit, both proximity and foreseeability of damage were present and it was therefore fair, just and reasonable to hold that a duty of care was owed to both the wife and husband.[60] So too, a duty of care has been held to exist in respect of an unsolicited email about

---

[55] 2013 ONCA 405 at [82].
[56] Lord Woolf in particular emphasises that the decision concerns references and that whether and how far it applies to supposedly analogous situations will have to be determined as they arise: [1995] 2 A.C. 296 at 354.
[57] [1995] 2 A.C. 296 at 319, 336, 345.
[58] *Aspin v Metric Group Ltd* [2004] EWHC 1265 (QB).
[59] [2013] EWHC 2 (QB). Cf. *Smeaton v Equifax Plc* [2013] EWCA Civ 108; [2013] 2 All E.R. 959 in which it was held that credit reference agencies do not assume a duty of care in tort, co-extensive with the duties that they owed under the Data Protection Act 1998, to all whose personal data they hold. Imposing a duty owed to members of the public generally would potentially give rise to an indeterminate liability to an indeterminate class. A co-extensive duty of care in tort would also be otiose, given that the Act provided a detailed code for determining the civil liability of credit reference agencies and other data controllers arising out of the improper processing of data (at [73]–[76]).
[60] Ibid. at [35].

a former employee sent to the employee's new employer.[61] *Spring* was also applied in Australia in respect of information given about the plaintiff's police service, some six years before, to a Criminal Justice Commission, which was investigating criminal involvement in gambling.[62]

Somewhat akin to the reference situation is that where D is engaged by X to make a report to X on the performance[63] or health of C. The mere fact that the defendant is commissioned to perform the service by a third party does not preclude his owing a duty to the claimant,[64] but it has been held that a doctor employed by an organisation to check on the health of prospective employees does not owe them a duty of care in the event that a negligent examination leads to refusal of employment.[65] Similarly a doctor making an examination on behalf of a life assurance company is under a duty not to damage the applicant in the course of the examination, but beyond that his duties are owed to the insurance company and not to the applicant.[66] In both these situations the defendant may be regarded as in the position of an investigator and the possibility of a conflict of interest points away from a duty of care being owed. Thus the district auditor in exercising his statutory reporting function does not owe a duty of care to officers of the local authority for:

"Parliament intended that [he] should be free to make his report whenever he considered it to be in the public interest to do so. Short of bad faith he must be free to criticise an officer of the local authority without fear of exposing himself to an action for negligence at the suit of that officer."[67]

---

[61] In *McKie v Swindon College* [2011] EWHC 469 (QB). H.H.J. Denyer QC held that a duty of care was owed to a former employee (the claimant) in respect of a defamatory email sent, unsolicited, to a university now employing him which led to his summary dismissal. Applying the principles articulated by the House of Lords in *Caparo v Dickman,* the judge held that economic loss was foreseeable to the claimant as a consequence of the sending of the negligent and defamatory email, that there was a sufficient relationship of proximity as a result of the defendants choosing to write the email they did, purportedly relying upon information derived from the time that the claimant worked for them and that it was fair just and reasonable to impose a duty of care (at [49]–[51]).

[62] *Wade v State of Victoria* [1999] V.R. 121. But it is not clear that *Spring* represents the law in Australia (see para.23.4, above) and *Wade* was doubted in *Cornwall v Rowan* [2004] SASC 384; 90 S.A.S.R. 269 at [694].

[63] Does *Thorne v University of London* [1966] 2 Q.B. 237 CA require reconsideration?

[64] *Phelps v Hillingdon LBC* [2001] 2 A.C. 619 HL.

[65] *Kapfunde v Abbey National* [1999] I.C.R. 1 CA.

[66] *X v Bedfordshire CC* [1995] 2 A.C. 633 HL at 752–753. *X v Bedfordshire* involved child abuse. It is now the case that a person involved in such a situation may owe a duty of care to the child but there is still no duty to the parents: *JD v East Berkshire etc NHS Trust* [2005] UKHL 23; [2005] 2 A.C. 373. This is therefore a situation in which there might be liability for defamation (subject to the protection of qualified privilege) but no duty of care in negligence: see *W v Westminster City Council* [2004] EWHC 2866 (QB).

[67] *West Wiltshire DC v Garland* [1995] Ch. 297 CA at 312; *South Pacific Manufacturing Co. v New Zealand Security Consultants and Investigations* [1992] 2 N.Z.L.R. 282 NZCA (no duty by insurance loss investigator to person making claim). Although this case follows the line on the relationship between negligence and defamation which was rejected in *Spring*, Lord Woolf approved the result because there "is not the same proximity between the parties as there is in the case of a reference given by an employer concerning an employee": [1995] 2 A.C. 350. It is not clear whether Lord Woolf is using "proximity" here in the broad sense of something which includes all the factors which go to make up fairness, justice and reasonableness.

Assumption of responsibility without reliance. In the reference situa-   **23.8**
tion the defendant will often, though not invariably, act with the express or
implied consent of the subject, or at least with his knowledge, so that in a
sense it may be said that the subject relies on the defendant's taking care[68]
There may be circumstances, however, when a duty may arise based on
assumption of responsibility without reliance by the claimant.[69] In *Young v
Bella*[70] the Supreme Court of Canada imposed liability in a case where an
error in interpreting a student's work led to her being suspected of child sex
abuse and this was communicated to the police and social workers.

> "Freedom of expression and the policies underlying qualified privilege can be taken
> into account in determining the appropriate standard of care in negligence.[71] . . .
> There is no reason in principle why negligence actions should not be allowed to
> proceed where (a) proximity and foreseeability have been established, and (b) the
> damages cover more than just harm to the plaintiff's reputation (i.e. where there are
> further damages arising from the defendant's negligence) . . . In fact all of the cases
> cited by the respondents as standing for the proposition that defamation had
> 'cornered the market' on reputation damages were cases in which (unlike here) there
> was no pre-existing relationship between the parties that gave rise to a duty of
> care."[72]

Even further removed from the facts of *Spring* is a case where the Court of
Appeal declined to strike out a claim brought by persons who had been denied
flights to England with the airline with which they had booked because an
employee of the Home Office had questioned their right of entry[73] (though of
course one cannot place too much weight on failed striking out applications).

---

[68] See Lord Goff at [1995] 2 A.C. 319. However, Lord Goff's reasoning emphasises *Hedley
Byrne* and assumption of responsibility more than the other members of the majority. Reliance
will of course be present in the classic reference cases but in *McKie* (above), *Wade v State of
Victoria* (above) and the situation where D is engaged by X to make a report to X on the
performance or health of C, there is no express reliance by the claimant on the defendant taking
care. These cases can only really be explained on the basis that there was a sufficient assumption
of responsibility to give rise to a duty of care on the part of the defendant.

[69] *White v Jones* [1995] 2 A.C. 207 HL. *Spring* was rejected in N.S.W. in *Sattin v Nationwide
News* (1996) 39 N.S.W.L.R. 32 but that was a case of publication of a photograph of the plaintiff
with a man who was not her husband, describing them as "newlyweds". The plaintiff's argument
really did amount to an attempt to use negligence a quite general alternative to libel. See also
Fulton v Globe & Mail (1997) 152 D.L.R. (4th) 377 (claim for defamation and a paragraph
claiming that the defendants were liable in addition, or in the alternative, "for doing shoddy
research"; paragraph struck out as not disclosing a cause of action) and *Yahong Bai v Sing Tao
Daily Ltd*, May 20, 2003, Ont. CA.

[70] [2006] SCC 3; [2006] 1 S.C.R. 108. Cf. *Sullivan v Moody* [2001] HCA 59; 207 C.L.R. 562
and *JD v East Berkshire Community Health NHS Trust* [2005] UKHL 23 HL; [2005] 2 A.C. 373;
[2005] 2 W.L.R. 993 in which the House of Lords held that claims in negligence brought by
parents against doctors and social workers who had wrongly determined that they had abused or
harmed their children had to be dismissed on public policy grounds (see para.23.4, above,
fn.42).

[71] The defendants were not required to investigate the matter themselves but on the facts they
did not have reasonable cause to make a report on the information available to them: at [34].

[72] [2006] SCC 3; [2006] 1 S.C.R. 108 at [56].

[73] *Farah v Home Office*, *The Times*, January 26, 2000, CA.

So too, in *Monk v Cann Hall Primary School*,[74] on an application for leave to amend her claim, the Court of Appeal accepted that it was arguable that a duty of care existed where psychiatric injury was caused to a school administrative assistant who had been made redundant and was then publicly escorted from the premises eight days before the end of term thereby giving the impression to those watching that she had committed an act of gross misconduct.

Although freedom of expression is commonly conceived of as a right or liberty of the defendant, it may also be necessary for the proper protection of the interests of society. The law of defamation has, in particular via the defence of privilege, attempted to strike a balance between this interest and protection of reputation, and that balance should not lightly be cast aside by extension of liability for negligence where the claimant is able to prove damage in the sense of that tort.[75]

23.9 Standard of care. If the statement is true, there can be no liability in negligence any more than for defamation[76]: there is no liability because the truth is revealed in an unfair manner or the investigations upon which it is based are not revealed in full.[77] The mere fact that the statement is untrue does not mean that the defendant is liable: the duty is one to take reasonable care and the defendant may be entitled to rely upon information supplied by others for whom he is not responsible. However, it is thought that in many cases factual inaccuracy will be virtually conclusive evidence of negligence.[78] Furthermore, where there has been reliance on inaccurate personal data falling within the Data Protection Act[79] there will be a claim for compensation for damage suffered thereby unless the data controller proves that he had taken such care in all the circumstances as was reasonably required.[80]

---

[74] [2013] EWCA Civ 826. A claim in defamation and for unfair dismissal had been compromised.

[75] In the extraordinary case of *Tame v New South Wales* [2002] HCA 35; 191 A.L.R. 449, the plaintiff was involved in a road accident and by administrative error the police recorded her as having a high blood alcohol level when in fact she had not been drinking at all. Although the error was corrected, the plaintiff became obsessed about the potential effect of this on her reputation and suffered a psychiatric disorder. The record was plainly defamatory but on the facts had done no harm to her reputation and was in any case presumably covered by qualified privilege. The court, while eschewing any rigid rules in Australian law that the plaintiff must be a person of normal fortitude or that the injury must occur from a sudden shock, held that the damage was not reasonably foreseeable. Gleeson C.J. and Gaudron and McHugh JJ. all adverted to the need for negligence liability to be restrained so that it did not disconform to the policies behind defamation law. See also para.23.4, above.

[76] *Spring v Guardian Assurance Plc* [1995] 2 A.C. 296 at 335–336, per Lord Slynn and at 347, per Lord Woolf.

[77] For this reason the case of *Bell-Booth Group v A-G* [1989] 3 N.Z.L.R. 148 NZCA, was rightly decided on its facts. The claim in *Lawton v BOC Transhield* [1987] I.C.R. 7 failed for the same reason.

[78] Tutor A in 2013 writes a reference on student B who graduated in 2003 and the records which he uses show incorrectly the student got a third rather than an upper second. Tutor A is not negligent but the university would find it hard to show that *it* was not (it is assumed that there is a duty of care in such a case).

[79] See para.22.19, above.

[80] Data Protection Act 1998, s.13.

The duty at common law is not confined to not telling an untruth, it also extends to not making misleading statements[81]; however, it does not extend to a duty to give a "full" reference.[82]

Liability in contract. In *Spring v Guardian Assurance* there had been a contractual relationship between the plaintiff and at least one of the defendants[83] and whether this was a contract of service or for services was not regarded as significant.[84] In either event there was an implied term in that contract (notwithstanding that all the duties of the plaintiff under it had ceased on his dismissal) that the former employer would ensure that reasonable care was exercised in the preparation of the reference,[85] though this would add nothing to the substance of a tort claim in respect of an inaccurate reference.[86] However, it is contemplated in *Spring's* case that the existence of a prior employment relationship may mean that during it or within a reasonable time after its termination the former employer is under a contractual duty to provide the reference.[87] Where there is no such duty by contract[88] an undertaking to the subject to provide a reference coupled with reliance by the subject might lead to liability under the current broad interpretation of *Hedley, Byrne v Heller & Partners.*[89]

23.10

Damage and causation. Negligence, unlike libel, is not actionable per se. Therefore the claimant is required to show on a balance of probabilities that he has suffered damage as a result of the defendant's negligence and mere general damage to reputation will not do.[90] Where the reference was a mere

23.11

---

[81] *Bartholomew v Hackney LBC* [1999] I.R.L.R. 246 CA. See also *Cox v Sun Alliance Life Ltd* [2001] EWCA Civ 649.

[82] *Kidd v Axa Equity and Law* [2000] I.R.L.R. 301.

[83] Corinium. It was uncertain whether there was any contractual relationship with Guardian: [1995] 2 A.C. 296 at 340.

[84] See para.23.3, above.

[85] [1995] 2 A.C. at 320, 340, 354. Cf. Lord Lowry at 327.

[86] Ibid. at 320.

[87] Most clearly by Lord Woolf at [1995] 2 A.C. 354. Lord Slynn at 339 said that: "even if here is no universal duty . . . contracts may exist when it is necessary to imply such a duty." On the facts of the case the LAUTRO rules required the defendants to provide a frank reference to the inquirers. But cf. *Aspin v Metric Group Ltd* [2004] EWHC 1265 (QB).

[88] Is a university under an enforceable duty to provide an academic reference at the request of a student? It is thought that if an employer is under such a duty the answer is yes. It is understood that in 1996 a student obtained a £50,000 settlement of a claim against a university in respect of an inaccurate reference. This is not of course the same thing as saying that an individual member of staff is under a duty enforceable by the student to give such a reference. Is a school under a similar duty? It might be more difficult to say there was a contract but it would be odd if the position were different.

[89] [1964] A.C. 465 HL. See *Henderson v Merrett Syndicates* [1995] 2 A.C. 145 HL and *White v Jones* [1995] 2 A.C. 207 HL.

[90] See paras 23.4 and 1.21, above. In *Young v Bella* [2006] SCC 3; [2006] 1 S.C.R. 108 (para.23.5, above) there was evidence to support loss of income and related matters but the SCC declined to interfere with an award of $430,000 general damages (higher than would have been made in the most serious case of personal injury) in a total award of $839,000.

confirmation of qualification the claimant may be able to show on a balance of probabilities that if an accurate one had been given he would have been able to obtain what he sought.[91] However, in a case where the claimant has failed to obtain employment it may be impossible to show that with an accurate reference the claimant would have got the job; e.g. references are commonly used only or primarily for the purpose of drawing up a short list of applicants from a large field and in such a case the best that the claimant can usually do is to show that he has lost a chance of obtaining the employment. Provided, however, that the chance is more than merely speculative this is not, in a case where the issue turns on what would have been done by a third party (i.e. the prospective employer in a reference case), a bar to the claimant's success and the court must value the lost chance as best it can.[92]

SECTION 2. HARASSMENT

23.12 The Protection from Harassment Act 1997. Harassment by unlawful means such as lies which is intended to cause and does cause injury to health may be tortious at common law.[93] However, even where there is no such injury there may be liability under the Protection from Harassment Act 1997. By virtue of s.1, a person must not pursue a course of conduct (1) which amounts to harassment of another and (2) which he knows or ought to know amounts to harassment of the other.[94] The question of whether he ought to know that his conduct amounts to harassment is determined by asking whether a reasonable person in possession of the information he has would think the course of conduct amounted to harassment.[95]

The Act does not attempt to define harassment but in its ordinary meaning it "describes conduct targeted at an individual which is calculated to produce the consequences described in section 7 of the Act[96] and which is oppressive

---

[91] Sometimes references are sought as a check on honesty after a conditional offer of employment has been made.

[92] *Allied Maples Group v Simmons & Simmons* [1995] 1 W.L.R. 1602 CA. This is not a reference case but the principle is supported by Lord Lowry in *Spring* [1995] 2 A.C. 296 at 327. Lord Lowry was in favour of remitting the case to the trial judge to determine damages but the majority favoured remitting the case to the CA on the issue of causation.

[93] *Wilkinson v Downton* [1897] 2 Q.B. 57 (despite the fact that there was clearly no "intention" in that case and despite Lord Hoffmann's criticisms of it in *Wainwright v Home Office* [2003] UKHL 53; [2004] 2 A.C. 406); *Janvier v Sweeney* [1919] 2 K.B. 316 CA; *Austen v University of Wolverhampton* [2005] EWHC 1635 (QB).

[94] S.1(1).

[95] S.1(2).

[96] S.7(2) "references to harassing a person include alarming the person or causing the person distress". Note "include": if the "harassee" is tough minded extreme annoyance might be the consequence. Is this within the Act? In *Potter v Price* [2004] EWHC 781 (QB), where threatening emails were sent from England to the claimant in Thailand and where there were concurrent claims under the 1997 Act and s.40 of the Administration of Justice Act 1970 (harassment of debtors), it was held that for the purposes of s.11 of the Private International Law (Miscellaneous Provisions) Act 1995 "significant elements" of the tort occurred in England, because the claimant frequently returned here and distress was an ongoing thing.

and unreasonable".[97] One cannot perhaps say much more than that there is a distinction between conduct which is "unattractive, even unreasonable, and conduct which is oppressive and unacceptable",[98] though the application of the distinction will be affected by the context in which the conduct takes place.[99] A "course of conduct" must involve conduct on at least two[100] occasions.[101] Harassment is primarily criminal[102] but it is also civilly actionable[103] by the person who is or may be the victim of it and both damages and an injunction may be obtained.[104] The origin of the Act is the phenomenon of "stalking",[105] but it is obviously capable of extending to directly intrusive

---

[97] *Thomas v News Group Newspapers Ltd* [2001] EWCA Civ 1233; [2002] E.M.L.R. 4 at [30].

[98] *Majrowski v Guy's and St Thomas's NHS Trusts* [2006] UKHL 34; [2007] 1 A.C. 224 at [30] per Lord Nicholls. The tormenting of a person by subjecting him to constant interference or intimidation will constitute harassment: *R v Curtis* [2010] EWCA Crim 123; [2010] W.L.R. 2770; [2010] 1 Cr. App. R. 31 (sporadic outbursts of violent temper over nine months). See also *Ferguson v British Gas Trading Ltd* [2009] EWCA Civ 46; [2010] 1 W.L.R. 785 (persistent, unjustified demands for payment even if unknown to management); *DPP v Hardy* [2008] EWHC 2874 (QB) (legitimate inquiry may become harassment by reason of the manner in which it was being pursued and its persistence); *James v CPS* [2009] EWHC 2925 (Admin) (continual abuse of person coming into contact with D even if contact voluntary).

[99] *Conn v Sunderland City Council* [2007] EWCA Civ 1492; [2008] I.R.L.R. 324.

[100] By s.1(1A), inserted by the Serious Organised Crime and Police Act 2005, where the harassment is of two or more persons there need only be conduct on one occasion in relation to each person but s.1(1A) does not give rise to a claim for damages, though an injunction may be obtained under s.3A.

[101] S.7(3). Hence the conduct in *Wilkinson v Downton* [1897] 2 Q.B. 57 would not be within the statute, nor, presumably, would that in *Johnson v Sampson*, 208 N.W. 814 (Minn., 1926) (long drawn out badgering of girl to get her to confess to immorality). However, the conduct in *Khorasandjian v Bush* [1993] Q.B. 727 CA, would. But see *Wainwright v Home Office* [2001] EWCA Civ 2081; [2002] Q.B. 1334 at [62] referring to "unresolved doubts" about the meaning of the phrase. The meaning of course of conduct has been considered in several criminal cases, e.g. *R. v Kellett* [2001] EWHC 1107 Admin (two telephone calls to the victim's work superior); *Kelly v DPP* [2002] EWHC 1428 Admin. The fewer the incidents to have occurred and the further apart in time, the less likely it would be that a finding of harassment could be reasonably made: *Lau v DPP* [2000] Crim. L.R. 580; *Pratt v DPP* [2001] EWHC 483 Admin. But cf. *Jones v Hipgrave* [2004] EWHC 2901 (QB); *Buckley v DPP* [2008] EWHC 136 Admin. There is no need for the complainant to have been harassed on every occasion that contributes to the course of conduct: *Howlett v Holding* [2006] EWHC 3758 at [22] (QB).

[102] S.2.

[103] Although civil liability under the 1997 Act is founded on conduct which amounts to a crime, the standard of proof in civil proceedings is the ordinary civil one of a balance of probabilities: *Jones v Hipgrave* [2004] EWHC 2901 (QB). Although there is some degree of overlap and similarity between the 1997 Act and the grounds for making an anti-social behaviour order under the Crime and Disorder Act 1998 ("that the person has acted . . . in an anti-social manner, that is to say, in a manner that caused or was likely to cause harassment, alarm or distress to one or more persons not of the same household as himself") and under the 1998 Act, although the proceedings are civil, the standard of proof is the criminal one, there are also significant differences between the purposes and scope of the two pieces of legislation.

[104] S.3. There are comparable provisions for Scotland in s.8. As to Northern Ireland, see s.13.

[105] After criticisms about the Act's ineffectiveness in dealing with this phenomenon a new offence directed specifically at "stalking" was added to the Act (s.2A) by the Protection of Freedoms Act 2012, s.111.

invasions of privacy like "doorstepping".[106] However, "conduct" includes speech,[107] so there is also a potential overlap with the areas of defamation[108] and invasion of privacy by publication of private information.[109] So the wrong may be committed by repeated accusations which were defamatory but not actionable, because, e.g. they were true, protected by privilege or they were not published to any third party.

There is no requirement that the conduct be in any way independently unlawful, though by s.1(3)(c) it is a defence (the burden of proof of which is on the defendant) that the conduct was in the particular circumstances reasonable.[110] The test here would seem to be whether it is objectively reasonable, not whether the defendant thinks it is.[111] *Thomas v News Group Newspapers*

---

[106] S.42 of the Criminal Justice and Police Act 2001 enables a police officer to direct persons to desist. The Act has been used on several occasions to obtain orders against members of the paparazzi.

[107] S.7(4).

[108] For examples of overlapping claims see *Cray v Hancock*, November 4, 2005, (QB) and *Sunderland Housing Co v Baines* [2006] EWHC 2359 (QB). In *Howlett v Holding* [2006] EWHC 41 (QB); *The Times*, February 8, 2000 at [22] the defendant had for some years conducted a vendetta against the claimant because of her opposition to a planning application by his company. The claimant had already obtained two jury verdicts against him in actions for defamation but he persisted in flying aircraft around the area towing defamatory banners and dropping leaflets. Eady J. granted an injunction to restrain harassment. In *R. v Debnath* [2005] EWCA Crim 3472 the court upheld a restraining order which indefinitely prohibited the defendant from publishing any information about the complainant or his fiancée. See also *Bloom v Robinson-Millar* [2013] EWHC 3918 (QB) (single award of damages made including aggravated damages, for libel and harassment against a leaseholder who had written numerous defamatory letters to residents of a block of flats and others making unfounded allegations against another resident who was a director of the management company); *ZAM v CFW* [2013] EWHC 662 (QB) (assessment of damages where there are overlapping claims); *The Law Society of England and Wales v Kordowski* [2011] EWHC 3185 (QB).

[109] But while a company may be libelled or subjected to a breach of confidence, it may not be the subject of harassment within the meaning of the Act: *Daiichi UK Ltd v Stop Huntington Animal Cruelty* [2003] EWHC 2337 (QB); [2004] 1 W.L.R. 1503.

[110] In addition, there is a defence for conduct pursued for the purpose of preventing or detecting crime (s.1(3)(a)) or pursued under any enactment or rule of law (s.1(3)(b)).

[111] See, *Majrowski v Guy's and St Thomas's NHS Trust* [2005] EWCA Civ 251; [2005] Q.B. 848 at [82] CA; *Banks v Ablex Ltd* [2005] EWCA Civ 173 at [26] CA; [2005] ICR 819; *Trimingham v Associated Newspapers Ltd* [2012] EWHC 1296 at [89] (QB); *Conn v City of Sunderland* [2007] EWCA Civ 1492; [2008] I.R.L.R. 324 at [18] CA. Compare the crime of blackmail: *R. v Harvey, Ulyett and Plummer* (1981) 72 Cr. App. R. 139 CA.

There is also a defence under s.1(3)(a) of the Act if the person who pursued the course of conduct shows "that it was pursued for the purpose of preventing or detecting crime". This defence has been stated by the Supreme Court (*Hayes v Willoughby* [2013] UKSC 17) to require for its application only that the defendant honestly and "rationally" believed that what he did was for purpose of preventing or detecting crime. It did not require proof that his conduct was objectively reasonable. The Supreme Court held that the defence was triggered where the prevention or detection of crime was the harasser's dominant (as distinct from sole) motive ([17]). However, a subjective belief on the part of defendant that would not justify the harasser's conduct: some control mechanism was required and that was to be found in the concept of "rationality".

"A test of rationality, applies a minimum objective standard to the relevant person's mental processes. It imports a requirement of good faith, a requirement that there should be some logical connection between the evidence and the ostensible reasons for the decision, and (which will usually amount to the same thing) an absence of arbitrariness, of capriciousness or of

Ltd^{112} was a civil action arising out of the Act. The claim concerned two articles and letters in a newspaper about the disciplining of police officers which had identified the claimant as the author of the complaint, identified her as black, given her name and place of work and, she alleged, caused her to receive hate mail. In dismissing an appeal from refusal of a defendant's striking out/summary judgment application,[113] the Court of Appeal held that ss.3 and 12 of the Human Rights Act 1998 are relevant to a claim under the 1997 Act; that it is for the defendant to show that his conduct is reasonable; but that unless the claimant's pleading alleges conduct by the defendant which is, at least, arguably unreasonable, it is unlikely to set out a viable plea of harassment.[114] To the argument that putting so much weight on reasonableness was unacceptably vague, the court responded that:

> "the test requires the publisher to consider whether a proposed series of articles, which is likely to cause distress to an individual, will constitute an abuse of the freedom of press which the pressing social needs of a democratic society require should be curbed. This is a familiar test and not one which offends against [Convention]'s requirement of certainty."[115]

Harassment and the media. There have been many cases brought under   **23.13** the 1997 Act for "stalking" and other persistent and unpleasant conduct but *Trimingham v Associated Newspapers Ltd*[116] was only the second full trial of a claim of alleged harassment by publication in the media.[117] The case offers

---

reasoning so outrageous in its defiance of logic as to be perverse" (per Lord Sumption at [14]).

[112] [2001] EWCA Civ 1233; [2002] E.M.L.R. 4.

[113] It was conceded that in principle the Act was capable of applying to press publications.

[114] "Subject to the law of defamation, the press is entitled to publish an article, or series of articles, about an individual, notwithstanding that it could be foreseen that such conduct was likely to cause distress to the subject of the article . . . . The 1997 Act has not rendered such conduct unlawful. In general, press criticism, even if robust, does not constitute unreasonable conduct and does not fall within the natural meaning of harassment. A pleading, which does no more than allege that the defendant newspaper has published a series of articles that have foreseeably caused stress to an individual, will be susceptible to a strike-out on the ground that it discloses no arguable case of harassment" (at [33]–[34]). See also *Sharma v Jay* [2003] EWHC 1230 (QB).

[115] At [50]. Before the Act, any claim for libel would presumably have been based on the implication that the claimant had behaved improperly in informing. From the report it looks likely that this would very arguably have been comment rather than fact so that in the absence of evidence that the opinion expressed was not that of the editor, no matter how unreasonable or racist, that, in the present state of the law of fair comment, would have been the end of the matter (para.12.25, above). So the decision does represent a restriction on press freedom greater than that posed by libel law.

[116] [2012] EWHC 1296 (QB).

[117] The first was the Northern Ireland case of *King v Sunday Newspapers Ltd* [2011] NICA 8; [2012] N.I. 1. In *King*, the claimant sued in respect of several newspaper articles. The articles made a number of allegations against Mr King, essentially accusing him of involvement in loyalist paramilitary crimes. One article revealed the identity of Mr King's partner, indicating that she was Catholic and that she and Mr King were bringing up their child in the Catholic faith. The defendant also published pictures of the claimant, including one in which Mr King and his partner were shown at a wedding. The claimant brought an action, inter alia, on the basis that the articles amounted to harassment within the meaning of the Protection from Harassment (Northern Ireland) Order 1997, art.3. The Northern Ireland Court of Appeal held that Mr King had not made

important insights into the approach to be taken to a claim in harassment brought by someone characterised by the judge as a "public figure" against a media defendant and makes it clear that it will be a rare case in which such a claim will succeed under the Act. The claimant, Ms Trimingham, had worked in journalism, communications and public relations for over 20 years. She had also been involved in politics as a party worker for several years and during the 2010 general election she was campaigns officer for the Electoral Reform Society, but worked on secondment as Mr Chris Huhne's press officer for his election campaign. Mr Huhne was re-elected and became a minister in the Coalition Government. In 2008, Ms Trimingham and Mr Huhne started an affair, unknown to both Mr Huhne's wife and Ms Trimingham's civil partner. The relationship became public in June 2010 when it was revealed by *The People* and *The Mail on Sunday*. Thereafter extensive coverage appeared in the defendant's newspapers about the relationship, which included the fact that the claimant was in a civil partnership with a woman and had deceived her civil partner. She sued in respect of interference with her rights to a private life under three statutes including under the Protection from Harassment Act 1997.[118] Although the articles were defamatory of the claimant, no claim for libel was brought as she did not dispute that what was published about her was substantially true. The relief claimed was for damages including aggravated damages and an injunction.

The judge held that the claim should fail. First, Ms Trimingham was not the purely private figure she claimed to be. Her reasonable expectation of privacy had become limited by reason of what she had herself disclosed in the past as well as by reason of her involvement with Mr Huhne, both professionally, as his press agent, and personally as his secret mistress.[119] Further, she was, as the defendant knew, a journalist who had herself disclosed information about other people for publication in the newspapers and so was a person who ought not reasonably to be expected to be distressed when such information was published about herself.[120] Secondly, it was true that the words complained of

---

out a case of harassment. The court emphasised that in approaching the question whether the defendant's conduct was unreasonable and oppressive it must take into account the right of the press to freedom of expression. Here there was no evidence that the articles constituted an abuse of freedom of the press which the pressing social needs of a democratic society required should be curbed. The claimant had not challenged the truth of the allegations, and the mere fact that the articles had caused him distress did not establish harassment. He had not shown that the defendant knew, or ought to have known, that it was harassing him. While the articles contained some factual errors and misused some private information, that did not show that the defendant had set out to harass Mr King as opposed to printing a story intended to expose aspects of his life in the public interest and in the exercise of its right of free expression (at [35]–[38]).

[118] The two other claims were for interference with her privacy right under the Copyright Designs and Patents Act 1988, s.85, in respect of two photographs (see para.23.19, below), and for misuse of private information pursuant to the Human Rights Act 1998, art.8 of the European Convention on Human Rights. Both these claims failed.

[119] [2012] EWHC 1296 (QB) at [249].

[120] Ibid. at [252].

included insults and other offensive matter, but that of itself did not suffice for her to succeed. As the judge explained, a course of conduct in the form of journalistic speech is reasonable under the Act unless, in the particular circumstances of the case, the course of conduct is so unreasonable that it is necessary (in the sense of a pressing social need) and proportionate to prohibit or sanction the speech in pursuit of one of the aims listed in art.10(2), including, in particular, for the protection of the rights of others under art.8[121]:

> "It would be a serious interference with freedom of expression if those wishing to express their own views could be silenced by, or threatened with, claims for harassment based on subjective claims by individuals that they feel offended or insulted. The test for harassment is objective. As Lord Phillips said in *Thomas* at para [35]: ' . . . before press publications are capable of constituting harassment, they must be attended by some exceptional circumstance which justifies sanctions and the restriction on the freedom of expression that they involve. It is also common ground that such circumstances will be rare'."[122]

To constitute harassment, the course of conduct must also cross a threshold of seriousness such that the gravity of the conduct must be of an order which would sustain criminal liability under s.2 of the Act.[123] In this case what the claimant complained of was not so unreasonable that it was necessary or proportionate to sanction or prohibit such publications in order to protect her rights. It was not the case that a reasonable person in the position of the defendant ought to have known that these articles, separately, or cumulatively, amounted to harassment of Ms Trimingham.

Thirdly, although the defendant referred to the claimant's sexuality in 65 articles over about 15 months, it only did so (a) when writing about matters of public interest, mainly developments in Mr Huhne's personal life which were relevant to his public life, and (b) when Ms Trimingham and her conduct (and other information about her) were within the range of what an editor could in good faith regard as relevant to the story. Finally, with regard to causation, the judge accepted that the claimant had indeed suffered the distress of which she complained but held that this was not caused by the course of conduct complained of.[124] Such distress as had been caused was the result of the publication by the defendant of the defamatory and true information concerning her, about which she did not make a complaint in defamation, and the actions of journalists and publishers for whom the defendant was not responsible.[125]

---

[121] Ibid. at [53].
[122] Ibid. at [267].
[123] Ibid. at [87]–[88].
[124] Ibid. at [253].
[125] Ibid. at [253]–[254].

23.14 Remedies and harassment. Damages under the Act "may be awarded for (among other things) any anxiety[126] caused by the harassment and any financial loss resulting from the statement"[127] but not, it is thought, for loss of reputation as such. By virtue of the Crime and Courts Act 2013,[128] the relevant provisions of which are not yet in force, aggravated and exemplary damages may also be available in a harassment claim brought against a "relevant publisher".

Although the 1997 Act says nothing on this matter, in accordance with general principle an employer is vicariously liable for conduct by an employee which contravenes the Act, including conduct directed at fellow employees, provided there is a sufficiently close connection between the conduct and the employment.[129]

---

[126] Provided it is not too remote, it would appear that damages might be recovered for more serious mental trauma, though the limitation period is six years, not three as in most personal injury cases: s.6.

[127] S.3(2).

[128] See paras 9.22–9.24 and 9.32–9.33, above.

[129] *Majrowski v Guy's and St Thomas's NHS Trusts* [2006] UKHL 34; [2007] 1 A.C. 224). And see *Daniels v MPC* [2006] EWHC 1622 (QB). In *Allen v Chief Constable of Hampshire* [2013] EWCA Civ 967 CA, the Court of Appeal struck out a claim brought against the chief constable based on vicarious liability for an alleged harassment campaign carried out by a police officer, as the facts did not reveal any, let alone a close, connection between the alleged acts and the tortfeasor's employment as a police officer. The acts of harassment involved telephone calls, arson and criminal damage but, even assuming that the police officer was responsible, there was nothing to connect these with the purported performance of police duties or functions. In addition to the 1997 Act, there are now various statutory provisions making it unlawful for an employer to subject a person to harassment in relation to employment. Details are beyond the scope of this work, but an important example is s.26 of the Equality Act 2010:

"(1) A person (A) harasses another (B) if—
    (a) A engages in unwanted conduct related to a relevant protected characteristic, and
    (b) the conduct has the purpose or effect of—
        (i) violating B's dignity, or
        (ii) creating an intimidating, hostile, degrading, humiliating or offensive environment for B.
(2) A also harasses B if—
    (a) A engages in unwanted conduct of a sexual nature, and
    (b) the conduct has the purpose or effect referred to in subsection (1)(b).
(3) A also harasses B if—
    (a) A or another person engages in unwanted conduct of a sexual nature or that is related to gender reassignment or sex,
    (b) the conduct has the purpose or effect referred to in subsection (1)(b), and
    (c) because of B's rejection of or submission to the conduct, A treats B less favourably than A would treat B if B had not rejected or submitted to the conduct.
(4) In deciding whether conduct has the effect referred to in subsection (1)(b), each of the following must be taken into account—
    (a) the perception of B;
    (b) the other circumstances of the case;
    (c) whether it is reasonable for the conduct to have that effect.
(5) The relevant protected characteristics are—
    age;
    disability;
    gender reassignment;
    race;
    religion or belief;

Section 3. False Statements Injuring Property

In *Emperor of Austria v Day and Kossuth*[130] the defendants printed in England　**23.15**
a large quantity of notes purporting to be legal tender in Hungary[131] with the
purpose of fomenting revolution in that country. The Court of Appeal in
Chancery upheld an injunction and an order for delivery up of the notes at the
suit of the Hungarian government. It is not clear what was the basis of the
decision but Turner L.J. referred to actual or prospective "injury to property".[132] However, that phrase was plainly being used in a somewhat loose
sense, since the risk presented by the defendants' actions was of debasement
of the currency. The case was referred to without disapproval in *RCA Corp v
Pollard*[133] and was applied in *Kingdom of Spain v Christie Manson &
Woods*[134] so as to hold that it was arguable that the Kingdom of Spain had a
right to restrain the use in England of forged export documents for Goya's *La
Marquesa de Santa Cruz*, the relevant damage being the diminution in value
of pictures in Spain for which proper documents could be obtained, the
increase in the attraction of illicit export and the expense to Spain of buying
back illicitly exported pictures. It would seem, therefore, that "injury to
property" may include pecuniary loss. However, these cases do not support a
general right not to have untruths told about oneself, for if that were the law
the torts of libel, malicious falsehood and passing off would not have developed as they did.[135]

Section 4. Passing Off

Nature of tort. The tort of passing off[136] is based upon the principle that a　**23.16**
person may not, by deceiving the public as to the origin of his goods or

---

sex;
　　sexual orientation."
[130] 45 E.R. 861; (1861) 3 De G.F. & J. 217.
[131] They were not fake copies of real Hungarian notes. Since a fairly liberal attitude is now
taken to the meaning of "trade" such conduct might now conceivably be passing off: para.23.14,
below.
[132] (1861) 3 De G. F. & J. 217 at 253–254.
[133] [1983] Ch. 135 CA. In *Mbasogo v Logo Ltd* [2006] EWCA Civ 1370 it is said at [27] that
Emperor of Austria
　　"is an authority which recognises the fundamental distinction between an action which
　　amounts to the exercise of sovereign authority in the territory of another and an action brought
　　to protect property rights, such as might be brought by an individual. It is this distinction which
　　founded the dismissal of the first two grounds of the bill (which related 2nd edn to the
　　protection of Hungary from revolution), but the upholding of the third ground (which the court
　　viewed as merely relating to the protection of property)."
[134] [1986] 1 W.L.R. 1120.
[135] Ibid.
[136] Wadlow, *Law of Passing Off*, 4th edn (2011); Kerly, *Trade Marks*, 15th edn (2011); Carty,
An Analysis of the Economic Torts (2010), Ch.8.

services, gain an unfair advantage over another. It is most commonly committed by the defendant representing that his goods or services are those of the claimant, but the principle is broader so that, e.g. it has been held to cover cases where the defendant showed the customer samples of the claimant's goods intending to fill the order with his own goods[137] or where he sought to take advantage of the generic reputation of goods of the type produced by the claimant, as by selling sparkling wine as "Spanish champagne".[138] The tort has been said in the House of Lords to have the following five elements: (1) a misrepresentation, (2) made by a trader in the course of trade, (3) to prospective customers of his or to ultimate consumers of goods or services supplied by him, (4) which is calculated (in the sense that this is a reasonably foreseeable consequence) to injure the business or goodwill of another trader and (5) which causes or threatens[139] actual damage to a business or goodwill of a trader by whom the action is brought.[140] More shortly (and perhaps preferably where the defendant represents his goods to be those of the claimant[141]) it has been said to involve (a) a goodwill or reputation attached to and recognised by the public as distinctive of the claimant's goods or services, (b) a misrepresentation by the defendant leading the public to believe that his goods or services are those of the claimant and (c) damage or likely damage.[142] It has been suggested that the tort is better referred to as "unfair competition",[143] but this has been strongly denied[144] and there remains a requirement of a false representation concerning the claimant or his goods.[145] In contrast to a copyright:

"The gist of an action for passing off is deceptive resemblance. The defendant is charged with deceiving the public into taking his goods as and for the goods of the plaintiff . . . . An action for infringement of artistic copyright, however, is . . . not concerned with the appearance of the defendant's work but with its derivation. The copyright owner does not complain that the defendant's work resembles his, his complaint is that the defendant has copied all or a substantial part of the copyright work. The reproduction may be exact or it may introduce deliberate variations . . . . Even where the copying is exact, the defendant may incorporate the copied features into a larger work much and perhaps most of which is original or derived from other sources. But while the copied features must be a substantial part of the

---

[137] *Bristol Conservatories v Conservatories Custom Build* [1989] R.P.C. 380 CA.
[138] *Bollinger v Costa Brava Wine Co. Ltd* [1960] R.P.C. 16; [1961] R.P.C. 116.
[139] I.e. for the purposes of a *quia timet* action.
[140] *Erwen Warnink BV v J. Townend & Sons (Hull)* [1979] A.C. 731 HL at 742, per Lord Diplock.
[141] *Consorzio de Prosciutto di Parma v Marks & Spencer* [1991] R.P.C. 351 CA at 368–369, per Nourse L.J.
[142] *Reckitt & Colman Products Ltd v Borden Inc.* [1990] 1 W.L.R. 491 at 511, per Lord Oliver.
[143] *Arsenal Football Club Plc v Reed* [2003] EWCA Civ 696 at [70]; [2003] 3 All E.R. 865 CA.
[144] *L'Oreal SA v Bellure NV* [2007] EWCA Civ 968; [2008] R.P.C. 9.
[145] Not merely a false representation "in the air": *Schulke & Mayr UK Ltd v Alkapharm UK Ltd* [1999] F.S.R. 161 (statement that defendants' antiseptic effective).

copyright work, they need not form a substantial part of the defendant's work. . . . Thus the overall appearance of the defendant's work may be very different from the copyright work, but it does not follow that the defendant's work does not infringe the plaintiff's copyright." [146]

Unlike defamation or malicious falsehood there is no element of denigration of the claimant or his wares, indeed the defendant typically lauds the claimant's wares and seeks to get the advantage of the claimant's good reputation. In practice there is a significant overlap between the law of passing off and the law of registered trade marks and the same facts will often give rise to causes of action under both heads. The Trade Marks Act 1994[147] removed certain restrictions on registrability of marks which formerly meant that the law of passing off was the only avenue to protection. Thus under the previous law it was not possible to register the shape of goods or their packaging[148] so that the manufacturers of lemon juice in plastic lemon-like containers had to sue for passing off.[149] This is no longer so[150] but the 1994 Act does not affect the law of passing off[151] and actions for this tort continue to be brought as an alternative to those for contravention of trade marks as well, of course, as in cases where a mark has not been (or cannot be) registered. The law of passing off is a large subject and only a bare outline is given here.

Goodwill. Goodwill has been described as "the benefit and advantage of the   **23.17** good name, reputation and connection of a business . . . the attractive force which brings in custom"[152] and damage to the value of goodwill is the key element in passing off, for the tort does not protect the claimant's name and reputation[153] but the goodwill associated with them.[154] If therefore that goodwill has not been established (because the claimant is only just starting out in

---

[146] . . . *Designers Guild Ltd v Russell Williams (Textiles) Ltd* [2000] 1 W.L.R. 2416; [2001] F.S.R. 113 HL at 123, per Lord Millett. But the law of passing off has been used to fill gaps in copyright law. Thus while there is copyright in a literary work there is probably no copyright in a title, but passing off may be committed by appropriating a title: see *Dicks v Yates* (1881) 18 Ch. D. 76 CA.

[147] Enacted to implement EC Directive 89/104.

[148] *Re Coca Cola* [1986] R.P.C. 421 HL.

[149] *Reckitt & Colman Products Ltd v Borden Inc.* [1990] 1 W.L.R. 491 HL.

[150] Trade Marks Act 1994, s.1(1). "A 'trade mark' means any sign capable of being represented graphically which is capable of distinguishing goods or services of one undertaking from those of other undertakings. A trade mark may, in particular, consist of words (including personal names), designs, letters, numerals or the shape of goods or their packaging." The law of trade marks was first applied to services by the Trade Marks (Amendment) Act 1984.

[151] Trade Marks Act 1994, s.2(2).

[152] . . . *IRC v Muller & Co.'s Margarine* [1901] A.C. 217 HL at 223–224, per Lord Macnaghten.

[153] The law of trade marks protects the first to some extent and the law of defamation the second.

[154] See e.g. *Diageo North America Inc. v Intercontinental Brands (ICB) Ltd* [2010] EWCA Civ 920 CA: [2012] Bus. L.R. 401 at [17] and [21]–[23].

that line of business[155]) or the goodwill has been abandoned[156] no action lies. Similarly, goodwill may be localised so that even though the activities of the claimant in country A may be well known to persons in England, there is no significant[157] goodwill (i.e. custom) here.[158] Goodwill may, however, be so to speak "collective" so that it may be damaged where the defendant falsely markets a product or services with a regional character in which a large number of producers share the goodwill, e.g. champagne or Parma ham.[159] The simplest case is that where, by imitating the claimant's product, the defendant diverts sales in his direction; but there may be damage to goodwill where, by marketing a different and inferior product under a name associated with the claimant, he dilutes or erodes the distinctiveness of that name.[160]

23.18 Misrepresentation and confusion. It is not necessary, whether the claim be one for an injunction or for damages, that the misrepresentation be intentional.[161] However the likelihood that persons (typically potential customers[162]) will be misled is of the essence of the tort.[163] Thus, to be actionable, the misrepresentation must have been such as to have led a substantial number[164] of potential customers to believe that goods or services offered by the defendant are the goods and services of the claimant or that what is done represents the defendant's goods or services to be connected with the claimant in such a way as would lead people to accept them on the faith of the claimant's reputation.[165] The situation of what is known as "merchandising" (selling products associated with some currently famous event or person) does

---

[155] See, e.g. *Marcus Publishing v Hutton-Wild Communications* [1990] R.P.C. 576 CA (defendant launching magazine with same name as plaintiff's intended magazine; result probably the same even if a mere spoiling operation).

[156] See *Norman Kark Publications v Odhams Press* [1962] 1 W.L.R. 380.

[157] *Athlete's Foot Marketing Asociates v Cobra Sports* [1980] R.P.C. 343.

[158] *Bernardin & Cie v Pavilion Properties* [1967] R.P.C. 581; but compare *Maxim's v Dye* [1977] 1 W.L.R. 1155.

[159] *HP Bulmer v J. Bollinger SA* [1978] R.P.C. 79; *Erwen Warnink BV v J. Townend & Sons (Hull)* [1979] A.C. 731; *Consorzio de Prosciutto di Parma v Marks & Spencer* [1991] R.P.C. 351 CA.

[160] *Taittinger v Allbev* [1993] F.S.R. 641 CA (elderflower champagne). The judgment of Millett L.J. in *Harrods v Harrodian School* [1996] R.P.C. 697 CA, should probably be regarded as concerned to emphasise the necessity of confusion in the public mind between the activities of the parties rather than denying that "dilution" can be damage.

[161] *Gillette UK v Eden West* [1994] R.P.C. 297. As to an account of profits see the remarks of Lord Parker in *Spalding & Bros v AW Gamage* (1915) 84 L.J. Ch. 449 HL.

[162] Not necessarily in all cases: see "endorsement", below.

[163] *Marengo v Daily Sketch & Sunday Graphic Ltd (1946)* [1992] F.S.R. 1:
"No one is entitled to be protected against confusion as such. Confusion may result from the collision of two independent rights or liberties, and where that is the case neither party can complain; they must put up with the results of the confusion as one of the misfortunes which occur in life. The protection to which a man is entitled is protection against passing off, which is quite [a] different thing from mere confusion" (at 2).

[164] *Neutrogena Corp v Golden Ltd (t/a Garnier)* [1996] R.P.C. 473.

[165] *Fine & Country Ltd v Okotoks Limited (formerly Spicerhaart Ltd)* [2012] EWHC 2230 at [74] (Ch).

not necessarily create any confusion in the public mind with the origin of
those goods,[166] for purchasers may have no concern at all about their origins.[167] However, in *Fenty v Arcadia Group Brands Ltd (t/a Topshop)*,[168] the
claimant, a well-known pop star with her own merchandising and endorsement operation, brought a claim for passing off in relation to the unauthorised
sale of t-shirts bearing her image that were being sold by the first defendant,
a well-known high street fashion retailer. Although authorised goods bearing
the claimant's name had been sold in another store which was part of the same
group as Topshop, Topshop had no licence to use the image in question. The
claimant had an agreement for her clothing designs to be sold in another high
street store and claimed that the public would be deceived into believing that
the t-shirts sold by Topshop were approved by her. The defendants argued that
customers bought the t-shirt because they liked the product and image; it was
a high quality fashion-led garment that was very different from standard pop
star merchandise, there was nothing which represented it as the claimant's
official merchandise and the public would not think it was. Birss J. gave
judgment for the claimant. The law of passing off required goodwill, misrepresentation and damage. While historically, merchandising and endorsement had given rise to problems in passing off cases,[169] provided the facts
supported it, there was nothing in the law to prevent a case of passing off
being made out in a false endorsement case, and the legal principles were the
same in a merchandising case.[170] The claimant had to have goodwill to
protect, and if goods were sold in circumstances in which purchasers understood there to be a representation that the goods were authorised, or were
"official" merchandise, and that representation was false, then as long as the
false representation was operative, the second element of passing off would be
satisfied. The claimant was regarded as a style icon and if seen to wear or
approve of an item of clothing, that was an endorsement of that item and she
had ample goodwill to succeed in a passing off action of the instant kind.
Furthermore, the fact that an item of clothing was a more design-led garment,

---

[166] *Elvis Presley Trade Mark* [1997] R.P.C. 543 and [1999] R.P.C. 567 CA. The tort is not based
on the plaintiff's proprietary right in the name or get up which the defendant has misappropriated
but the goodwill and reputation of his business which is likely to be harmed by the defendant's
misrepresentation: *Harrods Ltd v Harrodian School Ltd* [1996] R.P.C. 697 CA at 711; *Premier
Luggage and Bags Ltd v Premier Co. (UK) Ltd* [2002] EWCA Civ 387; [2003] F.S.R. 5 CA at
[37].

[167] But see the criticism of the first instance decision in *Arsenal Football Club Plc v Reed*
[2003] EWCA Civ 696 at [70] CA.

[168] [2013] EWHC 2310 (Ch).

[169] See e.g. *Tavener Rutledge v Trexapalm* [1977] RPC 275 (Kojak Lollipops, the "unauthorised" local lollipop retailer succeeded against the makers of the television programme);
Lyngstad v Anabas [1977] F.S.R. 62 (goods carrying photographs of the pop group Abba,
injunction refused); *Wombles v Womble Skip Hire* [1975] F.S.R. 488 (skips for collecting rubbish
branded Womble, injunction refused) A change in approach, however, came with *Mirage Studios
v Counterfeat Clothing* [1991] F.S.R. 145.

[170] [2013] EWHC 2310 (Ch) at [31].

rather than a lower quality simple plain t-shirt, would not rule out, in the mind of a purchaser, the idea that it was a product endorsed by the claimant or authorised merchandise. The scope of her goodwill was not only as a music artist but also in the world of fashion, as a style leader.[171]

So far as misrepresentation was concerned, while there was no evidence from the defendant's website that customers thought they were buying official merchandise, this was not determinative. The nature of the image was a fairly strong indication that it might be an authorised product. The fact that it was a fashion garment did not point for or against authorisation but the fact that it was sold by Topshop, which had many public links with famous stars, enhanced the likelihood in the purchaser's mind that the garment was authorised by her. While some purchasers might not have given much thought to whether the image was authorised, many would have been induced to think that it was, a view reinforced by the fact that the image was associated with a recent album issued by the claimant. Many fans would buy a product because they thought she had approved it; others would buy it because of the value of the perceived authorisation. In both cases a misrepresentation had been made and purchasers had been deceived and that deception obviously was damaging to the claimant's goodwill. It would amount to sales lost to her merchandising business and a loss of control over her reputation in the fashion world.[172]

Whether there is the likelihood of confusion[173] by the public is a question of fact, depending, e.g. on the similarity of the products,[174] the prominence with which the manufacturer's name or logo is displayed[175] and the degree of care which may be expected in a transaction of that kind.[176]

In the great majority of cases, where the defendant passes off his goods as those of the claimant, the parties are of necessity engaged in a common field

---

[171] Ibid. at [38-[46].

[172] Ibid. at [70]–[73].

[173] The distinction between mere confusion and unintentional deception is recognised as elusive. See, e.g. *Reed Executive v Reed Business Information* [2004] RPC 767 at 797; *Phones 4U Ltd v Phone4U.co.uk Internet Ltd* [2006] EWCA Civ 244; [2007] R.P.C. 5.

[174] Thus the public is unlikely to be confused between a television company and a motor car of the same name: *Granada Group v Ford Motor Co.* [1972] F.S.R. 103. See also, *Claude Ruiz-Picasso v OHIM, DaimlerChrysler AG* Case C-361/04 P, ECJ, January 12, 2005 (DaimlerChrysler applied to register as a Community trade mark the word 'Picaro' for vehicles and the application was opposed by the Pablo Picasso estate. The European Court of Justice upheld the decision of the Court of First Instance, ruling that the distinctiveness of the surname Picasso would lead to consumers being less, not more, likely to confuse the marks at issue).

[175] See Lord Oliver in *Reckitt & Colman Products Ltd v Borden Inc.* [1990] 1 W.L.R. 491 HL, for a warning against equating the conditions of the court room with those of the supermarket. The mere fact that the claimant's name is used does not mean there is a likelihood of confusion, it may simply connote that the goods are suitable for use with the claimant's goods: *Gledhill v British Perforated* (1911) 28 R.P.C. 429.

[176] *Hodgkinson & Corby Ltd v Wards Mobility Services Ltd* [1994] 1 W.L.R. 1564; *HFC Bank Plc v Midland Bank Plc* [2000] F.S.R. 176.

of activity as competitors and some of the cases appear to make this a necessary element in a case of passing off.[177] However, this view is now discredited[178] and a common field of activity[179] is simply a factor which makes it likely that there is a risk of confusion. Thus a claim for passing off by a newspaper company lay against a person who placed "inserts" in the newspapers after they had been sold to newsagents because the public might get the impression that the defendant was associated with the newspaper company and its goodwill might suffer because, although it had no control over the defendant, it was well known that the newspaper accepted only carefully vetted advertisements.[180] The practice of "endorsement"[181] of products and services by people who are famous in the worlds of sport and entertainment is now widespread and has been held to be covered by passing off. So in *Irvine v Talksport Ltd*[182] the defendants were held liable when they issued leaflets visually associating the claimant, a racing driver, with their radio station. It was enough for him to show that he had a substantial reputation or goodwill and that the defendant's conduct gave the false impression to a significant section of his market that he had endorsed their product. On the basis of unchallenged evidence that the claimant would have demanded £25,000 to endorse the station and that this was at the lower end of the fees he could command, that sum was awarded as damages.[183]

Trade. Passing off has been most closely associated with "trade". But it extends further than the normal meaning of that word. Thus Lord Byron succeeded in an action for a false representation that a book was his work[184]   **23.19**

---

[177] Of course even if the parties are competitors and the defendant's goods have features reminiscent of the claimant's it does not mean that confusion is likely: *Financial Times v Evening Standard* [1991] F.S.R. 7. It is not actionable in English law to take a free ride in a market created by the defendant's efforts (*Cadbury-Schweppes Pty v Pub Squash Co. Pty* [1981] 1 W.L.R. 193 PC) nor to imitate the style of the claimant's product if there is no breach of copyright and no risk of confusion as to origin (*Gordon Fraser Gallery v Tatt* [1966] R.P.C. 505).

[178] *Harrods v Harrodian School* [1996] R.P.C. 697 CA at 714.

[179] An issue which may need careful consideration: *Teleworks Ltd v Telework Group Plc* [2002] R.P.C. 27.

[180] *Associated Newspapers Plc v Insert Media Ltd* [1991] 1 W.L.R. 571 CA. For different opinions on how far in such "association" cases the public need to be believe that the claimant is "responsible" for the defendant see Millett L.J. in *Harrods v Harrodian School*, above, and *Dawnay Day & Co. Ltd v Cantor Fitzgerald International* [2000] R.P.C. 669 CA.

[181] As to "character merchandising" see above.

[182] [2003] EWCA Civ 423; [2003] 1 W.L.R. 1576. The detailed consideration of the law is in the first instance decision [2002] EWHC 539 (Ch); [2002] 1 W.L.R. 2355.

[183] Laddie J. followed *Henderson v Radio Corp Pty* [1960] N.S.W.R. 576. So a latter-day Tolley might have an action, given that the rigid controls on amateur sport have broken down. But that very breakdown would deprive him of his action for libel: *Tolley v Fry* [1931] A.C. 323 HL. In both *Henderson* and *Irvine* the contexts of the use were fields (dancing and sport) in which the plaintiffs were active, whereas Tolley had nothing to do with marketing chocolate, but that would not seem to matter.

[184] *Lord Byron v Johnson* (1816) 2 Mer. 29. See now para.23.23, below.

and the same is true of musicians,[185] artists[186] and "style-leaders".[187] *Clark v Associated Newspapers Ltd*[188] concerned the application of the law of passing off to a newspaper column which parodied the author's published diaries. In finding for the plaintiff, Lightman J. held that (1) a substantial number of readers must be likely to be misled as to authorship in more than a momentary or inconsequential way; (2) readers must be taken as they are found and not judged by too high a standard of perspicacity, but the authorship must be a matter of moment to them; (3) the work must be judged as a whole to decide whether a substantial body of readers may be misled. Professional[189] and trade associations,[190] fund raising charities[191] (including religious bodies[192]) and professional persons[193] have also succeeded, but an action was denied to a political party[194] and to an actor in respect of a claim by a newspaper that it had an exclusive interview with him.[195] The latter case, however, seems to depend on the facts and probably does not mean that an actor is wholly outside the protection of this tort.[196] Attempts to use the law of passing off to restrain the adoption by a neighbour of the same house name as that of the plaintiff[197] and by a peer to restrain the use of a title by his former wife after her remarriage[198] have failed, but the position may be different if the use of a non-trader's name could expose him to law suits.[199]

---

[185] *Hines v Winnick* [1947] Ch. 708; *Tam Wing Lun v Tam Kwok Hung* [1991] 2 H.K.C. 384; *Fenty v Arcadia Group Brands Ltd (t/a Topshop)* [2013] EWHC 2310 (Ch).

[186] *Marengo v Daily Sketch and Sunday Graphic* (1948) 65 R.P.C. 242. It is no obstacle that the name by which the claimant is known is an assumed one.

[187] *Fenty v Arcadia Group Brands Ltd (t/a Topshop)* [2013] EWHC 2310 (Ch).

[188] [1998] R.P.C. 261.

[189] *Society of Accountants and Auditors v Goodway* [1907] 1 Ch. 489.

[190] *Lagos Chamber of Commerce v Registrar of Companies* (1955) 72 R.P.C. 263 PC.

[191] *British Diabetic Association v Diabetic Society* [1995] 4 All E.R. 812.

[192] In the *British Diabetic* case Robert Walker J. was prepared to follow Australian, South African and US cases to this effect: *Holy Apostolic and Catholic Church etc. v Att-Gen, ex rel. Elisha* (1989) 18 N.S.W.L.R. 291; *Old Apostolic Church of Africa v Non-White Old Apostolic Church of Africa* 1975 (2) S.A. 684; *Purcell v Sowler*, 145 F.2d 979 (1944). However, it does not follow that the same will apply where the charity raises funds predominantly from its own members: [1995] 4 All E.R. at 821.

[193] *Dockrell v Douglas* (1899) 80 L.T. 556.

[194] *Kean v McGiven* [1982] F.S.R. 119 CA. In *Burge v Haycock* [2001] EWCA Civ 900; [2002] R.P.C. 28 CA, *Kean's* case was distinguished and an interim injunction granted to representatives of the Countryside Alliance to restrain a person standing in a local election under their name. The Alliance was not a registered political party under the current legislation.

[195] *Kaye v Robertson* [1991] F.S.R. 62.

[196] There is very little discussion of the point. Glidewell L.J. simply said, "I think that the plaintiff is not in the position of a trader in relation to his interest in his story about his accident and his recovery." If it is actionable to use the picture of a racing driver to promote a sport radio station it is presumably also actionable to use the picture of an actor to promote "talking books". However, a single interview is obviously far removed from an ongoing "endorsement" relationship.

[197] *Day v Brownrigg* (1878) 10 Ch. D. 294 CA.

[198] *Earl Cowley v Countess Cowley* [1901] A.C. 450 HL.

[199] *Routh v Webster* (1847) 10 Beav 561.

SECTION 5. MATTERS CONNECTED WITH COPYRIGHT

Moral rights. No attempt is made here to deal with the general law of the   **23.20**
protection of copyright,[200] though it may be relevant to cases based on other
causes of action, in particular breach of confidence or misuse of private
information.[201] However, Ch.IV of Pt I of the Copyright, Designs and Patents
Act 1988 deals with a number of rights (known as "moral rights") which fall
outside copyright but are connected therewith. Three of these, the rights to
object to derogatory treatment of a literary, dramatic, musical or artistic work,
to object to false attribution of authorship or directorship and the right to
privacy in relation to certain photographs and films, have some affinity with
reputation and with the matters discussed in the preceding chapter and are
therefore outlined here.[202] Infringement of the moral rights is actionable as a
breach of statutory duty.[203] Like the right to sue for defamation they are
personal rights and are not assignable[204] but they may pass on succession.[205]
In the case of the right to object to derogatory treatment and the right of
privacy in photographs and films they subsist for the period of the copyright.[206] The right not to have work falsely attributed to one continues for 20
years after the author's death.[207]

Objection to derogatory treatment of work. The author of a copyright   **23.21**
literary, dramatic, musical or artistic work, and the director of a copyright
film, has the right not to have his work subjected to derogatory treatment.[208]
"Treatment" of a work means any addition to, deletion from or alteration to
or adaptation of the work, other than (1) a translation of a literary or dramatic
work, or (2) an arrangement or transcription of a musical work involving no

---

[200] Copinger and Skone James, *Copyright*, 16th edn (2013).

[201] See, e.g. *A v B* [2000] E.M.L.R. 1007.

[202] The fourth moral right is to be identified as author or director of a literary, dramatic, musical or artistic work: Copyright, Designs and Patents Act 1988, s.77.

[203] Ibid. s.103. The claim of copyright infringement is one of strict liability: *Delves-Broughton v House of Harlot Ltd* [2012] EWPCC 29; *Clark v Associated Newspapers Ltd* [1998] 1 W.L.R. 1558 at 1568.

[204] Ibid. s.94.

[205] It has been said that the rights of successors should not necessarily be evaluated in the same way as those of the original creator: *Fuensanta v Antena3 TV* [2001] E.C.D.R. 23 Madrid CA.

[206] Ibid. s.86(1). The period is now generally author's life plus 70 years: SI 1995/3297.

[207] Copyright, Designs and Patents Act 1988, s.86(2).

[208] Ibid. s.80(1). "Treatment" was said in *Harrison v Harrison* [2010] EWPCC 3; [2010] E.C.D.R. 12 at [60] to be a "broad, general concept; de minimis acts apart, it implies a spectrum of possible acts carried out on a work, from the addition of say, a single word to a poem to the destruction of the entire work". It does not require that the original work shall remain recogni-sable as such (at [59]). The right conferred by this section extends to the treatment of parts of a work resulting from a previous treatment by a person other than the author or director, if those parts are attributed to, or are likely to be regarded as the work of, the author or director: s.80(7).

more than a change of key or register.[209] The treatment of a work is derogatory[210] if it amounts to distortion or mutilation[211] of the work or is otherwise prejudicial[212] to the honour or reputation[213] of the author or director.[214] In the case of a literary, dramatic or musical work the right is infringed[215] by a person who (a) publishes commercially, performs in public, broadcasts or

---

[209] Ibid. s.80(2)(a).

[210] The conditions of "distortion", mutilation" and "prejudicial to the honour or reputation" of the claimant were said to be alternatives in *Delves-Broughton v House of Harlot Ltd* [2012] EWPCC 29. However, in the earlier decision of *Pasterfield v Denham* [1999] F.S.R. 168 H.H.J. Overend concluded that the claimant must establish that the treatment accorded to his work was either a distortion or a mutilation that prejudices his honour or reputation as an artist. In the judge's view, the presence of the word "otherwise" in s.80 of the Act indicates that the words "prejudicial to the honour or reputation" also govern the first part of the definition, namely distortions and mutilations of the work. Thus, a "distortion" ("the twisting or perversion of words so as to give them a different sense") or "mutilation" ("the fact of rendering a thing imperfect by excision or destruction of one or more of its parts") only gave rise to liability if it also could be said to be prejudicial to the honour or reputation of the claimant. *Pasterfield* was not referred to in *Delves-Broughton*. There is something to be said for the view expressed in *Pasterfield* as the effect of treating "distortion" as sufficient in itself would mean that any change, beyond de minimis, would give rise to a claim.

In *Delves-Broughton* the judge found that considerable work had been put into the composition of the photographs which had been altered and in particularly to the creation of the "forest background". The changes were not "prejudicial to the honour or reputation of the author or director", nor had the originals been subject to "mutilation". However, removal of the forest background amounted to "distortion" and this was sufficient to amount to "derogatory treatment" (at [24]). In *Harrison v Harrison* [2010] EWPCC 3; [2010] F.S.R. 25 (see para.23.23, below) H.H.J. Fysh QC held the claim of prejudice to professional honour or reputation was not made out. The complaints raised by the claimant were "very modest" and focused mainly on the omission in the second edition of the book of relatively minor details. Where, as in the instant case, the work was a technical one, it will be inherently difficult to show that an omission of some inessential detail could amount to a prejudicial treatment of an antecedent work and on the facts the claimant failed to do so (at [84]–[85]).

[211] In *Sehgal v Union of India* [2005] F.S.R. 39, Delhi HC, under the similar provisions of s.57 of the Indian Copyright Act 1957, damages and an order for delivery were awarded to a sculptor whose mural had been pulled down, damaged and placed in storage. Cf. *Pasterfield v Denham* [1999] F.S.R. 168.

[212] In *Harrison v Harrison* [2010] EWPCC 3; [2010] F.S.R 25, H.H.J. Fysh Q.C. said with regard to the meaning of the word "prejudicial": "If all a claimant can find to support his case for derogatory treatment is a miscellany of arguable trivia, that is not enough. Still less cogent is for a claimant to amass a mound of extracted trivia and submit, *absent relevant evidence,* that the vice lies in its cumulative effect upon a reader. That seems to me impractical and largely to rob the section of its utility" (at [66]).

[213] This does not seem to have quite the same meaning as "reputation" in the context of defamation. While it is probably defamatory to suggest that an author is incompetent to say that he is not of the highest ability would not be: para.2.17, above (and see e.g. *Dee v Telegraph Group Ltd* [2010] EWHC 924 (QB); [2010] E.M.L.R. 20: professional tennis player). In s.80 the sense is the standing he enjoys in the public eye. The sense of "prejudicial to honour" is more difficult to pin down, but it would seem to mean something like insult, i.e. it would cover the case which would fall outside passing off because the defendant made it very plain that he had no co-operation from the plaintiff.

[214] See *Morrison Leahy Music Ltd v Lightbond Ltd* [1993] E.M.L.R. 144; *Pasterfield v Denham* [1999] F.S.R. 168.

[215] However, the concept of infringement is extended by s.83, which provides that certain other acts constitute an infringement, e.g. possession in the course of a business of an article infringing the right under s.80 or distribution otherwise than in the course of a business of such an article so as to affect prejudicially the honour or reputation of the author or director.

includes in a cable programme service a derogatory treatment of the work; or (b) issues to the public copies of a film or sound recording of, or including, a derogatory treatment of the work.[216] There are similar provisions for artistic works[217] for works of architecture, sculpture and artistic craftsmanship[218] and for films.[219]

Exceptions and qualifications to the right. The right to object to   **23.22**
derogatory treatment does not extend to certain articles which are subject to the general law of copyright, namely a computer program or any computer-generated work[220] or a work made for the purpose of reporting current events,[221] nor does it apply to the publication in a newspaper, magazine or similar periodical, or an encyclopaedia, dictionary, yearbook or other collective work of reference, of a literary, dramatic, musical or artistic work made for the purposes of such publication or made available with the consent of the author for the purposes of such publication.[222] The right is not infringed in cases where there would be no infringement of copyright by copying because it is not possible to ascertain the identity of the author and it is reasonable to assume that copyright has expired.[223] The right is not infringed by anything done for the purpose of (1) avoiding the commission of an offence, (2) complying with a duty imposed by or under an enactment, or (3) in the case of the British Broadcasting Corporation, avoiding the inclusion in a programme broadcast by them of anything which offends against good taste or decency or which is likely to encourage or incite to crime or to lead to disorder or to be offensive to public feeling, in these cases provided, where the author or director is identified at the time of the relevant act or has previously been identified in or on published copies of the work, that there is a sufficient disclaimer.[224] The right does not apply, where the copyright originally vested in the author's or director's employer,[225] to anything done in relation to the work by or with the authority of the copyright owner unless the author or director (a) is identified at the time of the relevant act, or (b) has previously been identified in or on published copies of the work; and where in such a case the right does apply, it is not infringed if there is a sufficient disclaimer.[226]

---

[216] Copyright, Designs and Patents Act 1988, s.80(4)(a).

[217] Ibid. s.80(4)(b).

[218] Ibid. s.80(4)(c).

[219] Ibid. s.80(6).

[220] Ibid. s.81(2).

[221] Ibid. s.81(3).

[222] Ibid. s.81(4).

[223] Ibid. s.81(5) and s.57. There are similar provisions for films in s.66A, added by SI 1995/3297.

[224] Copyright, Designs and Patents Act 1988, s.81(6).

[225] Similarly where there is Crown or Parliamentary copyright or where the copyright originally vested in an international organisation: ibid., s.82(1)(b), (c).

[226] Ibid. s.82.

23.23 False attribution of authorship or directorship. False attribution of authorship may be actionable at common law[227] but under s.84 of the Copyright, Designs and Patents Act 1988, a person has the right[228] not to have a literary, dramatic, musical or artistic work falsely attributed to him as author and not to have a film falsely attributed to him as director.[229] The section is not confined to professional authors and would therefore apply to the situation where a newspaper published an article purporting to have been written by the claimant.[230] A work is "attributed" to the claimant when there is a statement (express or implied)[231] that he is the author or director.[232] In *Harrison v Harrison*,[233] a second edition of a book, the first edition of which had been written by the claimant, was published by the defendants with no author's name being given (though it had been written by one of the defendants). The second edition contained substantial verbatim sections from the first edition which breached the claimant's copyright. On the back cover of the book were several laudatory quotes about the first edition. H.H.J. Fysh QC held that there had been a breach of s.84 of the Act. The "single message"[234] to a reader from the back cover of what was stated to be a second edition was: "here is the updated second edition of the excellent first edition of this book. Praise is for the author responsible for its creation and not for [the defendant publisher]

---

[227] See para.23.19, above.

[228] Infringement of which is actionable as a breach of statutory duty: Copyright, Designs and Patents Act 1988, s.103.

[229] There were similar provisions (but not for films or sound recordings) in the Copyright Act 1956, s.43.

[230] *Moore v News of the World* [1972] 1 Q.B. 441 CA (decided under s.43 of the 1956 Act).

[231] S.84 is narrower than the law of passing off in that a claimant must establish that the work in question contains what is a false attribution of authorship, and not merely what is or may be understood by some or more people to be, a false attribution: *Clark v Associated Newspapers Ltd* [1998] 1 W.L.R. 1558.

[232] Copyright, Designs and Patents Act 1988, s.84(1). The right is infringed by a person who (a) issues to the public copies of a literary, dramatic, musical or artistic work or a film in or on which there is a false attribution, or (b) exhibits in public an artistic work, or a copy of an artistic work, in or on which there is a false attribution: s.84(2). The right is also infringed (1) by a person who (a) in the case of a literary, dramatic or musical work, performs the work in public, broadcasts it or includes it in a cable programme service as being the work of a person, or (b) in the case of a film, shows it in public, broadcasts it or includes it in a cable programme service as being directed by a person, knowing or having reason to believe that the attribution is false: s.84(3) (2) by the issue to the public or public display of material containing a false attribution in connection with any of the acts mentioned in subs.(2) or (3): s.84(4) (3) by a person who in the course of a business (a) possesses or deals with a copy of a literary, dramatic, musical or artistic work or a film in or on which there is a false attribution, or (b) in the case of an artistic work, possesses or deals with the work itself when there is a false attribution in or on it, knowing or having reason to believe that there is such an attribution and that it is false: s.84(5) (4) in the case of an artistic work by a person who in the course of a business (a) deals with a work which has been altered after the author parted with possession of it as being the unaltered work of the author, or (b) deals with a copy of such a work as being a copy of the unaltered work of the author, knowing or having reason to believe that that is not the case: s.84(6).

[233] [2010] EWPCC 3; [2010] F.S.R. 25.

[234] In *Clark v Associated Newspapers Ltd* [1998] 1 W.L.R. 1558 it was held that a claimant had to establish "the single meaning" which the literary work would convey to a notional, reasonable reader (at 1568).

who produce a slew of books on different subjects. In the absence of any indication to the contrary, the reader of the back cover would . . . assume that the author of the title had not changed. But that is of course contrary to the fact."[235]

The right is infringed where the claimant is the author of some of the words used but there are material alterations or additions,[236] but very brief statements standing alone may not qualify as a "work" for the purposes of the Act.[237]

Right to privacy of certain photographs and films.   23.24

"(1) A person who for private and domestic purposes commissions[238] the taking of a photograph or the making of a film has, where copyright subsists in the resulting work, the right not to have (a) copies of the work issued to the public,[239] (b) the work exhibited or shown in public, or (c) the work broadcast or included in a cable programme service."[240]

The right is not, however, infringed by use in the following contexts which, under the Act, would not infringe copyright: incidental inclusion of the work in an artistic work, film, broadcast or cable programme; parliamentary or judicial proceedings; Royal Commissions and statutory inquiries; acts done under statutory authority; and acts done in relation to anonymous or pseudo-nymous works on assumptions as to the expiry of copyright.[241]

---

[235] Ibid. at [55].

[236] *Noah v Shuba* [1991] F.S.R. 14 (decided under s.43 of the 1956 Act. The wording is different but not, it seems, materially so). Note that in this case there was a parallel successful claim for libel because the inaccurate part of the article attributed views to the claimant which would not have been held by a competent doctor. The damages were £7,250 for libel and £250 for false attribution.

[237] Ibid. (two sentences, 17 words).

[238] In *Trimingham v Associated Newspapers Ltd* [2012] EWHC 1296 (QB).Tugendhat J. held that "commissioning" means that there must have been an obligation on the part of the commissioned party to produce the work and an obligation on the part of the commissioning party to pay money or money's worth (at [334]). As Ms Trimingham did not "commission" the photographs complained within the meaning of s.85 she could have no claim.

[239] Under the present law the copyright is generally in the photographer. Compare *Williams v Settle* [1960] 1 W.L.R. 1072: para.22.5, above.

[240] Copyright, Designs and Patents Act 1988, s.85(1).

[241] Ibid. s.85(2).

Part Four

THE ACTION

CHAPTER 24

THE INITIAL STAGES

SECTION 1. INTRODUCTION

General. No libel action should be brought without the most careful con- **24.1**
sideration of all the circumstances.

First, are the words clearly defamatory? Individuals are often aggrieved
over allegations about them in the press or media which are plainly false and
have undoubtedly caused them damage. It is hard for them to understand that
the law of defamation offers them no remedy unless the words are defamatory.[1] Furthermore, the new statutory definition of "defamatory" (publication
must have caused or be likely to cause serious harm to the claimant's
reputation)[2] may well raise the bar, and inevitably brings with it, at least in the
short term, a new uncertainty.

Secondly, can the defendant raise any defence which is likely to succeed at
the trial? That is often a question of great difficulty. Unless the claimant's
solicitor is an experienced defamation litigator, it is usually wise to consult
specialist counsel before sending a letter before action, and certainly before
issuing proceedings. These days it is also possible to instruct a barrister
directly, provided that he or she is licensed to accept instructions on this
basis.

Thirdly, what are the financial implications of litigation? In the event of
success, what damages is the claimant likely to recover? Much will depend on

---

[1] Under certain circumstances, the publication of false words may, however, be actionable in
malicious falsehood, conspiracy or under the Data Protection Act 1998.

[2] Defamation Act 2013, s.1(1): see para.2.5, above. That follows Tugendhat J.'s decision in
Thornton v Telegraph Media Group Ltd [2010] EWHC 1414 (QB); [2010] E.M.L.R. 25, itself
following Lord Atkin's speech in *Sim v Stretch* [1936] T.L.R. 669; [1936] 2 All E.R. 1237 in
stating the need for a threshold of seriousness, so as to exclude trivial claims. See also *Cammish
v Hughes* [2012] EWCA Civ 1655, [2013] E.M.L.R. 13, and *Euromoney Institutional Investor Plc
v Aviation News Ltd* [2013] EWHC 1505 (QB) at [24] (and see the cases there cited), where
Tugendhat J. suggested that the hurdle is already higher for the corporate than for the personal
claimant.

his own character and conduct. If he has attacked or provoked the defendant, or if his own unwise behaviour has given rise to the publication of which he complains, he is unlikely to receive much sympathy at the hands of a jury. If he is not altogether blameless he may be well advised not to bring an action.[3] And the potential consequences of failure may be disastrous.

A person who brings an action in defence of his reputation must be prepared to go into the witness box and deny the charge made against him. If he fails to do so the jury may express their opinion by awarding him nominal or contemptuous damages. If he does go into the box he must expect to be cross-examined on his conduct and credit, particularly if the defendant has pleaded justification (truth), and in the result may suffer a much greater injury than that which he has sustained from the defamatory words themselves.[4] Moreover, enthusiastic media coverage, which has to be expected in any case involving a public figure, and in many which do not, will tend to exacerbate the damage. A successful plea of justification has sometimes led to the institution of criminal proceedings, and the ultimate conviction of the claimant for the offence alleged.[5]

---

[3] See for instance *Pamplin v Express Newspapers (Note)* [1988] 1 W.L.R. 116; the plaintiff registered his car in the name of his young son, hoping to avoid liability for illegal parking by relying on the rule that a child under 10 cannot be guilty of a criminal offence. After his behaviour began to attract attention, the *Sunday Express* printed a leading article which accused Mr Pamplin of behaving like an unscrupulous "spiv" and of meriting disgust for making such use of his son. After an earlier verdict was quashed for misdirection, the jury rejected the defences of justification and fair comment but awarded Mr Pamplin only 1/2p. That is not to say that a man loses his right to damages because his character is not free from reproach: see per Greer L.J. in *Hobbs v Tinling* [1929] 2 K.B. at 46:

"A man with a damaged character is entitled to have his damaged character protected and if newspapers for their own purposes falsely allege that he had been guilty of crimes and misconduct the jury might well consider that even a man of bad character ought not to have his character made out to be blacker than the proved facts warrant."

In *Hamaizia v Comr of Metropolitan Police* [2013] EWHC 848 (QB), where two serving prisoners, convicted of grievous bodily harm and false imprisonment, complained of an allegation that they were involved in a murder, Tugendhat J. warned that their prospects of achieving any substantial award of damages were "seriously compromised" by their convictions. See also *Williams v MGN Ltd* [2009] EWHC 3150 (QB), where a convicted murderer attempted to bring a claim in libel.

[4] Examples are *Taylforth v News Group*, 1994, in which the defendant's counsel was able to attack the credit of the plaintiff, an actress in the television series "Eastenders", to great effect by cross-examination about her behaviour at a party, as evidenced by a video tape supplied to the defendant by a member of the public in the course of the trial; and *Jani Allan v Channel Four*, 1992, another case in which evidence appeared in the course of a trial and proved highly damaging on credit. In *Aitken v Guardian Newspapers*, 1997, the plaintiff, a well known politician, abandoned his action in the course of trial when it became clear that the defendant had unearthed new and highly damaging evidence. The consequences, in terms of costs and his public career, were ruinous (see fn.5, below).

[5] In *Johnson v Browning* (1705) 6 Mod. at 217, Lord Holt refers to a case where the plaintiff brought an action of slander in respect of an imputation that he was a highwayman. At the trial it was proved that he was one. He was arrested in court, committed at Newgate and hanged. The ruinous prosecution of Oscar Wilde (*R. v Wilde, The Times*, April 30 and May 1, 2, 1895), was the consequence of Wilde's proceedings against the Marquess of Queensberry for criminal libel (Queensberry had accused Wilde of "posing as a somdomite" [*sic*]) in which justification was successfully pleaded. In *R. v O'Toole, The Times*, October 16 and December 8, 1925, the evidence

Risks. The risks and potential costs of defamation proceedings have on any   **24.2**
view been substantially increased, at least in the short term, by the 2013
Defamation Act, which will create uncertainty as to the effect of the new
provisions. Even before the new law was passed, it was a truism that the only
person who could contemplate with equanimity bringing an action for libel or
slander was one with ample means, whose prior reputation was unblemished,
whose complaint was of a damaging and clear public misstatement of a
specific fact, and whose past contained no skeletons.[6] A good example of such
a claimant is provided by the case of Lord McAlpine, who was falsely accused
of child molestation both in the established media and by bloggers and
"Tweeters" such as Mrs Bercow.[7] A private communication may be privileged, even when quite widely published,[8] and a media story may attract
Reynolds (or "public interest") privilege,[9] and if the misstatement is not clear,
it may either be held to be honest comment[10] or give rise to a prolonged trial.
The proceedings, whether interlocutory, at the trial, or on appeal, tend to be
complex and expensive. In 1972 it was said that the aggregate bill that an
unsuccessful party would have to bear in the case of *Broome v Cassell*[11] might

---

given by the plaintiff in an action of slander led to his arrest and conviction for perjury. There
have also been more recent libel actions in which the plaintiff's evidence has been referred, after
trial, for consideration of prosecution for perjury. Notoriously, Jonathan Aitken was sentenced to
18 months' imprisonment in June 1999 for perjury and attempting to pervert the course of justice
(by persuading his daughter to give a false witness statement) during his 1997 libel action against
the *Guardian* ; in July 2001 Jeffrey Archer was convicted of two counts of perjury and two counts
of perverting the course of justice during his 1987 libel action against the *Daily Star*, and
sentenced to four years' imprisonment; and in January 2011 Thomas Sheridan, a Scottish
politician, was convicted by a Glasgow jury of five counts of perjury committed during his libel
action against News Group Newspapers in 2006, and sentenced to three years' imprisonment.

[6] That rule is not absolute, as shown by *Polanski v Condé Nast*, in which the Paris-based
claimant was awarded £50,000 by a jury on July 22, 2005 despite not being able to give evidence
in person because of the risk of extradition to the United States in respect of a conviction for
under-age sex. That difficulty led to an interlocutory appeal to the House of Lords: [2005] UKHL
10; [2005] 1 W.L.R. 637. The defendants' application to Strasbourg was rejected as inadmissible:
Condé Nast v UK, App. No.29746/05.

[7] *McAlpine v Bercow* [2013] EWHC 1342 (QB).

[8] See *Kearns v General Council of the Bar* [2003] EWCA Civ 331; [2003] 1 W.L.R. 1357 in
which the Court of Appeal upheld qualified privilege in respect of a publication to 10,132 barristers.

[9] *Reynolds v Times Newspapers Ltd* [2001] 2 A.C. 127, and most recently *Flood v Times
Newspapers Ltd* [2012] UKSC 11; [2012] 2 A.C. 273; [2012] E.M.L.R. 21. By s.4 Defamation
Act 2013, the common law *Reynolds* defence has been prospectively abolished and replaced by
a defence of publication on a matter of public interest. See generally Ch.15, above.

[10] See now Defamation Act 2013, s.3, which has prospectively abolished the common law
defence of honest comment and replaced it with a statutory defence of honest opinion.

[11] [1972] A.C. 1027 at 1113, where Lord Wilberforce referred to the English legal system as
"extravagant and punitive as to costs" in civil cases. In that case the trial at first instance lasted
17 days, the hearing in the Court of Appeal lasted 10 days, and the House of Lords heard
argument on 13 days. The appeal turned on disputed questions of law, but the length of the trial
is not unusual. The trial of the action in *McDonald's v Steel* (reported at [1995] 3 All E.R. 615
on an interlocutory point) lasted some 313 days. It may safely be assumed that the plaintiffs'
costs, which will have been irrecoverable (the defendants were litigants in person and not people
of means), will have run well into seven figures.

be more than £60,000; in June 1997 a plaintiff agreed to pay a defendant £765,000, representing 80 per cent of the defendant's costs assessed on the standard (not indemnity) basis, as a term of an agreement by which he was permitted to discontinue his action after several weeks of trial.[12] Such burdens result not only from prolonged inquiries into difficult facts, but often also reflect the uncertainties of the law and disagreements between judges for which the unsuccessful litigant is expected to pay. Even a successful party will find that he has incurred substantial costs which cannot be recovered from his opponent on detailed assessment.

24.3 **Finding out the actual words.** The words are the essence of an action in libel or slander. If at all possible, it is essential to obtain a copy of the document containing the libel, or (if it is a slander) to obtain statements from those who heard the actual words spoken, and record their recollection in direct speech. It is very difficult to give useful advice without knowing the exact words, for a great deal will turn on their exact meaning and context.[13] The client should be told not just to preserve a copy of the document containing the libel, but also all other documents which might conceivably be disclosable in the action, including electronic documents.[14]

24.4 **Defences.** It is important to advise the intending claimant as accurately as possible of the defences which are likely to be pleaded and the probable outcome of the action. However, it may be very difficult (e.g.) to advise on the likelihood of proof of justification (truth).[15] The question is not made any easier by the fact that the claimant cannot rely on choosing his own ground.[16] He may be concerned about part of an article, or may understand the words to

---

[12] *Nixon v Channel Four*, tried in June 1997.

[13] For pleading purposes it is essential to know the actual words. The claimant cannot guess at the words of a libel which he has not seen (*Collins v Jones* [1955] 1 Q.B. 564), and the words must be set out with reasonable certainty and precision (*British Data Management v Boxer Commercial Removals* [1996] 3 All E.R. 707 CA; *Best v Charter Medical of England Ltd* [2002] E.M.L.R. 335 CA). The words of CPR PD 53 para.2.4 ("In a claim for slander the precise words used . . . must, so far as possible, be set out in the particulars of claim") do not remove the requirement that a claimant must plead his case in slander with sufficient particularity to enable the defendant to know how to formulate his case (*Best v Charter Medical of England Ltd*, above). Before the advent of the CPR, the slander plaintiff was sometimes able to interrogate after acknowledgement of service as to the words spoken (*Atkinson v Fosbrooke* (1866) L.R. 1 Q.B. 628), and presumably the same result can be achieved by use of the power to order further information under CPR r.18.1. Pre-trial disclosure of a libel may in principle be obtained under CPR r.31.16, but he courts will require clear evidence of publication of a libel and "fishing" applications will receive short shrift. See further para.31.2, below.

[14] CPR 31BPD para.7.

[15] The common law defence of justification has been prospectively abolished by s.2, Defamation Act 2013, and replaced by a statutory defence of substantial truth.

[16] It is rarely possible to bring an action on one part of a statement and prevent the defendant from pleading the truth of another part of it. Generally, that will only be possible where there are two or more separate and distinct defamatory statements: in that situation, the claimant will be entitled to select one for complaint and the defendant will not be entitled to justify the others. See *Polly Peck v Trelford* [1986] Q.B. 1000 at 1032, per O'Connor L.J.; *Templeton v Jones* [1984] 1 N.Z.L.R. 448 CA of New Zealand; *Stonor v Daily Telegraph*, unreported, July 19, 1976, CA;

bear a particular meaning; but the defendant may be able to justify a different (but not separate and distinct) part of the article,[17] or to justify the part complained of, but in a different defamatory meaning,[18] or to justify a general sting by an example of behaviour by the claimant which was not even included in the article complained of.[19] What is more, if the defendant can prove the sting of the libel, or can prove the truth of one or more distinct charges, when those not proved to be true do not materially affect the claimant's reputation having regard to those which are proved to be true, he will succeed in the action[20]; and even a partial justification may reduce damages almost to vanishing point.[21] Even if the defendant cannot plead the truth of any part of the statement complained of, he can still show in mitigation of damages that the claimant has a bad reputation in a relevant sector of his life.[22]

It may be that there is an arguable defence of honest (formerly fair) comment.[23] If so, it should be remembered that the limits of comment are very wide indeed.[24] This is especially so in the case of those who seek or hold

---

S&K Holdings v Throgmorton [1972] 1 W.L.R. 1036 CA; *US Tobacco International Inc. v BBC* [1998] E.M.L.R. 816; *Cruise v Express Newspapers Plc* [1999] Q.B. 931; *Bennett v BBC* [2003] EWHC 553, Gray J; *Warren v Random House Group Ltd* [2008] EWCA Civ 834, [2009] Q.B. 600. See also para.11.5, above.

[17] *Polly Peck v Trelford* (above); *Warren v Random House Group Ltd* (above). See para.11.5, above and para.27.8, below.

[18] A defendant may justify any meaning which a properly directed jury may reasonably find to be the real meaning of the words complained of: *Prager v Times Newspapers* [1988] 1 W.L.R. 77 CA; *Williams v Reason (Note)* [1988] 1 W.L.R. 96 CA.

[19] *Rothschild v Associated Newspapers Ltd* [2013] EWCA Civ 197, [2013] E.M.L.R. 18.

[20] See the discussion in Ch.11, above and (on pleading the defence of justification) paras 27.8–27.9, below. Note that s.5, Defamation Act 1952 has been prospectively repealed and replaced by s.2(3), Defamation Act 2013.

[21] *Pamplin v Express Newspapers (Note)*, above, per Neill L.J. at 120.

[22] See paras 33.29–33.46, below. The defendant may now show that the claimant should only receive derisory damages because of bad conduct causally connected or "germane" to the libel (*Godfrey v Demon Internet (No.2)*, unreported, April 23, 1999), or put forward "directly relevant background context" in mitigation of damages, which may include evidence of specific misconduct on the claimant's part (*Burstein v Times Newspapers Ltd* [2001] 1 W.L.R. 579 CA; *Turner v News Group Newspapers Ltd* [2006] EWCA Civ 540; [2006] 1 W.L.R. 3469).

[23] The Supreme Court in *Joseph v Spiller* [2010] UKSC 53, [2011] 1 A.C. 852 expressed a preference for the term "honest comment". However, Defamation Act 2013, s.3 has prospectively abolished the common law defence of honest comment and replaced it with a statutory defence of "honest opinion".

[24] The test of honest comment has always been a partly objective and partly subjective one: could any person, however prejudiced and obstinate, honestly hold the view expressed, on the basis of the facts actually known to them? See *Tse Wai Chen v Chung* [2001] E.M.L.R. 31; *Joseph v Spiller*, above, and Ch.12. The new statutory defence of honest opinion in s.3(4), Defamation Act 2013 is perhaps even wider. It is an entirely objective defence: provided facts existed at the time the statement complained of was published (even if those facts were not known to the defendant at the time he expressed the opinion), there is a defence if an honest-minded person could have held the opinion based on those facts. An allegation that a claimant "happily promotes bogus treatments" was found to be a statement of opinion, defensible as comment: see *British Chiropractic Association v Singh* [2010] EWCA Civ 350; [2011] 1 W.L.R. 133.

public office or positions of public responsibility,[25] and in the case of businesses and companies which deal with the public.[26] Unless there is some clear evidence of malice or a significant misstatement of fact,[27] it is generally unwise to start an action where there is a reasonably arguable defence of honest opinion, however severe the terms of the criticism may be.[28]

If there is a possible defence of qualified privilege, intending claimants should be alive to the width and continuing uncertainty of the privilege for publication to the world at large first confirmed in *Reynolds v Times Newspapers Ltd*.[29] Although *Reynolds* privilege was initially stated to be an application of the traditional duty-interest test for qualified privilege, the defence has grown a long way from its roots, and the range of factors to be taken into account in deciding whether or not publication took place on a privileged occasion[30] is such that except in unusual, clear-cut cases, it will often be very difficult to advise a prospective claimant on the likely outcome. The position was made no easier by the development in *Loutchansky v Times Newspapers Ltd* of the test of responsible publication. That view was regarded as "despondent" in *Jameel v Wall Street Journal (No.2)*[31] by Eady J., who had in mind Lord Nicholls' words in *Reynolds v Times Newspapers Ltd*[32]:

> " . . . the extent of this uncertainty should not be exaggerated. With the enunciation of some guidelines by the court, any practical problems should be manageable".

However, the difficulties of giving practical advice in *Reynolds* privilege cases were not eased by the liberalising decision of the House of Lords in *Jameel (Mohammed) v Wall Street Journal*.[33] The approach of the majority appeared to subsume duty and interest in the larger question of whether publication of the article was in the public interest, but it was not clear to many practitioners by what objective canon that issue was to be resolved. Some assistance is now provided by the Supreme Court decision in *Flood v Times Newspapers Ltd*,[34] though the case raises further questions about the

---

[25] "Those who fill public positions must not be too thin-skinned in reference to comments made upon them": *Seymour v Butterworth* (1862) 3 F. & F. 372 at 377, per Cockburn C.J.

[26] E.g. *Broadway Approvals v Odhams* [1965] 1 W.L.R. 805 CA.

[27] Even if the defendant is mistaken as to one or some of the facts on which he comments, he has the protection of the Defamation Act 1952, s.6, but that section is prospectively repealed by s.3(8), Defamation Act 2013, which states the conditions for the new statutory defence of honest opinion, and appears (s.3(4)) to lower the bar for proof of supporting facts.

[28] For an example of the scope for strongly held and wholly contrasting views which experienced judges can take on the question of comment or statement of fact, see *Waterson v Lloyd* [2013] EWCA Civ 136; [2013] E.M.L.R. 17, where Tugendhat J. (at first instance) and Richards L.J. found the words complained of to be statements of fact, and McCombe and Laws L.JJ. reached the opposite conclusion with equal confidence.

[29] [2001] 2 A.C. 127. See Ch.15, above.

[30] As to which, see [2001] 2 A.C. 127 at 205, per Lord Nicholls.

[31] [2004] EWHC 37 (QB); [2004] E.M.L.R. 11.

[32] [2001] 2 A.C. 127 at 202.

[33] [2007] 1 A.C. 359.

[34] *Flood v Times Newspapers Ltd* [2012] UKSC 11, [2012] 2 A.C. 273; [2012] E.M.L.R. 21.

relative importance of public interest and responsible journalism for the purposes of the defence.

The task of advising prospective claimants will not be made easier when the prospective abolition of the *Reynolds* defence takes effect and is replaced by s.4, Defamation Act 2013, a new statutory defence of publication on a matter of public interest. While the Explanatory Notes to the Act suggest that s.4 is intended to reflect the law as laid down in *Flood*,[35] the conditions for the statutory defence are in different terms.

Stress of litigation. Apart from the uncertainty of the result, and the   **24.5** possibility of an outcome worse for the claimant's reputation than the publication complained of, the claimant should be aware of the time, effort, strain and anxiety involved in preparing for an action over what may be a period of a year or perhaps even years. It is remarkable how often a claimant's enthusiasm for litigation will evaporate as the sting of the libel fades and the strain and expense of the action grow. He should bear in mind the possibility of answering the defamer in an appropriate forum with the protection of qualified privilege, or, if he has been defamed in the media, of resorting to one of the procedures for making complaint which are described in this chapter. For all this, there are occasions where an individual is defamed publicly or in a quarter in which his reputation is important to him, or damaging rumours have been widely circulated, and an action for defamation may be the only way of clearing his name.

Letter before action: Defamation Pre-Action Protocol. It is now   **24.6** almost always essential[36] to send a letter before action (known in the Defamation Pre-Action Protocol as a "letter of claim"). The Defamation Pre-Action Protocol sets out the essential information that a letter before action should contain and lays down a timetable for the defendant's response. Its guidance, which is intended to encourage the exchange of full information at an early stage, the early resolution of disputes and the efficient management of proceedings where litigation cannot be avoided, should be followed in every case except those where the urgency of the situation is such that immediate issue of proceedings is unavoidably necessary.

A primary purpose of the Protocol is to allow the parties to make an informed judgment on the merits, through earlier access to the information they need. The Protocol marks a policy shift from the old practice of keeping cards close to the chest, and the old-fashioned "attack dog" approach to pre-action correspondence is best consigned to history. Nowadays, the claimant

---

[35] Para.29 of the Explanatory Notes.
[36] Contrast the position before the advent of the Pre-Action Protocols: see, e.g. *Goldsmith v Sperrings* [1977] 1 W.L.R. 478 at 509, per Bridge L.J. (who described the omission to send a letter before action as a discourtesy).

should state his case clearly and frankly,[37] preferably in terms which are consistent with those of any particulars of claim that ensue, and should not demand more than he is entitled to, still less proceed to litigation having substantially received his entitlement in the course of correspondence.[38] Failure to send a properly formulated letter before action may have adverse costs consequences.[39]

24.7 *Information to be contained in letter before action.* The Protocol requires that the following information be contained in the letter before action:

(1) the name of the claimant;

(2) sufficient details to identify the publication or broadcast which contained the words complained of;

(3) the words complained of and, if known, the date of publication; where possible, a copy or transcript of the words complained of should be enclosed;

(4) factual inaccuracies or unsupportable comment within the words complained of: the claimant should give a sufficient explanation to enable the defendant to appreciate why the words are inaccurate or unsupportable[40];

(5) the nature of the remedies sought by the claimant;
    and, where relevant:

(6) any facts and matters which make the claimant identifiable from the words complained of;

(7) details of any special facts relevant to the interpretation of the words complained of and/or any particular damage caused by them.

24.8 *Identification of meanings.* The Protocol states that it is desirable for the claimant to identify the meaning or meanings that he attaches to the words. That is salutary advice, but it is vital to ensure that any meanings canvassed in the letter do not conflict with the meanings later pleaded in the particulars of claim. For that reason, if specialist counsel is to be instructed to settle the particulars of claim, it is always wise to ask them to settle the letter before action also. Serious embarrassment (at the least) can arise if an unsound meaning is advanced in the letter before action and later abandoned.[41]

---

[37] *Rothschild v Associated Newspapers Ltd* [2011] EWHC 3462 (QB) at [60].

[38] *Citation Plc v Ellis Whittam Ltd* [2012] EWHC 764 (QB); *Euromoney Institutional Investor PLC v Aviation News Ltd* [2013] EWHC 1505 (QB), esp. at [142].

[39] See CPR r.44.2(5)(a), r.44.4(3)(a)(i) and Defamation Pre-Action Protocol, para.2.

[40] See *Rothschild v Associated Newspapers Ltd*, above, at [48] and [60].

[41] See for instance the judge's observations in *Dell'Olio v Associated Newspapers Ltd* [2011] EWHC 3472 (QB) at [30]–[31], where the meaning advanced in the letter of claim differed significantly from that pleaded in the particulars of claim (but neither was held to be capable of being a defamatory meaning).

Remedies. When dealing with remedies, the letter should normally ask for   **24.9**
payment of costs and (in appropriate cases) for an undertaking not to repeat
the libel or slander, and will usually ask for the defendant's proposals for
compensation, although if possible the demand for compensation should be
subordinated to the requirement for a proper apology and retraction. The
Protocol does not suggest this, but it is usually convenient to include a draft
of a proposed apology. For obvious reasons, the letter should not be headed
"without prejudice", although if there is a risk that it may be published, it
should be headed "Not for publication".[42]

Defendant's response. As soon as the prospective defendant receives a   **24.10**
letter before action he must quickly decide what attitude to adopt. His
response will largely depend on whether he is confident that he has a good
defence. As this may involve difficult questions of law he should immediately
consult his solicitors who should ideally, unless they are defamation specialists, instruct specialist counsel.[43] If the defendant is a newspaper or media
organisation, it may have worked on the story and gathered at least some
evidence, and may have taken pre-publication legal advice: but in every case
the defendant's immediate object, and that of his solicitor, should be to
investigate the facts of the case, to consider what defences are available, and
to obtain as much time as possible from the complainant to decide what course
to adopt. If the publication complained of is continuing online, the defendant
may wish to consider suspending it, at least while he completes his enquiries.
Where the defendant is an internet service provider, doing so may of itself
furnish a complete defence.[44]

Defamation Pre-Action Protocol. However, such considerations must be   **24.11**
reconciled with the Protocol, which obliges the defendant to provide a full
response to the letter before action as soon as possible, and to tell the claimant,
if it seems likely that he will not be able to respond within 14 days or the
period specified by the claimant, the date by which he intends to respond. His
response should say whether or to what extent the claim is accepted (if so,
stating what remedies he is prepared to offer) or rejected (if so, giving reasons,
including a sufficient indication of the facts which he is likely to rely on in
support of a substantive defence), and whether he needs more information (if
so, stating precisely what information is needed and why). The authors of the
Protocol suggest that it is "desirable" for the defendant to say what meaning

---

[42] *Private Eye*, for instance, has published letters before action, which may make the claimant
look foolish.
[43] On the circumstances in which it may be reasonable from a costs assessment perspective to
instruct specialist London solicitors as against a provincial firm, see *Gazley v News Group
Newspapers* [2004] EWHC 2675 (QB).
[44] Whether under the Electronic Commerce (EC Directive) Regulations 2002 or Defamation
Act 1996, s.1: see generally *Tamiz v Google Inc.* [2013] EWCA Civ 68; [2013] 1 W.L.R.
2151.

or meanings he puts on the words, but defendants may be wise to be a little cautious in following this advice unless they are very confident of their evidence and what it proves. It is common experience that when it is considered in detail, the evidence available to support a plea of justification fails to justify the published words at the high level of meaning hoped for, and to state a position in open correspondence about the actual meaning of the words, before establishing what meaning one is able to justify, may give rise to real embarrassment.

24.12 *Compensation.* If the decision is made to offer the claimant compensation, there is no longer any reason not to mention the amount. If a defendant takes this course, it will usually be done in a letter written "without prejudice save as to costs", but there may be advantages in making an open offer.[45] If the complainant has demanded a withdrawal or correction and apology, the defendant (if he has no defence)[46] should comply with the request. A prompt correction or apology may put a complete stop to any proceedings, and if it does not it can only benefit the defendant. If the defendant intends to make an offer of amends in accordance with s.2 of the Defamation Act,[47] he must do so before service of his defence.[48]

24.13 **Proportionality and ADR.** The Defamation Pre-Action Protocol stresses that in formulating letters of claim and of response and in taking subsequent steps, the parties should act reasonably to keep costs proportionate to the nature and gravity of the case and the stage the complaint has reached. The parties are also urged to consider whether some form of alternative dispute resolution procedure would be "more suitable" than litigation, and may be required by the court to produce evidence that alternative means of resolving their dispute have been considered. Failure to do so will be considered when the court determines costs.[49]

SECTION 2. CHOICE OF DEFENDANTS

24.14 **Introduction.** Who is liable and may be sued for publication of a defamatory statement has been earlier discussed.[50] In many cases there are likely to

---

[45] There was a resistance to allowing figures to go before juries (*Kiam v Neil* [1995] E.M.L.R. 1, and *John v MGN Ltd* [1997] Q.B. 586). However, trial by jury is now almost a dead letter (Defamation Act 2013, s.11), and an open offer might in the right case form the basis of an application for a stay: see the defendants' application in *Adelson v Associated Newspapers Ltd* [2008] EWHC 278 (QB); [2009] E.M.L.R. 10.

[46] Or, it may be, even if there is a defence of qualified privilege or, when it comes into effect, public interest privilege (on the latter, see Defamation Act 2013, s.4): an admission of an inaccuracy will not jeopardise that defence, and may be helpful in mitigating damage and resisting a plea of malice.

[47] See generally paras 19.1–19.6, above, and para.29.28–29.40, below.

[48] Defamation Act 1996, s.2(5).

[49] Defamation Pre-Action Protocol, para.3.7. See para.29.41, below.

[50] See Ch.8, above.

be several persons against whom legal action can be taken and who can be joined as defendants in the same action. However, it may be neither necessary, appropriate nor tactically prudent to commence proceedings against all those parties against whom a cause of action technically lies.

Person with strong defence. It would clearly be unwise to include as a   **24.15**
defendant a person who, though prima facie responsible with others for the publication complained of, has a strong defence of his own distinct from that of other defendants.

Examples. A person other than the author, editor or publisher of the defama-   **24.16**
tory statement may be able to establish that he is not liable as he took reasonable care in relation to the publication of the statement and did not know, or have reason to believe, that what he did caused or contributed to the publication of a defamatory statement.[51] A newspaper which has reported fairly and accurately a defamatory speech made at a public meeting, or a defamatory statement included in a circular relating to the dismissal of a director issued by a public company, is likely to have a statutory defence of privilege.[52] Where there is joint publication by a number of persons in circumstances which will enable each individual to maintain that he has an independent or derivative defence of privilege, the action will only succeed and should as a rule only be brought against those against whom malice can be proved.[53] For similar reasons, if the author of a maliciously motivated defamatory statement in, say, a newspaper, which might otherwise attract the defence of honest comment (honest opinion), is an independent contributor,[54] the editor or publishers should only be joined as defendants with the author if there is evidence of malice against them.[55]

Liability for aggravated and exemplary damages. Whilst it is clearly   **24.17**
desirable to ensure that at least one defendant has sufficient financial resources to meet the likely aggregate of the judgment for damages and costs, the choice of defendants could limit or restrict the damages recoverable. This is because of the rule that there is only one award of damages for publication of a libel.[56]

---

[51] See s.1 of the Defamation Act 1996 and paras 6.31 et seq., above. Moreover, Defamation Act 2013, s.10 prospectively shuts off any claim against a person who is not the author, editor or publisher unless the court is satisfied that it is not reasonably practicable to sue the author, editor or publisher (see para.6.45, above).

[52] See s.15 and paras 12 and 13(2) and (3) of Pt II of Sch.1 to the Defamation Act 1996. The newspaper must have published a reasonable letter or statement by way of explanation or contradiction: s.15(2). See paras 16.17–16.22, above. The person making the speech, or the company issuing the circular, might not have a defence.

[53] See *Egger v Chelmsford* [1965] 2 Q.B. 248; and para.17.24, above.

[54] Rather than a staff journalist for whom his superiors would be vicariously liable.

[55] See paras 12.36–12.37, above.

[56] *Hayward v Thompson* [1982] Q.B. 47 at 62h, 70e-g, 73–74, *Veliu v Mazrekaj* [2006] EWHC 1710 (QB); [2007] 1 W.L.R. 495.

That principle applies to exemplary damages. In an action against two or more defendants in which exemplary damages are claimed the sum awarded by way of exemplary damages has to be the lowest sum for which any of the defendants can be held liable.[57] Thus, if by reason of lack of resources or peripheral involvement with the publication, one of the defendants deserves punishment less than others, exemplary damages will be assessed against all defendants on the basis of what is the appropriate award against the former. If the conduct of that defendant does not merit any award of exemplary damages, there will be no award against any defendant. The same approach probably governs aggravated damages.[58] If matters relied upon as aggravating the damages cannot be proved as against a particular defendant, and he is not vicariously liable for the other defendants, then joining that defendant might result in the judge declining to award any sum by way of aggravated damages.[59]

24.18 Advantages of joining defendants. Even though orders for disclosure may be made against non-parties, the greater ease of the disclosure process as against a party to the action may be a reason for joining an individual as a defendant. Prospective problems of proof, or uncertainties as to who is responsible for the publication of the offending words, may also influence decisions as to the appropriate defendants. For example, the person who made a public speech defamatory of the claimant, later reported in a newspaper, might contend that he had not been reported accurately, or that his remarks had been quoted out of context, and that on those grounds he was not liable for what appeared in the newspaper. In such circumstances the sensible course would usually be to join both the publisher of the newspaper and the maker of the speech as defendants, as either the former will prove the accuracy of the report (and thus the liability of the speaker), or the latter establish that he has been misreported (in which case the publisher will be in difficulty).

---

[57] *Broome v Cassell* [1972] A.C. 1027 at 1063 (per Lord Hailsham) and at 1090 (per Lord Reid). See para.9.36, above.

[58] *Broome v Cassell*, above, at 1063; though Lord Denning disagreed in *Hayward v Thompson* [1982] Q.B. 47 at 62, at least so far as newspaper cases were concerned. See also *Veliu v Mazrekaj*, above, at [12]. In *Berezovsky v Russian Television and Radio Broadcasting Co.* [2010] EWHC 476 (QB) at [174]–[175], Eady J. considered *Broome v Cassell* and *Hayward v Thompson* and concluded that the question of whether any joint tortfeasor should be liable for aggravation of damages only to the extent of his joint liability, that is, at the lowest common denominator, could not be definitively answered. He decided, nonetheless, that the lowest common denominator approach was likely to be preferred by a modern appellate court, not least because it was likely to be more compatible with art.10, and therefore left individual aggravating factors out of account. In the event, he awarded damages only in respect of one meaning for which both defendants could be shown to be responsible, to avoid penalising the personal defendant for allegations which he could not be shown to have published.

[59] There would perhaps be an argument for a different result in a newspaper case. That would be founded on Lord Denning's lone view in *Hayward v Thompson*, above, at 62–63, that at least in newspaper cases it is impossible to draw a distinction between one defendant and another, so that if the court takes a poor view of the conduct of any of the defendants, it can award whatever sum it thinks fit in aggravation of damages without distinguishing between them.

Repeated statements. The common law principle is that each publication   **24.19**
of a defamatory statement gives rise to a separate cause of action.[60] Thus, a
newsworthy allegation could be sued on in separate actions against all newspapers that published the story, but to do that might be very burdensome, and
certainly very expensive; and with a one-year limitation period there is usually
little opportunity to pick defendants off one by one. Moreover, there are perils
in starting multiple actions against different defendants, as shown by the
decision in *Pedder v News Group Newspapers*,[61] in which a claim was struck
out as an abuse after an almost identical claim against another newspaper had
been litigated to trial and lost. It is likely to be more practical to identify and
proceed against the person originally responsible for disseminating the allegation, and perhaps include a claim for damages for repetition of the story by
others.[62] Alternatively, the action could be limited to the defendant who
published the allegation most prominently and in the most sensational and
indefensible terms, with a view to obtaining a large sum of damages and an
effective vindication. A further alternative may be to start proceedings against
all the intended targets and then apply for a stay of all actions but one until that
action is resolved by trial or settlement.

Section 3. Jurisdiction

Publication with a foreign element. If the defamatory publication has a   **24.20**
foreign element, consideration must be given as to whether litigation can be
pursued in the English courts. Within the term "foreign element" there are
included cases where the publisher of the defamatory statement is not present
in England and Wales and has no place of business here, publication which
takes place outside the jurisdiction of the English courts, and publication
about persons who have little or no connection with this country.

Publisher of defamatory statement not present in England or   **24.21**
Wales. Proceedings *in personam* are only possible against persons who can
be served with a claim form.[63] As a general rule service must be effected
within the geographical jurisdiction of the court, namely in England and
Wales.[64] Save where service is to be effected in an EU member state or a
Lugano Convention contracting state (Norway, Iceland, Switzerland), the

---

[60] That principle is now prospectively qualified, for limitation purposes at any rate, by
Defamation Act 2013, s.8. In broad terms s.8 provides that time runs from the first instance of
publication by a particular person, and does not re-start with a subsequent publication by that
same person unless the subsequent publication is materially different.

[61] [2004] E.M.L.R 19.

[62] See *Slipper v BBC* [1991] 1 Q.B. 283.

[63] See Dicey and Morris on *Conflict of Laws*, 15th edn (2012), Ch.11.

[64] It does not matter that the defendant's presence here is only fleeting: *Colt Industries v Sarlie*
[1966] 1 W.L.R. 440.

court's permission is required before a claim form can be served outside the jurisdiction.[65] The Civil Procedure Rules describe the categories of cases in which permission may be granted. They include claims founded on tort where the damage was sustained, or resulted from an act committed, within the jurisdiction.[66] Damage is presumed in libel,[67] and the damage is sustained and the act resulting in the damage is committed at the place or places of publication.[68] Publication occurs at the place where the statement is seen or received by another person, a rule which has particular importance for internet publication.[69] Thus, a defamatory internet page hosted by a foreign-based service provider is published in England if it is read here, and a foreign newspaper with an English circulation is (to that extent) published in this country: both cases, therefore, will come within the rule for the purposes of seeking leave to serve outside the jurisdiction.

24.22 *Procedure.* The application for permission to serve outside the jurisdiction is made by application notice stating the grounds of the application, the claimant's belief that his claim has a reasonable prospect of success, and the defendant's address, or, if not known, in what place the defendant is, or is

---

[65] See para.24.23, below.

[66] CPR r.6.36 and CPR 6 PD B para.3.1(9). Also where the person out of the jurisdiction is a necessary or proper party in a claim brought against a person who has been or will be served within or out of the jurisdiction and between whom and the claimant there is a real issue which it is reasonable for the court to try: CPR 6 PD B para.3.1(3). Under this head leave might be sought to serve a claim form on the writer of a defamatory book, resident abroad, where the book's publishers have already been served.

[67] The presumption is (or has been) a factor of central importance in cases where a claimant wishes to have his action against a foreign publisher tried in England, and was challenged (unsuccessfully) in two related cases. The arguments in each case were quite different. In *Jameel (Mohammed) v Wall Street Journal Sprl* [2006] UKHL 44; [2007] 1 A.C. 359, it was argued that English law, to be compatible with art.10 of the ECHR, had to require proof of special damage as an essential element of a cause of action in libel by a corporation. By a majority, that argument was rejected. S.1, Defamation Act 2013 prospectively changes the law to the extent of setting a threshold (higher in the case of a company) before a statement will be found to be defamatory. That is not the same as abolishing the presumption of damage: see the discussion at para.3.7, above. In *Jameel (Yousef) v Dow Jones* [2005] EWCA Civ 75; [2005] Q.B. 946, it was accepted by the defendant that damage could be presumed in a claim by a corporation where there had been significant publication of a defamatory article: the argument was that this was very different from presuming damage irrebuttably as a matter of law, and that if a defendant could show that no damage had been done, it ought to be able to do so. That argument also was rejected, but from the defendant's point of view it hardly mattered, since the action was stayed as an abuse.

[68] *Pullman v Hill* [1891] 1 Q.B. 524 at 527; *Hebditch v MacIlwaine* [1894] 2 Q.B. 54 at 61; *Bata v Bata* [1948] W.N. 366; *Shevill v Presse Alliance* [1996] A.C. 959; *King v Lewis* [2004] EWCA Civ 1329; [2005] E.M.L.R. 45.

[69] See *Godfrey v Demon Internet* [2001] Q.B. 201; *King v Lewis* (above); *Richardson v Schwarzenegger* [2004] EWHC 2422 (QB), and the important decision of the High Court of Australia in *Gutnick v Dow Jones & Co. Inc.* [2002] HCA 56, 210 C.L.R. 575. There is no rebuttable presumption of law that an article placed on an internet website open to general access has been published to a substantial number of people within the jurisdiction. The claimant bears the burden of proving that the material in question has been accessed and downloaded: *Al Amoudi v Brisard* [2006] EWHC 1062 (QB); [2007] 1 W.L.R. 113. For the law on publication generally, see Ch.6, above.

likely, to be found.[70] The applicant must be full and frank with the court. Permission will not be granted unless the court is satisfied that England or Wales is the proper place in which to bring the claim.[71] The court has power to make an order on the defendant's application within 14 days of acknowledgement of service declaring that the court has no jurisdiction and to set aside the claim form and its service, and to stay the proceedings notwithstanding that permission has been given under the above procedure.[72]

It is important to note that the bar will be raised when Defamation Act 2013, s.9 is brought into force, for the court will then not have jurisdiction to determine an action for defamation brought against a person not domiciled in the UK or another EU member state or a country which is a contracting party to the Lugano Convention (currently Norway, Iceland and Switzerland), unless it is satisfied that of all the places in which the statement complained of has been published, England and Wales is clearly the most appropriate place in which to bring an action in respect of the statement.

The Brussels Regime Leave is not required[73] to serve a claim form out of   **24.23**
the jurisdiction where the court has power to hear and determine the case by virtue of the Civil Jurisdiction and Judgments Acts 1982 or the Lugano Convention[74] or the Judgments Regulation (Council Regulation (EC) No.44/2001 of December 22, 2000 on jurisdiction and the recognition and enforcement of judgments in civil and commercial matters), otherwise known as Brussels I, which superseded the original 1968 Brussels Convention for all EU Member States.[75]

Service. Under CPR r.6.33, for service to be effected without leave, the   **24.24**
claim must be one which the court has the power to determine under the Judgments Regulation or the Lugano Convention (as a defamation claim undoubtedly is: see Art.1 of each instrument), the defendant must be domiciled in the United Kingdom or another EU member state or a Lugano Convention country (Norway, Iceland and Switzerland), and no proceedings between the same parties concerning the same claim must be pending in the courts of other parts of the United Kingdom or of any other member state or Convention territory.

Jurisdictional regime. As far as defamation is concerned, the jurisdictional   **24.25**
regime under the Judgments Regulation and the 2007 Lugano Convention is

---

[70] CPR r.6.37(1).71 CPR r.6.37(3).

[71] CPR r.6.37(3).

[72] CPR r.11.1.

[73] CPR r.6.33.

[74] The Lugano Convention of 2007 was designed to follow the procedures of the Judgments Regulation. It regulates the mutual recognition and enforcement of judgments as between EU members and the three Lugano Convention countries, Iceland, Norway and Switzerland.

[75] Denmark, which had previously remained subject to the original Brussels Convention, submitted to the Judgments Regulation from July 1, 2007: Civil Jurisdiction and Judgments Regulations 2007, SI 2007/1655.

broadly similar to that which held good under the 1968 Brussels and 1988 Lugano Conventions. The general rule is that persons domiciled in a Member State[76] shall (whatever their nationality) be sued in the courts of that state (art.2(1)), and may be sued in the courts of another Member State only by virtue of the rules as to special jurisdiction (art.3(1)). Article 5(3) provides by way of special jurisdiction that a person domiciled in a Member State may be sued in matters relating to tort in the courts for the place where the harmful event occurred or may occur.[77] The application of art.5(3) of the 1968 Brussels Convention to a libel claim was considered by the European Court of Justice in *Shevill v Presse Alliance*.[78] The plaintiff, a United Kingdom national resident in Yorkshire, brought proceedings in England in respect of an alleged libel in *France Soir*, a newspaper published in France with a very small circulation in England and Wales. The claim was limited to the few copies distributed there. The defendants applied to have the action stayed on the grounds that the place where the "harmful event" occurred within the meaning of art.5(3) of the Convention was France, where the newspaper was published, and the French courts alone had jurisdiction. The European Court decided that the victim of a libel by a newspaper article distributed in several Contracting States could bring an action for damages against the publisher either before the courts of the Contracting State where the publisher of the defamatory publication was established, which had jurisdiction to award damages for all the harm caused by the publication, or before the courts of each Contracting State in which the publication was distributed and where the victim claimed to have suffered injury to his reputation, which had jurisdiction to rule solely in respect of harm caused in the state where the action had been commenced.[79] The criteria for establishing whether a "harmful event" had occurred in a particular state were to be decided by the substantive laws of that state, so as regards England and Wales the plaintiff could rely on the presumption of damage.[80] Thus where a person is libelled in a foreign newspaper or magazine originating in an EU member state or in a Lugano Convention state,[81] but with a circulation in this country, he has the choice of commencing

---

[76] A dispute as to whether a defendant to a libel claim is domiciled within the jurisdiction for the purposes of the Judgments Regulation requires that the notion of domicile be construed in accordance with s.41 of the Civil Jurisdiction and Judgments Act 1982: the defendant must reside in the UK and the nature and circumstances of his residence must indicate that he has a substantial connection with the UK. "Residence" connotes a settled or usual place of abode: see *High Tech International v Deripaska* [2006] EWHC 3276 (QB)· [2007] E.M.L.R. 15, where residence was not established.

[77] Note that the Judgments Regulation has been prospectively amended with effect from January 10, 2015 (Regulation (EU) No.1215/2012 of the European Parliament and of the Council). The general jurisdictional rule (new art.4) and the rule for special jurisdiction in matters of tort (new art.7(2)) are unchanged.

[78] [1995] 2 A.C. 18 (Case C-68/93).

[79] The position is different in misuse of private information cases: *eDate Advertising GmbH v X* [2012] Q.B. 654 (Case C-509/09).

[80] See the House of Lords application of the ECJ decision: [1996] A.C. 959.

[81] That is to say Iceland, Norway and Switzerland.

proceedings in the courts of the European country or in the English courts, but if he chooses the latter his claim will be limited to such damages as are warranted by the extent of its circulation here.[82]

Publication by English publisher outside the jurisdiction. If pub-   24.26
lication is caused by a person domiciled in England and takes place in a member state of the EU (Judgments Regulation) or Norway, Iceland or Switzerland (Lugano Convention), the English courts must accept jurisdiction.[83] Thus, the English courts will hear and determine any defamation claim brought in this country against an English publisher or broadcaster in respect of distribution or transmission of the alleged libel in European Union countries.[84] That will be the case even if the claimant has little or no connection with this jurisdiction. The European Court of Justice decided in 2005 that

---

[82] Even so, a claimant which is a corporation may need to show a trading or business reputation in this country at the date of publication: see *Jameel (Mohammed) v Wall Street Journal Sprl* [2006] UKHL 44; [2007] 1 A.C. 359 at [93], per Lord Hope, and *Atlantis World Group of Companies NV v Gruppo Editoriale L'Espresso SpA* [2008] EWHC 1323 (QB); [2009] E.M.L.R. 15, where a claimant incorporated in the Netherlands Antilles sued an Italian publisher for publication in England and Wales, but failed to show that it had a trading or business reputation here. It might have had such a reputation even if it had never traded here (see per Sir Charles Gray at [49]). The decision of the Court of Appeal in *McDonald's Corp v Steel & Morris* (unreported, March 31, 1999) offers some obiter support for a distinction between individuals and corporations. Note that s.1(2) of the Defamation Act 2013 prospectively prevents corporations which trade for profit from suing unless the harm done to their reputation has caused or is likely to cause them serious financial loss. As far as individuals are concerned, the position is quite different. In *Jameel (Yousef) v Dow Jones* [2005] EWCA Civ 75; [2005] 1 Q.B. 946 at [28]–[29], the Court of Appeal saw no reason why a publication should not simultaneously create and besmirch the reputation of an individual: "To take an extreme example, imagine that an unknown American who was about to visit an English town was erroneously described in the town's local paper as a paedophile. Manifestly the law ought to afford him a cause of action in libel." The court approved Eady J.'s observations to the same effect in *Multigroup Bulgaria Holding AD v Oxford Analytica Ltd* [2001] E.M.L.R. 28, although the observations apparently approved encompassed a company as well as an individual: at [24], Eady J. referred to the hypothetical case of a small trader in Shanghai who wished to provide services for an influx of English tourists arriving for some sporting or cultural event.
"Suppose . . . that the company was libelled on English television just before the tourists left, in such a way as to discourage them from using the services contemplated by the Shanghai trader. I am by no means persuaded that such a trader (individual or corporate) would, or should, have no cause of action just because he, or it, had never been mentioned in England before".
[83] Art.2(1), Judgments Regulation; art.2(1), Lugano Convention.
[84] However, the double actionability rule still applies, apparently even where Judgment Regulation states are involved. For the rule generally, see *Boys v Chaplin* [1971] A.C. 356, and Dicey & Morris, *The Conflict of Laws*, 15th edn (2012), para.35R-099, r.256(3). Defamation survived the abolition of the double actionability requirement for tort enacted by the Private International Law (Miscellaneous Provisions) Act 1995 (see ss.10, 13), and generally its effect is to prevent recovery in the English courts for defamatory statements published abroad which are not actionable here. The purpose of the retention of the rule in defamation appears to have been: "to preserve the barrier of the *lex fori* so as, at least as a general rule, to prevent foreign liabilities in defamation and related claims being enforceable in the English courts unless the events giving rise to those liabilities give rise to an actionable claim in English domestic law" (Dicey & Morris, above, para.35–101), or, to put it another way, to discourage forum-shopping (as Eady J. observed in *Komarek v Ramco Energy Plc* [2002] EWHC 2501 (QB) at [39]).

where the English court had jurisdiction under art.2 over a UK-domiciled defendant, it had no power to stay proceedings on *forum conveniens* grounds in favour of the courts of a non-contracting state.[85] It appears to follow that a claimant from a non-Regulation or Convention country, who may have little if any connection with England and Wales, is entitled to sue in this jurisdiction for a libel published in his own country, simply on the basis that the defendant is domiciled within this jurisdiction, albeit that he would have to satisfy the double actionability rule.[86]

24.27 *Forum conveniens.* In cases which are not governed by the Judgments Regulation or the Lugano Convention, though the claim may come within CPR r.6.36 and para.3.1(9) of CPR 6B PD in that publication took place within the jurisdiction, the court may refuse permission to serve the claim form outside the jurisdiction or, after the claim form has been served, set it aside or its service on the defendant or stay the proceedings,[87] if it is satisfied that there is some other tribunal having competent jurisdiction "in which the case may be tried more suitably for the interests of all the parties and for the ends of justice".[88] This is known as the principle of *forum conveniens*, the constituents of which were authoritatively collated in *Spiliada Maritime Corp v Cansulex*.[89] They can be summarised as follows:

> (1) A stay will only be granted where there is some other available forum which is the appropriate forum for the trial of the action. This involves showing not only that England is not the natural or appropriate forum for the trial but that there is another available forum "which is clearly or distinctly more appropriate than the English forum".[90]

---

[85] *Owusu v Jackson* [2005] 1 Q.B. 801 ECJ. That was a Brussels Convention case, but there is no reason to suppose that the court's analysis would be any different for cases decided under the Judgments Regulation or the Lugano Convention. But for the ECJ's ruling, the competing forum would have been Jamaica, the place where the claimant suffered personal injury.

[86] The result in *Oraro v The Observer* would now be different (unreported, April 10, 1992, Drake J). A prominent lawyer living and practising in Kenya sued *The Observer* newspaper in respect of an article about a commission of inquiry set up in Kenya into the death of the plaintiff's brother. The action was stayed, notwithstanding that the newspaper's distribution in Kenya was very small as compared with its circulation in England. The judge placed emphasis on the subject of the article which he described as "all about Kenyan politics and Kenyan personalities", and upon the fact that the damage to the plaintiff's reputation, of high standing in Kenya, occurred "very substantially" in Kenya. The English court would now be unable to decline jurisdiction.

[87] The court will not give permission unless satisfied that England and Wales is the "proper place" in which to bring the claim: CPR r.6.37(3). This involves an exercise of the court's discretion, taking into account all the circumstances of the case (*Berezovsky v Michaels* [2000] 1 W.L.R. 1004 at 1018). For challenging the jurisdiction, see CPR Pt 11.

[88] Lord Kinnear in *Sim v Robinow* (1892) 19 R. 665 at 668.

[89] [1987] A.C. 460, per Lord Goff.

[90] Ibid. at 477. In *Berezovsky v Forbes* [1999] E.M.L.R. 278 CA, Hirst L.J. observed (at 299) that where, as in a case like *Kroch v Rossell* [1937] 1 All E.R. 725, there is no complaint of substance as regards an English tort at all, either because there is only insignificant English circulation, or because the plaintiff has no connection with or reputation to protect in this country, he will inevitably fail the *Spiliada* test. The Court of Appeal's decision was affirmed by a majority of the House of Lords as *Berezovsky v Michaels* [2000] 1 W.L.R. 1004. In *Berezovsky*, only 1,900

(2) In general the burden of proof rests on the defendant to persuade the court to exercise its discretion to grant a stay.[91]

(3) In deciding the natural and appropriate forum the court will have regard to "connecting factors", that is to say, matters which indicate the country with which the action has the most real and substantial connection.

> "These will include not only factors affecting convenience or expense (such as availability of witnesses), but also other factors such as the law governing the relevant transaction . . . and the places where the parties respectively reside or carry on business."

(4) If the court concludes that there is no other available forum which is clearly more appropriate for the trial of the action, it will ordinarily refuse a stay.

(5) If, on the other hand, it appears that there is some other available forum which prima facie is clearly more appropriate it will ordinarily grant a stay unless there are circumstances by reason of which justice requires that a stay should not be granted; if, e.g. it is established that the claimant will not obtain justice in the foreign jurisdiction.

If the defendant is English-domiciled, the English courts must accept jurisdiction and *forum conveniens* considerations have no application.[92]

The *forum conveniens* principle in defamation cases. The phenomenon of internet publication has contributed substantially to the number of defamation cases in which problems of *forum conveniens* have arisen in recent years. However, a new test for claims brought against defendants not domiciled in the United Kingdom, the EU or the Lugano Convention states

24.28

---

copies of the *Forbes* magazine were sold in England and Wales, as opposed to 785,000 in the United States and Canada and 13 in Russia, the claimants' own country. However, the claim was limited to the publication in England, and the claimants had significant connections with England and significant reputations to protect there. (In this context it is worth noting that a claimant who seeks permission to serve out of the jurisdiction in respect of publication within the jurisdiction is guilty of an abuse of the process if he seeks to include in the same action publications occurring elsewhere: see per Lord Steyn at 1012H, citing *Diamond v Sutton* (1866) L.R.1.Ex 130 at 132, where the court ordered a writ served out of the jurisdiction to be set aside unless the plaintiff gave an undertaking to confine himself to a cause of action arising within the jurisdiction.)

[91] However, where the application is for leave to serve out of the jurisdiction under CPR r.6.36, rather than a stay, the burden rests on the claimant: *Spiliada Maritime Corp v Consulex* [1987] A.C. 460 at 480. In *Chadha v Dow Jones* [1999] E.M.L.R. 724, concerned with whether service of the writ should be set aside, it was stated (by Roch L.J. at 732) that the plaintiff bore the onus of showing that he had sufficient connection with and a sufficient reputation to protect in this country. In *Schapira v Ahronson* [1999] E.M.L.R. 735 it was pointed out that in respect of any matter relied on by a party which will assist in persuading the court to exercise its discretion in his favour the evidential burden rests on that party (at 744). However, in *Berezovsky v Michaels* [2000] 1 W.L.R. 1004, another case of an application to serve out, the House of Lords, while reiterating that the burden lay on the claimant to show that England was clearly the appropriate forum in which the case should be tried in the interests of all the parties and the ends of justice, upheld the principle that the jurisdiction in which a tort is committed is prima facie the natural forum for the dispute (see per Lord Steyn at 1013–1014).

[92] See para.24.26 and fn.85, above.

(Norway, Iceland, Switzerland) has been prospectively introduced by Defamation Act 2013, s.9.[93]

Several factors have contributed to the apparent popularity of England and Wales as a forum for internet claims: among them are the presumption of damage in libel[94] (an attraction on its way out for trading companies)[95] and the rule that publication takes place where the defamatory material is read or heard, that is to say—in internet terms—downloaded (not the jurisdiction where the server is sited or that which the publisher intended to reach),[96] as well, no doubt, as the presumption of falsity and the absence of a "public figure" defence of the kind which inhibits prominent claimants in the USA.[97] It has been observed[98] that the rigour of these rules is mitigated by the requirement that to establish jurisdiction, a tort committed within the jurisdiction must be a real and substantial one.[99]

The starting-point for ascertainment of the appropriate forum is to identify the place where the libel has been committed, which by definition will be England in a case where permission to serve out has been given on the basis of publication here. Although the burden is on the claimant (in seeking permission to serve out) to show that England is clearly the appropriate forum in which the case should be tried in the interests of the parties and the ends of justice, regard must be had to the principle that the jurisdiction in which the tort was committed is prima facie the natural forum for the dispute.[100]

However, the more tenuous the claimant's connection with this jurisdiction (and the more substantial any publication abroad), the weaker this consideration becomes.[101] Even a substantial connection with England will not suffice

---

[93] See para.24.29, below.

[94] *Ratcliffe v Evans* [1892] 2 Q.B. 524 at 529; *Jameel (Mohammed) v Wall Street Journal* [2006] UKHL 44; [2007] 1 A.C. 359; *Jameel (Yousef) v Dow Jones* [2005] EWCA Civ 75; [2005] Q.B. 946. Note, however, that there is no presumption in a claimant's favour of substantial publication on an internet website: the claimant must prove publication, which in a proper case may be established by inference (*Al-Amoudi v Brisard* [2006] EWHC 1062 (QB); [2007] 1 W.L.R. 113. See also *Loutchansky v Times Newspapers Ltd (No.2)* [2001] E.M.L.R. 876).

[95] When s.1(2) Defamation Act 2013 is brought into force, a company which trades for profit will have no claim in defamation unless the harm done to its reputation by publication of the words complained of "has caused or islikely to cause the body serious financial loss".

[96] *Bata v Bata* [1948] W.N. 366; *Lee v Wilson & Mackinnon* (1934) 51 C.L.R. 276; *Godfrey v Demon Internet* [2001] Q.B. 201; *King v Lewis* [2004] EWCA Civ 1329; [2005] E.M.L.R. 45, *Richardson v Schwarzenegger* [2004] EWHC 2422 (QB); *Gutnick v Dow Jones & Co. Inc.* [2002] HCA 56, 210 C.L.R. 575. In *King v Lewis* the Court of Appeal rejected "out of hand" [34] a submission that the intention of the defendant as to the particular jurisdiction which he had targeted should be a factor in ascertaining the appropriate forum.

[97] *New York Times v Sullivan* 376 US 254.

[98] *Berezovsky v Michaels (No.1)* [2000] 1 W.L.R. 1004 at 1012, per Lord Steyn.

[99] As to which, see *Kroch v Rossell* [1937] 1 All ER 725, CA; *Jameel (Yousef) v Dow Jones & Co. Inc.* [2005] EWCA Civ 75, [2005] Q.B. 946; *Mardas v New York Times Co.* [2008] EWHC 3135 (QB); [2009] E.M.L.R. 8.

[100] *Berezovsky v Michaels*, above.

[101] *King v Lewis* [2004] EWCA Civ 1329; [2005] E.M.L.R. 45 at [27]. For examples of tenuous connections, see: *Kroch v Rossell* [1937] 1 All E.R. 725 C.A., in which the plaintiff sued in England on articles in a Belgian paper, *Le Soir*, which had an English circulation of less than 50, and in a French paper, *Le Petit Parisien*, of which 401 copies out of a million and a half came

if the harm done to the claimant in this jurisdiction is slight.[102] Nonetheless, the courts have shown reluctance to stay actions brought by claimants resident in England seeking amends for injury to reputation suffered in this country, even when publication here has been small.[103] Moreover, where the claimant's connection with the jurisdiction is substantial, and there has been substantial

---

to England, mainly for a French readership. Service of the writ was set aside on the basis that the plaintiff had no reputation in England and no connection with it beyond occupation of a furnished room taken for the purpose of the litigation; *Jeyaretnam v Mahmood*, January 11, 1991 unreported, where Brooke J. set aside a writ issued by a citizen of Singapore, who had lived and worked there for nearly all his life, against a Singapore newspaper which distributed about 12 copies in England; *Pillai v Sarkar, The Times*, July 21, 1994, where Drake J. held that India was clearly the more appropriate forum for determining a claim for damages for an alleged libel published in an English language periodical which had a circulation of 73,000 in India and 15 in England even though the plaintiffs only sought to claim for injury suffered in England; *Chadha v Dow Jones* [1999] E.M.L.R. 724 C.A. where Californian plaintiffs complained of English publication of the New York-based *Barrons Magazine* (total sales were 283,520 in the United States and 1,257 in the United Kingdom): service out of the jurisdiction was set aside, apparently because the evidence that the plaintiffs had reputations in England at the time of publication was vague and imprecise, and because there was not sufficient evidence that such reputations as they had were harmed by the English publication. In *Oraro v Observer Ltd*, unreported, April 10, 1992, the plaintiff was not allowed to proceed in this jurisdiction, although circulation of the offending article was much larger in England than in his native Kenya. Drake J. emphasised that the article was "all about Kenyan politics and Kenyan personalities", and that the damage to the plaintiff's high reputation occurred very substantially in Kenya. In the light of *Owusu v Jackson* [2005] 1 Q.B. 801 E.C.J, the court would now be unable to decline jurisdiction, because the publisher of the Observer was of course English-domiciled.

[102] E.g. *Wyatt v Forbes Inc.*, unreported, December 2, 1997, in which Morland J. held that Texas was the most suitable forum for a libel claim by Oscar Wyatt, the Texas-based oilman, because he had a pending libel claim in Texas against a different publisher but concerning the same allegations, and because Texas was the centre of his business and social life, even though he had family and business connections in England also. Any harm to Mr Wyatt's reputation was done by publication in America to Americans, while the English publication was incidental and small. See also *Jameel (Yousef) v Dow Jones* [2005] EWCA Civ 75; [2005] Q.B. 946, where although the claimant had English connections, it appeared that there were probably only five English-based subscribers to the offending publication (the *Wall Street Journal On-Line*): two of those did not know the claimant, and the other three were in the claimant's camp. It was not legitimate for the claimant to justify the English proceedings by praying in aid the effect that they might have in vindicating his reputation outside England, so on any view the damage and vindication would be minimal. The Court of Appeal used the new CPR-inspired language of abuse of process:

"The cost of the exercise will have been out of all proportion to what has been achieved. The game will not merely not have been worth the candle, it will not have been worth the wick . . It would be an abuse of process to continue to commit the resources of the English court, including substantial judge and possibly jury time, to an action where so little is now seen to be at stake." (at [69]–[70]).

No real and substantial tort had been committed within the jurisdiction.

[103] In *Schapira v Ahronson* [1999] E.M.L.R. 735 C.A. a stay was refused in an action brought by an Israeli citizen who had lived and worked in London for many years (and was also a British citizen) against an Israeli newspaper printed in Hebrew with an English circulation of only 141 copies.

"Where the tort of libel is allegedly committed in England against a person resident and carrying on business in England by foreigners who were aware that their publication would be sent to subscribers in England, that English resident is entitled to bring proceedings here against those foreigners and to limit his claim to publication in England, even though the circulation of the article alleged to be defamatory was extremely limited in England and there was a much larger publication elsewhere" (per Peter Gibson L.J. at 748–749).

publication here, proceedings are unlikely to be stayed even where the claimant lives abroad and sues publishers based in the same or another foreign jurisdiction.[104]

24.29 "Libel tourism" and Defamation Act 2013, s.9. Parliament has enacted s.9 of the Defamation Act to meet what it regarded as the problem created by those who have used the English legal system to recover damages against foreign publishers responsible for publication of defamatory statements in this jurisdiction, when the same libel may have been more widely published in other jurisdictions. The new section, which has not yet been brought into force, will apply to defamation actions against persons not domiciled in the UK, in any other EU member state or in a Lugano Convention state (i.e. Norway, Iceland and Switzerland). By s.9(2), the court will

---

Similarly, in *Harrods Ltd v Dow Jones & Co. Inc.* [2003] EWHC 1162 (QB), Harrods Ltd sued on the tiny English publication of some 10 copies of the US edition of the *Wall Street Journal* (plus a few hits on the online edition), yet was allowed to serve out of the jurisdiction. Even though the real damage (if any) must have been done in the United States, where the *Wall Street Journal* has a national distribution of 1.8 million copies, the claimant was an English company with a clear connection with the jurisdiction and a well-established reputation in England, and it was entitled to demonstrate to an English audience that the allegations were not true. In *Reuben v Time Inc.* [2003] EWHC 1430 (QB), Morland J. refused a stay of a claim by two British brothers, one resident in Monaco, and their two companies (one Bahamian, one British) for publication in England of Fortune magazine. There was substantial publication in England and Wales (13,087 copies), although the US/Canada sale (966,856) was of course far larger. See also *Richardson v Schwarzenegger* [2004] EWHC 2422 (QB), where a stay was refused to an American defendant sued for words attributed by the *Los Angeles Times* to a spokesman for Arnold Schwarzenegger during the 2003 Californian gubernatorial campaign. The claimant sued on publication in hard copies distributed in England and on English internet publication. Factors relevant to the judge's decision included the facts that the claimant, a UK citizen who was resident in England, worked there and was widely known there, but had no comparable reputation elsewhere, including in the USA. Moreover, the underlying events (relevant if justification was pleaded) took place in London. Nonetheless, the judge had some sympathy for the submissions of counsel for the applicant, who identified the question for the court as follows:
"This case is about whether a spokesman for a foreign politician in a local election campaign who was asked by a foreign newspaper to respond on behalf of the foreign electoral candidate to allegations concerning the past conduct of that candidate, and who provided a response that is immune from suit under local law and is protected by qualified privilege under our system of law in circumstances in which malice is not and could not reasonably be alleged, should nevertheless be amenable to the exorbitant jurisdiction of the English court . . . This summary was seductively put as though it were a new scenario free from authority. But it would seem to ignore . . . clear and recently stated principles of English law" (see per Eady J. at [28]).
[104] *King v Lewis* [2004] EWCA Civ 1329; [2005] E.M.L.R. 45 at [31]. In that case, an American boxing promoter, resident in Florida, sued a New York lawyer for words spoken on two Californian websites about New York litigation. The Court of Appeal found no error of law in Eady J.'s conclusion that leave to serve out had been rightly given, the claimant having a substantial reputation and a financial and business connection in England, and the evidence having shown that the two websites were popular in England and frequently accessed by English residents.
"The global publisher should not be too fastidious as to the part of the globe where he is made a libel defendant. We by no means propose a free-for-all for claimants libelled on the Internet. The court must still ascertain the most appropriate forum; the parties' connections with this or that jurisdiction will still have to be considered; there will be cases (like the present) where only two jurisdictions are really in contention. We apprehend that . . . in an Internet case the court's

have no jurisdiction to hear and determine an action to which the section applies unless it is satisfied that, of all the places in which the statement complained of has been published, England and Wales is "clearly the most appropriate place" in which to bring an action in respect of the statement.[105]

It appears that it will be for the claimant to satisfy the court that the domestic jurisdiction is clearly the most appropriate place to bring an action. That broadly accords with the current position, whereby the claimant has the burden of persuading the court to grant leave to serve outside the jurisdiction, by showing that he has sufficient connection with this country and a sufficient

---

discretion will tend to be more open-textured than otherwise; for that is the means by which the court may give effect to the publisher's choice of a global medium."
In *Berezovsky v Michaels* [2000] 1 W.L.R. 1004 HL (the case was reported as *Berezovsky v Forbes* in the Court of Appeal [1999] E.M.L.R. 278), Russian claimants were permitted to maintain a claim in England for English publication of the US magazine *Forbes* (sales were 785,710 in the United States and Canada, 1,915 in England and Wales and 13 in Russia), but they had significant connections with and reputations in England, and satisfied the burden of showing that England was clearly the most appropriate forum in which the case should be tried in the interests of all the parties and the ends of justice, regard being had to the principle that the jurisdiction in which a tort is committed is prima facie the natural forum for the dispute. The House of Lords rejected the submission that trans-national publications—whether by internationally circulating newspapers, or trans-border or satellite broadcasts or internet postings—should be regarded for the purposes of applying the *Spiliada* principles as giving rise to one cause of action. In *Mardas v New York Times Co.* [2008] EWHC 3135 (QB); [2009] E.M.L.R. 8 the defendants asked the court to stay two actions or strike them out as an abuse. The claimant complained of publication within the jurisdiction of hard copy and internet articles published by the *New York Times* and the *International Herald Tribune*. Eady J. allowed an appeal from the master's order striking the actions out. He held that what mattered was whether there had arguably been a real and substantial tort within the jurisdiction, and that could not depend on a "numbers game, with the court fixing an arbitrary minimum according to the facts of the case". The scale of publication was uncertain and would have to be determined at trial. The allegations (of lying and charlatanry) were not trivial, and the claimant was well known within the jurisdiction, where his children lived: there was no artificiality about protecting his reputation in England and Wales. It was obvious that given the increasing recognition in the Strasbourg jurisprudence that the right to protect honour and reputation was protected by art.8, care must be taken on such applications not to deprive a litigant too readily of his art.6 right of unimpeded access to the courts in pursuit of his remedies. The Court of Appeal refused permission to appeal: [2009] EWCA Civ 633. Note also that in *Polanski v Condé Nast Publications Ltd* [2005] UKHL 10; [2005] 1 W.L.R. 637 at [12], the House of Lords did not question the propriety of Roman Polanski's action against Condé Nast in respect of the English publication of 53,000 copies of *Vanity Fair*, even though the principal circulation was in the United States (1.13 million copies), and even though he was a French citizen, resident in France, who had not set foot in England since February 1978. Lord Nicholls observed that, given his international reputation, there was no question of his libel action being an abuse of the process of the court. Indeed, Condé Nast did not suggest otherwise. See also *Baturina v Times Newspapers Ltd* [2011] EWCA Civ 308, [2011] 1 W.L.R. 1526, where an unsuccessful attempt was made to strike out a claim by the wife of the mayor of Moscow for publication of a libel in England and Wales (where some 400,000 Russians resided) and in Russia. The libel was dependent on proof of knowledge of facts which gave rise to an innuendo meaning.
[105] By s.9(3), references in s.9(2) to the statement complained of include references to any statement which conveys the same, or substantially the same, imputation as the statement complained of.

reputation to protect here and that England is clearly the most appropriate forum in the interests of all the parties and the ends of justice.[106]

As matters stand, any claimant applying under CPR r.6.36 for leave to serve out must confine himself to suing in respect of English publication only. It is an abuse of process to do otherwise.[107] England and Wales is therefore the jurisdiction where the tort was committed, and hitherto has thus been prima facie the natural forum for the determination of the action.[108] By contrast, the effect of s.9 will be to oblige the court to consider all the jurisdictions where the defamatory statement has been published, in order to determine whether the domestic jurisdiction is clearly the most appropriate place in which to bring the action. As the Explanatory Notes to the Act make clear, " . . . if a statement was published 100,000 times in Australia and only 5,000 times in England that would be a good basis on which to conclude that the most appropriate jurisdiction in which to bring an action . . . was Australia[109] rather than England". However, the extent of publication in different jurisdictions may have little bearing on where the claimant's reputation mainly lies and on where that reputation has been most seriously damaged, and the Explanatory Notes rightly suggest that the court would wish to take into account such matters as the amount of damage to the claimant's reputation in England and Wales compared with elsewhere, the extent to which publication was targeted at a readership in England and Wales compared with elsewhere, and whether there was reason to think that the claimant would not receive a fair hearing elsewhere. No doubt the court will also wish to consider such factors as the convenience of witnesses and the relative expense of suing in different jurisdictions. It would be unsurprising if claimants resident in England and Wales were to surmount the new threshold more readily than foreign claimants.

The new section appears to contemplate a single most appropriate jurisdiction in which the claimant may sue,[110] and that jurisdiction may well not be England. It is not wholly clear what the position will be if the claimant wishes to sue in England in respect of English publication of a libel and (for instance) in New South Wales also, in respect of publication there of the same libel. The

---

[106] *Spiliada Maritime Corp v Consulex* [1987] A.C. 460 at 480; *Chadha v Dow Jones* [1999] E.M.L.R. 724, 732; *Berezovsky v Michaels* [2000] 1 W.L.R. 1004. See generally paras 24.27–24.28, above.

[107] *Diamond v Sutton* (1866) L.R.1.Ex 130 at 132; *Eyre v Nationwide News Pty Ltd* [1967] N.Z.L.R. 851; *Berezovsky v Michaels* [2000] 1 W.L.R 1004 at 1012H.

[108] In *Berezovsky v Michaels* [2000] 1 W.L.R. 1004 at 1013–1014 the H.L. upheld the principle that the jurisdiction in which a tort is committed is prima facie the natural forum for the dispute. See also (e.g.) *Mardas v New York Times Co.* [2008] EWHC 3135 (QB); [2009] E.M.L.R. 8 at [39], per Eady J.: "The approach has long been to recognise that where a tort has been committed the appropriate forum will usually be that of the jurisdiction where it took place."

[109] *Sic*: Australia is an unfortunate example, since it is not, of course, a single jurisdiction.

[110] Contrast the scheme of the Judgments Regulation and the Lugano Convention, whereby persons domiciled in an EU or Lugano member state may by way of special jurisdiction be sued for defamation in the courts for the place where the harmful event occurred, that is to say in each country where the claimant has been defamed: see para.24.25, above.

libel need not have been published in the mass media: take, for instance, a highly damaging allegation sent by a malicious rival domiciled in New York to the claimant's professional clients in London and in Sydney. He might have been caused grave damage in both jurisdictions, and vindication in one might not be effective vindication in the other. To sue here he would have to satisfy the court that England and Wales was clearly the most appropriate place in which to bring an action in respect of the statement. Suppose that he persuaded the court that England and Wales was clearly the most appropriate place to bring an action, and was permitted to sue in England on the English publication. If he then sued in New South Wales on the publication there, would he expose himself to an application for a stay of the English proceedings? Or if he issued proceedings in NSW first, in respect of the publication there, would he have difficulty in surmounting the s.9(2) threshold when seeking to issue in England and Wales? If so, there would be an argument that in those circumstances the court was denying him access to justice to vindicate his Art.8 right to reputation.[111] This seems not to be the object which the Act was intended to address.[112]

Problems over US enforcement of English judgments. Claimants **24.30** seeking to sue US publishers in the English courts should bear in mind the difficulties of enforcement of English judgments in the United States. The US First Amendment emphasis on the primacy of free speech[113] is not tolerant of common law models which seek a balance between the protection of free speech and the protection of reputation. There has for at least two decades been resistance in the United States to the enforcement of English libel judgments,[114] but one case attracted enough media attention to impel New

---

[111] See e.g. *Mardas v New York Times Co.*, above, at [13]. Such an outcome would also run counter to the scheme of the Judgments Regulation and the Lugano Convention, whereby persons domiciled in an EU or Lugano member state may by way of special jurisdiction be sued for defamation in the courts for the place where the harmful event occurred, that is to say in each country where they have been defamed: see para.24.25, above.

[112] The Lord Chancellor, the Rt Hon Kenneth Clarke MP, told the House of Commons when introducing the Bill on second reading that he was concerned by the use of the English courts by wealthy foreigners and public figures to stifle investigation and reporting. He gave the example of
"a Saudi businessman, say, threatening an American publication with an action because of an article that has had tiny circulation in the United Kingdom. This is a hypothetical case, but the Saudi would be using the nature of British law (*sic*) to threaten a publication in an entirely different jurisdiction. That is the evil we are trying to address." *Hansard,* HC cols 182–3 (June 12, 2012).

[113] The First Amendment to the US Constitution:
"Congress shall make no law respecting an establishment of religion, or prohibiting the free exercise thereof; or abridging the freedom of speech, or of the press; or the right of the people peaceably to assemble, and to petition the government for a redress of grievances".
See para.15.31.

[114] In *Bachchan v India Abroad Publications Inc.* 585 N.Y.S.2d 661 at 664 (Sup. Ct. N.Y. County 1992). the plaintiff, who lived in London, sued *India Abroad*, a small New York-based publication, in respect of 1,000 copies distributed in England. He obtained judgment and applied to enforce in New York. The state court concluded that although England and the US shared many common law principles, England's lack of an equivalent to the First Amendment formed a

York State politicians to introduce a law preventing New York courts from enforcing a foreign libel judgment unless the country where it was decided maintained standards of free speech at least equal to those in the United States.[115] New York was followed by several other states, and ultimately by the US Congress, which in 2010 passed the SPEECH Act.[116] Its effect is to prevent any US domestic courts (i.e. Federal or state courts) from recognising or enforcing a foreign judgment for defamation unless the domestic court determines that the judgment is consistent with the First Amendment.[117]

24.31 Scotland and Northern Ireland. Permission is not required to serve a claim form on a defendant in Scotland or Northern Ireland who has published a libel in England and Wales.[118] There is jurisdiction to order a stay of

---

significant difference between the jurisdictions, and that the protections offered by the First Amendment would be "seriously jeopardised" if foreign libel judgments were enforced which had been granted in accordance with standards accepted in England but "considered antithetical to the protections afforded the press by the US constitution". In the better known English case of *Matusevitch v Telnikoff* (reported in England on the fair comment point decided by the House of Lords: [1992] 2 A.C. 243), Telnikoff, who obtained a jury award of £240,000, applied to enforce his English libel judgment in Maryland, where Matusevitch was living, and Matusevitch countered by applying to the US District Court for the District of Columbia. The Supreme Court of Maryland and the federal court agreed with the conclusions of the New York court in *Bachchan* that First Amendment protections would be seriously jeopardised by enforcement of the English judgment: 347 Md. 561, 702 A.2d 230 (Md. 1997).

[115] This was the curiously named Libel Terrorism Protection Act 2008, which followed an unsuccessful attempt to persuade the New York Court of Appeals (*Ehrenfeld v Bin Mahfouz* 9 N.Y.3d 501) to declare that a judgment obtained against the applicant in England under the s.8 Defamation Act 1996 summary procedure was unenforceable, she having chosen not to defend the application in England (after earlier stating that the English action provided an opportunity to prove the truth of her allegations): *Mahfouz v Ehrenfeld* [2005] EWHC 1156 (QB). Her application in New York appears to have foundered on the court's finding (on a question certified to it by the US Court of Appeals, 2nd Circuit) that the New York courts had no personal jurisdiction over Mr Mahfouz.

[116] H.R. 2765 (111th): Securing the Protection of our Enduring and Established Constitutional Heritage Act.

[117] The Act was hailed in the US as a victory over "libel tourists". However, for a corrective to the media coverage of the "libel tourism" issue both in the UK and in the US, see Lord Hoffmann's Dame Ann Ebsworth Memorial Lecture, delivered on February 2, 2010 at Inner Temple (an edited version of the speech is available on the website of Index on Censorship, at *http://www.indexoncensorship.org/2010/02/the-libel-tourism-myth*). Lord Hoffmann observed that

"Complaints about libel tourism come entirely from the Americans and are based upon a belief that the whole world should share their view about how to strike the balance between freedom of expression and the defence of reputation. Naturally the American view is enthusiastically supported by the media in this country . . . It is only if you think, as many Americans do, that an American should only have to say *civis Americanus sum* to cloak himself in the immunity of the First Amendment against liability for injury which he has caused in a foreign country, or, as much of media in this country does, that we ought to become the second country in the world to adopt the *New York Times v Sullivan* rule, that there can be any basis for criticism . . . But before we are stampeded into changing our law, we should bear in mind that the points about which complaint is made are either binding on us as a matter of European law, as in the *Shevill* case, or have been approved by the Strasbourg court as compliant with the right to freedom of speech under the Convention."

[118] CPR r.6.32. However, there must be no proceedings between the parties for the same libel pending in the courts of any part of the United Kingdom (r.6.32(1)(a)).

proceedings brought in England against a defendant domiciled in Scotland or Northern Ireland on *forum conveniens* grounds.[119] Defamation Act 2013, s.9 will not change that, for it will only apply to actions for defamation against defendants who are not domiciled in the United Kingdom (or other EU members or Lugano convention states).

SECTION 4. OTHER COMPLAINTS PROCEDURES

General. There are many situations in which a person who is aggrieved by   **24.32**
what has been said about him in the press or other media may prefer (perhaps because he cannot contemplate the expense of litigation), or be compelled (e.g. because his complaint is of a damaging but non-defamatory inaccuracy) to make a complaint to a body charged with policing the branch of the press or media responsible for the publication. The principal bodies in this area are the Press Complaints Commission, Ofcom and the Advertising Standards Authority in conjunction with the Committee of Advertising Practice (CAP).

Press Complaints Commission. The Press Complaints Commission   **24.33**
(PCC) is the successor to the old Press Council, and was set up by press interests in 1991. Its shortcomings were comprehensively identified by the Leveson Report in November 2012.[120] Given that the PCC is unlikely to continue in its present form for very much longer, and given the current climate of uncertainty as to the form which its successor body will take, the reader is referred to the 11th edition of this work for a discussion of the PCC Code of Practice, and to the PCC website[121] for the current form of the Code.

Ofcom. By virtue of the Communications Act 2003, from December 29,   **24.34**
2003 the functions of the Broadcasting Standards Commission, the Independent Television Commission and the Radio Authority (together with the Office of Telecommunications (Oftel) and the Radiocommunications Agency) (the

---

[119] See *Lennon v Scottish Daily Record* [2004] EWHC 359 (QB); [2004] E.M.L.R. 18, following *Cumming v Scottish Daily Record* [1995] E.M.L.R. 538, and s.16 and Sch.4 of the Civil Jurisdiction and Judgments Act 1982, as amended by the Civil Jurisdiction and Judgments Order 2001, SI 2001/3929, together with s.49 of the 1982 Act. In *Lennon*, the claimant was a Celtic footballer who sued the *Daily Record* over English sales of an article about his supposed misbehaviour in Newcastle, and the defendant newspaper applied to stay the action on the ground that Scotland was the more appropriate forum. The case makes clear that no legislation allocating jurisdiction within the United Kingdom will be inconsistent with the Brussels Convention, or the Lugano Convention, or the Judgments Regulation, because those instruments allocate jurisdiction between member states. Scotland and England and Wales and Northern Ireland are separate jurisdictions but not separate member states.

[120] The Leveson Inquiry: Culture, Practices and Ethics of the Press, November 29, 2012 (see in particular Pt J, ch.4, paras 8.1–8.13).

[121] *http://www.pcc.org.uk.*

so-called legacy regulators), were vested in the Office of Communications (Ofcom).

24.35 Ofcom's Broadcasting Code. The current Broadcasting Code applies to television and radio programmes broadcast on and after March 21, 2013.[122] Ofcom will consider complaints about partiality, inaccuracy, offensiveness, harmfulness, unfairness and breach of privacy. In the case of the BBC, it will consider issues relating to fairness and privacy, and harm and offence (complaints about partiality and inaccuracy should be directed to the BBC Trust). There does not appear to be any provision for oral hearings: complaints are resolved by written submissions. Ofcom has the power to uphold complaints, and also (but only in the most serious cases) to order that the programme should not be repeated, to order the broadcast of a correction or a summary of the decision, or to impose a fine. Indeed, it can even shorten or withdraw a licence (though not in the case of the BBC, S4C or Channel 4), although this must be supposed to be a sanction of last resort.

24.36 Ofcom: privacy. Section 8 of the Code (Privacy) requires that any infringement of privacy in the making or broadcasting of a programme needs consent (unless the infringement is warranted), and it proscribes surreptitious filming or recording (which includes the use of long lenses, and recording telephone conversations without the other party's knowledge), again unless warranted. The definition of "warranted" is very general,[123] but it emphasises the importance of the public interest. Under the heading "Private lives, public places and legitimate expectation of privacy", the Code sets out the practices which broadcasters are to follow. "Legitimate expectation of privacy" will vary:

> "according to the place and nature of the information, activity or condition in question, the extent to which it is in the public domain (if at all) and whether the individual concerned is already in the public eye. There may be circumstances where people can reasonably expect privacy even in a public place. Some activities and conditions may be of such a private nature that filming or recording, even in a public place, could involve an infringement of privacy. People under investigation or in the public eye, and their immediate family and friends, retain the right to a private life, although private behaviour can raise issues of legitimate public interest."

---

[122] See *http://stakeholders.ofcom.org.uk/broadcasting/broadcast-codes/broadcast-code/*. Previous versions of the Code may be found at *http://stakeholders.ofcom.org.uk/broadcasting/broad cast-codes/*.

[123] By section 8.1 of the Code, "warranted"

"means that where broadcasters wish to justify an infringement of privacy as warranted, they should be able to demonstrate why in the particular circumstances of the case, it is warranted. If the reason is that it is in the public interest, then the broadcaster should be able to demonstrate that the public interest outweighs the right to privacy. Examples of public interest would include revealing or detecting crime, protecting public health or safety, exposing misleading claims made by individuals or organisations or disclosing incompetence that affects the public."

Broadcasters are obliged to pay particular attention to the privacy of children under the age of 16, who do not lose their rights to privacy because of the fame or notoriety of their parents or because of events in their schools. Consent must be obtained from a parent or guardian where a child under 16 is featured in a way that infringes privacy, unless the subject matter is trivial or uncontroversial and the participation minor, or it is warranted to proceed without consent.

Ofcom: fairness. The Fairness section of the Code (s.7) aims to ensure that **24.37** broadcasters avoid unjust or unfair treatment of individuals or organisations in programmes. That generally entails giving potential contributors full details of the nature and purpose of the programme, the kind of contribution which they are expected to make, and the areas of questioning which they will face, with the broad object of ensuring that an informed consent is given. However, there is provision for withholding some of that information when justifiable in the public interest. There is an obligation to take reasonable care in factual programmes to ensure that material facts have not been presented, disregarded or omitted in an unfair way, and that anyone whose omission could be unfair has been offered an opportunity to contribute, and programmes such as dramas and factually based dramas should not portray facts, events, individuals or organisations in an unfair way. If a programme alleges wrongdoing or incompetence or makes other "significant allegations", those concerned should normally be given an appropriate and timely opportunity to respond. Misrepresentation and deception (including surreptitious filming or recording) should not normally be used, unless it is in the public interest to use material obtained in that way and it cannot reasonably be obtained by other means.

Advertising. Complaints about advertising should be made to the Advertis- **24.38** ing Standards Authority (ASA), which considers complaints of breach of the two advertising codes drafted by the Committee on Advertising Practice (CAP). The two codes are the UK Code of Non-Broadcast Advertising, Sales Promotion and Direct Marketing (the CAP Code),[124] and the UK Code of Broadcast Advertising (the BCAP Code).[125]

The CAP Code applies to advertisements in (among others) newspapers, magazines, brochures, leaflets, circulars, mailings, catalogues and other printed publications, posters and aerial announcements, cinema and video promotions, and in non-broadcast media such as computer games and view-data services. It does not apply to (inter alia) TV and radio advertising, the contents of premium rate telephone calls, advertisements in foreign media or flyposting. The Code's first principle remains that all advertisements should be "legal, decent, honest and truthful". Marketing communications (i.e. advertisements and all other forms of communication covered by the Code)

---

[124] *http://www.cap.org.uk/Advertising-Codes/Non-broadcast-HTML.aspx.*
[125] *http://www.cap.org.uk/Advertising-Codes/Broadcast-HTML.aspx.*

should not materially mislead, and there are provisions designed to protect privacy. Advertisers are urged to obtain written permission in advance if they portray or refer to individuals or their identifiable possessions in any advertisement (except, possibly, crowd scenes and general public locations), or if they refer to people with a public profile, and they should not claim or imply an endorsement where none exists.[126]

The BCAP Code applies to all advertisements and programme sponsorship credits on radio and television services licensed by Ofcom. Its main principles are that advertisements should not mislead or cause serious or widespread offence or harm. Broadcasters are expected to ensure that advertisements comply with both the spirit and the letter of the Code. Advertisements should not be harmful or offensive, and there are provisions to protect privacy: in particular, subject to limited exception (e.g. brief and incidental appearances in crowd scenes), living persons should not be featured, caricatured or referred to in television advertisements without their permission.

SECTION 5. ISSUE OF CLAIM FORM

24.39 Commencement of action. Proceedings in an action of libel or slander must be issued in the High Court. They may not be started in a county court unless the parties have agreed in writing: CPR PD 7, para.2.9(1). A defamation claim, though in principle "suitable" for trial in the Royal Courts of Justice (see CPR PD 29, para.2.6(4)), may be transferred from the High Court to a county court under s.40 of the County Courts Act 1984, but the criteria for transfer (as to which see CPR r.30.3(2)) will tend to militate against an order for transfer except in small and simple cases. Once started, a defamation claim will almost invariably be allocated to the multi-track (the low financial values for the other tracks, together with the one day trial limit for fast track claims, will rule them out: see CPR r.26.6).

24.40 Indorsement of claim form. Before the introduction of the CPR, the writ in a slander action had only to be indorsed with the bare words "The Plaintiff's claim is for damages for slander", while a libel plaintiff was required to give sufficient particulars to identify the publication complained of. At least in cases where the libel or slander was not widely published, plaintiffs were usually well advised to limit themselves to a short general

---

[126] Although the case long pre-dated the Code, implying an endorsement where none existed was the mistake of the chocolate manufacturers Fry, *Tolley v Fry* [1931] A.C. 333: they published newspaper advertisements showing a caricature of Tolley, a well-known amateur golfer, in full golfing gear having just completed a drive. A packet of Fry's chocolate was protruding from his pocket and his caddie was holding others. The caption was a limerick in these terms: "The caddie to Tolley said, 'Oh Sir,/Good shot, Sir! That ball, see it go, Sir,/My word how it flies,/Like a cartet of Fry's/They're handy, they're good, and priced low, Sir' ". Tolley's consent was not sought, and the advertisement was found to mean that he had prostituted his amateur status.

indorsement, and thus to avoid repeating the libel in the writ—a public document—and giving further publicity to an already damaging defamation. The pre-CPR libel regime is preserved by CPR PD 53, para.2.2(1), which requires only that the publication the subject of the claim should be identified in the claim form, so that the pleading of the actual words can be left to the particulars of claim. However, para.2.2(2) requires, bizarrely, that in a claim for slander the claim form should, so far as possible, contain the words complained of, as well as identifying the person to whom they were spoken and when, which obliges the slander claimant to repeat the slander in the claim form which (like its predecessor the writ) has always been a public document.[127]

However, the modern default rule is that the pleadings have become public, and not just the claim form. A non-party may obtain a copy of any statement of case from court records unless the court orders otherwise, as long as the defendant has filed an acknowledgement of service of a defence: CPR r.5.4C(1). Any statement of case extracted from the court in this way will be a "document required by law to be open to public inspection" under s.15 of and Sch.1, para.5 to the Defamation Act 1996, and publication of an extract from it will be protected by statutory qualified privilege.[128] If a claim relates to a highly damaging libel or slander published to a small group of people, public availability of the particulars of claim may lead to its publication in the media on a far wider basis and with even more damaging effect. A claimant concerned about such a consequence should employ CPR r.5.4C(4), which enables a party or anyone identified in a statement of case to apply for an order that non-parties should not obtain a copy of the statement of case under 5.4C(1), or that they should obtain a copy only if it is edited in accordance with the directions of the court.

Damages. It used to be regarded as bad practice to claim a specific sum as general damages. That is because a claim for damages for defamation is unquantifiable except by a judge or jury at trial or by a judge on summary disposal, and because if a larger sum is awarded, a claimant cannot recover judgment for more than the sum claimed[129] unless he can obtain leave to amend.[130] However, in the smaller cases it may be desirable to limit the claim to £50,000 in order to reduce the amount payable on issue of the claim   **24.41**

---

[127] Gray J., in a libel case, described it as "unwise" to set out the words complained of in the writ (or claim form): *Carpenter v Associated Newspapers*, unreported, November 26, 2001.

[128] See *Qadir v Associated Newspapers Ltd* [2012] EWHC 2606 (QB); [2013] E.M.L.R. 15 and para.16.12, above.

[129] *Chattell v Daily Mail* (1900) 18 T.L.R. 165 CA.

[130] CPR r.17.1(2), 17.3; *Wyatt v Rosherville* (1885) 2 T.L.R. 282, where a jury awarded the plaintiff £300 more than he had claimed for injuries sustained when a bear at the Rosherville Pleasure Gardens "munched and crunched" at his arm. On amendment after judgment, see *Stewart v Engel* [2000] 1 W.L.R. 2268.

form.[131] It is misconceived to add a claim for interest on general damages for defamation, since damages are assessed as at the date of trial (taking account as they do of the defendant's conduct up to and including trial),[132] not as at the date on which the cause of action arose (namely the date of publication of the libel or slander).[133] If the claimant has reason to believe that the defendant intends to continue publishing the words complained of, he should add a claim for an injunction.[134] Final injunctions are commonplace in defamation proceedings.[135]

---

[131] The Civil Proceedings Fees (Amendment No.2) Order 2013, SI 2013/1410, provides for fees of (inter alia) £395 on issue of proceedings where the claim does not exceed £50,000, £685 where it does not exceed £100,000, £885 where it does not exceed £150,000, £1,080 where it does not exceed £200,000, £1,275 where it does not exceed £250,000, £1,475 where it does not exceed £300,000, and £1,670 where it is unlimited. Unless there is a substantial special damage claim, damages in even the most serious case are unlikely to exceed £300,000: see e.g. *Cairns v Modi* [2012] EWCA Civ 1382, [2013] 1. W.L.R. 1015 at [25].

[132] See, e.g. *John v MGN* [1997] Q.B. 586 at 607–608. That rule holds good despite the power of the court under CPR r.36.21(4) to order interest on damages where the claimant beats his own Protocol offer: see *McPhilemy v Times Newspapers Ltd* [2002] 1 W.L.R. 934; [2001] E.M.L.R. 35 at [17]–[18] (per Chadwick L.J.).

[133] It is submitted that the same must apply a fortiori to exemplary damages, which are also assessed as at the date of trial (because in awarding them the jury must take into account general damages: *John v MGN*, above, at 619), and which are punitive rather than compensatory in nature (so that there can be no question of awarding interest, which is in its nature designed to mitigate the loss incurred by a plaintiff in being kept out of his compensation). A claim for interest is entirely proper in the case of a claim for special damage.

[134] Omission of a claim for an injunction from the claim form does not prevent its inclusion in the particulars of claim (CPR r.16.2(5)), nor does it have any bearing on the claimant's entitlement to apply for an interim injunction: CPR r.25.1(4).

[135] *ZAM v CFW* [2013] EWHC 662 at [22] (per Tugendhat J.).

CHAPTER 25

INTERIM INJUNCTIONS

SECTION 1. GENERAL PRINCIPLES

Jurisdiction. The power to grant interim[1] injunctions is embodied in **25.1** s.37(1) of the Senior Courts Act 1981: "The High Court may by order (whether interlocutory or final) grant an injunction . . . in all cases in which it appears to be just and convenient to do so." This is a statement of established law.[2] Though the wording of the section is extremely wide, the power to grant interim injunctions is circumscribed by authority.[3] Generally, such an injunction can only be granted where a party to an action has invaded or threatens to invade a legal or equitable right of the other party, which can be enforced by the court, or when one party has behaved or threatens to behave in an unconscionable manner.[4] The latter does not include publication of false or defamatory statements. Accordingly the jurisdiction to grant interim injunctions in the field of defamation and malicious falsehood arises where there has been, or there is threatened, a publication of a defamatory

---

[1] Prior to the introduction of the CPR the term used for an injunction granted otherwise than at trial or in consequence of an adjudication establishing a right in law was "interlocutory". In the CPR an interim injunction is defined as "an injunction granted by interlocutory order" (r.25.1.9).

[2] The statutory power originates from s.25 of the Supreme Court of Judicature Act 1873, re-enacted in s.45(1) of the Supreme Court of Judicature Act 1925. The wording of s.37(1) of the 1981 Act is different from the earlier Acts, leading Lord Denning to conclude that it conferred a new and extensive jurisdiction to grant interlocutory injunctions (*Chief Constable of Kent v V* [1983] 1 Q.B. 34 at 42). This view was not accepted by the majority in *South Carolina Co. v Assurantie NV* [1987] A.C. 24 (see Lord Brandon at 39–40) and expressly disapproved in *Pickering v Liverpool Daily Post and Echo* [1991] 2 A.C. 370 at 420.

[3] *South Carolina Co. v Assurantie NV,* above, per Lord Brandon at 40. Regarding the limits of the court's powers to grant injunctions in general, see also *Mercedes Benz A.G. v Leiduck* [1996] A.C. 284 PC, *Broadmoor Special Hospital Authority v R* [2000] Q.B. 775 CA, *Fourie v Le Roux* [2007] UKHL 1; [2007] 1 W.L.R. 320, and *Masri v Consolidated Contractors International Co. SAL* [2008] EWCA Civ 625; [2009] Q.B. 503.

[4] *South Carolina Co. v Assurantie NV,* above, and see Donaldson L.J. in *Chief Constable of Kent v V,* above, at 45.

statement or a false statement which would give rise to a claim for malicious falsehood. The injunction would restrain the threatened or repeated publication of defamatory statements about the claimant. Exceptionally a publisher might be ordered to withdraw, say, a book or pamphlet containing the defamatory statements from distribution or circulation, or, if it was in his power to cause copies he had distributed to be returned to him. But that is probably the limit to which a court will go in making a mandatory order.[5]

25.2 Delicate nature of jurisdiction. The jurisdiction to grant interim injunctions to restrain publication of defamatory statements is "of a delicate nature", which "ought only to be exercised in the clearest cases".[6] That was stated by Lord Esher M.R. in *Coulson v Coulson*,[7] and it encapsulates the general approach of the court. The reluctance to grant peremptory injunctions is rooted in the importance attached to the right of free speech,[8] and the

---

[5] In *Chin Bay Ching v Merchant Ventures Pte Ltd* [2005] S.G.A. 29; [2005] S.L.R. 142 the Singapore Court of Appeal indicated, albeit making no express ruling, that in an appropriate case a mandatory interim injunction ordering a defendant to publish a correction might be granted. In support of this view the court cited *TV3 Network Ltd v Eveready New Zealand Ltd* [1993] 3 N.Z.L.R. 435 in which Gault J. had stated (in a defamation case) that there was "no jurisdictional bar to an injunction cast in mandatory form". Gault J. had observed that such an injunction had been granted in *Hermann Loog v Bean* (1884) 26 Ch. D. 306 though it would seem that the order in this case was made to effect the redelivery to the plaintiff of some letters which the defendant had wrongly directed the Post Office to deliver to him, rather than to obtain the publication of a correction of a defamatory statement. As the court's statutory powers under the offer to make amends procedure and the summary disposal procedure do not extend as far as ordering the defendant to publish a correction, it seems unlikely that any judge would consider that by virtue of his general powers to grant injunctions contained in s.37(1) of the Senior Courts Act 1981 he was enabled to make such an order. This argument is leant further support by the consideration that s.12, Defamation Act 2013, when it comes into force, will confer on the court in defamation cases a new power, when judgment is given for a claimant, to order the defendant to publish a summary of the court's judgment, but not a correction. Note also, however, the new powers the courts have under s.13, Defamation Act 2013, in cases where judgment has been given for a claimant, to order the operator of a third party website on which the defamatory statement is posted to remove the statement (s.13(1)(a)), and to order any person who was not the author, editor or publisher of the statement (as those terms are defined in s.1 Defamation Act 1996) to stop distributing, selling or exhibiting material containing the statement (see para.9.47, above). It is conceivable that the exercise of these powers may give rise to fresh interim injunctive proceedings between the claimant and a third party, say, where the operator of a third party website declines or fails to remove the statement in question.

[6] "It is well known that it is rare for the court to grant injunctions on interim applications in defamation cases. However, the court has jurisdiction to do so and will do so in an appropriate case": *ZAM v CFW* [2011] EWHC 476 (QB) per Tugendhat J. at [23].

[7] [1887] 3 T.L.R. 846.

[8] "The importance of leaving free speech unfettered is a strong reason in cases of libel for dealing most cautiously and warily with the granting of interim injunctions": Lord Coleridge in *Bonnard v Perryman* [1891] 2 Ch. 269 at 284, and see *Herbage v Pressdram Ltd* [1984] 1 W.L.R. 1160, Griffiths L.J. at 1162. These sentiments are underpinned by art.10 of the European Convention for the Protection of Human Rights and Fundamental Freedoms to which effect has been given in English law by the Human Rights Act 1998. See also *Greene v Associated Newspapers Ltd* [2004] EWCA Civ 1462; [2005] Q.B. 972 (the leading case in the modern era) at [57].

consideration that damages are liable to be an adequate remedy.[9] Thus the Court will only grant an interim injunction where[10]:

(1) the statement is unarguably defamatory;
(2) there are no grounds for concluding the statement may be true;
(3) there is no other defence which might succeed;
(4) there is evidence of an intention to repeat or publish the defamatory statement.[11]

To these conditions, which will be examined in turn below, there must be added a procedural requirement imposed by s.12(2) of the Human Rights Act 1998 that the person against whom the injunction is sought must be present or represented at the application, or notified about it, unless there are good reasons for not doing so.[12] The practice established in applications for interim

---

[9] *Greene v Associated Newspapers Ltd*, above, at [57], [78] and *Mosley v News Group Newspapers Ltd* [2008] EWHC 1777 (QB); [2008] E.M.L.R. 20 at [230] per Eady J.: "Whereas reputation can be vindicated by an award of damages, in the sense that the claimant can be restored to the esteem in which he was previously held, that is not possible where embarrassing personal information has been released for general publication". This feature may furnish a rationale for the radical difference between the court's approach to the grant of interim injunctions in defamation and its approach to cases for misuse of private information; an unfairly tarnished reputation may be vindicated, whereas a wrongful disclosure of private information can never meaningfully be put right. See in this connection the speech given by Sir David Eady on November 10, 2009 at the University of Hertfordshire (*http://www.judiciary.gov.uk/docs/ speeches/justice-eady-univ-of-hertfordshire-101109.pdf*) in which he observed that this "question of principle needs to be addressed and resolved". At the time of writing, this is still to occur.
[10] The four conditions as set out were applied by Tugendhat J. in *Coys Ltd v Autocherish Ltd* [2004] EWHC 1334 (QB); [2004] E.M.L.R. 25.
[11] The authoritative statement of Hunt J. in *Church of Scientology v Readers Digest* [1980] 1 N.S.W.L.R. 344 at 350A could also be regarded as a succinct summary of English law:
"I accept as settled law that the power to grant interlocutory injunctions in defamation cases must be exercised with great caution, and only in very clear cases. A plaintiff must establish that a subsequent finding by a jury that the matter complained of was not defamatory of him would be set aside as unreasonable, that there is no real ground for supposing that the defendant may succeed on any defence of justification, privilege or comment, and that he, the plaintiff, is likely to recover more than nominal damages. In particular questions of privilege and malice are not normally appropriate to be decided upon an interlocutory application. Nor will an injunction go which will have the effect of restraining the discussion in the press of matters of public concern".
S.12 Human Rights Act 1998 applies "if a court is considering whether to grant any relief which, if granted might affect the exercise of the Convention right to freedom of expression." S.12(3) stipulates that an injunction to restrain publication before trial is not to be granted unless the applicant is likely to establish that publication should not be allowed. If the four conditions listed above are fulfilled it will follow that the applicant will be able to satisfy the court that he is likely to establish at trial that publication should not be allowed. For further discussion of s.12, see paras 25.19–25.23, below.
[12] The full wording of s.12(2) is:
"If the person against whom the application for relief is made ('the respondent') is neither present nor represented, no such relief is to be granted unless the court is satisfied—(a) that the applicant has taken all practicable steps to notify the respondent; or (b) that there are compelling reasons why the respondent should not be notified."
Regarding this requirement of notice, now see the *Practice Guidance (Interim Non-Disclosure Orders)* [2012] 1 W.L.R. 1003 issued by Lord Neuberger M.R. on August 1, 2011, at [18]–[23]. The Guidance "sets out recommended practice regarding any application for interim injunctive

injunctions by *American Cyanamid v Ethicon*,[13] of not considering the merits of the case once it had been shown there was a serious issue to be tried, but determining where the balance of convenience lay between the parties as regards the imposition of a restraining order, has been rejected as inappropriate in defamation cases,[14] as has the rights 'balancing' approach which has been adopted in privacy and harassment cases.[15]

25.3 Statement unarguably defamatory. The reason for this pre-condition was forcefully explained by Lord Esher in the passage in his judgment in *Coulson v Coulson*[16] from which we have already quoted:

" . . . the question of libel or no libel was for the jury. It was for the jury and not for the Court to construe the document, and to say whether it was a libel or not. To

---

relief in civil proceedings to restrain the publication of information: an interim non-disclosure order": at [1]. Though directed primarily at privacy and confidentiality cases, the Guidance also applies to applications "made in respect of . . . a threatened libel or malicious falsehood": at [1]. The only circumstances in which the court is now liable exceptionally to grant an interim non-disclosure where the respondent has not been given advance notice of the application are (a) if there is a real prospect that were the respondent to be notified he would take steps to defeat the purpose of the injunctive proceedings, (b) where there is convincing evidence that the respondent is seeking to blackmail the applicant, or (c) if there has literally been no time to give notice before the injunction is required to prevent the threatened unlawful act: at [21], and see also the observations of Lord Hoffmann in *National Commercial Bank of Jamaica Ltd v Olint Corpn Ltd* [2009] UKPC 16; [2009] 1 W.L.R. 1405, at [13], as follows:

" . . . there appears to have been no reason why the application for an injunction should have been made ex parte, or at any rate, without some notice to the bank. Although the matter is in the end one for the discretion of the judge, audi alterem partem is a salutary and important principle. Their Lordships therefore consider that a judge should not entertain an application of which no notice has been given unless *either* giving notice would enable the defendant to take steps to defeat the purpose of the injunction (as in the case of a *Mareva* or *Anton Piller* order) *or* there has been literally no time to give notice before the injunction is required to prevent the threatened wrongful act. These two alternative conditions are reflected in rule 17.4(4) of the Supreme Court of Jamaica Civil Procedure Rules 2002. Their Lordships would expect cases in the latter category to be rare, because even in cases in which there was no time to give the period of notice required by the rules, there will usually be no reason why the applicant should not have given shorter notice or even made a telephone call. Any notice is better than none."

See also, to similar effect, *AB v Barristers Benevolent Association Ltd* [2011] EWHC 3413 (QB) at [28] (Tugendhat J.). Considerations (a) and (b) were germane in *ZAM v CFW* [2011] EWHC 476 (QB) at [4], [14]. If none of these conditions is satisfied, and an applicant fails to give advance notice, the application is likely to be dismissed on this ground alone.

[13] [1975] A.C. 396. The decision has been subjected to reinterpretation by Laddie J. in *Series 5 Software v Philip Clarke* [1996] 1 All E.R. 853, who adjudged that it did not exclude consideration of the relative strength of the parties' cases and if the court could come to a clear view it was a factor that could be taken into account.

[14] *Trevor v Solomon* [1977] 248 E.G. 779 CA; *Bestobell Paints Ltd v Bigg* [1975] 1 F.S.R. 421; *Herbage v Pressdram Ltd* [1984] 1 W.L.R. 1160, 1163 CA; *Khashoggi v IPC Magazines* [1986] 1 W.L.R. 1412 CA; *Ron West Motors v BCBZ (No.2)* [1989] 3 N.Z.L.R. 520 and 540; *Greene v Associated Newspapers Ltd*, above, at [55].

[15] *Greene v Associated Newspapers Ltd*, above, at [76]–[81]. For the rights 'balancing' approach, see *S (A Child) (Identification: Restrictions on Publication), Re* [2005] 1 A.C. 593 at [17] and the other authorities referred to in para.1.15, above and fn.99, below. See also *Re BBC* [2009] UKHL 34; [2010] 1 A.C. 145.

[16] [1887] 3 T.L.R. 846.

justify the Court in granting an interim injunction it must come to a decision upon the question of libel or no libel, before the jury decided whether it was a libel or not. Therefore the jurisdiction was of a delicate nature. It ought only to be exercised in the clearest cases, where any jury would say that the matter complained of was libellous, and where if the jury did not so find the Court would set aside the verdict as unreasonable."[17]

Thus it is not sufficient for a claimant to establish that the words are capable of being defamatory; the court must be satisfied that a jury would inevitably come to the conclusion that they were defamatory.[18]

Precise words unknown. This should not pose a problem in the case of a   **25.4**
continuing publication on the internet,[19] but clearly a claimant who does not know precisely what words the defendant intends to publish is in some difficulty in establishing the imminent publication of plainly defamatory statements.[20] In such circumstances the claimant's best course is usually to seek an injunction directed at a specific allegation, unarguably defamatory of him, which he can show the defendant threatens or is likely to publish.[21] In exceptional cases it may be possible to obtain an order for the production of the proposed article, story or script for the purposes of later seeking an injunction.[22]

---

[17] The use of the words "libel" and "libellous" rather than "defamation" and "defamatory" is perhaps potentially confusing, as technically a libel is a defamatory statement which is untrue or not otherwise defensible. However, it is clear from the context that Lord Esher's observations quoted above were directed to the issue whether the words were defamatory.

[18] *Kaye v Robertson* [1991] F.S.R. 62 at 67, and see *Herbage v Times Newspapers*, unreported, *The Times*, May 1, 1981. Regarding what allegations will properly be considered defamatory in the modern era, see *Thornton v Telegraph Media Group Ltd* [2010] EWHC 1414 (QB); [2011] W.L.R. 1985.

[19] Unless what is at issue is an internet publication whose meaning and status as defamatory is uncertain, owing to the unfixed and evolving nature of its context, e.g. on a bulletin board or a social networking site such as Facebook.

[20] "How can the Court judge whether documents which are not yet in existence will be libellous?" per Cotton L.J. in *Liverpool Household Stores Association v Smith* [1887] L.R. 37 Ch.D. 170 at 180. And the claimant is confronted with the additional problem arising from s.12(3) of the Human Rights Act (see above). In *Dickson Minto v Bonnier Media*, unreported, Ct of Sess, May 11, 2003, Lord Carloway refused an injunction when the exact terms of a proposed (defamatory) article were not known, and in a reference to s.12(3) stated: "It is difficult to assert that the petitioner will succeed in circumstances in which it is not known what exactly is to be published." See also *Spelman v Express Newspapers* [2012] EWHC 355 (QB) at [59].

[21] The allegation must be specified with some precision and particularity. In *British Data Management Plc v Boxer Commercial Removals Plc* [1996] E.M.L.R. 349 CA, the court disapproved of a claim for a *quia timet* injunction restraining the defendants from:
"publishing any statement concerning the plaintiffs or any of them to the effect that they are guilty of civil wrongs or criminal offences in relation to the contents of company accounts, annual reports or the prospectus in March 1992 ... "
as being insufficiently precise. Though it was not necessary to set out verbatim the very words of which the plaintiff complains, there must (said Hirst L.J.) be reasonable certainty as to the actual words of which the plaintiff prospectively complains and seeks to restrain. See also *Collins v Jones* [1955] 1 Q.B. 564, and para.26.11, below.

[22] The court has power to order disclosure and production of a document arising or likely to arise in an intended claim even before proceedings have started (s.33(2) of the Senior Courts Act 1981 and CPR r.31.16, or under the principle in *Norwich Pharmacal* (as to which, see paras 31.4–31.5, below)). Where proceedings have been started an order for specific disclosure of a

25.5 No grounds for the truth of the statement. In some of the earlier cases—following the Supreme Court of Judicature Act 1873—it was stated that the plaintiff must produce evidence of the untruth of the allegations: "As a general rule the plaintiff who applies for an interlocutory injunction must shew the statement to be untrue".[23] However, this requirement is not easily reconcilable with the principle that a prima facie cause of action is established once the claimant proves that defamatory words have been published about him; he does not have to prove that the defamatory words are false, for the law presumes this in his favour.[24] In practice, it is customary, if not invariable, for there to be some evidence of the falsity of the allegations,[25] for in the absence of such evidence the court may, in the exercise of its discretion,[26] and having regard to the "delicate nature" of the jurisdiction, refuse an injunction. It is not usual for the claimant to be able to prove on an application for an interlocutory injunction that the words are plainly false.

25.6 Defence of justification. The general rule has been that where the defendant contends that the words complained of are true, and asserts that he will plead and seek at trial to prove the defence of justification, the court will not grant an interim injunction, unless, exceptionally, the court is satisfied that such a defence is one that cannot succeed. This was the decision in *Bonnard v Perryman*.[27] Lord Coleridge explained[28]:

> "The right of free speech is one which it is for the public interest that individuals should possess and, indeed, that they should exercise without impediment, so long as no wrongful act is done; and, unless an alleged libel is untrue, there is no wrong committed; but, on the contrary, often a very wholesome act is performed in the

---

material document may be made under CPR r.31.12, though orders under this rule are usually made after standard disclosure has proved inadequate (see PD 31 paras 5.1 to 5.4). Disclosure against a non-party, however, can be obtained under CPR r.31.17: see para.31.10, below. In *Auckland Area Health Service v Television NZ* [1992] 3 N.Z.L.R. 456 the jurisdiction to order the production of a proposed script was described as "a wholly exceptional jurisdiction to be exercised only in cases where there is a well-grounded fear that the publication will be clearly unlawful".

[23] Per Jessel M.R., *Quartz Hill Consolidated Mining Co. v Beal* [1882] 20 Ch D 501 at 508; and in *Coulson v Coulson*, above, Lord Esher stated that "the Court must also be satisfied that in all probability the alleged libel was untrue". Further, in *Bestobell Paints Ltd v Bigg* [1975] 1 F.S.R. 421, Oliver J., having reviewed the authorities, stated, "an interlocutory injunction will not be granted in the absence of proof to the satisfaction of the court of the falsity of the statement". However, apart from the claim being one for malicious falsehood (which the judge discounted), the defendant had announced that he intended to justify. It is therefore submitted that the case is an example of a recent application of the rule in *Bonnard v Perryman* (see below) rather than authority for the proposition that a claimant, even in the absence of any indication by the defendant that he contends the words are true, must prove the untruth of the words to obtain an interim injunction.

[24] See para.11.4, above.

[25] See e.g. *ZAM v CFW* [2011] EWHC 476 (QB) at [12], [20].

[26] See para.25.24, below.

[27] [1891] 2 Ch. 269.

[28] [1891] 2 Ch. 269 at 284.

publication and repetition of an alleged libel. Until it is clear that an alleged libel is untrue, it is not clear that any right at all has been infringed".

This statement of the law has been endorsed and applied consistently since 1891.[29] In recent times the rigidity of the rule has been criticised as incompatible with the proper application of ECHR law, which requires the court to strike a balance between competing rights, notably art.8 (respect for private life) and art.10 (freedom of expression). But though it has been judged that it is not enough for a defendant in the face of a statement of the claimant that the words are untrue merely to assert that the words are true[30] or to state that he intends to justify without identifying the ambit or extent of that defence,[31] the Court of Appeal[32] has unequivocally re-asserted the absolute nature of the rule in defamation cases which it held was unaffected by the Human Rights Act 1998. For the moment, therefore, the proposition that a claimant cannot obtain an interim injunction to restrain the publication of defamatory words in the face of a statement from the defendant, verified as true,[33] that he can and will justify the alleged libel, can be regarded as an invariable rule,[34] unless it is plain that the plea of justification is bound to fail.[35] The claimant need not

---

[29] E.g. *Monson v Tussauds Ltd* [1894] 1 Q.B. 671; *Burns v Associated Newspapers* [1926] 42 T.L.R. 37; *Fraser v Evans* [1969] 1 Q.B. 349 at 360, per Lord Denning M.R.; *Crest Homes Ltd v Ascott* [1980] F.S.R. 396, per Lord Denning M.R. (at 398), "this case comes within the general rule that an interlocutory injunction will not be granted in a libel case where the defendant says he is going to justify"; *Khashoggi v IPC Magazines* [1986] 1 W.L.R. 1412. In *Holley v Smyth* [1998] Q.B. 726 the plaintiff alleged that the defendant had threatened to defame him to obtain money as the price of silence. The Court of Appeal reversed the order of the judge granting an injunction:
"There may be exceptions to the [*Bonnard v Perryman*] rule, but neither the would-be libeller's motive nor the manner in which he threatens publication nor the potential damage to the plaintiff is normally a basis for making an exception"
(Auld L.J. at 744A-B). In *Moran v Heathcote*, unreported, January 15, 2001 Eady J. rejected the submission that a different approach should be taken in the light of the introduction of the power to grant summary relief under s.8 of the Defamation Act 1996.

[30] See e.g. *ZAM v CFW* [2011] EWHC 476 (QB) at [19], [22].

[31] Eady J. in *Sunderland Housing Co. v Baines* [2006] EWHC 2359 (QB). See also Jacob L.J. in *Boehringer Ingelheim Ltd v Vetplus Ltd* [2007] EWCA Civ 583; [2007] F.S.R. 29 at [43], though the injunction was not being sought in defamation.

[32] *Greene v Associated Newspapers Ltd* [2004] EWCA Civ 1462; [2005] Q.B. 972.

[33] An affidavit used to be required but under the CPR the general rule is that at interim hearings evidence is by witness statement: r.32.6(1). In the *Sunderland Housing* (see above) there was no statement of truth.

[34] It has been argued that one effect of s.12(3) of the Human Rights Act 1998 is to reduce the inflexibility of the rule, but it is not an argument that the courts have so far accepted: see para.25.21, below.

[35] *Robins v Kordowski* [2011] EWHC 981 (QB) at [21]. But see by contrast *A, B, and C v Thames Television Ltd*, CA, March 3, 1987 where an interlocutory injunction granted to restrain the broadcasting of material referring to the plaintiffs as war criminals was upheld even though the defendants had stated their intention of justifying whatever it was they were going to broadcast. But the defendants refused to disclose the contents of the intended broadcast and were not asserting the truth of any statement that the plaintiffs were guilty of war crimes, in contradistinction to the statement that they were reasonably suspected of being guilty. In *Williams v Wolman*, CA, unreported, January 30, 1990, Stocker L.J. said that where there was an intended plea of justification "the plaintiffs can only be entitled to an injunction, if the court is satisfied that a plea of justification must fail if put before a jury which was not perverse."

state that he will justify the particular words or allegation comprising the alleged libel: it is sufficient for him to declare his intention to justify the core or sting of the alleged libel,[36] provided, of course, that the core or sting is a wider or more general meaning than that conveyed by the particular matters described in the words complained of, and is a meaning the words are capable of bearing.[37]

25.7 The application of *Bonnard v Perryman* in other jurisdictions. In Australia it has been said that the rule does not apply.[38] But more recently the rule has come under scrutiny by the High Court[39] in considering the legal principles applicable to the grant of interim injunctions in defamation cases. The court undertook an extensive review of both English and Australian case law, demonstrating how the latter had absorbed in large measure the reasoning behind the rule in *Bonnard v Perryman*, that freedom of speech was paramount, without converting it into a rigid and inflexible maxim. However, Heydon J., in a powerful and polemical dissenting judgment argued for the abandonment of the rule as being wholly inappropriate in the modern world:

> "Attention could be given to the significance of changed social conditions—to the fact that the judges who decided the cases which culminated in *Bonnard v Perryman* had just finished living through an era when the leading political journalists were Robert Cecil and Walter Bagehot; the name of Harmsworth was unknown; there were no relatively cheap mass circulation newspapers operated by large publicly owned companies and no radio or television outlets were operated by those companies and by the state . . . Those who had decided *Bonnard v Perryman* had lived through a time when there was no electronic media and no problem of cross-media ownership; the print organs were much more fragmented than now, were directed to a population with much lower literacy than now, were much less able to reach most of the adult population, and were much less able speedily to disseminate defamatory material. In short, attention would have to be directed to whether in modern conditions the mass media are more able to inflict harm which is not also grave but irreparable, and if so, whether it ought to be less difficult for plaintiffs to obtain urgent interlocutory relief to prevent such harm" (at [280]).

The position in New Zealand is colourably the same as in this jurisdiction.[40]

25.8 Other defences which might succeed. The court will not normally grant an interim injunction where the threatened publication will on its face be privileged.[41] The exception is where the defendant is clearly malicious:

---

[36] *Khashoggi v IPC Magazines Ltd*, above.
[37] Cf. *Bookbinder v Tebbit* [1989] 1 W.L.R. 640 CA.
[38] *National Mutual Life Association of Australasia v GTV Corp Pty* [1989] V.R. 747.
[39] *Australian Broadcasting Corp v O'Neill* [2006] HCA 46; 229 A.L.R. 457.
[40] *Chen v Carter* [2013] NZHC 869 citing *Bonnard v Perryman*, above, *NZ Mortgage Guarantee v Wellington Newspapers* [1989] 1 N.Z.L.R. 4, and *Television New Zealand Ltd v Rogers* [2007] 1 N.Z.L.R. 156 at [111]–[112]. See also *TV3 Network Services Ltd v Fahey* [1999] 2 N.Z.L.R. 129: "Any prior restraint of free expression requires a much higher threshold than the arguable case standard." Per Richardson P.
[41] *Quartz Hill Consolidated Mining Co. v Beal* [1882] 20 Ch D 501, applied in *Harakas v Baltic Mercantile and Shipping Exchange Ltd* [1982] 1 W.L.R. 958.

"[W]hen an occasion is protected by qualified privilege this court never grants an injunction to restrain a slander or libel—to prevent a person from exercising that privilege—unless it be shown that what the defendant proposes to say is known by him to be untrue so that it is clearly malicious."[42]

However, the issue of malice is not one that can be conveniently tried on an interim application.[43] It has been said that where a claimant must prove malice to succeed in the action the evidence of malice has to be "absolutely overwhelming" for the court to intervene to restrain publication by way of an interim injunction.[44]

Honest comment. Where the intended defence is honest comment it seems   **25.9** that the position is similar to where the intended defence is that of justification. If the defendant asserts that he will raise such a defence and prove the truth of the facts supporting the comment, then if the matter appears to be one of public interest and the claimant cannot establish an overwhelming case of malice,[45] an interim injunction will not be ordered.[46]

Where there is evidence that the claimant may have consented to the publication the court will not grant an interim injunction restraining continuance of the publication,[47] and an injunction could be refused on the grounds that by reason of the general character of the claimant he might well not obtain more than nominal damages at trial.[48]

Evidence of an intention to repeat or publish. The court will not grant   **25.10** an interim injunction unless there is some evidence, or there are some reasonable grounds to infer, that the defendant threatens or intends to publish, or to continue the publication of, the words.[49] However, where there has not

---

[42] Per Lord Denning in *Harakas v Baltic Mercantile and Shipping Exchange Ltd*, above, at 960.

[43] See Jessel M.R. in *Quartz Hill Consolidated Gold Mining Co. v Beall*, above, at 509.

[44] Griffiths L.J. in *Herbage v Pressdram Ltd* [1984] 1 W.L.R. 1160 at 1164.

[45] See the preceding paragraph.

[46] Per Lord Denning in *Fraser v Evans*, above, at 360, repeated in *Bryanston Finance Ltd v De Vries* [1975] Q.B. 703 at 724; *Ron West Motors v BCNZ* [1989] 3 N.Z.L.R. 520.

[47] *Monson v Tussauds*, above.

[48] *Bonnard v Perryman*, above, per Lord Coleridge at 284. By parity of reasoning, a plea of partial justification which might reduce the damages "almost to vanishing point" (*Pamplin v Express Newspapers Ltd* [1988] 1 W.L.R. 116 at 120, Neill L.J.) would be a reason for refusing an injunction in respect of defamatory allegations which are not fully covered by the plea.

[49] Per Jessel M.R. in *Quartz Hill Consolidated Mining Co. v Beal* [1882] 20 Ch D 501 at 508–509; and see *New Musical Express v Cardfont Publishers* [1956] R.P.C. 211. More generally, see Fry L.J. in *Proctor v Bayley* (1889) 42 Ch D 390:

"Now an injunction is granted for prevention, and where there is no ground for apprehending the repetition of a wrongful act there is no ground for an injunction. It was pressed on us that Mr Hares insisted on their having a right to do what they had done, but, looking at all the circumstances of the case, this foolish attempt to justify a past act does not raise any presumption that they intend to repeat it".

More recently, see *Martin v Channel Four Television Corp* [2009] EWHC 2788 (QB); *Terry (formerly 'LNS') v Persons Unknown* [2010] EWHC 119 (QB); [2010] E.M.L.R. 16, at [11]–[14], [65], [68]–[69], [149]; *Ambrosiadou v Coward* [2011] EWCA Civ 409; [2011] E.M.L.R. 21 (a privacy case) at [42]; and *APW v WPA* [2012] EWHC 3151 (QB) at [43]–[51] (a harassment and privacy case).

as yet been any publication of defamatory words, but there is a threat of publication, the claimant need not wait for publication to take place; he may seek to restrain publication, by means of a quia timet order, before it has taken place:

> "But no one can obtain a *quia timet* order by merely saying 'Timeo'; he must aver and prove that what is going on is calculated to infringe his rights."[50]

Thus there must be evidence that a defamatory statement concerning the claimant is about to be published.[51]

25.11 Slander. The claimant must establish that defamatory words have been spoken[52] and are liable to be repeated, or are threatened to be spoken, in circumstances that give rise, or will give rise, to a cause of action in slander. This involves either satisfying the court that the words come within one of the categories of cases where the words are actionable without proof of special damage,[53] or proving the likelihood of loss.[54]

25.12 Malicious falsehood. An interim injunction is obtainable to restrain the further or threatened malicious publication of false statements which are calculated to cause pecuniary damage to the claimant.[55] As the onus is upon a claimant to prove the falsity of the statement there clearly must be evidence of this before the court will entertain an application.[56] However, the rule in

---

[50] Per Lord Dunedin in *Att-Gen for Canada v Ritchie Contracting* [1919] A.C. 999 at 1005.

[51] Regarding the potential difficulties that may be associated with establishing this, see para.25.4, above. A defendant may be able to refute the claimant's allegation of intention to publish a defamatory allegation by offering an undertaking not to publish without giving notice to the claimant. This course was followed in *Fayed v Observer, The Times*, July 14, 1986, Mann J.

[52] Or otherwise communicated in transitory form; see para.3.6, above.

[53] See Ch.4, above.

[54] In *White v Mellin* [1895] A.C. 154 it was stated that as special damage was necessary to make up a cause of action (for slander of goods), and none was shown, a tort was not disclosed, and no injunction would be granted. However, where the injunction is sought quia timet, it would seem that it will suffice to show the likelihood of damage if the threatened publication takes place (see *Emerald Construction Co. Ltd v Lowthian* [1966] 1 W.L.R. 691). If this were not so, it is hard to see how an interim injunction could ever be granted to restrain the future publication of a slander not actionable per se: by definition, no actual loss will have been sustained. However, it may be the policy of the law not to permit injunctions in such circumstances. The point is moot, but in the current climate (see in particular s.1, Defamation Act 2013) the likelihood is that an injunction would be refused as an unnecessary and disproportionate interference with freedom of expression.

[55] Cf. Defamation Act 1952, s.3.

[56] *Bestobell Paints Ltd v Bigg* [1975] F.S.R. 421 at 439. The falsity of a statement will depend on its meaning. The "single meaning rule" does not apply to malicious falsehood (see *Ajinomoto Sweeteners Europe SAS v Asda Stores Ltd* [2010] EWCA Civ 609; [2010] Q.B. 204 and also para.21.5, above). Accordingly, it is submitted, the judge would have to assess the issue of meaning in the first instance as a question of whether a reasonable reader *could* interpret the statement sought to be enjoined in the manner contended for, but would also need to consider, as part of the analysis of whether the applicant was "likely to establish that publication should not be allowed" mandated by s.12(3) Human Rights Act 1998, whether it was an interpretation that was likely to prevail at trial.

Bonnard v Perryman[57] still applies, and an injunction will not be granted where the defendant states that he intends to justify.[58] Thus the court on an interlocutory application will not seek to resolve or make any provisional assessment of the rival contentions of falsity and truth, save to this extent, that if it is satisfied that no judge or jury could reasonably conclude that the statement was true, it may grant an injunction.[59] The claimant has to show that the defendant was (or, would be, if the threatened publication took place) acting maliciously. This is often in practice not such a burden as confronts a claimant seeking an interim injunction in a libel action faced by, say, a plea of qualified privilege.[60] If the words are clearly false, and it is established that, notwithstanding, the defendant intends to continue to publish them, that may be sufficient evidence of malice.[61]

Infringement of trade mark. Where the action arises from the false **25.13**
description of the contents of a product the name of which is a registered trade mark, and the application for an interim injunction is based upon the claim of infringement of trade mark the rule in *Bonnard v Perryman* does not apply.[62]

Injunctions based on other causes of action. The difficulties in obtain- **25.14**
ing interim injunctions in defamation in the face of the virtual bar imposed by *Bonnard v Perryman* have led litigants to base their claims on other causes of action, such as breach of confidence, misuse of private information and harassment.[63] Generally, judges have been cautious in granting injunctions in cases not founded in defamation but which have the effect of restraining publication of defamatory material, which the publisher maintains is true. If it is clear that the true nature of the complaint is defamation, that is to say injury to reputation, an injunction is unlikely to be granted.[64]

---

[57] [1891] 2 Ch. 269.

[58] *Bestobell Paints v Bigg*, above; *Boehringer Ingelheim Ltd v Vetplus Ltd* [2007] EWCA Civ 583; [2007] F.S.R. 29 at [14]. In Australia there is a different approach though the end result may be the same: in *Animal Liberation (Vic.) v Gascar* [1991] 1 V.R. 51 the single judge granted an injunction in injurious falsehood, although he acknowledged he could not do so in defamation, because the defendants asserted their statements were true. On appeal the decision was reversed, the court stating that the judge did not give sufficient weight to the right of free speech, and that in malicious falsehood, as in defamation, injunctions will only be granted in clear cases.

[59] *Kaye v Robertson* [1991] F.S.R. 62, adopted by Aldous J. in *Compaq Computer Corp v Dell Computer Corp Ltd* [1992] F.S.R. 93. This is surely no more than stating (using different phraseology) the proviso to the rule in *Bonnard v Perryman*, namely, that it does not apply where it appears the plea of justification is bound to fail.

[60] See para.25.8, above.

[61] *Horrocks v Lowe* [1975] A.C. 137 at 149. Note *Animal Liberation (Vic.) v Gascar*, above, where statements by defendants that they believed the allegations to be true were decisive in the reversal of the judge's decision to grant an injunction.

[62] *Boehringer Ingelheim Ltd v Vetplus Ltd*, above, which also confirms that the rule in *Bonnard v Perryman* does not apply to the tort of passing off.

[63] Under the Protection from Harassment Act 1997; see para.25.17, below.

[64] *Terry (formerly 'LNS') v Persons Unknown* [2010] EWHC 119 (QB); [2010] E.M.L.R. 16, in which Tugendhat J. decided on the evidence that it was likely that the nub of the applicant's complaint was the protection of his reputation in particular with commercial sponsors rather than

25.15 *Examples (1).* In *Sim v HJ Heinz Co. Ltd*[65] the plaintiff, an actor, sought to restrain television advertisements using a voice resembling his own. The plaintiff complained of libel, but abandoned that claim when it became clear that in view of such authorities as *Bonnard v Perryman* he could not obtain an injunction on that ground. He then founded his application on passing off. It was refused. The issue to be tried in the libel action was broadly the same as the issue to be tried in the passing-off action, and in the circumstances it was adjudged inappropriate to grant an injunction on the basis of passing off, while refusing an injunction on the basis of libel.

An injunction was refused to a group of pop stars who complained that articles about them in a newspaper written by their former press agent were in breach of the agent's duty of confidence (as well as libellous), partly on the grounds that the allegation of breach of confidence was so interwoven with the claim for libel that the balance of convenience was against granting an interim injunction.[66]

In *Service Corp International v Channel Four Television* Lightman J. refused to grant an injunction restraining the broadcasting of a film secretly taken by an employee working for a television company of the practices at a funeral home. The application was based on claims of trespass and breach of copyright, but the judge described it as an attempt to circumvent the rule preventing the grant of an interlocutory injunction where the claim was in defamation and the defendant intended to plead justification.[67]

25.16 *Examples (2).* There is, however, far from a rigid rule:

> "I can well see that there may be cases where it would be wrong to grant an injunction on breach of confidence when it would not be granted on libel: but I can equally well see that there are some cases of breach of confidence which are defamatory, where the court might intervene, even though the defendant says he intends to justify."[68]

An example of the latter would be *Francome v Mirror Group Newspapers*[69] where the plaintiff, a jockey, was granted an injunction restraining a newspaper from publishing articles based on illicit recordings of his private telephone conversations. The action was one for breach of confidence, but it

---

of his private life, and, as such, the rule in *Bonnard v Perryman* applied and precluded the grant of an interim injunction: see at [124]–[132].

[65] [1959] 1 W.L.R. 313.

[66] *Woodward v Hutchins* [1977] 1 W.L.R. 760. In *Brabourne v Hough* [1981] F.S.R. 79, Slade J. refused an injunction in claims based on passing off and unlawful interference with trade because they were closely allied to claims based on malicious falsehood and were governed by the principle that the court will not restrain publication of defamatory statements the defendant intends to justify.

[67] [1999] E.M.L.R. 83. To like effect, see *Tillery Valley Foods Ltd v Channel Four Television Corpn* [2004] EWHC 1075 (Ch), per Mann J. See also *Viagogo Ltd v Myles* [2012] EWHC 433 (Ch).

[68] Per Lord Denning M.R. in *Fraser v Evans* [1969] 1 Q.B. 349 at 362.

[69] [1984] 1 W.L.R. 892.

was clear the articles would have been defamatory. How to distinguish between the two types of cases described by Lord Denning has perhaps been indicated by Griffiths L.J.[70]:

> "If the court were to conclude that though the plaintiff had framed his claim in a cause of action other than defamation but nevertheless his principal purpose was to seek damages for defamation, the court will refuse interlocutory relief.[71] If, on the other hand, the court is satisfied that there is some serious interest to be protected such as confidentiality, and that outweighs considerations of free speech then the court will grant an injunction."[72]

It was argued in *McKennitt v Ash*,[73] a breach of confidence or privacy action, that as the judge had found that most or all of the allegations in the defendant's book on one aspect, namely her property dispute with the claimant, were false there could be no claim in breach of confidence, as whatever the position in defamation the falsity of what the defendant had written was a complete defence. Buxton L.J. pointed out that falsity was relevant only because it undermined the public interest defence, not because an allegation of falsity was inherent in the basic claim itself. He then commented:

> "[i]f it could be shown that a claim in breach of confidence was brought where the nub of the case was a complaint of the falsity of the allegations, and that was done to avoid the rules of the tort of defamation, then objections could be raised in terms of abuse of the process. That might be so at the interlocutory stage in an attempt to avoid the rule in *Bonnard v Perryman* . . . I would hold that provided the matter complained of is by its nature such as to attract the law of breach of confidence the defendant cannot deprive the claimant of his art.8 protection simply by demonstrating that the matter is untrue."[74]

In *Boehringer Ingelheim Ltd v Vetplus Ltd*[75] an interim injunction was granted (by the Court of Appeal) for infringement of trade mark, where the essence of the claim was allegedly false descriptions of the contents of a product in a comparative advertisement which, it was acknowledged, also gave rise to claims in libel and malicious falsehood in respect of which, because of the rule in *Bonnard v Perryman,* there could be no interim injunction. Jacob L.J.

---

[70] In *Microdata Information Services v Rivendale* [1991] F.S.R. 681 at 688. The judgment was given in September 1984.

[71] This would appear to be the ratio of *Terry (formerly 'LNS') v Persons Unknown*, above.

[72] The correctness of the decision was doubted (though applied) by Peter Gibson J. in *Western Front Ltd v Vestron Inc.* [1987] F.S.R. 66, and followed in *Essex Electric (Pte) Ltd v IPCs Computers (UK) Ltd* [1991] F.S.R. 690.

[73] [2006] EWCA Civ 714; [2008] Q.B. 73.

[74] At [79]–[80]. The point was expressed with greater trenchancy by Longmore L.J. in the same case:

> "The truth or falsity of the [private] information is an irrelevant inquiry in deciding whether the information is entitled to be protected and judges should be chary of becoming side-tracked into that irrelevant inquiry."

(at [86]).

[75] Reference above.

pointed out[76] that a trade mark infringement was not merely a claim to protect the claimant's reputation: it was a claim to protect a property right. And Longmore L.J. explained[77]:

> "The rule that no injunction will be given if there is an intention to justify has developed in the law of defamation (and been extended to malicious falsehood) for historical reasons apposite to those causes of action. No such reasons apply to trade mark infringement actions which seek to protect a particular form of intellectual property which is, to my mind, different in kind from a right to one's reputation or that of one's goods."[78]

25.17 Protection from Harassment Act. The Supreme Court has confirmed that the Protection from Harassment Act 1997 applies to harassing campaigns conducted by means of publication.[79] In *Georgallides v Etzin*,[80] G made an application under the Protection from Harassment Act 1997 for an order restraining E, who alleged he was owed money by G, from organising protests with placards and leaflets outside G's restaurant. Gray J. granted a limited injunction, commenting that though the words on the placards were defamatory of G he was satisfied that the application was not an attempt to circumvent the rule in *Bonnard v Perryman* but to prevent G from being harassed. And in *Howlett v Holding*[81] Eady J. granted a permanent injunction under the Act against a defendant who was pursuing a "campaign of public vilification" of the claimant by flying banners from an aircraft and dropping leaflets referring to the claimant in abusive and derogatory terms. The judge stated that it was important to identify the true nature of the claimant's complaint and of the conduct complained of, which was an endeavour to make the claimant's life "living hell".[82]

25.18 Conspiracy. The rule in *Bonnard v Perryman* was circumvented in *Gulf Oil (Great Britain) Ltd v Page*[83] by the formulation of the claim as one for damages for conspiracy. The plaintiff obtained an injunction prohibiting the defendant from flying an aeroplane over a racecourse towing a sign bearing a

---

[76] At [36].

[77] At [56].

[78] The Court upheld the judge's refusal to grant an injunction as it agreed with his decision, applying s.12(3) of the Human Rights Act 1998, that the claimant had not shown that it was more likely than not to succeed at trial.

[79] *Hayes v Willoughby* [2013] UKSC 17; [2013] 1 W.L.R. 935. See also *The Law Society v Kordowski* [2011] EWHC 3185 (QB); *Trimingham v Associated Newspapers Ltd* [2012] EWHC 1296 (QB); [2012] 4 All E.R. 717 and *ZAM v CFW* [2013] EWHC 662 (QB); [2013] E.M.L.R. 27. For some other recent interim injunction cases involving the alleged harassment of the claimant, see *Ting Lan Hong v XYZ* [2011] EWHC 2995 (QB), *EWQ v GFD* [2012] EWHC 2182 (QB), *SKA v CRH* [2012] EWHC 2236 (QB) and *APW v WPA* [2012] EWHC 3151 (QB).

[80] July 12, 2005, unreported.

[81] [2006] EWHC 41 (QB). The judge also observed that if the claim had been for an interim injunction based on libel there was insufficient material to warrant a plea of justification so *Bonnard v Perryman* would not have availed the defendant.

[82] Ibid. at [7].

[83] [1987] Ch. 327.

message defamatory of the plaintiff. It was not disputed that the words were true. The court said that the principle established in *Bonnard v Perryman* was not a complete answer to the claim for an interlocutory injunction, for in a conspiracy to injure the wrong arose from the sole or dominant purpose of the participants and the publication causing injury to the plaintiff. The same route was sought to be followed in *Femis-Bank v Lazar*[84] where the plaintiff confronted by a series of defamatory allegations published by the defendants claimed a conspiracy to injure and applied for an injunction. It was refused on the grounds that freedom of speech was an important factor to be taken into account and:

> "only in the very clearest cases such as existed in the *Gulf Oil* case would the interference with that public interest be justified by the grant of an injunction".[85]

It seems unlikely that the courts will allow the rule in *Bonnard v Perryman* to be regularly avoided by the device of alleging conspiracy to injure.

Section 12 of the Human Rights Act 1998. This section applies   **25.19**

> "if a court is considering whether to grant any relief which, if granted, might affect the exercise of the Convention right to freedom of expression".[86]

It must therefore apply to applications for interim injunctions to restrain publication of defamatory statements. Section 12(2) sets out a stringent procedural requirement. No injunction will be granted when the person against whom the injunction is sought is neither present nor represented unless the court is satisfied that the applicant has taken all practicable steps to notify that person or there are compelling reasons why that person should not be notified.[87] As a matter of practice, a claimant should give notice to the person he wants to injunct that he intends to apply for an injunction in sufficient time to enable that person to attend the application. In a breach of confidence or privacy case (where the *Spycatcher* principle[88] applies), a claimant should also give advance notice to any other person whom he proposes to notify of the order if granted because that person is known to have a pre-existing interest in the information whose publication is to be prevented, and the

---

[84] [1991] Ch. 391.
[85] Sir Nicolas Browne-Wilkinson V.-C. at 400.
[86] S.12(1) of the Act.
[87] For wording of the subsection and other germane observations, see fn.12, above.
[88] *Att-Gen v Guardian Newspapers Ltd (No.2)* [1990] 1 A.C. 109. See also *Ambrosiadou v Coward* [2011] EWCA Civ 409; [2011] E.M.L.R. 21, *OPQ v BJM* [2011] EWHC 1059 (QB); [2011] E.M.L.R. 23 (final injunction *contra mundum* granted, to cater for the problem identified in *Jockey Club v Buffham* [2002] EWHC 1866 (QB); [2003] Q.B. 462, that the *Spycatcher* principle does not bind third parties on notice of final injunctions) and *Hutcheson v Popdog Ltd* [2011] EWCA Civ 1580; [2012] 1 W.L.R. 782 (in which the Court of Appeal queried if *Jockey Club v Buffham* is correctly decided).

claimant intends him to be bound by it.[89] This rule has no role in defamation: the *Spycatcher* principle does not apply, and interim injunctions will bind only respondents, not third parties.

25.20 **Section 12(3).** Section 12(3) expressly relates to pre-publication injunctions and ordains that they are not to be granted "unless the court is satisfied that the applicant is likely to establish that publication should not be allowed". In short the court must be satisfied that a permanent injunction is "likely" to be obtained at trial or earlier conclusion of the case. In *Cream Holdings Ltd v Banerjee*[90] the House of Lords decided that "the general approach should be that the courts will be exceedingly slow to make interim restraint orders where the applicant has not satisfied the court he will probably ("more likely than not") succeed at trial", but the term "likely" was not to be given a single, inflexible definition, but applied pragmatically to the circumstances of each individual case.[91] Lord Nicholls explained:

> "Section 12(3) makes the likelihood of success at the trial an essential element in the court's consideration of whether to make an interim order. But in order to achieve the necessary flexibility the degree of likelihood needed to satisfy section 12(3) must depend on the circumstances. There can be no single, rigid standard governing all applications for interim restraint orders. Rather, on its proper construction the effect of section 12(3) is that the court is not to make an interim restraint order unless satisfied the applicant's prospects of success at the trial are sufficiently favourable to justify such an order being made in the particular circumstances of the case. As to what degree of likelihood makes the prospect of success 'sufficiently favourable' the general approach should be that the courts will be exceedingly slow to make interim restraint orders where the applicant has not satisfied the court he will probably ('more likely than not') succeed at trial. In general, that should be the threshold an applicant must cross before the court embarks on exercising its discretion, duly taking into account the relevant jurisprudence on Art. 10 and any countervailing Convention rights. But there will be cases where it is necessary for a court to depart from this general approach and a lesser degree of likelihood will suffice as a prerequisite."[92]

---

[89] *Practice Guidance (Interim Non-Disclosure Orders)* [2012] 1 W.L.R.1003, at [19], relying on *X v Persons Unknown* [2006] EWHC 2783 (QB); [2007] E.M.L.R. 10. See also *TUV v Persons Unknown* [2010] EWHC 853 (QB); [2010] E.M.L.R. 19, where, in connection with the obligation to notify non-party media entities on which an applicant might wish to serve the order, Eady J. stated that applicants should not be required to speculate or guess which media bodies might have an interest in the story, but if there were "solid grounds in the light of the available evidence" to believe that a particular media organisation had shown an interest in the material, that organisation should be notified.

[90] [2004] UKHL 44; [2005] 1 A.C. 253.

[91] The flexibility of the pragmatic approach in *Cream Holdings Ltd v Banerjee* has been valuable in the context of applications for interim injunctions made without notice, where the ring has to be held until the inter partes hearing. In that context, the question is whether there is a sufficient likelihood that the claimant will succeed at trial to justify granting an injunction for the short period until an inter partes hearing: *ASG v GSA* [2009] EWCA Civ 1574 at [5], per Waller L.J.

[92] At [22].

The effect of section 12(3) on the rule in Bonnard v Perryman. The   **25.21**
general principle that an interim injunction will not be granted in defamation
cases where the defendant expresses an intention to justify remains undis-
turbed by the restriction imposed by s.12(3). In *Cream Holdings Ltd v
Banerjee* in the Court of Appeal,[93] two members of the court referred to the
rule in *Bonnard v Perryman* in terms which indicated they thought the rule
was unaffected. In *Greene v Associated Newspapers Ltd,*[94] where direct
attention was given to this point, the conclusion was that the section could not
be construed as having abrogated the rule by a side-wind: the well-established
principle that "a rule of common law is not extinguished by a statute unless
the statute makes this clear by express provision or by clear implication had
to be applied".[95] The court had "no hesitation in holding that there was
nothing in s.12(3) . . . that can properly be interpreted as weakening in any
way the force of the rule in *Bonnard v Perryman.*"[96]

This ruling would seem to exclude an argument—short of Supreme court
level, at any rate—that s.12(3) requires a court to carry out an enquiry into the
merits of the defamation complaint because it has to be satisfied that the claimant
is likely to establish at trial that publication should not be allowed, i.e. is as a
matter of fact unlawful, and therefore that a mere assertion by the defendant that
he intends to plead, and will be able to prove, the truth of the defamatory
allegations is insufficient to see off an interim injunction application.[97]

The effect of the recognition of reputation as an Art.8 ECHR   **25.22**
right. The Court of Appeal in *Greene v Associated Newspapers Ltd,* in
deciding to retain the rule in *Bonnard v Perryman* in defamation, indicated
that it was content to assume for that purpose that a person's right to protect
his reputation was among the rights guaranteed by art.8 of the Convention.[98]
However, the potential consequences of that assumption did not receive
detailed attention in the court's judgment, specifically the possible impact of
a new situation whereby reputation (art.8) had to be treated as having equal
weight and value to free speech (art.10).[99] Since then, reputation has been

---

[93] [2003] EWCA Civ 103; [2003] Ch. 650.
[94] [2004] EWCA Civ 1462; [2005] Q.B. 972.
[95] A principle articulated in *R (Rottman) v Comr of Police of the Metropolis* [2002] 2 A.C. 692,
relied on in *Greene v Associated Newspapers Ltd,* above, at [64].
[96] At [66].
[97] The matter can be put this way: in terms of protecting freedom of expression, s.12(3) creates
a 'floor' but not a 'ceiling'.
[98] At [68].
[99] There is some discussion of the point towards the end of the judgment in *Greene* ([79]–[81]),
but as those paragraphs show, the landmark decision of the House of Lords in *Re S (A Child)
(Identification: Restrictions on Publication)* [2004] UKHL 47; [2005] 1 A.C. 593, in which Lord
Steyn at [17] first described the 'rights' balancing exercise ("First, neither article has *as such*
precedence over the other. Secondly, where the values under the two articles are in conflict, an
intense focus on the comparative importance of the specific rights being claimed in the individual
cases is necessary. Thirdly, the justifications for interfering with or restricting each right must be
taken into account. Finally, the proportionality test must be applied to each.") had emerged after
oral argument had concluded and before judgment was handed down. Thus, not only had there

ruled authoritatively to be an art.8 right both by the UK Supreme Court in *Re Guardian News & Media Ltd*[100] and by Grand Chambers of the European Court of Human Rights in *Axel Springer A.G. v Germany*[101] and *Von Hannover v Germany (No.2)*.[102] It thus remains to be seen whether the rule in *Bonnard v Perryman*, which proceeds integrally on the footing that priority is to be given to freedom of expression, is able to withstand these developments in authority at the highest level.[103]

25.23 Section 12(4). Section 12(4) imposes an obligation on the court to have particular regard to the importance of the Convention right of freedom of expression[104] and, where the proceedings relate to material which is claimed, or which appears to the court, to be journalistic, literary, or artistic material (or to conduct connected with such material), to:

(1) the extent to which the material has, or is about to, become available to the public, or it is, or would be, in the public interest for the material to be published; and

(2) any relevant privacy code.

This sub-section seems primarily directed at claims based on breach of confidence (or privacy) in which consideration of the extent to which material is in the public domain would be relevant.[105] The reference to public interest must add strength to a newspaper's resistance to an injunction on the grounds of public interest privilege.[106] "[C]onduct connected with such material" is

---

been only a short period of time to absorb the full implications of *Re S*, but the Court of Appeal in *Greene* did not have the benefit of argument on the point. Since then, several judges have spoken of the "necessity", consequential on the recognition of reputation as an art.8 right, of applying to defamation cases the "ultimate balancing test". See e.g. *Flood v Times Newspapers Ltd* [2009] EWHC 2375 (QB); [2010] E.M.L.R. 8. (Tugendhat J.'s decision was overturned in part, but not in that respect, by the Court of Appeal at [2010] EWCA Civ 804; [2011] 1 W.L.R. 153.) But see the observations of Lord Phillips in this connection at [44]–[46]: [2012] UKSC 11; [2012] 2 A.C. 273. See also, *Clift v Slough Borough Council* [2009] EWHC 1550 (QB); [2010] E.M.L.R. 4 (affirmed by Court of Appeal at [2010] EWCA Civ 1484; [2011] 1 W.L.R. 1774); and *Hunt v Times Newspapers Ltd* [2012] EWHC 1220 (QB):

"What seems to be emerging clearly is that the 'new methodology' sanctioned by the House of Lords in 2004, both in *Campbell v MGN Ltd* and in *Re S (A Child)*, originally in the context of privacy, where we had little established jurisprudence of our own, is now finding its way inexorably into the application of our well known principles of defamation" (per Eady J. at [13]).

[100] [2010] UKSC 1; [2010] 2 A.C. 697.
[101] [2012] E.M.L.R. 15.
[102] [2012] E.M.L.R. 16.
[103] Regarding this debate, see further fn.9, above.
[104] This has been interpreted as meaning that the court must pay regard to the right to freedom of expression, not that the right must be given priority: see *Ashdown v Telegraph Group Ltd* [2001] EWCA Civ 1142; [2002] Ch. 149; *Imutran Ltd v Uncaged Campaigns Ltd* [2001] All E.R. 385; *S (A Child) (Identification: Restrictions on Publication), Re*, above, at [16]–[17].
[105] For a discussion of the public domain doctrine see Warby, Moreham & Christie (eds), *The Law of Privacy and The Media*, 2nd edn (2011), Ch.4, paras 6–94–6–102.
[106] See *Reynolds v Times Newspapers* [2001] 2 A.C. 127.

intended to cover journalistic inquiries before a story is written.[107] Potentially relevant privacy codes include the Press Complaints Commission Editors' Code of Practice, the Ofcom Broadcasting Code.[108]

Discretion. An interim injunction is an equitable remedy and subject to the discretion of the court.[109] Thus the maxim "he who comes into equity must come with clean hands" is applicable.[110] Delay in making the application is a ground for refusing an injunction[111]; so too is conduct amounting to acquiescence.[112]   **25.24**

SECTION 2. PRACTICE AND PROCEDURE

Introduction. As the *Practice Guidance on Interim Non-Disclosure Orders*[113] issued by the Master of the Rolls (Lord Neuberger M.R.) in August 2011 makes clear at [29]–[32], in practical procedural terms, those who seek interim injunctions which, if granted, will affect another's freedom of expression, bear a particularly exacting burden: **25.25**

"29. The onus is on the applicant to satisfy the court that an interim non-disclosure order is justified. Where the applicant seeks derogations from open justice reference should be made to paragraphs 8–13 of this Guidance.
   30. Particular care should be taken in every application for an interim non-disclosure order, and especially where an application is made without-notice, by applicants to comply with the high duty to make full, fair and accurate disclosure of all material information to the court and to draw the court's attention to significant factual, legal and procedural aspects of the case. The applicant's advocate, so far as it is consistent with the urgency of the application, has a particular duty to see that the correct legal procedures and forms are used; that a written skeleton argument and a properly drafted order are prepared personally by her or him and lodged with the court before the oral hearing; and that, at the hearing, the court's attention is drawn to unusual features of the evidence adduced, to the applicable law and to the

---

[107] See *Hansard*, HC (6th series) Vol.315 (July 2, 1998); Home Secretary, the Rt. Hon. Mr Jack Straw M.P.

[108] See *Jameel v Wall Street Journal Europe Sprl* [2006] UKHL 44; [2007] 1 A.C. 359 in which Lord Hoffmann said,
   " . . . the standard of responsible journalism is made more specific by the code of practice which has been adopted by the newspapers and ratified by the Press Complaints Commission. This too . . . can provide valuable guidance." (at [55]).
As to the Ofcom Broadcasting Code, see para.24.35, above.

[109] *Hadmor Productions v Hamilton* [1983] 1 A.C. 191.

[110] E.g. the fact that the plaintiff misled the defendant and attempted to mislead the court are grounds for refusing (or discharging) an injunction: *Armstrong v Sheppard & Short* [1959] 2 Q.B. 384 at 397; *Dar Al Arkan Real Estate Development Co. v Al Refai* [2012] EWHC 3539 (Comm) (Andrew Smith J.).

[111] *Att-Gen v Sheffield Gas* (1852) 3 De G.M. & G. 304; *Greer v Bristol Tanning* (1885) 2 R.P.C. 268; per Cotton L.J. in *Poulett v Chatto & Windus* (1887) 4 T.L.R. at 142.

[112] *Monson v Tussauds* [1894] 1 Q.B. 671 at 697. This can also be regarded as a case where the possible defence of consent excluded the grant of an injunction.

[113] [2012] 1 W.L.R. 1003.

formalities and procedure to be observed including how, if at all, the order submitted departs from the model order.

31. Applications, especially those which seek derogations from open justice, must be supported with clear and cogent evidence which demonstrates that without the specific exception, justice could not be done.

32. Each application shall be subject to intense scrutiny. The need for intense scrutiny is particularly acute on without-notice applications, or where non-parties are or have been served with orders containing restrictions on access to documents, because, for instance, the order contains derogations from CPR PD 25A 9."

If an applicant fails to follow the recommended practice described in this document, the risk is that an otherwise meritorious application will be dismissed for that reason. Matters are apt to be finely balanced in any event. Lawyers considering acting for a client on such an application would therefore be well advised to acquaint themselves with the *Practice Guidance* and its detailed requirements. The procedural obligations are summarised at para.17 of the *Practice Guidance*.[114] Save in urgent cases an application for an interim injunction is to be made by an application notice.[115] Evidence is required to support the application[116] which must be set out either in a witness statement, or a statement of case, or the application, provided that in the latter instances they are verified by a statement of truth.[117] Evidence which is not contained in the application itself should be served with the application.[118] The application should also be accompanied by a draft of the order being sought,[119] which ought to be based on the model interim non-disclosure that accompanies the *Practice Guidance*.[120]

---

[114] "The applicant should prepare (a) the application / claim form; (b) a witness statement or statements justifying the need for an order; (c) legal submissions; (d) a draft order; and (e) an Explanatory Note (see paragraph 33, below). In the rare or urgent case where it is not possible to prepare such documentation prior to the hearing, the applicant should file a statement at the earliest practicable opportunity, setting out the information placed orally before the court".

Paras.33–34 of the Practice Guidance provide as follows:

"It is helpful if applications and orders are accompanied by an Explanatory Note, from which persons served can (a) readily understand the nature of the case, (b) ascertain whether they wish to attend the application hearing, and/or be legally represented at it, or, (c) where the application was heard without-notice, whether they wish to challenge the order. Where an interim non-disclosure order contains restrictions on access to documents it must be accompanied by an Explanatory Note when served on any non-party who was not present at the hearing of the application".

[115] CPR Pts 25 and 23.

[116] CPR r.25.3(2). Unless the court orders otherwise.

[117] CPR r.32.6(2)(b).

[118] CPR 23 PD, para.9.3.

[119] CPR 25A PD, para.2.4. A disk containing the draft of the order should also be made available.

[120] This is implicit in [30] of the *Practice Guidance*, which states that the applicant's advocate—so far as is consistent with the urgency of the application—has a particular duty (*inter alia*) to draw the court's attention to "the applicable law and to the formalities and procedure to be observed including how, if at all, the order submitted departs from the model order". See *ABK v KDT* [2013] EWHC 1192 (QB) at [12]. Nonetheless, the model order is in substance an order that

Urgent applications. An order for an interim injunction may be obtained   **25.26**
at any time including before proceedings are started, i.e. before a claim form
has been issued.[121] However, such an order will only be made if the matter is
genuinely urgent, or is otherwise necessary in the interests of justice.[122] This
means in practice that the intended claimant is required to demonstrate with
evidence that there is an imminent threat of the publication of defamatory
allegations likely to cause serious harm or damage. This will normally be
achieved by a witness statement or the draft of a witness statement, though
exceptionally the court may be prepared to accept an oral statement from the
intended claimant's advocate together with an undertaking to verify the
statement in a witness statement.[123] Except in the most urgent cases, the
advocate should prepare and lodge with the court before the hearing a skeleton
argument and a draft of the order sought.[124]

Attention must be given to s.12(2) of the Human Rights Act 1998 and the
need to pre-notify the intended defendant, unless there are compelling reasons
for not doing so.[125] If the intended defendant has not been notified or is not
present there is a duty on the intended claimant's advocate to disclose to the
court all material facts, and to refer to all relevant propositions of law and
rules of practice,[126] and failure to comply with this duty may result in the
injunction being set aside without regard to the merits.[127] The CPR provide for
the possibility of urgent applications being made by telephone.[128]

The Rules also specify the undertakings that must form part of the order,
unless the court orders otherwise, which will include undertakings as to
procedural steps required if the injunction has been obtained prior to the issue
of a claim form or application notice.[129] The order should also identify a
return date for a further hearing at which the intended defendant can be

---

is apposite to an application for an interim injunction restraining disclosure of private information, so if the application is one to restrain the publication of defamatory words, the precedent will
need to be modified significantly on that ground alone.

[121] CPR r.25.2(1).

[122] CPR r.25.2(2)(b). Where neither requirement is satisfied, it appears that there is no discretion to make an order—the court simply has no jurisdiction to do so: *Martin v Channel Four
Television Corp* [2009] EWHC 2788 (QB).

[123] See fn.114, above, setting out the text of [17] of the *Practice Guidance*, which explicitly
contemplates such a possibility.

[124] *Practice Guidance*, [17] and [30]; *Memory Corp v Sidhu (No.1)* [2000] 1 W.L.R. 1443 at
1460B–C, per Mummery L.J.

[125] See paras 25.2 and 25.19, above, and *Practice Guidance*, at [18]–[28].

[126] See *Memory Corp v Sidhu*, above, and n.25.3.5 in Vol.1 of *Civil Procedure* (*The White
Book*), where the topic is discussed at length. It may be noted that the first sentence of [30] in the
Practice Guidance appears to proceed on the footing that this obligation of 'full and frank
disclosure' applies on all applications for interim non-disclosure orders, not just applications
made without notice, but quaere whether this reflects the purpose of the rule, or the law.

[127] *R. v Kensington Income Tax Commissioners* [1917] 1 K.B. 486 at 514; *Brink's Mat Ltd v
Elcombe* [1988] 1 W.L.R. 1350, and cases referred to n.25.3.6 of Vol.1 of *The White Book*.

[128] CPR 25A PD, para.4.5.

[129] CPR 25A PD, para.5.1. In the case of without-notice applications, the claimant will also be
required to prepare a detailed note of the hearing and to undertake to serve a copy of it on the
respondent, and, in some cases, will also be required to undertake to commission and serve a

present and apply to vary or discharge the order if so advised.[130] The emphasis is on expedition and active case management[131]: extensions of time will not readily be granted[132] and delay, especially where it involves breaching undertakings[133] or missing court-appointed deadlines, will not be tolerated.[134] Parties will certainly not be permitted to 'warehouse' claims indefinitely.[135]

25.27 Open justice and derogations therefrom. The overarching principle is that hearings are held in public, and judgments and orders of the court are given publicly.[136] This principle applies to interim hearings, including applications for interim non-disclosure orders.[137] Even in claims for privacy and confidentiality, there is no general exception.[138] Derogations from open justice will only be justified in exceptional circumstances, where they are strictly necessary to secure the proper administration of justice. In order to secure the proper administration of justice in proceedings whose purpose is the protection of art.8 rights, the court may need to adopt procedures which seek to ensure that the vindication of those rights is not undermined by the way in which the court has processed an interim application.[139] Thus, applications for

---

transcript: see e.g. *RST v UVW* [2009] EWHC 2448 (QB); [2010] E.M.L.R. 13 at [32]; *G v Wikimedia Foundation Inc.* [2009] EWHC 3148 (QB); [2010] E.M.L.R. 14, at [28]–[32]; *Practice Guidance*, at [43]. In such cases, the claimant should also produce and serve an Explanatory Note: see *Practice Guidance*, at [33].

[130] CPR 25A PD para.5.1(3); *Practice Guidance*, at [38] and [40]. Where an injunction is made at a hearing of which all persons intended to be bound by it had notice, e.g. at the hearing of an application issued and served in the ordinary way in compliance with CPR Pt 23—particularly CPR rr.23.4 and 23.7—and the *Practice Guidance* following the issue of proceedings, there is no need for a return date: CPR 25A PD para.5.2; *Gold v Cox* [2012] EWHC 272 (QB), at [3].

[131] See *Practice Guidance*, [37]–[41]; *Hutcheson v Popdog Ltd* [2011] EWCA Civ 580; [2012] 1 W.L.R. 782; *AVB v TDD* [2013] EWHC 1705 (QB).

[132] *Giggs (previously known as CTB) v News Group Newspapers Ltd* [2012] EWHC 431 (QB); [2013] E.M.L.R. 5 at [108]–[111].

[133] See *Gray v UVW* [2010] EWHC 2367 (QB) at [36], [65]–[66], where the court emphasised that undertakings had to be honoured and if they were not, absent cogent explanation, sanctions would follow; *Goldsmith v BCD* [2011] EWHC 674 (QB).

[134] See *Giggs (previously known as CTB) v News Group Newspapers Ltd*, above, in which Tugendhat J. declined to reinstate injunctive proceedings which had been automatically struck out after the claimant failed to comply with the judge's direction to attend before the clerk of the lists on a particular date.

[135] See *JIH v News Group Newspapers Ltd* [2012] EWHC 2179 (QB) in which the court, of its own initiative, convened a hearing in a number of privacy cases in which interim injunctions had been granted in order to consider the approach to be taken where the parties had not taken steps to progress the claim towards settlement or trial. Now see CPR r.3.1(8) (in force with effect from April 1, 2013), which gives the court the power to contact the parties from time to time in order to monitor compliance with directions. The parties must respond promptly to any such enquiries from the court.

[136] *Scott v Scott* [1913] A.C. 417; *Re Guardian News & Media* [2010] UKSC 1; [2010] 2 A.C. 697.

[137] *Micallef v Malta* [2009] E.C.H.R. 1571, at [75] et seq.; *Donald v Ntuli* [2010] EWCA Civ 1276; [2011] 1 W.L.R. 294 at [50]; *Practice Guidance*, at [9].

[138] *Ambrosiadou v Coward* [2011] EWCA Civ 409; [2011] E.M.L.R. 21, at [50]–[54]; *Practice Guidance*, at [12].

[139] *Donald v Ntuli*, above, at [52]–[53]; *JIH v News Group Newspapers Ltd* [2011] EWCA Civ 42; [2011] 1 W.L.R. 1645, at [6]; *Practice Guidance*, at [10], [14].

derogations from open justice are more likely to be appropriate in confidence and privacy cases, where the very purpose of the claim is to prevent the disclosure of confidential or private information. Applications for interim injunctions will only be heard in private if and to the extent that the court is satisfied that by nothing short of the exclusion of the public can justice be done.[140] Anonymity will only be granted to one party or another where it is strictly necessary, and then only to that extent.[141] Anonymity was conferred on the parties to an application for an interim injunction in a defamation case where it appeared to the court that it would frustrate the purpose of the injunction if the application had the effect of making public the very allegations in respect of which the claimant was seeking relief, where there was evidence of blackmail, and where, overall, it was considered that the public interest in open justice would be best served by granting anonymity and revealing a suitable level of detail in a public judgment.[142] If an application is heard in private, an anonymity order may not be necessary, and vice versa.[143] Applications for derogations from open justice must be supported by evidence.[144] When considering a proposed derogation, the court will have regard to the rights not only of the parties but of any non-parties liable to be affected by the grant of a derogation and of the public at large, and furthermore it will take into account the general public interest in open justice and in the public reporting of court proceedings.[145] As such, interim non-disclosures containing derogations from the principle of open justice will not be granted simply because the parties consent.[146] Probably the only situation in which it will be appropriate for the court to grant an interim non-disclosure order that includes a prohibition on reporting the fact of the proceedings (a super-injunction) is where there is a risk that the respondent will act to defeat the injunction if notified of the application and short-term secrecy is necessary to enable the applicant safely to notify the respondent of the order.[147] The court's obligation to ensure open justice is a continuing one, so any derogations granted at a without-notice must be reviewed on the return date, and at any subsequent hearing.[148]

---

[140] *Ambrosiadou v Coward*, above.

[141] *Practice Guidance*, at [12]. See also *Goodwin v News Group Newspapers Ltd* [2011] EWHC 1437 (QB); [2011] E.M.L.R. 27 (concerning the anonymity order in respect of the woman with whom the claimant was alleged to be having an affair).

[142] *ZAM v CFW* [2011] EWHC 476 (QB) (Tugendhat J.). Anonymity was continued permanently following the trial of the action, on the blackmail ground: [2013] EWHC 662 (QB); [2013] E.M.L.R. 27, at [39]–[52] (Tugendhat J.).

[143] *JIH v News Group Newspapers Ltd*, above.

[144] *Practice Guidance*, at [13].

[145] *JIH v News Group Newspapers Ltd*, above, at [21]; *Practice Guidance*, at [14].

[146] *JIH v News Group Newspapers Ltd*, above, at [21(7)]; *Practice Guidance*, at [16].

[147] *DFT v TFD* [2010] EWHC 2335 (QB); *Terry (formerly LNS) v Persons Unknown*, above, at [137]–[139]; *Practice Guidance*, at [17].

[148] *Gray v UVW*, above.

25.28 **Undertaking.** Since an order for an interim injunction must normally contain an undertaking by the claimant to pay any damages which the defendant sustains as a result of the injunction which the court considers the claimant should pay,[149] the claimant's evidence should include evidence of his ability to meet any liability for damages as might arise by virtue of the undertaking.[150]

25.29 **Terms of order.** It is customary to seek to prohibit by the order repetition or further publication of the defamatory allegation complained of, or words to the same or similar effect. The addition of these general words should prevent a defendant publishing an allegation couched in different words but conveying the same defamatory sting as the original allegation. Thus in *Bentinck v Associated Newspapers*[151] an article conveying the meaning that the plaintiff had been mean in making no capital provision for his divorced wife was held to be in breach of an undertaking not to publish the words complained of—"[the plaintiff] is trying to divorce her without a penny, what a creep" —or words to similar effect, as the sting of the second article, culpable meanness, was substantially similar to that of the words complained of in the first article.

25.30 **Costs.** Traditionally, where an interim injunction is granted to hold the ring until the substantive dispute between the parties has been adjudicated upon at trial, the court would normally reserve the costs of the application to the trial judge, or order costs to be in the case.[152] However, costs are entirely in the discretion of the court, and in recent times judges have shown themselves willing to apportion the costs conclusively following the grant or refusal of an interim injunction.[153] Meanwhile, if an injunction is sought in circumstances where it clearly could not be granted (because, e.g. the defendant avers that he

---

[149] CPR 25A PD para.5.1(1).

[150] But note *Allen v Jambo Holdings Ltd* [1980] 1 W.L.R. 1252 CA in which it was said that the court would not deny a legally aided claimant an interlocutory injunction simply on the ground that his undertaking in damages would be of limited value, since questions of financial stability ought not to affect the question of the essential justice of the case. Such considerations are only likely to have greater force in circumstances where the claimant is concerned to protect his human rights and the court is under a statutory duty (s.6, Human Rights Act 1998) not to act incompatibly with those rights.

[151] [1999] E.M.L.R. 556.

[152] *Desquenne et Giral UK v Richardson* [2001] F.S.R. 2; *Kickers International S.A. v Paul Kettle Agencies Ltd* [1990] F.S.R. 436 (Hoffmann J.).

[153] That the Court of Appeal has no issue of principle with this approach can be seen from *Donald v Ntuli* [2010] EWCA Civ 1276; [2011] 1 W.L.R. 294 at [40]–[42], where the Court declined to interfere with an order of Eady J. whereby he had ordered the defendant to pay two thirds of the claimant's costs of and occasioned by the interim injunction application. The principle in *Desquenne et Giral UK v Richardson*, above, was said not to be a "hard and fast rule".

intends to plead and prove justification), the claimant is likely to be ordered to pay the costs of the application.[154]

Injunctions against persons whose identities are unknown. It is   **25.31**
permissible in an appropriate case to join a party to a claim by description rather than by name and for an injunction to be granted against such a person. This approach was sanctioned in *Bloomsbury Publishing Group v News Group Newspapers Ltd*[155] which was concerned with the theft, and attempted sale of extracts to newspapers, of an unpublished *Harry Potter* book. It was followed in *X v The Person or Persons Unknown,* the full title continuing, *who have offered and/ or provided the publishers of the Mail on Sunday, Mirror and Sun newspapers information about the status of the Claimant's marriage.*[156] As is evident from the title the injunction applied for was directed at unknown persons who were endeavouring to sell to newspapers a story about a celebrity's marriage, but the media were served with the injunction so that they would have knowledge of it and thus be bound on a *Spycatcher* basis[157] not to publish any such story which came into their possession. The newspapers complained about the lack of notice they had been given. Eady J. stated[158] that where a litigant intended to serve a prohibitory injunction upon one or more media publishers, intending that they should be bound by it, they should each

---

[154] See observations of Neuberger J. in *Picnic at Ascot v Kalus Derigs* [2001] F.S.R. 8 at [12]:
   "There may be cases where . . . the outcome of the hearing of the application for the interlocutory injunction should be so plain to the parties that the court should conclude that an order should be made against the defendant for wasting time and money in fighting the issue."
In a hopeless application by a claimant in a defamation action it would of course be the claimant who was wasting time and money. See also *Ascension Securities Ltd v Motley Fool Ltd* [2005] EWHC 3064 (Ch).
[155] [2003] EWHC 1205; [2003] 1 W.L.R. 1633.
[156] [2006] EWHC 2783 (QB); [2007] E.M.L.R. 290. Interim orders against persons unknown are now commonplace: see e.g. *TUV v Persons Unknown* [2010] EWHC 853 (QB); [2010] E.M.L.R. 19; *Terry (formerly LNS) v Persons Unknown* [2010] EWHC 119 (QB); [2010] E.M.L.R. 16 and *Contostavlos v Mendahun* [2012] EWHC 850 (QB). However, they are unlikely to be permitted to continue in perpetuity. Having regard to the importance in this field of active case management, if after a reasonable period of time an individual defendant cannot be identified, the interim injunction is likely to be discharged. See in this regard, *Terry,* above, at [134]–[136], [143], the *Practice Guidance,* at [41], and the commentary in the *Practice Guidance* on Clause 5(a) of the Model Order, as follows:
   "Where the respondent or defendant's identity is not known, or their whereabouts are unknown, there may be considerable problems in locating them in order to serve the claim form. This may necessitate an extension of time for service beyond the four month period. The court, by way of active case management, is required to ensure that the action is pursued with expedition. Indefinite extensions of time for service cannot be granted: *Terry* at [143]. A long-stop date may be inserted instead."
Nevertheless, see *AMP v Persons Unknown* [2011] EWHC 3454 (TCC) (a privacy and harassment case) at [20]–[21] (Ramsey J.) where it was envisaged that the proceedings would continue to trial without a named defendant.
[157] As to which, see para.25.19, above.
[158] At [18]. The applicant's obligation has now been explained as a duty to serve those media organisations which (so the applicant has solid grounds to believe) have displayed an interest in publishing the story, so that they have an opportunity to be heard: see fn.89, above.

be given a realistic opportunity to be heard on the appropriateness of the injunction and the scope of its terms. Procedures designed to bring about this result are now embodied in the *Practice Guidance on Interim Non-Disclosure Orders*.

25.32 Appeal. To appeal to the Court of Appeal from an order granting or refusing an interim injunction requires the permission of the judge or the Court of Appeal.[159] If permission is granted, the appeal may be expedited.[160]

SECTION 3. INJUNCTIONS TO RESTRAIN MISUSE OF PRIVATE INFORMATION

25.33 This section is concerned with interim injunctions directed against the publication of words or images which it is claimed constitute the misuse of private information relating to the claimant or an interference with his right to privacy protected by art.8 of the ECHR.[161] A pre-publication injunction,[162] if one can be obtained, is undoubtedly the preferred remedy in this field, and is sometimes said to be the only truly effective remedy, as the privacy of the information will cease to exist once it is widely disseminated and an award of damages, which is likely to be modest, will not put matters right.[163] The

---

[159] CPR r.52.3.

[160] *Unilever Plc v Chefaro Proprietaries Ltd (Practice Note)* [1995] 1 W.L.R. 243, 246–247; *Practice Guidance*, at [46]. It will depend on the circumstances of each case whether, and to what extent, expedition is necessary.

[161] This cause of action is discussed in detail in Ch.22, above.

[162] Or an injunction which arrests a continuing publication on the internet.

[163] The Court of Appeal in *A v B Plc* [2003] Q.B. 195 described an injunction as "the only remedy which is of any value" in a privacy case: at [11(ii)]. See also *Douglas v Hello Ltd* [2005] EWCA Civ 595; [2006] Q.B. 125 at [251]–[259]. The claimants had commenced an action in respect of the publication of unauthorised photographs taken at their wedding. Part of their claim was invasion of privacy. An interim injunction was obtained but it was discharged by the Court of Appeal. At the trial of the action the claimants were successful, a decision which was appealed by the defendant. The Court of Appeal, which dismissed the appeal against the judgment in favour of the claimants based on privacy, concluded its judgment by "revisiting" the decision to lift the interim injunction. It considered the decision was wrong:

"the award of damages [£14,600] eventually made to the [claimants], although unassailable in principle, was not at a level which, when measured against the effect of refusing them an interlocutory injunction, can fairly be characterized as adequate or satisfactory. Only by grant of an interlocutory injunction could the [claimant's] rights have been satisfactorily protected."

These sentiments were echoed by Eady J., in *Mosley v News Group Newspapers Ltd* [2008] EWHC 1777 (QB); [2008] E.M.L.R. 20 at [236]: " . . . it has to be accepted that an infringement of privacy cannot ever be effectively compensated by a monetary award . . . [N]o amount of damages can fully compensate the Claimant for the damage done. He is hardly exaggerating when he says that his life was ruined". The award of damages was £60,000. Eady J. also put the matter as follows in *Mosley* at [209]: "Once the cat is out of the bag, and the intrusive publication has occurred, most people would think that there was little to gain." But cf. *Mosley v UK* [2012] E.M.L.R. 1 in which the European Court of Human Rights rejected Mr Mosley's arguments to the effect that a legal system which failed to enable individuals to seek a pre-publication injunction to protect their privacy was at odds with art.8 (his proposal was that the media should be under a legal obligation to notify in advance those whose private information they intended to disclose).

principles governing the grant or refusal of an interim injunction to restrain misuse of private information are now well-settled.[164] The procedural requirements for making such an application are described in detail in the *Practice Guidance on Interim Non-Disclosure Orders*[165]; indeed, the *Practice Guidance* (including the Model Order attached to it) is principally directed to this topic.

Evidence. The claimant will have to show, as he would if seeking a defamation injunction, that the defendant was threatening to publish, or repeat the publication of, information which he claims is private.[166] He will also have to explain the grounds, if they are not self evident, for claiming that he has a reasonable expectation of privacy in respect of such information.[167] Information in the public domain will not generally be private,[168] and information that may have been private is likely to lose its character of privacy once it is in the public domain. This does not mean that any release or publication of private information will result in the information no longer qualifying for the purposes of legal proceedings for injunctive protection,[169] but the court will have to be satisfied that the information is not publicly available so that it cannot

25.34

See also the discussion in *Spelman v Express Newspapers* [2012] EWHC 355 (QB) at [109]–[118] per Tugendhat J.

[164] An authoritative account of the relevant principles may be found in *Hutcheson (previously 'KGM') v News Group Newspapers Ltd* [2011] EWCA Civ 808; [2012] E.M.L.R. 2 at [17]–[35].

[165] [2012] 1 W.L.R. 1003; see para.25.25ff, above.

[166] "So far as the burden of proof is concerned, it is, in my judgment, unnecessary to take time over a somewhat theoretical discussion as to legal, evidentiary and shifting burdens. Suffice to say that it is for the applicant for interim relief to make out the case of an infringement of his art.8 rights and for the respondent to raise a case of freedom of expression under art.10. But, ultimately, in a matter such as this, it is plain that the burden rests on the applicant to satisfy the requirements of s.12(3) of the HRA, or fail.": *Hutcheson (previously 'KGM') v News Group Newspapers Ltd* [2011] EWCA Civ 808; [2012] E.M.L.R. 2, per Gross L.J. at [31] with whom Lord Neuberger M.R. and Etherton L.J. agreed. See further, para.25.25, above.

[167] *Campbell v MGN Ltd* [2004] UKHL 22; [2004] 2 A.C. 457, Lord Nicholls at [20]–[21]: "essentially the touchstone of private life is whether in respect of the disclosed acts the person in question had a reasonable expectation of privacy". " . . . [T]he question whether there is a reasonable expectation of privacy is a broad one, which takes account of all the circumstances of the case." *Murray v Big Pictures (UK) Ltd* [2008] EWCA Civ 446; [2009] Ch. 481 at [36]. The test as to whether the applicant has a reasonable expectation of privacy or whether the respondent is under an enforceable obligation of confidence in respect of the relevant information is an objective one: *Author of a Blog v Times Newspapers Ltd* [2009] EWHC 1358 (QB); [2009] E.M.L.R. 22.

[168] *Att-Gen v Guardian Newspapers (No.2)* [1990] 1 A.C. 109, per Lord Goff at 282: "Once [information] has entered what is called the public domain . . . then, as a general rule, the principle of confidentiality can have no application to it."

[169] See Eady J. in *McKennitt v Ash* [2005] EWHC 3003 (QB); [2006] E.M.L.R. 10 at [199]: "it does not necessarily follow that because personal information has been revealed impermissibly to one set of newspapers, or to readers within one jurisdiction, that there can be no further intrusion upon a claimant's privacy by further revelations. Fresh revelations to different groups of persons can still cause distress and damage to an individual's emotional well-being."

sensibly be regarded as private,[170] and that an injunction will serve some purpose in protecting the claimant's asserted rights.[171] Unless it is plainly unnecessary, the claimant should provide some evidence to indicate that the information is not in the public domain, or that the extent or manner of public knowledge of the information is not such as to compromise his claim to privacy in respect of it. The fact that a court will refuse an injunction which serves no useful function is a compelling reason for seeking an interim injunction, particularly where the national media are the anticipated publishers, without delay.

The evidence required from a defendant contesting the application will, of course, depend on the grounds of his opposition. The defence that the information is in the public domain will require its widespread dissemination and availability to be demonstrated.[172] If it is contended on other grounds that the information is not private or is not information in respect of which the claimant has a reasonable expectation of privacy[173] that will almost certainly necessitate disclosure of how the information was obtained.[174] Thus, if the information is in the form of a photograph the court should be informed of where and in what circumstances it was taken. If it is alleged that the claimant has consented to the publication of the information, details of such consent should be given, which would have to negative any suggestion that the information was disclosed to, say a journalist or a friend, confidentially. The fact that there are two persons involved, as is the case, for example, in a 'kiss and tell' story, does not mean that one of those persons has an inalienable right to disclose information which may transgress the other's right to privacy.[175] A defendant may claim that the information in question related to an aspect of the claimant's private life about which he had given false publicity, and the defendant was entitled to publish what was the truth.[176] Evidence of the false

---

[170] The test suggested by Eady J. in *McKennitt v Ash*, derived from Lord Goff's definition of "public domain" in *Att-Gen v Guardian Newspapers (No.2)*, above, was whether the information in question was so generally accessible that, in all the circumstances, it could not be regarded as confidential (at [81]).

[171] In *Mosley v News Group Newspapers Ltd* [2008] EWHC 681 (QB) Eady J. refused an injunction restraining continued publication about the claimant's private life on the defendant's website on the grounds that the story had received massive coverage in newspapers and websites throughout the world, and the online version on the defendant's website had received nearly two million visits. "The dam had burst" remarked the judge, and the injunction would be a "futile gesture". See also *Re East Sussex County Council* [2009] EWHC 935 (Fam); [2009] 2 F.L.R. 852 and *TSE v News Group Newspapers Ltd* [2011] EWHC 1308 (QB).

[172] See fn.168, above.

[173] See fn.167, above.

[174] See *Murray v Big Pictures (UK) Ltd*, above at [36].

[175] "It does not follow, because one can reveal one's own private life, that one can expose confidential matters in respect of which others are entitled to protection if their consent is not forthcoming." Eady J. in *McKennitt v Ash*, above at [77]; See also *Re Angela Roddy (A Minor)* [2003] EWHC 2927 (Fam); [2004] E.M.L.R. 8; *CC v AB* [2006] EWHC 3083 (QB); [2007] E.M.L.R. 11; *CTB v News Group Newspapers Ltd* [2011] EWHC 1232 (QB) at [34]–[38]; *McClaren v News Group Newspapers Ltd* [2012] EWHC 2466 (QB); [2012] E.M.L.R. 33.

[176] See *Campbell v MGN*, above, in which the claimant accepted that she could not complain of the publication of the statement that she was receiving treatment for drug addiction, as she had

publicity would have to be provided. This kind of defence can be regarded as falling within the general bracket of public interest, the ground most commonly relied upon by the media when seeking to defend publication of articles or stories claimed to breach rights of privacy or confidentiality. Evidence of the factual basis of the public interest would have to be put before the court.

Balancing competing rights under articles 8 and 10. An injunction to restrain publication of private information is frequently resisted on the grounds that it would involve interference with the defendant's rights of freedom of expression under art.10 ECHR, and that is invariably the contention where it is claimed that dissemination of the information is in the public interest. In such cases the court has the task of striking a balance between the competing rights under art.8 and art.10, neither of which has primacy.[177] This requires the court to undertake "an intense focus on the comparative importance of the specific rights being claimed in the individual case".[178] This will not often be an exercise which can satisfactorily be carried out on an interim application, but the court must do its best on the evidence presented to it to decide whether the claim is of sufficient strength to surmount the threshold imposed by s.12(3) of the Human Rights Act 1998.[179] Provided that this threshold is crossed, a court will be inclined to protect claimed private information from publication by injunctive relief until trial: judges will no doubt have in mind the ultimate verdict of the Court of Appeal in *Douglas v Hello! Ltd* that an interim injunction should have been granted.[180]   **25.35**

Truth. It is no answer to an application for an injunction to restrain publication of private information that the information is true (the rule in *Bonnard v Perryman* does not apply), or, subject to the court taking the view that the nub of the applicant's complaint is libel, that it is untrue.[181] But truth or falsity   **25.36**

---

repeatedly asserted in public that she did not take drugs. See also *Spelman v Express Newspapers* [2012] EWHC 355 (QB) and *McClaren v News Group Newspapers Ltd*, above.

[177] See *Campbell v MGN*, above.

[178] Per Lord Steyn in *Re S* [2004] UKHL 47; [2005] 1 A.C. 593 at [17]. See also *BBC, Re* [2010] UKHL 34; [2010] 1 A.C. 145.

[179] See para.25.21, above.

[180] See fn.163, above and [257] of the judgment: " . . . the refusal of an interlocutory judgment in a case such as this represents a strong disincentive to respect for aspects of private life, which the Convention intends should be respected."

[181] "The foundation for the application for an interim injunction in cases of this kind is the (alleged) infringement of privacy. By contrast with the law of defamation (perhaps more familiar, at least to common lawyers), the fact that the information is true is, of itself, no bar to the obtaining of an injunction; instead and often, if not invariably, the fact that the information is true is the reason why injunctive relief is sought":
Hutcheson (previously 'KGM') v News Group Newspapers Ltd [2011] EWCA Civ 808; [2012] E.M.L.R. 2 at [33] per Gross L.J. See also paras 25.14 and 25.16 (concerning *McKennitt v Ash* above. As such, nor will it be a bar to relief if the applicant declines to tell the court whether the information is true or false: see *WER v REW* [2009] EWHC 1029 (QB); [2009] E.M.L.R. 17 at [9].

may be a relevant factor in deciding whether relief ought to be granted, or in relation to any ancillary orders sought.[182]

SECTION 4. INJUNCTIONS TO RESTRAIN FALSE STATEMENTS ABOUT PARLIAMENTARY, MUNICIPAL OR EUROPEAN PARLIAMENTARY CANDIDATES

25.37 Representation of the People Act 1983, section 106. Under this section of the Act[183] it is an illegal practice for a person before or during an election,[184] for the purpose of affecting the return of any candidate at the election, to make or publish any false statement of fact in relation to the candidate's personal character or conduct, unless he can show he had reasonable grounds for believing, and did believe, the statement to be true.[185] A person making or publishing such a statement may be restrained by interim or perpetual injunction by the High Court or a county court[186] from any repetition of that false statement or a false statement of similar character and, for the purpose of granting an interim injunction, prima facie proof of the falsity of the statement shall be sufficient.[187]

25.38 Proof. On an application for an injunction under this Act the burden lies on the claimant to prove that the statement is false,[188] and the remedy is by injunction only. As prima facie proof is sufficient for an interim injunction, it would seem that the rule in *Bonnard v Perryman* does not apply. If the defendant cannot displace the prima facie case of falsity, an injunction may be granted notwithstanding the defendant's insistence that he can and will prove at trial the statement to be true.

25.39 Statement calculated to influence the electors. In order to come within the Act "the false statement may or may not be such as would sustain an action of defamation".[189] It is sufficient if it is calculated to influence the electors, as, for instance, a statement that a candidate in a county constituency had "shot a fox or that a candidate, who is a temperate man, had been seen

---

[182] See e.g. *XJA v News Group Newspapers Ltd* [2010] EWHC 3174 (QB), at [15].

[183] The Act replaced the Representation of the People Act 1949. S.106 substantially re-enacts s.91 of the 1949 Act, which re-enacted ss.1 and 3 of the Corrupt and Illegal Practices Prevention Act 1895.

[184] Defined as "a parliamentary election or an election under the Local Government Act": s.202(1).

[185] S.106(1).

[186] An appeal lies to the High Court from any order made by a county court: s.106(9).

[187] S.106(3).

[188] A statement may be false by reason of what is omitted: *R. v Kylsant* [1932] 1 K.B. 442; *R. v Bishirgian* [1936] 1 All E.R. 586. Economy with the truth thus may result in a false statement.

[189] Per Madden J. in *North Louth Case* [1911] 6 O'M. & H. at 166.

taking a glass of sherry".[190] The statement complained of must be a statement of fact, and not merely of opinion:

> "A mere argumentative statement of the conduct of a public man, although it may be in respect of his private life, is not always, and in many cases certainly would not be, a false statement of fact".[191]

The statement must relate to the "personal character or conduct" of the claimant. It was held that calling a person a communist was not such a statement.[192] However, the dividing line between what is personal and what is political is not always readily apparent. For example, if a candidate at an election who professed to have been a consistent supporter by his vote of old age pensions or of trade unions were falsely charged with having opposed them by his votes, such statement could be said to affect his veracity and honour as well as his political character.[193] It is irrelevant whether the statement complained of has or has not been provoked by a statement of a similar character made by the claimant.[194]

European Parliament. The section now applies in European Parliamentary elections.[195]   **25.40**

---

[190] Per Pollock B. in *Borough of Sunderland Case* [1896] 5 O'M. & H. 53 at 62.

[191] *Borough of Sunderland Case*, above; *Ellis v National Union* [1900] 109 L.T.J. 493, where it was held that "radical traitors" was a statement of opinion and not of fact. Cf. Ch.12 concerning honest comment.

[192] *Burns v Associated Newspapers* [1926] 42 T.L.R. 37.

[193] Cf. Gibson J. in *North Louth Case*, above, at 158.

[194] Per Kennedy J. in *Monmouth Boroughs Case* [1901] 5 O'M. & H. at 174; per Madden J. in *North Louth* Case at 171.

[195] S.3, Sch.1, para.2(3), (4) of the European Parliamentary Elections Act 1978 and European Parliamentary Elections Regulations 1986, SI 1986/2209, reg.5(1), Sch.1.

SECTION 1. INTRODUCTION

Generally. Statements of case in an action for defamation are extremely **26.1** important. Due in part to the ambiguity of words and their capacity for inference and implication, pleadings, particularly in relation to the issues of meaning and reference to the claimant, can on occasion become tortuous and complex.[1] The increasing tendency has been to require the parties to set out

---

[1] In *Polly Peck Plc v Trelford* [1986] Q.B. 1000 at 1020, O'Connor L.J. commented that pleadings in libel actions had become an artificial minuet. Three years later May L.J. disagreed: he thought that an "archaic sarabande" was closer to the mark, since to call libel pleading a minuet was "to give it too delicate and attractive a description" (*Morrell v International Thomson Publishing Ltd*, C.A., unreported, May 16, 1989). In *Singh v Gillard* [1988] N.L.J.R. 144 Lord Donaldson M.R. said that the practice and procedure attendant upon the administration of justice in the context of claims for defamation was the last refuge of complexity and technicality in the law. See Kirby J. in *Favell v Queensland Newspapers Pty Ltd* [2005] HCA 52 at [21]–[22], to like effect. In *Lait v Evening Standard Ltd* [2011] EWCA Civ 859; [2011] 1 W.L.R. 2973 Laws L.J. said at [27],

"it is almost a commonplace that the law of defamation has become mired in technicality (see for example Diplock L.J.'s rueful reference to "this protracted exercise in logical positivism" in *Slim v Daily Telegraph Ltd* [1968] 2 Q.B. 157, 171E); and that is no service to litigants or the general public. However, in justice to practitioners in the field (and, with respect, the judges who have developed the law), this is an area where there are bound to be subtle distinctions. The reason is that . . . the foundation of the law of defamation is the concept of meaning: and the idea of meaning has over the centuries scratched the heads of the philosophers, never mind the lawyers. But it was the philosopher Ludwig Wittgenstein who said that everything that can

their respective cases with as much clarity[2] and openness as possible. The Practice Direction supplementing CPR Pt 53 on Defamation Claims provides that statements of case should be confined to the information necessary to inform the other party of the case he has to meet.[3] Such information should be set out precisely and in a manner proportionate to the subject matter of the claim.[4]

26.2 Material facts. The particulars of claim must contain a concise statement of the material facts on which the claimant relies, but not the evidence by which they are to be proved.[5] The claimant should state all the facts necessary for the

---

be said, can be said clearly (though he comprehensively broke his own rule); and we owe a duty to get this chapter of the common law, as much as any other, as clear as it can be made."

[2] See *Ashcroft v Foley* [2012] EWCA Civ 423; [2012] E.M.L.R. 25.

In *Burrows v Knightley* (1987) 10 N.S.W.L.R 651, Hunt J. commented as follows: at 658,

"Pleaders in defamation actions should not overlook either the nature of the litigation in which their clients are involved (which is already sufficiently, if necessarily, complicated) or the nature of the tribunal which will be deciding its result (a jury). The issues in a defamation action should always, so far as possible, be made simple and straightforward, not perplexing and pedantic or convoluted and confusing."

In *McPhilemy v Times Newspapers Ltd* [1999] 3 All E.R. 775, Lord Woolf M.R. made the following observations at 792 in relation to libel pleadings:

"I do not . . . suggest that the existing pleadings are other than in the form which is commonly adopted by libel practitioners. However, undoubtedly considerable time, energy and money have been incurred in producing those pleadings and the question arises whether this scale of expenditure is necessary or desirable. An indication of the scale is provided by the fact that the reply is already in a reamended form . . . As well as their expense, excessive particulars can achieve directly the opposite result from that which is intended. They can obscure the issues rather than providing clarification . . . [this] case is overburdened with particulars and simpler and shorter statements of case would have been sufficient."

In *Radu v Houston* [2009] EWHC 398 (QB) Eady J. observed at [15] that nothing in *McPhilemy* should be taken to sanction any relaxation of the basic rule that a claimant is entitled to know the case he has to meet.

[3] In *Lucas-Box v News Group Ltd* [1986] 1 W.L.R. 147 Ackner L.J. stated at 151:

"It is axiomatic that the function of pleadings is to define the issues between the parties, so that both the plaintiff and the defendant know what is the other side's case and thus everyone, counsel, judge and jury, are able to focus upon the real nature of the dispute. Although to some it may be a startling observation, we can see no reason why libel litigation should be immune from ordinary pleading rules."

"The ultimate purpose of one party's pleading is to inform the other party of the case that is being made out against him":

Conticorp SA v The Central Bank of Ecuador [2007] UKPC 40 at [38].

[4] CPR PD 53, para.2.1. In *McPhilemy v Times Newspapers Ltd* [1999] 3 All E.R. 775, Lord Woolf M.R. observed that pleadings were:

"required to mark out the parameters of the case that is being advanced by each party. In particular, they are still critical to identify the issues and the extent of the dispute between the parties. What is important is that the pleadings should make clear the general nature of the case of the pleader."

However, he noted that, after disclosure and the exchange of witness statements, pleadings frequently become only of historic interest and that in the majority of proceedings identification of the documents upon which a party relies, together with copies of that party's witness statements, will make the details of the nature of the case which the other side has to meet obvious and will reduce the need for particulars.

[5] CPR r.16.4(1)(a); *Glossop v Spindler* (1885) 29 S.J. 556. In *Ontulmus v Collett* [2013] EWHC 980 (QB) the defendants applied to strike out parts of the Particulars of Claim said to be "background". They submitted that CPR r.16.4(1)(a) requires the particulars of claim to include

purpose of formulating a complete cause of action. These facts are the publication by the defendant,[6] the words published,[7] that they were published of the claimant,[8] (where necessary) the facts relied on as causing them to be understood as defamatory[9] or as referring to the claimant and knowledge of these facts by those to whom the words were published,[10] and, where the words are slander not actionable per se, any additional facts making them actionable,[11] such as that they were calculated to disparage the claimant in an office held by him or that they have caused special damage.[12] When s.1(2), Defamation Act 2013 comes into force, a body that trades for profit will have to set out how the publication has caused or is likely to cause serious financial loss.

Particulars. The degree of particularity required will of course depend **26.3** upon the facts of each case. However, as a general rule, as much certainty and particularity must be insisted on as is reasonable having regard to the circumstances and to the nature of the acts alleged.[13] The CPR contain express requirements that particulars be given of certain allegations.[14] While particulars usually set out specific matters intended to be proved, a party may, in an appropriate and proper case, also aver that he intends to rely on an inference from facts which he can prove.[15] The court may at any time order a party to

---

a concise statement of the facts on which the claimant relies and nothing more. Tugendhat J. agreed. The Judge said at [27], " . . . pleading matters which are not those on which a claimant relies is contrary to the overriding objective . . . ".

[6] See Ch.6, above.

[7] See paras 3.1–3.5, above.

[8] See Ch.7, above.

[9] Note that s.1(1), Defamation Act 2013 (not yet in force) prospectively provides that a statement is not defamatory unless its publication has caused or is likely to cause serious harm to the reputation of the claimant. Where the claimant is a body that trades for profit, harm will not be serious harm unless it has caused or is likely to cause the body serious financial loss: s.1(2). It is already established that there is a threshold of seriousness which must be surmounted before words will be considered to be defamatory: see *Thornton v Telegraph Media Group Ltd* [2010] EWHC 1414 (QB); [2011] 1 W.L.R. 1985; *Cammish v Hughes* [2012] EWCA Civ 1655; [2013] E.M.L.R. 13 at [38].

[10] See paras 7.2–7.4, above. This is sometimes referred to as a "reference innuendo"; see, e.g. *Birchwood Homes Ltd v Robertson* [2003] EWHC 293 (QB), per Eady J.

[11] See Ch.5, above.

[12] For the requirements of pleading where aggravated or exemplary damages are claimed, see paras 26.29, 26.33, below. For the requirements of pleading where the claim is for malicious falsehood see para.26.42, below.

[13] *Ratcliffe v Evans* [1892] 2 Q.B. 524 at 532, per Bowen L.J.; *Tesla Motors Ltd v British Broadcasting Corp* [2013] EWCA Civ 152.

[14] See, e.g. CPR r.16.4(1)(b) (interest); CPR r.16.4(1)(c) and CPR PD 53, para.2.10 (damages); CPR PD 53, para.2.3(2) (innuendo meaning).

[15] *Fullam v Newcastle Chronicle* [1977] 1 W.L.R. 651 at 659, per Scarman L.J. In *Mills v MGN Ltd* [2002] EWHC 1384 (QB), in which one of the issues was pleading an inference of "mercenary calculation" in the context of a claim for exemplary damages, Eady J. applied *Scrutton v Bone*, unreported, November 20, 2001, (Ch), per Sir Andrew Morritt V-C in holding that the court was entitled to scrutinise at the pre-trial stage whether or not on the pleaded facts an inference was viable or not and, if not, could rule out the inference contended for. Moreover, in reliance upon *Turner v Metro-Goldwyn-Mayer Pictures Ltd* [1950] 1 All E.R. 449 and *Alexander v Arts Council of Wales* [2001] EWCA Civ 514; [2001] 1 W.L.R. 1840, Eady J. held

clarify any matter which is in dispute in the proceedings or give additional information in relation to any such matter.[16]

Section 2. Introductory Facts

26.4 Introductory facts. It is customary to give a short account of who the parties are. In the normal case this will be limited to a brief description of their occupations and (if appropriate) their relationship, e.g. where they are trade rivals. This is a convenient practice, especially where personal details of one or other party are, or may become, material to specific issues in the action: the relevant part of the introductory averment can later be incorporated by reference into the particulars pleaded in relation to that issue. In cases where the claimant's standing to sue, e.g. whether a corporation trades for profit or has a reputation which is capable of being damaged by the alleged libel, may be in issue,[17] the claimant should provide sufficient details of his standing in his prefatory averments. The defendant will be entitled to such additional information in relation to any prefatory averment as may be reasonably necessary and proportionate to enable the defendant to prepare his own case or understand the case he has to meet.[18]

Section 3. Publication

26.5 Details of publication: libel. The general principle demands only that the defendant be given due notice of the case he has to meet, and there is no fixed rule as to what amounts to a sufficient averment of publication.[19] However,

---

that "equivocal facts pleaded will not suffice when the key to the claim is necessarily an inference as to the defendant's subjective state of mind ... ". If, therefore, a pleader wishes to set up a case based on inference, he should take care to set out clearly both the inference contended for and the alleged factual basis for it. See also *Three Rivers DC v Bank of England (No.3)* [2003] 2 A.C. 1, in which Lord Hobhouse at [161] observed:

"Dishonesty is not to be inferred from evidence which is equally consistent with mere negligence. At the pleading stage the party making the allegation of dishonesty has to be prepared to particularise it and, if he is unable to do so, his allegation will be struck out. The allegation must be made upon the basis of evidence which will be admissible at the trial",

a passage relied upon by Tugendhat J. in *Bray v Deutsche Bank AG* [2008] EWHC 1263 (QB); [2009] E.M.L.R. 12 at [35], in relation to a plea of malice in a libel claim.

[16] See CPR r.18.1(1) and para.26.44, below.

[17] See Ch.8. In *Abbey v Gilligan* [2012] EWHC 3217 (QB); [2013] E.M.L.R. 12 one of the reasons the claimant failed in his breach of confidence and misuse of private information claims was because he was held not to have title to sue in respect of the emails that were the subject of the action.

[18] See *Gaston v United Newspapers* (1915) 32 T.L.R. 143 CA.

[19] CPR PD 53, para.2.1(1) specifies no more than that: "In a claim for libel the publication the subject of the claim must be identified in the claim form." But note also the more detailed requirements of para.3.2 of the Pre-Action Protocol for Defamation. More generally, in *Wallis v Valentine* [2002] EWCA Civ 1034; [2003] E.M.L.R. 8, the Court of Appeal upheld the striking out of a claim on the footing there was no evidence of publication fit to be left to a jury save to the claimant's partner and to continue the action in respect of those alleged publications alone would be an abuse of the process. In *Bataille v Newland* [2002] EWHC 1692 (QB), by contrast, Eady J. allowed to proceed to trial a substantially inferential case that one of the defendants had participated in publishing the words complained of, as did Tugendhat J. in *Bray v Deutsche Bank*

unless there are good grounds for variance,[20] the particulars of claim should allege, in respect of each publication relied on as a cause of action, that the words were published by the defendant on a specific occasion[21] to a named person or persons[22] other than the claimant.[23] Where the publication complained of is in a newspaper, book or other publication "to the world at large", the claimant is not expected to plead particular acts of publication, the court accepting that publication in such cases is to be inferred.[24] Where the publication complained of is on the internet, the claimant must identify the individual readers or plead a platform of facts from which an inference of publication can be drawn.[25] Where the defendant is an internet service provider, the claimant should also plead the basis on which it is alleged that the defendant is a publisher of the words complained of, and, as appropriate, specify the facts of

---

AG [2008] EWHC 1263 (QB); [2009] E.M.L.R. 12. In *Campbell v Safra* [2006] EWHC 819 (QB), Eady J. entered summary judgment for the defendant in a libel claim on the ground that there was no evidential basis to support the claimant's case that the defendant was responsible for publication of the article complained of, and the inherent probabilities pointed against the defendant's involvement. At [22], it was observed that "Bare assertion [of publication] is not enough. Nor is the claimant's suspicion or belief".

[20] For the way to proceed where the claimant lacks definite information about the publication, see para.26.7, below.

[21] The time and place of publication are generally essential, so that the defendant can identify the case made against him and, in particular, consider whether the action is time-barred or not. It is not proper to allege publication of defamatory matter in certain places "and elsewhere"; the claimant should specifically identify all the alleged locations of publication, *Webb v Bache* (1993) 117 F.L.R. 126.

[22] *Bradbury v Cooper* (1883) 12 Q.B.D. 94; *Roselle v Buchanan* (1886) 16 Q.B.D. 656; *Davey v Bewtinck* [1893] 1 Q.B. 185 CA.

[23] Particulars of claim which do not allege publication to some third person disclose no cause of action: *Hall v Geiger* (1929) 41 B.C.R. 481.

[24] *Fullam v Newcastle Chronicle* [1977] 1 W.L.R. 651 CA at 654–655 and 657; *Lazarus v Deutsche Lufthansa* (1985) 1 N.S.W.L.R. 188 at 193, per Hunt J.:

" . . . in both oral and written defamation cases, particulars should be supplied of the identity of the persons to whom the publication is alleged to have been made when that identity is relevant to the plaintiff's or the defendant's case. That identity will usually be relevant in oral defamation cases and in written defamation cases where it was not published in the mass media; but that identity will not usually be relevant in mass media case".

See also *McLean v David Syme* (1970) 92 W.N. (N.S.W.) 611 at 625:

"Although our courts have not adopted expressly the theory of the single publication rule, it has not been the practice in action for defamation arising out of the publication of an issue of a newspaper that the plaintiff should plead and prove each separate publication of the newspaper. Defamation actions of this kind have been dealt with on the footing that the plaintiff may recover damages in respect of the entire issue of a newspaper so long as he proves a publication on one occasion, notwithstanding that there may be multiple publications".

[But note s.8 of the Defamation Act 2013 for its effect on subsequent publications of the same or substantially the same material by the same person].

Caution should be exercised where complaint is made in respect of the publication of an issue of a newspaper in more than one jurisdiction. In such a case, the proper form of pleading is to plead the publication in each jurisdiction as a separate cause of action (see per Asprey J.A. in *McLean v David Syme* at 617). In addition, where an innuendo meaning is relied on, it may be necessary to plead the identity of the persons alleged to have had knowledge of the extrinsic facts, even in the case of a widely disseminated publication; see para 26 23, below.

[25] *Al Amoudi v Brisard* [2006] EWHC 1062 (QB); [2007] 1 W.L.R. 113; *Carrie v Tolkien* [2009] EWHC 29 (QB); [2009] E.M.L.R. 9 at [17]–[19]. See para.6.3, above.

his case on notification.[26] By virtue of s.10 of the Defamation Act 2013 (when it comes into force), where a claim is brought against a person who is not the author, editor or publisher[27] of the statement complained of, the claimant ought to state why it is not reasonably practicable for an action to be brought against the author, editor or publisher.

26.6 Details of publication: slander. The actual words must be ascertained and pleaded.[28] It is important to plead the names of the persons to whom they were spoken, when they were spoken and in what circumstances[29]:

> "Slander uttered to one person might not be actionable if uttered to another person; in that sense, therefore, it becomes essential to see to whom it is uttered, and that is part of the case which has to be stated, and which the other side is entitled to know for the purpose of meeting the charge."[30]

If the slander was uttered in a public room the defendant is entitled to "the best particulars the plaintiff can give of the persons present when the alleged slander was uttered".[31] The court will not order particulars where it would be unreasonable or oppressive to do so, e.g. where the slander is alleged to have been uttered in the public street[32] or where the claimant cannot recall the precise date.[33]

26.7 Publication to persons unknown. If the claimant does not know the name of the person or persons to whom publication is alleged, they must nevertheless be sufficiently described as to enable them to be identified. In very exceptional cases, particulars of claim may be permitted to stand notwithstanding that they fail adequately to identify the circumstances in which

---

[26] See para.6.20, above. In *Tamiz v Google* [2013] EWCA Civ 68; [2013] 1 W.L.R. 2151 the Court of Appeal upheld Eady J.'s conclusion that the defendant was not a primary publisher of the allegedly defamatory comments at common law since, although it facilitated publication of the blog and the comments posted on it, it had no prior knowledge of or control over the content of the blog. However, the Court of Appeal held, *contra* Eady J., that the defendant arguably became responsible as a publisher after it had been notified of the comments and allowed them to continue to be published. While it is for the defendant to raise, as appropriate, any of the various statutory defences that relate to publication on the internet, a claimant would be well advised to set out the basis on which he alleges that the defendant is responsible as a publisher.

[27] As those terms are defined in Defamation Act 1996, s.1.

[28] See para.26.13, below.

[29] CPR PD 53, para.2.4; see also CPR PD 53, para.2.2(2). Regarding the "public" status of statements of case, see *Qadir v Associated Newspapers Ltd* [2013] EWHC 2606 (QB); [2013] E.M.L.R. 15 at [27]–[40].

[30] *Bishop v Bishop* [1901] P. 325 at 328, per Jeune P; *Freer v Zeb* [2008] EWHC 212 (QB) at [27].

[31] *Williams v Ramsdale* (1887) 36 W.R. 125; *Ellison v Taioroa* (1898) 16 N.Z.L.R. 63; *Meredith v Dalton* [1944] O.W.N. 676.

[32] *Wingard v Cox* [1876] W.N. 106, Denman J.

[33] *Garnaut v Bennett (No.2)* (1909) 29 N.Z.L.R. 381: " . . . in the absence of special circumstances riveting the date in the memory, very few persons could fix the date of a conversation . . . "; *White v Barry* [1947] O.W.N. (Ont.) 755.

or the person or persons to whom the defamatory words are alleged to have been published. This may arise, for example, where the particulars of publication are essentially within the knowledge of the defendant and not of the claimant.[34] The proper course for the claimant in such a case is to plead the best particulars which he can give and to await disclosure or to seek or apply for further information from the defendant as to the identity of the person or persons to whom the words were published.[35] The court will not, however, entertain an action of a speculative nature and such a course will only be permitted where the claimant can show by uncontradicted evidence that publication by the defendant has taken place.[36] If he cannot do this, the court will order particulars of the names and addresses of the person or persons to whom publication is alleged, or in default that the allegation be struck out.[37] It will not in such circumstances postpone the provision of further information until after disclosure.[38]

Republication. Where the claimant seeks to make an original publisher responsible for the republication or repetition by a third person of defamatory words (either in addition to or without alleging liability for the original publication), he must make clear in his pleading the basis on which he claims **26.8**

---

[34] *Gourand v Fitzgerald* (1888) 37 W.R. 55 at 265; *Keogh v Incorporated Dental Hospital* [1910] Ir.R. 166; *Peck v La Valley* [1929] 2 D.L.R. 370; *Paquette v Cruji* (1979) 26 O.R. (2d) 294.

[35] CPR r.18.1; the intention behind the court's power under Pt 18 to order clarification and further information is that it will be used to afford a claimant the same opportunity to examine the defendant as he was afforded under the court's former power under RSC Ord.26 to order interrogatories, subject, of course, to considerations of necessity and proportionality. A response to a request for further information must be verified by a statement of truth. A claimant may also be able to take advantage of the provisions in the CPR by which a party may apply for disclosure before proceedings start or against a person not party to the proceedings, see CPR rr.31.16 and 31.17. For a more detailed discussion of further information and interrogatories in defamation, see Ch.31, section 2, below.

[36] *Best v Charter Medical of England Ltd* [2001] EWCA Civ 1588; [2002] E.M.L.R. 18; *Russell v Stubbs* [1913] 2 K.B. 200n; *CHC Software Care v Hopkins & Wood* [1993] F.S.R. 241 where Mummery J. held that discovery of names and addresses of recipients analogous to interrogatories would be ordered in the court's discretion where there was uncontradicted evidence of publication in similar terms to persons other than the particular ones identified in the statement of claim; *Lazarus v Deutsche Lufthansa* (1985) 1 N.S.W.L.R. 188:
> "A plaintiff in an action for oral defamation is obliged to identify the persons to whom it is alleged that the matter complained of was published. The names of those persons must be given unless he does not know them and thus is unable to give such particulars. In that case, provided that the plaintiff is able to establish a prima facie case of publication, it will be sufficient for him to give the best particulars he can identifying those persons"
at 194–195; *Borella v Penfolds Wines* (1992) 7 W.A.R. 492; *Freer v Zeb* [2008] EWHC 212 (QB) at [31].

[37] *Mutual Life v National Mutual* [1909] V.L.R. 445; *Barham v Huntingfield* [1913] 2 K.B. 193 at 197, 199, where the case of *Russell v Stubbs* [1913] 2 K.B. 200n is discussed and distinguished; see also *Citation plc v Ellis Whittan Limited* [2013] EWCA Civ 155 at [17]; *Davies v Rolleston* (1920) 149 L.T.J. 84; [1920] W.N. 29 CA; *McCarter Burr v Harris* [1922] 1 W.W.R. 677; *Irish Society v City of Dublin Assurance* [1928] Ir.R. 204; *Quann v Chatham* (1991) 107 N.B.R. 392 at 406.

[38] *Wesson v Campbell River and District Branch* (1985) 63 B.C.L.R. 327.

that the original publisher is liable for the subsequent publication.[39] The same principles apply to the pleading of an act of republication as to the pleading of an original publication.[40] The claimant may choose not to make the defendant liable for republication but to treat further publications which repeat the defamatory sting as relevant to the assessment of damages flowing from the original publication, and plead accordingly.[41]

26.9 Vicarious liability. In circumstances where the claimant seeks to make a defendant liable on the basis of that defendant's responsibility for the acts of an agent or employee, he should plead the necessary factual averments, namely that the agent or employee was acting on behalf of the defendant within the scope of his authority and set out any additional facts and matters on which he relies in support of such averments.[42]

26.10 Form of words. It is usual to describe in the particulars of claim the mode of publication (e.g. speech, publication in a newspaper, broadcast) and the basis on which an individual defendant is said to be responsible for it. The practice in a libel or slander claim of alleging that the defendant published the words "falsely and maliciously" is archaic and should not be used.[43] The modern practice is to plead simply that the defendant published "the following words defamatory of the claimant", thus indicating beyond doubt that the claim is brought in defamation. (Where the claimant wishes to allege express malice on the part of the defendant in order to defeat a plea of honest comment or qualified privilege, he will have to plead to this effect and give particulars of facts and matters from which he alleges the malice is to be inferred, but this should be done in a reply and not in the particulars of claim.[44] A claimant may,

---

[39] See paras 6.37–6.46, above, for the ways in which a defendant may be held liable for republication.

[40] *Unterberger v Prospectors Airways* [1962] O.W.N. 212.

[41] *Slipper v BBC* [1991] 1 Q.B. 283 CA, where the plaintiff brought an action in respect of a film broadcast by the defendant. The court declined to strike out the plaintiff's contention in his statement of claim that the defendant knew that the film was likely to be reviewed in the national press and that accordingly passages from several specified reviews which repeated the allegedly defamatory sting of the film should be taken into account in the assessment of damages; *McManus v Beckham* [2002] EWCA Civ 939; [2002] 1 W.L.R. 2982 CA. In *Berezovsky v Terluk* [2011] EWCA Civ 1534 one of the grounds on which the Court of Appeal dismissed the appeal was that the appellant was not liable for republication. Laws L.J. declined to rule on the proper test but said, obiter, at [28] he was "inclined to think that the modern law in this area should more visibly occupy the legal territory of privacy and free expression, and the tensions between them; and to that end the tort of defamation should excoriate not carelessness, but knowing or deliberate action." See para.6.47, above.

[42] In general, see para.8.30ff, above but see also *Burch v Parkinson* [2010] TASSC 42 at [13]–[16].

[43] *Motel Holdings Ltd v The Bulletin* (1963) 63 N.S.W.S.R. 208: "'Falsely and maliciously' may now be regarded as surplusage." The reason why this form of words is otiose lies in the fact that it is presumed in the claimant's favour that the defamatory words are false and their publication is malicious.

[44] See CPR PD 53, para.2.9. In actions for slander of title and malicious falsehood the claimant must always allege in the particulars of claim that the words were published falsely and maliciously, see para.26.42, below.

in an appropriate case, allege malice against a defendant in his particulars of claim in aggravation of damages,[45] and of course malice must be pleaded in the particulars of claim where the action is in malicious falsehood, because in that case it is an essential component of the cause of action.[46])

SECTION 4. THE WORDS PUBLISHED

Setting out words complained of: libel. In a libel claim the words used   **26.11**
are material facts and they must therefore be set out verbatim in the particulars of claim, preferably in the form of a quotation: it is not enough to describe their substance, purport or effect.[47]

> "The law requires the very words of the libel to be set out in the declaration in order that the court may judge whether they constitute a ground of action."[48]
>
>   "A plaintiff is not entitled to bring a libel action on a letter which he has never seen and of whose contents he is unaware. He must in his pleading set out the words with reasonable certainty . . . The court will require him to give particulars so as to

---

[45] See para.26.28, below.

[46] See Ch.21, above, and para.26.42, below.

[47] Although there is now an express rule of procedure requiring a claimant in a claim for slander to set out, so far as possible, the precise words used, if not already contained in the claim form (CPR PD 53, para.2.4), curiously there is no equivalent express procedural requirement in the case of a claim for libel. However, the requirement is so well-established that its omission from the CPR must have been inadvertent, and certainly cannot have been intended to have the effect that a claimant need no longer set out the actual words of a libel in the particulars of claim. See *Best v Charter Medical of England Ltd* [2001] EWCA Civ 1588; [2002] E.M.L.R. 18 for pleading requirements that are applicable to both slander and libel claims. In *Bunt v Tilley* [2006] EWHC 407 (QB); [2007] 1 W.L.R. 1243 at [4], Eady J. made the following observation:
  "It is notable that the claimant takes the stance that the words complained of in this litigation form only a small part of the totality of defamatory allegations published about him through the internet. He regards it as an on-going problem. He claims that ' . . . it is a precursor to a pandemic scale infection that is already widespread and festering just below the surface'. Nevertheless, he has to recognise that there is no mechanism in this kind of litigation for proceeding on the basis of 'sample' publications. If a claimant wishes to sue over defamatory allegations, and to recover compensation and other remedies in respect of them, they must be set out clearly in the particulars of claim."
It is unnecessary for the claimant to add to the words set out in the particulars of claim "or words to the like effect" for he is entitled to have it put before the jury that the words proved "are substantially to the same effect as the words alleged"; per Bankes and Atkin L.JJ. in *Tournier v National Provincial Bank* [1924] 1 K.B. 461 at 469, 487; or "a material and defamatory part of the words complained of": at 478, per Scrutton L.J.; *Conway v Westwood* (1936) N.P.D. 245. See also *Harris v Warre* (1879) 4 C.P.D. 125 at 127, 129; *Wood v Brown* (1815) 6 Taunt. 169; *Wright v Clements* (1820) 3 B. & Ald. 503; *Darbyshire v Leigh* [1895] 1 Q.B. 554 at 587, per Lord Esher M.R., per Lopes L.J. at 588; *Hay v Bingham* (1902) 5 O.L.R. 224; *Berry v Retail Merchants* (1924) 18 Sask.L.R. 283; *Shannon v King* [1931] 4 D.L.R. 438; *Collins v Jones* [1955] 1 Q.B. 564 CA; *Rosen v Alberta Motor Association Insurance* [1994] 1 W.W.R. 719; *Kerr v Haydon* [1981] 1 N.Z.L.R. 449.

[48] Per Abbott C.J. in *Wright v Clements* (1820) 3 B. & Ald. 503 at 506, and per Holroyd J. at 509; *Capital and Counties Bank v Henty* (1882) 7 A.C. 741 at 771, 772, per Lord Blackburn; "In libel you must declare upon the words; it is not sufficient to state their substance"; per Palles C.B. in *Fitzsimmons v Duncan Ltd* [1908] 2 Ir.R. 483 at 499.

ensure that he has a proper case to put before the court and is not merely fishing for one."[49]

The rigours of this rule may be slightly relaxed when the matter complained of is part of a television, film or other audio-visual presentation, where the combinations and permutations available are endless and the material is not easily susceptible to a detailed description of its defamatory aspects.[50] Some flexibility may also be permitted where the claimant is seeking an interim pre-publication injunction. In such a case, it is not invariably necessary for the claimant to set out the precise words, but the particulars of claim must be pleaded with sufficient particularity to enable the defendant not only to understand what it is the claimant alleges the words mean, but also to enable him to decide whether they have that meaning, as well as to enable the court to frame an injunction with sufficient precision.[51]

26.12 **Only relevant passages to be set out.** The particular passages complained of should be clearly identified and set out.[52] The claimant cannot confine the material of which he complains to an extract from a single publication when it is obvious that no reasonable reader would have read that extract in isolation and any reader who read beyond it could not possibly have drawn an inference defamatory of the claimant.[53] Where the claimant intends to allege that the meaning of words is affected by the context in which they were written or spoken, he should include this contextual material in the particulars of claim.[54] However, surrounding material which is genuinely

---

[49] *Collins v Jones* [1955] 1 Q.B. 564 at 571, per Denning L.J. For possible methods of coping with this difficulty, see para.26.16, below.

[50] *Lougheed v CBC* [1978] 4 W.W.R. 358:
    "In my view a plaintiff, in a defamation case involving an audio-visual presentation, should not be bound by the same strict rules as to particulars which apply to a written document or a verbal statement. However, this privilege granted to such a plaintiff should not be extended to permit the pleading merely of general conclusions that the plaintiff has been defamed. The plaintiff must, through his pleadings, clearly indicate to the defendant which portions of the television play give rise to the allegations of defamation ... "
    per Miller J. at 379.

[51] *British Data Management v Boxer Commercial Removals Plc* [1996] E.M.L.R. 349 CA.

[52] *Sydenham v Man* (1617) Cro.Jac. 407; *R. v Brereton* (1725) 8 Mod. 329; *Rubenstein v Truth and Sportsman Ltd* [1960] V.R. 479; *Ron Hodgson v Belvedere Motors* [1971] N.S.W.L.R. 472.

[53] *Charleston v News Group Newspapers Ltd* [1995] 2 A.C. 65, where it was held that a claim for libel could not be founded on a headline or photograph alone where the ordinary reader could not have failed to read further and to see at once that the headline and pictures were not to be taken at face value.

[54] *Bookbinder v Tebbit* [1989] 1 W.L.R. 640 at 647, per Ralph Gibson L.J.; *Gordon v Amalgamated Television Services* [1980] 2 N.S.W.L.R. 410:
    "Where the publication sued upon is in written form, a plaintiff is obliged to include within his pleading every passage which materially alters or qualifies the complexion of the imputation complained of", per Hunt J. at 413.
Cases based on the publication of defamatory material on the internet raise new issues about what matter, either linked to the words complained of by means of "hyperlinks" or otherwise, can properly be regarded as context: e.g. see *Buddhist Society of Western Australia Inc. v Bristile Ltd* [2000] WASCA 210 and *Budu v BBC* [2010] EWHC 616 (QB).

irrelevant to the claimant's complaint should be omitted. This is particularly important where the claimant is suing in respect of words contained in a book or a long "feature" article in a newspaper. Save in the exceptional circumstances where the sting of the matter can properly be said to derive from the publication read as a whole,[55] it will not be appropriate to set out the article or book in its entirety.[56] The indiscriminate inclusion of every word of a lengthy publication is not only potentially embarrassing, it may also assist the defendant to enter a plea of justification which goes beyond the specific meanings of which the claimant complains.[57]

Where the matter complained of consists of related material published by the defendant on different occasions, and where it appears from the face of the material itself that the defendant intended that it be read together or there are direct internal references one to the other so that the reader might reasonably be expected to read it together, it has been held to be an acceptable practice to plead all of the material in the one paragraph of the particulars of claim and

---

[55] *Killingsworth v Scott Knitting Co. Ltd* [1943] O.W.N. 520; *Churchill Forest Industries v Finkel* [1971] 1 W.W.R. 745; *Hadzel v De Waldorf* (1970) 16 F.L.R. 174:
"A plaintiff in defamation may set out the whole of some lengthy written or spoken matter, notwithstanding that there are parts which are not defamatory, either because it is desired to rely upon an imputation to be derived from the whole or because the meanings of separate defamatory parts can only be ascertained by reference to the whole context. In the latter case the pleader is obliged to set out or incorporate the necessary context in his statement of claim ... If unnecessary matter is pleaded, it may be ordered to be struck out", per Fox J. at 176;
Wharton v Vopni Press [1983] 1 W.W.R. 161;
  Dougherty v Nationwide News (1968) 88 W.N. (Pt. 1) (N.S.W.) 146 at 150:
" ... where the plaintiff claims that the libellous imputations emerge in their full force and extent only by a reading of the whole article, and the court is not convinced that this claim is ill-founded, then whether the defendant is embarrassed or not I would think that the court would be slow to interfere and tamper with the article ... ";
Hepburn v TCN Channel Nine [1983] 2 N.S.W.L.R. 682.
[56] *DDSA v The Times* [1973] 1 Q.B. 21 CA; *Lougheed v CBC* [1979] 3 W.W.R. 334 (where the plaintiff was ordered to designate each episode of a television play alleged to be defamatory by reference to the time frame set out in the transcript and to assign to such episode the nature of the defamation alleged); *Kerney v Optimus Holdings* [1976] V.R. 399; *Vulcan Industrial Packaging v CBC* (1979) 94 D.L.R. (3d) 729;
  Moffat v BCTV System [1985] 1 W.W.R. 271:
"What words are of themselves false? What false innuendoes arise from the words? What words taken with what pictures, graphs, charts and sounds give rise to false innuendoes? The plaintiff must isolate those portions, as numerous as they may be, of the broadcasts which the plaintiff says answer those questions" per Low L.J.S.C at 277;
Scott v Fourth Estate [1986] 1 N.Z.L.R. 336:
" ... it must be a rare case where a plaintiff can plead a whole article without particularising the passages in the article that he complains of. It may be appropriate to plead the whole article in order to claim that certain passages or libellous statements take their meaning from the article as a whole, but in order to focus the dispute it is important that the allegedly defamatory passages be sufficiently identified" per Williamson J. at 339–340.
[57] However, it should be borne in mind that a claimant does not necessarily restrict the breadth of a plea of justification by limiting his complaint to certain selected passages. A defendant is entitled to consider the publication as a whole in order to aver that the words, in their correct context, bear a meaning different from that alleged by the claimant and to plead that in that meaning the words are true: *Polly Peck Plc v Trelford* [1986] Q.B. 1000.

to identify the imputations said to have been conveyed by the material as a whole.[58] Where possible the claimant should give the page reference of the book or newspaper where the allegedly defamatory material is to be found. In cases in which the offending material is so long that it cannot conveniently be pleaded in the particulars of claim, the material should be pleaded in a schedule.[59]

26.13 Setting out words complained of: slander. As in libel, so in slander: the words are material facts. In slander, there is now an express procedural requirement that the precise words used be set out in the particulars of claim, so far as possible and if not already contained in the claim form.[60] This reflects the pre-existing law that the actual words spoken had to be set out verbatim "in order that the defendant may know the certainty of the charge, and may be able to shape his defence".[61] It is not sufficient to allege that the slanderer used such-and-such words, or words to an alleged effect.[62] If the claimant has joined claims for slanders uttered by separate defendants in one action he must allege each slander in a separate paragraph of his particulars of claim, the reason being that there can be no joint liability in cases of slander.[63]

---

[58] *Burrows v Knightley* (1987) 10 N.S.W.L.R 651.

[59] Under the RSC, the recommended course was to seek the leave of the court to plead the relevant material by schedule: Supreme Court Practice 1999, 18/6/3. Although it is not expressly endorsed under the CPR, it would still seem to be a sensible approach and the court is likely to be flexible in this respect, see CPR PD 16, para.13.3(3).

[60] CPR PD 53, para.2.4. It had been held that the inclusion of the words "so far as possible" do not have the effect of relieving the claimant of his obligation to plead his claim in slander with sufficient particularity to enable the defendant to know how to formulate his case: see *Best v Charter Medical of England Ltd* [2001] EWCA Civ 1588; [2002] E.M.L.R. 18. See also *Jennings v Buchanan* [2004] UKPC 36; [2005] 1 A.C. 115 at [5].

[61] Per Lord Ellenborough C.J. in *Cook v Cox* (1814) 3 M. & S. 110 at 113. Although precise words must be alleged in the particulars of claim, it is not necessary to prove that those exact words were in fact published. It is sufficient if the claimant proves at trial words which are substantially to the same effect. Where the claimant acknowledges that the alleged defamatory statements are not necessarily precisely those published by the defendants and that some of the witnesses to publication are not able to recall exactly what was said, the claimant may be required to adduce evidence setting out exactly what information the witnesses have given concerning the alleged slander: *Ferguson v McBee Technographics* [1988] 6 W.W.R. 716; [1989] 2 W.W.R. 499.

[62] *Maitland v Goldney* (1802) 2 East 426; *Gutsole v Mathers* (1836) 1 M. & W. 495 (slander of title); *Phelps v Kemsley* (1943) 168 L.T. at 20 CA; *Breen v McDonald* (1872) 22 Up.Can.C.P. 298; *Harris v Clayton* (1881) 21 N.B.R. 237; *Mackay v Stomp* [1992] 5 W.W.R. 475, where it was held that the fact that a defence had been served, and examinations for discovery had been held, did not constitute a waiver of the defect. For possible methods of coping with this difficulty, see para.26.17, below.

[63] *Chamberlain v White* (1623) Cro.Jac. 647, followed in *Bannigan v Callaghan* (1897) 33 Ir.L.T. 58. See also *Burcher v Orchard* (1652) Style 349; *Coryton v Lithbye* (1670) 2 Wms. Saund. 115 at 117c; *Chamberlain v Willmore* (1623) Palmer K.B. 313; *Carrier v Garrant* (1873) 23 Up.Can.C.P. 276; *Messervey v Simpson* (1912) 22 Manitoba R. 421. The decision to the contrary in *Robb v Morrison* (1920) N.S.W.S.R. 163 cannot be supported. "The words of one defendant are not the words of the other. The act of each constitutes an entire and distinct offence," per curiam in *Webb v Cecil* (1848) 46 K.R. 199. But the concept of "offence" is archaic, given that criminal libel has been abolished in many jurisdictions, including England and Wales.

Forms of slander. If the slanderous words were spoken affirmatively in 26.14
answer to a question, they should be alleged to have been spoken affirmatively,[64] but where the damaging meaning is to be collected from question and
answer together, both question and answer must be set out verbatim in the
particulars of claim.[65]

> "In an action for words you cannot out of a question and answer make an affirmative
> proposition. You must state the question and answer."[66]

If the slander was conveyed in the form of a question it must be set out as such
and not alleged to have been spoken affirmatively, for "there is a manifest
distinction between the same idea conveyed by words spoken affirmatively
and put interrogatively".[67] So where the words are virtually a continuation of
a conversation held at two different times, and neither conversation taken
separately is slanderous, both conversations must be set out.[68] If the slander
takes the form of the defendant repeating the defamatory words of someone
else, it must still be set out in the form of the actual words used by the
defendant, as for example: "Smith told me that Jones (the plaintiff) was a
card-sharper", and not as though what was spoken was the defendant's
original allegation, e.g. "Jones is a card-sharper".[69]

Ironic remarks, gestures and cartoons. Sometimes it will be necessary 26.15
to plead matter additional to the publication of words. For instance, if the
slander was conveyed by signs or gestures, the particular signs or gestures
must be described.[70] If the words were spoken ironically they must be set out
precisely as spoken, together with an averment that they were spoken ironically.[71] In appropriate cases, e.g. where the libel is contained in a cartoon or
collage, a photocopy can be appended in place of a description.

Words unknown to claimant: libel. Sometimes the claimant will have 26.16
real difficulty in ascertaining the precise words of the libel. The court has the

---

[64] *Yeates v Read* (1838) 4 Blackf. (Indiana) R. 463.
[65] Chit.Pl. 405; *Hams v Clayton* (1881) 21 N.B.R. 237; *Sonier v Brean* (1912) 41 N.B.R.
177.
[66] Per Littledale J. in *Bromage v Prosser* (1825) 4 B. & C. 247 at 252.
[67] Per curiam in *Barnes v Holloway* (1799) 8 T.R. 150; *Jackson v Adams* (1835) 2 Bing. N.C.
402.
[68] *Harris v Clayton* (1881) 21 N.B.R. 237 at 242, 250, 251.
[69] *Bell v Byrne* (1811) 13 East 554 at 562, 563. Cf. *Cartwright v Wright* (1823) 5 B. & Ald. 615;
Rainy v Bravo (1872) L.R. 4 P.C. 287.
[70] Per curiam in *Gutsole v Mathers* (1836) 1 M. & W. 495 at 501. It will generally be necessary
also to plead the innuendo meaning of the signs or gestures, together with particulars relied on as
showing that the signs or gestures were understood to refer to the claimant, see para.26.23,
below.
[71] See the declaration in *Boydell v Jones* (1838) 4 M. & W. 446, and *R. v Browne* (1707) 11
Mod. 86.

power to grant pre-action disclosure, but that will not be ordered to enable the claimant to fish for a case.[72] If he is unable to set out the very words of the libel, the best course is to insert in the particulars of claim the closest approximation which he can make of the actual words used. In due course he should apply for disclosure or serve the holder of the document (if he is a stranger to the action) with a witness summons under CPR r.34.2.[73] He may also seek or apply for further information from the defendant as to whether he published the words complained of or words to like effect.[74] This latter course will be useful if the relevant documentary evidence has become lost or destroyed. As soon as he is aware of a variance between the words alleged in the particulars of claim and the words actually used, the claimant should apply for permission to amend,[75] but at all stages the court will require to be convinced that the claimant has not been proceeding on a speculative basis and that he had material with which to launch the action with sufficient certainty in the first place.[76]

26.17 Words unknown to the claimant: slander. The problem of ascertaining the precise words published is usually even greater in the case of slander, which is by its nature transitory. As with cases of libel, the best course is for the claimant to set out as best he can in the particulars of claim the words which he believes to have been spoken by the defendant. If the exact words cannot be pleaded, the words must at least be set out with reasonable precision.[77] He should then seek or apply for further information from the defendant as to the actual words used on the occasion in question. Such an application is only likely to be allowed where the claimant can show by uncontradicted evidence that the defendant has at a certain place and in the presence of certain persons made against him a slanderous imputation of a definite character. The court will only assist a claimant who can demonstrate that he has a good cause of action but is unable to find out the precise form in which to frame it.[78]

---

[72] See para.31.2, below and CPR r. 31.16.

[73] If, for some reason, the claimant has not been able to obtain disclosure of the document in the hands of a non-party, the claimant may be able to obtain sight of the document prior to the trial by applying under CPR r.34.3(2)(b) for a summons to be issued for the witness to attend court to produce the document on a date earlier than the date fixed for trial. This rule formally recognises the possibility of a *"Khanna"* hearing: see *Khanna v Lovell White Durrant* [1995] 1 W.L.R. 121.

[74] *Dalgleish v Lowther* [1899] 2 Q.B. 590.

[75] *Harris v Ware* (1879) 4 C.P.D. 125 at 127, per Lord Coleridge C.J.; also per Reynolds J. in *Oswin v Radio 2UE* [1968] 1 N.S.W.R. 461 at 463.

[76] *Collins v Jones* [1955] 1 Q.B. 564.

[77] *Best v Charter Medical of England Ltd* [2001] EWCA Civ 1588; [2002] E.M.L.R. 18

[78] *Atkinson v Fosbroke* (1866) L.R. 1 Q.B. 628; and see *Russell v Stubbs* [1913] 2 K.B. 200n. The law is the same in Ontario: see *Campbell v Scott* (1890) 14 O.P.R. 203; and in British Columbia: see *Shannon v King* [1931] 4 D.L.R. 438 CA at 440; and in Alberta: *Rosen v Alberta Motor Association Insurance Co.* [1994] 1 W.W.R. 719.

"I think it would be a sad day if an individual who felt that another person had said something unflattering about him could issue a Statement of Claim and thereby commence a fishing

On receipt of the answer the claimant will have to consider his position. If there is a variance between the words which the claimant has pleaded and the words which the defendant admits speaking, the claimant should generally apply to amend his particulars of claim, provided of course the admitted words constitute an actionable slander. Where the defendant does not admit speaking words which constitute an actionable slander, the claimant will have to give serious consideration as to whether he can sensibly continue the action on the evidence available to him. Alternatively, the claimant might consider issuing a witness summons under CPR Pt 34 for the person to whom the words were allegedly spoken to attend court to give evidence, if that person is known but will not assist voluntarily. Under CPR r.34.3(2)(b) or (c), the claimant could apply for a witness summons to be issued for the relevant individual to give evidence on a date earlier than the date fixed for the trial or at a hearing other than the trial.

SECTION 5. FOREIGN PUBLICATION

Publication in a foreign language. Where the libel or slander was published in a foreign language, it must be set out in the particulars of claim in that language and followed by a literal translation: it is not enough to set out a translation without setting out the original or vice versa.[79] The pleader should include an averment to the effect that the translation is a true interpretation of the foreign language used. It would also be necessary to plead that the persons who read or heard the words understood the foreign language,[80]   **26.18**

---

expedition, placing the onus upon the defendant to disgorge all that might have been said. I am also mindful of the plaintiffs' problems in confronting as intimidating an opponent as the insurance industry. I think I would have been willing to go some way to ease their burden if there had been something in the pleadings that indicated to me that the plaintiffs were acting in good faith, were not on a fishing expedition and the defamatory words had actually been published. I might have been prepared to relax the strict rules if a summary of the words had been specified with an indication of the dates or times or people by and to whom the communications were made"
per Fruman J. at 723–724).

[79] *Zenobio v Axtell* (1795) 6 T.R. 162, where judgment for the plaintiff was arrested on the ground that a translation of the words, and not the original French words, was set out in the declaration; *Pirie v Carroll* (1931) 4 M.P.R. (Canada) 127, where a verdict for the plaintiff was set aside as the court was not satisfied that the words were spoken in the language in which they were laid in the statement of claim; *Jenkins v Phillips* (1841) 9 C. & P. 766, where the judge allowed the declaration setting out the words in English to be amended on proof that they were spoken in Welsh; *R. v Goldstein* (1821) 3 Brod. & Bing. 201; *Polehyki v Cromik* (1920) 15 Alberta R. 274. For the position in Malaysia, see *Dato' Seri Tiong King Sing v Datuk Justine Jinggut* [2003] 6 M.L.J. 433 (a decision of the High Court in Miri), albeit that in *Ng Kim Ho v Chai Sze Shin* [2006] M.L.J. 87, Clement Skinner J. sitting in the High Court in Kuching declined to follow it.

[80] *Jones v Davers* (1597) Cro.Eliz. 496; *Price v Jenkins* (1602) Cro.Eliz. 865: such knowledge is a "material fact"; *Fleetwood v Curley* (1619) Hob. at 268. American cases have held that the declaration must contain such an averment: *Wormouth v Cramer* (1829) 3 Wend. (N.Y.) R. 394; *Rich v Scalio* (1904) 115 Ill.App.R. 166; unless the foreign language is in the vernacular of the place where the words were published: *Bechtell v Shatler* (1832) Wright (Ohio) R. 107; *Rhodes v Naglee* (1885) 6 Pac.R. 863. See also *Parshotam v Lallou* (1917) Cape P.D. 288, and *Williamson*

thus avoiding the objection that there is no cause of action unless the hearers or readers of the defamatory words understood them in the language in which they were published.[81]

26.19 **Foreign publication.** Where the words have been published elsewhere than in this jurisdiction, the claimant should include in his particulars of claim an averment to the effect that the publication of the words was actionable under the law of the country in which publication took place.[82] In such circumstances, it has been held at first instance that it is sufficient for the claimant to plead and rely on the presumption that the laws of foreign countries are the same as domestic law.[83]

SECTION 6. THE MEANING OF THE WORDS

26.20 **Pleading meanings.** The claimant must plead in the particulars of claim the defamatory[84] meaning or meanings which he claims were borne by the

---

v Macpherson (1922) 43 Natal L.R. 200, where an averment was not necessary, as the declaration alleged that the words were addressed in the native language to natives. Although s.22(1) of the Welsh Language Act 1993 provides that in any legal proceedings in Wales the Welsh language may be spoken by any party, witness or other person who desires to use it, there has been no provision for the use of pleadings in the Welsh language (see s.22(2) of the Act). Thus, even if everyone in court understands Welsh, it would still seem that an English translation of Welsh words will be needed in the particulars of claim, and a party standing on his rights could require an interpretation and evidence that the translation in the pleadings was accurate.

[81] See the observations of Williams J. in the course of argument in *Amann v Damm* (1860) 8 C.B. (N.S) 597 at 600.

[82] The common law rule of double actionability is retained for defamation claims: s.13 of the Private International Law (Miscellaneous Provisions) Act 1995, and para. 24.26 (and fn.84 thereto), above. There is no reason in principle why this rule should not apply equally to cases where a claimant relies upon a foreign republication in relation to the assessment of damages.

[83] *University of Glasgow v The Economist* [1997] E.M.L.R. 495, per Popplewell J.; *Lazarus v Deutsche Lufthansa* (1985) 1 N.S.W.L.R. 188. Where the claimant raises the presumption, the burden of proving that the foreign law is different from domestic law passes to the defendant. It is to be noted, however, that the Report on Practice and Procedure in Defamation by the Supreme Court Procedure Committee (July 1991) strongly disapproved this rule of pleading, describing it as "quite unrealistic and curiously egocentric in the post-imperial age". The Report advocated that the onus rest on the plaintiff to establish actionability under foreign law. See also *Mother Bertha Music Ltd v Bourne Music Ltd*, unreported, July 31, 1997, Ferris J. Nevertheless, in *Gaddafi v Telegraph Group Ltd*, unreported, March 12–14, 2002, (QB), Sir Oliver Popplewell held that the principle remained good law. Where the claimant complains of publication in more than one jurisdiction, the proper course is to plead the publication in each jurisdiction as a separate cause of action (see *McLean v David Syme* (1970) 92 W.N. (N.S.W.) 611 at 617). See also the observations of Gray J. in *HH Sheikha Mouza Al Misnad v Azzaman Ltd* [2003] EWHC 1783 (QB).

[84] Note that s.1, Defamation Act 2013 (not in force at the time of writing) states that a statement is not defamatory unless its publication has caused or is likely to cause serious harm to the reputation of the claimant.

words or other publication of which he complains.[85] He should do so as

---

[85] *Lucas-Box v News Group Newspapers Ltd* [1986] 1 W.L.R. 146:
" . . . it has become the settled practice for a plaintiff, where the meaning of the words complained of is not clear and explicit, to plead the meanings which he says the words bear. This enables the defendant to know what case he has to meet and to prepare his defence accordingly. Such a practice is, further, of considerable assistance to the court since it thus clearly provides to the trial judge the meanings upon which he must rule in deciding whether the words published are capable of being so understood"
(per Ackner L.J. at 151–152).
In *Jameel v Times Newspapers Ltd* [2004] EWCA Civ 983; [2004] E.M.L.R. 31, Sedley L.J. observed at [12]:
"No issue arises before us about the need for a claimant to situate at least his highest pleaded meaning at one of these three levels: see now the judgment of Brooke L.J. in *Chase v News Group Newspapers Ltd* [2003] E.M.L.R. 11 at [45]."
So much is uncontroversial. However, Sedley L.J. went on to say:
"For my part I would think it high time that claimants were required to plead their levels of meaning in the alternative, especially since the decision in *Bennett* [*v News Group Newspapers Ltd* [2002] E.M.L.R. 39]."
Longmore L.J. expressly echoed this view at [43].
This view *is* controversial, and problematic. First, both the decisions invoked in support of it were concerned principally with *Lucas-Box* particulars, that is, particulars of meaning which it might be open to a defendant to plead in the context of a defence of justification, and not the manner in which a claimant might frame his case on meaning. Secondly, in practical terms, it is difficult to see what interest a claimant could have in pleading "levels of meaning in the alternative", rather than identifying the single highest or gravest defamatory meaning he contends a particular allegation bears. This has long been standard practice, and for good reason: it is unlikely to be in the claimant's interest to be equivocal about the "level of meaning" at trial.
In these circumstances, it is suggested that the "*Jameel* requirement" of pleading alternative meanings in particulars of claim should be confined to cases where the claimant is uncertain about the level of meaning attributable to the allegation in question. In such cases, in compliance with CPR PD 53, para.2.3(1), the claimant ought to plead alternative levels of meaning expressly. In cases where the claimant has a clear-cut case on what has been alleged against him, it is contended that there is no reason to depart from the standard practice of pleading the single, highest meaning.
In *Charman v Orion Publishing Group Ltd* [2005] EWHC 2187 (QB), Gray J. at [13], commenting upon Sedley L.J.'s observations in *Jameel v Times Newspapers Ltd* [2004] EWCA Civ 983; [2004] E.M.L.R. 31, rejected the defendant's contention that it was not nowadays open to a claimant to rely on a lower meaning than that asserted in his or her statement of case: "The Court of Appeal in *Slim* treated the Claimant's pleaded meaning in that case as the high water mark, leaving it open to the Claimant to contend for and for the jury to find some lesser meaning at trial." Also, at [17] Gray J. appeared to endorse the concerns expressed above about the applicability of *Chase* to particulars of claim.
However, when s.11, Defamation Act 2013 is brought into effect and jury trial in defamation is effectively abolished, this practice is likely to change. It will then be for the judge to determine meaning, probably at an early stage of proceedings, and the practice of putting meaning as high as possible will become counterproductive, for there will be a risk of the meaning being struck out. It may be that in future pleaders of particulars of claim in England will find it convenient in cases where the meaning is ambiguous to adopt a practice akin to the Australian system of pleading a number of alternative "imputations", on the footing that the judge will light upon one and rule out the others. Regarding the Australian system, see further fn.86, below.
In recent determinations of the actual meaning of the words complained of, the courts have stressed that they are not bound to accept the pleaded meanings and the decision on meaning is for them, see e.g. *Lord McAlpine of West Green v Bercow* [2013] EWHC 1342 (QB) at [42] and *Modi v Clarke* [2011] EWCA Civ 937 where the Court of Appeal said at [23] that on an application under CPR PD 53, para.4.1 the courts must consider any meanings that can properly be advanced.

precisely as possible[86] because properly pleaded meanings are key to the determination and proper conduct of all aspects of defamation litigation from the first stages through to trial.[87] The claimant needs to set out not only his case as to the natural and ordinary meaning of the words but also (where appropriate) as to any innuendo meaning (i.e. any meaning alleged to be conveyed to some person by reason of that person's knowledge of facts extraneous to the words complained of).[88] It is good practice also to make clear in appropriate cases (e.g. where the words complained of are very lengthy or difficult to comprehend) the part or parts of the words complained of from which each alleged meaning is derived.[89] Pleading a meaning is rarely an easy exercise. There will frequently be room for disagreement or uncertainty as to precisely what meaning or meanings may reasonably be drawn

---

[86] Australian courts have taken a particularly rigorous approach to the pleading of meanings (or "imputations").

"In this jurisdiction, as in every other jurisdiction in Australia, [the meaning] particularises the cause of action. The primary purpose of precision in this jurisdiction is to confine the issues which otherwise might arise and to notify the defendant of the case to be met. It is important for a defendant, for instance, to know what level of justification will meet the plaintiff's case":

Aboriginal Nations Pty Ltd v John Fairfax Publications Pty Ltd [1998] ACTSC 125 at [25]; see also *Drummoyne MC v ABC* (1990) 21 N.S.W.L.R. 135; *Cohen v Sir Moses Montefiore Jewish Home* [2003] N.S.W.S.C. 502; *Piggins v Denton* [2006] N.S.W.S.C. 954. Imprecise or ambiguous meanings are liable to be struck out: *Allworth v John Fairfax Group Pty Ltd* (1993) 113 F.L.R. 254; *Singleton v Ffrench* (1986) 5 N.S.W.L.R. 425; *Amalgamated Television Services v Marsden* (1998) 43 N.S.W.L.R. 158. True to say, pleaded imputations have played a more important role in Australian defamation actions over the last 30 years or so than in this jurisdiction—the imputations, rather than the words alleged to be defamatory, were the cause of action in certain Australian jurisdictions, including New South Wales, until the coming into force of the uniform Australian defamation legislation which restored the common law position, e.g. in New South Wales's case, see s.8 of the Defamation Act 2005 (NSW)—but a similar degree of punctiliousness in pleading meanings is desirable nonetheless. It seems unlikely that the Australian statutory reforms will result in courts there taking a more lax approach to the pleading of meaning: in *Holmes v Fraser* [2008] N.S.W.S.C. 570, the court held at [58] that the Uniform Civil Procedure Rules still require the plaintiff to specify each imputation upon which he relies. For recent examples, see *Habib v Radio 2UE Sydney Pty Ltd* [2010] NSWDC 244 and *Gant v The Age Co. Ltd* [2011] VSC 169.

[87] *Ashcroft v Foley* [2012] EWCA Civ 423; [2012] E.M.L.R. 25 per Pill L.J. and Sharp J. at [35]. See also *Rothschild v Associated Newspapers Ltd* [2012] EWHC 177 (QB) at [15] where Tugendhat J. said at trial at [15]:

" . . . Meaning is a central issue in most libel actions for two main reasons. First, if the claimant succeeds, the meaning of the words complained of determines how seriously the claimant has been defamed, and so the measure of any damages the claimant may be entitled to. Second, a defendant who is sued for libel has a complete defence if he can prove that the words complained of are substantially true (the defence is known as "justification" or "truth"). To determine whether or not words are true, or substantially true, it is first necessary to determine what those words mean".

The judgment was upheld on appeal: [2013] EWCA Civ 197; [2013] E.M.L.R. 18.

[88] CPR PD 53, para.2.3(1).

[89] *Hadzel v De Waldorf* (1970) 16 F.L.R. 174; *Magnifax Publishers Pty Ltd v Incentive Pty Ltd* (1970) 18 F.L.R. 100 (necessity to relate defamatory meanings to specific publications); *Moffat v BCTV System* [1985] 1 W.W.R. 271; *Rubenstein v Truth and Sportsman Ltd* [1960] V.R. 473 (where libels alleged are not common to all defendants). See *Mobb v Philbey* [1998] TASSC 58, where the court declined to order the plaintiff to identify the precise words of the document giving rise to the defamatory imputations alleged.

from the words used in the light of the ordinary man's knowledge.[90]

Surmounting the threshold of seriousness. When Defamation Act   **26.21**
2013, s.1(1) comes into force, it will provide that a statement is not defamatory unless its publication has caused or is likely to cause serious harm to the
reputation of the claimant.[91] It is likely to become good practice for the
claimant to plead the facts relied on to satisfy that threshold requirement,
which are likely to include such matters as the gravity of the defamation, the
number of publishees, and the significance of those publishees in respect of
the claimant's reputation.[92] Furthermore, by s.1(2), if the claimant is a body
that trades for profit, harm to its reputation will not be "serious harm" unless
it has caused or is likely to cause the body serious financial loss. A claimant
corporation will certainly have to plead its case on serious financial loss,
which (if the loss has already been caused) will presumably be in effect a plea
of special damage.

Pleading the natural and ordinary meaning. In setting out the natural   **26.22**
and ordinary meaning of the words, the claimant should be as specific as he
can be and should avoid ascribing too strained a meaning.[93] He should
exercise care since a meaning which is pleaded excessively widely may cause
subsequent embarrassment. An extravagant meaning runs the risk of an
adverse ruling under CPR PD 53, para.4.1, if it is not withdrawn by amendment. Alternatively, it may assist the defendant to introduce into a plea of
justification acts of misconduct other than those referred to in the words

---

[90] See e.g. *Lait v Evening Standard* [2011] EWCA Civ 859; [2011] 1 W.L.R. 2973 at [27] per
Laws L.J.

[91] These are not new concepts. They have emerged in the common law as a result of the new
rights-based jurisprudence that flows from the Human Rights Act 1998. See in particular
Thornton v Telegraph Media Group Ltd [2010] EWHC 1414 (QB); [2011] 1 W.L.R. 1985;
Cammish v Hughes [2012] EWCA Civ 1655; [2013] E.M.L.R. 13 at [38]. The new threshold of
seriousness has already been given particular emphasis in the case of companies. See for instance
per Tugendhat J. in *Euromoney Institutional Investor plc v Aviation News Ltd* [2013] EWHC 1505
(QB) at [24] (and the cases there cited):
    " . . . the likely effect upon a corporate claimant of any words complained of by it may not be
    sufficiently serious to provide the necessary justification for an interference with freedom of
    expression, even if they would have provided a sufficient justification for interference with the
    defendant's rights if the claimant were an individual."

[92] For example, it may be that particular damage will or may have been caused by publication
to a particular person or class of person.

[93] *Lewis v Daily Telegraph* [1964] A.C. 234:
    "I do not mean that ingenuity should be expended in devising and setting out different shades
    of meaning. Distinct meanings are what should be pleaded, and a reasonable test of distinctness
    would be whether the justification would be substantially different"
(per Lord Devlin at 282). See the lament of Sedley L.J. in *Halford v Chief Constable of
Hampshire Constabulary* [2003] EWCA Civ 102:
    "As May L.J. remarked in *Alexander v Arts Council of Wales* [2001] 1 W.L.R. 1853 at [41],
    libel pleaders never seem content to say that the words in issue mean what they say; a pyramid
    of insulting paraphrases has to be erected on them."

complained of.[94] The important point is to identify what the claimant is said to have done, not the opinion expressed by the defendant as to the quality of the act.[95]

26.23 Pleading innuendoes. Where the claimant relies on an innuendo meaning, he must plead particulars of the facts and matters on which he relies in support of that sense.[96] These facts or matters will generally incorporate either a special definition of the words known only to a limited class of persons (such

---

[94] *Maisel v Financial Times Ltd (No.1)* (1915) 84 L.J.K.B. 2145; *London Computer Training v BBC* [1973] 1 W.L.R. 424 CA at 427; *McGrath v Black* (1926) 95 L.J.K.B. 951 CA: "This case should be taken as a warning against imaginative innuendoes in actions for libel where no innuendo is required": per Scrutton L.J. at 953; *SA Associated Newspapers v Yutar* 1967 (3) S.A. 454, where the plaintiff complained that a poster alleging misconduct by him as a prosecutor in the course of a particular trial meant that he was unfit for the office of a prosecutor in a court of law, Steyn C.J. commented:

> "The correctness of the equation of these words with a meaning of such general import may be open to question, but that is the signification into which the plaintiff himself has translated them and that is the meaning to be justified by the defendants in substantiation of their plea"

(at 457); *Allworth v John Fairfax Group* (1993) 113 F.L.R. 254:

> "It has been said on numerous occasions that it is most important that false issues are avoided in defamation actions. False issues are most encouraged when a plaintiff pleads exaggerated or ambiguous imputations. Precision is required to avoid inappropriate attempts by the defendants to plead justification. . . . Precision in pleading tends also to reduce the need for the defendants to introduce contextual implications. Nevertheless, it is important not to take too restrictive a view of what imputations should be permitted to go forward to a tribunal of fact. . . . Pleading a serious, then a less serious 'fall-back' imputation is permissible. . . . That enables the defendant to focus more particularly on the imputations to which it can arguably plead justification."

(per Higgins J. at 258 et seq.). Cf. *Bookbinder v Tebbit* [1989] 1 W.L.R. 640 where the plaintiff sued on the allegation that the spending of £50,000 by the council (of which he was the leader) on overprinting school stationery with anti-nuclear statements had been a "damn fool" idea. It was held that the plaintiff had properly amended his statement of claim to delete the meaning that he had acted irresponsibly in causing large scale squandering of public funds since the ordinary man would regard the defamatory charge, if there was any, as limited to the spending of the stated sums on the stated project. The court accordingly struck out the paragraphs in the defendant's plea of justification which dealt with other occasions of alleged squandering of public money by the council under the leadership of the plaintiff. In *McPhilemy v Times Newspapers Ltd* [1999] 3 All E.R. 775, in which the claimant brought proceedings over an article claiming that a television programme alleging the existence of a conspiracy to murder republicans in Northern Ireland was a hoax, the defendant was allowed to introduce particulars challenging the existence of the alleged conspiracy in part because the truth or falsity of the main thesis of the programme had been a battleground in the proceedings from the start. Lord Woolf M.R. commented that the claimant could, from the outset, have made clear that he was confining his complaint about the article to the issue of whether the article alleged wrongly that he had been grossly irresponsible in permitting the broadcast. It should be noted, however, that, since the defendant is entitled to justify any meaning which the words complained are capable of bearing in their proper context, the claimant does not necessarily restrict the scope of a plea of justification by keeping his pleaded meanings narrow: see *Polly Peck v Trelford* [1986] Q.B. 1000. See also *Carlton Communications Plc v News Group Newspapers Ltd* [2002] EWHC 1650 (QB), [2002] E.M.L.R. 16 CA.

[95] *Botham v Khan, The Times*, July 15, 1996. A similar point was made in *Cruddas v Calvert* [2013] EWHC 2298 (QB). See e.g. at [82], the "defence must be based on what Mr Cruddas did or offered to do at the meeting, because that is how the articles are written."

[96] CPR PD 53, para.2.3(2); *Federal Capital Press v Edwards* (1992) 108 F.L.R. 118. The extrinsic facts and matters which are said to give rise to a defamatory meaning must be given

as slang or technical terms) or facts extrinsic to the libel which, if known about, affect the way the words complained of are understood.[97] In either case, the claimant must identify the person or persons to whom the words were published and who are alleged to have had knowledge of the special meaning or the extrinsic facts.[98] In default of compliance with the requirements for pleading innuendo meanings, the pleaded meaning may be struck out.[99]

Borderline cases. There may be cases in which the claimant is not certain whether he should rely on the natural and ordinary meaning of the words complained of or on a true or legal innuendo. For example, it may not always be easy to decide whether an extrinsic fact relied on is a matter of special knowledge, or whether it is just general knowledge in the light of which the   **26.24**

---

separately in relation to each pleaded meaning: *Gumina v Williams (No.1)* (1990) 3 W.A.R. 342:

> "It is not satisfactory to set out several imputations and then to plead all the particulars in one batch, leaving it for the other party to ask the plaintiff to sort out which particulars relate to which imputation . . . "

(at 350). See also *Winnel v Snow* [2003] ACTSC 94.

[97] See generally para.3.21, above. *Loughams v Odhams Press Ltd* [1963] 1 Q.B. 299; *Grubb v Bristol United Press* [1963] 1 Q.B. 309 at 320, 325, per Pearce L.J.; *Lewis v Daily Telegraph* [1964] A.C. 234. Since the cause of action arises when the words are published, the extrinsic facts must be facts known to the reader or hearer of the words at the time of publication: *Grappelli v Derek Block (Holdings) Ltd* [1981] 1 W.L.R. 822 "The inferences which were put upon the statements *after* the publication (by facts subsequently learnt) do not render them defamatory in the beginning" (per Lord Denning M.R. at 825). For a failed attempt to put an innuendo meaning on a newspaper headline on the basis that it was calculated to refer readers back to an earlier defamatory article, see *Greenslade v Swaffer* [1955] 1 W.L.R. 1109. Cf. *Burrows v Knightley* (1987) 10 N.S.W.L.R. 651, where it was held that where the plaintiff's complaint concerns related material published on separate occasions and it is apparent from the publication that the defendant intended the material to be read together, the plaintiff may plead all of the material in the one paragraph and it is not necessary to plead each part separately and to add true legal innuendoes. Where, however, there is no serialisation and nothing from which it might reasonably be assumed that the reader would have read the article in question together with its predecessor or predecessors, the pleader is obliged to plead the existence of one or more of the other articles as an extrinsic fact which, taken together with the article referred to, gives rise to an additional imputation: see *Interval Resort Networks v West* [1999] WASC 2.

[98] *Fullam v Newcastle Chronicle and Journal Ltd* [1977] 1 W.L.R. 651. Although Lord Denning M.R. (at 655) seems to allow no exceptions in such cases, Scarman L.J. (at 659) would have allowed the plaintiff in a proper case to rely on an inference that some readers must have known the special facts. In *Grappelli v Derek Block (Holdings) Ltd* [1981] 1 W.L.R. 822, the Court of Appeal emphasised that where a legal innuendo was relied on the plaintiff must specify the persons with the particular knowledge, though Dunn L.J. expressed agreement (at 830) with the judgment of Scarman L.J. that there might be an exception where the only reasonable inference was that some of the readers of a national newspaper must have the particular knowledge. *Grapelli* and *Fullam* were applied in *Baturina v Times Newspapers Ltd* [2011] EWCA Civ 308; [2011] 1 W.L.R. 1526 (CA).

[99] *Grubb v Bristol United Press* [1963] 1 Q.B. 309: "One can recollect that in practice thirteen and more years ago statements of claim frequently contained innuendoes unsupported by anything except the pleader's ingenuity. In those days a statement of claim lacked savour if it had no innuendo. But the present practice is for such innuendoes, if pleaded, to be struck out" (per Pearce L.J. at 326).

ordinary, though indirect, meaning of the words has to be ascertained.[100] In such cases, the best course is to plead in the alternative.[101]

26.25 Miscellaneous considerations. Save where he is permitted to amend, the general rule is that a claimant is bound by his pleading as to meaning, at least to the extent that he is not allowed at trial to contend that the words bear a more injurious meaning than that pleaded.[102] In the case of an innuendo, the rule is that the claimant is pinned precisely to his pleaded meaning and proof of a lesser meaning will not assist him.[103] Where a claimant relies on an innuendo meaning he raises a cause of action which is distinct from that based on the natural and ordinary meaning.[104] At any time after the service of the particulars of claim either party may apply to a judge for an order determining

---

[100] Difficulty will only usually arise where there is doubt as to whether the facts relied on are matters of general knowledge. If the facts relied on are a matter of general knowledge, an innuendo will not be required: *O'Brien v Wilson & Horton* [1971] N.Z.L.R. 386: "general knowledge is not an extrinsic fact for the purpose of [this rule] but is matter not requiring to be proved, in the light of which the jury can interpret the publication". Where a claimant relies upon extrinsic facts alternatively as being within the general knowledge of the community and as supporting an innuendo, he will not be ordered to supply particulars of the persons having knowledge of those facts unless it is obvious that the first alternative must fail: *Hughes v Mirror Newspapers* (1985) 3 N.S.W.L.R. 504. On the meaning of "general knowledge", see Bean J. in *Fox v Boulter* [2013] EWHC 1435 (QB) at [16].

[101] *Lewis v Daily Telegraph* [1964] A.C. 234 at 281, per Lord Devlin:
"I do not think that this should present any difficulty in practice. The pleader must ask himself whether he contemplates that evidence will be called in support of the allegation: if he does, it is a legal innuendo, and if he does not, it is not. If he is in doubt, he can plead in two paragraphs; and then if at the trial his opponent agrees or the judge rules that it is a matter of general knowledge, the legal innuendo can be dropped."
This approach was approved of by the Court of Appeal of Hong Kong in *Oriental Press Group Ltd v Next Magazine Publishing Ltd (No.2)* [2000] H.K.L.R.D. L15.

[102] *Slim v Daily Telegraph* [1968] 2 Q.B. 157 at 175, per Diplock L.J.:
" . . . the plaintiff is, in effect, estopped from contending that the words do bear a *more* injurious meaning and claiming damages on that basis. But the averment does not of itself prevent the plaintiff from contending at trial that even if the words do not bear the defamatory meaning alleged in the statement of claim to be the natural and ordinary meaning of the words, they nevertheless bear some other meaning *less* injurious to the plaintiff's reputation"
and per Salmon L.J. at 184–185 (as applied, for example, by Gray J. in *Charman v Orion Publishing Group Ltd* [2005] EWHC 2187 (QB) and Tugendhat J. in, among others, *Lord McAlpine of West Green v Bercow* [2013] EWHC 1342 (QB) at [42]). In *Chakravarti v Advertiser Newspapers Ltd* (1998) C.L.R. 519, the view was expressed that there will generally be no disadvantage in permitting reliance on a meaning which is simply a variant of the pleaded meaning but that there may be a disadvantage if a plaintiff is allowed to rely on a substantially different meaning or, even, a meaning which focuses on some different factual basis. But see *Taylor v Jecks* (1993) 10 W.A.R. 309: "Perhaps the answer might be that whereas, as regards the conduct of his case, the plaintiff will be held to the substance of his pleading, neither the judge in his charge to the jury, nor the jury, will be so confined"; *Broadcasting Corp of New Zealand v Crush* [1988] 2 N.Z.L.R. 234:
"There is a good deal to be said for the view that [the plaintiff] cannot [fall back at the trial on some lesser defamatory meaning]—at least unless his pleadings make it clear that he is reserving the right" (at 239).

[103] *Truth (NZ) Ltd v Holloway* [1960] 1 W.L.R. 997; *Singh v Gillard* [1988] N.L.J.R. 144.

[104] *Grubb v Bristol United Press* [1963] 1 Q.B. 309 at 327, per Pearce L.J.

whether or not the words complained of are capable of bearing a particular meaning or meanings attributed to them.[105]

SECTION 7. IDENTIFICATION OF THE CLAIMANT

Averment of reference to the claimant. It is an essential part of the   **26.26**
claimant's case to show that he is the person referred to by the defamatory words. Accordingly, where it is not absolutely clear on the face of the words that they refer to the claimant, e.g. where he is described by his initial letters, or by a fictitious name, or by the name of somebody else, or where he is not mentioned at all, the claimant should make clear in his particulars of claim the basis on which he claims to have been identified as the subject of the words complained of. He should set out the connecting facts which establish the link between himself and the words used,[106] and he should make plain his case as to the existence of a person or persons who in fact linked him with the words by reason of their knowledge of those connecting facts.[107] These matters are

---

[105] CPR PD 53, para.4.1. When the jury ceases to be the presumptive tribunal of fact in defamation cases upon the coming into force of s.11, Defamation Act 2013, there will be no inhibition on judges determining the actual meaning of words complained of at an early stage in the proceedings. As such, the question of whether words are or are not capable of bearing a particular meaning is liable to become an academic one. See paras 30.14–30.16, below.

[106] *Bruce v Odhams Press* [1936] 1 K.B. 697:
"Defamatory statements which are in the air, as it were, and do not by their words appear to refer to the plaintiff, have got to be made referable to the plaintiff by reason of special facts and circumstances which show that the words can reasonably be construed as relating to the plaintiff"
(per Greer L.J. at 705, also per Slesser L.J. at 708); *Clement v Fisher* (1827) 7 B. & C. 459; *Turner v Bulletin Newspaper Co. Pty Ltd* (1974) 131 C.L.R. 69 at 80; *Morgan v Odhams Press* [1971] 1 W.L.R. 1239 at 1242 and 1248; *Magnifax Publishers Pty Ltd v Incentive Pty Ltd* (1970) 18 F.L.R. 100:
"In the present case, the pleading does not identify the plaintiff with any particular words in the articles; reliance is placed simply on the general allegation that the words were published 'of and concerning the plaintiff'. In the present case, the allegation is inadequate. There should be something which enables the defendants to see which words are relied upon as constituting a reference, or references, to the plaintiff"
(per Fox J. at 104).

[107] *Fullam v Newcastle Chronicle & Journal Ltd* [1977] 1 W.L.R. 651. This case is about pleading legal innuendo meaning, but it is submitted that the same principle will apply in this context: see *Hayward v Thomson* [1982] 1 Q.B. 47 at 60, *Gumina v Williams (No.1)* (1990) 3 W.A.R. 342: " . . . there is no justification for distinguishing innuendoes as to identity from other true innuendoes" (at 344). Whether the claimant must plead and identify particular individuals who understood the publication to refer to him or whether he can rely on a case based on inference will probably depend on the circumstances of the case; see *Fullam v Newcastle Chronicle & Journal Ltd* [1977] 1 W.L.R. 651 at 659; *Grappelli v Derek Block* [1981] 1 W.L.R. 822 at 830 and *Cairns v Modi* [2013] EWCA Civ 1382; [2013] 1 W.L.R. 1015. In *C v MGN* (the second of the cases reported sub nom. *Cairns v Modi*) the Court of Appeal allowed an appeal reducing the amount of compensation to be paid to a claimant who had not been named where an offer of amends had been made, because the judge had attached too much importance to the large circulation and readership figures for the defendant's newspaper, and not to the numbers who would have identified the claimant. See also *Budu v BBC* [2010] EWHC 616 (QB) at [40].

In *Mouammar v Bruner* (1978) 84 D.L.R. (3rd) 121 (where the plaintiff alleged that members of the Canadian Arab community would identify him with the words complained of, it was held that it was not appropriate to order the plaintiff to identify specifically members of the general

material facts which must be pleaded.[108] If the claimant does not plead such facts sufficiently, his claim will be struck out.[109] Where a claimant is identified in a defamatory newspaper article not by his real name but by a pseudonym under which he had written a best-selling book, he should plead details of the class of people who read the newspaper in question and who (1) knew that the pseudonym was a pseudonym of the claimant, (2) knew that the claimant wrote the book in question and (3) knew that the words of the article referred to the claimant.[110] The claimant may face the difficulty that at the initial stage of pleading he is not aware of every person who read or heard the defamatory words and identified him as their subject. In such cases the claimant may be

---

public who identified him with those words on the basis that, as there was a significant Arab population in Canada within the circulation of the defendant newspaper, it would be open to a jury to find that members of that community would reasonably associate the plaintiff with the words. However, as the plaintiff alleged that his career with his employer had been adversely affected as a result of publication, he was ordered to disclose the names of the persons at his place of employment who he alleged had identified him with the words). *Gumina v Williams (No.1)* (1990) 3 W.A.R. 342:

> "A court will not order particulars to be given of facts which identify the plaintiff where it is obvious that a large number of readers will identify him, that is, the extrinsic facts, 'are of sufficient notoriety'."

(at 344–345). See also *Vitale v Bednall* [2000] WASC 207, in which it was held that the material facts had been sufficiently pleaded by describing the people having the special knowledge as those parents, staff and students with knowledge that the plaintiff was one of a small group of students who had been disciplined. "Lookalike" defamation claims will not be permitted: *O'Shea v MGN Ltd* [2001] E.M.L.R. 40. See also *Dwek v Macmillan Publishers Ltd* [2000] E.M.L.R. 284 CA, in which it was held that it was possible as a matter of law for it to be inferred that many old friends and acquaintances would have recognised the claimant without the need to identify individuals who had done so:

> "It is a matter of degree. Some people are very well known and it is obvious that a photograph would be recognised as being of them. In other cases, it might be that, absent particular evidence, it would not be possible to infer that any single person had understood the publication as referring to the claimant. There will be cases in between these two extremes."

(per May L.J. at 293–294).

[108] *Morgan v Odhams Press* [1971] 1 W.L.R. 1239; *Marathon Mutual Ltd v Waters* [2009] EWHC 1931; [2010] E.M.L.R. 3 In New South Wales extrinsic facts relied on to identify the plaintiff are not "material facts", but must nevertheless be pleaded in particulars: *Dawson Bloodstock Agency v Mirror Newspapers* [1979] 2 N.S.W.L.R. 733, applying *Turner v Bulletin Newspapers Co.* (1974) 131 C.L.R. 69.

[109] *Bruce v Odhams Press* [1936] 1 K.B. 697 at 713–714, per Scott L.J.; *Vadic v Ballarat News Pty Ltd* [1981] V.R. 213 (the plaintiffs, the Bishop and executive members of the Serbian Orthodox Church in Australia, sued over a publication which did not mention them by name but alleged in effect that the Serbian Orthodox Church was "communist-controlled" and "a front for Yugoslavia's Secret Police": the claim was struck out on the basis that the plaintiffs did not say what meaning was to be placed on the words so as to make any libel referrable to them); *Seafarers Int'l Union of Canada v Lawrence* (1980) 97 D.L.R. (3rd) 324, esp. at 327 (plaintiffs' claim to bring an action on their own behalf struck out because they did not plead sufficient facts to disclose a personal cause of action; claim on behalf of every member of the union also struck out because, inter alia, it was shown that at least some of the union members were unable to establish a personal cause of action). In *Budu v BBC* [2010] EWHC 616 (QB), the claim was struck out for want of evidence that readers of an article archived on the BBC website would have understood that he was referred to.

[110] *McNab v Associated Newspapers*, QBENI 95/0925/E, May 17, 1996, Otton L.J., CA.

allowed subsequently to expand his case, provided there is no prejudice to the defendant.[111]

Section 8. Actions for Slander

Actions for slander. Where the action is for slander, the claimant must also   **26.27**
show either that it was actionable per se, or that special damage flowed from it. If he wishes to allege that the words complained of impute a criminal offence punishable corporally, he should say so expressly and set out the common law or statutory offence[112] which he contends is imputed. Similarly, where the allegation is of a contagious disease, the disease should be specified, if its nature is not clear on the face of the words complained of, and where the claimant is a woman and the charge was one of unchastity express reference should be made to the Slander of Women Act 1891 (but not for much longer, given its pending repeal by the Defamation Act 2013).[113] Where the imputation was calculated to disparage the claimant in his office, profession, calling, trade or business, the claimant should plead that[114] and also allege[115] that he held the office or carried on the profession, calling, trade or business at the time when the words were published. In all other cases, the claimant must allege that special damage followed the speaking of the words: he must give particulars of the damage, and show sufficient nexus between the slander and the damage, otherwise the particulars of claim will disclose no cause of action.[116]

Section 9. Damages

General damages. In an action for libel the claimant need not allege that   **26.28**
actual damage has resulted from the words complained of. "The law presumes

---

[111] *Hayward v Thompson* [1982] 1 Q.B. 47 at 61; *Morgan v Odhams Press Ltd* [1936] 1 K.B. 697 (plaintiff given leave to supplement the particulars at any time up to 20 days before the trial of the action).

[112] The pleading should usually refer to both the Act and section which apply and, where there is any doubt, show that the offence is punishable by imprisonment. In *Noorani v Calver (No.2)* [2009] EWHC 561 (QB) Coulson J. accepted at [15]–[17] that an allegation of being an Islamic terrorist was sufficient to relate to the commission of serious and specific criminal offences.

[113] When it comes into the force, s14(1), Defamation Act 2013 will repeal the Slander of Women Act 1891 and s.14(2) will require proof of special damage where the imputation is that a person has a contagious or infectious disease.

[114] I.e. in the terms of the Defamation Act 1952, s.2. Since 1952 it has been unnecessary to plead that the words were spoken of the claimant in reference to his character or conduct in his trade, etc. For the extent of particularity required, see para.26.29, below.

[115] Probably in the prefatory averments.

[116] *Ward v Lewis* [1955]1 W.L.R. 9 CA: "It does not seem to me that there is any sufficient allegation in the pleading of connection between the conspiracy and the pleaded special damage" (per Morris L.J. at 12); *Knox v Spencer* (1922) 50 N.B.R. 69: an allegation that "in consequence of the premises the plaintiff has been and is greatly injured and damnified" is not a sufficient allegation of special damage to sustain an action for words not actionable per se. For the pleading of special damage, see para.28.29, below.

that *some* damage will flow in the ordinary course of things from the mere invasion of his absolute right to reputation",[117] and he is entitled to such general damages as the court may properly award, although he neither pleads nor proves any actual damage. The same rule applies in the case of slander actionable per se.

"The very speaking of the words, apart from all damage, constitutes a wrong and gives rise to a cause of action. The law in such a case, as in the case of libel, presumes and in theory allows proof of general damage."[118]

While it may not be strictly necessary to plead that the claimant has suffered damage when he relies only on the presumption of law in his favour, it would be ill-advised not to include at least the bare allegation that he has been caused distress and injury to his reputation.[119] Unless there is some doubt about the scope of the claimant's claim for damages, he will not be required to give particulars of a simple averment of this sort.[120] Thus, where, in an action by a bank for a libel imputing insolvency, which resulted in a run on the bank and liquidation, the plaintiff simply claimed "damages", an order for particulars as to the quantum of damages was refused.[121] Moreover where a newspaper averred that it had been "greatly injured in its business credit and reputation", this was held to be a sufficiently pleaded claim for general damages only, and the defendant was not entitled to further particulars of loss or damage.[122]

26.29 **Where damage must be pleaded.** However, where the claimant claims to have suffered an injury going beyond the normal damage which is presumed

---

[117] Per Bowen L.J. in *Ratcliffe v Evans* [1892] 2 Q.B. 524 at 528. Under the common law this principle applies just as much to corporations as it does to individuals: *Jameel (Mohammed) v Wall Street Journal Europe SPRL (No.2)* [2005] EWCA Civ 74; [2005] Q.B. 904. However, see now, s.1, Defamation Act 2013 for the prospective position governing bodies that trade for profit, though the presumption of damage is not apparently abolished. Whether the claimant is an individual or a corporation, where the defendant can demonstrate that the publication at issue caused the claimant's reputation no or minimal actual damage, an action based on such a publication may be stayed as an abuse of the process: *Jameel (Yousef) v Dow Jones & Co. Inc.* [2005] EWCA Civ 75; [2005] Q.B. 946. See para.30.48, below.

[118] *Ratcliffe v Evans*, above, at 530; followed in *Worsley v Cooper* [1939] 1 All E.R. 290.

[119] After the Defamation Act 2013, s.1 comes into force, it will become necessary to plead that serious harm to reputation has been, or is likely to be, caused to the claimant and provide particulars of the facts and matters relied on to support that. Where the claimant is a "body that trades for profit", the claimant will be required to plead and prove that serious financial harm has been, or is likely to be, caused by the statement complained of (s.1(2)). However, this is not a matter so much of pleading damages as of surmounting a threshold without which the claimant will have no cause of action. See para.26.21, above.

[120] *NZ Times v Wellington Publishing Co.* (1914) 33 N.Z.L.R. 907 at 909; *L & N Bank v George Newnes* (1900) 16 T.L.R. 433; *Bligh v Router* [1968] Q.W.N. 9. When the particulars of claim include a bare allegation of damage, it may nevertheless be a prudent course to obtain confirmation from the claimant that his case is limited to reliance on the presumption of damage.

[121] *L & N Bank v George Newnes* (1900) 16 T.L.R. 433: particulars were ordered of the period for which the run was alleged to have lasted.

[122] *NZ Times v Wellington Publishing Co.* (1914) 33 N.Z.L.R. 907. But note the position now under s.1, Defamation Act 2013 (not yet in force).

to follow in the ordinary course from a defamatory publication, he must give particulars of the facts and matters relied upon in support of that claim, including details of any conduct by the defendant which it is alleged has increased the loss suffered and of any loss which is peculiar to the claimant's own circumstances.[123] The purpose of this rule is to ensure that the defendant has adequate warning of the case which he has to meet and is assisted in computing the monetary element of any Pt 36 offer which he may choose to make.[124] A claimant is accordingly required to give details of any matters on which he will rely in aggravation of damages,[125] such as malicious conduct on the part of the defendant,[126] that the publication complained of was also a violation of his privacy or personal life[127] or that the defendant has failed to retract or apologise for the defamatory allegation.[128] The claimant must also give details of any idiosyncratic feature of the case which has caused him to be more adversely affected by the publication than might ordinarily have been expected.[129] A claimant should therefore ensure that he has included in the particulars of claim every matter which is distinct to the circumstances of his case and which he will seek to contend at trial has particularly contributed to

---

[123] CPR PD 53, para.2.10(1); *Adelson v Associated Newspapers Ltd* [2007] EWHC 997 (QB) at [82].

[124] *Perestrello Ltd v United Paint Co. Ltd* [1969] 1 W.L.R. 570.

[125] When the Crime and Courts Act 2013, s.39 is brought into effect, aggravated damages will only be awarded against a "relevant publisher" within the Act to compensate the claimant for mental distress, and not for purposes of punishment. See the general discussion at paras 9.20–9.22, 9.31–9.32 and 9.37–9.38, above.

[126] Damages are aggravated by the defendant's conduct at or after the time of publication: see *Lait v Evening Standard* [2010] EWHC 642 at [20] (QB). In *Henry v News Group Newspapers* [2011] EWHC 1058 (QB) Eady J. re-iterated that the purpose of aggravated damages was to compensate the claimant for any injury caused by the defendant's actions over and above the injury caused by the defamatory publication(s) complained of, and it followed that the aggravating conduct had to have been known to the claimant. What mattered was the impact of any conduct complained about on the claimant's feelings. Malice should only be alleged on proper grounds, see fn.152 to para.26.30, below, the observations in which are applicable to any allegation of malice, in whatever context within a defamation claim such a case is pleaded; *Warren v The Random House Group Ltd* [2008] EWCA Civ 834; [2009] Q.B. 600 at [91].

[127] See paras 9.16–9.19, above. It is certainly arguable that where a libel also violates the claimant's privacy, that should sound in an increased award of damages. See also the discussion in *The Law of Privacy and the Media*, Tugendhat and Christie (2nd edn., OUP, 2011), at para.7.25.

[128] See para.32.56, below.

[129] The claimant may, e.g. seek to contend that the defendant knew that other publications repeating the defamatory sting would follow from the original publication and that such publications are relevant to the assessment of damages: see *Slipper v BBC* [1991] 1 Q.B. 283 CA and *McManus v Beckham* [2002] EWCA Civ 939; [2002] 1 W.L.R. 2982 CA. However, case management considerations may mean that reliance upon other articles in support of aggravation of damage may make such a plea vulnerable to a strike out: *Clarke (t/a Elumina Iberica UK) v Bain* [2008] EWHC 2636 (QB) and *Lewis v Comr of Police for the Metropolis* [2011] EWHC 781 (QB) at [102] where Tugendhat J. dismissed on proportionality grounds an application by the claimant to amend to rely upon alleged republications in aggravation of damage.
In the case of internet publications, the Court of Appeal has said that the "percolation" phenomenon, or the propensity that such stories have to "go viral" is a legitimate factor to be taken into account in the assessment of damages: *Cairns v Modi* [2012] EWCA Civ 1382; [2013] 1 W.L.R. 1015 at [27].

his mental suffering or the injury done to his reputation. He runs the risk that, if he does not include such matters in his pleaded case, he will be not be allowed to refer to them at trial.[130] A claimant should not, however, plead an additional meaning to the one he says the words bear whether for the purposes of aggravated damages or any other reason.[131]

When pleading a claim for aggravated damages in an action against two or more persons in respect of a joint libel, the claimant should bear in mind that the award must be assessed at the lowest figure for which any of them can be held liable.[132] Unless he makes out a case for aggravated damages against each of the joint tortfeasors, aggravated damages cannot be assessed. Where a claimant is seeking aggravated damages, he must include a statement to that effect in his particulars of claim and set out his grounds for claiming them.[133] A corporate claimant may not claim aggravated damages in respect of conduct by the defendant alleged to have aggravated or exacerbated the defamation because such damages required injury to feelings, which a corporation could not suffer.[134]

26.30   **Special damage.**   Where the claimant claims to have suffered financial loss, he must allege such damage, including a general falling-off of business,[135] with reasonable particularity, otherwise he will not be able to give evidence of such damage at the trial.[136] The defendant is entitled to particulars of any

---

[130] Some matters on which the claimant may wish to rely in aggravation of damages may not take place until after the particulars of claim have been served. In this event, the claimant should make a prompt application to amend his particulars of claim in order to ensure that such matters are introduced at the earliest opportunity. Of course, the court is unlikely to insist that aggravating events taking place during the trial (such as aggressive and prolonged cross-examination) be formally pleaded if they are to be relied on. In this context, see the discussion in *Adelson v Associated Newspapers Ltd* [2007] EWHC 997 (QB), per Tugendhat J. at [75] et seq and *Cairns v Modi*, above at [32]. Note also that a claimant will not generally be permitted to expand his claim for damages after accepting an offer of amends under s.3 of the Defamation Act 1996: *Nail v News Group Newspapers Ltd* [2004] EWCA Civ 1708; [2005] 1 All E.R. 1040 at [15].

[131] *Lait v Evening Standard* [2010] EWHC 642 (QB) at [30] per Eady J.

[132] See para.9.29, above. The rule may be different in newspaper and certain other cases: see *Hayward v Thompson* [1982] 1 Q.B. 47 and *Woods v Chaleff* [1999] C.L.Y. 500 CA (where the acts relied on in aggravation of damages are part of a joint endeavour by all the defendants and it would be artificial to draw a distinction of blameworthiness).

[133] CPR r.16.4(c) and CPR PD 53, para.2.10(2).

[134] *Collins Stewart Ltd v The Financial Times Ltd (No.2)* [2005] EWHC 262 (QB); [2006] E.M.L.R. 5 at [31]; *Oriental Daily Publisher Ltd v Ming Pao Holdings Ltd* [2012] HKFCA 59; [2013] E.M.L.R. 7.

[135] *Calvet v Tomkies* [1963] 1 W.L.R. 1397:
" . . . if evidence of actual loss of earnings or decline in business, even without any figures mentioned, is to be put forward in a case such as this, as at present advised, I for my part am inclined to think that it should be pleaded with consequential discovery"
(per Russell L.J. at 1400); *Ashdown v Manitoba Free Press* (1891) 20 S.C.R. 43; *Blachford v Green* (1892) 14 O.P.R. 424. For the position of a sole director of a company not party to the claim, see *Monks v Warwick District Council* [2009] EWHC 959 (QB).

[136] *Geare v Britton* (1746) Buller N.P. 7; *Browning v Newman* (1726) 1 Str. 666, per Lord Raymond C.J.; *Westwood v Cowne* (1816) 1 Stark. 172; *Ratcliffe v Evans* [1892] 2 Q.B. 524 at 529; *Hayward v Pullinger and Partners* [1950] 1 All E.R. 581; *Calvet v Tomkies* [1963] 1 W.L.R. 1397; *Silver v Dominion Telegraph* (1882) 10 S.C.R. (Canada) 238 at 263; *Bank of New Zealand*

special financial damage alleged so that he may know what case he will have to meet, and have an opportunity of inquiring into the allegation of damage before he comes into court.[137] It may be permissible to include a claim for damages for personal injury.[138]

Degree of particularity necessary. The precise degree of particularity **26.31** necessary in alleging special financial damage depends on the circumstances of each case. As far as possible, the claimant should identify specific losses which he claims to have suffered. Such allegations will obviously require greater particularity than an allegation of general loss of custom. The names of any customers or prospective customers, friends, neighbours or associates who have been lost should be included in the particulars of claim.[139] If it is impossible for the claimant to give the names of any customers who have ceased to deal with him, e.g. his customers are persons who deal with him over the counter, or consist of a "floating or transitory class", such as the frequenters of a theatre or travellers using a hotel, he can allege a loss of business or custom generally[140]; and so where the minister of a dissenting chapel alleged that in consequence of the defendant's words churchgoers refused to permit him to preach and withdrew their support, Lord Kenyon C.J.

---

v *Fleming* (1889) 18 N.Z.L.R. 1, affirmed on this point [1900] A.C. 577. In *Collins Stewart Ltd v The Financial Times Ltd* [2004] EWHC 2337 (QB); [2005] E.M.L.R. 5, a claim for special damages was struck out on the grounds that a fall in the market capitalisation of the claimant company was considered too uncertain a basis for an assessment by the court of the quantum of damages occasioned by an alleged libel.

[137] Per Lord Halsbury L.C. in *The Mediana* [1900] A.C. 113 at 118. See also *Tesla Motors Ltd v BBC* [2013] EWCA Civ 152 and *Euromoney Institutional Investor Plc v Aviation News Ltd* [2013] EWHC 1505 (QB), where issues of particularity were considered in the malicious falsehood context.

[138] *Sattin v Nationwide News Pty* (1996) 39 N.S.W.L.R. 32. But see fn.241 to para.32.54, below.

[139] *Bluck v Lovering* (1885) 1 T.L.R. 497; *Cross v Bain, Pooler and Co.* [1937] O.W.N. 220; *Roche v Meyler* [1896] 2 Ir.R. 35; *Ashdown v The Manitoba Free Press Co.* (1891) 20 S.C.R. 43 at 50.; *Berscht v The Toronto Star Ltd* [1945] O.W.N. 8; *Trenton Mutual Life & Fire Ins v Perrine*, 23 N.J.Law 402:

"The general rule certainly is, that where the plaintiff alleges, by way of special damage, the loss of customers in the way of his trade, or the refusal of friends or acquaintances to associate with him, or the loss of marriage or the loss of service, the names of such customers or friends, or the name of the person with whom marriage would have been contracted, or service performed, must be stated."

[140] *Hargrave v Le Breton* (1769) 4 Burr. 2423 at 2424; *Hartley v Herring* (1799) 8 T.R. 130 at 133, per Lord Kenyon C.J.; *Ingram v Lawson*, 6 Bing. N.C. 212; *Bradley v Youlden* (1867) W.W. & A'B. (Victoria) 205; *Catson v Gleatson* (1891) 14 O.R. 222; *Ratcliffe v Evans* [1892] 2 Q.B. 524; *Worsley v Cooper* [1939] 1 All E.R. 290; *George v Blow* (1899) 20 N.S.W.L.R. 395 at 400; *Erick Bowman Remedy Co. v Jensen Salsbery Laboratories*, 17 F. (2d) 255:

"If the plaintiff desired to predicate its right to recover damages upon general loss of custom, it should have alleged facts showing an established business, the amount of sales for a substantial period preceding the publication, the amount of sales subsequent to the publication, facts showing that such loss in sales were the natural and probable result of such publication, and facts showing that the plaintiff could not allege the names of particular customers who withdrew or withheld their custom"

(per District Judge Phillips at 261).

held this sufficient, asking, "How could he have stated the names of all his congregation?"[141] The degree of certainty and particularity with which the damage ought to be pleaded will vary from case to case and is regulated by the character of the acts themselves and the circumstances under which they are done.[142]

26.32 Requirement to plead *nexus* between loss and publication. Since special financial loss is only recoverable where it is the natural and probable result of the publication, there must be a pleaded allegation to this effect which makes clear the claimant's case as to causation.[143] In certain cases it may be necessary to plead extrinsic facts which will be relied on to demonstrate that the diminution in the claimant's business was brought about by the defamatory publication and not by other extraneous causes, e.g. the fact that other businesses in the same field have not suffered a similar diminution.[144]

26.33 Miscellaneous considerations. It is possible, of course, for a claimant to include in his pleading a claim both for the loss of particular custom *and* for a general decline in business.[145] It is also possible to advance a claim in

---

[141] *Hartley v Herring* (1799) 8 T.R. 130 at 133.

[142] *Ratcliffe v Evans* [1892] 2 Q.B. 524 at 532, 533, per Bowen L.J.:
"As much certainty and particularity must be insisted on, both in pleading and proof of damage, as is reasonable, having regard to the circumstances and to the nature of the acts themselves by which the damage is done. To insist upon less would be to relax old and intelligible principles. To insist upon more would be the vainest pedantry."
See also *Tesla Motors Ltd v British Broadcasting Corp* [2013] EWCA Civ 152 and fn.171, below.

[143] *Tesla Motors Ltd v British Broadcasting Corp* [2013] EWCA Civ 152.

[144] *Burnham v Hornaday*, 223 N.Y.S. 750 (1927), modified and affirmed 228 N.Y.S. 246:
"When the words are not prima facie actionable, the complaint must not only contain an averment of special damages, but it must set forth precisely in what way such damages resulted from the publication"
(per Heffernan J. at 758); *Kee v Armstrong, Byrd & Co.* 151 Pac. 572:
"The plaintiff attempted to establish its case by showing the volume of business immediately prior to the appearance of this article and the volume immediately following its appearance, and to ascribe the decrease in the volume of business to the baneful effect this article had upon the public mind. But that was entirely too indefinite. There are many things that will cause a business to fluctuate, and many times business fluctuates without any apparent cause"
(per Brett C. at 575); *Erick Bowman Remedy v Jensen Salsbery Laboratories*, 17 F. (2d) 255:
"It was therefore necessary for the plaintiff to allege either the loss of particular customers by name, or a general diminution in its business, and extrinsic facts showing that such special damages were the natural and direct result of the false publication"
(per District Judge Phillips at 261). See also *Brady v Express Newspapers* [1994] T.L.R. 690 (a malicious falsehood claim).

[145] *Kruse v Lindner* (1978) 19 A.L.R. 85:
"But if the plaintiff desires to rely on any particular actual loss of the kind presumed to flow from the injury to his reputation he may give evidence of it provided it is alleged in the statement of claim or otherwise particularised. Thus where it is alleged in the statement of claim the plaintiff may give evidence of general loss of business profits and where he has pleaded loss of business specially, either in addition to or without the allegation of a general loss of business, he may prove loss of particular earnings or customers"
(per Smithers J. at 91).

respect of expenditure which the claimant has reasonably incurred in mitiga-tion of his loss.[146] However, he should in all cases be astute to ensure that there is no impermissible mix or overlap between the various heads of damage claimed.[147] Where a claimant takes advantage of s.3 of the Defamation Act 1952 and merely pleads that the words complained of are calculated to cause pecuniary damage, he is confined to that allegation and cannot introduce evidence that he has in fact suffered special damage. A claimant's pleaded claim for loss of income should be supportable in law.[148] He must also, in an appropriate case, particularise his case under s.3.[149] Where the claimant relies on a loss of income as special damage, he should give particulars of his taxable income and allowances over the relevant period, as he is entitled to be compensated only for the amount he would have received after tax.[150] Sim-ilarly, where a limited company is claiming for loss of profits, its potential tax liability on those profits should be taken into account in assessing the recover-able loss.[151]

Where distinct causes of action are alleged, some against one defendant or one set of defendants, and the others against other defendants, the damages claimed in respect of the causes of action alleged against different defendants or sets of defendants should be separately pleaded.[152] Similarly, where there is more than one claimant, the pleading should make clear precisely what damages are claimed by each claimant, not least so that the defendant can be adequately informed in the event that he decides to make a CPR Pt 36 offer or offers in respect of some or all of the claimants.

Exemplary damages.[153] The claimant must specifically plead a claim for   **26.34**
exemplary damages, together with his grounds for claiming them and the facts

---

[146] In *Spalding v Gamage* (1917) 34 R.P.C. 289 (a passing off action) Younger J. awarded the plaintiff the cost of counter-advertisements inserted in the press. Although the Court of Appeal ((1918) 35 R.P.C. 101) overturned the award at first instance, it did so on the basis that the judge had erred in failing to give sufficient weight to the damage done to the plaintiff's reputation. There seems no reason in principle why the costs of counter-advertisements could not be claimed in a proper case. It is submitted, however, that such a head of loss could not be used to render actionable a claim for slander actionable only on proof of special damages. See para.5.3, above.

[147] Computation of damage in this respect can be complex: see, e.g. *Cullinane v British "Rema" Manufacturing Co.* [1954] 1 Q.B. 292 CA.

[148] *Calvet v Tomkies* [1963] 1 W.L.R. 1397.

[149] *Tesla Motors Ltd v BBC* [2013] EWCA Civ 152 and *Euromoney Institutional Investor Plc v Aviation News Ltd* [2013] EWHC 1505 (QB). See further fn.171, below.

[150] *Phipps v Orthodox Unit Trusts* [1958] 1 Q.B. 314 CA.

[151] *Lewis v Daily Telegraph* [1964] A.C. 234 at 262.

[152] *Rubenstein v Truth and Sportsman Ltd* [1960] V.R. 473.

[153] When ss.34–39 of the Crime and Courts Act 2013 are brought into effect, which will be one year after the day on which a body is established by Royal Charter to carry on activities relating to the recognition of independent regulators of "relevant publishers", as defined, exemplary damages will generally not be awarded against a defendant publisher if it was a member at the material time of an approved regulatory body. For a full discussion, see paras 9.31–9.32, above.

on which he relies in his particulars of claim.[154] When pleading a claim for exemplary damages in an action against two or more persons in respect of a joint libel, the claimant should bear in mind that the award must be assessed at the lowest figure for which any of them can be held liable.[155] Unless he makes out a case for exemplary damages against each of the joint tortfeasors, exemplary damages may not be assessed.

Section 10. Other Relief

26.35 Injunction. If he proposes to ask for an injunction to restrain further publication of the words complained of, the claimant should plead as a fact that the defendant "threatens and intends" to continue to publish the words complained of. A claim for an injunction may be included in the particulars of claim even if it is not included in the claim form.[156] It is, however, good and common practice to include the claim for an injunction in the claim form, particularly where it is a substantial object of the action.

26.36 Declaration. Although it seems a declaration may be made notwithstanding that it has not been sought in the claim form or particulars of claim,[157] a claimant who seeks this form of relief would be well advised to specify it in his particulars of claim. A claim for declaratory relief is likely to arise only in actions for slander of title,[158] A declaration of falsity is not a remedy available at common law in libel or slander.[159]

26.37 Order for a summary of judgment to be published. When it comes into force, s.12, Defamation Act 2013 will give the court the general power to order a defendant to publish a summary of its judgment where it has given judgment to the claimant. If a claimant is seeking this remedy he should probably include a claim for an order in the claim form, or at least in the particulars of claim.

26.38 Order to remove a statement or cease distribution. When it comes into force, s.13, Defamation Act 2013, will give the court the power to order

---

[154] CPR r.16(4)(c) and CPR PD 53, para.2.10(2); For the requirements of a claim for exemplary damages, see Ch.9, section 3.

[155] See para.9.29, above, for a fuller explanation.

[156] CPR r.16.2(5).

[157] *Hulton v Hulton* [1916] 2 K.B. 642; affirmed [1917] 1 K.B. 813; *Harrison-Broadley v Smith* [1964] 1 W.L.R. 456. CPR Pt 16 does not require a claimant to specify in his particulars of claim that he seeks a declaration, and see CPR r.40.20 which simply provides that, "The court may make binding declarations whether or not any other remedy is claimed."

[158] *Re Lewis' Declaration of Trust* [1953] 1 All E.R. 1005.

[159] *Loutchansky v Times Newspapers Ltd*, unreported, January 16, 2001 (QB), per Gray J. The Court of Appeal endorsed this view of the law in *Jameel (Yousef) v Dow Jones & Co. Inc.* [2005] EWCA Civ 75; [2005] Q.B. 946 at [67].

the operator of a website on which the defamatory statement is posted to remove the statement or any person who was not the author, editor or publisher of the defamatory statement to stop distributing, selling or exhibiting material containing the statement. Whilst this is a power to make an order against a non-party, it seems unlikely that the claimant would be criticised for including a claim for an order in the claim form and particulars of claim.

Interest. Since damages for non-pecuniary loss are awarded to compensate **26.39** a claimant up until and including the trial, a claim for interest is only appropriate where the claimant is claiming damages for financial loss. Where the claimant seeks interest, the particulars of claim must contain a statement to that effect and certain other prescribed details such as the basis for his claim to interest and the percentage rate at which interest is claimed.[160]

SECTION 11. THE PRAYER AND STATEMENT OF TRUTH

The prayer. The practice in libel and slander actions, as with other actions, **26.40** is for the prayer for the relief or remedy to come at the end of the particulars of claim and to start "The claimant claims . . . ". The claimant should then set out separately and distinctly in numbered paragraphs the items of relief or remedy which are claimed. Where there are several defendants, he should specify the relief sought against each defendant or group of defendants. Although both parties are entitled to indicate to the court at trial the level of award of general damages which they respectively contend to be appropriate,[161] it is not usual for the claimant to specify the amount which he claims in his particulars of claim and he is certainly not bound to do so.[162] A claimant need not ask for costs or for general or other relief. No claim for a retraction can be made.[163]

Statement of truth. Particulars of claim which are not included in a claim **26.41** form must be verified by a statement of truth, the form of which is as follows: "[I believe] [The claimant believes] that the facts stated in these particulars of claim are true."[164] Attention is drawn to CPR r.32.14, which sets out the

---

[160] CPR r.16.4(1)(b) and r.16.4(2).

[161] *John v MGN Ltd* [1997] Q.B. 586 CA at 615. See para.9.11, above.

[162] *L & N Bank v George Newnes* (1900) 16 T.L.R. 433 at 434. However, the cost of issuing a claim form is scaled according to the amount of damages claimed. Some claimants accordingly now choose to specify a maximum figure of damages (e.g. "not exceeding £50,000").

[163] *Burnett v The Queen* (1979) 94 D.L.R. (3d) 281. See also *TV3 Network v Eveready New Zealand* [1993] 3 N.Z.L.R. 435.

[164] CPR r.22.1 and CPR PD 16, para.3.4.

consequences of verifying a statement of case containing a false statement without an honest belief in its truth.[165]

Section 12. Malicious Falsehood

26.42 **Generally.**[166] Where the claimant pursues a claim for slander of goods, slander of title or other malicious (or injurious) falsehood, there are different requirements of pleading. The claimant must plead the issue of publication with equal particularity as in libel or slander, and although he is not required by the rules of court to plead the meaning or meanings of the published words,[167] it will usually be appropriate to do so.[168] The claimant must also specifically allege that the words were false[169] and that they were published maliciously. He should set out the factual respects in which the words complained of are alleged to be untrue and he should give particulars of the facts and matters on which he relies to support the allegation of malice. Before settling any document containing an allegation of malicious falsehood, a pleader should satisfy himself not only that he has clear instructions to make the allegation but also that the material on which it is based is of such a character as to lead a responsible lawyer exercising an objective professional judgment to conclude that serious allegations could properly be based upon it.[170] Finally, the claimant must allege either that the words were calculated to

---

[165] CPR PD 16, para.3.5.

[166] See Ch.21, above.

[167] The question whether words can be untrue in an innuendo meaning for the purposes of an action for slander of goods or other malicious falsehood is unsettled. Where the claimant in such an action wishes to contend that there was an innuendo meaning, it is submitted that he should plead the extrinsic facts relied on, since they are arguably "material facts", notwithstanding that CPR PD 53, para.2.3(2) does not apply.

[168] See paras 21.5 and 21.7, above. The Court of Appeal held in *Ajinomoto Sweeteners SAS v Asda Stores Ltd* [2010] EWCA Civ 609; [2011] Q.B. 497 that the single meaning rule did not apply to malicious falsehood claims. It is therefore open to a claimant to complain about a range of meanings which it contends a substantial number of people would consider the publication to bear. For two recent cases where the court was required to differentiate between the position in libel and malicious falsehood see *Cruddas v Calvert* [2013] EWCA Civ 748 and at trial, [2013] EWHC 2298 (QB), and *Euromoney Institutional Investor Plc v Aviation News Ltd* [2013] EWHC 1505 (QB).

[169] In *Thornton v Telegraph Media Group Ltd* [2011] EWHC 159 (QB); [2011] E.M.L.R. 25 Tugendhat J. said that the only relevant question was whether the claimant had established that the words were false. There was no occasion to enquire whether or not they were comment. In *Euromoney Institutional Investor Plc v Aviation News Ltd* [2013] EWHC 1505 (QB) the same judge ruled that the words complained of in an advertisement were only capable of being an expression of opinion or a value judgment and a statement of opinion could not be complained of as a falsehood for the purpose of a claim in malicious falsehood.

[170] In *Cornwall Gardens Pte Ltd v RO Garrard & Co. Ltd* [2001] EWCA Civ 699; *The Times*, June 19, 2001, the Court of Appeal, following *Medcalf v Mardell* [2001] Lloyd's Rep. PN 146 CA, which concerned pleading allegations of fraud, had imposed a more stringent test, namely that before alleging malice, the pleader had to have evidence supporting that charge before him in admissible form. The House of Lords, however, reversed the latter decision (see [2002] UKHL 27; [2003] 1 A.C. 120), substituting the test set out in the text as the appropriate one for pleading fraud. While the *Cornwall* case was not referred to the House of Lords in *Medcalf v Mardell*, it follows from their Lordships' decision, it is submitted, that the same test should be applied to

cause pecuniary damage and must give particulars of the nature of the alleged probable damage and the grounds relied on for saying that damage is more likely than not[171] or that they did in fact cause such damage and again particularise that loss. In the latter case, the claimant should give particulars of the damage and show sufficient nexus between the publication of the words and the damage.[172] In an appropriate case a claimant suing for malicious

---

allegations of malice. Note also, though, that if it becomes clear at any later stage of the proceedings that the material on which the pleader relied is not going to be put before the court, the allegation should not be maintained. See also Eady J.'s observations on and application of these principles in *Hewitt v Grunwald* [2004] EWHC 2959 (QB) at [23]–[27].

[171] The pleading should follow the terms of s.3(1) Defamation Act 1952. Such a plea does not constitute an allegation of special damage and, where his pleading is so limited, the claimant cannot introduce evidence of special damage nor can he be obliged to give discovery of financial documents, *Calvet v Tomkies* [1963] 1 W.L.R. 1397.

The leading case is now *Tesla Motors Ltd v BBC*. At first instance ([2012] EWHC 310 (QB)), Tugendhat J. said at [66],

"In my judgment if a trader, such as each of the claimants in this case, makes a claim for malicious falsehood and, as he is entitled to do, he relies not on any actual damage, but on probable damage such as is referred to in the 1952 Act, s.3, the claimant must nevertheless give particulars of the nature of the allegedly probable damage and the grounds relied on for saying that it is more likely than not. For example, if what is relied on is the probability of such a trader having to incur expenses in advertising and other forms of publicity in order to counter the effects of the alleged falsehoods, then the Particulars of Claim should identify that probable damage. On the other hand, the damage which, it is said, is more likely than not to be a consequence of the alleged falsehood, may be delay in sales of a given number of vehicles, or loss of sales of a given number of vehicles, or the difference between the price at which vehicles will be saleable following publication of the falsehood complained of and the higher price at which it is said they would probably have been saleable but for the publication of the falsehood complained of. In such cases, then the Particulars of Claim should likewise identify that probable damage."

On appeal, [2013] EWCA Civ 152, Moore-Bick L.J. said at [37]

"All that is required in order to make the nature of the case clear is identification of the nature of the loss and the mechanism by which it is likely to be sustained. In the ordinary course of things derogatory statements about any commercial product are likely to put off some potential customers with a consequent loss of revenue from sales and (depending on the nature of the business) increases in unit costs of manufacturing, storage and distribution."

Moore-Bick L.J. (with whom Rimer and Maurice Kay L.JJ. agreed) went on at [45] to cite [66] of Tugendhat J.'s judgment and agreed that the claim was insufficiently particularised because the pleading did not attempt to identify what part of the loss was caused by the actionable statement.

On s.3(1) generally, see *Cruddas v Calvert* [2013] EWHC 2298 (QB) at [191]–[193] citing *Ferguson v Associated Newspapers Limited*, unreported, December 3, 2001, (QB) (followed in *IBM v Web-Sphere*, unreported, March 17, 2004 (Lewison J.)) where Gray J. said that in light of art.10 of the European Convention on Human Rights which requires any restriction on freedom of expression to be strictly justified 'calculated' should be interpreted as meaning 'likely' or 'probable' in an objective sense and whilst the purpose of s.3(1) was to relieve a claimant of having to prove actual damage it was not designed to enable a claimant to advance a speculative case on damage. Meanwhile, in *Fage UK Limited v Chobani UK Ltd* [2013] EWHC 630 (Ch); [2013] E.T.M.R. 28 Briggs J. dismissed a counter-claim in malicious falsehood on the basis that a letter sent to trading standards was not malicious and had not been calculated to cause damage: see at [151]–[152].

[172] *Brady v Express Newspapers* [1994] T.L.R. 690, where the court held that a prisoner could not sustain a case of malicious falsehood against a newspaper on the ground that the alleged untruths it had published would be likely to result in loss of prison privileges (including a discretionary weekly allowance) as no reasonable prison authority would withdraw such privileges without holding an inquiry.

falsehood may make a claim for aggravated damages in respect of injury to feelings.[173]

Section 13. Misuse of Private Information

26.43 Generally.[174] Where the claim is for misuse of private information,[175] the gist of the claim is that the claimant's right[176] to keep information that is private to him private has been interfered with by the defendant without justification.[177] Accordingly, the claimant must identify the information which he alleges is private to him and has been misused by the defendant. The claimant should plead the basis upon which he claims the relevant information is private and is private to him.[178] The claimant must also aver that he had a reasonable expectation[179] that the relevant information would be kept private by the defendant, pleading all the facts and circumstances alleged to support that averment.[180] The claimant should plead how this expectation of privacy arose; by reason, for example, of a pre-existing relationship of trust and confidence between the claimant and the defendant[181] or, where no such relationship existed, because the defendant knew or had reason to believe that the information at issue was private to the claimant, by reason, for instance, of the information being self-evidently private or on account of the claimant,

---

[173] *Joyce v Sengupta* [1993] 1 W.L.R. 337 CA.

[174] See generally Ch.22, above.

[175] *Campbell v MGN Ltd* [2004] UKHL 22; [2004] 2 A.C. 457; *Douglas v Hello! Ltd (No.3)* [2005] EWCA Civ 595; [2005] Q.B. 972; *McKennitt v Ash* [2006] EWCA Civ 1714; [2008] Q.B. 73; *Murray v Big Pictures (UK) Ltd* [2008] EWCA Civ 446; [2009] Ch. 481.

[176] The right to respect for private and family life under art.8(1) of the European Convention on Human Rights, incorporated into domestic law by the Human Rights Act 1998.

[177] The interference may be justified because, for example, publication was in the public interest (e.g. because it corrected a false statement made publicly by the claimant: see *Campbell v MGN Ltd*, above) or with reference to the defendant's right to freedom of expression under art.10(1) of the Convention more generally: *Re S (A Child) (Identification: Restrictions on Publication)* [2004] UKHL 47; [2005] 1 A.C. 593.

[178] I.e. because it is of an intrinsically private character (e.g. medical or sexual) or because it is derived from and relates to a private event (e.g. photographs taken at a private wedding reception: *Douglas v Hello! Ltd (No.3)*, above, or of a family trip to a café: *Murray v Big Pictures (UK) Ltd*, above. See *Browne v Associated Newspapers Ltd* [2007] EWCA Civ 295; [2008] Q.B. 103 at [29]–[32] and *McKennitt*, above. In *Abbey v Gilligan* [2012] EWHC 3217 (QB); [2013] E.M.L.R. 12 the claimant complained that emails obtained by the newspaper were published in breach of confidence and that their publication was a misuse of his private information. Tugendhat J., applying *Browne* and *McKennitt*, held that it was not sufficient for a claimant to assert that the emails and their contents were inherently private. The claimant had to set out why the information in the emails was private to him, and to show that he had a reasonable expectation of privacy in respect of that information. (But note also contra, *Imerman v Tchenguiz* [2010] EWCA Civ 908; [2011] Fam. 116.) Tugendhat J. also held that the claimant had no title to sue over company emails where he was not acting or purporting to act as a principal.

[179] *Campbell v MGN Ltd*, above.

[180] *Murray v Big Pictures (UK) Ltd*, above, at [36].

[181] *McKennitt v Ash*, above; *HRH The Prince of Wales v Associated Newspapers Ltd* [2006] EWCA Civ 1776; [2008] Ch. 57.

to the defendant's knowledge, having taken specific steps to keep the relevant information private. Any such averment of knowledge needs to be properly particularised, including by identifying any individual said to have possessed the alleged knowledge.[182] Importantly, the claimant should give proper particulars of why his expectation that the relevant information would remain private was reasonable. The claimant must also particularise how the relevant information was misused in breach of his expectation of privacy; for instance, that it was disclosed without his permission to third parties, paradigmatically to the world at large by a media publisher. In the latter case, the relevant media publication should be identified with the same degree of particularity as in libel or slander. In terms of remedies, the claimant is likely to want an injunction restraining further disclosure or publication of the private material, particularly where the claim concerns photographs or video footage.[183] If the claimant wishes to claim damages to compensate him for any distress, offence or similarly hurt feelings or loss of dignity alleged to have been caused by the defendant's misuse of his private information, such should be pleaded.[184] Likewise, any claim for special damages.[185] Aggravated[186] damages are in principle available and, if sought, the factual basis for the claim must be particularised.[187] It is less clear whether exemplary damages are available.[188]

---

[182] CPR PD 16, para.8.1(5).

[183] On the footing that the court has recognised that each further publication of a private photograph may amount to a fresh intrusion: *D v L* [2004] E.M.L.R. 1 at [23]; *Douglas v Hello! Ltd (No.3)*, above, at [105]; but see *Mosley v News Group Newspapers Ltd* [2008] EWHC 687 (QB), in which Eady J. dismissed the claimant's application for an interim injunction to restrain the defendant from further publishing extracts of a video depicting him taking part in sex acts with prostitutes on the ground that to do so would be futile.

[184] For a list of damages awards in misuse of private information cases, see, Appendix 1.

[185] See e.g *Cornelius v de Taranto* [2001] E.M.L.R. 329 (cost incurred by claimant in retrieving copies of medical report at issue recovered); *Douglas v Hello! Ltd (No.3)*, above, (award of damages in respect of cost of additional labour and expense incurred by personal claimants in expediting selection of authorised photographs pursuant to their contract with the corporate claimant upheld by the Court of Appeal).

[186] Morland J. awarded the claimant in *Campbell v MGN Ltd*, above, £1,000 by way of aggravated damages, an award reinstated by the House of Lords. In *Mosley v News Group Newspapers Ltd* [2008] EWHC 1777 (QB), Eady J. held at [222] that: "It must be recognised that it may be appropriate to take into account any aggravating conduct in privacy cases on the part of the defendant which increases the hurt to the claimant's feelings or "rubs salt in the wound". See also *Various Claimants v News Group Newspapers Ltd* (the voicemail interception litigation) [2012] EWHC 2692 (Ch), at [14] to [19].

[187] CPR r.16.4(1)(c).

[188] Eady J. concluded that, as a matter of law, exemplary damages were not available for misuse of private information: *Mosley v News Group Newspapers Ltd* [2008] EWHC 1777 (QB); [2008] E.M.L.R.20 at [172]–[197]. However, it may be noted that in *Douglas v Hello! Ltd* [2003] E.M.L.R. 601, Morritt V.-C. permitted the claimants to introduce at a late stage a claim for exemplary damages (which failed at trial: [2003] 3 All E.R. 996 at [272]–[273] per Lindsay J. In *Various Claimants v News Group Newspapers*, above, the judgment records that the claimants dropped their claims for exemplary damages after the first day of argument: [2]) In addition to *Mosley*, the defendant relied upon the Supreme Court decision in *R (on the application of Lumba) v Secretary of State for the Home Department* [2011] UKSC 12; [2012] 1 A.C. 245 where it was held that exemplary damages were not available in group litigation where not all the claimants were before the court.

In an appropriate case, the claimant might, alternatively, seek an account of the profits[189] the defendant has made by reason of the misuse of his private information.

Section 14. Claims under the Human Rights Act 1998

26.44 Generally. A person who claims that a public authority has acted (or proposes to act) in a way which is made unlawful by s.6(1) may bring proceedings against the authority under the Human Rights Act 1998 if he is the victim of the unlawful act.[190] The court may grant such relief or remedy within its powers as it considers just and appropriate, including damages.[191] It is now common to see claims for libel against public authorities accompanied by a claim under the Human Rights Act. The most likely claim of relevance to this book, will be in respect of an alleged infringement of art.8 of the Convention, which encompasses the right to reputation.[192] The claimant must plead that he is a victim of an act by a defendant which is a public authority; that publication has engaged his art.8 right and that the publication of the identifiable information has interfered with his art.8 right.[193]

Section 15. Amendment of Particulars of Claim

26.45 Permission unnecessary. A claimant may only amend his particulars of claim without agreement or permission if the particulars have not yet been served on any party.[194]

26.46 Permission necessary. If the particulars of claim have been served, a party may amend the particulars only with the written consent of all the parties or with the permission of the court.[195] If the amendment involves the addition,

---

[189] *Att-Gen v Guardian Newspapers Ltd (No.2)* [1990] 1 A.C. 109 at 262, per Lord Keith; *Att-Gen v Blake* [2001] 1 A.C. 268 at 278–280, per Lord Nicholls; *Kuddus v Chief Constable of Leicestershire Constabulary* [2001] UKHL 29; [2002] 2 A.C. 122 at [109] per Lord Scott.

[190] Human Rights Act 1998, s.7;

[191] Human Rights Act 1998, s.8; see *McLaughlin v London Borough of Lambeth* [2010] EWHC 2726 (Q.B); [2011] E.M.L.R 8 at [8].

[192] *Re Guardian News and Media Ltd* [2010] UKSC 1; [2010] 2 A.C. 697.

[193] The unlawful interference will depend upon the act of the defendant and regard must be had to whether or not any behaviour could be said to be proportionate. For instance, it may be that an initial publication could be justified but continued publication once on notice of the falsity of the allegations could not be so regarded. In *McLaughlin, above*, Tugendhat J. set out the claim pleaded on behalf of the claimant at [16]–[17] which he described as '*commendably brief.*' For another example, see *Clift v Slough Borough Council* [2010] EWHC 1550 (QB); E.M.L.R. 4 at [50] (affirmed on appeal: [2010] EWCA Civ 1484; [2011] 1 W.L.R. 1774).

[194] CPR r.17.1(1). If a party has amended his statement of case where permission of the court was not required, the court may disallow the amendment: see CPR r.17.2.

[195] CPR r.17.1(2).

substitution or removal of a party, an application to the court must be made in accordance with CPR r.19.4. When making an application to amend his particulars of claim, the claimant should file with the court the application notice and a copy of the statement of case with the proposed amendments.[196] It is a convenient practice to underline the proposed amendments in red. When permission to amend is given, the claimant should, within 14 days of the date of the order, file with the court the amended statement of case and must serve a copy of the order and the amended document on every other party, unless the court orders otherwise.[197] If the substance of the statement of case has been changed by reason of the amendment, the statement of case should be re-verified by a statement of truth.[198] A claimant who is granted permission to amend his particulars of claim is not required to retain the superseded text, unless the court directs him to do so.[199] Whilst there is no rule on the number of times a party can amend a pleading, the Court of Appeal in *Ashcroft v Foley* stressed that repeated satellite litigation concerning the state of pleadings was not a good use of court resources and there had to come a point at which repeated attempts at amendment became an abuse of process.[200]

Although there is no longer a procedural rule to the effect that the claimant must bear the costs of and occasioned by the amendment, unless there is good reason for the court to order otherwise, this is likely to continue in practice.[201] It is also possible that an amendment will affect the order for costs which is made at the conclusion of the trial, e.g. where a claim would have failed but for a late amendment which substantially altered the case which the defendant has to meet.

Permission may be granted at any stage of the proceedings, even after judgment or on appeal. However, as a general rule the later the application to amend, the more it is likely to be inquired into and the greater the risk that it will be refused.[202] An amendment may be allowed notwithstanding that the effect will be to add or substitute a new cause of action outside the relevant

---

[196] CPR PD 17, para.1.2. Permission will not be granted unless the new plea is in adequate form: *Ward v Lewis* [1955] 1 W.L.R. 9 (no nexus between the alleged slander and special damage) and *O'Dwyer v ITV Plc* [2012] EWHC 3321 (QB) at [12]. The general rule is that amendments in general ought to be allowed so that the real dispute between the parties can be adjudicated upon, provided that any prejudice to the other party or parties can be compensated by an order as to costs and the public interest in the efficient administration of justice is not harmed, see *Cobbold v Greenwich LBC*, unreported, August 9, 1999, C, a dictum of Peter Gibson L.J. relied upon in a number of cases.

[197] CPR PD 17, paras 1.3 and 1.5.

[198] CPR PD 17, para.1.4.

[199] CPR PD 17, para.2.2.

[200] [2012] EWCA Civ 423; [2012] E.M.L.R. 25 at [43].

[201] This point is made at the top of the PD to CPR, Part 17 ("A party applying for an amendment will usually be responsible for the costs of and arising from the amendment.").

[202] *Swain-Mason v Mills & Reeve LLP (Practice Note)* [2011] EWCA Civ 14; [2011] 1 W.L.R. 2735, CA. The Court of Appeal cited with approval an earlier decision of the court, *Worldwide Corp Ltd v GPT Ltd*, December 2, 1998, CA where Waller L.J. said,

"Where a party has had many months to consider how he wants to put his case and where it is not by virtue of some new factor appearing from some disclosure only recently made, why,

period of limitation if the new cause of action arises out of the same facts or substantially the same facts as a cause of action in respect of which relief has already been claimed.[203] It has been held that articles covering the same news story but published to different audiences (in addition to their common market area) by separate newspapers, whose defences may differ, do not arise out of the same occurrence or transaction.[204] An amendment may also be allowed to add or substitute (including partially to substitute) a claimant after the expiry of the limitation period, where the new claimant is to be substituted for a claimant named in the claim form in mistake for the new party, even if the substitution involves the introduction of a new claim.[205] Although it is not required by the rules, a witness statement should generally be prepared in

---

one asks rhetorically, should he be entitled to cause the trial to be delayed so far as his opponent is concerned and why should he be entitled to cause inconvenience to other litigants."
In *Woods v Chaleff* [1999] C.L.Y. 500, the Court of Appeal refused to allow an amendment raising a new particular of malice only six days before the trial of a libel action on the ground that the amendment should have been made earlier. Otton L.J. stated that:
"It would seem to me to be totally wrong, both in the spirit of the old regime and in particular of the new Woolf regime, to allow an amendment at this late stage and to create a risk of real prejudice to the defendant and embarrassment in preparation and conduct of the defence ... Late amendments will not readily be granted by the court and should not be because that is not considered to be part of the level playing field ... ".
Pell v Express Newspapers [2003] EWHC 1649 (QB), in which Eady J. refused to give the claimant permission to amend his particulars of claim to seek an award of exemplary damages five days before the trial of the action was due to start. In *Creative Resins International Ltd v Glasslam Europe Ltd* [2006] EWHC 182 (QB), Tugendhat J. refused permission to amend in a libel claim where the claim sought to be introduced was weak and there was no material demonstrating the need for the amendments or justifying the complexity and cost that would be added to the case if the amendments were permitted. In *Adelson v Associated Newspapers Ltd* [2007] EWHC 997 (QB) at [75] et seq., Tugendhat J. refused the claimant permission to amend to introduce new particulars of aggravated damages because (at [86]):
"the time and costs that would be required to investigate at trial the new matters sought to be introduced is not proportionate to the amount of money involved in any possible increased award of aggravated damages, is not proportionate given the financial position of Mr Adelson, and would distract the jury from concentrating on the already complex issues which they will have to decide".
(There was no appeal from this aspect of Tugendhat J.'s decision.). See also *Lewis v Comr of Police for the Metropolis* [2011] EWHC 781 (QB) (at [102]), where an application by the claimant to amend to rely upon alleged republications in aggravation of damage was dismissed by Tugendhat J. on proportionality grounds.
[203] CPR r.17.4(2). See *Komarek v Ramco Energy Plc*, unreported, November 21, 2002, (QB) at [57] et seq. See also *Wood v Chief Constable of the West Midlands Police* [2004] EWCA Civ 1638; [2005] E.M.L.R. 20, where May L.J. at [66]–[86] gave detailed consideration to the question of whether the trial judge (Tugendhat J.) had been right to permit the claimant to amend his case at trial to introduce a new claim for slander, a cause of action in respect of which the limitation period had long since expired. (The Court of Appeal concluded that the judge had and dismissed the defendant's appeal against that decision.)
[204] *Dickhoff v Armadale Communications Ltd* [1994] 1 W.W.R. 468; *Herron v King Broadcasting Co.*, 746 P.2d 295 (Wash., 1987) (an amendment raising a new time-barred cause of action based on a rewritten version of the original story broadcast over five hours later was disallowed). But see the observations of the Court of Appeal in *Reuben v Time Inc.* [2003] EWCA Civ 6, in particular, Keene L.J. at [17].
[205] See *Adelson v Associated Newspapers Ltd* [2007] EWCA Civ 701; [2008] 1 W.L.R. 585 at [61]–[66]. The appeal (against a decision refusing permission to amend) was dismissed, however, on the ground that the claimants had not proved with evidence that the existing corporate claimant

support of an application to amend, particularly if it is likely to be resisted and especially if it is made at a late stage of the proceedings (a matter that requires explanation).[206] Permission may be granted after judgment to allow the pleadings to conform with the amount of the jury's award.[207]

SECTION 16. DEFAULT IN SERVICE OF PARTICULARS OF CLAIM

Consequences of default in service. If the claimant fails to serve his **26.47** particulars of claim in due time, the defendant may apply for an order to dismiss the action.[208] Time for serving the particulars of claim may be extended with permission[209] or with written agreement.[210] Before applying for permission to extend the time, the claimant should first ask the defendant for his written agreement to such extension. Although there is no longer a procedural rule to the effect that a party seeking an extension of time must bear the costs of, and occasioned by, the application, unless there is a good reason for the court to order otherwise, this is the order that is likely to be made.

SECTION 17. APPLICATION FOR FURTHER INFORMATION

The court may at any time order the claimant to clarify any matter which is **26.48** in dispute in the proceedings or give additional information in relation to any such matter, whether or not the matter is contained or referred to in a statement of case.[211] Clarification or additional information will not be ordered before defence, unless it is necessary or desirable to enable the defendant to plead, or

---

had been named in the claim form in mistake for two new proposed claimants, in respect of part of the libel claim sought to be advanced by the existing claimant: [67]–[76].

[206] *Lawrence v Lord Norreys* (1888) 39 Ch D 213:

"If there had been a miscarriage in the first instance on the part of the pleader by omitting to plead fraud, an affidavit might have said so, and explained how the statement of claim came to be launched in such a form. He would not have been expected to put forward the evidence in support of his case. No court would have required him to do so, but the court naturally would expect him to show some ground for the faith that was in him, to satisfy them that the case of fraud was not a simple creation of his own imagination" (per Bowen L.J. at 235).

[207] *Dougherty v Nationwide News* [1971] 1 N.S.W.L.R. 313; *Hill v Church of Scientology* (1992) 7 O.R. 489. Permission to amend a proposed claim in respect of special damages will not be granted after a final judgment, unless there are grounds to set the judgment aside: see *Kirby v Telegraph Plc* [1999] E.M.L.R. 303 CA.

[208] CPR r.3.4(2)(c).

[209] CPR r.3.1(2)(a).

[210] CPR r.2.11.

[211] CPR r.18.1(1); *Dee v Telegraph Media Group Limited* [2009] EWHC 2546 (QB) at [17].

ought for any other special reason to be provided at that time.[212] If the claimant objects to complying with the request or part of it or is unable to do so within the time stated in the request, he must inform the defendant promptly and in any event within that time.[213] Where the claimant considers that a request can only be complied with at disproportionate expense and objects to comply for that reason, he should say so in his reply and explain briefly why he takes that view.[214] An application for clarification or additional information should be made promptly.[215]

The proper course is to apply in the first instance by letter before making a formal application to the court.[216] Conventionally the letter is served on the claimant with the defence. On such applications it is usual for the application notice to ask that, in default of the requested information being provided, the relevant allegations be struck out of the particulars of claim.[217] If the defendant is entitled to the information sought, the order may be made, even though the claimant may thereby disclose the names of the persons whom he intends to call as witnesses at the trial.[218] The claimant may say that, through loss of memory or for some other reason, he cannot give any further information. If satisfied that this objection is genuine and the claimant is not merely setting out a case of which he knows nothing, the court will generally either decline to make an order[219] or will order that he serve the best information he can

---

[212] The defendant will generally be able to obtain an order for clarification or additional information before the service of his defence where he can show that he needs the clarification or additional information in order to know how to plead, or whether to defend or to pay money into court and if so how much: *Fullam v Newcastle Chronicle* [1977] 1 W.L.R. 651 at 659, per Scarman L.J (particulars of publication); *Roselle v Buchanan* (1886) 16 Q.B.D. 656; *British Legal v Sheffield* [1911] Ir.R. 69. By contrast, the court will not order a claimant to provide information prior to service of the defence to enable the defendant to advance or supplement a defence: see the observations of Eady J. about the burden of proof in *Granada Television v News Group Newspapers Ltd*, unreported, July 30, 1999, (QB).

[213] CPR PD 18, para.4.1(1).

[214] CPR PD 18, para.4.2(2).

[215] *Gourand v Fitzgerald* (1889) 37 W.R. 55 CA, per Pollock B.:
"It is useless for the defendants to come at the last moment to discuss particular facts, such as the several occasions of publication, which are immaterial to the real issue, and that only cause delay."

[216] CPR PD 18, para.1.1. In the absence of such a letter the court may refuse an order unless of the opinion that there were sufficient reasons for an application by letter not having been made. Where the text of a request for clarification or information is so long that it cannot conveniently be contained in a letter, or the reply is likely to be lengthy, the request should not be made by letter, but in a separate document. Whether made by letter or in a separate document, the request should follow the form prescribed by CPR PD 18, para.1.6. Where the request is made by letter, the letter should, in order to distinguish it from any other that might routinely be written in the course of the case, state that it contains a request under Pt 18 and deal with no matters other than the request: see CPR PD 18, para.1.5. A request should be concise and strictly confined to matters which are reasonably necessary and proportionate to enable the defendant to prepare his own case or to understand the case he has to meet: see CPR PD 18, para.1.2.

[217] *Davey v Bewtinck* [1893] 1 Q.B. 185.

[218] *Marriott v Chamberlain* (1886) 17 Q.B.D. 154 at 164; *Humphries v Taylor* (1889) 39 Ch D 693; *Zierenberg v Labouchere* [1893] 2 Q.B. 183 at 187, 188; *Bishop v Bishop* [1901] P. 325; *Wootton v Sierver* [1913] 3 K.B. 499 CA.

[219] *Garnaut v Bennett (No.2)* (1909) 29 N.Z.L.R. 381.

give,[220] and may give liberty to supplement it not less than a fixed time before the trial. The court will not require the claimant in a defamation action to provide information about what is alleged to be untrue in the words complained of.[221]

---

[220] *Williams v Ramsdale* (1887) 36 W.R. 125.
[221] *Gouzenko v Rasky* [1959] O.W.N. 185. The court will not order particulars of an immaterial averment or of one as to which the burden of proof lies on the party applying for particulars.

CHAPTER 27

DEFENCE

SECTION 1. GENERAL PRINCIPLES

Defamation Act 2013 The Defamation Act 2013, which is not yet in force, **27.1** has replaced a number of common law defences with statutory defences. For instance, justification has been abolished and replaced with a defence of truth under s.2, Defamation Act 2013 and s.5, Defamation Act 1952 will be repealed.[1] Honest comment has been replaced with a defence of honest opinion under s.3, Defamation Act 2013 and s.6, Defamation Act 1952 will be repealed.[2] The common law defence of qualified privilege to the world at large established in *Reynolds v Times Newspapers Ltd*[3] is replaced with a defence of publication on a matter of public interest under s.4. There are also new defences for peer-reviewed statements in a scientific or academic journal[4] and for website operators.[5]

Many of these new defences are intended broadly to reflect the common law while simplifying and clarifying certain elements.[6] The common law

---

[1] S.2(4), Defamation Act 2013.
[2] S.3(8), Defamation Act 2013.
[3] [2001] 2 A.C. 127.
[4] S.6, Defamation Act 2013.
[5] S.5, Defamation Act 2013.
[6] See the Explanatory Notes to the Defamation Act 2013.

defences remain part of the law in many jurisdictions. Much of the case law that has built up, directed at how to plead these defences, therefore remains relevant both outside and inside England and Wales, where the case law should assist in the interpretation of these new defences.[7] Moreover, no changes are currently proposed to CPR Pt 53 which governs defamation actions, sets out various pleading requirements[8] and is designed to reflect the common law.[9]

27.2 General denial insufficient. The defendant must not plead a general denial of the allegations in the particulars of claim, but must take each allegation separately, and either admit it, or deny it, or say that he is unable to admit or deny it, but requires the claimant to prove it.[10] Where the defendant denies an allegation, he must state his reasons for doing so, and, if he intends to put forward a different version of events from that given by the claimant, he must state his own version.[11] The defendant must plead with sufficient precision and clarity so as to enable the claimant to know what he will be obliged to prove and what case he must prepare to meet,[12] while also paying due regard to the requirement of proportionality in the manner in which he advances his case.[13]

27.3 Specific denials. In a defamation action, the defendant may simply contest the claim on the basis that the claimant will be unable to establish the essential

---

[7] The Explanatory Notes state at paras 18, 27 and 35 that
"where a defendant wishes to rely on the new statutory defence the court would be required to apply the words used in the statute, not the current case law. In cases where uncertainty arises the current case law would constitute a helpful but not binding guide to interpreting how the new statutory defence should be applied."

[8] The Practice Direction still refers to 'justification' and 'fair comment on a matter of public interest'.

[9] In *Ashcroft v Foley* [2012] EWCA Civ 423; [2012] E.M.L.R. 25 which is now the leading case on pleading justification and honest comment the Court of Appeal held that Eady J. had been entitled to strike out defences of justification and honest comment, and to have refused the defendants permission to amend their defence, where the defences and proposed amendments were pleaded without sufficient and proper particularity, and the intended *Lucas-Box* meanings were vague, unclear and incoherent. In a joint judgment, Pill L.J. and Sharp J. said at [35]:
"Though the obligation on defendants to "specify" the defamatory meaning or meanings they intend to justify is now contained in CPR Practice Direction 53 para.2.5(1), the rule in the sub-paragraph accords with the pre-existing practice laid down in *Lucas Box v News Group Newspapers Ltd* [1986] 1 W.L.R. 147 and subsequent cases, by which defendants were required to inform the claimant and the court in their pleadings precisely and clearly what meaning they intended to justify, without "circumlocution or obfuscation" (see for example, *Viscount de L'Isle v Times Newspapers* [1987] 3 All E.R. 499 and *Morrell v International Thompson Publishing* [1989] 3 All E.R. 733).

[10] CPR r.16.5(1).

[11] CPR r.16.5(2).

[12] "It is critically important for the plaintiffs to know what the defendants are saying and will seek to prove at trial. I think the pleas, as drawn, leave the plaintiffs uncertain and confused": per Cameron J.A. at 138 in *Loos v Leader-Post Ltd* (1982) 15 Sask. R. 127. This sentence from the 11th edition was cited in *Hunt v Times Newspapers* [2012] EWHC 110 (QB) at [23]. See also *Ashcroft v Foley*, above.

[13] CPR r.1.1(2)(c) and r.1.3; CPR PD 53, para.2.1; *Tancic v Times Newspapers Ltd*, *The Times*, January 12, 2000, CA.

requirements of the cause of action. The defendant will succeed if the claimant fails to prove that the words are defamatory[14] or, if defamatory, that they were published by the defendant to a third party,[15] or, if published by the defendant, that they would be understood by reasonable people to refer to the claimant. The defendant is entitled to put the claimant to proof of all the facts alleged in the particulars of claim. Accordingly, where appropriate, the defendant should deny, or not admit, that he published the words complained of. The defendant should not, however, deny or refuse to admit "that he wrote or published the same falsely or maliciously as alleged",[16] for this might be construed as an indirect plea of justification. (A defendant should no longer, in any event, be placed by a claimant in the position of having to plead to such an averment.[17]) If the defendant proposes to contend that the words do not refer or, for some reason, are not capable of referring to the claimant, he should plead accordingly. Further, if the defendant contends that the words do not bear the defamatory meaning alleged by the claimant or are incapable of bearing that or any other defamatory meaning, or that they do not satisfy the common law threshold of seriousness[18] or the (pending) statutory threshold, he should say so.[19] The defendant must state in his defence what he alleges the meaning of the words is if it is relevant to some substantive defence he wishes to raise, such as justification or truth,[20] honest comment or honest opinion,[21] qualified privilege,[22] or to the quantification of damages, and it may be

---

[14] Under s.1, Defamation Act 2013 (not yet in force) a statement will not be defamatory unless its publication has caused or is likely to cause serious harm to the reputation of the claimant. If the claimant is a body trading for profit, harm to its reputation will not be "serious harm" unless it has caused or is likely to cause the body serious financial loss.

[15] See, e.g. *Bowe-Griffith v Sharp*, unreported, June 25–27, 2003 (QB), a slander claim based on allegations of dishonesty said to have been uttered by employees of a DIY store in which the defendant simply put the claimant to proof of her case of publication. The jury at trial found against the claimant on this issue and judgment was entered for the defendant.

[16] *Belt v Lawes* (1882) 51 L.J.Q.B. 359; *Penryhn v Licensed Victuallers* (1890) 7 T.L.R. 1; *Lowry v NZ Times* (1910) 29 N.Z.L.R. 570; *Leersnyder v Truth (NZ) Ltd* [1963] N.Z.L.R. 129; *Walcott v Hinds* (1964) 8 W.L.R. 50; *Stredwick v Wiseman* [1966] N.Z.L.R. 263; *Clines v Australian Consolidated* [1965] N.S.W.R. 604 (F Ct); *O'Sullivan v Schubert* [1963] V.R. 143.

[17] See para.26.10, above.

[18] *Thornton v Telegraph Media Group Ltd* [2010] EWHC 1414 (QB); [2011] 1 W.L.R. 1985; *Cammish v Hughes* [2012] EWCA Civ 1655; [2013] E.M.L.R. 13 at [38].

[19] See paras 30.2–30.5 for an explanation of the difference between a statement not bearing a particular meaning and not being capable of doing so. Once s.11 of the Defamation Act 2013 is in force and the possibility of jury trial has gone the issue of capability will become academic.

[20] See *Lucas-Box v News Group Ltd* [1986] 1 W.L.R. 147 at 152; *Prager v Times Newspapers* [1988] 1 W.L.R. 77 at 86; *Viscount De L'Isle v Times Newspapers* [1987] 3 All E.R. 499 at 507; *Finnamore v Sun Publishing* (1993) 77 B.C.L.R. (2d) 293. The defendant will generally be reluctant to confine himself to a pleaded meaning. However, where a defendant puts forward a plea of justification, he is obliged to state the meaning of the words which he is purporting to justify, see para.27.7, below.

[21] *Control Risks Ltd v New English Library Ltd* [1990] 1 W.L.R. 183.

[22] *Loveless v Earl* [1999] E.M.L.R. 530 CA; *Bonnick v Morris* [2003] 1 A.C. 300 PC.

desirable for him to do so in any event to enable the claimant and the court to understand his case on meaning.[23]

The defendant should consider with some care his response to the meanings pleaded by the claimant. While it is open to a defendant both to deny that the words bear a defamatory meaning and to advance a plea of justification, such an approach may be difficult to sustain forensically. Where words are capable of bearing the meaning attributed to them by the claimant, the right course may be to admit as much and to plead whatever substantive defences are available to the defendant.[24] Before serving any defence, the defendant should consider whether to make a general or qualified offer of amends under s.2 of the Defamation Act 1996. An offer to make amends cannot be made after service of the defence.[25]

27.4 Substantive defences. Either in addition to or alternatively to his denial of all or some of the claimant's pleaded case, the defendant may put forward one or more substantive defences which defeat the claimant's claim. The defendant may plead as many different, alternative defences as he wishes, even though the allegations are inconsistent, although it may not always be prudent for him to do so.[26] He must, however, arrange his defences so as not to confuse the issues and embarrass the claimant.[27]

---

[23] *Armstrong v Times Newspapers Ltd* [2006] EWHC 1614 (QB), per Gray J. at [15]:
"In the defence it is denied that the words bore the meaning attributed to them in the particulars of claim. The defence does not as such set out the meaning for which the defendants contend. (Although this conforms with current practice, I think it would be desirable if defendants were to identify in the defence the meaning for which they contend, in the same way that claimants are required to do)."
[24] It is possible that an obstinate refusal to admit in the defence what is obvious, i.e. that the words complained of are plainly defamatory or that they plainly bear the defamatory meaning attributed to them by the claimant, might be taken into account in aggravation of damages. But see fn.18, above.
[25] Defamation Act 1996, s.2(5).
[26] See, e.g. *Hackett v Tierney* [1952] Ir.R. 185 (commented on in *O'Hanlon v Electricity Supply Board* [1969] I.R. at 96), where the defendant was held entitled to deny having used the words complained of and also to claim qualified privilege in respect of them; *Casey v ABC* [1981] 1 N.S.W.L.R. 305; but see also *Alderman v French* (1823) 18 Mass.R. 1 at 8–9 for trenchant comments on the propriety of denying publication and pleading justification. In *McKeown v Attheraces Ltd* [2011] EWHC 3232 (QB) the defendant sought permission to amend to include a *Reynolds* defence. The claimant submitted that the amendment should only be allowed on the basis that the defendant was required to elect to plead the defence in substitution of defences already pleaded. At [10] Eady J. described this submission as "novel" and said "if the proposed defence is arguable, it seems to me right in principle to allow it to go forward".
[27] Although there is no longer a procedural requirement that allegations be set out in separate paragraphs, such an approach obviously remains desirable: see CPR PD 5, para.2.2; *Dryden v Smith* (1897) 17 O.P.R. 505:
"[the plaintiff] is entitled to have [the defences] set forth in such manner as will enable him upon reading them to form a fairly correct judgment as to their scope and meaning and as to what is intended to be relied upon under them. . . . I think the proper order should be to direct the defendant to amend, rearranging the paragraphs of the defence so as to group the separate defences under their appropriate heads . . . "
per Moss J.A. at 512; *Burnham v Hornaday* (1928) 228 N.Y.S. 246, where it was held that since the defences in the libel action were so commingled and jumbled with irrelevancies and redundancies that it was impossible to separate them without redrafting the pleading, all defences

Damages. The defendant must respond specifically to any claim for dam-   **27.5**
ages. Where special damage is required to be alleged in support of a claim for
words actionable only on proof of special damage, the defendant should,
where appropriate, object that none is pleaded or that the special damage
pleaded is too remote or that it is insufficient in point of law. Facts and matters
relied on in mitigation of, or otherwise in relation to, the amount of damages
should be expressly identified.[28] It should be noted that a bare denial that the
claimant suffered distress arising out of the publication is not sufficient if the
defendant intends to raise a positive case of alternative cause of distress. If the
defendant wishes to raise a positive case putting causation in issue, he must do
so expressly and with full particularity in his defence.[29]

Section 2. Plea of Justification[30]

When to plead this defence. If the defendant intends to justify he must   **27.6**
raise a plea of justification specifically in his defence.[31] A pleader should not
put a plea of justification on the record lightly or without careful consideration. Before pleading justification, a defendant should (1) believe that the
words complained of (in some defamatory meaning they are reasonably
capable of bearing) are true, (2) intend to support the defence at trial and (3)
have reasonable evidence to support the plea or reasonable grounds to suppose
that sufficient evidence to prove the allegations will be available at trial.[32] It

---

would be struck out and leave would be given to the defendant to replead. See also *Armstrong v
Times Newspapers Ltd* [2004] EWHC 2928 (QB) at [94] per Eady J., approved on appeal: [2005]
EWCA Civ 1007; [2005] E.M.L.R. 33 at [25]; *McKeith v News Group Newspapers* [2005]
EWHC 1162 (QB); [2005] E.M.L.R. 32 at [44], [53].

[28] See para.27.39, below.

[29] *Bennett v Guardian Newspapers Ltd* [1997] E.M.L.R. 301. However, bear in mind the rule
in *Associated Newspapers v Dingle* [1964] A.C. 371 that it is not open to a defendant to allege
that other publications to the same effect as the publication sued on have already tarnished the
claimant's reputation; see para.33.58, below; *Rath v Guardian News and Media Ltd* [2008]
EWHC 398 (QB), per Tugendhat J. at [98]–[99]. In this regard, see also *Television New Zealand
Ltd v Ah Koy* [2002] 2 N.Z.L.R. 616.

[30] See para.27.1, above.

[31] CPR r.2.5; *M'Pherson v Daniels* (1829) 10 B. & C. 263 at 272; *Belt v Lawes* (1882) 51
L.J.Q.B. 359.

[32] *McDonald's Corp v Steel* [1995] 3 All E.R. 615, where Neill L.J. held that the test of "clear
and sufficient evidence" (referred to approvingly by Lord Denning M.R. in *Associated Leisure v
Associated Newspapers Ltd* [1970] 2 Q.B. 450 at 456) was not appropriate as a threshold test
since, if applied literally, it would impose an unfair and unrealistic burden on a defendant who
will, provided he has entered a properly particularised plea of justification, be able to seek support
for his case from documents revealed in the course of discovery or from answers to interrogatories. In *B v J* [1999] E.M.L.R. 490, it was held that, while there was no special threshold of "clear
and sufficient evidence" for a plea of justification, that did not entitle a defendant to make
damaging counter-assertions at will or on the basis of only inconclusive evidence. In *Hunt v Times
Newspapers Ltd* [2012] EWHC 110 (QB) on a wide-ranging application to amend, Eady J.
re-iterated that it is clear from inter alia the decision in *McDonald's* that grave allegations of
criminal misconduct should not be pleaded on the basis of bare assertion. The defence of
justification was later upheld at trial: [2013] EWHC 1868 (QB). See also *Ashcroft v Foley* [2012]
EWCA Civ 423; [2012] E.M.L.R. 25. Similarly, it is not open to a defendant to reserve the right
to plead justification "after discovery and further investigations", *Bridle v Jones*, unreported,

is often the case that the defendant is unable to compile all the necessary evidence to mount a plea of justification and serve his defence within the prescribed time. In such cases, it is the usual course for the defendant to apply to extend the time for service of his defence. A reasonable extension of time will generally be granted where the defendant is able to give adequate reasons for requiring it.[33] Where the court refuses an extension of time, the defendant should serve whatever defence he can at that time and seek to amend his defence to introduce a plea of justification at the earliest possible opportunity after the necessary evidence has become available.[34] The defendant should bear in mind that it is possible that a failure to establish a plea of justification at the trial will be permitted to be taken in aggravation of damages.[35] However, a failure to plead justification is not to be taken as an admission of the falsity of the allegations made for the purposes of a claim for an injunction to restrain their repetition.[36]

27.7 Exact words in the particulars of claim must be justified. The defendant must justify the precise words set out in the particulars of claim.[37] He is not entitled to set out his own version of the words and then plead that those words are true.[38] To do so would be "like pleading to a statement of

---

December 9, 1997 (QB), per Morland J. See also *Hewitt v Grunwald* [2004] EWHC 2959 (QB) at [23]–[27] per Eady J. and *Adelson v Associated Newspapers Ltd (No.3)* [2008] EWHC 278 (QB); [2009] E.M.L.R. 10, per Tugendhat J. If after further investigations, the defendant is in a position to plead justification, he may apply for permission to amend.

[33] As to extending time for service of the defence, see para.27.50, below.

[34] The granting of permission to amend is discretionary and the defendant should not assume that he will be permitted to introduce a plea of justification, particularly if his application is made at a late stage. However,

> "it is well established that the court will be reluctant to refuse permission to add or extend a plea of justification solely for reasons of delay, because it is not in the public interest that claimants should recover damages and thereby achieve a public vindication of reputation which is not deserved":

see, e.g. *Basham v Gregory*, unreported, February 21, 1996, CA, and *Mackenzie v Business Magazines Ltd*, unreported, January 18, 1996, CA. Nonetheless, as Sir Thomas Bingham M.R. emphasised in *Basham v Gregory*, this consideration should not be regarded as a trump-card and it is always necessary to have regard to the overriding objective of the CPR and the consequences of a late amendment in terms of delay, cost and stress for the claimant: see *Cook v News Group Newspapers Ltd* [2002] EWHC 1070 (QB), per Eady J. See also *Foster v Associated Newspapers Ltd* [2002] EWHC 1885 (QB), per Gray J. For the practice relating to amendment, see paras 27.48–27.49, below.

[35] See para.34.57, below.

[36] *Bryanston Finance v De Vries* [1975] Q.B. 703 at 725, 740–741 (Diplock L.J. dissenting on this point at 735–736). However, Lawton L.J. (at 741) thought that "this form of defence necessarily provides some evidence of an admission, but it does not provide conclusive evidence".

[37] *Heap v Green* [1926] N.Z.L.R. 302, where a plea that "such words as may be admitted or proved to have been used by the defendant are true in substance and in fact" was held to be a bad plea.

[38] *Rassam v Budge* [1893] 1 Q.B. 571 CA; *Kordowski v Hudson* [2011] EWHC 2667 (QB) at [20].

claim alleging that the defendant has said that the plaintiff stole a pair of boots, that what the defendant said was that the plaintiff's footman stole the boots, and that was true".[39] If the words which the defendant published are materially different from those alleged in the particulars of claim, he should simply deny publication. If the claimant fails to prove that the words he alleges were in fact published, he fails to prove his case.[40]

Justifying the words in their natural and ordinary meaning. Where **27.8** a claimant complains that words are defamatory of him in their natural and ordinary meaning, the defendant is entitled to justify those words in any meaning which those words are capable of conveying to a reasonable man.[41] In all cases where a defendant alleges that the words complained of are true, he is required to specify the defamatory meaning or meanings he intends to justify.[42] This is because properly pleaded meanings are key to the determination and proper conduct of all aspects of defamation litigation from the first stages through to trial. A vague and general meaning is liable to lead to a loose and ineffective pleading with excessive and irrelevant particulars.[43] The

---

[39] per A. L. Smith L.J. in *Rassam v Budge* [1893] 1 Q.B. 571 at 577.

[40] per Lord Coleridge C.J. in *Rassam v Budge* at 576. Also see judgment of Hood J. in *Edgar v Freeman* [1915] V.L.R. 16 at 20 and *Kordowski*, above at [20].

[41] *Prager v Times Newspapers Ltd* [1988] 1 W.L.R. 77 per Purchas L.J. at 86
" . . . it is still open to a defendant to plead so as to justify any reasonable meaning of the words published which a jury, properly directed, might find to be the real meaning. . . . At the heart of this case, of course, is the proposition which asserts that the scope of the defence of justification should not depend upon the way the plaintiff pleads his case, but on the meanings which the words published are capable of bearing".
It would seem that the defendant is entitled to justify any meaning which the claimant himself puts on the words complained of, however outlandish that meaning may be: *Maisel v Financial Times* (1915) 31 T.L.R. 193. However, where a claimant amends his particulars of claim to withdraw an allegation that the words bore a general charge of wrongdoing, which meaning the words were in fact incapable of bearing, the defendant is not entitled to retain on his pleading a defence of justification based on the general charge of wrongdoing: *Bookbinder v Tebbit* [1989] 1 W.L.R. 640. While this remains the position at common law, the effect of s.11, Defamation Act 2013, removing the presumption in favour of jury trial may change in practice how a defendant approaches a defence of truth. For an example of the difficulties a defendant seeking to justify can face when meaning is ruled upon as a preliminary issue, see *Cruddas v Calvert* [2013] EWHC 2298 (QB) at [158]–[161], [170]–[173], [183]

[42] CPR PD 53, para.2.5(1). In *Ashcroft v Foley* [2012] EWCA Civ 423; [2012] E.M.L.R. 25 Pill L.J. and Sharp J. said at [35]:
"Though the obligation on defendants to 'specify' the defamatory meaning or meanings they intend to justify is now contained in CPR 53PD para.2.5(1), the rule in the sub-paragraph accords with the pre-existing practice laid down in *Lucas Box v News Group Newspapers Ltd* [1986] 1 W.L.R. 147 and subsequent cases, by which defendants were required to inform the claimant and the court in their pleadings precisely and clearly what meaning they intended to justify, without 'circumlocution or obfuscation' (see for example, *Viscount de L'Isle v Times Newspapers* [1987] 3 All E.R.499 and *Morrell v International Thompson Publishing* [1989] 3 All E.R. 733).
For discussion on the three "tiers" or levels of gravity of defamatory meaning, see *Chase v News Group Newspapers Ltd* [2002] EWCA Civ 1772; [2003] E.M.L.R. 11 at [45], per Brooke L.J., para.11.13, above and para.30.6, below.

[43] *Ashcroft v Foley* [2012] EWCA Civ 423; [2012] E.M.L.R. 25 where Pill L.J. and Sharp J. said at [49]:
"So far as the particulars are concerned, the vice of a vague and general meaning is that it is

meaning in which a defendant seeks to justify defamatory words must, however, be a *defamatory* meaning.[44] If the claimant has selected certain words from a publication and pleaded that in their natural and ordinary meaning they are defamatory of him, the defendant is entitled to look at the whole of the publication in order to aver that in their context the words bear a meaning different from that alleged by the claimant and to plead that in that meaning the words are true.[45] In giving particulars in support of his plea, the defendant is entitled to cull some or all of the facts and matters from parts of the publication of which the claimant has chosen not to complain, provided that he does not attempt to justify separate and distinct defamatory statements contained in the publication, which do not share a common sting with the defamatory allegations contained in the words complained of.[46]

---

liable to lead to a loose and ineffective pleading with excessive and irrelevant particulars, a state of affairs which is not permissible and which has been deprecated, particularly in libel actions, for many years: see for example, *Associated Leisure v Associated Newspapers Ltd* [1970] 2 Q.B. 450 and *Atkinson v Fitzwalter* [1987] 1 All E.R. 483. Particulars provided in support of a plea of justification must be both sufficient and pleaded with proper particularity. The former requirement is met if the (properly pleaded) particulars are capable of proving the truth of the defamatory meaning sought to be justified. The latter requirement is a factor to be judged not by the number of particulars provided, but by the pleading of a succinct and clear summary of the essential (and relevant) facts relied on, enabling a claimant to know the precise nature of the case against him, and providing him with sufficient detail so he can meet it. As Lord Woolf pointed out in *McPhilemy v Times Newspapers Ltd* [1999] All E.R. 775 at 793c, a loose and ineffective pleading can achieve directly the opposite effect from that which is intended by obscuring the issues rather than providing clarification."

[44] *Broadcasting Corp of NZ v Crush* [1988] 2 N.Z.L.R. 234 at 237 (proving the truth of a non-defamatory statement would be a "pointless exercise"). Note that CPR PD 53, para.2.5(1) requires the defendant to "specify the *defamatory* meanings he seeks to justify".

[45] *Polly Peck Plc v Trelford* [1986] Q.B. 1000 CA. It is likely that s.11, Defamation Act 2013, removing the presumption in favour of jury trial, will also impact upon whether *Polly Peck* remains relevant in England under the statutory defence of truth. If the single meaning is determined before justification is litigated then there may be no proper reason to allow a defendant to defend a capable meaning rather than the meaning found to be the true one. But see *Cruddas v Calvert* [2013] EWCA Civ 748.

[46] *Polly Peck Plc v Trelford* [1986] Q.B. 1000 at 1032, per O'Connor L.J.; *S & K Holdings Ltd v Throgmorton Publications Ltd* [1972] 1 W.L.R. 1036; *London Computer Operators Training Ltd v BBC* [1973] 1 W.L.R. 424; *Mintoff v Associated Newspapers Group, The Times,* April 26, 1989, CA, where it was held that allegations of acts of violence and murder were not severable from allegations involving government mismanagement and oppression and the defendants were entitled to include particulars of justification going to the latter allegations in defending a claim brought by a former Prime Minister of Malta over an article which amounted to a wide-ranging attack on his policies, notwithstanding that he had confined his complaint to the allegations of violence and murder; *Templeton v Jones* [1984] 1 N.Z.L.R. 448, where the plaintiff brought proceedings in respect of a speech by the defendant in which he described the plaintiff as a man who despised "bureaucrats, civil servants, politicians, women, jews and professionals". The plaintiff complained only of the allegation that he despised Jews and the court struck out all the particulars of justification advanced by the defendant other than those referrable to Jews on the ground that, although many of the allegations in the speech were illustrations of a theme that the plaintiff indulged in the politics of hatred, they were separate and several allegations. With regard to *Templeton v Jones* [1984] 1 N.Z.L.R 448, now see *TV New Zealand v Haines* [2006] 2 N.Z.L.R. 433. In *Polly Peck v Trelford* [1986] Q.B. 1000, O'Connor L.J. doubted that the allegation in *Templeton* that the plaintiff despised Jews was clearly severable from the rest of the passage and expressed his view that the defendant should have been entitled to introduce the particulars which were rejected; *Cruise v Express Newspapers Plc* [1999] Q.B. 931; *Carlton Communications Plc*

The preferred and usual practice is to set out the meaning or meanings at the start of the plea of justification.[47] When a properly drafted plea of justification is included in the defence, it is permissible to rely on any facts that are proved in order to support it to reduce the damages, even though those facts by themselves turn out to be insufficient to make good the defence as a whole.[48] However, it is not permissible to plead, under the guise of particulars of justification, alleged facts and matters with a view to leading evidence about such matters solely to support an argument that the claimant should receive a smaller sum by way of damages.[49] To adopt this latter course is an abuse of the process of the court.[50] The court will be careful to distinguish between a defendant genuinely seeking to justify a lesser, and different, defamatory meaning which the words are capable of bearing and one who is impermissibly trying to obtain a partial justification of the whole sting of the libel pleaded by the claimant.[51] It is also not permissible to plead a *Lucas-Box* meaning in the form of a hearsay statement, e.g. to seek to justify a defamatory publication in the meaning that "A said that B murdered C" (where B is the claimant).[52] It is permissible to defend an opinion under justification but if a defendant chooses to do so he must prove that the opinion is in fact true.[53]

---

v News Group Newspapers Ltd [2001] EWCA Civ 1644; [2002] E.M.L.R. 16; *Birchwood Homes Ltd v Robertson* [2003] EWHC 293 (QB); *Rath v Guardian News and Media Ltd* [2008] EWHC 398 (QB). The Court of Appeal addressed the question of general and specific stings in *Rothschild v Associated Newspapers* [2013] EWCA Civ 197; [2013] E.M.L.R. 18 upholding Tugendhat J's decision at trial and set out a series of interlocking principles.

[47] Per May L.J. at 738 in *Morrell v International Thomson Publishing*, above. This is standard practice. See the order of the words in CPR r.53 PD 2.5.

[48] *Pamplin v Express Newspapers* [1988] 1 W.L.R. 116; *Turner v News Group Newspapers Ltd* [2006] EWCA Civ 540; [2006] 1 W.L.R. 3469.

[49] *Atkinson v Fitzwalter* [1987] 1 W.L.R. 201 at 210.

[50] *Dunn v Pressdram Ltd*, April 19, 1985, unreported, CA: per Lord Donaldson M.R.:
"Little wonder that defendants are tempted to take an optimistic view of what they can legitimately place before the jury in support of a plea of justification. They may well fail, but they will have evidence before the jury upon which they can rely in reduction of the amount of damages which will be awarded. This is clearly an abuse of the process of the court, but it is extremely difficult to prevent."

[51] *Prager v Times Newspapers Ltd* [1988] 1 W.L.R. 77 CA at 88; and see following paragraph headed "Partial justification". It has been held in New Zealand that, at least where a plaintiff accepts that he is bound by the alleged natural and ordinary meaning pleaded by him, the defendant is not entitled to justify a lesser defamatory meaning: *Broadcasting Corp of New Zealand v Crush* [1988] 2 N.Z.L.R. 234. However, the position may change when s.11, Defamation Act 2013 comes into force.

[52] To do so would be to infringe the "repetition rule", which is a rule governing not only what facts and matters a defendant is entitled to plead and prove in support of a defence of justification, but that also circumscribes the permissible range of *meanings* a defendant can seek to justify: *Shah v Standard Chartered Bank* [1999] Q.B. 241 at 263; *Mark v Associated Newspapers Ltd* [2002] E.M.L.R. 839; *Hamilton v Clifford* [2004] EWHC 1542 (QB) at [33] per Eady J.; *Curistan v Times Newspapers Ltd* [2008] EWCA Civ 432; [2009] Q.B. 231 at [53] and [80]. For an account of how the repetition rule constrains the pleading of particulars of justification, see para.27.11, below.

[53] In *Cruddas v Calvert* [2013] EWHC 2298 (QB) Tugendhat J. said at [56]:
"Where the defamatory words complained of contain statements of both fact and opinion, the

27.9 Partial justification. Where there is, in effect, a single broad defamation made by a single publication, the attack must be justified as a whole and it cannot be justified by saying that the publication was partly true.[54] However, where the claimant complains about a number of defamatory allegations contained in a publication, the defendant may justify some only, provided the charge or charges which he justifies can be divided from the rest, and convey a distinct and separate imputation on the claimant.[55] If the defendant takes this course, he must make the separation so that the court may see quite clearly which charges he justifies and which he does not.[56] If he leaves it doubtful, his defence may be struck out as embarrassing.[57] Before pleading justification of any individual charge, the pleader is under a duty to satisfy himself that evidence is available to justify the plea.[58] Where the defendant considers that he may wish to rely on s.5 of the Defamation Act 1952 in respect of one or

---

defendant has a right to defend the statements of opinion either as honest opinion, or as true. Some statements of opinion may be value judgments which cannot be said to be true or false, but other statements of opinion may be either true or false. But if he chooses to defend an opinion by the defence of truth, a defendant must prove that the opinions are in fact true. See Gatley on Libel and Slander 11th edn, para.11.7. A defence of truth in respect of an opinion may succeed where a defence of honest opinion would not succeed, because a defence of honest opinion may be defeated by malice (that is, proof by the claimant that the defendant did not hold the opinion in question), whereas malice is irrelevant to a plea of truth."

[54] *Mann v Mackay Television* [1992] 2 Qd. R. 136 at 139: "It is not open to a defendant to publish something which in form does not lend itself to being justified and yet attempt to justify it in part by relying on something which neither language nor in substance was what was published"; *Becker v Smith's Newspapers Ltd* [1929] S.A.S.R. 469: "The defendants are not entitled to assert any fact which does not alone or in conjunction with other facts asserted meet the substance of the claim as a whole or in some severable part or imputation." Sometimes it will be a nice question whether the justification meets the substance of the claim. In *Plato Films v Speidel* [1961] A.C. 1090, Lord Denning considered the situation where a newspaper alleges that a man has been convicted six times for dishonesty but, on being sued, finds that he has only been convicted twice: "Although the newspaper cannot justify in whole it can justify in part. It can plead that, in so far as the words meant that he had been convicted twice, they were true and thus bring the convictions before the jury" (at 1142).

[55] *Howden v Truth & Sportsman Ltd (No.2)* (1938) 38 N.S.W.S.R. 287; *Cohen v Mirror Newspapers* [1971] 1 N.S.W.L.R. 623. See paras 11.11–11.12, above.

[56] *Stiles v Nokes* (1806) 7 East 493:
"A plea of justification may be good with a general reference to certain parts of the libel set forth in the declaration if the court can see with certainty which parts are referred to; as if the reference be to so much of the libel as imputes to the plaintiff such a crime (e.g. perjury) that would be sufficient, without repeating all those parts again, which would lead to prolixity of pleading and ought to be avoided."
(per Le Blanc J. at 507); *Clarkson v Lawson* (1830) 6 Bing 266 at 587: "a plea which professes to justify the whole, if in effect it justifies only a part, is bad" per Tindall C.J. at 273.

[57] *Fleming v Dollar* (1889) 23 Q.B.D. 388 CA:
"Admitting, therefore, that the defendant may sever his justification where the alleged libel is divisible, we now have to see what application should be made of that principle to this case. Now I have stated what the pleader has here tried to do. He admits that the defendant has gone too far, but he does not mention in what respect, or to what extent he has gone too far. . . . In my opinion this defence is extremely embarrassing to the plaintiff . . . "
(per Lord Coleridge C.J. at 393).

[58] *Prager v Times Newspapers Ltd* [1988] 1 W.L.R. 77 at 89. See fn.32, above.

more distinct defamatory charges, he should expressly plead that section in his defence.[59]

Justifying an innuendo meaning. Where the claimant relies on a true　**27.10** legal innuendo, he sets out a separate cause of action.[60] It is submitted that a defendant wishing to meet this separate cause of action with a plea of justification must confine himself to the legal innuendo meaning contended for by the claimant. The reason for this is that, in such a case, the claimant's complaint is peculiarly tied to the extended meaning which he seeks to place on the words "created by a conjunction of the words with something outside them".[61] The claimant's case depends on his being able to establish precisely this extended meaning and the defendant who seeks to justify some other meaning will not meet the claimant's case.[62]

Pleading particulars of justification. While it used to be acceptable, on　**27.11** very rare occasions where the defamatory words themselves contained very specific and detailed charges, for the defendant to allege generally that the words were true without giving any particulars,[63] it is now necessary in order to comply with the rules of pleading for the defendant to give details of the matters on which he relies in support of his plea of justification.[64] Thus, where a general

---

[59] *Moore v News of the World* [1972] 1 Q.B. 441 at 448–449. Note that s.2(4), Defamation Act 2013, when it comes into force, will abolish s.5, Defamation Act 1952 but s.2(3) should have a similar effect. See paras 11.16–11.17, above.

[60] *Grubb v Bristol United Press* [1963] 1 Q.B. 309. The claimant may plead such a cause of action either with or without a cause of action based on the natural and ordinary meaning of the words complained of. Where a claimant raises both causes of action, the defendant may justify in the natural and ordinary meaning of the words or in the legal innuendo meaning or both.

[61] *Grubb v Bristol United Press* [1963] 1 Q.B. 309 at 327, per Holroyd Pearce L.J.

[62] "Once the plaintiff had acknowledged that the words were not defamatory of him when taken in their natural and ordinary meaning, then it was absolutely incumbent on him to prove they bore the meaning alleged in the innuendo. If he only proved a lesser meaning, he would fail. A good illustration was given in the course of argument. The innuendo in this case imputed that the plaintiff 'has acted and is prepared to act dishonourably'. That is an imputation of *guilt*. If the jury thought that the words conveyed, not an imputation of *guilt*, but only of *suspicion*, the plaintiff would fail to prove his innuendo, with the result that he would fail in his action. . . . The reason is this: If the plaintiff had by his innuendo said the words only imputed *suspicion*, it would be open to the defendant to plead justification if it had sufficient evidence at its disposal to warrant suspicion: but as the plaintiff says the words impute *guilt*, the defendant cannot justify that meaning unless it has sufficient evidence to prove guilt, which is, of course, a higher burden than proving suspicion. So as matter of pleading, in order not to put the defendant to any disadvantage, the plaintiff is pinned to his innuendo",
per Lord Denning in *Truth (NZ) Ltd v Holloway* [1960] 1 W.L.R. 997 at 1000.

[63] *Marks v Wilson-Boyd* [1939] 2 All E.R. 605 per Goddard L.J. at 608.

[64] CPR PD 53, para.2.5(2). The leading case is now *Ashcroft v Foley* [2012] EWCA Civ 423; [2012] E.M.L.R. 25 where the Court of Appeal held that Eady J. had been entitled to strike out defences of justification and honest comment, and to have refused the defendants permission to amend their defence, where the defences and proposed amendments were pleaded without sufficient and proper particularity, and the intended *Lucas-Box* meanings were vague, unclear and incoherent. Pill L.J. and Sharp J. (with whom Elias L.J. agreed) said at [49]:
"Particulars provided in support of a plea of justification must be both sufficient and pleaded with proper particularity. The former requirement is met if the (properly pleaded) particulars are capable of proving the truth of the defamatory meaning sought to be justified. The latter

charge of misconduct is made and the defendant seeks to enter a plea of justification, he must plead the specific instances of misconduct with which he seeks to justify the charge with sufficient particularity as to enable the claimant to know precisely what are the facts to be tried.[65] For example, where the claimant is accused of incompetence, administrative or financial mismanagement and dereliction of duty, the defendant must give a clear indication of what he suggests the claimant did or did not do.[66] Similarly, where the defendant says that the claimant's workmanship is shoddy, he must provide examples of specific work claimed to be shoddy.[67] The defendant should, however, ensure that, in particularising his plea of justification, each sub-paragraph of the particulars is relevant to and supportive of one or more of the defamatory meanings sought to be justified[68] and he confines himself strictly to the issues

---

requirement is a factor to be judged not by the number of particulars provided, but by the pleading of a succinct and clear summary of the essential (and relevant) facts relied on, enabling a claimant to know the precise nature of the case against him, and providing him with sufficient detail so he can meet it. . . . ."

For a useful summary of the principles, see *Radu v Houston* [2009] EWHC 398 (QB) at [9]–[15].

[65] See *Ashcroft v Foley*, above, at [53]–[60]. Previous editions have referred to the statement by Alderson B. in *Hickinbotham v Leach* (1842) 10 M. & W. 361 at 363, that: "The plea ought to state the charge with the same precision as an indictment" and cited cases where that statement was approved: *Zierenberg v Labouchere* [1893] 2 Q.B. 183 at 187; *Wootton v Sievier* [1913] 3 K.B. 499. In *Ashcroft v Foley*, the defendants argued that the statement was out of date and did not reflect modern pleading practice. Pill L.J. and Sharp J. (with whom Elias L.J. agreed) disagreed. They said,

"the "precision of an indictment" rule if it can be so described, does no more than require a defendant to comply with the well-established principle that in pleading a defence of justification he must identify the acts which the claimant is said to have committed and which are relied on to justify whichever imputation they are directed to support."

The Court of Appeal said that it had "particular resonance when the charges are serious ones" and also held that the rule is just as applicable to a defence of honest comment as it was to a defence of justification.

In *J'Anson v Stuart* (1787) 1 T.R. 748 at 752, Ashurst J. said:

"When [the defendant] took upon himself to justify generally the charge of swindling, he must be prepared with the facts which constitute the charge in order to maintain his plea: then he ought to state those facts specifically, to give the plaintiff an opportunity of denying them; for the plaintiff cannot come to the trial prepared to justify his whole life".

In *Hunt v Times Newspapers* [2012] EWHC 110 (QB) Eady J. said at [25] that Ashurst J.'s statement could be justified by reference to the right to a fair trial guaranteed under art.6. The judge also addressed in detail in his judgment the specific instances pleaded to meet the general allegations that the claimant was, amongst other things, a senior crime figure.

See also *Devereux v Clarke* [1891] 2 Q.B. 582:

"The degree of fullness and precision which ought to be required in an action for libel from a defendant who has pleaded a justification and has been ordered to give particulars under that plea, is not infrequently a matter which admits of reasonable debate. Certain general propositions are now, I think, not open to controversy. In every case in which the defence raises an imputation of misconduct against him, a plaintiff ought to be enabled to go to trial with knowledge not merely of the general case he has to meet, but also of the acts which it is alleged he has committed and upon which the defendant wishes to rely as justifying the imputation . . ."

[66] *Loos v Leader-Post* [1982] 2 W.W.R. 459. *Ashcroft v Foley*, above.

[67] *Ad-West Neon Inc. v High-Line Construction* [1992] 3 W.W.R. 445.

[68] See e.g. *Hunt v Times Newspapers Ltd* [2013] EWHC 110 (QB) at [23].

necessary for a fair determination of the dispute between the parties[69] and does not act oppressively.[70] Where a serious allegation of dishonesty is made against the claimant, there is a particular obligation on the defendant to plead full details of that allegation, setting out what was alleged to have been known by whom.[71] However, it remains an open question whether the pleading of such allegations by way of justification is subject to less stringent requirements than those applied in other contexts, such as pleading malice to defeat a defence of

---

[69] *Polly Peck Plc v Trelford* [1986] Q.B. 1000 at 1021; *Rechem International Ltd v Express Newspapers Plc, The Times*, June 19, 1992, CA. *McPhilemy v Times Newspapers Ltd* [1999] 3 All E.R. 775:

"As with all actions, libel actions should, by proper case management, be confined within manageable and economic bounds. They should not descend into uncontrolled and wide-ranging investigations akin to public inquiries, where that is not necessary to determine the real issue between the parties. The court will . . . strive to manage the case so as to minimise the burden on litigants of slender means. This includes excluding all peripheral material which is not essential to the just determination of the real issues between the parties, and whose examination would be disproportionate to its importance to those issues."

(per May L.J.); *Tancic v Times Newspapers Ltd, The Times*, January 12, 2000, CA:

"the question whether an addition to a substantial plea of justification raises matters which are essential or central to a defence, or are merely peripheral, is pre-eminently one for the discretion of the judge who hears the application . . . "

(per Brooke L.J.). See also *Macintyre v Phillips* [2003] EWCA Civ 1087; [2003] E.M.L.R. 9, in which the Court of Appeal upheld a case management decision of Gray J. refusing the defendant permission to amend his defence of justification to rely on particulars based on "similar fact" evidence; the observations of the Court of Appeal in *O'Brien v Chief Constable of the South Wales Police* [2003] EWCA Civ 1085 (a claim for malicious prosecution and misfeasance in public office) at [66]–[71] in relation to "managing" similar fact evidence in civil claims, particularly in cases that will be tried by a jury; *McKeith v News Group Newspapers Ltd* [2005] EWHC 1162 (QB); [2005] E.M.L.R. 32; *Warren v The Random House Group (No.3)* [2007] EWHC 3062 (QB), per Eady J. at [8]: "A governing principle is that the court should ensure, so far as possible, that the case is confined to the real issue between the parties."

[70] *Polly Peck Plc v Trelford* [1986] Q.B. 1000 at 1032. Whether a defendant is acting oppressively depends not only on the facts of each case, but also on the attitude of the claimant, who may be able to limit the extent and cost of the inquiry at trial by making timely admissions of fact or by behaving in a way from the outset which makes clear that he is conducting the proceedings in a manner which demonstrates a desire to limit the expense so far as practice: see *McPhilemy v Times Newspapers Ltd* [1999] 3 All E.R. 775.

[71] *Carlton Communications Plc v News Group Newspapers Ltd*, unreported, June 14, 2001, (QB), Eady J. This case and a subsequent decision in the same action, albeit recorded as *Cook v News Group Newspapers Ltd* [2002] EWHC 1070 (QB), also support the proposition that where a defendant wishes to justify an allegation of dishonesty against a corporate claimant, he must identify an individual or individuals who had the state of mind alleged and whose guilty knowledge can be imputed to the corporate claimant. See also *McKeith v News Group Newspapers Ltd* [2005] EWHC 1162 (QB); [2005] E.M.L.R. 32 at [26]–[27], per Eady J.:

"If it had truly been intended . . . to accuse the claimant of dishonesty in respect of her theories and nutritional advice, it would surely have been spelt out as such a serious accusation requires . . . It is, of course, elementary that a person can mislead innocently or negligently or dishonestly. If such an allegation is to be made in a plea of justification, it behoves the pleader to identify whether a culpable state of mind is said to be applicable to the instant case. Moreover, if there is to be an allegation that misleading statements or representations had been made dishonestly, it would be necessary to set out the facts from which that state of mind is to be inferred."

and to similar effect, *Purnell v Business F1 Magazine Ltd*, unreported, March 14, 2006, (QB) at [6], per Eady J.

qualified privilege or honest comment.[72] Further,

> "There is a rule of general application in defamation (dubbed the 'repetition rule' . . .) whereby a defendant who has repeated an allegation of a defamatory nature about the claimant can only succeed in justifying it by proving the truth of the underlying allegation not merely the fact that the allegation has been made."[73]

In the case of a defence of justification of reasonable suspicion,[74] it is usually a requisite of such a defence that the particulars of justification should focus on some conduct of the claimant giving rise to reasonable suspicion.[75] It is also necessary for the defendant to plead the primary facts and matters which, *objectively judged*, are said to have given rise to reasonable grounds of suspicion.[76] In this regard, it is impermissible to plead as a primary fact the proposition that some person or persons announced, suspected or believed the claimant to be guilty. It may be open to a defendant to adduce hearsay evidence to establish a primary fact, but that in no way undermines the rule that statements (still less the beliefs) of any individual cannot themselves

---

[72] In *Ashcroft v Foley* [2012] EWCA 423; [2012] E.M.L.R. 25 the respondent argued that allegations of fraud, bad faith or deliberate misconduct are subject to the same requirements whether they appear in a plea of justification, or a plea of malice or anywhere else. As the Court of Appeal noted at [79], at first instance, Eady J. recorded the competing arguments but did not expressly accept either argument. Pill L.J. and Sharp J. did not consider it was necessary to resolve the issue. Elias L.J. agreed that it was not necessary to resolve the point but said, obiter, that his strong preliminary view was that the pleading of fraud in the context of a plea of justification should be subject to the same stringent requirements as applied in other contexts: see [93]. For the requirements for pleading malice see para.28.6, below.

[73] per Eady J. in *Musa King v Telegraph Group Ltd* [2003] EWHC 1312 (QB) at [32] and in *Al Rahji Banking & Investment Corp v The Wall Street Journal Europe SPRL* [2003] EWHC 1358 (QB) at [27] (in which he identifies "certain principles which are intended to discipline those who seek to justify any defamatory allegation on the basis that the particular claimant is only involved in wrongdoing, if at all, at one or two removes. They need to be stated because the court should always be alert against any form of pleading designed to by-pass those disciplines"), citing *Shah v Standard Chartered Bank* [1999] Q.B. 241 and *Chase v News Group Newspapers Ltd* [2002] EWCA Civ 1772; [2003] E.M.L.R. 11 CA. The repetition rule is not inconsistent with *Thoma v Luxembourg* (2003) 36 EHRR 21: *Mark v Associated Newspapers Ltd* [2002] EWCA Civ 772; [2002] E.M.L.R. 38 CA. "The repetition rule applies to [justification of] all levels of meaning": *Sharma v Singh* [2007] EWHC 2988 (QB), at [31] per Tugendhat J., citing *Jameel v Times Newspapers Ltd* [2004] EWCA Civ 983; [2004] E.M.L.R. 31 at [28]–[30]. It has no application to defences of *Reynolds* qualified privilege: see *Al-Fagih v HH Saudi Research & Marketing (UK) Ltd* [2001] EWCA Civ 1634; [2002] E.M.L.R. 13 at [34]–[38], per Simon Brown L.J., or statutory reporting privilege: see *Curistan v Times Newspapers Ltd* [2008] EWCA Civ 432; [2009] Q.B. 231.

[74] Now also known as a *Chase* level 2 meaning: see *Chase v News Group Newspapers Ltd* [2002] EWCA Civ 1772; [2003] E.M.L.R. 11 CA and fn 71.

[75] *Shah v Standard Chartered Bank* [1999] Q.B. 241; *Miller v Associated Newspapers* [2012] EWHC 3721 (QB). In *Miller* Sharp J. said at [14], citing *Shah*:

> "it is an essential requisite of a defence of justification to such a charge that it should focus on some conduct on the claimant's part giving rise to reasonable suspicion, albeit it may be necessary in a complicated case to portray some of the background and to set out the material which connects the main facts relied on. But the essential question remains whether the claimant has by his conduct brought suspicion upon himself."

[76] See *Miller*, above.

serve as primary facts.[77] Further, it is not permitted to justify a reasonable ground for suspicion meaning with reference to post-publication events since the issue falls to be judged as at the time of publication.[78] It is, however, permissible for a defendant to rely upon pre-publication events of which he was unaware at the time he published the material complained of.[79] Where a defendant seeks to prove the truth of a relevant fact by way of justification and the claimant makes an admission in respect of that fact, the court may in a particular case decline to allow the defendant to continue to maintain his allegation in the face of the admission, even where it does not match exactly the defendant's allegation.[80]

---

[77] In *APN & TVNZ v Simunovich Fisheries Ltd* [2009] NZSC 93 the New Zealand Supreme Court said at [34]:

"Circumstantial evidence cannot contribute to reasonable grounds for suspicion unless it gives rise to an available inference concerning the conduct of the plaintiff. The circumstantial evidence suggestion was first made by Brooke L.J. himself in Chase [at para.51] where he said that a defendant could 'rely on strong circumstantial evidence implicating [the plaintiff]' as grounds for reasonable suspicion. The circumstantial evidence could hardly have any value unless it 'implicated' the plaintiff by means of an available inference as to the plaintiff's conduct. That is why we have said that our elaboration represents something which was already implicit in the sixth principle."

Sharp J. agreed with his paragraph in *Miller v Associated*, above, at [15].

[78] However, see *Miller, above*, at [19]–[21] on whether explanations relating to the claimant's state of mind at the time can be given at trial.

[79] *Musa King v Telegraph Group Ltd* [2003] EWHC 1312 (QB) at [32] (quoted by the Court of Appeal in the appeal from that decision with apparent approval: [2004] EWCA Civ 613; [2004] E.M.L.R. 23 at [22]) and *Al Rajhi Banking & Investment Corp v The Wall Street Journal Europe SPRL* [2003] EWHC 1358 (QB) at [27], relying on *Evans v Granada Television* [1996] E.M.L.R. 429; *Shah v Standard Chartered Bank* [1999] Q.B. 241, following *Stern v Piper* [1997] Q.B. 123; *Bennett v News Group Newspapers Ltd* [2002] E.M.L.R. 39; *Chase v News Group Newspapers Ltd*, above; *Loutchansky v Times Newspapers Ltd* [2002] EWHC 2726 (QB) and *Miller*, above. This approach is not incompatible with arts 6 and 10 of the ECHR, see *Berezovsky v Forbes Inc.* [2001] EWCA Civ 1251; [2001] E.M.L.R. 45. See also *Hamilton v Clifford* [2004] EWHC 1542 (QB) at [36]–[52], per Eady J. for a detailed analysis and application of the principles governing level 2 justification, including the requirement that the grounds pleaded must be objectively reasonable, and *Fallon v MGN Ltd* [2006] EWHC 783 (QB); [2006] E.M.L.R. 19 and *Hunt v Times Newspapers* [2012] EWHC 110 (QB), which provides an example of the approach the court will take when scrutinising pleas of this kind. In *Joseph v Spiller* [2010] UKSC 53; [2011] 1 A.C. 852 Lord Phillips PSC at [89] said

"The courts have always held that the only defence to a bare comment which infers the existence of discreditable conduct but does not identify it is justification: see for example Bingham L.J. in *Brent Walker Group plc v Time Out Ltd* [1991] 2 QB 33, 44h. In justifying a bare defamatory comment the defendant is entitled, in accordance with the principles that govern that defence, to plead any fact, whether or not it was known to him when he made the comment in order to show that the comment was justified."

In *Armstrong v Times Newspapers Ltd* [2004] EWHC 2928 (QB), Eady J. put a stop to what he perceived to be an attempt by a defendant to circumvent the disciplines that govern the pleading of a level 2 meaning by pleading a level 3 meaning in the alternative: see [27]–[28]. Having ruled that the publication at issue was not capable of bearing any meaning lower than a level 2 meaning, he proceeded to excise from the lengthy particulars of justification (102 paragraphs' worth) all the material that failed to comply with the principles governing level 2 justification. These rulings were not challenged by the defendant on appeal ([2005] EWCA Civ 1007; [2005] E.M.L.R. 33 at [36]).

[80] *US Tobacco International Inc. v BBC* [1998] E.M.L.R. 816 CA:

"In carrying out that exercise the court will have regard to all the circumstances, including the

27.12 Similar fact evidence and justification. Where a defendant is pleading to a general sting then he must plead in the defence of justification all the matters upon which he relies. However, where he is seeking to justify a specific sting with reference to matters not directly in issue but by way of similar fact evidence it is not a requirement to plead the evidence relied upon. The general rule is that evidence should not be pleaded. However, it would be wise to notify the claimant of the matters upon which there is an intention to rely by way of similar fact evidence.

In *Desmond v Bower*[81] the defendant sought to defend the specific defamatory sting by pleading matters relating to other incidents than the one referred to in the words complained of. The claimant successfully applied to strike out those particulars of justification on the basis that they did not support the specific sting. Eady J. left open the question whether evidence of those incidents could come back into the case at trial as similar fact evidence under the principles outlined by the House of Lords in *O'Brien v Chief Constable of South Wales Police*.[82] In the course of his judgment the judge said "One does not introduce into the pleading evidence which is intended to support and make out [the] pleaded facts. That is not the purpose of a pleading" and added that a decision could not be made whether or not the material was probative and admissible until the witness statements were served. Later, the defendant applied for permission to serve a witness summons in respect of one other incident. Eady J. refused permission. That decision was subsequently appealed.[83]

27.13 Miscellaneous considerations. Where the defendant wishes to rely on s.13 of the Civil Evidence Act 1968, the defendant should plead the relevant conviction, notwithstanding that the rule relating to the pleading of convictions in reliance upon other sections of that Act[84] does not expressly extend to pleading a criminal conviction in a defamation action in reliance upon s.13.

---

nature of the allegation, its importance in the action, the extent of the admission, and the effect that the inclusion or exclusion of the allegation would be likely to have on the length and complexity of the trial"
(per Nicholls L.J.); applied in *Cruise v Express Newspapers Plc* [1999] Q.B. 931; but see *Carlton Communications Plc v News Group Newspapers Ltd* [2001] EWCA Civ 1644; [2002] E.M.L.R. 16, where the claimant had offered to make certain admissions in relation to matter at issue which the defendant wished to justify. For a detailed analysis of the Court of Appeal's decision in *US Tobacco*, see *Warren v The Random House Group Ltd (No.3)* [2007] EWHC 3062 (QB), per Eady J. at [14] et seq. and Court of Appeal's review of that analysis at [2008] EWCA Civ 834 at [103] et seq. (appeal dismissed).

[81] [2008] EWHC 2952 (QB).
[82] [2005] UKHL 26, [2005] 2 A.C. 534.
[83] [2009] EWCA Civ 667.
[84] CPR PD 16, para.9.1. Note the amendment to s.13 of the 1968 Act brought about by s.12 of the Defamation Act 1996.

Section 3. Defence of Truth under Defamation Act 2013, Section 2

Defence of truth. Section 2 of the Act will abolish the common law **27.14** defence of justification and replace it with a statutory defence of truth.[85] Under s.2(1) it will be a defence to an action for defamation for a defendant to show that the imputation[86] conveyed by the statement complained of is substantially true. If the statement conveys two or more distinct imputations and one or more of them is not shown to be substantially true then the defence will not fail if, having regard to the imputations which are shown to be substantially true, the imputations which are not shown to be substantially true do not seriously harm the claimant's reputation.[87]

At the present time there is no guidance on how to plead a defence of truth **27.15** outside the general requirements set out in CPR Pts 15 and 16. The Practice Direction to Pt 53 that applies to defamation claims refers to the common law defences and not to the new statutory defences. Following the wording of the Act, a pleader must identify and plead the imputation conveyed by the statement and show that the imputation conveyed is substantially true. That should mean that he should identify the meaning or imputation and then plead particulars in support of that imputation. It would be sensible, until further guidance is provided by the courts, for those particulars to respect the common law rules.[88]

Section 4. Plea of Honest Comment

The name of the defence. The Court of Appeal in *British Chiropractic* **27.16** *Association v Singh*[89] said that the defence should be re-named "honest opinion" because it "better reflects the realities." The statutory defence under s.3, Defamation Act 2013 will now be known as honest opinion and contains no requirement that the defence is on a matter of public interest. However, the Supreme Court in *Joseph v Spiller*[90] preferred "honest comment". Consequently, the common law defence will be referred to as "honest comment".

---

[85] S.2(4), Defamation Act 2013.

[86] The Explanatory Notes state that the use of the word 'imputation' is intended to preserve the repetition rule by focussing upon the imputations conveyed by the statement complained about.

[87] The Explanatory Notes state at paragraph 18 that
'where a defendant wishes to rely on the new statutory defence the court would be required to apply the words used in the statute, not the current case law. In cases where uncertainty arises the current case law would constitute a helpful but not binding guide to interpreting how the new statutory defence should be applied.'

[88] See paras 27.6–27.13, above.

[89] [2010] EWCA Civ 350, [2011] 1 W.L.R. 133 at [36].

[90] [2010] UKSC 53; [2011] 1 A.C. 852.

No change has been made to CPR Pt 53 PD paras 2.6 and 2.8 which still refer to "fair comment on a matter of public interest".

27.17 Defence must be specially pleaded. The defence of honest comment must always be specially pleaded.[91] The defendant should not, however, enter a plea of honest comment unless he is satisfied that the facts which are relied upon in support of the plea are true and he has reasonable evidence to support them or reasonable grounds for supposing that sufficient evidence to prove them will be available at the trial, at which he intends to support the defence.[92] Where a defendant alleges that the words complained of are honest comment on a matter of public interest, he must specify the defamatory meaning which he seeks to defend as comment.[93] This rule derives from the somewhat uncertain requirement which existed prior to the introduction of the CPR.[94] The defendant should specify, usually at the start of his pleading of the defence of honest comment, the comment in the words complained of, which he will contend falls within this defence. In advancing a plea of honest comment, the defendant is entitled to look at the whole of the publication and he may cull facts on which he alleges the comment to be based from parts of

---

[91] CPR PD 14, para.2.6; *Littleton v Hamilton* (1975) 4 O.R. (2d) 283 at 286. For a full account of what is permissible by way of a defence of honest comment, see Ch.12 and the leading case of *Joseph v Spiller* [2010] UKSC 53; [2011] 1 A.C. 852 at [2]–[7] per Lord Phillips PSC.

[92] *McDonald's Corp v Steel* [1995] 3 All E.R. 615 at 621, also per Neill L.J. at 622:
"It is to be remembered that the defences of justification and fair comment form part of the framework by which free speech is protected. It is therefore important that no unnecessary barriers to the use of these defences are erected, while at the same time the court is able to ensure that its processes are not abused by irresponsible and unsupported pleadings."

[93] CPR PD 53, para.2.6(1). See *Burstein v Associated Newspapers Ltd* [2007] EWCA Civ 600; [2007] 4 All E.R. 319 at [7]–[8], approving *Lowe v Associated Newspapers Ltd* [2006] EWHC 320 (QB); [2007] 2 W.L.R. 595, per Eady J. In *British Chiropractic Association v Singh* [2010] EWCA Civ 350, without making reference to *Burstein v Associated Newspapers* (where a differently constituted Court of Appeal had held that the court must find the single meaning of the words before considering whether the words complained of were fact or comment) the Court of Appeal said at [32]:
"It may be said that the agreed pair of questions which the judge was asked to answer . . . . was based on a premise, inherent in our libel law, that a comment is as capable as an assertion of fact of being defamatory, and that what differ are the available defences; so that the first question has to be whether the words are defamatory even if they amount to no more than comment. This case suggests that this may not always be the best approach, because the answer to the first question may stifle the answer to the second."
A defendant is bound by the requirements of CPR Pt 53 PD 2.6(1) and (2) to set out the defamatory meaning he seeks to defend as honest comment and to give particulars. It will then be a matter for the court to decide the order to determine the question of the natural and ordinary meaning of the words and whether or not they are fact or comment upon an application by a party. For the position in New Zealand, see *TV New Zealand v Haines* [2006] 2 N.Z.L.R. 433. And in New South Wales, *Breen v Nationwide News Pty Ltd* [2007] NSWDC 192 at [17]. And in South Africa see *Citizen 1978 (Pty) Ltd v McBride* 31 B.H.R.C. 147.

[94] *Control Risks Ltd v New English Library Ltd* [1990] 1 W.L.R. 183:
" . . . when fair comment is pleaded the defendant must spell out, with sufficient precision to enable the plaintiff to know what case he has to meet, what is the comment which the defendant will seek to say attracts the fair comment defence"
(per Nicholls L.J. at 189). For the position in Western Australia, see *Cock v Hughes* [2002] WASC 108.

the publication of which the claimant has not complained, provided those facts cannot be said to be separate and distinct defamatory statements.[95]

Pleading honest comment. If the pleader is in any doubt as to whether   **27.18** words which he seeks to defend by way of a plea of honest comment are indeed comment, as opposed to defamatory statements of fact, he should include a plea of justification in his defence.[96] By contrast, if the words complained of are plainly comment, there may be advantages for a defendant in limiting himself to a defence of honest comment.[97]

---

[95] *Polly Peck Plc v Trelford* [1986] Q.B. 1000: "What I have said in the context of justification can be applied by a parity of reasoning to fair comment . . . " (per O'Connor L.J. at 1032). See *Anderson v Nationwide News Pty Ltd (No.2)* (2002) 3 V.R. 639.

[96] *Broadway Approvals v Odhams Press* [1964] 2 Q.B. 683; *Telnikoff v Matusevitch* [1992] 2 A.C. 343:

"Since justification was not pleaded the plaintiff would necessarily succeed if the jury, the issue being left to them, were to decide that these paragraphs contained statements of fact"

(per Lord Keith at 351). Honest comment is not available as a defence to a mere implication, *Broadcasting Corp of New Zealand v Crush* [1988] 2 N.Z.L.R. 234. The defendant might also consider raising as a preliminary issue the question whether the words complained of are allegations of fact or expressions of opinion. In *Branson v Bower* [2001] EWCA Civ 791; [2001] E.M.L.R. 32 CA, it was held that the judge had been entitled to decide that the defendant was expressing his opinion, not making allegations of fact, when ascribing motives to the claimant other than those which he had publicly asserted, although an assertion of motive could be capable of amounting to an assertion of fact, depending on its context.

[97] If the words sued on are unarguably comment and a comment that an honest person could make, it is open to a defendant to apply for a summary determination of these issues under CPR Pt 24: see *Branson v Bower* [2001] EWCA Civ 791; [2001] E.M.L.R. 32; *Branson v Bower (No.2)* [2002] Q.B. 737; *Keays v Guardian Newspapers Ltd* [2003] EWHC 1565 (QB). For a defendant in such a case to rely alternatively on a defence of justification would inevitably undermine the argument that the words could not reasonably be interpreted otherwise than as comment. Where a defendant obtains such summary rulings in his favour, the claimant, to succeed, will have to establish that the defendant did not honestly believe in the truth of his comment: an uphill struggle: see *Tse Wai Chun v Cheng* [2001] E.M.L.R. 31, Court of Final Appeal of Hong Kong; *Sugar v Associated Newspapers Ltd*, unreported, February 6, 2001, (QB), per Eady J.; *Branson v Bower (No.2)* [2002] Q.B. 737. See also *Hamilton v Clifford* [2004] EWHC 1542 (QB) at [53]–[62] for a useful gloss on the principles to be derived from the line of recent authority on the defence of honest comment starting with *Branson v Bower* [2001] EWCA Civ 791; [2001] E.M.L.R. 32. In terms of the interrelationship between the defences of honest comment and justification, Eady J. stated at [60] that:

"It should perhaps be emphasised that nothing in the *Branson* decisions was intended to conflict with or undermine the repetition rule. They were not supposed to provide a way round the disciplines which the law imposes in respect of factual allegations which are objectively verifiable . . . For reasons of policy . . . one is not permitted to seek shelter behind a defence of fair comment when the defamatory sting is one of verifiable fact. Depending on the meaning of the particular words complained of, a defendant has either to justify the primary factual allegation . . . or comply with the necessary disciplines to establish 'reasonable grounds to suspect'. Fair comment does not provide an escape route in such circumstances."

In *Cruddas v Calvert* [2013] EWHC 2298 (QB) Tugendhat J. said at [56],

"Where the defamatory words complained of contain statements of both fact and opinion, the defendant has a right to defend the statements of opinion either as honest opinion, or as true. Some statements of opinion may be value judgments which cannot be said to be true or false, but other statements of opinion may be either true or false. But if he chooses to defend an opinion by the defence of truth, a defendant must prove that the opinions are in fact true."

27.19 Pleading particulars. The defendant must give details of the matters on which he relies in support of the allegation that the words complained of are honest comment on a matter of public interest.[98] He must give particulars of all the facts upon which the comment is legitimately based, "that is, of the facts which go to the pith and substance of the matter".[99] He must make the issue clear and unmistakeable, stating what are the facts which are alleged to be true and what expressions of opinion are the subject of honest comment.[100] The defendant can and should give such particulars notwithstanding that they are defamatory and he has not raised a plea of justification.[101] Where the defendant considers that he may wish to rely on s.6 of the Defamation Act 1952 in respect of his plea of honest comment, he should expressly plead that section in his defence.[102]

27.20 Pleading honest comment on privileged statements. Where a defendant contends that his comment was based on a statement previously made on a privileged occasion, he need not aver that the facts in the statement were

---

[98] CPR PD 53, para.2.6(2). Even before this rule was introduced, a pleader was obliged to give particulars of the facts on which the comment was based (*Cunningham-Howie v Dimbleby* [1951] 1 K.B. 360; *Lord v Sunday Telegraph* [1971] 1 Q.B. 235). In *Ashcroft v Foley* [2012] EWCA Civ 423; [2012] E.M.L.R. 25 the Court of Appeal said at [60] that the requirement that the facts relied upon be pleaded with the 'precision of an indictment' (see para.27.10, above) was just as applicable to a defence of honest comment as it was to a defence of justification where the charges are serious. It stressed that defendants were required by CPR 53 PD para.2.6(2) to set out the facts relied on as warranting the comment. Those facts had to be properly applied and the acts which the claimant was alleged to have committed had to be specified.

The former RSC contained a complicated requirement applying to what was described as "the rolled-up plea", a formerly popular form of pleading to the effect that "in so far as the words complained of consist of statements of fact, they are true in substance and in fact, and in so far as they consist of expressions of opinion, they are fair comment on those facts, which are a matter of public interest". This form of pleading, which had been held to amount only to a plea of fair comment and not one of justification also (*Sutherland v Stopes* [1925] A.C. 47), had become extinct by the time of the introduction of the CPR, which sensibly left no room for it. In *Joseph v Spiller* [2010] UKSC 53; [2011] 1 A.C. 852 Lord Phillips PSC said at [102] "It is a requirement of the defence that it should be based on facts that are true. This requirement is better enforced if the comment has to identify, at least in general terms, the matters on which it is based."

[99] Per Denning L.J. in *Cunningham-Howie v Dimbleby* [1951] 1 K.B. 360 at 364; see *Ashcroft v Foley*, above, at [60]

[100] *Barnes v Sykes* [1926] 3 W.W.R. 476 per Macdonald J.

[101] *Burton v Board* [1929] 1 K.B. 301:
"In my view, in alleging facts on which he relies he is asserting that these are facts, that he will prove them—not that he will justify them—and ask the jury to say that the comments are fair. From that point of view I think the particulars should stand. They are simply an allegation of fact which the defendant proposes to prove, not an allegation that the facts and inferences which would necessarily be drawn from them are true"
(per Scrutton L.J. at 306),
"The plea is that the words are fair comment made in good faith without malice upon a matter of public interest. Under a plea of that character the defendant is entitled to show, and indeed he must show, what the facts were upon which he commented . . . "
(per Sankey L.J. at 306).

[102] S.3(8) of the Defamation Act 2013 will repeal s.6. The Explanatory Notes explain that it is no longer considered necessary.

true, but he must allege and prove both that the statement was made on a privileged occasion and that his report of it was fair and accurate.[103]

Pleading matter of public interest. The defendant should specify the **27.21** matters which he alleges to be of public interest.[104] Where he contends that the matter is of public interest because the claimant invited criticism or comment, he should plead all facts and matters relied upon in support of such allegation.

Miscellaneous considerations. It is not appropriate for the defendant to **27.22** aver that the comment was expressed without malice and in good faith.[105]

Section 5. Defence of Honest Opinion Under Defamation Act 2013, Section 3[106]

Section 3 of the Defamation Act 2013 prospectively abolishes the common **27.23** law defence of fair or honest comment and repeals s.6, Defamation Act 1952[107] and replaces it with a statutory defence of honest opinion. To establish the defence under s.3, a defendant will have to show that three conditions are met. First, that the statement complained of was an opinion.[108] Second, that the statement complained of indicated, whether in general or specific terms, the basis of the opinion[109] and, third, that an honest person could have held the

---

[103] *Brent Walker Group Plc v Time Out Ltd* [1991] 2 Q.B. 33.

[104] The plea that the comment is on a matter of public interest is essential, notwithstanding that it is not an express requirement of the CPR: *Henry Fook v John Lee* [1976] 1 Malayan L.J. 231 FC:

"I think that it is well established that the defence of fair comment cannot be on any matter but must be on some matter of public interest . . . As the defence pleaded here is one simply of fair comment and not one of fair comment on a matter of public interest, I would with respect agree . . . that the learned judge should have allowed [the] application to strike out . . . This should not however prevent the defendants from applying to amend their defence before this matter comes to trial." However, whilst this remains the position at common law, it is not a requirement under s.3 of the Defamation Act 2013.

(per Suffian L.P. at 232). See also *Anderson v Ah Kit* [2004] WASC 194.

[105] *Hill v Comden* [1993] 1 Qd. R. 603 at 606: "the allegation that the statements were made in good faith and without malice is . . . an unnecessary allegation".

[106] See para.27.1, above.

[107] S.3(8), Defamation Act 2013.

[108] S.3(1), Defamation Act 2013. This is said in the Explanatory Notes to reflect the current law and embrace the requirement established in *Cheng v Tse Wai Chun Paul* (2000) 10 BHRC 525.

[109] S.2(3), Defamation Act 2013. The Explanatory Notes explain that this condition reflects the test approved by the Supreme Court in *Joseph v Spiller* [2010] UKSC 53; [2011] 1 A.C. 852 that "the comment must explicitly or implicitly indicate, at least in general terms, the facts on which it is based". Both conditions 2 and 3 are intended to retain the broad principles of the current common law defence as to the necessary basis for the opinion expressed but avoid the complexities which have arisen in case law. However, by omitting the requirement of the existing law that the defendant must have been aware of the facts on which he based his comment (*Lowe v Associated Newspapers Ltd* [2006] EWHC 320 (QB); [2007] Q.B. 580), s.3 creates an entirely objective defence that enables the defendant to rely on the defence, provided facts existed that would have justified the comment even if those facts were entirely unknown to the defendant. Presumably, the defendant will still be able to rely on the defence even if the facts on which he

opinion on the basis of (a) any fact which existed at the time the statement complained of was published; (b) anything asserted to be a fact in a privileged statement published before the statement complained of.[110] If the defendant can show the three conditions are met the defence can still be defeated if the claimant shows that the defendant did not hold the opinion.[111] A claimant would have to plead that case in a reply. There is no requirement under s.3 that the comment or opinion must be on a matter of public interest.

27.24 At the present time there is no guidance on how to plead a defence of honest opinion outside of the general requirements set out in CPR Pts 15 and 16. The Practice Direction to Pt 53 that applies to defamation claims refers to the common law defences and not to the new statutory defences. A pleader will have to plead expressly to each of the three conditions identified in the section. It will be necessary to identify the statement sought to be defended as an opinion (the first condition); to show that the statement identified the basis of the opinion (the second condition); and to identify the facts, whether true or published in a privileged statement, that existed at the time the comment was made (the third condition). It would be sensible, until further guidance is provided by the courts, for those particulars to respect the common law rules.[112]

SECTION 6. PLEA OF PRIVILEGE

27.25 Defence must be specially pleaded. Where a defendant alleges that the words complained of were published on a privileged occasion, he must specify the circumstances he relies on in support of that contention.[113]

27.26 Basis of privilege to be stated. Where he is required specifically to raise the defence of privilege, the defendant should allege and prove the facts and

---

based his comment would not have justified the comment so long as facts that would have justified him making the comment existed at the time he made the comment.

[110] S.3(4)(a) and (b), Defamation Act 2013. A privileged statement is defined in s.3(7) of the Act. The Notes explain that condition 3 is an objective test and consists of two elements. It is enough for one to be satisfied.

[111] S.3(5), Defamation Act 2013. This is intended to reflect the current law whereby the defence will fail if the claimant can show that the defendant did not honestly hold the opinion. For a recent and rare example where the court found that the defendant, in this case a Pt 20 defendant, did not hold the opinions sought to be defended see *Thompson v James* [2013] EWHC 515 (QB) at [351]–[359], [398]

[112] But note fn.109, above.

[113] CPR PD 53, para.2.7. For a full account of the factual situations giving rise to an occasion of absolute or qualified privilege, see Chs.13–16, above. In *Jameel (Mohammed) v Wall Street Journal Europe SPRL (No.2)* [2005] EWCA Civ 74; [2005] Q.B. 904 at [18], the Court of Appeal observed that the pleading requirement imposed by CPR PD 53, para.2.7 "can be a weighty one where a defendant relies on *Reynolds* privilege, for there may be many different circumstances relied upon in support of the defence". For the matters which a defendant is required to plead in support of this species of qualified privilege, see para.27.27, below.

circumstances which he claims bring him within the protection of the privilege.[114] Thus, where the defendant alleges that a privilege arises from corresponding interests and duties:

> "[i]t must appear that the subject-matter of the communication complained of is one in which the defendant and the party to whom he made the communication had corresponding interests or duties."[115]

Similarly, where the plea of privilege is founded on legitimate self-defence, the defendant must aver such facts as will enable the court to determine whether the statement complained of is sufficiently connected with, and relevant to, the attack or charges made by the claimant to bring it within the privilege.[116] The plea of privilege should be directed at the actual publication, and not at the various meanings or innuendoes which the claimant claims to arise from the words of the publication.[117] An averment that the words were published "bona fide and without malice" is not essential to the validity of a plea of qualified privilege and should not be pleaded, as in such a case there is a presumption of bona fides on the part of the defendant.[118] Where such an immaterial allegation is made, no particulars of it will be ordered.[119]

---

[114] *Stallworthy v Geddis* (1909) 28 N.Z.L.R. 366: "It is, I think, clear that . . . not only must the defence be specially pleaded, but the facts and circumstances must also be stated showing why and how the occasion is privileged" (per Edwards J. at 369); *Pierce v Ellis* (1856) 6 Ir.C.L.R. 55 at 62, per Pigot C.B.: " . . . the defendant in an action for libel or slander, who rests his defence upon the ground that the defamatory matter was published upon an occasion which makes it privileged, must set forth the facts which constitute the occasion".

[115] Per curiam in *Simmonds v Dunne* (1871) Ir.R. 5 C.L. 358 at 362; *Praeger v Shaw* (1855) 4 Ir.C.L.R. 660; *Elkington v London Association* (1911) 27 T.L.R. 329 CA where Farwell L.J. ordered that the defendants should give particulars with sufficient precision to enable the claimant to test the question whether the inquiry was made by a member of the defendant association. In the case of a newspaper or other publisher claiming a duty to disseminate material to the public and a reciprocal interest on the part of the public in receiving that material, the defendant must set out the circumstances of the publication giving rise to the duty and interest, such as the seriousness of the allegation, the extent to which it was a matter of public concern, the source and status of the information, the steps taken to verify it, the urgency of the matter and the steps taken to obtain and print the claimant's side of the story, see *Reynolds v Times Newspapers* [2001] 2 A.C. 127; *Gaddafi v Telegraph Group Ltd* [2000] E.M.L.R. 431, where it was held that in the new climate created by *Reynolds* it was very important that the claimant should have adequate particulars in order to evaluate the prospects of the defence succeeding. However, the defendant will not be required to elaborate on the status or identity of his sources where to do so would infringe the important principles which protect a defendant from revealing his source. In *Loutchansky v Times Newspapers Ltd (Nos 2–5)* [2001] EWCA Civ 536; [2002] Q.B. 321 CA, it was held that a media defendant who claims to have been entitled to publish in the public interest may not rely on matters about which it did not know at the time of publication.

[116] *O'Brien v Freeman's Journal* (1907) 41 Ir.L.T. 35. See *Vassiliev v Frank Cass & Co. Ltd* [2003] EWHC 1428 (QB) and *Blackwell v News Group Newspapers Ltd* [2007] EWHC 2098 (QB), both per Eady J.

[117] *Gration v Queensland Newspapers* [1989] 1 Qd. R. 381.

[118] *Clark v Molyneux* (1877) 3 Q.B.D. 237; *Jenoure v Delmége* [1891] A.C. 73; *Motel Holdings v Bulletin Newspapers* [1963] N.S.W.R. 1446: "It is a principle of the common law system of pleading that 'it is not necessary to state matter which would come more properly from the other side' " (per Sugerman J. at 1448); *Bates v Queensland Newspapers* [1996] 1 Qd. R. 13.

[119] *Cave v Torre* (1886) 54 I.,T. 515 CA: irrelevant allegation that defendant had reasonable and probable cause for believing that the libel was true.

27.27 Pleading Reynolds qualified privilege. Where a defendant newspaper or other publisher[120] claims that its dissemination of defamatory material[121] to the public[122] is covered by the species of qualified privilege explained by the House of Lords in *Reynolds v Times Newspapers Ltd*,[123] it must demonstrate why the nature of the subject matter of the publication was such that it was in the public interest for it to be published[124] and, where, for instance, it remains available on the internet following complaint, for it to continue to be published.[125] It is the publication *as a whole* that has to be assessed when considering the public interest, not merely the particular defamatory allegations of which the claimant complains.[126] The defendant must also set out the circumstances of the publication said to support publication in public interest,[127]

---

[120] The defence was originally formulated in a case where a defendant was a newspaper but it applies to anyone, including individuals who are not reporting, but speaking from their own knowledge: *Thompson v James* [2013] EWHC 515 (QB) at [272]; *Seaga v Harper* [2009] 1 A.C. 1 (PC); *Flood v Times Newspapers Ltd* [2012] UKSC 11; [2012] 2 A.C.273 at [44].

[121] The publication at issue need not be an investigative media report: *Seaga v Harper* [2008] UKPC 9; [2009] 1 A.C. 1; *Flood v Times Newspapers Ltd* [2012] UKSC 11; [2012] 2 A.C. 273 at [44]; *Thompson v James* [2013] EWHC 515 (QB) at [272].

[122] Where the publication at issue is to the world at large, save in exceptional circumstances (see *Malik v Newspost Ltd*, above, at [9], [13]; *Seray-Wurie v The Charity Commission of England & Wales* [2008] EWHC 870 (QB) at [17]–[19], [23] and *Bray v Deutsche Bank AG* [2008] EWHC 1263 (QB), at [98]), the defendant seeking to set up a defence of qualified privilege must satisfy the requirements of *Reynolds*: *Seaga v Harper* [2008] UKPC 9; [2008] 1 All E.R. 965; *Trumm v Norman* [2008] EWHC 116 (QB), per Tugendhat J.

[123] *Reynolds v Times Newspapers Ltd* [2001] 2 A.C. 127; see Ch.15, above.

[124] *Jameel v Wall Street Journal Europe SPRL* [2006] UKHL 44; [2007] 1 A.C. 359; *Flood v Times Newspapers* [2012] UKSC 11; [2012] 2 A.C. 273. This brief summary was set out without comment in *Hunt v Times Newspapers Ltd* [2012] EWHC 110 (QB) at [31]. For a full discussion of the defence see Ch.15, above.

[125] In *Flood v Times Newspapers* [2010] EWCA Civ 804, [2010] E.M.L.R. 26, the Master of the Rolls at [59] accepted the submission that whilst the subject-matter of the article, alleged police corruption, was a matter of public interest, it did not follow that there was a public interest in continuing to publish allegations online when the facts changed. The point was not addressed in the Supreme Court.

[126] See *Jameel v Wall Street Journal Europe SPRL* [2006] UKHL 44; [2007] 1 A.C. 359 at [34]; [48]–[52]; and [107]–[108].

[127] See CPR PD 53, para.2.7 and the observations on its application to *Reynolds* privilege defences in fn.103, above. The plea of the circumstances of publication should, where appropriate, focus on, and, at least, address Lord Nicholls's non-exhaustive list of relevant circumstances in *Reynolds* at [205]. In *Jameel v Wall Street Journal Europe SPRL* [2006] UKHL 44; [2007] 1 A.C. 359, Lord Bingham observed at [33] that Lord Nicholls had intended his non-exhaustive list:

"as pointers which might be more or less indicative [of whether the publication was privileged], depending on the circumstances of a particular case, and not, I feel sure, as a series of hurdles to be negotiated by a publisher before he could successfully rely on qualified privilege".

In *Miller v Associated Newspapers Ltd* [2003] EWHC 2799 (QB); [2004] E.M.L.R. 33, Eady J. at [7] sounded a salutary warning with regard to pleading *Reynolds* qualified privilege:

"Since the decision of their Lordships in *Reynolds* . . . there has been something of a tendency to plead qualified privilege in rather waffly generalities and these require close scrutiny. There is an undesirable trend to plead in rather vague terms and then to try to avoid the sanctions of Pt 24 by resorting to the dicta of Sir Thomas Bingham M.R. in *E (A Minor) v Dorset County Council* [1995] 2 A.C. 233 to the effect that in an area of developing jurisprudence an order

existing at the date of publication,[128] such as the seriousness of the allegation, the extent to which it was a matter of public concern, the source[129] and the status of

---

striking out should not be made. That is an important principle, but it is not to be regarded as a mantra that will guarantee a way round the disciplines of pleading."

In *Armstrong v Times Newspapers Ltd* [2005] EWCA Civ 1007; [2005] E.M.L.R. 33, the Court of Appeal observed at [74] that Eady J. was "right to direct himself that such defences required close scrutiny".

The "repetition rule" (see para.27.11, above) does not apply to the defence of *Reynolds* qualified privilege (*Galloway v Telegraph Group Ltd* [2004] EWHC 2786 (QB); [2005] E.M.L.R. 7 at [36], citing *Mark v Associated Newspapers Ltd* [2002] EWCA Civ 772; [2002] E.M.L.R. 38 at [33]–[35] and *Al-Fagih v HH Saudi Research Marketing (UK) Ltd* [2001] EWCA Civ 1634; [2002] E.M.L.R. 13 at [36]). For the interrelationship between the "repetition rule" and defence of *Reynolds* qualified privilege for "reportage", see *Roberts v Gable* [2007] EWCA Civ 721; [2008] 2 W.L.R. 129.

In *Armstrong v Times Newspapers Ltd* [2004] EWHC 2928 (QB), Eady J. at [94] emphasised the importance of considering and pleading particulars of *Reynolds* qualified privilege separately from particulars of justification and not confusing the two. In cases where both defences were relied on by a defendant, the two ought not to be treated as "interchangeable". As the judge observed:

"[The claimant's counsel] took particular issue with the first paragraph of the particulars, which merely purports to include all the preceding particulars which have gone to support the particulars of justification . . . If I may say so, it is a somewhat sloppy approach to use this cross-over technique as though particulars of justification were simply interchangeable with a case on *Reynolds* privilege."

The Court of Appeal endorsed the judge's criticism of this pleading technique on the (successful) appeal from the decision to strike out the defence of qualified privilege ([2005] EWCA Civ 1007; [2005] E.M.L.R. 33 at [25]). For another plea of qualified privilege that was found to be unsatisfactory for similar reasons, see *McKeith v News Group Newspapers* [2005] EWHC 1162 (QB); [2005] E.M.L.R. 32 at [44], [53].

[128] See *Loutchansky v Times Newspapers Ltd (Nos 2–5)* [2001] EWCA Civ 536; [2002] Q.B. 321, where it was held that a media defendant who claims to have been entitled to publish in the public interest may not rely on matters in support of that plea which arose after publication or about which it did not know at the time of publication. See also *McKeith v News Group Newspapers Ltd* [2005] EWHC 1162 (QB); [2005] E.M.L.R. 32 at [36] and [43]–[47].

[129] See *Gaddafi v Telegraph Group Ltd* [2000] E.M.L.R. 431, where it was held that in the new climate created by *Reynolds* it was very important that the claimant should have adequate particulars in order to evaluate the prospects of the defence succeeding. However, the defendant will not be required to elaborate on the status or identity of his sources where to do so would infringe the important principles which protect a defendant from revealing his source. In *Gaddafi* itself, Hirst L.J. expressed disquiet at allowing a *Reynolds* defence to go forward in which the defendant had not identified the sources of the article complained of. The Court of Appeal nevertheless considered that to refuse to do so would offend against the fundamental rule that journalists should not, without good reason, be compelled to reveal their sources. However, in *Reynolds v Times Newspapers Ltd* [2001] 2 A.C. 127, Lord Hope at 230 warned that:

" . . . care should be taken not to give the benefit of the privilege too readily to persons or organisations whose sources of information are themselves protected to an extent which renders the issue of malice inscrutable".

For further information and observations on how the court should approach cases where a defendant, in support of a plea of *Reynolds* privilege, seeks to rely on sources he declines to identify, see CPR r.53.3, Gray J. in *Loutchansky v Times Newspapers Ltd (No.4)* [2001] E.M.L.R. 38 at [50] and in *Loutchansky v Times Newspapers Ltd (No.7)* [2002] EWHC 2490 (QB) at [31]; Eady J. in *Jameel v The Wall Street Journal Europe SPRL* [2003] EWHC 2302 (QB) at [18]–[20], quoted and substantially approved by the Court of Appeal in the appeal from that decision (*Jameel v The Wall Street Journal Europe SPRL* [2003] EWCA Civ 1694; [2004] E.M.L.R. 6); see at [4] and [32]; *Berezovsky v The Russian Television and Radio Broadcasting Co.* [2008] EWHC 1918 (QB) at [22].

the information, the steps taken to verify it,[130] the urgency of the matter and the steps taken to obtain and print the claimant's side of the story. Responsible journalism or authorship, in all the circumstances, must be demonstrated.[131] In an appropriate case, it may be necessary or at least admissible for a defendant to plead and prove a subjective belief in the truth of its publication, formed as a result of a reasonable investigation,[132] in order to establish a defence of *Reynolds* privilege.[133] In such a case, the defendant should expressly identify the meaning it contends the individuals responsible for the publication understood it to

---

[130] In *Charman v Orion Publishing Group Ltd* [2007] EWCA Civ 972; [2008] 1 All E.R. 750, Ward L.J. was of the view at [66(2)] that, "Taking steps to verify the information" had been "given added emphasis" by the House of Lords in *Jameel v Wall Street Journal Europe SPRL* [2006] UKHL 44; [2007] 1 A.C. 359.

[131] *Jameel v Wall Street Journal Europe SPRL* [2006] UKHL 44; [2007] 1 A.C. 359 at [53]–[57] per Lord Hoffmann (see also [79]–[80]); at [107]–[109] per Lord Hope; at [134]–[138] per Lord Scott; at [147]–[149] per Lady Hale. At [32], Lord Bingham stated that "the rationale of the test" of responsible journalism, as he understood it, was that:

"there is no duty to publish and the public have no interest to read material which the publisher has not taken reasonable steps to verify. As Lord Hobhouse observed [in *Reynolds*] with characteristic pungency (p.238), 'No public interest is served by publishing or communicating misinformation'. But the publisher is protected if he has taken such steps as a responsible journalist would take to try and ensure that what is published is accurate and fit for publication."

The same point was re-iterated in *Flood v Times Newspapers Ltd* [2012] UKSC 11; [2012] 2 A.C. 273. See [75] per Lord Phillips PSC:

"Not all the items in Lord Nicholls's list in the *Reynolds case* [2001] 2 A.C. 127, 205 were intended to be requirements of responsible journalism in every case. The first question is whether, on the facts of this case, the requirements of responsible journalism included a duty of verification and, if so, the nature of that duty. I should insert a word of warning at the outset. Each case turns on its own facts. I use the phrase 'duty of verification' as shorthand for a requirement to verify in the circumstances of this case. My comments should not be treated as laying down principles to be applied in cases of different facts."

See also *Loutchansky v Times Newspapers Ltd (Nos 2–5)* [2001] EWCA Civ 1805; [2002] Q.B. 783 and *Jameel (Mohammed) v Wall Street Journal Europe SPRL (No.2)* [2005] EWCA Civ 74; [2005] Q.B. 904 at [87] for the views of the Court of Appeal. It will not be responsible journalism to leave an article online without some qualification once further information has come to light which qualifies or undermines it: see *Flood v Times Newspapers Ltd* [2009] EWHC 2375 (QB), [2010] E.M.L.R. 8, upheld in that respect on appeal ([2010] EWCA Civ 804, [2010] E.M.L.R. 26). The defendant sought to argue that once the result of an official investigation into the allegations was known, it made reasonable proposals to the claimant for alterations to the internet article which were rejected, and reasonably assumed that the claimant would not require any change unless he said otherwise. However, Lord Neuberger M.R. rejected that submission, stating at [81] that

" . . . the fact that the claimant's refusal [to agree a form of follow-up publication] is unreasonable will, save perhaps in the most unusual circumstances, not be enough to justify the defendant doing nothing if responsible journalism would require him to retract or modify a website publication if further relevant information comes to light. The essential point is that it is for a defendant to decide on the appropriate course to take."

The Supreme Court overturned the Court of Appeal but did not address this point.

[132] *Flood v Times Newspapers Ltd* [2012] 2 A.C. 273 at [79] per Lord Phillips.

[133] *Jameel (Mohammed) v Wall Street Journal Europe SPRL (No.2)* [2005] EWCA Civ 74; [2005] Q.B. 904 at [27]–[29]:

"It seems to us that, in seeking to demonstrate that a publication accords with the requirements of responsible journalism, a publisher will almost certainly wish to adduce evidence of the subjective belief of those responsible for the publication . . . Issues of subjective belief which hitherto have only been relevant where malice is in issue now become relevant to the inquiry

bear.[134] The Supreme Court in *Flood v Times Newspapers*[135] reiterated that reasonable steps have to been taken before publishing to verify if the allegations were true and the author must have a reasonable belief that there were grounds

---

of whether responsible journalism has been exercised . . . [this] suggest[s] that it may be necessary or at least admissible for a defendant to allege and prove subjective belief in order to establish a defence of *Reynolds* privilege."

For this reason, so the Court of Appeal proceeded to state, at [31]:

"It is important that the pleadings should make clear where a defendant is relying on reasonable belief in the truth of matters published, or their implications, and where he is not. It is also important that the claimant should make clear whether or not he denies that the belief was held, or whether he merely contends that the belief was not reasonable."

In *McKeith v News Group Newspapers Ltd* [2005] EWHC 1162 (QB); [2005] E.M.L.R. 32, Eady J. observed at [38] that: "More targeted pleadings in these respects would, apart from anything else, assist the parties in identifying individual issues of fact requiring an answer from the jury." In striking out the pleaded defence of qualified privilege in the *McKeith* case, Eady J. also stated at [39]:

" . . . there seems to be force in the submission that a defendant's advisers need to comply with these disciplines [as identified in *Jameel (Mohammed) v Wall Street Journal Europe SPRL (No.2)* at [29]–[31]] in order to set up a defence of *Reynolds* privilege, the pleading of which can so often descend into woolly generalities."

In this context, see also *McKeith* at [50].

A situation in which it would not be appropriate for a defendant to plead a subjective belief in the truth of its publication is where it was asserting that its publication constituted "reportage", as to which, see *Jameel (Mohammed) v Wall Street Journal Europe SPRL (No.2)*, above at [19]–[20], citing *Al-Fagih v HH Saudi Research Marketing (UK) Ltd*, above; *Galloway v Telegraph Group Ltd* [2006] EWCA Civ 17; [2006] E.M.L.R. 11; *Roberts v Gable* [2007] EWCA Civ 721; [2008] 2 W.L.R. 129; *Charman v Orion Publishing Group Ltd* [2007] EWCA Civ 972; [2008] 1 All E.R. 750 and *Radu v Houston* [2007] EWHC 2735 (QB) (upheld on appeal: [2008] EWCA Civ 921). In *Charman v Orion Publishing Group Ltd*, Sedley L.J. at [91] appeared to take the view that defences of reportage and responsible journalism were incompatible:

"It is the very dependence of a reportage defence on the bald retailing of libels which makes it forensically problematical to fall back upon an alternative defence of responsible journalism. Pleaders may need to decide which it is to be".

This view also seems to be supported by the observations of Eady J. in *McKeith v News Group Newspapers Ltd*, above at [37].

[134] The notion that it might be sensible for a defendant relying on *Reynolds* privilege, in appropriate circumstances, to identify the meaning he attributed to the publication at issue seemed implicit in the decision of the Privy Council in *Bonnick v Morris* [2002] UKPC 31; [2003] 1 A.C. 300; see, in particular, at [22]–[25]. Now, where a defendant seeking to rely on a defence of *Reynolds* privilege pleads the subjective belief the persons responsible for the publication at issue had in the truth of its contents and explains why that belief was reasonable (see fn.92, above), pleading the meaning the defendant understood the article to bear would appear to be integral to this exercise. Explicit support for this proposition can be derived from *McKeith v News Group Newspapers Ltd*, above, at [40]–[41]. Nonetheless, in this context, the salutary observations of Tugendhat J. in *Bray v Deutsche Bank AG* [2008] EWHC 1263 (QB); [2009] E.M.L.R. 12 at [42] ought to be noted:

" . . . in the normal course the publisher can be expected to perceive the meaning an ordinary, reasonable reader is likely to give the publication. And the more obvious that the words are defamatory of the complainant, the less weight a court will attach to other possible meanings when considering the state of mind of the publisher".

But see the discussion in *Flood v Times Newspapers Ltd* [2012] 2 A.C. 273 at [49]–[51] where *Reynolds* was determined as a preliminary issue before meaning. In *Flood,* Lord Phillips P.S.C. said at [79] that verification involves both a subjective and objective element. The responsible journalist would have to form a view on what he considered the allegations he was intended to make meant in order to ensure that he was satisfied such grounds existed.

[135] [2012] UKSC 11; [2012] 2 A.C. 273.

for believing that they were true. If the defence is of the "reportage" variety, where it is not the content of a reported allegation that is of interest but the fact that the allegation has been made, the verification requirement is to take proper steps to verify the making of the allegation, which must not be adopted.[136]

27.28 **Pleading privilege on behalf of a public authority.** If art.8 of the Convention, which encompasses reputation,[137] is engaged, a public authority must respect that right unless the interference can be justified under art.8(2). Where the defendant is a public authority with public duties to perform and is seeking to rely upon a defence of qualified privilege, regard must be had to the question whether there was a public law duty to communicate the material complained of. To support a defence of privilege a public authority must plead and prove the public duty relied upon and set out the legitimate aim of the publication and aver why publication was necessary and proportionate to that aim.[138] The same factors will need to be considered when defending a claim brought under the Human Rights Act.[139]

27.29 **Pleading privilege in relation to incidental publication.** Where a defendant contends that the communication in question was protected in law

---

[136] Ibid., [77], per Lord Phillips. For reportage, see fn.133, above.

[137] *Re Guardian News and Media Ltd* [2010] UKSC 1; [2010] 2 A.C. 697.

[138] *Wood v Chief Constable of the West Midlands Police* [2005] E.M.L.R. 20; *Clift v Slough Borough Council* [2010] EWCA Civ 1171; [2011] 1 W.L.R. 1774 per Ward L.J. at [19] applying *Huang v Home Secretary* [2007] 2 A.C. 167 at [19].

In *Morrison v Buckinghamshire County Council* [2011] EWHC 3444 (QB) H.H.J. Parkes Q.C. (sitting as a High Court judge) considered the position where art.8 had not been raised in the particulars of claim. The judge said at [75]:

"The difficulty with this is that it involves the defendant setting up and then knocking down a point which may not be raised against it, which is not the way in which the process of pleading works. The defendant can hardly be expected to plead that Art.8 is not engaged: that would be to anticipate a case which may not be made . . . Equally, the claimant cannot be expected to raise the point in her Particulars of Claim, before it is known whether the defendant will plead privilege. As Ward L.J. made clear in *Clift* at [39], the defence remains the common law defence of qualified privilege, and the public authority must plead that it is under a duty to communicate the information to those who have a corresponding duty or interest in receive it. That is what has been pleaded. If the claimant wishes to plead in response that for public law/ HRA reasons there was in fact no duty and thus no qualified privilege, that is in principle a matter for her to raise in her Reply, as she now seeks to do. It may be worth noting Lord Bingham's observation in *Kay v Lambeth BC* [2006] UKHL 10; [2006] 2 A.C. 465 at [29] that it would be burdensome and futile for a local authority to plead and prove that a possession order was justified in terms of art.8: it would be enough for it to assert its claim in accordance with domestic property law. It would then be for the occupier to raise an art.8 defence. Of course, in the possession context the local authority can then answer the art.8 defence in its Reply, whereas in defamation, the art.8 argument (if the nettle is not grasped by the defendant in the defence) can only be raised in the Reply. It may be that that defunct species of pleading, the rejoinder, will have to be disinterred."

In practice, many claimants are now including a stand alone claim under ss.6 and 7 of the Human Rights Act 1998 where the defendant is a public authority: see e.g. *Clift*, above; *McLaughlin v Lambeth LBC* [2010] EWHC 2726 (QB); [2011] E.M.L.R. 8; *Thompson v James* [2013] EWHC 515 (QB).

[139] See para.26.43, above.

because it was made incidentally to a privileged communication,[140] he should expressly aver that the incidental publication was reasonable or necessary in order to bring the document to the notice of those to whom it was his duty or interest to communicate it.[141]

Section 7. Defence of Publication on a Matter of Public Interest Under Defamation Act 2013, Section 4[142]

Section 4 of the Defamation Act 2013 will abolish the *Reynolds* qualified privilege defence.[143] It will be a defence to an action for defamation for the defendant to show that the statement complained of, whether it is a fact or a comment,[144] was, or formed part of, a statement on a matter of public interest[145]; and the defendant reasonably believed that publishing the statement complained of was in the public interest.[146] The court must have regard

27.30

---

[140] For an account of the substantive law relating to this aspect of the law of privilege see paras 14.66–14.73, above.

[141] *Robinson v Jones* (1879) 4 L.R.Ir. 391 at 395:

"To bring the present case, however, within this privilege, there should have been an allegation that communication by means of a post-card was a reasonable mode of communicating with the plaintiff. There is no such statement here"

(per Palles C.B.); *Moran v O'Regan* (1907) 38 N.B.R. 189:

"These pleas do not allege that the letter was written in the ordinary course of the defendant's business, nor do they allege any circumstances from which such fact could be inferred. If the pleas in their present form could be sustained, they would establish the proposition that in any and all cases a person could dictate to his confidential clerk a defamatory letter in reference to a third party, give it to the clerk to copy, and forward it, and, in the absence of malice, escape liability on the ground of privilege. That proposition is altogether too broad."

(per Barker J. at 206–207).

[142] See para. 27.1, above. The Explanatory Notes to the defence explain that it is based on the existing common law defence established in *Reynolds v Times Newspapers* [2001] 2 A.C. 127 and in subsequent case law. The notes explain that the 'statutory defence is intended essentially to codify the common law defence.' They go on to say that the 'current case law would constitute a helpful (albeit not binding) guide to interpreting how the new statutory defence should be applied. It is expected the courts would take the existing case law into consideration where appropriate.'

[143] S.4(6), Defamation Act 2013.

[144] S.4(5), Defamation Act 2013.

[145] Public interest is not defined but is said in the Explanatory Notes, para. 30, to be a concept which is well established in the English common law.

[146] S.4(1)(a) and (b), Defamation Act 2013. The intention of this provision, according to the Notes, is to reflect the existing common law as set out most recently in *Flood v Times Newspapers Ltd* [2012]] UKSC 11; [2012] 2 A.C. 273. Specific reference is made in the Notes to [113] of the judgment of Lord Brown in *Flood* where it is said:

"In deciding whether Reynolds privilege attaches (whether the Reynolds public interest defence lies) the judge, on true analysis, is deciding but a single question: could whoever published the defamation, given whatever they knew (and did not know) and whatever they had done (and had not done) to guard so far as possible against the publication of untrue defamatory material, properly have considered the publication in question to be in the public interest? In deciding this single question, of course, a host of different considerations are in play. One starts with the (expressly non-exhaustive) list of ten factors identified by Lord Nicholls of Birkenhead in the Reynolds case itself. As the present case well illustrates, however, depending on the particular publication in question, there are likely to be other relevant considerations too."

to all the circumstances of the case[147] provided that when determining whether it was reasonable for the defendant to believe that publishing the statement complained of was in the public interest, it must make such allowance for editorial judgment as it considers appropriate.[148] It must also disregard any omission of the defendant to take steps to verify the truth of the imputation if the statement complained of was or formed part of an accurate and impartial account of a dispute to which the claimant was a party,[149] that is to say if the circumstances are such as to give rise to what is currently known as a "reportage" defence.

27.31   The defendant will have to identify the statement complained of and the public interest. While there is no express reference to responsible journalism the defendant would still need to establish why he reasonably believed that publishing that statement was in the public interest. Since the court must have regard to all the circumstances of the case, all relevant matters should be pleaded and particularised. It is worth noting that the Explanatory Notes to the new Act, para.29, explain that the new defence is based on the existing common law defence "established" in the case of *Reynolds*, and "is intended to reflect the principles established in that case and in subsequent case law".

SECTION 8. DEFENCE FOR PEER-REVIEWED STATEMENTS UNDER
DEFAMATION ACT 2013, SECTION 6

27.32 When it comes into force, s.6 Defamation Act 2013 will provide a qualified privilege defence where a statement in a scientific or academic journal, whether published in electronic form or otherwise, relates to a scientific or academic matter and an independent review of the statement's scientific or academic merit was carried out by the editor of the journal and one or more persons with expertise in the scientific or academic matter concerned.[150] The defence does not require investigation into the circumstances of the case. Hence, the pleader only needs to plead that the statement related to an academic or scientific matter and that it was published following an independent review by the editor of the journal or an expert in the field. The privilege will also attach to publication in the same journal of any assessment of the statement's scientific or academic merit, if written by one or more of the people who carried out the independent review, and if the assessment was written in the course of that review.[151]

---

[147] S.4(2), Defamation Act 2013.
[148] S.4(4), Defamation Act 2013.
[149] S.4(3), Defamation Act 2013. This sub-section is, according to the Notes, intended to encapsulate the common law doctrine of reportage.
[150] S.6(1)–(3), Defamation Act 2013.
[151] S.6(4), Defamation Act 2013.

There will be a further secondary defence for the publication of a fair and **27.33**
accurate copy of, extract from or summary of the statement itself or an
assessment of its scientific or academic merit.[152]

SECTION 9. OTHER PLEAS

Offer of amends. A person wishing to rely by way of defence on the fact **27.34**
that he has made an offer of amends under s.2 of the Defamation Act 1996
should do so expressly.[153] He should specifically state that he is relying on the
offer in accordance with s.4(2) of the Defamation Act 1996 and that it has not
been withdrawn by him or been accepted. He may wish to attach to his
defence a copy of the offer which he has made. He need not, however, plead
that he did not know nor have reason to believe that the statement complained
of referred to the claimant or was likely to be understood as referring to him
and was both false and defamatory of the claimant, since these matters are
presumed in the defendant's favour until the contrary is shown.[154] It should be
borne in mind that a defendant who has made an offer of amends under s.2 is
not obliged to rely on it by way of defence, but if he does so, he may not rely
on any other defence.[155]

Secondary publication and innocent dissemination.[156] A printer, dis- **27.35**
tributor, seller, broadcaster, service provider or other person seeking to rely on
the statutory defence under s.1 of the Defamation Act 1996[157] should plead (1)
that he was not the author, editor or publisher of the statement complained of,
(2) that he took reasonable care in relation to its publication and (3) that he did
not know, and had no reason to believe, that what he did caused or contributed
to the publication of a defamatory statement. The defendant should identify

---

[152] S.6(5), Defamation Act 2013.

[153] CPR PD 53, para.2.11. The fact that the offer was made is a defence to defamation
proceedings in respect of the publication in question by that party against the person making the
offer (s.4(2), Defamation Act 1996), unless that person knew or had reason to believe that the
statement complained of (1) referred to the aggrieved party or was likely to be understood as
referring to him, and (2) was both false and defamatory of that party (s.4(3), Defamation Act
1996). If the offer was a qualified offer, the defence applies only in respect of the meaning to
which the offer related (s.4(4), Defamation Act 1996). An offer of amends under s.2 of the
Defamation Act 1996 must be made before the service of the defence (s.2(5), Defamation Act
1996).

[154] Defamation Act 1996, s.4(3); *Milne v Express Newspapers* [2002] EWHC 2564 (QB);
[2003] 1 W.L.R. 927, per Eady J.

[155] Defamation Act 1996, s.4(4) .

[156] Note that under s.10, Defamation Act 2013 a court will not have jurisdiction to hear and
determine an action for defamation brought against a person who was not the author, editor or
publisher of the statement complained of unless the court is satisfied that it is not reasonably
practicable for an action to be brought against the author, editor or publisher. This is not a defence
to a claim and the point should be taken before a defence is pleaded.

[157] For a full account of this defence see paras 6.22–6.29, above and *Tamiz v Google* [2013]
EWCA Civ 68; [2013] 1 W.L.R. 2151.

those facts and matters on which he will rely in support of the averment as to reasonable care. It is no longer necessary to rely on the common law defence of innocent dissemination, which is effectively superseded by this statutory defence.[158]

27.36 Operators of websites defence under Defamation Act 2013, s.5. There will be an additional defence available to operators of websites under this Act where a statement published on a website is complained about and a defendant can show that it was not the operator who posted the statement on the website.[159] All that an operator needs to plead in a defence is that it did not post the statement complained of. An operator will, however, have to comply with certain Regulations to be published by statutory instrument and a failure to comply may result in a loss of this defence.[160]

27.37 Limitation Act. Where the defendant wishes to raise the statute of limitations, he should do so expressly in his defence.[161]

27.38 Other defences making the claim not maintainable. Similarly, the defendant must plead specifically any other matter such as release, consent, accord and satisfaction or res judicata or abuse of process,[162] which he alleges makes the claimant's claim not maintainable. If the defendant wishes to raise a defence based on foreign law he must expressly plead the relevant law in his defence.[163] A defendant who seeks to rely on any provision of a right arising under the Human Rights Act 1998 or seeks a remedy available under that Act must state that fact in his defence and set out various other prescribed matters.[164]

---

[158] The common law would appear to be materially different in one respect, namely that it requires the defendant to show that he did not know that the publication was of a character likely to contain a *libel*, as opposed to a defamatory statement. See discussion at para.6.29, above.

[159] S.5(2), Defamation Act 2013. See para.6.30, above.

[160] S.5(3), Defamation Act 2013.

[161] CPR PD 16, para.14.1. See paras 19.13–19.21, above.

[162] The leading case on whether abuse of process can be found at trial is *Fairclough Homes Ltd v Summers* [2012] UKSC 26; [2012] 1 W.L.R. 2004 where the Supreme Court reached the conclusion that the court does have jurisdiction to strike out a statement of case at trial but should only do so in very exceptional circumstances. Nonetheless there are categories of abuse where findings of fact need to be made a trial: see *Broxton v McLelland* [1995] E.M.L.R. 485 and *Abbey v Gilligan* [2012] EWHC 3217 (QB); [2013] E.M.L.R. 12 at [132]–[134]. In *Abbey* abuse of process was relied upon as a defence and found as a matter of fact but Tugendhat J. considered it was not necessary to decide whether the action should be dismissed for abuse after trial because the substantive claim failed. In *Joseph v Spiller* [2012] EWHC 2958 (QB) Tugendhat J. held that the deliberate pursuit of a false claim for special damages was an abuse of process. While it did not affect the whole claim it led to an award of nominal damages: see [177]–[178]. See paras 19.22–19.28, above.

[163] I.e. where the claimant relies on a foreign publication: see para.28.19, above; *Meckiff v Simpson* [1968] V.R. 62; *Lazarus v Deutsche Lufthansa* (1985) 1 N.S.W.L.R. 188, 190.

[164] CPR PD 16, para.16.1.

SECTION 10. MITIGATION OF DAMAGES

Mitigation of damages. The well-established practice is for the defendant   **27.39**
specifically to plead in his defence particulars of any facts on which he relies
in mitigation of, or otherwise in relation to, the amount of damages
claimed.[165] The plea must be clear and precise.[166] Matters pleaded may
include[167] the fact that there has been an offer or a publication of a unilateral
correction or apology[168] or they may relate to the circumstances under which
the libel or slander was published, e.g. that the claimant provoked the publication by previously attacking the defendant.[169] A defendant may in certain
circumstances rely on the failure of the claimant to take up an offer to respond
to the material published or to be published.[170] A defendant may also plead in
mitigation of damages the claimant's general bad reputation[171] or the fact that

---

[165] Curiously, there is no express requirement to this effect in the CPR, notwithstanding that the
former RSC required either party to plead particulars of any facts on which he relied in mitigation
of, or otherwise in relation to, the amount of damages claimed. The CPR impose an obligation
only on the claimant to set out in his particulars of claim any facts on which he wishes to rely
relating to mitigation of loss or damage, see CPR PD 16, para.9.2. Having regard to the CPR's
emphasis on the identification of issues at an early stage, it seems likely that the absence of any
equivalent duty on the defendant in the current rules is attributable to oversight rather than any
deliberate intention to alter the pre-existing requirement.

[166] *Grant v McRae* (1906) 8 O.W.R. 304 at 305: "If the defendant wishes . . . to plead in
mitigation of damages, he must do so plainly"; *Meeker v Post Printing & Publishing* (1913) 135
Pac. 457:

"One reason for the rule requiring a defendant to plead his facts in mitigation of damages is
that the plaintiff may be advised as to what facts the defendant relies upon as his defense in that
respect, and in order that issues may be framed thereon so as to prevent surprise at the trial
concerning the facts upon which the defendant intends to prove in order to sustain this defense.
It is based upon the same necessity which requires written pleadings in all cases of courts of
record."

(per Hill J. at 459).

[167] For a full account of what may or may not be relied on by way of mitigation see paras
33.29–33.60, below.

[168] Where an apology is incorporated into the pleading, it should not mention any CPR Pt 36
payment which may have been made, or the amount of such payment (*Weber v Birkett* [1925] 1
K.B. 720 at 724–725), save in the unlikely event that the defendant is pleading the defence
provided for in s.2 of Lord Campbell's Act 1843. Where the defendant has made an offer of
amends under s.2 of the Defamation Act 1996, he may rely on it in mitigation of damages whether
or not it was relied on as a defence (s.4(5), Defamation Act 1996). A retraction of a defamatory
allegation which is not accompanied by an apology for the harm done to the claimant's reputation
will not necessarily be insufficient to mitigate damage and the sufficiency of such a retraction will
in each case be a matter for the jury or judge, where he is the trier of fact, *Pine v Macmillan, The
Times*, November 25, 1987. See *Voon Lee Shan v Sarawak Press Sdn Bhd* [2003] 690 M.L.J. 1
for a case in which the Malaysian equivalent of the defence under s.2 of the English Libel Act
(Lord Campbell's Act) 1843 was considered.

[169] *Kelly v Sherlock* (1866) L.R. 1 Q.B. 686. See also *Godfrey v Demon internet (No.2)*,
unreported, April 23, 1999, (QB), per Morland J., approved by May L.J. in *Burstein v Times
Newspapers Ltd* [2001] 1 W.L.R. 579 at [27].

[170] *Roux v ABC* [1992] 2 V.R. 577.

[171] Matters pleaded under the head of general bad reputation must not extend to specific acts
of misconduct: *Pamplin v Express Newspapers (No.2)* [1988] 1 W.L.R. 116n; *Scott v Sampson*
(1882) 8 Q.B.D. 491; *Plato Films v Speidel* [1961] A.C. 1090. The Report on Practice and
Procedure in Defamation by the Supreme Court Procedure Committee (July 1991) recommended
the abolition of this rule and a reform to this effect was included in the draft Defamation Bill but

he had pursued a false claim for special damages.[172] The defendant may at trial rely in mitigation of damages on any evidence properly before the court, including evidence which has been primarily directed to an unsuccessful plea of justification or fair comment.[173] It is increasingly the practice for a defendant to include in his defence an averment to the effect that he will rely (if and in so far as it is necessary) on such evidence at trial in mitigation of damages. A defendant may also plead in mitigation of damages "directly relevant background context" material.[174] Where a defendant makes an offer to make amends under s.2 of the Defamation Act 1996, should the defendant wish, if the offer is accepted, to rely at any subsequent hearing to assess the compensation due to the claimant under s.3(5) of the Defamation Act 1996 on any background contextual material, he should serve on the claimant a statement of case setting out the facts and matters on which he intends to rely.[175] A defendant may not rely in mitigation of damages on the fact that there have been other publications to the same or similar effect as the publication complained of about which the claimant has not complained,[176] whether the other publications were made by the defendant or not.[177]

---

was dropped at the Committee stage, having been described as a potential "muckrakers' charter" (*Hansard*, HC Vol.280, col.133). But, now see *Burstein v Times Newspapers Ltd* [2001] 1 W.L.R. 579 CA. For the position in New South Wales, see *Australian Broadcasting Corp v McBride* [2001] NSWCA 322. Where the defendant relies on a relevant criminal conviction as evidence of the claimant's bad reputation (see *Goody v Odhams Press* [1967] 1 Q.B. 333), he should plead particulars of the conviction, notwithstanding that, since he is seeking to prove merely the fact of conviction and not commission of the underlying offence, he does not need to take advantage of the provisions of ss.11–13 of the Civil Evidence Act 1968.

[172] In *Joseph v Spiller* [2012] EWHC 2958 (QB) Tugendhat J. held that the deliberate pursuit of a false claim for special damages was an abuse of process. Whilst it did not affect the whole claim it led to an award of nominal damages: see [177]–[178].

[173] *Pamplin v Express Newspapers* [1988] 1 W.L.R. 116; *Turner v News Group Newspapers Ltd* [2006] EWCA Civ 540; [2006] 1 W.L.R. 3469. The principle is stated sufficiently widely in *Pamplin v Express Newspapers* to encompass reliance in mitigation on matters deployed primarily in support of a plea of *Reynolds* qualified privilege.

[174] *Burstein v Times Newspapers Ltd* [2001] 1 W.L.R. 579; *Turner v News Group Newspapers Ltd* [2006] EWCA Civ 540; [2006] 1 W.L.R. 3469; *Warren v The Random House Group Ltd* [2008] EWCA Civ 834; [2009] Q.B. 600 at [78]–[79]:
"There is no substitute for examination in each case of whether the material qualifies as background context directly relevant to the assessment of the damage sustained by the claimant as a result of the publication, in particular the damage to his reputation in the sector of his life to which it relates and the injury to his feelings."
For fuller discussions of *Burstein* and its progeny, see para.11.16, above and para.35.43, below.

[175] *Abu v MGN Ltd (Practice Note)* [2002] EWHC 2345 (QB); [2003] 1 W.L.R. 2201 at [8]–[10], [21]; approved in *Nail v News Group Newspapers Ltd* [2004] EWCA Civ 1708; [2005] 1 All E.R. 1040 at [15]; *Turner v News Group Newspapers Ltd* [2005] EWHC 892 (QB); [2005] E.M.L.R. 25; see, in particular, at [18]; *Turner v News Group Newspapers Ltd* [2006] EWCA Civ 540; [2006] 1 W.L.R. 3469 at [98]; *Loughton Contracts Plc v Dun & Bradstreet Ltd* [2006] EWHC 1224 (QB); *SD Marine Ltd v Powell* [2006] EWHC 3095 (QB).

[176] *Dingle v Associated Newspapers Ltd* [1964] A.C. 371.

[177] *Rath v Guardian News and Media Ltd* [2008] EWHC 398 (QB), per Tugendhat J. at [98]–[99].

Section 12 of the Defamation Action 1952. Where a defendant pro- **27.40**
poses in accordance with s.12 of the Defamation Act 1952 to give evidence in
mitigation of damages that the claimant has recovered damages, or has
brought actions for damages, for libel or slander in respect of the publication
of words to the same effect as the words on which the action is founded, or
has received or agreed to receive compensation in respect of any such
publication, he should plead the relevant events, giving particulars of the
occasions on which he relies.

SECTION 11. STATEMENT OF TRUTH

Statement of truth. A defence must be verified by a statement of truth.[178] **27.41**
Proceedings for contempt of court may be brought against a person if he
makes, or causes to be made, a false statement in a document verified by a
statement of truth without an honest belief in its truth.[179]

SECTION 12. COUNTERCLAIM

Making a counterclaim. In an action for defamation, a defendant who **27.42**
alleges that he has been libelled or slandered by the claimant (or who has any
other claim against the claimant) may, instead of bringing a separate action,
make a counterclaim (whether it involves a claim for damages or not) by
adding the counterclaim to his defence and the court is entitled to pronounce
a final judgment in the same action on claim and counterclaim[180]; but if the
claimant persuades the court that the counterclaim should be dismissed or
dealt with separately from the main claim the court may at any time rule
accordingly.[181] The defendant may raise a counterclaim against the claimant
along with some person not a party to the action.[182]

---

[178] CPR r.22.1; CPR PD 16, para.12.1. The form of the statement of truth is as follows: "[I
believe] [the defendant] believes that the facts stated in this defence are true."

[179] CPR r.32.14.

[180] Under the CPR, such a counterclaim is included within the definition of a "Part 20 claim",
see CPR rr.20.2 and 20.3. A defendant may make a counterclaim against a claimant without the
court's permission if he files particulars of counterclaim with his defence. If the defendant wishes
to make a counterclaim at any other time, he requires the court's permission, see CPR
r.20.4(2).

[181] CPR r.20.9. which contains a non-exhaustive list of matters to which the court may have
regard when considering whether to dismiss a Pt 20 claim or to require it to be dealt with
separately from the claim by the claimant against the defendant. They include the connection
between the Pt 20 claim and the claim being made by the claimant against the defendant. The
fundamental question is whether dealing with the claim and counterclaim together is the "most
convenient and effective" way of managing the claims involved: see CPR r.20.1. See also CPR
r.3.1(2)(e).

[182] CPR r.20.5. A defendant who wishes to counterclaim against a person other then the
claimant must apply to the court for an order that that person be added as defendant to the
counterclaim. Where a court makes such an order, it will give directions as to the management
of the case.

27.43   **Pleading the counterclaim.** A counterclaim is governed by the same rules of pleading as particulars of claim.[183] The defendant should state the facts in numbered paragraphs under the heading "Part 20 claim" so as to distinguish them from the facts alleged by way of defence. If any of the facts on which the counterclaim is founded have already been pleaded in the defence, they need not be pleaded again in the counterclaim, but may be incorporated by reference.

Section 13. Contribution

27.44   **Tortfeasors liable for the same damage.** The defendant may, if he wishes, claim a contribution from any other person who is liable in respect of the same damage, whether jointly or otherwise.[184] The amount of the contribution recoverable from any person under the Act shall be such as may be found by the court to be just and equitable having regard to the responsibility of that person for the damage[185]; and the court is empowered to exempt any person from liability to make contribution, or to direct that the contribution to be recovered from any person shall amount to a complete indemnity.[186]

27.45   **Indemnities.** Under s.11 of the Defamation Act 1952, an agreement for indemnifying any person against civil liability for libel in respect of the

---

[183] The defence and counterclaim should normally form one document with the counterclaim following on from the defence, see CPR PD 15, para.15.1 and CPR PD 20, para.6.1. The contents of a Pt 20 claim should be verified by a statement of truth, see CPR PD 20, para.4.1.

[184] Civil Liability (Contribution) Act 1978, s.1(1). A person is liable to make contribution notwithstanding that he has ceased to be liable since the damage occurred unless the right on which the claim against him was based has been extinguished by a statute of limitation or prescription: Civil Liability (Contribution) Act 1978, s.1(3). A person who has made a bona fide settlement or compromise has a similar right to contribution if he would have been liable "assuming the factual basis of the claim against him could be established": Civil Liability (Contribution) Act 1978, s.1(4). A person who has been released from liability as part of a bona fide compromise may thus claim contribution from a joint tortfeasor notwithstanding that the effect of the release would have been to extinguish the claim for the joint tort against both of them. Similarly, a third party who ceases to be liable to the claimant, by reason of an agreed settlement of the claimant's claim against him, may still be liable to make contribution to the defendant. It has been held, however, that s.1(1) is directed to the payment of money by way of damages, so that a party who has settled with the claimant on the basis that he pay the latter's legal costs cannot recover that money (or other expenditure he may have incurred) by way of contribution: *Eastwood v Ryder*, *The Times*, July 31, 1990. For a discussion of this topic in the context of settlement, see paras 29.11–29.13, below. See, e.g. *Skrine & Co. v Euromoney Publications Plc* [2001] EWCA Civ 1479; [2002] E.M.L.R. 15 CA. For the position regarding third party claims in the Australian Capital Territory, see *Lamont v Dwyer* [2007] ACTSC 47.

[185] Civil Liability (Contribution) Act 1978, s.2(1). This subsection confers on the court a wide discretion to apportion the damages according to the measure of the relative responsibility or fault of the parties: *Weaver v Commercial Process* (1947) 63 T.L.R. 466; *Whitby v Burt, Boulton and Hayward* [1947] K.B. 918; *Mihaka v Wellington Publishing* [1975] 1 N.Z.L.R. 10 at 19 ("with due regard to relative blameworthiness and causative potency, with due observance of what is just and equitable").

[186] Civil Liability (Contribution) Act 1978, s.2(2).

publication of any matter shall not be unlawful unless at the time of the publication that person knows that the matter is defamatory and does not reasonably believe there is a good defence to any action brought upon it. Such a term is common in agreements for broadcasting, or the publication of books,[187] and a claim under it, if the term is lawful, is for indemnity, and not for contribution under the 1978 Act. However, unless protected by s.11 of the Defamation Act 1952, an express promise by A to indemnify B if he will publish a libel is void,[188] and it seems unlikely that it would be allowed to found a claim for contribution under the 1978 Act.[189]

Procedure and pleading. A claim by a defendant against any person (whether or not already a party) for contribution or indemnity is included within the definition of a Pt 20 claim under the CPR.[190] A defendant who has filed an acknowledgment of service or a defence may make a Pt 20 claim for contribution or indemnity against another defendant by filing a notice containing a statement of the nature and grounds of his claim and serving it on the other defendant.[191] A claim for contribution or indemnity against a person who is not already a party is made when the court issues a Pt 20 claim form, which must be in the prescribed form.[192] Particulars of the claim must be contained in or served with the Pt 20 claim form.[193] A defendant may make such a claim without the court's permission if the Pt 20 claim is issued before or at the same time as he files his defence.[194] At any other time, the court's permission is required.[195] An application for permission may be made without notice. Where the court gives permission to make a Pt 20 claim, it will at the same time give directions as to the service of the Pt 20 claim.[196]

27.46

---

[187] Distributors apparently have a common law right of indemnity from the publishers of a magazine: *Goldsmith v Sperrings* [1977] 1 W.L.R. 478 at 507. However, it has been held that a contract between a magazine and the author of a book arranging for the publication of extracts from the book in the magazine does not include an implied term of indemnity by virtue of custom and usage in the newspaper and periodical publishing business: *Eastwood v Ryder, The Times*, July 31, 1990.

[188] *Shackell v Rosier* (1836) 2 Bing. N.C. 634; *WH Smith v Clinton and Harns* (1908) 99 L.T. 840; *Bradstreets British v Harold Mitchell* [1933] Ch. 190; *Weld-Blundell v Stephens* [1920] A.C. 956 at 998, per Lord Wrenbury.

[189] It may be argued that the existence of such a term in an agreement should be taken into consideration in determining what is "just and equitable" under s.2(1) of the 1978 Act but to do so is tantamount to treating the term as enforceable and s.7(3) of the Civil Liability (Contribution) Act 1978 provides that nothing in the Act shall render enforceable any agreement for indemnity or contribution which would not be enforceable apart from the Act.

[190] CPR r.20.2.

[191] CPR r.20.6.

[192] CPR rr.20.7(2) and 4.1 (Form N211).

[193] CPR r.20.7(4).

[194] CPR r.20.7(3)(a). Where a Pt 20 claim for contribution or indemnity may be served without the court's permission, the Pt 20 claim form must be served on the person against whom it is made within 14 days after the date on which the party making the Pt 20 claim files his defence, see CPR r.20.8(1)(b).

[195] CPR r.20.7(3)(b).

[196] CPR r.20.8(3).

Section 14. Misuse of Private Information

27.47 **Generally.** As in claims for defamation, the defendant must take each allegation in the particulars of claim separately, and either admit it, or deny it, or say that he is unable to admit or deny it, but requires the claimant to prove it. Where the defendant denies an allegation, he must state his reasons for doing so, and, if he intends to put forward a different version of events from that given by the claimant, he must state his own version.[197] The defendant must plead with sufficient precision and clarity so as to enable the claimant to know what he will be obliged to prove and what case he must prepare to meet. So, for instance, if the defendant denies that the relevant information was private to the claimant or that the claimant had a reasonable expectation that the information would be kept private by the defendant, he should plead as much. Similarly, if the defendant wishes to deny an allegation in the particulars of claim that he had a pre-existing relationship of trust and confidence with the claimant or that he was, for some other alleged reason, on notice that the information was private to the claimant. Further, the defendant may put forward one or more substantive defences in answer to the claimant's claim, e.g. that the claimant gave his consent to his use of the relevant information, that the information was in the public domain[198] or that his publication or other use of the information was justified in the public interest[199] or with reference to the defendant's right to freedom of expression more generally.[200] The defendant should respond specifically in his defence to any facts and matters pleaded in the particulars of claim in support of a claim for general

---

[197] CPR r.16.5(1)-(2).

[198] *Att-Gen v Guardian Newspapers (No.2)* [1990] 1 A.C. 109 at 282 ("the principle of confidentiality only applies to information to the extent that it is confidential. In particular, once it has entered what is usually called the public domain (which means no more than that the information in question is so generally accessible that, in all the circumstances, it cannot be regarded as confidential) then, as a general rule, the principle of confidentiality can have no application to it . . . "). Quaere the extent to which public domain presents an answer to a claim based upon misuse of private information, particularly where the private information in question consists of a photograph or a video: *D v L* [2004] E.M.L.R. 1 at [23]; *Douglas v Hello! Ltd (No.3)* [2005] EWCA Civ 595; [2005] Q.B. 972 at [84] and [105]; see also *A v M (Family Proceedings: Publicity)* [2000] 1 F.L.R. 562.

[199] *Att-Gen v Guardian Newspapers (No.2)*, above, at 282; *Campbell v MGN Ltd* [2004] UKHL 22; [2004] 2 A.C. 457; *Mosley v News Group Newspapers Ltd* [2008] EWHC 1777 (QB); [2008] E.M.L.R.20 at [110]–[171]; also see, e.g. *Francome v Mirror Group Newspapers Ltd* [1984] 1 W.L.R. 892; *Lion Laboratories v Evans* [1985] Q.B. 526; *London Regional Transport Ltd v The Mayor of London* [2001] EWCA Civ 1491; [2003] E.M.L.R. 4; *Jockey Club v Buffham* [2002] EWHC 1866; [2003] Q.B. 462; *LNS v Persons Unknown* [2010] EWHC 119 (QB); [2010] E.M.L.R. 16; *Hutcheson v News Group Newspapers Ltd* [2011] EWCA Civ 808; [2012] E.M.L.R.2; *Ferdinand v MGN Ltd* [2011] EWHC 2454 (QB); *Abbey v Gilligan* [2012] EWHC 3217; [2013] E.M.L.R. 12; *AAA v Associated Newspapers Ltd* [2012] EWCA Civ 554.

[200] Under arts 8(2) and 10(1) of the European Convention on Human Rights. Where a claimant's rights under art.8(1) conflict with a defendant's under art.10(1), an "intense focus" upon the comparative importance of the specific rights being claimed in the individual case is necessary and the court must take into account the justification for interfering with or restricting each, having regard, ultimately, to proportionality: *Re S (A Child) (Identification: Restrictions on Publication)* [2004] UKHL 47; [2005] 1 A.C. 593.

compensatory or aggravated damages and should also set out any facts and matters upon which he wishes to rely in mitigation of damages.

SECTION 15. AMENDMENT OF DEFENCE AND COUNTERCLAIM

Amendment. After a defendant has served his defence, he may only amend   **27.48**
it with the written consent of all the parties or with the permission of the court.[201] If the amendment involves the removal, addition or substitution of a party, the permission of the court is required.[202] Where the defendant seeks permission to amend his defence, he should apply under CPR Pt 23 by application notice. A copy of the proposed amended statement of case should be filed with the application notice.[203]

Granting of permission in discretion of court. Permission to amend   **27.49**
will normally be given freely if the overriding objective requires it and there is no element of surprise or prejudice which cannot be compensated by an appropriate order as to costs or otherwise.[204] However, whilst there is no rule on the number of times a party can amend a pleading, the Court of Appeal in *Ashcroft v Foley* stressed that repeated satellite litigation concerning the state of pleadings was not a good use of court resources and there had to come a point at which repeated attempts at amendment, necessary because of the defendants' wish to keep the pleading as general as they can, became an abuse of process.[205] Moreover, the court has shown itself less willing to grant a defendant permission to amend his defence where the application is made late in the day, either at, or close to, the trial[206]; in particular, when a defendant

---

[201] CPR r.17.1(2).

[202] CPR r.17.1(3).

[203] CPR PD 17, para.1.2(2).

[204] For the general principle under the CPR, see *Cobbold v Greenwich LBC*, unreported, August 9, 1999, CA:

"Amendments in general ought to be allowed so that the real dispute between the parties can be adjudicated upon provided that any prejudice to the other party caused by the amendment can be compensated for in costs, and the public interest in the administration of justice is not significantly harmed";

"The essential principle is sometimes encapsulated by the proposition that it is never too late to amend, provided that there is no prejudice to the other party which cannot be cured by an appropriate order for costs":

Warren v Random House Group Ltd [2008] EWCA Civ 834; [2009] Q.B. 600 at [19]; see also *Cropper v Smith* (1884) 26 Ch D 700 at 710–711; *Cadam v Beaverbrook Newspapers Ltd* [1959] 1 Q.B. 413 at 423; per Morris L.J.; *Associated Leisure v Associated Newspapers* [1970] 2 Q.B. 450. But see *Swain-Mason v Mills and Reeve LLP (Practice Note)* 2011 EWCA Civ 14; 2011 1 W.L.R. 2735, CA on lateness.

[205] [2012] EWCA Civ 423; [2012] E.M.L.R. 25 at [43].

[206] *Plummer v Charman* [1962] 1 W.L.R. 1469 CA:

"The plea, if allowed, would have completely altered the scope of the action . . . In those circumstances it is quite clear, in accordance with ordinary principles, that the proposed amendment made at the eleventh hour must be looked at with great particularity to see whether in fact it has the slightest prospect of success",

(per Upjohn L.J. at 1473). The court will be particularly reluctant to allow a change from a deliberately adopted line of defence: *Sanders v Anderson* [1968] N.Z.L.R. 172. But see *W v Westminster City Council* [2004] EWHC 2812 (QB) at [32]–[43]. Despite the fact the defendants

seeks to introduce or expand a plea of justification at a late stage, his conduct will be closely inquired into, and the court will expect him to have shown due diligence in making his inquiries and investigations.[207] But a failure by a claimant to set out its case in pre-action correspondence may lead a court to be more willing to grant permission for a late amendment to a defence of justification.[208] A late application to add a defence of *Reynolds* qualified privilege will also be closely scrutinised by the court.[209] It has been held that where delay has been due to the defendant's own default, that factor should be taken into consideration by the judge as part of the matters to be weighed in deciding whether or not to allow an amendment. The mere fact that delay may be capable of being compensated in money is not conclusive of the question whether the amendment should or should not be permitted.[210] In particular,

---

delayed for four months after the proposed amendments had first been discussed until the eve of the date fixed for the trial of the action before making their application for permission to revise their defences of qualified and absolute privilege, Tugendhat J. considered at [41] he "really [had] . . . no choice" but to permit the amendment. A key factor telling in favour of this conclusion (at [42]) was that the second defendant's entitlement to a fair trial could "only be met" by permitting her to respond to the claimant's case of malice against her in the manner envisaged in her amended case. See *Swain-Mason*, above fn.204.

[207] per Lord Denning M.R. in *Associated Leisure v Associated Newspapers* [1970] 2 Q.B. 450 CA at 455–456:

" . . . the pleading ought to be scrutinised closely. The defendants ought to give proper particulars. They ought not to be allowed to put in a loose, ineffective pleading at the last hour."

Allworth v John Fairfax Group (1993) 113 F.L.R. 254; *Al Rajhi Banking & Investment Corp v The Wall Street Journal Europe SPRL*, above. See also *Cook v News Group Newspapers Ltd* [2002] EWHC 1070 (QB), per Eady J. and *Foster v Associated Newspapers Ltd* [2002] EWHC 1885 (QB), per Gray J. See also *Al Fayed v Condé Nast Publications Ltd*, unreported, May 23, 1997, per Morland J.

[208] In *Rothschild v Associated Newspapers Ltd* [2011] EWHC 3462 (QB) Tugendhat J. said at [60]:

" . . . there has been a significant change in the way in which libel proceedings (amongst others) are now conducted since the introduction of the CPR and the Pre-Action Protocols. These procedural changes have not of course altered the substantive law of libel, namely that a claimant is entitled to rely on the presumption of falsity. But the days when major libel trials could be conducted without either party knowing in advance the substance of the evidence to be adduced by the other have long since gone. The arguments advanced by [Leading Counsel for ANL] on the basis of the Pre-Action Protocol letters, and the availability of new information from the witness statements served by Mr Rothschild, are arguments which could not have been advanced to a court before the introduction of these new procedural changes. No case has been cited to me in which these arguments have been advanced in a similar context before now."

[209] See *Field v Local Sunday Newspapers Ltd*, unreported, November 28, 2001, (QB), in which Gray J. refused a late application by the defendant for permission to rely on *Reynolds* qualified privilege. Cf. *McKeown v Attheraces Ltd* [2011] EWHC 3232 (QB) where Eady J. allowed a defendant to amend to plead *Reynolds* qualified privilege and rejected the claimant's submission that a condition should be attached to the grant of permission requiring that the defendant elect whether to plead the defence in substitution of defences already pleaded: see [10].

[210] *Bower v Maxwell*, unreported, May 8, 1989, 89/472, CA:

" . . . viewed in the context, in particular of what Lord Griffiths said in the *Ketteman* case ([1987] 1 A.C. 189), it is my view that the learned judge rightly came to the conclusion that the defendant was in default with regard to his application for leave to amend, in default in the sense that he could and should have made the application for leave to amend earlier. It was

although there is no rule that allegations of fraud must be pleaded at the outset and cannot be added by amendment, the court must be clearly satisfied that the opposing party is not prejudiced, and that any inconvenience can be compensated, before it allows a late amendment involving a serious allegation such as fraud or criminality for the first time.[211] A belated application to amend should not, however, be refused on the ground that the proposed amendments would substantially increase the costs of the action which the claimant, if successful, would be unlikely to recover, unless there is also evidence to suggest that the amendments are shadowy or not bona fide.[212]

The court will be reluctant to refuse permission to add or extend a plea of justification solely for reasons of delay, because it is not in the public interest that defamation claimants should recover damages and thereby achieve a public vindication of reputation which is not deserved.[213] However, this consideration should not be regarded as a "trump card" and it is always necessary to have regard to the overriding objective of the CPR and the

---

open to the learned judge, in exercising his discretion, to come to the conclusion that there were factors in this case which justified his refusing leave to amend",
(per Woolf L.J.); *Edelman v Times Newspapers*, unreported, January 7, 1991, Drake J.:
"At the end of the day the question has to be asked whether the plaintiff has shown some unconscionable conduct on the part of the defendants or their advisers. If it does exist the defendants should plainly not be allowed to take advantage of it; and if it exists, though the discretion still remains, the case for disallowing the amendment would be virtually unanswerable.";
Perkins v Nationwide News Pty (1992) 106 F.L.R. 368, where it was held that the court would not lightly entertain an application to amend where to allow the proposed amendment would require vacating the time set aside for the hearing of the trial.
[211] *Atkinson v Fitzwalter* [1987] 1 W.L.R. 201 CA:
" . . . it must be remembered that fraud is a very serious allegation to make against a person, as for instance would be an allegation of a criminal offence, and may, if not raised at the outset be difficult, if not impossible, properly to investigate at a later stage in the proceedings. Further, the more serious the allegation that is made, then the more clearly satisfied must a court be that indeed no prejudice is being caused which cannot be compensated for in some satisfactory way or another before allowing the amendment."
(per May L.J. at 210).
"A plea of justification should not be allowed by amendment in circumstances in which the statement alleged to be defamatory unequivocally involves an assertion that the plaintiff has been fraudulent. In such circumstances, it behoves a defendant to be in possession of all the relevant facts in support of the contention before he makes the defamatory statement and he cannot be allowed to amend on the basis that his statement was unsupported by evidence known to him at that time."
(per Stocker L.J. at 221). *B v J* [1999] E.M.L.R. 490, where it was held that, although it was not normally appropriate for a court, on an application for permission to amend a pleading settled by counsel or a solicitor, to evaluate the strength of the case pleaded, in the context of plea seeking to justify allegations of fraud it might become necessary for the court to satisfy itself that the defendant had reasonable evidence to support the plea or reasonable grounds to believe that sufficient evidence to prove the allegations would be available at trial. While the support for such a plea did not have to amount to a complete case, it had to be sufficient to enable the allegation of fraud to be made.
[212] *Mackenzie v Business Magazines Ltd*, unreported, January 18, 1996, CA.
[213] per Eady J. in *Al Rajhi Banking & Investment Corp v The Wall Street Journal Europe SPRL*, above, at [14], citing *Basham v Gregory*, unreported, February 21, 1996, CA, and *Mackenzie v Business Magazines Ltd*, unreported, January 18, 1996, CA.

consequences of a late amendment in terms of delay, cost and stress for the claimant.[214] The court, by contrast, will not hesitate at any stage to rule out, as a matter of case management, proposed particulars of justification which are only of peripheral relevance to the central case in support of which they are sought to be advanced.[215] The matter fundamentally is for the discretion of the court in all the circumstances,[216] and, where it allows an amendment, it will usually do so on terms and subject, of course, to any adjournment which may be granted to allow the claimant an opportunity of meeting the amended defence.[217] Conversely, where an application to amend is refused, a defendant may in an appropriate case be given liberty to apply for permission to make a different properly framed amendment.[218]

Although it is not required by the rules, a defendant making a late application to amend ought to put in a witness statement explaining the lateness.[219] Where a defendant applied to amend his defence by raising a plea of privilege after the evidence was concluded, and the jury had retired, it was held that the judge had rightly refused to allow such amendment.[220] Where the defendants applied to amend their defence to raise a plea of justification following a trial

---

[214] per Eady J. in *Cook v News Group Newspapers Ltd* [2002] EWHC 1070 (QB), relying on *Basham v Gregory*, above, per Sir Thomas Bingham M.R. See also *Rothschild v Associated Newspapers Ltd* [2011] EWHC 3462 (QB)

[215] *McPhilemy v Times Newspapers Ltd*, above, at 789; *Cook v News Group Newspapers Ltd*, above.

[216] *Proetta v Times Newspapers Ltd*, unreported, February 21, 1991, Drake J.:
" . . . despite the change of direction indicated in *Ketteman* and in *Bower v Maxwell* . . . , I do not think that the former approach has been entirely superseded. It seems to me that the question I must finally decide in exercising discretion whether to allow an amendment is whether a greater injustice will be done by refusing than allowing the amendment."
Proetta v Times Newspapers Ltd, unreported, February 27, 1991, CA, per Taylor L.J.:
"If through lack of earlier insight or a change of mind a defendant realises, albeit at a late stage, that the pleadings do not set out his real case, there must be some measure of injustice should he not be allowed to plead and argue it. The extent of the injustice and how it compares with the injustice to the plaintiff of allowing a late amendment is a matter for the judge's discretion."

[217] *M'Carthy v Fitzgerald* [1909] 2 Ir.R. 445. However, the court will not impose conditions on the grant of permission requiring a defendant to drop other defences where it seeks to amend to plead *Reynolds* privilege. See *McKeown*, above at 110,

[218] *Atkinson v Fitzwalter* [1987] 1 W.L.R. 201 CA.

[219] *Associated Leisure v Associated Newspapers* [1970] 2 Q.B. 450:
"But when the defendant seeks to plead justification at a late stage, his conduct will be closely inquired into. The court will expect him to have shown due diligence in making his inquiries and investigations"
(per Lord Denning M.R. at 456); *Atkinson v Fitzwalter* [1987] 1 W.L.R. 201:
"I should say that if there were any reasonable basis for a belief that the defendants' delay in seeking leave for their amendment was deliberate in order to overreach the plaintiff or to obtain some tactical advantage I should come to the opposite conclusion, but there is here evidence on affidavit to the contrary sworn by a solicitor"
(per Stocker L.J. at 223).

[220] *Shea v O'Connor* (1894) 26 N.S.R. 205. See also *Meier v Klotz* (1928) 22 Sask.L.R. 385 where a defendant who had not pleaded privilege was not allowed to raise the defence for the first time in the Court of Appeal.

of qualified privilege determined in favour of the claimant, the judge dismissed the application because the factors in favour of permitting the amendment were outweighed by factors against allowing it, in particular the fact that the pleaded case was on its face insufficiently strong to warrant permission being granted to advance it at such a late stage.[221]

Section 16. Default in Service of Defence

Generally. If the defendant fails to serve his defence within the proper **27.50** time,[222] the claimant may obtain judgment in default.[223] The defendant and the claimant may agree that the prescribed period for filing a defence shall be extended by up to 28 days.[224] Where the defendant requires longer than 28 days for service of the defence, the defendant must apply to the court for an order extending time, even where the extension is agreed between the parties. Even after time for service of the defence has expired the defendant can still serve a defence at any time before judgment in default is signed and such defence cannot be treated as a nullity.[225]

Judgment for an amount to be decided by the court. Where the **27.51** claimant's claim is for damages only, the claimant may obtain a default judgment by filing a request in the relevant practice form.[226] The default judgment obtained in such circumstances will be for an amount to be decided by the court and costs.[227] On the entry of the judgment, the court will list a disposal hearing.[228] At the disposal hearing the court will give directions or decide the amount payable.[229] Where the claimant applies for default judgment against one of two or more defendants, the court may enter a default judgment on the claim against that defendant and the claimant may continue the proceedings against the other defendants, provided that the claim can be

---

[221] Before such a case could be permitted to go forward, the defendant would have to satisfy the requirements of *Ladd v Marshall* [1954] 1 W.L.R. 1489: see *Loutchansky v Times Newspapers Ltd* [2002] EWHC 2726 (QB).

[222] The period for filing a defence is 14 days after service of the particulars of claim or 28 days after service of the particulars of claim if the defendant serves an acknowledgment of service under CPR Pt 10, see CPR r.15.4.

[223] CPR r.12.3(2).

[224] CPR r.15.5(1). Where this happens, the defendant must notify the court in writing.

[225] *Gill v Woodfin* (1884) 15 Ch D 707; *Montagu v Land Corp* (1887) 56 L.T. 730.

[226] CPR r.12.4(1).

[227] CPR r.12.5(3).

[228] CPR PD 26, para.12.7.

[229] CPR PD 26, para.12.8. See, e.g. *Olafsson v Gissurarson* [2008] EWCA Civ 152 at [8] (in which the Court of Appeal dismissed an appeal by the defendant against an order dispensing with service of the claim form upon him). The court will not order that the amount payable is to be decided there and then unless any written evidence on which the claimant relies has been served on the defendant at least three days before the disposal hearing. Unless the court otherwise directs, a master or district judge may decide the amount payable: see CPR PD 26, para.12.10.

dealt with separately from the claim against the other defendants.[230] If it cannot be dealt with separately, the court will not enter a default judgment and it must deal with the claimant's application at the same time as it disposes of the claim against the other defendants.[231]

27.52 **Where an injunction is claimed.** If the claimant's claim consists of, or includes, a claim for an injunction, the claimant must make an application in accordance with CPR Pt 23 if he wishes to obtain a default judgment, unless he abandons that claim in his request for judgment.[232] On an application for default judgment, judgment shall be such judgment as it appears to the court that the claimant is entitled to on his statement of case.[233]

Section 17. Application for Further Information

27.53 **Application for further information.** Where the defendant has not provided adequate particulars of his case in his defence, the claimant should apply by letter for the particulars before making a formal application to the court.[234] When the application is made to the court,[235] the application notice may, where appropriate, ask that in default of provision of clarification and further information the allegations should be struck out of the defence.[236] The advantage of obtaining particulars is that the claimant will know precisely what case the defendant is going to make at the trial and be enabled to prepare accordingly.[237] Moreover, the issues will be defined by the matters specified in the particulars and the defendant may not be permitted at trial (without amendment) to go into matters not fairly included within them.[238]

---

[230] CPR r.12.8(2)(a).

[231] CPR r.12.8(2)(b).

[232] CPR rr.12.4(2) and 12.4(3).

[233] CPR r.12.11.

[234] For the rules and principles governing requests and applications for further information under CPR Pt 18; see para.26.48, above.

[235] The request should be made by letter if the text of the request is brief and the reply is likely to be brief. Otherwise, the request should be in a separate document: see CPR PD 18, para.1.4. If the request is made by letter, the letter should state that it contains a request made under CPR Pt 18, and should deal with no matters other than the request: see CPR PD 18, para.1.5.

[236] For the form of the request and the response, see CPR PD 18, paras 1.5 and 2.3.

[237] *Toronto Star v Globe* [1941] 4 D.L.R. 113: "More than in any class of action, pleadings are of the utmost importance in actions for defamation, and their regularity should be insisted upon" (per Hope J. at 118).

[238] *Cadam v Beaverbrook Newspapers Ltd* [1959] 1 Q.B. 413 CA: "It is quite clear that in giving particulars of justification the defendants are bound by the particulars that they have given: they cannot go beyond those particulars" (per Morris L.J. at 425). But see per Lord Woolf M.R. in *McPhilemy v Times Newspapers Ltd* [1999] 3 All E.R. 775 as regards the inter-relation between pleadings and witness statements *post* the introduction of the CPR and the latitude that might be accorded to defendants with regard to matters not specifically pleaded in the defence.

Demand must not be disproportionate. The court will be careful to see   **27.54**
that the demand for particulars is not disproportionate or otherwise oppressive, e.g. that the claimant is not covertly endeavouring to get something to
which he is not entitled, namely, the disclosure of the evidence in the
defendant's possession.[239] The rule is that a party is entitled to an order for
further particulars only for the purpose of ascertaining the nature of his
opponent's case that he has to meet, and not for the purpose of obtaining
advance notice of the evidence by which his opponent proposes to prove it.[240]
Where the claimant's application for particulars of justification is otherwise
proper it is no answer that in giving such particulars the defendant may be
compelled to disclose the names of persons he intends to call as witnesses.[241]

---

[239] *Wootton v Sievier* [1913] 3 K.B. 499 CA at 504. See also the observations of the Court of
Appeal in *Musa King v Telegraph Group Ltd (Practice Note)* [2004] EWCA Civ 613; [2005] 1
W.L.R. 2282 (reported as *King v Telegraph Group Ltd (Practice Note)*) at [63], and see the
discussion at para.31.39ff, below.

[240] *Aga Khan v The Times* [1924] 1 K.B. 675 at 679; *Toronto Star v Globe* [1941] 4 D.L.R.
113.

[241] *Wootton v Sievier* [1913] 3 K.B. 499; *Zierenberg v Labouchere* [1893] 2 Q.B. 183 at 188;
Humphries v Taylor (1888) 39 Ch D 693; *Bishop v Bishop* [1901] P. 325.

CHAPTER 28

REPLY AND DEFENCE TO COUNTERCLAIM

SECTION 1. INTRODUCTION

Generally. Save where the defendant has pleaded a defence of honest   **28.1**
comment or justification, it is not necessary for the claimant to serve a reply
if he merely denies the defence, for all material statements of fact in the
defence will automatically be deemed to have been denied and put in
issue.[1]

SECTION 2. PLEADING TO A DEFENCE OF HONEST COMMENT OR JUSTIFICATION

Admission or denial of facts pleaded in support of a plea of honest   **28.2**
comment or justification. Where a defendant alleges that the words
complained of are true, or are honest comment, the claimant must serve a
reply specifically admitting or denying the allegation and giving the facts on
which he relies.[2] Prior to the introduction of this rule, it had been recognised

---

[1] CPR rr.15.8 and 16.7. A reply is optional. A claimant need not serve one unless he wishes to
raise matters in answer to the defence which were not included in his particulars of claim. If a
claimant files a reply to the defence, he must file his reply when he files his allocation
questionnaire and serve his reply on the other parties at the same time as he files it: see CPR
r.15.8.

[2] CPR PD 53, para.2.8. Although the rule does not on its face contemplate a non-admission on
the part of the claimant, it seems unlikely that it was intended to exclude this form of response,
bearing in mind that the general rule permits a claimant simply to require a matter to be proved:
see CPR r.16.7(2)(b) and cf. CPR r.16.5(1)(b). However, non-admissions ought not to be made in
a reply by a claimant in respect of matters raised in a plea of justification or fair comment which
are within his knowledge. To do so would be to obfuscate rather than define the issues and
therefore contrary to the overriding objective. In such a case, the court may order the claimant to
provide further information: see, e.g. *Gaddafi v Telegraph Group Ltd*, unreported, December 20,
2000 (QB), per Eady J. In *Moss v Channel Five Broadcasting Ltd*, unreported, February 3, 2006
(QB), Eady J., having held that the defendant was entitled to justify the broadcast complained of
in the general meaning that the claimant was "a serious cocaine abuser", ordered the claimant
specifically to plead in her reply her case in answer to the particular instances of cocaine abuse
relied upon by the defendant in its defence.

that the failure of the court to exercise with sufficient frequency its acknowledged power to order a claimant to plead properly to particulars of justification often left defendants in genuine ignorance as to the nature of the claimant's case.[3] However, the court will be astute to ensure that this requirement of pleading does not weaken the position which the claimant enjoys as regards to the burden of proof.[4]

SECTION 3. PLEADING TO A DEFENCE UNDER SECTIONS 2 AND 3,
DEFAMATION ACT 2013

28.3 Admission or denial of facts pleaded in support of a plea under sections 2 and 3 of the Defamation Act 2013. No changes are currently proposed to the wording of CPR Pt 53. It is assumed that the court will require a claimant to reply to these defences in the same way that he is currently required to reply to the common law defences of honest comment and justification.

SECTION 4. PLEADING AN AFFIRMATIVE CASE IN REPLY GENERALLY

28.4 Pleading an affirmative case. Quite apart from the express requirement applying where the defendant pleads justification or honest comment, *in any case* where the claimant wishes to set up an affirmative case which is not included in his particulars of claim, he must serve a reply specifically pleading the matter or matters on which he relies.[5] It is good practice, e.g. for a claimant to respond in a reply to a defence of qualified privilege, particularly a plea of *Reynolds* privilege, with the same specificity as one is required to in

---

[3] See the Report on Practice and Procedure in Defamation (1991).

[4] *Morrell v International Thompson Publishing Ltd*, July 18, 1990, unreported, CA. Whilst the law has not changed, Tugendhat J. said in *Rothschild v Associated Newspapers Ltd* [2011] EWHC 3462 (QB) at [60]:

"... there has been a significant change in the way in which libel proceedings (amongst others) are now conducted since the introduction of the CPR and the Pre-Action Protocols. These procedural changes have not of course altered the substantive law of libel, namely that a claimant is entitled to rely on the presumption of falsity. But the days when major libel trials could be conducted without either party knowing in advance the substance of the evidence to be adduced by the other have long since gone. The arguments advanced by [Leading Counsel for ANL] on the basis of the Pre-Action Protocol letters, and the availability of new information from the witness statements served by Mr Rothschild, are arguments which could not have been advanced to a court before the introduction of these new procedural changes. No case has been cited to me in which these arguments have been advanced in a similar context before now."

[5] CPR r.16.7.

response to a defence of justification or honest comment.[6] When responding in a reply to a defence of qualified privilege, the pleader should take care to distinguish matters only relevant to the question of whether the publication at issue attracts a privilege from matters only germane to malice, and not to confuse the two.[7] Where a defendant is a public authority and pleads that the publication was privileged, the claimant should, if art.8 is engaged, respond to that plea by taking issue with whether or not the publication was necessary and proportionate and pursued a legitimate aim.[8] A reply must be verified by a statement of truth.[9]

Other illustrations. Thus, for instance, where the defendant has pleaded   **28.5** that the claimant's cause of action has been lost by reason of a release given to a joint tortfeasor, if the claimant wishes to rely on the fact that the alleged release was given without authority or on the terms that the cause of action against the defendant should be preserved, he should serve a reply pleading all the relevant underlying facts on which he relies.[10] Similarly, where a defendant has sought to rely by way of defence on the making of an offer of amends under s.2 of the Defamation Act 1996, and the claimant contends that the defendant is has no defence because he knew or had reason to believe that the statement complained of (1) referred to the claimant or was likely to be understood as referring to him and (2) was false and defamatory of the claimant, the claimant should plead as much in reply, setting out the facts and matters on which he relies in support of his contention.[11] Or, if the defendant

---

[6] In *Charman v Orion Publishing Group Ltd* [2007] EWCA Civ 972; [2008] 1 All E.R. 750, Hooper L.J. took the claimant to task for failing to plead in the reply criticisms of the defendant journalist's conduct in response to a defence of *Reynolds* qualified privilege: see [101], [122], [219], [228] and [230]–[231]. In particular, at [228], Hooper L.J observed:
 "I do not agree with Mr Tomlinson . . . that McLagan's failure to say that Smith was profoundly tainted was 'a fact which was of great importance in considering these events' and therefore undermines the defence of responsible journalism. I should add that this is one of the complaints which was to be found in neither the reply nor the amended reply, albeit . . . it was raised in the skeleton and in the opening. If it was seen as a fact of such great importance, one might expect to see it in the pleadings."
Whilst it is not necessary to respond to a defence of statutory qualified privilege unless raising malice, if a defendant raises a statutory qualified privilege defence and the claimant challenges fairness and accuracy or that the words complained of were of public concern and for the public benefit it would be sensible to raise those points in a reply: see *Qadir v Associated Newspapers Ltd* [2012] EWHC 2606 (QB); [2013] E.M.L.R. 15 for an example where such points were pleaded and succeeded. Note s.7(2), Defamation Act 2013 substitutes 'public interest' for 'public concern' under s.15(3), Defamation Act 1996.
[7] For a discussion of this distinction, see *Oliver v Chief Constable of Northumbria* [2003] EWHC 2417 QBD; [2004] E.M.L.R. 32 at [34]–[42].
[8] *Wood v Chief Constable of the West Midlands Police* [2005] E.M.L.R. 20; *Clift v Slough Borough Council* [2010] EWCA Civ 1171; [2011] 1 W.L.R. 1774 per Ward L.J. at [19]. See para.28.8, below.
[9] CPR r.22.1.
[10] *Gardiner v Moore* [1969] 1 Q.B. 55, esp. at 70–72.
[11] S.4(3) of the Defamation Act 1996: the defendant is presumed not to have known or had reason to believe these facts until the contrary is shown. See *Milne v Express Newspapers* [2004] EWCA Civ 664; [2005] 1 W.L.R. 772 in which the Court of Appeal, dismissing the claimant's appeal from the decision of Eady J. ([2002] EWHC 2564; [2003] 1 W.L.R. 927), held that a

has pleaded a conviction, the claimant should plead in reply, if relevant, s.8 of the Rehabilitation of Offenders Act 1974 and the relevant particulars of length of sentence, lapse of time and malice.[12] Where a defendant operator of a website raises a defence under s.5, Defamation Act 2013, the claimant should, if appropriate, plead in his reply that it was not possible for the claimant to identify the person who posted the statement, the claimant had given the operator notice of complaint in relation to the statement and the operator failed to respond to the notice of complaint in accordance with any provision contained in regulations.[13]

SECTION 5. MALICE

28.6 Malice. There is a specific rule of pleading that whenever it is intended to allege in answer to a plea of honest comment or qualified privilege[14] that the defendant was actuated by express malice, the claimant must serve a reply giving particulars of the fact and matters from which the malice is to be inferred.[15] Malice is a very serious allegation of intentional impropriety or bad faith and the rules of pleading allegations of this kind are strict. It is not sufficient merely to plead that the defendant acted maliciously. The plea must be more consistent with the presence of malice than with its absence; if it is

---

claimant who wished to rebut the defence under s.4 of the Defamation Act 1996 by establishing that the defendant had had reason to believe the statement complained of was false within the meaning of s.4(3) of the Act needed to plead and prove that the defendant was recklessly indifferent to the truth or falsity of the relevant statement.

[12] For a full account of the implications of the Rehabilitation of Offenders Act 1974, see Ch.18, above. The claimant should also probably plead in reply, if he wishes so to contend, that the conviction is irrelevant to any issue, cf. CPR PD 16, para.9.1.

[13] S.5(3)(a), (b), (c), Defamation Act 2013.

[14] Including the privilege defence for peer-reviewed statements in scientific or academic journals: see s.6(6), Defamation Act 2013.

[15] CPR PD 53, para.2.9. For matters which may be relied upon in support of a plea of malice, see Ch.17, above, and para.32.33ff, below. Note that the test for malice now varies depending upon the defence. In the context of traditional common law qualified privilege the test derives from *Horrocks v Lowe* [1975] A.C. 135. For honest comment see *Tse Wai Chun Paul v Albert Cheng* [2001] E.M.L.R. 777 and *Flood v Times Newspapers Ltd* [2012] UKSC 11; [2012] 2 A.C. 273. In relation to malice to defeat statutory qualified privilege defence see *Qadir v Associated Newspapers Ltd* [2012] EWHC 2606 (QB); [2013] E.M.L.R. 15 in which Tugendhat J. held that where a defendant relied on qualified privilege for a fair and accurate extract from a register or other document required by law to be open to public inspection, it was a good plea of malice to allege misuse of the privileged occasion, that is, use of the occasion for a purpose other than that for which the privilege was accorded, as long as it was also pleaded that misuse of the occasion was the dominant purpose or motive of the defendant. However, it was not necessary to plead or prove dominant improper motive in addition, since that was implicit in the plea of misuse of the occasion.

Whilst the defence under s.5, Defamation Act 2013 cannot be described as either a privilege or comment defence it too can be defeated by showing that an operator of a website acted with malice and a claimant would be expected to raise that plea in a reply: see s.5(11).

not, it is liable to be struck out.[16] Generalised or formulaic statements will not be permitted.[17] The plea of malice must focus upon what the defendant did or said or knew.[18] The court will be sceptical about pleas of malice in which the claimant pitches the meaning high and then asserts that the defendant did not or could believe that high meaning to be true, and so is malicious.[19] The claimant must allege specific facts from which it is alleged the inference is to be drawn.[20] Where there are several defendants and the claimant relies on malice to defeat a defence of qualified privilege, he must, in order to succeed,

---

[16] See for example, *Henderson v London Borough of Hackney* [2010] EWHC 1651 (QB) at [34]–[35] where Eady J. said,
"It has been confirmed by the Court of Appeal in *Telnikoff v Matusevitch* [1991] 1 Q.B. 102 and in *Alexander v Arts Council of Wales* [2001] 1 W.L.R. 1840 that, in order for a claimant to succeed in proving malice, it is necessary both to plead and prove facts which are more consistent with the presence of malice than with its absence. This is one of the reasons why, in practice, findings of malice are extremely rare. It is thus reasonably clear, as a matter of pleading practice, that allegations of malice must go beyond that which is equivocal or merely neutral. There must be something from which a jury, ultimately, could rationally infer malice; in the sense that the relevant person was either dishonest in making the defamatory communication or had a dominant motive to injure the claimant."
See also *Bray v Deutsche Bank AG* [2008] EWHC 1263 (QB), per Tugendhat J. at [35], relying upon *Three Rivers DC v Bank of England (No.3)* [2003] 2 A.C. 1 at [160]–[161] per Lord Hobhouse.

[17] The last three sentences in the 11th edition were endorsed by Eady J. in *Hughes v Risbridger* [2009] EWHC 3244 at [14]. Similarly, see *NRMA Insurance v Flanagan* [1982] 1 N.S.W.L.R. 585 per Hunt J. at 603:
"What the allegation amounts to is a conclusion from unspecified facts and matters . . . I have on many occasions criticised particulars in this bald form, which appear to be no more than verbal formulae, perhaps hallowed by long usage, but nevertheless producing more heat than light upon the nature of the case which the defendant has to meet."
See also *King v John Fairfax* [1983] 1 N.S.W.L.R. 31, *Henderson v London Borough of Hackney*, above, and *Thompson v James* [2013] EWHC 585 at [16]. For the position in Scotland see *Lyons v Chief Constable of Strathclyde Police* [2012] CSOH; 2012 Rep. L.R. 108 at [21]–[24], [49] affirmed by the Inner House, Extra Division: [2013] CSIH 46; 2013 G.W.D. 20–401.

[18] It is not permitted to plead what a reasonable person in the position of the defendant would have done. Malice is solely concerned with the actual state of mind of the individual alleged to be malicious: see *Horrocks v Lowe* [1975] A.C. 135 at 149 and *Loveless v Earl* [1999] E.M.L.R. 530 at 538 where the Court of Appeal said, "Malice is a subjective test, entirely dependent on the defendant's state of mind and intention."

[19] See *Crossland v Wilkinson Hardware Stores Ltd* [2005] EWHC 481 (QB), per Tugendhat J., citing *H v Chief Constable of H* [2003] EWCA Civ 102 at [56] and [63], where the Court of Appeal said that the court should be ready to find that the words complained of mean what they say and no more. In a similar vein, see Tugendhat J.'s observations in *Bray v Deutsche Bank AG* [2008] EWHC 1263 (QB); [2009] E.M.L.R. 12 at [42].

[20] *Komarek v Ramco Energy Plc*, unreported, November 21, 2002, (QB); *Beasley v St Mary's Hospital of Centralia* (1990) 558 N.E.2d 677. Equivocal facts will not do: *Alexander v Arts Council of Wales* [2001] EWCA 514; [2001] 1 W.L.R. 1840, citing *Turner v Metro-Goldwyn-Mayer Pictures Ltd* [1950] 1 All E.R. 449; *Sharma v Jay*, unreported, April 15, 2003, QBD; see also *Next Magazine Publishing Ltd v Ma Ching Fat* [2003] H.K.L.R.D. 75. In *Sugar v Associated Newspapers Ltd*, unreported, February 6, 2001, QBD, Eady J. held as follows:
"The fact, if it be a fact that the defence have . . . failed to apologise and persisted in their defence . . . is [not] evidence from which a lack of belief in the honesty of the comment can be inferred. On the contrary, it is said it is more consistent, or at least equally consistent, with honesty of belief . . . certainly the absence of apology, for reasons I have already given, is not capable of supporting a plea of malice".
The court's powers to dispose of cases of malice summarily under CPR Pt 24 and s.8, Defamation

aver and prove malice against each defendant.[21] It is not so clear that the same is true where the claimant seeks to rebut a plea of honest comment,[22] but it would nevertheless be prudent in such a situation for the pleader, if he properly can, to plead a case of malice against each defendant. Where the defendant is a corporation, the claimant should give particulars of the person or persons through whom it is intended to fix the corporation with the necessary malicious intent, as well as pleading the facts from which malice is to be inferred. However, malice cannot be proved by amalgamating states of minds of different individuals within an organisation.[23]

SECTION 6. DEFENCE TO COUNTERCLAIM

28.7 Where a counterclaim is pleaded. A defence to counterclaim is necessary if the defendant has pleaded a counterclaim, and must be pleaded in accordance with the rules applicable to defences.[24] The claimant must deal specifically with each allegation of fact of which he does not admit the truth.[25] A defence to counterclaim must be served within 14 days after receipt of the counterclaim. Permission is not required.[26]

Act 1996, have been much used. See the cases referred to in paras 30.19 and 30.35, below. "Dishonesty is not to be inferred from evidence which is equally consistent with mere negligence": *Three Rivers DC v Bank of England (No.3)* [2003] 2 A.C. 1 at [161] per Lord Hobhouse. "Carelessness of expression or carelessness in making a defamatory statement never provides a ground for inferring malice" (*Roberts v Bass* (2002) 194 A.L.R. 161 at [103], cited with approval by Gray J. in *Oliver v Chief Constable of Northumbria* [2003] EWHC 2417 QBD; [2004] E.M.L.R. 32 at [135].

[21] *Egger v Chelmsford* [1965] 1 Q.B. 248:

"If the plaintiff seeks to rely on malice to aggravate damages, or to rebut a defence of qualified privilege, or to cause a comment, otherwise fair, to become unfair, then he must prove malice against each person who he charges with it. A defendant is only affected by express malice if he himself was actuated by it: or if his servant or agent concerned in the publication was actuated by malice in the course of his employment."

(per Lord Denning M.R. at 265).

[22] *Egger v Chelmsford* [1965] 1 Q.B. 248: "If a publication has been held not to be fair comment, then all concerned in publishing it have published an unfair comment and no question of individual malice or bona fides can arise." (per Davies L.J. at 269). See also paras 12.26 and 12.42, above.

[23] *Webster v British Gas Services Ltd* [2003] EWHC 1188 (QB) at [30] per Tugendhat J.; *Akinleye v East Sussex Hospitals NHS Trust* [2008] EWHC 63 (QB) at [25]; *Bray v Deutsche Bank AG* [2008] EWHC 1263 (QB) at [16]); *Huish v Church Publishing* [1966] 2 N.S.W.R. 748.

[24] CPR r.20.3.

[25] CPR r.16.5. A claimant who entirely fails to deal with an allegation in the counterclaim shall be taken to admit that allegation.

[26] CPR r.15.4(1)(a). However, where the date by which the claimant must file his reply is later than the date by which he must file his defence to counterclaim, the court will normally order that the defence to counterclaim must be filed by the same date as the reply: see CPR PD 15, para.3.2A. Where the court does not make such an order, the reply and defence to counterclaim may form separate documents. The normal rule is that the reply and defence to counterclaim should form one document with the defence to counterclaim following on from the reply: see CPR PD 15, para.3.2 and CPR PD 20, para.6.2.

Section 7. Other Statements of Case

Other statements of case. No party may file or serve a statement of case   **28.8**
after reply without the court's permission.[27] There may be occasions when it
might be necessary in defamation proceedings to seek permission to serve a
rejoinder.[28]

---

[27] CPR r.15.9.

[28] In *Morrison v Buckinghamshire County Council* [2011] EWHC 3444 (QB) H.H.J. Parkes QC
(sitting as a High Court judge) considered the position where art.8 had not been raised in the
particulars of claim. The judge said at [75]:
    "The difficulty with this is that it involves the defendant setting up and then knocking down
    a point which may not be raised against it, which is not the way in which the process of
    pleading works. The defendant can hardly be expected to plead that Art.8 is not engaged: that
    would be to anticipate a case which may not be made . . . . Equally, the claimant cannot be
    expected to raise the point in her Particulars of Claim, before it is known whether the defendant
    will plead privilege. As Ward L.J. made clear in *Clift* at [39], the defence remains the common
    law defence of qualified privilege, and the public authority must plead that it is under a duty
    to communicate the information to those who have a corresponding duty or interest in receive
    it. That is what has been pleaded. If the claimant wishes to plead in response that for public law/
    HRA reasons there was in fact no duty and thus no qualified privilege, that is in principle a
    matter for her to raise in her Reply, as she now seeks to do. It may be worth noting Lord
    Bingham's observation in *Kay v Lambeth BC* [2006] UKHL 10; [2006] 2 A.C. 465 at [29] that
    it would be burdensome and futile for a local authority to plead and prove that a possession
    order was justified in terms of Art.8: it would be enough for it to assert its claim in accordance
    with domestic property law. It would then be for the occupier to raise an Art.8 defence. Of
    course, in the possession context the local authority can then answer the Art.8 defence in its
    Reply, whereas in defamation, the Art.8 argument (if the nettle is not grasped by the defendant
    in the defence) can only be raised in the Reply. It may be that that defunct species of pleading,
    the rejoinder, will have to be disinterred."
In practice, many claimants are now including a stand alone claim under ss.6 and 7 of the Human
Rights Act 1998 where the defendant is a public authority: see e.g. *Clift*, above; *McLaughlin v
Lambeth LBC* [2010] EWHC 2726 (QB); [2011] E.M.L.R. 8; *Thompson v James* [2013] EWHC
515 (QB).

CHAPTER 29

APOLOGY, OFFER OF AMENDS AND COMPROMISE

SECTION 1. APOLOGY

Apology: mitigation and defence. An adequate and properly publicised **29.1** apology will invariably go a long way to achieving vindication for a claimant. As such, a defendant may rely in mitigation of damages on the fact that he has apologised to the claimant for publishing the matter complained of.[1] Indeed, an offer of an apology, unreasonably refused, could also be put forward as grounds for mitigation of damages. Publication of a "full apology" is an element in the statutory defence under s.2 of Lord Campbell's Libel Act 1843,[2] while a component of an offer of amends under s.2 of the Defamation Act 1996 is an offer "to make a suitable correction of the statement complained of and a sufficient apology to the aggrieved party".[3] An offer to make amends which is not accepted may be relied upon in mitigation of damages whether or not it is relied on as a defence.[4] In certain circumstances, the publication of an apology may even form the basis of an argument that for the claimant to commence or continue defamation proceedings would be an abuse of process.[5]

Nature of an apology. The purpose of an apology is to appease the injured **29.2** feelings of the person defamed and to undo the harm done to his reputation in consequence of the publication. Its terms will depend upon the nature of the

---

[1] See para.33.55, below.
[2] For which see, paras 19.7–19.9, above; the plea is now in disuse.
[3] S.2(4)(a). See paras 19.2–19.6, above.
[4] Defamation Act 1996, s.4(5).
[5] On the ground that there is nothing of value that can legitimately be achieved by the proceedings: see *Hays Plc v Hartley* [2010] EWHC 1068 (QB), at [60] (Tugendhat J.) applying *Jameel v Dow Jones & Co. Inc.* [2005] EWCA Civ 75; [2005] Q.B. 946.

defamatory statement, but it should invariably include "a full and frank withdrawal of the charges or suggestions conveyed".[6] Further, the apology would be unlikely to be regarded as adequate without some expression of regret that such charges or suggestions were ever published.[7] A hypothetical apology, e.g. "If that is how my words were understood, then I apologise", may be sufficient, provided it is admitted that the defamatory charge is untrue.[8] Merely repeating another person's retraction is unlikely to be regarded as a proper withdrawal or apology.[9] The sufficiency of an apology is a matter to be decided at trial[10]; for the purpose of assessing compensation under the offer to make amends procedure it will be a matter for the judge.[11] A requirement that the defendant publishes an apology, and the content and mode of publication of that apology, are likely to be crucial terms of a settlement of defamation proceedings, and if they have not been agreed a settlement agreement is liable to be regarded as incomplete.[12]

29.3 Publicising the apology. The apology should be given similar publicity to the original libel, so that it is likely to come to the attention of those who read the libel:

---

[6] Per Cockburn C.J. in *Risk Allah Bey v Johnstone* (1868) 18 L.T. 620 at 621. In *Adelson v Associated Newspapers Ltd* [2008] EWHC 278 (QB); [2009] E.M.L.R. 11, Tugendhat J. observed with reference to this statement of Cockburn C.J. that, "The court expects an apology to be frank. It does not expect a claimant to accept an apology which is not full and frank, and which the defendant does not believe in." (at [74]). In *Winslet v Associated Newspapers Ltd* [2009] EWHC 2735 (QB); [2010] E.M.L.R. 11, an important aspect of Eady J.'s reasoning in permitting the claimant to make a unilateral statement in open court was that the defendant had chosen to put its own "spin" on the settlement by publishing its apology in a dismissive way. In such circumstances, there was no reason why the claimant should not also be allowed to publicise her understanding of the settlement, provided she did so in a fair and proportionate way.

[7] It might be said that "withdrawal" and "expression of regret" are the essential components of an apology, adopting the reasoning of Lord President Kinross in *Malcolm v Moore* (1901) 4 F. 23 at 26:

> "If a person is charged with having made a calumnious statement, and by way of tender or retraction only says 'I withdraw it', or 'I regret that I made it', that will not suffice, because such an expression of regret and retraction is quite consistent with his continuing to believe what he said, and the person against whom the calumny is uttered is not placed in the same position as if it had never been uttered. But when a man not only unreservedly withdraws what he has said, but expresses his regret for having said it and admits there was no ground for it, the position is wholly different, because when it is admitted that there is no ground for the statement, or in other words, that it is untrue, the person injured is put, in so far as the person who made the statement can do it, in the same position as if the statement has never been made".

[8] Where the words are clearly defamatory on their face, a hypothetical apology is unlikely to appear sincere.

[9] See *Associated Newspapers v Dingle* [1964] A.C. 371 per Lord Radcliffe at 400: "In my view the newspaper, having contributed its defamatory statements, was too much the reporter of other people's exculpations and too little concerned in putting its own authority and its own regrets behind the required vindication of the [plaintiff]."

[10] *Risk Allah Bey v Johnstone*, above.

[11] Defamation Act 1996, s.3(5).

[12] *Western Broadcasting Services v Seaga* [2007] UKPC 19 PC; [2007] E.M.L.R. 18.

"Inserting an apology means effectually inserting it; not so that people would not be likely to see it; but in such a manner as to counteract as far as possible the mischief done by the libel." [13]

Thus if the libel appeared in a newspaper, the apology should be inserted in the same newspaper, ideally with a type size and a prominence as similar as possible to the libel. The extent to which this is feasible in practice will vary, though if the apology is to be published as part of an agreed settlement, such details will ordinarily be the subject of negotiation. Nonetheless, in *Nail v News Group Newspapers*, Eady J. stated in the offer of amends context[14]:

" . . . there is no point in endlessly haggling or niggling about the size or location of an apology. The important thing is to achieve vindication as quickly and effectively as possible . . . I believe the important elements of the apology are that it was published relatively quickly after the proceedings were issued, at the top of the page, and that it was relatively eye-catching".

Third parties. An apology for the publication of defamatory words often **29.4** explains how they came to be published, even though they were not true; the purpose is to preserve the reputation both of the person defamed and of the publisher. The publisher should take care in such circumstances not to defame a third party,[15] though the occasion of a proper apology may well be privileged.[16]

Section 2. Settlement

Purposes of settlement. Since the costs of litigation and trial are liable to **29.5** be heavy and the outcome uncertain, the parties may well wish to settle their dispute before or after commencement of litigation. For the claimant, settlement offers the advantage of obtaining a vindication beyond that which a court can or is likely to grant,[17] and the use of litigation to achieve that end will not be an abuse of the process[18]:

---

[13] Per Bramwell B. in *Lafone v Smith* (1858) 3 H. & N. 735. The apology in this case, where s.2 of Lord Campbell's Libel Act 1843 had been raised as a defence, was inserted amongst notices addressed only to particular correspondents, where ordinary readers of news would not see it.

[14] [2004] EWHC 647 (QB); [2004] E.M.L.R. 20 at [69].

[15] See *Tracy v Kemsley Newspapers*, *The Times*, April 9, 1954, where an apology by the publishers of a newspaper for an article published by them rendered them liable in an action brought by the writer of the article.

[16] The subject was examined in *Watts v Times Newspapers* [1997] Q.B. 650 CA, in which it was held that a newspaper could not claim privilege for an apology inserted at the request of solicitors acting for the defamed party, which libelled a third party, but that the solicitors, though joint tortfeasors, were protected by privilege. See also *Oversea-Chinese Banking Corp v Wright* [1994] 3 S.L.R. 760, cited in *Watts v Times Newspapers*. For a fuller discussion see para.14.58, above.

[17] For instance, publication of an apology in terms drafted by the claimant, an agreed statement in court, or payment of indemnity costs.

[18] *Goldsmith v Sperrings* [1977] 1 W.L.R. 478 CA.

"Neither wealth nor power entitles a man to censor the press. If, however, his purpose be to vindicate and protect his reputation, the use of all remedies offered by the law for that purpose cannot be an abuse of the court's process . . . equally a man, while pursuing the remedies offered by the law, may negotiate to secure by arrangement with the parties sued terms more favourable than, or different from, what he would get in the absence of agreement. Such a negotiation, undertaken by properly advised parties, each of whom may have a legitimate interest in avoiding litigation and may be prepared to concede more than the law requires of them to achieve that end, does not mean that the plaintiff by his litigation is reaching out to secure a collateral advantage. In the context of libel, he may reasonably see in settlement a more effective way of protecting his reputation than by action; and whether he pursues his litigation to judgment, or settles it, he may in either case be seeking no more than the way he thinks best in the circumstances to protect his reputation."[19]

29.6 CPR and settlement. The court's duty under the Civil Procedure Rules is to further the overriding objective of enabling cases to be dealt with justly and at proportionate cost by actively managing cases, and that includes by helping the parties to settle the whole or part of the case.[20] The parties are under a duty to assist the court in this endeavour.[21] Moreover, quite apart from offers to settle made in the course of proceedings (see below), any offer to settle before proceedings are begun will be taken into account by the court when making any order as to costs.[22] If a party wishes to take advantage of the Rules specifically relating to "Offers to Settle" the offer should comply with CPR

---

[19] [1997] 1 W.L.R. 478 CA at 498–500, per Scarman L.J. Sir James Goldsmith started numerous actions against distributors of *Private Eye* (which he contended was running a campaign of libel against him), and settled many of them on terms that they ceased to handle the magazine. The remaining distributors applied to have the actions against them dismissed as an abuse of the process in that the plaintiff's purpose in pursuing the actions was not to protect his reputation but to destroy *Private Eye* by cutting off its retail outlets. The application failed. Regarding collateral purpose abuse, see further *Broxton v McClelland* [1995] E.M.L.R. 485 CA, *Wallis v Valentine* [2002] EWCA Civ 1034; [2003] E.M.L.R. 8, *Hays Plc v Hartley* [2010] EWHC 1068 (QB), and para.30.47, below.

[20] CPR r.1.4(2)(f). Active case management also includes encouraging the parties to use an alternative dispute resolution (ADR) procedure if the court considers that appropriate: r.1.4(2)(e). The Pre-Action Protocol for Defamation at paras 3.7–3.8 requires the parties to

"consider whether some form of alternative dispute resolution procedure would be more suitable than litigation, and if so, endeavour to agree which form to adopt . . . The Court takes the view that litigation should be a last resort, and that claims should not be issued prematurely when a settlement is still actively being explored".

The Protocol goes on to refer specifically to the possibilities of discussion and negotiation, early neutral evaluation by an independent third party, mediation, and referring the dispute to the Press Complaints Commission. ADR is discussed further at para.29.41, below.

[21] CPR r.1.3.

[22] CPR r.44.2(4)(c):

"In deciding what order (if any) to make about costs, the court must have regard to all the circumstances, including . . . any . . . admissible offer to settle made by a party which is drawn to the court's attention which is not an offer to which costs consequences under Part 36 apply."

See in this regard *KC v MGN Ltd* [2013] EWCA Civ 3; [2013] 2 Costs L.R. 269 which highlights the potential dangers for a claimant in not accepting an open, pre-action offer of settlement.

Pt 36.[23] A Pt 36 offer can be made at any time including before the commencement of proceedings.[24]

Subject-matter of settlement. Any settlement agreement should contain   **29.7**
provisions as to any statement, correction or apology which the defendant is
to make,[25] any sum which he is to pay in damages, how the costs which have
been incurred should be borne,[26] and how publicity should be given to the
settlement.[27] However, in particular cases, the terms may cover more, such as
the way in which those to whom the defamatory words have been published
should be notified of the complaint and its outcome, and what should be done
with, e.g. existing copies of books containing the offending material.[28] In
proper cases the terms may also include undertakings by the defendant not to
publish further matter defamatory of the claimant,[29] or by a distributor not to
distribute the periodical which contained the words complained of.[30]

Methods of settlement.[31] It is common for settlement to be effected by an   **29.8**
exchange of letters between the parties, although if the terms have been agreed
orally this is not strictly necessary. Where a claimant wishes to accept an offer
made by the defendant in correspondence to resolve the proceedings between
them, he should do so promptly, or run the risk that the offer will be construed
by the court as having expired.[32] Where the terms are complex they may be

---

[23] See r.36.2.

[24] CPR r. 36.3(2)(a).

[25] The content and publication of the apology can be critical terms: *Western Broadcasting Services v Seaga*, above. In *McLaughlin v Newall* [2009] EWHC 1925 (QB), it was observed obiter that a defamation settlement which left open the wording of a proposed apology was at grave risk of being found unenforceable.

[26] In *Adelson v Associated Newspapers Ltd* [2008] EWHC 278 (QB); [2009] E.M.L.R. 10 it was decided (at [93]) that the part of the defendant's open offer to settle the claim that related to costs, which envisaged that the costs of the litigation would "be decided by the judge according to ordinary principles", was too uncertain to be capable of binding acceptance by the claimant.

[27] Usually a statement in (open) court (as to which see para.29.10, below) achieves the widest possible publicity, for it attracts the attention of the media. The usual practice is for the claimant's solicitor to hand out copies of the statement to the press, or at least to the court representative of the Press Association, after it is read.

[28] A publisher defendant may not have any control over copies of books already distributed to wholesalers or retailers, but that need not prevent him undertaking to use his best endeavours to secure their return.

[29] An undertaking is a common term of settlement even where the defendant has not shown any particular intention of repeating the defamatory words or of continuing to defame the claimant, because the claimant will be determined to ensure that there is no recurrence, and a defendant's refusal to give an undertaking is likely (unless rationally explained) to be taken by the claimant as a pointer to probable repetition. Any undertaking will be contractual, unless given to the court, and a claimant faced with threatened breach would have to apply to the court for an injunction to enforce the undertaking.

[30] *Goldsmith v Sperrings*, above.

[31] This is a general topic which is here covered only in outline. For a detailed explanation and review, see Foskett, *The Law and Practice of Compromise*, 7th edn (London: Sweet & Maxwell, 2010).

[32] *Wakefield (t/a Wills Probate and Trusts of Weybridge) v Ford* [2009] EWHC 122 (QB) (Eady J.).

recorded in a deed or memorandum of agreement signed by or on behalf of the parties. The agreement may be executory.[33] It is a matter of interpretation whether the agreement itself extinguishes any liability in tort or does so only on being executed.[34] If the compromise is not carried out, the only remedy in the former case is on the agreement, while in the latter it is possible to sue on the original cause of action. It is also a matter of interpretation whether a settlement amounts to a release, which discharges joint tortfeasors, or a covenant not to sue, which reserves rights against joint tortfeasors.[35]

29.9 Terms incorporated in a judgment. Where an action has been commenced, the terms of settlement may, by consent, be incorporated in a judgment or order, either after application to the court, or, where the terms of the judgment or order are within those specified by the rules, and none of the parties is a litigant in person, without an application.[36] It may also be proper to commence proceedings for the purpose of obtaining a consent order compromising a dispute, e.g. where the claimant requires and is entitled to an injunction. The cause of action against those defendants against whom judgment is given will then be extinguished, and the judgment alone will be the source of the claimant's rights. It is common practice to set out the terms of settlement in a schedule appended to a simple order staying the proceedings except for the purpose of carrying the terms into effect.[37] The terms should not be so vague as to be unenforceable.[38]

29.10 Statements in court.[39] It was formerly the practice, on the settlement of an action for libel or slander, to allow the plaintiff to say on oath that the statements about him were untrue.[40] The current practice, however, enables a statement which has been approved by a judge to be made in court by either party to an action for libel or slander where there has been an acceptance of a Pt 36 offer, or the action has otherwise settled before trial.

> "The importance of the making of a statement in open court is, first, that it is likely to come to the attention of the press, who will give to it such attention as its public

---

[33] See *British Russian Gazette v Associated Newspapers* [1933] 2 K.B. 616 at 643–645.

[34] Ibid.

[35] *Cutler v MacPhail* [1962] 2 Q.B. 292; *Gardiner v Moore* [1969] 1 Q.B. 55; *Watts v Aldington* [1999] L. & T.R. 578; *Ansari v Knowles* [2012] EWHC 3137 (QB). See para.19.28, above.

[36] The detailed rules applying to consent judgments and orders are to be found in CPR r.40.6 and CPR 40B PD, para.3.

[37] This is known as a "Tomlin" order and is substantially in these terms:
"And the claimant and the defendant having agreed to the terms set forth in the schedule hereto, it is ordered that all further proceedings in this action be stayed except for the purpose of carrying such terms into effect, with liberty to apply for such purpose".
For further information about Tomlin orders, see *Civil Procedure* (*The White Book*), Vol.1, n.40.6.2 to CPR r.40.6.

[38] See *Wilson & Whitworth v Express and Independent Newspapers* [1969] 1 W.L.R. 197.

[39] This is the term employed in CPR 53 PD para.6, the practice direction which governs such statements, but the old coinage "statements in open court" continues to be used.

[40] Per Lord Reading in *Siever v Wootton*, *The Times*, February 13, 1920.

interest is seen by them to merit and, secondly, since the statement is part of a judicial proceeding, it is made on an occasion of absolute privilege."[41]

The statement may be unilateral, usually by the claimant,[42] but in an appropriate case by the defendant,[43] or bilateral, where the defendant joins in the making of a statement on agreed terms. A bilateral statement is usually more effective in publicising a withdrawal and apology of an untrue defamatory allegation, because it publicly commits the defendant to acceptance of its terms. Before the statement can be read it is necessary to apply for permission to make it, and its terms must be approved by the court[44]: if the application is granted, a date will be arranged for the statement to be read, usually before the judge in charge of the jury list.[45] If a defendant makes an offer to settle proceedings under CPR Pt 36, it will generally be the case that the costs of any formal application by the claimant for permission to make a unilateral statement and those of making the statement would fall to be paid by the defendant

---

[41] Per Ralph Gibson L.J. in *Barnet v Crozier* [1987] 1 W.L.R. 272 at 276.

[42] A unilateral statement is usually made where the defendant makes an offer to settle, which does not include a joint statement, but which the claimant nonetheless wishes to accept. However, the offer of amends procedure contemplates a unilateral statement by a defendant where the parties cannot agree the steps to be taken by way of correction, apology and publication: see s.3(4)(a), Defamation Act 1996. CPR PD 53, para.6 does not explicitly cover statements made under this subsection of the Act, but in *Winslet v Associated Newspapers Ltd* [2009] EWHC 2735 (QB); [2009] E.M.L.R. 11 Eady J. held that the wording of para.6.1 was very broad and was intended to provide for the possibility of a statement in court following any form of settlement in defamation proceedings.

[43] *CTB v News Group Newspapers Ltd* [2011] EWHC 3099 (QB).

[44] The practice is to make the application to the Senior Master under CPR Pt 23, but the judge retains control over whether a proposed statement will or will not be read, since it is read in the judge's court. If there is a dispute as to the terms of the statement, the Senior Master will usually refer it to the judge. If the statement is agreed, once the Senior Master gives permission, the order is sealed and a setting down number obtained from the Clerk of the Lists. A date convenient to both parties is arranged between counsels' clerks or between solicitors, and the signed statement is released to the judge for mention. If the proposed statement is unilateral, and is opposed or not agreed, the Senior Master will generally refer it to the judge. If it is known to be opposed, the application should be made direct to the judge. The court will not give permission for a bilateral statement to be read if it is reliably informed that the defendant is proposing to join in the making of a statement which he believes to be false: *Adelson v Associated Newspapers Ltd* [2008] EWHC 278 (QB); [2009] E.M.L.R. 10 at [70].

[45] The seriousness of the libel, the nature of the defence, the amount of the payment in, and the fact that the payment in of itself implies no admissions of the merits of the claim, were all matters to be taken into consideration (see *Jones v Rohrer*, *The Times*, February 23, 1984, Balcombe J., cited in *Barnet v Crozier* [1987] 1 W.L.R. 272 and approved by Drake J. in *Honeyford v The Comr for Equality & Race*, (unreported, April 17, 1991). Generally, however, the court will be slow to refuse a claimant leave to make a statement, especially where the matter complained of has received wide publicity, as it may be his only opportunity to vindicate his reputation. One of the factors which may be a ground for refusing leave is the smallness of the sum offered, when compared to the seriousness of the libel: see *Church of Scientology v Borth News*, below. Where there had been a substantial payment-in the claimant was entitled to a statement which wholly vindicated and exonerated him in respect of all the allegations, and the defendants could not require that the statement included anything which might detract from that vindication: see *Charlton v EMAP*, below. ("Payments-in" can no longer be made, but the sum offered as part of the settlement offer must continue to have a bearing on the terms of the statement.)

as an integral part of the costs of the action.[46] It is open to a claimant to apply to make a unilateral statement in open court after accepting an offer of amends: to do so is not to "continue" defamation proceedings for the purpose of the Defamation Act 1996, s.3(2) but to bring them to an end.[47]

The judge will consider the interests of third parties and is unlikely to approve a statement which contains unnecessary references to, or imputations against, such persons.[48] A fortiori, the defendant will be heard in opposition to the making of a unilateral statement.[49] Where a claimant settles with one defendant but continues the action against another, the making of a statement will be permitted before the trial of the action unless there is a real risk that a fair trial might be prejudiced.[50] As the attitude of the court is to encourage and facilitate the settlement of actions, parties who have made a bona fide settlement of a defamation action and wish to make a statement will normally be allowed to do so.[51] Statements in court may now be made not only in claims for libel and slander, but for malicious falsehood, breach of confidence and misuse of private information.[52]

29.11 Joint defendants. Where several defendants are sued jointly for a libel, the claimant can settle the action against one or more of them, and at the same time reserve his rights to continue the action against the other defendants.[53] Such a reservation may be express, or implied from an apparent intention that

---

[46] *Phillips v Associated Newspapers Ltd* [2004] EWHC 190 (QB); [2004] 1 W.L.R. 2106.

[47] *Winslet v Associated Newspapers Ltd* [2009] EWHC 2735 (QB); [2009] E.M.L.R. 11.

[48] "The court should be vigilant to see that the benefit of the procedure of making a statement in open court is not used to the unfair disadvantage of a third party"; per Ralph Gibson L.J. in *Barnet v Crozier* (above) at 282. It is submitted that a third party affected by a statement has standing to apply to the judge not to approve the statement. In *Virgin Atlantic Airways v British Airways*, unreported, January 11, 1993, Drake J. permitted a third party about whom adverse references were made in a proposed statement to make representations about the content of the statement, and to make a statement himself challenging what was said against him.

[49] See, e.g. *Charlton v EMAP, The Times*, June 11 1993, where the defendant was not allowed to insist on a reference being included to the fact that his payment-in had been made "for commercial reasons"; *Wolseley v Associated Newspapers* [1934] 1 K.B. 448. Subject to a defendant's objections, the court will usually give permission for a statement to be read, although permission may be refused where a payment into court has been accepted which is very small in comparison with the gravity of the libel: *Church of Scientology v Borth News* (1973) 117 Sol. Jo. 566, where the plaintiff accepted a payment-in of £50 and was refused leave to make a statement.

[50] *Barnet v Crozier*, above. CPR 53PD, para.6.4 includes a provision empowering the court to postpone the time for making the statement if other claims relating to the subject-matter of the statement are still proceeding; but this discretion will surely be exercised in accordance with the guidance given in *Barnet v Crozier*. This will not be an issue once the jury ceases to be the presumptive tribunal of fact in defamation actions: see s.11, Defamation Act 2013.

[51] See *Barnet v Crozier*, above, at 280.

[52] See CPR 53 PD, para.6.1, as amended with effect from April 6, 2011. The amendment reflects the former practice under RSC Ord.82, r.5(3) whereby a statement which referred to causes of action other than defamation could be approved by the judge for making in open court. Note also the availability of publicity orders in intellectual property cases: see *Samsung Electronics (UK) Ltd v Apple Inc. (Nos. 1 and 2)* [2012] EWCA Civ 1339; [2013] E.M.L.R. 10 and [2012] EWCA Civ 1430; [2013] E.M.L.R. 11.

[53] *Duck v Mayeu* [1892] 2 Q.B. 511 CA; *Apely Estates v De Bernales* [1947] Ch. 217 CA.

the action should continue against the other defendants.[54] If the claimant reserves his rights in this manner, the settlement will be construed as a covenant not to proceed further with the action against the party with whom the settlement is made.[55] If the claimant does not reserve his rights as against the other defendants, and the settlement is not in the form of a covenant not to sue or to continue proceedings, it may be construed as a release of the cause of action, and the effect will be to release all those jointly liable for the same publication.[56] Conversely, one of several defendants who wishes to settle may do so separately by agreement or by Pt 36 offer[57]; if he wishes to claim contribution or indemnity from his co-defendants or any of them he is not concerned with whether they are discharged by the form of settlement, for he may claim contribution from another liable for the same damage notwithstanding that that other has ceased to be liable for the same damage.[58] A defendant who has settled could still be in jeopardy of a claim for contribution made by another defendant against whom the claimant is continuing his action,[59] but this is unlikely if settlement was by means of a Pt 36 offer, as if he has been sued jointly or in the alternative the claimant will have to discontinue his claims against other defendants if he is to accept the offer.[60]

Under the offer of amends procedure provided by the Defamation Act 1996, the acceptance of an offer by one person to make amends does not affect any cause of action against another person in respect of the same publication.[61]

Contribution and indemnity. Under the Civil Liability (Contribution) Act 1978 a person liable in respect of any damage may recover from any other person liable in respect of the same damage such contribution as may be just and equitable having regard to the extent of that person's responsibility for the damage in question.[62] The right extends to a person who has made a bona fide **29.12**

---

[54] *Gardiner v Moore* [1969] 1 Q.B. 55; *Watts v Aldington* [1999] L. & T.R. 578; *Ansari v Knowles* [2012] EWHC 3137 (QB). See para.19.28, above.

[55] However, in *Watts v Aldington*, above, the Court of Appeal avoided categorising the agreement as a release or covenant not to sue, but concluded that the agreement was plainly subject to the implied term that the plaintiff's rights would be reserved against the person not a party to the settlement.

[56] As in *Cutler v McPhail* [1962] 2 Q.B. 292; but in *Bryanston Finance v De Vries* [1975] 1 Q.B. 703 at 732, Lord Diplock stated:

"... courts nowadays are reluctant to construe an agreement with one tortfeasor as a release rather than a covenant not to sue him, unless it is plain that the agreement was intended by the plaintiff to operate as a release of the other joint tortfeasors from their liability."

See also *Ansari v Knowles* [2012] EWHC 3137 (QB) and para.19.28, above.

[57] See para.29.20, below for Pt 36 offer when there are several defendants.

[58] See Civil Liability (Contribution) Act 1978, s.1(3). For the right to claim contribution after settlement, see para.29.12, below.

[59] *Logan v Uttlesford UDC* (1984) C.A.T. 263; (1984) 134 N.L.J. 500.

[60] CPR r. 36.12(2). See para.29.20, below.

[61] S.3(7).

[62] Ss.1(1) and 2(1). For an example of a finding of what is just and equitable, see *Adams v Associated Newspapers* [1999] E.M.L.R. 26, fn.64, below. Note that where A is vicariously liable

settlement or compromise,[63] if he would have been liable "assuming the factual basis of the claim against him could be established".[64] Thus a person who has settled a claim can claim contribution from another person liable in respect of the same damage, if the facts alleged in the original claim would have imposed liability on the person who has settled,[65] but not if they gave rise to no claim in law. It is submitted that if there is a dispute as to whether matter published was defamatory or referred to the original claimant or was fact rather than comment, or whether a printer or distributor knew or had reason to believe the matter was defamatory, a person making a bona fide settlement or compromise can claim under this provision. However, if there is a dispute over a matter of law, for instance, as to whether the occasion of publication was privileged, or as to whether the malice of a joint tortfeasor defeated a defence of honest comment, the claim for contribution would fail unless the claimant could show that he would be liable.[66]

---

for B he is "identified" with B's conduct for the purpose of assessing contribution: *Dubai Aluminium v Salaam* [2002] UKHL 48; [2003] 2 A.C. 366.

[63] Payment in bona fide settlement would include payment of costs: per Brooke L.J. in *Adams v Associated Newspapers* [1999] E.M.L.R. 26 at 36.

[64] S.1(4). In *Adams v Associated Newspapers*, above, the defendant sought a 100 per cent contribution from the third party which it claimed had provided it with the information contained in the article complained of, which alleged that the plaintiff had been "ousted after his self-confessed autocratic style of management saw morale plummet". The Court of Appeal decided that although the judge had held that the real damage was caused by the allegation that the plaintiff had been ousted by reason of his autocratic management style and that the defendant had not established that the third party had used the word "ousted", the allegation taken as a whole (without the expression "ousted") was defamatory and the third party was liable for the same damage as that which the plaintiff claimed. However, having regard to the judge's findings it was not just and equitable to order the third party to make any contribution to the settlement sum.

[65] If the allegations of fact were weakly supported and the person claiming contribution settled on a totally inappropriate assessment of the strength of the case, it is submitted that this could be taken into account in deciding what is equitable. It should be noted that he still has to show that the party from whom he is claiming contribution was liable. See *Skrine v EuroMoney Publications Plc* [2001] EWCA Civ 1479; [2002] E.M.L.R. 15, where the court considered what liability issues in Malaysian libel proceedings (settled there for £2.9 million) against individuals quoted in an article could be considered in English proceedings in which the claimants (the Malaysian defendants) sought contribution from the author, editor and publisher of the article. It was held, inter alia, that the English judge had to determine the meaning of the words without second-guessing the approach of a Malaysian judge.

[66] The application of s.1(4) to defamation claims raises one special difficulty, that is, that prima facie liability in defamation is established by proof of the publication of the defamatory matter by the defendant concerning the claimant (with the exception of certain instances of slander). It is arguable that the words "the factual basis of the claim against him" refer only to the matters relevant to such prima facie liability, and that if a claim was settled on showing such prima facie liability, a subsequent claim for contribution could not be defeated by showing that there was a defence in law to the original claim. But on this basis contribution could be claimed after settlement of a claim on a defamatory statement made on a clear occasion of absolute privilege, and this seems contrary to the intention of the legislation. It is submitted that the words "the factual basis of the claim against him" should be construed to include all matters of defence and reply, such as whether the defendant was malicious on an occasion of qualified privilege. However, these problems may be more imagined than real, as there is no known instance where an issue has arisen between defendants as to how s.1(4) should be applied.

Contribution and offer of amends. Where an offer of amends made **29.13**
under s.2 of the Defamation Act 1996 has been accepted, for the purposes of
the Civil Liability (Contribution) Act 1978 the amount of compensation paid
under the offer is to be treated as paid in bona fide settlement or compromise
of the claim.[67] Further, in any future contribution proceedings by or against
another person jointly liable, the person whose offer of amends was accepted
is not required to pay a greater amount than the amount of compensation
payable in pursuance of the offer.[68]

Authority to settle.[69] Express authority may be granted by a client to his **29.14**
barrister or solicitor to conclude a compromise. Nowadays it is unusual for
such an agreement to be made on behalf of a client without such authority.
However, a solicitor has implied authority to compromise a dispute on behalf
of his client in respect of extant proceedings.[70] A barrister's implied authority
is similar, but less extensive in that it will probably only arise when at court
or instructed to appear and conduct the client's case. There is a division of
opinion as to whether a solicitor or barrister can effectively conclude a
settlement contrary to the express instructions of the client which are not
known to the other party.[71] The better view, and the one in accord with the
normal principles of agency law, appears to be that such a settlement would
be binding.[72] However, provided application is made before the judgment or
order is perfected, the court has a discretion to set aside or refuse to enforce
a compromise concluded contrary to the express instructions of the client.[73]
Such a discretion may also be exercised where counsel consents to a compromise under a misapprehension as to its effect or where it is evident that
counsel for the parties were not *ad idem* as to the effect of the compromise.[74]

Infants and protected parties. If the claimant or defendant is an infant or **29.15**
protected party, no compromise is valid unless it is approved by the
court.[75]

---

[67] Defamation Act 1996, s.3(8)(a).

[68] Defamation Act 1996, s.3(8)(b).

[69] This is a general topic which does not have features peculiar to defamation cases. For
detailed explanation and review, refer to Foskett, *The Law and Practice of Compromise*, 7th edn
(2010), Pt 4.

[70] *Fray v Voules* (1859) 1 E. & E. 839; *Re Newen* [1903] 1 Ch. 812; *Little v Spreadbury* [1910]
2 K.B. 658; *Waugh v Clifford* [1982] 1 Ch. 374.

[71] See, e.g. *Mathews v Munster* [1887] 20 Q.B.D. 141; *Little v Spreadbury* [1910] 2 K.B.
658.

[72] *The Law and Practice of Compromise*, above, paras 21.04–21.21.

[73] *Neale v Gordon-Lennox* [1902] A.C. 465; *Shepherd v Robinson* [1919] 1 K.B. 474; *Marsden
v Marsden* [1972] Fam. 280.

[74] *Hickman v Berens* [1895] 2 Ch. 638.

[75] CPR r.21.10.

Section 3. Part 36 Offers

29.16 General. One of the objectives of the Civil Procedure Rules is to encourage and facilitate settlement of cases. Thus they include detailed provisions enabling claimants and defendants to make formal offers to settle, and expressly state the likely costs consequences where the offer is not accepted and the eventual award or judgment is no more advantageous to the party who has been made the offer than the terms of the offer.[76] The Rules are set out in Pt 36 and apply generally to all actions. The subject is covered only in outline, except in so far as there is special provision for defamation actions.

29.17 When an offer or payment may be made. An offer under Pt 36 may be made at any time, including before the commencement of proceedings.[77] The offer can, and normally will, include an offer to pay or accept a sum of money. Where a Pt 36 offer by a defendant which includes an offer to pay money is accepted, that sum must be paid to the claimant within 14 days of acceptance, and if it is not so paid the claimant may enter judgment for the unpaid sum.[78] The Pt 36 offer can, and usually should, cover other terms of settlement normally included where the complaint is defamation, like apologies and undertakings not to repeat the imputations complained of. There are obvious advantages in making the offer at an early stage: if the claimant fails to obtain a judgment "more advantageous" than the defendant's offer he will usually be ordered, unless it is unjust to do so, to pay the costs from a period (not less than 21 days after the offer was made or such longer period as the parties agree) specified in the offer ("the relevant period") and interest on those costs.[79] As for a claimant's early offer, there can be huge benefits in that if the claimant achieves the same or better[80] at trial he may be awarded interest on the damages running from the date on which the relevant period expired, costs from such date on an indemnity basis, interest on those costs, and (since April 2013) an additional amount calculated as a percentage either of damages or costs, not exceeding £75,000.[81] These provisions do not apply to a Pt 36 offer

---

[76] Pt 36 is a self-contained code prescribing the manner in which an offer may be made and the consequences flowing from accepting or failing to accept one. Although basic concepts of offer and acceptance underpin Pt 36, it is not to be understood as incorporating all the rules governing the formation of contracts. Certainty is to be commended in a procedural code which has to be understood by ordinary citizens, and it was with that in mind that Pt 36 had been drafted. Pt 36 was to be read and understood according to its own terms without importing other rules derived from the general law, save where that was clearly intended: *Gibbon v Manchester City Council* [2010] EWCA Civ 726; [2010] 1 W.L.R. 2081.

[77] R.36.3(2)(a). The phrase "more advantageous" is considered at para.29.25, below; it covers more than just the money element of the offer.

[78] R.36.11(6) and (7).

[79] R.36.14(2).

[80] The phrase used is "judgment against the defendant [which] is at least as advantageous as the proposals" contained in the claimant's offer: r.36.14(1)(b).

[81] R.36.14(3), as amended by the Civil Procedure (Amendment) Rules 2013, SI 2013/262. See also the Offers to Settle in Civil Proceedings Order 2013, SI 2013/93.

made less than 21 days before trial unless the court orders otherwise. A Pt 36 offer is made when it is served upon the other party.[82]

Form and content of a Part 36 offer. The offer must be in writing, state **29.18** that it is intended to have the consequences of Section I of Pt 36, specify a period of not less than 21 days within which the defendant will be liable for the claimant's costs in accordance with CPR r.36.10 ("the relevant period"[83]) if the offer is accepted,[84] state whether it relates to the whole of the claim or only part of it or to an issue that arises in it and if so to which part or issue, and state whether it takes into account any counterclaim.[85] The identification of the relevant period is important as during the currency of that period the offer cannot be withdrawn or made "less advantageous" without the court's permission.

Acceptance of offer. A claimant may accept a defendant's Pt 36 offer, and **29.19** a defendant may accept a claimant's offer, without needing permission of the court, by serving at any time before start of the trial, written notice of acceptance on the offeror, provided the offeror has not served notice of withdrawal of the offer.[86] However, if a claimant accepts an offer after the expiry of the "relevant period" his automatic entitlement to costs will be lost.[87] Once the offer is accepted, the claim, or that part of it the subject of the offer, is stayed.[88] As already mentioned, after acceptance of the defendant's offer by the claimant, the defendant has 14 days to pay the money element of the offer; the remedy for the claimant where the defendant does not honour the terms of his offer is to apply to the court to enforce the terms of the offer.[89] Where there is acceptance within the relevant period the claimant will be entitled to his costs of the proceedings on the standard basis up to the date of serving notice of acceptance.[90] In other instances the court will make an order as to costs unless liability for costs is agreed.[91]

In *Pell v Express Newspapers*[92] the defamation action was settled by the claimant's acceptance of a Pt 36 offer. Almost a year later the claimant sought to challenge an interlocutory costs order made against him before settlement when he had been refused permission to amend. The Court of Appeal refused permission to appeal, declaring that, assuming the settlement was not a formal

---

[82] R.36.7(1).
[83] "relevant period" is defined in r.36.3(1)(c) (by reference to r.36.2(2)(c)).
[84] Unless the offer is made less than 21 days before the start of the trial: CPR r.36.2(3).
[85] R.36.2(2).
[86] R.36.9.
[87] R.36.10(4)(b).
[88] R.36.11(1).
[89] R.36.11(8).
[90] R.36.10(1) and (2).
[91] R.36.10(4).
[92] [2004] EWCA Civ 46. See also *Pell v Express Newspapers* [2009] EWHC 118 (QB).

bar to challenging the judge's order for costs, what the claimant was attempting to do was wholly disproportionate and contrary to the interests of justice. If interlocutory orders could be challenged by way of appeal on the ground of alleged deceit, without the result of the trial or settlement being disturbed then the finality of judgments would be gravely undermined and the appeal process subverted.

29.20 Several defendants. Part 36 provides for different procedures and consequences where the claimant wishes to accept a payment or offer made by one or more, but not all, defendants, dependent on whether the defendants are sued jointly or in the alternative on the one hand, or are alleged to have several liability on the other. In the former case the claimant may accept the offer, without needing the court's permission, if he discontinues his claim against those defendants who have not made an offer and they give written consent to the acceptance. Where several liability is alleged, the claimant may accept the offer (without permission) and continue with his claims against the other defendants; in all other cases the claimant must obtain permission of the court to accept the offer.[93] Most defamation claims against multiple defendants will fall into the first category of defendants sued jointly or in the alternative, and for such claims this rule has changed the position significantly from what it was under RSC. Formerly there was a rule whereby, in an action against several defendants sued jointly, the plaintiff could accept money paid in by one or more defendants and continue his action against those defendants who had not paid in, although the amount paid in and accepted had to be taken into account when calculating the amount of damages which the plaintiff could recover. That rule no longer survives.

29.21 Withdrawal of offer. As already noted[94] the court's permission is required during the period specified in the offer, which cannot be less than 21 days, within which the defendant will be liable for the claimant's costs, or such longer period as the parties agree, to withdraw the offer or to change it to make it less advantageous. After the expiry of this period, provided written notice of acceptance has not been received, the offer can be withdrawn or changed by serving written notice.[95]

29.22 Part 36 offer and offer of amends. There would seem to be no bar against a defendant who has made an offer to make amends under s.2 of the Defamation Act 1996 also making a Pt 36 offer, but there could be little point in doing so until the response of the claimant to the offer to make amends is

---

[93] R.36.12.
[94] In para.29.18, above.
[95] R.36.3.

known. If the offer is accepted and compensation cannot be agreed there is no reason why the defendant should not make a Pt 36 offer, including or consisting solely of an offer of payment of a named sum, in respect of the anticipated determination of compensation, with a view to obtaining a favourable order for costs if compensation is assessed at a figure at or below the offer.

Statement in court. A party wishing to accept a Pt 36 offer in a libel or slander claim may apply before or after he accepts the offer to make a statement in open court.[96] **29.23**

Infants and patients. If the claimant (or defendant) is an infant or patient a Pt 36 offer may be accepted only with the approval of the court.[97] **29.24**

Verdict or judgment and costs. Under Pt 36 where a defendant's or claimant's offer is not accepted and the case continues until the completion of the trial, the costs consequences hinge on whether the eventual judgment is more advantageous to the claimant than the defendant's offer or at least as advantageous to the claimant as the proposals contained in the claimant's offer.[98] In the former case if the judgment is not more advantageous to the claimant the court will order, unless it considers it is unjust to do so, that the defendant is entitled to his costs from the date the relevant period expired and interest on those costs.[99] In the latter circumstances, where the judgment against the defendant is at least as advantageous to the claimant as the claimant's offer the court will, unless it considers it unjust to do so,[100] order that the claimant is entitled to interest, at a rate not exceeding 10 per cent above base rate, on the whole or any part of any sum of money for some or all of the period starting with the date on which the relevant period expired, costs on an indemnity basis from the date on which the relevant period expired, interest on those costs, and (from April 2013) an additional amount, calculated as a percentage either of damages or costs, not exceeding £75,000.[101] In relation to any money claim or money element of a claim, "more advantageous" now means better in money terms by any amount **29.25**

---

[96] CPR 53 PD, para.6.1. In relation to para.6.1 generally, see *Winslet v Associated Newspapers Ltd*, above.

[97] See r.21.10.

[98] R.36.14(1).

[99] R.36.14(2).

[100] See *Rackham v Sandy* [2005] EWHC 1354 (QB) in which an unsuccessful defendant who had rejected the claimant's Pt 36 offer escaped an indemnity costs order because of the financial consequences on him, which in the judge's view made it unjust to make such an order.

[101] R.36.14(3), as amended by the Civil Procedure (Amendment) Rules 2013, SI 2013/262. See also the Offers to Settle in Civil Proceedings Order 2013, SI 2013/93.

however small, and "at least as advantageous" is to be construed accordingly.[102] There are set out[103] considerations the court will take account when judging whether it is unjust to make these orders. They include the terms of the Pt 36 offer, the stage in the proceedings when the offer was made, the information available to the parties at the material time and the conduct of the parties with regard to the giving or refusing to give information for the purposes of enabling the offer to be made or evaluated. Thus a claimant who withheld information about specific loss attributable to a libel or a defendant who refused to give details of the extent of publication might find a court denying them the benefits awardable under r.36.14.

29.26 **Indemnity costs in favour of defendant.** Under r.36.14 a defendant whose Pt 36 offer is not accepted and which is not bettered by the judgment, in the sense of being more advantageous to the claimant, is only entitled to costs on a standard basis (together with interest on those costs).[104] As was pointed out in *McPhilemy v Times Newspapers (No.2)*[105] the possibility of indemnity costs was intended to provide an incentive to claimants to make offers of settlement when otherwise they would obtain no particular advantage in doing so, and such an incentive was unnecessary for defendants who were sufficiently encouraged by the existing normal costs orders to make sensible offers. Thus a defendant whose offer has not been bettered and who wishes to obtain indemnity costs must do so under Pt 44. Such an order will only normally be made where the claimant had acted unreasonably in refusing the defendant's offer,[106] or where there was something in the conduct of the action

---

[102] R.36.14(1A), added with effect from October 1, 2011. The purpose of this addition was to reverse the effect of the decision of the Court of Appeal in *Carver v BAA Plc* [2008] EWCA Civ 412; [2009] 1 W.L.R. 113. It has the same effect on the decision of Eady J. in *Jones v Associated Newspapers Ltd* [2007] EWHC 1489 (QB); [2008] E.M.L.R. 6. In *Jones*, the claimant had offered to settle on payment of £4,999 damages and costs together with an apology and an undertaking not to repeat. At trial the jury awarded £5,000 damages. The judge rejected the claimant's contention that r.36.14 applied, principally on the grounds that the offer had been made nearly a year before trial and the claimant would have suffered concern and distress in that period which was not compensated by any increased award, and whereas the offer included an unqualified apology, facts were revealed in the course of the trial which put the claimant in a less favourable light than would have the unqualified apology. If the same circumstances arose today, the court would be compelled by CPR r.36.14(1A) to hold that the damages award of £5,000 was "at least as advantageous to the claimant" as his Pt 36 offer of £4,999. Nonetheless, it is submitted that the judge would still be at liberty to take such considerations into account in deciding whether it was just or "unjust" to confer on the claimant the benefits to which he was presumptively entitled under r.36.14(3): see r.36.14(4) ("the court will take into account all the circumstances of the case").

[103] In r.36.14(4).

[104] See *Excelsior Commercial Holdings v Salisbury Hamer Apsden & Johnson* [2002] EWCA Civ 879 per Lord Woolf at [10].

[105] [2001] EWCA Civ 933; [2002] 1 W.L.R. 934.

[106] *Kiam v MGN Ltd (No.2)* [2002] EWCA Civ 66; [2002] 1 W.L.R. 2810, explaining *Reid Minty v Taylor* [2001] EWCA Civ 1723; [2002] 1 W.L.R. 2800, and see *Miller v Associated Newspapers* [2005] EWHC 773 (QB).

or some circumstance of the case which took it out of the norm so as to justify an order for indemnity costs.[107]

Non-disclosure of offer or payment. The fact that a Pt 36 offer has been **29.27** made must not be communicated to the trial judge until the case has been decided.[108] It must of course follow that the jury cannot be told. The embargo applies to the judge allocated in advance to conduct the trial, but not otherwise to interim proceedings. So parties should be careful to refrain from referring to an offer at a pre-trial review or other interim hearings before a judge who has been or might be allocated to preside at the trial. Nonetheless, the parties (or more precisely "the offeror and offeree") can agree in writing that this rule should not apply.[109] As to what happens if by inadvertence or otherwise the rule is broken, guidance may be provided by previous case law as the equivalent RSC rule[110] was in similar terms. The effect of the relevant decisions,[111] none of which involved jury trials, was that it was not mandatory to order a new trial before a different judge, but that the judge to whom disclosure had been made had a discretion whether or not to continue to hear the case. It is submitted that where a jury is involved it would be unsatisfactory and unfair to the party whose offer has been disclosed to continue the trial with the same jury once the fact of the offer and its detail had been made known. Where a defendant made a written offer in an open letter to pay a specific sum by way of compensation, it was held that such an offer could not be revealed at trial to the jury.[112] A Pt 36 offer will be treated as "without prejudice" except as to costs.[113]

Section 4. Offer of Amends

Objective. The procedure introduced by ss.2 and 3 of the Defamation Act **29.28** 1996[114] can be regarded as a means of settlement provided by statute in which the court is given a role in enforcing the settlement and determining suitable compensation. Its objective is to enable defamation defendants who accept they have made a mistake to avoid prolonged and expensive litigation in circumstances where they are prepared to acknowledge the wrong and to

---

[107] *Excelsior Commercial Holdings*, above.

[108] R.36.13(2). In *Adelson v Associated Newspapers Ltd* [2008] EWHC 278 (QB); [2009] E.M.L.R. 10, at [1], Tugendhat J. made an order to achieve this purpose.

[109] R.36.13(3)(c).

[110] RSC Ord.22, r.7.

[111] See *Millensted v Grosvenor House* [1937] 1 K.B. 717 CA; *Gaskins v British Aluminium* [1976] Q.B. 524 and *Garratt v Saxby* [2004] EWCA 341; [2004] 1 W.L.R. 2152.

[112] *Kiam v Neil* [1995] E.M.L.R. 1. In relation to open offers and the costs consequences thereof generally, see *Adelson v Associated Newspapers Ltd*, above.

[113] R.36.13(1).

[114] The origins of the regime introduced by the 1996 Act lie in Sir Brian Neill's Committee on Practice and Procedure in Defamation, which reported in July 1991. See also para.19.1, above.

make reasonable amends.[115] The procedure has proved much more popular than its cumbersome predecessor.[116]

29.29 The offer. An offer of amends under this procedure is defined as an offer:

(a) to make a suitable correction of the statement complained of and a sufficient apology to the aggrieved party,

(b) to publish the correction and apology in a manner that is reasonable and practicable in the circumstances, and

(c) to pay the aggrieved party such compensation (if any) and such costs as may be agreed or determined to be payable.[117]

The offer must be in writing, must be expressed to be an offer to make amends under s.2 of the 1996 Act, and must state whether it is a qualified offer,[118] and, if so, set out the defamatory meaning in relation to which it is made.[119] A defendant may make an offer of amends in respect of part of a publication.[120] No offer may be made after service of defence.[121] If an offer is confusing or equivocal, it will not be treated as an offer falling within the 1996 Act.[122] Nor

---

[115] *Abu v MGN Ltd* [2002] EWHC 2345 (QB); [2003] 1 W.L.R. 2201, per Eady J. at [4]. As the Court of Appeal (Lord Judge C.J., Lord Neuberger M.R., and Eady J.) summarised the position in *KC v MGN Ltd* [2013] EWCA Civ 3; [2013] 2 Costs L.R. 269 at [13]:
"Without attempting to rewrite the terms of ss.2–4 of the 1996 Act, it is plain that its purpose was to enable those who had been wrongly traduced to be vindicated by an apology and an appropriate offer of amends, and to provide those responsible for the defamatory statement with a means of acknowledging their error and making an offer of compensation to provide appropriate amends. The objective, to the advantage of both sides, is vindication without litigation. . . . As Eady J. observed in *Cleese v Clarke* [2004] E.M.L.R. 37, 'the purpose of the offer of amends procedure is to reduce delay and expense', a view endorsed by this court in *Warren v Random House Group Ltd* [2008] EWCA Civ 834; [2009] Q.B. 600, which underlined that ss.2–4 of the 1996 Act provided 'an exit route for a defendant who is unwilling or unable to advance a substantive defence" while providing the claimant with an opportunity 'to achieve an economical and rapid resolution of his complaint or part of it'."
See also per Eady J. in *Milne v Express Newspapers* [2002] EWHC 2564 (QB); [2003] 1 W.L.R. 927 at [41]: "The main purpose of the statutory regime is to provide an exit route for journalists who have made a mistake and are willing to put their hands up and make amends."
[116] The procedure under s.4 of the Defamation Act 1952, which according to the Neill Report (see fn.114, above) was hardly, if ever, used.
[117] S.2(4).
[118] A qualified offer is an offer in relation to a specific defamatory meaning which the defendant accepts that the statement conveys: s.2(2). Hence if the defendant offeror believes that the claimant has over-stated the meaning, he can make an offer predicated on his own preferred reading of the sense of the words.
[119] S.2(3).
[120] *Warren v Random House Group Ltd* [2007] EWHC 2856 (QB); [2009] Q.B. 600, [42] (Gray J.) (the defendant's appeal against this decision was dismissed: [2008] EWCA Civ 834; [2009] Q.B. 600); *Club La Costa (UK) Plc v Gebhard* [2008] EWHC 2552 (QB).
[121] S.2(5).
[122] *SD Marine Ltd v Powell* [2006] EWHC 3095 (QB).

will a purported offer of amends be treated as an offer falling within the Act
if it is accompanied by a reservation to the effect that the offeror does not
admit that the words complained of refer to the aggrieved party.[123]

Acceptance and non-acceptance. It is a curiosity of the offer of amends   **29.30**
regime that there is no provision for rejection of the offer. It is either accepted
or not accepted. But when does failure to accept become non-acceptance? The
consequences of non-acceptance are likely to be disastrous for the claimant
(who will face an all but irresistible defence under s.4(2) and recover no
damages),[124] so if he hesitates or needs further information before accepting,
is there a risk that he will be found to have "not accepted", so as to set in train
the consequences provided by s.4? There have been conflicting views. Gray J.
has held that the claimant is obliged to decide promptly whether or not to
accept it, which (as he recognised) may be a difficult decision, especially
when there is genuine uncertainty as to whether (for example) special damage
has been suffered[125]; but a decision by Eady J.[126] suggests a more flexible
approach, whereby—the judge regarding it as wholly unrealistic to suggest
that the offer could be kept open indefinitely at the claimant's option[127]—the
claimant should be allowed a "reasonable period" to decide whether to accept
or not accept (i.e. reject)[128] the offer. What is reasonable will depend on the
circumstances of the case. Sometimes it may be reasonable for a claimant to
explore an offer and its consequences,[129] which might involve an application
for disclosure, but only to evaluate the offer, not to explore the defendants'
state of knowledge of the facts or the quality of their journalism.[130]

Consequences of acceptance. Once the offer is accepted, a number of   **29.31**
consequences follow. The main consequence is that the party accepting the
offer may not bring or continue proceedings in respect of the publication

---

[123] *Club La Costa (UK) Plc v Gebhard* [2008] EWHC 2552 (QB).
[124] See para.29.39, below.
[125] *Loughton Contracts Plc v Dun & Bradstreet Ltd* [2006] EWHC 1224 (QB). For the very
much less stringent Scottish view of what amounts to non-acceptance, see *Moore v Scottish Daily
Record* [2007] CSOH 24 (but note that Eady J. has found the reasoning in that case unpersuasive:
Tesco Stores Ltd v Guardian News & Media Ltd [2009] E.M.L.R. 5, at [47]).
[126] *Tesco Stores Ltd v Guardian News & Media Ltd,* above.
[127] "There comes at some point a fork in the road. A claimant has to go to the right or the left
and, depending on that choice, either . . . s.3 or s.4 will come into operation. That choice cannot
be postponed indefinitely": ibid. at [47]–[48].
[128] *Tesco Stores Ltd v Guardian News & Media Ltd,* above, at [29].
[129] See, e.g. *Rigg v Associated Newspapers Ltd* [2003] EWHC 710 QBD; [2004] E.M.L.R.
4.
[130] *Tesco Stores Ltd v Guardian News & Media Ltd,* above, at [42]–[43]. The claimant's
argument relied on the absence of any time limit for acceptance in the statute, so enabling the
claimant to accept at any stage, subject only to the offer not being withdrawn: this was said to
involve no prejudice for the defendant which could not be compensated in costs.

concerned against the person making the offer.[131] However, he is entitled to enforce the offer, and he may apply to the court for an order that the other party fulfil his offer by taking any steps which have been agreed,[132] and for determination of the amount to be paid by way of compensation and costs if that cannot be agreed.[133] If there is no agreement on the steps to be taken by way of correction, apology and publication, the party making the offer may take such steps as he thinks appropriate, and in particular may make the correction and apology by a statement in court.[134] It has been observed that Parliament and the draftsmen of the CPR intended that once an offer has been validly accepted, informal discussions should take place between the parties so as to avoid if possible any need to apply to the court: there should be a spirit of compromise on both sides.[135] The party accepting the offer may, if needs be, apply to read a unilateral statement in open court. To do so is not to "continue" defamation proceedings for the purposes of s.3(2) of the Act, but to bring them to an end.[136]

29.32 Procedure for enforcement of offer of amends. The rules governing the enforcement of offers of amends are set out in CPR PD 53, para.3. If the offer has been made and accepted before any proceedings are begun then a claim must be made under Pt 8. If proceedings are in existence there must be an application in those proceedings under Pt 23. In either event there must be written evidence which must include[137]:

(1) a copy of the offer of amends;
(2) details of the steps taken to fulfil the offer of amends;
(3) a copy of the text of the correction and apology[138];
(4) details of the publication of the correction and apology[139];
(5) a statement of any amount paid as compensation;
(6) a statement of any amount paid for costs;

---

[131] S.3(2). It is noteworthy that he may not even obtain an injunction: see *Warren v Random House Group Ltd* [2008] EWCA Civ 834; [2009] Q.B. 600 at [12]. But he may—or was permitted to in 2001, at any rate—accept an offer of amends in respect of hard copy publication of an article, and reject it in the case of internet publication, with a view to proceeding to trial by judge and jury: *Green v Times Newspapers Ltd*, January 17, 2001, Gray J. However, Gray J. dealt with that obviously unsatisfactory situation by ordering summary disposal of the internet claim, so that one tribunal could assess damages in respect of both publications. It might be thought that the claimant's conduct would now be stigmatised as an abuse, a conclusion which Gray J. was unwilling to reach in 2001.

[132] S.3(3).
[133] S.3(5) and (6).
[134] S.3(4)(a). He may also give an undertaking to the court as to the manner of publication: s.3(4)(b). As to statements, see para.29.10, above.
[135] *Cleese v Clark* [2003] EWHC 137 QB; [2004] E.M.L.R. 3 per Eady J. at [21]–[24].
[136] *Winslet v Associated Newspapers Ltd* [2009] EWHC 2735 (QB); [2010] E.M.L.R. 11.
[137] PD 53, para.3.3.
[138] This could have a significant bearing on assessment of compensation: see s.3(5) of the Act.
[139] As fn.138, above.

(7) why the offer is unsatisfactory.

Where any step specified in s.2(4) of the Act[140] has not been taken, then the evidence must state what steps are proposed by the party to fulfil the offer of amends, and when they will be fulfilled, and, if none, that no proposal has been made to take that step.[141]

Compensation: general. If the parties cannot agree on the amount of   **29.33** compensation, the court will assess it on the same principles as damages in defamation proceedings,[142] except that the assessment will be made without a jury.[143] How the court should go about this exercise was examined in some detail in *Abu v MGN Ltd*.[144] As the Defamation Act obliges the court to determine compensation on the "same principles" as apply to the assessment of defamation damages, it follows that all evidence going to aggravation or mitigation which is admissible in a normal defamation trial will be equally admissible in this context. Thus the party making the offer may seek to show that the complainant is a person of general bad reputation, or that the background context or broad circumstances relating to the defamatory allegation reflect adversely upon him, or that some element of the damage has been caused by some extraneous factor, e.g. a different libel published by someone else.[145] But if he seeks to mitigate "offensively", by attacking the complainant's character for instance, he risks aggravating the situation and increasing the level of compensation due.[146] As for the claimant, he may draw attention to all matters that can be taken into account when determining general damages for defamation, such as his status and reputation, the mode and extent of publication, the conduct of the publisher and any injury to the complainant's feelings the result of the defamation or a consequence of high-handed, oppressive or insulting behaviour by the publisher.[147] However, fairness dictates that defendants must specify any particular mitigating factors to be relied on before or when making an offer, and claimants any aggravating factors before accepting one.[148] The claimant may also be able to claim

---

[140] See para.29.29, above.
[141] PD 53, para.3.3(3).
[142] Defamation Act 1996, s.3(5).
[143] Defamation Act 1996, s.3(10).
[144] [2002] EWHC 2345 (QB); [2003] 1 W.L.R. 2201, Eady J.
[145] Ibid. at [14]–[19].
[146] *Nail v News Group Newspapers Ltd* [2004] EWHC 647 (QB); [2004] E.M.L.R. 20 per Eady J. at [35]–[36] (the claimant's appeal was dismissed: [2004] EWCA Civ 1708; [2005] 1 All E.R. 1040).
[147] *Abu v MGN Ltd*, above, at [16].
[148] Ibid. at [8]–[10], [21], approved in *Nail v News Group Newspapers Ltd* [2004] EWCA Civ 1708; [2005] 1 All E.R. 1040 at [15]. See also *Turner v News Group Newspapers Ltd* [2005] EWHC 892 (QB); [2005] E.M.L.R. 25 at [22]–[23] and [2006] EWCA Civ 540; [2006] 1 W.L.R. 3469 at [98], and *Bowman v MGN Ltd* [2010] EWHC 895 (QB) at [19] (in which it was held to be impermissible for a claimant first to accept an offer of amends and then to contend, in support of his claim for compensation, that the words complained of had been published dishonestly).

special damages, or specific loss arising from the defamation, and for that purpose there may need to be some exchange of pleading and disclosure of documents.[149] It is likely that there will have to be witness statements, and if the statements are challenged, cross-examination. In short, the offer of amends procedure "is by no means always going to lead to speedy and cheap resolution in any ordinary sense",[150] and assessment of compensation as part of the offer to make amends procedure will be little different from an assessment of damages in a contested defamation action, except that the assessment will definitely be carried out by a judge and not a jury. However, there is no damages cap under the offer of amends procedure (by contrast with the summary disposal regime),[151] some very serious cases may be dealt with under it, and the claimant has in practical terms been denied a jury trial, so as the judge concluded in *Abu v MGN Ltd*:

> "There should be thus nothing in any sense 'rough and ready' about the assessment of a claimant's reputation under the offer of amends procedure. It would clearly be inappropriate to deprive either party of a proper analysis of his case. Naturally, due regard to case management considerations will generally ensure that time and money is not wasted, but proportionality does not always mean that corners need to be cut. In the case of grave allegations, where the defendant has recognised that he has made a serious error, it may be that justice requires that significant time and money be spent at arriving at the right answer."[152]

29.34 Argument about meaning following acceptance of an unqualified offer. In *Nail v News Group Newspapers Ltd* an important point of practice was raised about the scope of argument as to meaning at the offer of amends hearing. Eady J. held that where there is an unqualified offer, the parties "generally need to work on the basis that the words complained of bore the [claimant's] pleaded meanings". He disagreed with counsel for the defendant, who submitted that it remained the task of the court to form its own view on the precise meanings. He agreed that any exaggerated or distorted meaning should be ignored, but he expected that if such circumstances arose, the defendant would have made the challenge clear by making a qualified offer. "It would seem unfair on a claimant who accepts an unqualified offer to find that the court dismisses his meanings as untenable when it comes to assessing the damages.[153] In the Court of Appeal, May L.J. approved this approach, and the judge's refusal to admit much of the evidence which the parties (primarily, if not entirely, the defendant) had sought to adduce in aggravation and mitigation. "Claimants should . . . plead the full substance for which they seek

---

[149] *Abu v MGN Ltd*, above, at [21]. For the limited role of disclosure in the offer of amends process, see *Rigg v Associated Newspapers Ltd* [2003] EWHC 710 (QB); [2004] E.M.L.R. 4.
[150] *Abu v MGN Ltd*, above, at [21].
[151] Defamation Act 1996, s.9(1)(c).
[152] *Abu v MGN Ltd* (above) at [22].
[153] [2004] EWHC 647 (QB); [2004] E.M.L.R. 20 at [26]

redress: defendants who wish to make amends for significantly less than that full substance should make appropriate qualifications to their offer."[154]

Discount on compensation for offer of amends. The question of how   **29.35** far the making of an offer of amends should go to mitigate the amount of compensation awarded to the claimant was considered by the Court of Appeal in *Nail v News Group Newspapers Ltd.*[155]

At first instance, Eady J. had assessed the proper level of compensation for libels in the *News of the World* and in a book published by HarperCollins. The libels were summed up by the claimant's counsel as mapping out a life in which the claimant had progressed "from being a dog meat eating yob, who engaged in grubby and obscene sexual behaviour, to heartless prima donna". The judge took the view that the offer of amends regime was a process of conciliation, so that the very adoption of the procedure had a major deflationary effect on the appropriate level of compensation. Media defendants who act promptly when confronted with a claim are entitled to expect that the level of compensation will be "healthily discounted". His starting point was to consider what he would have awarded for the libels following a notional trial at which there had been no significant aggravation (such as a plea of justification) and no significant mitigation (such as an apology); to assess how much the particular libel was worth on the scale of gravity, having regard to what he called the current conventional ceiling of £200,000; and then to make a significant reduction to take account not only of any actual apology but also of the defendant's very willingness to use the offer of amends route. In the event, he settled on £45,000 as the notional trial award for the newspaper libel, and reduced that figure by half to £22,500.

This approach was endorsed by the Court of Appeal.[156] The court accepted that if an early unqualified offer to make amends is offered and accepted, and an agreed apology published, there is bound to be substantial mitigation (which May L.J. regarded as a less colourful synonym of Eady J.'s "healthy discount"), for the defendant has capitulated at an early stage, the claimant knows that his reputation has been repaired as far as it can be, and he is relieved of the anxiety and the costs risk of contested proceedings. There was

---

[154] [2004] EWCA Civ 1708; [2005] 1 All E.R. 1040 per May L.J. at [15].

[155] [2004] EWCA Civ 1708; [2005] 1 All E.R. 1040.

[156] As it was subsequently in *Turner v News Group Newspapers Ltd* [2006] EWCA Civ 540; [2006] 1 W.L.R. 3469 at [23], [66] and in *Cairns v Modi; KC v MGN Ltd* [2012] EWCA Civ 1382; [2013] 1 W.L.R. 1015 at [45]. In the *KC v MGN Ltd* section of the latter judgment (*KC v MGN Ltd* was an offer of amends case, *Cairns v Modi* was not; both were defendant's appeals in respect of awards damages/compensation), the Court of Appeal reduced the starting point figure from £150,000 to £100,000 (i.e. before applying the discount) partly by reference to the defendant's "early apology": [49]. It is submitted that it was in error to do so: it was at odds with the very approach the Court had endorsed at [45] (whereby the notional starting point figure is arrived at without reference to the fact of an apology) and, unfairly to the claimant, the defendant was given double credit for its apology, i.e. at both the "notional starting point figure" and the "discount" stage of the calculation.

a hint from May L.J. that the award might have been higher ("The possibility that another judge might have reached a somewhat higher amount does not mean that Eady J.'s conclusion was wrong"), but there was no error of principle, and no basis for the court to interfere.[157]

If the defendant treats a serious complaint casually, and publishes an apology which is late or off-hand, the discount for making an offer of amends will be less.[158] Similarly, ill-founded claims in correspondence for a substantive defence or for a plea of general bad reputation will result in a reduced discount.[159]

29.36 Burstein particulars. As s.3(5) of the 1996 Act requires the court to determine compensation on the "same principles" as apply to the assessment of defamation damages, all evidence going to aggravation or mitigation which would be admissible in a normal defamation trial will be equally admissible on the assessment of compensation following offer of amends. The offeror may therefore rely on the wider scope of mitigation sanctioned by the Court of Appeal in *Burstein v Times Newspapers*.[160] The *Burstein* principle was applied for the first time in the offer of amends context in *Turner v News Group Newspapers Ltd*,[161] which (in the Court of Appeal) supplied the opportunity for a frontal assault on the decision in *Burstein*, arguing that it could not be squared with the decision of the House of Lords in *Speidel v*

---

[157] In *Bowman v MGN Ltd*, above, Eady J. applied a discount of 50 per cent to a starting figure of £8,500 in respect of a libel adjudicated (at [14]) to be "at the less serious end of the scale", "because of the early apology, the willingness to remove the offending words immediately and the very prompt reliance on the offer of amends regime" (see [20]), leaving the claimant with compensation of £4,250.

[158] In *Campbell-James v Guardian Newspapers Ltd* [2005] EWHC 893 (QB); [2005] E.M.L.R. 24, Eady J. considered that the starting-point for a very grave libel on a distinguished British soldier, of whom it was falsely suggested that he had been in some way linked to the abuses at Abu Ghraib prison in Baghdad, was £90,000, which (in view of the newspaper's dismissive attitude) he reduced by 35 per cent for offer of amends purposes to a figure of £58,500. Similarly, in *Veliu v Mazrekaj* [2006] EWHC 1710 (QB); [2007] 1 W.L.R. 495, where the claimant was treated in a dismissive and insulting fashion, Eady J. allowed a 30 per cent discount on a starting point of £180,000, for an extremely serious libel imputing close involvement in the July 2005 terrorist attacks in London.

In *Turner v News Group Newspapers Ltd* [2005] EWHC 892 (QB); [2005] E.M.L.R. 25, the court applied the principle in *Burstein v Times Newspapers Ltd* [2001] 1 W.L.R. 579 CA for the first time in an offer of amends context, and admitted evidence of directly relevant background context. Eady J. decided (at [48]) that such material went not to the discount applicable to the offer of amends procedure but to the notional starting point figure (somewhat curiously, given the hypothesis of the calculation described in *Nail*: see para.29.35, above), which was £15,000. Taking into account the fact that Mr Turner was first treated dismissively and then told that the newspaper had no reason to believe that its allegations were false, the discount was set at 40 per cent and the award at £9,000. The Court of Appeal upheld Eady J.'s decision ([2006] EWCA Civ 540; [2006] 1 W.L.R. 3469).

[159] *Angel v Stainton* [2006] EWHC 637 (QB).

[160] [2001] 1 W.L.R. 579 (and see per Gray J. in *Carpenter v Associated Newspapers*, unreported, January 16, 2001). See also the fuller discussion at paras 33.43ff below.

[161] [2005] EWHC 892 (QB); [2005] E.M.L.R. 25.

Plato Films[162] and was unworkable in practice. This argument was rejected, and the outcome was that the Court of Appeal held[163] that defendants can properly rely on *Burstein* material in offer of amends, because fairness requires that a defendant should not be called on to pay compensation which is unmerited or to vindicate a claimant on a false basis—although of course if material is improperly put forward it may increase rather than reduce the compensation. Indeed, the introduction of *Burstein* material is particularly appropriate in offer of amends cases because there will have been no opportunity for evidence of specific acts of misconduct to have been put before the court in support of a plea of justification or honest comment or to show lack of malice. But the defendant may not rely on any material which is tantamount to introducing a substantive defence such as justification or honest comment.[164]

Position where only one of several defendants makes an   **29.37**
offer. Where one defendant makes an offer of amends, and the other plays no part in the proceedings, several rules of practice are in play. There cannot be separate awards against different defendants responsible for the same libel, because they are jointly and severally liable; any factors which tend to aggravate damages can only be taken into account in so far as they represent the lowest common denominator, that is to say the extent to which all defendants can be held responsible[165]; and by virtue of s.3(8)(b) of the Defamation Act 1996, where there are two defendants, one of whom has made an offer of amends and the other of whom has not, the liability of the defendant who has made the offer will be capped at the level of the compensation determined by the judge in accordance with the offer of amends regime. Hence in *Veliu v Mazrekaj*,[166] where the extremely grave libel was published in a Kosovan newspaper sold in London, one person responsible for its publication made an offer of amends, and another took no part in the proceedings, the overall figure for damages was set by Eady J. at £175,000, but the amount payable by the first defendant under the offer of amends procedure was £120,000. Both defendants remained jointly and severally liable for the whole sum, subject to the first defendant's statutory entitlement under s.3(8)(b) to have his liability capped at £120,000.

Steps taken in fulfilment of the offer, etc. The Act specifically requires   **29.38**
the court to take account of any steps taken in fulfilment of the offer and (so far as not agreed between the parties) of the suitability of the correction, the sufficiency of the apology, and whether the manner of their publication was

---

[162] [1961] A.C. 1090.
[163] [2006] EWCA Civ 540; [2006] 1 W.L.R. 3469. See also the discussion in *Warren v Random House Group Ltd* [2008] EWCA Civ 834; [2009] Q.B. 600 at [78] et seq.
[164] *Abu v MGN Ltd*, above, at [17], and *Cleese v Clark* (above) at [7].
[165] *Broome v Cassell* [1972] A.C. 1027 at 1063, 1089–90, 1105 and see para.9.36, above.
[166] [2006] EWHC 1710 (QB); [2007] 1 W.L.R. 495.

reasonable in the circumstances. The compensation may be reduced or increased accordingly.[167]

29.39 Rejection of offer of amends.[168] If the offer is not accepted, the fact that it was made is a defence to defamation proceedings in respect of the publication complained of by that claimant against the offeror,[169] subject to an important reservation. There is no such defence if the offeror knew or had reason to believe that words complained of (1) referred to the claimant or was likely to be understood as referring to him, and (2) were both false and defamatory of him, but it is to be presumed until the contrary is shown that the offeror did not know and had no reason to believe that was the case.[170] That reservation is not to be construed as denying the defence to journalists who have been negligent, but is:

> "only intended to shut out those who have acted in bad faith; that is to say, where a defendant knows that what he is alleging is untrue . . . . or where he has reason to believe that the words are false. What this means is that he has chosen to ignore or shut his mind to information which should have led him to *believe* (not merely suspect) that the allegation is false."[171]

---

[167] Defamation Act 1996, s.3(5).

[168] "Rejection" is a misnomer: the offer of amends regime makes no provision for rejection of the offer, which is either accepted or not accepted (as to which, see para.29.30, above). For the difficulties which this may raise, see *Loughton Contracts Plc v Dun & Bradstreet Ltd* [2006] EWHC 1224 (QB), where the problem was analysed in contractual terms of offer and counter-offer and the onus was placed squarely on the claimant to decide promptly whether or not to accept, and (for a sharp contrast) *Moore v Scottish Daily Record* [2007] CSOH 24, where even the pursuer's issue of proceedings after the offer of amends had been made was held not to amount to non-acceptance. In *Warren v Random House Group Ltd*, above, the Court of Appeal considered that the statutory scheme was not in fact contractual, because it contained express provisions as to what should or should not happen next and the court retained a role, but that the court would permit a party to resile from acceptance of an offer of amends only on "one of the traditional contractual grounds" or in rare and special circumstances: see [17], [27] and para.29.40, below. The question of how long a claimant has to accept or reject an offer of amends was considered by Eady J. in *Tesco Stores Ltd v Guardian News & Media Ltd* [2009] E.M.L.R. 5 discussed at para.29.30, above. In short, he held that the claimant must accept or reject the offer within a reasonable time, and that what is reasonable would depend on the circumstances of each case. He did not find the reasoning in the Scottish case of *Moore* (above) persuasive.

[169] Defamation Act 1996, s.4(2). A rejected qualified offer is a defence only in respect of the meaning to which the offer related.

[170] Ibid. s.4(3).

[171] *Milne v Express Newspapers* [2002] EWHC 2564 (QB); [2003] 1 W.L.R. 927, Eady J. The claimant's appeal from Eady J.'s judgment was dismissed by the Court of Appeal ([2004] EWCA Civ 664; [2005] 1 W.L.R. 772) which considered that his construction of s.4(3) was entirely correct, for the reasons that he gave. See *Thornton v Telegraph Media Group Ltd* [2011] EWHC 1884 (QB); [2012] E.M.L.R. 8 for an example of a case in which the claimant defeated a defence of offer of amends and established liability by proving that the defendant's journalist had acted dishonestly. In *John v Associated Newspapers Ltd* [2006] EWHC 1740 (QB), Eady J. refused an application by the defendant for summary judgment under CPR r.24 or to strike out the claim, mounted on the basis that the claimant had no real prospect of satisfying the s.4(3) test. On the facts pleaded by the claimant, the judge held that he could not say that a jury would be perverse if its members concluded (at [22]) that the journalist in question was recklessly indifferent to the truth of what he had written.

Where the defence of offer of amends is pleaded, the defendant may not rely on any other defence.[172] The offer may be relied on in mitigation of damages whether or not it is pleaded as a defence.[173]

Resiling from an accepted offer of amends. When an offer of amends   **29.40**
has been accepted, a party will be allowed to resile from it only on one of the traditional contractual grounds for impugning a contract, such as misrepresentation or mutual mistake,[174] or where there are "special circumstances", in the sense of circumstances so different from those contemplated that it is just to allow one party to be released from its obligation under the statutory scheme and to deprive the other of the benefit of the bargain which had been made. Such circumstances would only arise very rarely.[175]

Section 5. Alternative Dispute Resolution[176]

The court is required to further the overriding objective of the CPR by active   **29.41**
case management,[177] which includes encouraging the parties to use an alternative dispute resolution (ADR) procedure if the court considers it appropriate, and facilitating the use of that procedure.[178] Moreover, parties are given the opportunity, when completing their directions questionnaires[179] prior to the first case management conference, to request a stay for one month while the parties try to settle the case by ADR. If all the parties make this request, the proceedings will be stayed for a month.[180] However, regardless of the parties' wishes, if the court considers that such a stay would be appropriate,

---

[172] Defamation Act 1996, s.4(4). In *Club La Costa (UK) Plc v Gebhard*, above, Tugendhat J. observed at [28] that the defendants had "rightly" acknowledged that a denial or non-admission that the statement complained of referred to the claimant was "any other defence" within the meaning of s.4(4) and so could not be relied upon if the defendants chose to rely on an offer of amends as a defence.

[173] Ibid. s.4(5).

[174] Even though, on analysis,
"While the statutory scheme has many of the attributes of a contract, and is certainly consensual, . . . it is not a contract in the sense of creating rights and obligations, because it contains express provisions as to what should or should not happen next and the court retains a role":
Warren v Random House Group Ltd [2008] EWCA Civ 834; [2009] Q.B. 600, at [17].

[175] *Warren v Random House Group Ltd*, above, at [23]–[27]. In *Warren,* an agreed statement in open court had been read in performance of the accepted offer, but the defendant sought to withdraw the offer of amends and amend to plead justification.

[176] For a valuable general discussion of this subject, see *Civil Procedure (The White Book)*, Vol.2, Section 14.

[177] R.1.4(1).

[178] R.1.4(2)(e).

[179] Formerly "allocation questionnaires"; the procedure has been substantially revised with effect from April 1, 2013: see CPR r.26.3.

[180] R.26.4(2), in force from April 1, 2013. The court may extend the stay as appropriate: r.26.4(3).

it will direct that the proceedings either in whole or in part be stayed for such period as it considers appropriate.[181] The parties are under a duty to help the court in furthering the overriding objective,[182] which obliges them to take the use of ADR seriously. Perhaps a more potent means of persuasion has been the costs sanction, because when the court comes to exercise its discretion on costs it must have regard to all the circumstances, including the parties' conduct.[183] If a party turns down out of hand the chance of ADR when suggested by the court, it may face "uncomfortable" costs consequences.[184] However, refusal to take part in ADR need not, if reasonable, be visited with costs sanctions.[185] It is difficult to know how successful ADR has proved in defamation cases or how widely used it has been, but anecdotal evidence suggests that it has the capacity to achieve a harmonious outcome even in apparently unpromising circumstances.[186]

---

[181] R.26.4(2A), in force from April 1, 2013.

[182] R.1.3.

[183] R.44.2(4)(a).

[184] *Dunnett v Railtrack Plc* [2002] EWCA Civ 303; [2002] 2 All E.R. 850, per Brooke L.J. at [14]–[15]. See also CPR rr.44.2(5)(a) and 44.4(3)(a)(ii), and the Pre-Action Protocol for Defamation, para.3.7. As a general rule, silence in response to an invitation to participate in ADR will be viewed as unreasonable irrespective of whether there was a good reason to refuse to engage in ADR: *PGF I SA v OMFS CO 1 Ltd* [2013] EWCA Civ 1288.

[185] *Société Internationale de Télécommunications Aeronautiques SC v Wyatt* [2002] EWHC 2401 (Ch); *Hurst v Leeming* [2002] EWHC 1051 (Ch), where Lightman J. held that the fact that a party believed he had a watertight case was no justification for refusing mediation, nor was the fact that a full and detailed refutation of his opponent's case had already been supplied, but that a party might be justified, on the facts, in deciding that given the character and attitude of the other party, mediation was not appropriate because it had no realistic prospect of success. The burden is on the losing party to show why there should be a departure from the general rule on costs (i.e. an order depriving the winner of some or all of his costs) on the basis that he refused to agree to ADR, and the basic principle is that an order will not be made unless it is shown that the winning party acted unreasonably in refusing to agree to ADR: *Halsey v Milton Keynes General NHS Trust* [2004] EWCA Civ 576; [2004] 1 W.L.R. 3002. A party who agrees to mediation but then takes an unreasonable position in the mediation will be treated as if he had unreasonably refused to mediate: *Carlton v Strutt & Parker* [2008] EWHC 424 (QB).

[186] E.g. it provided an amicable resolution of the litigation in *Fayed v Telegraph Group Ltd*, reported on a different point at [2002] EWHC 1631 (QB). A not-for-profit company, Early Resolution (founded by former legal manager of Times Newspapers, Alastair Brett, and retired High Court judge, Sir Charles Gray) offers a range of ADR services specifically tailored to defamation disputes. The core scheme is a process of binding arbitration which involves the parties in making written submissions to a defamation QC or experienced junior, or a retired High Court judge, who rules on them with the assistance of two lay colleagues (if the dispute concerns meaning) or without (if the dispute is about fact/comment or quantum): see *http://www.early resolution.co.uk*.

PRE-TRIAL APPLICATIONS

SECTION 1. INTRODUCTION

Generally. This chapter addresses the principal interlocutory matters which **30.1** arise in the course of defamation litigation. The great majority of actions settle before trial, and defamation remains a field in which a sound grasp of interlocutory tactics is frequently of crucial importance in determining the outcome, whether by forcing a favourable settlement before trial or by ensuring that if trial comes the litigant's case is thoroughly prepared and his opponent's properly understood.[1]

SECTION 2. RULINGS ON MEANING

Rulings on meaning: CPR PD 53, paragraph 4(1).[2] The jurisdiction **30.2** to obtain a ruling on whether or not words are capable of bearing a particular

---

[1] As the Neill Committee observed in 1991:
" . . . more time is spent on preliminary skirmishing in defamation actions than in other forms of litigation, either at the interlocutory stage or at the beginning of the trial before the jury is empanelled. This is in our opinion, and experience, largely because of the nature of the cause of action. In no other area of the law is there so much divergence in the circumstances from one case to another. It is hardly possible to imagine a 'standard' libel action."
(Supreme Court Procedure Committee, Report on Practice and Procedure in Defamation, July 1991, para.1.13).
Almost 20 years later the same phenomenon prompted Lord Phillips of Worth Matravers to suggest the abandonment of trial by jury in defamation: "Finally, and fundamentally, has not the time come to recognise that defamation is no longer a field in which trial by jury is desirable? he issues are often complex and jury trial simply invites expensive interlocutory battles, such as the one before this court, which attempts to pre-empt issues from going before the jury" (*Joseph v Spiller* [2010] UKSC 53; [2011] 1 A.C. 852 at [116]). Parliament has since answered Lord Phillips's question in the affirmative: see s.11 of the Defamation Act 2013 ("Trial to be without a jury unless the court orders otherwise"). It remains to be seen whether this development will significantly reduce the frequency of interlocutory battles in this field of law.
[2] "Ruling on Meaning. 4.1 At any time the court may decide–(1) whether a statement complained of is capable of having any meaning attributed to it in a statement of case; (2) whether

meaning, whether they are capable of being defamatory of the claimant, and whether they are capable of bearing any other meaning defamatory of the claimant[3] has proved extremely valuable.

> "The whole purpose of the new rule[4] is to enable the court to fix in advance the ground rules on permissible meanings, which are of such cardinal importance in defamation actions, not only for the purpose of assessing the degree of injury to the plaintiff's reputation, but also for the purpose of evaluating any defences raised, in particular justification or fair comment. This applies with particular force . . . where there is a defence of justification of a lesser meaning than that pleaded in the statement of claim."[5]

Nevertheless, when the jury ceases to be the presumptive tribunal of fact in defamation cases upon the coming into force of s.11, Defamation Act 2013, there will be no inhibition on judges determining the actual meaning of words complained of at an early stage in the proceedings. As such, the question of whether words are or are not capable of bearing a particular meaning is liable to become an academic one. This is a process that is already well underway,[6] with ever fewer defamation actions being tried by jury.[7]

30.3 Background. Until 1991, the court could not be asked to rule whether words were capable of bearing a particular pleaded meaning (which is a question of law for the judge)[8] until the trial of the action. If a party wished to attack his opponent's pleaded meaning, whether it was the meaning put on the words complained of in the statement of claim or the *Lucas-Box* meaning

---

the statement is capable of being defamatory of the claimant; (3) whether the statement is capable of bearing any other meaning defamatory of the claimant". For pleading the meaning, see paras 26.20–26.24, above.

[3] Regarding this third limb of CPR PD 53, para.4(1) (ruling on whether words are capable of bearing "any other meaning defamatory of the claimant"), however, Tugendhat J. in *Dell'Olio v Associated Newspapers Ltd* [2011] EWHC 3472 (QB) discouraged the consideration or upholding of hypothetical defamatory meanings of which the claimant had made no complaint. At [31] the judge accepted the defendant's submission that "it would be futile for the court to consider every possible defamatory meaning of the words complained of", adding at [30] that

> "[a] court considering 'whether the statement is capable of bearing any other meaning defamatory of the claimant' cannot be required to proceed in a vacuum. There may be obvious potentially defamatory meanings . . . which it would be pointless for the court to consider, if the claimant does not raise them".

But see also *Church v MGN Ltd* [2012] EWHC 693 (QB); [2013] 1 W.L.R. 284 at [36] where the court's obligation to consider possible alternative meanings was held to militate against the defendant's proposal that applications for rulings on meaning should ordinarily be determined without a hearing.

[4] RSC Ord.82, r.3A, the antecedent of CPR PD 53, para.4(1).

[5] *Mapp v News Group Newspapers Ltd* [1998] Q.B. 520, 526, per Hirst L.J.

[6] See paras 30.14–30.16, below in relation to trials of meaning as a preliminary issue.

[7] At the time of writing (September 2013) it is believed that only two defamation cases have been tried by jury in England and Wales during the last four years: *Cooper v Evening Standard Ltd* (in June 2012) and *Boyle v MGN Ltd* (in October 2012).

[8] *Jones v Skelton* [1963] 1 W.L.R. 1362, 1370, per Lord Morris; *Lewis v Daily Telegraph* [1964] A.C. 234, 260, per Lord Reid; *Morgan v Odhams Press* [1971] 1 W.L.R. 1239, 1251H, per Lord Morris.

stating in the defence what the defendant sought to justify,[9] he could only do so by invoking the jurisdiction under RSC Ord.18, r.19. This entailed arguing that the meaning was one which the words were not even *arguably* capable of bearing.[10] It was also established in 1991 that there was jurisdiction under RSC Ord.33, r.3 to try as a preliminary issue the question whether the words complained of were capable of bearing a particular meaning,[11] but there was still a clear need for a simplified procedure. This was provided in 1994 by RSC Ord.82, r.3A. Since the coming into force of Pt 53 of the Civil Procedure Rules in February 2000, the jurisdiction is to be found in CPR PD 53, para.4(1).

Conceptual problems. The underlying intellectual tensions of the exercise   **30.4** of determining meaning were well expressed by Diplock L.J.:

> "Everyone outside a court of law recognises that words are imprecise instruments for communicating the thoughts of one man to another. The same words may be understood by one man in a different meaning from that in which they are understood by another and both meanings may be different from that which the author of the words intended to convey. But the notion that the same words should bear different meanings to different men and that more than one meaning should be 'right' conflicts with the whole training of a lawyer. Words are the tools of his trade. He uses them to define legal rights and duties. They do not achieve that purpose unless there can be attributed to them a single meaning as the 'right' meaning. And so the argument between lawyers as to the meaning of words starts with the unexpressed major premise that any particular combination of words has one meaning which is not necessarily the same as that intended by him who published them or understood by any of those who read them but is capable of ascertainment as being the 'right' meaning by the adjudicator to whom the law confides the responsibility of determining it."[12]

Principles to be applied. Nonetheless, the rules for determining whether   **30.5** words are capable of bearing a particular meaning are well established and

---

[9] *Lucas-Box v News Group Newspapers Ltd* [1986] 1 W.L.R. 147 CA.

[10] See *Drummond-Jackson v BMA* [1970] 1 W.L.R. 688 CA; *Morgan v Odhams Press*, above, at 1257h–1258c, 1267g–1268c. It is no longer permissible to mount such an argument: by s.7 of the Defamation Act 1996, the court shall not be asked to rule whether a statement is arguably capable, as opposed to capable, of bearing a particular meaning or meanings attributed to it. But given the breadth of the court's powers under para.4.1 there is no fathomable reason why a litigant might wish to do so.

[11] *Keays v Murdoch Magazines* [1991] 1 W.L.R. 1184 CA.

[12] *Slim v Daily Telegraph* [1968] 2 Q.B. 157 at 171–172. Diplock L.J. was articulating what has become known as the "single meaning" rule. For a more recent exposition of the rule, see *Lait v Evening Standard Ltd* [2011] EWCA Civ 859; [2011] 1 W.L.R. 2973. Significant inroads have been made into the rule: see *Curistan v Times Newspapers Ltd* [2008] EWCA Civ 432; [2009] Q.B. 231 in the statutory qualified privilege context (see para.3.16, above); *Bonnick v Morris* [2002] UKPC 31; [2003] 1 A.C. 300 and *Flood v Times Newspapers Ltd* [2012] UKSC 11; [2012] 2 A.C. 273 in the *Reynolds* privilege context; *Loveless v Earl* [1999] E.M.L.R. 530 and *Cammish v Hughes* [2012] EWCA Civ 1655; [2013] E.M.L.R. 13 at [49] in relation to malice, while in *Ajinomoto Sweeteners Europe SAS v Asda Stores Ltd* [2010] EWCA Civ 609; [2010] Q.B. 204, the Court of Appeal criticised the artificiality and potential injustice of the rule in deciding that it had no role to play in the tort of malicious falsehood.

rarely controversial. The starting point is that the judge's function is to delimit the range of meanings of which the words are reasonably capable of bearing[13] and to rule out any meanings outside that range[14]: the role of the tribunal of fact, conventionally the jury,[15] is to decide what meaning within that permissible range the words actually bear.[16] An authoritative summary of the principles is to be found in *Jeynes v News Magazines Ltd*[17]:

(1) The governing principle is reasonableness. (2) The hypothetical reasonable reader[18] is not naïve but he is not unduly suspicious. He can read between the lines.

---

[13] A helpful formulation of "the proper role of the judge" on such applications was constructed by Eady J. in *Gillick v Brook Advisory Centres*, described by Lord Phillips M.R. on appeal ([2001] EWCA Civ 1263 at [7]) as an "impeccable synthesis" of the authorities, as follows:
"The proper role for the judge when adjudicating a question of this kind is to evaluate the words complained of and to delimit the range of meanings of which the words are reasonably capable, exercising his or her own judgment in the light of the principles laid down in the authorities and without any of the former Order 18 Rule 19 overtones. If the judge decides that any pleaded meaning falls outside the permissible range, then it will be his duty to rule accordingly. In deciding whether words are capable of conveying a defamatory meaning, the court should reject those meanings which can only emerge as the produce of some strained or forced or utterly unreasonable interpretation. The purpose of the new rule is to enable the court to fix in advance the ground rules and permissible meanings, which are of cardinal importance in defamation actions, not only for the purpose of assessing the degree of injury to the claimant's reputation but also for the purpose of evaluating any defences raised, in particular, justification and fair comment."
[14] This is "an exercise in generosity, not in parsimony", per Sedley L.J., *Berezovsky v Forbes* [2001] EWCA Civ 1251; [2001] E.M.L.R. 45 at [16]. However, in *John v Guardian News & Media Ltd* [2008] EWHC 3066 (QB) Tugendhat J. said at [16] that he did not read Sedley L.J.'s observation as meaning that a judge may more safely err on one side than the other: "If a judge does err in holding words to be incapable of bearing a meaning pleaded by a claimant, then he deprives the claimant of his right to vindicate his reputation before a court. If the judge errs in holding words to be capable of a meaning pleaded by a claimant, then the defendant is wrongly burdened with defending libel proceedings. This can be a very onerous burden and one which interferes with the right of freedom of expression". See also *Jameel v Wall Street Journal Sprl* [2003] EWCA Civ 1694; [2004] E.M.L.R. 6 at [6], [9]–[16].
[15] But increasingly in recent years, the judge, hence the increasing number of preliminary trials of meaning: see paras 30.14–30.16, below.
[16] *Mapp v News Group Newspapers Ltd* [1998] Q.B. 520, CA. According to *Mapp*, it is open to a claimant at trial to rely on any lesser defamatory meanings within the permissible range. But this presupposes that meaning remains a live issue at that stage: logically, an early preliminary ruling on the actual meaning of the words must preclude this possibility. For the approach to be adopted to determination of meaning by a judge sitting alone without a jury, see *Skuse v Granada Television Ltd* [1996] E.M.L.R 278 CA; *Waterson v Lloyd* [2013] EWCA Civ 136; [2013] E.M.L.R. 17; *Charman v Orion Publishing Group Ltd* [2005] EWHC 2187 (QB) at [11] per Gray J.; *Miller v Associated Newspapers* [2005] EWHC 557 (QB) at [24] et seq.
[17] [2008] EWCA Civ 130 at [14] (per Sir Anthony Clarke M.R.).
[18] In a well-known passage, Neill L.J. described the ordinary reasonable reader in these terms:
"The hypothetical reasonable reader is not naïve but he is not unduly suspicious. He can read between the lines. He can read in an implication more readily than a lawyer, and may indulge in a certain amount of loose thinking. But he must be treated as being a man who is not avid for scandal and someone who does not, and should not, select one bad meaning where other non-defamatory meanings are available"
(*Hartt v Newspaper Publishing Plc*, unreported, October 26, 1989, CA). Lord Reid made a similar point in *Lewis v Daily Telegraph* [1964] A.C. 234 at 259–260:
"Ordinary men and women have different temperaments and outlooks. Some are unusually suspicious and some are unusually naïve. One must try to envisage people between these two

He can read in an implication more readily than a lawyer[19] and may indulge in a certain amount of loose thinking[20] but he must be treated as being a man who is not avid for scandal and someone who does not, and should not, select one bad meaning where other non-defamatory meanings are available.[21] (3) Over-elaborate analysis is best avoided. (4) The intention of the publisher is irrelevant.[22] (5) The article must be read as a whole,[23] and any 'bane and antidote'[24] taken together. (6) The

---

extremes and see what is the most damaging meaning they would put on the words in question . . . ".

In *Lennon v Scottish Daily Record* [2004] EWHC 359 (QB); [2004] E.M.L.R. 18, Tugendhat J. suggested that the ordinary reader should now be credited with having achieved a level of education not accessible to earlier generations, and should therefore be taken as being more discriminating and better able to understand what he or she reads. The judge founded that proposition, which may be thought controversial, on an observation of Eady J. in *Lukowiak v Unidad Editorial SA* [2001] E.M.L.R. 46, to the effect that ordinary citizens are now perceived by the courts to have stronger stomachs and more discriminating judgment than was traditionally recognised. However, Eady J.'s observation was made in the context of discussion of the defence of *Reynolds* qualified privilege and the social changes which have given rise to a right in the general public to be kept informed by the media about matters of public interest. As to the ordinary, reasonable Australian reader, see *Radio 2UE Sydney Pty Ltd v Chesterton* [2009] HCA 16; (2009) 238 C.L.R. 460. The concept of the ordinary reasonable reader is discussed further in paras 3.26–3.27, above.

[19] As Lord Devlin stated in *Lewis v Daily Telegraph*, above, at 277:

" . . . the natural and ordinary meaning of words ought in theory to be the same for the lawyer as for a layman, because the lawyer's first rule of construction is that words are to be given their natural and ordinary meaning as popularly understood. The proposition that ordinary words are the same for the lawyer as for the layman is as a matter of pure construction undoubtedly true. But it is very difficult to draw the line between pure construction and implication, and the layman's capacity for implication is much greater than the lawyer's. The lawyer's rule is that the implication must be necessary as well as reasonable. The layman reads in an implication much more freely; and unfortunately, as the law of defamation has to take into account, is especially prone to do so when it is defamatory."

[20] See also *Morgan v Odhams Press*, above, at 1245F-G, per Lord Reid, adopted by Hirst L.J. in *Aiken v Police Review*, unreported, April 12, 1995, CA:

"If we are to follow *Lewis*' case and take the ordinary man as our guide, then we must accept a certain amount of loose thinking. The ordinary man does not formulate reasons in his mind: he gets a general impression".

[21] "It seems to me unreasonable that when there are a number of good interpretations the only bad one should be seized on to give a defamatory sense to the document.": per Brett L.J. in *Capital & Counties Bank v Henty* (1880) 5 C.P.D. 514 at 541, cited with approval by Lord Halsbury L.C. in *Nevill v Fine Arts & General Insurance* [1897] A.C. 68 at 73.

[22] It should of course be remembered that the words are to be construed not by reference to the publisher's intention, although this can colour their meaning, but by the reader's reaction to them: *Berkoff v Burchill* [1996] 4 All E.R. 1008 CA. See also, *Bowker (t/a Lagopus Services) v The Royal Society for the Protection of Birds* [2011] EWHC 737 (QB) at [39]–[40].

[23] *Skuse v Granada Television Ltd* [1996] E.M.L.R. 278 CA; *Gillick v BBC* [1996] E.M.L.R. 267 CA; *Jameel v Times Newspapers Ltd* [2004] EWCA Civ 983; [2004] E.M.L.R. 31 at [12]. In terms of what might constitute the "whole" article, Sharp J. in *Dee v Telegraph Media Group Ltd* [2010] EWHC 924 (QB); [2010] E.M.L.R. 20 held, applying *Charleston v News Group Newspapers Ltd* [1995] 2 A.C. 65, that the ordinary reasonable reader was to be taken to have read the whole article before reaching a conclusion on meaning, and that this was so whether the article appeared on one page of a publication or across several pages. Where more than one article was under consideration, the key issue was whether the articles were sufficiently closely connected as to be regarded as a single publication. See para.3.33, above.

[24] *Charleston v News Group Newspapers Ltd* [1995] 2 A.C. 65; *Chalmers v Payne* (1835) 2 Cr. M. & R. 156 at 159, per Alderson B.; *Sergi v Australian Broadcasting Commission* [1983] 2 N.S.W.L.R. 669 at 670, per Hutley J.A. ("the bane and antidote theory . . . is merely a vivid way of stating that the whole publication must be considered, not a segment of it"). But it is unlikely

hypothetical reader is taken to be representative of those who would read the publication in question.[25] (7) In delimiting the range of permissible defamatory meanings, the court should rule out any meaning which "can only emerge as the product of some strained, or forced, or utterly unreasonable interpretation".[26] . . . (8) It follows that "it is not enough to say that by some person or another the words might be understood in a defamatory sense."[27]

The words complained of must also be read in context.[28] Furthermore, for words to be defamatory, the allegation they comprise must cross a threshold of seriousness, so as to exclude trivial claims.[29] It has been acknowledged that

---

that the mere printing of a denial will ever constitute an antidote sufficient to neutralise the bane: *Mark v Associated Newspapers* [2002] EWCA Civ 772; [2002] E.M.L.R. 38, per Simon Brown L.J. at [42]. In *Jameel v Times Newspapers Ltd* [2004] EWCA Civ 983; [2004] E.M.L.R. 31, Sedley L.J. referred at [16] to the "unaddressed tension" between the principle that the range of possible meanings is to be derived from the article as a whole, read through the eyes of a reasonable reader, and the principle that if the article contains a defamatory statement (the bane), that will define its meaning unless it is very plainly cancelled out (the antidote) in the same article. However, it is questionable whether these are really two discrete principles, let alone two principles in "tension" with one another. The point has received no further attention in the authorities.

[25] The court is concerned with the ordinary reasonable reader (or viewer) of the publication in question, who naturally will differ according to the character of the publication; see e.g. *John v Guardian News & Media Ltd* [2008] EWHC 3066 (QB) at [32] and *Cruddas v Calvert* [2013] EWHC 1427 (QB) at [22] (Tugendhat J.): "The hypothetical reader must be taken to be a reasonable representative of readers of *The Sunday Times*. What the characteristics of such people might be is a matter of public knowledge. It is a newspaper directed to readers with an interest and general knowledge of politics." (The Court of Appeal did not disagree: [2013] EWCA Civ 748.) See also *Flood v Times Newspapers Ltd* [2013] EWHC 2182 (QB) at [12] where Tugendhat J. made similarly complimentary remarks about the average reader of *The Sunday Times*.

[26] The text of the judgment here cites *Gillick v Brook Advisory Centres* [2001] EWCA Civ 1263 at [7].

[27] The text of the judgment here cites *Neville v Fine Arts & General Insurance* [1897] A.C. 68 per Lord Halsbury L.C. at 73.

[28] As regards what might amount to context when one is considering internet publications, see *Islam Expo Ltd v Spectator (1828) Ltd* [2010] EWHC 2011 (QB).

[29] *Thornton v Telegraph Media Group Ltd* [2010] EWHC 1414 (QB); [2011] W.L.R. 1985 (Tugendhat J.); see *Dell'Olio v Associated Newspapers Ltd* [2011] EWHC 3472 (QB) for an application of the principle. The principle finds expression in s.1(1) Defamation Act 2013, which provides as follows: "1. Serious Harm (1) A statement is not defamatory unless its publication had caused or is likely to cause serious harm to the reputation of the claimant." As para.11 of the Explanatory Notes to the Act explains:

"This section builds on the consideration given by the courts in a series of cases to the question of what is sufficient to establish that a statement is defamatory. A recent example is *Thornton v Telegraph Media Group Ltd* . . . in which a decision of the House of Lords in *Sim v Stretch* [1936] 2 All E.R. 1237] was identified as authority for the existence of a 'threshold of seriousness' in what is defamatory".

As regards the juristic status of the *Thornton* principle at common law, in *Euromoney Institutional Investor Plc v Aviation News Ltd* [2013] EWHC 1505 (QB), Tugendhat J. observed as follows at [19]

"The Court of Appeal has not considered whether (as held in *Thornton* . . .) words are only defamatory at common law if they satisfy a test of seriousness, and in the light of the Defamation Act 2013, s.1 (which introduces a new statutory test) it may now never have occasion to do so. But that court proceeded on the assumption that the claimant's complaint must surmount a threshold of seriousness. See *Cammish v Hughes* [2012] EWCA Civ 1655; [2013] E.M.L.R. 13 para [38]."

applications for rulings on meaning may have implications under art.10 of the European Convention on Human Rights.[30]

"Chase" levels of meaning. Forensic consideration of the meaning of **30.6** defamatory words—of a factual character, at any rate—has acquired its own shorthand as a result of the decisions of the Court of Appeal in *Bennett v News Group Newspapers Ltd*[31] and *Chase v News Group Newspapers Ltd*,[32] which have introduced the language of level (or "tier") 1, 2 and 3 meanings into legal debate. In very broad terms, they may be understood as meanings which impute (1) guilt, (2) reasonable grounds to suspect the claimant of guilt, and (3) grounds to investigate the claimant. As Sedley L.J. pointed out in a subsequent case[33]:

"The elevation of this taxonomy of meanings into legal categories is recent. It is correct to say that as long ago as 1963, in *Lewis v Daily Telegraph Ltd* [1964] A.C. 234, a libel action arising out of an article headlined 'Fraud squad probe firm', it was recognised, at least by Lord Devlin, that such an allegation might operate on any of three levels, each distinctly capable of justification: the fact of an inquiry, the existence of reasonable grounds for suspicion, and guilt. But, although the practice (criticised by Lord Devlin, *loc. cit.*, 287) has persisted of letting a claimant plead only his highest meaning and then argue for any lesser one, it was not until the decision of this court in *Bennett v News Group Newspapers* that recognition was accorded to these three classes as being legally distinct."

More recently, there has been a recognition that more than three levels of meaning may be required: for example, Gray J. has observed that there is a considerable gulf between the imputation of guilt of a criminal offence (level 1) and the imputation of the existence of grounds—even reasonable grounds —for suspicion of guilt (level 2), because the degree of reasonable suspicion may vary greatly from case to case; and in one case he found (on the hearing of a preliminary issue) that the true meaning was somewhere in between ("cogent grounds to suspect").[34]

---

[30] In *John v Guardian News & Media Ltd*, above, Tugendhat J. observed at [17] that the principle derived from Strasbourg jurisprudence to the effect that an adverse finding for express- ing honest value judgements was likely to involve a violation of art.10 of the Convention "must also apply to rulings on meaning":
"... the Strasbourg cases show that a claimant can make an action more difficult to defend by characterising an impugned statement as fact rather than as value judgment. A claimant can also do that by attributing to an impugned statement a meaning that is on any view high. There is a real risk of violation of art.10 if a claimant strains to attribute to words complained of a high factual meaning, which cannot be defended as true, and at the same time claims aggravated damages on the footing that the defendant knew the words to be false in that meaning".
For further observations on the relationship between art.10 and the issue of meaning, see *Ecclestone v Telegraph Media Group Ltd* [2009] EWHC 2779 (QB) at [10], *Dee v Telegraph Media Group Ltd*, above, at [29], and *Thornton v Telegraph Media Group Ltd* [2010] EWHC 1414 (QB); [2011] W.L.R. 1985 at [60]–[62] and [93]–[94].
[31] [2002] E.M.L.R. 39.
[32] [2002] EWCA Civ 1772; [2003] E.M.L.R. 11.
[33] *Jameel v Times Newspapers Ltd* [2004] EWCA Civ 983; [2004] E.M.L.R. 31 at [10].
[34] *Charman v Orion Publishing Group Ltd* [2005] EWHC 2187 (QB).

Jargon apart, the underlying principles have not changed, and indeed the *Skuse* and *Gillick* formulations have been repeatedly followed and endorsed, e.g. in *Jeynes*. Moreover, as Eady J. acutely observed in *Fallon v MGN Ltd*,[35] the *Chase* levels of meaning:

> "may be a somewhat artificial scale in the sense that defamatory words are capable of bearing an infinite variety of meanings and implications and, correspondingly, a range of levels of gravity which do not necessarily lend themselves to classification in one or other of these three categories".

Pigeonholing defamatory words or meanings attributed to those words—particularly defendants' *Lucas-Box* meanings—within one or other of the *Chase* levels of meaning (often artificially, as Eady J. implies in *Fallon*) has been used principally as a means of evaluating and keeping within proper bounds at the interim stage a pleaded defence of justification, bearing in mind that the case was to be tried by a jury susceptible to being prejudiced and led into error by the introduction of irrelevant extraneous material.[36] Accordingly, once s.11 of the Defamation Act 2013 is in force and the possibility of jury trial effectively gone, and judges have full control over proceedings from the outset, the utility of the *Chase* "levels of meaning" concept is liable to diminish. Judges, particularly if they have already determined the actual meaning of the words—or, to adopt the argot of the new Act, the actual "imputation conveyed by the statement complained of"[37]—will be at liberty to address in a more direct way whether any matter pleaded in support of a defence of truth is or is not relevant to establish the truth of the imputation in question.

30.7   **The high threshold for exclusion of meaning.** The Court of Appeal has indicated that first instance judges should be slower to rule out than to rule in pleaded meanings, particularly where the issue is whether words are capable of falling within one *Chase* level or another. In *Jameel v Wall Street Journal Sprl*,[38] which concerned the claimant's pleaded meaning, the point was approached from two different directions.

---

[35] [2006] EWHC 783 (QB); [2006] E.M.L.R. 19 at [1].

[36] See e.g. the principles governing justification of *Chase* level 2 meanings endorsed by the Court of Appeal in *Musa King v Telegraph Group Ltd* [2004] EWCA Civ 613; [2004] E.M.L.R. 23 at [22], set out in para.11.13, above. See also Eady J.'s remarks in *Flood v Times Newspapers Ltd* [2009] EWHC 411 (QB); [2009] E.M.L.R. 18 at [3]–[4] concerning justification of a *Chase* level 3 meaning:

> "The defendant wishes to justify the allegations about the claimant by reference to the *Lucas-Box* meaning that he was the subject of an internal police investigation and that there were grounds which, objectively regarded, justified a police investigation . . . This corresponds with what is nowadays sometimes referred to as a *Chase* level three meaning . . . In my experience, pleas of justification on this basis are rare and require careful scrutiny, in order to ensure that the particulars are properly confined."

[37] Defamation Act 2013, s.2(1).

[38] [2003] EWCA Civ 1694; [2004] E.M.L.R. 6 at [19].

First, at [10] Simon Brown L.J. advised judges to bear in mind the observations of Lord Nicholls in *Bonnick v Morris*[39] on the imprecision of language:

"Language is inherently imprecise. Words and phrases and sentences take their colour from their context. The context often permits a range of meanings, varying from the obvious to the implausible. Different readers may well form different views on the meaning to be given to the language under consideration."

Secondly, at [14], Simon Brown L.J. emphasised the high threshold of exclusion which must be satisfied:

" . . . every time a meaning is shut out (including any holding that the words complained of either are, or are not, capable of bearing a defamatory meaning) it must be remembered that the judge is taking it upon himself to rule in effect that any jury would be perverse to take a different view on the question. It is a high threshold of exclusion. Ever since Fox's Act 1792 the meaning of words in civil as well as criminal libel proceedings has been constitutionally a matter for the jury. The judge's function is no more and no less than to pre-empt perversity. That being clearly the position with regard to whether or not words are capable of being understood as defamatory or, as the case may be, non-defamatory, I see no basis on which it could sensibly be otherwise with regard to differing levels of defamatory meaning".

Injustice is also apt to result when a defendant's *Lucas-Box* meaning is ruled out, given that the effect of such rulings is to preclude the defendant from seeking to justify the words in that—usually lower—meaning, and thus, in the majority of cases, of justifying what he has published at all.

Another factor militating against the exclusion of pleaded meanings, to which Simon Brown L.J. adverted in *Jameel v Wall Street Journal Sprl*,[40] was the scope for the border between levels of meaning to be blurred and indistinct. The point was further accentuated in *Jameel v Times Newspapers Ltd*[41] in which Sedley L.J. remarked, in allowing an appeal from Gray J. (who had ruled out a level 2 meaning), that the distinction between level 2 and level 3 meanings was a fine one.[42]

Moreover, judges should be wary of ruling out a meaning unless there is sound reason to do so.[43]

---

[39] [2002] UKPC 31; [2003] 1 A.C. 300 at [20].

[40] Ibid. at [19].

[41] [2004] EWCA Civ 983; [2004] E.M.L.R. 31 at [18].

[42] Notwithstanding this conclusion, Gray J. at first instance ([2003] EWHC 2609 (QB)) set out the "real distinguishing features" of the two levels of meaning in terms which were cited without disapproval by Simon Brown L.J. in *Jameel v Wall Street Journal Sprl*, above, at [20], and by Sedley L.J. in *Jameel v Times Newspapers Ltd*, above, at [19] and [23].

[43] E.g. where a defence of justification depends on it, and the ruling would have the effect of limiting the evidence that might properly be adduced at trial: *Jameel v Wall Street Journal Sprl*, above, at [16]; *Armstrong v Times Newspapers Ltd* [2004] EWHC 2928 (QB) (this aspect of Eady J.'s ruling was not challenged when the case went to the Court of Appeal ([2005] EWCA Civ 1007)).

30.8 Meaning and the repetition rule. It is important to note the particular role that the repetition rule may play in ruling out a pleaded meaning even when the meaning may not be perverse. The repetition rule is a rule of law designed to prevent a jury from deciding that a particular class of publication, conveying rumour, hearsay or repetition of an allegation, is true or alter natively carries some lesser meaning than the original allegation would bear.[44] If a defendant endorses or repeats a defamatory allegation made by a third party, he cannot be heard to say that his words bear some lesser meaning than that borne by the words which he is repeating. The repetition rule thus:

> " . . . necessarily circumscribes the considerable latitude a jury otherwise has in relation to ascribing a meaning or meanings to defamatory words. Where it so operates, it might be more accurate to describe the role of the judge in delimiting the possible meanings as not so much 'pre-empting perversity' as precluding an otherwise possible meaning through the implementation of a rule of public policy. It may not be 'perverse' to ascribe to a particular article the meaning 'A said that B murdered C'. It is nonetheless not permitted to plead it as a *Lucas-Box* meaning for the reason that a defendant is required, if choosing to justify, to plead and prove that 'B murdered C'".[45]

Given that the stated purpose and justification of the repetition rule is to avoid the risk of a jury, in resolving the issues of meaning and substantial truth, reaching a conclusion that is unjust to a claimant, the rule may not need to be retained when the jury ceases to be the tribunal of fact in defamation cases upon the coming into force of s.11, Defamation Act 2013.

In *Curistan v Times Newspapers Ltd*,[46] the court decided that where one part of an article is privileged as a report of proceedings in Parliament and another part is not, the meaning of the privileged part was to be determined on a different basis from the meaning of the remainder: so far as the privileged words were concerned, the repetition rule was to be disapplied. In consequence, a reported (privileged) allegation is to be treated as meaning only that the allegation has been made, and as not to bear any connotation that the matter alleged is true. Moreover, this novel approach will apply only if a plea of privilege is upheld—which often will not be known until trial. If, for instance, the words for which privilege is claimed are ultimately held not to be a fair and accurate report, then no special rule will be applied. The full consequences of this iconoclastic approach to the determination of meaning remain to be seen: no cases possessing similar facts have arisen since.

30.9 Meaning: fact or comment. Although CPR PD 53, para.4(1) does not refer to the possibility of a decision being made by the court as to whether the words are only capable of being a statement of fact, or only a comment, this omission does not limit the court's powers to make such a ruling where

---

[44] See *Stern v Piper* [1997] Q.B. 123 at 135–136 and para.11.4, above.
[45] *Hamilton v Clifford* [2004] EWHC 1542 (QB) per Eady J. at [33]).
[46] [2008] EWCA Civ 432; [2009] Q.B. 231.

appropriate.[47] For instance, it may be desirable in a suitable case for a claimant to seek a ruling that the words are (only capable of being) factual in nature in order to exclude a pleaded defence of honest comment, or for a defendant to invite a determination that the words can only reasonably be construed as comment, for the purpose of eliminating any suggestion that he must justify the words in order to see off the claim.[48] An application for summary judgment under CPR r.24.2 would appear to be the most convenient route to obtaining such a ruling.[49]

Jurisdiction. The jurisdiction under CPR PD 53, para.4(1) is not limited to **30.10** rulings on meanings pleaded in the particulars of claim. Either party may apply for an order determining whether the words complained of are capable of bearing a meaning attributed to them in a statement of case (para.4.1(1)). The wording is wide enough[50] to embrace a ruling as to whether the words complained of are capable of bearing a particular *Lucas-Box* meaning[51] pleaded in the defence,[52] and a ruling on the meaning pleaded by the party making the application.[53]

Appeals. Except in cases which are clearly fit for argument in that court, the **30.11** Court of Appeal discourages appeals from rulings on meaning.[54] However, it will be less reluctant to interfere with a judge's decision where the judge has ruled out a meaning once and for all,[55] or where the judge has erred on the side of unnecessary restriction of meaning[56]; and even where the judge has upheld a meaning rather than ruled it out, it will intervene in a proper case: "no self-denying ordinance can absolve this court from its responsibility to act in such

[47] *Euromoney Institutional Investor Plc v Aviation News Ltd* [2013] EWHC 1505 (QB) per Tugendhat J. at [34].

[48] This was the thrust of the defendant's applications in *British Chiropractic Association v Singh* [2010] EWCA Civ 350; [2011] 1 W.L.R. 133 and in *Cammish v Hughes* [2012] EWCA Civ 1655; [2013] E.M.L.R. 13, albeit that they were both applications for the determination of meaning as a preliminary issue.

[49] See *Branson v Bower* [2002] Q.B. 737 (QB).

[50] As was RSC Ord.82, r.3A.

[51] *Lucas-Box v News Group Newspapers Ltd* [1986] 1 W.L.R. 147 CA.

[52] Such are usually coupled with applications for summary judgment under CPR Pt 24 or to strike out under CPR r.3.4(2), *viz.* in respect of the accompanying plea of justification or honest comment.

[53] As happened (in the RSC Ord.82, r.3A era) in *Parry v Express Newspapers*, unreported, March 9, 1995, CA. In *Jameel v Wall Street Journal* [2003] EWCA Civ 1694; [2004] E.M.L.R. 6, both parties invited the judge to rule on the meaning pleaded by the claimant.

[54] *Hinduja v Asian TV Ltd* [1998] E.M.L.R. 516; *Gillick v Brook Advisory Centres* [2001] EWCA Civ 1263 at [5]–[6].

[55] *Geenty v Channel Four* [1998] E.M.L.R. 524; *Cruise v Express Newspapers* [1999] Q.B. 931 at 936. See *Jameel v Wall Street Journal Europe* [2003] EWCA Civ 1694; [2004] E.M.L.R. 6; *Jameel v Times Newspapers Ltd* [2004] EWCA Civ 983; [2004] E.M.L.R. 31.

[56] *Berezovsky v Forbes Inc.* [2001] EWCA Civ 1251; [2001] E.M.L.R. 45.

cases".[57] It is particularly willing to look again at exclusionary rulings by first instance judges on the blurred frontier between level 2 and level 3 meanings.[58]

30.12 Procedure. Until the introduction of the CPR, applications for a ruling on meaning were listed before the judge in charge of the jury list, because the original wording of the rule required applications to be made to the judge in chambers, and because the function of the rule was to bring forward the determination of an issue which was otherwise for the trial judge to decide. On the face of para.4(1) of the CPR PD 53, it appears to be open to an applicant to apply either to the master or the judge. However, since the ruling is a substantive one which binds the trial judge, the correct practice is to list applications for, or involving, a ruling on meaning before the judge in charge of the jury list or another designated judge.[59] Applications for a ruling on meaning should be made promptly after the service of the relevant statement of case.[60] Ordinarily they will be determined following a hearing in open court: an argument to the effect that they should be decided routinely on paper was rejected.[61] Following a ruling on meaning, where it is held that the words are incapable of bearing the meaning or meanings attributed to them, the court may exercise its powers to strike out the pleading under CPR r.3.4, or may if appropriate (where there is a case to be salvaged) give the respondent the opportunity to re-plead.

30.13 Malicious falsehood. Although CPR PD 53, para.4(1) relates only to defamation, the court has the power[62] in malicious falsehood, applying the same principles as in defamation, to rule on whether words are reasonably

---

[57] *ICN Photonics Ltd v Patterson* [2003] EWCA Civ 343; *Burstein v Associated Newspapers* [2007] EWCA Civ 600 at [11]–[12].

[58] See para.30.7, above.

[59] This is the practice prescribed in the Queen's Bench Guide, at para.8.2.2 (see *Civil Procedure (The White Book)*, Vol.2, Section 1B); *Church v MGN Ltd* [2012] EWHC 693 (QB); [2013] 1 W.L.R. 284 at [19].

[60] CPR PD 53, para.4(2). The application notice must state that it is an application for a ruling on meaning under the Practice Direction supplementing CPR Pt 53 and the notice or the evidence contained or referred to in it, or served with it, must identify precisely the statement, and the meanings attributed to it, that the court is being asked to consider: see CPR PD 53, paras 4.3 and 4.4.

[61] In *Horlick v Associated Newspapers Ltd* [2010] EWHC 1544 (QB), Eady J. remarked at [10] that in determining the issue of meaning "a judge should be wary of allowing his impression of a newspaper article to be coloured by the detailed submissions of counsel". However, in *Church v MGN Ltd* [2012] EWHC 693 (QB): [2013] 1 W.L.R. 284 Tugendhat J. rejected the defendant's invitation to decide an application for a ruling on meaning (under CPR PD 53, para.4) on paper, holding that such applications should ordinarily be disposed of on the basis of submissions at a hearing in open court.

[62] Under CPR r.3.4(2)(a) ("the statement of case discloses no reasonable grounds for bringing or defending the claim") or CPR r.24.2.

capable of bearing a particular pleaded meaning and to exclude any unreasonable meanings.[63]

Section 3. Trial of Meaning as a Preliminary Issue

Meaning and preliminary issue. An increasing number of decisions on **30.14** meaning have recently been made on applications for the trial of a preliminary issue,[64] rather than by way of a ruling on capability under CPR PD 53, para.4(1), in actions which are not going to be tried by a jury.[65] Indeed, in *Bercow v Lord McAlpine of West Green (No.1)*, Tugendhat J. held that "in very many libel actions, furthering the overriding objective requires that the actual meaning of words complained of be determined at as early a stage in the litigation as is practical".[66] The procedure is likely to be invoked more frequently once the jury ceases to be the tribunal of fact for defamation

---

[63] "The Court of Appeal in *Ajinomoto Sweeteners Europe SAS v Asda Stores Ltd* [2010] EWCA Civ 609; [2010] Q.B. 204 held that any meaning which a reasonable reader could understand the words complained of to bear should go forward. But there was no suggestion that there should also go forward any meaning which the court has held only an unreasonable reader could understand . . . Nor does the judgment of the Court of Appeal in that case cast any doubt on the correctness of importing the principles set out in *Jeynes* into a decision on meaning in a malicious falsehood claim, in order to exclude an unreasonable meaning (as (Tugendhat J.) did: [2009] EWHC 1717 (QB); [2010] Q.B. 204 at para 28)": per Tugendhat J. in *Cruddas v Calvert* [2013] EWHC 1427 (QB) at [63]–[64]. See also *Euromoney Institutional Investor Plc v Aviation News Ltd* [2013] EWHC 1505 (QB) at [96]–[99] to like effect. The Court of Appeal in *Cruddas v Calvert* implicitly endorsed this approach: [2013] EWCA Civ 748 at [30]–[33].

[64] See e.g. *British Chiropractic Association v Singh* [2010] EWCA Civ 350; [2011] 1 W.L.R. 133 in which Eady J.'s preliminary ruling as to the meaning of the words ([2009] EWHC 1101 (QB)) was found to have been in error; *Cook v Telegraph Media Group Ltd* [2011] EWHC 1134 (QB); *Miller v Associated Newspapers Ltd* [2011] EWHC 2677 (QB); *Cammish v Hughes* [2012] EWCA Civ 1655; [2013] E.M.L.R. 13; *Auladin v Shaikh* [2013] EWHC 157 (QB); *Waterson v Lloyd* [2013] EWCA Civ 136; [2013] E.M.L.R. 17 (CA allowing an appeal against Tugendhat J.'s preliminary ruling on meaning); *Cruddas v Calvert* [2013] EWCA Civ 748 (ditto); *Bercow v Lord McAlpine of West Green (No.2)* [2013] EWHC 1342 (QB); *Fox v Boulter* [2013] EWHC 1435 (QB) (Bean J.); *Flood v Times Newspapers Ltd* [2013] EWHC 2182 (QB) (determination of meaning of internet publication).

[65] I.e. where no application has been made under CPR r.26.11 for trial by jury (see *Cook v Telegraph Media Group Ltd* [2011] EWHC 763 (QB), *Thornton v Telegraph Media Group Ltd* [2011] EWCA Civ 748; [2011] E.M.L.R. 29, *McKeown v Attheraces Ltd* [2011] EWHC 3232 (QB) at [13] and *Rothschild v Telegraph Media Group Ltd* [2011] EWHC 3462 (QB) at [63]), or by consent, or where the court has ordered trial by judge alone under s.69(3), Senior Courts Act 1981. If an action is to be tried by a jury, the meaning of the words complained of (and whether they are defamatory at all) is an issue of fact for the jury: see para.32.26, below. See also *Cruddas v Calvert* [2013] EWHC 1427 (QB) at [1] where Tugendhat J. speaks of the parties' agreement to trial by judge alone "making possible" the trial of a preliminary issue to determine the actual meaning of the words complained of.

[66] [2013] EWHC 981 (QB) at [40].

claims,[67] given the narrowing of the issues and the consequent saving in costs that such rulings are apt to produce. Applications for an order that meaning be tried as a preliminary issue are rarely contentious.[68] While the trial of meaning itself ought to be heard by a judge, since it is a determination as if at trial,[69] there is no reason why an application for an order that meaning be tried as a preliminary issue should not be decided by a master.[70] On the hearing of a preliminary issue, the judge[71] is determining the actual single meaning of the words, not delimiting the meanings which the words are capable of bearing. As for the approach to be adopted:

> "It appears to me to be particularly important where, as here, a judge is providing written reasons for his conclusion as to the meaning to be attributed to the words sued upon, that he should not fall into the trap of conducting an over-elaborate analysis[72] of the various passages relied on by the respective protagonists. The parties are entitled to a reasoned judgment but that does not mean that the court should overlook the fact that it is ultimately a question of the meaning which would be put on the words . . . by the ordinary reasonable reader . . . The exercise is essentially one of ascertaining the broad impression made on the hypothetical reader by the (words) taken as a whole."[73]

---

[67] "One of the greatest concerns today is the cost of all litigation in general, and the cost of libel actions in particular. One of the measures which the court has adopted to try to limit the costs is to order the trial of preliminary issues on meaning. These will be more frequent after the Defamation Act 2013 has brought into force the amendment to s.69(1) of the Senior Courts Act, to abolish the right to trial with a jury in a libel action": *Cruddas v Calvert* [2013] EWHC 1427 (QB) at [100], referring to s.11 Defamation Act 2013.

[68] "Such applications have become increasingly common in recent years and, so far as the court and counsel are aware, there has not previously been a report of a contested application, although since the hearing I handed down my reasons for not ruling on actual meaning in *Hamaizia v Comr for Police of the Metropolis* [2013] EWHC 848 (QB). In other cases the parties have in effect agreed, either that there should, or that there should not, be the trial of such a preliminary issue": per Tugendhat J. in *Bercow v Lord McAlpine of West Green (No.1)* [2013] EWHC 981 (QB) at [1].

[69] Note also the reasons why applications under CPR PD 53, para.4(1) for rulings on meaning are heard by a judge rather than a master: see para.30.12, above. These considerations would appear to be of even greater force where what is being sought is a final determination of what the words actually mean.

[70] See, for instance, *Qadir v Associated Newspapers Ltd* [2012] EWHC 2606 (QB); [2013] E.M.L.R. 15 at [2], which records that it was the master who directed that all issues of privilege and malice be tried as preliminary issues.

[71] So far it almost always has been a judge, the sole exception being *Marks & Spencer Plc v Granada Television*, unreported, February 23, 1998, in which Popplewell J. empanelled a jury to decide what the programme complained of meant. But in *Armstrong v Times Newspapers Ltd* [2005] EWHC 2816 (QB), Eady J. decided not to follow this approach: he was troubled by the prospect of the jury drafting in committee, each member contributing his or her own views to produce a special verdict. An appeal against his decision was dismissed: see *Armstrong v Times Newspapers Ltd* [2006] EWCA Civ 519; [2006] 1 W.L.R. 2462.

[72] See *Jeynes v News Magazines Ltd* [2008] EWCA Civ 130 at [14], extracted in para.30.5, above, principle (3).

[73] *Charman v Orion Publishing Group Ltd* [2005] EWHC 2187 (QB) at [11], per Gray J. See also *Miller v Associated Newspapers Limited* [2005] EWHC 557 (QB) at [24] et seq. In *Waterson v Lloyd* [2013] EWCA Civ 136; [2013] E.M.L.R. 17 the Court of Appeal concluded by a majority (McCombe and Laws L.JJ.) that Tugendhat J. had fallen into the trap of analysing the words as a judge rather than as an ordinary reader and of conducting an over-elaborate analysis, and

The principles governing the ascertainment of how the ordinary reasonable reader would interpret a publication are the same whether the judge is addressing the question of its actual meaning or the range of meanings of which it might reasonably be capable.[74] Meaning may also be determined as a preliminary issue in malicious falsehood,[75] albeit that the court will be determining the range of meanings the words in fact bear.[76]

Preliminary issue: fact or comment. The court also has the power to   **30.15**
determine as a preliminary issue whether the words complained of are allegations of fact or comment (or opinion).[77] Where an application is made for a

---

allowed the defendant's appeal against his determination of the meaning. Laws L.J. expressed the view at [66] that the circumscription of over-elaborate analysis when deciding meaning had "a particular resonance in the context of political speech".

[74] In *Waterson v Lloyd*, above, at [17] Richards L.J. confirmed that the principles governing ascertainment of meaning were the same regardless of whether the judge was determining the range of capable meanings or the actual meaning: "As to the court's general approach towards determining the meaning of a publication, it is common ground that the judge was correct to refer to the guidance in *Skuse v Granada Television Ltd* [1996] E.M.L.R. 278 as summarised by Sir Anthony Clarke M.R. in *Jeynes v News Magazines Ltd* [2008] EWCA Civ 130 at [14]." It may be observed that *Skuse* itself was an appeal from a decision of Brooke J. on the actual meaning of the words complained of and whether they were defamatory of the plaintiff. See also *Cruddas v Calvert* [2013] EWCA Civ 748 at [15].

[75] "The Court of Appeal held in *Ajinomoto Sweeteners Europe SAS v Asda Stores Ltd* [2010] EWCA Civ 609; [2010] Q.B. 204 that the single meaning rule does not apply to malicious falsehood. But that was the only point on which the Court of Appeal overturned my judgment. The court did not hold, and was not asked to hold, that the exercise of determining meaning by a trial of a preliminary issue should have been conducted differently, or should not have taken place at all":
Cruddas v Calvert [2013] EWHC 1427 (QB) at [58], per Tugendhat J. See the same judgment at [112] where the judge held that
"subject to one point, the meanings pleaded by the Claimant in . . . the Amended Particulars of Claim, and the meanings pleaded by the Defendants in . . . the Amended Defence, are all meanings within the range of meanings which reasonable readers could understand the words complained of to bear. Given the large circulation of *The Sunday Times*, the words complained of probably were so understood by a substantial number of readers."
The Court of Appeal agreed: [2013] EWCA Civ 748 at [31] and [33].

[76] The single meaning rule does not apply to malicious falsehood: *Ajinomoto Sweeteners Europe SAS v Asda Stores Ltd*, above, as explained further in *Cruddas v Calvert* [2013] EWHC 1427 (QB).
"[In malicious falsehood] the duty of the judge at trial is to indicate the reasonably available meanings, decide if a substantial number of persons would reasonably have understood the words to have such a meaning and then decide, in respect of a meaning which is in fact false and damaging, whether the author was actuated by malice":
Cruddas v Calvert [2013] EWCA Civ 748, per Longmore L.J. (with whom Rafferty L.J. and Sir Stephen Sedley agreed) at [30].

[77] See *British Chiropractic Association v Singh* [2010] EWCA Civ 350; [2011] 1 W.L.R. 133 in which the Court of Appeal allowed the defendant's appeal against a decision that the words consisted of an imputation of fact and substituted its view that they represented an expression of opinion, and *Cammish v Hughes* [2012] EWCA Civ 1655; [2013] E.M.L.R. 13 in which the Court of Appeal took a similar approach: the judge had not determined the issue of fact or comment, but the Court of Appeal held that the words were unarguably comment. In *Euromoney Institutional Investor Plc v Aviation News Ltd* [2013] EWHC 1505 (QB), Tugendhat J. at [34] observed that:
"The court's case management powers under CPR r.3 are wide enough to permit the court to proceed in the manner in which the Court of Appeal proceeded in *Singh* and *Cammish*. And the

preliminary trial of meaning, and there is an issue in the case as to whether the words are fact or comment, the court ought to be invited to rule on this issue too.[78] The court will normally determine meaning first, then decide whether in that meaning the words are fact or comment. But the court's approach to such an application, including as to the order in which it should decide the issues, may vary according to the facts of case.[79] If there is any room for debate about the right approach for the court to take, the parties ought to canvas their respective positions in their skeleton arguments.

30.16 Appeals. In principle, the Court of Appeal should be slow to overturn the reasoned decision of a judge that the words complained of bear or do not bear a particular meaning: it should not disturb his finding unless it is quite satisfied that he was wrong.[80] If the words are capable of the defamatory meaning which the judge has found them to bear, the Court of Appeal will not interfere lightly with his finding of fact. An appellate court ought not to conclude that the judge was wrong unless it is clear that some other meaning applies.[81] Nevertheless, if the appellate tribunal is quite satisfied that the judge's conclusion on meaning is wrong, it is its duty to reverse him.[82] It need not send the issue back to a judge for a retrial: it is in as good a position as a judge to

---

court's duty to have regard to the overriding objective in CPR r.1 may require it to proceed in this way, as the court held in *Cammish*."
See also *Cook v Telegraph Media Group Ltd* [2011] EWHC 1134 (QB) for another instance of the court ruling conclusively on whether the words complained of were fact or comment.

[78] "If the judge is going to make a definitive determination of meaning, he should normally deal with comment at the same time": *Cammish v Hughes*, above, at [43].

[79] In *Burstein v Associated Newspapers Ltd* [2007] EWCA Civ 600; [2007] E.M.L.R. 21 the Court of Appeal took the view that the court should determine meaning first then go to decide the issue of fact or comment: see at [7]–[8] per Keene L.J. (with whom Dyson and Waller L.JJ. agreed), relying upon *Lowe v Associated Newspapers Ltd* [2006] EWHC 320 (QB); [2007] Q.B. 580. In *British Chiropractic Association v Singh*, above, by contrast, the Court of Appeal suggested at [16] and [23] that in some cases the question of whether the words at issue are fact or comment should precede any determination of meaning, and offered no view on what the words actually meant. In *Euromoney Institutional Investor Plc*, above, Tugendhat J. summarised the somewhat uncertain position as follows at [31]:
"In *British Chiropractic Association v Singh* . . . the Court of Appeal held that in some cases the court considering a meaning application may decide first what meaning the words are capable of bearing, and then go on to consider whether that is a statement of fact or opinion. That is what Eady J. did in that case, at the invitation of the parties. But the Court of Appeal made clear that that is not always the best approach. In fact, in *Singh* the Court of Appeal unusually did not make any order on what the words complained of actually meant".

[80] "The Court of Appeal should be slow to differ from any conclusion of fact reached by a trial judge. Plainly this principle is less compelling where his conclusion is not based on his assessment of the reliability of witnesses or on the substance of their oral evidence and where the material before the appellate court is exactly the same as was before him. But even so, we should not disturb his finding unless we are quite satisfied he was wrong":
Skuse v Granada Television Ltd [1996] E.M.L.R 278, 286 per Sir Thomas Bingham M.R.

[81] *Cammish v Hughes* [2012] EWCA Civ 1655; [2013] E.M.L.R. 13 at [31].

[82] *Slim v Daily Telegraph* [1968] 2 Q.B. 157, 186–7 per Salmon L.J. ("If, however, the appellate tribunal is satisfied that the judge's finding of fact is wrong, it is its duty to reverse him. There is no reason why a judge's finding of fact in a libel action should be more sacrosanct than in any other action."), as applied in *Cruddas v Calvert* [2013] EWCA Civ 748 at [18]–[23].

determine what the meaning of the words is.[83] If in a claim for libel and malicious falsehood, the judge selects as the single meaning for libel purposes one of the peripheral meanings in the range relevant to malicious falsehood, the Court of Appeal may very well be satisfied that he has erred, since the single meaning generally speaking has to be the, or a, dominant one.[84]

Section 4. Summary Disposal and Summary Judgment

Introduction. This section is concerned with both the routes by which a defamation claim or issue may be disposed of summarily. These are, first, the procedure introduced by the Defamation Act 1996 for the summary disposal of defamation claims,[85] under which the court is empowered at any stage of the proceedings to consider the strength of the claim and the defences raised, and to dispose of the claim summarily in favour of either party. Thus the claim may be dismissed, or the claimant may obtain judgment and be granted relief including damages, without a trial. The second employs the summary judgment provisions of CPR Pt 24, which provide a route to summary determination in defamation cases for both claimants and defendants.[86] It is the latter route which has been employed most frequently over the last decade or so, notwithstanding the constraints imposed upon its operation by the continuing (if in practice ever less important) right to jury trial.[87]   **30.17**

(a) *Summary disposal under the Defamation Act 1996*

Origins and purpose of Defamation Act procedure. The genesis of the new procedure was a Bill drafted on his own initiative by Lord Hoffmann,[88] and sent to the Lord Chancellor in 1989. The Bill provided a person   **30.18**

---

[83] *Slim v Daily Telegraph*, above, at 177 per Diplock L.J., as applied in *British Chiropractic Association v Singh* [2010] EWCA Civ 350; [2011] 1 W.L.R. 133 at [15].

[84] *Cruddas v Calvert* [2013] EWCA Civ 748 at [32].

[85] The summary procedure is enacted in ss.8, 9 and 10 of the Act, which came into force on February 28, 2000. The rules of court provided for by s.10 are included in CPR Pt 53, namely r.53.2 and PD 53 paras 5.1 to 5.3.

[86] CPR Pt 24 replaced RSC Ord.14. By RSC Ord.14 r.1(2)(a), an application for summary judgment could be made in every action begun by writ other than an action which included a claim by the plaintiff for libel, slander, malicious prosecution, false imprisonment or seduction.

[87] See paras 30.33–30.34, below. It seems that there have only been four judgments arising out of the statutory summary disposal procedure since the last edition of this work was completed in September 2008: *Hughes v Alan Dick & Co. Ltd* [2008] EWHC 2695 (QB), *Supreme Events Ltd v Anderson*, unreported, December 17, 2009, *Robins v Kordowski* [2011] EWHC 1912 (QB), and *Jon Richard Ltd v Gornall* [2013] EWHC 1357 (QB). There have been innumerable CPR Pt 24 applications and judgments in defamation cases during the same period. The chief advantage of opting for the statutory procedure would appear to be the availability of the remedy of a declaration of falsity.

[88] At the time Hoffmann J.

libelled with a means of clearing his reputation quickly, and a defendant, who had inadvertently published defamatory matter, with a route by which a costly "gold-digging" claim could be avoided.[89] The suggested Bill did not obtain the support of the Neill Committee,[90] which raised various objections to its proposals.[91] It was said in particular that there was not a significant number of trivial libels fit for summary disposal, and that a new defence of offer of amends would deal with the problem of newspapers confronted by a "gold-digging" plaintiff seeking to exploit a publishing error by the defendant. However, Lord Hoffmann's proposals were in broad measure included in the draft Defamation Bill issued by the Lord Chancellor's Department for consultation in July 1995. In the introduction to the draft Bill, it was stated that the new summary procedure was "one of the most innovative parts" of the Bill's package of reforms; it not only brought defamation into line with most other proceedings (though by the time it was brought into force this had already been achieved by CPR Pt 24) but created "an entirely new regime, under which every defamation action must come before the judge at an early stage, so that he can decide if the claim is suitable for summary disposal, whether or not the parties have asked him to do so."[92] The provisions relating to summary disposal were incorporated in substance into the eventual Defamation Bill that was placed before Parliament (albeit they made no provision for defamation actions to come before a judge at an early stage), and they were enacted without amendment.

30.19 **Dismissal of claim.** Under the summary disposal procedure the court may dismiss the claim if it appears that it has no realistic prospect of success and there is no reason why it should be tried.[93] In the exercise of this jurisdiction the court has dismissed one claim on the grounds that the words complained of did not bear a defamatory meaning,[94] and another on the grounds that the claimant had no reasonable prospect of establishing malice in reply to a defence of qualified privilege[95]; in another, the court decided that the claimants had no reasonable prospect of establishing that there were persons within the jurisdiction who would either have read the words complained of (published in a German magazine with a small English circulation) or would have

---

[89] See Lord Hoffmann's speech in the debate on the Defamation Bill, House of Lords, March 8, 1996.
[90] The Working Group of the Supreme Court Procedure Committee, chaired by Lord Justice Neill, which examined practice and procedure in defamation.
[91] See the Working Group Report (July 1991), Ch.XVII.
[92] "Reforming Defamation Law and Procedure. Consultation on Draft Bill" (July 1995), para.6.1.
[93] S.8(2). The matters which the court should consider in deciding whether the claim should be tried are set out in s.8(4): see para.30.23, below. "Prospects of success" and "reason to be tried" are distinct tests and the criteria in s.8(4) apply only to the latter: *Mosley v Focus Magazin Verlag GmbH* [2001] EWCA Civ 1030, per Pill L.J. at [2].
[94] *Gillick v Brook Advisory Centres* [2002] EWHC 829 (QB), though Gray J.'s decision was reversed on appeal: [2001] EWCA Civ 1263.
[95] *Fox v Wokingham DC* [2003] EWCA Civ 499.

understood the words to refer to them.[96] A court might conclude that the claim has no reasonable prospect of success because of the strength or merits of a defence.

Judgment for claimant. The court may give judgment for the claimant[97] **30.20** and grant him summary relief[98] if it appears that there is no defence to the claim which has a realistic prospect of success, and that there is no other reason why the claim should be tried.[99]

Defendants' applications. In the first years of the procedure there were a **30.21** number of defendants' applications for summary disposal, sometimes in order to have the claim dismissed,[100] but as often to compel the claimant to have his claim determined under the summary procedure rather than by full jury trial, in accordance with the policy underlying this part of the 1996 Act, namely to ensure that suitable libel actions are inexpensively and speedily disposed of.[101] In such a case, the court must be satisfied that summary relief will adequately compensate the claimant for the wrong which he has suffered.[102]

---

[96] *Mosley v Focus Magazin Verlag GmbH*, above.

[97] A successful claimant's application was made in *James Gilbert Ltd v MGN Ltd* [2000] E.M.L.R. 680, while in *Loutchansky v Times Newspapers Ltd (No.5)* [2001] E.M.L.R. 39 an application for summary disposal of the claimant's damages claim after liability had already been determined in his favour succeeded (see para.30.21, below). In *Downtex v Flatley* [2003] EWCA Civ 1282, the claimant persuaded the Court of Appeal to hold that a defence of qualified privilege was bound to fail. The court accepted that the summary procedure (as under CPR Pt 24) should not involve the conduct of a mini-trial where the defence is fact-sensitive and there is reason to think that further facts may emerge or require investigation at trial before a fair or final conclusion can be reached, but held that it would be wrong to shy away from a determination where there is sufficient material before the court (on the pleadings or in evidence) to allow the court to form a confident view on the prospects of success, and where there is no reason to suppose that the defendant will be able to advance his case significantly better at trial (per Potter L.J. at [31]). In *Lloyd v Ratnatunga* (unreported, March 7, 2007, Eady J.) the cricketer Clive Lloyd obtained the maximum £10,000 damages and a declaration of falsity on his application for the summary disposal of his claim against a Sri Lankan newspaper. For some recent examples of (successful) claimants' applications, see *Robins v Kordowski* [2011] EWHC 1912 (QB) and *Jon Richard Ltd v Gornall* [2013] EWHC 1357 (QB).

[98] Defined in s.9(1).

[99] S.8(3).

[100] See, e.g. *Mosley v Focus Magazin Verlag GmbH*, above; *Gillick v Brook Advisory Centres*, above; and *Fox v Wokingham DC*, above.

[101] *Loutchansky v Times Newspapers Ltd (No.5)* [2001] E.M.L.R. 39 at [25] (affirmed [2002] Q.B. 783 CA).

[102] S.8(3). This effectively means that the court must be satisfied that £10,000 or less (or such other limit as is prescribed under s.9(1)(c)) is an adequate amount of damages. However, the court should consider the adequacy of this level of damages in the context of the other measures of relief that may be granted under s.9(1): see *Burstein v Times Newspapers Ltd* [2001] 1 W.L.R. 579 at 601, per May L.J. That principle was applied in *Mawdsley v Guardian Newspapers Ltd* [2002] EWHC 1780 (QB) at [16] and [56], where Morland J. observed that although an award of £30,000 from a jury might be inadequate compensation on its own, it did not follow that an award of £10,000 by way of summary relief, together with a declaration and an apology, would not be adequate.

A defendant can (indeed probably must)[103] waive an otherwise tenable defence to enable the court to grant a claimant summary relief.[104] The summary disposal process has since fallen out of fashion with defendants, in favour of applying for summary judgment under CPR Pt 24 (and, if appropriate, for a determination of meaning under CPR PD 53 para.4.1) and/or to strike out under CPR Pt 3.4(2).[105]

30.22 Realistic prospect of success. The test to be applied in the assessment of the strength or weakness of the claim and defence is the same, namely existence or absence of realistic prospect of success.[106] This phrase has become familiar not just in the summary judgment context[107] but in other areas also.[108] It has been accepted that the test under s.8 of the Defamation Act 1996 is the same as that under CPR Pt 24.[109] Thus the explanations of Lord Woolf M.R. in *Swain v Hillman*[110] as to the meaning of "no real prospect", and as to the circumstances when the summary procedure should be employed, offer material guidance. He said that:

> "[t]he words 'no real prospect of succeeding' do not need any amplification, they speak for themselves. The word 'real' distinguishes fanciful prospects of success . . . (the words 'no real prospect of succeeding') direct the court to the need to see whether there is a 'realistic' as opposed to a 'fanciful' prospect of success".[111]

---

[103] Otherwise it would not be possible to say that there is no defence to the claim which has a realistic prospect of success within s.8(3).

[104] *Milne v Telegraph Group Ltd* [2001] E.M.L.R. 30; *Green v Times Newspapers Ltd*, unreported, January 17, 2001, Gray J.; *Gillick v Brook Advisory Centres* [2002] EWHC 829 (QB), where the defendants abandoned defences of fair comment and qualified privilege in order to obtain an order that the claim was suitable for summary disposal: in the event, however, they obtained a ruling that the words were not defamatory of the claimant, so the claim was dismissed.

[105] For the likely reasons for this, see para.30.32, below.

[106] In the draft Bill of July 1995 whereas a claim might be dismissed if it appeared to have no realistic prospect of success, the court could not give judgment for the plaintiff if it appeared there was an "arguable defence" of justification or fair comment, or under s.1 (responsibility for publication) or ss.3 or 4 (offer of amends), or that there was no other defence which had a reasonable prospect of success (cl.7 of the draft Bill). In the Defamation Bill all defences had to pass the "realistic prospect of success" test.

[107] CPR r.24.2(a).

[108] E.g. setting aside a default judgment (CPR r.13.3 (1)) and obtaining permission to appeal (see CPR r.52.3 (6)).

[109] *James Gilbert v MGN* [2000] E.M.L.R. 680 at 690–691; *Downtex v Flatley* [2003] EWCA Civ 1282 at [30].

[110] [2001] 1 All E.R. 91.

[111] Ibid. at 92J. Lord Woolf's words were cited with approval by Lord Hope in *Three Rivers DC v Bank of England (No.3)* [2003] 2 A.C. 1 at 260, [94]–[95]. His Lordship said this:
"For the reasons which I have just given, I think that the question is whether the claim has no real prospect of succeeding at trial and that it has to be answered having regard to the overriding objective of dealing with the case justly. But the point which is of crucial importance lies in the answer to the further question that then needs to be asked, which is—what is to be the scope of that inquiry? The method by which issues of fact are tried in our courts is well settled. After the normal processes of discovery and interrogatories have been completed, the parties are allowed to lead their evidence so that the trial judge can determine where the truth lies in the light of that evidence. To that rule there are some well-recognised exceptions. For example, it may be clear as a matter of law at the outset that even if a party were to succeed

The party resisting an application for summary judgment has to have a case which is better than merely arguable.[112]

Reasons why the claim should be tried. The matters which the court   **30.23**
shall have regard to in considering whether a claim should be tried and not disposed of summarily are:

(1) whether all the persons who are or might be defendants in respect of the publication complained of are before the court;

(2) whether summary disposal of the claim against another defendant would be inappropriate;

(3) the extent to which there is a conflict of evidence;

(4) the seriousness of the alleged wrong (as regards the content of the statement and the extent of publication); and

(5) whether it is justifiable in the circumstances to proceed to a full trial.[113]

It follows that claims against two or more defendants (or possible defendants) are unlikely to be the subject of summary disposal unless all defendants are before the court (and not, e.g. beyond the jurisdiction, or not as yet served with proceedings) and it is appropriate so to dispose of the proceedings against all of them. Nor would cases where there is a conflict of evidence usually be regarded as suitable for summary disposal, at least where the conflict relates to issues which are critical or important to the determination of the claim or defence.[114] Moreover, the court will be cautious about ordering summary disposal where the claimant sues on foreign publication and relies

---

in proving all the facts that he offers to prove he will not be entitled to the remedy that he seeks. In that event a trial of the facts would be a waste of time and money, and it is proper that the action should be taken out of court as soon as possible. In other cases it may be possible to say with confidence before trial that the factual basis for the claim is fanciful because it is entirely without substance. It may be clear beyond question that the statement of facts is contradicted by all the documents or other material on which it is based. The simpler the case the easier it is likely to be to take that view and resort to what is properly called summary judgment. But more complex cases are unlikely to be capable of being resolved in that way without conducting a mini-trial on the documents without discovery and without oral evidence. As Lord Woolf said in *Swain v Hillman*, at p.95, that is not the object of the rule. It is designed to deal with cases that are not fit for trial at all."

[112] *International Finance Corp v Utexafrican SRPL* [2001] L.T.L. May 16, Moore-Bick J, citing *Alpine Bulk Transport v Saudi Eagle Shipping Co.* [1986] 2 Lloyd's Rep. 221, on the test for setting aside a default judgment under CPR r.13.3(1), where the defendant has a real prospect of defending the claim. As regards s.8 this approach would be in line with the intentions of Lord Hoffmann. In debate on the Bill in Committee of House of Lords (April 2, 1996) he rejected the "arguable defence" test, and observed that the object of the wording "realistic prospect of success" was to encourage judges to use the power to grant summary relief "in a vigorous, humane and commonsense way".

[113] Defamation Act 1996, s.8(4).

[114] Where such a conflict exists the court would be unable to conclude that the claim or defence had no realistic prospect of success. See, e.g. *HH Sheikha Mouza Al Misnad v Azzaman Ltd* [2003] EWHC 1703 at [33], [42]–[48], and *Downtex v Flatley* [2003] EWCA Civ 1282.

on the presumption of the identity of English and foreign law, where issues of law are raised which arise from a developing area of jurisprudence, and where art.10 ECHR is engaged and summary disposal would interfere with journalists' rights to freedom of expression.[115] The Act would appear to contemplate that in some cases the imputations complained of may be of such gravity, or have achieved such notoriety, that a trial, with its attendant publicity, is necessary, even though the defence to the claim has no realistic prospect of success.[116] Trivial or petty claims, however, are likely to be a target for summary disposal.[117]

30.24 Time for application. The Act enabled provision to be made by rules of court authorising a party to apply for summary disposal at any stage of the proceedings,[118] and by CPR PD 53, para.5.2 an application can be made at any time after the service of particulars of claim. Thus an attempt to obtain summary disposal may be launched well before there has been disclosure of documents or exchange of witness statements, and a party faced with such an application will have to consider whether he should seek an adjournment on the grounds that discovery might elicit information necessary for a precise evaluation of the merits of the claim or defence.[119] Though the court is obliged to consider an early application for summary relief on the material before it, before disposing of a claim summarily it will also wish to be satisfied that evidence is unlikely to emerge which will crucially affect the claimant's prospects of success or the defendant's prospects of successfully defending.[120]

30.25 Summary disposal after decision on liability. In view of the origins of s.8 and its wording it might be thought that applications for summary disposal would have to be made before trial. However, in *Loutchansky v Times Newspapers Ltd*[121] the claimant applied for summary disposal of the remainder of his claim after the jury had found in his favour on liability. There was not enough time for the jury empanelled on the issue of liability to assess damages and the claimant offered to limit his claim to £10,000. The judge

---

[115] *HH Sheikha Mouza Al Misnad v Azzaman Ltd*, above. In that case the developing area of law was *Reynolds* privilege.

[116] In those circumstances, unless the claimant asks for summary relief, summary disposal is likely to be refused on the grounds that such relief will not provide him with adequate compensation. But even if the claimant does apply for summary relief, it is possible, although perhaps somewhat improbable, that the court might still say that the action concerned such a well-publicised and serious libel that it should only be disposed of in a full trial before a jury.

[117] In appropriate circumstances they might be struck out as an abuse of the process: see *Wallis v Valentine* [2002] EWCA Civ 1034; [2003] E.M.L.R. 8 and *Jameel v Dow Jones & Co. Inc.* [2005] EWCA Civ 75; [2005] Q.B. 946.

[118] S.10(2).

[119] *Mosley v Focus Magazin Verlag GmbH*, above, at [19].

[120] *McDonald's Corp v Steel* [1995] 3 All E.R. 615; *S v Gloucester CC* [2000] 3 All E.R. 346 at 373 d–g, May L.J.; *Downtex v Flatley* [2003] EWCA Civ 1282 at [31].

[121] [2001] E.M.L.R. 39.

allowed the application. His reasoning (later upheld by the Court of Appeal)[122] is summarised in these passages:

> "[27] I accept that the word 'claim' which is to be found in section 8 (1) and elsewhere in this section will often be synonymous with 'cause of action', i.e. that it will embrace both liability and damages. But it is, in my judgment, important not to lose sight of the fact that section 8 does not speak of determination of a claim but, rather, of its disposal. A claim is not disposed of by the court until both liability and quantum have been decided.
>
> [28] Bearing in mind the policy of the Act and the wording of section 10, it appears to me that the meaning to be ascribed to the term 'claim' where it appears in section 8 is 'so much of the plaintiff's claim as remains to be disposed of when the application of section 8 is made'."[123]

No jury. Proceedings relating to summary disposal of a claim are to be heard   **30.26**
and determined without a jury.[124]

Summary relief. Where the claimant is granted summary relief the reme-   **30.27**
dies he will obtain will include such of the following as may be appropriate:

(1) a declaration that the statement of which he complains was false and
    defamatory;
(2) an order that the defendant publish or cause to be published a suitable
    correction and apology[125];
(3) damages not exceeding £10,000[126];
(4) an order restraining the defendant from publishing or further publishing
    the matter complained of.[127]

Publication of correction and apology or summary of judg-   **30.28**
ment. Clearly it was considered undesirable that the court should take an
active role in formulating the terms of a correction and apology. Thus the Act
provides for the parties to agree the content of the correction and apology, as
well as the time, manner, form and place of publication.[128] So where there is
a libel in a newspaper for which the claimant is granted summary relief, it is

---

[122] [2001] EWCA Civ 1805; [2002] Q.B. 321. The court did not think that s.10 could be used as an aid to construction of s.8 ([96]), and indicated that an order for publication of an apology would not be appropriate ([100]).

[123] [2001] E.M.L.R. 39 at [27]–[28].

[124] S.8(5).

[125] But this has to be agreed between the parties, and if not agreed the court can only direct publication of a summary of the court's judgment: see para.30.28, and fn.129, below.

[126] The maximum figure is subject to change by order of the Lord Chancellor made by statutory instrument: s.9 (1)(c) and 9(3) of the Act

[127] S.9(1)(d).

[128] S.9(2). Under CPR PD 53, para.5.3(1) the court has power to order the defendant to agree and publish a correction and apology, and to specify the date by which the parties should reach agreement about the content, time, manner, form and place of publication of the correction and apology.

for the parties to agree the wording of the correction and apology and also the issue of the newspaper, and the page, and place on the page, where the correction and apology is to appear, and possibly even its typeface and layout. If the parties cannot reach agreement on the content of the correction of the apology then the court has power to direct the publication of a summary of the court's judgment (by which summary relief was granted).[129] If such a summary cannot be agreed it will be settled by the court.[130] If the parties cannot agree the time, manner, form or place of publication of the correction and apology, the court can intervene by directing the defendant to take such reasonable and practicable steps as the court considers appropriate.[131]

30.29 Practice and procedure. The rules governing the practice and procedure for applications for summary disposal are contained in CPR Pt 53. They incorporate most of the basic rules applying to applications for summary judgment under CPR Pt 24.[132] The application is by notice which must state that it is an application for summary disposal under s.8 of the Act[133] and the contents of the notice or evidence contained or referred to in it or served with it must identify concisely any point of law or provision in a document on which the applicant relies and/or state that the application is made because the applicant believes that on the evidence the respondent has no real prospect of succeeding on the claim or successfully defending the claim and that the applicant knows of no other reason why the disposal of the claim should await trial.[134] The notice must also state whether or not the defendant has made an offer of amends under s.2 of the Act.[135] Section 10(2) of the Act provides for rules authorising the court at any stage of the proceedings to take the initiative and to treat any application or step in the proceedings as an application for summary disposal or to order summary disposal without an application. No such rule has been made. It was probably considered that the court's wide powers of case management under CPR Pt 3 were sufficient to enable the court summarily to dispose of a claim without such an application being made by a party.[136] If a s.8 application is outstanding and has not been disposed of,

---

[129] S.9(2). Now see s.12 Defamation Act 2013. When it comes into force, it will give the court a general power to order the publication of a summary of its judgment when judgment is given for the claimant, but s.8(5) of the 1996 Act remains unaffected: s.12(5), Defamation Act 2013. As the Explanatory Notes to the 2013 Act indicate (para.75): "The summary disposal procedure is a separate procedure which can continue to be used where this is appropriate". See para.9.46, above.

[130] S.9(2). The parties must file with the court drafts of the summary of the court's judgment showing the revisions they (respectively) wish to make, and apply to the court to settle the summary: CPR PD 53, para.5.3(4).

[131] S.9(2). This power must surely extend to the publication of a summary of the judgment, either agreed or settled by the court.

[132] CPR r.53.2(2).

[133] CPR PD 53, para.5.1(1).

[134] CPR PD 53, para.5.1(2) and PD 24 para.2(3).

[135] CPR PD 53, para.5.1(3).

[136] See CPR r.3.1(2) and r.1.4(2)(c).

the rules provide that a summary judgment application under CPR Pt 24 may not be made.[137] On the face of it, the rule would appear to preclude combining the two applications, and Gray J. has doubted the propriety of making successive applications under s.8/Pt.53 and Pt 24.[138] The fact is, however, that in practice applications under each head have been combined without comment.[139]

Offer to make amends. The Act provides for rules of court authorising the court to require a defendant to elect whether or not to make an offer to make amends under s.2.[140] CPR r.53.2(4) is such a rule. The court may direct the defendant to elect whether or not to make an offer to make amends on any application for summary disposal.[141] Under PD 53, para.5.1(3) the application notice must state whether or not the defendant has made such an offer and whether or not it has been withdrawn. The fact that an offer has been made, and has neither been withdrawn nor accepted, does not preclude a court from granting the claimant summary relief on the defendant's application.[142]   **30.30**

(b) *Summary judgment under CPR Part 24*

The Part 24 rubric. Under CPR Pt 24 the court may give summary judgment against a claimant or defendant on the whole of a claim or on a particular issue if: **30.31**

(1) it considers that—
   (a) that the claimant has no real prospect of succeeding on the claim or issue; or
   (b) that the defendant has no real prospect of successfully defending the claim or issue[143]; and

---

[137] CPR r.53.2(3)(a).

[138] *HH Sheika Mouza al Misnad v Azzaman Ltd* [2003] EWHC 1783 (QB) at [15]. It is true that in *Downtex v Flatley* [2003] EWCA Civ 1282 at [3] the practice of combining a s.8 application with one under Pt 24 was noted by the Court of Appeal without disapproval, but the point was not argued. Nevertheless, the s.8 application must be heard and disposed of before that under Pt 24 can be heard. By contrast, in *Hassan v Holburn* [2004] EWCA Civ 789, Sedley L.J. referred to the defendants as having been obliged at first instance (before Mitting J.) to elect between seeking summary disposal under s.8 and summary judgment under Pt 24. However, it is unclear whether the point was argued before the judge.

[139] See e.g. *Blackwell v Bates* [2007] EWHC 3098 (QB).

[140] S.10(2)(f).

[141] Presumably such a direction could not be given when the application for summary relief is made after service of the defence, since s.2(5) of the Act provides that an offer of amends cannot be made after service of the defence.

[142] *Green v Times Newspapers Ltd*, unreported, January 7, 2001, Gray J.

[143] A real prospect of success is one that is more than fanciful: *Swain v Hillman* [2001] 1 All E.R. 91 CA, per Lord Woolf M.R., approved in *Three Rivers DC v Bank of England (No.3)* [2003] 2 A.C. 1 at [94]–[95].

(2) there is no other compelling reason why the case or issue should be disposed of at trial.[144]

This general rule applies against claimants in any type of proceedings, and against defendants in nearly all cases.[145] The governing principles are now very well settled.[146] In particular, it should be noted that Pt 24 is not meant to dispense with the need for a trial where there are issues which should be investigated at the trial, and should not lead to the judge conducting a mini-trial.[147]

30.32 Advantages of CPR Part 24 over section 8, Defamation Act. There is no question that during the last decade or so defamation litigants have been using CPR Pt 24 far more often than the s.8 summary disposal route. This is probably because under s.8 the court can only adjudicate on the whole of the claim or defence, whereas under CPR Pt 24 the application for summary judgment can be confined to a particular issue, for instance the extent of publication, responsibility for publication, qualified privilege, honest comment or malice. A successful application may not be decisive of the action but it will often emasculate the claim or defence and lead to a favourable settlement. Furthermore, the attraction to a claimant of proceeding under CPR Pt 24 rather than s.8 is that he is not confined, if successful, to a limit of £10,000 on an award of damages. He can seek judgment for damages to be assessed. There is in addition a potentially valuable power under Pt 24 to order the claimant or the defendant to pay money into court if the court regards it as possible but improbable that the claim or defence (as the case may be) will succeed.[148]

---

[144] R.24.2. "Compelling" was added by Civil Procedure (Amendment No.3) Rules 2000.

[145] R.24.3. The exceptions as regards defendants are not material.

[146] See in particular *Three Rivers DC v Bank of England (No.3)* [2003] 2 A.C. 1 at [94]–[95] per Lord Hope of Craighead, *ED&F Man Liquid Products Ltd v Patel* [2003] EWCA Civ 472, and for some useful, recent syntheses of the relevant principles see *Easyair Limited v Opal Telecom Limited* [2009] EWHC 339 (Ch) per Lewison J. at [15] and *Credit Suisse International v Ramit Plana OOD* [2010] EWHC 2759 (Comm) per Hamblen J. at [23]–[25].

[147] *Swain v Hillman* [2001] 1 All E.R. 91 CA, per Lord Woolf M.R. at [95]; *Bataille v Newland* [2002] EWHC 1692 (QB), where Eady J. was concerned not to conduct a mini-trial to decide a factual dispute when there was a possibility that cross-examination might undermine the case advanced by a defendant; *Three Rivers DC v Bank of England (No.3)* [2003] 2 A.C. 1 at [94]–[95]; *Armstrong v Times Newspapers Ltd* [2005] EWCA Civ 1007.

[148] PD 24 paras 4, 5. See para.31.45, below; *Olatawura v Abiloye* [2002] EWCA Civ 998; [2003] 1 W.L.R. 275; *Bataille v Newland* [2002] EWHC 1692 (QB). Eady J. refused to make a conditional order for security in *Musa King v Telegraph Group Ltd* [2002] EWHC 1312 (QB). On appeal from Eady J., the power to make a conditional order for security for costs under r.24.6 was considered by the Court of Appeal (*King v Telegraph Group Ltd (Practice Note)* [2004] EWCA Civ 613; [2005] 1 W.L.R. 2282) but the appeal against Eady J.'s refusal to make an order was not pursued. Nonetheless, Brooke L.J. stated at [91] that he had no doubt that Eady J. had been right. The court will discourage misguided applications for summary judgment aimed at obtaining conditional orders for security (*Olatawura*, above, at [22]), and will be reluctant to be drawn into an assessment of the merits beyond what is strictly necessary for summary judgment purposes (at [26]).

CPR Part 24 and the right to trial by jury. The question arose at an   **30.33**
early stage as to how the power to grant summary judgment in defamation
cases could be reconciled with s.69(1) of (what is now) the Senior Courts Act
1981,[149] which grants a party a right to trial by jury where he has applied for
such a trial[150] and the court is satisfied that there is in issue a claim in respect
of (among other causes of action) libel or slander. This point was at the heart
of *Safeway Stores v Tate*,[151] in which the Court of Appeal allowed the
defendant's appeal from a judgment against him under CPR Pt 24, founded on
the judge's conclusion that the defendant had no real prospect of succeeding
on the issue of whether the words complained of were defamatory. Otton L.J.
stated that the right to trial by jury in libel and slander claims provided by
s.69(1) of the Senior Courts Act 1981 was not overridden by the Civil
Procedure Rules,[152] and accordingly CPR r.24.2 did not permit a judge alone
to determine questions of fact which should be decided by a jury. Whether the
words complained of were defamatory was such a question of fact. There was
clearly some judicial apprehension that this decision might be misunderstood
and construed as drastically restricting the operation of CPR Pt 24 in defamation cases, and it was explained some months later by a differently constituted
Court of Appeal in the case of *Alexander v Arts Council of Wales*.[153] The court
pointed out that the basis of the decision in *Safeway Stores* was that there was
a material issue of fact fit to be placed before the jury, namely, whether the
words were defamatory. It would have been different if there had not in reality
been an issue to go to the jury.

> "If the judge had . . . properly come to the conclusion that the words were only
> capable of having a defamatory meaning then it is difficult to see what objection
> there could be to his giving summary judgment on an issue on which there was no
> room for argument . . . The court, that is the judge, would not be 'satisfied that there
> is an issue', whether the words were defamatory, as required by s.69 of the [Senior
> Courts] Act 1981."[154]

---

[149] Formerly, the Supreme Court Act 1981. By s.11 Defamation Act 2013, s.69 of the Senior
Courts Act 1981 is to be amended to exclude the references to libel and slander, which will have
the effect of abrogating the right to jury trial in defamation claims.

[150] In accordance with CPR r.26.11, a provision which has been enforced more rigorously in
recent years: *Thornton v Telegraph Media Group Ltd* [2011] EWCA Civ 748; [2011] E.M.L.R.
29.

[151] [2001] Q.B. 1120.

[152] [2001] Q.B. 1120 at 1131 E–G.

[153] [2001] EWCA Civ 514; [2001] 1 W.L.R. 1840.

[154] Lord Woolf C.J. at [56]. In a similar vein, see the President of the Queen's Bench Division
(Sir Anthony May) in *Khader v Aziz* [2010] EWCA Civ 716; [2011] E.M.L.R. 2 at [23]:
"It is of course axiomatic that, in defamation proceedings, questions of law are for the judge,
but questions of fact are for the jury; so that neither the judge nor this court should presume
to make decisions dependant on issues of fact which ought properly to be left to the jury. But
that does not mean that a claimant can secure a full jury trial simply by asserting that there are
issues of fact."

However, where there are issues fit to be placed before a jury CPR Pt 24 "does not and should not be regarded as giving a right to summary judgment".[155]

30.34 Burden on applicant for summary judgment. The effect of these decisions is to place a considerably higher burden on a party seeking Pt 24 summary judgment in a defamation action than in other actions, at least where there are issues of fact involved (but not, of course, where it has already been decided that the trial will be held before a judge alone).[156] The test is not confined to "no real prospect of success", since the applicant must also establish that there is not, or there will not be, any evidence fit to be left to the jury on the issue in question. In *Alexander v Arts Council of Wales* the question for determination by the Court of Appeal was whether the trial judge was entitled to withdraw the issue of malice from the jury, and this required some definition of what constituted evidence fit to be left to the jury. The decision was that the judge had acted correctly as he rightly concluded that the evidence, taken at its highest, was such that a jury properly directed could not properly reach a necessary factual conclusion: " . . . If the judge had left the issue of malice to the jury and they had found in the claimant's favour, this court would have set that decision aside as being perverse."[157] Buxton L.J. in *Spencer v Sillitoe*[158] described the position post-*Alexander* as follows:

---

[155] *Alexander v Arts Council of Wales*, above, at [58]. In those circumstances the judge should conclude that there is a compelling reason why the case or issue should be disposed of at trial: see per Lord Woolf C.J. at [57].

[156] See *Bray v Deutsche Bank AG* [2008] EWHC 1263 (QB); [2009] E.M.L.R 12 at [28] et seq. which also provides a useful summary of the principles applicable to a claim in defamation which is *not* going to be tried by a jury.

[157] May L.J. at [44]. In discussing what was the appropriate test the Lord Justice referred to the test applied in criminal cases, and cited a passage from *R. v Galbraith* [1981] 1 W.L.R. 1039 at 1042c:

"Where however the prosecution evidence is such that its strength or weakness depends on the view to be taken of a witness's reliability, or other matters which are generally speaking within the province of the jury and where on one possible view of the facts there is evidence upon which a jury could properly come to the conclusion that the defendant is guilty, then the judge should allow the matter to be tried by the jury."

Following May L.J.'s reference in *Alexander v Arts Council of Wales* to the *Galbraith* test in criminal proceedings, Tugendhat J. has expressed the test in these terms:

"Because this is a libel action, where the claimant has a right to trial by jury, the test I must apply on these applications is closely analogous to the test used in criminal trials in the light of *R. v Galbraith* [1981] 1 W.L.R. 1039. This is re-emphasised by May L.J. in *Alexander v Arts Council of Wales* [2001] 1 W.L.R. 1840 at 1852. It is: Could a jury properly directed, and seeking dutifully to comply with the relevant directions, conscientiously reach a conclusion that the applicants were actuated by malice or not? If so, I should leave it to the jury, or at least to a later stage, to determine. But if I am able to conclude that a properly directed and conscientious jury could only decide the issue in favour of the appellant, then it will be my duty to close off that issue so as to save time and money in accordance with the objectives of the Civil Procedure Rules. If that is established, then there is no issue for a jury to decide"

(*Meade v Pugh & Hamilton* [2004] EWHC 408 (QB) at [18]).

[158] [2002] EWCA Civ 1579; [2003] E.M.L.R. 10 at [23]. See also *Wallis v Valentine* [2002] EWCA Civ 1034; [2003] E.M.L.R. 175.

"The question . . . comes down to whether there is an issue of fact on which, on the evidence so far available, the jury could properly, and without being perverse, come to a conclusion in favour of the claimant."

He pointed out that before trial it was unlikely that a judge would be able to find that a witness would necessarily be disbelieved by a jury however implausible his account.[159]

Subject-matter of applications under Part 24. Applications under   **30.35** CPR Pt 24 have become a commonplace feature of defamation litigation. The jurisdiction is flexible and there appears to be no limit to the range of issues typically arising in a defamation action that may properly be made the subject of an application for summary judgment. For example, defendants' applications have been made on the following grounds:

(1) the claimant has no real prospect of proving publication or that a particular person is responsible for publication[160];

(2) the claimant has no real prospect of showing that the words complained of are defamatory of him[161];

(3) the claimant has no real prospect of proving reference[162];

---

[159] [2002] EWCA Civ 1579; [2003] E.M.L.R. 10 at [24]. Simon Brown L.J. observed in the same case at [31]
"I do not think that the court's power properly extends to denying a claimant the chance of persuading a jury, albeit against all the odds, that his account of the meeting is the truth and his adversary's is not. Were the jury in this case actually to find for the claimant, I do not think that this court could then strike down their verdict as perverse; and that, as I believe, is the touchstone by which the r.24 power falls to be exercised in a case like this . . . "
In *Miller v Associated Newspapers Ltd* [2003] EWHC 2799 (QB); [2004] E.M.L.R. 33 at [13], Eady J. directed himself in these terms:
"Specifically in the context of the right to jury trial, judgment should not be given at any stage which has the effect of depriving the parties of a jury decision in any case where the defence may depend at least in part on a finding of fact which would be properly open to that tribunal: see, e.g. *Wallis v Valentine* [2003] E.M.L.R. 8 at [13] and *Branson v Bower* [2002] 2 Q.B. 737 at 744. Thus, even if a judge thinks that a particular factual conclusion for which one side contends is somewhat far-fetched, it is the jury's credulity rather than the judge's that must be kept in mind. The parties should therefore be given the benefit of the doubt: see, e.g. *Spencer v Sillitoe* [2003] E.M.L.R. 10 at [31] and *Bataille v Newland* [2002] EWHC 1692 (QB) at pp.6–7."
(So also in *McKeith v News Group Newspapers Ltd* [2005] EWHC 1162 (QB); [2005] E.M.L.R. 32 at [50].)
[160] Applications succeeded in *Wallis v Valentine* [2002] EWCA Civ 1034; [2003] E.M.L.R. 8, *Campbell v Safra* [2006] EWHC 819 (QB) ("bare assertion (that D has caused publication) is not enough", per Eady J. at [22]), *Khader v Aziz* [2010] EWCA Civ 716; [2011] E.M.L.R. 2, and *Budu v BBC* [2010] EWHC 616 (QB), but failed in *Bataille v Newland* [2002] EWHC 1692 (QB), *Bray v Deutsche Bank AG*, above (a renewed application in the same case, mounted on the same basis, was also unsuccessful: [2009] EWHC 1356 (QB)), and in *Dar Al Arkan Real Estate Development Co. v Al Refai* [2013] EWHC 1630 (Comm).
[161] See e.g. *Baturina v Times Newspapers Ltd* [2010] EWHC 696 (QB); [2010] E.M.L.R. 18 (application mounted on this basis failed); the argument was not pursued by the defendant at the appeal: [2011] EWCA Civ 306; [2011] 1 W.L.R. 1526.
[162] See e.g. *Budu v BBC*, above, in which the defendant's application for summary judgment in respect of one of the articles complained of also succeeded on this ground.

(4) the claimant has no real prospect of establishing that the defendant is responsible for an alleged republication[163];

(5) the claimant has no real prospect of resisting a defence of qualified privilege,[164] honest comment,[165] absolute privilege,[166] justification,[167] or under reg.19 of the Electronic Commerce (EC Directive) Regulations 2002[168];

(6) the claimant has no real prospect of establishing malice.[169]

---

[163] *Baturina v Times Newspapers Ltd*, above.

[164] Applications succeeded in *Regan v Taylor* [2000] E.M.L.R. 549 (CA); *Alexander v Arts Council of Wales*, above; *Kearns v General Council of the Bar* [2003] EWCA Civ 331; [2003] 1 W.L.R. 1357; *Crossland v Wilkinson Hardware Stores Ltd* [2005] EWHC 481 (QB), *Bray v Deutsche Bank AG*, above, *Seray-Wurie v Charity Commission*, above, and *Bowker v Royal Society for the Protection of Birds* [2011] EWHC 737 (QB) and failed in *Spencer v Sillitoe* [2002] EWCA Civ 1579; [2003] E.M.L.R. 10, and *W v H* [2008] EWHC 399 (QB); [2009] E.M.L.R. 11.

[165] *Branson v Bower* [2002] Q.B. 737, *Keays v Guardian Newspaper Ltd* [2003] EWHC 1565 (QB), *Waterson v Lloyd* [2013] EWHC 2201 (QB). In *Burstein v Associated Newspapers Ltd* [2007] EWCA Civ 600; [2007] 4 All E.R. 319; [2007] E.M.L.R. 21 the defendant's application failed at first instance but succeeded in the Court of Appeal.

[166] Successful applications were made in *Gray v Avadis* [2003] EWHC 1830 (QB) (complaint to Office for the Supervision of Solicitors); *Tufano v Vincenti* [2006] EWHC 1496 (QB) (psychiatrist's report for family proceedings); *Buckley v Dalziel* [2007] EWHC 1025 (QB); [2007] 1 W.L.R. 2933 (witness statement given to police) and *Westcott v Westcott* [2008] EWCA Civ 818; [2009] Q.B.407 (oral complaint and subsequent written statement to police).

[167] Applications succeeded in *Johnson v Perot Systems Europe Ltd* [2005] EWHC 2450 (QB), *H v Tomlinson* [2008] EWCA Civ 1258; [2009] E.L.R. 14, *Ali v Associated Newspapers Ltd* [2010] EWHC 100 (QB), *Budu v BBC*, above, *Dee v Telegraph Media Group Ltd* [2010] EWHC 924 (QB); [2010] E.M.L.R. 20, and *King v Grundon* [2012] EWHC 2719 (QB). Applications failed in *Musa King v Telegraph Newspapers Ltd* (above); *Pedder v Associated Newspapers Ltd* [2003] EWHC 1219 (QB), and in *Jameel v Times Newspapers Ltd* [2003] EWHC 2609 (QB). (This part of Gray J.'s judgment was not taken to the Court of Appeal: [2004] EWCA Civ 983; [2004] E.M.L.R. 31.) For some pre-CPR precursors of these authorities, see *Levene v Roxhan* [1970] 1 W.L.R. 1322 (CA) and *Robson v News Group Newspapers Ltd*, unreported, October 9, 1995.

[168] *Kaschke v Gray* [2010] EWHC 690 (QB); [2011] 1 W.L.R. 452. Stadlen J. concluded that it would be inappropriate to grant summary judgment to the defendant information society service provider who operated the website blog where the article complained of had been published where there was a real prospect that he might not establish at trial that he could avail himself of the reg.19 defence because his control over the blog arguably went beyond mere storage of information.

[169] Applications seeking summary judgment in respect of pleas of malice are (at a high level of generalisation) more apt to succeed owing to the special, more exacting, pleading requirement, applicable only to pleas of malice and other species of dishonesty, that a claimant must plead a case which is more consistent with the presence of malice than its absence: see *Bray v Deutsche Bank AG* [2008] EWHC 1263 (QB); [2009] E.M.L.R 12 at [35], citing *Telnikoff v Matusevitch* [1991] 1 Q.B. 102 and *Three Rivers DC v Bank of England (No.3)* [2001] UKHL 16; [2003] 2 A.C. 1, and *Ashcroft v Foley (No.2)* [2012] EWHC 2214 (QB); [2012] E.M.L.R. 32 at [10]–[14] (special rule does not apply to pleas of justification). Applications succeeded in *Alexander v Arts Council of Wales* [2001] EWCA Civ 514; [2001] 1 W.L.R. 1840; *Milne v Express Newspapers* [2004] EWCA Civ 664; [2005] 1 W.L.R. 772 (in the context of offer of amends); *Webster v British Gas* [2003] EWHC 1188 (QB), *Seray-Wurie v Charity Commission* [2008] EWHC 870 (QB), *Bray v Deutsche Bank AG* [2009] EWHC 1356 (QB), *Khader v Aziz* [2010] EWCA Civ 716; [2011] E.M.L.R. 2, *Henderson v London Borough of Hackney* [2010] EWHC 1651 (QB), *France v Freemans Solicitors* [2010] EWHC 3291 (QB) and *Bowker v Royal Society for the Protection of Birds* [2011] EWHC 737 (QB), but failed in *Clarke v Davey* [2002] EWHC 2342

Similarly, claimant's applications for summary judgment have proceeded on the following grounds:

(1) the defendant has no real prospect of making good a pleaded defence of qualified privilege,[170] justification,[171] or honest comment[172];

(2) the defendant has no real prospect of making good a case that the words complained of did not refer to the claimant,[173] or of defeating an argument for a presumption of substantial publication on the internet;[174]

(3) the defendant has no real prospect of defeating a case of malice pleaded in response to a defence of qualified privilege (i.e. that his case of malice is bound to be upheld at trial).[175]

(QB), *Komarek v Ramco Energy Plc* [2002] EWHC 2501 (QB), *Branson v Bower* [2002] Q.B. 737 (an honest comment case), *John v Associated Newspapers Ltd* [2006] EWHC 1740 (QB) (where D sought to attack C's plea of malice under s.4(3) of the Defamation Act 1996 in answer to a defence of offer of amends: cf. *Milne v Express Newspapers* (above)) and *Hughes v Risbridger* [2009] EWHC 3244 (QB).

[170] Applications succeeded in *Miller v Associated Newspapers Ltd* [2003] EWHC 2799 (QB); [2004] E.M.L.R. 33, and in *McKeith v News Group Newspapers Ltd* [2005] EWHC 1162 (QB); [2005] E.M.L.R. 32, both cases of *Reynolds* privilege, and in the non-*Reynolds* case of *Wood v Chief Constable of West Midlands* [2004] EWCA Civ 1638; [2005] E.M.L.R. 20. Applications to rule out *Reynolds* privilege are less likely to succeed than those where the privilege is the traditional common law kind, because they will tend to be more fact-sensitive: *Seray-Wurie v Charity Commission*, above, at [22]. The claimant's application for summary judgment in a *Reynolds* privilege case failed before the Court of Appeal in *Armstrong v Times Newspapers Ltd* [2005] EWCA Civ 1007 (having succeeded at first instance). A claimant's application failed in *Hamilton v Clifford* [2004] EWHC 1542 (QB). It is noteworthy that in *Miller v Associated Newspapers Ltd*, above, Eady J. criticised the tendency to plead *Reynolds* privilege in vague terms and then to try to avoid Pt 24 sanctions by resorting to the dicta of Bingham M.R. in *E v Dorset County Council* [1995] 2 A.C. 233, to the effect that in an area of developing jurisprudence an order striking out should not have been made: "That is an important principle, but it is not to be regarded as a mantra which will guarantee a way around the disciplines of pleading" at [7]. He would have been surprised

"if their Lordships believed, after the exposition of the law and practical guidance offered in *Reynolds* itself and shortly afterwards in *Turkington*, that the law itself was still in a state of development" (at [33]).

[171] Successfully in *Hamilton v Clifford*, above, *Jameel v Times Newspapers Ltd* [2005] EWHC 1219 (QB) and *Gregg v O'Gara* [2008] EWHC 658 (QB); unsuccessfully in *Hewitt v Grunwald* [2004] EWHC 2959 (QB). In *Berezovsky v Russian Television and Radio Broadcasting Co.* [2009] EWHC 1733 (QB), Eady J., in acceding to a defendant's application to set aside a judgment which had been entered against him in default of acknowledgement of service, rejected the claimant's argument that the defendant's defence of justification had no real prospect of success.

[172] *Hamilton v Clifford*, above.

[173] *Club La Costa (UK) Plc v Gebhard* [2008] EWHC 2552 (QB). The application failed. Tugendhat J. held that he was not in a position to determine whether or not D's "no reference" defence had a real prospect of success.

[174] The argument and the application failed: *Al Amoudi v Brisard* [2006] EWHC 1062 (QB); [2007] 1 W.L.R. 113.

[175] Nevertheless, no application mounted on this basis has (ultimately) succeeded. In *Hayter v Fahie* [2008] EWCA Civ 1336 the judge had granted summary judgment to C on the footing that a jury would be perverse to conclude that D had not acted maliciously in publishing the words complained of. The Court of Appeal set aside this order and directed a trial, observing that an

30.36 The approach which the court will take. Eady J. provided a helpful example of how the courts should approach applications for summary judgment in defamation actions which are to be tried by jury, when he ruled on a defendant's Pt 24 application founded on the contention that the claimant had no real prospect of succeeding in proving publication[176]:

"First, it seems that I should address the primary facts relied upon by the claimant for establishing the defendant's responsibility for the publication of the 12th January letter. The burden is upon the claimant to establish those facts at trial. At this stage, I should make all assumptions in favour of the claimant so far as pleaded facts are concerned.[177]

Again, in so far as evidence has been introduced for the purpose of the present application, I should assume that those facts will be established, save in so far as it can be demonstrated on written evidence that any particular factual allegation is indisputably false.[178]

The next question is whether, on the facts assumed, a properly directed jury could draw the inference for which the claimant contends. In this case, of course, the inference is that the second defendant was, in some sense, a participant in the publication of the letter. I should only rule out the case against the second defendant if I am satisfied that a jury would be perverse to draw that inference . . .

If the defendant's case is so clear that it cannot be disputed, there would be nothing left for a jury to determine. If, however, there is room for legitimate argument, either on any of the primary facts or as to the feasibility of the inference being drawn, then a judge should not prevent the claimant having the issue or issues resolved by a jury. I should not conduct a mini trial or attempt to decide the factual dispute of first appearances when there is the possibility that cross-examination might undermine the case that the defendant is putting forward."[179]

---

issue concerning D's state of mind should not have been determined summarily. The court reached the same conclusion in *Hughes v Alan Dick & Co. Ltd* [2008] EWHC 2695 (QB) at [16].

[176] *Bataille v Newland* [2002] EWHC 1692 (QB). There were concurrent applications to strike out under CPR r.3.1(2)(k) and r.3.4(2)(a) and (b).

[177] Unless the facts being contended for are inherently improbable: see *Fashion Gossip Ltd v Esprit Telecoms UK Ltd* [2000] EWCA 235, and the (minority) remarks of Carnwath L.J. in *Khader v Aziz* [2010] EWCA Civ 716; [2011] E.M.L.R. 2 at [46]–[48]

("We were asked, by both parties, to assume that it could be proved at trial that these nonsensical words were indeed spoken by Mr Dowd. This was said to be the correct approach to an application for summary judgment under CPR Part 24 . . . Eady J. proceeded on the same basis. For my part, I am unable to see why the court should be so constrained. This was not an application under the 'striking-out' provisions, which direct attention to whether the statement of case itself discloses reasonable grounds for bringing the claim (rule 3.4(2)(a)). The issue under rule 24.2 is simply whether the claimant has a 'real prospect of succeeding on the claim' (rule 24.2(a)(i)). Under that rule there seems to be no reason why the court should be required to assume proof of allegations, merely because they are pleaded.").

[178] That the approach outlined by Eady J. in the first two paragraphs of this extract from *Bataille* is in substance the correct one for the court to take is supported by the decision of the Court of Appeal in *Campbell v Frisbee* [2002] EWCA Civ 1374; [2003] E.M.L.R. 3 at [11] per Lord Phillips M.R. giving the judgment of the court; see also *Bray v Deutsche Bank AG* [2008] EWHC 1263 (QB); [2009] E.M.L.R. 12 per Tugendhat J. at [38]–[39].

[179] Eady J. also suggested that he could not be confident that "all the cards are on the table" and that would prevent him from granting summary judgment; see also *Dar Al Arkan Real Estate Development Co. v Al Refai* [2013] EWHC 1630 (Comm). Similarly,

"On an application for summary judgment the court cannot resolve disputed questions of fact, although if it is clear beyond question that the respondent to the application will not be able to

Practice and procedure. An application for summary judgment may be   **30.37**
made as soon as the defendant has filed acknowledgment of service[180]: cf.
summary disposal applications under s.8 of the 1996 Defamation Act, which
may be made after service of the particulars of claim, whether or not service
has been acknowledged.[181] An application under CPR Pt 24 may not be made
if an application has been made for summary disposal under s.8 of the
Defamation Act 1996, and that application has not been disposed of, or has
been granted.[182] In practice, joint s.8 and Pt 24 applications have been made
without attracting adverse comment,[183] although current practice is generally
to proceed under Pt 24 only. Where a party makes an application under Pt 24,
it is usual practice to accompany it with a (contingent) application under CPR
r.3.4(2), in order to achieve the striking out of the relevant part of the
statement of case in the event that summary judgment is granted. Furthermore,
it is not uncommon for applications for summary judgment under Pt 24 and
to strike out under CPR r.3.4(2)(a) or (b) to be advanced in tandem (i.e. in a
"further or alternatively" format).[184]

The summary judgment application should be listed before the master,
although the master may refer it to a judge.[185] However, if it is combined with
an application for a ruling on meaning under CPR PD 53, para.4(1), it should
be listed before the judge in charge of the jury list or another designated
judge.[186]

In the light of the decision in *Armstrong v Times Newspapers Ltd*,[187] the
grounds for the application should be set out in clear terms either in the
application notice or in the supporting evidence: generalities risk taking
the respondent by surprise, and ambushes will not be tolerated. In *Armstrong*,
the claimant's notice of application had given only the most general grounds
for the application, namely that the defendants had no real prospect of
successfully establishing a *Reynolds* defence, so the defendants decided that

---

establish the facts on which he relies (which may be because there is some inherent improbabil-
ity in what is being asserted or some extraneous evidence which contradicts it) the court may
enter summary judgment"
(*Bezant v Rausing* [2007] EWHC 1118 (QB), per Gray J., citing *Celador Productions Ltd v Boone*
[2004] EWHC 2362 (Ch) at [6]–[7], approved by the CA in *Doncaster Pharmaceuticals v The
Bolton Pharmaceutical Co.* [2006] EWCA Civ 661 at [4]).

[180] CPR r.24.4(1).
[181] CPR PD 53, para.5.2.
[182] CPR r.53.2 (3).
[183] See fn.138, above.
[184] Although it is commonplace for applicants to proceed in this way, the logic of doing so is
questionable. Assuming that there is a sound basis for an application under CPR Pt 24, there
would appear to be no reason to proceed under either CPR r.3.4(2)(a) or (b): CPR Pt 24 is a more
flexible power, and the condition for striking out is more difficult to satisfy, such that it is hard
to conceive of an application succeeding under CPR r.3.4(2)(a) or (b) which failed under Pt 24.
Under these circumstances, does this frequently employed practice constitute good practice? See
further para.30.38, below.
[185] CPR PD 24, para.3.
[186] See para.30.12, above.
[187] [2005] EWCA Civ 1007.

there was no need to put in evidence. Shortly before the hearing, the claimant served a substantial skeleton argument which raised issues as to the truth of a number of matters asserted in the defence. Had the claimant set out the grounds of the application for summary judgment in the notice, the defendants would have been able to decide what evidence to adduce, in order to show the judge that there were evidential issues fit for trial, but as it was, the claimant's approach was "entirely unsuitable",[188] and the defendants faced a mini-trial for which they were inevitably unprepared. The Court of Appeal allowed their appeal and restored the defence of qualified privilege.

SECTION 5. STRIKING OUT STATEMENTS OF CASE

30.38 Striking out statements of case: CPR rule 3.4(2). This rule[189] enables the court to strike out a statement of case (or of course a part of it) if it (1) discloses no reasonable grounds for bringing or defending the claim, (2) is an abuse of the court's process or otherwise likely to obstruct the just disposal of the proceedings, or if (3) there has been a failure to comply with a rule, practice direction or court order. The jurisdiction to strike out is frequently invoked in defamation, although it is now common practice for applications under r.3.4(2)(a) to be combined with applications for summary judgment under Pt 24, which has become the weapon of choice for the litigant seeking to shut out an issue.[190] It is unclear what, if anything, such "double-barrelled" applications achieve (or whether it makes any sense to proceed in this way[191]): the court tends to decide such applications under Pt 24,[192] though sometimes the basis on which judgment is given borders on the ambiguous.[193]

When such applications are made, the court will take a different approach to the two limbs: on the application to strike out, the court will assume the truth of facts which appear from the pleadings to be common ground, but in the case of facts which are in dispute, the court must act on the assumption that the facts are correctly stated in the statement of case which is under attack.[194] It is not entirely clear how far evidence is admissible on an application to strike out, but it is submitted that where the application is founded on

---

[188] For the reasons given by Lord Hope in *Three Rivers DC v Bank of England (No.3)* [2003] 2 A.C. 1 at [95].

[189] CPR r.3.4(2) is the descendent of the old RSC Ord.18 r.19.

[190] See para.30.35, above.

[191] See fn.184, above.

[192] See for instance *Sharma v Jay* [2003] EWHC 1230 (QB); *Bataille v Newland* [2002] EWHC 1692 (QB); *Dar Al Arkan Real Estate Development Co. v Al Refai* [2013] EWHC 1630 (Comm).

[193] See, e.g. the language used in *Wood v Chief Constable of West Midlands Police* [2003] EWHC 2971 (QB); [2004] E.M.L.R. 17 [59]: "No useful purpose would be achieved by not giving summary judgment that the plea of qualified privilege be struck out", and by the Court of Appeal in the same case ([2004] EWCA Civ 1638; [2005] E.M.L.R. 20 at [17])).

[194] *Sharma v Jay*, above, at [15]–[16]; *Collins Stewart v Financial Times Ltd* [2004] EWHC 2337 (QB); [2005] E.M.L.R. 5 at [24]. This distinction is reflected in the remarks of Carnwath L.J. in *Khader v Aziz* [2010] EWCA Civ 716; [2011] E.M.L.R. 2 at [46]–[48], quoted in full in fn.177, above. The corollary of Carnwath L.J.'s observations concerning CPR Pt 24 is that for the

a pleading point—that is, on the basis that the statement of case discloses no reasonable grounds for bringing or defending the claim (under CPR r.3.4(2)(a))—evidence will be irrelevant and inadmissible,[195] whereas the position will plainly be different where the application is founded on abuse, failure to comply with a rule or one of the other grounds identified in r.3.4(2)(b) and (c). By contrast, on the application for summary judgment, evidence is admissible and is almost invariably adduced.[196]

Management of cases: the impact of the CPR. While technical plead-   **30.39** ing points have been received less enthusiastically by the courts since the advent of the CPR,[197] the power to strike out has been given extra potency by CPR case management principles. It was authoritatively observed pre-CPR that:

> "The trial of [an] action should concern itself with the essential issues and the evidence relevant thereto and . . . public policy and the interest of the parties require that the trial should be kept strictly to the issues necessary for a fair determination of the dispute between the parties".[198]

---

purpose of CPR r.3.4(2)(a) the court *should* "assume proof of allegations merely because they are pleaded".

[195] No evidence was admissible on an application under Ord.18, r.19(1)(a), the predecessor of CPR r.3.4(2)(a), but there is no equivalent provision in the CPR. For indications of current judicial thinking, see *Sharma v Jay* (above) at [15]–[16] and the words of Eady J. in *Bataille v Newland* (above):

> "I must focus on the claimant's pleaded case in the first instance. That is all I am permitted to do for the purposes of the strike-out application . . . . As to the Part 24 application, however, I can have regard also to evidence for determining whether the claimant's case has no realistic prospect of success".

[196] A reminder of the usual practice is found in *Hewitt v Grunwald* [2004] EWHC 2959 (QB), where it was agreed that the strike-out application under r.3.4(2), on which evidence was not admissible, would be dealt with first, while the Pt 24 application would be adjourned to give the defendants an opportunity, if they wished, to put in evidence. Occasionally it will not be necessary to adduce evidence in support of an application under CPR Pt 24: if the application rests on admissions in the pleadings of the party whose case is under challenge, for instance. Otherwise, if there is any room for doubt concerning the facts relied on in support of an application for summary judgment, evidence ought to be proffered.

[197] Note the words of Sedley L.J.:

> " . . . defamation practitioners may do well to accustom themselves to that fact that the wind of change in civil procedure is blowing on them as it blows on everybody else. The kind of pleading issue that (counsel) . . . has run before us today is now history. It is perfectly plain what this case is about. What it requires is trial or settlement, not interlocutory jockeying for forensic advantage"

(*Dwek v MacMillan Publishers* [2000] E.M.L.R. 284 at 294). Note also Lord Woolf M.R.'s exhortation in *McPhilemy v Times Newspapers Ltd* [1999] 3 All E.R. 775 at 793:

> "Unless there is some obvious purpose to be served by fighting over the precise terms of a pleading, contests over their terms are to be discouraged. In this case the distinct impression was given by the parties that both sides were engaged in a battle of tactics. Each side was seeking to fight the action on, what from that party's perspective appeared to be, the most favourable ground. The dispute over particulars was just being used as a vehicle for that purpose."

[198] *Polly Peck v Trelford* [1986] Q.B. 1000 at 1021, per O'Connor L.J.; *Rechem International Ltd v Express Newspapers Ltd*, unreported, June 12, 1992, CA; *US Tobacco v BBC* [1998] E.M.L.R. 816 at 828–829, per Nicholls L.J.

Since the implementation of the CPR, the court has been expressly charged with a duty to manage cases actively,[199] allotting to each an appropriate share of the court's resources[200] and dealing with each proportionately,[201] in particular by identifying the issues at an early stage and deciding promptly which need full investigation and trial and disposing summarily of the others.[202] In managing cases the court may exclude an issue from consideration.[203] Indeed, proportionality requires the court to limit a case strictly to the central issues necessary for its fair resolution and to exclude all peripheral side-issues and disputes.[204] The courts are eager to keep libel actions within manageable and economic bounds, and will strive to manage cases so as to minimise the burden on litigants and the court which:

> "includes excluding all peripheral material which is not essential to the just determination of the real issues between the parties, and whose examination would be disproportionate to its importance to those issues".[205]

Even where a defendant is putting forward an allegation central to his defence, the court will exercise control over the manner in which that is done and limit the costs involved.[206] In these circumstances, the parties to litigation, discharging their own obligation to help the court to further the overriding objective,[207] should take care not to raise any unnecessary issues in their statements of case.[208]

30.40 Applications by claimant. The defence is subject to the general rules of pleading and, if it, or any part, of it discloses no reasonable defence, the claimant may apply to have it struck out.[209] The court should, however, only

---

[199] CPR r.1.4(1).

[200] CPR r.1.1(2)(e).

[201] CPR r.1.1(2)(c).

[202] CPR r.1.4(2)(b), (c).

[203] CPR r.3.2(k). In defamation cases judges have been particularly keen to put this principle to work in relation to issues of damages: see e.g. *Adelson v Associated Newspapers Ltd* [2007] EWHC 997 (QB), at [89]–[98]; *Clarke (t/a Elumina Iberica UK) v Bain* [2008] EWHC 2636 (QB), at [35]–[68]; *El Naschie v Macmillan Publishers Ltd* [2011] EWHC 1468 (QB) at [30]–[36].

[204] *McPhilemy v Times Newspapers Ltd* [1999] 3 All E.R. 775 at 791, per May L.J.; *Cook v News Group Newspapers Ltd* [2002] EWHC 1070 (QB), Eady J.

[205] *McPhilemy v Times Newspapers Ltd* [1999] 3 All E.R. 775 at 791, per May L.J. See also *Tancic v Times Newspapers Ltd, The Times,* January 12, 2000, CA, and *McKeith v News Group Newspapers Ltd* [2005] EWHC 1162 (QB); [2005] E.M.L.R. 32 at [17]. Note also Eady J.'s determination in *Armstrong v Times Newspapers Ltd* [2004] EWHC 2928 (QB) to isolate the "real issues" in the action and to excise superfluous material. The judge's decision in *Armstrong* was later reversed ([2005] EWCA Civ 1007), but in this respect his approach was commended by the Court of Appeal at [53].

[206] *McPhilemy v Times Newspapers Ltd,* above, at 794.

[207] CPR r.1.3.

[208] *Ontulmus v Collett* [2013] EWHC 980 (QB), per Tugendhat J. at [23]–[28].

[209] CPR r.3.4(2)(a). See paras 27.6, 27.16 and 27.25, above for the general pleading requirements for the defences of justification, honest comment and qualified privilege. The leading case is now *Ashcroft v Foley* [2012] EWCA Civ 423; [2012] E.M.L.R. 25 in which the Court of Appeal held that Eady J. had been entitled to strike out defences of justification and honest comment, and to have refused the defendants permission to amend their defence, where the defences and

exercise its power to strike out in a clear case.[210] Thus, a plea of justification and other substantive defences will only be struck out in a plain and obvious case, where the defendant's position is unarguable.[211] Where the material complained of is not capable of bearing a *Lucas-Box* meaning attributed to it by the defendant, that meaning will be struck out, although the correct route to achieving this result will be to make an application for a ruling on meaning under CPR PD 53, para.4(1), coupled with a contingent application to strike out.[212] Particulars of justification will not be struck out on the ground that there will be no evidence to support them unless they meet the test of being "incurably bad".[213] They will be struck out where they are not capable of

---

proposed amendments were pleaded without sufficient and proper particularity, and the intended *Lucas-Box* meanings were vague, unclear and incoherent. For another recent example of the court striking out the whole of a plea of justification, having found that it was defective in a number of discrete ways, see *Radu v Houston* [2009] EWHC 398 (QB).

[210] *Kemsley v Foot* [1952] A.C. 345; *Cadam v Beaverbrook* [1959] 1 Q.B. 413; *Buttes Gas & Oil Co. v Hammer* [1975] 1 Q.B. 557.

" . . . this is a striking-out application, and in relation to any striking-out application two things at least are clear. First, in considering any application to strike out, the courts will not go outside the pleadings themselves. Secondly, the courts will only exercise their undoubted right to strike out all or part of the pleadings in a very clear case"
(per Roskill L.J. at 577).

[211] *Waters v Sunday Pictorial Newspapers* [1961] 1 W.L.R. 967: the power to strike out:
"is only to be exercised where it is clear that the defences which have been put forward cannot really succeed, so that it may be proper to strike them out at such an early stage in the action. But, unless that is reasonably plain, it is a jurisdiction which in practice is not exercised, and it is a jurisdiction which is exercised only with the greatest care"
(per Danckwerts L.J. at 974). See *Aspro Travel Ltd v Owners Abroad Group* [1996] 1 W.L.R. 132 CA at 140: "The test when it is sought to strike out a pleading is whether the facts there alleged are arguably capable of supporting the plea." By way of example of cases in which a defence of justification was struck out, see *Howden v Truth and Sportsman* (1937) 58 C.L.R. 416:
"The imputation contained in a statement that a man has been convicted of an indictable offence and sentenced to imprisonment is not, in my opinion, sustained by proof of a conviction and sentence quashed on appeal, and no finding that the imputation was true should be allowed to stand . . . To leave the pleas standing in their present form would cause an embarrassment at the trial and a danger of miscarriage which can only be avoided by striking them out"
(per Dixon J. at 421); *Davis v Stewart* (1868) 18 Up.Can.C.P. 482; *Cuddington v Wilkins* (1616) Hobart 67 at 81; *Alexander v N.E. Ry* (1865) 6 B. & S. 340 at 344: "Any person who asserted that the plaintiff was convicted, knowing that the conviction had been quashed, would publish a libel." (per Blackburn J.); *Leyman v Latimer* (1878) 3 Ex.D. 15 at 21:
"It is not true to say of the plaintiff that he is a convicted felon; he is a convicted felon who is in the position of a pardoned felon, and the felony is at the time extinguished."

[212] See paras 30.2–30.3, above and Section 1 of this chapter more generally. For comparative purposes, see *JWH Group Pty Ltd v Buckeridge (No.3)* [2009] WASC 271 in which Le Miere J., in the Supreme Court of Western Australia, struck out certain imputations advanced by the defendant as part of a plea of justification.

[213] *McDonald's Corp v Steel* [1995] 3 All E.R. 615:
"The power to strike out is a draconian remedy which is only to be employed in clear and obvious cases . . . I anticipate therefore that it will only be in a few cases where it will be possible to say at an interlocutory stage and before full discovery that a particular allegation is *incapable* of being proved".
(per Neill L.J. at 623).

Note, however, that the court will not investigate at the interlocutory stage whether a defendant has a proper evidential basis for a defence of justification: *Ashcroft v Foley (No.2)* [2012] EWHC 2214 (QB); [2012] E.M.L.R. 32, per Eady J.

supporting a pleaded *Lucas-Box* meaning.[214] They will also be struck out where the meaning sought to be justified is one of "reasonable grounds for suspicion" and they relate to matters which occurred after the publication complained of,[215] or if they offend against any of the other special rules which govern what can be pleaded in justification of such a meaning.[216] A plea of qualified privilege will not be struck out where it is arguable whether the sender and recipient of the allegedly defamatory communication had corresponding interests in its contents.[217] A plea of qualified privilege will, however, be struck out where the defendant plainly had no obligation to put the relevant defamatory allegations into the public domain and a wide publication was clearly not fairly warranted by the occasion.[218] Facts alleged in support of a defence of qualified privilege which arose or came to the attention of the defendant after the publication of the material complained of will be struck out on the grounds that they cannot have had any bearing on the defendant's alleged duty to publish.[219] The same goes for facts alleged in support of a defence of honest comment which arose after the publication of the relevant comment.[220] Furthermore, a defence of honest comment will be struck out

---

[214] "Each sub-paragraph of the particulars of justification should be relevant to and supportive of one or more of the defamatory meanings sought to be justified. Of course, it is right that some material may appear as necessary background, but it must genuinely form part of the narrative for the purpose of achieving that ultimate objective. It is obviously not appropriate to include allegations merely with a view to creating a climate of prejudice":
Hunt v Times Newspapers Ltd [2012] EWHC 110 (QB), per Eady J. at [24]. See also *Jameel v Times Newspapers Ltd* [2005] EWHC 1219 (QB) for an example of a case where a plea of justification based on a level 3 *Lucas-Box* meaning was struck out because it was inadequately supported by the pleaded particulars.

[215] *Bennett v News Group Newspapers Ltd* [2002] E.M.L.R. 39; *Chase v News Group Newspapers Ltd* [2002] EWCA Civ 1772; [2003] E.M.L.R. 11. This rule is not incompatible with the jurisprudence of the ECHR: *Chase v News Group Newspapers Ltd*, above.

[216] See, for example, the rules derived from *Musa King v Telegraph Group Ltd* [2004] EWCA Civ 613; [2004] E.M.L.R. 23 at [22] governing justification of a *Chase* level 2 *Lucas-Box* meaning, set out in para.11.13 above.

[217] *Aspro Travel Ltd v Owners Abroad Group* [1996] 1 W.L.R. 132 (CA); *Clancy v Roland* [1923] 2 D.L.R. 288, where it was held that defendants should be allowed to establish their plea of privilege in any legal way they could, that they should not be hampered in their defence and that the court would not strike out a pleading as embarrassing unless it appeared on merely reading the pleadings through that it was one which did not admit of plausible argument. But see *Lucas & Son v O'Brien* [1978] 2 N.Z.L.R. 289, where it was held that the defence of qualified privilege was "so clearly untenable that it could not possibly succeed" (per Richmond P. at 303); and *Howlett v Holding* [2003] EWHC 286 (QB), in which Eady J. struck out a defence of qualified privilege where there was no prospect of the defendant establishing at trial that he had the necessary duty to pronounce to the world at large (to some extent, by means of aerial banners flown behind an aeroplane) that the claimant was guilty of shoplifting, when the information available to him at the time of publication could create no more than a reasonable suspicion of shoplifting.

[218] *Joseph v Spiller* [2009] EWHC 1152 (QB). (While the defendants successfully appealed other aspects of the judge's decision (ultimately: [2010] UKSC 53; [2011] 1 A.C. 852), they did not try to appeal against the striking out of their defence of qualified privilege.)

[219] *Loutchansky v Times Newspapers Ltd* [2001] EWCA Civ 536; [2002] Q.B. 321 at [40]–[44].

[220] *Cohen v Daily Telegraph* [1968] 1 W.L.R. 916; *Lowe v Associated Newspapers Ltd* [2006] EWHC 320 (QB); [2007] Q.B. 580 at [74].

where the comment is not on a matter of public interest, but on a private topic.[221]

There can be no doubt that pleas of *Reynolds* qualified privilege alleged in circumstances where the defendant cannot possibly have satisfied the obligations of responsible journalism will be struck out.[222] A plea of honest comment will not be struck out where there is sufficient doubt in law and fact as to whether or not the subject-matter of the comment is a matter of public interest[223] or where it is open to a jury reasonably to find that a comment to the effect contended for by the defendant is to be found in the words complained of.[224] On the other hand, where a defence of honest comment is utterly insupportable, it will be struck out.[225] In malicious falsehood, a pleaded defence of honest comment will be struck out as impertinent.[226] In *Al Amoudi v Brisard*[227] an application was made to strike out a defence which denied that there had been substantial publication of an article on an internet website, on the grounds that there was a rebuttable presumption of substantial internet publication within the jurisdiction: the application failed, because the judge found that there was no such presumption, and that it was for the claimant to prove publication.

In an appropriate case, the court may adjourn an application to strike out in order to give the defendant a final chance of pleading in accordance with the rules,[228] or permit the application to strike out while giving the pleader an

---

[221] *Andre v Price* [2010] EWHC 2572 (QB) at [93].

[222] Although given the intrinsically fact-dependent nature of pleas of *Reynolds* privilege, an application to strike out will usually have to be combined with one under CPR Pt 24: see e.g. *Miller v Associated Newspapers* [2003] EWHC 2799 (QB); [2004] E.M.L.R. 33; *Wood v Chief Constable of West Midlands Police* [2003] EWHC 2971 (QB); [2004] E.M.L.R. 17, affirmed [2004] EWCA Civ 1638; [2005] E.M.L.R. 20; *McKeith v News Group Newspapers Ltd* [2005] EWHC 1162 (QB); [2005] E.M.L.R. 32 (all three of which may have been decided on a summary judgment basis); by contrast, see *Armstrong v Times Newspapers Ltd* (in which the judge's decision to rule out qualified privilege was overturned by Court of Appeal ([2005] EWCA Civ 1007)). Meanwhile, in *Grobbelaar v News Group Newspapers Ltd* [2001] EWCA Civ 33; [2001] 2 All E.R. 437, a *Reynolds* privilege defence was held by the CA to have been correctly ruled out at trial (the issue of qualified privilege was not considered in the claimant's subsequent appeal to the House of Lords). See also *Hunt v Times Newspapers Ltd* [2012] EWHC 110 (QB) and [2012] EWHC 1220 (QB).

[223] *Morton v Arbuckle* [1918] V.L.R. 657.

[224] *Control Risks v New English Library* [1989] 3 All E.R. 577.

[225] *Gaddafi v Telegraph Group Ltd* [2000] E.M.L.R. 431 CA; *Baldwin v Rusbridger* [2001] E.M.L.R. 47; *Hamilton v Clifford* [2004] EWHC 1542 (QB); *Thornton v Telegraph Media Group Ltd* [2009] EWHC 2863 (QB) (Sir Charles Gray). In *Joseph v Spiller* [2010] UKSC 53; [2011] 1 A.C. 852, the Supreme Court allowed the defendants' appeal against the CA's decision to uphold (on different grounds from Eady J.) the striking out of the defence of fair (honest) comment.

[226] See the reasoning in *Thornton v Telegraph Media Group Ltd* [2011] EWHC 159 (QB); [2011] E.M.L.R 25 and *Euromoney Institutional Investor Plc v Aviation News Ltd* [2013] EWHC 1505 (QB) at [102]–[103], both decisions of Tugendhat J.

[227] [2006] EWHC 1062 (QB); [2007] 1 W.L.R. 113.

[228] *Morrell v International Thompson Publishing* [1989] 3 All E.R. 733.

opportunity to recast his pleading,[229] or allow the pleading to stand subject to certain aspects of it being reformulated.[230]

30.41 Applications by defendant. If the particulars of claim disclose no reasonable cause of action, the defendant can apply to have them struck out and the action dismissed.[231] He should, however, only take such a step where it is "plain and obvious . . . that the statement of claim as it stands is insufficient"[232] and "there is no reason to suppose that the plaintiff can improve it by amendment".[233] Examples of cases where it would be appropriate to make such an application include cases where it is clear that the words were published on an occasion which was absolutely privileged,[234] or where the claimant plainly lacks standing to maintain the proceedings,[235] or where the defendant is not a publisher at common law,[236] or, in slander, where the words

---

[229] See, e.g. *Howe v Burden* [2004] EWHC 196 (QB).

[230] See e.g. *Ashcroft v Foley* [2011] EWHC 1710 (QB); [2011] E.M.L.R. 30.

[231] CPR r.3.4(2)(a).

[232] *Hubbuck v Wilkinson* [1899] 1 Q.B. at 91, applied by Harman L.J. in *Merricks v Nott-Bower* [1965] 1 Q.B. 57 at 70. "In a very clear case": per Denman J. in *Kellaway v Bury* (1892) 66 L.T. at 600; "In all cases which are clear beyond all doubt": per Lindley L.J. ibid. at 602; "The pleading will not be struck out unless it is demurrable and something worse than demurrable": per Chitty L.J. in *Republic of Peru v Peruvian Guano* (1887) 36 Ch D at 496; "unless the court is satisfied that it would be impossible for the plaintiff to win his action", per Salmon L.J. in *Merricks v Nott-Bower* [1965] 1 Q.B. 57 CA at 72. See *Shendish Manor Ltd v Coleman* [2001] EWCA Civ 913, where it was held that there was a need for caution when deciding to strike out a claim on the basis of witness statements exchanged in advance of trial (a path illuminated by *McDonald's Corp v Steel* [1995] 3 All E.R. 615). A witness statement might be sufficiently ambiguous as to require elaboration orally. However, where a defendant sought summary judgment in his favour, it behoved a claimant to ensure that his evidence was in sufficiently clear terms to show a realistic prospect of success. With regard to applications to strike out at this stage of the proceedings more generally, see para.30.42, below.

[233] Per Lindley M.R. in *Hubbuck v Wilkinson* [1899] 1 Q.B. 86 at 94.

[234] See e.g. *Gray v Avadis* [2003] EWHC 1830 (QB) (complaint to Office for the Supervision of Solicitors), *Tufano v Vincenti* [2006] EWHC 1496 (QB) (psychiatrist's report for family proceedings), *Buckley v Dalziel* [2007] EWHC 1025 (QB); [2007] 1 W.L.R. 2933 (witness statement given to police); *Westcott v Westcott* [2008] EWCA Civ 818; [2009] Q.B. 407 (oral complaint and subsequent written statement to police); *Karim v Newsquest Ltd*, unreported, October 27, 2009 (website article summarising a hearing in the Solicitors Disciplinary Tribunal absolutely privileged under s.14 Defamation Act 1996 as being a fair, accurate and contemporaneous report of legal proceedings); *Vaidya v GMC* [2010] EWHC 984 (QB) (letter to GMC); *White v Southampton University Hospitals NHS Trust* [2011] EWHC 825 (QB) (letter to GMC); *Mayer v Hoar* [2012] EWHC 1805 (QB) (barrister's response to BSB following C's complaint); *Iqbal v Dean Manson Solicitors & Co.* [2013] EWCA Civ 149 (witness statements made in course of legal proceedings). See also *Baxendale-Walker v Middleton* [2011] EWHC 998 (QB) in which claims for conspiracy and malicious falsehood were struck out inter alia on grounds of absolute privilege (but cf. *Adams v Law Society* [2012] EWHC 980 (QB), a misfeasance in public office and Human Rights Act claim, and the references at [150]–[156] to *Autofocus Ltd v Accident Exchange Ltd* [2010] EWCA Civ 788).

[235] E.g. where the action is brought by a governmental entity (*Derbyshire CC v Times Newspapers Ltd* [1993] A.C. 534; cf. *McLaughlin v Lambeth LBC* [2010] EWHC 2726 (QB); [2011] E.M.L.R. 8) or a political party (*Goldsmith v Bhoyrul* [1997] E.M.L.R. 407).

[236] See *Bunt v Tilley* [2006] EWHC 407 (QB); [2007] 1 W.L.R. 1243 (mere conduits in the internet context); *Metropolitan International Schools Ltd v Designtechnica Corp* [2009] EWHC 1765 (QB); [2009] E.M.L.R. 27 (operators of search engines); but cf. *Tamiz v Google Inc.* [2013] EWCA Civ 68; [2013] 1 W.L.R. 2151 (platform providers arguably publishers at common law

are actionable only on proof of special damage and the special damage alleged
is insufficient in law to sustain the action,[237] or where the words are clearly not
calculated to disparage the claimant in respect of any office, profession,
calling, trade or business held or carried on by him at the time of publication
for the purpose of s.2 Defamation Act 1952.[238] Furthermore, if some
specific aspect of the particulars of claim or reply fails to disclose a reasonably
viable case—for example, a claim for aggravated[239] or special[240]
damages[241] or a plea of malice in answer to a defence of qualified privilege[242]—the defendant may apply to strike out that specific part of the
claimant's pleaded case alone.[243] On any application to strike out, the court
decides no more than that the claimant's pleaded case is arguable or unarguable and it does not follow from a decision to allow the pleading to stand that
the trial judge is bound to leave the claimant's case to the jury.[244] If the
question is one "requiring serious argument and careful consideration", the
defendant should not apply to have the particulars of claim struck out, but
raise an objection in point of law in his defence and apply to have it tried as
a preliminary issue.[245] If the particulars of claim are insufficient owing to the
omission of some material averment, e.g. the words are actionable only on

---

post-notification) (and for comparative purposes, *Trkulja v Google Inc. LLC (No.5)* [2012] VSC
533, *Wishart v Murray* [2013] NZHC 540, *Oriental Press Group Ltd v Fevaworks Solutions Ltd*
[2013] HKCFA 47).

[237] *Michael v Spiers and Pond* (1909) 101 L.T. 52.

[238] *Andre v Price* [2010] EWHC 2572 (QB) at [103].

[239] See e.g. *Collins Stewart Ltd v Financial Times Ltd* [2005] EWHC 262 (QB); [2006]
E.M.L.R. 5; *Adelson v Associated Newspapers Ltd* [2007] EWHC 997 (QB), at [89]–[98]; *Clarke
(t/a Elumina Iberica UK) v Bain* [2008] EWHC 2636 (QB), at [35]–[68]; *Lait v Evening Standard
Ltd* [2010] EWHC 642 (QB), at [17]–[30] (particulars in aggravation of damages struck out as
being reliant upon defamatory meanings different from the meaning attributed to the words
complained of for the purposes of the case on liability); *Blakeney-Williams v Cathay Pacific
Airways Ltd* [2012] HKCFA 61; [2013] E.M.L.R. 6; *Oriental Daily Publisher Ltd v Ming Pao
Holdings Ltd* [2012] HKCFA 59; [2013] E.M.L.R. 7; *ZAM v CFW* [2013] EWHC 662 (QB);
[2013] E.M.L.R. 27.

[240] See *Collins Stewart Ltd v Financial Times Ltd*, above, at [24] (application to strike out part
of a special damage plea based on the loss of value in shares of one claimant corporation—the
parent company of the other claimant—upheld on grounds that it represented a measure of
damages which was unsound in law, and that the claim was untriable and a waste of the court's
resources); *Monks v Warwick DC* [2009] EWHC 959 (QB) (pleaded claim for special damages
struck out where the claimant sought to recover losses said to have been incurred by his company).

[241] Notwithstanding the express wording of CPR r.3.4(2)(a), which arguably relates only to
liability ("that the statement of case discloses no reasonable grounds for bringing . . . the claim");
but note the condition for striking out in CPR r.3.4(2)(b): "that the statement of case . . . is
otherwise likely to obstruct the just disposal of the proceedings".

[242] See e.g. *Monks v Warwick DC*, above.

[243] See CPR r.3.4(1): "In this rule . . . , reference to a statement of case includes reference to
a part of a statement of case."

[244] *Morgan v Odhams Press* [1971] 1 W.L.R. 1239 at 1242 (Lord Reid), at 1253 (Lord Morris),
at 1257 (Lord Guest), at 1263 (Lord Donovan) and at 1268 (Lord Pearson).

[245] CPR r.3.1(2)(i): see s.7 of this Chapter, below. See the judgment of Lindley M.R. in
Hubbuck v Wilkinson [1899] 1 Q.B. 86 at 91; *Worthington v Belton* (1902) 18 T.L.R. 438;
Marchant v Ford [1936] 2 All E.R. 1510:
"All we have to decide in this case is whether use can be made of the rules with regard to the

proof of special damage, and no special damage is alleged, or if the claimant attempts to plead a true legal innuendo without setting out the extrinsic facts on which he relies, the defendant can apply to have the particulars of claim struck out, though the claimant, if he has a sustainable case, will generally, upon terms, obtain permission to amend.[246] The practice sometimes adopted of withholding any objection until the trial is, however, a risky one and may involve adverse repercussions in respect of costs.[247]

30.42 After exchange of witness statements. The practice of exchanging witness statements before trial has given rise to the possibility of applying, at or before trial (i.e. at the pre-trial review), to strike out parts of an opponent's pleading if it is apparent from the witness statements served that the party will not be able to prove part of his pleaded case. This was the course adopted in *McDonald's Corp v Steel*,[248] where (in pre-CPR days) the plaintiff applied before trial and before discovery had been completed, but after service of witness statements, to strike out parts of the defence and particulars of justification and fair comment. On the defendants' appeal, Neill L.J. stated that when an application is made before trial, the correct approach is to consider whether or not the defendants' case in relation to a particular passage in the defence is incurably bad: at an interlocutory stage, and before full discovery, the court will seldom be able to say that a particular allegation is incapable of being proved.[249] However, he saw considerable merit in applying at the close of evidence at trial to strike out allegations for which there is no

striking out of a statement of claim to determine in advance an arguable question which is partly one of law and partly one of fact. It seems to me that the learned judge took upon himself to decide a matter which could only properly be decided when the whole evidence was before the court."
(per Greer L.J. at 1512). Where the defendant alleges that there has been a binding settlement by way of compromise which, if established, would dispose of the action, he should raise the issue in the pleadings and apply for an order staying the proceedings and for determination before trial of the question whether the alleged compromise amounts to a binding settlement of the claimant's claims: *Eyre v Wilson & Morton* [1967] N.Z.L.R. 769.

[246] *Aqua Vital Australia Ltd v Swan Television* [1995] Aust. Torts Reports 62,709, where it was held that it would be a rare case in which a court would strike out a plea of true innuendo on the ground that there were no extrinsic facts to support the innuendo, without giving the plaintiff every reasonable opportunity properly to particularise the plea; *Church of Scientology v Globe & Mail* (1978) 19 O.R. (2d) 62:
" . . . drafting pleadings in libel actions is a difficult and technical process. The order striking out the pleading will be without prejudice to the plaintiff's rights to file a fresh statement of claim within 15 days of this order. It may be that the plaintiff will benefit by further consideration of the form the statement of claim should take in this case"
(per Cory J. at 65); *Quann v Chatam* (1991) 107 N.B.R. 392:
" . . . the court should endeavour to achieve substantive justice rather than procedural justice, and in cases where defective pleadings are struck out, leave to amend should be given if the pleadings can be improved and no injustice is done by the amendment"
per Riordon J. at 399.

[247] In this context, see *Burstein v Times Newspapers Ltd*, unreported, March 3, 2000, per H.H.J. Richard Walker sitting as a judge of the High Court.

[248] [1995] 3 All E.R. 615 CA. For a more recent example, see *Andre v Price* [2010] EWHC 2572 (QB).

[249] [1995] 3 All E.R. 615 at 623.

evidence for the jury to consider, and he regarded the practice of applying at the start of trial as a sensible one in an appropriate case, where it was likely to shorten the trial, but warned that there may be cases where the defendant hopes (and, he implied, should be permitted) to prove his case by eliciting favourable answers in cross-examination.[250]

Abuse of process. The CPR r.3.4(2) regime is often employed for the purpose of applications to strike out or stay for abuse of the process, coupled with the jurisdiction to stay under r.3.1(2)(f) and what Lord Diplock called the: **30.43**

> "inherent power which any court of justice must possess to prevent misuse of its procedure in a way which, although not inconsistent with the literal application of its procedural rules, would nevertheless be manifestly unfair to a party to litigation before it, or would otherwise bring the administration of justice into disrepute among right-thinking people. The circumstances in which abuse of process can arise are very varied; those which give rise to the instant appeal must surely be unique. It would, in my view, be most unwise if this House were to use this occasion to say anything that might be taken as limiting to fixed categories the kinds of circumstances in which the court has a duty (I disavow the word discretion) to exercise this salutary power".[251]

Categories of application. Certain established categories of abuse can tentatively be stated, but it is important to remember that, as Lord Diplock warned, the categories of abuse of process are not fixed or limited, and even to speak of "categories" creates a misleading illusion of self-containment, when in reality the facts of given cases will cross and overlap such boundaries as exist.   **30.44**

Inadequate or embarrassing statements of case. The court will generally intervene where either party's statement of case is seriously unclear or confusing or otherwise likely to add unnecessarily to the cost and complexity of proceedings.[252] The CPR provide in terms that if a statement of case is an abuse of the court's process or is otherwise likely to obstruct the just disposal   **30.45**

---

[250] Ibid.

[251] *Hunter v Chief Constable of the West Midlands Police* [1982] A.C. 529 at 536.

[252] See *Ashcroft v Foley* [2012] EWCA Civ 423; [2012] E.M.L.R. 25 in relation to defences of justification and honest comment, and, more generally, *Ontulmus v Collett* [2013] EWHC 980 (QB) per Tugendhat J. at [24]–[28]

("CPR r.16.4(1)(a) states that particulars of claim must include a concise statement of the facts on which the claimant relies . . . [Counsel for the defendant] submits that particulars of claim should not include anything else. If they do, then it will not be clear to a defendant what the claim is, and a defendant has to plead to them, and that will be wasteful . . . In my judgment [the submission] is correct. Pleading matters which are not those on which a claimant relies is contrary to the overriding objective . . . a history of previous matters in dispute between the parties has no place in a claim for libel, unless it is relevant to a constituent of the cause of action.")

of the proceedings, an application may be made to have it struck out.[253] Thus, where a defendant is unclear as to what parts of a severable charge he is justifying or where he seeks to justify part of an indivisible charge, his plea may be struck out as embarrassing.[254] So also if the defendant, instead of pleading to the version of the words complained of in the particulars of claim, sets out his own version of the words and then justifies them, the plea will be struck out as irrelevant and embarrassing.[255] Similarly, if a defendant seeks to justify a non-defamatory meaning or to rely for the purposes of a defence of honest comment on a non-defamatory comment.[256] Likewise, a defendant cannot assert, either by way of justification or in mitigation of damages, the truth of a separate charge or charges which are made in the publication containing the words complained of but which the claimant has omitted from his complaint, and such a plea will be struck out.[257] Generally, matters pleaded in mitigation of damage which are inadmissible for that purpose will be struck out.[258] Where a defence is so confused and cluttered with irrelevancies that it is impossible clearly to make out the individual defences being advanced, the defence may be struck out, with liberty to the defendant to re-plead. However,

---

[253] CPR r.3.4(2)(b). Although the rule does not contain the express references to matter which is scandalous, frivolous or vexatious or to the possibility of prejudice, embarrassment or delay to the fair trial of the action (which were formerly included in its predecessor under RSC Ord.18, r.19 as grounds for striking out), it is submitted that there has been no substantive change to the court's ability to strike out and the court will continue to strike out on the same grounds as before. See, e.g. *Spencer v Sillitoe (No.2)* [2003] EWHC 1651 (QB), per Eady J. art.6(1) of the ECHR, which provides for a fair and public hearing in the determination of a person's civil rights and obligations, may require caution in the exercise of the discretion to strike out. But:
"it is no part of the court's function to proceed to trial if to do so would give rise to a substantial risk of injustice. The function of the court is to do justice between the parties; not to allow its process to be used as a means of achieving injustice. A litigant who has demonstrated that he is determined to pursue proceedings with the object of preventing a fair trial has forfeited his right to take part in a trial. His object is inimical to the process he purports to invoke":
per Chadwick L.J. in *Arrow Nominees Inc. v Blackledge* [2000] 2 B.C.L.C. 167 at [54]. Now see *Summers v Fairclough Homes Ltd* [2012] UKSC 26; [2012] 1 W.L.R. 2004.
[254] *Fleming v Dollar* (1889) 23 Q.B.D. 388 CA; *Davis v Billing* (1891) 8 T.L.R. 58 CA; *Mann v Mackay Television* [1992] 2 Qd. R.136.
[255] *Rassam v Budge* [1893] 1 Q.B. 571 CA; *Selfridge v Financial Telegraph Ltd, The Times*, January 14, 1931, CA; *Mutual Assurance v Abbott* (1893) 19 V.L.R. 456; *Fulford v Wallace* (1901) 1 O.L.R. 278; *Edgar v Freeman* [1915] V.L.R. 16.
[256] *Broadcasting Corporation of New Zealand v Crush* [1988] 2 N.Z.L.R. 234, 237 (proving the truth of a non-defamatory meaning would be a "pointless exercise"); *Maxwell v Bower*, unreported, April 10, 1990, per Michael Davies J.
[257] *Plato Films v Speidel* [1961] A.C. 1090:
"I cannot think that the appellants should be entitled to give evidence of particular facts tending to show the character and disposition of the respondent merely because those alleged facts are said to be asserted or presented in some parts of the film itself"
(per Lord Morris at 1147); *Polly Peck Plc v Trelford* [1986] Q.B. 1000 CA:
"Where a publication contains two or more separate and distinct defamatory statements, the plaintiff is entitled to select one for complaint, and the defendant is not entitled to assert the truth of the others by way of justification."
(per O'Connor L.J. at 1032).
[258] *Plato Films v Speidel* [1961] A.C. 1090. For the current law governing matters admissible in mitigation of damages, see *Burstein v Times Newspapers Ltd* [2001] 1 W.L.R. 579, *Turner v News Group Newspapers Ltd* [2006] EWCA Civ 540; [2006] 1 W.L.R. 3469 and paras 27.39 and

the court has shown itself reluctant to strike out a statement of claim by a litigant in person which was wordy and prolix but nevertheless pleaded a cause of action.[259] A plea in particulars of claim describing the alleged "unfairness and inaccuracy" of a report may be struck out as tending to delay the fair trial of the action.[260] In determining whether to strike out material pleaded in a defence of justification or honest comment, the court will seek to strike a balance between the legitimate defence of free speech and free comment on the one hand and on the other hand the costs which might be involved if every peripheral issue was examined and debated at the trial.[261]

The need for finality. The court will be alert to ensure that its process is   **30.46** not abused by attempts to litigate issues which have been[262] or should have been[263] previously determined, or to undermine existing decisions by flank attack. Hence, an action may be stayed as an abuse of the process where the claimant has already instituted proceedings in another forum against the same defendant in respect of the publication of the same material.[264] A claim may also be struck out where the essential facts and matters going to liability would be the same as those already raised in earlier proceedings which were brought by the same claimant against another defendant in respect of a similar publication and which either failed or were abandoned by the claimant,[265] or

---

29.36, above. In *Rath v Guardian News and Media Ltd* [2008] EWHC 398 (QB), a plea that the claimant had not complained of other *Guardian* articles to similar effect was struck out.

[259] *Morris v Wiltshire, The Times*, February 15, 1994, CA.

[260] For the onus of proving fairness and accuracy lies on the defendant: *Kimber v Press Association* [1893] 1 Q.B. 65, 71.

[261] *Rechem International Ltd v Express Newspapers Plc, The Times*, June 19, 1992, CA. See also the other authorities referred to in fn.198, above.

[262] In *Crossley v Wallace* [2009] EWHC 2846 (QB), Openshaw J. held that a libel action had been properly struck out where the proceedings were an obvious attempt to re-litigate issues already determined between the parties in a nuisance action. For res judicata generally, see paras 19.22–19.23, above. The principle includes cases which might fall outside a strict application of res judicata, as for instance *Macdougall v Knight* (1890) 25 Q.B.D. 1 CA, where the plaintiff brought a first action over certain words in a pamphlet, failed, and then brought a second action over other words to the same effect in the same pamphlet. The second action was stayed as an abuse. In this latter context, now see the broader approach taken by the court in *Schellenberg v BBC* [2000] E.M.L.R. 296, approved by the CA in *Jameel v Dow Jones & Co. Inc.* [2005] EWCA Civ 75; [2005] Q.B. 946. See also *Baxendale-Walker v Middleton* [2011] EWHC 998 (QB) in which claims for conspiracy and malicious falsehood were struck out inter alia on grounds that they were improper attempts to mount a collateral attack on a final decision of a court of competent jurisdiction.

[263] *Henderson v Henderson* (1843) 3 Hare 100; *Bradford & Bingley Building Society v Seddon* [1999] 1 W.L.R. 1482; *Johnson v Gore-Wood & Co.* [2002] 2 A.C. 1; *Aldi Stores Ltd v WSP Group Ltd* [2007] EWCA Civ 1260; [2008] 1 W.L.R. 748.

[264] *Maple v David Syme* [1975] 1 N.S.W.L.R. 97; *Cumming v Scottish Daily Record* [1995] E.M.L.R. 538, departing from an earlier decision by the same judge, *Foxen v Scotsman Publications* [1995] E.M.L.R. 145. It is not an abuse of the process to bring libel proceedings where matters have already been the subject of industrial (employment) tribunal proceedings which were based purely on irregularities in the dismissal process, *Friend v Civil Aviation Authority* [1998] I.R.L.R. 253 CA.

[265] *Oates v Mirror Group Newspapers*, unreported, May 19, 2000, CA; *Pedder v News Group Newspapers Ltd* [2003] EWHC 2442 (QB); [2004] E.M.L.R. 19; *Schellenberg v BBC* [2000] E.M.L.R. 296, per Eady J.:

where a fresh action has been brought against a joint publisher on the same publication as has been found not defamatory of the claimant in an action brought by him against another of the publishers.[266] However, the court declined to strike out defences of justification and fair comment on grounds of abuse and issue estoppel where some of the issues raised by them had been litigated previously in the small claims court.[267] If a defendant argues its appeal on the basis that another decision against it, which it has not appealed, is wrong, that is not an abuse of process unless the defendant's object is to obtain a favourable decision from the Court of Appeal and then apply out of time for leave to appeal the other decision. There is no abuse in seeking to argue an appeal on its merits without being handicapped by what may or may not have been a correct decision in another, unappealed, case.[268]

30.47   **Impermissible collateral objective.** If a claimant can be proved to have had a collateral purpose in initiating litigation, "one which the law does not recognise as a legitimate use of the remedy sought", the court may stay the action as an abuse of its process.[269] Thus, it has been held to be an abuse of

---

"The pursuit of the present action in the hope of salvaging something from the disastrous outcome of the previous action can only, in my view, be characterised as a desperate exercise in damage limitation. It represents one last throw of the dice. In all the circumstances I am afraid I cannot accept that there is any realistic prospect of a trial yielding any tangible or legitimate advantage such as to outweigh the disadvantage for the parties in terms of expense, and the wider public in terms of court resources"
See also *Vassiliev v Amazon Inc.* [2003] EWHC 2302 (Comm). For the approach taken to such matters by the New South Wales Court of Appeal, see *Habib v Radio 2UE Sydney Pty Ltd* [2009] NSWCA 231.

[266] *Burtonshaw v BBC* (1978) 128 N.L.J. 483.

[267] *Tanner v Filby*, unreported, January 28, 2003 (QB). Eady J. observed that there was no reason why the defendants should be under a permanent ban by reason of the small claims court proceedings from criticising the claimant and held that they had every right to defend themselves in the High Court in respect of their exercise of the right of free speech. See also *Arul Chandran v Chew Chin Aik Victor* [2001] 1 S.L.R. 505.

[268] *Jameel v Wall Street Journal Europe* [2003] EWCA Civ 1694; [2004] E.M.L.R. 6. The defendant appeared to be contending that an unappealed decision by Eady J. in *Al Rajhi v Wall Street Journal* [2003] EWHC 1776 (QB) was wrong, thus prompting a vigorous intervention by counsel for Mr Al Rajhi, whereupon the defendant hastened to explain that it did not intend to secure a decision of the Court of Appeal that the unappealed decision in *Al Rajhi* was wrong. Counsel for the claimant argued that it would be an abuse of process for the defendant to argue the appeal before the court on any basis other than that Eady J. had been right to rule as he did in *Al Rajhi*; but Simon Brown L.J. disagreed, at [26]. He had no doubt that it would be an abuse of process for the defendant to succeed in the present appeal and then apply out of time for permission to appeal the *Al Rajhi* decision, but that was not the defendant's intention: it sought only to argue the appeal on its merits without being handicapped by what may or may not have been a correct decision in *Al Rajhi*, and there was no objection to that.

[269] *Goldsmith v Sperrings* [1977] 1 W.L.R. 478. The majority (Lord Denning M.R. dissenting) held that suing distributors of a magazine and seeking to settle on the basis that they would no longer distribute the magazine did not amount to an abuse of the process of the court, even if what was obtained by the settlement went beyond any remedy the court could award and beyond what was necessary for the plaintiff's protection. See also *Packer v Meagher* [1984] 3 N.S.W.L.R. 486, where the action was struck out as an abuse of the process on the finding by the court that the proceedings were brought for a dominant ulterior and collateral purpose of investigating the conduct of a Royal Commission and not to vindicate the plaintiff's own reputation; *Broxton v McClelland* [1995] E.M.L.R. 485 CA; *Wallis v Valentine* [2002] EWCA Civ 1034; [2003]

the process of the court to issue a claim and maintain libel proceedings in being in order to gag discussion.[270] The institution of proceedings with an ulterior motive is not of itself enough to constitute an abuse[271]: it is necessary that the court's processes should be misused to achieve something not properly available to the claimant in the course of properly conducted proceedings.[272] Two distinct categories have been noted: cases where a collateral advantage is sought which is beyond the proper scope of the action,[273] and cases where the proceedings have been conducted:

> "in a manner designed to cause the defendant problems of expense, harassment, commercial prejudice or the like beyond those ordinarily encountered in the course of properly conducted litigation".[274]

So, a claim in libel and contract was struck out when its object was to obtain a collateral advantage (compensation for the claimant's dismissal, to which an employment tribunal had already ruled that he was not entitled) by harassing the defendant and causing him disproportionate trouble and expense.[275] A claimant can be expected to wish his action to be heard as soon as possible in order to clear his name and where a claimant has delayed in prosecuting a libel action and can give no valid explanation for his delay, the court may infer that his motive for the delay is not a proper one and constitutes an abuse of the process.[276] The court will:

E.M.L.R. 8; *Powell v Boladz* [2003] EWHC 2160 (QB), where the defendant applied unsuccessfully to strike out a claim on the grounds, inter alia, that the claimant sought not to vindicate his reputation but to achieve a collateral purpose; *Bezant v Rausing* [2007] EWHC 1118 (QB); and the account given in *Hays Plc v Hartley* [2010] EWHC 1068 (QB), per Tugendhat J. at [33]–[45]. See further, in a different context, *JSC BTA Bank v Ablyazov* [2011] EWHC 1136 (Comm); [2011] 1 W.L.R. 2996.

[270] *Wallersteiner v Moir* [1974] 1 W.L.R. 991 CA. In that case the plaintiff had caused inordinate and inexcusable delay.

[271] See, e.g. *Ashley v Chief Constable of Sussex* [2008] UKHL 25; [2008] 1 A.C. 962 at [70] per Lord Rodger of Earlsferry.

[272] *Wallis v Valentine* [2002] EWCA Civ 1034; [2003] E.M.L.R. 8; *Broxton v McClelland* [1995] E.M.L.R. 485 at 497–498.

[273] See the discussion by Bridge L.J. in *Goldsmith v Sperrings Ltd* (above) at 503 D-H.

[274] *Wallis v Valentine* (above), at [31], following *Broxton v McClelland* [1995] E.M.L.R. 485 at 497–498; *Freer v Zeb* [2008] EWHC 212 (QB).

[275] *Bezant v Rausing* [2007] EWHC 1118 (QB), following *Wallis v Valentine* [2002] EWCA Civ 1034; [2003] E.M.L.R. 8.

[276] *Grovit v Doctor* [1997] 1 W.L.R. 640. Such applications failed in *Gaddafi v Telegraph Group Ltd*, unreported, July 27, 2000, per Eady J., in *Powell v Boladz* [2003] EWHC 2160 (QB) (where Tugendhat J. considered in detail the law so far as concerns the proper purpose of proceedings in defamation, delay in prosecution of an action, and the requirements of art.6 of the ECHR for the requirement of a fair trial within a reasonable time) and in *Morrissey v McNicholas* [2011] EWHC 2738 (QB) (Tugendhat J.), but succeeded in *Adelson v Anderson* [2011] EWHC 2497 (QB) (also Tugendhat J.). In *Desmond v MGN Ltd* [2008] IESC 56, the Supreme Court of Ireland (by a majority, Kearns J. dissenting) dismissed the defendant's appeal against Hanna J.'s decision not to strike out a libel action for want of prosecution. The court held that, although the plaintiff's delay had been both inordinate and inexcusable, the balance of justice favoured the plaintiff being allowed to proceed with his action given the nature of the defence that had been filed (which included a plea of justification).

In pre-CPR days, when delay in litigation was a much greater problem than it is today, delay was more usually advanced not as an indicator of abuse but as a ground for an application to strike

"need strong evidence that the plaintiff was in fact seeking something beyond the protection and vindication of his reputation before the court could stay his action as an abuse of process",[277]

and only in the most clear and obvious cases will it be appropriate to strike out proceedings as an abuse of process so as to prevent a claimant from bringing an apparently proper cause of action to trial.[278]

30.48 Proceedings which are not "worth the candle": *Jameel* **abuse of process.**[279] A novel ground on which a defendant may apply to strike out a defamation claim[280] as an abuse of process has emerged over recent years. It is a jurisdiction that has been invoked many times in defamation cases, and latterly in other types of claim engaging the right to freedom of expression[281]:

---

out for want of prosecution. In one case where such an application was made, the plaintiff was able (on appeal) to defeat the application on most unusual grounds. He had won substantial damages at trial in May 1988, but the newspaper defendants obtained new evidence which suggested that he had lied to the jury: a re-trial was ordered. The most important of the new witnesses thereafter retracted his evidence, and then retracted the retraction, no fewer than seven times. The Court of Appeal asked itself whether it would ever have ordered a new trial had it realised just how unreliable this principal witness was, and allowed the plaintiff's appeal against an order striking his claim out. Justice required that the evidence should be explored fully at trial. As Ward L.J. put it:

"Three very important pillars which support the due and proper administration of justice fall for consideration in this case. The first is that there should be an end to litigation. The second is that justice delayed is justice denied. The third, to quote from the speech of Lord Hailsham of St Marylebone, is 'the general importance of the principle that in all cases before them the court should insist on parties and witnesses disclosing the truth, the whole truth and nothing but the truth . . . .' (*D v NSPCC* [1978] A.C. 171) . . . . In this case there has been an affront to justice by the lies and perversions of one or more than one person. Since the court's own integrity has been assaulted in this manner, it is, in my judgment, all the more important that the truth must out"

(*Gilberthorpe v Hawkins (No.2)* CA, March 15, 1995, unreported).

[277] *Goldsmith v Sperrings* [1977] 1 W.L.R. 478 at 500, per Scarman L.J. Where a claimant genuinely seeks vindication, but that vindication will be minimal in view of the tiny publication of the libel in this jurisdiction, and achieved at a cost out of all proportion to the result, the claim may be dismissed as an abuse (*Jameel v Dow Jones & Co. Inc.* [2005] EWCA Civ 75; [2005] Q.B. 946).

[278] *Wallis v Valentine* (above), at [31], following *Broxton v McClelland* [1995] E.M.L.R. 485 at 497–498.

[279] After *Jameel v Dow Jones & Co. Inc.* [2005] EWCA Civ 75; [2005] Q.B. 946.

[280] The question that lies at the heart of the *Jameel* jurisdiction is whether, if the court were to allow the proceedings to continue, it would be sanctioning an interference with freedom of expression which was unnecessary for the protection of reputation, since it was plain that the claimant could not have suffered more than minimal damage to reputation: see *Jameel*, above, at [40] and [55]. On their face, such considerations are of course only relevant to defamation, but see the cases referred to in fn.281, below, where the *Jameel* principle has been considered in the context of other causes of action.

[281] E.g. in malicious falsehood (*Tesla Motors Ltd v BBC* [2013] EWCA Civ 152, *Citation Plc v Ellis Whittam Ltd* [2013] EWCA Civ 155) and in breach of confidence (*Abbey v Gilligan* [2012] EWHC 3217 (QB); [2013] E.M.L.R. 12). This despite the point made in the preceding footnote. But see also *Sullivan v Bristol Film Studios Ltd* [2012] EWCA Civ 570; [2012] E.M.L.R. 27, in which the Court of Appeal rejected an attempt to apply the *Jameel* principles to a claim for infringement of copyright, in particular the obiter remarks of Lewison L.J. at [29] and [32]: "If I am entitled to recover a debt of £50 I should, in principle, have access to justice to enable me to recover it if my debtor does not pay. It would be an affront to justice if my claim were simply struck out."

"recent cases demonstrate that each of the three judges who are currently hearing most of the defamation cases are applying the principle of *Jameel v Dow Jones* with some frequency, and in a number of different, but related, contexts in defamation actions".[282] While the central principles are now tolerably clear,[283] the precise nature and reach of the jurisdiction is not. Despite it being axiomatic that it is only in the most clear and obvious cases that it will be appropriate to strike out proceedings as an abuse of process, it may be difficult to predict with confidence in any particular case whether the court will or will not agree that the claim is a *Jameel* abuse. Moreover, an incorrect prediction may prove costly: it is not unusual for *Jameel*-based applications to involve in-depth scrutiny of the germane facts, circumstances and evidence. Nevertheless, what unifies the authorities that make up the relevant jurisprudence[284] is that in each case it was open to the defendant, generally at an early stage, to present the claim as one that was, for one reason or another, trivial or pointless, such that it would be disproportionate to permit it to proceed any further. The question of whether it is or is not proportionate for the proceedings to continue is answered by the court with reference to what is in essence a cost—benefit calculation, "cost" in terms of the parties' costs and, perhaps more importantly, the impact upon the court's increasingly hard-pressed resources, and "benefit" in terms of the true value to the claimant of any realistically available remedy.

---

[282] Per Tugendhat J. in *Thornton v Telegraph Media Group Ltd* [2010] EWHC 1414 (QB); [2011] 1 W.L.R. 1985 at [62].

[283] The key appellate authorities are: *Jameel* itself; *Khader v Aziz* [2010] EWCA Civ 716; [2011] E.M.L.R. 2; *Lait v Evening Standard Ltd* [2011] EWCA Civ 859; [2011] 1 W.L.R. 2973, and *Cammish v Hughes* [2012] EWCA Civ 1655; [2013] E.M.L.R 13.

[284] As Tugendhat J. suggested in *Thornton v Telegraph Media Group Ltd*, above, at [62] (see fn.282, above), the corpus of first instance authority concerned with the application of the principles in *Jameel* is now substantial. Among the more interesting and significant of these authorities (in addition to the ones that went on appeal: see fn.283, above) are the following (in chronological order): *Bezant v Rausing* [2007] EWHC 1118 (QB); *Adelson v Associated Newspapers Ltd* [2008] EWHC 278 (QB); [2009] E.M.L.R. 10; *Ewing v News International Ltd* [2008] EWHC 1390 (QB); *Mardas v New York Times Co.* [2008] EWHC 3135 (QB); [2009] E.M.L.R. 8 (note also the CA's refusal of permission to appeal: [2009] EWCA Civ 633); *Carrie v Tolkien* [2009] EWHC 29 (QB); [2009] E.M.L.R. 9; *Haji-Ioannou v Dixon* [2009] EWHC 178 (QB); *Noorani v Calver* [2009] EWHC 561 (QB); *Sanders v Percy* [2009] EWHC 1870 (QB); *Lonzim Plc v Sprague* [2009] EWHC 2838 (QB); *Williams v MGN Ltd* [2009] EWHC 3150 (QB); *Budu v BBC* [2010] EWHC 616 (QB); *Baturina v Times Newspapers Ltd* [2010] EWHC 696 (QB); [2010] E.M.L.R. 18 (see also on appeal: [2011] EWCA Civ 308; [2011] 1 W.L.R. 1526); *Kaschke v Osler* [2010] EWHC 1075 (QB); *Hays Plc v Hartley* [2010] EWHC 1068 (QB); *Henderson v London Borough of Hackney* [2010] EWHC 1651 (QB); *Taylor v Associated Newspapers Ltd* [2010] EWHC 2494 (QB); *Ronaldo v Telegraph Media Group Ltd* [2010] EWHC 2710 (QB); *Daniels v BBC* [2010] EWHC 3057 (QB); *Wallis v Meredith* [2011] EWHC 75 (QB); *Kordowski v Hudson* [2011] EWHC 2667 (QB); *Davison v Habeeb* [2011] EWHC 3031 (QB); [2012] 3 C.M.L.R. 6; *Tamiz v Google Inc.* [2012] EWHC 449 (QB); [2012] E.M.L.R. 24 (see also on appeal: [2013] EWCA Civ 68; [2013] 1 W.L.R. 2151); *Jeeg Global Ltd v Hare* [2012] EWHC 773 (QB); *King v Grundon* [2012] EWHC 2719 (QB); *University of Salford v Duke* [2013] EWHC 196 (QB); [2013] E.L.R. 259; *Caborn-Waterfield v Gold* [2013] EWHC 440 (QB); *Hamaizia v Comr of Police for the Metropolis* [2013] EWHC 848 (QB); *Euromoney Institutional Investor Plc v Aviation News Ltd* [2013] EWHC 1505 (QB); *Tamiz v Guardian News & Media Ltd* [2013] EWHC 2339 (QB); *Mama Group Ltd v Sinclair* [2013] EWHC 2374 (QB).

The notion that certain proceedings are simply not worth the court time and costs which they entail is very much a product of the new climate engendered by the Civil Procedure Rules. The starting-point of the genre is *Schellenberg v BBC*,[285] which was decided only a matter of months after the CPR came into effect. In that case, Eady J. struck out a libel action against the BBC after the claimant's actions against the *Guardian* and *Sunday Times* had settled on disadvantageous terms some five weeks into the hearing of the *Guardian* action. Applying the overriding objectives of the CPR and making robust use of case management principles, the judge held that the pursuit of the action in the hope of salvaging something from the disastrous outcome of the previous action could only be characterised as a desperate exercise in damage limitation, and could not accept that there was "any realistic prospect of the trial yielding any tangible or legitimate advantage such as to outweigh the disadvantages for the parties in terms of expense, and the wider public in terms of court resources".[286] Nor was it an insuperable objection that there was a right to trial by jury[287]:

> "Even in a jury action it is regarded under the C.P.R. as a judge's duty to take a realistic and practical attitude. He or she is expected to be more proactive even in areas where angels have traditionally feared to tread. I have seen nothing to suggest that the C.P.R. are to be applied any less rigorously, or the judges are to be less interventionist, in litigation of the kind where there is a right to trial by jury. That important right is sometimes described as a 'constitutional right', although the meaning of that emotive phrase is a little hazy. Nevertheless I see no reason why such cases require to be subjected to a different pre-trial regime. It is necessary to apply the overriding objective even in those categories of litigation and in particular to have regard to proportionality. Here there are tens of thousands of pounds of costs at stake and several weeks of court time. I must therefore have regard to the possible benefits that might accrue to the claimant as rendering such a significant expenditure potentially worthwhile."[288]

Eady J.'s words were endorsed by the Court of Appeal in *Wallis v Valentine*,[289] and then in *Jameel v Dow Jones*,[290] the leading decision, and the one

---

[285] [2000] E.M.L.R. 296. The application was also made under Pt 24.

[286] Ibid. at 318–319.

[287] The Court of Appeal in *Wallis v Valentine* agreed with Eady J.'s words, warning, however, that the judge must not usurp the jury: [2002] EWCA Civ 1034; [2003] E.M.L.R. 8 at [33].

[288] *Schellenberg*, above, at 318.

[289] [2002] EWCA Civ 1034; [2003] E.M.L.R. 8 at [33], dismissing the claimant's appeal against the striking out of his claim by H.H. Judge Previté QC. The judge had found that damages were likely to be modest or nominal (the only publication having been technical, namely to the claimant's partner, who lived with him and would not have thought the worse of him), the issues were complex, the claimant had no means of paying the defendants' costs if he lost, the interlocutory proceedings and the trial would be lengthy and wholly disproportionate to the importance of the case, and the claim had been brought for the dominant motive of causing harassment and expense to the defendants. Note that in *Jameel* at [58] the Court of Appeal regarded *Wallis* as an "extreme" case. The principle stated in *Wallis* has nonetheless been followed: see e.g. *Hussein v William Hill* [2006] EWHC 25 (QB) and *Bezant v Rausing* [2007] EWHC 1118 (QB).

[290] [2005] EWCA Civ 75; [2005] Q.B. 946.

which has given the jurisdiction its name. The latter was a case where a libel had been published to a minimal extent in England and Wales by a foreign publisher, and it was held that no substantial tort had been committed within the jurisdiction. Two developments made the court in *Jameel* more receptive to a submission that pursuit of a libel action might be an abuse of process: one was the introduction of the CPR, which required a more flexible and pro-active approach of the court, and the other was the coming into force of the Human Rights Act 1998, which (by s.6) required the court to administer the law in a manner compatible with Convention rights:

"Keeping a proper balance between the Article 10 right to freedom of expression and the protection of individual reputation must . . . require the court to bring to a stop as an abuse of process defamation proceedings that are not serving the legitimate purpose of protecting the claimant's reputation".[291]

Even if the claimant had succeeded at trial, there would have been a gross disproportion between the minimal vindication achieved and the huge cost which would have been entailed. Elaborating upon a remark of Eady J.'s in *Schellenberg*,[292] the court found that "The game would not merely not have been worth the candle, it will not have been worth the wick".[293] So, a claim in which no jury, properly directed, could award more than nominal damages,

---

[291] Ibid. at [55]. Since the English court's power to strike out applying *Jameel* rests in part on the Human Rights Act 1998 and art.10 of the European Convention on Human Rights, it has not found favour in Australia. As was noted in *Calabro v Zappla* [2010] NSWDC 127 at [66]: "no proceedings have been struck out on this basis in Australia. Courts have merely expressed concern at the disproportionate costs as opposed to vindication in very limited publications where the parties know each other well . . . ". See also the obiter remarks of Basten J.A. in *Bristow v Adams* [2012] NSWCA 166 at [41] that, "had a stay been sought prior to trial, there would have needed to be careful attention to the differences between English and Australian law" and "account might need to be taken of the separate defence provided by s.33 [of the Uniform Defamation Acts 2005], described as a defence of 'triviality', and its relationship to the power to stay for abuse of process based on a disproportion between the likely costs of the trial and the possible outcome."

[292] At 318: "I am therefore . . . bound to ask whether, in the old colloquial phrase, the game is worth the candle." For an account of the origins of this phrase, see the judgment of H.H. Judge Chambers QC (sitting as a Judge of the High Court) in *Cammish v Hughes* [2012] EWHC 976 (QB) at [61]: "The expression is derived from a French saying which is much to the same effect except that it may be a little more precise. Thus, *jeu* meaning a play rather than a game, the question was whether the presentation of the play was worth the (often considerable) expense of its illumination. Libel cases immediately come to mind as candidates for such a test." (The judge's dismissal of the defendant's *Jameel*-based application was later overturned on appeal: [2012] EWCA Civ 1655; [2013] E.M.L.R 13.)

[293] *Jameel*, above, at [69]. It is mildly ironic that the Court of Appeal's ringing endorsement of Eady J.'s "game not worth the candle" metaphor, not to mention the sheer quantity of jurisprudence to which the application of the phrase has given rise, came after the judge himself had disavowed it as an "off the cuff remark in an *ex tempore* judgment . . . specifically with reference to the very unusual facts of that case", and as one which it would "not be right to elevate . . . into a general principle of some kind to be applied in other libel actions": *Howe v Burden* [2004] EWHC 196 (QB).

is liable be struck out.[294] It may be noted that the enactment of s.1 of the Defamation Act 2013, whereby a statement will be treated as non-defamatory "unless its publication has caused or is likely to cause serious harm to the reputation of the claimant", was influenced by the decision in *Jameel*, although the precise nature of the relationship between the two is unclear.[295]

30.49 Further examples of abuse. It has been held to be an abuse to launch an action for libel based on a document disclosed in a previous action,[296] and to commence libel proceedings knowing they could not be fairly tried by reason of a term insisted upon by that claimant in settlement of earlier proceedings brought over substantially the same defamatory charge, thereby disabling a key witness from giving evidence for the defendant.[297] Where the defendant shows that the claimant's cause of action is statute barred and must inevitably fail for that reason, the action will be struck out.[298]

30.50 Developing jurisprudence. It should be remembered that the courts have warned against the dangers of striking out claims which raise questions of law which are in a state of development.[299] In an area of the law which is uncertain and developing it is not normally appropriate to strike out, and it is important to ensure that such development should be on the basis of actual facts found at trial not on hypothetical facts assumed (possibly wrongly) to be true for the purpose of the strike out. While the bulk of the common law of defamation, including the law of *Reynolds* qualified privilege (its most significant recent innovation),[300] would be treated by the court as settled for this purpose, the principle is liable to have an increased significance after the Defamation Act 2013, which introduces among other things new statutory defences of truth (s.2), honest opinion (s.3) and publication on a matter of public interest (s.4), has come into force.

---

[294] *Pedder v Associated Newspapers Ltd* [2003] EWHC 1219 (QB); [2004] E.M.L.R. 19 at [36], per Gray J.; see also *Wallis v Valentine,* above, *Bezant v Rausing* [2007] EWHC 1118 (QB) at [144], and *Freer v Zeb* [2008] EWHC 212 (QB).

[295] See para.11 of the Explanatory Notes to the Act, which concerns s.1, as follows: "The section builds on the consideration given by the courts in a series of cases to the question of what is sufficient to establish that a statement is defamatory. A recent example is *Thornton v Telegraph Media Group Ltd* [[2010] EWHC 1414 (QB); [2011] 1 W.L.R. 1985] . . . There is also currently potential for trivial cases to be struck out on the basis that they are an abuse of process because so little is at stake. In *Jameel* . . . it was established that there needs to be a real and substantial tort. This section raises the bar for bringing a claim so that only cases involving serious harm to the claimant's reputation can be brought."

[296] *Riddick v Thames Board Mills* [1977] Q.B. 881 (CA), and see para.31.13, below.

[297] *Carpenter v Associated Newspapers Ltd*, unreported, November 26, 2001, (QB), per Gray J. See also *Raab v Associated Newspapers Ltd* [2011] EWHC 3375 (QB) in which *Carpenter* was distinguished (D's application to strike out or alternatively to stay proceedings on the ground that C declined to release a witness from a confidentiality undertaking was dismissed).

[298] *Riches v DPP* [1973] 1 W.L.R. 1019 (CA). See, more recently, *Zinda v ARK Academies* [2011] EWHC 3394 (QB).

[299] *E v Dorset County Council* [1995] 2 A.C. 233, per Sir Thomas Bingham M.R.

[300] See in this regard *Miller v Associated Newspapers Ltd* [2003] EWHC 2799; [2004] E.M.L.R. 33 per Eady J. at [33].

SECTION 6. STAY OF PROCEEDINGS

Power to order stay. The court has an inherent jurisdiction, recognised by **30.51**
s.49(3) Senior Courts Act 1981[301] and restated by CPR r.3.1(2)(f),[302] to stay
proceedings before it. Where a defendant contests the court's jurisdiction to
hear the claim, there is also a power to stay under CPR r.11(6)(d). The burden
lies on the applicant seeking a stay to show, by cogent evidence, that there are
sound reasons for a stay in the particular case,[303] and that it would be just and
convenient to order one in all the circumstances.[304]

Situations in which stay ordered. In the defamation context, the power **30.52**
to stay is probably exercised most regularly in the context of abuse of
process.[305] Abuse apart, the jurisdiction has most often been invoked in
circumstances in which there are parallel proceedings, whether civil (including employment proceedings), criminal, or disciplinary, and the question
arises whether the defamation action should be stayed pending the resolution
of the other proceedings. Underlying the exercise of the jurisdiction in the
defamation field is the proposition that the essence of a genuine complaint in
defamation is prompt action, both because a claimant with a serious claim will
want prompt vindication,[306] and because it is important that defendants should
not have "the anxiety, expense and inconvenience of a defamation action

---

[301] S.49(3): "Nothing in this Act shall affect the power of the Court of Appeal or the High
Court to stay any proceedings before it, where it thinks fit to do so, either of its own motion or
on the application of any person, whether or not a party to the proceedings."

[302] R.3.1(2): "Except where these Rules provide otherwise, the court may . . . (f) stay the whole
or part of any proceedings or judgment either generally or until a specified date or event."

[303] *Wakefield v Channel Four Television* [2005] EWHC 2410 (QB) at [11].

[304] "The appropriate course in any case depends on what is just and convenient on the facts":
Vaughan v London Borough of Lewisham [2013] EWHC 795 (QB) at [40] per Sharp J.

[305] As to which, see in particular paras 30.43–30.50, above.

[306] It was this consideration that also prompted in part the progressive reduction in the
limitation period in defamation from six years (Limitation Act 1980, s.2) to three (Limitation Act
1980, s.4A, added by Administration of Justice Act 1985, s.57(2)), and from three years to one
(Limitation Act 1980, s.4A, added by Defamation Act 1996, s.5(2)). But that is not to say that
there may not be occasions when it is wholly legitimate to delay issue of a claim form. David
Steel J. recalled in *Steedman v BBC* [2001] EWCA Civ 1534; [2002] E.M.L.R. 17 at [20] the
words of the Supreme Court Procedure Committee (under the chairmanship of Neill L.J.) in 1991,
suggesting that the issue of a claim form might appropriately be delayed:
" . . . because the subject of the libel is being investigated by some other means and they wish
to await the outcome, rather than have two such enquiries proceeding in parallel. For example,
newspaper allegations may be the subject of a disciplinary inquiry by a professional or sporting
body; there may be criminal proceedings in progress, touching upon the same issues; or a
Department of Trade investigation may be on foot. Again, we can see that delay might be
justified in such cases, although there would generally be no reason to keep the potential
defendants completely in the dark"
(Neill Report, para.VIII.5). To that, one might add the case where a claimant has several claims
against different newspapers, which he is unwilling or unable to sue simultaneously. But with the
limitation period a mere year, as opposed to the three years in 1991 when the Neill Committee
reported, it might now be better to issue and serve the claim forms, proceed with one and apply
to stay the others pending determination of the first. Moreover, potential defendants should under
no circumstances be kept in the dark."

hanging over them for an unnecessarily long period."[307] Moreover, there is acknowledged to be a "chilling effect" on journalists' rights under art.10 of the European Convention if, when sued for defamation, they are prevented from putting forward their defence for any significant period of time;[308] and the entitlement of any litigant under art.6 to have a fair and public hearing "within a reasonable time"[309] is a major consideration.[310] Therefore the need for swift progress in defamation litigation will be a matter of particular concern to the court. Nevertheless, "there is no easy rule of thumb" to assist the court to decide which of two parallel proceedings should go first: it is for the court to decide, on the fullest possible information, and having regard to the particular facts and circumstances and the likely timetable of the individual case, where the balance of justice lies.[311] So in *Fallon v MGN*, where the newspaper sought a stay of a libel action pending determination of related criminal proceedings, but no defence of justification had been pleaded and the claimant had not even been charged with criminal wrongdoing, an application for a stay was premature. The judge held that it was important that the issues should at least be crystallised in properly pleaded form.[312] By contrast, in a case where the defendant applied to dismiss for want of prosecution, the Court of Appeal held that a libel claimant had acted reasonably in delaying until the outcome of related French proceedings was known.[313] There may be good reason to stay libel proceedings in favour of parallel criminal proceedings to avoid prejudice to the criminal trial.[314]

Much will depend on which proceedings were started first, how far the defamation action has progressed, whether the overlapping issues are more suitable for determination in the defamation or in the parallel proceedings, and the extent to which (if at all) the parallel proceedings will assist in the

---

[307] *Oyston v Blaker* [1996] 2 All E.R. 106 per Henry L.J. at 108, 118; and in *Grovit v Doctor*, unreported, October 28, 1993 C.A., Glidewell L.J. said:
"The purpose of a libel action is to enable the plaintiff to clear his name of the libel, to vindicate his character. In an action for defamation in which the plaintiff wishes to achieve this end, he will also wish the action to be heard as soon as possible".
Similarly, in *Steedman v BBC* [2001] EWCA Civ 1534; [2002] E.M.L.R. 17, the Court of Appeal noted that:
"Delay itself, whether or not it is established to have been prejudicial to the defendant, is rightly treated as prejudicial to the administration of justice".
For delay as abuse of process, see also *Grovit v Doctor* [1997] 1 W.L.R. 640 HL, *Powell v Boladz* [2003] EWHC 2160 (QB), *Adelson v Anderson* [2011] EWHC 2497 (QB), and *Morrissey v McNicholas* [2011] EWHC 2738 (QB).
[308] *Wakefield v Channel Four Television*, above, at [29].
[309] Art.6.1: "Everyone is entitled to a fair and public hearing within a reasonable time and by an independent and impartial tribunal established by law."
[310] *Fallon v MGN Ltd* [2005] EWHC 1572 (QB) at [16].
[311] *Fallon v MGN Ltd*, above, at [17]–[18].
[312] [2005] EWHC 1572 (QB) at [28].
[313] *Khalili v Bennett* [2000] E.M.L.R. 996. In *Grobbelaar v News Group Newspapers*, (reported on appeal to the House of Lords from the jury's verdict at [2002] 1 W.L.R. 3024) the claimant agreed not to progress his libel action until criminal proceedings had been concluded.
[314] *Wakefield v Channel Four Television* [2005] EWHC 2410 (QB) at [23].

determination of issues in the defamation proceedings.[315] Where the parallel proceedings are criminal and the defendant is the libel claimant, a conviction will be conclusive evidence of his commission of the offence,[316] but in disciplinary cases the conclusions of tribunals will not usually be admissible, and even if admissible not determinative, on any issue in the defamation proceedings.[317] In *Gee v BBC*[318] the judge found it almost impossible to decide whether libel proceedings or disciplinary proceedings before the General Medical Council should be heard first, but ultimately concluded that proceedings in courts of law must in the interests of justice take priority over even the hearings of a tribunal of such importance as the GMC. In *Sharma v Jay (No.2)*,[319] another GMC case, the defendants sought a stay of a slander action pending resolution of GMC enquiries into the claimant's activities, but their application was refused: the GMC had not formulated any charges against the claimant, the slander action had been started well before the GMC investigation, so had "seniority", a date for trial had been fixed, and the issues were not such that the GMC should determine them first.[320] Moreover, findings made by the GMC would not be dispositive of any issues in the slander action. Unusually, it was the claimant who sought a stay pending determination of GMC proceedings in the case of *Wakefield v Channel Four Television*.[321] The application was refused, partly because the judge concluded that the claimant was trying to extract what advantage he could from the existence of the libel proceedings while not wishing to progress them, but also because (inter alia) the conclusions of the GMC would not be relevant or admissible on justification, there was no power in the GMC to compel disclosure of documents, and allegations which went to undermine fundamentally the claimant's professional integrity and honesty were best determined in court.

---

[315] For example, where both sets of proceedings involve the same parties or their privies, an issue decided in the first might become res judicata for the purposes of the second.

[316] Civil Evidence Act 1968, s.13(1), as amended by Defamation Act 1996, s.12(1). Note that in *Khalili v Bennett* (above) Hale L.J., at [41] indicated that, in the light of the fact that a conviction in a UK court is conclusive proof that the convicted person committed the offence, she did "not follow the argument that therefore the defamation trial should come on before the criminal trial. The chances of injustice resulting from it seem to me to be considerable in the circumstances".

[317] On the footing that ss.11 and 13, Civil Evidence Act 1968 only render criminal convictions, not prior tribunal findings, conclusive evidence in subsequent defamation proceedings. Furthermore, unless the relevant regulatory body or prosecutor is the defendant in the defamation proceedings, there will not be an identity of parties as between the disciplinary and defamation proceedings: see *McKeown v Attheraces Ltd* [2011] EWHC 179 (QB).

[318] Michael Davies J., unreported, July 30, 1984.

[319] Eady J., unreported, February 11, 2004.

[320] As Eady J. said in *Sharma v Jay (No.2)* (above) at [10]:
" . . . one pays the greatest respect to the expertise of the GMC in resolving matters of a professional nature and in particular of a medical nature, but here . . . there are very serious allegations of dishonesty on both sides. It cannot seriously be suggested that priority should be given to GMC proceedings for the resolution of issues of that kind".

[321] [2005] EWHC 2410 (QB).

Tesco Stores Ltd v Guardian News & Media[322] involved a claim in libel and malicious falsehood where an offer of amends had been made in response to the libel claim, but the claimant declined to say whether or not the offer was accepted. The defendants asked the judge to stay the malicious falsehood claim on the basis that it added nothing legitimate to the libel action, interfered with the proper working of the offer of amends procedure and (if the offer of amends was accepted) should not as a matter of principle or policy be allowed to proceed. This attempt to impose a permanent stay on a properly pleaded cause of action was stoutly resisted by the claimant, which argued that the court's case management powers could not, absent abuse of process, be used to stay a properly constituted cause of action, and relied on *Ashley v Chief Constable of Sussex Police*[323] for the proposition that case management powers should not be used to prevent a claimant bringing to trial a viable claim simply because he could recover no damages additional to those recoverable from another cause of action on which liability had been conceded: moreover, it argued that it was entitled to a public vindication of its right not (as it was put) "to be subjected to a series of false, malicious and damaging statements about its tax affairs". The interrelated questions which Eady J. had to resolve were whether the claimant should be compelled to elect to accept or reject the offer of amends, and whether the malicious falsehood claim should be stayed as serving no useful purpose. The judge distinguished *Ashley* on the basis that in that case there was a legitimate potentially vindicatory purpose in permitting the second cause of action to proceed, notwithstanding the chief constable's admission of liability as far as the other cause of action was concerned. In the present case there was no legitimate objective in pressing on with the malicious falsehood claim, which would have driven a "coach and four" through the statutory offer of amends regime enacted by Parliament, and the judge stayed it forthwith.[324]

In *Blake v Associated Newspapers Ltd*,[325] Gray J. ordered a stay of a libel action on the ground that certain key issues which had to be decided in the

---

[322] [2009] E.M.L.R. 5.
[323] [2008] 1 A.C. 962. In that case Lord Bingham said at [4]:
" . . . it is ordinarily for the claimant, properly advised of the litigation risk, to decide what claim, being arguable and legally unobjectionable, he wishes to pursue, and case management, legitimately used to ensure that the court's process is efficiently and justly used, gives no warrant to extinguish the autonomy of the individual litigant".
Lord Rodger stated at [70] that:
"Case management is intended to assist, not to frustrate, the administration of justice between the parties. Where parties have a valid cause of action, justice is unlikely to be served by preventing them from advancing their cause of action on the ground that their motive for doing so is somehow improper".
[324] Eady J. gave the claimant a fixed period in which to accept or reject the offer of amends.
[325] [2003] EWHC 1960 (QB). See also *His Holiness Sant Baba Jeet Singh Ji Maharaj v Eastern Media Group Ltd* [2010] EWHC 1294 (QB) and *Shergill v Purewal* [2010] EWHC 3610 (QB) in which Eady J. and Sir Charles Gray respectively stayed libel proceedings on similar grounds. *Shergill v Purewal*. A similar problem arose in *Hamilton & Greer v Hencke* (unreported,

case (which related to the validity of a consecration of a bishop outside the mainstream churches) were not justiciable in a civil court.

It is not unusual for defamation claims to be stayed pending mediation or some other form of alternative dispute resolution, as is common in other types of civil litigation[326]: the policy of encouraging settlement supersedes even the imperative of progressing defamation cases to trial as expeditiously as possible.

SECTION 7. THE TRIAL OF ISSUES

Generally. Lord Scarman once warned: "Preliminary points of law are too often treacherous short cuts. Their price can be, as here, delay, anxiety, and expense".[327] However, the CPR encourage the trial of preliminary issues, whether of law or of mixed law and fact, and CPR r.3.1(2)(i) and (j) give the court a flexible power to direct the separate trial of any issue and to decide the order in which issues are to be tried.[328] In deciding whether to exercise the power by directing the trial of a specific issue or issues, the concerns articulated by Lord Scarman will nonetheless be at forefront of judge's mind: is the holding of a preliminary trial likely to save time, expense and court resources and thereby further the overriding objective in CPR r.1.1, or is it liable to produce the opposite result? The answer to this question will vary from case to case depending particularly on whether one or more issues can be separated out from the others, and the extent to which the early determination of those **30.53**

July 21, 1995), May J., where (before s.13 of the Defamation Act 1996, was passed) the area of non-justiciability consisted of matters the subject of parliamentary privilege.

[326] See CPR r.26.4 for the court's powers to stay proceedings on this basis. Indeed, as of April 1, 2013, if both parties request a month's stay for ADR in their directions questionnaires, it will be granted automatically.

[327] *Tilling v Whiteman* [1980] A.C. 1 at 25C (a landlord and tenant case). See also Lord Denning M.R.'s earlier remarks to the same effect in *Richards v Naum* [1967] 1 Q.B. 620 at 626.

[328] Despite the existence of so flexible a power, there are certain practical limits to its operation in defamation, which traditionally has been tried by a jury. It has been said that in a libel action issues of liability and damages should not be tried separately, particularly when a jury is involved (*Lewis v Daily Telegraph (No.2)* [1964] 2 Q.B. at 621, per Pearson L.J.), and as a general proposition that must be right, since questions of liability and of damages are in practice very closely connected: for instance, partial proof of justification, though insufficient to meet the sting of the charge, may nonetheless have a dramatic impact on damages (see for instance *Pamplin v Express Newspapers* [1988] 1 W.L.R. 116 at 120, per Neill L.J.:

> "There may be many cases . . . where a defendant who put forward a defence of justification will be unable to prove sufficient facts to establish the defence at common law and will also be unable to bring himself within the statutory extension of the defence contained in s.5 of the Defamation Act 1952. Nevertheless the defendant may be able to rely on such facts as he has proved to reduce the damages, perhaps almost to vanishing point".

Conversely, aggressive cross-examination of the claimant on issues of justification may properly be taken into consideration in aggravation of damages if the plea fails. Nevertheless, see para.31.68, below and the discussion of *Collins-Stewart v Financial Times Ltd* [2004] EWHC 2337; [2005] E.M.L.R. 5 to be found there.

issues is apt to have a substantial benefit for the litigation. Ideally, the perceived benefit will be the possibility that the preliminary trial is dispositive of the claim as a whole, but it may be sufficient if the procedure promises to narrow the issues, or even merely to enable the parties to obtain a better idea of where they stand. The potential downside is that adopting such a procedure may turn out to have been an expensive waste of time.

Accordingly, at the heart of a decision to direct the trial of a preliminary issue rests a reasonably elaborate cost-benefit calculation. Some issues will be relatively inexpensive to try, and the benefit of doing so obvious: for example, an early determination of an issue of meaning or of fact or comment may have the consequence of ruling in or out, in part or as a whole, a defence of justification or honest comment. But by contrast, where the costs of trying the preliminary issue are likely to be significant—for instance, the trial of a contentious defence of *Reynolds* privilege—the court will require more persuasion that there is a saving to be had. In particular, in a case where the defendant is relying on more than one substantive defence, most typically *Reynolds* privilege and justification, the principal risk in costs terms is that a preliminary trial of one of the defences will be determined in favour of the claimant, with the result that the other defence has to be tried too. By this stage, especially if witnesses who were called at the first trial are being recalled to give evidence on different topics at the second, the court may wonder why it did not order all the issues to be tried at once. *A fortiori* if the first trial has generated interlocutory appeals, which happens not infrequently in defamation cases.

In spite of these concerns, orders for the separate trial of issues have become common in defamation, particularly as the role of the jury has diminished,[329] and although unlikely to be made before service of defence,[330]

---

[329] In *Kirby-Harris v Baxter* [1995] E.M.L.R. 516 CA, it was held wrong to direct trial by judge alone of a preliminary issue involving a question of fact which for practical purposes amounted to deciding whether the defendants were motivated by malice, when the plaintiff was entitled to have the issue determined by a jury. But for all sorts of reasons, judges have not been attracted to the idea of empanelling a jury to determine a preliminary issue. For instance, were a jury to be empanelled to decide the factual aspects of *Reynolds* privilege defence in a case where the defendant relied on that defence and justification, and they ruled on that issue in favour of a claimant, either the same jury would then need to go on to hear a second trial of justification or a fresh jury would have to be empanelled to decide that issue. (In this connection, see further fn.333, below.) Neither seems ideal. Generally speaking, therefore, either the parties have agreed that a preliminary issue should be tried by judge alone, or the court has made an order to that effect in its discretion: see Senior Courts Act 1981, s.69(4) which specifically provides that "different questions of fact arising in any action" may "be tried by different modes of trial". One notable exception is the pioneering order made by Popplewell J. in *Marks & Spencer Plc v Granada Television*, unreported, February 23, 1998, whereby he directed that the actual meaning of the words complained of to be determined by a jury. The jury rejected the defendant's *Lucas-Box* meaning, which was the premise of the defence of justification, with the result that several weeks of trial were saved. Although the judge's approach was later endorsed by Hirst L.J. in *Shah v Standard Chartered Bank* [1999] Q.B. 241 at 265–266, the experiment has never been repeated. Cf. Eady J.'s attitude in *Armstrong v Times Newspapers Ltd* [2005] EWHC 2816 (QB).

[330] When it is likely to be premature, because the issues have not crystallised: *Turkot v Oxus Gold Plc* [2006] EWHC 3361 (QB).

may be made at an early stage of the litigation, for instance at the case management conference. Indeed, if it has become evident by this juncture that such a direction might be desirable, the matter ought to be canvassed with the court: where it is decided to direct a preliminary trial, there may be significant contingent costs savings by reason of the reduction in the scope of disclosure, and of factual and expert witness evidence. Nevertheless, matters may not have become sufficiently clear at this stage, and it is open to the court to exercise the power to direct a preliminary issue at any time before the full trial of all the issues.

Qualified privilege. An issue which has often been tried separately and   **30.54** first in defamation is qualified privilege. In an early CPR-era case, *GKR Karate v Yorkshire Post*, Sir Oliver Popplewell made an order at trial for determination of preliminary issues of qualified privilege and malice. The Court of Appeal dismissed the claimant's appeal, May L.J. observing that libel actions are especially amenable to the culture of the Civil Procedure Rules and require novel and imaginative case management. He believed that "a fair means of determining privilege and malice expeditiously . . . without having to trudge expensively through the mire of justification" achieved the over-riding objective.[331] Another division of the Court of Appeal suggested that qualified privilege "ordinarily falls to be judged as a preliminary issue",[332] and in a later case[333] Brooke L.J. stated that it might very well be, now that the ground rules for *Reynolds* qualified privilege had become fairly settled, that judges might think it wise to direct a preliminary issue on qualified privilege in such a case, on the basis that a decision in favour of the defendants would avert a long trial on justification; but he warned of the potential injustice of delaying the ultimate trial while preliminary issues are fought over, perhaps all the way to the House of Lords. In *Henry v BBC*,[334] the issue of *Reynolds* privilege was decided against the BBC, so that justification still had to be tried at a later date. The same occurred in *Qadir v Associated Newspapers Ltd*,[335] following a preliminary trial of issues of statutory report-ing and common law privilege and malice. Had the Court of Appeal's decision in *Flood v Times Newspapers Ltd*[336] been allowed to stand, it would have

---

[331] [2000] E.M.L.R. 396 at 404.

[332] *Loutchansky v Times Newspapers Ltd (No.2)* [2001] EWCA Civ 1805; [2002] Q.B. 783 at [41]. Lord Phillips encouraged the determination of *Reynolds* privilege as a preliminary issue in *Flood v Times Newspapers Ltd* [2012] UKSC 11; [2012] 2 A.C. 273 at [49], describing it as "commonplace and sensible".

[333] *Macintyre v Chief Constable of Kent* [2002] EWCA 1087 at [35]–[36]. At first instance, Gray J. had refused to order the trial of preliminary issues because of the risk that the issues would throw up wide-ranging factual inquiries, and because it would be unsatisfactory for one jury to decide the issue of malice in favour of the claimant and for another jury to have to be empanelled at a later date to decide the remaining issues, including justification.

[334] [2005] EWHC 2787 (QB).

[335] [2012] EWHC 2606 (QB); [2013] E.M.L.R. 15.

[336] [2010] EWCA Civ 804; [2011] 1 W.L.R. 153.

produced the same undesirable result, but the Supreme Court[337] preferred Tugendhat J.'s conclusion, which was in favour of the defendant. The issue of *Reynolds* privilege was ultimately decided in favour of the defendants in *Charman v Orion Publishing Group Ltd.*[338] In *Roberts v Gable*,[339] Eady J.'s ruling that an article was protected by *Reynolds* qualified privilege of the reportage variety was upheld by the Court of Appeal. Meanwhile, in *McKeown v Attheraces Ltd*,[340] Eady J. declined to order that *Reynolds* privilege be tried as a preliminary issue on the ground that there was no clear advantage in doing so. The facts were heavily in dispute and the privilege issues could not be determined in a vacuum. Furthermore, if a preliminary issue of *Reynolds* privilege were to be decided in favour of the claimant, the evidence would have to be considered in detail for the purposes of justification and honest comment, after this had already been done for the purpose of privilege. There was liable to be substantial duplication and no saving of time or costs.

30.55 Other issues. Issues have been tried as to absolute privilege[341] and qualified privilege by report of proceedings in Parliament,[342] and as to whether words were comment or fact.[343] There have also been several trials of preliminary issues as to the meaning of the words complained of, which in some cases have served to narrow very substantially the matters in issue in justification.[344] By contrast, in *Cairns v Modi*,[345] Tugendhat J. declined to order the trial of an issue as to the extent of publication within the jurisdiction of the tweet complained of. The object of the proposed exercise was to lay the ground for a submission, if warranted, that the action was a *Jameel*-abuse of process. But the judge held that, even if the number of publishees turned out to have been very limited, it would not have been determinative of the question of abuse of process. Likewise, in *Price v Powell*, a misuse of private information

---

[337] [2012] UKSC 11; [2012] 2 A.C. 273. That said, the litigation continues in relation to the online publication of the article complained of: see [2013] EWHC 2182 (QB).

[338] The Court of Appeal decided to reverse the judge's decision that no privilege was made out: [2007] EWCA Civ 972; [2008] 1 All E.R. 750.

[339] [2007] EWCA Civ 721; [2008] Q.B. 502.

[340] [2011] EWHC 3232 (QB) at [27]–[31].

[341] *Freer v Glover* [2005] EWHC 3341 (QB).

[342] *Curistan v Times Newspapers Ltd* [2008] EWCA Civ 432; [2008] 3 All E.R. 923.

[343] *Branson v Bower* [2001] EWCA Civ 791; [2001] E.M.L.R. 32; *British Chiropractic Association v Singh* [2010] EWCA Civ 350; [2011] 1 W.L.R. 133; *Euromoney Institutional Investor Plc v Aviation News Ltd* [2013] EWHC 1505 (QB).

[344] These decisions include *Charman v Orion Publishing Group Ltd* [2005] EWHC 2187 (QB); *Armstrong v Times Newspapers Ltd* [2006] EWHC 1614 (QB); and *Curistan v Times Newspapers Ltd*, above; *Cruddas v Calvert* [2013] EWCA Civ 748, in which the Court of Appeal allowed the defendant's appeal against Tugendhat J.'s determination of the meaning, reinstating the plea of justification which had been struck out contingently upon the judge's ruling on meaning. See further paras 30.14–30.16, above.

[345] [2010] EWHC 2859 (QB). Bean J. went on to award the claimant £90,000 damages at the trial of the action ([2012] EWHC 756 (QB)) in respect of a publication to some 65 people, an award upheld by the Court of Appeal: [2012] EWCA Civ 1382; [2013] 1 W.L.R. 1015.

case, the same judge refused to direct a preliminary trial of the question of whether certain germane text messages and images stored on a mobile telephone were authentic: the application was ruled premature.[346]

---

[346] *Price v Powell* [2013] EWHC 1325 (QB).

CHAPTER 31

INTERLOCUTORY MATTERS

SECTION 1. DISCLOSURE

General. The purpose of this section is to highlight those few aspects of **31.1** disclosure which have a particular bearing on defamation litigation. The reader is referred to specialist publications for a full account of the principles and practice of disclosure.[1]

Disclosure before action. Senior Courts Act 1981, s.33(2) and CPR **31.2** r.31.16 permit pre-action disclosure where the applicant and respondent are likely to be parties to subsequent proceedings,[2] where if proceedings had started, the respondent's duty of standard disclosure would extend to the documents sought, and where, most importantly, disclosure before action is necessary in order to dispose fairly of the anticipated proceedings, to assist the

---

[1] See in particular Matthews and Malek, *Disclosure*, 4th edn (London: Sweet & Maxwell 2012), and Sweet & Maxwell's *Civil Procedure* (*The White Book*), Vol.1, notes to CPR Pt 31.

[2] I.e. the persons concerned are likely to be—meaning "may well be"—parties in proceedings if those proceedings are issued: *Black v Sumitomo Corp* [2001] EWCA Civ 1819; [2002] 1 W.L.R. 1562 per Rix L.J. at [71]–[72]:

"Where the future has to be predicted, but on an application which is not merely pre-trial but pre-action, a high test requiring proof on the balance of probability will be both undesirable and unnecessary: undesirable, because it does not respond to the nature and timing of the application; and unnecessary, because the court has all the power it needs in the overall exercise of its discretion to balance the possible uncertainties of the situation against the specificity or otherwise of the disclosure requested".

dispute to be resolved without proceedings, or to save costs.[3] However, it should not be thought that r.31.16 gives carte blanche to libel litigants to fish for a case, either by obtaining disclosure of documents thought to contain defamatory words or by finding evidence to support a prospective defence. Given that disclosure will only be ordered where the court can say that the documents sought would have to be disclosed at the stage of standard disclosure, the court would have to be clear what the issues in the action are likely to be before it can form a view as to whether pre-action disclosure is desirable for one or other of the reasons set out in the rule.[4] It will not be possible, therefore, for a defendant to a libel action to seek pre-action disclosure to support a hoped-for plea of justification,[5] or for a claimant to fish for a case of malice in anticipation of a defence of qualified privilege or honest comment. However, it should not be forgotten that a purpose of pre-trial disclosure is to assist not only those who can already plead a cause of action to improve their pleadings, but also those who need disclosure as a vital step in deciding whether to litigate at all or as a vital ingredient in the pleading of their case.[6]

31.3 Disclosure of document shown to a third person. It may be that a prospective libel claimant who can show that a particular document containing words defamatory of him was shown by the prospective defendant to a third party on a particular occasion—so can resist a charge of fishing—will be able to invoke r.31.16 to obtain pre-action disclosure of the libel.[7] That would not be a major extension of the principle which has long allowed slander plaintiffs to interrogate before service of particulars of claim as to the precise words spoken.[8] Without disclosure of the actual words of the libel, the

---

[3] But note that s.35(1) prevents the court from making an order under s.33 if it considers that compliance with the order would be likely to be injurious to the public interest. For the position in New South Wales, see *Hatfield v TCN Channel Nine Pty Ltd* [2010] NSWCA 69, in which the state Court of Appeal dismissed the applicant's appeal against a decision of the first instance judge whereby he refused to order preliminary discovery of "any episode of, and the transcript of any episode of, the television series known as '*Underbelly: The Golden Mile*' . . . in which the applicant is named, depicted (by an actor or picture or otherwise) and/or referred to" in order that the applicant might, if so advised, sue the respondent for defamation.

[4] So an order was made in a case involving causes of action under the Data Protection Act 1998 and in confidence and privacy, where it was clear that the documents sought would be in issue in subsequent proceedings: *Hughes v Carratu International Plc* [2006] EWHC 1791 (QB).

[5] *Granada Television v News Group Newspapers Ltd*, unreported, July 30, 1999.

[6] *Black v Sumitomo Corp* [2001] EWCA Civ 1819; [2002] 1 W.L.R. 1562 per Rix L.J. at [68]; *Mitsui v Nexen Petroleum* [2005] EWHC 625 (Ch); [2005] 3 All E.R. 511 at [27].

[7] Note also the jurisdiction of the court under s.33(1), Senior Courts Act 1981, and (to an extent) CPR r.25.1(1)(c) to make an order providing for the inspection, photographing, preservation, custody or detention of property which appears to the court to be property which may become the subject-matter of subsequent proceedings before the court, or as to which any question may arise in any such proceedings. A physical document is a species of property: *Lord Ashburton v Pape* [1913] 2 Ch. 469; *ITC Film v Video Exchange* [1982] 1 Ch. 431.

[8] *Atkinson v Fosbroke* (1866) L.R. 1 Q.B. 628, and see paras 31.18 and 31.23, below.

claimant is in grave difficulty because of the obligation to plead actual words and not their gist,[9] and because of the embargo on guesswork.[10]

Norwich Pharmacal orders. The *Norwich Pharmacal*[11] route is in some **31.4** cases an alternative means of obtaining pre-action disclosure of documents and information for the purpose of bringing defamation proceedings. However, the jurisdiction only provides a right of action in discovery against a person who has become mixed up in the wrongdoing of others.[12] In *Rugby Football Union v Consolidated Information Services Ltd (formerly Viagogo Ltd) (in liquidation)*,[13] the Supreme Court restated the principles governing the *Norwich Pharmacal* jurisdiction. The relevant authorities emphasise the need for flexibility and discretion in considering whether the remedy should be granted,[14] but the basic conditions for the exercise of the jurisdiction can be summarised as follows:

  (a) an arguable wrong must have been carried out against the applicant by an alleged wrongdoer;

  (b) the person against whom the order is sought must (i) be mixed up in the arguable wrongdoing,[15] and (ii) be able or likely to be able to provide information which would enable the applicant to take action against the alleged wrongdoer;

---

[9] *British Data v Boxer Removals* [1996] 3 All E.R. 707 CA; *Best v Charter Medical of England* [2001] EWCA Civ 1588; [2002] E.M.L.R. 18.

[10] *Collins v Jones* [1955] 1 Q.B. 564 CA.

[11] *Norwich Pharmacal v Customs & Excise* [1974] A.C. 133:
"If through no fault of his own a person gets mixed up in the tortious acts of others so as to facilitate their wrongdoing he may incur no personal liability but he comes under a duty to assist the person who has been wronged by giving him full information and disclosing the identity of the wrongdoers. I do not think that it matters whether he became so mixed up by voluntary action on his part or because it was his duty to do what he did. It may be that if this causes him expense the person seeking the information ought to reimburse him. But justice requires that he should co-operate in righting the wrong if he unwittingly facilitated its perpetration",
per Lord Reid at 175. The court's power to grant orders on this basis is preserved by CPR r.31.18.

[12] [1974] A.C. 133 at 175. In *Norwich Pharmacal*, the wrongdoing was tortious, but it is now clear that it need not be: see *Ashworth Hospital Authority v MGN Ltd* [2001] 1 W.L.R. 515 at [66] and [2002] UKHL 29; [2002] 1 W.L.R. 2033 at [34]; *Carlton Film Distributors v VCI* [2003] EWHC 616 (Ch); [2003] F.S.R. 47. Furthermore, despite Lord Reid's wording in *Norwich Pharmacal* at 175 (see fn.11, above), it is not a necessary condition of the exercise of the jurisdiction that the respondent has facilitated the alleged wrongdoing in question: *Various Claimants v News Group Newspapers Ltd* [2013] EWHC 2119 (Ch) at [52] per Mann J.

[13] [2012] UKSC 55; [2012] 1 W.L.R. 3333 at [14]–[17].

[14] *Ashworth Hospital Authority v MGN Ltd* [2002] UKHL 29; [2002] 1 W.L.R. 2033 per Lord Woolf C.J. at [57]; *Koo Golden East Mongolia v Bank of Nova Scotia* [2007] EWCA Civ 1443; [2008] Q.B. 717 per Sir Anthony Clarke M.R. at [37]–[38].

[15] It is sufficient if the respondent is innocently mixed up in the alleged wrongdoing, but it is no bar to the exercise of the jurisdiction if he is more culpably involved: *X Ltd v Morgan-Grampian Publishers Ltd* [1991] 1 A.C. 1, 54 per Lord Lowry.

So the respondent to an application must be more than a spectator or the mere possessor of some relevant document. As Lord Reid observed[16]:

" . . . a person might know that a particular person is in possession of a libellous letter which he has good reason to believe defames him but the author of which he cannot discover. I am satisfied that it would not be proper in either case to order discovery in order that the person who has suffered damage might be able to find and sue the wrongdoer. Neither authority, principle nor public policy would justify that."

Furthermore, by what is known as the "mere witness" rule, no order may be made against a person who will in due course be compellable to supply the information, whether orally or by disclosure:

"It has been clear at least since the time of Lord Hardwicke that information cannot be obtained by discovery from a person who will in due course be compellable to give that information either by oral testimony as a witness or on a subpoena duces tecum. Whether the reasons justifying that rule are good or bad it is much too late to inquire: the rule is settled. But the foundation of the rule is the assumption that eventually the testimony will be available either in an action already in progress or in an action which will be brought later".[17]

    (c) there must be a need for an order to enable action to be brought against the alleged wrongdoer, although that action need not be legal proceedings in respect of the arguable wrong; any form of redress (for example disciplinary action or the dismissal of an employee) will suffice[18]; the applicant must genuinely intend to try to seek redress for the arguable wrong[19];

    (d) an order will only be granted if it is proportionate to do so in all the circumstances,[20] having particular regard to the privacy and data protection rights of the alleged wrongdoers and the terms of the order

---

[16] *Norwich Pharmacal v Customs & Excise* [1974] A.C. 133 at 174D. So in *Ricci v Chow* [1987] 1 W.L.R. 1658 CA, where the plaintiff sought *Norwich Pharmacal* discovery against someone who had no involvement in publication of the libel, that individual could not be ordered to disclose the names of those responsible for publication, even if he knew them. For a detailed contemporary analysis of the "mere witness" rule, see *Various Claimants v News Group Newspapers Ltd* [2013] EWHC 2119 (Ch) per Mann J.

[17] [1974] A.C. 133 at 174a-b, per Lord Reid. In *Mitsui v Nexen Petroleum* [2005] EWHC 625 (Ch); [2005] 3 All E.R. 511, an order was refused because the information could have been obtained by pre-action disclosure, not from the respondent to the application, but from a prospective defendant to anticipated proceedings.

[18] *British Steel Corp v Granada Television Ltd* [1981] A.C. 1096 per Lord Fraser of Tullybelton at 1200.

[19] *Golden Eye (International) Ltd Telefonica UK Ltd* [2012] EWCA Civ 1740; [2013] R.P.C. 18 at [7(iii)] (issue as formulated by Arnold J.; implicitly approved by Court of Appeal).

[20] *Ashworth Hospital Authority v MGN Ltd* [2002] UKHL 29; [2002] 1 W.L.R. 2033 per Lord Woolf C.J. at [36], [57]; *Golden Eye (International) Ltd v Telefonica UK Ltd*, above, at [15]. "The essential purpose of the remedy is to do justice. This involves the exercise of discretion by a careful weighing of all relevant factors. Various factors have been identified in the authorities as relevant. These include (i) the strength of the possible cause of action contemplated by the applicant . . . ; (ii) the strong public interest in allowing an applicant to vindicate his legal rights . . . ; (iii) whether the making of the order will deter similar wrongdoing in the future . . . ; (iv) whether the information could be obtained from another source . . . ; (v)

sought, although the test of necessity does not require the remedy to be one of last resort[21]; and

(e) discretionary factors favour granting disclosure.

The *Norwich Pharmacal* jurisdiction extends to cases "where there is a good indication of wrongdoing, but not every piece of what the claimant needs to plead a case is fully in position".[22] Indeed, it may be available even when the applicant is unsure that he has a viable cause of action, as happened in *P v T Ltd*.[23] In that case the respondent, the applicant's former employer, was ordered to give discovery to enable the applicant to identify and bring libel or malicious falsehood proceedings against a third party whose allegations formed the basis for his summary dismissal. The employer would not specify the nature of the allegations or identify their source, and the applicant was dismissed after a disciplinary hearing which the judge described as a "farce". Since (the applicant claimed) it was generally known in the industry that he had been dismissed for misconduct of a kind which he could not explain, he could not obtain employment. His only course was to find out the nature of the allegations and the identity of their source, in the hope of clearing his name by litigation. Remarkably, the employer appears to have been in the position of a mere bystander, akin to the person whom Lord Reid envisaged as being in possession of a libellous letter.[24] It is true that the employer acted on the allegations by dismissing the applicant, but the tort, if any, was complete when the libel was published to the employer, and so that the employer was not on the face of it caught up in the third party's tortious acts.[25] The answer may lie

---

whether the respondent to the application knew or ought to have known that he was facilitating arguable wrongdoing . . . or was himself a tortfeasor . . . ; (vi) whether the order might reveal the names of innocent persons as well as wrongdoers, and if so whether such innocent persons will suffer any harm as a result . . . ; (vii) the degree of confidentiality of the information sought . . . ; (viii) the privacy rights under article 8 of the European Convention on Human Rights . . . of the individuals whose identity is to be disclosed . . . ; (ix) the rights and freedoms under the EU data protection regime of the individuals whose identity is to be disclosed . . . ; (x) the public interest in maintaining the confidentiality of journalistic sources, as recognised in section 10 of the Contempt of Court Act 1981 and the European Convention on Human Rights . . . ":
Rugby Football Union v Consolidated Information Serviced Ltd (formerly Viagogo Ltd) (in liquidation), above, at [17].

[21] *R (Mohamed) v Secretary of State for Foreign and Commonwealth Affairs (No.1)* [2008] EWHC 2048 (Admin); [2009] 1 W.L.R. 2579 DC, at [94].

[22] *Carlton Film Distributors v VCI* [2003] EWHC 616 (Ch); [2003] F.S.R. 47 at [11], per Jacob J.

[23] [1997] 1 W.L.R. 1309, Sir Richard Scott V-C. The judge's order was not appealed.

[24] See para.31.4, above in relation to the 'mere witness' rule.

[25] Compare, for instance, *X v Morgan-Grampian* [1991] 1 A.C. 1, where a journalist came into possession of confidential information stolen by his source; he wrote an article based on the information, and was held to have been mixed up, albeit innocently, in the source's tortious acts. It may be that the judge had in mind Lord Reid's words in *Norwich Pharmacal* at 175d to the effect that where the person in possession of the information "has to any extent incurred any liability to the person wronged", that is a fortiori a case for full disclosure: in *P v T Ltd*, there was an admitted liability to the applicant for unfair dismissal. The applicant did argue that point, relying also on *CHC Software v Hopkins & Wood* [1993] F.S.R. 241 per Mummery J. at 250.

in the suggestion that the mere innocent receipt of a piece of information may be sufficient involvement, if that receipt facilitates the wrong.[26] *P v T Ltd* was cited with approval in *Ashworth Hospital Authority v MGN Ltd*, where Lord Woolf C.J. referred to it as a case where relief was granted because it was necessary in the interests of justice albeit that the claimant was not able to identify without discovery what would be the appropriate cause of action.[27]

31.5 Internet cases. Applications for *Norwich Pharmacal* orders have become common in internet cases.[28] It is important to note the possible ramifications in such cases of the rights of the third party (alleged wrongdoer) to privacy under art.8 ECHR, his rights of free speech under art.10 ECHR, his data protection rights under art.8 of the Charter of Fundamental Rights of the European Union[29] and other national and EU legislation, and his potential rights under s.10 of the Contempt of Court Act 1981. In *Totalise Ltd v Motley Fool Ltd*,[30] an internet service provider successfully applied for an order for discovery against operators of a website containing bulletin boards on which members of the public were able to post defamatory material. On appeal (on costs) the Court of Appeal warned against making an order unless it has first considered whether the disclosure is warranted having regard to the rights and freedoms or the legitimate interests of the data subject,[31] and stressed the need to be careful not to make an order which unjustifiably invades the right of an individual to respect for his private life under art.8. That is easier said than done:

> "It is difficult to see how the court can carry out this task if what it is refereeing is a contest between two parties, neither of whom is the person most concerned, the data subject; one of whom is the data subject's prospective antagonist; and the other of whom knows the data subject's identity, has undertaken to keep it confidential so far as the law permits, and would like to get out of the cross-fire as rapidly and as cheaply as possible."

---

[26] *Campaign Against Arms Trade v BAE Systems Plc* [2007] EWHC 330 (QB) at [13]. This analysis would seem to be supported by the reasoning and conclusions of Mann J. in *Various Claimants v News Group Newspapers Ltd* [2013] EWHC 2219 (Ch).

[27] [2002] UKHL 29; [2002] 1 W.L.R. 2033 at [57].

[28] See e.g. *Totalise Ltd v Motley Fool Ltd* [2001] EWCA Civ 1897; [2002] 1 W.L.R. 1233, *Smith v ADVFN plc* [2008] EWCA Civ 518, *G v Wikimedia Foundation Inc.* [2009] EWHC 3148 (QB); [2010] E.M.L.R. 14, *Lockton Companies International v Persons Unknown* [2009] EWHC 3423 (QB) (permission granted to serve *Norwich Pharmacal* order on Google Inc. out of the jurisdiction); *Golden Eye (International) Ltd v Telefonica UK Ltd*, above, and *Bacon v Automattic Inc.* [2011] EWHC 1072 (QB); [2012] 1 W.L.R. 753 (permission granted to serve *Norwich Pharmacal* order on US-based defendants including ISPs by alternative method, i.e. email).

[29] As to which see the *Rugby Football Union* case, above, at [26]–[31].

[30] [2001] E.M.L.R. 29, Owen J.

[31] [2001] EWCA Civ 1897; [2002] 1 W.L.R 1233 at [24]–[25]. (The court must have meant to limit that particular observation to a case where the condition at para.6 of Sch.2 to the Data Protection Act 1998 is engaged.) Now see *Golden Eye (International) Ltd v Telefonica UK Ltd*, above, and the *Rugby Football Union* case, above, at [19]–[46].

The court suggested that one solution would be for the website operator, where appropriate, to tell the user what is going on and to offer to pass on in writing to the claimant and the court any worthwhile reason that the user wants to put forward for not having his or her identity disclosed, and the court could require that to be done before making an order. Doing so would:

> "enable the court to do what is required of it with slightly more confidence that it is respecting the law laid down in more than one statute by Parliament and doing no injustice to a third party, in particular not violating his convention rights."[32]

However, there is little evidence in the authorities of this having been done in practice. The reality is that such applications are almost invariably consented to by the respondent internet service provider or web host, which usually does not even appear before the court (safe in the knowledge that its costs of complying with the order will be borne by the applicant in any event), but instead contents itself with maintaining a position of neutrality and indicating that it will abide by any order that the court thinks it right to make. This renders it difficult for the court properly to take into account the rights of the unrepresented third parties whose identification is sought,[33] but nonetheless this is what it must endeavour to do. Some applications have sought such extensive details of users of bulletin boards and discussion groups that it must have been almost impossible to give proper consideration to third party rights.[34] However, the court always has a discretion whether or not to make a *Norwich Pharmacal* order, even where the necessary pre-conditions are satisfied,[35] and is entitled to decline to make an order where the defamation

---

[32] [2001] EWCA Civ 1897; [2002] 1 W.L.R. 1233 at [26].

[33] "It is, of course, in the nature of these applications that the respondent to the disclosure application has no position on whether the order should be made and will usually (as in this case) consent to the relief being granted subject in appropriate cases to the payment of the costs incurred in making the disclosure. Wider and more fundamental issues such as whether the relief is excessive, a disproportionate invasion of the users' Article 8 and data protection rights, or is unjustified by the evidence or the status of the claimants will usually be a matter for the judge to consider unaided by any adversarial argument.":
Golden Eye (International) Ltd v Telefonica UK Ltd, above, at [6]. In the *Golden Eye* case itself, the court at first instance heard representations from Consumer Focus, a statutory body set up under the Consumers, Estate Agents and Redress Act 2007 to represent the interests of consumers, and in the Court of Appeal, from the Open Rights Group.

[34] See for example the difficulties which Mackay J. found in dealing with an application for the disclosure of the identities of users responsible for hundreds of postings: *Smith v ADVFN Plc* [2008] EWHC 577 (QB). On appeal from that decision, the Court of Appeal sounded a note of warning to applicants: the judge has a discretion to decline to address line by line an "indiscriminate and disorganised mass of material", and applicants should be selective and discriminating: [2008] EWCA Civ 518 at [14].

[35] In *Totalise v Motley Fool Ltd* at first instance ([2001] E.M.L.R. 750 at [27]), Owen J. identified the following matters as relevant to the exercise of the discretion: the strength of the claimants' prima facie case against the wrongdoer; the gravity of the defamatory allegations; whether the wrongdoer was waging a concerted campaign against the claimant; the size and extent of the potential readership; the fact that the wrongdoer was hiding behind the anonymity which the website allowed; whether the claimant had any other practical means of identifying the wrongdoer; and whether the defendant had a policy of confidentiality for users of the website. The existence of the discretion is also evident from the decision of the Court of Appeal: see [2001] EWCA Civ 1897; [2002] 1 W.L.R 1233 at [27], where the court envisaged that a judge might

complained of consists of mere abuse or is otherwise trivial,[36] or where the mooted claim has no real prospect of success,[37] such that the claimant's concern in seeking the order is outweighed by the countervailing rights of the unrepresented third parties.[38] Since a *Norwich Pharmacal* order is a species of injunction, unless the order is being made by consent, in which case a master may deal with the matter, only a judge has the power to grant one.[39] Where the court has granted a *Norwich Pharmacal* order but there is reason to believe that it has not been complied with for reasons of lack of technical understanding, the court has power to make such further order as is necessary and proportionate to enable the respondent to comply and to ensure that the earlier order is not frustrated by an innocent failure to understand the technical issues.[40]

---

refuse disclosure of the identity of an alleged wrongdoer whose attacks, though legally defamatory, were so obviously designed merely to insult as not to carry a realistic risk of doing the claimant quantifiable harm. Now see also the list of relevant factors set out by the Supreme Court in the *Rugby Football Union* case, above, at [17] and extracted in fn.20, above. Although Lord Kerr of Tonaghmore speaks there of "the exercise of discretion by a careful weighing of all relevant factors", some of the factors to which he refers are probably better described as going to the question of proportionality than discretion.

[36] On the question of the meaning of website postings, it is interesting to note Eady J.'s observations in *Smith v ADVFN Plc* [2008] EWHC 1797 (QB) at [16]–[17]:

" . . . communications of this kind are much more akin to slanders . . . than to the usual, more permanent kind of communications found in libel actions. People do not often take a 'thread' and go through it as a whole like a newspaper article. They tend to read the remarks, make their own contributions if they feel like inclined, and think no more about it. It is this analogy with slander which led me . . . to refer to 'mere vulgar abuse', which used to be discussed quite often in the heyday of slander actions. It is not so much a defence that is unique to slander as a means of interpreting the meaning of words. From the context of casual conversations, one can often tell that a remark is not to be taken literally or seriously and is rather to be construed merely as abuse. That is less common in the case of more permanent written communications, although it is by no means unknown. But in the case of a bulletin board thread it is often obvious to casual observers that people are just saying the first thing that comes into their heads and reacting in the heat of the moment. The remarks are often not intended, or not to be taken, as serious." See also *Clift v Clarke* [2011] EWHC 1164 (QB), to like effect.

[37] *Nordeen v Hill* [2012] EWHC 2847 (QB) (application dismissed (1) on the ground that there was no reasonable basis for concluding that a defamation action could succeed: the publication in issue was prima facie time barred and, assuming that what was said was defamatory, qualified privilege would apply and there was no apparent arguable case of malice; (2) as a matter of discretion).

[38] This course was envisaged by Owen J. and the Court of Appeal in *Totalise v Motley Fool Ltd* (above), and adopted in *Sheffield Wednesday Football Club Ltd v Hargreaves* [2007] EWHC 2375 (QB) and *Clift v Clarke* [2011] EWHC 1164 (QB).

[39] CPR PD 2B, paras 2.2 and 2.3(a) and CPR PD 25A, para.1.2(1). Having regard to the considerations concerning the rights of third parties mentioned earlier in this paragraph, it is suggested that the proper course for the claimant to adopt in relation to the listing of *Norwich Pharmacal* orders proposed to be made by consent is as follows: (i) in cases where it appears that there may be a significant issue concerning the rights of third parties, to list the matter before the judge; or (ii) in cases where there does not appear to be such an issue, to list the application in the first instance before the master, on the footing that if things should turn out otherwise, it is open to him to refer the matter to a judge.

[40] *Patel v UNITE* [2012] EWHC 92 (QB) in which the applicant was granted an order requiring the respondent to permit an independent computer expert to take an image of its database with a view to preparing a report on the extent to which the data it contained (including deleted data) identified the persons responsible for certain allegedly defamatory and harassing postings.

Scope of disclosure in defamation: Justification. It is well established **31.6**
that, subject always to CPR r.31.6, a claimant is only obliged to give disclosure in relation to the matters alleged in the particulars of justification, because the defendant is not entitled to fish for some other defence in the claimant's papers.[41] However, the defendant cannot necessarily limit his disclosure to the matters raised in the particulars, since subject to CPR Pt 31 and r.31.6 specifically he must disclose all documents relevant to matters put in issue by his plea of justification.[42] In *Evans v Granada*,[43] the defendant sought to justify a meaning that there were reasonable grounds to suspect that the plaintiff had committed the acts alleged, and the plaintiff, who would have been entitled to lead evidence to rebut the case that there were reasonable grounds to suspect him, and to support that case with contemporary documents, successfully obtained an order for discovery of documents which tended to show that he was innocent of the charge or that there were no reasonable grounds to suspect him of it.

Qualified privilege. Equally, where the defendant has pleaded qualified **31.7**
privilege, he will have to disclose all documents which support or undermine his case that he was under a duty to publish, or had an interest in publishing, the words complained of. In the case of a plea of *Reynolds* privilege, that is liable to include disclosure of journalists' notes and other material relied on as

---

[41] *Metropolitan Saloon v Hawkins* (1859) 4 H.& N. 146; *Zierenberg v Labouchère* [1893] 2 Q.B. 183 CA; *Yorkshire Provident v Gilbert* [1895] 2 Q.B. 148 CA; *Arnold and Butter v Bottomley* [1908] 2 K.B. 151 CA; *Goldschmidt v Constable* [1937] 4 All E.R. 293 CA; *Evans v Granada* [1996] E.M.L.R. 429 CA. Cf. *McDonald's Corp v Steel* [1995] 3 All E.R. 615 per Neill L.J. at 621:
> "... there will be cases where, provided a plea of justification is properly particularised, a defendant will be entitled to seek support for his case from documents revealed in the course of discovery".

There is of course no rule that the defendant may not amend to plead justification after disclosure (*Edelman v Times Newspapers Ltd*, unreported, January 17, 1991, CA): it is commonplace to do so. In *Taranissi v BBC* [2008] EWHC 2486 (QB), Eady J. observed at [13] that the principle in *Yorkshire Provident Life Assurance Co. v Gilbert*, above, "is as sound today as it was at that time", the principle being that:
> "[t]he defendant's right ... is to have discovery of all matters relating to the questions in issue as narrowed by the particulars. I do not think in a libel action he is entitled to get anything more ... I think it would be a very bad precedent to suggest that a person can simply by libelling another obtain access to all his books and see whether he can justify what he has said or not. I think it would be very lamentable if we should say when a person has libelled another and has justified and given particulars, that he is entitled to more than discovery of that which relates to those particulars (per Lindley L.J. at 152)".

Applying the principle, Eady J. dismissed the defendant's application whereby it sought specific disclosure from the claimant of documents which it believed would support a case of justification that it had not yet pleaded.

[42] *Evans v Granada* [1996] E.M.L.R. 429 CA. In *Campbell v Associated Newspapers Ltd*, unreported, May 25, 1995, CA, the allegation which the defendant intended to justify had been admitted by the plaintiff in correspondence, so discovery relating to that allegation was not necessary nor, presumably, relevant to any issue. For a modern case involving a defendant's application for specific disclosure where justification was pleaded, see *Beckham v News Group Newspapers Ltd* [2005] EWHC 2252 (QB).

[43] [1996] E.M.L.R. 429.

giving rise to the existence of a duty to publish and as supporting a case of responsible journalism.

31.8 Malice. Where the claimant has pleaded malice in his reply in rebuttal of a defence of qualified privilege or honest comment, the parties must give disclosure of all documents which support or undermine the claimant's case on the defendant's state of mind.[44] But where the claimant relies on the defendant's motivation or state of mind in publishing the words in aggravation of damages,[45] he is not entitled to disclosure from the defendant.[46]

31.9 Offer of amends.[47] There may need to be disclosure of documents as part of the process of determining compensation under the offer of amends procedure,[48] and in cases where *Burstein* particulars[49] are pleaded by the defendant to show background context which is directly relevant to the subject matter of the libel, or to the claimant's reputation or sensitivity in the relevant part of his life,[50] extensive disclosure of such material may be necessary. Disclosure may also be ordered to enable a claimant to make up his or her mind whether or not to accept an offer of amends: *Rigg v Associated Newspapers Ltd*.[51] However, *Rigg* was a case where the claimant needed access to a single specific identified document which was relevant to a pleaded issue and highly material to the decision which she had to make, and should not be treated as

---

[44] In *Maudling v Granada*, unreported, November 20, 1975 (May J.), it was held that a plaintiff who had pleaded malice was not confined to discovery only in relation to the pleaded particulars of malice, since the defendant's state of mind was in issue and discovery of all documents relevant to that state of mind should be given under established *Peruvian Guano* principles. It is submitted that the authority remains sound, save that "chain of inquiry" discovery principle has been supplanted by the CPR r.31.6 standard disclosure test. See also *Fiddes v Channel 4 Television Corp* [2010] EWCA Civ 516, in which the Court of Appeal dismissed an appeal by the claimant against a decision of Tugendhat J. whereby he refused to order the defendant to carry out a search of back-up tapes of computer records in order to retrieve certain deleted emails which, if retrieved, the claimant contended, were likely to bear materially on the correctness or otherwise of his case on malice, which was being advanced in response to the defendant's defence of fair comment. The Court of Appeal decided that the judge had correctly considered the various factors that were relevant to a decision on whether to order the defendant to carry out such a search, and that he had been entitled to conclude that there was no sufficient likelihood of the retrieval of emails that were significant and relevant to the issues in the case.

[45] See for instance *Broxton v McLelland (No.2)* [1997] E.M.L.R. 157 CA. CPR PD 53, para.2.10 requires the claimant to plead all the matters relied on in support of his damages claim.

[46] *Henry v News Group Newspapers Ltd* [2011] EWHC 1058 (QB) (Eady J.).

[47] For the offer of amends procedure, see generally paras 29.28ff above, and for the issues which arise in connection with compensation and might potentially give rise to a need for disclosure, see in particular para.29.33, above.

[48] *Abu v MGN Ltd* [2002] EWHC 2345 (QB); [2003] 1 W.L.R. 2201, per Eady J. at [21].

[49] *Burstein v Times Newspapers Ltd* [2001] 1 W.L.R. 579. See para.29.36, above.

[50] *Turner v News Group Newspapers Ltd* [2006] EWCA Civ 540; [2006] 1 W.L.R. 3469.

[51] [2003] EWHC 710 (QB); [2004] E.M.L.R. 4, Gray J. The newspaper had refused to allow the claimant to see the journalist's notes until she had accepted the offer of amends. She applied for inspection on the footing that the notes were "mentioned" in the defence within r.31.14 (held, quoting from a document which is not referred to as such is not "mentioning" it), and alternatively for accelerated specific disclosure under r.31.12.

approving on a routine or wide-scale basis applications for disclosure by claimants faced with a decision whether or not to accept offers of amends.[52] In a similar vein, it has been said that it is wrong to plead a "bad faith" allegation[53] in answer to an offer of amends defence in the hope that something may be "fished" up in the course of disclosure.[54] Nor will disclosure be ordered to explore the defendants' state of knowledge of the facts or the quality of their journalism before those questions are put in issue.[55]

Non-party disclosure. A party to proceedings may also obtain access to   **31.10** documents in the control of a non-party by seeking an order for non-party disclosure under CPR r.31.17,[56] although the conditions for the exercise of this jurisdiction are exacting. The court may order non-party disclosure only where the documents of which disclosure is sought are likely[57] to support the case of the applicant or adversely affect the case of one of the other parties to the proceedings,[58] and where it can be shown that disclosure is necessary in order to dispose fairly of the claim or to save costs. The applicant must also demonstrate to the court that the documents, or classes of documents, that are being sought in fact exist; non-parties will not be required to investigate whether there are any documents which happen to fit the relevant description.[59] Furthermore, the court has no power to make an order for non-party disclosure in respect of a class of documents where it is established that there are individual documents within the class that do not satisfy the relevance condition: the threshold condition cannot be circumvented by an order which puts upon the non-party the task of identifying those documents within a

---

[52] Ibid. at [25].

[53] Under s.4(3) of the Defamation Act 1996.

[54] *Milne v Express Newspapers Ltd* [2002] EWHC 2564 (QB); [2003] 1 W.L.R. 927 per Eady J. at [28], upheld [2004] EWCA Civ 664; [2005] 1 W.L.R. 772.

[55] *Tesco Stores Ltd v Guardian News & Media Ltd* [2009] E.M.L.R. 5 per Eady J. at [43].

[56] Statutory licence for the granting of such orders is to be found in s.34, Senior Courts Act 1981 and s.53, County Courts Act 1984.

[57] "The word 'likely' in this context has been considered in the Court of Appeal and is taken to mean that the document or documents 'may well' assist: see e.g. *Three Rivers DC v Bank of England (Disclosure) (No.1)* [2003] 1 W.L.R. 210 CA.": per Eady J. in *Flood v Times Newspapers Ltd* [2009] EWHC 411 (QB); [2009] E.M.L.R. 18 at [23].

[58] In this regard,

"[i]t is elementary . . . as in relation to the disclosure of documents more generally, that in determining whether a document or class of documents has a potentially relevant bearing on one or more of the live issues in the case, one should focus narrowly on the pleadings as they stand, in order to see how the issues have been defined up to that point. Thus . . . one cannot be guided by speculation as to how a different case might be pleaded, after a new source of documents is investigated, or as to matters which are merely canvassed in evidence—without being incorporated into a pleading.":

Flood v Times Newspapers Ltd, above, at [36]; see also at [10] ("In relation to any third party disclosure application, it is always necessary to focus carefully on the pleaded issues in the case."). In *Briscoe Mitchell v Hodder & Stoughton Ltd* [2008] EWHC 2852 (QB), Tugendhat J. dismissed an application for non-party disclosure where the documents sought appeared to be relevant only to the credit of individuals who were due to be called as witnesses at trial.

[59] *Howglen Ltd (Application for Disclosure), Re* [2001] 1 All E.R. 376, 382 (Pumfrey J.); *Flood v Times Newspapers Ltd*, above, per Eady J. at [34].

composite class which do, and those which do not, meet the condition.[60] Moreover, as with *Norwich Pharmacal* applications, even where these conditions are satisfied, the court has a discretion whether or not to make an order. In exercising this discretion, the court will take into account where the public interest lies and the rights and interests of third parties, in particular the extent to which ordering disclosure would infringe such persons' rights of privacy or confidentiality.[61] The court has an obligation to ensure, if necessary of its own motion, that the jurisdiction to order non-party disclosure is not used inappropriately, even where an application is made by consent, and carrying out that responsibility, the court will hear submissions from any non-party whose interests need to be considered.[62] Under the circumstances, disclosure against non-parties should be regarded as the exception rather than the rule: it will not be ordered as a matter of routine.[63] Since the merits of a *Reynolds* defence fall to be assessed against the background of the material available to the journalists before publication, a defendant is most unlikely to obtain an order for non-party disclosure in support of such a defence.[64] So far as costs are concerned, the general rule is that the applicant will be ordered to pay the respondent's costs of the application and of complying with any order made.[65]

31.11 Release of privileged documents to enable plea of justification. Where a newspaper, which was a defendant in a libel action brought by two police officers over an article which suggested that they had tampered with evidence concerning the prosecution of B, applied to the Court of Appeal for disclosure of documents which were privileged by public interest immunity and had been supplied to B by the Police Complaints Authority for the purposes of his successful appeal against conviction, the Court of Appeal permitted the release of the documents and the variation of B's implied undertaking in order to enable the newspaper to plead justification. The public interest in winning the co-operation of witnesses for the purpose of investigating police complaints was, on the facts, outweighed by the "imperative" public interest in ensuring that the newspaper had a proper opportunity of

---

[60] *Flood v Times Newspapers Ltd*, above, at [35], citing *Three Rivers DC v Bank of England (Disclosure) (No.1)* [2002] EWCA Civ 1182; [2003] 1 W.L.R. 210 and *American Home Products Corp v Novartis Pharmaceuticals UK Ltd (Application for Disclosure)* [2001] F.S.R. 41 CA.

[61] *Flood v Times Newspapers Ltd*, above, at [25]. But see also *Henry v News Group Newspapers Ltd* [2011] EWHC 296 (QB) at [12] where Tugendhat J. observed that third party rights and interests may *support* the grant of the order.

[62] *Flood v Times Newspapers Ltd*, above, at [29].
" . . . both *Frankson v Home Office* [2003] 1 W.L.R. 1952 and *Flood v Times Newspapers Limited . . .* [2009] E.M.L.R. 18 are authority for the proposition that a third party, whose interests are obviously affected by an application such as this, should be served or at least notified of the claim and/or the hearing":
Brady v PKF (UK) LLP [2011] EWHC 3178 (QB) per Coulson J. at [26].

[63] *Flood v Times Newspapers Ltd*, above, at [22], citing *Frankson v Secretary of State for the Home Department* [2003] EWCA Civ 655; [2003] 1 W.L.R. 1952.

[64] *Flood v Times Newspapers Ltd*, above, at [40].

[65] CPR r.48.1(2).

obtaining the evidence that it needed so that the grave allegations which it made against the officers could be properly tested in the courts.[66]

Restrictions on disclosure to protect sources. The law protects dis- **31.12**
closure of sources of information by the long-established common law "news-paper rule", by s.10 of the Contempt of Court Act 1981, and by art.10 of the European Convention on Human Rights.[67]

Use of disclosed documents. Questions have often arisen about the extent **31.13**
to which a party who discovers material defamatory of him in a disclosed document may use it as the basis of a defamation claim. Before the CPR, the courts used the language of "implied undertaking" to describe the obligations of the parties to respect the limited purpose for which disclosure is given.[68] (The concept of implied undertaking survives in a criminal context, where it prevents the use of documents disclosed by the prosecution in criminal proceedings for any purpose except the conduct of the defence, thus prevent-ing their use for a claim in defamation, and where in any event an absolute immunity against such claims extends to out of court statements made as part of the process of investigating a crime or possible crime with a view to prosecution.)[69] The CPR now provide simply that a party to whom a docu-ment is disclosed may use it only for the purpose of the proceedings in which it is disclosed, except where the document has been read to or by the court, or referred to, at a hearing held in public, or the court gives permission, or the party who disclosed the document and the person to whom it belongs agree.[70]

However, even in those circumstances, the court may make an order restricting or prohibiting the use of a disclosed document.[71] The exercise of

---

[66] *Ex p. Coventry Newspapers Ltd* [1993] Q.B. 278 CA. Tugendhat J. distinguished *Ex p. Coventry Newspapers Ltd* in *Raab v Associated Newspapers Ltd* [2011] EWHC 3375 (QB) in dismissing the defendant's application to strike out or stay defamation proceedings on the ground that it was being prevented from justifying, and therefore the claim could not be fairly tried, by reason of the claimant's refusal to release a witness from a confidentiality undertaking: unlike in the *Coventry Newspapers* case, the defendant was not inhibited from pleading justification by reason of the undertaking.

[67] These provisions are discussed at paras 31.32–31.37, below.

[68] The implied undertaking was stated as being not to use disclosed documents for any purpose other than those of the action in which they were disclosed: *Alterskye v Scott* [1948] 1 All E.R. 469; *Distillers v Times Newspapers Ltd* [1975] Q.B. 613; *Riddick v Thames Board Mills* [1977] Q.B. 881 CA (where the plaintiff brought a libel action on a document disclosed by the defendant on discovery in an earlier action: held, the action was an abuse and must fail). However, as Lord Fraser pointed out in *Rank Film v Video Information Centre* [1982] A.C. 380 at 447, that statement of principle did not cover cases such as *Norwich Pharmacal v Customs & Excise* [1974] A.C. 133, where an order was made for discovery so that it should be used in another action: he re-stated the principle as being that information is not to be used by the party who gets discovery for purposes other than that for which production was ordered.

[69] *Taylor v Serious Fraud Office* [1999] 2 A.C. 177; *Westcott v Westcott* [2008] EWCA Civ 818; [2009] Q.B. 407.

[70] CPR r.31.22(1).

[71] CPR r.31.22(2).

that jurisdiction was considered by Eady J. in *McBride v Body Shop International Plc*,[72] where the defendant applied to the court under CRP r.31.22(2) to prevent the claimant from suing in libel on an email disclosed during Employment Tribunal proceedings. Relevant considerations include (1) the facts that compulsory disclosure involves an infringement of privacy and that public policy requires the encouragement of full disclosure in litigation (factors which underlay the old implied undertaking) and (2) the extent to which the document in question played a central role in the litigation in which it was disclosed (the more tangential its role, the less necessary it might be for an understanding of the case and the less relevant to the process of public scrutiny of litigation; yet the starting point should be an assumption of necessity and relevance). The court will balance the competing interests, public and private. Eady J. concluded that the balance of justice lay in favour of prohibiting the use of a disclosed document which had not been read out in the Employment Tribunal, which entailed an attack on the good faith of the defendant's employees in circumstances where qualified privilege applied and there was no evidence of malice, and which was published on an extremely limited basis. Similar public policy factors underlay an application by the General Medical Council to prevent inspection of confidential documents listed by a libel claimant who had obtained the documents in the course of disclosure in GMC disciplinary proceedings against him.[73] The basis of the GMC's concern was that its efforts to persuade patients and other complainants to follow through allegations against doctors would be undermined if it was not able to promise them confidentiality. However, the documents were relevant to the defendants' plea of justification, they were needed to defend rather than to commence litigation, there was a risk that the parallel proceedings before the GMC and the High Court might, if inspection was not permitted, reach inconsistent outcomes, there was a public interest in ensuring so far as possible that claimants in defamation actions did not obtain misleading or false vindication, art.6 ECHR was engaged, and in any event measures could be put in place to ensure that confidentiality was protected.

SECTION 2. FURTHER INFORMATION AND INTERROGATORIES

31.14   **Introduction.** For well over a century, interrogatories played a very important part in defamation litigation, but the very word "interrogatory" has now disappeared from the English rules of procedure, and the old Ord.26 has been swallowed up in CPR Pt 18, an amalgam of the former procedures for interrogatories and further and better particulars, designed to provide a quick

---

[72] [2007] EWHC 1658 (QB).
[73] *Wakefield v Channel Four Television Corp* [2006] EWHC 3289 (QB).

and simple mechanism for clarifying the issues in dispute.[74] Under r.18.1(a), the court may order a party to (1) clarify any matter which is in dispute in the proceedings, or (2) give additional information in relation to any such matter, whether or not the matter is contained in or referred to in a statement of case.[75] It is the latter provision—namely that information may be ordered to be given about a matter in dispute which is not contained or referred to in the statements of case—which has superseded, and preserved the concept, of the interrogatory,[76] which was a form of oral discovery, not confined to the facts directly in issue on the pleadings. The Practice Direction supplementing Pt 18 stipulates that requests should be "concise and strictly confined to matters which are reasonably necessary and proportionate to enable the first party to prepare his own case or to understand the case he has to meet",[77] which recalls the necessity test for interrogatories.[78] Accordingly, the interrogatory remains alive under another name, subject to the principles set out in *Hall v*

---

[74] The interrogatory prospers in other common law jurisdictions and has explicitly survived CPR-style reformulations of civil procedure: see for example Pt 22 of the NSW Uniform Civil Procedure Rules 2005. See *Zaetta v Nationwide News Pty Ltd* [2009] N.S.W.S.C. 508 for an example of a decision concerning an application under Pt 22 that a defendant in a libel action be ordered to answer certain interrogatories and to give better answers to others. See also *Metcash Trading Ltd v Bunn (No.4)* [2008] FCA 1607 for the approach of the Federal Court of Australia to a wide-ranging request for further and better particulars by a defendant in proceedings for, inter alia, libel: the court ordered the plaintiffs to give further and better particulars of their case as to (inter alia) (a) which part or parts of the publications complained of gave rise to the pleaded imputations, (b) their trading reputation, and (c) in relation to that part of their claim which rested upon a true innuendo imputation.

[75] *Dee v Telegraph Media Group Ltd* [2009] EWHC 2546 (QB) stands as an example of the court taking a non-technical approach to an application for further information in a defamation case and ordering a party to provide further information concerning a matter which was not, strictly speaking, in issue on the pleadings. Eady J. ordered the claimant to answer two questions posed by the defendant the purpose of which was to comprehend the scope of the issues that would be outstanding at trial if the defendant succeeded on its arguments as to the meaning of the words complained of (the question to be resolved on the facts of the case was whether or not certain tennis matches played by the claimant in Spanish tournaments were matches on the "international professional tennis circuit"). The court's reasoning at [17] was as follows:

"I see no reason why the claimant should not offer further clarification on these matters. It has not been suggested that he is unable to do so. It is important to place as many cards as possible on the table at this stage. There is nothing to be gained from arguments about whether a request for further information is the right mechanism to adopt. I shall simply direct that the questions are to be answered constructively, rather than merely by way of non-admission, so that the defendant can know the full extent of the real dispute".

[76] "The making of a Pt 18 Request, as here, that is not directed at a matter in a statement of case, has taken the place of interrogatories under the RSC": *National Grid Electricity Transmission Plc v ABB Ltd* [2012] EWHC 869 (Ch) (an unlawful competition claim), per Roth J. at [73]. The judge went on to hold at [74] that the principles laid down by Sir Thomas Bingham M.R. in *Hall v Sevalco Ltd* [1996] P.I.Q.R. 344 (the reference to Lord Woolf M.R. in Roth J.'s judgment is in error) concerning the administration of interrogatories under RSC Ord.26, r.1 applied mutatis mutandis to the making of a CPR Pt 18 request that did not seek further information about a statement of case.

[77] CPR PD 18, para.1.2.

[78] See *Rowland v Fayed* [2000] C.P. Rep. 35, Arden J., a case in which the requests were expressly referred to as interrogatories (which they were), and in which the judge derived assistance from pre-CPR authority in the shape of *Hall v Sevalco Ltd*, above (in the same way that the Court of Appeal later did in *Swain-Mason v Mills & Reeve* [2011] EWCA Civ 14; [2011] 1

Sevalco Ltd[79] and the overriding objective of the CPR,[80] and limited in its scope to matters in dispute in the proceedings, albeit that it is unclear how far the criteria for allowing or disallowing interrogatories under the old regime continue to be valid now. In all the circumstances, it still seems appropriate to retain this section, which remains in point when it is desired to obtain further information about a matter which, perhaps because not directly in issue on the statements of case, is not susceptible to a simple request for clarification.[81] However, the section has been much cut down[82] and generally limited to a statement of the criteria which have in the past been applied to interrogatories in defamation cases.

(a) *General*

31.15   **The need for interrogatories and requests for information to relate to a matter in dispute in the action.** Interrogatories were a form of oral discovery and, as with any discovery, it was a fundamental precondition that they should relate to a matter in question in the action. That requirement appears to chime with the restriction of further information at CPR r.18.1(1) to clarification of "any matter . . . in dispute in the proceedings" or to "additional information in relation to any such matter". If it did not relate to a matter in dispute, it could not be administered even if it might be admissible in cross-examination of a witness: in other words, it was not enough for the

---

W.L.R. 2735 at [74] in the context of late applications for permission to amend). For the necessity test for interrogatories, see para.31.17, below.

[79] [1996] P.I.Q.R. 344, as held in *National Grid Electricity Transmission Plc v ABB Ltd*, above, to be applicable to a CPR Pt 18 request that did not seek further information regarding a statement of case. Sir Thomas Bingham M.R., giving the judgment of the court (in a case in which 17 interrogatories had been served on the same day as a 51-page request for further and better particulars of the statement of claim), stated as follows:

"The guiding principle in this field must be that laid down in RSC Ord.26, r.1(1), that interrogatories must be necessary either for disposing fairly of the cause or matter or for saving costs. Necessity is a stringent test. It cannot be necessary to interrogate to obtain information or admissions which are or are likely to be contained in pleadings, medical reports, discoverable documents or witness statements unless, exceptionally, a clear litigious purpose will be served by obtaining such information or admissions on affidavit. As a general statement we would agree with the statement . . . endorsed by Coleman J. that, 'Suitable times to interrogate (if at all) will probably be after discovery and after exchange of witness statements.' Interrogatories should not be regarded as a source of ammunition to be routinely discharged as part of an interlocutory bombardment preceding the main battle. The interrogator must be able to show that his interrogatories, if answered when served, will serve a clear litigious purpose by saving costs or promoting the fair and efficient conduct of the action."

[80] See *Rowland v Fayed*, above, and (for the approach of the Court of Appeal to a request for further information) *Toussaint v Mattis* [2001] C.P.Rep. 61.

[81] See *Rowland v Fayed*, above.

[82] By comparison with the account given in Ch.30 of the 9th edition of this work (published in 1998).

interrogatory to go solely to credit.[83] Beyond this, by comparison with interrogatories, how far does the right to "further information" go? The requirement that it be limited to clarification and information about matters in dispute makes it unlikely that it extends as far as the right to interrogate. Historically, the right to interrogate was not confined to the facts directly in issue, but extended to any facts the existence or non-existence of which was relevant to the existence or non-existence of the facts directly in issue[84]: and it was not necessary that answers to the interrogatories should be conclusive on the question in issue, as long as they had some bearing on the question and might form a step in establishing liability.[85] It seems unlikely that the court would sanction such requests for information, which recall the old "train of enquiry" discovery. By contrast, other functions of interrogatories seem more compatible with the aim of further information: for instance, the function of interrogatories was not limited to giving the claimant a knowledge of that which he did not already know, but included the getting an admission of anything which he had to prove on any issue which was raised between him and the defendant,[86] and they were generally admissible if they tended to destroy the case of the party interrogated,[87] so that, for instance, the plaintiff could interrogate the defendant as to any facts which, if proved, would be material evidence to destroy a plea of justification.[88]

Particulars. In principle, if a party has delivered particulars in support of a   **31.16**
plea, the issues are limited to the matters specified in the particulars.[89] However, a defendant who has pleaded justification cannot necessarily limit his obligation to give disclosure, or to answer interrogatories, or, it is submitted, to supply further information, to the matters pleaded in his particulars, if other matters are put in issue by the plea.[90]

---

[83] *Parnell v Walter* (1890) 24 Q.B.D. 441, 452 per Denman J.; *Kennedy v Dodson* [1895] 1 Ch. 334, 342 per A. L. Smith L.J. (but note the explanation of the second sentence of A. L. Smith L.J.'s judgment at 341 by Falconer J. in *Rockwell Corp v Serck Industries* [1988] F.S.R. 187 at 202–203); *Re Howell Morgan* (1888) 39 Ch.D. 316, 321 per Lopes L.J.; *Caryll v Daily Mail* (1904) 90 L.T. 307, 308 per Romer L.J.

[84] *Marriott v Chamberlain* (1886) 17 Q.B.D. 154, 163 per Lord Esher M.R. Lord Esher's words were approved in *Nash v Layton* [1911] 2 Ch. 71 CA at 76, 83, and *Osram Lamp Works Ltd v Gabriel Lamp Co.* [1914] 2 Ch. 129 CA. See also *Cleland v Neill* [1951] N.I. 61 (permitting interrogatories by plaintiff about malice, and about matters within plaintiff's own knowledge).

[85] *Blair v Haycock* (1917) 34 T.L.R. 39 HL.

[86] *Att-Gen v Gaskill* (1882) 20 Ch.D. 519, 528 per Cotton L.J. The observation of A. L. Smith L.J. in *Kennedy v Dodson* [1895] 1 Ch. 334 at 341, that the only legitimate use of interrogatories is to obtain from the other party admissions of facts which the party interrogating must prove in order to establish his case, was obiter: see per Falconer J. in *Rockwell Corp v Serck Industries* [1988] F.S.R. 187 at 202–203. Note in this connection that serving a notice to admit facts pursuant to CPR r.32.18 may offer another route to achieve this result.

[87] Per Lord Esher M.R. in *Hennessy v Wright (No.2)* (1890) 24 Q.B.D. 445n at 447.

[88] See, e.g. *Marriott v Chamberlain* (1886) 17 Q.B.D. 154 CA at 163, 164.

[89] *Yorkshire Provident Co. v Gilbert* [1895] 2 Q.B. 148 CA at 152; *Arnold v Bottomley* [1908] 2 K.B. 151 CA.

[90] *Evans v Granada* [1996] E.M.L.R. 429 CA.

31.17 Necessity. Requests for further information must be concise and strictly confined to matters which are reasonably necessary and proportionate to enable the first party to prepare his own case and to understand the case he has to meet. That recalls, but does not precisely echo, the requirement that interrogatories must be necessary either for disposing fairly of the cause or matter, or for saving costs.[91] The need to avoid extravagant use of requests for further information was considered by the Court of Appeal in *Musa King v Telegraph Group Ltd*, where Brooke L.J. observed[92] that the emphasis in the Practice Direction to Pt 18 was "on confining this part of any litigation (in which costs tended to get out of control in the pre-CPR regime) strictly to what is necessary and proportionate and to the avoidance of disproportionate expense". Moreover, there are some clear limits. Details of a party's insurance arrangements will not be ordered to be provided under Pt 18.[93] Nor will disclosure of documents provided to a judge when he was counsel in order to support an allegation of apparent bias against that judge arising out of the fact that he was involved in unrelated litigation while a barrister involving one of the parties.[94]

31.18 Further information before defence. Generally, leave to serve interrogatories was not given before defence, for until the defence had been served it was impossible to say what the matters in question in the action were.[95] It seems equally unlikely that requests for further information will be sanctioned before defence, for the same reason. However, this rule (which was not invariable) had a particular exception in cases of slander. If the claimant can clearly show that the defendant, at a certain place and in the presence of certain persons, has made a slanderous imputation of a definite character against him, but that he is unable to frame his particulars of claim because the persons present have refused to inform him of the words spoken, the court will, it is submitted, allow him to obtain further information from the defendant as to the precise words used, just as it used to allow him to interrogate the defendant.[96]

31.19 Time for requests for further information. It was said in the early 1990s, at a time when the courts were striving to reduce the costs of litigation under the straitjacket of the RSC, that unless the answers were essential for the preparation of the requesting party's case for trial and could not reasonably be

---

[91] See fn.78, above.
[92] [2004] EWCA Civ 613; [2005] 1 W.L.R. 2282 (reported as *King v Telegraph Group Ltd (Practice Note)*) at [63]. Brooke L.J. recalled Lord Woolf M.R.'s remarks in *McPhilemy v Times Newspapers Ltd* [1999] 3 All E.R. 775 at 792–794, *q.v.*
[93] *West London Pipeline & Storage Ltd v Total UK Ltd* [2008] EWHC 1296 (Comm). Details of insurance are a private arrangement between the insured and insurer, routine production of which would encourage speculative "deep pocket" litigation.
[94] *Mireskandari v Associated Newspapers Ltd* [2010] EWHC 967 (QB).
[95] *Mercier v Cotton* (1876) 1 Q.B.D. 442 CA at 445; *Hancock v Guerin* (1878) 4 Ex.D. 3.
[96] *Atkinson v Fosbroke* (1866) L.R. 1 Q.B. 628, where the plaintiff's affidavit evidence of the circumstances of publication was uncontradicted. (See also *Russell v Stubbs* [1913] 2 K.B. 200n

expected to emerge from requests for further and better particulars and further discovery or witness statements, interrogatories would not normally be ordered, and that for this reason the service of interrogatories before exchange of witness statements was almost always premature.[97] The Court of Appeal endorsed that approach, emphasising that interrogatories must be necessary either for disposing fairly of the cause or matter or for saving costs, and agreeing as a general statement with the proposition that suitable times to interrogate (if at all) will probably be after discovery and after exchange of witness statements.[98] It is open to the courts to raise precisely the same objections to requests for further information, given the overriding objective of the CPR.[99] However, it is not at all difficult to think of situations in defamation cases where further information before disclosure or witness statements will continue to be necessary. One example might be the case where a claimant wishes to know the identities of all persons to whom the damaging publication has been sent, in order to take steps to mitigate damage by setting the record straight.[100] Another is the *Atkinson v Fosbroke* type of case.[101] Moreover, it will often be unrealistic in defamation cases, where

---

(Court of Appeal and House of Lords); but cf. *Barham v Huntingfield* [1913] 2 K.B. 193 CA, and *Re Whitworth, O'Rourke v Darbishire* [1919] 1 Ch. 320 per Scrutton L.J. at 348).

[97] *Det Danske Hedeselskabet v KDM International Plc* [1994] 2 Lloyd's Rep. 534 per Colman J. at 537.

[98] *Hall v Sevalco Ltd,* above: see fn.79, above for the relevant passage in the judgment of Sir Thomas Bingham M.R. By contrast, in *UCB Bank v Halifax* (*The Times*, July 15, 1996), the judge ordered interrogatories before completion of discovery, finding a "clear litigious purpose" in the plaintiff's desire to know what was in the second defendant valuer's mind when he produced an allegedly excessive valuation, and pointing to the modern tendency to encourage openness. It seems from the short *Times* report that the defendants did not suggest that the plaintiff would be receiving a witness statement from the valuer, and were therefore not in a position to argue that interrogatories were unnecessary or premature. See also *Thrombosis Research Institute v Demeliou-Mason* [1996] F.S.R. 785 and (for the distinction between the functions of interrogatories and witness statements, and a critique of the school of thought that the latter made the former redundant); *Parfums Yves Saint Laurent v Ritz Hotel* [1990] F.S.R. 36 CA of Hong Kong.

[99] CPR r.1.1. Cf. *McPhilemy v Times Newspapers Ltd* [1999] E.M.L.R. 751 at 776, where Lord Woolf M.R. said this, in the context of particulars of justification:

"The need for extensive pleadings including particulars should be reduced by the requirement that witness statements are now exchanged. In the majority of proceedings identification of the documents upon which a party relies, together with copies of that party's witness statements, will make the detail of the nature of the case the other side has to meet obvious. This reduces the need for particulars in order to avoid being taken by surprise. This does not mean that pleadings are now superfluous. Pleadings are still required to mark out the parameters of the case that is being advanced by each party. In particular they are still critical to identify the issues and the extent of the dispute between the parties. What is important is that the pleadings should make clear the general nature of the case of the pleader. This is true both under the old rules and the new rules. The Practice Direction to CPR 16, paragraph 9.3 requires, in defamation proceedings, the facts on which a defendant relies to be given. No more than a *concise* statement of those facts is required. As well as their expense, excessive particulars can achieve directly the opposite result from that which is intended. They can obscure the issues rather than providing clarification. In addition, after disclosure and the exchange of witness statements pleadings frequently become of only historic interest."

[100] See *CHC Software v Hopkins & Wood* [1993] F.S.R. 241.

[101] (1866) L.R. 1 Q.B. 628: see para.31.23, below. A similar order for interrogatories was made in *Western Provident v Norwich Union* (Sir Michael Davies, July 4, 1996), where the plaintiff

witness statements are seldom exchanged long before trial, to expect that there will be time after exchange to obtain (let alone act on) the answers to any further information which may still be necessary.

31.20 Grounds for refusing to order further information. The grounds on which the court used to refuse to order interrogatories are likely to be grounds for refusal to order further information under the CPR, so it is worth setting out the pre-CPR position. The court could refuse leave to serve, or could disallow, an interrogatory on the ground that it was oppressive,[102] scandalous,[103] irrelevant to the issue in the action, or not put bona fide for the purposes of the action but for some collateral purpose, e.g. to obtain materials for an action against someone else.[104] A "fishing" interrogatory would be disallowed, i.e. one which did not relate to a matter in question in the action; fishing interrogatories included those asked "in order to enable the party [interrogating] to see if he can find out a case, either of complaint or defence, of which at present he knows nothing",[105] e.g. to obtain evidence in support of a plea that the words were published to "divers other persons whose names the plaintiff is at present unable to specify",[106] or to obtain evidence to bolster an inadequately particularised plea of justification,[107] and they also included those which asked about facts which supported (rather than impeached) the other party's case.[108] Interrogatories might not be put merely to discover the

---

pleaded libels to sales staff by internal email, which encouraged staff to make defamatory allegations about the plaintiff, and invited the very strong inference (arising from a number of factors) that the defendant's sales staff must have made such allegations to the plaintiff's customers or potential customers. The plaintiff was permitted to interrogate the defendant as to whether any of its sales staff did make such allegations, and if so which of them, to whom and in what words. In that case neither witness statements nor discovery was likely to be productive of the information sought, and there was little question on the facts of "fishing" for a case.

[102] *Kennedy v Dodson* [1895] 1 Ch. 344 CA; *White v Credit Reform Association Ltd* [1905] 1 K.B. 653 at 659, 660 (per Collins M.R. and Mathew L.J.). In *White's* case, the plaintiff wanted to ask the defendant to go through its books to find out the names of those to whom the offending publication (a book) had been shown: that was held to be obviously oppressive.

[103] "Nothing can be scandalous which is relevant": per Cotton L.J. in *Fisher v Owen* (1878) 8 Ch.D 645 at 653.

[104] *White v Credit Reform Association Ltd* [1905] 1 K.B. 653 per Collins M.R. at 658–659; *Edmondson v Birch* [1905] 2 K.B. 523; *Plymouth Mutual v Traders' Publishing Association* [1906] 1 K.B. 403 at 414, per Vaughan Williams L.J.

[105] Per Lord Esher M.R. in *Hennessy v Wright (No.2)* (1890) 24 Q.B.D. 445n at 448; adopted by Kennedy L.J. in *Russell v Stubbs* [1913] 2 K.B. 200n at 204. And see *Barham v Huntingfield* [1913] 2 K.B. 193 CA at 199, for a "striking example of fishing interrogatories". See also *Tangyes v Inman Steamship Co.* (1889) 88 L.T.J. 32, where interrogatories were disallowed which asked the plaintiff who had supplied him with copies of the circular complained of. For a modern application of this principle, see *Trader Publishing Ltd v Autotrader.com Inc.* [2010] EWHC 142 (Ch) (Vos J.).

[106] *Barham v Huntingfield* [1913] 2 K.B. 193 CA.

[107] *Gourley v Plimsoll* (1873) L.R. 8 C.P. 362; *Arnold v Bottomley* [1908] 2 K.B. 151 CA; and see para.31.40, below. Of course, where the plea of justification is properly particularised, no difficulty arises: see, e.g. *McDonald's Corp v Steel* [1995] 3 All E.R. 615 per Neill L.J. at 621ff.

[108] *Rockwell International Corp v Serck Industries* [1988] F.S.R. 187.

evidence by which the other party intended to prove his case,[109] or the names of the witnesses he would call at the trial.[110] Nor would interrogatories be ordered against a mere witness, not involved in the printing or publication of an article, to discover the identities of the printers and publishers.[111]

Privilege against self-incrimination. There is a general rule that no-one will be compelled, in the course of civil proceedings, to answer any question or produce any document if to do so would tend to expose them to proceedings for an offence or for the recovery of a penalty.[112] However, there was no privilege against self-incrimination in the case of interrogatories aimed at finding out the identity of the proprietor, publisher or printer of a newspaper under s.19 of the Stamp Duties on Newspapers Act 1836 (as re-enacted by s.1 of and Sch.2 to the Newspapers, Printers and Reading Rooms Repeal Act 1869),[113] and the same will no doubt apply to such requests for further information. The objection to answering on grounds of self-incrimination may of course be taken by way of response to a request for further information, and for it be taken, it is enough that the answer or disclosure "may tend to bring (the party) into the peril and possibility of being convicted as a criminal".[114] How real must the possibility be? Historically, the question has been considered in the context of criminal libel[115]: privilege has been claimed in the past on the basis that answering interrogatories as to publication of libels might expose the party to proceedings for criminal libel.[116] The mere unlikelihood of prosecution is not enough to prevent reliance on privilege, but:

"cases may . . . arise in which the court is satisfied that no reasonable man could possibly be in apprehension of a prosecution, as, for instance, where the offence is

31.21

---

[109] *Bidder v Bridges* (1885) 29 Ch.D. 29 CA; *Benbow v Low* (1880) 16 Ch.D 93 CA; *Ridgway v Smith* (1890) 6 T.L.R. 275; *Lever v Associated Newspapers Ltd* [1907] 2 K.B. 626 CA; *Hooton v Dalby* [1907] 2 K.B. 18 CA; *Knapp v Harvey* [1911] 2 K.B. 725 CA at 730, 732.

[110] *Eade v Jacobs* (1877) 3 Ex.D. 335, more fully reported in 37 L.T. 621; *M'Colla v Jones* (1887) 4 T.L.R. 12; *Hooton v Dalby* [1907] 2 K.B. 18 CA; *Knapp v Harvey* [1911] 2 K.B. 725 CA; *Rockwell International Corp v Serck Industries* [1988] F.S.R. 187. The position is different where the names form part of the material facts in the case: *Marriott v Chamberlain* (1886) 17 Q.B.D. 154 CA. The burden of showing this lies on the party interrogating: per Vaughan Williams L.J. in *Knapp v Harvey* at 730. Cf. *Wootton v Sievier* [1913] 3 K.B. 499 CA, in the context of an order for particulars.

[111] *Ricci v Chow* [1987] 1 W.L.R. 1658 CA.

[112] Although note the exception to the privilege against self-incrimination where the proceedings constitute "proceedings for infringement of rights pertaining to any intellectual property" within the meaning of s.72(2), Senior Courts Act 1981, which has been held to extend to proceedings for breach of confidence where the confidential information in question is "technical or commercial" in nature (as per s.72(5) of the same Act): *Phillips v News Group Newspapers Ltd* [2012] UKSC 28; [2013] 1 A.C. 1.

[113] *Ricci v Chow*, above.

[114] *Lamb v Munster* (1882) 10 Q.B.D. 110 per Field J. at 111, cited with approval by Stuart-Smith L.J. in *Bishopsgate Investment Ltd v Maxwell* [1993] Ch. 1 at 38–39.

[115] The offence of criminal libel was abolished by s.73 of the Coroners and Justice 2009 which came into effect on January 12, 2010.

[116] *Lamb v Munster* (1882) 10 Q.B.D. 110; *Triplex Safety Glass v Lancegaye* [1939] 2 K.B. 395 CA.

trivial or was committed many years ago . . . and then it may be that the judge . . . might insist on an answer".[117]

The required degree of risk of prosecution must be "real and appreciable" (even if proceedings are in fact improbable).[118] It is not appropriate to plead privilege where the risk of a charge is remote.[119] In *Re Westinghouse (No.2)* Lord Denning M.R. expressed the view that the privilege should not be allowed in a libel case where there is no real risk of the defendant being prosecuted; and Roskill L.J. echoed those doubts.[120]

(b) *The practical scope of interrogatories and requests for further information by claimants*

31.22 General. The purpose of the paragraphs which follow is to describe the areas in which the law has in the past permitted interrogatories to be administered by the claimant. There is no reason to suppose that the court will not, in the same situations, adopt the same approach to the supply of further information at the claimant's request as it has in the past done to the administration of interrogatories.

31.23 Publication—slander. In a slander action the claimant has long been permitted to interrogate the defendant as to whether he spoke the words pleaded, or words to that effect[121] (the object of adding those words being to prevent the defendant from "swearing by the card").[122] If the plaintiff obtained an admission that words similar to those pleaded were used, he could then seek leave to amend to plead the admitted words,[123] but the plaintiff could only interrogate as to the words pleaded, and (with one exception) could not otherwise interrogate in order to discover what precise words were

---

[117] *Triplex Safety Glass v Lancegaye*, above, per Du Parcq L.J., giving the judgment of the court, at 405.

[118] *Re Westinghouse (No.2)* [1978] A.C. 547 per Lord Denning M.R at 574. This test was approved by Viscount Dilhorne at 627. Roskill L.J. asked whether the risk could be regarded as "so far beyond the bounds of reason as to be a fanciful possibility" (at 579) and Shaw L.J. required "a degree of risk which cannot be dismissed as tenuous or illusory or so improbable as to be virtually without substance" (at 581). All three formulations of the Court of Appeal were regarded by Lord Fraser (at 647) as following *Triplex*. Viscount Dilhorne repeated his approval of Lord Denning's test in *British Steel v Granada* [1981] A.C. 1096 at 1177–1178 (Lords Fraser and Russell agreed).

[119] *Renworth v Stephenson, The Times,* January 16, 1996.

[120] *Re Westinghouse (No.2)* [1978] A.C. 547 at 573, 580.

[121] *Dalgleish v Lowther* [1899] 2 Q.B. 590 CA; *Saunderson v von Radeck* (1905) 119 L.T.J. 33 HL.

[122] *Dalgleish v Lowther*, above, per Sir F. H. Jeune at 594.

[123] *Phelps v Kelmsley* (1943) 168 L.T. 18 at 20, per Goddard L.J.; and see *Zameen Investments v Brazier*, March 20, 1990, CA, for the consequences of not establishing in advance of trial exactly what words were spoken: there, the trial judge declined to leave the plaintiff's claim to the jury.

spoken. The exception arose when he could clearly show that the defendant, at a certain place and in the presence of certain persons, had made a slanderous imputation of a definite character against him, but that he was unable to frame his statement of claim because the persons present had refused to inform him of the words spoken. In that event, the court would allow him to interrogate the defendant as to the precise words used.[124]

Publication to a third person—slander. The plaintiff was also per-   **31.24**
mitted to interrogate the defendant as to whether the words were spoken and published to, or in the presence of, the particular person or persons named in the statement of claim,[125] but if he had alleged publication to, or in the presence of, other persons whose names were unknown to him, he would not be allowed to interrogate the defendant on this issue[126] unless he could show that there had in fact been a publication to other persons unknown, and that the interrogatories were not fishing.[127] The mere fact that the defendant had not applied to have the allegation (i.e. of publication to persons unknown) struck out made no difference.[128]

Publication—libel. The claimant has always had to plead in his statement   **31.25**
of case the actual words complained of,[129] but there seems no reason why he should not ask the defendant whether he published the words pleaded, or words to the same effect, on the principle in *Dalgleish v Lowther*.[130] Where the libel is contained in an anonymous or pseudonymous letter the defendant may be asked whether he wrote the letter,[131] but before he answered an interrogatory which asked whether he was the author of a document that he did not have in his possession he was entitled to see it, and no doubt the court would take the same view today.[132] If the defendant denied having written the letter, he could be interrogated, for the purpose of comparing the handwriting, as to whether he wrote other letters.[133] However, the plaintiff could not interrogate the defendant as to the contents of an alleged libellous letter which

---

[124] *Atkinson v Fosbroke* (1866) L.R. 1 Q.B. 628. In that case, the plaintiff's affidavit evidence of the circumstances of publication was uncontradicted.

[125] *Dalgleish v Lowther*, above.

[126] *Barham v Huntingfield* [1913] 2 K.B. 193 CA.

[127] *Barham v Huntingfield*, above, distinguishing *Russell v Stubbs* [1913] 2 K.B. 200n CA and HL. See para.31.26, below.

[128] *Barham v Huntingfield*, above, at 198, per Kennedy L.J.

[129] See *Best v Charter Medical of England Ltd* [2001] EWCA Civ 1588; [2002] E.M.L.R. 335.

[130] [1899] 2 Q.B. 590 CA.

[131] *M'Loughlin v Dwyer* (1875) Ir.R. 9 C.L. 170: interrogatories allowed by Keogh J. as to whether the defendant was responsible for writing and publishing a letter which was in fact pseudonymous, though bearing the plaintiff's signature. (The defendant's objection to answer on grounds of self-incrimination was rejected because the libel would not have justified criminal proceedings).

[132] *Dalrymple v Leslie* (1881) 8 Q.B.D. 5.

[133] *Jones v Richards* (1885) 15 Q.B.D. 439 DC.

actually existed and could be produced.[134] Moreover, the plaintiff could not compel the defendant to answer from memory an interrogatory as to the contents of a letter of which the defendant had kept no copy and had no accurate recollection.[135]

31.26 Publication to unknown person—libel. If the plaintiff alleged publication to other persons whose names were unknown to him, he was not allowed to interrogate the defendant on this issue, because it amounted to fishing for a further cause of action, unless a strong foundation could be laid for some wider publication: *Barham v Huntingfield*,[136] where the Court of Appeal distinguished its earlier decision (upheld in a few short sentences by the House of Lords) in *Russell v Stubbs*.[137] *Russell v Stubbs* was a claim in libel on a circular sent out by the defendants (the proprietors of *Stubbs' Weekly Gazette*) who provided financial information about businesses for the benefit of their subscribers. The defendants applied to strike out from the statement of claim the words:

> "The plaintiffs believe that the said libel was published to some other persons whom they cannot specify, but they will rely on the publication thereof to every person to whom they may discover it was published."

and the Court of Appeal treated the application as being in substance the plaintiff's application for interrogatories, since that was bound to follow if the pleading stood. The plaintiff's uncontradicted affidavit showed that the circular had been published to one company and its principal, and that on request it had been sent out to the plaintiff firm also, which made it probable that the circular had been published to other third parties; moreover, the plaintiff knew the exact words published. On those facts, the court took the view that interrogatories directed to the identities of other publishees would not amount to a fishing expedition.[138]

In *Barham v Huntingfield*, by contrast, there was no sworn evidence of other publications, but a mere unsupported allegation that the slander had been published to others apart from the person identified in the statement of

---

[134] *Fitzgibbon v Greer* (1875) Ir.R. 9 C.L. 294, distinguished in *Cleland v Neill* [1951] N.1. 61, where the interrogatories were directed to what was said at a meeting, not to the contents of minutes of the meeting; *Norton v Hoare (No.2)* (1913) 17 C.L.R. 348.

[135] *Dalrymple v Leslie* (1881) 8 Q.B.D. 5.

[136] [1913] 2 K.B. 193 CA.

[137] *Barham v Huntingfield*, above, distinguishing *Russell v Stubbs* [1913] 2 K.B. 200n CA and HL.

[138] *Russell v Stubbs* was followed in New South Wales in a case where the defendant credit agency alleged that the plaintiff was bankrupt: *Kaiser v George Laurens* [1982] 1 N.S.W.L.R. 294. There, Hunt J. was prepared to infer that, by reason of its business, the defendant credit agency would have published the words complained of (alleging that the plaintiff was bankrupt) to others apart from the one company alleged in the statement of claim, and allowed extensive interrogatories asking whether the defendant had published the allegation to any other persons, who the publishees were, and what words were used. Cf. *White v Credit Reform* [1905] 1 K.B. 653 CA, where such interrogatories were refused as oppressive.

claim.[139] In a malicious falsehood action Mummery J. ordered discovery analogous to interrogatories of the identities of all persons to whom a damaging letter was sent.[140] As in *Russell v Stubbs*, there was uncontradicted evidence that letters in identical or similar terms to the one set out in the statement of claim had been sent to other persons. The statement of claim alleged publication to such other persons, five of whom were named. Mummery J. held that copies of the letters sent to other persons, and the distribution list, were documents relevant to the issues in the action, and that the plaintiff's purpose (to write to all the publishees in order to set the record straight and mitigate damage, rather than to obtain documents on which to base a cause of action against third parties) was a proper one.

Reference. It is generally immaterial (except in relation to damages and in   **31.27**
the context of the offer of amends procedure)[141] whether a defendant intended to refer to the claimant[142]: what matters is whether reasonable persons would have understood the words complained of to refer to him. For that reason, the plaintiff was not entitled to interrogate the defendant as to whether he intended to refer to the claimant,[143] unless the interrogatory could be justified as going to malice or damages.[144]

Meaning. Similarly, the meaning of the words (at least where there is no   **31.28**
legal innuendo) is a matter exclusively for the jury, and the defendant's views on meaning cannot be admissible.[145] Hence a request for further information as to the meaning which the defendant intended his words to bear would not be allowed.[146]

---

[139] See also *Dalgleish v Lowther*, above, where the plaintiff was allowed to interrogate as to whether the defendant spoke the slander in the presence of any persons apart from the two named in the statement of claim, even though (as in *Barham*) there was no obvious basis for the plea: however, the plaintiff in *Dalgleish* only wanted to discover who else had been present on the one occasion of publication pleaded, rather than (as in *Barham*) to fish for other occasions of publication.

[140] *CHC Software v Hopkins & Wood* [1993] F.S.R. 241.

[141] See s.4(3) of the Defamation Act 1996 and para.29.39, above.

[142] *Hulton v Jones* [1910] A.C. 20; but see *Hayward v Thompson* [1982] Q.B. 47 per Lord Denning M.R. at 60. See Ch.7, above.

[143] *Hulton v Jones* [1909] 2 K.B. 444; [1910] A.C. 20; *Heaton v Goldney* [1910] 1 K.B. 754 CA (meaning rather than reference); *Simson v Tribune* (1911) 31 N.Z.L.R. 953; *Gordon v NZ Times* (1912) 31 N.Z.L.R. 1060. Cf. *Spiers & Pond v John Bull* (1916) 85 L.J.K.B. 992 CA.

[144] In *Franklin v Daily Mirror Newspapers Ltd* (1933) 149 L.T. 433; [1933] W.N. 187, the Court of Appeal disallowed interrogatories about the defendant's intention to refer to the plaintiff, even though the interrogatories were apparently relevant to the issue of malice (pleaded in reply to a defence of fair comment). The court expressly stated that it was laying down no general rule; Lord Hanworth M.R.'s reasoning is unclear from the reports; and it seems unlikely that the decision would be followed today. Cf. *Morley v Patrick* (1910) 21 O.L.R. 240 and *Norton v Hoare (No.2)* (1913) 17 C.L.R. 348 (High Court of Australia), which the Court of Appeal declined to follow, and *Erwin v Southdown Press* [1976] V.R. 353.

[145] See para.32.26, below.

[146] *Heaton v Goldney* [1910] 1 K.B. 754 CA, disapproving *Foster v Perryman* (1891) 8 T.L.R. 115. In *Heaton v Goldney* the argument that the interrogatories went to damages was rejected. Malice was not in issue. Similarly in Canada: *McCrea v Canada Newspapers* (1993) 109 D.L.R. (4th) 396 CA of Nova Scotia.

31.29 Damages. Interrogatories relating to quantum of damages were generally admissible in defamation actions.[147] Further information relating to quantum will be ordered, because the CPR oblige the claimant to plead any matters relied on by the claimant in aggravation of damages,[148] and it is well established that the defendant must plead all matters relied on in mitigation of damage, which may be extensive,[149] so that the parties' contentions are clearly pleaded as material facts. The defendant's failure to apologise can be relevant to aggravation of damages,[150] and no doubt should be pleaded; therefore further information might be ordered which goes to the defendant's refusal or failure to apologise.[151]

31.30 Defendant's state of mind. Where the defence of qualified privilege or honest comment is raised, and the claimant has pleaded express malice, or the state of mind of the defendant when he published the words is otherwise in issue (e.g. because a newspaper has pleaded *Reynolds*[152] privilege), the claimant may in principle ask for further information about it.[153] However, and this is of particular importance in cases of *Reynolds* privilege where there is often reliance on un-named sources, no further information will be ordered which goes to the identity of the defendant's sources of information, unless the court orders otherwise.[154] The issue of the defendant's state of mind will also arise under the defence of offer of amends. If an offer of amends under s.2 of the 1996 Act is not accepted by the aggrieved party, the fact that the offer was made is a defence, but not if the person making the offer knew or had reason to believe that the statement complained of (1) referred to the aggrieved party or was likely to be understood as referring to him, and (2) was both false and defamatory of that party (although it is presumed until the contrary is shown that he did not know and had no reason to believe that was the case).[155] There seems no reason why further information should not be ordered which goes to the defendant's knowledge of the falsity of his statement, or to his knowledge

---

[147] *Marriott v Chamberlain* (1886) 17 Q.B.D. 154 CA at 162, 164; *Scaife v Kemp* [1892] 2 Q.B. 319, more fully reported at (1892) 61 L.J.Q.B. 515; and see *Heaton v Goldney* [1910] 1 K.B. 754 at 758, per Vaughan Williams L.J.

[148] PD 53, para.2.10.

[149] See, e.g. *Burstein v Times Newspapers Ltd* [2001] 1 W.L.R. 579, and para.29.36, above. There is no longer an express provision in the rules requiring a defendant to plead to the claimant's case in damages (cf. the old RSC Ord.18 r.12(1)(c), replacing the earlier Ord.82, r.7), but it is no doubt implicit in CPR r.16.5 that he must do so. See para.27.39, above.

[150] *Rantzen v MGN Ltd* [1994] Q.B. 670 CA at 683; and see para.26.29, above.

[151] *Clark v Ainsworth* (1996) 40 N.S.W.L.R. 463 CA.

[152] *Reynolds v Times Newspapers Ltd* [2001] 2 A.C. 127.

[153] *Elliott v Garrett* [1902] 1 K.B. 870 CA; *White v Credit Reform* [1905] 1 K.B. 653 CA; *Plymouth Mutual v Traders' Publishing Association* [1906] 1 K.B. 403 CA at 412–413; *Dawson v Dover Chronicle* (1913) 108 L.T. 481 per Farwell L.J. at 484: "It is established that the plaintiff can interrogate a defendant who sets up a plea of privilege as to the facts from which an inference of malice may be drawn."

[154] CPR r.53.3. See also para.31.36, below, for s.10 of the Contempt of Court Act 1981.

[155] Defamation Act 1996, s.4(2), (3). Offer of amends is discussed at paras 29.28ff, above.

of reference to the claimant, although not before bad faith under s.4(3) Defamation Act 1996 has been pleaded.[156]

Actions against newspapers: identities of those responsible for publication. **31.31**

If the libel was contained in a newspaper, the plaintiff was permitted to interrogate the defendant as to whether he was the printer, publisher or proprietor at the time when the words were published,[157] and to interrogate the printer or publisher to find out the name of the proprietor[158] and the publisher to find out the name of the printer, even though the object was to enable the claimant to bring an action against the person whose name is sought.[159] However, the plaintiff could not ask the defendant whether he was the editor of the newspaper[160] or the author of the alleged libel.[161] Note that the Stamp Duties on Newspapers Act 1836[162] does not confer a right of discovery; it merely removes the privilege against self-incrimination.[163] Hence no order for interrogatories lay against a person who had no responsibility at all for publication of the words complained of so was not a defendant to the defamation claim,[164] and who could not be brought within the scope of the *Norwich Pharmacal* principle.[165] Interrogatories were generally not allowed which related to the possession or contents of the manuscript on which the article was based.[166]

Sources. **31.32**

The law protects disclosure of sources of information by data protection legislation, by the long-established common law "newspaper rule",

---

[156] See *Tesco Stores Ltd v Guardian News & Media Ltd* [2009] E.M.L.R. 5 per Eady J. at [43], and para.31.8, above.

[157] Stamp Duties on Newspapers Act 1836, s.19, re-enacted by Newspapers, Printers, and Reading Rooms Repeal Act 1869, s.1; *Lefroy v Burnside (No.1)* (1879) 4 L.R.Ir. 340 (proprietor); *Carter v Leeds Daily News* [1876] W.N. 11 (publisher). However, in the light of Defamation Act 1996, s.1, it should be remembered that a printer or (if distinct from the publisher) a proprietor is now unlikely to be sued.

[158] *Dixon v Enoch* (1871) L.R. 13 Eq. 394. But note the effect of Defamation Act 1996, s.1: see previous note.

[159] *Hillman's Airways v Société Anonyme* [1934] 2 K.B. 356 (du Parcq J.).

[160] *Carter v Leeds Daily News*, above.

[161] *Wilton v Brignell* [1875] W.N. 239; *Carter v Leeds Daily News*, above.

[162] See fn.157, above.

[163] *Ricci v Chow* [1987] 1 W.L.R. 1658 CA; *British Steel Corp v Granada* [1981] A.C. 1096 per Lord Wilberforce at 1172.

[164] *Ricci v Chow*, above.

[165] *Norwich Pharmacal v Customs & Excise* [1974] A.C. 133.

[166] *Hennessy v Wright (No.2)* (1890) 24 Q.B.D. 445n CA; *Hope v Brash* [1897] 2 Q.B. 188 CA (a case on inspection of documents). However, the defendant could be interrogated about alterations and deletions to the text before publication: *McNab v Wellington Publishing* (1914) 33 N.Z.L.R. 1362, where this appears to have been relevant to damages; *Isbey v NZBC (No.2)* [1975] 2 N.Z.L.R. 237, where the differences between the original manuscript and the broadcast text were material. Malice was in issue; that is not clear from the report of Cooke J.'s judgment, but does appear from an earlier interlocutory application in the case, reported at [1975] 1 N.Z.L.R. 721.

by s.10 of the Contempt of Court Act 1981, by art.10 of the European Convention on Human Rights, and (in the case of requests for further information) by CPR r.53.3.

31.33 Data Protection. Applications which entail the disclosure of sources may fall foul of the provisions of the Data Protection Act 1998, for it has been said (obiter) that in the light of Sch.2, para.2 of that Act no order should be made for the disclosure of a data subject's identity, whether under the *Norwich Pharmacal* jurisdiction or otherwise, unless the court has first considered whether disclosure is warranted having regard to the rights and freedoms or legitimate interests of the data subject.[167]

31.34 The newspaper rule. There is a very well-established common law rule, the so-called "newspaper rule", whereby discovery (whether of documents or by interrogatories) will not be ordered in libel actions[168] against newspapers, so as to force them to disclose their sources of information before trial.[169] It is submitted that if the rule is invoked in answer to a request for further information, the courts will continue to respect it, although for the reasons advanced below it is probably now redundant in the United Kingdom.[170] The reasons for the rule are obscure, but are probably founded in considerations of public policy.[171] The rule only applies at interlocutory stages, and not at the

---

[167] *Totalise Ltd v Motley Fool Ltd* [2001] EWCA Civ 1897; [2002] 1 W.L.R. 1233 at [24]. For a full discussion of the Data Protection Act, see Warby, Christie & Moreham (eds), *The Law of Privacy and the Media*, 2nd edn (Oxford: Oxford University Press, 2010), Ch.6: and see also paras 22.19ff. and 31.5, above.

[168] It has been applied also to slander of title: *Broadcasting Corp of New Zealand v Alex Harvey Industries Ltd* [1980] 1 N.Z.L.R. 163 CA.

[169] *Hennessy v Wright (No.2)* (1890) 24 Q.B.D. 445 CA; *Parnell v Walter* (1890) 24 Q.B.D. 441 CA; *Hope v Brash* [1897] 2 Q.B. 188 CA; *Elliott v Garrett* [1902] 1 K.B. 870 CA; *Plymouth Mutual v Traders' Publishing Association* [1906] 1 K.B. 403 CA; *Adams v Fisher* (1914) 30 T.L.R. 288 CA; *Lyle-Samuel v Odhams* [1920] 1 K.B. 135 CA; *South-Suburban Co-operative Society v Orum* [1937] 2 K.B. 690 CA; *McGuinness v Att-Gen for Victoria* (1940) 63 C.L.R. 73; *Korda v Odhams* [1948] W.N. 376; *Lawson v Odhams* [1949] 1 K.B. 129 CA; *Georgius v Oxford University Press* [1949] 1 K.B. 729 CA; *Att-Gen v Clough* [1963] 1 Q.B. 773 CA; *Att-Gen v Mulholland* [1963] 2 Q.B. 477 CA; *Isbey v New Zealand Broadcasting Corp (No.2)* [1975] 2 N.Z.L.R. 237; *Brill v Television Service One* [1976] 1 N.Z.L.R. 683; *Andrews v John Fairfax* [1978] 2 N.S.W.L.R. 300; *Trigg v Incorporated News Agencies* [1978] 2 N.S.L.R. 302n; *Broadcasting Corp of New Zealand v Alex Harvey Industries* [1980] 1 N.Z.L.R. 163; *British Steel Corp v Granada* [1981] A.C. 1096. See also the discussion in *Wran v ABC* [1984] 3 N.S.W.L.R. 241; *Fairfax v Cojuangco* (1988) 165 C.L.R. 346; and *Herald and Weekly Times v Guide Dog Owners* [1990] V.R. 451; and contrast *Kerrisk v North Queensland Newspaper* (1992) 2 Qd.R. 398. See also *Bond v Western Australian Newspapers Ltd* [2009] WASCA 127.

[170] It was considered, and implicitly regarded by the Court of Appeal as alive although of little continuing value, in *Gaddafi v Telegraph Group Ltd* [2000] E.M.L.R. 431 per Hirst L.J. at 455–458.

[171] *McGuinness v Att-Gen for Victoria* (1940) 63 C.L.R. 73 per Dixon J. at 104; *D v NSPCC* [1978] A.C. 171 at 227–228; *British Steel v Granada* [1981] A.C. 1096 per Lord Fraser of Tullybelton at 1197–1198.

trial of the action.[172] It has repeatedly been said to be subject to unspecified exceptions,[173] but there seems to be no reported English case where an exception has been held to apply,[174] and in New Zealand it has been suggested that the rule should be regarded as absolute.[175] The protection of the newspaper rule extends to journalists in the full time employment of a newspaper,[176] to trade periodicals,[177] but not to the authors of letters published in newspapers[178]; it is doubtful whether it extends to freelance journalists[179] or to the publishers of *Crockford*, the annual clerical directory,[180] but it almost certainly applies to broadcasters.[181]

CPR rule 53.3. However, more certain and effective source protection is available. First, CPR r.53.3 provides that unless the court orders otherwise, a party to a defamation claim will not be required to provide further information about the identity of the defendant's sources of information.[182] Unlike its predecessor, RSC Ord.82, r.6, it is not limited to cases where qualified privilege or fair (honest) comment are in issue. It is perhaps an oddity given the new importance in common law qualified privilege of the source of the defendant's information, the status of that information and the steps taken to verify it,[183] and may debar claimants from obtaining further information about what may be a critical part of a defendant's case. Given the statutory protection of journalists' sources under s.10, Contempt of Court Act 1981, and the discretionary control over further information which Pt 18 gives to the court, it is arguable that further protection of sources was unnecessary. However, the

31.35

---

[172] *British Steel v Granada* [1981] A.C. 1096.

[173] See, e.g. *Hope v Brash* [1897] 2 Q.B. 188 CA at 191–192.

[174] See, e.g. per Lord Fraser in *British Steel v Granada* [1981] A.C. 1096 at 1199. However, Lord Fraser referred to one Scots case as an exception: *Cunningham v Duncan and Jamieson* (1889) 16 R. 383.

[175] *Broadcasting Corp of New Zealand v Alex Harvey Industries* [1980] 1 N.Z.L.R. 163 at 169, per Woodhouse P. However, in *Lange v Atkinson* [2000] NZCA 95 [55]–[57] it was suggested that this view may require reconsideration, and that the rule should not be regarded as being set in stone. In Australia it may yield to necessity in the interests of justice (cf. s.10 of the Contempt of Court Act 1981): *Fairfax v Cojuangco* (above). For an authoritative statement of the applicable principles concerning protection of journalistic sources in Canada, see the decision of the Supreme Court of Canada in *R v National Post* 2010 SCC 16.

[176] *Lawson v Odhams Press Ltd* [1949] 1 K.B. 129 CA.

[177] *Georgius v Oxford University Press* [1949] 1 K.B. 729 CA.

[178] *South-Suburban Co-operative Society v Orum* [1937] 2 K.B. 690 CA.

[179] *British Steel v Granada* [1981] A.C. 1096 per Lord Fraser at 1198.

[180] *Plymouth Mutual v Traders' Publishing Association* [1906] 1 K.B. 403 CA.

[181] *Isbey v NZBC (No.2)* [1975] 2 N.Z.L.R. 237; *Brill v Television Service One* [1976] 1 N.Z.L.R. 683; *Broadcasting Corp of New Zealand v Alex Harvey Industries Ltd* [1980] 1 N.Z.L.R. 163 CA; *British Steel v Granada* [1981] A.C. 1096 per Lord Wilberforce at 1172–1173.

[182] Curiously, the wording of the rule appears to contemplate that no party, whether or not a defendant, may be ordered to give further information about the defendant's sources.

[183] *Reynolds v Times Newspapers Ltd* [2001] 2 A.C. 127; *Loutchansky v Times Newspapers Ltd* [2001] EWCA Civ 1805; [2002] Q.B. 783; *Jameel v Wall Street Journal* [2007] 1 A.C. 359; *Flood v Times Newspapers Ltd* [2012] UKSC 11; [2012] 2 A.C. 273. See *Gaddafi v Telegraph Group Ltd* [2000] E.M.L.R. 431, where this particular conundrum is confronted.

court does now have a discretion to make an order, where before it had none, and the rule applies to all litigants, not just journalists.

31.36 Contempt of Court Act 1981, section 10.[184] More to the point, the common law position has been overtaken by s.10 of the Contempt of Court Act 1981.[185] The section offers a far more extensive protection than the newspaper rule provided. It applies to all causes of action, not just libel, and to evidence at trial as much as to applications at interlocutory stages, including applications for disclosure, interrogatories and further information.[186] It is for the applicant for disclosure of a source of information to satisfy the court that disclosure is necessary in one of the specified interests, although there are circumstances in which it may be desirable for a media defendant, pleading a *Reynolds* defence, to consider whether disclosure may be preferable to anonymity.[187] Since the Human Rights Act 1998 came into force, the court must so far as possible equate the purposes for which disclosure is permitted under s.10 with the legitimate aims listed by art.10(2) ECHR as allowing derogation from the right to freedom of expression, and apply the same test of necessity as that which the ECHR applies when considering art.10.[188]:

> "The approach of the European Court to the question of whether disclosure of a source is 'necessary' involves a single exercise in which the court considers not merely whether, on the facts of the particular case, disclosure of the source is

---

[184] This is not the place for a full consideration of s.10, for which see Arlidge, Eady & Smith, *Contempt of Court*, 4th edn (2011), Ch.9, and *The Law of Privacy and the Media*, 2nd edn (Oxford: Oxford University Press, 2010), Ch.16.

[185] The section provides as follows:
"No court may require a person to disclose, nor is any person guilty of contempt of court for refusing to disclose, the source of information contained in a publication for which he is responsible, unless it be established to the satisfaction of the court that disclosure is necessary in the interests of justice or national security or for the prevention of disorder or crime."

[186] *Secretary of State for Defence v Guardian Newspapers* [1985] A.C. 339 per Lord Diplock at 345, 347.

[187] In *Reynolds v Times Newspapers Ltd* [2001] 2 A.C. 127 at 205 Lord Nicholls said: "In general a newspaper's unwillingness to disclose the identity of its sources should not weigh against it." But Gray J., wrestling with the difficulty of assessing the reliability of anonymous sources, has suggested that media defendants may need to consider "carefully and conscientiously" whether non-disclosure of the identity of sources is justified and necessary.
"I accept that it would be wrong to draw any inference adverse to the newspaper from the mere fact of the withholding of information as to the identity of its sources. That is, however, not to say that every claim made by the journalist as to the reliability of his unnamed source is to be taken at face value":
Loutchansky v Times Newspapers Ltd (No.4) [2001] E.M.L.R. 38 at [50]–[52]. The European Court of Human Rights has accepted the reasoning of the Norwegian courts that where it is impossible for the court to verify the extent to which a journalist has acted with due care in relying on an anonymous source, the defamatory allegation ought to be regarded as the newspaper's own, and that a stricter duty of care applies where anonymous sources are used: *Tønsbergs Blad AS and Haukom v Norway*, App. No.510/04, at [95].

[188] *Ashworth Hospital Authority v MGN Ltd* [2001] 1 W.L.R. 515 at 532, per, Lord Phillips M.R.

necessary to achieve the legitimate aim but, more significantly, whether the achievement of the legitimate aim on the facts of the instant case is so important that it overrides the public interest in protecting journalistic sources in order to ensure free communication of information to and through the press".[189]

"The question in each case to which s.10 of the 1981 Act or art.10 of the Convention applies is thus whether the claimant has shown that it is both necessary, in the sense of there being an overriding interest amounting to a pressing social need, and proportionate for the Court to order the journalist to disclose the name of his source . . . the requirements of necessity and proportionality are separate but substantially cover the same area."[190]

In answering that question, the judge must balance the interests of the claimant on the one hand and the interests of the journalist on the other hand.[191] The principles governing the interplay between arts 8 and 10, stated by Lord Steyn in *Re S*, apply equally in the context of source protection.[192] The court cannot determine in any given case whether an encroachment upon

---

[189] Ibid. at 535. Art.10 requires that any interference with the right to freedom of expression must be necessary in a democratic society in the interests, inter alia, of the protection of the reputation and rights of others: "necessary" implies a pressing social need, and interference with freedom of expression should be no more than proportionate to the legitimate aim pursued. In that context it has been held that:
"Having regard to the importance of the protection of journalistic sources for press freedom in a democratic society and the potentially chilling effect an order of source disclosure has on the exercise of that freedom, such a measure cannot be compatible with Article 10 of the Convention unless it is justified by an overriding requirement in the public interest":
Goodwin v UK [1996] E.H.H.R. 123 at 143. This was Mr Goodwin's appeal from the decision of the House of Lords in *X v Morgan-Grampian* [1991] 1 A.C. 1. The European Court of Human Rights held that given the existence of an injunction restricting dissemination of the confidential information by the press, the further purposes served by an order for disclosure did not amount to an overriding requirement in the public interest. Now see *Financial Times Ltd v UK* [2010] E.M.L.R. 21 in which the Strasbourg court determined that the applicant media organisations' rights under art.10 had been violated by an order requiring them to disclose documents which might lead to the identification of a journalistic source (see *Interbrew SA v Financial Times Ltd* [2002] EWCA Civ 274; [2002] E.M.L.R. 24). The Strasbourg court concluded at [71] that Interbrew SA's interests in taking proceedings against the source to prevent damage from further dissemination of confidential information "were, even if considered cumulatively, insufficient to outweigh the public interest in the protection of journalists' sources". See also *Sanoma Uitgevers BV v The Netherlands* (App. No.38224/03); [2011] E.M.L.R. 4, a Grand Chamber decision of the European Court of Human Rights.
[190] *Mersey Care NHS Trust v Ackroyd (No.2)* [2007] EWCA Civ 101; [2008] E.M.L.R. 1 at [17].
[191] *Mersey Care NHS Trust v Ackroyd* (above), [18].
[192] *Mersey Care NHS Trust v Ackroyd* (above), applying *Re S (A Child) (Identification: Restrictions on Publication)* [2005] 1 A.C. 593 at [17]:
"The interplay between articles 8 and 10 has been illuminated by the opinions in the House of Lords in *Campbell v MGN Ltd* . For present purposes the decision of the House on the facts of Campbell and the differences between the majority and the minority are not material. What does, however, emerge clearly from the opinions are four propositions. First, neither article has as such precedence over the other. Secondly, where the values under the two articles are in conflict, an intense focus on the comparative importance of the specific rights being claimed in the individual case is necessary. Thirdly, the justifications for interfering with or restricting each right must be taken into account. Finally, the proportionality test must be applied to each. For convenience I will call this the ultimate balancing test. This is how I will approach the present case."

the confidentiality of a source is necessary and proportionate, until the competing interests have been balanced one against the other.[193]

31.37 Responsible person. The protection of the section is not restricted to journalists, broadcasters and newspaper proprietors, but extends to any person who is "responsible" for a publication,[194] which:

> "includes any speech, writing, broadcast, programme included in a programme service or other communication in whatever form, which is addressed to the public at large or any section of the public".[195]

Despite the apparent limitation to information "contained in" a publication, s.10 applies even where the information has not actually been published, as long as it was communicated and received for the purpose of publication.[196] Furthermore, the defendant need not show that delivery up of a document (or, presumably, answering a request for further information) will certainly reveal a source of information: it is enough that it may do so.[197]

31.38 Circulation. Where the libel is published in a well-known newspaper with which the jury is likely to be familiar, there is authority that the plaintiff cannot interrogate (or, it must follow, obtain an order for further information from) the proprietors as to the number of copies which were printed and published, because the exact circulation figure is unlikely to be important and the jury will be well enough aware of the general type and extent of circulation to be able to assess damages.[198] The position is different where the newspaper is comparatively obscure, in which case information as to circulation will be relevant to damages.[199] In practice, however, disclosure of

---

[193] *Inner West London Assistant Deputy Coroner v Channel 4 Television Corp* [2007] EWHC 2513 (QB); [2008] 1 W.L.R. 945 at [25].

[194] This definition may include a person who has supplied information to a newspaper and then worked with its journalists to produce a story (*John Reid Enterprises Ltd v Pell* [1999] E.M.L.R. 675, Carnwath J.), and the deputy editor of a newspaper (*O'Mara Books v Express Newspapers Ltd* [1998] E.M.L.R. 383, Neuberger J.)

[195] Contempt of Court Act 1981, ss.2(1) and 19.

[196] *X v Morgan-Grampian* [1991] 1 A.C. 1.

[197] *Secretary of State for Defence v Guardian Newspapers Ltd* [1985] A.C. 339 at 349 (Lord Diplock).

[198] *Whittaker v Scarborough Post* [1896] 2 Q.B. 148 CA, disapproving on this point *Parnell v Walter* (1890) 24 Q.B.D. 441, *The Times*; *Rumney v Walter* (1891) 61 L.J.Q.B. 149, *The Times*; *James v Carr* (1890) 7 T.L.R. 4, *The Western Mail*. In *Whittaker*, the newspaper was *The Scarborough Post*, which the court regarded as likely to be familiar to a Leeds jury. The position would have been different had the case been tried by a London jury. In *Garrett v Nationwide News* (1965) 8 F.L.R. 415, the Supreme Court of the Australian Capital Territory held that an interrogatory about the circulation of *The Australian* should be allowed, because, inter alia, the defendant publisher denied that it had a large circulation, and the newspaper was only one year old, so that it was not yet well known although sold throughout Australia.

[199] *Whittaker v Scarborough Post*, above, per Lord Esher M.R. at 150 and per Kay L.J. at 151. The court suggested that even in that case, an answer that the circulation was "considerable" should be sufficient.

circulation is routinely given and evidence of circulation (and readership) is invariably admitted at trial.

(c) *The practical scope of interrogatories and requests for further information by defendants*

General. The paragraphs which follow describe the areas in which the law   **31.39**
has in the past permitted interrogatories to be administered by the defendant.
There seems no reason why the court should not in the same situations adopt
the same approach to the supply of further information at the request of
defendants as it has in the past done to the administration of interrogatories.

Justification. Where justification was pleaded and properly particularised,   **31.40**
the defendant was allowed to interrogate the plaintiff as to any facts which, if
proved, would be material evidence in support of the plea (and vice versa: the
plaintiff could interrogate the defendant as to facts which would be material
evidence to destroy the plea).[200] However, the defendant was not allowed to
serve interrogatories in order to fish for a defence of justification.[201] Any
interrogatories directed by the defendant to the plaintiff were limited to the
issues as defined by the particulars of justification.[202] Needless to say, if the
defendant had not pleaded justification he could not interrogate the plaintiff as
to any matters which tended to establish the truth of the allegations complained of.[203]

Claimant's state of mind. Where the defendant pleaded privilege or fair   **31.41**
comment and the plaintiff pleaded malice, the defendant was allowed to
interrogate the plaintiff as to facts which went to substantiate his honest belief
in the truth of the statement complained of at the time when he published it,

---

[200] *Marriott v Chamberlain* (1886) 17 Q.B.D. 154 CA: *McDonald's Corp v Steel* [1995] 3 All
E.R. 615 CA at 621f. It is not unreasonable to view the decision in *Dee v Telegraph Media Group
Ltd* [2009] EWHC 2546 (QB) as a modern application of this principle. See further para.31.14,
above.

[201] *Gourley v Plimsoll* (1873) L.R. 8 C.P. 362; *Buchanan v Taylor* [1876] W.N. 73; *Zierenberg
v Labouchere* [1893] 2 Q.B. 183 CA at 188–190; *Yorkshire Provident v Gilbert* [1895] 2 Q.B. 148
CA; *Arnold v Bottomley* [1908] 2 K.B. 151 CA; *Goldschmidt v Constable* [1937] 4 K.B. 293 CA.
"The moment it appears that questions are asked and answers insisted upon in order to enable the
party to see if he can find a case, either of complaint or defence, of which at present he knows
nothing . . . the rule against 'fishing' interrogatories applies": *Hennessy v Wright (No.2)* (1890) 24
Q.B.D. 445n per Lord Esher M.R. at 448; adopted by Kennedy L.J. in *Russell v Stubbs* [1913] 2
K.B. 200n at 204.

[202] *Yorkshire Provident v Gilbert* [1895] 2 Q.B. 148 CA. See further fn.41, above. *Evans v
Granada* [1996] E.M.L.R. 429 CA, shows that the converse does not necessarily hold good. That
is to say, interrogatories by the plaintiff to the defendant will not be limited to the matters put in
issue by the particulars of justification, but will extend to matters relevant to the plaintiff's
rebuttal of the defence.

[203] *Hindlip v Mudford* (1870) 6 T.L.R. 367; *Aldridge v Fairfax* [1984] 2 N.S.W.L.R. 544.

although those facts might incidentally prove the truth of the statement.[204] However, the defendant could not interrogate the plaintiff as to the objective truth of what was published, since that (as opposed to his honest belief in its truth) was not in issue.[205]

31.42 Fair (honest) comment. A defendant who had pleaded fair comment was allowed to interrogate the plaintiff as to the truth of the facts on which his comments were based.[206]

31.43 Damages. The claimant is now obliged to plead all matters relied upon in relation to damages,[207] so that the issues on damages should be clearly set out. The defendant may in principle ask for further information on any issue relating to damages.

Section 3. Security for Costs and Maintenance

31.44 General. The regime for obtaining security for costs in civil litigation is governed principally by CPR rr.25.12 and 25.13. Where, on the defendant's application, supported by written evidence, the court is satisfied, having regard to all the circumstances of the case, that it is just to make an order, and one or more conditions applies, or an enactment permits the court to require security, then it may make an order for security for costs under r.25.12. The relevant conditions are[208]:

> (a) the claimant is resident out of the jurisdiction, but not resident in a Brussels or Lugano Contracting State or a Regulation State,[209] as defined by section 1(3), Civil Jurisdiction and Judgments Act 1982;

---

[204] *McKergow v Comstock* (1906) 11 O.L.R. 637 (Ontario DC).

[205] *Redmond v Uebergang* [1984] 1 N.S.W.L.R. 311, Hunt J., where both qualified privilege and malice were pleaded; *Aldridge v Fairfax* [1984] 2 N.S.W.L.R. 544, Hunt J., where in the absence of a plea of justification or reliance by the plaintiff on falsity of the words in support of a claim for aggravated damages, the defendant could not interrogate as to the truth of the words.

[206] *Peter Walker v Hodgson* [1909] 1 K.B. 239 CA. That was a case of the "rolled up" plea of fair comment, now extinct in England. However, the authority holds good for the plea in its modern form, as it was a case in which particulars were supplied of the facts relied on in support of the plea of fair comment.

[207] CPR PD 53, para.2.10 and r.16.4(1)(c).

[208] See CPR r.25.13(2).

[209] The Civil Jurisdiction and Judgments Acts 1982 and 1991 give the force of law to the Brussels Convention of 1968, the Lugano Convention of 1988 and other related treaties. The practical importance of the Brussels Convention for UK purposes has been much reduced by Council Regulation 44/2001 of December 22, 2000 (known as the Brussels or Judgments Regulation) which supersedes the Brussels Convention for all EU Member States. The Lugano Convention signatories which are not EU members are Iceland, Norway and Switzerland. See also para.24.23, above.

(b) . . .[210]

(c) the claimant is a company or other body (whether incorporated inside or outside Great Britain) and there is reason to believe that it will be unable to pay the defendant's costs if ordered to do so;

(d) the claimant has changed his address since the claim was commenced with a view to evading the consequences of the litigation;

(e) the claimant failed to give his address, or gave an incorrect address, in the claim form;

(f) the claimant is acting as a nominal claimant (other than as a representative claimant under Pt 19) and there is reason to believe that he will be unable to pay the defendant's costs if ordered to do so[211];

(g) the claimant has taken steps in relation to his assets that would make it difficult to enforce an order for costs against him.

Although the CPR contain a number of other rules enabling the court to direct payments tantamount to orders for security for costs in a variety of circumstances outside these provisions, this section focuses on Pt 25 and on questions of maintenance, which are of more direct concern to defamation litigants.[212]

The scope of security under the CPR. The court's general powers of   **31.45**
management include a jurisdiction to make orders which are tantamount to orders for security for costs outside the provisions of Pt 25.[213] CPR r.3.1(3)(a) provides that when the court makes an order it may make it subject to conditions, including a condition to pay a sum of money into court, and r.3.1(5) enables the court to order a party to pay a sum of money into court if that party has, without good reason, failed to comply with a rule, practice direction or a relevant pre-action protocol (although in practice that failure would have to amount to the regular flouting of proper court procedures).[214] Moreover, r.3.1(2)(m) allows the court to take any other step or make any other order for the purpose of managing the case and furthering the overriding

---

[210] (b) has been repealed.

[211] Lack of means is made expressly relevant in the case of nominal claimants, for which see *Orme v Associated Newspapers Ltd*, unreported, November 10, 1980, CA, where the plaintiff in a libel action was the director of the Unification Church in Britain, and the defendant sought (and obtained) security on the basis that the real plaintiff was the Unification Church.

[212] For a full discussion of Pt 25 security, see the notes to Pt 25 in Sweet & Maxwell's *Civil Procedure (The White Book)*, Vol.1. For the approach in Scotland to security for costs—or "caution" as it is referred to in that jurisdiction—in a defamation action, see *Ewing v Times Newspapers Ltd* [2008] CSOH 169.

[213] *Olatawura v Abiloye* [2002] EWCA Civ 998; [2003] 1 W.L.R. 275 at [18]–[19].

[214] *Olatawura v Abiloye* (above) at [25]. In *Sarayiah v Suren* [2004] EWHC 1981 (QB) Tugendhat J. declined ([112]–[115]) to make an order under CPR r.3.1(3) or (5) for a defendant to bring money into court because of alleged failures to comply with rules of court: following *Olatawura v Abiloye*, he held that there was no want of good faith on the defendant's part and that the failures alleged, even if made good, did not amount to the repeated breaches required before the court will exercise this jurisdiction.

objective, and such an order may include an order for security.[215] When exercising the power under r.3.1(5), the court must have regard to (1) the amount in dispute, and (2) the costs which the parties have incurred or which they may incur.[216] Where a party pays money into court under r.3.1(3) or (5), the money shall be security for any sum payable by that party to any other party to the proceedings.[217] In addition, on an application for summary judgment under Pt 24, when it appears possible that a claim or defence may succeed but improbable that it will do so, the court may make a conditional order which requires a party to pay a sum of money into court.[218] This means that although security for costs under Pt 25 cannot be ordered against a defendant, even though he resides out of the jurisdiction,[219] a defendant may be the subject of an order on a Pt 24 summary judgment application, or be ordered to pay money into court under CPR r.3.1(3) or (5), orders which are undoubtedly tantamount to security for costs.[220]

31.46 **Modern principles for the exercise of the wider jurisdiction to order security.**[221] The court has a wide discretion under the CPR to ensure that justice can be done, and relevant considerations, besides the ability of the party concerned to pay, will be (1) his conduct of the proceedings (including in particular his compliance or otherwise with any applicable rule, practice direction or protocol) and (2) the apparent strength of his case (whether claim or defence).[222] That does not mean that the court should ordinarily penalise breaches of the rules by making orders for payment in under r.3.1(5), although such an order might be appropriate if the party is regularly flouting proper court procedures or otherwise demonstrating a want of good faith:

> "good faith for this purpose consisting of a will to litigate a genuine claim or defence as economically and expeditiously as reasonably possible in accordance with the overriding objective".[223]

Nor will an order for security be appropriate in every case where a party seems to have a rather weak claim or defence, and misguided applications for summary judgment[224] aimed at obtaining conditional orders for security are to be discouraged. The court will be reluctant to be drawn into an assessment of

---

[215] Ibid. at [25].

[216] R.3.1(6).

[217] Subject to the right of a defendant under r.37.2 to treat all or part of any money paid into court as a Pt 36 payment: r.3.1(6A).

[218] CPR PD 24, paras 4 and 5.

[219] *Re Percy Co.* (1876) 2 Ch.D. 531 at 532, per Jessel M.R.; *Naamlooze v Bank of England* [1948] 1 All E.R. 465 CA. But a defendant may, of course, be ordered to give security for the costs of his counterclaim or other Pt 20 claim, which is treated as if it were a claim for the purposes of the CPR.

[220] *Olatawura v Abiloye* [2002] EWCA Civ 998; [2003] 1 W.L.R. 275 at [18]–[19], [23].

[221] *Olatawura v Abiloye*, above.

[222] Ibid. at [24].

[223] Ibid. at [25].

[224] CPR 24 PD paras 4 and 5.

the merits beyond what is strictly necessary for summary judgment purposes, and security will rarely be ordered solely because a case appears weak.[225] However, a claim which appears highly likely to succeed will not attract an order for security.[226]

Difficulty of enforcement. No assumption must be made that an order for security will follow from proof of residence in a non-contracting state.[227] Instead, it must be established that any costs order made in favour of the defendant would not be enforceable, or would be substantially more difficult and therefore more expensive to enforce, in that jurisdiction.[228] Furthermore, if the court finds that it may be effectively impossible to enforce an order for costs, that would provide an objective justification for the court to make an order for payment of the costs likely to ordered against a claimant if unsuccessful, that is to say, the full amount of the defendant's approved costs budget.[229] If the claimant has entered into a conditional fee agreement, such security payment can include the costs uplift permitted to be recovered under such an arrangement, which may amount to 100 per cent of the base costs.[230]

31.47

Impecuniosity and the risk of stifling a genuine claim. The fact that the claimant is impecunious is not a ground for awarding security, but it is a factor which must be relevant to the likely difficulty of enforcement. On the other hand, the court must be alert to prevent the power to order security from being used as an instrument of oppression by stifling a genuine claim, so (as

31.48

---

[225] Ibid. at [26].

[226] *Keary Developments Ltd v Tarmac Constructions Ltd* [1995] 3 All E.R. 534 at 540; *Al-Koronky v Time Life Entertainment Group Ltd* [2006] EWCA Civ 1123 at [24].

[227] *Nasser v United Bank of Kuwait* [2001] 1 W.L.R. 1868 CA; *Al-Koronky v Time Life Entertainment Group Ltd* [2006] EWCA Civ 1123 at [24].

[228] *Al-Koronky v Time Life Entertainment Group Ltd* [2005] EWHC 1688 (QB), a case in which the claimants resided out of the jurisdiction in Sudan, which is not a contracting state (i.e. a party to the Brussels or Lugano Conventions or a Regulation state). The judgment of Eady J. was upheld by the Court of Appeal: [2006] EWCA Civ 1123. See also *Kahangi v Nourizadeh* [2009] EWHC 2451 (QB), at [10]–[20], concerning the possibility of enforcement in Iran, another non-contracting state.

[229] *Texuna International Ltd v Cairns Energy Plc* [2004] EWHC 1102 (Com), Gross J. In *Al-Koronky v Time Life Entertainment Group Ltd* (above) there was uncontradicted evidence that enforcement in Sudan would fail, and in the exercise of his discretion (taking account, in particular, of the failure of the claimant to state clearly that the claim would be stifled if security was ordered) the judge ordered security for costs in the sum of £375,000 down to the conclusion of disclosure. That amounted to 87 per cent of the sum sought. The Court of Appeal regarded the judge's exercise of discretion as unappealable, although it was observed that he might equally legitimately have settled on a substantially lower figure ([49]). See also *Mengi v Hermitage* [2012] EWHC 2045 (QB); [2012] 5 Costs L.O. 641. In relation to costs budgets, now see Section II of CPR Pt 3 and CPR PD 3E (in force from April 1, 2013). Defamation claims were previously subject to a costs budgeting pilot scheme which, subject to contrary order, continues to apply to any action commenced prior to April 1, 2013 involving a claim for libel or slander: CPR PD 51D (as to which, see *Henry v News Group Newspapers Ltd* [2013] EWCA Civ 19; [2013] 2 All E.R. 840) and the Civil Procedure (Amendment) Rules 2013, SI 2013/262 (L.1), para.22(12).

[230] *Mengi v Hermitage*, above.

stated above) security will not be ordered where a claim appears highly likely to succeed.[231] The court will not order security in a sum which it knows the claimant cannot afford.[232] The party's ability to raise money will be a prime consideration, not least in the light of art.6, but "paradoxically, the more difficult it appears to be for the person concerned to raise the money, the more obvious becomes the need for an order for security to protect the other party against the risk of incurring irrecoverable costs. The court will have to resolve that conundrum as best it may."[233] However, it cannot be assumed in the claimant's favour that an order for security will have a stifling effect: that must turn on the evidence, which the court may expect to include evidence that there do not exist third parties who can reasonably be expected to put up security for the defendant's costs,[234] and that evidence should be full and candid, and should be scrutinised with a critical eye by the court, which will be prepared to draw adverse inferences from unexplained lacunae.[235]

31.49 Conditional fee agreements. In contrast with most other types of civil claim, the conditional fee agreement ("CFA") funding regime as constituted prior to April 1, 2013 continues to govern defamation cases. It was originally intended, as part of the Jackson costs reforms,[236] that litigants who entered into CFAs in order to fund the pursuit or defence of a defamation case—in common with most other areas of civil litigation—would no longer be permitted to seek to recover from the losing party in the event of success a costs uplift or any amount in respect of the obtaining of after-the-event ("ATE") insurance. However, as a result of the concerns articulated by Leveson L.J. in his Report into the Culture, Practices and Ethics of the Press (Part I)[237]and by the Joint Parliamentary Committee scrutinising the Defamation Bill[238] regarding the particular importance of ensuring that ordinary people had access to justice in cases involving the press, Parliament has decided for the time being to retain the *status quo ante* in defamation and other types of "publication and privacy proceedings".[239] This is somewhat ironic given that the previous

---

[231] See fn.226, above.

[232] *Al-Koronky v Time Life Entertainment Group Ltd* (above) at [24]–[25]. "The making of an order for security is not intended to be a weapon by which a defendant can obtain a speedy summary judgment without a trial": *Radu v Houston* [2006] EWCA Civ 1575 per Waller L.J. at [18].

[233] *Olatawura v Abiloye* (above) per Simon Brown L.J. at [22].

[234] *Brimko Holdings Ltd v Eastman Kodak Co.* [2004] EWHC 1343 (Ch).

[235] *Al-Koronky v Time Life Entertainment Group Ltd* (above) at [27].

[236] See Jackson L.J.'s *Review of Civil Litigation Costs: Final Report*, published January 2010 (*http://www.judiciary.gov.uk/publications-and-reports/review-of-civil-litigation-costs/index*).

[237] Published on November 29, 2012.

[238] Published on December 4, 2012.

[239] See the Legal Aid, Sentencing and Punishment of Offenders Act 2012 (Commencement No.5 and Saving Provision) Order 2013, SI 2013/77 (C.4), arts 1 and 4. "Publication and privacy proceedings" are defined in art.1 as proceedings for defamation, malicious falsehood, breach of confidence involving publication to the general public, misuse of private information, and harassment where the defendant is a news publisher. (Notably, claims under the Data Protection Act 1998 and the Human Rights Act 1998 are not included.) "News publisher" is defined in art.1

government proposed (but ultimately abandoned) secondary legislation designed to bring about a reform of the use of CFAs in defamation cases alone, and that the ECHR ruled in *MGN Ltd v UK*[240] that the CFA regime which continues to govern media law cases is at odds with art.10 of the Convention.[241]

The fact that a party has entered into a CFA, of itself, has no impact on the case for or against making an order for security, although a claimant with satisfactory ATE insurance may be able to resist an order on the basis that his insurance provides enough protection for the defendant.[242] In *King v Telegraph Group Ltd*[243] the defendant sought Pt 24 summary judgment, arguing that if the claimant should "squeak past" the summary judgment test he should be permitted to continue with his claims only on payment into court of a sum by way of security for the defendant's costs. This argument was reinforced by the fact that the claimant was funded by a CFA, a species of funding which, the defendant submitted, created a particularly chilling effect on media defendants given the fact that such defendants are likely to have to pay their own costs even if they are successful, and a substantial uplift on the claimant's costs if they are not, thus creating an enormous incentive to buy out of the litigation regardless of the merits.[244] The defendant argued that, given that the CFA regime presupposes that lawyers will only take on litigation where the prospects of success are 50 per cent or more, if the judge hearing a summary judgment application forms the view that the chances are in fact less than 50 per cent, he should be on guard against this "ransom" effect and bring some discipline to bear by ordering a modest payment into court. Eady J. rejected these arguments, refusing to be drawn into an assessment of the merits beyond what was necessary for establishing whether the Pt 24 test had been met, querying what the point would be of requiring the claimant to make a modest payment into court, where anything larger would be likely to bring the proceedings to an abrupt end, thereby denying the claimant access to

---

as meaning "a person who publishes a newspaper, magazine or website containing news or information about or comment on current affairs".

[240] [2011] E.M.L.R. 11, an application arising out of Naomi Campbell's claim against the publisher of the *Mirror* newspaper for misuse of private information, and specifically the CFA funding arrangements for the case, focussing on the manifest lack of proportionality between the damages recovered and the costs the defendant was ordered to pay; see also *Campbell v MGN Ltd (No.2)* [2005] UKHL 61; [2005] 1 W.L.R. 3394 for the decision of the House of Lords with which MGN Ltd took issue.

[241] For a comprehensive account of the events that led to the retention of the pre-existing CFA regime for "publication and privacy proceedings", and some proposals for the future, see the Final Report of the Civil Justice Council's Working Group on Defamation Costs, published on April 18, 2013. The Working Group was established in December 2012, following the publication of Leveson L.J.'s Report (Pt I), in order to consider potential reform of costs arrangements in defamation and privacy cases.

[242] *Al-Koronky v Time Life Entertainment Group Ltd* (above) at [35].

[243] [2003] EWHC 1312 (QB).

[244] Such arguments found favour with the European Court of Human Rights in *MGN Ltd v UK*, above.

justice and working against the policy underlying CFAs.[245] On the hearing of
the appeal, the Court of Appeal had no doubt that Eady J. had been right, for
the reasons that he gave:

> "While experience has shown that courts can readily detect on paper those cases
> which have no real prospect of success—and also those where it is possible that a
> claim may succeed but improbable that it will do so—to go any further than this in
> the pre-trial assessment of the merits of an action, at whatever early stage of the
> proceedings the application is made, would be to lure the court into dangerous
> territory and to open the way to very undesirable satellite litigation".[246]

Instead, the Court of Appeal suggested that the solution to cases where a
claimant is funding litigation by conditional fee agreement without after the
event insurance is to make a prospective costs capping order under CPR
r.3.2(m).[247] The court now has a specific power to make costs capping
orders.[248]

31.50 Maintenance: "pure funders". Attempts are sometimes made to obtain
security from claimants of whom there is reason to believe that their litigation
is being funded by third parties. In the past, defendants faced with such

---

[245] Ibid. at [15]–[17].

[246] [2004] EWCA Civ 613; [2005] 1 W.L.R. 2282 per Brooke L.J. at [91].

[247] "In my judgment the only way to square the circle is to say that when making any costs
capping order the court should prescribe a total amount of recoverable costs which will be
inclusive, so far as a CFA-funded party is concerned, of any additional liability. It cannot
be just to submit defendants in these cases, where their right to freedom of expression is at
stake, to a costs regime where the costs they will have to pay if they lose are neither
reasonable nor proportionate and they have no reasonable prospect of recovering their
reasonable and proportionate costs if they win" (per Brooke L.J. at [101]).

Brooke L.J.'s words were endorsed by Lord Hoffmann in *Campbell v MGN Ltd (No.2)*, above,
at [31] to [34]. In *Henry v BBC* [2005] EWHC 2503 (QB), a CFA case with a substantial success
fee, Gray J. reluctantly refused to make an order just days before the trial of the action, because
a cost capping order must operate prospectively, with the purpose of enabling the capped party
to plan ahead so that the case can be brought to trial within the limit allowed. To make an order
at a very late stage would simply operate to penalise the claimant's legal advisers. However, an
order was made by McCombe J. in *Tierney v News Group Newspapers Ltd* [2006] EWHC 50
(QB), a CFA case with no legal costs insurance. The judge rejected the claimant's argument that
a cost capping order should only be made where there is demonstrable extravagance by the party
in question, and that the discipline of post-trial detailed assessment of costs was a sufficient
constraint. He held that the case was one where the issues of fact and law were neither complex
nor novel, and ordered that the level of cap should be determined by the costs judge. Master
Campbell duly set the cap at a level well below the estimate of costs prepared by the claimant's
solicitor, on the basis that in his view there was no need for the claimant to instruct leading
counsel at trial. On appeal (*Tierney v News Group Newspapers Ltd (No.2)* [2006] EWHC 3275
(QB)), Eady J., sitting with Senior Costs Judge Hurst as assessor, held that Master Campbell's
order had not exceeded the ambit of his discretion. The court would be loath to endorse a decision
that prevented the claimant from instructing leading counsel while the defendant was free to do
so, because that would not be consistent with the principle of equality of arms, but the defendant
had conceded that it would instruct only junior counsel at trial. See also *Peacock v MGN Ltd*
[2009] EWHC 769 (QB), a costs capping decision under CPR rr.44.18 to 44.20, which came into
force on April 6, 2009 (which, in turn, preceded the reformulated CPR Pt 3 that came into effect
on April 1, 2013).

[248] See CPR Pt 3, section III, and CPR PD 3F, which came into force on April 1, 2013.

claimants have demanded an undertaking that the maintainer will pay their costs if the action fails.[249] A stout refusal often proved effective, no doubt because of the general uncertainty among practitioners about the existence and extent of the jurisdiction, but in one case, where the French company maintaining the plaintiff offered a limited undertaking, an action was stayed pending the provision of a fuller undertaking.[250] However, it is now clear that where litigation is maintained by what have been termed "pure funders" (defined by Simon Brown L.J. as those with no personal interest in the litigation, who do not stand to benefit from it, are not funding it as a matter of business, and in no way seek to control its course),[251] no order for costs will generally be made against the maintainer under s.51, Senior Courts Act 1981. That being so, a fortiori there can be no basis for an application for security against such a maintainer before trial, when no costs liability has crystallised.

Other maintainers. There is no obvious reason why "professional" main-   **31.51**
tainers, such as trade unions, medical defence societies and legal expenses insurers, should be in a different position from "pure funders". Costs orders are not normally made against such maintainers, but it is taken for granted that they will meet the costs ordered against their members, and if they did not, the court would probably make a costs order against them unless there was a good reason not to do so,[252] even though a trade union or medical defence maintainer is simply providing a service for its members and has no stake in the outcome of the litigation.[253] The distinction is difficult to understand.[254]

---

[249] These demands may have been prompted by the cases—in particular *Hill v Archbold* [1968] 1 Q.B. 686—in which Lord Denning M.R. suggested that a stranger who funded litigation should be required to undertake to pay the costs of the other side, and that if they refused, the proceedings should be struck out. In so far as the mischief which Lord Denning identified was that proceedings might be financed by a party who was immune from personal liability for an adverse order for costs, that mischief has now been remedied by s.51 of the Senior Courts Act 1981 (see per Millett L.J. in *Abraham v Thompson* [1997] 4 All E.R. 362 at 378).

[250] *Broxton v McClelland*, unreported, November 6, 1992, Drake J.

[251] *Hamilton v Al Fayed (No.2)* [2002] EWCA Civ 665; [2003] 2 W.L.R. 128 at [40]. Chadwick L.J. at [71] preferred this formulation:
   "I use the expression 'pure funder' to denote a person who provides funds to meet the litigation costs of a claimant in circumstances in which he, himself, has no collateral interest in the outcome of the claim—other than as a source of reimbursement of the funds which he has provided".
See further *Dymocks Franchise Systems (NSW) Pty Ltd v Todd* [2004] UKPC 39; [2004] 1 W.L.R. 2807.

[252] See *Hamilton v Al Fayed (No.2)* (above) per Hale L.J. at [75], and *Singh v Observer Ltd* [1989] 2 All E.R. 751 per Macpherson J. at 757.

[253] As for legal expenses insurers, see *Murphy v Young* [1997] 1 W.L.R. 1591 CA, where the plaintiff was supported by such insurance: held, no ground for an order for costs against the insurer under s.51, Supreme Courts Act 1981. Despite being founded on a commercial agreement, legal insurance is in principle in the public interest and may benefit both parties (see per Phillips L.J. at 1603–1604).

[254] "It is quite difficult to understand why there should be any difference between 'pure' funders such as those in this case and trade union funders. It is true that trade unions will not fund cases which they consider unmeritorious and exercise a degree of control over the

Commercial funders, by contrast, who do stand to gain financially from the outcome of the litigation, are liable to be ordered to pay the successful party's costs if the claim fails.[255] However, the last category apart,[256] the fact that a costs order is likely to be made against such a maintainer after trial under s.51, Senior Courts Act 1981, if the maintained litigant is not good for an order for costs against him, provides no justification for an order for security against the maintainer before the costs liability has crystallised, nor even for a fishing expedition for disclosure of the identity of the maintainer: such orders flow from a jurisdiction which should only be exercised where a clear case of abuse of process is established.[257] Where there is no question of conduct which amounts to abuse of process, generally the preferable course will be to let the action proceed to trial, and seek an order under s.51 of the Senior Courts Act 1981 against the third party maintainer (or, if his identity is not known, for disclosure of his name).[258] This was the approach adopted by Mr Fayed in the litigation brought against him by Neil Hamilton, although ultimately his application failed.[259]

31.52 **Security where there is assignment or champerty.** CPR r.25.14 makes express provision for security for costs to be ordered against persons other than the claimant in circumstances where the person has assigned his right to the claim to the claimant with a view to avoiding the possibility of a costs order being made against him, or has contributed to or agreed to contribute to

---

litigation they do fund. But it could well be said that 'pure' funders ought to be more discriminating in deciding what to fund. They should not be able to put their heads in the sand and support unmeritorious litigation at no risk of further cost to themselves just because they happen to sympathise with the unsuccessful litigant. Sympathy for a person or his cause may be understood: but we would not in other contexts regard it as any substitute for a hard-headed assessment of the legal and factual merits of his case"
(per Hale L.J. in *Hamilton v Al Fayed (No.2)*, above, at [76]).

[255] *Dymocks Franchise Systems (NSW) Pty Ltd v Todd*, above, and *Arkin v Borchard Lines Ltd* [2005] EWCA Civ 655; [2005] 1 W.L.R. 3055.

[256] As to which, see para.31.52, below.

[257] *Abraham v Thompson* [1997] 4 All E.R. 362 CA. The same applies where a stay is applied for: *Faryab v Naz Smith (2001)*, unreported, August 28, 1998, CA. The position is different where a costs order has been made in favour of one litigant and it is clear that the loser must have been funded by a third party: in that case, the court has a power, necessarily ancillary to s.51, to order disclosure of the name of the funder (*Raiffeisen Zentralbank Osterreich AG v Crosseas Shipping Ltd* [2003] EWHC 1381 (Comm), Morison J.). It will also be different if there is reason to believe that the maintainer is not bona fide: see per Kennedy L.J., *Condliffe v Hislop* [1996] 1 W.L.R. 753 at 762, and *Abraham v Thompson*, above.

[258] *Aiden Shipping v Interbulk* [1986] A.C. 965; *Condliffe v Hislop*, above; *Abraham v Thompson*, above. Once the occasion has arisen for the exercise of that power, the court will investigate the identity of the loser's third party maintainer and its liability to pay the winner's costs: *Singh v Observer* [1989] 2 All E.R. 751, as explained by Potter L.J. in *Abraham v Thompson*. See also Phillips L.J.'s analysis of the principles for the application of s.51 to maintainers in *Murphy v Young* [1997] 1 All E.R. 518 CA, where the fact that plaintiff was supported by legal expenses insurance did not justify an order for costs against the insurer under s.51, Senior Courts Act 1981. For the relevant procedure when seeking a costs order against a non-party, see CPR r.48.2.

[259] *Hamilton v Al Fayed (No.2)* (above).

the claimant's costs in return for a share of any money or property which the claimant might recover in the proceedings. That express formulation of a power to order security against assignors seeking to avoid cost liabilities, and those who have entered into champertous agreements, plainly excludes simple maintainers.

SECTION 4. CONSOLIDATION, JOINDER AND SEVERANCE

Consolidation: general. In defamation and malicious falsehood, the par- **31.53** ties may apply for consolidation either under statute or under the Civil Procedure Rules. However, the CPR machinery is far more flexible and convenient, and the statutory route, although still available, has in practice fallen into disuse.[260]

Consolidation under statute. Section 5 of the Law of Libel Amendment **31.54** Act 1888 provides that the court may, on application by two or more defendants in actions brought by one plaintiff in respect of the same (or substantially the same) libel, make an order for the consolidation of the actions, so that they shall be tried together.[261] It also entitles defendants, to new actions brought by the same plaintiff over (substantially) the same libel, to be joined into the consolidated action if, before trial of the consolidated action, they apply jointly with the existing defendants. Despite the preoccupation of the 1888 Act with newspapers, s.5 is not confined to newspaper libels, and it applies to actions for slander and malicious falsehood as well as to actions for libel.[262]

Apportionment of damages. There are complex provisions for the appor- **31.55** tionment of damages in actions consolidated under s.5 of the 1888 Act. The section requires the jury to assess the whole amount of damages awarded (if any) in one sum, but a separate verdict must be taken for or against each

---

[260] For the position in the state of Victoria, where the guiding principle is whether ordering consolidation is likely to expose a plaintiff to a substantial risk of real prejudice, see *Buckley v Herald and Weekly Times Pty Ltd* [2009] VSCA 118.

[261] Before the 1888 Act, it appears that no order for consolidation could be obtained by any defendant to separate actions brought by the same plaintiff in respect of the same libel. For the oppressive consequences, see the judgments in *Stone v Press Association* [1897] 2 Q.B. 159 CA, where the plaintiff brought separate actions against the Press Association and 16 different newspapers which repeated the PA story:

"It was precisely for the purpose of meeting such a state of things and relieving newspaper proprietors from oppressive litigation of this kind that section 5 of the Act was passed":
per A. L. Smith L.J. at 162. The whole object of the section is to prevent:

"the multiplication of pleadings, and the consequent multiplication of costs, and the burthen hereby thrown upon defendants who may have inadvertently copied a libel, the real libellers being those who first published it":
per Lord Esher M.R. at 162.

[262] Defamation Act 1952, s.13.

defendant in the same way as if the actions had been tried separately; and if the jury finds a verdict against the defendant or defendants in more than one of the consolidated actions, it must then apportion the damages between those defendants, and if the trial judge awards the plaintiff the costs of the action, the costs will be apportioned between them.[263]

31.56 Consolidation by rule. The old and relatively detailed provisions of RSC, Ord.4, r.9(1) were swept away by CPR r.3.1(2)(g), which in the most laconic terms asserts that the court may—except where the Rules provide otherwise —consolidate proceedings. Under the old rule, consolidation of two or more actions could be ordered if it appeared to the court that some common question of law or fact arose in them,[264] or that the rights to the relief claimed were in respect of or arose out of the same transaction or series of transactions, or that for some other reason it was desirable to make an order. Given that in making an order under this rule the court will be seeking to give effect to the overriding objective, these considerations are likely to remain highly relevant to the exercise of the court's discretion, even though they no longer appear in the rule. In contrast to the regime under the 1888 Act,[265] either the claimant or the defendant may apply.

31.57 Consolidation, etc. of claimants and defendants. Consolidation may be ordered where the claimants and the defendants are the same, or where they are all different.[266] While it is not possible to consolidate two actions where the claimant in one is the defendant in the other, that difficulty can be avoided if one action could be ordered to stand as a Pt 20 claim in the other.[267]

31.58 Consolidation, etc. of actions. Under the old rule the court could order two actions to be tried at the same time, or one immediately after the other, or could stay one until the determination of others. Those powers are now part

---

[263] These provisions appear to apply also to a judge sitting alone: *Mitchell v Hirst* [1936] 3 All E.R. 872.

[264] Thus, if the defendant defamed the plaintiff on different occasions (*Bridgmont v Associated Newspapers Ltd* [1951] 2 K.B. 578 CA, a decision that causes of action in slander should not be severed from a claim in libel), or defamed two or more persons in the same libel (*Horwood v Statesman Publishing* (1929) 141 L.T. 54 CA; *Lewis v Daily Telegraph (No.2)* [1964] 2 Q.B. 601 CA), or if different defendants (e.g. the editor, publishers and printers of a newspaper) had been separately sued for defaming two or more persons in the same libel (see, e.g. *Horwood v Statesman Publishing*, above, where the printers, who sought consolidation, had apologised and paid money into court, while the publisher and editor pleaded fair comment), the court might order the separate actions to be consolidated. Conversely, where the only common issue was whether the words were defamatory, consolidation was unlikely to be justifiable (*Daws v Daily Sketch* [1960] 1 W.L.R. 126 CA).

[265] S.5 allows only defendants to apply.

[266] *Horwood v Statesman Publishing*, above, per Sankey L.J. at 59.

[267] *Reynolds v Mole, The Times*, May 16, 1908. The plaintiff brought an action for libel against the defendant, and the defendant brought a separate counter-action for libel against the plaintiff: the court ordered that the two actions should be consolidated, and that the defendant should counterclaim in his defence to the first action.

of the case management armoury of CPR r.3.1(2). Rule 3.1(2)(h) enables the court to order two or more claims to be tried on the same occasion,[268] a form of wording which (it is submitted) is flexible enough to permit trial of one immediately after the other, and r.3.1(2)(f) permits an order for a stay of the whole or part of the proceedings either generally or until a specified date or event, for instance the determination of a related claim.

Objections to consolidation. An order for consolidation would not be   **31.59**
made under the old rule where it would embarrass the parties or the court, and it is submitted that this consideration will continue to weigh heavily with the court in the exercise of its discretion. Embarrassment may arise, e.g. out of the different defences pleaded by different defendants and the difficulties which the jury may find in disentangling the issues,[269] or from the nature of the libels and the relationship of the claimants.[270] Moreover, it is generally impossible to order consolidation if different solicitors are instructed for different claimants.[271]

Time for application. An application for consolidation may be made at   **31.60**
any time, but it should be made as soon as possible, and unjustified delay may

---

[268] For a recent example, see *Cooper v Turrell* [2011] EWHC 3269 (QB) in which three actions between the same parties involving claims for defamation, breach of confidence and misuse of private information were tried together.

[269] *Sun Life v British International Press, The Times*, December 1, 1932, in which the plaintiff sued the proprietors, printers and editor of a newspaper for libel, and brought another action against newsagents who had sold the paper and displayed a poster calling attention to the article. The newspaper defendants intended to plead justification, privilege and fair comment, while the newsagents intended to plead innocent dissemination. The Court of Appeal set aside an order for consolidation on the grounds that the issues between the newspaper defendants and the plaintiffs in the first action were different in kind and nature from those which the newsagent defendants sought to set up in the second action, that it would be difficult for the jury to disentangle these issues if the actions were tried at the same time, and that the newsagents would be embarrassed by the joinder. Cf. *Eddison v Dalziel* (1893) 9 T.L.R. 334 CA, where three actions were consolidated under s.5 of the 1888 Act: in two, the defendants pleaded justification, and in the third, they pleaded an apology and paid into court. The report gives no reason for the decision.
Conversely, where actions are consolidated before defence, it appears that different defendants are entitled to put in different defences, and that their entitlement to do so should not be interfered with by the consolidation: see per Rigby L.J. in *Stone v Press Association* [1897] 2 Q.B. 159 CA at 164. That said, if their defences gave rise to questions of embarrassment or other difficulty, it would no doubt be a reason for severance. This was the basis on which Sharp J. declined to direct that libel actions brought by the claimant against two different newspaper groups over articles making similar allegations should be tried together: *Ronaldo v MGN Ltd* [2009] EWHC 2862 (QB) at [25]–[26].

[270] *Marchant v Ford* [1936] 3 All E.R. 104 CA. The plaintiffs in the two actions were father and daughter: both sued on allegations contained in a single book. In the daughter's case, the libel was that she was grossly immoral; in the father's, that he was a coarse brute who had driven his daughter into an immoral life. The passages complained of were different in each case. It appears that in this case the embarrassment anticipated by the Court of Appeal was of a literal kind.

[271] *Lewis v Daily Telegraph (No.2)* [1964] 2 Q.B. 601.

be a factor in refusal of an application.[272] It appears that an application notice should be issued in each action,[273] and served on all parties.[274] Alternatively, it may still be acceptable for one application notice to be issued bearing the full title of each action. The court may make an order for consolidation before service of defences,[275] or even before service of the claim form.[276]

31.61 Joinder and severance. Under the old rules, it was necessary to read RSC Ord.4, r.9(1) (consolidation) closely with the similar wording of the provisions for joinder of causes of action and parties (Ord.15, rr.1 and 4) and severance (Ord.15, r.5). The current provision for joinder of causes of action is CPR r.7.3, which allows a claimant to use a single claim form to start all claims which can conveniently be disposed of in the same proceedings. The test is simply convenience. If joinder turns out to be inconvenient, the court has the power to direct that any part of the proceedings be dealt with as separate proceedings or to order separate trials.[277] It is now common practice for the claimant to sue the defendant in the same action in libel and/or slander and/or malicious falsehood and/or misuse of private information and/or breach of confidence and/or harassment. Representative actions under CPR r.19.6 are unlikely to be allowed in defamation.[278]

31.62 Addition and substitution of parties. As for addition and substitution of parties, in place of the old Ord.15, r.4(1), which permitted joinder of two or more persons as plaintiffs or defendants where (if separate actions were brought by or against each of them) some common question of law or fact would arise in all the actions, and where all rights to relief claimed in the action were in respect of or arose out of the same transaction or series of transactions,[279] the new r.19.1 states simply that any number of claimants or

---

[272] See, e.g. *Campbell v Associated Newspapers Ltd*, unreported, May 25, 1995, CA, where the defendant's application for leave to appeal from the judge's refusal to order consolidation was heard by the Court of Appeal about two weeks before one of the two actions was due to come on for hearing (the second action not having been set down).

[273] *Daws v Daily Sketch* [1960] 1 W.L.R. 126.

[274] Pre-CPR, service on all parties was the normal, but not invariable, practice: see *Arab Monetary Fund v Hashim (No.4)* [1992] 1 W.L.R. 553 at 559, per Hoffmann J.

[275] *Stone v Press Association*, above. In practice, it was unusual under the old rule to make an order before the pleadings had closed and the issues were defined, and the same constraints are likely to hold good under the CPR.

[276] *Arab Monetary Fund v Hashim (No.4)* [1992] 1 W.L.R. 553 CA (Hoffmann J.) and 1176.

[277] CPR r.3.1(2)(e),(i): cf. the former RSC Ord.15, r.5.

[278] *The Law Society v Kordowski* [2011] EWHC 3185 (QB) at [166]–[169].

[279] In an old Victorian case, *Smith v Foley* (1912) V.L.R. 314, decided on a rule identical with the predecessor of Ord.15, r.4(1), it was held that in defamation cases "the same transaction" meant the same publication. Hence if the defendant defamed the first plaintiff and the second plaintiff in the same libel or slander, the first plaintiff and the second plaintiff could join in one action, since common questions of law or fact would arise if they sued the defendant separately, and their respective rights to relief arose out of the same publication. (See, e.g. *Booth v Briscoe* (1877) 2 Q.B.D. 496 CA; *Horwood v Statesman Publishing* (1929) 141 L.T. 54 CA: cf. *Daws v Daily Sketch* [1960] 1 W.L.R. 126, where the only common question of law or fact was whether the words were defamatory). But if the defendant defamed the first plaintiff in one libel, and the

defendants may be joined as parties to a claim. That, however, is implicitly subject to the r.7.3 convenience test, and in addition r.19.2(3) enables the court to order any person to cease to be a party if his being a party is not "desirable".[280] In practice, the defamation claimant will usually join as co-defendants, in one action, all those jointly responsible for publication of the libel or slander, and if he decides to sue them separately, they can apply for consolidation.

Expiry of limitation period. It is necessary to read the provisions of the **31.63** Civil Procedure Rules (CPR r.17.4: amendments to statements of case after expiry of limitation period) and r.19.5: special provisions for addition and substitution of parties after expiry of limitation period) in the light of the jurisprudence which grew up around R.S.C. O.20 r.5.[281] Once the relevant limitation period has expired, a party may be added or substituted only if the limitation period was current when the proceedings were started, and if the addition or substitution is necessary, which means necessary for that action.[282] The addition or substitution is necessary only if the court is satisfied that the new party is to be substituted for a party who was named in the claim form in mistake for the new party, or the claim cannot properly be carried on by or against the original party unless the new party is added or substituted as claimant or defendant, or the original party has died or had a bankruptcy order made against him and his interest or liability has passed to the new party.[283] In cases of mistake, it must be proved that the person responsible for the issue of the claim form had made a mistake as to the name rather than the identity of the party, but for which the new party would have been named in the claim form.[284]

---

[280] Joinder was set aside under r.19.2(3) in *Sarayiah v Suren* [2004] EWHC 1981 (QB), a slander action in which three defendants had been joined ex parte notwithstanding that they had good limitation defences and notwithstanding that joinder was (as Tugendhat J. found) unnecessary.

second plaintiff in another libel, the first plaintiff and the second plaintiff could not without leave sue the defendant in the same action, even though the libels were identical, unless they could be described as part of the "same series" of transactions (see, e.g. *Sandes v Wildsmith* [1893] 1 Q.B. 771).

[281] *Adelson v Associated Newspapers Ltd* [2007] EWCA Civ 701; [2008] 1 W.L.R. 585 at [26].

[282] *Edwards v Golding* [2007] EWCA Civ 416, where joinder of a defendant was misconceived given that following a discontinuance there was no more than a shell of an action in existence, and given that it could not be said to be "necessary" within CPR r.19.5 (the limitation period having expired), "necessary" meaning necessary for that existing action, that the party should be joined.

[283] CPR r.19.5(3).

[284] *Adelson v Associated Newspapers Ltd* [2007] EWCA Civ 701; [2008] 1 W.L.R. 585. *Adelson* was a case of mistake as to the structure of a group of companies, with the consequence that (as the claimants argued) the second claimant, a non-trading company with two operating subsidiaries, was joined instead of the subsidiaries. However, the mistake which must be established to bring a claimant within CPR r.19.5(3)(a) is one as to the party's name rather than as to its identity, and it was not established on the evidence that those responsible for issuing the claim were under any misapprehension as to the true corporate structure of the second claimant's group of companies, but for which they would have added the subsidiaries.

Section 5. Mode of Trial

31.64 General. As matters stand, either party to an action for libel or slander has a right to trial by jury, unless the court is of opinion that the trial requires any prolonged examination of documents or accounts, or any scientific or local examination, which cannot conveniently be made with a jury.[285] A party wishing to exercise this right must apply for trial by jury within 28 days of service of the defence.[286] If he does not, the right is lost, and the court will only order jury trial if it is persuaded to do so in the exercise of its discretion.[287] It is highly unlikely to do so.[288] The right to jury trial applies equally

---

[285] Senior Courts Act 1981, s.69(1). S.69 provides as follows:

"(1) Where, on the application of any party to an action to be tried in the Queen's Bench Division, the court is satisfied that there is in issue— . . . (b) a claim in respect of libel (or) slander, . . . the action shall be tried with a jury, unless the court is of opinion that the trial requires any prolonged examination of documents or accounts or any scientific or local investigation which cannot conveniently be made with a jury.

(2) An application under subsection (1) must be made not later than such time before the trial as may be prescribed.

(3) An action to be tried in the Queen's Bench Division which does not by virtue of subsection (1) fall to be tried with a jury shall be tried without a jury unless the court in its discretion orders it to be tried with a jury.

(4) Nothing in subsections (1) to (3) shall affect the power of the court to order, in accordance with rules of court, that different questions of fact arising in any action be tried by different modes of trial; and where any such order is made, subsection (1) shall have effect only as respects questions relating to any such charge, claim, question or issue as is mentioned in that subsection."

[286] CPR r.26.11, and Senior Courts Act 1981, s.69(2). In recent years, courts have been taking a much more rigorous approach to CPR r.26.11 than they did previously. In *Cook v Telegraph Media Group Ltd* [2011] EWHC 763 (QB), Tugendhat J. concluded that a party who wished to exercise his right to jury trial under s.69(1) needed to apply to the court in accordance with r.26.11, or the right was irretrievably lost. In *Thornton v Telegraph Media Group Ltd* [2011] EWCA Civ 748; [2011] E.M.L.R. 29, the Court of Appeal (Leveson and Carnwath L.JJ.) proceeded on the footing that *Cook* was correctly decided, observing that the judgment marked a "sea-change" in the court's approach to s.69(1).

[287] Under s.69(3), Senior Courts Act 1981. Whether the court is being asked, as a matter of its discretion, to extend time under CPR r.3.1(2)(a) for an application to be made under CPR r.26.11 or to make an order under s.69(3), Senior Courts Act 1981, the exercise is the same and the same factors will be taken into account: *Thornton v Telegraph Media Group Ltd* [2011] EWCA Civ 748; [2011] E.M.L.R. 29, as applied by Eady J. in *McKeown v Attheraces Ltd* [2011] EWHC 3232 (QB) at [13], by Tugendhat J. in *Rothschild v Telegraph Media Group Ltd* [2011] EWHC 3462 (QB) at [63], and by Nicola Davies J. in *McGrath v Independent Print Ltd* [2013] EWHC 2202 (QB) at [24]. In parenthesis, the loss of a right to jury trial by failing to make an application under r.26.11 within the prescribed time was not a "sanction" against which a party might seek "relief" by reference to CPR r.3.9(1): see *Cook v Telegraph Media Group Ltd* [2011] EWHC 763 (QB) at [87].

[288] " . . . an action which does not come within section 69(1) has to be tried without a jury, unless the court in its discretion orders it to be tried with a jury. The discretion is now very rarely exercised, reflecting contemporary practice. Contemporary practice has an eye, among other things, to proportionality; the greater predictability of the decision of a professional judge; and the fact that a judge gives reasons . . . The overriding objective in rule 1.1 and rule 3.1(2)(m) are there for general case management purposes."

per May L.J. in *Armstrong v Times Newspapers Ltd* [2006] EWCA Civ 519; [2006] 1 W.L.R. 2462 at [15], [19]. In a similar vein, see Lord Phillips of Worth Matravers in *Joseph v Spiller* [2010] UKSC 53; [2011] 1 A.C. 852 at [116]:

"Finally, and fundamentally, has not the time come to recognise that defamation is no longer

to assessment of damages, where (for instance) liability has been conceded or an interlocutory default judgment obtained.[289] However, the effect of the newly enacted s.11 Defamation Act 2013 is to remove from s.69(1), Senior Courts Act 1981 the references to libel and slander. When this provision comes into force, the right to jury trial in defamation will be abolished, with the result that actions for libel and slander, in common with most other civil claims proceeding in the Queen's Bench Division,[290] will fall to be tried by judge alone, unless exceptionally the court orders otherwise.[291]

Prolonged examination of documents. When considering whether the **31.65** trial will require any prolonged examination of documents or accounts which cannot conveniently be made with a jury, the court must first consider whether the trial will involve prolonged examination of documents or accounts, secondly whether the examination can conveniently be done with a jury, and thirdly whether in the exercise of the court's discretion there should nonetheless be trial by jury, even though the proviso to s.69(1) is satisfied.[292] Such documents include written directions on points of law prepared by the judge.[293] The question of whether the trial will involve prolonged examination of documents will depend on such factors as the extent to which counsel will be able to simplify the issues for the jury, and whether or not the real issues involve broad-brush questions or close analysis of detail.[294] "Examination" is not limited to the documents which contain the actual evidence in the case and

---

a field in which trial by jury is desirable? The issues are often complex and jury trial simply invites expensive interlocutory battles, such as the one before this court, which attempts to pre-empt issues from going before the jury."
This clear preference for judge-alone trials is reflected in a number of recent decisions: see e.g. *Cook v Telegraph Media Group Ltd* [2011] EWHC 763 (QB), *Rothschild v Telegraph Media Group Ltd* [2011] EWHC 3462 (QB), *Lewis v Comr of Police for the Metropolis* [2012] EWHC 2391 (QB) and *Bento v Chief Constable of Bedfordshire Police* [2012] EWCA Civ 956.

[289] *Beta Construction v Channel Four* [1990] 1 W.L.R. 1042 CA. However, if damages are to be assessed under the Defamation Act 1996, s.8 summary disposal procedure, they will be assessed by judge alone: s.8(5); so also if compensation has to be determined under the offer of amends procedure: s.3(10).

[290] Actions for malicious prosecution and false imprisonment being the only remaining exceptions.

[291] Under s.69(3), Senior Courts Act 1981; as to which, see para.31.67, below.

[292] See *Goldsmith v Pressdram Ltd* [1988] 1 W.L.R. 64 CA; *Beta Construction v Channel Four* [1990] 1 W.L.R. 1042 CA at 1047, 1055. For the residual discretion granted by s.69(3), see para.31.67, below.

[293] *Field v Local Sunday Newspapers Ltd*, unreported, December 10, 2001, Gray J.

[294] *Rothermere v Times Newspapers Ltd* [1973] 1 W.L.R. 448 at 451 and 457; *De L'Isle v Times Newspapers Ltd* [1988] 1 W.L.R. 49 at 60 (where May L.J. contrasted the broad-brush approach which would be appropriate in that case with the position in *Goldsmith v Pressdram*). In *Maccaba v Liechtenstein* [2004] EWHC 1580 (QB), where although the documents included Hebrew phrases and required some expert evidence on Jewish law, it was not apparent that the jury would have to examine a large number of the documents, and any problems of comprehension were surmountable. This was a classic case for trial by jury, since the main issue at trial would be which account of events was true. By contrast, in *W v Westminster City Council* [2004] EWHC 2866 (QB); (2005) 1 F.L.R. 816, the substantial volume of documents in the trial bundle was likely to require careful study, and trial by judge alone was ordered; similarly, in *Turkot v Oxus Gold Plc* [2006] EWHC 3361 (QB), the documents were lengthy and complex and mainly legal in nature.

includes documents which are likely to be introduced in cross-examination.[295] The question of convenience concerns the efficient administration of justice rather than the probable difficulty of any issue involved, and the word "conveniently" means without substantial difficulty in comparison with carrying out the same process with a judge alone.[296] The inconvenience to be considered is exclusively that arising from "the prolonged examination of documents".[297] It is not enough that the trial will be long and complicated.[298] In *Beta Construction v Channel Four*[299] Stuart-Smith L.J. identified four main areas in which the efficient administration of justice might be made less than convenient if trial takes place with jury: (1) the physical problem of handling large numbers of documents in the jury box, (2) substantial prolongation of the trial because of the number and complexity of the documents, (3) significantly increased expense, both by the added length of trial and extra copying, and (4) the risk that the jury may not understand the documents, especially accounts and commercial documents.[300] Nonetheless, the number

---

"Prolonged examination" can be equated to "careful reading": *Culla Park Ltd v Richards* [2007] EWHC 1687 (QB) at [26]; *Gentoo Group Ltd v Hanratty* [2008] EWHC 2328 (QB).

[295] *Goldsmith v Pressdram Ltd*, above. Where counsel diverge widely in their assessment of the likely course of cross-examination, the court will take note of the fact that counsel who will be conducting a cross-examination is in a stronger position to predict its course than his opponent: *Gregson v Channel Four* [2002] EWCA Civ 941 per Waller L.J. at [14]. See also *Fiddes v Channel Four Television Corp* [2010] EWCA Civ 730; [2010] 1 W.L.R. 2245 in which the Court of Appeal reviewed and refined the applicable principles (upholding Tugendhat J.'s decision to dispense with the jury).

[296] *Goldsmith v Pressdram Ltd*, above, at 74; *De L'Isle v Times Newspapers Ltd* [1988] 1 W.L.R. 49 CA at 59; *Beta Construction v Channel Four*, above; *Taylor v Anderton* [1995] 1 W.L.R. 447 CA. Convenience must be assessed not by reference to the likelihood of repeated judicial rulings on the admissibility and relevance of documents, with the jury having to come in and out of court as each ruling is considered and given, but by reference to the examination of such documents as are judged to be admissible and relevant and therefore have to be considered by the jury: *Culla Park Ltd v Richards* [2007] EWHC 1687 (QB) at [17]. But note the caveat in *Fiddes v Channel Four Television Corp*, above, at [18]:

> "We would like to emphasise the need for caution when invoking the additional length, and (even more) the additional cost, of a jury trial as factors to be taken into account on the second, convenience, section 69 question. Jury trial will almost always take longer, and cost more, than trial by judge alone. The extra time taken, and the extra costs involved, in a jury trial may often be a useful sort of quantitative cross-check of what might otherwise be a purely qualitative assessment of the extra inconvenience of a jury trial (as was done in *Beta Construction* [1991] 1 W.L.R. 1042). However, it would be dangerous if those two factors were given much independent weight, as it would risk undermining the important right to a jury trial which section 69(2) gives—to defendants as well as to claimants—in libel actions".

[297] "[I]t is important to appreciate that the inconvenience to be considered in the second [convenience] section 69 question is that arising from 'the prolonged examination of documents': the court should not, at that stage, look at any other inconvenience which may arise as a result of a jury trial, although it could well be relevant when considering the third [residual discretion to order jury trial] question": *Fiddes v Channel Four Television Corp*, above, at [21] per Lord Neuberger M.R.

[298] *Rothermere v Times Newspapers Ltd*, above.

[299] [1990] 1 W.L.R. 1042 at 1048–1049. See also at 1055–1056, per Neill L.J.

[300] The provisions of the uniform Australian legislation for jury trial include a similar exception for prolonged examination of documents (and for scientific and technical issues). For example, s.21 of the Defamation Act 2005 (NSW) is in these terms:

of documents is not, of itself, the issue.[301] The fact that juries in criminal trials sometimes have to consider complex documentation is irrelevant to the questions posed under s.69.[302]

Scientific or local investigation. The same principles apply, mutatis   **31.66**
mutandis, to cases involving scientific (and local) investigation: would the investigation be such that it could conveniently be made with a jury, having regard to the criteria identified in *Beta Construction v Channel Four?*[303]

Residual discretion. Under s.69(3) an action to be tried in the Queen's   **31.67**
Bench Division, which does not by virtue of s.69(1) fall to be tried with a jury, shall be tried by a judge alone unless the court in its discretion orders it to be tried with a jury. Whereas the wording of s.69's predecessor, s.6(1) of the Administration of Justice (Miscellaneous Provisions) Act 1933, held an even balance between judge and jury, the emphasis, and presumption, in s.69(3) is

---

"(1) Unless the court orders otherwise, a plaintiff or defendant in defamation proceedings may elect for the proceedings to be tried by jury.
(2) An election must be:
(a) made at the time and in the manner prescribed by the rules of court for the court in which the proceedings are to be tried, and
(b) accompanied by the fee (if any) prescribed by the regulations made under the Civil Procedure Act 2005 for the requisition of a jury in that court.
(3) Without limiting subsection (1), a court may order that defamation proceedings are not to be tried by jury if:
(a) the trial requires a prolonged examination of records, or
(b) the trial involves any technical, scientific or other issue that cannot be conveniently considered and resolved by a jury."
In New South Wales, "conveniently" means not merely physical inconvenience, but requires the applicant to establish that there are circumstances of "unusual difficulty" from the point of view of the jury's understanding of the issues, and (to a lesser extent) from the point of view of the judge in summing up: *Peck v Email Ltd* (1987) 8 N.S.W.L.R. 430; *Mallik v McGeown* [2008] N.S.W.S.C. 129.
    [301] "The number of documents is not the issue when it comes to the first [prolonged examination of documents] and second [convenience] section 69 questions. As Slade L.J. said [in *Goldsmith v Pressdram Ltd* [1988] 1 W.L.R. 65, 74–75] in a passage cited by the Judge, '[t]here may be many cases where numerous documents will be required to be looked at, but no substantial practical difficulties are likely to arise in their examination being made with a jury', and, by contrast, there can be cases where 'relatively few documents will require examination, but nevertheless long and minute examination of them is likely to be required'":
Fiddes v Channel Four Television Corp, above, at [21].
    [302] "The fact that juries in criminal trials (especially those trials involving allegations of complex financial fraud and the like) sometimes have to consider complex documentation does not really bear on the three section 69 questions. It may well be that, in some such criminal trials, the section 69 questions would result in the conclusion that the trial should be by judge alone, but the questions do not arise in the criminal field even in relation to such cases: there is an absolute right to a jury trial, save in circumstances which are very different from those covered by section 69":
Fiddes v Channel Four Television Corp, above, at [22].
    [303] *Hope Technical Developments v BBC*, unreported, March 28, 1996, CA, per Hirst L.J.

against trial with jury.[304] Furthermore, in the current climate, the discretion is highly unlikely to be exercised in favour of jury trial.[305] In exercising it, a consideration in favour of a jury arises where the case involves prominent figures in public life[306] and issues of national interest,[307] or where the defendant is a public authority[308]; another is the fact that the case involves issues

---

[304] *Goldsmith v Pressdram Ltd* [1988] 1 W.L.R. 49 CA at 68, 72 and 76; *Aitken v Preston* [1997] E.M.L.R. 415 CA; *Fiddes v Channel Four Television Corp*, above, at [15(iii)(1)]; *McKeown v Attheraces Ltd* [2011] EWHC 3232 (QB) at [13]; *Bento v Chief Constable of Bedfordshire Police* [2012] EWCA Civ 956 at [11].

[305] See the authorities referred to in fn.288, above, in particular *Bento v Chief Constable of Bedfordshire Police*, above, in which the Court of Appeal, in dismissing the defendant Chief Constable's appeal against Tugendhat J.'s refusal to accede to his application for jury trial, roundly rejected the argument that the judge had erred by failing to give due weight to the status of Bedfordshire Police as a public authority:

" . . . [T]he appellant Chief Constable has not shown that the judge reached a conclusion which no reasonable judge could reach. He was entitled to give weight to the factors to which he referred, and in particular the advantages of a reasoned judgment. He was entitled to give more weight to those factors than to the factors relied upon by the appellant, particularly to the advantages to the Chief Constable, as a public authority, of having the issue . . . whether the respondent killed his girlfriend tried by a jury"(per Hooper L.J. at [26], with whom Maurice Kay L.J. and Henderson J. agreed). See also the multiplicity of reasons given by Hooper L.J. at [23]–[24] for why it was reasonable for the judge to exercise his discretion against jury trial notwithstanding that the defendant was a public authority. In particular, the judge had been entitled to regard the seriousness of the defendant's accusations against the claimant by way of justification as a factor which told *against* jury trial. Having regard to the Court of Appeal's reasoning, and its paean to the virtues of reasoned judgments, it is difficult to conceive of a situation in which it would be obviously *right* for a judge to direct a jury trial as an exercise of discretion.

[306] The rationale being that a judge may have an involuntary bias towards those of "his own rank and dignity": see *Cook v Telegraph Media Group Ltd* [2011] EWHC 763 (QB) at [101], [108]. *Rothermere v Times Newspapers Ltd*, above (decided on the 1933 Act); *Aitken v Preston*, above; *Gentoo Group Ltd v Hanratty* [2008] EWHC 2328 (QB) at [7]. "An important consideration in favour of a jury arises where, as here, the case involves prominent figures in public life and questions of great national interest . . . [T]he fact that one party is a public figure may often be a reason for favouring a jury trial . . . ": *Fiddes v Channel Four Television Corp*, above, at [15(iii)(2)], [20].

[307] However, note that in *Lewis v Comr of Police for the Metropolis* [2012] EWHC 1391 (QB) at [29(iii)], Tugendhat J., in deciding not to order a jury trial, concluded that: "the significant national interest in this case makes it all the more important that there should be a reasoned judgment".

[308] The rationale here being that a judge may have an involuntary bias towards the government or the Crown, that is to say, the entity which appointed him: see *Cook v Telegraph Group Ltd* [2011] EWHC 763 (QB), (obiter) per Tugendhat J. at [91]–[108] (citing at [98] Blackstone's *Commentaries on the Laws of England* Book IV(1769), pp.342–343: "The trial by jury . . . is also that trial by the peers of every Englishman, which, as the grand bulwark of his liberties, is secured to him by [Magna Carta] . . . in times of difficulty and danger, more is to be apprehended from the violence and partiality of judges appointed by the crown, in suits between the king and the subject than, than in disputes between one individual and another . . . "). But see also *Lewis v Comr of Police for the Metropolis*, above, in which Tugendhat J. considered *Racz v Home Office* [1994] 2 A.C. 45 (in which the HL upheld the CA's decision not to order jury trial in an action for assault, battery and misfeasance in public office where exemplary damages were claimed), and declined to order jury trial. See also the Court of Appeal's treatment of this issue in *Bento v Chief Constable of Bedfordshire*, above, where it was the defendant public authority which wanted jury trial (on the ground that the reputation of a public authority was of great public interest and that it was entitled "in defence of a serious criminal charge laid publicly by it at the claimant's door,

of credibility and that a party's honour and integrity are under attack.[309] However, even when these factors are present, they may well be outweighed by other countervailing considerations.[310] The overriding objective under the CPR is relevant to the exercise of that discretion: since it is concerned inter alia with dealing with cases at proportionate cost and saving expense, it will almost certainly tell against jury trial.[311] The desirability of a reasoned judgment is liable to be a weighty factor in favour of judge alone.[312] The difficulties of demarcation between the roles of judge and jury in a case of *Reynolds* privilege are a reason for exercising the discretion in favour of trial by judge alone.[313]

Separate trial of liability and quantum. It is possible, in appropriate   **31.68** circumstances, to split the issues of liability and quantum, with one being tried with a jury and the other by judge alone.[314] So in *Collins Stewart v Financial Times Ltd*,[315] a case with complex general and special damage claims, Tugendhat J. ordered a split trial, with liability to be tried by judge and jury and damages (general and special) by judge alone. It was common ground that a judge alone should try the special damage claim, which would undoubtedly involve prolonged examination of documents. As for general damages, the judge held that the necessary directions to the jury on the law would be difficult to understand and would require prolonged consideration. Moreover, he found that, since juries do not give reasons, it would be impossible for the judge trying the special damage claim to know what view the jury had taken on the issues of fact in assessing general damages, and therefore there would be a risk of double or under compensation and of inconsistent verdicts.

---

to seek to prove its truth to the satisfaction of a jury" (see at [22])): Tugendhat J. found such arguments unpersuasive, and the Court of Appeal found no fault with his approach.

[309] *Goldsmith v Pressdram*, above; *Aitken v Preston*, above; *Gentoo Group Ltd v Hanratty*, above. *Fiddes v Channel Four Television Corp*, above, at [15(iii)(3)].

[310] See e.g. *Lewis v Comr of Police for the Metropolis, above,* and *Bento v Chief Constable of Bedfordshire*, above.

[311] See May L.J. in *Armstrong v Times Newspapers Ltd* [2006] EWCA Civ 519; [2006] 1 W.L.R. 2462 at [15], [19] (quoted in fn.288, above); *W v Westminster City Council* [2004] EWHC 2866 (QB); (2005) 1 F.L.R. 816; *Cook v Telegraph Media Group Ltd*, above, at [113] ("A trial by judge alone is in general, and is in this case, much more likely to satisfy the overriding objective, in every element of it listed in the CPR.")

[312] *Aitken v Preston*, above, at 422; *Foster v Associated Newspapers Ltd* [2002] EWHC 1885 (QB) at [23], Gray J. See also *Fiddes v Channel Four Television Corp*, above, at [15(iii)(4)], *Lewis v Comr of Police for the Metropolis, above,* and *Bento v Chief Constable of Bedfordshire*, above.

[313] *Gregson v Channel Four Television Corp* [2002] EWCA Civ 941. See *Jameel (Mohammed) v Wall Street Journal* [2005] EWCA Civ 74; [2005] Q.B. 904 at [70], where the Court of Appeal observed that the division between the role of the judge and that of the jury where *Reynolds* privilege is in issue is not an easy one, and questioned whether jury trial was desirable at all in such cases. The decision of the Court of Appeal was later overturned ([2006] UKHL 44; [2007] 1 A.C. 359), but nothing in the speeches in the House of Lords detracts from the force of that observation.

[314] Senior Courts Act 1981, s.69(4); CPR r.3.1(1)(i), (m); *Phillips v Metropolitan Police Comr* [2003] EWCA Civ 382 at [17].

[315] [2004] EWHC 2337; [2005] E.M.L.R. 5.

31.69 Separate modes of trial for different issues. In *Armstrong v Times Newspapers*,[316] where the parties had agreed that the action should be tried by judge alone, the defendant nonetheless argued that the preliminary issue of meaning should be tried by a jury. At first instance Eady J. refused to make that order, influenced in particular by the problems which would arise for the jury, drafting in committee, in applying the single meaning doctrine and the repetition rule and delivering a special verdict. The defendant's appeal was dismissed, but the Court of Appeal confirmed that the effect of s.69(4) of the Senior Courts Act 1981 was to give the court an open discretion to order that different questions of fact—such as meaning—should be tried by a different mode of trial from the action as a whole: in other words, there was jurisdiction to order that meaning be tried by jury while the trial of the action was in the hands of a judge sitting alone. Given the difficulties to which Eady J. adverted, such an order is unlikely to be made in practice,[317] except, perhaps, in a case (if it can be imagined) where the issue of meaning presents no shades of grey but a stark choice between black and white. However, the Court of Appeal warned[318] that s.69(4) could only be used to fillet out questions of fact, and not issues of mixed law and fact, and that the *obiter* assumption to the contrary by the court in *Phillips v Comr of Police of the Metropolis*[319] was wrong.[320]

31.70 Chancery Division. The right to jury trial only arises if the action is to be tried in the Queen's Bench Division. A party to a defamation action in the Chancery Division, wanting trial by jury, can apply to the court for a transfer under CPR r.30.5(1), but there is no right to require transfer.[321]

---

[316] [2006] EWCA Civ 519; [2006] 1 W.L.R. 2462.

[317] Since the Court of Appeal's decision in *Armstrong*, no such order has ever been made.

[318] [2006] EWCA Civ 519; [2006] 1 W.L.R. 2462, at [19].

[319] [2003] EWCA Civ 382 at [17].

[320] Gray J. seems to have thought that s.69(4) could be used for that purpose in the later case of *Turkot v Oxus Gold Plc* [2006] EWHC 3361 (QB) (*Armstrong* is not referred to in his judgment) but he declined to order trial by jury of preliminary issues of mixed law and fact on the ground that they involved prolonged examination of documents and that trial of the issues was in any event premature.

[321] *Stafford Winfield Cook v Winfield* [1981] 1 W.L.R. 458 CA; *CHC Software v Hopkins & Wood* [1993] F.S.R. 241.

CHAPTER 32

THE TRIAL: THE CLAIMANT'S CASE

SECTION 1. COMMENCEMENT OF TRIAL

Jury. Jury trial has been a rarity for some years, and will become extremely **32.1** unusual once Defamation Act 2013, s.11 is brought into effect.[1] However, if the action is to be tried by a jury, the trial will commence with the selection and swearing of jurors. The jury will consist of 12 persons if proceedings are in the High Court, and eight persons if in a county court.[2] The jury will be selected by ballot in open court from the panel of jurors summoned to attend.[3] The jury so selected shall try only one issue, save that the trial of two or more issues by the same jury may take place if the trial of the second or last issue begins within 24 hours from the time when the jury is constituted.[4] The parties may challenge the array, i.e. the whole panel,[5] or may challenge individual jurors for cause.[6] There is no right of peremptory challenge.[7] Challenges for

---

[1] S.11 will remove the presumption in favour of jury trial in defamation cases. See para.31.64ff, above for issues arising in respect of mode of trial.

[2] County Courts Act 1984, s.67.

[3] Juries Act 1974, s.11(1).

[4] Juries Act 1974, s.11(5). An "issue" in this context must mean a claim: see s.69 of the Senior Courts Act 1981. This provision would seem to require that two actions giving rise to common questions of fact but which cannot be consolidated should be tried at the same time, rather than one after another (see CPR r.3.1(2)(g) and (h)), for in the latter event there cannot be the same jury.

[5] This is now almost unheard of. Valid grounds would be that the summoning officer was in a position inconsistent with impartiality, or was suspected of holding such a position: *O'Connell v R.* (1844) 11 Cl. & Fin. 155.

[6] The grounds are few, e.g. that the juror lacks mental capacity, or is suspected of bias, or has committed some crime which disqualifies him from serving (see Juries Act 1974, s.1, Sch.1 Pt II).

[7] *Creed v Fisher* (1854) 9 Exch. 472.

cause should be made before the juror is sworn. Any outstanding procedural matters or applications should normally be dealt with before the jury is sworn in.[8]

32.2 Opening statement. Though the conduct of the trial and the order of speeches is a matter for the trial judge,[9] the trial will normally commence with an opening statement on behalf of the claimant. However, where the burden of proof of all the issues in the action lies on the defendant, the defendant will usually be allowed to begin.[10] The purpose of the claimant's opening statement is to explain the nature of his case,[11] and to outline the evidence upon which he relies.[12] If the admissibility of evidence is disputed it should not be mentioned, for if it is later ruled inadmissible there may be grounds for discharging the jury, with the likely consequence of an order for payment of the costs thrown away. Thus documents which are not agreed and which the defendant contends are inadmissible should not at this stage be shown to the jury.[13] Where the claimant considers it is necessary to include references to disputed evidence in his opening, he should seek a ruling from the judge as to its admissibility beforehand. In his opening the claimant must keep within the ambit of his pleaded case. It would not be proper, for instance, to suggest to the jury that the words complained of bore a fundamentally different or more serious meaning than that contended for in the particulars of claim. It should also be borne in mind that the terms of the opening statement may raise issues about which the defendant may be entitled to cross-examine the claimant.[14] It is not uncommon for the defendant to be permitted to make a short speech following that of the claimant.[15]

---

[8] Queen's Bench Guide para.10.2.4.

[9] The conduct of the trial and the order of speeches come within the judge's general powers of case management.

[10] Under the Rules of the Supreme Court, a defendant upon whom fell the burden of proof of all the issues in the action was entitled to begin (Ord.35 r.7(6)). There is no such absolute rule in the CPR, but in such a situation one would expect the judge to accede to an application that the defendant should open the case. Thus a defendant pleading, say, justification, who has admitted publication of the words complained of, that they refer to the claimant, and are defamatory of him in the meanings contended for by the claimant, and further admits all the matters relied upon in support of the claim for damages, will generally be allowed to begin. The defendant opened and called its evidence first in *Nixon v Channel Four*, June 1997, and the same happened in *Hamilton v Al Fayed*, December 1999, Morland J.

[11] He should provide a written summary of his opening speech unless the points are covered in a skeleton argument: Queen's Bench Guide para.10.2.3.

[12] For a description of the advantages provided by an opening statement, particularly as regards influencing a jury as to meaning, see *John Fairfax Publications Pty v Rivkin* [2003] HCA 50; 201 A.L.R. 77 McHugh J. at [74].

[13] It is the parties' responsibility to provide sufficient bundles of documents for the use of the jury: Queen's Bench Guide para.10.2.7. In practice, the parties' counsel liaise over the contents of the jury bundle, which is usually agreed, or substantially so, and the claimant's solicitors generally prepare it.

[14] E.g. see *Delaney v News Media* [1976] 1 N.Z.L.R. 322 at 326.

[15] See Queen's Bench Guide para.10.2.3.

SECTION 2. EVIDENCE FOR THE CLAIMANT: INTRODUCTION

General. The claimant must call evidence[16] on all matters alleged in the   **32.3**
particulars of claim, essential to his claim, which are not admitted by the
defendant, or presumed in the claimant's favour, or for the decision of the jury
without the assistance of evidence. Thus evidence may be required to establish
the introductory averments as to the claimant's status, to prove publication of
the words set out in the particulars of claim, and to show that they refer to the
claimant. There should be evidence of the facts and matters relied upon in
support of the claim for damages,[17] and to sustain any claim for exemplary
damages. Further, the claimant will need to call evidence to prove allegations
made in the reply, e.g. that the defendant was actuated by express malice or
by way of answer to, or rebuttal of, a plea of justification.

Evidence by video link. CPR r.32.3 provides that the court may allow a   **32.4**
witness to give evidence through a video link or by other means. When the use
of video conferencing (VCF) is being considered a judgment must be made
not only as to whether it will achieve an overall cost saving but as to whether
its use is likely to be beneficial to the efficient, fair and economic disposal of
the litigation.[18] In *Polanski v Condé Nast Publications* the claimant in a libel
action was allowed to give his evidence at trial by VCF. from Paris, since if
he came to England he was at risk of extradition to the USA, from which he
had fled before sentencing after pleading guilty to having unlawful sexual
intercourse with a minor. The judge made an order permitting the claimant to
give evidence by VCF, but his order was reversed by the Court of Appeal. The
House of Lords[19] restored the judge's order, holding (by a majority of three to
two) that although there was a public interest in not assisting a fugitive from
justice to escape his just deserts, the claimant would in fact do so whether or
not a video link order was made, and there was a strong public interest in
allowing a claim properly brought in England to be properly and fairly
litigated. Moreover, if the administration of justice was not brought into
disrepute by the claimant bringing proceedings in England, it would not be
brought into disrepute by allowing him recourse to the procedural facility of
video conference link. The general rule was that in respect of proceedings
properly brought in England a party's unwillingness to come into this country
because of his fugitive status was a valid reason for making a VCF. order.[20]

---

[16] In civil proceedings the rule is that where a witness is called to give oral evidence his witness statement shall stand as his evidence in chief unless the court otherwise orders (r.32.5(2)), but in jury actions the court will always order that evidence in chief be given orally.

[17] They must be pleaded in the particulars of claim: CPR PD 53, para.2.10.

[18] CPR PD 32,PD para. 29.1 and Annex 3.

[19] [2005] UKHL 10; [2005] 1 W.L.R. 637.

[20] A complaint by the defendant to the ECHR that this decision was contrary to arts 6 and 10 of the Convention was ruled inadmissible on the grounds that it was "manifestly ill founded" (*Condé Nast v United Kingdom,* App. No.29746/05).

The majority were also of the view that the court was not bound to make an order excluding a witness's statement as evidence if he did not attend for cross-examination. Such an order should be made only if, exceptionally, justice so required. The principle underlying the Civil Evidence Act 1995 was that in general the preferable course was to admit hearsay evidence, and let the court attach to the evidence whatever weight might be appropriate. This applied to jury trial as well as trials by judge alone.

32.5 Introductory averments. The opening paragraph(s) of the particulars of claim, which generally record the professional and social status of the claimant, or his occupation or office, are rarely a matter of dispute, and they can usually be proved by the evidence of the claimant himself. Where in claims for slander or malicious falsehood the claimant is relying on ss.2 or 3 of the Defamation Act 1952 to avoid the need to prove special damage, it will be essential to prove, if not admitted, that the office, profession, calling, trade or business was held or carried on by him at the time of publication. To prove that the claimant held a public office, it is sufficient to prove that he acted in the office, without proof of appointment.[21] However, there is no such presumption in the case of a private office, for instance that of an executor or trustee in bankruptcy, appointment to which must be strictly proved.[22] Where it is sought to prove that the claimant was carrying on a profession it is usually sufficient to show that the claimant was practising at the relevant date, but where the words impute want of qualification to exercise the profession a strict proof of professional qualification is necessary.[23]

SECTION 3. PROOF OF PUBLICATION

32.6 Production of document. What is required is evidence that the defamatory statement was communicated by or on behalf of the defendant to persons other than the claimant. In cases of libel this usually[24] presents little difficulty. Production of the document containing the statement will in many cases be sufficient evidence. Thus where the statement is in a newspaper, production of

---

[21] Per Buller J. in *Berryman v Wise* (1791) 4 T.R. 366; *Cannell v Curtis* (1835) 2 Bing. N.C. 228; *M'Ganey v Alston* (1836) 2 M. & W. 206; *Doe d. Bowley v Barnes* (1846) 8 Q.B. 1037; *Dexter v Hayes* (1860) 11 Ir. C.L.R. 106, affirmed sub nom. *Hayes Dexter* (1861) 13 Ir. C.L.R. 22.

[22] *Short v Lee* (1821) 2 Jac. & W. 464 at 468 (collector of titles); *Bright v Legerton* (1860) 2 de G.F. & J. 606 at 614.

[23] *Pickford v Gutch* (1787) 8 T.R. 305n; *Moises v Thornton* (1799) 8 T.R. 303. Both these cases concerned alleged slanders arising from statements that the plaintiff was a "quack". It was held that the plaintiffs had to prove strictly their medical qualifications. This must have been considered necessary in order to establish a cause of action in slander. For as regards the truth or falsity of the statement the onus is on the defendant to prove the latter.

[24] Libels disseminated online arguably stand as an exception to this general rule. For the difficulties that a claimant may encounter in proving a substantial internet-based publication, see e.g. *Lonzim Plc v Sprague* [2009] EWHC 2838 (QB). See further para.32.9, below.

a copy of the paper will generally be accepted as prima facie evidence of publication by the journalist named in the byline, and by the editor, publishers and printers of the newspaper. Production of a copy of a book would provide evidence of publication by the named author and publishers of the book of a defamatory statement contained in the book.

Publication by the defendant. It must be proved that the defendant was   **32.7** responsible for the publication. Where an action was brought over a report in a newspaper describing the defendant's allegedly defamatory objections to a book written by the claimant, the claim was struck out, for the allegation that the defendant had authorised publication of the words complained of was no more than bare assertion.[25]

Inferences. It is not necessary in all cases to prove that the libellous matter   **32.8** was actually seen and read by some third party. If it is a matter of reasonable inference that this happened, a prima facie case of publication will be established.[26] Thus, proof that a libellous letter was sent through the post is prima facie evidence of publication to the person to whom it was addressed.[27] The same must surely be true where it is proved that an email was sent to stated addressees. The sending of a libellous postcard has been held to be prima facie evidence of publication to the persons who handled the postcard.[28] Again in the case of a libel contained in a telegram, the contents "are necessarily communicated to all clerks through whose hands it passes".[29] It is suggested that the same reasoning must apply to the transmission of a defamatory fax, at least where it is not to a private line. There is no presumption that a letter in an unsealed envelope will be read by anyone other than the addressee.[30]

---

[25] *Campbell v Safra* [2006] EWHC 1062 (QB). Similarly in slander: *Khader v Aziz* [2010] EWCA Civ 716; [2011] E.M.L.R. 2. See also *SMEC Holdings Ltd v Boniface* [2005] N.S.W.S.C. 1099 in which one of the issues was whether certain defamatory emails, undoubtedly transmitted from various computers, were sent and published by the defendant. The judgment considered whether there was sufficient evidence of publication by the defendant to leave the issue to the jury. Similarly, in *Applause Store Productions Ltd v Raphael* [2008] EWHC 1781 (QB), the issue was whether the defendant (or some stranger) was responsible for making defamatory postings on Facebook.

[26] However, where the publication is only to a small number of people, any claim risks being struck out as an abuse of process (see further para.6.2, above). Further, once the Defamation Act 2013, s.1, comes into effect in England and Wales, a claimant will have to establish that the statement complained of has caused, or is likely to cause, serious harm to his reputation, which may be difficult where the publication is limited (para.6.3).

[27] *Warren v Warren* (1834) 1 C.M. & R. 250. See also *Bezant v Rausing* [2007] EWHC 1118 (QB) in which the claimant complained of a letter from the defendant's solicitor to the claimant, which it was alleged, though marked "private and confidential" was opened by, and therefore published to, the claimant's daughter. Gray J. ruled that the mere assertion by the claimant that the defendant knew that family members opened each other's mail was not enough to establish liability.

[28] *Robinson v Jones* (1879) 4 L.R.Ir. 391; *Sadgrove v Hole* [1901] 2 K.B. 1; *Huth v Huth* [1915] 3 K.B. 82.

[29] *Williamson v Freer* (1874) L.R. 9 C.P. 393 at 395.

[30] *Huth v Huth*, above. It is always open to a claimant to seek to prove that in the particular case it was a natural and probable consequence of sending the letter, sealed or unsealed, that it would

32.9 **Internet publication.**[31] It has been decided that where defamatory material is posted on a website by an internet service provider there is publication of that material to any person who accesses that site and reads the material.[32] The place of publication is the place or places where the material is downloaded.[33] The same reasoning must apply to email, which is published to the persons to whom it is transmitted at the place where it is received. Production of a printout of the offending material is likely to be regarded as sufficient evidence of publication to the addressees of email.[34] However, as regards material posted on the internet there is no presumption that it will have been downloaded by a significant number of persons, or indeed anyone. In *Al Amoudi v Brisard*[35] Gray J. rejected a submission that once a posting on the world wide web had been established it was a rebuttable presumption of law that there had been publication to a significant number of identifiable persons in the jurisdiction who had downloaded the material. It was a matter of inference, and the claimant must prove a sufficient "platform of facts" for the inference reasonably to be drawn.[36]

32.10 **Handwriting.** Proof that a libel, which has been published, is in the handwriting of the defendant, is prima facie evidence that the publication was by the defendant.[37] The claimant can prove the handwriting of the defendant by calling a witness who had seen the defendant write,[38] or who has received

---

be opened and read by a third party: see *Theaker v Richardson* [1962] 1 W.L.R. 151. Or that the defendant knew that a letter addressed to the the claimant was likely to be opened by his clerk or secretary, and that is what happened: *Gomersall v Davies* (1898) 14 T.L.R. 430.

[31] See paras 6.25 et seq., above for discussion on the position of service providers under common law, under s.1 of the Defamation Act 1996, and under Electronic Commerce (EC) Regulations 2002.

[32] *Godfrey v Demon Internet* [2001] Q.B. 201.

[33] *Gutnick v Dow Jones* [2002] HCA 56, 210 C.L.R. 575, a decision of the High Court of Australia which reviewed common law principles and rejected the concept of single publication. The proposition that internet material is published at the place where it is downloaded was accepted without argument in *King v Lewis* [2004] EWCA Civ 1329, [2005] E.M.L.R. 4. See also *Carter v B C Federation of Foster Parents Association* [2005] BCCA 398.

[34] A statement in very similar terms which appeared in the 9th edition was approved in *Bristile v Buddhist Society of Western Australia* [1999] W.A.S.C. 259.

[35] [2006] EWHC 1062 (QB); [2007] 1 W.L.R. 113. In *Jameel (Yousef) v Dow Jones & Co. Inc.* [2005] EWCA Civ 75; [2005] Q.B. 946 the words complained of were posted on a subscription website. The particulars of claim alleged that there were between 5,000 and 6,000 subscribers within the jurisdiction. The defendant was able to show that the offending material had only been accessed by five subscribers within the jurisdiction, two of whom did not know the claimant and had no recollection of reading his name and the other three were connected with the claimant. The Court of Appeal struck out the claim as an abuse of the process. See para.30.48ff for the concept of a real and substantial tort.

[36] See also *Baturina v Times Newspapers Ltd* [2010] EWHC 696 (QB); [2010] E.M.L.R. 18 at [38] (reversed on appeal [2011] EWCA Civ 308; [2011] 1 W.L.R. 1526, but this point was unaffected); *Trumm v Norman* [2008] EWHC 116 (QB); *Brady v Norman* [2008] EWHC 2481 (QB) [23]–[26]; *ZAM v CFW* [2013] EWHC 662 (QB) at [108].

[37] "Where a libel is produced written by a man's hand, and the author is not known, he is taken in the mainer, and that throws proof upon him, and if he cannot show the composer the verdict is against him": per Holt C.J. in *R. v Beare* (1698) 1 Ld. Raym. at 417.

[38] *Doe d. Mudd v Suckermore* (1836) 5 A. & E. 703 at 731.

documents purporting to be written or signed by the defendant in reply to letters addressed to him,[39] or who has seen in the ordinary course of business documents purporting to be in the defendant's handwriting.[40] If a witness is asked if he has seen the defendant write, and he answers yes, the subsequent question as to whether he believes the libel to be in the defendant's handwriting may then be put.[41] Whether the witness has seen the defendant write more or less frequently affects the weight but not the admissibility of the evidence. If the witness has ever seen the defendant write, even though it was only once, or many years before, it is enough to introduce the subsequent question whether he believes the libel to be in the defendant's handwriting.[42]

Criminal Procedure Act 1865, section 8. Another mode of proof is provided by s.8 of the Criminal Procedure Act 1865, which enacts that: **32.11**

> "Comparison of a disputed writing with any writing proved to the satisfaction of the judge to be genuine shall be permitted to be made by witnesses, and such writings, and the evidence of witnesses respecting the same, may be submitted to the court and jury as evidence of the genuineness, or otherwise, of the writing in dispute."

Under this section (which is not limited to criminal trials) any other document admitted,[43] or proved to the satisfaction of the judge,[44] to be in the defendant's handwriting, though not otherwise relevant to the case, is admissible for the purpose of comparison. It is not essential for the original of the disputed writing to be available for comparison. Expert evidence based upon a comparison of a photocopy of the disputed writing with genuine writing is admissible under the Act.[45]

Experts. Although under the common law any person familiar with the defendant's handwriting can testify that the libel is in the same handwriting, and under the Criminal Procedure Act 1865 anyone can make a comparison between the disputed writing and the writing which the judge accepts is that of the defendant, it is common practice where handwriting is in dispute to call an expert. It has been stated that a jury should not be left to decide questions   **32.12**

---

[39] *Lord Ferrers v Shirley* (1731) Fitz. 195; *Doe d. Mudd v Suckermore* at 731.

[40] *Doe d. Mudd v Suckermore* at 731; *Re Clarence Hotel* (1909) 54 S.J. 117.

[41] *Eagleton v Kingston* (1803) 8 Ves. 438 at 473.

[42] *Eagleton v Kingston* at 473; *Doe d. Mudd v Suckermore* at 730.

[43] The claimant may interrogate or cross-examine the defendant to obtain such admission: *Jones v Richard* (1885) 15 Q.B.D. 439, though interrogatories as such have been replaced by the procedure under CPR Pt 18 obtaining further information. Those who understood the value of the interrogatory should not despair, for there is reason to suppose that it survives under a new name: see para.31.14, above.

[44] On the balance of probabilities: see *R. v Ewing* [1983] 1 Q.B. 1039 at 1047.

[45] *Lockheed-Arabia v Owen* [1993] Q.B. 806 CA. It is for the judge or jury to decide what weight should be given to such evidence.

of disputed handwriting without the assistance of expert evidence.[46] Juries should be warned not to make unaided comparisons between disputed and genuine handwriting,[47] nor should the judge appear to be a handwriting expert by comparing examples of signatures.[48]

32.13 Action for slander. Where there is no admission by the defendant that he spoke the words complained of or words to like effect,[49] the claimant must call evidence of what the defendant said and of who heard him. The actual words spoken must be proved; it is not sufficient for witnesses to state what they believe to be the substance or effect of the words, or their impression of what was said.[50] The burden is of course on the claimant to do so.[51] The witnesses will usually be those who were present, but hearsay evidence is in principle admissible of what the witness was told by someone present that the defendant said.[52] Evidence as to the presence of other people when the words were spoken may be insufficient, as the fact that there were other people in the vicinity does not of itself entitle anyone to draw the conclusion that those people must have heard what was said.[53] A tape recording of the slander would be admissible.[54]

32.14 Variance between words alleged and words proved. The requirement to prove the actual words spoken does not mean that there must be complete correspondence between the words pleaded and the words proved, whether in a slander action or a libel action where the oral evidence of witnesses is the only proof available.[55] In practice, the words proved in a slander action will often differ, to a greater or lesser degree, from those pleaded. As long as the words proved are a material and defamatory part of the words alleged, or words which are substantially to the same effect, the claimant is entitled to have it decided, or left to the jury to decide, whether the words alleged or words to the like effect have been proved, or of course he could seek leave to

---

[46] *R. v Rickard* (1918) 13 Cr.App.R. 140.

[47] *R. v Tilley* [1961] 1 W.L.R. 1309; *R. v O'Sullivan* [1969] 1 W.L.R. 497.

[48] *R. v Tilley*, above; *R. v Simbodyal, The Times*, October 10, 1991, CA.

[49] In the defence or in his witness statement.

[50] *Maitland v Goldney* (1802) 2 East 426; *Harrison v Bevington* (1838) 8 Carr. & P. 708 per Lord Abinger C.B. at 710; *Phelps v Kemsley* [1942] 168 L.T. 18; *Zameen Investments & Rafiuddin v DF Brazier Builders & O'Hara-Smith*, unreported, March 20, 1990, CA.

[51] For a relatively recent example of a claimant who was unable to persuade the judge to rely on his evidence of publication, see *Hussein v Farooq* [2008] EWHC 2487 (QB).

[52] Civil Evidence Act 1995, s.1.

[53] *Moberly v Comr of Police*, unreported, May 13, 1987, CA.

[54] *R. v Ali and Hussain* [1966] 1 Q.B. 688. The tape would be proved by its production, or a copy of it, authenticated in such manner as the court may approve: s.8(1) of the Civil Evidence Act 1995. If the tape is lost or the recording erased, evidence from someone who listened to it is admissible: *Taylor v Chief Constable of Cheshire* [1986] 1 W.L.R. 1479.

[55] Two centuries ago, the courts were less tolerant. In *Walters v Mace* (1819) 2 B. & Al. 756, 106 E.R. 541, a claimant who complained of the words: "This is my umbrella, and he stole it from my back door," and proved: "It is my umbrella, and he stole it from my back door" was nonsuited.

amend his particulars of claim.[56] In such a case, if the words proved convey to the mind of a reasonable man practically the same meaning as the words set out, the variance will be immaterial.[57]

> "The plaintiff is entitled to put before the jury his case that the words proved though not the very words pleaded are words substantially to the like effect. Whether this be done by amending the pleading, by framing the question to the jury so as to raise the point, or by directing the jury that the words pleaded would be proved by proof of words substantially to the same effect, seems to me immaterial. No slander of any complexity could ever be proved if the *ipsissima verba* of the pleading had to be established."[58]

Thus, where the words set out in the declaration, "Ware Hawk! You must take care of yourself there; mind what you are about", were alleged to have been spoken of the plaintiff to a person about to supply him with goods, it was held that the failure to prove the words "you must take care of yourself there", was not a material variance, for such words contained no qualification of the charge.[59]

Fatal variance. However if the words proved materially alter or qualify the sense of those set out in the particulars of claim, the variance will be fatal to the claimant,[60] unless he can persuade the judge to grant him permission to amend the particulars of claim.[61] If the amendment would require the defendant to plead and prove new grounds of defence, it is unlikely that leave would be granted except perhaps on terms as to the costs thrown away, as it would   **32.15**

---

[56] *Harris v Warre* (1879) 4 C.P.D.125, 128; *Tournier v National Provincial Bank* [1924] 1 K.B. 461 at 469, 478, 487.

[57] "Where an oral statement is complained of, it is rarely possible (in the absence of a recording, a transcript or a very careful note) for a plaintiff to establish the precise words used by the defendant. But the law does not demand a level of precision which is unattainable in practice. The plaintiff must plead the words complained of, but it is enough if the tribunal of fact is satisfied that those words accurately express the substance of what was said";
Buchanan v Jennings [2004] UKPC; [2005] 1 A.C. 115 at [5]. See also *Orpwood v Barkes* (1827) 4 Bing. 261; *Rutherford v Evans* (1830) 6 Bing. 451 at 458; *Harris v Warre* (1879) 4 C.P.D. 125 at 128.

[58] Per Atkin L.J. in *Tournier v National Provincial Bank* [1924] 1 K.B. 461 at 487, 488. "The jury should be directed that if they think the defendant used, in substance, the words, or a material and defamatory part of the words complained of, they should say so and he is liable": per Scrutton L.J. at 478.

[59] *Orpwood v Barkes*, above. "Hawk" was short for "hawker" and it was considered that with or without the words not proved, the effect in context was "Beware of the sharper". In the same case Park J. stated (at 263) that "if a man were to say, "You are a thief, for you stole a woman's heart", the latter words, as explaining the meaning of the charge, could not be omitted".

[60] *Hancock v Winter* (1816) 7 Taunt. 205; *Cartwright v Wright* (1822) 5 B. & Ald. 615; *Zameen Investments & Rafiuddin v DF Brazier Builders & O'Hara-Smith*, unreported March 20, 1990, CA.

[61] Under CPR Pt 17 the court has a general power to grant permission to amend a statement of case at any time provided the limitation period has not expired. If that has occurred the power is limited to the circumstances stated in r.17.4 unless the court is able to exercise its discretion to extend or exclude the limitation period under ss.28 or 32A of the Limitation Act 1980.

entail a lengthy adjournment of the trial.[62] It might be fairer to dismiss the action, leaving the claimant the option to start a fresh action based on the words he can prove were published.[63]

32.16 Foreign language. Where the words complained of are in a foreign language the claimant must prove, if not admitted, first, the actual words published, and secondly, their English translation.[64] If the English translation of the words allegedly published cannot be agreed, it will be necessary for the claimant to call an interpreter.[65] The claimant must also prove that persons who heard or read the words understood the foreign language, for clearly if defamatory words are communicated in a language altogether unknown or incomprehensible to those who hear or read them there is no publication[66]; but understanding can often be inferred. Thus a foreign language newspaper published or circulating in this country will be assumed to have a readership which understands the language, although the claimant would be wise to call evidence of its circulation here. In the case of a foreign language website which has been read and hence published in this country, the same assumption might be less readily made,[67] and the claimant would be wise to call evidence from those who read and understood it, or at least to prove that a substantial number of those who understand the language live here.

32.17 Production of the libel. If it is the core of the claimant's claim that defamatory words have been published about him in a document, he should produce the document, or the material part of it, as primary evidence of the

---

[62] Cases cited in previous editions of this book where leave was granted, e.g. *Smith v Knowelden* (1841) 2 M. & Gr. 561, *Huckle v Reynolds* (1859) 7 C.B. (N.S.) 114 and *Saunders v Bate* (1856) 1 H. & N. 402 would appear to be cases where there was no substantial variation.

[63] The one-year limitation period (s.5 of the Defamation Act 1996) may preclude this.

[64] This will be set out in the particulars of claim. This rule was held not to be essential in *Sing v Jinggut* (2003) 6 M.L.J. 433, where the court refused to strike out particulars of claim in which only the translation of the words complained of had been included and not the words in the language in which they had been published (Mandarin). However, in *Ng Kim Cho v Chai Sze Shin* [2006] MLJU 0087 Clement Skinner J. declined to follow this decision and ruled that the failure to set out the words complained of in the language in which they were published was fatal to the plaintiff's case.

[65] S.22 of the Welsh Language Act 1993 provides for the Welsh language to be spoken in legal proceedings in Wales by any party, witness or other person who desires to use it. The section does not extend to written use of the Welsh language, but that appears to be envisaged by the CPR Practice Direction relating to the Use of the Welsh language in cases in the civil courts in Wales, subject to the giving of proper notice. Presumably, therefore, there would be no objection in principle to pleading a Welsh slander in Welsh, without a translation into English.

[66] Cf. *Fleetwood v Curley* (1619) Hob. 267 at 268, where Lord Hobart observed:
"... the slander and damage consist in the apprehension of the hearers, and therefore slanderous words in Welsh bear no action, except you affirm, that they were spoken in the hearing of them that understood the Welsh tongue".
The passage was referred to in *Fullam v Newcastle Chronicle* [1977] 1 W.L.R. 651 at 658.

[67] There is no rebuttable presumption of law that an article placed on an internet website open to general access has been published to a substantial number of people within the jurisdiction. The claimant bears the burden of proving that the material in question has been accessed and downloaded: *Al Amoudi v Brisard* [2006] EWHC 1062 (QB); [2007] 1 W.L.R. 113.

libel. Where the original libel cannot be produced, because it has been lost, or is in the possession of a third party, or because it is physically impossible to produce it,[68] secondary evidence of the contents of the document may be given.[69] A statement in a document may be proved by production of a copy of that document authenticated in such manner as the court may approve.[70]

Section 4. Identification of Claimant

Introduction.   **32.18**

> "The plaintiff to succeed in the action must prove a publication of and concerning him, and if he does not satisfy the onus of proof which is on him in this respect there is no cause of action."[71]

In other words, the claimant must prove that he was the subject of the libel. The position is slightly different in malicious falsehood, where it is enough that there should be a reference, direct or indirect, to the claimant's business, even if the claimant himself is not identified in the minds of those to whom the words are published.[72]

Claimant not expressly named.[73] Where the claimant is named in the   **32.19**
libel no difficulty will usually arise. Unless the claimant's name is a common name[74] no evidence that there were readers who identified the claimant is necessary, as the claimant only has to establish that persons could have identified him from the words used, which plainly they could if his name was not common and he was expressly named. Where the claimant's name is generally a common name, but not in the context in which it is mentioned, it would also seem unnecessary to lead evidence that the claimant was identified as the person referred to.[75] However where the libel does not *ex facie* refer to

---

[68] E.g. a tombstone or a placard on a building.
"Suppose that . . . a witness were to say that he saw a man chalk certain [defamatory] words up, and that these were in the handwriting of AB, surely that would be good evidence against AB as the production of the writing itself would be impossible":
Sayer v Glossop (1848) 2 Exch. at 411.
[69] For an explanation of what types of secondary evidence are admissible and in what circumstances, see *Phipson on Evidence*, 17th edn (London: Sweet & Maxwell, 2012), Ch.41.
[70] Civil Evidence Act 1995, s.8(1)(b).
[71] Per A. L. Smith M.R. in *Sadgrove v Hole* [1901] 2 K.B. 1 at 4; cited by Lord Donovan in *Morgan v Odhams Press* [1971] 1 W.L.R. 1239 at 1263. See Ch.7, above.
[72] *Marathon Mutual Ltd v Waters* [2009] EWHC 1931 (QB); [2010] E.M.L.R. 3.
[73] See para.7.2, above.
[74] "Where a common name is included in an article, the name itself will not suffice to identify any individual who bears that name": (*Jameel (Yousef) v Dow Jones* [2005] EWCA Civ 75; [2005] Q.B. 946; at [45]).
[75] E.g. If an article about corrupt bank managers named a manager called Smith, or an article about incompetent surgeons named a surgeon called Jones; and there were few, if any, bank managers or surgeons with those names.

the claimant, e.g. where he is described by his initial letters, or by a nickname, or by a fictitious name,[76] or by the name of another, extrinsic evidence must be given "to connect the libel with the [claimant]",[77] evidence from which it would be reasonable to deduce that the defamatory words "implicated" the claimant.[78] For this purpose witnesses can be called to testify that they understood, from reading the libel in the light of the facts and circumstances narrated and described, and their acquaintance with, and knowledge of, the claimant, that he was the person referred to.[79] In *Morgan v Odhams Press* the plaintiff, who complained about an article in a newspaper which stated that a named woman had been kidnapped by members of a dog-doping gang and kept in a house near Finchley, was able to prove it referred to him by calling evidence of various people who at the material time had seen the woman, who had been staying at the plaintiff's flat in Willesden (some three miles from Finchley), in company with the plaintiff, and who had read the article and

---

[76] An action has been brought by a plaintiff suing in the *nom de plume* he adopted as an author. It was held that the court had power to waive the apparent breach of RSC Ord.6, r.1 (requiring the plaintiff's name to be contained on the writ) but the Court of Appeal declined to rule (it was an interlocutory appeal) whether the plaintiff could maintain a libel action in a fictitious name: *Andy McNab v Associated Newspapers Ltd*, unreported, May 17, 1996, CA. It is most unlikely that a defamation claimant in the position of Andy McNab, who is known by his nom de plume and is unwilling for good reason to disclose his real name, would now be prevented from suing, and obtaining vindication, in the name in which he is known. Were it otherwise, he would be prevented from asserting his art.8 reputation right. Indeed, defamation claimants who have good reason to need anonymity have been permitted to sue and to obtain judgment under the cloak of anonymity: see *Cairns v Modi* [2012] EWCA Civ 1382, [2013] 1 W.L.R. 1015 (where to have named KC would have been to exacerbate the damage caused by a libel understood by relatively few people to refer to him) and *ZAM v CFW* [2013] EWHC 662 (QB), where the principles are considered (in that case, the claimant was being blackmailed). Anonymity is relatively common-place in actions involving privacy or breach of confidential information: for the principles, see *JIH v News Group Newspapers Ltd* [2011] EWCA Civ 42; [2011] 1 W.L.R. 1645. See also para.25.27, above.
    Under the CPR the claim form should state the full name of each party (PD 7A, para.4.1(1)), which has been held to be a direction that parties should, but not must, be named (*Bloomsbury Publishing Group Ltd v News Group Newspapers Ltd* [2003] EWHC 1205 Ch; [2003] 1 W.L.R. 1633, a claim in copyright, confidence and conversion against persons described but not known by name). See further para.25.31, above.
[77] *Fournet v Pearson* (1897) 14 T.L.R. 82; and see *Lawrence v Newberry* (1891) 64 L.T. 797. In *Budu v BBC* [2010] EWHC 616 (QB), the claimant failed to adduce any evidence that readers of an article archived on the BBC website, which contained no express reference to him, would have understood that he was referred to.
[78] *Morgan v Odhams Press Ltd* [1971] 1 W.L.R. 1239 at 1263. In *Channel Seven Sydney v Parras* [2002] NSWCA 202, it was held that where the defamatory material did not refer to the plaintiff by name but to his business, evidence that it was understood to refer to the plaintiff and not just to his business was required. However, it was also held that where the business of a corporate plaintiff is described (e.g. hotel, night club) it is sufficient to prove that some recipients of the defamatory publication knew who the owners of the business were even though they were unaware of the company's formal title.
[79] *Broome v Cosden* (1845) 1 C.B. 728; *Hulton v Jones* [1909] 2 K.B. 404; [1910] A.C. 20; *Cassidy v Daily Mirror* [1929] 2 K.B. 331; *Youssoupoff v Metro-Goldwyn- Mayer Pictures Ltd* (1934) 50 T.L.R. 581 CA; *Hough v London Express* [1940] 2 K.B. 507; *Morgan v Odhams Press Ltd*, above.

understood it to refer to the plaintiff.[80] Even if the witnesses are accepted as honest witnesses, their evidence is not conclusive. The test is an objective one, whether on the evidence an ordinary sensible man would draw the inference that the words referred to the claimant, and the tribunal of fact is entitled to form its own opinion about this.[81] Where the identity of the claimant would be known only to those with knowledge of special circumstances it is necessary for the claimant to prove that the words were published to persons with such knowledge,[82] though in certain circumstances this could be a matter of inference.[83] It is immaterial that the persons who identified the claimant as the subject of the libel did not believe it to be true.[84]

Other evidence that claimant was identified. Evidence may be admissible that the claimant has been identified as the subject of the article, even though the means of identification, or the reason why the claimant was connected with the libel, is not established. Thus evidence that the claimant was pointed out and made the subject of ridicule and laughter at a public meeting shortly after the publication of the libel is admissible "as identifying the subject of the libel and as a proof of the consequences necessarily resulting from its publication".[85] The claimant can give evidence about persons who made contact with him and by their conduct or statements showed that they had identified him as the subject of the libel.[86] Evidence of anonymous telephone communications to the claimant after the publication of the libel is also admissible, although such evidence should be treated with caution.[87]   **32.20**

Identification from a subsequent publication. Although as a general rule a claimant cannot rely on events subsequent to publication to establish that the words referred, or would have been understood to refer, to him,[88] in   **32.21**

---

[80] The House of Lords, reversing the Court of Appeal, found that it would not have been unreasonable for a hypothetical sensible reader who knew the special facts to infer that the article referred to the plaintiff.

[81] *Morgan v Odhams Press Ltd*, above, at 1245.

[82] *Bruce v Odhams Press Ltd* [1936] 1 K.B. 697; *Consolidated Trust Co. Ltd v Browne* (1948) 49 S.R. (N.S.W.) 86, where the statement was defamatory of the (unnamed) owners of a building but the action failed for want of any evidence that the statement had been published to any persons who knew the claimants to be the owners.

[83] Where a photograph of the claimant taken 20 years ago was published in a book and a national newspaper it could be inferred that some readers of the book and newspaper would have been old friends and acquaintances of the claimant who would have recognised him from the photograph: *Dwek v Macmillan Publishers Ltd* [2000] E.M.L.R. 284 CA. But no inference could be drawn where publication of the words complained of was in a German magazine with a small English circulation and the matters relied upon to prove identification of the claimants not expressly named were the contents of articles in English newspapers: *Mosley v Focus Magazin Verlag GmbH* [2001] EWCA Civ 1030.

[84] *Morgan v Odhams Press*, above, at 1252.

[85] *Cook v Ward* (1830) 6 Bing. 409 per Tindall C.J. at 415.

[86] *Hayward v Thompson* [1982] Q.B. 47 at 57.

[87] *Jozwiak v Sadek* [1954] 1 W.L.R. 275.

[88] *Grappelli v Derek Block (Holdings) Ltd* [1981] 1 W.L.R. 822.

certain circumstances evidence may be admissible of a subsequent publication naming the claimant for the purposes of identifying the claimant as the subject of defamatory allegations in which he is not named. In *Hayward v Thompson*[89] the plaintiff complained of two articles published in a Sunday newspaper on consecutive Sundays, in the first of which he was not mentioned by name. The judge's ruling that the jury could look at the second article, to see to whom the first article referred, was upheld on appeal.[90] This ruling has been applied and extended in Australia to allow a plaintiff claiming in respect of a defamatory item in a morning newspaper (which did not name him) to rely upon a television programme in which he featured, which was broadcast later that day.[91]

32.22   The claimant a member of a group. Where the claimant is only identified as a member of a group, body or class, he must lead evidence that he was a member and that the fact of his membership was known by persons to whom the words were published. It is common in these cases to call evidence from persons who can state that they understood the libel to refer to the claimant.[92]

32.23   Slander. Where a slander is not communicated in direct terms, but by expressions, gestures and intonations of the voice, it may be competent for witnesses, who heard the expressions, or saw the gestures, to state to whom they understood them to apply.[93]

---

[89] [1982] Q.B. 47.

[90] The judge apparently relied on *Russell v Kelly* (1972) 13 Am. Rep. 169, which was cited with little enthusiasm in *Grappelli v Derek Block*, above, at 830, CA. In *Grappelli* it was held that the plaintiff could not rely on facts coming to the knowledge of persons after publication to support an innuendo meaning on the grounds that the cause of action must be complete at the time of publication. In *Hayward v Thompson* Lord Denning M.R. distinguished *Grappelli* by stating (at 60) that it did not apply where the words were defamatory on the face of them, "were aimed at" or "intended to refer" to the plaintiff, and the only question was one of identification. In principle it is difficult to distinguish between cases where extrinsic facts are relevant to identification, and cases where they are relevant to defamatory meaning. The conclusion must be that there is in English law some conflict of authority on the issue whether subsequent publications can be referred to in order to establish identification or meaning. It has to be said that Lord Denning's emphasis of intention is somewhat in conflict with the established principle that save in the context of malice the intention of the publisher of a libel is irrelevant to liability. In relation to meaning this topic is discussed in para.3.33, above, and see also para.32.27, below.

[91] *Baltinos v Foreign Language Publications* [1986] 6 N.S.W.L.R. 85: the defendant was a morning newspaper that previewed a television programme to be broadcast later that day in an article including the words "Migrant victims of rapacious con-men". Hunt J. permitted the plaintiff to rely on the TV programme for the purposes of identification, holding that the jury might have regard to the naming of the plaintiff in a subsequent publication, even though the defendant was not responsible for it, when the matter complained of was interpreted by the ordinary reasonable reader as inviting him to ascertain the identity of the person to whom the defendant intended to refer from that subsequent publication.

[92] But such evidence is not essential: *Vlasic v Federal Capital Press* [1976] 9 A.C.T.R. 1.

[93] *Leonard v Allen* (1853) 65 Mass. R. 241; *Blakeman v Blakeman* (1884) 31 Minn. R. 396.

Evidence of reputation. It is generally unnecessary, and possibly imper-   **32.24**
missible, to lead evidence to show that the claimant has a reputation, for that
is presumed.[94] However, such evidence may be required in respect of a
corporate claimant which is not trading or carrying on business within the
jurisdiction of the place where the defamatory statement was published.[95]
Indeed, once Defamation Act 2013, s.1(2)[96] has been brought into effect, such
evidence will no doubt play an important part in showing that the words
complained of have caused or are likely to cause the company serious
financial loss. An action brought by an overseas corporation which did not
itself trade but acted as the holding company of a number of trading subsidiaries, where there was no evidence that the existence of the corporation was
known in any of the four jurisdictions where the words complained of were
published, was withdrawn from the jury and dismissed at the end of the
claimant's case on the grounds that no jury could conclude that the claimant
was defamed or damaged in any trading or business reputation within any of
the relevant jurisdictions.[97]

SECTION 5. DEFAMATORY MEANINGS

Defamation Act 2013, s.1 The Act prospectively introduces a statutory   **32.25**
threshold, by which a statement is not defamatory unless its publication has
caused or is likely to cause serious harm to the reputation of the claimant. It
gives statutory effect to the concept of a threshold of seriousness already
recognised by the common law,[98] a threshold which is of particular relevance

---

[94] This must be the corollary of the rule that no evidence need be called of damage to
reputation, as a presumption arises to this effect upon proof of publication of a defamatory
statement referring to the claimant: *Shevill v Presse Alliance* [1996] A.C. 959 at 983; *Jameel
(Yousef) v Dow Jones & Co. Inc. (*above) at [27]. "I do not believe it to be seriously suggested
that under English law an individual human being has to surmount a preliminary hurdle in order
to bring defamation proceedings by showing an established reputation": Eady J. in *Multigroup
Bulgaria Holding AD v Oxford Analytica Ltd* [2001] E.M.L.R. 737. In *Jameel* the Court of Appeal
approved as "sound sense" Eady J.'s view expressed in *Multigroup* that an article defaming an
identifiable individual would give rise to a cause of action even where no one reading the article
had prior knowledge of the victim. See also para.32.62, below.
[95] See *McDonald's Corp v Steel*, unreported, March 1999, CA. But Eady J. in *Multigroup
Bulgaria Holding AD v Oxford Analytica Ltd*, above, considered any observations to this effect
obiter.
[96] Defamation Act 2013, s.1 provides as follows:
"(1) A statement is not defamatory unless its publication has caused or is likely to cause serious
harm to the reputation of the claimant. (2) For the purposes of this section, harm to the
reputation of a body that trades for profit is not "serious harm" unless it has caused or is likely
to cause the body serious financial loss."
[97] *Multigroup Bulgaria Holding AD v Oxford Analytica Ltd*, above.
[98] See *Thornton v Telegraph Media Group Ltd* [2010] EWHC 1414 (QB); [2011] 1 W.L.R.
1985; *Cammish v Hughes* [2012] EWCA Civ 1655; [2013] E.M.L.R. 13 at [38].

where the claimant is a company.[99] However, given the form of the statutory provision, except where it is obvious, it will be important for a claimant to adduce evidence showing the damage which the defamatory words have caused, or are likely to cause, damage which will or should have been pleaded.[100] A higher corporate threshold has been prospectively introduced by s.1(2), by which harm to the reputation of a body that trades for profit is not "serious harm" unless it has caused or is likely to cause the body serious financial loss. This will also have to be proved with evidence.

32.26 **Natural and ordinary meaning.** Where the claimant is relying on the natural and ordinary meaning of the words complained of, no evidence of their meaning is admissible or of the sense in which they were understood,[101] or of any facts giving rise to inferences to be drawn from the words used.[102] It is for the jury to determine the sense in which the words would reasonably have been understood by an ordinary man in the light of generally known facts and meanings of words.[103] Thus evidence of the meaning of a slang expression which has passed into common use would not be admissible.[104]

---

[99] See for instance per Tugendhat J. in *Euromoney Institutional Investor plc v Aviation News Ltd* [2013] EWHC 1505 (QB) at [24] (and see the cases there cited):
"... the likely effect upon a corporate claimant of any words complained of by it may not be sufficiently serious to provide the necessary justification for an interference with freedom of expression, even if they would have provided a sufficient justification for interference with the defendant's rights if the claimant were an individual."

[100] See paras 2.5 et seq., above.

[101] A rule described as "well settled" by Lord Bridge in *Charleston v News Group Newspapers* [1995] 2 A.C. 65 at 70; and see Diplock L.J. in *Slim v Daily Telegraph Ltd* [1968] 2 Q.B. 157 at 173. This passage was approved in *John Fairfax v Hook* (1983) 72 F.L.R. 190.

[102] Cf. *Tolley v Fry* [1931] A.C. 333, where evidence was given without objection which came close to stating the sense in which the advertisement complained of would have been understood. Generally, if evidence of facts is necessary to establish a defamatory inference, that would not be a natural and ordinary meaning but one arising from extrinsic facts, *ergo* an innuendo meaning.

[103] In *Favell v Queensland Newspapers* [2005] HCA 52, 221 A.L.R. 186, Kirby J. at [23] criticized what he called "the fiction of the ordinary reasonable reader". And at [24] he suggested: "It would be preferable to drop this fiction altogether. Judges should not hide behind their pretended reliance on the fictitious reasonable recipient of the alleged defamatory material attributing to such person the outcome that the judges actually determine for themselves".
The judge encouraged the emergence of a new formulation to explain more precisely why one imputation is held defamatory and another is not.
In *Nikowitz v Verlagsgruppe* (App. No.5266/03) the Austrian court had held that a satirical article was defamatory, but the ECHR (February 22, 2007) disagreed, ruling that it was plainly meant to be humorous, and that the applicants' conviction for defamation was a breach of their art.10 rights. The ordinary reasonable reader is not prone to misunderstanding.

[104] In 1858 the term "blackleg" was considered to have passed into common use (per Pollock C.B. in *Barnett v Allen* (1858) 3 H. & N. 376 at 379); but its meaning at that time was associated with gambling, not strike-breaking. In *Bass v TCN Channel Nine Pty* [2006] NSWCA 343 part of the words complained of was that the plaintiff was a "shonky operator". "Shonky" was an expression which had apparently in the course of time undergone various changes of meanings, albeit all derogatory (see Hunt A.J.A. at [5] and [6]), but no evidence seems to have been given as to its current meaning.

Context. As the natural and ordinary meaning has to be obtained from a   **32.27**
consideration of the words in their context,[105] the claimant must put in any
document which forms part of the context.[106] In the case of a libel in a
newspaper, the claimant should put in the whole of the article containing the
words complained of, and any other article or item in the same issue which he
contends lends colour, emphasis or meaning to the words. Where either party
relies for meaning on more than one article in the same newspaper, the key
issue is whether the articles are sufficiently closely connected to be regarded
as a single publication, and it makes no difference of principle whether the
articles are on continuation pages or a different part of the same newspaper.[107]
So also in the case of an internet libel, where it may be appropriate to put in
any other page from which the reader would have proceeded (e.g. by hyperlink) to the words complained of. Articles in other issues of a newspaper,
before or after the article complained of, may on occasion be properly
regarded as part of the context, for instance where the article is part of a
series.[108] Where the libel is contained in a letter, a previous letter (referred to
in the letter complained of and read by the publishee of the alleged libel), may
be put in evidence.[109] In slander cases, evidence can be given of the surrounding words, for instance the form of the question to which the words were given
in answer, or the general course of the speech of which the words complained

---

[105] *Nevill v Fine Art* [1897] A.C. 68 at 72; *Charleston v News Group Newspapers Ltd*,
above.

[106] The claimant will be restricted to documents which he has pleaded as part of the context:
Bookbinder v Tebbit [1989] 1 W.L.R. 640 at 647.

[107] *Dee v Telegraph Media Group Ltd* [2010] EWHC 924 (QB); [2010] E.M.L.R. 20, where the
words complained of were on the front page of the newspaper, where the words: "Full story: S20"
appeared. The claimant made no complaint about the article in S20 (part of a sport supplement),
but the defendant relied on it, arguing that the front page article had to be read together with S20.
Sharp J. held that the ordinary reasonable reader was to be taken to have read the passages to
which he was directed on subsequent pages, so that the two articles had to be read together to
ascertain the meaning of the front page article complained of.

[108] See *Burrows v Knightley* (1987) 10 N.S.W.L.R. 651 where Hunt J. permitted material, i.e.
serialisation of a book in a newspaper, published on different days to be pleaded in one paragraph
of the statement of claim on the grounds that there was either an intention on the part of the
defendants that the material be read together or the reader might reasonably be expected to read
it together. Evidence of previous articles was admitted in *English and Scottish Co-operative v
Odhams Press* [1940] 1 K.B. 440, but it seems there was no objection. In many situations, the
reasoning in *Telnikoff v Matusevitch* [1992] 2 A.C. 343 may be applicable: readers of the words
complained of may not have seen the other article in a previous issue or had it in mind. And it
has been observed that subsequent articles can hardly affect the meaning of words at the time they
were published. See *Simons Proprietary Ltd v Riddell* [1941] N.Z.L.R. 913; *Grappelli v Derek
Block (Holdings) Ltd* [1981] 1 W.L.R. 822; but compare *Hayward v Thompson* [1982] Q.B. 47,
where a subsequent article was relied upon for identification. In *Galloway v Telegraph Group*
[2004] EWHC 276 (QB); [2005] E.M.L.R. 7 Eady J. directed a jury who had to consider parts of
newspaper articles spread over two days that the first day's article could be borne in mind when
considering the meaning of the second day's article, but not the other way round. This topic is also
discussed in para.3.33, above and (in relation to identification of the claimant) in para.32.21,
above. In some cases subsequent articles are admitted on the issue of damages, to show repetition
of the libel: e.g. *Darby v Ouseley* (1856) 1 H. & N. 1.

[109] *White v Bourgin* (1917) 204 Ill.App.R. 83.

of formed a part.[110] It has been stated that what properly forms part of the context should be decided by reference to what ordinary reasonable readers would regard as part of the context.[111]

32.28 Innuendo. Where the claimant relies on an innuendo meaning, that is to say a meaning derived from special facts extrinsic to the words, he can give evidence of facts pleaded in support of the innuendo meaning which he contends would have led reasonable persons to understand the words in that meaning. The claimant must prove that the relevant facts and circumstances were known to those persons to who the words were published.[112] Thus evidence of facts or circumstances unknown to those persons to whom the words were published could not be led, for they could not have been influenced in their understanding of the words by facts and circumstances of which they were unaware.[113] Further, for the evidence to be admissible, the facts and circumstances must have existed at or before the time when the words were published. Thus, where a company published an advertisement in a newspaper naming two persons who, it was announced, were no longer in the company's employment, evidence of a news item published a week later, that one of the persons had been convicted on a charge of fraud, was ruled inadmissible to support a defamatory meaning.[114] There is no need for the claimant to prove that the defendant knew or should reasonably have foreseen that the words complained of bore the innuendo meaning alleged.[115]

32.29 Interpretation of words. It has long been an established practice that where the claimant has pleaded an innuendo he may, in addition to calling

---

[110] *Bookbinder v Tebbit*, above, per Ralph Gibson L.J. at 647. The context may be crucial: for instance, in *Thompson v Bernard* (1807) 1 Campbell 48, 170 E.R. 872, the defendant said that the plaintiff "is a damned thief; and so was his father before him; and I can prove it". However, evidence was given that he then added, "Thompson received the earnings of the ship, and ought to pay the wages". In context, the words did not impute the felony of theft.

[111] See *Australian Broadcasting Corp v Obeid* [2006] NSWCA 231, where the words complained of were broadcast at various times in the course of a three hour programme and there was a dispute as to what parts of the broadcast should be considered as part of the context for the purpose of deciding the meaning of the words complained of.

[112] "The evidence required is evidence of special facts causing the words to have a meaning revealed to those who knew the special facts, but not revealed by the words used in the absence of such knowledge," per Greer L.J. in *Tolley v Fry* [1930] 1 K.B. 467 at 480, applied by Slesser L.J. in *Hough v London Express* [1940] 2 K.B. at 514. See also *Baturina v Times Newspapers Ltd* [2011] EWCA Civ 308, [2011] 1 W.L.R. 1526; *Capital and Counties Bank Ltd v Henty* (1882) 7 A.C. 741 at 771 and *Fullam v Newcastle Chronicle* [1977] 1 W.L.R. 651. This may be a matter of inference, e.g. "where the publication is in a national newspaper with a very wide circulation, and the only reasonable inference is that some of the readers of that newspaper must have knowledge of the facts which are said to give rise to the innuendo": Dunn L.J in *Grappelli v Derek Block (Holdings) Ltd* [1981] 1 W.L.R. 822 at 880, and see *Fullam v Newcastle Chronicle*, above, per Scarman L.J. at 659.

[113] Per Brett L.J. in *Capital and Counties Bank v Henty* (1880) 5 C.P.D. at 539, 542; per Russell L.J. in *Cassidy v Daily Mirror* [1929] 2 K.B. 331 at 353.

[114] *Simons Proprietary Ltd v Riddell* [1941] N.Z.L.R. 913. And see *Capital and Counties Bank v Henty* (1882) 7 A.C. 741 and *Grappelli v Derek Block (Holdings) Ltd* [1981] 1 W.L.R. 822.

[115] *Baturina v Times Newspapers Ltd* [2011] EWCA Civ 308; [2011] 1 W.L.R. 1526.

evidence of the extrinsic facts on which he relies, call witnesses who know the extrinsic facts to state the meaning in which they understood the words. The practice seems to stem from the same source as that which applies to evidence concerning the identification of the claimant.[116] As with identification evidence, the jury are not bound to adopt the opinions of witnesses as to the meanings in which the words would be understood by those with knowledge of the extrinsic facts, or to accept evidence as to how the words were understood: they are entitled to reach their own conclusions. Under this rule, evidence is admissible as to the meaning of slang expressions, or local or special terms, not in general use but familiarly known and employed by certain people in a certain district or region.[117] This would clearly extend to trade or technical jargon in use by those engaged in the material activity. The meaning of the expression is regarded as an extrinsic fact, and pleaded as such, as are the persons or categories of persons who know the meaning.[118] The critical test as to whether evidence of meaning is admissible is the extent to which the expression is known or in use.[119] Where the slang expression "has been used long enough to be understood, not only by experts in slang, but by the public at large, no such evidence is admissible".[120] The meaning is then a natural and ordinary meaning, which cannot be explained by any witness.[121] However, doubt has been cast on the practice of calling witnesses

---

[116] See paras 32.20–32.22, above, and, e.g. *Broome v Gosden* (1845) 1 C.B. 728, 135 E.R. 728. Some practitioners speak of "reference innuendos" and "meaning innuendos", i.e. identification of the unnamed claimant by reference to facts, and defamatory meanings arising by virtue of extrinsic facts.

[117] *Barnett v Allen* 157 E.R. 516, (1858) 3 H. & N. 376; and see e.g. *Thaarup v Hutton Press* (1943) 169 L.T. 309 ("pansy"); *Fields v Davis, The Times*, May 25, 1955 ("tramp"); and *Winyard v Tatler Publishing Co.*, unreported, June 16, 1991, CA ("the international boot", Scots slang which was explained to the jury by a sergeant in the Strathclyde Police as meaning "a whore"). The 8th edition of this book suggested that the rule applies where the words are foreign words. This seems incorrect: it is suggested that where the words complained of are in a foreign language, evidence should be given of their English translation, but not, if a natural and ordinary meaning is complained of, of the defamatory meanings in which they were understood: see para. 32.16, above.

[118] *Fullam v Newcastle Chronicle* [1977] 1 W.L.R. 651. In *Bovis v Thorne, The Times*, July 14, 1926, Horridge J. ruled that evidence that the words bore a special meaning different from the natural and ordinary meaning was inadmissible as no such meaning had been pleaded.

[119] In *Fox v Boulter* [2013] EWHC 1435 (QB) at [16], Bean J. said this:
"I regard 'general knowledge' as referring to what Lord Mansfield CJ in *R v Horne* [1775–1802] All E.R. Rep. 390 at 393E called 'matters of universal notoriety'—that is to say, matters which any intelligent viewer or reader may be expected to know. Anything which requires assiduous reading and a good memory so as to recall the facts of a story dating back several weeks or months cannot fall within that definition. To give the term 'general knowledge' such a wide interpretation would erode the distinction between ordinary and natural meaning on the one hand and innuendo meaning on the other, and would breach the well established rule that evidence is inadmissible on the issue of the natural and ordinary meaning of the words complained of."

[120] Per Pollock C.B. in *Barnett v Allen*, above, at 379.

[121] See para.32.26, above. Cf. *Daines v Hartley* (1848) 3 Exch. 200, 154 E.R. 815; *Duke of Brunswick v Harmer* (1849) 3 Carr. & K. 10, 175 E.R. 441 (witness not allowed to explain the meaning of word "natural"). In *Daines v Hartley* the question "What did you understand by those words?" was ruled inadmissible by Pollock C.B. For the question properly to be put it was

of extrinsic fact to explain how they understood the words by Sedley L.J. in the case of *Baturina v Times Newspapers Ltd*,[122] where an innuendo meaning depended on proof that readers would have been aware of a provision of Russian law. In an apparently obiter passage at [56], Sedley L.J. said this:

> "My other chief misgiving, though possibly a misplaced one, arises from what appeared from time to time to be an assumption that it will be open to Mrs Baturina to call witnesses to testify to how they reacted to the Sunday Times story in the light of their extrinsic knowledge. It will of course be for the trial judge to decide what evidence is admissible, but in principle it is the jury or, absent a jury, the judge whose task is to decide what a reasonable reader will have made of a publication. Where an innuendo is relied on, their judgment will of course be informed by evidence of what the reasonable reader will additionally have known. But it is not the case that a claimant is entitled without more to put into the witness box a series of witnesses to say on oath what they made of the publication. It may be otherwise where for example a special and limited class of reader is relied on, or where it is necessary to prove damage of a particular kind. But in principle the meaning and effect of the published words, either by themselves or when married with proven extraneous facts, is what the court itself is there to decide."

32.30 Claimant's interpretation of the words. Where the claimant relies on the natural and ordinary meaning he is equally subject to the rule that evidence cannot be given as to meaning. Thus he cannot be asked what he understood the words to mean.[123] The claimant may be able to give evidence on meaning, if he has pleaded an innuendo:

> "I do not see that the evidence of either party as to what is (or is not) the slang meaning should be excluded. To prevent the parties giving evidence when any other witness can would be to return to the days of *Bardell v Pickwick*."[124]

32.31 Damaging nature of a statement. Evidence has been admitted to show that a statement bearing a particular meaning is damaging to the claimant's

---

adjudged necessary to ask first of all, "Was there anything to prevent those words from conveying the meaning which ordinarily they would convey?" and for evidence to be given of that. But Pollock C.B. would seem to have in mind context rather than extrinsic facts:

> "Something may have previously passed which gives a peculiar character and meaning to some expression, and some word which ordinarily or popularly is used in one sense may, from something that has gone before be restricted and confined to a particular sense, or may mean something different from that which it ordinarily and usually does mean."

It is submitted that neither question would now be regarded as proper unless a meaning arising from extrinsic facts was pleaded.

[122] [2011] EWCA Civ 308; [2011] 1 W.L.R. 1526. Hooper L.J. agreed with Sedley L.J.'s judgment (and that of the Master of the Rolls).

[123] He can, however, be asked, in the context of damages, about the effect of the publication of the libel upon him (see para.32.54), and an intelligible answer usually involves some reference to the claimant's understanding of the meaning of the words. But the jury are usually warned that this is not evidence of meaning, and it should be ignored in relation to that issue. See *Hughes v Mirror Newspapers Ltd* [1985] 3 N.S.W.L.R. 504.

[124] Per Staughton L.J. in *Winyard v Tatler Publishing Co. Ltd*, above. The 8th and earlier editions of this book maintained, on the authority of *Wood v Mackey* (1881) 21 N.B.R. 109, that the plaintiff could not give evidence as to meaning even where an innuendo meaning was relied upon. It is submitted that Staughton L.J.'s is the more rational approach.

reputation.[125] Thus, where the words complained of suggested that the plaintiff had consented to the use of his name in advertisements, evidence was admissible of the effect that this would have on his reputation as an amateur golfer,[126] and where a story was published not written by the plaintiff but carrying his name as the author, evidence was given of the inferior quality of the writing causing the attribution of authorship to convey a defamatory meaning.[127] When s.1, Defamation Act 2013 is brought into force, evidence that serious harm to reputation has been caused or is likely to be caused will be essential except in obvious cases.[128]

Burden of proof. "Burden of proof" is perhaps an inapt phrase to use with **32.32** reference to an issue upon which evidence is not admissible unless it is alleged that the words are defamatory by virtue of an innuendo meaning. However, the burden is generally upon the claimant to satisfy the jury that the words in their natural and ordinary meaning convey a defamatory imputation.[129] With an innuendo meaning the burden is on the claimant to prove the existence of extrinsic facts, that such facts caused the words to bear a defamatory meaning to reasonable persons with knowledge of the facts, and that there were one or more persons amongst those to whom the words were published who had such knowledge.[130] It is unnecessary to prove that anyone did in fact understand the words in the defamatory sense alleged.[131]

Section 6. Evidence of Malice

Introduction. Proof of express malice is necessary to defeat the defences of **32.33** qualified privilege, whether under common law or statute, and to establish a cause of action for malicious falsehood. However, it need not be proved in the case of a plea of *Reynolds* privilege, where "the propriety of the defendant's

---

[125] See also para.32.53, below.

[126] *Tolley v Fry* [1931] A.C. 333. In *Reader's Digest Services v Lamb* [1982] 150 C.L.R. 500, Brennan J. stated (at 507) that it could be proved that a defamatory imputation had an especially adverse impact on the plaintiff's reputation in the eyes of some group or class in the community.

[127] *Ridge v English Illustrated* (1913) 29 T.L.R. 592; and see *Moraes v Electric Pavilion, The Times*, October 30, 1925 (singer mistakenly included in programme).

[128] See para.32.25, above.

[129] *Capital and Counties Bank v Henty* (1882) 7 A.C. 741 at 782; *Jones v Skelton* [1963] 1 W.L.R. 1362 at 1377. Nowadays the meaning would be that pleaded in the particulars of claim, or a less injurious meaning of the same kind: see Ch.26, s.6, above, and *Slim v Daily Telegraph* [1968] 2 Q.B. 157. If the defendant seeks to justify different meanings then it must be for him to persuade the jury that those are the meanings borne by the words.

[130] *Capital and Counties Bank v Henty*, above; *Nevill v Fine Arts* [1897] A.C. 68 at 79; *Frost v London JS Bank* (1906) 22 T.L.R. 760; *Hough v London Express* [1940] 2 K.B. 507; *Horrocks v Lowe* [1975] A.C. 135.

[131] *Hough v London Express*, above.

conduct is built in to the conditions under which the material is privileged".[132] Malice in honest comment requires proof that the defendant did not hold the view that he expressed.[133] Express malice may be a ground for claiming aggravated damages. Further, if malice is proved against the defendant he may not rely in support of a plea of justification (truth) upon convictions in respect of which the claimant has become rehabilitated under the Rehabilitation of Offenders Act 1974.[134]

32.34 Definition. As has been explained earlier in this work,[135] express malice is not susceptible to a single definition which is broadly applicable to the varying circumstances where it arises as an issue. In the context of qualified privilege[136] it can be described as acting not out of a sense of duty giving rise to the privilege but from some improper motive. Where express malice has been alleged in response to the defence of honest comment the claimant will have to show that the defendant (if the author of the comment) did not honestly hold the views expressed.[137] Malice as an ingredient of the tort of malicious falsehood has been stated to be the same as malice for the purpose of defeating a defence of qualified privilege in libel and slander cases.[138] As for malice

---

[132] *Jameel (Mohammed) v Wall Street Journal Sprl* [2006] UKHL 44; [2007] 1 A.C. 359, per Lord Hoffmann at [46]. Reynolds privilege is prospectively abolished by Defamation Act 2013, s.4 and replaced by the defence of publication on a matter of public interest. See para.15.21, above.

[133] "It is important to note . . . that the significance of malice in (the context of fair comment) has been significantly reduced in recent years by the recognition that motive is largely irrelevant in the context of the expression of honest opinions and that, essentially, the important question for the purposes of fair comment is whether or not the commentator honestly held the opinion expressed"
(per Eady J., *Crossley v Newsquest* [2008] EWHC 3054 (QB) at [48]). Lord Nicholls' judgment in *Tse Wai Chun v Cheng* [2000] HKCFA 86 [2001] E.M.L.R. 31 shows that malice in fair comment is a subjective question, and entails proof that the defendant did not genuinely hold the view he expressed. Thus if the defendant knew that his comments were untrue, or was recklessly indifferent to the truth or falsity of his comments, that would constitute malice. The fact that the defendant was actuated by spite, animosity, intent to injure, intent to arouse controversy or other motivation, even if it was the dominant or sole motive, would not of itself defeat the defence, but might be compelling evidence from which lack of genuine belief in the view expressed could be inferred. See also *Joseph v Spiller* [2010] UKSC 53, [2011] 1 A.C. 852 at [108], and *Cammish v Hughes* [2012] EWCA Civ 1655, [2013] E.M.L.R. 13.
Note that the common law defence of fair comment, already renamed "honest comment" by the Supreme Court in *Joseph v Spiller* [2010] UKSC 53, [2011] 1 A.C. 852, has been prospectively abolished by Defamation Act 2013, s.3, and replaced by the statutory defence of honest opinion, which will be defeated by proof that the defendant did not hold the opinion claimed or (where the statement complained of was published by the defendant but made by someone else) that the defendant knew or ought to have known that the author did not hold that opinion. For analysis of the new provision, see para.12.4, above.

[134] S.8(5) of the Act. The term is not defined.

[135] See Ch.17 and para.12.36, above.

[136] But not *Reynolds* or public interest privilege: see para.15.21, above.

[137] *Tse Wai Chun v Cheng* [2000] HKCFA 86 [2001] E.M.L.R. 31.

[138] *Spring v Guardian Assurance* [1993] 2 All E.R. 273 CA at 288. Glidewell L.J. quoted extensively from the speech of Lord Diplock in *Horrocks v Lowe* [1975] A.C. 135 at 150, and he clearly had in mind Lord Diplock's explanation of what constitutes malice where qualified privilege is claimed. The decision was reversed on the issue of negligence, but the ruling on

which aggravates the damage, it would primarily involve spite, or ill-will, or a desire to injure the claimant as the motivating factor for publishing the defamatory material.[139]

This section will chiefly focus on evidence of malice which will defeat the defence of qualified privilege.

No honest belief. In whatever context malice is raised, evidence tending to show, or from which it can be inferred, that the defendant had no honest belief in the truth of the defamatory statement will usually be powerful evidence of malice.

32.35

> "If it be proved that (the defendant) did not believe that what he published was true this is generally conclusive evidence of express malice, for no sense of duty to protect his own legitimate interests can justify a man in telling deliberate falsehoods about another, save in the exceptional case where a person may be under a duty to pass on without endorsing, defamatory reports made by some other person".[140]

There is a division of view as to whether it is absence of honest belief (as suggested by Lord Diplock in the above passage) or improper motive which is definitive of malice,[141] though the better view is probably the latter.[142] As was pointed out by Gray J. in *Rackham v Sandy*,[143] the point will usually be of limited practical significance, since knowledge of falsity will in nearly every instance establish the existence of an improper motive.[144] So also in the context of comment,

---

malicious falsehood was not appealed. The rationale of the decision is questionable. In the majority of malicious falsehood cases no question of a "privilege"—capable of being mis-used—arises: publishers are simply exercising the right of speech or expression freely available to all. For a more recent case on the same topic, see *Quinton v Peirce* [2009] EWHC 912 (QB), [2009] F.S.R. 17 at [83].

[139] See Lord Devlin in *Rookes v Barnard* [1964] A.C. 1129 at 1221.

[140] Per Lord Diplock in *Horrocks v Lowe* [1975] A.C. 135 at 149–150.

[141] The latter is the Australian view. See for instance *Roberts v Bass* [2002] HCA 57; 212 C.L.R. 1 at [78]: "In the law of qualified privilege, the common law has always regarded malice as the publishing of defamatory material with an improper motive. Knowledge of falsity is "almost conclusive evidence" that the defendant had some improper motive in publishing the material and that it actuated the publication. That judges have treated knowledge of falsity as almost conclusive evidence of malice is no ground, however, for treating it as a separate head of, or equivalent to, malice." (per Gaudron, McHugh and Gummow JJ). At [76], it was said by the same judges that "leaving aside the special case of knowledge of falsity, mere proof of the defendant's ill-will, prejudice, bias, recklessness, lack of belief in truth or improper motive is not sufficient to establish malice". See also the statement of Graham J. derived from *Roberts v Bass* in *National Auto Glass Supplies (Australia) Pty v Nielsen* [2007] FCA 1625 at [259]: "malice means a motive for, or a purpose of, defaming the plaintiff that is inconsistent with the duty or interest that protects the occasion of the publication. It is the motive or purpose for which the occasion is used that is ultimately decisive, not the defendant's belief in the truth of the matter." See also *Marshall v Megna* [2013] NSWCA 30 and *Cush v Dillon* [2011] HCA 30, 243 C.L.R. 298.

[142] See para.17.4, above.

[143] [2005] EWHC 482 (QB).

[144] But not, according to *Gross v Weston* [2007] NSWCA 1, if there is no more proved than mere absence of a positive belief in the truth of what was published.

"A comment which falls within the objective limits of the defence of fair comment can lose its immunity only by proof that the defendant did not genuinely hold the view he expressed. Honesty of belief is the touchstone."[145]

Thus evidence of inconsistent or contradictory statements by the defendant would be admissible; so too evidence of conduct by the defendant which is not readily reconcilable with a belief in the truth of the defamatory allegation he has made.[146] If the words complained of convey a defamatory meaning which the defendant knew to be untrue but he did not intend to convey, and the intended meaning was believed by the defendant to be true, that does not amount to malice.[147]

In privilege cases proof that the defendant honestly believed that the false statement was true does not necessarily exclude a finding of malice if there is evidence that the statement was made with the intention of harming the claimant.[148] Where there is likely to be a defence of fair and accurate report under the Defamation Act 1996, s.15, evidence of actual knowledge by the defendant of the falsity or unfairness of the report (or reckless indifference) will be good evidence of malice.[149]

32.36 Recklessness. Recklessness as to the truth of a defamatory statement, not caring whether it be true or false, is treated as equivalent to knowledge that it is false.[150] Thus evidence may be led which indicates such a disposition on the part of the defendant, that, e.g. he deliberately abstained from availing himself of means of information readily to hand which would have shown the

---

[145] Per Lord Nicholls in *Tse Wai Chun v Cheng* [2000] HKCFA 86 [2001] E.M.L.R. 31 at [79]. The reason for this, as far as fair or honest comment is concerned, is that the defence exists to further and facilitate freedom of expression by conferring legitimacy on the voicing of opinions on matters of public interest; it is in the public interest that everyone should be free to express his own honestly held views on such matters. If they are not the defendant's honestly held views there are no grounds to afford him such a defence. See also *Crossley v Newsquest* [2008] EWHC 3054 (QB) at [48], *Joseph v Spiller* [2010] UKSC 53, [2011] 1 A.C. 852 at [108], and *Cammish v Hughes* [2012] EWCA Civ 1655, [2013] E.M.L.R. 13.

[146] In *Fountain v Boodle* (1842) 3 Q.B. 5, where the complaint arose from an allegation by the defendant that the plaintiff, formerly in the defendant's employ as a governess, had been incompetent and not "ladylike nor good tempered", evidence was left to the jury that the defendant had kept the plaintiff in her service for a year without complaint about her competence, temper or manners, and that she had recommended the plaintiff to other persons for a similar situation. It was held that such evidence was rightly admitted on the issue whether the defendant believed her unfavourable reference was true.

[147] *Loveless v Earl* [1999] E.M.L.R.27; *Alexander v Arts Council of Wales* [2001] EWCA Civ 242; [2001] 1 W.L.R. 1840. In *Crossland v Wilkinson Hardware Stores* [2005] EWHC 481 (QB) Tugendhat J. pointed out that meaning and malice were often linked as it was common for a claimant to pitch the meaning high and then say that the defendant could not have believed that meaning. In such cases it was important that the words were given their ordinary meaning. See also para.17.20, above.

[148] *Wilts United Dairies v Thomas Robinson* [1957] R.P.C. 220 at 237.

[149] *Qadir v Associated Newspapers Ltd* [2012] EWHC 2606 (QB); [2013] E.M.L.R. 327.

[150] *Horrocks v Lowe*, above. So too if the defendant was recklessly indifferent to the truth or falsity of his comment: *Tse Wai Chun v Cheng*, above, at [40].

imputation to be groundless.[151] Recklessness is not, however, to be equated with "carelessness, impulsiveness, or irrationality".[152] Thus, if the defendant honestly believed his statement to be true, it may not matter that he failed to investigate it beforehand. Omission to make any inquiry in such circumstances is not itself evidence of malice.[153] It has been suggested that malice could arise if the defamatory charge was made, not on the evidence of the defendant's own senses, and a slight inquiry would have shown that the charge was unfounded.[154] Wilful blindness to the real facts has been said to be a test by which a jury may be led to consider whether the defendant did or did not really believe his statement to be true[155]; recently, it has been treated as effectively synonymous with indifference to the truth and as pointing clearly to malice.[156]

Sources of evidence. Apart from evidence tending to show absence of honest belief or recklessness, the sources of evidence of malice[157] can be placed in four categories: **32.37**

> (1) extrinsic evidence, that is to say, "something outside the [libellous] statement itself"[158];

---

[151] See *Royal Aquarium v Parkinson* [1892] 1 Q.B. 431: the defendant had accused the plaintiff of putting on a performance which included "the most indecent action" between a male and a female figure. There was evidence of the innocent nature of the performance by two figures representing not a male and female, but two males dressed as a clown and a pantaloon. Lord Esher M.R. stated (at 44) that the defendant had "allowed his mind to get into such a reckless state of prejudice that he was regardless of the interests of other persons, and whether what he was saying was true or false". That justified the jury in finding malice. For a discussion of the concept of recklessness, see para.17.16, above.

[152] See *Horrocks v Lowe*, above, at p.150. There must be a "genuine indifference" to the truth or falsity of the words: *Hughes v Risbridger* [2010] EWHC 491 (QB) at [24]. Carelessness, impulsiveness or irrationality plainly could not suffice, because a finding of malice is akin to a finding of dishonesty or fraud (*Hughes v Risbridger* [2010] EWHC 491 (QB) at [24]; *Monks v Warwick DC* [2009] EWHC 959 (QB) at [27], citing *Three Rivers DC v Bank of England* [2003] 2 A.C. 1 at [161], per Lord Hobhouse: "Dishonesty is not to be inferred from evidence which is equally consistent with mere negligence"). For that reason, findings of malice are rare, whether at trial or (a fortiori) on summary application, where it has been said that although such a finding might in theory be possible, "It could scarcely be so where a real issue turns on the defendant's state of mind and a credibility judgment is required": *Hayter v Fahie* [2008] EWCA Civ 1336 at [23], per Sir Anthony May P. See also *Hughes v Alan Dick & Co. Ltd* [2008] EWHC 2695 (QB) at [16].

[153] *Clark v Roe* (1854) 4 Ir. C.L.R. 1 at 9; *Clark v Molyneux* (1877) 3 Q.B.D. 237 at 249; *Cook v Brogden* (1885) 1 T.L.R. 497 at 498; *A B v X Y*, 1917 S.C. 15; *Horrocks v Lowe* [1975] A.C. 135.

[154] Per Lord Salvesen in *A B v X Y*, 1917 S.C. 15 at 23; *Uren v John Fairfax* (1966) 117 C.L.R. 118 at 125. But failing to make inquiry through carelessness is not evidence of malice: *Cooke v Brogden* (1885) 1 T.L.R. 497.

[155] Per Brett L.J. in *Clark v Molyneux*, above, at 248.

[156] *Cambridge v Makin* [2012] EWCA Civ 85; [2012] E.M.L.R. 19 at [62]–[63], where the defendant had in his hands the documents on which he relied as substantiating his charge but had closed his eyes to the obvious, namely that they did no such thing. It was found that he did not care whether his allegation was true or false.

[157] The term is here used in the broad sense as explained in *Horrocks v Lowe*, above.

[158] *Nevill v Fine Arts and General Insurance Co. Ltd* [1895] 2 Q.B. 156 at 171, per Lopes L.J.; *Horrocks v Lowe*, above, at 151, per Lord Diplock.

(2) intrinsic evidence, that is to say, "something contained in the [libellous] statement itself"[159];

(3) the circumstances of the publication; and

(4) the conduct of the defendant in the course of the litigation and at trial.

The existence of malice at the time of, and actuating, publication must be proved, but almost invariably this can only be proved by inference which the jury can be asked to draw from evidence concerning acts and conduct of the defendant both before and after publication.

32.38 Extrinsic evidence.

"There may be evidence of the defendant's conduct upon occasions other than that protected by the privilege which justify the inference that upon the privileged occasion too his dominant motive in publishing what he did was personal spite or some other improper motive."[160]

Thus evidence of the defendant's expressions of personal spite or ill will towards the claimant,[161] evidence that the defendant had some previous quarrel with the claimant,[162] or brought unsuccessful actions against him, or had spoken disparagingly about him is relevant. "Anything that shows that the plaintiff and the defendant lived on bad terms may bear on the issue of malice".[163]

32.39 Other defamatory words and repetition. Other defamatory words published by the defendant about the claimant can be relied upon as evidence of malice,[164] even though they are not the subject of an action, and were published after the action began.[165] Repetition of a slander may be evidence

---

[159] Ibid.

[160] *Horrocks v Lowe*, above, at 151, per Lord Diplock.

[161] Per Parke B. in *Wright v Woodgate* (1835) 2 C.M. & R. 573 at 577. Though personal spite or ill will motivating publication of the defamatory comment will not in itself be malice defeating the defence of fair comment it may be evidence, "sometimes compelling evidence", from which lack of genuine belief in the view expressed may be inferred, and therefore admissible: *Tse Wai Chun v Cheng* [2000] HKCFA 86; [2001] E.M.L.R. 31 at [79].

[162] *Simpson v Robinson* (1848) 12 Q.B. 511.

[163] Per Denman C.J. in *Simpson v Robinson* (1848) 12 Q.B. 511, above, at 515.

[164] "You may give in evidence any words as well as any act of the defendant to show *quo animo* he spoke the words which are the subject of the action", per Lord Ellenborough in *Rustel v Macquister* (reported as a note to *Thompson v Bernard* (1807) 1 Campbell 48, 170 E.R. 872). It seems that it would be open to the defendant to prove the truth of the words: *Warne v Chadwell* (1819) 2 Stark. 457.

[165] *Pearson v Lemaitre* (1843) 5 M. & Gr. 700: "If the evidence given for that purpose [to prove the existence of a malicious motive] establishes another cause of action, the jury should be cautioned against giving any damages in respect of it"; per Tindall C.J. at 720. Furthermore, the jury must be satisfied that it is possible to impute malice from the *subsequent* publication at the time of publication of the words complained of, and not just malice at a subsequent time: *Hemmings v Gasson* (1858) E.B. & E. 346. See also *Herald v McGregor* (1928) 41 C.L.R. 254: malice at the time of the subsequent publication may be grounds for aggravated damages, and *ZAM v CFW* [2013] EWHC 662 (QB): subsequent publication may be relied on as evidence of malice, and (even if not complained of as a further cause of action) as adding to the claimant's distress, and therefore as aggravating damages.

of malice.[166] So too, evidence that the defendant inserted in a subsequent edition of the same newspaper a paragraph reasserting the truth of the libel,[167] or published subsequent articles attacking the claimant and alluding to the libel action,[168] or procured the publication of the same, or substantially the same, libel in some other newspaper.[169]

Intrinsic evidence. Malice may be inferred from the terms of the words complained of.[170]   **32.40**

> "It may be that the language used in a libel, though under other circumstances justifiable, may be so much too violent for the occasion and circumstances . . . as to form strong evidence of malice . . . and that an inference of actual malice may be drawn from its use".[171]

However, though unnecessarily strong language disproportionate to the occasion may be some evidence of malice,[172] or a matter from which malice might be inferred,[173] the tendency of the courts is not to be over-critical of the force or warmth of language used on a privileged occasion,[174] especially where it is used in self-defence or in vindication of character,[175] and it appears that where the only evidence of improper motive lies in the language used, the claimant must show affirmatively that the defendant did not believe it to be true or was indifferent to its truth or falsity.[176]

---

[166] *Defries v Davis* (1835) 7 Carrington and Payne 112, 173 E.R. 50.

[167] *Barwell v Adkins* (1840) 1 M. & Gr. 807. "Suppose", said Sir James Mansfield C.J. in *Finnerty v Tipper* (1809) 2 Camp. 72 at 74 "a man published a libel, and afterwards published a paper saying that everything in the libel was true, that . . . might be read at the trial to prove the malice of the original publication".

[168] *Chubb v Westley* (1834) 6 Carr. & P. 436.

[169] *Delegal v Highley* (1837) 8 Carr. & P. 444.

[170] *Thomas v Bradbury, Agnew* [1906] 2 K.B. 627 at 637.

[171] Per Cockburn C.J. in *Spill v Maule* (1869) L.R. 4 Ex. 232 at 235.

[172] E.g. *Robertson v McDougal* (1824) 4 Bing. 670; *Cooke v Wildes* (1855) 5 E. & B. 328; *George v Goddard* (1861) 2 F. & F. 689 at 691; *Oddy v Paulet* (1865) 4 F. & F. 1009.

[173] *Khader v Aziz* [2012] EWCA Civ 716; [2011] E.M.L.R. 2; *Turner v MGM* [1950] 1 All E.R. 449 at 455.

[174] See *Spill v Maule* (1869) L.R. 4 Ex. 232; Pollock B. in *Nevill v Fine Arts* [1895] 2 Q.B. 156 at 162: "The mere use of words that are stronger than the occasion demands ought not to make that a libel which if expressed in milder terms would not be so". And Tindall C.J. in *Shipley v Todhunter* (1836) 7 C. & P. 680 at 690: "It is not because strong and angry language is used that a letter is a libel. Persons differ in their expressions. We must go further, and see not merely whether the expressions are angry, but whether they are malicious." In an action between two politicians over the contents of a leaflet, the use of expressions such as "misleading and disgraceful insinuations", "total misrepresentation", "blatant distortion", and "outrage" were adjudged contemporary political rhetoric rather than evidence of malice: *Mayes v Hudson* [1993] 79 L.G.E.R.A. 65 (S.A. Sup Ct), Perry J. "To submit the language of privileged communications to a strict scrutiny and hold all excess beyond the exigency of the occasion to be evidence of malice, would in effect greatly limit, if not altogether defeat, that protection which the law throws over privileged communications": *Laughton v Bishop of Sodor and Man* (1872) L.R. 4 P.C. 495 at 508, quoted with approval in *Nevill v Fine Arts Co.*, above, at 172.

[175] *Laughton v Sodor and Man*, above; *Adam v Ward* [1917] A.C. 309.

[176] *Khader v Aziz*, above, at [29].

32.41 Irrelevant material. The claimant may cite the inclusion of irrelevant defamatory material in the words protected by privilege as evidence of malice.[177] The test is not whether the material is logically relevant, but whether in all the circumstances it can be inferred that the defendant realised that it had nothing to do with the particular duty or interest on which the privilege was based, but nevertheless "seized the opportunity to drag in irrelevant defamatory matter to vent his personal spite, or for some other improper motive".[178] Judges and juries should be slow to draw this inference.

32.42 Circumstances of publication. The deliberate adoption on a privileged occasion of a mode of communication which is more damaging than the occasion and circumstances require is evidence of malice. Thus, although a customer may use words of reasonable complaint to a tradesman whom he believes to have acted unfairly or dishonestly, and the words, though defamatory, may be excused by the occasion, it would be evidence of malice if he were to do so outside the shop and in so loud a voice as to call attention or persons passing by to his remarks.[179] A defamatory communication sent by postcard, when it might have been sent by closed letter, has been held to be evidence of malice, if the communication refers, or would be taken to refer, to a particular individual, but not if the imputation was conveyed in words which would not enable those through whose hands the postcard passed to identify the claimant.[180]

32.43 Presence of third persons. The mere fact that a slanderous communication—prima facie privileged—is made in the hearing of third persons with no legitimate interest in its subject-matter is not evidence of malice where their presence is casual and not sought by the defendant.[181] Nor would the privilege be lost if the presence of third persons was the result of an arrangement between them and the claimant,[182] but where the defendant seeks an opportunity for making before others a charge which might have been made in private,[183] or raises his voice so that others may hear what he has to say, that would be clear evidence of malice. Further:

---

[177] *Adam v Ward* [1917] A.C. 309; *Horrocks v Lowe* [1975] A.C. 135.
[178] *Horrocks v Lowe*, above, at 151; *Thompson v James* [2013] EWHC 585 (QB), at [17]–[19].
[179] *Oddy v Paulet* (1865) 4 F. & F. 1009 (although this case can be read as addressing the issue of the existence of privilege rather than evidence of malice); *Jones v Thomas* (1889) 53 L.T. 678 at 680.
[180] *Sadgrove v Hole* [1901] 2 K.B. 1 at 5, 6; and see *Williamson v Freer* (1874) L.R. 9 C.P. 393 (telegram). It may well be that nowadays no presumption would be made that postal staff read postcards, but similar reasoning would apply to a fax or a letter not marked "private and confidential" sent to the claimant's office.
[181] *Toogood v Spyring* (1834) 1 C.M. & R. 181 at 194; *Padmore v Lawrence* (1840) 11 A. & E. 380; *Jones v Thomas* (1885) 53 L.T. 678.
[182] Per Hosking J. in *Hall v Balkind* (1918) 37 N.Z.L.R. 740 at 744.
[183] Per Parke B. in *Toogood v Spyring*, above, at 194.

"If a person whose duty it is to make a statement to certain persons calls in other persons to whom he owes no duty to make the statement, in order that those other persons may hear it, . . . it would not become his duty to refrain from making his statement to the proper persons, but . . . there would be evidence of malice in his making it in the presence of others who might promulgate it".[184]

It is otherwise, however, if in calling in a third person the defendant is only doing what a prudent man would do to protect his own interests.[185]

Volunteered statements. There is some uncertainty as to whether the fact   **32.44**
that information was volunteered on a privileged occasion can be evidence of malice.[186] The existence of privilege cannot be affected by whether the statement was made voluntarily or in answer to a request.[187] However, in *Greenlands v Wilmhurst*[188] Hamilton L.J. stated:

" . . . the fact that a communication is volunteered is material on the question of malice—was the defendant a fussy busybody acting ultroneously, or a person discharging a genuine social duty?"[189]

The fact that the defamatory statement was volunteered may be capable of supporting a case that the defendant was motivated by a desire to injure the claimant or some other ulterior purpose, and was therefore malicious.

Defendant's conduct in litigation and at trial. As malice can be   **32.45**
inferred from the defendant's conduct at any time, whether before or after publication, his actions during the course of litigation, and his demeanour and attitude at trial, may be relied upon as indicative of malice. Thus malice proved to have existed at the time of trial may be believed to have existed at the time the words were published.[190] Putting forward a defence of justification is not by itself evidence of malice, since pleading truth is consistent with a belief in the truth of the words.[191] It is difficult to see how the defence could give rise to an inference of malice unless it is put forward recklessly,[192] or the defendant refuses to withdraw the defence at trial having called no evidence to support it,[193] or it is abundantly plain that the defamatory statement is

---

[184] Per Lord Esher in *Pittard v Oliver* [1891] 1 Q.B. 474 at 477, 478; and see Pollock B. in *Jones v Thomas*, above.
[185] *Taylor v Hawkins* (1851) 16 Q.B. 308 at 318, 325.
[186] *Gardener v Slade* (1849) 18 L.J.Q.B. 334 has been cited as authority for the proposition that a volunteered statement is in itself no evidence of malice.
[187] *Macintosh v Dun* [1908] A.C. 390 at 399.
[188] [1913] 3 K.B. 507.
[189] [1913] 3 K.B. 507 at 535.
[190] *Simpson v Robinson* (1848) 12 Q.B. 511; 116 E.R. 959 at 514.
[191] *Broadway Approvals v Odhams Press* [1965] 1 W.L.R. 805 at 814 and 825.
[192] *Herald v McGregor* (1928) 41 C.L.R. 254.
[193] *Simpson v Robinson*, above.

untrue.[194] Similarly, a refusal to apologise may be consistent with a belief in the truth of the defence case, and is not of itself evidence of malice.[195] However, answers given by the defendant in the course of his evidence at trial, and his demeanour in the witness box, displaying, e.g. overt hostility towards the claimant, can be urged upon the jury as indicating malice.[196] So too, that the defendant has lied whilst giving evidence,[197] but some caution should be exercised before basing a finding of malice on these grounds.[198] The way in which defendant's counsel has conducted the case at trial, though no doubt a factor that may aggravate the damages (and in practice often has),[199] cannot be regarded as evidence of malice to defeat a defence otherwise available.[200]

32.46 Refusal to apologise. The mere fact that a defendant, who has uttered an erroneous defamatory statement on a privileged occasion, declines to meet a demand for an apology, or to withdraw the statement, is not evidence that the statement was made maliciously.[201] Nor is a refusal to apologise, nor to retract a criticism which is found to be fair comment, nor to persist in a plea of justification which is not made good.[202] However, where a defendant becomes

---

[194] *Mangena v Lloyd Ltd* (1908) 98 L.T. 640 at 643; *Simpson v Robinson*, above; and see Gibson J. in *Sevenoaks v Latimer* (1920) 54 Ir. L.T. 11 at 14. In *Broadway Approvals Ltd v Odhams Press* [1965] 1 W.L.R. 805 at 815, Sellers L.J. observed that "Malice is not established by forensic imagination however eloquently expressed." That may still be true, but counsel's forensic imagination is now subject to the lay client's statement of truth (CPR r.22.1), by which the litigant must state his belief that the facts stated in the pleading are true. See also *Caulfield v Whitworth* (1868) 18 L.T. (N.S.) 527 and *Hayford v Forrester-Paton*, 1927 S.C. 740 at 749. Similarly, mere persistence in a reasonable plea of justification ought not to aggravate damages, unless the defence is completely insupportable: *Blakeney-Williams v Cathay Pacific Airways Ltd* [2010] HKCFA 61; [2013] E.M.L.R. 6 at [105], per Lord Neuberger of Abbotsbury N.P.J.

[195] *Broadway Approvals v Odhams Press* [1965] 1 W.L.R. 805 at 814 and 825: "The failure to apologise or retract and persistence in a plea of justification are in themselves not evidence of malice. They may be in certain circumstances but more frequently they would show sincerity and belief in what had been said and establish the best reason for the publication" (per Sellers L.J. at 814).

[196] See *Thomas v Bradbury Agnew* [1906] 2 K.B. 627.

[197] *Turner v MGM Pictures Ltd* [1950] 1 All E.R. 449.

[198] In *Turner v MGM Pictures*, above, it was said to be "a dangerous line of argument" (per Lord Porter at 460).

[199] For a recent example, see *Cairns v Modi* [2012] EWCA Civ 1382; [2013] 1 W.L.R. 1015, where the trial judge's decision to add to a general damages award of £75,000 a further £15,000 by way of aggravated damages, to reflect the conduct of the defendant's counsel at trial, was upheld by the Court of Appeal.

[200] *Brown v Citizen's Life* (1902) 2 N.S.W.S.R. 202 and cf. *Broadway Approvals v Odhams Press*, above, in which pleadings settled by counsel were not evidence of malice. But modern litigation has moved on. Nowadays, the litigant is obliged to verify the pleadings served in his name, whether or not they have been settled by counsel: CPR r.22.1. If the litigant verifies a pleading which he does not believe to be true, that, it is submitted, will be potent evidence of malice.

[201] *Horrocks v Lowe* [1972] 1 W.L.R. 1625, per Lord Denning at 1630; and see Lord Diplock [1975] A.C. 135 at 152: "a refusal to apologise is at best tenuous evidence of malice, for it is consistent with a continuing belief in the truth of what one has said". See fn.195, above.

[202] *Broadway Approvals v Odhams Press* [1965] 1 W.L.R. 805 at 814, 825. In the light of *Tse Wai Chun v Cheng* [2000] HKCFA 86 [2001] E.M.L.R. 31, persistence in a plea of justification

aware that the statement is false but thereafter still refuses to withdraw or apologise, that may be evidence from which a jury can infer malice.[203]

Evidence to defeat offer of amends defence. The fact that an offer of amends has been made and not withdrawn is a defence unless the defendant knew or had reason to believe that the statement complained of referred to the claimant or was likely to be understood as referring to him, and was false and defamatory of him.[204] The onus of establishing this is on the claimant[205]: it involves proving bad faith on the part of the defendant.[206] As regards the falsity of the statement, it is not sufficient to show that there were reasonable grounds to suspect the statement was untrue, or that the defendant ought to have ascertained that it was untrue (constructive knowledge). "The defendant had reason to believe the statement was false" means that "he has chosen to ignore or shut his mind to information which should have led him to *believe*, not merely to suspect, that the allegation is false".[207] That amounts to recklessness as that term is used in the context of malice.   **32.47**

SECTION 7. EVIDENCE DIRECTED AT DEFENDANT'S CASE OF PRIVILEGE

General principles. Where the facts of a plea of privilege are in dispute, the claimant must be permitted to lead evidence in opposition to the factual basis of the defendant's case. Thus if it is contended that the defamatory statement was written by the defendant as a former employer of the claimant who had been asked to supply a reference to the claimant's new employer, the claimant could introduce evidence to show that the defendant was never his employer, or that he had not been asked for a reference, or that the person to whom the reference was sent was not his new employer.   **32.48**

***Reynolds* privilege cases (public interest defence).** Where *Reynolds* privilege is raised the position is not quite so clear. In principle, the claimant must of course be able to lead evidence as to any factual matter in issue on the *Reynolds*/public interest defence. The question has often been: what exactly is in issue?   **32.49**

---

should probably be considered as consistent with the comment being the genuinely held opinion of the defendant and therefore a contra-indicator of malice in the sense in which it defeats the honest comment defence.

[203] See *Matheson v Schneideman* [1930] N.Z.L.R. 151.

[204] Defamation Act 1996, s.4.

[205] The effect of the presumption included in s.4(3) of the Act.

[206] *Milne v Express Newspapers* [2002] EWHC 2564 (QB); [2003] 1 W.L.R. 927. The decision was upheld in the Court of Appeal: [2004] EWCA Civ 664; [2005] 1 W.L.R. 772, where it was said that the words "had reason to believe the statement complained of . . . was . . . false" were to be construed as importing the concept of recklessness from *Horrocks v Lowe,* namely indifference to the truth or falsity of the words complained of.

[207] Ibid. at [41].

So in *Jameel v Wall Street Journal (No.1)*[208] it was not relevant to qualified privilege whether the publication was true or not; nor was it relevant to speculate what further information the publisher might have discovered if he had made more extensive inquiries. However, evidence was admissible to show that the defendant's sources were in fact unlikely to have told the defendant what it alleged it was told, or at least unlikely to have conveyed the information as clearly as the defendant alleged. In *Jameel*, Simon Brown L.J. distinguished between evidence to that effect, and evidence which sought to show that the defendant's sources were not in fact as objectively reliable as was claimed, which would have been inadmissible.[209]

The source of the defendant's information is one of the ten circumstances in Lord Nicholls' non-exhaustive list of circumstances to be taken into account when determining whether publication attracted *Reynolds* privilege.[210] The claimant, it is submitted, must be able to lead evidence on other matters on Lord Nicholls' list, if they are in dispute, such as whether comment was sought from him, and whether the article contained the gist of his side of the story.

In *Flood v Times Newspapers Ltd*,[211] the claimant was permitted to lead evidence relevant to the context in which the issues relevant to *Reynolds* privilege arose, although much of it was not only unchallenged but common ground. In the event, however, Tugendhat J. drew on his evidence only in so far as it was uncontroversial, save in one respect. He held that it was relevant to the assessment that had to be made as to whether the interference with the claimant's right to reputation under art.8 was proportionate.[212] The test was whether the interference was proportionate, not whether the journalists believed it to be so.[213]

The area of admissible claimant's evidence may have been widened by the Court of Appeal's observations in *Jameel v Wall Street Journal (No.3)*[214] that the presumption of falsity should not be applied when considering issues of fact that were relevant to *Reynolds* privilege, a proposition which was endorsed when the case was considered by the House of Lords.[215]

The House of Lords in *Jameel (No.3)* took the view that in assessing whether publication is in the public interest the defamatory statement should not be considered in isolation but in the context of the article as a whole. Lord Bingham stated[216]:

---

[208] *(No.1)* [2003] EWCA Civ 1694; [2004] E.M.L.R. 6, applying *GKR Karate (UK) Ltd v Yorkshire Post Newspapers Ltd* [2000] 1 W.L.R. 2571.

[209] *Jameel (No.1)*, at [31].

[210] *Reynolds v Times Newspapers Ltd* [2001] 2 A.C. 127 at 205.

[211] [2009] EWHC 2375 (QB); [2010] E.M.L.R. 8.

[212] Ibid. at [197].

[213] The decision was ultimately upheld in the Supreme Court: [2012] UKSC 11, [2012] 2 A.C. 273.

[214] [2005] EWCA Civ 74; [2005] Q.B. 904.

[215] [2006] UKHL 44; [2007] 1 A.C. 359, see Lord Hoffmann at [62].

[216] At [34].

" . . . consideration should be given to the thrust of the article which the publisher has published. If the thrust of the article is true, and the public interest condition is satisfied, the inclusion of an inaccurate fact may not have the same appearance of irresponsibility as it might if the whole thrust of the article is untrue."

It must be doubted whether Lord Bingham intended by those words to open up the question of whether the article as a whole was true or false, or even the truth or falsity of significant facts in the article which would diminish or eliminate the public interest in the article's publication as a whole. It is generally not the truth of the allegations as such that is in issue in a *Reynolds/ public interest case*,[217] but what steps the journalists took to verify the allegations. The public interest in a non-reportage case does of course lie in the fact that the information is or may be true, and the publisher will therefore be obliged to take reasonable steps to satisfy himself that the allegation is true (the subjective element) and his belief must be the result of a reasonable investigation, and must be a reasonable belief to hold (the objective element).[218] There is no reason why the claimant should not lead evidence to show that the journalist failed to take the steps that he should have done to investigate the matter and to satisfy himself of its truth. Indeed, that was what Simon Brown L.J. envisaged in *Jameel (No.1)* when he held that evidence would be admissible if tending to show that the defendant's sources had not given it the information claimed.

Necessity of evidence. In many cases where there is a *Reynolds* or public interest defence, evidence from the claimant on this issue will be unnecessary. For example, in *Charman v Orion Publishing Group*[219] there was a trial of the issue of privilege, including *Reynolds* privilege, and the claimant was not called to give evidence nor was anyone called to give evidence on his behalf. Gray J. described this as "entirely appropriate", and further commented at [76]:   **32.50**

"Where, as here, the issue is whether an author or journalist conducted himself responsibly in relation to the publication complained of, it will rarely be necessary for factual evidence to be called on behalf of the claimant".

This was despite service of a reply containing 27 pages of particulars. The aptness of the judge's observation seems unaffected by the reversal of his decision on appeal.[220] Similarly, much of the evidence which the claimant was

---

[217] As was made clear by the Court of Appeal in *Jameel v Wall Street Journal Sprl (No.1)* [2003] EWCA Civ 1694; [2004] E.M.L.R. 6 at [31] and *GKR Karate (UK) Ltd v Yorkshire Post Newspapers Ltd* [2000] 1 W.L.R. 2571, per May L.J.

[218] *Flood v Times Newspapers Ltd* [2012] UKSC 11, [2012] 2 A.C. 273 at [78]–[79]. Precisely what the journalist must satisfy himself of will of course depend on the meaning of the published article. The responsible journalist will have regard to the full range of meanings that a reasonable reader might put on the article (see [51]).

[219] [2006] EWHC 1756 (QB); [2007] 1 All E.R. 622.

[220] [2007] EWCA Civ 972.

allowed to lead in *Flood v Times Newspapers Ltd*[221] was almost entirely uncontroversial, and not the subject of cross-examination, but it was nonetheless evidence which was properly given about the claimant's background and about the impact on him of the internal police investigation which the defendant reported, and of the article sued on. Moreover, it was relevant to the assessment as to whether the interference with his art.8 right to reputation was proportionate.[222]

SECTION 8. EVIDENCE TO SUPPORT CLAIM FOR DAMAGES

32.51 Damage presumed. As a general proposition, the claimant in cases of libel or slander actionable per se need not prove actual damage, for:

> "The law presumes that *some* damage will flow in the ordinary course of things from the mere invasion of his absolute right to reputation".[223]
> "There is no obligation on the plaintiffs to show that they have suffered actual damage . . . In every case (a plaintiff) is entitled to say that there has been a serious libel upon him, that the law assumes he must have suffered damage, and that he is entitled to substantial damages."[224]

More recently, the Court of Appeal held that the presumption of damage was not incompatible with Art.10 ECHR, and confirmed that it remained part of English law.[225]

However, that presumption of damage must now be qualified in two respects, one statutory and the other the product of application of the European Convention on Human Rights.

The statutory qualification was introduced by s.1, Defamation Act 2013 (not yet in force), which provides that a statement is not defamatory unless its publication has caused or is likely to cause serious harm to the reputation of the claimant. Thus far, the section gives statutory effect to the concept of a threshold of seriousness already recognised by the common law.[226] The common law threshold of seriousness that applies is of particular relevance to a corporate claimant.[227] Furthermore, a higher corporate threshold has been

---

[221] [2009] EWHC 2375 (QB); [2010] E.M.L.R. 8.

[222] Ibid. at [197]

[223] *Ratcliffe v Evans* [1892] 2 Q.B. 524 at 528, per Bowen L.J.

[224] *English and Scottish Co-operative v Odhams Press Ltd* [1940] 1 K.B. 440 at 461, per Goddard L.J.

[225] *Jameel (Yousef) v Dow Jones* [2005] EWCA Civ 75; [2005] Q.B. 946.

[226] See *Thornton v Telegraph Media Group Ltd* [2010] EWHC 1414 (QB); [2011] 1 W.L.R. 1985; *Cammish v Hughes* [2012] EWCA Civ 1655; [2013] E.M.L.R. 13 at [38].

[227] See for instance per Tugendhat J. in *Euromoney Institutional Investor plc v Aviation News Ltd* [2013] EWHC 1505 (QB) at [24] (and see the cases there cited):
" . . . the likely effect upon a corporate claimant of any words complained of by it may not be sufficiently serious to provide the necessary justification for an interference with freedom of expression, even if they would have provided a sufficient justification for interference with the defendant's rights if the claimant were an individual."

prospectively introduced by s.1(2), by which harm to the reputation of a body that trades for profit is not "serious harm" unless it has caused or is likely to cause the body serious financial loss. Once that threshold is met, damage will still be presumed.[228] The other qualification was firmly established by the decision of the Court of Appeal in *Jameel (Yousef) v Dow Jones*,[229] where the Court of Appeal decided that if a claimant brought an action in circumstances where his reputation had suffered no, or minimal, actual damage, it might constitute an interference with freedom of expression that was not necessary for the protection of the claimant's reputation, which might render the action susceptible to being struck out as an abuse of the process.

It follows that trading companies should expect to lead evidence of actual or likely serious financial loss, and other claimants, including individuals, would be well advised (at least where there has been limited publication) to lead evidence of damage to reputation or evidence from which such damage may be inferred.

Extent of publication. The extent of publication is highly relevant to damages[230]; as are the numbers who would recognise the claimant as the subject of the libel.[231] Thus there is usually evidence of the circulation of the newspaper carrying the libel, or of the copies sold of the offending book, or of the number of website hits or readers of the blog or "Tweet". Where the claimant is not expressly named, or an innuendo meaning is relied upon, there should be evidence from which the jury can deduce the number of persons likely to identify the claimant as the person defamed or to understand the words in a defamatory sense.[232] If the claimant is seeking damages for repetition by others of the defamatory statement originally published by the defendant, there must be evidence that such repetition was intended or authorised by the defendant, or was the foreseeable, or natural and probable, consequence of the original publication.[233] **32.52**

Injury to reputation. The claimant can call evidence of the effect of the defamation on his reputation.[234] It is unlikely that direct evidence from a **32.53**

---

[228] In other words, the common law of presumption of damage is not abolished: it is simply that a higher threshold must be satisfied before the presumption operates. See para.3.7, above.

[229] [2005] EWCA Civ 75; [2005] Q.B. 946. See generally para.30.48, above.

[230] *Jameel (Yousef) v Dow Jones* [2005] EWCA Civ 75; [2005] Q.B. 946; *John v MGN* [1997] Q.B. 586 at 607; *Cairns v Modi* and *KC v MGN Ltd* [2012] EWCA Civ 1382; [2013] E.M.L.R. 8. The importance of the extent of publication is very long established: in *Gathercole v Miall* (1846) 15 M. & W. 319, 153 E.R.872, Parke B. observed that "surely the proprietor of a newspaper, with a very large circulation, is to be visited with larger damages for a libel published in it than one of a more limited circulation".

[231] *Morgan v Odhams Press* [1971] 1 W.L.R. 1239; *KC v MGN Ltd* (above).

[232] *Fullam v Newcastle Chronicle and Journal* [1977] 1 W.L.R. 651; *Baturina v Times Newspapers Ltd* [2011] EWCA Civ 308; [2011] 1 W.L.R. 1526.

[233] *Slipper v BBC* [1991] 1 Q.B. 283; *McManus v Beckham* [2002] EWCA Civ 939; [2002] 1 W.L.R. 2982.

[234] See *Cornwell v Myskow* [1987] 1 W.L.R. 631 at 635. See also para.32.31, above, concerning evidence of the damaging nature of the defamation.

witness in whose estimation the claimant's reputation has been diminished will often be available, but evidence that the claimant had been called names as a result of the libel has been permitted,[235] and evidence of this kind is nowadays not uncommon at libel trials.[236] Evidence that the libel has rendered the claimant unemployable is admissible.[237] Further, the claimant can give evidence that the words complained of are likely to cause him pecuniary loss, either in support of a claim for general damages or in a claim for malicious falsehood where advantage is taken of s.3 of the Defamation Act 1952.[238]

32.54 Injury to feelings. In assessing damages the jury can take into account the distress, hurt and humiliation that the defamatory publication has caused to the claimant.[239] Thus the claimant can describe his reactions and feelings upon learning of the publication.[240] Evidence is commonly given by those who know the claimant well as to his mood and demeanour after the defamatory statement came to his attention. Whether this could be extended to evidence of the claimant's physical health is an unsettled question.[241] Evidence of mental suffering or illness caused by the publication, not to the claimant, but to his wife is not admissible if its purpose is to prove injury to the wife,[242] but

---

[235] *Garbett v Hazel Watson* [1943] 2 All E.R. 359 CA.

[236] In *Bishop v New York Times*, 233 N.Y.R. 446 (1922) it was held that the plaintiff might prove that he had been shunned and avoided by former friends and acquaintances, and in *Cook v Ward* (1830) 6 Bingham 409, 130 E.R. 1338, it was said that evidence that the plaintiff had been made the subject of ridicule was admissible as proof of the consequence necessarily resulting from publication. In *Hughes v Mirror Ltd* [1985] 3 N.S.W.L.R. 504 evidence was permitted from the host of a radio talk show concerning a number of listeners who called his programme having read the defamatory words in the defendant's newspaper and made statements which demonstrated a hostile view of the plaintiff.

[237] *Miller v Mirror Group Newspapers*, unreported, December 19, 1990, CA. This would require to be pleaded: CPR PD 53, para.2.10(1).

[238] *Calvet v Tomkies* [1963] 1 W.L.R. 1397.

[239] *John v MGN Ltd* [1997] Q.B. 586.

[240] This may well involve an explanation of the claimant's understanding of the defamatory meaning conveyed by the publication; but the evidence is not on that ground excluded. See *Hughes v Mirror Group Newspapers* [1985] 3 N.S.W.L.R. 504. The judge will usually warn the jury that the evidence is relevant to damages but not to meaning.

[241] Save for one decision at first instance in Hong Kong (*Chu Siu Kuk Yuen, Jesssie v Apple Daily Ltd* [2002] 1 H.K.L.R.D. 1), there is no reported case of a claimant recovering in defamation for injury to health. In *Wheeler v Somerfield* [1966] 2 Q.B. 94 at 104 Lord Denning M.R. said: "A libel action concerns injury to reputation and not injury to health. I can imagine that there might be cases in which a libel might cause injury to health. I would not exclude the possibility of such an action". There are cases where such phrases as "mental suffering" (*Goslin v Corry* (1844) 7 M. & Gr. at 346), "mental pain" (*Lynch v Knight* (1861) 9 H.L.C. at 598) and "great pain of body and mind" (*Rigby v Mirror Newspapers* (1963) 64 N.S.W.S.R. 34) are used, but these could be explained as descriptive of injury to feelings. However, in *Sattin v Nationwide News* (1996) 39 N.S.W.L.R. 32 an amendment claiming damages for personal injury was allowed, and Levine J. (at 45) referred to an unreported state case (*Clough v Mirror Newspapers*, November 28, 1983) where evidence was admitted that the publication had caused an aggravation of the plaintiff's duodenal ulcer. In *Marsden v Amalgamated Television Services* [2001] NSWCA damages for injury to health would have been awarded had such loss been proved. See also *McCrae v SA Telecasters* (1976) 14 S.A.S.R. 162.

[242] *Guy v Gregory* (1840) 9 Car. & P. 584, 173 E.R. 966.

the claimant can give evidence of the effect upon him of such distress as he observed of his wife and daughter.[243]

Actual damages. The claimant can lead evidence of actual loss, whether it   **32.55** be general loss of business or profits, or loss of particular earnings, customers, clients or patients, provided the details have been properly pleaded.[244]

Where there is a loss to a company owned or controlled by the claimant, that loss will not be recoverable by the claimant unless and to the extent that he is able to show an indirect loss to himself.[245] A public limited company cannot claim special damages on the basis of the difference between its actual market capitalisation following publication of the alleged libel and its potential market capitalisation without the alleged libel.[246]

Slander not actionable per se. In the cases of slander not actionable per   **32.56** se the "actual damage done is the very gist of the action"[247]: the claimant must prove that he has suffered special damage as the direct and natural result of the words complained of, otherwise the action will fail.

> "As much certainty and particularity must be insisted upon, both in pleading and proof of damage, as is reasonable, having regard to the circumstances and to the nature of the acts themselves by which the damage is done."[248]

Special damage must be specifically pleaded and the claimant will only be permitted to prove the kind of special damage alleged in the particulars of claim.[249] The claimant must lead evidence to connect the special damage with the words complained of.[250] If, for instance, the claimant pleads the names of persons whose custom has been lost as the result of the publication of the

---

[243] Morland J. in *Nixon v Channel Four Television*, unreported, April 11, 1997; Eady J. in *Nail v News Group Newspapers* [2004] EWHC 647 (QB); [2004] E.M.L.R. 362 at [27]; *ZAM v CFW* [2013] EWHC 662 (QB) at [74].

[244] *Ratcliffe v Evans* [1892] 2 Q.B.D. 524; and see *Harrison v Pearce* (1859) 32 L.T. (O.S.) 298. All losses must now be properly pleaded and particularised: see CPR PD 53, para.2.10(1).

[245] See e.g. *Monks v Warwick DC* [2009] EWHC 959 (QB) at [28]–[30].

[246] *Collins Stewart Ltd v Financial Times Ltd* [2004] EWHC 2337 (QB); [2005] E.M.L.R. 5. There might have been many factors influencing fluctuations in the market capitalisation, and the measure of damages was too uncertain to be acceptable as a legal basis for assessing damages. Further, the investigation required to assess the loss in market value attributable to the alleged libel would have rendered the case untriable. In this case Tugendhat J. struck out a claim for £230,626,320 damages based on the fall in the market value of the shares of the second claimant, Collins Stewart Plc. As for the proposition that the losses suffered by the first claimant, Collins Stewart Ltd, a wholly owned subsidiary of Collins Stewart plc, and the subject of the defamatory article, would be reflected in the losses suffered by the shareholders of the second claimant, the judge found that not sustainable.

[247] *Ratcliffe v Evans*, above, at 531.

[248] *Ratcliffe v Evans*, above, at 532.

[249] *Hayward v Pullinger & Partners* [1950] 1 All E.R. 581; *Ilkiw v Samuels* [1963] 1 W.L.R. 991 CA.

[250] Per Hannen J. in *Salmon v Isaac* (1869) 20 L.T. 885 at 886. In *Taylor v Hamilton* (1927) S.A.S.R. 314 the plaintiff failed because there was no evidence that his inability to obtain employment was caused by the words complained of.

words complained of, evidence must be adduced that they did so as a result of the defendant's words.[251] If called to give evidence, such witnesses may be challenged in cross-examination as to whether they ceased to deal with or employ the claimant on account of what other persons said, and they may also be asked what those other persons did say.[252]

32.57 Aggravated damages. Where the claimant has alleged that the damage has been aggravated by the conduct of the defendant and given details of such conduct in the particulars of claim,[253] evidence of such matters may be led by the claimant (if an individual and not a company).[254] It can cover a broad ambit, since "the jury in assessing damages are entitled to look at the whole conduct of the defendant from the time the libel was published down to the time they give their verdict".[255] Evidence has been held to be admissible which shows that the defendant has published other defamatory words about the claimant, whether such words were or were not connected with the subject-matter of the action,[256] and whether publication took place before[257] or after the publication giving rise to the action.[258] The reason was explained by Tindal C.J.:

> "Either party may with a view to damages, give evidence to prove or disprove the existence of a malicious motive in the mind of a publisher of defamatory matter".[259]

But subsequent publications which shed light on the defendant's motive or state of mind, and thus go to prove malice and consequent injury to the claimant's feelings, should not be confused with publications relied on to increase damages for injury to reputation. In *Collins Stewart v Financial Times Ltd (No.2)*, a case of corporate claimants, Gray J. expressed the view

---

[251] *Tilk v Parsons* (1825) 2 C. & P. 201; *Hallock v Miller* (1848) 2 Barb. (N.Y.) R. 630; *McCann v Keasney* (1880) 20 N.B.R. 84.

[252] *King v Watts* (1838) 8 Car. & P. 614, 173 E.R. 642.

[253] CPR PD 53, para.2.10(1). But plainly the claimant is not expected to plead aggravating matters which occur at a late stage, in particular during the trial itself.

[254] Aggravated damages are not available to a corporate claimant: *Collins Stewart v Financial Times Ltd (No.2)* [2005] EWHC 262 (QB); [2006] E.M.L.R. 5 at [28]–[31]; *Oriental Daily Publisher Ltd v Ming Pao Holdings Ltd* [2012] HKFCA 59; [2013] E.M.L.R. 7.

[255] Per Lord Esher in *Praed v Graham* (1889) 24 Q.B.D. 53 at 55.

[256] E.g. *Hemmings v Gasson* (1858) E.B. & E. 346, 120 E.R. 537; and see *Kiam v MGN* [2002] EWCA Civ 43; [2003] Q.B. 281 at [8], where the other articles, which did cover the same area as the words complained of, were accepted to have been factually incorrect.

[257] There are few examples of prior publications: *Barrett v Long* (1851) 3 H.L.C. 395, 10 E.R. 154 is one.

[258] *Pearson v Lemaitre* (1843) 5 M. & Gr. 700, 134 E.R. 742; *Kiam v MGN Ltd*, above; *ZAM v CFW* [2013] EWHC 662 (QB). If the evidence establishes another cause of action the jury should be warned against giving any damages in respect of it: *Pearson v Lemaitre*; although an omission on the part of the judge to give such a caution to the jury is not necessarily a ground for granting a new trial: *Darby v Ouseley* (1856) 1 H. & N. 1; *Anderson v Calvert* (1908) 24 T.L.R. 399; *Williams v MGN Ltd*, December 19, 1990, CA. The defendant may in principle prove the truth of the defamatory words in mitigation.

[259] *Pearson v Lemaitre*, above, at 719–720.

that there were sound reasons both of principle and of practice why a claimant, whether an individual or a corporation, should not be permitted to seek to recover increased damages in respect of the publication of subsequent articles which were not themselves the subject of complaint (at [27]).[260]

Even where evidence is in principle admissible of other publications, not sued upon, it may be doubted whether a modern court, applying the overriding objective of the CPR, would be tolerant of protracted exploration of the truth or falsity of other defamatory words relied in in aggravation. Such matters must be kept within limits or there is a risk that the work involved in determining them may become disproportionate.[261]

Nonetheless, evidence of matters tending to establish malice on the part of the defendant is, as a general rule, admissible to support a claim for aggravated damages.[262] As the damages are compensation for the additional injury to the claimant's feelings,[263] it is submitted that the conduct of the defendant from which malice is to be inferred must have been known to or have come to the knowledge of the claimant.[264]

Persistence at trial in a plea of justification can be taken into account in assessing damages if the plea fails,[265] and the same applies if the defendant does not attempt to establish the defence at the trial but does not abandon it.[266] It is uncertain whether denial that the words are defamatory, or refer to the claimant, can have an aggravating effect.[267] It has been doubted whether mere

---

[260] [2005] EWHC 262 (QB); [2006] E.M.L.R. 5. Given that the judge envisaged both individual and corporate claimants, he cannot have had in mind increased damages for injury to feelings. That decision was followed by Tugendhat J. in *ZAM v CFW* [2013] EWHC 662 (QB).

[261] *Clarke (t/a Elumina Iberica UK) v Bain* [2008] EWHC 2636 (QB), where Tugendhat J. noted, at [41], that even if evidence of subsequent publications was in principle admissible "the court may, in exercise of its case management powers, determine to exclude such evidence".

[262] See paras 9.18 et seq, above and Section 6 of this chapter. Simon Brown L.J. in *Kiam v MGN*, above, when listing aggravating factors, said "complete indifference to the truth was amply demonstrated": at [6].

[263] See *Rookes v Barnard* [1964] A.C. 1129 at 1221, per Lord Devlin.

[264] See Pearson L.J. in *McCarey v Associated Newspapers* [1965] 2 Q.B. 86 at 104. In *Syme v Mather* (1977) V.R. 516 at 526 it was said "Aggravated damages may be awarded in defamation if the defendant's conduct aggravates the subjective hurt to the plaintiff."

[265] *Herald v McGregor* [1928] V.L.R. 189 FC; approved 41 C.L.R. 254; *Broome v Cassell* [1972] A.C. 1027 at 1125, per Lord Diplock. *John v MGN* [1997] Q.B. 586 at 608, per Bingham M.R. But cf. *Singleton v Ffrench* (1986) 5 N.S.W.L.R. 425: vigorous persistence in a legitimate defence, if bona fide, cannot be used to increase damages; and *Coyne v Citizen Finance Ltd* (1991) 172 C.L.R. 211 at 237 (Toohey J.), referred to in *Rantzen v MGN* [1994] Q.B. 670 at 683. However, "it is wrong in principle to award aggravated damages . . . solely because the defendant has decided in good faith to run a defence of justification, which is then run in a reasonable way. The fact that the defence fails, even in a case where the court regards it as not merely wrong but weak, is not enough, on its own, to bring aggravated damages into play": per Lord Neuberger, giving the leading judgment of the Hong Kong Final Court of Appeal in *Blakeney-Williams v Cathay Pacific Airways Ltd* [2012] HKFCA 61, [2013] E.M.L.R. 6 at [105].

[266] *Simpson v Robinson* (1848) 12 Q.B. 511, 116 E.R. 959.

[267] In *Syme v Mather* (1977) V.R. 516, it was ruled that a denial in the defence that the words were defamatory of, or referred to, the plaintiff, was incapable of being aggravation. But in *Kiam v MGN Ltd* [2002] EWCA Civ 43; [2003] Q.B. 281 at [10], the fact that the defendant's case to the end was that the offending article though untrue was simply not defamatory seems to have been regarded as a potentially aggravating factor.

failure to make an apology can ever justify aggravation of damages,[268] and it has long been accepted that a well-judged apology will mitigate damage,[269] but the weight of recent authority is to the effect that the absence of an apology can, depending on the facts of the case, increase injury to feelings.[270] Conduct calculated to deter the claimant from pursuing his claim has been given as an example of aggravation.[271]

When the Crime and Courts Act 2013, s.39 is brought into effect, aggravated damages will only be awarded against a relevant publisher within the Act to compensate the claimant for mental distress, and not for purposes of punishment.[272] But s.39(4) states that nothing in the section is to be read as implying that aggravated damages would otherwise be awardable for the purposes of punishment. Nor indeed should they be awarded for such purposes.[273]

32.58 **Aggravated damages and corporations.** Corporate claimants may not recover aggravated damages.

---

[268] Per Lord Reid in *Morgan v Odhams Press* [1971] 1 W.L.R. 1239 at 1247 and Lord Guest at 1262. See also *Coyne v Citizen Finance Ltd* (1991) 172 C.L.R. 211 at 237, referred to in *Rantzen v MGN* [1994] Q.B. 670 at 683, per Toohey J.: "Mere persistence, or even vigorous persistence, in a bona fide defence, in the absence of improper or unjustifiable conduct, cannot be used to aggravate compensatory damages." See also per Lord Neuberger, *Blakeney-Williams v Cathay Pacific Airways Ltd* [2012] HKFCA 61, [2013] E.M.L.R. 6 at [106]:
"... I do not consider that (the absence of an apology) can take matters any further in a case ... where the defendant has decided in good faith to raise a defence of justification, which is then run in a reasonable way.... it is hardly consistent for a defendant to apologise if he is running a defence of justification: it would positively undermine the defence."

[269] *Collins Stewart v Financial Times Ltd (No.2)* [2005] EWHC 262, [2006] E.M.L.R. 5 at [34], per Gray J: "The reason why an apology has the effect of reducing compensatory damages is that the apology, to a greater or lesser extent depending on its terms, reduces or repairs the original damage to reputation. If there is no apology, the appropriate compensatory award is unaffected. A failure to apologise (where an apology was called for) introduces an entirely new element, that is, an entitlement on the part of the claimant to extra damages which are not for injury to reputation but for the additional separate element of injury to feelings.

[270] A passage in the speech of Lord Hailsham L.C. in *Broome v Cassell & Co. Ltd* [1972] A.C. 1027 at 1071 was regarded by the Court of Appeal in *Rantzen* (below) as strong support for the proposition that the absence of an apology can be taken into account in aggravation of damages. See also *Sutcliffe v Pressdram* [1991] 1 Q.B. 153 per Nourse L.J. at 184.; *Rantzen v MGN Ltd* [1994] Q.B. 670 at 683; *John v MGN Ltd* [1997] Q.B. 586, per Bingham M.R; *Kiam v MGN Ltd*, above, per Simon Brown L.J. at [7]. The rationale may be that, as Gray J. suggested in *Collins Stewart v Financial Times Ltd (No.2)* (see fn.269, above), there is aggravation where an apology is called for but not forthcoming. Cf. *Andrews v John Fairfax* [1980] 2 N.S.W.L.R. 225: "It was only a failure to apologise which the jury are entitled to regard as unjustified which would support the award of aggravated damages"; and *Carson v John Fairfax* (1993) 113 A.L.R. 577. In *Syme v Mather*, above, it was said that an inadequate apology could exacerbate the claimant's sense of injury.

[271] Per Nourse L.J. in *Sutcliffe v Pressdram*, above, at 184.

[272] By s.61, ss.34–39 will not come into force until one year after the establishment by Royal Charter of a body charged "with the purpose of carrying on activities relating to the recognition of independent regulators of relevant publishers (as defined by s.41)". See the general discussion at paras 9.22–9.24, 9.32–9.33 and 9.38–9.39, above.

[273] See e.g. *Khodaparast v Shad* [2000] 1 W.L.R. 618 at 632, per Otton L.J.

"The defining characteristic of an award of aggravated damages is that its function is to provide a claimant with compensation for injury to his or her feelings caused by some conduct on the part of the defendant or for which the defendant is responsible. . . . It seems to me to follow that aggravated damages are in principle not available to a corporate claimant . . . . The reason is that . . . a company has no feelings to injure and cannot suffer distress".[274]

This reasoning would appear to apply to other impersonal institutions having capacity to sue for defamation, such as a firm (where the action is brought in the firm's name and not in the names of the partners).

Conduct of case at trial. How the case is conducted on behalf of the **32.59** defendant at trial can also be relied upon as aggravating the damage. The court can take into account that the claimant has been cross-examined in a wounding or insulting way,[275] or has been personally criticised in the course of counsel's closing speech,[276] or has been the subject of defamatory allegations made by the defendant in the course of proceedings.[277] Even "turgid speeches to the jury" in support of a plea of justification which is bound to fail can be aggravation.[278]

Exemplary damages. To support a claim for exemplary damages there **32.60** must be evidence that the claimant knew that what he proposed to publish was defamatory and untrue, or that he was reckless, not caring whether the publication was true or false[279]; and that he decided to publish because the prospects of material advantage outweighed the prospects of material loss.[280] Evidence that a newspaper failed to check a story could be sufficient, but only where the failure to check could be stigmatised as so crass as to be capable of

---

[274] *Collins Stewart v Financial Times Ltd (No.2)* [2005] EWHC 262, [2006] E.M.L.R. 5 at [28]–[31], per Gray J.; *Oriental Daily Publisher Ltd v Ming Pao Holdings Ltd* [2012] HKFCA 59; [2013] E.M.L.R. 7.

[275] Per Bingham M.R. in *John v MGN*, above, at 608. In *Sallows v Griffiths* [2001] F.S.R. (malicious falsehood and malicious procurement of arrest) the CA approved an award of £1000 as aggravated damages for repeating allegations of theft in the course of cross-examination. In *Cairns v Modi* [2012] EWCA Civ 1382; [2012] 1 W.L.R. 1015, the trial judge awarded an extra £15,000 (on top of £75,000 compensatory damages) by way of aggravated damages to reflect the conduct of the defendant's leading counsel during the trial. The Court of Appeal dismissed an appeal against the award.

[276] *Kiam v MGN Ltd*, above, at [9], e.g. "no amount of money will satisfy [the claimant]"; the claimant had wanted "his day in court".

[277] *Khodarparast v Shad* [2000] 1 W.L.R. 618 CA; a malicious falsehood case. It was held that the defendant's unjustified endeavours to blacken the plaintiff's character to show that she was an unreliable witness attracted an award of aggravated damages.

[278] Per Nourse L.J. in *Sutcliffe v Pressdram*, above, at 184.

[279] In *John v MGN* [1997] Q.B. 586 at 618G-H, Sir Thomas Bingham M.R. considered that "not caring whether the publication was true or false", though an accurate formulation of the test of recklessness, was capable of leading to confusion and recommended a direction that the jury must be satisfied that the publisher had no genuine belief in the truth of what he published.

[280] *Rookes v Barnard* [1964] A.C. 1129 at 1226; *Broome v Cassell* [1972] A.C. 1027 at 1079, per Lord Hailsham; *John v MGN*, above. The topic of exemplary damages is examined in depth in Ch.9, above.

amounting to recklessness.[281] The mere fact that a libel is published in the course of a business carried on for profit does not entitle a claimant to an award of exemplary damages.[282] The publication must have been motivated by mercenary considerations, by the publisher's belief that he would better off financially if he violated the claimant's rights than if he did not.[283] The prominence given by a newspaper to the libel could in this regard be a critical factor.[284] As the damages are punitive, the means of the defendant are relevant and evidence of the defendant's financial resources is therefore in principle admissible.[285] Where there is more than one defendant the damages will be assessed by reference to the least guilty.[286]

32.61 **Statutory restrictions on awards of exemplary damages** When ss.34–39 of the Crime and Courts Act 2013 are brought into effect, which will be one year after the day on which a body is established by Royal Charter to carry on activities relating to the recognition of independent regulators of relevant publishers, as defined,[287] exemplary damages will generally not be awarded against a defendant publisher if it was a member at the material time of an approved regulatory body.[288]

SECTION 9. EVIDENCE OF CLAIMANT'S GOOD CHARACTER OR
REPUTATION

32.62 **Whether such evidence necessary or relevant.** It was stated in an earlier edition of this book[289] that evidence of the claimant's good character or reputation[290] is, as a rule, neither relevant nor necessary in an action of

---

[281] *John v MGN*, above, at 623.

[282] See *Manson v Associated Newspapers Ltd* [1965] 1 W.L.R. 1038, approved in *Broome v Cassell*, above, at 1079.

[283] *John v MGN*, above, at 619.

[284] *Riches v News Group* [1986] Q.B. 256 at 272B: an eye-catching headline including "exclusive" on the front page was a matter from which the jury could infer a cynical calculation that the sales of the newspaper with the article on the front page would justify any risk of paying damages.

[285] *Rookes v Barnard* [1964] A.C. 1129 at 1228, per Lord Devlin. In *John v MGN*, above, there was no evidence of the defendant newspaper's means, but the judge's direction, "Do not because you may think the Mirror Group are very wealthy go over the top on that account" could not in the view of the Court of Appeal be faulted. In *McCartney v Sunday Newspapers Ltd* [1988] N.I. 565 detailed evidence of a newspaper's financial position was not allowed.

[286] Per Lord Hailsham and Lord Reid in *Broome v Cassell*, above, at 1063 and 1090 respectively. Lord Hailsham regarded the same principle as holding good for aggravated damages. That was the approach of Eady J. in *Berezovsky v Russian Television and Radio Broadcasting Co* [2010] EWHC 476 (QB) where (in the context of a claim for aggravated damages) he adopted the lowest common denominator approach, which he regarded as more compatible than the alternative with art.10.

[287] S.61(7).

[288] For a full discussion, see paras 9.32–9.33, above. See also fn.272, above.

[289] 8th edition.

[290] In this context the expressions probably have the same meaning: see *Plato Films v Speidel* [1961] A.C. 1090 at 1137–1138, Lord Denning.

defamation, for the law presumes that his character is good until the contrary is proved, and he can safely rest on that assumption. However, this statement attracted criticism that the authorities cited in support were "old and unsatisfactory",[291] and that the presumption was on analysis not as to good character or reputation, but as to injury to reputation resulting from defamation.[292] Even if there is a presumption that the claimant is of good character, it has been pointed out that it must be a rebuttable presumption, and "a party is never prevented from leading evidence to establish an issue upon which he has a rebuttable presumption in his favour".[293] It is submitted that an accurate statement of the law is that evidence of the claimant's good character or reputation is generally unnecessary, but not necessarily irrelevant.[294] However, unless rebutting a plea of justification, its relevance would relate to damages, and the evidence should be directed at the claimant's general character or reputation, and should not include particular instances of good conduct.[295] In the absence of a plea of justification the claimant cannot lead evidence as to his enhanced or undiminished reputation at the time of trial.[296]

Character in issue. Where the defendant has imputed that the general character of the claimant is bad, the claimant can adduce evidence of his general good character,[297] but just as a defendant cannot cite particular instances of the claimant's misconduct to diminish the damages, so the claimant cannot give evidence of particular facts in support of his claim to have a good character.[298]

32.63

---

[291] Hunt J. in *Bickel v John Fairfax* [1981] 2 N.S.W.L.R. 474 at 482. The authorities cited were *Cornwall v Richardson* (1825) Ry. & M. 305 and *Guy v Gregory* (1840) 9 C. & P. 584.

[292] Ibid. at 483.

[293] Ibid. at 483. The same judge, Hunt J. (in *Anderson v Mirror Newspapers (No.2)* (1986) 5 N.S.W.L.R. 735) said that it was now generally accepted that evidence of the plaintiff's good reputation was admissible. In *Cornwell v Myskow* [1987] 1 W.L.R. 630, evidence of the plaintiff's qualities and reputation as an actress at the time of publication was held to be admissible. However, evidence of an undiminished or enhanced reputation at the time of trial, called with a view to increasing damages, was not admissible relevant to, and could have confused the jury when considering, the issues of fair comment and malice.

[294] For an example of where there was voluminous evidence of good reputation, even though no defence of justification, see *Jensen v Clark* [1982] 2 N.Z.L.R. 268. This topic was discussed at length in *Marsden v Amalgamated Television Services* [1999] N.S.W.S.C. 1119. The judge decided that evidence of the plaintiff's good reputation as a legal practitioner and former President of the Law Society should be admitted where the defamatory statements were allegations that the plaintiff had sexual intercourse with young boys. The arguments principally focused on whether the evidence should be limited to that sector of the plaintiff's reputation affected by the defamatory imputation and how that sector should be defined.

[295] See *Anderson v Mirror Newspapers (No.2)*, above.

[296] *Cornwell v Myskow*, above, at 635.

[297] *King v Waring* (1803) 5 Esp. 13; *Fountain v Boodle* (1842) 3 Q.B. 5; and see Civil Evidence Act 1995, s.7(3).

[298] Per Greer L.J. in *Hobbs v Tinling* [1929] 2 K.B. 1 at 9; *Anderson v Mirror Newspapers (No.2)*, above. In so far as the rule about particular instances of misconduct has been modified by *Burstein v Times Newspapers* [2001] 1 W.L.R. 579 (see paras 33.43 et seq, below) it must possible

SECTION 10. EVIDENCE IN REBUTTAL OF JUSTIFICATION OR A
COMPOSITE PLEA OF HONEST COMMENT

32.64 Practice. Where there is a plea of justification on the record, the claimant will want to give and to lead evidence in answer to the allegations that are made in that plea. So too if there is a defence of honest comment and the facts, the basis of the comment, are disputed. How and when such evidence is given and led will fall within the general powers of the court under the CPR to control the evidence, and of case management.[299] Hitherto it was said to be within the discretion of the court to allow the claimant either to give at the outset all the evidence he intends to offer in rebuttal, or to postpone giving such evidence and leave it to the defendant to make out his plea, and then to give evidence of any matters which are properly admissible to rebut the plea.[300] That discretion must survive under the new Rules, albeit that for some time it has been the almost invariable practice for the claimant to give evidence relating to justification or honest comment at the outset before the defendant presents his case. It would be quite exceptional for the claimant to be permitted to call some evidence in rebuttal, and to reserve the remainder until the defendant's evidence was complete. Of course, if the claimant is taken by surprise by some evidence introduced by the defendant, which ought not to happen if the defendant's case has been properly pleaded and witness statements served, the court is likely to allow the claimant thereafter to call evidence in rebuttal.

Although there is a general rule that, if a party who has served a witness statement does not call that witness or put in his statement, then any other party may put in the statement as hearsay evidence,[301] this does not permit a claimant at the conclusion of the defendant's case to put in witness statements, served by the defendant, of witnesses not called by the defendant, where parts of the statements, which the claimant proposes to invite the jury to reject, substantially conflict with the claimant's case.[302]

32.65 Evidence must disprove specific charge. The evidence tendered in rebuttal of a plea of justification must go to disprove the specific charge made by the defendant. If the charge, whether in the words complained of or in the particulars of justification, imputes a particular act of misconduct, evidence of the claimant's general good character in that respect is not admissible in

---

for the claimant to introduce evidence to challenge allegations put forward as part of the relevant background context.

[299] CPR r.32.1 and r.1.4 respectively.

[300] *Browne v Muray* (1825) Ry. & M. 254, 171 E.R. 1012.

[301] CPR r.32.5(5).

[302] *McPhilemy v Times Newspapers (No.2)* [2000] E.M.L.R. 575, where the principle was stated that there was no absolute rule of law which prohibited a party from asserting that evidence given in chief by a witness whom he had called was untruthful. Nevertheless, as matter of discretion a judge should ordinarily not permit a party to impugn the honesty of his own witness without giving that witness an opportunity to be heard.

rebuttal of the plea.[303] Thus where the plaintiff was accused of cowardice in the field on a particular occasion, it was held that evidence of gallantry on other occasions was inadmissible,[304] but if the charge is broadly expressed, e.g. one of general dishonesty, evidence of the claimant's general good character for honesty is admissible, for in such a case the claimant's general good character for honesty is put in issue by the plea.[305] Likewise a general charge of cowardice would admit instances of bravery. However, evidence of the claimant's good reputation in the area defamed may be relevant and admissible in relation to damages.[306]

SECTION 11. EVIDENCE IN CLAIM OF MISUSE OF PRIVATE INFORMATION[307]

General.[308] The burden on the claimant will be to prove the factual basis of **32.66** his claim which will be set out in the particulars of claim. The essential contents of this pleading have been earlier explained[309] and what is alleged in the particulars will determine what evidence will be required of the claimant. There are some common elements in relation to evidence between this cause of action and defamation. "Misuse" of private information, in the context in which the subject is covered in this book, usually consists of actual or threatened publication. Thus, the claimant will have to prove that the information for which privacy is claimed has been published by the defendant. In many cases, such as a tabloid "exclusive", this will not be an issue. But there have been instances where the identity of the publisher, or the extent of the publication, is not self-evident. For example, the information might be contained in an anonymous leaflet or circular, or disseminated online in an anonymous blog or email.[310] The claimant will have to adduce evidence proving directly or by inference the responsibility of the defendant for the

---

[303] *Cornwall v Richardson* (1825) Ry. & M. 305; *Edmondson v Amery, The Times,* January 28, 1911; *Lim v Lawless,* unreported, April 26, 1990, CA; and *Brine v Bazalgette* (1849) 3 Exch. 692, 154 E.R. 1024 (where it was said that evidence of the plaintiff's general competence as a surveyor could not be led, given that what had been impugned was his competence in one transaction). In *Anderson v Mirror Newspapers (No.2)* (1986) 5 N.S.W.L.R. 735, the general principle stated was that the claimant was not allowed to lead evidence in reply to demonstrate falsity which was irrelevant to what was published, or did not meet the defendant's pleaded case.

[304] *Edmondson v Amery,* above, per Phillimore J.

[305] *Doe d. Farr v Hicks,* cited in *Doe v Walker* (1801) 4 Esp. at 51; *King v Waring* (1803) 5 Esp. 13; *Fountain v Boodle* (1842) 3 Q.B. 5; *Lim v Lawless,* above.

[306] See para.32.62, and *Marsden v Amalgamated Television Services,* above.

[307] For a general discussion of this cause of action see Ch.22, above.

[308] See also evidence in support of applications for interim injunctions: para.25.34, above.

[309] See para.26.43 above.

[310] For example, in the case of *Terry (formerly LNS) v Persons Unknown* [2010] EWHC 119 (QB); [2010] E.M.L.R. 16, the claimant did not know the identity of the proposed defendants at the stage when he was applying for interim relief.

publication. That may involve a *Norwich Pharmacal* application against an internet service provider.[311]

32.67 Reasonable expectation of privacy. That the information is such as to give rise to a reasonable expectation of privacy is a crucial element of the claimant's case. This has been described as a broad question which takes account of all the circumstances of the case.[312] Those circumstances include

> "The nature of the activity in which the claimant was engaged, the place at which it was happening, the nature and purpose of the intrusion, the absence of consent and whether it was known or could be inferred, the effect on the claimant and the circumstances in which and the purposes for which the information came into the hands of the publisher."[313]

Many of these matters will be known to the claimant, and he or his friends, family and associates will be able to give evidence about them. But it is not enough for the claimant simply to assert that the relevant information is private: it is essential that he should set out why it is private and show that he had a reasonable expectation of privacy in respect of it.[314]

32.68 "Intense focus". This phrase[315] has now become the shorthand description of the investigation that the court must carry out when balancing the competing rights of privacy under art.8 ECHR and freedom of expression under art.10. It is not in every case that this exercise must be undertaken as the defence may not raise any issues that bring rights under art.10 into play.[316] However, public interest is the most common ground of resistance where publication is by the media and art.10 is then engaged. The "intense focus" is on the individual facts of the particular case.[317] Thus the claimant should seek to introduce any evidence which supports his case that the threatened level of intrusion into his private life would be substantial and damaging, and which undermines any claim to public interest.

32.69 Rebutting the defence. The most common responses in privacy claims are that the information is in the public domain, or otherwise was not information

---

[311] See for example *G v Wikimedia Foundation Inc.* [2009] EWHC 3148 (QB); [2010] E.M.L.R. 14.

[312] *Murray v Big Pictures (UK) Ltd* [2008] EWCA Civ 446; [2009] Ch. 481 at [36].

[313] *Murray v Big Pictures (UK) Ltd*, above.

[314] *Abbey v Gilligan* [2012] EWHC 3217 (QB); [2013] E.M.L.R. 12.

[315] First used by Lord Steyn in *Re S* [2004] UKHL 47; [2005] 1 A.C. 593 at [17]: the court must undertake "an intense focus on the comparative importance of the specific rights being claimed in the individual case". See also *Re BBC* [2009] UKHL 34; [2010] 1 A.C. 145.

[316] E.g. *P & Others v Quigley* [2008] EWHC 1051 (QB): "no conceivable public interest in making ... scurrilous allegations [against claimants]". Similar considerations apply in cases involving demands for money, such as *OPQ v BJM* [2011] EWHC 1059 (QB); [2011] E.M.L.R. 23.

[317] See *Mosley v News Group Newspapers Ltd* [2008] EWHC 1777 (QB), [2008] E.M.L.R.20 at [10].

in respect of which the claimant had a reasonable expectation of privacy, that the claimant gave his consent to the use of the information, and that publication was justified in the public interest. In most cases the evidence that the claimant will call or produce to establish his claim will cover these points, but specific allegations made by the defendant will have to be addressed.

Damages. The principal subjects of damages are distress, hurt feelings and loss of dignity suffered by the claimant as a consequence of the infringement of his privacy.[318] These are matters about which the claimant, and probably the claimant alone, can give evidence.[319] There may also be aggravating conduct by the defendant, like further intrusions into privacy after the incident the subject of the action. Advancing a case of public interest which fails may be aggravating conduct, but not (apparently) attacks on the claimant's character during the trial.[320] The award should take account of the fact that a right of the claimant has been infringed, and this requires more than a nominal amount.[321]   **32.70**

---

[318] Ibid. at [216].

[319] As in defamation cases, evidence of those who know the claimant well might also be admissible: see para.32.54, above.

[320] *Mosley v News Group Newspapers*, above at [223]. Eady J. said:

"There have, it is true, been attacks on the claimant's character (references to 'depravity' and so forth), but this is not a defamation case and reputation is not in issue. It would not be right to increase damages because of attacks on character which the defendant, if sued for libel, would wish to defend."

An alternative view is that an attack on a claimant's character based on what has been revealed by infringement of privacy must exacerbate the distress suffered by the claimant as a result of the infringement.

[321] *Mosley v News Group Newspapers* at [216]–[217].

CHAPTER 33

THE TRIAL: THE DEFENDANT'S CASE

SECTION 1. SUBMISSION OF NO CASE

Introductory. At the close of the claimant's case the defendant may be in   **33.1**
a position to ask the judge to dismiss the action on the ground that there is no
case to answer. Historically, trial of defamation claims by jury has been the
norm in England and Wales, but such trials are now rare and will soon be
rarer.[1] But where there is a jury, there is a high threshold to surmount before
the judge can take the case away from them. It is the same test as that applied
in criminal jury trials.[2] Where the evidence is such that its strength or
weakness depends on the view taken of a witness's reliability, or to other
matters which are generally speaking within the province of the jury, and on

---

[1] The law has been prospectively amended by s.11, Defamation Act 2013, to remove the
presumption in favour of jury trial in defamation cases.

[2] *Alexander v Arts Council of Wales* [2001] EWCA Civ 514; [2001] 1 W.L.R. 1840 per May
L.J. at [37]:
" . . . it is open to the judge in a libel case to come to the conclusion that the evidence, taken
at its highest, is such that a jury properly directed could not properly reach a necessary factual
conclusion. In those circumstances, it is the judge's duty, upon a submission being made to
him, to withdraw that issue from the jury. This is the test applied in criminal jury trials: see *R
v Galbraith* [1981] 1 W.L.R. 1039 at 1042c. In my view, it applies equally in libel actions."
In a jury trial, the defendant is not put to his election to call no evidence: *Young v Rank* [1950]
2 K.B. 510.

one possible view of the facts there is evidence upon which a jury could properly, and without being perverse, come to a conclusion in favour of the claimant, then the judge should allow the matter to be left to the jury.[3] The position is different where trial is by judge alone, where the defendant will generally be put to his election to call no evidence.[4] If he is, with the result that his evidence is left out of account, the judge's role is not so much to rule on a submission of no case as to decide whether the claimant has proved his case on a balance of probabilities, which in the circumstances is unlikely to be a heavy burden.[5]

However, if the defendant decides to make a submission, he may argue that there is no evidence of publication, or no evidence that the words complained of or words to similar effect were published, or that no evidence has been given on which the court could properly find that the words would be understood by reasonable persons to refer to the claimant. He may submit that the words complained of were incapable of defaming or harming the particular claimant.[6] He may contend that the words are not in their natural and ordinary meaning capable of being defamatory,[7] and, if a true innuendo meaning is pleaded, that there is no evidence on which the court could properly find that the words would be understood by reasonable persons in that meaning. Again, it may be clear that the words were published on a privileged occasion, and there may be no evidence of malice or (with the same consequence) the evidence may be equally consistent with the existence or non-existence of malice. Where honest comment has been pleaded, the defendant may urge that the matter is one of public interest and that there is no evidence of malice. If the action is one for slander of the claimant in the way of his office, profession or trade, there may be no evidence that the claimant held such an office, or carried on a profession or trade, at the date when the words were published, or there may be no evidence that the words were calculated to disparage him in his office, profession or trade.[8] In a case of

---

[3] This proposition is adapted from the well-known passage in *R. v Galbraith* [1981] 1 W.L.R. 1039 at 1042C.

[4] The general rule before a judge alone is that the defendant should be put to his election to call no evidence whatever the outcome of the submission: see comments in *Alexander v Rayson* [1936] 1 K.B. 169 at 178; *Benham Ltd v Kithira Investments* [2003] EWCA Civ 1794; *Graham v Chorley Borough Council* [2006] EWCA Civ 92. Where such an election is made, a new trial will only be ordered on appeal in exceptional circumstances: *Portland Management v Harte* [1977] Q.B. 306 CA. For a fuller discussion of this topic, particularly in the light of the court's powers under the CPR, reference should be made to para.32.1.6 of *Civil Procedure* Vol.1.

[5] See *Benham Ltd v Kithira Investments* (above) per Simon Brown L.J. at [30].

[6] *Multigroup Bulgaria Holding AD v Oxford Analytica Ltd* [2001] E.M.L.R. 737. Eady J. dismissed the claim at the end of the claimant's case, holding that the corporate claimant, a Bulgarian holding company, as it did not trade or exercise any management role in any of its subsidiaries, could not have been defamed or damaged with regard to any business or trading reputation in the eyes of reasonable readers.

[7] An application would now normally be made before trial under CPR 53PD, paras 4.1 to 4.4 ("Ruling on Meaning"). See Ch.30, s.2. If such an application were left until trial, there would probably be costs consequences.

[8] Defamation Act 1952, s.2.

alleged slander actionable only on proof of special damage, the defendant may be in a position to contend that there is no evidence of it, or that the special damage proved is insufficient in law to maintain the action, or is too remote.[9]

Judge's ruling postponed. Where in a jury trial a submission of no case   **33.2**
is made after the claimant has called his evidence, the judge has a discretion whether to rule on the matter at that stage or to defer ruling until the whole of the evidence has been called.[10] Indeed, he can, if he wishes, postpone his ruling until after verdict, and in a proper case give judgment for the defendant, even if a jury has returned a verdict in the claimant's favour.[11] It has been pointed out that the practice of taking the verdict of the jury before ruling whether there is evidence of malice has serious disadvantages where a number of disconnected circumstances by which malice is said to be established come into question,[12] but such a course can be convenient, for if the Court of Appeal should think that the judge's ruling was erroneous it will be unnecessary to send the case for retrial to another jury.[13] If the judge, at the end of the claimant's case, does rule that there is some evidence for the jury, he is entitled at the conclusion of the whole case, to reconsider his ruling, and enter judgment for the defendant if he is then of the opinion that the claimant's evidence fails to disclose any cause of action,[14] or is so weak that a verdict in his favour would be set aside by the Court of Appeal as unreasonable,[15] or perverse.[16]

SECTION 2. OPENING STATEMENT ON BEHALF OF THE DEFENDANT

Defendant's opening speech. If the defendant intends to call evidence, he   **33.3**
may, after the claimant has concluded his evidence, open his case to the jury.[17]

---

[9] See para.32.55, above.
[10] *Marbé v George Edwardes* [1928] 1 K.B. 269; *Cleghorn v Sadler* [1945] K.B. 325 at 328–329; *Young v Rank* [1950] 2 K.B. 510; but see *Parry v Aluminium Corporation* (1940) 162 L.T. 236, per Goddard L.J.
[11] See, e.g. *Adams v Coleridge* (1884) 1 T.L.R. 84 at 87.
[12] Per Lord Porter in *Turner v Metro-Goldwyn-Mayer Pictures Ltd* [1950] 1 All E.R. 449 at 453–454. The court will not know what matters the jury have relied upon for their finding of malice. Lord Porter's dicta covered taking the verdict of the jury before ruling whether the words are capable of a defamatory meaning, but as the court can now rule on this at an interim stage (CPR PD 53, paras 4.1 to 4.4) it is highly improbable that such an issue would be left for determination even until trial, let alone until the trial's end.
[13] *Skeate v Slaters* [1914] 2 K.B. 429. The benefit of following this course was pointed out in *Alexander v Arts Council of Wales*, above, at [45].
[14] *Skeate v Slaters*, above, at 434.
[15] Per Buckley L.J. in *Skeate v Slaters*, above, at 438; cf. *Banbury v Bank of Montreal* [1918] A.C. 626.
[16] See *Alexander v Arts Council of Wales*, above, at [36].
[17] This is subject to the overall discretion of the judge exercising his case management powers. He is unlikely to permit an opening speech if the defendant has already made a statement after the claimant's opening speech.

In doing so, he has no right to suggest to the jury that they could stop the case and say they had heard enough, or that they could send the claimant away at that stage with a derisory award of damages.[18]

SECTION 3. EVIDENCE FOR THE DEFENDANT: GENERAL

33.4 Context of alleged libel or slander. For the purpose of showing that the words are not defamatory, or do not bear the meaning put upon them by the claimant, the defendant is entitled (if he has pleaded the point)[19] to have put before the jury the whole article containing the alleged libel or to give in evidence the whole speech, dialogue or conversation in which the alleged slander was spoken.[20] If the alleged libel appeared in a newspaper, the defendant may be entitled to put in evidence any other article in the same issue which is referred to in the article containing the alleged libel or is otherwise connected with the article, on the basis that it is part of the context.[21] The question is whether the relevant articles (which may be on different pages or in different parts of the newspaper) are sufficiently closely connected to be regarded as a single publication.[22] However, if the passage on which the defendant wishes to rely is on a different page and there is no reference to it in the article, it may be regarded as too remote to have any bearing on the meaning of the words complained of.[23] The same principles are applied to internet publication,[24] where there may be questions as to whether different

---

[18] *Alexander v H Burgoine & Sons Ltd* [1939] 4 All E.R. 568; *Beevis v Dawson* [1957] 1 Q.B. 195 at 208–209, Singleton L.J.

[19] *Bookbinder v Tebbit* [1989] 1 W.L.R. 640 CA at 647.

[20] *Cooke v Hughes* (1824) Ry. & M. 112; *Chalmers v Payne* (1835) 2 Cr. M. & R. 156, Alderson B.; *Polly Peck v Trelford* [1986] 1 Q.B. 1000 at 1020; *Charleston v News Group Newspapers Ltd* [1995] 2 A.C. 65.

[21] *Dee v Telegraph Media Group Ltd* [2010] EWHC 924 (QB); [2010] E.M.L.R. 20; *Galloway v Telegraph Group Ltd* [2004] EWHC 2786 (QB); [2005] E.M.L.R. 7. In *Galloway*, Eady J. accepted as part of the context two documents found in the Foreign Ministry of Baghdad reproduced in full in the defendant's newspaper on the same day as one of the articles complained of, but not the subject of complaint. The judge agreed it was necessary to take them into account when considering meaning. The rule is hallowed by antiquity: see *Thornton v Stephen* (1837) 2 Moo. & R. 45, 174 E.R. 209.

[22] *Dee v Telegraph Media Group Ltd*, above. The words complained of were on the front page of the newspaper, where the words: "Full story: S20" appeared. The claimant made no complaint about the article in S20 (part of a sport supplement), but the defendant relied on it, arguing that the front page article had to be read together with S20. Sharp J. held that the ordinary reasonable reader was to be taken to have read the passages to which he was directed on subsequent pages, so that the two articles had to be read together to ascertain the meaning of the front page article complained of.

[23] In *R. v Lambert* (1810) 2 Camp. 398, 170 E.R. 1196, a case of seditious libel, a different passage in the paper was allowed to be put before the jury, albeit "disjoined from the passage complained of", seemingly because it was relevant to the issue of the defendant's intention. Lord Ellenborough ruled that "If there be any parts of the same paper upon the same topic with the libel, or fairly connected with it, the defendants have a right to their being read, although locally disjoined from it".

[24] See the discussion at para.3.34, above.

pages on a website, perhaps linked by a hyperlink, should be read together. Articles contained in different daily issues of the same newspaper, but connected with the subject-matter of the libel, may properly be regarded as part of the context, for example when they are part of a series.[25] Context may assume special importance to a defendant relying upon *Reynolds* privilege. Public interest will be assessed on an evaluation of the interest of the whole article or matter complained of and not wholly by reference to the defamatory statement.[26]

Reference to claimant. Where an alleged libel does not unambiguously   **33.5**
refer to the claimant, and the claimant has called witnesses to prove that the words refer to him, the defendant can call witnesses to state that they read the libel and did not understand it to refer to the claimant.[27] In such a case, however, if the jury are satisfied that a number of sensible and honest persons reasonably understood the libel to refer to the claimant it affords no answer to say that other persons did not think the same, and understood the words to refer to someone else.[28]

Slander. In cases of slander the defendant can call any persons who were   **33.6**
present to say that they did not hear the words alleged to have been spoken. The defendant can give evidence himself that there was nobody in earshot other than the claimant when he spoke the words.[29]

> "The evidence [however], of one person who swears that he heard the defendant utter the words complained of is, if the jury are satisfied that he is an honest witness, of greater weight than that of a number of persons who were present and did not hear the words."[30]

---

[25] In *Burrows v Knightley* (1987) 10 N.S.W.L.R. 651, material was serialised on different days, and Hunt J. allowed material published on different days to be pleaded in one paragraph of the statement of claim on the grounds that there was either an intention on the part of the defendants that the material be read together or the reader might reasonably be expected to read it together. Evidence of previous articles was admitted in *English and Scottish Cooperative v Odhams Press* [1940] 1 K.B. 440, but it seems there was no objection. In many situations, the reasoning in *Telnikoff v Matusevitch* [1992] 2 A.C. 343 may be applicable: readers of the words complained of may not have seen the other article in a previous issue or had it in mind. And it has been observed that subsequent articles can hardly affect the meaning of words at the time they were published. See *Simons Proprietary Ltd v Riddell* [1941] N.Z.L.R. 913; *Grappelli v Derek Block (Holdings) Ltd* [1981] 1 W.L.R. 822; but compare *Hayward v Thompson* [1982] Q.B. 47, where a subsequent article was relied upon for identification. In *Galloway v Telegraph Group Ltd* [2004] EWHC 276 (QB); [2005] E.M.L.R. 7 Eady J. directed a jury who had to consider parts of newspaper articles spread over two days that the first day's article could be borne in mind when considering the meaning of the second day's article, but not the other way round. In some cases subsequent articles are admitted on the issue of damages, to show repetition of the libel: e.g. *Darby v Ouseley* (1856) 1 H. & N. 1. See also the discussion at para.3.33, above.

[26] *Jameel (Mohammed) v Wall Street Journal Sprl* [2006] UKHL 44; [2007] A.C. 359.

[27] See *Godhard v Inglis* (1904) 2 C.L.R. 78 at 82.

[28] Per Avory J. in *Youssoupoff v Metro-Goldwyn-Mayer Pictures Ltd*, *The Times*, March 6, 1934.

[29] *Moberly v Comr of Police*, unreported, May 13, 1987, CA.

[30] Per Swift J. in *Silverman v Stein*, *The Times*, March 18, 1926.

33.7 Meaning of words. If the claimant relies on the natural and ordinary meaning of the words, no evidence is admissible by the defendant (or the claimant) as to their meaning. In theory at least, he may seek to displace the natural and ordinary meaning of the words by giving evidence of circumstances known to all those who read or heard the words which show that they would not have been understood in their natural and ordinary meaning, but in some other lesser defamatory or innocuous meaning.[31] If the claimant relies on an innuendo meaning, the defendant may lead evidence contradicting the extrinsic facts on which the claimant relies, or showing that they were not known to those to whom the words were published.

33.8 Claimant's office, profession, etc. Where the words are only actionable if they are calculated to disparage the claimant in any office, profession, calling, trade, or business, the defendant may give evidence to show that the claimant did not hold the office or carry on the profession, calling, trade or business at the time of the publication of the words complained of.

33.9 Defamation Act 2013, s.1 The Defamation Act prospectively introduces a statutory threshold, by which a statement is not defamatory unless its publication has caused or is likely to cause serious harm to the reputation of the claimant. A higher corporate threshold will apply (s.1(2)), by which harm to the reputation of a body that trades for profit is not "serious harm" unless it has caused or is likely to cause that body serious financial loss. The Act thus gives statutory effect to the concept of a threshold of seriousness already recognised by the common law.[32] If the defendant is in a position to adduce evidence to show (perhaps most probably in the case of a corporate claimant) that its reputation has not suffered or is not likely to suffer serious harm or financial loss, then there seems no reason why that should not be done.

SECTION 4. PROOF OF JUSTIFICATION[33]

33.10 Evidence confined to particulars. The evidence that the defendant can lead in support of a plea of justification is governed by the particulars of

---

[31] As happened in *Hankinson v Bilby* 175 E.R. 182 (1847) 2 Car. & K. 440. See also *Chiam See Tong v Xin Zhang Jiang Restaurant* [1995] 3 S.L.R. 196 mentioned at para.3.23, fn.260, above.

[32] See *Thornton v Telegraph Media Group Ltd* [2010] EWHC 1414 (QB); [2011] 1 W.L.R. 1985; *Cammish v Hughes* [2012] EWCA Civ 1655; [2013] E.M.L.R. 13 at [38]. The threshold already applies with particular force to a company: see for instance per Tugendhat J. in *Euromoney Institutional Investor plc v Aviation News Ltd* [2013] EWHC 1505 (QB) at [24]:

"... the likely effect upon a corporate claimant of any words complained of by it may not be sufficiently serious to provide the necessary justification for an interference with freedom of expression, even if they would have provided a sufficient justification for interference with the defendant's rights if the claimant were an individual."

[33] The common law defence of justification is prospectively abolished by s.2, Defamation Act 2013, which replaces it with a statutory defence of truth. The new section "is intended broadly to reflect the current law" (pace the Explanatory Notes to the Act, para.13), so it is suggested that existing practice will be substantially unchanged, at least in the short term.

justification, and the ambit of admissible evidence will be defined by the content of these particulars.[34] If he wishes to give evidence of matters not pleaded he must seek leave to amend to add fresh particulars.[35] Furthermore, the plea of justification will specify the defamatory meanings the defendant seeks to justify,[36] and he will be confined to establishing the truth of that meaning or meanings.

Exclusion of evidence. Whereas in criminal proceedings the court has a general discretion to exclude relevant evidence because of the adverse effect it is judged to have on the fairness of the proceedings,[37] it is doubted that a judge has any similar power under common law in a civil jury action.[38] However, under the CPR the trial judge does have the power to exclude evidence that would otherwise be admissible[39] and may properly do so in support of, and subject to, the overriding objective of ensuring that cases are dealt with expeditiously and justly.[40]   **33.11**

Onus and standard of proof. If the trial is by judge alone, it is likely that the meaning of the words will have been determined in advance of the trial.   **33.12**

---

[34] *Yorkshire Provident Co. v Gilbert* [1895] 2 Q.B. 148; and see CPR PD 53, para.2.5(2). This chapter attempts to focus on the trial of the action, not on issues of pleading, which should have been resolved well before trial. It is therefore not appropriate here to go into the rules of justification, such as the repetition rule or the so-called *Chase* levels of meaning. For a full analysis, see para.11.13, above.

[35] *Williams v Reason* [1988] 1 W.L.R. 96n per Stephenson L.J. at 100. However, the defendant may seek to introduce similar fact evidence on the basis that it is probative of a pleaded issue. The general rule is that facts, not evidence, are pleaded, but to avoid ambush the claimant should be notified in advance of trial of the intention to rely on similar fact evidence. Usually that will be achieved by service of witness statements. In *Desmond v Bower* [2008] EWHC 2952 (QB), the defendant's attempt to plead matters relating to other incidents apart from the one referred to in his book failed when the particulars were struck out as not going to the specific sting. However, Eady J. left open the question of whether evidence of those incidents could come back into the case as similar fact evidence (on the principles set out in *O'Brien v Chief Constable of South Wales Police* [2005] UKHL 26; [2005] 2 A.C. 534), deferring a decision on admissibility until witness statements were served. In the event, the defendant was refused permission by Eady J. a few days before trial to issue a witness summons with a view to leading evidence about another such incident: that decision was successfully appealed ([2009] EWCA Civ 667; [2010] E.M.L.R. 5).

[36] CPR PD 53, para.2.5(1); known as *Lucas-Box* particulars after *Lucas-Box v News Group Newspapers Ltd* [1986] 1 W.L.R. 49.

[37] Police and Criminal Evidence Act 1984, s.78.

[38] See *Phipson on Evidence*, 17th edn (London: Sweet & Maxwell, 2012), para.39–34, and *Arab Monetary Fund v Hashim (No.2)* [1990] 1 All E.R. 673 at 681.

[39] CPR r.32.1(2).

[40] *Polly Peck (Holdings) plc v Trelford* [1986] Q.B. 1000 per O'Connor L.J. at 1021; *Grobbelaar v News Group Newspapers Ltd* [2001] 2 All E.R. 437, C.A. In *O'Brien v Chief Constable of South Wales* [2003] EWCA Civ 1085, the Court of Appeal gave guidance on the exercise of the discretion to exclude in the context of similar fact evidence: see Brooke L.J. at [71]. In *Desmond v Bower (No.2)* [2009] EWCA Civ 857 the trial judge had excluded evidence which the defendant had sought to put in, on account of the unfairness which would result to the claimant, the material not having been put to the claimant in cross-examination and his case having closed. However, the Court of Appeal allowed the defendant's appeal, since (in its view) the question to be asked was whether it was manifestly unjust to exclude the evidence.

If there is a jury, then of course meaning will not be determined until the end of the case. The onus is upon the defendant to prove the truth of the words in their natural and ordinary meaning, whatever the jury find that to be, or in any innuendo meaning contended for by the claimant and accepted by the jury. The plea of justification will succeed if the defendant proves that the sting or substance of the defamatory words is true,[41] or, if the words contain two or more distinct charges, the defendant proves some of the charges to be true and those not so proved do not materially injure the claimant's reputation having regard to the truth of the other charges.[42] The standard of proof is the civil standard, on the balance of probabilities, and this is so even where the defamatory words and the plea of justification allege the commission of a criminal offence.[43] However:

> "The gravity of the issue becomes part of the circumstances which the court has to take into consideration in deciding whether or not the burden of proof has been discharged. The more serious the allegation the more cogent is the evidence required to overcome the unlikelihood of what is alleged and thus to prove it."[44]

33.13 Evidence of justification in mitigation if defence not pleaded. It is a long established rule that in the absence of a plea of justification the defendant cannot, in order to mitigate damages, give evidence of any facts tending to prove the truth of the libel.[45] Nor can he achieve that purpose by

---

[41] *Turcu v News Group Newspapers Ltd* [2005] EWHC 799 (QB) per Eady J. at [109]–[111]:
  " . . . English law is generally able to accommodate the policy factors underlying the Article 10 jurisprudence by means of established common law principles; for example that a defamatory allegation need only be proved, on a balance of probabilities, to be *substantially* true. The court should not be too literal in its approach or insist upon proof of every detail where it is not essential to the sting of the article. . . . In deciding whether any given libel is substantially true, the court will have well in mind the requirement to allow for exaggeration, at the margins, and have regard in that context also to proportionality. In other words, one needs to consider whether the sting of a libel has been established having regard to its overall gravity and the relative significance of any elements of inaccuracy or exaggeration."
  See also *Chase v News Group Newspapers Ltd* [2002] EWCA Civ 1772, [2003] E.M.L.R. 11 at [34].
[42] Defamation Act 1952, s.5. This provision is prospectively repealed by the Defamation Act 2013, s.2(4).
[43] *Hornal v Neuberger Products* [1957] 1 Q.B. 247.
[44] Per Ungoed-Thomas J. in *Re Dellow's Will Trust* [1964] 1 W.L.R. 451 at 455, approved in *Re H (minors)* [1996] A.C. 563 per Lord Nicholls at 586D. Similarly, see in the libel context *Chase v News Group Newspapers Ltd* [2002] EWCA Civ 1772, [2003] E.M.L.R. 11 per Brooke L.J. at [35]:
  "The burden of proving justification rests on the defendant. Although the standard of proof is the balance of probabilities, the more improbable an allegation the stronger must be the evidence that it did occur before, on the balance of probabilities, its occurrence will be established."
[45] *Smith v Richardson* (1737) Willes 20; *Underwood v Parks* (1744) 2 Str. 1200; *Waithman v Weaver* (1822) Dowl. & Ry. (N.P.) 10; *Rumsey v Webb* (1842) Car. & M. 104; *Watt v Watt* [1905] A.C. 115; *Hobbs v Tinling* [1929] 2 K.B. 1; *Speidel v Plato Films* [1961] A.C. 1090 per Lord Denning at 1133–1134.

cross-examination as to such facts, even if he expressly disavows justification, and states that he tenders the evidence merely in mitigation of damages.[46]

> "It is a principle as old as my recollection of Westminster Hall, that matter of justification cannot be given in evidence in an action in order to mitigate damages."[47]
> "Even in mitigation of damages it is well settled that you cannot go into evidence which, if proved, would constitute a justification. Nor does it appear to me that it makes any difference that the evidence is offered in cross-examination."[48]

Indeed, any attempt to give evidence of facts tending to prove the truth, or to elicit them by cross-examination of the claimant or his witnesses, when there is no plea of justification on the record, is a factor which the jury would be entitled to regard as aggravating the damages.[49]

However, some modification of these bare principles was achieved by the decision in *Burstein v Times Newspapers*.[50] To avoid the jury being put "in blinkers" when they came to assessing damages, the defendant may (though he has not sought to justify) lead evidence of directly relevant background facts in mitigation of damages, even though the facts might have been the ingredients of a defence of justification.

Evidence before the court on unsuccessful plea of justification or   **33.14**
honest comment. Where a defendant who has put forward a defence of justification or honest comment is unable to prove sufficient facts to establish the defence, he can still rely on such facts as he has proved to reduce the damages, "perhaps almost to vanishing point".[51] However, a defendant will be strictly limited to evidence that can truly be said to go to the pleaded defence and will not be allowed, under the guise of justification, to lead evidence, damaging to the claimant in other respects, which does not in reality go to justification at all.[52] This approach was confirmed in *Burstein v Times*

---

[46] Per Byles and Willes JJ. in *Bracegirdle v Bailey* (1859) 1 F. & F. 536 at 537; per Scrutton L.J. in *Hobbs v Tinling* [1929] 2 K.B. 1 at 18; per Greer L.J. ibid. at 39; per Sankey L.J. ibid. at 50.

[47] Per Lord Abinger in *Speck v Phillips* (1839) 5 M. & W. 279 at 281. This was a wrongful dismissal action, but it would seem the observation was intended generally.

[48] Per Lord Halsbury L.C. in *Watt v Watt* [1905] A.C. 115 at 118.

[49] See *Risk Allah Bey v Whitehurst* (1868) 18 L.T. (N.S.) 615 at 620; *Watt v Watt*, above, at 118. See also *Galloway v Telegraph Group Ltd* [2004] EWHC 2786 (QB); [2005] E.M.L.R. 7 per Eady J. at [203].

[50] [2001] 1 W.L.R. 579. This case is more fully discussed at para.33.43, below.

[51] Per Neill L.J. in *Pamplin v Express Newspapers Ltd* [1988] 1 W.L.R. 116 at 120; *Jones v Pollard* [1997] E.M.L.R. 233; *Turner v News Group Newspapers Ltd* [2006] EWCA Civ 540; [2006] 1 W.L.R. 3469, at [43]–[46]; *McKenna v MGN Ltd* [2007] EWHC 1996 (QB).

[52] Per Parker L.J. in *Atkinson v Fitzwalter* [1987] 1 W.L.R. 201 at 214:
"A defendant is entitled to rely in mitigation of damages on any evidence which is properly before the jury and this can include evidence in support of an unsuccessful plea of justification: see the judgment of Neill L.J. in *Pamplin v Express Newspapers Ltd* . . . It therefore appears to me to be of considerable importance that defendants should be strictly limited to evidence which can truly be said to go to justification and should not be allowed, under the guise of justification, to lead evidence which does not in reality go to justification at all."

Newspapers, where disapproval was expressed of the practice of seeking to put forward a weak case of justification so as to be able to use the facts pleaded in support of it in reduction of damages. This was described as "unsatisfactory tactical manoeuvring".[53]

33.15 Evidence admissible on other issues. Evidence which tends to prove some issue properly raised in the action is still admissible even though its effect may be to prove the truth of a libel to which no justification has been pleaded.[54] For example, where there is a defence of privilege, and the defendant wishes to refute an allegation of express malice, he may well want to establish that he honestly believed the statement to be true and to introduce evidence of the grounds of his belief: he will be permitted to do so. However, the jury would have to be directed that the evidence could not be treated as proving the truth of the defamatory allegation.

33.16 Other defamatory words. Where the claimant, in order to show malice, gives evidence of other defamatory words published by the defendant (not being mere repetition of the libel or slander charged), the defendant may prove the truth of such other words.[55]

33.17 Convictions. Where it is necessary to decide whether the claimant committed a criminal offence, proof that he stands convicted of that offence is conclusive evidence that he committed that offence, and his conviction is admissible accordingly.[56] For the purpose of identifying the facts on which the conviction was based, the contents of any document admissible as evidence of the conviction, and the contents of the information, complaint, indictment, or charge-sheet on which the claimant was convicted, are admissible in evidence, "without prejudice to the reception of any other admissible evidence for the purpose of identifying the facts on which the conviction was based".[57] The

---

Russell L.J. used almost identical words in *Prager v Times Newspapers Ltd* [1988] 1 W.L.R. 77 at 93.

[53] May L.J. at [22]. A claimant would be well advised to seek to strike out before trial such a weak or unsustainable case of justification.

[54] *Manning v Clement* (1831) 7 Bing. 362 (evidence directed at disproving plaintiff's assertion as to the nature of his business); and see *Peatling v Watson* [1909] V.L.R. 198 at 203, per Madden C.J., and *Delaney v News Media Ownership* [1976] 1 N.Z.L.R. at 326.

[55] *Warne v Chadwell* (1819) 2 Stark. 457; 171 E.R. 704. There may be the pleading difficulty that the claimant is likely to have pleaded the other defamatory words in his reply. In that event, it is suggested that the defendant should seek leave to put in a rejoinder (see CPR r.15.9).

[56] S.13(1), Civil Evidence Act 1968 as amended by s.12 (1) of the Defamation Act 1996. Thus particulars of claim that set out, as the words complained of, only those matters which appear in the certificate of conviction may be struck out as an abuse of the process of the court; but this will not be the case where the allegations include matters which go beyond the circumstances relating to the conviction: *Levene v Roxhan* [1970] 1 W.L.R. 1322. The section now only applies as against a claimant; if a conviction of a defendant or a person not a party to the action is relevant, proof of the conviction is not conclusive evidence of the commission of the offence, but upon such proof he will be taken to have committed the offence unless the contrary is proved.

[57] S.13(2), Civil Evidence Act 1968.

obvious alternative evidence, and the most comprehensive account of the facts, would be the trial judge's summing up, which may be proved by the shorthand writer's transcript.[58]

Spent convictions. Evidence of a spent conviction as defined by the Reha- **33.18**
bilitation of Offenders Act 1974[59] is not generally admissible.[60] This does not prevent a defendant in a defamation action from relying on such a conviction in support of a defence of justification, honest comment, or absolute or qualified privilege.[61] However, a plea of justification in those circumstances would be defeated by proof of malice.[62]

SECTION 5. PROOF OF FAIR OR HONEST COMMENT

Supporting facts. Evidence to sustain the defence of fair comment (now to **33.19**
be known briefly as honest comment),[63] will be largely directed to establishing the facts and matters relied upon as the basis of the comment.[64] Details of

---

[58] It was suggested by Phillimore L.J. in *Levene v Roxhan*, above, at 1326, that the transcript of some of the evidence given at the trial or of the summing-up might be introduced as evidence of the facts upon which the conviction was based. In *Brinks Ltd v Abu-Saleh and Others (No.2)* [1995] 1 W.L.R. 1487, the plaintiff brought civil proceedings in conversion against those involved in the Brink's Mat bullion robbery, whether as robbers, or conspirators, or handlers of stolen goods or the proceeds. The certificate of the conviction of one defendant stated baldly that he had been convicted of one count of conspiracy to handle stolen goods, and no connection with the robbery was stated. It was therefore necessary for the plaintiff to prove the facts on which the conviction had been based. It was held by Rimer J. that the shorthand writer's transcript of the trial judge's summing up would be admissible under s.4(1), Civil Evidence Act 1968. In *Taylor v Taylor* [1970] 1 W.L.R. 1148, C.A., a transcript of criminal proceedings was held to be admissible in evidence under ss.2(1) and 4(1) of that Act.

[59] The Act is fully explained in Ch.18, above.

[60] S.4(1), Rehabilitation of Offenders Act 1974.

[61] S.8(3) of the Act, which has been prospectively amended by the Defamation Act 2013, s.16(2) to replace the reference to justification and honest comment with a reference to the new defences under s.2 (truth) and s.3 (honest opinion).

[62] S.8(5) of the Act, which has been prospectively amended by the Defamation Act 2013, s.16(3) to replace the reference to justification with a reference to the new defence under s.2 (truth). For what constitutes malice in this context, see para.18.17, above.

[63] That is the Supreme Court's preferred name for the defence: *Joseph v Spiller* [2010] UKSC 53; [2011] 1 A.C. 852. However, this common law rebranding has been overtaken by Parliament, which has prospectively abolished the defence of fair comment and replaced it with a new statutory defence of honest opinion: s.3, Defamation Act 2013. That had been the name proposed by the Court of Appeal, because recent legislation in other common law jurisdictions (New Zealand, Australia and Ireland) now describes the defence as honest opinion, and because "to describe the defence for what it is would lend greater emphasis to its importance as an essential ingredient of the right to free expression, . . . (and) better reflects the realities": *British Chiropractic Association v Singh* [2010] EWCA Civ 350; [2011] 1 W.L.R. 133 at [35]–[36].

[64] What facts qualify as supporting facts for the comment were summarised by Eady J. in *Lowe v Associated Newspaper* Ltd [2006] EWHC 320 (QB); [2007] 2 W.L.R. 595. Included in the requirements are that they must have (1) existed at the time of publication, and (2) have been known, at least in general terms to the commentator at the time the comment was made, albeit that he may have forgotten them.

such matters have to be included in the defence.[65] Clearly the evidence will be confined to these particulars,[66] and (if malice has been pleaded) to the issue of whether the defendant honestly held the view expressed.[67] Where the comment is based on a statement made on a privileged occasion,[68] the defendant must demonstrate that his report of the statement was fair and accurate.[69]

33.20 Fact or comment. (1) The question whether the words the subject of the claim are statements of fact or expressions of opinion is decided upon a consideration of the words themselves.[70] It is not permissible to have regard to some other article, letter, document or publication in response to which the words were written which have not been repeated or summarised in the defendant's words.[71] It is submitted, however, that the words must be appraised within their entire relevant context in adjudicating whether they are fact or comment.[72] No oral evidence is admissible on this issue.[73]

33.21 Fairness of comment. (2) As this is to be judged objectively, applying the test whether any man, however prejudiced and obstinate, could honestly hold the view expressed by the defendant on the facts known to him,[74] it is unnecessary for the defendant (absent a plea of malice) to state in evidence that he did indeed hold the opinion stated,[75] although his evidence should state what facts were known to him.

(3) However, if malice is alleged it will of course be essential for the defendant to give evidence to rebut the charge. Since honesty of belief is the

---

[65] CPR PD 53, para.2.6(2); *Cunningham-Howie v Dimbleby* [1951] 1 K.B. 360; *Lord v Sunday Telegraph* [1971] 1 Q.B. 235. See para.27.19, above.

[66] As with justification: *Yorkshire Provident v Gilbert* [1895] 1 Q.B. 148 at 152; and see *Aga Khan v Times Publishing Co.* [1924] 1 K.B. 675 per Sargent L.J. at 684; *Cunningham-Howie v Dimbleby*, above.

[67] *Tse Wai Chun v Cheng* [2000] HKCFA 86 [2001] E.M.L.R. 31.

[68] See *Mangena v Wright* [1909] 2 K.B. 958; *Grech v Odhams Press* [1958] 2 Q.B. 275.

[69] *Brent Walker Group v Time Out* [1991] 2 Q.B. 33.

[70] It is instructive to consider the analysis of the Court of Appeal in *British Chiropractic Association v Singh*, above, in which the court was able to find that the assertion that there was "not a jot of evidence" for the claims of chiropractic was, in context, a value judgment; and that undertaken by Gray J. in *Oliver v Chief Constable of Northumbria* [2003] EWHC 2417 (QB); [2004] E.M.L.R. 32 at [22]–[33]. See also *Haines v Television New Zealand* [2004] NZAR 513: " . . . a statement of fact without reference to any other facts on which it was based could not be opinion or comment."

[71] *Telnikoff v Matusevitch* [1992] 2 A.C. 343.

[72] This proposition was confirmed by Sir Philip Otton in *Branson v Bower (No.1)* [2001] EWCA Civ 791; [2001] E.M.L.R. 800 at [16] when he stated—upholding the ruling of Eady J.—that "the words complained of *when taken in the context of the article as a whole* are such that no reasonable jury could conclude other than that they were comment" (emphasis added).

[73] See *Cornwell v Myskow* [1987] 1 W.L.R. 630 CA at 637–638; *Jeyaretnam v Goh Chok Tong* [1989] 1 W.L.R. 1109 PC at 1113.

[74] *Tse Wai Chun v Cheng* [2000] HKCFA 86; [2001] E.M.L.R. 31; *Telnikoff v Matusevitch*, above (and see Lloyd L.J. in CA [1991] 1 Q.B. 102 at 105); *Pervan v N. Queensland Newspaper Co.* [1993] 178 A.L.R. 301; *Merivale v Carson* (1887) 20 Q.B.D. 275.

[75] In a clear case the judge can rule, without hearing evidence, that the comment must be considered as fair: see *Branson v Bower (No.2)* [2001] E.M.L.R. 809.

critical factor,[76] the defendant's evidence will be required to establish this or to rebut the allegation that the opinion he expressed was not one genuinely held by him.

It is worth noting that Defamation Act 2013, s.3, by which honest comment is prospectively abolished and replaced with a statutory defence of honest opinion, makes some significant changes to the common law. One of them is that, by s.3(4), there will be a condition that an honest person could have held the opinion on the basis of any facts which existed at the time when the statement was published. Crucially, by contrast with the common law, there is no requirement that the facts should have been known to the commentator. Presumably the result is that provided facts exist, even if not known to the defendant, then if an honest-minded person could have held the opinion on those facts (the facts that existed even if not known to the defendant) he is protected.

Matter of public interest. This is a question for the judge to decide[77] and **33.22** he is unlikely to be assisted by, or to require, the opinion of others. The surrounding circumstances about which evidence may be given as part of the factual substratum of the comment may bear upon the issue whether the subject-matter of the comment is one of public interest, which is not to be confined within narrow limits.[78] S.3 of the Defamation Act prospectively removes any public interest element from the new statutory defence of honest opinion.

Section 6. Proof of Privilege

Facts creating privilege must be proved. Where the defendant relies on **33.23** the defence of privilege, he must prove the facts and circumstances necessary for the existence of the privilege unless they are not in dispute or are already in evidence, e.g. he has elicited them in cross-examination of the claimant or his witnesses. In these instances, the advocate for the defendant will be in a position to submit that the occasion was privileged and that there is no evidence of malice to go to the jury, and, if successful in his submission, will avoid the necessity of calling the defendant to establish the privilege and avoid also the risk of affording in cross-examination evidence of malice which might defeat the privilege.[79]

---

[76] *Tse Wai Chun v Cheng* [2000] HKCFA 86 [2001] E.M.L.R. 31.

[77] *Jones v Skelton* [1963] 1 W.L.R. 1362 per Lord Morris at 1378.

[78] *Tse Wai Chun v Cheng*, above.

[79] The judge is not bound to rule on either issue at this juncture; and even if the judge does make a ruling which disposes of the case, the jury may still be invited to return a verdict, in case the ruling is disturbed on appeal: see Bingham L.J. in *Kingshott v Associated Kent Newspapers Ltd* [1991] 1 Q.B. 88 at 101; and also *Alexander v Arts Council of Wales* [2001] EWCA Civ 514; [2001] 1 W.L.R. 1840 per May L.J. at [45].

33.24 Facts only need be proved. The defendant need only prove the facts and circumstances necessary for the existence of the privilege, and it will then normally be for the judge to rule whether there is a reciprocity of duty or interest or other ground of privilege, but the defendant may also lead evidence to show that an interest or duty exists.[80] Such evidence may not carry much impact unless given by a witness other than the defendant himself, as the defendant's belief that he had an interest or duty in making the statement or communicating the information is irrelevant to the question whether the occasion is privileged.[81] Where privilege is claimed on the grounds that the publication is a fair and accurate report of public proceedings or of an official document,[82] the defendant will have to lead evidence as to what was stated in the material part of the proceedings or document so that the jury can consider the fairness and accuracy of the publication.[83] Where statutory privilege is claimed under s.15 of the Defamation Act 1996, evidence may be called to support the defendant's case that publication of the matter was of public concern and for the public benefit.[84]

33.25 *Reynolds* or public interest privilege. Where *Reynolds*[85] or public interest privilege is pleaded, there is likely to be a heavy evidential burden on the defendant,[86] as it is an essential ingredient of the privilege, which it is for the defendant to establish, that the publisher or journalist has acted responsibly. As regards the common law defence at any rate, the evidence will no doubt focus on the "non-exhaustive list of circumstances" set out in the speech of

---

[80] e.g. *Winstanley v Bampton* [1943] K.B. 319, where evidence was given by naval and military officers that a commanding officer in H.M. Forces had an interest in seeing that junior officers serving under him did not incur debts they were unable to discharge, which led to the judge ruling that a letter written by a creditor of a junior officer to his commanding officer to secure payment of a debt was written on a privileged occasion.

[81] *Stuart v Bell* [1891] 2 Q.B. 341; *Hebditch v MacIlwaine* [1894] 2 Q.B. 54.

[82] See Sch.1 to the Defamation Act 1996.

[83] See, e.g. *Kingshott v Associated Newspapers Ltd* [1991] 1 Q.B. 88.

[84] S.15(3), Defamation Act 1996; *Kingshott v Associated Newspapers* [1991] 1 Q.B. 88; *Qadir v Associated Newspapers Ltd* [2012] EWHC 2606 (QB); [2013] E.M.L.R. 15, where the judge held that although public concern and public benefit were objective questions for the judge, on which the defendant's belief was immaterial, it was relevant to consider what the defendant said about his belief.

[85] [2001] 2 A.C. 127. The defence is fully discussed at para.15.2, above. However, it must be noted that the common law defence known as *Reynolds* privilege has been prospectively abolished by s.4, Defamation Act 2013, which will create a new defence of publication on a matter of public interest, intended to reflect the principles established by case law. The court will be obliged by s.4(2) to have regard to all the circumstances in determining whether the defendant has shown that the statement complained of was, or formed part of, a statement on a matter of public interest, and that he reasonably believed that publishing the statement complained of was in the public interest.

[86] The difficulties to which this evidential burden can give rise are illustrated by the judge's analysis of the defendant's evidence in the early case of *Loutchansky v Times Newspapers Ltd (No.4)* [2001] E.M.L.R. 38. (The case was later remitted to the judge by the Court of Appeal for reconsideration in respect of one misdirection of law: [2001] EWCA Civ 1805; [2002] Q.B. 783).

Lord Nicholls in *Reynolds*,[87] with particular attention being given to the source of the journalist's information, the steps taken to verify the information, the urgency of the matter, whether comment was sought from the claimant, and the circumstances of the publication. Some of the circumstances will not be relevant in every case, since each case turns on its own facts. Verification is likely to be an important factor in most cases: the responsible journalist must take reasonable steps to satisfy himself that the allegation is true. That, according to Lord Phillips, has a subjective and an objective element: not only must he satisfy himself of the truth of what he intends to publish, but his belief must be the result of a reasonable investigation and must have been a reasonable belief to hold.[88] Much will depend on the meaning of the material to be published: the duty of verification will attach to whichever *Chase* level of meaning the allegation bears,[89] and the journalist ought to have had regard to the meanings that a reasonable reader might attribute to the material.[90] The journalist will therefore have to be prepared to explain in evidence what range of meanings was contemplated and why. Moreover, there will generally need to be evidence that the journalist or the editor has, in forming a judgment about publication, weighed the public interest in knowing the information (if it is true) against the harm likely to be caused to the claimant by publication of damaging allegations.[91] Since the new statutory defence under the Defamation Act 2013, s.4 is intended to

---

[87] "Depending on the circumstances, the matters to be taken into account include the following. The comments are illustrative only. 1. The seriousness of the allegation. The more serious the charge, the more the public is misinformed and the individual harmed, if the allegation is not true. 2. The nature of the information, and the extent to which the subject matter is a matter of public concern. 3. The source of the information. Some informants have no direct knowledge of the events. Some have their own axes to grind, or are being paid for their stories. 4. The steps taken to verify the information. 5. The status of the information. The allegation may have already been the subject of an investigation which commands respect. 6. The urgency of the matter. News is often a perishable commodity. 7. Whether comment was sought from the plaintiff. He may have information others do not possess or have not disclosed. An approach to the plaintiff will not always be necessary. 8. Whether the article contained the gist of the plaintiff's side of the story. 9. The tone of the article. A newspaper can raise queries or call for an investigation. It need not adopt allegations as statements of fact. 10. The circumstances of the publication, including the timing. This list is not exhaustive. The weight to be given to these and any other relevant factors will vary from case to case."
([2001] 2 A.C. 127 at 205).

[88] *Flood v Times Newspapers Ltd* [2012] UKSC 11; [2012] 2 A.C. 273 per Lord Phillips at [78]–[79]. "In most cases [the exception being "reportage"] the *Reynolds* defence will not get off the ground unless the journalist honestly and reasonably believed that the statement was true . . . ": per Lord Hoffmann, *Jameel (Mohammed) v Wall Street Journal Europe Sprl* [2006] UKHL 44; [2007] A.C. 359 at [62].

[89] Ibid., particularly at [79]–[80].

[90] The full range of meanings, according to Lords Phillips and Brown (ibid. at [51] and [111]); but cf. Lord Mance at [129]—quaere whether the journalist should have in mind the least damaging of the possible meanings (referring to *Bonnick v Morris* [2002] UKPC 31; [2003] 1 A.C. 300).

[91] Ibid. at [66], [68], [113], [184].

reflect the common law,[92] it seems that substantially the same matters will need to be addressed in evidence.

33.26 Reportage. "Reportage" cases may broadly be defined as those in which the public interest lies in knowing that the allegations have been made, and in their being reported fairly and disinterestedly, rather than in the content or truth of the allegations.[93] It is "a special kind of responsible journalism, but with distinctive features of its own".[94] In such cases, there is no need for the publisher to concern itself with whether the allegations are true or false, so there is no obligation to verify where the truth lies.[95] Similarly, it may be unrealistic in such cases to expect the journalist to seek comment from the parties. That said, all the circumstances (including those on Lord Nicholls' non-exhaustive list)[96] should be considered, adjusted as necessary for the special nature of reportage.[97] The journalists involved should normally give evidence as to what their intentions were in reporting the story, although the test is objective, not subjective; and their evidence should cover all the circumstances surrounding the gathering of the information, the manner of its reporting and the purpose to be served. In the words of Ward L.J.: "Protection will be lost if the journalist adopts the report and makes it his own or if he fails to report the story in a fair, disinterested and neutral way."[98]

SECTION 7. REBUTTAL OF MALICE

33.27 Presumption of good faith. If the occasion is privileged, it is presumed in the defendant's favour that he acted without malice.[99]

> "It is clear that it was not for the defendant to prove that he was acting from a sense of duty, but for the plaintiff to satisfy the jury that the defendant was acting from some other motive than a sense of duty."[100]

---

[92] See the Explanatory Notes to the Act, para.29. See also fn.85 and para.15.4, above.

[93] The common law reportage doctrine will be abolished as part of the abolition of the *Reynolds* privilege defence when the Defamation Act s.4(6) comes into effect. S.4(3) of the Act is intended to "encapsulate the core of . . . the doctrine": Explanatory Notes to the Act, para.32. However, it is notable that the statutory provision seems significantly narrower in its potential application than its common law antecedent. For one, it is confined to accounts of disputes to which the claimant was a party. See further para.15.4, above.

[94] *Roberts v Gable* [2007] EWCA Civ 721; [2008] Q.B. 502 per Ward L.J. at [60].

[95] *Flood v Times Newspapers Ltd*, above, at [34]; *Roberts v Gable*, above, per Ward L.J. at [61(2), (3)].

[96] See fn.87, above.

[97] *Roberts v Gable* at [61(6)].

[98] Ibid., [61(4)–(5)].

[99] *Clark v Molyneux* (1877) 3 Q.B.D. 237; *Jenoure v Delmouge* [1891] A.C. 73.

[100] Per Cotton L.J. in *Clark v Molyneux*, above, at 251.

Similarly, if the words complained of are honest comment, it is for the claimant to prove that the defendant was malicious, in the sense that he did not honestly believe that his comment was justified or did not honestly hold the opinion expressed.[101]

Allegation of express malice. Where privilege (or honest comment) is   **33.28**
raised as a defence it is common for the claimant to allege by way of reply that the defendant was actuated by express malice. In that situation, the defendant will wish to give evidence to rebut the allegation of malice. The nature of that evidence will obviously depend on the way in which the claimant puts his case on malice, which must be fully pleaded in his reply.[102] If it is alleged that the defendant had no honest belief in the truth of the defamatory statement, or published it recklessly without considering or caring whether it be true or not, the defendant would give evidence as to his belief in the truth of the statement and the grounds of his belief,[103] notwithstanding that the effect of such evidence might be to prove the truth of the statement.[104] Further, a defendant who is the author of the defamatory statement can give evidence that he did not intend or believe his words to convey the defamatory meaning attributed to them, and that in the meaning which he intended and believed the words to convey he believed them to be true.[105] Similarly, if the allegation is that the defendant did not believe that his honest comment was justified, then the defendant must adduce evidence to show that he did honestly hold the relevant opinion.[106]

---

[101] *Tse Wai Chun Paul v Albert Cheng* [2000] HKCFA 35; [2001] E.M.L.R. 777 per Lord Nicholls at [75]; *Joseph v Spiller* [2010] UKSC 53; [2011] 1 A.C. 852 at [68], [69], [108].

[102] CPR PD 53, para.2.9.

[103] For example, the sources of his information, and why he felt it right to rely on them. See e.g. *Cockayne v Hodgkisson* (1833) 5 C. & P. 543 at 545, 546; 172 E.R. 1091.

[104] This proposition, for which there was little authority (although *Pearson v Lemaitre* (1843) 5 M. & Gr. 700 at 710; 134 E.R. 742 provided some guidance) was approved by the Court of Appeal in *Warren v Random House* [2008] EWCA Civ 834; [2009] Q.B. 600 at [91]. However, as the court emphasised, what is admissible is evidence as to state of mind, not as to the truth of the allegation. *Cockayne v Hodgkisson*, above, is instructive: the plaintiff, a gamekeeper, complained of a letter accusing him of covertly selling his employer's game. The judge allowed the defendant, on the issue of his good faith, to call evidence about representations made to the defendant before he wrote the letter about the plaintiff associating with poachers, but not evidence to prove that the plaintiff did associate with poachers.

[105] *Loveless v Earl* [1999] E.M.L.R. 530, CA. As Hirst L.J. said at 538–9,
" . . . it is very important to contrast the test for meaning on the one hand and the test for malice on the other. Meaning is an objective test, entirely independent of the defendant's state of mind or intention. Malice is a subjective test, entirely dependent on the defendant's state of mind and intention. Thus, in a case where words are ultimately held objectively to bear meaning A, if the defendant subjectively intended not meaning A but meaning B, and honestly believed meaning B to be true, then the plaintiff's case on malice would be likely to fail".
See also *Bonnick v Morris* [2002] UKPC 31; [2003] 1 A.C. 300, where the Privy Council considered a journalist's understanding of the meaning of the words complained of in a case of *Reynolds* privilege.

[106] See fn.101, above.

SECTION 8. EVIDENCE IN MITIGATION OF DAMAGES

33.29 Categories of evidence. Admissible evidence that can be given in mitigation of damages can be placed in the following categories:

(1) claimant's bad reputation;
(2) facts relevant to the contextual background in which the defamatory publication came to be made;
(3) evidence properly before the court on some other issue;
(4) facts which tend to disprove malice;
(5) claimant's own conduct;
(6) apology or other amends;
(7) damages already recovered for same libel.

To those categories may be added another, applicable where the allegations have low credibility: evidence that readers did not believe the words complained of, and evidence that the originator of the allegations (*ex hypothesi* not the defendant) had low credibility, may be capable of reducing general damages.[107]

The decision of the European Court of Human Rights in *Steel & Morris v United Kingdom* appeared to point to a further category, namely, the defendant's means.[108] Relying on that decision, it was argued in *Gur v Avrupa Newspapers Ltd*[109] that the judge should have taken into account the means of the defendant. Dyson L.J. expressed the view, albeit obiter, that it was a fundamental and long established principle of English law that the means of a defendant were irrelevant to the assessment of damages for a tort, and if that was to be changed following the *Steel & Morris* decision the change would have to be made by the House of Lords.[110] For the moment, therefore, it does not seem that the income and resources of the defendant would be regarded as admissible on the issue of damages.

Nothing is admissible in evidence for the purpose of mitigating damages if the defendant has introduced it on the understanding that it should not be so used, or disclaiming any intention so to use it.[111]

---

[107] *Oriental Daily Publisher Ltd v Ming Pao Holdings Ltd* [2012] HKFCA 59; [2013] E.M.L.R. 7, where the leading judgment was given by Ribeiro P.J., with whom Lord Neuberger agreed. See also *Morgan v Odhams Press Ltd* [1971] 1 W.L.R. 1239 at 1252, per Lord Morris of Borth-y-Gest.

[108] (2005) App. no.64816/01; [2005] E.M.L.R. 15. The court held that the award of damages in the case (a total of £76,000) was disproportionate and amounted to a breach of art.10 because although moderate by contemporary standards in England and Wales, it was very substantial when compared to the modest income and resources of the defendants.

[109] [2008] EWCA Civ 594; [2009] E.M.L.R. 4.

[110] At [25]. Tuckey and Buxton L.JJ. agreed with Dyson L.J.'s judgment.

[111] Per Lord Radcliffe in *Associated Newspapers Ltd v Dingle* [1964] A.C. 371 at 395–396: "I think in this sort of case courts should be strict on such a point"; and see Lord Morris at 416.

(a) *Claimant's bad reputation*

Evidence of general bad reputation. The admissibility of evidence of **33.30**
bad reputation in mitigation of damages in actions for defamation was fully
considered in *Scott v Sampson*,[112] and the judgment of Cave J., with which
Mathew J. concurred, has been accepted as an accurate statement of the
law.[113] After an exhaustive review of the authorities, the judgment divided the
evidence which it was suggested might be given in mitigation of damages into
three heads:

(1) evidence of general bad reputation;
(2) evidence of rumours that the plaintiff had done what was charged in the
    libel;
(3) evidence of particular acts of misconduct on the part of the plaintiff
    tending to show his character and disposition.

The court held that evidence of general bad reputation was admissible in
mitigation of damages; but that evidence falling within classes (2) and (3) was
not admissible.[114]

The reasoning supporting the admissibility of such evidence was explained by **33.31**
Cave J.[115];

"Speaking generally, the law recognises in every man a right to have the estimation
in which he stands in the opinion of others unaffected by false statements to his
discredit; and if such false statements are made without lawful excuse, and damage
results to the person of whom they are made, he has a right of action. The damage,
however, which he has sustained must depend almost entirely on the estimation in
which he was previously held. He complains of an injury to his reputation; and it
seems most material that the jury who have to award those damages should know,
if the fact is so, that he is a man of no reputation. 'To deny this would' as is observed
in Starkie, *Evidence*, 'be to decide that a man of the worst character is entitled to the
same measure of damages with one of unsullied and unblemished reputation. A
reputed thief would be placed on the same footing with the most honourable
merchant, a virtuous woman with the most abandoned prostitute. To enable the jury
to estimate the probable quantum of injury sustained a knowledge of the party's
previous character is not only material, but seems to be absolutely essential.' It is
said that the admission of such evidence will be a hardship upon the plaintiff, who
may not be prepared to rebut it; and under the former practice, where the damages
could not be pleaded to, and general evidence of bad character was allowed to be

---

[112] (1882) 8 Q.B.D. 491.
[113] *Hobbs v Tinling* [1929] 2 Q.B. 1; *Plato Films v Spiedel* [1961] A.C. 1090; *Associated Newspapers Ltd v Dingle* [1964] A.C. 371.
[114] The Working Group on Practice and Procedure in Defamation under the chairmanship of Neill L.J. recommended in July 1991 the abolition of the rule in *Scott v Sampson* so as to enable a defendant to plead and prove specific acts, to a plaintiff's discredit, by way of mitigating damages. The Defamation Bill 1996 included a clause to implement this recommendation (cl.13) but the clause was lost at the Committee stage in the House of Commons.
[115] (1882) 8 Q.B.D. 491 at 503.

given under a plea of not guilty, there was something in this objection, which, however, is removed under the present system of pleading,[116] which requires that all material facts shall be pleaded, and a plaintiff who has notice that general evidence of bad character will be adduced against him, can have no difficulty whatever if he was a man of good character in coming prepared with friends who have known him to prove that his reputation has been good. On principle, therefore, it would seem that general evidence of reputation should be admitted, and on turning to the authorities it will be found that it has been admitted in a great majority of those cases and that its admission has been approved by a great majority of the judges who have expressed an opinion on the subject."[117]

33.32 Admissible evidence. While "It is, no doubt, true that in practice it may be difficult to define exactly . . . the borderline between evidence of general bad reputation and that of specific conduct which has led to it",[118] it is settled that only evidence of general bad reputation is admissible.[119] However, it has been held that conviction of a serious crime is evidence that the claimant has a bad reputation,[120] and it may still be open to argument that evidence of the claimant's involvement in a single notorious event is admissible as tending to prove general bad reputation.[121] It would seem that the claimant may make an admission of bad reputation.[122]

---

[116] It is good practice to set out in the defence details of any matters relied upon in mitigation of damages, and thoroughly bad practice not to do so, but although since the introduction of the CPR there has been no express rule to that effect. The RSC required both parties to plead matters relied on in relation to damages, but the CPR now requires only the claimant to do so (CPR 53, PD para.2(10)). This can only have been an oversight. See fn.165 in Ch.27, above.

[117] Such evidence was admitted by Heath J. in *Kirkmam v Oxley* (1811–1816); by Holroyd J. in *Ellershaw v Robinson*, Lanc.Sp. Ass. 1824; by Lord Tenterden C.J. in *Mawby v Barber*, Linc. Summ. Ass. 1826; by Lord Denham (after consulting Parke B). in *Moore v Oastler*, York Sp. Ass. 1836; and by Coltman J. in *Hardy v Alexander*, Liv. Summ. Ass. 1837. These cases are cited in Starkie, *Evidence*, 3rd edn, pp.306, 641, 642.

[118] Per Viscount Simonds in *Plato Films v Speidel* [1961] A.C. 1090 at 1124–1125.

[119] *Plato Films v Speidel*, above. Lord Radcliffe expressed the opinion (1131) that it would be wrong to hold that general evidence of reputation could not include evidence citing particular incidents, if they were of sufficient notoriety to be likely to contribute to current reputation, since "such incidents are, after all, the basic material upon which the reputation rests". This view was not endorsed by any of the members of the Appellate Committee. Nevertheless, Lord Radcliffe tentatively repeated his proposition in *Associated Newspapers Ltd v Dingle* [1964] A.C. 371 at 399–400: "It may still be that in a proper case a man's bad reputation can be proved by giving evidence of some incident of notoriety", though he acknowledged that the law might have confined itself to "hazy generalities (such) as 'a well-known pickpocket' or a 'notorious prostitute'". In *Hunt v Evening Standard Limited* [2011] EWHC 272 (QB) Tugendhat J. refused to strike out a plea of general bad reputation which alleged that the claimant's reputation among law enforcement agencies was as the head of one of the most notorious organised crime groups in the country, and that he was regarded as extremely dangerous and violent.

[120] *Goody v Odhams Press* [1967] 1 Q.B. 333. However, that would not apply to all convictions, e.g. where they occurred long ago or are irrelevant to the imputation complained of: see Salmon L.J. in *Goody v Odhams Press* at 344. Convictions which are spent under the Rehabilitation of Offenders Act 1974 would not be admissible.

[121] In addition to Lord Radcliffe in *Associated Newspapers Ltd v Dingle* [1964] A.C. 371, see Lord Cohen at 406, and Salmon L.J. in *Goody v Odhams Press*, above, at 343; but Lord Denning in *Dingle* said, "Nor can the report of a single incident, even if it be notorious, be brought up against the plaintiff" (at 412).

[122] Per Lord Denning in *Associated Newspapers Ltd v Dingle* [1964] A.C. 371 at 412, citing *Hawkins v Express Dairy* (1940) 163 L.T. 147, although what the plaintiff did in that case was to

Reputation in relevant sector. Evidence of general bad reputation must   **33.33**
be confined to the sector of the claimant's character relevant to the libel.[123] If
the libel charges the claimant with treachery, evidence that he has a reputation
for loose morals would be inadmissible in mitigation of damages.[124] However,
in *Wood v Cox*[125] the plaintiff, a jockey, brought an action for libel charging
him with having pulled a particular horse on two specified occasions; evidence was admitted from four officials of the Jockey Club about the plaintiff's
reputation for foul riding and not trying to win.

Evidence of subsequent bad character. The evidence must be confined   **33.34**
to the general bad character of the claimant before, or at the time of, the
publication of the libel.[126] Evidence of bad character after that time is not
admissible in mitigation of damages, otherwise "a person might slander
another and then call some of the neighbours to say that they had heard
imputations which he had himself set afloat".[127]

Rumours. As to evidence of rumours that the claimant had done what was   **33.35**
charged in the libel, Cave J. indicated why such evidence could not be led:

---

admit to particular acts of misconduct as grave as those alleged in the libel (there must be doubt
as to whether the judge was entitled to take the admission into account in assessing damages,
particularly as *Scott v Sampson* was not referred to). Further, in *Plato Films v Speidel* Lord
Denning said: "The plaintiff cannot speak as to his own character and reputation because he does
not know what other people think of him, or, at any rate he cannot give evidence of what they
think of him" (at 1143). In *Jones v Pollard* [1997] E.M.L.R. 233 CA, there was a reference to the
"plaintiff's acknowledgement of his own bad reputation" (at 252).

[123] Per Lord Radcliffe in *Plato Films v Speidel* [1961] A.C. 1090 at 1131; also Lord Denning
at 1140.

[124] Per Devlin L.J. in *Plato Films v Speidel*, above, at 1102 CA. In *Jorgensen v New Zealand
Newspapers* [1974] 2 N.Z.L.R. 45, previous convictions were ruled irrelevant as having no
bearing upon that aspect of the plaintiff's reputation affected by the libel.

[125] (1888) 4 T.L.R. 652. By contrast, in *Shave v West Australian Newspapers* [2003] WASC 83,
where the plaintiff was a government minister and the defamatory allegation was that he had
given misleading evidence at an official inquiry, the court refused to strike out a plea that the
plaintiff had a reputation as a minister who had inadequately and incompetently discharged his
duties. It was stated that the scope of the relevant sector of a plaintiff's reputation was not limited
by the scope of the imputations pleaded, and that the various facets of a politician's life were
constantly under scrutiny.

[126] The evidence admissible is of his reputation as accumulated from one source or another
over the period of time that precedes the occasion of the libel: per Lord Radcliffe in *Associated
Newspapers Ltd v Dingle* [1964] A.C. 371 at 399. See also *Rochfort v John Fairfax* [1972] 1
N.S.W.L.R. 16 at 22–23 (subsequent convictions irrelevant). In Australia at least there is some
doubt as to whether this is a rule strictly applicable in all circumstances: see review of case law
and discussion in *Anderson v Ah Kit* [2004] WASC 194.

[127] Per Patterson J. in *Thompson v Nye* (1850) 16 Q.B. 175. Cf. *Hughes v Mirror Newspapers*
[1985] 3 N.S.W.L.R. 504, where the plaintiff's attempt to introduce evidence of his bad reputation
after publication was disallowed. However, such evidence was admitted in *Television New
Zealand v Quinn* [1996] 3 N.Z.L.R. 24. In *Australian Broadcasting Corp v McBride* [2001]
NSWCA 322, doubts were expressed as to whether the rule should survive, the argument being
that as damages were assessed on the basis of injury to reputation up to the time of the award, a
bad reputation acquired after the publication and before the award was a material factor.

"It would seem that on principle such evidence is not admissible as only indirectly tending to affect the plaintiff's reputation. If these rumours and suspicions have, in fact, affected the plaintiff's reputation, that may be proved by general evidence of reputation. If they have not affected it they are not relevant to the issue . . . Unlike evidence of general reputation, it is particularly difficult for the plaintiff to meet and rebut such evidence; for all that those who know him best can say is that they have not heard anything of these rumours. Moreover, it may be that it is the defendant himself who started them . . . Both the weight of authority and principle seem against the admission of such evidence."[128]

33.36 Other publications. Other publications to the same effect as the words complained of, or relating to the same incident as is referred to in the words, are inadmissible,[129] and this rule covers previous publications by the same defendant.[130] Nor is it permissible to avoid this rule by alleging that such publications have already tarnished the claimant's reputation.[131]

---

[128] *Scott v Sampson* (1882) 8 Q.B.D. 491 at 504. See also *Plato Films v Speidel* [1961] A.C. 1090 at 1136; *Associated Newspapers Ltd v Dingle* [1964] A.C. 371 at 410–411.

[129] *Associated Newspapers Ltd v Dingle*, above, applying *Saunders v Mills* (1829) 6 Bing. 213, 130 E.R. 1262. To the same effect see also *French v Triple M Melbourne Pty Ltd* [2008] VSC 550, Forrest J. However, note s.12, Defamation Act 1952, where the claimant has sued on other publications to the same effect: see para.33.60, below.

[130] *Rath v Guardian Newspapers Ltd* [2008] EWHC 398 (QB). In mitigation of damages the defendant relied on the fact that claimant had made no complaint about earlier articles in the defendant's newspaper which made similar allegations to those complained of in the action. This part of the pleading was struck out as contrary to the ruling in *Dingle*. However, Tugendhat J. left open the possibility that failure by a claimant to point out to a newspaper an error in a prior publication would be relevant to mitigation of damage where the error was later repeated.

[131] *Associated Newspapers Ltd v Dingle* [1964] A.C. 371 at 398, 406, 412, 413, 417. See also *Jensen v Clark* [1982] 2 N.Z.L.R. 268, but in assessing damages in that case the judge took into account that the publication complained of was but one incident in a sustained campaign. In *Bennett v Guardian Newspapers Ltd* [1997] E.M.L.R. 301 the Court of Appeal upheld the judge's decision to exclude evidence of and cross-examination about events subsequent to publication which it was suggested by the defendants caused distress to the plaintiffs, on the grounds that the evidence was irrelevant. See also *Television New Zealand v Ah Koy* [2002] 2 N.Z.L.R. 616, in which the principle of "isolation of damages" was examined, and explained as confining damage to that resulting from the words published by the defendant whilst excluding evidence of damage to reputation caused by other publications.

In *Bass v TCN Channel Nine Pty Ltd* [2006] NSWCA 343 the New South Wales Court of Appeal had to consider an unusual situation relating to the admissibility of evidence on damages. The plaintiff complained of defamation in the course of a TV programme which he said contained two imputations against him: (1) that he was a "shonky" (i.e dishonest) operator; and (2) that he could not be relied upon to pay his employees their due wages. The defendant justified the first imputation and pleaded privilege in relation to the second. The jury found the shonky allegation true, and the judge upheld the plea of privilege, ruling that there was no evidence of malice. On appeal, the judge's ruling on malice was held to be in error, and a retrial was ordered in respect of the second imputation. At the retrial the judge allowed the defendant to introduce evidence of the finding by the jury that the shonky operator allegation was true. This was the subject of appeal. The Court of Appeal held that the evidence was admissible on two grounds: first, applying the principles stated in *Dingle v Associated Newspapers Ltd* [1964] A.C. 371, the jury would have to be directed that the sum awarded for the second imputation must represent the injury caused by that imputation, isolating any injury caused by the "shonk" imputation (see [20]); and secondly, the finding that the plaintiff was a shonky operator was relevant to the plaintiff's credit [22], particularly as the imputation was in the forefront of his case at the second trial ("his evidence of his reaction to the programme when he first saw it gave particular and repeated emphasis to the shonk imputation" at [26]). It should perhaps be noted that the truth of the shonk imputation was pleaded in mitigation of damages but it was not left to the jury on this basis as it would have

Particular acts of misconduct. As to evidence of particular acts of **33.37** misconduct on the part of the claimant tending to show his character and disposition, Cave J. summarised his reasoning and conclusions for excluding such evidence as follows[132]:

> "Both principle and authority seems equally against its admission . . . It would give rise to interminable issues which would have but a very remote bearing on the question in dispute, which is to what extent the reputation which he actually possesses has been damaged by the defamatory matter complained of.[133] Among all the cases which have been reviewed there is not one which can be cited in support of the admissibility of this evidence. In *Bracegirdle v Bailey*[134] such evidence was rejected . . . and in *Jones v Stevens*[135] the evils attending its admission are eloquently pointed out."

Particular facts and circumstances tending to show the disposition of the claimant now must be distinguished from particular facts directly relevant to the context in which a defamatory publication came to be made.[136]

Sources of evidence of reputation. According to Lord Denning, the most **33.38** likely source is persons who know the claimant well:

> "In order to show that a man has a bad reputation, you should call *those who know him* and have had dealings with him. They are in a position to judge his worth. If they consider he has a bad reputation, they are very likely right, and he has nothing very much to lose. If it is a settled reputation which has been accumulated over a period by a series of misdeeds, they will know of it. If it is a reputation which has been destroyed at one blow by a single conviction, they will know of it too. Either way, if you call those who know him well, you are likely to get at the truth . . . But if you go beyond these, you immediately get into the realms of reports and rumours, often enough spread by busybodies who know nothing of the man, or indulged in by newspapers for the benefit of their circulation . . . "[137]

The witness would be unlikely to be able in chief to state the underlying reasons for the claimant's bad reputation because he could not describe particular incidents giving rise to the reputation, but he could be asked in cross-examination the grounds of his belief, and on what it was based.[138] A

---

transgressed the decision in *Speidel v Plato Films Ltd* [1961] A.C. 1090, and the established rule that "evidence of particular facts tending to show the "character and disposition" of the plaintiff is not admissible on the issue of damages" (see [28]).

[132] *Scott v Sampson* (1882) 8 Q.B.D. 491 at 505.

[133] This is an early reference to what would now be called case management, as May L.J. observed in *Burstein v Times Newspapers Ltd* [2001] 1 W.L.R. 579 at 592H.

[134] (1859) 1 F. & F. 536, 175 E.R. 842.

[135] (1882) 11 Price 235 at 265.

[136] *Burstein v Times Newspapers Ltd* [2001] 1 W.L.R. 579. per May L.J. at 592H; and see para.33.43, below.

[137] *Associated Newspapers Ltd v Dingle* [1964] A.C. 371 at 402.

[138] Per Lord Denning in *Plato Films v Speidel* [1961] A.C. 1090 at 1140. The dangers of asking such questions are obvious: "The floodgates may be opened through which streams of details and particular facts may flow"; ibid. per Lord Morris at 1147.

police officer could no doubt give evidence if the claimant had a criminal reputation.[139]

33.39 Cross-examination as to particular acts of misconduct. Although evidence led to support an unsuccessful plea of justification can be considered in connection with damages,[140] where justification is not pleaded, the defendant cannot under the guise of giving evidence of the claimant's general bad character, adduce evidence in chief of, or endeavour by cross-examination of the claimant or his witnesses to elicit, any facts or incidents in the claimant's life which tend to prove the truth of the libel. Just as a defendant cannot prove in evidence in chief specific instances of misconduct, as distinguished from general reputation, to mitigate damages, so he cannot achieve that purpose by cross-examination to such specific instances.[141] Any attempt to give evidence of such facts in chief or to elicit them in cross-examination is a fact which the jury are entitled to take into account as a ground for aggravating the damages,[142] but a claimant can no doubt be cross-examined about facts relevant to the context in which the defamatory publication came to be made.[143]

33.40 Cross-examination as to credit permitted. Although the defendant cannot, in the absence of a plea of justification, give evidence of any incidents in the claimant's past life which tend to establish the truth of the libel, he can, if the claimant goes into the witness box, always cross-examine him as to credit even though such cross-examination may incidentally elicit such incidents.[144] Further, such cross-examination might also elicit other discreditable incidents in the claimant's life.

> "When a witness has given evidence material to the issues in a case you can cross-examine him on matters not directly material to the case in order to ask the jury to infer from his answers that he is not worthy of belief, and that they should not accept his answers on questions material to the case as true. This is cross-examination as to credit."[145]

---

[139] See Lord Denning in *Plato Films v Speidel* [1961] A.C. 1090 at 1139.

[140] See para.33.13, above.

[141] Per Scrutton L.J. in *Hobbs v Tinling* [1929] 2 K.B. 1 at 18; *Plato Films v Speidel*, above, per Lord Denning at 1143; and see *Watt v Watt* [1905] A.C. 115 per Lord Halsbury at 118; *Bass v TCN Channel Nine Pty Ltd* [2006] NSWCA 343.

[142] *Watt v Watt*, above.

[143] *Burstein v Times Newspapers* [2001] 1 W.L.R. 579: see para.33.43ff, below.

[144] *Horne v Milne* (1881) 7 V.L.R. 297; *Peatling v Watson* [1909] V.L.R. 198 at 203; *Hobbs v Tinling* [1929] 2 K.B. 1 and *Williams v Mirror Group Newspapers Ltd*, December 19, 1990, CA, where this passage in the 8th ed. was referred to. (There is a short report of the case in the *Independent*, February 12, 1991.) See also *TCN Channel Nine v Antoniadis* [1998] N.S.W.S.C. 543, in which the NSW Court of Appeal stated:

> "(The defendant) was entitled to cross-examine the plaintiff as to credit on matters which might have been, but were not, particularised under the defence of justification. However, the evidence so obtained would be relevant only to the plaintiff's credibility, and the defendant could not lead evidence to contradict the plaintiff's answers". (at 53).

See also *Bass v TCN Channel Nine Pty Ltd*, above.

[145] Per Scrutton L.J. in *Hobbs v Tinling*, above, at 18–19.

However this cross-examination as to credit is subject to the discretion of the judge.[146] Its justification is that it may elicit facts tending to show that the claimant's evidence is not worthy of belief. Except in so far as it can be so justified it may be properly disallowed.[147] If the claimant does no more, in a case where justification is not pleaded, than give evidence as to his background, the falsity of the libel and its effect upon him, he can only be cross-examined as to credit with a view to showing that his evidence is untrue on those matters which are in issue, which do not include the falsity of the libel.[148]

Claimant's denial. If incidents about which the claimant has been cross-   **33.41**
examined are denied by him, no further evidence can usually be called to rebut the denials.[149] It is incumbent on the judge and vital to a proper trial to explain clearly to the jury the legal effects of such cross-examination, namely, (1) that, while they are not bound to accept the claimant's denials, those denials, though unaccepted, afford no evidence that the incidents have taken place[150]; (2) that the answers given to such cross-examination (if disbelieved or in any event) are not relevant on the issue of mitigation of damages, but only destroy the claimant's credibility in respect of other evidence.[151]

> "Cross-examination as to credit has one legitimate object only, and that is to cut away the effect of the evidence given by the plaintiff, to induce the jury to refuse to accept it—in other words to destroy it. In a case where there has been such cross-examination, it is the duty of the judge to warn the jury that the answers given by the plaintiff are not to be taken into account in mitigation of damages but must only be used as a test as to their acceptance of testimony. It is only as to truthfulness that the character of the plaintiff comes into question."[152]

---

[146] Now buttressed by powers under CPR Pt 32 to control evidence, and in particular r.32.1(3), which entitles to court to limit cross-examination. However, that power must be exercised in accordance with the overriding objective of dealing with cases justly. See *O'Brien v Chief Constable of South Wales* [2005] UKHL 26; [2005] 2 A.C. 534 particularly at [54].

[147] *Mutch v Sleeman* (1928) 29 N.S.W.S.R. 125 at 134, 135. The considerations to which the court should have regard were listed by Sankey L.J. in *Hobbs v Tinling*, above, at 51 quoting s.153 of the Indian Evidence Act of 1872 which, he stated, was an accurate summary of English law. Note also Lord Denning's observations in *Plato Films v Speidel* [1961] A.C. 1090 at 1143: "It is not good for the law that a judge admit a "roving" cross-examination to credit and then go on to tell the jury to ignore it when they come to assess damages, knowing that it is an impossible thing to ask them to do. Better not to have it introduced at all."

[148] Per Stuart-Smith L.J. in *Williams v Mirror Group Newspapers Ltd*, above.

[149] There are three recognised exceptions, namely (1) where a witness has been convicted of a crime; (2) previous inconsistent statements; and (3) evidence to show the witness is biased in favour of the party calling him: see *Phipson on Evidence*, 17th edn (London; Sweet & Maxwell, 2012), para.12–14.

[150] Famously illustrated by Scrutton L.J. in *Hobbs v Tinling*, above, at 21:
"If by cross-examination to credit you prove that a man's oath cannot be relied upon, and he has sworn he did not go to Rome on May 1, you do not, therefore, prove that he did go to Rome on May 1; there is simply no evidence on the subject."

[151] *Hobbs v Tinling*, above, at 19, 21, 32, 39, 46, 51. *Judd v Sun Newspapers* (1930) 30 N.S.W.S.R. 294.

[152] Per Halse-Rogers J. in *Judd v Sun Newspapers*, above, at 316.

33.42 Restrictions on jury. The jury are not entitled to intervene during the claimant's cross-examination to credit with an intimation they have heard enough and desire to find for the defendant. If they do so, the judge should tell them that they must hear the claimant's case to the end, and that they must suspend their judgment until the claimant's case is complete, and when it is completed he should direct them as to the issues they have to try.[153]

(b) *Facts relevant to the contextual background in which the defamatory publication was made*

33.43 The *Burstein* case. This category of admissible evidence arises from the decision of the Court of Appeal in *Burstein v Times Newspapers*.[154] The defamatory allegation complained of was that the claimant had organised bands of hecklers to go about wrecking performances of modern atonal music. There was no defence of justification and the plea of fair comment was struck out by the trial judge. The judge did not permit the defendant to seek to prove in mitigation of damages certain facts about the claimant, including that he had formed a group of campaigners against modernist atonal music which styled itself "The Hecklers", that they had issued a manifesto calling upon the public to join them in booing at the end of a performance at the Royal Opera House of Gawain, an opera by Sir Harrison Birtwistle, and that the claimant and The Hecklers had greeted the end of the performance of the opera with boos and hisses.

The leading judgment of the Court of Appeal was given by May L.J., who reviewed the major authorities on mitigation in defamation actions, and in particular *Scott v Sampson*[155] and *Plato Films v Speidel*,[156] and concluded that Cave J.'s third head of inadmissible evidence in *Scott v Sampson*, namely facts and circumstances tending to show the disposition of the plaintiff, did not extend to exclude evidence of particular facts directly relevant to the context in which the defamatory publication came to be made. Further, he held that in *Plato Films v Speidel* the main concern of the House of Lords had been in essence one of case management, to prevent libel trials from becoming roving inquiries into the plaintiff's reputation, character or disposition, and that what had been held to be inadmissible was evidence of particular facts said to be relevant to the plaintiff's general reputation and disposition. However, the House of Lords did not decide that particular facts directly relevant to the context in which a defamatory publication came to be made were inadmissible. Thus May L.J. concluded that he was not constrained by authority from holding that "evidence of directly relevant background context" was

---

[153] *Hobbs v Tinling*, above.
[154] [2001] 1 W.L.R. 579.
[155] (1882) 8 Q.B.D. 491.
[156] [1961] A.C. 1090.

admissible in mitigation. The evidence about the claimant's activities, excluded by the judge, fell within this description, and accordingly should have been admitted.[157] As matters stood, the jury had been invited to assess damages in blinkers. However, in the event the appeal was dismissed, because the court held that even had the evidence been admitted, it would not have affected the jury's award of damages.

***Burstein* reviewed.** The *Burstein* decision was considered by the Court of   **33.44**
Appeal in *Turner v News Group Newspapers Ltd.*[158] The claimant complained of an article about couples who indulged in "swinging", defined as "hooked on sex with strangers". The article featured the claimant and one of his former wives (the second defendant) who (so it was alleged) was pressurised by the claimant to have sex with strangers at a Coventry club. The defendant acknowledged that this was untrue and made an offer of amends under ss.2–4 of the Defamation Act 1996, which was accepted. The court was required to assess compensation under s.3(5) of the Act. The defendant sought to rely on three categories of material in mitigation of damages under the *Burstein* rule: the involvement of the claimant and his former wife in fetish functions at a Coventry club; the claimant's encouragement of his former wife in her career as a model to pose for explicit photos; and the fact that the claimant had "slagged off" his former wife in a newspaper feature. Eady J. held[159] that the *Burstein* rule should be applied in assessment of compensation under the offer of amends procedure. He considered that the first two categories came within the term "directly relevant background context" of which, according to *Burstein*, evidence was admissible, and the third category of evidence—the "slagging off" of his former wife in a newspaper—was relevant to the issue of the extent of his hurt feelings "by tabloid exposure on the subject of his marital relations".

The Court of Appeal rejected the claimant's appeal. The court held that while majority judgments in *Plato Films v Speidel* endorsed the basic principle originating from *Scott v Sampson*, that a claimant cannot be subjected to a roving enquiry into aspects of his life unconnected with the subject-matter of the defamatory publication,[160] that principle had never been absolute—for instance, it had long been accepted that evidence of specific acts properly before the court in support of pleas of justification or fair comment could be taken into account in assessment of damages. The principles expressed by Cave J. in *Scott v Sampson* and in *Speidel* sprang from concerns about the

---

[157] The evidence could have been stigmatised as particular acts of discreditable conduct; but in so far as the court diverged from previous authority, much emphasis was placed on the introduction of the CPR and the obligation of the court to further the overriding objective by exercising its powers of case management. The admissibility of mitigating evidence was described as essentially a case management question: [39]–[41].

[158] [2006] EWCA Civ 540; [2006] 1 W.L.R. 3469.

[159] [2006] EWHC 892 (QB); [2006] 1 W.L.R. 3469.

[160] At [42].

risks of a trial within a trial, with which the new powers of case management equipped the courts to deal. *Burstein* was not irreconcilable with *Speidel*, and was binding on the court. The court upheld the decision of Eady J. that the *Burstein* rule applied to the assessment of compensation in offer of amends cases, and it was said that the application of the rule might be particularly appropriate in such cases as there would be no opportunity for evidence of specific acts of misconduct to be put before the court in support of a plea of justification or fair comment, and evidence of past conduct might be of special importance in assessing injury to the claimant's feelings which could be an important factor in offer of amends cases where there is likely to have been an apology, repairing injury to reputation.

33.45 Guidance given in *Turner v News Group*. The Court of Appeal stated that:

— There was no requirement for a causal connection between acts sought to be relied upon in a *Burstein* plea and the publication of the libel[161];

— There was no need for the defendant to show that he had the directly relevant facts in mind when publishing the words complained of[162];

— It was not a requirement of the *Burstein* principle that the claimant had deliberately sought for himself a particular kind of reputation (as suggested by Sir Christopher Slade in *Burstein*)[163];

— If a *Burstein* plea contained hurtful allegations which could not ultimately be made out, that additional hurt would be reflected in the award of damages or compensation; so too if the judge concluded that the allegations were made improperly[164];

— The courts should apply *Burstein* with some caution, and should guard against extending too creatively the concept of "directly relevant background"[165];

— A *Burstein* plea was likely to be particularly appropriate in cases where an offer of amends had been made.

33.46 What evidence is admissible under the *Burstein* principle. Pill L.J. followed Sir Christopher Slade in *Burstein* in preferring to define what was admissible as being directly relevant background facts, which were admissible because they were directly relevant to the damage to the claimant's reputation suffered by him as a result of the publication.[166] Keene L.J. appeared to accept

---

161 For example, that the libel was provoked by the matters to be relied on in the *Burstein* plea: Keene L.J. at [53].
162 Ibid. at [54].
163 Ibid. at [55].
164 Ibid. at [59].
165 Ibid. at [56].
166 Ibid. at [94].

the term "directly relevant background context".[167] Keene and Pill L.JJ. agreed that if evidence was to qualify under the principle spelt out in *Burstein's* case, it had to be evidence which was so clearly relevant to the subject matter of the libel or to the claimant's reputation or sensitivity in that part of his life that there would be a real risk of the jury assessing damages on a false basis if they were kept in ignorance of the facts to which the evidence related.[168] Moses L.J., by contrast, questioned the value of much of that terminology, preferring the formulation that a defendant might seek to reduce damages by adducing evidence which was directly relevant to a claimant's conduct or reputation in the particular sector to which the defamatory material related.[169]

The scope of the *Burstein* principle was considered again by the Court of Appeal in *Warren v Random House Group Ltd*,[170] where the court preferred the phrase "directly relevant background context" as the best encapsulation of the criterion for admissibility, but agreed with the observations of Moses L.J. in *Turner*, to the effect that, taken on its own, it would give insufficient guidance to judges called upon to apply it. In the court's view, there was no substitute for examination in each case of whether the material qualified as background context directly relevant to the assessment of the damage sustained by the claimant as a result of the publication, in particular the damage to his reputation in the sector of his life to which it related and the injury to his feelings. The Court in *Warren* upheld the decision of the judge to strike out certain particulars of a *Burstein* plea, pointing out that the essence of the defamatory allegation complained of was that the claimant had secured a contract for a low fee by fraudulent misrepresentation, whereas the material in the *Burstein* particulars did not necessarily entail dishonesty on the part of the claimant. Further, the events relied upon occurred some time after the alleged misrepresentation and though "background" did not necessarily confine admissibility to material occurring prior to, or at the time of, the events giving rise to the defamatory allegation, the "temporal factor" raised "a substantial question-mark as to the strength of [their] connection to the libel".[171]

It appears, therefore, that a degree of connection between the subject matter of the libel and the *Burstein* particulars is required, both in terms of similarity of allegation and in terms of closeness in time; or, at least, that the more different the allegations are from the libel, and the further away in time, the less likely the *Burstein* particulars are to be allowed. That is hardly surprising, because an allegation of some entirely distinct behaviour, especially taking place at a long remove from the matters alleged in the libel, could not easily be described as directly relevant background context.

---

[167] Ibid. at [56].
[168] Ibid. at [56] and [94].
[169] Ibid. at [87]–[91].
[170] *Warren v Random House Group Ltd* [2008] EWCA Civ 834; [2009] Q.B. 600 at [79].
[171] Ibid. at [86].

(c) *Evidence properly admitted before the court on some other issue*

33.47 Admissible evidence on some other issue. The court may be entitled to take into account, in mitigation of damages, evidence which has been properly admitted as relevant to some other issue arising in the case.[172] Thus evidence which has been led to support a defence of justification or honest comment, which was not sufficient to make good the defence, can be relied upon to reduce the damages.[173] Hence partial justification can have a major impact on damages.[174] In *Joseph v Spiller*,[175] the conduct of the first claimant in falsifying a special damage claim and thereby abusing the process of the court had the result that, despite succeeding on the merits on both justification and honest comment, the claimants were awarded only nominal damages.

(d) *Facts which tend to disprove malice*

33.48 General principles. The defendant may, with a view to mitigation of damages, give evidence of any facts or circumstances which show the absence of any malicious motive or intention on his part.[176]

33.49 Intention of the defendant. Although it is no defence that the defendant did not intend to refer to the claimant, or intend the words to be understood in any defamatory sense, the defendant can give such fact in evidence in

---

[172] But this proposition should not be taken too far. If, in rebuttal of an allegation of express malice, a defendant gave evidence that he believed the libellous allegations to be true, and stated the grounds of his belief, that, say, there were widespread rumours that the claimant had acted as alleged, it is submitted that the defendant could not rely upon the existence of such rumours in mitigation of damages.

[173] This topic has already been discussed at para.33.13, above. See in particular *Pamplin v Express Newspapers Ltd* [1988] 1 W.L.R. 116 at 120; *Jones v Pollard* [1997] E.M.L.R. 233; *Turner v News Group Newspapers Ltd* [2006] EWCA Civ 540; [2006] 1 W.L.R. 3469 at [43]–[46]; *McKenna v MGN Ltd* [2007] EWHC 1996 (QB).

[174] See Lord Denning in *Plato Films v Speidel* [1961] A.C. 1090 at 1141–1142; and *Pamplin v Express Newspapers Ltd* [1988] 1 W.L.R. 116 CA.

[175] [2012] EWHC 2958 (QB). This was the trial by Tugendhat J. of the action which had previously gone to the Supreme Court on the issue of honest comment: [2010] UKSC 53; [2011] 1 A.C. 852.

[176] This statement has appeared in previous editions of this book, and is amply supported by dicta, albeit chiefly in nineteenth century cases (e.g. per Tindal C.J. in *Pearson v Lemaitre* 134 E.R. 742, (1843) 5 M. & Gr. 700 at 719–720; *Smith v Scott* 175 E.R. 241, (1847) 2 C. & K. 580 at 585–6; per Blackburn J. in *Campbell v Spottiswoode* 122 E.R. 288, (1863) 3 B. & S. 769 at 781; per Farwell L.J. in *Hulton v Jones* [1909] 2 K.B. 444 at 479). However, whereas evidence which disproves malice is clearly material to refute an allegation of motive which might otherwise aggravate the injury, it is less apparent why the absence of malice should necessarily serve to lessen the injury to the claimant. In many cases, it will make no difference to the claimant, or at least not reduce the injury to his reputation or feelings, that the defendant acted bona fide and believed the libel to be true. (Of course, if the defendant apologised as soon as he realised it was untrue, that would be strong mitigation.) The extent to which, and circumstances in which, absence of express malice can of itself mitigate damage, when no malice is alleged by the claimant, is a topic which would perhaps benefit from a contemporary review.

mitigation of damages "as negativing express malice on his part".[177] Further, it has been stated that the defendant may urge in mitigation any facts which go to show that he honestly believed, and had reasonable grounds for believing, that what he said or wrote was true, although such belief is no defence in the absence of privilege.[178]

Defendant not the original author. The fact that the defendant was not the original author of the libel or slander, but only published it by way of repetition, is no defence. It may, however, be regarded as a less damaging act (and possibly less malicious) to repeat rather than to originate a defamatory statement. Thus it has been held that a defendant in a slander action can prove in mitigation of damages that he said at the time that he heard the slanderous matter from another named person.[179] Similarly, a defendant has been allowed to prove in mitigation that it derived its information from a company report,[180] or that he copied words from a newspaper[181] or based his libellous allegations expressly on a newspaper report.[182] However, there are plainly limits to evidence of this nature. In the first place, there is potentially a conflict with the rule that other publications of the libel are inadmissible in mitigation of damages.[183] Further, where the libel or slander did not disclose the source of the information, but was stated "as a fact of the defendant's own knowledge", evidence that the defendant merely repeated or republished information which he derived from some other source was not admitted in mitigation of damages.[184] It is submitted, therefore, that unless it is apparent on the face of the

33.50

---

[177] Per Farwell L.J. in *Hulton v Jones*, above, at 479, and the cases cited in the previous footnote. Although it is not entirely clear from the report, it does not appear that express malice can have been in issue in the case, which was about reference to the plaintiff and did not involve a defence of qualified privilege or fair comment.

[178] See the observation of Blackburn J. in *Campbell v Spottiswoode* 122 E.R. 288; (1863) 3 B. & S. 769 at 781; and per Huddleston B. in *Bryce v Rusden* (1886) 2 T.L.R. 435 at 440.

[179] *Bennett v Bennett* 172 E.R. 1377; (1834) 6 C. & P. 588.

[180] *Davis v Cutbush* 175 E.R. 820; (1859) 1 F. & F. 487 (newspaper report of a company report to shareholders).

[181] *Saunders v Mills* 130 E.R. 1262; (1829) 6 Bing. 213, where the defendant, a newspaper publisher, copied the story from another newspaper, and it was said "that evidence might weigh with the jury, as shewing there was less of malice than if the defendant had been the original composer of this libel" (but he was not allowed to show that the story had also been published in other newspapers). It is not clear from the report that the defamatory article acknowledged on its face that it was sourced from another newspaper, but that may be thought unlikely. However, in *Talbutt v Clark* 174 E.R. 300; (1840) 2 Mood. & R. 312, where the court refused to admit evidence in mitigation at the instance of the defendant editor, to the effect that the libel was simply published as a letter from a correspondent, Denman C.J. said that the decision (i.e. *Saunders v Mills*, although he did not identify it by name) had been very much questioned.

[182] *Mullett v Hulton* 170 E.R. 708; (1803) 4 Esp. 248, where the defendant was allowed to adduce evidence of a newspaper report as having been the source of his libel (although he then failed to produce it). It may have been relevant that the libellous letter referred on its face to the newspaper report.

[183] *Associated Newspapers Ltd v Dingle* [1964] A.C. 371.

[184] *Mills v Spencer* 171 E.R. 331; (1817) Holt N.P. 533 at 534. Gibbs C.J. suggested that the position might have been different had the defendant made it clear when uttering the slander that he had been given the information by another. See also *Talbutt v Clark*, above.

libel or from the words of the slander that it was copied from, or was a repetition of, another publication, evidence of the source will not as a rule be admitted in mitigation of damages.[185] However, where the libel was copied from another newspaper, but the defendant omitted several passages which strongly reflected on the claimant, he was allowed to prove that in mitigation of damages.[186]

(e) *Claimant's own conduct*

33.51 Relevance in assessment of damages. The conduct of the claimant is a factor that the court can take into account when assessing damages,[187] but "conduct" in this context relates in particular (but not exclusively) to activities that can be causally connected to the publication of the libel of which the claimant complains, such as direct provocation.[188] It might exceptionally

---

[185] The exception would appear to be *Saunders v Mills*, above, which was strongly doubted on this point by Denman C.J. in *Talbutt v Clark*, above (see fn.181). However, so much of the decision in *Saunders v Mills* as decided that the defendant could not adduce evidence that the libel was also published in other newspapers, was applied by the House of Lords in *Associated Newspapers Ltd v Dingle* (above). Moreover, both Lord Radcliffe (396–397) and Lord Morris referred in terms to the defendant having been allowed to prove that he copied the story, without expressing disapproval of that part of the decision. Lord Radcliffe explained it on the basis that it "would tend not only to disprove express malice but also to show the comparative innocence of his conduct, to palliate it". It may be interesting to note that in *Hays Plc v Hartley* [2010] EWHC 1068 (QB), Tugendhat J. took the view that the fact that the defendant was an intermediary, a news agency rather than the author of the article complained of, was one of several factors which were likely to result in a modest award of damages.

[186] *Creevy v Carr* 173 E.R. 29; (1835) 7 Car. & P. 64.

[187] *Associated Newspapers Ltd v Dingle* [1964] A.C. 371 per Lord Radcliffe at 395; *Broome v Cassell* [1972] A.C. 1027 per Lord Hailsham of St Marylebone L.C. at 1071; and see *Kelly v Sherlock* (1866) L.R. 1 Q.B. 686.

[188] See *Watts v Fraser* 174 E.R. 154, (1835) 1 Moody and Robinson 449, and *Moore v Oastler*, reported as a note to *Watts v Fraser*. Both cases involved provocation by earlier libels on the defendant by the plaintiff. See also *Broome v Cassell* [1972] A.C. 1027 per Lord Hailsham L.C. at 1071. In *Campbell v News Group Newspapers Ltd* [2002] EWCA Civ 1143; [2002] E.M.L.R. 43, where Lord Hailsham's observations were applied, the Court of Appeal stated at [33] that
"It would be an affront to justice if a claimant's own disreputable conduct—here established in, and directed to improving materially the outcome of, the litigation itself—had to be ignored in assessing the damages that the claimant would otherwise merit for a defamation which could be shown to have injured his reputation prior to the libel".
In *Joseph v Spiller* [2012] EWHC 2958 (QB), the trial judge awarded only nominal damages, notwithstanding the claimants' success on the merits, to reflect the first claimant's conduct in falsifying a special damage claim.
Kelly v Sherlock (above) was not a case of direct provocation, nor causally connected to the publication of the libel, but it was a case where the behaviour of the plaintiff, an Anglican clergyman who had not conducted himself attractively, seems to have been the main factor in his award of one farthing. As Blackburn J. put it,
"Now, there can be no set-off of one libel or misconduct against another; but in estimating the compensation for the plaintiff's injured feelings, the jury might fairly consider the plaintiff's conduct and the degree of respect which the plaintiff himself had shewn for the feelings of others; and finding on the evidence, that he published in the local press sermons reflecting on the local authorities, that he published a statement (which I own I think borne out by the articles) that the defendant's paper was so conducted as to justify the epithet of 'the dregs of provincial journalism;' and, above all, that he delivered from the pulpit, and published in the provincial papers, a statement to the effect that some of his opponents (no matter, in my

include more broadly provocative actions by the claimant.[189] It may also include behaviour which is an abuse of the process of the court.[190]

Provocation by claimant's defamation. The fact that the claimant has **33.52** himself published some libel or slander on the defendant has been accepted as admissible evidence in mitigation of damages, provided that such libel or slander was published so shortly before as fairly to raise the presumption that it provoked the defendant to publish the libel complained of.[191]

> "It is undoubtedly settled law that a defendant cannot justify, or even excuse, the publication of slander by merely showing that the plaintiff had himself been guilty of similar conduct . . . But where the defamatory matter alleged to have been published by the plaintiff has been spoken at such time and under such circumstances as to raise the fair presumption that the defendant's defamation may have been provoked by the plaintiff's, I certainly think the evidence should not be excluded."[192]

Limits of this area of mitigation. Whether the limits of this area of **33.53** mitigation should be defined narrowly is uncertain. It has been held that the defendant must show that the libel published by the plaintiff came to his (the defendant's) knowledge before he published the libel complained of,[193] that

---

opinion, whether including the defendant or not) had been guilty of subornation of perjury, and would, as he charitably hoped, repent on their deathbeds and confess their guilt, I cannot say that I think the jury were bound to give him substantial damages".

[189] In *Godfrey v Demon (No.2)*, unreported, April 23, 1999, an action based on defamatory postings on the internet, the defendant was permitted to put forward the allegation that the plaintiff had himself posted "deliberately provocative, offensive, obnoxious and frequently puerile comments about other countries, their citizens and cultures" with a view to provoking others to trade insults which he then could claim to be defamatory. Morland J. decided that this was bad conduct causally connected to the libel sued upon. His decision was approved in *Burstein v Times Newspapers Ltd*, above, but May L.J. stated that "the ambit of this class of admissible conduct should be confined to exceptional cases in which provocative conduct of the claimant would be admissible even though it did not directly or exclusively provoke the defendant" (at [26]).

[190] *Joseph v Spiller* [2012] EWHC 2958 (QB), where the trial judge awarded only nominal damages, notwithstanding the claimants' success on the merits, to reflect the first claimant's conduct in falsifying a special damage claim.

[191] *Tarpley v Blabey* 132 E.R. 171, (1835) 2 Bing. N.C. 437; *Moore v. Oastler*, reported as a note to *Watts v Fraser* at 174 E.R. 154; (1835) 1 Mood. & R. 449; for a much fuller report of *Watts v Fraser*, see 112 E.R. 455; (1837) 7 A. & E. 223; *News Media v Finlay* [1970] N.Z.L.R. 1089 at 1102; *Broome v Cassell* [1972] A.C. 1027 at 1071, where Lord Hailsham L.C. stated "The bad conduct of the plaintiff himself may also enter into the matter, where he has provoked the libel, or where perhaps he has libelled the defendant in reply". Lord Hailsham's observations were applied by the Court of Appeal in *Campbell v News Group Newspapers Ltd* [2002] EWCA Civ 1143; [2002] E.M.L.R. 43. In *Trumm v Norman* [2008] EWHC 116 (QB), Tugendhat J. took into account, when assessing damages for defamatory statements about the claimant published in a Trade Union circular and on its website, "provocative and offensive postings" on the claimant's website which "set a low level for the tone of discussion about the affairs of the Union." Damages were reduced by 50 per cent.

[192] Per Lord Campbell C.J. in *Moore v Oastler*, above.

[193] *Watts v Fraser* 112 E.R. 455 (1837) 7 A. & E. 223.

evidence of a subsequent libel by the claimant is inadmissible,[194] and that general evidence that the claimant has been in the habit of defaming the defendant, or unrelated third parties, is inadmissible.[195]

33.54 Other conduct of the claimant. The conduct of the claimant during the course of, and in relation to, the litigation, may be of relevance in assessing damages.[196] It is suggested that the type of conduct which might lead a jury to reduce the damages would be acting in an oppressive manner calculated to cause the defendant harassment and expense beyond that ordinarily encountered in the course of proceedings. The fact that the claimant was being maintained in the action by a business competitor of the defendant might be a material consideration.[197] A refusal by the claimant to accept an offer by the defendant of a statement in open court cannot be regarded as a failure to mitigate the damage.[198] The offer to the claimant of an interview or the chance of replying in kind appears not to be a mitigating factor, so presumably his refusal of such an offer would not tell against him on assessment of damages.[199]

(f) Apology or other amends

33.55 Effect of apology. Although apology is no defence to an action for libel or slander, the prompt offer of a sincere apology can be substantial mitigation of damages.[200] The right of the defendant to give evidence that he made or offered an apology is statutorily enacted,[201] but in practice this statute is never invoked as it has long been recognised that evidence of an apology is admissible in mitigation of damages. The sooner an apology is published the

---

[194] *Tarpley v Blabey*, above.

[195] *Wakley v Johnson* (1826) Ry. & M. 422, per Best L.J.; *Judd v Sun Newspapers* (1930) 30 N.S.W.S.R. 294; but *Godfrey v Demon (No.2)* is a decision the other way: see fn.189, above.

[196] See Lord Hailsham in *Broome v Cassell*, above, at 1071; and *Campbell v News Group Newspapers Ltd* [2002] EWCA Civ 1143; [2002] E.M.L.R. 43.

[197] See *Broxton v McClelland (No.2)* [1997] E.M.L.R. 157.

[198] *Kiam v Neil* [1995] E.M.L.R. 1.

[199] In *Roux v Australian Broadcasting* [1992] 2 V.R. 577, the defendant was permitted to plead by way of mitigation that the plaintiff had not responded to an invitation to a television interview after the broadcast of the defamatory allegations in which he could have replied to the allegations. However, the point was not decided to be anything more than arguable. But see *Dawes v News* [1935] S.A.S.R. 312 (cited in *McCree v SA Telecasters* (1976) 14 S.A.S.R. 162) where it was stated that offering the plaintiff the opportunity of replying in kind did not amount to making amends. In *Television New Zealand v Ah Koy* [2002] 2 N.Z.L.R. 616, the plea that the offer to the plaintiff of a broadcast interview was a mitigating factor was struck out.

[200] See generally paras 29.1ff above. The proposition is uncontentious, but by way of example see *Houston v Smith*, unreported, CA. transcript no.91/1516/6, December 16, 1993, where Hirst L.J. in reducing damages to £50,000 stated that "If the defendant had promptly apologised, the appropriate figure would have been a very small fraction of £50,000".

[201] Lord Campbell's Libel Act 1843, s.1.

greater its mitigating effect,[202] but an apology offered or published after the commencement of the action, or even in the course of trial,[203] may be put forward as mitigation.

The quality and effect of an apology has come under close scrutiny in assessments of compensation under the offer of amends procedure. In *Cleese v Clark*[204] the judge described the apology as published without "great enthusiasm or generosity of spirit" and therefore it had done little to mitigate the hurt to the claimant's feelings. In *Nail v News Group Newspapers*[205] Eady J. stated:

> " . . . there is no point in endlessly haggling or niggling about the size or location of an apology. The important thing is to achieve vindication as quickly and effectively as possible . . . I believe that the important elements of the apology are that it was published relatively quickly after the proceedings were issued, at the top of the page, and that it was relatively eye-catching".

The mitigating effect of an apology will also depend upon whether it is a genuine apology, that is to say, full and frank, expressing the beliefs of the defendant.[206]

Retraction. An apology will almost certainly include a retraction or with-   **33.56**
drawal of the defamatory statement complained of. However, a retraction on its own, or any form of correction, may qualify as some measure of mitigation. A jury have been directed to take into consideration the fact that the defendant had offered to open the columns of his newspaper to the plaintiff, and had published several letters which the plaintiff had written contradicting or explaining the imputations contained in the libel.[207]

---

[202] In *Kiam v Neil (No.2)* [1996] E.M.L.R. 493 at 509, Beldam L.J. commenting on *Houston v Smith*, above, said: "Of course an immediate apology given by the defendant in that case, from which it might be inferred that what had been said was said in the heat of the moment, would be a factor which considerably reduced the extent of the injury."
As to the necessary constituents of a sufficient apology, see para.29.2, above. It has been said that an inadequate apology can exacerbate the plaintiff's sense of injury: *Syme v Mather* [1977] V.R. 516.
[203] See e.g. *Fairbairn v John Fairfax* [1977] 21 A.C.T.R. 1.
[204] [2003] EWHC 137 (QB); [2004] E.M.L.R. 37.
[205] [2004] EWHC 647 (QB); [2004] E.M.L.R. 20 at [69]. In *Campbell James v Guardian Media Group Ltd* [2005] EWHC 893 (QB); [2005] E.M.L.R. 24 the judge remarked that it was a case for a speedy, unequivocal and prominent apology, but what the claimant obtained was an apology published three months after the offending article which the claimant might have considered "off-hand" in its terms. He therefore assessed the right discount "for the belated offer of amends and apology" was 35 per cent. See also *Angel v Stainton* [2006] EWHC 637 (QB) where a grudging and insufficiently conciliatory response to the complaint diminished the discount applicable.
[206] See *Adelson v Associated Newspapers Ltd* [2008] EWHC 278 (QB), [2009] E.M.L.R. 10 at [71]–[74].
[207] *Harle v Catherall* (1866) 14 L.T. 801. The report does not make clear to what issue the judge told the jury these matters were relevant, but it is submitted they could properly be taken into account in assessment of damages.

33.57 Offer of amends. An offer of amends made under s.2 of the Defamation Act 1996, which is not accepted, may be relied upon in mitigation of damages whether or not it was relied upon as a defence.[208]

(g) *Damages already recovered for same libel*

33.58 General rule. As earlier stated, the defendant cannot prove in mitigation of damages that some other person or persons have on previous occasions published the same libel or other account of the facts alleged in the libel, for the fact that others have defamed the claimant is wholly irrelevant.[209] Such evidence is inadmissible, even when coupled with evidence that on such occasions the claimant did not sue or prosecute,[210] or take any steps to contradict the charges made against him.[211]

33.59 At common law. Moreover, at common law the defendant could not in mitigation of damages, give any evidence to show that the claimant had already commenced an action,[212] or recovered damages against,[213] some other person or persons for other publications of the same libel.

33.60 Defamation Act 1952, section 12. The Defamation Act 1952, s.12 provides that:

> "In any action for libel or slander the defendant may give in evidence in mitigation of damages that the plaintiff has recovered damages, or has brought actions for damages, for libel or slander in respect of the publication of words to the same effect as the words on which the action is founded, or has received or agreed to receive compensation in respect of any such publication."

This can provide a dilemma for a defendant, for evidence of damages already recovered, if substantial, may be treated by the jury as a benchmark for their assessment in the instant case, and if modest, may cause them to react by awarding a much larger sum on the basis that the claimant was in their view undercompensated in the earlier case.

Section 9. Evidence in Defence of Misuse of Private Information Claim[214]

33.61 General. The evidence required by the defendant will, naturally enough, depend on what is alleged in the particulars of claim, and challenged in the

---

[208] Defamation Act 1996, s.4(5).

[209] *Saunders v Mills* 130 E.R. 1262, (1829) 6 Bing. 213; *Associated Newspapers Ltd v Dingle* [1964] A.C. 371. However, the defendant is only to pay damages for the defamatory words he has himself used, not for defamatory words published by others: see *Harrison v Pearce* 175 E.R. 855, (1858) 1 F. & F. 567 as explained by Lord Denning in *Associated Newspapers Ltd v Dingle* at 397–398. See also *French v Triple M Melbourne Pty Ltd* [2008] VSC 550, Forrest J.

[210] *R. v Holt* 101 E.R. 245, (1793) 5 T.R. 436.

[211] *Pankhurst v Hamilton* (1886) 2 T.L.R. 682.

[212] *Harrison v Pearce*, above.

[213] *Creevy v Carr* 173 E.R. 29, (1835) 7 C. & P. 64; *Tucker v Lawson* (1886) 2 T.L.R. 593.

[214] For a full discussion of this cause of action, see Ch.22, above.

defence, and what substantive defences are put forward in the defence.[215] The most common assertions made by a defendant are that the information is not private, or does not give rise to a reasonable expectation of privacy, that the claimant gave his consent to the publication of the information, that the information is in the public domain, or that publication of the information is in the public interest, or is a justifiable exercise of the right of freedom of expression under art.10 of ECHR. These pleas where raised will, of course, be the matters to which the defendant's evidence will be directed. Where art.10 is engaged the court has to undertake the exercise of balancing in the particular case the competing rights of privacy under art.8 and freedom of expression under art.10 which requires an "intense focus" on the individual facts of the case. A defendant should therefore endeavour to call or produce evidence which will demonstrate the high level of public interest in the information published, as compared with the degree of intrusion, if any, into the claimant's privacy, and which makes such intrusion and any interference with the claimant's rights proportionate.

Reasonable expectation of privacy. Reference has earlier been made[216] **33.62** to the description in *Murray v Big Pictures (UK) Ltd*[217] of the circumstances which can be relevant to the question whether there is a reasonable expectation of privacy. Those circumstances (which particularly relate to photographs but are applicable to any kind of information), about which the defendant or his witnesses may be able to give evidence, include the nature of the activity in which the claimant was engaged, the place at which it was happening, the nature and purpose of the intrusion, whether the claimant consented, whether it was known that he had not consented, and the circumstances in which and the purposes for which the information came into the hands of the publisher.

Damages. In *Mosley v News Group Newspapers Ltd*[218] the judge considered **33.63** that it may be appropriate to take into account the conduct of the claimant:

> " . . . [T]he extent to which [the claimant's] own conduct has contributed to the nature and scale of his distress *might* [judge's emphasis] be a relevant factor on causation. Has he, for example, put himself in a predicament by his own choice which contributed to his distress and loss of dignity?"[219]

---

[215] See para.27.47 above for what may or should be included in the defence in a claim for misuse of private information. Reference should also be made to para.25.34, above concerning evidence on interim injunction applications, and paras 32.66 et seq., above about the claimant's evidence in a privacy claim.

[216] See para.32.67, above.

[217] [2008] EWCA Civ 446; [2009] Ch. 481.

[218] [2008] EWHC 1777 (QB), [2008] E.M.L.R. 20.

[219] At [224].

The judge also ruled that exemplary damages could not be awarded in claim for infringement of privacy.[220] However, when the relevant provisions of the Crime and Courts Act 2013 enter into force, exemplary damages may in principle, albeit only in exceptional circumstances, be available in a claim for misuse of private information brought against a "relevant publisher".[221]

---

[220] At [197].
[221] See paras 9.20–9.21 and 9.30–9.31, above.

CHAPTER 34

THE TRIAL: FUNCTIONS OF JUDGE AND JURY

The slow demise and statutory abolition of jury trial. The trial of **34.1**
defamation actions by judge and jury is already a rarity, and is about to fade
away into history. Lord Denning's words no longer resonate as once they
did:

> "It [trial by jury] has been the bulwark of our liberties too long for any of us to seek
> to alter it. Whenever a man is on trial for serious crime, or when in a civil case a
> man's honour or integrity is at stake . . . then trial by jury has no equal."[1]

At the time of writing, there have been two jury trials of defamation actions
in England and Wales since July 2009.[2] There are a number of reasons for this.
Reynolds privilege cases, which represent a substantial proportion of actions
defended by the media, are peculiarly unsuited to trial by jury, by reason of the
confused division of functions of judge and jury,[3] and by the jury having to
find specific facts, sometimes necessitating an "exam paper" of questions for
the jury to answer[4]; jury trials take longer, particularly as witnesses give their
evidence in chief orally, whereas before a judge alone the statement of the
witness will usually stand as his evidence in chief, and there will be a
consequential saving of costs[5]; and judges are becoming increasingly concerned about the inconvenience and practical difficulties of managing trials

---

[1] *Ward v James* [1966] 1 Q.B. 273 at 295.

[2] *Cooper v Associated Newspapers Ltd*, award of £60,000 in June 2012; *Boyle v MGN Ltd*,
award of £54,650 in October 2012.

[3] "The division between the role of judge and that of the jury when *Reynolds* privilege is in
issue is not an easy one; indeed it is open to question whether jury trial is desirable at all in such
a case": Lord Phillips M.R. in *Jameel (Mohammed) v Wall Street Journal Sprl* [2005] EWCA Civ
74; [2005] Q.B. 904 at [70]. In *Radu v Houston* [2007] EWHC 2328 (QB) in which Eady J.
refused to allow a jury in the trial of a preliminary issue of privilege (including *Reynolds*
privilege), one of his reasons was that a jury would be unlikely to perform any useful function as
there were unlikely to be many contentious facts for them to resolve. In *Flood v Times
Newspapers Ltd* [2012] UKSC 11; [2012] 2 A.C. 273, at [49] Lord Phillips, faced with the
problem that the judge considering a claim for *Reynolds* privilege as a preliminary issue will
generally have to determine meaning, which is normally a matter for the jury, could only suggest
that the parties should agree to trial by judge alone.

[4] There were, for instance, fifteen questions in *Loutchansky v Times Newspapers* [2001]
E.M.L.R. 38, where the jury played a very occasional bit part as the need for them arose. There
was reason to suppose that they would have preferred a more conventional role.

[5] However, in *Fiddes v Channel Four Television Corp* [2010] EWCA Civ 730; [2010] 1 W.L.R.
2245, the Court of Appeal warned that giving too much independent weight to the additional
length and cost of jury trial would risk undermining the important right to jury trial: "Jury trial
will almost always take longer, and cost more, than trial by judge alone", per Lord Neuberger
M.R. at [18]. Nonetheless, Tugendhat J.'s decision to order trial by judge alone was upheld.

with juries, especially when there are large files of documents. Consequently, where the parties are not agreed on mode of trial, judges have been very much more open to persuasion that one of the exceptions to a mandatory jury trial listed in s.69 of the Senior Courts Act 1981 applies[6]; and when the right to jury trial has been lost,[7] the residual discretion under s.69(3) to order jury trial is very rarely exercised in favour of a jury.[8]

34.2 Statutory abolition of presumption in favour of jury trial. By s.11, Defamation Act 2013, which at the time of writing has not been brought into force, the right to jury trial in defamation actions has been abolished. The result will be that actions for libel and slander, like most other civil claims proceeding in the Queen's Bench Division or the county court, will be tried by judge alone, unless exceptionally the court orders otherwise. In reality, jury trial for defamation will be a thing of the past. It follows that this chapter is about to become almost wholly redundant. However, it is unclear when it is proposed that s.11 should be brought into force, so for the moment there may be some merit in continuing to set out the position as it currently stands.

34.3 Basic rules. It is trite that the judge decides questions of law and the jury all issues of fact. In defamation, where is the line drawn? The general rule is well known: it is for the judge to rule whether there is any, or any sufficient, evidence of a fact in issue for the jury to consider; and if there is, it is for the jury to decide whether that fact has been established by the evidence. Thus where there is a plea of justification, a claimant can apply to the judge at the conclusion of the evidence to strike out the plea, or part of it, or to withdraw that defence, or part of it, from the jury on the grounds that there is insufficient evidence upon which a jury could properly conclude that the plea, or part of

---

[6] Some of the problems of jury trial in complex cases are well exemplified by the final observations of Auld L.J. when giving judgment on an appeal in a libel action brought by a solicitor against his clients who had accused him in a letter to a firm of estate agents of breach of fiduciary duty and breach of confidence, which was tried by a judge and jury:
"Before leaving this case I should express my sympathy to the judge and to the jury on the enormous burdens imposed on both of them in this case, given the unhappy divide of responsibility between them on supposedly self-contained issues of law and fact. In fact the critical issues, particularly as to fiduciary relationship and matters of confidence, and the ingredients of malice as distinct from justification, were in truth more matters of mixed law and fact. It is, in my view, no advertisement for our system of jury trial in civil cases—where it applies—for such complex issues to be tried in this way. A Martian on learning of it would be amazed, as would the ordinary person in the street."
(*Ratiu v Conway* [2005] EWCA Civ 1302; [2006] 1 All E.R. 571 at [185].)
[7] For example, because of failure to comply with the requirement of CPR r.26.11 that an application for jury trial must be made within 28 days of service of defence (after which the right is irretrievably lost: *Cook v Telegraph Media Group Ltd* [2011] EWHC 763 (QB); and see *Thornton v Telegraph Media Group Ltd* [2011] EWCA Civ 748; [2011] E.M.L.R. 29)
[8] See paras 31.64 and 31.67 and Ch.31 fn.288, above; and a good example of judicial reluctance to order jury trial as a matter of discretion is supplied by *Bento v Chief Constable of Bedfordshire Police* [2012] EWCA Civ 956.

it, was made out.[9] The threshold to be crossed before the issue can be withdrawn from the jury is a high one: the evidence, taken at its highest, must be such that the jury properly directed could not properly reach the necessary factual conclusion.[10] In that event, it is the judge's duty, once a submission is made to him, to withdraw the issue from the jury.

The proper construction of a deed or other document having legal effect is a matter for the judge; and any issue that arises as to what is the law of another country is for the judge's decision.[11]

Defamatory meaning. In times past the general practice was not to grant   **34.4** the jury any role in adjudicating whether the words complained of were defamatory. That was regarded as a question of law for determination by the judge.[12] However, since Fox's Act 1792, it has been recognised that a critical function of the jury is to decide whether the claimant has been defamed.[13] "Libel or no libel, since Fox's Act, is of all questions peculiarly one for the jury."[14] So it has long been accepted that whether the words carry a defamatory meaning is an issue of fact.

> "In general the meaning of words is a matter of law . . . But in defamation the meaning of words is a question of fact, that is, there is libel or no libel according to the impression the words convey to the jury, and not according to the construction put upon them by the judge."[15]

The question of fact involves two elements; what the words mean, and whether that meaning is defamatory.

Are the words capable of bearing a defamatory meaning? The   **34.5** jury's role in determining meaning is subject to one important pre-condition, namely that it is for the judge to decide whether the words are capable of bearing a defamatory meaning. That question has been described as a question of law, but in truth that means simply that it is a question reserved to the judge.[16] If the words are so capable then it is a question for the jury to decide

---

[9] *McDonalds Corp v Steel* [1995] 3 All E.R. 615 at 623.

[10] *Alexander v Arts Council of Wales* [2001] EWCA Civ 514; [2001] 1 W.L.R. 1840 at [37]. This is the test on a half time submission in a criminal trial: see *R. v Galbraith* [1981] 1 W.L.R. 1039 at 1042.

[11] Senior Courts Act 1981, s.69(5).

[12] It would appear that the jury could decide meaning, but not whether that meaning was defamatory: see the judgment of Lord Mansfield in *R. v Shipley* (1784) 4 Doug 73.

[13] The 1792 Act related to criminal prosecutions, but it was said to be "only declaratory of the common law": see Scrutton L.J. in *Broome v Agar* (1928) 44 T.L.R. 339. It has been repealed by the Coroners and Justice Act 2009, s.178 and Sch.23.

[14] Per Lord Coleridge C.J. in *Saxby v Easterbrook* (1878) 3 C.P.D. 339.

[15] Per Lord Devlin in *Lewis v Daily Telegraph* [1964] A.C. 234 at 258.

[16] See *Jones v Skelton* [1963] 1 W.L.R. 1362 P.C. at 1371, per Lord Morris:
> "It is well settled that the question whether words complained of are capable of conveying a defamatory meaning is a question of law and is therefore one calling for the decision of the court. If the words are so capable then it is a question for the jury whether the words do in fact convey a defamatory meaning."

But Diplock L.J. in *Slim v Daily Telegraph* [1968] 2 Q.B. 157 at 174, said that the decision as to defamatory meanings which words are capable of bearing is called a question of law "for this

whether the words do in fact convey a defamatory meaning. In the normal course of things, the question of whether the words are capable of bearing the pleaded meanings, or any defamatory meaning, should have been decided long before trial under the CPR 53PD, para.4.1 procedure.

34.6 Task of the judge. The judge's function is to delimit the range of meanings that the words are capable of bearing (and which a properly directed jury could therefore find them to bear), and rule out any meanings falling outside that range.[17] Eady J. has expressed the judge's role in a passage described by Lord Phillips M.R. on appeal[18] as an "impeccable synthesis" of the authorities:

> "The proper role for the judge when adjudicating a question of this kind is to evaluate the words complained of and to delimit the range of meanings of which the words are reasonably capable . . . If the judge decides that any pleaded meaning falls outside the permissible range, then it will be his duty to rule accordingly. In deciding whether words are capable of conveying a defamatory meaning, the court should reject those meanings which can only emerge as the produce of some strained or forced or utterly unreasonable interpretation. . . . The court should give the article the natural and ordinary meaning which it would have conveyed to the ordinary reasonable reader reading the article once. Hypothetical reasonable readers should not be treated as either naive or unduly suspicious. They should be treated as being capable of reading between the lines and engaging in some loose thinking, but not as being avid for scandal. The court should avoid an over-elaborate analysis of the article, because an ordinary reader would not analyse the article as a lawyer or accountant would analyse documents or accounts. Judges should have regard to the impression the article has made upon them themselves in considering what impact it would have made on the hypothetical reasonable reader. The court should certainly not take a too literal approach to its task."

It is important to avoid over-elaborate judicial analysis,[19] particularly in the context of political speech.[20]

34.7 Two or more meanings reasonably possible. Where the words complained of are reasonably capable of either an innocent or a defamatory meaning, it is a question of fact for the jury to determine which of the two

---

reason, and no other" that it is reserved to the judge. Similarly, Lord Reid in *Morgan v Odhams Press* [1971] 1 W.L.R. 1239 at 1243: "I have more than once stated my view that the meaning of words is not a question of law in the true sense . . . It is simply a question which our law reserves for the judge." Hence, no doubt, the tendency to refer to the question of whether the defamatory meaning alleged by the claimant is within the range of possible meanings as one "regarded" as a question of law: see *British Chiropractic Association v Singh* [2010] EWCA Civ 350; [2011] 1 W.L.R. 133 at [13].

[17] "An exercise in generosity, not in parsimony", according to Sedley L.J., *Berezovsky v Forbes* [2001] EWCA Civ 1251; [2001] E.M.L.R. 45 at [16].

[18] *Gillick v Brook Advisory Centres* [2001] EWCA Civ 1263 at [7].

[19] *Jeynes v News Magazines Ltd* [2008] EWCA Civ 140 at [14].

[20] *Waterson v Lloyd* [2013] EWCA Civ 136; [2013] E.M.L.R. 17 per Laws L.J. at [66].

meanings the words actually bore.[21] Indeed it is accepted that a passage of text may bear several meanings:

> "Everyone outside a court of law recognises that words are imprecise instruments for communicating the thoughts of one man to another. The same words may be understood by one man in a different meaning from that which they are understood by another... Different men would not be unreasonable in ascribing different meanings to the same words. Hence the distinction between defamatory meanings which words are capable of bearing and *the* particular defamatory meaning which, for the purposes of the tort of libel, they bear."[22]

The task of the jury is to decide which of the possible meanings is the "right" meaning, that is to say the single natural and ordinary meaning of the words.[23] "Their various views would coalesce in one combined (and perhaps compromise) view of the natural and ordinary meaning, and whether it was defamatory."[24]

Where words are susceptible of a number of innocent interpretations, and only one defamatory meaning, that meaning must be left to the jury, if it is a meaning the words are capable of bearing. Whether the context of words, which, when read in isolation, are defamatory, removes the sting or transforms the meaning so as to render the words incapable of being defamatory,[25] is as a general rule a matter for the jury.

> "Only in the clearest cases would it be proper for a judge to rule that the sting of words, which are *ex hypothesi* capable of a defamatory meaning in themselves, is drawn by the surrounding context, so that in the result those words cease to be capable of a defamatory meaning. In my judgment the general though perhaps not

---

[21] *Hart v Wall* (1877) 2 C.P.D. 146.
"The question is not whether the letters are susceptible of an innocent interpretation, but whether no libellous construction can reasonably be put upon them; for if such a construction can reasonably be given to them, it is for the jury to say whether or not that is the true interpretation of them":
per Lord Coleridge C.J. at 149. *Simmons v Mitchell* (1880) 6 A.C. 156; *Cassidy v Daily Mirror* [1929] 2 K.B. 331 at 339, Scrutton, L.J.: "I do not agree with some dicta to the effect that if words are capable of several meanings, some defamatory and some innocent, they should not be left to the jury."
[22] Per Diplock L.J. in *Slim v Daily Telegraph* [1968] 2 Q.B. 157 at 171, 174.
[23] *Slim v Daily Telegraph*, above, at 174. The rule is no longer the same in malicious falsehood cases, which are not tried by jury: *Ajinomoto Sweeteners Europe SAS v Asda Stores Ltd* [2010] EWCA Civ 609; [2011] Q.B. 497 (and most recently *Cruddas v Calvert* [2013] EWCA Civ 748). For a recent discussion of the single meaning rule in the context of honest comment, see *Lait v Evening Standard Ltd* [2011] EWCA Civ 859; [2011] 1 W.L.R. 2973 at [34]–[35], [50], [52]. It may be wondered, given the importance of jury trial as a justification for the single meaning rule (see per Diplock L.J. in *Slim* at 174), how long it will survive the end of jury trial in defamation.
[24] Per Hirst L.J. in *Mitchell v Book Sales*, unreported, March 24, 1994, CA.
[25] I.e. "bane and antidote" cases: see Alderson B in *Chalmers v Payne* (1835) 2 Cr.M. & R. 156.

universal rule should be that this is a matter for the jury and not for the judge to decide."[26]

34.8 Meanings in the statements of case. Though the claimant must set out in the particulars of claim the defamatory meaning or meanings he contends are borne by the words complained of,[27] the judge is not confined to ruling whether the words are capable of bearing those meanings.[28] His ruling may cover any lesser defamatory meaning that might possibly be conveyed by the words.[29] The judge may also rule whether the words are capable of bearing a meaning contended for by the defendant as part of the defences of justification or fair comment. He may even rule as to whether words relied on not as being defamatory of the claimant but as being relevant to the issue of malice are capable of bearing the meaning attributed to them.[30]

34.9 Innuendo meanings. Where the claimant is relying upon an innuendo meaning, that is to say, a meaning arising from extrinsic facts,[31] the judge must rule whether there is evidence of such facts fit to be left to the jury,[32] and if there is, must then consider whether, if the jury find such facts proved, the words are capable of bearing the innuendo meanings attributed to them.[33]

> "If the judge, taking into account the manner and the occasion of the publication and all other facts which are properly in evidence, is not satisfied that the words are capable of the meaning ascribed to them, then it is not his duty to leave the question raised by the innuendo to the jury."[34]

Further, the judge ought not to leave the issue to the jury unless there is evidence that someone to whom the words were published knew the extrinsic

---

[26] Per Hirst L.J. in *Mitchell v Faber and Faber* [1998] E.M.L.R. 284; *Mark v Associated Newspapers* [2002] E.M.L.R. 839; *Charleston v News Group Newspapers Ltd* [1995] 2 A.C. 65 is perhaps an example of an exception. See also the observations of Sedley L.J. in *Jameel v Times Newspapers Ltd* [2004] EWCA Civ 983; [2004] E.M.L.R. 31 at [16].

[27] CPR 53PD, para.2.3(1)(a).

[28] Despite what O'Connor L.J. said in *Polly Peck v Trelford* [1986] 1 Q.B. 1000 at 1033.

[29] CPR 53PD, para.4.1(3), and see *Slim v Daily Telegraph*, above, per Diplock L.J. at 175; *Skuse v Granada Television* [1995] E.M.L.R. 278. The judge is only likely to rule on a lesser meaning if it is in the same class or range of meanings as that set out in the particulars of claim, and not some wholly different meaning. Thus, e.g. a judge might find that the words were capable of bearing the meaning that the claimant was suspected of theft, rather than, as had been pleaded, had committed theft, and reserve the former meaning to the jury; but he would not leave the case to the jury on the basis that the words were only capable of bearing the meaning that the claimant had been drunk, when neither that nor any similar meaning had been alleged. The judge's decision would surely be that such a meaning was not part of the claimant's case.

[30] *Bray v Deutsche Bank* [2009] EWHC 1356 (QB). It does not appear that CPR 53PD para.4(1) had been used for this purpose before.

[31] Explained in paras 3.20 et seq., above. For recent discussion of the varieties of innuendo meaning, see *Lord McAlpine of West Green v Bercow* [2013] EWHC 1342 (QB); *Fox v Boulter* [2013] EWHC 1435 (QB).

[32] See Lord Hodson in *Lewis v Daily Telegraph* [1964] A.C. 234 at 271.

[33] *Lewis v Daily Telegraph*, above, at 259.

[34] Per Lord Selbourne L.C. in *Capital and Counties Bank v Henty* (1882) 7 A.C. 741 at 744. This was not a case where a true innuendo was pleaded.

facts on which the claimant relies to support his innuendo.[35] An innuendo gives rise to a separate cause of action,[36] so where both an innuendo meaning and a natural and ordinary meaning are put forward by the claimant, a ruling that the words are incapable of bearing the innuendo meaning will only bring the action to an end if there is a similar ruling in respect of the natural and ordinary meaning.

Incapable of innocent meaning. Before CPR Pt 24 brought summary judgment to defamation, it would have been exceptional for a judge to rule that words were incapable of bearing any meaning other than a defamatory meaning, or to direct the jury that they must find the words defamatory.[37] In *Broome v Agar*[38] the Court of Appeal refused to reverse a finding that the allegation made by the defendant that the plaintiff (a chauffeur) was giving "joy rides" to women in the defendant's car, was not defamatory.   **34.10**

> "It is a long step to pass from the power of a judge to withdraw the case from a jury on the ground that he thinks that the words are not capable of a defamatory meaning to the position that, if a judge or judges think that words are only capable of a defamatory meaning, he or they can enter judgment for the plaintiff without a finding of the jury, or direct the jury to find that the words are defamatory, or keep on ordering a new trial, because the jury will not return the verdict which the judges think they ought to find."[39]

However, the position now is that if the words are only capable of a defamatory meaning the judge is entitled—indeed it is his duty—so to rule, and to give summary judgment on the issue of meaning:

> "If the judge had . . . properly come to the conclusion that the words were only capable of having a defamatory meaning, then it is difficult to see what objection there could be to his giving summary judgment on an issue on which there was no room for argument. The judge would have been doing no more than what the trial judge could have done if the action had proceeded to trial. The court, that is the judge, would not be 'satisfied that there is in issue', whether the words were defamatory, as required by section 69 of the Supreme Court Act 1981."[40]

---

[35] See para.3.22, above. This may be a matter of inference: see *Dwek v Macmillan Publishers* [2000] E.M.L.R. 284, a "reference innuendo" case, but the principle is the same. See *Fullam v Newcastle Chronicle* [1977] 1 W.L.R. 651 and *Baturina v Times Newspapers Ltd* [2011] EWCA Civ 308, [2011] 1 W.L.R. 1526, in neither of which was an inference sustainable; rather, the claimant was ordered to give particulars of those who would have known the special facts.

[36] See *Lewis v Daily Telegraph*, above.

[37] In *Mitchell v Book Sales*, cited above, counsel's contention that the words were incapable of anything other than a defamatory meaning, and that the trial judge should have positively directed the jury to find in the plaintiff's favour, was described by Hirst L.J. as "a most extravagant submission".

[38] (1928) 44 T.L.R. 339.

[39] Per Scrutton L.J. in *Broome v Agar*, above, at 340. Cf. *Lockhart v Harrison* (1928) 139 L.T. 521.

[40] *Alexander v Arts Council of Wales* [2001] EWCA Civ 514; [2001] 1 W.L.R. 1840 per Lord Woolf C.J. at [56], who was explaining the decision of another division of the Court of Appeal (*Safeway Stores v Tate* [2001] Q.B. 1120). That court had allowed an appeal from the trial judge of a libel action who had granted the claimant summary judgment after striking out the defence of justification and ruling that the defendant had no real prospect of success on the issue of defamatory meaning. The CA had held that it was for the jury to decide what meanings the words

34.11 **Time for ruling on meanings.** Until quite recently,[41] rulings as to meanings were normally given in the course of trial.[42] The judge could even delay his decision until after the jury had delivered their verdict,[43] but this has not been the modern practice.[44] Now an application for a ruling as to whether the words are capable of bearing a particular meaning or meanings may be made at any time after service of the particulars of claim,[45] and should be made promptly.[46] In most cases there will thus have already been a decision on this issue prior to the trial. The respective roles of judge and jury in relation to determination of meaning remain the same whether the ruling is given at an interim hearing or at trial.

34.12 **Slanders.** Where the slander is alleged to be actionable without proof of special damage on the ground that it suggests the commission of a criminal offence, it is a question of law for the judge whether the acts and conduct which the words are capable of imputing to the claimant amount to a crime punishable with imprisonment. In cases where s.2 of the Defamation Act 1952 is relied upon, it must be for the jury to decide whether the words complained of were calculated to disparage the claimant in any office, profession, calling, trade or business held or carried on by him at the time of the publication.[47] When special damage has to be proved, it is a question of law for the judge whether any damage proved constitutes special damage, and, if it does, whether such special damage was the natural and probable result of the words complained of, or is too remote. It is a question of fact for the jury what (if any) damage has been proved, and also whether such damage did or did not result from the publication of the words complained of.

---

bore. Lord Woolf's remarks were to the effect that the CA in *Safeway* was only ruling that summary judgment could not be granted where there was an issue as to whether the words were defamatory, in which case it must be left to the jury; it was not excluding summary judgment when the words were only capable of a defamatory meaning.

[41] September 1994 when RSC Ord.82, r.3A was introduced.

[42] Unless it was such an improbable meaning that an application to strike out could be made under RSC Ord.18, r.19, but that required the judge to find that the words complained of were not even arguably capable of bearing a defamatory meaning.

[43] In *Liberace v Daily Mirror, The Times*, June 17–18, 1959 the ruling on meaning was given after the jury's verdict. The plaintiff, an American entertainer, complained of an article in the *Daily Mirror* which described him as "the summit of sex—the pinnacle of Masculine, Feminine and Neuter. Everything that He, She, or It can ever want" and "this deadly, winking, sniggering, snuggling, chromium-plated, scent-impregnated, luminous, quivering, giggling, fruit-flavoured, mincing, ice-covered heap of mother-love". Salmon J. left these passages (with the exception of the expression "fruit-flavoured") to the jury to decide whether they connoted homosexuality, and accepted the jury's verdict that they did, saying on the question of law he had come to the conclusion that the words were just capable of the meaning which the jury had found, although he was by no means certain that he would have come to the same conclusion of fact. In present times it is unlikely to be defamatory to call a person a homosexual.

[44] In theory it could still be done, as the judge may rule on whether words are capable of bearing a defamatory meaning "at any time": CPR 53PD, para.4.1.

[45] CPR 53 PD, para.4.2. See further Ch.30, s.2, above.

[46] Ibid.

[47] The judge's task is to rule whether the words are capable of so disparaging the claimant.

Publication. Whether the facts as proved constitute a publication is a   **34.13**
question of law for the judge to determine. Where this question of law
depends upon doubtful or contradictory evidence the jury should be left to
decide the issues of fact, and the legal decision can be deferred until they have
made their findings.[48]

Reference to claimant. It is a question of law for the judge whether there   **34.14**
is any evidence to be left to the jury that the words complained of would be
understood by reasonable persons to refer to the claimant. If there is, it is for
the jury to decide whether the words were or would be so understood.[49]

> "There are two questions involved in the attempt to identify (the plaintiff) as the
> person defamed. The first question is a question of law—can the article, having
> regard to its language, be regarded as capable of referring to (the plaintiff)? The
> second question is a question of fact—does the article, in fact, lead reasonable
> people, who know (the plaintiff), to the conclusion that it does refer to him? Unless
> the first question can be answered in favour of (the plaintiff) the second question
> does not arise, and where the trial judge went wrong was in treating evidence to
> support the identification in fact as governing the matter, when the first question is
> necessarily, as a matter of law, to be answered in the negative."[50]

In nearly every case where the claimant is not expressly referred to, the
claimant will rely on extrinsic facts, and knowledge of those facts by some of
those to whom the words were published,[51] to establish that the words referred
to him; and as with an innuendo meaning, it is the task of the judge to decide
that there is sufficient evidence of those facts, that they were known to some
of those who heard or read the words, and that persons with such knowledge
could reasonably identify the claimant, to leave the matter to the jury. Knowledge of those facts by some of those to whom the words were published may
in appropriate circumstances be a matter of inference,[52] and it would be the
judge's task to decide whether the primary facts are sufficient to enable a jury
to draw the inference.

Malicious falsehood. A claim for malicious falsehood could be tried by a   **34.15**
judge sitting with a jury where it is joined in an action for libel or slander.[53]

---

[48] For examples see *Powell v Gelston* [1916] 2 K.B. 615; and *Theaker v Richardson* [1962] 1
W.L.R. 151 CA, where the jury were asked whether the defendant anticipated that someone other
than the plaintiff would open and read the defendant's letter and whether it was a natural and
probable consequence of the defendant's acts that the plaintiff's husband should open and read it,
and these questions were approved (by Harman L.J.) as "just the kind of questions of fact which
ought to be left to a jury". The jury could, alternatively, be directed as to what findings of fact
are required for there to be publication.
[49] *Knupffer v London Express* [1944] A.C. 116; *Morgan v Odham's Press* [1971] 1 W.L.R. 1239
at 1246, 1254, 1269.
[50] Per Viscount Simon L.C. in *Knupffer v London Express*, above, at 121.
[51] E.g. *Morgan v Odham's Press* [1971] 1 W.L.R. 1239.
[52] *Dwek v Macmillan Publishers* [2000] E.M.L.R. 284.
[53] See s.69 of the Senior Courts Act 1981; a malicious falsehood claim joined in an action for
malicious prosecution or false imprisonment would also qualify.

It would then be for the judge to decide whether the words were capable of being an actionable disparagement of the claimant's goods.

> "If it is clear that what is complained of is a mere puffing of his own goods by the defendant then there is no question for a jury.[54] Whether the words are false, were published maliciously and were calculated to cause the claimant pecuniary damage are questions of fact for the jury."[55]

34.16 Justification. As earlier stated,[56] the judge must determine whether the words are capable of bearing the defamatory meaning (if different from the meaning contended for by the claimant) which the defendant seeks to justify. The judge will further have to rule on whether there is sufficient evidence to enable the jury to find that that meaning (or the claimant's defamatory meaning) has been justified. The application of s.5 of the Defamation Act 1952 is a matter for the jury.

34.17 Honest comment. It is for the judge to decide whether the matter commented on is one of public interest.[57] It is for the jury to decide whether the words complained of are allegations of fact or comment,[58] and if expressions of opinion, whether such comments are honest comment or not.[59] However in every case it is first of all the duty of the judge to determine whether the words are capable of being comment,[60] or conversely were not capable of being statements of fact,[61] and whether there is any material which would entitle the jury to find that the comment was unfair,[62] that is to say that the opinions expressed were such that they could not honestly be held on the clearly

---

[54] *Alcott v Millar's Karri Ltd* (1904) 91 L.T. 722 at 723.

[55] See s.3 of the Defamation Act 1952. It must be for the judge to rule that the words are capable of causing pecuniary damage of the kind prescribed by the section. Where special damage is alleged the position is the same as with slanders actionable on proof of special damage: see para.34.12, above.

[56] See para.34.8, above.

[57] Per Lopes L.J. in *South Hetton v N.E. News* [1894] 1 Q.B. 133 at 141, 143; *Jones v Skelton* [1963] 1 W.L.R. 1362 at 1378; *London Artists v Littler* [1969] 2 Q.B. 375. In *Anderson v Ah Kit* (2004) WASC 194 there was a ruling that the welfare of animals kept privately and not open for public inspection was not a matter of public interest for the purposes of fair comment.

[58] Per Bankes L.J. in *Aga Khan v Times Co.* [1924] 1 K.B. 675 at 680; *Turner v MGM Pictures* [1950] 1 All E.R. 449 at 461; *Jones v Skelton*, above, at 1379.

[59] *Hunt v Star* [1908] 2 K.B. 309; *Dakhyl v Labouchere* [1908] 2 K.B. 325n at 329; *Jones v Skelton*, above, at 1379. The jury will apply the objective test, whether the comment is one that an honest person could have made, albeit that that person may have been prejudiced or had exaggerated obstinate views: *Tse Wai Chun v Cheng* [2000] HKCFA 86; [2001] E.M.L.R. 31.

[60] *Turner v MGM Pictures*, above; *Jones v Skelton*, above; *London Artists v Littler*, above; *British Chiropractic Association v Singh* [2010] EWCA Civ 350; [2011] 1 W.L.R. 133.

[61] *Branson v Bower* [2001] EWCA Civ 791; [2001] E.M.L.R. 800, in which on a preliminary issue there was a ruling that the words were comment and were not capable of being statements of fact.

[62] *McQuire v Western Morning News* [1903] 2 K.B. 100; *Sutherland v Stopes* [1925] A.C. 47; *London Artists v Littler*, above; and cf. *Telnikoff v Matusevitch* [1991] 1 Q.B. 102, where the Court of Appeal implicitly approved the judge's decision to withdraw the case from the jury on the grounds, inter alia, that it was not open to the jury to find the comment unfair (decision reversed on other grounds in the House of Lords: [1992] 2 A.C. 343).

established or uncontroversial facts.[63] But it would appear that the initial exercise for the judge is to decide what meanings the words are capable of bearing; only then can the judge determine whether the words complained of, in those meanings, are capable of being comment.[64] The fairness of the comment must in part depend upon what facts pleaded as the basis of the comment are proved or admitted. Whether, and which of, such facts have been proved is for the jury to decide, subject to the judge's ruling as to the sufficiency of evidence for the issue to be left to the jury. Thus the judge will be unable to rule on the objective fairness of the comment if there are disputed issues of fact for the jury to resolve, unless on the undisputed facts the objective test is satisfied to the extent that it would be perverse for the jury not to find the comment honest.[65] It is for the jury to apply s.6 of the Defamation Act 1952.

Qualified privilege. The respective functions of judge and jury where privilege is claimed have been succinctly explained by Lord Esher M.R.[66]:   **34.18**

"The question whether the occasion is privileged, if the facts are not in dispute, is a question of law only, for the judge, not for the jury. If there are questions of fact in dispute upon which this question depends, they must be left to the jury, but, when the jury have found the facts, it is for the judge to say whether they constitute a privileged occasion."[67]

Reynolds **or public interest privilege.** The same division of roles was confirmed by Lord Nicholls in *Reynolds v Times Newspapers*[68]:   **34.19**

"Any disputes of primary fact[69] will be a matter for the jury, if there is one. The decision on whether, having regard to the admitted or proved facts, the publication was subject to qualified privilege is a matter for the judge".[70]

---

[63] See *Branson v Bower* [2002] Q.B. 737 at [54]. The decision was made not at trial, but on an application for summary judgment under CPR Pt 24.

[64] *Associated Newspapers v Burstein* [2007] EWCA Civ 600; [2007] 4 All E.R. 319 per Keene L.J. at [7]. However, the practice of determining first whether words are defamatory, and then whether they are comment, was questioned by the Court of Appeal in *British Chiropractic Association v Singh* [2010] EWCA Civ 350; [2011] 1 W.L.R. 133 at [32], which wondered whether it was necessarily the best approach, given that the answer to the first question might "stifle" the answer to the second. But that had been a trial of preliminary issues by judge alone. The same flexibility is not available if a jury is determining meaning.

[65] *Branson v Bower* [2002] Q.B. 737.

[66] In *Hebditch v MacIlwaine* [1894] 2 Q.B. 54 at 58.

[67] See also Lord Finlay in *Adam v Ward* [1917] A.C. 309 at 318:
"It is for the judge and the judge alone to determine as a matter of law whether the occasion is privileged unless the circumstances attending it are in dispute, in which case the facts necessary to raise the question of law should be found by the jury."

[68] [2001] 2 A.C. 127 at 205G.

[69] Gillard A.J.A. in *Herald & Weekly Times v Popovic* (2003) VSCA 161 defined "primary facts" in this context as "the actual happening of a particular event, what was said or done, but not the inferences or conclusions to be drawn from those primary facts" [111]. Thus whether the conduct of the publisher was reasonable—an ingredient of the statutory defence of qualified privilege under the law of the State of Victoria—was for the judge to decide as it was not a primary fact.

[70] In *Loutchansky v Times Newspapers (No.4)* [2001] E.M.L.R. 38 Gray J. left 15 questions of primary fact to the jury.

The difficulties that arise in distinguishing what are factual issues for the jury and what are matters for the judge led Lord Phillips M.R. to express the remarks quoted in the opening paragraph of this chapter.[71] In *Flood v Times Newspapers Ltd*,[72] Lord Phillips P.S.C. made it plain that in his view issues of public interest privilege are not suited to jury trial. Before the court can balance the public interest in publication against the public interest in ensuring a reputation, and in particular the reputation of a public figure, is not falsely besmirched, and before the court can determine what it is that the journalist should have verified, it is necessary to determine the meaning of the words complained of. But that, of course, is a function of a jury. Lord Phillips suggested that a sensible way of avoiding this difficulty would be for the parties to agree to trial by judge alone.[73] That, of course, is not always what the parties want. The difficulty is compounded by the fact that it is often desirable to determine public interest privilege by way of preliminary issue, well before the trial of the action proper.

The reality is that it is unlikely that an English jury will ever again be involved in making findings of fact in a public interest privilege case. But if it happens, the jury will have to face an "exam paper" of the kind imposed on the jury in *Loutchansky v Times Newspapers Ltd*.[74] They will have to decide meaning and all the relevant factual issues, most of them no doubt from Lord Nicholls's non-exhaustive list in *Reynolds*,[75] and once they have found all the facts necessary to enable the judge to rule on privilege, their function will be performed.

---

[71] See fn.3, above: *Jameel (Mohammed) v Wall Street Journal SPRL* [2005] EWCA Civ; [2005] Q.B. 904 at [70].

[72] [2012] UKSC 11; [2012] 2 A.C. 273.

[73] Ibid. at [49].

[74] [2001] E.M.L.R. 38: see fn.4, above.

[75] *Reynolds v Times Newspapers Ltd* [2001] 2 A.C. 127 at 205:
"Depending on the circumstances, the matters to be taken into account include the following. The comments are illustrative only. 1. The seriousness of the allegation. The more serious the charge, the more the public is misinformed and the individual harmed, if the allegation is not true. 2. The nature of the information, and the extent to which the subject matter is a matter of public concern. 3. The source of the information. Some informants have no direct knowledge of the events. Some have their own axes to grind, or are being paid for their stories. 4. The steps taken to verify the information. 5. The status of the information. The allegation may have already been the subject of an investigation which commands respect. 6. The urgency of the matter. News is often a perishable commodity. 7. Whether comment was sought from the plaintiff. He may have information others do not possess or have not disclosed. An approach to the plaintiff will not always be necessary. 8. Whether the article contained the gist of the plaintiff's side of the story. 9. The tone of the article. A newspaper can raise queries or call for an investigation. It need not adopt allegations as statements of fact. 10. The circumstances of the publication, including the timing. This list is not exhaustive. The weight to be given to these and any other relevant factors will vary from case to case. Any disputes of primary fact will be a matter for the jury, if there is one. The decision on whether, having regard to the admitted or proved facts, the publication was subject to qualified privilege is a matter for the judge. This is the established practice and seems sound. A balancing operation is better carried out by a judge in a reasoned judgment than by a jury. Over time, a valuable corpus of case law will be built up."

The so-called "reportage" cases depend for their public interest not on the content of the reported allegation but the fact that the allegation has been made, and the publisher is protected as long as he has taken proper steps to verify the making of the allegation (i.e the fact that it was made), provided that he does not adopt it.[76] It would seem that it is for the judge to rule on whether the article amounts to reportage, and that must be judged on the merits of the story at the time of publication. Given the generally narrower scope for examining the steps taken to verify the story, and the reduced significance of the journalist's belief in the truth of the story (since the story is the fact of the allegations being made, not their truth or falsity) it would seem that there is even less opportunity in reportage cases for the jury to play a meaningful role.[77]

Absolute privilege. If such a case reaches trial the position as to the respective roles of judge and jury would appear to be the same as in qualified privilege cases.[78]   34.20

Fair and accurate reports. If the existence of privilege, either at common law or by virtue of statute, is dependent on the words being a fair and accurate report, the fairness and accuracy of the report containing the words is a question of fact for the jury.[79] The judge can withdraw the question from the jury if no reasonably minded jury properly directed could have come to any other conclusion than that the report was fair and accurate.[80] No regard should be given to minor inaccuracies or omissions of a trifling character.[81] It would seem that it is for the judge to decide whether the matter complained of can   34.21

---

[76] Per Lord Phillips, *Flood v Times Newspapers Ltd* [2012] UKSC 11; [2012] 2 A.C. 273 at [77].

[77] For the matters to be taken in account in establishing reportage, see per Ward L.J. at [61] in *Roberts v Gable* [2007] EWCA Civ 721; [2008] Q.B. 502.

[78] It is usual for this question to be determined before trial, e.g. after service of particulars of claim, if the facts alleged disclose an occasion of absolute privilege; e.g. *Law v Llewellyn* [1906] 1 K.B. 487; *Burr v Smith* [1909] 2 K.B. 306. More recent examples are *Waple v Surrey CC* [1998] E.M.L.R. 503, though the decision to strike out the action on the grounds of absolute privilege was reversed on appeal, *Smeaton v Butcher* [2000] E.M.L.R. 985 and *Westcott v Westcott* [2008] EWCA Civ 818; [2009] Q.B. 407.

[79] *Turner v Sullivan* (1862) 6 L.T.(N.S.) 130; *Street v Licensed Victuallers Society* (1874) 22 W.R. 553; *Milissich v Lloyds* (1877) 46 L.S.C.P. 404; *Kingshott v Associated Kent Newspapers* [1991] 1 Q.B. 88 at 97. For burden of proof, see paras 13.49 and 16.4, above.

[80] *Kimber v Press Association* [1893] 1 Q.B. 65 at 72, 74, 77; *Hope v Leng* (1907) 23 T.L.R. 243; *Cook v Alexander* [1974] Q.B. 279; and see *Leslie v Mirror Newspapers* (1971) 45 A.L.S.R. 700 referred to in *Kingshott v Associated Kent Newspapers*, above, at 98. In *Street v Licensed Victuallers*, above, it was said that the judge should hesitate before withdrawing the case from the jury.

[81] *Kimber v Press Association*, above; *Hope v Leng*, above; it would be "wrong to judge the report by the exact standard of accuracy which would be expected in a report purporting to come from the hand of a trained lawyer", per Collins M.R. at 244, and *Leslie v Mirror Newspapers*, above, at 701. See also *Qadir v Associated Newspapers Ltd* [2012] EWHC 2606 (QB); [2013] E.M.L.R. 15.

be regarded as "a report".[82] It is within the judge's discretion as to whether he rules on the sufficiency of evidence of unfairness or inaccuracy before or after the jury have given their verdict.[83]

34.22 **Qualified privilege under statute.** Whether the occasion that was reported, or the document that was copied or published, or from which extracts were published, fall within those specified in the Schedule to s.15 of the Defamation Act 1996, are matters of law for the judge to decide. Thus whether a meeting is a "public meeting" is a question which the judge has to determine,[84] and it was for the judge to rule whether a statement made by a civil servant at a press conference, later amplified in a telephone conversation with a journalist, was "a notice or other matter issued for the information of the public by or on behalf of any government department".[85] Presumably it would also be for the judge to rule whether or not material sued on was an "extract" from a register required by law to be open to public inspection (while it would be for the jury to decide whether that extract was fair and accurate).[86] However, questions raised by s.15(3) of the Defamation Act 1996, whether the matter is "not of public concern" or its publication is "not for the public benefit",[87] it has now been held, raise factual issues to be resolved by the jury.[88]

---

[82] In *Morriss v News of The World, The Times*, May 17, 1929, part of the article complained of purported to be extracted from evidence given in court but was inserted not as being a report of a judicial proceeding in the ordinary sense but as part of a descriptive account given by the author not only of what he heard and saw in court but also of the plaintiff's house, the character of his friends, the crowd which had assembled to see him and a number of other things extraneous to the proceedings; Swift J. ruled that the article could not be defended as a report of judicial proceedings. In *Cook v Alexander*, above, the CA held that though a "parliamentary sketch" was a different thing from a report of proceedings in Parliament, it was nonetheless a "report" for the purposes of attracting privilege. See also *Tsikata v Newspaper Publishing Ltd* [1997] 1 All E.R. 655; *Curistan v Times Newspapers Ltd* [2008] EWCA Civ 432, [2009] Q.B. 231; *Qadir v Associated Newspapers Ltd* [2012] EWHC 2606 (QB); [2013] E.M.L.R. 15.

[83] See *Kingshott v Associated Kent Newspapers* [1991] 1 Q.B. 88 at 101.

[84] *Khan v Ahmed* [1957] 2 Q.B. 149.

[85] Certainly the judge ruled on the matter in *Blackshaw v Lord* [1984] Q.B. 1 with no suggestion from the Court of Appeal that he should not have done so (although his conclusion was found to be erroneous: see at 23). It was para.12 in Pt II of the Sch. to the Defamation Act 1952 that was under consideration, later extended by para.15 of Pt II of Sch.1 of the 1996 Act. It may not, however, be entirely a question of law: see Dunn L.J. at 38, adopting Jordan C.J. in *Campbell v Associated Newspapers* (1948) 48 N.S.W.S.R. 301 at 303.

[86] *Qadir v Associated Newspapers Ltd*, above.

[87] In *Crossley v Newsquest* [2008] EWHC 3054 (QB) at [23] Eady J. observed that the apparent requirement of s.15(3) that a defendant must show, even in the case of a court report untainted by malice, that the report was of public concern *and* for the public benefit, was an onerous burden, although the court's construction of the provision would have to take into account the requirements of art.10. See also Tugendhat J.'s analysis of public concern and benefit in *Qadir v Associated Newspapers Ltd*, above.

[88] *Kingshott v Associated Kent Newspapers* [1991] 1 Q.B. 88; contrary to the widely held view (e.g. *Boston v Bagshaw* [1966] 1 W.L.R. 1126) that these were matters for the judge: see Bingham L.J. at 99–101. The decision was on s.7(3) of the 1952 Act but it must apply to s.15(3) of the 1996 Act. However the correctness of this decision has been doubted: *McCartan Turkington Breen v Times Newspapers* [2001] 2 A.C. 277, per Lord Cooke at [26].

Malice. Whether the defendant was actuated by malice is a question of fact **34.23** for the jury, provided always there is evidence from which malice can be reasonably inferred. Whether there is any such evidence is a question of law for the judge to determine. "In order to enable the plaintiff to have the question of malice left to the jury, it is necessary that the evidence should raise a probability of malice and be more consistent with its existence than with its non-existence. It is not sufficient if it falls short of that and is consistent only with a mere possibility. To direct a jury to consider mere possibilities in such a case would be practically to destroy the protection which the law throws over privileged communications".[89]

There has been some debate about the requirement that the evidence should be more consistent with the existence than the non-existence of malice, and discussion as to whether it amounts to a more demanding test than that there should be sufficient evidence upon which a reasonably minded jury properly directed could reach a finding of malice.[90] Ultimately, the test to be applied is

---

[89] *Alexander v Arts Council of Wales* [2001] 1 W.L.R. 1840 at [32] per May L.J. (a statement of the law taken with approval from the 8th edition of *Gatley*, which in turn quoted *Walton v Denton* (1930) 31 N.S.W.S.R. at 400, per Street C.J. and Halse Rogers J.), followed in *Ratiu v Conway* [2005] EWCA Civ 1302; [2006] 1 All E.R. 571 and *Telnikoff v Matusevitch* [1991] 1 Q.B. 102 CA at 120. Eady J. observed in *Ashcroft and Foley (No.2)* [2012] EWHC 2214 (QB); [2012] E.M.L.R. 32 at [11] that the rule has the effect of reinforcing rights of defendants under art.10 ECHR, and "presents a significant hurdle to any claimant seeking to undermine a defence of qualified privilege (and, perhaps, . . . also a defence of fair comment)".

See also *Adam v Ward* [1917] A.C. 309 at 318; *Somerville v Hawkins* 138 E.R. 231 (1851) 10 C.B. 583 at 590; *Taylor v Hawkins* (1851) 16 Q.B. 308; *Harris v Thompson* (1853) 13 C.B. 333; *Turner v MGM Pictures* [1950] 1 All E.R. 449 at 455. As Scrutton L.J. observed in *Lionel Barber v Deutsche Bank* (1918) House of Lords Printed Cases at 317 (but reversed on appeal: [1919] A.C. 304):

"There is hardly any case of privilege in which there is not some circumstance which is consistent with malice, and which a jury not sufficiently directed and desiring to find against the defendant may use to found a verdict of express malice; but which yet is equally consistent with no improper motive, and which cannot therefore properly be treated as evidence of either."

[90] In the 9th edition of *Gatley* the editors, having quoted the passage from Maule J.'s judgment in *Somerville v Hawkins*, above, continued (at para.34.18):

"It is submitted this is another method of formulating the proposition that there must be sufficient evidence upon which a reasonably minded jury properly directed could reach a finding of malice before the issue is left for their consideration."

In *Next Magazine v Ma Ching Fat* [2003] H.K.L.R.D. 751 Lord Cooke (at [131]) said he preferred the views of the 9th edition to the 8th edition and that he thought the test was "whether on the evidence as a whole a reasonable jury could find that lack of honest belief is proved" (it was a fair comment case).

However, in *Alexander v Arts Council of Wales* [2001] EWCA Civ 514; [2001] 1 W.L.R. 1840 May L.J. indicated (at [32]) that he approved of the statement of the law in the 8th edition (see fn.89, above). He also described the test in these terms:

"The critical question for the judge was whether there was any evidence, taken at its highest, on which a jury properly directed could properly infer that the defendant subjectively did not honestly believe that what she intended to say in the publications relied on was true." (at [42]).

In *Ratiu v Conway* [2005] EWCA Civ 1302; [2006] 1 All E.R. 571 Auld L.J. adopted May L.J.'s "succinct formula" and commented that it was "of a piece" with the proposition in the 8th edition of *Gatley*. See also *Telnikoff v Matusevitch* [1991] 1 Q.B. 102, CA, at 120.

this: "The critical question for the judge (is) whether there (is) any evidence, taken at its highest, on which a jury properly directed could properly infer that the defendant subjectively did not honestly believe that what she intended to say in the publications relied on was true".[91]

Where the defamatory statement is untrue and describes the conduct of the claimant in blacker and stronger terms than those in which they should have been described, the existence of malice is eminently one for the jury.[92] So too, of course, if there is evidence that the defendant did not believe what he said or wrote was true, or was indifferent to its truth or falsity.[93] If there is no evidence, or insufficient evidence, the judge ought (subject to any other outstanding issues) to withdraw the issue from the jury and give judgment for the defendant.[94]

34.24 Damages. "The assessment of damages is peculiarly the province of the jury in an action for libel."[95] Subject to guidance and directions of the judge,[96] the jury will consider and determine all matters relating to the assessment of damages. These will include such actions and conduct of the defendant as are relied upon as aggravating the damage and any claim for exemplary damages, though the judge will rule whether any particular incident, if proved, can give rise to aggravated damages, and whether there is sufficient evidence of those

---

[91] *Alexander v Arts Council of Wales*, above, per May L.J. at [32].

[92] See per Lord Phillimore in *Lionel Barber v Deutsche Bank* [1919] A.C. 304 at 332.

[93] *Horrocks v Lowe* [1975] A.C. 135 at 150.

[94] *Stuart v Bell* [1891] 2 Q.B. 341 at 345, 352.

[95] Per curiam in *Davis v Shepstone* (1886) 11 App. Cas. 187 P.C. at 191; *Broome v Cassell* [1972] A.C. 1027 at 1065–1066.

[96] As explained in *Rantzen v Mirror Group Newspapers (1986) Ltd* [1994] Q.B. 670 and *John v MGN Ltd* [1997] Q.B. 586. It was said in *John* that jurors could properly be informed as to earlier libel awards approved or substituted by the Court of Appeal, and also take into account brackets suggested by counsel or by the judge as appropriate to the facts before them; and that jurors could be told of the current conventional scale of compensatory damages being awarded for pain and suffering in personal injury cases, as a check on the reasonableness of any figure being considered as an award of damages. Since that time, it has become conventional to inform jurors of the existence of a "ceiling" for general damages, which is currently around £275,000, according to the Court of Appeal in *Cairns v Modi* [2012] EWCA Civ 1382, [2013] 1 W.L.R. 1015, where there is a helpful discussion of the elements and objects of an award of general damages in defamation. The effect of *Simmons v Castle* [2012] EWCA Civ 1039, as amended [2012] EWCA Civ 1288; see [2013] 1 W.L.R 1239 for both judgments, would appear to be that with effect from April 1, 2013, the proper level of general damages for (inter alia) "social discredit" and "mental distress" will be increased by 10 per cent, unless the claimant had entered into a conditional fee agreement (CFA) before that date. It is unclear whether "social discredit" simply means "defamation", which was the term employed by the CA in its first decision, or, if not, what exactly it means. It is also unclear whether the 10 per cent increase will in fact be applied until ss.44–46, Legal Aid Sentencing and Punishment of Offenders Act 2012 are brought into force in relation to proceedings for defamation, malicious falsehood, breach of confidence involving publication to the general public, misuse of private information, and harassment where the defendant is a news publisher. The introduction of those sections, which prospectively deprive successful claimants whose claim has been funded by a CFA of the right to recover success fees and ATE insurance premiums from defendants, has been delayed in respect of those categories of proceedings by the Legal Aid, Sentencing and Punishment of Offenders Act 2012 (Commencement No.5 and Saving Provision) Order 2013, SI 2013/77, para.4.

facts and matters which would entitle a jury to make an award of exemplary damages.[97] The jury may in some cases have to take into account any vindication the claimant may have obtained by a "merits" judgment already given in the case, e.g. striking out the defence of justification.[98] The jury must exclude from their consideration the question of costs, which is a matter entirely for the judge.[99]

Defamation Act 1996, section 1: responsibility for publica- **34.25**
tion. Whether a person is "the author, editor or publisher" of the statement complained of, within the meaning of s.1(1)(a), must be primarily a question of law for the judge, although his ruling may depend upon facts,[100] which, if in dispute, will be for the jury to find. Questions of reasonable care and knowledge[101] must be questions of fact for the jury.

Defamation Act 1996, sections 2 to 4: offer to make amends. There **34.26**
may be matters for both the judge and jury to determine if an offer of amends is not accepted and is relied upon by the defendant as a defence or in mitigation of damages.[102] It is suggested that whether an offer constitutes an offer to make amends under s.2 is for the judge to decide. If the claimant seeks to defeat the defence of offer of amends by proving that the defendant knew or had reason to believe that the statement complained of referred or was likely to be understood as referring to the claimant, and was false and defamatory of him,[103] issues of fact are raised which are clearly the function of the jury to determine, subject to the judge's ruling on the sufficiency of the evidence.

---

[97] See Section 3 of Ch.9, above.
[98] See *Purnell v Business Magazine Ltd* [2007] EWCA Civ 744, [2008] 1 W.L.R. 1 at [24], [29], more fully discussed in para.9.2, above.
[99] See direction given by Bramwell B. in *Kelly v Sherlock* (1866) L.R. 1 Q.B. 686 at 690, 691.
[100] E.g. what is the person's responsibility in relation to the decision to publish the statement: see s.1(2).
[101] See s.1(1)(b), (c), (5).
[102] See s.4(2) and (5).
[103] S.4(3). See *Milne v Express Newspapers* [2004] EWCA Civ 664; [2005] 1 W.L.R. 772.

THE TRIAL: THE FINAL STAGES[1]

SECTION 1. SPEECHES

Generally. The order of speeches is within the discretion of the judge.[2] As **35.1** a general rule the claimant will have the last word, unless the defendant elects not to adduce evidence.[3] If a submission is made in the course of the final speech of the party who has the last word, which is a new submission that could not have been anticipated, the other party can apply to the judge for a right to reply.[4] An advocate making his final speech should take care not to

---

[1] Substantial parts of this chapter, and in particular sections 2 and 3, will become wholly or largely redundant once Defamation Act 2013, s.11 is brought into force. By s.11, the right to jury trial in defamation actions has been prospectively abolished. The result will be that actions for libel and slander, like most other civil claims proceeding in the Queen's Bench Division or the County Court, will be tried by judge alone, unless exceptionally the court orders otherwise. In reality, jury trial for defamation will be a thing of the past.

[2] The discretion comes within the ambit of the judge's case management powers.

[3] The RSC effectively provided that where the defendant elected not to adduce evidence but put in a document in the course of cross-examination, the defendant still had the last word (Ord.35, r.7(3)). The CPR do not contain any express rules about order of speeches, but the practice has not changed. In *John Fairfax Publications v Rivkin* 2003 HCA 50; (2003) 20 A.L.R. 77 a complaint was made that the trial had been unfair as the judge had not allowed plaintiff's counsel to reply to the defendant's final speech, where the defendant had called no evidence. The complaint was rejected. McHugh J. stated, "It is a fundamental rule of common law jury trial of a civil cause that, if counsel for the defendant does not call evidence, he or she has the last address" (at [71]). But that must be subject to the court's overriding discretion.

[4] *Mitchell v Book Sales*, unreported, March 24, 1994, CA. Counsel for the defendant had suggested in his final speech that the racist terms which the plaintiff claimed he had been accused of using were inoffensive and commonplace at the time (in the 1960s) when he was said to have used them. The complaint by the plaintiff on appeal, that defendant's counsel had in effect been giving evidence, was rejected, and it was stated that counsel for the plaintiff could have asked to be allowed to reply to a submission he had not anticipated. "The order of speeches is not sacrosanct since (the Order) which gives the defendant the last word where he calls no evidence is subject to the overriding power of the judge ... to give directions as to the order of speeches."

mislead the jury,[5] should not give evidence,[6] or draw attention to wholly irrelevant matters or evidence,[7] and should not make unfounded suggestions likely to have "a very serious effect in inflaming the damages".[8] Where an advocate's final address includes unjustifiable criticism of the other party's decision not to call a witness, which could result in incurable unfairness to that other party, the judge may discharge the jury.[9] An advocate for either party may now indicate to the jury the level of award of damages which he contends would be appropriate, and defence counsel will sometimes refer to conventional personal injury awards.[10] It would seem an advocate can also refer to awards in other defamation cases which have been approved or made by the Court of Appeal,[11] though it has been said that counsel should not refer to comparables and that the only detailed guidance on figures should come from the judge.[12]

---

[5] See *Praed v Graham* (1889) 24 Q.B.D. 53 at 55.

[6] Although "forensic elaboration and hyperbole" is permissible: *Mitchell v Book Sales*, above. See also *Habib v Nationwide News Pty Ltd* [2007] NSWCA 91, in which one of the grounds of appeal was that counsel for the defendant made "misleading impermissible and unjustifiable" submissions to the jury. The article complained of reported that the plaintiff had participated in a well-known road race when he was claiming to be clinically depressed, and one of the defamatory meanings alleged was that the plaintiff was falsely claiming a disability pension when he was not in fact disabled. The jury found that this meaning was not conveyed by the article. Defence counsel submitted in his final speech that the plaintiff could be clinically depressed "to quite a serious degree" and still be able to run in the race, "otherwise you would have to say that anybody who is a good runner could not be clinically depressed [and] that is complete nonsense". The majority of the New South Wales Court of Appeal considered that the submissions of counsel would have been understood by the jury to be submissions as to the views that would be held by the ordinary reasonable reader, and thus not objectionable, and (per Basten J.A.) that whilst counsel for the defendant did use colourful language, it was unlikely that the jury "was necessarily impressed or distracted by advocacy". However, Handley A.J.A., dissenting, took the view that what was asserted by counsel was medical fact, was not based on evidence and could not have been within the general knowledge of the ordinary reasonable reader.

[7] In *Nationwide News v Heggie* [2001] N.S.W.C.A. 257, where the jury had been empanelled to decide the meaning of the words complained of, counsel addressed the jury on the truth of the imputations alleged and the intentions of the publisher. The judge discharged the jury, a decision upheld on appeal. In *Buck v Jones* [2002] N.S.W.C.A. it was ruled impermissible for counsel to refer to what had been said incidentally by a witness about meaning in the course of her evidence, which concerned identifying the plaintiff as the subject of the words complained of.

[8] Per Collins M.R. in *Chattell v Daily Mail* (1901) 18 T.L.R. 165 at 167. Counsel (Mr Marshall-Hall K.C.) had suggested that the defendants had asked for three weeks to deliver a defence so that they could "ransack all England" to find, if they could, something against the claimant which might prevent her going into the witness box.

[9] *Gladding v Channel 4 Television* [1999] E.M.L.R. 475. The plaintiff's counsel, having notified the defendant that objection was taken to the entire statement of one of the defendant's witnesses who was not then called, pilloried that witness in his final speech accusing him of cowardice in not giving evidence. The Court of Appeal upheld the judge's decision that he could not satisfactorily remedy the situation by direction or in the course of summing-up and the jury should be discharged.

[10] *John v MGN* [1997] Q.B. 586 at 615–616; *Cairns v Modi* [2012] EWCA Civ 1382; [2013] 1 W.L.R. 1015 at [25]

[11] *Rantzen v Mirror Group* [1994] Q.B. 670; *John v MGN*, above; *Cairns v Modi*, above. The judge must control "the risk of over citation" (*Rantzen v Mirror Group*, at 694) and, it is submitted, citation of inappropriate and wholly different cases.

[12] Per Simon Brown L.J. in *Kiam v MGN* [2002] EWCA Civ 43; [2003] Q.B. 281 at [55]–[56].

SECTION 2. SUMMING-UP

Summing-up. After speeches the judge will sum the case up to the jury.   **35.2**
This will include an explanation of the respective functions of judge and jury.
The judge will direct the jury as to the relevant law, identify and explain the
issues of fact which are for the jury's decision, will explain which party bears
the burden of proof on each issue, and the standard of proof, and will
summarise the evidence which goes to each of those issues.[13] The judge may
express his opinion on the facts provided he leaves the decision to the jury:

> " . . . the judge is entitled to make such comments on fact as he thinks right, either
> during the trial, or in the summing-up, provided he makes clear to the jury that they
> are judges of fact, and not the judge, and that his observations are only submitted for
> their consideration and guidance and may be disregarded if the jury do not agree
> with them."[14]

Guidance on damages. The judge will tell the jury the factors which are   **35.3**
relevant to assessment of damages, such as the gravity of the libel, the extent
of its publication, and the absence of an apology.[15] He can now give further
guidance by:

(1) referring to awards in other defamation cases which have either been
    approved or made by the Court of Appeal;

(2) drawing the jury's attention to the current conventional scale of com-
    pensatory damages being awarded for pain and suffering in actions for
    personal injuries[16];

---

[13] " . . . the jury shall be authoritatively told what the issues are on which the case depends, and
the principles of law which cause those issues to be the lines of determination and, where at
all events the evidence is voluminous or complicated, that it shall be arranged to the jury
according to the aspects on which its several relevancies touch the issues":
per Madden C.J., in *Holford v The Melbourne Tramway* [1909] V.L.R. 497 at 507.

[14] Per Scrutton L.J. in *Hobbs v Tinling* [1929] 2 K.B. 1 at 33. But cf. *Mears v R.* [1993] 1
W.L.R. 818 PC, in which it was held (in a criminal appeal) that the proper test in relation to
comments made by a judge in his directions to the jury was not whether he had usurped the jury's
function but whether he had commented in such a way as to make the summing-up fundamentally
unbalanced, and, if he had, repetition of the direction that it was a matter for the jury would not
remedy the unfairness. So also in *R. v Wood* [1996] 1 Cr.App. R. 207, C.A., where passages in
the summing up were said to be "the stuff of advocacy".

[15] This subject is explored in Ch.9, above.

[16] This practice attracted some criticism by the Privy Council when considering an appeal on
libel damages from the Court of Appeal of Jamaica: *The Gleaner Co. v Abrahams* [2003] UKPC
55; [2004] 1 A.C. 628. Eady J. in *Mosley v News Group Newspapers Ltd* [2008] EWHC 1777
(QB) pointed out the "obvious incongruities" when trying to make comparisons between libel
and personal injury awards. Similarly, Lord Neuberger, giving the leading judgment of the Hong
Kong Final Court of Appeal in *Blakeney-Williams v Cathay Pacific Airways Ltd* [2012] HKFCA
61, [2013] E.M.L.R. 6 at [101], agreed with Lord Hoffmann's observations in *The Gleaner* about
the significant policy and practical differences between awards of general damages for defamation
and for personal injury, considerations which
"emphasise the very limited extent to which the level of personal injury awards can assist a
court when it is assessing general damages for defamation. I doubt that personal injury
damages would be of any legitimate assistance beyond providing a sort of cross-check in a case
where a judge is minded to award a relatively large amount by way of general damages for

(3) suggesting to the jury what in figures might be an appropriate award, or what are the upper and lower figures of an appropriate bracket[17]; and

(4) if appropriate, telling the jury the current effective ceiling for general damages in defamation.[18]

Where a judgment has already been given in a case which might be regarded as having provided a measure of vindication to the claimant (e.g. striking out a defence of justification) the jury should be directed that they can take this into account, but it is open to them to conclude that the judgment had no, or only, marginal, effect on vindication.[19]

The jury should be asked to ensure that any award they make is proportionate to the damage that the claimant has suffered.[20]

35.4 Deficiencies in the summing-up. If there have been errors or omissions in the course of the summing-up, they should be drawn to the attention of the judge before the jury retires. Failure to do so may weigh against an appellant in a complaint to the Court of Appeal that there has been a misdirection occasioning a substantial wrong or miscarriage of justice.[21]

SECTION 3. VERDICT

35.5 Questions for the jury. The jury can be asked to answer a series of questions relating to the factual issues which arise in the case, or, in other

---

defamation (and even then I am far from saying that a judge should, as opposed to may, find such an exercise helpful)".

That was very much the basis on which reference to conventional personal injury awards was suggested in *John v MGN* (above)—as a check on the reasonableness of the figure being considered.

[17] *John v MGN* [1997] Q.B. 586. In *Kiam v MGN*, above, it was suggested that before the judge recommends a bracket to the jury it should be formally discussed with counsel, "each side being given a proper opportunity to argue the matter after having exchanged authorities and skeleton submissions": per Simon Brown L.J. at [56]. Earlier (in *Sutcliffe v Pressdram* [1991] 1 Q.B. 153 at 178–179) it had been suggested that improved guidance to juries on damages could be provided by the judge inviting them to consider the investment income resulting from an award placed in a building society deposit account, or what could be bought with the sum awarded. These proposals were supplanted by the practice sanctioned in *John v MGN*.

[18] Currently of the order of £275,000: see *Cairns v Modi* [2012] EWCA Civ 1382; [2013] 1 W.L.R. 1015 at [25].

[19] *Purnell v Business Magazine Ltd* [2007] EWCA Civ 744; [2008] 1 W.L.R. 1. In *Cruddas v Adams* [2013] EWHC 145 (QB), Eady J. suggested at [43] that vindication in a reasoned judgment will count for little in the eyes of most people, who will simply want to know "How much did he get?" (following *Cairns v Modi* [2012] EWCA Civ 1382; [2013] 1 W.L.R. 1015 at [31], which is to the same effect).

[20] *Rantzen v Mirror Group*, above, at 696; *Cairns v Modi*, above, at [34] and [41]. In *Sutcliffe v Pressdram Ltd* [1991] 1 Q.B. 153 CA at 179, it was suggested that the judge should ask them to consider, once they had a particular sum in mind, how much it might earn if invested, or what they could buy with it in terms of a home, a car, or a holiday. In more recent times that kind of guidance is thought to have been rare.

[21] See *Kiam v Neil (No.2)* [1996] E.M.L.R. 493 at 500; it was pointed out that there was a time when absence of any complaint to the judge about a deficiency in the summing-up would disqualify a party from seeking a new trial on appeal, as stated by Lord Halsbury in *Nevill v Fine Art* [1897] A.C. 68 at 76. See further para.36.4, fn.41, below.

words, to give a special verdict. This is particularly appropriate where the jury's tasks include resolving disputes of fact upon which the judge's ruling on law may be dependent, as with qualified privilege.[22] Where malice is an issue in relation to liability it is common practice to leave that as a separate question to be answered by the jury. In more simple cases, where meaning or justification are the areas of dispute, the most convenient procedure is often to invite the jury to find a general verdict by submitting just two questions for them to answer, namely: "1. Do you find for the claimant or for the defendant? 2. If for the claimant, what sum do you award by way of damages?" If there is a claim for exemplary damages that the judge rules can be left to the jury, it is the practice for the jury to be asked specific questions relating to that claim.[23] It has not been the practice for the jury to be required to state what sum, if any, they have awarded by way of aggravated damages, though this is now encouraged in actions for malicious prosecution and false imprisonment.[24]

Several libels or slanders alleged. In an action in respect of two or more   **35.6**
libels or slanders alleged in separate paragraphs of the claim form and particulars of claim, or where both a natural and ordinary meaning and an innuendo meaning are put forward, it is within the discretion of the judge whether the jury are asked to give one award of damages or several awards in respect of each cause of action.[25] In exercising his discretion, the judge will take account of how the parties have formulated their statements of case and the manner in which they have conducted the action or the defence, which may have made it essential that there should be more than one verdict in order that justice between the parties may be done.[26]

---

[22] In *Loutchansky v Times Newspapers (No.4)* [2001] E.M.L.R. 38, Gray J. left 15 questions of primary fact, relating to the plea of privilege, to be answered by the jury. (The Court of Appeal [2001] EWCA Civ 1805; [2002] Q.B. 783 later allowed the defendants' appeal on *Reynolds* privilege, which was remitted to the judge for a fresh determination). Such "exam papers" have the disadvantage that they may complicate matters for the jury, and may give rise to inconsistencies (e.g. one defendant malicious, the other not, on precisely the same evidence). However, in some cases they are unavoidable, and there is an advantage of individual questions on the principal issues of fact in that a retrial may be avoided if, on appeal, the judge's ruling on legal issues is reversed.

[23] See e.g. *Manson v Associated Newspapers* [1965] 1 W.L.R. 1038 at 1046.

[24] *Comr of Police v Thompson* [1998] Q.B. 498. The Court of Appeal set out the directions that should be given to a jury in malicious prosecution and false imprisonment cases, but there are practical reasons why the observations about the desirability of a separate award for aggravated damages should not apply to defamation cases. See para.9.21, above. However, judges sitting without a jury will often make clear the value of that part of the award which represents aggravated damages: see e.g. *ZAM v CFW* [2013] EWHC 662 (QB) at [122] and *Cruddas v Calvert* [2013] EWHC 2298 (QB) at [305] (both decisions of Tugendhat J.).

[25] *Barber v Pigden* [1937] 1 K.B. 664; distinguishing *Weber v Birkett* [1925] 2 K.B. 152, in which it was stated that a verdict awarding a lump sum without apportionment between several causes of action was not a valid verdict; *Hayward v Thompson* [1982] 1 Q.B. 47.

[26] Per Scott L.J. in *Barber v Pigden*, above, at 683. If there has been a payment into court in respect of one cause of action, or separate payments in respect of each cause of action, there would be compelling reasons for separate awards of damages, but there are formidable problems arising under CPR r.36.13(2), which prohibits communication of the fact of payment-in to the trial

35.7 Consolidated actions. In the vanishingly rare case when actions have been consolidated under s.5 of the Law of Libel Amendment Act 1888,[27] rather than under the court's general powers of case management,[28] the jury should assess the whole amount of the damages (if any) in one sum, but a separate verdict must be taken for or against each defendant in the same way as if the actions consolidated had been tried separately; and if the jury find a verdict against the defendant or defendants in more than one of the actions so consolidated, they must proceed to apportion the amount of the damages between or against the last mentioned defendants. The application of this section was explained by Lord Esher M.R.[29]:

> "The meaning seems to be that, if there are several actions consolidated, the jury need not necessarily find against the defendants in some of them; and they must find against those defendants in one sum and then apportion the one sum which they have found among them. If they think that the defendants in one of the actions are the principal libellers [and the other defendants merely copiers] or that there are headings or expressions used by some of the defendants in their newspaper that make the libel stronger in their case, they may apportion the sum so that such defendants may have to bear a larger proportion than the others."

Where actions have been consolidated under the court's general powers of case management,[30] no question of apportionment arises, and the jury should be directed to award a separate sum of damages in respect of each libel against each defendant.

35.8 Verdicts. The jury should give their verdict by their foreman in open court in the presence of the other jurymen.[31] If this is done, and none of the jury protest, there is a presumption that they all assented to it.[32] The judge may allow an alteration to the verdict even after the jury have been formally discharged provided the interests of justice made it appropriate for him to do so.[33] If the verdict is for the claimant, there must be an award of damages,

---

judge until the case has been decided. Curiously, perhaps, there is no exception made for a trial judge sitting with a jury. A solution might be to obtain a direction for separate awards at a pre-trial review.

[27] S.13 of the Defamation Act 1952 extended the application of s.5 of the 1888 Act to actions for slander, slander of title, and slander of goods or other malicious falsehood.

[28] CPR r.3.1(2)(g).

[29] *Stone v Press Association* [1897] 2 Q.B. 159 at 162.

[30] CPR r.3.1(2)(g).

[31] *Ellis v Deheer* [1922] 2 K.B. 113. Owing to shortage of space in court only the foreman and two or three of the jury were able to get into the body of the court, the rest of the jury remaining in the passage. Some of those outside were unable to hear the announcement of the verdict and complained that the verdict announced was not one with which they had agreed. A new trial was granted.

[32] Per Atkin L.J. in *Ellis v Deheer*, at 120. The presumption is rebuttable.

[33] *Igwemma v Chief Constable of Manchester* [2001] EWCA Civ 953; [2001] 4 All E.R. 751 (claim for malicious prosecution).

however small. A verdict for the claimant with no award of damages has been ruled as void in law.[34]

Where two claimants sue on a libel by which they have been separately defamed, the jury should make a separate award of damages in respect of each claimant.[35] As against defendants in the same action sued in respect of a joint libel the jury must give one verdict and one award for the total damages.[36] They have no power or authority to apportion the damages between co-defendants.[37] That is true also of an award that includes an element of aggravated damages or exemplary damages (although in that event the sum awarded by way of exemplary[38] or aggravated[39] damages must reflect the lowest common denominator of culpability of any of the defendants).

Majority verdicts. The jury are asked initially to return a unanimous verdict, for the court cannot accept a majority verdict unless the jury have had a reasonable time for deliberation.[40] What is reasonable will depend upon the nature and complexity of the case.[41] Once such time has elapsed, a majority verdict is acceptable, although in practice the judge will always want to hear from counsel before deciding to give a majority direction. A majority verdict means: (1) where there are not less than 11 jurors, 10 are agreed; or (2) where there are 10 jurors, nine of them are agreed.[42] With the consent of the parties the verdict can be by a lesser majority.[43] The judge has a discretion to continue the trial where a juror has to be discharged (e.g. by reason of ill health).[44] **35.9**

---

[34] *Clement v Lewis* 129 E.R.1299; (1822) 3 Brod. & Bing. 297. If the jury return a verdict for the claimant but fail to assess damages, it is open to the trial judge to send them back to make an assessment: *Wisdom v Brown* (1885) 1 T.L.R. 412. However, in *Broxton v McLelland* [1997] E.M.L.R. 157, the jury answered the question as to how much they awarded the plaintiff by way of damages, "zero", and judgment was entered for the defendant. Counsel did not argue on appeal that there was any distinction to be drawn between an award of no damages and a nominal award.

[35] See *Booth v Briscoe* (1877) 2 Q.B.D. 496, but not where the claimants have been jointly defamed, e.g. as partners.

[36] *Heydon's Case* (1613) 11 Co.Rep. 56; *Dawson v McClelland* [1899] 2 Ir.R. 486; *Greenlands v Wilmshurst* [1913] 3 K.B. 507, CA; *Broome v Cassell* [1972] A.C. 1027 at 1089 (Lord Reid), and 1105 (Viscount Dilhorne); *Veliu v Mazrekaj* [2006] EWHC 1710 (QB); [2007] 1 W.L.R. 495.

[37] *Greenlands v Wilmhurst*, above.

[38] Per Lord Hailsham L.C. in *Broome v Cassell & Co. Ltd* [1972] A.C. 1027 at 1063.

[39] *Veliu v Mazrekaj* [2006] EWHC 1710 (QB); [2007] 1 W.L.R. 495 at [11]; *Berezovsky v Russian Television and Radio Broadcasting Co.* [2010] EWHC 476 (QB) at [175].

[40] S.17(4) of the Juries Act 1974. In the Crown Court, there is a statutory minimum time of two hours, with ten minutes added for the time that the jury take to get to and from their retirement room.

[41] S.17(4) of the Juries Act 1974.

[42] S.17(1) of the Juries Act 1974. In a county court, where there is a jury of eight, a verdict agreed by seven is acceptable: s.17(2).

[43] S.17(5) of the Juries Act 1974. Where it appears from the length of their deliberations, or from what the foreman says when the jury come back into court, that the jury may not be able to reach a verdict on which at least ten of them agree, the parties will always consider whether it might be preferable to accept (say) a majority verdict by consent, rather than endure the expense and strain of a second trial.

[44] As happened in *Hamilton v Al Fayed*, unreported, December 20, 1999.

SECTION 4. JUDGMENT

35.10 Generally. Where there is a general verdict the successful party will ask for judgment in accordance with the jury's verdict.[45] A special verdict may be decisive in favour of one party or another and enable that party to seek judgment. It may only resolve issues of fact, the legal implications of which then have to be argued and adjudicated upon.[46] It is for the judge to decide in the light of the verdict whether an injunction should be granted.[47] The judgment will include an appropriate order for the payment of costs.[48] If the unsuccessful party wishes to apply for a stay of execution in respect of the whole or part of the judgment pending appeal, he should first apply to the judge.[49] Any application for leave to appeal should be made to the judge in the first instance.[50]

SECTION 5. COSTS

35.11 Introduction. Lord Justice Jackson's Review of Civil Litigation Costs, published in December 2009, recommended that success fees and After The Event (ATE) insurance premiums should no longer be recoverable from the losing party, so that lawyers' success fees (if agreed) would have to be paid by their successful clients on the basis of a percentage of their base costs, capped at an agreed percentage of damages. By way of a quid pro quo for claimants, the Review proposed that general damages for defamation and misuse of private information (among others) should rise by 10 per cent. The claimant would also be able to enhance his recovery substantially by means of a realistic claimant's offer to settle which, if not accepted (but ultimately proving sufficient) would result in an order (unless unjust) for indemnity costs and additional damages. Moreover, there would be a regime of what is called "qualified one way costs shifting" (QOCS), by which the costs ordered against a claimant should not exceed a reasonable amount, having regard to the financial resources of all the parties and their conduct in connection with the dispute.

35.12 LASPO 2012. The Legal Aid, Sentencing and Punishment of Offenders Act 2012 (LASPO) contains provisions designed to bring into effect a number of

---

[45] Thus if the jury find for the claimant and award him £X damages, the claimant will ask for judgment in that sum. If the jury find for the defendant, the defendant will ask for an order that the action be dismissed.

[46] E.g. whether in the circumstances the occasion is privileged; as in *Loutchansky v Times Newspapers (No.4)* [2001] E.M.L.R. 38 (above).

[47] See para.9.41, above.

[48] See s.5, below.

[49] CPR r.52.7.

[50] CPR r.52.3(2).

reforms following Jackson L.J.'s recommendations. Section 44 contains provisions designed to prevent the claimant from recovering a success fee or his ATE premium from the defendant. S.44(4) amends s.58A(6), Courts and Legal Services Act 1990, preventing any order for costs that requires the payment by one party of all or part of a success fee payable by another party under a conditional fee agreement (CFA). In other words, the winner's success fee will not be payable by the loser. However, that provision is not retrospective. By s.44(6), s.44(4) will generally not prevent such a costs order if the success fee is payable under a CFA entered into before date when s.44(4) comes into force.[51] Similarly, s.46(1) inserts a new s.58C in the Courts and Legal Services Act 1990, by which a costs order in favour of a party to proceedings who has taken out a costs insurance policy may not include provision requiring the payment of an amount in respect of all or part of the premium of the policy. In other words, the winner's ATE premium will not be recoverable from the losing party.

It was originally envisaged that the provisions of ss.44 and 46 would come into effect for all purposes on April 1, 2013. So it was that the Court of Appeal stated in its amended decision in *Simmons v Castle*,[52] giving effect to Jackson L.J.'s proposed damages uplift, that

> " . . . with effect from 1 April 2013, the proper level of general damages in all civil claims for (i) pain and suffering, (ii) loss of amenity, (iii) physical inconvenience and discomfort, (iv) social discredit, or (v) mental distress, will be 10% higher than previously, unless the claimant falls within section 44(6) of the 2012 Act. It therefore follows that, if the action now under appeal had been the subject of a judgment after 1 April 2013, then (unless the claimant had entered into a CFA before that date) the proper award of general damages would be 10% higher than that agreed in this case, namely £22,000 rather than £20,000."[53]

Delay in bringing LASPO, ss.44, 46 into force in publication and privacy cases. However, widespread concerns about the effect of ss.44 and 46 LASPO,[54] and in particular about the importance of ensuring that ordinary   **35.13**

---

[51] The CFA must have been entered into specifically for the purposes of the provision to the litigant of advocacy or litigation services in connection with the matter that is the subject of the proceedings in which the costs order is made, or advocacy or litigation services must have been provided to the litigant under the agreement in connection with that matter before the commencement day (i.e. the date when s.44(4) comes into force).

[52] *Simmons v Castle (No.1)* [2012] EWCA Civ 1039; [2013] 1 W.L.R. 1239; *Simmons v Castle (No.2)* [2012] EWCA Civ 1288; [2013] 1 W.L.R. 1239 at [50].

[53] In the earlier of the two *Simmons v Castle* decisions (above), which it later amended, the CA had applied the uplift to general damages for "(i) pain, suffering and loss of amenity in respect of personal injury, (ii) nuisance, (iii) defamation, and (iv) all other torts which cause suffering, inconvenience or distress to individuals". The change of wording was due to the court deciding in the second case to extend the uplift beyond torts to other causes of action, such as breach of contract, but it does not appear that the removal of the reference to defamation was the subject of argument. It appears that the expression "social discredit" was intended to include defamation.

[54] Explained in the Final Report of the Civil Justice Council Defamation Costs Working Group 2013, at paras 1.8–1.17.

people had access to justice in cases involving the press, have had the result that in certain areas of this field of law their commencement has been delayed. By statutory instrument made on January 18, 2013,[55] ss.44 and 46 were brought into effect from April 1, 2013 except as regards "publication and privacy proceedings", which means proceedings for (a) defamation, (b) malicious falsehood, (c) breach of confidence involving publication to the general public, (d) misuse of private information, and (e) harassment, where the defendant is a news publisher.

According to the Final Report of the Civil Justice Council Defamation Costs Working Group 2013,[56] it is anticipated that the LASPO-based changes will come into effect later in 2013, to coincide with the commencement of complementary measures in the Defamation Act. For the time being, therefore, the winning party's success fee and ATE premium continue to be recoverable from the losing party.[57]

35.14 Conditional Fee Agreements (CFAs). Owing to the decision to delay bringing LASPO, ss.44 and 46 into force in publication and privacy cases, the CFA funding regime as constituted before April 1, 2013 continues to thrive in the defamation sphere.[58] It is unclear what the effect on CFAs of the new legislation will be once the sections have been brought into force, but it seems likely that the popularity of the CFA as a means of litigation funding will be reduced. The Review of Civil Litigation Costs envisaged that the proposed 10 per cent increase in damages would enable any success fee payable to the claimant's lawyers to be paid out of the damages award, but no success fee large enough to attract lawyers to act on a CFA basis could be payable out of that element of a defamation damages award. Given that the claimant will also in future be unable to recover his ATE premium from the defendant, it is not surprising that the future commercial viability of the CFA model has been doubted.

---

[55] The Legal Aid, Sentencing and Punishment of Offenders Act 2012 (Commencement No.5 and Saving Provision) Order 2013, SI 2013/77.

[56] Para.1.17. The Report was published on April 18, 2013.

[57] By the new CPR r.48.2, the existing provisions of CPR Pts 43–48 will continue to apply in relation to a pre-commencement funding arrangement, i.e. one which relates to publication and privacy proceedings (which includes defamation) where the agreement was entered into before the relevant date, i.e. the date on which ss.44 and 46 of LASPO come into force for such proceedings, and where one of two conditions is satisfied, namely, either (a) where it was entered into specifically for the purposes of the provision of advocacy or litigation services to the person to whom the success fee is payable in relation to the matter that is the subject of the proceedings in which the costs order is to be made, or (b) where the advocacy or litigation services were provided to that person under the agreement in connection with that matter before the relevant date (r.48.2(2)). "Funding arrangement" is as defined at CPR r.43.2(1)(k)(i) and (ii).

[58] CFAs are the subject of statutory provisions in Pt II of Courts and Legal Services Act 1990, as amended by the Access to Justice Act 1999, and now the Conditional Fee Agreements Order 2013, SI 2013/689. They have produced a considerable amount of case law. Practitioners should refer to sections 7A and 7B of Vol.2 of *Civil Procedure*, which includes extracts from the relevant statutes, summarises relevant decisions, and provides extensive and detailed information about CFAs.

The legitimacy of CFAs in defamation and privacy cases was reviewed by the   **35.15**
House of Lords in *Campbell v MGN Ltd*,[59] in which it was submitted by the
defendant newspaper that it should not be liable to pay any part of the
claimant's success fees on the grounds that such a liability was so disproportionate as to infringe its rights to freedom of expression under art.10 of the
European Convention of Human Rights. This argument was rejected by the
House of Lords, as the underlying purpose of CFAs was not only to provide
a means of funding the particular action, but also by requiring unsuccessful
defendants to pay a success fee, a method of funding other litigation which
other litigants might be unable to afford. That was a proportionate measure
which it was open to the legislature to choose to fund access to justice.
Further, there was no obligation on a solicitor, before entering into a CFA, to
satisfy himself that the client could not fund the litigation himself. However
the "chill factor" and "blackmailing effect" arising from impecunious claimants using CFAs to bring defamation proceedings against the media was
recognised. In the event, the case went to the Strasbourg court, which held
unanimously[60] that the requirement for MGN Ltd to pay Campbell's success
fees (calculated at twice the base costs) of two appeals to the House of Lords
was a disproportionate interference with its art.10 rights.[61] The proposed
changes to the CFA regime to be brought in by ss.44 and 46 of LASPO 2012
are designed to meet the criticisms of the ECtHR.

Defamation Proceedings Costs Management Scheme. This scheme   **35.16**
ran (initially as a pilot) from October 1, 2009 to March 31, 2013 at the Royal
Courts of Justice in London and in the Manchester District Registry, and
applied to all proceedings in libel, slander or malicious falsehood started in
either centre between October 1, 2009 and April 1, 2013. It continues to apply
to proceedings issued before 1 April 2013.[62]

The provisions of the Costs Management Scheme are set out in CPR PD51D.[63]   **35.17**
Its object is to manage litigation so that the costs of each party are proportionate to the value of the claim and the reputational issues at stake and so that

---

[59] [2005] UKHL 61; [2005] 1 W.L.R. 3394.

[60] [2011] E.M.L.R. 20.

[61] In *Turcu v News Group Newspapers* [2005] EWHC 799 (QB) at [6]–[7], Eady J. anticipated
the Strasbourg court's concerns when he described the defendant's position when faced with a
claimant with the benefit of a CFA as "wholly unenviable", and remarked, ". . . there must be a
significant temptation for media defendants to pay up something, to be rid of the litigation for
purely commercial reasons, without regard to the true merits of the litigation."

[62] By para.22(12), Transitional Provisions under the Civil Procedure (Amendment) Rules 2013,
SI 2013/262,

   "(12) Any defamation proceedings commenced before 1 April 2013 within the scope of the
   Defamation Proceedings Costs Management Scheme provided for by Practice Direction 51D
   supporting Part 51 will proceed and be completed in accordance with that scheme."

[63] Now revoked.

the parties are on an equal footing.[64] It provides for the court to manage the costs of the litigation as well as the case itself, and for each party to produce a costs budget in a standard form in advance of any case management or costs management conference. At any case or costs management conference or pre-trial review, the court will have before it the detailed costs budgets of both parties to the litigation, and is obliged to take into account the costs involved in each proposed procedural step: armed with that information, it will record approval or disapproval of each side's budget,[65] and when doing so will consider whether the budgeted totals for each stage of the work are within the broad range of reasonable and proportionate costs. Solicitors are expected to liaise monthly to check that their respective budgets are not being exceeded and, if they are, either party may apply to bring the case back to court for a case management conference.[66] By para.5.6, the court is bound, when assessing costs on the standard basis, to have regard to the receiving party's last approved budget, and will not depart from that approved budget unless satisfied that there is good reason to do so.

> "The starting point must be that the approved budget is intended to provide the financial limits within which the proceedings are to be conducted, and the court will not allow costs in excess of the budget unless something unusual has occurred. Whether there is good reason to depart from the approved budget in any given case, therefore, is likely to depend on, among other things, how the proceedings have been managed, whether they have developed in a way that was not foreseen when the relevant case management orders were made, whether the costs incurred are proportionate to what is in issue and whether the parties have been on an equal footing."[67]

35.18 The new CPR provisions for costs management. Defamation proceedings starting on or after April 1, 2013 are now governed by a new procedure governing all claims allocated to the multi-track.[68] This is not the place to do more than offer a brief overview of the CPR provisions, for which the reader is referred to *Civil Procedure*.[69]

35.19 New overriding objective. The key to the new provisions lies in the amendment to the overriding objective of the CPR. That objective is now to

---

[64] CPR PD 51D, para.1.3. The need to ensure that the parties are on an equal footing is concerned with the unfair exploitation of superior resources rather than with the provision of information about how expenditure was progressing: *Henry v News Group Newspapers Ltd* [2013] EWCA Civ 19, [2013] 2 All E.R. 840 at [20].

[65] CPR PD 51D, para.5.3.

[66] CPR PD 51D, para.5.5.

[67] *Henry v News Group Newspapers Ltd*, above, per Moore-Bick L.J. at [18]. Compliance with all the requirements of the Practice Direction is not a prerequisite of asking the court to depart from the approved budget: see [21].

[68] Note that there are transitional provisions for proceedings involving CFAs and ATE policies entered into before LASPO, ss.44 and 46 come into force: see the new r.48.2 and fn.57, above. In essence, the pre-existing CPR Pts 43–48 will continue to apply in the case of such funding arrangements, and for those parts and a commentary the reader is referred to *Civil Procedure (The White Book)* (London: Sweet & Maxwell, 2013).

[69] *Civil Procedure (The White Book)* (London: Sweet & Maxwell, 2013).

enable the court to deal with cases justly *and at proportionate cost*.[70] Central to the new regime is CPR r.44.3, the new basis of assessment (whether detailed or summary). On standard basis assessment, the court will only allow costs which are proportionate to the matter in issue. Costs which are disproportionate in amount may be disallowed or reduced even if they were reasonably or necessarily incurred.[71] Costs are proportionate if they bear a reasonable relationship to the sums in issue in the proceedings, the value of any non-monetary relief in issue in the proceedings, the complexity of the litigation, any additional work generated by the conduct of the paying party, and any wider factors involved in the proceedings, "such as reputation or public importance".[72]

Rules for costs management. A central pillar of the new provisions is the rules for costs management, which differ in some important respects from the provisions of the Defamation Proceedings Costs Management Scheme. All parties (except litigants in person) must now file and exchange budgets by the date specified in the directions questionnaire[73] or otherwise seven days before the first case management conference.[74] The default rule is that failure to file a budget will be visited with a draconian penalty, for the party in default will be treated (unless the court otherwise orders) as having filed a budget comprising only the applicable court fees.[75] The court may at any time make a costs management order, by which it will record the extent to which the budgets are agreed between the parties and, in so far as they are not agreed, will record the court's approval after making appropriate revisions. Once such an order has been made, the court will thereafter control the parties' budgets in respect of recoverable costs.[76] The court is to have regard to the available budgets of the parties in making any case management decision, regardless of whether or not it has made a costs management order, and will take into account the costs involved in each procedural step.[77] Moreover, in any case where a costs management order has been made, the court will, when assessing costs on the standard basis, have regard to the receiving party's last approved or agreed budget for each phase of the proceedings, and not depart from that approved or agreed budget unless satisfied that there is good reason to do so.[78]

35.20

That provision at once recalls the very similar wording of para.5.6 of the Defamation Proceedings Costs Management Scheme, which the Court of

35.21

---

[70] CPR r.1.1(1), r.1.1(2).
[71] CPR r.44.3(2).
[72] CPR r.44.3(5).
[73] CPR r.26.3(1).
[74] CPR r.3.13.
[75] CPR r.3.14. Master McCloud made such an order against the claimant in June 2013 in the case of *Mitchell v News Group Newspapers Ltd*. That order is understood to be under appeal.
[76] CPR r.3.15.
[77] CPR r.3.17.
[78] CPR r.3.18.

Appeal considered in *Henry v News Group Newspapers Ltd.*[79] In that case, Moore-Bick L.J. turned to consider the new cost management rules, and gave this guidance:

> "Those rules, which will become effective from 1 April 2013, differ in some important respects from the practice direction with which this appeal is concerned. In particular, they impose greater responsibility on the court for the management of the costs of proceedings and greater responsibility on the parties for keeping budgets under review as the proceedings progress. Read as a whole they lay greater emphasis on the importance of the approved or agreed budget as providing a *prima facie* limit on the amount of recoverable costs. In those circumstances, although the court will still have the power to depart from the approved or agreed budget if it is satisfied that there is good reason to do so, and may for that purpose take into consideration all the circumstances of the case, I should expect it to place particular emphasis on the function of the budget as imposing a limit on recoverable costs. The primary function of the budget is to ensure that the costs incurred are not only reasonable but proportionate to what is at stake in the proceedings. If, as is the intention of the rule, budgets are approved by the court and revised at regular intervals, the receiving party is unlikely to persuade the court that costs incurred in excess of the budget are reasonable and proportionate to what is at stake."

35.22 Costs capping orders. Cost-capping orders grew out of the unhappy situation where a defendant was faced with a CFA-funded claimant with no after the event (ATE) insurance policy. In *Musa King v Telegraph Group Ltd*,[80] the defendant asked the Court of Appeal to make an order capping the costs of the action. The court accepted that the case had exposed a situation which was a cause of concern, namely that in defamation actions, particularly where the litigation was extravagantly conducted, CFA funding could result in obvious unfairness to defendants which was bound to have a chilling effect on a newspaper exercising its art.10 rights to freedom of expression. The court therefore indicated how the court's powers might be exercised to deal with the problem. In summary, where defamation proceedings were initiated without ATE cover, the defendant could apply at the allocation stage for a "costs capping order", which would be a direction that the recoverable costs would be limited to a specified amount. A costs judge would determine the sum which was reasonable and proportionate to fix as the recoverable costs of the action. The power of the court to make such orders was derived from s.51 of the Supreme Court Act 1981 and CPR r.3.1(2)(m).[81]

---

[79] [2013] EWCA Civ 19, [2013] 2 All E.R. 840.
[80] [2004] EWCA Civ 613; [2005] 1 W.L.R. 2282.
[81] In *Tierney v News Group Newspapers Ltd* [2006] EWHC 50 (QB); [2006] 4 Costs L.R. 606, a libel action, McCombe J. said that it was almost a presumption that a costs capping order was appropriate where the claimant was impecunious, was funded by CFA and there was no ATE insurance. In the same case, after the Master had assessed and capped prospective costs, Eady J. (on appeal from the Master's order) discussed the applicable principles and considerations when assessing the appropriate costs figures: *Tierney v News Group Newspapers Ltd* [2006] EWHC 3275 (QB). But such an order was refused by Gray J. in *Henry v BBC* [2005] EWHC 2503 (QB); [2006] 1 All E.R. 154 because the application was made but a few days before trial and was therefore too late.

The current regime is set out at CPR rr.3.19–3.20, and in Practice Direction **35.23**
3F, which starts with the warning that the court will make a costs capping
order only in exceptional circumstances.[82] Subject to that stern proviso, the
rule enables the court at any stage of the proceedings to make a costs capping
order against all or any of the parties if it is in the interests of justice to do so,
if there is a substantial risk that without such an order costs would be
disproportionately incurred, and if it is not satisfied that that risk can be
adequately controlled by case management directions or detailed assessment
of costs.[83] In deciding whether to exercise its discretion under the rule, the
court will consider all the circumstances of the case, including whether there
is a substantial imbalance between the financial position of the parties,
whether the costs of determining the amount of the cap are likely to be
proportionate to the overall costs of the litigation, the stage which the proceedings have reached,[84] and the costs incurred to date and to be incurred in the
future.[85] Once made, an order will limit the costs recoverable by the party
subject to the order unless it applies successfully for a variation, which will
not be made unless there has been a material and substantial change of
circumstances since the order was made or there is some other compelling
reason why a variation should be made.[86]

The basic principles. The costs of the proceedings are in the discretion of   **35.24**
the court, which has full power to determine by whom, in what amount and
when costs are to be paid.[87] If the court decides to make an order about costs
the general rule is that the unsuccessful party will be ordered to pay the costs
of the successful party,[88] but this is subject to a qualification expressed in the
widest possible terms: "the court may make a different order".[89] In deciding
what order to make the court must have regard to all the circumstances,
including the conduct of all the parties, whether a party has succeeded on part
of his case, even if not wholly successful, and any admissible offer to settle

---

[82] CPR 3FPD, para.1.1. For a somewhat critical view of that restrictive wording, see *Peacock
v MGN Ltd* [2009] EWHC 769 (QB); [2009] 4 Costs L.R. 584, where Eady J. was inhibited by
the exceptionality principle from making an order which he would otherwise have been strongly
tempted to make.
[83] CPR r.3.19(5).
[84] An order is unlikely to be made against a claimant close to trial: *Henry v BBC* (above).
[85] CPR r.3.19(6).
[86] CPR r.3.19(7).
[87] CPR r.44.2(1).
[88] CPR r.44.2(2)(a). There may well be an issue as to who has been successful. In *Roache v
News Group Newspapers* [1998] E.M.L.R. 161 CA. Sir Thomas Bingham M.R. suggested the
following test:
  "Who, as a matter of substance and reality has won? Has the plaintiff won anything of value
  which he could not have won without fighting the action through to a finish? Has the defendant
  substantially denied the plaintiff the prize which the plaintiff fought the action to win?"
The case was a libel action in which the plaintiff failed to beat the payment in but sought costs
on the grounds that he obtained an injunction which had not been offered. The plaintiff was
awarded costs by the trial judge but the decision was reversed on appeal.
[89] CPR r.44.2(2)(b).

which is drawn to the court's attention, which is not an offer to which the costs consequences under Pt 36 apply.[90] The conduct to be considered includes the conduct before as well as during the proceedings, and the extent to which the parties have followed the pre-action protocol,[91] whether it was reasonable for a party to raise, pursue or contest a particular allegation or issue, the manner in which a party has pursued or defended its case or a particular allegation or issue and whether a claimant exaggerated its claim.[92]

Where a court order makes no mention of costs, as a general rule no party is entitled to costs.[93]

35.25 Juries' views on costs. Juries are not concerned with costs.[94] The judge is under no obligation to give effect to any views the jury may have expressed about the award of costs.[95]

"The judge must exert his discretion as to costs not only unfettered by, but wholly independently of, any view expressed by the jury on that particular matter."[96]

35.26 Derisory or nominal damages. Where the court awards only a penny or some other nominal sum of damages, the usual practice has been for the judge to make no order as to costs,[97] although this has not been an invariable rule.[98] An exception might be a case where the claimant has throughout only asked for nominal damages, having brought the action solely for the purpose of clearing his name. On the other hand, if liability is admitted, or the trial is one for assessment of damages only, and the jury award only nominal damages, the costs of the trial are likely to be the defendant's regardless of whether there has been an offer to settle.[99]

---

[90] CPR r.44.2(4).

[91] See para.24.6, above.

[92] CPR r.44.2(5). Eady J. when ruling on costs in *McKenna v MGN Ltd*, (July 17, 2007) awarded the defendant (which lost the action) the costs of defending the claim, abandoned by the claimant in the course of litigation, that the defendant had published the article maliciously. Such an allegation, the Judge remarked, was sometimes made for tactical reasons, and if those tactics failed it would be likely that costs consequences would follow.

[93] CPR r.44.10(1).

[94] See para.32.24 and fn.99, above.

[95] *Robert v Jones* [1891] 2 Q.B. 189 at 198, per Hawkins L.J.

[96] *Martin v Benson* [1927] 1 K.B. 771 at 774, per McCardie J.

[97] See *Martin v Benson* [1927] 1 K.B. 771, where many of the earlier cases are summarised; *Dering v Uris* [1964] 2 Q.B. 669, (plaintiff awarded 1/2d damages); *Pamplin v Express Newspapers* [1988] 1 W.L.R. 116 at 122, Neill L.J.; *Reynolds v Times Newspapers*, November 21, 1996 (plaintiff awarded "zero pounds" which the judge decided should be understood as an award of one penny; no order as to costs to date of payment in).

[98] Some examples of cases where the plaintiff was awarded costs are given in *Martin v Benson*, above, and included cases where the defendant was found to have acted maliciously. In *Hiles v Davies*, *The Times*, June 20, 23, 1964, the judge described the verdict of a halfpenny damages as "remarkable" and awarded the plaintiff his costs.

[99] See *Anglo-Cyprian Trade Agencies v Paphos Wine Industries* [1951] 1 All E.R. 873; *Alltrans Express v CVA Holdings* [1984] 1 W.L.R. 394 CA.

Costs for the defendant. There is nothing in CPR Pt 44 indicating that the   **35.27**
court should adopt a different approach where it is the defendant who is
successful. The rationale for a differentiated approach has been expressed in
these terms:

> "Considerations sufficient to justify a refusal of costs to a plaintiff are not neces-
> sarily sufficient in the case of a defendant, for the former initiates the litigation while
> the latter is brought into it against his will."[100]

However, such considerations will not impinge on the importance laid by the
CPR, as regards the exercise of the court's discretion, on the conduct of the
parties and the other factors specified.[101] It may be that the pre-CPR authorities,[102] supporting the proposition that a successful defendant may be
deprived of his costs if he has been guilty of conduct which led the claimant
into believing that he had a good cause of action, could still be regarded as
offering guidance as to how the court's discretion might now be exercised.
However, statements to the effect that there could not be any circumstances
that would enable a judge properly to order a successful defendant to pay all
the costs of the action[103] can no longer be regarded as authoritative, albeit the
circumstances in which such an order might properly be made would be
exceptional.[104]

Costs against a non-party. Under s.51(3) of the Senior Courts Act 1981   **35.28**
the court is empowered to determine by whom the costs are to be paid.[105]
There is not to be implied into this section any limitation restricting orders as
to costs to orders made against parties to the relevant proceedings.[106] However, an order for payment of costs by a non-party should be regarded as
exceptional and the judge should treat any application for such an order with
considerable caution.[107] A non-party maintaining the claimant's libel action

---

[100] Per Lord Sterndale M.R. in *Ritter v Godfrey* [1920] 2 K.B. 47 at 53.

[101] CPR r.44.2(4), 44.2(5).

[102] *Bostock v Ramsey* [1900] 2 Q.B. 616; *Ritter v Godfrey*, above.

[103] See *Dicks v Yates* (1881) 18 Ch. D. 76 at 85, per Jessel M.R. and James L.J.; *Foster v G.W. Ry* (1882) 8 Q.B.D. 515 at 521, 522, per Brett L.J.; *Andrew v Grove* [1902] 1 K.B. 625.

[104] In *Daniels v Walker*, unreported, May 3, 2000, CA, the defendant, although successful, was ordered to pay the costs because of the way the matter had been conducted in the court below. In *Ford v GKR Construction* [2000] 1 W.L.R. 1397 CA, the court upheld an order of the trial judge that the defendant should pay all the claimant's costs even though the claimant had failed to beat the payment in. The defendant had failed to disclose until trial evidence which had a substantial impact on damages.

[105] As amended by s.4 of the Courts and Legal Services Act 1990. The relevant words appear in s.51(3). S.51(1) of the 1981 Act reproduced s.50(1) of the Supreme Court of Judicature (Consolidation) Act 1925, which was virtually identical to s.5 of the Supreme Court of Judicature Act 1891.

[106] *Aiden Shipping v Interbulk* [1986] A.C. 965.

[107] See *Symphony Group Plc v Hodgson* [1993] Q.B. 179, where the Court of Appeal laid down principles for the guidance of judges in respect of orders for costs against non-parties, and more recently *Dolphin Quays Developments Ltd v Mills* [2008] EWCA Civ 385; [2008] 1 W.L.R. 1829. It was stated in *Globe Equities v Globe Legal Services* [1999] B.L.R. 232, CA, that "ultimately the test is whether in all the circumstances it is just to exercise the power [under s.51]" (per Morritt L.J. at 240).

may be at risk of an order for payment of the successful defendant's costs,[108] but not (even if a solicitor acting for the party) if the maintainer is agreeing to run the risk of a loss by indemnifying the client against having to pay the opponent's costs under a CFA, without any prospect of a gain.[109] The maintainer will not be liable if he is a "pure funder", that is to say, paying or contributing to a party's costs as an act of charity, to enable that party to bring or defend the action without a direct interest in the result or any part in the control and management of the litigation.[110] A person against whom a costs order is sought under s.51 should be added as a party for the purpose of costs only.[111]

The court may order the legal or other representative of a party to meet the whole or part of "wasted costs", that is to say, costs incurred as a result of any improper, unreasonable or negligent act on the part of the legal or other representative.[112]

35.29 Amount of costs. A person in whose favour an order for costs has been made will have such costs assessed either on a standard basis or an indemnity basis.[113] Where the court does not indicate the basis of assessment, the costs will be assessed on a standard basis.[114] The principal differences between the two methods of assessment are that on an assessment on a standard basis the court will only allow costs that are proportionate to the matter in issue, and any doubts about whether costs have been reasonably incurred will be resolved in favour of the paying party.[115]

35.30 Indemnity costs. With the introduction of the CPR, the threshold for an assessment on an indemnity basis was lowered. It does not require a finding of lack of moral probity or of conduct deserving of moral condemnation on the part of the paying party.[116] It is sufficient if the litigation has been

---

[108] See *Singh v Observer* [1989] 2 All E.R. 751, reversed on appeal on an issue of fact: [1989] 3 All E.R. 777; and *McFarlane v EE Caledonia* [1995] 1 W.L.R. 366. See generally paras 31.50—31.51, above.

[109] *Sibthorpe v Southwark London Borough Council* [2011] EWCA Civ 25; [2011] 1 W.L.R. 2111.

[110] *Hamilton v Al Fayed (No.2)* [2002] EWCA Civ 665; [2003] Q.B. 1175, in which there was an extensive review of the authorities. The conclusion was based on policy considerations, that it was in the public interest that persons should have access to the courts, and the unfunded party's ability to recover his costs had to yield to the funded party's right of access to the courts.

[111] CPR r.46.2.

[112] S.51(6), (7), Senior Courts Act 1981. This topic is beyond the ambit of this book. Readers should refer to *Civil Procedure*, Vol.1, r.46.8 and 46PD.5.

[113] CPR r.44.3(1).

[114] CPR r.44.3(4).

[115] See r.44.3(2). In *Gazley v Wade & News Group Newspapers Ltd* [2004] EWHC 2675 (QB) it was held that the costs judge was correct to rule that it was not reasonable for the claimant to instruct London libel specialists as his solicitors rather than a local firm in Norwich in respect of his defamation claim against a local newspaper.

[116] *Reid Minty v Taylor* [2001] EWCA Civ 1723; [2002] 1 W.L.R. 2800. May L.J. said that the pre-CPR authorities were no longer helpful in considering the test for an indemnity costs order under the new procedural code.

conducted in a way that is unreasonable,[117] though the unreasonableness must be of a high degree, not merely wrong or misguided.[118] So in *Wakefield v Ford*,[119] Eady J. ordered indemnity costs against a claimant on discontinuance where he had acted completely unreasonably in launching and persisting in litigation in which he sought vindication which was clearly unwarranted, in that he sued on an allegation of negligence which he must have known was justified. In *Noorani v Calver (No.2)*[120] Coulson J. made a similar order against a discontinuing claimant whom he found to have brought what the claimant well knew to have been a hopeless claim.

Pt 36: indemnity costs and other sanctions. Although indemnity costs **35.31** will still be granted to a claimant where the defendant fails to accept a Pt 36 offer that should have been accepted, there are now additional post-judgment benefits available to claimants in such circumstances in the light of Jackson L.J.'s *Review of Civil Litigation Costs*. These are designed to redress what was seen as a defendant-weighted imbalance in sanctions for failing to beat an opponent's offer to settle, such that there was less incentive for a defendant to accept a claimant's reasonable offer to settle than vice versa.[121] The new rule provides, as before, that where the claimant fails to obtain a judgment more advantageous[122] than the defendant's Pt 36 offer, then the court (unless it considers it unjust to do so) will order that the defendant is entitled to his costs from the date on which the relevant period expired[123]: that provision is

---

[117] *Reid Minty v Taylor*, above. In *Miller v Associated Newspapers Ltd* [2005] EWHC 773 (QB) indemnity costs were ordered against the unsuccessful claimant after a Pt 36 payment was not accepted on the grounds that the claimant had been unreasonable in not accepting the payment. But see *Rackham v Sandy* [2005] EWHC 1354 (QB); [2006] 1 Costs L.R. 34 where in similar circumstances indemnity costs were refused because of the financial consequences on the defendant.

[118] *Kiam v MGN (No.2)* [2002] EWCA Civ 66; [2002] 1 W.L.R. 2810.

[119] [2009] EWHC 122 (QB).

[120] [2009] EWHC 592 (QB).

[121] The perceived imbalance has now been righted by LASPO, s.55, which enables rules of court to be made for civil proceedings involving a claim for money, to permit a court to order an additional amount to be paid to a claimant by a defendant, where the defendant does not accept the claimant's offer to settle, and the court subsequently gives judgment for the claimant which is at least as advantageous to the claimant as the claimant's offer, and empowers the Lord Chancellor to prescribe, as a percentage of the amount awarded to the claimant by the court, the additional amount that may be paid by the defendant in such cases. The Offers to Settle in Civil Proceedings Order 2013, SI 2013/93, sets out the scale of prescribed percentages, which does not entirely accord with that set out in the new rule, CPR r.36.14.

[122] "More advantageous", in relation to a money claim or the money element of a claim, now means better in money terms by any amount, and "at least as advantageous" will be construed accordingly: CPR r.36.14(1A). See *Jones v Associated Newspapers Ltd* [2007] EWHC 1489 (QB); [2008] E.M.L.R. 6 for the meaning and application of the words "at least as advantageous". (Otherwise this decision needs to be treated with caution. Owing the subsequent introduction of CPR r.36.14(1A), if the same circumstances were to arise today, it would not be open to the court to reach the conclusion that it did in *Jones* by the same route: see further para.29.25, above).

[123] The "relevant period" is defined at CPR r.36.3(1)(c).

unchanged.[124] But where judgment against the defendant is at least as advantageous to the claimant as the proposals contained in the claimant's Pt 36 offer, then the court (again unless it considers it unjust to do so) will order that the claimant is entitled to interest on the sum of money awarded at 10 per cent above base rate for some or all of the period starting with the date on which the relevant period expired, costs on the indemnity basis from the date on which the relevant period expired, interest on those costs at a rate not exceeding 10 per cent above base rate, and an additional amount, not exceeding £75,000.[125] In deciding whether or not it would be unjust to make such an order, the court will take into account all the circumstances, including the terms of any Pt 36 offer, the stage of the proceedings at which the offer was made, the information available to the parties at the time the offer was made, and the conduct of the parties in giving or refusing to give information to enable the offer to be made or evaluated.[126] However, no such order can be made in relation to a Pt 36 offer which has been withdrawn, or changed so that its terms are less advantageous to the offeree (and the offeree has beaten the less advantageous offer), or offered less than 21 days before trial (unless the court has abridged the relevant period).[127] Presumably, notwithstanding the new encouragements for claimants to make and for defendants to accept settlement offers, the courts will continue to take the view that the application of this rule carries no moral stigma or implied disapproval of the defendant's conduct, but simply has the function of bringing discipline to bear on litigants and encouraging reasonable offers of settlement.[128]

35.32 Costs of separate issues. Prior to the introduction of the CPR it was most unusual for the court to award the costs of a particular issue to the party who had succeeded on that issue notwithstanding that that party has lost the action, and the practice was discouraged.[129] Such a division of costs is one of several

---

[124] CPR r.36.14(2).

[125] CPR r.36.14(3). The amount is to be calculated by applying the "prescribed percentage" either (where the claim is or includes a money claim) to the sum awarded to the claimant by the court, or (where the claim is only a non-monetary claim) to the sum awarded to the claimant in respect of costs. The "prescribed percentage" will be 10 per cent of the amount awarded up to £500,000, and where the award is above £500,000 up to £1 million, it will be 10 per cent up to £500,000 and 5 per cent of any amount above that figure.

[126] CPR r.36.14(4).

[127] CPR r.36.14(6).

[128] See *McPhilemy v Times Newspapers (No.2)* [2001] EWCA Civ 933; [2002] 1 W.L.R. 934, and the observations of Simon Brown L.J. in *Kiam v MGN (No.2)* [2002] EWCA Civ 66; [2002] 1 W.L.R. 2810 at [6]–[8], explaining that the underlying rationale of CPR r.36.21 (replaced by r.36.14) was to encourage claimants to make Pt 36 offers. "(The claimant's) position is . . . quite different from that of the defendant who plainly has every incentive to make a settlement offer, generally by way of payment into court, irrespective of the basis on which any costs order will be made."

[129] *Cinema Press v Pictures and Pleasures* [1945] K.B. 356 where the problems caused by making separate orders on different issues were described; and see *Wheeler v Somerfield* [1966] 2 Q.B. 94.

possible orders available under the CPR,[130] which also permit the court to penalise the successful party who has failed on a particular issue, or who has only been partially successful, by awarding him only a proportion of his costs.[131]

Costs against co-defendants. As a general rule where two or more **35.33** persons are joined as co-defendants in respect of a tortious act for which they are jointly liable and judgment is given against them with costs, each is liable to the claimant for all the costs.[132] However, this may not apply where separate defences are raised. Thus in a libel action in which the plaintiff recovered damages against both defendants, one of whom admitted liability and pleaded an apology, but the other pleaded justification, it was held that the defendant who pleaded justification was alone liable for the costs occasioned to the plaintiff by that plea.[133]

Law of Libel Amendment Act 1888. It is vanishingly rare for consolida- **35.34** tion to be ordered under s.5 rather than under CPR r.3.1(2)(g), but when two or more actions have been consolidated under that section, "the judge at trial, if he awards the plaintiff the costs of the action, shall thereupon make such order as he shall deem just for the apportionment of such costs between and against such defendants". The wording of the statute would not seem to affect the general rules.

Summary assessment. The CPR enable the court to make a summary **35.35** assessment of the costs when ordering a party to pay costs to another party.[134] As a general rule summary assessment is required to be made only in respect of fast track cases and at the conclusion of other cases which have lasted not more than one day.[135] So summary assessment in defamation cases normally arises only on interim hearings.

Payment on account. When the court has ordered a party to pay costs **35.36** subject to detailed assessment at the end of the trial, it will order payment of a reasonable sum on account, unless there is good reason not to do so.[136] The

---

[130] CPR r.44.2(6).

[131] An order employed well before the advent of the CPR: *Wheeler v Somerfield* [1966] 2 Q.B. 94; *John Richardson Computers v Flanders (No.2)* [1994] F.S.R. 144.

[132] The converse will apply where an action fails against both defendants. In *Rackham v Sandy*, [2005] EWHC 1354 (QB); [2006] 1 Costs L.R. 34, the claimant was ordered to pay the costs of the successful defendants as it had been his choice to join them.

[133] *Hobson v Leng* [1914] 3 K.B. 1245 CA. No specific order had been made by the trial judge, who had simply granted judgment with costs. See also *Stumm v Dixon* (1889) 22 Q.B.D. 529, where a similar decision was made in a non-libel case, Lord Esher commenting, "I cannot help saying that to compel the other defendant to pay those costs [of an alternative separate defence raised by the first defendant] would be absolutely contrary to natural justice" (at 531).

[134] CPR r.44.6(1).

[135] CPR 44PD para.9.2.

[136] CPR r.44.2(8).

presumption in favour of a payment on account is new.[137] It has been stated that the court should normally order an interim payment in favour of the successful party for an amount less than the likely full amount of assessed costs, but in exercising its discretion the court will take into account all the circumstances of the particular case.[138]

35.37 Costs in action under Slander of Women Act 1891. The Act has been prospectively repealed by s.14, Defamation Act 2013. In an action for words spoken and published imputing unchastity or adultery to a woman or girl under the Slander of Women Act 1891,[139] "a plaintiff shall not recover more costs than damages unless the judge shall certify that there was reasonable ground for bringing the action". It has been held that a counterclaim for such an imputation is an "action" within the meaning of the Act.[140] The judge may give a certificate on an application subsequent to the trial.[141]

35.38 Appeal against costs orders. An appeal against any order relating to costs requires permission to appeal to be granted either by the trial judge or the Court of Appeal.[142]

---

[137] Compare the previous rule, the former r.44.3(8): "Where the court has ordered a party to pay costs, it may order an amount to be paid on account before costs are assessed". Even under that rule, though, orders for payment on account of costs were becoming the standard practice (see e.g. per Eady J. in *Wakefield v Ford* [2009] EWHC 122 (QB) at [31]).

[138] For examples of the court's approach see *Mars UK v Teknowledge* [2000] F.S.R. 138; *Allason v Random House UK Limited* [2002] EWHC 1030 (Ch); *Noorani v Calver (No.2)* [2009] EWHC 592 (QB).

[139] The editors know of no action brought under this Act in the last 35 years.

[140] *Croft v Hewitt, The Times*, July 28, 1911.

[141] *Russo v Cole* [1966] 1 W.L.R. 248.

[142] The general rule applies: CPR r.52.3.

CHAPTER 36

APPEAL[1]

Section 1. General Principles

Application for permission to appeal. All appeals from judgments of a **36.1** judge and jury or a judge alone in respect of claims for libel require permission.[2] Permission to appeal will only be given where the court considers that the appeal would have a real prospect of success or where there is some other compelling reason why the appeal should be heard.[3] Permission may be sought from the lower court at the hearing at which the decision to be appealed was made, or from the appeal court.[4] Where the lower court refuses

---

[1] Only matters in respect of which there is specific authority from the field of defamation practice are covered in any depth in this chapter. For guidance on points of general application the reader should refer elsewhere, specifically to the entry for CPR Pt 52 in the most up-to-date edition of *Civil Procedure* (*The White Book*), Vol.1. It is important to appreciate that Pt 52 was amended as of October 1, 2012 and new practice directions came into force on the same day.

[2] CPR r.52.3(1).

[3] CPR r.52.3(6). For an example of a decision in a libel context, see *Irving v Penguin Books Ltd* [2001] EWCA Civ 1197, in which permission to appeal was refused. See, similarly, *Fox v Wokingham DC* [2003] EWCA Civ 499; *Pell v Express Newspapers* [2004] EWCA Civ 46 and *Jameel (Mohammed) v Wall Street Journal Europe SPRL (No.2)* [2005] EWCA Civ 74; [2005] Q.B. 904 at [54]–[68]. For an example of a libel case where permission to appeal was granted on the basis that there was some other compelling reason why the appeal should be heard see *North London Mosque Trust v Policy Exchange and another* [2010] EWCA Civ 526. The case settled before the hearing.

[4] CPR r.52.3(2). Although applying to the lower court for permission to appeal is not mandatory, a litigant with arguable grounds for appeal should generally apply to the lower court at the time of judgment for five reasons: (1) the judge below is seized of the matter and so the application will take minimal time; indeed the judge may have already decided that the case raises questions fit for an appeal; (2) an application at this stage does not cause either party additional costs; (3) there is nothing to lose if the application fails; the litigant may have two bites at the cherry if he so wishes; (4) no harm is done if the application succeeds but the litigant subsequently decides not to appeal; (5) if the application succeeds and the litigant subsequently decides to appeal, he avoids the expensive and time-consuming permission stage in the Court of Appeal.

an application for permission to appeal, a further application may be made to the appeal court.[5] Where permission is sought from the appeal court, the application should be made in an appellant's notice.[6] Such notice must be filed at the appeal court within 21 days of the date of the decision of the lower court, unless the lower court has specified a different period.[7] The notice must be served on each respondent as soon as practicable and in any event not later than seven days after filing.[8]

The grounds of appeal given must set out clearly why the decision of the lower court was wrong or was unjust because of a serious procedural or other irregularity in the proceedings of the lower court.[9] At the appeal hearing, except with the permission of the appeal court, a party may not rely on a matter not contained in his appeal notice.[10] Further, an appeal notice may not be amended except with the permission of the appeal court.[11] Every appellant who is represented is also required to lodge and serve a skeleton argument at the same time as filing of the appellant's notice.[12] The above time limits cannot be extended by agreement of the parties; an application must be made to the appeal court.[13]

Permission is required from the Court of Appeal for any appeal to that court from a decision of a county court or the High Court which was itself made on appeal.[14] Permission will only be granted in such circumstances where the case raises an important point of principle or practice or where there is some other compelling reason for the Court of Appeal to hear it.[15] Permission to appeal will also be granted more sparingly against case management decisions having regard to whether the issue is of sufficient significance to justify the costs of an appeal; the procedural consequences of an appeal and whether it would be more convenient to determine the issue at or after trial.[16] A respondent should only file submissions at the permission stage if they are addressed to the point that the appeal does not meet the relevant threshold test or that there is some material inaccuracy in the papers that the applicant has placed before the court.[17] Unless the court directs otherwise, a respondent

---

This guidance was endorsed by the Court of Appeal in *T (A Child)* [2002] EWCA Civ 1736 at [12]–[13].

[5] CPR r.52.3(3).
[6] CPR r.52.4(1).
[7] CPR r.52.4(2).
[8] CPR r.52.4(3); CPR 52C, para.7.1.
[9] CPR PD 52C, para.5(1).
[10] CPR r.52.11(5).
[11] CPR r.52.8.
[12] CPR PD 52C, para.3(3)(g).
[13] CPR r.52.6.
[14] CPR r.52.13(1).
[15] CPR r.52.13(2). In relation to second appeals generally, see *Tanfern Ltd v Cameron-MacDonald (Practice Note)* [2000] 1 W.L.R. 1311 at [41]–[46] and *Clark (Inspector of Taxes) v Perks* [2001] 1 W.L.R. 17 CA. See also *Uphill v BRB (Residuary) Ltd* [2005] EWCA Civ 60; [2005] 1 W.L.R. 2070.
[16] CPR PD 52A, para.4.6.
[17] *Jolly v Jay* [2002] EWCA Civ 277 at [44]–[47].

need not take any action when served with an appellant's notice until such time as notification is given to him that permission to appeal has been granted.[18]

Where permission to appeal is granted.[19] An order giving permission   **36.2**
to appeal may limit the issues to be heard by the appellate court.[20] Where limited permission is granted, the court will either refuse permission on any remaining issues or reserve the question of permission on any remaining issues to the appeal court.[21] An order giving permission to appeal may also be made subject to conditions.[22] The appeal court has the power to strike out the whole or part of an appeal notice and to set aside permission to appeal in whole or in part, although it will exercise these powers only where there is a compelling reason for doing so.[23] Where permission to appeal is granted, if the respondent's position is that the decision of the court below was correct for the reasons it gave, he is not obliged to put in a respondent's notice.[24] If, however, the respondent wishes the appeal court to vary the lower court's decision in any respect, he must seek permission to appeal[25] and file and serve

---

[18] CPR PD 52, para.5.22.
[19] For the procedure after permission is obtained generally, see CPR PD 52, paras 6.1–6.3A.
[20] CPR r.52.3(7)(a).
[21] CPR PD 52C, para.18.
[22] CPR r.52.3(7)(b). The power is expressed broadly. It may, for example, be just for the court to impose a condition that the appellant pays the respondent's costs of the appeal in any event where the appellant is seeking by his appeal to clarify a particular point of general principle, whereas the respondent has no interest in the wider issues: see *Morris v Wrexham BC* [2001] EWHC 697 (Admin). The appeal court has the specific power to impose or vary conditions upon which an appeal may be brought (CPR r.52.9(1)(c)) but will only exercise this power where there is a compelling reason for doing so (CPR r.52.9(2)). Note that in *Lloyd Jones v T Mobile (UK) Ltd* [2003] EWCA Civ 1162; (2003) 49 E.G. 130 at [26], the Court of Appeal granted permission to appeal on condition that the appellant should not be entitled to the costs of the appeal, even if it succeeded. The appellant was a large corporation which had incurred substantial costs in relation to the appeal because the matter was important to its business. The respondents, by contrast, were individual objectors to the installation of a telephone mast. The ostensible rationale of this decision was to prevent the respondents being caused financial oppression by the appeal and thereby to ensure that the parties were on an even footing.
[23] CPR r.52.9(1)(a), (b) and r.52.9(2). The court will not permit these provisions to be used as a vehicle for tactical skirmishing or unnecessary satellite litigation. Save in exceptional circumstances, it will be a misuse of court's resources for a party to require the court to consider the substance of an appeal on some intermediate date between the grant of permission and hearing of the appeal: see *Nathan v Smilovitch* [2002] EWCA Civ 759 at [8]–[9]. What will amount to a "compelling reason"? A reason will only be compelling if the materials put before the judge to obtain permission were so inaccurate or incomplete, either by reason of the omission of some decisive authority or statutory provision or otherwise, that the judge granted permission when he otherwise would not have done so, i.e. the court was misled and the matter not brought to the court's attention would have been decisive: *Nathan v Smilovitch*, above; *Hertsmere BC v Harty* [2001] EWCA Civ 1238; *Barings Bank Plc (in liquidation) v Coopers & Lybrand* [2002] EWCA Civ 1155. Note also that where a party was present at the hearing at which permission was given, he may not subsequently ask the court to exercise its powers under CPR r.52.9(1): CPR r.52.9(3).
[24] CPR r.52.5(1).
[25] CPR r.52.3(1) and PD52C, para.8(1).

a respondent's notice.[26] In such a case, where the respondent seeks permission from the appeal court to mount an appeal, such permission must be requested in the respondent's notice.[27] If the respondent merely wants the appeal court to uphold the order of the lower court for reasons different from or additional to those given by the lower court, he does not require permission to appeal and need only file and serve a respondent's notice.[28]

A respondent's notice must be filed within the time directed by the lower court or, if no such direction has been given, within 14 days from either (1) where the lower court has given permission to appeal, the date the respondent is served with the appellant's notice or (2) the date the respondent is served with notification that the appeal court has given permission or ordered that the application for permission and the substantive appeal are to be heard together.[29] Unless the appeal court orders otherwise, the respondent's notice must be served on the appellant and any other respondent as soon as practicable and, in any event, no later than 7 days after it is filed.[30] The respondent must also provide a skeleton argument in all cases where he proposes to address arguments to the court.[31] If not included in the respondent's notice, the respondent's skeleton argument should be filed and served on the appellant 42 days after the date of the listing window notification.[32]

Every appeal will be limited to a review of the decision of the lower court unless a practice direction provides otherwise or the court considers that it would be in the interests of justice to hold a re-hearing.[33] Unless the appeal court or the court whose decision is being appealed orders otherwise, an appeal does not operate as a stay of any order or decision of the lower court.[34] The Court of Appeal has no power to make a quite different type of order from the order the judge was asked to make if it is satisfied that the judge's approach cannot be faulted, unless the parties agree to such a procedure being adopted.[35]

36.3 Security for costs. Where an order granting permission to appeal is made, the appeal court can order the appellant, or a respondent who also appeals, to give security for the costs of the appeal where, having regard to all the circumstances of the case, the court is satisfied that it is just to make such an order and where one or more of seven specified conditions applies, or where

---

[26] CPR r.52.5(2) and r.52.5(6).
[27] CPR r.52.5(3).
[28] CPR PD 52C, para.8(3).
[29] CPR r.52.5(4) and (5).
[30] CPR r.52.5(6).
[31] CPR PD 52C, para.13(1).
[32] CPR PD 52C. There is a Timetable in CPR PD 52C to which reference should be made.
[33] CPR r.52.11(1) and see CPR PD 52, para.9.1.
[34] CPR r.52.7.
[35] *Musa King v Telegraph Group Ltd (Practice Note)* [2004] EWCA Civ 613; [2005] 1 W.L.R. 2282 (reported as *King v Telegraph Group Ltd (Practice Note)*) at [54].

an enactment permits the court to make the order.[36] In exercising its discretion in this respect, the court will take into consideration the whole subject-matter and character of the action as well as the merits of the appeal.[37] When security is ordered, the conventional form of order provides that unless the security is given as ordered within the time limited (usually 28 days), the appeal is struck out with costs without further order.[38]

Raising a point not taken below. As a general rule, neither party can **36.4**
raise on appeal a point which he could have taken, but did not take, at the trial.[39] It is not, however, a question of jurisdiction but of discretion and the

---

[36] CPR r.25.15(1) and see CPR r.52.3(7)(b). As to the seven specified grounds, see CPR r.25.13(2). The application may be made either in the respondent's notice or subsequently by a separate application notice, in which case it should be made promptly, as soon as the facts justifying the order are known. The Court of Appeal has power under CPR r.52.10 to make an order for security in respect of the costs of the proceedings below: *Dar International FEF Co. v Aon Ltd* [2003] EWCA Civ 1833; [2004] 1 W.L.R. 1395. See *His Holiness Sant Baba Jeet Singh Ji Maharaj v Eastern Media Group* [2011] EWCA Civ 139.

[37] *Usil v Brearly* (1878) 3 C.P.D. 206 at 207; *Aldington v Watts, Independent,* July 20, 1990, and *Guardian,* July 27, 1990. The court held that it had a discretion in such a case and would consider whether ordering security would amount to a denial of justice to the appellant. In considering that question, the court would take into account the merits of the appeal. In order to avoid giving security, the appellant must satisfy the court that his grounds of appeal are real and substantial. If a party is looking for substantial security for costs, the application must be supported by detailed evidence usually in the form of a draft bill of costs to support the claim: per Tuckey L.J. in *Turkan and Co. (a firm) v Toplum Postasi Ltd* [2001] EWCA Civ 99.

[38] CPR PD 4, para.4.4, PF44.

[39] *Hughes v Dinorben* (1859) 32 L.T.(O.S.) 271:
"It would be very dangerous if parties were allowed to stand by without making objections [as to the admissibility of evidence], and, when the result was unfavourable to them, apply to set aside the verdict"
(per Lord Campbell C.J. at 272); *Warham v Selfridge and Co.* (1914) 30 T.L.R. 344; *Moore v News of the World* [1972] 1 Q.B. 441:
"Now section 5 [of the Defamation Act 1952] was not pleaded. It was not raised by counsel in the court below. Naturally enough the judge did not refer to it. As it was not raised below, I am of the opinion that it cannot be made any ground of complaint here"
(per Lord Denning M.R. at 448); *Delaney v News Media Ownership Ltd* [1976] 1 N.Z.L.R. 322.
See also *Jones v MBNA International Bank,* unreported, June 30, 2000, per May L.J. at [52]:
"Civil trials are conducted on the basis that the court decides the factual and legal issues which the parties bring before the court . . . Normally a party cannot raise in subsequent proceedings claims or issues which could and should have been raised in the first proceedings. Equally, a party cannot, in my judgment, normally seek to appeal a trial judge's decision on the basis that a claim, which could have been brought before the trial judge but was not, would have succeeded if it had been so brought. The justice of this as a general principle is, in my view, obvious. It is not merely a matter of efficiency, expediency and cost, but of substantial justice. Parties to litigation are entitled to know where they stand. The parties are entitled, and the court requires, to know what the issues are. Upon this depends a variety of decisions, including, by the parties, what evidence to call, how much effort and money it is appropriate to invest in the case, and generally how to conduct the case; and, by the court, what case management and administrative decisions to make and give, and the substantive decision of the case itself. Litigation should be resolved once and for all, and it is not, generally speaking, just if a party who successfully contested a case advanced on one basis should be expected to face on appeal, not a challenge to the original decision, but a new case advanced on a different basis. There may be exceptional cases in which the court would not apply the general principle which I have expressed."

rule is thus not absolute.[40] Nevertheless, an attempt by a party to introduce for the first time on appeal a point which was open to him below will be carefully scrutinised and is only likely to succeed on rare occasions. A defendant who has pleaded that the words are not defamatory, or, alternatively, that they were published on a privileged occasion, and who is content to let the case go to the jury on the first issue alone, is most unlikely to be permitted on appeal to raise the defence of privilege. Similarly, if a party at the time takes no objection to a non-direction by the judge or to a misdirection as to a matter of fact or to a question put to the jury, he will generally be deemed to have waived the point and thus to have debarred himself from raising that matter on appeal.[41] It is not, however, appropriate to object to directions as to the law and a failure

---

See also *Jameel (Mohammed) v Wall Street Journal Europe SPRL (No.2)* [2005] EWCA Civ 74; [2005] Q.B. 904 at [54]–[57].

[40] *Burchett v Kane* [1980] 2 N.S.W.L.R. 266n:
"To grant or refuse a new trial is always a matter of discretion. . . . The exercise of discretion, in the present case, is complicated by the fact that the point upon which the appellant now seeks to rely was never taken at trial. This omission does not of itself necessarily preclude his obtaining the relief which he seeks; but it is, beyond question, an obstacle which it may be difficult for him to surmount"
(per Samuels J.A. at 271); applied in *Andrews v John Fairfax* [1980] 2 N.S.W.L.R. 225; *Hickman v Kent Sheep Breeders* (1920) 37 T.L.R. 163. In *UK Learning Academy Ltd v Leeds City Council* [2011] EWCA Civ 1513 the Court of Appeal tentatively suggested that it had the power to decide new issues which were capable of being determinative of an appeal without making factual findings, but if the court took that course it would be turning itself into a tribunal of first instance and there would be no recourse to the Court of Appeal for a further appeal, if required.

[41] *Nevill v The Fine Art and General Insurance Co.* [1897] A.C. 68:
" . . . where you are complaining of a non-direction of the judge, or that he did not leave a question to the jury, if you had the opportunity of asking him to do it and you abstained from asking for it, no Court would ever have granted you a new trial . . . "
(per Lord Halsbury L.C. at 76);
Kiam v Neil (No.2) [1996] E.M.L.R. 493, per Beldam L.J.:
"It seems to me difficult to accept that misdirections singly or cumulatively can be so significant that a substantial wrong or miscarriage of justice has occurred if counsel experienced in this branch of the law failed to draw the judge's attention to the mistakes or omissions", (at 500);
Macdougall v Knight (1889) 14 A.C. 194:
"Now I think it is the duty of those who are suggesting that other questions ought to have been asked and other issues raised to have intervened at this point, and to have requested Baron Huddleston definitely and distinctly to put the questions that they now insist ought to have been submitted to the jury. But nothing of the sort was done. The parties took their chance of what the jury would do, and I think nothing could be more mischievous than to allow litigants to raise new questions when, under such circumstances, the jury have decided against them. If such a course were permitted no end could possibly be found to litigation" (per Lord Halsbury L.C. at 199–200);
Speight v Syme (1895) 21 V.L.R. 672:
" . . . it is no less the duty as it is the right of counsel, if he thinks that the Judge has passed over any circumstance that deserved to be noticed, or has given a wrong version of any piece of evidence, to request him, at the first convenient opportunity before the verdict is returned, to add to or amend his charge. If this right is not availed of, the Judge's charge cannot afterwards be impeached on that score"(per Holroyd J. at 681);
Jones v Skelton [1963] 1 W.L.R. 1362 at 1375; *Barber v Pigden* [1937] 1 K.B. 664; *Brown v Citizens' Life Assurance* (1902) 2 N.S.W.S.R. 202: "Where there has been a non-direction by a Judge a party cannot complain unless the attention of the Judge is drawn to it at trial" (at 216, per G. B. Simpson J.).

to do so will not count against the appellant.[42] Above all, however, an appellate court is not bound by the premise on which a case is argued before it.[43]

Retrial. Formerly, the appeal court was not bound to order a retrial unless it   **36.5**
was of the opinion that some substantial wrong or miscarriage of justice had been occasioned.[44] Thus, where, in an action for libel, the jury found for the

Failure to invite the judge to withdraw a question from the jury does not prevent an appellant from arguing that the jury's verdict was perverse: *Banbury v Bank of Montreal* [1918] A.C. 628; *Grobbelaar v News Group Newspapers Ltd* [2001] All E.R. 437 CA. However, where a party expressly invites the judge to leave a question to the jury, he is debarred from contending that the jury's verdict was demonstrably perverse: *McPhilemy v Times Newspapers Ltd* [2001] EWCA Civ 871; [2001] E.M.L.R. 34. See also *Jameel (Mohammed) v Wall Street Journal Europe SPRL (No.2)* [2005] EWCA Civ 74; [2005] Q.B. 904 at [64]:

"[Counsel for the claimants] referred us to a substantial body of authority in footnote 40 to paragraph 36.4 of the 10th Edition of *Gatley on Libel and Slander*. This gives strong support to the proposition that this court will not entertain a complaint of misdirection in a defamation action if counsel has failed to avail himself of the chance of raising the matter at trial. We consider that this principle is particularly significant in the present case. The only remedy for a misdirection is a re-trial . . . We would be very reluctant to permit a point to be raised on appeal which could and should have been taken below in circumstances such as this. Were it plain that the misdirection had resulted in a miscarriage of justice we might have been persuaded to grant permission to appeal none the less. But that is far from the case . . . ".

[42] *Herald v McGregor* (1928) 41 C.L.R. 255 at 269, per Isaacs J.; *Broome v Cassell* [1972] A.C. 1027 at 1119: "I cannot accept that acquiescence by counsel validates the defect" (per Lord Wilberforce). A party may not be entitled to a new trial where the acceptance of its submissions was an operative cause of the error of law made at the trial, *Petritsis v Hellenic Herald* [1978] 2 N.S.W.L.R. 174.

[43] *Grobbelaar v News Group Newspapers Ltd* [2002] UKHL 40; [2002] 1 W.L.R. 3024 HL, per Lord Millett at [68]. See also the trenchant observations of Lord Hobhouse on the subject of "concessions" at [56] in the same case:

"The so-called 'concession' [on behalf of the plaintiff, that in awarding damages of £85,000 the jury must have been satisfied not only that no match-fixing had taken place but that the plaintiff had not been party to any corrupt agreement] has now been advanced as a reason for dismissing the plaintiff's appeal to your Lordships' House. It is said that the 'concession' having been made, the plaintiff should be held to it (although no prejudice to the defendants is suggested) and the decision of the Court of Appeal upheld without further examination. To accede to this submission would serve no greater purpose than to compound the Court of Appeal's error. Your Lordships have been shown the passages in the transcript of the Court of Appeal upon which the argument is based. To my reading they are of very limited significance and do not extend beyond what would be expected in exchanges which take place when an advocate is being subjected to close questioning by an unsympathetic court. It is a misuse of the privilege of having an oral hearing with oral arguments for a court to try to decide the case by obtaining 'concessions' from counsel. The purpose of oral arguments is to inform, clarify and enlighten the minds of the court (hopefully in favour of the advocate's client). It is not right to seek to decide cases upon the tenacity of the advocate or 'concessions' forced out of the advocate in the course of oral argument . . . Still less is it right to decide appeals upon the basis of upholding wrong decisions arrived at using legally mistaken 'concessions' by counsel."

On the same issue, see further Lord Bingham at [21].

[44] RSC Ord.59, r.11(2). For the principles which governed the application of this rule, see *Bray v Ford* [1896] A.C. 44; *Lionel Barber v Deutsche Bank* [1919] A.C. 304; *Braddock v Bevins* [1948] 1 K.B. 580 CA; *Tedlie v Southam Ltd* [1950] 1 W.W.R. 1009; *Moore v News of the World* [1972] 1 Q.B. 441: "There were left out of the summing-up, as out of every summing-up which deserves the name, some of the things which one party and probably both parties would have liked put in; but there was no omission which could have led to a misunderstanding or injustice" (per Stephenson L.J. at 453); *Hayward v Thompson* [1982] 1 Q.B. 47:

defendants, notwithstanding that there was no substantive defence and it was substantially agreed that the words were defamatory and referred to the plaintiff, the court declined to allow an appeal in circumstances where it appeared that there had been a payment into court of more than the jury could have reasonably awarded as damages. The court held that, as a new trial could only produce a result which was in practical terms the same as the original trial, there had been no substantial wrong or miscarriage of justice.[45] The wording of this proviso was held to afford a guide to the exercise generally of the discretion in ordering or refusing a new trial, even where the rule of court was not in terms applicable.[46] Although CPR Pt 52 contains no direct equivalent to RSC Ord.59, r.11(2), CPR r.52.10(3) provides that in an appeal from a claim tried with a jury, the Court of Appeal may, instead of ordering a new trial, make an order for damages or vary an award of damages made by the jury. It has also been held that no change to the law was intended.[47] Where the Court of Appeal could remedy the flaw in the result of the trial proceedings by exercising one of its powers under CPR r.52.10(3), consistently with the overriding objective, it seems likely that it would do so. Under CPR r.52.11(3) the court will allow an appeal where the decision of the lower court was either wrong or unjust because of a serious procedural or other irregularity in the

---

"To my mind in an action for libel a Court of Appeal should pay no regard to any supposed misdirection by the judge—on law or on fact—unless it was plainly such as to lead to a substantial miscarriage of justice"

(per Lord Denning M.R. at 63); *Pamplin v Express Newspapers Ltd* [1988] 1 W.L.R. 116n:
"What constitutes a miscarriage of justice in these circumstances? The fact that the court would, had it been the jury, have given the same verdict cannot be sufficient to negative a miscarriage, for that would be to usurp the function of the jury. If there is a misdirection and the jury, properly directed, *might* have returned a different verdict there is authority for the proposition that this is a miscarriage of justice"

(per Purchas L.J. at 130).

[45] *Poliakoff v News Chronicle Ltd* [1939] 1 All E.R. 390:
"Whatever criticism may be made of the conduct of the trial below, and whatever suggestion of misdirection may be urged upon a critical examination of the summing up, it is manifest that no substantial wrong or miscarriage was thereby occasioned. . . . it is manifest to me that, if we did order a new trial, it would only cause the waste of a good deal of money in costs . . . ″

(per MacKinnon L.J. at 394–395). Cf. *Pratten v The Labour Daily Ltd* [1926] V.L.R. 115:
" . . . it must be remembered that in many libel actions . . . the plaintiff may merely wish to vindicate his character; and a verdict for even nominal damages might be all-important to him, and entirely serve his purpose, by establishing that the imputations made against him were false: and to deprive him of the opportunity of obtaining such a verdict would, I think, obviously be a substantial wrong or miscarriage of justice" (per McArthur J. at 132–133).

[46] *Holdsworth v Associated Newspapers* (1937) 53 T.L.R. 1029 CA at 1032.

[47] See *Hamilton v Al Fayed (No.2)* [2001] E.M.L.R. 15 CA:
"We consider that Ord.59, r. 11 reflected a principle of general application. We do not believe that this principle has changed with the new Rules. A new trial should be ordered when the interests of justice so demand. Where a party has behaved fraudulently, been guilty of procedural impropriety or some other irregularity has affected the fairness of the trial the vital question to be asked is whether there is a real danger that this has influenced the outcome. If there is, a retrial should normally be ordered."

(per Lord Phillips M.R.). With regard to the Court of Appeal's powers under CPR r.52.10(3), see also para.38.30, below.

proceedings of the lower court, and if it does so, will consider its power inter alia to order a new trial under CPR r.52.10(2)(c). Accordingly, except in cases where exercise of one of the Court of Appeal's powers under CPR r.52.10(3) will cure the error or injustice in the proceedings below, it is anticipated that the Court of Appeal and, indeed, the Supreme Court, will order a new trial in the same circumstances as they did prior to the introduction of the Civil Procedure Rules.[48]

Section 2. Improper Admission or Rejection of Evidence[49]

Discretion of the trial judge. The admission or rejection[50] of evidence is   **36.6** a matter falling within the discretion of the trial judge. The exercise of that discretion will not generally be disturbed unless it has been wrongly exercised

---

[48] But, in this regard, see *Jameel v Wall Street Journal Europe SPRL* [2006] UKHL 44; [2007] 1 A.C. 359, in which the House of Lords took a robust approach to the error it discerned in the Court of Appeal's application of the law of *Reynolds* privilege: it held the article complained of to be privileged and entered judgment for the defendant. Although Lord Bingham agreed with the majority that the Court of Appeal had gone wrong, at [36] he expressed doubt about whether the majority's response to this error was the right one:

"The House has not, like the judge and jury, heard the witnesses and seen the case develop day after day. It has read no more than a small sample of the evidence. It seems to me a large step for the House, thus disadvantaged, to hold that the publication was privileged. But I find myself in a minority, and it serves no useful purpose to do more than express my doubt".

See also *Flood v Times Newspapers Ltd* [2012] UKSC 11; [2012] 2 A.C. 273 at [102]–[103]. In the Court of Appeal in *Flood v Times Newspapers* [2010] EWCA Civ 804; [2011] 1 W.L.R. 153, Lord Neuberger M.R. made reference to this paragraph and the proper approach on appeal when considering the Reynolds defence. Lord Phillips P.S.C. said,

"The extent to which the trial judge is at an advantage over the Court of Appeal will depend on the circumstances of the particular case. The greater the advantage of the trial judge, the greater the weight to be attached to his decision and the more cogent must be the basis for finding that his decision was wrong."

[49] CPR r.52.11(3) introduces new wording to describe the circumstances in which an appeal may be allowed, namely where a decision was (1) wrong or (2) was unjust because of a serious procedural or other irregularity. Nevertheless, this and each of the next seven sections below, which reflect typical grounds of appeal from verdicts in defamation cases prior to the introduction of the CPR, falls within one or other limb of the CPR r.52.11(3) test. For this reason, the existing structure of these sections is retained. As regards the extent to which pre-CPR case law remains applicable, the authors of *Civil Procedure*, Vol.1 (2008) (*The White Book*) write at fn.52.0.8 (at p.1383) under the heading "Pre-2000 authority" that:

"The changes made in 2000 are so fundamental that citation of authority on the former rules is of limited assistance in resolving questions which arise concerning Pt 52. This does not, however, mean that experience gained from the old rules or judicial analysis of those rules should be ignored. The commentary to RSC Ords 55, 56, 58 and 59 in the Supreme Court Practice 1999 neatly distils the authorities and learning which accumulated over the last 125 years of the second millennium."

[50] See now CPR r.32.1(2) which confers on the court a specific power to exclude evidence and *GKR Karate (UK) Ltd v Yorkshire Post Newspapers Ltd (No.1)* [2000] 1 W.L.R. 2571. The court's power to exclude evidence must be exercised in accordance with the overriding objective of dealing with a case justly: *Grobbelaar v Sun Newspapers Ltd*, *The Times*, August 12, 1999, CA.

and a substantial wrong has occurred.[51] Where evidence is found to have been wrongly excluded, the court will not interfere with an award of damages if it is not persuaded that the award of the jury would have been different had the evidence been admitted.[52]

36.7 Admission of evidence. A new trial was granted where evidence of special damage was admitted, although there was no allegation of such damage in the statement of claim.[53] Similarly, an appeal was allowed where evidence of the truth of defamatory imputations in the words complained of was admitted under a plea of fair comment.[54] Where evidence was admitted for the defendant of a defamatory article, published by the plaintiff after the alleged libel and making no reference to the defendant, a new trial was granted on the ground that such evidence had been wrongly admitted.[55] So far as the relevance of matters raised by a defendant in support of his plea of justification is concerned, this is a question of degree for the trial judge, who should consider the evidence in the light of the issues raised by the statements of case and the scope of matters put before the jury.[56]

36.8 Exclusion of evidence. A new trial has been granted where evidence relevant to publication was excluded,[57] and also where the occasion was

---

[51] The principles upon which the Court of Appeal can properly interfere with the exercise of the trial judge's discretion are set out in *Hadmor Productions v Hamilton* [1983] 1 A.C. 191 per Lord Diplock at 220; *Proetta v Times Newspapers Ltd*, unreported, February 27, 1991: "Whether this court would have exercised its discretion in the same way is entirely another matter and an irrelevant matter" (per Taylor L.J.). As regards what constitutes a sufficient error in the exercise of discretion to warrant interference by the appeal court, see *Tanfern Ltd v Cameron-MacDonald (Practice Note)* [2000] 1 W.L.R. 1311 at [32]. Brooke L.J. suggested that guidance might be gained from the speech of Lord Fraser in *G v G (Minors: Custody Appeal)* [1985] 1 W.L.R. 647 at 652. In the latter part of the passage cited by Brooke L.J., Lord Fraser stated:

" . . . the appellate court should only interfere when they consider that the judge of first instance has not merely preferred an imperfect solution which is different from an alternative imperfect solution which the Court of Appeal might or would have adopted, but has exceeded the generous ambit within which a reasonable disagreement is possible."

For an example of a case where a judge's exercise of discretion was overturned, see *Desmond v Bower* [2009] EWCA Civ 857. In this interlocutory appeal (involving the admissibility of a taped telephone conversation) Hooper L.J. said at [57] "In my view this is not a case of interfering with a case management decision or interfering with some discretionary decision of the judge. It is taking steps to ensure a possible miscarriage of justice does not occur." See also Pill L.J. at [31]–[32].

[52] *Burstein v Times Newspapers Ltd* [2001] 1 W.L.R. 579 CA.

[53] *Dominion Telegraph v Silver* (1882) 10 S.C.R. (Canada) 238; *Miles v Commercial Banking* (1904) 1 C.L.R. 470.

[54] *Brown v Moyer* (1893) 20 O.A.R. 509; *Manitoba Free Press v Martin* (1893) 21 S.C.R. 518 (Canada).

[55] *Downey v Armstrong* (1901) 1 O.L.R. 237. Cf. *Broxton v McClelland, (No.2)* [1997] E.M.L.R. 157, where it was held that the trial judge had properly admitted evidence as to the ongoing dispute between the plaintiff's financial backer and the defendants on the basis that it was relevant to the assessment of the extent to which the plaintiff had really suffered hurt feelings.

[56] *Lim v Lawless, Independent*, August 22, 1991, CA. See *Desmond v Bower* at [2009] EWCA Civ 667 and [2009] EWCA Civ 857.

[57] *Curneen v Sweeney* (1969) 103 I.L.T.R. 29.

privileged and the judge refused to admit evidence to show the defendant's motives in publishing the words.[58] Similarly, an appeal was allowed in a case where the judge let in for the defence evidence outside the particulars delivered in mitigation of damages but refused to allow the plaintiff to adduce evidence in rebuttal.[59] Also, in a case where the plaintiff sought to go beyond the presumption of falsity and to give a better account of himself than that to which the presumption entitled him, it was held to be wrong for the trial judge to refuse the defendant an opportunity to cross-examine the plaintiff on the point.[60] Further, the failure by a trial judge to rule before the retirement of the jury as to whether the plaintiff could give evidence in rebuttal of a plea of justification, has been held to be a good ground of appeal.[61] An appeal was not allowed where the verdict of the jury would in all probability have been the same had the rules of evidence been correctly observed or an alternative means of adducing the evidence pursued.[62]

Miscellaneous considerations. It should be borne in mind that the wrongful admission of evidence may give rise to an additional or alternative ground of appeal concerning the directions of the judge in relation to such evidence.[63]   **36.9**

Section 3. Wrong Conclusion of Law

Wrongly withdrawing a question from the jury.[64] It is the duty of the judge to rule whether the words are capable of bearing a defamatory meaning,[65] or of referring to the claimant, or whether the words were published on   **36.10**

---

[58] *Miller v Green* (1899) 32 N.S.R. 129.

[59] *Maclaren v Davis* (1890) 6 T.L.R. 372. Cf. *Martin v Manitoba Free Press* (1892) 8 Manitoba R. 51; affirmed (1893) 21 S.C.R. 518 (Canada).

[60] *Williams v Mirror Group Newspapers, Independent*, February 12, 1991. In this case the court held there had been no substantial wrong or miscarriage of justice.

[61] *Beevis v Dawson* [1957] 1 Q.B. 195 CA; *Hobbs v Tinling* [1929] 2 K.B. 1, where it was held that, in a case where, before the conclusion of the cross-examination of the plaintiff, the jury intervened to say that they desired to find for the defendant, the judge should have told them that the intervention was premature, that they must hear the claimant's case to the end and be directed as to the issues they had to try.

[62] *Snowden v Branson*, unreported, July 6, 1999, CA.

[63] *Cornwell v Myskow* [1987] 1 W.L.R. 630:

"It is hardly necessary to say that this evidence went to financial damage, although none was pleaded, to the meaning of the article, to whether the comment, if comment, was fair, to whether it was comment at all, and to malice. ... That this was all both inadmissible and highly prejudicial cannot, in our view, be doubted and one would have expected the judge so to direct the jury in his summing up. He did not do so."

(per Parker L.J. at 637–638).

[64] Note that s.11, Defamation Act 2013 removes the presumption that the trial will be heard by a jury. In the future these passages are likely to be of academic interest only to English practitioners.

[65] A judge should leave the issue of defamatory meaning to the jury if he concludes that the jury could reasonably come to the decision that the words are defamatory. *Turner v Metro-Goldwyn-Mayer* [1950] 1 All E.R. 449 HL at 454:

"If [the judge] comes to the conclusion that a reasonable jury would be justified in finding that [the words] had a libellous tendency, he must leave it to them even though the words might also

an occasion of privilege, or whether there is sufficient evidence for the jury to reach a finding on a particular factual issue. If the judge has wrongly withdrawn an issue from the jury, the court should order a new trial.[66] Thus, where the judge wrongly holds that a jury must find a report fair,[67] or where he wrongly fails to leave to them the question whether an imputation of improper motives is fact or comment,[68] the court will grant a new trial.

36.11 Insufficient evidence. "No evidence" means no evidence that a reasonable man could act upon. If the evidence was such that no reasonable man acting carefully could find for the party upon whom the burden of proof rested, then there was no evidence to go to the jury. If, e.g. no facts in support of an innuendo meaning are proved, the judge must not allow the case to go to the jury; and, if he does so, the Court of Appeal will set aside a verdict for the claimant.[69] Similarly, if the evidence adduced in support of an allegation of malice is equally consistent with either its existence or non-existence, the judge must not allow the case to go to the jury.[70] If he does so, and the jury find a verdict for the claimant, the Court of Appeal will set aside the verdict

---

bear an innocent interpretation, or, to put it from the point of view of an appellate court, the question of libel or no libel should have been left to the jury if it cannot be said that twelve men could not reasonably have come to the conclusion that the words were defamatory."

[66] For this reason, in *Alexander v Arts Council of Wales* [2001] EWCA Civ 514; [2001] 1 W.L.R. 1840, the Court of Appeal reminded judges of the possibility of leaving such questions to the jury notwithstanding their view on matters of law, to avoid the need for expensive retrials. See also *McPhilemy v Times Newspapers Ltd* [2001] EWCA Civ 871; [2001] E.M.L.R. 34:

"Only when it is plain that one verdict alone would be rational and any other perverse should the issue be withdrawn. The risk of a successful appeal and the disproportionate expense of a retrial is otherwise too great."

(per Simon Brown L.J.). Conversely, in *Downtex v Flatley* [2003] EWCA Civ 1282, the Court of Appeal decided that the judge had wrongly *failed* to rule out a defence of qualified privilege. At [38], Potter L.J. expressed concern that:

"it would be an inappropriate exercise in this court to reverse the considered view of a first instance judge in a specialist jurisdiction in that there were insufficient facts before him . . . to justify the giving of summary judgment . . . In such cases, the approach of this court is usually, and rightly, to refuse to become engaged in the detail of a matter in which (as in the case of the exercise of a judicial discretion), the outcome largely depends on a process of evaluation in relation to which opinions may vary from judge to judge."

Nonetheless, in the *Downtex* case itself the Court of Appeal did not let this concern stand in its way, decided that the judge *had* had sufficient facts before him to rule summarily on the viability of the defence of qualified privilege, and so determined it in favour of the first claimant. For an account of why *Downtex* is a problematic case, see para.14.4, above.

Similarly, in *Burstein v Associated Newspapers Ltd* [2007] EWCA Civ 600; [2007] 4 All E.R. 319, the Court of Appeal held that Eady J. had been wrong to allow a libel claim to go to the jury on the ground that the pleaded defence of fair comment might not succeed, and instead should have entered judgment summarily for the defendant, which it proceeded to do itself.

[67] *Leslie v Mirror Newspapers* (1971) 45 A.L.J.R. 700 HC.

[68] *O'Shaughnessy v Mirror Newspapers* (1970) 125 C.L.R. 166 HC.

[69] *Capital and Counties Bank v Henty* (1882) 7 A.C. 741; *Nevill v Fine Arts* [1897] A.C. 68; *Frost v London Stock Bank* (1906) 22 T.L.R. 760 CA.

[70] See *Alexander v Arts Council of Wales* [2001] EWCA Civ 514; [2001] 1 W.L.R. 1840: a judge has a duty to withdraw a question from the jury if the evidence, taken at its highest, is such that a jury properly directed could not properly reach a necessary factual conclusion. In this context, see also Buxton L.J.'s approval at [26] in *Fox v Wokingham DC* [2003] EWCA Civ 499 of Simon Brown L.J.'s dictum to this effect in *Spencer v Sillitoe* [2002] EWCA Civ 1579; [2003]

and (assuming the defendant has a defence which the claimant bore the burden of rebutting by establishing malice) order judgment to be entered for the defendant.[71] In assessing whether there was sufficient evidence to go to the jury, the duty of the appellate court is to approach the matter realistically and to consider the entirety of the evidence, not just the evidential position as it stood, e.g. when a submission of no case to answer was made.[72] The fact that the trial judge and the judges on appeal are dissatisfied with the verdict is not enough to justify the court in setting aside and entering judgment for the defendant if there was evidence fit to be considered by the jury.[73]

Section 4. Misdirection[74]

Misdirection as to defamatory meaning. Where the words are capable		**36.12**
of a defamatory meaning, the judge must always leave it to the jury to decide whether they are or are not a libel, except in a wholly extraordinary case where the fact is already admitted.[75] The proper course is for the judge to instruct the jury as to what amounts to a libel in point of law, and then leave it to them, as persons of ordinary intelligence, to say whether the words fall within that definition or not.[76] The judge is not bound to, but he may, express to the jury his own view of the meaning of the words, provided that he makes

---

E.M.L.R. 10 at [32]. It appears that in exceptional cases this duty may legitimately be subordinated to other considerations, e.g. where a judicial decision runs the risk of being represented as a judicial prevention of a jury response: *McPhilemy v Times Newspapers Ltd* [2001] EWCA Civ 871; [2001] E.M.L.R. 34.

[71] *Turner v Bowley* (1896) 12 T.L.R. 402 CA; *Dobson v Donkin* [1975] B.L.T 253.

[72] *Payne v Harrison* [1961] 2 Q.B. 403:

" . . . there is authority for the proposition that the defendant has no right until all the evidence is concluded to have a ruling on a submission that there is no case to answer. . . . Even assuming that the judge did rule incorrectly, the defendant was thereby left in a position in which at least the judge had every right to place him, namely, he was compelled to elect. Either he could call no evidence and stand on his submission before the judge, and if necessary before this court, or he could call evidence. He took the latter course. He cannot now, when it has proved disadvantageous, revert to the former choice. Events have moved on since he made his choice. Truth has superseded hypothesis."

(per Holroyd Pearce L.J. at 413–414).

[73] Per Collins M.R. in *Hope v Leng* (1907) 23 T.L.R. 243 at 244. See also *Riches v News Group Newspapers Ltd* [1986] 1 Q.B. 256 per Stephenson L.J. at 270: "I share the judge's belief, expressed to the jury in leaving the issue of exemplary damages to them, that as much should be left to a jury as possible in these cases and they should not be turned into a lawyer's chess table."; and *Grobbelaar v News Group Newspapers Ltd* [2002] UKHL 40; [2002] 1 W.L.R. 3024 HL, generally.

[74] See also Ch.35, above concerning the trial judge's summing up.

[75] *Maclaren v Davis* (1890) 6 T.L.R. 372.

[76] *Parmiter v Coupland* (1840) 6 M. & W. 105; *Grant v Yates* (1886) 2 T.L.R. 368; *Youssoupoff v Metro-Goldwyn-Mayer* (1934) 50 T.L.R. 581 at 584. It would usually be a misdirection for which the claimant could ask for a new trial if the judge were to direct the jury that defamatory words were, in the old formula, words "calculated to expose the plaintiff to hatred, ridicule or contempt": *Tournier v National Provincial Bank* [1924] 1 K.B. 461; *Pratten v Labour Daily* [1926] V.L.R. 115 FC.

it quite clear that the ultimate decision rests with them.[77] In an ordinary case it will be a good ground of appeal if the judge goes further than this.[78] If he directs the jury as a matter of law that the words are libellous, or directs them as to the meaning of the words in such a way that there must be a verdict for the claimant, he is determining a question which is not within his province to determine, and the court will grant a new trial on the ground of misdirection, unless a verdict contrary to the judge's direction would have been perverse.[79] Conversely, a new trial will be ordered if the judge has left to the jury, as a possible meaning of the words complained of, a meaning of which they are not capable.[80] When the action is tried by a judge alone, his finding of fact as to the meaning of words may be reversed on appeal.[81]

---

[77] See per Parke B. in *Parmiter v Coupland* (1840) 6 M. & W. 105 at 108; per Lord Denman C.J. and Patteson J. in *Baylis v Lawrence* (1840) 11 A. & E. 920 at 925 and at 926; *Holroyd v Parkes* (1856) 10 N.S.W.L.R. 166n; *Knott v Telegram Printing* (1916) 27 Manitoba R. 336; affirmed [1917] 3 W.W.R. 335; *Thompson v Truth* (1931) 31 N.S.W.S.R. 292 CA; affirmed (1934) 34 N.S.W.S.R. 21 PC.

[78] "If he were to take it upon himself to say that it was a libel he would be wrong in so doing": per Alderson B. in *Parmiter v Coupland* (1840) 6 M. & W. 105 at 109; "A judge is not entitled to say to the jury; 'I direct you that the words are defamatory and your duty is to assess damages'": per Sankey L.J. in *Broome v Agar* (1928) 138 L.T. 698 at 702; *Dakhyll v Labouchere* [1908] 2 K.B. 325n; 77 L.J.K.B. 728. The judgments of the Court of Appeal are reported in *The Times*, July 29, 1904, and in House of Lords Printed Cases (1907) at 592–609. The judge in summing up directed the jury that the word "quack" meant "a pretender to skill which the pretender does not possess". As Collins M.R. pointed out:
> "the direction was calculated to suggest to the jury that if a man had an adequate qualification he cannot be a quack. It is perfectly conceivable that a man of the very highest attainment can bring himself under the imputation of being a quack if he carries on his profession by quack methods and lends himself to a class of practice which might fairly be described as the practice of a quack";

Rhodenizer v Rhodenizer (1919) 50 D.L.R. 344; *Barrett v Independent Newspapers* [1986] I.L.R.M. 601:
> "Because the community standard represented by the jury may differ radically from the individual standard of the judge in determining what is defamatory, it would be a usurpation of the jury's function in the matter if the judge were to take upon himself to rule conclusively that the words were defamatory" (per Henchy J. at 607).

See also the judgment of Otton L.J. in *Safeway Stores Plc v Tate* [2001] 2 W.L.R. 1377 at 1385 et seq.

[79] "The written or printed words may be so plainly and necessarily defamatory that the judge should instruct the jury that they are calculated to bring the plaintiff into hatred or contempt and should forthwith proceed to direct their attention to the question of damages. Where a judge does so direct a jury if the jury should find a verdict contrary to his direction it may be deemed perverse and may be set aside and a new trial ordered": per Lord Phillimore in *Lockhart v Harrison* (1928) 139 L.T. 521 at 524.

[80] *Lewis v Daily Telegraph* [1964] A.C. 234.

[81] Subject, of course, to the strictures described in para.36.24, below. See per Salmon L.J. in *Slim v Daily Telegraph* [1968] 2 Q.B. 157 CA at 186–187 and *Curistan v Times Newspapers Ltd* [2008] EWCA Civ 432; [2008] 3 All E.R. 923. In *British Chiropractic Association v Singh* [2010] EWCA Civ 350; [2011] 1 W.L.R. 133, the Court of Appeal overturned Eady J.'s conclusions on meaning and as to whether the words were fact or comment at a trial of preliminary issues. On the question of fact or comment, Hodgson JA sitting in the Supreme Court of New South Wales in *Griffith v Australian Broadcasting Corporation* [2010] NSWCA 257 said at [53]–[55]:
> "There are statements in the authorities to the effect that, although the distinction between a statement of fact and a comment is difficult to draw, a decision has to be made as to whether

Misdirection as to the intention of the defendant and reference to   **36.13**
the claimant. The court will grant a new trial if the judge directs the jury
that the issue of libel or no libel depends on what the defendant meant and
intended by the words.[82] The test is not what the defendant meant by the
words, but what the reasonable reader would have understood to be their
meaning.[83] Similarly, the court will grant a new trial if the judge, on the issue
of identity, were to direct the jury that the question depended on whether the
defendant meant to refer to the claimant.[84]

Misdirection as to privilege and honest comment. Where the judge   **36.14**
misdirected the jury that the existence of privilege was contingent upon
whether, in their opinion, the defendant honestly believed his words to be true
and that the burden of proof to that effect was on him, a new trial was
granted.[85] Where the judge directed the jury that the defendant would be
within the privilege of the occasion "if as a reasonable man he had a right to
think that the charge was true", a new trial was granted. The question was not

---

an imputation is one or the other. For example, in *John Fairfax Publications v O'Shane* [2005]
NSWCA 164; (2005) Aust Torts Rep 81–789 at [27], Giles JA said this:
> [27] There can not be a clear line between comment and statement of fact. Many
> defamatory words have elements of fact, conclusion from facts and expression of opinion.
> A characterisation must nonetheless be made, and the context and circumstances of the use
> of the words will be important. In my opinion, where a primary judge has reached a
> conclusion as to the standard of a work, the appeal court should only attempt to reach its own
> conclusion if it is satisfied that the primary judge's conclusion is vitiated by error."

In *Cruddas v Calvert* [2013] EWCA Civ 748 the Court of Appeal overturned in part Tugendhat
J.'s conclusions on meaning at a trial of preliminary issues. Longmore L.J. said at [18]–[19]:
> "[Counsel for the Claimant] relied heavily on a supposed principle that the meaning of words
> was a jury question (and thus a question of fact) and that the judge was the best person qualified
> to reach the right conclusion which should not be "second-guessed" by this court. . . . There
> is, of course, considerable force in this argument. On the other hand imputations of criminal
> conduct are extremely serious and, if an appellate court thinks that an article just does not bear
> that imputation, it should say so."

[82] *Donoghue v Hayes* (1831) Hayes (Ir.Exch.) R. 265; *O'Brien v Salisbury* (1889) 54 J.P.215;
Johnston v Ewan (1893) 24 O.R. 116.

[83] *Haire v Wilson* (1829) 9 B. & C. 643; *Clement v Fisher* (1830) 10 B. & C. 472; *Capital and
Counties Bank v Henty* (1882) 7 A.C. 741, per Lord Selborne L.C. at 745; per Lord Blackburn
at 772; and per Lord Bramwell at 790; *Hulton v Jones* [1910] A.C. 20 at 24, per Lord Loreburn
L.C.

[84] *Godhard v Inglis* (1905) 2 C.L.R. 78.

[85] *Jenoure v Delmege* [1891] A.C. 73; *Clark v Molyneux* (1877) 3 Q.B.D. 237, where the judge
used language which must have misled the jury into believing that the burden of proof lay on the
defendant to show that he was not actuated by malice rather than on the plaintiff to show that he
was: per Brett L.J. at 247, and per Cotton L.J. at 251; *Siopolosz v Taylor* [1944] 2 D.L.R. 92;
Netupsky v Craig (1972) 28 D.L.R. (3d) 742, SC:
> "failure to tell the jury that when words are spoken or written on an occasion of qualified
> privilege the *bona fides* of the defendant and his honesty of belief in the truth of his statements
> is presumed and the burden then lies on the plaintiff to rebut that presumption constitutes
> serious non-direction amounting to misdirection . . . "

(per Ritchie J., quoting Schroeder J.A., at 746). A new trial was also ordered in a fair comment
case where the judge misdirected the jury that a distinction could be drawn between acceptable
and unacceptable motives, thereby supplanting genuineness of belief as the determining factor, in
deciding whether the defendant was actuated by malice: *Tse Wai Chun v Cheng* [2001] E.M.L.R.
31 Court of Final Appeal of Hong Kong.

whether an ordinary reasonable man would have believed the charge, but whether the defendant did in fact believe it, regardless of his degree of intelligence or credulity; the only thing to be considered was the state of the defendant's mind.[86] A retrial was ordered where the trial judge failed to explain to the jury that they should be slow to infer an improper motive in relation to qualified privilege and failed to make it clear that an allegation of actual knowledge was no longer being pursued and failed to specify which evidence was relevant to a finding of malice.[87] Where a judge in effect directed the jury that if comment tended to charge the plaintiff with improper conduct it could not be fair comment, it was held by the Court of Appeal that the question of fair comment had not been properly left to the jury as a separate issue, and that there must be a new trial on the ground of misdirection.[88]

36.15 Misdirection as to compensatory damages. It is the duty of the trial judge to direct the jury as to any rule of law by which they ought to be governed in their assessment of damages.[89] If he does not do so the court may grant a new trial, even though the damages assessed are not excessive,[90]

---

[86] *Morton v Dean* [1921] 2 W.W.R. 847 (Canada); *Collins v Cooper* (1902) 19 T.L.R. 118; *Clark v Molyneux* (1877) 3 Q.B.D. 237 at 244, per Bramwell L.J., and per Brett L.J. at 248; *Horrocks v Lowe* [1975] A.C. 135 HL, where the judge was held to have applied a wrong test.

[87] *Halpin v Oxford Brookes University*, [1996] C.L.Y. 5658, (November 30, 1995) CA, Neill L.J. A retrial was also ordered where, inter alia, the judge failed to direct the jury that certain evidence was relevant only to malice and not to the issue of justification: *Reynolds v Times Newspapers Ltd* [2001] 2 A.C. 127 CA.

[88] *Hunt v Star* [1908] 2 K.B. 309 CA. This case is considered and explained in *Kemsley v Foot* [1952] A.C. 345 at 359–360.

[89] *Knight v Egerton* (1852) 7 Exch. 407; *English and Scottish Co-operative Society v Odhams Press Ltd* [1940] 1 K.B. 440 CA; *Rookes v Barnard* [1964] A.C. 1129; *Miles v Commercial Banking* (1904) 1 C.L.R. 470; *Holmes v Jones* (1907) 4 C.L.R. 1692 at 1696; *Ling v Thompson* [1935] Q.R. 37 FC. Cf. *Holloway v Truth (NZ) Ltd* [1959] N.Z.L.R. 1121; *Riddick v Thames Board Mills* [1977] Q.B. 881 CA: failing to give direction on what was irrelevant; *Andrews v John Fairfax* [1980] 2 N.S.W.L.R. 225 at 234. While the Court of Appeal in *Purnell v Business F1 Magazine Ltd* [2007] EWCA Civ 744; [2008] 1 W.L.R. 1 (as to which decision, see para.9.2, above) accepted that a prior reasoned judgment, rejecting a justification defence, is capable of providing some vindication of a claimant's reputation (at [27]), it rejected the contention that Gray J. had erred "in not directing the jury in terms to consider whether [the prior] judgment was sufficient to constitute all the vindication to which the respondent was entitled" (at [34]). To like effect, see *Coates v Harbour Radio Pty Ltd* [2008] N.S.W.S.C. 292, in which Adams J. at [200] observed:

"The damages to which the plaintiff is entitled is such sum as will place him in the same position as he would have been in had he not been wronged, to the extent that money can do this. This requires consideration, not only of his injured feelings but the amount that will vindicate his reputation. To some extent, this judgment should do so, but it is unreal to suppose that it will be read, or even come to the attention, of many. A substantial sum [A$360,000; £175,000] must be awarded, in my view, to satisfy the purposes of the law".

The Court of Appeal in *Cairns v Modi* [2012] EWCA Civ 1382; [2013] 1 W.L.R. 1015 rejected the submission that damages should be less following a trial by judge alone than after the verdict of the jury on the basis that the judge would provide a reasoned judgment.

[90] *Edmondson v Allen* (1910) 40 N.B.R. 299. *Reynolds v Times Newspapers Ltd* [2001] 2 A.C. 127 CA:

although, if the Court of Appeal considered it could solve the problem by exercising its powers under CPR r.52.10(3), no doubt it would take that path.[91] In the context of the jury's assessment of compensatory damages, it has been stated that the members of the jury should be given some guidance which will assist them to appreciate the real value of large sums,[92] and be invited to consider the purchasing power of any award they made. They should be required to ensure that their award was proportionate to the damage which the claimant suffered and necessary to provide adequate compensation and to re-establish his reputation.[93] The fact that the jury have been referred by way of comparison to the conventional compensatory scales in personal injury cases as well as to previous libel awards made or approved by the Court of Appeal is perfectly proper and will not in the normal course afford grounds for appeal.[94] The judge may in his directions also have indicated to the jury the level of award which he considered appropriate, although, if he did so, he must also have directed the jury to make up their own mind and not to regard themselves as bound by the submission of counsel or the indications of the judge.[95] Such a direction may take the form of a suggested range or "bracket" of appropriate damages.[96] If other libels were given in evidence to prove

---

"It was incumbent on [the judge] to explain to the jury the purpose of damages in a libel action, and to tell them of matters which they might properly take into account when seeking to assess an appropriate award."

[91] As to these powers, see para.36.5, above. See *Campbell v News Group Newspapers Ltd* [2002] EWCA Civ 1143; [2002] E.M.L.R. 43.

[92] *Sutcliffe v Pressdram* [1991] 1 Q.B. 154.

[93] *Rantzen v Mirror Group Newspapers* [1994] Q.B. 670. On guidance to the jury generally, see paras 9.5–9.12, above.

[94] *John v MGN Ltd* [1997] Q.B. 586 CA, but see *Gur v Avrupa Newspaper Ltd* [2008] EWCA Civ 594; 2009] E.M.L.R. 4, in which Dyson L.J. stated that a detailed comparison with personal injury awards was to be avoided, albeit that regard could be had to them "in a general way" as a check for reasonableness; *Carson v John Fairfax* (1993) 178 C.L.R. 44:

"... we see no significant danger in permitting trial judges to provide to the jury an indication of the ordinary level of the general damages component of personal injury awards for comparative purposes, nor in counsel being permitted to make a similar reference"

(per Mason C.J. at 61); *Ali v Nationwide News Pty Ltd* [2008] NSWCA 183, per Basten J.A. at [226]. The practice approved in England and Wales of taking guidance from personal injury awards is, nevertheless, a matter of policy, not a requirement of law. The view of courts in other common law jurisdictions that no rational assistance could be obtained from them has been found by the Privy Council to be entirely legitimate: see *The Gleaner Co. Ltd v Abrahams* [2003] UKPC 55; [2004] 1 A.C. 628 an appeal from Court of Appeal of Jamaica at [62], and the similar views expressed by appellate courts in New Zealand (*Television New Zealand Ltd v Quinn* [1996] 3 N.Z.L.R. 24 at 47) and Ireland (*Proinsias de Rossa v Independent Newspapers Plc* [1999] 4 I.R. 432) cited in the *Gleaner* case at [61].

[95] *John v MGN Ltd*, above, at 616.

[96] *John v MGN Ltd*, above, at 615–616. In *Kiam v MGN Ltd* [2002] EWCA Civ 43; [2003] Q.B. 281 at [56], Simon Brown L.J. observed that if a judge is going to suggest a bracket of damages to the jury, it would be preferable for the bracket to be formally discussed before it was fixed, with each side being given an opportunity to argue the matter after having exchanged authorities and brief skeleton arguments indicating how they proposed to argue the matter. Furthermore:

"If, as in the present case, either side suggests that there is a close comparable in point, consideration should be given to handing the jury an agreed note identifying the particular points which each side wishes to emphasise. Otherwise, counsel should not generally refer to

malice, the judge should have directed the jury not to give any damages in respect of them[97]; but an omission to give such direction is not necessarily a ground for a new trial.[98]

Where the defamatory effect of a word depends on a slang meaning which may be known to only a few readers of the publication in question, the jury should have been reminded by the judge that this fact is relevant to the amount of damages to be awarded in compensation.[99] Likewise, it is relevant to the assessment of damages that a claimant is not named in a newspaper and would only be identified by a few readers.[100] Where the plaintiff relied on alleged misconduct on the part of the defendant as aggravating damages, but where there was no claim for exemplary damages, the judge should have told the jury that, however great their indignation, they were not allowed to take account of that misconduct so as to include an exemplary element in their award.[101] Similarly, where a defence of justification to the whole libel has been set up, and was clearly proved as to a separate part or parts, it is the duty of the judge to direct the jury not to give damages in respect of such part or parts, and, if he omits to do so, a new trial will be ordered.[102] Where the action is against several defendants in respect of a joint libel, the judge should not have directed the jury to assess the damages separately and enter separate judgments in accordance with their verdict, even where the defendants have put in separate defences.[103]

---

comparables and, if they do, the judge should be alert to explain to the jury how these are being properly taken into account in his own bracket."
These suggestions were approved by Lord Hoffmann as "eminently practical" in *The Gleaner Co. Ltd v Abrahams* [2003] UKPC 55; [2004] 1 A.C. 628 at [48].

[97] *Pearson v Lemaltre* (1843) 5 M. & Gr. 700. Similarly, where the claimant relies for aggravated damages on other articles published by the defendant, the trial judge should caution the jury against the danger of treating such articles as a separate cause of action and awarding damages in respect of them: *Williams v Mirror Group Newspapers*, *Independent*, February 12, 1991. Failure to do so may not, however, occasion a substantial wrong or miscarriage of justice.

[98] *Darby v Ouseley* (1856) 1 H. & N. 1; *Anderson v Calvert* (1908) 24 1.L.R. 399 CA.

[99] *Winyard v Tatler Publishing*, *Independent*, August 16, 1991.

[100] *Cairns v Modi; KC v MGN Ltd* [2012] EWCA Civ 1382; [2013] 1 W.L.R. 1015.

[101] *Sutcliffe v Pressdram* [1991] 1 Q.B. 153 at 187. In the context of claims in respect of unlawful conduct by the police, it has been held that a jury should be told that, if they considered the case was one for the award of damages other than basic damages, then they should usually make a separate award for each category. The Court of Appeal stated that although this was contrary to the practice to date, it would result in greater transparency as to the make-up of the award: see *Thompson v Comr of the Police of the Metropolis* [1998] Q.B. 498 CA. But see Lord Hoffmann's speech in *The Gleaner Co. Ltd v Abrahams*, above, in which he observed at [41] that:
"Ever since the distinction between compensatory and exemplary damages was formulated by Lord Devlin in *Rookes v Barnard* [1964] A.C. 1129 it has been recognised that compensatory damages may also have a punitive, deterrent or exemplary function."

[102] *Wilson v Mutual Stores* (1889) 25 V.L.R. 262; *Anderson v Calvert* (1908) 24 T.L.R. 399.

[103] *Dawson v M'Clelland* [1899] 2 Ir.R. 486; *Greenlands v Wilmshurst* [1913] 3 K.B. 507 CA.

Misdirection as to exemplary damages. Where the claimant claims   **36.16**
exemplary damages, the Court of Appeal may intervene if the judge did not
direct the jury that before such damages could be awarded they must be
satisfied that the publisher had no genuine belief in the truth of what was
published and that he acted in the hope or expectation of material gain.[104] He
should also direct them as to the need to ensure that the defendant would not
be sufficiently punished by the total amount of compensation awarded and that
the total award was reasonable[105] and no more than the minimum sum
necessary to meet the public purpose underlying such damages.[106] He should
also give the jury guidance as to the proper distribution of exemplary damages
if there is more than one claimant.[107]

Miscellaneous misdirections. Any important matter of law must be the   **36.17**
subject of a direction by the judge.[108] The judge may express his personal
view of the facts to the jury, but should warn the jury that the decision is for
them.[109] It is not generally fatal if the judge has failed to direct the jury that
the more serious the allegation made, the higher the standard of proof, save in
exceptional cases.[110] If the jury raised a question as to costs, the judge should

---

[104] *John v MGN Ltd*, above. This remains the orthodox view of the law, but see *Kuddus v Chief Constable of Leicestershire Constabulary* [2001] UKHL 29; [2002] 2 A.C. 122 and *A v Bottrill* [2002] UKPC 44; [2003] 1 A.C. 449, the effect of which, arguably, is that a defamation claimant no longer needs to establish a mercenary calculation on the part of the defendant as a precondition for claiming exemplary damages.

[105] *Riches v News Group Newspapers* [1986] Q.B. 256 at 278, 287.

[106] *John v MGN Ltd* [1997] Q.B. 586.

[107] *Riches v News Group Newspapers* [1986] Q.B. 256 at 277–278.

[108] *Riches v News Group Newspapers*, above, at 280. See *Ratiu v Conway* [2005] EWCA Civ 1302; [2006] 1 All E.R. 571, for an example of a case in which the Court of Appeal allowed an appeal on the basis that the trial judge had made misdirections of law and fact. Auld L.J. at [185] expressed sympathy with the judge and jury on account of:
"the enormous burdens imposed on both of them in this case, given the unhappy divide of responsibility between them on supposedly self-contained issues of law and fact. In fact, the critical issues, particularly as to fiduciary relationship and matters of confidence and the ingredients of malice as distinct from justification were in truth more matters of mixed law and fact. It is, in my view, no advertisement for our system of jury trial in civil cases—where it applies—for such complex issues to be tried in this way. A Martian, on learning of it, would be amazed, as would the ordinary person in the street".

[109] *Lefolii v Gouzenko* [1969] S.C.R. 3 at 7, 11.

[110] *Lawrence v Chester Chronicle, The Times*, February 8, 1986. It was held that in most cases it was a matter for the jury's common sense. With regard to exemplary damages, it has been held that the jury should be told that as the charge is grave, so should the proof be clear: *John v MGN Ltd* [1997] Q.B. 586 at 619. But now see the observations of the House of Lords in *In re B (Children) (Care Proceedings: Standard of Proof) (CAFCASS intervening)* [2009] 1 A.C. 11. Lady Hale, who delivered the leading speech and considered the standard of proof in the care context, said at [70] that
"the standard of proof in finding the facts necessary to establish the threshold under section 31(2) or the welfare considerations in section 1 of the 1989 Act is the simple balance of probabilities, neither more nor less. Neither the seriousness of the allegation nor the seriousness of the consequences should make any difference to the standard of proof to be applied in determining the facts. The inherent probabilities are simply something to be taken into account, where relevant, in deciding where the truth lies".
Lord Hoffmann, agreeing with Lady Hale, rejected the notion of a "heightened" civil standard of

have directed them that they were not to be concerned with costs at all, although a failure to do so clearly may not necessarily occasion a miscarriage of justice.[111] A claimant is entitled to have his factual case on an issue squarely put before the jury by the judge.[112]

36.18 Onus of proof. Where a new trial is applied for on the ground of misdirection, traditionally the onus of showing that the alleged misdirection did not cause a substantial miscarriage of justice lies on the respondent, and he must show it by authentic evidence.[113] In determining whether a substantial wrong or miscarriage of justice has been occasioned by reason of the judge's misdirection, the court will not speculate what might have been the result if the judge had rightly directed the jury.[114] In determining whether there is such misdirection as to warrant an order for a new trial, the summing-up will be considered as a whole.[115] Too much weight will not be attached to isolated or detached expressions, nor will a single sentence be separated from its context, unless it dominates the reasoning on which that part of the summing-up is based.[116]

The question to be considered is not whether every expression in the summing-up is perfectly accurate, but whether there is reason to believe that a verdict which is not warranted by the evidence may have been caused or induced by an erroneous enunciation of the law by the judge.[117] Where, if there was a deficiency in the direction of the trial judge, it could only enure to the benefit of the appellant, the court will not grant a new trial.[118] Similarly, a new trial will not be granted if the court is of the opinion that the same

---

proof. There was only one civil standard of proof, and that was proof that the fact in issue more probably occurred than not.

[111] *Pamplin v Express Newspapers* [1988] 1 W.L.R. 116.

[112] *Reynolds v Times Newspapers Ltd* [2001] 2 A.C. 127 CA.

[113] *White v Barnes* [1914] W.N. 74; *Lionel Barber v Deutsche Bank* [1919] A.C. 304 at 323.

[114] Per Lord Halsbury L.C. in *Bray v Ford* [1896] A.C. 44 at 48; per Lord Herschell ibid. at 53; *Braddock v Bevins* [1948] 1 K.B. 580 CA at 600.

[115] See, e.g. *Reynolds v Times Newspapers Ltd* [2001] 2 A.C. 127 CA.

[116] *Clark v Molyneux* (1877) 3 Q.B.D. 237 at 243, per Bramwell L.J.; *Turner v Metro-Goldwyn-Mayer* [1950] 1 All E.R. 449 HL at 462; *Truth (NZ) Ltd v Holloway* [1960] 1 W.L.R. 997 PC at 1003; *Knott v Telegram Printing* (1916) 27 Manitoba R. 336; *Wade & Wells v Laing* (1957) 11 D.L.R. (2d) 276:
> "It seems to me it was unnecessary for the trial Judge in instructing the jury to review specifically every factor and every element, every *indicia* that may have been stressed by counsel from which the jury was asked by counsel to draw an inference of malice ... "
(at 281); *Rantzen v Mirror Group Newspapers* [1994] Q.B. 670 at 684:
> "In our judgment there was no misdirection of any significance in this case. In any event, even if one assumes that there may be some merit in some of the individual complaints, we are quite satisfied that there is no possibility that any misdirections led to the risk of injustice of any 'substantial wrong or miscarriage'." (per Neill L.J.).

[117] *Wells v Lindop* (1888) 15 O.A.R. 695; *Riches v News Group Newspapers* [1986] 1 Q.B. 256:
" ... more than niceties of analysis are required and the defendants have to show misdirections substantial enough to invalidate a jury's verdict" (per Stephenson L.J. at 272–273).

[118] *Doyle v Sparrow* (1980) 27 O.R. (2d) 206 at 208.

verdict must inevitably have been found if the jury had been rightly directed.[119]

SECTION 5. UNREASONABLE VERDICT

Very strong grounds necessary. Only on very strong grounds will the　**36.19** court in an action for defamation interfere or set aside a verdict or grant a new trial on the ground that the verdict is unreasonable or perverse. An appellate court ought not to find the verdict of a jury on liability to be perverse unless there was no rational explanation for it.[120] An inference of perversity should not be drawn lightly.[121] The jury are the constitutional tribunal for the decision of libel or no libel, and only in an extreme case will their verdict be set aside as unreasonable.[122] If the words complained of are capable of a defamatory

---

[119] *Merivale v Carson* (1887) 20 Q.B.D. 275 at 281, per Lord Esher M.R.; *Simpson v Malcom* (1914) 43 N.B.R. 79, where it was held that the court is not warranted in granting a new trial on the ground of misdirection in a case where, if the verdict had been for the opposite party on a proper direction, it would be set aside.

[120] *Grobbelaar v News Group Newspapers Ltd* [2002] UKHL 40; [2002] 1 W.L.R. 3024 HL, per Lord Millett at [67].

[121] In *Grobbelaar v News Group Newspapers Ltd*, above, Lord Hobhouse castigated the reasoning of the Court of Appeal which had led it to set aside as perverse the jury's verdict of £85,000 damages for the plaintiff and to enter judgment for the defendant. With regard, e.g. to the Court of Appeal's reasoning that because the jury had gone astray on damages then its verdict on liability must have been perverse, Lord Hobhouse had the following to say at [53]:

"This reasoning is remarkable: it reasons that because the jury has gone wrong on verdict No 2, it has gone wrong on verdict No 1—perversely wrong. This is simply a non sequitur. Verdict No 1 is not dependent upon the correctness of Verdict No 2."

Lord Hobhouse then went on, at [57], to address the principle that an appellate court ought not to draw an inference of perversity where other explanations of the jury's verdict were available and to illustrate how the Court of Appeal had gone wrong in that case:

"A further criticism to be made of the Court of Appeal's decision in the present case is that they chose to make a questionable inference in preference to adopting the ordinary and obvious explanation of the jury's second verdict. The ordinary explanation is that the jury went wrong in some way in deciding upon the amount of their award. It is a commonplace that juries, even after an impeccable direction from the judge, may make such a mistake. Why should one not infer that that is what occurred in the present case? I will come to the factors which may have led the jury to overassess the damages. But, first, there are factors which militate against their having delivered a perverse verdict on liability. The jury were properly directed. It should not lightly be assumed that, in failing to be satisfied that a burden of proof had been discharged, a jury had acted perversely. There is no evidence that the jury were behaving irrationally during the trial. The verdicts were unanimous. Their third verdict was that the plaintiff should not recover exemplary (penal) damages. At criminal trials in 1997, the plaintiff was tried on two counts, the first of conspiring corruptly with Lim and others and accepting money to fix or for having fixed matches, the second for accepting a bribe of £2,000 from Vincent to fix or for having fixed matches. At the first criminal trial, the jury was unable to agree on either count. The jury was discharged and a retrial was ordered. At the retrial, the plaintiff was unanimously acquitted on the first count and the jury was again unable to agree on the second count. It has not been suggested on this appeal that the criminal juries were acting perversely . . . The question why one should infer that the civil jury was perverse remains unanswered."

[122] *Odger v Mortimer* (1873) 28 L.T. 472; *Broome v Agar* (1928) 138 L.T. 698 CA; *Lockhart v Harrison* (1928) 139 L.T. 521 HL at 523, per Lord Buckmaster:

"It is of course not true to say that a jury's verdict in these circumstances can never be assailed. A plain and obvious defamation incapable of any innocent explanation, if found by the jury to be non-libellous, would certainly be set aside, but such cases occur so rarely that within the last

meaning and the jury have found in fact that the words do bear that meaning, the court will not set aside the verdict and where, though the words are capable of a defamatory meaning, the jury have found in fact that the words do not bear that meaning, the verdict will not be set aside unless it is unreasonable.[123] Likewise, where the meaning of the words is capable of bearing two distinct stings, and where the defendant has advanced scant evidence to justify one of those stings, a verdict for the claimant should not be stigmatised as perverse.[124] In the absence of any misdirection the appellate

---

century there are only two to which our attention has been drawn in which this power has been exercised".

See also per Lord Phillimore at 524; *Broome v Cosden* (1845) 1 C.B. 728: a new trial ought not to be granted:

"unless the court can see that the jury have done manifestly wrong in not finding the alleged libel to bear the meaning that the plaintiff has thought fit to put upon it by the innuendo":

(per Tindal C.J. at 731); *Gwynne v Wairarapa Times-Age* [1972] N.Z.L.R. 586; *Ryan v Ross* (1916) 22 C.L.R. 1; followed in *Thompson v Truth (No.1)* (1929) 31 N.S.W.S.R. 129; *M'Inerney v Clareman* [1903] 2 Ir.R. 347 at 395, 405:

"A finding of 'libel' or 'no libel' is not necessarily final. It is liable to be set aside like other verdicts if it is a conclusion to which reasonable men could not, or ought not to, have come. This is now the well-settled rule in all causes of action; and if it is but rarely acted on in cases of libel, this . . . is due to the difficulty of applying the principle to a finding that is to a considerable extent a matter of opinion";

Massey v NZ Times (1911) 30 N.Z.L.R. 929:

"All the cases show that, on a verdict for the defendant, in an action for libel, the court will not interfere unless the grounds for interference are overwhelmingly strong"

(per Williams J. at 951). Nevertheless, the task of the appellate court is to seek to interpret the jury's decision and not, because of justifiable dissatisfaction at the outcome, to take upon itself the determination of factual issues which lay within the exclusive province of the jury: *Grobbelaar v News Group Newspapers Ltd*, above, per Lord Bingham at [26]. As regards how the appellate court should go about this task, see Lord Bingham in the same case at [7]:

"How, then, is the jury's verdict to be understood? . . . While speculation about the jury's reasoning and train of thought is impermissible, the drawing of inevitable or proper inferences from the jury's decision is not, and is indeed inherent in the process of review."

[123] Per curiam in *Australian Newspaper v Bennett* [1894] A.C. 284 at 287; *Beamish v Dairy Supply* (1897)13 T.L.R. 484 CA; *Walkinshaw v Drew* [1936] 4 D.L.R. 685; *Cairns v John Fairfax & Sons* [1983] 2 N.S.W.L.R. 708:

"This court must determine whether it was open to the jury in the present proceedings to hold that the statement that the plaintiffs were involved in the relevant sexual association was not defamatory of them. . . . There is, I think, a distinction to be drawn between the cases . . . where the issue is the meaning of words and cases, such as the present, which depend upon community standards. . . . There is, I think, more difficulty in the court holding that a jury could not form a particular view as to general community standards than in deciding whether a word is capable of a non-defamatory meaning"

(per Mahoney J.A. at 720); *Kelly v Daily Telegraph* (1897) 18 N.S.W.L.R. 358: "If the words used are by any possible construction which can be put upon them susceptible of an innocent meaning then the verdict of the jury for the defendant is conclusive", (at 361); *Grant v Yates* (1886) 2 T.L.R. 368.

[124] See *Grobbelaar v News Group Newspapers Ltd*, above, per Lord Hobhouse at [49]–[51]:

"It is said that the jury misunderstood the gravamen of the accusation . . . There are two straight forward and obvious answers to this line of argument. The first is that it was a matter for the jury and the Court of Appeal should have accepted the jury's verdict on this point unless they were prepared to decide that there was no issue to go to the jury on this point. It was correctly decided that there was an issue to go to the jury and that the agreed meaning and the publication were capable of having the significance contended for by the plaintiff. The second is that, for the purposes of the law of defamation, what is relevant is the effect of the publication upon the

court will only interfere with a finding of the jury if it was one which a jury, viewing the whole of the evidence reasonably, could not properly find.[125] Where the jury finds a general verdict, it is not permissible to ask their grounds and then found an appeal on the submission that there was no evidence in support of the ground mentioned in the subsequent response.[126]

Where the verdict would be set aside. Where the words are obviously incapable of any but a defamatory meaning, and there is no question but that they were published of the claimant, and the jury have nevertheless found a verdict for the defendant, the court will set aside the verdict as perverse and unreasonable and order a new trial,[127] but the position must be clear and

36.20

---

perceptions of the ordinary reader of the 'Sun' newspaper, not upon those of a judge of the Court of Appeal, and how it would alter such a reader's view of the plaintiff. Thus, the Court of Appeal not only confused the respective roles of judge and jury but also confused what might be relevant in other legal contexts with what is relevant in relation to defamatory publications . . . The Lord Justice [Simon Brown L.J.] was seriously in error when he summed up his own view of the case, supplanting the principled approach to the issues and usurping the function of the jury. The judgment of the Court of Appeal set aside the first verdict of the jury as perverse . . . Thus, they decided that it was perverse of the jury to remain unpersuaded that the agreed meaning of the defamatory material had been proved to be substantially true. This was a remarkable decision since it was always open to the jury to remain unpersuaded upon an issue which has been properly left to them by the trial judge and of which the burden of proof rested upon the party *against* whom they are finding, as was the case here."

[125] *Australian Newspaper v Bennett* [1894] A.C. 284 at 287:
"Their Lordships have not, any more than the court below had, to determine in the present case what is the conclusion at which they would have arrived, or what is the verdict they would have found. The only point to be determined is, whether the verdict found by the jury, for whose consideration essentially it was, was such as no jury could have found as reasonable men".
O'Brien v Salisbury (1889) 6 T.L.R. 137:
"The jury are the appointed tribunal for the decision of the question libel or no libel, and the Court ought not to invade their province unless it can plainly be seen that the verdict is *perverse* and *so unreasonable* as to lead to the conclusion that the jury have not honestly taken the matters into their consideration."
See *M'Inerney v Clareman* [1903] 2 Ir.R. 347 CA, where it was laid down that no higher or more rigorous test is to be applied in cases of libel than in other actions of tort. See also *Grobbelaar v News Group Newspapers Ltd* [2002] UKHL 40; [2002] 1 W.L.R. 3024 HL:
"If the jury's finding in favour of the appellant could not be explained on any ground not indicative of perversity, the Court of Appeal would have been not only entitled but bound to quash it."
(per Lord Bingham at [26]) and Lord Millett in the same case at [67]: "an appellate court ought not to find the verdict of a jury on liability to be perverse unless there is no rational explanation for it."
[126] *Barnes v Hill* [1967] 1 Q.B. 579 CA: "All the discussion after the verdict was surplusage and ought to be ignored", (at 588). See also *Evans v Davies* [1991] 2 Qd. R. 498:
"It is the jurors' formal answers on which they have reached agreement and which they unanimously agree shall be brought in as their answers which, on being announced, are paramount. . . . They are not later to be cajoled into making a retraction or permitted to be questioned by the parties in an attempt to introduce some variation, disharmony or disagreement into the previous picture of unanimity"
(per Macrossan C.J. at 501).
[127] *Levi v Milne* (1827) 4 Bing. 195; *Hakewell v Ingram* (1854) 2 C.L.R. 1397; *Rocke Tompsitt v Wilson* (1887) 13 V.L.R. 833; *Blashki v Smith* (1891) 17 V.L.R. 634; *Sydney Post v Kendall* (1910) 43 S.C.R. 461 (Canada) (Davies and Duff JJ. dissenting on the ground that it was impossible to say that the words were incapable of an innocent construction); *Lumsden v Spectator* (1913) 29 O.L.R. 293; *Doyle v Mcintosh* (1917) 17 N.S.W.R. 402; *Ryan v Ross* [1915]

beyond argument.[128] Some authorities suggest that the court will not order a new trial where it is clear that if the verdict had been for the claimant it would have been a verdict for a nominal amount only.[129]

36.21 Jury not bound to accept evidence called only by one side. Where the claimant, in order to establish that the words referred to him, had to rely entirely on the opinion of witnesses, the court held that, though no witnesses were called for the defence, the jury was not bound to accept the opinions of the claimant's witnesses; that as soon as the jury had before them the facts on which the opinions were based they were entitled to act upon their own judgment, and that their verdict, unless so unreasonable as to be really perverse, was conclusive.[130]

36.22 Substituting an alternative verdict. Where all the facts are before the court, and the court is satisfied that a verdict in favour of the claimant is clearly unreasonable, the court is not bound to order a new trial, but may, under CPR r.52.10(2)(a), affirm, set aside or vary any order or judgment made

---

Queensland L.R. 56; affirmed (1916) 22 C.L.R. 1 (Isaacs and Gavan Duffy JJ. dissenting on the grounds that the words were not incapable of a non-defamatory construction); *Leech v Leader* (1926) 20 Sask.L.R. 337 CA; *Rofe v Smith* (1927) 27 N.S.W.S.R. 313 PC; *Thompson v Truth (No.1)* (1929) 31 N.S.W.S.R. 129; *Lockhart v Harrison* (1928) 139 L.T. 521 HL at 523–524; *Evans v Davies* [1991] 2 Qd.R. 498:
"The fact that the subject matter of the jury's deliberations in such a case is a matter involving the law of defamation and of fact finding in that area does not involve some special magic. In this as in any other area of fact a jury are capable of arriving at a conclusion which is incontrovertibly wrong and which can be set aside on appeal"
(per Macrossan C.J. at 511); *Hartt v Newspaper Publishing, The Times*, November 9, 1989 (judge sitting without a jury by agreement of the parties); *Barrett v Independent Newspapers* [1986] I.L.R.M. 601:
"It is clear from all the authorities that if a jury enters a verdict holding that words complained of were not defamatory, that verdict can, in exceptional and rare cases, it is stated, be set aside, on appeal, on the grounds that the words were incapable of an innocent interpretation . . . "
(per Finlay C.J. at 603). For the position in New South Wales, see *John Fairfax Publications Pty Ltd v Rivkin* [2003] HCA 50; (2003) 201 A.L.R. 77.

[128] Per Sankey L.J. in *Broome v Agar* (1928) 138 L.T. 698 at 702.

[129] *Wilson v London Free Press* (1918) 42 O.L.R. 12, per Riddell J. citing *Milligan v Jamieson* (1902) 4 O.L.R. 650; *Simonds v Chesley* (1891) 20 S.C.R. (Canada) 174; *Scammel v Clarke* (1894) 23 S.C.R. 307 (Canada); *Alteman v Ferguson* (1919) 47 D.L.R. 618 (Man.); *Dennison v Sanderson* [1946] 4 D.L.R. 314; *Vidal v Temperley* (1899) 20 N.S.W.L.R. 223; *Friend v Smith* (1884) 5 N.S.W.L.R. 59; *Griffiths v Johnston* (1903) 3 N.S.W.S.R. 107; *Sunkissed Bananas v Banana Growers* (1935) 35 N.S.W.S.R. 526, though the point was left open in *Lang v Australian Consolidated* [1970] 2 N.S.W.R. 408 and see also *Pratten v The Labour Daily Ltd* [1926] V.L.R. 115.

[130] *Peat v Greymouth* (1916) 36 N.Z.L.R. 40. A party will be debarred from contending that the jury's verdict was perverse where he has expressly invited the judge to leave the question to the jury, and it is open to the other party to contend in his closing speech that the jury should return an answer in his favour, notwithstanding that he cannot ask the jury to disbelieve any witness whose truthfulness he has not specifically challenged: *McPhilemy v Times Newspapers Ltd* [2001] EWCA Civ 871; [2001] E.M.L.R. 34 CA.

or given by the lower court.[131] This power ought, however, to be exercised with the greatest caution, otherwise it would lead to the practice of judges substituting themselves for juries.[132] If there is a doubt in the matter the case should be left to the decision of another jury.[133]

Perverse verdict for the defendant. Where in an action for libel the **36.23** court is satisfied that the verdict returned for the defendant is perverse, and clearly against the weight of evidence, conventionally the court would direct a new trial.[134] While, it appears, that the Court of Appeal in such circumstances has the power, at least in theory, to enter judgment for the claimant and to assess the damages,[135] it would have to take care before exercising it that it was not trespassing on matters within the exclusive province of the jury.

Verdict by judge alone. Where the case is tried by a judge alone the **36.24** appeal is by way of a review of the decision, unless the court considers that

---

[131] *Skeate v Slaters* [1914] 2 K.B. 429 CA:
"We are entitled, upon the evidence as a whole, to say whether the evidence is such as that twelve reasonable men could properly arrive at the conclusion that the plaintiff was entitled to a verdict. If we are of the opinion that they could not, the Court has, I think full power to enter judgment for the defendants, not because they find facts, for that is the province of the jury, but because they find there are no facts sufficient to support a verdict in favour of the plaintiff", (at 439);
Parker v John Fairfax [1980] A.C.L.R. 558; *Black v Mackenzie* (1917) 37 N.Z.L.R. 235 CA.
The House of Lords in *Jameel v Wall Street Journal Europe SPRL* [2006] UKHL 44; [2007] 1 A.C. 359 substituted its view for that of the judge in holding that the publication at issue attracted *Reynolds* privilege, notwithstanding the reservations about taking this course expressed by Lord Bingham at [36]. In *Flood v Times Newspapers Ltd*, the Court of Appeal ([2010] EWCA Civ 804, [2010] E.M.L.R. 26) had also substituted its own view for that of the judge on the issue of *Reynolds* privilege. The court disagreed with the view taken by a different constitution of the court in *Galloway v Telegraph Group Ltd* [2006] EWCA Civ 17, [2006] E.M.L.R. 11 at [68], namely that whether or not *Reynolds* privilege applied was in effect an exercise of discretion. The court considered that although the issue involved a value judgment or balancing exercise, it raised a question of law to which as a matter of principle there was only one answer: see Lord Neuberger M.R. at [45] to [49] and Moore-Bick L.J. at [107]. In the Supreme Court [2012] UKSC 11; [2012] 2 A.C. 273, Lord Phillips agreed that a decision on *Reynolds* did not involve the exercise of a discretion, but—not having heard argument on the point—declined to lay down any general principle as to the approach to be adopted by an appellate court to an issue of *Reynolds* privilege ([104]–[106]). The same self-denying ordinance was adopted by Lords Mance, Clarke and Dyson ([182], [186], [203]).
[132] *Skeate v Slaters* [1914] 2 K.B. 429 at 437, 443; *Cooke v Wilson* (1916) 85 L.J.K.B. 889 at 896, 897. See 131, above for *Flood v Times Newspapers Ltd* [2010] EWCA Civ 804, [2010] E.M.L.R. 26, in particular at [48].
[133] *Skeate v Slaters* [1914] 2 K.B. 429 at 443.
[134] *Jacobs v Miles (No.2)* (1900) 25 V.L.R. 511 CA: "It is the function of the jury to assess the damages, and the court cannot usurp that function" (per Madden J. at 512); *Toulmin v Millar* (1887) 12 A.C. 746 at 747, per Lord Halsbury; *Skeate v Slaters* [1914] 2 K.B. 429 at 440, per Buckley L.J.
[135] See CPR r.52.10(3)(a) which confers upon the Court of Appeal the power "to make an order for damages" instead of ordering a new trial. Nonetheless, before exercising this power in the circumstances described, the Court of Appeal would also have to be satisfied that a jury would be perverse *not* to find that the words complained of were defamatory, bore a particular meaning, were not susceptible to any pleaded defence, etc.

in the circumstances of an individual appeal it would be in the interests of justice to hold a rehearing.[136] However, the judge has had the benefit of seeing and hearing the witnesses and a litigant has an uphill task in seeking to overturn a finding of fact by the judge[137] or, as in a case involving a defence of *Reynolds* privilege, an evaluative decision of law which (though not one of discretion)[138] is heavily fact dependent and value laden.[139] Where the judge is

---

[136] CPR r.52.11(1).

[137] In cases which have been tried by a judge sitting alone, where the appellant alleges that the judge has made errors of fact, in *Assicurazioni Generali SpA v Arab Insurance Group (BSC) (Practice Note)* [2002] EWCA Civ 1642; [2003] 1 W.L.R. 577, the Court of Appeal gave useful guidance as to the correct approach to such appeals: see at [6]–[23], per Clarke L.J. and at [193]–[197], per Ward L.J. Where the judge's evaluation of the facts is under challenge, such cases may be closely analogous to exercise of discretion cases and the appellate court should approach them in a similar way. See also *Cambridge v Makin* [2012] EWCA Civ 85; [2012] E.M.L.R. 19 at [62] per Tomlinson L.J. For a case in which the House of Lords held that the Court of Appeal had erred in substituting its own assessment of the evidence for that of the trial judge (in relation to an issue of substantiality in a copyright claim), see *Designers Guild Ltd v Russell Williams (Textiles) Ltd* [2000] 1 W.L.R. 2416; cf. *Jameel v Wall Street Journal Europe Sprl* [2006] UKHL 44; [2007] 1 A.C. 359. See also *Flood v Times Newspapers Ltd* [2012] UKSC 11; [2012] 2 A.C. 273 and fn.131, above.

[138] See fn.131, above.

[139] "As I have said, in this appeal the court is concerned to review an evaluative judgment of a very experienced judge. As the Master of the Rolls, Sir Anthony Clarke, said in *Mersey Care NHS Trust v Ackroyd* [2007] EWCA Civ 101; [2008] E.M.L.R. 1, decisions of this kind involve a balancing of different factors and, although it can be said to involve a question of law, it is a question of law which is heavily fact-dependent and value-laden and upon which many factors may be relevant on both sides. The Master of the Rolls likened the exercise in that case to the exercise performed by a judge in balancing the various factors identified by Lord Nicholls in *Reynolds* as being relevant to the issue of *Reynolds* privilege . . . The balance is a matter for the judge. It is not a matter for the appellate court. This court will not interfere with a judge's conclusion after weighing all the circumstances in the balance unless he had erred in principle or reached a conclusion which is plainly wrong":

Radu v Houston [2008] EWCA Civ 921, per May L.J. at [20]. However, the Supreme Court in *Flood v Times Newspapers Ltd* [2012] UKSC 11; [2012] 2 A.C. 273 declined to rule upon the circumstances in which an appellate court should interfere with the assessment of the lower court on an issue such as whether a publication should be protected by *Reynolds* privilege and criticised the Court of Appeal for having done so. See fn.131, above.

In *Fiddes v Channel 4* [2010] EWCA Civ 730; [2010] 1 W.L.R. 2245 the Court of Appeal considered a decision by Tugendhat J., shortly before trial, to dispense with a jury pursuant to section 69(1) of the Senior Courts Act 1981. The Court acknowledged the experience of the judge and his close familiarity with the case at [11] and went on to say at [12], "Nonetheless, this does not mean that this court should rubber stamp his decision. That would be fundamentally inconsistent with the existence of a right to appeal . . . ." In the event, the appeal was dismissed, since there was no error of law: [44]. In *Hayter v Fahie* [2008] EWCA Civ 1336 the Court of Appeal overturned an order granting summary judgment in a libel action where the judge found malice even though he had not heard evidence from the defendant. Sir Anthony May P. said at [24]

"I consider that summary judgment should not have been given where there was, as I have explained, an issue of credibility as to Mr Fahie's state of mind both as to his understanding of the material meaning of what he wrote and as to his belief as to whether the statement was true in that meaning".

He reserved the question of whether a contested issue of malice could properly be determined in summary judgment proceedings, accepting that it might in theory be possible, but not where a real issue turned on the defendant's state of mind and a credibility judgment was required [23].

required to carry out a balancing exercise the appellate court should not interfere unless satisfied that the judge was wrong.[140] Where a procedural decision had been taken by a judge the appellate court was concerned with what was fair in the circumstances identified and evaluated by the judge.[141] An appellate tribunal will not lightly interfere with a judge's finding where the words complained of are capable of the defamatory meaning which they have been found to bear or where the judge has determined the actual meaning of the words complained of or whether the words are fact or comment. However, whilst the court should be slow to differ from any conclusion of fact reached by a trial judge, that principle was less compelling where the judge's conclusion was not based on his assessment of the reliability of witnesses or on the substance of their oral evidence and where the material before the appellate court was exactly the same as had been before the judge.[142] If the appellate tribunal is satisfied that the judge's finding of fact is wrong, it is its duty to reverse him.[143] Not giving adequate reasons for a decision may furnish sufficient grounds for allowing an appeal.[144]

SECTION 6. EXCESSIVE OR INADEQUATE DAMAGES

Province of the jury. The jury is entrusted with the task of assessing   **36.25** damages and the appellate court is slow to interfere with an award on the ground that it is either too great or too small.[145] The mere fact that the verdict

---

[140] *Lait v Evening Standard* [2011] EWCA Civ 859; [2011] 1 W.L.R. 2973 at [63] per Lord Neuberger M.R.

[141] In *Berezovsky v Russian Television and Radio Broadcasting Co.* [2010] EWCA Civ 1345 the defendant, Terluk, made a last-minute application to adjourn a hearing on the basis that legal funding had been available. Eady J. refused the application. The Court of Appeal dismissed the appeal applying *Gillies v Secretary of State for Work and Pensions* [2006] UKHL 2; [2006] 1 W.L.R. 781. Whilst it knew what the judge did not know, that funds had materialised to enable representation on the appeal, the appellate court was concerned with what was fair in the circumstances identified and evaluated by the judge.

[142] *Skuse v Granada Television* [1996] E.M.L.R. 278 at 286; *Cammish v Hughes* [2012] EWCA Civ 1655; [2013] E.M.L.R. 13 at [31].

[143] *Slim v Daily Telegraph* [1968] 2 Q.B. 157 at 186–187. *British Chiropractic Association v Singh* [2010] EWCA Civ 350; [2011] 1 W.L.R. 133 at [13] to [15] and [31], *Modi v Clarke* [2011] EWCA Civ 937; *Cruddas v Calvert* [2013] EWCA Civ 748 where Longmore L.J. said at [18]–[19], [21]:

"[Counsel for the Claimant] relied heavily on a supposed principle that the meaning of words was a jury question (and thus a question of fact) and that the judge was the best person qualified to reach the right conclusion which should not be "second-guessed" by this court. . . . There is, of course, considerable force in this argument. On the other hand imputations of criminal conduct are extremely serious and, if an appellate court thinks that an article just does not bear that imputation, it should say so . . . if one is satisfied that judge's finding is wrong, it is one's duty to reverse him."

[144] *English v Emery Reimbold & Strick Ltd* [2002] EWCA Civ 605; [2002] 1 W.L.R. 2409; *In the matter of S (Children)* [2007] EWCA Civ 694.

[145] *Davis v Shepstone* (1886) 11 A.C. 187 at 191:

"The only question which remains is as to the amount of damages. The assessment of these is peculiarly the province of the jury in an action for libel. The damages are not limited to the amount of pecuniary loss which the plaintiff is able to prove. And their Lordships see no reason

is for a larger sum than the judges of the Court of Appeal would have given is not of itself a sufficient reason for upsetting the award.[146] Even where the Court of Appeal considered that the bracket of damages suggested by the judge had been entirely reasonable and the sum awarded by the jury was in excess of it, it did not condemn the award as unreasonable or excessive since it was not out of all proportion to what could sensibly have been awarded.[147]

---

for saying that the award of damages awarded were excessive or for interfering with the finding of the jury in this respect"
(per Lord Herschell L.C.); *Sutcliffe v Pressdram* [1991] 1 Q.B. 153:
"In all the circumstances, it is not surprising that such a challenge to a jury's assessment of damages can very rarely succeed . . . "
(per Lord Donaldson M.R. at 176); *Ley v Hamilton* (1935) 153 L.T. 384 HL at 386, per Lord Atkin:
"So far as my own experience goes, the duties of juries in assessing damages even in libel cases are performed as reasonably and as efficiently as they have always been. . . . It is precisely because the real damage cannot be ascertained and established that the damages are at large. It is impossible to track the scandal, to know what quarters the poison may reach: it is impossible to weigh at all closely the compensation which will recompense a man or a woman for the insult offered or the pain of a false accusation. No doubt in newspaper libels juries take into account the vast circulations which are justly claimed in present times";
Broome v Cassell [1972] A.C. 1027 HL:
"It may very well be that, on the whole, judges, and the legal profession in general, would be less generous than juries in the award of damages for defamation. But I know of no principle of reason which would entitle judges, whether of appeal or at first instance, to consider that their own sense of the proprieties is more reasonable than that of a jury, or which would entitle them to arrogate to themselves a constitutional status in this matter which Parliament has deliberately withheld from them, for aught we know, on the very ground that juries can be expected to be more generous on such matters than judges"
(per Lord Hailsham L.C. at 1066); *Jones v Hulton* [1909] 2 K.B. 444 at 483. In Scotland there is a historical working rule of thumb that a higher court should not interfere with a jury award of "non-pecuniary loss" damages on the ground that it is excessive unless it is at least double what the higher court would have awarded: see *Baigent v BBC* 2001 S.C. 281, referring to *Girvan v Inverness Farmers Dairy (No.2)* [1997] UKHL 47; 1998 S.C. (H.L.) 1.
[146] *Duberley v Gunning* (1792) 4 T.R. 651; *Youssoupoff v Metro-Goldwyn-Mayer* (1934) 50 T.L.R. 581: "It is extremely rare for the Court of Appeal to interfere with the verdict (of a jury) as to the amount of damages when the libel is established" (per Scrutton L.J. at 585); *Snyder v Montreal Gazette* (1978) 87 D.L.R. (3d) 5 at 17:
"In this field, juries are especially apt at determining the propriety of a compensation. They represent the views of a cross-section of society and should mirror the generally accepted opinion as to the value of the reputation of an honest public man. Indeed in the United Kingdom as well as in Canada, the assessment of those damages by juries has been consistently higher than that by Judges, either at trial or on appeal. Now that is the very function and purpose of the institution of the jury . . . ".
Coyne v Citizen Finance Ltd (1991) 172 C.L.R. 211, (per Toohey J. at 239):
" . . . assuming that the jury has been properly directed, if the members of an appellate court can say no more than that the damages are considerably higher than they themselves would have awarded, there is no justification for interfering with the verdict of the jury".
[147] *Kiam v MGN Ltd* [2002] EWCA Civ 43; [2003] Q.B. 281. In the *Kiam* case itself, the factors the Court of Appeal took into consideration in deciding that the award of £105,000 was proportionate and not excessive were the great deference to be shown to jury awards in defamation cases, the large percentage differences between jury awards and those substituted for them in the few cases in which the Court of Appeal had been prepared to intervene under s.8 of the Courts and Legal Services Act 1990, and the fact that the increase in the maximum award of general damages in personal injury cases had had the effect of raising the ceiling for juries' libel awards to almost twice the sum under appeal. Sedley L.J., dissenting, considered that no award of general damages over £60,000 was sustainable. He took the view that the jury most probably

Similarly, the Court of Appeal is very reluctant to overturn an award on the ground of inadequacy of damages, and will not do so merely because they think that "a more complete measure of justice would have been attained if the jury had given higher damages".[148]

> "It is not because a judge thinks that the jury would have done fuller justice by awarding higher damages that he is entitled to disturb their verdict, and order a new trial, when the action is one entirely for the consideration of the jury acting as reasonable men."[149]

Criteria for interfering with an award. For many years, the court **36.26** would only overturn an award if it was clearly of the opinion that, having regard to all the circumstances of the case, the damages were either so large or so small that no jury, properly applying their minds to the relevant evidence, could reasonably have given them.[150] To justify interference with

---

reached the conclusion it did by wrongly including an element of punitive damages in what should have been a purely compensatory award: see at [73]–[76]. The issue of exemplary damages had been withdrawn from the jury at trial. But see *The Gleaner Co. Ltd v Abrahams* [2003] UKPC 55; [2004] 1 A.C. 628 in which Lord Hoffmann at [41]–[42] held that:

"Ever since the distinction between compensatory and exemplary damages was formulated by Lord Devlin in *Rookes v Barnard* [1964] A.C. 1129 it has been recognised that compensatory damages may also have a punitive, deterrent or exemplary function. What distinguishes exemplary damages for the purpose of the *Rookes v Barnard* dichotomy is that they do not have a compensatory function . . . In the case of tort, liability to pay damages as compensation for loss or harm is capable of having some deterrent or exemplary effect and this is particularly true of defamation; first, because it is an intentional tort and secondly because the conduct of the defendant is capable of aggravating the damages."

In this context, see also per Lord Hoffmann at [53]–[56], to achieve a just result as to damages in defamation cases:

"[Some] might prefer . . . to compromise the purity of the distinction [between general and exemplary damages] . . . Oil and vinegar may not mix in solution but they combine to make an acceptable salad dressing."

The result of this appeal was that the Privy Council declined to interfere with the Court of Appeal of Jamaica's substituted award of J$35 million (at the time it was made, equivalent to £533,000).

[148] Per Tindal C.J. in *Rendall v Haywood* (1839) 5 Bing. N.C. 424; *Kelly v Sherlock* (1866) L.R. 1 Q.B. 686 at 697, per Mellor J. For the position in Ontario, see *Barrick Gold Corp v Lopehandia* (2004) 71 O.R. (3d) Ont. CA. See also *Ali v Nationwide News Pty Ltd* [2008] NSWCA 183 in which the New South Wales Court of Appeal substituted an award of A$275,000 (£128,000) for general compensatory damages for the A$125,000 (£58,000) which had been awarded by the trial judge. The Court held, applying *Carson v John Fairfax & Sons Ltd* (1993) 178 C.L.R. 44 and *Rogers v Nationwide News Pty Ltd* [2003] HCA 52; (2003) 216 C.L.R. 327, that an appellate court should intervene to prevent a miscarriage of justice if it is convinced that the damages are so high or so low that it is outside the range of what could reasonably be regarded as appropriate to the circumstances of the case: at [86]–[88].

[149] Per Barton J. in *Davies Brothers v Bond* (1912) 13 C.L.R. 518 at 526; *McLeod v Trott* [1933] N.Z.L.R. 42 at 43, per Myers C.J.; *MacDonagh v Tarpey* [1933] Ir.R. 666 at 674.

[150] *Praed v Graham* (1889) 24 Q.B.D. 53; *Sutcliffe v Pressdram* [1991] 1 Q.B. 153:

"The various tests which have been stated in the past can be summarised by saying that a jury's award will only be interfered with on appeal if it is so large or so small as to be irrational; that is to say, incapable of having been arrived at by a process of reason and necessarily arrived at through emotion, prejudice, caprice or stupidity, or simply on a wrong basis"

(per Nourse L.J. at 184); *Hicks v Gregory* (1904) 6 Western Australia L.R. 100; *Miles v Commercial Banking* (1904) 1 C.L.R. 470; *Falcke v Herald* [1925] V.L.R. 56:

"In my opinion the amount of damages awarded by the jury is much greater than any

the award, the court had to be satisfied that the jury had awarded a sum which no set of reasonable men could have fixed by way of damages.[151] In judging the reasonableness of the amount it was held that "a reasonable proportion must exist between the sum awarded and the circumstances of the case",[152]

reasonable body of men could have awarded, and I am therefore of the opinion that the verdict should be set aside on the ground that the damages are excessive . . . By finding that the words were published maliciously without any reasonable evidence to support it and by awarding damages to an amount which is grossly excessive and entirely out of proportion to the circumstances of the case, the whole of the jury's verdict is, in my opinion, discredited and the whole trial has been unsatisfactory"
(per McArthur J. at 79–80); *News Media v Finlay* [1970] N.Z.L.R. 1089 at 1099:
"The test which a Court should apply in considering whether the damages in a libel suit in particular are excessive is well established. In this class of case the assessment of damages is peculiarly the province of the jury and unless it is manifest that the jury have made an award out of all proportion to the injury suffered by the plaintiff so that it may be inferred that the jury could not properly have applied their minds to the relevant evidence the award of the jury will not be set aside."
Mihaka v Wellington Publishing [1975] 1 N.Z.L.R. 10; *Lees v Evans* (1891) 12 N.S.W.L.R. 7, where the court set aside a verdict for £200 damages on the ground that, as the plaintiff was a man of infamous reputation, the jury acted unreasonably in awarding anything more than nominal damages; *Blackshaw v Lord* [1984] Q.B. 1 at 27:
"We cannot reduce (or increase) the sum awarded by the jury unless it was one which no 12 reasonable jurors could have awarded if they had properly directed their minds to the evidence and been properly directed as to the relevant considerations and principles by the judge";
English and Scottish Co-operative v Odhams Press Ltd [1940] 1 K.B. 440 CA; *Maling v Bennett* (1929) 29 N.S.W.S.R. 280.
[151] *Broome v Cassell* [1972] A.C. 1027: "I think it was much too large, but that is not the test" (per Lord Reid at 1090, HL):
"When one looks at a jury's award in such a case one has to ask, whether it could have been made by sensible people acting reasonably, or whether it must have been arrived at capriciously, unconscionably or irrationally"
(per Lord Kilbrandon at 1135); *M'Carthy v Maguire* [1899] 2 Ir.R. 802; *Butler v Black* [1920] N.Z.L.R. 17; *Robs v Lamport* (1956) 2 D.L.R. (2d) 225; (1957) 9 D.L.R. (2d) 585 at 586–587; *Quinlan v Moloney* [1942] Q.S.R. 87; *Abraham v Advocate Ltd* [1946] 2 W.W.R. 181 PC:
"While the assessment is particularly within the province of the jury the amount must bear some relation to the damage suffered. Where it is so excessively high or so inadequate as to amount to a wholly incorrect estimation an appellate tribunal will interfere"
(per Lord Goddard at 1886); *Triggell v Pheeney* (1951) 82 C.L.R. 497; *David Syme v Mather* [1977] V.R. 516 at 518, 531; *Australian Consolidated Press v Uren* (1966) 117 C.L.R. 185 at 203, per Windeyer J.: "A grossly excessive verdict in a libel case can be set aside"; applied *Andrews v John Fairfax* [1980] 2 N.S.W.L.R. 225 at 245. In Canada the court will not interfere unless the amount of the damages is such as to shock the sense of justice and it is shown that they have been assessed on a wrong principle: *Levi v Reed* (1880) 6 S.C.R. 482 (Canada); *Nagy v Webb* [1930] 1 W.W.R. 357; *Brenner v Cisek* [1929] 2 W.W.R. 158; *Allan v Bushnell TV* (1969) 4 D.L.R. (3d) 212 at 223 (so excessive that no jury fully sensible of its duty and acting judicially could have given them); *Netupsky v Craig* [1971] 1 O.R. 51 at 70 (same test); affirmed (1972) 28 D.L.R. (3d) 742; *Coyne v Citizen Finance Ltd* (1991) 172 C.L.R. 211 at 239, per Toohey J.:
"There will be awards by juries that are so large or so small that there is an instinctive reaction by the appellate court that something must have gone wrong in the jury's deliberations. . . . But that is not to say that an appellate court should begin with its instinctive reaction and test the award against that. Rather the court should first look at the evidence, assume that the jury took a view of the evidence most consistent with the verdict it returned, and then ask whether, in the light of that evidence, the award is sustainable."
[152] *Harris v Arnott (No.2)* (1890) 26 L.R.Ir. 55, per Palles C.B. and Dowse B. ("there must be a reasonable proportion between the facts of the case and the sum given") at 68, per O'Brien C.J. at 74; *Miles v Commercial Banking* (1904) 1 C.L.R. 470; *Greenlands v Wilmshurst* [1913] 3 K.B.

and that the verdict "should be set aside if the court cannot find any reasonable proportion between the amount awarded and the loss sustained".[153] However, the Court of Appeal, in the context of an appeal against an award on the ground that it was excessive, has held that its power to intervene should be interpreted so as to give proper weight to the guidance given by the House of Lords[154] and by the European Court of Human Rights[155] as to the consistency between the common law and art.10 of the European Convention for the Protection of Human Rights and Fundamental Freedoms.[156] As a result it held that the test which had previously been regarded as the barrier against intervention should be lowered and that the courts should subject large awards of damages to a more searching scrutiny than had been customary in the past. The question, as expounded by the Court of Appeal, has become:

"Could a reasonable jury have thought that this award was *necessary* to compensate the claimant and to re-establish his reputation?"[157]

The court will ask itself whether the award was excessive as judged by objective standards of reasonable compensation, necessity and proportionality.

Wrong measure of damages. An award of damages will further be set aside if the court—although not in a position to say that no reasonable jury could have awarded such a sum or could have thought that it was necessary to compensate the claimant and to restore his reputation—nevertheless comes to the conclusion that the jury must have taken into consideration irrelevant matters, omitted to consider some relevant matter or applied a wrong measure of damages.[158] Also where there has been some mistake in point of law or on

36.27

---

507 at 532, per Hamilton L.J. ("there must be some reasonable relation between the wrong done and the solatium applied"); *Tolley v Fry* [1930] 1 K.B. 467 CA at 476 ("the damages must have some reasonable relation to the facts of the case"); *Scott v Musial* [1959] 2 Q.B. 429 at 437; *Lewis v Daily Telegraph* [1963] 1 Q.B. 340 at 380 ("out of all proportion to the facts").

[153] *Taff Vale v Jenkins* [1913] A.C. 1 per Lord Atkinson at 7; *Knupffer v London Express* [1943] K.B. 80 at 91; *Broadway Approvals v Odhams Press* [1965] 1 W.L.R. 805 at 818 ("extravagantly out of proportion to any possible injury"). Such considerations are now supported by the case law of the European Court of Human Rights: *Tolstoy Miloslavsky v UK* (1995) 20 EHRR 442 and *Steel & Morris v UK* (2005) 41 EHRR 22.

[154] *Ex p. Brind* [1991] 1 A.C. 696; *Att-Gen v Guardian Newspapers Ltd (No.2)* [1990] 1 A.C. 109; *Derbyshire CC v Times Newspapers Ltd* [1993] A.C. 670.

[155] *The Sunday Times v UK (No.2)* (1991) 14 EHRR 229.

[156] *Rantzen v Mirror Group Newspapers* [1994] Q.B. 670. Also, see s.6(1), Human Rights Act 1998.

[157] [1994] Q.B. 670 at 692; see also *John v MGN Ltd* [1997] Q.B. 586; *Kiam v MGN Ltd* [2002] EWCA Civ 43; [2003] Q.B. 281.

[158] *Sentinel Review v Robinson* (1927) 61 O.L.R. 62; *WA Newspaper v Salter* (1916) 8 Western Australia L.R. 103; *Chapman v Ellesmere* [1932] 2 K.B. 431 at 455, 456, 472, 477; *Morgan v Odhams Press* [1971] 1 W.L.R. 1239 HL; *Farrell v Kramer* (1963) 159 Me. 387; *Syme v Mather* [1977] V.R. 516.

the elements of damage to the claimant[159] on the part of the trial judge, or mistake in the calculation of figures by the jury, an award will be set aside.[160] Where, e.g. particulars of claim allege the publication of two separate libels, and the defendant is proved to have published one libel but not the other, the jury cannot award any damages for the libel which the defendant is not proved to have published, and if they do so their verdict will be set aside and a new trial ordered, whether they acted against the direction of the judge, or by his direction, or without any direction at all.[161] So also where the jury were allowed to take into account a meaning which the words could not bear, and must, from the size of their verdict, have done so, a new trial was ordered.[162] The court will also overturn an award of damages where it is "satisfied that the jury have not acted reasonably upon the evidence, but have been misled by prejudice or passion into awarding excessive damages".[163]

36.28 Nominal or contemptuous damages. Provided there is no ground for suspecting misconduct on the part of the jury and they have decided the issue of liability, the court will not interfere with an award simply on the ground that it is nominal in amount.[164] There is no necessary inconsistency in a jury finding a verdict for a claimant for a penny's damages, even though they find that the libel was maliciously written, for "the jury may have thought there was some ill feeling, and yet that the plaintiff suffered no real damage".[165]

---

[159] *Dingle v Associated Newspapers* [1964] A.C. 371 HL; *Holt v Sun Publishing* (1979) 100 D.L.R. (3d) 447 (failure to consider effects on constituents or potential voters); *Sallows v Griffiths* [2001] F.S.R. 15 CA (malicious falsehood); *Campbell v News Group Newspapers Ltd* [2002] EWCA Civ 1143; [2002] E.M.L.R. 43.

[160] *Rendall v Hayward* (1839) 5 Bing. N.C. 424; *Forsdike v Stone* (1868) L.R. 3 C.P. 607; *English and Scottish Co-operative v Odhams* [1940] 1 K.B. 440 CA; *Poliakoff v News Chronicle* [1939] 1 All E.R. 390; *Davies Brothers v Bond* (1912) 13 C.L.R. 519; *Pat v Illinois* [1929] 2 W.W.R. 14.

[161] *Lionel Barber v Deutsche Bank* [1919] A.C. 304 per Lord Atkinson at 320.

[162] *Lewis v Daily Telegraph* [1964] A.C. 234. Cf. *Riddick v Thames Board Mills* [1977] Q.B. 881.

[163] *Watt v Watt* [1905] A.C. 115 at 118, per Lord Halsbury L.C.; *Chapman v Ellesmere* [1932] 2 K.B. 431; *Lefolii v Gouzenko* [1969] S.C.R. 3 (the summing-up must have confused the jury).

[164] It is, however, contrary to principle and authority for a jury to find that a claimant has been libelled but to award no damages whatsoever: "a plaintiff who is successful in a libel action must be awarded some damages, even if they amount to no more than the smallest coin of the realm." (*Reynolds v Times Newspapers Ltd* [2001] 2 A.C. 127 CA, per Lord Bingham C.J.).

[165] *Cooke v Brogden* (1885) 1 T.L.R. 497 at 499, per Lord Coleridge C.J.; *McCullogh v Robinson* [1930] 3 W.W.R. 534 (CA Sask.); *Dennison v Sanderson* [1946] O.R.601:
"A jury is not necessarily perverse if it refuses to regard as seriously as the party assailed may do, the seemingly venomous attacks made [in the course of a heated election campaign]. No monetary loss is involved, and a jury is not likely to regard as serious the damage, if any, done by rough words applied to a political opponent ... "
(per Robertson C.J.O. at 616); *Kelly v Sherlock* (1866) L.R.1 Q.B. 686: " ... no one, who in these unhappy controversies was not already prejudiced against the plaintiff, would think worse of him in consequence of the vulgar abuse of the defendant"; *Webb v Louis* (1907) 7 N.S.W.S.R. 734; *Butcher v Payton* (1890) 9 N.Z.L.R. 240; *Bekker v Wrack* [1937] N.Z.L.R. 549:
"Upon the evidence before them, it was open to the jury to consider that the defendant was a

Alternatively, the jury may have been reasonably inclined to the view that the claimant did not seek financial reward.[166]

Exemplary damages. An appellate court has no more control over the size **36.29** of an award of exemplary damages than it does over the size of an award of compensatory damages.[167] It has been held that principle requires that an award of exemplary damages should never exceed the minimum sum necessary to meet the public purpose underlying such damages, that of punishing the defendant, showing that tort does not pay and deterring others.[168] There is some suggestion in the authorities that, in assessing the appropriateness of an award of exemplary damages, the court should have regard to the ratio which the award bears to the amount of compensatory damages awarded.[169]

Substituting a new award. Where an award of damages by a jury is set **36.30** aside on appeal on the ground that it is excessive or inadequate, the Court of Appeal has power, instead of ordering a new trial, to substitute what it considers to be a proper sum by way of damages.[170] It is to be expected that

---

foolish old man whose defamatory statements would not impress his hearers with any adverse opinion of the plaintiff."

[166] *Geddie v Rink* [1935] 1 W.W.R. 87 CA:

"Apart, however, from the single fact that the jury at first assessed no damages and eventually no more than nominal damages, there is nothing I can find on the record to suggest that their verdict was a compromise verdict or to show that there was any misconduct on their part in coming to it. On the contrary the verdict may be sustained as a reasonable one even if the slanders were gross when it is borne in mind that there is no evidence that the plaintiff suffered any pecuniary loss, while there is good ground for the conclusion that the jury might very well have thought that he was not seeking pecuniary gain by the litigation but simply to clear his character"

(per Mackenzie J.A. at 101).

[167] *Broome v Cassell* [1972] A.C. 1027 at 1090; *Coyne v Citizen Finance* (1991) 172 C.L.R. 211:

"The proper performance by the appellate court of the functions entrusted to it will require that it intervene to prevent miscarriage of justice. It is true that the somewhat unprincipled common law rules relating to the nature and limits of defamation damages may, in cases in those jurisdictions where exemplary or punitive damages are still available, make the task of the appellate court in reviewing a jury's award an unusually difficult one. The reason for the difficulty is that the interaction of sometimes competing notions of compensation, vindication, retribution and even deterrence may give rise to a wide variety of possible components of the jury's overall award. Even in such cases, the inability to identify specific components will not absolve the appellate court of the responsibility of determining whether the overall award is within the limits of what could reasonably be regarded as appropriate in the circumstances of the particular case"

(per Mason C.J. at 216).

[168] *John v MGN Ltd* [1997] Q.B. 568 at 619.

[169] *Broome v Cassell* [1972] A.C. 1027; *Riches v News Group Newspapers* [1996] 1 Q.B. 256 at 282–283, per Parker L.J. In the context of claims in respect of unlawful conduct by the police, it has been held that it would be unusual for an award of exemplary damages to produce a result more than three times the basic damages being awarded, as the total of the basic, aggravated and exemplary damages: see *Thompson v Comr of the Police of the Metropolis* [1998] Q.B. 498 CA. See also *Sallows v Griffiths* [2001] F.S.R. 15 CA.

[170] CPR r.52.10(3).

the Court of Appeal will follow this course rather than put the parties to the expense of a further trial at first instance, unless to do so would be, for some reason, unjust.[171] Awards made by the Court of Appeal under this power are intended over a period of time to provide a corpus to which reference may be made in subsequent cases and on which reliance may be placed as establishing some standards as to what are "proper" awards.[172] The Appellate Committee of the House of Lords also had the power to substitute for a sum of damages awarded by a jury such sum as appeared to it to be proper instead of ordering a new trial.[173] It is presumed that the Supreme Court has the same power, for its jurisdiction corresponds to that of the Appellate Committee under the Appellate Jurisdiction Acts 1876 and 1888.[174]

36.31 **Ordering a new trial.** The Court of Appeal is not bound to substitute its own award where it sets aside an award of damages on the ground that it is excessive or inadequate and it may order a new trial instead. The new trial will generally be limited to the issue of quantum.[175] However, a general new trial will be ordered where it is not possible to say that justice could be done between the parties by directing a new trial as to damages alone,[176] e.g. where

---

[171] See per Lord Diplock in *Broome v Cassell* [1972] A.C. 1027 at 1122–1123:
"This involves the parties, through no fault of their own, in greatly increased costs which, particularly in libel actions, are, to the discredit of our legal system, out of all proportion even to the large compensatory awards in the instant case. . . . the consideration of costs involved is one which it would be unrealistic and unjust to ignore."
This case was decided under the former rule which required the appellate court to order a new trial, unless the parties otherwise agreed.
[172] *Rantzen v Mirror Group Newspapers* [1994] Q.B. 670 at 694, 695–696; *John v MGN Ltd* [1997] Q.B. 586 at 612: "As and when a framework of awards is established this will provide a valuable pointer to the appropriate level of award in the particular case." For a list of the awards substituted or approved by the Court of Appeal see Appendix 3, below.
[173] The House of Lords found it had this power by reason of s.4 of the Appellate Jurisdiction Act 1876 (to "determine what of right, and according to the law and custom of this realm, ought to be done in the subject-matter of such appeal") and by virtue of its inherent jurisdiction to exercise any power vested in the Court of Appeal in the absence of statutory or judicial restriction: *Grobbelaar v News Group Newspapers Ltd*, above, at [25], per Lord Bingham. Exercising this power in *Grobbelaar*'s case, the House of Lords quashed the jury's award of £85,000 damages, and substituted it with a nominal award of £1.
[174] Constitutional Reform Act 2005, s.40 and Sch.9; UKSC Practice Direction 1, para.1.1.1.
[175] E.g. *McCarey v Associated Newspapers Ltd (No.2)* [1965] 2 Q.B. 86; *Andrews v John Fairfax & Sons* [1980] 2 N.S.W.L.R. 225; *English and Scottish Co-operative v Odhams* [1940] 1 K.B. 440:
"I think it would be wrong if, in ordering a new trial, we were to put [the plaintiffs] in jeopardy once more as to the whole of the case. They have established to the satisfaction of the jury that an article has been written containing, according to the meaning which a normal man would put on it, these injurious reflections on them. It seems to me, therefore, that the only matter left . . . is the question of damages, and on that, as I say, there will have to be a new trial . . . limited to the quantification and assessment of damages"
(per Slesser L.J. at 456); *Sutcliffe v Pressdram* [1991] 1 Q.B. 153 at 179–181, per Lord Donaldson M.R. and at 193, per Russell L.J.
[176] *Uren v Australian Consolidated Press* (1965) 66 S.R. (N.S.W.) 271, per Walsh J. (dissenting but approved in *Australian Consolidated Press v Uren* (1966) 117 C.L.R. 185).

the question of damages cannot be easily separated from the other evidence in the case.[177]

Damages awarded by judge. Where the damages have been awarded by   **36.32**
a judge sitting alone or by a master, the Court of Appeal has power to alter the figure itself,[178] but as the damages in defamation are essentially a matter of "impression and of common sense",[179] the Court of Appeal will not readily interfere, unless the judge has misapprehended the facts[180] or has taken into account irrelevant factors[181] or applied a wrong principle of law.[182] It will otherwise reject his figure only in "very special" or "very exceptional" cases, when he has made a wholly erroneous estimate of the damage suffered.[183] The Court of Appeal will adopt the same approach under s.3(5) of the Defamation Act 1996.[184]

SECTION 7. MISCONDUCT

Misconduct by the jury. The Court of Appeal will grant a new trial if the   **36.33**
jury have behaved in a way which has denied a fair and impartial trial to either party. Where, e.g. the smallness of the damages shows that the jury have made a compromise, and, instead of deciding the issue of liability, have agreed to

---

[177] *The Herald and Weekly Times Ltd v McGregor* (1928) 41 C.L.R. 254 at 270–271.

[178] CPR r.52.10(2)(a).

[179] Per Lord Wright in *Davies v Powell Duffryn* [1942] A.C. 601 at 616.

[180] *United Printers v Bernard* (1969) 11 W.I.R. 269 (wrong meaning of words); *McDonald's Corp v Steel*, unreported, March 31, 1999, CA.

[181] Or failed to take into account relevant ones: in *C v MGN Ltd*, decided and reported with *Cairns v Modi* [2012] EWCA Civ 1382; [2013] 1 W.L.R. 1015, the CA accepted at [49] that it should not interfere unless the judge's evaluation was "plainly wrong or followed a misdirection", but found the figure excessive because the judge had given insufficient weight to the limited publication and early apology. See fn.184, below.

[182] *Grabareuic v Northwest Publications* (1968) 67 D.L.R. (2d) 748; *SA Associated Newspapers v Samuels*, 1980 (1) S.A. 24, AD; or has failed to take into account relevant factors: *Truth (NZ) Ltd v Bowles* [1966] N.Z.L.R. 303 (plaintiff's character and a prompt apology); *Pat v Illinois Publishing* [1929] 2 W.W.R. 14:
"The Court, however, must act upon well understood principles when considering whether the amount awarded should be increased or otherwise, and unless it appears that the trial Judge failed to take into consideration some element of damage which he should have considered, I do not think his decision should be disturbed"
(per Martin J.A. at 16–17). But a failure to consider an apology is irrelevant if the award is correct: *Advocate v Husbands* (1969) 15 W.L.R. 180; *Steel v McDonald's Corp (No.4)*, *Independent*, May 10, 1999 CA (words fair comment not statements of fact).

[183] Per Lord Radcliffe in *Associated Newspapers v Dingle* [1964] A.C. 371 at 393, see also at 404, 405, 408, at 418 (award too small); *Fielding v Variety Inc.* [1967] 2 Q.B. 84 CA (excessive damages awarded by a master, reduced on appeal); *McElroy v Cowper-Smith* [1967] S.C.R. 425; *Nkrumah v Ataa* [1972] 2 G.L.R. 21.

[184] *Cairns v Modi; C v MGN Ltd* [2012] EWCA Civ 1382; [2013] 1 W.L.R. 1015. An offer of amends had been made in *C* and the judge had assessed the appropriate starting point to be £150,000 before applying a 50 per cent discount. The Court of Appeal reduced the initial sum from £150,000 to £100,000 before applying the (unchallenged) 50 per cent discount: see [49].

find for the claimant for nominal damages only, a new trial will be granted, such a case being in effect as if the jury had been discharged without a verdict.[185] If the words complained of are grossly defamatory and the claimant has not done anything to provoke or give the least ground for the imputation cast upon him or to show that he has disentitled himself to a verdict sufficient to vindicate his character, a penny in damages may be treated as a species of compromise and no true verdict at all, even though the claimant may not have proved any actual damage.[186] Also, where there are grounds to suppose that the jury have reduced or otherwise decided on a figure for damages, not by considering the evidence relevant to the question of compensation, but by taking into consideration which party would ultimately have to pay the costs, that would be reason for setting the verdict aside, but only if the court takes the view that there must necessarily have been a substantial wrong.[187] Further, if a jury or juror demonstrates a closed mind before the completion of the evidence, that may be ground for ordering a new trial. Thus, where, before the conclusion of the cross-examination of the plaintiff, the jury intervened with an intimation that they desired to find for the defendants and then did so without any summing up, it was held that the judgment entered for the defendants must be set aside and a new trial ordered.[188] However, the mere communication by the jury of an opinion in favour of the claimant during or at the close of the claimant's case, before the defendant's evidence is heard, is not of itself such misconduct on the part of the jury as will justify counsel for the defendant in refusing to go on with the case, and entitle the defendant to a new trial.[189] Moreover, the mere fact that a conversation has taken place

---

[185] Per Blackburn J. in *Kelly v Sherlock* (1866) L.R.1 Q.B. 686 at 697–698; *Hall v Poyser* (1845) 13 M. & W. 600; *Falvey v Stanford* (1874) L.R.10 Q.B. 54 at 56; *Chilweli v Webster* (1918) 37 N.Z.L.R. 369.

[186] See *Falvey v Stanford* (1874) L.R. 10 Q.B. 54:

"There is no obligation on the plaintiffs to show that they have suffered actual damage. A plaintiff may, if he can, by way of aggravating damages, prove that he has suffered actual damage. But in every case he is perfectly entitled to say that there has been a serious libel upon him, that the law assumes he must have suffered damage, and that he is entitled to substantial damages":

per Goddard L.J. in *English and Scottish Co-operative v Odhams* [1940] 1 K.B. 440 at 461.

[187] *Pamplin v Express Newspapers* [1988] 1 W.L.R. 116n:

" . . . in my judgment, it is impossible to be sure that the jury had not assessed the quantum of damages appropriate to reflect the injury to the plaintiff's already impaired reputation at some small figure in excess of 12p but then decided to reduce it to that sum because of the heavy burden of costs which they assumed would be placed on the defendants"

(per Purchas L.J. at 130).

[188] *Hobbs v Tinling* [1929] 2 K.B. 1: "I am further of the opinion that the jury ought to have been told that their intervention was premature, that they must keep an open mind until the conclusion of the plaintiff's case . . . " (per Greer at 46); *Biggs v Evans* (1912) 106 L.T.

[189] *Campbell v Hackney Furnishing* (1906) 22 T.L.R. 318; *Peat v Greymouth* (1916) 36 N.Z.L.R. 40:

"The general rule appears to be that misconduct with which the successful party has had nothing to do will not form a ground for granting a new trial unless such misconduct was calculated to influence the verdict, or was such as to raise a well-grounded suspicion that it may have influenced the result"

(per Sim J. at 47).

between a juryman and one of the parties to the action, or his representatives, is not of itself a ground for a new trial, unless there is reasonable ground for believing that the course of justice has been, or was likely to be, substantially affected.[190]

Misconduct by counsel. A new trial will only be granted on the ground of **36.34** misconduct of counsel where such misconduct was serious and obvious, and must, in the opinion of the court, have led to an erroneous determination by the jury.[191]

> "It would be a very serious thing to hold that every indiscretion or extravagance of counsel in addressing a jury, every allusion to matters not actually in evidence, every rhetorical exaggeration, would subject his client to the loss of his verdict because it might possibly have influenced the jury prejudicially to the other side."[192]

But when the court is clearly of opinion that the jury must have been influenced by a speech made by counsel,[193] or by the way the case was conducted,[194] into finding an erroneous verdict, a new trial will be granted.

---

[190] *David Syme v Swinburne* (1909) 10 C.L.R. 43.

[191] *Peat v Greymouth* (1916) N.Z.L.R. 40:
" . . . unless there is some reasonable ground for supposing that the observations might have had some influence in leading the jury to the conclusion at which they arrived the verdict, in our opinion, cannot be disturbed"
(per Sim J. at 46); *Croll v McRae* (1930) 30 N.S.W.S.R. 137 at 143.

[192] Per Denniston J. in *Norton v Stringer* (1909) 29 N.Z.L.R. 249 at 258. The judge further observed that it would be inequitable to allow counsel's misconduct to form a ground of appeal where it had been unnoticed or unobjected to; *Justin v Associated Newspapers* [1967] 1 N.S.W.R. 61; *Andrews v John Fairfax* [1980] 2 N.S.W.L.R. 225 at 237:
"The mere fact that counsel in his address misunderstood or even misrepresented the law or the facts does not justify the withdrawal of the case from the jury unless the trial judge considers that the conduct of counsel has created a situation which cannot be rectified in his summing-up",
(per Hutley J.A.).

[193] *Praed v Graham* (1889) 24 Q.B.D. 53 at 55, per Lord Esher M.R.; *Chattell v Daily Mail* (1901) 18 T.L.R. 165; *Australian Consolidated Press v Uren* (1966) 117 C.L.R. 185 at 200. If a judge discharges the jury due to concern that a closing speech made by counsel may have had a prejudicial effect on the jury, the Court of Appeal has jurisdiction to consider an appeal from that decision, but the circumstances in which it will interfere with the decision are "rare in the extreme": per Judge L.J., *Gladding v Channel 4 Television Corp* [1999] E.M.L.R. 475 CA.

[194] *Watt v Watt* [1905] A.C. 115; *Beevis v Dawson* [1957] 1 Q.B. 195 CA, where, in a case in which justification was pleaded, counsel for the defendants, uncorrected by the judge, told the jury that the burden of proof was upon the plaintiff to prove that the statements complained of were false, and further invited the jury to stop the case and find for the plaintiff with a farthing's damages, and the jury did so, a new trial was ordered:
"There began, almost from the commencement of the case, a wrangling or quarrelling or bickering between counsel, and it lasted throughout the case. . . . If a case is conducted as this was, the judge is deprived of the assistance which he is entitled to expect from counsel. Continuous bickering becomes a burden for everyone in court—for judge and for jury—and it is almost impossible for justice to be done. It is not surprising if, in such circumstances, a judge gets tired or if the jury get tired; sometimes it leads to confusion."
(per Singleton L.J. at 201).

36.35 Misconduct by a party. If a favourable decision has been obtained by the misconduct of the successful party, the court will be ready to grant a new trial.[195]

> "Where a party deliberately misleads the court in a material matter, and that deception has probably tipped the scale in his favour (or even, as I think, where it may reasonably have done so), it would be wrong to allow him to retain the judgment thus unfairly procured."[196]

36.36 Misconduct by the judge. Misconduct by the trial judge, such as constant interruption or intervention in a manner which is prejudicial to one or other of the parties, may afford good grounds for appeal.[197]

SECTION 8. SURPRISE

36.37 Verdict obtained by surprise. A new trial will be granted where a verdict was obtained against a party in circumstances where, as a result of surprise, he was not prepared either to advance his own case or to meet the case presented against him. However, where a party alleges that the evidence given at the trial took him by surprise but did not apply for an adjournment to enable him to meet the evidence and instead took his chance of obtaining a verdict, a new trial will not be granted.[198]

SECTION 9. DISCOVERY OF FRESH EVIDENCE

36.38 Criteria for allowing new trial on basis of discovery of fresh evidence. The Court of Appeal will not receive fresh evidence, oral or written, "unless it orders otherwise".[199] Under the RSC, the Court of Appeal

---

[195] Per Denning L.J. in *Tombling v Universal Bulb* [1951] 2 T.L.R. 289 at 297. For the limits of the principle and as to verdicts obtained by fraud or misconduct generally, see *Hamilton v Al Fayed (No.2)* [2001] E.M.L.R. 15 CA.

[196] Per Pearce L.J. in *Meek v Fleming* [1961] 2 Q.B. at 379; *Hip Foong Hong v H Neoria & Co.* [1918] A.C. 888 at 894; *Skone v Skone* [1971] 1 W.L.R. 812 HL at 817.

[197] See *Cornwell v Myskow* [1987] 1 W.L.R. 630, where the conduct of the judge was raised as a ground of appeal, but, in the event, not dealt with.

[198] *Isaacs v Hobhouse* [1919] 1 K.B. 398 CA.

[199] CPR r.52.11(2). In *Terluk v Berezovsky* [2011] EWCA Civ 1534 the Court of Appeal held that it was not appropriate to introduce witness statements in an appeal against a finding of defamation where the statements were made four years after the defamation complained of. It said that whilst the primary rule as to the admission of fresh evidence was expressed in CPR r.52.11(2)(b), the three criteria set out in *Ladd v Marshall* [1954] 1 W.L.R. 1489 constituted the relevant considerations in deciding on the exercise of discretion. See also *Tamiz v Google* [2013] EWCA Civ 68; [2013] 1 W.L.R. 2151 at [12]; *Hertfordshire Investments Ltd v Bubb* [2000] 1 W.L.R. 2318 CA; *Hamilton v Al Fayed (No.2)* [2001] E.M.L.R. 15 CA; *Mann v Eccott* [1998] N.S.W.S.C. 364. The principles upon which a new trial may be ordered on the ground of the discovery of fresh evidence are the same as those which apply where the Court of Appeal is asked to hear the new evidence itself: see Ord.59, r.10(2). It is to be borne in mind that, where a new trial is ordered on some ground other than the discovery of fresh evidence, the fresh evidence may in any event be adduced at the new trial, providing it is admissible: see *Williams v Reason* [1988] 1 W.L.R. 96n at 111. The Court of Appeal's approach in *Hamilton v Al Fayed (No.2)* [2001] E.M.L.R. 15 was followed in *Riyad Bank v Ahli United Bank (UK) Plc* [2005] EWCA Civ 1419 and in *Toth v Jarman* [2006] EWCA Civ 1028; [2006] 4 All E.R. 1276. In *Al-Koronky v Time Life*

only granted a new trial on the ground that fresh evidence had been discovered since the trial of the first action where the evidence proposed to be adduced was of such a character as to justify the court in saying that the verdict could not, in the interests of justice, be relied on, because it was based on mistake, surprise or fraud. A number of "special grounds"[200] had to be made out: (1) that the new evidence could not have been obtained with reasonable diligence for use at the trial[201]; (2) that the evidence was such that, if given, it would probably have had an important influence on the result of the case,[202] although it need not be decisive[203]; and (3) it was such as was presumably to be believed, although it need not be incontrovertible.[204] The CPR do not retain the former requirement for special grounds, but the principles remain relevant:

Entertainment Group Ltd [2006] EWCA Civ 1123 the Court of Appeal refused to admit fresh evidence in an appeal against an order for security for costs in a libel action.

[200] See RSC Ord.59, r.10(2).

[201] *Williams v Reason* [1988] 1 W.L.R. 96n:

"... it is, in my judgment, important to discourage litigants from seeking to put before this court evidence that they have made no attempt to obtain in order to support a new case that they hope will succeed when the case that they have made has failed. It is only in clear cases that this court will allow an unsuccessful litigant, who has not tried to obtain the fresh evidence, to be excused the attempt and to adduce the evidence"

(per Stephenson L.J. at 100),

"In almost every case it must be incumbent on an applicant to make some effort, albeit unsuccessfully, before coming to the court and attempting to establish that the evidence was not available within the first criterion in *Ladd v Marshall*"

(per Purchas L.J. at 114).

[202] See *Hamilton v Al Fayed (No.2)* [2001] E.M.L.R. 15 CA: thus "the court has to consider the implications of the fresh evidence in order to decide whether to admit it" (per Lord Phillips M.R.). Fresh evidence as to the credit of a witness will rarely satisfy this requirement unless the court has been deliberately deceived in relation to the credibility of that witness (ibid.).

[203] *Young v Kershaw* (1899) 81 L.T. 531:

"The party asking for the new trial must show that there was no remissness on his part in adducing all possible evidence at the trial. Then again, as to the class of new evidence, the rule is that the new evidence must be such that, if adduced, it would be practically conclusive—that is, evidence of such a class as to render it probable almost beyond doubt that the verdict would be different"

(per Collins L.J. at 532); *Garnaut v Bennett (No.3)* (1910) 29 N.Z.L.R. 565. Where the new evidence is directed to the credibility of a witness, it may only be adduced where the court is satisfied that it "*must* have led a reasonable jury to a different conclusion from that actually arrived at in the case": per Cohen L.J. in *Braddock v Tillotsons Newspapers* [1950] 1 K.B. 47 at 56; *Gilberthorpe v News Group Newspapers, Independent*, June 15, 1989, CA, where the court held that, although it was normally slow to deprive a litigant of a judgment on account of the discovery of new evidence, it would do so where the new evidence raised such high doubts about the soundness of the trial verdict that it would be unjust to permit it to stand.

[204] *Sutcliffe v Pressdram* [1991] 1 Q.B. 153:

"The nature of the evidence which is being tendered must be set out very clearly in the application and normally takes the form of a signed statement or affidavit by the potential witness, together with an explanation of why the evidence could not have been obtained for use at the trial. It would be possible, albeit less persuasive, to submit an affidavit by a third party stating, on information supplied by the potential witness, what evidence that witness would give. What, so far as I am aware, has never before been attempted is to ask this court to order a new trial on the footing that *if* two witnesses were compelled to give evidence at a new trial and *if* they told the truth, their evidence would be credible and would have an important influence upon the result of the case."

(per Lord Donaldson M.R. at 172).

they are matters which the Court of Appeal must consider in the exercise of its discretion when deciding whether or not to receive fresh evidence.[205] A new trial will be more readily ordered where it is alleged that there has been deception or impropriety or other culpable conduct on the part of the party opposing the application.[206]

SECTION 10. COSTS

36.39 **Costs.** The costs of a successful application for a new trial are in the discretion of the Court of Appeal,[207] but, in the absence of special circumstances, will be given to the applicant.[208] The costs of both trials, i.e. the costs of the first trial and of the new trial, will, in the absence of any special order to the contrary, abide the event of the new trial.[209] Where, therefore, a nonsuit was set aside, and a new trial was ordered which resulted in the plaintiff's favour, he was held entitled to the costs of the first trial as part of the costs of the action.[210] So also where at the first trial the jury disagreed.[211] However where the costs of the first trial were ordered to "abide the result of a new trial", and at the new trial the jury returned a verdict for one farthing damages, and the judge refused to give the plaintiff a certificate for costs, it was held that "the result of the new trial" meant the result of that trial as to costs, and therefore the plaintiff was not entitled to any costs of the first trial.[212]

---

[205] *Hertfordshire Investments Ltd v Bubb* [2000] 1 W.L.R. 2318 at 2325, per Hale L.J., approved by the Court of Appeal in *Hamilton v Al Fayed (No.2)*, above, at [11]. Another procedural appeal point in relation to which the court, post-CPR, has followed the old RSC practice is the question of when the court will permit fresh evidence to be admitted concerning matters *that have occurred* since the date of the trial or hearing under appeal. CPR r.52.11(2), unlike its predecessor in the RSC, RSC Ord.59, r.10(2), contains no express qualification permitting the admission of such evidence only in the most exceptional of circumstances (having regard to the need for finality in litigation). See *Hughes v Singh*, The Times, April 21, 1989, for the position under the RSC. However, in *Bentley and Skinner (Bond Street Jewellers) Ltd v Searchmap Ltd* [2003] EWHC 1621 (Ch) at [20], Lightman J. treated the principles stated in *Hughes v Singh* as continuing in effect post-CPR.

[206] *Williams v Reason* [1988] 1 W.L.R. 96 at 99.

[207] CPR r.44.3(1). *Hamilton v Seal* [1904] 2 K.B. 262, discussing *Bray v Ford* [1896] A.C. 44 at 56; *Jones v Richards* (1899) 15 T.L.R. 398. Cf. *Dakhyl v Labouchere* (1904) 39 L.J. Newspaper at 410.

[208] CPR r.44.3(2)(a). Cf. *Stevens v Economic Builders* [1938] W.N. 55.

[209] *Creen v Wright* (1877) 2 C.P.D. 354, approved in *Field v G.N. Ry* (1878) 3 Ex.D. 261; *Jones v Richards* (1899) 15 T.L.R. 398 CA. A modern example is *McCartan Turkington Breen (a firm) v Times Newspapers Ltd* [2001] 2 A.C. 277 HL. Cf. *O'Reilly v McCall* [1910] 2 Ir.R. 42 HL: the costs may in a proper case be given to the appellant in any event. If the claimant takes money out of court before the new trial, he may be awarded the costs of the first trial: *Rookes v Barnard (No.2)* [1966] 1 Q.B. 176.

[210] *Creen v Wright*, above.

[211] *Copeland v Corporation of Blenheim* (1885) 11 O.P.R. 54.

[212] *Brotherton v Metropolitan District* [1894] 1 Q.B. 666 CA.

Costs budgeting. An appeal lies to the Court of Appeal from the decision **36.40**
of the Senior Costs Judge under the Defamation Proceedings Costs Management Scheme.[213]

---

[213] *Henry v News Group Newspapers* [2013] EWCA Civ 19; [2013] C.P. Rep. 20. The Costs
Management Scheme has since April 2013 been replaced with the New Costs Rules and Practice
Directions following Lord Justice Jackson's recommendations: see para.35.18, above.

Appendix 1

Forms and Precedents[1]

---

[1] The Forms and Precedents set out in this Appendix are designed to be read alongside Chs 26–28 and the relevant Civil Procedure Rules and Practice Directions. At the time of going to press the provisions of the Defamation Act 2013 have not yet come into force, nor has any date been set for when they will. All the precedents in this book have therefore been drafted on the basis of existing law and, where appropriate, suggested wording changes for when the provisions of the new Act do come into force have been added in square brackets (non-italicised text).

[2] In previous editions of this book, precedents were provided for applications for interim injunctive relief in privacy claims. However, in all cases where an interim injunction is sought to restrict freedom of expression the position is now governed by the Master of the Rolls' Practice Guidance which contains a Model Order that practitioners must use. These documents can be found in *Civil Procedure*, Vol. 1 (2013), at B13–001 onwards, or online at *http://www.judiciary .gov.uk/Resources/JCO/Documents/Guidance/practice-guidance-civil-non-disclosure-orders-july2011.pdf*.

[3] Note that all statements of case filed with the court since October 2, 2006 are public documents in the sense that the public can, in general, copy them as of right, CPR r.5.4C(1). The court does, though, have power, upon the application of a party or of any person named in a statement of case, to restrict access to and copying of a statement of case: CPR r.5.4C(4). In an appropriate case a claimant might apply for an order under CPR r.5.4C(4).

DEFENCES

REPLIES

C SETTLEMENT OF ACTION

---

⁴ Note that there is no replacement for s.6 Defamation Act 1952 ("fair comment"). Para.28 of the Explanatory Notes to the Defamation Act 2013 states that such a provision is no longer necessary given the new approach to the honest opinion defence under s.3(4) of that Act. A defendant will be able to show that the three conditions to be satisfied for the honest opinion defence (those required under s.3(2)–(4), Defamation Act 2013) have been met without needing to prove the truth of every single allegation of fact relevant to the statement complained of.

FORMS AND PRECEDENTS

A. Steps up to and Including Issue of Proceedings   A1.1

Letter Of Claim[5]

(a) **Letter of Claim**—libel in newspaper—seeking apology, statement in court and inviting proposals as to damages

The Editor
[*name of relevant publication*]
[*address of relevant publication*]

[*name of complainant*]

Dear Sir/Madam,

We act for [*set out the name and a brief description of the client*]

On [*date*] you published on page [*x*] of [*name of relevant publication*] an article entitled [*name of article*] which referred to our client. The article contained the following defamatory words about our client [*set out the words complained of*]. A full copy of the article is attached to this letter.

The allegations you published meant and were understood to mean [*set out meaning the intended claimant attributes to the words complained of*]. These charges amount to a very serious libel on him and have caused him considerable distress and embarrassment. [*After s.1 Defamation Act 2013 comes into force, give details of why (unless obvious) publication has caused or is likely to cause serious harm to the complainant's reputation; where the complainant is a body trading for profit, explain how that serious harm is likely to cause or has caused the complainant serious financial loss.*] The allegations made against him are false and your attack on him was unjustified [*set out factual inaccuracies or unsupportable comment within the words complained of giving sufficient explanation to enable the intended defendant to appreciate why the words are inaccurate or unsupportable*].

In the circumstances, our client requires from you as a matter of urgency a full and unequivocal public retraction and apology in terms to be approved by us, a statement in open court and an undertaking not to repeat these allegations. We have also advised him that he is entitled to substantial compensation for the injury to his reputation and feelings, as to which we invite your proposals. In respect of damages our client will

---

[5] The pre-action protocol for defamation (Civil Procedure, Vol.1 (2013) C6–001) governs the standards for efficient conduct of pre-action litigation. The protocol sets out the information that should be included in the letter of claim and the defendant's response to the letter of claim: see the observations of Tugendhat J. in *Rothschild v Associated Newspapers Ltd* [2012] EWHC 177 (QB) at [16]–[18]. It is particularly important that a letter of claim sets out all the remedies sought where an offer of amends might be made in response: see *Abu v MGN Ltd* [2002] EWHC 2345 (QB); [2003] 1 W.I.R. 2201 at [8]–[10], and fn.7 below.

point to the following facts and matters [*set out matters relied upon in support of damages claim*]. Our client will also require payment by you of all the legal costs he has incurred in this matter.

This letter is written in accordance with the pre-action protocol for defamation. We look forward to hearing from you without delay. If we have not received a satisfactory reply by [*date*], our instructions are to issue a claim form. In the meantime, our client reserves all his rights.

Yours faithfully,

(b) **Letter of Claim**—libel published on internet—seeking apology and inviting proposals as to damages (see para.A1.4, below for Offer to Make Amends pursuant to Defamation Act 1996, s.2; para.A1.18, below for Defence).

Mr C.D.
[*address*]

In the Matter of an Intended Action Between A.B. v You

Dear Sir,

We act for A.B., the internationally renowned historian.

On [*date*], on your "Modern History Bulletin Board", a website set up or caused to be set up by you on the internet at the address http://www.[*insert website address*].co.uk, you published the following words which are defamatory of our client, "A.B., the famous historian, recently left the country after it was announced that his affairs had come under police investigation for alleged tax evasion."

These words meant and would have been understood to mean that our client is guilty of tax evasion. This allegation is entirely false. He has never been suspected of any impropriety in relation to his tax affairs, let alone been the subject of police investigation into an evasion by him of his tax liabilities. Your publication of these allegations on the internet at a website which is readily accessible to users of the system constitutes a very serious libel and has caused him considerable embarrassment and distress. The extent of the damage caused to our client's reputation is evidenced by the fact that, since the date upon which the passage complained of was published, your website has (at the time of writing) been accessed some 2,000 times, as is indicated by the number of "hits" recorded on the website's title page. [*Alternatively where publication is unknown, set out a platform of facts from which it can be inferred that the article has been read in this jurisdiction and request that all weblogs and publication data are retained.*][6]

In the circumstances, our client requires from you as a matter of urgency a full and unequivocal retraction and apology in terms to be approved by us, and an undertaking not to repeat these allegations. We have also advised him that he is entitled to substantial compensation for the injury to his reputation and feelings, as to which we invite your proposals. Our client will also require payment by you of all the legal costs he has incurred in this matter.

We look forward to hearing from you without delay. If we have not received a satisfactory reply by [*date*], our instructions are to issue a claim form. We would therefore be obliged if you could indicate to us as soon as is practicable, the name and

---

[6] See fn.25 under para.26.5, above.

address of a solicitor who will accept service of proceedings on your behalf should that eventuality arise. In the meantime, our client reserves all his rights.

Yours faithfully,

Forms of Correction and Apology   A1.2

(a) An article appeared on page [x] of the issue of this newspaper for [date] under the heading "[x]" to the effect that Mr A.B. was guilty of [set out the meaning of the passage in respect of which the apology is being made]. The report published by us was based upon information that we believed to be reliable. We have, however, subsequently looked into the matter and now recognise that there was no foundation to these allegations and we regret that they were ever made. We are happy to take the earliest opportunity of correcting our error and of expressing to Mr A.B. our regret for any distress or embarrassment caused to him by the publication of the original article.

(b) In yesterday's issue of [name of publication], there appeared on page [x] a paragraph under the heading "[x]". It has been pointed out to us that this could have been read by some readers as suggesting that [set out the meaning of the passage in respect of which the apology is being made]. No such suggestion was ever intended, and it would, of course, have been totally unfounded. We greatly regret any distress or embarrassment which the wording of this paragraph may have caused to A.B., and we are glad to take the opportunity of apologising to him and correcting any misunderstanding.

Response to Letter of Claim—Libel in newspaper—seeking apology,   A1.3
statement in court and inviting proposals as to damages (see para.A1.1, above)

Dear Sir/ Madam,

We act on behalf of [the potential defendant] and are in receipt of your Letter of Claim dated [. . .]. Our client admits having published the article. We do not consider that the words complained of are defamatory of your client or could have been understood in the meaning you have set out. If the article is defamatory then the article meant that [set out the meaning the defendant alleges the words complained of to mean, if desirable to do so]. In that meaning the words are true and our client will rely upon the defence of justification. In particular, [set out the points that the defendant is likely to rely upon]. Accordingly we are instructed to reject your claim and, if proceedings are issued intend to defend them vigorously.

Offer to Make Amends: Qualified Offer to Make Amends Pursuant   A1.4
to Defamation Act 1996, s.2[7]

Messrs Smith & Co

[address]

---

[7] See fn.5 above. A defendant will be tied, when it comes to compensation, to reliance on points he made known to the claimant before the offer of amends was accepted. For this reason it is important to raise any matters in mitigation in the letter making the offer: *Nail v News Group Newspapers Ltd* [2005] 1 All E.R. 1040 per May L.J. at [15]; *Abu v MGN Ltd* [2003] 1 W.L.R. 2201 at [8]–[10].

[Date]

In the Matter of an Intended Action Between A.B. v C.D.

Dear Sirs,

We act for Mr C.D. in the above-mentioned matter and write this letter in response to your letter before action dated [*date*].

In the letter, you made reference to a statement published by Mr C.D. at a website on the internet at the address http://www.[*website address*].co.uk, and entitled "Modern History Bulletin Board".

Our client now accepts in relation to the statement of which Mr A.B. makes complaint that in so far as it meant and was understood to mean that he was under suspicion of committing the offence of tax evasion and behaved in a manner so as to give rise to such a suspicion,[8] it is defamatory and untrue.

Accordingly, we are instructed to make on behalf of our client a qualified offer to make amends pursuant to Defamation Act 1996, s.2 in relation to that defamatory meaning which, it is accepted, the statement complained of conveys.[9]

The terms of our client's offer to make amends are as follows:

    (1) he will publish on his website at http://www.[*website address*].co.uk with similar prominence and in the same font size as the statement complained of, a correction of the said statement, in the following terms[10]:

        "For those of you who have been to this page before, especially between [*relevant dates*], you may have seen a passage at the foot of the screen in which I suggested that A.B. was under suspicion of tax evasion and had behaved in such a manner as to give rise to such a suspicion. I now recognise that this allegation was wrong and caused A.B. considerable embarrassment and distress. I wish to take this opportunity to clarify the situation to all those who read that statement and to withdraw the allegation unreservedly. I express my sincere regret and apologies to A.B. for any embarrassment or distress caused to him by my publication of this statement at my website on the internet";

    (2) he will undertake not further to publish or cause to be published whether by himself his servants agents or otherwise howsoever the words complained of or any similar words defamatory of your client;

    (3) he will undertake to pay the legal costs which your client has reasonably incurred by reason of making this complaint;

    (4) he will pay compensation for any damage which your client may have sustained by reason of the said publication, the amount of which shall be agreed between the parties.[11]

---

[8] In order to be a qualified offer to make amends the defamatory meaning in relation to which the qualified offer is being made must be set out: s.2(3)(c), Defamation Act 1996. Otherwise the offer will be taken to refer to the words in the meaning complained of by the claimant.

[9] The offer must be in writing, must be expressed to be an offer to make amends under s.2, Defamation Act 1996, and must state if it is a qualified offer: s.2(3)(a)–(c), Defamation Act 1996.

[10] S.2(4)(a) and (b), Defamation Act 1996.

[11] In relation to compensation and costs in the context of an offer to make amends under Defamation Act 1996, see ss.2(4)(c) and 3(5).

Where a defendant's offer to make amends is accepted by the claimant before the issue of proceedings, but the parties require a court order that the offer be fulfilled (s.3(3) Defamation Act 1996) or the parties do not agree on the steps to be taken by way of correction, apology and publication, the amount of compensation or costs (s.3(4)–(6) Defamation Act 1996), a claim for such relief should be made under CPR Pt 8: see para.3 of the practice direction supplementing CPR Pt 53.

We look forward to hearing your response to these proposals and, in the meantime, expressly reserve all our client's rights.

Yours faithfully,

Claim Form[12]   **A1.5**

(a) Claim Form—common form—slander and libel—telephone conversations containing slander—same words subsequently transmitted by electronic mail—damages—injunction

The claimant's claim is for:

(1) Damages,[13] including aggravated damages, for slander in respect of the following words spoken and published by sales agents and other representatives of the second defendant with reference to the claimant in the course of telephone conversations with actual and potential trade customers of the claimant between [*relevant date(s)*][14]: "A.B. is a thief and a liar and is not to be trusted."

(2) Damages for libel in respect of words contained in an electronic mail ("e-mail") message published or caused to be published by the first and/or the second defendant to sales agents and other representatives of [*X*] Limited on an e-mail system on [*relevant date(s)*].

(3) An injunction to restrain the first defendant whether by himself, his servants or agents or otherwise and the second defendant whether by its officers, directors, servants or agents or otherwise from further publishing or causing to be published the words complained of or any similar words defamatory of the claimant.

Value
The Claimant cannot say how much he intends to recover
The Claimant wishes his claim to be issued in the High Court because by law his claim must be commenced in the High Court by way of the County Courts Act 1984, section 15(2)(c) and CPR PD 7A, para.2.9

[I believe] [the (*claimant*) believes] that the facts stated in this Claim Form are true.[15]

(b) Claim Form—common form—libel in book about to be published

The claimant's claim is for:

---

[12] In general with regard to claim forms, see CPR Pt 7 and form N1.

[13] The claimant is not required to state that he is claiming aggravated, exemplary or special damages in the claim form, but it remains good practice to do so.

[14] In relation to the requirement that the claim form adequately identify the publication complained of, see paras 2.1, 2.2 and 2.4 of the practice direction to CPR Pt 53. In respect of a claim for slander the claim form must as far as possible contain the words complained of (in direct speech) and identify the person to whom they were spoken and when. See paras 26.5–6, above.

[15] All statements of case must be verified by a statement of truth as well as other documents such as witness statements. See, generally CPR Pt 22.

(1) Damages, including aggravated damages, for a libel contained on page 150 of the book "[*title of book*]" caused to be printed and published by the defendants in or about April 2002.

(2) An injunction restraining the first defendant by himself, his servants, agents or otherwise howsoever and the second defendant by its directors, servants or agents or otherwise howsoever from printing or publishing or causing to be printed or published the words complained of by the claimant on page 150 of the book "[*title of book*]" or any similar words defamatory of the claimant.

Value

The Claimant cannot say how much he intends to recover
The Claimant wishes his claim to be issued in the High Court because by law his claim must be commenced in the High Court by way of the County Courts Act 1984, section 15(2)(c) and CPR PD 7A, para.2.9

B. STATEMENTS OF CASE[16]

PARTICULARS OF CLAIM, ETC[17].

A1.6 Particulars of Claim—Libel—common form—reference—natural and ordinary meanings/innuendo meanings—damages—injunction

IN THE HIGH COURT OF JUSTICE   HQ

QUEEN'S BENCH DIVISION
[....... DISTRICT REGISTRY]
BETWEEN:

A.B.

Claimant

And

1. C LIMITED
2. D
3. E

Defendants

PARTICULARS OF CLAIM

1. The claimant is [*set out sufficient particulars to identify the claimant and any relevant background facts, focusing on the sector of his reputation which it is claimed has been affected by the libel; and, after s.1 Defamation Act 2013 comes into force, give details of why (unless obvious) publication has caused or is likely to cause serious harm to the complainant's reputation; where the complainant is a body trading for profit, explain how that serious harm is likely to cause or has caused the complainant serious financial loss. It may be more convenient to plead those matters after the meaning and reference paragraphs,*

---

[16] With regard to statements of case generally, see CPR Pt 16.
[17] With regard to particulars of claim, see Ch.26 above.

because meaning and reference will be highly relevant to the issue of serious harm].[18]

2. The first defendant is the publisher of [*name of publication*], a [*daily/weekly*] newspaper with a considerable circulation and readership throughout the jurisdiction of this court.[19] The second defendant is the editor [*/proprietor*] of the said newspaper and the third defendant is a journalist who at all material times was employed [and/or retained] by the first defendant.

3. On the front and third pages of [*name of publication*] for [*date*], in an article headlined "[*name of article*]" under the byline of and/or written by the third defendant, the defendants and each of them published the following words defamatory of the claimant:
[*set out words complained of as appropriate, including headlines, text of article, captions to photographs*]

4. The said words referred and were understood to refer to the claimant.

Particulars of Reference

4.1   The claimant repeats paragraph 1 above.

4.2   [*set out all material facts and matters which (i) identify the claimant as the subject of the words complained of and (ii) establish that those reading the words complained of would have known that they referred to the claimant*].

4.3   By reason of their knowledge of the said facts and matters, the claimant was identified by a large but unquantifiable number of readers of the words complained of as the individual referred to by the said words. Without limiting the generality of this averment, these persons included [*set out the relevant publishees, where appropriate*].

5. In their natural and ordinary meaning the words meant and were understood to mean that [*set out natural and ordinary meaning of words complained of*].[20]

---

[18] By s.1, Defamation Act 2013 (not yet in force), a statement will not be defamatory unless its publication has caused or is likely to cause serious harm to the reputation of the claimant. In the case of a body that trades for profit, harm to its reputation will not be "serious harm" unless it has caused or is likely to cause the claimant serious financial loss. That will plainly entail examining the statement in itself, but it is likely to involve also a careful investigation of the inherent gravity of the allegation, the nature and status of the claimant, the publisher and the publishee(s), and a number of other circumstances (see discussion at para.2.6 above). That is a very different process from the determination of whether a statement is defamatory to which practitioners are accustomed, and it is submitted that claimants (and certainly claimants which are bodies trading for profit) should set out these factors in their Particulars of Claim. In the case of a body trading for profit which alleges that the harm to its reputation has caused (as opposed to is likely to cause) it serious financial loss, that will often take the form of traditional particulars of special damage.

[19] At this juncture, claimants should put forward their case as to the breadth of publication (circulation and/or readership) of the journal containing the libel complained of and, if appropriate, the influence the publication commands with the individuals to whom it is published. If liability is established, these matters will have an impact on the level of damages.

[20] "(1) The claimant must specify in the particulars of claim the defamatory meaning which he alleges that the words or matters complained of conveyed, both (a) as to their natural and ordinary meaning; and (b) as to any innuendo meaning . . . (2) in the case of an innuendo meaning, the claimant must also identify the relevant extraneous facts.": see para.2.3 of the practice direction to CPR Pt 53. On pleading meaning, see the discussion at paras 26.20ff, above.

6. Further or alternatively, by way of innuendo the said words meant and were understood to mean [*set out innuendo meaning of words complained of*].

Particulars

6.1 [*set out the factual basis of the knowledge possessed by the readers of the words who understood the words complained of in the innuendo meaning contended for which renders the words understandable in that innuendo meaning*]

6.2 In the premises, the said facts and matters would have been known to a substantial but unquantifiable number of unidentifiable readers of [*name of publication*] and these readers would have understood the words complained of herein to bear the meaning set out in paragraph 6 above.

7. By reason of the publication of the said words, the claimant has been gravely damaged in his character and reputation, has suffered considerable distress and embarrassment,[21] and has suffered special damage.[22]

Particulars of Special Damage

[*set out full particulars of any special damage alleged*]

8. Further, the claimant claims interest pursuant to section 35A of the Senior Courts Act 1981 on the amount of special damages found to be due to him at such rate and for such period as the Court thinks fit.[23]

9. Further or alternatively, in support of his claim for general, aggravated and/or exemplary damages the claimant will rely on the following facts and matters: [*set out facts and matters relied upon*].[24]

---

[21] The plea of general damage should be tailored to suit the type of injury the claimant is said to have sustained. The version used in the text is commonplace and is a more modern formulation of a plea of general damage than the traditional plea that the claimant: "has been brought into public scandal, odium and contempt and injured in his character, credit and reputation." There may, nevertheless, be factual situations to which the traditional form is still appropriate. Moreover, although damage is presumed and the above paragraph is sufficient, para.2.10(1) of the practice direction to CPR Pt 53 provides, "A claimant must give full details of the facts and matters on which he relies in support of his claim for damages". That is likely to become particularly important given the prospective statutory hurdle (s.1, Defamation Act 2013), by which a statement will not be defamatory unless its publication has caused or is likely to cause serious harm to the claimant's reputation; *a fortiori* in the case of a claimant which is a body trading for profit, where harm to its reputation will not amount to "serious harm" unless it has caused or is likely to cause the body serious financial loss, which may of course be capable of being pleaded as special damage.

[22] See fn.18, above.

[23] If the claimant is seeking special damages as part of his defamation claim, CPR r.16.4 makes detailed provision for what information must be given in the particulars of claim of the sum claimed and any interest sought thereon. See para.26.39, above.

[24] CPR r.16.4 requires a claimant seeking aggravated or exemplary damages as part of any claim to state as much in the particulars of claim together with the grounds for the claim. Para.2.10(2) of the practice direction to CPR Pt 53 expressly emphasises that in defamation claims: "Where a claimant seeks aggravated or exemplary damages he must provide the information specified in rule 16.4(1)(c)."

10. Unless restrained the defendants and each of them will further publish the words complained of or similar words defamatory of the claimant.

AND the claimant claims:

(1) Damages, including special, aggravated and exemplary damages, for libel;
(2) Interest on the special damages pursuant to section 35A of the Senior Courts Act 1981 to be assessed;
(3) An injunction to restrain the first defendant whether by its directors, servants or agents or otherwise howsoever and the second and third defendants whether by themselves their servants or agents or otherwise howsoever from publishing or causing to be published the said or any similar words defamatory of the claimant.

[I believe] [the (*claimant*) believes] that the facts stated in these Particulars of Claim are true.

Particulars of Claim—Libel—damages—aggravating factors—injunction **A1.7** (see para.A1.16, below, for Defence; para.A1.24, below, for Reply)[25]

IN THE HIGH COURT OF JUSTICE HQ

QUEEN'S BENCH DIVISION
[....... DISTRICT REGISTRY]
BETWEEN:

A.B.

Claimant

And

C LIMITED

Defendant

PARTICULARS OF CLAIM

1. The claimant is the Member of Parliament for [   ] and one of Her Majesty's Privy Councillors. Between May 2002 and April 2007, he served in Her Majesty's Government as an Under-Secretary of State for [   ].
2. The defendant is the publisher of *The Sunday Correspondent*, a national weekly newspaper with an enormous circulation and readership throughout this jurisdiction.
3. On pages 6 and 7 of the issue of *The Sunday Correspondent* for May 3, 2013, the defendant published or caused to be published the following words defamatory of the claimant: [*set out words complained of*].
4. In their natural and ordinary meaning, the said words meant and were understood to mean that:

   4.1 despite his considerable personal wealth, the claimant has deliberately and callously caused his son, John, and his son's mother Ms Jan Smith to live on social security payments;

---

[25] See fn.18 above.

    4.2   the claimant is a hypocrite who is prepared to complain publicly about the social problem of single-parent families, but privately refuses to fulfil his own paternal responsibilities towards his son.

5. The publication of the words complained of has gravely injured the reputation of the claimant, has exposed him to public scandal and contempt and caused him embarrassment and distress.
6. In support of his claim for general damages and/or in aggravation of damages, the claimant will rely on the fact that, despite the gravity of the allegations being made by the defendant, and the description of the article containing the words complained of as a "Special Investigation", the defendant prepared and published the article without making any attempt to verify the facts with him or afford him any opportunity to comment on the proposed publication.
7. Unless restrained by injunction, the defendant will further publish or cause to be published the said or some similar libels of the claimant.

AND the claimant claims:

    (1) Damages, including aggravated damages, for libel;
    (2) An injunction to restrain the defendant whether by its officers, servants or agents or otherwise howsoever from further publishing or causing to be published the words complained of or any other words to the same or any similar effect defamatory of the claimant.

[I believe] [the (*claimant*) believes] that the facts stated in these Particulars of Claim are true.

A1.8 Particulars of Claim—Libel—special damages—injunction (see para. A1.17, below, for Defence)[26]

IN THE HIGH COURT OF JUSTICE   HQ

QUEEN'S BENCH DIVISION
[....... DISTRICT REGISTRY]
BETWEEN:

A.B.

Claimant

And

1. C LIMITED
2. D
3. E

Defendants

PARTICULARS OF CLAIM

1. The claimant is a financier. Between January 1975 and June 1988, he was employed by International Finances Incorporated, a United States corporation incorporated in the state of Wyoming in the United States, in its London office

---

[26] See fn.18 above.

as a Vice-President. Thereafter until May 2005, he carried on business from New York as a freelance adviser to a number of major financial institutions in the United States including [—]. From June 7, 2005 until [*date*], he was employed by Jodrow Bank Limited in London as its Chief Executive.

2. The first defendant is the publisher of *What's Happening in Finance*, a weekly journal which is principally concerned with financial and business matters and has an enormous circulation and influence in the business community within this jurisdiction. The second defendant is a journalist employed by the first defendant.

3. In the issue of *What's Happening in Finance* for [*date*], the defendants published or caused to be published of and concerning the claimant, and of and concerning him in the way of his profession, the following defamatory words: [*set out words complained of*].

4. In their natural and ordinary meaning the said words meant and were understood to mean that the claimant was guilty of fraudulently disposing of assets belonging to International Finances Incorporated to his own financial advantage.

5. In consequence, the claimant has been injured in his personal and professional reputation, has undergone extreme embarrassment and hurt to his feelings, and has suffered special damage:

Particulars of Damage

5.1 On [*date*], after a meeting was held by the board of directors of the Jodrow Bank to discuss the charges made in the article complained of herein, the claimant was summarily dismissed from his employment on account of the said charges.

5.2 By reason of the publication of the article complained of, the claimant has lost his employment and his future prospects in the job market have been severely diminished.

5.3 The claimant is presently unable to quantify and/or particularise the loss he has sustained. In so far as such loss is quantifiable, the claimant will serve particulars of special damage separately when they become available.

6. Further the claimant claims interest pursuant to section 35A of the Senior Courts Act 1981 on the amount of special damages found to be due to him at such rate and for such period as the Court thinks fit.

7. Unless restrained, the defendants and each of them will further publish the said or similar words defamatory of the claimant.

AND the claimant claims:

(1) Damages, including special damages, for libel;

(2) Interest on the special damages pursuant to section 35A of the Senior Courts Act 1981 to be assessed;

(3) An injunction to restrain the first defendant, whether by its directors its servants or agents or otherwise howsoever, and to restrain the second defendant, whether by himself his servants or agents or otherwise howsoever from further publishing or causing to be published the said or any similar words defamatory of the claimant.

[I believe] [the (*claimant*) believes] that the facts stated in these Particulars of Claim are true.

A1.9 Particulars of Claim—Libel published on the internet (see para.A1.1(b), above, for Letter of Claim; para.A1.4, above, for Offer to Make Amends pursuant to Defamation Act 1996, s.2; para.A1.18, below, for Defence; para. A1.25, below, for Reply)[27]

IN THE HIGH COURT OF JUSTICE   HQ

QUEEN'S BENCH DIVISION
[....... DISTRICT REGISTRY]
BETWEEN:

A.B.

Claimant

And

C

Defendant

PARTICULARS OF CLAIM

1. The claimant is a renowned historian and Reader in Modern British History at the University of Christminster.
2. The defendant is a self-employed journalist specialising in post-war European history and the author and/or editor[28] of a website which he set up or caused to be set up in or about [*date*] on the internet. The said website is entitled "Modern History Bulletin Board" and its address is http://www.[*website address*].co.uk. At all material times the said website has been open to general access by any user of the internet. In the circumstances, it is to be inferred from the open access of the site and the wide interest in modern history amongst large sections of the population including history pupils, students and lecturers, that the words complained of in paragraph 3 were published to a substantial but unquantifiable number of readers.[29]
3. On a date presently unknown between [*date*] and [*date*], on the said website, the defendant published or caused to be published (and continues to publish or cause to be published) the following words defamatory of the claimant: "A.B., the world renowned historian, recently left the country after was it announced that his affairs had come under police investigation for alleged tax evasion."
4. In their natural and ordinary meaning the words meant and were understood to mean that the claimant is guilty of tax evasion.
5. By reason of the publication of the words complained of the claimant has been injured in his reputation and has been caused acute distress and hurt to his feelings.
6. Unless restrained the defendant will further publish or cause to be published the same or similar words defamatory of the claimant.

AND the claimant claims:

---

[27] See fn.18 above.

[28] Defamation Act 1996, s.1, defines the law relating to responsibility for publication. See also ss.5 and 10, Defamation Act 2013 and Ch.6 above.

[29] In cases where the publication complained of is alleged to have been published via the internet, see para.26.5 above.

(1) Damages for libel;
(2) An injunction restraining the defendant whether by himself his servants, agents or otherwise howsoever from further publishing or causing to be published the same or any similar words defamatory of the claimant.

[I believe] [the (*claimant*) believes] that the facts stated in these Particulars of Claim are true.

Particulars of Claim—Slander—imputing criminal offence—in foreign **A1.10** language—foreign publication—publication to known and to unknown persons—words calculated to disparage claimant in his business reputation —damages: special loss of specific customers/general loss of business—injunction[30]

IN THE HIGH COURT OF JUSTICE   HQ
QUEEN'S BENCH DIVISION
[....... DISTRICT REGISTRY]
BETWEEN:

A.B.
Claimant

And

1. C
2. D LIMITED
Defendants

PARTICULARS OF CLAIM

1. The claimant is a sole trader carrying on the business of [*set out sufficient particulars to identify the claimant, the relevant background facts, and his relevant business reputation*].
2. The first defendant, who is domiciled in England, is and was at all material times an employee of the second defendant [(*i*) *identify the defendants and the relationship between them, and (ii) explain the relationship, if any, between the claimant and the defendants*]. The second defendant is a company which is registered in England, has its offices in London and carries on the same business as the claimant.[31]
3. At all material times the first defendant was acting in the course of his employment and/or for and on behalf of the second defendant, which is accordingly vicariously liable for his actions and defaults pleaded herein.
4. On or about [*date*], in the course of a telephone conversation with M. Antoine Reno, who at the material time was in France, the first defendant spoke and

---

[30] See para.26.6 above and para.2.4 of the practice direction to CPR Pt 53: "In a claim for slander the precise words used and the names of the persons to whom they were spoken and when must, so far as possible, be set out in the particulars of claim, if not already contained in the claim form." For a case on the proper interpretation of para.2.4, see *Best v Charter Medical of England*, [2002] E.M.L.R. 18. On the effect of s.1 Defamation Act 2013, see fn.18 above.

[31] Notwithstanding that the words were published in France, the defendants can be sued in England because they are domiciled here: see *Shevill v Presse Alliance SA* [1996] A.C. 959 and para.24.25 above.

published to M. Reno and/or to Mme Emiline Cousteau and/or to Mme Sophie Monclain, the latter two of whom were present in the room with M. Reno at the material time, listening to the conversation by means of the telephone's speakerphone facility, of and concerning the claimant and of and concerning him in the way of his business: "Cet homme est un criminel résolu et fut même incriminé pour le chantage dans les années 70s en cours de négotiations avec compagnie [X]".

5. Further or alternatively, the claimant has grounds to believe that the said words were also published to some other persons whom he cannot presently identify and will not be able to identify until after the completion of disclosure, the exchange of witness statements and/or the service of requests for further information herein, but who were also in M. Reno's room at the material time listening to the said conversation by means of the speakerphone ("the Unknown Publishees"). The grounds for the claimant's belief are comments to this effect made to him by M. Reno during a telephone conversation with him on [*date*]. While M. Reno recollects that there were other such persons in his room at the said time, he is unable to remember who they were. In any event, the claimant will rely at trial upon the publication of the words complained of to each and every person to whom he may ascertain the said words have been published.

6. The publishees and each of them speak French fluently and understood the words complained of.

7. The following is a true and literal translation of the said words: "This man is a determined crook and was even convicted of blackmail in the 1970s in relation to a deal he did with [X] Limited".

8. In their natural and ordinary meaning, the said words meant and were understood to mean that the claimant is a determined crook who, in the course of conducting his business with [X] Limited, was found guilty and convicted of the criminal offence of blackmail.[32]

9. The publication of the said words in France is actionable by the law of France. The claimant will rely on the presumption of English law that the law of France is the same as that of England.[33]

10. By reason of the publication of the said words, the claimant has been seriously injured in his personal reputation, business reputation and goodwill, and M. Reno, Mme Cousteau and Mme Monclain who had formerly dealt with him have ceased to do so, and he has thereby lost the profits and gains which he would have otherwise acquired[34]:

Particulars of Special Damage

[*set out full particulars of any special damage alleged*]

10. By reason of the publication of the said words, the claimant has been seriously injured in his personal reputation business reputation and goodwill, and has suffered a general loss of business.

---

[32] In an action for slander, words which impute to the claimant the commission of a crime for which he can be made to suffer "corporally" (i.e. physically by way of punishment), are actionable without proof of special damage.

[33] Reliance on this presumption has been deprecated as anachronistic (see para.26.19 above), but unless the claimant wishes to take on the burden of proving foreign law it remains a sensible course, not least because the defendant may not dispute that the words were actionable under the laws of the jurisdiction where the words were published.

[34] In an action for slander, where the words complained of are "calculated to disparage the claimant in any office, profession, calling, trade or business held or carried on by him at the time

Particulars of General Loss of Business

[*Set out full particulars of the claimant's loss of business*]

11. Unless restrained the defendants and each of them will further publish the said or similar words defamatory of the claimant.

AND the claimant claims:

(1) Damages for slander;
(2) An injunction restraining the first defendant whether by himself, his servants, agents, or otherwise, or the second defendant whether by its officers, directors, or servants, agents or otherwise from further publishing the said or any similar words defamatory of the claimant.

[I believe] [the (*claimant*) believes] that the facts stated in these Particulars of Claim are true.

Particulars of Claim—Slander—delivery of defamatory speech—words **A1.11** calculated to disparage the claimant—Defamation Act 1952, s.2 (see para.A1.20, below, for Defence and Counterclaim)[35]

IN THE HIGH COURT OF JUSTICE   HQ

QUEEN'S BENCH DIVISION
[....... DISTRICT REGISTRY]
BETWEEN:

A.B.
Claimant

And

C
Defendant

PARTICULARS OF CLAIM

1. The claimant is a barrister by profession, called to the bar in 1970. Between June 2003 and the present date, the claimant has served as an elected local councillor on the Rockford County Council.
2. The defendant is a retired schoolteacher who has served as an elected local councillor during the same period.
3. In the afternoon of [*date*], the claimant and the defendant were present in the Debating Chamber of Rockford County Council, Taggart Road, Rockford and there attended a debate held in private concerning the sale of residential homes owned by the said Council.
4. In the course of a speech delivered during the said debate at or about 4.30 p.m., the defendant spoke and published to the members of the Council present at the

---

of publication" (Defamation Act 1952, s.2), they need not allege or prove special damage. However, if special damages are to be recovered, they must be pleaded and proved. See paras 26.29 and 26.30, above.

[35] See fn.18 above.

material time the following words defamatory of the claimant calculated to disparage him in his office as a councillor and in his profession as a barrister: "Mr A.B.'s bandying around of these baseless allegations about me is a sorry attempt to redress the damage caused by his being made the subject of High Court bankruptcy proceedings last year."

5. In their natural and ordinary meaning the words meant and were understood to mean that the claimant is a bankrupt and/or is unable to discharge all his just debts as and when they fall due for payment.

6. By reason of the publication of the words complained of, the claimant has been caused serious injury to his personal and professional reputation and has suffered considerable embarrassment and distress.

7. Unless restrained by this Court, the defendant will further publish or cause to be published the words complained of or similar words defamatory of the claimant.

AND the claimant claims:

(1) Damages for slander;

(2) An injunction to restrain the defendant whether by himself, his servants or agents or otherwise howsoever from further publishing and/or causing to be published the said or any similar words defamatory of the claimant.

[I believe] [the (*claimant*) believes] that the facts stated in these Particulars of Claim are true.

A1.12 **Particulars of Claim**[36]—Malicious falsehood—trade rivals—Defamation Act 1952, s.3/special damages—injunction (see para.A1.22, below, for Defence)

IN THE HIGH COURT OF JUSTICE   HQ

QUEEN'S BENCH DIVISION
[....... DISTRICT REGISTRY]
BETWEEN:

A LIMITED
Claimant

And

B LIMITED
Defendant

PARTICULARS OF CLAIM

1. The claimant is a company incorporated in Scotland which carries on business as a manufacturer and supplier of birdseed for sale to farmers throughout the United Kingdom and the European Union.

2. The defendant is a company incorporated in England engaged in the same business in direct competition with the claimant in the United Kingdom.[37]

---

[36] Generally, for requirements when pleading malicious falsehood, see para.26.42, above.

[37] The claimant should also set out particulars of all facts and matters bearing on the relationship between the claimant and the defendant and the circumstances in which the words complained of came to be published.

3. In or about May 2013, the defendant published or caused to be published in its marketing brochure entitled *Fancy Birds—Summer 2013*, copies of which were issued in particular to Mr William Miller and Mr John Barleymow and to the farming community at large, the following words of and concerning the claimant and its business: "Since a finding by government scientists that A Ltd's birdseed contains hazardous toxins which may be poisonous to farmyard animals other than birds, their customers may want to try us instead."

4. The said words were false in the following respects[38]:

Particulars of Falsity

4.1 There has been no investigation by any governmental department into products manufactured or supplied for sale to the public by the claimant;

4.2 No product manufactured or supplied for sale to the public by the claimant contains toxins hazardous or poisonous to any farmyard animal.

5. The defendant published or caused the said words to be published maliciously:

Particulars of Malice

5.1 The defendant is a trade rival of the claimant . . .
[*set out full particulars of malice relied upon. To support a plea of malice, the defendant's state of mind in publishing the words complained of must have been as set out in 5.x below*]

5.x In the premises, the defendant published or caused to be published the words complained of knowing them to be false, or recklessly, not caring whether they were true or false and/or with no honest belief that they were true. In so doing, the defendant was actuated by the dominant motive of damaging the claimant and its business.

6. The publication of the said words was calculated to cause pecuniary damage to the claimant in respect of its said business because the words were disparaging of the claimant's goods and encouraged customers to purchase the defendant's goods instead of the claimant's.[39] [*alternatively, where the claimant has evidence of quantifiable pecuniary loss state*] By reason of the publication of the said words, the claimant has suffered loss of damage:

Particulars of Special Damage

[*set out the particulars of loss occasioned by the publication of the said words*]

7. Further, the claimant claims interest pursuant to section 35A of the Senior Courts Act 1981 on the amount of damages found to be due to it at such rate and for such period as the Court thinks fit.

---

[38] At this point, all particulars identifying the respects in which the words complained of were false, should be set out.

[39] For pleading requirements where the claimant relies upon s.3 Defamation Act 1952 see *Tesla Motors Ltd v British Broadcasting Corporation* [2013] EWCA Civ 152; (2013) 163 N.L.J. 290 and para.26.42, fn.171, above. A case that the words were calculated to cause loss must be particularised. It should be noted that a claimant who relies upon s.3 is precluded from advancing a case that he is entitled to special damages: *Calvet v Tomkies* [1963] 1 W.L.R. 1397.

8. Unless restrained the defendant will continue to publish the said or similar false statements of and concerning the claimant and its business.

AND the claimant claims:

(1) Damages, including special damages [*if special damages are being claimed*], together with interest thereon pursuant to section 35A of the Senior Courts Act 1981 to be assessed];
(2) An injunction to restrain the defendant by itself its directors, officers, servants or agents or otherwise howsoever from further publishing the said or any similar falsehood of and concerning the claimant.

[I believe] [the (*claimant*) believes] that the facts stated in these Particulars of Claim are true.

A1.13 Particulars of Claim—privacy—misuse of private information[40] (see A1.23 for the Defence)

IN THE HIGH COURT OF JUSTICE   HQ

QUEEN'S BENCH DIVISION
[....... DISTRICT REGISTRY]
BETWEEN:

A.B.

Claimant

And

1. C.D.
2. E LIMITED

Defendants

PARTICULARS OF CLAIM

1. The claimant is a well-known politician who is married with two children aged 8 and 12.
2. The first defendant is a journalist, employed by the second defendant, the publisher of The Daily News, a daily newspaper with a substantial circulation and readership within the jurisdiction.
3. The defendants on [*date*] published and/or caused to be published on the front page of the newspaper an article containing the following information: that the claimant, a married man, was having an extra-marital affair, with a Ms X and was, or there were reasonable grounds to suspect that he was, the father of her 2-year-old child. The defendants also published alongside the article a photograph of the claimant together with Ms X and the child. The full article is annexed hereto as Schedule 1.
4. The claimant had, at all material times, a reasonable expectation that the information set out in paragraph 3 above and the images in the photograph

---

[40] For guidance on pleading in a misuse of private information action generally see para.26.43, above. For guidance on pleading an application for interim injunctive relief in this context see fn.2 above.

would remain private and/or confidential. The claimant will rely upon the following facts:

4.1 the information related to aspects of his personal life which were self-evidently confidential;

4.2 the information came from a confidential source;

4.3 the information related to aspects of the personal life of a child and her mother including speculation about the likely father of the child;

4.4 neither the claimant nor Ms X consented to the publication of the information or the photograph of themselves or the child.

5. In disclosing the information in paragraph 3 to the world at large the defendants misused the private information and/or breached the claimant's right to privacy.

6. As a result of the misuse of the claimant's private information and/or the breach of his privacy he has suffered hurt, distress and embarrassment. The claimant will rely upon the following in support of his claim for damages including aggravated damages: [*fill in relevant information here*].

7. Unless restrained by injunction, the defendants will further publish or cause to be published the said or similar private information.

AND the claimant claims:

(1) Damages, including aggravated damages, for misuse of private information, and/or for the breach of his privacy;

(2) An injunction restraining the first defendant whether by himself or howsoever and the second defendant whether by itself its directors, servants or agents from publishing or cause to be published the said or similar private information.

[I believe] [the claimant believes] that the facts stated in these Particulars of Claim are true.

Application for a Ruling on Meaning[41] A1.14

IN THE HIGH COURT OF JUSTICE HQ

QUEEN'S BENCH DIVISION
[....... DISTRICT REGISTRY]
BETWEEN:

A.B.

Claimant

And

C LIMITED

Defendant

APPLICATION NOTICE

---

[41] Note that this precedent will have no further value once s.11, Defamation Act 2013 (which removes the presumption in favour of jury trial) comes into force, because the court will no longer have the task of deciding whether the words complained of are capable of bearing a particular or any defamatory meaning. See Ch.30 above.

(We) [*Solicitors*] (on behalf of) (the defendant)
intend to apply for an order (a draft of which is attached) that

(1) Pursuant to CPR part 53 Practice Direction 4.1(1) the article sued upon is not capable of bearing the meanings pleaded at paragraphs X(a) and (b) of the Particulars of Claim and such paragraphs be struck out and judgment be entered for the defendant;

(2) Pursuant to CPR part 53 Practice Direction 4.1 (2) and/or (3) the article is not capable of bearing any meaning defamatory of the claimant and such paragraphs be struck out and judgment be entered for the defendant.

Because
the words complained of are not capable of bearing the meanings pleaded and/or they are not capable of being defamatory of the claimant.

DEFENCES

A1.15 Common Form Defences

(a) Slander

1. Paragraph 1 of the Particulars of Claim [*i.e. the prefatory averments*] is admitted.
2. It is denied that the defendant spoke and published the words set out in paragraph 2 of the Particulars of Claim.
(*or*)
It is admitted that the defendant spoke and published the words set out in paragraph 2 of the Particulars of Claim to the persons identified therein, but denied that he spoke and published them of and concerning the claimant or of or concerning him in the way of his profession or in relation to his conduct therein.
3. The said words do not and are not capable of being understood to refer to the claimant.
4. The said words do not and were not understood to bear the meanings alleged in paragraph 2 of the Particulars of Claim or any defamatory meaning.[42]
5. The said words were not calculated to disparage the claimant in his profession [*or office, trade, calling or business*] as alleged in paragraph 3 of the Particulars of Claim or at all.
6. It is denied that the claimant sustained the loss and damage alleged in paragraph 4 of the Particulars of Claim or any loss or damage by reason of the publication of the words complained of herein.

(b) Libel

1. Save that no admissions are made as to the circulation or readership of the said newspaper, paragraph 1 of the Particulars of Claim is admitted.

---

[42] In *Armstrong v Times Newspapers Ltd* [2006] EWHC 1614 (QB), Gray J. at [15] made the following observation: "In the Defence it is denied that the words bore the meaning attributed to them in the Particulars of Claim. The Defence does not as such set out the meaning for which the Defendants contend. (Although this conforms with current practice, I think it would be desirable if defendants were to identify in the Defence the meaning for which they contend, in the same way that claimants are required to do)." See the discussion at para.27.3, above.

2. The defendant denies that he wrote, printed or published or caused to be written, printed or published the words set out in paragraph 2 of the Particulars of Claim or any of them.
3. It is denied that the said words referred or were understood to refer to the claimant.
4. It is denied that the said words bore or were understood to bear or were capable of bearing the meanings set out in paragraph 2 of the Particulars of Claim or any defamatory meaning.

[I believe] [the (*defendant*) believes] that the facts stated in this Defence are true.

Defence— Libel—justification [alternatively, truth]—honest comment [alter- **A1.16** natively, honest opinion]—honest comment on privileged material [alternatively honest opinion on privileged material]—ss.5 and 6, Defamation Act 1952 [alternatively, s.2(3), Defamation Act 2013[43]]—response to claim for aggravated damages—mitigation—s.12 Defamation Act 1952 (see para.A1.7, above, for Particulars of Claim; para.A1.24, below, for Reply)

IN THE HIGH COURT OF JUSTICE   HQ

QUEEN'S BENCH DIVISION
[....... DISTRICT REGISTRY]
BETWEEN:

A.B.

Claimant

And

C LIMITED

Defendant

DEFENCE

1. Save that the defendant does not admit the word "enormous", paragraphs 1 and 2 of the Particulars of Claim are admitted.
2. It is admitted that on pages 6 and 7 of *The Sunday Correspondent* for May 3, 2008, the defendant published an article which included the words pleaded in paragraph 3 of the Particulars of Claim. The said words formed part of a much longer article to the whole of which the defendant will refer for the context and true meaning of the words complained of.
3. It is denied that in their natural and ordinary meaning the said words, in their proper context, bore or were capable[44] of bearing the meanings or either of them pleaded in paragraph 4 of the Particulars of Claim.
4. If and in so far as the said words in their natural and ordinary meaning bore and were understood to bear the meanings set out below, they were true in substance

---

[43] See fn.4 above re the position concerning the repeal of s.6 Defamation Act 1952.
[44] See fn.42, above.

and in fact[45] [alternatively, when s.2 Defamation Act 2013 comes into force: If and in so far as the said words bore the imputations set out below then the statement is substantially true]:

4.1   that the claimant has been guilty of a reprehensible lack of parental responsibility by abandoning the child he had by his mistress;
4.2   that the claimant is a hypocrite for making public pronouncements which are not matched by his own private behaviour.

Particulars of Justification [alternatively, Particulars of Truth]

(1)   [*Set out all relevant facts and matters which support the plea that the words are true in substance and in fact, e.g.:*]
      The claimant has been a Member of Parliament since 1984. As pleaded in paragraph 1 of the Particulars of Claim, between May 2002 and April 2007, he served in the government as an Under-Secretary of State for [   ]. In that capacity, he made a number of speeches in Parliament[46] and in public in which he espoused the cause of "Back to Basics", a social policy which called for a return by society to traditional family values and placed a strong emphasis on parental responsibility: [*set out relevant content of speeches*].

(2)   The claimant published a book containing autobiographical memoirs, entitled *Personal Reflections*, in or about [*date*]. In the said book, there are a number of passages in which the claimant articulated his conviction that the "root-cause of various forms of social malaise was the dereliction by parents of their duties towards their children. Parents must be accountable to society." (p. 120). The defendant will refer to and rely upon all these passages at trial, but for present purposes simply refers to the page and paragraph number of the relevant extracts.

(3)   At a press conference held on April 1, 2012, the claimant announced that he had had a sexual relationship with his former employee, a researcher named Ms Jan Smith (now Mrs Brown), and that on June 7, 2009, she had given birth to a son, John, of whom he was the father.

---

[45] The defendant is required clearly to identify the meaning of the words which he seeks to justify: *Lucas-Box v News Group Newspapers Ltd* [1986] 1 W.L.R. 147 at 153; *Viscount De L'Isle v Times Newspapers Ltd* [1987] 1 W.L.R. 49. See para.7.8, above. For pleading requirements when justifying, see para.2.5 of the practice direction to CPR Pt 53 and paras 27.6 to 27.13 above for explanations of the repetition and conduct rules and the professional obligations placed on a pleader. For the defence of truth under s2, Defamation Act 2013, see para.27.14, above.

[46] It should be noted that a plea of justification which challenges matters said or done within Parliament is prohibited by art.9 of the Bill of Rights 1689: *Prebble v Television New Zealand* [1995] 1 A.C. 321. However, in *Allason v Haines* [1996] E.M.L.R. 143, on the application of the defendants for a stay of the action on the grounds that the enforcement of the privilege deprived them of what was probably their only defence, it was held that to refuse a stay would be unjust. Defamation Act 1996, s.13, now provides the machinery for the waiver of Parliamentary privilege "where the conduct of a person in or in relation to proceedings in Parliament is in issue in defamation proceedings" (Defamation Act 1996, s.13(1)). It is submitted that were the situation in *Allason* to arise again, the court would grant a stay of the action unless and until the claimant waived his privilege in accordance with s.13. With regard to Defamation Act 1996, s.13, and Parliamentary privilege generally, see *Hamilton v Al-Fayed* [2001] 1 A.C. 395 HL.

(4) Notwithstanding and in flat contradiction of his previously adopted stance, at a further press conference on April 15, 2013, the claimant stated that he intended neither to take an active role in the upbringing of his son nor to make any financial provision for him. The purported ground for this conduct was that he did not wish to interfere in the relationship of Mrs Brown with her husband who "were happy to treat the child as their own".

5. Further or alternatively, in so far as the said words made or contained the following comment or expression of opinion, namely that the claimant had behaved in a callous, hypocritical and reprehensible manner towards Mrs Brown and his son,[47] the defendant contends that the said words constituted honest comment on a matter of public interest [alternatively, when s.3 Defamation Act 2013 comes into force: the said words were a statement of opinion], namely the propriety or otherwise of the conduct of a member of the government whose private behaviour towards his own family stood in stark contrast to his public pronouncements on the issue, at a time when he had direct responsibility for governmental policy on issues relating to social security.

Particulars of Fact Upon Which Comment is Based [alternatively, Upon Which the Statement of Opinion is Based]

(1) The defendant repeats paragraphs 4(1) to (4) above.

6. Further or alternatively, in so far as the words contained the comment or expression of opinion set out in paragraph 5 above, they were honest comment upon a matter of public interest [alternatively, they were a statement of opinion] based upon the following facts which were stated to have been found proved in the judgment of Mr Justice Just given in open court on May 8, 2012 in wardship proceedings in the Family Division of the High Court of Justice in London in the case of *Re J (A Minor)* which related to the claimant's son, a fair and accurate report of which was published on page 5 of the same issue of the said newspaper.

Particulars of Fact Upon Which Comment [alternatively, the Statement of Opinion] *is Based*

6.1 In his judgment dated May 8, 2012, Mr Justice Just found that: [*set out particulars of all relevant facts found to have been proved*]

---

[47] The defendant is under an obligation clearly to identify the comment which he contends is "fair" (or, now, "honest"): *Control Risks Group Ltd v New English Library* [1990] 1 W.L.R. 183. For pleading requirements when setting up a defence of honest comment, see para.2.6 of the practice direction to CPR Pt 53 and paras 27.17 to 27.24 above.

7. The defendant will rely, if necessary, upon the provisions of sections 5 and/or 6 of the Defamation Act 1952[48] [alternatively, section 2(3) Defamation Act 2013[49]].

8. No admissions are made in respect of paragraph 5 of the Particulars of Claim.

9. If the claimant is entitled to any award of general damages (which is denied), it is denied that the claimant is entitled to an award of aggravated damages thereon by reason of the facts and matters alleged in paragraph 6 of the Particulars of Claim or otherwise. The defendant will rely upon the following in answer to the matters alleged in paragraph 6 of the Particulars of Claim:

[set out all relevant matters which (i) meet and answer the allegations being advanced by the claimant in support of his claim for aggravated damages, or (ii) demonstrate that the claim is misconceived in fact and/or in law, e.g.:]

9.1 It is untrue that the defendant prepared and published the article without making any attempt to verify the facts with the claimant or afford him any opportunity to comment on the proposed publication. On four separate occasions on Friday, May 1, 2013, Ms Peterson of the defendant telephoned the claimant at his office in Millbank at Westminster to seek the claimant's comments on the proposed publication. Ms Peterson was informed through the claimant's secretary that he was not willing to discuss his personal life with the media.

9.2 Further, even if those attempts had not been made, the alleged failure to contact the claimant would not have been a justified ground of criticism of the defendant because the claimant stated at the press conference held on April 15, 2013 that he was not prepared to discuss his private life further, in particular, the arrangements he had made for his son with Mrs Brown, with the media.

10. If (which is denied) the claimant is entitled to any damages, in mitigation of those damages, the defendant will rely upon the fact that the claimant has brought a claim and has received compensation for damages for libel in respect of the publication in *The Rockford Times* newspaper of *[date]* of words to the same effect as those complained of in this action.[50]

11. By reason of the matters pleaded above, it is denied that the claimant is entitled to the injunctive relief he claims against the defendant in paragraph 7 of the Particulars of Claim.

[I believe] [the *(defendant)* believes] that the facts stated in this Defence are true.

A1.17 **Defence**—Libel—qualified privilege (statutory) pursuant to Defamation Act 1996, s.15 (fair and accurate report of proceedings in public before a court anywhere in the world) [alternatively s.15 as amended by s.7, Defamation Act 2013]—justification [alternatively, truth]—mitigation of damages: evidence of bad reputation—Civil Evidence Act 1968, s.13 (see para.A1.8, above, etc. for Particulars of Claim)

---

[48] Note that these sections will be repealed by ss.2(4) and 3(8), Defamation Act 2013.
[49] See again fn.4 above. As the new section 2(3) will only relate to the truth defence, it may be preferable to move this part to a new paragraph at 4.3 in the above example.
[50] See Defamation Act 1952, s.12.

IN THE HIGH COURT OF JUSTICE   HQ

QUEEN'S BENCH DIVISION
[....... DISTRICT REGISTRY]
BETWEEN:

A.B.

Claimant

And

C LIMITED

Defendant

DEFENCE

1. Save that the defendant avers that the claimant was summarily dismissed from his employment with International Finances Incorporated on June 7, 1988 and from Jodrow Bank on [*date*], in each case for gross misconduct, paragraph 1 of the Particulars of Claim is admitted.
2. Save that no admissions are made as to the precise size of the circulation or the influence commanded by *What's Happening in Finance*, paragraphs 2 and 3 of the Particulars of Claim are admitted.
3. It is admitted that the defendant published in the issue of the said journal for [*date*] the words set out in paragraph 4 of the Particulars of Claim.
4. It is admitted that the words complained of bore and were understood to bear the meaning alleged in paragraph 4 of the Particulars of Claim.
5. The words complained of consisted of a fair and accurate report of legal proceedings in public brought against the claimant and accordingly were published on an occasion of qualified privilege.[51]

Particulars

5.1 In criminal proceedings which came on for trial at the Central Criminal Court, Old Bailey, London on May 31, 2008, the claimant was prosecuted for fifteen separate counts of theft contrary to section 1 of the Theft Act 1968 in connection with the disposal of International Finances Incorporated's assets to a number of bank accounts held offshore in Bermuda in his name and/or in the name of shell companies incorporated by him.

5.2 On June 25, 2008, the claimant was convicted on two of the said counts of theft which related to the misappropriation by him of some £120,000 of his clients' investments, and was sentenced to 2 years' imprisonment, suspended for 2 years.

5.3 To the extent that the words complained of referred to the said criminal proceedings against the claimant, namely, the headline, paragraphs 1 to 12, and 20 to 23 of the article complained of, they constituted a fair and

---

[51] S.15, Defamation Act 1996, expanded the defence of statutory qualified privilege, and it will be further expanded by ss.4 to 11 of the Defamation Act 2013. For pleading requirements when relying on a defence of qualified privilege, see para.2.7 of the practice direction to CPR Pt 53. In this context, see also *McCartan Turkington Breen v Times Newspapers Ltd* [2001] 2 A.C. 277 HL.

accurate report of the said proceedings which took place in public before a court in the United Kingdom. Accordingly, the said words are protected by qualified privilege under section 15 of the Defamation Act 1996 and Part I (2) of Schedule 1 thereto.[52]

6. Further or alternatively, in the natural and ordinary meaning contended for by the claimant and admitted by the defendants in paragraph 4 above, the words complained of are true in substance and in fact [alternatively, that the imputation conveyed by the statement complained of is substantially true].

Particulars of Justification [alternatively, Particulars of Truth]

[set out facts and matters which establish that the words complained of are true in the meaning which the Defendants have accepted they bear or, under s.2 Defamation Act 2013 in the imputation the statement is said to convey]

6.1 The defendant repeats paragraphs 5.1 and 5.2 above.

7. Further, if and in so far as may be necessary, the defendants will rely in mitigation of damages on the following facts and matters:

7.1 The claimant has at all material times borne a general bad reputation as a dishonest fraudster. In support of this allegation, the defendant will rely upon the conviction of the claimant referred to in paragraph 5.2 above, and upon section 13 of the Civil Evidence Act 1968, in support of the contention that the said conviction of the claimant is conclusive evidence that he committed that offence.[53]

8. It is accordingly denied that the claimant has suffered the damage specified in paragraph 6 of the Particulars of Claim or any damage by reason of the publication by the defendants of the words complained of or that the defendants are liable for any embarrassment or hurt to the claimant's feelings, as to which, no admissions are made.

9. Further, by reason of the foregoing, it is denied that the claimant is entitled to the relief sought in paragraph 7 of the Particulars of Claim or any relief.

[I believe] [the (*defendant*) believes] that the facts stated in this Defence are true.

A1.18 **Defence**—Libel—offer to make amends (Defamation Act 1996, ss.2–4)—qualified offer, not accepted by claimant—mitigation of damages (Defamation Act 1996, s.4(5)) (see para.A1.1(b), above, etc. for Letter of Claim; para.A1.4, above, for Offer to Make Amends pursuant to Defamation

---

[52] An absolute privilege will attach *inter alia* to fair and accurate reports of proceedings in public in any court in the UK, if the report is published contemporaneously with the proceedings. Accordingly, if the report in this precedent had been published contemporaneously, it will be absolutely privileged: see para.13.35, above.

[53] See in this context s.12 Defamation Act 1996, which amends s.13 of the Civil Evidence Act 1968. In relation to what facts a defendant can rely on in mitigation of damages, see para.27.39 above.

Act 1996, s.2; para.A1.9, above, for Particulars of Claim; para.A1.25, below, for Reply)

IN THE HIGH COURT OF JUSTICE HQ

QUEEN'S BENCH DIVISION
[....... DISTRICT REGISTRY]
BETWEEN:

A.B.

Claimant

And

C.D.

Defendant

DEFENCE

1. Save that it is denied that the defendant continues to cause the words complained of in paragraph 3 of the Particulars of Claim to be published, paragraphs 1, 2 and 3 of the Particulars of Claim are admitted.
2. It is denied that the words complained of bore or were understood to bear or are capable of bearing the meaning alleged in paragraph 4 of the Particulars of Claim.
3. In so far as the words complained of meant and were understood to mean that the claimant was under suspicion of committing the offence of tax evasion and had behaved in such a manner as to give rise to such a suspicion, the defendant has duly made to the claimant an offer to make amends pursuant to section 2 of the Defamation Act 1996 ("the 1996 Act"), which has not been withdrawn by the defendant and has not been accepted by the claimant.[54]

Particulars of Qualified Offer

3.1 The defendant first received notice of the claimant's complaint herein by letter from his solicitors dated [*date*]. As soon as practicable thereafter on [*date*], having accepted that the words complained of bore the specific defamatory meaning set out herein and were false, the defendant made the claimant a qualified offer in accordance with sections 2(2) and 2(4) of the 1996 Act.

3.2 The said offer has not been withdrawn by the defendant and is relied upon by the Defendant pursuant to section 4(2) Defamation Act 1996.

3.3 By a letter from the claimant's solicitors dated [*date*], it was indicated on behalf of the claimant that he did not accept the said offer.

4. Further or alternatively, if and in so far as is necessary, the defendant will rely at trial on the facts and matters set out under paragraph 3 above in mitigation of damages.

---

[54] Defamation Act 1996, ss.2–4 introduced the "Offer to Make Amends" defence. For pleading requirements when relying upon an offer of amends as a defence see para.27.34, above.

5. By reason of the foregoing, it is denied that the defendant is liable to compensate the claimant for any damage or hurt he may have suffered (as to which no admissions are made) by reason of the words complained of, as alleged in paragraph 5 of the Particulars of Claim or at all.
6. Paragraph 6 of the Particulars of Claim is denied.

[I believe] [the (*defendant*) believes] that the facts stated in this Defence are true.

A1.19   Defence—Absolute privilege

(a) Statements made by an advocate in judicial proceedings

The said words were published on an occasion of absolute privilege.

Particulars of Absolute Privilege

(1) The defendant is a barrister;
(2) The said words were spoken by the defendant in open court [*on date*] in the European Court of Human Rights in Strasbourg in proceedings brought against the government of the United Kingdom by A.B. for whom, at all material times, the defendant was acting;
(3) The said words were spoken by the defendant in his capacity as advocate for the said A.B., and in the course of the said proceedings.

(b) Statements made by Officer of State in official report

The said words were written and published by the Defendant in his capacity as Permanent Under-Secretary of State to the Ministry of [   ] in an official report made to the Minister of [   ], and were therefore absolutely privileged.

(c) Fair and accurate report of proceedings in public published contemporaneously pursuant to Defamation Act 1996, s.14

The said words are absolutely privileged pursuant to section 14(3)(a) of the Defamation Act 1996, being a fair and accurate report of proceedings in public before the Central Criminal Court, Old Bailey, London and published contemporaneously with those proceedings.[55]

Particulars of Absolute Privilege

(1) On [*date*], A.B. went on trial for the offence of rape contrary to section 1 of the Sexual Offences Act 1956;
(2) On the same date, at the outset of the said trial, the trial judge Mr Justice John made an order pursuant to section 4(2) of the Contempt of Court Act 1981

---

[55] Defamation Act 1996, s.14 (as will be amended by Defamation Act 2013, s.7(1)) provides that "a fair and accurate report of proceedings in public before a court to which this section applies, if published contemporaneously with the proceedings, is absolutely privileged". See A2.23, Appendix 2.

postponing the publication of any report of the said proceedings until the proceedings were concluded or further order;

(3) No further order was made during the course of the said trial and on [*date*], the claimant was convicted;

(4) The defendant published the report of the said proceedings in its newspaper the day after the said conviction of the claimant;

(5) In the premises, in so far as the said report was published as soon as practicable after publication was permitted, it was published contemporaneously[56] and accordingly is protected by absolute privilege.

[I believe] [the (*defendant*) believes] that the facts stated in this Defence are true.

Defence and Counterclaim—Slander—qualified privilege (common **A1.20** law—duty/interest & response to an attack)—counterclaim (defamatory words spoken and published by claimant)—repetition of slander in local and national press (see para.A1.11, above for Particulars of Claim.)

IN THE HIGH COURT OF JUSTICE　　　　　　　　　　　　　HQ

QUEEN'S BENCH DIVISION
[....... DISTRICT REGISTRY]
BETWEEN:

A.B.

Claimant

And

C

Defendant

DEFENCE

1. Paragraphs 1 and 2 of the Particulars of Claim are admitted.
2. Save that it is admitted that on the afternoon of [*date*], the claimant and the defendant attended a debate in the Debating Chamber of Rockford County Council, during which the defendant made a speech, paragraph 3 of the Particulars of Claim is not admitted.
3. The defendant denies that he spoke or otherwise published or caused to be published the words set out in paragraph 4 of the Particulars of Claim on the date alleged or at all. In support of this contention, the defendant will rely on the official transcript of the proceedings of the said debate.
4. Further or alternatively, if (which is denied) the said words were spoken and published by the defendant, it is denied that the said words were calculated to disparage the claimant in his profession or his office as alleged in paragraph 4 of the Particulars of Claim or at all. The defendant avers that the said words are not actionable without proof of special damage and none is alleged.

---

[56] Defamation Act 1996, s.14(2).

5. Further or alternatively, if (which is denied) the said words were published, they were published on an occasion of qualified privilege.[57]

Particulars

5.1   [*set out all facts and matters which give rise to the privilege, in this case (i) the duty/interest situation and (ii) the claimant's attack on the character of the defendant to which the defendant was responding*]
In the course of the said debate on [*date*], as is recorded in the official transcript of the proceedings on page [*x*], line [*y*], at or about 3.15 p.m., the claimant interjected during the speech of Councillor John Smith and spoke and thereby published the following words of and concerning the defendant: "Mr C knows very well, although he continues to deny it, that he is up to his neck in the 'Homes for Votes' scandal. He has sold council houses to the people living in his ward on the cheap, as long as they pledge their continued support."

5.2   In speaking these words, the claimant wrongfully and unjustly attacked the defendant as behaving improperly in the discharge of his duties as a Councillor, and falsely accused him of cynically and unscrupulously selling residential homes owned by the Council to private purchasers below their market value to his own political advantage.

5.3   In the circumstances, the defendant was under a duty and/or it was his proper and legitimate interest to communicate to those to whom the said allegations were published by the claimant his defence to those claims and the true facts as to the same and the motives of the claimant in making them, and all those who heard the words spoken by the defendant had a corresponding and legitimate interest in receiving such communication. It is further averred that the communication by the defendant was reasonable in all the circumstances, its dissemination being no wider than the attack by the claimant, and no wider than was necessary in order to inform those interested.

6. Further or alternatively, the said words do not and were not understood to bear the meaning alleged in paragraph 4 of the Particulars of Claim.

7. Paragraphs 6 and 7 of the Particulars of Claim are denied. In the premises, it is denied that the claimant is entitled to the relief claimed in the Particulars of Claim or any relief.

8. Further or alternatively, the defendant has a Counterclaim herein and will seek to set off the same in extinction or diminution of the claimant's claim.

Counterclaim[58]

9. On [*date*], at [*time*], the claimant, having called a press conference held outside the Town Hall, substantially repeated the allegations he had previously made in

---

[57] While the overriding objective of the CPR in general requires conciseness in defamation pleading (see *McPhilemy v Times Newspapers* [1999] 3 All E.R. 775 CA, for example) it is submitted that there will still be cases in which CPR r.16.4 and para.2.1 of the practice direction to CPR Pt 53 demand a greater degree of specificity and detail in defamation pleading than in other causes of action, e.g. when particularising a *Reynolds v Times Newspapers Ltd* [2001] 2 A.C. 127-type qualified privilege. See Ch. 27 generally above for detail on pleading the various different libel defences.

[58] With regard to counterclaims, see CPR r.15.7 and CPR Pt 20 and practice directions to those parts. Para.3.1 of the practice direction to CPR Pt 15, in particular, provides: "The defence and

the Debating Chamber set out in paragraph 5.1 above and thereby spoke and published the following words defamatory of the defendant, calculated to disparage him in the way of his office as a Councillor: [*set out words complained of*].

10. The said words in their natural and ordinary meaning meant and were understood to mean that the defendant has cynically and unscrupulously sold residential homes owned by the Council to private purchasers below their market value to his own political advantage.

11. Further, as the claimant knew and could and did foresee by calling a press conference and speaking the said words to reporters from the local and/or national press, they were likely to be reported and repeated in the local and/or national press; alternatively, it was the natural and probable consequence of the publication of the words at the said press conference that they would be rehearsed in the local and/or national press. In the premises, the defendant contends that the claimant is liable for the publication of the following passages from reports in the local and/or national press which repeat the defamatory sting of the words complained of and should be taken into account in the assessment of general damages[59]: [*set out the relevant reports*].

12. By reason of the publication of the said words by the claimant, the defendant has suffered injury to his reputation and has been caused serious distress and injury to his feelings.

13. Unless restrained, the claimant will further publish the said or similar words defamatory of the defendant.

AND the defendant counterclaims:

(1) Damages for slander;
(2) An injunction restraining the claimant whether by himself his servants, or agents or otherwise from further publishing or causing to be published the said or any similar words defamatory of the defendant.

[I believe] [the (*defendant*) believes] that the facts stated in this Defence and Counterclaim are true.

Defence—Libel—common law qualified privilege [alternatively, statutory   **A1.21**
defence of publication on a matter of public interest] —responsible journalism—*Reynolds v Times Newspapers Ltd* [2001] 1 A.C. 127[60] [alternatively, under s.4 Defamation Act 2013] (see Reply at A1.26)

---

counterclaim should normally form one document with the counterclaim following on from the defence."

[59] This was the form of pleading approved by the Court of Appeal in *Slipper v BBC* [1991] 1 Q.B. 283.

[60] The most important development in the law of common law qualified privilege in recent times was the House of Lords' decision in *Reynolds v Times Newspapers Ltd*, above, in which their Lordships redefined the conditions on which publications to the world at large may attract qualified privilege. See also the re-statement of the defence in *Jameel v Wall Street Journal Europe SPRL* [2006] UKHL 44; [2007] 1 A.C. 359, and the Supreme Court's most recent consideration of the defence in *Flood v Times Newspapers Ltd* [2012] UKSC 11; [2012] 2 A.C. 273. The pleading requirements imposed by para.2.7 of the practice direction to CPR Pt 53 are of great importance when the defendant is setting up a *Reynolds*-type qualified privilege defence. See para.27.27, above for the requirements of a plea of *Reynolds* qualified privilege and Ch.15 for further discussion about the defence. Whilst there is as yet no guidance on how the changes being introduced by the Defamation Act 2013 will impact on pleading, see para.27.31 above.

IN THE HIGH COURT OF JUSTICE   HQ

QUEEN'S BENCH DIVISION

[....... DISTRICT REGISTRY]

BETWEEN:

A.B.

Claimant

And

C LIMITED

Defendant

DEFENCE

1. Paragraph 1 of the Particulars of Claim is admitted. It is averred that [*set out any relevant facts and matters about the claimant as to why he is a subject of public concern.*]
2. Paragraph 2 is admitted.
3. As to paragraphs 3 and 4 it is admitted that the words complained of were published by the defendant. However, it is denied that the articles bore or were capable of bearing the meanings pleaded. The article was not concerned exclusively with the claimant but dealt with wider political issues. Without prejudice to the generality of the defendant's case on meaning it is averred that the article did not allege that the claimant was guilty but called for an investigation into his (and other people's) conduct. The tone of the article was measured and responsible.
4. The words complained of were published on an occasion of qualified privilege [alternatively, were a statement on a matter of public interest].

Particulars

(1) The article was about matters of public and general concern and interest [*set out why.*]

(2) It was justifiable to include the defamatory allegations in the article [*explain why*] [alternatively, the statement complained of was, or formed part of a statement on a matter of public interest for the following reasons: [*explain reasons*]].

(3) The steps taken to publish the information were fair and reasonable [alternatively, the defendant reasonably believed that publishing the statement complained of was in the public interest for the following reasons:]. In or about [*date*] the author first learnt about allegations being made about the claimant and others connected with the claimant and decided to conduct research into these matters. By the time the article came to be published the writer had conducted extensive research into the subject matter. In particular, [*set out all investigations undertaken by the journalist such as interviews with individuals, attending conferences, reading books and articles*].

(4) The information obtained by the journalist was of a high quality. In particular, [*set out any facts to support the contention that the nature, status and sources of the information were to be relied upon*].

(5) Upon receiving the information relied upon in the article it was checked, considered and, where necessary, corroborated. [*set out any facts to support this contention such as querying any answers given in interviews at a later date*].

(6) Prior to publication the defendant took reasonable steps to contact the claimant, to put the allegations to him and to obtain his response. [*set out all efforts made to contact the claimant or his representative*].

(7) The article was published on [*date*] because the subject-matter was one of current concern [*set out the circumstances and timing of publication*].

(8) The article, when published, contained the gist of the claimant's side of the story.

(9) [*Where the defendant's subjective belief is relevant include an assertion to that effect together with the basis of that belief*][61]

(10) In the circumstances the defendant had a moral and/or social duty to publish the words complained of and the public at large had a corresponding legitimate interest in receiving the information. [*or, in the circumstances, the publication to the world at large was in the public interest*] [alternatively, the words complained of were published pursuant to section 4, Defamation Act 2013[62]].

[I believe] [the (*defendant*) believes] that the facts stated in this Defence are true.

Defence—Malicious falsehood (see para.A1.12, above, for Particulars of Claim)   **A1.22**

IN THE HIGH COURT OF JUSTICE   HQ

QUEEN'S BENCH DIVISION
[....... DISTRICT REGISTRY]
BETWEEN:

A LIMITED

Claimant

And

B LIMITED

Defendant

DEFENCE

1. Save that it is admitted that the claimant is a company which carries on the business of the manufacture and supply of bird seed, paragraph 1 of the Particulars of Claim is not admitted.

---

[61] The Court of Appeal in *Jameel (Mohammed) v Wall Street Journal Europe SPRL (No.2)* [2005] EWCA Civ 74; [2005] Q.B. 904 at [18] directly addressed the question: "What must a defendant plead and prove to establish Reynolds privilege?" and at [31] expressed the view that the pleadings should make clear that where a defendant was relying upon the reasonable belief in the truth of the matters published such matters should be pleaded. On appeal, the House of Lords did not address the point. Where the defendant wishes to rely on having taken reasonable steps to verify the allegation, that may entail (as Lord Phillips suggested in *Flood v Times Newspapers Ltd* (above)) showing that the responsible journalist satisfied himself that the allegation was true, that his belief was the result of a reasonable investigation, and that it was a reasonable belief to hold. Note what is required under s.4, Defamation Act 2013: to explain why the defendant reasonably believed that publishing the statement was in the public interest. See paras 27.30–27.31, above.

[62] Their Lordships in *Jameel v Wall Street Journal Europe SPRL* [2006] UKHL 44; [2007] 1 A.C. 359 differed on whether or not a defendant needed to be under a duty to publish. It appears from *Flood* (above) that the concept of duty has gone, and that the question is whether publication is justified in the public interest: See the discussion of the common law defence at para.27.27.

2. Paragraph 2 of the Particulars of Claim is admitted.
3. Save that the defendant makes no admissions in relation to whom its marketing brochure was published, paragraph 3 of the Particulars of Claim is admitted.
4. It is denied that the said words were false as alleged in paragraph 4 of the Particulars of Claim or at all. Without limiting the generality of this denial, in response to the Particulars of Falsity set out under Paragraph 4 of the Particulars of Claim, the defendant pleads as follows: [*set out in as much detail as possible, the facts and matters relied upon to rebut the allegation that the words were false*].
5. The defendant denies that any publication of the words by the defendant complained of (as to which no admissions are made, save as admitted in paragraph 3 above) was malicious as alleged in paragraph 5 of the Particulars of Claim. With regard to the Particulars of Malice set out thereunder, the defendant pleads as follows: [*set out all facts and matters relied upon to rebut the allegations of malice and/or improper motive*].
6. Paragraph 6 of the Particulars of Claim is denied. [Alternatively, if the claimant alleges that he has sustained actual pecuniary loss by reason of publication of the falsehoods complained of state: *with regard to paragraphs 6 and 7 of the Particulars of Claim, if, which is denied, the cause of any loss sustained by the claimant was the publication complained of by the claimant, no admissions are made as to the quantum of such damages.*]
7. Paragraph 7 of the Particulars of Claim is denied.

[I believe] [the (*defendant*) believes] that the facts stated in this Defence are true.

A1.23 **Defence**—privacy/misuse of private information (see A1.13 for Particulars of Claim)[63]

IN THE HIGH COURT OF JUSTICE   HQ

QUEEN'S BENCH DIVISION
[....... DISTRICT REGISTRY]
BETWEEN:

A.B.

Claimant

And

1. C.D.
2. E LIMITED

Defendants

DEFENCE

1. Paragraph 1 is admitted.
2. Save that no admissions are made as to the extent of publication or circulation, paragraph 2 is admitted.
3. It is admitted that the defendant published the information set out in paragraph 3 save that it is denied that the defendant published information that could be understood to mean that the claimant was the father of Ms X's child.

---

[63] See para.27.47, above for the requirements when responding to a claim for misuse of private information.

4. It is denied, as pleaded in paragraph 4, that the defendant had a reasonable expectation that the information would remain private and/or confidential. In respect of sub-paragraphs 4.1 to 4.4:

4.1　It is admitted that neither the claimant nor Ms X consented to the publication. However, neither the claimant nor Ms X took any steps to keep their relationship confidential [*set out particulars*].

4.2　It is further admitted that the information came from a source but the information from the source was that the source had seen the claimant and Ms X conducting their relationship in public.

4.3　Even though the claimant is married with two children he conducted his relationship with Ms X in public. Ms X and the claimant dined together in restaurants in London, where the claimant lived away from his wife during the week. The claimant also stayed over at Ms X's house and allowed him to be seen in the street with Ms X and her child.

4.4　It is admitted that some of the information related to a child. The claimant made no efforts to protect the confidentiality or privacy of the child.[64]

5. For the reasons set out above, it is denied that the defendant misused the information.

6. If, which is denied, the claimant had a reasonable expectation of privacy, there was a public interest in revealing the information. In support of its case, the defendant will rely upon the following facts and matters:

6.1　The claimant is a well-known politician.

6.2　The claimant has allowed himself to be seen having a relationship with a single mother, whilst married.

6.3　Sub-paragraph 4.3 above is repeated.

6.4　The claimant published an article in *The Daily News*, five years ago, headlined, "Why families should stay together". He set out his opposition to changes in the divorce laws and commented that the country would be a better place if marriages did not fail and families did not break up.

6.5　The claimant made a speech in Parliament, two years ago, in the course of a debate about family values, in which he said it would be better for society if children were brought up by both their parents.

6.6　In the circumstances, the defendant was entitled to correct the impression given out to the public by the claimant that he was a happily married man and a politician who spoke about family values which he did not adhere to in his own life.

7. If, which is denied, the claimant has been distressed and embarrassment, it is denied that the defendant is liable for any damage caused.

8. It is denied, for the reasons set out above, that the claimant is entitled to an injunction.

The defendants believe that the facts stated in this Defence are true.

---

[64] For the position relating to photographs of children see *Murray v Big Pictures (UK) Ltd* [2008] EWCA Civ 446; [2009] Ch 481 and, more recently, *AAA v Associated Newspapers Ltd* [2012] EWHC 2103 (QB); [2013] E.M.L.R. 2.

REPLIES[65]

A1.24 Reply—Libel—reply to plea of justification [alternatively, reply to a plea of truth] and honest comment [alternatively, honest opinion]—express malice (see para.A1.7, above, for Particulars of Claim; para.A1.16, above, for Defence)

IN THE HIGH COURT OF JUSTICE   HQ

QUEEN'S BENCH DIVISION
[....... DISTRICT REGISTRY]
BETWEEN:

A.B.

Claimant

And

C LIMITED

Defendant

REPLY

1. The claimant joins issue with the defendant on its Defence save for the admissions it contains and those averments therein which are expressly admitted below.
2. It is denied that the words complained of in the meanings pleaded in paragraph 4 of the Defence are true. As to the particulars of justification [alternatively, truth] set out thereunder, the claimant pleads as follows:

   2.1 *[set out the claimant's response to the particulars set out by the defendant in support of its plea of justification/truth, admitting and denying as appropriate. As far as possible, the claimant should put forward a positive case as to his version of the facts and matters which form the basis of the plea of justification/truth.]*

3. It is denied that the words complained of were honest comment on a matter of public interest [alternatively, an honest opinion] as alleged in paragraph 5 of the Defence or at all:

   3.1 The words set out in paragraph 5 did not convey the comment set out therein and are not capable of conveying that comment.
   3.2 Further, it is denied that any comment conveyed by the articles was based upon the facts alleged in the particulars under paragraph 5 of the Defence. Without limiting the generality of that denial, it is averred that: *[set out the basis for the claim that the alleged comment could not have been based on the facts].*
   3.3 Further, the allegations relied on in support of the comment are false and unfounded in the respects set out under paragraph 2 above and the true

---

[65] See generally Ch. 28, above.

facts do not support, and are incapable of supporting, the alleged comment.

3.4   Further, and in any event, it is denied that the alleged comment concerns any matter of public interest. The comment does not concern the claimant's conduct as a government minister, but his conduct as a husband and a father. The claimant's conduct as a husband and a father is a private matter and not a matter of public interest. [Alternatively, once the Defamation Act 2013 is in force, this paragraph becomes unnecessary.[66]]

4. Further and alternatively, the said words were published maliciously.[67]

Particulars of Malice

[*e.g.*]

4.1   The author of the article is a journalist who at all material times was employed by the defendant. As such the defendant is vicariously liable for the actions of its journalist.

4.2   The journalist had no honest belief in publishing the words complained of. [*set out the material facts on which the claimant relies in support of the contention that the identifiable controlling mind within the corporate defendant (in this case the journalist), at the time of publication, had no honest belief in the allegations he was making of the claimant. For instance*]

[*e.g.*]   (i)   It is evident from the terms in which the article was published that the journalist could only have had two sources for the article, namely Mr and Mrs Brown. Mr and Mrs Brown have confirmed to the claimant that they did not supply the journalist with any information relating to the allegations made in the said article which are complained of by the claimant. The journalist had no, or no reliable alternative source of information in that regard.

(ii)   The journalist nevertheless proceeded to allege that Mr and Mrs Brown considered that the claimant's behaviour towards Mrs Brown and her son was shameful. He did so in a manner which was calculated to suggest and must have been intended to suggest to readers that these were allegations which Mr and/or Mrs Brown themselves had made to the newspaper. They had not.

(iii)   In the premises, at no time did the journalist have any or any sufficient grounds for honestly believing that those allegations were true.

(iv)   Notwithstanding the foregoing, and although it is now well aware that the fundamental factual basis of all the articles complained of is false, the defendant has not made or offered any correction or apology to the claimant in respect of any of the words complained of, but has instead sought to defend its

---

[66] This is due to the removal of the requirement that the opinion be on a matter of public interest in order to benefit from the honest opinion defence under s.3 Defamation Act 2013.

[67] Malice is a very serious allegation and specific rules apply. For the requirements when pleading malice, see para.28.6, above.

articles by pleas of justification [alternatively, truth] and honest comment [alternatively, honest opinion] which are inaccurate and unfounded in the respects specified above.

(v) In the premises, if (which is denied), the words in question conveyed the comment [alternatively, the statement of opinion] alleged, they were published maliciously with an absence of honest belief.

5. Save and in so far as expressly admitted above, the claimant denies each and every allegation contained in the Defence as if set out herein and separately traversed.

[I believe] [the (*claimant*) believes] that the facts stated in this Reply are true.

A1.25 Reply—Reply to defence of qualified offer to make amends (see para.A1.1(b), above, etc. for Letter of Claim; para.A1.4, above, for Offer to Make Amends pursuant to Defamation Act 1996, s.2; para.A1.9, above, for Particulars of Claim; para.A1.18, above, for Defence)

IN THE HIGH COURT OF JUSTICE   HQ

QUEEN'S BENCH DIVISION
[....... DISTRICT REGISTRY]
BETWEEN:

A.B.

Claimant

And

C LIMITED

Defendant

REPLY

1. The claimant joins issue with the defendant on his Defence save for the admissions it contains and those averments therein which are expressly admitted below.

2. The claimant denies that the defendant is entitled to rely on his purported offer to make amends to the claimant as a defence to the claimant's claim herein as alleged in paragraph 4 of the Defence or at all. Without limiting the generality of this denial, the claimant pleads to the said paragraph and to the Particulars thereunder, as follows:

2.1 It is admitted that on [*date*], the claimant received a letter dated [*date*] from the solicitors for the defendant purporting to contain a qualified offer to make amends to the claimant, as alleged in paragraph 4.1 of the Defence.

2.2 In relation to the specific defamatory meaning of the words complained of relied upon by the defendant in paragraph 5 of the Defence and upon which his qualified offer is predicated, the claimant repeats paragraph 2 above. In the premises and pursuant to section 4(4) of the 1996 Act, it is averred that the qualified offer made by the defendant is only a defence in respect of the meaning to which the offer related and, accordingly, is not a defence to the meaning which the claimant contends the words complained of bore or were understood to bear.[68]

2.3   Further or alternatively, at all material times the defendant knew or had reason to believe that the words complained of:

2.3.1 referred to or were likely to be understood as referring to the claimant:

Particulars of Knowledge of Reference

[set out all facts and matters which support the contention that the defendant knew or had reason to believe that the words complained of referred to the claimant; e.g.:]

(i)   The claimant repeats the first and second sentences of paragraph 1 of the Particulars of Claim;

(ii)   The defendant has attended and reported on many of the public lectures given by the claimant on historical matters at the University of Christminster and, on several occasions, has met with and otherwise corresponded with the claimant in relation to matters of mutual professional interest;

(iii) The words complained of refer to the claimant by name and expressly identify him as "the world renowned historian";

(iv)   By reason of the foregoing, the defendant knew or had reason to believe that the words complained of referred to the claimant and/or that in publishing the said words, they were likely to be understood by a substantial but unquantifiable number of those who accessed the website of the defendant as referring to the claimant; and

2.3.2 were false and defamatory of the claimant:

Particulars of Knowledge that Words are False and Defamatory of the Claimant[69]

[set out all facts and matters which support the contention that the defendant knew or had reason to believe that the words complained of were false and defamatory of the claimant; e.g.:]

(i)   The words complained of are defamatory on their face.

(ii)   On [date], a fortnight or thereabouts before the publication by the defendant of the words complained of herein, in response to an article entitled "Don flees after tax dodge", which had been published in the issue of *The Christminster Gazette* dated [date] and related to the tax affairs of the claimant, the Press Office of the University of Christminster, with the express authority of the claimant, caused to be issued to the public generally and to the press in particular, a press release detailing the response of the claimant to the defamatory charges which had been made therein which demonstrated that the said charges were false.

---

[68] The averment contained in this paragraph is arguably unnecessary because the point would be covered by the implied joinder of issue.

[69] See *Milne v Express Newspapers Plc* [2004] EWCA Civ 664; [2005] 1 W.L.R. 772.

(iii) On page 10 of the subsequent issue of *The Christminster Gazette* dated [*date*], in an article entitled "A.B.—an apology", the editor of the said journal published a full and unequivocal retraction of and apology for the allegations that had been made of the claimant. It was expressly accepted in the said article that the allegations made about the claimant in the previous issue were without any foundation in fact whatsoever;

(iv) The defendant is a postal subscriber to *The Christminster Gazette* and on [*date*] was sent a copy of the press release referred to in paragraph 2.3.2(ii) above;

(v) In the premises, the claimant will rely on the inference that the defendant read *The Christminster Gazette* dated [*date*] in which the apology to the claimant was published and/or the press release, both of which set out the true factual position in relation to defamatory charges published by the defendant of which complaint is made herein;

(vi) Accordingly, at all material times prior to his publication of the words complained of, the defendant knew or had reason to believe that the said words were defamatory of the claimant and false.

2.4　Paragraphs 4.2 and 4.3 of the Defence are admitted.

[I believe] [the (*claimant*) believes] that the facts stated in this reply are true.

A1.26 **Libel**—common law qualified privilege [alternatively, statutory defence of publication on a matter of public interest]—responsible journalism—*Reynolds v Times Newspapers Ltd* [2001] 1 A.C. 127 [alternatively, s.4 Defamation Act 2013] (see para.A1.21, above for Defence)

IN THE HIGH COURT OF JUSTICE   HQ

QUEEN'S BENCH DIVISION
[....... DISTRICT REGISTRY]
BETWEEN:

A.B.

Claimant

And

C LIMITED

Defendant

REPLY

1. The claimant joins issue with the defendant save for the admissions it contains and the averments therein which are expressly admitted below.

2. It is denied that the words complained of were published on an occasion of qualified privilege [alternatively, that they formed part of a statement on a matter of public interest]. As to the particulars of qualified privilege [alternatively, the defence under section 4 of the Defamation Act 2013]
[*set out the claimant's response to the particulars set out by the defendant in support of its plea of qualified privilege, admitting or denying where appropriate. It should be possible for the claimant to plead in respect of the information relied upon by the defendant (unless the sources are confidential) and the steps taken to verify the information or obtain comment from the claimant. For instance,*]

2.1 It is admitted that the subject matter was of public concern. However it was unnecessary to include the defamatory passages about the claimant or to allege that the claimant was guilty.

2.2 It is not admitted that the defendant undertook extensive research into the subject-matter. The defendant is put to strict proof in respect of the research alleged to have been undertaken.

2.3 It is denied that the information relied upon was of a high quality. Part of the information relied upon by the defendant came from Mr X who had an axe to grind in that he was the former business partner of the claimant until the two men parted company acrimoniously. As such his evidence should have been treated with the utmost caution.

2.4 It is denied that the defendant took all possible steps to contact the claimant. The claimant first learnt that this article was to be published [*set out all facts and matters to show that the claimant was not given an adequate opportunity to respond properly to the defendant's inquiries, if there were any.*] There was no public interest in the article being published at that time. It is to be inferred that the words complained of were only published on that date so as to obtain a scoop and not because there was any pressing concern to the public.

2.5 It is not admitted that the defendant held the belief pleaded. Alternatively, it is not admitted that the belief held was a reasonable one for the following reasons: [*set out reasons*].

2.6 In the circumstances it is denied that the words complained of are protected by qualified privilege [alternatively, under section 4 of the Defamation Act 2013].[70]

3. [I believe] [the (*claimant*) believes] that the facts stated in this reply are true.

C. Settlement of Action

Settlement—minute of order—compromise of libel action on terms making   **A1.27**
provision for payment of liquidated sum of damages, costs and the reading of a statement in court—undertaking by defendants to claimant not to repeat defamatory words

IN THE HIGH COURT OF JUSTICE   HQ

QUEEN'S BENCH DIVISION
[....... DISTRICT REGISTRY]
BETWEEN:

A.B.

Claimant

And

1. C LIMITED
2. D.E.

Defendants

MINUTE OF ORDER

---

[70] Malice is not necessary in response to a defence of *Reynolds* qualified privilege or under s.4, Defamation Act 2013: see para.15.21, above.

UPON HEARING Counsel for the claimant and for the defendants

AND UPON the first defendant undertaking not further to publish whether by its directors, officers, servants, agents or otherwise howsoever and the second defendant undertaking not further to publish whether by himself his servants agents or otherwise howsoever the words complained of in this action or any similar words defamatory of the claimant[71]

AND the parties having agreed to the terms set forth in the Schedule hereto

BY CONSENT

IT IS ORDERED AND DIRECTED that all further proceedings in this action be stayed except for the purpose of carrying the said terms into effect

AND the parties have permission to apply for the purpose of carrying the said terms into effect.

Dated the *x*th day of *x* 20[*x*]

We hereby consent to an Order in the above terms

                 Solicitors for the defendants   *Solicitors for the claimant*

SCHEDULE

1. The defendants agree to pay to the claimant an agreed sum of £ [*insert sum*] in full and final settlement of (i) the claimant's claim for damages and (ii) the claimant's costs of this action.
2. The defendants agree to join with the claimant in the making of a Statement in Court (subject only to the approval of the High Court Judge) in the terms of the Statement signed by the claimant's and the defendants' solicitors dated [*x*] and annexed hereto at Annex 1.

                 Solicitors for the defendants   *Solicitors for the claimant*

A1.28 Statement in Open Court[72]—libel broadcast—retraction and apology by defendants—agreed sum of damages—payment of costs

STATEMENT IN COURT

Claimant's counsel: The claimant in this action for libel is a well-known novelist and writer and the author of a novel entitled *Sense and Sensitivity*, published earlier this year. The first defendant is the broadcaster of the weekly television series, *Literary World*, and Mr Smith, the second defendant, is the presenter of the programme and a renowned literary critic.

In the course of a feature on *Literary World* entitled, *Pride and Plagiarism*, broadcast by the first defendant on [*date*] which dealt as its subject with the claimant

---

[71] An undertaking by the defendant to the court provides maximum security to the claimant who can enforce its breach by commencing proceedings for contempt of court. Alternatively, it is commonplace for the defendant to undertake contractually not to repeat the allegations complained of. In that case, the undertaking would not appear in the body of the consent order but would be one of the terms in the Schedule setting out the agreement between the parties. The remedy available to the claimant if the defendant breached its undertaking would be proceedings for enforcement.

[72] For rules of practice relevant to Statements in Court, see para.6 of the practice direction to CPR Pt 53.

and his novels, a number of statements were made by Mr Smith suggesting that the claimant in writing *Sense and Sensitivity* had been guilty of systematic plagiarism. These allegations were entirely without foundation. As such, they represent a grave slur on the claimant's personal and professional integrity, and have caused him considerable distress.

The defendants now accept their serious error in publishing these libels on television and recognise the considerable damage they have done to the claimant. The defendants are here today by their counsel to withdraw the imputations unreservedly and to apologise publicly to the claimant. The defendants have also agreed to pay to the claimant a substantial sum by way of damages and in settlement of his legal costs.

Defendants' counsel: I wish to associate myself on behalf of the defendants with all that has been said by counsel for the claimant and to repeat the defendants' regret that these statements were ever broadcast.

Claimant's counsel: I ask for leave to withdraw the record.

Appendix 2

Statutes

(* Statutory provisions which are the subject of prospective repeal or amendment are indicated in italics and square brackets)

Bill of Rights 1688   A2.1

(1 Will. & Mar. Sess. 2 c. 2)

1.[1]

[. . .]

(25) Freedom of Speech

That the Freedome of Speech and Debates or Proceedings in Parlyament ought not to be impeached or questioned in any Court or Place out of Parlyament.

---

[1] As amended by Accession Declaration Act 1910 (c.29), s.1.

Parliamentary Papers Act 1840

[3 & 4 Vict. c. 9]

1. **Proceedings, criminal or civil, against persons for publication of papers printed by order of Parliament, to be stayed upon delivery of a certificate and affidavit to the effect that such publication is by order of either House of Parliament**

It shall and may be lawful for any person or persons who now is or are, or hereafter shall be, a defendant or defendants in any civil or criminal proceeding commenced or prosecuted in any manner soever, for or on account or in respect of the publication of any such report, paper, votes, or proceedings by such person or persons, or by his, her, or their servant or servants, by or under the authority of either House of Parliament, to bring before the court in which such proceeding shall have been or shall be so commenced or prosecuted, or before any judge of the same (if one of the superior courts at [the Royal Courts of Justice][2]), first giving twenty-four hours' notice of his intention so to do to the prosecutor or plaintiff in such proceeding, a certificate under the hand of [the Speaker of the House of Lords][3], or of the clerk of the Parliaments, or of the speaker of the House of Commons, or of the clerk of the same house, stating that the report, paper, votes, or proceedings, as the case may be, in respect whereof such civil or criminal proceeding shall have been commenced or prosecuted, was published by such person or persons, or by his, her, or their servant or servants, by order or under the authority of the House of Lords or of the House of Commons, as the case may be, together with an affidavit verifying such certificate; and such court or judge shall thereupon immediately stay such civil or criminal proceeding; and the same, and every writ or process issued therein, shall be and shall be deemed and taken to be finally put an end to, determined, and superseded by virtue of this Act.

2. In case of any civil or criminal proceeding hereafter to be commenced or prosecuted for or on account or in respect of the publication of any copy of such report, paper, votes, or proceedings, it shall be lawful for the defendant or defendants at any stage of the proceedings to lay before the court or judge such report, paper, votes, or proceedings, and such copy, with an affidavit verifying such report, paper, votes, or proceedings, and the correctness of such copy, and the court or judge shall immediately stay such civil or criminal proceeding; and the same, and every writ or process issued therein, shall be and shall be deemed and taken to be finally put an end to, determined, and superseded by virtue of this Act.

3. It shall be lawful in any civil or criminal proceeding to be commenced or prosecuted for printing any extract from or abstract of such report, paper, votes, or proceedings, to give in evidence . . . [4] such report, paper, votes, or proceedings, and to show that such extract or abstract was published bona fide and without malice; and if such shall be the opinion of the jury, a verdict of not guilty shall be entered for the defendant or defendants.

4. Provided always, that nothing herein contained shall be deemed or taken, or held or construed, directly or indirectly, by implication or otherwise, to affect the privileges of Parliament in any manner whatsoever.

---

[2] Words substituted by virtue of the Supreme Court of Judicature (Consolidation) Act 1925, s.224(1).

[3] Words substituted by the Constitutional Reform Act 2005, Sch.6, para.2.

[4] The words omitted were repealed by the Statute Law Revision Act 1958 and the reference to printing includes a reference to including in a programme service; see the Broadcasting Act 1990, s.203(1), Sch.20, para.1.

Libel Act 1843 (Lord Campbell's Act) A2.3

[6 & 7 Vict. c. 96]

1. . . . In any action for defamation it shall be lawful for the defendant (after notice in writing of his intention so to do, duly given to the plaintiff at the time of filing or delivering the plea in such action) to give in evidence, in mitigation of damages, that he made or offered an apology to the plaintiff for such defamation before the commencement of the action, or as soon afterwards as he had an opportunity of doing so, in case the action shall have been commenced before there was an opportunity of making or offering such apology.

2. In an action for a libel contained in any public newspaper or other periodical publication, it shall be competent to the defendant to plead that such libel was inserted in such newspaper or other periodical publication without actual malice, and without gross negligence, and that before the commencement of the action, or at the earliest opportunity afterwards, he inserted in such newspaper or other periodical publication a full apology for the said libel, or, if the newspaper or periodical publication in which the said libel appeared should be ordinarily published at intervals exceeding one week, had offered to publish the said apology in any newspaper or periodical publication to be selected by the plaintiff in such action; . . . and . . . ,[5] to such plea to such action it shall be competent to the plaintiff to reply generally denying the whole of such plea.

4. . . . [6]

Libel Act 1845 A2.4

[8 & 9 Vict. c. 60]

2. It shall not be competent to any defendant in such action, whether in England or in Ireland, to file any such plea,[7] without at the same time making a payment of money into court by way of amends . . . , but every such plea so filed without payment into court shall be deemed a nullity and may be treated as such by the plaintiff in the action.

Newspaper Libel and Registration Act 1881 A2.5

[44 & 45 Vict. c. 60]

1. In the construction of this Act, unless there is anything in the subject or context repugnant thereto, the several words and phrases hereinafter mentioned shall have and include the meanings following; (that is to say,) [The word "registrar" means—

    (a) in England and Wales, the registrar of companies for England and Wales, and

    (b) in Northern Ireland, the registrar of companies for Northern Ireland.][8]

---

[5] The words omitted were repealed by the Statute Law Revision Acts 1891 and 1892.

[6] Ss.4–6 of 1843 Act were repealed by s.178 of and Sch.2 (Part 2) to the Coroners and Justice Act 2009.

[7] A plea as permitted by the Libel Act 1843. The effect of the section is to make payment into court an obligatory part of the statutory defence created by the 1843 Act.

[8] Definition substituted by the Companies Act 2006 (Consequential Amendments, Transitional Provisions and Savings) Order 2009/1941, Sch.1, para.1(2).

The word "newspaper" shall mean any paper containing public news, intelligence, or occurrences, or any remarks or observations thereon printed for sale, and published in England or Ireland periodically, or in parts or numbers at intervals not exceeding 26 days between the publication of any two such papers, parts, or numbers.

Also any paper printed in order to be dispersed, and made public weekly or oftener, or at intervals not exceeding 26 days, containing only or principally advertisements.

The word "occupation" when applied to any person shall mean his trade or following, and if none, then his rank or usual title, as esquire, gentleman.

The phrase "place of residence" shall include the street, square, or place where the person to whom it refers shall reside, and the number (if any) or other designation of the house in which he shall so reside.

The word "proprietor" shall mean and include as well the sole proprietor of any newspaper, as also in the case of a divided proprietorship the persons who, as partners or otherwise, represent and are responsible for any share or interest in the newspaper as between themselves and the persons in like manner representing or responsible for the other shares or interests therein, and no other person.

4. A court of summary jurisdiction [in Northern Ireland][9], upon the hearing of a charge against a proprietor, publisher, or editor, or any person responsible for the publication of a newspaper, for a [blasphemous][10] libel published therein, may receive evidence . . . [11] as to any matter which under this or any other Act, or otherwise, might be given in evidence by way of defence by the person charged on his trial on indictment, and the court, if of opinion after hearing such evidence that there is a strong or probable presumption that the jury on the trial would acquit the person charged, may dismiss the case.

7. Where, in the opinion of the Board of Trade, inconvenience would arise or be caused in any case from the registry of the names of all the proprietors of the newspaper (either owing to minority, coverture, absence from the United Kingdom, minute subdivision of shares, or other special circumstances), it shall be lawful for the Board of Trade to authorise the registration of such newspaper in the name or names of some one or more responsible "representative proprietors."

8. A register of the proprietors of newspapers as defined by this Act shall be established under the superintendence of the registrar.

9. It shall be the duty of the printers and publishers for the time being of every newspaper to make or cause to be made to [the registrar][12] in the month of July in every year, a return of the following particulars according to the Schedule A hereunto annexed; that is to say,

    (a) The title of a newspaper;

    (b) The names of all the proprietors of such newspaper together with their respective occupations, places of business (if any), and places of residence.

10. If within the further period of one month after the time hereinbefore appointed for the making of any return as to any newspaper such return be not made, then each printer and publisher of such newspaper shall, on conviction thereof, be liable to a

---

[9] Words inserted by the Coroners and Justice Act 2009, s.177, Sch.21(4).

[10] Word inserted by the Coroners and Justice Act 2009, s.177, Sch.21(4).

[11] The words that previously appeared here ("*as to the publication being for the public benefit, and as to the matters charged in the libel being true, and as to the report being fair and accurate, and published without malice, and*") were repealed by the Coroners and Justice Act 2009, s.178, Sch.23(2).

[12] Words substituted by the Companies Act 2006 (Consequential Amendments, Transitional Provisions and Savings) Order 2009/1941, Sch.1, para.1(3).

penalty not exceeding level 2 on the standard scale,[13] and also to be directed by a summary order to make a return within a specified time.

11. Any party to a transfer or transmission of or dealing with any share of or interest in any newspaper whereby any person ceases to be a proprietor or any new proprietor is introduced may at any time make or cause to be made [to the registrar][14] a return according to the Schedule B hereunto annexed and containing the particulars therein set forth.

12. If any person shall knowingly and wilfully make or cause to be made any return by this Act required or permitted to be made in which shall be inserted or set forth the name of any person as a proprietor of a newspaper who shall not be a proprietor thereof, or in which there shall be any misrepresentation, or from which there shall be any omission in respect of any of the particulars by this Act required to be contained therein whereby such return shall be misleading, or if any proprietor of a newspaper shall knowingly and wilfully permit any such return to be made which shall be misleading as to any of the particulars with reference to his own name, occupation, place of business (if any), or place of residence, then and in every such case every such offender being convicted thereof shall be liable to a penalty not exceeding level 3 on the standard scale.[15]

[13.—**Registrar to enter returns in register**

(1) It is the duty of the registrar forthwith to register every return made under this Act in the register of newspaper proprietors.

(2) Any person may—

    (a) inspect the register, or

    (b) require a copy of any material on the register.

(3) The registrar may specify the form and manner—

    (a) in which application is to be made for any such inspection or copy, and

    (b) in which copies are to be provided.

(4) The applicant may require any copy so provided to be certified by the registrar as a true copy.

(5) The Secretary of State may make provision by regulations (to be made by statutory instrument) as to the manner in which such a certificate is to be provided in a case where the copy is provided in electronic form.

(6) Copies provided by the registrar may, instead of being certified in writing to be an accurate record, be sealed with the registrar's official seal.][16]

[15.—**Certified copy of material on register to be admissible in evidence**

A copy provided under section 13, certified by the registrar (whose official position it is unnecessary to prove) to be an accurate record of the contents of the original document, is in all legal proceedings admissible in evidence—

    (a) as of equal validity with the original document, and

    (b) as evidence of any fact stated in the original document of which direct oral evidence would be admissible.][17]

16. All penalties under this Act may be recovered before a court of summary jurisdiction in manner provided by the Summary Jurisdiction Acts.

Summary orders under this Act may be made by a court of summary jurisdiction.

---

[13] The Criminal Justice Act 1982, s.37(2) which sets out the amounts of the standard scale, as substituted by the Criminal Justice Act 1991, s.17(1).

[14] Words substituted by the Companies Act 2006 (Consequential Amendments, Transitional Provisions and Savings) Order 2009/1941, Sch.1, para.1(3).

[15] The subsection is printed as amended.

[16] Substituted by the Companies Act 2006 (Consequential Amendments, Transitional Provisions and Savings) Order 2009/1941, Sch.1, para.1(4).

[17] Substituted by the Companies Act 2006 (Consequential Amendments, Transitional Provisions and Savings) Order 2009/1941, Sch.1, para.1(6).

18. The provisions as to the registration of newspaper proprietors contained in this Act shall not apply to the case of any newspaper which belongs to a [company formed and registered under the Companies Act 2006 or incorporated in another EEA state][18].

19. This Act shall not extend to Scotland.

20. This Act may for all purposes be cited as the Newspaper Libel and Registration Act 1881.

The Schedules to which this Act refers:

SCHEDULE A

Return made pursuant to the Newspaper Libel and Registration Act 1881.

Title of the Newspaper	Names of the Proprietors	Occupations of the Proprietors	Places of Business (if any) of the Proprietors	Places of Residence of the Proprietors

SCHEDULE B

Return made pursuant to the Newspaper Libel and Registration Act 1881.

Title of Newspaper	Names of Persons who cease to be Proprietors	Names of Persons who become Proprietors	Occupation of new Proprietors	Places of Business (if any) of new Proprietors	Places of Residence of new Proprietors

A2.6

Law of Libel Amendment Act 1888

[51 & 52 Vict. c. 64]

1. In the construction of this Act the word "newspaper" shall have the same meaning as in the Newspaper Libel and Registration Act 1881.

---

[18] Words substituted by the Companies Act 2006 (Consequential Amendments, Transitional Provisions and Savings) Order 2009/1941, Sch.1, para.1(7).

3 . . . [19]
4 . . . [20]

5. It shall be competent for a judge or the court, upon an application by or on behalf of two or more defendants in actions in respect to the same, or substantially the same, libel brought by one and the same person, to make an order for the consolidation of such actions, so that they shall be tried together, and after such order has been made, and before the trial of the said actions, the defendants in any new actions instituted in respect to the same, or substantially the same, libel shall also be entitled to be joined in a common action upon a joint application being made by such new defendants and the defendants in the actions already consolidated.

In a consolidated action under this section the jury shall assess the whole amount of the damages (if any) in one sum, but a separate verdict shall be taken for or against each defendant in the same way as if the actions consolidated had been tried separately; and if the jury shall have found a verdict against the defendant or defendants in more than one of the actions so consolidated, they shall proceed to apportion the amount of damages which they shall have so found between and against the said last-mentioned defendants; and the judge at the trial, if he awards to the plaintiff the costs of the action, shall thereupon make such order as he shall deem just for the apportionment of such costs between and against such defendants.

. . .

8. No criminal prosecution shall be commenced against any proprietor, publisher, editor, or any person responsible for the publication of a newspaper for any libel published therein without the order of a judge at chambers being first had and obtained. Such application shall be made on notice to the person accused, who shall have an opportunity of being heard against such application.

. . .

10. This Act shall not apply to Scotland.
11. This Act may be cited as the Law of Libel Amendment Act 1888.

[Slander of Women Act 1891[21]   **A2.7**

[54 & 55 Vict., c. 51]

1. Words spoken and published which impute unchastity or adultery to any woman or girl shall not require special damage to render them actionable. Provided always that in any action for words spoken and made actionable by this Act, a plaintiff shall not recover more costs than damages, unless the judge shall certify that there was reasonable ground for bringing the action.

This Act may be cited as the Slander of Women Act 1891 and shall not apply to Scotland.]

Defamation Act 1952   **A2.8**

[15 & 16 Geo. 6 & 1 Eliz. 2, c. 66]

1 . . . [22]

---

[19] Repealed by the Defamation Act 1996, s.16, Sch.2.
[20] Repealed by the Coroners and Justice Act 2009, s.178, Sch.23(2).
[21] This Act is prospectively repealed by the Defamation Act 2013, s.14(1).
[22] S.1 (broadcast statement) has been repealed. See now Broadcasting Act 1990.

Slander affecting official, professional or business reputation

2. In an action for slander in respect of words, calculated to disparage the plaintiff in any office, profession, calling, trade or business held or carried on by him at the time of the publication, it shall not be necessary to allege or prove special damage, whether or not the words are spoken of the plaintiff in the way of his office, profession, calling, trade or business.

Slander of title, etc.

3.—(1) In an action for slander of title, slander of goods or other malicious falsehood, it shall not be necessary to allege or prove special damage—
    (a) if the words upon which the action is founded are calculated to cause pecuniary damage to the plaintiff and are published in writing or other permanent form, or
    (b) if the said words are calculated to cause pecuniary damage to the plaintiff in respect of any office, profession, calling, trade or business held or carried on by him at the time of the publication.

(2) Section one of this Act shall apply for the purpose of this section as it applies for the purpose of the law of libel and slander.[23]

[Justification

5. *In an action for libel or slander in respect of words containing two or more distinct charges against the plaintiff, a defence of justification shall not fail by reason only that the truth of every charge is not proved if the words not proved to be true do not materially injure the plaintiff's reputation having regard to the truth of the remaining charges.*[24]

Fair comment

6. *In an action for libel or slander in respect of words consisting partly of allegations of fact and partly of expression of opinion, a defence of fair comment shall not fail by reason only that the truth of every allegation of fact is not proved if the expression of opinion is fair comment having regard to such of the facts alleged or referred to in the words complained of as are proved.*[25]*]*

Extension of certain defences to broadcasting

9.—(1) Section three of the Parliamentary Papers Act 1840 (which confers protection in respect of proceedings for printing extracts from or abstracts of parliamentary papers) shall have effect as if the reference to printing included a reference to broadcasting by means of wireless telegraphy.

Limitation on privilege at elections

10. A defamatory statement published by or on behalf of a candidate in any election to a local government authority, to the National Assembly for Wales, to the Scottish Parliament or to Parliament shall not be deemed to be published on a privileged

---

[23] Though not expressly repealed, this subsection is superseded by the Broadcasting Act 1990.

[24] Defamation Act 1952, s.5 is prospectively repealed by the Defamation Act 2013, s.2(4).

[25] Defamation Act 1952, s.6 is prospectively repealed by the Defamation Act 2013, s.3(8).

occasion on the ground that it is material to a question in issue in the election, whether or not the person by whom it is published is qualified to vote at the election.

Agreements for indemnity

11. An agreement for indemnifying any person against civil liability for libel in respect of the publication of any matter shall not be unlawful unless at the time of the publication that person knows that the matter is defamatory, and does not reasonably believe there is a good defence to any action brought upon it.

Evidence of other damages recovered by plaintiff

12. In any action for libel or slander the defendant may give evidence in mitigation of damages that the plaintiff has recovered damages, or has brought actions for damages, for libel or slander in respect of the publication of words to the same effect as the words on which the action is founded, or has received or agreed to receive compensation in respect of any such publication.

Consolidation of actions for slander, etc.

13. Section five of the Law of libel Amendment Act 1888 (which provides for the consolidation, on the application of the defendants, of two or more actions for libel by the same plaintiff) shall apply to actions for slander and to actions for slander of title, slander of goods or other malicious falsehood as it applies to actions for libel; and references in that section to the same, or substantially the same, libel shall be construed accordingly.

Application of Act to Scotland

14. This Act shall apply to Scotland subject to the following modifications, that is to say:

    (a) sections one, two, eight and thirteen shall be omitted;

    (b) for section three there shall be substituted the following section—

        "3. *Actions for verbal injury.*—In any action for verbal injury it shall not be necessary for the pursuer to aver or prove special damage if the words on which the action is founded are calculated to cause pecuniary damage to the pursuer";

    (c) subsection (2) of section four shall have effect as if at the end thereof there were added the words "Nothing in this subsection shall be held to entitle a defender to lead evidence of any fact specified in the declaration unless notice of his intention so to do has been given in the defences"; and

    (d) for any reference to libel, or to libel or slander, there shall be substituted a reference to defamation; the expression "plaintiff" means pursuer; the expression "defendant" means defender; for any reference to an affidavit made by any person there shall be substituted a reference to a written declaration signed by that person; for any reference to the High Court there shall be substituted a reference to the Court of Session or, if an action of defamation is depending in the sheriff court in respect of the publication in question, the sheriff; the expression "costs" means expenses; and for any reference to a defence of justification there shall be substituted a reference to a defence of veritas.

Interpretation

16.—(1) Any reference in this Act to words shall be construed as including a reference to pictures, visual images, gestures and other methods of signifying meaning.

Proceedings affected and saving

17.—(1) This Act applies for the purposes of any proceedings begun after the commencement of this Act, whenever the cause of action arose but does not affect any proceedings begun before the commencement of this Act.

(2) . . . [26]

Short title, commencement, extent and repeals

18.—(1) This Act may be cited as the Defamation Act 1952 and shall come into operation one month after the passing of this Act.

(2) This Act shall not extend to Northern Ireland.

Public Bodies (Admission to Meetings) Act 1960

[8 & 9 Eliz. 2 c. 67]

Admission of public to meetings of local authorities and other bodies

1.—(1) Subject to subsection (2) below, any meeting of a . . . body exercising public functions, being a body to which this Act applies, shall be open to the public.[27]

(2) and (3) [Provide for the body to have power to exclude the public in certain circumstances when publicity would be prejudicial to the general interest.]

(4) Where a meeting of a body is required by this Act to be open to the public during the proceedings or any part of them, the following provisions, shall apply, that is to say,—

>   (a) public notice of the time and place of the meeting shall be given by posting it at the offices of the body (or, if the body has no offices, then in some central and conspicuous place in the area with which it is concerned) three clear days at least before the meeting or, if the meeting is convened at shorter notice, then at the time it is convened;

>   (b) there shall, on request and on payment of postage or other necessary charge for transmission, be supplied for the benefit of any newspaper a copy of the agenda for the meeting as supplied to members of the body (but excluding, if thought fit, any item during which the meeting is likely not to be open to the public), together with such further statements or particulars, if any, as are necessary to indicate the nature of the items included or, if thought fit

---

[26] Repealed by the Coroners and Justice Act 2009, s.178, Sch.23(2).

[27] The amendments made by the Local Government (Access to Information) Act 1985 are incorporated. The bodies to which the Act applies are set out in the Schedule, as amended by, inter alia the above Act, the Local Government Act 1985, Community Land Act 1975, Health Authorities Act 1995, and the Water Act 1989, and include parish or community councils, the parish meetings of rural parishes, health authorities, advisory committees established under the Water Resources Act 1991, and customer services committees maintained under s.28 of the Water Industry Act 1991. Pt VA of the Local Government Act 1972 (inserted by the Local Government (Access to Information) Act 1985) governs access to meetings and documents of "principal councils" (for definition see ss.100J and 270). Section 100H(5) provides:

Where any accessible document for a meeting to which this subsection applies:

>   (a) is supplied to, or open to inspection by, a member of the public; or

>   (b) is supplied for the benefit of any newspaper, in pursuance of s.100B(7) above; the publication thereby of any defamatory matter contained in the document shall be privileged unless the publication is proved to be made with malice.

"Accessible documents" are defined in subs.(6).

in the case of any item, with copies of any reports or other documents supplied to members of the body in connection with the item;

(c) while the meeting is open to the public, the body shall not have power to exclude members of the public from the meeting and duly accredited representatives of newspapers attending for the purpose of reporting the proceedings for those newspapers shall, so far as practicable, be afforded reasonable facilities for taking their report and, unless the meeting is held in premises not belonging to the body or not on the telephone, for telephoning the report at their own expense.

(5) Where a meeting of a body is required by this Act to be open to the public during the proceedings or any part of them, and there is supplied to a member of the public attending the meeting, or in pursuance of paragraph (b) of subsection (4) above there is supplied for the benefit of a newspaper, any such copy of the agenda as is mentioned in that paragraph, with or without further statements or particulars for the purpose of indicating the nature of any item included in the agenda, the publication thereby of any defamatory matter contained in the agenda or in the further statements or particulars shall be privileged, unless the publication is proved to be made with malice.[28]

Parliamentary Commissioner Act 1967   **A2.10**

[1967 c. 13]

Reports by Commissioners

10.—(1) In any case where the Commissioner conducts an investigation under this Act or decides not to conduct such an investigation, he shall send to the member of the House of Commons by whom the request for investigation was made (or if he is no longer a member of that House, to such member of that House as the Commissioner thinks appropriate) a report of the results of the investigation or, as the case may be, a statement of his reasons for not conducting an investigation.

(2) In any case where the Commissioner conducts an investigation under section 5(1) of this Act, he shall also send a report of the results of the investigation to the principal officer of the department or authority concerned and to any other person who is alleged in the relevant complaint to have taken or authorised the action complained of.

(2A) In any case where the Commissioner conducts an investigation pursuant to a complaint under section 5(1A) of this Act, he shall also send a report of the results of his investigation to the person to whom the complaint relates.[29]

(5) For the purposes of the law of defamation, any such publication as is hereinafter mentioned shall be absolutely privileged, that is to say—

(a) the publication of any matter by the Commissioner in making a report to either House of Parliament for the purposes of this Act;

(b) the publication of any matter by a member of the House of Commons in communicating with the Commissioner or his officers for those purposes or by the Commissioner or his officers in communicating with such a member for these purposes;

(c) the publication by such a member to the person by whom a complaint was made under this Act of a report or statement sent to the member in respect of the complaint in pursuance of subsection (1) of this section;

---

[28] Subs.(7) provides that any reference to a newspaper applies to a news agency systematically supplying reports to newspapers or broadcasters.

[29] Added by the Domestic Violence, Crime and Victims Act 2004, Sch.7, para.5(3).

(d) the publication by the Commissioner to such a person as is mentioned in subsection (2) [or (2A)]³⁰ of this section of a report sent to that person in pursuance of that subsection.

A2.11   **Theatres Act 1968**

[1968 c. 54]

Amendment of law of defamation

4.—(1) For the purposes of the law of libel and slander (. . . ³¹) the publication of words in the course of a performance of a play shall, subject to section 7 of this Act, be treated as publication in permanent form.

(2) The foregoing subsection shall apply for the purposes of section 3 (slander of title, etc.) of the Defamation Act 1952 as it applies for the purposes of the law of libel and slander.

(3) In this section "words" includes pictures, visual images, gestures and other methods of signifying meaning.

(4) This section shall not apply to Scotland.

Exceptions for performances given in certain circumstances

7.—(1) Nothing in sections 2 to 4 of this Act shall apply in relation to a performance of a play given on a domestic occasion in a private dwelling.

(2) Nothing in sections 2 to 6 of this Act shall apply in relation to a performance of a play given solely or primarily for one or more of the following purposes, that is to say—

(a) rehearsal; or
(b) to enable—
  (i) a record or cinematograph film to be made from or by means of the performance; or
  (ii) the performance to be broadcast; or
  (iii) the performance to be included in a programme service (within the Broadcasting Act 1990) other than a sound or television broadcasting service³²;

. . .

(3) In this section—

"broadcast" means broadcast by wireless telegraphy (within the meaning of the Wireless Telegraphy Act 2006), whether by way of sound broadcasting or television;

"cinematograph film" means any print, negative, tape or other article on which a performance of a play or any part of such a performance is recorded for the purposes of visual reproduction;

"record" means any record or similar contrivance for reproducing sound, including the "sound-track" of a cinematograph film;

18. *Interpretation.* (1) In this Act . . .

"play" means—

(a) any dramatic piece, whether involving improvisation or not, which is given wholly or in part by one or more persons actually present and

---

³⁰ Words inserted by the Domestic Violence, Crime and Victims Act 2004, Sch.7, para.5(6).
³¹ Repealed by the Coroners and Justice Act 2009, s.178, Sch.23(2).
³² Substituted by the Broadcasting Act 1990 s.203(1), Sch.20, para.13.

(b) any ballet given wholly or in part by one or more persons actually present and performing, whether or not it falls within paragraph (a) of this definition; . . .

Civil Evidence Act 1968   **A2.12**

[1968 c. 41]

Convictions as evidence in civil proceedings[33]

11.—(4) Where in any civil proceedings the contents of any document are admissible in evidence by virtue of subsection (2) above, a copy of that document, or of the material part thereof, purporting to be certified or otherwise authenticated by or on behalf of the court or authority having custody of that document shall be admissible in evidence and shall be taken to be a true copy of that document or part unless the contrary is shown.

(5) Nothing in any of the following enactments, that is to say—

(a) section 14 of the Powers of Criminal Courts (Sentencing) Act 2000 (under which a conviction leading to . . . [34] discharge is to be disregarded except as therein mentioned);

(aa) section 187 of the Armed Forces Act 2006 (which makes similar provision in respect of service convictions)[35];

(b) section 191 of the Criminal Procedure (Scotland) Act 1975 (which makes similar provision in respect of convictions on indictment in Scotland); and

(c) section 8 of the Probation Act (Northern Ireland) 1950 (which corresponds to the said section 12) or any corresponding enactment of the Parliament of Northern Ireland for the time being in force,

shall affect the operation of this section; and for the purposes of this section any order made by a court of summary jurisdiction in Scotland under section 383 or section 384 of the said Act of 1975 shall be treated as a conviction.

(7) In this section—

"service offence" has the same meaning as in the Armed Forces Act 2006;

"conviction" includes anything that under section 376(1) and (2) of that Act is to be treated as a conviction, and "convicted" is to be read accordingly.[36]

Conclusiveness of convictions for purposes of defamation actions[37]

13.—(1) In an action for libel or slander in which the question whether the plaintiff did or did not commit a criminal offence is relevant to an issue arising in the action, proof that, at the time when that issue falls to be determined, he stands convicted of that offence shall be conclusive evidence that he committed that offence; and his conviction thereof shall be admissible in evidence accordingly.

---

[33] The subsections are printed as amended.
[34] Words repealed by the Criminal Justice Act 1991, Sch.11, para.5.
[35] Added by the Armed Forces Act 2006, Sch.16, para.51(4).
[36] S.11(7) was substituted for s.11(6) by the Armed Forces Act 2006, Sch.16, para.51(5).
[37] This section is printed as amended by the Defamation Act 1996, s.12.

(2) In any such action as aforesaid in which by virtue of this section the plaintiff is proved to have been convicted of an offence, the contents of any document which is admissible as evidence of the conviction, and the contents of the information, complaint, indictment or charge-sheet on which he was convicted, shall, without prejudice to the reception of any other admissible evidence for the purpose of identifying the facts on which the conviction was based, be admissible in evidence for the purpose of identifying those facts.

(2A) In the case of an action for libel or slander in which there is more than one plaintiff:

    (a) the references in subsections (1) and (2) above to the plaintiff shall be construed as references to any of the plaintiffs; and

    (b) proof that any of the plaintiffs stand convicted of an offence shall be conclusive evidence that he committed that offence so far as that fact is relevant to any issue arising in relation to his cause of action or that of any other plaintiff.

(3) For the purposes of this section a person shall be taken to stand convicted of an offence if but only if there subsists against him a conviction of that offence by or before a court in the United Kingdom or [(in the case of a service offence) a conviction (anywhere) of that service offence].[38]

(4) [Subsections (4) to (7) of section 11][39] of this Act, shall apply for the purposes of this section as they apply for the purposes of that section, but as if in the said subsection (4) the reference to subsection (2) were a reference to subsection (2) of this section.

Rehabilitation of Offenders Act 1974[40]

[1974 c. 53]

Rehabilitated persons and spent convictions

1.—(1) Subject to subsection[s (2), (5) and (6)][41] below, where an individual has been convicted, whether before or after the commencement of this Act, of any offence or offences, and the following conditions are satisfied, that is to say—

    (a) he did not have imposed on him in respect of that conviction a sentence which is excluded from rehabilitation under this Act; and

    (b) he has not had imposed on him in respect of a subsequent conviction during the rehabilitation period applicable to the first-mentioned conviction in accordance with section 6 below a sentence which is excluded from rehabilitation under this Act;

then, after the end of the rehabilitation period so applicable (including, where appropriate, any extension under section 6(4) below of the period originally applicable to the first-mentioned conviction) or, where that rehabilitation period ended before the commencement of this Act, after the commencement of this Act, that individual shall for the purposes of this Act be treated as a rehabilitated person in respect of the first-mentioned conviction and that conviction shall for those purposes be treated as spent.

---

[38] Words substituted by the Armed Forces Act 2006, Sch.16, para.52(a).

[39] Words substituted by the Armed Forces Act 2006, Sch.16, para.52(b).

[40] Ss.1, 4, 7 of this Act are subject to prospective amendment by the Tribunals, Courts and Enforcement Act 2007, Sch.13 (s.1 only; date to be appointed) and by the Legal Aid, Sentencing and Punishment of Offenders Act 2012, Sch.25 (ss.1, 4 and 7; date to be appointed).

[41] As substituted by the Protection of Freedoms Act 2012, Sch.9(9), para.134(2).

(2) A person shall not become a rehabilitated person for the purposes of this Act in respect of a conviction unless he has served or otherwise undergone or complied with any sentence imposed on him in respect of that conviction; but the following shall not, by virtue of this subsection, prevent a person from becoming a rehabilitated person for those purposes—

    (a) failure to pay a fine or other sum adjudged to be paid or imposed on a conviction, or breach of a condition of a recognizance or of a bond of caution to keep the peace or be of good behaviour;

    (b) breach of any condition or requirement applicable in relation to a sentence which renders the person to whom it applies liable to be dealt with for the offence for which the sentence was imposed, or, where the sentence was a suspended sentence of imprisonment, liable to be dealt with in respect of that sentence (whether or not, in any case, he is in fact so dealt with);

    (c) failure to comply with any requirement of a suspended sentence supervision order.

(2A) Where in respect of a conviction a person has been sentenced to imprisonment with an order under section 47(1) of the Criminal Law Act 1977, he is to be treated for the purposes of subsection (2) above as having served the sentence as soon as he completes service of so much of the sentence as was by that order required to be served in prison.

[(2B) In subsection (2)(a) above the reference to a fine or other sum adjudged to be paid by or imposed on a conviction does not include a reference to an amount payable under a confiscation order made under Part 2 or 3 of the Proceeds of Crime Act 2002.][42]

(3) In this Act "sentence" includes any order made by a court in dealing with a person in respect of his conviction of any offence or offences, other than—

    [(za) a surcharge imposed under section 161A of the Criminal Justice Act 2003;]

    (a) an order for committal or any other order made in default of payment of any fine or other sum adjudged to be paid by or imposed on a conviction, or for want of sufficient distress to satisfy any such fine or other sum;

    (b) an order dealing with a person in respect of a suspended sentence of imprisonment.

(4) In this Act, references to a conviction, however expressed, include references—

    (a) to a conviction by or before a court outside Great Britain; and

    (b) to any finding (other than a finding linked with a finding of insanity) . . . in any criminal proceedings . . . [43] that a person has committed an offence or done the act or made the omission charged;

and notwithstanding anything in [section 247 of the Criminal Procedure (Scotland) Act 1995 (c.46)][44] or section 14 of the Powers of Criminal Courts (Sentencing) Act 2000 [or section 187 of the Armed Forces Act 2006][45] (conviction of a person . . . [46] discharged to be deemed not to be a conviction) a conviction in respect of which an order is made discharging the person concerned absolutely or conditionally shall be treated as a conviction for the purposes of this Act and the person in question may become a rehabilitated person in respect of that conviction and the conviction a spent conviction for those purposes accordingly.

---

[42] As added by the Proceeds of Crime Act 2002, Sch.11 para.7.
[43] Omitted words repealed by the Children Act 1989, s.108(7), Sch.15.
[44] Words substituted by the Criminal Justice and Licensing (Scotland) Act 2010 asp 13 (Scottish Act), s.24(1).
[45] Words inserted by the Armed Forces Act 2006, Sch.16, para.63.
[46] Omitted words repealed by the Criminal Justice Act 1991, s.101(2), Sch.13.

[(5) This Act does not apply to any disregarded conviction or caution within the meaning of Chapter 4 of Part 5 of the Protection of Freedoms Act 2012.

(6) Accordingly, references in this Act to a conviction or caution do not include references to any such disregarded conviction or caution.][47]

Effect of rehabilitation

4.—(1) Subject to sections 7 and 8 below, a person who has become a rehabilitated person for the purposes of this Act in respect of a conviction shall be treated for all purposes in law as a person who has not committed or been charged with or prosecuted for or convicted of or sentenced for the offence or offences which were the subject of that conviction; and, notwithstanding the provisions of any other enactment or rule of law to the contrary, but subject as aforesaid—

    (a) no evidence shall be admissible in any proceedings before a judicial authority exercising its jurisdiction or functions in Great Britain to prove that any such person has committed or been charged with or prosecuted for or convicted of or sentenced for any offence which was the subject of a spent conviction; and

    (b) a person shall not, in any such proceedings, be asked, and, if asked, shall not be required to answer, any question relating to his past which cannot be answered without acknowledging or referring to a spent conviction or spent convictions or any circumstances ancillary thereto.

(2) Subject to the provisions of any order made under subsection (4) below, where a question seeking information with respect to a person's previous convictions, offences, conduct or circumstances is put to him or to any other person otherwise than in proceedings before a judicial authority—

    (a) the question shall be treated as not relating to spent convictions or to any circumstances ancillary to spent convictions, and the answer thereto may be framed accordingly; and

    (b) the person questioned shall not be subjected to any liability or otherwise prejudiced in law by reason of any failure to acknowledge or disclose a spent conviction or any circumstances ancillary to a spent conviction in his answer to the question.

    [(bb) in any proceedings under Part 2 of the Sexual Offences Act 2003, or on appeal from any such proceedings;][48]

    [(bc) in any proceedings on an application under section 2, 4 or 5 of the Protection of Children and Prevention of Sexual Offences (Scotland) Act 2005 (asp 9) or in any appeal under section 6 of that Act;][49]

    [(c) in any proceedings relating to parental responsibilities or parental rights (within the meaning of section 1(3) and section 2(4) respectively of the Children (Scotland) Act 1995), guardianship, adoption or the provision by any person of accommodation, care or schooling for children under the age of 18 years;

    (cc) in any proceedings under Part II of the Children (Scotland) Act 1995;][50]

    [(d) in any proceedings relating to the variation or discharge of a youth rehabilitation order under Part 1 of the Criminal Justice and Immigration Act 2008, or on appeal from any such proceedings;][51]

---

[47] As added by the Protection of Freedoms Act 2012, Sch.9(9), para.134(3).

[48] Substituted by the Sexual Offences Act 2003, Sch.6, para.19.

[49] Added by the Criminal Justice and Licensing (Scotland) Act 2010 asp 13 (Scottish Act), s.104.

[50] Substituted by the Children (Scotland) Act 1995, Sch.4, para.23(4)(a).

[51] Substituted by the Criminal Justice and Immigration Act 2008, Sch.4(1), para.22.

...

[(f) in any proceedings in which he is a party or a witness, provided that, on the occasion when the issue or the admission or requirement of the evidence falls to be determined, he consents to the determination of the issue or, as the case may be, the admission or requirement of the evidence notwithstanding the provisions of section 4(1)[52]; or

...

[(h) in any proceedings brought under Part 7 of the Coroners and Justice Act 2009 (criminal memoirs etc.).][53]

(3) Subject to the provisions of any order made under subsection (4) below,—

(a) any obligation imposed on any person by any rule or law or by the provisions of any agreement or arrangement to disclose any matter to any other person shall not extend to requiring him to disclose a spent conviction or any circumstances ancillary to a spent conviction (whether the conviction is his own or another's); and

(b) a conviction which has become spent or any circumstances ancillary thereto, or any failure to disclose a spent conviction or any such circumstances, shall not be a proper ground for dismissing or excluding a person from any office, profession, occupation or employment, or for prejudicing him in any way in any occupation or employment.

(4) The Secretary of State may by order—

(a) make such provision as seems to him appropriate for excluding or modifying the application of either or both of paragraphs (a) and (b) of subsection (2) above in relation to questions put in such circumstances as may be specified in the order;

(b) provide for such exceptions from the provisions of subsection (3) above as seem to him appropriate, in such cases or classes of case, and in relation to convictions of such a description, as may be specified in the order.[54]

(5) For the purposes of this section and section 7 below any of the following are circumstances ancillary to a conviction, that is to say—

(a) the offence or offences which were subject of that conviction;

(b) the conduct constituting that offence or those offences; and

(c) any process or proceedings preliminary to that conviction, any sentence imposed in respect of that conviction, any proceedings (whether by way of appeal or otherwise) for reviewing that conviction or any such sentence, and anything done in pursuance of or undergone in compliance with any such sentence.

(6) For the purposes of this section and section 7 below "proceedings before a judicial authority" includes, in addition to proceedings before any of the ordinary courts of law, proceedings before any tribunal, body or person having power—

(a) by virtue of any enactment, law, custom or practice;

(b) under the rules governing any association, institution, profession, occupation or employment; or

(c) under any provision of an agreement providing for arbitration with respect to questions arising thereunder;

---

[52] Added by the Coroners and Justice Act 2009, s.158(1).

[53] Added by the Coroners and Justice Act 2009, s.158(1).

[54] The powers conferred on the Secretary of State by this subsection and by s.7(4) have been exercised in the Rehabilitation of Offenders Act 1974 (Exceptions) Order 1975, as amended, which makes exceptions to the provisions of s.4(1), (2), and (3)(b) in relation to various types of work, licences, certificates and permits, proceedings, and action taken for the purpose of safeguarding national security. See also the Banking Act 1987.

to determine any question affecting the rights, privileges, obligations or liabilities of any person, or to receive evidence affecting the determination of any such question.

Limitations on rehabilitation under this Act, etc.

7.—(1) Nothing in section 4(1) above shall affect—

    (a) any right of Her Majesty, by virtue of Her Royal prerogative or otherwise, to grant a free pardon, to quash any conviction or sentence, or to commute any sentence;

    (b) the enforcement by any process or proceedings of any fine or other sum adjudged to be paid by or imposed on a spent conviction;

    (c) the issue of any process for the purpose of proceedings in respect of any breach of a condition or requirement applicable to a sentence imposed in respect of a spent conviction; or

    (d) the operation of any enactment by virtue of which, in consequence of any conviction, a person is subject, otherwise than by way of sentence, to any disqualification, disability, prohibition or other penalty the period of which extends beyond the rehabilitation period applicable in accordance with section 6 above to the conviction.

(2) Nothing in section 4(1) above shall affect the determination of any issue, or prevent the admission or requirement of any evidence, relating to a person's previous convictions or to circumstances ancillary thereto—

    (a) in any criminal proceedings before a court in Great Britain (including any appeal or reference in a criminal matter);

    (b) in any service disciplinary proceedings or in any proceedings on appeal from any service disciplinary proceedings;

    (bb) in any proceedings under Part 2 of the Sexual Offences Act 2003, or on appeal from any such proceedings;

    (c) in any proceedings relating to adoption, the marriage of any minor, [or the formation of a civil partnership by any minor,][55] the exercise of the inherent jurisdiction of the High Court with respect to minors or the provision by any person of accommodation, care or schooling for minors;

    (cc) in any proceedings brought under the Children Act 1989;

    [(d) in any proceedings relating to the variation or discharge of a youth rehabilitation order under Part 1 of the Criminal Justice and Immigration Act 2008, or on appeal from any such proceedings;][56]

    (e) in any proceedings before a children's hearing under the Social Work (Scotland) Act 1968 or on appeal from any such hearing; or

    (f) in any proceedings in which he is a party or a witness, provided that, on the occasion when the issue or the admission or requirement of the evidence falls to be determined, he consents to the determination of the issue or, as the case may be, the admission or requirement of the evidence notwithstanding the provisions of section 4(1); or

    [(h) in any proceedings brought under Part 7 of the Coroners and Justice Act 2009 (criminal memoirs etc.).][57]

In the application of this subsection to Scotland, "minor" means a child under the age of eighteen.

(3) If at any stage in any proceedings before a judicial authority in Great Britain (not being proceedings to which, by virtue of any of paragraphs (a) to (e) of subsection (2)

---

[55] Words inserted by the Civil Partnership Act 2004, Sch.27, para.53.
[56] Substituted by the Criminal Justice and Immigration Act 2008, Sch.4(1), para.22.
[57] Added by the Coroners and Justice Act 2009, s.158(1).

above or of any order for the time being in force under subsection (4) below, section 4(1) above has no application, or proceedings to which section 8 below applies) the authority is satisfied, in the light of any considerations which appear to it to be relevant (including any evidence which has been or may thereafter be put before it), that justice cannot be done in the case except by admitting or requiring evidence relating to a person's spent convictions or to circumstances ancillary thereto, that authority may admit or, as the case may be, require the evidence in question notwithstanding the provisions of subsection (1) of section 4 above, and may determine any issue to which the evidence relates in disregard, so far as necessary, of those provisions.

(4) The Secretary of State may by order exclude the application of section 4(1) above in relation to any proceedings specified in the order (other than proceedings to which section 8 below applies) to such extent and for such purposes as may be so specified.

(5) No order made by a court with respect to any person otherwise than on a conviction shall be included in any list or statement of that person's previous convictions given or made to any court which is considering how to deal with him in respect of any offence.

Defamation actions

8.—(1) This section applies to any action for libel or slander begun after the commencement of this Act by a rehabilitated person and founded upon the publication of any matter imputing that the plaintiff has committed or been charged with or prosecuted for or convicted of or sentenced for an offence which was the subject of a spent conviction.

(2) Nothing in section 4(1) above shall affect an action to which this section applies where the publication complained of took place before the conviction in question became spent, and the following provisions of this section shall not apply in any such case.

(3) Subject to subsections (5) and (6) below, nothing in section 4(1) above shall prevent the defendant in an action to which this section applies from relying on any defence *of justification or fair comment* [under section 2 or 3 of the Defamation Act 2013 which is available to him or any defence of][58] of absolute or qualified privilege which is available to him, or restrict the matters he may establish in support of any such defence.

(4) Without prejudice to the generality of subsection (3) above, where in any such action malice is alleged against a defendant who is relying on a defence of qualified privilege, nothing in section 4(1) above shall restrict the matters he may establish in rebuttal of the allegation.

(5) A defendant in any such action shall not by virtue of subsection (3) above be entitled to rely upon *the defence of justification* [a defence under section 2 of the Defamation Act 2013][59] if the publication is proved to have been made with malice.

(6) Subject to subsection (7) below a defendant in any such action shall not, by virtue of subsection (3) above, be entitled to rely on any matter or adduce or require

---

[58] By s.16(2) of the Defamation Act 2013, the words "of justification or fair comment or" in the Rehabilitation of Offenders Act 1974, s.8(3) are prospectively substituted by the words "under section 2 or 3 of the Defamation Act 2013 which is available to him or any defence".

[59] By s.16(3) of the Defamation Act 2013, the words "the defence of justification" in s.8(5) of the 1974 Act are prospectively substituted by the words "a defence under section 2 of the Defamation Act 2013".

any evidence for the purpose of establishing (whether under section 14 of the Defamation Act 1996[60] or otherwise) the defence that the matter published constituted a fair and accurate report of judicial proceedings if it is proved that the publication contained a reference to evidence which was ruled to be inadmissible in the proceedings by virtue of section 4(1) above.

(7) Subsection (3) above shall apply without the qualifications imposed by subsection (6) above in relation to—

(a) any report of judicial proceedings contained in any bona fide series of law reports which does not form part of any other publication and consists solely of reports of proceedings in courts of law; and

(b) any report or account of judicial proceedings published for bona fide educational, scientific or professional purposes, or given in the course of any lecture, class or discussion given or held for any of those purposes.

[(8) In the application of this section to Scotland—

(a) for the reference in subsection (1) to libel and slander there shall be substituted a reference to defamation;

(b) for references to the plaintiff and the defendant there shall be substituted respectively references to the pursuer and the defender; and

(c) for references to the defence of justification there shall be substituted references to the defence of veritas.[61]]

A2.14   **Civil Liability (Contribution) Act 1978**

[1978 c. 47]

Proceedings for contribution

Entitlement to contribution

1.—(1) Subject to the following provisions of this section, any person liable in respect of any damage suffered by another person may recover contribution from any other person liable in respect of the same damage (whether jointly with him or otherwise).

(2) A person shall be entitled to recover contribution by virtue of subsection (1) above notwithstanding that he has ceased to be liable in respect of the damage in question since the time when the damage occurred, provided that he was so liable immediately before he made or was ordered or agreed to make the payment in respect of which the contribution is sought.

(3) A person shall be liable to make contribution by virtue of subsection (1) above notwithstanding that he has ceased to be liable in respect of the damage in question since the time when the damage occurred, unless he ceased to be liable by virtue of the expiry of a period of limitation or prescription which extinguished the right on which the claim against him in respect of the damage was based.

(4) A person who has made or agreed to make any payment in bona fide settlement or compromise of any claim made against him in respect of any damage (including a payment into court which has been accepted) shall be entitled to recover contribution in accordance with this section without regard to whether or not he himself is or ever

---

[60] As amended by the Defamation Act 1996, s.14(4).

[61] S.8(8) is prospectively repealed by the Legal Aid, Sentencing and Punishment of Offenders Act 2012, Sch.25(1) (date to be appointed).

was liable in respect of the damage, provided, however, that he would have been liable assuming that the factual basis of the claim against him could be established.

(5) A judgment given in any action brought in any part of the United Kingdom by or on behalf of the person who suffered the damage in question against any person from whom contribution is sought under this section shall be conclusive in the proceedings for contribution as to any issue determined by that judgment in favour of the person from whom the contribution is sought.

(6) References in this section to a person's liability in respect of any damage are references to any such liability which has been or could be established in an action brought against him in England and Wales by or on behalf of the person who suffered the damage; but it is immaterial whether any issue arising in any such action was or would be determined (in accordance with the rules of private international law) by reference to the law of a country outside England and Wales.

Assessment of contribution

2.—(1) Subject to subsection (3) below, in any proceedings for contribution under section 1 above the amount of the contribution recoverable from any person shall be such as may be found by the court to be just and equitable having regard to the extent of that person's responsibility for the damage in question.

(2) Subject to subsection (3) below, the court shall have power in any such proceedings to exempt any person from liability to make contribution, or to direct that the contribution to be recovered from any person shall amount to a complete indemnity.

(3) Where the amount of the damages which have or might have been awarded in respect of the damage in question in any action brought in England and Wales by or on behalf of the person who suffered it against the person from whom the contribution is sought was or would have been subject to—

   (a) any limit imposed by or under any enactment or by any agreement made before the damage occurred;

   (b) any reduction by virtue of section 1 of the Law Reform (Contributory Negligence) Act 1945 or section 5 of the Fatal Accidents Act 1976; or

   (c) any corresponding limit or reduction under the law of a country outside England and Wales;

the person from whom the contribution is sought shall not by virtue of any contribution awarded under section 1 above be required to pay in respect of the damage a greater amount than the amount of those damages as so limited or reduced.

Proceedings against persons jointly liable for the same debt or damage

3. Judgment recovered against any person liable in respect of any debt or damage shall not be a bar to an action, or to the continuance of an action, against any other person who is (apart from any such bar) jointly liable with him in respect of the same debt or damage.

Successive actions against persons liable (jointly or otherwise) for the same damage

4. If more than one action is brought in respect of any damage by or on behalf of the person by whom it was suffered against persons liable in respect of the damage (whether jointly or otherwise) the plaintiff shall not be entitled to costs in any of those actions, other than that in which judgment is first given, unless the court is of the opinion that there was reasonable ground for bringing the action.

Interpretation

6.—(1) A person is liable in respect of any damage for the purposes of this Act if the person who suffered it (or anyone representing his estate or dependants) is entitled to recover compensation from him in respect of that damage (whatever the legal basis of his liability, whether tort, breach of contract, breach of trust or otherwise).

Savings

7.—

(3) The right to recover contribution in accordance with section 1 above supersedes any right, other than an express contractual right, to recover contribution (as distinct from indemnity) otherwise than under this Act in corresponding circumstances; but nothing in this Act shall affect—

　　(a) any express or implied contractual or other right to indemnity; or

　　(b) any express contractual provision regulating or excluding contribution;

which would be enforceable apart from this Act (or render enforceable any agreement for indemnity or contribution which would not be enforceable apart from this Act).

A2.15 <center>**Limitation Act 1980**</center>

[1980 c. 58]

Time limits under Part I subject to extension or exclusion under Part II

1.—(1) This Part of this Act gives the ordinary time limits for bringing actions of the various classes mentioned in the following provisions of this Part.

(2) The ordinary time limits given in this Part of this Act are subject to extension or exclusion in accordance with the provisions of Part II of this Act.

Time limit for actions founded on tort

2. An action founded on tort shall not be brought after the expiration of six years from the date on which the cause of action accrued.

Time limit for actions for defamation or malicious falsehood

4A. The time limit under section 2 of this Act shall not apply to an action for (a) libel or slander, or (b) slander of title, slander of goods or other malicious falsehood, but no such action shall be brought after the expiration of one year from the date on which the cause of action accrued.[62]

Extension of limitation period in case of disability

28.—(1) Subject to the following provisions of this section, if on the date when any right of action accrued for which a period of limitation is prescribed by this Act, the person to whom it accrued was under a disability, the action may be brought at any time before the expiration of six years from the date when he ceased to be under a disability or died (whichever first occurred) notwithstanding that the period of limitation has expired.

---

[62] Substituted by the Defamation Act 1996, s.5(2).

(4A) If the action is one to which section 4A of this Act applies, subsection (1) above shall have effect—

    (a) in the case of an action for libel or slander, as if for the words from "at any time" to "occurred" there were substituted the words "by him at any time before the expiration of one year from the date on which he ceased to be under a disability"; and

    (b) in the case of an action for slander of title, slander of goods or other malicious falsehood, as if for the words "six years" there were substituted the words "one year".[63]

Discretionary exclusion of time limit for actions for defamation or malicious falsehood

32A.—(1) If it appears to the court that it would be equitable to allow an action to proceed having regard to the degree to which—

    (a) the operation of section 4A of this Act prejudices the plaintiff or any person whom he represents, and

    (b) any decision of the court under this subsection would prejudice the defendant or any person whom he represents,

the court may direct that that section shall not apply to the action or shall not apply to any specified cause of action to which the action relates.

(2) In acting under this section the court shall have regard to all the circumstances of the case and in particular to—

    (a) the length of, and the reasons for, the delay on the part of the plaintiff;

    (b) where the reason or one of the reasons for the delay was that all or any of the facts relevant to the cause of action did not become known to the plaintiff until after the end of the period mentioned in section 4A—

      (i) the date on which any such facts did become known to him, and

      (ii) the extent to which he acted promptly and reasonably once he knew whether or not the facts in question might be capable of giving rise to an action; and

    (c) the extent to which, having regard to the delay, relevant evidence is likely—

      (i) to be unavailable, or

      (ii) to be less cogent than if the action had been brought within the period mentioned in section 4A.

(3) In the case of an action for slander of title, slander of goods or other malicious falsehood brought by a personal representative—

    (a) the references in subsection (2) above to the plaintiff shall be construed as including the deceased person to whom the cause of action accrued and any previous personal representative of that person; and

    (b) nothing in section 28(3) of this Act shall be construed as affecting the court's discretion under this section.

(4) In this section "the court" means the court in which the action has been brought.[64]

Equitable jurisdiction and remedies

36.—(1) The following time limits under this Act, that is to say—

  . . .

---

[63] Substituted by the Defamation Act 1996, s.5(3).
[64] Substituted by the Defamation Act 1996, s.5(4).

(aa) the time limit under section 4A for actions for libel or slander

. . .

shall not apply to any claim for . . . an injunction or for other equitable relief, except in so far as any such time limit may be applied by the court by analogy in like manner as the corresponding time limit under any enactment repealed by the Limitation Act 1939 was applied before 1st July 1940.[65]

A2.16 ## Contempt of Court Act 1981

[1981 c. 49]

The strict liability rule

1. In this Act "the strict liability rule" means the rule of law whereby conduct may be treated as a contempt of court as tending to interfere with the course of justice in particular legal proceedings regardless of intent to do so.

Limitation of scope of strict liability

2.—(1) The strict liability rule applies only in relation to publications, and for this purpose "publication" includes any speech, writing, programme included in a cable programme service or other communication in whatever form, which is addressed to the public at large or any section of the public.[66]

(2) The strict liability rule applies only to a publication which creates a substantial risk that the course of justice in the proceedings in question will be seriously impeded or prejudiced.

(3) The strict liability rule applies to a publication only if the proceedings in question are active within the meaning of this section at the time of the publication.

(4) Schedule 1 applies for determining the times at which proceedings are to be treated as active within the meaning of this section.

(5) In this section "programme service" has the same meaning as in the Broadcasting Act 1990.

Defence of innocent publication or distribution

3.—(1) A person is not guilty of contempt of court under the strict liability rule as the publisher of any matter to which that rule applies if at the time of publication (having taken all reasonable care) he does not know and has no reason to suspect that relevant proceedings are active.

(2) A person is not guilty of contempt of court under the strict liability rule as the distributor of a publication containing any such matter if at the time of distribution (having taken all reasonable care) he does not know that it contains such matter and has no reason to suspect that it is likely to do so.

(3) The burden of proof of any fact tending to establish a defence afforded by this section to any person lies upon that person.

Contemporary reports of proceedings

4.—(1) Subject to this section a person is not guilty of contempt of court under the strict liability rule in respect of a fair and accurate report of legal proceedings held in public, published contemporaneously and in good faith.

---

[65] Para.(aa) substituted by the Defamation Act 1996, s.5(5). The limitation amendments made by the 1996 Act apply to causes of action arising after September 3, 1996: ss.5(6), 19(2).

[66] Amendments effected by the Broadcasting Act 1990 s.203(1), Sch.20, para.31(1) have been incorporated.

(2) In any such proceedings the court may, where it appears to be necessary for avoiding a substantial risk of prejudice to the administration of justice in those proceedings, or in any other proceedings pending or imminent, order that the publication of any report of the proceedings, or any part of the proceedings, be postponed for such period as the court thinks necessary for that purpose.

(2A) Where in proceedings for any offence which is an administration of justice offence for the purposes of section 54 of the Criminal Procedure and Investigations Act 1996 (acquittal tainted by an administration of justice offence) it appears to the court that there is a possibility that (by virtue of that section) proceedings may be taken against a person for an offence of which he has been acquitted, subsection (2) of this section shall apply as if those proceedings were pending or imminent.[67]

(3) For the purposes of subsection (1) of this section a report of proceedings shall be treated as published contemporaneously—

    (a) in the case of a report of which publication is postponed pursuant to an order under subsection (2) of this section, if published as soon as practicable after that order expires;

    (b) in the case of a report of allocation or sending proceedings of which publication is permitted by virtue only of subsection (6) of section 52A of the Crime and Disorder Act 1998 ("the 1998 Act"), if published as soon as practicable after publication is so permitted;

    (c) in the case of a report of an application of which publication is permitted by virtue only of sub-paragraph (5) or (7) of paragraph 3 of Schedule 3 to the 1998 Act, if published as soon as practicable after publication is so permitted.[68]

Discussion of public affairs

5. A publication made as or as part of a discussion in good faith of public affairs or other matters of general public interest is not to be treated as a contempt of court under the strict liability rule if the risk of impediment or prejudice to particular legal proceedings is merely incidental to the discussion.

Savings

6. Nothing in the foregoing provisions of this Act—

    (a) prejudices any defence available at common law to a charge of contempt of court under the strict liability rule;

    (b) implies that any publication is punishable as contempt of court under that rule which would not be so punishable apart from those provisions;

    (c) restricts liability for contempt of court in respect of conduct intended to impede or prejudice the administration of justice.

Consent required for institution of proceedings

7. Proceedings for a contempt of court under the strict liability rule (other than Scottish proceedings) shall not be instituted except by or with the consent of the Attorney General or on the motion of a court having jurisdiction to deal with it.

Sources of information

10. No court may require a person to disclose, nor is any person guilty of contempt of court for refusing to disclose, the source of information contained in a publication

---

[67] Added by the Criminal Procedure and Investigations Act 1996, s.57(3)

[68] Text of subsections 4(3)(b) and (c) substituted by the Criminal Justice Act 2003, Sch.3(2), para.53 (with effect from June 18, 2012).

for which he is responsible, unless it be established to the satisfaction of the court that disclosure is necessary in the interests of justice or national security or for the prevention of disorder or crime.

Publication of matters exempted from disclosure in court

11. In any case where a court (having power to do so) allows a name or other matter to be withheld from the public in proceedings before the court, the court may give such directions prohibiting the publication of that name or matter in connection with the proceedings as appear to the court to be necessary for the purpose for which it was so withheld.

Tribunals of Inquiry

20.—(1) In relation to any tribunal to which the Tribunals of Inquiry (Evidence) Act 1921 applies, and the proceedings of such a tribunal, the provisions of this Act (except subsection (3) of section 9) apply as they apply in relation to courts and legal proceedings; and references to the course of justice or the administration of justice in legal proceedings shall be construed accordingly.

(2) The proceedings of a tribunal established under the said Act shall be treated as active within the meaning of section 2 from the time when the tribunal is appointed until its report is presented to Parliament.

SCHEDULES

Section 2

SCHEDULE 1

TIMES WHEN PROCEEDINGS ARE ACTIVE FOR PURPOSES OF

SECTION 2

Preliminary

2. Criminal, appellate and other proceedings are active within the meaning of section 2 at the times respectively prescribed by the following paragraphs of this Schedule; and in relation to proceedings in which more than one of the steps described in any of those paragraphs is taken, the reference in that paragraph is a reference to the first of those steps.

Other proceedings at first instance

12. Proceedings other than criminal proceedings and appellate proceedings are active from the time when arrangements for the hearing are made or if no such arrangements are previously made, from the time the hearing begins, until the proceedings are disposed of or discontinued or withdrawn; and for the purposes of this paragraph any motion or application made in or for the purposes of any proceedings, any pre-trial review in the county court, is to be treated as a distinct proceeding.

13. In England and Wales or Northern Ireland arrangements for the hearing of proceedings to which paragraph 12 applies are made within the meaning of that paragraph—

    (a) in the case of proceedings in the High Court for which provision is made by rules of court for setting down for trial, when the case is set down;

    (b) in the case of any proceedings, when a date for the trial or hearing is fixed.

Senior Courts Act 1981

A2.17

[1981 c. 54]

Trial by jury

69.—(1) Where, on the application of any party to an action to be tried in the Queen's Bench Division, the court is satisfied that there is in issue—

    (a) a charge of fraud against that party; or

    (b) a claim in respect of *libel, slander,*[69] malicious prosecution or false imprisonment; or

    (c) any question or issue of a kind prescribed for the purposes of this paragraph,

the action shall be tried with a jury unless the court is of opinion that the trial requires any prolonged examination of documents or accounts or any scientific or local investigation which cannot conveniently be made with a jury.

(2) An application under subsection (1) must be made not later than such time before the trial as may be prescribed.

(3) An action to be tried in the Queen's Bench Division which does not by virtue of subsection (1) fall to be tried with a jury shall be tried without a jury unless the court in its discretion orders it to be tried with a jury.

(4) Nothing in subsections (1) to (3) shall affect the power of the court to order, in accordance with rules of court, that different questions of fact arising in any action be tried by different modes of trial; and where any such order is made, subsection (1) shall have effect only as respects questions relating to any such charge, claim, question or issue as is mentioned in that subsection.

(5) Where for the purpose of disposing of any action or other matter which is being tried in the High Court by a judge with a jury it is necessary to ascertain the law of any other country which is applicable to the facts of the case, any question as to the effect of the evidence given with respect to that law shall, instead of being submitted to the jury, be decided by the judge alone.

Representation of the People Act 1983

A2.18

[1983 c. 2]

False statements as to candidates

106.—(1) A person who, or any director of any body or association corporate which—

    (a) before or during an election,

    (b) for the purpose of affecting the return of any candidate at the election,

makes or publishes any false statement of fact in relation to the candidate's personal character or conduct shall be guilty of an illegal practice, unless he can show that he had reasonable ground for believing, and did believe, the statement to be true.

---

[69] By the Defamation Act 2013, s.11(1) the words "libel, slander," are prospectively omitted from the Senior Courts Act 1981, s.69(1)(b).

(2) A candidate shall not be liable nor shall his election be avoided for any illegal practice under subsection (1) above committed by his agent other than his election agent unless—

(a) it can be shown that the candidate or his election agent has authorised or consented to the committing of the illegal practice by the other agent or has paid for the circulation of the false statement constituting the illegal practice; or

(b) an election court find and report that the election of the candidate was procured or materially assisted in consequence of the making or publishing of such false statements.

(3) A person making or publishing any false statement of fact as mentioned above may be restrained by interim or perpetual injunction by the High Court or the county court from any repetition of that false statement or of a false statement of a similar character in relation to the candidate and, for the purpose of granting an interim injunction, prima facie proof of the falsity of the statement shall be sufficient.

(5) Any person who, before or during an election, knowingly publishes a false statement of a candidate's withdrawal at the election for the purpose of promoting or procuring the election of another candidate shall be guilty of an illegal practice.

(6) A candidate shall not be liable, nor shall his election be avoided, for any illegal practice under subsection (5) above committed by his agent other than his election agent.

(7) In the application of this section to an election where a candidate is not required to have an election agent, references to an election agent shall be omitted and the reference in subsection (6) above to an illegal practice committed by an agent of the candidate shall be taken as a reference to an illegal practice committed without the candidate's knowledge and consent.

(9) Article 60 of the County Courts (Northern Ireland) Order 1980 (appeals from county courts) shall apply in relation to any order of a county court in Northern Ireland made by virtue of subsection (3) above as it applies in relation to any such decree of a county court as is mentioned in paragraph (1) of that Article.

A2.19

County Courts Act 1984

[1984 c. 28]

General jurisdiction in actions of contract and tort

15.—(1) Subject to subsection (2), a county court shall have jurisdiction to hear and determine any action founded on contract or tort.

(2) a county court shall not, except as in this Act provided, have jurisdiction to hear and determine—

(c) any action of libel or slander.

Jurisdiction by agreement in certain actions

18.—If the parties to any action, other than an action which, if commenced in the High Court, would have been assigned to the Chancery Division or to the Family Division or have involved the exercise of the High Court's Admiralty jurisdiction, agree, by a memorandum signed by them or by their respective [legal representatives],[70] that a county court specified in the memorandum shall have jurisdiction in the

---

[70] Words substituted by the Courts and Legal Services Act 1990, s.125(3), Sch.18.

action, that court shall have jurisdiction to hear and determine the action accordingly.

Transfer of proceedings to county court

40.—(1) Where the High Court is satisfied that any proceedings before it are required by any provision of a kind mentioned in sub-section (8) to be in a county court it shall—

    (a) order the transfer of the proceedings to a county court; or

    (b) if the court is satisfied that the person bringing the proceedings knew, or ought to have known, of that requirement, order that they be struck out.

(2) Subject to any such provision, the High Court may order the transfer of any proceedings before it to a county court.

(3) An order under this section may be made either on the motion of the High Court itself or on the application of any party to the proceedings.

(4) Proceedings transferred under this section shall be transferred to such county court as the High Court considers appropriate, having taken into account the convenience of the parties and that of any other persons likely to be affected and the state of business in the courts concerned.

(5) The transfer of any proceedings under this section shall not affect any right of appeal from the order directing the transfer.

(6) Where proceedings for the enforcement of any judgment or order of the High Court are transferred under this section—

    (a) the judgment or order may be enforced as if it were a judgment or order of a county court; and

    (b) subject to subsection (7), it shall be treated as a judgment or order of that court for all purposes.

(7) Where proceedings for the enforcement of any judgment or order of the High Court are transferred under this section—

    (a) the powers of any court to set aside, correct, vary or quash a judgment or order of the High Court, and the enactments relating to appeals from such a judgment or order, shall continue to apply; and

    (b) the powers of any court to set aside, correct, vary or quash a judgment or order of a county court, and the enactments relating to appeals from such a judgment or order, shall not apply.

(8) The provisions referred to in subsection (1) are any made—

    (a) under section 1 of the Courts and Legal Services Act 1990; or

    (b) by or under any other enactment.

(9) This section does not apply to family proceedings within the meaning of Part V of the Matrimonial and Family Proceedings Act 1984.[71]

Trial by jury

66.—(1) In the following proceedings in a county court the trial shall be without a jury—

(Admiralty proceedings and those arising under certain statutes)

(2) In all other proceedings in a county court the trial shall be without a jury unless the court otherwise orders on an application made in that behalf by any party to the proceedings in such manner and within such time before the trial as may be prescribed.

(3) Where, on any such application, the court is satisfied that there is in issue—

---

[71] S.40 was substituted by the Courts and Legal Services Act 1990, s.2(1).

... (b) a claim in respect of *[libel, slander,]*[72] malicious prosecution or false imprisonment ...

the action shall be tried with a jury, unless the court is of the opinion that the trial requires any prolonged examination of documents or accounts or any scientific or local investigation which cannot conveniently be made with a jury.

A2.20　　　　　　　**Copyright, Designs and Patents Act 1988**

[1988 c. 48]

Right to object to derogatory treatment of work

80.—(1) The author of a copyright literary, dramatic, musical or artistic work, and the director of a copyright film, has the right in the circumstances mentioned in this section not to have his work subjected to derogatory treatment.

(2) For the purposes of this section—

    (a) "treatment" of a work means any addition to, deletion from or alteration to or adaptation of the work, other than—

        (i) a translation of a literary or dramatic work, or

        (ii) an arrangement or transcription of a musical work involving no more than a change of key or register; and

    (b) the treatment of a work is derogatory if it amounts to distortion or mutilation of the work or is otherwise prejudicial to the honour or reputation of the author or director;

and in the following provisions of this section references to a derogatory treatment of a work shall be construed accordingly.

(3) In the case of a literary, dramatic or musical work the right is infringed by a person who—

    (a) publishes commercially, performs in public, broadcasts or [communicates to the public][73] a derogatory treatment of the work; or

    (b) issues to the public copies of a film or sound recording of, or including, a derogatory treatment of the work.

(4) In the case of an artistic work the right is infringed by a person who—

    (a) publishes commercially or exhibits in public a derogatory treatment of the work, or broadcasts or [communicates to the public][74] a visual image of a derogatory treatment of the work,

    (b) shows in public a film including a visual image of a derogatory treatment of the work or issues to the public copies of such a film, or

    (c) in the case of—

        (i) a work of architecture in the form of a model for a building,

        (ii) a sculpture, or

        (iii) a work of artistic craftsmanship,

issues to the public copies of a graphic work representing, or of a photograph of, a derogatory treatment of the work.

(5) Subsection (4) does not apply to a work of architecture in the form of a building; but where the author of such a work is identified on the building and it is the subject of derogatory treatment he has the right to require the identification to be removed.

---

[72] By the Defamation Act 2013, s.11(2) the words "libel, slander," are prospectively omitted from the County Courts Act 1984, s.66(3).

[73] Words substituted by the Copyright and Related Rights Regulations 2003/2498, Sch.1(1), para.10(1)(a).

[74] Words substituted by the Copyright and Related Rights Regulations 2003/2498, Sch.1(1), para.13(2).

(6) In the case of a film, the right is infringed by a person who—
    (a) shows in public or [communicates to the public][75] a derogatory treatment of the film; or
    (b) issues to the public copies of a derogatory treatment of the film.

(7) The right conferred by this section extends to the treatment of parts of a work resulting from a previous treatment by a person other than the author or director, if those parts are attributed to, or are likely to be regarded as the work of, the author or director.

(8) This section has effect subject to sections 81 and 82 (exceptions to and qualifications of right).

Exceptions to right

81.—(1) The right conferred by section 80 (right to object to derogatory treatment of work) is subject to the following exceptions.

(2) The right does not apply to a computer program or to any computer-generated work.

(3) The right does not apply in relation to any work made for the purpose of reporting current events.

(4) The right does not apply in relation to the publication in—
    (a) a newspaper, magazine or similar periodical, or
    (b) an encyclopaedia, dictionary, yearbook or other collective work of reference,
of a literary, dramatic, musical or artistic work made for the purposes of such publication or made available with the consent of the author for the purposes of such publication.

Nor does the right apply in relation to any subsequent exploitation elsewhere of such a work without any modification of the published version.

(5) The right is not infringed by an act which by virtue of section 57 or 66A (acts permitted on assumptions as to expiry of copyright etc.) would not infringe copyright.

(6) The right is not infringed by anything done for the purpose of—
    (a) avoiding the commission of an offence,
    (b) complying with a duty imposed by or under an enactment, or
    (c) in the case of the British Broadcasting Corporation, avoiding the inclusion in a programme broadcast by them of anything which offends against good taste or decency or which is likely to encourage or incite to crime or to lead to disorder or to be offensive to public feeling,
provided, where the author or director is identified at the time of the relevant act or has previously been identified in or on published copies of the work, that there is a sufficient disclaimer.

Qualification of right in certain cases

82.—(1) This section applies to—
    (a) works in which copyright originally vested in the author's or director's employer by virtue of section 11(2) (works produced in course of employment),
    (b) works in which Crown copyright or Parliamentary copyright subsists, and

---

[75] Words substituted by the Copyright and Related Rights Regulations 2003/2498, Sch.1(1), para.10(1)(b).

(c) works in which copyright originally vested in an international organisation by virtue of section 168.

(2) The right conferred by section 80 (right to object to derogatory treatment of work) does not apply to anything done in relation to such a work by or with the authority of the copyright owner unless the author or director—

(a) is identified at the time of the relevant act, or

(b) has previously been identified in or on published copies of the work;

and where in such a case the right does not apply, it is not infringed if there is a sufficient disclaimer.

Infringement of right by possessing or dealing with infringing article

83.—(1) The right conferred by section 80 (right to object to derogatory treatment of work) is also infringed by a person who—

(a) possesses in the course of a business, or

(b) sells or lets for hire, or offers or exposes for sale or hire, or

(c) in the course of a business exhibits in public or distributes, or

(d) distributes otherwise than in the course of a business so as to affect prejudicially the honour or reputation of the author or director,

an article which is, and which he knows or has reason to believe is, an infringing article.

(2) An "infringing article" means a work or a copy of a work which—

(a) has been subjected to derogatory treatment within the meaning of section 80, and

(b) has been or is likely to be the subject of any of the acts mentioned in that section in circumstances infringing that right.

False attribution of work

84.—(1) A person has the right in the circumstances mentioned in this section—

(a) not to have a literary, dramatic, musical or artistic work falsely attributed to him as author; and

(b) not to have a film falsely attributed to him as director; and in this section an "attribution", in relation to such a work, means a statement (express or implied) as to who is the author or director.

(2) The right is infringed by a person who—

(a) issues to the public copies of a work of any of those descriptions in or on which there is a false attribution, or

(b) exhibits in public an artistic work, or a copy of an artistic work, in or on which there is a false attribution.

(3) The right is also infringed by a person who—

(a) in the case of a literary, dramatic or musical work, performs the work in public, or communicates it to the public as being the work of a person, or

(b) in the case of a film, shows it in public, or communicates it to the public as being directed by a person,

knowing or having reason to believe that the attribution is false.

(4) The right is also infringed by the issue to the public or public display of material containing a false attribution in connection with any of the acts mentioned in subsection (2) or (3).

(5) The right is also infringed by a person who in the course of a business—

(a) possesses or deals with a copy of a work of any of the descriptions mentioned in subsection (1) in or on which there is a false attribution, or

(b) in the case of an artistic work, possesses or deals with the work itself when there is a false attribution in or on it, knowing or having reason to believe that there is such an attribution and that it is false.

(6) In the case of an artistic work the right is also infringed by a person who in the course of a business—

    (a) deals with a work which has been altered after the author parted with possession of it as being the unaltered work of the author, or

    (b) deals with a copy of such a work as being a copy of the unaltered work of the author,

knowing or having reason to believe that that is not the case.

(7) References in this section to dealing are to selling or letting for hire, offering or exposing for sale or hire, exhibition in public, or distributing.

(8) This section applies where, contrary to the fact—

    (a) a literary, dramatic or musical work is falsely represented as being an adaptation of the work of a person, or

    (b) a copy of an artistic work is falsely represented as being a copy made by the author of the artistic work,

as it applies where the work is falsely attributed to a person as author.

Right to privacy of certain photographs and films

85.—(1) A person who for private and domestic purposes commissions the taking of a photograph or the making of a film has, where copyright subsists in the resulting work, the right not to have—

    (a) copies of the work issued to the public,

    (b) the work exhibited or shown in public, or

    (c) the work broadcast or communicated to the public;

and, except as mentioned in subsection (2), a person who does or authorises the doing of any of those acts infringes the right.

(2) The right is not infringed by an act which by virtue of any of the following provisions would not infringe copyright in the work—

    (a) section 31 (incidental inclusion of work in an artistic work, film, [or broadcast]);

    (b) section 45 (parliamentary and judicial proceedings);

    (c) section 46 (Royal Commissions and statutory inquiries);

    (d) section 50 (acts done under statutory authority);

    (e) section 57 or 66A (acts permitted on assumptions as to expiry of copyright, etc.)

Duration of rights

86.—(1) The rights conferred by section 77 (right to be identified as author or director), section 80 (right to object to derogatory treatment of work) and section 85 (right to privacy of certain photographs and films) continue to subsist so long as copyright subsists in the work.

(2) The right conferred by section 84 (false attribution) continues to subsist until 20 years after a person's death.

Consent and waiver of rights

87.—(1) It is not an infringement of any of the rights conferred by this Chapter to do any act to which the person entitled to the right has consented.

(2) Any of those rights may be waived by instrument in writing signed by the person giving up the right.

(3) A waiver—

(a) may relate to a specific work, to works of a specified description or to works generally, and may relate to existing or future works, and

(b) may be conditional or unconditional and may be expressed to be subject to revocation;

and if made in favour of the owner or prospective owner of the copyright in the work or works to which it relates, it shall be presumed to extend to his licensees and successors in title unless a contrary intention is expressed.

(4) Nothing in this Chapter shall be construed as excluding the operation of the general law of contract or estoppel in relation to an informal waiver or other transaction in relation to any of the rights mentioned in subsection (1).

Application of provisions to joint works

88.—(1) The right conferred by section 77 (right to be identified as author or director) is, in the case of a work of joint authorship, a right of each joint author to be identified as a joint author and must be asserted in accordance with section 78 by each joint author in relation to himself.

(2) The right conferred by section 80 (right to object to derogatory treatment of work) is, in the case of a work of joint authorship, a right of each joint author and his right is satisfied if he consents to the treatment in question.

(3) A waiver under section 87 of those rights by one joint author does not affect the rights of the other joint authors.

(4) The right conferred by section 84 (false attribution) is infringed, in the circumstances mentioned in that section—

(a) by any false statement as to the authorship of a work of joint authorship, and

(b) by the false attribution of joint authorship in relation to a work of sole authorship;

and such a false attribution infringes the right of every person to whom authorship of any description is, whether rightly or wrongly, attributed.

(5) The above provisions also apply (with any necessary adaptations) in relation to a film which was, or is alleged to have been, jointly directed as they apply to a work which is, or is alleged to be, a work of joint authorship.

A film is "jointly directed" if it is made by the collaboration of two or more directors and the contribution of each director is not distinct from that of the other director or directors.

(6) The right conferred by section 85 (right to privacy of certain photographs and films) is, in the case of a work made in pursuance of a joint commission, a right of each person who commissioned the making of the work, so that—

(a) the right of each is satisfied if he consents to the act in question, and

(b) a waiver under section 87 by one of them does not affect the rights of the others.

Application of provisions to parts of works

89.—(1) The rights conferred by section 77 (right to be identified as author or director) and section 85 (right to privacy of certain photographs and films) apply in relation to the whole or any substantial part of a work.

(2) The rights conferred by section 80 (right to object to derogatory treatment of work) and section 84 (false attribution) apply in relation to the whole or any part of a work.

<h2 style="text-align:center">Broadcasting Act 1990   A2.21</h2>

[1990 c. 42]

Defamatory material

166.—(1) For the purposes of the law of libel and slander [. . .][76] the publication of words in the course of any programme included in a programme service shall be treated as publication in permanent form.

(2) Subsection (1) above shall apply for the purposes of section 3 of each of the Defamation Acts (slander of title etc.) as it applies for the purposes of the law of libel and slander.

(4) In this section "the Defamation Acts" means the Defamation Act 1952 and the Defamation Act (Northern Ireland) 1955.

(5) Subsections (1) and (2) above do not extent to Scotland.

Private International Law (Miscellaneous Provisions) Act 1995   A2.22

[1995 c. 42]

Purpose of Part III

9.—(1) The rules in this Part apply for choosing the law (in this Part referred to as "the applicable law") to be used for determining issues relating to tort or (for the purposes of the law of Scotland) delict.

(2) The characterisation for the purposes of private international law of issues arising in a claim as issues relating to tort or delict is a matter for the courts of the forum.

(3) The rules in this Part do not apply in relation to issues arising in any claim excluded from the operation of this Part by section 13 below.

(4) The applicable law shall be used for determining the issues arising in a claim, including in particular the question whether an actionable tort or delict has occurred.

(5) The applicable law to be used for determining the issues arising in a claim shall exclude any choice of law rules forming part of the law of the country or countries concerned.

(6) For the avoidance of doubt (and without prejudice to the operation of section 14 below) this Part applies in relation to events occurring in the forum as it applies in relation to events occurring in any other country.

(7) In this Part as it extends to any country within the United Kingdom, "the forum" means England and Wales, Scotland or Northern Ireland, as the case may be.

(8) In this Part "delict" includes quasi-delict.

Abolition of certain common law rules

10. The rules of the common law, in so far as they—
- (a) require actionability under both the law of the forum and the law of another country for the purpose of determining whether a tort of delict is actionable; or
- (b) allow (as an exception from the rules falling within paragraph (a) above) for the law of a single country to be applied for the purpose of determining the issues, or any of the issues, arising in the case in question,

---

[76] Words repealed by the Coroners and Justice Act 2009, s.178, Sch.23(2).

and hereby abolished so far as they apply to any claim in tort or delict which is not excluded from the operation of this Part by section 13 below.

Choice of applicable law: the general rule

11.—(1) The general rule is that the applicable law is the law of the country in which the events constituting the tort or delict in question occur.

(2) Where elements of those events occur in different countries, the applicable law under the general rules is to be taken as being—

(a) for a cause of action in respect of personal injury caused to an individual or death resulting from personal injury, the law of the country where the individual was when he sustained the injury;

(b) for a cause of action in respect of damage to property, the law of the country where the property was when it was damaged; and

(c) in any other case, the law of the country in which the most significant element or elements of those events occurred.

(3) In this section "personal injury" includes disease or any impairment of physical or mental condition.

Choice of applicable law: displacement of general rule

12.—(1) If it appears, in all the circumstances, from a comparison of—

(a) the significance of the factors which connect a tort or delict with the country whose law would be the applicable law under the general rule; and

(b) the significance of any factors connecting the tort or delict with another country,

that it is substantially more appropriate for the applicable law for determining the issues arising in the case, or any of those issues, to be the law of the other country, the general rule is displaced and the applicable law for determining those issues or that issue (as the case may be) is the law of that other country.

(2) The factors that may be taken into account as connecting a tort or delict with a country for the purposes of this section include, in particular, factors relating to the parties, to any of the events which constitute the tort or delict in question or to any of the circumstances or consequences of those events.

Exclusion of defamation claims from Part III

13.—(1) Nothing in this Part applies to affect the determination of issues arising in any defamation claim.

(2) For the purposes of this section "defamation claim" means—

(a) any claim under the law of any part of the United Kingdom for libel or slander or for slander of title, slander of goods or other malicious falsehood and any claim under the law of Scotland for verbal injury; and

(b) any claim under the law of any other country corresponding to or otherwise in the nature of a claim mentioned in paragraph (a) above.

A2.23 ## Defamation Act 1996

[1996 c. 31]

Responsibility for publication

1.—(1) In defamation proceedings a person has a defence if he shows that—

(a) he was not the author, editor or publisher of the statement complained of,

    (b) he took reasonable care in relation to its publication, and

    (c) he did not know, and had no reason to believe, that what he did caused or contributed to the publication of a defamatory statement.

(2) For this purpose "author", "editor" and "publisher" have the following meanings, which are further explained in subsection (3)—

"author" means the originator of the statement, but does not include a person who did not intend that his statement be published at all;

"editor" means a person having editorial or equivalent responsibility for the content of the statement or the decision to publish it; and

"publisher" means a commercial publisher, that is, a person whose business is issuing material to the public, or a section of the public, who issues material containing the statement in the course of that business.

(3) A person shall not be considered the author, editor or publisher of a statement if he is only involved—

    (a) in printing, producing, distributing or selling printed material containing the statement;

    (b) in processing, making copies of, distributing, exhibiting or selling a film or sound recording (as defined in Part I of the Copyright, Designs and Patents Act 1988) containing the statement;

    (c) in processing, making copies of, distributing or selling any electronic medium in or on which the statement is recorded, or in operating or providing any equipment, system or service by means of which the statement is retrieved, copied, distributed or made available in electronic form;

    (d) as the broadcaster of a live programme containing the statement in circumstances in which he has no effective control over the maker of the statement;

    (e) as the operator of or provider of access to a communications system by means of which the statement is transmitted, or made available, by a person over whom he has no effective control.

In a case not within paragraphs (a) to (e) the court may have regard to those provisions by way of analogy in deciding whether a person is to be considered the author, editor or publisher of a statement.

(4) Employees or agents of an author, editor or publisher are in the same position as their employer or principal to the extent that they are responsible for the content of the statement or the decision to publish it.

(5) In determining for the purposes of this section whether a person took reasonable care, or had reason to believe that what he did caused or contributed to the publication of a defamatory statement, regard shall be had to—

    (a) the extent of his responsibility for the content of the statement or the decision to publish it,

    (b) the nature or circumstances of the publication, and

    (c) the previous conduct or character of the author, editor or publisher.

(6) This section does not apply to any cause of action which arose before the section came into force.

Offer to make amends

2.—(1) A person who has published a statement alleged to be defamatory of another may offer to make amends under this section.

(2) The offer may be in relation to the statement generally or in relation to a specific defamatory meaning which the person making the offer accepts that the statement conveys ("a qualified offer").

(3) An offer to make amends—

(a) must be in writing,

(b) must be expressed to be an offer to make amends under section 2 of the Defamation Act 1996, and

(c) must state whether it is a qualified offer and, if so, set out the defamatory meaning in relation to which it is made.

(4) An offer to make amends under this section is an offer—

(a) to make a suitable correction of the statement complained of and a sufficient apology to the aggrieved party,

(b) to publish the correction and apology in a manner that is reasonable and practicable in the circumstances, and

(c) to pay to the aggrieved party such compensation (if any), and such costs, as may be agreed or determined to be payable.

The fact that the offer is accompanied by an offer to take specific steps does not affect the fact that an offer to make amends under this section is an offer to do all the things mentioned in paragraphs (a) to (c).

(5) An offer to make amends under this section may not be made by a person after serving a defence in defamation proceedings brought against him by the aggrieved party in respect of the publication in question.

(6) An offer to make amends under this section may be withdrawn before it is accepted; and a renewal of an offer which has been withdrawn shall be treated as a new offer.

Accepting an offer to make amends

3.—(1) If an offer to make amends under section 2 is accepted by the aggrieved party, the following provisions apply.

(2) The party accepting the offer may not bring or continue defamation proceedings in respect of the publication concerned against the person making the offer, but he is entitled to enforce the offer to make amends, as follows.

(3) If the parties agree on the steps to be taken in fulfilment of the offer, the aggrieved party may apply to the court for an order that the other party fulfil his offer by taking the steps agreed.

(4) If the parties do not agree on the steps to be taken by way of correction, apology and publication, the party who made the offer may take such steps as he thinks appropriate, and may in particular—

(a) make the correction and apology by a statement in open court in terms approved by the court, and

(b) give an undertaking to the court as to the manner of their publication.

(5) If the parties do not agree on the amount to be paid by way of compensation, it shall be determined by the court on the same principles as damages in defamation proceedings.

The court shall take account of any steps taken in fulfilment of the offer and (so far as not agreed between the parties) of the suitability of the correction, the sufficiency of the apology and whether the manner of their publication was reasonable in the circumstances, and may reduce or increase the amount of compensation accordingly.

(6) If the parties do not agree on the amount to be paid by way of costs, it shall be determined by the court on the same principles as costs awarded in court proceedings.

(7) The acceptance of an offer by one person to make amends does not affect any cause of action against another person in respect of the same publication, subject as follows.

(8) In England and Wales or Northern Ireland, for the purposes of the Civil Liability (Contribution) Act 1978—

(a) the amount of compensation paid under the offer shall be treated as paid in bona fide settlement or compromise of the claim; and

(b) where another person is liable in respect of the same damage (whether jointly or otherwise), the person whose offer to make amends was accepted is not required to pay by virtue of any contribution under section 1 of that Act a greater amount than the amount of the compensation payable in pursuance of the offer.

(9) In Scotland—

(a) subsection (2) of section 3 of the Law Reform (Miscellaneous Provisions) (Scotland) Act 1940 (right of one joint wrongdoer as respects another to recover contribution towards damages) applies in relation to compensation paid under an offer to make amends as it applies in relation to damages in an action to which that section applies; and

(b) where another person is liable in respect of the same damage (whether jointly or otherwise), the person whose offer to make amends was accepted is not required to pay by virtue of any contribution under section 3(2) of that Act a greater amount than the amount of compensation payable in pursuance of the offer.

(10) Proceedings under this section shall be heard and determined without a jury.

Failure to accept offer to make amends

4.—(1) If an offer to make amends under section 2, duly made and not withdrawn, is not accepted by the aggrieved party, the following provisions apply.

(2) The fact that the offer was made is a defence (subject to subsection (3)) to defamation proceedings in respect of the publication in question by that party against the person making the offer.

A qualified offer is only a defence in respect of the meaning to which the offer related.

(3) There is no such defence if the person by whom the offer was made knew or had reason to believe that the statement complained of—

(a) referred to the aggrieved party or was likely to be understood as referring to him, and

(b) was both false and defamatory of that party;

but it shall be presumed until the contrary is shown that he did not know and had no reason to believe that was the case.

(4) The person who made the offer need not rely on it by way of defence, but if he does he may not rely on any other defence.

If the offer was a qualified offer, this applies only in respect of the meaning to which the offer related.

(5) The offer may be relied on in mitigation of damages whether or not it was relied on as a defence.

Limitation of actions: England and Wales

5. [Subsections (1) to (5) contain textual amendments of the Limitation Act 1980. They have been incorporated in the text of that Act (above)].

(6) The amendments made by this section apply only to causes of action arising after the section comes into force.

Limitation of actions: Northern Ireland

6.—(1) The Limitation (Northern Ireland) Order 1989 is amended as follows.

(2) In Article 6 (time limit: certain actions founded on tort) for paragraph (2) substitute—

"(2) Subject to Article 51, an action for damages for—
  (a) libel or slander; or
  (b) slander of title, slander of goods or other malicious falsehood, may not
      be brought after the expiration of one year from the date on which the
      cause of action accrued.".

(3) In Article 48 (extension of time limit, for paragraph (7) substitute—
"(7) Where the action is one to which Article 6(2) applies, paragraph (1) has
effect—
  (a) in the case of an action for libel and slander, as if for the words from "at
      any time" to "occurred" there were substituted the words "by him at any
      time before the expiration of one year from the date on which he ceased
      to be under a disability"; and
  (b) in the case of an action for slander of title, slander of goods or other
      malicious falsehood, as if for the words "six years" there were substi-
      tuted the words "one year".".

(4) For Article 51 substitute—

*"Court's power to override time limit: actions for defamation or
malicious falsehood.*

51.—(1) If it appears to the court that it would be equitable to allow an action
to proceed having regard to the degree to which—
  (a) the provisions of Article 6(2) prejudice the plaintiff or any person whom
      he represents; and
  (b) any decision of the court under this paragraph would prejudice the
      defendant or any person whom he represents,
the court may direct that those provisions are not to apply to the action, or are not
to apply to any specified cause of action to which the action relates.

(2) In acting under this Article the court is to have regard to all the circumstances of the case and in particular to—
  (a) the length of, and the reasons for, the delay on the part of the plain-
      tiff;
  (b) in a case where the reason, or one of the reasons, for the delay was that
      all or any of the facts relevant to the cause of action did not become
      known to the plaintiff until after the expiration of the period mentioned
      in Article 6(2)—
        (i) the date on which any such facts did become known to him, and
       (ii) the extent to which he acted promptly and reasonably once he knew
            whether or not the facts in question might be capable of giving rise
            to an action; and
  (c) the extent to which, having regard to the delay, relevant evidence is
      likely—
        (i) to be unavailable, or
       (ii) to be less cogent than if the action had been brought within the time
            allowed by Article 6(2).

(3) In the case of an action for slander of title, slander of goods or other
malicious falsehood brought by a personal representative—
  (a) the references in paragraph (2) to the plaintiff shall be construed as
      including the deceased person to whom the cause of action accrued and
      any previous personal representative of that person; and
  (b) nothing in Article 48(3) shall be construed as affecting the court's
      discretion under this Article.

(4) In this Article "the court" means the court in which the action has been
brought.".

(5) The amendments made by this section apply only to causes of action arising after the section comes into force.

Ruling on the meaning of a statement

7. In defamation proceedings the court shall not be asked to rule whether a statement is arguably capable, as opposed to capable, of bearing a particular meaning or meanings attributed to it.

Summary disposal of claim

8.—(1) In defamation proceedings the court may dispose summarily of the plaintiff's claim in accordance with the following provisions.

(2) The court may dismiss the plaintiff's claim if it appears to the court that it has no realistic prospect of success and there is no reason why it should be tried.

(3) The court may give judgment for the plaintiff and grant him summary relief (see section 9) if it appears to the court that there is no defence to the claim which has a realistic prospect of success, and that there is no other reason why the claim should be tried.

Unless the plaintiff asks for summary relief, the court shall not act under this subsection unless it is satisfied that summary relief will adequately compensate him for the wrong he has suffered.

(4) In considering whether a claim should be tried the court shall have regard to—

- (a) whether all the persons who are or might be defendants in respect of the publication complained of are before the court;
- (b) whether summary disposal of the claim against another defendant would be inappropriate;
- (c) the extent to which there is a conflict of evidence;
- (d) the seriousness of the alleged wrong (as regards the content of the statement and the extent of publication); and
- (e) whether it is justifiable in the circumstances to proceed to a full trial.

(5) Proceedings under this section shall be heard and determined without a jury.

Meaning of summary relief

9.—(1) For the purposes of section 8 (summary disposal of claim) "summary relief" means such of the following as may be appropriate—

- (a) a declaration that the statement was false and defamatory of the plaintiff;
- (b) an order that the defendant publish or cause to be published a suitable correction and apology;
- (c) damages not exceeding £10,000 or such other amount as may be prescribed by order of the Lord Chancellor;
- (d) an order restraining the defendant from publishing or further publishing the matter complained of.

(2) The content of any correction and apology, and the time, manner, form and place of publication, shall be for the parties to agree.

If they cannot agree on the content, the court may direct the defendant to publish or cause to be published a summary of the court's judgment agreed by the parties or settled by the court in accordance with rules of court.

If they cannot agree on the time, manner, form or place of publication, the court may direct the defendant to take such reasonable and practicable steps as the court considers appropriate.

(3) Any order under subsection (1)(c) shall be made by statutory instrument which shall be subject to annulment in pursuance of a resolution of either House of Parliament.

Summary disposal: rules of court

10.—(1) Provision may be made by rules of court as to the summary disposal of the plaintiff's claim in defamation proceedings.

(2) Without prejudice to the generality of that power, provision may be made—
- (a) authorising a party to apply for summary disposal at any stage of the proceedings;
- (b) authorising the court at any stage of the proceedings—
    - (i) to treat any application, pleading or other step in the proceedings as an application for summary disposal, or
    - (ii) to make an order for summary disposal without any such application;
- (c) as to the time for serving pleadings or taking any other step in the proceedings in a case where there are proceedings for summary disposal;
- (d) requiring the parties to identify any question of law or construction which the court is to be asked to determine in the proceedings;
- (e) as to the nature of any hearing on the question of summary disposal, and in particular—
    - (i) authorising the court to order affidavits or witness statements to be prepared for use as evidence at the hearing, and
    - (ii) requiring the leave of the court for the calling of oral evidence, or the introduction of new evidence, at the hearing;
- (f) authorising the court to require a defendant to elect, at or before the hearing, whether or not to make an offer to make amends under section 2.

Summary disposal: application to Northern Ireland

11. In their application to Northern Ireland the provisions of sections 8 to 10 (summary disposal of claim) apply only to proceedings in the High Court.

Evidence of convictions

12.—(1) [Subsection (1) contains textual amendments of the Civil Evidence Act 1968. They have been incorporated in the text of that Act (above).]

The amendments made by this subsection apply only where the trial of the action begins after this section comes into force.

(2) In section 12 of the Law Reform (Miscellaneous Provisions) (Scotland) Act 1968 (conclusiveness of convictions for purposes of defamation actions), in subsections (1) and (2) for "a person" substitute "the pursuer" and for "that person" substitute "he"; and after subsection (2) insert—

"(2A) In the case of an action for defamation in which there is more than one pursuer—
- (a) the references in subsections (1) and (2) above to the pursuer shall be construed as references to any of the pursuers, and
- (b) proof that any of the pursuers stands convicted of an offence shall be conclusive evidence that he committed that offence as far as that fact is relevant to any issue arising in relation to his cause of action or that of any other pursuer.".

The amendments made by this subsection apply only for the purposes of an action begun after this section comes into force, whenever the cause of action arose.

(3) In section 9 of the Civil Evidence Act (Northern Ireland) 1971 (conclusiveness of convictions for purposes of defamation actions), in subsections (1) and (2) for "a person" substitute "the plaintiff" and for "that person" substitute "he"; and after subsection (2) insert—

"(2A) In the case of an action for libel or slander in which there is more than one plaintiff—

(a) the references in subsections (1) and (2) above to the plaintiff shall be construed as references to any of the plaintiffs, and

(b) proof that any of the plaintiffs stands convicted of an offence shall be conclusive evidence that he committed that offence so far as that fact is relevant to any issue arising in relation to his cause of action or that of any other plaintiff.".

The amendments made by this subsection apply only where the trial of the action begins after this section comes into force.

Evidence concerning proceedings in Parliament

13.—(1) Where the conduct of a person in or in relation to proceedings in Parliament is in issue in defamation proceedings, he may waive for the purposes of those proceedings, so far as concerns him, the protection of any enactment or rule of law which prevents proceedings in Parliament being impeached or questioned in any court or place out of Parliament.

(2) Where a person waives that protection—

(a) any such enactment or rule of law shall not apply to prevent evidence being given, questions being asked or statements, submissions, comments or findings being made about his conduct, and

(b) none of those things shall be regarded as infringing the privilege of either House of Parliament.

(3) The waiver by one person of that protection does not affect its operation in relation to another person who has not waived it.

(4) Nothing in this section affects any enactment or rule of law so far as it protects a person (including a person who has waived the protection referred to above) from legal liability for words spoken or things done in the course of, or for the purposes of or incidental to, any proceedings in Parliament.

(5) Without prejudice to the generality of subsection (4), that subsection applies to—

(a) the giving of evidence before either House or a committee;

(b) the presentation or submission of a document to either House or a committee;

(c) the preparation of a document for the purposes of or incidental to the transacting of any such business;

(d) the formulation, making or publication of a document, including a report, by or pursuant to an order of either House or a committee; and

(e) any communication with the Parliamentary Commissioner for Standards or any person having functions in connection with the registration of members' interests.

In this subsection "a committee" means a committee of either House or a joint committee of both Houses of Parliament.

Reports of court proceedings absolutely privileged

14.—(1) A fair and accurate report of proceedings in public before a court to which this section applies, if published contemporaneously with the proceedings, is absolutely privileged.

(2) A report of proceedings which by an order of the court, or as a consequence of any statutory provision, is required to be postponed shall be treated as published contemporaneously if it is published as soon as practicable after publication is permitted.

[(3) This section applies to—

(a) any court in the United Kingdom,

(b) the European Court of Justice or any court attached to that court,

(c) the European Court of Human Rights, and

(d) any international criminal tribunal established by the Security Council of the United Nations or by an international agreement to which the United Kingdom is a party.]

In paragraph (a) "court" includes any tribunal or body exercising the judicial power of the State.

[(3) This section applies to—

(a) any court in the United Kingdom;

(b) any court established under the law of a country or territory outside the United Kingdom;

(c) any international court or tribunal established by the Security Council of the United Nations or by an international agreement;

and in paragraphs (a) and (b) "court" includes any tribunal or body exercising the judicial power of the State.][77]

(4) In section 8(6) of the Rehabilitation of Offenders Act 1974 and in Article 9(6) of the Rehabilitation of Offenders (Northern Ireland) Order 1978 (defamation actions: reports of court proceedings), for "section 3 of the Law of Libel Amendment Act 1888" substitute "section 14 of the Defamation Act 1996".

Reports, etc., protected by qualified privilege

15.—(1) The publication of any report or other statement mentioned in Schedule 1 to this Act is privileged unless the publication is shown to be made with malice, subject as follows.

(2) In defamation proceedings in respect of the publication of a report or other statement mentioned in Part II of that Schedule, there is no defence under this section if the plaintiff shows that the defendant—

(a) was requested by him to publish in a suitable manner a reasonable letter or statement by way of explanation or contradiction, and

(b) refused or neglected to do so.

For this purpose "in a suitable manner" means in the same manner as the publication complained of or in a manner that is adequate and reasonable in the circumstances.

(3) This section does not apply to the publication to the public, or a section of the public, of matter which is not of *[public concern]* [public interest][78] and the publication of which is not for the public benefit.

(4) Nothing in this section shall be construed—

(a) as protecting the publication of matter the publication of which is prohibited by law, or

(b) as limiting or abridging any privilege subsisting apart from this section.

---

[77] By the Defamation Act 2013, s.7(1), this subsection of the Defamation Act 1996 is prospectively substituted by the alternative text set out in square brackets.

[78] By the Defamation Act 2013, s.7(2) the words "public concern" in s.15(3), Defamation Act 1996 are prospectively substituted by the words "public interest".

Repeals

16. The enactments specified in Schedule 2 are repealed to the extent specified.

Interpretation

17.—(1) In this Act—

"publication" and "publish", in relation to a statement, have the meaning they have
for the purposes of the law of defamation generally, but "publisher" is specially
defined for the purposes of section 1;

"statement" means words, pictures, visual images, gestures or any other method of
signifying meaning; and

"statutory provision" means—

(a) a provision contained in an Act or in subordinate legislation within the
meaning of the Interpretation Act 1978,

[(aa) a provision contained in an Act of the Scottish Parliament or in an
instrument made under such an Act, or]

(b) a statutory provision within the meaning given by section 1(f) of the
Interpretation Act (Northern Ireland) 1954.

(2) In this Act as it applies to proceedings in Scotland—

"costs" means expenses; and

"plaintiff" and "defendant" mean pursuer and defender.

General provisions

Extent

18.—(1) The following provisions of this Act extend to England and Wales—
section 1 (responsibility for publication),
sections 2 to 4 (offer to make amends), except section 3(9),
section 5 (time limit for actions for defamation or malicious falsehood),
section 7 (ruling on the meaning of a statement),
sections 8 to 10 (summary disposal of claim),
section 12(1) (evidence of convictions),
section 13 (evidence concerning proceedings in Parliament),
sections 14 and 15 and Schedule 1 (statutory privilege),
section 16 and Schedule 2 (repeals) so far as relating to enactments extending to
England and Wales,
section 17(1) (interpretation), this subsection,
section 19 (commencement) so far as relating to provisions which extend to
England and Wales, and
section 20 (short title and saving).

(2) The following provisions of this act extend to Scotland—
section 1 (responsibility for publication),
sections 2 to 4 (offer to make amends), except section 3(8),
section 12(2) (evidence of convictions),
section 13 (evidence concerning proceedings in Parliament),
sections 14 and 15 and Schedule 1 (statutory privilege),
section 16 and Schedule 2 (repeals) so far as relating to enactments extending to
Scotland,
section 17 (interpretation), this subsection,
section 19 (commencement) so far as relating to provisions which extend to
Scotland, and

section 20 (short title and savings).
(3) The following provisions of this Act extend to Northern Ireland—
section 1 (responsibility for publication),
sections 2 to 4 (offer to make amends), except section 3(9),
section 6 (time limit for actions for defamation or malicious falsehood),
section 7 (ruling on the meaning of a statement),
sections 8 to 11 (summary disposal of claim),
section 12(3) (evidence of convictions),
section 13 (evidence concerning proceedings in Parliament),
sections 14 and 15 and Schedule 1 (statutory privilege),
section 16 and Schedule 2 (repeals) so far as relating to enactments extending to Northern Ireland,
section 17(1) (interpretation), this subsection,
section 19 (commencement) so far as relating to provisions which extend to Northern Ireland, and
section 20 (short title and saving).

Commencement

19.—(1) Sections 18 to 20 (extent, commencement and other general provisions) come into force on Royal Assent.[79]
(2) The following provisions of this act come into force at the end of the period of two months beginning with the day on which this Act is passed—
section 1 (responsibility for publication),
sections 5 and 6 (time limit for actions for defamation or malicious falsehood),
section 12 (evidence of convictions),
section 13 (evidence concerning proceedings in Parliament),
section 16 and the repeals in Schedule 2, so far as consequential on the above provisions, and
section 17 (interpretation), so far as relating to the above provisions.
(3) The provisions of this Act otherwise come into force on such day as may be appointed—
    (a) for England and Wales or Northern Ireland, by order of the Lord Chancellor, or
    (b) for Scotland, by order of the Secretary of State.
and different days may be appointed for different purposes.
(4) Any such order shall be made by statutory instrument and may contain such transitional provisions as appear to the Lord Chancellor or Secretary of State to be appropriate.

Short title and saving

20.—(1) This act may be cited as the Defamation Act 1996.
(2) . . . [80]

SCHEDULES

Section 15

---

[79] 4 July 1996.
[80] Repealed by the Coroners and Justice Act 2009, s.178, Sch.23(2).

SCHEDULE 1

QUALIFIED PRIVILEGE

PART I

STATEMENTS HAVING QUALIFIED PRIVILEGE WITHOUT EXPLANATION OR CONTRADICTION

1. A fair and accurate report of proceedings in public of a legislature anywhere in the world.
2. A fair and accurate report of proceedings in public before a court anywhere in the world.
3. A fair and accurate report of proceedings in public of a person appointed to hold a public inquiry by a government or legislature anywhere in the world.
4. A fair and accurate report of proceedings in public anywhere in the world of an international organisation or an international conference.
5. A fair and accurate copy of or extract from any register or other document required by law to be open to public inspection.
6. A notice or advertisement published by or on the authority of a court, or of a judge or officer of a court, anywhere in the world.
7. A fair and accurate copy of or extract from matter published by or on the authority of a government or legislature anywhere in the world.
8. A fair and accurate copy of or extract from matter published anywhere in the world by an international organisation or an international conference.

PART II

STATEMENTS PRIVILEGED SUBJECT TO EXPLANATION OR CONTRADICTION

[9.—(1) A fair and accurate copy of or extract from a notice or other matter issued for the information of the public by or on behalf of—
  (a) a legislature in any member State or the European Parliament;
  (b) the government of any member State, or any authority performing govern-mental functions in any member State or part of a member State, or the European Commission;
  (c) an international organisation or international conference.
(2) In this paragraph "governmental functions" includes police functions.
10. A fair and accurate copy of or extract from a document made available by a court in any member State or the European Court of Justice (or any court attached to that court), or by a judge or officer of any such court.]

[9 (1) A fair and accurate copy of, extract from or summary of a notice or other matter issued for the information of the public by or on behalf of—
  (a) a legislature or government anywhere in the world;
  (b) an authority anywhere in the world performing governmental functions;
  (c) an international organisation or international conference.
(2) In this paragraph "governmental functions" includes police functions.

10. A fair and accurate copy of, extract from or summary of a document made available by a court anywhere in the world, or by a judge or officer of such a court.][81]

11.—(1) A fair and accurate report of proceedings at any public meeting or sitting in the United Kingdom of—

    (a) a local authority, local authority committee or in the case of a local authority which are operating executive arrangements the executive of that authority or a committee of that executive;

    (aa) in the case of a local authority which are operating executive arrangements, the executive of that authority or a committee of that executive;

    (b) a justice or justices of the peace acting otherwise than as a court exercising judicial authority;

    (c) a commission, tribunal, committee or person appointed for the purposes of any inquiry by any statutory provision, by Her Majesty or by a Minister of the Crown, a member of the Scottish Government, the Welsh Ministers or the Counsel General to the Welsh Assembly Government or a Northern Ireland Department;

    (d) a person appointed by a local authority to hold a local inquiry in pursuance of any statutory provision;

    (e) any other tribunal, board, committee or body constituted by or under, and exercising functions under, any statutory provision.

(1A) In the case of a local authority which are operating executive arrangements, a fair and accurate record of any decision made by any member of the executive where that record is required to be made and available for public inspection by virtue of section 22 of the Local Government Act 2000 or of any provision in regulations made under that section.

(2) In sub-paragraph (1)(a), (1)(aa) and (1A)—

"local authority" means—

    (a) in relation to England and Wales, a principal council within the meaning of the Local Government Act 1972, any body falling within any paragraph of section 100J(1) of that Act or an authority or body to which the Public Bodies (Admission to Meetings) Act 1960 applies,

    (b) in relation to Scotland, a council constituted under section 2 of the Local Government etc. (Scotland) Act 1994 or an authority or body to which the Public Bodies (Admission to Meetings) Act 1960 applies,

    (c) in relation to Northern Ireland, any authority or body to which sections 23 to 27 of the Local Government Act (Northern Ireland) 1972 apply; and

"local authority committee" means any committee of a local authority or of local authorities, and includes—

    (a) any committee or sub-committee in relation to which sections 100A to 100D of the Local Government Act 1972 apply by virtue of section 100E of that Act (whether or not also by virtue of section 100J of that Act), and

    (b) any committee or sub-committee in relation to which sections 50A to 50D of the Local Government (Scotland) Act 1973 apply by virtue of section 50E of that Act.

(2A) In sub-paragraphs (1) and (1A)—

"executive" and "executive arrangements" have the same meaning as in Part II of the Local Government Act 2000.

---

[81] By s.7(4) of the Defamation Act 2013, paras 9 and 10 of Sch.1 to the Defamation Act 1996 are prospectively substituted by the alternative text set out in square brackets.

(3) A fair and accurate report of any corresponding proceedings in any of the Channel Islands or the Isle of Man or in another member State.

[11A A fair and accurate report of proceedings at a press conference held anywhere in the world for the discussion of a matter of public interest.][82]

12.—(1) A fair and accurate report of proceedings at any public meeting held *in a member State* [anywhere in the world].[83]

(2) In this paragraph a "public meeting" means a meeting bona fide and lawfully held for a lawful purpose and for the furtherance or discussion of a matter of *public concern* [public interest],[84] whether admission to the meeting is general or restricted.

13.—(1) A fair and accurate report of proceedings at a general meeting of a *UK public company* [listed company].[85]

[(2) A fair and accurate copy of or extract from any document circulated to members of a UK public company—
  (a) by or with the authority of the board of directors of the company,
  (b) by the auditors of the company, or
  (c) by any member of the company in pursuance of a right conferred by any statutory provision.

(3) A fair and accurate copy of or extract from any document circulated to members of a UK public company which relates to the appointment, resignation, retirement or dismissal of directors of the company.

(4) In this paragraph "UK public company" means—
  (a) a public company within the meaning of section 1(3) of the Companies Act 1985 or Article 12(3) of the Companies (Northern Ireland) Order 1986, or
  (b) a body corporate incorporated by or registered under any other statutory provision, or by Royal Charter, or formed in pursuance of letters patent.

(5) A fair and accurate report of proceedings at any corresponding meeting of, or copy of or extract from any corresponding document circulated to members of, a public company formed under the law of any of the Channel Islands or the Isle of Man or of another member State.]

[(2) A fair and accurate copy of, extract from or summary of any document circulated to members of a listed company—
  (a) by or with the authority of the board of directors of the company,
  (b) by the auditors of the company, or
  (c) by any member of the company in pursuance of a right conferred by any statutory provision.

(3) A fair and accurate copy of, extract from or summary of any document circulated to members of a listed company which relates to the appointment, resignation, retirement or dismissal of directors of the company or its auditors.

(4) In this paragraph "listed company" has the same meaning as in Part 12 of the Corporation Tax Act 2009 (see section 1005 of that Act).][86]

---

[82] Para.11A of Sch.1 to the Defamation Act 1996 is prospectively inserted by s.7(5), Defamation Act 2013.

[83] By s.7(6), Defamation Act 2013 the words "in a member State" in para.12(1) of Sch.1 to the Defamation Act 1996 are prospectively substituted by the words "anywhere in the world".

[84] By s.7(6), Defamation Act 2013, the words "public concern" in para.12(2) of Sch.1 to the Defamation Act 1996 are prospectively substituted by the words "public interest".

[85] By s.7(7)(a), Defamation Act 2013, the words "UK public company" in para.13(1) of Sch.1 to the Defamation Act 1996 are prospectively substituted by the words "listed company".

[86] By s.7(7)(b), Defamation Act 2013, paras 13(2) to (5) of Sch.1 to the Defamation Act 1996 are prospectively substituted by the alternative text set out in square brackets.

14. A fair and accurate report of any finding or decision of any of the following descriptions of association, formed *[in the United Kingdom or another member State]* [anywhere in the world][87], or of any committee or governing body of such an association—

    (a) an association formed for the purpose of promoting or encouraging the exercise of or interest in any art, science, religion or learning, and empowered by its constitution to exercise control over or adjudicate on matters of interest or concern to the association, or the actions or conduct of any person subject to such control or adjudication;

    (b) an association formed for the purpose of promoting or safeguarding the interests of any trade, business, industry or profession, or of the persons carrying on or engaged in any trade, business, industry or profession, and empowered by its constitution to exercise control over or adjudicate upon matters connected with that trade, business, industry or profession, or the actions or conduct of those persons;

    (c) an association formed for the purpose of promoting or safeguarding the interests of a game, sport or pastime to the playing or exercise of which members of the public are invited or admitted, and empowered by its constitution to exercise control over or adjudicate upon persons connected with or taking part in the game, sport or pastime;

    (d) an association formed for the purpose of promoting charitable objects or other objects beneficial to the community and empowered by its constitution to exercise control over or to adjudicate on matters of interest or concern to the association, or the actions or conduct of any person subject to such control or adjudication.

[14A A fair and accurate—

    (a) report of proceedings of a scientific or academic conference held anywhere in the world, or

    (b) copy or extract from or summary of matter published by such a conference.][88]

[15.—(1) A fair and accurate report of, or copy of or extract from, any adjudication, report, statement or notice issued by a body, officer or other person designated for the purposes of this paragraph—

    (a) for England and Wales or Northern Ireland, by order of the Lord Chancellor, and

    (b) for Scotland, by order of the Secretary of State.

(2) An order under this paragraph shall be made by statutory instrument which shall be subject to annulment in pursuance of a resolution of either House of Parliament.]

[15 (1) A fair and accurate report or summary of, copy of or extract from, any adjudication, report, statement or notice issued by a body, officer or other person designated for the purposes of this paragraph by order of the Lord Chancellor.

(2) An order under this paragraph shall be made by statutory instrument which shall be subject to annulment in pursuance of a resolution of either House of Parliament.][89]

---

[87] By s.7(8), Defamation Act 2013, the words "in the United Kingdom or another member State" in para.14 of Sch.1 to the Defamation Act 1996 are prospectively substituted by the words "anywhere in the world".

[88] Para.14A of Schedule 1 to the Defamation Act 1996 is prospectively inserted by s.7(9), Defamation Act 2013.

[89] By s.7(10), Defamation Act 2013, para.15 of Sch.1 to the Defamation Act 1996 is prospectively substituted by the alternative text set out in square brackets.

PART III

SUPPLEMENTARY PROVISIONS

[16.—(1) In this Schedule—

"court" includes any tribunal or body exercising the judicial power of the State;

"international conference" means a conference attended by representatives of two or more governments;

"international organisation" means an organisation of which two or more governments are members, and includes any committee or other subordinate body of such an organisation; and

"legislature" includes a local legislature.

(2) References in this Schedule to a member State include any European dependent territory of a member State.

(3) In paragraphs 2 and 6 "court" includes—

　(a) the European Court of Justice (or any court attached to that Court) and the Court of Auditors of the European Communities,

　(b) the European Court of Human Rights,

　(c) any international criminal tribunal established by the Security Council of the United Nations or by an international agreement to which the United Kingdom is a party, and

　(d) the International Court of Justice and any other judicial or arbitral tribunal deciding matters in dispute between States.

(4) In paragraphs 1, 3 and 7 "legislature" includes the European Parliament.

17.—(1) Provision may be made by order identifying—

　(a) for the purposes of paragraph 11, the corresponding proceedings referred to in sub-paragraph (3);

　(b) for the purposes of paragraph 13, the corresponding meetings and documents referred to in sub-paragraph (5).

(2) An order under this paragraph may be made—

　(a) for England and Wales or Northern Ireland, by the Land Chancellor, and

　(b) for Scotland, by the Secretary of State.

(3) An order under this paragraph shall be made by statutory instrument which shall be subject to annulment in pursuance of a resolution of either House of Parliament.]

[16 In this Schedule—

"court" includes—

　(a) any tribunal or body established under the law of any country or territory exercising the judicial power of the State;

　(b) any international tribunal established by the Security Council of the United Nations or by an international agreement;

　(c) any international tribunal deciding matters in dispute between States;

　　"international conference" means a conference attended by representatives of two or more governments;

　　"international organisation" means an organisation of which two or more governments are members, and includes any committee or other subordinate body of such an organisation;

　　"legislature" includes a local legislature; and

　　"member State" includes any European dependent territory of a member State.][90]

---

[90] By s.7(11), Defamation Act 2013, paras 16 and 17 of Sch.1 to the Defamation Act 1996 are prospectively substituted by the alternative text set out in square brackets.

Section 16

Schedule 2

Chapter	Title	Extent of repeal
1888, c. 64.	Law of Libel Amendment Act 1888.	Section 3.
1952, c. 66.	Defamation Act 1952.	Section 4. Sections 7, 8 and 9(2) and (3). Sections 16(2) and (3). The Schedule.
1955, c. 20.	Revision of the Army and Air Force Acts (Transitional Provisions) Act 1955.	In Schedule 2, the entry relating to the Defamation Act 1952.
1955, c. 11 (N.I.).	Defamation Act (Northern Ireland) 1955.	Section 4. Sections 7, 8 and 9(2) and (3). Section 14(2). The Schedule.
1972, c. 9 (N.I.).	Local Government Act (Northern Ireland) 1972.	In Schedule 8, paragraph 12.
1981, c. 49.	Contempt of Court Act 1981.	In section 4(3), the words "and of section 3 of the Law of Libel Amendment Act 1888 (privilege)".
1981, c. 61.	British Nationality Act 1981.	In Schedule 7, the entries relating to the Defamation Act 1952 and the Defamation Act (Northern Ireland) 1955.
1985, c. 43.	Local Government (Access to Information) Act 1985.	In Schedule 2, paragraphs 2 and 3.
1985, c. 61.	Administration of Justice Act 1985.	Section 57.
S.I. 1986 No. 594 (N.I. 3).	Education and Libraries (Northern Ireland) Order 1986.	Article 97(2).
1990, c. 42.	Broadcasting Act 1990.	Section 166(3). In Schedule 20, paragraphs 2 and 3.

A2.24   **Broadcasting Act 1996**

[1996 c. 55]

Publication of OFCOM's findings

119.—(1) Where OFCOM have considered and adjudicated upon a fairness complaint, they may direct the relevant person to publish the matters mentioned in subsection (3) in such manner, and within such period, as may be specified in the directions.

(3) Those matters are—

    (a) a summary of the complaint;

    (b) OFCOM's findings on the complaint or a summary of them.

121. Certain statements etc. protected by qualified privilege for purposes of defamation[91]

121.—(1) For the purposes of the law relating to defamation—

    (a) publication of any statement in the course of the consideration by OFCOM of, and their adjudication on, a fairness complaint,

    (b) publication by OFCOM of directions under section 119(1) relating to a fairness complaint, or

    (c) publication of a report of OFCOM, so far as the report relates to fairness complaints,

is privileged unless the publication is shown to be made with malice.

(2) Nothing in subsection (1) shall be construed as limiting any privilege subsisting apart from that subsection.

Data Protection Act 1998   **A2.25**

[1998 c. 29]

1.—Basic interpretative provisions

(1) In this Act, unless the context otherwise requires—

"data" means information which—

    (a) is being processed by means of equipment operating automatically in response to instructions given for that purpose,

    (b) is recorded with the intention that it should be processed by means of such equipment,

    (c) is recorded as part of a relevant filing system or with the intention that it should form part of a relevant filing system,

    (d) does not fall within paragraph (a), (b) or (c) but forms part of an accessible record as defined by section 68; or

    (e) is recorded information held by a public authority and does not fall within any of paragraphs (a) to (d);

"data controller" means, subject to subsection (4), a person who (either alone or jointly or in common with other persons) determines the purposes for which and the manner in which any personal data are, or are to be, processed;

"data processor", in relation to personal data, means any person (other than an employee of the data controller) who processes the data on behalf of the data controller;

"data subject" means an individual who is the subject of personal data;

"personal data" means data which relate to a living individual who can be identified—

---

[91] "Fairness complaint" means a complaint to OFCOM of unjust or unfair treatment in a BBC programme or programme under a television or radio licensed service; or unwarranted infringement of privacy in, or in connection with the obtaining of material included in, such programmes: ss.110(4) and 107(1).

(a) from those data, or

(b) from those data and other information which is in the possession of, or is likely to come into the possession of, the data controller,
and includes any expression of opinion about the individual and any indication of the intentions of the data controller or any other person in respect of the individual;

"processing", in relation to information or data, means obtaining, recording or holding the information or data or carrying out any operation or set of operations on the information or data, including—

(a) organisation, adaptation or alteration of the information or data,

(b) retrieval, consultation or use of the information or data,

(c) disclosure of the information or data by transmission, dissemination or otherwise making available, or

(d) alignment, combination, blocking, erasure or destruction of the information or data;

"public authority" means a public authority as defined by the Freedom of Information Act 2000 or a Scottish public authority as defined by the Freedom of Information (Scotland) Act 2002;

"relevant filing system" means any set of information relating to individuals to the extent that, although the information is not processed by means of equipment operating automatically in response to instructions given for that purpose, the set is structured, either by reference to individuals or by reference to criteria relating to individuals, in such a way that specific information relating to a particular individual is readily accessible.

(2) In this Act, unless the context otherwise requires—

(a) "obtaining" or "recording", in relation to personal data, includes obtaining or recording the information to be contained in the data, and

(b) "using" or "disclosing", in relation to personal data, includes using or disclosing the information contained in the data.

(3) In determining for the purposes of this Act whether any information is recorded with the intention—

(a) that it should be processed by means of equipment operating automatically in response to instructions given for that purpose, or

(b) that it should form part of a relevant filing system,

it is immaterial that it is intended to be so processed or to form part of such a system only after being transferred to a country or territory outside the European Economic Area.

(4) Where personal data are processed only for purposes for which they are required by or under any enactment to be processed, the person on whom the obligation to process the data is imposed by or under that enactment is for the purposes of this Act the data controller.

(5) In paragraph (e) of the definition of "data" in subsection (1); the reference to information "held" by a public authority shall be construed in accordance with section 3(2) of the Freedom of Information Act 2000 or section 3(2), (4) and (5) of the Freedom of Information (Scotland) Act 2002.

(6) Where

(a) section 7 of the Freedom of Information Act 2000 prevents Parts I to V of that Act or

(b) section 7(1) of the Freedom of Information (Scotland) Act 2002 prevents that Act

from applying to certain information held by a public authority, that information is not to be treated for the purposes of paragraph (e) of the definition of "data" in subsection (1) as held by a public authority.

2. Sensitive personal data

In this Act "sensitive personal data" means personal data consisting of information as to—

    (a) the racial or ethnic origin of the data subject,

    (b) his political opinions,

    (c) his religious beliefs or other beliefs of a similar nature,

    (d) whether he is a member of a trade union (within the meaning of the Trade Union and Labour Relations (Consolidation) Act 1992),

    (e) his physical or mental health or condition,

    (f) his sexual life,

    (g) the commission or alleged commission by him of any offence, or

    (h) any proceedings for any offence committed or alleged to have been committed by him, the disposal of such proceedings or the sentence of any court in such proceedings.

3. The special purposes

In this Act "the special purposes" means any one or more of the following—

    (a) the purposes of journalism,

    (b) artistic purposes, and

    (c) literary purposes.

4.—The data protection principles

(1) References in this Act to the data protection principles are to the principles set out in Part I of Schedule 1.

(2) Those principles are to be interpreted in accordance with Part II of Schedule 1.

(3) Schedule 2 (which applies to all personal data) and Schedule 3 (which applies only to sensitive personal data) set out conditions applying for the purposes of the first principle; and Schedule 4 sets out cases in which the eighth principle does not apply.

(4) Subject to section 27(1), it shall be the duty of a data controller to comply with the data protection principles in relation to all personal data with respect to which he is the data controller.

10.—Right to prevent processing likely to cause damage or distress.

(1) Subject to subsection (2), an individual is entitled at any time by notice in writing to a data controller to require the data controller at the end of such period as is reasonable in the circumstances to cease, or not to begin, processing, or processing for a specified purpose or in a specified manner, any personal data in respect of which he is the data subject, on the ground that, for specified reasons—

    (a) the processing of those data or their processing for that purpose or in that manner is causing or is likely to cause substantial damage or substantial distress to him or to another, and

    (b) that damage or distress is or would be unwarranted.

(2) Subsection (1) does not apply—

    (a) in a case where any of the conditions in paragraphs 1 to 4 of Schedule 2 is met, or

    (b) in such other cases as may be prescribed by the Secretary of State by order.

(3) The data controller must within twenty-one days of receiving a notice under subsection (1) ("the data subject notice") give the individual who gave it a written notice—

(a) stating that he has complied or intends to comply with the data subject notice, or

(b) stating his reasons for regarding the data subject notice as to any extent unjustified and the extent (if any) to which he has complied or intends to comply with it.

(4) If a court is satisfied, on the application of any person who has given a notice under subsection (1) which appears to the court to be justified (or to be justified to any extent), that the data controller in question has failed to comply with the notice, the court may order him to take such steps for complying with the notice (or for complying with it to that extent) as the court thinks fit.

(5) The failure by a data subject to exercise the right conferred by subsection (1) or section 11(1)[92] does not affect any other right conferred on him by this Part.

13.—**Compensation for failure to comply with certain requirements**

(1) An individual who suffers damage by reason of any contravention by a data controller of any of the requirements of this Act is entitled to compensation from the data controller for that damage.

(2) An individual who suffers distress by reason of any contravention by a data controller of any of the requirements of this Act is entitled to compensation from the data controller for that distress if—

(a) the individual also suffers damage by reason of the contravention, or

(b) the contravention relates to the processing of personal data for the special purposes.

(3) In proceedings brought against a person by virtue of this section it is a defence to prove that he had taken such care as in all the circumstances was reasonably required to comply with the requirement concerned.

14.—**Rectification, blocking, erasure and destruction.**

(1) If a court is satisfied on the application of a data subject that personal data of which the applicant is the subject are inaccurate, the court may order the data controller to rectify, block, erase or destroy those data and any other personal data in respect of which he is the data controller and which contain an expression of opinion which appears to the court to be based on the inaccurate data.

(2) Subsection (1) applies whether or not the data accurately record information received or obtained by the data controller from the data subject or a third party but where the data accurately record such information, then—

(a) if the requirements mentioned in paragraph 7 of Part II of Schedule 1 have been complied with, the court may, instead of making an order under subsection (1), make an order requiring the data to be supplemented by such statement of the true facts relating to the matters dealt with by the data as the court may approve, and

(b) if all or any of those requirements have not been complied with, the court may, instead of making an order under that subsection, make such order as it thinks fit for securing compliance with those requirements with or without a further order requiring the data to be supplemented by such a statement as is mentioned in paragraph (a).

(3) Where the court—

---

[92] S.11(1) of the Act confers a right on individuals to give notice to a data controller to require the data controller at the end of such period as is reasonable in the circumstances to cease, or not to begin, processing for the purposes of direct marketing personal data in respect of which they are the data subject.

    (a) makes an order under subsection (1), or

    (b) is satisfied on the application of a data subject that personal data of which he was the data subject and which have been rectified, blocked, erased or destroyed were inaccurate, it may, where it considers it reasonably practicable, order the data controller to notify third parties to whom the data have been disclosed of the rectification, blocking, erasure or destruction.

(4) If a court is satisfied on the application of a data subject—

    (a) that he has suffered damage by reason of any contravention by a data controller of any of the requirements of this Act in respect of any personal data, in circumstances entitling him to compensation under section 13, and

    (b) that there is a substantial risk of further contravention in respect of those data in such circumstances, the court may order the rectification, blocking, erasure or destruction of any of those data.

(5) Where the court makes an order under subsection (4) it may, where it considers it reasonably practicable, order the data controller to notify third parties to whom the data have been disclosed of the rectification, blocking, erasure or destruction.

(6) In determining whether it is reasonably practicable to require such notification as is mentioned in subsection (3) or (5) the court shall have regard, in particular, to the number of persons who would have to be notified.

Exemptions

27.—**Preliminary.**

(1) References in any of the data protection principles or any provision of Parts II and III to personal data or to the processing of personal data do not include references to data or processing which by virtue of this Part are exempt from that principle or other provision.

(2) In this Part "the subject information provisions" means—

    (a) the first data protection principle to the extent to which it requires compliance with paragraph 2 of Part II of Schedule 1, and

    (b) section 7.

(3) In this Part "the non-disclosure provisions" means the provisions specified in subsection (4) to the extent to which they are inconsistent with the disclosure in question.

(4) The provisions referred to in subsection (3) are—

    (a) the first data protection principle, except to the extent to which it requires compliance with the conditions in Schedules 2 and 3,

    (b) the second, third, fourth and fifth data protection principles, and

    (c) sections 10 and 14(1) to (3).

(5) Except as provided by this Part, the subject information provisions shall have effect notwithstanding any enactment or rule of law prohibiting or restricting the disclosure, or authorising the withholding, of information.

32.—**Journalism, literature and art.**

(1) Personal data which are processed only for the special purposes are exempt from any provision to which this subsection relates if—

    (a) the processing is undertaken with a view to the publication by any person of any journalistic, literary or artistic material,

    (b) the data controller reasonably believes that, having regard in particular to the special importance of the public interest in freedom of expression, publication would be in the public interest, and

    (c) the data controller reasonably believes that, in all the circumstances, compliance with that provision is incompatible with the special purposes.

(2) Subsection (1) relates to the provisions of—
  (a) the data protection principles except the seventh data protection principle,
  (b) section 7,
  (c) section 10,
  (d) section 12,
  (e) section 14(1) to (3).

(3) In considering for the purposes of subsection (1)(b) whether the belief of a data controller that publication would be in the public interest was or is a reasonable one, regard may be had to his compliance with any code of practice which—
  (a) is relevant to the publication in question, and
  (b) is designated by the Secretary of State by order for the purposes of this subsection.

(4) Where at any time ("the relevant time") in any proceedings against a data controller under section 7(9), 10(4), 12(8) or 14 or by virtue of section 13 the data controller claims, or it appears to the court, that any personal data to which the proceedings relate are being processed—
  (a) only for the special purposes, and
  (b) with a view to the publication by any person of any journalistic, literary or artistic material which, at the time twenty-four hours immediately before the relevant time, had not previously been published by the data controller,
the court shall stay the proceedings until either of the conditions in subsection (5) is met.

(5) Those conditions are—
  (a) that a determination of the Commissioner under section 45 with respect to the data in question takes effect, or
  (b) in a case where the proceedings were stayed on the making of a claim, that the claim is withdrawn.

(6) For the purposes of this Act "publish", in relation to journalistic, literary or artistic material, means make available to the public or any section of the public.

SCHEDULE 1

THE DATA PROTECTION PRINCIPLES

PART I

THE PRINCIPLES

1. Personal data shall be processed fairly and lawfully and, in particular, shall not be processed unless—
  (a) at least one of the conditions in Schedule 2 is met, and
  (b) in the case of sensitive personal data, at least one of the conditions in Schedule 3 is also met.

2. Personal data shall be obtained only for one or more specified and lawful purposes, and shall not be further processed in any manner incompatible with that purpose or those purposes.

3. Personal data shall be adequate, relevant and not excessive in relation to the purpose or purposes for which they are processed.

4. Personal data shall be accurate and, where necessary, kept up to date.

5. Personal data processed for any purpose or purposes shall not be kept for longer than is necessary for that purpose or those purposes.

6. Personal data shall be processed in accordance with the rights of data subjects under this Act.

7. Appropriate technical and organisational measures shall be taken against unauthorised or unlawful processing of personal data and against accidental loss or destruction of, or damage to, personal data.

8. Personal data shall not be transferred to a country or territory outside the European Economic Area unless that country or territory ensures an adequate level of protection for the rights and freedoms of data subjects in relation to the processing of personal data.

PART II

INTERPRETATION OF THE PRINCIPLES IN PART I

The first principle

1.(1) In determining for the purposes of the first principle whether personal data are processed fairly, regard is to be had to the method by which they are obtained, including in particular whether any person from whom they are obtained is deceived or misled as to the purpose or purposes for which they are to be processed.

(2) Subject to paragraph 2, for the purposes of the first principle data are to be treated as obtained fairly if they consist of information obtained from a person who—

    (a) is authorised by or under any enactment to supply it, or

    (b) is required to supply it by or under any enactment or by any convention or other instrument imposing an international obligation on the United Kingdom.

2.(1) Subject to paragraph 3, for the purposes of the first principle personal data are not to be treated as processed fairly unless—

    (a) in the case of data obtained from the data subject, the data controller ensures so far as practicable that the data subject has, is provided with, or has made readily available to him, the information specified in sub-paragraph (3), and

    (b) in any other case, the data controller ensures so far as practicable that, before the relevant time or as soon as practicable after that time, the data subject has, is provided with, or has made readily available to him, the information specified in sub-paragraph (3).

(2) In sub-paragraph (1)(b) "the relevant time" means—

    (a) the time when the data controller first processes the data, or

    (b) in a case where at that time disclosure to a third party within a reasonable period is envisaged—

        (i) if the data are in fact disclosed to such a person within that period, the time when the data are first disclosed,

        (ii) if within that period the data controller becomes, or ought to become, aware that the data are unlikely to be disclosed to such a person within that period, the time when the data controller does become, or ought to become, so aware, or

        (iii) in any other case, the end of that period.

(3) The information referred to in sub-paragraph (1) is as follows, namely—

    (a) the identity of the data controller,

    (b) if he has nominated a representative for the purposes of this Act, the identity of that representative,

(c) the purpose or purposes for which the data are intended to be processed, and

(d) any further information which is necessary, having regard to the specific circumstances in which the data are or are to be processed, to enable processing in respect of the data subject to be fair.

3.(1) Paragraph 2(1)(b) does not apply where either of the primary conditions in sub-paragraph (2), together with such further conditions as may be prescribed by the Secretary of State by order, are met.

(2) The primary conditions referred to in sub-paragraph (1) are—

(a) that the provision of that information would involve a disproportionate effort, or

(b) that the recording of the information to be contained in the data by, or the disclosure of the data by, the data controller is necessary for compliance with any legal obligation to which the data controller is subject, other than an obligation imposed by contract.

4.(1) Personal data which contain a general identifier falling within a description prescribed by the Secretary of State by order are not to be treated as processed fairly and lawfully unless they are processed in compliance with any conditions so prescribed in relation to general identifiers of that description.

(2) In sub-paragraph (1) "a general identifier" means any identifier (such as, for example, a number or code used for identification purposes) which—

(a) relates to an individual, and

(b) forms part of a set of similar identifiers which is of general application.

The second principle

5. The purpose or purposes for which personal data are obtained may in particular be specified—

(a) in a notice given for the purposes of paragraph 2 by the data controller to the data subject, or

(b) in a notification given to the Commissioner under Part III of this Act.

6. In determining whether any disclosure of personal data is compatible with the purpose or purposes for which the data were obtained, regard is to be had to the purpose or purposes for which the personal data are intended to be processed by any person to whom they are disclosed.

The fourth principle

7. The fourth principle is not to be regarded as being contravened by reason of any inaccuracy in personal data which accurately record information obtained by the data controller from the data subject or a third party in a case where—

(a) having regard to the purpose or purposes for which the data were obtained and further processed, the data controller has taken reasonable steps to ensure the accuracy of the data, and

(b) if the data subject has notified the data controller of the data subject's view that the data are inaccurate, the data indicate that fact.

The sixth principle

8. A person is to be regarded as contravening the sixth principle if, but only if—

(a) he contravenes section 7 by failing to supply information in accordance with that section,

(b) he contravenes section 10 by failing to comply with a notice given under subsection (1) of that section to the extent that the notice is justified or by failing to give a notice under subsection (3) of that section,

(c) he contravenes section 11 by failing to comply with a notice given under subsection (1) of that section, or

(d) he contravenes section 12 by failing to comply with a notice given under subsection (1) or (2)(b) of that section or by failing to give a notification under subsection (2)(a) of that section or a notice under subsection (3) of that section.

The seventh principle

9. Having regard to the state of technological development and the cost of implementing any measures, the measures must ensure a level of security appropriate to—

(a) the harm that might result from such unauthorised or unlawful processing or accidental loss, destruction or damage as are mentioned in the seventh principle, and

(b) the nature of the data to be protected.

10. The data controller must take reasonable steps to ensure the reliability of any employees of his who have access to the personal data.

11. Where processing of personal data is carried out by a data processor on behalf of a data controller, the data controller must in order to comply with the seventh principle—

(a) choose a data processor providing sufficient guarantees in respect of the technical and organisational security measures governing the processing to be carried out, and

(b) take reasonable steps to ensure compliance with those measures.

12. Where processing of personal data is carried out by a data processor on behalf of a data controller, the data controller is not to be regarded as complying with the seventh principle unless—

(a) the processing is carried out under a contract—

(i) which is made or evidenced in writing, and

(ii) under which the data processor is to act only on instructions from the data controller, and

(b) the contract requires the data processor to comply with obligations equivalent to those imposed on a data controller by the seventh principle.

The eighth principle

13. An adequate level of protection is one which is adequate in all the circumstances of the case, having regard in particular to—

(a) the nature of the personal data,

(b) the country or territory of origin of the information contained in the data,

(c) the country or territory of final destination of that information,

(d) the purposes for which and period during which the data are intended to be processed,

(e) the law in force in the country or territory in question,

(f) the international obligations of that country or territory,

(g) any relevant codes of conduct or other rules which are enforceable in that country or territory (whether generally or by arrangement in particular cases), and

(h) any security measures taken in respect of the data in that country or territory.

14. The eighth principle does not apply to a transfer falling within any paragraph of Schedule 4, except in such circumstances and to such extent as the Secretary of State may by order provide.

15.(1) Where—

(a) in any proceedings under this Act any question arises as to whether the requirement of the eighth principle as to an adequate level of protection is met in relation to the transfer of any personal data to a country or territory outside the European Economic Area, and

(b) a Community finding has been made in relation to transfers of the kind in question, that question is to be determined in accordance with that finding.

(2) In sub-paragraph (1) "Community finding" means a finding of the European Commission, under the procedure provided for in Article 31(2) of the Data Protection Directive, that a country or territory outside the European Economic Area does, or does not, ensure an adequate level of protection within the meaning of Article 25(2) of the Directive.

SCHEDULE 2

CONDITIONS RELEVANT FOR PURPOSES OF THE FIRST PRINCIPLE: PROCESSING OF ANY PERSONAL DATA

1. The data subject has given his consent to the processing.

2. The processing is necessary—

(a) for the performance of a contract to which the data subject is a party, or

(b) for the taking of steps at the request of the data subject with a view to entering into a contract.

3. The processing is necessary for compliance with any legal obligation to which the data controller is subject, other than an obligation imposed by contract.

4. The processing is necessary in order to protect the vital interests of the data subject.

5. The processing is necessary—

(a) for the administration of justice,

(aa) for the exercise of any functions of either House of Parliament,

(b) for the exercise of any functions conferred on any person by or under any enactment,

(c) for the exercise of any functions of the Crown, a Minister of the Crown or a government department, or

(d) for the exercise of any other functions of a public nature exercised in the public interest by any person.

6.(1) The processing is necessary for the purposes of legitimate interests pursued by the data controller or by the third party or parties to whom the data are disclosed, except where the processing is unwarranted in any particular case by reason of prejudice to the rights and freedoms or legitimate interests of the data subject.

(2) The Secretary of State may by order specify particular circumstances in which this condition is, or is not, to be taken to be satisfied.

SCHEDULE 3

CONDITIONS RELEVANT FOR PURPOSES OF THE FIRST PRINCIPLE: PROCESSING OF SENSITIVE PERSONAL DATA

1. The data subject has given his explicit consent to the processing of the personal data.

2.(1) The processing is necessary for the purposes of exercising or performing any right or obligation which is conferred or imposed by law on the data controller in connection with employment.

(2) The Secretary of State may by order—
    (a) exclude the application of sub-paragraph (1) in such cases as may be specified, or
    (b) provide that, in such cases as may be specified, the condition in sub-paragraph (1) is not to be regarded as satisfied unless such further conditions as may be specified in the order are also satisfied.

3. The processing is necessary—
    (a) in order to protect the vital interests of the data subject or another person, in a case where—
        (i) consent cannot be given by or on behalf of the data subject, or
        (ii) the data controller cannot reasonably be expected to obtain the consent of the data subject, or
    (b) in order to protect the vital interests of another person, in a case where consent by or on behalf of the data subject has been unreasonably withheld.

4. The processing—
    (a) is carried out in the course of its legitimate activities by any body or association which—
        (i) is not established or conducted for profit, and
        (ii) exists for political, philosophical, religious or trade-union purposes,
    (b) is carried out with appropriate safeguards for the rights and freedoms of data subjects,
    (c) relates only to individuals who either are members of the body or association or have regular contact with it in connection with its purposes, and
    (d) does not involve disclosure of the personal data to a third party without the consent of the data subject.

5. The information contained in the personal data has been made public as a result of steps deliberately taken by the data subject.

6. The processing—
    (a) is necessary for the purpose of, or in connection with, any legal proceedings (including prospective legal proceedings),
    (b) is necessary for the purpose of obtaining legal advice, or
    (c) is otherwise necessary for the purposes of establishing, exercising or defending legal rights.

7.(1) The processing is necessary—
    (a) for the administration of justice,
    (aa) for the exercise of any functions of either House of Parliament,
    (b) for the exercise of any functions conferred on any person by or under an enactment, or
    (c) for the exercise of any functions of the Crown, a Minister of the Crown or a government department.

(2) The Secretary of State may by order—
    (a) exclude the application of sub-paragraph (1) in such cases as may be specified, or
    (b) provide that, in such cases as may be specified, the condition in sub-paragraph (1) is not to be regarded as satisfied unless such further conditions as may be specified in the order are also satisfied.

7A.(1) The processing—
    (a) is either—
        (i) the disclosure of sensitive personal data by a person as a member of an anti-fraud organisation or otherwise in accordance with any arrangements made by such an organisation; or
        (ii) any other processing by that person or another person of sensitive personal data so disclosed; and

(b) is necessary for the purposes of preventing fraud or a particular kind of fraud.

(2) In this paragraph "an anti-fraud organisation" means any unincorporated association, body corporate or other person which enables or facilitates any sharing of information to prevent fraud or a particular kind of fraud or which has any of these functions as its purpose or one of its purposes

8.(1) The processing is necessary for medical purposes and is undertaken by—
    (a) a health professional, or
    (b) a person who in the circumstances owes a duty of confidentiality which is equivalent to that which would arise if that person were a health professional.

(2) In this paragraph "medical purposes" includes the purposes of preventative medicine, medical diagnosis, medical research, the provision of care and treatment and the management of healthcare services.

9.(1) The processing—
    (a) is of sensitive personal data consisting of information as to racial or ethnic origin,
    (b) is necessary for the purpose of identifying or keeping under review the existence or absence of equality of opportunity or treatment between persons of different racial or ethnic origins, with a view to enabling such equality to be promoted or maintained, and
    (c) is carried out with appropriate safeguards for the rights and freedoms of data subjects.

(2) The Secretary of State may by order specify circumstances in which processing falling within sub-paragraph (1)(a) and (b) is, or is not, to be taken for the purposes of sub-paragraph (1)(c) to be carried out with appropriate safeguards for the rights and freedoms of data subjects.

10. The personal data are processed in circumstances specified in an order made by the Secretary of State for the purposes of this paragraph.

A2.26

Human Rights Act 1998

[1998 c. 42]

Arrangement of Sections

Introduction

Legislation

Public Authorities

8. Judicial remedies.
9. Judicial acts.

Remedial Action

10. Power to take remedial action.

Other Rights and Proceedings

11. Safeguard for existing human rights.
12. Freedom of expression.
13. Freedom of thought, conscience and religion.

Derogations and Reservations

14. Derogations.
15. Reservations.
16. Period for which designated derogations have effect.
17. Periodic review of designated reservations.

Judges of the European Court of Human Rights

18. Appointment to European Court of Human Rights.

Parliamentary Procedure

19. Statements of compatibility.

Supplemental

20. Orders etc. under this Act.
21. Interpretation, etc.
22. Short title, commencement, application and extent.

SCHEDULES

Schedule 1—The Articles.
    Part I—The Convention.
    Part II—The First Protocol.
    Part III—The Sixth Protocol.
Schedule 2—Remedial Orders.
Schedule 3—Derogation and Reservation.
    Part I—Derogation.
    Part II—Reservation.
Schedule 4—Judicial Pensions.

An Act to give further effect to rights and freedoms guaranteed under the European Convention on Human Rights; to make provision with respect to holders of certain judicial offices who become judges of the European Court of Human Rights; and for connected purposes.

[9TH NOVEMBER 1998]

BE IT ENACTED by the Queen's most Excellent Majesty, by and with the advice and consent of the Lords Spiritual and Temporal, and Commons, in this present Parliament assembled, and by the authority of the same, as follows:

Introduction

1.—The Convention Rights.

(1) In this Act "the Convention rights" means the rights and fundamental freedoms set out in—
    (a) Articles 2 to 12 and 14 of the Convention,
    (b) Articles 1 to 3 of the First Protocol, and
    (c) Article 1 of the Thirteenth Protocol,
as read with Articles 16 to 18 of the Convention.

(2) Those Articles are to have effect for the purposes of this Act subject to any designated derogation or reservation (as to which see sections 14 and 15).

(3) The Articles are set out in Schedule 1.

(4) The Secretary of State may by order make such amendments to this Act as he considers appropriate to reflect the effect, in relation to the United Kingdom, of a protocol.

(5) In subsection (4) "protocol" means a protocol to the Convention—
    (a) which the United Kingdom has ratified; or
    (b) which the United Kingdom has signed with a view to ratification.

(6) No amendment may be made by an order under subsection (4) so as to come into force before the protocol concerned is in force in relation to the United Kingdom.

2.—Interpretation of Convention rights.

(1) A court or tribunal determining a question which has arisen in connection with a Convention right must take into account any—
    (a) judgment, decision, declaration or advisory opinion of the European Court of Human Rights,
    (b) opinion of the Commission given in a report adopted under Article 31 of the Convention,
    (c) decision of the Commission in connection with Article 26 or 27(2) of the Convention, or
    (d) decision of the Committee of Ministers taken under Article 46 of the Convention,
whenever made or given, so far as, in the opinion of the court or tribunal, it is relevant to the proceedings in which that question has arisen.

(2) Evidence of any judgment, decision, declaration or opinion of which account may have to be taken under this section is to be given in proceedings before any court or tribunal in such manner as may be provided by rules.

(3) In this section "rules" means rules of court or, in the case of proceedings before a tribunal, rules made for the purposes of this section—
    (a) by the Lord Chancellor or the Secretary of State, in relation to any proceedings outside Scotland;
    (b) by the Secretary of State, in relation to proceedings in Scotland; or
    (c) by a Northern Ireland department, in relation to proceedings before a tribunal in Northern Ireland—

(i) which deals with transferred matters; and

(ii) for which no rules made under paragraph (a) are in force.

Legislation

3.—Interpretation of legislation.

(1) So far as it is possible to do so, primary legislation and subordinate legislation must be read and given effect in a way which is compatible with the Convention rights.

(2) This section—

    (a) applies to primary legislation and subordinate legislation whenever enacted;

    (b) does not affect the validity, continuing operation or enforcement of any incompatible primary legislation; and

    (c) does not affect the validity, continuing operation or enforcement of any incompatible subordinate legislation if (disregarding any possibility of revocation) primary legislation prevents removal of the incompatibility.

4.—Declaration of incompatibility.

(1) Subsection (2) applies in any proceedings in which a court determines whether a provision of primary legislation is compatible with a Convention right.

(2) If the court is satisfied that the provision is incompatible with a Convention right, it may make a declaration of that incompatibility.

(3) Subsection (4) applies in any proceedings in which a court determines whether a provision of subordinate legislation, made in the exercise of a power conferred by primary legislation, is compatible with a Convention right.

(4) If the court is satisfied—

    (a) that the provision is incompatible with a Convention right, and

    (b) that (disregarding any possibility of revocation) the primary legislation concerned prevents removal of the incompatibility,

it may make a declaration of that incompatibility.

(5) In this section "court" means—

    (a) the Supreme Court;

    (b) the Judicial Committee of the Privy Council;

    (c) the Court-Martial Appeal Court;

    (d) in Scotland, the High Court of Justiciary sitting otherwise than as a trial court or the Court of Session;

    (e) in England and Wales or Northern Ireland, the High Court or the Court of Appeal;

    (f) the Court of Protection, in any matter being dealt with by the President of the Family Division, the Vice-Chancellor or a puisne judge of the High Court.

(6) A declaration under this section ("a declaration of incompatibility")—

    (a) does not affect the validity, continuing operation or enforcement of the provision in respect of which it is given; and (b) is not binding on the parties to the proceedings in which it is made.

5.—Right of Crown to intervene.

(1) Where a court is considering whether to make a declaration of incompatibility, the Crown is entitled to notice in accordance with rules of court.

(2) In any case to which subsection (1) applies—

(a) a Minister of the Crown (or a person nominated by him),

(b) a member of the Scottish Executive,

(c) a Northern Ireland Minister,

(d) a Northern Ireland department,

is entitled, on giving notice in accordance with rules of court, to be joined as a party to the proceedings.

(3) Notice under subsection (2) may be given at any time during the proceedings.

(4) A person who has been made a party to criminal proceedings (other than in Scotland) as the result of a notice under subsection (2) may, with leave, appeal to the Supreme Court against any declaration of incompatibility made in the proceedings.

(5) In subsection (4)—

"criminal proceedings" includes all proceedings before the Court-Martial Appeal Court; and

"leave" means leave granted by the court making the declaration of incompatibility or by the Supreme Court.

Public authorities

6.—Acts of public authorities.

(1) It is unlawful for a public authority to act in a way which is incompatible with a Convention right.

(2) Subsection (1) does not apply to an act if—

(a) as the result of one or more provisions of primary legislation, the authority could not have acted differently; or

(b) in the case of one or more provisions of, or made under, primary legislation which cannot be read or given effect in a way which is compatible with the Convention rights, the authority was acting so as to give effect to or enforce those provisions.

(3) In this section "public authority" includes—

(a) a court or tribunal, and

(b) any person certain of whose functions are functions of a public nature,

but does not include either House of Parliament or a person exercising functions in connection with proceedings in Parliament.

(4) . . .

(5) In relation to a particular act, a person is not a public authority by virtue only of subsection (3)(b) if the nature of the act is private.

(6) "An act" includes a failure to act but does not include a failure to—

(a) introduce in, or lay before, Parliament a proposal for legislation; or

(b) make any primary legislation or remedial order.

7.—Proceedings.

(1) A person who claims that a public authority has acted (or proposes to act) in a way which is made unlawful by section 6(1) may—

(a) bring proceedings against the authority under this Act in the appropriate court or tribunal, or

(b) rely on the Convention right or rights concerned in any legal proceedings,

but only if he is (or would be) a victim of the unlawful act.

(2) In subsection (1)(a) "appropriate court or tribunal" means such court or tribunal as may be determined in accordance with rules; and proceedings against an authority include a counterclaim or similar proceedings.

(3) If the proceedings are brought on an application for judicial review, the applicant is to be taken to have a sufficient interest in relation to the unlawful act only if he is, or would be, a victim of that act.

(4) If the proceedings are made by way of a petition for judicial review in Scotland, the applicant shall be taken to have title and interest to sue in relation to the unlawful act only if he is, or would be, a victim of that act.

(5) Proceedings under subsection (1)(a) must be brought before the end of—

    (a) the period of one year beginning with the date on which the act complained of took place; or

    (b) such longer period as the court or tribunal considers equitable having regard to all the circumstances,

but that is subject to any rule imposing a stricter time limit in relation to the procedure in question.

(6) In subsection (1)(b) "legal proceedings" includes—

    (a) proceedings brought by or at the instigation of a public authority; and

    (b) an appeal against the decision of a court or tribunal.

(7) For the purposes of this section, a person is a victim of an unlawful act only if he would be a victim for the purposes of Article 34 of the Convention if proceedings were brought in the European Court of Human Rights in respect of that act.

(8) Nothing in this Act creates a criminal offence.

(9) In this section "rules" means—

    (a) in relation to proceedings before a court or tribunal outside Scotland, rules made by the the Lord Chancellor or Secretary of State for the purposes of this section or rules of court,

    (b) in relation to proceedings before a court or tribunal in Scotland, rules made by the Secretary of State for those purposes,

    (c) in relation to proceedings before a tribunal in Northern Ireland—

        (i) which deals with transferred matters; and

        (ii) for which no rules made under paragraph (a) are in force,

rules made by a Northern Ireland department for those purposes,

and includes provision made by order under section 1 of the Courts and Legal Services Act 1990.

(10) In making rules, regard must be had to section 9.

(11) The Minister who has power to make rules in relation to a particular tribunal may, to the extent he considers it necessary to ensure that the tribunal can provide an appropriate remedy in relation to an act (or proposed act) of a public authority which is (or would be) unlawful as a result of section 6(1), by order add to—

    (a) the relief or remedies which the tribunal may grant; or

    (b) the grounds on which it may grant any of them.

(12) An order made under subsection (11) may contain such incidental, supplemental, consequential or transitional provision as the Minister making it considers appropriate.

(13) "The Minister" includes the Northern Ireland department concerned.

8.—Judicial remedies.

(1) In relation to any act (or proposed act) of a public authority which the court finds is (or would be) unlawful, it may grant such relief or remedy, or make such order, within its powers as it considers just and appropriate.

(2) But damages may be awarded only by a court which has power to award damages, or to order the payment of compensation, in civil proceedings.

(3) No award of damages is to be made unless, taking account of all the circumstances of the case, including—

    (a) any other relief or remedy granted, or order made, in relation to the act in question (by that or any other court), and

    (b) the consequences of any decision (of that or any other court) in respect of that act, the court is satisfied that the award is necessary to afford just satisfaction to the person in whose favour it is made.

(4) In determining—

    (a) whether to award damages, or

    (b) the amount of an award,

the court must take into account the principles applied by the European Court of Human Rights in relation to the award of compensation under Article 41 of the Convention.

(5) A public authority against which damages are awarded is to be treated—

    (a) in Scotland, for the purposes of section 3 of the Law Reform (Miscellaneous Provisions) (Scotland) Act 1940 as if the award were made in an action of damages in which the authority has been found liable in respect of loss or damage to the person to whom the award is made;

    (b) for the purposes of the Civil Liability (Contribution) Act 1978 as liable in respect of damage suffered by the person to whom the award is made.

(6) In this section—

"court" includes a tribunal;

"damages" means damages for an unlawful act of a public authority; and

"unlawful" means unlawful under section 6(1).

9.—*Judicial acts.*

(1) Proceedings under section 7(1)(a) in respect of a judicial act may be brought only—

    (a) by exercising a right of appeal;

    (b) on an application (in Scotland a petition) for judicial review; or

    (c) in such other forum as may be prescribed by rules.

(2) That does not affect any rule of law which prevents a court from being the subject of judicial review.

(3) In proceedings under this Act in respect of a judicial act done in good faith, damages may not be awarded otherwise than to compensate a person to the extent required by Article 5(5) of the Convention.

(4) An award of damages permitted by subsection (3) is to be made against the Crown; but no award may be made unless the appropriate person, if not a party to the proceedings, is joined.

(5) In this section—

"appropriate person" means the Minister responsible for the court concerned, or a person or government department nominated by him;

"court" includes a tribunal;

"judge" includes a member of a tribunal, a justice of the peace (or, in Northern Ireland, a lay magistrate) and a clerk or other officer entitled to exercise the jurisdiction of a court;

"judicial act" means a judicial act of a court and includes an act done on the instructions, or on behalf, of a judge; and

"rules" has the same meaning as in section 7(9).

Remedial action

10.—*Power to take remedial action.*

(1) This section applies if—

    (a) a provision of legislation has been declared under section 4 to be incompatible with a Convention right and, if an appeal lies—

        (i) all persons who may appeal have stated in writing that they do not intend to do so;

    (ii) the time for bringing an appeal has expired and no appeal has been brought within that time; or

    (iii) an appeal brought within that time has been determined or abandoned; or

  (b) it appears to a Minister of the Crown or Her Majesty in Council that, having regard to a finding of the European Court of Human Rights made after the coming into force of this section in proceedings against the United Kingdom, a provision of legislation is incompatible with an obligation of the United Kingdom arising from the Convention.

(2) If a Minister of the Crown considers that there are compelling reasons for proceeding under this section, he may by order make such amendments to the legislation as he considers necessary to remove the incompatibility.

(3) If, in the case of subordinate legislation, a Minister of the Crown considers—

  (a) that it is necessary to amend the primary legislation under which the subordinate legislation in question was made, in order to enable the incompatibility to be removed, and

  (b) that there are compelling reasons for proceeding under this section,

he may by order make such amendments to the primary legislation as he considers necessary.

(4) This section also applies where the provision in question is in subordinate legislation and has been quashed, or declared invalid, by reason of incompatibility with a Convention right and the Minister proposes to proceed under paragraph 2(b) of Schedule 2.

(5) If the legislation is an Order in Council, the power conferred by subsection (2) or (3) is exercisable by Her Majesty in Council.

(6) In this section "legislation" does not include a Measure of the Church Assembly or of the General Synod of the Church of England.

(7) Schedule 2 makes further provision about remedial orders.

Other rights and proceedings

11. Safeguard for existing human rights.

A person's reliance on a Convention right does not restrict—

  (a) any other right or freedom conferred on him by or under any law having effect in any part of the United Kingdom; or

  (b) his right to make any claim or bring any proceedings which he could make or bring apart from sections 7 to 9.

12.—Freedom of expression.

(1) This section applies if a court is considering whether to grant any relief which, if granted, might affect the exercise of the Convention right to freedom of expression.

(2) If the person against whom the application for relief is made ("the respondent") is neither present nor represented, no such relief is to be granted unless the court is satisfied—

  (a) that the applicant has taken all practicable steps to notify the respondent; or

  (b) that there are compelling reasons why the respondent should not be notified.

(3) No such relief is to be granted so as to restrain publication before trial unless the court is satisfied that the applicant is likely to establish that publication should not be allowed.

(4) The court must have particular regard to the importance of the Convention right to freedom of expression and, where the proceedings relate to material which the respondent claims, or which appears to the court, to be journalistic, literary or artistic material (or to conduct connected with such material), to—

    (a) the extent to which—

        (i) the material has, or is about to, become available to the public; or

        (ii) it is, or would be, in the public interest for the material to be published;

    (b) any relevant privacy code.

(5) In this section—

"court" includes a tribunal; and

"relief" includes any remedy or order (other than in criminal proceedings).

13.—*Freedom of thought, conscience and religion.*

(1) If a court's determination of any question arising under this Act might affect the exercise by a religious organisation (itself or its members collectively) of the Convention right to freedom of thought, conscience and religion, it must have particular regard to the importance of that right.

(2) In this section "court" includes a tribunal.

Derogations and reservations

14.—*Derogations.*

(1) In this Act "designated derogation" means any derogation by the United Kingdom from an Article of the Convention, or of any protocol to the Convention, which is designated for the purposes of this Act in an order made by the Secretary of State.

(2) . . .

(3) If a designated derogation is amended or replaced it ceases to be a designated derogation.

(4) But subsection (3) does not prevent the Secretary of State from exercising his power under subsection (1) to make a fresh designation order in respect of the Article concerned.

(5) The Secretary of State must by order make such amendments to Schedule 3 as he considers appropriate to reflect—

    (a) any designation order; or

    (b) the effect of subsection (3).

(6) A designation order may be made in anticipation of the making by the United Kingdom of a proposed derogation.

15.—*Reservations.*

(1) In this Act "designated reservation" means—

    (a) the United Kingdom's reservation to Article 2 of the First Protocol to the Convention; and

    (b) any other reservation by the United Kingdom to an Article of the Convention, or of any protocol to the Convention, which is designated for the purposes of this Act in an order made by the Secretary of State.

(2) The text of the reservation referred to in subsection (1)(a) is set out in Part II of Schedule 3.

(3) If a designated reservation is withdrawn wholly or in part it ceases to be a designated reservation.

(4) But subsection (3) does not prevent the Secretary of State from exercising his power under subsection (1)(b) to make a fresh designation order in respect of the Article concerned.

(5) The Secretary of State must by order make such amendments to this Act as he considers appropriate to reflect—

  (a) any designation order; or

  (b) the effect of subsection (3).

16.—Period for which designated derogations have effect.

(1) If it has not already been withdrawn by the United Kingdom, a designated derogation ceases to have effect for the purposes of this Act, at the end of the period of five years beginning with the date on which the order designating it was made.

(2) At any time before the period—

  (a) fixed by subsection (1), or

  (b) extended by an order under this subsection,

comes to an end, the Secretary of State may by order extend it by a further period of five years.

(3) An order under section 14(1) ceases to have effect at the end of the period for consideration, unless a resolution has been passed by each House approving the order.

(4) Subsection (3) does not affect—

  (a) anything done in reliance on the order; or

  (b) the power to make a fresh order under section 14(1).

(5) In subsection (3) "period for consideration" means the period of forty days beginning with the day on which the order was made.

(6) In calculating the period for consideration, no account is to be taken of any time during which—

  (a) Parliament is dissolved or prorogued; or

  (b) both Houses are adjourned for more than four days.

(7) If a designated derogation is withdrawn by the United Kingdom, the Secretary of State must by order make such amendments to this Act as he considers are required to reflect that withdrawal.

17.—Periodic review of designated reservations.

(1) The appropriate Minister must review the designated reservation referred to in section 15(1)(a)—

  (a) before the end of the period of five years beginning with the date on which section 1(2) came into force; and

  (b) if that designation is still in force, before the end of the period of five years beginning with the date on which the last report relating to it was laid under subsection (3).

(2) The appropriate Minister must review each of the other designated reservations (if any)—

  (a) before the end of the period of five years beginning with the date on which the order designating the reservation first came into force; and

  (b) if the designation is still in force, before the end of the period of five years beginning with the date on which the last report relating to it was laid under subsection (3).

(3) The Minister conducting a review under this section must prepare a report on the result of the review and lay a copy of it before each House of Parliament.

Judges of the European Court of Human Rights

18.—Appointment to European Court of Human Rights.

(1) In this section "judicial office" means the office of—
- (a) Lord Justice of Appeal, Justice of the High Court or Circuit judge, in England and Wales;
- (b) judge of the Court of Session or sheriff, in Scotland;
- (c) Lord Justice of Appeal, judge of the High Court or county court judge, in Northern Ireland.

(2) The holder of a judicial office may become a judge of the European Court of Human Rights ("the Court") without being required to relinquish his office.

(3) But he is not required to perform the duties of his judicial office while he is a judge of the Court.

(4) In respect of any period during which he is a judge of the Court—
- (a) a Lord Justice of Appeal or Justice of the High Court is not to count as a judge of the relevant court for the purposes of section 2(1) or 4(1) of the Senior Courts Act 1981 (maximum number of judges) nor as a judge of the Senior Courts for the purposes of section 12(1) to (6) of that Act (salaries etc.);
- (b) a judge of the Court of Session is not to count as a judge of that court for the purposes of section 1(1) of the Court of Session Act 1988 (maximum number of judges) or of section 9(1)(c) of the Administration of Justice Act 1973 ("the 1973 Act") (salaries etc.);
- (c) a Lord Justice of Appeal or judge of the High Court in Northern Ireland is not to count as a judge of the relevant court for the purposes of section 2(1) or 3(1) of the Judicature (Northern Ireland) Act 1978 (maximum number of judges) nor as a judge of the Court of Judicature of Northern Ireland for the purposes of section 9(1)(d) of the 1973 Act (salaries etc.);
- (d) a Circuit judge is not to count as such for the purposes of section 18 of the Courts Act 1971 (salaries etc.);
- (e) a sheriff is not to count as such for the purposes of section 14 of the Sheriff Courts (Scotland) Act 1907 (salaries etc.);
- (f) a county court judge of Northern Ireland is not to count as such for the purposes of section 106 of the County Courts Act (Northern Ireland) 1959 (salaries etc.).

(5) If a sheriff principal is appointed a judge of the Court, section 11(1) of the Sheriff Courts (Scotland) Act 1971 (temporary appointment of sheriff principal) applies, while he holds that appointment, as if his office is vacant.

(6) Schedule 4 makes provision about judicial pensions in relation to the holder of a judicial office who serves as a judge of the Court.

(7) The Lord Chancellor or the Secretary of State may by order make such transitional provision (including, in particular, provision for a temporary increase in the maximum number of judges) as he considers appropriate in relation to any holder of a judicial office who has completed his service as a judge of the Court.

(7A) The following paragraphs apply to the making of an order under subsection (7) in relation to any holder of a judicial office listed in subsection (1)(a)—
- (a) before deciding what transitional provision it is appropriate to make, the person making the order must consult the Lord Chief Justice of England and Wales;
- (b) before making the order, that person must consult the Lord Chief Justice of England and Wales.

(7B) The following paragraphs apply to the making of an order under subsection (7) in relation to any holder of a judicial office listed in subsection (1)(c)—

(a) before deciding what transitional provision it is appropriate to make, the person making the order must consult the Lord Chief Justice of Northern Ireland;

(b) before making the order, that person must consult the Lord Chief Justice of Northern Ireland.

(7C) The Lord Chief Justice of England and Wales may nominate a judicial office holder (within the meaning of section 109(4) of the Constitutional Reform Act 2005) to exercise his functions under this section.

(7D) The Lord Chief Justice of Northern Ireland may nominate any of the following to exercise his functions under this section—

(a) the holder of one of the offices listed in Schedule 1 to the Justice (Northern Ireland) Act 2002;

(b) a Lord Justice of Appeal (as defined in section 88 of that Act).

Parliamentary procedure

19.—Statements of compatibility.

(1) A Minister of the Crown in charge of a Bill in either House of Parliament must, before Second Reading of the Bill—

(a) make a statement to the effect that in his view the provisions of the Bill are compatible with the Convention rights ("a statement of compatibility"); or

(b) make a statement to the effect that although he is unable to make a statement of compatibility the government nevertheless wishes the House to proceed with the Bill.

(2) The statement must be in writing and be published in such manner as the Minister making it considers appropriate.

Supplemental

20.—Orders etc. under this Act.

(1) Any power of a Minister of the Crown to make an order under this Act is exercisable by statutory instrument.

(2) The power of the Lord Chancellor or the Secretary of State to make rules (other than rules of court) under section 2(3) or 7(9) is exercisable by statutory instrument.

(3) Any statutory instrument made under section 14, 15 or 16(7) must be laid before Parliament.

(4) No order may be made by the Lord Chancellor or the Secretary of State under section 1(4), 7(11) or 16(2) unless a draft of the order has been laid before, and approved by, each House of Parliament.

(5) Any statutory instrument made under section 18(7) or Schedule 4, or to which subsection (2) applies, shall be subject to annulment in pursuance of a resolution of either House of Parliament.

(6) The power of a Northern Ireland department to make—

(a) rules under section 2(3)(c) or 7(9)(c), or

(b) an order under section 7(11),

is exercisable by statutory rule for the purposes of the Statutory Rules (Northern Ireland) Order 1979.

(7) Any rules made under section 2(3)(c) or 7(9)(c) shall be subject to negative resolution; and section 41(6) of the Interpretation Act (Northern Ireland) 1954 (meaning of "subject to negative resolution") shall apply as if the power to make the rules were conferred by an Act of the Northern Ireland Assembly.

(8) No order may be made by a Northern Ireland department under section 7(11) unless a draft of the order has been laid before, and approved by, the Northern Ireland Assembly.

21.—Interpretation, etc.

(1) In this Act—

"amend" includes repeal and apply (with or without modifications);

"the appropriate Minister" means the Minister of the Crown having charge of the appropriate authorised government department (within the meaning of the Crown Proceedings Act 1947);

"the Commission" means the European Commission of Human Rights;

"the Convention" means the Convention for the Protection of Human Rights and Fundamental Freedoms, agreed by the Council of Europe at Rome on 4th November 1950 as it has effect for the time being in relation to the United Kingdom;

"declaration of incompatibility" means a declaration under section 4;

"Minister of the Crown" has the same meaning as in the Ministers of the Crown Act 1975;

"Northern Ireland Minister" includes the First Minister and the deputy First Minister in Northern Ireland;

"primary legislation" means any—

    (a) public general Act;

    (b) local and personal Act;

    (c) private Act;

    (d) Measure of the Church Assembly;

    (e) Measure of the General Synod of the Church of England;

    (f) Order in Council—

        (i) made in exercise of Her Majesty's Royal Prerogative;

        (ii) made under section 38(1)(a) of the Northern Ireland Constitution Act 1973 or the corresponding provision of the Northern Ireland Act 1998; or

        (iii) amending an Act of a kind mentioned in paragraph (a), (b) or (c);

and includes an order or other instrument made under primary legislation (otherwise than by the Welsh Ministers, the First Minister for Wales, the Counsel General to the Welsh Assembly Government, a member of the Scottish Executive, a Northern Ireland Minister or a Northern Ireland department) to the extent to which it operates to bring one or more provisions of that legislation into force or amends any primary legislation;

"the First Protocol" means the protocol to the Convention agreed at Paris on 20th March 1952;

"the Eleventh Protocol" means the protocol to the Convention (restructuring the control machinery established by the Convention) agreed at Strasbourg on 11th May 1994;

"the Thirteenth Protocol" means the protocol to the Convention (concerning the abolition of the death penalty in all circumstances) agreed at Vilnius on 3rd May 2002;

"remedial order" means an order under section 10;

"subordinate legislation" means any—

   (a) Order in Council other than one—
      (i) made in exercise of Her Majesty's Royal Prerogative;
     (ii) made under section 38(1)(a) of the Northern Ireland Constitution
         Act 1973 or the corresponding provision of the Northern Ireland
         Act 1998; or
    (iii) amending an Act of a kind mentioned in the definition of primary
         legislation;
   (b) Act of the Scottish Parliament;
  (ba) Measure of the National Assembly for Wales;
  (bb) Act of the National Assembly for Wales;
   (c) Act of the Parliament of Northern Ireland;
   (d) Measure of the Assembly established under section 1 of the Northern
      Ireland Assembly Act 1973;
   (e) Act of the Northern Ireland Assembly;
   (f) order, rules, regulations, scheme, warrant, byelaw or other instrument
      made under primary legislation (except to the extent to which it oper-
      ates to bring one or more provisions of that legislation into force or
      amends any primary legislation);
   (g) order, rules, regulations, scheme, warrant, byelaw or other instrument
      made under legislation mentioned in paragraph (b), (c), (d) or (e) or
      made under an Order in Council applying only to Northern Ireland;
   (h) order, rules, regulations, scheme, warrant, byelaw or other instrument
      made by a member of the Scottish Executive, Welsh Ministers, the First
      Minister for Wales, the Counsel General to the Welsh Assembly Gov-
      ernment, a Northern Ireland Minister or a Northern Ireland department
      in exercise of prerogative or other executive functions of Her Majesty
      which are exercisable by such a person on behalf of Her Majesty;
"transferred matters" has the same meaning as in the Northern Ireland Act 1998;
    and
"tribunal" means any tribunal in which legal proceedings may be brought.

(2) The references in paragraphs (b) and (c) of section 2(1) to Articles are to Articles of the Convention as they had effect immediately before the coming into force of the Eleventh Protocol.

(3) The reference in paragraph (d) of section 2(1) to Article 46 includes a reference to Articles 32 and 54 of the Convention as they had effect immediately before the coming into force of the Eleventh Protocol.

(4) The references in section 2(1) to a report or decision of the Commission or a decision of the Committee of Ministers include references to a report or decision made as provided by paragraphs 3, 4 and 6 of Article 5 of the Eleventh Protocol (transitional provisions).

(5) . . .

22.—Short title, commencement, application and extent.

(1) This Act may be cited as the Human Rights Act 1998.

(2) Sections 18, 20 and 21(5) and this section come into force on the passing of this Act.

(3) The other provisions of this Act come into force on such days as the Secretary of State may by order appoint; and different days may be appointed for different purposes.

(4) Paragraph (b) of subsection (1) of section 7 applies to proceedings brought by or at the instigation of a public authority whenever the act in question took place; but otherwise that subsection does not apply to an act taking place before the coming into force of that section.

(5) This Act binds the Crown.
(6) This Act extends to Northern Ireland.
(7) . . .

SCHEDULE 1 THE ARTICLES

PART I THE CONVENTION

RIGHTS AND FREEDOMS

Right to life

Article 2

1. Everyone's right to life shall be protected by law. No one shall be deprived of his life intentionally save in the execution of a sentence of a court following his conviction of a crime for which this penalty is provided by law.

2. Deprivation of life shall not be regarded as inflicted in contravention of this Article when it results from the use of force which is no more than absolutely necessary:

    (a) in defence of any person from unlawful violence;
    (b) in order to effect a lawful arrest or to prevent the escape of a person lawfully detained;
    (c) in action lawfully taken for the purpose of quelling a riot or insurrection.

Prohibition of torture

Article 3

No one shall be subjected to torture or to inhuman or degrading treatment or punishment.

Prohibition of slavery and forced labour

Article 4

1. No one shall be held in slavery or servitude.

2. No one shall be required to perform forced or compulsory labour.

3. For the purpose of this Article the term "forced or compulsory labour" shall not include:

    (a) any work required to be done in the ordinary course of detention imposed according to the provisions of Article 5 of this Convention or during conditional release from such detention;
    (b) any service of a military character or, in case of conscientious objectors in countries where they are recognised, service exacted instead of compulsory military service;
    (c) any service exacted in case of an emergency or calamity threatening the life or well-being of the community;
    (d) any work or service which forms part of normal civic obligations.

Right to liberty and security

Article 5

1. Everyone has the right to liberty and security of a person. No one shall be deprived of his liberty save in the following cases and in accordance with a procedure prescribed by law:

(a) the lawful detention of a person after conviction by a competent court;

(b) the lawful arrest or detention of a person for non-compliance with the lawful order of a court or in order to secure the fulfilment of any obligation prescribed by law;

(c) the lawful arrest or detention of a person effected for the purpose of bringing him before the competent legal authority on reasonable suspicion of having committed an offence or when it is reasonably considered necessary to prevent his committing an offence or fleeing after having done so;

(d) the detention of a minor by lawful order for the purpose of educational supervision or his lawful detention for the purpose of bringing him before the competent legal authority;

(e) the lawful detention of persons for the prevention of the spreading of infectious diseases, of persons of unsound mind, alcoholics or drug addicts or vagrants;

(f) the lawful arrest or detention of a person to prevent his effecting an unauthorised entry into the country or of a person against whom action is being taken with a view to deportation or extradition.

2. Everyone who is arrested shall be informed promptly, in a language which he understands, of the reasons for his arrest and of any charge against him.

3. Everyone arrested or detained in accordance with the provisions of paragraph 1(c) of this Article shall be brought promptly before a judge or other officer authorised by law to exercise judicial power and shall be entitled to trial within a reasonable time or to release pending trial. Release may be conditioned by guarantees to appear for trial.

4. Everyone who is deprived of his liberty by arrest or detention shall be entitled to take proceedings by which the lawfulness of his detention shall be decided speedily by a court and his release ordered if the detention is not lawful.

5. Everyone who has been the victim of arrest or detention in contravention of the provisions of this Article shall have an enforceable right to compensation.

Right to a fair trial

Article 6

1. In the determination of his civil rights and obligations or of any criminal charge against him, everyone is entitled to a fair and public hearing within a reasonable time by an independent and impartial tribunal established by law. Judgment shall be pronounced publicly but the press and public may be excluded from all or part of the trial in the interest of morals, public order or national security in a democratic society, where the interests of juveniles or the protection of the private life of the parties so require, or to the extent strictly necessary in the opinion of the court in special circumstances where publicity would prejudice the interests of justice.

2. Everyone charged with a criminal offence shall be presumed innocent until proved guilty according to law.

3. Everyone charged with a criminal offence has the following minimum rights:

(a) to be informed promptly, in a language which he understands and in detail, of the nature and cause of the accusation against him;

(b) to have adequate time and facilities for the preparation of his defence;

(c) to defend himself in person or through legal assistance of his own choosing or, if he has not sufficient means to pay for legal assistance, to be given it free when the interests of justice so require;

(d) to examine or have examined witnesses against him and to obtain the attendance and examination of witnesses on his behalf under the same conditions as witnesses against him;

(e) to have the free assistance of an interpreter if he cannot understand or speak the language used in court.

No punishment without law

Article 7

1. No one shall be held guilty of any criminal offence on account of any act or omission which did not constitute a criminal offence under national or international law at the time when it was committed. Nor shall a heavier penalty be imposed than the one that was applicable at the time the criminal offence was committed.

2. This Article shall not prejudice the trial and punishment of any person for any act or omission which, at the time when it was committed, was criminal according to the general principles of law recognised by civilised nations.

Right to respect for private and family life

Article 8

1. Everyone has the right to respect for his private and family life, his home and his correspondence.

2. There shall be no interference by a public authority with the exercise of this right except such as is in accordance with the law and is necessary in a democratic society in the interests of national security, public safety or the economic well-being of the country, for the prevention of disorder or crime, for the protection of health or morals, or for the protection of the rights and freedoms of others.

Freedom of thought, conscience and religion

Article 9

1. Everyone has the right to freedom of thought, conscience and religion, this right includes freedom to change his religion or belief and freedom, either alone or in community with others and in public or private, to manifest his religion or belief, in worship, teaching, practice and observance.

2. Freedom to manifest one's religion or beliefs shall be subject only to such limitation as are prescribed by law and are necessary in a democratic society in the interests of public safety, for the protection of public order, health or morals, or for the protection of the rights and freedoms of others.

Freedom of expression

Article 10

1. Everyone has the right to freedom of expression. This right shall include freedom to hold opinions and to receive and impart information and ideas without interference by public authority and regardless of frontiers. This Article shall not prevent States from requiring the licensing of broadcasting, television or cinema enterprises.

2. The exercise of these freedoms, since it carries with it duties and responsibilities, may be subject to such formalities, conditions, restrictions or penalties as are prescribed by law and are necessary in a democratic society, in the interests of national security, territorial integrity or public safety, for the prevention of disorder or crime, for the protection of health or morals, for the protection of the reputation or rights of others, for preventing the disclosure of information received in confidence, or for maintaining the authority and impartiality of the judiciary.

Freedom of assembly and association

Article 11

1. Everyone has the right to freedom of peaceful assembly and to freedom of association with others, including the right to form and to join trade unions for the protection of his interests.

2. No restrictions shall be placed on the exercise of these rights other than such as are prescribed by law and are necessary in a democratic society in the interests of national security or public safety, for the prevention of disorder or crime, for the protection of health or morals or for the protection of the rights and freedoms of others. This Article shall not prevent the imposition of lawful restrictions on the exercise of these rights by members of the armed forces, of the police or of the administration of the State.

Right to marry

Article 12

Men and women of marriageable age have the right to marry and to found a family, according to the national laws governing the exercise of this right.

Prohibition of discrimination

Article 14

The enjoyment of the rights and freedoms set forth in this Convention shall be secured without discrimination on any ground such as sex, race, colour, language, religion, political or other opinion, national or social origin, association with a national minority, property, birth or other status.

Restrictions on political activity of aliens

Article 16

Nothing in Articles 10, 11 and 14 shall be regarded as preventing the High Contracting Parties from imposing restrictions on the political activity of aliens.

Prohibition of abuse of rights

Article 17

Nothing in this Convention may be interpreted as implying for any State, group or person any right to engage in any activity or perform any act aimed at the destruction of any of the rights and freedoms set forth herein or at their limitation to a greater extent than is provided for in the Convention.

Limitation on use of restrictions on rights

Article 18

The restrictions permitted under this Convention to the said rights and freedoms shall not be applied for any purpose other than those for which they have been prescribed.

PART II THE FIRST PROTOCOL

Protection of property

Article 1

Every natural or legal person is entitled to the peaceful enjoyment of his possessions. No one shall be deprived of his possessions except in the public interest and subject to the conditions provided for by law and by the general principles of international law.

The preceding provisions shall not, however, in any way impair the right of a State to enforce such laws as it deems necessary to control the use of property in accordance with the general interest or to secure the payment of taxes or other contributions or penalties.

Right to education

Article 2

No person shall be denied the right to education. In the exercise of any functions which it assumes in relation to education and to teaching, the State shall respect the right of parents to ensure such education and teaching in conformity with their own religious and philosophical convictions.

Right to free elections

Article 3

The High Contracting Parties undertake to hold free elections at reasonable intervals by secret ballot, under conditions which will ensure the free expression of the opinion of the people in the choice of the legislature.

PART III ARTICLE 1 OF THE THIRTEENTH PROTOCOL

Abolition of the death penalty

The death penalty shall be abolished. No one shall be condemned to such penalty or executed.

SCHEDULE 2 REMEDIAL ORDERS

ORDERS

1.—(1) A remedial order may—
    (a) contain such incidental, supplemental, consequential or transitional provision as the person making it considers appropriate;
    (b) be made so as to have effect from a date earlier than that on which it is made;
    (c) make provision for the delegation of specific functions;
    (d) make different provision for different cases.
  (2) The power conferred by sub-paragraph (1)(a) includes—

(a) power to amend primary legislation (including primary legislation other than that which contains the incompatible provision); and

(b) power to amend or revoke subordinate legislation (including subordinate legislation other than that which contains the incompatible provision).

(3) A remedial order may be made so as to have the same extent as the legislation which it affects.

(4) No person is to be guilty of an offence solely as a result of the retrospective effect of a remedial order.

Procedure

2. No remedial order may be made unless—

(a) a draft of the order has been approved by a resolution of each House of Parliament made after the end of the period of 60 days beginning with the day on which the draft was laid; or

(b) it is declared in the order that it appears to the person making it that, because of the urgency of the matter, it is necessary to make the order without a draft being so approved.

Orders Laid in draft

3.—(1) No draft may be laid under paragraph 2(a) unless—

(a) the person proposing to make the order has laid before Parliament a document which contains a draft of the proposed order and the required information; and

(b) the period of 60 days, beginning with the day on which the document required by this sub-paragraph was laid, has ended.

(2) If representations have been made during that period, the draft laid under paragraph 2(a) must be accompanied by a statement containing—

(a) a summary of the representations; and

(b) if, as a result of the representations, the proposed order has been changed, details of the changes.

Urgent cases

4.—(1) If a remedial order ("the original order") is made without being approved in draft, the person making it must lay it before Parliament, accompanied by the required information, after it is made.

(2) If representations have been made during the period of 60 days beginning with the day on which the original order was made, the person making it must (after the end of that period) lay before Parliament a statement containing—

(a) a summary of the representations; and

(b) if, as a result of the representations, he considers it appropriate to make changes to the original order, details of the changes.

(3) If sub-paragraph (2)(b) applies, the person making the statement must—

(a) make a further remedial order replacing the original order; and

(b) lay the replacement order before Parliament.

(4) If, at the end of the period of 120 days beginning with the day on which the original order, was made, a resolution has not been passed by each House approving

the original or replacement order, the order ceases to have effect (but without that affecting anything previously done under either order or the power to make a fresh remedial order).

DEFINITIONS

5. In this Schedule—

"representations" means representations about a remedial order (or proposed remedial order) made to the person making (or proposing to make) it and includes any relevant Parliamentary report or resolution; and

"required information" means—

(a) an explanation of the incompatibility which the order (or proposed order) seeks to remove, including particulars of the relevant declaration, finding or order; and

(b) a statement of the reasons for proceeding under section 10 and for making an order in those terms.

CALCULATING PERIODS

6. In calculating any period for the purposes of this Schedule, no account is to be taken of any time during which—

(a) Parliament is dissolved or prorogued; or

(b) both Houses are adjourned for more than four days.

CALCULATING PERIODS

7.—(1) This paragraph applies in relation to—

(a) any remedial order made, and any draft of such an order proposed to be made,—

(i) by the Scottish Ministers; or

(ii) within devolved competence (within the meaning of the Scotland Act 1998) by Her Majesty in Council; and

(b) any document or statement to be laid in connection with such an order (or proposed order).

(2) This Schedule has effect in relation to any such order (or proposed order), document or statement subject to the following modifications.

(3) Any reference to Parliament, each House of Parliament or both Houses of Parliament shall be construed as a reference to the Scottish Parliament.

(4) Paragraph 6 does not apply and instead, in calculating any period for the purposes of this Schedule, no account is to be taken of any time during which the Scottish Parliament is dissolved or is in recess for more than four days.

SCHEDULE 3 DEROGATION AND RESERVATION

PART I DEROGATION

Repealed on: **April 8, 2005**

[. . .]

Part II RESERVATION

At the time of signing the present (First) Protocol, I declare that, in view of certain provisions of the Education Acts in the United Kingdom, the principle affirmed in the second sentence of Article 2 is accepted by the United Kingdom only so far as it is compatible with the provision of efficient instruction and training, and the avoidance of unreasonable public expenditure.

Dated 20 March 1952. Made by the United Kingdom Permanent Representative to the Council of Europe.

Schedule 4 JUDICIAL PENSIONS

Duty to make orders about pensions

1.—(1) The appropriate Minister must by order make provision with respect to pensions payable to or in respect of any holder of a judicial office who serves as an ECHR judge.

(2) A pensions order must include such provision as the Minister making it considers is necessary to secure that—

  (a) an ECHR judge who was, immediately before his appointment as an ECHR judge, a member of a judicial pension scheme is entitled to remain as a member of that scheme;

  (b) the terms on which he remains a member of the scheme are those which would have been applicable had he not been appointed as an ECHR judge; and

  (c) entitlement to benefits payable in accordance with the scheme continues to be determined as if, while serving as an ECHR judge, his salary was that which would (but for section 18(4)) have been payable to him in respect of his continuing service as the holder of his judicial office.

Contributions

2. A pensions order may, in particular, make provision—

  (a) for any contributions which are payable by a person who remains a member of a scheme as a result of the order, and which would otherwise be payable by deduction from his salary, to be made otherwise than by deduction from his salary as an ECHR judge; and

  (b) for such contributions to be collected in such manner as may be determined by the administrators of the scheme.

Amendments of other enactments

3. A pensions order may amend any provision of, or made under, a pensions Act in such manner and to such extent as the Minister making the order considers necessary or expedient to ensure the proper administration of any scheme to which it relates.

Definitions

4. In this Schedule—
"appropriate Minister" means—

(a) in relation to any judicial office whose jurisdiction is exercisable exclusively in relation to Scotland, the Secretary of State; and

(b) otherwise, the Lord Chancellor;

"ECHR judge" means the holder of a judicial office who is serving as a judge of the Court;

"judicial pension scheme" means a scheme established by and in accordance with a pensions Act;

"pensions Act" means—

(a) the County Courts Act (Northern Ireland) 1959;

(b) the Sheriffs' Pensions (Scotland) Act 1961;

(c) the Judicial Pensions Act 1981; or

(d) the Judicial Pensions and Retirement Act 1993; and

"pensions order" means an order made under paragraph 1.

A2.27

Electronic Commerce (EC Directive) Regulations 2002

[SI 2002/2013]

Mere conduit

17.—(1) Where an information society service is provided which consists of the transmission in a communication network of information provided by a recipient of the service or the provision of access to a communication network, the service provider (if he otherwise would) shall not be liable for damages or for any other pecuniary remedy or for any criminal sanction as a result of that transmission where the service provider—

(a) did not initiate the transmission;

(b) did not select the receiver of the transmission; and

(c) did not select or modify the information contained in the transmission.

(2) The acts of transmission and of provision of access referred to in paragraph (1) include the automatic, intermediate and transient storage of the information transmitted where—

(a) this takes place for the sole purpose of carrying out the transmission in the communication network, and

(b) the information is not stored for any period longer than is reasonably necessary for the transmission.

Caching

18. Where an information society service is provided which consists of the transmission in a communication network of information provided by a recipient of the service, the service provider (if he otherwise would) shall not be liable for damages or for any other pecuniary remedy or for any criminal sanction as a result of that transmission where—

(a) the information is the subject of automatic, intermediate and temporary storage where that storage is for the sole purpose of making more efficient onward transmission of the information to other recipients of the service upon their request, and

(b) the service provider—

(i) does not modify the information;

(ii) complies with conditions on access to the information;

(iii) complies with any rules regarding the updating of the information, specified in a manner widely recognised and used by industry;

(iv) does not interfere with the lawful use of technology, widely recognised and used by industry, to obtain data on the use of the information; and

(v) acts expeditiously to remove or to disable access to the information he has stored upon obtaining actual knowledge of the fact that the information at the initial source of the transmission has been removed from the network, or access to it has been disabled, or that a court or an administrative authority has ordered such removal or disablement.

Hosting

19. Where an information society service is provided which consists of the storage of information provided by a recipient of the service, the service provider (if he otherwise would) shall not be liable for damages or for any other pecuniary remedy or for any criminal sanction as a result of that storage where—

(a) the service provider—
  (i) does not have actual knowledge of unlawful activity or information and, where a claim for damages is made, is not aware of facts or circumstances from which it would have been apparent to the service provider that the activity or information was unlawful; or
  (ii) upon obtaining such knowledge or awareness, acts expeditiously to remove or to disable access to the information, and
(b) the recipient of the service was not acting under the authority or the control of the service provider.

Protection of rights

20.—(1) Nothing in regulations 17, 18 and 19 shall—
(a) prevent a person agreeing different contractual terms; or
(b) affect the rights of any party to apply to a court for relief to prevent or stop infringement of any rights.

(2) Any power of an administrative authority to prevent or stop infringement of any rights shall continue to apply notwithstanding regulations 17, 18 and 19.

Notice for the purposes of actual knowledge

22. In determining whether a service provider has actual knowledge for the purposes of regulations 18(b)(v) and 19(a)(i), a court shall take into account all matters which appear to it in the particular circumstances to be relevant and, among other things, shall have regard to—

(a) whether a service provider has received a notice through a means of contact made available in accordance with regulation 6(1)(c), and
(b) the extent to which any notice includes—
  (i) the full name and address of the sender of the notice;
  (ii) details of the location of the information in question; and
  (iii) details of the unlawful nature of the activity or information in question.

Crime and Courts Act 2013   A2.28

[2013 c. 22]

Publishers of news-related material: damages and costs

34 Awards of exemplary damages

(1) This section applies where—
(a) a relevant claim is made against a person ("the defendant"),

    (b) the defendant was a relevant publisher at the material time,

    (c) the claim is related to the publication of news-related material, and

    (d) the defendant is found liable in respect of the claim.

(2) Exemplary damages may not be awarded against the defendant in respect of the claim if the defendant was a member of an approved regulator at the material time.

(3) But the court may disregard subsection (2) if—

    (a) the approved regulator imposed a penalty on the defendant in respect of the defendant's conduct or decided not to do so,

    (b) the court considers, in light of the information available to the approved regulator when imposing the penalty or deciding not to impose one, that the regulator was manifestly irrational in imposing the penalty or deciding not to impose one, and

    (c) the court is satisfied that, but for subsection (2), it would have made an award of exemplary damages under this section against the defendant.

(4) Where the court is not prevented from making an award of exemplary damages by subsection (2) (whether because that subsection does not apply or the court is permitted to disregard that subsection as a result of subsection (3)), the court—

    (a) may make an award of exemplary damages if it considers it appropriate to do so in all the circumstances of the case, but

    (b) may do so only under this section.

(5) Exemplary damages may be awarded under this section only if they are claimed.

(6) Exemplary damages may be awarded under this section only if the court is satisfied that—

    (a) the defendant's conduct has shown a deliberate or reckless disregard of an outrageous nature for the claimant's rights,

    (b) the conduct is such that the court should punish the defendant for it, and

    (c) other remedies would not be adequate to punish that conduct.

(7) Exemplary damages may be awarded under this section whether or not another remedy is granted.

(8) The decision on the question of—

    (a) whether exemplary damages are to be awarded under this section, or

    (b) the amount of such damages,

must not be left to a jury.

35 Relevant considerations

(1) This section applies where the court is deciding whether the circumstances of the case make it appropriate for exemplary damages to be awarded under section 34.

(2) The court must have regard to the principle that exemplary damages must not usually be awarded if, at any time before the decision comes to be made, the defendant has been convicted of an offence involving the conduct complained of.

(3) The court must take account of the following—

    (a) whether membership of an approved regulator was available to the defendant at the material time;

    (b) if such membership was available, the reasons for the defendant not being a member;

    (c) so far as relevant in the case of the conduct complained of, whether internal compliance procedures of a satisfactory nature were in place and, if so, the extent to which they were adhered to in that case.

(4) The reference in subsection (3)(c) to "internal compliance procedures" being in place is a reference to any procedures put in place by the defendant for the purpose of ensuring that—

    (a) material is not obtained by or on behalf of the defendant in an inappropriate way, and

    (b) material is not published by the defendant in inappropriate circumstances.

(5) The court may regard deterring the defendant and others from similar conduct as an object of punishment.

(6) This section is not to be read as limiting the power of the court to take account of any other matters it considers relevant to its decision.

36 Amount of exemplary damages

(1) This section applies where the court decides to award exemplary damages under section 34.

(2) The court must have regard to these principles in determining the amount of exemplary damages—

    (a) the amount must not be more than the minimum needed to punish the defendant for the conduct complained of;

    (b) the amount must be proportionate to the seriousness of the conduct.

(3) The court must take account of these matters in determining the amount of exemplary damages—

    (a) the nature and extent of any loss or harm caused, or intended to be caused, by the defendant's conduct;

    (b) the nature and extent of any benefit the defendant derived or intended to derive from such conduct.

(4) The court may regard deterring the defendant and others from similar conduct as an object of punishment.

(5) This section is not to be read as limiting the power of the court to take account of any other matters it considers relevant to its decision.

37 Multiple claimants

(1) This section applies where a relevant publisher—

    (a) is a defendant to a relevant claim, and

    (b) is found liable to two or more persons in respect of the claim ("the persons affected").

(2) In deciding whether to award exemplary damages under section 34 or the amount of such damages to award (whether to one or more of the persons affected), the court must take account of any settlement or compromise by any persons of a claim in respect of the conduct.

(3) But the court may take account of any such settlement or compromise only if the defendant agrees.

(4) If the court awards exemplary damages under section 34 to two or more of the persons affected, the total amount awarded must be such that it does not punish the defendant excessively.

(5) If the court awards exemplary damages under section 34 to one or more of the persons affected, no later claim may be made for exemplary damages as regards the conduct.

38 Multiple defendants

(1) Any liability of two or more persons for exemplary damages awarded under section 34 is several (and not joint or joint and several).

(2) Subsection (1) has effect subject to the law relating to the liability of a partner for the conduct of another partner.

(3) Where the liability of two or more persons for exemplary damages is several, no contribution in respect of the damages may be recovered by any of them under section 1 of the Civil Liability (Contribution) Act 1978.

39 Awards of aggravated damages

(1) This section applies where—
    (a) a relevant claim is made against a person ("the defendant"),
    (b) the defendant was a relevant publisher at the material time,
    (c) the claim is related to the publication of news-related material, and
    (d) the defendant is found liable in respect of the claim.

(2) Aggravated damages may be awarded against the defendant only to compensate for mental distress and not for purposes of punishment.

(3) In this section, "aggravated damages" means damages that were commonly called aggravated before the passing of this Act and which—
    (a) are awarded against a person in respect of the person's motive or exceptional conduct, but
    (b) are not exemplary damages or restitutionary damages.

(4) Nothing in this section is to be read as implying that, in cases where this section does not apply, aggravated damages may be awarded for purposes of punishment.

40 Awards of costs

(1) This section applies where—
    (a) a relevant claim is made against a person ("the defendant"),
    (b) the defendant was a relevant publisher at the material time, and
    (c) the claim is related to the publication of news-related material.

(2) If the defendant was a member of an approved regulator at the time when the claim was commenced (or was unable to be a member at that time for reasons beyond the defendant's control or it would have been unreasonable in the circumstances for the defendant to have been a member at that time), the court must not award costs against the defendant unless satisfied that—
    (a) the issues raised by the claim could not have been resolved by using an arbitration scheme of the approved regulator, or
    (b) it is just and equitable in all the circumstances of the case to award costs against the defendant.

(3) If the defendant was not a member of an approved regulator at the time when the claim was commenced (but would have been able to be a member at that time and it would have been reasonable in the circumstances for the defendant to have been a member at that time), the court must award costs against the defendant unless satisfied that—
    (a) the issues raised by the claim could not have been resolved by using an arbitration scheme of the approved regulator (had the defendant been a member), or
    (b) it is just and equitable in all the circumstances of the case to make a different award of costs or make no award of costs.

(4) The Secretary of State must take steps to put in place arrangements for protecting the position in costs of parties to relevant claims who have entered into agreements under section 58 of the Courts and Legal Services Act 1990.

(5) This section is not to be read as limiting any power to make rules of court.

(6) This section does not apply until such time as a body is first recognised as an approved regulator.

41 Meaning of "relevant publisher"

(1) In sections 34 to 40, "relevant publisher" means a person who, in the course of a business (whether or not carried on with a view to profit), publishes news-related material—

    (a) which is written by different authors, and

    (b) which is to any extent subject to editorial control.

This is subject to subsections (5) and (6).

(2) News-related material is "subject to editorial control" if there is a person (whether or not the publisher of the material) who has editorial or equivalent responsibility for—

    (a) the content of the material,

    (b) how the material is to be presented, and

    (c) the decision to publish it.

(3) A person who is the operator of a website is not to be taken as having editorial or equivalent responsibility for the decision to publish any material on the site, or for content of the material, if the person did not post the material on the site.

(4) The fact that the operator of the website may moderate statements posted on it by others does not matter for the purposes of subsection (3).

(5) A person is not a "relevant publisher" if the person is specified by name in Schedule 15.

(6) A person is not a "relevant publisher" in so far as the person's publication of news-related material is in a capacity or case of a description specified in Schedule 15.

(7) But a person who is not a "relevant publisher" as a result of paragraph 8 of that Schedule (micro-businesses) is nevertheless to be regarded as such if the person was a member of an approved regulator at the material time.

42 Other interpretative provisions

(1) This section applies for the purposes of sections 34 to 41.

(2) "Approved regulator" means a body recognised as a regulator of relevant publishers.

(3) For the purposes of subsection (2), a body is "recognised" as a regulator of relevant publishers if it is so recognised by any body established by Royal Charter (whether established before or after the coming into force of this section) with the purpose of carrying on activities relating to the recognition of independent regulators of relevant publishers.

(4) "Relevant claim" means a civil claim made in respect of any of the following—

    (a) libel;

    (b) slander;

    (c) breach of confidence;

    (d) misuse of private information;

    (e) malicious falsehood;

    (f) harassment.

(5) For the purposes of subsection (4)—

    (a) the reference to a claim made in respect of the misuse of private information does not include a reference to a claim made by virtue of section 13 of the Data Protection Act 1998 (damage or distress suffered as a result of a contravention of a requirement of that Act);

    (b) the reference to a claim made in respect of harassment is a reference to a claim made under the Protection from Harassment Act 1997.

(6) The "material time", in relation to a relevant claim, is the time of the events giving rise to the claim.

(7) "News-related material" means—
   (a) news or information about current affairs,
   (b) opinion about matters relating to the news or current affairs, or
   (c) gossip about celebrities, other public figures or other persons in the news.

(8) A relevant claim is related to the publication of news-related material if the claim results from—
   (a) the publication of news-related material, or
   (b) activities carried on in connection with the publication of such material (whether or not the material is in fact published).

(9) A reference to the "publication" of material is a reference to publication—
   (a) on a website,
   (b) in hard copy, or
   (c) by any other means;

and references to a person who "publishes" material are to be read accordingly.

(10) A reference to "conduct" includes a reference to omissions; and a reference to a person's conduct includes a reference to a person's conduct after the events giving rise to the claim concerned.

   . . .

61 Short title, commencement and extent

(1) This Act may be cited as the Crime and Courts Act 2013.

(2) Subject as follows, this Act comes into force on such day as the Secretary of State may by order appoint; and different days may be appointed for different purposes . . .

   . . .

(7) Sections 34 to 39 come into force at the end of the period of one year beginning with the day on which a body is established by Royal Charter with the purpose of carrying on activities relating to the recognition of independent regulators of relevant publishers (as defined by section 41).

   . . .

(12) Subject as follows, this Act extends to England and Wales, Scotland and Northern Ireland.

(13) The following extend to England and Wales only—

   . . .

   (d) sections 34 to 42 . . .

   . . .

SCHEDULE 15

Section 41

EXCLUSIONS FROM DEFINITION OF "RELEVANT PUBLISHER"

Broadcasters

1 The British Broadcasting Corporation.
2 Sianel Pedwar Cymru.
3 The holder of a licence under the Broadcasting Act 1990 or 1996 who publishes news-related material in connection with the broadcasting activities authorised under the licence.

Special interest titles

4 A person who publishes a title that—
- (a) relates to a particular pastime, hobby, trade, business, industry or profession, and
- (b) only contains news-related material on an incidental basis that is relevant to the main content of the title.

Scientific or academic journals

5 A person who publishes a scientific or academic journal that only contains news-related material on an incidental basis that is relevant to the scientific or academic content.

Public bodies and charities

6 (1) A public body or charity that publishes news-related material in connection with the carrying out of its functions.

(2) "Public body" means a person or body whose functions are of a public nature.

Company news publications etc.

7 A person who publishes a newsletter, circular or other document which—
- (a) relates to a business carried on by the person, and
- (b) only contains news-related material on an incidental basis that is relevant to the person's business.

Micro-businesses

8 (1) A person who, in carrying on a micro-business, publishes news-related material where either condition A or condition B is met.

(2) Condition A is that the news-related material is contained in a multi-author blog.

(3) Condition B is that the news-related material is published on an incidental basis that is relevant to the main activities of the business.

(4) "Micro-business" means a business which—
- (a) has fewer than 10 employees, and
- (b) has an annual turnover not exceeding £2,000,000.

(5) The number of employees is to be calculated as follows—
- (a) find the total number of hours per week for which all the employees of the business are contracted to work;
- (b) divide that number by 37.5.

(6) "Employee" has the same meaning as in the Employment Rights Act 1996 (see section 230 of that Act).

(7) "Multi-author blog" means a blog that contains contributions from different authors.

Book publishers

9 (1) A person who is the publisher of a book.

(2) "Book" does not include any title published on a periodic basis with substantially different content.

Crime and Courts Act 2013
EXPLANATORY NOTES

. . .

Sections 34 to 42: Publishers of news-related material: damages and costs

56. On 29th November 2012 *the Report of An Inquiry into the Culture, Practices and Ethics of the Press* was presented to Parliament (HC 780) ("the Leveson Report"). In the report, the Rt. Hon. Lord Justice Leveson makes a range of recommendations to reform the regulatory framework for the press, creating a new framework for press regulation, with the principle of industry self-regulation at its heart. The new framework proposed is for a system of voluntary self-regulation, overseen by a recognition body established by Royal Charter and strengthened by a series of incentives for members of the press in the application of costs and exemplary damages, encouraging them to join a recognised regulator. Sections 34 to 42 and Schedule 15 set out the new system for exemplary damages and costs, as well as defining those who meet the definition of a 'relevant publisher' to whom the new system of exemplary damages will apply.

A2.29   **Defamation Act 2013**

[2013 c. 26]

CONTENTS

Requirement of serious harm

Summary of court judgment

12. Power of court to order a summary of its judgment to be published

Removal, etc. of statements

13. Order to remove statement or cease distribution etc.

Slander

14. Special damage

General provisions

15. Meaning of "publish" and "statement"
16. Consequential amendments and savings etc.
17. Short title, extent and commencement

An Act to amend the law of defamation.

[25th April 2013]

BE IT ENACTED by the Queen's most Excellent Majesty, by and with the advice and consent of the Lords Spiritual and Temporal, and Commons, in this present Parliament assembled, and by the authority of the same, as follows:—

Requirement of serious harm

1. Serious harm

(1) A statement is not defamatory unless its publication has caused or is likely to cause serious harm to the reputation of the claimant.

(2) For the purposes of this section, harm to the reputation of a body that trades for profit is not "serious harm" unless it has caused or is likely to cause the body serious financial loss.

Defences

2. Truth

(1) It is a defence to an action for defamation for the defendant to show that the imputation conveyed by the statement complained of is substantially true.

(2) Subsection (3) applies in an action for defamation if the statement complained of conveys two or more distinct imputations.

(3) If one or more of the imputations is not shown to be substantially true, the defence under this section does not fail if, having regard to the imputations which are shown to be substantially true, the imputations which are not shown to be substantially true do not seriously harm the claimant's reputation.

(4) The common law defence of justification is abolished and, accordingly, section 5 of the Defamation Act 1952 (justification) is repealed.

3. Honest opinion

(1) It is a defence to an action for defamation for the defendant to show that the following conditions are met.

(2) The first condition is that the statement complained of was a statement of opinion.

(3) The second condition is that the statement complained of indicated, whether in general or specific terms, the basis of the opinion.

(4) The third condition is that an honest person could have held the opinion on the basis of—

    (a) any fact which existed at the time the statement complained of was published;

    (b) anything asserted to be a fact in a privileged statement published before the statement complained of.

(5) The defence is defeated if the claimant shows that the defendant did not hold the opinion.

(6) Subsection (5) does not apply in a case where the statement complained of was published by the defendant but made by another person ("the author"); and in such a case the defence is defeated if the claimant shows that the defendant knew or ought to have known that the author did not hold the opinion.

(7) For the purposes of subsection (4)(b) a statement is a "privileged statement" if the person responsible for its publication would have one or more of the following defences if an action for defamation were brought in respect of it—

    (a) a defence under section 4 (publication on matter of public interest);

    (b) a defence under section 6 (peer-reviewed statement in scientific or academic journal);

    (c) a defence under section 14 of the Defamation Act 1996 (reports of court proceedings protected by absolute privilege);

    (d) a defence under section 15 of that Act (other reports protected by qualified privilege).

(8) The common law defence of fair comment is abolished and, accordingly, section 6 of the Defamation Act 1952 (fair comment) is repealed.

4. Publication on matter of public interest

(1) It is a defence to an action for defamation for the defendant to show that—

    (a) the statement complained of was, or formed part of, a statement on a matter of public interest; and

    (b) the defendant reasonably believed that publishing the statement complained of was in the public interest.

(2) Subject to subsections (3) and (4), in determining whether the defendant has shown the matters mentioned in subsection (1), the court must have regard to all the circumstances of the case.

(3) If the statement complained of was, or formed part of, an accurate and impartial account of a dispute to which the claimant was a party, the court must in determining whether it was reasonable for the defendant to believe that publishing the statement was in the public interest disregard any omission of the defendant to take steps to verify the truth of the imputation conveyed by it.

(4) In determining whether it was reasonable for the defendant to believe that publishing the statement complained of was in the public interest, the court must make such allowance for editorial judgement as it considers appropriate.

(5) For the avoidance of doubt, the defence under this section may be relied upon irrespective of whether the statement complained of is a statement of fact or a statement of opinion.

(6) The common law defence known as the Reynolds defence is abolished.

5. Operators of websites

(1) This section applies where an action for defamation is brought against the operator of a website in respect of a statement posted on the website.

(2) It is a defence for the operator to show that it was not the operator who posted the statement on the website.

(3) The defence is defeated if the claimant shows that—

    (a) it was not possible for the claimant to identify the person who posted the statement,

(b) the claimant gave the operator a notice of complaint in relation to the statement, and

(c) the operator failed to respond to the notice of complaint in accordance with any provision contained in regulations.

(4) For the purposes of subsection (3)(a), it is possible for a claimant to "identify" a person only if the claimant has sufficient information to bring proceedings against the person.

(5) Regulations may—

(a) make provision as to the action required to be taken by an operator of a website in response to a notice of complaint (which may in particular include action relating to the identity or contact details of the person who posted the statement and action relating to its removal);

(b) make provision specifying a time limit for the taking of any such action;

(c) make provision conferring on the court a discretion to treat action taken after the expiry of a time limit as having been taken before the expiry;

(d) make any other provision for the purposes of this section.

(6) Subject to any provision made by virtue of subsection (7), a notice of complaint is a notice which—

(a) specifies the complainant's name,

(b) sets out the statement concerned and explains why it is defamatory of the complainant,

(c) specifies where on the website the statement was posted, and

(d) contains such other information as may be specified in regulations.

(7) Regulations may make provision about the circumstances in which a notice which is not a notice of complaint is to be treated as a notice of complaint for the purposes of this section or any provision made under it.

(8) Regulations under this section—

(a) may make different provision for different circumstances;

(b) are to be made by statutory instrument.

(9) A statutory instrument containing regulations under this section may not be made unless a draft of the instrument has been laid before, and approved by a resolution of, each House of Parliament.

(10) In this section "regulations" means regulations made by the Secretary of State.

(11) The defence under this section is defeated if the claimant shows that the operator of the website has acted with malice in relation to the posting of the statement concerned.

(12) The defence under this section is not defeated by reason only of the fact that the operator of the website moderates the statements posted on it by others.

6. Peer-reviewed statement in scientific or academic journal etc.

(1) The publication of a statement in a scientific or academic journal (whether published in electronic form or otherwise) is privileged if the following conditions are met.

(2) The first condition is that the statement relates to a scientific or academic matter.

(3) The second condition is that before the statement was published in the journal an independent review of the statement's scientific or academic merit was carried out by—

(a) the editor of the journal, and

(b) one or more persons with expertise in the scientific or academic matter concerned.

(4) Where the publication of a statement in a scientific or academic journal is privileged by virtue of subsection (1), the publication in the same journal of any assessment of the statement's scientific or academic merit is also privileged if—

    (a) the assessment was written by one or more of the persons who carried out the independent review of the statement; and

    (b) the assessment was written in the course of that review.

(5) Where the publication of a statement or assessment is privileged by virtue of this section, the publication of a fair and accurate copy of, extract from or summary of the statement or assessment is also privileged.

(6) A publication is not privileged by virtue of this section if it is shown to be made with malice.

(7) Nothing in this section is to be construed—

    (a) as protecting the publication of matter the publication of which is prohibited by law;

    (b) as limiting any privilege subsisting apart from this section.

(8) The reference in subsection (3)(a) to "the editor of the journal" is to be read, in the case of a journal with more than one editor, as a reference to the editor or editors who were responsible for deciding to publish the statement concerned.

7. Reports etc. protected by privilege

(1) For subsection (3) of section 14 of the Defamation Act 1996 (reports of court proceedings absolutely privileged) substitute—

"(3) This section applies to—

    (a) any court in the United Kingdom;

    (b) any court established under the law of a country or territory outside the United Kingdom;

    (c) any international court or tribunal established by the Security Council of the United Nations or by an international agreement;

and in paragraphs (a) and (b) "court" includes any tribunal or body exercising the judicial power of the State."

(2) In subsection (3) of section 15 of that Act (qualified privilege) for "public concern" substitute "public interest".

(3) Schedule 1 to that Act (qualified privilege) is amended as follows.

(4) For paragraphs 9 and 10 substitute—

"9 (1) A fair and accurate copy of, extract from or summary of a notice or other matter issued for the information of the public by or on behalf of—

    (a) a legislature or government anywhere in the world;

    (b) an authority anywhere in the world performing governmental functions;

    (c) an international organisation or international conference.

(2) In this paragraph "governmental functions" includes police functions.

10. A fair and accurate copy of, extract from or summary of a document made available by a court anywhere in the world, or by a judge or officer of such a court."

(5) After paragraph 11 insert—

"11A A fair and accurate report of proceedings at a press conference held anywhere in the world for the discussion of a matter of public interest."

(6) In paragraph 12 (report of proceedings at public meetings)—

    (a) in sub-paragraph (1) for "in a member State" substitute "anywhere in the world";

    (b) in sub-paragraph (2) for "public concern" substitute "public interest".

(7) In paragraph 13 (report of proceedings at meetings of public company)—

(a) in sub-paragraph (1), for "UK public company" substitute "listed company";

(b) for sub-paragraphs (2) to (5) substitute—

"(2) A fair and accurate copy of, extract from or summary of any document circulated to members of a listed company—

(a) by or with the authority of the board of directors of the company,

(b) by the auditors of the company, or

(c) by any member of the company in pursuance of a right conferred by any statutory provision.

(3) A fair and accurate copy of, extract from or summary of any document circulated to members of a listed company which relates to the appointment, resignation, retirement or dismissal of directors of the company or its auditors.

(4) In this paragraph "listed company" has the same meaning as in Part 12 of the Corporation Tax Act 2009 (see section 1005 of that Act)."

(8) In paragraph 14 (report of finding or decision of certain kinds of associations) in the words before paragraph (a), for "in the United Kingdom or another member State" substitute "anywhere in the world".

(9) After paragraph 14 insert—

"14A A fair and accurate—

(a) report of proceedings of a scientific or academic conference held anywhere in the world, or

(b) copy of, extract from or summary of matter published by such a conference."

(10) For paragraph 15 (report of statements etc. by a person designated by the Lord Chancellor for the purposes of the paragraph) substitute—

"15 (1) A fair and accurate report or summary of, copy of or extract from, any adjudication, report, statement or notice issued by a body, officer or other person designated for the purposes of this paragraph by order of the Lord Chancellor.

(2) An order under this paragraph shall be made by statutory instrument which shall be subject to annulment in pursuance of a resolution of either House of Parliament."

(11) For paragraphs 16 and 17 (general provision) substitute—

"16 In this Schedule—

"court" includes—

(a) any tribunal or body established under the law of any country or territory exercising the judicial power of the State;

(b) any international tribunal established by the Security Council of the United Nations or by an international agreement;

(c) any international tribunal deciding matters in dispute between States;

"international conference" means a conference attended by representatives of two or more governments;

"international organisation" means an organisation of which two or more governments are members, and includes any committee or other subordinate body of such an organisation;

"legislature" includes a local legislature; and

"member State" includes any European dependent territory of a member State."

8. Single publication rule

(1) This section applies if a person—

(a) publishes a statement to the public ("the first publication"), and

(b) subsequently publishes (whether or not to the public) that statement or a statement which is substantially the same.

(2) In subsection (1) "publication to the public" includes publication to a section of the public.

(3) For the purposes of section 4A of the Limitation Act 1980 (time limit for actions for defamation etc.) any cause of action against the person for defamation in respect of the subsequent publication is to be treated as having accrued on the date of the first publication.

(4) This section does not apply in relation to the subsequent publication if the manner of that publication is materially different from the manner of the first publication.

(5) In determining whether the manner of a subsequent publication is materially different from the manner of the first publication, the matters to which the court may have regard include (amongst other matters)—

    (a) the level of prominence that a statement is given;

    (b) the extent of the subsequent publication.

(6) Where this section applies—

    (a) it does not affect the court's discretion under section 32A of the Limitation Act 1980 (discretionary exclusion of time limit for actions for defamation etc.), and

    (b) the reference in subsection (1)(a) of that section to the operation of section 4A of that Act is a reference to the operation of section 4A together with this section.

Jurisdiction

9. Action against a person not domiciled in the UK or a Member State etc.

(1) This section applies to an action for defamation against a person who is not domiciled—

    (a) in the United Kingdom;

    (b) in another Member State; or

    (c) in a state which is for the time being a contracting party to the Lugano Convention.

(2) A court does not have jurisdiction to hear and determine an action to which this section applies unless the court is satisfied that, of all the places in which the statement complained of has been published, England and Wales is clearly the most appropriate place in which to bring an action in respect of the statement.

(3) The references in subsection (2) to the statement complained of include references to any statement which conveys the same, or substantially the same, imputation as the statement complained of.

(4) For the purposes of this section—

    (a) a person is domiciled in the United Kingdom or in another Member State if the person is domiciled there for the purposes of the Brussels Regulation;

    (b) a person is domiciled in a state which is a contracting party to the Lugano Convention if the person is domiciled in the state for the purposes of that Convention.

(5) In this section—

"the Brussels Regulation" means Council Regulation (EC) No 44/2001 of 22nd December 2000 on jurisdiction and the recognition and enforcement of judgments in civil and commercial matters, as amended from time to time and as applied by the Agreement made on 19th October 2005 between the European

Community and the Kingdom of Denmark on jurisdiction and the recognition and enforcement of judgments in civil and commercial matters (OJ No L299 16.11.2005 at p.62);

"the Lugano Convention" means the Convention on jurisdiction and the recognition and enforcement of judgments in civil and commercial matters, between the European Community and the Republic of Iceland, the Kingdom of Norway, the Swiss Confederation and the Kingdom of Denmark signed on behalf of the European Community on 30th October 2007.

10. Action against a person who was not the author, editor etc.

(1) A court does not have jurisdiction to hear and determine an action for defamation brought against a person who was not the author, editor or publisher of the statement complained of unless the court is satisfied that it is not reasonably practicable for an action to be brought against the author, editor or publisher.

(2) In this section "author", "editor" and "publisher" have the same meaning as in section 1 of the Defamation Act 1996.

Trial by jury

11. Trial to be without a jury unless the court orders otherwise

(1) In section 69(1) of the Senior Courts Act 1981 (certain actions in the Queen's Bench Division to be tried with a jury unless the trial requires prolonged examination of documents etc.) in paragraph (b) omit "libel, slander,".

(2) In section 66(3) of the County Courts Act 1984 (certain actions in the county court to be tried with a jury unless the trial requires prolonged examination of documents etc.) in paragraph (b) omit "libel, slander,".

Summary of court judgment

12. Power of court to order a summary of its judgment to be published

(1) Where a court gives judgment for the claimant in an action for defamation the court may order the defendant to publish a summary of the judgment.

(2) The wording of any summary and the time, manner, form and place of its publication are to be for the parties to agree.

(3) If the parties cannot agree on the wording, the wording is to be settled by the court.

(4) If the parties cannot agree on the time, manner, form or place of publication, the court may give such directions as to those matters as it considers reasonable and practicable in the circumstances.

(5) This section does not apply where the court gives judgment for the claimant under section 8(3) of the Defamation Act 1996 (summary disposal of claims).

Removal, etc. of statements

13. Order to remove statement or cease distribution etc.

(1) Where a court gives judgment for the claimant in an action for defamation the court may order—

    (a) the operator of a website on which the defamatory statement is posted to remove the statement, or

(b) any person who was not the author, editor or publisher of the defamatory statement to stop distributing, selling or exhibiting material containing the statement.

(2) In this section "author", "editor" and "publisher" have the same meaning as in section 1 of the Defamation Act 1996.

(3) Subsection (1) does not affect the power of the court apart from that subsection.

Slander

14. Special damage

(1) The Slander of Women Act 1891 is repealed.

(2) The publication of a statement that conveys the imputation that a person has a contagious or infectious disease does not give rise to a cause of action for slander unless the publication causes the person special damage.

General provisions

15. Meaning of "publish" and "statement"

In this Act—

"publish" and "publication", in relation to a statement, have the meaning they have for the purposes of the law of defamation generally;

"statement" means words, pictures, visual images, gestures or any other method of signifying meaning.

16. Consequential amendments and savings etc.

(1) Section 8 of the Rehabilitation of Offenders Act 1974 (defamation actions) is amended in accordance with subsections (2) and (3).

(2) In subsection (3) for "of justification or fair comment or" substitute "under section 2 or 3 of the Defamation Act 2013 which is available to him or any defence".

(3) In subsection (5) for "the defence of justification" substitute "a defence under section 2 of the Defamation Act 2013".

(4) Nothing in section 1 or 14 affects any cause of action accrued before the commencement of the section in question.

(5) Nothing in sections 2 to 7 or 10 has effect in relation to an action for defamation if the cause of action accrued before the commencement of the section in question.

(6) In determining whether section 8 applies, no account is to be taken of any publication made before the commencement of the section.

(7) Nothing in section 9 or 11 has effect in relation to an action for defamation begun before the commencement of the section in question.

(8) In determining for the purposes of subsection (7)(a) of section 3 whether a person would have a defence under section 4 to any action for defamation, the operation of subsection (5) of this section is to be ignored.

17. Short title, extent and commencement

(1) This Act may be cited as the Defamation Act 2013.

(2) Subject to subsection (3), this Act extends to England and Wales only.

(3) The following provisions also extend to Scotland—

(a) section 6;

    (b) section 7(9);

    (c) section 15;

    (d) section 16(5) (in so far as it relates to sections 6 and 7(9));

    (e) this section.

(4) Subject to subsections (5) and (6), the provisions of this Act come into force on such day as the Secretary of State may by order made by statutory instrument appoint.

(5) Sections 6 and 7(9) come into force in so far as they extend to Scotland on such day as the Scottish Ministers may by order appoint.

(6) Section 15, subsections (4) to (8) of section 16 and this section come into force on the day on which this Act is passed.

Defamation Act 2013
EXPLANATORY NOTES

Introduction

1. These explanatory notes relate to the Defamation Act 2013, which received Royal Assent on 25 April 2013. They have been prepared by the Ministry of Justice in order to assist the reader in understanding the Act. They do not form part of the Act and have not been endorsed by Parliament.

2. The notes need to be read in conjunction with the Act. They are not, and are not meant to be, a comprehensive description of the Act. So where a section or part of a section does not seem to require any explanation or comment, none is given.

Summary

3. The Defamation Act 2013 reforms aspects of the law of defamation. The civil law on defamation has developed through the common law over a number of years, periodically being supplemented by statute, most recently the Defamation Act 1952 ("the 1952 Act") and the Defamation Act 1996 ("the 1996 Act").

Background

4. The Government's Coalition Agreement gave a commitment to review the law of defamation, and on 9 July 2010 the Government announced its intention to publish a draft Defamation Bill. The *Draft Defamation Bill* (Cm 8020) was published for full public consultation and pre-legislative scrutiny on 15 March 2011.

5. The public consultation closed on 10 June 2011. The Ministry of Justice received 129 responses from a range of interested parties. A comprehensive summary of the responses received was published on 24 November 2011 (*Draft Defamation Bill Summary of Responses to Consultation CP(R) 3/11*). In addition to the Government consultation, pre-legislative scrutiny of the draft Bill was undertaken by a Parliamentary Joint Committee. The committee held oral evidence sessions between April and July 2011 and its final report was published on 19 October 2011 (*The Joint Committee on the Draft Defamation Bill Report* Session 2010–2012, HL 203, HC 930-I).

6. The Government response to the Joint Committee's report was published on 29 February 2012 (*The Government's Response to the Report of the Joint Committee on the Draft Defamation Bill* Cm 8295) and set out the Government's conclusions including on certain matters raised in the public consultation but not specifically addressed in the Committee's report.

Territorial Extent and Application

7. Most of the Act's provisions extend to England and Wales only, but certain provisions also extend to Scotland:

Section 6 relates to the publication of peer-reviewed statements in scientific or academic journals.

Section 7(9) extends qualified privilege to fair and accurate reports of proceedings of a scientific or academic conference.

Section 15 defines the terms "publish" and "statement".

Section 16(5) is a saving provision which relates in part to sections 6 and 7(9).

Section 17 determines the extent and commencement of the Act.

8. In relation to Wales, the Act does not relate to devolved matters or confer functions on the Welsh Ministers.

9. The Act amends a number of enactments which extend to Scotland and Northern Ireland as well as to England and Wales. These amendments, apart from that made by section 7(9) which extends to Scotland, will extend to England and Wales only.

Commentary on Sections

Section 1: Serious harm

10. *Subsection (1)* of this section provides that a statement is not defamatory unless its publication has caused or is likely to cause serious harm to the reputation of the claimant. The provision extends to situations where publication is likely to cause serious harm in order to cover situations where the harm has not yet occurred at the time the action for defamation is commenced.

Subsection (2) indicates that for the purposes of the section, harm to the reputation of a body that trades for profit is not "serious harm" unless it has caused or is likely to cause the body serious financial loss.

11. The section builds on the consideration given by the courts in a series of cases to the question of what is sufficient to establish that a statement is defamatory. A recent example is *Thornton v Telegraph Media Group Ltd*[1] in which a decision of the House of Lords in *Sim v Stretch*[2] was identified as authority for the existence of a "threshold of seriousness" in what is defamatory. There is also currently potential for trivial cases to be struck out on the basis that they are an abuse of process because so little is at stake. In *Jameel v Dow Jones & Co*[3] it was established that there needs to be a real and substantial tort. The section raises the bar for bringing a claim so that only cases involving serious harm to the claimant's reputation can be brought.

12. *Subsection (2)* reflects the fact that bodies trading for profit are already prevented from claiming damages for certain types of harm such as injury to feelings, and are in practice likely to have to show actual or likely financial loss. The requirement that this be serious is consistent with the new serious harm test in *subsection (1)*.

Section 2: Truth

13. This section replaces the common law defence of justification with a new statutory defence of truth. The section is intended broadly to reflect the current law while simplifying and clarifying certain elements.

14. *Subsection (1)* provides for the new defence to apply where the defendant can show that the imputation conveyed by the statement complained of is substantially true. This subsection reflects the current law as established in the case of *Chase v News Group Newspapers Ltd*[4], where the Court of Appeal indicated that in order for the defence of justification to be available "the defendant does not have to prove that every word he or she published was true. He or she has to establish the "essential" or "substantial" truth of the sting of the libel".

15. There is a long-standing common law rule that it is no defence to an action for defamation for the defendant to prove that he or she was only repeating what someone else had said (known as the "repetition rule"). Subsection (1) focuses on the imputation conveyed by the statement in order to incorporate this rule.

16. In any case where the defence of truth is raised, there will be two issues: i) what imputation (or imputations) are actually conveyed by the statement; and ii) whether the imputation (or imputations) conveyed are substantially true. The defence will apply where the imputation is one of fact.

17. *Subsections (2) and (3)* replace section 5 of the 1952 Act (the only significant element of the defence of justification which is currently in statute). Their effect is that where the statement complained of contains two or more distinct imputations, the defence does not fail if, having regard to the imputations which are shown to be substantially true, those which are not shown to be substantially true do not seriously harm the claimant's reputation. These provisions are intended to have the same effect as those in section 5 of the 1952 Act, but are expressed in more modern terminology. The phrase "materially injure" used in the 1952 Act is replaced by "seriously harm" to ensure consistency with the test in section 1 of the Act.

18. *Subsection (4)* abolishes the common law defence of justification and repeals section 5 of the 1952 Act. This means that where a defendant wishes to rely on the new statutory defence the court would be required to apply the words used in the statute, not the current case law. In cases where uncertainty arises the current case law would constitute a helpful but not binding guide to interpreting how the new statutory defence should be applied.

Section 3: Honest opinion

19. This section replaces the common law defence of fair comment[5] with a new defence of honest opinion. The section broadly reflects the current law while simplifying and clarifying certain elements, but does not include the current requirement for the opinion to be on a matter of public interest.

20. *Subsections (1) to (4)* provide for the defence to apply where the defendant can show that three conditions are met. These are condition 1: that the statement complained of was a statement of opinion; condition 2: that the statement complained of indicated, whether in general or specific terms, the basis of the opinion; and condition 3: that an honest person could have held the opinion on the basis of any fact which existed at the time the statement complained of was published or anything asserted to be a fact in a privileged statement published before the statement complained of.

21. Condition 1 (in *subsection (2)*) is intended to reflect the current law and embraces the requirement established in *Cheng v Tse Wai Chun Paul*[6] that the statement must be recognisable as comment as distinct from an imputation of fact. It is implicit in condition 1 that the assessment is on the basis of how the ordinary person would understand it. As an inference of fact is a form of opinion, this would be encompassed by the defence.

22. Condition 2 (in *subsection (3)*), reflects the test approved by the Supreme Court in *Joseph v Spiller*[7] that "the comment must explicitly or implicitly indicate, at least in general terms, the facts on which it is based". Condition 2 and Condition 3 (in *subsection (4)*) aim to simplify the law by providing a clear and straightforward test. This is intended to retain the broad principles of the current common law defence as to the necessary basis for the opinion expressed but avoid the complexities which have arisen in case law, in particular over the extent to which the opinion must be based on facts which are sufficiently true and as to the extent to which the statement must explicitly or implicitly indicate the facts on which the opinion is based. These are areas where the common law has become increasingly complicated and technical, and where case law has sometimes struggled to articulate with clarity how the law should apply in particular circumstances. For example, the facts that may need to be demonstrated in relation to an article expressing an opinion on a political issue, comments made on a social network, a view about a contractual dispute, or a review of a restaurant or play will differ substantially.

23. Condition 3 is an objective test and consists of two elements. It is enough for one to be satisfied. The first is whether an honest person could have held the opinion on the basis of any fact which existed at the time the statement was published (in *subsection (4)(a)*). The subsection refers to "any fact" so that any relevant fact or facts will be enough. The existing case law on the sufficiency of the factual basis is covered by the requirement that "an honest person" must have been able to hold the opinion. If the fact was not a sufficient basis for the opinion, an honest person would not have been able to hold it.

24. The second element of condition 3 (in *subsection (4)(b)*) is whether an honest person could have formed the opinion on the basis of anything asserted to be a fact in a "privileged statement" which was published before the statement complained of. For this purpose, a statement is a "privileged statement" if the person responsible for its publication would have one of the defences listed in *subsection (7)* of the section if an action was brought in respect of that statement. The defences listed are the defence of absolute privilege under section 14 of the 1996 Act; the defence of qualified privilege under section 15 of that Act; and the defences in sections 4 and 6 of the Act relating to publication on a matter of public interest and peer-reviewed statements in a scientific or academic journal.

25. *Subsection (5)* provides for the defence to be defeated if the claimant shows that the defendant did not hold the opinion. This is a subjective test. This reflects the current law whereby the defence of fair comment will fail if the claimant can show that the statement was actuated by malice.

26. *Subsection (6)* makes provision for situations where the defendant is not the author of the statement (for example where an action is brought against a newspaper editor in respect of a comment piece rather than against the person who wrote it). In these circumstances the defence is defeated if the claimant can show that the defendant knew or ought to have known that the author did not hold the opinion.

27. *Subsection (8)* abolishes the common law defence of fair comment. Although this means that the defendant can no longer rely on the common law defence, in cases where uncertainty arises in the interpretation of section 3, case law would constitute a helpful but not binding guide to interpreting how the new statutory defence should be applied.

28. *Subsection (8)* also repeals section 6 of the 1952 Act. Section 6 provides that in an action for libel or slander in respect of words consisting partly of allegations of fact and partly of expression of opinion, a defence of fair comment shall not fail by reason only that the truth of every allegation of fact is not proved if the expression of opinion is fair comment having regard to such of the facts alleged or referred to in the words complained of as are proved. This provision is no longer necessary in light of the new approach set out in *subsection (4)*. A defendant will be able to show that conditions 1, 2 and 3 are met without needing to prove the truth of every single allegation of fact relevant to the statement complained of.

Section 4: Publication on matter of public interest

29. This section creates a new defence to an action for defamation of publication on a matter of public interest. It is based on the existing common law defence established in *Reynolds v Times Newspapers*[8] and is intended to reflect the principles established in that case and in subsequent case law. *Subsection (1)* provides for the defence to be available in circumstances where the defendant can show that the statement complained of was, or formed part of, a statement on a matter of public interest and that he reasonably believed that publishing the statement complained of was in the public interest. The intention in this provision is to reflect the existing common law as most recently set out in *Flood v Times Newspapers*[9]. It reflects the fact that the common law test contained both a subjective element—what the defendant believed was in the

public interest at the time of publication—and an objective element—whether the belief was a reasonable one for the defendant to hold in all the circumstances.

30. In relation to the first limb of this test, the section does not attempt to define what is meant by "the public interest". However, this is a concept which is well-established in the English common law. It is made clear that the defence applies if the statement complained of "was, *or formed part of*, a statement on a matter of public interest" to ensure that either the words complained of may be on a matter of public interest, or that a holistic view may be taken of the statement in the wider context of the document, article etc. in which it is contained in order to decide if overall this is on a matter of public interest.

31. *Subsection (2)* requires the court, subject to subsections (3) and (4), to have regard to all the circumstances of the case in determining whether the defendant has shown the matters set out in subsection (1).

32. *Subsection (3)* is intended to encapsulate the core of the common law doctrine of "reportage" (which has been described by the courts as "a convenient word to describe the neutral reporting of attributed allegations rather than their adoption by the newspaper"[(10)]. In instances where this doctrine applies, the defendant does not need to have verified the information reported before publication because the way that the report is presented gives a balanced picture. In determining whether for the purposes of the section it was reasonable for the defendant to believe that publishing the statement was in the public interest, the court should disregard any failure on the part of a defendant to take steps to verify the truth of the imputation conveyed by the publication (which would include any failure of the defendant to seek the claimant's views on the statement). This means that a defendant newspaper for example would not be prejudiced for a failure to verify where *subsection (3)* applies.

33. *Subsection (4)* requires the court, in considering whether the defendant's belief was reasonable, to make such allowance for editorial judgement as it considers appropriate. This expressly recognises the discretion given to editors in judgments such as that of *Flood*, but is not limited to editors in the media context.

34. *Subsection (5)* makes clear for the avoidance of doubt that the defence provided by this section may be relied on irrespective of whether the statement complained of is one of fact or opinion.

35. *Subsection (6)* abolishes the common law defence known as the Reynolds defence. This is because the statutory defence is intended essentially to codify the common law defence. While abolishing the common law defence means that the courts would be required to apply the words used in the statute, the current case law would constitute a helpful (albeit not binding) guide to interpreting how the new statutory defence should be applied. It is expected the courts would take the existing case law into consideration where appropriate.

Section 5: Operators of websites

36. This section creates a new defence for the operators of websites where a defamation action is brought against them in respect of a statement posted on the website.

37. *Subsection (2)* provides for the defence to apply if the operator can show that they did not post the statement on the website. *Subsection (3)* provides for the defence to be defeated if the claimant can show that it was not possible for him or her to identify the person who posted the statement; that they gave the operator a notice of complaint in relation to the statement; and that the operator failed to respond to that notice in accordance with provision contained in regulations to be made by the Secretary of State. *Subsection (4)* interprets *subsection (3)(a)* and explains that it is possible for a claimant to "identify" a person for the purposes of that subsection only if the claimant has sufficient information to bring proceedings against the person.

38. *Subsection (5)* provides details of provision that may be included in regulations. This includes provision as to the action which an operator must take in response to a notice (which in particular may include action relating to the identity or contact details of the person who posted the statement and action relating to the removal of the post); provision specifying a time limit for the taking of any such action and for conferring a discretion on the court to treat action taken after the expiry of a time limit as having been taken before that expiry. This would allow for provision to be made enabling a court to waive or retrospectively extend a time limit as appropriate. The subsection also permits regulations to make any other provision for the purposes of this section.

39. *Subsection (6)* sets out certain specific information which must be included in a notice of complaint. The notice must specify the complainant's name, set out the statement concerned and where on the website the statement was posted and explain why it is defamatory of the complainant. Regulations may specify what other information must be included in a notice of complaint.

40. *Subsection (7)* permits regulations to make provision about the circumstances in which a notice which is not a notice of complaint is to be treated as a notice of complaint for the purpose of the section or any provision made under it.

41. *Subsection (8)* permits regulations under this section to make different provision for different circumstances.

42. *Subsection (11)* provides for the defence to be defeated if the claimant shows that the website operator has acted with malice in relation to the posting of the statement concerned. This might arise where, for example, the website operator had incited the poster to make the posting or had otherwise colluded with the poster.

43. *Subsection (12)* explains that the defence available to a website operator is not defeated by reason only of the fact that the operator moderates the statements posted on it by others.

Section 6: Peer-reviewed statement in scientific or academic journal etc.

44. This section creates a new defence of qualified privilege relating to peer-reviewed material in scientific or academic journals (whether published in electronic form or otherwise). The term "scientific journal" would include medical and engineering journals.

45. *Subsections (1)* to *(3)* provide for the defence to apply where two conditions are met. These are condition 1: that the statement relates to a scientific or academic matter; and condition 2: that before the statement was published in the journal an independent review of the statement's scientific or academic merit was carried out by the editor of the journal and one or more persons with expertise in the scientific or academic matter concerned. The requirements in condition 2 are intended to reflect the core aspects of a responsible peer-review process. *Subsection (8)* provides that the reference to "the editor of the journal" is to be read, in the case of a journal with more than one editor, as a reference to the editor or editors who were responsible for deciding to publish the statement concerned. This may be relevant where a board of editors is responsible for decision-making.

46. *Subsection (4)* extends the protection offered by the defence to publications in the same journal of any assessment of the scientific or academic merit of a peer-reviewed statement, provided the assessment was written by one or more of the persons who carried out the independent review of the statement, and the assessment was written in the course of that review. This is intended to ensure that the privilege is available not only to the author of the peer-reviewed statement, but also to those who have conducted the independent review who will need to assess, for example, the papers originally submitted by the author and may need to comment.

47. *Subsection (5)* provides that the privilege given by the section to peer-reviewed statements and related assessments also extends to the publication of a fair and accurate copy of, extract from or summary of the statement or assessment concerned.

48. By *subsection (6)* the privilege given by the section is lost if the publication is shown to be made with malice. This reflects the condition attaching to other forms of qualified privilege. *Subsection (7)(b)* has been included to ensure that the new section is not read as preventing a person who publishes a statement in a scientific or academic journal from relying on other forms of privilege, such as the privilege conferred under section 7(9) to fair and accurate reports etc. of proceedings at a scientific or academic conference.

Section 7: Reports etc. protected by privilege

49. This section amends the provisions contained in the 1996 Act relating to the defences of absolute and qualified privilege to extend the circumstances in which these defences can be used.

50. *Subsection (1)* replaces subsection (3) of section 14 of the 1996 Act, which concerns the absolute privilege applying to fair and accurate contemporaneous reports of court proceedings. Subsection (3) of section 14 currently provides for absolute privilege to apply to fair and accurate reports of proceedings in public before any court in the UK; the European Court of Justice or any court attached to that court; the European Court of Human Rights; and any international criminal tribunal established by the Security Council of the United Nations or by an international agreement to which the UK is a party. *Subsection (1)* replaces this with a new subsection, which extends the scope of the defence so that it also covers proceedings in any court established under the law of a country or territory outside the United Kingdom, and any international court or tribunal established by the Security Council of the United Nations or by an international agreement.

51. *Subsection (2)* amends section 15(3) of the 1996 Act by substituting the phrase "public interest" for "public concern", so that the subsection reads "This section does not apply to the publication to the public, or a section of the public, of matter which is not of public interest and the publication of which is not for the public benefit". This is intended to prevent any confusion arising from the use of two different terms with equivalent meaning in this Act and in the 1996 Act. *Subsection (6)(b)* makes the same amendment to paragraph 12(2) of Schedule 1 to the 1996 Act in relation to the privilege extended to fair and accurate reports etc. of public meetings.

52. *Subsections (3)* to *(10)* make amendments to Part 2 of Schedule 1 to the 1996 Act in a number of areas so as to extend the circumstances in which the defence of qualified privilege is available. Section 15 of and Schedule 1 to the 1996 Act currently provide for qualified privilege to apply to various types of report or statement, provided the report or statement is fair and accurate, on a matter of public concern, and that publication is for the public benefit and made without malice. Part 1 of Schedule 1 sets out categories of publication which attract qualified privilege without explanation or contradiction. These include fair and accurate reports of proceedings in public, anywhere in the world, of legislatures (both national and local), courts, public inquiries, and international organisations or conferences, and documents, notices and other matter published by these bodies.

53. Part 2 of Schedule 1 sets out categories of publication which have the protection of qualified privilege unless the publisher refuses or neglects to publish, in a suitable manner, a reasonable letter or statement by way of explanation or correction when requested to do so. These include copies of or extracts from information for the public published by government or authorities performing governmental functions (such as the police) or by courts; reports of proceedings at a range of public meetings (e.g. of

local authorities) general meetings of UK public companies; and reports of findings or decisions by a range of associations formed in the UK or the European Union (such as associations relating to art, science, religion or learning, trade associations, sports associations and charitable associations).

54. In addition to the protection already offered to fair and accurate copies of or extracts from the different types of publication to which the defence is extended, amendments are made by *subsections (4)*, *(7)(b)* and *(10)* of the section to extend the scope of qualified privilege to cover fair and accurate summaries of the material. For example, *subsection (4)* extends the defence to summaries of notices or other matter issued for the information of the public by a number of governmental bodies, and to summaries of documents made available by the courts.

55. Currently qualified privilege under Part 1 of Schedule 1 extends to fair and accurate reports of proceedings in public of a legislature; before a court; and in a number of other forums anywhere in the world. However, qualified privilege under Part 2 only applies to publications arising in the UK and EU member states. *Subsections (4)*, *(6)(a)*, *(7)*, and *(8)* extend the scope of the defence to cover the different types of publication to which the defence extends anywhere in the world. For example, *subsection (6)* does this for reports of proceedings at public meetings, and *subsection (8)* for reports of certain kinds of associations.

56. *Subsection (5)* provides for qualified privilege to extend to a fair and accurate report of proceedings at a press conference held anywhere in the world for the discussion of a matter of public interest. Under the current law as articulated in the case of *McCartan Turkington Breen v Times Newspapers Ltd*[11], it appears that a press conference would fall within the scope of a "public meeting" under paragraph 12 of Schedule 1 to the 1996 Act. This provision has been included in the Act to clarify the position.

57. Currently Part 2 qualified privilege extends only to fair and accurate reports of proceedings at general meetings and documents circulated by UK public companies (paragraph 13). *Subsection (7)* of the section extends this to reports relating to public companies elsewhere in the world. It achieves this by extending the provision to "listed companies" within the meaning of Part 12 of the Corporation Tax Act 2009 with a view to ensuring that broadly the same types of companies are covered by the provision in the UK and abroad. It also extends a provision in the 1996 Act (which provides for qualified privilege to be available in respect of a fair and accurate copy etc. of material circulated to members of a listed company relating to the appointment, resignation, retirement or dismissal of directors of the company) to such material relating to the company's auditors.

58. *Subsection (9)* inserts a new paragraph into Schedule 1 to the 1996 Act to extend Part 2 qualified privilege to fair and accurate reports of proceedings of a scientific or academic conference, and to copies, extracts and summaries of matter published by such conferences. It is possible in certain circumstances that Part 2 qualified privilege may already apply to academic and scientific conferences (either where they fall within the description of a public meeting in paragraph 12, or where findings or decisions are published by a scientific or academic association (paragraph 14)). The amendments made by *subsection (9)* will however ensure that there is not a gap.

59. *Subsection (11)* substitutes new general provisions in Schedule 1 to reflect the changes that have been made to the substance of the Schedule. It also removes provisions allowing for orders to be made by the Lord Chancellor identifying "corresponding proceedings" for the purposes of paragraph 11(3) of the Schedule, and "corresponding meetings and documents" for the purposes of paragraph 13(5). The provision relating to paragraph 13(5) no longer has any application in the light of the amendments made to that paragraph by *subsection (7)*, while the power in relation to paragraph 11(3) has never been exercised and the amendment leaves the provision to take its natural meaning.

Section 8: Single publication rule

60. This section introduces a single publication rule to prevent an action being brought in relation to publication of the same material by the same publisher after a one year limitation period from the date of the first publication of that material to the public or a section of the public. This replaces the longstanding principle that each publication of defamatory material gives rise to a separate cause of action which is subject to its own limitation period (the "multiple publication rule").

61. *Subsection (1)* indicates that the provisions apply where a person publishes a statement to the public (defined in *subsection (2)* as including publication to a section of the public), and subsequently publishes that statement or a statement which is substantially the same. The aim is to ensure that the provisions catch publications which have the same content or content which has changed very little so that the essence of the defamatory statement is not substantially different from that contained in the earlier publication. Publication to the public has been selected as the trigger point because it is from this point on that problems are generally encountered with internet publications and in order to stop the new provision catching limited publications leading up to publication to the public at large. The definition in *subsection (2)* is intended to ensure that publications to a limited number of people are covered (for example where a blog has a small group of subscribers or followers).

62. *Subsection (3)* has the effect of ensuring that the limitation period in relation to any cause of action brought in respect of a subsequent publication within scope of the section is treated as having started to run on the date of the first publication.

63. *Subsection (4)* provides that the single publication rule does not apply where the manner of the subsequent publication of the statement is "materially different" from the manner of the first publication. *Subsection (5)* provides that in deciding this issue the matters to which the court may have regard include the level of prominence given to the statement and the extent of the subsequent publication. A possible example of this could be where a story has first appeared relatively obscurely in a section of a website where several clicks need to be gone through to access it, but has subsequently been promoted to a position where it can be directly accessed from the home page of the site, thereby increasing considerably the number of hits it receives.

64. *Subsection (6)* confirms that the section does not affect the court's discretion under section 32A of the Limitation Act 1980 to allow a defamation action to proceed outside the one year limitation period where it is equitable to do so. It also ensures that the reference in subsection (1)(a) of section 32A to the operation of section 4A of the 1980 Act (section 4A concerns the time limit applicable for defamation actions) is interpreted as a reference to the operation of section 4A together with section 8. Section 32A provides a broad discretion which requires the court to have regard to all the circumstances of the case, and it is envisaged that this will provide a safeguard against injustice in relation to the application of any limitation issue arising under this section.

Section 9: Action against a person not domiciled in the UK or a Member State etc.

65. This section aims to address the issue of "libel tourism" (a term which is used to apply where cases with a tenuous link to England and Wales are brought in this jurisdiction). *Subsection (1)* focuses the provision on cases where an action is brought against a person who is not domiciled in the UK, an EU Member State or a state which is a party to the Lugano Convention. This is in order to avoid conflict with European jurisdictional rules (in particular the Brussels Regulation on jurisdictional matters[12].

66. *Subsection (2)* provides that a court does not have jurisdiction to hear and determine an action to which the section applies unless it is satisfied that, of all the

places in which the statement complained of has been published, England and Wales is clearly the most appropriate place in which to bring an action in respect of the statement. This means that in cases where a statement has been published in this jurisdiction and also abroad the court will be required to consider the overall global picture to consider where it would be most appropriate for a claim to be heard. It is intended that this will overcome the problem of courts readily accepting jurisdiction simply because a claimant frames their claim so as to focus on damage which has occurred in this jurisdiction only. This would mean that, for example, if a statement was published 100,000 times in Australia and only 5,000 times in England that would be a good basis on which to conclude that the most appropriate jurisdiction in which to bring an action in respect of the statement was Australia rather than England. There will however be a range of factors which the court may wish to take into account including, for example, the amount of damage to the claimant's reputation in this jurisdiction compared to elsewhere, the extent to which the publication was targeted at a readership in this jurisdiction compared to elsewhere, and whether there is reason to think that the claimant would not receive a fair hearing elsewhere.

67. *Subsection (3)* provides that the references in *subsection (2)* to the statement complained of include references to any statement which conveys the same, or substantially the same, imputation as the statement complained of. This addresses the situation where a statement is published in a number of countries but is not exactly the same in all of them, and will ensure that a court is not impeded in deciding whether England and Wales is the most appropriate place to bring the claim by arguments that statements elsewhere should be regarded as different publications even when they are substantially the same. It is the intention that this new rule will be capable of being applied within the existing procedural framework for defamation claims.

Section 10: Action against a person who was not the author, editor etc.

68. This section limits the circumstances in which an action for defamation can be brought against someone who is not the primary publisher of an allegedly defamatory statement.

69. Subsection (1) provides that a court does not have jurisdiction to hear and determine an action for defamation brought against a person who was not the author, editor or publisher of the statement complained of unless it is satisfied that it is not reasonably practicable for an action to be brought against the author, editor or publisher.

70. Subsection (2) confirms that the terms "author", "editor" and "publisher" are to have the same meaning as in section 1 of the 1996 Act. By subsection (2) of that Act, "author" means the originator of the statement, but does not include a person who did not intend that his statement be published at all; "editor" means a person having editorial or equivalent responsibility for the content of the statement or the decision to publish it; and "publisher" means a commercial publisher, that is, a person whose business is issuing material to the public, or a section of the public, who issues material containing the statement in the course of that business. Examples of persons who are not to be considered the author, editor or publisher are contained in subsection (3) of section 1 of the 1996 Act.

Section 11: Trial to be without a jury unless the court orders otherwise

71. This section removes the presumption in favour of jury trial in defamation cases.

72. Currently section 69 of the Senior Courts Act 1981 and section 66 of the County Courts Act 1984 provide for a right to trial with a jury in certain civil proceedings (namely malicious prosecution, false imprisonment, fraud, libel and slander) on the

application of any party, "unless the court considers that the trial requires any prolonged examination of documents or accounts or any scientific or local investigation which cannot conveniently be made with a jury".

73. *Subsection (1)* and *subsection (2)* respectively amend the 1981 and 1984 Acts to remove libel and slander from the list of proceedings where a right to jury trial exists. The result will be that defamation cases will be tried without a jury unless a court orders otherwise.

Section 12: Power of court to order a summary of its judgment to be published

74. In summary disposal proceedings under section 8 of the 1996 Act the court has power to order an unsuccessful defendant to publish a summary of its judgment where the parties cannot agree the content of any correction or apology. The section gives the court power to order a summary of its judgment to be published in defamation proceedings more generally.

75. *Subsection (1)* enables the court when giving judgment for the claimant in a defamation action to order the defendant to publish a summary of the judgment. *Subsection (2)* provides that the wording of any summary and the time, manner, form and place of its publication are matters for the parties to agree. Where the parties are unable to agree, *subsections (3)* and *(4)* respectively provide for the court to settle the wording, and enable it to give such directions in relation to the time, manner, form or place of publication as it considers reasonable and practicable. *Subsection (5)* disapplies the section where the court gives judgment for the claimant under section 8(3) of the 1996 Act. The summary disposal procedure is a separate procedure which can continue to be used where this is appropriate.

Section 13: Order to remove statement or cease distribution etc.

76. This section relates to situations where an author may not always be in a position to remove or prevent further dissemination of material which has been found to be defamatory. *Subsection (1)* provides that where a court gives judgment for the claimant in an action for defamation, it may order the operator of a website on which a defamatory statement is posted to remove the statement, or require any person who was not the author, editor or publisher of the statement but is distributing, selling or exhibiting the material to cease disseminating it. This will enable an order for removal of the material to be made during or shortly after the conclusion of proceedings.

77. *Subsection (3)* ensures that the provision does not have any wider effect on the jurisdiction of the court to grant injunctive relief.

Section 14: Actions for slander: special damage

78. This section repeals the Slander of Women Act 1891 and overturns a common law rule relating to special damage.

79. In relation to slander, some special damage must be proved to flow from the statement complained of unless the publication falls into certain specific categories. These include a provision in the 1891 Act which provides that "words spoken and published . . . which impute unchastity or adultery to any woman or girl shall not require special damage to render them actionable". *Subsection (1)* repeals the Act, so that these circumstances are not exempted from the requirement for special damage.

80. *Subsection (2)* abolishes the common law rule which provides an exemption from the requirement for special damage where the imputation conveyed by the statement complained of is that the claimant has a contagious or infectious disease. In case law dating from the nineteenth century and earlier, the exemption has been held to apply in the case of imputations of leprosy, venereal disease and the plague.

Section 15: Meaning of "publish" and "statement"

81. This section sets out definitions of the terms "publish", "publication" and "statement" for the purposes of the Act. Broad definitions are used to ensure that the provisions of the Act cover a wide range of publications in any medium, reflecting the current law.

Section 16: Consequential amendments and savings etc.

82. *Subsections (1) to (3)* make consequential amendments to section 8 of the Rehabilitation of Offenders Act 1974 to reflect the new defences of truth and honest opinion. Section 8 of the 1974 Act applies to actions for libel or slander brought by a rehabilitated person based on statements made about offences which were the subject of a spent conviction.

83. *Subsections (4) to (8)* contain savings and interpretative provisions.

Section 17: Short title, extent and commencement

84. This section sets out the territorial extent of the provisions and makes provision for commencement.

Commencement

85. Section 15, the savings related provisions in subsections (4) to (8) of section 16 and section 17 (short title, commencement and extent) come into force on the day on which the Act is passed. Otherwise, the Act will come into force on such day as the Secretary of State may specify by order (section 17(4)) or, in so far as provisions extend to Scotland, on such day as the Scottish Ministers may by order appoint (section 17(5)).

Hansard References

86. The following table sets out the dates and Hansard references for each stage of the Act's passage through Parliament.

Stage	Date	Hansard reference
House of Commons		
Introduction	10 May 2012	Vol. 545 Col. 164 http://www.publications.parliament.uk/pa/cm201213/ cmhansrd/cm120510/debtext/ 120510-0001.htm#12051029000012
Second Reading	12 June 2012	Vol. 546 Cols. 177–267 http://www.publications.parliament.uk/pa/cm201213/ cmhansrd/cm120612/debtext/ 120612-0001.htm#12061240000002
Committee	19 June 2012	Public Bill Committee: Defamation Bill
	21 June 2012	
	26 June 2012	

Stage	Date	Hansard reference
Report and Third Reading	12 September 2012	Vol. 505 Cols. 309–381 http://www.publications.parliament.uk/pa/cm201213/ cmhansrd/cm120912/debtext/ 120912-0002.htm#12091223000002
House of Lords		
Introduction	8 October 2012	Vol. 739 Col. 828 http://www.publications.parliament.uk/pa/ld201213/ ldhansrd/text/121008-0001.htm#1210084000451
Second Reading	9 October 2012	Vol. 739 Cols. 932–986 http://www.publications.parliament.uk/pa/ld201213/ ldhansrd/text/121009-0001.htm#12100930000316
Committee	17 December 2012	Vol. 741 Cols. GC413–GC468
	19 December 2012	Vol. 741 Cols. GC521–GC578
	15 January 2013	Vol. 742 Cols. GC181–GC240
	17 January 2013	Vol. 742 Cols. GC307–GC372
Report	5 February 2013	Vol. 743 Cols. 140–254 http://www.publications.parliament.uk/pa/ld201213/ ldhansrd/text/130205-0001.htm#13020546001351
Third Reading	25 February 2013	Vol. 743 Cols. 848–852 http://www.publications.parliament.uk/pa/ld201213/ ldhansrd/text/130225-0001.htm#13022512000429
Ping Pong		
Commons Consideration of Lords Amendments	16 April 2013	Commons: Vol. 561 Cols. 266–288 http://www.publications.parliament.uk/pa/cm201213/ cmhansrd/cm130416/debtext/ 130416-0003.htm#13041655000001
Lords Consideration of Commons Reasons	23 April 2013	Lords: Vol. 744 Cols. 1362–1387 http://www.publications.parliament.uk/pa/ld201213/ ldhansrd/text/130423-0001.htm#13042379000292
Consideration of Lords message	24 April 2013	Vol. 561 Cols. 913–923 http://www.publications.parliament.uk/pa/cm201213/ cmhansrd/cm130424/debtext/ 130424-0002.htm#13042446000003
Royal Assent	25 April 2013	http://www.publications.parliament.uk/pa/ld201213/ ldhansrd/text/130425-0001.htm#13042554000435 http://www.publications.parliament.uk/pa/cm201213/ cmhansrd/cm130425/debtext/ 130425-0002.htm#13042550000004

(1) [2010] EWHC 1414.

(2) [1936] 2 All ER 1237.

(3) [2005] EWCA Civ 75.

(4) [2002] EWCA Civ 1772 at para.34.

(5) The Supreme Court in *Spiller v Joseph* [2010] UKSC 53 referred to this as honest comment.

(6) (2000) 10 BHRC 525.

(7) [2010] UKSC 53 (at para.105).

(8) [2001] 2 A.C. 127.

(9) [2012] UKSC 11. See, for example, the judgement of Lord Brown at 113.

(10) Per Simon Brown in *Al-Fagih* [2001] EWCA Civ 1634.

(11) [2001] 2 A.C. 277.

(12) Council Regulation (EC) 44/2001 on jurisdiction and the recognition and enforcement of judgments in civil and commercial matters.

Appendix 3

Damages Awards

Part 1: Awards of libel damages approved or made by the Court of Appeal or the Supreme Court (or formerly the House of Lords) to which reference may be made in other actions[1]

A3.1 Gorman v Mudd, unreported, October 15, 1992
A3.2 Rantzen v Mirror Group Newspapers [1994] Q.B. 670
A3.3 Houston v Smith, December 16, 1993, unreported C.A. Transcript No. (Civil Division) 1544 of 1993
A3.4 John v MGN Ltd [1997] Q.B. 586
A3.5 Kiam v Neil (No. 2) [1996] E.M.L.R. 493
A3.6 Jones v Pollard [1997] E.M.L.R. 233
A3.7 Steel & Morris v McDonald's Corp, unreported, March 31, 1999
A3.8 Khodaparast v Shad [2000] 1 W.L.R. 618
A3.9 Burstein v Times Newspapers Ltd [2000] EWCA Civ 338; [2001] 1 W.L.R. 579
A3.10 Kiam v MGN Ltd [2002] EWCA Civ 43; [2003] Q.B. 281
A3.11 Campbell v News Group Newspapers Ltd [2002] EWCA Civ 1143; [2002] E.M.L.R. 43
A3.12 Grobbelaar v News Group Newspapers Ltd [2002] UKHL 40; [2002] 1 W.L.R. 3024
A3.13 Wood v Chief Constable of West Midlands Police [2004] EWCA Civ 1638; [2005] E.M.L.R. 20
A3.14 Galloway v Telegraph Group Ltd [2006] EWCA Civ 17; [2006] E.M.L.R. 11
A3.15 Purnell v Business F1 Magazine Ltd [2007] EWCA Civ 744; [2008] 1 W.L.R. 1
A3.16 Gur v Avrupa Newspaper Ltd [2008] EWCA Civ 594; [2009] E.M.L.R. 4
A3.17 Berezovsky v Terluk [2011] EWCA Civ 1534
A3.18 Cairns v Modi; KC v MGN [2012] EWCA Civ 1382; [2013] 1 W.L.R. 1015

Part 2: Non-jury Damages Awards from 2000

A3.19 Cunningham v Essex CC, unreported, June 2000
A3.20 Lillie v Newcastle City Council [2002] EWHC 1600 (QB)
A3.21 English v Hastie, unreported, January 2002
A3.22 Field v Local Sunday Newspapers, unreported, March 2002
A3.23 Greenaway v Poole [2003] EWHC 1735 (QB)
A3.24 The Gleaner Company Ltd v Abrahams [2003] UKPC 55; [2004] 1 A.C. 628
A3.25 Downtex v Flatley [2004] EWHC 333 (QB)
A3.26 Walsh v Carpenter, unreported, April 25, 2005
A3.27 Rackham v Sandy [2005] EWHC 482 (QB)
A3.28 Cray v Hancock, unreported, November 4, 2005

---

[1] In contrast to the views of Pill L.J. in *Kiam v Neil (No. 2)* [1996] E.M.L.R. 493 (see A3.5) Dyson L.J. in *Gur v Avrupa Newspaper Ltd* [2008] EWCA Civ 594, said that all judge alone damages awards could be used as comparators. See A3.16.

A3.29 Keith-Smith v Williams [2006] EWHC 860 (QB)
A3.30 Murray v Motor Schools Association, unreported, June 12, 2006
A3.31 Creative Resins International Ltd v Glasslam Europe Ltd [2006] EWHC 3159 (QB)
A3.32 Culla Park Ltd v Richards [2007] EWHC 1850 (QB)
A3.33 Ghannouchi v Al Arabiya, unreported, November 8, 2007
A3.34 Seafresh Ltd v Shaw, unreported, 2008
A3.35 Trumm v Norman [2008] EWHC 116 (QB)
A3.36 Applause Store Productions Ltd v Raphael [2008] EWHC 1781 (QB); [2008] Info. T.L.R. 318
A3.37 Galloway v Jewish Communications Ltd, unreported, July 31, 2008
A3.38 Keating v Large, unreported, August 13, 2008
A3.39 Gregg v O'Gara [2008] EWHC 658 (QB)
A3.40 Coad v Cruze [2009] EWHC 3782 (QB)
A3.41 Levi v Bates [2009] EWHC 1495 (QB)
A3.42 Emlick v Gulf New, unreported, July 23, 2009
A3.43 Warren v Madugqu, unreported, July 27, 2009
A3.44 Bloom v Robinson-Millar [2013] EWHC 3918 (QB)
A3.45 Supreme Events Ltd v Anderson, unreported, December 17, 2009
A3.46 Bryce v Barber, unreported, July 26, 2010
A3.47 Metropolitan International Schools Ltd v Designtechnica Corp [2010] EWHC 2411 (QB)
A3.48 Phillips v Kordowski, unreported, October 12, 2010
A3.49 Cambridge v Makin [2011] EWHC 12 (QB)
A3.50 Can Say (t/a Corbe Café) v British Gas Trading Ltd [2010] EWHC 3946 (QB)
A3.51 Farrall v Kordowski [2011] EWHC 2140 (QB)
A3.52 Clynes v O'Connor [2011] EWHC 1201(QB)
A3.53 Robins v Kordowski [2011] EWHC 1912 (QB)
A3.54 Thornton v Telegraph Media Group Ltd [2011] EWHC 1884 (QB); [2012] E.M.L.R. 8
A3.55 Al-Amoudi v Kifle [2011] EWHC 2037 (QB)
A3.56 Cooper v Turrell [2011] EWHC 3269 (QB)
A3.57 Bento v Chief Constable of Bedfordshire [2012] EWHC 1525 (QB)
A3.58 Joseph v Spiller [2012] EWHC 2958 (QB)
A3.59 Miller v Associated Newspapers Ltd [2012] EWHC 3721 (QB)
A3.60 Hussein v Hamilton Franks & Co Ltd [2013] EWHC 462 (QB)
A3.61 Cruddas v Adams [2013] EWHC 145 (QB)
A3.62 Thompson v James [2013] EWHC 515 (QB)
A3.63 ZAM v CFW and TFW [2013] EWHC 662 (QB); [2013] E.M.L.R. 27
A3.64 Jon Richard Ltd v Gornall [2013] EWHC 1357 (QB)
A3.65 Cruddas v Calvert, Blake and Times Newspapers Ltd [2013] EWHC 2298 (QB)

Part 3: Compensation awards under the Offer of Amends Scheme (ss.2–4 Defamation Act 1996)

A3.66 Cleese v Clark [2003] EWHC 137 (QB); [2004] E.M.L.R. 3
A3.67 Nail v News Group Newspapers Ltd [2004] EWCA Civ 1708; [2005] 1 All E.R. 1040
A3.68 Campbell-James v Guardian Media Group Plc [2005] EWHC 893 (QB); [2005] E.M.L.R. 24
A3.69 Turner v News Group Newspapers Ltd [2006] EWCA Civ 540; [2006] 1 W.L.R. 3469

A3.70 Angel v Stainton [2006] EWHC 637 (QB)
A3.71 Veliu v Mazrekaj [2006] EWHC 1710 (QB); [2007] 1 W.L.R. 495
A3.72 Bowman v MGN Ltd [2010] EWHC 895 (QB)

Part 4: Damages awards in misuse of personal information and harassment cases involving speech (since 2000)[2]

A3.73 Cornelius v de Taranto [2001] E.M.L.R. 12
A3.74 Campbell v MGN Ltd [2002] EWHC 499 (QB); [2002] E.M.L.R. 30
A3.75 Peck v United Kingdom (2003) 36 E.H.R.R. 41; [2003] E.M.L.R. 15
A3.76 Lady Archer v Williams [2003] EWHC 1670 (QB); [2003] E.M.L.R. 38
A3.77 W v Westminster City Council (No.2) [2005] EWHC 102 (QB); [2005] 4 ALL E.R. 96 (Note)
A3.78 Douglas v Hello! Ltd [2005] EWCA Civ 595; [2006] Q.B. 125
A3.79 Cray v Hancock, unreported, November 4, 2005
A3.80 McKennitt v Ash [2005] EWHC 3003 (QB); [2006] E.M.L.R. 10
A3.81 Mosley v News Group Newspapers Ltd [2008] EWHC 1777 (QB); [2008] E.M.L.R. 20
A3.82 Applause Store Productions Ltd v Raphael [2008] EWHC 1781 (QB); [2008] Info. T.L.R. 318
A3.83 Bloom v Robinson-Millar, October 7, 2009, [2013] EWHC 3918 (QB)
A3.84 Cooper v Turrell [2011] EWHC 3269 (QB)
A3.85 AAA v Associated Newspapers Ltd [2012] EWHC 2103 (QB); [2013] E.M.L.R. 2
A3.86 WXY v Gewanter, Positive Profile and Burby [2013] EWHC 589 (QB)
A3.87 ZAM v CFW and TFW [2013] EWHC 662 (QB); [2013] E.M.L.R. 27

Part 1

Awards of libel damages approved or made by the Court of Appeal or the Supreme Court (or formerly the House of Lords) to which reference may be made in other actions

Gorman v Mudd October 15, 1992, unreported C.A.   A3.1

The plaintiff, the Conservative M.P. for Billericay, complained of a "mock press release" written and circulated by the defendant, a prominent member of the Billericay community, to 91 persons which conveyed the meaning (in summary) that the plaintiff had opposed and sought to destroy the Billericay Conservative Businessman's Association and to humiliate the defendant out of personal spite. A plea of qualified privilege was upheld. Thus the jury had to find express malice if the plaintiff was to succeed. There was no apology.

The Court of Appeal reduced the jury's award of £150,000 to £50,000.

(Note: The Court of Appeal's jurisdiction to substitute its own figure of damages only arose because the parties consented: the power of the court to intervene in fixing damages without the consent of the parties could only be exercised in appeals set down on or after February 1, 1991. Furthermore there had been no consideration of the

---

[2] For further non-pecuniary damages awards made by the European Court of Human Rights in art.8 cases, see Scorey & Eicke *Human Rights Damages: Principles and Practice* (London: Sweet & Maxwell, 2003).

impact of Article 10 of the European Convention on Human Rights on the assessment of libel damages (see Rantzen v. MGN, below). However, the test the court had to apply in substituting its own figure, "such sum as appears to the Court to be proper", was the same as under the former Order 59 r.11(4). The Court now has a wide power under the current CPR 52.10(3) to make an order for damages or vary an award. It is therefore submitted that this is an award made by the Court of Appeal to which the jury can be referred.)

A3.2   Rantzen v Mirror Group Newspapers [1994] Q.B. 670

The subject of the action was four articles in the same issue of *The People*, including one on the front page and a leading article, covering the same story and theme that the plaintiff who had set up an organisation, Childline, to protect children from sexual abuse, had kept secret the fact that a teacher, who had revealed to Childline abuses of children occurring at a school at which he taught, was himself a pervert, unfit to have any child in his care. One of the meanings contended for by the plaintiff, and left to the jury was that she had protected the teacher as a reward for his help. The defendants pleaded justification and fair comment, which were maintained at trial, and the plaintiff replied by alleging express malice. The Court of Appeal reduced the jury's award of £250,000 to £110,000.

A3.3   Houston v Smith, December 16, 1993, unreported C.A. Transcript No. (Civil Division) 1544 of 1993

The plaintiff, a doctor, complained of an accusation made by the defendant, a lady doctor, heard by a number of patients in the waiting room, that he had sexually harassed the defendant and female staff at the surgery. A statement which carried similar implications was made by the defendant orally a day later. There was no apology. The defendant raised and persisted in a limited plea of justification. The jury awarded £150,000 damages. The Court of Appeal reduced the award to £50,000.
(Hirst L.J.:
"I should add that this amount is in my judgment at the very top of the range for a slander of this kind, and is only appropriate because of the very grave and exceptional aggravating factors to which I have already referred. Had the slander remained within the confines of the waiting room and, still more, if the defendant had promptly apologised, the appropriate sum would have been a very small fraction of 50,000.")

A3.4   John v MGN Ltd [1997] Q.B. 586

The action concerned an article in *The Sunday Mirror*, covering two inside pages, but introduced on the front page with words in capital letters, "Elton's diet of death", accompanied by a photograph of the plaintiff. The article stated that the plaintiff had suffered from bulimia and was now hooked on a bizarre new diet which could kill him, describing his behaviour at a party in California where he was seen to put food in his mouth, chew it and then spit it out. The plaintiff had never been at the party. He gave evidence that he had been "incensed" by the article because he had had eating and drug and alcohol addiction problems, but had cured himself, and had publicised as much on television. The newspaper had offered an apology but its terms had not been agreed and none was published. The claim was defended on the grounds that the words were not defamatory.

    The Court of Appeal reduced the jury's award of general damages from £75,000 to £25,000 (*"Though the article was false, offensive and distressing it did not attack (the plaintiff's) personal integrity or damage his reputation as an artist."* per Sir Thomas Bingham M.R.), and the award of exemplary damages from £275,000 to £50,000.

Kiam v Neil (No.2) [1996] E.M.L.R. 493   A3.5

The plaintiff was a businessman well known for his appearance in television advertisements for the product made by the company he owned. *The Sunday Times* published an article in which it was alleged that he was being sued after defaulting on a £13.5 million loan and had filed in the USA for bankruptcy protection. ("*It would be hard to imagine a more damaging allegation against a successful entrepreneur*", per Beldam L.J. at p.498). Three weeks later an apology in agreed terms was published, but the parties could not agree on compensation. The Court of Appeal refused to interfere with the jury's award of £45,000.

(Note: Pill L.J. at p.516:

"*The danger I foresee in inviting juries to make comparisons with other cases, comparisons which would inevitably become elaborate as each party emphasises particular but different features of those other cases, is that the jury will be distracted from their central duty to consider the circumstances of the case in hand and make an award based on their conscientious assessment of what is involved. I agree with the Master of the Rolls' call (in John v. MGN) for discretion in citing awards. In this context, a 'battle of comparables' in front of a jury may produce its own injustice, as well as being time consuming and costly.*")

Jones v Pollard [1997] E.M.L.R. 233   A3.6

The plaintiff complained of two articles in consecutive issues of *The Sunday Mirror* which accused him of assisting the KGB by organising sex with Russian prostitutes for British businessmen visiting Russia who could then be blackmailed. The defendants pleaded justification. The plaintiff conceded in evidence that he was a persistent womaniser, but denied procuring prostitutes, though a tape of a conversation with a journalist in which the plaintiff was apparently arranging an assignment between the journalist and a prostitute was introduced in evidence (the plaintiff's explanation was that he was either drunk or fantasising). The defendants called no evidence and the judge withdrew from the jury such parts of the plea of justification which mentioned or suggested contact with the KGB. The Court of Appeal held that the jury must have concluded that the charge of procuring prostitutes was made out in part.

The jury's award of £100,000 general damages was reduced to £40,000. ("*I can see no justification for an award which is comparable with Rantzen*": Hirst L.J. at p.259.)

Steel & Morris v McDonald's Corporation, unreported, March 31, 1999   A3.7

Two McDonalds companies sued two individuals in respect of allegations made in a Greenpeace pamphlet. After a very lengthy trial Bell J. upheld the McDonalds companies' claims for libel in respect of many but not all the allegations made in the pamphlet and awarded £60,000 damages, £30,000 to each plaintiff corporation. The appellants appealed and the Court of Appeal reduced the awards to £20,000 each because it had differed from the Judge on one issue pertaining to justification and another in respect of fair comment. The European Court of Human Rights held that the awards were disproportionate to the aim served because the awards were "*very substantial when compared to the modest income and resources of the two applicants*": [2005] E.M.L.R. 15, at page 314 at [96]. (NB: The Court of Appeal in *Gur v Avrupa Newspaper Ltd* [2008] EWCA Civ 594 (see A3.16 below) said that the means of a party were irrelevant.)

Khodaparast v Shad [2000] 1 W.L.R. 618   A3.8

This was an action for malicious falsehood in which the plaintiff, a teacher at an Iranian religious school, sued the defendant, her former lover, for publishing certain documents throughout the Iranian community in London. The documents appeared to be pages from pornographic magazines containing photographs of the plaintiff. As a result of the publications, she lost her job. The documents were false. The plaintiff had at no time been involved in the sex industry in any way. At trial the judge awarded £20,000. The Court of Appeal dismissed the defendant's appeal. Otton L.J. commented that this was a blatant malicious falsehood that was persisted in and aggravated by the defendant's cruel, ruthless and relentless attack on the plaintiff's character. He agreed with the trial judge's view that had the plaintiff's cause of action been defamation then a proper sum by way of compensation would have been £50,000.

A3.9 Burstein v Times Newspapers Ltd [2000] EWCA Civ 338; [2001] 1 W.L.R. 579

The claimant, a composer of modern romantic music, sued over a diary piece published in *The Times* alleging that he "*used to organise bands of hecklers to go about wrecking performances of modern atonal music, particularly anything by Harrison Birtwhistle.*" At trial the claimant applied to strike out various particulars pleaded in mitigation of damages relating to his activities as co-founder of 'The Hecklers', which included a notorious occasion of booing at the end of a performance of Birtwhistle's 'Gawain' at the Royal Opera House. The defendant applied for summary disposal of the claim under s.8 of the 1996 Act on the ground that the damages should be limited to £10,000. The judge acceded to the claimant's application and refused the defendant's. The jury awarded £8,000. The defendant appealed, arguing that the judge should not have struck out the particulars pleaded in mitigation of damages. The Court of Appeal held that some of the particulars should not have been struck out. The jury had been left to assess damages in blinkers. However, the jury's award would stand as the Court was not persuaded that it would have been any lower if the material had not been excluded.

A3.10 Kiam v MGN Ltd [2002] EWCA Civ 43; [2003] Q.B. 281

The claimant was a businessman well-known for his appearance in television advertisements for the product made by the company he owned (see A3.5). The *Daily Mirror* published an article which alleged, amongst other things, that his marketing and entrepreneurial ability had deserted him and that the imminent financial collapse of a company which he had taken over was due to his own professional failures. The claimant sued for libel and malicious falsehood. The article was untrue in numerous respects, was written without any attempt to check the facts and involved some distortion of the materials on which it was based. An apology was only offered three days before trial, and shortly before trial the defendant had published three further articles which contained unchecked and inaccurate factual matter. A defence of not defamatory was persisted in at trial and the defendants also suggested to the jury that the claimant was impossible to satisfy and that no amount of money would do so. The Court of Appeal, by a majority, upheld the jury's award of compensatory and aggravated damages in the sum of £105,000. It did so although the judge had suggested to the jury a bracket of between £40,000 and £75,000–£80,000, which the Court of Appeal described as an "*entirely reasonable*" bracket (per Simon Brown L.J. at para.53(i)).

A3.11 Campbell v News Group Newspapers Ltd [2002] EWCA Civ 1143; [2002] E.M.L.R. 43

The action concerned an article in *The Sun* published in 1995 which alleged that the claimant was an active paedophile who (a) sexually abused children whom he had lured into his house with the promise of money; (b) made videos of the abuse and marketed those videos; (c) demanded money for the return of a video; (d) admitted enjoying watching teenagers through peep-holes in public lavatories; and (e) generally had a perverted interest in children. The defendants pleaded justification and relied upon a video which featured the claimant and a young (but not under-age) man engaging in sexual activity and allegedly discussing watching children in public lavatories. It was common ground that if the video was genuine the defendants would have partially justified the allegations made against the claimant, and that if it had been doctored and the defendants were aware of it, then this would aggravate the damages awarded to the claimant. The defendants argued that the claimant's conduct up to and including trial should mitigate the damages awarded to him. The jury awarded the claimant £350,000. The Court of Appeal considered that the defendants did not have a fair trial but, at the request of the parties, substituted their own figure instead of remitting the matter. The Court of Appeal considered that had the libel been made good in full, without any partial justification—in other words, had the videotape been dubbed and falsified—the libel would have been near the top of the range of seriousness. The claimant's poor sexual reputation would not have gone very far to diminish the damages. However the tape was genuine and provided substantial justification. Furthermore the claimant had engaged during the litigation in an elaborate and long-lasting attempt to pervert the course of justice. The Court of Appeal reduced the award of general damages to £30,000 and published an appendix discussing authorities on quantum of libel damages.

Grobbelaar v News Group Newspapers Ltd [2002] UKHL 4; [2002] 1   A3.12 W.L.R. 3024

The action concerned a series of articles published in *The Sun* in 1994 accusing the claimant, a well-known goalkeeper, of corruption. The claimant sued for libel. At trial the parties agreed that the articles meant that the claimant had dishonestly taken bribes and had fixed or attempted to fix the result of football matches in which he had played and that he had dishonestly taken bribes with a view to fixing the result of games in which he would play. In relation to damages the judge indicated that an award at the top end of the scale would be £150,000 but that if a significant part of the defence of justification was made out, even if the defence did not succeed, the award might be very small indeed. The jury found for the claimant and awarded him £85,000 by way of compensatory damages. The newspaper appealed. The Court of Appeal set aside the jury's decision finding that it could have been consistent only with the jury having found the claimant innocent of all corruption. The award of £85,000 was unsustainable. The Court of Appeal held that the jury's verdict was perverse and entered judgment for the defendants. The claimant appealed. The House of Lords held that the correct interpretation of the jury's verdict was that it found that the claimant had made a corrupt agreement and corruptly accepted money, as it would have been perverse to do otherwise, but accepted the claimant's version of the sting of the articles as extending to actually fixing matches, as the judge had directed was open to it, and found that that sting had not been justified. The House of Lords had inherent power to reduce the award of damages to a nominal sum of £1 to reflect the conduct of the claimant in the allegations against him which had been justified.

Wood v Chief Constable of West Midlands Police [2004] EWCA Civ 1638;   A3.13 [2005] E.M.L.R. 20

The claimant and H, trading as VSG, were in the motor salvage business for the insurance industry. H was arrested and charged with handling stolen motor vehicles, unconnected with VSG. Prior to H's trial, a senior police officer wrote letters to members of the insurance world, including to a client of VSG, advising of H's arrest and of his attempt "to disguise his criminal activities with a veil of legitimacy", thereby referring to VSG. The letters did not name the claimant, but he sued in libel complaining that the letters implicated him, as H's partner in VSG and its public face, in the alleged criminal activity of H. The police unsuccessfully raised qualified privilege. At the trial, the client of VSG to whom a letter was sent gave unexpected evidence that the letter was never received and an amendment to plead slander was sought and allowed. The jury awarded £45,000. The Court of Appeal dismissed the appeal and upheld the jury award.

A3.14 Galloway v Telegraph Group Ltd [2006] EWCA Civ 17; [2006] E.M.L.R. 11

The defendant published articles on April 22 and 23, 2003 said to have been based on documents found in badly damaged government buildings in Baghdad, accusing the claimant, a former Labour Member of Parliament and prominent anti-war campaigner, of having received money from Saddam Hussein's regime and having been granted special deals in the United Nations oil-for-food programme. The articles published on April 23 also reported that the documents indicated that the claimant had demanded more money from Saddam Hussein's regime but had been rebuffed and also raised questions about his ownership of various properties including a villa in the Algarve. The defendant disputed the meaning attributed to the articles by the claimant and pleaded *Reynolds* qualified privilege. Eady J., sitting without a jury, held that the articles were not protected by qualified privilege. Since there was no plea of justification it was not part of the court's function to rule directly upon the truth or otherwise of the underlying allegations and it had to presume that the words were false. The allegations were serious; there had been no apology; and some of the conduct at trial had been aggravating. The claimant was awarded £150,000 in December 2004. The Court of Appeal dismissed the defendant's appeal in January 2006. It held that given the seriousness of the key allegation that the claimant had taken money from Iraq for his personal profit, there was no basis upon which it could interfere with the amount of damages awarded by the judge.

A3.15 Purnell v Business F1 Magazine Ltd [2007] EWCA Civ 744; [2008] 1 W.L.R. 1

The claimant sued the publisher and author of an article alleging that he bribed a journalist using his employer's money. At an interim hearing the defence of justification was struck out on the basis that no reasonable jury could conclude that the article was true. At trial the jury awarded £75,000 for injury to feelings, injury to reputation and vindication. The defendants appealed contending that since the defence had been struck out the judge was wrong to leave the issue of damages for vindication to the jury. The Court of Appeal dismissed the appeal holding that there could be no criticism of the judge's direction on vindication and no criticism of the jury's award of damages.

A3.16 Gur v Avrupa Newspaper Ltd [2008] EWCA Civ 594; [2009] E.M.L.R. 4

The claimant, a Turkish businessman living in London, sued a Turkish language newspaper after it published three articles, one on the front page, alleging that he was guilty of defrauding the Turkish authorities by diverting funds intended for a UK charity and misstating the costs of a building project in order to pocket the surplus. The defendant entered no defence and judgment in default was granted. At a hearing to assess damages, Victoria Sharp QC (sitting as a Deputy High Court Judge) made one award for £85,000 for all three articles. An appeal was dismissed in April 2008. The Court of Appeal expressed the view that any change to the long established principle in the law of libel that courts cannot take account of a losing defendant's means when assessing the damages to be paid to the successful claimant is a matter which must be dealt with by the House of Lords.

In the course of his judgment in the Court of Appeal Dyson L.J. said, *"I can, however, see no reason why a judge or jury should not be able to take account of previous awards made by a judge, which will be reasoned and often are fully reasoned. Like the decisions of the Court of Appeal, so too awards made by judges sitting alone can provide a corpus to which reference can be made"*. Tuckey L.J. agreed and Buxton L.J. delivered a concurring judgment. (However, see the comments of Pill L.J. in Kiam v. Neil (No. 2) [1996] E.M.L.R. 493 above.)

Berezovsky v Terluk [2011] EWCA Civ 1534

A3.17

The claimant was a wealthy Russian businessman who lived in the United Kingdom, having claimed political asylum. The defendants to the original action were the state-owned Russian Television and Radio Broadcasting Company and Mr Terluk, an individual who the trial judge found had provided an interview for an episode of *Vesti Nedeli*, a news programme broadcast on a channel operated by the first defendant. The theme of the programme was the murder of a former KGB agent, Alexander Litvinenko, by radioactive poisoning some years earlier in the United Kingdom. The judge found that the words spoken by the interviewee meant that the claimant was part of a criminal conspiracy and had attempted to pay the interviewee huge amounts, and if that did not work drug him, to procure a false admission which would help the claimant. There was no truth in any of the allegations. The allegations were serious and calculated to put the claimant's refugee status in the United Kingdom at risk. The libel went uncorrected for almost three years, and the defendants had maintained a justification defence at trial. Damages of £150,000 were awarded against each defendant, and would have been higher had the meaning that the claimant was implicated in the murder of Litvinenko been made out. There had been aggravation, but the judge took a 'common denominator' approach, rather than trying to identify the aggravating features of each individual defendant's conduct.

Mr Terluk appealed against the level of award. The first defendant played no part in the appeal. The Court of Appeal explained that Eady J. had considered all the relevant factors when arriving at the amount of the damages award, including the seriousness of the libel and the amount of time it went uncorrected. Whilst the award "was certainly a high one" it did not "substantially [exceed] the most that any jury could reasonably have thought appropriate" (as per *Kiam v MGN* [2002] EWCA Civ 43). *John v MGN* [1997] Q.B. 586 was not intended to prescribe a precise correlation of damages in libel with damages for personal injury [69]; the argument that an award of £150,000 was apt only for a case of catastrophic personal injury, which it was contended was much more grave than this libel, was rejected.

Cairns v Modi; KC v MGN [2012] EWCA Civ 1382; [2013] 1 W.L.R. 1015

A3.18

The claimant in *Cairns* was an international cricketer. He sued over an allegation of match fixing published on Twitter by the defendant, who had been the Chairman of the Indian Premier League and the Vice President of the Board of Cricketing Control for India. No apology was ever made and the defendant pursued an aggressive and baseless justification defence at trial. The number of publishees of the original tweets was limited; fewer than 100 (although the tweets had been repeated, albeit in a less grave form, on another website, where about 1,000 people had read them). Damages of £90,000 were awarded. The starting point had been £75,000, and an additional £15,000 had been awarded by the trial judge in respect of aggravated damages, due to the way the defendant had conducted his case. The Court of Appeal rejected the appeal over the level of the award, holding that the sums were proportionate to the seriousness of the allegation and its "direct impact on the claimant and would serve to vindicate his reputation" [41].

The claimant in *KC* was the biological father of Baby P. He had been wrongly referred to as a child rapist in an article published by the defendant in its *People* magazine. The defendant had offered a swift apology and made an offer of amends under the procedure in the Defamation Act 1996, which had been accepted. The level of damages was left to be decided by the court. Bean J. said that the nature of the allegations was very serious, worse than in *Terluk v Berezovsky* ([2011] EWCA Civ 1534), *Houston v Smith* (December 16, 1993, unreported C.A. Transcript No. (Civil Division) 1544 of 1993), *Nail v News Group Newspapers Ltd* ([2005] 1 All E.R. 1040) or *Angel v Stainton* ([2006] EWHC 637 (QB)). The *People* magazine had a circulation of about half a million copies, and an estimated readership of 1,200,000 people. Taking into account these factors the judge had used a starting point of £150,000, which he reduced by 50% to factor in the apology and use of the offer of amends scheme. The defendant appealed, claiming that the judge's starting point was too high. The Court of Appeal agreed, and said it should have been £100,000. The trial judge had placed too much weight on the circulation and readership figures of the magazine in coming to the starting point, and insufficient focus was given to the number of people who would have read the article and actually identified KC as being the man referred to (he was not named in the article; he was only identifiable to those who knew that he was the father of Baby P). The correct award was therefore £50,000, taking account of the 50% discount. The new starting point would be consistent "with the limited publication and early apology, [but] would nevertheless adequately reflect the abhorrent nature of the crime falsely alleged against KC and the damage done to and its impact on him" [49].

Part 2

Non-jury Damages Awards (from 2000)

A3.19 Cunningham v Essex County Council, June 2000

The claimant, a teacher who had been employed by the defendants, sued them for various torts including libel. The libel claim was in respect of a letter which included accusations of theft by the claimant. The letter was passed onwards from the original recipient, by someone within the first defendant council, to another department. The Court held that the onward transmission of the letter was the responsibility of the first defendant and not protected by qualified privilege and therefore the claimant was entitled to damages in the sum of £9,500.

A3.20 Lillie v Newcastle City Council [2002] EWHC 1600 (QB)

The claimants were qualified nursery workers at a Social Services-run day nursery in Newcastle. In 1995 Newcastle City Council commissioned a report into allegations of child abuse at the nursery. The report was written and published to the council by its authors in November 1998. On November 12, 1998 the council held a sub-committee meeting at which the report was presented to members of the sub-committee, the press and the public. It concluded that the claimants were guilty of sexually, physically and emotionally abusing children in their care both inside and outside the nursery, sometimes acting alone and sometimes involving other people. The claimants were given no forewarning about the date on which it would be published, its contents or the details of the complaints made against them. The conclusions were widely reported in the local and national press and the claimants were forced to flee from their homes, go into hiding and change their names. All of the defendants pleaded qualified privilege. Four of the defendants pleaded justification. The case lasted seven months. Eady J. held that the allegations were untrue and that four of the defendants were motivated by malice which vitiated their defences of qualified privilege. The first defendant's defence of qualified privilege was upheld. Each claimant was awarded general and aggravated damages of £200,000, the maximum level the Court considered was permitted (with special damages to be determined at a later date). Eady J. considered that each of the claimants had merited an award at the highest permitted level and both had earned it several times over because of the scale, gravity and persistence of the allegations and of the aggravating factors.

English v Hastie, January 2002   **A3.21**

The claimants, insurance underwriters working for a company called Trenwick, sued the defendants, the publisher and editor of a monthly subscription newsletter circulated among the insurance industry in London and internationally. The article reported that a writ had been issued against Trenwick by another company called Fairmont which the claimants alleged meant that they had unlawfully interfered in Fairmont's business and wrongly diverted about £200,000 and that one of the claimants had resigned and the other was suspended pending an inquiry. The defendants relied upon the defence of *Reynolds* qualified privilege. A jury held that the article was defamatory and answered some factual questions relevant to the privilege defence. Gray J. dismissed that defence, held that the article meant that there existed reasonable grounds to suspect that the claimants had unlawfully interfered with the business of another company and had failed to disclose a financial interest, and awarded the claimants £10,000 each.

Field v Local Sunday Newspapers, March 2002   **A3.22**

The chief executive of Bedford Borough Council, Shaun Field, the borough solicitor, Michael Gough, and a barrister employed by BBC, Andy Darkoh, sued the *Bedfordshire on Sunday* newspaper and Stewart Lister, the local agent of the Conservative Party, in respect of publications relating to their conduct during council elections that took place in the borough in 2000. Mr Field was the returning officer and in one ward it was discovered that an envelope containing postal ballots had not been counted. The council sought a court ruling for an order to allow a recount to take place. The County Court Judge adjourned the application on various grounds. Mr Lister produced a critical press release about the steps taken by the council which led to an article being published in the local newspaper. The claimants sued for libel. The defendants disputed the meanings pleaded and relied upon defences of justification, fair comment, absolute and qualified privilege. At trial Gray J. held that, having published the press release, Mr Lister was also liable for the re-publication of parts of the press release that appeared in the articles. The Judge dismissed the defences of privilege and comment in respect of all three claimants. The Judge upheld the defence of justification in respect of Mr Gough and Mr Darkoh and ruled that it failed in respect of Mr Field. The Judge held that Mr Field, who was supposed to be apolitical, had been libelled to the effect that he had authorised the spending of public funds in order to further the aims of one political party, and awarded him £27,500 in damages for two publications. In 2003 Mr Gough successfully appealed the Judge's decision on justification in relation to his responsibilities in the election with damages to be assessed at a later hearing.

Greenaway v Poole [2003] EWHC 1735 (QB)   **A3.23**

The defendant, a councillor, published a newsletter in October 1998 and two pamphlets in April 1999 that contained allegations of dishonesty, corruption and misappropriation on the part of the claimants, one of whom was a parish council clerk and the other a former councillor. So far as one of the publications was concerned the Court ruled that s.10 Defamation Act 1952 removed any possibility of privilege. The defendant failed in his plea of justification and the claimants proved that the defendant was motivated by malice. Jack J., sitting without a jury, held that the allegations, although not published nationally, were serious and unjustified and had caused real damage in the community where the claimants were well known and that the defendant had succeeded in preventing the second claimant being re-elected and causing the first claimant to resign. Jack J. took into account the level of damages in personal injuries cases and awarded each claimant £25,000.

A3.24 The Gleaner Company Ltd v Abrahams [2003] UKPC 55; [2004] 1 A.C. 628

The plaintiff, a former Jamaican Minister of Tourism, had been accused of taking bribes. A plea of justification had stood on the record for some seven years before it was struck out in the absence of pleaded facts to support it. An apology was then published, but the plaintiff produced strong evidence of a ruined career, public humiliation and prolonged stress. The Privy Council declined to interfere with an award of the equivalent of £533,000 general damages made by the Jamaican Court of Appeal in substitution of a jury award of £1.2m. The Jamaican Court of Appeal declined to follow the English practice derived from *John v MGN Ltd* [1997] Q.B. 586 of using personal injuries damages as a reference point in the quantification of libel damages, and the Privy Council held that they had not erred in this respect. It was a question of policy "open to legitimate differences of opinion" and did not, in Lord Hoffmann's view, involve any question of legal principle.

A3.25 Downtex v Flatley [2004] EWHC 333 (QB)

The claimant, a company, sued the defendant for libel in respect of two letters that alleged that the claimant was or was close to being insolvent and its directors might have been guilty of misconduct in distorting and manipulating the financial figures. The pleaded defence of qualified privilege had been struck out on appeal at an earlier hearing and the action came before Tugendhat J. for summary disposal under s.8 Defamation Act 1996. Tugendhat J. considered that, without the cap of £10,000 imposed by the Defamation Act 1996, the damages award would not have been less than £30,000 which was the least which was required to compensate for the damage done; but it could have been higher.

A3.26 Walsh v Carpenter, unreported, April 25, 2005

The claimant sued for libel over an allegation made in an email published to one person to the effect that he had been dismissed from his employment for 'financial irregularities'. Eady J., sitting without a jury, awarded damages of £18,000. The allegations were serious; the defendant had been motivated by malice and had refused to retract the allegation; and he had repeated the allegation in his evidence, even though he had made no attempt to justify it.

A3.27 Rackham v Sandy [2005] EWHC 482 (QB)

The claimant sued over a letter written by three defendants in their capacities as the CEO, finance director and legal director of a company, and sent to four members of the board of the company. The letter made allegations of poor corporate governance by the claimant. The defendants had first raised their concerns with the chairman of the company, but he had not dealt with them. The defendants obtained and followed legal advice from solicitors on the letter before it was sent. The second defendant was not involved in the writing of the letter. He approved it after it was read over the telephone to him while he was on holiday. The defendants relied on the defence of qualified privilege. The claimant admitted that the publication was made on an occasion of qualified privilege. Gray J., sitting without a jury, held that this was a case where there was an established relationship between the publishers and the publishees and the court should be slower to find malice in such cases. The judge found that the second and third defendants had not been actuated by any improper motive in sending the letter. The first defendant was found to have written the letter in order to procure the removal of the claimant from the board and to save his own position. The claimant was awarded judgment against the first defendant and £2,000 damages. Gray J. considered that the allegations in the letter complained of were of some gravity but the circulation of the letter had been very limited. The judge also considered that the action was brought because no acceptable apology was offered to him rather than because his feelings had been hurt by the libel and that, in the circumstances, the reasoned judgment in his favour would provide vindication.

Cray v Hancock, unreported, November 4, 2005   **A3.28**

The claimant was a solicitor who had acted for the defendants, a husband and wife, in a dispute with a bathroom firm. In April 2003, the wife terminated the solicitor's instructions, complaining about delay in the execution of a consent order and the level of the claimant's firm's fees. In early January the husband sent a letter and two faxes to the claimant's offices which were seen by other members of the claimant's firm. The claimant contended that the husband had embarked on a 2-year campaign of harassment by sending e-mails and letters (mostly anonymously) and by posting material, again anonymously, on various websites and internet forums. A claim for libel and harassment was commenced by the claimant in August 2003 and the defendants counterclaimed for negligence in the conduct of their case against the bathroom firm. H.H.J. Previté (sitting as a High Court Judge) found for the claimant and dismissed the counterclaim. The Judge awarded £9,000 for the libel claims and £10,000 for the harassment.

Keith-Smith v Williams [2006] EWHC 860 (QB)   **A3.29**

The claimant, a candidate of the UK Independence Party in 2005, sued the defendant in respect of a series of offensive comments alleging sexual perversions and racism made by her anonymously on an internet discussion group. Only members could contribute to discussions but anyone could access the site over the internet. The purpose of the site was to engage in political discussion. The allegations were untrue and the defendant refused to apologise. H.H.J. MacDuff QC awarded £5,000 compensatory and £5,000 aggravated damages. The Judge said that the damages were modest because the remarks had fortunately not been disseminated widely and were in all probability disbelieved.

Murray v Motor Schools Association, unreported, June 12, 2006   **A3.30**

The claimant, a former driving instructor, sued the defendant over allegations in its monthly magazine that he had deliberately failed driving test candidates and had distorted the Driving Standards Agency's percentage rates. The libel was admitted, a front page apology was published and a statement in open court made. At a damages hearing Eady J. awarded the claimant £30,000.

Creative Resins International Ltd v Glasslam Europe Ltd [2006] EWHC   **A3.31**
3159 (QB)

The claimant, a company producing glass products, sued three defendants in respect of two publications, a letter and an article published online and in hard copy in a trade magazine. By the time the matter came to a hearing before Eady J. only the third defendant, who was sued only in respect of the article, remained in the case. He was resident in the United States and did not wish to take part in the proceedings but was aware of their existence. The Court held that the article meant that the claimant had been guilty of flagrant acts of copyright infringement and had deliberately ignored an order of a German court. Since the claimant was a corporate entity the Court was required to fix general damages which did not include damages for hurt feelings. The publication had been malicious, but in the circumstances this was not directly relevant; however, the allegations had never been withdrawn and the award needed to leave no doubt in the minds of anyone who had read the article that they were false. The Judge awarded £15,000.

A3.32 Culla Park Ltd v Richards [2007] EWHC 1850 (QB)

Four claimants who ran an activity centre and a restaurant in Carmarthenshire sued the four defendants in for alleging (by means of signs) that the claimants were dumping rubbish and toxic waste at their site. At an interim hearing Eady J. struck out the defences, on the ground of non-payment of costs orders and because no substantive defences were available. At trial, where the defendants did not appear, the Court held that all four defendants were liable. Eady J. had to determine damages in respect of four claimants and how much each defendant was liable to pay. The Judge did not award separate damages for each publication. He awarded £24,000 in general damages to each of the three personal claimants who had each suffered their own anxiety and lived with the distress suffered by the others, and £39,000 in special damages to the corporate claimant.

A3.33 Ghannouchi v Al Arabiya, unreported, November 8, 2007

The claimant, a Tunisian exile given political asylum in England in 1993, sued the defendant, a Dubai-based television broadcaster, in respect of a broadcast that described him as an extremist Islamic figure with links to, and as being identified with, Al Qaeda. The defendant was aware of the proceedings but chose not to defend them save to suggest that publication was minimal in England and Wales. Eady J., in assessing damages, took into account the seriousness of the allegation; the behaviour of the defendant and the security and safety of the claimant if people did not believe he had no links to terrorism. The Judge awarded £165,000.

A3.34 Seafresh Ltd v Shaw, unreported, 2008

The claimant company sued a former agent who had left to work for a rival company in respect of allegations in a leaflet that the claimant had taken advantage of its customers by inflating its prices. Publication was limited but damaging, because the Court found that the leaflet had been sent to customers of the claimant. The defendant did not take part in the proceedings and judgment was entered in default. At a damages hearing, H.H.J. Curran, sitting in the County Court in Cardiff, awarded £20,000.

A3.35 Trumm v Norman [2008] EWHC 116 (QB)

The claimant, a train driver and former member of ASLEF, sued the defendant, the acting general secretary of ASLEF. The words complained of were published in a circular sent to about 18,000 people, not all of whom were members of ASLEF, and on the union's website. The circular alleged that the claimant was guilty of disreputable conduct, untruthful and an obsessive. Qualified privilege protected publication to members but not other publishees, who numbered about 100 people. In assessing damages Tugendhat J. took into account the tone of the claimant's own website reports about ASLEF, which provoked the circular, and the claimant's robust personality, and awarded £7,500, half the amount the Judge said he would have awarded had it not been for the claimant's own conduct and personality.

Applause Store Productions Ltd v Raphael [2008] EWHC 1781 (QB);   **A3.36**
[2008] Info T.L.R. 318

The claimants alleged that the defendant set up a Facebook profile in the name of the
second claimant containing personal information about him and a group page alleging
that the claimants owed a substantial amount of money and were not to be trusted in
the financial conduct of their business. The defendant, a former friend of the second
claimant, denied that he was responsible for setting up the profile or the group page.
At trial Richard Parkes QC (sitting as a Deputy High Court Judge without a jury) held
that the defendant was responsible for setting up and, hence, publishing the profile and
the group page. The extent of publication was estimated at fewer than 100 people. The
Deputy Judge awarded the second claimant £15,000 for libel and the first claimant
company £5,000. He also awarded the second claimant £2,000 for breaches of his
privacy.

Galloway v Jewish Communications Ltd, unreported, July 31, 2008   **A3.37**

The claimant, the Respect Party MP, complained about a broadcast on a local and
internet radio show that twice featured a fictitious Middle Eastern correspondent
named 'Georgie Galloway', who spoke the words 'Kill the Jews!' The defendant
admitted the claim in full and at a damages hearing Eady J. held that the feature was
a spoof but bore the serious defamatory meaning that the claimant held anti-semitic
views. The Judge took into account the apology made by the defendant on its website
and the relatively small scale of publication and awarded the claimant £15,000
damages.

Keating v Large, unreported, August 13, 2008   **A3.38**

The claimant, the national chairman of the staff association of the Ministry of Defence,
sued Roy Large, the operator of the Ministry of Defence Police's 'unofficial' website,
over allegations relating to the granting of legal assistance to the claimant's partner.
The postings alleged that the claimant had personally granted his partner Police
Defence Federation legal assistance to pursue a spurious and unfounded employment
tribunal claim. The allegations were false. At a quantum hearing Richard Parkes QC,
sitting as a Deputy High Court Judge, awarded the claimant £45,000 damages.

Gregg v O'Gara [2008] EWHC 658 (QB)   **A3.39**

The claimant was head of the West Yorkshire Police Homicide and Major Enquiry
team which was involved in the investigation into the Yorkshire Ripper hoax letters.
This was a case review of the hoaxes which had misled the police investigation of the
1978 and 1979 murders, and led to the conviction in March 2006 of John Humble for
perverting the course of justice. The defendant had published a series of allegations in
an email and on websites, which suggested that the claimant had knowingly brought
about the conviction of an innocent man (i.e. Humble), and had been party to
tampering with DNA evidence and mistreating the accused during the investigation.
The defence relied upon was justification. The claimant applied for summary judgment
on the basis that there was no real prospect of the defence succeeding. The claimant
showed that the defamatory allegations complained of were indisputably false. He
relied upon the fact that John Humble had admitted to the 1970s hoaxes and pleaded
guilty, and had continued to assert his responsibility for the hoaxes after he was
convicted. The defendant had posted a letter on his own website from John Humble in
which Humble had admitted responsibility. The claimant had played no part in the
forensic process leading to the conviction of Humble and his only involvement in the
police station interviewing process had been to monitor it remotely. The evidence that
there had been substantial internet publication in the jurisdiction was uncontradicted.

There was no credible evidence to support the plea of justification and no other viable defence. The judge awarded the claimant £50,000.

A3.40   Coad v Cruze [2009] EWHC 3782 (QB)

The claimant was a Conservative councillor. She brought claims against two members of a local political organisation over libels contained in an election leaflet distributed in 2007 and a non-election political leaflet published in 2008. The first defendant compromised the action. The second defendant made an unsuccessful application to adjourn the trial of damages, judgment having been entered in default. The judge found that the pleaded meanings contended for by the claimant were unsustainable. He assessed damages on the basis of the meanings that he had determined, namely that there were reasonable grounds to suspect that the Electoral Commission was investigating the claimant for suspected election expense irregularities and that there were strong grounds to suspect voting fraud on the part of the claimant. Although the defence of justification had been struck out, the second defendant had persisted in his allegations. Evidence of publication was lacking, but the judge accepted that the leaflets had been distributed in the claimant's ward and must at least have been read by a few hundred constituents. The admissible evidence as to distress was extremely limited. However, the second defendant had never apologised or offered a retraction. The judge awarded £15,000.

A3.41   Levi v Bates [2009] EWHC 1495 (QB)

The claimant, a former director of Leeds United Football Club, brought a claim in relation to comments published in three match programmes for club home fixtures and in a letter to club members by the defendant chairman of the club, Ken Bates. The defendant had referred to the claimant's behaviour as devious and dishonourable. The defendant relied on defences of meaning, fair comment, qualified privilege and justification. The judge determined that the allegations in their actual meanings could not be justified and that whilst the allegations were in the nature of comment, the substratum of fact which underlay them was insufficient for the defence to succeed. Qualified privilege protected the defendant's letter but the match programmes were distributed to those with no immediate interest in club affairs, such as corporate guests, PR people and visiting fans. The defendant had sought to justify the allegations at a public trial lasting many days. The gratuitous inclusion of personal address details in one of the match programmes was an aggravating factor. The judge awarded £50,000 in respect of the three match programmes where the defences had failed, and subdivided that award publication by publication.

A3.42   Emlick v Gulf News, unreported, July 23, 2009

The claimant was a property developer in the United Arab Emirates. He brought a claim in relation to an article published in a newspaper based in the UAE in April 2008 but sued only in relation to the damage caused by the publication in England and Wales. He pleaded that the article meant that he was an unscrupulous property developer who had defrauded investors and evaded those pursuing him. The publisher did not take part in the proceedings but asserted in writing to the court that UAE was the correct jurisdiction and that publication data suggested that there were only 100 readers of the publication in England and Wales. The claimant's case on the extent of publication was that he had been contacted by dozens of people based within the jurisdiction who had read the article and relied on its reproduction on 14 third party websites—republications for which the judge held the defendant responsible. The judge accepted that the claimant had been subject to a serious and damaging libel and awarded £25,000 damages. If the whole publication had been within the jurisdiction he would have awarded £100,000.

Warren v Madugqu, unreported, July 27, 2009   **A3.43**

The defendant, otherwise known as Herbie Hyde, made a series of claims in a television interview that the claimant, a boxing promoter, had manipulated boxers and bribed them to give up titles. The specific allegation that the claimant complained of was that he had dishonestly persuaded one boxer to retire and give up his title so that a younger boxer promoted by the claimant would gain the title from him. The defendant took no part in the proceedings and judgment in default was entered against him. The claimant contended that the publication, particularly the allegation of bribery, had been a serious attack on his integrity, as his promoter role required that he should behave fairly and honestly. The judge awarded £35,000.

Bloom v Robinson-Millar, October 7, 2009, [2013] EWHC 3918 (QB)   **A3.44**

The claimant, an accountant, sued his neighbour over seven different publications which alleged that he had committed serious criminal offences including fraud, perjury and criminal damage in his role as director of the management company of the block of flats in which both parties lived. The claimant and others had told the defendant that the allegations were unfounded but she persisted in making them over many years. The defendant's substantive defences were struck out prior to trial. The claimant was entitled to the law's protection from behaviour which was obsessive and irrational and which reasonable people would have realised amounted to harassment. The number and gravity of the allegations, over a considerable period, justified a global damages award of £30,000. The judge said that if she had thought it appropriate to make separate awards she would have awarded £25,000 for the claim in libel and £5,000 for the claim in harassment.

Supreme Events Ltd v Anderson, unreported, December 17, 2009   **A3.45**

The claimant was a wedding planning company which brought a claim in respect of an internet posting alleging that it had been taken to court on numerous occasions and that readers of the posting should therefore avoid dealing with it. The defendant denied responsibility for publication but admitted that she had been aware of the statements in question. Under s.8 of the Defamation Act 1996 the Master summarily disposed of the claim, awarding the maximum figure of £10,000 permitted under the statutory scheme.

Bryce v Barber, unreported, July 26, 2010   **A3.46**

The defendant, a chef, had fallen out with the claimant, a certified bailiff who was studying law at Stafford University. The defendant had posted an indecent image of a child on an internet social network site alongside a statement which suggested that the claimant was a paedophile. Judgment was entered against the defendant. The claimant adduced evidence on the assessment of damages that the posting had caused him great distress and would have been visible to more than 800 people. The judge found the posting to have been malicious. There was no apology or expression of remorse, and damages were assessed at £10,000.

Metropolitan International Schools Ltd v Designtechnica Corp [2010]   **A3.47**
EWHC 2411 (QB)

The claimant was a distance learning company based in the United Kingdom. It brought claims in respect of two separate internet forum threads, each of which discussed one of the claimant's products. The defendant was a US-based IT industry consumer affairs website operator. The forum threads alleged that there were reasonable grounds to suspect that the claimant offered courses which infringed copyright, were sold in a cavalier manner with improper and fraudulent credit checking procedures and were, in sum, a fraud. The forum threads were extensive, running to hundreds of webpages. The defendant took no part in the proceedings and judgment in default was entered against it, the claims against two other internet intermediaries having been either settled or resolved. On the assessment of damages the claimant chose not to rely on the presumption of falsity in its favour but adduced positive evidence refuting the allegations. The claim was only made in relation to damage sustained within the jurisdiction. There was evidence that the threads were accessed by readers within the jurisdiction, the claimant's business was overwhelmingly UK-based, and its courses were marketed there. The award was £50,000.

A3.48 Phillips v Kordowski, unreported, October 12, 2010

The defendant ran a website, "Solicitors from Hell", which encouraged internet users to post statements anonymously naming and shaming UK solicitors for shoddy work or disreputable conduct. The defendant did not attempt to verify the material that was uploaded to the website, but offered to remove postings if aggrieved subjects paid a £299 administration fee. The specific post on the website to which the claimant objected had received 50,000 hits. It alleged that the claimant was of dubious professional competence. In the absence of any substantive defence the claimant applied for summary judgment. The demand for payment to ensure that the libel was taken down was an aggravating factor. Damages were assessed at £17,500.

A3.49 Cambridge v Makin [2011] EWHC 12 (QB)

Both parties were professional interpreters. The claimant was also a non-executive director of a not-for-profit company (NRPSI) controlled by the Chartered Institute of Linguists (CIL), which administered a register of professional linguists for use by the police and public service organisations who used interpreters. NRPSI had granted a licence to access the register to a third party commercial agency. The defendant sent an email to a distribution list which included, among others, members of the CIL who had registered with NRPSI. It criticised the claimant, alleging that she had abused her position as a director by acting in conflict with the interests of those she was bound to protect, because she had granted a licence from which she stood to gain personally. The statement was found to be untrue: there was no real possibility of a conflict of interest, given the claimant's limited connection with the third party agency. While the defendant's plea of qualified privilege would have been successful in respect of a number of the publishees, a finding of malice ultimately defeated it in any event. The libel was a serious one, published initially to about 1,000 members of the claimant's own profession, and had caused great distress. It was particularly humiliating given that the claimant worked voluntarily for the NRPSI and had reached a distinguished position in her profession. Damages were assessed at £30,000. This took account of a £30,000 settlement that had already been received from GMB trade union, which had been the second defendant to the claim.

A3.50 Can Say (t/a Corbe Café) v British Gas Trading Ltd [2010] EWHC 3946 (QB)

The claimant was the new owner and operator of a café business that he had taken over from his son, who had defaulted on the payment of several electricity bills. The defendant was the electricity provider. The son had been operating the business through a limited company, so the debt was in the company's name. Despite notifying the defendant of these facts, one of its employees arrived at the claimant's premises to disconnect the supply because of non-payment. Whilst attending he remarked to one of the claimant's customers that he was doing so because "this chap did not pay his electricity bill", clearly referring to the claimant, who successfully sued for slander. The statement was untrue: he had not failed to pay the account. The failure was the company's. There was no evidence of any pecuniary loss, but the slander was actionable per se as it was calculated to disparage the claimant in his business. It had caused him distress, although it was not published widely. General damages were assessed at £12,750.

Farrall v Kordowski [2011] EWHC 2140 (QB)   A3.51

The defendant was the operator of the "Solicitors from Hell" website (see A3.48 above). An anonymous poster had published an entry on the website seriously criticising the claimant's professional competence as a solicitor. The claimant was not given the chance to comment on the posting, but was only offered the opportunity to delete it, for a fee of £299. Following pre-action correspondence between the parties the listing had been removed but, as at the date of the hearing, it was still possible to know there had been a critical posting about the claimant by performing a simple internet search. The precise extent of hits on the post was not known. Judgment in default had been entered against the defendant, and a permanent injunction granted. He had played no part in the proceedings at any stage. Lloyd Jones J. found that the libel had been very distressing for the claimant, a young solicitor, with potentially very serious consequences for her career. The allegations were made without foundation and were malicious. They were aggravated by the fact there was no attempt to verify them before publication or ask the claimant for comment, nor was any attempt made to apologise. The defendant's attempts to pressurise the claimant into paying him to remove the allegations and his conduct when dealing with the claimant's complaint were described by the judge as "arrogant and disreputable". The duration of publication was limited; it was posted online in full for only around a month. Damages were assessed at £10,000.

Clynes v O'Connor [2011] EWHC 1201 (QB)   A3.52

The parties were neighbours. The defendant slandered the claimant by shouting various insults at him including that he was a 'wife beater', 'drug dealer' and a 'pervert', which was witnessed by a small audience of people standing nearby (a handful of adults, and several children). The defendant failed to engage meaningfully in the legal process. There was no evidence of actual injury to reputation or any need for public vindication. Damages were assessed at £1,500. The judge observed that the matter should have "been disposed of by a prompt apology at the outset" and that "the parties should quite simply have got on with their lives".

Robins v Kordowski [2011] EWHC 1912 (QB)   A3.53

The claimant was a partner of a law firm who, together with the firm, sued the operator of the "Solicitors from Hell" website (see A3.48 and A3.51 above). The claim was brought over a post alleging that he had lied and acted in his own interests while disregarding the interests of a former client. The claim was initially brought against two defendants but subsequently settled against the second, leaving only Mr Kordowski. Judgment had been granted in default of defence, which Tugendhat J. refused to set aside. He offered no correction or apology, and gave every indication that he sought to prove the allegations true. The claimants successfully applied for summary disposal of the claim under s.8 Defamation Act 1996, under which damages are capped at a maximum of £10,000. An injunction was ordered and a damages award of £10,000 was made. At [86] the judge stated that: "In my judgment an award of less than £10,000 for so serious an allegation as that of lying and dishonesty made against the claimant solicitors would not adequately reflect the vindication that they have achieved."

A3.54 Thornton v Telegraph Media Group Ltd [2011] EWHC 1884 (QB); [2012] E.M.L.R. 8

The claimant had written a book about the art world based on many interviews she had conducted, and acknowledged Ms Lynn Barber, a journalist, as one such interviewee. The defendant, the publisher of a national newspaper, had published a book review of the claimant's book, both in print and online, written by Ms Barber. The review implied that Ms Barber had not been interviewed by the claimant and alleged that the claimant had given her interviewees copy approval, i.e. the right to read what was said about them and to alter it. The claimant brought a libel claim over the interview allegation, and a malicious falsehood claim concerning the copy approval allegation. A qualified offer of amends was made in respect of the interview allegation, but was rejected by the claimant. The claimant succeeded in full: the interview allegation was held to be false, and the malicious falsehood claim was made out. The former was the more serious allegation: it was an attack on the claimant's honesty. Although an apology was published in respect of that allegation, it was not prompt. The qualified offer of amends provided no defence to the libel claim as malice had been established. Damages were aggravated by the finding of malice, together with the manner in which the defendant had dealt with the claimant's complaint. The approach taken by counsel in the cross-examination of the claimant at trial, which was aggressive and unnecessarily intrusive, had also increased the sum. The award was £65,000, which the judge would, if necessary, have apportioned as to £50,000 for the libel, and £15,000 for the malicious falsehood, splitting the award equally between the print and online publications. The website publication was more limited in terms of publishees, but lasted much longer, and was likely to have been picked up by searches for the claimant's name online.

A3.55 Al-Amoudi v Kifle [2011] EWHC 2037 (QB)

The claimant was a wealthy Ethiopian businessman with business connections in the United Kingdom. The defendant was the publisher and editor of an Ethiopian news website, on which an article was published which made several very serious defamatory allegations against the claimant. These were that there were reasonable grounds to suspect him of having knowingly financed international terrorism, that he had married his young daughter off to an elderly Saudi royal as a gift, that he was probably responsible for murdering the person with whom his daughter had an affair, and that he had been hunting his daughter and his supposed granddaughter across London in order to ensure their execution in Saudi Arabia, by way of flogging, stoning to death or otherwise. The judge accepted on the evidence that the readership of the article was likely to be in the several thousands. The article was freely available on the internet for about three months, and was subsequently available on a password-protected basis to those who registered with the site. The defendant played no part in the proceedings, but continued to repeat the allegations, and maintained their truth. Judgment in default was entered, and damages were assessed at £175,000. The allegations were of a very serious nature, and the impact on those reading them was likely to have been substantial. The defendant's unrepentant stance had also aggravated the damages: far from apologising, he had continued to repeat the libels and had abused the claimant and his lawyers.

A3.56 Cooper v Turrell [2011] EWHC 3269 (QB)

The claimants were a public company and one of its directors. The defendant was the former CEO of the company whose employment had been terminated. He subsequently went on to make various libellous allegations against the claimants online and in emails to the company's regulator, accusing them of dishonesty and criminal conduct, and questioning the director's fitness to continue in his role. The defendant had, whilst his contract was being terminated, made recordings of various confidential discussions, including one in which the director had disclosed private medical information to a third party, and discussions amongst company board members while they were taking advice from the company's solicitors. As part of his campaign against the company, he subsequently uploaded the recording to his website. Tugendhat J. found that the defendant had acted maliciously and dishonestly, knowing that the libels were false. The claimants were entitled to damages and injunctive relief. There had been substantial publication aimed at those doing business with the company. The company was awarded £30,000 in respect of the libels and £10,000 for the breach of confidence. The director was awarded £50,000 for the libels and £30,000 for the misuse of his private information.

Bento v Chief Constable of Bedfordshire [2012] EWHC 1525 (QB)   A3.57

The claimant had been convicted of murder but, following fresh evidence, an application to quash the conviction and order a retrial was granted, although the CPS ultimately decided not to pursue the prosecution. The defendant, upset with that decision, issued a press release criticising the CPS, which was held to mean that the decision was wrong because the claimant was "probably guilty of the offence". The defendant pleaded justification and qualified privilege, but failed on both counts. The statement was untrue because the defendant could not establish that the claimant killed the deceased on the balance of probabilities. The qualified privilege defence was also rejected because the public interest was not served by the police issuing statements suggesting that a decision of the CPS was wrong because the individual concerned was probably guilty. An attempt to rely on reply to attack privilege also failed: it was premature if it was intended to rebut an attack on the defendant's conduct, and would have been disproportionate in any event. There was no evidence of publication on a national scale, but various local media had been emailed the statement. £125,000 damages were awarded, with aggravation attributable to the pursuit of the justification defence at trial.

Joseph v Spiller [2012] EWHC 2958 (QB)   A3.58

The claimants were members of a Motown tribute act that was promoted by the defendants, a musical events booking agency and its owner. The claimants sued over a posting on the agency's booking website which questioned their professionalism and their ability to adhere to the terms of contracts they signed, which had been written following a dispute between the parties over a repeat booking at a venue. The defendants pleaded justification and honest comment, claiming that the leader of the band, the first claimant, had conducted himself in an unprofessional, contemptuous and cavalier manner towards contractual obligations. Judgment was given for the claimants in part; whilst the first claimant had acted unprofessionally he had not demonstrated a contemptuous or cavalier attitude to contractual relations, and the first defendant had not believed what he had written (namely there being a risk that the claimants might not abide by all the terms of a contract they signed). However, only nominal damages were awarded because of an attempt by the first claimant to deceive the court by fabricating a part of the claim for special damages. Although it did not affect the whole claim, it was very serious, and amounted to an abuse of the court's process.

Miller v Associated Newspapers Ltd [2012] EWHC 3721 (QB)   A3.59

The claimant was a management consultant who co-founded an IT consultancy, whose clients included large businesses and public bodies. He sued the defendants over a front page article appearing in the *Daily Mail*. It alleged there were reasonable grounds to suspect that he was a willing beneficiary of improper conduct and cronyism because of his friendship with the then Deputy Commissioner of the Metropolitan Police, over the award of multi-million pound publicly-funded police contracts to his consultancy. The newspaper had a circulation in the millions. The defendant had made an open offer, but it was rejected by the claimant. It did not contain an apology and the offer of damages was low. The defendant lost on its justification defence at trial and failed to make good its argument that continuation of the claim amounted to an abuse of process. Damages were assessed at £65,000, substantially aggravated by the failure to publish any apology or retraction, the pursuance of the justification defence, and the contention that continuance of the claim amounted to an abuse of process. The cross-examination of the claimant at trial (which, though courteous, was lengthy and tenacious) also exacerbated the damages, as did the prominence of the article and the failure to contact the claimant prior to publication.

A3.60 Hussein v Hamilton Franks & Co Ltd [2013] EWHC 462 (QB)

The claimants were doctors who had originally trained in the United Kingdom, but subsequently moved to the United States, together with their son, a businessman. The parents had family connections in the United Kingdom, and the son had business connections. The defendant was a UK-registered company that operated a business website containing a section marked 'black list'. The claimants' details were added to that list and under the relevant entry it was alleged they had acted in a fraudulent and deceptive manner in relation to business transactions. The defendant failed to file a defence, and judgment was entered in default. An injunction was granted and damages were assessed at £40,000; £10,000 for each of the parents, and £20,000 for the son. While the United Kingdom was not the main locus of their reputations, the allegations were severe and the ambit of publication sufficiently large to justify that sum.

A3.61 Cruddas v Adams [2013] EWHC 145 (QB)

The claimant was a wealthy businessman and philanthropist, who subsequently became the co-treasurer of the Conservative party. The defendant was a lobbyist and political blogger. The claimant had been the subject of a series of articles, the result of an undercover exposé, about his alleged role in the 'cash for access' scandal (namely that he had offered for sale the opportunity to influence government policy to foreign donors in breach of electoral law). The claimant had sued the newspaper that published the original allegations for libel and malicious falsehood (in which he was, subsequent to this claim, wholly successful). He had also sued another national newspaper that repeated them, which settled the claim against it, apologising and withdrawing the allegations by way of a statement in open court. The defendant in this case repeated the allegations to similar effect through blog posts and tweets, specifically contending that the claimant was a criminal, and challenging him to sue. He refused to acknowledge the falsity of his claims, and took every opportunity to aggravate the original publications until, at the last moment, he finally acknowledged that the criminality allegations were false. No defence was filed, and judgement in default was entered. At the assessment of damages hearing he offered a last-minute apology and sought to withdraw the allegations of criminality. An award of £45,000 was made by Eady J. who said that the award might have been higher, but he took into account that, by the time of this hearing, a significant number of readers who were following the subject would have come to recognise that the defendant's allegations were silly and not to be taken seriously.

A3.62 Thompson v James and Carmarthenshire County Council [2013] EWHC 515 (QB)

The claimant, a self-styled political blogger, sued her local council and its Chief Executive for libel over an open letter published on a blog. It had accused the claimant and her family of running a campaign of harassment, intimidation and defamation of council staff. There was a lengthy and complex history between the parties, originating from the rejection of planning applications made by the claimant's brother-in-law. More recently, there had been a dispute concerning the filming of council meetings by the claimant, which had, on one occasion, resulted in her being arrested (the police having been called by the council). An open letter had been written by a member of the public criticising the council's actions, which had been posted on a public blog, and urged a reply. This came in the form of the Chief Executive's open letter, criticising the claimant and her family's behaviour, which was the subject-matter of her claim. The claimant had throughout been criticising the council on her blog, alleging *inter alia* that the chief executive operated a "slush fund" and was guilty of corruption. Five of these postings formed the basis of his counterclaim in libel against her. On the claim, judgment was entered for the defendants. Their justification defence succeeded. On the counterclaim, judgment was entered for the Chief Executive who succeeded in respect of three out of the five postings complained about. Suggestions that the chief executive's counterclaim had been an abuse of process were without foundation. Damages were assessed at £25,000, of which £5,000 represented aggravated damages awarded because of the way the chief executive was cross-examined at trial, and because the claimant's dominant motive had been to injure him. The award was limited because of the small number of publishees who would have seen the claimant's blog (there had been only around 200 hits).

ZAM v CFW and TFW [2013] EWHC 662 (QB); [2013] E.M.L.R. 27   **A3.63**

The claimant was a senior businessman and school governor whose immediate family were the beneficiaries of substantial family trusts. The first defendant was the claimant's wife's sister, who was also a beneficiary of the trusts, and the second defendant was her husband. The defendants had made entirely false allegations to the claimant's employer and family members, that he had mismanaged and misappropriated the family trusts, and was a paedophile. They further attempted to blackmail him. When demands made of the claimant were not met, they repeated the allegations, in breach of an interim injunction, to others, including those responsible for a school of which the claimant was a governor. The claimant sued for slander, libel and harassment. The first defendant denied liability for having made the statements and the second defendant played no part whatsoever in the proceedings. The number of publishees, although initially very limited, was subsequently estimated to be in the hundreds or, at most, the low thousands. The proceedings against the first defendant had been settled. Summary judgment had been granted against the second defendant. The aggravating features were particularly grave. He was ordered to pay damages of £100,000 with a further £20,000 to compensate the claimant for the distress and harassment suffered. No separate award was made for harassment, since the harassment consisted in the making of the defamatory publications. Tugendhat J. added at [119] that "If a national newspaper had published the allegations complained of . . . the damages would have been towards the upper end of the range in which a court can award in general damages for libel."

Jon Richard Ltd v Gornall [2013] EWHC 1357 (QB)   **A3.64**

The claimant was a jewellery retailer that conducted most of its business with one major department store. The defendant was a former employee of the claimant who had her employment terminated following a disciplinary investigation. The claim was brought over anonymous letters sent to the department store, alleging that the claimant had inflated invoices over the years, and perpetrated a £300,000 fraud on it. The evidence adduced showed conclusively that the defendant was responsible for the letters, after which she indicated she did not intend to continue to defend the claim. Publication was limited, but there were significant aggravating features: (1) the company did not have a standing such that people would instantly recognise that any wrongdoing was entirely uncharacteristic of it; (2) the gravity of the allegations; (3) the nature of the recipients of the letters: the department store was central to the survival of the claimant's business and some of the letters were sent to senior personnel within it; and (4) the presentation of the letters (their being headed "Whistleblowing" was designed to clothe the sender as "well intentioned" with "genuine concerns"). The declarations sought by the claimant under the Defamation Act 1996, s.8 were granted, together with an injunction and damages of £10,000. Whilst the proper award was £75,000, a cap was imposed by the summary procedure under s.9(1)(c) of the Act.

A3.65 Cruddas v Calvert, Blake and Times Newspapers Ltd [2013] EWHC 2298 (QB)

This case was related to that described at A3.61 above. The claimant was a millionaire businessman, and formerly a co-treasurer of the Conservative party. The defendants were undercover reporters working for the *Sunday Times*, and the newspaper's publisher. The claimant sued in libel and malicious falsehood over a series of articles published both in print and online accusing him of corruption and breach of electoral law. Justification was pleaded in defence of the libel claim, and the defendants denied the journalists had acted with malice. The articles had received the maximum possible publicity: one had been on the front page of the newspaper. The claimant succeeded in full, with a finding of malice made against the two reporters, for whom the newspaper was held vicariously liable. The articles were untrue to the extent they alleged corruption, and there was no evidence to support the meaning of breach of electoral law. The allegations were grave and went to the claimant's honour and integrity. He suffered great distress and public humiliation, and had to resign from his post as co-treasurer of the party. The conduct of the defendants both in contesting the matter and at trial had been "offensive". The trial had not received much press attention so the libels were not further circulated in that way, but that the judge explained that meant that it was "all the more important that the award of damages should be one that (would) receive publicity". Damages of £180,000 were ordered, which included £15,000 for damages aggravated by the defendants' conduct. No separate damages were awarded for the malicious falsehood: the claimant could not recover twice for the same damage.

Part 3

Compensation awards under the Offer of Amends Scheme (ss.2–4 Defamation Act 1996)

A3.66 Cleese v Clark [2004] E.M.L.R. 37

The claimant, the well-known comedian, actor and writer, sued the author of a defamatory article about him in the *Evening Standard*, and the paper's publisher. The article alleged that the claimant faced humiliation after his latest television series proved to be a flop in the United States. The defendants made an offer of amends and the case came before Eady J. to determine compensation under s.3(5) of the Defamation Act 1996. The Court held that the allegations were very much at the lower end of gravity and that whilst the claimant had been attacked personally and professionally he was not accused of anything criminal or cruel or anti-social. The Judge awarded £13,500.

A3.67 Nail v News Group Newspapers Ltd [2004] EWCA Civ 1708; [2005] 1 All E.R. 1040

In 1998 Harper Collins published a biography of the claimant entitled "Nailed". He decided not to sue at that time, on legal advice. In 2002 extracts from "Nailed" were published in the *News of the World* newspaper and the book attracted new consumer interest, selling about a hundred copies. The claimant sued the *News of the World* over the offending article and, separately, Harper Collins in respect of the editions of the book sold in 2002. An offer to make amends having been accepted by the claimant, Eady J. awarded the claimant £7,500 in compensation for the book and £22,500 for the article after applying a discount of 50% for the offer of amends. The claimant appealed. The appeal was dismissed.

Campbell-James v Guardian Media Group Plc [2005] EWHC 893 (QB);   **A3.68**
[2005] E.M.L.R. 24

The claimant complained about an article published in *The Guardian* newspaper in September 2004 headed "UK officers linked to torture jail" which falsely linked him with the notorious abuses at Abu Ghraib prison in Iraq in 2003. Colonel Campbell-James accepted an offer to make amends made by the defendant under s.2 Defamation Act 1996. Eady J. considered the allegation to be very serious: "*Anyone who truly bore a degree of responsibility for such atrocious abuse of power, even indirectly, would rightly be reviled and made the subject of criminal charges or, at least, military discipline*". The judge also noted Col Campbell-James's distress at being accused of something which he found "*personally abhorrent*". There was solid evidence before the court of a serious security risk to Col Campbell-James and his family following the article. *The Guardian* was criticised for waiting three months before publishing an apology and correction, when there should have been "*an immediate and generous acknowledgment of error*". Its attitude was described as "*remarkably casual*". Eady J. considered £90,000 to be the correct notional starting point for damages which would have been awarded at trial and 35% to be the appropriate percentage reduction taking into account the offer of amends and apology. The claimant was accordingly awarded £58,500 in compensation.

Turner v News Group Newspapers Ltd [2006] EWCA Civ 540; [2006] 1   **A3.69**
W.L.R. 3469

A former wife of the claimant was featured in an article in the *News of the World* newspaper concerning 'swinging' and sex parties. It was said that she had been introduced to the swinging scene by her husband (who was not named but was identifiable to some readers) and that their marriage broke up after he pressured her to have sex with other men. An offer to make amends was made by the defendant, coupled with a lengthy '*Burstein*' mitigation plea. An apology was published but compensation not agreed. At the compensation hearing, the defendant relied on an amended '*Burstein*' plea in mitigation while the claimant relied on both forms of the '*Burstein*' plea as matters aggravating the injury, disentitling the defendant from any, let alone a 'healthy' discount, for the offer of amends. Eady J. awarded the claimant £9,000 in compensation after applying a discount of 40% for the offer of amends. In May 2006 the Court of Appeal dismissed the claimant's appeal, holding that the Judge made no error.

Angel v Stainton [2006] EWHC 637 (QB)   **A3.70**

The claimant, an 81-year-old director of an aircraft and defence equipment company, sued a rival company and its managing director for alleging that he had been convicted and imprisoned for illegal arms dealing. The accusation had been contained in a letter written by the defendants to the receivers of the claimant's former business, which both the claimant's current company and the defendants were competing to purchase. The letter was also copied to four other organisations, all of whom were connected with the claimant's ability to conduct his business. Although accepting that the specific allegation was false, the defendants did not make an offer of amends until the issue of proceedings, since they sought to exploit a prosecution which had apparently been brought many years earlier but subsequently abandoned. Although all other steps were agreed, the parties could not agree on the issue of compensation. Eady J. held that the right starting figure was £40,000. Although there was a limited publication and no evidence of any lasting actual damage, this was a very serious allegation touching upon the claimant's core attributes. The defendants had not only failed to capitulate at an early stage, their attitude had been grudging and not sufficiently conciliatory. They had also aggravated the hurt to the claimant by persisting until a late stage in the suggestion that the claimant's character might be attacked in court. Eady J. made a discount of 40%, awarding £24,000.

A3.71 Veliu v Mazrekaj [2006] EWHC 1710 (QB); [2007] 1 W.L.R. 495

The Claimant, a journalist who had lived and worked in the UK for 8 years, sued in respect of an article in an Albanian language newspaper published in the jurisdiction that alleged that he had been implicated in the London terrorist bombings. An apology appeared 5 months later. The first defendant, the publisher, made an offer of amends that was accepted. The second defendant, the editor, failed to acknowledge service and judgment was entered against him. Eady J. held that the libel was of exceptional gravity. The starting point for damages was £180,000. The appropriate discount against the starting point bearing in mind the publisher's conduct was one third. Compensation payable by the first defendant was assessed at £120,000. Given the slight mitigating effect of the apology, damages against the second defendant were set at £175,000.

A3.72 Bowman v MGN Ltd [2010] EWHC 895 (QB)

The claimant sued on articles published on the newspaper's website which suggested that he had had a romantic relationship with a fellow actor. Because the claimant was in a serious, committed relationship with another woman, the article would have been understood in a defamatory sense by those who knew of his relationship. The article was removed from the internet after 27 hours. The defendant offered an immediate apology and a correction was promptly published on the website. Compensation could not be agreed and an application was made for the court to determine compensation under s.3(5) of the Defamation Act 1996. It was part of the claimant's case that the journalist had been given the correct information before the article went live online. The court awarded the relatively modest sum of £4,250, less than earlier without prejudice offers, for several reasons. Firstly, in the absence of concrete evidence as to the number of readers who would have understood the defamatory innuendo, a conservative approach to damages was appropriate. Secondly, the allegation was essentially celebrity gossip and there was no strong evidence of an adverse effect on the claimant's relationship. Thirdly, he had not proved that the pre-publication conversation with the journalist had actually taken place. Fourthly, the mitigating effect of the newspaper's conduct was worth a 50% discount on the notional starting figure for damages, £8,500. However, the defendant was criticised by the judge for adopting a "take it or leave it" approach to its offers, rather than facilitating negotiation by answering enquiries from the claimant.

Part 4

Damages awards in misuse of personal information and harassment cases involving speech (since 2000)[3]

A3.73 Cornelius v de Taranto [2001] E.L.M.R. 12

The claimant, a teacher, was suffering stress at work and with a view to taking legal action obtained an expert report. She was interviewed by the defendant, a senior

---

[3] See fn.2, above.

registrar, who prepared a report. The report was sent to a consultant and to the claimant's GP, she said without her consent. It also became part of her NHS records and she was unable to secure its removal. The claimant sued the defendant for libel and breach of confidence. Morland J. dismissed the claim in libel, upholding the defence of justification. The Judge held that the report had been disclosed without the claimant's consent to the GP and the consultant and that the claimant was entitled to damages for mental distress caused by the breach of confidence. The Judge awarded the "modest" sum of £3,000 in damages for distress and £750 for the expense incurred to retrieve copies of the report from the NHS records. The Court of Appeal upheld the finding of liability and did not consider the damages issue: [2001] EWCA Civ 1511; [2002] E.M.L.R. 6.

Campbell v MGN Ltd [2002] EWHC 499 (QB); [2002] E.M.L.R. 30   **A3.74**

The claimant, an internationally known fashion model and celebrity, was revealed in two articles in *The Mirror* newspaper, contrary to her previous false assertions, to be a drug addict who was attending meetings of Narcotics Anonymous ('NA'). The articles were accompanied by covertly taken photographs of the claimant leaving a NA meeting. The claimant sued for breach of confidence and under the Data Protection Act 1998. At trial Morland J. held that, notwithstanding concessions made by the claimant, there had been a breach of confidence and invasion of her privacy in revealing private information about her. She was awarded £2,500 in damages for distress and injury to feelings having been reported to have said, "I saw the piece and got upset for 5 minutes" [133]. An additional £1,000 was awarded in aggravated damages over a subsequent article published about her claim. The Court of Appeal allowed an appeal by the defendant against this decision and the House of Lords allowed an appeal from the Court of Appeal's decision, re-instating the original judgment and award: [2004] UKHL 22; [2004] 2 A.C. 457.

Peck v United Kingdom (2003) 36 E.H.R.R. 41; [2003] E.M.L.R. 15   **A3.75**

The applicant was filmed on CCTV walking alone at night down Brentwood High Street with a knife in his hand. He was seen attempting to commit suicide by cutting his wrists. The police were notified by the CCTV operator and the applicant was disarmed and taken for treatment. The local council decided to publish press releases concerning the CCTV system in local papers. As a result of the local press coverage, the footage was used by television companies, subject to conditions being attached by the council. The applicant lodged complaints to the BSC, the ITC and the PCC about the use of the footage. He sought judicial review of the council's disclosure of the CCTV which was rejected by the High Court. The applicant complained to the European Court of Human Rights, alleging a breach of article 8. The ECtHR held that there had been a breach of article 8 and considered that the applicant must have suffered significant distress, embarrassment and frustration, which would not be sufficiently compensated by a finding of a violation. He was awarded 11,800 euros in respect of non-pecuniary damage.

Lady Archer v Williams [2003] EWHC 1670 (QB); [2003] E.M.L.R. 38   **A3.76**

The claimant was a scientist who had held a number of senior academic positions, and was also the wife of a famous former politician. She employed the defendant as her secretary and personal assistant. The defendant disclosed confidential details about the claimant to a newspaper, including information about a medical procedure that she had allegedly undergone. The information had been gleaned from her time in employment with the claimant, and was disclosed in breach of her employment contract. The disclosures resulted in a number of newspaper articles concerning the confidential information. The claimant successfully sued for a breach of confidence, obtaining damages and an injunction. There was no overriding public interest in the disclosure of sensitive personal information relating to the claimant. At trial Jackson J. awarded the claimant the sum of £2,500 in damages for breach of confidence and injury to feelings caused by the defendant's disclosures. Jackson J. considered at [76] that, *"general damages for injury to feelings should be kept to a modest amount and should be proportionate to the injury suffered. Such awards should be well below the level of general damages suffered for serious physical or psychiatric injury."*

A3.77 W v Westminster City Council (No.2) [2005] EWHC 102 (QB); [2005] 4 All E.R. 96

The claimant sued the first defendant, a public authority, and two of its social workers, over statements published in a report to a Child Protection Conference where five people were present. The concern was that the claimant was a predatory paedophile who was grooming an 11-year-old girl for sexual abuse and prostitution. At an earlier hearing Tugendhat J. dismissed an application on behalf of the defendants that publications made in a child protection conference were covered by absolute privilege, stated the test to be applied to determine whether or not any of the defendants were malicious and granted the claimant permission to amend his particulars of claim to include a claim under s.7 of the Human Rights Act 1998. At trial Tugendhat J. dismissed the libel claim on the basis that the defence of qualified privilege succeeded and the defendants were not malicious. However, he held that the disclosure of concerns about the claimant at the conference was an improper interference with his article 8 rights and made a declaration to that effect. Damages were not required to afford just satisfaction but had they been the Court would have awarded £1,000 (see [352]).

A3.78 Douglas v Hello! Ltd [2005] EWCA Civ 595; [2006] Q.B. 125

The first and second claimants, well-known film actors, sold the rights to publish photographs of their wedding to the third defendant, OK! magazine. The first defendant, the publisher of Hello! magazine, obtained and published unauthorised photographs of the wedding. At trial, following various interim hearings, Lindsay J. held that the first and second claimants were entitled to damages and a perpetual injunction against Hello! on the grounds that the publication of the unauthorised photographs constituted a breach of confidence. The Judge held that OK! was entitled to damages from Hello! on substantially similar grounds. He rejected OK!'s case in respect of other torts. He assessed the damages due to the first and second claimants at £3,750 each for the distress occasioned by the publication of the unauthorised photographs and £7,000 between them for the costs and inconvenience of having to deal hurriedly with the selection of authorised photographs. He awarded nominal damages under the Data Protection Act 1998, and awarded OK! £1,026,706 in respect of their loss of profit from the exploitation of the authorised photographs, attributable to the publication of the unauthorised photographs and £6,450 in respect of wasted costs. The Court of Appeal upheld the awards in respect of the first and second claimants, describing the sums awarded as *"very modest"* ([2005] EWCA Civ 595, [2006] Q.B. 125 at [110]), but allowed the appeal against OK!. The House of Lords reversed the judgment of the Court of Appeal in respect of the third claimant: [2007] UKHL 21; [2008] 1 A.C. 1.

A3.79 Cray v Hancock, unreported, November 4, 2005

See A3.28 above. The Judge awarded £10,000 for the harassment.

A3.80 McKennitt v Ash [2005] EWHC 3003 (QB); [2006] E.M.L.R. 10

The first claimant, a composer and performer of folk music, and two companies owned and operated by her, sued the first defendant, the author of a book about the first claimant, and the second defendant, the corporate publisher of the book, for breach of confidence/invasion of privacy. Certain allegations of confidential information were held to invade the first claimant's privacy and at trial Eady J. awarded a sum of £5,000 for hurt feelings and distress over the publication of personal and intimate details which the defendant had acquired over the course of her friendship with the claimant. The Judge described the sum at [162] as '*relatively modest*'. Nominal damages were awarded to the corporate claimants. The award was upheld on appeal: [2006] EWCA Civ 1714; [2008] Q.B. 73.

Mosley v News Group Newspapers Ltd [2008] EWHC 1777 (QB); [2008]   **A3.81**
E.M.L.R. 20

The claimant, the President of the Federation Internationale de l'Automobile, the governing body of motor sport worldwide, was covertly filmed engaging in sado-masochistic activities with five dominatrices in a private flat. An edited version of the footage was made available on the defendant's website in connection with a *News of the World* article entitled 'F1 boss has sick Nazi orgy with 5 hookers'. The claimant accepted that the events shown occurred but claimed that their disclosure infringed his right to privacy and the publication of them to the world at large was a misuse of personal information. He also denied any Nazi element. Eady J. held that the claim-ant's article 8 rights to privacy were engaged and there was no evidence that the sexual role play was intended to be an enactment of Nazi behaviour or adoption of any of its attitudes. Though the sexual activities were unconventional there was no public interest or other justification for the clandestine recording, for the publication of the footage and images or for the placing of the video extracts on the defendant's website. The Judge awarded the claimant £60,000 in general damages, but held that exemplary damages were not recoverable in a claim for infringement of privacy.

Applause Store Productions Limited v Raphael [2008] EWHC 1781 (QB);   **A3.82**
[2008] Info T.L.R. 318

See A3.36 above for report. The Deputy Judge awarded £2,000 for breach of pri-vacy.

Bloom v Robinson-Millar, October 7, 2009, [2013] EWHC 3918 (QB)   **A3.83**

See A.3.44 above for report. The judge said that had she considered it appropriate to make separate awards, she would have awarded £5,000 for the claim in harassment.

Cooper v Turrell [2011] EWHC 3269 (QB)   **A3.84**

See A3.56 above for the report. The judge awarded the first claimant £30,000 for a misuse of his private medical information in addition to an award for the libels against him. The judge explained that since damages for libels included compensation for distress, double counting had to be avoided. Had the award for misuse of private information been the sole award, it would have been £40,000 [107].

AAA v Associated Newspapers Ltd [2012] EWHC 2103 (QB); [2013]   **A3.85**
E.M.L.R. 2

The claimant was a young child whose birth was the result of an extra-marital affair between a famous married male politician and the claimant's mother. The defendant was the publisher of the *Daily Mail*, which produced a series of articles that speculated as to the claimant's paternity, and were illustrated by an unpixelated photograph of the claimant, with her face clearly visible. The photograph had been taken covertly, in a public place, without her mother's consent, at a time when the claimant was less than one-year-old. Through her litigation friend she sued for a breach of privacy over the articles and the multiple publications of the photograph. The defendant successfully defended the articles on the basis of public interest. However, publication of the photographs was not reasonable, nor justified. The unpixelated photograph had been published three times, and on the third occasion the defendant was aware that the claimant's family took issue with it. Damages of £15,000 were awarded. Nicola Davies J. explained that the level of award should serve as notice of "how seriously the court regards infringements of a child's rights" [127]. An appeal by the claimant against the dismissal of her claim for damages in respect of private information and the refusal to grant an injunction was dismissed: [2013] EWCA Civ 554.

A3.86 WXY v Gewanter, Positive Profile and Burby [2013] EWHC 589 (QB)

The claimant was a wealthy woman with close connections to a foreign head of state and his family. The defendants were a PR consultant, his company, and a client of theirs who had published private and confidential information concerning the claimant online. The information included allegations about the claimant's sexual conduct and details of private discussions between her and a third party in which she allegedly made sensitive disclosures about the head of state. Although the claimant was not named, she was identifiable. The defendants threatened to make further postings. The postings were online for about three and a half months, but no findings were made at trial as to the number of hits on the website in this jurisdiction. The claimant successfully sued for a breach of privacy and for harassment. The judge found the material was posted with the intention of securing a financial benefit for the third defendant. An award of £24,950 was made for the privacy breach, which included £5,000 of aggravated damages. No separate award was made for the harassment element of the claim because the trial judge found that the claimant's distress had been caused by the website postings and the threats of further postings, and it would therefore be wrong to assess damages in respect of the harassment as well, because that would be to double-count.

A3.87 ZAM v CFW and TFW [2013] EWHC 662 (QB); [2013] E.M.L.R. 27

See A3.63 above for the report. Whilst the claim in harassment succeeded, no separate award was made under that heading because the making of the defamatory statements (in respect of which an award of £120,000 had already been made) constituted the harassment.

INDEX

INDEX

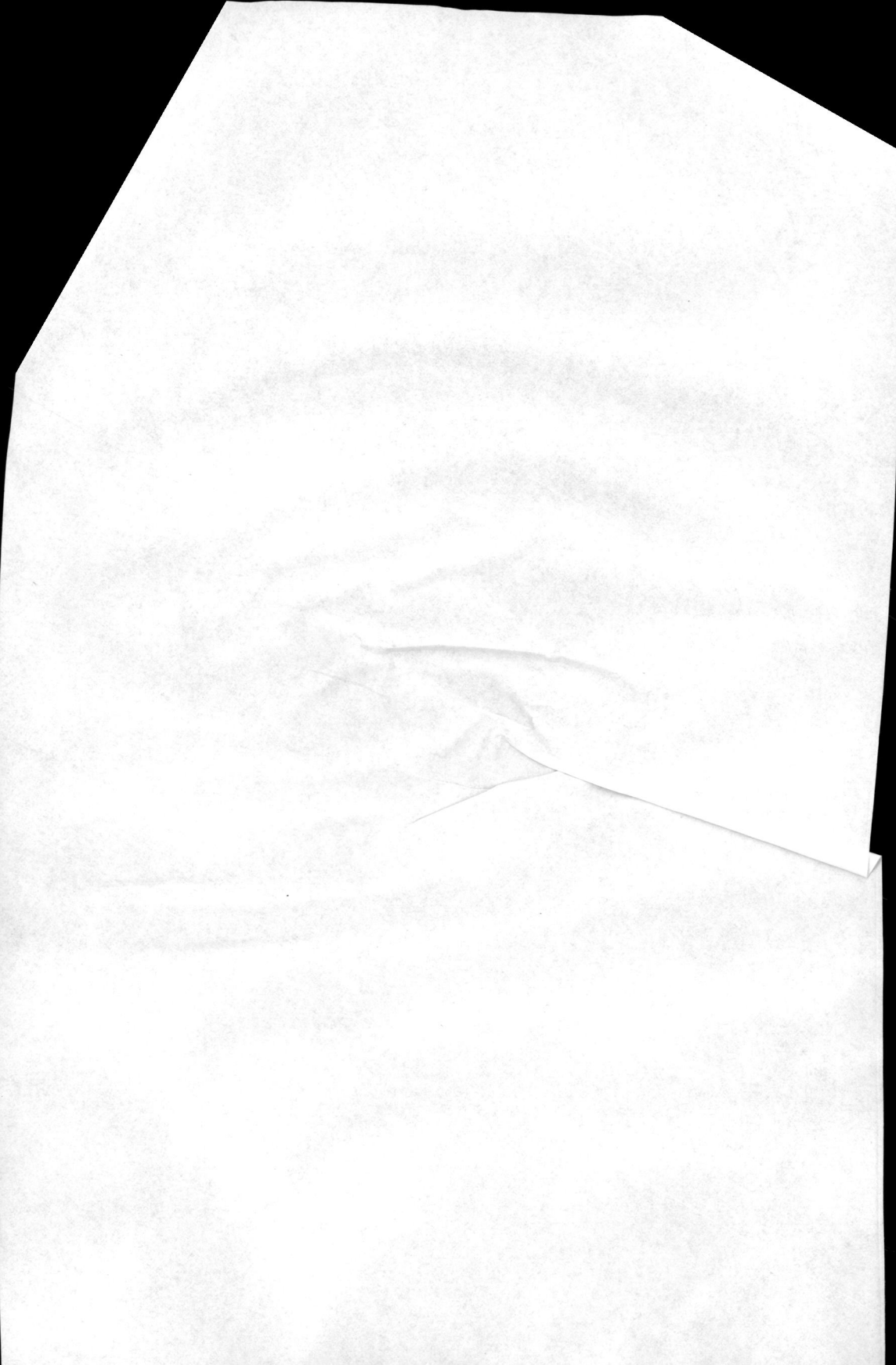